3 1192 01289 0883

Oxford Dictionary of National Biography

Volume 42

Oxford Dictionary of National Biography

IN ASSOCIATION WITH

The British Academy

From the earliest times to the year 2000

Edited by

H. C. G. Matthew

and

Brian Harrison

Volume 42

Osborne–Pate

UNIVERSITY PRESS

Great Clarendon Street, Oxford OX2 6DP

Oxford University Press is a department of the University of Oxford.
It furthers the University's objective of excellence in research, scholarship,
and education by publishing worldwide in

Oxford New York

Auckland Bangkok Buenos Aires Cape Town
Chennai Dar es Salaam Delhi Hong Kong Istanbul Karachi
Kolkata Kuala Lumpur Madrid Melbourne Mexico City Mumbai Nairobi
São Paulo Shanghai Taipei Tokyo Toronto

Oxford is a registered trade mark of Oxford University Press
in the UK and in certain other countries

Published in the United States
by Oxford University Press Inc., New York

First published 2004

British Library Cataloguing in Publication Data
Data available

Library of Congress Cataloging in Publication Data
Data available: for details see volume 1, p. iv

ISBN 0-19-861392-X (this volume)
ISBN 0-19-861411-X (set of sixty volumes)

Text captured by Alliance Phototypesetters, Pondicherry
Illustrations reproduced and archived by
Alliance Graphics Ltd, UK
Typeset in OUP Swift by Interactive Sciences Limited, Gloucester
Printed in Great Britain on acid-free paper by
Butler and Tanner Ltd,
Frome, Somerset

LIST OF ABBREVIATIONS

1 *General abbreviations*

AB	bachelor of arts
ABC	Australian Broadcasting Corporation
ABC TV	ABC Television
act.	active
A$	Australian dollar
AD	*anno domini*
AFC	Air Force Cross
AIDS	acquired immune deficiency syndrome
AK	Alaska
AL	Alabama
A level	advanced level [examination]
ALS	associate of the Linnean Society
AM	master of arts
AMICE	associate member of the Institution of Civil Engineers
ANZAC	Australian and New Zealand Army Corps
appx *pl.* appxs	appendix(es)
AR	Arkansas
ARA	associate of the Royal Academy
ARCA	associate of the Royal College of Art
ARCM	associate of the Royal College of Music
ARCO	associate of the Royal College of Organists
ARIBA	associate of the Royal Institute of British Architects
ARP	air-raid precautions
ARRC	associate of the Royal Red Cross
ARSA	associate of the Royal Scottish Academy
art.	article / item
ASC	Army Service Corps
Asch	Austrian Schilling
ASDIC	Antisubmarine Detection Investigation Committee
ATS	Auxiliary Territorial Service
ATV	Associated Television
Aug	August
AZ	Arizona
b.	born
BA	bachelor of arts
BA (Admin.)	bachelor of arts (administration)
BAFTA	British Academy of Film and Television Arts
BAO	bachelor of arts in obstetrics
bap.	baptized
BBC	British Broadcasting Corporation / Company
BC	before Christ
BCE	before the common (*or* Christian) era
BCE	bachelor of civil engineering
BCG	bacillus of Calmette and Guérin [inoculation against tuberculosis]
BCh	bachelor of surgery
BChir	bachelor of surgery
BCL	bachelor of civil law
BCnL	bachelor of canon law
BCom	bachelor of commerce
BD	bachelor of divinity
BEd	bachelor of education
BEng	bachelor of engineering
bk *pl.* bks	book(s)
BL	bachelor of law / letters / literature
BLitt	bachelor of letters
BM	bachelor of medicine
BMus	bachelor of music
BP	before present
BP	British Petroleum
Bros.	Brothers
BS	(1) bachelor of science; (2) bachelor of surgery; (3) British standard
BSc	bachelor of science
BSc (Econ.)	bachelor of science (economics)
BSc (Eng.)	bachelor of science (engineering)
bt	baronet
BTh	bachelor of theology
bur.	buried
C.	command [identifier for published parliamentary papers]
c.	*circa*
c.	*capitulum pl. capitula*: chapter(s)
CA	California
Cantab.	Cantabrigiensis
cap.	*capitulum pl. capitula*: chapter(s)
CB	companion of the Bath
CBE	commander of the Order of the British Empire
CBS	Columbia Broadcasting System
cc	cubic centimetres
C$	Canadian dollar
CD	compact disc
Cd	command [identifier for published parliamentary papers]
CE	Common (*or* Christian) Era
cent.	century
cf.	compare
CH	Companion of Honour
chap.	chapter
ChB	bachelor of surgery
CI	Imperial Order of the Crown of India
CIA	Central Intelligence Agency
CID	Criminal Investigation Department
CIE	companion of the Order of the Indian Empire
Cie	Compagnie
CLit	companion of literature
CM	master of surgery
cm	centimetre(s)

Cmd	command [identifier for published parliamentary papers]
CMG	companion of the Order of St Michael and St George
Cmnd	command [identifier for published parliamentary papers]
CO	Colorado
Co.	company
co.	county
col. *pl.* cols.	column(s)
Corp.	corporation
CSE	certificate of secondary education
CSI	companion of the Order of the Star of India
CT	Connecticut
CVO	commander of the Royal Victorian Order
cwt	hundredweight
$	(American) dollar
d.	(1) penny (pence); (2) died
DBE	dame commander of the Order of the British Empire
DCH	diploma in child health
DCh	doctor of surgery
DCL	doctor of civil law
DCnL	doctor of canon law
DCVO	dame commander of the Royal Victorian Order
DD	doctor of divinity
DE	Delaware
Dec	December
dem.	demolished
DEng	doctor of engineering
des.	destroyed
DFC	Distinguished Flying Cross
DipEd	diploma in education
DipPsych	diploma in psychiatry
diss.	dissertation
DL	deputy lieutenant
DLitt	doctor of letters
DLittCelt	doctor of Celtic letters
DM	(1) Deutschmark; (2) doctor of medicine; (3) doctor of musical arts
DMus	doctor of music
DNA	dioxyribonucleic acid
doc.	document
DOL	doctor of oriental learning
DPH	diploma in public health
DPhil	doctor of philosophy
DPM	diploma in psychological medicine
DSC	Distinguished Service Cross
DSc	doctor of science
DSc (Econ.)	doctor of science (economics)
DSc (Eng.)	doctor of science (engineering)
DSM	Distinguished Service Medal
DSO	companion of the Distinguished Service Order
DSocSc	doctor of social science
DTech	doctor of technology
DTh	doctor of theology
DTM	diploma in tropical medicine
DTMH	diploma in tropical medicine and hygiene
DU	doctor of the university
DUniv	doctor of the university
dwt	pennyweight
EC	European Community
ed. *pl.* eds.	edited / edited by / editor(s)
Edin.	Edinburgh
edn	edition
EEC	European Economic Community
EFTA	European Free Trade Association
EICS	East India Company Service
EMI	Electrical and Musical Industries (Ltd)
Eng.	English
enl.	enlarged
ENSA	Entertainments National Service Association
ep. *pl.* epp.	*epistola(e)*
ESP	extra-sensory perception
esp.	especially
esq.	esquire
est.	estimate / estimated
EU	European Union
ex	sold by (*lit.* out of)
excl.	excludes / excluding
exh.	exhibited
exh. cat.	exhibition catalogue
f. *pl.* ff.	following [pages]
FA	Football Association
FACP	fellow of the American College of Physicians
facs.	facsimile
FANY	First Aid Nursing Yeomanry
FBA	fellow of the British Academy
FBI	Federation of British Industries
FCS	fellow of the Chemical Society
Feb	February
FEng	fellow of the Fellowship of Engineering
FFCM	fellow of the Faculty of Community Medicine
FGS	fellow of the Geological Society
fig.	figure
FIMechE	fellow of the Institution of Mechanical Engineers
FL	Florida
fl.	*floruit*
FLS	fellow of the Linnean Society
FM	frequency modulation
fol. *pl.* fols.	folio(s)
Fr	French francs
Fr.	French
FRAeS	fellow of the Royal Aeronautical Society
FRAI	fellow of the Royal Anthropological Institute
FRAM	fellow of the Royal Academy of Music
FRAS	(1) fellow of the Royal Asiatic Society; (2) fellow of the Royal Astronomical Society
FRCM	fellow of the Royal College of Music
FRCO	fellow of the Royal College of Organists
FRCOG	fellow of the Royal College of Obstetricians and Gynaecologists
FRCP(C)	fellow of the Royal College of Physicians of Canada
FRCP (Edin.)	fellow of the Royal College of Physicians of Edinburgh
FRCP (Lond.)	fellow of the Royal College of Physicians of London
FRCPath	fellow of the Royal College of Pathologists
FRCPsych	fellow of the Royal College of Psychiatrists
FRCS	fellow of the Royal College of Surgeons
FRGS	fellow of the Royal Geographical Society
FRIBA	fellow of the Royal Institute of British Architects
FRICS	fellow of the Royal Institute of Chartered Surveyors
FRS	fellow of the Royal Society
FRSA	fellow of the Royal Society of Arts

FRSCM	fellow of the Royal School of Church Music
FRSE	fellow of the Royal Society of Edinburgh
FRSL	fellow of the Royal Society of Literature
FSA	fellow of the Society of Antiquaries
ft	foot *pl.* feet
FTCL	fellow of Trinity College of Music, London
ft-lb per min.	foot-pounds per minute [unit of horsepower]
FZS	fellow of the Zoological Society
GA	Georgia
GBE	knight or dame grand cross of the Order of the British Empire
GCB	knight grand cross of the Order of the Bath
GCE	general certificate of education
GCH	knight grand cross of the Royal Guelphic Order
GCHQ	government communications headquarters
GCIE	knight grand commander of the Order of the Indian Empire
GCMG	knight or dame grand cross of the Order of St Michael and St George
GCSE	general certificate of secondary education
GCSI	knight grand commander of the Order of the Star of India
GCStJ	bailiff or dame grand cross of the order of St John of Jerusalem
GCVO	knight or dame grand cross of the Royal Victorian Order
GEC	General Electric Company
Ger.	German
GI	government (*or* general) issue
GMT	Greenwich mean time
GP	general practitioner
GPU	[Soviet special police unit]
GSO	general staff officer
Heb.	Hebrew
HEICS	Honourable East India Company Service
HI	Hawaii
HIV	human immunodeficiency virus
HK$	Hong Kong dollar
HM	his / her majesty('s)
HMAS	his / her majesty's Australian ship
HMNZS	his / her majesty's New Zealand ship
HMS	his / her majesty's ship
HMSO	His / Her Majesty's Stationery Office
HMV	His Master's Voice
Hon.	Honourable
hp	horsepower
hr	hour(s)
HRH	his / her royal highness
HTV	Harlech Television
IA	Iowa
ibid.	*ibidem*: in the same place
ICI	Imperial Chemical Industries (Ltd)
ID	Idaho
IL	Illinois
illus.	illustration
illustr.	illustrated
IN	Indiana
in.	inch(es)
Inc.	Incorporated
incl.	includes / including
IOU	I owe you
IQ	intelligence quotient
Ir£	Irish pound
IRA	Irish Republican Army
ISO	companion of the Imperial Service Order
It.	Italian
ITA	Independent Television Authority
ITV	Independent Television
Jan	January
JP	justice of the peace
jun.	junior
KB	knight of the Order of the Bath
KBE	knight commander of the Order of the British Empire
KC	king's counsel
kcal	kilocalorie
KCB	knight commander of the Order of the Bath
KCH	knight commander of the Royal Guelphic Order
KCIE	knight commander of the Order of the Indian Empire
KCMG	knight commander of the Order of St Michael and St George
KCSI	knight commander of the Order of the Star of India
KCVO	knight commander of the Royal Victorian Order
keV	kilo-electron-volt
KG	knight of the Order of the Garter
KGB	[Soviet committee of state security]
KH	knight of the Royal Guelphic Order
KLM	Koninklijke Luchtvaart Maatschappij (Royal Dutch Air Lines)
km	kilometre(s)
KP	knight of the Order of St Patrick
KS	Kansas
KT	knight of the Order of the Thistle
kt	knight
KY	Kentucky
£	pound(s) sterling
£E	Egyptian pound
L	lira *pl.* lire
l. *pl.* ll.	line(s)
LA	Lousiana
LAA	light anti-aircraft
LAH	licentiate of the Apothecaries' Hall, Dublin
Lat.	Latin
lb	pound(s), unit of weight
LDS	licence in dental surgery
lit.	literally
LittB	bachelor of letters
LittD	doctor of letters
LKQCPI	licentiate of the King and Queen's College of Physicians, Ireland
LLA	lady literate in arts
LLB	bachelor of laws
LLD	doctor of laws
LLM	master of laws
LM	licentiate in midwifery
LP	long-playing record
LRAM	licentiate of the Royal Academy of Music
LRCP	licentiate of the Royal College of Physicians
LRCPS (Glasgow)	licentiate of the Royal College of Physicians and Surgeons of Glasgow
LRCS	licentiate of the Royal College of Surgeons
LSA	licentiate of the Society of Apothecaries
LSD	lysergic acid diethylamide
LVO	lieutenant of the Royal Victorian Order
M. *pl.* MM.	Monsieur *pl.* Messieurs
m	metre(s)

m. *pl.* mm.	membrane(s)
MA	(1) Massachusetts; (2) master of arts
MAI	master of engineering
MB	bachelor of medicine
MBA	master of business administration
MBE	member of the Order of the British Empire
MC	Military Cross
MCC	Marylebone Cricket Club
MCh	master of surgery
MChir	master of surgery
MCom	master of commerce
MD	(1) doctor of medicine; (2) Maryland
MDMA	methylenedioxymethamphetamine
ME	Maine
MEd	master of education
MEng	master of engineering
MEP	member of the European parliament
MG	Morris Garages
MGM	Metro-Goldwyn-Mayer
Mgr	Monsignor
MI	(1) Michigan; (2) military intelligence
MI1c	[secret intelligence department]
MI5	[military intelligence department]
MI6	[secret intelligence department]
MI9	[secret escape service]
MICE	member of the Institution of Civil Engineers
MIEE	member of the Institution of Electrical Engineers
min.	minute(s)
Mk	mark
ML	(1) licentiate of medicine; (2) master of laws
MLitt	master of letters
Mlle	Mademoiselle
mm	millimetre(s)
Mme	Madame
MN	Minnesota
MO	Missouri
MOH	medical officer of health
MP	member of parliament
m.p.h.	miles per hour
MPhil	master of philosophy
MRCP	member of the Royal College of Physicians
MRCS	member of the Royal College of Surgeons
MRCVS	member of the Royal College of Veterinary Surgeons
MRIA	member of the Royal Irish Academy
MS	(1) master of science; (2) Mississippi
MS *pl.* MSS	manuscript(s)
MSc	master of science
MSc (Econ.)	master of science (economics)
MT	Montana
MusB	bachelor of music
MusBac	bachelor of music
MusD	doctor of music
MV	motor vessel
MVO	member of the Royal Victorian Order
n. *pl.* nn.	note(s)
NAAFI	Navy, Army, and Air Force Institutes
NASA	National Aeronautics and Space Administration
NATO	North Atlantic Treaty Organization
NBC	National Broadcasting Corporation
NC	North Carolina
NCO	non-commissioned officer
ND	North Dakota
n.d.	no date
NE	Nebraska
nem. con.	*nemine contradicente*: unanimously
new ser.	new series
NH	New Hampshire
NHS	National Health Service
NJ	New Jersey
NKVD	[Soviet people's commissariat for internal affairs]
NM	New Mexico
nm	nanometre(s)
no. *pl.* nos.	number(s)
Nov	November
n.p.	no place [of publication]
NS	new style
NV	Nevada
NY	New York
NZBS	New Zealand Broadcasting Service
OBE	officer of the Order of the British Empire
obit.	obituary
Oct	October
OCTU	officer cadets training unit
OECD	Organization for Economic Co-operation and Development
OEEC	Organization for European Economic Co-operation
OFM	order of Friars Minor [Franciscans]
OFMCap	Ordine Frati Minori Cappucini: member of the Capuchin order
OH	Ohio
OK	Oklahoma
O level	ordinary level [examination]
OM	Order of Merit
OP	order of Preachers [Dominicans]
op. *pl.* opp.	opus *pl.* opera
OPEC	Organization of Petroleum Exporting Countries
OR	Oregon
orig.	original
OS	old style
OSB	Order of St Benedict
OTC	Officers' Training Corps
OWS	Old Watercolour Society
Oxon.	Oxoniensis
p. *pl.* pp.	page(s)
PA	Pennsylvania
p.a.	per annum
para.	paragraph
PAYE	pay as you earn
pbk *pl.* pbks	paperback(s)
per.	[during the] period
PhD	doctor of philosophy
pl.	(1) plate(s); (2) plural
priv. coll.	private collection
pt *pl.* pts	part(s)
pubd	published
PVC	polyvinyl chloride
q. *pl.* qq.	(1) question(s); (2) quire(s)
QC	queen's counsel
R	rand
R.	Rex / Regina
r	recto
r.	reigned / ruled
RA	Royal Academy / Royal Academician

RAC	Royal Automobile Club
RAF	Royal Air Force
RAFVR	Royal Air Force Volunteer Reserve
RAM	[member of the] Royal Academy of Music
RAMC	Royal Army Medical Corps
RCA	Royal College of Art
RCNC	Royal Corps of Naval Constructors
RCOG	Royal College of Obstetricians and Gynaecologists
RDI	royal designer for industry
RE	Royal Engineers
repr. *pl.* reprs.	reprint(s) / reprinted
repro.	reproduced
rev.	revised / revised by / reviser / revision
Revd	Reverend
RHA	Royal Hibernian Academy
RI	(1) Rhode Island; (2) Royal Institute of Painters in Water-Colours
RIBA	Royal Institute of British Architects
RIN	Royal Indian Navy
RM	Reichsmark
RMS	Royal Mail steamer
RN	Royal Navy
RNA	ribonucleic acid
RNAS	Royal Naval Air Service
RNR	Royal Naval Reserve
RNVR	Royal Naval Volunteer Reserve
RO	Record Office
r.p.m.	revolutions per minute
RRS	royal research ship
Rs	rupees
RSA	(1) Royal Scottish Academician; (2) Royal Society of Arts
RSPCA	Royal Society for the Prevention of Cruelty to Animals
Rt Hon.	Right Honourable
Rt Revd	Right Reverend
RUC	Royal Ulster Constabulary
Russ.	Russian
RWS	Royal Watercolour Society
S4C	Sianel Pedwar Cymru
s.	shilling(s)
s.a.	*sub anno*: under the year
SABC	South African Broadcasting Corporation
SAS	Special Air Service
SC	South Carolina
ScD	doctor of science
S$	Singapore dollar
SD	South Dakota
sec.	second(s)
sel.	selected
sen.	senior
Sept	September
ser.	series
SHAPE	supreme headquarters allied powers, Europe
SIDRO	Société Internationale d'Énergie Hydro-Électrique
sig. *pl.* sigs.	signature(s)
sing.	singular
SIS	Secret Intelligence Service
SJ	Society of Jesus
Skr	Swedish krona
Span.	Spanish
SPCK	Society for Promoting Christian Knowledge
SS	(1) Santissimi; (2) Schutzstaffel; (3) steam ship
STB	bachelor of theology
STD	doctor of theology
STM	master of theology
STP	doctor of theology
supp.	supposedly
suppl. *pl.* suppls.	supplement(s)
s.v.	*sub verbo* / *sub voce*: under the word / heading
SY	steam yacht
TA	Territorial Army
TASS	[Soviet news agency]
TB	tuberculosis (*lit.* tubercle bacillus)
TD	(1) *teachtaí dála* (member of the Dáil); (2) territorial decoration
TN	Tennessee
TNT	trinitrotoluene
trans.	translated / translated by / translation / translator
TT	tourist trophy
TUC	Trades Union Congress
TX	Texas
U-boat	*Unterseeboot*: submarine
Ufa	Universum-Film AG
UMIST	University of Manchester Institute of Science and Technology
UN	United Nations
UNESCO	United Nations Educational, Scientific, and Cultural Organization
UNICEF	United Nations International Children's Emergency Fund
unpubd	unpublished
USS	United States ship
UT	Utah
v	verso
v.	versus
VA	Virginia
VAD	Voluntary Aid Detachment
VC	Victoria Cross
VE-day	victory in Europe day
Ven.	Venerable
VJ-day	victory over Japan day
vol. *pl.* vols.	volume(s)
VT	Vermont
WA	Washington [state]
WAAC	Women's Auxiliary Army Corps
WAAF	Women's Auxiliary Air Force
WEA	Workers' Educational Association
WHO	World Health Organization
WI	Wisconsin
WRAF	Women's Royal Air Force
WRNS	Women's Royal Naval Service
WV	West Virginia
WVS	Women's Voluntary Service
WY	Wyoming
¥	yen
YMCA	Young Men's Christian Association
YWCA	Young Women's Christian Association

2 *Institution abbreviations*

All Souls Oxf.	All Souls College, Oxford
AM Oxf.	Ashmolean Museum, Oxford
Balliol Oxf.	Balliol College, Oxford
BBC WAC	BBC Written Archives Centre, Reading
Beds. & Luton ARS	Bedfordshire and Luton Archives and Record Service, Bedford
Berks. RO	Berkshire Record Office, Reading
BFI	British Film Institute, London
BFI NFTVA	British Film Institute, London, National Film and Television Archive
BGS	British Geological Survey, Keyworth, Nottingham
Birm. CA	Birmingham Central Library, Birmingham City Archives
Birm. CL	Birmingham Central Library
BL	British Library, London
BL NSA	British Library, London, National Sound Archive
BL OIOC	British Library, London, Oriental and India Office Collections
BLPES	London School of Economics and Political Science, British Library of Political and Economic Science
BM	British Museum, London
Bodl. Oxf.	Bodleian Library, Oxford
Bodl. RH	Bodleian Library of Commonwealth and African Studies at Rhodes House, Oxford
Borth. Inst.	Borthwick Institute of Historical Research, University of York
Boston PL	Boston Public Library, Massachusetts
Bristol RO	Bristol Record Office
Bucks. RLSS	Buckinghamshire Records and Local Studies Service, Aylesbury
CAC Cam.	Churchill College, Cambridge, Churchill Archives Centre
Cambs. AS	Cambridgeshire Archive Service
CCC Cam.	Corpus Christi College, Cambridge
CCC Oxf.	Corpus Christi College, Oxford
Ches. & Chester ALSS	Cheshire and Chester Archives and Local Studies Service
Christ Church Oxf.	Christ Church, Oxford
Christies	Christies, London
City Westm. AC	City of Westminster Archives Centre, London
CKS	Centre for Kentish Studies, Maidstone
CLRO	Corporation of London Records Office
Coll. Arms	College of Arms, London
Col. U.	Columbia University, New York
Cornwall RO	Cornwall Record Office, Truro
Courtauld Inst.	Courtauld Institute of Art, London
CUL	Cambridge University Library
Cumbria AS	Cumbria Archive Service
Derbys. RO	Derbyshire Record Office, Matlock
Devon RO	Devon Record Office, Exeter
Dorset RO	Dorset Record Office, Dorchester
Duke U.	Duke University, Durham, North Carolina
Duke U., Perkins L.	Duke University, Durham, North Carolina, William R. Perkins Library
Durham Cath. CL	Durham Cathedral, chapter library
Durham RO	Durham Record Office
DWL	Dr Williams's Library, London
Essex RO	Essex Record Office
E. Sussex RO	East Sussex Record Office, Lewes
Eton	Eton College, Berkshire
FM Cam.	Fitzwilliam Museum, Cambridge
Folger	Folger Shakespeare Library, Washington, DC
Garr. Club	Garrick Club, London
Girton Cam.	Girton College, Cambridge
GL	Guildhall Library, London
Glos. RO	Gloucestershire Record Office, Gloucester
Gon. & Caius Cam.	Gonville and Caius College, Cambridge
Gov. Art Coll.	Government Art Collection
GS Lond.	Geological Society of London
Hants. RO	Hampshire Record Office, Winchester
Harris Man. Oxf.	Harris Manchester College, Oxford
Harvard TC	Harvard Theatre Collection, Harvard University, Cambridge, Massachusetts, Nathan Marsh Pusey Library
Harvard U.	Harvard University, Cambridge, Massachusetts
Harvard U., Houghton L.	Harvard University, Cambridge, Massachusetts, Houghton Library
Herefs. RO	Herefordshire Record Office, Hereford
Herts. ALS	Hertfordshire Archives and Local Studies, Hertford
Hist. Soc. Penn.	Historical Society of Pennsylvania, Philadelphia
HLRO	House of Lords Record Office, London
Hult. Arch.	Hulton Archive, London and New York
Hunt. L.	Huntington Library, San Marino, California
ICL	Imperial College, London
Inst. CE	Institution of Civil Engineers, London
Inst. EE	Institution of Electrical Engineers, London
IWM	Imperial War Museum, London
IWM FVA	Imperial War Museum, London, Film and Video Archive
IWM SA	Imperial War Museum, London, Sound Archive
JRL	John Rylands University Library of Manchester
King's AC Cam.	King's College Archives Centre, Cambridge
King's Cam.	King's College, Cambridge
King's Lond.	King's College, London
King's Lond., Liddell Hart C.	King's College, London, Liddell Hart Centre for Military Archives
Lancs. RO	Lancashire Record Office, Preston
L. Cong.	Library of Congress, Washington, DC
Leics. RO	Leicestershire, Leicester, and Rutland Record Office, Leicester
Lincs. Arch.	Lincolnshire Archives, Lincoln
Linn. Soc.	Linnean Society of London
LMA	London Metropolitan Archives
LPL	Lambeth Palace, London
Lpool RO	Liverpool Record Office and Local Studies Service
LUL	London University Library
Magd. Cam.	Magdalene College, Cambridge
Magd. Oxf.	Magdalen College, Oxford
Man. City Gall.	Manchester City Galleries
Man. CL	Manchester Central Library
Mass. Hist. Soc.	Massachusetts Historical Society, Boston
Merton Oxf.	Merton College, Oxford
MHS Oxf.	Museum of the History of Science, Oxford
Mitchell L., Glas.	Mitchell Library, Glasgow
Mitchell L., NSW	State Library of New South Wales, Sydney, Mitchell Library
Morgan L.	Pierpont Morgan Library, New York
NA Canada	National Archives of Canada, Ottawa
NA Ire.	National Archives of Ireland, Dublin
NAM	National Army Museum, London
NA Scot.	National Archives of Scotland, Edinburgh
News Int. RO	News International Record Office, London
NG Ire.	National Gallery of Ireland, Dublin

NG Scot.	National Gallery of Scotland, Edinburgh
NHM	Natural History Museum, London
NL Aus.	National Library of Australia, Canberra
NL Ire.	National Library of Ireland, Dublin
NL NZ	National Library of New Zealand, Wellington
NL NZ, Turnbull L.	National Library of New Zealand, Wellington, Alexander Turnbull Library
NL Scot.	National Library of Scotland, Edinburgh
NL Wales	National Library of Wales, Aberystwyth
NMG Wales	National Museum and Gallery of Wales, Cardiff
NMM	National Maritime Museum, London
Norfolk RO	Norfolk Record Office, Norwich
Northants. RO	Northamptonshire Record Office, Northampton
Northumbd RO	Northumberland Record Office
Notts. Arch.	Nottinghamshire Archives, Nottingham
NPG	National Portrait Gallery, London
NRA	National Archives, London, Historical Manuscripts Commission, National Register of Archives
Nuffield Oxf.	Nuffield College, Oxford
N. Yorks. CRO	North Yorkshire County Record Office, Northallerton
NYPL	New York Public Library
Oxf. UA	Oxford University Archives
Oxf. U. Mus. NH	Oxford University Museum of Natural History
Oxon. RO	Oxfordshire Record Office, Oxford
Pembroke Cam.	Pembroke College, Cambridge
PRO	National Archives, London, Public Record Office
PRO NIre.	Public Record Office for Northern Ireland, Belfast
Pusey Oxf.	Pusey House, Oxford
RA	Royal Academy of Arts, London
Ransom HRC	Harry Ransom Humanities Research Center, University of Texas, Austin
RAS	Royal Astronomical Society, London
RBG Kew	Royal Botanic Gardens, Kew, London
RCP Lond.	Royal College of Physicians of London
RCS Eng.	Royal College of Surgeons of England, London
RGS	Royal Geographical Society, London
RIBA	Royal Institute of British Architects, London
RIBA BAL	Royal Institute of British Architects, London, British Architectural Library
Royal Arch.	Royal Archives, Windsor Castle, Berkshire [by gracious permission of her majesty the queen]
Royal Irish Acad.	Royal Irish Academy, Dublin
Royal Scot. Acad.	Royal Scottish Academy, Edinburgh
RS	Royal Society, London
RSA	Royal Society of Arts, London
RS Friends, Lond.	Religious Society of Friends, London
St Ant. Oxf.	St Antony's College, Oxford
St John Cam.	St John's College, Cambridge
S. Antiquaries, Lond.	Society of Antiquaries of London
Sci. Mus.	Science Museum, London
Scot. NPG	Scottish National Portrait Gallery, Edinburgh
Scott Polar RI	University of Cambridge, Scott Polar Research Institute
Sheff. Arch.	Sheffield Archives
Shrops. RRC	Shropshire Records and Research Centre, Shrewsbury
SOAS	School of Oriental and African Studies, London
Som. ARS	Somerset Archive and Record Service, Taunton
Staffs. RO	Staffordshire Record Office, Stafford
Suffolk RO	Suffolk Record Office
Surrey HC	Surrey History Centre, Woking
TCD	Trinity College, Dublin
Trinity Cam.	Trinity College, Cambridge
U. Aberdeen	University of Aberdeen
U. Birm.	University of Birmingham
U. Birm. L.	University of Birmingham Library
U. Cal.	University of California
U. Cam.	University of Cambridge
UCL	University College, London
U. Durham	University of Durham
U. Durham L.	University of Durham Library
U. Edin.	University of Edinburgh
U. Edin., New Coll.	University of Edinburgh, New College
U. Edin., New Coll. L.	University of Edinburgh, New College Library
U. Edin. L.	University of Edinburgh Library
U. Glas.	University of Glasgow
U. Glas. L.	University of Glasgow Library
U. Hull	University of Hull
U. Hull, Brynmor Jones L.	University of Hull, Brynmor Jones Library
U. Leeds	University of Leeds
U. Leeds, Brotherton L.	University of Leeds, Brotherton Library
U. Lond.	University of London
U. Lpool	University of Liverpool
U. Lpool L.	University of Liverpool Library
U. Mich.	University of Michigan, Ann Arbor
U. Mich., Clements L.	University of Michigan, Ann Arbor, William L. Clements Library
U. Newcastle	University of Newcastle upon Tyne
U. Newcastle, Robinson L.	University of Newcastle upon Tyne, Robinson Library
U. Nott.	University of Nottingham
U. Nott. L.	University of Nottingham Library
U. Oxf.	University of Oxford
U. Reading	University of Reading
U. Reading L.	University of Reading Library
U. St Andr.	University of St Andrews
U. St Andr. L.	University of St Andrews Library
U. Southampton	University of Southampton
U. Southampton L.	University of Southampton Library
U. Sussex	University of Sussex, Brighton
U. Texas	University of Texas, Austin
U. Wales	University of Wales
U. Warwick Mod. RC	University of Warwick, Coventry, Modern Records Centre
V&A	Victoria and Albert Museum, London
V&A NAL	Victoria and Albert Museum, London, National Art Library
Warks. CRO	Warwickshire County Record Office, Warwick
Wellcome L.	Wellcome Library for the History and Understanding of Medicine, London
Westm. DA	Westminster Diocesan Archives, London
Wilts. & Swindon RO	Wiltshire and Swindon Record Office, Trowbridge
Worcs. RO	Worcestershire Record Office, Worcester
W. Sussex RO	West Sussex Record Office, Chichester
W. Yorks. AS	West Yorkshire Archive Service
Yale U.	Yale University, New Haven, Connecticut
Yale U., Beinecke L.	Yale University, New Haven, Connecticut, Beinecke Rare Book and Manuscript Library
Yale U. CBA	Yale University, New Haven, Connecticut, Yale Center for British Art

3 *Bibliographic abbreviations*

Adams, *Drama* — W. D. Adams, *A dictionary of the drama*, 1: *A–G* (1904); 2: *H–Z* (1956) [vol. 2 microfilm only]

AFM — J O'Donovan, ed. and trans., *Annala rioghachta Eireann / Annals of the kingdom of Ireland by the four masters*, 7 vols. (1848–51); 2nd edn (1856); 3rd edn (1990)

Allibone, *Dict.* — S. A. Allibone, *A critical dictionary of English literature and British and American authors*, 3 vols. (1859–71); suppl. by J. F. Kirk, 2 vols. (1891)

ANB — J. A. Garraty and M. C. Carnes, eds., *American national biography*, 24 vols. (1999)

Anderson, *Scot. nat.* — W. Anderson, *The Scottish nation, or, The surnames, families, literature, honours, and biographical history of the people of Scotland*, 3 vols. (1859–63)

Ann. mon. — H. R. Luard, ed., *Annales monastici*, 5 vols., Rolls Series, 36 (1864–9)

Ann. Ulster — S. Mac Airt and G. Mac Niocaill, eds., *Annals of Ulster (to AD 1131)* (1983)

APC — *Acts of the privy council of England*, new ser., 46 vols. (1890–1964)

APS — *The acts of the parliaments of Scotland*, 12 vols. in 13 (1814–75)

Arber, *Regs. Stationers* — F. Arber, ed., *A transcript of the registers of the Company of Stationers of London, 1554–1640 AD*, 5 vols. (1875–94)

ArchR — *Architectural Review*

ASC — D. Whitelock, D. C. Douglas, and S. I. Tucker, ed. and trans., *The Anglo-Saxon Chronicle: a revised translation* (1961)

AS chart. — P. H. Sawyer, *Anglo-Saxon charters: an annotated list and bibliography*, Royal Historical Society Guides and Handbooks (1968)

AusDB — D. Pike and others, eds., *Australian dictionary of biography*, 16 vols. (1966–2002)

Baker, *Serjeants* — J. H. Baker, *The order of serjeants at law*, SeldS, suppl. ser., 5 (1984)

Bale, *Cat.* — J. Bale, *Scriptorum illustrium Maioris Brytannie, quam nunc Angliam et Scotiam vocant: catalogus*, 2 vols. in 1 (Basel, 1557–9); facs. edn (1971)

Bale, *Index* — J. Bale, *Index Britanniae scriptorum*, ed. R. L. Poole and M. Bateson (1902); facs. edn (1990)

BBCS — *Bulletin of the Board of Celtic Studies*

BDMBR — J. O. Baylen and N. J. Gossman, eds., *Biographical dictionary of modern British radicals*, 3 vols. in 4 (1979–88)

Bede, *Hist. eccl.* — *Bede's Ecclesiastical history of the English people*, ed. and trans. B. Colgrave and R. A. B. Mynors, OMT (1969); repr. (1991)

Bénézit, *Dict.* — E. Bénézit, *Dictionnaire critique et documentaire des peintres, sculpteurs, dessinateurs et graveurs*, 3 vols. (Paris, 1911–23); new edn, 8 vols. (1948–66), repr. (1966); 3rd edn, rev. and enl., 10 vols. (1976); 4th edn, 14 vols. (1999)

BIHR — *Bulletin of the Institute of Historical Research*

Birch, *Seals* — W. de Birch, *Catalogue of seals in the department of manuscripts in the British Museum*, 6 vols. (1887–1900)

Bishop Burnet's History — *Bishop Burnet's History of his own time*, ed. M. J. Routh, 2nd edn, 6 vols. (1833)

Blackwood — *Blackwood's [Edinburgh] Magazine*, 328 vols. (1817–1980)

Blain, Clements & Grundy, *Feminist comp.* — V. Blain, P. Clements, and I. Grundy, eds., *The feminist companion to literature in English* (1990)

BL cat. — *The British Library general catalogue of printed books* [in 360 vols. with suppls., also CD-ROM and online]

BMJ — *British Medical Journal*

Boase & Courtney, *Bibl. Corn.* — G. C. Boase and W. P. Courtney, *Bibliotheca Cornubiensis: a catalogue of the writings … of Cornishmen*, 3 vols. (1874–82)

Boase, *Mod. Eng. biog.* — F. Boase, *Modern English biography: containing many thousand concise memoirs of persons who have died since the year 1850*, 6 vols. (privately printed, Truro, 1892–1921); repr. (1965)

Boswell, *Life* — *Boswell's Life of Johnson: together with Journal of a tour to the Hebrides and Johnson's Diary of a journey into north Wales*, ed. G. B. Hill, enl. edn, rev. L. F. Powell, 6 vols. (1934–50); 2nd edn (1964); repr. (1971)

Brown & Stratton, *Brit. mus.* — J. D. Brown and S. S. Stratton, *British musical biography* (1897)

Bryan, *Painters* — M. Bryan, *A biographical and critical dictionary of painters and engravers*, 2 vols. (1816); new edn, ed. G. Stanley (1849); new edn, ed. R. E. Graves and W. Armstrong, 2 vols. (1886–9); [4th edn], ed. G. C. Williamson, 5 vols. (1903–5) [various reprs.]

Burke, *Gen. GB* — J. Burke, *A genealogical and heraldic history of the commoners of Great Britain and Ireland*, 4 vols. (1833–8); new edn as *A genealogical and heraldic dictionary of the landed gentry of Great Britain and Ireland*, 3 vols. [1843–9] [many later edns]

Burke, *Gen. Ire.* — J. B. Burke, *A genealogical and heraldic history of the landed gentry of Ireland* (1899); 2nd edn (1904); 3rd edn (1912); 4th edn (1958); 5th edn as *Burke's Irish family records* (1976)

Burke, *Peerage* — J. Burke, *A general* [later edns *A genealogical*] *and heraldic dictionary of the peerage and baronetage of the United Kingdom* [later edns *the British empire*] (1829–)

Burney, *Hist. mus.* — C. Burney, *A general history of music, from the earliest ages to the present period*, 4 vols. (1776–89)

Burtchaell & Sadleir, *Alum. Dubl.* — G. D. Burtchaell and T. U. Sadleir, *Alumni Dublinenses: a register of the students, graduates, and provosts of Trinity College* (1924); [2nd edn], with suppl., in 2 pts (1935)

Calamy rev. — A. G. Matthews, *Calamy revised* (1934); repr. (1988)

CCI — *Calendar of confirmations and inventories granted and given up in the several commissariots of Scotland* (1876–)

CClR — *Calendar of the close rolls preserved in the Public Record Office*, 47 vols. (1892–1963)

CDS — J. Bain, ed., *Calendar of documents relating to Scotland*, 4 vols., PRO (1881–8); suppl. vol. 5, ed. G. G. Simpson and J. D. Galbraith [1986]

CEPR letters — W. H. Bliss, C. Johnson, and J. Twemlow, eds., *Calendar of entries in the papal registers relating to Great Britain and Ireland: papal letters* (1893–)

CGPLA — *Calendars of the grants of probate and letters of administration* [in 4 ser.: *England & Wales*, *Northern Ireland*, *Ireland*, and *Éire*]

Chambers, *Scots.* — R. Chambers, ed., *A biographical dictionary of eminent Scotsmen*, 4 vols. (1832–5)

Chancery records — chancery records pubd by the PRO

Chancery records (RC) — chancery records pubd by the Record Commissions

CIPM	*Calendar of inquisitions post mortem*, [20 vols.], PRO (1904–); also *Henry VII*, 3 vols. (1898–1955)
Clarendon, *Hist. rebellion*	E. Hyde, earl of Clarendon, *The history of the rebellion and civil wars in England*, 6 vols. (1888); repr. (1958) and (1992)
Cobbett, *Parl. hist.*	W. Cobbett and J. Wright, eds., *Cobbett's Parliamentary history of England*, 36 vols. (1806–1820)
Colvin, *Archs.*	H. Colvin, *A biographical dictionary of British architects, 1600–1840*, 3rd edn (1995)
Cooper, *Ath. Cantab.*	C. H. Cooper and T. Cooper, *Athenae Cantabrigienses*, 3 vols. (1858–1913); repr. (1967)
CPR	*Calendar of the patent rolls preserved in the Public Record Office* (1891–)
Crockford	*Crockford's Clerical Directory*
CS	Camden Society
CSP	*Calendar of state papers* [in 11 ser.: *domestic*, *Scotland*, *Scottish series*, *Ireland*, *colonial*, *Commonwealth*, *foreign*, *Spain* [at Simancas], *Rome*, *Milan*, and *Venice*]
CYS	Canterbury and York Society
DAB	*Dictionary of American biography*, 21 vols. (1928–36), repr. in 11 vols. (1964); 10 suppls. (1944–96)
DBB	D. J. Jeremy, ed., *Dictionary of business biography*, 5 vols. (1984–6)
DCB	G. W. Brown and others, *Dictionary of Canadian biography*, [14 vols.] (1966–)
Debrett's Peerage	*Debrett's Peerage* (1803–) [sometimes *Debrett's Illustrated peerage*]
Desmond, *Botanists*	R. Desmond, *Dictionary of British and Irish botanists and horticulturists* (1977); rev. edn (1994)
Dir. Brit. archs.	A. Felstead, J. Franklin, and L. Pinfield, eds., *Directory of British architects, 1834–1900* (1993); 2nd edn, ed. A. Brodie and others, 2 vols. (2001)
DLB	J. M. Bellamy and J. Saville, eds., *Dictionary of labour biography*, [10 vols.] (1972–)
DLitB	Dictionary of Literary Biography
DNB	*Dictionary of national biography*, 63 vols. (1885–1900), suppl., 3 vols. (1901); repr. in 22 vols. (1908–9); 10 further suppls. (1912–96); *Missing persons* (1993)
DNZB	W. H. Oliver and C. Orange, eds., *The dictionary of New Zealand biography*, 5 vols. (1990–2000)
DSAB	W. J. de Kock and others, eds., *Dictionary of South African biography*, 5 vols. (1968–87)
DSB	C. C. Gillispie and F. L. Holmes, eds., *Dictionary of scientific biography*, 16 vols. (1970–80); repr. in 8 vols. (1981); 2 vol. suppl. (1990)
DSBB	A. Slaven and S. Checkland, eds., *Dictionary of Scottish business biography, 1860–1960*, 2 vols. (1986–90)
DSCHT	N. M. de S. Cameron and others, eds., *Dictionary of Scottish church history and theology* (1993)
Dugdale, *Monasticon*	W. Dugdale, *Monasticon Anglicanum*, 3 vols. (1655–72); 2nd edn, 3 vols. (1661–82); new edn, ed. J. Caley, J. Ellis, and B. Bandinel, 6 vols. in 8 pts (1817–30); repr. (1846) and (1970)
DWB	J. E. Lloyd and others, eds., *Dictionary of Welsh biography down to 1940* (1959) [Eng. trans. of *Y bywgraffiadur Cymreig hyd 1940*, 2nd edn (1954)]
EdinR	*Edinburgh Review, or, Critical Journal*
EETS	Early English Text Society
Emden, *Cam.*	A. B. Emden, *A biographical register of the University of Cambridge to 1500* (1963)
Emden, *Oxf.*	A. B. Emden, *A biographical register of the University of Oxford to AD 1500*, 3 vols. (1957–9); also *A biographical register of the University of Oxford, AD 1501 to 1540* (1974)
EngHR	*English Historical Review*
Engraved Brit. ports.	F. M. O'Donoghue and H. M. Hake, *Catalogue of engraved British portraits preserved in the department of prints and drawings in the British Museum*, 6 vols. (1908–25)
ER	The English Reports, 178 vols. (1900–32)
ESTC	*English short title catalogue, 1475–1800* [CD-ROM and online]
Evelyn, *Diary*	*The diary of John Evelyn*, ed. E. S. De Beer, 6 vols. (1955); repr. (2000)
Farington, *Diary*	*The diary of Joseph Farington*, ed. K. Garlick and others, 17 vols. (1978–98)
Fasti Angl. (Hardy)	J. Le Neve, *Fasti ecclesiae Anglicanae*, ed. T. D. Hardy, 3 vols. (1854)
Fasti Angl., 1066–1300	[J. Le Neve], *Fasti ecclesiae Anglicanae, 1066–1300*, ed. D. E. Greenway and J. S. Barrow, [8 vols.] (1968–)
Fasti Angl., 1300–1541	[J. Le Neve], *Fasti ecclesiae Anglicanae, 1300–1541*, 12 vols. (1962–7)
Fasti Angl., 1541–1857	[J. Le Neve], *Fasti ecclesiae Anglicanae, 1541–1857*, ed. J. M. Horn, D. M. Smith, and D. S. Bailey, [9 vols.] (1969–)
Fasti Scot.	H. Scott, *Fasti ecclesiae Scoticanae*, 3 vols. in 6 (1871); new edn, [11 vols.] (1915–)
FO List	*Foreign Office List*
Fortescue, *Brit. army*	J. W. Fortescue, *A history of the British army*, 13 vols. (1899–1930)
Foss, *Judges*	E. Foss, *The judges of England*, 9 vols. (1848–64); repr. (1966)
Foster, *Alum. Oxon.*	J. Foster, ed., *Alumni Oxonienses: the members of the University of Oxford, 1715–1886*, 4 vols. (1887–8); later edn (1891); also *Alumni Oxonienses … 1500–1714*, 4 vols. (1891–2); 8 vol. repr. (1968) and (2000)
Fuller, *Worthies*	T. Fuller, *The history of the worthies of England*, 4 pts (1662); new edn, 2 vols., ed. J. Nichols (1811); new edn, 3 vols., ed. P. A. Nuttall (1840); repr. (1965)
GEC, *Baronetage*	G. E. Cokayne, *Complete baronetage*, 6 vols. (1900–09); repr. (1983) [microprint]
GEC, *Peerage*	G. E. C. [G. E. Cokayne], *The complete peerage of England, Scotland, Ireland, Great Britain, and the United Kingdom*, 8 vols. (1887–98); new edn, ed. V. Gibbs and others, 14 vols. in 15 (1910–98); microprint repr. (1982) and (1987)
Genest, *Eng. stage*	J. Genest, *Some account of the English stage from the Restoration in 1660 to 1830*, 10 vols. (1832); repr. [New York, 1965]
Gillow, *Lit. biog. hist.*	J. Gillow, *A literary and biographical history or bibliographical dictionary of the English Catholics, from the breach with Rome, in 1534, to the present time*, 5 vols. [1885–1902]; repr. (1961); repr. with preface by C. Gillow (1999)
Gir. Camb. opera	*Giraldi Cambrensis opera*, ed. J. S. Brewer, J. F. Dimock, and G. F. Warner, 8 vols., Rolls Series, 21 (1861–91)
GJ	*Geographical Journal*

Gladstone, *Diaries*	*The Gladstone diaries: with cabinet minutes and prime-ministerial correspondence*, ed. M. R. D. Foot and H. C. G. Matthew, 14 vols. (1968–94)
GM	*Gentleman's Magazine*
Graves, *Artists*	A. Graves, ed., *A dictionary of artists who have exhibited works in the principal London exhibitions of oil paintings from 1760 to 1880* (1884); new edn (1895); 3rd edn (1901); facs. edn (1969); repr. [1970], (1973), and (1984)
Graves, *Brit. Inst.*	A. Graves, *The British Institution, 1806–1867: a complete dictionary of contributors and their work from the foundation of the institution* (1875); facs. edn (1908); repr. (1969)
Graves, *RA exhibitors*	A. Graves, *The Royal Academy of Arts: a complete dictionary of contributors and their work from its foundation in 1769 to 1904*, 8 vols. (1905–6); repr. in 4 vols. (1970) and (1972)
Graves, *Soc. Artists*	A. Graves, *The Society of Artists of Great Britain, 1760–1791, the Free Society of Artists, 1761–1783: a complete dictionary* (1907); facs. edn (1969)
Greaves & Zaller, *BDBR*	R. L. Greaves and R. Zaller, eds., *Biographical dictionary of British radicals in the seventeenth century*, 3 vols. (1982–4)
Grove, *Dict. mus.*	G. Grove, ed., *A dictionary of music and musicians*, 5 vols. (1878–90); 2nd edn, ed. J. A. Fuller Maitland (1904–10); 3rd edn, ed. H. C. Colles (1927); 4th edn with suppl. (1940); 5th edn, ed. E. Blom, 9 vols. (1954); suppl. (1961) [see also *New Grove*]
Hall, *Dramatic ports.*	L. A. Hall, *Catalogue of dramatic portraits in the theatre collection of the Harvard College library*, 4 vols. (1930–34)
Hansard	*Hansard's parliamentary debates*, ser. 1–5 (1803–)
Highfill, Burnim & Langhans, *BDA*	P. H. Highfill, K. A. Burnim, and E. A. Langhans, *A biographical dictionary of actors, actresses, musicians, dancers, managers, and other stage personnel in London, 1660–1800*, 16 vols. (1973–93)
Hist. U. Oxf.	T. H. Aston, ed., *The history of the University of Oxford*, 8 vols. (1984–2000) [1: *The early Oxford schools*, ed. J. I. Catto (1984); 2: *Late medieval Oxford*, ed. J. I. Catto and R. Evans (1992); 3: *The collegiate university*, ed. J. McConica (1986); 4: *Seventeenth-century Oxford*, ed. N. Tyacke (1997); 5: *The eighteenth century*, ed. L. S. Sutherland and L. G. Mitchell (1986); 6–7: *Nineteenth-century Oxford*, ed. M. G. Brock and M. C. Curthoys (1997–2000); 8: *The twentieth century*, ed. B. Harrison (2000)]
HJ	*Historical Journal*
HMC	Historical Manuscripts Commission
Holdsworth, *Eng. law*	W. S. Holdsworth, *A history of English law*, ed. A. L. Goodhart and H. L. Hanbury, 17 vols. (1903–72)
HoP, *Commons*	*The history of parliament: the House of Commons* [*1386–1421*, ed. J. S. Roskell, L. Clark, and C. Rawcliffe, 4 vols. (1992); *1509–1558*, ed. S. T. Bindoff, 3 vols. (1982); *1558–1603*, ed. P. W. Hasler, 3 vols. (1981); *1660–1690*, ed. B. D. Henning, 3 vols. (1983); *1690–1715*, ed. D. W. Hayton, E. Cruickshanks, and S. Handley, 5 vols. (2002); *1715–1754*, ed. R. Sedgwick, 2 vols. (1970); *1754–1790*, ed. L. Namier and J. Brooke, 3 vols. (1964), repr. (1985); *1790–1820*, ed. R. G. Thorne, 5 vols. (1986); in draft (used with permission): *1422–1504*, *1604–1629*, *1640–1660*, and *1820–1832*]
IGI	*International Genealogical Index*, Church of Jesus Christ of the Latterday Saints
ILN	*Illustrated London News*
IMC	Irish Manuscripts Commission
Irving, *Scots.*	J. Irving, ed., *The book of Scotsmen eminent for achievements in arms and arts, church and state, law, legislation and literature, commerce, science, travel and philanthropy* (1881)
JCS	*Journal of the Chemical Society*
JHC	*Journals of the House of Commons*
JHL	*Journals of the House of Lords*
John of Worcester, *Chron.*	*The chronicle of John of Worcester*, ed. R. R. Darlington and P. McGurk, trans. J. Bray and P. McGurk, 3 vols., OMT (1995–) [vol. 1 forthcoming]
Keeler, *Long Parliament*	M. F. Keeler, *The Long Parliament, 1640–1641: a biographical study of its members* (1954)
Kelly, *Handbk*	*The upper ten thousand: an alphabetical list of all members of noble families*, 3 vols. (1875–7); continued as *Kelly's handbook of the upper ten thousand for 1878* [1879], 2 vols. (1878–9); continued as *Kelly's handbook to the titled, landed and official classes*, 94 vols. (1880–1973)
LondG	*London Gazette*
LP Henry VIII	J. S. Brewer, J. Gairdner, and R. H. Brodie, eds., *Letters and papers, foreign and domestic, of the reign of Henry VIII*, 23 vols. in 38 (1862–1932); repr. (1965)
Mallalieu, *Watercolour artists*	H. L. Mallalieu, *The dictionary of British watercolour artists up to 1820*, 3 vols. (1976–90); vol. 1, 2nd edn (1986)
Memoirs FRS	*Biographical Memoirs of Fellows of the Royal Society*
MGH	Monumenta Germaniae Historica
MT	*Musical Times*
Munk, *Roll*	W. Munk, *The roll of the Royal College of Physicians of London*, 2 vols. (1861); 2nd edn, 3 vols. (1878)
N&Q	*Notes and Queries*
New Grove	S. Sadie, ed., *The new Grove dictionary of music and musicians*, 20 vols. (1980); 2nd edn, 29 vols. (2001) [also online edn; see also Grove, *Dict. mus.*]
Nichols, *Illustrations*	J. Nichols and J. B. Nichols, *Illustrations of the literary history of the eighteenth century*, 8 vols. (1817–58)
Nichols, *Lit. anecdotes*	J. Nichols, *Literary anecdotes of the eighteenth century*, 9 vols. (1812–16); facs. edn (1966)
Obits. FRS	*Obituary Notices of Fellows of the Royal Society*
O'Byrne, *Naval biog. dict.*	W. R. O'Byrne, *A naval biographical dictionary* (1849); repr. (1990); [2nd edn], 2 vols. (1861)
OHS	Oxford Historical Society
Old Westminsters	*The record of Old Westminsters*, 1–2, ed. G. F. R. Barker and A. H. Stenning (1928); suppl. 1, ed. J. B. Whitmore and G. R. Y. Radcliffe [1938]; 3, ed. J. B. Whitmore, G. R. Y. Radcliffe, and D. C. Simpson (1963); suppl. 2, ed. F. E. Pagan (1978); 4, ed. F. E. Pagan and H. E. Pagan (1992)
OMT	Oxford Medieval Texts
Ordericus Vitalis, *Eccl. hist.*	*The ecclesiastical history of Orderic Vitalis*, ed. and trans. M. Chibnall, 6 vols., OMT (1969–80); repr. (1990)
Paris, *Chron.*	*Matthaei Parisiensis, monachi sancti Albani, chronica majora*, ed. H. R. Luard, Rolls Series, 7 vols. (1872–83)
Parl. papers	*Parliamentary papers* (1801–)
PBA	*Proceedings of the British Academy*

Pepys, *Diary*	*The diary of Samuel Pepys*, ed. R. Latham and W. Matthews, 11 vols. (1970–83); repr. (1995) and (2000)
Pevsner	N. Pevsner and others, Buildings of England series
PICE	*Proceedings of the Institution of Civil Engineers*
Pipe rolls	*The great roll of the pipe for* . . ., PRSoc. (1884–)
PRO	Public Record Office
PRS	*Proceedings of the Royal Society of London*
PRSoc.	Pipe Roll Society
PTRS	*Philosophical Transactions of the Royal Society*
QR	*Quarterly Review*
RC	Record Commissions
Redgrave, *Artists*	S. Redgrave, *A dictionary of artists of the English school* (1874); rev. edn (1878); repr. (1970)
Reg. Oxf.	C. W. Boase and A. Clark, eds., *Register of the University of Oxford*, 5 vols., OHS, 1, 10–12, 14 (1885–9)
Reg. PCS	J. H. Burton and others, eds., *The register of the privy council of Scotland*, 1st ser., 14 vols. (1877–98); 2nd ser., 8 vols. (1899–1908); 3rd ser., [16 vols.] (1908–70)
Reg. RAN	H. W. C. Davis and others, eds., *Regesta regum Anglo-Normannorum, 1066–1154*, 4 vols. (1913–69)
RIBA Journal	*Journal of the Royal Institute of British Architects* [later *RIBA Journal*]
RotP	J. Strachey, ed., *Rotuli parliamentorum ut et petitiones, et placita in parliamento*, 6 vols. (1767–77)
RotS	D. Macpherson, J. Caley, and W. Illingworth, eds., *Rotuli Scotiae in Turri Londinensi et in domo capitulari Westmonasteriensi asservati*, 2 vols., RC, 14 (1814–19)
RS	Record(s) Society
Rymer, *Foedera*	T. Rymer and R. Sanderson, eds., *Foedera, conventiones, literae et cuiuscunque generis acta publica inter reges Angliae et alios quosvis imperatores, reges, pontifices, principes, vel communitates*, 20 vols. (1704–35); 2nd edn, 20 vols. (1726–35); 3rd edn, 10 vols. (1739–45), facs. edn (1967); new edn, ed. A. Clarke, J. Caley, and F. Holbrooke, 4 vols., RC, 50 (1816–30)
Sainty, *Judges*	J. Sainty, ed., *The judges of England, 1272–1990*, SeldS, suppl. ser., 10 (1993)
Sainty, *King's counsel*	J. Sainty, ed., *A list of English law officers and king's counsel*, SeldS, suppl. ser., 7 (1987)
SCH	Studies in Church History
Scots peerage	J. B. Paul, ed. *The Scots peerage, founded on Wood's edition of Sir Robert Douglas's Peerage of Scotland, containing an historical and genealogical account of the nobility of that kingdom*, 9 vols. (1904–14)
SeldS	Selden Society
SHR	*Scottish Historical Review*
State trials	T. B. Howell and T. J. Howell, eds., *Cobbett's Complete collection of state trials*, 34 vols. (1809–28)
STC, 1475–1640	A. W. Pollard, G. R. Redgrave, and others, eds., *A short-title catalogue of … English books … 1475–1640* (1926); 2nd edn, ed. W. A. Jackson, F. S. Ferguson, and K. F. Pantzer, 3 vols. (1976–91) [see also Wing, *STC*]
STS	Scottish Text Society
SurtS	Surtees Society
Symeon of Durham, *Opera*	*Symeonis monachi opera omnia*, ed. T. Arnold, 2 vols., Rolls Series, 75 (1882–5); repr. (1965)
Tanner, *Bibl. Brit.-Hib.*	T. Tanner, *Bibliotheca Britannico-Hibernica*, ed. D. Wilkins (1748); repr. (1963)
Thieme & Becker, *Allgemeines Lexikon*	U. Thieme, F. Becker, and H. Vollmer, eds., *Allgemeines Lexikon der bildenden Künstler von der Antike bis zur Gegenwart*, 37 vols. (Leipzig, 1907–50); repr. (1961–5), (1983), and (1992)
Thurloe, *State papers*	*A collection of the state papers of John Thurloe*, ed. T. Birch, 7 vols. (1742)
TLS	*Times Literary Supplement*
Tout, *Admin. hist.*	T. F. Tout, *Chapters in the administrative history of mediaeval England: the wardrobe, the chamber, and the small seals*, 6 vols. (1920–33); repr. (1967)
TRHS	*Transactions of the Royal Historical Society*
VCH	H. A. Doubleday and others, eds., *The Victoria history of the counties of England*, [88 vols.] (1900–)
Venn, *Alum. Cant.*	J. Venn and J. A. Venn, *Alumni Cantabrigienses: a biographical list of all known students, graduates, and holders of office at the University of Cambridge, from the earliest times to 1900*, 10 vols. (1922–54); repr. in 2 vols. (1974–8)
Vertue, *Note books*	[G. Vertue], *Note books*, ed. K. Esdaile, earl of Ilchester, and H. M. Hake, 6 vols., Walpole Society, 18, 20, 22, 24, 26, 30 (1930–55)
VF	*Vanity Fair*
Walford, *County families*	E. Walford, *The county families of the United Kingdom, or, Royal manual of the titled and untitled aristocracy of Great Britain and Ireland* (1860)
Walker rev.	A. G. Matthews, *Walker revised: being a revision of John Walker's Sufferings of the clergy during the grand rebellion, 1642–60* (1948); repr. (1988)
Walpole, *Corr.*	*The Yale edition of Horace Walpole's correspondence*, ed. W. S. Lewis, 48 vols. (1937–83)
Ward, *Men of the reign*	T. H. Ward, ed., *Men of the reign: a biographical dictionary of eminent persons of British and colonial birth who have died during the reign of Queen Victoria* (1885); repr. (Graz, 1968)
Waterhouse, *18c painters*	E. Waterhouse, *The dictionary of 18th century painters in oils and crayons* (1981); repr. as *British 18th century painters in oils and crayons* (1991), vol. 2 of *Dictionary of British art*
Watt, *Bibl. Brit.*	R. Watt, *Bibliotheca Britannica, or, A general index to British and foreign literature*, 4 vols. (1824) [many reprs.]
Wellesley index	W. E. Houghton, ed., *The Wellesley index to Victorian periodicals, 1824–1900*, 5 vols. (1966–89); new edn (1999) [CD-ROM]
Wing, *STC*	D. Wing, ed., *Short-title catalogue of … English books … 1641–1700*, 3 vols. (1945–51); 2nd edn (1972–88); rev. and enl. edn, ed. J. J. Morrison, C. W. Nelson, and M. Seccombe, 4 vols. (1994–8) [see also *STC, 1475–1640*]
Wisden	*John Wisden's Cricketer's Almanack*
Wood, *Ath. Oxon.*	A. Wood, *Athenae Oxonienses … to which are added the Fasti*, 2 vols. (1691–2); 2nd edn (1721); new edn, 4 vols., ed. P. Bliss (1813–20); repr. (1967) and (1969)
Wood, *Vic. painters*	C. Wood, *Dictionary of Victorian painters* (1971); 2nd edn (1978); 3rd edn as *Victorian painters*, 2 vols. (1995), vol. 4 of *Dictionary of British art*
WW	*Who's who* (1849–)
WWBMP	M. Stenton and S. Lees, eds., *Who's who of British members of parliament*, 4 vols. (1976–81)
WWW	*Who was who* (1929–)

Osborne, Sir Cyril (1898–1969), politician, was born on 19 June 1898 in Hucknall Lane, Bulwell, Nottingham, the son of Thomas Osborne, a coalminer, and his wife, Ann, formerly Bonser (*née* Carnell). Brought up in what he recalled was 'a very stern puritan home' (*Hansard 5C*, 632, 12 Dec 1960, 66), he was educated at the local elementary school, began work at the age of fourteen, and undertook a variety of arduous manual jobs before enlisting as a private with the Royal Field Artillery. He served in France, Belgium, Italy, and Egypt. Thereafter, as a former serviceman, he was able to read economics at University College, Nottingham. He then became a successful businessman and stockbroker, and eventually a director of a number of textile and wholesale grocery companies. Following the death of his first wife (whose name is not known), he married on 4 December 1935 Joyce Lawrence (*b.* 1908/9), daughter of Ernest Louis Feibusch, a solicitor, of Wolverhampton. They had two sons and two daughters. During the Second World War he was a welfare adviser in the midlands and assisted the Ministry of Information. In 1945 he was elected Conservative MP for the Louth division of Lincolnshire, a seat he held until his death.

Osborne is chiefly associated with the campaign to limit immigration into Britain from the new Commonwealth. He first raised the issue in 1950, asking for separate figures for non-white immigration, and in 1952 he began a campaign for controls. While insisting that he was not racially prejudiced, he called for restrictions on entry on several grounds: the sheer volume of actual or potential immigrants; the abuse of the welfare state ('the honey pot'); overcrowding; crime, especially drug trafficking and prostitution; unemployment; and health, especially tuberculosis and leprosy. Inclined to lose his temper, and to reveal openly his wish to keep Britain white, he was sometimes an embarrassment in the Commons. Several MPs judged that his extreme, provocative manner did a disservice to the cause he was advocating.

In many ways, however, Osborne's campaign was successful. In 1958, for instance, the Conservative Party conference called for restrictions on entry, and the 1959 general election saw the return of many more MPs, including twelve from Birmingham, who wished to abandon the 'open door' policy. He distributed to delegates at the 1961 conference copies of a letter he had written to the *Daily Telegraph*, in which he urged immediate restrictions, warning that in time there would be more non-white than white people in Britain: 'We shall cease to be a European nation and become a mixed Afro-Asian society' (*Daily Telegraph*, 11 Oct 1961). Shortly afterwards R. A. Butler, the home secretary, introduced the Commonwealth Immigrants Bill into the Commons, and Osborne was dubbed by *The Times* 'the spirit, if not the architect, of the Bill' (*The Times*, 17 Nov 1961). Symbolically, it was in 1961 that he was knighted. Thereafter he maintained better relations with the party. In March 1965 he was persuaded by the shadow home secretary to moderate a motion about to be put to the Commons: instead of calling for a ban on all future immigration, except for those whose parents or grandparents had been born in Britain, he called instead for 'periodic and precise limits' to be fixed—and he was supported by the votes of the whole shadow cabinet. His demand for assisted repatriation also found its way into official Conservative policy. In many ways Osborne's views prefigured those which Enoch Powell articulated in 1968, though Osborne had none of Powell's subtlety.

Osborne was also noted for his opposition to generally progressive causes. E. M. Forster, a fellow member of the Reform Club, remembered him as always 'denouncing something' (Williams, 129). He was opposed to extending the licensing laws, to the creation of football pools and premium bonds, to the abolition of corporal punishment and of the death penalty, and to the decriminalization of homosexuality. Leo Abse judged that the driving force in him was a rigid puritanism, consequent upon an unusually repressed childhood (Abse, 148–9). Certainly he often referred to his stern Victorian upbringing. He was the only MP to oppose the pay rise which the House of Commons voted itself in 1964, and, characteristically, the politician for whom he professed the most complete admiration was Stafford Cripps. Osborne had genuine fears of a world population explosion, of economic collapse, and of decadence in the West. He was chairman of the Anglo-Soviet parliamentary group, a justice of the peace in Leicester, a governor of Leicester Royal Infirmary, and, for twenty years, chairman of the Leicester chamber of commerce. He died of natural causes at the Royal Infirmary, Leicester, on 31 August 1969, having lived in his later years at Kinchley House, Rothley, Leicestershire. His second wife survived him. ROBERT PEARCE

Sources *The Times* (1 Sept 1969) · *Hansard 5C* (1945–69) · L. Abse, *Private member* (1973) · F. Williams, *Nothing so strange* (1970) · *The Times House of Commons: 1966* (1966) · b. cert. · m. cert. [Joyce Feibusch] · d. cert.
Archives FILM BFI NFTVA, documentary footage
Likenesses photograph, repro. in *Times House of Commons*
Wealth at death £186,968: probate, 23 Dec 1969, *CGPLA Eng. & Wales*

Osborne, Dorothy [*married name* Dorothy Temple, Lady Temple] (**1627–1695**), letter writer, was the youngest daughter and tenth child of Sir Peter *Osborne (1584/5–1653) [*see under* Osborne, Peter (1521–1592)], royalist lieutenant-governor of Guernsey, and Dorothy, *née* Danvers (1590–1650/51) of Dauntsey, Wiltshire. With the outbreak of the civil war Dorothy's mother took the children from the family home of Chicksands Abbey, Bedfordshire, to stay in Chelsea, perhaps with her brother, the parliamentarian (and future regicide) Sir John Danvers. From there, about 1642 or early 1643, the family travelled to St Malo, France, to be near to their father, and Lady Osborne got into debt sending provisions to her besieged husband in Castle Cornet, Guernsey. In 1644, when Dorothy was seventeen, they finally returned to Chelsea (Chicksands had been sequestrated). Two of Dorothy's brothers were killed during the civil war: Henry at Naseby (1645); Charles at Hartland, Devon (1646).

Sir Peter held Castle Cornet until August 1646, when he

Dorothy Osborne (1627–1695), by Gaspar Netscher, 1671

was forced into retreat and exile in St Malo. Dorothy and a brother (probably Robin) set out to meet their father there. *En route* they met Sir William *Temple (1628–1699) who was just embarking on a tour of the continent. They set off for St Malo together and their lengthy courtship began. There were oppositions on both sides. In part Dorothy's father objected to her marrying the son of Sir John Temple, master of the rolls in Ireland, seen by some as willing to serve irrespective of the politics of the administration. But her father had also hoped for a more lucrative match for Dorothy to restore the family finances which had been much depleted after the heavy fines imposed by the parliamentary government. Dorothy's brother Henry (1618–1675), who was one of the small group of peers who escorted Charles II back to England, also strongly objected to the match, and kept a diary, partly in code, detailing his opposition to Temple.

Temple left for Paris about summer 1648 and was abroad for most of the following five years. He and Dorothy met briefly in London in winter 1650–51, before she was taken back to Chicksands. In December 1652 Dorothy received a letter from Temple announcing his return from the Netherlands and asking whether he owed her the £10 that he had once promised to pay her on her marriage. Their famous correspondence began with her reply: 'But for the ten pounde hee [Temple] Claimes it is not yett due, and I think you may doe well … to putt it in the Number of his desperate debts, for 'tis a very uncertaine one' (*Letters*, ed. Moore Smith, 3).

Osborne's letters to Temple record her family's opposition to their engagement, and their careful surveillance of her, mostly on Henry's part. At Chicksands she was introduced to suitor after suitor; the letters provide an itemized assessment of their shortcomings, and describe how each new one was sent on his way. The letters were smuggled out of Chicksands to Temple, who kept them in a cabinet that is still on display at Moor Park, Surrey. Only one of his letters to her survived from their courtship, the rest were destroyed as soon as she had read them.

In November 1654 Osborne suffered from a severe attack of smallpox which nearly killed her, and left her permanently scarred. One month later, on Christmas day, Dorothy and William were married before a justice of the peace according to the vows promulgated in the previous year by Barebone's Parliament. The details are recorded in the marriage register in St Giles-in-the-Fields, London. The marriage did not end her problems with her family, and in February she and Temple brought a suit against her brother in chancery for refusing to pay her portion. The dispute was settled that June.

Initially Dorothy and her husband lived with his maternal uncle, Robert Hammond, in Reading, where their first son, John, was born, on 18 December 1655. In May 1656 they moved to Ireland where they had eight or possibly nine children, six of whom died in infancy. (In 1679 their fourteen-year-old daughter Diana died of smallpox, and their son John drowned himself in April 1689.) They returned to London in 1663. From the relative penury of the early years of their marriage they found themselves in much grander surroundings when Temple was made ambassador in the Netherlands in June 1665. He was recalled in 1670, and Dorothy returned in September 1671. With her husband she later played a part in arranging the marriage of William of Orange and Mary, daughter of James, duke of York, acting as go-between, and remained her confidante until Mary's death a few months before her own. She and Temple retired to Moor Park, near Farnham, Surrey, an estate bought by Temple in 1680.

Dorothy died at Moor Park on 7 February 1695 and was buried in Westminster Abbey, the place marked by a plaque on the wall of the south aisle, and stone set in the floor. Her fame was secured by the publication of her letters—first in extracts in Courtenay's biography of her husband in 1836, and then in various editions through the nineteenth and twentieth centuries. While Temple's biographers have tended to pay tribute to her as a helpmeet, recent rereadings of the letters (held in the British Library, Add. MS 33975) emphasize Osborne's wider range. In her letters she comments on political events (the ejection of Algernon Sidney from the Commons; or the plot against Cromwell); on religious controversies (on the sermons of Stephen Marshall and William Erbury, for example; or declaring herself a 'devote' of Jeremy Taylor); and on the art of writing, as well as on her own wide range of reading (from the French romances she read in the original, to her dismissal of Margaret Cavendish's writing). Nevertheless, it is for the elegance and wit of the letters that Osborne will be remembered, and for the sparkling personality that shines through her writing. KENNETH PARKER

Sources D. Osborne, *Letters to Sir William Temple, 1652–1654*, ed. K. Parker (1987); rev. edn (2001) • *The letters of Dorothy Osborne to William Temple*, ed. G. C. Moore Smith (1928); reproduced lithographically (1947–59) • E. A. Parry, *My own way: an autobiography* (1932) • T. P. Courtenay, *Memoirs of the life, works and correspondence of Sir William Temple*, 2 vols. (1836) • H. E. Woodbridge, *William Temple: the man and his work* (1940) • D. Cecil, *Two quiet lives* (1947); repr. (1967), (1988) • K. H. D. Haley, *An English diplomat in the Low Countries: Sir William Temple and John de Witt* (1986) • V. Woolf, *The common reader: second series* (1932) • *DNB* • C. Hintz, '"Desire and renunciation": the letters of Dorothy Osborne', diss., Toronto, 1988

Archives BL, letters to Sir William Temple, Add. MS 33975

Likenesses G. Netscher, oils, 1671, NPG [*see illus.*] • P. Lely, oils, Moor Park, Surrey • P. Lely, oils, Broadlands, Hampshire

Osborne, Sir Edward (*c*.1530–1592), merchant and local politician, was one of the four children of Richard Osborne, of Ashford, Kent, and his wife, Jane, the daughter of John Broughton. Both parents probably came from minor gentry families, although Richard is described only as a yeoman in his son's apprenticeship records.

William Hewett's apprentice and heir His father's lands at Ashford passed to another son, Thomas, while Edward was apprenticed in 1544 or 1545 to William *Hewett, master of the Clothworkers' Company. Hewett was an overseas merchant whose premises included The Rose in Fish Street on the approach to London Bridge, and the story was preserved in the Hewett and Osborne families that the young apprentice made his fortune by leaping gallantly into the Thames to save his master's little daughter when a careless maid let her fall in. Between 1560 and 1562 he married Anne Hewett (1543/4–1585), by then the only child of the wealthy lord mayor. The romantic tale of the rescue and their courtship was first published in 1720 by John Strype: 'Sir William was pleased to say, Osborn saved her, and Osborn should enjoy her' (Stow, 2.v.133–4), and became the subject of a popular Victorian novel, *The Colloquies of Edward Osborne* by Anne Manning.

Hewett died in 1567, leaving the Osbornes heirs partly by settlement and partly by bequest to the greater part of his real and personal estate, although his nephew and partner Henry Hewett was left his main business premises at the Three Cranes in Candlewick Street. Anne and Edward Osborne acquired the Fish Street premises, a mansion house with adjoining buildings in Philpot Lane, The Crown in Fenchurch Street, and other London properties, as well as extensive estates in Hewett's native Yorkshire and nearby parts of Derbyshire and Nottinghamshire. The lands in the southern tip of the West Riding—at Harthill, Thorpe Salvin, Todwick, Waleswood, Woodall, and Woodsetts—and adjacent lands at Killamarsh, Derbyshire, would later form the nucleus of the Kiveton estate of the dukes of Leeds. The manor of Parsloes in Dagenham, Essex, where the Osbornes built themselves a country house, was not (as often stated) inherited from Hewett, but bought several years after his death from another master of the Clothworkers' Company, Sir Rowland Hayward, and Thomas Wilbraham.

City politics Osborne had become a freeman of the Clothworkers' Company in 1553, a week after Queen Mary's accession. He then disappears from the record for the rest of her reign. He took his own first apprentice in 1559, was admitted to the livery in 1560, and was elected steward in 1562 and a warden in 1565 and 1569, but rather surprisingly never went on to serve as master, although he remained closely associated with the company and left money for a memorial dinner to be held there after his death. Instead he sought city office, and served as alderman for Castle Baynard ward (1573–6) and Candlewick ward (from 1576), sheriff (1575–6), and lord mayor (1583–4; he was knighted on 2 February 1584). He was also MP for London in the parliament of 1586, where the only record of his activity is as a member of the committee attending the queen to present reasons for executing Mary, queen of Scots. From 1586 until his death he was president of St Thomas's Hospital (having been treasurer in 1571–3), and from 1590 surveyor-general of hospitals. From 1587 he was a commissioner of sewers for the River Lea.

Osborne was also called on by the privy council to arbitrate in disputes concerning the wholesale cloth trade, maritime insurance, foreign contracts, patent infringements, and the mining industry (he had his own coal pit in Yorkshire). He was evidently regarded as a fair-minded man, in spite of occasional accusations of sharp practice. In 1566 he was indicted in the court of exchequer, together with a broker married to Lady Hewett's sister, for fraudulent conveyancing designed to circumvent the laws against usury, but the case was dismissed for lack of evidence. After this he was careful only to lend at interest if repayment was in another currency, when it was legitimate to charge a fee for money-changing. This made him unpopular with acquaintances such as the earl of Shrewsbury and his family, who expected an interest-free loan of ready money and were offered instead an expensive bill of exchange payable in Antwerp. And even internationally agreed loans could give rise to prolonged disputes, as Osborne and other lenders discovered when a debt incurred in 1561–2 by the Swedish ambassador Guildenstern was later disowned by the Swedish king's usurping brother.

It was probably characteristic that Osborne made interest-free loans to close relatives but recorded them all in a ledger. At his death he subtracted from their legacies the small sums owed by his two brothers, his brother-in-law, and a cousin. Humane views, however, emerge in connection with the education of his sons. Both were sent to learn Latin and Greek at the boarding-school kept by Elias Newcomen and went on to Cambridge and the Inner Temple. In a testimonial written in 1586 for Newcomen when he applied for a post at Merchant Taylors' School, Osborne not only praised the schoolmaster's 'skill and longe Experience in teachinge', his being of a sincere religion, 'a thinge in a teacher muche to be respected', and his daily catechism of the children in the same, but also 'the great Lenitie and gentlenes which he useth towardes his schollers' (Merchant Taylors' Company, court minutes, vol. 3, fol. 149). Osborne's closest personal friend was not another businessman but the deputy recorder of London, William Daniell, a man with a reputation for learning and wisdom who was later knighted and made a justice of the common pleas.

Trading activities It was as a merchant, however, that Osborne made his own reputation. The first surviving record of his trading activities is in 1559, when he exported thirteen unfinished cloths to Antwerp. He must therefore have belonged then to the Company of Merchant Adventurers, but he had ceased to be actively involved by the time they were incorporated in 1564 and fell out with the Clothworkers' Company in 1565–6. Instead he became a pioneer in sending to more distant outlets cloths and kerseys which had been dyed and dressed in England. The port books show that from 1567 to 1577 he exported these mainly to Spain and Portugal, importing in exchange oil and raisins from Spain, spices from Portugal, and wine, vinegar, and canvas from France. When he used a partner it was at first his brother-in-law Lawrence Mellowe, a clothworker married to his sister Julian or Gillian. Later it was Mellowe's regular partner, Richard Staper, a younger clothworker who joined the family in 1567 by marrying Henry Hewett's sister Dionis. In 1577 Osborne and Staper were both named as assistants in the charter of the new Company of Spain and Portugal. In 1578 they were the first merchants to be approached with a project to open up the trade with Brazil. In 1579 Osborne's name was the first of sixty-five in the charter of the Eastland Company, the new regulated company granted a monopoly of much of the Baltic trade, with Staper another charter member, and within a few months they exported cloths and kerseys worth over £1000 to Danzig. The Russia Company became another interest; in 1584 Osborne was the first signatory of a petition from Muscovy House demanding reimbursement of sums laid out by the company for Sir Jerome Bowes during his embassy to Russia.

Above all Osborne is to be credited with the revival of direct trade on a large scale between England and the Levant. Antwerp had been the entrepôt in recent decades for Levant goods, but was in decline by the 1570s; the Turks, after Lepanto, were desperate for English tin and lead, and they represented a huge potential market for English cloth. Osborne and Staper seized this favourable conjunction by sending out to Constantinople through Poland in 1575 two agents who procured a safe conduct for a more substantial emissary, William Harborne. Osborne had obtained his freedom of the Clothworkers' Company and subsequently employed him in Spain. Now unofficially backed by the English government as well as the merchants, he arrived in Constantinople late in 1578 and within a few months had persuaded the sultan to write to Queen Elizabeth offering security of trade to all her subjects. This was not what Osborne and Staper had had in mind. By the time the letter's Latin translation reached the queen, crucial phrases had been rewritten to convert it into a monopoly for themselves and Harborne. The queen then replied asking for the privileges to be extended to all her nationals, and the Turks responded in 1580 by issuing a more specific charter of liberties, which became the model for all later renewals of the capitulations under which the English continued to trade in the Ottoman empire until 1923. The enterprise was nearly sabotaged at the outset by French machinations and English piracy, but the Turks accepted Elizabeth's apology for the latter and allowed Harborne to return as a fully accredited ambassador. As was to remain the pattern for two centuries, he acted both as the crown's representative and as the salaried agent of the London merchants granted the monopoly of the trade. These were led by Osborne, who was named in the Turkey Company's charter of September 1581 as its governor for the seven years of its monopoly, 'in consideration that the said Edward Osborne hath bene the principall setter foorth and doer in the opening and putting in use of the said trade'. He was given wide powers over the company, which was known to the customs as Edward Osborne, Richard Staper & Co., and traded from his own premises in Philpot Lane. At his death it was still paying him £20 a year to store its bulky bales in 'certayne warehouses, vaults and chambers' attached to his mansion. Nevertheless it was no family business, but was conceived from the outset on the grand scale required for success. The heavy initial outlay was subsidized in part by a loan of 10,000 lb in silver from the queen—the New World fuelling development of the Old—and contributions to the joint stock were broadly based. Consulates were quickly established in Chios, Tripoli in Syria, Alexandria, Algiers, and Patras, and soon convoys of richly laden English merchantmen had become a familiar sight in the eastern Mediterranean. The main exports were cloth and tin, the main imports raw silk, cotton yarn and cotton wool, grograms and camlets (mohair/silk and mohair fabrics respectively), carpets, currants, galls, and a wide range of spices and drugs. This was to remain the basic pattern of the Levant trade until the nineteenth century.

Expansion of the Levant trade Within a generation this influx of raw material was to revolutionize the silk and cotton manufacturing industries in England. In the 1580s these were still in their infancy, and there was therefore a large re-export trade in Levant goods for which there was as yet no home market. This in turn encouraged further expansion, in which Osborne and Staper again played a leading part. They exported Cretan wine via London to the Baltic. They took advantage of the detention of their ship the *Bark Reynolds* at Malta on its way back from Syria in 1582 to negotiate a trading agreement there, together with the use of Maltese harbour facilities on the Levant voyage. They re-exported opium, mastic, cotton yarn, and cotton cloth to the Barbary coast, Osborne using Harborne's influence at the Porte to try to secure a friendly reception from the Ottoman regencies of Algiers, Tunis, and Tripoli, while Staper was heavily involved in the earl of Leicester's partnership trading to Morocco. And Osborne had for some time been looking further east. With Mellowe and others he imported £1437 worth of East India goods in the *Mildred* from Bombay in 1575. He sponsored John Newbery's expedition to Persia in 1580–82, as well as the longer exploration of the land route to the East

Indies undertaken by Newbery between 1583 and 1591, partly in the company of Ralph Fitch and John Eldred. Eldred returned from Syria in 1588 in the *Hercules*, billed (with some justice) as 'the richest ship of English merchants' goods that ever was known to come into this realm' by the Turkey Company's invaluable publicist Richard Hakluyt, for whom Osborne and Staper had secured the award and continuation of a Clothworkers' exhibition at Oxford. This success was well timed. The Venice Company, which controlled the valuable trade in currants, wine, and oil with the Ionian Islands and the Morea, was already co-operating with the Turkey Company in freighting ships to the Levant, and when the charters of the two companies expired close together in 1588–9 their members quickly agreed to seek a new combined charter as Merchants of the Levant.

This was issued on 7 January 1592. From this time in practice a regulated company, not a joint stock, the Levant Company was granted a twelve-year monopoly of trade with the Venetian and the Ottoman dominions, and also with the vast territories on the land route to the East Indies, although these were transferred eight years later to the first East India Company. Osborne, who was again named as governor (for the first year) in the charter, might well be regarded as the founding father of both great national enterprises. He had certainly earned the tribute paid by the Levant Company's historian A. C. Wood: 'With argosies on all the seas and ventures in every clime he was in fact the prototype of the merchant prince of the modern world.'

Death and succession Osborne died just four weeks later, in London on 4 February 1592. He was buried on 15 February at St Dionis Backchurch, where a monument was erected near his usual seat, as requested in his will. This was written on 18 January, properly witnessed on the 20th (by the future ambassador Henry Lello, among others), and cited in the inquisitions post mortem carried out in York and London, as well as in his son's will seven years later. Two fair copies survive among the family papers in Leeds, one annotated by a lawyer. Nevertheless there is no record of probate in the Prerogative Court of Canterbury or any other likely court. Unless this was a simple clerical error, the explanation may be connected with Osborne's second marriage.

Anne Osborne had died in 1585, leaving five children—Alice, Hewett, Anne, Edward, and Jane—who all survived to marry and have children. On 15 September 1588 Sir Edward Osborne married secondly, at St Dionis Backchurch, Margaret (*c*.1554–1602), the daughter and coheir of Charles Pratt, citizen and leatherseller, and the widow firstly of John Midleton, citizen and merchant tailor, and secondly of Edmond Chapman, squire joiner to Queen Elizabeth and yeoman of the royal armouries at Greenwich. She already had three sons and three daughters from her first marriage and a son from her second (and was to have two more daughters from her fourth), but had none from her marriage to Osborne. She had inherited a third of her father's moveable property and of his substantial real estate in Southwark and Lambeth, and both her husbands had left her a life interest in their own leasehold and freehold property, as well as being generous with their moveable estate. Osborne followed their example by settling the Philpot Lane houses on her for life a fortnight before their marriage. In his will he confirmed this and also left her a life interest in other London and Essex properties in lieu of dower, including the Fish Street premises, now called the Rose and Pomegranate. His eldest son inherited the northern estates, but burdened with an annuity of £63, which Osborne calculated would bring his widow's total income from his estate up to £200. By the custom of London she also received a third of his moveable property. His three 'unadvanced' children—Hewett, Edward, and Jane—received another third (Alice and Anne had been well dowered on marriage and were left only silver dishes), and the remaining third was to be divided in equal fourths between his widow and the three unadvanced children. After Margaret's death Hewett Osborne was to have all the real property held by her except Philpot Lane; the reversion of this was to be sold immediately after Osborne's death, and the proceeds divided among all five children. Although the three eldest were over twenty-one, their stepmother was named as sole executor for the third time. Osborne's cousin Edward Osborne of the Inner Temple was to give her legal assistance in return for a £50 legacy, and William Daniell, Richard Staper, and Osborne's Levant merchant son-in-law Robert Offley were named as overseers.

None of this depended on Margaret's continued widowhood, and she lost no time in marrying again, on 10 April 1592 at St Dionis Backchurch, as his third wife, Robert Clarke, of Pleshey, Essex, a baron of the exchequer. Later deeds and wills suggest that a deal was eventually made with her stepchildren whereby she dropped most of her other claims on the estate in exchange for having her interest in the Philpot Lane property extended from life to 1900 years. After her death in 1602 her interest was inherited by Sir Robert Clarke, who brought his fourth wife to live there.

This arrangement allowed the Osbornes to consolidate their estates elsewhere, especially after the Essex lands were sold by Hewett Osborne's son Edward, the first baronet, to finance further purchases in Yorkshire. In the next generation the rapid rise through the peerage of Sir Edward Osborne's great-grandson Thomas Osborne, first duke of Leeds, was made possible not only by his own abilities and opportunities but also by the foresight of ancestors who had built up an estate capable of supporting a dynasty. Like the Levant Company, the dukedom was to survive for a quarter of a millennium.

Sonia P. Anderson

Sources W. Yorks. AS, Leeds, Yorkshire Archaeological Society, DD5/3/302–354, 360 • W. Yorks. AS, Leeds, Yorkshire Archaeological Society, DD5/4/231–240 • W. Yorks. AS, Leeds, Yorkshire Archaeological Society, DD5/5/150 • W. Yorks. AS, Leeds, Yorkshire Archaeological Society, DD5/23/37 • W. Yorks. AS, Leeds, Yorkshire Archaeological Society, DD5/38/1 • PRO, C 142/234/17 • PRO, C 142/236/73 • PRO, E 159/353, m. 28 • PRO, E 179/45/252, m. 23 • PRO, PROB 11/49, fol. 9 • PRO, PROB 11/56, fol. 19 • PRO, PROB 11/65, fol. 15 • PRO, PROB 11/69, fol. 65 • PRO, PROB 11/73, fol. 6 • PRO, PROB

11/91, fol. 12 • PRO, PROB 11/96, fol. 43 • PRO, PROB 11/110, fol. 49 • PRO, PROB 11/111, fol. 12 • PRO, SP 12/6, fol. 52 • PRO, SP 12/239, fol. 44 • PRO, SP 91/1, fol. 30 • A. B. Beaven, ed., *The aldermen of the City of London, temp. Henry III–[1912]*, 2 vols. (1908–13) • HoP, *Commons* • records, Worshipful Company of Clothworkers • J. L. Chester, ed., *The reiester booke of Saynte De'nis Backchurch parishe … begynnynge … 1538*, Harleian Society, register section, 3 (1878) • S. A. Skilliter, *William Harborne and the trade with Turkey, 1578–1582* (1977) • *CSP dom.*, 1547–94 • *CSP for.*, 1569–92 • *APC*, 1571–92 • R. Hakluyt, *The principal navigations, voyages, traffiques and discoveries of the English nation*, 2nd edn, 3 vols. (1598–1600); repr. 12 vols., Hakluyt Society, extra ser., 1–12 (1903–5) • B. Dietz, ed., *The port and trade of early Elizabethan London: documents*, London RS, 8 (1972) • D. Fischer, 'The development and organisation of English trade to Asia, 1553–1605', PhD diss., U. Lond., 1970 • BL, Lansdowne MS 29, fol. 125 • BL, Lansdowne MS 38, fol. 40 • BL, Lansdowne MS 53, fol. 168 • BL, Lansdowne MS 60, fols. 8, 90 • BL, Lansdowne MS 110, fol. 188 • R. E. C. Waters, *Genealogical memoirs of the extinct family of Chester of Chicheley*, 1 (1878) • R. Cooke, *Visitation of London, 1568*, ed. H. Stanford London and S. W. Rawlins, [new edn], 2 vols. in one, Harleian Society, 109–10 (1963) • G. E. Cokayne, 'Pedigrees of the families of Osborne and Buckby', *The Genealogist*, new ser., 24 (1907–8), 1–14 • J. Stow, *A survey of the cities of London and Westminster and the borough of Southwark*, ed. J. Strype, new edn, 2 vols. (1720) • Merchant Taylors' Company, court minutes, vol. 3, fol. 149 • A. C. Wood, *A history of the Levant Company* (1935) • *VCH Essex*, 5.277 • S. J. Madge, ed., *Abstracts of inquisitiones post mortem relating to the City of London*, 2: *1561–1577*, British RS, 26 (1901), 98–9

Archives W. Yorks. AS, Leeds, Yorkshire Archaeological Society, papers

Wealth at death PRO, C 142/234/17 (York, 5 Oct 1592); C 142/236/73 (London, 19 May 1593), calendared in British Record Society, Index Library, 36 (1908), 174–5 • at last assessment, eighteenth equal among Londoners, but assessment remained at £250 for last fifteen years of his life: lay subsidy assessments, 1577, PRO E 179/45/252, m. 23; 1582, R. G. Lang, ed., *Two Tudor subsidy assessment rolls for the city of London: 1541 and 1582*, London Record Society, 29 (1993), no. 354; 1589, Cooke, *Visitation of London*, 161 • bequeathed mostly cloth; £100 and £50 to brothers; £10 p.a. to sister after her husband's death; £3 to William Harborne for a ring; £10 each to St Thomas's and Christ's hospitals; £5 to petty debtors in the two London compters: will, W. Yorks. AS, Leeds, Yorkshire Archaeological Society, DD5/23/37 • lands in Harthill and Woodall: survey, W. Yorks. AS, Leeds, Yorkshire Archaeological Society, DD5/3/342a

Osborne, Ethel Elizabeth (1882–1968), industrial hygienist and medical practitioner, was born on 30 January 1882 in Cedar Avenue, Armley, Leeds, Yorkshire, the second of four children and elder daughter of James Goodson, butcher and later businessman, and his wife, Elizabeth, *née* Lockley, who was of Welsh descent. Small, with dark hair and deep-blue eyes, she was judged beautiful as well as intelligent. She retained a strong regional accent throughout her life. Ethel attended the Leeds Central higher grade school, the first school to provide state secondary education in Leeds. Her education at Yorkshire College (then part of the federated Victoria University, and later the University of Leeds) was reflected in her commitment in later life to a view of the necessary relationships between pure and applied science, and between science and industry. She was one of the minority who graduated (BSc honours in physics, 1902) and of the very few to proceed to the further degree of MSc, also in physics (1907).

On 10 December 1903, at Armley parish church, Ethel Goodson married Irish-born William Alexander Osborne

Ethel Elizabeth Osborne (1882–1968), by unknown photographer

(1873–1967), then assistant professor at University College, London. Soon after, they sailed to Australia, where he had been appointed professor of physiology and histology at the University of Melbourne. Both were multilingual and their first joint project was a German grammar for science students (1906). They shared interests in applied science, but Ethel was committed to improving the status of women. An original member from 1910 of an informal but long-lasting group of university-educated Melbourne women, the Catalysts, her fact-finding visit in the same year to the London-based Lyceum Club provided the model for the Melbourne Lyceum Club, of which she was elected a foundation vice-president in 1912. The Melbourne club had a young membership, not confined to academics, and unlike London it declined to admit women on the basis of the distinction of husbands or male relatives.

With her three children Ethel Osborne returned to Leeds in 1916 after her brother Godfrey was killed in France. Unable to return to Australia she served with enthusiasm in the local munitions factories in night welfare work and as head supervisor under the Health of Munitions Workers Committee (HMWC). By mid-August 1916 her research interests in relation to the health of women munition workers included weight loss, menstrual changes, dermatitis and other 'contact' conditions, time lost through illness, and the causes of accidents, particularly heat and cold. Her lengthy studies were published as two reports for the HMWC's successor, the Industrial Fatigue Research Board: *The Output of Women Workers in Relation to Hours of Work in Shell-Making* (1919) and (with H. M. Vernon and B. Muscio) *Two Contributions to the Study of Accident Causation* (1922). These reports related directly to the board's central concern with the relationships between shorter working hours, the working environment, efficiency, and the development of such managerial concepts as accident-proneness. On her return to Melbourne in 1919, Ethel Osborne was invited to advise the commonwealth court of conciliation and arbitration on conditions of employment in the clothing industry, for a case which won some women workers a forty-hour week.

Pursuing a long-held ambition Osborne qualified in medicine at the University of Melbourne (MB BS, 1923; DPH, 1931), sharing the Fulton prize in obstetrics and gynaecology. Although more than a hundred women had graduated in medicine at Melbourne since the first did so in 1891, it was unusual for them to be married or to have experienced childbirth. Ethel Osborne practised medicine in public hospitals and privately, while developing her interest in industrial health and hygiene. In 1924 she published a union-commissioned report on the health of women workers in the printing and allied trades, and was a Commonwealth delegate to the international congresses on industrial diseases at Amsterdam (1925) and Budapest (1928).

Osborne's interest in the education of women was lifelong. Of her three daughters, the eldest was the second woman to graduate in agricultural science at the University of Melbourne and later specialized in dietetics; the second qualified in medicine; and the third was prominent in local government. Institutionally, Osborne was chiefly associated with the Emily McPherson College of Domestic Economy, Melbourne, which she served as a foundation councillor (1912–37), treasurer, vice-president, and president (1915–17, 1919–28). She developed a major interest in dietetics, the study of diet and nutrition, and collaborated with her husband on a textbook and in writing, lecturing, and broadcasting on the subject. In 1928 and 1930 she represented Australia at the Pan-Pacific Women's Conference in Honolulu, and she liaised with the League of Nations and the International Labour Office about welfare in industry. Between 1931 and 1937 she attended a number of European congresses on health and industrial relations, sometimes as a senior representative.

Osborne enjoyed both the motor car and the aeroplane during the war years; she was an early, if erratic, motorist, and took part in record-breaking passenger flights. An absent-minded housekeeper and mother of four, she allowed her children to roam out of doors, with bare feet and wearing rational dress. She retired in 1938 with her husband to their property at Kangaroo Ground, Victoria, where they lived frugally off their own produce. Her unconventionality, strong will, and boundless energy blended with warmth and humour to make her a formidable fighter for the causes she espoused, which included work creation during the depression. However, her later years were blighted by alcoholism; she became domineering, her eccentricity of behaviour and dress grew more marked, and her health declined. She died after many years in an East Melbourne hospital on 3 December 1968, and was cremated two days later at the Springvale crematorium, Melbourne. Her three daughters and son survived her. DIANE LANGMORE

Sources *The Argus* [Melbourne] (24 July 1928) · *The Argus* [Melbourne] (15 Aug 1928) · *The Argus* [Melbourne] (27 Sept 1928) · *The Argus* [Melbourne] (2 Feb 1929) · *The Argus* [Melbourne] (15 Sept 1930) · *The Argus* [Melbourne] (6 Aug 1931) · *The Argus* [Melbourne] (21 Aug 1931) · *The Argus* [Melbourne] (8 Sept 1931) · *The Argus* [Melbourne] (15 Dec 1932) · *The Argus* [Melbourne] (20 Dec 1932) · *Warrandyte Historical Society Newsletter*, 51 (Oct 1986) · J. Docherty, *The Emily Mac: the story of the Emily McPherson College* [1981] · J. M. Gillison, *A history of the Lyceum Club* (1975) · *Commonwealth Arbitration Reports*, 13 (1919) · University of Melbourne Archives, W. A. Osborne MSS · NL Aus., Bessie Rischbieth MSS · A. Mackinnon, *Love and freedom: professional women and the reshaping of personal life* (1997) · b. cert. · m. cert. · d. cert. · private information [U. Leeds] · private information (2004) [Mary Gordon, niece]

Archives NL Aus., MSS | NL Aus., Bessie Rischbieth MSS · University of Melbourne, W. A. Osborne MSS

Likenesses photograph, priv. coll. [*see illus.*]

Wealth at death A$188,951

Osborne, Francis (1593–1659), writer, was born on 26 September 1593, the fifth and youngest son of Sir John Osborne (1551–1628), administrator, of Chicksands Priory, Shefford, Bedfordshire, and his wife, Dorothy, daughter and coheir of Richard Barlee of Elsenham Hall, Essex. Osborne's early years were divided between Chicksands and his father's house in London; he was educated privately, 'bred mostly at home, not so much as in a free-school or university' (Wood, *Ath. Oxon.*, 1.706). He may have travelled abroad in his late teens, and refers in a later work to experiences 'beyond sea' (Potter, vii).

After going to London 'at ripe years', writes Wood, Osborne 'frequented the court, became a servant in the Pembrochian family, and at length master of the horse to that most Noble Count William earl of Pembroke' (Wood, *Ath. Oxon.*, 1.706). For a time he held a minor post in the office of the lord treasurer's remembrancer, the office presided over by his father and eldest brother successively. The deaths of his father in 1628 and of the third earl in 1630 probably ended his ambitions of holding public office, and his writing often reveals a tone of disappointment in his failure to obtain preferment. His earliest biographer finds no record of his subsequent career until 1641, when he 'ran with the times, having been puritanically educated, [and] had public employments then, and under Oliver, conferr'd upon him' (ibid.). He married Anna Draper (*d.* 1657), sister of William Draper of Nether Worton, Oxfordshire, who became a colonel in the parliamentary army, and by 1647 Osborne was a 'new made Justice and a Committee-man for this County' as well as a parliamentary visitor for the University of Oxford (Wood, *History and Antiquities*, 2.501, 511).

About 1650 Osborne removed to Oxford; Wood notes

that 'in his last days [he] lived in Oxon purposely to print certain books of his composition that then lay by him, and to have an eye on his son John' (Wood, *Ath. Oxon.*, 1.706). The only son among Osborne's four children, John was registered as a demy of Magdalen College, Oxford, in 1648, and, with Draper's assistance, was installed as fellow of All Souls College in 1650, after an altercation between the parliamentary visitors at Oxford and the parliamentary committee for university business in London. By 1653, also through Draper's influence, Francis Osborne was appointed 'one of the seven for the countie and city of Oxon, that was a judge as to all prisons and persons committed to any prisons in comitatu vel civitate Oxon 1653' (*Life and Times of Anthony Wood*, 1.185). He sympathized with parliament in politics and religion. During the last eight years of his life he published a series of historical, political, and moral works, which were read widely during the Restoration and early eighteenth century. His thinking shows the influence of Hobbes, whose 'great acquaintance' he was (*Brief Lives*, 1.370).

Osborne's son, John, received the degree of BCL in 1654 and proceeded to the Inner Temple in 1657; he married his first cousin, Elizabeth Draper, and served as prime serjeant-at-law in Ireland from 1680 until 1686. It was for John that Osborne wrote in two parts his chief publication, the *Advice to a Son*. Part 1 was issued anonymously in late 1655. Its pragmatic and apothegmatic observations appeared under the headings: 'Studies', 'Love and marriage', 'Travel', 'Government', and 'Religion'. The work gained immediate popularity, passing through several editions in two years. In 1658 Osborne issued an enlarged edition of part 1, with his name on the title-page, and at the same time brought out a more discursive second part, inferior to the first, dedicated to Draper.

The book's pragmatism and cynicism may have furthered its rapid acceptance. Its frank and practical aim was to guide the reader to material success in a treacherous, self-seeking world. Popular with Oxford scholars, it enjoyed a wide readership outside the university as well. In 1658 there appeared two curious replies by London hack writers. Misogynistic passages in *Advice to a Son* ostensibly prompted the scurrilous parody, *Advice to a Daughter*, by John Heydon in 1658; as Eugenius Theodidactus, Heydon attacked Osborne as 'the unconquered enemy of Women' (sig. A4). Heydon was attacked in return by Thomas Pecke in *Advice to Balaam's Ass* (1658), which asserted that Heydon's book was a collection of plagiarisms. Heydon answered in a second edition of the *Advice to a Daughter* (1659), with an added section: 'Thomas Peck, Counsellor, examined, turn'd over the Bar and sent to Bedlam for his madness'.

The tone of worldliness in the *Advice* contributed to Osborne's reputation for atheism. In 1658, after complaints from local ministers that the *Advice* 'did instil principles of Atheism into young Gentlemen', a formal complaint was brought to the vice-chancellor and a proposal put forward to have Osborne's books publicly burned (Wood, *History and Antiquities*, 2.684). 'But it taking no effect', Wood records, 'July the 27., the vice-cancellor [Dr John Conant] caused all the booksellers to appeare before him, and commanded them not to sell any of Mr. [Francis] Osborne's booke': as might be expected, 'The book afterwards sold the more' (*Life and Times of Anthony Wood*, 1.257).

In later years Pepys fondly called the author 'my father Osborne' and recorded that Sir William Petty listed the *Advice* with Browne's *Religio medici* and Butler's *Hudibras* as the works 'most esteemed and generally cried up for wit in the world' (Pepys, *Diary*, 19 Oct 1661; 27 Jan 1664). Swift complained that Osborne affected phrases fashionable at court, quickly rendering his writing unintelligible (*Tatler*, no. 230). Johnson denounced Osborne as 'A conceited fellow'. 'Were a man to write so now, the boys would throw stones at him'; Boswell defended his work as 'shrewd and lively' and 'somewhat quaint', a book with 'an air of originality. We figure to ourselves an ancient gentleman talking to us' (Boswell, *Life*, spring 1772).

After the *Advice*, Osborne is best-known for the *Historical Memoires of Q. Elizabeth and James I* (1658), reprinted in Sir Walter Scott's *Secret History of the Court of James I* (1811). Other works include *A Persuasive to a Mutual Compliance under the Present Government* (February 1652), Osborne's contribution to the engagement controversy, dedicated to Cromwell and printed anonymously for the purpose of offering services as a secret agent; attached to it was *A Plea for a Free State Compared with Monarchy*, both reprinted by Sir Walter Scott in 1811 in *Scarce and Valuable Tracts … Lord Somers* (6.153–77). Also appearing anonymously in 1652 was *A Seasonable Expostulation with the Netherlands*. Neither *A Persuasive* nor *A Seasonable Expostulation* was included in editions of Osborne's collected *Miscellaneous Works*.

Other works include *Political Reflections upon the Government of the Turks* (1656) and *Miscellany of sundry essayes, paradoxes, and problematicall discourses, letters and characters, together with politicall deductions from the history of the earl of Essex* (1659); the latter was dedicated to his niece, Elizabeth Draper. An unattributed, undated manuscript of a play, 'The True Tragicomedy', in the British Library (Add. MS 25348) may be the work of Francis Osborne.

Osborne's publications made him a celebrity, and he paid many visits to London; but his later life was one of straitened circumstances owing to the unhappy result of a legal battle over property. At the death of Osborne's father in 1628, the four youngest Osborne brothers inherited the North Fambridge estate in Essex, the eldest brother, Sir Peter, having received the family seat at Chicksands. Because Sir Peter fought for the king in the civil war he was fined, and he sued Francis for the North Fambridge manor. The first judgment came in favour of Sir Peter in 1653; an appeal also favoured Sir Peter's claim in March 1655, the property proceeding to his son Henry; by then Francis was the only surviving Osborne brother. Published letters place Francis at Kelvedon, Essex, in 1657; after the death of his wife, Anna, in that year he sold his remaining property and appears to have lived the rest of his life in the homes of others, with his publisher Thomas Robinson in Oxford and with William Draper at Nether Worton. He died at Draper's house on 4 February 1659 and was buried in Nether Worton chapel. His epitaph is recorded in the 1722 *Works*.

On 13 March 1676 Osborne's *Miscellaneous Works* (1673; 7th edn) was brought before the House of Lords as a seditious publication, apparently without consequence, for 'denouncing a monarchy and saying that the commonwealth is the best government' (*Ninth Report*, HMC; Parry, xxii). The complainant, a Captain John Seymour, and the bookseller, Samuel Mearn, were brought before a committee of the house, but no recorded result of the proceeding exists. Further editions of the *Miscellaneous Works* were issued in 1682, 1689, 1701, and 1722, the last containing previously unpublished letters from Francis to his brother-in-law and his wife, written between 1653 and 1658, and a memoir of his life by an anonymous editor, based on Wood's account of 1691. No manuscripts in his hand remain, with the possible exception of 'The True Tragicomedy'. MARIE C. HENSON

Sources E. A. Parry, 'Introduction', in F. Osborne, *Advice to a son*, ed. E. A. Parry (1896), iii–xxii, and notes, 136–48 • *The miscellaneous works of … Francis Osborne*, 1 (1722), iii–xxi, 1–35 • L. Potter, 'Introduction', in F. Osborne, *The true tragicomedy formerly acted at court*, ed. L. Potter (1983), vol. 3 of *The Renaissance imagination*, i–xxxvii • Wood, *Ath. Oxon.*, 2nd edn, 1.705–7 • *The letters of Dorothy Osborne to William Temple*, ed. G. C. Moore Smith (1928), appx 9, 311–17 • F. F. Madan, 'Some notes on the bibliography of Francis Osborne', *Oxford Bibliographical Society Publications*, new ser., 4 (1950), 55–60 • F. Madan, *Oxford literature, 1651–1680* (1931), vol. 3 of *Oxford books: a bibliography of printed works* (1895–1931); repr. (1964) • Burke, *Peerage* (1970) • A. Wood, *The history and antiquities of the University of Oxford*, ed. J. Gutch, 2 (1796), 501, 511, 684 • *The life and times of Anthony Wood*, ed. A. Clark, 1–2, OHS, 19, 21 (1891–2) • J. M. Wallace, 'The engagement controversy of 1649–1652: an annotated list of pamphlets', *Bulletin of the New York Public Library*, 68 (1964), 384–405 • *Brief lives, chiefly of contemporaries, set down by John Aubrey, between the years 1669 and 1696*, ed. A. Clark, 1 (1898), 370 • S. A. E. Betz, 'Francis Osborn's *Advice to a son*', *Seventeenth-Century Studies* [ed. R. Shafer], 2nd ser. (1937), 3–67 • M. Burrows, ed., *The register of the visitors of the University of Oxford, from AD 1647 to AD 1658*, CS, new ser., 29 (1881) • J. R. Bloxam, *A register of the presidents, fellows … of Saint Mary Magdalen College*, 8 vols. (1853–85) • *DNB* • J. N. D. Bush, *English literature in the earlier seventeenth century, 1600–1660*, 2nd edn (1962), 626 [bibliography] • L. B. Wright, introduction, in *Advice to a son: precepts of Lord Burghley, Sir Walter Raleigh, and Francis Osborne*, ed. L. B. Wright (1962), ix–xxvi • H. R. Plomer and others, *A dictionary of the booksellers and printers who were at work in England, Scotland, and Ireland from 1641 to 1667* (1907), 156 • W. K. Jordan, 'The laymen and the moderates', *The development of religious toleration in England*, 2 (1936), 240–49 • W. Scott, ed., *A collection of scarce and valuable tracts … Lord Somers*, 2nd edn, 6 (1811) • *Ninth report*, 3 vols., HMC, 8 (1883–4)

Likenesses B. van der Helst, print (after portrait by E. Walker), NPG

Wealth at death in 1655 lost estate of North Fambridge, Essex, to eldest brother and his son in lawsuit; in 1657 sold remaining property on wife's death; spent last years in the home of brother-in-law: *Letters of Dorothy Osborne*, ed. Moore Smith; *Miscellaneous works*, vol. 1, pp. 31, 35

Osborne, Francis, fifth duke of Leeds (1751–1799), politician, was born and baptized on 29 January 1751 in the parish of St James's, Westminster, the only surviving son of Thomas Osborne, fourth duke of Leeds (1713–1789), politician, and Lady Mary Godolphin (*d.* 1764), daughter and eventual heir of Francis *Godolphin, second earl of Godolphin. Styled marquess of Carmarthen, he was educated

Francis Osborne, fifth duke of Leeds (1751–1799), by Sir Thomas Lawrence, early 1790s

at Westminster School (1764–7), and matriculated from Christ Church, Oxford, on 11 June 1767; he was created MA on 30 March 1769 and DCL on 7 July 1773. A member of the Royal Society from 1773, he was also proud of his literary knowledge and even dabbled in amateur playwriting. 'If his knowledge was not profound it was miscellaneous and extensive', noted one memorialist (*Political Memoranda*, ii); another that he was 'most polite and pleasing in his manners, with a sweet temper and an excellent understanding, happily cultivated' (Doran, 258). On 29 November 1773, at Holdernesse House, Hertford Street, London, he married Lady Amelia D'Arcy (1754–1784), daughter and heir of Robert *D'Arcy, fourth earl of Holdernesse, and Mary Doublet, countess of Mertola (*d.* 1801). They had two sons and a daughter, but the marriage ended in scandal in December 1778 when the marchioness ran off with Captain Jack Byron (*d.* 1791), father by a subsequent marriage of the poet Byron. After obtaining a divorce on 31 May 1779, Carmarthen married, on 11 October 1788, at Hanwell, Middlesex, Catherine (1764–1837), daughter of Thomas Anguish, master in chancery, and Sarah Henley; they had a son and a daughter.

Early career, 1774–1783 In 1774 Carmarthen was returned at a by-election for the borough of Eye in Suffolk. The seat was made available as compensation for his father's surrendering of the office of chief justice on eyre north of

Trent. 'My father', he noted, 'did not much approve the plan; but seeing my wish to come into the House of Commons, merely to oblige me consented'. In view of the burgeoning American crisis, Carmarthen was 'convinced of the necessity of strengthening government' and 'had no scruple in voting uniformly with them', the sole exception being a vote in the minority on 28 April over the Massachusetts petition, as he 'could by no means approve of the rejecting it unheard'. He spoke four times in favour of the bills to regulate the government of Massachusetts during May, but did not attend the debates on the Quebec Bill. At the general election of 1774 he took advantage of an electoral interest at Helston in Cornwall which he had inherited from his grandfather Lord Godolphin. He was returned only to be unseated on petition on 15 March 1775. Of this second brief spell in the Commons he recalled that 'I took no active part … on account of the uncertainty of my situation; however, I voted with the government except upon Lord North's conciliatory plan' on 20 February 1775 (*Political Memoranda*, 1–4).

Carmarthen had already decided that in the event of losing his seat in the Commons he would request elevation to the Lords. On 15 May 1776 he was called up in his father's barony as Lord Osborne of Kiveton. He held court appointments as a lord of the bedchamber (1776–7) and lord chamberlain of the queen's household (1777–80). Having been made a privy councillor in 1777, he was also appointed lord lieutenant of the East Riding of Yorkshire the following year. He gradually became dissatisfied with Lord North's administration, and dated his change of heart to the time of Admiral Keppel's court martial in January 1779. Having also become a convert to economic reform, he resigned his place at court on 31 December and was summarily dismissed from his lord lieutenancy on 8 February 1780. Now an active member of the parliamentary opposition, he was on friendly terms with lords Shelburne and Rockingham, though belonging to the faction of neither. He published two political pamphlets advocating changes in men and measures, entitled *A Letter to the Right Honourable, Ld. Th[urlo]w* (1780) and *An Address to the Independent Members of both Houses of Parliament* (1782). He was restored to the lord lieutenancy at the insistence of the Rockingham administration in March 1782, and with the further change of ministry in July was appointed by Shelburne as ambassador-extraordinary and minister-plenipotentiary at Paris. He did not proceed to France, however, and resigned in April 1783 in the wake of Shelburne's fall.

Foreign secretary, 1783–1791 As an opponent of the Fox–North coalition of 1783 Osborne was ideally placed to be recruited by William Pitt, who was desperately short of cabinet material as he tried to establish a viable ministry during the constitutional crisis precipitated by the defeat of the East India Bill. On 23 December 1783 Osborne was appointed secretary of state for foreign affairs in Pitt's administration. He succeeded his father as fifth duke of Leeds on 23 March 1789, and was elected a knight of the Garter on 15 December 1790, though for some reason he was never formally invested with this honour. Within Pitt's cabinet he remained something of a makeweight, proving an undistinguished foreign secretary. It was widely believed that the prime minister was the driving force behind foreign policy, as had clearly been the case in the commercial treaty with France of 1787. Conversely, Leeds's guiding principle was hostility to France. He was therefore delighted by the revolutionary turmoil of 1789. 'I defy the ablest heads in England', he wrote in July, 'to have planned, or its whole wealth to have purchased, a situation so fatal to its rival, as that to which France is now reduced by her own intestine commotions' (duke of Leeds to duke of Dorset, 31 July 1789, BL, Add. MS 28064).

The duke of Leeds resigned as foreign secretary over the Ochakov affair of 1791. This complicated episode has often been glossed over as a minor incident. Indeed a contemporary journal described the affair shortly afterwards as being probably 'of small importance in the eyes of posterity' and 'already almost forgotten at home' (*Annual Register*, 1793, 33). But the dispute over Russian retention of Ochakov—a Black Sea port captured from the Turks in 1788—nevertheless marked an early appearance of the Eastern question in British diplomacy. Pitt, supported by Leeds, aimed at a complex diplomatic realignment involving Prussia and Poland, with additional support from Denmark. The scheme encountered difficulties because the true objectives could not be revealed in public for fear of undermining confidential negotiations still under way. It was naïvely hoped that Russia would back down in the face of a show of British naval force in the Baltic, and that Ochakov would be returned to Turkish control. This would open up new trade routes from Poland, in turn smoothing the path for her cession of Danzig to Prussia. The overriding objective was the strengthening of the British–Prussian relationship, but the brinkmanship involved proved unpopular. The parliamentary opposition led by Charles James Fox adopted an anti-war and pro-Russian stance, so Pitt wisely decided to back down. Leeds resigned in a fit of pique, believing his position to have been seriously undermined by the change in policy. Yet, the absurdity of continuing bellicosity towards Russia became apparent when Denmark refused to open her ports to the British navy, thus negating a key strategic element in the original scheme.

Later career, 1792–1799 Although he retained precious little political influence, Leeds suffered occasional delusions of grandeur, the most notable of which occurred in the summer of 1792, when he convinced himself that he might form a ministry of national unity as first lord of the Treasury, with Pitt and Fox serving under him as secretaries of state. The affair ended in a farcical interview with George III on 14 August. The notion of appointing a neutral figure to the Treasury struck the king as absurd: 'it would be awkward for Mr Pitt … to descend to an inferior situation … and that whoever was the First Lord must either be a cipher or Mr Pitt appear as a *commis*' (*Political Memoranda*, 189). In fact Leeds had been the dupe of an elaborate plan by Fox to counter the equally devious machinations of Lord Loughborough that were destabilizing the whig opposition. When Leeds reported that

George III had also informed him that Pitt had not recently broached the subject of coalition, this confirmed the suspicions of the opposition leadership and simultaneously exposed Loughborough's self-seeking ambition. The affair was terminated by a confrontation between the duke and the prime minister. Leeds was astonished at Pitt's brazen assertion that 'there had been no thoughts of any alteration in the government, that circumstances did not call for it, nor did the people wish it, and that no new arrangement, either by change or coalition, had ever been in contemplation' (ibid., 194). Once Leeds had relayed this information to members of the opposition, they supplied him with sufficient details of the earlier approaches to Loughborough to confirm beyond 'all doubt that Mr Pitt's saying "No change had been in contemplation" was not strictly true' (ibid., 196). The duke of Portland concluded that the affair had demonstrated that Leeds did not have 'any weight with Pitt, or in the Closet, or anywhere' (Portland to Fox, 21 July 1792, BL, Add. MS 47561, fol. 120). Lord Malmesbury noted acerbically that Leeds had been 'carried away more by his imagination and sanguine hopes, in which his string of toad-eaters encourage him, than by reason and reflection' (Harris, 2.470–73).

Leeds spoke for the last time in the Lords on 30 May 1797, during the debate on the duke of Bedford's motion for the dismissal of the Pitt ministry. On this occasion he gave limited support to the notion of a change in administration, ridiculing the idea that 'the existence of the constitution was inseparably connected with the continuation of the present ministry in power', but he also distanced himself from the more radical opponents of government by declaring that parliamentary reform was 'a most dangerous remedy to resort to' (Cobbett, *Parl. hist.*, 32.762–3).

Leeds died of erysipelas at his house in St James's Square, London, on 31 January 1799, aged forty-eight, and was buried in All Saints' Church, Harthill, Yorkshire. George William Frederick (1775–1838), his elder son by his first marriage, succeeded as sixth duke. One obituary commended the late duke's amiable manners and personal integrity, but inadvertently drew attention to the shortcomings of his political career by describing him as a man of 'higher talents than he was generally supposed to possess' (*GM*, 1st ser., 69/1, 1799, 169). Indeed, his vanity had long been a standing joke in society. So frequent were his references to his time at the Foreign Office that some acquaintances had taken to placing bets on how long it would be before he mentioned it in conversation.

David Wilkinson

Sources *The political memoranda of Francis, fifth duke of Leeds*, ed. O. Browning, CS, new ser., 35 (1884) • J. Ehrman, *The younger Pitt*, 3 vols. (1969–96) • D. Wilkinson, 'The political career of William Henry Cavendish-Bentinck, third duke of Portland, 1738–1809', PhD diss., U. Wales, Aberystwyth, 1997 • *The later correspondence of George III*, ed. A. Aspinall, 5 vols. (1962–70) • *Diaries and correspondence of James Harris, first earl of Malmesbury*, ed. third earl of Malmesbury [J. H. Harris], 2nd edn, 4 vols. (1845) • *The journal and correspondence of William, Lord Auckland*, ed. [G. Hogge], 4 vols. (1861–2) • J. Doran, *A lady of the last century* (1873) • Cobbett, *Parl. hist.* • *Annual Register* (1793) • *GM*, 1st ser., 69 (1799), 168–9 • GEC, *Peerage* • *DNB* • J. Brooke, 'Osborne, Francis Godolphin', HoP, *Commons, 1754–90*

Archives BL, corresp. and papers, Add. MSS 27914–27918, 28059–28068, 28570; Egerton MSS 3498–3507 | BL, corresp. with Lord Auckland, Add. MSS 34421–34436, *passim* • BL, corresp. with Sir William Hamilton, Add. MSS 41198–41199 • BL, corresp. with Sir Robert Keith, Add. MSS 35518–35570, *passim* • BL, corresp. with Robert Liston, Add. MS 34465 [copies] • BL, letters to duke and duchess of Newcastle, Add. MSS 32991, 33031, 33071–33083, *passim* • CKS, corresp. with third duke of Dorset • East Riding of Yorkshire Archives Service, Beverley, letters to Thomas Grimston • N. Yorks. CRO, corresp. with Christopher Wyvill • NA Scot., corresp. relating to foreign affairs • NL Scot., corresp. with Robert Liston • NRA, priv. coll., letters to Lord Lansdowne • PRO, Chatham papers, PRO 30/8 • PRO, corresp. with Lord Hervey, FO 528 • PRO, letters to William Pitt, PRO 30/8 • Royal Arch., letters to George III

Likenesses J. Reynolds, group portrait, oils, 1777–9 (*The society of the dilettanti*), Brooks's Club, London • T. Lawrence, portrait, 1790–94, priv. coll. [*see illus.*] • attrib. G. Knapton, oils (after J. Reynolds), NPG • R. M. Meadows, stipple (after T. Lawrence), BM, NPG • J. M. W. Turner, engraving (after J. Reynolds) • photogravure (after stipple by T. Lawrence, 1792), NPG

Osborne, George (1690?–1762?), journalist and journal editor, was probably born in 1690; details of his parents are unknown. He was clearly well educated and appears to have been a lawyer by training. The crypto-Jacobite journal the *Mitre and Crown* (1748–51), for which he was the editor and principal writer, was described as being 'By a Gentleman late of the Temple' (*Mitre and Crown*, September 1748, frontispiece). He had one son, possibly named Marcellus, who practised law in chambers, 'over the seal office in the Inner Temple', and who, in 1753, seems to have married 'a very good fortune' (BL, Add. MS 28236, fols. 22, 60). Osborne's earlier writing career remains largely obscure, though he claimed to have had great success with his 'Creed of a rationalist', winning approbation from both the bishop of London and the archbishop of Canterbury (*True Briton*, 5/16, 375).

The *Mitre and Crown* was launched as a fortnightly political journal 'in which Our Constitution in Church and State will be explain'd and defended' with 'a short Account of most valuable Books' and an abstract of 'several Publick Papers, with the usual Common News' (*Mitre and Crown*, 1, September 1748). From February 1749 it was published monthly. The journal appeared at a time when Jacobitism appeared an all but spent force in the aftermath of the disaster at Culloden. It seems to have been an attempt to rally tories to the 'legitimate' cause and to prevent their defection to a pro-Hanoverian opposition led by Frederick, prince of Wales. Osborne and his contributors preached a divine-right theory of kingship which denied 'the imaginary Natural Rights all men are said to be equally entitled to', and rejected the idea of an organized contract between the king and his people (Monod, 33). In this respect Osborne's work differed from some earlier, more popular Jacobite journals, such as those by Nathaniel Mist and George Flint, in its return to an older mainstream of Jacobite ideas, owing more to the writing of Robert Filmer than John Locke. The *Mitre and Crown* was reprinted in two volumes (the second including three editions of a third volume) and was on sale in 1751, as advertised in his second journal, the *True Briton* (1751–3).

Osborne's involvement in producing the *True Briton*

brought him into close collaboration with the Roman Catholic landowner John Caryll, Edward Gibbon (father of the historian), and General James Oglethorpe. This weekly journal was generally written from an opposition standpoint but mostly eschewed open criticism of the administration, though sympathy for the Stuart royal family was fairly often revealed. He was trenchant in his defence of Alexander Murray and the independent electors of Westminster. In the final two editions Osborne was unswerving. He altered the publication day of the penultimate issue in 1753 so as to celebrate Restoration day, a long-standing Jacobite rhetorical device. In the final number he included lines celebrating 'Prince Charles':

> The Christian Hero's martial Looks here shine,
> Mixt with the Sweetness of the Stuart Line.
> (*True Briton*, 5/20, 471)

This journal was also printed in collected form, in five volumes.

Osborne's personal difficulties are well documented in his frequent correspondence with John Caryll, who supplied him with sympathy, encouragement, advice, and a little money. Osborne was involved in a bitter and long-lasting lawsuit with the Aston family, and he blamed their spite for a series of conflicts with his creditors. In July 1752 he was writing to Caryll from the house of Warren, 'a Sheriffs Officer in Grays Inn Lane' (BL, Add. MS 28236, fol. 1), and from there he seems to have moved, within a few weeks, to the Fleet prison. In gaol he was able to carry on writing and publishing the *True Briton*, albeit with considerable difficulty. His letters to Caryll lament the unreliability of supposed assistants, publishers, and booksellers, and especially the non-appearance of funds he claims were promised him by a partner (apparently General Oglethorpe), who was to assist by bearing half of the expenses of the *True Briton* from summer 1752 onwards. Little money was forthcoming from Oglethorpe, and Osborne also fell out with Edward Gibbon, complaining on 1 April 1753 of 'the deceit, treachery, falsehood, ill nature and expense, which I have experienc'd from or been cast upon by, My pretended Friends, real Enemies or pretended warm Patriots and Party Men' (BL, Add. MS 28236, fol. 29).

Despite some necessarily limited financial aid from the indebted Caryll, Osborne ended the *True Briton* in April 1753. Thereafter he wrote and published occasional pamphlets, newspaper entries, and collections, often calling on Caryll for advice. His wife, of whom details are unknown, died in 1762, at a time when his legal disputes seemed to be drawing to a favourable conclusion. Osborne, who from 1755 lived in Marsham Street, London, seems to have died soon after, probably also in 1762.

PAUL CHAPMAN

Sources BL, Add. MS 28236 • P. K. Monod, *Jacobitism and the English people, 1688–1788* (1989) • *Mitre and Crown*, 2 vols. (1748–51) • *True Briton*, 5 vols. (1751–3)
Archives BL, letters and MSS, Add. MS 28236

Osborne, George Alexander (1806–1893), pianist and composer, born on 24 September 1806 at Limerick, was the third son of the organist and a vicar-choral of Limerick Cathedral, and his wife, a member of the MacMahon family. As a boy he received organ lessons from his father, and when barely fourteen he was able to take the latter's place occasionally on the organ bench. With no definite idea of adopting the profession of music, when he was about eighteen he was sent by his father to Brussels to visit a sick aunt. A spirited account of his journey was published in the *Proceedings of the Musical Association* (9, 1882–3, 95–113), in a paper entitled 'Musical coincidences and reminiscences'. Osborne remained in Brussels for several years, which he recollected as 'wearisome years of study and anxiety' (*Proceedings of the Musical Association*, 9.97). At first he was intended for holy orders, and, with this in view, he attended the classes at Prince's classical academy. While he was a pupil there his skill as a musician attracted the attention of several prominent persons, among whom was the prince de Chimay, an able and enthusiastic musical amateur, and husband of the former Madame Tallien, of French Revolution fame. Osborne soon became a frequenter of the prince's château, where he met many prominent writers and musicians, including George Sand, F.-J. Fétis, Luigi Cherubini, and Daniel Auber, and where he benefited from a study of the music in the prince's library. At the Château de Chimay he often conducted performances of his own and other compositions by the prince's private orchestra, which included masses by Cherubini in the chapel.

Meanwhile Osborne's theological studies were pursued with lessening interest, and when he was twenty years old he finally decided to adopt music as his profession. In this step he was warmly supported by the prince de Chimay, who procured for him the appointment of instructor to the eldest son of the prince of Orange, who was later to become king of Holland. In Brussels, as chapel-master to the prince of Orange, Osborne directed many successful concerts, at one of which he met the violinist Charles Auguste de Bériot and accompanied the singer Maria Malibran, who in 1836 became Bériot's wife. Bériot and Osborne became close friends, and together they composed thirty-three duets for violin and piano, many of which enjoyed a great vogue for a time.

During the Belgian revolution of 1830 Osborne figured as a volunteer on the royalist side, and it is related that an attempt to shoot him was frustrated only by a defect in his assailant's gun. He was, however, made a prisoner, but released at the intercession of the prince. In 1831 Osborne went to Paris, where he lived for years in close contact with Cherubini, Auber, Stephen Heller, Liszt, and the violinist Heinrich Wilhelm Ernst. With Berlioz and Chopin he was particularly well acquainted, and he published his reminiscences of them, as well as some autobiographical matter, in two papers read before the Musical Association on 3 February 1879 and 5 April 1880 (*Proceedings of the Musical Association*, 5, 1879–80, 60–75, 6, 1880–81, 91–105). Osborne was one of the four pianists who played the accompaniments to Chopin's F minor concerto on the piano (the composer playing the solo part) at the famous concert in Paris on 26 February 1832. When Berlioz and

Chopin visited England, Osborne spent much time with them.

While living in Paris, Osborne continued his musical studies under Johann Peter Pixis, Fétis, Antoine Reicha, and Friedrich Kalkbrenner. At the same time he wrote a large number of compositions, chiefly piano music of a light character. His sister Bessie Osborne, later Mrs Hampton, an amateur singer, visited him in Paris and became fashionable for her renditions of Irish melodies at social gatherings. In 1844 and 1845 Osborne spent some time in London and gave several concerts there. He made the city his permanent home from the end of 1847, when the threat of revolution forced him to relinquish his house in Paris. He paid a brief visit to Ireland in 1848. By the time of his establishment in London, Osborne had already published his piano piece *La pluie de perles*, which was said to have brought him several thousand pounds, twelve different publishers being licensed by him to produce editions of it. Its popularity gained for him numerous pupils in London, where his vogue as a teacher lasted almost until his death. Osborne also played frequently in public, making tours of the provinces with distinguished artists. Although upwards of eighty years of age, he made his last appearance in public at a concert of the Wind Instrument Society on 15 November 1889. He died at his residence, 5 Ulster Terrace, Regent's Park, on 16 November 1893, and was buried in Highgate cemetery. He left at least one son, George.

Osborne excelled in his performances of Bach, and many young musicians sought his advice as to the correct manner of playing Chopin. He was one of the first English musicians to recognize the importance of the music of Schumann and Brahms, and to present a positive critical response to Wagner; he conducted the first performance in England of a work by Wagner, an orchestral arrangement made from the piano score of the march from *Tannhäuser*, at a concert of the Amateur Musical Society at the Hanover Square Rooms in April 1854. In 1876 he visited Bayreuth. Besides numerous piano fantasias and transcriptions, mostly derived from well-known operas, Osborne composed three overtures (one of which, *The Forest Maiden*, was written for the Brighton festival of 1875 and performed at the Alexandra Palace in 1876), two operas (of which *Sylvia* was rehearsed at Drury Lane but never performed), a few songs, and some accomplished chamber music, including a sextet (op. 63, for piano, flute, oboe, horn, cello, and double bass, published in Paris *c*.1840), three piano trios and several string quartets (all unpublished), and a cello sonata (published in London in 1876). His music lacks originality, but is accomplished and possessed considerable popular appeal. While living in Belgium, Osborne was decorated by the king with the order of the Oak-Crown. He was also a member of the Philharmonic Society of London, a director of the Royal Academy of Music, and for years a prominent member of the Musical Association. He was a genial and kind friend to young musicians, and an admirable public speaker, especially when speaking extemporaneously. His cheerful nature, delightful sense of humour, and pleasant Irish brogue were all noted by his contemporaries, and Charles Villiers Stanford described him as 'that most excellent of men and most delightful of companions' (Stanford, *Studies and Memories*, 123).

R. H. LEGGE, *rev.* ROSEMARY FIRMAN

Sources Brown & Stratton, *Brit. mus.* • J. Mongrédien, 'Osborne, George Alexander', *New Grove* • *A love of life and music: the memoirs of Hector Berlioz*, ed. and trans. D. Cairns (1977); repr. (1987) [Fr. orig., *Mémoires de Hector Berlioz* (1870)] • A. W. Ganz, *Berlioz in London* (1950) • C. V. Stanford, *Studies and memories* (1908) • C. V. Stanford, *Pages from an unwritten diary* (1914) • *The Times* (22 Nov 1893) • *MT*, 34 (1893), 739 • *MT*, 35 (1894), 16–17 • private information (1894) • P. A. Scholes, *The mirror of music, 1844–1944: a century of musical life in Britain as reflected in the pages of the Musical Times*, 1 (1947), 252 • d. cert. • Grove, *Dict. mus.*

Wealth at death £2307 9*s*. 10*d*.: resworn probate, March 1894, *CGPLA Eng. & Wales* (1893)

Osborne, Henry. *See* Osborn, Henry (*bap*. 1694, *d*. 1771).

Osborne, John James (1929–1994), playwright and autobiographer, was born on 12 December 1929 at 2 Cookham Road, Fulham, west London, the only son of Thomas Godfrey Osborne (*d*. 1942), a commercial artist and advertising copywriter, and Nellie Beatrice Grove.

Early years and education The Osbornes were from south Wales, gentle and genteel poor, with a sense, according to Osborne, that they had been done some social injustice. Osborne adored his father, who died of tuberculosis when Osborne was twelve. The Groves were tough, noisy, and indestructible cockneys who ran a string of pubs across London. Osborne's mother was a barmaid all her life. He hated her. A family diet of virulence and *Schadenfreude* nourished a dramatist and commentator who combined, to a degree rare in modern England, unsparing truthfulness with devastating wit.

Thomas Osborne left an insurance policy which paid for John to go to St Michael's, Barnstaple, a minor Devon public school, in 1943. He was expelled in the summer term of 1945 after thumping the headmaster, who had struck him for listening to a proscribed broadcast by Frank Sinatra. School certificate was the only formal qualification he acquired, but his intelligence was sharp and streetwise from the start, and he was stage-struck. As an actor in local amateur theatre, he took dancing lessons at the Gaycroft School of Dancing and Drama and Speech in North Cheam, Surrey, whose director recommended him as an assistant stage manager and children's teacher to a company setting up a 'number two' tour of England with a popular melodrama of the day, *No Room at the Inn*.

Acting on the road, *c*.1947–1955 A number two tour went to the smaller towns where live drama was hanging by a thread. It was the toughest practical training for a life in the theatre, with no time for fine-tuning or second thoughts. (Some of Osborne's greatest successes were later written at high speed—*Look Back in Anger* in nine days, *The Entertainer* in eleven—and he rarely rewrote.) He remained a touring jobbing actor for seven years. For a playwright whose chief subject would be England and the English, he acquired a priceless experience of English attitudes on the ground. He wrote his first play in 1949.

John James Osborne (1929–1994), by Daniel Farson, 1956

Far from Huddersfield, Ilfracombe, Kidderminster, or Frinton, British theatre was enjoying a golden age of great acting. British playwrights came a poor second, and all new work was read for perceived improprieties and sedition by the lord chamberlain's office. Shaftesbury Avenue took its passion from Broadway (Tennessee Williams, Arthur Miller), and its cleverness from France (Anouilh, Cocteau, Giraudoux, Sartre). It remained blissfully blind to the complexities of the Britain in which Osborne had served his apprenticeship. The country was recovering from a war for survival with a mixture of relief, hardship, exhaustion, and complacency. The empire was being broken up. Osborne was one of the first writers in any medium to address Britain's purpose in the post-imperial age.

To attract the best new writers into the theatre was a prime aim of the English Stage Company, founded in 1955 at the Royal Court Theatre in Sloane Square. George Devine, the artistic director, and Tony Richardson, his deputy, invited scripts, and Osborne sent *Look Back in Anger*. It was his seventh play: written in May–June 1955, partly on the pier at Morecambe, where he was appearing in *Seagulls over Sorrento*, and partly on the Chiswick barge he shared in near poverty with a fellow actor and writer, Anthony Creighton. Richardson told him that it was the best play since the war. Devine scheduled it for the first season, and gave him work as a script reader and actor in the new company. For the first time in his life Osborne felt valued and secure.

Look Back in Anger: transforming British theatre, 1956–1966

One of many myths which gathered around the first night of *Look Back in Anger* on 8 May 1956 was that it was savaged by all the theatre critics except Kenneth Tynan in *The Observer*. The truth is that most influential reviewers acknowledged its stunning vitality and emotional power.

Osborne's cruel comedy of Jimmy Porter, under siege in an attic flat with wife Alison, mistress Helena, and chum Cliff, on a series of provincial Sundays, offered the very un-English spectacle of private grief in a public place. It restored rhetoric to the English stage for the first time since Shaw. It rescued language from its fashionably high-minded role in the verse plays of the day and allowed it back at the heart of the drama where it could drive both character and action. Osborne's ear for the evasiveness behind the clichés, banalities, and non sequiturs of contemporary English was exceptionally keen, and he gave judgment without quarter. English inertia and what he saw as cunning reluctance to give fight never ceased to exasperate him. 'Peace!' explodes Jimmy at one point. 'God! She wants peace! My heart is so full, I feel ill—and she wants peace!' (*Look Back in Anger*, II.1).

Osborne reached his peak in the decade between 1956 and 1966, when he followed *Look Back* with *The Entertainer* (1957), *Luther* (1961), *Inadmissible Evidence* (1965), and *A Patriot for Me* (1965). He was the first to question the point of the monarchy on a prominent public stage and to treat male homosexuality—a criminal condition at the time—as a subject about which it was possible to be at once sympathetic, bracing, and lewd. He ran up the black flag for contempt as an honest and healthy emotion, and for the purgative wisdom of bad behaviour and bad taste. 'The real revelation', wrote Devine's biographer Irving Wardle 'was that a character could behave like a rat and still speak the truth' (Wardle, 'Tragedy'). Audiences relished the chastisement of the plays like hell-fire sermons packed with firecracker jokes.

Look Back in Anger became a best-seller in the bookshops, selling hundreds of thousands of copies and reviving the entire business of play publishing and buying in Britain. It was the single stone that started an avalanche of new writing in the British theatre. Events soon confirmed that the English Stage Company had indeed found the writer for the hour. Autumn 1956 saw the Suez and Hungarian crises, which both entered the bloodstream of *The Entertainer*, Osborne's next play. Laurence Olivier was the first of the established guard to 'cross over' to the Court: he fastened on the role of the vicious comedian Archie Rice with a feral snap, and enjoyed one of the juiciest triumphs of his career.

Since childhood Osborne had loved the danger and rudeness of music-hall—'abiding and cruel, like the English spirit itself'—and set his state-of-the-nation play in this tacky deteriorating world. Archie's dreadful gags and songs are interspersed with Archie failing at home with wife, father, daughter, son. The theatre becomes Britain itself, coming out of 'Suez' and empire with nothing but shame—'Don't clap too hard', cries Archie on cue, for the 5000th time, 'It's a very old building'. Britannia appeared stark naked, but forbidden, by law, to move.

The phrase 'angry young man' was quickly slapped on Osborne, Kingsley Amis, Jimmy Porter, and any other male under thirty who was perceived to question the *status quo*. Like all such labels, it was used by grateful news editors to arouse the reader, defuse a perceived threat to society, and detox its fumes. Osborne became a celebrity, and appeared in a high-profile anthology of work by young writers, *Declarations* (1957), where he wrote, 'I want to make people *feel*, to give them lessons in feeling. They can think afterwards'.

Fleet Street sniffed hubris. Despite the Court success of *Epitaph for George Dillon* (1958), a play written earlier with

Creighton, Osborne was due for his first fall. As he changed wives for the first time, his private life became an open book in the pseudonymous gossip columns of the day, 'Paul Tanfield' of the *Daily Mail* and 'William Hickey' of the *Daily Express*. He hit back with a state-of-the-nation musical in a big West End theatre, bypassing Devine. Though often rudely funny, *The World of Paul Slickey* offered so self-gnawing and relentlessly bitter a view of British corruptibility that it commended itself to almost nobody: it ended the first act of Osborne's career.

Osborne took up with a pugilist German monk. 'I am alone', cries Martin Luther, 'I am alone and against myself'. Here was a kindred spirit, 'sucking up cares like a leech'. Osborne took from Wittenberg the lessons that revolution brings disorder, that men make a mob in no time, and that faith is more important than works. For 'faith', read also 'passion', of which Osborne suffered a lifelong, corrosive excess. *Luther* (1961) restored his critical reputation overnight. His absorption and understanding of the material is impressive, even if some of the writing sounds hard won by homework; the hero's sermons and tormented prayers to a perhaps unlistening God are as grand and moving as Verdi arias. Luther was played by Albert Finney, the first genuine working-class star of the new British theatre and cinema, and the play was a hit.

The matter of Britain had not disappeared. The emotional and political unrest of 1956 had been smoothed away by Harold Macmillan. The Berlin Wall went up in August 1961; the West did little, the arms race gathered speed. On holiday in the south of France, Osborne fired off to *Tribune* a 'Letter to my fellow countrymen' (18 August) which machine-gunned the entire British electorate and those they had elected to lead them into what seemed like an imminent Armageddon. At times barely coherent with distress, it climaxes in the memorable, if Byronically melodramatic 'Damn you, England'. He would not be allowed to forget that he had flung his curse from that most un-Osborne of countries, Abroad.

A member of the Campaign for Nuclear Disarmament since 1959, Osborne returned home and on 17 September joined Doris Lessing, Herbert Read, and hundreds more in an illegal, sit-down protest in Trafalgar Square. Expecting at least a month in prison, he was fined £1 after a night in the cells. He was already disillusioned with the campaign, and it was his last gesture of this kind. Like Philip Larkin, he drifted to the libertarian, unorganized right, considering himself 'a radical who hates change'. With hindsight, it is clear to see that, as he tore up the polite fictions of a century and a half, John Osborne was a patriot reconnecting England with its earlier, more violent, and emotional self.

Posterity will probably decide that *Inadmissible Evidence* (1965) is Osborne's best play—it is the most intensely sustained in feeling, and technically the boldest, often proceeding simultaneously on two levels of both place and time. A solicitor spiralling into breakdown, Bill Maitland has all the strikes against him—lecher, insomniac, mean boss, failed father, terrified husband, and lover—yet his displacement by nothing more or less than his own nature is truly tragic. It is also horribly funny. As he lays about his staff and office in the descent to limbo, Bill glories in the Osborne version of the third beatitude. Blessed the meek most certainly are not. Bad enough that they show the rest of humanity up so badly; why should they also inherit the earth?

After the meek, the hypocrites of censorship. The lord chamberlain's office treated the script of *A Patriot for Me* (1965) like a whore-house in need of fumigation by nuns, snipping words and phrases ('clap', 'crabs', 'Tears of Christ!'), pulling men out of beds, removing three scenes crucial to the emotional credibility of the play, including the dazzling and dangerous drag ball. Osborne resisted all the changes, and Devine turned the Court into a 'club' theatre for the run of the show. The playwright paid half of the production costs himself. The play is long and uneven, but contains some of Osborne's best writing, including scenes of tenderness rare in the rest of his work. From the true story of the homosexual Austrian Colonel Redl, blackmailed into spying for Russia and forced to shoot himself, Osborne created a brilliant panorama of sexual, racial, and class themes. *A Patriot for Me* enjoyed, naturally, a tremendous *succès de scandale*. At the end of 1966 Osborne gave detailed, sobering evidence to the joint parliamentary committee on censorship of the theatre. Censorship was abolished in 1968.

Film, television, and later plays The much loved Devine died of overwork in 1965. Under William Gaskill the Royal Court moved on, although all Osborne's plays were premièred there up to *A Sense of Detachment* (1972). In *The Hotel in Amsterdam* (1968) and *West of Suez* (1971) he wrote marvellous concerto roles for, respectively, Paul Scofield and Ralph Richardson. But these fluent, well-crafted plays are more narrowly metropolitan and less adventurous than their predecessors, and in *A Sense of Detachment* he appeared coldly to deconstruct himself and his actors, critics, and audience entirely.

The cumbersome *Watch it Come Down* (1975) was the National Theatre's last new play at the Old Vic and its first in the new Lasdun building on the South Bank—fondly described by Osborne as 'Colditz-on-Thames'. *Déjavu* (1989) was a peppery, genial retake of *Look Back in Anger*, thirty-seven years on. Some of the sparring was laboured, but there was much unchanging wisdom and force.

With Tony Richardson and the American producer Harry Saltzman, Osborne founded Woodfall Films in 1958, to put *Look Back in Anger* on screen, with Richard Burton as Jimmy, followed by *The Entertainer* (1959), with Olivier. Woodfall produced many of the best British movies of the 1960s, above all the glorious *Tom Jones* (1962), for which Osborne won an Oscar for best screenplay. (Richardson took Oscars for best picture and best director.) His television plays—among them *A Matter of Scandal and Concern*, *Ms*, and *God Rot Tunbridge Wells*, a play about Handel with Trevor Howard—were sharply scaled to an intimate medium.

Marriages and friendships In appearance Osborne was tall and lean, with a bony elegance, high cheekbones, and delicate, feminine lips. It was a witty face which on camera could accommodate pipes, cigarettes, or cigars, sulk moodily, burst into wicked laughter or a sparkling smile. A complex and byzantine personal life—countless friendships, loyal and betrayed, five marriages, four broken, one lasting—informed his work. *The Hotel in Amsterdam*, best and most Chekhovian of his later plays, resembles Noel Coward's *Present Laughter* in being entirely about the friendship of kindred souls in the long shadow cast by a single, absent, monster ego. If Osborne seemed to feel a real regret that women could not be friends with chaps as chaps can—the designer Jocelyn Rickards being an exception—there is also a near obsession with homosexuality in men.

'Where does friendship end and where do people become queer?' Osborne asked in 1968. He describes his quarrelsome friendship with the bisexual Richardson as a 'mariage blanc', and in the memoirs and journalism loses few opportunities to show that he could attract homosexuals, but was never a 'poof'. 'How queer are you?' asked Coward, precisely to the point at their first meeting. 'About 20 per cent', replied the young dandy. On other occasions, the figure varied considerably, but in 1992 he told Lynn Barber of the *Independent on Sunday* (2 February 1992) that he had never had sex with another man. Attempts to prove otherwise after his death, drawing on the evidence of the openly gay Creighton, were inconclusive, and by then the world cared a lot less.

More interesting is the theatrical use he made of his obsession. In one interview he described homosexuality as 'a metaphor of ambiguity and pain'. Homosexuals lived in an alternative society, 'like sinners in church'. Before the decriminalizing of male homosexual acts in 1967, Osborne could see being queer in England as a heroic, subversive condition; as soon as they began to join the visible world, gays became just another pressure group, prone to cant, and, as such, fair game.

Three of Osborne's wives were actresses, two journalists on *The Observer*. The first two marriages—from 1951 to 1957 to Pamela Elizabeth Lane, who inspired the character Alison Porter, and from 1957 to 1963 to Mary Eileen *Ure (1933–1975), the first Alison on stage—both ended in divorce but apparently without much public bitterness. The third—to the writer and critic Penelope Ann Douglass *Gilliatt, *née* Conner (1932–1993), whom he married on 25 May 1963—also ended in divorce but was lived out more publicly, since her first husband had been best man at the wedding of Princess Margaret and Tony Armstrong-Jones. Osborne and Gilliatt had a daughter, Nolan; when she grew up, Osborne rejected her as 'devotedly suburban'. In her prime, Gilliatt was a brilliant critic and gifted fiction writer, but she moved in rather posh circles and seemed to arouse the bully in Osborne. He also learned what it was like to be married to someone whose first marriage was to her newspaper. The competition was unwelcome.

In 1968 Osborne divorced Gilliatt and married the actress Jill Bennett (1929–1990), formerly married to Willis Hall. One director friend remembered them walking down the King's Road in Chelsea: tall, stylish, competing wits, like Beatrice and Benedick. After a few years, Shakespeare soured into Strindberg, and the marriage performed a dance of death with bilious acrimony for anyone who would watch. In 1977 they divorced. 'She was the most evil woman I have come across', Osborne told Barber, and his contempt for Bennett's suicide in 1990 showed that his fury had lost none of its power to shock.

Indian summer and the art of revenge, 1989–1991 Osborne's fifth and last marriage (from 1978 to his death), to the former arts journalist and critic of *The Observer* Helen Dawson, was devoted and comparatively private. In the redoubtable Dawson he finally met an intelligent partner with no competing ambitions. They settled in Shropshire, near Craven Arms. She organized and typed for him, and encouraged him to write his memoirs. It was the best advice he received since the death of George Devine. On these irresistible two volumes—as much as on the plays—his reputation will rest.

Osborne's *A Better Class of Person* (1989) and *Almost a Gentleman* (1991) are among the best—and funniest—memoirs of their time. (A third volume was commissioned, but never finished.) Few writers have described more brilliantly the banal hermetic smugness of lower middle-class suburban life. In the account of his career up to 1966, not many are spared, but they include Devine, Dawson, Robert Stephens, John Dexter, and Vivien Leigh. His mother emerged as the most baleful—but also the greatest—influence on his life. She taught him 'The fatality of hatred … She is my disease, an invitation to my sick room' (Osborne, *A Better Class of Person*, 271). She embodied all the things he most disliked about England in her 'hypocritical, self-absorbed, calculating and indifferent' self. But if her sin was indifference in his childhood, her crimes were cunning pathos and sweet reasonableness before his rage. Nellie Beatrice was indestructible. She revelled in the attention, particularly from the *Daily Mail*. Attempting matricide, Osborne instead made a creature of whom Dickens would have been proud.

Through the 1980s Osborne played the role of Shropshire squire with great pleasure and a heavy slosh of irony. He wrote a diary for *The Spectator*. He opened his garden to raise money for the church roof, from which he threatened to withdraw covenant-funding unless the vicar restored the Book of Common Prayer. Defying 'frivolously rabid, churchless wives', he had returned to the Church of England about 1974. Everything he wrote was fired by the fierce belief that 'We really do live in a very wicked world' ('Intellectuals and just causes: a symposium', *Encounter*, vol. 29, no. 3 Sept 1967).

Osborne had a serious liver crisis in 1987 and became a diabetic, injecting twice a day. He died at his home, The Hurst, Clunton, near Craven Arms, Shropshire, of heart failure and diabetes complications on Christmas eve 1994. He was buried in St George's churchyard, Clun. He would have been unsurprised to learn that the end, when it came, was as a *Daily Mail* scoop. 'Angry Man of Theatre Dies', tolled the great enemy solemnly on Boxing day 1994. It had been a quiet Christmas, no one else had the story, and they gave him the front page. Next day, the *Daily Express* lost no time in reminding its readers what a bad boy he had been as they kicked the corpse into its grave.

MICHAEL RATCLIFFE

Sources J. Osborne, *A better class of person* (1981) • J. Osborne, *Almost a gentleman* (1991) • J. Osborne, *Damn you, England* (1994) • cuttings from many sources, 1956–2000, *Guardian* library • I. Wardle, 'The tragedy of John Osborne', *Independent on Sunday* (1 Jan 1995) • I. Wardle, *The theatres of George Devine* (1978) • W. Gaskill, *A sense of direction* (1988) • T. Richardson, *Long distance runner* (1993) • K. Tynan, *A view of the English stage* (1984) • R. Stephens, *Knight errant* (1995) • J. Dexter, *The honourable beast* (1993) • *WWW*, 1980–90 • *WWW*, 1991–5 • b. cert. • d. cert. • L. Barber, interview, *Independent on Sunday* (2 Feb 1992)
Archives Indiana University, Bloomington, Lilly Library, corresp. and literary papers • U. Texas, diaries, letters, notebooks, literary MSS | FILM priv. coll.?, filmed scene of Osborne and Jill Bennett in *A patriot for me* at a fundraising event, 1960s
Likenesses D. Farson, bromide print, 1956, NPG [*see illus.*] • photographs, 1956–77, Hult. Arch. • J. Bown, photograph, 1959, repro. in *The Observer* (17 May 1959) • D. Stock, photograph, 1963, repro. in *Sunday Times* (13 July 1963) • Z. Dominic, photograph, 1965, repro. in *The Times* (1993) • photograph, 1968, repro. in *The Guardian* (6 June 1992) • Douglas Brothers, photograph, 1992, repro. in *Independent on Sunday* (2 Feb 1992) • A. Armstrong-Jones, group portrait, photograph, repro. in *Vogue* (1958?) • Snowdon, photograph, repro. in Osborne, *Damn you, England*, cover • F. Topolski, photograph, NPG
Wealth at death £585,764: probate, 9 Feb 1995, *CGPLA Eng. & Wales*

Malcolm Osborne (1880–1963), by Dorothy Webster Hawksley, 1959

Osborne, Malcolm (1880–1963), printmaker and teacher of printmaking, was born on 1 August 1880 at 2 Waterloo, Frome, Somerset, one of three sons of Alfred Arthur Osborne, a schoolmaster, and his wife, Sarah Elizabeth, *née* Biggs. Osborne was educated in Bristol at the Merchant Venturers' School, then at the Queen's Road School of Art; in 1901 he won a scholarship to the Royal College of Art, intending to be a sculptor. After the mandatory term in the school of architecture Osborne—encouraged by Charles Lethaby, the professor of design—changed to graphic art. In Frank Short's etching class Osborne learned all forms of copper printmaking, integrating an innate sense of form and design with technical craftsmanship.

Osborne's first original etching came after a British Institute scholarship in 1904; this was followed by landscapes and other work in drypoint for which he was elected associate of the Royal Society of Painter-Printmakers in 1906; he became a full member in 1909 and served as president in 1938. His pre-war work is of mixed quality: the acclaim that greeted the etching *My Mother* and the mezzotint *William Morris* after G. F. Watts is difficult to sustain now; of the London streetscapes *National Gallery Portico* is much the best, with the city full of Edwardian vigour and bustle; while the *Timber Haulers* after C. W. Furse, although reproductive, is magnificent. The landscapes similarly display a disparity in accomplishment: for example, the gentle delicateness of *After the Storm, Amberley* with the dull heaviness of *Stirling Bridge*.

Osborne joined the Artists' Rifles in 1914, was commissioned in 1915, and was continuously in action in France, Macedonia, and Palestine. He was informed of his election as an associate of the Royal Academy while in command of a trench mortar company outside Jerusalem waiting to attack. Demobbed in July 1919, he taught at the Central School of Arts and Crafts in London and produced the first of a series of justly distinguished portraits with *The Problem* (of his friend Arnold Mason). In 1921 this was followed by another of equal worth, *Nathaniel Sparks*, and *Trekkers of the Plain, Salonica*, one of only two etchings of wartime experience.

In 1924 Osborne succeeded Frank Short at the Royal College of Art as professor of etching and engraving; he reorganized the school, appointing as assistant teachers Job Nixon (etching) and Robert Wright Stewart (lithography). He continued his own printmaking and is remembered by his students not only as a superb craftsman but as a conscientious and caring teacher. On 19 July 1927 he married in St Luke's Church, Kensington, London, Amy Margaret Stableford (*b.* 1882/3). In 1940 he evacuated the school to Ambleside in the Lake District, returning to London in 1945. He retired in 1948 to be succeeded by Robert Austin; during his retirement he produced many prints. He died at his home, 44 Redcliffe Gardens, West Brompton, on 22 September 1963, survived by his wife.

Osborne was elected Royal Academician in 1926 and created CBE in 1948, but his reputation has been eclipsed by the generation of artist-printmakers a decade his junior who formed the vanguard of the modern movement, just as etching itself fell out of favour after 1930. It is no surprise that the last critical work on Osborne was published in 1929, and that many authorities since have repeated the formula that after 1925 his work generally loses its quality and refinement. There are many fine prints after this period, however, including the late landscapes of the Lake District such as *The Veil of Spring, Windermere* (aquatint, 1947), and portraits such as *Frank Short* (1931) and *Douglas Cockerell* (1948). Prints by Osborne are in the Ashmolean Museum, Oxford, and the British Museum and the Victoria and Albert Museum, London. HAL BISHOP

Sources M. C. Salaman, 'Etchings of Malcolm Osborne ARA, RE', *Print Collectors' Quarterly*, 12 (1925), 285–313 • M. C. Salaman, *Malcolm Osborne* (1929) • K. M. Guichard, *British etchers, 1850–1940* (1981) • private information (2004) [J. Bostock] • A. Jarman and others, eds., *Royal Academy exhibitors, 1905–1970: a dictionary of artists and their work in the summer exhibitions of the Royal Academy of Arts*, 6 vols. (1973–82) • C. Frayling, *The Royal College of Art: one hundred and fifty years of art and design* (1987) • M. C. Salaman, 'Etchings and engravings of Malcolm Osborne ARA, RE', *The Studio*, 75 (1919), 110–17 • R. Garton, introduction, *British printmakers, 1855–1955* (1992) • G. M. Waters, *Dictionary of British artists, working 1900–1950* (1975) • D. Buckman, *The dictionary of artists in Britain since the war* (1998) • prints and catalogues, BM, department of prints and drawings • b. cert. • m. cert. • d. cert. • *CGPLA Eng. & Wales* (1963)

Likenesses D. W. Hawksley, chalk and watercolour drawing, 1959, NPG [*see illus.*]

Wealth at death £254 19*s*. 7*d*.: probate, 30 Oct 1963, *CGPLA Eng. & Wales*

Osborne, Peregrine, **second duke of Leeds** (*bap*. **1659**, *d*. **1729**), naval officer, was baptized on 29 December 1659 at Harthill, Yorkshire, fifth of the eleven children of Thomas *Osborne, first duke of Leeds (1632–1712), and his wife, Bridget (*bap*. 1629, *d*. 1704), daughter of Montagu *Bertie, second earl of Lindsey, and his first wife, Martha. Osborne was tutored privately and, to complete his education, on 16 March 1671 accompanied his eldest brother to France for nine months. His father secured for him in 1673 reversions to the clerkship of the patents in the court of chancery and the lucrative auditorship of the exchequer, but he never obtained either office. On 15 December 1674, after his father became earl of Danby, Thomas Osborne's former Scottish title of Viscount Osborne of Dunblane was regranted to his son; in the new patent the title was given as Viscount Dumblane, by which Osborne was known until 1689. Though under age he was elected MP for Berwick upon Tweed in 1677, and spent a month attached to Ralph Montagu's Paris embassy, to learn the art of diplomacy. As a member of the court party, he was classed by Shaftesbury as 'thrice vile' (Cruickshanks, 184). He became MP for Corfe Castle, Dorset, on 26 February 1679, only to be unseated in April on petition. From 1679 to 1682 he actively sought his father's release from the Tower.

Danby aimed to marry his son to a wealthy heiress, Bridget (1662–1734), daughter of Sir Thomas Hyde, second baronet, of Aldbury, Hertfordshire, and stepdaughter of the goldsmith-banker Sir Robert Viner, one of Danby's foremost business allies. Unfortunately, when aged twelve she had allegedly married her cousin John Emerton. While Danby was occupied in protracted legal and financial proceedings to get this marriage annulled, Dumblane wooed the heiress into a private marriage at St Marylebone Church on 25 April 1682. They had two sons (the elder died of smallpox in 1711) and two daughters; Dumblane also had an illegitimate son, who was a midshipman in 1729.

In June 1685 Dumblane was slightly wounded in Feversham's army at the battle of Sedgemoor. He became a feckless spendthrift and, having squandered most of his wife's fortune and accumulated debts of £10,000, fled to the continent, only ten days after his wife miscarried, to avoid his creditors. On his return to England in January 1687 his financial affairs were put firmly under his father's control. In April 1688 he carried letters for Danby to William of Orange and, anticipating William's invasion, in November raided Welbeck, home of the duke of Newcastle, for arms. Elected MP for York in the Convention Parliament (January 1689), Dumblane, though nominal leader of his father's tory group, showed little interest in parliamentary matters. Although he voted on 5 February against declaring the throne vacant, the next day he followed Danby's change of heart in pledging loyalty to William, publicly recanting in the House of Commons. He was rewarded by a warrant for the office of postmaster-general; inexplicably it went to John Wildman, the veteran ex-republican. On his father's elevation to the marquessate on 20 April 1689, Dumblane was styled earl of Danby.

His naval career developed from his hobby of designing yachts. In the summer of 1689 the new earl of Danby fitted out a privateer, an action which caused his father to seek a warrant for his arrest for treason; he was released after House of Commons protests at this breach of its privileges. On 3 March 1690 he was summoned to the House of Lords in his father's barony as Lord Osborne of Kiveton; for a time he attended with exemplary regularity, but he rarely spoke. In the same year he used one of his speedy yachts to arrest Lord Preston and other Jacobite conspirators *en route* for France. He fought gallantly as second in command of the naval force in the unsuccessful attack on Brest, and commanded a regiment of dragoons raised by the City of London after the Anglo-Dutch defeat off Beachy Head on 30 June. This loyalty secured him the post of colonel commanding the first regiment of marines ever formed. His impulsive generosity and unpredictability endeared him to his ships' crews.

After showing conspicuous gallantry at Barfleur in 1692, Danby was allowed to fly a special swallowtail pennant. If his offer to reconnoitre Brest had been taken up, French capture of the merchant fleet bound for Smyrna might have been avoided. On 12 July 1693 he was promoted to rear-admiral of the red, and given command of a special flotilla of bomb-vessels and fireships for an attack on St Malo. He became rear-admiral of the blue in January 1694, and the Admiralty backed his views on the girdling of ships against Navy Board opposition. After his father became duke of Leeds on 4 May, Peregrine became known as marquess of Carmarthen. His spirited exploits at Camarets Bay in 1694 were followed by publication of his

Journal of the Brest Expedition. In the summer of 1695 he was escorting home the eighty-sail Cadiz merchant fleet when he mistook eighteen East Indiamen for the French Brest squadron; considering himself outnumbered he retired to Milford Haven, where, wind-bound, he failed to prevent five of the East Indiamen falling into French hands. Summoned back to London, he was sacrificed by the Admiralty to mercantile ire, though a committee of the House of Lords praised his courage and fidelity.

In the autumn of 1697 William III presented Tsar Peter the Great, in the Netherlands, with the *Royal Transport*, a heavily armed yacht designed by Carmarthen, and described (Luttrell, 4.290) as the 'best sailer' in the fleet. Peter was so pleased with the vessel that on his visit to England in 1698 he sought out Carmarthen, who had further improved its sailing performance. A model of the ship in the St Petersburg naval museum shows it to have had a schooner rig, so that it could sail closer to the wind than any contemporary square-rigged warship. Russian sources suggest that Carmarthen had a large collection of ships' models, and that Tsar Peter bought similar models on his advice. The marquess became quite intimate with Peter, and introduced him to his favourite tipple, brandy laced with peppers. He helped organize a mock battle at Portsmouth in Peter's honour, and gave him directions for the creation of a modern Russian navy. He even recommended personnel to achieve this: Henry Farquarson, later professor of mathematics at the St Petersburg naval academy; John Perry, who supervised the building of Russian dockyards and canals; and shipbuilders Nye and Dean. As a reward Carmarthen was given by the tsar the sole privilege of importing tobacco into Russia, which he immediately assigned to the Heathcotes and other London merchants in return for a lump sum of 1000 guineas and £1500 per annum for life. He received little of either grant.

In 1699 Carmarthen was assigned a special galley, the 190 ton *Peregrine*, built at his direction and at royal expense, in lieu of £9000 arrears of a Charles II pension; however, William III refused to part with her, and a further compensatory pension of £1000 per annum was never paid. Although some aristocratic naval appointments under Anne were clearly 'dormant', Carmarthen rose to be nominally vice-admiral of the red in 1703. In 1705 he led the squadron that shipped Marlborough to the Southern Netherlands, and wrote a pamphlet, *Method for the Speedy Manning Her Majesty's Royal Navy*. His naval career culminated in his appointment on 21 December 1708 as admiral of the red. At the trial of Dr Sacheverell in March 1710 he voted with a minority of the lords for acquittal. On the death of his father he became duke of Leeds, though most of his father's estates went to his own son, on whom he became financially dependent. He was lord lieutenant of the East Riding of Yorkshire in 1713–14.

After 1714 Leeds seems to have reverted to his earlier political loyalties. During the 1715 Jacobite rising he declared, 'I had not a thought when I engaged in [the 1688–9 revolution] … that the Prince of Orange's landing would end in deposing the King' (GEC, *Peerage*, new edn, 7.511). 1716–17 saw him plotting with Jacobites in France as Mr Laurence. Although Bolingbroke termed him a 'madman' (ibid.), in correspondence with the Jacobite King James III he was promised (on 6 April 1716) £200,000, an earldom, and command of the fleet. While his wife, 'ruined by her cruel lord's inhuman usage' (ibid., 513), appealed in 1717 to the crown for assistance, Leeds remained in exile until pardoned in 1723. He died, in indigent circumstances, on 25 June 1729 and was buried at Aldbury, Hertfordshire on 4 July; his wife was buried with him on 16 March 1734. He was succeeded, as third duke of Leeds, by his second son, Peregrine (1691–1731), who married as his first wife the daughter of Edward Harley, earl of Oxford.

A short, fair-complexioned, wiry figure, who in his youth played the violin well, Leeds was fiery (he fought at least three duels in 1693–8), 'bold, volatile and somewhat eccentric' (Macaulay, 4.1966). Undoubtedly something of a rake, he was permanently impecunious, though unlucky in office and pension (and he spent considerable amounts in the interests of the crown and starving marines). Yet he was a committed and not unsuccessful naval commander, and innovative in ship design. His father's political influence probably helped in his pursuit of yachting experiments, in the face of considerable Admiralty opposition; but one modern authority goes as far as to suggest that 'if [tsar] Peter [the Great] is known … as the "Father of the Russian Fleet" … then surely [Osborne] can be regarded as at least its godfather' (Ryan, 81).

Basil Morgan

Sources A. Browning, *Thomas Osborne, earl of Danby and duke of Leeds, 1632–1712*, 3 vols. (1944–51) · W. F. Ryan, 'Peter the Great's English yacht: Admiral Lord Carmarthen and the Russian tobacco monopoly', *Mariner's Mirror*, 69 (1983), 65–84 · J. S. Bromley, ed., 'The manning of the Royal Navy: selected pamphlets, 1693–1873', *Navy Records Society*, 119 (1976), 42–5, 374–6 · GEC, *Peerage*, new edn, 7.507–13 · E. Cruickshanks, 'Osborne, Peregrine', HoP, *Commons, 1660–90* · *DNB* · *CSP dom., 1670–71; 1673–5; 1677–8; 1689–91; 1693–1704* · A. Grey, ed., *Debates of the House of Commons, from the year 1667 to the year 1694*, 10 vols. (1763) · N. Luttrell, *A brief historical relation of state affairs from September 1678 to April 1714*, 6 vols. (1857) · E. Hamilton, *The backstairs dragon*, US edn (1970) · *The Sergison papers*, ed. R. D. Merriman, Navy RS, 89 (1950), 73ff. · T. B. Macaulay, *The history of England from the accession of James II*, new edn, ed. C. H. Firth, 6 vols. (1913–15)

Archives W. Yorks. AS, Leeds, Yorkshire Archaeological Society, papers | BL, letters to William Blathwayt, Add. MS 34351 · BL, letters to his son, Egerton MS 3385a · NRA, priv. coll., letters to his wife

Likenesses stipple, pubd 1806 (after Petitot), NPG · engraving, repro. in H. Walpole, *A catalogue of the royal and noble authors of England, Scotland, and Ireland* (1806), vol. 4

Osborne, Peter (1521–1592), administrator, was the second son of Richard Osborne of Tyld Hall, Lachingdon, Essex, and his wife, Elizabeth Coke. His family had long been settled at Purleigh in Essex. Osborne was possibly educated at Cambridge University. He entered Lincoln's Inn in 1543, becoming associate bencher in 1566 and assistant governor in 1570.

Osborne probably married, before 1551, Anne (*d.* 1615),

daughter of Dr John Blythe, regius professor of physic at Cambridge, and niece of Sir John Cheke. The couple had eleven sons, including John (1551–1628), Christopher (1557/8–1600), who were both MPs, and Henry Osborne (*b.* 1557/8, *d.* in or after 1648), and eleven daughters. John Osborne was the father of Sir Peter Osborne [*see below*] and the writer Francis *Osborne (1593–1659). Peter Osborne's political success is probably attributable to his connection with two important men, William Cecil, Lord Burghley, and Cheke. Marriage ties and religious convictions established and reinforced his friendships with both men. Cecil became Osborne's parliamentary patron, turning to his fellow protestant Francis Russell, second earl of Bedford, to secure a seat for him. Osborne was returned as MP for Tregony in Cornwall in 1559, although he may have been elected to Bridport in Dorset as early as March 1553, when he was described as 'toward the Pryve Chamber, and a great officer in the Eschequier, being also of right good estymacion & lernyng, and one who in that place maye doe your towne mouche good' (*Sixth Report*, HMC, 1.497). Cheke's position at court as chamberlain of the exchequer and principal secretary ensured that Osborne obtained lucrative offices in the exchequer under Edward VI. In 1551 Osborne was appointed clerk of the faculties and keeper of the privy purse. From 1552 to 1553, and again from 1559 until his death, he was the lord treasurer's remembrancer in the exchequer. He probably supported Lady Jane Grey in July 1553, for he was reported to have been in prison at some time during Mary I's reign. This seems probable because of his close association with John Dudley, duke of Northumberland, from autumn 1552. Cheke and Osborne were certainly close friends, even after Mary's accession: Cheke appointed him one of his executors and died at his house in Wood Street, London, in September 1557. Osborne's daughter Katherine later married Cheke's grandson Sir Thomas Cheke.

Osborne again rose to prominence in the country's financial affairs under Elizabeth I, because he was considered 'an authority upon commercial matters' (*DNB*). In 1560, the same year in which he became involved in royal minting activities, the queen granted him the manor of South Fambridge, Essex. By 1562 Osborne had relocated from Wood Street to Ivy Lane, London, possibly to accommodate his growing household. In 1562 he became an ecclesiastical commissioner. He was added to the quorum of the peace for Middlesex at about the same time. His other posts included deputy governor of the Society of Mineral and Battery Works in 1568. Osborne was commissioner for disputes with Portugal in 1573 and for piracy in 1580. Burghley continued to be Osborne's primary patron, ensuring that he was elected as MP for Horsham, Sussex, in 1563, Guildford, Surrey, in 1571, Plympton Eagle, Devon, in 1572, Aldeburgh, Suffolk, in 1584 and 1586, and Burghley's own borough, Westminster, in 1589. During Elizabeth's reign, Osborne corresponded with Burghley, principally about commercial matters. They discussed merchant contractors, wine transport from the Netherlands to Spain, and contracts for the carriage of salt. By January 1578 Burghley had secured the reversion of lord treasurer's remembrancer to Osborne's eldest son, John Osborne. Peter Osborne was triumphant, for he considered that office the 'stay of his house, his wife and his children' (*Salisbury MSS*, 2.177).

Beginning in 1576 Osborne began to purchase from Edward Snowe parts of the priory of Chicksands in Bedfordshire, a house of the Gilbertine order with two cloisters. He never established a residence there, leaving this task instead to John Osborne. He died on 7 June 1592 and was buried at St Faith's under St Paul's. His widow died in 1615.

Sir Peter Osborne (1584/5–1653), administrator, was the eldest of five sons of Sir John Osborne (1551–1628), administrator, of Chicksands, and his wife, Dorothy (1561/2–1638), eldest daughter and heir of Richard Barlee of Elsenham Hall, Essex. He had one sister and was named after his grandfather. Sir John Osborne purchased Chicksands outright before 1600, making it his principal residence. There he restored Campton church, built a vicarage, and constructed a family mausoleum. His other sons included Christopher (*d.* 1635x40), Thomas (*d.* 1651), and Richard Osborne (*d.* 1634). Peter Osborne was admitted as a fellow-commoner of Emmanuel College, Cambridge, on 11 July 1603. On 20 February 1610 he married Dorothy (1590–1650/51), the sixth and youngest daughter of Sir John Danvers of Dauntsey, Wiltshire, and his wife, Elizabeth. His wife's brothers were Henry *Danvers, first Baron Danvers of Dauntsey and first earl of Danby (1573–1644), and Sir John *Danvers (1584/5–1655), of Chelsea. Osborne was knighted on 7 January 1611. In 1621 he was appointed lieutenant-governor of Guernsey, with the governorship reverting to him on Danvers of Dauntsey's death. He thereafter took up residence at Castle Cornet, a small fort guarding the approach to the harbour of St Peter Port. It is doubtful that his wife and children ever lived there with him. He was MP for Corfe Castle, Dorset, in 1623–4 and 1625. On his father's death on 2 November 1628, he succeeded to the office of lord treasurer's remembrancer and his family took up residence at Chicksands. At this time he had nine children: Thomas (1609–1637), Elizabeth (*b.* 1610, *d.* in or after 1631), Ann (1613–1642), Henry (1614–1645), Sir John Osborne, baronet (*c.*1615–1699), Sir Henry Osborne (1619–1675), Charles (1620–1642), Robert (1626–*c.*1653), and Dorothy *Osborne, married name Temple (1627–1695). There were other children, who all died young. Sir Peter Osborne spent most of his time away from his family, fulfilling his duties at Guernsey, where he was in charge of 200 soldiers. When he did go to London to report to the council of war, he often visited his wife and her relations at the earl of Danby's house. From November 1640 to August 1641 he was possibly resident in Chelsea. On 23 April 1640 he advanced £1000 to Charles I, who was desperate for money.

When hostilities began between king and parliament in 1642, Osborne determined to take his family to the safety of Guernsey. However, Guernsey chose to side with parliament and Osborne held Castle Cornet for the king. Robert

*Rich, second earl of Warwick (1587–1658), became the governor of Guernsey in 1643 and several times ordered Osborne to surrender Castle Cornet. Osborne refused his old friend and kinsman in the most courteous terms and continued to hold out for aid from Charles. This assistance never materialized despite many assurances. Osborne and his men were in dire straits after the castle was besieged from March 1643, for they had always relied on Guernsey's residents for their sustenance. When he took over at Castle Cornet, his wife had retreated with her children to the safety of St Malo. She was soon forced to sell her plate and to contract heavy debts in order to aid her husband's plight. She became ill towards the end of 1643 and left St Malo with her children on a Dutch ship for England. Since Chicksands had been sequestered by order of the parliamentary committee for delinquencies on 27 April 1643, Dorothy Osborne took her children to live with her brother Sir John Danvers, a parliamentarian. There they met Oliver Cromwell, who reportedly favoured Osborne's youngest daughter, Dorothy. In early 1646 Osborne retreated exhausted to exile in St Malo after Sir Thomas Fanshawe was given command of Castle Cornet. His daughter Dorothy visited him there from 1648 until summer 1649. *En route* she stayed on the Isle of Wight, where she met her future husband, William *Temple (1628–1699). At the time of her marriage in 1654 she recorded that her father's income exceeded £4000 per annum. Her own portion may have been up to £4000.

Sir Peter Osborne concealed some 41 per cent of the real value of his Chicksands estate and his fine was more manageable at £2440. In April 1649 his fourth son, Henry Osborne, attempted to compound for delinquency in order to regain Chicksands. On 29 May 1649 Sir Peter Osborne compounded for his delinquency for 'bearing arms in the first war against Parliament' (Green, *Calendar of the Proceedings of the Committee for Compounding*, 3.1974). His estate was discharged after the payment of a fine on 4 June 1650. There was also some trouble after his death over the reversion of Pickering rectory, Yorkshire, and over the manor of North Fambridge, Essex. Osborne effectively overturned his father's wishes regarding Chicksands and North Fambridge. Sir John Osborne's will of 1626 stipulated that his widow should enjoy possession of Chicksands for life, with reversion to Osborne, and that North Fambridge was to be divided between his four younger sons. After his father's death in 1628, Sir Peter Osborne convinced his mother to live in London with his brother Thomas Osborne and entered into the manor of North Fambridge and his father's other estates in Essex. He dispossessed his brothers. His youngest brother, Francis Osborne, and his nephew Richard Osborne initiated a chancery suit against his son Sir Henry Osborne. The chancery verdict of 27 March 1655 was for Sir Henry Osborne, and Francis Osborne was left the embittered author of *Advice to a Son* (1656).

Sir Peter Osborne made his will on 26 February 1650. A previous conveyance had already disposed of all his lands and the will allocated his personal goods, which he left, primarily to his wife and his heir, as his executors. Osborne also gave bequests of £10 each to two male servants, the poor of Campton, and the men to whom he had entrusted his estates. He directed that several of the hangings, two portraits (which had belonged to his grandfather Sir Peter Osborne), and his entire library at Chicksands should be handed down in perpetuity through the male line as heirlooms. He died in March 1653.

J. G. Elzinga

Sources BL, Add. MS 5297, fol. 34*r* • Burke, *Peerage* (1999) • *CPR*, *1560–63* • *CSP dom.*, *1547–80* • *JHC*, 1.120 • Cooper, *Ath. Cantab.*, 3.26 • S. R. Gardiner, *History of the great civil war, 1642–1649*, 3 vols. (1886–91) • M. A. E. Green, ed., *Calendar of the proceedings of the committee for advance of money, 1642–1656*, 3 vols., PRO (1888) • M. A. E. Green, ed., *Calendar of the proceedings of the committee for compounding … 1643–1660*, 5 vols., PRO (1889–92) • F. Heal and C. Holmes, *The gentry in England and Wales, 1500–1700* (1994) • *Fourth report*, HMC, 3 (1874) • *Seventh report*, HMC, 6 (1879) • *Sixth report*, HMC, 5 (1877–8) • *Calendar of the manuscripts of the most hon. the marquis of Salisbury*, 1–2, HMC, 9 (1883–8) • HoP, *Commons*, *1558–1603*, 3.156–9 • Clarendon, *Hist. rebellion* • *DNB* • *Letters from Dorothy Osborne to Sir William Temple*, *1652–1654*, ed. E. A. Parry (1888) • *The letters of Dorothy Osborne to William Temple*, ed. G. C. Moore Smith (1928) • F. B. Tupper, *The chronicles of Castle Cornet, Guernsey* (1851) • Venn, *Alum. Cant.*

Archives BL, account of work in exchequer, Egerton MS 3369, fols. 1b–37 [copies] • BL, certificate relating to sequestration of his estate, 1644, Add. MS 61681, fol. 181 • BL, Lansdowne MSS 14, 18, 24, 26, 52, 56, 146, *passim* • BL, Lansdowne MSS 52, fol. 90; 66, fol. 217 • BL, letters, Add. MS 46367, fols. 51b, 57b, 58b • BL, opinions chiefly upon commercial questions, Lansdowne MS Xi.17, *passim* • PRO, C 142/249/59 • PRO, letters | BL, Add. MS 5297, fol. 34 • BL, list of persons present at his wife's funeral, Cotton MS Vespasian C. xiv, fol. 196 • BL, register of his corresp. with Lord Warwick, Stowe MS 184, fols. 114–20 • BL, Lansdowne MS 106, fol. 1 [relating to Christopher Osborne] • Hatfield House, Hertfordshire, letters to Burghley, Hatfield MS 223/7 • PRO, chancery proceedings, C. 6, bundle 121, no. 95

Wealth at death valued at £4000 p.a.; fined by committee for compounding for estate at a third (£2666): PRO, SP 02

Osborne, Sir Peter (1584/5–1653). *See under* Osborne, Peter (1521–1592).

Osborne, Ralph Bernal (1808?–1882), politician, the eldest son of Ralph *Bernal (*d.* 1854) and his first wife, Anne Elizabeth, *née* White, added Osborne to his name by royal licence in 1844 when he married (on 20 August) Catherine Isabella, only daughter of Sir Thomas Osborne, eighth baronet, and heir to his estates in counties Wicklow and Tipperary. He was vague about his early life. At his funeral his birth date was given as 26 March 1808. He was at Charterhouse School from 1819 to 1826. According to the admissions register of Trinity College, Cambridge, he was admitted on 17 February 1826 'at the age of twenty'. He signed the university matriculation register for 3 November 1827. At Cambridge he claimed to have received not education but 'instruction in all the vices for which the place was notorious'. He was a contemporary of Arthur Hallam, Alfred Tennyson, Richard Monckton Milnes, and Alexander William Kinglake, the last of whom became a close friend. In 1830 Bernal's father (having remarried and thus reduced the young man's financial prospects)

Ralph Bernal Osborne (1808?–1882), by Alfred, Count D'Orsay, 1846

obtained for him a commission in the 71st regiment of foot. Transferring into the 7th in 1833, he served in Ireland, becoming an additional aide-de-camp to the whig earl of Mulgrave, who was created marquess of Normanby in 1838 and was viceroy from 1835 to 1839.

In 1841 Bernal won a seat at High Wycombe as an advanced Liberal, against the national trend and in opposition to the hitherto dominant Carrington interest. He remained an MP with short breaks until 1874, sitting for Middlesex (1847–57), Dover (1857–9), Liskeard (1859–65), Nottingham (1866–8), and Waterford City (1870–74). He called himself a Liberal but in the 1840s and 1850s was ranked as a radical. He worked with Joseph Hume and J. A. Roebuck, denouncing jobbery and government expenditure, declaring that 'the influence of the aristocracy has increased, is increasing and ought to be diminished', supporting free trade, the secret ballot, triennial parliaments and further franchise extension, voluntaryism in education, and the abolition of flogging in the army. His experience at Dublin Castle and as an active Irish landlord led him to advocate, in and out of season, a wide range of Irish reforms. He defended the union but argued for the suppression of the viceroyalty, for state provision to Maynooth College (thus attracting the hostility of the 'protestant' party), and for the drastic reform of both Irish land law and the Church of Ireland.

Osborne was one of those radicals who, having previously denounced Palmerston's assertive foreign policy, backed him strongly in the Don Pacifico affair of 1850. He afterwards presided at a dinner in the foreign secretary's honour at the Reform Club and became identified as a Palmerstonian. He refused Russell's offer of minor office in 1851. With Derby and Disraeli in power he was in his element. *The Times* wrote on 22 July 1852: 'To no man more than to Mr. Osborne do we owe it that the middle and lower classes of this country have clearly understood and justly appreciated the shabby manoeuvring and hollow casuistry of the Derby Government'.

When the Aberdeen coalition was formed at the end of 1852 Osborne became secretary of the Admiralty, a post he held until 1858. Office muzzled him, but in January 1855 he made a slashing contribution to the debate on Roebuck's motion censuring the government's conduct of the war. He castigated the entire military system as archaic and corrupt, while refusing to accept that this was the fault of the government: parliament and aristocratic society bore the responsibility because they refused to allow the army to be reformed. After 1858 he never held office, partly because of the offence he had given to so many, including the queen. But he played an important role in the Commons at certain junctures, making a notable speech in the debate on the Danish question in 1864 and assisting Disraeli in carrying parliamentary reform in 1867. In his last entry in *Dod's Parliamentary Companion*, after the passage of the Ballot Act in 1872, he specified no reforms which he wished to promote.

Osborne's reputation rested on his wit and force as a speaker. His friend Sir John Trelawny called him 'the House's jester'; Disraeli, another friend, described him as 'the chartered libertine of debate'; White as 'the rollicking merryman of the House'. He had a 'strong-built frame', 'smooth, sallow face', 'falcon eye', and 'powerful voice'. 'His manner was that of a consummate comic actor', and he peppered his speeches with picturesque, if often crude, ridicule of other speakers. He said of Henry Goulburn that, whenever Peel changed his party, 'there was that miserable old tin kettle fastened to his tail'. The killjoy Lord Robert Montagu and Cobden allied together were like 'Righteousness and peace kissing each other'. During other members' speeches he kept up a running fire of invariably audible asides, 'more diverting than Senatorial'.

Osborne was one of the most conspicuous of the self-consciously independent MPs who flourished during the period of weak party alignment in the mid-nineteenth century. But even then, as he himself put it, voters did not relish disloyalty to party—hence his numerous enforced changes of constituency. He was a welcome figure in the Commons and in the clubs, and on the country-house circuit, in the hunting-field, and at the races both in England and Ireland; but he became so much the jester of politics that he ceased to be taken seriously. John Bright said after dining with him: 'Osborne prefers jokes and ridicule and nonsense to any useful and agreeable conversation'. If he was warm towards friends, he was often overbearing and had a violent temper. He was a good singer and actor, and a prolific writer of political and social doggerel.

Osborne's wife predeceased him, and at his death his two daughters shared his estate which included more than 13,000 acres around his house at Newtown Anner, Clonmel, co. Tipperary, that brought in more than £5000 per annum. He died of cancer on 4 January 1882 at Bestwood Lodge, Arnold, Nottinghamshire, the house of the duke of St Albans, husband of his younger daughter, and was buried at Bestwood. DEREK BEALES

Sources P. H. Bagenal, *The life of Ralph Bernal Osborne, MP* (1884) • *DNB* • *The parliamentary diaries of Sir John Trelawny, 1858–1865*, ed. T. A. Jenkins, CS, 4th ser., 40 (1990) • *The Times* (5 Jan 1882) • *The Times* (11 Jan 1882) • *Parliamentary Pocket Companion* (1841–74) • W. White, *The inner life of the House of Commons*, ed. J. McCarthy, [another edn], 2 vols. (1915) • Trinity College, Cambridge, Admissions register (1800–50) [consulted by Dr D. J. McKitterick] • University of Cambridge, matriculation register [consulted by Dr E. S. Leedham-Green] • R. L. Arrowsmith, ed., *Charterhouse register, 1769–1872* (1974) • J. Bateman, *The great landowners of Great Britain and Ireland*, 4th edn (1883) • W. Fraser, *Disraeli and his day* (1891) • *The diaries of John Bright*, ed. R. A. J. Walling [1930] • *The Guardian* (11 Jan 1882), 47 • *Army List*

Archives BL, letters to Sir C. Napier, Add. MSS 40024, 40032

Likenesses Count D'Orsay, engraving, 1846, NPG [*see illus.*] • Aτη [A. Thompson], caricature, chromolithograph, NPG; repro. in *VF* (28 May 1870) • Count D'Orsay, lithograph, BM • C. Pellegrini, portrait, Reform Club, London

Wealth at death £37,861 5*s*. 6*d*.: probate, 30 Nov 1882, *CGPLA Eng. & Wales*

Osborne [*née* Haggenson], **Ruth** (**1682–1751**), alleged witch, details of whose upbringing are unknown, lived with her husband, John Osborne (*b*. 1695, *d*. in or after 1751), a labourer, at Gubblecote, a small settlement near Tring, Hertfordshire. For many years the couple were rumoured to be Jacobites and witches by many in the neighbourhood. It was believed by some that Ruth Osborne had even bewitched her own brother, a man named Haggenson, who lived in a neighbouring parish. Because of such rumours the Osbornes found it difficult to get work and they were reliant on poor relief. In 1745 Ruth went to the farm of one John Butterfield to beg for buttermilk. The farmer angrily told her to be off as 'he had not enough for his hogs', and Ruth retorted that 'the pretender would have him and his hogs too'. When, several months later, some of his calves died Butterfield concluded that Osborne must have bewitched them. Butterfield was eventually forced out of farming and by 1751 he was running the Black Horse alehouse at Gubblecote Cross. He believed he was still under a spell, however, as he suffered from recurring fits. Some of his customers, including one Thomas Colley, suggested he consult a cunning-woman. He followed this advice and she told him that he had been bewitched by 'two of his neighbours, a man and a woman'. This served to confirm Butterfield's suspicions about the Osbornes. It was decided that the community should consider their guilt at a witch swimming, a popular trial introduced in England in the early seventeenth century and which continued after the repeal of the statutes against witchcraft in 1736.

The swimming of Ruth Osborne and her husband was well planned. The town criers of three neighbouring towns, Winslow, Leighton Buzzard, and Hemel Hempstead, announced that a man and a woman were to be 'publickly duck'd at Tring' on 22 April. Tring's overseer of the poor, Matthew Barton, knew the Osbornes and lodged them in the town's workhouse for protection. However, in the expectation of serious trouble on the day the workhouse master, Jonathan Tomkins, had them removed to the vestry of the church. His fears were confirmed as a frustrated mob, estimated to be several thousand strong, began to demolish the workhouse and threatened to burn it down if the Osbornes were not handed over. Tomkins gave in and Ruth and her husband were escorted out of town by the mob to a pool at Long Marston, near Gubblecote. There Ruth was partially stripped, her thumbs tied to her toes, and a rope placed under her armpits, before she was thrown into the water. According to the custom of witch swimming she would be judged guilty if she floated and innocent if she sank. She floated, and to confirm this outcome Thomas Colley pushed her under several times with a stick. Ruth Osborne died minutes after being dragged back on to the bank having 'been suffocated with Water and Mud'. Though not the last person to undergo this trial, Osborne was the last person in England to die as a result. Thomas Colley was subsequently hanged for his part in her death. OWEN DAVIES

Sources *The tryal of Thomas Colley* (1751) • *The remarkable confession, and last dying words of Thomas Colley* (1751) • *GM*, 1st ser., 21 (1751), 186, 198 • W. B. Carnochan, 'Witch-hunting and belief in 1751: the case of Thomas Colley and Ruth Osborne', *Journal of Social History*, 4 (1971), 389–403

Osborne, Sarah (*d*. **1692**). *See under* Salem witches and their accusers (*act*. 1692).

Osborne, Lord Sydney Godolphin (**1808–1889**), philanthropist, third son of Francis Godolphin Osborne, first Baron Godolphin (1777–1850), and Elizabeth Charlotte (*d*. 1847), daughter of William Eden, first Baron Auckland, was born at Stapleford in Cambridgeshire on 5 February 1808. When in 1859 his elder brother, George Godolphin (1802–1872), succeeded his cousin, Francis Godolphin D'Arcy Osborne, as eighth duke of Leeds, he obtained the rank of a duke's son.

Osborne was educated at Rugby School and from 1824 at Brasenose College, Oxford. He was awarded a BA in 1830, and, having taken holy orders, was appointed rector of Stoke Poges in Buckinghamshire in 1832. In 1841 he accepted the living of Durweston in Dorset, which was in the gift of Lord Portman, and he occupied that incumbency until 1875. Osborne married on 29 May 1834 Emily (*d*. 1875), daughter of Pascoe Grenfell of Taplow Court, Buckinghamshire, and was thus brother-in-law of Charles Kingsley (1819–1875) and James Anthony Froude (1818–1894). The couple had two sons and two daughters.

Osborne is best known for his series of 'lay sermons' delivered from the pulpit of *The Times* under the signature S. G. O., which gained him something of a national reputation in his day. A militant and controversial philanthropist, in his published letters (1844–84) he addressed matters as diverse as free trade, education, sanitation, women's rights, cattle plague, and cholera. Despite his relationship to Kingsley and his link, through him, to the Christian socialists, Osborne was essentially a tory paternalist, although he kept clear of party politics.

Lord Sydney Godolphin Osborne (1808–1889), by John Watkins

During the Crimean War, Osborne travelled to the East, made an unofficial inspection of the hospitals under Florence Nightingale's care, and published the results in *Scutari and its Hospitals* (1855). He was publicly thanked in parliament for his self-appointed task.

On the Irish question, in which he took a special interest after a visit to the west of Ireland during the famine of 1849, Osborne was a strong unionist, and in ecclesiastical matters he was an opponent of Tractarianism. His special cause was the plight of the agricultural labourer, of whom his knowledge was unrivalled, while his forecast of the villager's social and political emancipation and its results was remarkably acute. The last letters of Osborne's series addressed to *The Times* were on the subject of the Whitechapel murders. A selection from the letters was published, with a brief introduction by Arnold White (2 vols., 1888). Osborne's other writings included *Gleanings in the West of Ireland* (1850), *Lady Eva: her Last Days: a Tale* (1851), *Hints to the Charitable* (1856), *Hints for the Amelioration of the Moral Condition of a Village* (1856), and *Letters on the Education of Young Children* (1866). In 1875 Osborne resigned his benefice and retired to Lewes, Sussex, where he died at his home, Pelham House, on 9 May 1889.

THOMAS SECCOMBE, *rev.* MARK CLEMENT

Sources *The letters of S. G. O.*, ed. A. White, 2 vols. (1888) • *Men of the time* (1887) • *Saturday Review*, 71 (1891), 115–16 • *Annual Register* (1889) • *The Times* (10 May 1889) • Boase, *Mod. Eng. biog.* • Burke, *Peerage* • Foster, *Alum. Oxon.* • *CGPLA Eng. & Wales* (1889)

Archives BL, letters to John Bright, Add. MS 43389 • CKS, letters to Edward Stanhope

Likenesses J. Watkins, carte-de-visite, NPG [*see illus.*] • J. & C. Watkins, carte-de-visite, NPG • portrait, repro. in White, ed., *Letters of S. G. O.* • wood-engraving (after photograph by J. & C. Watkins), BM; repro. in *ILN* (25 May 1889)

Wealth at death £12,601 8*s.* 10*d.*: probate, 31 May 1889, *CGPLA Eng. & Wales*

Osborne, Thomas, first duke of Leeds (1632–1712), politician, best known under his earlier titles of earl of Danby and marquess of Carmarthen, was born on 20 February 1632, and baptized eight days later, the second son of Sir Edward Osborne (1596–1647) of Kiveton, Yorkshire, and his second wife, Anne (*d.* 1666), widow of William Middleton of Stockeld, Yorkshire. He became his father's heir in 1638 when a chimney in the family house at York collapsed, killing his elder brother, Edward. Thomas avoided a similar fate only because he had stopped to play with the family cat which had crawled under a table, an early instance perhaps of his strong survival instinct as well as his persistent dancing with danger. He was well connected on both sides of his family. His father, the grandson of a lord mayor of London, Sir Edward Osborne, had been created a baronet in 1620 and risen under the patronage of Strafford to become vice-president of the council of the north in 1632, a post in which he displayed unswerving loyalty to the king. In 1639 and 1640 Sir Edward superintended the dispatch of troops to the border to take part in the threatened war with the Scots, resigning as MP for Berwick in 1640 because of his military responsibilities, and subsequently became lieutenant-general of the royalist forces raised at York. Sir Edward's first wife was Margaret Belasyse, daughter of Thomas Belasyse, Viscount Fauconberg. Thomas's mother was Sir Edward's second wife, the second daughter of Thomas Walmesley of Dunkenhalgh, Lancashire, and Elizabeth Danvers, who was the sister of Henry *Danvers, earl of Danby, and descended from John Neville, fourth Baron Latimer. These connections gave Thomas impeccable royalist credentials and a network of influential relatives, both of which he was to exploit to the full during his later career.

Early career After defeat at Marston Moor in 1644 Sir Edward Osborne played no further part in the war, but the sequestration of his estate left a legacy of impoverishment that Thomas was later very keen to reverse. The war had also disrupted Thomas's education, for although he appears to have received some tuition in York he did not attend university or an inn of court. Two years after his father's death he left England to tour Europe, accompanied for some time by Sir William Temple, on whose knowledge of international affairs he was later to rely. Having visited Italy Osborne spent 1650 in Paris, where he and other exiles met at the house of Sir Richard Browne, with whose son-in-law, John Evelyn, he became 'intimately acquainted' (Evelyn, 4.14). The diarist's assessment that his one-time friend was 'haughty' captures something of Osborne's personality, for his pride was commented on by

Thomas Osborne, first duke of Leeds (1632–1712), by Robert White, *c.*1694

others (ibid., 4.20). In 1652 he was back in London, courting a distant cousin, Dorothy *Osborne, but the match was vetoed by his mother. The following year, however, he married a much better connected bride, Lady Bridget Bertie (*bap.* 1629, *d.* 1704), daughter of Montague Bertie, second earl of Lindsey. Dorothy Osborne dismissed the match as a piece of fortune-hunting but it seems to have been a loving marriage, which produced three sons, including Edward (*d.* 1689), the eldest son, and Peregrine *Osborne, the third son, the only one who survived his father, and eight daughters. Lady Bridget was depicted by her enemies as a domineering woman responsible for some of her husband's greed if not his success. Thomas and his wife returned to Kiveton, only 6 miles from Welbeck, the seat of the Cavendishes, with whom he became friends. But it was probably not until the Restoration that Osborne secured a connection with George Villiers, second duke of Buckingham, who was to be his political patron. In 1661, presumably due to Buckingham's influence, he served as high sheriff of Yorkshire, and his decision to carve out a local career may have resulted from a rebuff to an attempt that year to recover a £1000 fine imposed on the family in the 1640s. Although he was offered 'some good peniworths' (Browning, 2.9) if he would follow Lord Ossory to Ireland he declined to do so. The local knowledge gained by remaining in Yorkshire was to stand him in excellent stead during his ministerial career. In 1662 he was part of a local commission for enforcing the Corporation Act against dissenters and the following year acquired considerable local standing as a result of his efforts to investigate and uncover a conspiracy, the so-called Yorkshire plot. Complaining to the government when he found others had been insufficiently zealous, he may have discerned the political mileage to be gained out of exploiting fears of rebellion. On 16 January 1665 he was elected as MP for York on Buckingham's interest, against a court candidate.

Osborne followed his patron's hostility to Edward Hyde, earl of Clarendon. Both he and Buckingham had been thwarted when Clarendon blocked a bill to restore the council of the north and Clarendon had also ruined Osborne's plan to farm the excise in Yorkshire, a project which he had presented to the king in 1665 and which marked his first foray into fiscal policy. It was therefore probably for factional reasons, rather than ideological ones, that in 1665 he opposed a proposal to extend to the whole nation an oath renouncing taking up arms against the king and promising not to alter the government in church and state. Certainly when there were renewed reports of a conspiracy in the north Osborne refused a commission to investigate, dismissing the danger to the government. His hostility to Clarendon proved the 'first step to … his future rise' (*Memoirs of Sir John Reresby*, 71) because Osborne used it to show his loyalty to Buckingham. This was confirmed when he resigned his deputy lieutenancy to share his patron's temporary disgrace after the mud-flinging which formed Clarendon's counter-attack and again when he opposed the king's attempt to set up his own commission to examine the public accounts, even though Charles attempted to include Osborne on it. Even a long personal conversation with the king on 8 June failed to persuade him. Buckingham's return to favour would therefore mean Osborne's rise.

According to Clarendon's own account Osborne told many before parliament sat that if the lord chancellor 'were not hanged he would be hanged himself' (*Life of … Clarendon*, 3.309) and he certainly began one of the lines of attack; but although he was appointed to the committee that drew up the formal charge against Clarendon and acted as teller of the house on important votes against him, Osborne's part was less prominent than others. Always a solid rather than inspiring speaker he seldom contributed to debates and was distracted by illness and the death of his eldest daughter, Elizabeth. In 1668 he reminded Buckingham of his usefulness by co-ordinating an attack on the duke of Ormond and by harrying Arthur Annesley, first earl of Anglesey. Anglesey was suspended from the treasurership of the navy, and Osborne was rewarded on 5 November 1668 when, on Buckingham's recommendation, he and Sir Thomas Littleton kissed the king's hand for the post. He now had a salary of £1250 p.a, invaluable if he was to make any headway into his £10,000 debt, and was one of Buckingham's key allies. Thus when Clarendon's remaining prop, Sir William Coventry, was removed from privy council Buckingham pressed for Osborne to replace him, but his candidature was blocked in turn by Henry Bennet, the earl of Arlington, who now posed the chief threat to Buckingham's power. Osborne concluded that the duke of York and Buckingham ought to work together and wrote his first survey of party organization to show the advantages of such a collaboration. Although there were defects inherent in the scheme, Buckingham's mishandling of it irritated Osborne who told the duke in December 1669 that he intended 'to retire only to the businesse of that imployment I am charged with' (Browning, 2.24). To some extent he did withdraw, for his only recorded intervention in 1670 was in favour of the new Conventicle Act, which Buckingham opposed. Osborne's name was still mentioned in March 1670 as a possible member of the new governing cabal, but when he unsuccessfully tried to persuade Buckingham out of his Francophile policy relations between them cooled. By November of that year Osborne told the duke that he found himself 'much estranged both from your trust and usuall kindnesse' and, assuring Buckingham of his continuing fidelity, resolved 'to retire from all publique employment, in which as I have never received any profitt, so have I been as far from any other satisfaction but that of doing your Grace service' (ibid., 2.25–6). In fact Osborne dedicated himself to understanding the navy, and both his ambition and his competence pushed him in the direction of rejecting both his patron and his co-treasurer. In the summer of 1671 he accused Littleton of 'great disservice to his Majestie' (ibid., 1.86) and on 11 July privy council resolved that in future there should be a single treasurer. Osborne was duly appointed on 20 September, with an increased salary of £2000.

Having rid himself of his rival Osborne set about using his post to replace the patronage offered by Buckingham with that of the crown. Indeed, he was to acquire the reputation of being false to his friends and to the nation; or, in the words of his enemy Shaftesbury, was 'cut out naturally for a courtier' (Christie, 2.312). His diary shows frequent visits with the king or duke of York to the fleet and these trips appear to have dispelled any bad impressions created by his earlier behaviour. On 29 April 1672 he was offered a seat on privy council, even though this was shortly after the stop of the exchequer, the declaration of indulgence, and the declaration of war against the Dutch, all of which he opposed. The tensions between Osborne and Buckingham over the direction of government policy were evident when Osborne sent him Slingsby Bethel's *The Present Interest of England*. It is unlikely that Osborne agreed with Bethel's plea for toleration as a way of promoting trade, but the tract did challenge the basis of the war with the Dutch and extol the virtues of the triple alliance of Britain, Sweden, and the Netherlands, positions with which Osborne agreed wholeheartedly. Buckingham replied in *A Letter to Sir Thomas Osborn*, which set out the government position and poked fun at the number-crunching Osborne by claiming that it was impossible to make all this 'as plain as that two and two make four' (p. 18). A reply, *Observations on the Letter Written to Sir Thomas Osborne*, in turn ridiculed the idea that the Dutch were suited to pursuing imperial ambitions and claimed that France had a 'universal design', thus posing by far the greater threat. The exchange is important, since it marks the foundations of the foreign policy which Osborne was to pursue throughout his career.

For most of the summer Osborne duly absconded from London. His attendance at several meetings of government supporters in late 1672 perhaps encouraged a bid to secure his support in the forthcoming session, for Osborne received, two days before parliament met, a warrant for his elevation to the Scottish peerage as Viscount Osborne of Dunblane. Although he was appointed to the committee drafting the address from the Commons against the declaration of indulgence and spoke against the bill to ease protestant dissenters, arguing that a relaxation of the requirement to renounce the solemn league and covenant would incite them to rebellion, Osborne was more an opponent of the religious policy than of the court itself. Thus although he supported the Test Bill, he sought to moderate some of its harsher clauses against Catholic officers serving in the army and the duke of York's household. On monetary matters, moreover, he argued the government case, urging for as much money for the navy as possible as the best safeguard against popery. This stance prompted a reconciliation between Osborne and the duke of York, an alliance that lasted until 1678 and which was partly behind his promotion on 19 June 1673 to the post of lord treasurer, though Buckingham's support was also instrumental. Lord Clifford had been forced to resign because of his Catholicism, but, according to Sir John Reresby, Osborne was to pay Clifford half of the salary of his office or, some said, a large one-off payment of £10,000–20,000. At his swearing-in Osborne was treated to a speech by the earl of Shaftesbury, who reminded him that the talents which allowed men to rise were often different from those needed to maintain themselves. Osborne thanked the earl at the time but, when the ambiguity sank in, 'sent a gentleman to desire him to return him the thanks he had given him' (Le Neve, 107). In explaining his friend's rise Evelyn acknowledged that he was 'a man of excellent natural parts' but thought he had 'nothing generous or gratefull' in him (Evelyn, 4.20).

Lord treasurer, 1673–1679 Promotion brought Osborne new status. On 15 August 1673 he was created Baron Osborne of Kiveton and Viscount Latimer of Danby in the English peerage, allowing him to resign his Scottish title to his son Peregrine. But his appointment did not bring immediate political dominance and there were plenty of obstacles in the way of his further success. Some of these, such as his rivalry with the secretary to the Treasury, Sir Robert Howard, and his own serious illness in the summer of 1673, were petty or personal. But the most important difficulty lay in the structural inadequacies of the king's finances: a shortfall in the revenue to the tune of an annual £500,000 deficit, debts increased by war, salaries in arrears, and advances paid by tax farmers that mortgaged future revenue. Latimer had never supported the war against the Dutch but recognized that on financial grounds alone it had to end. He immediately began disbanding troops and transferring others to the pay of England's ally, France, in order to transfer cost. His guiding principles were set down in a memorandum of October in which he noted his policy 'in all things to promote the Protestant interest both att home and abroad' and to maintain fiscal competence (Browning, 2.63). Latimer further promised he would either break the French alliance or his own white staff. In order to achieve these aims Latimer had finally to ditch Buckingham and create his own following in parliament. He began to foster close ties with the groups around Edward Seymour, whose rising fortunes had mirrored his own, and Sir Heneage Finch. Towards the close of the year the new treasurer submitted a stark assessment to the king: the crown's fortunes 'cannot bee amended but by force or by compliance', he argued (ibid.). Clearly showing the weakness or rather impracticability of the former course, Latimer highlighted the need to secure the latter, which meant accommodation with parliament over religion. The state of the finances thus reinforced, or were used to reinforce, Latimer's personal convictions about state and church.

The final breach with Buckingham came in 1674 when the duke was attacked in parliament by the earl of Arlington. Although Latimer did attempt to rescue Buckingham's mastership of the horse his inability to do so provoked accusations of ingratitude from the duke and encouraged a rumour that Latimer might resign. Certainly Arlington appeared to emerge a strengthened rival, especially as he took most of the credit for negotiating the peace. But in the longer run Arlington's factionalism had reduced his usefulness to the king and the peace gave Latimer the opportunity to introduce a series of financial reforms. As a memorandum of 17 March 1674 put it, everything depended on Latimer's fiscal skills: 'the sinewes of the monarchy are to bee recovered in these three yeares or niver' (Browning, 2.65). Latimer urged retrenchment and asked, impossibly, for the king's 'steddy and unalterable resolutions to assist him' (ibid.). Using the money from salaries and pensions, Latimer paid off the armed forces and renegotiated the tax farms at more favourable rates. A settlement was also reached with the bankers affected by the 1672 stop of the exchequer. These early successes brought reward. On 27 June 1674 he was promoted to an earldom, using the title of his granduncle Danby. In the same year he was made lord lieutenant of the West Riding and a Scottish privy councillor. More importantly in September 1674 Arlington resigned as secretary of state. At last Danby seemed free of rivals.

Between 1675 and 1678 Danby attempted to consolidate his power in a number of interlinking ways which were summarized in the maxim 'to settle the church and state; to defend the one against schismaticks and papists, and the other against commonwealthsmen and rebels' (*Supplementary Lindsey MSS*, 377). First, he sought to rely on the Church of England for political as well as religious support. Second, he used propaganda to attract support for the court by appealing to the cavalier mentality, vilifying his enemies as republicans and dissenters. Third, he sought by these means to cultivate a party in parliament that was loyal to the court. Fourth, he employed the resources of the Treasury to achieve his aims while retaining sound financial policies. Fifth, for both ideological and financial reasons he sought to divert the king from a Francophile foreign policy. Vigour in the first four objectives, and ambiguity over the fifth, helped polarize English politics into embryonic parties.

Danby's alliance with the Church of England was forged early. From October 1674 onwards Danby began meeting with senior clerics to consider how to suppress popery and support the church, and in January 1675 measures were agreed which included the repression of conventiclers and the formal voiding of the 1672 licences under the declaration of indulgence. A further appeal to Anglican cavalier loyalty was made by a plan to erect a statue of Charles I at Charing Cross and re-inter his body. More significantly, in the 1675 session of parliament Danby introduced in the Lords a Test Bill which would have confined political power to Anglican royalists by requiring officeholders and MPs to take an oath against resistance to the king and promise never to endeavour to alter the government of church or state. The bill was debated for seventeen days in the upper house, with Lord Chancellor Finch as the principal court speaker, before Danby allowed it to be dropped. Even then he continued to promote a strict alliance with, and political power for, churchmen. In 1676 he directed each bishop to prepare a census of papists and nonconformists in their diocese. Although known as the Compton Census the idea originated with Danby, who believed the results should persuade the king of the viability of suppressing both papists and dissenters without provoking rebellion. Danby also allied with the bishops in the Lords to construct a formidable church–court axis.

Defence of the church and reviving memories of the civil war and its aftermath also figured prominently in a brilliant propaganda campaign. Danby, in alliance with secretary Joseph Williamson and licenser of the press Roger L'Estrange, fully appreciated the power of the press, perhaps because he had witnessed how effective William of Orange's propaganda had been during the Dutch war but also because the treasurer was himself the victim of many libels. Perhaps the most famous of these, the *Letter from a Person of Quality*, attacked the court for attempting to construct 'a distinct party from the rest of the Nation of the High Episcopal Men and the Old Cavalier' (p. 1). Danby's administration replied with a barrage of tracts, often publicized in the government sponsored *London Gazette*, which harped on the themes of the church and civil war. But the most effective reply, sponsored by the treasurer and published on the eve of the 1677 session, was *A Paquet of Advices and Animadversions*, which undermined the reputation of the earl of Shaftesbury by warning that he sought to lead the nation back along the steps of 1641.

Although ostensibly appealing to moderation, Danby's propaganda and policies were divisive and provoked opposition. In 1675 an attempt was made, supported by Arlington, to impeach him. Although he knew of the attack in advance and it found weak support, it may have prompted Danby to consider the need for a more disciplined court party. During summer 1675 he increased the number of MPs in receipt of a pension from the excise farm, and shortly before parliament reassembled Danby sent out more than 100 letters inviting MPs to attend. The government worked up lists of supporters which reckoned on about 100 loyal members. The scale of such management was new and resented, so that by creating one party Danby was helping to consolidate another: an anti-court or country party. Despite, or perhaps because of, Danby's methods the court suffered defeats on important supply motions and only very narrowly defeated a motion to address the king to dissolve parliament. These failures of management led Charles and Danby to different conclusions. While the king sought refuge in alliance with France, the minister pressed his master to ally with the Dutch and to renew efforts to construct a court party. Between the prorogation in November 1675 and the new session in February 1677 Danby and his manager Sir Richard Wiseman worked hard to increase the number of court dependants. As Bishop Burnet pointed out, where his predecessors had sought to buy off leading opponents, Danby 'reckoned that the major number was the surer game; so he neglected the great men who he thought raised the price too high, and reckoned he could gain ten ordinary men cheaper than one of those' (*Bishop Burnet's History*, 2.71). Alternatively, he first made opponents the lowest offer that there was any chance of them accepting; if they agreed, he won his man, but if not he gave out that £100 more would have bought them and thereby 'made them odious … so that take or leave he gain'd his point' (Le Neve, 26–7). Danby later admitted to spending £252,467 in the three years 1676–9 as 'secret service' money and was alleged to have spent almost another £50,000 more. Danby's attempt to build a court party was thus more organized and on a more ambitious scale than anything undertaken before. Initially his methods seemed very successful. Lists compiled between the spring of 1675 and early 1676 named 137 court voters, and when parliament did reassemble the treasurer was able to head off claims made in the House of Lords that it had been dissolved by the long prorogation. The four ring-leading peers, including Buckingham, were sent to the Tower, and on the back of that success the treasurer secured supply. Paper calculations of support in 1678 even put the number of adherents at over 200. Danby's pensioners were nevertheless far from being a reliable or effective block of votes. Moreover, inside the house his methods inspired the country party to new levels of sophistication, and outside it they created the belief that, as Andrew Marvell put it, he sought 'the growth of popery and arbitrary government' (Marvell, *An Account of the Growth of Popery and Arbitrary Government*, 1677).

Danby's chief difficulty, however, lay in the king's fondness for alliance with France. In 1677, pursuing a wholly different policy, Danby successfully manipulated parliament into making addresses promising aid if Charles declared war against France. When ambassador Ralph Montagu wrote suggesting that the alarm these caused in Paris could be used to extract money from Louis XIV, Danby suppressed the letter and on 4 April drew up his own statement for the king in which he argued that the success of the session was in part due to MPs' belief in Charles's firmness against France. He went so far as to suggest that failure to continue this policy would not only ruin future sessions but also alienate the nation so far that it would imperil the government. By contrast, he saw in the current situation 'the greatest conjunction of honour, wisedome, glory and nationall advantages that ever offered itselfe in any age to any prince or nation'. He added that a stance of war against France would gain arms and money for the crown by the consent of the people, force which 'might incourage you to speake boldly' if parliament refused to negotiate a healthy financial settlement (Browning, 2.66–9). Charles accepted this most important of policy statements; but his insistence on seeing the colour of parliament's money revealed the weaknesses in Danby's parliamentary management, for mistrust of the court put strings on the support for the war. Aware that Charles resented the attitude of MPs, Danby drafted a memorandum in June 1677 in which he desperately pleaded with the king that only 'unsteadinesse of resolution in those steps hee has begun' could spoil his domestic affairs. Danby put the situation as bluntly as he felt able:

> Till hee can fall into the humour of the people [the king] can never bee great nor rich, and while differences continue prerogative must suffer, unlesse he can live without Parliament. That the condition of his revenue will not permitt that. (ibid., 2.69–71)

Charles, however, had already decided that his revenue could be improved by underhand deals with France. Danby had little option but to try to wreck the negotiations or, which might have the same effect, maximize the king's demands. Fatefully, he chose the latter, pressing the French for more money in return for a long adjournment of parliament. Aware of the weakness of his position, particularly after the destructive Buckingham was released in July, Danby declared to the duke of York that it was impossible to serve a king who treated his faithful ministers in this way and threatened to retire from public life. Although James appeased him, both men must have known that in order to save his power Danby had conceded one of his major policy objectives. Attempting to salvage something from the situation he continued to haggle with the French for more money and made one last bid to win back the king to his policy by reviving the idea of a marriage between William of Orange and James's daughter Mary. Charles's agreement in October 1677 raised the stakes all round. The match laid the foundations for an important relationship between William and Danby that would have long-lasting consequences, and in the short term Danby gained considerable prestige. But the gambler's throw also provoked French anger against him. A formal offensive league between England and the Netherlands failed to materialize, allowing France to resume its assault on the king's vacillating mind and forcing an adjournment of parliament from 15 to 28 January 1678. This, Danby noted in a letter to Montagu, meant 'that nobody will now beleeve other then that the peace is concluded by concert betwixt us and France' (Browning, 2.332). Such forebodings were abundantly proved right during the subsequent session. When news of Louis XIV's victory at Ghent reached the Commons on 22 February 1678 a motion to draft an address calling for the removal of evil councillors was only narrowly defeated and, despite Danby's pleadings, a motion was passed to address for an immediate war with France. Ironically the treasurer had been forced into opposing a war which he had been trying for years to persuade the king to undertake and in doing so he lost the trust of both Charles and parliament. Moreover, since parliament had granted no supply and had stopped lucrative custom revenues from French goods, the treasurer was in no position to resist a French proposal to give the king money in return for an alliance. On 25 March Danby sent a letter to Montagu, later brandished against him, confirming English demands, though ironically, as he had predicted, the French offers dissolved.

Danby's policies now lay in tatters. When parliament reassembled on 29 April 1678 it attacked him and proved so intractable that Charles had to prorogue it on 13 May without having been granted any money. The treasurer was all too aware that the king, who had been forced to raise troops without supply, was acutely short of money. He had hitherto maintained financial stability by maximizing revenue from the custom and excise farmers; but he had failed to make major innovations elsewhere and an outline of his fiscal policies shows a rather uncreative approach (Browning, 3.27–31). Thus although Danby refused to sign France's latest treaty on 17 May, he must have been glad of the money it offered. Even then on 18 June, with parliament back in session, he had to declare that the king could not live without an additional supply of £300,000 a year, but the motion for relief was again mishandled by Danby's parliamentary managers and rejected. It was probably an indication of how desperate he had become that the treasurer considered the possibility of using the army that had been raised to maintain royal authority, though it is also clear that he misread the international scene and expected the peace negotiations to fail. Either way, he failed to disband, flying in the face of direct parliamentary provisions to do so and thereby exacerbating fears about his intentions. By the autumn of 1678 Danby had earned the enmity of both France and the English opposition.

Impeachment and the Tower, 1678–1684 The revelation of the Popish Plot, an alleged Catholic conspiracy to murder the king and massacre protestants, therefore offered Danby an opportunity to resurrect his fortunes. Ignoring Charles's desire to avoid bringing the plot before parliament, the treasurer hoped that he could benefit by proving the plot to be true, even though the duke of York's interests lay in proving it to be false. Thus while Danby wanted a parliamentary investigation in order to restore his anti-popish credentials, York wanted a quick examination before privy council. Danby was even prepared to sacrifice the duke for his own advantage, actively considering a bill of limitations 'to paire the nailes … of a popish successor' (*Memoirs of Sir John Reresby*, 157). Such tensions led inevitably to a rupture, which was only temporarily patched up when it became clear to Danby that the plot threatened to backfire on him as well. Such a breach was dangerous, for Danby had few friends, and his enemies now numbered Ralph Montagu, whose ambition to become secretary of state had been frustrated by the treasurer. Supported by France, Montagu intended to reveal what he knew of Danby's role in the secret negotiations with Louis XIV. Danby knew of this plan and attempted to forestall it by seizing Montagu's papers. But at the end of the debate on 19 December 1678 Montagu informed MPs about a casket containing important letters which were then fetched and read. After hearing the letter of 25 March 1678, in which a proposal for money had been made to Louis only five days after the passage of an act authorizing the raising of money for war against France, the house resolved to impeach. On 21 December the committee reported the charges. These were that Danby had 'encroached to himself regal power' through his conduct of foreign affairs, that he had endeavoured to introduce arbitrary power by raising an army on pretence of a war, and that he was 'popishly affected' and had concealed the plot (Browning, 2.74–5). For the next six months Danby attempted, without success, to extricate himself from these legal proceedings.

Danby's immediate response was to persuade the king to add an authorization to the drafts of the offending letters, to allow him to hide behind the power of royal command and neutralize the first and perhaps most damaging of the charges. On 23 December he duly made a defence, during which he ridiculed his concealment of the plot, declaring that 'this is the first time that any man was accused to be the concealer of that plot whereof he hath been a principal means of procuring the discovery' (*Memoirs Relating to the Impeachment*, appendix, 40–48). He even tried to use the occasion to re-state his fundamental hostility to France. He then successfully made his case one of principle between the houses, ensuring that the Lords refused to order him into custody. To break the deadlock the session was prorogued on 30 December. Subsequent discussions between the king and leaders of the opposition offered the prospect that the prosecution might be dropped if Danby resigned, and he may therefore have leant his weight behind the dissolution of 24 January 1679 which was necessary for the deal's success; but in any case the minister had more positive plans. Having already purged his administration of those who had joined his enemies, the treasurer remodelled it further and came to an understanding with York, securing for him a declaration of the illegitimacy of the duke of Monmouth in return for James's temporary exile. He also sought to influence public opinion by publishing *Two Letters from Mr Montagu*, which contained his vindicating speech, and *An*

Explanation of the Lord Treasurer's Letter to Mr Montagu. Nevertheless the general election proved disastrous for Danby's pensioner MPs. On 1 March the king granted him a pardon for all offences committed before 27 February 1679, but he had still not resigned by the time parliament met on 6 March, and a paralysing dispute over the speakership erupted between him and Sir Edward Seymour, another former ally with whom he had fallen out. Seymour claimed that the king did not 'valew the Treasurer's power of a fiddlestick' (Browning, 1.320), but after much wrangling Charles did back Danby, and the house was adjourned in order to choose another candidate. Only then, on 13 March, did Charles ask Danby to resign and he softened the blow with the offer of a pension of £5000 a year for life and a marquessate. The manner in which Danby resigned ruined any chances that the prosecution against him would be dropped. In an attempt to quell the dissatisfaction Charles assured the Lords on 22 March that Danby was innocent of the charges made against him, but, fearful of what might come out in a full-scale trial, urged him into hiding. From his refuge Danby sent the white staff to the king on 25 March, formally ending his period in office.

The impeachment process continued unabated, but first parliament needed to find Danby. On 26 March a bill was introduced in the Lords to ban him from entering the royal presence, from holding any public office or grants, and banishing him unless he surrendered himself by 1 May. Greater pressure was added by the Commons when, on 1 April, a bill of attainder was passed on the grounds that his absence confirmed the treason charges. Danby therefore surrendered himself and was committed to the Tower of London, where he remained until 1684. Having secured their quarry MPs turned their attention to other matters, but on 25 April he pleaded his pardon in an attempt to block further proceedings. This infuriated MPs since it undermined the whole impeachment process and the Commons voted the pardon illegal. This put the two houses in conflict, as Danby may have hoped, and relations were further soured by demands that the bishops should not be allowed to sit during the impeachment because it was a matter of blood. From the Tower Danby poured oil on the flames by warning that the Commons aimed at complete sovereignty and 'must either bee shortly dismiss't' or the king would be ruined (Browning, 2.82–3). Even after Charles prorogued parliament on 27 May, Danby continued to press for a dissolution. With remarkable foresight he also advised the king to issue a declaration and hold the next parliament outside London, policies which he would adopt two years later.

Although Danby could bombard the king with written advice prison limited his influence, so he pressed Charles for his release. The king promised his continuing favour but either feared the reaction or was secretly quite glad to have Danby at arm's length, for the next five years were a continuous round of blocked appeals. For some the length of his imprisonment must have seemed only natural justice for a man who had vindictively locked up Shaftesbury for a year. Thus when Danby canvassed to secure his release in the autumn of 1680 Shaftesbury declared he would 'not abate him an ace' (BL, Add. MS 28053, fol. 203). Danby again petitioned the parliament which met at Oxford in March 1681 but its early dissolution deprived him of a hearing. The longevity of his captivity was also due to allegations, which went further than the impeachment charge, that Danby had not only tried to stifle the plot but was also responsible for the murder of Sir Edmund Berry Godfrey, the justice to whom Titus Oates had revealed the Popish Plot (*Some Reflections upon the Earl of Danby in Relation to Sir Edmund Berry Godfrey's Murder*, 1679). On 16 May 1681 Edward Fitzharris attempted to free himself from a charge of treason by directly implicating Danby in the murder, and on this evidence a Middlesex grand jury (composed of a number of hostile MPs) indicted the earl. Danby petitioned the king to arrange for an immediate trial so that he could clear his name, but the execution of Fitzharris left him without such an opportunity. On 19 May 1681 he moved king's bench to take action against the publishers of Fitzharris's accusations but these proceedings also proved abortive. On 27 May and 29 June 1682 Danby had his plea for habeas corpus heard but refused at king's bench; the lord chief justice's speech made his ears 'tingle' (Le Neve, 98), prompting him to canvass for the case to be referred to the judges rather than parliament, a move disliked by the king. Despite these setbacks and a series of family disasters, including a near-fatal accident for his wife, whom he was nevertheless refused permission to visit, Danby remained resilient. On 17 August 1683 William Longueville found him 'pretty well, and ye same good company, and temperate in what he said' about the Rye House Plotters who had been executed (Thompson, 2.35).

Danby spent much of his time in the Tower preparing vindications of his administration. *An Impartial State of the Case of the Earl of Danby* (1679) was a spirited defence. But he had also to engage with Sir Robert Howard, who accused him in *An Examination of the Impartial Case* (1679) of gross fiscal mismanagement. There was some truth to these allegations, for the gap between income and expenditure was probably greater at the beginning of 1679 than it had been when he took office. On the other hand it was clear that the king's foreign policy had wrecked smooth relations with parliament that might have yielded supply, in return for only about £300,000 of French aid, and that the treasurer had not decreased the revenue. Danby's reply, *The Answer of the Earl of Danby to a Late Pamphlet* (1680), sparked a further exchange: Howard attacked in print again in October 1680, in turn provoking *The Earl of Danby's Answer to Sr Robert Howard's Book* (1680), in which he floated the proposal that offering incentives to the managers of taxes, as he had done in the case of the excise, would greatly improve the revenue. Vindication of his administration spilt over into a vindication of the king's conduct since Danby had lost office, for in 1681 he also penned a draft declaration for the king to issue after the abrupt dissolution of the third Exclusion Parliament. Although rejected in favour of a shorter version, the text contained the earl's characteristic appeal to memories of the civil war.

Release and revolution The immediate cause of Danby's release was the king's decision in 1684 not to summon a new parliament as the law required. According to Danby's eldest son, Edward, Viscount Latimer, the king said in February 'that if the judges would not baile you (which hee would see and speake with the judges tomorrow) hee would by God free you himself' (BL, Add. MS 28049, fol. 214). This proved unnecessary, for on 12 February the judges declared that the earl could be bailed. Once free, Danby immediately sought to regain influence, but although fêted by members of a loyalist club the earl received a much more frosty reception from the duke of York. He also found it difficult to persuade the king to show favour, despite a private interview and a pleading memorandum (Browning, 2.110–12). He therefore withdrew from court and retired to his Yorkshire estate. Illness prevented him from playing any more of an active role but in December he went back to London in an unsuccessful attempt to secure the mastership of the rolls for his son. Rumours that he himself might gain office in a remodelled ministry were crushed by the death of Charles. Yet James's accession did signal a turn in Danby's fortunes. He found 'the king and ministers outwardly very civill' (ibid., 2.128) and on the first day of the new parliament he presented a petition about his impeachment. Three days later the Lords, annulling a decision of 19 March 1679, declared that the impeachment had lapsed. Danby therefore sent James a new memorandum on 6 July reiterating his call for compensation. This time James summoned him, but the discussions about the Test Act, which the king sought to repeal, were evidently unsatisfactory. James called him again in November, perhaps with a view to him replacing the dismissed Halifax, and the king showed him the provocative speech he proposed to make about the Test Act and army officers. But again the earl's response appears not to have pleased the king. Danby nevertheless avoided open confrontation. He made no recorded speech in the second session, though he did draft a speech proposing to refer the king's dispensing power to the judges. For the next two years he retired into private life.

During this time Danby renewed his links with William of Orange. In 1686 the king refused him permission to travel abroad, and for much of that year the earl was preoccupied with the fall-out from the collapse of the marriage of his son, Peregrine, Viscount Dumblane. But in 1687, when many of his relatives were deprived of their posts as the king purged office-holders, Danby received a visit from William's agent Dykvelt. On 30 May 1687 William was sent a letter in which the earl declared proudly that 'no competitor can pretend an equall share' in his service (Browning, 2.117). When a second agent, Zuylestein, visited in August he brought a letter for Danby from William and carried one back from the earl. Danby became a key figure in William's plans. On 28 January 1688 Danby was so far identified with the opposition that he received an anonymous letter threatening his life unless he made peace with the king, but such intimidation did nothing to deter him. Danby was nevertheless careful to cultivate Princess Mary as well as her husband William, attempting to place his daughter, Lady Plymouth, in Mary's bedchamber. Danby was one of the first to consider the idea of inviting William, and was the most important tory signatory to the letter that was drawn up in the wake of the acquittal of the seven bishops, whose trial he had attended.

Danby played a key role in the conspiracy against James. He advised William to land in the north, hoping thereby to have 'a share in the whole management by the interest he believed he had in that country' (*Bishop Burnet's History*, 3.303). Certainly towards the end of August he was sending large sums of money to the continent and was soliciting gentry support among the tory Anglicans. He was also formally reconciled with the earl of Devonshire, the manager of his earlier impeachment but a fellow Williamite. Danby set up his headquarters at Ribston Hall in Yorkshire, where on 1 October he and Devonshire arranged the final details of their planned rising. Danby was summoned by the king to London but excused himself and moved to Kiveton, leaving his son Dumblane at York. While waiting for the invasion Danby played an important part in keeping up the spirits of the Williamites. The invasion force landing in the west both surprised Danby's plans and forced him and his allies into action. Danby took up arms on 20 November and wrote to the prince requesting further direction, though he also lamented William's neglect of the north. On 22 November Danby arranged a bloodless coup at York, riding at the head of horsemen shouting for 'a free parlament and the protestant religion and noe popery' (*Memoirs of Sir John Reresby*, 529). Even if he was probably not its author, as the British Library catalogue implies, *Some Thoughts of a Private Person* was published to justify the actions at York in terms of a right of resistance to defend legal rights and a denial that this infringed scriptural injunctions.

Having been excluded from the principal share in William's glory, Danby had already begun to fear that complete victory by either James or William would be undesirable, but the prince's call for the forces marshalled at Nottingham under the command of the earl of Devonshire to march south and Princess Anne's departure from Nottingham destroyed any hopes the earl may have had of using his position in the north to act as mediator. It may be significant that James seriously considered the possibility of retreating to the north and throwing himself on Danby; but his flight confirmed Danby's intention to reach London as soon as possible. This he was unable to do because a fear of Irish soldiers seized the north and Danby decided to move westward to meet any threat. Danby did not reach the capital until 28 December, in time to hear William accept provisional control of the government. While the revolution consolidated Danby's power in the north he felt aggrieved by the prince's neglect and the favour shown to Halifax. But his followers did well at the elections to the Convention and the struggle transferred to the parliamentary arena. Danby chaired an address of thanks for William's administration but his supporters were quiet, absent, or perhaps confused in the early debates about the throne. On 29 January, after the Commons had decided on a vacancy, and with Danby in the chair, the Lords heard a proposal for a regency as 'the best and safest way to preserve the Protestant religion and the laws of this kingdom' (*JHL*, 1685–1691, 14.110). Yet Danby spoke 'strenuously' (Le Neve, 113) and duly voted against this, thereby securing its defeat, even though Halifax thought he favoured the project; and then voted against giving William and Mary the crown. He appears to have been attempting to set up an interest for Mary as sole monarch, since he urged her to come to England. Under his influence the Lords therefore objected to the word 'vacancy' in the Commons resolution because that implied an elective monarchy. When the resulting conference between the houses reopened the debate in the Commons Danby's followers there voted against the vacancy of the throne. But Mary herself warned that 'she would take it extreme unkindly if any, under a pretence of their care of her, would set up a divided interest between her and the prince' (*Bishop Burnet's History*, 3.393) and Danby was among those summoned to hear William declare that he would return to the Netherlands if he did not receive the kingship for life. The earl had no alternative but to submit. He broadcast his change of heart via Lord Dumblane who apologized on 7 February 1689 in the Commons for not voting in favour of the vacancy. Even so, the earl remained acutely sensitive to tory sensibilities and favoured a rewording of the oath of allegiance so that there was no recognition of the new monarchs as 'rightful and lawful', and when Halifax opposed this Danby 'schooled him so shamefully that my Lord Hallifax did not open his mouth' (Bodl. Oxf., MS Ballard 45/27a).

Return to office Despite the differences over the crown, William and Mary seemed to owe much to Danby, who therefore hoped for reward. In February 1689 he was nevertheless offered only the presidency of the council, not the treasurership he desired, while his rival Halifax became lord privy seal. Such was his reluctance to accept the presidency that he later told Reresby it had been 'forced … upon him' (*Memoirs of Sir John Reresby*, 557). Moreover Danby felt compelled to write a remonstrance to the new king only five days into his reign to urge rewards for his followers who had been overlooked. His son, Lord Latimer, was refused the post of gentleman of the bedchamber, which he had held under Charles II, and Lady Plymouth equally failed to enter the queen's bedchamber. On 28 February 1689 Reresby was subjected to a dinner-table indictment by Danby of the government, particularly of its religious policy, and for the following month the earl hardly ventured into parliament, returning only to block the intended repeal of the Test Acts. When confronted he told the king he 'would serve him in everything but against the Church' (Foxcroft, 2.211). He was appointed on 1 April as governor of Hull, though he told Reresby it was 'as a place of retreat, and whereby to make his terms, shoud there be a change of times' (*Memoirs of Sir John Reresby*, 571). Not surprisingly the king exclaimed that 'as for my Lord Danby hee knew not what to make of him' (Foxcroft, 2.206). It was only with difficulty that, on 6 April 1689, he was created marquess of Carmarthen, taking his title from property in Wales granted in 1674. The truth was that William resented Carmarthen's imperiousness and remembered his naïvety in the all-important European sphere. He was a useful if limited statesman but he was also a man with a divisive past. According to Halifax, Carmarthen's heart was never really in the compromise ministry that the king appointed and had allegedly advised that William had as well put himself in the hands of the fanatics as continue his trimming policy.

Carmarthen's awkwardness was clear from his absence from council and parliament for much of May, perhaps a silent protest at what he perceived to be the inadequate financial settlement. But he was forced back when Oates, attempting to reverse the judgments made in 1685 against him, attacked him. Carmarthen declared that the sentence ought to be reversed in so far as Oates had formerly been whipped from Newgate to Tyburn and now ought to be whipped back again. Such rash language provoked the king to wonder whether the marquess was mad when he made the speech. Carmarthen, however, went further and had Oates sent to prison, an act which reanimated animus against him, resulting in a pointed resolution that a pardon was not pleadable to bar an impeachment. In June his son Peregrine, now styled the earl of Danby, was investigated over a privateer which he had fitted out, and John Howe moved that an address be presented to the king requesting that all persons who had ever been impeached by the Commons might be dismissed; from the beginning of the session Carmarthen was thought to be vulnerable to another impeachment. The request for the removal of impeached ministers nevertheless struck at Halifax as much as Carmarthen, and when on 2 August the house attacked the former, Carmarthen's son and followers joined the fray. It may have been the case that he was working with the whigs to overthrow his rival; if so, it merely disgusted William who, in his more exasperated moods, wanted to be rid of the earl. But Carmarthen refused to go unless dismissed and this the king was reluctant to do, for Halifax was deeply unpopular and events were pushing the king towards, not against, the churchmen whom the lord president represented.

Carmarthen's credit rose in the remainder of 1689. The constant bickering between Halifax and the whigs in the second session of the Convention reduced the usefulness of both and alienated the king. By December there were even reports that Carmarthen might be reappointed as treasurer and he was generally held responsible for the dissolution of parliament on 12 January 1690. Halifax's resignation less than a month later signalled Carmarthen's victory in the factional struggle. But it was much more than a personal triumph. He brought ideological allies into government, and on the back of successful elections, in which the church became a rallying cry, Carmarthen returned to the business of creating a court party. Counting on a majority in the upper house but only a core of fifty supporters in the lower, he came to an understanding with Speaker Sir John Trevor to manage the court interest. The lord president also set about restoring financial probity, gaining the excise revenue for the life of the king and the customs for four years. Attempts were made by the whigs to wrongfoot him over the recognition of the king and queen as 'rightful and lawful', which they sought to include in an abjuration bill, and a motion was made calling for Carmarthen's removal. But these actions only confirmed the fact that he was now regarded as the king's principal adviser, a position consolidated when Shrewsbury resigned as secretary of state in June. Always pallid, he was nicknamed 'the White Marquis' (Thompson, 2.149) and for the next three years he appeared to head the government.

But if Carmarthen's power had always been slightly illusory in his first ministry, it was even more so in his second. He now had no department to act as a power base, had a number of strong colleagues to counter-balance him, was an object of suspicion for those with long memories, and in his relations with the new king could not domineer. William's absences on campaign, however, provided a pretext for Carmarthen to try to engross power by cutting out Mary and thinking 'little by little to do all' (Dalrymple, vol. 2, appendix, 2.122). In her private memoirs Mary noted that he was 'of a temper I can never like' (Doebner, 29). Although he worked assiduously in the summer of 1690, he was peculiarly ill-suited to his role as power-broker and alienated both political extremes. The high-church leader the earl of Rochester thus thought him 'quite struck up with the Dissenters' (Browning, 1.481), while the whigs were alienated by his refusal to press for the dissolution of the tory-dominated parliament. When parliament resumed in October the lord president was thus again attacked. Carmarthen had nevertheless resorted to old techniques and been forming a body of 'managers of the king's directions', led by Sir John Lowther and Sir Henry Goodricke (ibid., 3.178–9). As a result of their and the king's pressure the Commons voted the unprecedented sum of £4 million supply. Carmarthen's position was boosted by his revelation of a Jacobite conspiracy, after Lord Preston was captured with incriminating papers. Thus when William left in January 1691 Carmarthen was again left as 'chief minister in his absence' (Luttrell, 2.137). He now received a pension of £3500 a year and rumours abounded that he would be created a duke.

In 1691 Carmarthen was, in the words of his most astute biographer, 'all pervasive rather than all-powerful' (Browning, 1.489). His position in the government meant that he suffered for any errors, and long before the October session both parties had begun to muster an attack on him. When it came it centred on the miscarriage of the naval forces, but this was diverted onto the earl of Nottingham (perhaps not altogether unwittingly by the earl of Danby), and Carmarthen used evidence from the Preston affair, which implicated malcontents of both parties, to 'break the teeth' of his opponents (ibid., 2.192). In a sense Carmarthen's power rested on division. He was disliked by both extremes, but so long as they were not powerful enough to topple him he was able to head a composite ministry. When, therefore, tory malcontents Rochester and Seymour entered the government in 1692 and sided with Nottingham, the lord president's position was threatened. The zealots attempted to wrest leadership from him by urging a more violent party line. Thus when Rochester advised the king to shift from a land to a sea war, Carmarthen dismissed such tactics as 'sitting still and letting the French king take what he will' (Dalrymple, 2.242). Whereas Halifax had been ideologically committed to a balanced ministry, Carmarthen sought only a pragmatic coalition. He therefore saw his problems in terms of the lack of a solid body of supporters to rely on. He marshalled the court block and supported William's opposition to the Place and Triennial Bill, both of which sought to limit royal power.

Carmarthen's second fall from power was, though not without drama in its final stages, a gradual process. Power shifted during late 1693 and 1694 towards the whigs, and the emerging manager was not Carmarthen but the earl of Sunderland. During the 1693–4 session the lord president was pushed into awkward compromises. He was active in rejecting the Treason Bill, an issue about which he felt strongly out of personal experience, but while disliking the scheme to create the Bank of England he argued for it in order to preserve supply for the military campaign. Such ambiguity meant that Carmarthen was increasingly irrelevant to both the king and the whigs, as the remodelling of the ministry in March 1694 showed. Although created duke of Leeds on 4 May 1694, he had effectively been sidelined. Aware of his incongruous position at the head of a predominantly whig ministry Leeds retreated into caution. In August, when asked his views about the fleet, he would 'give no opinion but managed his arguments so well for and against' that Shrewsbury could not fathom his opinion, but was 'sure he has left himself latitude enough to be of either, as the event shall give occasion' (*Private and Original Correspondence of … Shrewsbury*, 66). As he must have suspected, it was only a matter of time before the whigs sought to be rid of him. In November 1694, perhaps in an attempt to stave off dismissal, he supported (against the king's wishes) the Triennial Act, which required general elections to be held at least every three years. According to his own later memoir, William told him that he 'should live to repent it' (*Copies and Extracts of some Letters*, xi). He now also advocated acceptance of the Treason Bill, albeit with a wrecking amendment. But in the spring of 1695 the House of Commons began to investigate corruption in the East India Company. A bill of penalties against one of the chief culprits, Sir Thomas Cooke, roused Leeds into daily attendance, for he had been accused of receiving £10,000 for speaking against the bill to grant the new East India Company a charter. Although Leeds denied this, with 'a most solemn protestation of his cleanness and innocence' (Le Neve, 121), the investigation revealed that Cooke had enlisted the duke's support through the agency of Sir Basil Firebrace and that a sum of 5500 guineas had been paid. Leeds, most unconvincingly, claimed that he told the intermediary to keep the money and was unaware that it had been left in his house. The Commons decided once again to impeach him.

Leeds immediately delivered a three-hour speech in his own defence. Reminding his audience of his ill treatment in 1678 he declared that the new charges were as baseless as the earlier ones and called for a quick trial. Articles were duly presented on 29 April but accused him only of betraying his trust as a privy councillor by receiving bribes. The following day Leeds entered a plea of not guilty, which seemed highly unlikely, but the key witness, Leeds's servant John Robart, had conveniently disappeared and no further action could be taken before the prorogation. In May he was nevertheless told to absent himself from the council, an order that rendered his position as lord president almost purely nominal. Although he continued to haunt the court his position must have appeared increasingly ridiculous. On his return from campaign William renewed his injunction against attending council, but in return the whigs agreed to call off any further investigation and the impeachment fell with the dissolution of parliament.

Dismissal and retirement His new semi-detached status allowed Leeds to create difficulties for the whigs in the session of 1695–6. When a Recoinage Bill came from the Commons Leeds proposed an amendment which would have declared coin to be valued by weight and compensation paid for the shortfall. The whig-guided Commons refused this and Leeds withdrew his opposition. But that he had not changed his mind was clear later in the session when he opposed fixing the rate of guineas at 22*s*., only to acquiesce once again when he suffered defeat. In the wake of the attempt in February 1696 to assassinate the king Leeds received a special summons to attend a cabinet council, but his main concern in parliament appears to have been to find a way to allow tories to escape the trap being set for them by the whig 'association', which bound subscribers to recognize William as 'rightful and lawful' king. Having failed to prevent its formulation entirely, Leeds proposed an alternative form of wording that recognized that William 'hath a right by law to the Crown and that no other person whatsoever hath any right to the same' (*House of Lords MSS*, new ser., 2.205). Leeds opposed a similar bill coming from the Commons that made the association compulsory for all office-holders. He took a bigger step into opposition when he intervened on behalf of one of the alleged assassination conspirators, Sir John Fenwick, protesting against his attainder and pleading for a milder penalty. Even then William did not dismiss his titular lord president. In the following session (of 1697–8) Danby continued to provoke the whigs by acting as a manager in the dispute between the houses over Charles Duncombe, a financier friend, whose attainder was rejected in the upper house on Leeds's casting vote. Moreover, when a bill to establish a new East India Company came up from the Commons, he denounced it as against the liberty of the subject and an infringement of the right of sovereignty.

As the tide began to turn against the whigs, Leeds pursued a vendetta against one of their leaders, the chancellor of the exchequer Charles Montagu, in the 1698–9 session. In part this was the result of pique when Montagu, not Leeds, secured the post of auditor of the exchequer; but it was also the residue of the duke's hostility to the whig's financial revolution. Leeds also exploited whig divisions over the standing army by opposing the retention of William's Dutch guards. It can scarcely have come as a surprise when, on 18 May 1699, he was finally dismissed as lord president and, subsequently, from his lord lieutenancies and governorship of Hull; the wonder was that he had held on to them for so long. Even then he may have lost his offices because the king believed him to be dying. After his recovery in the autumn of 1699 Leeds played a very irregular role in public life. In 1700 he was active in parliament about the Darien affair and the issue of royal grants, and in 1701 joined the tories in denouncing the partition treaties; but his distaste for impeachment proceedings was sufficiently strong to cause him to desert them when they went further and attacked the whig ministers. He was rewarded for his moderation when his own 1695 impeachment was finally dismissed along with those against the Junto.

Although he had been courted for his support by the king in 1700 and 1701, it was the accession of Queen Anne in 1702 that brought Leeds back into favour at Whitehall. Although he accepted the post of privy councillor, he 'declined being put into any other public post' (Le Neve, 145), perhaps because he was too moderate for the high-churchmen who gained power but also because he was by now seventy. But defence of his family and the church, two of his abiding principles, could bring him out of retirement. In 1703 he sought, and failed, to obtain legal redress against Montagu (now—ironically—Lord Halifax), and supported the occasional conformity bills that were promoted in the first three sessions of Anne's reign, though not the attempt to tack the measure to supply. During one debate he rashly told Halifax that 'his family was raised by rebellion, but his own suffered by it' (*Beaufort MSS*, 96), leading to the challenge of a duel between Halifax and Carmarthen (as Leeds's son and heir, Peregrine, now was) that was stopped only when the House of Lords intervened. In 1705 Leeds told the upper house that the greatest danger to the church came from the practice of occasional conformity, and entered his protest against the resolution that it was in a 'safe and flourishing condition' (Cobbett, *Parl. hist.*, 6.507). Consequently another potential duel between Halifax and Carmarthen had to be stopped by order of the Lords. But such vehemence was only a sign that once again the whigs were regaining influence. During 1705 most of Leeds's relatives lost their posts.

Soon after the loss of his wife on 7 January 1704 Leeds appears to have contemplated settling down to writing his memoirs. Perhaps as an aid he also began to keep a diary. But family affairs, principally worries about his unstable and impecunious son Carmarthen, seem to have distracted him. In any case a further political shift in 1709–10, in the form of the Sacheverell affair, renewed his activity for the defence of the church. Regularly attending the trial, he signed repeated protests against the resolutions adopted by the whig-dominated Lords against the doctor. Allegedly weeping during Sacheverell's eloquent self-defence, Leeds voted for his acquittal. Leeds was himself prompted into speech, using the occasion to vindicate his own actions at the revolution, claiming he:

> never thought, that things would have gone so far, as to settle the Crown on the Prince of Orange, whom he had often heard say that he had no such thoughts himself. That they ought to distinguish between resistance and revolution; for vacancy or abdication was the thing they went upon, and therefore resistance was to be forgot; for had it not succeeded it had certainly been rebellion, since he knew of no other but hereditary right. (Cobbett, *Parl. hist.*, 6.847)

Nevertheless, while the Sacheverell affair encouraged some into dallying with James Francis Edward Stuart, the Pretender, Leeds opened correspondence with Hanover. His attempt to represent the past in the way he wished to be remembered was also evident in the publication of *Copies and Extracts of some Letters Written to and from the Earl of Danby* (1710), which contained a vindicatory introduction. Although calculated to 'shew how faithfully I acted to the best of my understanding for the interest of my countrey' in the 1670s (p. xiii), many of the letters were not accurately reprinted, containing many revisions and omissions in order to minimize his connections with the French negotiations. Leeds also republished, in book form, the collected pamphlets against Howard (*Memoirs Relating to the Impeachment of Thomas Earl of Danby*, 1710). These publications prompted a revival of what one defender called printed 'calumnies' against him (*A Vindication of his Grace*, 1711), including the accusation that he had only dared publish Ralph Montagu's letters once the latter died.

Death and reputation Leeds himself died from convulsions on 26 July 1712 at Easton Neston, Northamptonshire, the seat of his daughter Lady Leominster, and was buried at Harthill, Yorkshire, with his ancestors. According to one account, he had lived the last twenty-five years 'without ever going once to stool, the excrementious parts of his food, after a due digestion in his stomach being discharg'd the same way it was taken in' (Le Neve, 145–6). His will expressly forbade that his body lie in state. The earl's third, unstable, surviving son, Peregrine, inherited the title but the estate was left to the first duke's grandson, also named Peregrine. Leeds had outlived most of his friends, contemporaries, and many of his close relatives. Few commentators, contemporary and modern, have been able to ignore the duke's flaws. He was proud, ambitious, and grasping from instinct as well as from the pressure of his own and his family's debts. He saw little wrong with bribery, whether it be designed to line his own pockets or those whom he sought to manage, so that he appeared to some as the epitome of a corrupt courtier. His capacity to misrepresent events and motives, including his own, was sometimes breathtaking. He was a stiff, formal politician, bombastic and domineering. Yet in some of these failings were also the keys to his success. His pride and ambition nurtured a remarkably resilient and persevering determination to be at the centre of affairs and to make political comebacks; such qualities also entailed a dedication to business that made him indispensable to more than one monarch. Indeed the longevity of his service to the crown must rank him alongside Walpole, who resembled him in many ways. Leeds's knowledge of the value of money attuned the treasurer in him and made him appreciate the power of a pension or office to buy favour. He was the first to recognize the power of the Treasury as the key to ministerial pre-eminence and hence, not coincidentally, his administration is found being referred to by contemporaries as a 'prime ministry' (Le Neve, 25). His domineering style dictated the need to create bodies of loyal supporters, while he appreciated that dominance in committee was as important as oratory on the floor of the house. Such skills at parliamentary management did much to pave the way for, and even create, party government. His own talent for misrepresentation gave him insights into the value of propaganda and the deception and intrigue demanded by partisan politics, and he skilfully used the language of moderation for party purposes.

Accused of disloyalty to his friends and patrons there were nevertheless a number of ideological tenets, aside from an unshakeable commitment to securing prominence for his family, from which Leeds could not be shifted. The first and most important was loyalty to the Church of England. Throughout his career, and no matter what offence it caused, he resolutely defended the church against the perceived twin dangers of popery and dissent. In this view he represented a very powerful strain of opinion, which he did all he could to encourage and sustain. This passion for the established church was sufficient to overcome his otherwise habitual loyalty to the Stuarts and his belief in non-resistance in 1688. His agonizing after the revolution on both accounts was also entirely typical of the trauma that many moderate tories suffered. It was this, as much as his political skills, that perhaps gave his place in the post-revolutionary government such importance. The church in danger was his rallying cry at all the high points in his career: in the 1670s, in 1688, and in the early 1690s. The second antipathy which he held throughout his career was towards France. He was hostile to the ambitions of Louis XIV throughout the 1670s and hostile to the threat posed by France after the revolution. Louis recognized as much by fostering the impeachment proceedings in 1678–9. It is thus ironic that Danby was perceived to have presided over the growth of popery and Francophile arbitrary government. In part this reflected a characteristic of both his ministries: his power was always rather illusory. Lacking great personal charm and unable to strike warm political relationships with MPs or monarchs, he tended to preside over, rather than direct, affairs. This figureheading pragmatism had its value, especially to Charles II but also to William, yet it left Danby vulnerable to events. Both in the 1670s and the 1690s he seems to have lacked control of the situation;

and it is no coincidence that in both decades his undeveloped sense of foreign affairs left him at a disadvantage. Danby lacked foresight. He was a remarkable, manipulative, and clever man; but he was not an imaginative one. It seems totally plausible, as he later claimed, that he had not foreseen William's coup for the crown. Then, as so often, Danby's pride and egotism obscured his perspicuity. Where he did have vision, in trying to persuade Charles to adopt a resolutely protestant, anti-French policy, he failed to discern that the complicity demanded by the king inevitably destroyed his own credibility. In part this lack of imagination was because Danby was a conviction politician whose policies lay rooted in the prejudices and assumptions of a significant section of the nation. In articulating their opinions Danby was a formidable force.

MARK KNIGHTS

Sources A. Browning, *Thomas Osborne, earl of Danby and duke of Leeds, 1632–1712*, 3 vols. (1944–51) [vol. 1 incl. most exhaustive biography; vols. 2 and 3 incl. extensive transcripts of Danby's papers] • BL, Add. MSS 28040–28095; described in *The manuscripts of the House of Lords*, 4 vols., HMC, 17 (1887–94), vol. 1; and in A. W. Thibaudeau, *Catalogue of the collection of autograph letters and documents formed by Alfred Morrison*, 6 vols. (1883–92) • BL, Egerton MSS 3324–3359 [a collection of Leeds family papers]; calendared in *The manuscripts of the duke of Leeds*, HMC, 22 (1888), 1–58 • C. G. O. Bridgeman and J. C. Walker, eds., *Supplementary report on the manuscripts of the late Montagu Bertie, twelfth earl of Lindsey*, HMC, 79 (1942) • J. Le Neve, *The lives and characters of the most illustrious persons … who died in the year 1712* (1714) [the longest near-contemporary life] • *Memoirs of Sir John Reresby*, ed. A. Browning (1936) • *Bishop Burnet's History* • Cobbett, *Parl. hist.* • E. M. Thompson, ed., *Correspondence of the family of Hatton*, 2 vols., CS, new ser., 22–3 (1878) • J. Dalrymple, *Memoirs of Great Britain and Ireland*, 3 vols. (1771–8) • *CSP dom.*, *1660–1702* • O. Airy, ed., *Essex papers*, CS, new ser., 47 (1890) • Evelyn, *Diary* • *The life and letters of Sir George Savile … first marquis of Halifax*, ed. H. C. Foxcroft, 2 vols. (1898) • R. Doebner, ed., *Memoirs of Queen Mary of England* (Leipzig and London, 1856) • *The complete works in verse and prose of Andrew Marvell*, ed. A. B. Grosart, 4 vols. (1872–5) • *The life of Edward, earl of Clarendon … written by himself*, new edn, 3 vols. (1827) • *The letters of Dorothy Osborne to William Temple*, ed. G. C. Moore Smith (1928) • *Private and original correspondence of Charles Talbot, duke of Shrewsbury*, ed. W. Coxe (1821) • *Copies and extracts of some letters written to and from the earl of Danby (now duke of Leeds)* (1710) • *Memoirs relating to the impeachment of Thomas earl of Danby (now duke of Leeds), in … 1678* (1710) • N. Luttrell, *A brief historical relation of state affairs from September 1678 to April 1714*, 6 vols. (1857) • S. Bethel, *The present interest of England* (1671) • M. Nedham, *A pacquet of advices and animadversions sent from London to the men of Shaftsbury* (1676) • [T. Osborne, duke of Leeds], *An explanation of the lord treasurer's letter to Mr Montagu* (1679) • [G. Villiers, second duke of Buckingham], *A letter to Sir Thomas Osborn* (1672) • *The answer of the … earl of Danby to a late pamphlet, entituled 'An examination of the impartial state of the case of the earl of Danby'* (1680) • *The earl of Danby's answer to Sr. Robert Howard's book entituled 'An account of the state of His Majesties revenue'* (1680) • *The manuscripts of the duke of Beaufort … the earl of Donoughmore*, HMC, 27 (1891) • A. Whiteman and M. Clapinson, eds., *The Compton census of 1676: a critical edition*, British Academy, Records of Social and Economic History, new ser., 10 (1986) • A. C. Wood, 'The revolution in the north of England', *Transactions of the Thoroton Society*, 44 (1940), 72–104 • E. S. De Beer, 'The development of parties during the ministry of Danby', MA diss., U. Lond., 1923 • J. Montano, 'Courting the moderates: ideology, propaganda and party, 1660–1678', PhD diss., Harvard U., 1987 • J. Pollock, *The Popish Plot* (1903) [appx incl. Danby's notes for a declaration] • GEC, *Peerage* • W. D. Christie, *A life of Anthony Ashley Cooper, first earl of Shaftesbury, 1621–1683*, 2 vols. (1871) • *BIHR*, 11 (1933–4), 137 • W. A. Speck, 'The revolution of 1688 in the north of England', *Northern History*, 25 (1989), 188–204 • *The manuscripts of the House of Lords*, new ser., 12 vols. (1900–77), vol. 2 • M. Goldie, 'Danby, the bishops, and the whigs', *The politics of religion in Restoration England*, ed. T. Harris, P. Seaward, and M. Goldie (1990), 75–106

Archives BL, corresp., papers, and journals, Add. MSS 28040–28054, 38849, 63650, Egerton MSS 3324–3508, Egerton charters 2290–2300 • Lincs. Arch., house and stable accounts • NRA, priv. coll., log relating to battle of Hogue • PRO, official records as lord high treasurer and as treasurer of navy; household and estate accounts, PRO 30/52 • W. Yorks. AS, Leeds, Yorkshire Archaeological Society, personal, family, and estate papers, DD5, 192 • Wellcome L., commonplace book • Yale U., Beinecke L., corresp. and papers | BL, letters to Lord Essex, Stowe MSS 201–212 • Bodl. Oxf., letters to principal officers of the ordnance • Cumbria AS, Carlisle, letters to Lord Lonsdale • Leics. RO, corresp. with earl of Nottingham • Sheff. Arch., corresp. with Sir Henry Bennet • U. Nott. L., corresp. with first earl of Portland

Likenesses S. Cooper, miniature, 1650–59, Buccleuch collection • N. Dixon, miniature, 1670–79, priv. coll. • R. White, engraving and drawing, *c.*1670–1679, BM; repro. in H. B. Butler, C. R. L. Fletcher, E. Walker, and C. F. Bell, *Historical portraits, 1600–1700* (1911) • P. Lely, oils, *c.*1673, NPG; repro. in Browning, *Thomas Osborne*, vol. 1, front pl.; on loan to Dover House • G. Kneller, oils, *c.*1680–1685, Holkham Hall, Norfolk • probably W. Claret, oils, *c.*1682, Marlborough House, London • J. Greenhill, oils, *c.*1682, Marlborough House, London • R. White, engraving, *c.*1694, NPG [*see illus.*] • J. Kerseboom and G. vander Vaart, oils, 1704, repro. in O. Airy, *Charles II* (1901); on loan to Lancaster House, London • A. Blooteling, line engraving (after P. Lely), BM, NPG • G. Kneller, oils; on loan to Treasury • portrait, priv. coll.

Wealth at death over £26,000—from sale of property; £11,500 to granddaughters; bulk of estate not estimable: will, PRO, PROB 11/537

Osborne, Thomas (*bap.* **1704**?, *d.* **1767**), bookseller, was the son of the London bookseller Thomas Osborne (*d.* 1744), who had established a bookselling business in Gray's Inn; he was probably the Thomas Osborne baptized in St Andrew, Holborn, London, on 13 April 1704 to Thomas and Brilliana Osborne. He was admitted as a freeman of the Stationers' Company by patrimony on 2 July 1728 and was made a liveryman four days later. In June 1738 he bought the lease from Mary Gooding of the ground chambers, 1 and 2 Page's Buildings, Field Court, Gray's Inn, and he continued at this location until his death. His father, whose will was proved on 7 March 1744, left his stock and copyright to Thomas, as well as property in London: a house in Fulwood's Rents where Thomas lived; the father also owned other houses and the ferry at Chelsea.

Just what the working relationship was between father and son is not clear, but in 1729 the first of a long series of trade catalogues was issued, presumably a practice begun by the younger Osborne. In 1854 Thomas Thorpe, the bookseller, offered for sale a collection of Osborne's catalogues from 1729 to 1768 in fifty-three volumes octavo. Only a fraction of the numerous catalogues issued by Osborne have survived, but it is evident that he purchased the libraries of the most eminent persons of the time.

The most important collection that Osborne purchased and then issued a catalogue for was the Harleian Library, the sale of which provides valuable insights into his business practices. Robert Harley, first earl of Oxford, chancellor of the exchequer, then lord treasurer, and head of the tory ministry under Queen Anne, and his son Edward Harley, the second earl, were among the greatest of English collectors of books and manuscripts. The Harleian books were sold after the death of the second earl in 1741 for £13,000 to Osborne, who engaged Samuel Johnson and William Oldys, literary secretary to the earl from 1738 to 1741, to prepare a catalogue of the books to attract possible purchasers. Proposals for printing the first two volumes of the catalogue by subscription, dated 1 November 1742, were written by Johnson and his 'Account of the Harleian Library' also prefaced the first volume of the catalogue, published with the second volume on 28 February 1743 to puff the library. The first two volumes of the catalogue were sold by subscription for 10s., half at the time of subscribing and half on the delivery of the two volumes. Osborne apparently anticipated that his marketing strategy for the library would create controversy; Johnson's 'Account', while giving a broad overview of the collection, is in large measure an apology for selling the catalogue. The haste with which Osborne had forced Johnson and Oldys to compile the catalogue meant that it was poorly organized in places and that many of the books did not receive commentary. Osborne attempted to forestall criticism by having Johnson write a notice for the beginning of the second volume admitting the shortcomings and promising a better performance in the future, a promise that would not be kept. These arguments were not accepted by everyone, and when issuing the third and fourth volumes of the catalogue on 4 January 1744 Osborne found it necessary to turn to Johnson again for a preface with further justification, not only for the price asked for the catalogue but for the prices of the books themselves. By this time the clamour was so loud that Osborne was forced to announce in the preface that he would either credit the price of the catalogue against the purchase of any of the books, or else refund it. At the same time it was announced that the annotations in the third and fourth volumes had been greatly reduced. A fifth volume of the catalogue appeared on 8 April 1745 but was 'nothing more than a catalogue of Osborne's old stock' (Hawkins, 133).

One reason for the reduced annotations in volumes 3 and 4 of the catalogue is that Johnson and Oldys were now involved in another scheme to help Osborne recoup his investment in the Harleian Library: selecting pamphlets of the sixteenth and seventeenth centuries, largely on political and religious subjects, and annotating them for the *Harleian Miscellany*, which appeared in eight quarto volumes (1744–6). Again, Osborne asked Johnson to assist him by writing the proposals for printing the work by subscription and contributing an introduction on the importance of small tracts and fugitive pieces to the first number published 24 March 1744.

About this time Osborne and Johnson had a confrontation. Sir John Hawkins, who knew Johnson at the time, recounts that Osborne was a sharp businessman, determined to get all of the work he could out of his employees, and ignorant of what scholarship entails. Johnson was poring over one of the pamphlets to decide whether it should be reprinted in the *Miscellany* when Osborne began to abuse him roughly for wasting time:

> Johnson's anger at so foul a charge was not so great as to make him forget that he had a weapon at hand: he seized a folio that lay near him, and with it felled his adversary to the ground, with some exclamation, which, as it is differently related, I will not venture to repeat. (Hawkins, 150)

The altercation made such an impression on Johnson that he told the story, with slight variations, to several people including James Boswell and Hester Lynch Thrale. Johnson also remembered Osborne in his life of Alexander Pope, as 'a man entirely destitute of shame, without sense of any disgrace but that of poverty'. The shafts of Pope's satire were directed in vain against Osborne as they were 'deadened by his impassive dullness' (Johnson, 187). Pope had complained that Osborne had pretended to sell the subscription copies of the *Iliad* at half price when in fact he had cut down the common folio copies to the size of the subscription quartos. As a result, when a revised version of *The Dunciad* appeared in 1743, Pope substituted Osborne's name for that of Samuel Chapman in the urinating contest with Edmund Curll in book 2.

Osborne's name appears in numerous imprints. *The British Librarian*, by Oldys, was published from January to June 1737 by Osborne. He was also involved in the publication of such large works as Robert James's *Medicinal Dictionary* (1743–5) and Richard Rolt's *A New Dictionary of Trade and Commerce* (1756). Between March 1754 and November 1763 he was active as a member of the Stationers' Company's court of assistants. But Osborne is primarily remembered for his great success in selling libraries. A 'catalogist', Nichols says, is one who 'distributes their Books at fixed prices, for ready money'; he continues:

> Among these Catalogists stands foremost Tom Osborne, who filled one side of Gray's-inn with his lumber, and, without knowing the intrinsic value of a single book, contrived such arbitrary prices as raised him to a country house and dog-and-duck huntings. (Nichols, *Lit. anecdotes*, 3.625)

Osborne was short and thick in stature, and generally spoke in a domineering manner to inferiors.

> In the latter part of his life his manners were considerably softened, particularly to the young booksellers who had occasion to frequent his shop in pursuit of their orders. If they were so fortunate as to call whilst he was taking wine after dinner, they were regularly called into the little parlour in Gray's Inn to take a glass with him. 'Young man,' he would say, 'I have been in business more than forty years, and am now worth more than 40,000*l*. Attend to your business, and you will be as rich as I am.' (Timperley, 716)

However, to assess Osborne's character properly is difficult. His undoubted success as a bookseller provoked an adverse reaction from other members of the trade who were eager to see his power and influence diminished. Most of the negative comments that have survived can be traced to Pope and Johnson. To be singled out by Pope is no distinction as the list of his satiric victims is extensive, while Johnson, whose lack of social skills is well documented, is a strange source for Osborne's failures in this regard although Boswell, Hawkins, Nichols, Piozzi, and other early biographers, William Cooke and William Shaw, all took their information from him. But Osborne was the bookseller for the Revd A. M. Toplady, who described him as a respectable man; Dibdin calls him 'the most celebrated bookseller of his day', and Timperley 'a bookseller of great eminence' (Dibdin, 334; Timperley, 716).

Osborne died on 21 August 1767, and was buried at St Mary's, Islington. His will was made on 8 July and proved on 26 August 1767. His estate was divided among his widow, Mary, his brother-in-law William Smith, and his nephew, William Toll. His stock was sold in 1768–9. The London booksellers John Osborne (*c.*1688–1734) of Lombard Street and then of The Ship, Paternoster Row, in partnership with Thomas Longman were apparently not related to the Thomas Osbornes; nor, apparently, were John Osborn (*d.* 1745) and his son John Osborn (*c.*1714–1775) of St Saviour's Dock and then (from 1733) of the Golden Ball, Paternoster Row. O. M. BRACK

Sources 'Memoir of William Oldys esq.', *N&Q*, 3rd ser., 1 (1862), 41–4 • W. C. B., 'Thomas Osborne, bookseller', *N&Q*, 7th ser., 12 (1891), 205 • Boswell, *Life*, 1.154, 158, 534; 3.158 • W. Cooke, 'The life of Samuel Johnson, LL.D.', *The early biographies of Samuel Johnson*, ed. O. M. Brack and R. E. Kelley (1974), 97–8 • T. F. Dibdin, *Bibliomania* (1809), new edn (1842), 348–9, 354–5 • *ESTC* • J. D. Fleeman, *A bibliography of the works of Samuel Johnson*, 2 vols. (2000) • J. Hawkins, *The life of Samuel Johnson, LL.D.*, 2nd edn (1787), 132–51 • S. Lewis, *History and typography of Islington* (1843), 250 • S. Johnson, 'Shenstone', *Lives of the English poets*, ed. G. B. Hill, [new edn], 3 (1905), 348–60 • D. F. McKenzie, ed., *Stationers' Company apprentices*, [3]: 1701–1800 (1978), 255 • Nichols, *Lit. anecdotes*, 1.151, 585; 2.282; 3.401–4, 601, 649–50, 654; 4.665; 5.352, 462, 471; 6.130; 8.286, 446, 463–4, 496, 699; 9.419 • Nichols, *Illustrations*, 2.109, 130; 4.143, 354 • 'Osborne's catalogues of books', *N&Q*, 3rd ser., 7 (1865), 324 • H. L. Piozzi, *Anecdotes of the late Samuel Johnson*, ed. A. Sherbo (1974), 137 • H. R. Plomer and others, *A dictionary of the printers and booksellers who were at work in England, Scotland, and Ireland from 1726 to 1775* (1932) • A. Pope, *The Dunciad*, ed. J. Sutherland (1943), vol. 5 of *The Twickenham edition of the poems of Alexander Pope*, ed. J. Butt (1939–69); 3rd edn [in 1 vol.] (1963); repr. (1965), 303–4 • W. Shaw, 'Memoirs of the life and writings of Samuel Johnson', *The early biographies of Samuel Johnson*, ed. O. M. Brack and R. E. Kelley (1974), 156 • C. H. Timperley, *Encyclopaedia of literary and typographical anecdote*, 2nd edn (1842), 716–17 • W. Winters, *Memoirs of the life and writings of the Rev. A. M. Toplady* (1872), 23, 45 • *IGI* • will, PRO, PROB 11/732, sig. 76 [will of T. Osborne the elder, father] • will, PRO, PROB 11/931, sig. 315

Osborne, Walter Frederick (1859–1903), painter, was born on 17 June 1859 at 6 Cornish Terrace, Rathmines, Dublin, the second of the three children of William Osborne RHA (1823–1901), an animal painter, and his wife, Anne Jane Woods, of O'Brien's Bridge, co. Clare. He was educated at Rathmines (Benson's) School (1870–75), in the schools of the Royal Hibernian Academy, Dublin (1876–81), and at the Koninklijke Academie voor Schone Kunsten, Antwerp (1881–3). In Antwerp he encountered the realist painting of French and Netherlandish artists, and the teaching of Charles Verlat at the academy introduced him to vigorous brushwork and bold colour. His small sketch *Moderke verhoft* (*c.*1882, National Gallery of Ireland, Dublin) is a good example of his developing style—a peasant-genre subject painted from life, boldly executed, and with accents of vivid colour. Among his classmates were a number of English students who were to become part of the British naturalist school to which the first half of his career belongs, and he met others in Brittany in 1883. Like them, he came under the influence of the French naturalist painter Jules Bastien-Lepage and for a time adopted his painting technique and grey-green palette.

After Brittany Osborne's life followed a pattern of winters spent in Dublin at his parents' house, 5 Castlewood Avenue, Rathmines, and the rest of the year in small villages in England with a few like-minded artists, painting landscape and rural genre scenes. His most characteristic pieces include children and animals and combine careful underlying drawing with painterly surfaces and sensitive colour. *An October Morning* (1885, corporation of London, Barbican) shows the beach and pier at Walberswick, Suffolk, and *Cherry Ripe* (exh. Institute of Painters in Oil Colours, London, 1889–90; Ulster Museum, Belfast), carefully put together from preparatory sketches and even a photograph, is set in the High Street at Rye, Sussex. Although he worked in remote rural areas, Osborne did not isolate himself. He made regular visits to the London galleries and sent work to exhibitions in London, Liverpool, and Birmingham. Throughout this time he was also actively involved in Dublin life. From 1877 he exhibited annually with the Royal Hibernian Academy and became an academician in 1886.

In the early 1890s family circumstances obliged Osborne to spend more time in Ireland. He lived at 5 Castlewood Avenue and, from 1895, had a large studio at 7 St Stephen's Green. He began to paint Dublin street life, especially the area of old Dublin around St Patrick's Cathedral, as in *Life in the Streets: Musicians* (1893, Hugh Lane Municipal Gallery of Modern Art, Dublin). *In a Dublin Park: Light and Shade* (exh. RA, 1895; National Gallery of Ireland, Dublin) is confident, broadly painted, and shows a preoccupation with rendering the effects of light which owes something to French impressionism. *The Lustre Jug* (exh. New English Art Club, 1901; National Gallery of Ireland, Dublin) is even more adventurous, the light from the small window being expressed in vivid touches of iridescent colour.

During the last ten years of his life Osborne turned increasingly to portrait painting—responsibility for the support of his parents and niece fell heavily on him, and portraits sold better than genre or landscape. One of his most successful was *Mrs Noel Guinness and her Daughter Margaret* (1898, priv. coll., Dublin), which won him a bronze medal at the Paris Universal Exhibition in 1900. While he kept up his connections outside Ireland, he was an active member of the lively Dublin cultural life of the period. Most of his friends were artists and writers, but he had a much wider acquaintance, and was a welcome visitor in many houses. Tall and athletic-looking, he bicycled round Dublin and was a keen cricketer. In town he dressed like a lawyer or a doctor, though he allowed himself to look more like an artist in the country. He never married, prevented, apparently, by his family responsibilities and lack of money. Held in great affection by a wide circle of friends and venerated by his students, he was considered to be Ireland's most distinguished artist, with a growing reputation abroad, when he died of pneumonia on 24 April 1903 at 5 Castlewood Avenue. He was buried in Mount Jerome cemetery, Harold's Cross, Dublin. The National Gallery of Ireland and the Hugh Lane Municipal Gallery of Modern Art, both in Dublin, have his paintings and drawings in their collections; the National Gallery of Ireland also holds his annotated sketchbooks.

JEANNE SHEEHY

Sources J. Sheehy, *Walter Osborne* (1974) · J. Sheehy, *Walter Osborne* (1983) [exhibition catalogue, NG Ire. and Ulster Museum, Belfast, 16 Nov 1983 – 29 Feb 1984] · J. Campbell, *The Irish impressionists* (1984) [exhibition catalogue, NG Ire.] · *DNB* · T. Bodkin, *Four Irish landscape painters* (1920) · S. Gwynn, 'An artist and his work', *Garden wisdom* (1921), 20–46 · parish records, St Peter's, Rathmines, Dublin, 11/9/1859 [baptism] · J. C. Benson, *Rathmines School roll, 1858–99* (1932)

Likenesses N. Hill, pencil drawing, *c.*1885, NG Ire. · B. Fletcher, drawing, 1888 · W. Osborne, self-portrait, oils, 1894, NG Ire. · photograph, NG Ire.

Wealth at death £3815 6*s.* 9*d.*: resworn administration, 6 June 1903, *CGPLA Ire.* · £134 5*s.* 0*d.*: Irish administration sealed in England, 27 June 1903, *CGPLA Eng. & Wales*

Osborne, Walter Victor (1870–1950), trade unionist, was born at Wilby, Norfolk, on 1 September 1870, the son of James Osborne (or Osborn), a shepherd, and his wife, Emily, *née* Frost. From about 1890 he worked for the Great Eastern railway, his employers for twenty-two years. On 15 October 1896, at the Wesleyan Methodist centenary chapel, York, he married Naomi Wright, a native of Norfolk who was working as a domestic servant in York; she was the daughter of John Wright, a farm labourer. At the time of his marriage Osborne was a foreman railway porter living in Stoke Newington, London; by 1901 the couple had settled with a two-year-old daughter in Walthamstow, their long-term residence.

As a young man Osborne had been a member of the extreme Social Democratic Federation at some time in the late 1880s or early 1890s, but had soon left and become a consistent anti-socialist. Among those who knew him personally he had a reputation for being honest and humorous, though somewhat lethargic and excessively devoted to his personal freedom, refusing, for example, to work overtime for the Great Eastern railway. However, he rose to the position of head porter at Clapton station in north London while remaining a member of the Amalgamated Society of Railway Servants, which he had joined in 1892. Indeed, in 1897 he organized a local branch of the union in Walthamstow and served as branch secretary. Along with many of his contemporaries in the trade union movement of the 1900s he combined approval for the labour representation committee (LRC) with a continued commitment to Liberalism, and was consequently a warm supporter of the railway servants' general secretary, Richard Bell, one of the first LRC candidates to be elected to parliament, where he worked closely with the Liberal Party.

Osborne, however, began to feel unhappy about developments in labour politics in 1903. In the first place the LRC decided to impose a pledge on its candidates to form a distinct group in parliament separate from other parties, a pledge which Bell refused to accept and in which he was supported by a majority at the railway servants' conference in 1904. In the second place the general meeting of the railway servants decided to make the political levy compulsory for all members, and the socialist dominated executive committee chose three socialists as the union's next candidates for parliament. Osborne carried a motion at the Walthamstow branch to discontinue paying the political levy and fifty-three other branches of the union called for a ballot on the question of affiliation to the LRC. However, when such a ballot was held in 1905, 81 per cent of those voting were in favour of maintaining the existing levy arrangements. Osborne seems to have had an exaggerated idea of the extent to which the emerging Labour Party was dominated by socialists, perhaps because of his experience of the executive of his own union, and although his views were not unique they were clearly shared by only a minority.

Osborne pressed stubbornly ahead with legal action against the railway servants' political levy in 1907, supported by money raised by readers of the tory newspaper, the *Daily Express*. His case was defeated in the High Court but was successful in the Court of Appeal in 1908 on the grounds that the definition of a trade union in the 1876 act did not include the support of a political party. This time Osborne was supported by money raised not only through the national press, but apparently also through small subscriptions from sympathetic union branches. The railway servants backed by the Trades Union Congress and the Labour Party, which stood to lose the bulk of its financial base if denied trade union support, then took the case to the House of Lords where the Osborne judgment was upheld in November 1909. Not satisfied with this Osborne instructed his solicitor to take legal action over the use of the railwaymen's already accumulated political fund; the union's executive retaliated by expelling him, but this only led Osborne to start another legal action for his reinstatement, which was dismissed in the High Court but upheld in the Court of Appeal. Once again the railwaymen prepared to take the case as far as the House of Lords, but reached a settlement with Osborne's solicitor before the hearing. Osborne was by then such a well-known figure that he was able to launch a brief career as a writer on trade union issues, publishing two books defending his activities, *My Case* (1910) and *Sane Trade Unionism* (1913), and also to secure appointment as the chief clerk of the anti-socialist British Constitution Association.

The success of Osborne's campaign was short-lived, however, for, while the Liberal government could hardly denounce one of its own supporters who had pursued his right to freedom of conscience, it was increasingly dependent on the Labour Party for its small majority in the House of Commons after the 1910 general election. As a result the Liberals softened the impact of the Osborne judgment by introducing the payment of MPs in the budget of 1911; and then reversed it in the Trade Union Act of 1913, by legalizing the financing of political action provided that the payments came from a special political fund from which individual members should have the right to contract out. The Labour Party meanwhile became the undisputed focus for trade union political representation as a result of its leading role in securing the legislation to remedy the Osborne judgment. In this way Osborne's activities may have strengthened the Labour Party and certainly initiated an important party division over British trade union law. In 1927 the Conservatives put the burden on those who wished to contract in to political levies. Labour repealed this legislation in 1946, thus restoring the 1913 position. The Conservatives imposed regular ballots on the continuation of union political funds in 1984.

During the 1920s Osborne continued to campaign against what he described, at a meeting of the National League of Liberal Trade Unionists and Cooperatives, as 'socialist tyranny'. By fighting Liberals, he complained, the Labour Party had divided the progressive vote (*Walthamstow Guardian*, 20 April 1928). By then, however, he had disappeared from national view. No obituary has been traced following his death, at the City General Hospital, York, on 15 June 1950. ALASTAIR J. REID

Sources G. W. Alcock, *Fifty years of railway trade unionism* (1922) • P. S. Bagwell, *The railwaymen: the history of the National Union of Railwaymen*, [1] (1963) • H. Pelling, 'The politics of the Osborne judgment', *HJ*, 25 (1982), 889–909 • b. cert. • m. cert. • d. cert. • census returns, 1901 • press cuttings book on the Osborne judgment, City of York Public Library • press cuttings, Walthamstow Local History Library • *CGPLA Eng. & Wales* (1950)

Wealth at death £593 6s. 9d.: probate, 1950, *CGPLA Eng. & Wal.*

Osborne, William. *See* Osborn, William (1736–1808).

Osburh [Osburga] (*fl.* **839**), consort of Æthelwulf, king of the West Saxons, married *Æthelwulf (*d.* 858), who was son of *Ecgberht, king of Wessex (*r.* 802–39), while he was sub-king of Kent (825–39). The marriage probably occurred well before 839, for, on Æthelwulf's succession to Wessex, their eldest son became sub-king of Kent, while their second son was attesting charters from *c.*840. Osburh's father, Oslac, according to Asser, the late ninth-century biographer of her youngest son, *Alfred (*d.* 899), was:

> King Æthelwulf's famous butler, … a Goth by nation, for he was sprung from Goths and Jutes, namely from the seed of Stuf and Wihtgar, two brothers who received control over the Isle of Wight from their uncle King Cerdic and Cynric his son. (*Life of Alfred*, chap. 2)

This story identified the roots of Osburh's family, her Scandinavian ancestors, and also their relationship to the Cerdicings. Osburh, as far as is known, was the mother of all Æthelwulf's offspring: a daughter, Æthelswith, and five sons: Æthelstan, who seems to have died *c.*851, and *Æthelbald (*d.* 860), *Æthelberht (*d.* 865), *Æthelred (*d.* 871), and Alfred, all four of whom were successively kings of Wessex. That Alfred bequeathed two of his three daughters (perhaps only a life-interest in) estates in the Isle of Wight may lend some colour to the story of Osburh's ancestral Wight-ish connections.

Osburh is not mentioned in the Anglo-Saxon Chronicle. No charter attestations of hers are known, though an 'Osric *princeps*', perhaps her brother, attested from the 840s to 860. According to the contemporary Frankish annals of St Bertin, s.a. 856, it was 'not customary for the West Saxon king or his people to confer [on the king's wife] the title of queen'. In 856, when Æthelwulf married the Carolingian princess Judith, and broke with custom by naming her queen, Osburh may already have been dead, or else she was repudiated.

Asser, apparently relying on Alfred's reminiscences, says '[Osburh was] an extremely pious woman, noble in character and by birth'. She is best known through Asser's story about the book of 'Saxon songs' (*carmina Saxonica*) which 'she showed to Alfred and his brothers, saying: "I shall give this book to whichever one of you can learn [that is, memorize] it the fastest"'; and when Alfred:

> attracted by the beauty of the book's initial letter, … asked, 'Will you really give this book to the one of us who can understand it the soonest and recite it to you?', she smiled with pleasure and, reassuring him, said, 'Yes, I will'. (*Life of Alfred*, chap. 23)

Asser's point was to highlight the special qualities of Osburh's youngest son, Alfred, who learned and recited the book first and presumably won the prize, and whose enthusiasm for 'Saxon songs', and for translations into the vernacular, was later to characterize his reign. The story finds a wider context in ninth-century manuscript evidence for the interest of high-status women in books, and for their role in educating their children.

JANET L. NELSON

Sources *Alfred the Great: Asser's Life of King Alfred and other contemporary sources*, ed. and trans. S. Keynes and M. Lapidge (1983) • P. A. Stafford, 'The king's wife in Wessex, 800–1066', *Past and Present*, 91 (1981), 3–27 • P. Stafford, *Queens, concubines and dowagers: the king's wife in the early middle ages* (1983) • J. L. Nelson, 'Reconstructing a royal family: reflections on Alfred, from Asser', *People and places in northern Europe, 500–1600: essays in honour of Peter Hayes Sawyer*, ed. I. Wood and N. Lund, [another edn] (1991), 47–66 • A. P. Smyth, *King Alfred the Great* (1995) • M. Brown, 'Female book-ownership in England during the ninth century: the evidence of the prayerbooks', *Reformed English women*, ed. D. Dumville and L. Abrams [forthcoming]

Osbwrn Wyddel [Osborn the Irishman] (*fl.* **1292–1293**), dynastic founder, is said to have come from Ireland to settle in the commote of Ardudwy in north-west Merioneth. According to tradition he was a member of the Geraldine (Fitzgerald) lineage and therefore a descendant of Gerald of Windsor and his wife, Nest, the daughter of the Welsh king Rhys ap Tewdwr (*d.* 1093). There is no firm evidence to confirm this but his name may suggest Norman antecedents. The only definite reference to him is in the 1292/3 Merioneth lay subsidy roll, in which he is listed as a substantial taxpayer in the township of Llanaber. His descendants included several prominent local families, including those of Corsygedol, Maes-y-neuadd, and Ynysmaengwyn. The Corsygedol family, descended from his son Cynwrig, played an active part in the affairs of the county in the later middle ages. Osbwrn's great-grandson Gruffudd ap Llywelyn ap Cynwrig and his great-great-grandson Einion ap Gruffudd held the office of sheriff in the late fourteenth century; Gruffudd also founded a hospice for travellers at Egryn in Llanaber and in 1391 was granted a papal licence to have masses celebrated in the oratory there. Another descendant was Dafydd ab Ieuan ab Einion, who conducted the epic Lancastrian defence of Harlech Castle during the Wars of the Roses. Osbwrn's significance is genealogical rather than historical and his own ancestry and the circumstances of his arrival in Merioneth must remain a mystery. A. D. CARR

Sources K. Williams-Jones, ed., *The Merioneth lay subsidy roll, 1292–3* (1976) • *DWB* • *An inventory*, 6: *Merionethshire*, Royal Commission on Ancient and Historical Monuments in Wales and Monmouthshire (1921) • J. E. Griffith, *Pedigrees of Anglesey and Carnarvonshire families* (privately printed, Horncastle, 1914); facs. edn (1985) • *DNB* • [W. W. E. Wynne ?], 'Pedigree of Osborn Wyddel etc.', *Archaeologia Cambrensis*, 3rd ser., 9 (1863), 56–9

Oscytel [Oskytel] (*d.* **971**), archbishop of York, was at least partly Danish by origin, and belonged to a powerful Anglo-Danish landowning family in the east midlands. His name is Anglo-Scandinavian; one of his two identifiable kinsmen, Abbot Thurcytel of Bedford, had a Danish name, while the other, Oswald, bishop of Worcester (961–92) and archbishop of York (971–92), was a nephew of Archbishop Oda of Canterbury (942–58), whose father, a Dane, had come to England in the *micel here* (great army) of 865. Oscytel, Thurcytel, and Oswald all owned land in the east midlands and the fens, and Oda was also influential there. Oscytel owned land at Beeby, Leicestershire, which he granted on his deathbed to Æthelwold, bishop of Winchester, probably to endow Ely; Æthelwold later gave it to Oscytel's kinsman Thurcytel in exchange for land at Doddington and 'Waeremere'. It can be presumed that Oscytel, as has been argued in the case of his kinsman Oswald, owed his promotion to the episcopate to the backing of his powerful family network and not to the patronage of courtiers. In the middle of the tenth century the Wessex dynasty, still uninfluential in the east midlands, would have found it advantageous to establish good relations with a powerful local family of partly Danish origin.

Oscytel's date of birth is not known, though it is unlikely to have been later than *c.*920; likewise nothing is known of his education or his early career in the church, though an 'Oscetel circweard' (sacrist or treasurer), who may perhaps be identifiable with him, occurs in a witness list of 949; the church where he was a dignitary is not stated. By 951 Oscytel was bishop of Dorchester, a diocese corresponding to the early Anglo-Saxon see of Leicester, and probably, in Oscytel's day, extending over the newly formed shires of Oxfordshire, Buckinghamshire, Hertfordshire, Bedfordshire, Cambridgeshire, Huntingdonshire, Northamptonshire, Leicestershire, and, almost certainly (though this has never before been acknowledged), Nottinghamshire; the see of Lindsey, later to be added to Dorchester, was a separate entity in Oscytel's lifetime. His predecessor, Æthelwald, occurs for the last time in 949, and the Anglo-Saxon Chronicle (texts B, C, s. a. 971) says that Oscytel had been bishop for twenty-two years by the time of his death in 971. This entry also states that he was made archbishop of York in the time of Eadred (*d.* 955), which would be chronologically impossible as Archbishop Wulfstan of York did not die until 26 December 956, but which might be a garbled reference to his original consecration as bishop of Dorchester, which is mentioned immediately beforehand.

Oscytel first occurs as bishop subscribing charters in 951, though he only did so frequently from 955. King Eadred, who died at the end of that year, bequeathed £400 to him and gave him a third share of 2000 gold mancuses to distribute within his diocese. During 956 and 957 Oscytel's name can be found in the subscription lists to the overwhelming majority of King Eadwig's charters, but from 958 he is to be found subscribing Edgar's. This change in allegiance followed Edgar's assumption of kingship in Mercia and Northumbria in 957, though probably not immediately. Both Eadwig and Edgar gave Oscytel estates in Nottinghamshire, Eadwig granting him Southwell in 956 and Edgar granting him Sutton in 958. Eadwig's charter, though dated 958, has the correct indiction for 956 and is subscribed by Edgar as Eadwig's brother, not as king. The text of the charter describes Oscytel as bishop, but he appears in the subscription list as archbishop: perhaps the date and the subscription list were altered at York subsequently. Edgar's charter is dated 958 and describes Oscytel as bishop. It is likely that both grants were made to Oscytel as bishop of Dorchester to strengthen his position in the extreme north of his diocese, and that it was only subsequently that Oscytel transferred them to the estates of the archbishopric of York—a move which evidently led to Nottinghamshire becoming part of the archdiocese of York, a change in diocesan boundaries which is described nowhere in contemporary sources but which can easily be assumed to have happened as a result of Oscytel's pluralism. He may well have been responsible for establishing (or refounding on a larger scale) the church of Southwell as a powerful minster community, to provide him with a point from which he and later archbishops of York could spread their influence in Nottinghamshire.

Oscytel became archbishop of York perhaps as late as the end of 958 or in 959, since he witnessed no genuine charters as archbishop earlier than 959. It has usually hitherto been assumed that he succeeded his predecessor Wulfstan immediately after the latter's death, but there may well have been a vacancy while Edgar tried to secure his political authority in the north. The Ramsey chronicle states that Oscytel went to Rome to collect his pallium, but no other source records this and the Ramsey chronicler may have assumed that he did so because his younger kinsman and eventual successor at York, Oswald, subsequently did. Oscytel probably retained control of the see of Dorchester even after his promotion to York, for the *Liber Eliensis* refers to him simply as bishop when describing him bequeathing his land at Beeby to Bishop Æthelwold of Winchester. It also shows him acting as bishop of Dorchester in a dispute concerning stolen charters for Horningsea in Cambridgeshire which erupted in Edgar's reign, possibly after 959. Oscytel's pluralism was uncanonical, but politically expedient both for himself, since he must have wanted to maintain his ties with the area where his family was powerful, and for Edgar, who wanted to ensure that no archbishop of York would be tempted to follow Wulfstan's example in defying West Saxon claims to hegemony in the north. Oscytel was certainly loyal to Edgar and witnessed many of his charters. He was also loyal to his own family. In 958 when Oswald returned to England to join Oda's household, only to learn of the latter's death, Oscytel welcomed him and recommended him to his friends, especially Dunstan. Moreover, it is likely that he gave at least moral support to Oswald in his foundation of Ramsey Abbey, and just possibly to Thurcytel in his refoundation of Crowland. His bequest to Æthelwold, which was doubtless intended for the latter's abbey at Ely, suggests that irrespective of family considerations he was generally in favour of the new monastic establishments in the fens, all lying in his diocese of Dorchester. Oscytel died on 31 October 971 at Thame, a manor of the bishops of Dorchester, and his body was taken to Bedford for burial by his kinsman Thurcytel, who was abbot there. He was succeeded at York by Edwald, who, however, resigned shortly afterwards, leaving the coast clear for Oswald, while Leofwine, bishop of Lindsey, took over the diocese of Dorchester. JULIA BARROW

Sources M. A. O'Donovan, 'An interim revision of episcopal dates for the province of Canterbury, 850–950 [pt 1]', *Anglo-Saxon England*, 1 (1972), 23–44, esp. 38–9 • *AS chart.*, S 550, 554, 557, 569, 574, 581–3, 587–8, 590–4, 596–8, 600–01, 603–4, 606–13, 615–16, 619–22, 624, 628, 630, 633–5, 637–8, 641, 643, 646, 649, 659, 661, 663, 669, 673–5, 677, 679–85, 687–90, 695–6, 698–703, 705–12, 714, 716–20, 722–4, 726, 731, 733–5, 737–9, 741, 744–5, 748, 750, 752, 754, 757–9, 762–3, 767–9, 771–3, 776, 778–9, 806, 808–9, 833, 1214, 1291, 1294, 1515, 1574, 1662 • D. Whitelock, 'The dealings of the kings of England with Northumbria in the 10th and 11th centuries', *The Anglo-Saxons: studies in some aspects of their history and culture presented to Bruce Dickins*, ed. P. Clemoes (1959), 70–88 • J. Raine, ed., *The historians of the church of York and its archbishops*, 3 vols., Rolls Series, 71 (1879–94), vol. 1, pp. 404, 420; vol. 2, p. 340 • D. Whitelock, 'The conversion of the eastern Danelaw', *Saga book of the Viking Society for Northern Research*, 12 (privately printed, London, 1937–45), 159–76, esp. 170, 173–5 • A. Wareham, 'St Oswald's family and kin', *St Oswald of Worcester: life and influence*, ed. N. Brooks and C. Cubitt (1996), 46–63 • W. Farrer and others, eds., *Early Yorkshire charters*, 12 vols. (1914–65), vol. 1, nos. 2–3 • E. O. Blake, ed., *Liber Eliensis*, CS, 3rd ser., 92 (1962), 96, 105–7 • *ASC*, s.a. 971 (texts B, C) • F. M. Stenton, 'The founding of Southwell Minster', *Preparatory to 'Anglo-Saxon England': being the collected papers of Frank Merry Stenton*, ed. D. M. Stenton (1970), 364–70 • John of Worcester, *Chron.*, 422, s.a. 972 • *Willelmi Malmesbiriensis monachi de gestis pontificum Anglorum libri quinque*, ed. N. E. S. A. Hamilton, Rolls Series, 52 (1870), 247–8 • Symeon of Durham, *Opera*, 2.127 • W. D. Macray, ed., *Chronicon abbatiae Rameseiensis a saec. x usque ad an. circiter 1200*, Rolls Series, 83 (1886), 24–5, 43 • Ordericus Vitalis, *Eccl. hist.*, 2.340–42

Osgar [Oscarus] (*d.* **984**), abbot of Abingdon, was one of the clerks who left Dunstan's community at Glastonbury to go with Æthelwold when he was appointed abbot of Abingdon, *c.*954. He was sent by Æthelwold to Fleury on the Loire to learn the Benedictine rule, and returned with a written account of it. When Æthelwold became bishop of Winchester in 963, he appointed Osgar his successor in the abbacy of Abingdon. Osgar was present at the expulsion of secular canons from Winchester, and made a speech on that occasion recorded by Wulfstan in his life of St Æthelwold. In a letter from Fleury, written partly in cipher, an abbot is blamed for not returning a copy of Florus's commentary on St Paul's epistles; the name 'Oscarus' fits the cipher, and the borrower is no doubt identical with the abbot of Abingdon. Osgar purchased and obtained large tracts of land for his monastery and his name is appended to a number of genuine charters of the years 967–74. He died at Abingdon in 984, having finished the buildings begun there by his mentor Æthelwold.

MARY BATESON, *rev.* MARIOS COSTAMBEYS

Sources J. Stevenson, ed., *Chronicon monasterii de Abingdon*, 2 vols., Rolls Series, 2 (1858) • Wulfstan, 'Vita S. Ethelwoldi', *Patrologia Latina*, 137 (1853), 79 • *Willelmi Malmesbiriensis monachi de gestis pontificum Anglorum libri quinque*, ed. N. E. S. A. Hamilton, Rolls Series, 52 (1870), 5, 725, 729, 731, 834, 835 • W. Stubbs, ed., *Memorials of St Dunstan, archbishop of Canterbury*, Rolls Series, 63 (1874)

Osgod Clapa (*d.* **1054**), landowner and exile, whose byname means 'a coarse, rough person', is usually assumed to be a Dane who followed King Cnut to England. He may, however, have been a descendant of Osgod, Eadulf's son, kinsman of Theodred, bishop of London (*d.* 951), for he had an estate at Pakenham, Suffolk, where Osgod, Eadulf's son, also held land. He attests charters of Cnut and Harthacnut from 1026 to 1042, often in association with *Tovi the Proud, and in the early 1040s he witnessed the will of Thurstan, Lustwine's son, as a member of the shire-court of Norfolk. The Anglo-Saxon Chronicle describes him as a staller (*ASC*, s.a. 1046, text D) and Hermann of Bury calls him *maior domus*, which suggests that he held some official position in the king's household. His office may have been connected with London, the home base of the royal fleet. He had an estate at Lambeth and in the 1030s attested a writ of Cnut (of dubious authenticity) in favour of St Paul's, signing at the head of the lay witnesses below the rank of earl (*AS chart.*, S 992). He is also addressed in a writ of Edward for Westminster Abbey, which (if genuine) must be dated 1044–6 (*AS chart.*, S 1121), after the bishop of London but before the sheriff of Middlesex.

In 1042 Osgod's daughter Gytha married Tovi the Proud, at Lambeth, which may have been her marriage portion, for Tovi gave land there to his church at Waltham, Essex. Osgod attests charters of Edward the Confessor between 1042 and 1046, but in 1046 he was exiled, for unspecified reasons. He fled to Flanders, where by 1049 he had gathered a fleet of ships at Wulpe, near Sluys. King Edward took this act seriously enough to dispatch a fleet against him, but Osgod, leaving his wife in safety at Bruges, ravaged around the Naze in Essex. Returning with their plunder, all but two (or four) of the ships were destroyed in a storm. John of Worcester claims that Osgod sought refuge in Denmark, but the Anglo-Saxon Chronicle merely records that he died 'suddenly, as he was lying in bed' in 1054 (*ASC*, s.a. 1054, text C); whether this implies that he had returned to England is a matter of opinion. No children other than Gytha are recorded. Osgod's lands were confiscated by the king on his exile, Pakenham being given by Edward to Bury St Edmunds (*AS chart.*, S 1074). He is commemorated in the *Liber vitae* of Thorney Abbey, and he may be the Osgod entered, with his wife, Æthelswyth, in the *Liber vitae* of the New Minster at Winchester. At Bury St Edmunds he was remembered in the first instance as a despoiler, though he had a change of heart; Hermann of Bury has a vivid (though perhaps imaginary) description of him, wearing his golden arm-rings and carrying a gilded axe slung from his shoulder. ANN WILLIAMS

Sources *ASC*, s.a. 1046, 1049, 1054 [texts C, D] • Hermann the Archdeacon, 'De miraculis Sancti Eadmundi', *Memorials of St Edmund's Abbey*, ed. T. Arnold, 1, Rolls Series, 96 (1890), 26–92 • F. E. Harmer, ed., *Anglo-Saxon writs* (1952) • John of Worcester, *Chron.* • S. Keynes, *An atlas of attestations in Anglo-Saxon charters, c.670–1066* (privately printed, Cambridge, 1993) • *AS chart.*, S 962–4, 967–70, 972, 975–6, 979, 982, 992–4, 999, 1001–8, 1010–13, 1044, 1074, 1121, 1531 • D. Whitelock, 'Scandinavian personal names in the *Liber vitae* of Thorney Abbey', *Saga-book of the Viking Society*, 12 (2) (1937–8), 127–53, repr. in *History, law and literature in tenth- and eleventh-century England* (1981) • S. Keynes, ed., *The Liber vitae of the New Minster and Hyde Abbey, Winchester* (Copenhagen, 1996) • P. Nightingale, 'The origin of the court of husting and Danish influence on London's development into a capital city', *EngHR*, 102 (1987), 559–78, esp. 565–6 • A. Williams, 'The king's nephew: the family, career, and connections of Ralph, earl of Hereford', *Studies in medieval history presented to R. Allen Brown*, ed. C. Harper-Bill, C. J. Holdsworth, and J. L. Nelson (1989), 327–43 • C. R. Hart, *The early charters of eastern England* (1966) • K. Mack, 'The stallers: administrative innovation in the reign of Edward the Confessor', *Journal of Medieval History*, 12 (1986), 123–34

Osgodby, Adam (*d.* 1316), administrator, came from Osgodby, near Selby in Yorkshire. Although his early career remains obscure, he is known to have acted as attorney for Stephen Mauley in 1286 and 1291, and for William Acon and Walter Percehaye during that period. From 1295 to 1316 he was keeper of the rolls of chancery, and probably owed his place in government to Edward I's long-serving clerk and sometime chancellor, William Hamilton (*d.* 1307). He was also closely associated with Robert Bardelby and the Airmyn brothers, especially William (*d.* 1336). From 1307 Osgodby was keeper of the Domus Conversorum, a house for converted Jews situated in Chancery Lane, which was customarily used to deposit chancery records and became a natural residence for chancery clerks visiting London. From 1310, while Walter Reynolds (*d.* 1327) was chancellor, Osgodby kept the household of the chancery, normally the chancellor's duty and right, and consequently received the usual yearly fee of £500. He was always the first named of those clerks temporarily having custody of the great seal, a task with which he was charged in 1302 (from 23 to 30 September and from 30 October), 1310 (from May to July), and 1311 (from 27 August to 28 September). In the five or so years before his death he was sometimes in charge of the seal for more lengthy periods, from December 1311 to before 5 October 1312; from 17 to 22 April and from 13 June to 16 July 1313; from 31 March until 26 September 1314; and on two occasions in 1315 (2 June and from 14 to 25 November).

Osgodby probably also owed his early ecclesiastical advancement to Hamilton. He was a canon of York from 1289, and in 1293 he was installed as parson of Gargrave. In December 1300 he was granted free warren in all the demesne lands of his prebend of Ulfshelf in Yorkshire and in March 1303 he had wardship of the manor of Drax in the same county by demise of the executors of Edmund, earl of Cornwall (*d.* 1300). He continued to hold Drax for at least another seven years, since the heir of Philip Paynell was still a minor. In May 1306 he was appointed with Robert Bardelby, a fellow canon and chancery employee, as a proctor for the archbishop of York to attend the king's council. In September 1310 he voted at the election of the new dean of York, Master William Pickering. In 1311 Osgodby was inducted to the church of Bubwith, Yorkshire, on the presentation of Lady Isabella de Vescy, although there was some dispute about her right in this. He also held the prebend of Burford in Shropshire.

Osgodby was no stranger to litigation. An inquest held on 23 August 1304 found that he and his servants were hindered by Hugh Skilhare and others in the field of Winterburn, north of Gargrave, from taking tithes of a yearly value of 100*s.*, which they later recovered in court Christian. In June 1308, as a mark of the special affection for his clerk and for good service to his father, Edward II issued letters to the pope and cardinals 'in as good and gracious a form as possible' in order to benefit Osgodby's business in the papal court. Three years later, following a judgment pronounced against them in the court of York, the abbot and convent of Selby appealed to the court of Rome concerning their case against Adam Osgodby. Although the abbot secured a mandate preventing the sheriff from exercising Osgodby's writ of *capias* pending the business of the appeal, the latter was able to have the appeal declared null. In March 1314, at Osgodby's instance, the abbot and convent of Sawley (within whose patronage the living of Gargrave lay) received absolution from an eight-year sentence of excommunication, no doubt benefiting from the former's influence at court. Osgodby himself served in a judicial capacity, holding assizes in York in 1314. He received a further assize commission in September 1315.

Osgodby died in August 1316. His brother, Walter, succeeded to his estate, and Henry Cliffe (*d.* 1334), another chancery clerk, was executor of his will.

A. J. MUSSON

Sources *Chancery records* • Tout, *Admin. hist.*, vols. 2–3, 6 • *The register of John le Romeyn … 1286–1296*, ed. W. Brown, 1, SurtS, 123 (1913) • *The register of William Greenfield, lord archbishop of York, 1306–1315*, ed. W. Brown and A. H. Thompson, 1–3, SurtS, 145, 149, 151 (1931–6) • J. R. Walbran, ed., *Memorials of the abbey of St Mary of Fountains*, 1, SurtS, 42 (1863) • Eyre rolls, assize rolls etc, PRO, JUST 1/1113 • *CIPM*, 1, no. 279

Wealth at death 68 acres of land, a house, a windmill, and rents valued at 6 marks and 10*s.*: *CIPM*, 1, no. 279

Osgood, James Ripley (1836–1892), publisher, was born on 22 April 1836 in Fryeburg, Oxford, Maine, USA, the son of Colonel Edward Lewis Osgood and his wife, Abigail Ripley Dana, the daughter of a distinguished Boston family. He was the brother of Kate Putnam Osgood (*b.* 1841), who later became a poet and wrote the famous civil war poem 'Driving home the cows'. He was educated at Bowdoin College, Brunswick, Maine, from 1850 to 1854, and in August 1855 became a clerk in the publishing firm of Ticknor & Fields. He was made a junior partner in 1864, and it was in this capacity that he travelled to London in 1867. He was commissioned with the task of soliciting contributions from Charles Dickens for the company's periodicals, but a more significant outcome was reported in the *American Literary Gazette* on 1 June 1867: 'One of the results of his successful tour is [that] … Charles Dickens … [has] decided to recognize Ticknor & Fields as the only authorized publisher of his works in America' (Moss and Moss, 84n.).

It was at this time that Dickens was considering a second reading tour of North America and was in contact with J. T. Fields, among others, about arrangements. Osgood became involved in these, travelling with George Dolby, the tour's general manager, on the initial inspection of venues. His extensive social connections were useful in this regard; Dolby called him 'one of the most popular men in America' (Dolby, 107). On the tour proper Osgood was engaged in administrative duties, including acting as treasurer—Dickens commented that the financial records were 'excellently kept by Mr. Osgood' (*Letters of Charles Dickens*, 12.12) and engaging in the constant battle against speculators, attempting (with limited success) to prevent ticket touts from obtaining and re-selling tickets. He was also a member of Dickens's unofficial 'bodyguard', conducting the novelist to and from his readings and protecting him during the performances, in one instance literally throwing a dog out of the room 'in a transport of presence of mind and fury' (ibid., 12.3, 41). Dickens described him in another letter with a combination of admiration and good-humoured fun: 'Osgood is on guard. He made a most brilliant appearance before the Philadelphia public, and looked hard at them. The mastery of his eye diverted their attention from his boots:—charming in themselves, but (unfortunately) two left ones' (ibid., 12.18).

Osgood and Dolby also paid particular attention to Dickens's morale, as he himself admitted to being 'often heavy, and rarely sleep[ing] much'. Osgood's place in Dickensian legend was secured by his role in a 'ridiculous', twelve-mile walking competition designed to keep Dickens in spirits; as the Boston Bantam, Osgood represented America, competing against Dolby, as the Man of Ross (*Letters of Charles Dickens*, 12.29–30, 714). Dickens drew up the articles of agreement for the contest, held on 29 February 1868, and Osgood emerged victorious by half a mile. Dickens later often referred to him as the 'Bantam', and he was fêted at a sumptuous dinner given by Dickens for eighteen friends in honour of the event. Upon his return from America, however, Dickens became caught up with business and a British reading tour, and neglected to correspond with Osgood for over a year. This led to a remonstrative letter from Osgood; Dickens admitted the fault, assuring Osgood in December 1868 that 'The remembrance of your ever ready interest and zeal, and of your cheery companionship in scorching railway cars and eccentric hotels, is never to be so lightly dealt with on my side' (ibid., 12.238).

Due largely to his success in dealing with Dickens's second reading tour Osgood became a senior partner of Fields, Osgood & Co. in 1868. Having accumulated sufficient publishing experience he set up on his own in 1871 as James R. Osgood & Co., a company that published Henry James's first volume of fiction, *A Passionate Pilgrim and other Tales* (1875), as well as some other early works by James, including *Roderick Hudson* (1875) and *The American* (1877). As director of this firm Osgood also arranged with Thomas Hardy for the American publication of some works first published in the *Cornhill Magazine*. In May 1885, however, Henry James noted that 'J. R. Osgood & Co., my dear Boston publishers, have failed' (James, 79). Although a 'man of integrity … he had apparently managed his business poorly' (Edel, 82), as his 'enthusiasm for literary publishing [had] unfortunately often remained unchecked by economic realities' (Winship, 23). After this bankruptcy Osgood left America and settled in London in 1886. There he acted as an agent for Harper & Brothers, where, while he had few further dealings with James, he continued to correspond with Hardy, this time about the printing of his work in *Harper's New Monthly Magazine*. In November 1890, with the assistance of Harpers, Osgood set up business again—as partner, with Clarence W. McIlvaine, in Osgood, McIlvaine & Co., at 45 Albemarle Street. In the following year they published Hardy's *A Group of Noble Dames* and the first edition in volume format of *Tess of the D'Urbervilles* (initially published in instalments in *The Graphic*)—commissions given to the new firm by Hardy probably '[i]n part as a gesture of friendship towards … Osgood' (Millgate, 308).

Osgood died at his home, 161A Piccadilly, London, on 18 May 1892; Hardy travelled up to the city for his funeral, on 22 May. The firm continued for a few years, publishing in 1895–6 the handsome and textually important 'first uniform and complete edition' of Hardy's Wessex novels, which included the first edition in book format of *Jude the Obscure* (1896 [1 November 1895]). Osgood, McIlvaine & Co., however, was soon afterwards absorbed by Harper & Brothers, with McIlvaine continuing to act as their representative in London. M. CLARE LOUGHLIN-CHOW

Sources *IGI* · *The letters of Charles Dickens*, ed. M. House, G. Storey, and others, 11 (1999) · Boase, *Mod. Eng. biog.* · G. Dolby, *Charles Dickens as I knew him*, 2nd edn (1912) · M. Winship, *American literary publishing in the nineteenth century: the business of Ticknor and Fields* (1995) · P. Schlicke, ed., *Oxford reader's companion to Dickens* (1999) · J. Forster, *The life of Charles Dickens*, ed. J. W. T. Ley (1928) · S. P. Moss and C. J. Moss, *American episodes involving Charles Dickens* (1999) · *The collected letters of Thomas Hardy*, ed. R. L. Purdy and M. Millgate, 1 and 2 (1978–80) · M. Millgate, *Thomas Hardy: a biography* (1982) · R. L. Purdy, *Thomas Hardy: a bibliographical study* (1954) · *Henry James: letters*, ed. L. Edel, 3: *1883–1895* (1980) · L. Edel, *Henry James*, 3 (1963) · d. cert. · *CGPLA Eng. & Wales* (1893)

Wealth at death £5869 12*s*. 4½*d*.: probate, 12 July 1893, *CGPLA Eng. & Wales*

Osgoode, William (1754–1824), judge in Canada, was born in March 1754 in London, the only son of William Osgood (*d*. 1767), a Leeds hosier who left an estate of £20,000. Perhaps because of his father's acquaintance with John Wesley, William was sent to the Methodist school at Kingswood, near Bath, from which he went to Christ Church, Oxford (BA, 1772; MA, 1777). He entered Lincoln's Inn in 1773 and was called to the bar in November 1779, the year in which he published *Remarks on the Law of Descent*, a response to William Blackstone's *Commentaries on the Laws* *of England*. Instead of practising as a barrister, Osgoode built a reputation as an accomplished draftsman in the courts of equity. In 1791, when Quebec was divided into two provinces, he secured appointment as chief justice of Upper Canada, with the promise of the same position in the senior colony of Lower Canada on the first vacancy. As an industrious administrator with tory and now Anglican sympathies, Osgoode enjoyed cordial relations with a like-minded lieutenant-governor, John Graves Simcoe, and leading British officials. Both an executive councillor and, as speaker of the legislative council, a manager of government business, Osgoode sought to adapt English civil law to the circumstances of an infant frontier colony. A controversial Judicature Act of 1794 scaled down the district courts of common pleas and created a central court of king's bench. He left largely unaltered English criminal law as introduced by the proclamation of 1763.

In 1794 Osgoode migrated to Quebec, where his career was less harmonious. He exchanged a loyalist province for an uncongenial French Catholic community at a time when Britain was at war with revolutionary France. Potential or imagined threats to the fragile social order and the colony's security, whether from invasion or subversion, alarmed Osgoode and a beleaguered English-speaking minority. In this fevered atmosphere the authorities enacted security legislation, enforced by an intelligence service and the active prosecution of rioters. Habeas corpus was suspended, and an elastic definition of sedition and treason, going far beyond British precedent, covered conspiracies hatched in an overseas territory and aimed at overturning the sovereignty of an absent king. In a show trial in 1797 an American undercover agent for revolutionary France, David McLane, was convicted and executed for high treason, a verdict guaranteed through proceedings manipulated by Osgoode and his fellow judges. In Lower Canada the judiciary was politicized, Osgoode himself combining the roles of chief justice, councillor, principal adviser to the governor, and head of political security.

The garrison mentality evinced by the ruling élite also strained French–British relations. Osgoode denounced the French Canadiens as ignorant, disloyal democrats. He found incomprehensible the earlier official endorsement of cultural toleration and argued that the security of British rule necessitated a vigorous policy of Anglicization. This stance exacerbated his fractious dealings with the experienced, masterful governor, Lord Dorchester, who had since the 1770s worked for ethnic accommodation. After a harmonious interlude in 1796–7, Osgoode also fell foul of Dorchester's successor, the irascible General Robert Prescott, by engineering opposition among councillors to the governor's regulations for accelerating settlement of the Eastern townships, adjacent to the American border, and curtailing land speculation. The governor accused his chief justice of being in league with speculators, a plausible charge since Osgoode acquired almost 12,000 acres. In 1799 Prescott was recalled following protests to London orchestrated by Osgoode. His bickering with Robert Shore Milnes, who arrived that year as lieutenant-governor, prompted him to resign in return for an £800 pension, and he left Quebec in 1801. In London, still concerned about Canadian affairs, Osgoode advised the Colonial Office in 1822 on the drafting of an abortive bill to reunite the Canadas. With an abiding interest in procedural reform, he served on two royal commissions on the courts of law which eventually led in 1832 to the Uniformity of Process Act. He died, unmarried, at the Albany, London, on 17 January 1824. Osgoode Hall, first built in York (Toronto) in 1829–32 as headquarters of the Law Society of Upper Canada, and now a law school associated with York University, was named after him.

PETER BURROUGHS

Sources Archives of Ontario, Toronto, Osgoode collection · NA Canada, William Osgoode collection, MG23-HI10 · original correspondence, Canada, 1791–1801, PRO, CO 42/89–101, 115–17, 316–19 · entry books, Canada, 1791–1801, PRO, CO 43/17–19, 37–8 · sessional papers, Canada, PRO, CO 45/18–19, 24, 126–7 · F. M. Greenwood, *Legacies of fear: law and politics in Quebec in the era of the French Revolution* (1993) · S. R. Mealing, 'Osgoode, William', *DCB*, vol. 6 · A. G. Doughty and D. A. McArthur, eds., *Documents relating to the constitutional history of Canada, 1791–1818* (Ottawa, 1914) · W. Colgate, 'Letters from the Hon. Chief Justice William Osgoode: a selection from his Canadian correspondence, 1791–1801', *Ontario History*, 46 (1954), 77–95, 149–68 · A. R. M. Lower, 'Three letters of William Osgoode, first chief justice of Upper Canada', *Ontario History*, 57 (1965), 181–7 · W. R. Riddell, 'William Osgoode, first chief justice of Upper Canada, 1792–1794', *Canadian Law Times* [*Toronto*], 41 (1921), 278–98, 345–58 · *The correspondence of Lieutenant Governor John Graves Simcoe*, ed. E. A. Cruikshank, 5 vols. (1923–31)

Archives NA Canada, MSS · Public Archives of Ontario, Toronto, corresp. | PRO, Colonial Office records · PRO, private letters to John King, CO 42/22

Likenesses G. T. Berthon, oils, Osgoode Hall Law School, Toronto, Canada

Osgyth [St Osgyth, Osyth, Osith] (*fl.* **late 7th cent.**), abbess of Chich, is an extreme illustration of the problems of elucidating the lives of the first generation of princess-saints from late hagiographies. In two twelfth-century lives, themselves known only from later and fragmentary versions, two distinct bodies of tradition, one apparently derived from Aylesbury, and the other from Chich, Essex, were conflated and confused with legends of St Modwenna of Burton and St Eadgyth of Polesworth. Furthermore, it remains uncertain whether the Aylesbury and Chich legends genuinely referred to one woman, or to different though near-contemporary women of the same name.

The essentials of the twelfth-century narrative are as follows. Osgyth was the daughter of a King 'Fredeswald' and his wife, Wilburh, daughter of Penda and sister of Wulfhere, king of the Mercians. She was born in her father's palace at Quarrendon, Buckinghamshire, and was brought up at Aylesbury in the nunnery of her aunt St Eadgyth. On a journey to visit another aunt, St Eadburh, at Adderbury, she drowned in the Cherwell, but was revived by the prayers of Eadburh and Eadgyth. Despite her wish to remain a virgin, her parents married her to King *Sigehere of the East Saxons [*see under* East Saxons, kings of the], but she was miraculously saved from consummating the marriage. Sigehere accepted the inevitable and gave Osgyth the vill of Chich, where she took the veil, gathered a community of nuns, and built a church and monastic buildings. She was kidnapped by pirates, who beheaded her after she refused to worship idols. In one version her parents collected the body for burial at Aylesbury; in the other it was buried at Chich, taken to Aylesbury for safe keeping for forty-six years, but then returned.

Both the Buckinghamshire and the Essex stories are consistent with known late seventh-century conditions. 'Fredeswald' can probably be identified with Frithuwald, the Mercian sub-king who endowed Chertsey Minster in 672–4 and whose kingdom may have extended from the lower Thames northwards across the Chilterns. Other daughters of Penda were abbesses, and Eadgyth may be the saint of that name later venerated at Bicester: the Buckinghamshire tradition embodied genuine memories of early local saints. Aylesbury can be identified archaeologically as an eighth-century religious site. There are also indications, both written and archaeological, that Chich was an Anglo-Saxon minster.

But were there two Osgyths, or merely one? Essex was within the Mercian ambit, and a marriage alliance between an East Saxon king and a niece of the Mercian overlord Wulfhere is wholly plausible; the chronology also fits well. The main difficulty is that there were two feast days (3 June at Aylesbury, 7 October at Chich) and two corpses. The saint's relics are located at Chich in the earlier part of the Old English list of resting places, but the later version in the Domesday Breviate has Osgyth entries for both Chich and Aylesbury. Furthermore, in 1501–2 the vicar of Aylesbury tried unsuccessfully to elevate a corpse of St Osgyth buried in his church. The story of the temporary removal of the relics from Chich to Aylesbury reads as an uneasy attempt to reconcile two distinct cults. The available evidence does not admit a confident solution.

JOHN BLAIR

Sources D. Bethell, 'The lives of St Osyth of Essex and St Osyth of Aylesbury', *Analecta Bollandiana*, 88 (1970), 75–127 · C. Hohler, 'St Osyth and Aylesbury', *Records of Buckinghamshire*, 18 (1966–70), 61–72 · R. P. Hagerty, 'The Buckinghamshire saints reconsidered … St Osyth and St Edith of Aylesbury', *Records of Buckinghamshire*, 29 (1987), 125–32 · K. Bailey, 'Osyth, Frithuwold and Aylesbury', *Records of Buckinghamshire*, 31 (1989), 37–48 · A. Campana, 'Santa Ositha', *Archivio Italiano per la storia della pietà*, 9 (1996), 95–121

O'Shanassy, Sir John (1818–1883), politician in Australia, was born at Ballinahow, near Thurles, co. Tipperary, Ireland, the son of John O'Shanassy, a surveyor, and his wife, Margaret Dwyer. After his father died in 1831 he left school and was apprenticed to a Tipperary draper and wine and spirits merchant. In 1839 he married Margaret McDonnell (*d.* 1887) of Thurles, and in July of that year the couple sailed for New South Wales, encouraged by a relative who had previously gone to Sydney. Their vessel called at Melbourne in the new settlement at Port Phillip. O'Shanassy was persuaded not to travel further and bought a small property, Windriet, near Western Port. The venture failed and in 1845 he commenced a more successful career as a draper in Melbourne. In 1849 he was able to buy cheaply some crown land in inner North Melbourne, which soon became very valuable.

Sir John O'Shanassy (1818–1883), attrib. Antoine Fauchery, *c.*1858

An intelligent, outspoken man, with a deceptive façade of popular radicalism in these early years which belied his true conservatism, O'Shanassy quickly gained public prominence. From 1845 to 1851 he was president of the St Patrick's Society, founded in 1842 to 'preserve in this colony' the memory of Ireland. In 1846 he briefly held a seat on the Melbourne council, and in the late years of the decade he was involved in opposition to the transportation of convicts to Port Phillip and in the campaign for separation of Port Phillip from New South Wales.

Upon separation in 1851 O'Shanassy was elected to the first Victoria legislative council and became effective leader of the opposition to the conservative official, nominee, and squatting members who dominated the council. In 1852 he was a member of the select committee on the goldfields, in 1853–4 of the committee which drew up the new Victoria constitution, and in November 1854 of another commission on goldfields. This last commission became more important following the Eureka rebellion of December 1854, and its major recommendations included the miners' right and provision for immediate miner representation on the legislative council.

O'Shanassy's business activities widened and prospered. He promoted building societies and was chairman of the Colonial Bank of Australasia from its formation in 1855 until 1870. He built a mansion, Tara, on a 16 acre property in the then outer suburb of Camberwell. He was the leading lay Roman Catholic in the colony, and one of the first trustees of the public library.

At the first elections under the new constitution in September 1856, O'Shanassy was elected to represent Kilmore, which he held until December 1865. He was a major figure in the unstable, faction-ridden early years of the Victoria parliament. He briefly held power from 11 March 1857 to 24 April 1857 and from 10 March 1858 to 27 October 1859, and more extensively and successfully in the second parliament, from 14 November 1861 to 27 June 1863. In these years he drifted towards more conservative positions on many issues, including free trade. He was greatly concerned to promote Catholic interests in matters such as state aid for religion and denominational education. His third government was notable for two pieces of legislation, the 1862 Common Schools Act and the 1862 Crown Lands Act, which was promoted by his lands minister and fellow Catholic, Charles Gavan Duffy.

Upon losing office for the third time O'Shanassy became part of the minority opposition to the McCulloch government, defending free trade and the powers of the legislative council during the early stage of the constitutional crises of the mid-1860s. He retired from parliament in December 1865 and left in May 1866 to travel to Europe, visiting Ireland and England, and Rome, where he was appointed a knight of the order of St Gregory for his services to Catholic education. He arrived back in Melbourne in July 1867.

By now O'Shanassy had begun acquiring significant pastoral interests in New South Wales and Queensland and was largely allied with those who had previously been his political enemies. Significantly, he became a member of the legislative council, having been elected in May 1868 for Central Province, a seat he held until April 1874. He was now at odds with Duffy, whose government of 1871–2 he strongly opposed and whose defeat ironically paved the way for the 1872 Education Act, which abolished state aid to church schools and introduced secular education to government schools, both anathema to O'Shanassy.

After another visit to Europe in 1874, in 1875 O'Shanassy chaired a royal commission on the volunteer forces. He twice tried unsuccessfully to re-enter the assembly before being elected for Belfast in May 1877. In parliament he focused on the fight to reintroduce state aid, and with a small group of followers with whom he held the balance of power contributed to a new period of political instability from 1878 to 1882. He lost his seat at the elections of March 1883.

O'Shanassy was created CMG in 1870 and KCMG in 1878. He died on 5 May 1883 at Camberwell, Victoria, survived by his wife, two of his three sons, and his three daughters. He was buried on 6 May at Hawthorn, Victoria. Ambitious and egocentric, he was none the less vigorous in promoting economic development and the interests of his church. DON GARDEN

Sources *AusDB* • G. Serle, *The golden age: a history of the colony of Victoria, 1851–1861* (1963) • G. Serle, *The rush to be rich* (1971) • P. O'Farrell, *The Irish in Australia* (1986) • W. H. Archer, 'Sir John O'Shanassy: a sketch', *Melbourne Review*, 8 (1883) • *The Argus* [Melbourne] (7 May 1883) • *The Times* (7–9 May 1883) • G. R. Bartlett, 'Political organization and society in Victoria, 1864–1883', PhD diss., Australian National University, 1964 • S. Dew, 'The Belfast electorate, 1803–1883', BA Hons diss., Monash University, 1969 • P. Mennell, *The dictionary of Australasian biography* (1892) • J. H. Heaton, *Australian dictionary of dates and men of the time* (1934)

Likenesses attrib. A. Fauchery, photograph, *c.*1858, State Library of Victoria, Australia [*see illus.*]

Wealth at death £75,000—New South Wales properties: *AusDB*

O Shannon, Cathal (1893–1969), Irish nationalist and trade unionist, was born on 9 June 1893 at Drumsough, near Randalstown, co. Antrim, the third of four children of Charles Shannon (*c.*1851–1908), a locomotive engine driver, and his wife, Alice (*c.*1850–1925), *née* McLarnon, of Draperstown, co. Derry. His parents were both Irish Roman Catholics, and O Shannon's upbringing inspired an interest in the Irish language, republicanism, and trade unionism, the 'three threads that have run together in one piece in me all through my life' (O Shannon MSS, COS 93/12/12B). When he was six months old the family moved to Draperstown, where he was educated at the national school, later going to St Columb's College, Derry, on a scholarship. In 1908 his father's death caused him to be sent to Belfast for grinding for the civil service, which he hated. By 1909 he was active in Sinn Féin, the Irish Republican Brotherhood (IRB), Fianna Éireann, and the Gaelic League, and began to correspond for various nationalist, and later labour, journals. In 1910 he abandoned his studies for a clerkship with Heysham Steamers, Belfast. Impressed by James Connolly's writings since 1908, he joined the Irish Transport and General Workers' Union (ITGWU) in 1912, and accepted Connolly's offer of a job with the union's Belfast staff in 1913.

After August 1914 O Shannon acted on behalf of Connolly with the IRB in the preparations for the Easter rising, and mobilized with about 100 insurgents at Coalisland, co. Tyrone, on Easter Saturday 1916. With the defeat of the rising, he was interned in Fron-goch, Wales. After the general amnesty at Christmas, and repeated arrest, he worked as an ITGWU official in Cork from July 1917 to March 1918. As the ITGWU enjoyed phenomenal growth, O Shannon acquired national influence, as intermittent editor, from March 1918, of the union's *Voice of Labour* (1918–19), *Watchword of Labour* (1919–21), and *Voice of Labour* (1921–7); member of the Labour Party and Trade Union Congress executive (1918–20 and 1922–3); a lynchpin of Labour's collusion with republicans during the War of Independence; and labour TD for Louth–Meath (1922–3). On the run in Britain in 1920, under the name Conor Hayes, he organized the Stockport, Cheshire, by-election campaign of the imprisoned ITGWU chief William O Brien, and met his future wife, Margaret Doris Finn, of Stockport, in Manchester's Free Trade Hall. Arrested in March 1920, he was released from Mountjoy gaol, Dublin, on 5 May after an eight-day hunger strike.

O Shannon's back-room role has confined him to passing historical treatment, and he remains enigmatic as a republican who endorsed Labour's neutrality on the Anglo-Irish treaty; and as the self-styled 'Irish Bolshevik' who promoted soviets and glorified violent strikes in the ITGWU press, yet defended the union leadership as it pursued a moderate wage policy and retreated from direct action after 1921. By 1923 the glory days were over. Recalled to an ITGWU reeling from economic recession and a split with James Larkin, O Shannon worked as political secretary (1924–6), and head of (wage) movements (1926–41). During these fractious years he produced several pamphlets attacking the ITGWU's rivals, and edited the Labour Party newspapers *The Irishman*, *Watchword*, and *Torch*. He married Margaret Doris Finn in 1924 and, small in frame, became familiar around Dublin as a 'slight, bent figure with the black broad-brimmed hat' (*Irish Times*, 6 Oct 1969), the hallmark of the Dublin literary man. Secretary of the Irish Trade Union Congress (1941–5), and the breakaway Congress of Irish Unions (1945–6), O Shannon served as a workers' representative on the labour court from its foundation in September 1946 to his retirement in 1969, continuing to write, notably as a columnist with the *Evening Press*, and editor of the commemorative *Fifty Years of Liberty Hall* (1959). He died in St Lawrence's Hospital, Dublin, on 4 October 1969, and was buried in Dean's Grange cemetery on 6 October, leaving a son, Cathal, and two daughters, Gráinne and Fionnuala. His wife predeceased him. EMMET O CONNOR

Sources Irish Labour History Archive, Dublin, O Shannon MSS · *Saothar*, 19 (1994), 107–9 · C. D. Greaves, *The Irish Transport and General Workers' Union* (1982) · J. A. Gaughan, *Thomas Johnson* (1980) · A. Mitchell, *Labour in Irish politics, 1890–1930* (1974) · *Liberty Jubilee Issue* [Special Commemorative Issue] (1959), 35–45 · *Irish Times* (6 Oct 1969) · *Irish Times* (7 Oct 1969) · H. Boylan, *A dictionary of Irish biography*, 2nd edn (1988) · D. J. Hickey and J. E. Doherty, *A dictionary of Irish history* (1980); pbk edn (1987) · private information (2004) · d. cert.

Archives Irish Labour History Archive, Dublin, MSS | FILM Radio Telefis Éireann, Dublin, 'Survivors', 1964 · RTÉ archive, Dublin, documentary footage | SOUND BBC Northern Ireland Archives, documentary footage · Radio Telefis Éireann, Dublin, 'Great lock out', 15 Sept 1963 · Radio Telefis Éireann, Dublin, '1916 in Ulster', 10 March 1964 · Radio Telefis Éireann, Dublin, 'Cathal O Shannon and Helena Moloney', 11 Nov 1964 · Radio Telefis Éireann, Dublin, 'Favourite records', 23 Nov 1968 · Radio Telefis Éireann, Dublin, 'C. O Shannon', 14 Nov 1969 · Radio Telefis Éireann, Dublin, 'Rock among men', 12 Sept 1971 · Radio Telifis Éireann, Dublin, 'First Dáil', 19 Jan 1969 · Ulster Folk and Transport Museum, Cultra, co. Down, BBC Northern Ireland Archives, 'Old Ireland free: Easter rising, 1916', Museum 3993

Likenesses group portrait, photograph, 1919, repro. in Mitchell, *Labour in Irish politics* · group portrait, photograph, *c.*1946, Services Industrial Professional & Technical Union, Liberty Hall, Dublin; repro. in F. A. D'Arcy and K. Hannigan, *Workers in union* (1988), 223 · photograph, 1946, repro. in Gaughan, *Thomas Johnson* · R. Pyke, ink and pencil with drypoint, NG Ire. · etching, Services Industrial Professional & Technical Union, Liberty Hall, Dublin; repro. in *Liberty Jubilee Issue*, 55

O'Shaughnessy, Arthur William Edgar (1844–1881), poet, was born at 46 Pembroke Square, London, on 14 March 1844, the son of Oscar William O'Shaughnessy, a painter of animal pictures who died of consumption in 1848, and his wife, Louisa Anne Deacon (1813–1896), a schoolteacher. Arthur and his younger brother, Oscar, grew up in Kensington, where the family lived together with Louisa's eldest sister, Caroline. The boys were educated privately.

In June 1861 Arthur O'Shaughnessy was appointed a transcriber in the department of printed books in the library of the British Museum, and in August 1863 he was promoted to an assistantship in the zoological department. Both positions, it seems, were attained partly through the patronage of Edward Bulwer-Lytton, a Conservative MP. The transfer gave great offence to naturalists and was condemned by a resolution passed at a meeting of the Zoological Society. O'Shaughnessy knew very little about natural history; in 1870 he narrowly escaped being sacked for his consistently bad work, but Bulwer-Lytton's intervention saved him. Thereafter, he became such a good authority on herpetology (the study of reptiles) that he was made responsible for that section of the annual zoological record. His death in 1881 was deplored as a loss to science by Dr Albert Günther, the head of the museum department to which O'Shaughnessy belonged.

Also in 1870, O'Shaughnessy published, to acclaim, his *Epic of Women and other Poems*, illustrated by his friend J. T. Nettleship. *Lays of France*, which appeared two years later, was chiefly adapted from the poems of the twelfth-century poet Marie de France. His work was heavily influenced by French romanticism and, fluent in the language, he spent most of his holidays in Paris.

In 1873 O'Shaughnessy's protector, Bulwer-Lytton, died. Finding him in tears at work, and remembering visits to Bulwer-Lytton by a very well-dressed woman who always wore a veil, O'Shaughnessy's friend Edmund Gosse, then a transcriber, leapt to the conclusion that Bulwer-Lytton was O'Shaughnessy's natural father. In fact, Bulwer-Lytton's interest in the young man arose from his relationship with O'Shaughnessy's aunt Laura, as, after his separation from Rosina Bulwer-Lytton, he and Laura were married in all but name. Nevertheless, the rumour was not laid to rest until after the deaths of all concerned.

O'Shaughnessy married Eleanor Kyme Marston, daughter of the playwright John Westland *Marston (1819–1890), on 26 June 1873. He published *Music and Moonlight* (1874) to lukewarm reviews, and then he and his wife wrote a book of tales for children: *Toyland* (1875). Their first child, Westland Kyme, was born 31 July 1874 but died two months later; a second son also died in infancy. On 8 February 1879 Eleanor herself died, of cirrhosis of the liver, and her husband deplored her death in an elegy of great beauty. He was working as the English correspondent of *Le Livre*, and planning to remarry, when, after a few days' illness, he died of a lung infection at his London home, 163 Golbourne Road, Notting Hill, on 30 January 1881. He was buried at Kensal Green cemetery in London on 3 February.

O'Shaughnessy's posthumously published poems, *Songs of a Worker* (1881), were, apart from a few poems on sculpture, criticized as repetitious. His contemporaries tended to agree that his reputation suffered from a lack of editorial rigour in selection. In general, though, his musicality was praised, but not his intelligence or imagination. His most lasting poem, set to music by Edward Elgar, is probably the 'Ode' from *Music and Moonlight*, which begins:

> We are the music makers
> And we are the dreamers of dreams.

RICHARD GARNETT, *rev.* JESSICA HININGS

Sources W. D. Paden, *Arthur O'Shaughnessy: the ancestry of a Victorian poet* (1964) • R. Garnett, 'Memoir', *The poets and the poetry of the century*, ed. A. H. Miles, 7 (1892), 189–90 • L. C. Moulton, *Arthur O'Shaughnessy: his life and his work with selections from his poems* (1894) • Ward, *Men of the reign* • Boase, *Mod. Eng. biog.* • *The Athenaeum* (5 Feb 1881), 196–7 • E. C. Stedman, *Victorian poets*, 13th edn (1887)
Archives Col. U., Butler Library, corresp. and literary MSS • Duke U., Perkins L., corresp., literary MSS, and papers • Queen's University, Belfast, poems and papers • University of Kansas, Lawrence | BL, corresp. with Helen Snee, Ashley MS 3720 • Bodl. Oxf., letters to D. G. Rossetti [copies] • Herts. ALS, corresp. with Lord Lytton • U. Leeds, Brotherton L., letters to Edmund Gosse
Wealth at death under £800: administration, 14 Feb 1881, *CGPLA Eng. & Wales*

O'Shaughnessy, William (1674–1744), army officer in the French service, son of Roger O'Shaughnessy (*d.* 1690) and his wife, Helen, daughter of Conor MacDonogh O'Brien of Ballynee, co. Meath, was born in Gort, co. Galway, Ireland, and on the death of his father in July 1690 he became the head of the O'Shaughnessys of Gort. In 1689, aged fifteen, he became captain of foot and afterwards acting colonel in James II's army. He went to France early in 1690 with the regiment of the Irish brigade commanded by Daniel O'Brien, afterwards third Viscount Clare, in which he was appointed captain by Louis XIV on 10 July 1691. He served in Italy in 1692 and was present at the battle of Marsaglia, in Piedmont, in 1693. In 1696 he witnessed the close of the operations at the back of the Alps by the siege of Valenza, where he became commandant of the 3rd battalion of his regiment, and he was appointed to the army of the Meuse.

When the 2nd and 3rd battalions of Clare were re-formed in 1698 O'Shaughnessy was appointed captain of the grenadiers of the battalion which was maintained from 1 April 1698. With his regiment, one of the most famous of the Irish brigade, he served in Germany in the campaigns of 1701–02; he was present at the reduction of Kehl and the first battle of Hochstedt in 1703, and at Blenheim the year after. In 1705 he served with the army of the Moselle. In 1706 he fought at Ramillies, and became major of Clare on 4 July, upon the death of Major John O Carroll, and lieutenant-colonel on 12 September. He served with his regiment in Flanders in 1707, at Oudenarde in 1708, at Malplaquet in 1709, and at the defence of the lines of Arleux, Denain, Douai, Bouchain, and Quesnoy in 1710–12. Subsequently he served in the campaigns in Germany, including the sieges of Landau and Freiberg. He became a brigadier-general on 3 April 1721 and was employed with the army of the Rhine in 1733 and in the campaigns of 1734–5, when he attained the rank of major-general (*maréchal de camp*) on 1 August 1734. He later served with the army in Flanders in 1742, and was in command at Cambray during the campaign of 1743. On 1 November of that year he was appointed to the command at Gravelines, where he died on 2 January 1744, aged seventy, the oldest Irish major-general in French service.

H. M. CHICHESTER, *rev.* D. M. BEAUMONT

Sources J. C. O'Callaghan, *History of the Irish brigades in the service of France*, [new edn] (1870) • House of Lords appeals, King's Inn Library, Dublin [Roger O'Shaughnessy estate] • M. J. Blake, 'Tabular pedigree of O'Shaughnessy of Gort, 1543–1783', *Journal of the Galway Archaeological and Historical Society*, 6 (1909–10), 64; 7 (1910–11), 53
Archives Bibliothèque Nationale, Paris, MS on career in France

O'Shaughnessy, Sir William Brooke. *See* Brooke, Sir William O'Shaughnessy (1808–1889).

O'Shea, John Augustus (1839–1905), journalist, was born on 24 June 1839 at Nenagh, co. Tipperary. His father was John O'Shea, a well-known journalist, who worked for the *Clonmel Guardian*. After receiving his elementary education in Nenagh, O'Shea was sent on 31 October 1856 to the Catholic University in Dublin. In 1859 he went to London to work as a journalist. He became a special correspondent to various newspapers. In 1860 he represented an American journal at the siege of Ancona, defended by the papal troops, and he described part of the Austro-Prussian War. Settling in Paris he acted for some time as a correspondent of Richard Pigott's *Irishman* newspaper. For this paper, and for *The Shamrock*, a magazine also owned by Pigott, O'Shea wrote many of his best stories and sketches, especially the *Memoirs of a White Cravat* (1868). His usual signature was the Irish Bohemian. In 1869 he joined the London *Standard*, and for twenty-five years was one of its most active special correspondents. He reported the Franco-Prussian War, when he was captured by the French and nearly executed as a spy. He was in the siege of Paris, and in Spain during the Carlist War of 1872, and reported the famine in Bengal in 1877. After leaving *The Standard* he continued to write occasional articles in various English and Irish papers, including the *Freeman's Journal* and the Dublin *Evening Telegraph*. He was a longstanding member of the staff of *The Universe*, a Roman Catholic paper published in London.

In 1885 he became president of the Southwark Irish Literary Club, an important centre for the Gaelic revival in London. He was injured in a traffic accident, which left him paralysed in his last years. He died in poverty at his home in Jeffreys Road, Clapham, on 13 March 1905, and was buried in Kensal Green Roman Catholic cemetery, on 18 March. He was twice married, his second wife and a daughter surviving him.

O'Shea's admirable sense of style, and his dash and wit, distinguish his writing. His contemporaries described him as the last of the bohemian journalists. His books are, in the main, made up of articles written during his working life. He was a witty conversationalist and raconteur, and an admirable public speaker.

D. J. O'DONOGHUE, *rev.* MARIE-LOUISE LEGG

Sources *Freeman's Journal* [Dublin] (14 March 1905) • *The Times* (14 March 1905) • J. A. O'Shea, *Leaves from the life of a special correspondent* (1885)

Likenesses photograph, repro. in O'Shea, *Leaves from the life of a special correspondent*, frontispiece

O'Shea, Katharine. *See* Parnell, Katharine (1845–1921).

O'Shea [*married name* Rollo]**, Teresa Mary** [Tessie] (**1913–1995**), singer and actress, was born on 13 March 1913 at 61 Plantagenet Street, Cardiff, the daughter of James Peter O'Shea, a labourer at a gasworks, and his wife, Nellie, *née* Carr. Her father was Irish, her mother Lancastrian; she inherited her mother's accent. A natural performer, she won a talent contest at the age of eight, tying for first place with an entire Welsh choir. A subsequent appearance in a charity show brought her to the attention of the Stoll organization, and at the legal minimum age of twelve she was appearing professionally at the Bristol Hippodrome. Within months she was appearing at a showcase venue, the Chiswick Empire. Her early act owed a great deal to the comedian Lily Morris, but O'Shea rapidly developed a voice of both power and sweetness and a unique rapport with her audience. She had a large body, weighing 17 stone at the peak of her career, and her signature tune in the 1940s gave her her best known sobriquet, Two Ton Tessie, but while her songs alluded to her lack of sexual success—'Nobody Loves a Fat Girl when she's Forty', 'I fell in love with an airman but I'm nobody's sweetheart now'—their tone was one of self-celebration, reinforced by high kicks and a brisk banjolele accompaniment.

In 1934 O'Shea moved to the Moss Empires circuit and throughout the decade she consistently topped variety bills throughout Britain, notably in Blackpool where her Lancashire roots made her a summer season favourite. During the Second World War she maintained this dominance on several fronts: as one of the most popular artistes with the Entertainments National Service Association, as a performer at royal private parties, and as a guest on the radio show *Happidrome*. On 31 July 1940 she married David Halsel Rollo (*b*. 1916/17), schoolmaster, son of David Rollo, a hotel manager in Blackpool. He was three years her junior, and at the time of their marriage was a second lieutenant in the Royal Artillery. There were no children of the marriage, which ended in divorce in 1950. In 1944 she and Max Miller jointly topped the bill at the Palladium; the contrast of their comic styles served to underline their high status in the profession. O'Shea appeared at the first royal variety performance of the peace in 1946; she closed the first half, descending like a *deus ex machina* in a glittering dress and singing 'Money is the Root of All Evil' as she flung banknotes into the audience. This surrealist note was echoed in several of her songs, such as the yodelling routine 'U are a Liarty', and the high-speed 'I met him by the withered weeping willows'.

As the end of the war approached O'Shea's film career began with *The Way Ahead* in 1944. In 1946 she had a seemingly career-changing opportunity with *London Town*, in which she played a pearly queen. However, the British film industry failed to find her a suitable follow-up role: John E. Blakeley cast her in two northern comedies, opposite Sandy Powell in *Holidays with Pay* and Frank Randle in *Somewhere in Politics*, but neither achieved the

Teresa Mary O'Shea (1913–1995), by John Capstack

wider exposure the performers deserved. It was in the 1949 film *The Blue Lamp* that the real power and charm of O'Shea was to be seen. She had a cameo role as herself in a murder story played across London nightlife—cinemas, dog tracks, and a variety theatre. 'Tessie O'Shea … she's good', remarked one of the protagonists, and the life-loving vigour with which she attacked her saucy but innocuous song contrasted with the callousness of the young armed robbers. The effectiveness of this juxtaposition was grounded in nostalgia: as the materialism of the 1950s, here symbolized by the brutal murder of a young policeman, had begun to erode the values that had orchestrated the welfare state, so live variety shows had largely given way to television. The warmth of O'Shea's performance, perhaps even more effectively than the idealized figure of the old-time bobby on the beat, incarnated an older England.

This element of outdatedness accounted, perhaps, for the slump in O'Shea's career that followed. In 1963, however, Nöel Coward cast her in his Broadway musical *The Girl who Came to Supper*, in a role that closely resembled her part as a cockney mother in *London Town*. This time, however, she won a Tony award and went on to appear as a guest on the Ed Sullivan show (with the Beatles) and in cabaret. She received a further Oscar nomination for her role in *The Russians are Coming, the Russians are Coming* in 1966, and an Emmy award for a television performance in *Doctor Jekyll and Mr Hyde*. She returned to Blackpool to play a summer season with Ken Dodd in 1970, and she launched her own series on British television, *As Good Cooks Go*. O'Shea's career, however, was now centred on

America, and in 1971 she made one of her best remembered film appearances in the Disney fantasy *Bedknobs and Broomsticks*. Two years later she starred in *London Revue* at the Sands Hotel in Las Vegas, Nevada, and she continued to make occasional appearances in Britain. She retired to Leesburg, Florida, where she died on 21 April 1995.

FRANCES GRAY

Sources *Moving picture guide* • *The Independent* (24 April 1995) • *The Times* (24 April 1995) • J. Richards, *Films and British national identity* (1995) • b. cert. • m. cert.
Archives FILM BFI NFTVA, performance footage
Likenesses J. Capstack, photograph, NPG [*see illus.*]

O'Shea, William Henry (1840–1905). *See under* Parnell, Katharine (1845–1921).

Oshere (*fl. c.*680–*c.*693). *See under* Hwicce, kings of the (*act. c.*670–*c.*780).

Oskytel. *See* Oscytel (*d.* 971).

Oslac (*fl. c.*760). *See under* South Saxons, kings of the (*act.* 477–772).

Oslac (*fl.* 963–975), magnate, is of unknown antecedents, but his name could be an Anglicized version of Old Norse Áslákr and it has been conjectured that he came from the eastern Danelaw; his son Thored was living in Cambridgeshire in the time of King Edgar. According to the chronicle attributed to John of Wallingford (a much later text of uncertain authority), the decision to divide Northumbria into two earldoms north and south of the River Tees was taken at a council held by King Edgar at York, on the death of Earl Osulf of Bamburgh. The reason given was the king's unwillingness to let the whole area come to be regarded as any one person's inheritance, 'lest this stir up discord due to the wishes of the Northumbrians to have their ancient liberties restored' (Vaughan, 54). The southern earldom, comprising the area from the Humber to the Tees (the old kingdom of Deira and the later county of York, with its three ridings) was given to Oslac.

Oslac first witnessed as earl three royal charters issued in 963, all relating to the northern Danelaw. Initially he seems to have been of only local importance and he was not in regular attendance at King Edgar's court. The Anglo-Saxon Chronicle (text D) says he was appointed as earl in 966, but the date is almost certainly mistaken. Apart from a group of three doubtful Abingdon charters which claim to be dated 965, Oslac does not witness surviving royal diplomas again until 968, but from that year onwards he became much more prominent nationally and witnessed many of Edgar's charters. John of Wallingford says that together with Ælfsige, bishop of Chester-le-Street, Oslac escorted Kenneth, king of the Scots, to King Edgar's court to receive the cession of Lothian. Roger of Wendover, however, names Earl Eadwulf of Bernicia in the place of Oslac when recording this event, the exact date of which is unknown. Wendover's account is to be preferred, but both earls may have been present on this historic occasion. From 971 until 975, only four ealdormen witness royal charters consistently: Ælfhere of Mercia, Æthelwine of East Anglia, Brihtnoth of Essex, and Oslac of southern Northumbria. All must have held power over wide territories; between them they were entrusted with the distribution of King Edgar's fourth law code over the whole of England. An entry dated 975 in the Anglo-Saxon Chronicle (text D) records that 'the famous earl' Oslac was banished from England. The B text of the chronicle (also in texts A and C) suggests that the banishment was due to the activity of the anti-monastic party after King Edgar's death. The entry concludes: 'The valiant man Oslac was driven from the country, over the tossing waves, the gannet's bath, the homeland of the whale; a grey-haired man, wise and skilled in speech, he was bereft of his lands' (*ASC*, s.a. 975, texts A, B, C).

CYRIL HART

Sources *ASC*, s.a. 966 [text D]; s.a. 975 [texts A, B, C, D] • *AS chart.*, S 712, 712a, 716, 732–4 • R. Vaughan, ed., 'The chronicle attributed to John of Wallingford', *Camden miscellany, XXI*, CS, 3rd ser., 90 (1958) • *Rogeri de Wendover liber qui dicitur flores historiarum*, ed. H. G. Hewlett, 3 vols., Rolls Series, [84] (1886–9) • C. Hart, *The Danelaw* (1992) • D. Whitelock, *History, law and literature in 10th–11th century England* (1981), chap. 3 • *English historical documents*, 1, ed. D. Whitelock (1955), 397–401 • S. Keynes, 'The additions in Old English', *The York gospels*, ed. N. Barker (1986), 81–99

Osler, Abraham Follett (1808–1903), glass manufacturer and meteorologist, was born on 22 March 1808, the eldest son of Thomas Osler, glass manufacturer of Birmingham, and his wife, Fanny Follett. From 1816 to 1824 he was educated at Hazelwood School, near Birmingham, which had been established on progressive lines by Thomas Wright Hill. On leaving school Osler joined his father's firm. In 1831 he took over its management and developed it with energy and ability, especially in the manufacture of fine decorative crystal glass. He married, in 1832, Mary, daughter of Thomas Clark, a Birmingham merchant and manufacturer. Three of their eight children survived him.

In 1835 the Birmingham Philosophical Institution purchased a set of conventional meteorological instruments which required an observer to take readings at certain times. Osler, recognizing the need for reliable self-recording instruments, designed and constructed an apparatus combining a pressure plate anemometer to register wind speed, a vane to register wind direction, and a siphon gauge to register rainfall. The working parts of each instrument were linked to pencils which traced their records continuously on a sheet of paper moved along by clockwork. Earlier attempts to record the meteorological elements had been ineffective, whereas Osler's apparatus, erected at the institution (where it ran for sixty-five years) and publicized at the British Association meeting of 1837, was recognized to be both cheap and effective, its records of considerable value to meteorology. Examples were installed in the temporary magnetic observatories established in 1840 at St Helena, Toronto, and the Cape of Good Hope. Osler continued to improve it and versions of his anemometer were installed at Greenwich observatory in 1841, at London's Royal Exchange, at Plymouth, Inverness, and Liverpool observatory. When Robinson cup anemometers came into use, after 1846, Osler fitted a self-recording mechanism, thus obtaining mean hourly velocities as well as total mileage of wind. Later, records of pressure, direction, velocity, and rainfall were caused to register on the same timed chart.

Encouraged and supported by the British Association, Osler developed the way in which the records were drawn, enhancing their characteristic features and pointing up the interaction of the meteorological elements. Thus he was able to show, by a series of monthly, quarterly, annual, and mean diurnal wind records, the average distribution of winds during each part of the day and for the different seasons. He also demonstrated the similar nature of the mean diurnal wind and temperature records, a feature which Sir David Brewster had independently discovered in 1840. Brewster paid tribute to Osler's labours, describing his results concerning anemometry as the most important since meteorology had taken its place among the physical sciences.

Osler himself urged the establishment of observatories in different latitudes, which he believed would show the importance of the sun in creating atmospheric turbulence. To the British Association meeting in 1865 he showed the interesting and valuable results that could be obtained by close comparisons of air movements recorded at Wrottesley, Liverpool, and Birmingham. On the grand scale, he showed the relation of atmospheric disturbances to the trade wind systems and the effect of the earth's rotation on northerly and southerly wind flows.

Other interests also occupied Osler: after delivering three lectures on chronometry and its history at the Birmingham Philosophical Institution in January 1842 he collected funds and set up a standard clock for Birmingham in front of the institution, and to regulate it he provided a transit instrument and an astronomical clock for its rooftop observatory. Subsequently, without telling anyone, he altered the clock from Birmingham to Greenwich time, and, though the difference was remarked on, one by one church and private clocks were adjusted to match it, while the rest of the country was keeping local time. Craniometry also attracted him: he devised and constructed an accurate instrument for brain measurements, which gave full-sized diagrams of the exact form of the skull.

Osler was elected FRS in 1855. He retired from business in 1876, devoting himself thereafter to scientific pursuits. He was elected fellow of the Royal Meteorological Society only in 1882. Osler was a generous benefactor to his native city, to which he presented a clock and bells, matching those on the law courts in London, for the new municipal buildings. His donations of £5000 to the Birmingham and Midland Institute, and a like sum to Mason's College, later Birmingham University, were anonymous. Osler died at his home, South Bank, Harborne Road, Edgbaston, on 26 April 1903, and was buried at Birmingham.

P. E. Dowson, *rev.* Anita McConnell

Sources *The Times* (28 April 1903), 10c • W. J. R., *PRS*, 75 (1905), 328–34 • [W. J. Russell], *Abraham Follett Osler, 1808–1903* (1904) • W. E. K. Middleton, *Invention of the meteorological instruments* (1969) • personal knowledge (1912) • *Symons's Meteorological Magazine*, 38 (1903–4), 118 • R. J. Charleston, *English glass and the glass used in England, circa 400–1940* (1984) • *Quarterly Journal of the Royal Meteorological Society*, 30 (1904), 238 • d. cert.

Likenesses W. T. Roden, portrait, 1863

Wealth at death £107,385 8*s.* 2*d.*: resworn probate, Feb 1904, *CGPLA Eng. & Wales* (1903)

Osler, Edward (1798–1863), newspaper editor and writer, born at Falmouth, Cornwall, on 30 January 1798, was the eldest son of Edward Osler (*d.* 1832) and his wife, Mary, daughter of Edward Paddy, master of a packet at Falmouth. She died in April 1864, aged ninety-one. Their son's early education was conducted by a Baptist minister, and as Osler was intended for the medical profession he was apprenticed to Carvosso, a surgeon at Falmouth, and trained at Guy's Hospital, subsequently qualifying in 1818 as MRCS. From about 1819 to 1825 he held the appointment of resident house surgeon at the Swansea Infirmary, and was also surgeon to the Swansea house of industry. At Swansea parish church, in February 1821, he married Jennette Powell, the daughter of a local architect. She died at Swansea about 1828, leaving a daughter and a son. During his residence in Swansea Osler became a great friend of Lewis Weston Dillwyn, and consequently enjoyed the advantage of a scientific library. Through his friend Osler was able to send two valuable papers on marine biology to the *Philosophical Transactions* in 1826 and 1832. He was duly elected a fellow of the Linnean Society.

Osler became a surgeon in the navy and visited the West Indies, writing during the passage and his term of duty there the poem 'The Voyage', published in 1830, as well as some papers on natural history. Although raised as a dissenter, Osler became a member of the Church of England, and on his return to England became associated with Prebendary William John Hall, editor of the *Christian Remembrancer*, in the production of *Psalms and Hymns Adapted to the Services of the Church of England* (1836), generally known in its later issues as the *Mitre Hymn-Book*. He contributed to this collection fifteen versions of the Psalms and fifty hymns, some of both sections being adapted from previous authors. He also published various other works on ecclesiastical subjects, and these were consolidated in *Church and King*, published in periodical form in 1836–7.

About this period in his life Osler was on the staff in London and Bath of the Society for the Promotion of Christian Knowledge, but was also taking a deep interest in secular matters. His most important publication, the *Life of Admiral Viscount Exmouth*, came out in 1835, and he drew up a small treatise, the 'Administration and improvement of the poor laws', which was published by the poor-law commission as an appendix to its report.

In 1837 Osler married, at Gluvias, Cornwall, his second wife, Sarah Atkinson of Leeds, and a few years later, about 1841, he was called to Truro in Cornwall as editor of the *Royal Cornwall Gazette*, the leading Conservative journal in the county, and remained in that position until his death. Several articles contributed by him to its columns, such as the 'Packet question: Falmouth or Southampton' and 'History of the Cornwall Railway', were reissued in a separate form. Osler's second wife died at Truro on 31 January 1842, aged thirty-seven, leaving four children. His third wife was Charlotte Free, niece and adopted daughter of Captain Brilton of Stralton Place, Falmouth. Her death occurred at Truro on 19 January 1868; she left no children. Osler died at the Parade, Truro, on 7 March 1863, and was buried at Kenwyn. One of the smaller painted-glass windows in the chancel of that church was erected by his friends to his memory. He was survived by a son and two daughters from his second marriage, his other three children having predeceased him.

W. P. COURTNEY, *rev.* NILANJANA BANERJI

Sources G. C. Boase, *Collectanea Cornubiensia: a collection of biographical and topographical notes relating to the county of Cornwall* (1890) • Boase & Courtney, *Bibl. Corn.* • J. Julian, ed., *A dictionary of hymnology*, rev. edn (1907) • *Royal Cornwall Gazette* (13 March 1863) • Allibone, *Dict.*

Osler, Sir William, baronet (1849–1919), physician, was born on 12 July 1849 at Bond Head, Tecumseh, Ontario, Canada, the sixth son and eighth child of the Revd Featherstone Lake Osler (1805–1895) and Ellen Free Pickton (1806–1906), daughter of a London merchant; both families were of Cornish origin. Featherstone Osler had spent several years in the Royal Navy before deciding to become an Anglican minister; he matriculated in 1833 at St Catharine's College, Cambridge, and following his graduation in 1836 he was ordained a deacon 'for the cure of souls in His Majesty's foreign possessions' and sent with his new bride as a missionary to Upper Canada. Although his initial appointment was for five years, the family stayed and thrived. Featherstone Osler was disappointed that none of his sons followed him into the ministry. However, they included a successful businessman, a lawyer, and a high-court judge.

Canadian childhood William Osler, known as Willie, was originally destined for a career in the church. He was educated at the grammar school in Dundas, Ontario, whence the family had moved in 1857; at nearby Barrie grammar school; and, from January 1866, at Trinity College School, Weston. Although he was always a good student and became a prefect at Trinity, the most distinguishing trait to emerge from his schooldays was a strong proclivity for jokes and pranks which frequently got him into trouble and even led to his expulsion from school in Dundas. The sense of fun and mischief never left him.

In 1867 Osler entered Trinity College, Toronto, where he came under the influence of two men who awakened his passion for natural history and encouraged his switch from divinity to medicine. The Revd W. A. Johnson (1816–1880), founder and warden of Trinity College, was an ardent field naturalist and microscopist; Dr James Bovell (1817–1880) was a devout medical practitioner and teacher at Trinity College and at the proprietary Toronto school of medicine. Under the guidance of these two local worthies, Osler acquired a taste for science. His early publications were on algae, parasites, and other natural historical topics. He also began acquiring medical skills by assisting Bovell and another local practitioner, and enrolled in the Toronto school of medicine. Bovell gave him free access to his fine personal library and encouraged Osler's fascination with gross and microscopic anatomy.

Sir William Osler, baronet (1849–1919), by John Singer Sargent, 1914

In 1870 Bovell returned to the West Indies, where he eventually became ordained, and Osler went to the better medical school at McGill University, Montreal. There he became a favourite of his third formative teacher, Palmer Howard (1823–1889), professor of medicine. Howard fostered Osler's interest in pathology and, like Bovell, shared his private library with his young protégé. Osler's thesis, now lost, analysed twenty post-mortem examinations, and included specimens and microscopic slides. It won Osler a prize, though his general academic record at McGill was good but not outstanding. He graduated MD CM from McGill in 1872.

Encouraged by Howard and the other McGill medical faculty to aspire to a teaching career in Montreal, Osler left in July 1872 for what was to be a two-year postgraduate stay in Europe, financed by his brother. His initial plan was to study ophthalmology and to return as a specialist. He spent his first year in London, attending clinics at University College Hospital and St Thomas's Hospital, and studying physiology and pathology at University College and the Brown Institute with John Scott Burdon-Sanderson, whom he was eventually to succeed as regius professor of physic at Oxford. His flirtation with ophthalmology ended on learning from Howard that three practitioners intended to set up in the specialty in Montreal. He declined an offer to return to McGill to teach materia medica. Instead he continued his study of pathology in Berlin and Vienna; back in Canada in 1874, he was offered a lectureship in the Institutes of Medicine at McGill. At the age of twenty-five, he was younger than some of his students.

Osler spent a decade on the faculty of his alma mater. He taught physiology, histology, and pathology at the medical school, and parasitology at a local veterinary college; he attended patients on the smallpox ward at Montreal General Hospital and gradually developed a private practice. He also began to publish widely, mostly case reports, clinical lectures, or pathological observations. He made friends easily, especially with the students, whom he could formally counsel after 1877, when he was made registrar of the medical school. The following year he was elected attending physician at Montreal General; he celebrated his success by spending the summer in London, where he passed his membership of the Royal College of Physicians. He returned to London with Palmer Howard in 1881 for the Seventh International Medical Congress, which attracted most of the medical élites of Europe. In 1884 he went back to Germany, where medical thinking had been transformed by the work of Robert Koch and others on bacteriology. Osler was cautiously receptive of the germ theory, but his own approach to disease continued to be clinical and pathological.

Teaching medicine in the United States While in Germany, Osler was invited to apply for the chair of clinical medicine at the University of Pennsylvania in the USA. He was interviewed by the doyen of Philadelphia physicians, Silas Weir Mitchell, who happened to be in Europe also. Mitchell and Osler immediately recognized each other as kindred spirits, and Mitchell's enthusiastic recommendation smoothed the way for Osler's move to the conservative and inbred medical community in Philadelphia. It offered even more outlets than Montreal for a man of Osler's clubbable instincts, and Osler quickly became part of Philadelphia's medical and cultural life. He took an active interest in the fine historical collections in the library of the College of Physicians of Philadelphia, and regularly attended the meetings of several local and national medical societies. He had been elected president of the Canadian Medical Association during his last year in Montreal; his presidential address in 1885, entitled 'The growth of a profession', elaborated themes that were to preoccupy him for the rest of his life. These included the notions that solidarity within the medical profession was an unmitigated good, that patients had nothing to fear from a powerful, well-educated, and self-regulating profession, and that the true future of medicine lay in the wise application of science. Earlier that year Osler delivered the Goulstonian lectures to the Royal College of Physicians in London. He was elected a fellow of the college in 1883, his first eligible year. He chose as his subject malignant endocarditis, a fatal disease that lent itself to close analysis of both its clinical and pathological dimensions. He also worked on diseases of the blood, the nervous system, typhoid fever, and, a recurring topic of interest to him, pneumonia.

During his Philadelphia years, Osler continued to perform frequent autopsies, but his skills as a clinical teacher also flourished. He was an excellent diagnostician with an admirable bedside manner and an ability to put patients at their ease. Although physically slight and possessed of an unimpressive, high-pitched voice, he nevertheless always commanded centre-stage in the ward or clinic. Medical students adored him, and he always had a few special favourites, whom he called his 'latchkeyers', students to whom he gave the key to his house so that they could use his personal library whenever they wanted. He was one of the founding members, in 1885, of the Association of American Physicians, devoted to improving the standards of medical practice and education. His private practice also grew, his consultations sometimes taking him as far afield as Chicago, Montreal, or Maine. Many of those he treated were doctors or medical students, who seemed to gravitate to him, but his patients included an increasing number of the rich and famous, including Walt Whitman, Sir Charles Tupper, and several occupants of the White House.

If Osler hesitated before leaving Montreal for Philadelphia, he had no difficulty accepting the call to Johns Hopkins in Baltimore. Johns Hopkins University had been opened in 1876, but the medical school and hospital were delayed as the building plans were complicated and the money from the original bequest of Mr Hopkins began to run short. The medical facilities were eagerly anticipated, expected as they were to incorporate the latest scientific advances in both patient care and student education. Osler agreed in 1888 to let his name be put forward as physician-in-chief at the hospital and professor of medicine at the medical school. The formal offer was made in September 1888, which allowed Osler to wind down his Philadelphia commitments and move to Baltimore in May 1889, in time for the official opening of the hospital. The medical school still required further endowment; this was eventually secured, somewhat controversially, from four wealthy women who attached the condition that the medical school admit women medical students. Osler himself believed that nursing was a more suitable occupation for women, but he was prepared to accept them into the medical profession. One of the benefactors, Mary Garrett, further stipulated the even more daring requirement that the medical school admit no one without an undergraduate degree. Despite fears that few students, male or female, would turn up, the faculty agreed to the conditions, and the school was finally opened in 1893.

During his first four years in Baltimore, Osler had relatively few duties. The routine work in the hospital being performed by his residents, he was free to devote more time to writing. The principal result was his *Principles and Practice of Medicine*, published to great acclaim in 1892. Dedicated to his early teachers, Johnson, Bovell, and Howard, it was one of the last single-authored textbooks to cover the whole of medicine. Although Osler later complained that effecting the revisions for subsequent editions was a millstone around his neck, it turned a national physician into an international figure. It was eventually translated into French, German, Spanish, and Chinese and went through eight editions during Osler's lifetime, the eighth (1912) with the help of Thomas McCrae, who continued to edit subsequent editions after Osler's death.

The Principles finished, Osler promptly proposed marriage to Grace Linzee Revere Gross (1854–1928), the wealthy widow of a prominent Philadelphia surgeon whom Osler had cared for during his final illness. Their first child, born almost exactly nine months after their marriage on 7 May 1892, died shortly after birth. They doted on their only other child, Edward Revere (1895–1917), and never really recovered from his death in the First World War. Osler himself loved children and always had many young friends, who brought out his natural sense of fun and mischief. Although Revere was never a particularly studious boy, he and his father had a close relationship, cemented by frequent fishing trips together after Revere (dubbed Isaak Walton junior by Osler) developed a passion for angling.

Osler's years at Johns Hopkins were the busiest of his life. Under his guidance there emerged the first organized clinical unit in the English-speaking world, containing the best features of English schools and German clinics. Osler was the most visible of the four foundation professors at the medical school who were famously commemorated in John Singer Sargent's painting, and the early success of the school owed much to his energy and clinical teaching. He continued to publish clinical papers at an astonishing rate: in 1897, for instance, he wrote articles *inter alia* on mitral stenosis, gallstones, typhoid fever, tics, tuberculosis, cretinism, leprosy, pneumonia, and malaria. He was a frequent contributor to *Johns Hopkins Hospital Bulletin* and *Johns Hopkins Hospital Reports*, periodicals with which he was intimately associated during his Hopkins years. At the same time he relied on his associates to keep things running smoothly during his frequent absences from Baltimore. These were occasioned by his extensive consulting practice, his increasing demand as a speaker, his active participation in national and international medical meetings, and his regular trips to Europe. He was an ardent spokesman on behalf of public health, devoting a good deal of time to efforts designed to control tuberculosis.

As his income from royalties and his practice increased, Osler began to devote more time and money to building his library. He had developed a love for the writings of Sir Thomas Browne as a student, and he always made time each day for non-medical reading. This influenced his own literary style which, especially for his public addresses at commencements, medical gatherings, and the like, was memorably littered with allusions to great authors of the past. His collection of addresses aimed at medical students and young practitioners, *Aequanimitas* (1904), achieved instant popularity, was twice reprinted with additional speeches, and long served as a formal presentation gift to graduates of many medical schools. Two such public occasions were especially controversial. Osler's Ingersol lecture at Harvard, delivered in May 1904 and entitled 'Science and immortality', argued for the separate realms of faith and science, before an audience which expected him to reveal the depths of his own Christian faith. Although Osler always quoted liberally from the Bible when the situation demanded, he became an infrequent churchgoer in his later years, and carefully hid whatever faith he retained from public view.

'The fixed period', his farewell address at Johns Hopkins in February 1905, inaccurately described Anthony Trollope's short story of the same name, and argued that men's best work is done before they reach forty and that perhaps it would be better for the world were they chloroformed at sixty. Although he later insisted that he was being light-hearted, the newspapers interpreted his speech as advocating forced euthanasia for the elderly. It was a curious way for a man in his sixth decade to end his American career and head for what he and his wife hoped would be a much quieter life at Oxford.

Regius chair at Oxford As a Canadian, Osler had always felt at least half-English, and he valued his association with the Royal College of Physicians and the Royal Society, to which he was elected a fellow in 1898. He had already turned down an approach to go to the University of Edinburgh, but the regius chair of medicine vacated by J. S. Burdon-Sanderson's retirement was too tempting to a man visibly tired by the hectic pace of his later American years. The chair carried prestige but little else: a modest salary of £400 per annum and few duties, since Oxford did not possess a clinical school. Osler was especially pleased that the regius chair carried a studentship at Christ Church, college of John Locke and Robert Burton, two of his favourite authors. He was already financially secure, and although he could not avoid seeing some private patients he was more in need of leisure than income.

In fact Osler's English years were busy, though more as a medical statesman and literary figure than an active clinician. He and Grace purchased a big Victorian house at 13 Norham Gardens (which Osler nicknamed the Open Arms, so frequently did they entertain). Books much preoccupied him, not only his own growing library, whose cataloguing he began, but the Bodleian Library of Oxford University, where he became an honorary curator, and the Oxford University Press, which he served as a delegate. He was in constant demand as an eponymous lecturer, delivering the Harveian lecture and Lumleian lectures to the Royal College of Physicians, the Linacre lecture at St John's College, Cambridge, and the Silliman lectures at Yale. The last, entitled *The Growth of Modern Medicine*, delivered in 1913 but not published until after his death, were typical in their historical focus and their concern with assessing the problems and prospects of modern medicine.

Although he did much, Osler also learned how to say no. He declined the invitation to stand for parliament, to serve on the royal commission on vivisection, or to become president of several medical organizations. His testimony to the Haldane commission on medical education encouraged the eventual establishment of academic medical, surgical, and obstetric units in some British medical schools, and he was instrumental in founding, in 1906, the Association of Physicians of Great Britain and Ireland, modelled on the American group. At the same time he was suspicious of what was called the 'full time' system, whereby academic clinicians would devote themselves entirely to research and teaching. He developed a close relationship with his brother regius at Cambridge,

Thomas Clifford Allbutt, and became the figurehead founding editor of the *Quarterly Journal of Medicine*. He edited (also with the help of Thomas McCrae) a massive, seven-volume *System of Medicine*, and gently encouraged the development of science and medicine teaching at Oxford. No one was surprised when he was created a baronet in 1911.

The First World War proved cataclysmic to the Oslers. Osler devoted a good deal of time to war work, both as a consultant to military hospitals and as a participant in relief agencies. The influx of friends and old students serving in the Canadian army medical corps kept the Open Arms busy. Osler's former surgical colleague at Johns Hopkins and future biographer, Harvey Cushing, joined an American volunteer medical unit; by coincidence, he was at Revere's bedside when Osler's son died of shrapnel wounds in August 1917. Osler consoled himself increasingly with the planned catalogue of his library, which he bequeathed to McGill. The catalogue was finished long after Osler's own death, by his nephew W. W. Francis, the first Osler librarian.

Osler's seventieth birthday, in July 1919, was celebrated widely, and included the publication of a two-volume Festschrift and a special issue of *Johns Hopkins Hospital Bulletin*. 'Pity I had not died—fine obituary flavor', he remarked. His own health had begun to fail during the latter years of the war, as he became subject to frequent pulmonary infections. One of these later in 1919 turned into a pulmonary abscess, from which he died on 29 December at his home in Norham Gardens, Oxford.

Reputation At the time of his death Osler was without doubt the most famous and revered anglophone doctor in the world. His reputation persists, despite the fact that he made no fundamental discoveries. He was, in his own terms, a transmitter rather than a transformer. The persistence of the Osler myth may be attributed to at least three factors.

First, Osler had a remarkably attractive personality. He had an infectious sense of humour, nowhere better seen than in the series of articles, some scurrilous, some semi-serious, which he published under the pseudonym Egerton Yorrick Davis, MD, Late US Army Surgeon. At the same time he could cope brilliantly with death and the dying, even if sometimes, like Uncle Toby, he whistled that he would not weep. Second, he was an outstanding teacher of clinical medicine who trained many of the academic leaders of the next generation. In an age when science increasingly influenced medical thinking and practice, Osler, with his commitment to the humanities, seemed to combine the science and art of medicine in a perfect mix. Third, he developed a graceful prose style which could make the commonplace sound profound, while espousing a vision of the medical profession which resonated with colleagues. Osler's vision of a literate, autonomous profession placing the needs of patients and of society more generally above those of self-interest seems idealistic and naïve in the modern world; it still finds a ready audience. W. F. Bynum

Sources H. Cushing, *The life of William Osler* (1925) • *Bulletin* [International Association of Medical Museums], 9 (1926) [*Sir William Osler memorial number: appreciations and reminiscences*, ed. M. E. Abbott] • M. Bliss, *William Osler: a life in medicine* (1999) • J. A. Barondess, J. P. McGovern, and C. G. Roland, eds., *The persisting Osler* (1985) • J. A. Barondess and C. G. Roland, eds., *The persisting Osler 2* (1994) • C. S. Bryan, *Osler: inspirations from a great physician* (1997) • R. L. Golden and C. G. Roland, eds., *Sir William Osler: an annotated bibliography with illustrations* (1997) • E. F. Nation, *An up-dated checklist of Osleriana* (1988) • W. Osler, *Aequanimitas*, 2nd edn (1922) • W. Osler, *An Alabama student and other biographical essays* (1908) • *DAB* • *The Times* (30 Dec 1919)

Archives Duke U., letters and papers • Johns Hopkins University, Baltimore, corresp. and papers • King's Lond., corresp. and papers • McGill University, Montreal, Osler Library of the History of Medicine, corresp. and papers • RCP Lond., papers • U. Cal., San Francisco, papers • University of British Columbia Library, Woodward Biomedical Library, letters • University of Toronto, papers • Wellcome L., letters • Yale U., papers | Wellcome L., letters to Sir Edward Sharpey-Schafer

Likenesses J. S. Sargent, oils, exh. RA 1906, Johns Hopkins University, Baltimore, Maryland • S. S. Thomas, oils, 1908, Christ Church Oxf. • J. S. Sargent, drawing, 1914, College of Physicians, Philadelphia [*see illus.*] • J. Russell & Sons, photograph, NPG; repro. in *National Photographic Record*, vol. 1

Wealth at death £15,865 7*s*. 5*d*.: probate, 20 April 1920, *CGPLA Eng. & Wales*

Osman, Efendi [*formerly* William Thomson] (*b.* before **1800**, *d.* **1835**), guide to travellers in Egypt, was originally William Thomson, a native of Scotland. Details of his life, gleaned from passing remarks by the many travellers who knew him in Cairo, are scant and occasionally contradictory. This sometimes leads to confusion, as with Osman's original identity: he signed his name both as William Thomson and as William Taylor, and he has been misidentified by others as Donald Thomson and Donald Donald.

Thomson enlisted in the 78th highlanders, a regiment that was sent to Egypt in 1807 as part of an unsuccessful expedition to suppress Mehmet Ali's newly established regime. Captured in a disastrous rear-guard action at Rosetta, Thomson was sold into slavery; he was subsequently compelled to profess Islam, forcibly circumcised, and given the name Osman. Though his initial years of servitude were harsh, his skills, including a reputation for medical knowledge, earned him better treatment. When he was making the *hajj*, or pilgrimage, in Arabia in 1814–15 Osman met the celebrated Swiss traveller John Louis Burckhardt, who later persuaded the British consul-general in Egypt, Henry Salt, to arrange Osman's freedom. A good businessman, Osman took an inheritance from a former master and managed it so successfully as to achieve affluence. He rose high in Egypt's élite Turkish society and was accorded the title of efendi, or gentleman. Hence it is not surprising that he refused to return to Scotland, though many of his British acquaintances encouraged him to do so. Osman also became a *dragoman*, or interpreter, at the British consulate in Cairo, but his life-style, manners, and religion remained thoroughly Eastern. He had several wives, sometimes concurrently, but no details of them are known.

What brought Osman to the attention of so many

British travellers in Egypt was his function as an intermediary between them and Egyptian society. As increasing numbers of British arrived in Egypt during the early nineteenth century, they frequently sought out Osman for aid in dealing with the myriad aspects of Eastern life, there being scant support services for travellers in those days. His help, for which he received commissions, was considered essential: 'In short', one traveller wrote, 'nothing is to be accomplished without Osman, who keeps the rogues in order' (Hay, fol. 37). Osman performed a great service to scholarship by helping the informal group of British orientalists and Egyptologists that assembled in Egypt during the early nineteenth century, a group that included Edward William Lane, Sir Gardner Wilkinson, Robert Hay, Joseph Bonomi, Frederick Catherwood, James Burton, Algernon Percy (Baron Prudhoe, who later became the fourth duke of Northumberland), Major Orlando Felix, and others. Without Osman, it is difficult to see how they could have accomplished as much as they did.

Osman Efendi died from dysentery on 8 November 1835 at his home in Suq al-Khushab, Cairo. His adherence to Islam had always fascinated his British acquaintances, many of whom doubted his sincerity, but in his final hours Osman refused Christian attention and died as a Muslim. He was buried shortly after his death in Cairo's Bab al-Nasir cemetery in the grave of his friend J. L. Burckhardt. JASON THOMPSON

Sources J. Thompson, 'Osman Effendi: a Scottish convert to Islam in early nineteenth-century Egypt', *Journal of World History*, 5 (1994), 99–123 • W. R. Dawson and E. P. Uphill, *Who was who in Egyptology*, 3rd edn, rev. M. L. Bierbrier (1995) • J. Thompson, *Sir Gardner Wilkinson and his circle* (1992) • A. K. Elwood, *Narrative of a journey overland from England*, 2 vols. (1830) • R. R. Madden, *Travels in Turkey, Egypt, and Palestine in 1824, 1825, 1826, and 1827*, 2 vols. (1829) • J. Madox, *Excursions in the Holy Land, Egypt, Nubia, Syria*, 2 vols. (1834) • J. M. Sherer, *Scenes and impressions in Egypt and Italy* (1824) • W. H. Yates, *The modern history and condition of Egypt*, 2 vols. (1843) • J. Carne, *Recollections of travels in the East* (1830) • *The Courier* (28 Dec 1835) • R. Hay, diary, AM Oxf.

Wealth at death wealthy; owned several houses in Cairo

Osman, Alfred Henry (1864–1930), promoter of pigeon racing, was born at 4 Albert Villas, Northumberland Park, Tottenham, London, on 12 July 1864, the second son in the large family of John Jonas Osman, civil servant, and his wife, Sarah Ann, *née* Patience, of Bushey, Hertfordshire. A pigeon fancier from youth, Osman overcame strong parental objections and pursued his hobby. His father in particular 'looked upon pigeon racing, like many others in those days, as a most degrading sport' (*Racing Pigeon*, 5 April 1930, 214). Young Osman nevertheless built his own loft in the garden of the family home and almost as soon as he left school he began writing about pigeons, contributing to *The Stock-Keeper*, *Homing News*, and the *Fanciers' Gazette*; from 1908 until his death he was a regular contributor to the *News of the World*.

Osman married in 1889 Ada Gertrude Jones, with whom he had a son and a daughter. He began his working life as a solicitor's clerk and pursued a successful career in law, but his true devotion was to pigeon racing. He would regularly rise before dawn and walk miles in order to toss the birds for a short homeward training flight. He conducted short-course 'flapping races' between pairs of birds on Wanstead flats and sometimes raced birds down the long city streets, where their relative agility became the subject of serious debate and betting. Later he became a chief promoter of the long-distance races that most people associate with the sport—the 500, 600, and 700 mile events—but in the early days races were held over short distances. Osman was fortunate in having as an employer an Admiralty barrister who was a devotee, and he was thus able to give more time than would have been usual to the sport. His first club was the Essex Homing Society, and in 1896 he founded the London North Road Federation, proudly serving as its first president.

As well as being a leading clubman, Osman was also one of the sport's great breeders. His world-famous Osman strain of racing pigeon began in spring 1888 with the birth of Old Billy, who 'from early youth upwards demonstrated that he was an uncommonly intelligent pigeon' (*Racing Pigeon*, 5 April 1930, 213). Old Billy did not enjoy special success as a racer but 'imparted wonderful homing qualities to his children' (ibid., 213). One of these, a hen called Mumpy, flew 200 miles in dreadful weather in a little over fourteen hours in 1891. Another descendant was Forlorn Hope, born in 1902, 'truly one of the pluckiest and most remarkable pigeons the sport has produced' (ibid., 214). A highly successful racer, it beat about 3000 other birds in the race from Newcastle in 1907, with a velocity of 806 yards per minute into a strong wind.

Through the sport Osman became friendly with John William Logan, the long-serving member of parliament for Market Harborough, and in 1897 they formed the National Flying Club, the object of which was to stage 'grand national' pigeon races. In 1899 Edward VII, then prince of Wales, won the club's race from Lerwick, with the duke of York, later George V, coming third, the successful royal birds having been trained at Sandringham. A trophy was subsequently presented to the club by the king to be competed for annually. In 1898 Osman and Logan, with the help of friends, founded the *Racing Pigeon* weekly in a small office in Temple Chambers, near Victoria Embankment. The first issue appeared that April and Osman, who was editor-in-chief, wrote from the outset the popular column 'Food for novices' under the pen-name Squills. Pigeon-fancying had great appeal for working men, and the pigeon was often called the poor man's racehorse. In fact the pigeon fancier had much greater contact with his animal than did the average racehorse (or indeed greyhound) owner, and he was to be considered 'not only owner but trainer, breeder and even jockey as well as stable lad' (C. Osman, *Racing Pigeons*, viii).

Amid an atmosphere of 'spy mania' engendered by the outbreak of war in August 1914, severe restrictions were placed on the movement of pigeons. Some birds had their wings clipped, while others were liberated and their lofts sealed, forcing them to fend for themselves in the wild. Osman helped to persuade the Home Office to introduce a permit system under the defence of the realm regulations, whereby owners were allowed to carry out limited training of their birds, thus preserving the lives of many thousands of racing and fancy pigeon. Homing birds were soon enlisted in the war effort. In November 1914 Osman was consulted about the possibility of employing pigeons on board trawlers and minesweepers at sea so that they could send reports to the Admiralty. He devised a scheme involving pigeon fanciers in coastal regions and the government pigeon service was born, later organized and controlled by F. Romer and Osman's son, Major William Osman. Not all the signals sent were urgent, and one skipper wrote: 'All well; having beef pudding for dinner' (A. H. Osman, 21). But other messages told of mines and even Zeppelin attacks, and the service grew to the point that the Royal Naval Air Service employed pigeons in all its machines reconnoitring over the sea.

Early in 1915 the War Office needed pigeons and men for the signal service in France, as well as for a home forces pigeon service as part of the defence against invasion. Osman accepted an army commission as captain (he was later styled lieutenant-colonel) but took no pay for his work, which involved setting up the home forces pigeon service and overseeing recruitment both of men and pigeons for the army. Towards the end of the war about 22,000 pigeons were at work on the French and Italian fronts, looked after by 400 'pigeoneers' in the British army carrier-pigeon service. In 1918 an air force carrier-pigeon service was set up, with lofts in every major aerodrome.

Osman was seconded to the intelligence corps to organize the use of pigeons in covert operations. Pigeons were dropped by parachute in baskets behind enemy lines with messages in French and Flemish, appealing for intelligence information. The obvious problem of enemy interception led to agents being parachuted behind the lines with a basket of pigeons attached to their backs. Osman recalled that the scheme was a success: 'except that at the outset great difficulty was experienced in getting the man to jump from the plane' (A. H. Osman, 48). This problem was solved by the invention of a collapsible seat which gave way when the pilot pulled a lever, allowing the pigeon-carrying agent 'gracefully to parachute to earth' (ibid., 48). At the end of the war more than 500 certificates for meritorious service were awarded to fanciers whose pigeons had served in the government pigeon service. Osman was appointed OBE for his efforts, and in January 1920 the National Homing Union presented him with a gift raised by subscription.

Osman later wrote a history of the carrier-pigeon service during the First World War, published in 1928 by the Racing Pigeon Publishing Company Limited. This imprint produced a number of 1*s.* and 2*s.* paperbacks aimed at pigeon fanciers. Osman's titles, some of which appeared under his pen-name Squills, included *The Production of a Strain* (1924), *The Secrets of Long-Distance Pigeon Racing* (1924), and *Pigeons and How to Keep Them* (1925). He used his editorials in the *Racing Pigeon* to promote long-distance racing, notably the San Sebastian, which he regarded as the sport's blue ribbon event. In the July 1924 race more than 600 birds participated: the successful ones would be highly valued as blood stock, and this race above all others emphasized the monetary aspect of the sport, which was undeniably one of its attractions. But there was some feeling in the pigeon-racing fraternity that long-distance races, and in particular those that involved a 'compulsory night out', meant cruelty to the birds, which were forced either to fly an exhausting distance non-stop or else to forage for food and water using skills that had, it was argued, largely been bred out of them. Osman, who had done all that he could to prevent cruelty in the sport, maintained that the birds were capable of racing the long distances and he pointed to the high rate of eventual return as proof.

Osman, who suffered ill health towards the end of his life, died at his home, Apsley House, 95 Cambridge Park, Wanstead, Essex, on 30 March 1930, and was survived by his wife and children. After his death the *Racing Pigeon* continued to be edited by his son and, later, his grandson, Colin, who published a comprehensive guide to the sport, *Racing Pigeons* (1957; reissued 1996). MARK POTTLE

Sources *The Times* (9 July 1925) · *The Times* (11 July 1925) · *The Times* (15 July 1925) · *The Times* (1 April 1930), 11e · *Racing Pigeon* (5 April 1930) · A. H. Osman, *Pigeons in the Great War: a complete history of the carrier-pigeon service during the Great War, 1914–1918* (1928) · C. Osman, *Racing pigeons: a practical guide to the sport* (1957) · C. A. E. Osman, *The widowhood book* (1952) · A. O'Hagan, 'Diary', *London Review of Books*, 18/24 (12 Dec 1996), 29 · b. cert. · d. cert. · *CGPLA Eng. & Wales* (1930)

Likenesses photograph (with George VI as duke of York), repro. in *Racing Pigeon*, 215 · portrait, repro. in *Racing Pigeon*, 213

Wealth at death £20,692 6*s.* 9*d.*: probate, 29 April 1930, *CGPLA Eng. & Wales*

Osmund (*fl.* 765–770x72). *See under* South Saxons, kings of the (*act.* 477–772).

Osmund (*d.* 805x11), bishop of London, succeeded Bishop Heathoberht, who died in 801, and was probably consecrated by Archbishop Æthelheard on his return from Rome in 802 or 803. He attended the council of 'Clofesho' in October 803, where he subscribed acts concerning the rights of the sees of Worcester and Canterbury and an ordinance against the appointment of laymen as heads of monasteries, and was attended by an abbot, three priests, and one other. He was also present at a synod held at 'Acleah' in August 805. His successor, Æthelnoth, appears as bishop in 811.

WILLIAM HUNT, *rev.* MARIOS COSTAMBEYS

Sources W. de G. Birch, ed., *Cartularium Saxonicum*, 1 (1885) · E. B. Fryde and others, eds., *Handbook of British chronology*, 3rd edn, Royal Historical Society Guides and Handbooks, 2 (1986)

Osmund [St Osmund] (*d.* **1099**), bishop of Salisbury, canonized in 1457, was the founder of a community of canons at the newly established see of Salisbury, and, after his death, came to be regarded as the founder also of the widely influential Salisbury liturgy, the use of Sarum.

Almost nothing is known of Osmund's family, date of birth, place of origin, or education, although it is generally assumed that he was of continental birth and came to England after the conquest. An *avunculus*, Arestaldus, was included in the names listed for commemoration in the martyrology that John Leland saw at Salisbury on the eve of the Reformation. Fifteenth-century tradition claimed that Osmund was William I's nephew, the son of an otherwise unrecorded sister; she and her husband are named variously as either Isabella and Henry, count of Séez (Jones and Macray, 373), or Margaret and Lucillus (Oxford, Jesus College, MS 114, fol. 27v). No support for such claims can be found in earlier sources; the bull of canonization of 1 January 1457 refers in less specific terms to Osmund as 'stirpe regia, ac etiam ducali nobilissima ortus prosapia' ('Of royal lineage, and indeed born into the most noble ducal family)' Malden, 227).

Before his elevation to the episcopate, Osmund was one of William I's chaplains, and from 1070 until 1078 was royal chancellor. His term as chancellor is important for the virtual abandonment of the use of the vernacular for royal writs, and the adoption of Latin as the usual language for royal executive and administrative instruments. Although relinquishing the post on becoming bishop of Salisbury in 1078, Osmund continued to be involved in royal administration during the reigns of both William I and William II. On 1 December 1088, for example, he summoned the disgraced William of St Calais, then awaiting permission to begin his exile, to attend the king's court that Christmas at London. He also allowed the scribal resources available to him as bishop of Salisbury to be drawn upon for secular administrative purposes: scribes who participated in the production of books for the community at Salisbury were also involved in copying geld accounts for the south-west, datable to 1086, and parts of the Exon Domesday, the draft return for the south-western circuit of the Domesday inquiry. Although no explicit evidence survives of Osmund's participation in the Domesday Survey, his previous experience as royal chancellor, and the known involvement of Salisbury scribes, make it highly probable that he too was involved, perhaps as a circuit commissioner.

Osmund's bishopric of Salisbury comprised the recently united sees of Sherborne and Ramsbury (Dorset, Wiltshire, and Berkshire). In 1075 his predecessor, Hermann, had been granted permission to move the see to Old Sarum, an episcopal manor and the site of a royal castle close to the present city of Salisbury, but he had been able to do little more than initiate the building of a cathedral, before dying on 20 February 1078. Osmund, therefore, came to be viewed as the true founder of the cathedral and its chapter. He introduced a community of canons, probably in 1089, and, in his foundation charter of 1091, granted an endowment comprising a substantial proportion of the episcopal lands. The cathedral, built just outside the inner fortifications of the royal castle, was completed in 1092, and was dedicated on 5 April 1092.

Rather less is known than used to be thought about the character of the community that Osmund established. The so-called *Institutio Osmundi*, purporting to date from 1091, which describes a secular cathedral chapter with a hierarchy of dignitaries and canons holding territorial prebends, and which appeared to establish a blueprint followed by other non-monastic cathedral chapters in England, has been demonstrated to have been a later compilation, begun in the mid-twelfth century and subsequently revised and elaborated. In his foundation charter, Osmund mentioned neither dignitaries nor prebends, but stated merely that he had made his grant to the canons *illis viventibus canonice* ('to those living canonically'; Greenway, 98). Although neither here nor elsewhere did Osmund spell out what he meant by 'living canonically', the early community appears to have had a less hierarchical structure, and to have led a more fully common life, than became the norm for secular cathedral chapters, including Salisbury, during the twelfth century. Evidence of communal activity is provided by the large number of manuscript books produced at Salisbury during the late eleventh century, the work of numerous scribes, often working in close collaboration. Some of these scribes may well have been canons, since William of Malmesbury records that Osmund himself copied and even bound books for his community. It has also been suggested that the assignation of a prebend to the bishop in the mid-twelfth century (a practice in England unique to Salisbury), may have had its roots in Osmund's own regular participation in the ministry of the high altar in the cathedral, since the income of the prebend was derived from a portion of the oblations of the high altar (*Fasti Angl., 1066–1300*, xxv).

The content and appearance of the books produced at Salisbury in the late eleventh century lend weight to William of Malmesbury's claim that Osmund's canons were renowned for the fame of their learning, and that he was able to attract learned clerks from far and wide. The books comprise one of the first substantial collections of patristic texts to have been formed in England since the eighth century, and bear witness to a level of interest in biblical and theological scholarship comparable with that of the leading centres of learning on the continent. The styles of handwriting suggest that those who wrote the books had come to Salisbury from many different centres, both in England and on the continent, while the textual affiliations of some of the works copied suggest direct contact with religious houses not only in Normandy but elsewhere in northern France, the Low Countries, and even further afield. Osmund's personal influence may well have been instrumental in acquiring from the continent exemplars of texts then rare in England.

William of Malmesbury drew attention to the fame not only of the Salisbury canons' intellectual prowess but also of their singing. Unfortunately the late-eleventh-century books which survive from Salisbury shed no light on the early history of the Salisbury liturgy with which Osmund has long been associated. By at least the mid-fourteenth century he had come to be regarded as the author of the Salisbury *Ordinale* and *Consuetudinarium* which summarize the procedural and liturgical custom of Salisbury, and which act as a general guide to the use of Sarum. But both texts were compiled a century after Osmund's death; an absence of contemporary evidence makes it very difficult to prove what part he may have played in laying the foundations for the customs that they describe.

The details of Osmund's activities within his diocese are also very poorly recorded; his only surviving *acta* are his episcopal profession to Archbishop Lanfranc and his foundation charter. He seems to have been in the forefront of efforts in England to exert episcopal authority more rigorously over the diocesan clergy and laity. Contemporary annotations in the late-eleventh-century Salisbury copy of the canon law compilation known as the *Collectio Lanfranci* (Salisbury Cathedral, MS 78), reveal a deep concern for the proper conduct of diocesan bishops and for matters of clerical discipline, and may well reflect Osmund's own concerns. He was certainly known as a stern disciplinarian, dealing harshly with those who failed to meet the high standards that he set himself. He promoted the cult of his most illustrious predecessor as bishop of the region, St Aldhelm, by attending the retranslation of his remains at Malmesbury, and acquiring a relic of the saint's left arm. This activity, reported in some detail by William of Malmesbury in his life of Aldhelm, may have been the source for Ranulf Higden's claim that Osmund *dictavit* a life of Aldhelm (*Polychronicon*, 7.294).

Osmund died in December 1099 after a long, lingering illness. His death was recorded by John of Worcester as Saturday 3 December, but the bull of canonization of 1457 gives 4 December, which was then assigned as his feast day. He was buried at Old Sarum. A new and more elaborate tomb was constructed in the second half of the twelfth century, which was relocated in 1226 to the newly completed lady chapel of the present Salisbury Cathedral.

Osmund's contemporaries acknowledged his outstanding qualities of holiness and moral probity. Unlike some of his fellow bishops, especially those who had been promoted from the royal curia as he himself had been, Osmund was noted for his chastity, for his lack of greed or worldly ambition, and for not extorting heavy exactions from the monasteries within his diocese. Faricius, monk of Malmesbury and later abbot of Abingdon, both monasteries within the Salisbury diocese, referred to him as 'an orthodox bishop, a man of humility, worthy to be honoured and praised for his wisdom and holiness' (*Patrologia Latina*, 89.84). His humility was also noted by Eadmer who recorded that Osmund was one of only two bishops who begged forgiveness of Anselm for their failure to take his part against William II at the Council of Rockingham in 1095. Apart from a reference to the accusation of parsimony which William of Malmesbury subsequently erased, the only criticism levelled against Osmund came from the pen of the hagiographer Goscelin, who had been a frequent associate of Osmund's predecessor, Bishop Hermann. He did not find the new incumbent so welcoming, but referred to Osmund bitterly as 'the king who knew not Joseph' (Exodus 1:8), and claimed that he was forced to leave by 'viperine envy and the barbarity of a step-father' (Goscelin, *Liber confortatorius*, 29, 82). It is not known what provoked this enmity.

Osmund's reputation for holiness and for instituting the cathedral chapter and its customs grew steadily from the middle of the twelfth century onwards, gathering pace during the early thirteenth century, and culminating in the first petition for his canonization in 1228. The earliest datable miracle at the site of his tomb dates from between 1155 and 1165, about the time that the *Institutio* associated with his name was first compiled, while the earliest surviving reference to him as 'saint' occurs in the treasurer's inventory of 1214. Although the commission ordered by Gregory IX on 30 May 1228 to inquire into Osmund's life and miracles came to nothing, Osmund's tomb continued to be venerated and, as the fame and influence of the cathedral and its customs spread throughout the province of Canterbury, so too was his name increasingly associated with the texts that set out the use of Sarum. Further unsuccessful petitions for his canonization were made during the episcopacies of Ralph Erghum (1375–88), Robert Hallum (1407–17), and John Chaundeler (1417–26). A final petition was submitted in 1452, which, after various delays, resulted in Calixtus III's bull of 1 January 1457 which formally proclaimed Osmund a saint. TERESA WEBBER

Sources *Willelmi Malmesbiriensis monachi de gestis pontificum Anglorum libri quinque*, ed. N. E. S. A. Hamilton, Rolls Series, 52 (1870) • *Fasti Angl., 1066–1300*, [Salisbury] • D. Greenway, 'The false *Institutio* of St Osmund', *Tradition and change: essays in honour of Marjorie Chibnall*, ed. D. Greenway, C. Holdsworth, and J. Sayers (1985), 77–101 • T. Webber, *Scribes and scholars at Salisbury Cathedral, c.1075–c.1125* (1992) • A. R. Malden, ed., *The canonization of Saint Osmund* (1901) • Fabricius of Malmesbury, 'Vita S. Aldhelmi', ed. J. A. Giles, *Patrologia Latina*, 89 (1850), 63–84 • C. H. Talbot, ed., 'The *Liber confortatorius* of Goscelin of Saint Bertin', *Studia Anselmia*, 37 (1955) • *Polychronicon Ranulphi Higden monachi Cestrensis*, ed. C. Babington and J. R. Lumby, 9 vols., Rolls Series, 41 (1865–86) • *Eadmeri Historia novorum in Anglia*, ed. M. Rule, Rolls Series, 81 (1884) • W. H. Rich Jones and W. Dunn Macray, eds., *Charters and documents illustrating the history of the cathedral, city, and diocese of Salisbury, in the twelfth and thirteenth centuries*, Rolls Series, 97 (1891) • D. Bates, ed., *Regesta regum Anglo-Normannorum: the Acta of William I, 1066–1087* (1998) • D. Stroud, 'The cult and tombs of St Osmund at Salisbury', *Wiltshire Archaeological and Natural History Magazine*, 78 (1984), 50–54 • John of Worcester, *Chron.* • W. H. Rich Jones, ed., *Vetus registrum sarisberiense alias dictum registrum S. Osmundi episcopi: the register of St Osmund*, 2 vols., Rolls Series, 78 (1883–4), 2.55 • Jesus College, Oxford, MS 114, fol. 27v • B. R. Kemp, ed., *Salisbury, 1078–1217*, English Episcopal Acta, 18 (1999)

Osorno. For this title name *see* O'Higgins, Ambrosio, marquess of Osorno in the Spanish nobility (*c*.1721–1801).

Osred I (696x8–716), king of Northumbria, was the son of *Aldfrith whose only known wife was *Cuthburh, sister of Ine, king of the West Saxons. An inconsistency in Bede's statements makes it uncertain whether Aldfrith died in 704 or 705, but the latter is the more likely. The Anglo-Saxon Chronicle assigns Aldfrith's death to 14 December, after which (according to Stephen of Ripon's life of Bishop Wilfrid) an otherwise unknown king called Eadwulf reigned for two months. He was expelled following military operations around Bamburgh by a coalition involving Bishop Wilfrid, the princess-abbess of Whitby, Ælfflæd, and the ealdorman Beorhtfrith. Osred then became king at the age of eight, and also Wilfrid's adopted son. This relationship did not result in Wilfrid's restoration to the see of York, however; at a synod held on the banks of the River Nidd in the first year of Osred's reign, Wilfrid was allowed to retain the churches of Ripon and Hexham and was apparently made bishop of the latter. Warfare with the Picts was continued in Osred's reign, for in 711 the ealdorman (*praefectus*) Beorhtfrith defeated them between the rivers Avon and Carron in southern Scotland. Osred was killed in 716, but no reliable details of the killing are known, apart from a remark in the northern recension of the Anglo-Saxon Chronicle that it took place 'south of the border' (*ASC*, s.a. 716, text D), possibly the border with the Picts. William of Malmesbury wrote of a conspiracy, but this was probably conjecture.

Writing while Osred was alive, Bede equated him with Josiah, the king of Judah responsible for purification of worship, but after the king's death he expressed the opinion that the standards of the church had declined since Aldfrith's time. Boniface, who shared this latter opinion, represented Osred as 'driven by the spirit of wantonness, fornicating, and in his frenzy debauching throughout the nunneries virgins consecrated to God' (Tangl, no. 73; *English Historical Documents*, 1, no. 177), while the author of the ninth-century Latin poem *De abbatibus* accused him of killing his nobles or forcing them into monasteries. In the late eleventh century, Folcard associated him with a miracle worked by John of Beverley and described him as a man of religion and faith, but to the extent that this was based on any authentic tradition it may have been inspired by some otherwise unknown donation made by Osred to Beverley. It is possible that Osred's treatment of the church and his nobles derived from financial problems, for he failed to maintain Aldfrith's high quality silver coinage. His death ended the near monopoly of the Northumbrian kingship exercised by the descendants of Æthelfrith (*d.* *c.*616) since the time of Oswald (*d.* 642), for Osred's successor was Cenred, son of Cuthwine, son of Leodwold, an alleged descendant of the founder of Bernicia, Ida, by a collateral line. No details are known of Cenred's reign, which lasted from 716 to 718.

DAVID ROLLASON

Sources E. Stephanus, *The life of Bishop Wilfrid*, ed. and trans. B. Colgrave (1927) • Bede, *Hist. eccl.*, 5.18–19, 22, 24 • *ASC*, s.a. 705, 716 [texts A, D, E] • E. Classen and F. E. Harmer, eds., *An Anglo-Saxon chronicle from British Museum, Cotton MS Tiberius B. IV* (1926) • *Bedas metrische 'Vita sancti Cuthberti'*, ed. W. Jaager (Leipzig, 1935) • M. Tangl, ed., *Die Briefe des heiligen Bonifatius und Lullus*, MGH Epistolae Selectae, 1 (Berlin, 1916), no. 73; trans. as 'Letter of Boniface and seven other missionary bishops to Æthelbald, king of Mercia, urging him to reform', *English historical documents*, 1, ed. D. Whitelock (1955), no. 177 • Æthelwulf, *De abbatibus*, ed. A. Campbell (1967) • *Willelmi Malmesbiriensis monachi de gestis regum Anglorum*, ed. W. Stubbs, 2 vols., Rolls Series (1887–9) • J. J. North, *English hammered coinage*, 3rd edn, 1: *Early Anglo-Saxon to Henry III, c.600–1272* (1994) • D. P. Kirby, 'Northumbria in the time of Wilfrid', *St Wilfrid at Hexham*, ed. D. P. Kirby (1974), 1–34 • D. P. Kirby, *The earliest English kings* (1991)

Osred II (*d.* 792), king of Northumbria, was the son of King *Alhred [*see under* Oswulf] and his queen, Osgifu, and thus descended from Ida, founder in 547 of the Bernician dynasty of Northumbrian kings, by two collateral lines: that is via Ida's son Ocga on his mother's side, and by Ida's son Eadric on his father's side. In view of the fact that his father married in 768, Osred is unlikely to have been more than nineteen years old when he came to the throne, after the murder of Ælfwald I, in 788. In 790 he was deposed, tonsured at York, and expelled, to be replaced by Æthelred I (*d.* 796), who had himself been exiled in 779. According to the Northumbrian annals, Osred was on the Isle of Man in 792 when he relied on the proffered support of certain nobles to attempt to return to Northumbria. He was deserted by his soldiers, however, and captured by King Æthelred who had him killed at a place called 'Aynburg' on 14 September. He was buried in the church of the monastery of Tynemouth, Northumbria.

DAVID ROLLASON

Sources Symeon of Durham, *Opera* • *ASC*, s.a. 789, 790, 792 [texts E, F] • D. P. Kirby, *The earliest English kings* (1991)

Osric (*d.* 634), king of Deira, was the son of Ælfric and cousin to his predecessor *Eadwine, who had ruled the whole kingdom of Northumbria. Osric became king of Deira, the southern part of Northumbria, in 633. As a member of the Deiran royal family he had been baptized by Paulinus *c.*627 during the first attempt to convert Northumbria by Italian missionaries based in Kent; he later renounced Christianity. Under Eadwine the kingdom had expanded, but Eadwine was slain in battle against an alliance of British and Mercian forces in October 633 and Northumbria split back into its constituent parts of Deira and Bernicia. Since Eadwine's sons had been killed, expelled, or captured, Osric took control of Deira, the southern part, but the northern area went to a member of the Bernician dynasty who had been exiled during Eadwine's reign. This king, Eanfrith, was also a recent convert, but he had been baptized by the Irish church. Northumbria was therefore split between two rivals, both now supposedly Christian, yet remained under attack by the British and Mercian alliance that had destroyed Eadwine, the first Christian king. As a result both Osric and Eanfrith apostatized. Loyalty to the ruler appears to have been the initial impetus behind acceptance of Christianity by the pagan Anglo-Saxon aristocracy and people, rather than a change of faith. On this occasion the perception of the ruler's access to divine favour and of whether Christianity offered more certain rewards than paganism probably proved less powerful than the fear of retribution for abandoning ancestral ties with the old gods. Bede, however, described the kings' apostasy as a betrayal of the faith of their people.

Osric was killed by the British king Cadwallon, himself a Christian, in the following summer, 634, after laying siege to his army in a fortified town; despite earlier claims, it has been shown that this is unlikely to have been York. As a result of their apostasy, Osric and Eanfrith, who was killed in the same year, were subsequently excluded from the Northumbrian king-lists and their regnal year assigned to Oswald (*d.* 642), their Christian successor, even though Osric's son *Oswine (*d.* 651), a model of Christian humility, later became king in Deira and Eanfrith was Oswald's brother. D. J. Craig

Sources Bede, *Hist. eccl.*, 3.1, 14 • *ASC*, s.a. 634 [text E] • J. Campbell, *Essays in Anglo-Saxon history* (1986) • P. H. Blair, 'The *Moore memoranda* on Northumbrian history', *The early cultures of north-west Europe: H. M. Chadwick memorial studies*, ed. C. Fox and B. Dickins (1950), 245–57 • M. Miller, 'The dates of Deira', *Anglo-Saxon England*, 8 (1979), 35–61 • S. Wood, 'Bede's Northumbrian dates again', *EngHR*, 98 (1983), 280–96 • J. M. Wallace-Hadrill, *Bede's Ecclesiastical history of the English people: a historical commentary*, OMT (1988) • N. J. Higham, *The convert kings* (1997), 202–3 • C. E. Stancliffe, 'Kings and conversion: some comparisons between the Roman mission to England and Patrick's to Ireland', *Frühmittelalterliche Studien*, 14 (1980), 59–94 • J. M. Wallace-Hadrill, *Early Germanic kingship in England and on the continent* (1971) • D. P. Kirby, 'Bede and Northumbrian chronology', *EngHR*, 78 (1963), 514–27

Osric (*fl.* **674–679**). *See under* Hwicce, kings of the (*act. c.*670–*c.*780).

Osric (*d.* **729**), king of Northumbria, began his reign in 718. He therefore ruled for eleven years of Bede's life, but no information other than his accession and death is given in the *Historia ecclesiastica*. There is no contemporary evidence for his paternity. Twelfth-century sources, including the history of the church of Durham attributed to Symeon of Durham and the *Series regum Northymbrensium*, claim that his father was *Aldfrith (*Oswiu's illegitimate Irish-born son), and therefore that he was brother to *Osred I. Alternatively, it has been suggested that he was the son of *Alchfrith (Oswiu's eldest son, who was subking in Deira but who fought against him). This theory has been extended to equating him with an Osric who is recorded as a king of the Hwicce between about 676 and 690 (Bede, *Hist. eccl.*, 4.23), but the suggestion that he ruled in this part of western Mercia thirty years before becoming king of Northumbria is based mainly on an equation of the two names and would mean that he became king for the second time at the age of sixty-five. The obscurity over Osric's background may conceal an irregularity in his birth, but he appears to have been the last of the old line of Northumbrian kings descended from Ida through Æthelfrith. A taint of illegitimacy may have opened the way for rival claimants to the throne.

The suggestion that Osric was young enough to be a puppet of Wilfrid's faction at the Northumbrian court seems unlikely, since it has also been shown that he must have been aged between fourteen and twenty when he came to the throne, if he was a son of Aldfrith, and much older if a son of Alchfrith. He is said by Bede to have nominated his successor, Ceolwulf (*d.* 764), although he was of a different lineage. William of Malmesbury in the twelfth century claimed that Osric and his predecessor, Cenred (*r.* 716–18), Ceolwulf's brother, were implicated in the death of Osred (*r.* 705/6–716), but if Osric was Aldfrith's son this would imply that he allied with a rival lineage to murder his own brother, and may strengthen the argument that his father was Alchfrith.

Osric's name is recorded in an eighth-century calendar under 9 May, which accords with the date of his death as given by Bede (*contra* Plummer in *Opera historica*, 1.349), though other commentators have tried to link this entry with the apostate *Osric (*d.* 634), whose name, Bede states, was excluded from the regnal lists. The entry reads *Depositio Osrici regis*. Bede simply states that he died, but the entries in the A, B, and C texts of the Anglo-Saxon Chronicle (under the year 731) claim that he was slain. D. J. Craig

Sources Bede, *Hist. eccl.*, 4.23; 5.23 • *ASC*, s.a. 716, 729, 731 [texts A, B, C, D, E] • Symeon of Durham, *Opera* • William of Malmesbury, *Gesta regum Anglorum / The history of the English kings*, ed. and trans. R. A. B. Mynors, R. M. Thomson, and M. Winterbottom, 2 vols., OMT (1998–9) • W. Levison, *England and the continent in the eighth century* (1946) • P. Grosjean, 'Un fragment d'obituaire Anglo-Saxon du VIIIe siècle naguère conservé à Munich', *Analecta Bollandiana*, 79 (1961), 320–45 • *Venerabilis Baedae opera historica*, ed. C. Plummer, 2 vols. (1896) • D. P. Kirby, 'Northumbria in the time of Wilfrid', *Saint Wilfrid at Hexham*, ed. D. P. Kirby (1974), 1–34 • D. P. Kirby, *Bede's Historia ecclesiastica gentis Anglorum: its contemporary setting* (1992) • W. Goffart, *The narrators of barbarian history* (1988) • D. N. Dumville, 'The Ætheling: a study in Anglo-Saxon constitutional history', *Anglo-Saxon England*, 8 (1979), 1–33 • C. S. Taylor, 'Osric of Gloucester', *Transactions of the Bristol and Gloucestershire Archaeological Society*, 26 (1903), 308–25

Ossian. *See* Oisín (*supp. fl.* 3rd–5th cent.).

Ossington. For this title name *see* Denison, (John) Evelyn, Viscount Ossington (1800–1873).

Ossory. For this title name *see* Butler, Piers, first earl of Ossory and eighth earl of Ormond (*b.* in or after 1467, *d.* 1539); Butler, Margaret, countess of Ossory and Ormond (*d.* 1542); Butler, James, ninth earl of Ormond and second earl of Ossory (*b.* in or after 1496, *d.* 1546); Butler, Thomas, tenth earl of Ormond and third earl of Ossory (1531–1614); Butler, Walter, eleventh earl of Ormond and fourth earl of Ossory (1559–1633); Butler, Thomas, sixth earl of Ossory (1634–1680).

Ostenaca [Oustenaca] (*d.* before **1780**?), leader of the Cherokee Indians, was born of unknown parentage into the Cherokee nation, which in the eighteenth century was a loose federation of towns that spanned modern Tennessee, Georgia, and North and South Carolina. He first became prominent in the 1730s. Also known as Judd's Friend or Judge's Friend, at that time he lived at Great Tellico in the Middle Towns of the Cherokee and became a significant supporter of the Tellico–Hiwassee alliance's usurpation of the traditional primacy of Chota, the main Overhill Cherokee settlement on the Little Tennessee River. In 1730 the British had recognized the Tellico warrior Moitoi as the Cherokee 'emperor'. But in the early 1750s the authority of Moitoi's successor collapsed. Chota reasserted its leadership and Ostenaca, apparently choosing the rising star, moved to nearby Tomotly, where he rose to become Outacité ('Mankiller').

There Ostenaca competed with *Attakullakulla, also known as Little Carpenter, to become the main channel for Cherokee dealings with South Carolina and Virginia. Attakullakulla was a gifted and wily statesman who—having visited London in 1730—could plausibly claim superior understanding of the British. Ostenaca, less talented,

Ostenaca (*d.* **before 1780?**), by unknown engraver, pubd 1762

far less devious, and overshadowed by his opponent in dealings with South Carolina, set about developing a special relationship with Virginia. The 1756 Broad River treaty, which offered Cherokee military aid for a Virginian fort and trade, was largely Attakullakulla's creation, but it was Ostenaca who did most to make it work. He threw himself into military and diplomatic expeditions, often staying with the family of Thomas Jefferson and once being given the use of the private carriage of Virginia's lieutenant-governor, Robert Dinwiddie.

But Dinwiddie betrayed Ostenaca: the fort was never garrisoned, there were never enough Virginian traders, and the Cherokee bands defending the frontier were poorly rewarded. In 1759 a series of clashes with the frontier settlers spread to the Carolinas as young warriors sought revenge on the whites. Warriors on their way home from fighting alongside British troops against the French and their American Indian allies were often accused of harassing and pillaging colonial American frontier homesteads. The frontiersmen in turn were accused of killing allied Cherokee in order to redeem their scalps for the high bounties the colonial governments had set on enemy Creek, Delaware, and Shawnee Indians. Even Ostenaca was so disillusioned and suspicious that he withdrew from an eleventh-hour embassy to Charles Town. It was a lucky escape: the emissaries were taken hostage by South Carolina governor William Henry Lyttelton, who then marched on the Cherokee towns with South Carolina militia, starting the Cherokee War. Forced into a humiliating treaty on behalf of the nation, Attakullakulla found himself isolated and discredited. Only a few Cherokee hostages were released and many more died of smallpox in Fort Loudoun. The remainder were massacred when Ostenaca and Oconostota, the Great Warrior, tried to rescue them. The two leaders, with Kanagatucko, the 'Fire King' of Chota, then joined or encouraged ferocious revenge raids on the white settlements. By spring the southern frontier had been swept back more than a hundred miles to the Atlantic.

But the triumvirate knew that ultimately they must negotiate peace. The Cherokees were heavily dependent on South Carolina traders for European goods, and even in peace time the French had been unable to provide even a fraction of their needs. Ultimately the nation would run out of ammunition and other essential trade goods, despite the activities of a handful of smugglers. For eighteen months the leaders kept in the background, leaving the open fighting to young hot-bloods such as Seroweh, the Young Warrior of Estatoe. But even in August 1761, with twenty towns and half the nation's crops destroyed, fear paralysed parley. Instead the duty fell to Little Carpenter who obtained a surprisingly moderate treaty with South Carolina. Attakullakulla's prestige was restored. Though (unlike Oconostota) he willingly embraced the peace, Ostenaca was now a secondary figure in Cherokee affairs.

Early in 1762 the appearance in Tomotly of a Virginian emissary, Ensign Henry Timberlake, offered Ostenaca an unexpected lifeline. He made Timberlake his personal guest, protected him against the suspicions of others, and at last—overcoming his remaining fears—agreed to escort him home. Virginia's lieutenant-governor Francis Fauquier, jealous of South Carolina and thinking Ostenaca more malleable than Attakullakulla, gave him a warm welcome. Ostenaca saw his opening. Hoping to trump Little Carpenter, he successfully demanded to go to London to meet the king.

The visit by Ostenaca and two Cherokee companions in the summer of 1762 was a great sensation. They were quickly received by Charles Wyndham, second earl of Egremont, then secretary of state, and after some delay by George III. Although Ostenaca's interpreter had died at sea, and no treaty was contemplated, the government saw that pleasing him was essential to a peaceful Cherokee frontier. The Cherokee were taken on official tours of St Paul's, the houses of parliament, and Woolwich dockyards—all designed to impress the visitors. Crowds followed them to Vauxhall, the Mansion House, and theatres, and even watched them dress. They dined with noblemen and were painted by Francis Parsons and Joshua Reynolds. Educated London earnestly debated

Ostenaca's status, Cherokee polity, and British obligations towards their late foes.

Both Ostenaca's and Egremont's objectives were fulfilled. Ostenaca returned to America a leading advocate of peaceful co-existence and having achieved a formidable prestige. Henceforth he aimed to preserve peace and slow down the advance of white settlement by negotiating orderly boundary adjustments, including the Hard Labour line of 1768. Although he did not quite displace Attakullakulla at the great American Indian congress of Augusta in 1763, his recent experience of London secured him the public deference of others. Through John Stuart, the sympathetic British superintendent of Indian affairs in the southern district, he pressed for a buffer zone of métis settlers and as late as 1771 complained of illegal intrusions by white hunters. This Cherokee–imperial dialogue, which Ostenaca worked so hard to sustain, ensured the nation's survival until the American Revolution. Ostenaca probably died before 1780. JOHN OLIPHANT

Sources H. Corkran, *The Cherokee frontier: conflict and survival, 1740–62* (Norman, OK, 1962) • J. Oliphant, *Peace and war on the Anglo-Cherokee frontier, 1756–1763* (2000) • J. Oliphant, 'The Cherokee embassy to London, 1762', *Journal of Imperial and Commonwealth History*, 27/1 (1999), 1–26 • T. Hatley, *The dividing paths: Cherokees and South Carolinians through the era of revolution* (1993) • J. P. Reid, *A law of blood: the primitive law of the Cherokee nation* (New York, 1970) • H. Timberlake, *The memoirs of Lieutenant Henry Timberlake* (1765)
Archives BL, Burney collection of newspapers • Hunt. L., Loudoun and Abercromby MSS • PRO, original corresp. of the secretaries of state and the board of trade, CO
Likenesses J. Reynolds, portrait, 1762 (of Ostenaca?) • engraving (after J. Reynolds?), repro. in *London Magazine* (Aug 1762) • engraving (of Ostenaca?), Bureau of American Ethnology • engraving, Bodl. Oxf.; repro. in *Royal Magazine* (July 1762) [*see illus.*] • group portrait, engraving (*The Cherokees in London, 1762*; after J. Reynolds?)

Österberg, Martina Sofia Helena Bergman- (**1849–1915**), feminist and promoter of women's physical education, was born on 7 October 1849 in Hammarlunda, a village near Malmö in the south of Sweden, one of the six children of Karl Bergman, a prosperous farmer, and his wife, Betty Lundgen. Even as a girl, it seems, she felt impatient of the restrictions imposed on women, and her family encouraged her independence. She was privately educated, and worked as a governess and as a librarian before enrolling in 1879 at the Royal Central Gymnastics Institute, founded in Stockholm in 1814 by the much-venerated pioneer of remedial gymnastics, Per Hendrick Ling. In an era when formal exercise was very largely military drill, Ling had explored its therapeutic potential. When he died, his exercise system—with its strong physiological base—remained the core of the institute's training of both men and women gymnastic teachers. Women needed health as well as men, Ling had stated, and Martina Bergman was to make it a tool of their emancipation.

Ling's system was virtually unknown in Britain before 1879, when the London school board set out to improve the poor physique of girls in its elementary schools by engaging a Swedish woman to introduce Ling's free exercises. As they required no apparatus, these could be performed in the classroom, if the teacher had a rudimentary training. The massive task of training teachers began, and was continued with great success by Martina Bergman when she took over the school board post in 1881. She also succeeded strikingly in her aim of publicizing the Swedish system by open practices and demonstrations (including one before royalty).

Called to give evidence in 1887 to the Cross commission on elementary schooling, Madame Bergman-Österberg (as she was known from her marriage in 1886 to Edvin Per Wilhelm Österberg, a Stockholm schoolmaster) said that where Ling's system had been introduced children held themselves better and were more alert. Privately, though, she had already decided that her ideal of a healthy womanhood could not be realized among the poor. Their physique, she told a friend, was so impaired by neglect, bad food, and bad living conditions that, unless these circumstances could be changed, no radical improvement could be effected. In 1885 she had launched her own college, the Hampstead Physical Training College, to prepare students from more privileged classes to teach in the new girls' secondary schools. In 1887 she left school board work, and in 1895 moved away from London to Dartford Heath in Kent, where she bought an estate with room for facilities such as playing fields and tennis courts for what was now known as Kingsfield College. Students took a rigorous 'Swedish' course of gymnastics, anatomy, and physiology, as well as English team games—an addition prompted by the fact that hockey, lacrosse, and cricket were growing popular with English schoolgirls.

Such a college was intensely novel. Visitors were dazzled by student displays, but also by the crusading zeal of the handsome, well-built, imperious woman who accounted for its success by saying that Ling's system was too good to fail. Madame Bergman-Österberg herself took care to see that it did not; not only, as she later said, training the teachers but creating a demand for them. Amid the apprehensions of national decline which prevailed around the turn of the century, she convinced the heads of countless high schools for girls that the gymnastics and games mistress—the specialist in health—had become essential. By 1905 five other colleges like hers existed to meet the demand, two of them having been launched by her own former students. In 1909 the Board of Education based its physical education syllabus for elementary schools on the work of Ling. His system was introduced in the navy and in some boys' public schools, and remained standard in girls' schools throughout Britain and the colonies.

Madame Bergman-Österberg died of cancer at her home, Kingsfield, in Dartford Heath, Kent, on 30 July 1915, struggling at the last to complete the formalities of leaving her college in trust to the nation. Sir George Newman, who had known her since his days as first medical director at the Board of Education, was to describe her, looking back, as 'the morning star' of that reformation in health which he had tried to promote by such means as school medical inspections. It must be said, though, that in later life she had been wrapped up in her college and at some remove from the kind of problems she encountered in her school board days.

Madame Bergman-Österberg's feminism, too, had its narrow streak. She did, indeed, endow a scheme in Sweden to educate women for enfranchisement, and she and her husband in 1914 donated their house in Bostad, south Sweden, to be made into a women's horticultural college. But in England, as the suffrage battle raged in the period up to the First World War, it was not she but one of her former students who launched the Gymnastic Teachers' Suffrage Society. The increasingly desperate fight for the vote evidently impinged on Madame Bergman-Österberg less than the fact that she herself had created for women a new profession that was to advance their economic and social freedom.

It was a profession that went with the grain of leadership culture in the last days of empire, invoking a sense of moral purpose and discipline which looked beyond the physical benefits of gym. The gym mistress, confident of what she was doing and with an authority which gave her poise, was central to the running of many girls' schools until the latter part of the twentieth century. Out of Madame Bergman-Österberg's new profession there also came a newer one: physiotherapy. SHEILA FLETCHER

Sources University of Greenwich, Dartford Campus, Oakfield Lane, Dartford, Kent, Bergman Osterberg Archive • A. Broman, 'In commemoration of Madame Bergman Osterberg', *Bergman Osterberg Union Magazine* (1995) • minutes, London school board, 1879–87, LMA • 'Royal commission to enquire into working of elementary education acts: minutes', *Parl. papers* (1887), 30.378, C. 5158 • J. May, *Madame Bergman Osterberg* (1969) • S. Fletcher, *Women first* (1984) • d. cert.

Archives University of Greenwich, Dartford, Kent, Dartford campus

Likenesses photographs, University of Greenwich, Dartford, Kent

Wealth at death £4430 14*s*. 6*d*.: probate, 28 Sept 1915, *CGPLA Eng. & Wales*

Osthryth [Ostrith] (*d.* 697), queen of the Mercians, consort of King Æthelred, was the daughter of *Oswiu (611/12–670), king of Northumbria, and his second wife, Eanflaed. Her marriage appears to have taken place some time before 679, in which year her husband fought with her brother *Ecgfrith, king of Northumbria since 670, near the River Trent. Another of her brothers, a youth named Ælfwine, was killed in the battle; he is said to have been beloved in both kingdoms, which suggests that he had been frequenting his sister's court in Mercia as well as his brother's in Northumbria. Ecgfrith's desire to avenge Ælfwine's death would have provoked further conflict between the two kingdoms, if Archbishop Theodore had not made peace. A sign of the subsequent co-operation between the Mercian and Northumbrian rulers is provided by the willingness of *Æthelred (*d.* after 704) and Osthryth to expel Wilfrid from their kingdom, allegedly to please Ecgfrith.

It seems to have been after the battle of the Trent that Osthryth carried out the pious action for which she is best remembered. She retrieved the remains of the body of her uncle, *Oswald, who had been killed by the Mercian king Penda at the battle of 'Maserfelth' in 642 (his head and arms had already been taken to Northumbria), and arranged for them to be transported to the monastery at Bardney in the province of Lindsey (modern Lincolnshire), of which she and her husband were generous patrons. The Bardney monks were at first reluctant to receive the remains of the hated king who had once conquered their land, although they acknowledged Oswald's sanctity; a timely miracle changed their minds, and the relics were reverently washed and placed in a shrine.

It has been speculated that Osthryth's promotion of her uncle's cult may have had a political motive. The veneration of Oswald was already developing into a dynastic cult in Northumbria, where his head was preserved at Lindisfarne and his arms at Bamburgh; perhaps the choice of Bardney as the resting-place for the other remains was intended to provide a focus for Northumbrian sympathies in Lindsey, which was a territory long disputed between Mercia and Northumbria. Whether for this or for some other reason, Osthryth does not seem to have been popular in her husband's kingdom: in 697 she was murdered by the Mercian nobles. She was probably buried at Bardney, where her husband Æthelred subsequently retired as a monk; a later list of saints' resting-places indicates that both of them were venerated there. Æthelred is known to have had one child, presumably with Osthryth: this was *Ceolred (*d.* 716), who became king of Mercia in 709.

S. E. KELLY

Sources Bede, *Hist. eccl.*, 3.11; 4.21; 5.24 • E. Stephanus, *The life of Bishop Wilfrid*, ed. and trans. B. Colgrave (1927), 80 • A. Thacker, '*Membra disjecta*: the divison of the body and the diffusion of the cult', *Oswald: Northumbrian king to European saint*, ed. C. Stancliffe and E. Cambridge (1995), 97–127 • D. W. Rollason, 'Lists of saints' resting-places in Anglo-Saxon England', *Anglo-Saxon England*, 7 (1978), 61–93

Ostler, William (*d.* 1614), actor, had a brief but notable career among the King's Men early in the seventeenth century. He first appears as a boy actor among the children of the Chapel Royal who performed Jonson's *Poetaster* at the Blackfriars playhouse in 1601. He was probably also a chorister, since he is not one of the seven chapel boys mentioned in December 1601 as actors not musicians. He next appears on 11 April 1609 as the first of three players, all recently or still belonging to the Chapel Royal, who performed a hastily arranged entertainment (published by J. Knowles in Butler, 1999), written by Jonson, mounted by Inigo Jones, and played before the king and the royal family at the opening of the New Exchange in the Strand. He played a shopkeeper and was by this time an adult, for he had a servant, Giles Gary, who played the boy in the shop (the other actor was Nathan Field, who played the key keeper). Probably later in that year Ostler was one of the players from the Chapel Royal whom the King's Men took on as adults 'to strengthen the Kings service' when the King's Men began to use the Blackfriars playhouse as well as the Globe (PRO, LC 5/133, p. 50).

Ostler soon became a principal member of the King's

Men. He appears in the cast lists of six of the company's plays: Jonson's *Alchemist* (1610) and *Catiline* (1611); Beaumont and Fletcher's *Captain* (*c*.1609–12), *Bonduca* (*c*.1609–14), and *Valentinian* (*c*.1610–14); and Webster's *Duchess of Malfi* (*c*.1612–14). In this last play he played Antonio, a virtuous hero surrounded by corruption, the only part he is known to have played in a regular play. In celebrating a brawl in which Ostler came off badly, John Davies called him in 1611, perhaps ironically, 'the Roscius of these times' and 'Sole King of Actors' (Davies, epigram 205). Ostler acquired the lease of a share in the Blackfriars playhouse on 20 May 1611, and he bought one in the Globe on 20 February 1612, so that he held a seventh of one playhouse and a fourteenth of the other, both leases to expire in 1629.

Ostler married Thomasin, daughter of the actor John *Heminges, who was the company's treasurer, about 1611, when she would have been sixteen. The Ostlers' child, Beaumont (named presumably for the playwright), was baptized on 18 May 1612 at St Mary Aldermanbury, London, where Heminges lived and Thomasin had been baptized on 15 January 1595. Ostler died intestate, apparently in his twenties, on 16 December 1614, leaving to his widow (who became his administratrix six days later) only his two shares 'for her relief and maintenance' along with debts of 'a very great value' (PRO, KB 27/1454/1/m. 692). She gave the shares to her father in trust and in 1615 brought a famous lawsuit against him when he would not return them or give her the income from them.

HERBERT BERRY

Sources E. K. Chambers, *The Elizabethan stage*, 4 vols. (1923), vol. 2, pp. 322, 331 • lawsuit, *T. Ostler* v. *J. Heminges*, PRO, KB 27/1454/1/m. 692 [partly transcribed and translated by C. Wallace, *The Times* (4 Oct 1909), 9] • Hatfield House, Cecil MSS, bills 35/1, 1a, 7; reported in *Calendar of the manuscripts of the most hon. the marquess of Salisbury*, 24, HMC, 9 (1976), 168 • PRO, LC 5/133, p. 50 • J. Davies, *A scourge of folly* (1611), epigram 205 • PRO, STAC 5/C. 46/39 • PRO, PROB 12/13, p. 176 • M. Butler, ed., *Re-presenting Ben Jonson: text, history, performance* (1999) • parish register, St Mary Aldermanbury, GL, MS 3572/1

Wealth at death £300 leases on share in Blackfriars Playhouse and the Globe, bequeathed to wife: lawsuit, *T. Ostler* v. *J. Heminges*, PRO, KB 27/1454/1/m. 692

Ostorius Scapula, Publius (*d*. AD 52), Roman governor of Britain, died in the province. His date of birth is unknown, but was probably about 1 BC at the earliest. His father, of the same names as himself, was a high-ranking Roman knight, who became prefect of Egypt in AD 10. His mother was perhaps called Sallustia Calvina. An uncle, Quintus Ostorius Scapula, was one of the first two prefects of the praetorian guard (2 BC). Scapula's son Marcus served in Britain under his father and became consul in AD 59. A grandson, also called Marcus, was proconsul of Asia in 114–15. The family had estates in northern Italy, perhaps near Novaria (Novara), but probably derived from central or eastern Italy.

Scapula arrived in Britain to take up his command as the second Roman governor of Britain late in AD 47 and had to take rapid action against free Britons who had attacked the province (between the Trent and Severn). In order to secure his rear, Scapula now ordered the surrender of weapons by the peoples under Roman control. This provoked a revolt by the Iceni of what is now East Anglia, who enjoyed the status of a client kingdom; they were joined by neighbouring peoples. Scapula's son won the highest Roman distinction for valour during the ensuing campaign. In AD 49 Scapula campaigned in north Wales against the Deceangli, reaching the Irish Sea, but failing to bring the enemy to a pitched battle. He had to abandon the campaign in order to suppress an anti-Roman movement in the client state of the Brigantes, who occupied most of what is now northern England. During the following year, AD 50, he attempted to subdue the Silures of south Wales, who were now led by the surviving British leader from the time of the Roman invasion, Caratacus. Again, Scapula's success was limited, and Caratacus escaped north to the Ordovices of Snowdonia. During this period Scapula transferred one, or two, of his four legions from Camulodunum (Colchester) to the frontier region, one new base being Viroconium (Wroxeter). The vacated fortress at Camulodunum was now turned into a *colonia* (a chartered new town for the settlement of retired veteran legionaries).

During AD 51, in the course of a campaign against the Ordovices, Scapula finally brought Caratacus to battle, somewhere in north Wales, and achieved a decisive victory. Caratacus fled to the Brigantes, but the Brigantian ruler, Queen Cartimandua, remained loyal to Rome and handed Caratacus over. He was sent with his wife, daughter, and brothers to Rome, where Claudius displayed them in a victory ceremony. Scapula was rewarded by an honorary triumph. Despite this success, British resistance continued, with the Silures wiping out several legionary cohorts which were engaged in building forts. Scapula took immediate steps and proclaimed his intention to 'extinguish the name of the Silures' (Tacitus, *Annals*, xii.39). But in the same year, AD 52, he died at his post, 'wearied by the irksomeness of his task' (ibid.), as Tacitus put it, at the end of his lengthy account of Scapula's governorship (he had already given a brief summary in the *Agricola*). Later in the *Annals* Tacitus also describes the murder of Scapula's son Marcus at the hands of Nero's assassins in AD 66.

A. R. BIRLEY

Sources C. Tacitus, *The histories [and] the annals*, ed. and trans. C. H. Moore and J. Jackson, 3 (1937), bk 12, pp. 31–40 • Tacitus, *Agricola*, ed. and trans. M. Mutton (1914), 14 • A. R. Birley, *The fasti of Roman Britain* (1981) • L. Petersen, ed., *Prosopographia Imperii Romani saeculi I. II. III*, 2nd edn, 5/3 (1897–8); repr. (1987), nos. 162–7, esp. 164

Ostrer, Isidore (1889–1975), financier and film producer, was born in the East End of London on 17 June 1889, the third surviving son of Nathan Ostrer (*d*. 1932), a jeweller's salesman, and his wife, Francesca (Fanny; *d*. 1932). His father had left Ukraine to escape antisemitic persecution in the 1870s, and came to England via Paris, where he met his future wife. Isidore was the most outstandingly intelligent of the six Ostrer children; the film actor James Mason later said that the five brothers had one opinion and one brain between them (*The Guardian*, 9 July 1996).

Ostrer began work as a stockbroker's clerk in the City of London. On 31 March 1914 he married Helen Dorothy, daughter of Lloyd Spear-Morgan, a solicitor, and granddaughter of the high sheriff of Carmarthenshire. The couple had six children. Ostrer was turned down for service in the army because of health reasons, but prospered sufficiently to set up the Lothbury Investment Corporation in 1919 and Ostrer Brothers Merchant Bank (with two of his brothers, Maurice and Mark) in 1921.

In the 1920s Ostrer and his brothers were responsible for a number of company flotations, the most important of which were Amalgamated Textiles in 1920 and the Gaumont-British Picture Corporation in 1927. The prospects opened up by the first Cinematograph Films Act and the coming of the 'talkies' encouraged Isidore to assume direct control of Gaumont-British. In August 1929 he became chairman, with Mark as vice-chairman and Maurice joint managing director.

Having created a circuit of over 350 cinemas, Ostrer turned his hand to film production. The old Gaumont studio at Lime Grove, Shepherd's Bush, was rebuilt and Ostrer encouraged his production chief, Michael Balcon, to make big budget films which would appeal to an international audience. Most ambitious of these was an adaptation of Leon Feuchtwangler's *Jew Suss* (1934) starring Conrad Veidt, Benita Hume, and one of Ostrer's three daughters, Pamela. However, the American market proved resistant to British films, substantial losses were made, and in 1937 Gaumont-British's production activities were severely curtailed.

Ostrer had encouraged American investment in Gaumont-British as early as 1929 when William Fox bought a substantial (though not, as he had thought, a controlling) interest in the company. In 1936 another deal was planned with the brothers Joseph and Nicholas Schenk—the heads respectively of Twentieth Century Fox and MGM—but it was disrupted by a hostile counterbid by John Maxwell of the rival Associated-British cinema circuit. In October 1941 Ostrer sold his shares to J. Arthur Rank, though it was not until 1944 that the conflicting interests in the corporation were sufficiently reconciled for Rank to assume complete control.

His first marriage having ended in divorce, on 27 April 1933 Ostrer married Marjorie, daughter of John William Ernest Roach. Because of his second wife's tuberculosis, Ostrer moved to South Africa; but his Jewish background and radical views made it difficult for him to condone a white supremacist society. He returned to England, but remained in touch with his wife, an actress and model, and their adopted daughter. Isidore Ostrer published two books on economics, *A New International Currency* (1921) and *The Conquest of Gold* (1932), displaying an idiosyncratic but strikingly progressive approach similar in spirit to that of J. M. Keynes. He also published two books of poetry, and was fond of telling people that money was only important to him in so far as it permitted him to write and paint.

Although Ostrer had divested himself of his film interests, he was not ready to retire, and he reinvolved himself with the textile industry. Since the launch of Amalgamated Textiles in 1920 he and his brothers had retained a twenty-three per cent stake in the company (which long since had been renamed Illingworth-Morris). Ostrer quickly built this up to over fifty per cent and took control of the company, attempting over the next twenty-four years to make it the dominant force in the woollen textiles industry. Guided by Ostrer's economic theories, Illingworth-Morris used its profits to expand by buying up its rivals. This policy was misguided, and by the time of Ostrer's death the company had become an unwieldy giant, supplying vestments to the papacy and tennis-ball cloth to Dunlop, but ill-equipped to withstand the harsh economic climate of the late 1970s and early 1980s. Ostrer's daughter Pamela Mason, the film actress, inherited his dominant shareholding in the company.

Isidore Ostrer's progressive views extended from economics to health and lifestyle. He believed that the secret of longevity lay in fasting—sometimes for as long as thirty days—and drinking only water. He was disappointed in his expectation that he would live until he was 130, but he managed to lead a healthy and active life until shortly before his death from cancer at the age of eighty-five on 3 September 1975 at his home, Hills End, Titlarks Hill, Sunningdale.

Mark Ostrer (1892–1958), financier and film producer, was born three years after Isidore, on 4 November 1892. He served very effectively as the public face of the Ostrers. It was Mark who attended film premières and hobnobbed with film stars and his amiability well qualified him as the envoy of the Gaumont-British Picture Corporation in its negotiations with Hollywood. When the corporation was taken over by J. Arthur Rank, Mark retained his place on the board because of his good relations with the heads of Twentieth Century Fox and MGM; he remained a popular and influential figure in the British film industry until his death. Mark Ostrer was married twice, first to Karen Peterson (*d.* 1940); and then in 1943 to Olivia May Venning, with whom he had two sons. Mark Ostrer died at 186 Charles Street, London, on 5 November 1958. He was survived by his second wife.

Maurice Ostrer (*d.* 1975), financier and film producer, was the youngest of the brothers. He was described by James Mason (who married Isidore's daughter Pamela) as Isidore's shadow. Certainly the brothers collaborated very closely throughout a long and adventurous business career and Maurice died within months of his older brother, in December 1975. Maurice's main achievement, other than helping to manage Isidore's affairs, was in running Gainsborough Studios. He was in charge of production from 1937 onwards, but the day-to-day running of the studio was left in the capable hands of Edward Black until November 1943, when the two men fell out and Black resigned. It was in the period between the end of 1943 and the beginning of 1946, when Maurice took direct charge of the studio, that Gainsborough's most successful films, such as *The Wicked Lady* (1945), were produced. After resigning from Gainsborough in May 1946, Maurice worked briefly as an independent producer, and then joined Isidore in Cannes. Until the early 1970s he spent most of his time there, returning to England only for Illingworth-Morris board meetings. But his last years were spent with Isidore in a large house in Sunningdale, where the brothers became increasingly reclusive, even from each other. Maurice Ostrer died on 3 December 1975 at Sunningdale. ROBERT MURPHY

Sources M. Balcon, *Michael Balcon presents … a lifetime of films* (1969) • A. Wood, *Mr Rank: a study of J. Arthur Rank and British films* (1952) • G. Macnab, *J. Arthur Rank and the British film industry* (1993) • R. Low, *The history of the British film*, 4: *1918–1929* (1971) • R. Low, *Film making in 1930s Britain* (1985) • P. Shearlock, 'The perils of Pamela', *Sunday Times* (11 Oct 1981), 63 • *The Times* (6 Nov 1958), 15 [obit. of Mark Ostrer] • private information • *CGPLA Eng. & Wales* (1976) [Isidore Ostrer and Maurice Ostrer] • *CGPLA Eng. & Wales* (1959) [Mark Ostrer] • m. certs. • d. cert. • d. cert. [Mark Ostrer]

Wealth at death £1,492,435: probate, 13 April 1976, *CGPLA Eng. & Wales* • £455,689 16s. 6d.—Mark Ostrer: probate, 21 May 1959, *CGPLA Eng. & Wales* • £579,331—Maurice Ostrer: probate, 27 April 1976, *CGPLA Eng. & Wales*

Ostrer, Mark (1892–1958). *See under* Ostrer, Isidore (1889–1975).

Ostrer, Maurice (*d.* 1975). *See under* Ostrer, Isidore (1889–1975).

Ostrith. *See* Osthryth (*d.* 697).

Ostrogorski, Moisei Yakovlevich (1854–1919), political analyst, was born in Semicatrez, in the district of Bielsk, Grodno, in Belorussia, on 3 March 1854, the eldest of the three children of Yakolev Ostrogorski, who belonged to a landowning family of Jewish origin. He studied law at the University of St Petersburg and, after obtaining his degree, took up employment in the legislative department of the ministry of justice where, in 1882, he became head of department. In 1884 the authoritarianism that gripped Russia following the murder of Alexander II caused him to emigrate to France. In Paris he enrolled in the École Libre des Sciences Politiques, the private university founded in 1871 by Emile Boutmy and Hippolyte Taine. Ostrogorski's Parisian period saw him passionately committed to democratic militancy in defence of Dreyfus but, above all, it marked the beginning of his career as an expert in public law. In 1892 his study, *Les femmes au point de vue du droit public*, was published in France, soon to be followed by translations published in England (*The Rights of Women: a Comparative Study in History and Legislation*, 1893) and Germany.

In 1887 Ostrogorski began his research into political parties, at first confining himself to American parties. In 1889, on the advice of James Bryce, whom he knew by correspondence, Ostrogorski went to London to extend his inquiry to British political parties. This was to be the first of a long series of visits to the United Kingdom, during which Ostrogorski stayed in a hotel in Russell Square, close to the British Museum, where he spent his days studying. Frequently he organized trips to areas outside London to round out his bibliographical research with direct observation of the new parties in operation and to ask questions of the organizers of the political machines. He concluded his research on Britain in 1895. The following year he went to the United States to observe American parties at first hand.

Preparation for the publication of this research lasted until December 1902, when Macmillan published *Democracy and the Organisation of Political Parties*, which was followed a few months later by a French edition. The work consisted of two volumes, the first on the subject of British parties and the second on American parties. It was the first book to be dedicated entirely to extra-parliamentary political parties. It aimed to show how the development of modern political machines would inevitably come into conflict with the principles and institutions of liberal democracies. The vicissitudes of the British parties had strengthened Ostrogorski's conviction of this. He maintained that, from the development of the caucus system in Birmingham in the 1870s, British parties had taken the same path as American parties. The caucus system, in Ostrogorski's view, severely diminished the role of the individual in politics: instead of a lively dispute about ideas and policies, organizations accompanied by material and moral corruption would predominate. To save democracy Ostrogorski proposed replacing the permanent parties with one-issue leagues which would unite individuals for a limited period on the basis of specific objectives. The collective life of the masses would thus be given merely short-term and non-constricting organization, compatible with the theory and practice of democratic liberalism. Ostrogorski's book was based on wide-ranging research in periodicals, newspapers, and local libraries, which makes it a fertile source of information. While his condemnation of the caucus seems exaggerated in the light of the twentieth-century party bureaucracies which succeeded it, many of his detailed observations of the British political system—for example, the role of local government—were, and remain, original.

On completion of his book, in March 1903 Ostrogorski returned to Russia. In 1906 he was elected to the first Duma—the first experiment in representative institutions in Russia—for the constituency of Grodno. In keeping with the ideas expressed in his academic works, he refused to belong to a party. However, he became a leading member of the Duma, and was influential on questions of constitutional law and parliamentary procedure. When the crisis of the first Duma took place in July 1906, he was in London as a member of the Russian delegation to the inter-parliamentary conference. He tried to get himself re-elected to the second Duma (February 1907) and the third (October 1907) as a representative of the opposition coalition, but he failed both times.

Political defeat brought Ostrogorski back to his studies, and his attention turned again to Britain. He had visited England in August 1905 to revise and update his analysis of British politics. On that occasion the fame of his researches won him the honorary title of temporary member of the National Liberal Club. He went back to England again in June 1908, in July 1909, and finally for a longer period in April 1910. He was convinced that in the years since his book had come out many things had changed in British politics and that his analysis needed radical revision, although he felt that his section on American politics was much more sound and still relevant. Therefore in 1910 he published *Democracy and the party system in the United States: a study in extra-constitutional government*, a revised and abbreviated version of the 1902 edition, exclusively concerned with American parties. The new research on the British situation became part of the French edition of 1912 entitled *La démocratie et les parties politiques*, which gave a revised and abbreviated version of the whole work. Ostrogorski examined the Labour Party at some length, whereas he had merely made passing reference to it in the 1902 edition, and made significant changes to his final assessment. In general, however, his interpretation was unchanged. He remained convinced that the extra-parliamentary parties had destroyed the classic constitutional balance, by destroying the model of virtue and temperance that European liberals had admired for so long. The details of this analysis were set out again in a series of four articles on the evolution of British institutions that he began to write in 1912 and which were published the following year in the Russian periodical, the *European Herald*, whose editor was the liberal jurist Maxime Kovalevski. Ostrogorski was invited to put the four articles together to form a book to be published in France, but, although tempted by the proposal, he declined because of his precarious health.

In September 1913 Ostrogorski was struck down with vascular thrombosis which paralysed the left side of his body. Despite a long and difficult convalescence he made a miraculous recovery. In 1916 he took up a post at the University of St Petersburg, teaching constitutional law. In the same year he put the four articles on Britain together into one volume, aimed at a Russian readership, under the title *Konstitutsionnaya evolyutsia Anglii* ('The evolution of the British constitution'). In the introduction he defined his objective once and for all: to declare Bagehot's classic analysis of the British system out of date from the moment the extra-parliamentary parties appeared. In Ostrogorski's view the new parties had destroyed the traditional balance and produced an intolerable supremacy of the executive over the other powers. The British model was thus rejected in favour of a system of assembly in which the theory of organized parties would not find room for manoeuvre. This was his last work. Moisei Ostrogorski died in Petrograd during 1919, although the exact date has been obscured by the revolution.

GAETANO QUAGLIARIELLO

Sources G. Quagliariello, *Politics without parties: Moisei Ostrogorski and the debate on political parties on the eve of the twentieth century* (1996) • G. Quagliariello, 'Contributo alla biografia di M. Y. Ostrogorski', *Ricerche di storia politica*, 10 (1995) • P. Pombeni, 'Starting in reason ending in passion: Bryce, Lowell, Ostrogorski and the problem of democracy', *HJ*, 37 (1994), 319–41 • G. Orsina, ed., *Contro i partiti: saggi sul pensiero di Moisei Ostrogorski* (1993) • G. Ionesco, *Moisei Ostrogorski (1854–1919) and the theory of the professional political organization, rediscoveries: some neglected modern European political thinkers* (1986), 139–60 • R. Barker and X. H. Johnston, 'The politics and political ideas of Moisei Ostrogorski', *Political Studies*, 4 (1974), 415–29 • S. M. Lipset, 'Ostrogorskii, Mosei', *International encyclopedia of social science* (1968) • A. Ronnay, *The doctrine of responsible party government* (1954) • E. R. A. Seligman, ed., *Encyclopaedia of the social sciences*, 15 vols. (1930–35)

Archives BL, Macmillan MSS • Bodl. Oxf., Bryce MSS • Institut des Études Politiques, Paris, Boutmy MSS • priv. coll., Levy-Bruhl MSS

Ó Súilleabháin, Amhlaoibh [Humphrey O'Sullivan] (1783–1838), poet and diarist, was born in Killarney, Kerry, Ireland, on 1 May 1783, the son of Donncha Ó Súilleabháin (Denis O'Sullivan; 1738–1808), a hedge schoolmaster, and his wife, Máire Ní Bhuachalla (Mary Buckley; 1748–1827), described in 1821 as a 'hugster' (small shopkeeper). He had at least three brothers and two sisters, and the family left Killarney in 1789, moving first to Waterford and then in 1790 to Rogerstown, a crossroads outside Callan, co. Kilkenny, where his father erected a schoolhouse in a single day. They finally settled in Callan where Amhlaoibh spent the rest of his life.

Amhlaoibh Ó Súilleabháin owes his place in literature to *Cín Lae Amhlaoibh uí Shúilleabháin*, his Gaelic diary or *cín lae* (it was edited by Michael McGrath and published in 1936–7 in four volumes). Use of Gaelic for contemporary writing at that time was unusual, although not unknown. Ó Súilleabháin derived his proficiency in written Gaelic from his father who taught him. The diary covers the years 1827 to 1835, and began in English as 'observations on the weather, herbs, plants, trees etc.', but the language soon changed to Gaelic (although practical, financial, and administrative details are often given in English).

The original interest in nature was maintained, but the diary expanded into a significant record of the lives of those provincial middle-class Catholics who supported the campaigns of Daniel O'Connell and aspired to replace the ruling élite of the established church as the dominant class in Irish society. A local leader of O'Connell's political campaigns, Ó Súilleabháin made a speech in Irish at a 'monster meeting' in favour of Catholic emancipation in 1828. He also collected local contributions to the O'Connellite campaigns (the 'Catholic rent'), and in 1828 led the Catholic side in an agitation to wrest the charitable Callan dispensary from protestant control.

The diary is equally valuable as a record of Gaelic intellectual life. Ó Súilleabháin's themes include popular pastimes, Irish and international politics, protestant extremism, the campaign against the payment of tithes to the established church, relief schemes for the poor, foreign wars, legal issues, local agrarian rebellions, medical matters, and traditional festivals. The extravagant meals enjoyed by the leading Catholics of Callan at the home of the parish priest are described in detail.

It is less forthcoming on the details of Ó Súilleabháin's personal life: a single sentence on 1 July 1829 records the death of his wife, Máire Ní Dhulachanta (Mary Delahunty). She probably came from the Kilkenny city area. The diary, however, makes occasional reference to his surviving children, Donncha (*b.* *c.*1814), Anastás (*b.* *c.*1820), Amhlaoibhín, and Séamas, as well as to three children who died. It describes in detail an unsuccessful attempt to negotiate a second marriage (27–9 December 1829), and also includes details of presumed paternity payments to a servant, Maraed Soinseán, to whom a daughter Máire was born on 10 July 1831.

Ó Súilleabháin maintained a school in Callan, with some breaks, until 1831 when its closure coincided with the establishment of a state system of education, but more particularly with the growth of his business as a 'linen draper' and shopkeeper. He travelled regularly to wholesalers in Dublin, which allowed him to keep abreast of contemporary intellectual developments, in particular those associated with the Royal Irish Academy. He copied, compiled, and collected manuscripts, wrote stories and poems, and maintained contact with an extensive intellectual network, comprising scholars, artists, antiquarians, medical practitioners, and Catholic clergy. None of his work was printed in his lifetime; instead it forms part of the Gaelic manuscript tradition. Ó Súilleabháin died in 1838 and was buried at Kilbride, Callan, co. Kilkenny.

PROINSIAS Ó DRISCEOIL

Sources T. de Bhaldraithe, ed., *Cín Lae Amhlaoibh* (1970) • T. de Bhaldraithe, 'Cín Lae Amhlaoibh', *The pleasures of Gaelic literature*, ed. J. Jordan (1977), 97–111 • M. McGrath, *Cínlae Amhlaoibh Uí Shúileabháin*, 4 vols. (1936–7) • M. O'Flanagan, ed., *Kilkenny ordnance survey letters*, 2 (1931), 16 • P. Ó Drisceoil, *Ar Scaradh Gabhail: An Fhéiniúlacht in Cín Lae AmhlaoibhUí Súilleabháin* (2000) • É. Ó hÓgáin, 'Amhlaoibh Ó Súilleabháin agus a mhuintir in 1821', *Old Kilkenny Review* (1985), 189–90 • É. Ó hÓgáin, 'Scríobhaithe lámhscríbhinní Gaeilge i gCill Chainnigh 1700–1870', *Kilkenny: history and society*, ed. W. Nolan and K. Whelan (1990), 405–36 • B. Ó Madagáin, *An Dialann Dúlra* (1978) • Royal Irish Acad., MSS 23 A 48, 23 L 23, 23 H 26 • 'Irish education inquiry: second report', *Parl. papers* (1826–7), vol. 12, no. 12 • census information for 1821 in Canon Carrigan's notebooks, St Kieran's College, Kilkenny, Carrigan papers • Ó Súilleabháin family tombstone, Kilbride, Callan, co. Kilkenny, Ireland • Delahunty family tombstone, Outrath, Kilkenny, Ireland • J. Pigot, *City of Dublin and Hibernian provincial directory* (1824), 137

Archives Royal Irish Acad., 23 A 48, 23 H 26, 23 I 21, 23 K 41, 23 K 46, 23 K 50, 23 L 20, 23 L 23 | St Kieran's College, Kilkenny, Carrigan notebooks

Ó Súilleabháin, Eoghan Rua [Owen Roe O'Sullivan] (*c.*1748–1784), poet, was born in Meentogues, co. Kerry. Meentogues, about 7 miles to the east of Killarney, is in the Slieve Luachra area of that county, a region which was famous for literature in the eighteenth century and is still famous for the quality of traditional music that can be heard there. Eoghan spent his short life mainly in this area working sometimes as a schoolmaster or as a tutor to the children of well-to-do local people. However, he also found work as an itinerant labourer or *spailpín* in co. Cork and co. Limerick. He seems never to have settled for long, and many of the stories about him refer to his tendency to lose posts because of his rakish behaviour. It is interesting that in these stories in which he transgresses the boundaries of acceptable behaviour he is invariably the hero and his traducers are the villains. A typical story is the one associated with one of his most celebrated poems 'An tArrachtach Sean' ('The old monster'). After one of his excursions from his home territory he returned at Christmas to find that there was a poetic contention concerning the virtues of the married men of the parish as opposed to those of the bachelors. Ó Súilleabháin's satire on the married men (the 'old monsters' who were married to the beautiful maidens) swept away the opposition and won the day for the bachelors. The whole episode has a ritual flavour in which a society delineates the boundaries by identifying and even glorifying those who go beyond them.

It seems also that Eoghan Rua spent some time in England after he joined the Royal Navy, either by his own volition or by being pressed into it. He served under Vice-Admiral Rodney and in April 1782 was present when he won his greatest victory off the coast of Dominica in the West Indies. A poem in English, 'Rodney's Glory', is attributed to Ó Súlleabháin, the last verse reading as follows:

Now may prosperity attend,
Brave Rodney and his Irishmen,
And may he never want a friend,
While he shall remain commander;
Success to our Irish officers,
Seamen bold and jolly tars,
Who like the darling sons of Mars
Take delight in the fight
And vindicate bold England's right
And die for Erin's glory.
(Ua Duinnín, *Amhráin*, xx)

The sentiments are interesting, even if this is not great poetry. At least one of his other poems was written while Ó Súilleabháin was in England, 'I Sacsaibh na séad i gcéin óm dhúchas' ('In England of the treasures far away from my native place'). This poem gives the idea that he may have been pressed into service as a number of lines refer to the fetters that tie him to England.

Generally speaking the subject matter of Ó Súilleabháin's poetry is unremarkable. The political content is anti-English and pro-Jacobite. He is the master of the political *aisling* or dream poetry in which the poet sees Ireland as a beautiful woman deserted by her rightful spouse, abused by strangers and awaiting the former's return from across the sea. It is usually acknowledged that this genre reaches its highest level with Ó Súilleabháin even though the political impulse, the return of the Jacobite pretenders to the throne, had long been an empty aspiration. His strength is in the mastery of language, metre, and style, and this virtuosity must have helped in making him a poet-hero among those who could understand his words whether they read them in manuscript or just heard them sung or recited. It is on account of this virtuosity that he was and is still known as 'Eoghan an Bhéil Bhinn' ('Sweet-Mouthed Owen'). Any of the twenty or so *aisling* poems attributed to him could be taken as an exemplar for the genre, and few have surpassed his 'Ceo Draíochta' ('Magic mist') or 'Im leabaidh aréir' ('Last night in my bed'). His output includes love poems, some of them earthy enough as one would expect, laments for friends and patrons, occasional poems, satires (including a number of poetical 'warrants'), and the aforementioned political *aislings* and other poems.

Of Ó Súilleabháin's career as a teacher relatively little is known. He seems to have been tutor to the children of the Nagles from near Fermoy, co. Cork, and is said to have left this employment pursued by Mr Nagle with a gun. It is speculated that this was the occasion of Ó Súilleabháin's joining the Royal Navy. When he returned from service in the navy he is said to have set up school in Knocknagree, near his birthplace in co. Kerry. He reputedly asked the parish priest, Father Ned Fitzgerald, to announce his school in the following terms:

Reverend Sir—
Please to publish from the altar of your holy Mass
That I will open school at Knocknagree Cross,
Where the tender babes will be well off,
For it's there I'll teach them their Criss Cross;
Reverend Sir, you will by experience find,
All my endeavours to please mankind,
For it's there I will teach them how to read and write;
The Catechism I will explain
To each young nymph and noble swain …

With compass and rule I will teach them
Bills and bonds and informations,
Summons, warrants, supersedes,
Judgement tickets good,
Leases, receipts in full,
And releases, short accounts,
With rhyme and reason,
And sweet love letters for the ladies.
(Ua Duinnín, *Amhráin*, xxii)

There is no record of the success or otherwise of this venture. In the summer of 1784 it seems Ó Súilleabháin was wounded in an affray at an alehouse in Killarney. He returned to Knocknagree wounded and with a fever and, as his editor paraphrased the demise of co. Kerry's most famous hero-poet, 'an act of self indulgence, it is said, brought on a relapse from which he never rallied' (Ua Duinnín, *Amhráin*, xxiii). He was buried probably in Muckross Abbey, Killarney, in 1784. ALAN HARRISON

Sources P. Ua Duinnín, *Amhráin Eoghain Ruaidh Uí Shúilleabháin* (Dublin, 1901) • P. Ua Duinnín, *Beatha Eoghain Ruaidh Uí Shúilleabháin* (Dublin, 1902) • D. Corkery, *The hidden Ireland* (1925) • S. Ó Tuama and T. Kinsella, *An duanaire: poems of the dispossessed* (Dublin, 1981) • S. Ó Tuama, *An grá in amhráin na ndaoine* (Dublin, 1960) • B. Ó Buachalla, *Aisling Ghéar* (Dublin, 1996) • D. Ó hÓgáin, *An file* (Dublin, 1982) • D. Ó hÓgáin, *The hero in Irish folk history* (Dublin, 1985) • J. O' Daly, *Poets and poetry of Munster* (Dublin, 1850)

Ó Súilleabháin, Muiris [Maurice O'Sullivan] (**1904–1950**), writer, was born on 19 February 1904 on the Great Blasket Island (An Blascaod Mór), co. Kerry, Ireland, the youngest child of Seán 'Lís' Ó Súilleabháin (*bap.* 1868) and his wife, Cáit Ní Ghuithín (*bap.* 1873, *d.* 1905). Ó Súilleabháin was the great-grandson of one of the island's *filí* (traditional versifiers), Mícheál Ó Súilleabháin (*fl.* 1810–1890), and the author Tomás Ó Criomhthain (1855–1937) was a great-uncle of Ó Súilleabháin on his mother's side. After the death of his mother Ó Súilleabháin spent six years in an orphanage in Dingle town on the mainland before returning in 1911 to the Blaskets where he attended the island school until 1918. It was his grandfather Eoghan Ó Súilleabháin who was to be the dominant person in young Muiris's life. Eoghan (Daideo) was a noted *seanchaí* (traditional lorist).

The Great Blasket Island is situated off the Kerry coast. It contained, at the time of Ó Súilleabháin's birth, an Irish-speaking community of 145 people (6 others lived on the adjacent island of Inis Icíleáin from whence Muiris Ó Súilleabháin's grandmother came). The island community and its lifestyle were essentially medieval in character, with a strong oral tradition of storytelling and *seanchas* (traditional lore) deeply rooted in the Gaelic tradition. The island became a focus for visiting scholars interested in

Muiris Ó Súilleabháin (1904–1950), by Vincent Henry Lines

Irish language and culture, and George Derwent Thomson (1903–1987) was one of those who visited, on the advice of Robin Flower (1881–1946), keeper of manuscripts at the British Museum. Thomson was a Greek scholar, later to become professor of Greek at Birmingham (1937–70). On his arrival at the island in 1923 he established a close friendship with Muiris Ó Súilleabháin and his family. He was later to dedicate his edition of the *Oresteia* (1938) to Muiris Ó Súilleabháin.

Thomson persuaded Ó Súilleabháin not to emigrate to America but rather to join the Gárda Síochána (the Irish civil police) in 1927. After training Ó Súilleabháin took up police duty in an Irish-speaking district at Indreabhán in west Galway and it was here that he first began to write. Thomson urged Ó Súilleabháin to write of his childhood on the island, and Ó Súilleabháin wrote a manuscript in sections, which were sent to Thomson who was then teaching at University College, Galway. Thomson edited the text as it arrived, and, with the assistance of Moya Llewelyn Davies, he also translated it into English. The translation was published as *Twenty Years a-Growing* in May 1933, one month after the Irish original *Fiche Blian ag Fás* had appeared. *Twenty Years a-Growing* covers the period of Muiris Ó Súilleabháin's early childhood on the Great Blasket Island, including an account of his schooling in the Dingle Orphanage, until his arrival in west Galway as a policeman. Its style is youthful and joyously exuberant, and gives a young man's point of view on the Blasket community at its strength. Its portrait may be tinged slightly with nostalgia, particularly in its moving recollections of Ó Súilleabháin's family and island friends and of his grandfather Eoghan, but its style and that of the English translation make island life accessible. From its success in translation (in French and German as well as in English), it clearly appealed to a readership interested in the romance of island life. E. M. Forster knew Ó Súilleabháin, and in his introduction to the 1933 English text he wrote:

> … and though he is pleased that his book should be translated, his main care is for the Irish original, because it will be read on the Blasket. They will appreciate it more than we can, for whom the wit and poetry must be veiled. On the other hand, we are their superiors in astonishment. They cannot possibly be as much surprised as we are, for here is the egg of a sea-bird—lovely, perfect, and laid this very morning.

Muiris Ó Súileabháin resigned from the Gárda Síochána on 5 July 1934 to become a full-time writer, and married Cáit Ní Chatháin of Doire Fheárta, An Cheathrú Rua in west Galway, on 10 July of that year. They had two children: Eoghan (*b.* 1935) and Máirín (*b.* 1944). Muiris wrote the second of what he had planned as an autobiographical trilogy—*Fiche Blian Faoi Bhláth* (*Twenty Years a-Flowering*)—between 1935 and 1940. Irish-language publishers showed no enthusiasm for it, however, and the text has remained unpublished. Freelance writing and journalism and broadcasting in Irish did not provide a living for the Ó Súilleabháin family and Muiris Ó Súilleabháin returned to the police in 1950. He died while swimming off Salthill on 25 June 1950 and was buried two days later at Barr an Doire, An Cheathrú Rua, co. Galway.

MUIRIS DIARMUID MAC CONGHAIL

Sources Fiche Blian ag Fás MS, NL Ire., MS Acc/4562 • series of interviews with Professor George Derwent Thomson • N. Ní Aimhirgín, *Muiris Ó Súilleabháin* (1983) • G. Thomson, *The Blasket heritage* (1988) • M. Mac Conghail, *The Blaskets: a Kerry island library* (1987) • parish register, Kerry, Ballyferriter [baptism: parents]
Archives NL Ire., MS of Fiche Blian Art Gallery Fás • priv. coll.
Likenesses V. H. Lines, pencil and ink drawing, NG Ire. [*see illus.*] • S. O'Sullivan, drawing, NG Ire. • photographs, priv. coll.

Ó Súilleabháin, Tadhg Gaelach [Timothy Sullivan] (*c.***1715**–*c.***1795**), poet, whose origins are obscure, is not mentioned in any documentary source and no manuscripts survive in his hand; what is known of his life is reconstructed largely from oral tradition and from the internal evidence of his poetry and the manuscripts in which it occurs. According to local tradition he was born in Tuar na Fola, co. Limerick. His earliest known poem is a eulogy of Tadhg McCarthy, bishop of Cork, written about 1740. To judge by the provenance of manuscripts containing his poems, and the place names mentioned in them, he was active in co. Cork until the mid-1760s, and in co. Waterford thereafter. Tradition maintains that, following a religious conversion, he led a life of piety, becoming in his later years a member of a confraternity in Dungarvan, co. Waterford, for which he composed a series of poems. This tradition is given some support by Ó Súilleabháin's surviving poetical corpus, which consists of thirty-four secular poems and thirty-three devotional poems, the former dating predominantly from before the 1760s, and the latter from after. The devotional poetry was collected together in a manuscript anthology in 1792 by Laurence Morrissey, later parish priest of Owning, co. Kilkenny, and first published as *The Pious Miscellany*, in Clonmel, co. Tipperary, in 1802. Over twenty editions were published in the first half of the nineteenth century, mostly in the towns of Munster, and it became the most frequently printed book in the Irish language before the twentieth century. Ó Súilleabháin died in Waterford city about 1795.

NIALL Ó CIOSÁIN

Sources T. Sullivan, *Irish pious miscellany* (1802) • Royal Irish Acad., MSS 109, 195, 304, 379, 413 • JRL, Irish MS 64 • R. Ó Foghludha, ed., *Tadhg Gaelach* (1929)

Osulf [Oswulf], **earl of Bamburgh** (*d.* **1067**), magnate, was the son of Eadulf, earl of Bamburgh (*d.* 1041), the younger son of Earl *Uhtred (*d.* 1016). Eadulf succeeded his brother Ealdred as earl in 1038 but was himself killed in 1041 by Earl Siward who then assumed control of the whole earldom of Northumbria from the Humber to the Tweed. In 1065 Morcar, successor to Tostig in the earldom, appointed Osulf, described as a young man, to rule that portion of his territory which lay to the north of the Tyne, thus revitalizing the comital power of the house of Bamburgh. Following the Norman conquest, Morcar was deposed and imprisoned and Tostig's former deputy, Copsi, was given Osulf's earldom. Early in February 1067 Copsi ventured north and drove Osulf into hiding while he attempted to secure his position as earl. Osulf took to the woods and mountains of the region suffering want and hunger but managing to gather together allies who had shared a similar fate. Some of his supporters were, according to William of Poitiers, disaffected members of Copsi's entourage who wanted their lord to oppose the Conqueror. Osulf's opposition to Copsi may also have been fuelled by the suspicion that Copsi may have been implicated in the deaths of Osulf's uncle Gospatric and other members and allies of the house of Bamburgh murdered at the behest of Tostig in the early 1060s. Five weeks after his appointment to the earldom, on 12 March 1067, Copsi was attacked by Osulf and his men as he feasted at the ancient comital manor of Newburn. Copsi escaped to the local church but when it was set on fire he was forced out of the burning building; as he emerged Osulf decapitated him. Osulf seems to have regained control of the earldom of Bamburgh and remained unthreatened by any other expeditions sanctioned by William the Conqueror. However, in the autumn of 1067, Osulf was run through by the spear of a bandit whom he had intercepted whether by chance or design. He was succeeded as earl by his kinsman *Gospatric who purchased the office from the king.

WILLIAM M. AIRD

Sources Symeon of Durham, *Opera*, vol. 2 • Guillaume de Poitiers [Gulielmus Pictaviensis], *Histoire de Guillaume le Conquérant / Gesta Gulielmus ducis Normannorum et regis Anglorum*, ed. R. Foreville (Paris, 1952) • Ordericus Vitalis, *Eccl. hist.*, vol. 2 • A. Williams, *The English and the Norman conquest* (1995) • F. S. Scott, 'Earl Waltheof of Northumbria', *Archaeologia Aeliana*, 4th ser., 30 (1952), 149–215 • W. M. Aird, 'St Cuthbert, the Scots and the Normans', *Anglo-Norman Studies*, 16 (1993), 1–20

O'Sullivan, Cornelius (**1841–1907**), brewing chemist, was born in Bandon, co. Cork, on 20 December 1841, one of three boys and four girls born to James O'Sullivan, merchant, and his wife, Elizabeth Morgan. His brief primary schooling was at Denny Holland's private school, followed by some years at Tommy Lordan's Cavendish School; he left the latter as a protest over indiscriminate corporal punishment. He attended evening classes of the Department of Science and Art in Bandon in 1861–2. On the strength of four prizes won at examinations in May 1862 he was awarded a scholarship at the Royal School of Mines, London. During his three-year course there he won further prizes, then briefly joined the teaching staff of the Royal College of Chemistry as a student assistant under Professor August Wilhelm von Hofmann. On Hofmann's appointment as professor of chemistry at Berlin University in 1865 O'Sullivan accompanied him as private assistant.

The following year Hofmann's influence secured O'Sullivan the post of assistant brewer and chemist to Bass, Ratcliff, and Gretton Ltd of Burton upon Trent. He remained with them as head of the scientific and analytical department until his death. In 1875 the company established a laboratory department; O'Sullivan's brother James became his assistant in 1876. O'Sullivan was among the first chemists to apply scientific principles specifically to brewing, and was quick to realize the value of Pasteur's work to the industry. It was particularly his work on the products of the hydrolysis of starch by acids and by diastase to which he owed his reputation. The results of his work on starch were published in numerous papers, chiefly in the *Journal of the Chemical Society*, between 1872 and 1879. His important work included his rediscovery of maltose (following Dubrunfaut in 1847) and the effect of temperature in determining the character of the products of the action of diastase on starch; on the sugars and other carbohydrates of certain cereals and germinated grain (such as his detection and isolation of raffinose in barley); on the chemistry of different gums; and on the enzymes of yeast.

On 2 February 1870 O'Sullivan married, at St Mary's Church, Derby, Edithe Nadin (*d.* 1904) of Barrow Hall, Barrow upon Trent, near Derby, the daughter of Joseph Nadin, co-proprietor of Stanton colliery. They had three sons, the youngest of whom died in childhood, and a daughter. The family lived at 140 High Street, Burton upon Trent, until 1897 when they moved to number 148 which was built by the company. There O'Sullivan installed a fully equipped chemical laboratory. The family took a holiday in Bandon almost every year for over thirty years. O'Sullivan's interests included music, fishing, and, latterly, motoring. He belonged to and gave several lectures to the Burton Natural History and Archaeological Society. Elected a fellow then vice-president of the Chemical Society in 1876, he served on its council from 1882 to 1885 and was awarded its Longstaff medal in 1884 chiefly for his researches on the chemistry of the carbohydrates. He was an original member of the Institute of Chemistry, the Society of Chemical Industry, on whose publication committee he served for ten years, and the Institute of Brewing, of which he was elected an honorary member in 1893; he served on the council of each. In 1885 he was elected a fellow of the Royal Society.

Edithe had long suffered from asthma, then from a weak heart, caused by rheumatic fever, from which she died in July 1904. O'Sullivan, after a bad attack of catarrhal jaundice, died at home on 8 January 1907. He was buried next to his wife and third son in Ballymodan graveyard near Bandon on 13 January.

T. E. JAMES, *rev.* ROBERT SHARP

Sources H. D. O'Sullivan, *The life and work of C. O'Sullivan, F.R.S.* (1934) · *Journal of the Institute of Brewing*, 13 (1907), 102–4 · *Nature*, 75 (1906–7), 277 · *Journal of the Society of Chemical Industry*, 26 (1907), 139–40 · *Proceedings of the Institute of Chemists of Great Britain and Ireland* (1907), 24 · *The Analyst*, 32 (1907), 74 · *The Times* (9 Jan 1907)
Wealth at death £70,360 2s. 3d.: resworn probate, 4 March 1907, *CGPLA Eng. & Wales*

O'Sullivan, Donall. *See* O'Sullivan Beare, Donnell Cam, count of Bearehaven in the Spanish nobility (1560–1618).

O'Sullivan, Humphrey. *See* Ó Súilleabháin, Amhlaoibh (1783–1838).

O'Sullivan, Maurice. *See* Ó Súilleabháin, Muiris (1904–1950).

O'Sullivan, Mortimer (1792/3–1859), Church of Ireland clergyman, was born at Clonmel, co. Tipperary, the second son of John O'Sullivan, a schoolmaster. He was educated with his elder brother, Samuel [*see below*], and his friend William Phelan at the Clonmel endowed school. The headmaster, Dr Richard Carey, a close friend of John O'Sullivan, was an earnest protestant, while the O'Sullivans were Roman Catholics. Carey was much revered by his pupils, and the realization that Catholic dogma pronounced him a reprobate first led Mortimer to begin the train of thought that led him to Anglicanism. He entered as a protestant scholar at Trinity College, Dublin, in 1813 (having first matriculated in 1811), and proceeded BA in 1816. He took his MA in 1832 and his BD and DD in 1837.

After six or seven years at the university O'Sullivan returned to the south, and became second master of the Tipperary endowed school, and curate of the parish of Tipperary. He was subsequently the first master of the Royal School at Dungannon and also lived in Waterford for a time. He was chaplain of St Stephen's Chapel, Dublin, and on 20 December 1827 was collated to the prebend of St Audoen's in St Patrick's Cathedral, Dublin. This office he resigned on 24 August 1830 on being presented to the rectory of Killyman, co. Armagh, in succession to William Phelan.

As a young man O'Sullivan became interested in the relations between the Catholic and protestant churches in Ireland. In 1824, in reply to Thomas Moore's *Captain Rock*, he wrote *Captain Rock Detected*. Here O'Sullivan refuted the charges of financial rapacity that Moore levied against the Anglican clergy and attributed the current disturbed state of the south of Ireland to excessive rents, absentee landlords, and the demoralizing influence of the Roman Catholic clergy. O'Sullivan gave evidence before the parliamentary select committee on the state of Ireland in spring 1825 and (with William Phelan) subsequently published *A Digest of Evidence on the State of Ireland in 1824–5* (1826). In 1834 he was sent with the Revd Charles Boyton as a deputation to England and Scotland from the Irish clergy to make known the condition of their church. O'Sullivan described with great eloquence and passion the insecurity of the Irish protestant clergy, in Liverpool on 22 November 1834, Exeter Hall, London, on 20 June and 11 July 1835, and also in many provincial towns. On 26 May 1835, when summoned to give evidence before the select committee on Orange lodges, O'Sullivan stated that the Orange societies were of importance in preserving the peace of Ulster. On his return to Ireland in October 1835 he engaged in a controversy with Dr Daniel Murray, the Roman Catholic archbishop of Dublin, who charged him with misreporting his words before the Lords' committee on the circulation of the Bible among the laity. The correspondence was published. In September 1836 O'Sullivan was again in Glasgow, and on 27 May 1837 a further enthusiastic meeting was held in Exeter Hall. Full reports of all the meetings from mid-1835 onwards, with correspondence, were published by O'Sullivan and the Revd Robert M'Ghee in *Romanism as it Rules in Ireland* (1840). In 1851 O'Sullivan was Donellan lecturer at Trinity College, taking as his theme 'The hour of the Redeemer', an examination of the redeeming and atoning work of Christ. O'Sullivan published numerous other sermons, tracts, and contributions to the debate on Roman Catholicism and the state of Ireland. In 1849 he became a prebendary of Armagh and in 1853 was made rector of Tandragee, co. Armagh. During the latter years of his life he resided in Lower Gloucester Street, Dublin, and officiated as chaplain to the earl of Carlisle, the lord lieutenant, and to the duke of Manchester. He died in Dublin on 30 April 1859, and was buried on 3 May in Chapelizod churchyard.

Samuel O'Sullivan (1790–1851), Church of Ireland clergyman, elder brother of Mortimer, was born at Clonmel on 13 September 1790, and educated with Mortimer at the Clonmel endowed school. He attended protestant services with his schoolmaster, and was powerfully attracted by the liturgy. When he obtained a scholarship at Trinity College, Dublin, in 1814 (having first matriculated in 1812), he was entered as a member of the Church of England. He graduated BA in 1818, MA in 1825, and BD and DD in 1837. He was an active member of the university historical society, and was awarded the medal for the best speaker in debates. He was ordained in 1818, serving initially as curate of St Catherine's, Dublin, and at the same time chaplain of the Marshalsea, Dublin. In 1827 he succeeded Dean Le Fanu as chaplain to the Royal Hibernian Military School in Phoenix Park, a position he held for the rest of his life. His time was chiefly devoted to literary pursuits. His first work, published in 1816, argued that the course of English history in the sixteenth and seventeenth centuries manifestly displayed the agency of divine providence. It greatly impressed his contemporaries. He contributed to *Blackwood's Edinburgh Magazine* and to *Fraser's Magazine*, and wrote extensively for the *Dublin University Magazine*. Towards the end of his life, in 1850, he compiled and published a well-received explanation of the catechism of the Anglican church. He died at the Royal Hibernian Military School on 6 August 1851 and was buried on 9 August in the churchyard at Chapelizod, Dublin. His wife, a son, Henry R. M. O'Sullivan, and a daughter, survived him.

CHARLOTTE FELL-SMITH, *rev.* JOHN WOLFFE

Sources J. C. Martin and M. O'Sullivan, eds., *Remains of the Rev. Samuel O'Sullivan, DD* (1853) • 'The late Rev. Samuel O'Sullivan', *Dublin University Magazine*, 38 (1851), 504–8 • J. Jebb, 'Biographical memoir', *The remains of William Phelan*, ed. M. Phelan (1832), 1–87 • *Memoirs, journal and correspondence of Thomas Moore*, ed. J. Russell, 8 vols. (1853–6) • *GM*, 2nd ser., 36 (1851), 438–9 • D. Bowen, *The protestant crusade in Ireland, 1800–70* (1978) • J. Wolffe, *The protestant crusade in Great Britain, 1829–1860* (1991)

Archives NL Scot., corresp. with Blackwoods

Likenesses J. Kirkwood, etching (after C. Grey), NPG

Wealth at death £5000: probate, 18 June 1859, *CGPLA Ire.*

O'Sullivan, Owen Roe. *See* Ó Súilleabháin, Eoghan Rua (*c.*1748–1784).

O'Sullivan, Samuel (1790–1851). *See under* O'Sullivan, Mortimer (1792/3–1859).

O'Sullivan, Seumas. *See* Starkey, James Sullivan (1879–1958).

O'Sullivan Beare, Donnell Cam, count of Bearehaven in the Spanish nobility (1560–1618), chieftain, was the son of Donnell, chief of the O'Sullivan Beare in co. Kerry, and Margaret O'Brien, daughter of the O'Brien of Thomond. In 1563 his father was killed by a McGillycuddy and was succeeded by Donnell's uncle Owen O'Sullivan Beare. Owen regarded his young nephew as a threat and banished Donnell to his mother's country, in Eyeries on the south side of the Kenmare River. He was educated in Waterford and learned to speak fluent English. When, in 1580, Owen was imprisoned in Limerick on suspicion of conspiring to rebel, he agreed to put Beare, in co. Cork, in Donnell's charge. In return, Donnell acknowledged Owen as his adopted father, a decision he subsequently regretted. During this confused period, as guardian of Beare, Donnell appears to have been in rebellion against the crown, probably on the advice of Owen's supporters. Certainly, in December 1581 he engaged and routed in battle at Carberry a raiding party composed mainly of Gaelic allies of the crown.

Owen was probably released early in 1582, and he granted Donnell a portion of land within his lordship. However, this accommodation soon broke down and Donnell was expelled once more. Donnell then turned to the English law of primogeniture as a means of regaining his father's country, and from 1584 appeared regularly in London to plead his case. Owen and Donnell vied to prove their loyalty to the crown, and each accused the other of involvement in the Desmond rebellion of 1579–83. Neither was entirely innocent, but Owen had much the longer record of disloyalty.

In May 1587 the case was heard before the lord deputy and privy council of Ireland, who recommended that Donnell receive a portion of Beare after Owen's death and be given a pension paid out of Owen's rents until then. However, Donnell, dissatisfied, appealed to the English privy council in London. When Donnell and Owen outlined their respective positions before the privy council in London in July 1591, it could not come to a decision because of a lack of reliable evidence and decided to send a commission to Beare to examine witnesses. Finally, on 5 June 1593 the privy council ruled that Beare be partitioned between Donnell, Owen, and Owen's brother Phillip. Crucially, although Owen was granted the bulk of the land, Donnell received the castle of Dunboy and its environs. Dunboy was probably the best harbour in south-west Ireland, enabling its possessor to levy tolls on Spanish and French fishermen who trawled the thriving fisheries off the coast of Cork and Kerry. The loss of these revenues undermined Owen's authority, and in 1594 Donnell was formally elected O'Sullivan Beare in his stead.

Donnell's gains were soon jeopardized by the growing political instability in Munster, caused mainly by the success enjoyed by Hugh O'Neill, earl of Tyrone, in his rebellion against the government. For the next seven years O'Sullivan appeared outwardly loyal, and when Tyrone marched triumphantly into Munster in 1600 O'Sullivan was one of the few chieftains who ignored his summons. However, his real attitude towards the crown may well have been more ambiguous. He was close to another ostensibly loyalist Gaelic chieftain, Florence McCarthy Reagh, who was secretly encouraging Spanish intervention in Ireland on behalf of the rebels. It should also be noted that sources of O'Sullivan's later years show him to have been a very zealous Catholic.

When the Spanish landed at Kinsale on 2 October 1601 O'Sullivan supported them enthusiastically and handed over Dunboy to a Spanish garrison. He led about 1000 men under Tyrone at the disastrous battle of Kinsale on 24 December 1601. Following the battle he attempted to submit to the government, but the English refused to pardon him. Before fleeing back to Ulster, Tyrone appointed O'Sullivan head of the rebel forces in Munster. O'Sullivan commanded about 2000 men and over the next year became the main symbol of continued Irish resistance.

Meanwhile, in January 1602 the leader of the Spanish expedition agreed terms with the English, which included the handing over of Dunboy. O'Sullivan hastened back to Beare, and through subterfuge managed to seize Dunboy from its Spanish garrison. He immediately dispatched letters to the king of Spain, apologizing for his actions and appealing for further aid. Some help did eventually arrive from Spain, but not enough to make a difference. The sheer inaccessibility of Dunboy and its surrounds enabled O'Sullivan to engage in a protracted, but hopeless, rearguard action. The strategic importance of Dunboy prompted Sir George Carew, lord president of Munster, to devote all his resources to taking it. The castle fell in late June 1602 after a skilfully conducted siege by Carew. During the latter half of 1602 O'Sullivan's allies melted away, and by year's end he was effectively cornered in Bantry. In late December a royal force of about 2000 engaged the remnants of his forces at Glengariff. After a fierce battle the English made off with O'Sullivan's cattle, leaving him with no means to sustain his army. Starved of supplies, he decided to march out of Munster, hoping to link up with Tyrone. In the epic march that followed his forces suffered terribly from almost continuous attacks from English forces and from Irish eager to prove their loyalty. They enjoyed a brief respite on crossing the Shannon at Portland, co. Tipperary, but on reaching Aughrim, in co. Galway, were confronted by numerically superior forces commanded by Captain Henry Malby and Henry Burke. O'Sullivan roused his men into a desperate assault, which routed their surprised enemies. On 14 January 1603 he and thirty-four survivors reached the relative safety of Leitrim, having traversed 200 miles in fourteen days in the depths of winter. After resting, O'Sullivan entered Ulster only to discover that Tyrone had already surrendered.

In June 1603 O'Sullivan accompanied Tyrone and Rory O'Donnell to London to speak with the newly crowned James I. However, he was refused a pardon. He returned to Ireland and, in spring 1605, sailed into La Corunna, Spain, with several hundred followers. There he helped found the Irish college at Santiago de Compostela in Galicia. Early in 1606 his men were shipped to Flanders, but he went to Madrid to pursue a career as a courtier. He was granted a pension, admitted to the prestigious Spanish order of Santiago in 1607, and created count of Bearehaven in 1617. Shortly before his death O'Sullivan was apparently involved in plans to initiate a rebellion in Munster. On 16 July 1618 O'Sullivan was killed by John Bathe outside Madrid, apparently after a dispute over money. The circumstances of his death are obscure and quite suspicious, given that Bathe was a spy for the English government. O'Sullivan had two sons with his wife, Elena, daughter of O'Sullivan Mor. TERRY CLAVIN

Sources *CSP Ire.*, 1585–1608 · *APC*, 1587–93, 1597, 1599–1600 · T. Stafford, *Pacata Hibernica* (1896), vol. 2, pp. 47–9, 118–28, 152, 156, 215, 281–5 · *AFM*, vols. 5–6 · P. O'Sullivan Beare, *Ireland under Elizabeth: chapters towards a history of Ireland in the reign of Elizabeth*, ed. and trans. M. J. Byrne (1903) · J. S. Brewer and W. Bullen, eds., *Calendar of the Carew manuscripts*, 4: *1601–1603*, PRO (1870) · R. A. Stirling, *The Spanish monarchy and Irish mercenaries* (1994), p. 65 · M. Kerney Walsh, *Spanish knights of Irish origin*, 1 (1960), 1–5 · J. J. Silke, *The Spanish intervention in Ireland* (1970), 111, 131–2, 153, 155–6, 159, 163, 175 · M. Kerney Walsh, *An exile of Ireland* (1996), 104–6 · P. Somerville-Large, *From Bantry Bay to Leitrim* (1980) · *Calendar of patent records, Elizabeth*, 2, pp. 295–8

Likenesses portrait, 1613, Maynooth, co. Kildare, Ireland

O'Sullivan Beare, Philip (*b. c.*1590, *d.* in or after 1634), historian and writer, was one of the seventeen children of Dermot O'Sullivan and his wife, Johanna MacSwiney. Born on Valentia Island off the Kerry coast in south-western Ireland, he belonged to the family that owned much of the remote peninsula. However, the O'Sullivans, headed by the O'Sullivan Beare, were under pressure from an English regime keen to advance alien systems of land tenure, inheritance, and agriculture, and from new planters established in the region. The Nine Years' War, ending in 1603, brought the defeat of the O'Sullivans and their allies. Many of those not killed in the warfare moved to continental Europe. Among the refugees were Philip

O'Sullivan Beare, his parents, some of his siblings, and his kinsman O'Sullivan Beare. The young O'Sullivan arrived in Corunna in northern Spain in 1602, and immediately received the protection of the local governor, Carazena. Educated at Santiago de Compostela, he joined kinsmen who opposed the Jesuits' annexation of the college in 1613. Unlike others in the institution, he was not destined for the priesthood, and soon secured commissions in the army and then the navy. However, this service was not congenial to a young man with scholarly and polemical inclinations. A bellicosity, which would later animate his writings, also marked his behaviour. At Madrid in 1618, he engaged in a sword fight with another fugitive from Ireland, Sir John Bathe, suspected as a spy sent to report on the schemes of the refugee community in Spain. In the ensuing mêlée, Bathe killed the O'Sullivan Beare, whom Philip III of Spain had ennobled as conde de Birhaven.

Philip O'Sullivan took sanctuary in the house of the French ambassador, but suffered no penalties. Thereafter his movements are obscure. The suggestion that he eventually returned to Ireland, to the Franciscan house of Kilcrea in co. Cork, is unsupported by any evidence. Nor is it known when he died. The last clear indication of his being alive is in 1634.

O'Sullivan's writings reveal something of the attitudes of the dispossessed Irish Catholics who had been forced to move to continental Europe. They were intended to secure diplomatic and military backing from the Habsburgs for the Irish Catholic cause. In addition, they were informed by Spanish historical fashions, emphasizing a Manichaean struggle between heretics and the faithful. In 1621 he published at Lisbon *Historiae catholicae Iberniae compendium*. This was a voluminous account of the tribulations of his own people, culminating in a detailed narrative of the campaigns and defeats in Munster in the 1580s and 1590s. Drawing on his intimate local knowledge and the recollections of his family, and written from the perspective of the defeated, it is a valuable corrective to the histories of the victors. In common with his later compositions, it extols Gaelic Ireland and seeks to rebut the contumely heaped on it by both the Old and New English conquerors. O'Sullivan was influenced by his mentor, Father Patrick Synott, and by two Jesuit historians, Michael Cantwell and Richard Conway. O'Sullivan's *Historiae*, first published during his life, was—in part—translated and republished in 1903. In addition, he drew on local traditions, mostly in the Irish language, to write saints' lives. That of St Mochna was included in Colgan's *Acta*. Others were criticized by fellow clerics for their tone and inaccuracies. More substantial and with longer lasting impact was a life of St Patrick, *Patritiana decas*, published in Madrid in 1629. This contributed to the contested process by which Patrick was promoted by Catholics and protestants alike as the national saint of Ireland.

As an exile, embittered by the loss of hereditary possessions, O'Sullivan inveighed against the apologists of and collaborators with the English and protestant order in Ireland. In his *Zoilomastix* he sought to refute the calumnies against the Irish of both Giraldus Cambrensis and (more recently) of Stanihurst. His defence included much incidental detail of indigenous habits as well as attacks on those of the interloping English. Known only in manuscript in the seventeenth century, *Zoilomastix* was judged by O'Sullivan's co-religionists to have been marred by its rhetorical extravagances. He also contributed through his 'Tenebriomastix' to the controversy associated with Thomas Dempster as to whether Ireland or Scotland was to be identified with Scotia. In 'Archicornigeromastix' he took on James Ussher, a foremost champion of protestantism in Ireland. O'Sullivan's offering suffered from the disadvantage that in Spain, where he was writing, Ussher's publications were banned and so known only by (hostile) report. However, O'Sullivan's compositions, despite their shortcomings, show how victims of the violent upheavals of the sixteenth century could construct a sympathetic record of what they had endured. TOBY BARNARD

Sources D. J. O'Doherty, 'Domnal O'Sullivan Bear and his family in Spain', *Studies*, 19 (1930), 211–26 · M. K. Walsh, *'Destruction by peace': Hugh O'Neill after Kinsale* (1986), 110 · P. O'Sullivan Beare, *Ireland under Elizabeth: chapters towards a history of Ireland in the reign of Elizabeth*, ed. and trans. M. J. Byrne (1903) · *Selections from the Zoilomastix of Philip O'Sullivan Beare*, ed. T. J. O'Donnell (Dublin, 1960) · W. F. T. Butler, 'The identity of Philip O'Sullivan Beare, the historian', *Journal of the Royal Society of Antiquaries of Ireland*, 55 (1925), 95–8 · C. Carroll, 'Irish and Spanish cultural and political relations in the work of O'Sullivan Beare', *Political ideology in Ireland, 1541–1641*, ed. H. Morgan (Dublin, 1999), 229–53 · A. Gwynn, 'An unpublished work of Philip O'Sullivan Bear', *Analecta Hibernica*, 6 (1934), 1–11 · B. Cunningham and R. Gillespie, '"The most adaptable of saints": the cult of St Patrick in the seventeenth century', *Archivium Hibernicum*, 49 (1995), 82–104

Oswald [St Oswald] (**603/4–642**), king of Northumbria, was the second son of *Æthelfrith (*d. c.*616), king of Bernicia and later of the Northumbrians, and his wife, Acha, the daughter of *Ælla, king of Deira.

Irish exile, conversion, and seizure of power Following Æthelfrith's death in battle against Acha's brother *Eadwine, who thus became king of both regions of Northumbria, Oswald was exiled at the age of about thirteen with his six brothers, including Eanfrith and *Oswiu (also Oslac, Oswudu, Oslaf, and Offa), and took refuge from his uncle in Scotland and Ireland.

During his exile Oswald learned to speak Irish fluently and is recorded as fighting on behalf of his hosts in Ireland, together with other Bernician nobles. While, with the exception of Eadwine, all the rulers of Bernicia and Deira up to that point had been pagan, Oswald was converted to Christianity at this time, and was probably baptized at the Columban monastery of Iona on the west coast of Scotland, in the Irish colony of Dál Riata. Both Bede and Adomnán, in his life of St Columba, show that Oswald maintained strong ties with Iona after he became king.

Oswald and his brothers were refugees for seventeen years, until King Eadwine, who had been converted to Christianity by a mission from Canterbury led by Paulinus, was overthrown in 633 by an alliance between the British king Cadwallon of Gwynedd and Penda of Mercia. Oswald's brother Eanfrith then became king in Bernicia for a year until he also was killed by Cadwallon; Osric of Deira, a cousin of Eadwine, was killed within the same year. One of Eadwine's sons had been slain along with his father, and another, Eadfrith, was taken hostage by Penda. Eadwine's widow, Æthelburh, and his remaining descendants fled with Bishop Paulinus to her brother's court in Kent.

In 634 Oswald returned from exile and avenged his father and brother in battle with Cadwallon near Hadrian's Wall, at a place known to Bede as Heavenfield and in British sources as Cantscaul. Cadwallon was killed near a stream called the Denisesburn (probably the Rowley Water, near Hexham), and Oswald became ruler of Bernicia at the age of thirty. He later reported to Ségéne, abbot of Iona, that this victory had been achieved through divine help, and that he had been granted a vision of St Columba before the battle, although there were only twelve baptized Christians in his army. By the time that Bede wrote, almost a century later, Oswald was said to have set up a cross before the battle, which he held firm until his soldiers fixed it in position, and then prayed with them for God's aid. A wooden cross at Heavenfield later became a focus for pilgrimage and miracle stories, but this image of devotion to the cross may suggest that Bede wished to portray Oswald as another Constantine.

Since most of the Deiran royal family had been killed or exiled, Oswald was able to take control of both kingdoms for eight years. Eadwine's son Eadfrith, who had been taken hostage by Penda, was murdered. This may have been at Oswald's instigation, since it brought Penda no political advantage. Eadwine's widow, Æthelburh, also felt her children and grandchildren threatened by Oswald and by her brother the king of Kent, again presumably at Oswald's instigation, and sent them abroad for protection. Oswald's influence can be shown to have later extended into several kingdoms south of the Humber, and he is the sixth king named in Bede's list of rulers who held sway (*imperium*) in this area. He was hated as an alien conqueror in Lindsey, and he also ruled over Sussex. He stood godfather to *Cynegils of Wessex at his baptism *c*.635, and married his daughter. He and Cynegils are named as joint donors of Dorchester-on-Thames to Bishop Birinus as an episcopal seat. His overlordship is also said by Bede to have included the Picts and the Scots to the north, and an entry in the Irish annals suggests that Edinburgh, the centre of the kingdom of the Gododdin, fell to the Angles during his reign, in 638.

Christian king Apart from Adomnán's version of what Oswald is supposed to have told the abbot of Iona about the battle of Heavenfield, and brief entries reporting his battles in the Irish and Welsh annals and in the *Historia Brittonum*, where he is nicknamed Lamnguin (Brightblade), all that is known of Oswald's life is derived from Bede, who was writing eighty-eight years after the king's death, when legends had already begun to accumulate. Oswald is one of the great heroes of Bede's *Historia ecclesiastica gentis Anglorum*, but very little is reported there about his secular career. His wife, the daughter of Cynegils of Wessex, is not named, and it only emerges in later chapters that he had a son, Oethelwald, who became king of Deira in 651 and allied with his father's killer, Penda, against his uncle Oswiu.

Bede's principal interest in Oswald is his role in the conversion of Northumbria, and the miracles associated with him after his death. Since Paulinus's mission had collapsed with the death of Eadwine and his subsequent retreat to Kent, Oswald sent to Iona for a bishop to convert his people. Following the failure of the first candidate, a second bishop, Áedán, was consecrated. Oswald donated to him the tidal island of Lindisfarne, which lay a short distance up the coast from the royal palace at Bamburgh, for his monastery and episcopal seat. Apart from Oswald's own background of exile among the Irish, it is probable that he did not wish to revive the Canterbury mission associated with the Deiran royal family, which was now in exile, though it is reported that he completed the church that Eadwine had started to build at York.

Bede ascribes to Oswald the Christian virtues of faith, humility, charity, and concern to establish the church. He was willing to act as interpreter for Áedán, and stood godfather to his father-in-law, Cynegils. He is said to have prayed at length in a distinctive way, with his palms upward, and when he was killed in battle, he was remembered as having said a prayer for the souls of his army, though not his opponents. Alcuin later claimed that he built and richly endowed many churches. Bede's most famous story emphasizes his generosity to the poor. While Oswald was holding a feast on Easter day, at which Bishop Áedán was present, a servant, with the official duty of providing for the needy, told the king that there was a press of people outside demanding alms. Oswald immediately ordered that the food should be taken out to them, and that the silver dish being used at the meal should be broken up and distributed. Bishop Áedán thereupon blessed his right hand, saying 'may this hand never perish' (Bede, *Hist. eccl.*, 3.6).

Death and cult Oswald was killed at the age of thirty-eight in battle against Penda of Mercia and his British allies on 5 August 642, at a place named by Bede as 'Maserfelth'. In British sources the site is variously given as 'Cocboi', 'Cocboy', or 'Cogwy'. This has been taken to be Oswestry in Shropshire, on the border between Mercia and Powys, since Reginald of Durham described the site in the twelfth century, although this identification has been disputed and other names, which place the battle in Lancashire or Lindsey, put forward. Oswald's body was ritually dismembered by the pagan Penda, and his head, arms, and hands displayed on stakes. A year later his brother and successor, Oswiu, came with an army and took these trophies back to Bernicia. Oswald's head was buried within the church at Lindisfarne, and his arms taken to St Peter's Church in the royal palace at Bamburgh. His right hand was found to be undecayed, in fulfilment of Bishop Áedán's prophecy, and was placed in a silver casket. Writing almost a hundred and fifty years later, Alcuin recorded that the hand was still supple, with nails that continued to grow. A chronicle entry in the *Historia regum* under the year 774 later noted that the hand was still in the church at Bamburgh, wrapped in a pall and placed in a costly shrine.

Although Bede does not claim that Oswald died a martyr's death, in the eighty-eight years between the battle and the time that Bede was writing, *c.*730, various popular legends had grown up around the site of his death. Bede records three miracle stories associated with this place, showing how the cult of Oswald's sanctity developed: in the first of these a horse is cured of convulsions by rolling on the ground; the owner of the horse then recognizes that a holy person has died at this place; and a girl is therefore cured of paralysis by being brought to the spot in a cart. The place is distinguished by the greenness of the grass there and becomes famous as a source of cures, which are transmitted through dust taken from the spot, to the extent that a hole is dug to the height of a man. It is not implied that Oswald was buried here, only that his blood had soaked the ground.

Parallel with this popular cult are three other miracle stories, which are associated with Hexham. Bede records that the monks undertook a pilgrimage each year, on the day before the anniversary of the king's death, to the wooden cross which Oswald had set up before the battle of Heavenfield in 634. (This cannot have taken place before the foundation of the monastery at Hexham by Wilfrid thirty years after Oswald's death, and may be an ecclesiastical takeover of a popular cult.) Splinters from the cross placed in water were said to have effected cures of both men and cattle, although Bede also gives the example of a Hexham monk cured of a fractured arm by moss taken from the wood of the cross. Bishop Acca of Hexham reported two more miracle stories to Bede, of a man in Ireland cured of the plague through drinking water flavoured with a splinter taken from the stake on which Oswald's head was displayed, and of the monastic community at Selsey in Sussex, again founded by Wilfrid, all but one of whom were spared from the plague by Oswald's intercession on the anniversary of his death, some forty years before, which the monks thereafter observed as a feast day.

The remains of Oswald's body were retrieved about half a century after his death by his niece *Osthryth, King Oswiu's daughter, after she married King Æthelred of Mercia and became queen, probably at some time between 675 and 679. It is not known what had happened to the body before this, after the head and arms had been cut off in 642. The bones were taken on a cart to the monastery of Bardney in Lindsey, but owing to the hostility of the monks, who remembered Oswald as an alien oppressor, these remained outside overnight under a tent. Bede records that a pillar of light above the tent was seen by both the local inhabitants and the monks, who therefore recognized Oswald's sanctity and allowed the body inside. The bones were then washed and enshrined within the church, beneath the king's gold and purple banner. Bede records two other miracles associated with Oswald's shrine here, in both of which a sick person was healed: one of a boy with an ague who spent a night by the shrine, the other of a monk from a neighbouring monastery who was cured by some dust which had absorbed the water used to wash Oswald's bones.

Despite Queen Osthryth's murder by the Mercians in 697, Oswald's body remained at Bardney, and the shrine was later adorned by the Mercian king Offa (*r.* 757–96) with 'silver, gold, gems and much finery', as Alcuin records (Alcuin, 35). This surprising Mercian royal interest in Oswald's sanctity was subsequently continued in the tenth century by Æthelflæd, lady of the Mercians, and her husband, Æthelred, who retrieved Oswald's bones from Bardney, which was by that stage within the Danelaw, and removed them to the church of St Peter at Gloucester in 909. They were translated again after the Norman conquest to a new shrine in Gloucester by Thomas (II), archbishop of York. But in the twelfth-century life of Oswald by Reginald of Durham, it is claimed that the bones of the body at Bardney had been reduced to three, as a result of the eagerness of relic hunters, and the only items taken to Gloucester were the left arm and some hair.

Reginald also records that the hand at Bamburgh had become neglected by the eleventh century, though this may be propaganda to justify the actions of a monk named Winegot, who stole the arm and took it to his own monastery at Peterborough in the time of Abbot Elsin (*d.* 1055). It is said to have been saved from the Danes in 1070 by Prior Æthelwold, who hid the arm in his bed. It was subsequently recorded at Peterborough in 1140 by the chronicler Hugh Candidus, where it was inspected by the bishop of Lincoln and others, and said to be still intact, with both flesh and skin.

Oswald's head appears to have remained in the church or cemetery at Lindisfarne for over two centuries, without being credited with any miracles, until the community of St Cuthbert was forced to leave the island in the face of Danish attacks, *c.*875. Reginald of Durham gives an alternative story, which has the head removed to Bamburgh by Oswald's relatives after being revealed by a miraculous light, although it was later retrieved from there by guile. Symeon of Durham says that Oswald's head was taken from the island inside the reliquary coffin of St Cuthbert, and Reginald similarly says that it was placed there after its retrieval. A skull with a sword cut was identified as that of Oswald when the tomb of St Cuthbert at Durham Cathedral was opened in 1104 for the translation of his relics. Oswald's head was said to be the only other skull placed in the new shrine. When the tomb of Cuthbert was reopened by James Raine in 1827, a piece of skull in poor condition was identified as Oswald's. The tomb was opened again in 1899 by William Greenwell, and at that stage a detailed debate occurred about the medical condition of the skull. The evidence, subsequently reviewed by Richard Bailey, shows that a skull with a sword cut was identified and returned to the shrine, and this is almost certainly that of Oswald. As a result of this association, in post-conquest iconography St Cuthbert is usually shown carrying St Oswald's head.

The growth of Oswald's cult in England can be followed in the increasing number of references in calendars and martyrologies, in various recastings of Bede's chapters on his life and miracles (in particular the extensive treatments in Alcuin's York poem in the late eighth century and Ælfric's homily in the late tenth century), as well as in numerous post-conquest writings. In addition, a major cult developed on the continent, particularly in Germany, the Low Countries, Switzerland, Italy, and Scandinavia. The beginnings of this can be seen in Bede, where the Anglo-Saxon missionary Willibrord is said to have told Acca and Wilfrid that many miracles linked to Oswald's relics had occurred among the Frisians. Oswald's feast day was noted in the eighth-century calendar associated with Willibrord and several sites in Europe later claimed to hold relics of Oswald, including at least four possible heads and several arms. The development of the cult on the continent moves far away from the historical figure of Oswald, and cannot be reviewed here, but it has been the subject of much modern research. The standard image in later continental iconography shifts from St Oswald carrying a covered cup, based on Bede's story of his charity, to an image of the saint with a raven, which sometimes carries a ring, derived not from Bede but from a Middle High German romantic epic, the *Münchener Oswald*.

D. J. CRAIG

Sources Bede, *Hist. eccl.*, 2.20; 3.1–3, 6, 9–13 • *Adomnán's Life of Columba*, ed. and trans. A. O. Anderson and M. O. Anderson, rev. edn, rev. M. O. Anderson, OMT (1991) • Alcuin, *The bishops, kings, and saints of York*, ed. and trans. P. Godman, OMT (1982) • E. Faral, ed., 'Historia Brittonum', *La légende Arthurienne, études et documents: les plus anciens textes*, 3: *Documents* (1929), 1–62 [Harleian recension] • *Ann. Ulster* • E. Phillimore, ed., 'The *Annales Cambriae* and Old Welsh genealogies', *Y Cymmrodor*, 9 (1888), 141–83 [version A] • 'Historia regum', Symeon of Durham, *Opera*, vol. 2 • *ASC*, s.a. 634, 635, 641 [text E]; s.a. 906 [text D] • Reginald of Durham, 'Vita sancti Oswaldi regis et martyris', Symeon of Durham, *Opera*, vol. 1 • 'Historia Dunelmensis ecclesiae', Symeon of Durham, *Opera*, vol. 1 • *Willelmi Malmesbiriensis monachi de gestis pontificum Anglorum libri quinque*, ed. N. E. S. A. Hamilton, Rolls Series, 52 (1870) • *The chronicle of Hugh Candidus, a monk of Peterborough*, ed. W. T. Mellows (1949) • Ælfric [abbot of Eynsham], 'Natale sancti Oswaldi regis et martyris', *Ælfric's Lives of saints*, ed. W. W. Skeat, 2, EETS, 94, 114 (1900), 125–43 • H. A. Wilson, ed., *The calendar of St Willibrord from MS Paris Lat. 10837*, HBS, 55 (1918) • C. Stancliffe and E. Cambridge, eds., *Oswald, Northumbrian king to European saint* (1995) • D. P. Kirby, *The earliest English kings* (1991) • H. Moisl, 'The Bernician royal dynasty and the Irish in the seventh century', *Peritia*, 2 (1983), 103–26 • K. H. Jackson, 'On the northern British section in Nennius', *Celt and Saxon: studies in the early British border*, ed. N. K. Chadwick (1963), 20–62 • P. Clemoes, *The cult of St Oswald on the continent* (1983) • T. M. Charles-Edwards, 'Bede, the Irish and the Britons', *Celtica*, 15 (1983), 45–52 • V. A. Gunn, 'Bede and the martyrdom of St Oswald', *Martyrs and martyrologies*, ed. D. Wood, SCH, 30 (1993), 57–66 • R. Foltz, 'Saint Oswald, roi de Northumbrie: étude d'hagiographie royale', *Analecta Bollandiana*, 98 (1980), 49–74 • *Venerabilis Baedae opera historica*, ed. C. Plummer, 2 vols. (1896)

Oswald [St Oswald] (*d.* 992), archbishop of York, was one of the leaders of the English monastic reformation of the tenth century. His cult was developed at his principal monastic foundation, Ramsey, and at his cathedral at Worcester, where he was bishop from 961 to 992. What is known of his career derives chiefly from an anonymous life, written between 997 and 1002, which is attributed to Byrhtferth of Ramsey, and from charters that were preserved in the medieval archives of Worcester Cathedral.

Origin and early life The names of Oswald's parents are unknown; but he was of Anglo-Danish extraction, a nephew of Archbishop *Oda (941–58) and grandson of one of the settlers who had come to Britain in the 'great' army of Ivarr and Ubbe. Other kinsmen, Archbishop Oscytel of York and Abbot Thurcytel of Bedford, had Scandinavian names, but his own name is English and it is possible that his mother came from the south-west midlands where Oswald later had many kinsmen with English names. During boyhood Oswald was trained in sacred letters by his uncle, Archbishop Oda, and was believed in the twelfth century, both at Ramsey and Canterbury, to have also been tutored by the West Frankish scholar, Frithegod of Canterbury. Enriched with numerous gifts from his uncle, Oswald is purported by Byrhtferth to have purchased a 'monastery' in Winchester, where, however, the luxurious lifestyle of the married secular clerks perturbed the pious adolescent. He was therefore sent by Oda to the pre-eminent monastery (*arcisterium*) of St Benedict at Fleury-sur-Loire, where the archbishop himself was said to have previously made his monastic profession and where the most perfect service of God in accord with Benedict's rule was believed to be observed. There, under Abbot Wulfhard (Wulfald), Oswald undertook for several years the full rigours of the monastic life, practising additional personal austerities; he also memorized monastic regulations and the office, so that he would be able to teach them in England.

Archbishop Oda, towards the end of his life, sought permission from the diocesan bishop of Orléans and from the community at Fleury for Oswald's release from his obligation of stability in order that he might return to England. The archbishop may have wished to install his nephew at Ely, a site he had just acquired from King Eadwig, perhaps in the hope of re-establishing monastic life there. But any such plans were dashed, first by King Eadwig's loss of control in 957 of all territories north of the River Thames and then by Oda's death (2 June 958) before Oswald had reached Dover. Oswald therefore sought instead the patronage of a more distant kinsman, Oscytel, who had become archbishop of York two years previously. The story in the twelfth-century Ramsey *Liber benefactorum* (in *Chronicon abbatiae Rameseiensis*, ed. W. D. Macray, Rolls Series, 1886) that Oswald, with his friend Germanus, then accompanied Oscytel to Rome to secure the pallium and that the two companions delayed at Fleury on the return journey should probably be accepted. Tenth-century English archbishops seem to have gone to Rome for their pall if they had been uncanonically translated to their metropolitan church from another see. Oscytel, who had been bishop of Dorchester before his elevation to York and who seems to have retained that see after his promotion, certainly fits that category. His journey, seemingly in late 958 or early 959, would have been the first time an archbishop of York had needed to go to Rome for that purpose. Oscytel's patronage of Oswald also led, according to

Byrhtferth, to an introduction to 'Bishop Dunstan', presumably also in 958 or 959 when Dunstan was bishop of both Worcester and London. It is recounted that after his elevation to Canterbury, Dunstan persuaded King Edgar to appoint Oswald to the vacant see of Worcester; Oswald was commended to the king by the magnates of the region and 'elected and honourably consecrated by the bishops' (Byrhtferth of Ramsey, 1.420), events which may be placed early in the year 961, to judge from his attestation as bishop in the bulk of the extant charters of that year.

Monastic revival The appointment of Oswald to the wealthy see of Worcester was part of a deliberate policy (with Dunstan's promotion to Canterbury and, in 963, Æthelwold's to Winchester) of putting reformed monks into the key positions in the English church in order that they might initiate the rapid adoption of ideas of monastic reform that had been current on the continent for a generation. Oswald therefore recalled from Fleury his friend Germanus, directing young clerks to be instructed by him in monastic customs; and he soon established him with twelve companions in the *parochia* (minster) at Westbury-on-Trym where they are said to have remained for some four years. Byrhtferth portrays King Edgar's support for the new monasticism with a highly imaginative account of an Easter witan attended by all Edgar's bishops, and even by all the abbots and abbesses with their monks and nuns, in which Edgar, acknowledging the fame of St Benedict through Oswald's narration, ordered the construction of more than forty monasteries and was urged by Æthelwold to expel clerks from these houses. It is difficult to know whether any more credence should be given to the ensuing story that when Oswald sought a more secure foundation for his monks, the king offered him a choice of three possible sites: St Albans, Ely, or Benfleet. That may have been designed to gratify Ramsey's self-importance, but it may surely be accepted from Byrhtferth that it was the Anglo-Saxon nobleman, Æthelwine, a son of Ealdorman Æthelstan Half-King, who offered Oswald the fenland island site of Ramsey, where three men seeking the monastic habit had already gathered.

Having accepted Ramsey, Oswald sent Eadnoth ('the elder') to oversee the construction of temporary accommodation there in the spring (some time between 965 and 969) and himself led the Westbury monks there on 29 August. The construction of the permanent buildings began in the following year and the monastery received handsome endowments from Oswald himself, from Æthelstan Mannessune (who was married to a kinswoman of Oswald), as well as from the founder, Ealdorman Æthelwine, and his brother, Ælfwold. Oswald retained control over Ramsey throughout his lifetime and Byrhtferth claims that he visited every year, though he only describes two visits. The day-to-day direction of the Ramsey monks was exercised by a dean (successively Germanus, Æthelnoth, and Eadnoth 'the younger'). Oswald was believed to have consecrated the completed church there in 974. Byrhtferth also describes a great gathering at Ramsey on 8 November 991, when the ailing Oswald seems to have rededicated the church, which had had to be extensively rebuilt after the original central tower had split. After Oswald's death, the dean Eadnoth (the son of Æthelstan Mannessune and therefore a kinsman of Oswald) became the first abbot of Ramsey.

After the transfer of the Westbury monks to Ramsey in the heart of the eastern Danelaw, where his paternal kin were based, Oswald turned to the revival of monasticism within his own diocese, first in his cathedral at Worcester and second at Winchcombe. Byrhtferth knew only of Ramsey's role in these events: namely that their dean, Germanus, had been appointed to head the house at Winchcombe and that the priest Wynsige (Wynsinus), who had been schooled at Ramsey, led a group of their choir monks to Worcester. Both the manner and the chronology of Oswald's introduction of monks to the cathedral community were the subject of conflicting interpretations in twelfth-century sources and have also occasioned controversy among modern historians. The best evidence is the series of nearly eighty leases issued by Oswald in the course of his pontificate to tenants of the church of Worcester, most of which are witnessed by members of the community. The leases show that the composition of Oswald's community (or at least of those senior enough to act as witnesses) changed gradually, but with influxes of new names in the 960s and 970s. They also show that the bulk of the community continued to be styled by their clerical grades (priest, deacon, or clerk) and that the style 'monk' was used occasionally, but irregularly, from the later 970s. There is a gap in the witnessed leases between 970 and 976, but from 977 to 985 the community is found headed by the priest Wynsige, who in one lease of the year 977 is styled 'monk' along with nine of the other twenty-six witnesses, though most of them revert to their clerical styles in subsequent leases. Nine of Oswald's leases were grants of properties to individual clerks, deacons, or priests of the church of Worcester, usually specifying their right to bequeath the land to two subsequent clerics; one such was the lease to the monk Wynsige of property which his father had previously held. There is no sign here, then, of the introduction of stricter rules of communal property following Oswald's reform. The leases also show that from the year 966 the church of Worcester was dedicated to St Mary, in addition to St Peter, and that in 983 Oswald had exceeded all expectation by completing the construction of the new church of St Mary.

All this accords with the belief, current at Worcester in the second decade of the twelfth century and reported both by Eadmer and by William of Malmesbury, that Oswald had introduced monks gradually to his see 'with most holy guile' (*De gestis pontificum*, 248) and had built the church of St Mary for them, immediately adjacent to the old cathedral church of St Peter, where the clerks continued to serve. On this interpretation, from 966 Oswald gradually built up a community of monks in the church of St Mary, who had an increasingly important role in the whole cathedral community; many of them proceeded beyond the minor clerical orders to be ordained as deacon and priest and may have had a full share of pastoral work alongside the clerks of St Peter's.

An alternative interpretation of Oswald's reform was current at Worcester by the 1130s, namely that on Edgar's orders Oswald had expelled all those Worcester clerks who refused to abandon their wives and to become monks, and that he appointed Wynsige from Ramsey as dean of the new monastic cathedral community. Both in a rewritten annal of John of Worcester's chronicle and in the dubious record of Bishop Wulfstan's synod of 1092, the supposed expulsion of the clerks is attributed to the year 969, the date of one of Oswald's unwitnessed leases into which a note of the 'witness of Wynsige and all the monks of Worcester' had already been inserted by the early eleventh century. About the middle of the twelfth century, however, an elaborate forged charter of King Edgar, known by its first word *Altitonantis*, was produced which placed the supposed expulsion in 964 (the year of the expulsion of clerks from Winchester). The purpose of the expulsion myths in twelfth-century Worcester (as of similar fabrications at Canterbury) was to exalt the status of the monastic chapter in relation to secular clergy at a time when the bishop was no longer a monk and when there were fears that he might therefore attempt to secularize the chapter.

The lordship of Worcester The church of Worcester was already richly endowed before Oswald's day, and neither his reputation, nor that of the monks he introduced, seems to have led to any substantial new acquisitions of property. The practice of leasing estates to prominent laymen was also long established at Worcester but no previous (or later) Anglo-Saxon bishop seems to have taken so much care to record leases in writing. The properties which Oswald leased were smaller (mostly of 1, 2, or 3 hides) than the great ecclesiastical manors that had long been in the hands of his church. But together the leased estates amounted to almost a third of the 600 hides in the possession of the church of Worcester. They were often on peripheral, inferior land or in underdeveloped wooded country and they supported fewer peasant ploughteams, probably being more dependent upon hired labour. By contrast Oswald seems to have reserved the best arable land for the demesnes of his great estates and there is reason to think that these demesnes were already associated with nucleated settlements and open fields and perhaps too with production for the market in Worcester and in the other nascent towns in the region.

Oswald's leases were normally granted for a period of three lives, after which the land was to revert to the church of Worcester; they thus respected the canons prohibiting the permanent alienation of any properties given to the church. The bulk of the lessees were lay nobles, that is local thegns (though one—Ælfwold—was a king's thegn); but there were also a number of retainers (*cnihtas*) and craftsmen. Some tenants were from families whose members had held lands from earlier bishops and in some instances Oswald can be seen granting a lease for three lives to the heir of the recipient of one of his earlier leases, thus extending the duration of the lease and virtually turning it into a hereditary holding. Almost a quarter of Worcester's leased estates were granted to members of Oswald's own family, to his brothers, Osulf and Æthelstan, and to a series of nephews, nieces, and more distant relatives. All Oswald's tenants were bound personally to the service of the bishop; many indeed received their leases in recognition of their 'faithful service'; others purchased them.

The leases do not themselves specify what services the bishop might require from his tenants. But a tripartite chirograph (*indiculum*) drawn up in the name of Oswald and addressed to King Edgar, of which the Worcester copy is preserved in Hemming's cartulary of the late eleventh century, purports to set down for the benefit of his successors in the see the terms which Oswald had agreed with his lessees. A great variety of obligations are specified as due from the tenants' estates: riding services, church-scot, toll, swine-scot and other church rights, lime burning and church building, erecting fencing for the bishop's hunt, and so forth. Much the most important, however, was the general demand for obedience to the bishop's commands: the tenants must both fulfil the service due to the bishop (as well as that due to the king) and be subject to the will of the bishop (*archiductor*) if they wished to retain their benefices. It is impossible to prove the authenticity of such a unique document in the absence of any of the three original copies; its terms do not seem improbable, though the insistence upon obedience and on the revocability of tenures would certainly have been of interest in the generation after 1066, when the third lives of Oswald's leases were coming to an end and when a Norman aristocracy was establishing itself in the diocese. Viewing the *indiculum* alongside the extant leases, we seem to see Oswald co-ordinating local notables and his own kinsmen into a network of *fideles* established throughout the diocese to support the bishop of Worcester's seigneurial standing at both national and local levels and to provide the expertise necessary for running a great landed lordship.

By the time of Domesday Book the bulk of the estates of the church of Worcester had been organized into a judicial and administrative unit known as the 'triple hundred' of Oswaldslow, which took its name from Oswald. Indeed, in the forged *Altitonantis* charter King Edgar is purported to have granted the monks of St Mary's a half-hundred of 'Cuthbergelaw' which he then formed into a whole hundred with estates already in their possession, to be held by their priest Wynsige and his successors; the charter goes on to claim to create or confirm two hundreds ('Wulfereslaw' and 'Winburgetreow') for Bishop Oswald, which were to form (along with the monks' hundred) a 'shipsoke' of three hundreds in the place to be called thenceforth Oswaldslow, in memory of the bishop. Within Oswaldslow the monks and the bishop were to enjoy a most extensive range of royal judicial rights and a comprehensive immunity excluding all royal officials. That was what the twelfth-century church of Worcester wished to be believed, but it is difficult to know whether any historical reality lies behind it. The judicial immunity excluding the king's agents is a feature of post-conquest rather than Anglo-Saxon law; and the definition of private hundreds from the estates of great ecclesiastical lords seems likewise to have been a product of the mid-eleventh century, rather than the mid-tenth. It remains equally uncertain whether the definition of shipsokes of 300 hides to raise ships' crews of sixty armed men was indeed the work of Edgar or rather of Æthelred the Unready a generation later; it seems very unlikely to have been a policy already established as early as 964. It may be concluded that Oswaldslow is more likely to have been an eleventh-century creation, given authority by its attribution to Worcester's great saint, rather than a personal achievement of Oswald himself.

The archbishopric of York On the death of Archbishop Oscytel of York on 1 November 971, a certain Edwald of unknown origin was nominated to succeed him, but withdrew before his consecration, purportedly preferring a quieter life. The elevation of Oswald in his place suggests (as with the raising of Dunstan to Canterbury in 959 even though Bishop Byrhthelm had already been translated there) that the king was determined to have his own man in the see of York and to continue the policy begun under Oscytel of having the northern metropolitanate filled by a man from the eastern Danelaw but whose loyalties and interests were anchored by the tenure of a southern bishopric. Oswald's appointment to York seems (from his attestation of charters) to belong to the last days of 971 or the first half of 972. In the summer or autumn of 972 Edgar sent him on an embassy, with Abbot 'Ætherius' (perhaps Æthelgar of the New Minster, Winchester) and Wulfmær, a king's thegn, to the court of the German emperor, Otto I, which returned, according to Byrhtferth, with even more notable gifts than those that they had taken. The German journey may have been designed to gain approval and expertise in relation to Edgar's long-delayed 'imperial' coronation at Bath on Whit Sunday in the following year, a ceremony where the two archbishops, Dunstan and Oswald, were to preside jointly and which is described at length by Byrhtferth with quotations from the second English coronation ordo. Oswald's German embassy may have been combined with his journey to Rome to obtain the pallium from Pope John XIII, which belongs to very much the same time. According to Byrhtferth, Oswald earned the praise of both God and men for the substantial payments of pennies which he made as alms at monasteries, and at villas, castles, country estates, and cities, before he returned with the pope's blessing. A generation later Archbishop Wulfstan of York (*d.* 1023) was to take a much more critical view of the monetary payments that were expected in Rome in order to secure the pall.

Very little is known of Oswald's management of his northern diocese and province. There has survived (from a Worcester manuscript) a copy of a declaration that he made listing the York properties that he or his predecessor, Oscytel, had recovered but which had been lost again in the unsettled conditions after Edgar's death and the succession of Earl Thored in 975; the endangered properties include over twenty vills dependent upon the great York estates of Otley, Ripon, and Sherburn in Elmet. This suggests that (as with the Worcester leases) Oswald was determined to ensure through written records that the property claims of his cathedral should not be forgotten but rather, as soon as political circumstances permitted, vigorously prosecuted.

Oswald is not known to have introduced any reform to the clergy of his cathedral at York. But Byrhtferth claims that at the ruined monastery of Ripon, Oswald discovered a great hidden treasure, namely the bones of St Wilfrid along with the relics of five succeeding abbots (Tatberht, Botwine, Albert, Sicgred, and Wildegel); he goes on to assert that in the church with Wilfrid's pontifical seat, where hitherto 'deacons and sparrows' had dwelt, Oswald arranged for monks to serve God. Since what were held to be the relics of Wilfrid had already been taken from Ripon to Canterbury a generation earlier by Archbishop Oda and since nothing is known in any later source of this revival of monastic life at Ripon, it has been doubted whether Oswald really attempted to build a monastic community there around a revived cult of Ripon's founder and early abbots. But the fact that some relics of all six Ripon saints were later to be found in the high altar at Peterborough is most easily explained by the suggestion that Oswald and Ripon were indeed directly involved in the revival of their cult in the world of reformed monasticism. It may rather be that Ripon is simply one of the houses where the revived Benedictine life did not outlast the first generation of monastic reform.

The anti-monastic reaction Byrhtferth's life of Oswald claims that seven monasteries had been constructed within the Mercian province of the Hwicce (that is, in the diocese of Worcester), under Oswald's control and with their heads appointed by King Edgar. To the already mentioned Worcester, Westbury, and Winchcombe, may readily be added Pershore (established under Abbot Foldbriht by 970) and Evesham (under Abbot Osweard from much the same time). If Byrhtferth's figure is accurate rather than symbolic, we may guess that the missing houses may have been at Deerhurst, where St Ælfheah was said to have received his monastic training, and conceivably at Gloucester, whose history is very dark at this time. Whatever the true number, however, the early years of Oswald's pontificate had certainly seen a remarkable transfer of landed resources in the diocese into the hands of reformed monks. In that process there are likely to have been losers, both among the local nobles and among the secular clerks previously associated with minster churches. The tension thereby created in Hwiccan society was exacerbated by the succession dispute that arose following Edgar's death on 8 July 975, when the powerful Mercian ealdorman, Ælfhere, supported the claims of Æthelred, the son of Edgar's third wife, Ælfthryth, while Oswald, together with the leading reformers and with Ramsey's founder, Ealdorman Æthelwine, backed Edward, the child of the first marriage. In the ensuing struggle for power, land, and followers, that was only finally resolved by the murder of Edward the Martyr and the accession of Æthelred the Unready in 978, the lands of the new monasteries associated with the opposing faction were an obvious target.

Byrhtferth describes these events in terms of a general expulsion of abbots and their monks and of the reintroduction of married clerks in their place. In particular he relates that Abbot Germanus and his monks were driven from Winchcombe by Ealdorman Ælfhere of Mercia; late traditions and breaks in the succession of abbots indicate that similar (but more temporary) expulsions occurred at both Evesham and Pershore. Byrhtferth believed that Ælfhere, 'the mad wind coming from the western territories', influenced others to follow his example of replacing monks by secular clerks (Byrhtferth of Ramsey, 1.443–6). Clearly Oswald's houses were particularly vulnerable since the bishop was known as one of Edward's leading supporters; Ramsey, however, lying within the ealdormanry of its founder, Æthelwine, was a safe refuge and the cathedral community at Worcester also seems to have survived intact. Whether the clerks of St Peter's and the monks of St Mary's were a sufficiently unified community to mean that there were at Worcester no ousted married clerks seeking to encourage the ealdorman to restore them by force, or whether Worcester's noble tenants were sufficiently influential to protect their lord's church from interference, are subjects for speculation. Most of the leases had originally been made with Ælfhere's consent and licence and this continued to be the pattern throughout Edward's reign, so it may be that bishop and ealdorman collaborated at least to preserve the cathedral. Moreover, one of the Worcester lessees was a king's thegn, Ælfwold, very possibly to be identified as the brother of Ealdorman Æthelwine, whom Byrhtferth singles out as the first man to resist the anti-monastic tide in Mercia. Oswald, it would seem, had provided his see with potent protectors.

Books and liturgy Like other English centres of monastic reform, Oswald's Worcester acquired books written on the continent and also developed its own distinctive version of the Carolingian minuscule script, which is first witnessed in the part of a charter of the year 961 which seems to have been written by Oswald himself. It is instructive, however, that (as at Canterbury) the new Anglo-Caroline script was practised at the same time, and even in the same volumes (for example, British Library, Royal MS 8 B.xi), as the traditional insular square minuscule. At Winchester, by contrast, Æthelwold's reform meant that from 964 for Latin texts only Caroline script was permitted. The coexistence of the two scripts at Worcester may reflect the collaboration of both monks of St Mary's and clerks of St Peter's in the production of books for the Worcester Library. Between 983 and 985 Oswald leased land at Bredicot to the priest Goding and Hemming's cartulary records that this grant was to enable him to serve as scribe and that he wrote many books for the monastery. His work for the community cannot be identified, but one Worcester scribe, Sistan, can be shown to have copied works by the Carolingian writers Smaragdus and Paschasius Radbertus for the Worcester Library at this time in the new script.

Byrhtferth records Oswald's gift to Ramsey of a 'glorious pandect', that is, a complete Bible, which sadly has not survived. But a number of high-quality volumes with illuminated initials and scripts in various registers from Oswald's houses are extant. The so-called Winchcombe sacramentary seems to have been produced in that house, or by Winchcombe monks after their flight to Ramsey, as a gift to the mother house of Fleury (Orléans, Bibliothèque Municipale, MS 127, 105). A huge and magnificently written and illuminated psalter (British Library, Harley MS 2904), once attributed either to Winchester or to Ramsey, seems likely to have been made for Oswald's own use at York or Worcester. The scribe of this psalter also wrote a pontifical (Cambridge, Sidney Sussex College, MS 100, part 2) intended for a bishop to carry around with him; it was probably made for Oswald's own use, either at Worcester or in his northern diocese; its ordination and other ceremonies represent a fascinating mixture of English and continental liturgical practices, perhaps typical of Oswald's eclectic and compromising instincts.

Death and cult After the rededication of the monastic church at Ramsey in November 991 and the great banquet that followed, Oswald returned to Worcester in failing health. Byrhtferth tells that despite weakening further that winter, he resumed in February 992 his Lenten custom of washing the feet of twelve poor men each day, accompanied by the singing of Psalms 120–34. After this task he passed away peacefully on 29 February, while singing the doxology. After being elaborately washed and laid out, the body was buried by the community next day within a mausoleum of wonderful workmanship which the community later claimed had been constructed by Oswald himself.

A cult developed very rapidly. Byrhtferth describes miraculous signs that accompanied the funeral and the working of wonders at Oswald's tomb. Probably within two years of his death, his feast (28 February) had already been entered into the York metrical calendar that was being extended at Ramsey. Ten years after his death an elaborate translation was masterminded by his successor, Bishop Ealdwulf, who had the bones solemnly enshrined on the south side of the altar of the cathedral church of St Mary on 15 April 1002. A series of miraculous cures and events then effectively established his sanctity. His deposition and translation were treated as major feasts in local calendars and less prominently in some other English texts and at Fleury. He is invoked in four or five Anglo-Saxon litanies, including the portable prayer book (or *portiforium*) of St Wulfstan (Cambridge, Corpus Christi College, MS 391) which also contains three hymns in his honour and a calendar that lists his second translation (8 October), occasioned by Wulfstan's rebuilding of the cathedral. Byrhtferth's life held the field for more than a century, but *c.*1115 the Canterbury hagiographer and historian, Eadmer, wrote at the request of the Worcester community an account of the life and miracles of St Oswald, which clarified and updated Byrhtferth's account and recounted miracles associated with the two translations. Nothing of significance is added by the life written by the late twelfth-century prior, Senatus, nor by the later medieval abbreviated versions. N. P. Brooks

Sources [Byrhtferth of Ramsey], 'Vita sancti Oswaldi auctore anonymo', *The historians of the church of York and its archbishops*, ed. J. Raine, 1, Rolls Series, 71 (1879), 399–475 • 'Liber benefactorum ecclesiae Rameseiensis', Ramsey Abbey, *Chronicon abbatiae Rameseiensis a saec. x usque ad an. circiter 1200*, ed. W. D. Macray, Rolls Series, 83 (1886) • Eadmer, 'Vita sancti Oswaldi' and 'Miracula sancti Oswaldi', *The historians of the church of York and its archbishops*, ed. J. Raine, 2, Rolls Series, 71 (1886), 1–59 • *AS chart.*, S 731, 1297–1375 • N. Brooks and C. Cubitt, eds., *St Oswald of Worcester: life and influence* (1996) • P. H. Sawyer, 'Charters of the reform movement: the Worcester archive', *Tenth-century studies*, ed. D. Parsons (1975), 84–102 • D. N. Dumville, *English Caroline script and monastic history* (1993) • M. Lapidge, *Anglo-Latin literature, 900–1066* (1993) • D. Knowles, *The monastic order in England*, 2nd edn (1963), 31–82 • E. John, *Land tenure in early England* (1958) • Senatus, 'Vita S. Oswaldi archiepiscopi', *The historians of the church of York and its archbishops*, ed. J. Raine, 2, Rolls Series, 71 (1886), 60–97 • *Willelmi Malmesbiriensis monachi de gestis pontificum Anglorum libri quinque*, ed. N. E. S. A. Hamilton, Rolls Series, 52 (1870) • E. John, *Orbis Britannie* (1966) • Hemming's cartulary, BL, Cotton MS Tiberius A.xiii

Archives Bibliothèque Municipale, Orléans, MS 127, 105 • BL, Harley MS 2904 • Sidney Sussex College, Cambridge, MS 100, pt 2

Oswald (*fl.* **1006–1042**), Benedictine monk and scholar, was the nephew of St *Oswald, archbishop of York. The earliest period of Oswald's life was spent as an oblate at Ramsey. According to the twelfth-century *Liber benefactorum* of Ramsey, he was one of the four schoolboys who, in the time of Abbot Eadnoth (992–1006), cracked one of the monastery's bells by pulling frivolously and inexpertly on the bell-ropes; their teachers (one of whom was probably Byrhtferth of Ramsey) and the monks threatened them with severe punishment, but they were pardoned by Eadnoth. Oswald subsequently travelled to the continent, visiting St Omer, Arras, Corbie, St Denis in Paris, and then Lagny; he ended up studying at Fleury (as his uncle had done before him). His travels and accomplishments at Fleury were recorded in a poem by Constantine, a monk of Fleury who later became abbot of Micy (*d.* 1021); although the poem is lost, it was composed in elegiacs and addressed to Bishop Oswald, and was seen in manuscript by John Leland (*d.* 1552), who made a note of its content. Oswald subsequently returned to Ramsey, where he led a life of quiet study, becoming a man 'renowned for his erudition and piety', according to the *Liber benefactorum* (*Chronicon abbatiae Rameseiensis*, 159–60); the same source records that he turned down the offer of a bishopric, preferring to pursue his literary studies at Ramsey. On the occasion of a visit by Edward the Confessor (*r.* 1042–66) to Ramsey, Oswald successfully petitioned the king for a grant of estates at Wimbotsham and Downham Market, Norfolk; the original charter does not survive, but the grant is recorded in a document dated 1060 but forged in the twelfth century by Osbert of Clare (*AS chart.*, S 1030).

Oswald's scholarly activity resulted in a substantial corpus of writing, most of which has unfortunately perished. The *Liber benefactorum* records that in the Ramsey library there was a volume of Oswald's poetry, which gave evidence of his 'multifarious learning and acute ingenuity', but this volume has not survived (*Chronicon abbatiae Rameseiensis*, 160). Leland was familiar with two further works: a *Liber sacrarum precationum* (said by Leland to be partly in verse, partly in prose), and a treatise *De componendis epistolis* cast in the form of a letter. John Bale (*d.* 1563) added to this list a work entitled *De edendis carminibus*. All of these have apparently been lost. Leland records that he had seen two manuscripts of Oswald's writings, one at Glastonbury, the other at Ramsey; but they have perished. However, two brief poems have been identified as the work of Oswald: both are preserved in a mid-eleventh-century manuscript from Canterbury (now in Cambridge University Library, MS Gg.5.35), and both are in an elaborate metrical form known as *versus retrogradi*: that is to say, the metre is preserved whether they are read forwards or backwards. The first, consisting of twenty-one hexameters, begins 'Centum concito sic qui nouit condere versus' ('he who knows how to compose quickly a hundred lines in this manner'). It contains an indication of Oswald's authorship in line 9: 'istos texuit Oswoldus, qui est nescius artis' ('Oswald, who is ignorant of the art, composed these [lines]'). The second, in four elegiac distichs, begins

> Terrigene bene nunc laudent, ut condecet, almum
> vocibus excelsis sic sibi perplacitis.
> ('Let earth-dwellers now duly praise the kindly God, as is
> fitting, with celestial voices pleasing to him.')

Michael Lapidge

Sources W. D. Macray, ed., *Chronicon abbatiae Rameseiensis a saec. x usque ad an. circiter 1200*, Rolls Series, 83 (1886) • *Commentarii de scriptoribus Britannicis, auctore Joanne Lelando*, ed. A. Hall, 1 (1709), 172 • M. Lapidge, 'The hermeneutic style in tenth-century Anglo-Latin literature', *Anglo-Saxon England*, 4 (1975), 67–111 • P. Dronke, M. Lapidge, and P. Stotz, 'Die unveröffentlichten Gedichte der Cambridger Liederhandschrift (CUL Gg.5.35)', *Mittellateinisches Jahrbuch*, 17 (1982), 54–95 • *AS chart.*, S 1030

Archives CUL, MS Gg.5.35

Oswald. *See* Corda, Oswald (*d.* 1434).

Oswald, George (**1735–1819**). *See under* Oswald, Richard (1705?–1784).

Oswald, James (**1703–1793**), Church of Scotland minister and philosophical writer, was born on 23 July 1703, the eldest of four children of George Oswald (1664–1726), minister of Dunnet, in Caithness, and his wife, Margaret Murray (*d.* 1747). A comment in one of his letters to his wealthy and influential brother Richard *Oswald implies that he studied at King's College, Aberdeen. James was attending the divinity class of William Hamilton at his father's alma mater, the University of Edinburgh, in 1723, but for how long is unknown; there is no record of his performing any ministerial exercises there. After his father's death in January 1726 the presbytery of Caithness expedited his pastoral trials. He was licensed on 9 March, called to the vacancy at Dunnet on 14 June, and ordained there on 30 August. On 15 January 1728 he married Elizabeth, daughter of James Murray of Clairdon; they had seven children.

In 1731 the manse was declared unsafe for habitation and substantial restoration was required. His wife died on 20 August 1746, and on 27 January 1749 he married Margaret, daughter of Sir Patrick Dunbar of Northfield. She died on 12 December 1779; there were no children.

At Dunnet, Oswald conducted weekly services in both English and Gaelic. Although it was the most northerly parish on the Scottish mainland he gained a more than local reputation. When in December 1748 he was presented to Methven in Perthshire, the patron of that parish, David Smyth, could claim in defence of his nomination that Oswald 'has often preach'd in the Largest Churches of Edinburgh & Glasgow, to the Satisfaction and hearing of the whole Congregation' while Oswald's own presbytery testified that he was 'of Excellent Piety, a fine Preacher, and Well Qualified to gain the Affection and Esteem of any people who will give him a fair Hearing' (assembly papers, NA Scot., CH1/2/90, fols. 111, 149). His translation to Methven was nevertheless delayed for two years by the presbytery of Perth, ostensibly out of regard for strong local hostility to the appointment. John Moncrieff of Tippermalloch, the son of the previous incumbent and himself minister of the nearby parish of Rhynd, who had inherited property in Methven through a maternal uncle, led a concerted opposition to the patron and remaining heritors by supporting the lay eldership of the parish who had united 'in favours of a man most unacceptable to those of the greatest Consideration in the parish' (ibid., fol. 110), and some of them faced civil charges for intimidation. In the presbytery the lay representatives supported *en bloc* their brethren in the parish, while the ministerial members were divided, making it impossible for the presentation to proceed. Oswald, who was not himself the major target, stayed above the fray. After the presbytery had been more than once rebuked his installation was finally carried out on 12 December 1750 by a riding committee appointed by the commission of the general assembly. The militants in the congregation seceded and formed a connection with the Anti-Burgher Secession Church. This suggests that Oswald owed his transfer to the duke of Argyll's ecclesiastical interest, then headed by another of Hamilton's former pupils, Patrick Cuming, who used riding committees as a way of enforcing the law of patronage without compromising the beliefs of defiant presbyters. When a younger generation of moderate ministers, led by William Robertson, forced a confrontation in the general assembly of 1752 by insisting upon a less conciliatory policy towards those who refused to carry out legally conducted presentations, Cuming and his associates went along, and the earliest publication attributed to Oswald, *Some thoughts relating to that submission and obedience due to the authority and decisions of the supreme judicature of the church* (1753), defended the stricter policy of the moderate party which he would later come to despise.

In late 1761 and early 1762 Oswald was a candidate for the chair of ecclesiastical history at the University of Glasgow at the same time that Cuming was attempting to secure the principalship of the University of Edinburgh. In a letter of 22 December 1761 (Caldwell papers, NL Scot., MS 4942, fol. 52), Principal Leechman told William Mure that most of the Glasgow professors preferred Oswald for the chair, which was in the gift of the crown, and on 1 January 1762 Oswald was formally recommended by the university. Oswald was in the habit of making annual excursions to the Glasgow area in late summer to visit his merchant sons George *Oswald [*see under* Oswald, Richard] and Alexander, and his brother Richard, and these visits probably strengthened his connections with professors, ministers, and politicians in the west. But the death of Argyll in April 1761 had weakened the prospects of Cuming and his friends. The new manager of Scottish affairs, the third earl of Bute, demonstrated his commitment to the younger generation of moderate clergy by selecting Robertson over Cuming for the Edinburgh position in February 1762 and William Wight over Oswald for the Glasgow chair three months later. Henceforth Oswald would have no hope of preferment in the Church of Scotland or the Scottish universities, other than honorific distinctions such as the moderatorship of the general assembly in May 1765 and the DD degree from Glasgow later the same year. His subsequent ecclesiastical career was defined largely by feelings of resentment towards Robertson and the moderates.

As co-author of a memorandum in a case of breach of contract that had come before the Caithness presbytery in 1732 Oswald had already set standards that informed the rest of his career. He derived from his father a strong sense of the dignity and probity of the clerical profession, and defended the binding nature of promises by appeal to a natural law founded in 'the common Sense of Mankind, and the generally received acceptation of terms' (Caithness minutes, 6 April 1732). In *Some Thoughts* he cited the same authorities to justify the parallel institutions of civil and church government. But it was at the height of his activity as an ecclesiastical politician in the mid-1760s that he made his name as an author, beginning in 1765 with a brief *Scripture Catechism, for the Use of Families*.

With his election as moderator Oswald and his friends set the stage for the general assembly of 1766 to take up the so-called schism overture, which was meant to embarrass the moderates by publicizing and condemning the large number of defections from the Church of Scotland that had allegedly occurred as a result of their rigorous enforcement of the law of patronage. The patronage in contention was patronage exercised by external authorities without the co-operation of persons of maturity and judgement within the parish. For Oswald, however, the issue of patronage and schism was closely connected with a series of other problems that he blamed on the moderates, including moral corruption, valuing intellectual accomplishments over piety, and above all tolerating 'free-thinking' and 'scepticism'. In the moderator's closing address to the assembly in 1765, he warned

> we have trifled too long with sceptics; let us remit their subtlety to the schools, and assuming the dignity which

> belongs to our office, let us present the human understanding with truth which no man of sense will gainsay, and the human heart with motives which no man of probity will resist. (Morren, 2.412)

Oswald expressed his views more forcefully in *A Sermon Preached at the Opening of the General Assembly of the Church of Scotland* (1766), to which he added fourteen letters that expanded his arguments. Although the schism overture was defeated in that assembly, and Oswald himself confided to his brother his 'immense fatigue' as a result of his involvement in church affairs (letter to Richard Oswald, 6 June 1766), he vowed to continue his struggle if the sermon was a success. The result was his anonymous *Letters concerning the present state of the Church of Scotland, and the consequent danger to religion and learning, from the arbitrary and unconstitutional exercise of the law of patronage* (1767). Although Robertson is not named, there is a scarcely veiled attack on him for his 'youth, inexperience and too great influence with clergymen and others of not the most respectable characters'; he is accused of defending fornicators and abortionists while surrendering the 'sacred office' to 'the mere will and pleasure of men in power' (36). Nevertheless, one of Robertson's allies would later refer to Oswald as 'a respectable clergyman of the Church of Scotland' (*Autobiography*, ed. Burton, 97).

Oswald's most substantial work, *An Appeal to Common Sense in Behalf of Religion*, was published in November 1766, his authorship being identified by a notice in the Edinburgh press. Several sizeable orders of the first edition from the London bookseller Thomas Cadell are recorded in the letter-book of one of the original publishers, John Bell, of the Edinburgh firm Kincaid and Bell, and a second edition appeared in London in 1768 under Oswald's own name. In 1772 he added an anonymous second volume, co-published by Cadell in London and Kincaid and Creech in Edinburgh. The work was favourably noticed in the *Monthly Review*, *Critical Review*, and *Göttingische Anzeigen*. A German translation of both volumes appeared at Leipzig in 1774. The English dissenter William Enfield commended the work in his controversy with Joseph Priestley. The Irish evangelical Philip Skelton curiously thought that Oswald showed skill in argumentation but undervalued revelation. Priestley's hostile *Examination of Dr Reid's 'Inquiry into the human mind on the principles of common sense', Dr Beattie's 'Essay on the nature and immutability of truth', and Dr Oswald's 'Appeal to common sense in behalf of religion'* (1774) created the notion of a Scottish school which was perpetuated in attacks by the English translator of Buffier's *First Truths* (1780) and became canonical through the critical work of Immanuel Kant. Oswald wrote independently of Thomas Reid and James Beattie, but he capitalized on the appeal to common sense contained in Reid's *Inquiry into the Human Mind* (1764) to reinforce a theme that had been part of his own thinking for over thirty years, and established contact with Reid after the latter's move to Glasgow. He particularly commended to Reid the theory of human nature of the Swiss protestant Béat de Muralt, author of *L'Instinct divin* (1727).

The argument of Oswald's *Appeal* is theologically motivated throughout, and must be seen in relation to his campaign against the fashionable philosophies that he considered to be encouraged by the social and intellectual contacts of the moderates. He criticized Francis Hutcheson's moral sense theory and the trend towards rational religion. The practical consequences, as he perceived them, of David Hume's scepticism were an important target, but he acknowledged Hume's logical acumen and avoided personalizing the debate. Oswald shared many of Hume's reservations about the power of reasoning, but considered common sense a universal, God-given remedy which could not be impugned without undermining sense and sanity, morals and society. This common sense was beyond any need of analysis: it was found in the same persons of judgement and authority as formed the mainstay of Scottish parish management. Oswald found nothing problematic in ascribing to a direct deliverance of our common human reason or cognitive faculty a knowledge of the maxims of both logic and metaphysics, the principles of natural and moral philosophy, the necessities of mathematics, the contingencies of human existence, and the existence, power, and attributes of deity. These things do not come through human education: they are more evident than anything that could be presented in evidence, but mental maturity, intelligent observation, repeated experience, and a temperate climate may still be necessary to our appreciation of them.

Already by 1767 Oswald was consulting his brother over draft papers for a continuation of the *Appeal*, but it was not until ill health in the early 1770s forced the delegation of his pastoral duties to others that he found time to complete the new volume. In June 1770 he preached before the Society in Scotland for Propagating Christian Knowledge, which published his sermon as *The Divine Efficacy of the Gospel-Dispensation*. Oswald's theology was orthodox but not narrowly Calvinistic. In 1773 he was contemplating twin studies of the external and internal evidences of Christianity, for which he had received encouragement from the *Critical Review*. He considered the expectation of divine favours, conferred through a worthy mediator, 'a dictat of common-sense', because of its universality and because the practice of those who petition for favours without mediation elicits such a natural resentment in us as to be 'a manifest offence against common-sense' (to Richard Oswald, 1 Nov 1773). In 1774 he published *Six Sermons on the General Judgement*. During the following winter he undertook a commission from his near neighbour Thomas Hay, earl of Kinnoull, and the earl's brother, the archbishop of York, to prepare something against 'the progress of a licentious way of thinking which has had a long course & hath now reached almost to the vulgar' (ibid., 22 May 1775). This seems to have formed the basis of *Hypocrisy Detestable and Dangerous: Four Sermons*, which appeared anonymously in Glasgow in the year of Oswald's death. He had nothing to do with a second anonymous work that is occasionally ascribed to him, *Alarming Progress of French Politics* (1787).

By November 1776 two of the heritors who supplied his

stipend, including the patron, were in financial difficulties and the rest took advantage of Oswald's forbearance, with the result that his brother helped to support him. On 24 April 1783 he demitted his charge and retired to Scotstoun, to the residence of his son George. Oswald, like Reid, was a founding member of the Glasgow Society for the Sons of the Clergy. He died on 2 August 1793, leaving £100 each to this and a corresponding society in Edinburgh, and charitable donations to his former parishes.

RICHARD B. SHER and M. A. STEWART

Sources MS correspondence of Richard Oswald, NA Scot., GD213/53, fols. 202–250 • Caithness and Perth presbytery minutes, NA Scot., CH2/47/3, CH2/299/16–17 • associate presbytery of Perth and Dunfermline minutes, 1752–4, NA Scot., CH3/261/1 • general assembly papers, NA Scot., CH1/2/90, fols. 82–159 • register of divinity students, Edinburgh UL, Da. 41 • Oswald to Thomas Reid, 16/10/1766, Aberdeen UL, MS 2131/3/III/17 • N. Morren, ed., *Annals of the general assembly of the Church of Scotland*, 2 vols. (1838–40) • *Edinburgh Evening Courant* (25 May 1768) • NL Scot., Caldwell MS 4942, fol. 52 [W. Mure of Caldwell] • John Bell letter-books (1764–73), Bodl. Oxf., MS Eng. lett. c. 20–21 • *The autobiography of Dr Alexander Carlyle of Inveresk, 1722–1805*, ed. J. H. Burton (1910) • *Fasti Scot.*, new edn, 4.223, 7.120 • J. Cooper, 'James Oswald (1703–93) and the application of the common sense philosophy to religion', PhD diss., U. Edin., 1948 • M. Kuehn, *Scottish common sense in Germany, 1768–1800* (1987), chap. 3 • J. Coutts, *A history of the University of Glasgow* (1909) • D. Hancock, *Citizens of the world: London merchants and the integration of the British Atlantic community, 1735–1785* (1995) • J. Fieser, ed., *Scottish common sense philosophy: sources and origins*, 5 vols. (2000)
Archives NA Scot., Church of Scotland, General Assembly papers, 1750, CH 1/2/90 • NA Scot., letters to his brother Richard, GD 213/53, fols. 202–50

Oswald, James (1710–1769), musician and publisher, was baptized on 21 March 1710 at Crail, Fife, the second son of John Oswald and Elspit Horn. His father was town drummer of Crail and later became leader of the town waits of Berwick upon Tweed, where he died in 1758 (buried there, 2 October). His younger brother Henry (*b*. Crail, 1714) also became a professional musician. Almost nothing is known of James Oswald before 12 August 1734, when he announced a collection of his own minuets in the *Caledonian Mercury*. He was by then a dancing-master in Dunfermline, but in 1735 moved to Edinburgh, where he remained until 1741. A *Collection of Minuets* (1736) brought him early success there, and he was also active as a cellist and teacher, and perhaps as a violinist: his talent with the bow was mentioned in an epistle, probably by Allan Ramsay, written on Oswald's departure for London in 1741 and published in the *Scots Magazine* for October that year. He was to remain in London until around 1763. About 1741 he eloped with Marion (sometimes Mary Ann) Melvill; they eventually married on 12 February 1744 at St James's, Westminster. The marriage produced four children—Mary, Agnes, Elizabeth, and Frances—and at some time Oswald also adopted a niece, the illegitimate daughter of Marion's brother Thomas.

While in Edinburgh Oswald had produced a first *Curious Collection of Scots Tunes* (1740). A revised edition with many new pieces was published in London by John Simpson, and was followed from 1742 by a second collection that included several pieces ascribed to 'David Rizo', which according to Ramsay were widely known to be Oswald's own. The dedication of the London volumes to Frederick, prince of Wales, suggests early patronage by royalty, which continued later with Oswald's appointment as chamber composer to George III in 1761.

In London Oswald contributed to, and profited from, a growing enthusiasm for Scots music, and followed up his *Scots Tunes* with the *Caledonian Pocket Companion*, an outstandingly successful production that probably accounted for much of his income after he set up his own publishing business in 1747. Some of his most intriguing publications were issued between 1747 and the early 1750s for the Society of the Temple of Apollo, which he may have founded. Lack of evidence has led to this society's being branded secret, even sinister. Frank Kidson called it mysterious, and listed Oswald, Charles Burney, Giuseppe Sammartini, John Reid, and Thomas Erskine as its members, while both Peter Holman and John Purser have suggested connections with freemasonry.

During the 1750s Oswald continued to publish his own music, particularly single-sheet songs. In 1755 he issued his *Airs for the Seasons* for melody instrument and continuo, comprising pieces devoted to the seasons of the year. A second set followed in the 1760s. Marion Oswald had died by 1764 and perhaps as early as the mid-1750s, and Oswald became close to Leonora, widow of his patron John Robinson-Lytton. They married and moved to Knebworth, Hertfordshire, following Oswald's sale of his music publishing business. In 1822 Richard Clark, in his *Account of the National Anthem*, claimed that towards the end of his life Oswald was responsible for setting the chime barrel of the bells at Windsor parish church with the tune of 'God Save the King', consequently known in those parts as 'Oswald's are [air]' and leading some to suppose he had composed it. Oswald died on 2 January 1769 at Knebworth, Hertfordshire, and was buried there on 9 January. His wife lived until 1790.

Although so little is known about him—there is no contemporary character sketch, or surviving likeness—Oswald seems to have enjoyed a solid reputation as a musician. A note in an edition from the 1770s of the *Comic Tunes in Queen Mab* states that his 'fine taste, his elegant compositions, his pathetic performance, were well known and justly admired' (Kidson, 'Temple of Apollo', 37). His fondness for anonymity, pseudonyms, and, consequently, mystery—a fondness also manifest, perhaps, in his elopement—suggests a secretive, impetuous, and characterful individual. Some of his manuscript compositions are in Glasgow University Library.

JOHN WAGSTAFF

Sources D. Johnson and H. Melvill, 'Oswald, James', *New Grove*, 2nd edn • J. Purser, *Scotland's music* (1992) • D. Johnson, *Scottish fiddle music in the 18th century: a music collection and historical study* (1984) • D. Johnson, *Music and society in lowland Scotland in the eighteenth century* (1972) • P. Holman, 'preface', in F. Geminiani and J. Oswald, *Trio sonatas on Scots tunes, for two violins and continuo* (1992) • J. Barlow, 'preface', in J. Oswald, *Airs for the seasons, for flute (or violin) and continuo* (1983) • H. G. Farmer, *A history of music in Scotland* (1947) • F. Kidson, 'Oswald, James', *British music publishers, printers and engravers* (1900), 84–7 • F. Kidson, 'James Oswald, Dr Burney, and "The temple of Apollo"', *Musical Antiquary*, 2 (1910–11), 34–41 •

R. Fiske, *Scotland in music: a European enthusiasm* (1983) • D. Baptie, 'Oswald, James', *Musical Scotland past and present: being a dictionary of Scottish musicians from about 1400 till the present time*, ed. D. Baptie (1894), 142–3 • R. Clark, *An account of the national anthem entitled 'God save the king!'* (1822) • *GM*, 1st ser., 39 (1769), 54 • *IGI*

Oswald, James (1715–1769), politician, eldest son of James Oswald, MP for Kirkcaldy (1702–7) and for Kirkcaldy burghs (1713–15), was born at Dunnikier, Dysart, Fife. His brother John later became bishop of Raphoe. He was educated at Kirkcaldy burgh school, where he became a good friend of one of his schoolfellows, Adam Smith. He entered the University of Edinburgh and was admitted as a student at Lincoln's Inn on 13 December 1733. After making a prolonged grand tour he was called to the Scottish bar in 1740. He did not practise, however, and on 2 June 1741 was returned to parliament for Kirkcaldy burghs, which he continued to represent until 1768 with the exception of the years from 1747 to 1754 during which he sat for Fife. On 19 January 1747 he married, in London, Elizabeth Reynardson (*née* Townsend), daughter of a London brewer and MP for Westbury, Joseph Townsend, and widow of Abraham Reynardson.

A strong whig, Oswald voted against the hiring of Hanoverian troops (10 December 1742). On the formation of the 'broad bottom' administration he received the office of Scottish commissioner of the navy (December 1744). His speeches, principally on economic and military matters, were always very able. He demonstrated his independence by supporting, on 28 October 1745, Hume Campbell's motion for an inquiry into the causes and progress of the Jacobite rising, the entire responsibility for which he laid at the door of the government, thus alienating Pitt the elder. He then ingratiated himself with the Leicester House party. Such tactics proved successful and he gained office: from December 1751 to December 1759 he sat on the Board of Trade, and from 22 December 1759 to 15 April 1763 on the Treasury board. On 4 May 1763 he was appointed joint vice-treasurer in Ireland, after having been sworn of the privy council on 20 April. He retired from parliament on grounds of ill health and was succeeded as MP by his son James Townsend Oswald.

Oswald was an able and industrious public servant, and also a man of literary and philosophical tastes. He was a close friend and an amiable critic not only of Adam Smith, but also of David Hume, Henry Home, Lord Kames, and John Home, the author of *Douglas*. He died in Hammersmith on 24 March 1769. J. M. Rigg, *rev.* J.-M. Alter

Sources E. Haden-Guest and E. Cruickshanks, 'Oswald, James', HoP, *Commons, 1715–54* • E. Haden-Guest, 'Oswald, James', HoP, *Commons, 1754–90* • *Memorials of the public life and character of James Oswald of Dunniker* (1825) • D. Stewart, *Biographical memoirs* (1811), 5 • A. F. Tytler, *Memoirs of the life and writings of the Honourable Henry Home of Kames*, 2nd edn, 3 vols. (1814) • *The diary of the late George Bubb Dodington* (1784) • J. H. Burton, *Life and correspondence of David Hume*, 2 vols. (1846) • J. Ramsay, *Scotland and Scotsmen in the eighteenth century*, ed. A. Allardyce, 2 vols. (1888) • H. Walpole, *Memoirs of the reign of King George the Second*, ed. Lord Holland [H. R. Fox], 2 vols. (1846) • H. Walpole, *Memoirs of the reign of King George the Third*, ed. D. Le Marchant, 4 vols. (1845) • *GM*, 1st ser., 14 (1744), 677 • *GM*, 1st ser., 17 (1747), 102 • *GM*, 1st ser., 39 (1769), 168 • Walpole, *Corr.*

Archives NRA, priv. coll., political corresp. and MSS | NA Scot., letters to Sir Hew Dalrymple; letters to Lord Kames
Likenesses W. H. Lizars, line engraving, NPG

Oswald, John (*c.*1760–1793), journalist and poet, was born in Edinburgh, where his father, also John Oswald, a goldsmith of 'great learning', kept John's Coffee House. Nothing is known of his mother. John learned Latin and Greek as a youth, and later studied Arabic, French, Italian, Spanish, and Portuguese. He was a goldsmith's apprentice, but joined the Royal Irish regiment in 1776 or 1777, serving from early 1781 as a lieutenant in India. Before embarking, he married his first wife, Louisa, in Deal. They had two sons. On the way to India, he duelled with Colonel Norman Macleod. Oswald was in Madras in the winter of 1782–3, but left India in 1783, returning by land to the Deal–Dover area. His wife having died, he married Bathesheba Fagge Owen (*bap.* 1759), a widow, on 1 June 1784 in Folkestone. They had one daughter, Jane, and an infant son.

Oswald worked in Grub Street, London, on the *Political Herald and Review* (1785–6), and published with James Ridgway the *British Mercury* (1787), with prints by Gillray and Rowlandson. He reported parliamentary debates for the *London Gazetteer* (1789–91), lectured and debated in London (Society of Free Debate at Coachmakers Hall, 1790), wrote poetry (*Euphrosyne: an Ode to Beauty*, 1788, under the pseudonym Sylvester Otway), love poems for *The World* (1790), and political pamphlets: *Review of the Constitution of Great Britain* (1784), *Ranae comicae evangelizantes* (1786), *The Alarming Progress of French Politics* (1787), and *The Cry of Nature* (1791). By now a friend of Tom Paine, John Horne Tooke, David Williams, James Mackintosh, and John and William Stone, Oswald was known as a revolutionary activist in England and France. His reputation may be sensed by his *Constitution for the Universal Commonwealth* (1793), which was recommended to Burke, with the works of Paine, Sieyès, Barlow, and Mirabeau, in 1792.

By May 1790 Oswald was resident in Paris. He watched the debates in the national assembly, where he presented an 'Ode to the Triumph of Freedom' on 4 September 1790. He met Thomas Cooper, Joel Barlow, Thomas Christie, Wolf Tone, Lord Edward Fitzgerald, Brissot, Danton, Desmoulins, the Rolands, Théroigne de Méricourt, and Henry Redhead Yorke, with whom he argued between 1792 and 1793. Oswald collaborated with Bonneville as editor of a monthly journal, *Chronique du Mois* (1791–3), of the Circle Social (founded in Paris in January 1790), which included Brissot, Condorcet, and Lanthenas among its authors. James Ridgway was its London bookseller (1791). Oswald also worked as secretary and reporter for a few months on the *Universal Patriot* (edition of 3 May 1790), the English newspaper printed in Paris, London, and Calais, hoping to cover debates on both sides of the channel. Late in 1792 the British Club was formed by some British men and women who met in White's Hotel in Paris to celebrate successes of the French army and national assembly. Oswald officiated as secretary. He spoke in the Jacobin Club (22 August 1792, 30 September 1792, 4 February 1793), wrote its *La tactique du peuple* (*c.*1792), and worked as its publisher and collaborating editor. He translated its *Almanach des Père Gérard* by Collot d'Herbois as *The Spirit of the French Constitution: the Almanach of Goodman Gérard* with a subsidy from the London Corresponding Society. He was named an honorary French citizen on 25 September 1792 and commander in the French revolutionary army. As commandant of the Parisian pikemen Oswald left Paris on 26 March 1793 with his battalion to fight and die at Thouars in the battle of La Vendée on 14 September 1793. His two sons (aged fourteen and seventeen) served as drummer boys, and were wounded but not killed in this same battle.

Oswald, a vegetarian and atheist, used the pseudonyms Ignotus (in the *Political Herald*, 1785–7), Sylvester Otway (London newspapers 1788–9), and H. K. He was of 'middle height … noble carriage, [had a] heroic and grave face, sober manners and [was] a bit stiff' (Lichtenberger, 483).

T. F. Henderson, *rev.* Ralph A. Manogue

Sources D. V. Erdman, *Commerce des lumières: John Oswald and the British in Paris, 1790–1793* (1986) • A. Lichtenberger, 'John Oswald: Ecossais, Jacobin et socialiste', *Revolution Française*, 32 (1897), 481–95
Archives Royal Literary Fund, London, archives, case file no. 15

Oswald, Sir John (1771–1840), army officer, son of James Townsend Oswald, was born at Dunnikier, Kirkcaldy, Fife, on 2 October 1771. For some years (from about 1785) he was at the military school at Brienne, France, just after Napoleon had left. With Louis-Antoine Fauvelet de Bourrienne, Napoleon's school companion and future secretary, Oswald contracted a lifelong friendship, and some of his holidays were spent in Paris. He thus acquired a command of the French language, which proved of great service to him in his profession, and a sympathy with the French, which was uncommon at that time. However, abhorrence of revolutionary principles, intensified by the loss of personal friends whom he had known in Paris in his youth, gave bias to his political views. He was appointed a second lieutenant in the 23rd foot (Royal Welch Fusiliers) on 1 February 1788, and first lieutenant in the 7th foot (Royal Fusiliers) on 29 January 1789. In June 1790 he embarked to join the Royal Fusiliers at Gibraltar, was appointed captain of an independent company on 24 January 1791, and on 23 March of that year became a captain in the 35th foot. While brigade major to Major-General John Leland, he resigned when the grenadier company of the 35th, which he commanded, was ordered to the West Indies. He served with the 2nd provisional battalion of grenadiers at the capture of Martinique, St Lucia, and Guadeloupe in 1794, and was afterwards in garrison at Port-au-Prince on San Domingo until his company was drafted and the officers and sergeants sent home to recruit. He became major in the 35th on 1 September 1795, lieutenant-colonel of the regiment on 30 March 1797, and lieutenant-colonel in the army on 29 December 1798.

Oswald commanded the 35th during the expedition to The Helder in the Netherlands in 1799, until severely wounded at Crabbenham, near Bergen aan Zee, on 19 September. In 1800 he embarked with the two battalions of his regiment among the troops dispatched under Major-General Richard Pigot, and landed with them at Minorca. He subsequently took part in the blockade of Valletta and capture of Malta, remaining there in command of the regiment until the peace of Amiens, when he went home on leave. On the renewal of the war he rejoined the regiment at Malta, and became brevet colonel on 30 October 1805. With the 35th he joined the troops under Lieutenant-General Sir James Craig in Sicily, was appointed commander at Melazzo, and commanded the advance of Major-General Sir John Stuart's force at the landing in Calabria in June of that year. He commanded the 3rd brigade of the army at the battle of Maida on 4 July 1806, and three days later marched with it into Lower Calabria, where he captured Scylla Castle after a siege of twenty days. On his return to Sicily he received the local rank of brigadier-general. In February 1807 he went with Major-General Alexander Mackenzie Fraser to Egypt, where the two battalions of the 35th were the first troops to land. He commanded the troops sent against Alexandria, and attacked and captured the western lines, taking many guns and driving the Turks within the walls. Alexandria capitulated two days later. Oswald was then sent to Rosetta, where he came under repeated attack for fifteen days before being withdrawn in the face of vastly superior enemy forces. He remained in Alexandria until the expedition returned to Sicily, where he was appointed commandant of Augusta. In June 1808 his local rank was extended to the Mediterranean generally, and in October he was appointed to command a large body of troops collected at Melazzo. In 1809 he led the reserve in the expedition to the coast of Italy, which ended in the capture of the islands of Ischia and Procida; of the latter he became commandant. He went back to Sicily in July 1809, and in September was sent to the Ionian Islands with an expeditionary force, which seized Zante (Zákynthos), Cephalonia, Ithaca, and Cerigo (Kithira).

In March 1810, recognizing the danger to the captured islands from the neighbouring French garrison in Santa Maura (Levkas), Oswald collected 2000 troops and landed there on 23 March. He drove the enemy behind their lines, personally leading the troops that stormed the strongest of the entrenchments, and secured the enemy's capitulation after eight days. He then administered the civil and military government of the captured islands. By his tact and judgement he confirmed the prepossessions of the Greeks in favour of British rule, and he also established advantageous relations with the neighbouring Turkish pashas. On 11 February 1811 Oswald was appointed colonel of the 1st Greek light infantry, consisting mostly of Greek brigands, who made very good soldiers. He left the administration of the Ionian Islands—which he nominally governed until 1815—to Richard Church and returned home to impress on the government their strategic importance. He was made a major-general on 4 June 1811 and appointed to command the western district. On 28 January 1812 he married Charlotte (*d.* 1827), eldest daughter of the Revd Lord Charles Murray-Aynsley, son of John Murray, third duke of Atholl. James Townsend, their son, served as an army officer from 1839 to 1848.

Oswald joined the staff of the Peninsular army on 22 October 1812, during the retreat from Burgos. He was present with Wellington during rearguard cavalry actions on 23–4 October, and on the 25th took command of the 5th division during the absence of Major-General James Leith. At the head of the division he had some sharp fighting at Villa Muriel and the passage of the River Carrión, and remained in charge of it until it went into winter quarters on the banks of the River Douro, though on one occasion during the withdrawal he incurred Wellington's displeasure for varying his line of march without authority. When the army took the field in May 1813, Oswald commanded the 5th division in its difficult march through the north of Portugal and the Spanish provinces of Zamora, León, and Palencia, as it drove the enemy back at Osma on 17 June, and, passing through a mountainous country previously considered impassable for troops with guns, joined Wellington at Vitoria on 20 June. He led the division at the battle of Vitoria on the 21st and the opening phase of the siege of San Sebastian. However, Leith resumed command of the division two days previous to the assault on San Sebastian on 31 August, Oswald reverting to a brigade until he was wounded on the 31st.

The death of an elder brother, and the failing health of his father, to whose estates he had become heir, now resulted in Oswald's recall to England. He received the thanks of parliament for his services at Vitoria and San Sebastian, and a gold medal with two clasps for Maida, Vitoria, and San Sebastian. He was made KCB on 4 June 1815. On the disbanding of the Greek light infantry he became colonel-commandant of one of the batteries of the rifle brigade, and on 9 October 1819 appointed colonel of the 35th, a post he retained until his death in 1840. He became a lieutenant-general on 12 August 1819 and a general on 10 January 1837, and was made GCB in 1824 and GCMG in 1838. In politics he was a staunch conservative and once, in the days before the first Reform Act, unsuccessfully contested the county of Fife. In October 1829 he married Emily Jane, daughter of Lord Henry Murray and cousin of his first wife, Charlotte; she survived him.

In person Oswald was a tall, handsome, powerful man, over 6 feet in height, who used his weapons well in hand-to-hand combat, notably in the attack on Scylla Castle in 1806. He had strong literary tastes, was a good and ready public speaker, and was popular in society. Oswald died at his seat, Dunnikier, Kirkcaldy, Fife, on 8 June 1840.

H. M. CHICHESTER, *rev.* JOHN SWEETMAN

Sources *Army List* • *A short history of the royal Sussex regiment, 1701–1926* (1941) • R. Trimen, ed., *An historical memoir of the 35th royal Sussex regiment of foot* (1873) • private information (1894)

Archives NRA, priv. coll., corresp. and papers | BL, corresp. with Sir Hudson Lowe, Add. MSS 20109–20110, 20164–20171, 20184–20186, 20191

Likenesses S. Watson, oils, repro. in *Short history*, facing p. 12; known to be in Dunniker House, Fife, in 1941 • group portrait (after engraving by Cardon; after de Loutherbourg), repro. in *Short history*, facing p. 8; known to be at the Officers' Mess at Dupont? in 1941

Oswald, Richard (1705?–1784), merchant and diplomat, was born, probably in 1705, in Dunnet, Caithness, Scotland, the second of the four children of George Oswald (1664–1726), the Presbyterian minister of Dunnet, and his wife, Margaret (*d.* 1747), of Pennyland, Caithness, the daughter of Richard Murray of Scotscalder, Caithness, and his wife, Jean Smythe. The suggestion in the *Dictionary of National Biography* that Richard Oswald was the unsuccessful candidate for the Thurso schoolmastership can be discarded on the grounds that, since the search took place in 1711, he would have been at most eleven years old when applying for the position. He left Caithness at the age of twenty after his father's death and apprenticed himself to his older cousins Richard (1687–1763) and Alexander Oswald (1694–1766), who had built a successful trade in Glasgow in tobacco, sugar, and wine. During the 1730s he travelled through southern North America and the Caribbean as their factor, distributing supplies to planters, collecting crops in payment, and dunning tardy debtors. He returned to Glasgow in 1741 and became a junior partner in his cousins' firm.

Assisted by several thousand pounds of prize profits reaped during the War of the Austrian Succession, Oswald moved to London in early 1746 and, from a counting-house at 17 Philpot Lane, commenced an ambitious shipping and merchandising operation. At first tobacco played an important role in his business, but he soon branched out into horses, slaves, and sugar. He undergirded his capital-intensive tobacco and slave adventures with a marriage on 12 November 1750, at St Martin-in-the-Fields to Mary Ramsay (1719–1788), the daughter of a wealthy Jamaica merchant, Alexander Ramsay (*d.* 1738), and his wife, Jean Ferguson, and a partnership with two fellow Scots who had moved to London in the 1740s, John Mill (1710–1771) and Robert Scott (*d.* 1771). With the support this cohort provided, Oswald began to exploit opportunities in two additional areas—government contracting and land speculation. Contracting came first, helped by the support of a cousin, James Oswald of Dunnikier, who sat on the Treasury board. Richard Oswald supplied summer encampments in southern England with bread, forage, straw, wood, and wagons in 1756, 1757, and 1758. In 1758 he agreed to supply the troops in Germany with bread. Over the course of the Seven Years' War he executed three separate contracts and held two separate commissions with the commissariat; in all, he cleared over £125,000. The end of the war in 1763 ushered in a new era of enterprise for Oswald, a period of large-scale land acquisition and development—activities which meshed neatly with ongoing slaving and shipping businesses. In the Caribbean he acquired title to four plantations, totalling 1566 acres. In North America, after false starts in Nova Scotia and South Carolina, he obtained 30,000 acres in East Florida near the confluence of the Halifax and Timoka rivers. His greatest investment occurred closer to home, however: between 1764 and 1784 he acquired and 'improved' roughly 7000 acres on the banks of the River Ayr in Ayrshire (the Auchincruive estate) and about the same amount in Kirkcudbrightshire and Dumfriesshire (the Cavens estate).

Oswald's global interests were sorely tested by the American War of Independence. During these years he curtailed his operations overseas. In 1780 he sold land he owned in Virginia, and the following year he began to withdraw from Florida. At the same time he stepped up his involvement in politics, which until then had been largely advisory. He wrote memoranda on military strategy, drawing on years of experience in and with the colonies, and submitted them to friends in Whitehall. In December 1781 he provided bail to release his old correspondent and friend Henry Laurens, who had previously used Oswald's counting-house as his own office whenever he was in London and who had been imprisoned in the Tower since September 1780. In March 1782 the marquess of Rockingham, on the advice of the earl of Shelburne, made Oswald his emissary in Paris to ascertain the American position on peace. There is no evidence to support the *Dictionary of National Biography*'s claim that Adam Smith had introduced Shelburne to Oswald, or that Smith's ideas became Oswald's own; the Oswald and Shelburne circles had overlapped for decades, and Oswald's thoughts on protected and free trade were more nuanced and self-serving than Smith's. Between April and June Oswald shuttled between London and Paris. His work was frustrated by the presence and conflicting claims of competing representatives appointed by Shelburne's rivals in the ministry. When Rockingham died in early July, Shelburne, who succeeded Rockingham as chief minister, removed the others and, in a commission dated 25 July 1782, appointed Oswald sole British representative charged with crafting an American peace. From the beginning to the end of the negotiations Oswald adhered to the belief that America's commercial dependence on Britain was the critical issue, and that political dependence meant comparatively little. These beliefs withstood the assistance provided by Henry Strachey and Alleyne Fitzherbert, who had been sent by Shelburne in the autumn to make sure Oswald did not give away too much. Oswald was too highly regarded by the Americans to consider his replacement. Five months after his appointment Oswald gave Shelburne a testament of these beliefs in the form of the preliminary articles of peace. This agreement, the first of the settlements to come out of Paris, raised a storm of protest at home and eventually brought down the Shelburne administration and, with it, the peacemaker. The preliminary articles proved more lasting than did the objections to it, however, and Oswald's terms were accepted without revision as the final treaty of Paris in September 1783.

After returning to London Oswald retreated to the comfort of his family and friends, dividing his days between his new town house, 9 Great George Street, and his mansion on the banks of the River Ayr designed and decorated by James Adam. When in London he entertained the American negotiators on their return to the United States. He occasionally dabbled in trade, although he passed the management of the firm on to his nephews John (1747–1808) and Alexander Anderson (1756–1832). He died in his bedroom at Auchincruive at 6 a.m. on 6 November 1784, and was buried in the High Church, Glasgow. With no legitimate children (he had fathered two illegitimate sons in the 1740s, but they had predeceased him), his substantial estate passed to his nephew **George Oswald** (1735–1819). His wife, Mary, died on 6 December 1788 and was buried alongside the peacemaker in the Oswald vault at St Quivox parish church.

Oswald's nephew George Oswald of Scotstoun, near Glasgow, was born on 30 July 1735 in Dunnet, Caithness, one of the eight children of his elder brother, the Revd James *Oswald (1703–1793), Presbyterian minister of Dunnet and (after 1750) Methven, Perthshire, and in 1765 moderator of the general assembly of the Church of Scotland, and his first wife, Elizabeth, the daughter of James Murray and his wife, Margaret Sinclair. George Oswald first worked for his father's cousins, Richard and Alexander Oswald, and in the late 1760s he established his own tobacco-trading firm on Virginia Street under the name of Oswald, Dennistoun & Co. He also served as a partner in Glasgow's Ship Bank. In January 1764 he married Margaret (1747–1791), the daughter of David Smythe of Methven; they had four sons and five or six daughters. He acquired the small estates of Scotstoun and Balshagray, near Glasgow, in 1766, after the deaths of Richard and Alexander Oswald, and in 1784 he inherited the estate of Auchincruive on the death of his uncle Richard. In 1797 he was elected the rector of Glasgow University. He died on 6 October 1819, and was succeeded by his son Richard Alexander Oswald (1771–1841). DAVID HANCOCK

Sources D. Hancock, *Citizens of the world: London merchants and the integration of the British Atlantic community, 1735–1785* (1995) • R. B. Morris, *The peacemakers: the great powers and American independence* (1965) • Burke, *Gen. GB* • *Memorials of the public life and character of the Right Honourable James Oswald of Dunnikier* (1825) • *The papers of Henry Laurens*, ed. P. M. Hamer and others, 15 vols. (1968–) • G. C. Rogers, 'The East Florida Society of London, 1766–1767', *Florida Historical Quarterly*, 54 (1976), 481–7 • *Journal of the commissioners for trade and plantations*, [14 vols.] (1920–38) [April 1704 – May 1782] • W. L. Grant and J. F. Munro, eds., *Acts of the privy council of England: colonial series*, 6 vols (1908–12) • *Fasti Scot.* • J. Paterson, *History of the counties of Ayr and Wigton*, 3 vols. (1863–6) • *Autobiography of the Rev. Dr. Alexander Carlyle … containing memorials of the men and events of his time*, ed. J. H. Burton (1860); repr. as *Anecdotes and characters of the times*, ed. J. Kinsley (1973) • *DNB* • *Glasgow Mercury* (6 Nov 1784) • *Glasgow Mercury* (18 Nov 1784) • *Morning Chronicle* (12 Nov 1784) • *The Times* (11 Jan 1785) • cashbook of George Oswald, NA Scot., GD 1/618/32–324 • U. Edin. L., Oswald MSS • kirk records (burials), Ayrshire, St Guivox • priv. coll., Oswald MSS • will, PRO, PROB 11/1125. sig. 37

Archives NA Scot., letter-books • NA Scot., corresp. • priv. coll. • U. Edin. L., special collections division, corresp. • U. Mich., Clements L., Richard Oswald memoranda • University of Virginia, Charlottesville, memoranda • Yale U., Beinecke L., letter-books | Ballindallach Castle, near Aviemore, General James Grant MSS • Hockworthy House, Wellington, Somerset, Oswald of Dunnikier MSS • Island RO, Spanishtown, Jamaica, deeds • NA Scot., register of Sasines • Spottes, near Castle Douglas, Herries MSS • U. Mich., Clements L., Shelburne MSS

Likenesses W. Denune, oils, 1749, priv. coll. • T. Gainsborough, oils, *c*.1770–1774 (George Oswald)

Wealth at death £250,000–£500,000: Henry Laurens to George Washington, 18 June 1778, L. Cong.; *The Times*, 3, col. 1

Oswell, (William) Cotton (1818–1893), explorer and hunter, was born at Leytonstone, Essex, on 27 April 1818, the elder son of William Oswell (1782–1822) and his wife, Amelia (*d.* 1848), the daughter of Joseph Cotton, deputy master of Trinity House and grandson of Dr Nathaniel Cotton. From 1833 to 1835 he was at Rugby School, under the headmastership of Thomas Arnold. He proceeded to East India College, Haileybury, where he was placed second among the students of his year. Having obtained an appointment through his uncle John Cotton, one of the East India Company's directors, in 1837 he went to Madras where, during his ten years' residence, he won celebrity as an elephant-catcher.

After serving as assistant to the principal collector of revenue at Arcot and as head assistant at Coimbatore, Oswell was ordered to South Africa for his health. There he spent two years in hunting and became acquainted with the missionary David Livingstone. When in 1849 Livingstone determined to investigate the truth of rumours as to a great lake in the Kalahari, Oswell and his friend Mungo Murray returned to South Africa from England in order to take part in the exploration, Oswell undertaking to defray the whole expense of the guides. The result was the discovery by Europeans of Lake Ngami, and the important practical demonstration that the Kalahari could be crossed by oxen and wagons. Livingstone freely acknowledged his indebtedness to the companionship of Oswell, who looked after the wagons and supplied the party with food, thus enabling the work of surveying, of making scientific collections, and of studying the African people to be carried on without anxiety or preoccupation. The kuabaoba, or straight-horned rhinoceros, was named Oswellii after Oswell, who also received the medal of the Societé de Géographie de Paris for his share in the journey. He again accompanied Livingstone in 1851, on an expedition to meet the Kololo paramount chief Sebituane. On that occasion they first sighted the Zambezi River.

Recalled from a life of adventure by family matters, Oswell returned to England in 1853. On the outbreak of the Crimean War he went to the front as the guest of some of his Indian friends, and rendered good service in the trenches, in the hospitals, and as the bearer of secret service money for Lord Raglan. He afterwards travelled through North and South America, and in 1860 married Agnes Frances (*d.* 1908), fourth daughter of Francis Rivaz; they settled at Groombridge in Kent. In his lifetime he was more celebrated as a gentleman sportsman than as an African explorer. His collection of hunting trophies was renowned as a private museum and, at the end of his life, he contributed chapters to C. P. Wolley's anthology *Big Game Shooting* (1894). To the regret of his contemporaries, Oswell published no accounts of his expeditions with Livingstone. His modesty, gentlemanly demeanour, and physical prowess were much admired. He died at his home, Hillside, Groombridge, on 1 May 1893, survived by his wife, three sons, and two daughters, and was buried at Groombridge.

After his death, much of his most important correspondence was published by his eldest son, Edward Oswell, together with a foreword by his friend Francis Galton, the propagandist of eugenics. Among these letters are some from Livingstone which credit Oswell with the initial conception of introducing European colonization and commerce to central Africa as an antidote to the slave trade.

THOMAS SECCOMBE, *rev.* NORMAN ETHERINGTON

Sources W. E. Oswell, *William Cotton Oswell*, 2 vols. (1900) • J. Listowel, *The other Livingstone* (1974) • A. Roberts, *A history of Zambia* (1976) • L. H. Gann, *A history of Northern Rhodesia* (1969) • T. Tlou and A. Campbell, *History of Botswana* (1984) • J. M. MacKenzie, *The empire of nature* (1988) • Burke, *Gen. GB* (1914) • *CGPLA Eng. & Wales* (1893)

Archives NL Scot., corresp. with David Livingstone

Wealth at death £21,294 16*s.* 6*d.*: resworn probate, May 1894, *CGPLA Eng. & Wales* (1893)

Oswen, John (*fl.* 1548–1553), printer, was active first at Ipswich, and afterwards at Worcester. He was one of only two printers known to have worked at Ipswich in the sixteenth century; the earlier, Anthony Scoloker, probably began work in 1547 and had moved his press to London by June 1548. Nine works printed at Ipswich by John Oswen survive, five of them dated 1548 and the others undated. A further two books, also from 1548, were listed as Oswen's by Andrew Maunsell in his 1595 *Catalogue of English Printed Books*, but no copies of either these or of a third, seen by William Herbert and described in his revision of Joseph Ames's *Typographical Antiquities* (1785–90, 3.1458), appear to survive. All twelve books were works by protestant reformers, including English translations of tracts by John Calvin, Christopher Hegendorff, Antoine Marcort, Philip Melanchthon, and Joannes Oecolampadius. Two Ipswich 'gospellers', Peter Moone and John Ramsey, provided the texts for two books of crude anti-papist verse, and the Henry Reiginalde named as translator of one Latin work was very likely Henry Reynolds of nearby Belstead.

Oswen's final Ipswich book may well have been Reiginalde's translation of Hegendorff's *Domestical Sermons* (1548), which ends with the promise that 'The rest of the sermons shalbe printed shortlye'. The continuation, dated 'the last daye of February 1549', in fact appeared at Worcester, where the printer had relocated by the turn of the year. Oswen is specifically named as 'of Worcester' in a patent of 6 January 1549 (2 Edward VI), the text of which he prefixed to his first Worcester book, Henry Hart's *Consultory for All Christians*, dated 30 January 1549. Oswen's privilege authorized him to print and sell, within the principality of Wales and the marches, both service and prayer books and 'al maner of bokes conteinyng any storye or exposition of Gods holy scripture'. He consequently issued at Worcester two editions of the Book of Common Prayer, dated 24 May 1549 (quarto) and 30 July 1549 (folio); these were followed on 1 September by a psalter, on 8 October by an edition of the homilies, and on 12 January 1550 by a New Testament, all in quarto. At the same time he continued with his programme of publishing English versions of tracts by such continental reformers as Heinrich Bullinger, Matteo Gribaldi, Jean Veron, and Ulrich Zwingli, alongside similar native works by Thomas Lever and Bishop John Hooper. In addition to the nineteen books surviving from Oswen's Worcester years a further three works of 1549–50, now lost, were assigned to his press by Maunsell or Herbert.

While at Worcester, Oswen apparently had an agent at Shrewsbury, for the colophons of several books indicate that they were 'also to sell' there. Both at Ipswich and at Worcester his printing was distinguished by the use of lively woodcut border pieces and initials; a number of these, as well as some of his types, were later used by the London printer John Tisdale. Oswen was made a freeman of the city of Worcester in 1553, but only two of his books with that year date survive, an edition of the statutes and Hooper's homily 'to be read in the tyme of pestylence', dated 18 May at the end of the text. This was probably Oswen's last book: no further record of him is known, and it is very likely that he left England following the accession of Mary in July 1553. With the closure of his press Worcester was without a printer until 1709; printing did not recommence at Ipswich until 1720.

JANET ING FREEMAN

Sources E. G. Duff, *The English provincial printers, stationers and bookbinders to 1557* (1912) • J. I. Freeman, 'Anthony Scoloker, the "*Just reckoning* printer", and the earliest Ipswich printing', *Transactions of the Cambridge Bibliographical Society*, 9 (1986–90), 476–96 • *STC, 1475–1640* • J. Ames, *Typographical antiquities, or, An historical account of the origin and progress of printing in Great Britain and Ireland*, ed. W. Herbert, 3 vols. (1785–90) • W. K. Sessions, *The first printers at Ipswich in 1547–1548 and Worcester in 1549–1553* (1984) • M. Cooper, *The Worcester book trade in the eighteenth century* (1997)

Oswine [St Oswine, Oswin] (*d.* **651**), king of Deira, was the last independent ruler of Deira, the southern part of Northumbria. His father was the apostate *Osric (*d.* 634), but Oswine is portrayed by Bede as a model of royal submission to the authority of the church. Following his father's overthrow in 634 he is said to have been taken to Wessex. His rival *Oswiu (*d.* 670), who became king of Bernicia in 642, appears to have been unable to establish his authority over Deira, despite marrying *Eanflæd, a member of the Deiran royal family and Oswine's second cousin. Oswine became king in Deira two years later (644 deduced from Bede, *Hist. eccl.*, 3.14; 643 in the E text of the Anglo-Saxon Chronicle). His attractive personality and appearance are described in unusual detail by Bede, who notes that his bounty attracted followers from other kingdoms. Despite his rule in the southern part of Northumbria, he appears to have accepted the authority of the Irish mission based in Bernicia.

Bede's principal story about Oswine concerns his complaint about Áedán's misuse of a gift he had given him, the bishop's reproof, and Oswine's acceptance of that criticism. This level of humility was inappropriate for an Anglo-Saxon ruler, and despite Bede's praise of his ability to attract a retinue, when Oswiu finally moved against him, Oswine was forced to dissolve an outnumbered army and was murdered in the company of a single follower, through the treachery of one of his thegns. The murder took place on 20 August 651, at a place called 'Ingetlingum'. As Bede says that the army was dissolved near Catterick, this has been taken to be Gilling West, north Yorkshire; the alternative identification, as Collingham, west Yorkshire, is based on a speculation by Daniel Haigh (*d.* 1879). Oswiu was induced by his wife, Eanflæd, to compensate for the murder by founding a monastery at Gilling, where another blood relative, Trumhere, became first abbot. Oswine was omitted from Alcuin's poem on the rulers and saints of York, but evidence for a growing cult is suggested by his inclusion in the eighth-century calendar of Willibrord, although on 19 rather than 20 August.

Bede does not directly state that Oswine's body was buried at the newly founded monastery. His cult was revived four centuries later when it was claimed that his body had been discovered on 11 March 1065 at Tynemouth, a former Bernician monastic site near Newcastle, after he had appeared in a vision to the priest there, named Ædmund. This claim is complicated by several factors. A later king of Northumbria, Osred (*d.* 792), is the only royal burial recorded at Tynemouth and the names may have been confused. Also, Tynemouth monastery was initially claimed by Durham, but later given to St Albans by the earl of Northumberland in 1090 following a dispute. The account of Oswine's rediscovery in 1065 appears in a life written about the year 1111 in the interests of St Albans (edited by J. Raine in 1839); but a rival account from early twelfth-century Durham claims that his bones were exposed by Ælfred Westou, a priest of Durham, and that in 1075 these were granted, together with the church at Tynemouth, to the Jarrow monks who subsequently formed the community at Durham (Symeon of Durham, *Opera*, 1.88, 124–5).

The St Albans life of St Oswine (BL, Cotton MS Julius A.x) was composed by an anonymous monk of St Albans, later prior of Wymondham, a year after the translation of Oswine's body to a new shrine in the newly completed church of St Mary at Tynemouth, which took place on 20 August 1110, the anniversary of his death. It includes a copious list of miracles ascribed to Oswine's intervention, with subsequent additions. The offices for his festival are given in a fourteenth-century abridgement of this life by John of Tynemouth (BL, Cotton MS Tiberius E.i; Oxford, Corpus Christi College, 134 edited by C. Horstmann in 1901). A now badly damaged psalter fragment bearing the inscription 'Liber Oswini Deiorum regis' ('the book of Oswine, king of the Deirans'; BL, Cotton MS Galba A.v) is certainly much later, probably dating from the revival of his cult in the twelfth and thirteenth centuries. Oswine's shrine was broken up at the Reformation in 1539.

D. J. CRAIG

Sources Bede, *Hist. eccl.*, 3.14, 24 • *ASC*, s.a. 644, 651 [text E] • H. A. Wilson, ed., *The calendar of St Willibrord from MS Paris Lat. 10837*, HBS, 55 (1918) • J. Raine, ed., 'Vita Oswini regis deirorum', *Miscellanea biographica*, SurtS, 8 (1838), 1–59 • Symeon of Durham, *Opera*, 1.88, 124–5 • 'De sancto Oswino rege et martire', *Nova legenda Anglie, as collected by John of Tynemouth, J. Capgrave, and others*, ed. C. Horstman, 2 (1901), 268–73 • T. D. Hardy, *Descriptive catalogue of materials relating to the history of Great Britain and Ireland*, 1, Rolls Series, 26 (1862), nos. 651–6 • D. W. Rollason, 'The cults of murdered royal saints in Anglo-Saxon England', *Anglo-Saxon England*, 11 (1983), 1–22 • M. Miller, 'The dates of Deira', *Anglo-Saxon England*, 8 (1979), 35–61 • J. M. Wallace-Hadrill, *Bede's Ecclesiastical history of the English people: a historical commentary*, OMT (1988) • *A history of Northumberland*, Northumberland County History Committee, 15 vols. (1893–1940), vol. 8 • D. H. Haigh, 'Yorkshire runic monuments', *Yorkshire Archaeological and Topographical Journal*, 2 (1871–2), 252–88 • Symeon of Durham, *Libellus de exordio atque procursu istius, hoc est Dunhelmensis, ecclesie / Tract on the origins and progress of this the church of Durham*, ed. and trans. D. W. Rollason, OMT (2000) • N. J. Higham, *The convert kings* (1997), 226–31 • C. Chase, '*Beowulf*, Bede, and St Oswine: the hero's pride in Old English hagiography', *The Anglo-Saxons: synthesis and achievement*, ed. J. D. Woods and D. A. E. Pelteret (1985), 37–48

Oswiu [Oswy] (**611/12–670**), king of Northumbria, permanently united the rival kingdoms of Bernicia and Deira into Northumbria over the course of his twenty-eight year reign, which culminated in the Synod of Whitby. Bede describes him as the seventh overlord who held the *imperium* south of the Humber. He was a younger son of King *Æthelfrith of Bernicia.

Exile and early life Following his father's death in battle about 616 against Eadwine of Deira, who became king of both regions, Oswiu was exiled at the age of five and taken to Scotland and Ireland together with his brothers, including Eanfrith and *Oswald, who became kings before him, and perhaps four others, named as Oslac, Oswudu, Oslaf, and Offa in text E of the Anglo-Saxon Chronicle. A sister, *Æbbe, later became abbess of Coldingham.

Doubts have been raised whether Æthelfrith's queen, Acha, who was a member of the Deiran royal family and King Eadwine's sister, was really Oswiu's mother, since with the approval of Bishop Áedán Oswiu subsequently married Eadwine's daughter, *Eanflæd, who would have been his first cousin. A late source, the *Vita Oswini*, describes him as a bastard. This may help to explain his difficulties in assuming control of Deira, despite the success of his brother Oswald in ruling both kingdoms.

Oswiu had probably been in exile for seventeen years, from the age of five until he was about twenty-one, when in 633 his brother Eanfrith regained the kingship of Bernicia for a year before his death at the hands of the British king Cadwallon, who had overthrown Eadwine. The subsequent victory of his brother Oswald over Cadwallon at the battle of Heavenfield in 634 gave Oswald control of both kingdoms. During this time Oswiu became a fluent Irish speaker and he and Oswald were baptized as Christians, either in Ireland or on Iona (the island of the monastery of St Columba off the west coast of Scotland), and this was to mould his religious outlook until the Synod of Whitby in 664. At this same period exiled Bernician princes, including Oswald, are recorded as fighting on behalf of their Irish hosts, and it is likely that Oswiu was among them. Subsequently he is one of the few English kings whose deeds are noted in the Irish annals.

Probably during his period of exile in Ireland (although this may have occurred later) Oswiu fathered a child, *Aldfrith (who was to become king of Northumbria in 686), apparently through a relationship with a princess of the Uí Néill dynasty, named as Fín in later genealogies. By Bede's standards this child was illegitimate, but Irish law required only that the father acknowledge the child. Aldfrith was later famed as a scholar in Irish sources, but was not apparently welcome in England until he became king, possibly because of the resentment of Oswiu's subsequent male offspring.

Oswiu seems to have legally married twice, although this is not apparent from Bede. In the *Historia Brittonum* he is said to have married Rhiainfellt, daughter of Rhwyth, the son of Rhun. Elsewhere in the same source Rhun is described as a son of Urien of Rheged. Rheged was a British kingdom, apparently in the area of Carlisle, and it is likely that Oswiu married a princess of this kingdom as part of his brother King Oswald's expansionist policy before his death in 642. Two of Oswiu's known children, his son *Alchfrith and his daughter Alhflæd, were of marriageable age in the early 650s, and Alchfrith fought beside him in 655. They therefore cannot have been the children of King Eadwine's daughter Eanflæd (*b.* 626), also mentioned in the *Historia Brittonum*, whom Oswiu married, probably between 643 and 645, after he had become king. Rhiainfellt appears to be the first queen commemorated in the *Liber vitae* of Lindisfarne and Durham, although the identification of her name has been doubted.

The war with Penda and the struggle for Deira Oswiu became king in 642, at the age of about thirty, after Oswald was slain by the armies of Penda of Mercia in alliance with the British, at a place recorded by Bede as 'Maserfelth'; this has been identified as possibly Oswestry in what is now Shropshire. Oswald's body was ritually dismembered by the pagan Penda and the head and arms were displayed on stakes. A year after his brother's overthrow King Oswiu came with an army and retrieved the undecayed limbs, which he took back to Bernicia. The head was buried in the cemetery at Lindisfarne and an arm and hand enshrined in the chapel of the royal palace at Bamburgh. Through dying in battle fighting a pagan king, Oswald had received a martyr's death and his brother's actions laid the basis for his subsequent cult and sanctification.

The first thirteen years of Oswiu's reign were dominated by the struggle with Penda, who continually attacked Bernicia, and is once recorded by Bede as ravaging right up to the walls of Bamburgh. Initially, Oswiu's position appears to have been greatly weakened, and he seems to have been driven back into his heartland of Bernicia. He was apparently unable to assert his authority over the extensive area in southern England which Oswald had ruled, and Deira returned to the control of Eadwine's dynasty through a cousin, *Oswine (*d.* 651), who is recorded by Bede as an attractive and popular king, and a friend of Áedán of Lindisfarne, who acted as bishop for both kingdoms despite the split.

The obstacle presented by Oswine to the revival of his fortunes was the first occasion on which Oswiu's capacity for ruthless political directness became apparent. He sent to Kent for Eadwine's daughter, Eanflæd, and married her. Four children were subsequently born to this union, and the eldest son, *Ecgfrith, eventually succeeded to both kingdoms in 670. But the marriage does not seem to have increased Oswiu's personal support in Deira, so in 651 he raised an army against Oswine, who dispersed his own troops and went into hiding; he was subsequently murdered at Oswiu's instigation. This hard-headed approach did not win the support of his wife, who persuaded him to found a monastery at Gilling in recompense for the death of her kinsman, nor of the Deiran nobility, who were still not prepared to accept him as king, nor of Bede, who admired Oswine's humility. Oswine was replaced as king of Deira by Oswald's son Oethelwald, possibly at Oswiu's instigation, but Oethelwald was soon following an independent line, hostile to his uncle, in co-operation with Penda.

Oswiu seems to have attempted to deal initially with Penda by promoting family ties with the Mercian royal dynasty, and by trying to detach Penda's subordinates from his sphere of influence by persuading them to accept Christianity, while Penda himself remained pagan. Most successfully, he persuaded Penda's son *Peada to become Christian as the price of marrying his daughter Alhflæd; similarly, Oswiu's own son Alchfrith married Penda's daughter Cyneburh. Oswiu also persuaded Sigeberht (the Good), king of the East Saxons and a personal friend, to become Christian. Both Peada and Sigeberht were persuaded to accept baptism in Oswiu's territory, near Hexham, from his own bishop, Finán of Lindisfarne, in 653, and Oswiu himself probably stood godfather.

The battle of the 'Winwæd' and Northumbrian supremacy It is likely that Penda took these as provocative acts and attacked Bernicia as a result. Oswiu was driven to the north of his territories; probably at Stirling he was forced to pay a huge tribute to Penda and his British allies, recorded in British sources as the 'Restitution of Iudeu'. Oswiu was also forced to let his son Ecgfrith, who was then aged ten, be taken hostage to Penda's court. Despite this humiliating compromise, a subsequent offer of tribute was refused by Penda, who was determined to destroy Bernicia, according to Bede. Oswiu, who was now about forty-three, and his son Alchfrith were forced to give battle in the face of daunting odds. In addition to thirty legions thirty times his strength ranged against him (an appropriately biblical number), his nephew Oethelwald of Deira had allied with Penda. In desperation Oswiu therefore pledged twelve estates to the church, and also his one-year-old daughter *Ælfflæd, in a request for divine aid against the pagan.

Bede records that battle was joined near the River 'Uinuaed' ('Winwæd') on 15 November 655. This has not been identified but appears to have been in the area of 'Loidis' where the campaign was concluded. This is assumed to be Leeds, in the southern part of Deira, although earlier commentators suggested a site in southern Scotland. In the *Historia Brittonum* the site is named as 'in campo Gai'. Despite his superiority of numbers, some of Penda's allies, including Oethelwald, appear to have deserted him, and he and much of his army were slaughtered or drowned in the swollen river. Oswiu beheaded him, probably in revenge for the mutilation of his brother. The earliest manuscript of Bede's *Historia ecclesiastica gentis Anglorum* is unclear at one point, but John Prestwich showed that it is probably Penda himself, rather than the East Anglian king Æthelhere, who is described as the author of the war.

In fulfilment of his vow before the battle, Oswiu did indeed give twelve estates for the founding of monasteries, six in Bernicia and six in Deira, one of which was used for the founding of Hartlepool, where his infant daughter Ælfflæd was sent initially, in fulfilment of his other pledge, into the care of Abbess Hild, a Deiran princess and cousin of the queen. Another was at Whitby, where Hild and Ælfflæd subsequently moved and where Oswiu himself was eventually buried. But Bede seems to contrast wryly the twelve estates promised before the battle with the twelve little estates actually given (Mayr-Harting, 99), although James Campbell has argued that Bede's word, *possessiunculis*, is a technical term meaning a single settlement rather than being deliberately dismissive (Campbell, *Essays*, 96, 112).

Bede, however, is rather grudging in his treatment of this victory and Oswiu in general; but later authors such as Alcuin recognized it as a major turning point in the triumph of Christianity among the Anglo-Saxons. Oswiu had secured his southern frontier, Bernicia and Deira were now free from pagan attack, and Mercia was under Northumbrian control for three years and became Christian, despite the subsequent revolt of the Mercian nobles who installed Penda's son Wulfhere as king. During this period Oswiu ruled the northern part of Mercia directly, and placed his son-in-law Peada in charge of the southern part until he was apparently assassinated through the machinations of his wife, Oswiu's daughter Alhflæd. This high-handed treatment, reminiscent of the murder of Oswine, may have provoked the revolt which re-established Mercian independence in 658. Although this period of Northumbrian power south of the Humber was fairly brief, it allowed Bede to recognize Oswiu as successor to the overlordship enjoyed by Oswald and five previous kings, in a famous passage later reused in the Anglo-Saxon Chronicle under the year 829, where the term *bretwalda* first appears.

Oswiu does not seem to have attempted to reimpose control over Mercia after Wulfhere became king, but instead turned his attention to the northern border of his kingdom, in the area which is now Scotland. Shortly before Oswiu's victory at the River 'Winwæd', Talorcan, son of his brother Eanfrith and a Pictish princess, had become king of the Picts, possibly at Oswiu's instigation. Talorcan died in 657, but Bede notes in two places that Oswiu subjected the Picts to Northumbrian domination and forced them to pay tribute, and it is probable that Oswiu took the offensive in the early 660s following his nephew's death. Oswiu may at this point have been acting in alliance with the Irish in western Scotland, among whom he was brought up, although with the death of his former patron it appears that he made these people tributary as well. It has been claimed that for this brief period in the late 650s Oswiu had wider power in Britain than any king until James I.

The Synod of Whitby and ecclesiastical politics Oswiu had been supported at the battle of the River 'Winwæd' by his son Alchfrith. Oswiu installed him as sub-king, apparently in Deira in succession to his traitorous nephew Oethelwald, who is not heard of again. In the early 660s, however, Alchfrith began following a different ecclesiastical policy to his father, who remained a supporter of the Columban church based at Lindisfarne and Iona. Having initially given Ripon to Irish monks, he ejected these in favour of the Roman party spearheaded by Wilfrid. Deiran separatism was associated with the Canterbury-backed mission of Paulinus which had introduced Christianity during Eadwine's reign. Oswiu's wife Eanflæd, Eadwine's daughter, had been baptized by Paulinus and brought up in Kent, and retained a circle of ecclesiastical advisers who followed the practices of the Roman church. At this period, therefore, owing to the attacks of those such as Wilfrid who wished to see the English church brought more closely in line with orthodox practice and papal authority, the Columban mission was being marginalized and its influence in England diminished.

Oswiu was therefore faced with behaviour by his son and co-ruler which increasingly challenged his authority, and by the rise of a centralizing movement which threatened to exclude him from influence in Deira, and in most other English kingdoms, as well as forgoing the spiritual and material support of the papacy as the heirs of St Peter. Bede famously claimed that there was a split in the royal household over the date of Easter, with Oswiu's court following Columban practice and thus celebrating Easter early, while the queen and her supporters were still fasting in Lent; but this absurd situation had already happened fourteen times in the twenty-two years of the marriage of Oswiu and Eanflæd, and it is clear that it was the increasing political pressure on Oswiu that required the situation to be resolved.

A synod of the Northumbrian church was therefore convened at Whitby in 664, possibly instigated by Alchfrith and supposedly under the joint authority of both kings, but Oswiu chaired the debate and made the final decision. Despite his personal affection for the spokesman of the Columban party, Colmán, bishop of Lindisfarne, Oswiu accepted the Roman method for calculating Easter. In doing so he outmanoeuvred his son, for his acceptance was based on the supremacy of St Peter over St Columba, rather than on the patronizing arguments for the dismissal of the Columban case put forward by Alchfrith's champion, Wilfrid. Wilfrid's biographer, unlike Bede, records that Oswiu smiled when he made his choice.

The fruits of this decision can be seen in a letter of 667 from Pope Vitalian in Rome in response to a letter sent by Oswiu, apparently acting in concert with the king of Kent, to propose a new archbishop of Canterbury. Up to this point the church and rulers of Northumbria do not seem to have recognized the authority of Canterbury, nor felt themselves able to influence such appointments. The pope addresses him as 'King of the Saxons', praises him, welcomes his embrace of orthodoxy, and prays for the extension of his rule throughout Britain, as well as sending a generous selection of relics to him and his queen and promising to send a bishop as he had requested. This letter must have been an extremely gratifying reward for Oswiu's new position.

The downside of this acceptance of Rome's authority emerged with the appointment of Theodore of Tarsus as the new archbishop of Canterbury. Following the Synod of Whitby and Colmán's departure to Ireland, Oswiu had appointed Tuda as bishop of Lindisfarne for Bernicia and had allowed Alchfrith to install Wilfrid at York, apparently as a separate bishop for Deira. But Tuda died of the plague and Wilfrid went abroad for consecration. In his absence Oswiu appointed Ceadda (Chad) to be bishop of both kingdoms, with his see at York. This seems to have been prompted by a final rebellion by Alchfrith against his father, who had denied him permission to go to Rome with Benedict Biscop, possibly fearing the opportunity for undue influence with the pope. Alchfrith is not heard of again, and it is probable that Wilfrid stayed away so as not to be caught up in his downfall. Oswiu, however, who was now at last unchallenged ruler of the united kingdom of Northumbria, unwisely allowed Ceadda to be consecrated to Wilfrid's see by the bishop of the West Saxons and two unorthodox British bishops. As a result Archbishop Theodore, when he arrived in Northumbria in 669, deposed Ceadda and reinstated Wilfrid as bishop of the whole kingdom, including the conquered territories to the north.

Surprisingly, as with the Mercian revolt of 658, Oswiu seems to have been prepared to accept this humiliation, and to accept Wilfrid too, since Bede records that he offered Wilfrid a considerable gift to escort him to Rome. Oswiu was now aged fifty-eight and ill, and this was probably intended to be his final pilgrimage, perhaps in response to Pope Vitalian's letter. Wilfrid, however, refused and Oswiu died on 15 February 670, to be succeeded as king of all Northumbria by his son Ecgfrith. He was buried in St Peter's Church at Whitby, which had become the mausoleum of the Deiran royal family, and where his daughter Ælfflæd would later succeed Hild as abbess. This was a fitting end to his struggle to amalgamate the two kingdoms and by the time that Alcuin wrote, at the end of the next century, he was acclaimed as one of the heroes of the church of York.

Oswiu was the father of at least seven children, with three different women. As shown above, the rebellious Alchfrith and Peada's murderous wife, Alhflæd, were probably both children of the British princess Rhiainfellt. Eanflæd, the Deiran princess whom he married at the beginning of his reign when she was about eighteen, had two sons, Ecgfrith, who eventually succeeded to both kingdoms following his father's death in 670, and Ælfwine, who was killed fighting the Mercians in 679. Oswiu and Eanflæd also had two daughters, Ælfflæd, who was dedicated by her father to the church before the battle of the 'Winwæd' and became joint abbess of Whitby in 680 together with her mother, and *Osthryth, who after her father's death married King Æthelred of Mercia and promoted the cult of her uncle Oswald. Aldfrith, Oswiu's son with the Irish princess Fín, attained the Northumbrian throne after his half-brother Ecgfrith was killed in 686, despite his illegitimacy, partly through the efforts of his half-sister Ælfflæd. Oswiu's dynasty thus controlled the Northumbrian throne until the beginning of the next century. D. J. Craig

Sources Bede, *Hist. eccl.*, 3.14–15, 21–2, 24–5, 28–9; 4.1, 3, 5 • Nennius, *'British history' and 'The Welsh annals'*, ed. and trans. J. Morris (1980) • E. Stephanus, *The life of Bishop Wilfrid*, ed. and trans. B. Colgrave (1927) • 'Historia abbatum auctore Baeda', *Venerabilis Baedae opera historica*, ed. C. Plummer, 1 (1896), 364–87 • Alcuin, *The bishops, kings, and saints of York*, ed. and trans. P. Godman, OMT (1982) • *ASC*, s.a. 617, 641, 650, 654, 656, 667, 670 [text E] • *Ann. Ulster* • John of Worcester, *Chron.* • H. Sweet, ed., *Liber vitae*, *The oldest English texts*, EETS, 83 (1885), 153–66 • J. Raine, ed., 'Vita Oswini regis deirorum', *Miscellanea biographica*, SurtS, 8 (1838), 1–59 • N. J. Higham, *The convert kings* (1997), 225–77 • D. P. Kirby, *The earliest English kings* (1991) • B. Yorke, *Kings and kingdoms of early Anglo-Saxon England* (1990) • K. H. Jackson, 'On the northern British section in Nennius', *Celt and Saxon: studies in the early British border*, ed. N. K. Chadwick (1963), 20–62 • H. Moisl, 'The Bernician royal dynasty and the Irish in the seventh century', *Peritia*, 2 (1983), 103–26 • M. Miller, 'The dates of Deira', *Anglo-Saxon England*, 8 (1979), 35–61 • H. Mayr-Harting, *The coming of Christianity to Anglo-Saxon England*, 3rd edn (1991) • R. Abels, 'The council of Whitby: a study in early Anglo-Saxon politics', *Journal of British Studies*, 23/1 (1983–4), 1–25 • J. Campbell, 'The first Christian kings', *The Anglo-Saxons*, ed. J. Campbell (1982), 45–69 • J. Campbell, *Essays in Anglo-Saxon history* (1986) • A. P. Smyth, *Warlords and holy men: Scotland, AD 80–1000* (1984) • D. P. Kirby, '… per universas Pictorum provincias', *Famulus Christi*, ed. G. Bonner (1976), 286–324 • J. O. Prestwich, 'King Æthelhere and the battle of the Winwaed', *EngHR*, 83 (1968), 89–95 • N. Brooks, *The early history of the church of Canterbury: Christ Church from 597 to 1066* (1984) • A. H. Smith, *The place-names of the West Riding of Yorkshire*, 7, English Place-name Society, 36 (1962) • P. Wormald, 'Bede, the "Bretwaldas" and the origins of the "gens Anglorum"', *Ideal and reality in Frankish and Anglo-Saxon society*, ed. P. Wormald, D. Bullough, and R. Collins (1983), 99–129 • D. P. Kirby, 'Northumbria in the time of Wilfrid', *Saint Wilfrid at Hexham*, ed. D. P. Kirby (1974), 1–34 • J. M. Wallace-Hadrill, *Bede's Ecclesiastical history of the English people: a historical commentary*, OMT (1988) • J. M. Wallace-Hadrill, *Early Germanic kingship in England and on the continent* (1971) • K. Harrison, 'The reign of King Ecgfrith of Northumbria', *Yorkshire Archaeological Journal*, 43 (1971), 79–84 • S. Wood, 'Bede's Northumbrian dates again', *EngHR*, 98 (1983), 280–96

Oswulf. *See* Osulf, earl of Bamburgh (*d.* 1067).

Oswulf (*d.* 759), king of Northumbria, was the son of *Eadberht (*d.* 768) and descendant of the founder of the Bernician royal house, Ida, via his son Ocga. He succeeded to the throne on his father's abdication in 758, only to be killed by his household (*familia*) on 24 July 759 at a place called 'Methil Wongtun', which has not been identified but may be identical with 'Medilwong', referred to in the anonymous life of St Cuthbert. His successor, **Æthelwold Moll** (*fl.* 759–765), was of unknown ancestry. If he was the same person as the Moll in whose favour, according to a letter of Pope Paul I, King Eadberht had alienated the monasteries of Coxwold and Stonegrave, in what is now Yorkshire, and the unidentified 'Donamuthe', he was presumably a leading official of that king, since the letter refers to him as a 'patrician' (*patricius*). Little is known of his reign. In 761 he defeated and killed a certain Oswin, perhaps a claimant to the throne, at Eildon, in modern Northumberland, and on 1 November 762 he married Æthelthryth at Catterick. In 765 he is recorded as having 'lost the kingdom of the Northumbrians' on 30 October at an unidentified place called 'Pincanheale' (Symeon of Durham, *Opera*, 2.43). Since this is elsewhere referred to as a meeting-place of Northumbrian councils, it is possible that Æthelwold Moll was deposed in such a body.

The next king, **Alhred** (*fl.* 765–774), claimed descent from another collateral branch of the family of Ida, deriving from the latter's son Eadric. That his family may have been connected with the Tyne area is suggested by the fact that his son *Osred II was buried at Tynemouth. Alhred minted coins and, in 768, he married Osgifu, apparently a daughter of the former king Oswulf, perhaps to strengthen his position. He patronized missionary activity on the continent and there has survived a letter from him and Osgifu to the Anglo-Saxon missionary bishop Lul, referring to the exchanging of names for commemoration in the mass between England and the continent, and asking particularly that Lul should 'help and care for our embassies to your lord the most glorious King Charles [Charlemagne], that you may make peace and amity, which are proper to all, to be firmly strengthened between us' (Tangl, no. 121; *English Historical Documents*, 1, no. 187). The letter also alludes, however, to disturbances in the churches and people of Northumbria, which seems consistent with a report in another source of how Liudger, the future bishop of Münster, had to return to Frisia because of civil disturbances at York, where he was studying. Finally, in 774, King Alhred was 'deprived of the society of the royal household and nobles, by the counsel and consent of all his people' (Symeon of Durham, *Opera*, 2.45), and fled first to Bamburgh, and then into exile in the kingdom of the Picts. As with Oswulf, his deposition hints at the power of the Northumbrian council.

The Northumbrians then accepted as king **Æthelred I** (*d.* 796), son of the former king Æthelwold Moll. In view of the fact that his father's marriage had taken place only in 762, he may have been a child at his accession. Little is known of his 'first' reign, and only one coin has been assigned to it. In 778 he ordered the killing of three ealdormen (*duces*) and in 779 he was driven into exile, to be replaced by a member of the line of Eadberht, **Ælfwald I** (*d.* 788), son of the former king Oswulf. In 786 Ælfwald received in his kingdom George, bishop of Ostia and legate of the pope, who held an important council, attended by Ælfwald and the secular and ecclesiastical magnates of Northumbria. This promulgated a series of decrees, including one requiring that kings be of legitimate birth and anathematizing any who conspired to kill a king. Ironically, Ælfwald himself was murdered. The killing occurred at a place called 'Scythlescester', near Hadrian's Wall, on 23 September 788 as a result of a conspiracy formed by his patrician Sicga, whose name had come at the head of the lay representatives at the 786 council. The king was buried at Hexham and apparently regarded as a martyr, for according to the annals a heavenly light was seen at the place of his death and a church constructed there. The reign had not been an altogether settled one, for the annals report the killing at Christmas 780 of Ælfwald's patrician Bearn at the hands of two ealdormen. Alcuin indeed regarded the reign as inaugurating a period of moral decline: 'From the days of King Ælfwald fornications, adulteries, and incest have flooded the land, so that these sins have been committed without any shame and even with the handmaids of God' (Dümmler, no. 16; *English Historical Documents*, 1, no. 193).

Following a short reign by Osred II, Æthelred I was restored to the throne in 789, and enjoyed a second reign. In 792 he married Ælfflæd, daughter of King *Offa of Mercia, at Catterick. He appears to have been a ruthless ruler: in 790 he captured, tonsured, and then exiled the former king Osred II; in the same year he made an unsuccessful attempt to execute the nobleman and future king *Eardwulf; in 791 he persuaded the sons of the former king Ælfwald I to leave their sanctuary in St Peter's, York, under false promises and had them drowned; and in 792 he had Osred killed after his abortive attempt to return from exile. In 796, however, Æthelred was himself murdered, at Corbridge according to one source, by two ealdormen. Although Æthelred had enjoyed the support of Charlemagne, who sent him gifts, he was severely criticized by Alcuin for luxurious living and immorality.

David Rollason

Sources Symeon of Durham, *Opera* • B. Colgrave, ed. and trans., *Two lives of Saint Cuthbert* (1940) • M. Tangl, ed., *Die Briefe des heiligen Bonifatius und Lullus*, MGH Epistolae Selectae, 1 (Berlin, 1916) • A. W. Haddan and W. Stubbs, eds., *Councils and ecclesiastical documents relating to Great Britain and Ireland*, 1 (1869) • E. Dümmler, ed., *Epistolae Karolini aevi*, MGH Epistolae [quarto], 4 (Berlin, 1895) • S. Lebecq, *Marchands et navigateurs frisons du haut moyen âge*, 2 vols. (1983) • J. J. North, *English hammered coinage*, 3rd edn, 1: *Early Anglo-Saxon to Henry III, c.600 1272* (1994) • D. P. Kirby, *The earliest English kings* (1991) • *English historical documents*, 1, ed. D. Whitelock (1955)

Oswy. *See* Oswiu (611/12–670).

Osyth. *See* Osgyth (*fl.* late 7th cent.).

Otho, Sir, de Grandson. *See* Grandson, Sir Otto de (*c.*1238–1328).

Otis, James, senior (1702–1778), merchant and politician in America, was born in Barnstable, Massachusetts, on 14 June 1702 to John Otis (1657–1727) and Mercy Bacon. The leading merchant of Barnstable county (Cape Cod), John Otis left his son a sizeable fortune, upon which he improved by practising law, beginning in 1730. About 1723 he married Mary Allyne (*b.* 1702) of Wethersfield, Connecticut; they had thirteen children, seven of whom survived infancy. Among these were the political leaders James *Otis junior (1725–1783), Samuel Allyne Otis (1740–1814), and Mercy Otis *Warren (1728–1814), one of the new nation's leading women writers, who was also passionately interested in affairs of state.

Otis held a series of town and county offices, starting with justice of the peace in 1734. Connected by both kinship and business interests to the handful of leading families that ran Barnstable county, by 1740 he was handling half the local litigation. In 1745 the town of Barnstable elected him to the Massachusetts house of representatives, a post he held until 1757. In the house Otis immediately became one of the leaders of the 'court party'

James Otis senior (1702–1778), by John Singleton Copley, *c.*1758

formed by Governor William Shirley that favoured a vigorous prosecution of King George's War (1744–8), the War of the Austrian Succession in Europe, and, later, the French and Indian War (the Seven Years' War in Europe) against the French Canadians and their American Indian allies, 1754–63. They also successfully retired the province's inflated paper money in favour of silver. Otis received handsome rewards for his efforts: he commanded the Barnstable militia as its colonel, though he saw no action, and received lucrative government contracts to provide provisions and transportation for the military. His greatest coup was to corner the market on whaleboats in the mid-1750s.

Otis aspired to higher political office than the house. In 1757 he resigned his seat to campaign for election to the upper house, or council, whose members were elected jointly by the outgoing council and the incoming house of representatives, subject to the governor's veto. Otis learned that he had been rejected because Thomas Hutchinson, who had been Shirley's chief adviser and had previously co-operated with Otis, had said that:

> [Otis] never Did Carry things while in the Court By any merit But only By Doing little Low Dirty things for Governor Shirley such as Persons of worth Refused to medle with and that Shirley made use of me only as a Tool for [their] purposes. (CUNY, Otis papers, Box 1, 44, memorandum, *c.*15 Aug 1757)

Thus began the feud between the Hutchinson and Otis clans and factional networks that played so crucial a role in Massachusetts's path to revolution.

Otis tried again for higher office in 1760, when the province's chief justiceship fell vacant. He hoped to convince the new governor, Francis Bernard (1760–69) that he deserved a seat on the superior court, which the two previous governors had promised him. However, given Otis's commercial reputation as 'an old Pirate and a Cursed old Rogue' (CUNY, Otis papers, Box 1, 67, examination of Ebenezer Chipman, 8 Aug 1758) Bernard doubted his willingness to enforce British laws restraining colonial trade and chose Thomas Hutchinson instead.

In 1760 Otis returned to the house of representatives, which chose him as its speaker. With his son James's election to the house from Boston the following year the Otises led a renewed 'popular party' that increasingly gained power as Hutchinson and Bernard were saddled with enforcing unpopular British measures. But the Otises were not firm in their opposition, for in 1764 Governor Bernard temporarily won their allegiance by appointing the elder Otis judge of probate and chief justice of the inferior court for Barnstable county. However, by 1766, Otis was again in the lead of protests against the Stamp Act, and between 1766 and 1769 Bernard regularly vetoed his election to the council.

When Hutchinson replaced Bernard as governor in 1770 he attempted to win back both Otises. He succeeded with the elder by allowing his election to the council beginning in 1771 and by bestowing upon him the lucrative guardianship of the American Indians in Plymouth. The younger Otis, however, remained loyal to the resistance during those increasingly rare instances when he retained his sanity, prompting his father to rebuke him thus: 'If you Continue to go on this way your family will be Ruined and you will Destroy yourself Both Soul and Body' (Gay–Otis papers, 1 Aug 1772 [draft]). The elder Otis's loyalty remained unimpeachable for several years; he was even chosen in 1774 to the royally appointed council that replaced Massachusetts's elected upper house.

With the coming of the revolution, however, the elder Otis realized that he needed to support the cause to retain his influence in overwhelmingly pro-revolutionary Massachusetts. Ironically Otis's hometown of Barnstable was a hotbed of loyalism, the only town in Massachusetts that refused to endorse independence. Until his death in 1778 Otis did much to ensure Barnstable's participation in the war and to make sure that its opponents failed to do much damage.

Otis embodied the political order of provincial Massachusetts, where leading members of local élites met in Boston to exchange favours and to ensure that they and their constituents benefited from government policies. To be sure he was useful to the Massachusetts resistance (especially in the 1760s). He was one of the few major politicians of his generation who did not actively embrace loyalism, and he assisted in sustaining the patriot cause in his county. But, in the words of family biographer John Waters, 'In the midst of the revolutionary crisis the old man remained a petty provincial horse trader' (Waters, 180). William Pencak

Sources J. J. Waters, *The Otis family in provincial and revolutionary Massachusetts* (1968) • Col. U., Butler Library, Otis papers • Col. U., Gay-Otis papers • Mass. Hist. Soc., Otis MSS • J. A. Schutz, *William Shirley: king's governor of Massachusetts* (1961) • H. Otis, 'Genealogical and historical memoir of the Otis family', *New England Historical and Genealogical Register*, 2 (1848), 281–96 • *IGI*

Archives Col. U., papers • Mass. Hist. Soc., papers

Likenesses J. S. Copley, portrait, *c.*1758, Wichita Art Museum, Kansas [*see illus.*]

Wealth at death substantial property left to children: Waters, *The Otis family*

Otis, James, junior (1725–1783), politician and revolutionary leader in America, was born on 2 February 1725 to James *Otis senior (1702–1778) and Mary Allyne (*b.* 1702) in Barnstable (Cape Cod), Massachusetts. The elder Otis, the cape's leading merchant, lawyer, and political figure, sent his son to Harvard College, where he graduated AB in 1743; Otis junior then entered legal practice. In 1755 he married Ruth Cunningham, a wealthy heiress; like her father, Captain Nathaniel Cunningham, she was a loyalist sympathizer during the American War of Independence. Their three children's politics reflected their parents' dissension: a son died in a British prison in 1777, one daughter married the son of the revolutionary general Benjamin Lincoln, and another daughter married a lieutenant in the British army.

All that was to come. The newly-weds soon moved to Boston, where Otis's father used his friendship with governors William Shirley and Thomas Pownal to obtain appointments for him as justice of the peace (1756) and deputy advocate-general of the Massachusetts vice-admiralty court (1757), an office worth £200 per annum. In this case the nepotism was justified. Both future revolutionary John Adams and loyalist Thomas Hutchinson praised Otis. Hutchinson 'never knew fairer or more noble conduct in a pleader than Otis', who 'defended his causes solely on their broad and substantial foundations' rather than on legal technicalities (Tudor, 36).

Otis's break with the 'court party' led by Hutchinson came in 1760. His father believed that he was entitled to the seat on the superior court made vacant by the death of Chief Justice Stephen Sewall. Despite the Otises' active campaigning the new governor, Francis Bernard, selected Hutchinson for the post, probably because he thought that he would take a stronger line on enforcing British customs regulations. A clash over precisely this issue, in 1761, brought Otis to the leadership of the 'popular party' in Boston and Massachusetts. Boston merchants, angry that customs commissioner Charles Paxton was seizing illegal goods, challenged his power to issue writs of assistance—warrants permitting him to search anywhere—in the superior court. Otis gave up his position at the vice-admiralty court to press the suit, which he handled free of charge. In February 1761 he presented his case. In a letter written over fifty years later future United States president John Adams, a young lawyer who witnessed the event, immortalized Otis's speech as critical in leading to the American War of Independence: 'Otis was a flame of fire! … American independence was then and there born' (*Works of John Adams*, 10.247). Adams's contemporaneous trial notes recall that Otis argued that the writs of assistance were 'the worst instrument of arbitrary power, the most destructive to English liberty, and the fundamental

James Otis junior (1725–1783), by Joseph Blackburn, 1755

principles of the [British] Constitution'. Otis insisted therefore that, much like the common law courts in England, Massachusetts's superior court had the obligation to declare the writs void and unconstitutional (*Legal Papers of John Adams*, 2.521–2).

Otis was grasping at a straw, for no other legal argument could question warrants granted by an act of parliament. Chief Justice Hutchinson responded by sending to England to find out if the courts there granted the warrants, which they did, implying that they were in fact constitutional and that Massachusetts's superior court could also issue them. Ironically when the British attorney-general finally ruled on the writs in 1766 he took a different tack altogether: parliament's legislation concerning the writs did not apply to the colonies. Even so, Otis's speech, though heard by only a small audience and never published, had an impact. He had revived natural rights theory, previously used concerning naval impressment during the great riot of 1747, to oppose a British policy that denied rights that the colonials perceived to be fundamental. Boston's appreciative town meeting elected him for the first time to the house of representatives in May 1761, a position that he held until 1769, and again in 1771, when insanity forced his retirement.

In the 1760s Otis was perhaps the most powerful advocate in America, both in his speeches and his pamphlets, for the position that Britain had no right to tax the colonies. *A Vindication of the Conduct of the House of Representatives* (1762) claimed that 'a House of Representatives, here at least, bears an equal proportion to the governor, as the House of Commons to the King'. The governor could not spend any money without the house's consent, even for trivial expenses during its recess. Otis's *The Rights of the British Colonies Asserted and Proved* (1764) anticipated the Virginian Patrick Henry's argument that 'taxation without representation is tyranny'. Otis insisted that 'the very act of taxing, except over those who are represented, appears to me to be depriving them of one of their most essential rights'. *A Vindication of the British Colonies* (1765) in turn denied that the colonies could be represented in parliament, 'virtually' or otherwise, as the British legislature as a whole had no knowledge of colonial Americans, a distinct society.

Otis's patriotism nevertheless was problematic. In the early 1760s he briefly supported the governor rather than the popular party, after his father had received important political appointments in Barnstable. He redeemed himself in 1765 by denouncing the Stamp Act, as a Massachusetts delegate at the intercolonial congress in Albany. By the late 1760s, however, Otis was suffering from alcoholism; he raved like a lunatic in public, broke the windows in the Boston townhouse, and shot off his gun at random. A savage beating that he received from customs officer James Robinson in September 1769 accelerated his pathetic decline. His relatives obtained guardianship over him and, despite occasional signs of rationality, he was unable to support the war of independence or even to take care of himself for the last decade of his life. His death came on 25 September 1783, when a bolt of lightning struck him while he was standing in the doorway of a friend's house in Andover, Massachusetts. WILLIAM PENCAK

Sources W. Pencak, 'Otis, James', *ANB* • W. Tudor, *The life of James Otis* (1823) • J. J. Waters, *The Otis family in provincial and revolutionary Massachusetts* (1968) • J. R. Ferguson, 'Reason in madness: the political thought of James Otis', *William and Mary Quarterly*, 36 (1979), 194–214 • C. K. Shipton, 'James Otis', *Sibley's Harvard graduates: biographical sketches of those who attended Harvard College*, 11 (1960), 247–87 • *Legal papers of John Adams*, ed. L. K. Wroth and H. B. Zobel, 3 vols. (1965) • *The works of John Adams, second president of the United States*, ed. C. F. Adams, 10 vols. (1850–56)

Archives Col. U., papers • Mass. Hist. Soc., papers | Col. U., Gay-Otis papers

Likenesses J. Blackburn, portrait, 1755, priv. coll. [*see illus.*]

Wealth at death estate given in guardianship to relatives after he went insane

O'Toole, Bryan (*d.* **1825**), army officer, was appointed cornet in a regiment of hussars raised by Friedrich, Baron Hompesch, in 1792, and served with it, under the duke of Brunswick, in the first campaign of that year in Champagne, including the taking of Verdun and the attack on Thionville. He was present at the battle of Jemappes, and later, under the prince of Condé, at Neerwinden, at the blockades of Condé and Maubeuge, and the battle of Charleroi. He then joined the British army under the duke of York, and commanded a squadron of Hompesch at Boxtel and Nijmegen, and in the winter retreat of 1794–5 from the Waal to Bremen. On his arrival in England he was appointed captain-lieutenant in one of the regiments of the Irish brigade, then in British pay, and on 25 March 1796 was made captain in the Hompesch hussars, with which he went to the West Indies. Baron Hompesch had two units in British pay (hussars and rifles). O'Toole served with the Hompesch hussars in San Domingo, and returned home with the remnants of the corps in 1797.

O'Toole was appointed to a troop in a new corps, Hompesch's mounted riflemen, with which he served in Ireland in 1798, and was present at Vinegar Hill and Ballynahinch. He was placed on half pay when the corps was disbanded in 1802. He was appointed captain in the 39th foot in 1803, and began a series of assignments in southern Europe. He was aide-de-camp to Major-General Broderick in the expedition to Naples in 1805, and to Sir Galbraith Lowry Cole in the expedition to Calabria and at the battle of Maida in 1806. After receiving the rank of brevet major in 1808, he commanded a light battalion at the capture of Ischia in 1809, and commanded the Calabrian Free Corps, in British pay, during Murat's threatened invasion of Sicily in 1810. He resigned his command to accompany the 39th to the Peninsula as captain, and was appointed major in the 2nd Portuguese cacadores, which he commanded at Ciudad Rodrigo, Badajoz, Salamanca, Madrid, and the siege of and retreat from Burgos. On 21 June 1813 he was appointed lieutenant-colonel, and received command of the 7th cacadores in Sir Lowry Cole's division, which took part in the battle of Vitoria, the blockade of Pampeluna, and the battles in the Pyrenees. During his Peninsular service O'Toole lost the use of one arm. He was placed on half pay of the Portuguese officers in 1816. He was made CB on 4 June 1815, and had the gold cross for Ciudad Rodrigo, Salamanca, Vitoria, and the Pyrenees. He died at Fairford, co. Wexford, on 27 February 1825. H. M. CHICHESTER, *rev.* GORDON L. TEFFETELLER

Sources Fortescue, *Brit. army* • W. F. P. Napier, *History of the war in the Peninsula and in the south of France*, rev. edn, 6 vols. (1876) • *Supplementary despatches (correspondence) and memoranda of Field Marshal Arthur, duke of Wellington*, ed. A. R. Wellesley, second duke of Wellington, 15 vols. (1858–72) • *Army List* • *GM*, 1st ser., 95/1 (1825), 567–8 • T. Bunbury, *Reminiscences of a veteran*, 3 vols. (1861)

O'Toole, Laurence. *See* Laurence (*c*.1128–1180).

Otté, Elise Charlotte (1818–1903), linguist and historian, was born in Copenhagen on 30 September 1818. Nothing is known of her father beyond his surname and the fact that he was Danish, nor of her mother save that she was English and called Mary Anne. In 1820 Elise's parents went to Santa Cruz in the Danish West Indies, where her father died. Her mother returned to Copenhagen, where she met the English philologist Benjamin *Thorpe who was studying in Denmark. She married Thorpe and they set up home with Elise in England. Thorpe taught Elise several modern languages and from a very early age she knew enough Anglo-Saxon and Icelandic to help him in his work. Edmund Gosse paints a particularly unattractive picture of Thorpe, 'a pedant of the narrowest description, and a captious taskmaster' whose 'demands upon his young stepdaughter's time and labour became more than her patience could endure' (Gosse, 15). According to him it was to escape Thorpe's tyranny that Miss Otté in 1840 fled secretly to Boston, Massachusetts. Gosse's picture of Thorpe is qualified by E. S. Day, of whose family Miss Otté was a long-standing friend (Day, 83). Whatever the cause, Miss Otté went to Boston to teach in a family. She became interested in the transcendental movement and was invited to join the Brook Farm experiment, but declined. Instead she turned to science and attended lectures on geology, physiology, and anatomy at Harvard. She then moved to Europe and settled at Frankfurt in the family of a professor for whom she translated English scientific monographs into German. After returning to England she resumed her work with her stepfather, whom she helped to prepare his translation of the elder or poetic Edda, *Edda Sæmundar hinns Frôða* (1866). According to Gosse she again found 'the bondage intolerable', and in 1849 went to St Andrews, to the family of Professor George Edward Day, for whom she translated scientific works and who helped her with the scientific aspects of her published translations. In 1863 she moved with Day and his wife to Torquay, and she helped to nurse Day during his final illness.

In 1872, after Day's death, Miss Otté moved to London, where she wrote for scientific periodicals and published literary works. Her *Scandinavian History* (1874), proved popular and was reprinted many times as *Norway, Sweden and Denmark* until as late as 1939. It and *Denmark and Iceland* (1881) show careful scholarship and are based on primary and secondary sources in several languages. Contemporary reviewers, knowing them to be by a woman, felt them too serious, and in 1912 Gosse remarked that she never acquired ease in literary expression (*DNB*). To a later reader, however, her style seems at once authoritative and pleasingly direct. She is entirely at ease with Scandinavian terms and writes with the lucid sparseness characteristic of good Scandinavian prose. Her loyalty to Scandinavia and her refusal to conform to feminine stereotypes come across forcefully in her scathing treatment of Queen Kristina and her meddlesome mother. She compiled grammars of Danish (1884) and of Swedish (1884) and textbooks for students of German (1859) and Danish (1879). In addition she translated from the German works by Alexander von Humboldt (*Views of Nature*, 1850, and *Cosmos*, 5 vols., 1849–58), Reinhold Pauli (*Pictures of Old England*, 1861), and J. M. Lappenberg (*A History of England under the Anglo-Saxon Kings*, 1881); and from the French a work on natural history by Quatrefages de Bréau (*The Rambles of a Naturalist on the Coast of Spain, France and Sicily*, 1857). The influence of her stepfather was ever present in her work: her translation of Pauli's work was dedicated to him and her edition of Lappenberg's work was a revision of Thorpe's earlier translation. Her translations of complex works in several academic disciplines represent a considerable intellectual achievement. Gosse considered her one of the most learned women of her time, whose erudition showed best in her 'copious and marvellously illuminating' conversation (Gosse, 15). For many years she was incapacitated by pain caused by curvature of the spine. She died unmarried at her home, 160 Sheen Road, Richmond, Surrey, on 20 December 1903. ELIZABETH BAIGENT

Sources E. Gosse, *The Athenaeum* (2 Jan 1904), 15 • Boase, *Mod. Eng. biog.* • *BL cat.* • *DNB* • *The Times* (21 Dec 1903) • E. S. Day, letter, *The Athenaeum* (16 Jan 1904), 82–3 • Allibone, *Dict.*

Wealth at death £853 4*s*. 4*d*.: probate, 27 Jan 1904, *CGPLA Eng. & Wales*

Otter, William (1768–1840), bishop of Chichester, born on 23 October 1768 at Cuckney, Nottinghamshire, was the fourth son of the seven children of Edward Otter (1724–1785), vicar of Cuckney, and also of the Derbyshire parishes of Bolsover, Scarcliffe, and Upper Langwith. His mother was Dorothy (*d*. 1772), daughter of John Wright of North Anston, Yorkshire. He went up to Jesus College, Cambridge, in 1785, where he was Rustat scholar, graduating BA as fourth wrangler in 1790. Otter was tutored by William Frend and, like his brother Edward (1764–1837), a fellow of the college, supported Frend in his dispute with the college in 1793. In that year Otter proceeded MA, and later, in 1836, BD and DD. In 1791 he was ordained to the curacy of Helston, Cornwall, where he was also master of the grammar school. Otter returned to Jesus College as a fellow in 1796, remaining until 1804, and for a time served as a committee member of the Cambridge Volunteers.

As an undergraduate Otter befriended Edward Daniel Clarke (of whom he published a *Life* in 1824) and Thomas Robert Malthus. Together with John Marten Cripps, they travelled to the continent in 1799. Otter alone accompanied Malthus onwards from Lake Vänern as he gathered supporting evidence for his *Essay on Population* in Sweden, Norway, Finland, and Russia, while Otter occupied himself with botanizing (he was later a fellow of the Linnean Society). Otter's memoir of Malthus, prefixed to the second edition of *The Principles of Political Economy* (1836), sought to create a more receptive climate for Malthus's works by highlighting his personal qualities, and remains an important source for Malthus's life.

Otter resigned his fellowship on his marriage in 1804 to Nancy Sadleir (*d*. 1860), daughter of William Bruere of Leatherhead, former secretary to the government and member of the supreme court of Calcutta. The couple had three sons and five daughters: among them William Bruere became archdeacon of Chichester after his father's death; his eldest daughter, Sophia, married Malthus's son, Henry; his second daughter, Caroline, married John (later the first Lord) Romilly; the fourth, Maria, married Lord Justice Sir William Milbourne James; and the fifth, Emily, married Edward Strutt, the first Lord Belper. Shortly before his own marriage Otter was presented by Bruere to the rectory of Colmworth, Bedfordshire. He resigned this living along with that of Sturmer, Essex, which he had held for only one year, on his appointment as rector of Chetwynd, Shropshire, in 1811, to which he added the vicarage of Kinlet in 1814. Otter supplemented his income through tutoring, numbering among his pupils sons of Sir Samuel Romilly, Sir John St Aubin, and Sir Roger Newdigate; in 1822 he moved his family to Oxford and acted as private tutor to the third Lord Ongley. In 1825 Otter acquired a third benefice, the vicarage of St Mark's, Kennington, through the patronage of George D'Oyly, the husband of his wife's sister.

Possibly through his association with D'Oyly, Otter was chosen as first principal of King's College, London (after John Lonsdale declined the post), in June 1831, and

William Otter (1768–1840), by John Linnell, 1841

resigned Kennington on his appointment; his whig connections helped prevent the college appearing too partisan. He was simultaneously appointed divinity lecturer, delivering weekly sermons and Monday discourses on theology throughout his tenure. Since the principal was excluded from the governing council, Otter's authority over the college was limited. While he won the confidence of his staff and safely saw the college through its first years, he did not develop any particular affection for the institution, having little contact with it after his resignation in 1836, and instead joining the senate of the University of London from that year.

Otter resigned from King's College and his Shropshire parishes when he was chosen by Lord Melbourne for the bishopric of Chichester: 'exactly the place for me', he observed to Samuel Butler (BL, Add. MS 34590, fols. 309–10). He was consecrated at Lambeth on 2 October 1836. Although Otter was already in indifferent health when appointed, he was an active and reforming diocesan. His most notable innovation was the diocesan association established in January 1838, intended to support the provision of church accommodation and to both augment endowments and fund the stipends of additional clergy. By December the association had raised £2732 for accommodation and £2085 for additional clergy, with another £1120 subscribed for special purposes. In 1839 the association absorbed a diocesan board of education founded earlier in the year, while the ruridecanal system was reinvigorated in order to provide support, with Otter encouraging his deans to revive the ruridecanal chapters. The training school for masters in parochial schools which began modest operations at Otter's initiative in

1840 provided the focus for a memorial subscription proposed by Julius Hare, which in 1849–50 bore fruit in the building of Bishop Otter College, Chichester.

Otter's commitment and lack of partisanship won him the affection and co-operation of both clergy and laity. He worked closely with the earl of Chichester and especially with the duke of Richmond. Most strikingly he took an interest in the careers of both Julius Hare and Henry Manning. In 1840 Otter appointed Hare archdeacon of Lewes, dismissing Hare's reservations regarding the liturgy and creed with the observation that 'my opinions on these points are just the same as your own' (N. M. Distall, *Guessing at Truth*, 1979, 138–9). Otter acknowledged Manning's promise in appointing him rural dean and secretary of the diocesan association, although he deplored his more controversial publications as liable to alienate evangelicals in the diocese, warning that 'the peace of the Church is of much more advantage than any advance even to a good cause, which can only be obtained at the expense of peace' (E. S. Purcell, *Life of Cardinal Manning*, 1895, 7.136). Otter's success in allaying doctrinal tensions in the diocese is apparent from the absence of controversy associated with the foundation at Chichester in 1838 of a theological college with the Tractarian Charles Marriott as principal, for which Otter shared responsibility with Manning and the dean of Chichester, George Chandler.

A tall, thin man, 'of very mild and amiable manners' (W. Sussex RO, Goodwood MS 1576), Otter was a liberal in theology and a moderate whig in politics; at times, however, both as a diocesan reformer and, at the end of his life, in his defence of cathedral institutions against the proposed reforms of the ecclesiastical commissioners, he stood comfortably alongside decided high-churchmen. Otter's first publications appeared in 1812, vindicating the British and Foreign Bible Society from the strictures of Herbert Marsh. After this date his writings mostly concerned pastoralia, notably the posthumously published *Pastoral Addresses*, which he had delivered while bishop. He advised his clergy to maintain their studies and reflect on their reading (his own favourite author was Robert Leighton, archbishop of Glasgow 1611–1684), and called on them to revive the practice of catechism as part of a wider stress on making Christian instruction more demanding in the light of the spread of education. Otter frequently referred to the works of his friend Malthus, and emphasized their implications for devising approaches to the problem of pauperism—in 1818 he described the provident society established in his own parish, and later welcomed the new poor law. Otter placed most stress on the importance of popular education in bringing the poor to an understanding of their own condition. He looked for close co-operation between the National Society and the government, and in 1839 took a more moderate position than most of his episcopal colleagues on the government plan for tighter control of the distribution of public subsidies for education. He was one of three bishops who did not support Archbishop Howley's resolution on the subject in parliament on 5 July 1839, although he remained opposed to many features of the government scheme as it developed. Otter died at Broadstairs, Kent, on 20 August 1840, and was buried in the retrochoir of Chichester Cathedral. ARTHUR BURNS

Sources R. Holtby, *Bishop William Otter* (1989) · L. J. Hodson, 'The diocese of Chichester, 1829–1929', typescript, W. Sussex RO, EPI/53/9/1 · F. J. C. Hearnshaw, *The centenary history of King's College, London, 1828–1928* (1929) · *GM*, 2nd ser., 14 (1840), 539–41 · *Miscellanea Genealogica et Heraldica*, new ser., 3 (1880), 304–5, 328–9 · *Educational Magazine*, 3rd ser., 2 (1840), 271–2 · A. Gray and F. Brittain, *A history of Jesus College, Cambridge*, rev. edn (1988), 143 · P. James, *Population Malthus: his life and times* (1979) · R. A. Soloway, *Prelates and people: ecclesiastical social thought in England, 1783–1852* (1969)

Archives Bodl. Oxf., corresp. with Henry Manning · W. Sussex RO, Goodwood MSS, letters to duke of Richmond

Likenesses J. Linnell, portrait, 1840–41, priv. coll. · J. Linnell, mezzotint, 1841, AM Oxf., BM [*see illus.*] · J. Towne, bust, 1844, Chichester Cathedral · J. Towne, bust, Bishop Otter College, Chichester

Otterbourne, Nicholas. *See* Otterburn, Nicholas (*c.*1400–1462).

Otterbourne, Thomas (*fl. c.*1340–1346), historian, is thought to have been a member of the Franciscan order. He has sometimes been confused with his namesake, Thomas *Otterbourne (*fl.* 1420). A man of that name was sixty-fifth lector in divinity at Oxford *c.*1340, had graduated DTh at Oxford by September 1343, and was licensed to hear confessions in the archdeaconry of Durham by Bishop Bury on 21 September 1343. From his name, and the diocese in which he was licensed, he was probably a native of north-east England.

Otterbourne's historical importance lies in his probable authorship of the continuation from 1297 of a Franciscan chronicle, now lost, but known in the sixteenth century as the chronicle of Richard of Durham. This chronicle was the source on which the Lanercost chronicler drew for much of his material; indeed, the Lanercost chronicle, which survives in only one manuscript, BL, Cotton MS Claudius D.vii, is in large part an adaptation of Richard of Durham's chronicle. In all probability the author of the Anonimalle chronicle of St Mary's Abbey, York, also made use of the continuation of Richard of Durham's chronicle. The evidence for Otterbourne's authorship of that continuation is provided by Sir Thomas Grey (*d.* 1369). In the prologue to his *Scalacronica* Grey states that he had made use of a chronicle by Thomas Otterbourne, a Franciscan friar and Oxford doctor of divinity. Although Grey does not say that Otterbourne had lived in Carlisle, it is unlikely that there were two Franciscan chroniclers writing in the far north of England at much the same time, and on the basis of Grey's evidence modern scholars have identified the author of the continuation of Richard of Durham with Otterbourne.

The section of what is now the Lanercost chronicle from 1297 to 1346 was written by an author interested in the history of the north of England in the first half of the fourteenth century, who shows particular knowledge of events in and around Carlisle. He gives a vivid account of the siege of Carlisle by the Scots in 1315, and a detailed and sympathetic description of the treason and execution of Andrew Harclay, earl of Carlisle, early in 1323. The warden of the Franciscan house in Carlisle heard Harclay's confession before his execution. His knowledgeable accounts of military matters have led to suggestion that the author may have been a knight before entering the Franciscan order. He writes about national politics in Edward II's reign from a pro-baronial standpoint, and shows little respect for Edward II, criticizing him for pursuing in his youth 'pointless and trivial occupations unsuitable for the son of a king' (*Chronicon de Lanercost*, 236). He also shows an interest in the history of the Franciscan order, and he observes, in discussing the deposition of Edward II, that Queen Isabella held the order in high regard.

ANTHONY TUCK

Sources J. Stevenson, ed., *Chronicon de Lanercost, 1201–1346*, Bannatyne Club, 65 (1839) • *Scalacronica, by Sir Thomas Gray of Heton, knight: a chronical of England and Scotland from AD MLXVI to AD MCCCLXII*, ed. J. Stevenson, Maitland Club, 40 (1836) • V. H. Galbraith, ed., *The Anonimalle chronicle, 1333 to 1381* (1927) • W. R. Childs and J. Taylor, eds., *The Anonimalle Chronicle, 1307 to 1334: from Brotherton collection MS 29*, Yorkshire Archaeological Society, 147 (1991) • J. S. Brewer, ed., *Monumenta Franciscana*, 1, Rolls Series, 4 (1858) • A. Gransden, *Historical writing in England*, 2 vols. (1974–82) • A. G. Little, 'The authorship of the Lanercost chronicle [pt 1]', *EngHR*, 31 (1916), 269–79 • H. Summerson, *Medieval Carlisle: the city and the borders from the late eleventh to the mid-sixteenth century*, 2 vols., Cumberland and Westmorland Antiquarian and Archaeological Society, extra ser., 25 (1993) • J. Taylor, *English historical literature in the fourteenth century* (1987)

Archives BL, Cotton MS Claudius D.vii

Otterbourne, Thomas (*fl.* **1420**), historian, has often been confused with his older namesake, Thomas *Otterbourne (*fl. c.*1340–1346). He was the author of a chronicle which was edited and printed by Thomas Hearne in 1732. Hearne discussed the evidence for the existence of a chronicler called Otterbourne, and cited the opinion of Thomas Tanner (*d.* 1735) that there were two chroniclers of this name. Tanner was almost certainly correct, but very little is known about the life of the second Thomas Otterbourne. He may be tentatively identified with the Thomas Otterbourne who was presented to the living of Haddiscoe, Norfolk, on 30 October 1383 and became rector of Chingford, Essex, in 1393. The family of Ros of Helmsley were the patrons of the living of Chingford, and this perhaps strengthens the assumption that, like his namesake, he was a native of north-east England. If so, he was perhaps the Thomas Otterbourne of Yorkshire who acted as a mainpernor for a number of different people several times between 1379 and 1382.

Otterbourne's chronicle exists in a fifteenth-century manuscript, BL, Harley MS 3643; a transcript (which differs only in a few details from the fifteenth-century manuscript) was made in the sixteenth century: this survives as BL, Cotton MS Vitellius F.ix. Hearne's edition was based on this latter manuscript, which was damaged in the fire of 1731. John Stow, working in the later sixteenth century, translated the sections of the chronicle that cover the Anglo-Saxon period and the years from 1400 to 1420: his translation survives as BL, Harley MS 6223, folios 122*r*–141*r*.

Although the chronicle starts with the legendary history of Britain, it provides detailed information only for the years from 1377 to 1420, when it ends. Even here, it is largely dependent on a manuscript of Thomas Walsingham's chronicle. V. H. Galbraith noted that nine-tenths of Otterbourne's text for the reigns of Henry IV (from 1406) and Henry V consists of 'word for word extracts' from Walsingham, and his account of Richard II's reign and the early years of Henry IV's is also substantially derived from Walsingham. Virtually all the rest of Otterbourne's material for Henry V's life and reign, including the story of the dauphin's gift of tennis balls to Henry, comes from the *Liber metricus* of Thomas Elmham. A few passages in the later part of his chronicle appear to be derived from other sources. His account of how Robert de Vere, duke of Ireland, met his death in 1392 seems to be independent of Walsingham, and his description of the siege of Berwick by Henry IV during the uprising of 1405 has a few details that do not derive from any known source. This may be further evidence for the author's north-eastern origins, though most of his coverage of northern affairs from 1377 onwards is derived from Walsingham.

Otterbourne can be regarded as an independent source for only a very small number of the events he describes, and he himself freely acknowledges his debt to others. In the introduction to his chronicle, he says that his work consists of extracts transcribed from other chronicles, for the benefit of those 'who do not possess many chronicles or cannot read those they have' (Hearne, 3). He explicitly acknowledges his dependence on Geoffrey of Monmouth, Bede, William of Malmesbury, Henry of Huntingdon, Roger of Howden, and 'Cestrensis polichronicon' (Ranulf Higden), but he does not admit to any borrowing from Walsingham. Although his chronicle survives while that of his namesake has been preserved only as a shadow behind the Lanercost chronicle, there can be little doubt that the first Thomas Otterbourne was a historian of much more significance than the second.

ANTHONY TUCK

Sources *Duo rerum Anglicarum scriptores veteres, Thomas Otterbourne et Joh. Whethamstede*, ed. T. Hearne, 1 (1732) • *Thomae Walsingham, quondam monachi S. Albani, historia Anglicana*, ed. H. T. Riley, 2 vols., pt 1 of *Chronica monasterii S. Albani*, Rolls Series, 28 (1863–4) • *Johannis de Trokelowe et Henrici de Blaneforde ... chronica et annales*, ed. H. T. Riley, pt 3 of *Chronica monasterii S. Albani*, Rolls Series, 28 (1866) • [T. Walsingham], *Chronicon Angliae, ab anno Domini 1328 usque ad annum 1388*, ed. E. M. Thompson, Rolls Series, 64 (1874) • T. Walsingham, *The St Albans chronicle, 1406–1420*, ed. V. H. Galbraith (1937) • *Elmhami 'Liber metricus de Henrico Quinto'*, ed. C. A. Cole, Rolls Series, 11 (1858) • *Chancery records* • C. L. Kingsford, *English historical literature in the fifteenth century* (1913) • A. Gransden, *Historical writing in England*, 2 (1982) • A. L. Martin, 'Chingford old church', *Bulletin of the Chingford Antiquarian and Historical Society*, 1 (Sept 1958)

Archives BL, Cotton MS Vitellius F.ix • BL, Harley MSS 3643, 6223

Otterburn, Sir Adam (*d.* **1548**), lawyer and diplomat, was possibly descended from the family which produced such notable legal figures in the fifteenth century as Nicholas Otterburn, clerk register, and John Otterburn, official of Lothian. Nothing certain is known of his parents, although it is possible that Marion Brown, the widow of Thomas Otterburn, in whose favour he resigned lands in

1515, was his mother, and Thomas his father. His sister may have been the Janet Otterburn who married John Laing in 1528, though Otterburn had a daughter of the same name. He was married twice—first to Janet Rhynd and then, before 1525, to Euphame Mowbray. With his second wife he had three sons: John, Robert, and Thomas. He also had three daughters: Margaret, Janet, and another whose name is unknown.

Having graduated MA, probably at a foreign university, Otterburn appeared in 1503 on the same witness list as James Henryson, king's advocate. Their relationship was a close one and in later years Otterburn maintained links with Henryson's widow and family. He was first nominated to appear as a procurator before the lords of council in 1505 and appeared regularly thereafter. Over the period 1504 to 1514 he was the fourth most popular procurator before the lords in terms of nominations by litigants. In 1514 he was constituted as procurator by more litigants than any other man of law, and his standing as a lawyer was such that in 1509 he acted on behalf of the king during the temporary absence of Henryson; in 1512 he succeeded Henryson as burgh clerk of Edinburgh, a post which he retained until about 1525.

On 5 January 1517 Otterburn was appointed a lord of council and thereafter was regularly on the council sederunt. He was also one of those appointed to act as receiver of Queen Margaret's rents in December 1518. In May 1523 he was authorized, in the absence of the justice-clerk, to subscribe all judicial deliverances in criminal cases provided he did so along with one of the regents. Despite becoming a member of the council, Otterburn—as was common practice—maintained his activity as an advocate both before the lords of council and in sheriff courts. He was also constituted one of the sheriffs-depute of Stirling by Lord Erskine in 1524.

As a burgess and common clerk of Edinburgh, Otterburn was heavily involved in burgh affairs. This was recognized on 27 November 1521 when he was promoted from ordinary burgess and admitted as honorary burgess and guild brother. In February 1518 the burgh community had vigorously supported his protest at an attempt by the provost, the first earl of Arran, to usurp his right of appointing a deputy clerk—a stand for burgh independence that ended with triumphant shouts of 'Otterburn, Otterburn'. Otterburn was himself provost of the burgh in 1521–2, 1528–32, 1543–4, and 1547–8, and also fulfilled the office occasionally at other times when the serving provost was absent, particularly during 1535–6. As provost he was active in 1530 during an outbreak of plague in the burgh, imposing sanitary regulations. Otterburn also acted on the burgh's behalf in legal matters before the lords of council, before and after the foundation of the college of justice in 1532. He devoted some of his assets to engaging in trade, and appears to have imported cloth and other products.

Appointment as king's advocate in 1524 as successor to James Wishart, though boosting his precedence in the council sederunt, did not end Otterburn's career as an advocate working for private clients. There is evidence that he continued to acquire significant client income as well as his annual fee from the king. For instance, in 1527 the earl of Cassillis acknowledged that he was 300 merks in debt to Otterburn, while in July 1533, following arbitration, it was agreed between Otterburn and Andrew Murray of Blackbarony that the latter should pay Otterburn 200 merks over five years in return for counsel and labour concerning Murray's lands and leases during that period. Otterburn also enjoyed a considerable career as a diplomat from January 1521, when he was a member of a commission sent to meet Lord Dacre, the English warden of the marches, to discuss measures against border raids. Other border commissions followed in August 1525, late 1528 (leading to the treaty of Berwick), 1533, and 1534 and Otterburn also attended days of truce. His early political stance was that of a supporter of the eighteenth earl of Angus, and he argued that the election of Archibald Douglas of Kilspindie as provost of Edinburgh in 1519 was conform to law and that to remove him would damage the burgh's privileges. The antagonism between Arran and the burgh was reversed by a compromise reached in January 1521 and from this time Otterburn modified his position somewhat in regard to Arran's enemy, Angus. In the following January the duke of Albany laid siege to Angus's castle at Tantallon and Otterburn's farm at Auldhame was damaged, though he subsequently received compensation from the exchequer.

Otterburn had frequent contact with the English ambassador Thomas Magnus, particularly in regard to the possible marriage of James V to Princess Mary Tudor. In letters of November 1524 Magnus described him as 'very favourable and foreward in our causes', and as 'one of the wisest men in Edinburgh, well lerned and of good experience and practise' (*State Papers, Henry VIII*, 4.232, 236). Otterburn was sent to London in 1533 by the king bearing a letter of credence to Henry VIII describing James's 'singular traist and confidence' in him as a man who had 'aye bene a sollistar of peace and concord to be betuix Us and our Realmes' (ibid., 664); while in England Otterburn was knighted, probably by Henry VIII. He returned to Scotland in May 1535 but was back in London the next year from March until June, discussing a proposed meeting between King James and King Henry. During this period, as in other periods of absence from the realm, Otterburn's role as king's advocate was taken up by interim substitutes appointed on a temporary basis.

Otterburn's first appearance in parliament, as representative of Edinburgh, came in 1523 when he was also elected one of the lords auditor of causes. He subsequently appeared on a regular basis as a commissioner to parliament for the burgh of Edinburgh, sometimes being appointed one of the lords of the articles. Service to crown, burgh, and private clients allowed Otterburn to build up considerable landed estates. By 1518 he held Auldhame, near Tantallon, of the archbishop of St Andrews. In 1527 he purchased the lands of Redhall in Edinburghshire from William, master of Glencairn. Two years later, as a reward for his services as ambassador, he was granted the lands of Orchardfield, near Kirknewton, Edinburghshire.

Prior to 1536 he apprised (obtained infeftment in, as secured creditor, following failure to repay a debt) the lands of Dirleton.

In 1538, because of his reported ability as a poet, Otterburn was involved in writing the speech in French which welcomed Mary of Guise to Edinburgh (though neither this speech nor any of his poetry has survived). Then in September of that year he was suddenly dismissed from office for communicating with the exiled earl of Angus. In the words of the English ambassador Sir Ralph Sadler, he was 'suspected to be over good an Englishe man' (Inglis, 68–9). He had not been in favour of the forfeiture of Angus in 1528 and he was rumoured to have been in contact with the exiled earl while he was in London in 1536. Warded in Dumbarton Castle for four months, he was released and exiled to Fife during the king's pleasure and fined £2000 before regaining his liberty towards the end of 1539. The Edinburgh burgess Nicol Cairncross gave caution for payment of £1000 of the fine to the treasurer, James Kirkcaldy of Grange. This fine led to financial difficulties that troubled Otterburn for the rest of his life. Despite his frequent contact with England, he did not favour the reformed religion and enjoyed close contacts with Cardinal David Beaton.

Otterburn was politically rehabilitated to some extent because of his skill in diplomacy. In 1542 he was sent to London, but the circumstances of this mission are unclear. On 16 February 1543 he resumed his place as a lord of session. He strongly opposed the proposal that the infant Queen Mary should marry Prince Edward of England, and the issue appears to have caused a shift in his view of foreign policy towards a closer understanding with France. Sir Ralph Sadler later attributed the remark to Otterburn that 'if your lad were a las, and our las were a lad, would you then be so earnest in the mateir?' (Clifford, 3, 326). During 1543 Otterburn was re-elected provost of Edinburgh, and English reports firmly portray him as a supporter of the pro-French Cardinal Beaton. However, he was again dismissed as provost following the successful attack on Edinburgh by the earl of Hertford in May 1544. He may have been imprisoned towards the end of the year for his continuing association with the Douglases, who were declared guilty of treason by Governor Arran, but after a reconciliation in the following February Otterburn was again sitting as a lord of session in April 1545.

Following Beaton's murder on 29 May 1546 Otterburn was part of an embassy sent to England in August to discuss an offer by Henry to include Scotland in the recent treaty of Campe. He did not return until August 1547. In July 1548 he was attacked in Edinburgh by John Muir of Annestoun and John Murray of Annestounheid; 'sore hurt on the head', he died there on 6 July (*CSP Scot.*, *1509–89*, 90). The motive is unknown but may have related to his pro-French political position. JOHN FINLAY

Sources J. D. Marwick, ed., *Extracts from the records of the burgh of Edinburgh, AD 1403–1528*, [1], Scottish Burgh RS, 2 (1869) • J. A. Inglis, *Adam Otterburn of Redhall: king's advocate, 1524–1538* (1935) • J. Finlay, 'Professional men of law before the lords of council, *c*.1500–*c*.1550', PhD diss., U. Edin., 1997 • M. H. B. Sanderson, *Cardinal of Scotland: David Beaton, c.1494–1546* (1986) • W. K. Emond, 'The minority of James V, 1513–1528', PhD diss., U. St Andr., 1988 • T. I. Rae, *The administration of the Scottish frontier, 1513–1603* (1966) • protocol book of Alexander Makneil, NA Scot., B22/22/18 • *The state papers and letters of Sir Ralph Sadler*, ed. A. Clifford, 3 vols. (1809) • *CSP Scot. ser.*, *1509–89* • *State papers published under … Henry VIII*, 11 vols. (1830–52), vol. 4 • NA Scot., C.S.1, 5, 6, 7; C.C.8 • *Reg. PCS*, 1st ser., vols. 1–3 • M. Livingstone, D. Hay Fleming, and others, eds., *Registrum secreti sigilli regum Scotorum / The register of the privy seal of Scotland*, 4–6 (1952–63) • J. M. Thomson and others, eds., *Registrum magni sigilli regum Scotorum / The register of the great seal of Scotland*, 11 vols. (1882–1914), vol. 4 • *APS*, *1424–1567* • R. K. Hannay, ed., *Acts of the lords of council in public affairs, 1501–1554* (1932) • C. B. B. Watson, ed., *Roll of Edinburgh burgesses and guild-brethren, 1406–1700*, Scottish RS, 59 (1929) • F. J. Grant, ed., *The Faculty of Advocates in Scotland, 1532–1943*, Scottish RS, 145 (1944)

Otterburn, Nicholas (*c*.1400–1462), administrator, is of unknown parentage, but was probably related to the other Otterburns active in fifteenth-century Scotland and was certainly uncle of Master John Otterburn, his likely successor as official of St Andrews within Lothian. Master Nicholas, who was of the diocese of Glasgow, was a student at St Andrews University *c*.1415–1419 and retained links with the arts faculty there in 1429–30. He matriculated at Louvain University in 1431. In due course he was licensed in canon law and graduated MA and bachelor in civil law. He was provided to his first benefice (the vicarage of Mearns, Glasgow diocese) in 1422, retaining it until at least 1436. He litigated for various other benefices, and obtained a canonry and prebend of Glasgow by 1442 and the vicarage of Edinburgh by 1455, both possibly held until his death. He was official of St Andrews within Lothian by 1441 until *c*.1458. In 1449 he became secretary to James II. It is not known who brought him into the administration, though the chancellor, William, Lord Crichton, Bishop Kennedy of St Andrews, and Bishop Turnbull of Glasgow are all possibilities. He remained in office until 1452 and was clerk of the rolls and register of Scotland from 1454 to 1460. In part because of his official posts he witnessed a number of crown charters and served on the king's council and in parliament in judicial matters. He was an ambassador to England and France several times, most notably in 1448–9, when he and two others travelled to Burgundy to arrange the marriage of James II to Mary, daughter of Arnold, duke of Gueldres. Otterburn is stated to have written 'Epithalamium Jacobi II', presumably to mark the occasion of the marriage. He died on 31 January 1462. ALAN R. BORTHWICK

Sources J. M. Thomson and others, eds., *Registrum magni sigilli regum Scotorum / The register of the great seal of Scotland*, 11 vols. (1882–1914), vol. 2 • *CEPR letters*, vols. 7–10, 12 • E. R. Lindsay and A. I. Cameron, eds., *Calendar of Scottish supplications to Rome*, 1: *1418–1422*, Scottish History Society, 3rd ser., 23 (1934) • A. I. Dunlop, ed., *Calendar of Scottish supplications to Rome*, 2: *1423–1428*, Scottish History Society, 3rd ser., 48 (1956) • A. I. Dunlop, ed., *Calendar of Scottish supplications to Rome*, 3: *1428–1432*, ed. I. B. Cowan, Scottish History Society, 4th ser., 7 (1970) • A. I. Dunlop, ed., *Calendar of Scottish supplications to Rome*, 4: *1433–1447*, ed. D. MacLauchlan (1983) • J. Kirk, R. J. Tanner, and A. I. Dunlop, eds., *Calendar of Scottish supplications to Rome*, 5: *1447–1471* (1997) • *CDS*, vol. 4 • *RotS*, vol. 2 • G. Burnett and others, eds., *The exchequer rolls of Scotland*, 5–6 (1882–3) • C. Innes, ed., *Registrum episcopatus Glasguensis*, 2 vols., Bannatyne Club, 75 (1843); also pubd as 2 vols., Maitland Club, 61 (1843) • *Thomae*

Dempsteri Historia ecclesiastica gentis Scotorum, sive, De scriptoribus Scotis, ed. D. Irving, rev. edn, 2 vols., Bannatyne Club, 21 (1829)

Otterburne, Sir Adam. *See* Otterburn, Sir Adam (*d.* 1548).

Otthen, Hippocrates (*d.* **1611**), physician, was related to the noble family of Otthens in Alsace, but was educated and became doctor of medicine at the University of Montpellier, France. He came to England with his father, the emperor's physician, who had been summoned by Elizabeth I. Pressed into the service of the earl of Leicester, 'who desired him to pertain unto him' (Stow, 4.113), he continued in the latter's service for many years, both at home and in the Low Countries. He was admitted a licentiate of the College of Physicians on 4 July 1589, being described as 'vir doctus et practicator bonus' ('a learned man and good practitioner'). On the death of Leicester he entered the service of the earl of Essex, and, by Elizabeth's command, attended him in the wars of France and the expedition to Cadiz. After his return to England he was ordered by Elizabeth to attend Lord Mountjoy, later earl of Devonshire, in Ireland. He subsequently accompanied, in the same capacity of physician, the earl of Hertford, the English ambassador to the archduke of Austria. The rest of his life was spent in private practice.

On either 16 March 1605 or 12 June 1609 Otthen was incorporated DM at Oxford. He married Dorothy, a daughter of Roger Drew of Densworth in Sussex, and spent his last years with her 'in great bliss and happiness' (Stow, 4.113). He died on 13 November 1611 and was buried in the church of St Clement Danes, London, where a monument, with inscription, was erected to his memory on the south side of the chancel. After his death his wife married Sir Stephen Thornhurst of Kent, and died on 12 June 1620, aged fifty-five. She was buried in Canterbury Cathedral, where a monument was erected to her memory.

W. A. SHAW, *rev.* PATRICK WALLIS

Sources Munk, *Roll* • Foster, *Alum. Oxon.* • J. Stow, *A survey of the cities of London and Westminster and the borough of Southwark*, ed. J. Strype, new edn, 2 vols. (1720) • Wood, *Ath. Oxon.*

Ottley, Adam (*bap.* **1655**, *d.* **1723**), bishop of St David's, was baptized at Pitchford, Shropshire, on 5 January 1655, the second surviving son of Sir Richard Ottley (1626–1670) of Pitchford, gentleman of the privy chamber to Charles II, and his wife, Lady Lettice, daughter of Robert Ridgeway, second earl of Londonderry. The Ottleys had been staunchly royalist in the civil war; the bishop's grandfather Sir Francis *Ottley (1600/01–1649) was Charles I's governor of Shrewsbury. Adam Ottley matriculated at Trinity College, Cambridge, in 1672, was made a scholar in 1674, and took his BA in 1676 and MA in 1679. He then migrated to Trinity Hall, Cambridge, where he was a fellow from 1680 to 1684, and was admitted DD in 1691. He served as rector of Prestbury, Shropshire, from 1682, as a prebendary of Hereford from 1686, and as archdeacon of Shropshire from 1687. He married Ann Baldwyn (*bap.* 1660?, *d.* 1720) at Stokesay church on 24 January 1688; she was probably the daughter of Sir Samuel Baldwyn, of Elsedge, serjeant-at-law, and thus sister of Elizabeth Baldwyn who married Ottley's elder brother Thomas and of Charles Baldwyn, whig MP for Ludlow in the 1681, 1685, and 1691 parliaments. The marriage seems to have been childless. She was buried at Pitchford on 14 April 1720.

Ottley appears to have had tory sympathies and emerged as a candidate for promotion under the ministry of Robert Harley, earl of Oxford. His nephews Acton Baldwyn, who had succeeded to the family seat in the Commons at Ludlow, and the younger Adam Ottley (1685–1752) both had tory inclinations. When the see of Hereford fell vacant some in the diocese canvassed for Ottley to become bishop, but instead, following the translation of Philip Bisse to the see of Hereford, Ottley was nominated on 11 December 1712 to succeed him as bishop of St David's. The younger Adam Ottley enthusiastically reported that 'the whole ministry' (Evans, 119) struggled for Ottley's appointment, but he particularly indicated the support of 'Mr Brydges'—probably the whig paymaster-general, James Brydges, later first duke of Chandos. Elected on 28 February 1713, Ottley was confirmed at Bow church on 14 March, consecrated at Lambeth on the following day, and enthroned at St David's Cathedral on 29 July. Although his penultimate predecessor, Philip Bull (1705–10), had been an effective reforming force the see of St David's had suffered from a long series of indifferent, often non-resident bishops, who (like Bisse) had used it merely as a stepping stone to greater things. From the beginning Ottley was determined to be an exception. He restored the episcopal palace at Abergwili, in Carmarthenshire, which had become uninhabitable, and did much to create the building that survived a devastating fire in 1903 and now houses the Carmarthenshire county museum. Ottley undertook three visitations of the diocese (in 1714, 1717, and 1723) and attempted to advance the careers of native Welsh clergymen. He was rigorous in enforcing clerical residence and in attempting to improve the quality of his diocesan clergy; he also tried to stamp out the itinerant preaching of the most popular of his clergy, Griffith Jones, rector of Llanddowror, whom he condemned for 'intruding himself into the churches of other ministers without their leave' (Jenkins, 14). His attempt to confine Jones, whose activities anticipated the growth of Welsh Methodism, within parochial boundaries was unsuccessful. Ottley was also recognized as a patron of Welsh literature; he was the dedicatee of Theophilus Evans's *Drych y prif oesoedd* in 1716 and subscribed to Evans's translations of English-language religious works into Welsh in 1719 and 1722. In 1724 he wrote to the SPCK, suggesting that they publish an English translation of Rhys Prichard's *Canwyll y Cymry*, but the scheme fell through.

Ottley fell ill on 23 September 1723 with 'a pain at my stomach, heart burning and an inclination to vomiting' (Evans, 128). He died at the episcopal palace, Abergwili, on 4 October and was buried at Abergwili—a choice that was extremely unusual for post-Reformation bishops of St David's and a fitting final proof of his commitment to his diocese. His library and collection of curiosities was auctioned at Paul's Coffee-House, London, on 19 April 1725. His nephew Adam was the chief beneficiary of his will, dated 5 September 1723, in which he passed on the estate that he had inherited in 1688 from his uncle and godfather Sir Adam Ottley, master of the chancery court. The nephew, registrar of St David's from 1713, was the writer of most of the materials in the Ottley papers, a substantial collection eventually deposited at the National Library of Wales. Generally regarded as one of the most effective eighteenth-century bishops in Wales, and one of the few bishops of St David's regularly resident and genuinely committed to his diocese, Ottley was even eulogized in verse:

O thou who dost the sacred mitre grace,
Thou the good star that rul'st St David's place …
Thee Ottley with new vigour wee behold
Enlivening statutes to their force of old,
A Palace which some thought no crime t'impair,
We see rebuilding by thy better care.
(Evans, 130)

J. D. Davies

Sources NL Wales, Ottley papers • G. E. Evans, 'Adam Ottley, bishop of St. David's, 1713–23', *Carmarthenshire Antiquary*, 28 (1938), 117–30 • 'Will of Adam Ottley, bishop of St David's', *Carmarthenshire Antiquary*, 26 (1936), 9 • A. Ottley, letters to Browne Willis, Bodl. Oxf., MS Willis 37 • Lord Hawkesbury, 'The family of Ottley of Pitchford' and 'Extracts from the parish registers of Pitchford', *Shropshire Archaeological and Natural History Society Transactions*, 2nd ser., 7 (1895), 361–74 • Venn, *Alum. Cant.*, 1/3.287 • *The manuscripts of his grace the duke of Portland*, 10 vols., HMC, 29 (1891–1931), vol. 5, p. 247 • G. H. Jenkins, *Literature, religion and society in Wales, 1660–1730* (1978) • will, PRO, PROB 11/594, fol. 114 • E. Cruickshanks, 'Baldwyn, Charles', 'Ottley, Sir Richard', HoP, *Commons, 1660–90* • J. B. Lawson, 'Baldwyn, Acton', HoP, *Commons, 1715–54* • *IGI*
Archives NL Wales, corresp. and papers | Bodl. Oxf., letters to Browne Willis, MS Willis 37
Wealth at death bequeathed (unspecified) residue of estate to nephew; £10 each to sister and two nieces; bequests ranging from 50s. to half a year's wages made to all servants: will, PRO, PROB 11/594, fol. 114

Ottley, Alice (1840–1912), headmistress, was born on 23 March 1840 at Acton, Suffolk, the fourth of the sixteen children (of whom two died in infancy, two when young) of Lawrence Ottley (1808–1861), vicar of Acton, and his wife, Elizabeth (*d.* 1902), daughter of the Revd John Bickersteth. In 1850 her father became rector of Richmond, North Riding of Yorkshire, holding a canonry from 1859. The family life was profoundly religious in the evangelical tradition and Alice was educated at home until after the death of her nearest sister, Bessie, in 1854, when she was sent away with two other sisters to a school in London kept by a former governess to the family. Unhappy there, she returned to Richmond in 1856 and devoted herself to her younger siblings, who included Henry Bickersteth Ottley (1850–1932), a clergyman prominent in sabbatarian organizations, Edward Bickersteth Ottley (1853–1910), canon of Rochester, Robert Lawrence Ottley (1856–1935), regius professor of moral and pastoral theology at Oxford, and Charles Langdale *Ottley (1858–1932), a rear-admiral.

Lawrence Ottley died in 1861, leaving twelve children, the youngest a boy of eighteen months. The family went south and settled in Hampstead, where Mrs Ottley took in pupils, and to these and to her family Alice gave up her next twenty years in the self-abnegating spirit that was always characteristic of her. In the 1870s she began attending lectures organized by the London Ladies' Educational Association at University College (doing much of the necessary reading on the bus since there was so little time at home), including those in English language and literature given by Henry Morley. In 1876 she gained her honours certificate in the Cambridge higher local exam. In 1877 she deputized for a few weeks for Ada Benson, first headmistress of Oxford high school, and enjoyed the experience, though at this stage she was not in favour of girls' day schools; they did not, she thought, provide enough scope for the character training that to her was the main aim of education.

Mrs Ottley gave up her school in 1880, and Alice, the following February, went to teach at the school in Warrington Crescent, Maida Vale, run by Miss Margaret Clarke, whom she had met through her association with the Revd William Henry Cleaver, curate of St Mary Magdalene, Paddington. Her religious sympathies were now high-church (even when she was a child her father had described her as a little Puseyite), and she assisted Miss Clarke in the foundation (1872) of the Society of the Holy Name, an association for church teachers. In 1899 she became superior of the society, which held retreats for teachers. In 1883 Canon W. J. Butler (1818–1894), looking for a headmistress for a new high school in Worcester run on Church of England lines, was told by the head of Oxford high school that Alice Ottley would be the ideal choice, and Miss Clarke herself persuaded her to leave Warrington Crescent to take up the appointment.

The school opened on 21 June 1883 in Britannia House, a fine early Georgian building, with ten children aged from ten to fifteen (later joined by one other) who were known as the First Brood. Two years later there were 125 pupils, whom she treated in those early days as an intimate family group and for whom she devised delightful treats. The school badge was a lily, the motto 'the white flower of a blameless life', and religious education and the spiritual development of the girls was Miss Ottley's paramount concern; she herself prepared them for confirmation. 'You are princesses in the Court of Heaven, and must behave as such', she told them (James, 70), and she insisted on very high standards of deportment and speech. Like Charlotte Yonge (though a generation junior to her) she upheld the ideals of a past generation, which wanted girls to be selfless home-daughters without personal ambition, ministering to their parents and family; the regime of the school was more like that of a convent than the ordinary high school. She became regarded as legendary in Worcester, though some thought her standards too high and her ideas visionary and unpractical. The school council, however, knew that she had a strong will and practical ambitions—such as the wish to put the science teaching on a satisfactory footing and to change the school's constitution so that it was no longer a commercial enterprise. (This was achieved the year after her death.)

Tiny, frail, exquisitely neat, white-haired, with an ivory white complexion, Alice Ottley had amazing powers of physical endurance despite poor health. She performed many good works outside the school, interesting herself in the Girls' Friendly Society, conducting Bible classes, caring one summer for the inmates of an almshouse, and lavishing hospitality not only on old members of the school but on the factory girls whom she entertained every Christmas. In 1884 she was elected a member of the Association of Head Mistresses, becoming vice-president in 1896 and representing the association on Worcestershire education authority after 1902. She became a member of the archbishops' central church council on secondary education in 1899.

Though dreading retirement, Miss Ottley had several times suggested to the school council that it was time she should go, but had always been persuaded to stay on. In 1912, however, after the opening of the summer term, she at last had to give in, exhausted and prematurely aged. Nevertheless, she helped appoint her successor, initiated her into the school's ways, and interviewed every member of the staff individually. Some she asked to stay on; others she advised to find new situations. She was not even well enough to attend the school's twenty-ninth birthday celebrations, though she sent lacrosse equipment as her present. She died at 47 Albany Street, London, of bronchial pneumonia on 18 September 1912, and was buried at Astwood cemetery, Worcester. On 7 February 1914 it was decided that the school's name should be changed to the Alice Ottley School. Two Alice Ottley scholarships, tenable by former pupils at the school, were established at St Hugh's College, Oxford. GILLIAN AVERY

Sources M. E. James, *Alice Ottley: first headmistress of the Worcester High School for girls, 1883–1912* (1914) · V. Noake, *History of the Alice Ottley School, Worcester* (1952) · *CGPLA Eng. & Wales* (1912)
Likenesses D. Adams, portrait, 1896, Alice Ottley School, Worcester · Norman May & Co. Ltd, photograph, 1897, repro. in James, *Alice Ottley*, frontispiece
Wealth at death £7992 4s. 6d.: probate, 9 Nov 1912, *CGPLA Eng. & Wales*

Ottley, Sir Charles Langdale (1858–1932), naval officer, was born at Richmond, Yorkshire, on 8 February 1858, the seventh son of Lawrence Ottley (1808–1861), rector of Richmond and canon of Ripon, and his wife, Elizabeth, the daughter of John Bickersteth, rector of Sapcote, Leicestershire, and the sister of Robert Bickersteth, bishop of Ripon. Robert Lawrence Ottley, canon of Christ Church, Oxford, was his elder brother. He entered the Royal Navy in 1871, and in 1877 was serving as a midshipman in the screw corvette *Amethyst*, when in company with the *Shah* she engaged the rebel Peruvian warship *Huascar* off the coast of Peru. He gained accelerated promotion to lieutenant in 1879 by obtaining first-class certificates in all his examinations, and in 1882, as lieutenant of the *Monarch*, under Captain George Tryon, was present at the bombardment of Alexandria. Later in that year he returned home in order to qualify as a torpedo officer, and while serving in the *Vernon* he displayed marked technical ability by devising a successful automatic mooring gear for submarine mines. In 1884–6 he was torpedo lieutenant of Rear-Admiral Tryon's flagship, the *Nelson*, on the Australia station; he was later appointed torpedo lieutenant of the *Camperdown* and afterwards of the *Victoria*, flagships of the commander-in-chief in the Mediterranean, Admiral Sir Anthony Hoskins, who was later relieved by Vice-Admiral Tryon. Ottley was promoted commander in June 1892, but remained in the ship in that rank as executive officer until early in 1893, when he returned home to become commander of the *Vernon* for two and a half years. In 1892 he married Kathleen Margaret, the daughter of Colonel Alexander Stewart, Royal Artillery; their son died of wounds in 1914. He resumed sea service in 1897, in command of the sloop *Nymphe* in the Mediterranean, and was employed chiefly as senior naval officer at Port Said (1897) and at Constantinople (1898).

Ottley relinquished command of the *Nymphe* on his promotion to captain in January 1899, and was then appointed naval attaché to various British embassies; he acted in that capacity during the next five years in Washington, Rome, Tokyo, St Petersburg, and Paris, thereby gaining unique knowledge and experience of foreign navies and foreign policy. Towards the end of his service as naval attaché he contemplated adopting a political career, and he was chosen in 1903 as prospective Conservative candidate for Pembroke Boroughs. But his special qualifications led to his appointment in 1904 to the staff of the recently established committee of imperial defence, and in 1905 to his selection, although a comparatively junior captain, to succeed Rear-Admiral Prince Louis of Battenberg (afterwards Louis Mountbatten, first marquess of Milford Haven) as director of naval intelligence, then the most important post, other than membership of the board, in the Admiralty; he then abandoned his parliamentary ambitions. This appointment made Ottley a key member of Admiral Sir John Fisher's inner planning élite. As director of naval intelligence he sat on a number of important commissions, notably that of 1906 on war risks to shipping. He favoured an amphibious strategy, and worked to secure the adoption of naval plans by the army. Fisher considered him a genius, but did not take him into his innermost confidence, on account of his well-known loquacity. Ottley opposed Fisher on the key issue of a naval staff, and by 1908 was arguing in private, to Arthur Balfour, that Fisher should be sacrificed to save his naval reforms.

In 1907 Ottley was the principal naval delegate to the second Peace Conference at The Hague, where he took a leading part in drawing up the convention limiting the use of submarine mines, to the development of which he had devoted so much ingenuity many years earlier. In that same year, when the original secretary of the committee of imperial defence, Sir George Clarke (afterwards Lord Sydenham), relinquished that office, owing chiefly to differences of view which had arisen between him and the first sea lord, Sir John Fisher, Ottley was selected, largely at Fisher's insistence, to relieve him. In 1908 he was a delegate to the International Maritime Conference of London, and accepted the dangerous limits that it placed on the use of Britain's greatest weapon, the economic blockade.

He reached the top of the captains' list in that year, but not having served at sea in that rank he was automatically placed on the retired list on promotion to rear-admiral (1908). However, he remained secretary to the committee of imperial defence until February 1912, when he had completed five years in office. Those five years, largely as a result of Ottley's unostentatious but skilful organization and guidance, allied to the efforts of his deputy, and later successor, Captain Maurice Hankey RM, formed the most important period in the development of the committee into a highly efficient instrument for the co-ordination of the nation's resources and forces in the preparation for, and conduct of, a total war.

Having lost the confidence of Fisher over economic warfare and other issues, Ottley left office in 1912 to take up the post of director of Armstrong, Whitworth & Co., of Newcastle upon Tyne. Their offer was financially very attractive, and, despite the best efforts of the prime minister, Asquith, the Treasury refused to match it. Churchill considered Ottley the best choice as his first chief of naval staff in October 1911, and in August 1912 tried to get the Treasury to meet his terms for leaving Armstrong Whitworth, where he was unhappy and ashamed of himself for having left the public service. Once again, nothing came of this approach, and Ottley remained with Armstrong Whitworth, taking an active part in the superintendence of that company's output of war material, particularly after the outbreak of war in 1914. He worked closely with the Admiralty over the Turkish battleship and dockyard contract of 1913.

On retirement from office in 1912, Ottley made his home at Coruanan, Fort William, Inverness-shire. He was appointed MVO in 1903, CB in 1911, and KCMG in 1907 for his services at The Hague Peace Conference. He retired from the board of Armstrongs in 1926 on the post-war reconstruction of the company when it amalgamated with Vickers after a financial crisis. A few days before his death he moved from Coruanan to Creag, Tarbert, Argyll, where he died on 24 September 1932. He was a man of much charm and no little literary ability, a good linguist, and a fluent, convincing, and persuasive speaker. Despite his many talents, however, he was not a leader. He made the committee of imperial defence a highly effective secretariat and co-ordinating body, but never achieved the influence or eminence of his successor. He was, like many of his contemporaries, exploited to further the aims of Lord Fisher, and then discarded when he was of no further use. H. G. Thursfield, *rev.* Andrew Lambert

Sources A. Offer, *The First World War: an agrarian interpretation* (1989) · F. Johnson, *Defence by committee* (1960) · R. F. MacKay, *Fisher of Kilverstone* (1973) · *Fear God and dread nought: the correspondence of Admiral of the Fleet Lord Fisher of Kilverstone*, ed. A. J. Marder, 2 (1956) · J. D. Scott, *Vickers: a history* (1962) · S. W. Roskill, *Hankey, man of secrets*, 1 (1970) · D. M. Schurman, *Julian S. Corbett, 1854–1922: historian of British maritime policy from Drake to Jellicoe*, Royal Historical Society Studies in History, 26 (1981) · R. S. Churchill, ed., *Winston S. Churchill*, companion vol. 2 (1969) · R. Williams, *Defending the empire: the conservative party and British defence policy, 1899–1915* (1991) · A. J. Marder, *The anatomy of British sea power*, American edn (1940) · *Navy List* · Venn, *Alum. Cant.*

Archives NMM, corresp. with Sir Julian Corbett · Tyne and Wear Archive Service, Newcastle upon Tyne, Rendel MSS

Wealth at death £2219 15*s.* 2*d.*: probate, 21 Dec 1932, *CGPLA Eng. & Wales*

Ottley, Sir Francis (1600/01–1649), politician, was the eldest son of Thomas Ottley of Pitchford, Shropshire, and Mary, daughter of Roger *Gifford (*d.* 1597), physician. He entered Shrewsbury School at the age of ten, matriculated from Lincoln College, Oxford, on 4 December 1618 aged seventeen (but took no degree), and in November 1619 entered the Inner Temple as a student. In 1621 he married Lucy, widow of Thomas Pope and daughter of Thomas Edwards, sheriff of Shropshire (1621).

Ottley was active in local affairs, and on the outbreak of the civil war became one of the leading royalists in Shropshire. He was a signatory of the loyal declaration of the grand jury sitting at the assizes at Shrewsbury on 8 August 1642 and was in touch with Sir Edward Hyde. On 10 September, the king wrote from Nottingham authorizing him to raise a force of 200 foot and to secure Shrewsbury for the royal interest; a few days later he was appointed captain of the troop. Ottley was knighted at Shrewsbury on 21 September 1642. He lobbied hard for the governorship of the town, and showed his loyalty on 2 January 1643 by issuing an order compelling the inhabitants to sign a declaration against parliament. But three days later, Hyde wrote that though the king had 'a very just sense of your merit', he:

> hath had of late ill luck in making governors of cities and towns: and though he hath always chosen loved and popular men for those places; yet private differences have so far grown, that he hath been in danger of losing the corporation. However, he resolves there shall be no other governor but you … (Owen and Blakeway, 1.432)

Ottley was confirmed in the position before the end of the month.

On Ottley's initiative the manufacture of muskets commenced in the town, but he seems to have had a difficult time. In July local inhabitants were found to be plotting to betray Shrewsbury to the enemy. Ottley received a letter from Oxford informing him that:

> There is a complaint here, that your press is idle, and doth the king no service; that the Parliament diurnals and pamphlets are in every body's hands, but no country work on the king's side to antidote their poison. If it shall please you to have an eye on the press, and to see our diurnals reprinted there, you wuld do the king and his cause good service, and Secretary Nichols shall thank you. (Owen and Blakeway, 1.437–8)

On 25 January 1644 Prince Rupert wrote to Ottley criticizing his failure to place the suspected traitors on trial 'so that the punishment may go to some, the example and terror to all' (Webb, 381); he himself was planning to make the town his headquarters, and demanded immediate arrangements be made for the secure housing of troops and military equipment. Rupert was convinced that Ottley was loath to court unpopularity with parliamentarian sympathizers in Shrewsbury. Late in 1644 he was removed from his position of governor, succeeded by Sir Michael Ernley, and was named instead as sheriff (though the parliamentarians claimed legitimacy for their own appointment, Thomas Mytton).

Ottley was not in Shrewsbury when it was surprised on 22 February 1645 because he had been captured the previous day, at a meeting with other commissioners of array at Apley, home of Sir William Whitmore, near Bridgnorth. He was one of four signatories of the articles of capitulation at the surrender of Bridgnorth Castle on 26 April 1646. By the terms of surrender, the occupants (who included Lady Ottley and her children) were allowed to return to their homes with horses and arms, but were then to choose between exile and peace. Ottley chose peace. On 16 June 1646 he petitioned to compound for delinquency, and on 25 June 1649 the fine was fixed at £1200. Ottley died in London a few weeks later, on 11 September 1649. He had carefully preserved the papers generated by his role in the civil war, and they are of great value in understanding the course of events in Shropshire and the neighbouring counties. His widow was granted administration of his estates. Their eldest son, Richard Ottley (1626–1670), who had been a captain in the royalist army, was knighted on 21 June 1660, was a gentleman of the privy chamber to Charles II, and sat as MP for Shropshire from 1661 until his death on 10 August 1670.

STEPHEN WRIGHT

Sources H. Owen and J. B. Blakeway, *A history of Shrewsbury*, 2 vols. (1825) • W. Phillips, ed., 'The Ottley papers relating to the civil war [pts 1–3]', *Transactions of the Shropshire Archaeological and Natural History Society*, 2nd ser., 6 (1894), 27–78; 2nd ser., 7 (1895), 241–360; 2nd ser., 8 (1896), 199–312 • W. J. Farrow, *The great civil war in Shropshire (1642–49)* (1926) • J. Webb, *Civil war in Herefordshire* (1879) • M. A. E. Green, ed., *Calendar of the proceedings of the committee for compounding … 1643–1660*, 5 vols., PRO (1889–92) • P. R. Newman, *Royalist officers in England and Wales, 1642–1660: a biographical dictionary* (1981) • E. Calvert, ed., *Shrewsbury School regestum scholarium, 1562–1635: admittances and readmittances* [1892], 226 • W. H. Cooke, ed., *Students admitted to the Inner Temple, 1547–1660* [1878] • will, PRO, PROB 6/24, fol. 122*r* • E. Cruickshanks, 'Ottley, Sir Richard', HoP, *Commons, 1660–90*, 3.188 • Foster, *Alum. Oxon.*

Archives NL Wales, official corresp. and family papers • Shrops. RRC, letters and papers

Likenesses P. Troueil, portrait, 1636, Rowley's House Museum, Shrewsbury [*see illus.*]

Wealth at death exact sum unknown: will, PRO, PROB 6/24, fol. 122*r*

Ottley, William Young (1771–1836), writer on art and collector, was born near Thatcham, Berkshire, on 6 August 1771, the son of a plantation owner, Richard Ottley. He was educated at a school near Richmond, Yorkshire, where he was a pupil of George Cuitt the elder before going on to Winchester College. He entered the Royal Academy Schools in 1787, studying briefly under John Brown (1749–1787), whose studio contents he purchased the same year. Brown's estate included 219 drawings, which formed the basis of Ottley's collection of old master drawings, prints, and paintings. Ottley added to his collection during a ten-year period of study and travel in Italy (1791–9), taking advantage, after the French invasion of 1796, of the desire of many prominent collectors to sell their family treasures before they were looted. He acquired pictures from the Aldobrandini, Colonna, Borghese, and Corsini families, for example Botticelli's *Mystic Nativity* (1500?) and Raphael's *Dream of Scipio* (*c*.1504; 'Vision of a Knight') both now in the National Gallery, London. The bulk of his collection of Italian old master drawings was sold in 1823 to Sir Thomas Lawrence for £8000. Among the highlights, which formed the core of Lawrence's magnificent drawings collection, were splendid groups of drawings by Michelangelo and Raphael assembled by and later stolen from the French painter Jean-Baptiste Wicar (1762–1834), superintendent of official French depredations. Ottley bought the stolen drawings from the Florentine painter Antonio Fedi (to whom they had been given by the thieves, a father and son Pampaloni), but the precise timing of

Sir Francis Ottley (1600/01–1649), by Petrus Troueil, 1636 [with members of his family]

their acquisition and Ottley's possible role in the theft remain open to suspicion (Scheller). Although Lawrence's collection was later largely dispersed (a cause of national regret), most of the drawings by Michelangelo and Raphael were acquired by national subscription for the University of Oxford and are now in the Ashmolean Museum, Oxford.

On his return to London in 1799 Ottley established himself as a writer, connoisseur, and *marchand-amateur*. He was elected a fellow of the Society of Antiquaries and, as a leading arbiter of taste, he advised others on the purchase of works of art. He married some time before 1802. His well-known art publications began with *The Italian School of Design* (1808), a series of facsimile prints engraved (often by himself) after drawings in his own collection. The second and third parts of this ambitious project—intended to provide 'a chronological sequence of the designs of the most eminent artists of Italy' (unpaginated 'Advertisement' to *The Italian School of Design*)—were published in 1813 and 1823 (when the whole work was issued in one volume). In 1816 he published *An Inquiry into the Origin and Early History of Engraving on Copper and Wood* (2 vols.), the companion to which, *An Inquiry into the Invention of Printing*, was published posthumously in 1863. In 1826–8 he published two volumes of facsimile engravings after rare incunabula and early prints. His projected monumental dictionary of engravers, the *Notices of Engravers and their Works*, was abandoned after the publication in 1831 of the first volume (covering A–Baldung). Among the collectors he advised was Granville Leveson-Gower, first marquess of Stafford, most of whose picture gallery he had recorded in four folio volumes of engravings (1818). Two other works devoted mainly to paintings appeared in 1826: *A Descriptive Catalogue of the Pictures in the National Gallery*, commissioned by Lawrence, and *A series of plates engraved after the paintings and sculptures of the most eminent masters of the early Florentine school*, which prompted a reassessment of thirteenth- to fifteenth-century Italian painting.

In 1833 Ottley became keeper of prints and drawings at the British Museum, a post that he accepted apparently for financial reasons, since the act abolishing slavery had reduced his income from the family's West Indies plantation. Although one of the best connoisseurs of his day, he was already in poor health and died in London on 26 May 1836 without having made much of a mark on the collection. He began a new catalogue, but his time at the museum was clouded by rows with the director and trustees about his working conditions. His own remarkable art collection was the subject of a number of private sales and public auctions in London, for which he did much of the research for the catalogues when alive.

NICHOLAS TURNER

Sources J. Gere, 'William Young Ottley as a collector of drawings', *British Museum Quarterly*, 18 (1953), 44–53 • E. K. Waterhouse, 'Some notes on William Young Ottley's collection of Italian primitives', *Italian Studies*, 17 (1962), 272–80 • D. Rodgers, 'Ottley, William Young', *The dictionary of art*, ed. J. Turner (1996) • J. Ingamells, ed., *A dictionary of British and Irish travellers in Italy, 1701–1800* (1997), 728–9 • C. Lloyd, *Art and its images: an exhibition of printed books containing engraved illustrations after Italian painting*, nos. 8, 34 [exhibition catalogue, Bod., April–June 1975] • H. Ottley, *A biographical and critical dictionary of recent and living painters and engravers* (1866) • A. A. [A. Atkinson], 'William Young Ottley', *N&Q*, 174 (1938), 236–9 • A. A. [A. Atkinson], 'Further notes on the Young and Ottley families', *N&Q*, 175 (1938), 326–30, 344–7 • R. W. Scheller, 'The case of the stolen Raphael drawings', *Master Drawings*, 11 (1973), 119–37 • A. Griffiths, 'Introduction: the department of prints and drawings of the British Museum and the history of print collecting', *Landmarks in print collecting: connoisseurs and donors at the British Museum since 1753*, ed. A. Griffiths (British Museum Press, 1996), 9–18 [exhibition catalogue, Museum of Fine Arts, Houston, TX, 1996, and elsewhere] • Bryan, *Painters* (1886–9), 2.236

Archives CUL, MSS relating to armour

Likenesses F. C. Lewis, stipple (after W. Rivière), BM • attrib. W. Rivière, oils, AM Oxf.

Ottobuono [Ottobuono or Ottobono Fieschi; *later* Adrian V] (*c.***1205–1276**), papal official and pope, was born into the Genoese family of the counts of Lavagna. Trained as a theologian and canonist, he acquired distinguished Savoyard connections through his sister, the second wife of Count Thomas (II), but more valuable to his career was the fact that his uncle, Sinibaldo Fieschi, became pope as Innocent IV in June 1243. In November that year Ottobuono was made a papal chaplain, and he subsequently held archdeaconries at Rheims and Parma, before he became cardinal-deacon of San Adriano in 1252. Following his uncle's death in 1254 he remained an important figure at the curia, where his part in the negotiations with Henry III over the throne of Sicily, and his support for Henry's brother Richard and second son, Edmund, doubtless helped to secure his appointment by Clement IV on 4 May 1265 as papal legate to England.

Ottobuono's commission was threefold: to bring about peace and reconciliation following the barons' war; to reform the clergy and the working of the church; and to preach crusade. He left Rome after 19 July 1265, and by 30 August had reached Paris, where he learned of Simon de Montfort's death at Evesham on 4 August. He arrived in England on 29 October. He lodged in the Tower of London for safety, and met Henry III in Canterbury on 1 November, on that day summoning a council for the clergy.

At his first legatine council, held at either Westminster or London on 1 December 1265, Ottobuono made public his commissions, together with the powers he had from the pope to resolve 'urgent and arduous matters'. Crusade and reform needed peace between the 'disinherited' rebels and Henry III's advisers. The council was to initiate the peace. Ottobuono denounced and suspended four bishops as baronial supporters, issuing a general excommunication of all the king's enemies. However, these actions confirmed the suspicions of the rebels about his Savoyard connections and made his task more difficult.

There was very widespread unrest in the months after Evesham, intensified by royalist vindictiveness against former Montfortians. The king's lengthy siege of Kenilworth Castle gave Ottobuono the opportunity to demand, at a parliament held at Kenilworth in August 1266, that negotiations be entered into with the rebels, and he then helped to establish a committee of bishops and barons to decide what was needed to restore peace in the realm. The legate himself was to be one of two arbiters when differences arose within the committee. The result was the dictum of Kenilworth, announced on 31 October, and then proclaimed by Ottobuono to a church council in Coventry the following day. But the dictum was widely rejected at first, in spite of Ottobuono's efforts to promote it at a parliament held at Bury St Edmunds in February 1267, until in April the earl of Gloucester occupied London in order to force the government to give better terms to its adversaries. The legate, who was in the capital at the time, did not resist the earl, though he retreated to the Tower for safety. While there he was entrusted with the Westminster and crown jewels, used by the king as pledges for loans. He later moved to the Cistercian monastery of Stratford Langthorne in Essex, where he was joined by the king in May. Urgent negotiations, in which the legate was closely involved, finally led to a settlement and to the acceptance of the dictum, helped by a tax on the clergy which Ottobuono arranged in order to assist those disinherited in the civil war to redeem their lands. A letter from Ottobuono to Clement IV, probably of June 1267, spoke of 'varying degrees of discord lasting from the beginning of Lent until 20 June, after which came reconciliation from the hand of God' (Graham, 'Letters of Cardinal Ottoboni', 118–19).

Ottobuono then proceeded to reconcile Llywelyn of Wales with the king. After four days of negotiations the treaty of Montgomery was agreed on 29 September 1267. Although his commission also covered Scotland and Ireland, Ottobuono visited neither country personally, operating instead through envoys. Alexander III, king of Scots, received one papal envoy, refused a second, a certain Master Maurice, entry to his court, and threatened a third with violence. Scottish bishops did attend the councils but, as regards Ireland, Ottobuono was more concerned to ensure that the crusade was preached there, arranging this through the bishop of Lismore. His commission for peace was concluded on 18 November 1267 by the Statute of Marlborough, which stressed a return to the rule of law and marked the success of his political work.

The resulting stability allowed Ottobuono to proceed with his commission on church reform. The exile of Boniface of Savoy, archbishop of Canterbury, enabled the legate to establish his authority over the English clergy. No election to a bishopric or abbacy could take place without his mandate. In April 1268 he convened a three-day council in London at St Paul's, at which all clergy were summoned to attend in person or by proctor. Having absolved excommunicate Montfortians, Ottobuono issued a set of fifty-three canons, based upon, and often specifically referring to, but none the less considerably amplifying, those issued in 1237 by the legate Otto. Surviving in some seventy versions, they remained fundamental to the law of the church in England until the sixteenth century—they were first printed in 1504.

Ottobuono's constitutions deal with a wide range of issues of conduct and jurisdiction, affecting both the secular and regular clergy. For instance, the former were forbidden to exercise secular jurisdiction, or to take part in lawsuits in which judgments of blood might be given. Simony was condemned, as were concubinage and the bearing of arms, and severe restrictions were placed upon pluralism. Ottobuono sought to improve the position of vicars, and also to ensure that vicars resided in their livings. Archbishops and bishops, too, were expected to reside among their flocks, and restrictions were placed upon demands for procurations and other exactions liable to abuse. Orders were given for the maintenance of church buildings, and rights of sanctuary were upheld. The last thirteen canons deal with the regulars. Ottobuono was clearly knowledgeable in matters monastic. This emerges with particular clarity from the constitutions he issued to individual monasteries following visitations by his commissaries. One such was Westminster Abbey, to which he directed constitutions on 17 April, a few days before the council. But the canons directed in general terms to monks and nuns, though they doubtless gained in force from the legate's knowledge of conditions in particular houses, are largely devoted to commonplace matters of discipline and organization. They are concerned, for instance, to maintain traditional bans or restrictions on the eating of meat, on the holding of private property, and on engagement in trade, and to ensure that monks and nuns care properly for their sick, and make confession and celebrate the eucharist with becoming frequency. The complete set of canons was to be made public by being recited word for word by bishops at their annual diocesan synods.

Ottobuono's third commission, to preach the crusade, was not neglected. Clement had specified that if English crusaders did not go to the Holy Land, funds so far collected—sufficient for 500 knights—would be used elsewhere. This followed an extension of crusade preaching to deal with the rebels in England and also the planned invasion from France in September 1266 by the younger Simon de Montfort. This invasion did not materialize, and the pope continued to complain about the general lack of support for the crusade. In October 1266 he urged Ottobuono to preach with even more vigour.

At first there were difficulties. When Ottobuono called for a crusade at the Bury parliament, the magnates expressed misgivings about the likely effects of denuding the country of its defenders. But the legate persevered, preaching in London and again in Lincoln (where he used interpreters), and at Northampton in June or July 1268 he finally had the satisfaction of seeing the Lord Edward and many barons take the cross. When his legation to England ended in July 1268, Ottobuono returned to Italy having largely achieved what he set out to do. He attended the Second Council of Lyons in 1274, and on 11 July 1276, with the support of Charles of Anjou, he was elected pope, as Adrian V. But he died in Viterbo on 16 August without having being ordained priest, consecrated, or crowned, and was buried there in the church of San Francesco. His final bequests included prayers for Henry III and his family, and a hospital, dedicated to St Thomas of Canterbury in his native Liguria, where English pilgrims were to be specially received. Among his personal effects was found a precious jewel belonging to the English crown.

BRENDA M. BOLTON

Sources R. Graham, 'Letters of Cardinal Ottoboni', *EngHR*, 15 (1900), 87–120 • R. Graham, 'Cardinal Ottoboni and the monastery of Stratford Langthorne', *EngHR*, 33 (1918), 213–25 • A. P. Bagliani, *I testamenti dei cardinali del duecento*, Miscellanea della Società Romana di Storia Patria, 25 (1980), 142–63 • F. M. Powicke and C. R. Cheney, eds., *Councils and synods with other documents relating to the English church, 1205–1313*, 2 vols. (1964), vol. 1, pt 2, 725–92 • A. P. Bagliani, *Cardinali di curia e 'familiae' cardinalizie dal 1227 al 1254*, 2 vols. (1972) • K. Hampe, 'Neues Archiv der Gesellschaft für altere deutsche Geschichtskunde', 12 (1897), 337–72 • N. Schopp, *Papst Hadrian V (Kardinal Ottobuono Fieschi)* (1916) • E. Martène and U. Durand, *Thesaurus novus anecdotorum*, 5 vols. (1717), vol. 2, pp. 402, 422–3 • *CEPR letters*, 1.437 • A. Lewis, 'The English activities of Cardinal Ottobuono', PhD diss., University of Manchester, 1937 • R. Brentano, *Rome before Avignon: a social history of thirteenth-century Rome* (1974) • L. Gatto, 'Adriano V', *Dizionario biografico degli Italiani*, ed. A. M. Ghisalberti, 1 (Rome, 1960) • A. Potthast, ed., *Regesta pontificum Romanorum, 1198–1304*, 2 vols. (1874–5), vol. 2, p. 1709 • L. Duchesne, ed., *Le Liber pontificalis*, 2 vols. (Paris, 1886–92), vol. 2, p. 457 • F. M. Powicke, *King Henry III and the Lord Edward: the community of the realm in the thirteenth century*, 2 vols. (1947)

Archives LPL, MS 499 fols. 257v–261

Likenesses A. di Cambio?, tomb, San Francesco, Viterbo, Italy

Wealth at death very rich indeed: Bagliani, *I testamenti*, 142–63

Ó Tuama, Seán [John O'Tuomey] (**1708–1775**), Irish-language poet, born at Baile an Fhantaigh, near Kilmallock, co. Limerick, was probably educated in a local hedge-school, which specialized in preparing young men for the priesthood. The curriculum would have consisted largely of Latin, with some Greek and Hebrew, together with English, science, and geography. He was also trained in Gaelic in a part of the country where there was vibrant scribal and poetic activity.

Ó Tuama became a teacher in Croom, co. Limerick, about 1734, probably at the behest of Father Nioclás Ó Dónaill, a Franciscan, and former president of the Irish College at Leuven. Ó Tuama's school was well regarded, as he had the sons of some local landlords among his pupils. Ó Tuama, who was styled *an Ghrinn* ('the Fun-Loving') because of his self-confessed love of song and carousing in convivial company, also established a tavern in Croom, where he proclaimed that customers of a Gaelic inclination were welcome, whether or not they had the capacity to pay. His wife, Muirinn, frowned upon such largesse and tried to prevent it, but it appears that the enterprise was never a financial success. The tavern became a meeting place or 'court' for many poets and literati in the region, who convened to compose and judge verse on prescribed themes. Unanimously acknowledged as chief among them was Seán Clárach Mac Dónaill, whose visit to Croom, probably in 1735, was celebrated in verse by Father Ó Dónaill, by Ó Tuama, and by Aindrias Mac Craith, *an Mangaire Súgach* ('the Merry Pedlar', a sobriquet bestowed by Ó Tuama), his close friend and fellow poet, with whom Ó Tuama's career is inextricably linked. They were born in the same townland and Mac Craith arrived in Croom shortly after Ó Tuama, perhaps to replace or assist him in the school. The two had a bitter falling-out about 1750. Thus began a poetic dispute in which each satirized the other with scurrilous verse. The reasons for the quarrel are not clear but there has been speculation that Mac Craith's drinking was a major contributing factor.

Aside from occasional verse, elegy, and the praise of patrons, the major preoccupations in Ó Tuama's poetry are hatred of the English hegemony, the poor state of the Catholic religion, and, concurrently, a fiercely anti-protestant, Jacobite vein. One set of poems by members of the group satirizes Donnchadh Ó hÉadromáin (Hederman), a Dominican monk who converted to protestantism in 1736. The invasion of Britain in 1745 by the Young Pretender (Charles Edward Stuart) was a major event, and Ó Tuama composed a number of poems about it. Another poem from this period bitterly attacks a certain Píotar (Peter) and four others of Gaelic origin who enlisted on the side of the state against the Pretender. The intriguing cross-dressing figure of Seán or Seon Anna Príor, provided the amusing theme for other verses, the earliest dating perhaps from 1743. The Maigue poets, as they were known, also used the *barántas* ('warrant') form, a mixture of prose and verse imitating certain legal terminology, an extension of metaphor of their poetic conclave as 'court'. The metaphor may also be read as a muted challenge to the oppressive legal regime of the time. Often the poet's theme was personal, such as the death of an Preabaire (Dasher), the favourite horse of Father Nioclás Ó Dónaill. Even these verses, however, as well as lamenting the loss of the beloved animal, also contain political and religious commentary. Ó Tuama moved to Mungret Gate near Limerick city in 1769 where he died on 30 August 1775. His remains were returned for burial in Croom churchyard. A headstone erected by his grandson and inscribed with his name and dates marks his grave.

LILLIS Ó LAOIRE

Sources R. Ua Foghludha, *Éigse na Máighe* (1952) • M. Comer Bruen and D. Ó hÓgáin, *An Mangaine Súgach: Beatha agus Saothar* (1996) • P. Ua Duinnín, *Filidhe na Máighe* (1906) • A. Heusaff, *Filí agus Cléir san Ochtú hAois Déag* (1992) • C. O'Flynn, *The Maigue poets* (1995) • B. Ó Buachalla, *Aisling Ghéar* (1996)

Ó Tuathail, Adam Dubh [Adam Duff O'Toole] (*d.* **1328**), reputed heretic, was a son of Walter Duff O'Toole. His place of origin and residence are unknown but the stronghold of the O'Tooles was in the Wicklow Mountains, south of Dublin. He was tried before an ecclesiastical court in Dublin in 1327 on charges of denying the incarnation and the doctrine of the Trinity, impugning the virtue of the Blessed Virgin, denying the resurrection of the dead, holding the scriptures to be fictitious, and accusing the apostolic see of falsehood. These errors he was said to have compounded by relapse and blasphemy before his spiritual judge. He was found guilty and pronounced a heretic, and was passed to the secular authorities for punishment. On 11 April 1328 he was publicly burnt at Hoggen Green, a common and public meeting-place to the east of the city walls of Dublin. Nothing is known of his early life but there is an isolated reference on an Irish patent roll which may refer to him. In 1303 a Brother Adam O'Toole was appointed to act for the abbot of the Cistercian house of Dunbrody in the latter's absence. ANNE R. NEARY

Sources J. T. Gilbert, ed., *Chartularies of St Mary's Abbey, Dublin: with the register of its house at Dunbrody and annals of Ireland*, 2 vols., Rolls Series, 80 (1884) · Barberini Latini, Vatican, MS 2126, fol. 125 *r* [printed in J. Watt, 'Negotiations between Edward II and John XXII concerning Ireland', *Irish Historical Studies*, 10 (1956), 1–20] · *Jacobi Grace, Kilkenniensis, Annales Hiberniae*, ed. and trans. R. Butler, Irish Archaeological Society (1842) · T. Leland, *The history of Ireland from the invasion of Henry II* (1773) · R. Holinshed and others, eds., *The chronicles of England, Scotlande and Irelande*, 2 vols. (1577) · E. Tresham, ed., *Rotulorum patentium et clausorum cancellariae Hiberniae calendarium*, Irish Record Commission (1828)

O'Tuomey, John. *See* Ó Tuama, Seán (1708–1775).

Otway, Caesar [*pseud.* Terence O'Toole] (**1780–1842**), religious journalist and writer on Ireland, was born in co. Tipperary, the son of Loftus Otway, a merchant. He entered Trinity College, Dublin, on 6 December 1796, aged sixteen, and graduated BA in 1801. After being ordained he was successively curate of a number of country parishes. In 1836 he was appointed to the assistant chaplaincy of Leeson Street Magdalen Chapel, Dublin, where he became one of the leading evangelical preachers. He was twice married, first to Frances, daughter of the Very Revd James Hastings, dean of Achonry, and second to Elizabeth, daughter of W. Digges La Touche of Sans Souci. Elizabeth and Caesar Otway had two sons and two daughters.

In 1825 Otway and Joseph Henderson Singer, later bishop of Meath, launched the *Christian Examiner*, the first Irish religious magazine to promote the cause of the established church. It was through Otway's encouragement that William Carleton began his literary career by writing for the periodical. Otway was an enthusiastic antiquary and an admirer of Irish scenery, and published *A Tour in Connaught* (1839) and *Sketches in Erris and Tyrawley* (1841). He co-operated with the landscape painter and antiquary George Petrie in the first volume of the *Dublin Penny Journal*, for which he wrote under the pseudonym Terence O'Toole and was also a contributor to the *Dublin University Magazine*. Ill health prevented him from writing his projected history of Ireland, and from editing the works of Sir James Ware. He died in Dublin on 16 March 1842.

D. J. O'DONOGHUE, *rev.* DAVID HUDDLESTON

Sources [A. P.], 'Our portrait gallery, no. I', *Dublin University Magazine*, 14 (1839), 396–7 · *Dublin University Magazine*, 19 (1842), 546–8 · J. B. Leslie, Biographical succession list of clergy for Dublin diocese · J. Wills, *Lives of illustrious and distinguished Irishmen*, 6 (1847), 446–9 · Burtchaell & Sadleir, *Alum. Dubl.* · *The Athenaeum* (2 April 1842), 294 · [J. H. Todd], ed., *A catalogue of graduates who have proceeded to degrees in the University of Dublin, from the earliest recorded commencements to … December 16, 1868* (1869), 444 · D. Bowen, *The protestant crusade in Ireland, 1800–70* (1978)

Likenesses J. Kirkwood, etching (after W. Stevenson), NPG, NG Ire.; repro. in *Dublin University Magazine*, 13 (1839)

Otway, Sir Loftus William (**1775–1854**), army officer, was born on 28 April 1775, the fourth son of the six children of Cooke Otway (*d.* December 1800), captain of horse, of Castle Otway, co. Tipperary, and his wife, Elizabeth (*d.* 1807), daughter of Samuel Waller of Lisbrian, co. Tipperary. Otway had three older brothers—Henry (*d.* 1815), Robert Waller (later Admiral Sir Robert; 1772–1846), and Samuel Jocelyn (*d.* 1855), in holy orders—one younger brother, George (*d.* 1804), an infantry major, and a sister, Martha (*d.* 1802). He joined the 5th dragoon guards as a cornet on 17 May 1796, and advanced to lieutenant on 2 September. Possibly he went to Ireland with the regiment in October; he was present during the defeat of rebels at Vinegar Hill on 21 June 1798. He became a captain on 27 October 1798, and obtained a majority on 24 February 1803, before transferring to the 8th light dragoons on 14 July 1804. Otway seems to have served as deputy adjutant-general in Canada at about this time. On 28 March 1805 he went on Irish half pay as lieutenant-colonel. Retaining that army rank, he obtained a majority in the 18th light dragoons on 12 February 1807.

Otway embarked with the regiment for Portugal in July 1808, but saw no action before peace the following month. The 18th light dragoons remained in the Peninsula with Lieutenant-General Sir John Moore's army which marched into Spain to confront the French. Heavily outnumbered, Moore ordered retirement northwards towards Corunna on 5 December 1808, Otway's regiment forming part of the rearguard. On 12 December 1808, in a night attack at Rueda, Otway distinguished himself by capturing 'the whole of the French Cavalry out-lying picquet' (*Army List*, 1840). Shortly afterwards near Valladolid he overwhelmed a strong French force, taking its colonel 'and more of his Chasseurs than he had dragoons to guard them, and brought them all into headquarters, horses, men, arms and baggage' (ibid.). Otway then led the regiment in the absence of its commanding officer in successful skirmishes at Sahagun. When it faced a superior enemy force at Benevente on 27 December the regiment held off six squadrons of the imperial guard for almost an hour, after which Otway's outlying picket captured a general and 150 prisoners.

The 18th light dragoons reached Corunna on 16 January 1809 and the regiment was back in England by 8 February, where it stayed for four years. However, Otway returned to the Peninsula to command a cavalry brigade in Marshal William Carr Beresford's Portuguese army, and fought at Busaco on 27 September 1810. When Beresford advanced on Badajoz, at Campo Mayor on 25 March 1811 Otway captured over 500 men and sixteen guns, but vigorous enemy counter-attacks restricted him to sixteen prisoners and one tumbril. During the subsequent withdrawal towards Lisbon his cavalry protected Beresford's left flank at Albuera on 16 May 1811, a day after formally going on English half pay. His proposal to raise a unit of lancers from non-French prisoners of war was rejected by the Horse Guards in London during September 1812. Otway remained in the Peninsula until 1814, almost certainly training Portuguese recruits. He advanced to colonel in the British army on 4 June 1813, was knighted by the prince regent on 15 January 1815, appointed CB on 4 June 1815, and, in 1822, made a knight of the order of Charles III of Spain. He had married Frances, only daughter of Sir

Charles Blicke of Caroon Park, Surrey; they had a son and a daughter.

Otway received the military general service medal with three clasps for Sahagun and Benevente, Busaco, and Albuera. He was promoted major-general on 12 August 1819 and lieutenant-general on 10 January 1837, and was colonel of the 84th foot from 30 December 1840 until his death. He was promoted general on 11 November 1851. Otway died at his residence, 13 Grosvenor Square, London, on 7 June 1854, and was buried in Highgate cemetery. His son, Loftus Charles (1815–1861), diplomat, was minister-plenipotentiary to Mexico (1858–9) and consul-general at Milan (1860–1). JOHN SWEETMAN

Sources *Army List* • Burke, *Peerage* • H. Malet, *The historical memoirs of the XVIIIth hussars* (1907) • R. L. Pomeroy, ed., *The story of a regiment of horse, being the regimental history from 1685 to 1922 of the 5th Princess Charlotte of Wales' Dragoon guards*, 1 (1924) • C. W. C. Oman, *A history of the Peninsular War*, 1, 3, 4 (1902–11) • *The Times* (9 June 1854) • Burke, *Gen. GB* (1858) • Boase, *Mod. Eng. biog.* • Foster, *Alum. Oxon.*
Archives NAM, letters and papers | U. Southampton L., letters to Lord Palmerston

Otway, Sir Robert Waller, first baronet (1770–1846), naval officer, the second son of Cooke Otway of Castle Otway, co. Tipperary, and Elizabeth, daughter of Samuel Waller of Lisbrian, co. Tipperary, was born in Ireland on 26 April 1770. His father intended him for an army career, but he entered the navy as a midshipman in April 1784 on the *Elizabeth*, guardship at Portsmouth, with Captain Robert Kingsmill. Between 1785 and 1789 he served twice in the Mediterranean, in the *Phaeton* and then the *Trusty*, before going in the *Blonde* to the West Indies, where, and off the coast of Africa, he remained in different ships until promoted into the brig *Falcon* as lieutenant on 8 August 1793. In December he was appointed to the *Impregnable* (98 guns), bearing the flag of Rear-Admiral Benjamin Caldwell. When the *Impregnable's* fore-topsail-yard was badly damaged in the battle of 1 June 1794, Otway, accompanied by a midshipman, went aloft and secured it so that the ship remained under control, for which Caldwell publicly thanked him. Caldwell took Otway as his first lieutenant in the *Majestic* when appointed commander-in-chief in the West Indies, and in the following January he promoted him to the command of the sloop *Thorn* (confirmed by the Admiralty 7 August 1795).

In April Otway captured *La Belle Créole*, a large schooner sent from Guadeloupe by Victor Hugues (who had been sent to capture Guadeloupe by the French Jacobin government). The schooner was sent to burn St Pierre, Martinique, whose royalist inhabitants gratefully presented Otway with a gold-hilted sword valued at 200 guineas. In May the *Thorn* (16 guns, 80 men) captured the sloop *Courrier National* (18 guns, 119 men) after a thirty-five minute action in which Otway and five of his crew were wounded (James, 1.321). He afterwards rendered important assistance against the insurgents in St Vincent and Grenada, and on 30 October 1795 was posted by Sir John Laforey, the new commander-in-chief, to the frigate *Mermaid*. In her, and afterwards in the *Ceres* and the *Trent*, he had an exceptionally adventurous and successful career. He played an important part in the capture of Grenada in 1796. In July 1799 he narrowly escaped capture in a daring raid into La Guayra, on the coast of Venezuela, in pursuit of the frigate *Hermione*. In his six years in the West Indies he was said to have captured or destroyed 200 enemy privateers or merchantmen. The *Trent*, in 1799 and 1800, 'is supposed to have made as many captures as ever fell to the lot of one vessel in the same space of time' (Brenton, 2.448). He earned his success, which made him rich, by intelligent ship management. Admiral Sir Thomas Ussher, a lieutenant on the *Trent*, declared that no captain was more attentive to the comfort of his officers and men and that there was so much method in his manner of carrying on the service that, though in a constant state of activity, they had as much leisure as any other ship's company. Without unnecessary display of polished bolts or nail heads, the *Trent* was the most perfect man-of-war on the station, ready to go into action in five minutes. Every rope and spar was kept in place and the decks clear. Otway inspected each gun after exercise and ensured it was ready and clear of encumbrance. Ussher added that Otway always accompanied his boats on dangerous raids but hid this in his reports where he gave the credit to his officers.

In November 1800 the *Trent* returned to England with the flag of Sir Hyde Parker, who took Otway as his flag captain in the *Royal George*, and, in February 1801, in the *London*, when Parker took command of the fleet sent to break the armed neutrality of the Baltic powers. It is said, apparently on Otway's authority, that it was at his suggestion that the fleet advanced against Copenhagen through the Sound (between Zealand and Sweden) instead of by the Great Belt (between Zealand and Fünen). During the battle which followed, when the commander-in-chief determined to hoist the celebrated signal to 'discontinue the action', Otway, opposing the signal, obtained permission to go to Admiral Nelson to ascertain his situation. He was sent home with dispatches, and, returning in August, was appointed to the *Edgar*, serving in the Baltic, the channel, and the West Indies, returning in July 1802. In late 1801 he married Clementina Holloway (*d.* 20 Oct 1851), eldest daughter and coheir of Admiral John Holloway: they had five sons and six daughters. His two eldest sons, both commanders in the navy, predeceased him.

Ill health and a severe domestic calamity prevented Otway from joining the *Culloden* at the resumption of hostilities in 1803, but during 1804–5 he commanded the *Montagu*, under Charles Cornwallis, off Brest, engaging the *Alexandre* in the dash at the French fleet on 22 August 1805. In the spring of 1806 he was part of Sir Richard Strachan's command in pursuit of the French squadron under Willaumez. In 1807 he was sent to the Mediterranean, where he served on the coast of Calabria, and in 1808 on the coast of Catalonia in co-operation with the Spanish patriots. After bringing the *Malta* to England, he returned in May 1809, commanding the *Ajax*, and then the *Cumberland*, in the blockade of Toulon and the French coast. In December 1811 his health failed and he was compelled to invalid. In May 1813 he returned to the *Ajax*, in the channel and the Bay of Biscay. In autumn he co-operated with the army in the siege of San Sebastian, and early in 1814 he convoyed a fleet of transports to Quebec, afterwards assisting in equipping the flotilla on Lake Champlain.

On 4 June 1814 Otway was promoted rear-admiral, and from 1818 to 1821 was commander-in-chief at Leith, Scotland. On 8 June 1826 he was made a KCB and appointed commander-in-chief in South America, where his watchfulness and tact at a time of political turmoil led the Brazilian government to award him its order of the Southern Cross. He returned to England in 1829. On 22 July 1830 he was promoted vice-admiral and on 15 September 1831 was created baronet. Groom of the bedchamber to both William IV and Victoria, he was promoted admiral on 23 November 1841 and was made a GCB on 8 May 1845. He died suddenly on 12 May 1846; his third son, George Graham Otway, succeeded him as second baronet, and his fourth son, Sir Arthur John Otway, as third baronet.

Ralfe's comment that '[Otway] is one of the fortunate few who have no enemies, no detractors, none who will admit a hint or insinuation to his disparagement' was backed by successive commanders. 'There is not an officer in his Majesty's navy of greater zeal and promise', wrote St Vincent, recalling particularly how well Otway preserved the *Montagu's* masts and spars in the Bay of Biscay in 1806, and Cornwallis declared that 'there is no officer whose services I should have preferred either as a captain or as admiral' (Ralfe, 4.19–20, 24).

J. K. LAUGHTON, *rev.* MICHAEL DUFFY

Sources J. Ralfe, *The naval biography of Great Britain*, 4 (1828), 1–24 • J. Foster, *The peerage, baronetage, and knightage of the British empire for 1882*, 2 [1882], 476 • J. Marshall, *Royal naval biography*, 1/2 (1823), 691–701 • O'Byrne, *Naval biog. dict.*, [2nd edn] • *Historical memoir of Sir Robert Waller Otway, bt, KCB, vice-admiral of the red* (privately printed, 1840) • W. James, *The naval history of Great Britain, from the declaration of war by France, in February 1793, to the accession of George IV in January 1820*, 5 vols. (1822–4) • E. P. Brenton, *The naval history of Great Britain, from the year 1783 to 1836*, 2 vols. (1837) • D. Syrett and R. L. DiNardo, *The commissioned sea officers of the Royal Navy, 1660–1815*, rev. edn, Occasional Publications of the Navy RS, 1 (1994)

Archives NMM | BL, corresp. with Sir R. Gordon, Add. MS 43214

Likenesses oils, 1843–6, NMM • J. W. Cook, engraving (after miniature), repro. in Ralfe, *Naval biography*, vol. 4, facing p. 1 • M. Gauci, lithograph (after M. Masquerier), BM, NPG

Otway, Thomas (1616–1693), Church of Ireland bishop of Ossory, was born at Alderbury, Wiltshire, on 1 November 1616, the son of George Otway, Church of England clergyman. He was educated at Winchester College, and was admitted a sizar of Christ's College, Cambridge, his father's old college, on 13 June 1632, 'aged 15'. He graduated BA in 1636 and MA in 1639, afterwards taking the degree of DD at Trinity College, Dublin. He subsequently became chaplain to Sir Ralph Hopton, and an active civil war royalist. He was taken prisoner during the war and banished to the West Indies, where he remained until the Restoration. On his return to England, he was at once marked out for preferment. He was rector of St Botolph, Billingsgate (June 1663–June 1664), and of Etchingham, Sussex (June 1664–1670). He never married.

In 1670 Otway became chaplain to John, first Baron Berkeley of Stratton, who took Otway with him to Ireland when he was made lord lieutenant. Lord Berkeley procured Otway's promotion to the see of Killala by patent dated 16 November in the same year. He was consecrated in Christ Church, Dublin, on 29 January 1671. As bishop of Killala he encountered opposition from Presbyterians and tories. He was translated to the see of Ossory by patent dated 7 February 1680, in spite of the objections raised against him on the grounds that he had executed a tory in his own house without legal warrant. He received *in commendam* the archdeaconry of Armagh and a rectory attached to it. In February 1686 the earl of Clarendon advocated his promotion to the see of Cashel, but his advice was not acted upon; no Church of Ireland episcopal vacancies were filled during James II's reign.

In May 1689 Otway sat in James II's Irish parliament, one of four Church of Ireland bishops in the House of Lords. After the battle of the Boyne, William ordered his suspension (21 July 1690) for his refusal to pray for the new monarchy. Otway, however, succeeded in laying the blame on the dean and chapter, and the suspension was never enforced; but shortly afterwards he declared that he had seen no sufficient justification for the late revolution, that James II was still lawful king, and no power of pope or people could dethrone him, and, recalling the persecutions he had suffered under Cromwell, professed his readiness, in spite of his advanced age, to undergo the same again. However, by November 1690 he could tell Bishop Anthony Dopping of Meath that he had resolved 'on a cheerful obedience to the present powers' (McGuire, 148). In October 1692 he sat in William's House of Lords, and was still in possession of his see when he died on 6 March 1693. He was buried in his cathedral church of St Canice, Kilkenny, near the west door, and over his grave was erected a marble stone with an inscription to his memory.

By his will, dated 8 December 1692, besides his legacy to Christ's College, Cambridge, and numerous other benefactions, Otway bequeathed £200 to Trinity College, Dublin, and a like sum to build a library in the churchyard of St Canice, Kilkenny, of which his own books were to form the nucleus. The library was incorporated during Anne's reign.

A. F. POLLARD, *rev.* JAMES MCGUIRE

Sources *The whole works of Sir James Ware concerning Ireland*, ed. and trans. W. Harris, 1 (1739), 430–31 • H. Cotton, *Fasti ecclesiae Hibernicae*, 2 (1848), 282; 4 (1850), 70 • J. B. Leslie, *Ossory clergy and parishes* (1933), 22–3 • R. Mant, *History of the Church of Ireland*, 2 (1840), v–vii • J. McGuire, 'The Church of Ireland and the "Glorious Revolution" of 1688', *Studies in Irish history presented to R. Dudley Edwards*, ed. A. Cosgrove and D. McCartney (1979), 137–49 • C. E. Pike, ed., *Selections from the correspondence of Arthur Capel, earl of Essex, 1675–1677*, CS, 3rd ser., 24 (1913), 92, 94, 97–9, 106, 113 • *CSP dom.*, 1686–7 • *Sixth report*, HMC, 5 (1877–8), esp. 725, 745, 759 [Marquess of Ormonde] • *Calendar of the manuscripts of the marquess of Ormonde*, new ser., 8 vols., HMC, 36 (1902–20), vol. 5 • *The manuscripts of the marquis of Ormonde, the earl of Fingall, the corporations of Waterford, Galway*, HMC, 14 (1885), 228 • *Second report*, HMC, 1/2 (1871); repr. (1874), appx, p. 227 [O'Conor Don MSS] • BL, Add. MS 28948, fol. 118 • *Memoirs of Ireland from the restoration …* (1716), 125, 225 • N. Luttrell, *A brief historical relation of state affairs from September 1678 to April 1714*, 3 (1857), 58 • *The correspondence of Henry Hyde, earl of Clarendon, and of his brother Laurence Hyde, earl of Rochester*, ed. S. W. Singer, 2 vols. (1828), vol. 1, pp. 252, 253, 257; vol. 2, pp. 48–50 • J. P.

Prendergast, *Ireland from the restoration to the revolution, 1660 to 1690* (1887), 83, 84, 138 • R. Lascelles, ed., *Liber munerum publicorum Hiberniae … or, The establishments of Ireland*, 2 vols. [1824–30] • J. Graves and J. G. A. Prim, *History, architecture, and antiquities of the cathedral church of St Canice, Kilkenny* (1857), 52, 315 • J. O'Phelan, *Epitaphs on the tombs in the cathedral church of St Canice* (1813), 45 • T. W. Moody and others, eds., *A new history of Ireland*, 9: *Maps, genealogies, lists* (1984), 429, 437

Archives NA Ire., copy of visitation of Ossory, M 2830 • NL Ire., account of the see of Ossory, MS 10203 [transcript] | Dublin City Library, Gilbert Collection, letters relating to Otway family, MS 224

Wealth at death approx. £1300—bequests in will: Leslie, ed., *Ossory clergy and parishes*, 22

Otway, Thomas (1652–1685), playwright and poet, was born on 3 March 1652 at Milland, Sussex, the only son of Humphrey Otway (1611–1671), curate of St George's, Trotton, and rector of nearby All Hallows, Woolbeding. Otway's mother may have been Elizabeth Otway, widow of Humphrey, who died in 1703 and named her daughter Susanna as her legatee. However, as Otway refers to both his parents in the past tense, and to himself as an 'onely' child in his semi-autobiographical poem *The Poet's Complaint of his Muse* (1680) it is possible that he was the son of a previous wife. If so, no records have yet been found of her existence.

In the *Poet's Complaint* Otway states that his parents gave him a 'generous Education, high'. Whatever other schools or tutors this may refer to, Otway spent a year at Winchester College in 1668 which coincided with the longer residence there of Anthony Cary, fifth Viscount Falkland (1656–1694). Whether or not Otway developed a close friendship with the aristocrat four years his junior during his brief passage though Winchester, he certainly did his best to cultivate the acquaintance later. His play *Caius Marius* (1679) is dedicated to Falkland and alludes to 'having had the honour to be near You, and bred under the same Discipline with You' (*Works*, 1.435). Falkland provided the prologue to Otway's play *The Souldiers Fortune* (1681), but there are no other signs of Falkland's patronage or friendship.

On leaving Winchester Otway was admitted as a commoner of Christ Church, Oxford, on 12 May 1669 (*Works*, 1.8). In *The Poet's Complaint* Otway states that he was a happy and talented student but that the idyllic period was terminated by the news of his 'good *Senander*'s' death. The term Senander is a Latin–Greek coinage for old man, and the lines must refer to the death of his father who was buried at Woolbeding on 9 February 1671 (ibid., 1.4). Without his father's financial support, Otway was unable to remain at Oxford and he left without a degree in 1671.

London and the theatre According to John Downes, bookkeeper for the Duke's Playhouse, Aphra Behn gave Otway the part of the king in her play *The Forc'd Marriage, or, The Jealous Bridegroom*. However, 'the full House put him to such a Sweat and Tremendous Agony' that he was 'dash't and spoiled as an actor' (Downes, 34). Since the first performance of *The Forc'd Marriage* was in December 1670, when presumably Otway was still at Oxford, he must have

Thomas Otway (1652–1685), by John Riley, *c.*1680–85

appeared in a revival. Downes's anecdote notwithstanding, there are references to Otway appearing on stage by Anthony Wood and Charles Gildon, as well as in the satire *A Session of the Poets*, about 1677 (Wood, *Ath. Oxon.*, 2.781; Gildon, 107). Probably Otway maintained himself as an actor during the early 1670s, learning in a very practical way the craft of writing plays. In 1675 his first play, *Alcibiades*, was performed by the Duke's Company at the Dorset Garden playhouse, probably in late September (and published that year).

Alcibiades, dedicated to Charles Sackville, earl of Middlesex, is a very competent work, following the fashion for rhymed plays and providing opportunities for the spectacular stage effects for which the Dorset Garden playhouse was particularly well equipped. The plot is loosely based on Plutarch's life of Alcibiades, and charts Alcibiades's banishment from Athens and alliance with Sparta, where he becomes the object of the lustful infatuation of the Spartan queen, Deidamia. Otway points out in the preface to his next play that Alcibiades 'was none of that squeamish Gentleman I make him' and would not have 'boggl'd' at an affair (*Works*, 1.173). His Alcibiades, however, is a model if weak hero. The play contains such standard Restoration tragic materials as attempted rape, regicide, murder, and suicide, and concludes in a general bloodbath. It was brilliantly cast with Thomas Betterton as Alcibiades; Mary Lee, who had played the fierce and lustful Empress of Morocco in Elkanah Settle's 1673 play of that name, took the role of Queen of Sparta. Elizabeth Barry, who was to create many of Otway's subsequent heroines, played the minor role of Draxilla. *Alcibiades* is a strong first play, and introduces many of the themes, character types, and plot structures that dominate Otway's writing: loss of place and coherence; male friendship; tyrannical and unnatural fathers; orphans; vacillating heroes; and open-ended conclusions. All Otway's plays were written for and first performed by the Duke's Company, and organized around the strengths of that company.

Otway's next play, *Don Carlos, Prince of Spain*, opened the following year on 9 June (and was published the same year). The play was dedicated to the duke of York, and the preface acknowledges the poet's 'unspeakable Obligations' to John Wilmot, earl of Rochester, who made it 'his business to establish it in the good opinion of the *King*, and his *Royal Highness*' (*Works*, 1.174). Briefly, at least, Otway was enjoying noble patronage and royal favour. The play contains echoes of John Dryden's *Tyrannick Love* (1669) and *Aureng-Zebe* (1675) as well as of Shakespeare's *Othello* and *Hamlet*. The main source, however, was the historical novella *Don Carlos* by César Vischard, l'abbé de St Réal, which had been published in France in 1672 and 'englished' by 'H. I.' in 1674. Otway condensed the action from many months to about twenty-four hours to create an intense tragedy of sexual rivalry between father and son, both of whom love the king's new wife, who was formerly engaged to the son. In the king's illegitimate brother, Don John of Austria, Otway created a cheerful libertine whose carefree sexuality provides a counterpoint to the frustrated sexual and political desires experienced by the triangle of father, son, and wife. Fashionably libertine and sexually charged, *Don Carlos* was a great success. John Downes noted that 'all Parts being admirably Acted, it lasted successively ten days; it got more Money than any preceding Modern Tragedy' (Downes, 36). The roles of King Philip, Don Carlos, and Elizabeth, were taken by Betterton, William Smith, and Mary Lee respectively. Elizabeth Barry did not appear in *Don Carlos*, but took leading roles in Otway's next productions, *Titus and Berenice* and *The Cheats of Scapin*, a short tragedy and comic companion piece performed together probably in December 1676.

This two-play form of entertainment was an innovation, and one that anticipated the eighteenth-century custom of accompanying a tragic work with a comic 'afterpiece'. Both plays had contemporary French sources: *Titus and Berenice* is a pared down version of Racine's *Bérénice* and *Cheats* is based on Molière's *Les fourberies de Scapin*. When printed in 1677 the plays were dedicated to Rochester. Clearly working very rapidly to build on the success of *Don Carlos*, Otway also trumped two playwrights from the rival King's Company. John Crowne was working on a ten-act version of *Bérénice*, and Edward Ravenscroft was writing a *commedia dell'arte* form of *Les fourberies*, works which were performed in 1677.

As with *Don Carlos*, *Titus and Berenice* dramatizes the parting of true lovers. Titus had just become emperor of Rome and by law and custom is debarred from marrying a foreign monarch—Berenice, queen of Palestine. Titus must decide between his conflicting desires for rule and glory and love and happiness:

> Should I to follow Love, from Glory fly,
> Forsake my Throne, in every Vassel's eye,
> How mean and despicable must I prove.
> (II. 110–12; *Works*, 1.273)

Unlike Racine's more resolved hero, Titus's eventual decision to repudiate Berenice is not treated as the triumph of duty over desire but rather as a sacrifice that distorts Titus's character. Alone and unhappy, he decides to 'make the world's as wretched as I am' (III. 479). Betterton and Barry took the leading roles and Barry appeared again in *Cheats* as Lucia, one of a quartet of lovers who have married without their fathers' permission. Above all, *Cheats* provided a vehicle for the Duke's Company's great comedian Anthony Leigh in the role of the contriving servant and scamp Scapin who undertakes a variety of disguises and plays a range of tricks in order to aid the lovers and cheat their greedy fathers. *Titus and Berenice* was Otway's last verse tragedy, and *Cheats* his last good-natured comedy. Serious drama was moving away from the courtly heroic verse toward blank verse and prose dramas that were bloodthirsty and less than chivalric. In comedy the trend of the 1670s was for harsh and witty sex dramas, with each dramatist vying to produce more shocking on-stage effects. These trends suited Otway's themes and preoccupations and he was to produce his finest dramas in the next eight years. There may also have been personal reasons for the increasingly savage and cynical nature of his dramatic output.

Affronts, duels, love, and war With a good début in 1675 and three plays staged successfully in 1676, Otway was at the start of an outstanding career. Nevertheless, he had no plays performed in 1677 although he was probably working that year on his savage comedy *Friendship in Fashion*, performed in April 1678. His disillusionment with the theatre is shown in the prologue as he advises parents to 'breed' their sons to 'wholesome Law, or give èm Trades' since poets

> by Critiques are worse treated here,
> Than on the Bank-side Butchers do a Bear.
> (ll. 20, 25–26; *Works*, 1.335)

The prologue also alludes to efforts that have been made to 'wrong him with his Friends', perhaps the earl of Middlesex and Dorset to whom the printed work is dedicated in an epistle which expresses concern lest something in the play has offended him. Otway, a staunch tory, was satirized in the anonymous *A Session of the Poets* (1680), which he believed to have been by Elkanah Settle (a whig). Pamphlets published in 1682 and 1683 describe Otway as challenging Settle to a duel and Thomas Shadwell's satire *The Tory-Poets* (1682) mocks allegations that 'S—le's a Coward, 'cause fool Ot—y fought him'. That Otway deeply resented the attack on him in *A Session* is clear, since he refers angrily to the satire in *The Poet's Complaint* (stanza 8). Personal satire was commonplace among Restoration writers, and unfortunately Otway seems to have been both thin-skinned and bellicose. These traits may have encouraged his attempt to change his career and join the army.

There is also a tradition that Otway was in love with

Elizabeth Barry, who gave birth to a daughter by Rochester in December 1677, and that he enlisted because of a broken heart. The evidence for a relationship between Otway and Barry is based on a series of love letters, alternately amorous, plangent, and angry, attributed to him in *Familiar letters: written by the … earl of Rochester, and several other persons of honour and quality*, first published in 1697. The validity of the letters is dubious: like many of the 'histories' of the time, familiar letters were a semi-fictional form of literature, and their editors, in this case the unscrupulous Thomas Brown, did not always correctly attribute or transcribe such materials. The letters, first published twelve years after Otway's early death in 1685, bear no superscription and are not given out as addressed to Barry until 1713, a year after her demise. William Oldys's manuscript notes in 1727 to Gerard Langbaine's *An Account of the English Dramatic Poets* (1691) refer to Elizabeth Barry's scorn for Otway's love. But there were no references to an amorous relationship during the lifetime of either the poet or the actress, which, given the frankness with which Elizabeth Barry's life and the lives of other actresses were treated, suggests there is little foundation for this particular romantic accretion—though a strong and productive professional relationship did clearly exist.

Whatever the reason, in February 1678 Otway obtained a commission as ensign in a foot regiment raised by the duke of Monmouth as part of Charles II's brief attempt to intervene in the hostilities between France and the Netherlands. The regiment was sent to Flanders in July, and in November 1678 Otway had obtained a lieutenancy (*Works*, 1.23). By early 1679 the forces were withdrawn and the troops disbanded. Otway refers wryly to his soldiering in the epilogue to *Caius Marius*: 'needs the Fool would be a Man at Arms' (l. 10). Although never more than a lieutenant, Otway seems subsequently to have promoted himself, and continued martial pursuits. A duel is described in a letter of June 1679 from John Verney to Sir Ralph Verney, this time with a more considerable opponent, John Churchill, later duke of Marlborough. Verney reports that 'Churchill, for beating an orange wench in the Duke's playhouse, was challenged by Capt. Otway (the poet), and both were wounded, but Churchill most' (ibid., 1.25).

Back to the stage In the prologue to *Friendship in Fashion* (which probably opened in April 1678, and was published that year), Otway untruthfully assures the 'Ladies' that the play has no 'Bawdy in't' (l. 7). In fact, the ironically titled play is a cruel and witty comedy, depicting betrayals in friendship and love as a set of remarkably unpleasant characters meet to cuckold, ridicule, and betray each other. The language of commerce dominates the sexual transactions and an insistent and degrading animal imagery is used to describe the characters. The play does not seem to have been particularly successful, but remains one of the most intelligent, if cynical and cold, plays of the period.

Otway's next play, *The History and Fall of Caius Marius*, performed in the autumn of 1679 (published 1680), is a political tragedy responding to a period of tense political and religious crisis brought about by Titus Oates's allegations of a popish plot to murder the king and impose Roman Catholicism on England. Otway freely adapted Plutarch's description of the life of Caius Marius and combined it with elements of Shakespeare's *Romeo and Juliet* to dramatize the contest for the war consulship of Rome between Metellus and Caius Marius. Caius Marius jun., son of Caius Marius, and Lavinia, daughter of Metellus, enact the Romeo and Juliet roles with variations that include Lavinia awakening before her husband's death, allowing the two lovers to commiserate briefly. Meanwhile, much of the play displays the corrupt electioneering efforts carried out by the two factions, and their confrontations, which lead to exile and violence. Caius Marius, ambitious and unscrupulous, who courts the 'plebs' may well be a portrait of the earl of Shaftesbury, leader of the whig faction. However, Metellus, leader of the patricians, is little better. Anti-whig though the play may be, neither faction displays any signs of political morality or responsibility. In Metellus and Caius Marius, Otway created two violent and cruel fathers who destroy their biological and political families. *Caius Marius* held the stage into the eighteenth century and performances of *Romeo and Juliet* often incorporated the revival of Juliet in the family vault.

Otway's *annus mirabilis* 1680 was a productive year for Otway and represents a high point in his career. *The Poet's Complaint of his Muse* was published and two new plays were performed, *The Orphan* in the spring, and *The Souldiers Fortune* in the summer. Otway seems to have gained the patronage of Nell Gwyn. The anonymous satire *An Essay of Scandall* (date not known) describes him as tutor to her son Charles Beauclerk and hopes, unkindly, that Otway will make him

> (if that's possible to be)
> A viler Poet, and more dull then he.
> (Harley MSS 6913, 6914, 7319)

Other evidence of a connection between Otway and Gwyn is his signature as witness to a power of attorney granted by Nell Gwyn to one James Frazier to receive her pension, dated 1 June 1680 (*Works*, 1.33). In the autumn of that year Otway received an MA degree from Cambridge. The reasons for this conferral are unclear. J. C. Ghosh speculates that he may have falsified his status at Oxford (ibid., 1.26). It is also possible that the degree represented an honour granted to a writer whose works satirized whigs and who was increasingly associated with the court and tory politics. Otway's loyalty to the Yorks is indicated by the final stanzas of *The Poet's Complaint*, which describe their exile, and by his dedication of *The Orphan* to the duchess of York.

The Orphan is a domestic tragedy set in a country estate in Bohemia. The play's main source is 'The History of Brandon' in *The English Adventures*, published in 1675 by a 'Person of Honour', probably Roger Boyle, earl of Orrery, and there are also 'borrowings' from Dryden and Nathaniel Lee. Twin brothers and close friends, Castalio and Polydore have fallen in love with the beautiful orphan Monimia who is their father's ward. Their father, Acasto, yet another of Otway's powerful and quixotic patriarchs, has set his face against their marrying. Castalio secretly weds Monimia, but on their wedding night, Polydore, who does not realize they are married, manages to substitute himself for his brother. The truth gradually emerges the following day: Polydore and Monimia are horrified, and kill themselves. Elizabeth Barry achieved lasting fame in the role of Monimia, in which, according to John Downes, 'she forc'd Tears from the Eyes of her Auditory' and gained the 'Name of Famous Mrs. Barry' (Downes, 38). Despite its idyllic setting, *The Orphan* is an anti-pastoral drama in which all the elements of the traditional pastoral, freedom from care, innocence, trust, closeness to nature, and simplicity of lifestyle are evoked, only to be cancelled.

The Souldiers Fortune is a fast-paced cuckolding comedy based on the efforts of two disbanded and poverty-stricken soldiers to find themselves sex and money. Barry played Beaugard's lost love Clarinda, Betterton took the role of the hero Beaugard, and in the pimp Sir Jolly Jumble and the elderly merchant Sir Davy Dunce the company's comic actors Anthony Leigh and James Noakes were given roles brilliantly suited to their abilities to portray lechery and perversity. The play concludes with Beaugard able to blackmail Sir Davy Dunce, who tried to have him murdered, into acquiescing to his liaison with his wife. Otway's position in the world of Restoration theatre without consistent and powerful patronage surely encouraged his cynical outsider's view of society and his characteristic refusal to provide a conventional conclusion.

The Souldiers Fortune, for example, was dedicated not to any great courtier but to his bookseller, Richard Bentley. Bentley, Otway perhaps unwisely remarks, pays 'honestly for the Copy' while 'a Person of higher Rank and Order' knowing he does not deserve the obsequious praise lavished in a dedication 'is very unwilling to part with ready Money for' it (*Works*, 2.91). Otway seems never to have secured consistent patronage. Otway's next play, *Venice Preserv'd* (1682), was dedicated to the duchess of Portsmouth, Charles II's powerful French mistress. However, whether she was pleased with a play featuring a foreign courtesan is open to question—Otway did not dedicate any further works to her. His last play, *The Atheist* (1683), was dedicated to Lord Elande, who died shortly thereafter. A mixture of tactlessness and bad luck marks Otway's relations with the nobility whose support was so essential for those seeking to make their career as writers.

Last works *Venice Preserv'd*, Otway's most famous play, was first staged in February 1682. It is a play about plots, a topical subject, and captures brilliantly a mood of civil discontent, suspicion, and betrayal. The main source is Saint-Réal's pseudo-history *A Conspiracy of the Spaniards Against the State of Venice* published in France in 1674 and translated in 1675. The hero, Jaffeir, has eloped with Belvidera, daughter of the senator Priuli, and as the play opens Priuli refuses to help the poverty-stricken family and curses the couple and their son. Jaffeir is induced to join a conspiracy against the state of Venice by his friend Pierre, an ideologue, a soldier, and a man who has lost his mistress, Aquilina, to the senator Antonio. Jaffeir offers his wife, Belvidera, to the conspirators as a pledge for his fidelity. However, after the conspirator Renault has tried to rape Belvidera, Jaffeir acquiesces to her insistence that they inform the Venetian senate of the conspiracy. In return for the information, the senate agrees to spare the lives of the conspirators but immediately breaks its word, only sparing Jaffeir and condemning the rest to death by torture. As Pierre awaits public execution, at his request Jaffeir stabs him and then stabs himself. Comic and outrageously perverse scenes between Aquilina and Antonio provided a major element in the play's immediate popularity and subsequent notoriety. The characters of Antonio and Renault may have been intended as a composite satiric portrait of the earl of Shaftesbury. Contemporaries certainly regarded the play as a triumphant tory work. There were performances on 21 April and 31 May 1682, each provided with new prologues and epilogues by Dryden and Otway, to celebrate the return of the duke and duchess of York from exile in Scotland. Modern scholars, however, have pointed out that neither the conspirators, nor the senators are admirable, and that neither group obviously represents either whigs or tories.

Despite the success of *Venice Preserv'd*, Otway's own success waned. After 1682, when the two London theatre companies, the King's and Duke's, united, there was less demand for new plays and he was lucky to get another play staged. Otway revived the leading characters of *The Souldiers Fortune* in his last play, *The Atheist, or, The Second Part of the Souldiers Fortune* (probably first acted no later than July 1683, and published 1684). The atheist of the title, Daredevil, is a satiric portrait of a freethinker, who in reality is both religious and deeply superstitious and 'never feels so much as an Ague-fit, but he's afraid of being damn'd' (I. 339–42; *Works*, 2.308). The libertinism that was admired in *Don Carlos* is now depicted as foolish. Irreverent, farcical, and outrageous, *The Atheist* is nevertheless the most socially mature of Otway's comedies.

Final years and death In the thin years that followed the performance of *The Atheist*, Otway contributed verses to friends' works and composed the elegy *Windsor Castle, in a Monument to our Late Sovereign K. Charles II of Ever Blessed Memory* (1685). According to Wood, shortly before his death he was engaged in composing a congratulatory poem on the accession of James II (Wood, *Ath. Oxon.*, 2.782). He was also credited with translating from French *The History of the Triumvirates*, published in 1686, though J. C. Ghosh does not include it in his definitive edition of the collected works. Otway appears to have been working on another play, since an advertisement in *The Observator* on 27 November and 4 December 1686 offers a reward from Betterton and Smith for 'Four Acts of a Play' written by Otway before his death.

Most accounts agree that Otway died in Tower Hill on 14 April 1685, probably in extreme poverty. Theophilus Cibber paints a pathetic picture of Otway choking to death on a roll bought with money he had begged (T. Cibber, *Lives of the Poets of Great Britain*, 2 vols., 1753, 2.334). Other accounts have Otway dying after pursuing the murderer of a friend (*Works*, 1.31; Ham, 214–15). John Dennis simply states that Otway died in an 'Alehouse … in

Adversity unpitied, and dy'd unlamented' (J. Dennis, *Remarks upon Mr. Pope's Translation of Homer*, 1717, 5–6). Otway was buried at St Clement Danes on 16 April 1685—aged thirty-three.

Reputation and significance Despite the occasional hostile lampoon, Otway was well thought of by his contemporaries. In *The Play-House*, 'A Satyr Writt in the Year 1685' (1689), for example, Robert Gould asserts that:

> Thy *Orphan* and *Venetian* piece Sublime
> Shall ever stand, and dare the Teeth of *Time*.

Gerard Langbaine described *The Orphan* as 'a very moving tragedy' (G. Langbaine, *An Account of the English Dramatick Poets*, 1691, 398) and in less generous vein the *Tory-Poets* asserted that 'he never writes a Verse but when he's drunk'. By Otway's own account in the *Poet's Complaint*, he was inclined to debauchery and his verse epistle to his friend Richard Duke (1684) extols the joys of 'a generous Bottle, and a Lovesome She' (1.63). According to the tract *Les soupirs de la Grande Britaigne* (1713), Otway died £400 in debt to his vintner. The anonymous 'Satyr upon Poets' (1703) also states that he used to borrow money from 'kind Banker Betterton' (*Poems on Affairs of State*, 1703, 2.142).

The Orphan and *Venice Preserv'd* were regularly performed throughout the eighteenth century and into the nineteenth, providing leading roles for the great actors of those ages. *Caius Marius* was performed into the eighteenth century and *The Cheats of Scapin* was regularly performed as an afterpiece. However, Otway's other comedies were rapidly considered 'loose and prophane' (*A Comparison between the Two Stages*, 1702, 58), and increasingly he was admired above all for *The Orphan* and *Venice Preserv'd*. Oliver Goldsmith famously stated that Otway was 'next to Shakespeare, the greatest genius England has produced in tragedy' (*Bee*, 8, 24 Nov 1759). However, the scenes between Aquilina and Antonio were rapidly excised from productions and publications of *Venice Preserv'd*. In his life of Otway, Samuel Johnson regretted the 'dispicable scenes of vile comedy' in *Venice Preserv'd*, but noted its popularity with the public and remarked that the 'striking passages are in every mouth' (Johnson, *Lives of the English Poets*, 1.444). The basic plot event of *The Orphan*, Monimia's 'rape' by her brother-in-law, came to be regarded as both improbable and indecent, and the play's popularity had waned by the nineteenth century. The comedies largely forgotten, and *Venice Preserv'd* bowdlerized, from the later eighteenth century onwards Otway came to be admired for pathos and tender depictions of friendship and love. By the mid-nineteenth century, however, the sensuality of his plays, even when cut, increasingly rendered them unacceptable for the stage.

Interest in Otway revived in the twentieth century with editions of his works by Montague Summer and J. C. Ghosh and productions of *Venice Preserv'd* and *The Orphan* at the Old Vic. These editions were reprinted in the 1960s and helped to stimulate new approaches to Otway. By this time the savagery, cynicism, and obscenity of Otway's works no longer disqualified them from serious attention and admiration; indeed, his harsh satires on political motives and frank treatment of sexual relations suited modern tastes. Late twentieth-century productions of *Venice Preserv'd*, *The Orphan*, and *The Atheist* have all demonstrated their strength and dramatic viability. Otway is currently regarded as a major Restoration dramatist, with *Venice Preserv'd* generally assessed as the best political tragedy of that period. JESSICA MUNNS

Sources *The works of Thomas Otway: plays, poems, and love-letters*, ed. J. C. Ghosh, 2 vols. (1968) • J. Downes, *Roscius Anglicanus, or, An historical review of the stage* (1708) • Wood, *Ath. Oxon.*, 1st edn, vol. 2 • [C. Gildon], *The lives and characters of the English dramatick poets … first begun by Mr Langbain* [1699] • *An essay of scandall*, [n.d.], BL, Harl. MSS 6913, 6914, 7319 • 'The lover's session', *Poems on affairs of state … by the greatest wits of the age*, 2 (1703), 156–65, esp. 159 • R. G. Ham, *Otway and Lee: biography from a baroque age* (1969) • S. Johnson, *The lives of the English poets*, 3 vols. (1780–81), 441–6 • J. Hagstrum, *Sex and sensibility: ideal and erotic love from Milton to Mozart* (1980) • H. M. Batzer Pollard, *From heroics to sentimentalism: a study of Thomas Otway's tragedies* (1974) • J. Munns, *Restoration politics and drama: the plays of Thomas Otway, 1675–83* (1995) • A. Mackenzie Taylor, *Next to Shakespeare: Otway's Venice preserv'd and The orphan and their history on the London stage* (1950) • J. M. Wallace, 'Otway's *Caius Marius* and the exclusion crisis', *Modern Philology*, 85 (1987–8), 364–6 • K. P. Warner, *Thomas Otway* (1982) • C. W. Holgate, ed., *Winchester long rolls, 1653–1721* (1899) • J. M. Armistead, *Four Restoration playwrights: a reference guide to Thomas Shadwell, Aphra Behn, Nathaniel Lee, and Thomas Otway* (1984), 261–387 • J. D. Canfield, 'Thomas Otway', *Restoration and eighteenth-century dramatists: first series*, ed. P. R. Backscheider, DLitB, 80 (1989), 146–71

Likenesses J. Riley, portrait, *c.*1680–1685, U. Lond. [*see illus.*] • W. Blake, tempera, *c.*1800, Man. City Gall. • Du Guernier, line engraving, repro. in *The works of Mr. Thomas Otway*, 2 vols. (1712) • attrib. W. Faithorne junior, engraving (after Soest), repro. in Ham, *Otway and Lee* • school of Hoskins, oils, Buccleuch collection • J. Houbraken, line engraving (after M. Beale), BM, NPG; repro. in T. Birch, *The heads and characters of illustrious persons of Great Britain*, 1 (1743) • attrib. J. Riley, oils, Christ Church Oxf. • Soest, oils, Courtauld Inst. • oils, Winchester College, Hampshire • oils, Winchester College, Hampshire • photograph (after Soest), NPG • photograph (after J. Riley?), NPG • photograph (after W. Blake), NPG • photograph (after school of Hoskins), NPG • portrait, Knole, Kent

Wealth at death died in poverty; probably in debt to his vintner: *Les soupirs de la Grande Britaigne, or, The groans of Great Britain* (1713)

Oudart, Nicholas (*d.* 1681), government official, was born at Malines, Brabant, in the Low Countries and styled himself 'Sieur de Rixtel au Pays de Kempen en Brabant' in later life. He moved to England as 'a little page' in the household of Sir Henry Wotton, who subsequently sponsored his education. Created MA at Oxford on 13 August 1636 and incorporated MA at Cambridge in 1639, Oudart studied medicine. He was licensed to practise medicine from St Catharine's College, Cambridge, in 1639, and took the degree of MB at Oxford on 31 January 1643. By September 1640 he was serving as secretary to Sir William Boswell, the English ambassador at The Hague, and two years later was in the employ of Sir Edward Nicholas, then acting secretary of state. He continued to serve Nicholas after the secretary left England for France in 1646, writing newsletters in invisible lemon-juice ink.

Oudart was first recorded as a member of Charles I's entourage in August 1647, although he had probably been with the king as a writing clerk before this, and compounded with parliament for a fine of £22. He remained with the confined king, handling correspondence, including a letter from Charles in early 1648 urging his son, the duke of York, to attempt escape which so incensed the House of Lords as to produce speculation that Oudart might have been executed had he not fled to the Netherlands. He took notes of the treaty negotiations in the Isle of Wight. Charles I may, however, have lost trust in him and Nicholas seems to have believed he was involved in betraying the king's escape plans.

By June 1649 Oudart was secretary to Charles I's daughter, Mary of Orange, the princess royal, in the Netherlands, and his services were lent to her brother, Charles II, whom Oudart accompanied to Scotland in 1650. Moving between the Orange court and the royalist exiles around Henrietta Maria, he earned the animosity of Sir Edward Hyde and of Nicholas, who was suspicious of his involvement with Nicholas's rival, Robert Long. In 1655 Oudart married 'a handsome gentlewoman', Eva Tortarolis, daughter of John Tortarolis of Leiden, who was rumoured to have a portion of £10,000. The marriage produced three daughters: Barbara, who married William Foster; Amelia Isabella, married to Bartholomew van Sittert; and Dorothy, who was unmarried at the time of her father's death. A member of the princess of Orange's council, Oudart remained in her employ until her death in 1661, was named an executor of her estate, and served her son William as Latin secretary and a member of his council. He was characterized by a contemporary as one who 'gettes his desires' through 'obsequious eye service' rather than 'sufficiency or integrity' (*Nicholas Papers*, 3.100), although the princess considered him honest and loyal.

Oudart sought rewards at the Restoration, but was granted only a reversion to a signet clerkship and admitted gentleman of the privy chamber on 18 November 1662. From at least January 1663 he was connected with the wine licence office, but lost money there. For years he shuttled to the Netherlands, settling the estate of the princess of Orange, undertaking minor diplomatic duties, and keeping an eye on his wife's property. In the summer of 1665 he was arrested there in retaliation for the English imprisonment of a member of the Dutch embassy in London and although an exchange was made in January 1666 he later claimed to have been racked and kept in prison after his counterpart's release. A warrant authorizing £500 compensation was issued in February 1666 but the incident marked the end of Oudart's position with William of Orange and led to the loss of his wife's Dutch estates. He was granted a patent as secretary for the Latin tongue on 19 July 1666, with a salary of £80. From 1667 he was a fellow of the Royal Society and an acquaintance of Samuel Pepys and of John Evelyn, who petitioned for the office of Latin secretary in 1670 when he heard Oudart was 'irrecoverably sick' (PRO, SP 29/273/106).

In 1675 Oudart petitioned Charles II for the lease of a crown estate on the grounds that he had served the crown since his youth, 'being a great sufferer, and being now with his family reduced to very great straits' (*CSP dom.*, 1675–6, 468). The following year he was once again in the Netherlands trying to regain estates there and in 1678 unsuccessfully petitioned to assume his reversion to a signet clerkship. In 1680 he requested permission to sell the office of Latin secretary, being too infirm to carry out its duties and badly needing money. He died in Little Dean's Yard, Westminster, and was buried in the west cloister of Westminster Abbey on 21 December 1681. His will, dated 5 March 1672, was proved on 13 July 1682 by his widow, Eva. She subsequently petitioned the crown for payment of moneys owed him, she and her family having gone to live off the charity of friends and relatives in the Netherlands. A manuscript copy of 'Eikon basilike', said to be in Oudart's hand, was used for Royston's printed edition, while a number of Oudart's papers came into the possession of the antiquary Francis Peck who printed some of them in his *Desiderata curiosa*.

W. W. WROTH, *rev.* S. A. BARON

Sources *The life and letters of Sir Henry Wotton*, ed. L. P. Smith, 2 vols. (1907) • *The Nicholas papers*, ed. G. F. Warner, 4 vols., CS, new ser., 40, 50, 57, 3rd ser., 31 (1886–1920) • *CSP dom.*, 1635–7, 108; *1640–41*, 93; *1642–3*, 444; *1648–9*, 38; *1655*, 358; *1660–61*, 365; *1661–2*, 84, 312; *1663–4*, 23, 580; *1665–6*, 159, 244, 303, 530; *1666–7*, 359; *1670*, 242; *1673*, 91; *1675–6*; *1676–7*, 130, 136, 182; *1678*, 61, 71, 110; *1680–81*, 85; *1682*, 522 • *Calendar of the Clarendon state papers preserved in the Bodleian Library*, ed. O. Ogle and others, 5 vols. (1869–1970) • F. Peck, ed., *Desiderata curiosa*, 2 vols. (1732–5) • PRO, SP 29 • [J. Hamilton, duke of Hamilton], *The Hamilton papers: being selections from original letters … relating to … 1638–1650*, ed. S. R. Gardiner, CS, new ser., 27 (1880) • Nichols, *Lit. anecdotes* • F. M. G. E. Higham, *The principal secretary of state: a survey of the office from 1558 to 1680* (1923) • W. Bray, ed., *Memoirs of John Evelyn, Esq., F.R.S.*, 5 vols. (1827) • J. L. Chester, ed., *The marriage, baptismal, and burial registers of the collegiate church or abbey of St Peter, Westminster*, Harleian Society, 10 (1876) • M. A. E. Green, ed., *Calendar of the proceedings of the committee for compounding … 1643–1660*, 5 vols., PRO (1889–92) • will, PRO, PROB 11/370, fol. 88

Wealth at death apparently impoverished in later years; widow dependent on support of friends and kin: will, PRO, PROB 11/370, fol. 88

Oudh, nawab wazirs of (*act.* 1754–1814), were Nishapuri Saiyids who ruled the major political system of north India (Oudh, or more correctly Awadh) from 1754 to 1814, during the era of its most robust influence. They were the third to the sixth in a dynasty of eleven that lasted from 1720 to 1856.

A major historical region from classical times until Indian independence in 1947, Oudh occupied a riverine plain defined by the Jumna River to the south-west, the Himalayas on the north, the Gandak River to the east, and Benares to the south-east. By 1775 it had grown to 90,000 square miles, bigger than England, Scotland, and Wales combined, and almost as large as the modern Indian state of Uttar Pradesh; it contained a population of some 21 million. Named for the city of Ayudhya ('Unconquerable') near modern Fyzabad, the land of Lord Rama and the setting for the Sanskrit epic *Ramayana*, this realm inherited much of the fading authority and prestige of Mughal Delhi after 1724. It was targeted by the English East India Company for greater control, until being annexed to the British empire in two stages, in 1801 and 1856, the latter being the immediate cause of the 1857 mutiny.

The nawabs of Oudh were Shiʿi Muslims whose ancestors came from Persia. In the process of consolidating and

Nawab wazirs of Oudh (*act.* 1754–1814), by Tilly Kettle, (1772) [Shuja ud-Daula (right), with his son Asaf ud-Daula]

expanding their political presence in the north, they invited a steady stream of scholars, poets, jurists, architects, and painters from Persia and other Indian cities. Throughout the eighteenth and early nineteenth centuries Oudh thus joined other regional political systems of India such as Hyderabad, Bengal, Bhopal, Bahawalpur, Arcot, Poona, Sind, and Mysore as fertile arenas for the development of a composite, pragmatic, and secular south Asian culture, the medium for which was increasingly Urdu, which gradually replaced Indo-Persian, the official language of the Mughals.

Shuja ud-Daula (*d.* 1775), nawab of Oudh, was born Mirza Jalal ud-Din Haidar, the son of Mirza Muhammad Muqim (known as Safdar Jang; *d.* 1754) and Sadr un-Nisa Begam (*d.* 1796). Because he was primarily a general—enlarging his realm dramatically, and losing only narrowly to British-led forces at Buxar in 1764—Shuja laid personal claim to neither poetry, philosophy, nor the fine arts, yet he and his courtiers supported a wide range of cultural and scholarly activity at his capital in Fyzabad. Realizing his value as an ally, the victorious East India Company reinstated him in 1765, and for the next half-century a process of mutual testing and political experimentation occurred. Through the subsidiary alliance system, under which he had to pay for the upkeep of British-officered Indian troops, the way was opened for increasing company intervention during subsequent reigns. Shuja none the less modernized his army during this period, closed Oudh to the disruptive and monopolistic effects of European trade, secured the treasury in the custody of his main consort, the Bahu Begam (*d.* 1816), realizing that only there would it be safe from British predation, and made large annexations in Etawah and Rampur, the latter with the hired use of company forces. Governor-General Warren Hastings treated him formally as an equal. He died in 1775 at Rohilkhand from blood poisoning.

Under **Asaf ud-Daula** (*d.* 1797), nawab of Oudh, born Mirza Amani, the son of Shuja and Bahu Begam, the favourite of Shuja's 700 wives and concubines, Oudh changed from a military patronage state to a mostly demilitarized protectorate under the subsidiary alliance. In contrast to his father, Asaf was neither a soldier nor an administrator. Most British dismissed him as extravagant, ineffectual, and effete. To Warren Hastings he was a 'cheerful, good tempered and pliant creature' with an 'excellent but unapplied understanding' (letter to John Macpherson, 6 Feb 1785, BL, Add. MS 29116, fol. 150). During Asaf's reign there was a marked erosion in the autonomy of the realm. By steadily coming to control Oudh's foreign relations, border security, army, and much of its revenues, the British profited immensely, while guaranteeing the survival of the regime against all external and internal enemies, in effect depriving it of all but cultural and internal administrative activity. Whereas this meant that Oudh's military-administrative aristocracy was now largely unemployed, Lucknow, Asaf's new capital, became the major patronage centre in all of north India, a haven for writers and artists fleeing unsettled conditions elsewhere. By 1800 it presented, via an admittedly eclectic set of architectural styles, an admirable array of mosques, palaces, gardens, inns, ceremonial buildings, and gateways. Shiʿi influence grew, the annual mourning of Muharram becoming a lavish sponsored festival for all communities, including non-Muslims, as well as a rite of cultural legitimization for the regime. Asaf died at Lucknow in 1797 from heart failure.

Asaf's proclaimed successor, **Vizir Ali** (*d.* 1817), was an adopted son of the former nawab. In 1780, at the height of pre-annexation British interference, Asaf had solved the problem of an heir (he was impotent, and never consummated his arranged marriage) by adopting Ali from a poor Muslim family and rearing him for the purpose. But he ruled for only four months during 1797 and 1798; his views, nurtured by the secluded but highly influential Begams (dowager widows, mainly of Shuja and his father, Safdar Jang) in Fyzabad, were overtly anti-British. His military preparations to oppose the company were met by Governor-General Sir John Shore, who personally led a military expedition into Oudh, deposed Vizir Ali, and installed Asaf's half-brother, Saadat Ali, in his place. A year later, still bristling at British interference in Oudh and other regional states, Vizir Ali organized a military coalition against them in and near Benares, which, although short-lived, gained the support of Indians from many classes in Benares, Nepal, and eastern Oudh, causing the alarmed British to accelerate the annexationist tendencies already present in their evolving system of indirect rule. Married to Hussaini Begam, Vizir Ali died at Calcutta in 1817 from unknown causes.

Saadat Ali (*d.* 1814), nawab of Oudh, was born Mirza Sa'adat Ali Khan. As Asaf's half-brother, he had hoped to topple Asaf's clearly ineffective rule in 1776, and almost succeeded; but when his plot failed, the British kept him under house arrest in Benares throughout Asaf's entire reign, as a possible successor. Shortly after being installed as nawab, following the fall of Vizir Ali, he came under great pressure from the new governor-general, Lord Wellesley, who suspected the designs of not only the Afghans but also the French, and who, in 'schoolmaster's language', took Saadat's declaration of inability to pay the now vastly increased subsidy as proof of unfitness to rule. Under great coercion from Henry Wellesley, Saadat was forced in 1801 to cede half of his territory, the remaining portion becoming surrounded on three sides by company lands, and on the fourth by the Himalayas. In exchange, the subsidiary alliance system was eliminated; Saadat henceforth retained all revenues from his reduced territory and never again had to rent British-officered troops for protection. He impressed British visitors with his administrative capacity and application. One described him as a 'man of talent and acquirements', which included a fluent and idiomatic mastery of English (R. Heber, *Narrative of a journey through the upper provinces of India*, 3 vols., 1828, 1.395–6). After 1801 the ruler and court of north India's major successor state were exempted from the need for defensive readiness, a situation which prevailed until Saadat's death in Lucknow from poison in 1814. In the protected, isolated situation created under Saadat's reign, Oudh's educated and ruling élites suffered increasing ennui and demoralization. Political and cultural forms arose which sterner British pro-consuls took as effeteness and decadence, justifying annexing the rest in 1856. Oudh's political and military importance had been eclipsed; its more lasting achievements lay in the realms of cultural patronage, social accommodation, literary conservation and renewal, and religious reform.

RICHARD B. BARNETT

Sources M. Alam, *The crisis of empire in Mughal north India: Awadh and the Punjab, 1707–1748* (1986) • R. B. Barnett, *North India between empires: Awadh, the Mughals, and the British, 1720–1801* (1980) • C. A. Bayly, *Indian society and the making of the British empire* (1988), vol. 2/1 of *The new Cambridge history of India*, ed. G. Johnson • A. L. Srivastava, *Shuja-ud-Daulah*, 2 vols. (1945–61) • P. J. Marshall, 'Economic and political expansion: the case of Oudh', *Modern Asian Studies*, 9 (1975), 465–82 • A. Halim Sharar, *Guzishta Lakhnau: Mashriqi Tamaddun ka aakhiri Namuna* (1965); trans. in part as E. S. Harcourt and F. Hussain, trans., *Lucknow: the last phase of an oriental culture* (1975) • G. Ali Khan Naqawi, 'Imad us-Sa'adat', MS, 1808, BL; lithographed, 1864 • S. Tasadduq Hussain, *Begumaat-i Awadh* [n.d.] • H. Singh, 'Nami', 'Tarikh-i Sa'adat'i Jawid', MS, 1806, BL, Or. 1820 • B. Stein, 'A decade of historical efflorescence', *South Asia Research*, 10/2 (1990), 125–38 • H. Goetz, *The crisis of Indian civilization in the 18th and early 19th century* (Calcutta, 1938) • A. Ray, *The rebel nawab of Oudh: revolt of Vizir Ali Khan (1799)* (1990)

Archives BL OIOC, Saadat Ali, *Lata'if us-Sa'adat* [Witticisms of Sa'adat], compiled by Saiyad Insha'allah, 2021
Likenesses T. Kettle, portrait, 1772 (Shuja ud-Daula and Asaf ud-Daula), Musée National du Château de Versailles, France [*see illus.*] • J. Zoffany, group portrait, 1786 (Asaf ud-Daula; *Colonel Mordaunt's cock-fight*), priv. coll. • portrait (Shuja ud-Daula), BL, Oriental Antiquities • portrait (Vizir Ali), Husainabad Imambara, Lucknow; repro. in Ray, *Rebel nawab of Oudh*, jacket • portrait (Saadat Ali), BL, Oriental Antiquities • portraits, Husainabad Imambara, Lucknow
Wealth at death £2,000,000—Shuja ud-Daula: Barnett, *North India between empires*

Oudney, Walter (1790–1824), naval surgeon and traveller in Africa, was born in December 1790 to humble parents, in Edinburgh. With some medical knowledge he became a surgeon's mate on a man-of-war, was appointed assistant surgeon and then surgeon in 1810, and was stationed in the East Indies. When peace was declared he returned on half pay to Edinburgh to join his mother and sisters. He attended classes at the university, graduated MD on 1 August 1817, and set up in private practice.

The course of the Niger was one of the most contentious questions of African geography and, after attempts to solve it by exploration from west Africa had failed, it was proposed that it be approached from Tripoli, where the British consul-general Hanmer Warrington had established cordial relations with the ruling Turkish pasha, Yusuf Karamanlı. After Joseph Ritchie's attempt using the new route in 1818 had ended in disaster, and when his companion George Francis Lyon had refused to make a second attempt, the Foreign Office was looking for suitable replacements. James Robinson Scott, a former lecturer in botany at the University of Edinburgh, recommended Oudney, whom he considered an accomplished surgeon and botanist. Oudney had become a member of the Wernerian Society and had studied chemistry and natural history, hoping to become a lecturer in botany at Edinburgh University, but he expressed himself keen to go to Africa. In 1821 he learnt that he had been appointed leader of the expedition with Hugh Clapperton, a naval officer on half pay, also from Edinburgh, who was appointed assistant at Oudney's request.

Oudney and Clapperton arrived in Tripoli in October 1821, to be joined by Dixon Denham, who had volunteered to join the expedition and had managed to get himself appointed its leader over both Oudney, the original leader, and Clapperton, his senior in service rank. Oudney, who had volunteered for a scientific expedition, found himself appointed permanent vice-consul at Bornu, and was charged with exerting a diplomatic presence to increase British standing; however, he also helped to open up new areas to trade, and to further exploration and the collection of natural historical specimens. The party was acrimonious and divided, though its relations with the hosts and guides were good. On 7 April 1822 it arrived in Murzuq in Fezzan, where it was delayed after finding that no preparations had been made for the expedition; Oudney and Clapperton explored the neighbourhood, and finally in November 1822, with the assurance of a military escort, the group set off southwards across the desert. Denham apparently despised his companions for their humble backgrounds. Oudney found himself required by Denham to investigate unfounded allegations about Clapperton's sexual behaviour. In February they reached Kuka (later Kukawa), the capital of Bornu, on Lake Chad. Here they were detained by the ruler Sheik Muhammad el Kanemi, who was afraid for their safety. Eventually Oudney and Clapperton left for Kano on 14 December 1823. In the extremely cold weather Oudney, who had been in poor health since arriving at Kuka, caught pneumonia; he died at Katagum in the Sudan on 12 January 1824 and was buried there.

Oudney was said to have been of middle height and slightly built, pale and grave. He was enterprising and determined, and was sympathetic to Africans. The account of the expedition was published by Denham in 1826 and, with Oudney dead and Clapperton in Africa, he was able to appropriate to himself most of the credit for the expedition which had very considerably advanced the state of geographical knowledge of the area as well as establishing cordial relations between the local rulers and Britain, and promising new avenues for trade. The Niger question, however, remained unsolved: Oudney's own (erroneous) theory was that it must terminate in the lakes of Nupe (which he called Nyffe). Some of Oudney's mineralogical notes and some geographical information are included in Denham's *Narrative* and some hundreds of his natural history specimens were brought back. None the less his part in the expedition was circumscribed by chronic illness and curtailed by his early death, and he is little remembered. ELIZABETH BAIGENT

Sources D. Denham and H. Clapperton, *Narrative of travels and discoveries in northern and central Africa* (1826) • A. Adu Boahen, *Britain, the Sahara and the western Sudan, 1788–1861* (1964) • E. W. Bovill, *The Niger explored* (1968) • E. W. Bovill, ed., *Missions to the Niger*, 4 vols., Hakluyt Society, 2nd ser., 123, 128–30 (1964–6) • R. Brown, *Observations on the structure and affinities of the more remarkable plants collected…in central Africa* (1826) • *DNB*

Oudoceus. *See* Euddogwy (*supp. fl.* late 6th cent.).

Oughton, Sir Adolphus, **baronet** (**1684/5–1736**). *See under* Oughton, Sir (James) Adolphus Dickenson (*bap.* 1719, *d.* 1780).

Oughton, Sir (**James**) **Adolphus Dickenson** (*bap.* **1719**, *d.* **1780**), army officer and antiquary, was baptized at St Giles-in-the-Fields, London, on 27 October 1719, the illegitimate son of Colonel **Sir Adolphus Oughton**, baronet (1684/5–1736), army officer and politician, and Miss Frances Dickenson (*b.* 1697) of St Giles-in-the-Fields. In his early years he was known as James Adolphus Dickenson. His father was the son of Adolphus Oughton (*d.* 1684) of Fillongley, Warwickshire, and Great Harborough, Leicestershire, and his wife, Mary, daughter of Richard Samwell of Upton, Northamptonshire. He matriculated at Trinity College, Oxford, on 19 March 1702, aged seventeen. He entered the Middle Temple in 1703, but did not follow a legal career. Oughton served under Marlborough at Blenheim in 1705 and was commissioned captain and lieutenant-colonel in the 1st foot guards in 1706, seeing further action at Oudenarde in 1708. About 1712 he married his cousin Frances Bagot (*d.* 1714), daughter of his mother's sister Frances and her husband, Sir Thomas Wagstaffe, and widow of Sir Edward Bagot. That year he accompanied Marlborough into exile, but he returned in 1714 at the accession of George I, when he became groom of the bedchamber to the prince of Wales (afterwards George II). He inherited a lease of twenty-five years on an estate in Bishop's Tachbrook in Warwickshire on his wife's death in 1714, and later married Elizabeth, daughter of John Baber and his wife, Mary Draper.

Oughton was promoted colonel and appointed first major of the Coldstream Guards in 1715, the year in which he was elected member of parliament for Coventry. In 1717 he was appointed regimental lieutenant-colonel of the Coldstream. He continued to support the ministry following the breach between George I and his son that year, and resigned from the prince's household in December; in 1718 he received a secret service payment of £500 from the government, and on 27 August he was created a baronet. Re-elected for Coventry in 1722 (after fighting a duel with William, third Baron Craven, brother of his opponent Fulwar Craven), Oughton remained a prominent ministerialist and senior army officer, serving in Ireland between 1729 and 1733. His ambition to be governor of Minorca may have been thwarted by his ambivalence on the excise question, where the militant opposition of his Coventry constituents to the Excise Bill led him to abstain rather than vote with Walpole's government. He was none the less appointed colonel of the 8th dragoons in 1733, and was again elected for Coventry in 1734. He became a brigadier-general in 1735, but died at Bishop's Tachbrook on 4 September 1736. He was a freemason and had something of a reputation as a rake.

The young Dickenson grew up on his father's estate at Bishop's Tachbrook, and attended Coventry grammar school from 1725 until 1729, after which he went to Charterhouse School until 1735, where he excelled in the classics. His place at Charterhouse was secured for him through the influence of Frederick, prince of Wales, a friend of his father and fellow freemason. Initially destined for an exhibition at Christ Church, Oxford, he instead attended Trinity College, Dublin, in 1736 and 1737. His father's death in 1736 removed his sole source of financial support, necessitated his departure from Trinity, and prompted him to seek a military career. In 1737 he was commissioned cornet in the 8th dragoons, of which his father had been colonel and which was then stationed in Ireland; he purchased a lieutenancy in 1741, the year he started to use his father's surname. Two of his abiding interests began while he was a subaltern: he became a freemason in London in 1737 and developed a passion for antiquities while serving in Ireland in the late 1730s.

The army's enlargement in 1742 provided Oughton with his captaincy, in the 37th regiment of foot, and that year he went to Flanders with his regiment, taking the opportunity to visit Rhineland cities, record antiquities, and collect medals. After returning to Britain in 1746 for the suppression of the Jacobite rising, he saw action at the battle of Falkirk and fought as a major of brigade at Culloden, being elected secretary of the Cumberland Society, which was formed in Inverness in April 1746. He experienced his third battle, Laffeldt, in 1747 as the 37th's major and was promoted, without purchase, to the regiment's lieutenant-colonelcy in 1749. Commanding the regiment on Minorca between 1749 and 1754 he acted as the island's provincial grand master mason and indulged his fondness for travel, visiting Algiers and spending several months in Italy in 1752—during which visit he acted as witness at Sir William Chambers's marriage in Rome and took copious notes on the Arsenale in Venice.

Stationed in Scotland in 1754 and 1755, Oughton met and in the latter year married the widowed mother of Hew Whitefoord *Dalrymple (1750–1830), Mary Dalrymple, *née* Ross (*d.* 1793). He also joined Edinburgh's Select Society and Revolution Society before returning to England in 1756 and taking the 1st battalion of his regiment to Flanders in 1758. On his return to Britain in 1759, following his command of the 37th at the battle of Minden, Oughton was rewarded with the colonelcy of the 55th regiment of foot; he was also left £1000 in the will of General James Wolfe. He settled in Bolton Street, Piccadilly, for the next eight years and, while militarily unemployed in London, Oughton was elected to its Society of Arts in 1762 and its Society of Antiquaries in 1767. At a time when many Britons were equivocal about the Hanoverian dynasty Oughton lost no opportunity to proclaim his allegiance to the protestant succession: among his other societal memberships were those of the Blew and Orange Society and the Antigallican Society. In 1762 he was promoted from the colonelcy of the 55th to that of the 31st regiment of foot. As colonel of the 31st he had and exercised such opportunities for patronage within his regiment that he became well known in the army not only for ensuring that officers were promoted within his regiment but also for supporting and sponsoring officers of slender means but great potential.

Oughton returned to Scotland in 1767 with the rank of major-general to fill the post of deputy to the commander-in-chief, north Britain, John Campbell, marquess of Lorne (later fifth duke of Argyll). His final promotion, to the rank of lieutenant-general, came in 1770 and he succeeded Lorne as commander-in-chief in 1778, having been created KB in 1773 and appointed to the sinecure post of lieutenant-governor of Antigua in 1772. The majority of his final thirteen years of life in Scotland were ones of uxorious tranquillity. With the nation at peace until 1775 Oughton was largely free to follow his own interests and he passed the time in learning Gaelic, in tours of inspection, in socializing in Edinburgh, and in active freemasonry, being elected grand master of the Scottish grand lodge in 1769 and 1770 and to the masonic royal order of Scotland in 1769. During his time in Scotland Oughton met both James Boswell and Samuel Johnson: Johnson's description of Oughton as 'a very extraordinary man; a man of boundless curiosity and unwearied diligence' (Boswell, 567) remains the best description of this remarkable military paragon. As the war in America intensified after 1778 so Oughton's workload increased. This undoubtedly affected his health and probably contributed to his early death, which occurred in Bath on 14 April 1780. He was buried in Bath Abbey two days later and a memorial tablet was erected in Westminster Abbey in 1781.

STEPHEN WOOD

Sources S. C. Wood, *By dint of labour and perseverance*, Society for Army Historical Research, special publication, 14 (1997) · W. Y. Carman, 'Lieutenant-General Sir Adolphus Oughton, KB', *Journal of the Society for Army Historical Research*, 271 (1989), 127–9 · A. Hayter, ed., *An eighteenth-century secretary at war* (1988) · GEC, *Baronetage*, vol. 5 · C. T. Atkinson, *Regimental history: the royal Hampshire regiment*, 1: *To 1914* (1950) · *Caledonian mercury* (14 April 1755) · J. Prebble, *Mutiny: highland regiments in revolt, 1743–1804* (1975) · parish register, St Giles-in-the-Fields, London, 27 Oct 1719 [baptism] · J. Ingamells, ed., *A dictionary of British and Irish travellers in Italy, 1701–1800* (1997) · parish register, Bath, Bath Abbey, 16 April 1780 [burial] · A. Oughton, memoirs and memoranda, c.1770, NAM, MSS 8808–8836 · A. Oughton, commonplace book and journals, 1729–58, National War Museum of Scotland, MSS M1990.660, 1–4 · J. Boswell, *The life of Samuel Johnson … to which is added the journal of a tour of the Hebrides*, ed. W. Wallace, new edn (1897), 567 · E. Cruickshanks, 'Oughton, Sir Adolphus', HoP, *Commons, 1715–54* · *GM*, 1st ser., 6 (1736), 552 · *GM*, 1st ser., 50 (1780), 203 · Foster, *Alum. Oxon., 1715–1886*, 3.1096

Archives BL, corresp., Add. MSS 21729, 21732 · Coventry Archives, corresp. · NA Scot., letters, GD 24/1/577 · NAM, journal and commonplace book, MSS 8808–8836 · National War Museum of Scotland, Edinburgh, commonplace book and journals (Italian journey and Hanoverian campaign), MSS M1990.660, 1–4 · NRA, priv. coll., notebook, relating to Flanders campaign | BL, corresp. with Edward Hopkins, Add. MS 64929 · Staffs. RO, corresp. with Lord Dartmouth

Likenesses G. Knapton, oils, 1753, NAM · J. Downman, oils, c.1778, Scot. NPG · R. Hayward, effigy on a monument, 1781, Westminster Abbey, London · print, BM

Oughton, Thomas (*b.* 1660), ecclesiastical lawyer and legal writer, born on 13 September 1660 in the parish of Holy Trinity Church, Coventry, Warwickshire, was the son of Thomas Oughton (*d.* 1695), registrar of the court of delegates, and his wife, Issable. The younger Oughton was a deputy registrar of the same court until about 1720, and remained on the list of proctors until about 1740.

Oughton achieved a lasting reputation for his treatise on procedure in the ecclesiastical courts—a work that had an unfortunate history. As early as 1713 Oughton completed a manuscript entitled *Processus judiciarius*, which he handed over to a printer; but the entire stock and also, it seems, the copy were destroyed by fire. Oughton then set about the painful task of rewriting the lost book, which occupied him for a further fifteen years. It finally appeared in 1728, in two volumes, under a new title, *Ordo judiciorum*, which the author borrowed from that of a book by the sixteenth-century Italian procedural writer Roberto Maranta. Dedicated to the judges and advocates of Doctors' Commons, the treatise began with a detailed account of the civilian profession and its customs. The author then described the procedure of the church courts, which still used Latin for both the written documents and the oral proceedings.

Only a few years after the first edition, parliament abolished the use of Latin in all the courts, a change which was not reflected in the second edition (1738) but which nevertheless seems not to have diminished the status of Oughton as the principal guide to the ecclesiastical courts before the nineteenth-century reforms. Sir William Scott said in 1820 that Oughton and Godolphin were 'the oracles of our practice' (*Phillimore's Reports*, 3.329). An attempt was made in 1831 to render Oughton's treatise more widely accessible by translating a considerable part of it into English. The new edition by James Thomas Law, chancellor of Lichfield and Coventry, was printed as *Forms of Ecclesiastical Law, or, The Mode of Conducting Suits in the consistory Courts*, and it enjoyed a second edition in 1844. It included material inserted at the appropriate points from other authors, rendering further recourse to the Latin proceduralists largely unnecessary for practical purposes. Nothing is known about Oughton's family life, or when and where he died. J. H. BAKER

Sources P. G. S. [P. G. Stein], 'Oughton, Thomas', *Biographical dictionary of the common law*, ed. A. W. B. Simpson (1984) • J. H. Baker, *Monuments of endlesse labours: English canonists and their work, 1300–1900* (1998), 89–94 • *Phillimore's reports*, 3 (1820), 329 • *IGI*

William Oughtred (*bap.* 1575, *d.* 1660), by Wenceslaus Hollar

Oughtred, William (*bap.* 1575, *d.* 1660), mathematician, was the son of Benjamin Oughtred (*d.* 1618), a writing-master and 'registrar' at Eton College, and was baptized there on 5 March 1575 (reputedly the day of his birth). After attending the school as a king's scholar and being taught arithmetic by his father, he went on to King's College, Cambridge, in 1592; he became a fellow there in 1595, graduating BA in 1596 and proceeding MA in 1600. He later said that it was during this period that he began to study mathematics intensively, and 'by inciting, assisting and instructing others, brought many in to the love and study of those Arts, not only in our own, but in some other Colledges also' (Oughtred, sig. [A4]*v*). His first known mathematical writings and instrument designs date from this period, although they appeared in print much later.

Having been ordained priest in 1603, Oughtred left the university in 1605 to become vicar of Shalford, in Surrey; he was rector of nearby Albury from 1610 until his death. The move to Shalford enabled him to marry Christsgift Caryll, baptized at Godalming, Surrey, on 21 April 1588, as a daughter of William Caryll or Carell and his wife, Doryty. The Carylls lived at Tangley in the parish of Wonersh (not far from Shalford), and Christsgift's marriage to Oughtred took place there on 20 February 1606. Oughtred also built up links with other local families, teaching mathematics to the son of Sir Francis Aungier and Latin to a member of the household of George Duncombe. This did not mean that his horizons narrowed; he mentions having met Edmund Gunter through the good offices of 'my honoured friend, Master Henry Briggs', while on a visit to London in 1618. About 1620 Oughtred first encountered one Captain Marmaduke Neilson or Nelson, who proposed an astronomical method of finding longitude at sea; Neilson seemed to admit that he was wrong, but was to reappear in the early 1630s making similar claims, with the backing of Lord Falkland. Oughtred was then consulted about the matter by Peter Heylin, and appointed to a commission consisting of several learned men set up to reconsider it in May 1636.

Meanwhile Oughtred was introduced to Thomas Howard, second earl of Arundel (1586–1646), as he described in 1633:

> About five yeares since, the Earle of Arundell my most honourable Lord in a time of his private retiring to his house … at West Horsley, foure small miles from me … hearing of me … was pleased to send for me: and afterward at London to appoint mee a chamber in his owne house [Arundel House, in the Strand]. (Oughtred, sig. B*v*)

There are hints that Oughtred hoped for more concrete benefits from the relationship, perhaps in terms of church preferments, but he was disappointed. His sole acquisition was the Heathfield prebend at Chichester Cathedral, bestowed upon him by Bishop Henry King, who lived in Surrey during the civil war period and was a cousin of George Duncombe; King allowed his son John to become one of Oughtred's pupils. The grant was made in or after 1644, so can only have been a purely nominal honour; it may have been intended as a compensation for Oughtred following his complaint, in 1647, that John King had seduced one of his daughters (Crum, 20).

In return for the earl's patronage Oughtred taught his second surviving son, William (later Viscount Stafford). It was for this pupil, he said, that he compiled his *Arithmeticae in numeris et speciebus institutio: quae … totius mathematicae quasi clavis est* (1631). In this he took algebraic methods from continental sources, especially Viète, and presented them in a concise form through the intensive use of symbols, some of which were invented by himself; the resulting volume was relatively small and inexpensive, in marked contrast to the rival work of Thomas Harriot (posthumous, also 1631). In presenting a copy to Peter Heylin, Oughtred described it as:

> but a mole-hyll, easily stept over. Some thinke it hard; it is indeed new to this our age; but either this, or els some such

> like, familiar to the ancients … and indeed analytice is the true way of invention … it is not hard: it is the way of nature, which is most plaine and easie, and free from anfractuous ambiguities, in all her workes. (Bodl. Oxf., MS Rawl. D.353, fol. 96)

An English edition of the *Clavis*, translated by Dr Robert Wood, appeared in 1647 as *The Key of the Mathematics New Forged and Filed*, with a preface in which Oughtred thanked Thomas Wharton, Jonas Moore, and others for helping to see the volume through the press. A number of his shorter mathematical writings were appended to the second and third Latin editions, which appeared under the title *Clavis mathematica(e)* in 1648 and 1652 respectively. The latter of these was produced in Oxford by a group including John Wallis (1616–1703), Seth Ward (1617–1689), and the young Christopher Wren (1632–1723). It reflects the unique status Oughtred had by then attained as a figurehead for contemporary English mathematicians.

Oughtred's position in the Howard household allowed him to make contact with other members of the mathematical community in London, including various instrument makers. He had a close relationship with Elias Allen, whose workshop by St Clement Danes was only a short distance down the Strand from Arundel House, and he was later in contact with Allen's apprentice and successor Ralph Greatorex. Allen was responsible for realizing various instrument designs for Oughtred—some devised during his time in Cambridge and some soon after his first encounter with logarithms. The latter instruments included the 'circles of proportion'—the earliest form of slide-rule—which allowed problems of multiplication and division to be reduced to addition and subtraction by the use of logarithms. Oughtred was persuaded by one of his pupils, William Forster, to publish an account of this device, despite his consistent wariness about promoting the use of instruments. He believed that their availability often kept people from studying the theoretical aspects of mathematics. *The Circles of Proportion and the Horizontal Instrument … Invented, and the Uses of Both Written in Latine by Mr W.O.*, Forster's translation, was published in 1632. The second instrument of the title, placed on the back of the circles of proportion, was a tool for demonstrating astronomical principles and for laying out sundials on any kind of plane. It was later adapted to make a garden sundial, of which Oughtred published an account in *The Description and Use of the Double Horizontall Dyall* (1636). The circles of proportion and especially the horizontal instrument involved Oughtred (and Forster) in a bitter dispute with Oughtred's former pupil Richard Delamain, who had also published accounts of both instruments as his own invention. Oughtred retaliated in a piece usually found bound with *The Circles of Proportion*: *To the English gentrie … the just apologie of Wil: Oughtred, against the slaunderous insimulations of Richard Delamain* [1633]. In this he made a scathing attack on those mathematical teachers who were more interested in the use of instruments than the study of mathematical theory, calling them 'doers of tricks' and 'Jugglers'. Here and elsewhere he defended the unity of mathematics, deploring the 'superficiall scumme and froth of Instrumentall tricks and practices' that emerged when practice was not based upon sound theoretical understanding.

Other instruments Oughtred developed included a straight slide-rule (described in the preface to *The Circles of Proportion* and in a letter to Elias Allen), a gauging rod (described in *The New Artificial Gauging Line*, 1633), and another sundial, which was to become one of the most popular of its type in the seventeenth and eighteenth centuries. This last instrument had already been available from Allen's workshop for about twenty years when an account of it was published in 'The description of the generall horologicall ring', appended to a new edition of *The Description and Use of the Double Horizontall Dyall* (1652).

Forster was one of the many men who went to Oughtred in London or at Albury to benefit from his tuition and from access to his unparalleled mathematical library. The list of his disciples includes many eminent contemporary mathematicians and scholars—Seth Ward, Christopher Wren, Laurence Rooke, and Jonas Moore being only the best known of them—though it is now difficult to be sure which were genuinely his pupils and which were simply admiring colleagues. Many of them made use of the *Clavis* as a teaching text: Ward is said to have employed the work in his university teaching at Cambridge in the early 1640s, and Rooke to have lectured upon it at Gresham College in the 1650s. The Savilian professor John Wallis also paid homage to Oughtred and produced another edition of the *Clavis* in 1667.

Other works by Oughtred are *The Solution of All Sphaerical Triangles by the Planisphere* (1651, ed. Christopher Brookes); *Trigonometria* (1657, Englished by Richard Stokes as *Trigonometrie*); and the posthumous *Opuscula mathematica* (1677) containing various previously unpublished short treatises. He is also credited, probably incorrectly, with an English translation (in 1633) of Jean Leurechon's *Recreations mathematiques* of 1629. The 'planisphere' mentioned in the first of these works was yet another of Oughtred's inventions, devised about 1610 along with an instrument 'giving the Prosthaphaereses of the Plannets according to the Theory of Copernicus' (W. Oughtred, *The Solution of All Sphaerical Triangles by the Planisphere*). Both instruments had astrological uses. Oughtred's interest in astronomy was inseparably bound up with belief in astrology; Aubrey reports that he was also deeply committed to the study of alchemy. The impression his neighbours gained of these activities may have reinforced the threat to his tenure of the Albury living when, in 1646, he was brought before a sequestration committee for his loyalty to the royalist cause. The parliamentarian astrologer William Lilly claimed credit for organizing his defence; Aubrey believed that the Surrey landowner Sir Richard Onslow was primarily responsible for its successful outcome and that this was why the 1647 *Key of the Mathematics* was dedicated to Onslow and his son.

Oughtred and his wife had thirteen children, according to Aubrey, or twelve according to a note of names and dates preserved by Ashmole: William, Henry (twice), Benjamin, Simon, Margaret, Judith, Edward, Elizabeth, Anne,

George, and John. Benjamin and John became watchmakers. The family connection with the instrument-making trade was further strengthened by the marriage of one of the daughters to Christopher Brookes, an apprentice of Elias Allen and the editor of Oughtred's treatise on spherical triangles. Oughtred died on 13 June 1660, probably at Albury, where he was buried on 15 June; Aubrey writes that he expired with joy on hearing of the king's restoration. The administration of his estate was granted to his son, Henry, on 24 July 1661. While some of his books were dispersed, others, with some of his papers, eventually reached the hands of the mathematician William Jones: the books were merged with other contents of a private library during the nineteenth century, and cannot now be separately identified.

FRANCES WILLMOTH

Sources F. H. Willmoth, *Sir Jonas Moore: practical mathematics and Restoration science* (1993), chap. 2 • H. K. Higton, 'Elias Allen and the role of instruments in shaping the mathematical culture of seventeenth-century England', PhD diss., U. Cam., 1996 • *Brief lives, chiefly of contemporaries, set down by John Aubrey, between the years 1669 and 1696*, ed. A. Clark, 2 (1898), 105–15 • A. J. Turner, 'William Oughtred, Richard Delamain and the horizontal instrument in seventeenth century England', *Annali dell' Istituto e Museo di Storia della Scienza di Firenze*, 6 (1981), 99–201 • W. Oughtred, *To the English gentrie … the just apologie of Wil: Oughtred against the slaunderous insimulations of Richard Delamain* [1633] • notes about Oughtred, Bodl. Oxf., MS Ashmole 1137, fol. 3v • H. C. Malden, ed., *The parish registers of Godalming*, pt 1 (1904), 9 • *IGI* • W. Sterry, ed., *The Eton College register, 1441–1698* (1943), 253 • G. L. Hennessy, *Chichester diocese clergy lists* (1900), 9 • D. Lloyd, *Memoires of the lives … of those … personages that suffered … for the protestant religion* (1668), 608 • W. Kennett, *A register and chronicle ecclesiastical and civil* (1728), 721 • *CSP dom.*, 1635–6 • G. Vernon, *The life of the learned and reverend Dr Peter Heylin* (1628), 43–9 • will, PRO, PROB 6/37, fol. 61 • *The poems of Henry King, bishop of Chichester*, ed. M. Crum (1965), 20 • private information (2004) • parish register (marriage), Wonersh, 20 Feb 1606

Archives NRA, priv. coll., books and papers

Likenesses W. Hollar, etching, 1644, BM; repro. in W. Oughtred, *Clavis mathematicae*, 2nd edn (1648), frontispiece • G. P. Harding, watercolour drawing (after W. Hollar), NPG • W. Hollar, drawing, BM [*see illus.*]

Ouida. *See* Ramée, Marie Louise de la (1839–1908).

Ould, Sir Fielding (*c.*1710–1789), man-midwife, was born at Galway, Ireland, one of two children of Captain Ould (1689–*c.*1715) of the Royal regiment of Welch fusiliers and Lettice Shawe, the daughter of the Revd Fielding Shawe, canon of Tagh Saxon. His father, who fought at the battles of the Boyne and Aughrim, was later assassinated in London, and Fielding and his brother, Abraham, were raised in Galway. Beginning about 1729 Ould spent five years as a dissector in the department of anatomy in Trinity College, Dublin, and attended courses in botany, chemistry, and natural philosophy, but left without a degree. He then studied in Paris under Gregoire the elder, the first Frenchman to give private lessons in midwifery. It was there that Ould made his greatest contribution to obstetrics when he was first to observe that in normal labour the foetal head entered the maternal pelvis in the lateral position and then rotated, prior to delivery. Ould married Gracia Walker in 1733, and they had several children. She was related by marriage to the Chamberlen family, who had introduced the obstetric forceps to midwifery practice in the previous century.

On his return to Dublin in 1736 or 1737 Ould resided at 21 Frederick Street South and developed a large midwifery practice in Golden Lane. He was granted a licence in midwifery by the King and Queen's College of Physicians in Ireland, on 16 August 1738, as he was found to be 'singularly well qualified' in the art of obstetrics. Four years later his famous book, *A Treatise of Midwifery, in Three Parts*, was published. Dedicated to the fellows of the College of Physicians, it also carried their imprimatur. Ould recommended the use of opiates in prolonged labour. He may have possessed a pair of obstetric forceps, and he wrote that 'The best adapted instrument is the large forceps, which is in general use all over Europe'. He described episiotomy and cautioned against premature extraction of the placenta. He opposed the use of caesarean section, which he argued would necessarily destroy the mother. His sound judgement and moral courage are evidenced by the fact that he advised professional consultation in difficult obstetric cases. His textbook was one of the first important works on obstetrics in English, and contained many new and important observations, including his original studies on the mechanism of normal labour. His caring attitude is evident throughout the book, as is his commitment to improve the quality of care for women in childbirth.

Ould was appointed assistant master of the Dublin Lying-in Hospital in 1745. In 1753 he received the degree of BA, 'speciali gratia' from Trinity College, and three years later applied to Trinity and the College of Physicians to be examined for a bachelor's degree in medicine. The College of Physicians refused as it was contrary to their by-laws, which stated that 'no man … shall have a licence to practise midwifery and physic together'. Trinity, however, conferred an honorary degree in medicine on Ould in 1761, causing the indignant physicians to dissolve their links with the university. Some twenty-four years later they relented and Ould was admitted as a licentiate in medicine of the College of Physicians on 3 October 1785.

In 1759 Ould became master of the lying-in hospital after the untimely death of its founder, Bartholomew Mosse, and devoted himself to lowering maternal mortality and improving patients' welfare and facilities. He proceeded with the building of a place of entertainment and fund-raising, known as the Round Rooms, thus giving rise to the hospital's alternative and soon-to-be-adopted name—The Rotunda. This, the first maternity hospital in Ireland and Great Britain, provided excellent facilities and developed a worldwide reputation for patient care, teaching, and clinical research. In May 1760 Ould was knighted by John Russell, the duke of Bedford and lord lieutenant of Ireland. A Dublin wit wrote the following epigram:

> Sir Fielding Ould is made a Knight,
> He should have been a lord by right;
> For then each lady's prayer would be,
> O Lord, Good Lord, deliver me!
> (Brody, 234–40)

During his professional career, which extended from 1736

to 1788, Ould was obstetrician not only to the destitute but also to the nobility, and he attended the countess of Wellesley at the birth of Arthur, duke of Wellington. He enhanced the reputation of the Dublin School of Midwifery and became acknowledged as one of Ireland's foremost obstetricians. Ould died at his home, 21 Frederick Street South, Dublin, of apoplexy on 29 November 1789 and was buried in the nearby St Ann's churchyard, Dawson Street. MICHAEL J. O'DOWD

Sources A. H. McClintock, 'On the rise of the Dublin school of midwifery; with memoirs of Sir Fielding Ould and Dr J. C. Fleury', *Dublin Quarterly Journal of Medical Science*, 25 (1858), 1–20 • S. A. Brody, 'The life and times of Sir Fielding Ould', *Bulletin of the History of Medicine*, 52 (1978), 228–50 • T. D. O'Donel Browne, *The Rotunda Hospital, 1745–1945* (1947) • T. P. C. Kirkpatrick, *The book of the Rotunda Hospital*, ed. H. Jellett (1913) • I. Campbell Ross, *Public virtue, public love* (1986) • J. F. Fleetwood, *The history of medicine in Ireland*, 2nd edn (1983) • T. P. C. Kirkpatrick, *History of the medical teaching in Trinity College, Dublin, and of the School of Physic in Ireland* (1912) • C. A. Cameron, *History of the Royal College of Surgeons in Ireland*, 2nd edn (1916) • J. D. H. Widdess, *A history of the Royal College of Physicians of Ireland, 1654–1963* (1963) • L. D. Longo, 'A treatise of midwifery in three parts', *American Journal of Obstetrics and Gynecology*, 172 (1995), 1317–19 • D. Coakley, *Irish masters of medicine* (1992) • E. O'Brien, A. Crookshank, and G. Wolstenholme, *A portrait of Irish medicine* (1984)
Archives Royal College of Physicians of Ireland, Dublin, Kirkpatrick collection
Likenesses T. Hickey, chalk and crayon drawing, 1759, NG Ire.; repro. in McClintock, 'On the rise of the Dublin school of midwifery' • lithograph (after T. Hickey), Royal College of Physicians of Ireland, Dublin; copy, Rotunda Hospital, Dublin

Ouless, Walter William (1848–1933), portrait painter, was born at St Helier, Jersey, on 21 September 1848, the third son of Philip John Ouless (1817–1885), marine painter, and his wife, Caroline Marguette Savage. He was educated at Victoria College, Jersey, and moved to London in 1864, entering the Royal Academy Schools the following year, at sixteen. In 1869, when he was not yet twenty-one, he made his first appearance at a Royal Academy exhibition, with two subject pictures, *Home Again* and *A Tender Passage*. He continued to exhibit regularly until 1928, when he was represented by a portrait of Sir Arthur Keith, which is now in the Royal College of Surgeons together with his portrait of Lord Lister, painted in 1897. He was elected ARA in 1877, before he was thirty, and RA in 1881, and in 1924 he became a senior academician.

At the beginning of his career Ouless painted subject pictures, and it was on the advice of Sir J. E. Millais that he concentrated on portraiture. Ouless was quickly recognized as one of the most trustworthy portrait painters of the day, sure of getting a good and sympathetic likeness with a high degree of technical skill. At the same time his earlier practice in figure composition enabled him to give to his portraits a broadly pictorial effect combined with veracity in detail. In his academy notes of 1875 Ruskin observed: 'Mr Ouless has adopted from Mr Millais what was deserving of imitation, and has used the skill he has learned to better ends. All his portraits here are vigorous and interesting' (Ruskin, 30–31). He proceeded to build an immensely successful career as a society portraitist, though he has been described as a 'competent' artist rather than an 'inspired' one (Wood).

One of Ouless's earliest portraits was of Charles Darwin, painted for the family in 1875. Other commissions soon followed, notably of Cardinal Newman (1880–81), for the Oratory in Birmingham, and Sir Frederick Roberts (1882), for the mess at Woolwich. He painted both Edward VIII (1900) and George V (1905) as prince of Wales, the latter for Lincoln's Inn. Among the other distinguished people who sat for him was Cardinal Manning (1888), a painting destroyed by enemy action in 1940, but represented by a replica at the Oratory, Birmingham. The portraits by Ouless in the National Portrait Gallery include *John Bright* (1879), *John Morley* (1891), and *Thomas Hardy* (1922). Ouless painted a self-portrait for the Uffizi Gallery, Florence, which was exhibited at the academy in 1918. In his later years he painted a few landscapes, mostly in the county of Dorset.

Ouless was for a long time active on the council of the Royal Academy. He was a governor of Dulwich College, and occupied himself a good deal with the affairs of the Dulwich Picture Gallery, which he helped to rehang. For many years he devoted much time to the Artists' General Benevolent Institution, both as honorary secretary and vice-president. Personally he was much liked, although during his later years partial deafness kept him from mixing much in general society. 'No man could have had a more loyal and steadfast friend, nor wiser counsellor, while he also possessed the charming courtesy of a great gentleman' (*The Times*, 1 Jan 1934).

Ouless was a chevalier of the Légion d'honneur and a member of the order of Leopold, and during his long life he received gold and silver medals for his work at Berlin, Paris, Munich, and Vienna. On 6 November 1878 he married Lucy Maitland (1847/8–1931), daughter of Thomas King Chambers MD, honorary physician to the prince of Wales, of Shrubs Hill House, Sunningdale. The eldest of their three daughters was Catherine Ouless (*b.* 1879), the landscape and portrait painter. He died after a short illness at his home, 12 Bryanston Square, London, on 25 December 1933.

CHARLES MARRIOTT, *rev.* MARK POTTLE

Sources *The Times* (27 Dec 1933) • *The Times* (1 Jan 1934) • J. Johnson and A. Greutzner, *The dictionary of British artists, 1880–1940* (1976), vol. 5 of *Dictionary of British art* • G. M. Waters, *Dictionary of British artists, working 1900–1950* (1975) • B. Stewart and M. Cutten, *The dictionary of portrait painters in Britain up to 1920* (1997) • Wood, *Vic. painters*, 3rd edn • *Men and women of the time* (1899) • *WWW* • private information (1949) • E. H. H. Archibald, *Dictionary of sea painters* (1980) • J. Ruskin, *Notes on some of the principal pictures exhibited in the rooms of the Royal Academy* (1875) • m. cert. • d. cert.
Likenesses W. W. Ouless, self-portrait, oils, 1883, Aberdeen Art Gallery • H. von Herkomer, group portrait, oils, 1908 (*The Council of the Royal Academy*), Tate collection • Elliott & Fry, photograph, 1914, NPG • W. W. Ouless, self-portrait, oils, 1918, Uffizi Gallery, Florence; replica, *Barreau Gallery, Jersey Museum, St Helier* • W. Stoneman, photograph, 1933, NPG • O. Edis, photograph, NPG • Lock & Whitfield, woodburytype photograph, NPG; repro. in T. Cooper, *Men of mark: a gallery of contemporary portraits* (1880) • G. G. Manton, group portrait, watercolour (*Conversazione at the Royal Academy, 1891*), NPG • C. Ouless, portrait; destroyed • R. W. Robinson, photograph, NPG; repro. in *Members and Associates of the Royal Academy of Arts, 1891* • J. Russell & Sons, photograph, NPG

Wealth at death £166,207 9*s.* 9*d.*: probate, 8 Feb 1934, *CGPLA Eng. & Wales*

Oulton, Walley Chamberlain (*fl.* 1783–1820), playwright and theatre historian, was born in Dublin, the son of Walley Oulton (*b. c.*1737) and his wife, Catherine, the daughter of Dr Chamberlen Walker, who himself came from the Chamberlen family of physicians who had invented obstetrical forceps. His great-grandfather, also named Walley Oulton, had settled in Dublin early in the eighteenth century, and set up as a glover in Nicholas Street. It is said that Walley Chamberlain Oulton lost his father during infancy, and on his mother's remarriage was left in the care of his grandfather Dr Walker, from whom he received a classical education. Other sources, however, state that he was educated privately in Dublin under Dr Ball. In any event, his first play, *The Haunted Castle*, was performed at the Capel Street theatre in December 1783, and was quickly followed by several other pieces. According to Stephen Jones, 'intoxicated with this success, he neglected his studies, and came to London' (Baker), where he married Ann Elizabeth Churchill on 5 November 1787 at St Luke's, Chelsea. They had at least two daughters and two sons, John Oulton and Thomas Walker Oulton, the latter of whom was baptized on 23 May 1796.

In London Oulton was soon embroiled in controversy. His burletta *Hobson's Choice* was staged in 1787 by John Palmer at the Royalty Theatre in Wellclose Square. Palmer's enterprise was opposed by the powerful lobby of supporters of London's patent theatres, and Oulton's light-hearted satire of the prevailing theatrical conditions (his subtitle was *Thespis in Distress*) gave disproportionate offence. Believing himself *persona non grata* at Drury Lane and Covent Garden, Oulton concealed his authorship of his next play, *As it should be*, which was performed under the Colman management at the Haymarket in June 1789. The younger Colman continued to support Oulton after the deception was discovered, and it was at the Haymarket that many of his plays were first performed. As a dramatist he was modestly content to gratify popular taste in a career that lasted until 1817. He was not, however, prolific (twenty-five known pieces in thirty-four years), and it may have been financial considerations that drew him into acting. His first recorded appearance was as Pierre in Otway's *Venice Preserv'd* at the Richmond Theatre on 18 September 1792, but he may have acted for Palmer at the Royalty as early as 1787 or 1788, as several of the Royalty playbills for those seasons are missing.

A minor playwright and a forgotten actor, Oulton was also a journalist and an industrious historian of the English theatre. The *Busy Body*, which he published three times a week during the first two months of 1787, was his attempt to establish himself as a periodical essayist in the tradition of Addison and Steele. Its twenty-five issues were collected for publication in book form in 1789. He also entered into controversy in 1795, with two pseudonymous pamphlets attacking the self-proclaimed prophet Richard Brothers and his disciple Nathaniel Halhed. Oulton's ill-judged defence of the authenticity of *Vortigern*, Samuel Ireland's Shakespeare forgery, appeared anonymously in 1796. The protection of anonymity did not last long, and Oulton shared the embarrassment of a gullible public, redeeming himself somewhat by the publication, also in 1796, of his two-volume updating of Benjamin Victor's *History of the Theatres of London*. It is as a theatre historian that he is best known, and his last major work, published in 1818, was a further updating of this *History* to 1817 in three volumes. His *Authentic memoirs of the green room (for 1799) containing the lives of all the performers of the theatres-royal* is not entirely reliable, but it was successful enough to merit expansion to two volumes in 1800 and to run to six further editions between 1801 and 1816. Oulton also edited, for publication in 1801, *Barker's Continuation of Egerton's Theatrical Remembrances, Baker's Biographia dramatica, etc.*, which had further editions in 1803 and 1814. His journeyman work included a shoddy edition of Shakespeare's poems (1804), anthologies of the writings of Kotzebue (1800) and Anna Seward (1813), a translation of Gessner's *Death of Abel* (1811), an English gazetteer (1805), and (his last known publication) a *Picture of Margate and its Vicinity* (1820). Nothing is known of Oulton after 1820, and no details of his private life have been preserved. Even in the memoirs of men who knew him, like George Colman the younger and James Boaden, his name is scarcely mentioned.

Sidney Lee, *rev.* Peter Thomson

Sources D. E. Baker, *Biographia dramatica, or, A companion to the playhouse*, rev. I. Reed, new edn, rev. S. Jones, 3 vols. in 4 (1812) · J. Boaden, *Memoirs of the life of John Philip Kemble*, 2 vols. (1825) · A. Nicoll, *A history of English drama, 1660–1900*, 6 vols. (1952–9), vols. 4–5 · Highfill, Burnim & Langhans, *BDA* · *IGI* · *A new biographical dictionary of 3000 cotemporary [sic] public characters, British and foreign, of all ranks and professions*, 2nd edn, 3 vols. in 6 pts (1825) · D. J. O'Donoghue, *The poets of Ireland: a biographical and bibliographical dictionary* (1912) · K. Drinkwater, 'Obstetrics and gynaecology', *Liverpool Medico-Chirurgical Journal*, 33 (July 1913), 451 · H. Drinkwater, 'The modern descendants of Dr Peter Chamberlen', *Liverpool Medico-Chirurgical Journal*, 36 (1916), 98 · private information (2004) [D. Oulton] · parish register, St Luke's, Chelsea [marriage]

Oulton, Wilfrid Ewart (1911–1997), air force officer, was born on 27 July 1911 at 2 Ellie Street, Monks Coppenhall, Nantwich, Cheshire, the eldest of eight children of schoolteacher Llewellin Oulton. His mother, Martha, *née* Wellings, died when Wilfrid was young and his father remarried. Educated at Abertillery county school, where his father was chemistry master, he won an open scholarship to University College, Cardiff, where he spent a period as an engineering student before moving to the RAF College, Cranwell. He graduated top of his entry as a pilot and was commissioned in July 1931. Flying Southampton, then Scarpa, flying boats with 204 squadron at Mount Batten, then 202 squadron in Malta, he demonstrated a marked aptitude for both the theory and the practice of air navigation. He subsequently completed the long postgraduate specialist navigation course at the air navigation school at RAF Manston (1933–5), and joined the staff as an instructor.

Oulton had married Sarah ('Terry') (*d.* 1990), daughter of the late Revd E. Davies of Pitsea, in Malta in 1935 when he was under the age qualifying for marriage allowance so, to supplement his income as his family grew, he qualified as an interpreter in German. On the outbreak of war in 1939, he was flying maritime patrol Anson aircraft over the western approaches with 217 squadron from Pembroke Dock but, with his engineering background, he was soon moved to technical development duties in the Ministry of Aircraft Production and sent to Washington to organize RAF navigation training in North America.

Oulton returned to maritime operations in 1943 commanding 58 squadron, flying Halifax bombers in an anti-submarine role. In May 1943 he and his crew operating over the Bay of Biscay destroyed two U-boats (U-663 and U-463) and crippled a third (U-563), which was sunk, Oulton having expended all of his depth charges, by the relieving aircraft. Awarded the DFC for these operations in late 1943, he took 206 and 220 squadrons, equipped with Flying Fortress aircraft, to Lajes in the Azores to establish a base to enable allied aircraft hunting German U-boats to cover the 'mid-Atlantic gap'. He was awarded a DSO for establishing and commanding this vital facility, and in January 1944, now a group captain, he was moved to Northern Ireland to command the flying boat base at RAF Castle Archdale. In March 1945 he was appointed deputy director of maritime operations in Ireland. He was mentioned in dispatches in 1940 and again in 1944 and 1945. At the end of the war he was, briefly, deputy director of flying (later air traffic) control, which involved him in establishing air traffic arrangements for the new airport at Heathrow. In 1946 he returned to Northern Ireland as the RAF director of the joint anti-submarine school at Londonderry. A very different posting came in 1950 when he was appointed air attaché in Argentina, Uruguay, and Paraguay. On his return to the Air Ministry in 1953 he was appointed CBE and joined the directorate of staff training before moving to the directorate of operations.

In 1955, and now an air commodore, Oulton was surprised to be tasked with establishing, then commanding, the tri-service base on Christmas Island in the Pacific Ocean, for the testing of the British megaton nuclear weapons. With his experience of establishing the Azores base twelve years earlier Oulton, as task force commander of operation Grapple, led the force, which eventually comprised some 4000 men, from 1956 to 1958. Oulton, whose father had been a student of Sir Ernest Rutherford at Manchester, was delighted to be working closely with Ministry of Supply scientists to complete the megaton nuclear weapons tests before the test ban treaty came into force.

On returning from the Pacific, Oulton was appointed CB and promoted to air vice-marshal to become senior air staff officer at Coastal Command headquarters at Northwood. This proved to be his final posting as, at his own request, he retired from the RAF in 1960. An honorary fellow of Cardiff University and a fellow of the Royal Institute of Navigation and of the Institute of Electronic and Radio Engineers, he joined EMI to advise on military projects. He travelled extensively, consulting and promoting export sales. He was chairman of Medsales Executive from 1982, again promoting export sales, particularly in south-east Asia. His memories of his time as task force commander were published in 1987 as *Christmas Island Cracker: an Account of the Planning and Execution of the British Thermonuclear Bomb Tests, 1957*, and in 1995 appeared *Technocrat*, the biography of his friend the American nuclear scientist Dr Allen Crocker, whom he had met in connection with the nuclear tests.

Throughout his life Oulton was physically very fit, and he had been RAF squash champion in 1938–9. He continued to play the game well into his eighties and similarly remained an enthusiastic and active Scottish country dancer. His wife, Sarah, died in 1990, and on 15 November 1991 he married Leticia Sara Malcolm (*b.* 1920/21), an Argentinian artist and family friend whom the Oultons had met in Buenos Aires. In retirement they lived in Lymington, Hampshire, where he died of bladder and prostate cancer at Oakhaven, Lower Pennington Lane, on 31 October 1997; his second wife survived him. His ashes were spread over the Bay of Biscay by an aircraft of 206 squadron.

ROBIN WOOLVEN

Sources *Daily Telegraph* (5 Nov 1997) · *The Independent* (21 Nov 1997) · *The Times* (1 Dec 1997) · *WW* (1957–97) · *Debrett's handbook: distinguished people in British life* [n.d.] · b. cert. · m. cert. · d. cert. · *Air Force List* (Dec 1932–1982) · *RAF retired list* (Dec 1932–1982) · private information (2004) [Robert Oulton, son; Wyneth Harrison, half-sister; squadron history officer, 206 squadron, RAF Kinloss, and members of 206 Squadron Association] · operational record for 58 squadron, 1943, PRO, file AIR27/544 · operational record for 206 squadron, 1943–4, PRO, file AIR27/1223

Likenesses photograph, repro. in *The Times* · photographs, repro. in W. E. Oulton, *Christmas Island cracker* (1987)

Wealth at death £352,901: probate, 15 Dec 1997, *CGPLA Eng. & Wales*

Ouseley, Sir Frederick Arthur Gore, second baronet (1825–1889), church musician, was born on 12 August 1825 in Grosvenor Square, London, the fourth and youngest surviving child of Sir Gore *Ouseley, first baronet (1770–1844), orientalist and diplomatist, and his wife, Harriet Georgina, daughter of John *Whitelocke (1757–1833). From the age of three he displayed remarkable musical gifts and he soon began to compose. However, he received no disciplined training in music, and after private education proceeded to Christ Church, Oxford, in 1843. He inherited his father's title in 1844 and took his BA degree in 1846.

Ouseley then prepared himself for ordination in the Church of England. At the same time he worked towards the degree of BMus (1850), for which he composed as his 'exercise' a sacred cantata. It was unprecedented for anyone of his class to take this degree, then anomalous in status and poorly esteemed. He later wrote that, together with ordination, this was part of his purpose 'to do something to raise the music of the Sanctuary'. Of high-church tendencies, he was also among the first and eventually the most influential of those who, following John Jebb, held that the services of the Book of Common Prayer should

Sir Frederick Arthur Gore Ouseley, second baronet (1825–1889), by Lewis Carroll (Charles Lutwidge Dodgson), 1860

properly be sung wherever possible, not only in cathedrals. Ouseley was made deacon in 1849 and became curate in the parish of St Paul's, Knightsbridge, London. He was personally insulted during the No Popery riots evoked by the so-called ritualism of its daughter church of St Barnabas, Pimlico. Disturbed by apparent signs of Erastianism in the Church of England, he resigned at the end of 1850. Eventually, after extensive travels in Europe, he decided that his vocation as clergyman lay in a country parish.

However, Ouseley was insistent on daily choral services. To meet this exceptional requirement he built at his own expense the parish church of St Michael just outside Tenbury, Worcestershire, together with adjoining buildings to accommodate a miniature foundation, St Michael's College, for the personnel required for the choral services and the education of the choristers. The church was consecrated in 1856, and, having taken priest's orders in 1855, Ouseley became incumbent of the parish and warden of the college, where he remained until his death. To the college, which he intended to 'form a model for the choral service of the Church in these realms', he devoted the whole of his means.

Meanwhile, in 1854 Ouseley had taken the degree of DMus, and when the following year the Oxford chair of music fell vacant he was appointed, only eight days after the death of Sir Henry Rowley Bishop. As he was unknown to the profession of music and without scholarly achievement behind him, this alacrity may be explained by the fact that he was the only DMus who, as an MA, was a member of convocation. The post, involving only part-time duties, was compatible with his work at Tenbury. In 1886 he became also a canon of Hereford Cathedral, having held the titular dignity of precentor from 1855, and it was at Hereford during a period of canonical residence that he died, unmarried and suddenly, on 6 April 1889. He was buried on 11 April at St Michael's Church, Tenbury.

As a composer, though an able contrapuntist, Ouseley lacked gifts of significant invention. Of two oratories, *The Martyrdom of St Polycarp* (DMus, 1854) is a mild essay after Mendelssohn, whereas *Hagar* (Hereford festival, 1873) is lifeless. His small secular output is unimportant. In church music his ideals lay in the past. From more than seventy-five anthems, large and small, some with orchestra, few have justified survival like the short, austere 'O Saviour of the world' and the bigger, livelier 'It came even to pass'. His thirteen services include two for double choir, of which one has orchestral accompaniment, but have nothing to say at the end of the twentieth century. His essential contribution to church music lies in the valuable influence exerted through St Michael's College on standards in both parish churches and cathedrals.

In scholarship, only Ouseley's edition of *The Sacred Compositions of Orlando Gibbons* (1873) requires mention. But as professor he improved the status of Oxford music degrees by introducing examinations in addition to the requirement of an original composition, and by providing that candidates must pass responsions, the preliminary examination for the BA degree. Though his syllabus was narrow and university residence was not required, these reforms (in step with Cambridge) proved the first stage towards establishing music as a university discipline. He also amassed a celebrated private library of antiquarian music and musical literature amounting to about 3500 volumes, including important manuscripts and many treatises, some rare. This passed to St Michael's College, upon the closure of which in 1985 its great substance became the property of the Bodleian Library, Oxford.

Reputedly short-tempered, Ouseley was nevertheless held in affection by former pupils and was not above a frolic. At leisure, he enjoyed singing Spanish and Italian national songs to his improvised guitar accompaniment.

WATKINS SHAW

Sources W. Shaw, ed., *Sir Frederick Ouseley and St Michael's, Tenbury* (1988) • F. W. Joyce, *The life of Rev. Sir F. A. G. Ouseley, Bart* (1896) • J. Stainer, 'The character and influence of the late Sir Frederick Ouseley', *Proceedings of the Musical Association*, 16 (1889–90), 25–39 • *The compositions of the Rev. Sir Frederick A. Gore Ouseley*, ed. J. S. Bumpus (privately printed, London, 1892) • W. Shaw, 'Sir Frederick Ouseley and his collection', *Brio*, 27 (1990), 45–7 • F. T. Havergal, *Memorials of Frederick Arthur Gore Ouseley* (1889) • E. H. Fellowes, *The catalogue of manuscripts in the library of St Michael's College, Tenbury* (1934) • d. cert. • Ouseley family bible, Hereford Cathedral

Archives Birm. CA, corresp. • U. Birm. L., letters | Bodl. Oxf., Tenbury MSS • Hereford Cathedral

Likenesses R. A. Lucas, oils, 1835, Royal School of Church Music, London • H. B. Ziegler, tinted drawing, *c*.1835, Royal School of Church Music, London • W. H. F. Hutchinson, oils, 1857, St Michael's Church, Tenbury • C. L. Dodgson [L. Carroll], photograph, 1860, NPG [*see illus.*] • T. Jones, photograph, *c*.1888, repro. in Havergal, *Memorials of Frederick Arthur Gore Ouseley*, frontispiece • A. Foster, oils, 1893 (posthumous), U. Oxf., faculty of music • Lock & Whitfield, woodburytype photograph, NPG; repro. in T. Cooper,

Men of mark: a gallery of contemporary artists (1883) · photographs, NPG
Wealth at death £6729 14*s.* 11*d.*: resworn probate, June 1890, *CGPLA Eng. & Wales* (1889)

Ouseley, Gideon (1762–1839), Methodist preacher, was the eldest son of John Ouseley (*b. c.*1735) of Kilticoghly, co. Galway, and his wife, Anne, daughter of Francis Surridge, of Fairyhill, co. Galway. He was born at Dunmore, co. Galway, the residence of his great-uncle William Ouseley, on 24 February 1762. Sir Ralph *Ouseley was his younger brother.

Ouseley was the son of a freethinking, anti-clerical father and a pious mother who introduced him to the family collection of Anglican and puritan literature. Despite his father's anti-clericalism he was bound for a career in the Church of Ireland and was tutored by the local Catholic priest, Father Keane, who had been educated in Europe. Ouseley, having failed to win a place at Trinity College, Dublin, studied with his cousins Sir Gore *Ouseley and Sir William *Ouseley under a private tutor, one Dr Robinson. His father inherited a farm in co. Roscommon, to where the family moved in 1781. Shortly after, he married Miss Harriet Wills (1762–1853) of Wills Grove, in 1783. They had no children. The marriage resulted in a small estate being settled on him by her father. However, the estate subsequently had to be surrendered, probably unnecessarily, after a lawsuit. Ouseley then entered a phase of dissolute living, which was dramatically brought to an end by a drunken shooting accident in which he lost an eye and very nearly his life. During his convalescence his wife read to him Edward Young's gloomy *Night Thoughts*, which, in conjunction with his near-death experience, resulted in a lasting preoccupation with death and eternity.

Ouseley's first experience of evangelical religion was in April 1791, at the meetings conducted in a local inn by Methodist quartermaster Robinet, attached to the Royal Irish Dragoons and stationed in Dunmore barracks. Thus began a long and psychologically painful conversion during which Ouseley encountered other Methodist itinerants and joined a local Methodist society. He soon decided to become an itinerant preacher but his work was undertaken as a freelance evangelist because of his suspicion of ecclesiastical institutions and their clergy. In 1797 he and his wife settled in the town of Sligo, and opened a girls' school. However, in 1799 he was invited by the Irish Methodist conference to be part of a team of Irish-speaking evangelists with a specific mission to the Irish Catholic poor in the wake of the rebellion of the United Irishmen.

Ouseley sang and preached, mostly in Irish, to large gatherings of people at county assizes, fairs, market days, funerals, and wakes, in prisons, and outside church services. His early reports for Dr Coke, the director of the Irish mission, capture the flavour of these occasions:

> On Monday we came to Baillieborough. The market people were assembled when we came into the street. We did not alight, but prepared to attack the devil's kingdom which still remained strong in the town. The Methodists wished us out of the street, when they saw the manner of our proceedings, riding on our horses, with our umbrellas over our heads, the day being wet, but a young girl was so alarmed that she feared the day of judgement was at hand. (Ouseley MSS, CR/6/3/F/10)

Gideon Ouseley (1762–1839), by T. A. Dean (after John Jackson)

Ouseley was not only characterized by his evangelical zeal but also by his anti-Catholicism, which predated his evangelical conversion and was part of a wider anti-clericalism. He drew a distinction between priests and the ordinary people, whom he regarded as victims of priestly tyranny and insupportable financial burdens. However, his anti-Catholicism underwent several phases of development and therefore by 1807 Ouseley was much more willing to engage in public controversies against Catholics. The thrust of his attacks also changed. Whereas earlier he had been more concerned with the social consequences of Catholic errors, after 1807 he unleashed a prolific pamphlet attack on Catholic dogma which continued until his death.

During the 1820s Ouseley, apart from his continuing commitment to preaching, spent much of the decade publishing his own highly individualistic solutions to Ireland's miseries. His remedies were for more responsible landlordism, a more equitable and rational assessment of tithes, the state payment of Catholic priests, and an electoral register based on minimum educational standards to ensure that landlords would have to provide schools for those over whom they exerted economic and political influence. He died in Dublin on 14 May 1839 and was buried at Mount Jerome cemetery, Harold's Cross, Dublin. There is a memorial church to him in Mountmellick, Queen's county, the town in which he preached his last sermon. At the heart of Ouseley's personality and work were a sincere religious faith and a genuine compassion for his country and countrymen. He was one of Ireland's most influential figures in the early nineteenth-century post-rebellion era. DAVID HUDDLESTON

Sources D. Hempton, 'Gideon Ouseley: rural revivalist, 1791–1839', *The religion of the people* (1996), 130–39 • W. Arthur, *The life of Gideon Ouseley* (1876) • W. Reilly, *Memorial of Gideon Ouseley* (1847) • N. B. Harmon, ed., *The encyclopaedia of world Methodism*, 2 (1974) • PRO NIre., Gideon Ouseley MSS, CR/6/3/F

Archives PRO NIre., papers, CR/6/3/F • Wesley Historical Society, Belfast, papers, MSS Box 1

Likenesses T. A. Dean, stipple (after J. Jackson), BM, NPG [*see illus.*] • engraving, repro. in Arthur, *Life of Gideon Ouseley* • engraving, repro. in Harmon, ed., *Encyclopaedia of world Methodism*

Ouseley, Sir Gore, first baronet (1770–1844), diplomatist, second son of Captain Ralph Ouseley (*d.* 1804) of Limerick, whose family had originated in Shropshire, and his first wife, Elizabeth, daughter of Henry Holland, also of Limerick, was born on 24 June 1770 at Limerick. He was educated at home with his brother, William *Ouseley, and his cousin Gideon *Ouseley, under a tutor, Dr Robinson. His father, to whom he was attached, took an active interest in the boys' education. Ouseley was an assiduous pupil, also possessed of athletic ability.

In 1787 Ouseley left for India, where he busied himself in commercial affairs. By 1792 he had settled at 'Bygonbarree' in the Dacca province of Bengal where, along the banks of the River Brahmaputra, he established a factory producing baftas (fine cloths) which were sold more cheaply than elsewhere in the province. He lived a relatively solitary existence and spent his leisure time studying Persian, Bengalese Hindi, Arabic, and Sanskrit. He became an elegant speaker and writer of Persian. In addition to his linguistic and literary pursuits he concerned himself deeply with music, an accomplishment he passed on to his son the composer Frederick Arthur Gore *Ouseley, and improved his skill at drawing. He made the acquaintance of the eminent orientalist Sir William James in 1794.

In the first years of the next century a move to Lucknow resulted in Ouseley's acquiring more insight into and experience of public and political service through his friendship with and attachment to Nawab Shuja ud-Daula, wazir of Oudh, as his major commandant and confidant. Anglo-French rivalry in India increased as a result of Napoleon's invasion of Egypt in mid-1798 when Marquess Wellesley took counter-measures to defend the British position, including a policy of subsidiary treaties with local princes. Within this strategic context, Ouseley earned Wellesley's approval for his well-judged attempts to cultivate good relations between the state of Oudh and the British power. This resulted crucially in Wellesley's later furthering of Ouseley's career. Ouseley returned to England in 1805. On 12 April 1806 he married Harriet Georgina, daughter of John *Whitelocke, army officer. They had two sons, Wellesley Abbas Ouseley and Frederick Arthur Gore *Ouseley, and three daughters, Mary Jane, Eliza Shirin, who died an infant, and Alexandrina Perceval. Ouseley was created baronet on 3 October 1808. In 1809, on the recommendation of Wellesley as secretary of state for foreign affairs, he was nominated *mehmendar*, guide and host to Mirza Abul Hasan, the Persian ambassador to Britain.

In 1810, following the British missions to Persia of John Malcolm and Harford Jones, Ouseley was appointed ambassador-extraordinary to the court of Fath Ali Shah. Accompanying Mirza Abul Hasan, Ouseley left England in July 1810 and reached Bombay before landing at Bushehr on 1 March 1811. He passed through Shiraz and Esfahan, and reached Tehran on 9 November where a treaty was signed on 14 March 1812. It had been preceded by many disagreements over etiquette and substance, but in spite of difficulties and misunderstandings Wellesley was pleased and entirely approved of Ouseley's conduct. Fath Ali Shah was no less enthusiastic and commended Ouseley to the prince regent. Ouseley received the decoration of the Lion and Sun. Because of some objections in London the treaty was not finally ratified until some further revisions had been negotiated by Meorier and Elis, the British plenipotentiaries, on 25 November 1814. There was further reciprocal respect when Ouseley met Abbas Muza, the prince royal, in Tabriz in 1812. Ouseley was instructed to use his good offices to mediate in the Perso-Russian hostilities. This culminated in the treaty of Gulistan on 13 October 1813. Ouseley left Tehran for Russia in mid-1814. He received the gratitude of the tsar, Alexander I, for his role and was honoured with the grand cordon of the order of St Alexander Nevsky.

Ouseley was sworn of the privy council on 10 October 1820. He enjoyed the favour of the prince regent, assisted at his coronation in 1820, and was made knight grand cross of the Royal Guelphic Order in 1831. Granted a pension of £2000 a year, he retired from public life, though he was appointed high sheriff of Buckinghamshire in 1835. Thereafter he devoted himself to family affairs and his literary and antiquarian interests. He was one of those responsible for the founding of the Royal Asiatic Society in London in 1823 and was associated with the formation of the oriental translation committee, of which he was elected chairman. He became president of the Society for the Publication of Oriental Texts, formed in 1842. In later life he suffered from ill health. He died of intestinal problems at his country residence, Hall Barn Park, Beaconsfield, which he had purchased in 1832, on 18 November 1844; he was survived by his wife. The place of his burial is unknown but his wife erected a monument to him in Hertingfordbury church.

Ouseley was a loyal, capable, and devoted practical public servant. He was also a notable oriental scholar at a time when that subject was in its infancy and he did much to encourage its emergence through his complementary literary and archaeological interests. It was not just his linguistic skill that was remarkable: his cultural sympathy was noticeable. He was attentive to those in his service and concerned for their welfare. Conciliatory and respectful, he was prepared to stand on his dignity when the occasion demanded it. Of middle stature, he was neat and trim in appearance. His spiritual integrity and moral behaviour were accompanied by a deep respect for the Anglican church and regular religious observances. His concern both for religion and for oriental scholarship was demonstrated by the assistance he gave, while at Shiraz, to Henry Martyn, missionary and first translator of the New Testament into Persian. R. W. FERRIER

Sources J. Reynolds, 'Memoir of the late Right Hon. Sir Gore Ouseley', in G. Ouseley, *Biographical notices of Persian poets* (1846) • J. Morier, *A second journey through Persia, Armenia, and Asia Minor to Constantinople between the years 1810 and 1816* (1818) • W. Ouseley, *Travels in various countries of the East, more particularly Persia*, 3 vols. (1819–23) • R. Greaves, 'Iranian relations with Great Britain and British India, 1798–1921', *Cambridge History of Iran*, ed. P. Avery, G. Hambly, and C. P. Melville, 7 (1991) • *The despatches, minutes and correspondence of the Marquess Wellesley … during his administration in India*, ed. M. Martin, 5 vols. (1836–40) • R. Savory, 'British and French diplomacy in Persia, 1800–10', *Iran Journal of the British Institute of Persian Studies*, 10 (1972), 31–44 • M. Atkins, *Russia and Iran, 1780–1828* (1980) • I. Amini, *Napoléon et la Perse* (1995) • R. K. Ramazani, *Foreign policy of Iran* (1966) • J. Malcolm, *History of Persia*, 2 vols. (1815) • H. J. Brudges, *An account of his majesty's mission to the court of Persia in the years 1807–1811*, 2 vols. (1834) • P. E. Roberts, *India under Wellesley* (1929) • *DNB*

Archives BL, Add. MS 19529 • BL OIOC • Bodl. Oxf., diary | BL, letters to Lord Wellesley, Add. MSS 37284–37313 • Bodl. Oxf., letters to Sir T. Phillipps • Herefs. RO, corresp. with Sir Harford Jones • PRO, letters to Stratford Canning, FO 352 • PRO, Foreign Office MSS • U. Southampton L., corresp. with Palmerston • U. Southampton L., letters to first duke of Wellington

Likenesses H. Cook, stipple, 1833 (after portrait by R. Rothwell), BM, NPG; repro. in W. Jerdan, *National portrait gallery of illustrious and eminent personages*, 5 vols. (1830–34), vol. 4 • W. Ridley, stipple (after portrait by S. Drummond), BM, NPG; repro. in *European Magazine* (1810)

Ouseley, Sir Ralph (1772–1842), army officer in the Portuguese service, was born at Kilticoghly, co. Galway, the second son of John Ouseley and his wife, Anne, daughter of Francis Surridge of Fairyhill, co. Galway. He was the younger brother of Gideon *Ouseley. On 25 November 1794 he was appointed lieutenant in the Leicester fencible infantry, one of many regiments of home-service regulars called 'fencibles'. He served gallantly with the forces in Ireland in 1798, commanded a detachment at the defeat of Lake's troops at Castlebar, and helped to force the surrender of the French at Ballinamuck. Ouseley was appointed to the 38th foot in March 1801. He commanded the grenadier company during Robert Emmet's insurrection in Dublin in 1803. For a year he was often detached to guard the powder mills near Rathcool. In 1804 Ouseley joined the 76th to go to India, and in succession was transferred to a company in the Royal African Corps in March 1805, the 82nd in August, and the staff of the army depot, Isle of Wight, in March 1807. In September 1809 he exchanged to the 63rd foot.

Ouseley then began a more continuous tenure by entering the Portuguese service under Marshal Beresford as major in the 18th infantry, with which he served during the campaigns of 1810–12. He became lieutenant-colonel of the regiment after the capture of Badajoz, and commanded it in the Pyrenees in 1813, where he distinguished himself in action against a superior force near Pampeluna on 30 July 1813. He was then transferred to the 8th Portuguese, and commanded that regiment in a night attack on the height in front of Urda. In this action, his modest force of 500 men drove off a French force of 3000. Philippart highlighted this event, but Napier merely stated that the French were on this occasion dislodged from the heights by two Portuguese brigades. Ouseley was carried from the field with a bayonet wound in the breast and a musket ball through the abdomen, which was extracted from the back. He received the Peninsular gold medal for the Pyrenees.

Ouseley attained the rank of major, the highest he held in the British service, on 25 November 1813, and was placed on half pay on 25 October 1814. He then went to Rio de Janeiro, where the king of Portugal renewed his Portuguese rank of lieutenant-colonel, and made him a knight of the order of the Tower and Sword. In 1817 he raised and organized at Rio de Janeiro the 1st regiment. He commanded it in the capture of Pernambuco and was made a knight of San Bento d'Avis. In October 1817 he was promoted colonel and placed on the staff. In 1818 he was sent from Rio to England with dispatches, which he had the acuity to rescue when the vessel was taken by pirates.

Ouseley retired from the British service in 1825. He attained the rank of major-general in the army of Portugal. He died at Lisbon on 3 May 1842, aged seventy. An autopsy showed that the musket ball which passed through his body at Urda caused a lesion of the intestines, which after an interval of nearly thirty years contributed to his death. Ouseley's foreign knighthood was not recognized in British army lists.

H. M. CHICHESTER, *rev.* GORDON L. TEFFETELLER

Sources *GM*, 2nd ser., 18 (1842), 206 • J. Philippart, ed., *The royal military calendar*, 3rd edn, 4 (1820) • Burke, *Peerage*

Ouseley, Sir William (1767–1842), orientalist, was born in Monmouthshire, the eldest son of Ralph Ouseley, army officer, and his first wife, Elizabeth, daughter of Henry Holland of Limerick. Sir Gore *Ouseley, diplomatist, was his brother. Ouseley was educated privately until 1787, when he went to Paris to study. The following year he became a cornet in the 8th regiment of dragoons. After serving in the 1794 campaign under the duke of York, he sold out and went to Leiden to resume the oriental, and especially Persian, studies which had already fascinated him during his time in Paris.

In 1795 Ouseley published *Persian miscellanies: an essay to facilitate the reading of Persian manuscripts … with engraved specimens*, a treatise on the various styles of Persian handwriting, enriched with many illustrations of manuscripts, and numerous notes showing considerable research. On his return to England in 1796 Ouseley was gazetted major in Lord Ayr's regiment of dragoons stationed at Carlisle, and there he married, on 6 March 1796, Julia, daughter of Lieutenant-Colonel John Irving. They had three daughters and six sons, including Sir William Gore *Ouseley (1797–1866), diplomatist and writer. Soon afterwards Ouseley took up residence at Crickhowell, Brecknockshire, where he remained until at least about 1820. In 1801 he wrote to the earl of Chichester dwelling on his ambition to become an envoy to some eastern court, and asking the earl to use his influence in procuring a government subsidy and approval for a proposed journey to Persia.

In 1797 Ouseley received the honorary degree of LLD at Trinity College, Dublin, and that of PhD from the University of Rostock. He was knighted in 1800. The Persian journey did not take place until 1810, when Sir William accompanied his brother, Sir Gore Ouseley, as private secretary, on his mission to the shah of Persia. By way of preparation for his eastern observations, he had lived some months in 1810 in the house of the Persian envoy, Mirza Abul Hasan, in London, where he learned to speak Persian. In July of that year they started from Portsmouth on HMS *Lion* for India and Persia, from where William Ouseley returned to Britain with the new treaty in July 1812. He published his account as *Travels in Various Countries of the East, More Particularly Persia* (3 vols., 1819–23), whose title-page states that the author was an honorary fellow of the royal societies of Edinburgh, Göttingen, and Amsterdam, and a member of the Asiatic Society of Bengal. His valuable collection of Persian manuscripts was offered for sale, and the catalogue, written by himself and printed in 1831, contains notices of 724 manuscripts. Ouseley died at Boulogne in September 1842.

Besides the works already mentioned Ouseley published numerous other books on oriental subjects, notably his *Oriental Collections* (3 vols., 1797–9). He translated several works from Persian, including an *Epitome of the ancient history of Persia, extracted from the Jehan Ara* of Ahmad al-Kazwini, the author of the *Nigaristan* (1799). He also edited volumes by J. L. Burckhardt and contributed extensively to the *Transactions* of the Royal Society of Literature. STANLEY LANE-POOLE, *rev.* PARVIN LOLOI

Sources *Encyclopaedia Britannica*, 9th edn (1875–89) · T. J. Mathias, *Pursuits of literature: a satirical poem in four dialogues*, 2nd edn (1797), 231–2 · 'Ouseley, Sir William', *Biographie des hommes vivants, ou, Histoire par ordre alphabétique*, 4 (1818), 577–8 · Burke, *Peerage* · A. J. Webb, *A compendium of Irish biography* (1878) · letter from William Ouseley to the earl of Chichester, 6 Dec 1801, BL, Add. MS 33108, fol. 425 · M. E. Yapp, *Strategies of British India: Britain, Iran and Afghanistan, 1798–1850* (1980) · Ward, *Men of the reign* · Watt, *Bibl. Brit.* · Allibone, *Dict.* · J. Haydn, *A dictionary of biography, past and present*, ed. B. Vincent (1877) · [J. Watkins and F. Shoberl], *A biographical dictionary of the living authors of Great Britain and Ireland* (1816); repr. (1966)
Archives Bodl. Oxf., letters to John Haddon Hindley
Likenesses H. R. Cook, stipple (after S. Drummond), BM, NPG; repro. in *European Magazine* (1811)

Ouseley, Sir William Gore (**1797–1866**), diplomatist and author, born in London on 26 July 1797, was the eldest son of Sir William *Ouseley (1767–1842), orientalist, and his wife, Julia Irving; Sir Gore *Ouseley, bt, also an orientalist, was his uncle. He entered the diplomatic service when very young, and in November 1817 was attached to the British embassy at Stockholm. After serving at other European courts he became, in November 1825, paid attaché at Washington, DC. He remained there for seven years, and in 1832 published *Remarks on the statistics and political institutions of the United States, with some observations on the ecclesiastical system of America, her sources of revenue, …*. The book, an edition of which was issued at Philadelphia during the same year under the auspices of Washington Irving, gave a highly favourable picture of American institutions. It was somewhat severely criticized by William Jacob in the *Quarterly Review* for December 1832, but was quoted with approval in Lord Brougham's *Political Philosophy* (1849, pt 3, 340).

In June 1832 Ouseley went to Rio de Janeiro as secretary of legation. He served as chargé d'affaires in Brazil in 1833 and again in 1836 and 1838–41. On 13 December 1844 he was sent to Buenos Aires as minister to the Argentine confederation, from where he was dispatched, in January 1846, on a special mission to Montevideo (see PRO, FO 6/114). In conjunction with M. Deffaudis, the representative of France, he secured the evacuation of Uruguay by the Argentine troops and the withdrawal of their fleet from the capital, which was occupied by English and French troops.

Some time after his return to England, in 1850, Ouseley published *Notes on the Slave Trade, with Remarks on the Measures Adopted for its Suppression*. It was directed against the proposals recently made in parliament by William Hutt for withdrawing the squadron employed on the west coast of Africa in checking the slave trade.

On 29 June 1852 Ouseley was created KCB. He was made DCL by Oxford University on 20 June 1855. On 30 October 1857 he was dispatched on a special mission to Central America. He afterwards travelled in the United States, and returned to England in 1860. He retired on a pension of £1000, but continued to take much interest in South American affairs, being chairman of the Falkland Islands' Company and other companies at his death.

Ouseley, besides speaking several modern languages, was a good classical scholar. In addition to the works mentioned, and some contributions to periodicals, he published *A description of views in South America, from original drawings made in Brazil, the River Plate, the Parana …* (1852). The drawings were selected for publication by Queen Victoria. He married, in 1829, Maria, daughter of M. Van Ness, governor of Vermont. She died on 18 January 1881, having borne two sons and a daughter. The elder son, William Charles, was attached to Sir Charles Hotham's mission to the River Plate in 1852, and died in Paraguay in 1858. The other son, a lieutenant in the navy, died during the Baltic operations in the same year. The daughter, Frances, married J. T. Fitzmaurice RN, fifth son of the earl of Orkney. Ouseley died from an abscess of the prostate at his London home, 31 Albemarle Street, on 6 March 1866.

G. LE G. NORGATE, *rev.* H. C. G. MATTHEW

Sources *GM*, 4th ser., 1 (1866), 588–9 · *ILN* (17 March 1866) · *FO List* (1866) · PRO, FO 6/114 · d. cert.
Archives BL, corresp. with Lord Aberdeen, Add. MSS 43127, 43152–43153 · Bodl. Oxf., letters to Benjamin Disraeli · Hants. RO, corresp. with third earl of Malmesbury · NL Scot., letters to John Ouseley · U. Southampton L., Palmerston MSS
Likenesses W. G. Ouseley, self-portrait, oils, Gov. Art Coll.
Wealth at death under £14,000: probate, 21 March 1866, *CGPLA Eng. & Wales*

Oustenaca. *See* Ostenaca (*d.* before 1780?).

Outlaw, Roger (*d.* **1341**), prior of the hospital of St John of Jerusalem in Ireland and administrator, belonged to a wealthy Kilkenny family. He is first mentioned as prior of the hospital in Kilmainham in August 1317 but had probably held the office for some time before that date. In 1330 the order's general chapter at Montpellier appointed him to hold office as prior for a further ten years from 1331.

Outlaw was first appointed chancellor of Ireland on 4 January 1322 and held this office until 1331, and again from 1332 to 1337 and from 1338 to his death. He acted as deputy to John Darcy, the justiciar, on several occasions between 1324 and 1341 and also as deputy to the treasurer, Walter Islip, a close associate, in 1317–18 and 1325–6. He was appointed to head the eyre of Meath in 1324 and was charged in 1333 with examining the state of the king's courts in Ireland and in 1338 with making a twice-yearly survey of the Irish exchequer and treasury.

As prior Outlaw had taken part in the resistance to the Scottish invasion and throughout his official career he participated in military expeditions against the rebel Irish, but he was also involved in attempts to restore peace by negotiation with the Irish. In 1332, in preparation for Edward III's proposed visit to Ireland, he was given power to treat with both English and Irish about coming into the king's peace, and was later instrumental in retaining Domnall Mac Murchadha in the king's service at an annual fee.

Outlaw probably used the resources of the hospital to help to meet his official expenses, and in return used his official position to increase the order's possessions. He received grants of lands, rents, and wardships from the crown and also benefited from licences to acquire property in mortmain. In 1327 he was accused by the justiciar, the earl of Kildare, of being too occupied with the affairs of the hospital to attend to the king's business, and of having divided the king's lands, wardships, and marriages between himself and Alexander Bicknor, archbishop of Dublin, but his official career was unaffected and the hospital continued to prosper. His efforts were greatly appreciated by his brethren, who in 1333 granted him three of the order's houses for his personal use during his lifetime, in recompense for his activities in promoting the hospital's interests and the consequent increase in its prosperity.

Roger Outlaw's family connections in Kilkenny involved him in an acrimonious dispute with Richard Ledred, bishop of Ossory. In 1324 Outlaw used his position as chancellor to obstruct the bishop's attempts to invoke the secular arm against Alice Kyteler and her son, and Roger's kinsman, William Outlaw, whom Ledred had accused of heresy. The prior was to be instrumental in arriving at a compromise with Ledred over the fate of William Outlaw, which included giving security for William's future good behaviour. The animosity broke out again in 1328 when the prior was active on behalf of Arnold Poer, who had been convicted of heresy by Ledred. As a result the bishop accused him of abetting Poer in his heretical depravity and Outlaw had to purge himself of the charge in the parliament held at Dublin in January 1329.

In addition to his official, family, and hospitaller interests Outlaw had close associations with certain of the nobility, being one of the executors of the will of William de Burgh, earl of Ulster, in 1333 and acting as attorney in Ireland for William Montagu, earl of Salisbury, in 1340. He visited England on several occasions, to inform the king of the state of the land of Ireland, and contributed financially to Edward III's expedition to the Low Countries in 1338.

Outlaw died on 6 February 1341 at the hospitallers' house at Any (now Hospital), Limerick, in the words of the Kilkenny chronicler, Friar Clyn, a prudent and a gracious man. PHILOMENA CONNOLLY

Sources C. McNeill, ed., *Registrum de Kilmainham: register of chapter acts of the Hospital of Saint John of Jerusalem in Ireland, 1326–1339*, IMC (1932) • H. G. Richardson and G. O. Sayles, *The administration of Ireland, 1172–1377* (1963) • F. de Ledrede, *A contemporary narrative of the proceedings against Dame Alice Kyteler*, ed. T. Wright, CS, 24 (1843) • J. T. Gilbert, ed., *Chartularies of St Mary's Abbey, Dublin: with the register of its house at Dunbrody and annals of Ireland*, 2, Rolls Series, 80 (1884) • PRO, E 101 • E. Tresham, ed., *Rotulorum patentium et clausorum cancellariae Hiberniae calendarium*, Irish Record Commission (1828) • *The annals of Ireland by Friar John Clyn and Thady Dowling: together with the annals of Ross*, ed. R. Butler, Irish Archaeological Society (1849) • *Chancery records*

Likenesses effigy, church, Hospital (formerly Any), co. Limerick

Outram, Benjamin (*bap.* **1764**, *d.* **1805**), civil engineer and ironmaster, was born at Alfreton, Derbyshire, where he was baptized on 1 April 1764, the eldest son of Joseph Outram (1732–1811), a local freeholder, and his second wife, Elizabeth. His father practised as a land agent and served as a turnpike trustee and enclosure commissioner; the tradition that he also had an ironworks at Ripley is unfounded. While he was still very young, Benjamin (who was probably named after an uncle who died in 1741, rather than the American Benjamin Franklin, as sometimes claimed) attracted the attention of Francis Beresford, a local attorney and a member of a leading west Derbyshire gentry family, who appears to have helped with his education and training. Outram became a land surveyor and both he and his father were early promoters of the Cromford Canal, authorized in 1789, which ran from the Erewash Canal at Langley Mill to Cromford and Pinxton, passing within a few miles of the Outrams' home at Alfreton.

While the canal was being built, a freehold estate of about 200 acres became available along its route at Butterley, between Alfreton and Ripley, which in 1790 Beresford bought in his own name and Outram's. Here Outram established an ironworks and within a few years the business had expanded to include a limestone quarry and limekilns, with collieries and ironstone pits spread over a wide area around Butterley Hall. In 1792 Beresford and Outram were joined by John Wright, a Nottingham banker who married Beresford's eldest daughter, and William Jessop (1745–1814), principal engineer of the Cromford Canal, of which Outram was resident engineer, and the four men together established Benjamin Outram & Co., with a nominal capital of £6000. Outram took up residence at Butterley Hall and was the only partner active in the management of the company, in which he was assisted by a younger brother, Joseph.

In addition, Outram built up a considerable civil engineering practice following his success with the Cromford Canal, completed in 1793. In Derbyshire he was responsible for the Derby and Nutbrook canals in the south-east of the county and the much more ambitious Peak Forest Canal in the north-west; further afield he was engineer to the Huddersfield Canal. He also reported on several schemes which did not go ahead.

More important than his canal work was Outram's contribution to the development of railways. Cast-iron rails had begun to replace wooden track after their first use at Coalbrookdale in 1767, and in 1787–8 a new type of L-section rail, with a flat tread and vertical inside flange, in place of rails designed to take wagons with flanged wheels, was introduced underground at Sheffield and on the surface at Wingerworth ironworks, near Chesterfield. Outram took up the idea of plate rails, as they became known, improved their design, and became the leading promoter of their use in many parts of the country, especially the east midlands and south Wales. In some cases he acted as engineer for canal companies seeking to build tram road branches; elsewhere he merely supplied rails made at Butterley ironworks, which thus became one of the country's main producers of castings of this sort outside south Wales. On the other hand, the notion that the words 'tram' or 'tram road' are derived from Outram's name has long been dismissed as untenable.

In 1800 Outram married Margaret (1778–1863), daughter of the Scottish political economist and writer James *Anderson (1739–1808), with whom he had five children: Francis, Anna, James *Outram, Margaret, and Elizabeth. Shortly afterwards he gave up most of his engineering commitments to devote more time to managing the works at Butterley, which by this date already employed more than 500 men. On 22 May 1805, however, while on a visit to London, Outram died after only a few days' illness, apparently from a stroke (his wife uses the phrase 'brain fever'). His sudden death, without leaving a will, led to the discovery of considerable confusion in his affairs and his dealings with the Butterley Company, as the business became known in 1807. Only in 1815, after four years of chancery litigation, was the partnership reconstructed and Mrs Outram released from obligations incurred by her husband. She returned to her native Aberdeen in 1810 with her children, of whom the second son, James Outram (1803–1863), was made a baronet in 1858 for his part in suppressing the Indian mutiny. She never remarried.

Evidence from the extensive surviving records of the Butterley Company confirms the view of Benjamin Outram—suggested by the letters and journals of his wife—that he was a man of great vigour and spirit, characteristics shared by his father, Joseph, with whom he did not get on. Mrs Outram wrote:

> My husband like many other men of great talent and comprehensive and generous mind, was hasty in his temper, feeling his own superiority over others. Accustomed to command, he had little toleration for stupidity and slowness, and none for meanness or littleness of any kind. (Outram, 101)

A temperament of this sort enabled Outram to create the largest coal, iron, and engineering business in the east midlands in barely fifteen years, while at the same time transforming the way in which railways were built. It also led to a situation in which his wife and family, far from benefiting from his success as both ironmaster and engineer, were reduced to near poverty when the rashness of some of his actions became clear after his death.

PHILIP RIDEN

Sources M. F. Outram, *Margaret Outram, 1778–1863, mother of the Bayard of India* [1932] • M. J. T. Lewis, *Early wooden railways* (1970) • P. Riden, 'The Butterley Company and railway construction, 1790–1830', *Transport History*, 6 (1973), 30–52 • P. Riden, *The Butterley Company, 1790–1830*, 2nd edn, Derbyshire RS (1990) • register, Derbys. RO [baptism]
Archives Derbys. RO, Butterley Co. MSS
Wealth at death see Riden, *Butterley Company*

Outram, Sir Benjamin Fonseca (1774–1856), surgeon and naval officer, son of Captain William Outram, was born in Kilham, near Bridlington, Yorkshire, and baptized at Gravesend, Kent. He was apprenticed to a Mr Coleman and later to Mr William Harvis, surgeon-apothecaries of Gravesend. He joined the Royal Navy as a surgeon's mate in 1794, serving in the frigate *Isis*. Promoted to the rank of surgeon in 1796, he served in the *Harpy*, *La Nymphe*, and *Boadicea*, where his medical competence and clinical acumen won high praise from Dr Thomas Trotter, physician of the fleet. He was surgeon in the *Superb* in her celebrated action off Algeciras, when Sir James Saumarez routed the French and Spanish fleets on 12 July 1801, and his presence of mind prevented an explosion on board. He received war medals and clasps for his services under Sir Richard Goodwin Keats during the war. The brief peace enabled him to undertake further surgical training at Guy's Hospital, London, and on the renewal of hostilities he served in the hospital ship *Matilda*, the frigate *Euryalus*, and the yachts *Royal Charlotte* and *Royal Sovereign*. During this period he studied intermittently in Edinburgh, where he graduated doctor of medicine on 24 June 1809, after presenting his inaugural thesis, 'De febre continua'. He was admitted a licentiate of the Royal College of Physicians, London, on 16 April 1810, and practised as a physician in London, where he lived more than forty years, from 1832 in Hanover Square. He also acted as physician to the Welbeck Street Dispensary. On 18 May 1811 he married Ann Scales, widow of Captain Richard Corne RN, with whom he travelled extensively, and they spent several years on the continent. She died suddenly at Clifton, near Bristol, in 1852.

On 3 May 1838 Outram was elected a fellow of the Royal Society, but was not the author of the geological paper published in its *Transactions* (1796), with which his name is associated in the list of fellows. He also became one of the earliest members of the Royal Geographical Society, where he proved a faithful friend and a kind and congenial colleague, contributing actively to its meetings.

In 1841 Outram became inspector of fleets and hospitals.

He was made a knight bachelor and companion of the bath on 17 September 1850, and was admitted a fellow of the Royal College of Physicians on 9 July 1852.

On 10 October 1855 Outram married Sally, the daughter of Joseph Outram, a near relative of General Sir James Outram. He contracted cholera while travelling to a scientific meeting and died on 18 February 1856 while convalescing at Brighton. He was buried with his first wife at Clifton.

A man of considerable affluence, Outram was an able clinician with wide scientific interests, and a generous philanthropist. His uncle Captain Sir Thomas Outram left him a small estate in Kilham.

Outram left legacies to his friends, £4000 to his domestics and £100 each to the Fistula Hospital, the Institution for the Widows of Medical Men of London, the Naval School for Boys at New Cross, the Naval Benevolent Institution, and the Distressed Governesses' Society.

Outram published a pamphlet, *Suggestions to Naval Surgeons Previous to, during, and after a Battle*, and 'An account of the action in the Straits of the Mediterranean on the night of the 12th of July 1801', published in *The Times* and used by T. S. Hughes in his continuation of Hume and Smollett's *History of England* (1857). D'A. POWER, *rev.* J. WATT

Sources Retired surgeons' register, PRO, ADM 104/12 • *Memoir of Sir Benjamin Outram … inspector of naval hospitals and fleets, Royal College of Physicians of London* [n.d.] [incl. Outram's 'An account of the action in the Straits of the Mediterranean on the night of the 12th of July 1801'] • T. Trotter, *Medicina nautica: an essay on the diseases of seamen*, 2nd edn, 3 (1804), 100–01, 121–3 • *GM*, 2nd ser., 45 (1856), 429 • *Proceedings* [Royal Geographical Society], 1 (1855–7), 126–7 • class lists of James Gregory and Professor J. Home, 1807–8, U. Edin. L., special collections division • Pupils entered under Mr Stocker; entry of physicians and surgeons; pupils and dressers, 1778–1813, Guy's Hospital Library, 51 • Munk, *Roll* • *The history of England … by Hume and Smollett: with the continuation from the accession of George III to the accession of Queen Victoria*, ed. T. S. Hughes, new edn, 18 vols. (1854–5)
Archives U. Edin. L., corresp. and papers

Outram, George (1805–1856), journalist, was born on 25 March 1805 at Clyde ironworks, Glasgow, second son of Joseph Outram (1771–1830), manager of the ironworks and later shipowner, and Elizabeth, daughter of George Knox of Craigleith. His uncle was the engineer Benjamin *Outram (*bap.* 1764, *d.* 1805). About 1807 Joseph Outram moved to Leith, where George attended the high school. He proceeded to the University of Edinburgh, and in 1827 he became a member of the Faculty of Advocates, but after ten years of a legal career he readily accepted the post of editor at the *Glasgow Herald*. Outram's attitude towards the law is reflected in the witty, satirical tones of *Legal Lyrics and Metrical Illustrations of the Scotch Form of Process*, initially printed for private circulation among friends and colleagues (1851), and ultimately reprinted several times after his death, reaching a wider readership in spite of its heavy dependence on Scottish dialect. *Legal Lyrics* was initially printed under the pseudonym Quizdom Rumfunidos. The work was published posthumously by Blackwoods under Outram's own name in 1874 as *Lyrics Legal and Miscellaneous*, introduced by Henry Glassford Bell. A new edition in 1887 was edited by J. H. Stoddard, a later editor of the *Glasgow Herald*. Additional pieces were added, and corrections made. A final edition appeared in 1916, published by Foulis Press. The best known of Outram's poems, 'The Annuity', was in the public domain far earlier, as it was anonymously published in the *Illustrated London Magazine* in December 1854. Outram also worked with John Wilson on his Christopher North articles, 'Dies boreales', in *Blackwood's Magazine* in the 1840s and early 1850s.

As a lawyer, Outram lived and worked in Edinburgh, where he was a member of the Edinburgh Angling Club. In Edinburgh he met his wife, Frances McRobbie, daughter of William McRobbie of Smallwood, Jamaica. They were married in Edinburgh on 28 November 1837. A few months after accepting the editorship of the *Glasgow Herald* in May 1837 (at £400 a year), Outram was offered a partnership in the business to which he gave his name, holding four of the twenty-eight shares, worth a nominal £100 each. He settled in Glasgow, where his family grew to four sons and one daughter. The daughter died in infancy, and the last of the sons died in 1887.

As an editor Outram was moderate in tone and conservative by nature, but moved to indignant support of causes he favoured, such as Scottish nationalism. He was a member of the National Association for the Vindication of Scottish Rights Movement, using his newspaper to advocate its cause, incidentally managing some gibes at *The Scotsman* (an Edinburgh publication) for its apparent lack of patriotism. Outram was also responsible for reversing the *Herald*'s anti-cornlaw policy. Under Outram's benign and stable editorship the circulation of the paper almost doubled to 4500 copies per issue.

Outram died on 16 September 1856, of liver disease, at Rosemore, on the Holy Loch, and was buried in Warriston cemetery, Edinburgh. He was survived by his wife. His name was perpetuated in the publishing firm of Outram (George) & Co. ROSEMARY SCOTT

Sources H. G. Bell, 'Introductory notice', in G. Outram, *Lyrics legal and miscellaneous* (1874) • Boase, *Mod. Eng. biog.* • m. cert. • d. cert. • A. Phillips, *Glasgow's Herald, 1783–1983* (1982) • *Glasgow Herald* (17 Sept 1856) • J. G. Wilson, ed., *The poets and poetry of Scotland*, 2 (1877) • Irving, *Scots.* • *ILN* (Dec 1854) • *Glasgow Chamber of Commerce Journal* (March 1976)
Archives NL Scot., letters to Blackwoods
Likenesses portrait, *c.*1840–1849, repro. in Phillips, *Glasgow's 'Herald'*

Outram, Sir James, first baronet (1803–1863), army officer in the East India Company, second son of Benjamin *Outram (*bap.* 1764, *d.* 1805), civil engineer and ironmaster, of Butterley Hall, Derbyshire, and his wife, Margaret (1778–1863), daughter of Dr James Anderson of Mounie, Aberdeenshire, was born at Butterley Hall on 29 January 1803. Mrs Outram, who by the sudden death of her husband was left in very straitened circumstances, was a woman of great self-reliance and independence. With her young family she resided for three years at Worksop, then

Sir James Outram, first baronet (1803–1863), by Thomas Brigstocke, *c.*1863

for two years at Barnby Moor, and in 1810 moved to Aberdeen.

Education and early career From 1814 Outram was educated in Aberdeen first at Udny School, then at Mr Esson's school, and finally (in 1818) at Marischal College. In 1819 he received a direct Indian cadetship, sailed for India in May, and arrived in Bombay on 15 August. He was temporarily posted to the 4th native infantry, with rank as ensign from 2 May 1819, and then was gazetted a lieutenant in the 1st grenadier native infantry, but was shortly afterwards transferred to the 12th regiment and became acting-adjutant in July 1820.

In November 1822 Outram arranged with his brother, Francis, a second lieutenant in the Bombay Engineers, that they should put by out of their pay as subalterns an allowance for their mother. At Rajkot, where his regiment was quartered, he became an enthusiastic sportsman; and his shikar-book for the seasons of 1822–3 and 1823–4 shows a record of seventy-four wild boars, four nilgai, two hyenas, and two wolves. In April 1824 he moved with his regiment to Malegaon in Khandesh.

India: war and administration, 1824–1856 For the next fourteen years Outram was engaged in a little-known, but vital, aspect of the establishment of British rule in western India: the subjugation of petty chieftains and tribal peoples in the region known as Khandesh and in the interior of Gujarat. The official reports speak of 'tribal rebellions', 'outrages' against the British, the lawlessness of marauding bands of tribal peoples, and the refusal of some of the chiefs to accept the new British order. While the contests were unequal, pitting poorly armed and undisciplined groups against the armies of the East India Company, the petty chiefs and the tribal leaders fought tenaciously.

Towards the end of 1824 Outram took part in an expedition against Kittur, a princely state which had lapsed to the British on the death without heirs of the ruler, but had resisted the British government and repulsed a small force sent to take possession. Outram's brother, Francis, served in the same expedition. Kittur was besieged, and surrendered on 5 December 1824. In March 1825 Outram was sent to seize the hill fort of Malair between Surat and Malegaon, when an insurrection broke out in the western districts of Khandesh. The garrison fled, the leader and many of his adherents were cut down, and the rest escaped to the hills completely disorganized. In recognition of his services and merit he was placed, on 22 April 1825, under the collector and political agent in Khandesh.

The province of Khandesh became British territory in 1818, after the defeat of the Marathas. At that time the Bhils, a people driven out of Mewar and Jodhpur and subsisting mainly on plunder, formed an eighth part of the whole population of the area. The Bhil agency was established in 1825 under the collector of Khandesh, with three agents: one in the north-west, one in the south, and Outram in the north-east. To the last was entrusted the duty of raising a Bhil light infantry corps, under native commissioned and non-commissioned officers of line regiments. He proceeded to Jatgaon, and led the detachment of his own regiment stationed there to dislodge some Bhils from the mountain fastnesses. Supported by reinforcements from Malegaon, the operation ended in the occupation of the Bhil lands. Outram commenced the formation of his corps by enlisting his captives who brought in their relatives. He also succeeded in gaining the confidence of the chief men by living unguarded among them, and persuaded five to join his corps. By July 1826 300 Bhils who were enrolled in his corps had become efficient soldiers. By 1828 the corps numbered 600 men. In 1829 Francis Outram killed himself in a fit of depression.

In 1830 the Bombay government decided to invade and subdue the Dang country, a tract of tangled forest on the west of Khandesh inhabited by marauding Bhils. Outram, after a fortnight's campaign, overran the country and subdued it, returning with the principal chiefs as his prisoners. In 1831 Outram was sent to investigate uprisings in the districts of Yàwal and Sauda, and to apprehend the offenders. He captured 469 suspected persons and, after inquiry, 158 were committed for trial. In 1833, the Bhils of the Barwani territory in the Satpura Mountains north of Khandesh having risen in rebellion, Outram, who had been promoted captain on 7 October 1832, took the field against them and struck a decisive blow, capturing the rebel chief Hatnia. During his residence in Khandesh Outram was always able to indulge his passion for hunting, and during the ten years from 1825 to 1834 he killed 191 tigers, 25 bears, 12 buffaloes, and 15 leopards.

Early in 1835 Outram accompanied the British resident

at Indore through Malwa and Nimar; then the government sent him to survey the neighbouring province of Gujarat, where, in the Mahi Kantha district, opposition to British rule had developed. Outram's report expressed his conviction that Mahi Kantha would not be peaceful until the unruly clans which occupied it had been subdued and the chiefs punished for opposition to British arms. Outram went on leave to Bombay in December, to be married to his cousin, Margaret Clementina (*d.* 12 July 1911), daughter of James Anderson of Bridgend, Brechin, Forfarshire. A fortnight after his wedding he returned to Mahi Kantha as political agent, with the general direction of affairs civil and military. Outram succeeded in Mahi Kantha but with the use of such violence that the governor of Bombay, Sir Robert Grant, and the court of directors reproved him, but complimented his military genius, energy, and sound judgement.

Outram's wife was invalided home, and in October 1838, when a British force was ordered to assemble for service in Afghanistan, Outram at once volunteered, and was appointed extra aide-de-camp to Sir John Keane. He was dispatched on a special mission to Cutch, to arrange for land and water transport for the expedition. Outram was associated with Lieutenant Eastwick (afterwards a director of the East India Company), the assistant resident, in a mission to the court of Hyderabad, to conclude a detailed treaty with the amir. The envoys, however, met with such unmistakable signs of hostility that they were compelled to return without effecting their object. Outram was sent on missions to Shah Shuja, the claimant to the Afghan throne, and General MacNaghten in February and March 1839. He took part at Kandahar in the installation of Shah Shuja. He left that city with the advanced column on 27 June, to attack Ghazni, which fell on 23 July. Outram was appointed to command an expedition for the capture of Dost Muhammad Khan, the deposed ruler who had fled towards Bamian and escaped beyond the Oxus.

On 21 August Outram was placed under the British envoy at Kabul, MacNaghten, to conduct an expedition into disturbed districts lying between Kabul and Kandahar. The object of the expedition was to defeat the Ghilzai people, to arrest four chiefs, to punish the inhabitants of the village of Maruf, who had destroyed a caravan *en route* for India, and to reduce the fort of Haji Khan. He attacked and demolished Haji Khan, and finally arrived at Quetta on 31 October, having accomplished his mission.

Outram accompanied General Willshire as aide-de-camp in November to the siege of Kalat. He was deputed to take a copy of the general's dispatch to the governor of Bombay by the direct route to Sonmiani Bundar, to find out whether the route would be practical for troops. Disguised as an Afghan, he started on this perilous journey through an enemy's country, accompanied by a private servant and two Saiyids of Shal as guides. After many adventures and hairbreadth escapes he reached Sonmiani on 23 November, having subsisted during the whole journey on dates and water. From Sonmiani he went by water to Karachi and Bombay. For his services at Kalat, Outram was promoted brevet major on 13 November 1839, while Shah Shuja bestowed on him the second-class order of the Durrani empire.

At the end of 1839 Lord Auckland appointed Outram political agent in Lower Sind, in succession to Colonel Pottinger. He arrived at Hyderabad on 24 February. The main features of his work in 1840 were the reduction of taxes on inland produce brought to the British camp at Karachi, the relief of the Indus traffic from excessive tolls, and the negotiations with Mir Sher Muhammad of Mirpur, whereby quasi-amicable relations were established. In 1841 he negotiated a satisfactory treaty with Mir Sher Muhammad. Soon afterwards Mir Nur Muhammad, the amir of Hyderabad, summoned Outram to his deathbed, and confided his brother, Mir Nasir Khan, and his youngest son, Mir Husain Ali, to Outram's protection. Outram regarded this as a sacred charge and the boy as an adopted son.

On 18 August 1841 Outram left Hyderabad for Quetta, having been appointed political agent in Upper Sind in addition to his charge of Lower Sind. He arrived at Quetta on 2 September, and the young Nasir, khan of Kalat, met him in durbar. On 6 October the khan was installed by Outram at Kalat, after signing the ratification to a treaty with the Indian government. At the end of November Outram heard that the British army, which had occupied Kabul, was under siege, and his energies were taxed to the utmost to support the failing prestige of the government.

In February 1842 Lord Ellenborough succeeded Lord Auckland as governor-general. Outram did his best to impress on the new governor-general the inadvisability of retiring from Afghanistan without first reasserting British power at Kabul. On 28 March 1842 General England was defeated at Haikalzai, in the Pishin valley. The general officially laid the blame upon Outram's assistant, Lieutenant Hammersley, for want of proper acquaintance with the disposition and movements of the enemy. Outram could not acquiesce in the censure, and his bold advocacy of Hammersley's cause brought him under the displeasure of Lord Ellenborough, who invested General William Nott with the chief political as well as military control in Kandahar and Sind, thus subordinating Outram to him as a political officer.

On 1 June Outram left Sukkur for Quetta, to assist General Nott in his preparations for an advance on Kabul. In October he accompanied General England in the withdrawal of his force to India through the dangerous part of the Bolan Pass. He then pushed on alone to Sukkur to report to Sir Charles James Napier, who in August had taken over the command of the troops in Sind and Baluchistan, with entire control over the political agents and civil officers. Outram was remanded to his regiment, and the political establishment dissolved. At a public dinner given to Outram at Sukkur, on 5 November 1842, Napier proposed his health in the following terms: 'Gentlemen, I give you the "Bayard of India", sans peur et sans reproche, Major James Outram of the Bombay army', and the epithet has since become permanently linked with his name.

Outram applied for furlough for two years, and was to

have sailed on 2 January 1843, when, on the application of Napier, he was appointed a commissioner for the arrangement of the details of a revised treaty with the amirs of Sind. He arrived at Sukkur on 3 January. This was the beginning of an association between the two men that ended in extraordinary bitterness, carried on through memoranda, books, and speeches. While part of the rancour on Outram's part may have been due to the loss of his independent position in Sind, and being brought under Napier's control, there were fundamental policy differences between them over the place of the Indian rulers, such as the amirs, in the new order. Napier believed the amirs were relics of oppressive feudalism that should be abolished, whereas Outram believed that before the British entered Sind, the people there were as happy as those under any government in Asia. When the governor-general ordered an even more rigorous treaty to be signed by the amirs, Outram became convinced that Napier would use it to goad the amirs into war, which would give him the opportunity to annex the whole of Sind. Knowing how the amirs' undisciplined, ill-armed tribesmen would be slaughtered by Napier's army, Outram wrote to him protesting that his policies were harsh and tyrannical, and that every life lost in consequence would be murder. Outram was no longer the Bayard of India; in correspondence Napier referred to him as 'son of a bitch'.

Outram accompanied Napier in his march across the desert to Imamgarh to destroy the amirs' great fort. After the fort was demolished Outram went to Khairpur to meet the chiefs of Upper Sind and the vakils of the amirs of Lower Sind, and on 8 February he arrived at Hyderabad. What happened at Hyderabad at this time was central to the dispute between Outram and Napier. Outram had asked for one more chance to negotiate the new treaty before attacking them, and Napier had agreed. According to Napier's version, while Outram was at the residency, he and his force of 100 men were attacked by 8000 men under Mir Shahdad Khan, one of the leading amirs, and after gallantly defending the residency, they escaped by boat up the River Indus under heavy fire. Napier then began the war in earnest against the amirs. Outram's version of events is very different. He said that the amirs had signed the treaty, and that he had written this to the governor-general, but that Napier had not sent the letter, not wanting to miss the excuse for attacking the amirs. While Outram's account seems plausible, Napier's was more heroic, and it became the accepted version.

On 16 February Outram joined Napier at Matiari, 16 miles above Hyderabad. Napier at once sent Outram off at his own request to burn the Miani and neighbouring forests (*shikárgáhs*), in which it was expected the enemy would collect, and from which it would be difficult to dislodge them. He was employed on this duty while Napier was fighting the battle of Miani, where, as Outram had predicted, Napier's well-trained troops slaughtered 6000 of the amirs' followers. On 18 February the amirs of Hyderabad, Mirs Hasan Khan, Shahdad, and Husain Ali Khan, surrendered. The two former were detained as prisoners, but the latter was released at Outram's request out of respect for the memory of his late father, Mir Nur Muhammad.

Outram's functions as commissioner having ceased on the outbreak of hostilities, he left on 20 February for Bombay, carrying dispatches. In April he was presented at Bombay with a sword of honour of the value of 300 guineas and a costly piece of plate. For his services in the Sind War he was promoted brevet lieutenant-colonel on 4 July 1843, and made a CB. Outram's share of the prize money amounted to £3000, but he declined to take the money for himself, and distributed it among charitable institutions in India.

Outram returned to England in May 1843 with his mind filled with the unfortunate condition of the amirs and people of Sind, and during his furlough was engaged in making representations on their behalf. He was also engaged in the great controversy on the annexation of Sind, and the difference of opinion between Napier and himself led to a serious rupture. The contest proved a long and costly one for Outram. For years the uncongenial paper warfare dragged on, and was the source of misrepresentations, misunderstandings, and aspersions on both sides.

News of upheaval at Lahore and the murder of the Maharaja Sher Singh was received in London in November, and Outram returned to India in December, armed with a letter from Wellington to the commander-in-chief in India. When Outram arrived at Sir Hugh Gough's camp at Fatehpur, Lord Ellenborough, who was there, refused, as a supporter of Napier, to grant him a personal interview, and objected to his joining Gough, but gave him the minor political charge of Minar in central India. There was not sufficient work to occupy him in Minar; he was worried with the Sind controversy, and in September he resigned his appointment, intending to return home. An outbreak, however, in the southern Maratha country between Bombay and Goa led Outram to offer his services. He was sent on special duty and on 13 October 1844 he was present at the capture of Samangarh. The rebellion spreading, he was attached to Major-General Delamotte's staff as head of the intelligence department. During the campaign he distinguished himself at the storming and capture of the forts of Pawangarh and Panala. Outram returned to Bombay in December, and was at once ordered to take part in the suppression of disturbances in Savantvadi, south of the country he had just left.

In May 1845 Outram was appointed resident at Satara, and he took up his appointment on 26 May; in May 1847 he was transferred to the British residency at Baroda, the highest position under the Bombay government. On 21 February 1848 he became a regimental major. Ill health compelled him in November to go for a change of air to Egypt and Syria, and he occupied himself there by writing an exhaustive memoir on Egypt for the East India Company, for which he received the thanks of government. Outram returned to his post at Baroda in May 1850. Here he set himself to work to put down *khatpat* or corruption. He sent in charges against Narsu Pant, head native agent at the residency, and in a full report, dated 31 October

1851, for submission to the court of directors, he dealt with the *khatpat* case without respect of persons. His report was considered by the Bombay government to be disrespectful both to itself and to the ruler of Baroda. The result was that Outram was removed from the office of resident at Baroda. He returned to England in March 1852. While the court of directors upheld the Bombay government, it expressed a hope that on Outram's return to India a suitable opportunity would be found of employing him.

In July 1853, having been promoted regimental lieutenant-colonel in the preceding month, Outram returned to India, arriving at Calcutta on 12 September. While at Calcutta, at the request of the governor-general, he wrote 'Memorandum on the invasion of India from the westward', which argued that the Indus River should be the western frontier of British India. The court of directors had written to the governor-general to find employment for Outram under the supreme government, and the transfer, towards the end of the year, of Baroda from the Bombay government to the government of India enabled Lord Dalhousie to reinstate Outram as resident there. Outram arrived at Baroda on 19 March 1854, and, after holding the office for a month, was appointed political agent and commanded at Aden. He embarked at Bombay in June, but the change to Aden in the hot season affected his health. In November Lord Dalhousie appointed him to the residency of Oudh, and he made his official entry into Lucknow on 5 December.

Outram was instructed to prepare at once a report on the condition of the country, and to state whether the improvement demanded by Lord Hardinge seven years previously had in any degree been effected. In March 1855 he submitted his report, which represented the condition of Oudh as deplorable, and reluctantly recommended annexation as the only remedy. Annexation took place in February 1856, but with harsher terms for the ruler than Outram had recommended. Outram was promoted major-general on 28 November 1854, and was made KCB in February 1856. Ill health compelled him to return home in May.

The Anglo-Persian War, 1857 On 13 November Outram was summoned to India House and informed that he had been appointed to the command of the army for the Anglo-Persian War. Outram was given the local rank of lieutenant-general, and invested with diplomatic powers. He left England at once, and landed at Bombay on 22 December 1856. He left Bombay on 15 January 1857, and arrived at Bushehr on 27 January. The Persian commander-in-chief was at Borazjan, and was collecting a large force there. Outram determined to attack this position and, after a march of 46 miles in forty-one hours, in cold, wet, and stormy weather, the camp was reached, and found to have been hastily abandoned on Outram's approach. Outram commenced his return march on the night of 7 February to Bushehr, carrying with him large stores of provision. On the march, at daybreak on 8 February, they were attacked at Khushab by some 6000 Persians, with a few guns. After a smart action, in which 700 Persians were killed and two guns captured, the Persian force fled.

It was not until 26 March that operations were commenced against the Persian stronghold, Muhammarah. The Persians abandoned their position and fled, leaving sixteen guns and all their baggage stores and ammunition behind them. Peace had already been concluded at Baghdad, and the war was at an end. Outram was sent to Baghdad in May to arrange the formation of a mission to see that the evacuation of Herat fortress and district was duly carried out by the Persians. He returned to Bombay on 26 June 1857. For his services Outram was made GCB.

The Indian mutiny, 1857–1858 Meanwhile the Indian mutiny had broken out, and Outram's son, who was stationed at Aligarh, and his wife had a narrow escape. Outram reached Calcutta on 31 July, and on 8 August was given command of two divisions of the Bengal army occupying the country from Calcutta to Cawnpore inclusive, while he was also made chief commissioner of Oudh in succession to Sir Henry Montgomery Lawrence, killed in the defence of Lucknow. He took with him Robert Napier as his military secretary and chief of staff, and arrived at Dinapore on 19 August. On 1 September he was at Allahabad, and on 15 September he reached Cawnpore.

Outram had already telegraphed from Benares to Havelock that he would shortly join him at Cawnpore with reinforcements, but that he would leave to Havelock the glory of the relief of Lucknow, accompanying him only in his civil capacity as commissioner, and placing his military services at Havelock's disposal as a volunteer. On 28 September Sir Colin Campbell confirmed Outram's temporary transfer of command by a general order, in which he called attention to the disinterested sacrifice made by Outram in favour of Havelock. On 19 September 1857 the force crossed the river and marched out of Cawnpore. On 23 September, in the action of the Alambagh, Outram, at the head of the volunteer and native cavalry, pursued the flying enemy to the Charbagh Bridge. On 25 September Havelock's force, after severe fighting, in which Outram received a flesh wound in the arm, won their way to the residency.

Outram resumed his military command by a general order on 26 September. He found that he had simply reinforced a beleaguered garrison, and was himself effectually besieged until November, when Sir Colin Campbell, the commander-in-chief, came to the rescue. On 12 November Outram, on his side, blew in the outer wall of the garden of the palace of Farid Bakhsh, and opened his batteries on the insurgent defences in front. The buildings were soon in his possession; but he was still half a mile from the most advanced post of Sir Colin Campbell's force, and the way was under the enemy's fire. Outram, however, determined to meet Sir Colin Campbell without delay and, with Havelock and seven others, set out. Four were struck down, but Outram, Havelock, and their surviving companions reached the Moti Mahal unhurt. After a short conference they made their way back. Sir Colin entrusted the withdrawal of the garrison and the evacuation of the residency to Outram.

After the evacuation of the residency Campbell left Outram with a field force at the Alambagh position to hold the city of Lucknow until Campbell had placed his convoy in safety and disposed of the Gwalior mutineers. For three months Outram's division, consisting of about 5000 men and 25 guns, kept in check 120,000 organized troops with more than 130 guns. The leader of the rebels at Lucknow was the famous Maulvi known as Ahmad Shah. He made determined efforts to sever Outram's communications, and continually harassed his outposts. From the end of December 1857 and through January and February 1858 sharp engagements were fought, in which Outram's troops were successful. The last and most desperate attack was made by the rebels on 25 February, and it was not until dawn the next day that they were completely routed and fell back on Lucknow.

On 1 March 1858 Campbell returned to take Lucknow. Outram was placed in command of a large force of picked troops on the north side of the Gumti River, and, crossing the river on 6 March, he pitched his camp near the Fyzabad Road. On 9 March he made his attack, seizing the Chakar Kothi, or yellow house, the key of the enemy's position in that quarter, and, driving the rebels to the river, threw up batteries on its bank to keep down the enemy's fire. The *kaisarbagh* fell to Sir Colin Campbell on the morning of 14 March. On 16 March Outram, having recrossed the Gumti, advanced through the Chattar Manzil and carried the residency. On the morning of 19 March Outram attacked the Musabagh, held by 5000 men and thirteen guns, and carried it, capturing twelve guns. So ended the capture of Lucknow.

Last years, 1858–1860 Outram was appointed military member of the governor-general's council, and, handing over the charge of Oudh to Robert Montgomery, left Lucknow on 4 April and joined Lord Canning at Allahabad. Many important matters, such as the reorganization of the Indian army, were under consideration during Outram's tenure of office, and he left many wise and carefully prepared minutes recording his views. A baronetcy was conferred upon him by the queen, and the House of Commons voted him an annuity of £1000, to be continued to his immediate successor. On 16 July Outram was promoted lieutenant-general. In October the City of London conferred upon him its freedom and presented him with a sword of honour.

In July 1860 Outram's health gave way. He resigned his seat in the council of the viceroy, and, after a public entertainment at Calcutta, left India for good. An equestrian statue of him by J. H. Foley RA was erected on the Maidan in Calcutta by public subscription. On the institution of the Order of the Star of India in 1861, Outram was one of the first to receive the KSI. In June 1862 he received an honorary DCL from Oxford University. In July a deputation headed by the duke of Argyll presented him with silver plate at his house, 10 Queen's Gate Gardens, South Kensington. He died at Pau in the south of France on 11 March 1863, his only child, Francis Boyd Outram (1836–1912), inheriting the title. His wife survived him. He was given a public funeral and was buried on 25 March in Westminster Abbey. The grave is near the centre of the nave, marked by a marble slab bearing the words 'The Bayard of India'. A statue by Noble was erected on the Thames Embankment.

Contemporary accounts suggest that Outram was kind-hearted and modest, but very stubborn and unwilling to change his mind once it was made up. Like his great opponent, Sir Charles Napier, he enjoyed fighting and the command of men, but, unlike him, was deeply attached to the traditional Indian leaders. He quickly saw and rewarded merit in young officers, and he seemed to have a genuine concern for the welfare of his soldiers. He spent much on books for regimental libraries in India, and he established at Dum-Dum a soldiers' club known as the Outram Institute.

Outram's publications included, in addition to his reports and minutes officially printed: *Rough Notes of the Campaign in Sinde and Afghanistan in 1838–9* (privately printed, 1840); *The Conquest of Scinde: a Commentary* (1846); and *Lieutenant-General Sir James Outram's Persian Campaign in 1857* (privately printed, 1860).

R. H. VETCH, *rev.* AINSLIE T. EMBREE

Sources F. J. Goldsmid, *James Outram: a biography*, 2 vols. (1880) · L. J. Trotter, *The Bayard of India: a life of General Sir James Outram* (1909) · J. W. Kaye and G. B. Malleson, *Kaye's and Malleson's History of the Indian mutiny of 1857–8*, new edn, 6 vols. (1909) · J. Outram, *The conquest of Scinde: a commentary* (1846) · J. Outram, letters and diary, BL OIOC, MSS Eur. B 330, E 0208, F 007 · M. F. Outram, *Margaret Outram, 1778–1863, mother of the Bayard of India* [1932] · *A memoir of the public services rendered by Lieut. Col. Outram* (1853) · *Lieut. General Sir James Outram's Persian campaign in 1857* (1860) · H. T. Lambrick, *Sir Charles Napier and Sind* (1952) · J. Outram, *A refutation of certain calumnies* (1845) · R. Huttenback, *British relations with Sind, 1799–1843* (1962) · Burke, *Peerage* (1959) · *CGPLA Eng. & Wales* (1863)

Archives BL OIOC, corresp. and papers · BL OIOC, letters and papers relating to Lucknow · BL OIOC, journals relating to Sind, MS Eur. B 330 · NAM, corresp. and papers | BL, corresp. with G. P. Badger, Add. MS 38775 · BL, letters to H. Bruce, Add. MS 43993 · BL, corresp. with Sir Charles Napier, Add. MSS 40522, 40864–40866, *passim* · BL, letters to Sir Henry Rawlinson, Add. MS 47662 · BL, corresp. with Lord Ripon, Add. MSS 40865–40866 · BL OIOC, letters to William Dalgairns, MS Eur. B 330 · BL OIOC, letters to Lord Elphinstone, MSS Eur. F 87–89 · BL OIOC, corresp. with John Jacob, MS Eur. F 75 · NA Scot., Murray, Ramsay MSS · NA Scot., letters to Lord Dalhousie · NA Scot., corresp. with Sir Charles Augustus Murray · PRO, corresp. with Lord Ellenborough, PRO 30/12 · W. Yorks. AS, Bradford, letters to Lord Canning

Likenesses C. Baugniet, lithograph, pubd 1858, NPG · T. J. Barker, oils, 1859, NPG · H. Baxter, oils, 1861; formerly at United Services and Royal Aero Club, London · J. H. Foley, marble bust, exh. RA 1861, Victoria Memorial Hall, Calcutta, India · P. Petit of Nice, photograph, 1862, NAM · T. Brigstocke, oils, *c.*1863, Oriental Club, London; study, NPG [*see illus.*] · C. G. Lewis, group portrait, engraving, pubd 1863 (*The relief of Lucknow*; after T. J. Barker), NPG · M. Noble, marble bust, 1866, Westminster Abbey · M. Noble, bronze statue, *c.*1871, Victoria Embankment Gardens, London · J. H. Foley, statue, 1873; formerly on Maidan, Calcutta · J. E. Breun, oils (after oil by unknown artist), East India and Sports Club, London · Kilburn, carte-de-visite, NPG · R. J. Lane, lithograph, BM · A. Y. Shortt, oils, East India and Sports Club, London · engravings (after photographs), NAM, NPG · group portrait, engraving (*The durbar of the rajah of Travencore: reception of General Outram and staff*), NPG · oils, Scot. NPG · photograph, NPG

Wealth at death under £30,000: administration, 4 May 1863, *CGPLA Eng. & Wales*

Ouvry, Frederic (1814–1881), antiquary and lawyer, born on 20 October 1814 at 6 Abingdon Street, Westminster, was the third son of Peter Aimé Ouvry, under-secretary at the Ordnance office, and Sarah Amelia Delamain, and was nephew of John Payne *Collier. He was descended from James Ouvry, a Huguenot refugee from the neighbourhood of Dieppe who arrived in England in 1683 and settled in Spitalfields.

Ouvry served five-year articles with George Hildyard King, was then admitted a solicitor in 1835, and joined the firm of Hildyard and King at 13 Tokenhouse Yard in the City of London. He became a partner in Farrer & Co. at 66 Lincoln's Inn Fields in 1855. His most famous client was his friend Charles Dickens, who instructed him to act on several occasions, including the drafting of the novelist's formal deed of separation from his wife, Catherine, in 1858. Ouvry was depicted as Mr Undery in 'The Haunted House' in *All the Year Round* (1859). Another client, Coutts & Co., bankers, presented him in 1869 with a portrait bust by Marshall Wood. Ouvry was also solicitor to the fifth duke of Newcastle and worked with W. E. Gladstone after the duke's death to administer Newcastle's complex estate. He was honorary solicitor to the Royal Institute of British Architects from 1862 and made an honorary fellow in 1877. He was also solicitor to the Royal Literary Fund from 1864 and treasurer from 1877. He achieved the highest office in his profession in 1871 as president of the Incorporated Law Society. The Ouvry family had a long association with the Weavers' Company; Frederic was upper bailiff in 1878, and presented the company with the badge worn by later upper bailiffs.

On 24 February 1848 Ouvry was elected fellow of the Society of Antiquaries of London, and from 1854 to 1874 he filled the office of treasurer. On his resignation he was made vice-president, and on 4 January 1876 he was unanimously elected president. He retired in 1878. He presented the society with many valuable books, and a portrait of William Oldys. He contributed two papers to *Archaeologia* (1853–5), but his tastes and collections were mostly concerned with literary history. He had a fine library of manuscripts, autograph letters, and printed books, including the first four folios of Shakespeare. A catalogue of his collection of old ballads, compiled by T. W. Newton, was issued in 1887. He frequently printed facsimiles of rare publications of which only one copy was known; the first was *The Cobler of Canterburie* (1862).

Ouvry married Emily Anna (Minnie) Procter on 28 September 1854, and lived at Riverside, Maidenhead, Berkshire, and 12 Queen Anne Street, Cavendish Square, London. They had no children. He died suddenly at his town house on 26 June 1881, and was buried at Acton. His library was sold in April 1882 for £6169 2*s*., and some items were acquired by the British Museum Library.

Bernard Nurse

Frederic Ouvry (1814–1881), by Marshall Wood, 1869

Sources S. Corke, 'Fields: a short history', 1991, Farrer & Co., solicitors, 66 Lincoln's Inn Fields [typescript] • J. G. Ouvry, 'The Ouvry family in the nineteenth century', *Proceedings of the Huguenot Society*, 24 (1983–8), 473–9 • [T. D. Kendrick and J. G. Mann], *The presidents of the Society of Antiquaries of London: with biographical notes*, Society of Antiquaries of London Occasional Papers, 2 (1945) • *DNB* • Gladstone, *Diaries* • *CGPLA Eng. & Wales* (1881)

Archives priv. coll. | BL, corresp. with W. E. Gladstone, Add. MSS 44414–44785 • Farrer & Co., London, company records • Sandon Hall, Staffordshire, Harrowby Manuscript Trust, corresp. with Lord Tweedmouth, George Robinson, and Baroness Burdett Coutts • St Deiniol's Library, Hawarden, letters to W. E. Gladstone • U. Edin. L., special collections division, corresp. with James Halliwell-Phillipps

Likenesses M. Wood, marble bust, 1869, S. Antiquaries, Lond. [*see illus.*] • photograph, repro. in Ouvry, 'The Ouvry family in the nineteenth century', pl. 37a

Wealth at death £45,683 15*s*. 7*d*.: probate, 24 Aug 1881, *CGPLA Eng. & Wales*

Oven, Joshua van (1766–1838), surgeon and educationist, was born in London, the son of Abraham van Oven (*d.* 1778), physician, who according to family tradition was of Spanish descent. He had settled in London from Holland shortly after qualifying at Leiden in 1759. Both were Hebrew scholars and each in turn combined private medical practice with service as honorary medical officer to the poor of the Great Synagogue, London. They were prominent in congregational counsels. Joshua van Oven, whose father died when he was twelve, was a man of high intellect, great industry, and robust self-confidence. He studied under Sir William Blizard, and qualified as licentiate of the Company of Surgeons in 1784.

Van Oven married Elizabeth Goodman (*d.* 1823), daughter of Hirsch Gutman, in 1791. There were two daughters and three sons, the youngest of whom, Barnard, was a licentiate of the Royal College of Surgeons. Van Oven conducted a large practice from home in Bury Street and thereafter successively at 14 Fenchurch Buildings, Fenchurch Street, and 12 Devonshire Square, Bishopsgate. For many years he was in partnership with his son Barnard. His father's advice and example reinforced Joshua van

Oven's interest in Jewish studies and in the Hebrew language and literature at a time of Jewish new learning in continental Europe. He corresponded with colleagues in Hebrew, wrote some Hebrew and English verse, and was a leading figure in periodic efforts to advance interest in Hebrew literature in Britain.

Van Oven was a founder of the Jews' Free School (1817) in London, where he long served as president and in which he encouraged the improvement of teaching methods and the extension of training in manual skills. He was also a prime mover in the establishment in 1799 in Highgate of the private Jewish boarding-school for Jewish boys under the headmastership of his friend and notable Hebraist, Hyman Hurwitz.

Van Oven's periodic English sermons at the Great Synagogue contributed to the movement for synagogal addresses in the vernacular. He frequently addressed the pupils at the Jews' Free School on Jewish life and faith, and was a strong advocate of the training of congregational readers and cantors in styles more attuned to English congregations. His pedagogic works include his English translation from the Hebrew (by S. J. Cohen) of *Elements of Faith* (1815) for use in schools by girls and boys and his *Manual of Judaism* (1835) for young people.

In 1795 the metropolitan magistrate, Patrick Colquhoun, published his report on policing and crime in London. In response to his strictures therein on the numbers of indigent, unskilled, and unemployed Jews in the streets, largely of comparatively recent German and Polish origin, van Oven in correspondence and subsequent meetings with Colquhoun, propounded an ambitious ameliorative scheme, including handicraft training for youth and care for the aged and infirm. It was to be financed by Jewish communal taxation and the transfer by certain parishes of parochial funds raised from their Jewish residents. The plan as finally submitted by van Oven and Colquhoun was rendered abortive by divisions within the Jewish community and opposition from the parishes. The opening of the Jews' Hospital in Mile End in 1807 through funds given and raised by the financier, Abraham Goldsmid, was acknowledged to be based upon van Oven's proposals.

The campaign for Jewish civic and political emancipation attracted van Oven's consistent public support. Barnard van Oven, with his father's encouragement, was a major pioneer pamphleteer in that cause. While van Oven's enthusiasm for Anglicized forms in Jewish public life was not unconnected with the emancipatory aspiration, he was certainly imbued in any event with the growing sense of need for a greater degree of professionalism in public administration. In some ways ahead of his time, he was typical, within his own community, of those elements in the society of his day, secular and religious, whose social reformist zeal proved a creative feature of the then new age.

In 1830 van Oven was heavily in debt through failed incautious speculation and was declared insolvent. It was a fall from grace which led him to leave London. He settled in Liverpool in 1831, living at 10 Great George Street and cared for by Harriet van Oven, to whom he bequeathed his possessions by will dated 5 October 1837 and to whom he therein referred as 'my daughter' towards whom he deemed himself 'under inexpressible obligation for support besides the use of her furniture'. On arrival in that city he joined the Liverpool Hebrew congregation, then in Seel Street, where, despite failing health, he was active in congregational life and occasionally delivered English sermons. He continued to be listed as surgeon. Van Oven died at 10 Great George Street on 3 February 1838 and was buried in the congregational cemetery, then in Deane Street, on 7 February 1838. ISRAEL FINESTEIN

Sources S. S. Levin, 'The origins of the Jews' Free School', *Transactions of the Jewish Historical Society of England*, 19 (1960), 97–114 • E. S. Conway, 'The origins of the Jewish Orphanage', *Transactions of the Jewish Historical Society of England*, 22 (1970), 53–66 • J. van Oven, *Letters on the present state of the Jewish poor in the metropolis* (1802) • T. M. Endelman, *The Jews of Georgian England, 1714–1830* (1979) • G. Black, *JFS: the history of the Jews' Free School, London, since 1732* (1998) • L. Wolf, 'The origin of the *Nevè Zedek*', *Essays in Jewish history*, ed. C. Roth (1934), 193–202 • registers, Great Synagogue, London • records, Liverpool Hebrew congregation • *Jewish Chronicle* [London] (13 Jan 1905) • *Jewish encyclopaedia*, 12 (1925), 400 • d. cert.

Archives Liverpool Hebrew Congregation, Princes Road, Liverpool, MSS • LMA, Great Synagogue, London MSS • priv. coll., Jews' Hospital archives

Likenesses S. Drummond, portrait, 1813, priv. coll.; copy by I. Solomon, Liverpool Hebrew Congregation, 1838 • T. Blood, engraving, 1815 (after S. Drummond), repro. in C. Roth, *History of the Great Synagogue* (1950), 220

Overall, Douglas (1892–1978), chartered surveyor and commercial property developer, was born on 9 May 1892 at 18 Clifton Street, Brighton, the son of Frank Harry Overall, furniture salesman, and his wife, Sarah Jane Millard. He attended Brighton College for a time, where he studied engineering, but in 1913 he joined the commercial estate agents Hillier and Parker, becoming right-hand man to one of its founders, Tom Parker. During the First World War he was commissioned in the Royal Garrison Artillery. Mentioned in dispatches, he retired with the rank of captain. In 1919 he was made a partner with Hillier and Parker, and played an important role in the firm's merger with another prominent shops agency, May and Rowden, in 1921.

Together with Walter Stanley Edgson, Overall developed the merged practice, Hillier, Parker, May, and Rowden, as one of Britain's most important commercial chartered surveyors. While Edgson specialized in the London property market, Overall concentrated on the provinces. He played an important part in the establishment of a national commercial property market, developing a system for assembling information on shopping centres throughout Britain in order to meet the property needs of rapidly expanding multiple retailers such as Marks and Spencer, Boots, and Woolworths. In 1937 Overall, together with Edgson, became joint senior partner of Hillier Parker.

In addition to his work for the firm, Overall was engaged in the commercial property market as principal, as well as agent. In 1927 he established the property company Sterling Estates, which built up a portfolio of high street shop properties. Sterling was acquired by Royal Insurance in 1973, though Overall remained chairman until his death, by which time Sterling's portfolio was worth at least £50 million. Overall also perceived the growing market for factories and built speculatively for letting on the industrial estates which mushroomed along London's arterial roads during the 1930s. He set up Industrial Estates, an offshoot of Sterling Estates, to develop and hold such factories.

Overall was also active in public life. During the war he was involved in the management of the air raid patrol, coordinating 1000 warden staff. He raised £100,000 for the pilots and crews funds of the RAF, served as a justice of the peace, an additional commissioner for taxes, a governor of Putney Hospital, a member of the boards of many charities, and as a member of Westminster city council. He also became chairman of the Association of London Property Owners and the London Auction Mart. Overall married Dorothy Grace Waters (1890–1978) about 1918. They had a son and a daughter.

Overall was a keen golfer. When he became a president of the Chartered Auctioneers and Estate Agents' Institute he was asked to open its golfing society. In front of a crowd of spectators he failed to hit an opening shot which was designed to mark the occasion. After he missed the ball a second time the crowd fell silent: Overall turned to his caddy and, with stiff upper lip, calmly remarked: 'That's a damn long course isn't it?' (private information). He retired from Hillier Parker in 1953, after which he devoted more of his time to running Sterling Estates. He died at his home, 102 Rivermead Court, Fulham, on 13 October 1978 at the age of eighty-six. His wife survived him by only five days. His son, Tony, also served as a director of Sterling Estates for fifteen years, before establishing his own property company. PETER SCOTT

Sources E. L. Erdman, *People and property* (1982) • *Chartered Surveyor*, 111 (1978) • O. Marriott, *The property boom* (1967) • private information (2004) • d. cert. • d. cert. [Dorothy Grace Overall] • b. cert.

Wealth at death £759,546: probate, 11 Dec 1978, *CGPLA Eng. & Wales*

Overall, John (*bap.* 1561, *d.* 1619), bishop of Norwich, was born at Hadleigh, Suffolk, and baptized there on 2 March 1561, the younger son of George Overall, who died that July. He was educated at the local grammar school in Hadleigh, where John Boys, son of the rector of West Stow, Suffolk, was one of his contemporaries. John Still, then Lady Margaret professor of divinity at Cambridge, and parish priest from 1571, took an interest in their education. Owing to his patronage and direction both applied to St John's College, Cambridge, when in 1575 he became master. When Still moved to become master of Trinity College, Overall followed him and on 18 April 1578 was admitted as a scholar, alongside Anthony Maxey. He graduated BA in 1579 and became a minor fellow on 2 October 1581. He proceeded MA the following year and on 30 March became a major fellow. Overall received other college preferments while Still was master and at the start

John Overall (*bap.* 1561, *d.* 1619), by Wenceslaus Hollar, 1657

of the academic year in 1586 he was made praelector Graecus: by October 1588 he was praelector mathematicus. He became seneschal on 17 December 1589 and junior dean on 14 October 1591; that year he was also ordained priest at Lincoln. He was briefly, in 1591–2, vicar of Trumpington, a college living just outside Cambridge. In 1592 Sir Thomas Heneage, on behalf of Elizabeth I, presented him to the vicarage of Epping, Essex.

In December 1595 Overall was appointed regius professor of divinity at the death of William Whitaker. He was popular with his pupils and although his election had the queen's support, it was the result of a vote of younger university men against the deterministic doctrines of Whitaker. Overall had publicly acquitted himself at a disputation with Anthony Wotton before the earl of Essex and his election may have been a snub for Archbishop John Whitgift, who had adopted the Calvinistic Lambeth articles with Whitaker's support. Overall, with Lancelot Andrewes, Samuel Harsnett, and others, had rejected these articles in support of Peter Baro, the Lady Margaret professor of divinity, when on 12 January 1596 he attacked them from the pulpit. This opposition cost Baro his chair, as he failed to be re-elected in 1596 and was succeeded by Thomas Playfere, but the style of Cambridge theology did not become monochrome. Overall was not as radical as Baro but in 1599 he clashed with the authorities when he maintained that the perseverance of a truly justified man was conditional upon repentance. There followed a year-long campaign against Overall which ultimately had little effect. In the summer of 1600 even his objection to Richard Neile's teaching on private confession was censured. None the less, he retained his chair until he resigned it in 1607.

As one of the chaplains-in-ordinary to the queen Overall was appointed by Whitgift in 1598 to preach before her on the third Wednesday of Lent, 15 March, in place of Bishop Godfrey Goldsbrough of Gloucester. Shortly afterwards, at Easter, his theological position was further endorsed in Cambridge when he was appointed master of St Catharine's College, with the support of Whitgift. Thereafter he was occasionally chosen to give Lenten sermons before the queen, but he was not happy in the pulpit. It was reckoned that years of classical lecturing in Latin had made it 'troublesome to him to speak English in a continued oration' (Fuller, *Worthies*, 61). John Manningham, a Magdalene graduate who would have heard Professor Overall in Cambridge, later complained that he 'discoursed verry scholastically' when he preached a Whitehall sermon at the dead queen's court on 6 April 1603 (BL, Harley MS 5353, fol. 120*v*).

In 1602 Overall was made rector of Algarkirk, Lincoln; he held the living for three years. With the support of Sir Fulke Greville he was nominated dean of St Paul's Cathedral in May the same year, in succession to the nonagenarian Elizabethan dean, Alexander Nowell. At his election on 29 May Bishop John Bancroft collated him to the prebend of Tottenhale in that cathedral. On 6 June Lawrence Barker, vicar of St Botolph, Aldersgate, and a former colleague at Trinity, spoke at Paul's Cross of the 'gravity & learning and life' (BL, Harley MS 5353, fol. 25*v*) of the new dean. The deanery itself became a haven for scholars like Scultetus who shared the house with him. Overall himself, according to the radical preacher Thomas Scott, emerged as something of a zealous ritualist. In 1603 he became rector of Clothall in Hertfordshire (which he held until 1615). He staffed that parish with a curate as he did also Therfield, his other Hertfordshire benefice from 1605, which he surrendered in 1614 to a Hadleigh contemporary, Bishop Still's nephew, William Alabaster, when he converted back to the Church of England.

At the Hampton Court conference Overall spoke on 16 January 1604 of predestination, using much material from his Cambridge disputes of the 1590s. In particular he questioned double predestination by considering those who lapsed, such as those who though previously considered justified had then committed adultery. Although his *Sententia ecclesiae Anglicanae praedestionibus* were not printed in his lifetime they circulated widely in manuscript and informed George Carleton's theological reading at the Synod of Dort. They were published several times from 1631. As a result of the conference Overall found himself responsible for adding a substantial section to the catechism, on the sacraments. This amplified catechism remained at the heart of Anglican teaching and praxis until the 1970s. When the controversial Edmund Reeve wrote *The Communion Book[e] Catechisme Expounded* in 1635 for his parishioners of Hayes, Middlesex, he paid tribute to both Overall and John Buckeridge for their work on the sacraments. Writing to Bishop Wright of Lichfield, Reeve claimed that Overall, 'that most greatly learned Divine', was the 'first instrument which God used for to instruct me in the Catholicke faith' (Reeve, sig. B3). Overall was also invited to join the Westminster team of ten biblical revisers under Lancelot Andrewes who worked to translate the first books of the Old Testament, up to 2 Kings inclusive, for the 1611 Authorized Version.

On 16 April 1604 at Mitcham, Surrey, Overall married Anne, daughter of Edward Orwell of Christ Church, Greyfriars Newgate, London, registrar of the court of arches, who came from a Lancashire family. Perhaps the Anne baptized at Christ Church on 11 May 1583, she was, according to John Aubrey, 'the greatest Beautie of her time in England' (*Brief Lives*, 226). Although she committed adultery with the notorious womanizer Richard Sackville, third earl of Dorset, and with Sir John Selby of Yorkshire, she was not subject to ecclesiastical censure. Her marriage to Overall was childless.

Following Thomas Ravis's promotion to the bishopric of Gloucester, in March 1605 Overall succeeded him as prolocutor of the lower house of the convocation of Canterbury. As such he worked closely with Archbishop Richard Bancroft. In the following year convocation produced canons in response to the outrage felt at the Gunpowder Plot and the need to circumscribe the actions of Catholics who upheld political resistance to tyrants. Although three books of canons were provided only the first passed both houses of convocation in both provinces, and James VI and I resisted their publication since he believed that the twenty-eighth canon, which spoke of 'bordering kings' who 'through ambition and malice' invade their neighbours, reduced his own title to kingship to being merely *de facto*. The remaining books of canons, ascribed to Overall, were not published until 1690, when Archbishop William Sancroft used them in an attempt to justify the position of the nonjurors although Anglican defenders of the 1688 revolution had seized upon the same objected phrases to countenance William III's illegal act.

Largely through the support of Sir Fulke Greville, whose family home was Warwick Castle, Overall became bishop of Coventry and Lichfield; he was elected on 14 March 1614 and consecrated on 3 April following. He spent most of his time in London, and seems only to have visited the diocese occasionally, first in 1614 and then during the royal progress south after James I's only visit to the Scottish kingdom in the summer of 1617 when the king arranged to meet his bishop at Coventry. The absence of his register makes it impossible to judge his role as a governor in the diocese but he maintained theological interests in his correspondence with the likes of Vossius and Grotius on the continent and provided for the clergy of his diocese by ordaining in the capital. Much of his time was spent working alongside Lancelot Andrewes and John Buckeridge in the court of high commission. He was involved in the deprivation and censure of four ministers (between

December 1614 and May 1617), and in examining Catholic priests in January 1618. Having avoided preaching at court between 1603 and 1615, he took a regular turn on the third Sunday in Lent in 1616, 1617, and 1618.

Following a *congé d'élire* dated 9 May 1618, on 21 May the dean and chapter of Norwich elected Overall as bishop, but this was not confirmed until the end of the summer, when he moved to Norwich Palace. His further preferment is something of a surprise, and cannot have been much to the liking of the primate: in November 1617 Archbishop Abbot wrote to Sir Dudley Carleton that he feared that Overall 'maketh no bones … to deliver doubtfull thinges for true and fained thinges for certaine' (PRO, SP 14/105/95, fol. 9*v*). Indeed, Overall was one of the remonstrants' proposed delegates to the Synod of Dort. However, he did not long survive his translation to his home diocese, as he died on 12 May 1619. He was buried in the south choir aisle of the cathedral. The monument above his tomb was put up in 1669 at the expense of his former secretary and amanuensis, John Cosin.

Overall's most enduring legacy, beyond his contribution to the revised catechism of the Church of England, was his visitation articles of 1619. At Lichfield the triennial visitations of 1614 and 1617 had been the excuse that took him to his diocese; although those articles do not seem to exist, presentments to his visitation suggest that he was concerned to encourage the appropriate provision of communion plate across his diocese. He did not live long enough to make a visitation of the Norwich diocese in person but his articles formed the antecedents of at least twenty other sets issued in the 1620s and 1630s, including those of Harsnett (1620) and of Andrewes (1625). Bishop Richard Neile at Durham even absorbed Overall's article about private confession, their old duelling ground. Their shape in part derived from those of John Jegon (1611). Within them Overall went well beyond the 1571 requirement on preachers not to treat of subjects not agreeable to scripture, making the churchwardens responsible for ensuring conformity in the pulpit. In insisting upon conformity he was more successful, even in a short space of time, across the diocese than had been his predecessor.

NICHOLAS W. S. CRANFIELD

Sources muniment book 15, Westminster Abbey · BL, Harley MS 5353 · CUL, Add. MS 48 · Fuller, *Worthies* (1662) · D. Wilkins, *Concilia*, 4 vols. (1737) · E. Reeve, *The communion book catechisme expounded* (1636) [1635 edn *The communion booke …*] · *Aubrey's Brief lives*, ed. O. L. Dick (1949) · PRO, C 66/2190; SP 14/90/101 · Venn, *Alum. Cant.* · K. Fincham, *Prelate as pastor: the episcopate of James I* (1990) · Norwich dean and chapter act book, Norfolk RO, DCN 24/2, fol. 20v · LPL, Register Abbot I, fols. 126–31 · N. R. N. Tyacke, 'Arminianism and English culture', *Britain and the Netherlands*, ed. A. C. Duke and C. A. Tamse (The Hague, 1981), 98 · D. Oldridge, *Religion and society in early Stuart England* (1998)

Likenesses oils, 1614–19, Trinity Cam.; version, Trinity Hall, Cambridge · W. Hollar, etching, 1657, NPG; repro. in A. Sparrow, *A rationale upon the book of common prayer of the Church of England* (1657) [*see illus.*] · oils, *c*.1660–1679, Auckland Castle, co. Durham · R. White, line engraving, BM, NPG; repro. in [W. Sancroft], ed., *Bishop Overall's convocation book* (1690)

Overall, William Henry (1829–1888), librarian, son of William Henry Overall, a messenger who died before 1857, and Rosetta Davey, was born on 18 January 1829 at St John's Wood, St Marylebone, Middlesex. Educated at a private school, he entered the office of the town clerk at Guildhall in 1847 as a messenger, and attended the metropolitan evening classes for young men at Crosby Hall, Bishopsgate (later City of London College). On 20 April 1851 he married Mary Anne Elizabeth Bailey; they had fourteen children. Overall purchased his freedom of the City in January 1857 and in March was appointed to the new post of sub-librarian of the corporation library. The library then consisted of a few straggling apartments in the front of the Guildhall, and the corporation was heavily criticized for the poor facilities.

In 1865, on the death of William Turner Alchin, Overall received the appointment of librarian, and superintended the removal of the collections to a spacious new building in Basinghall Street, opened in 1872. The following year the public was admitted for reference and use increased dramatically. In 1874 a museum opened in the basement and Overall, as curator, rapidly expanded the collections with notable acquisitions, especially of Roman remains found in the City. His knowledge of the historical topography of the City of London and its suburbs was extensive and accurate, and the ready help which he afforded in his official position to all enquirers made his services widely appreciated. The library committee (2 July 1888) acknowledged 'his devotion to his duties, and urbanity of manner' (Library Committee Minutes, Corporation of London Records Office). He was elected a fellow of the Society of Antiquaries of London in May 1868, and was for many years a member of the councils of the Library Association and the London and Middlesex Archaeological Society.

Overall's first publication was the *Catalogue of Sculpture … Belonging to the Corporation* (1867–8), and he subsequently compiled several other catalogues of special collections. In 1877 he was presented with the honorary freedom and livery of the Clockmakers' Company, of whose library and museum of clocks and watches, deposited in the Guildhall Library, he prepared a printed catalogue in 1875, which was followed in 1881 by his *History* of the company. His particular scholarly interest was the City in the early modern period. Among other publications he edited, in 1874, a facsimile of the sixteenth-century map of London attributed to Agas, and with his cousin, H. C. Overall, he compiled an index to the Remembrancia series of records (1579–1664) in the corporation archives. This work was the outcome of a joint examination of the corporation records and an elaborate report on their nature and condition.

Overall lived at 27 Queen Margaret's Grove, Mildmay Park, before 1872, and at 24 Grosvenor Road, Highbury *c*.1872–1885. He died at his home, Shaxted, 1 Crouch Hall Road, Crouch End, Hornsey, London, on 28 June 1888 after a long illness and was buried in St Pancras cemetery, Finchley, on 3 July. He was survived by his wife and nine of their children.

CHARLES WELCH, *rev.* BERNARD NURSE

Sources *Proceedings of the Society of Antiquaries of London*, 2nd ser., 12 (1887–9), 391 • C. Welch and P. Norman, *Modern history of the City of London* (1896) • F. Sheppard, *Treasury of London's past* (1991) • Library Committee minutes, 1857–88, CLRO • freedom certificate, 22 Jan 1857, CLRO
Archives V&A, letters to T. Williams
Wealth at death £3770 16*s*. 11*d*.: probate, 21 July 1888, *CGPLA Eng. & Wales*

Overbury, Sir Thomas (*bap.* 1581, *d.* 1613), courtier and author, was born at the manor house in Compton Scorfen (Compton Scorpion), near Ilmington, Warwickshire, and baptized on 18 June 1581 at Barton on the Heath. He was the third of the ten children of Sir Nicholas Overbury (*c.*1549–1643), judge and MP, and his wife, Mary (*c.*1565–1617), daughter of Giles Palmer of Compton Scorfen and his wife, Muriella.

Education and rise to prominence The Overbury family had not been substantial landowners until Nicholas Overbury in 1598 bought the manor of Bourton on the Hill from John Palmer, to whom he was already related by marriage. However, the family finances made it possible for Thomas Overbury to go up as a gentleman commoner to Queen's College, Oxford, in 1595. In 1598 he entered the Middle Temple, London, his father's inn. There he became a friend of John Manningham, who recorded some of Overbury's sayings in his diary: some were witticisms, but also included were such remarks as: 'He would not have the bishops to have anie temporalities, or temporall jurisdicion, but live upon tithes, and nothing but preach' and 'Sir Rob. Cecile followed the E of Ess[ex's] death not with a good mynde' (*Diary of John Manningham*, 236). The combination of verbal creativity, moderate puritanism, and a degree of sympathy for the second earl of Essex adumbrate later achievements and attitudes of Overbury's. So does the first reference to him in print, in a highly complimentary epigram in the *Affaniae* (1601) of his Oxford contemporary Charles Fitz-Geffrey, a collection in which many of the other epigrams are addressed either to wits or to godly protestants. Fitz-Geffrey was not Overbury's only literary friend: Overbury knew Ben Jonson well enough to gossip about him to Manningham as early as 1603, and Jonson later wrote an epigram complimenting Overbury on raising the moral tone of the court. They subsequently became enemies; Jonson claimed many years later and somewhat implausibly, in conversation with Drummond of Hawthornden, that this was because Overbury had tried to use him as a go-between in an attempted adulterous relationship with the countess of Rutland (*Ben Jonson*, 1.138).

During Overbury's time at the Middle Temple, in his father's words:

> hee and John Guilby, his father's chiefe clerke, were sent (upon a voyage of pleasure) to Edinburgh, with 60 li between them. There Thom: met with Sir Wm. Cornwallis, one who knew him in Queene's colledge at Oxford. Sir Wm. commended him to diverse, & among the rest to Robin Carr, then page to the earle of Dunbarre: so they two came along to England together, & were great friends. (Oldisworth, fol. 92*v*)

This journey was made around 1601, and thereafter Overbury returned to the Middle Temple for at least two years. A letter of Overbury's to Carr in 1613 refers to their 'love' as of nine years' standing (*Memorials of Affairs of State*, 3.479), which suggests that after their first meeting in Edinburgh their friendship was renewed and became more intimate in 1604, presumably on Carr's arrival in England. When his friend came to the personal notice of the king, Overbury benefited. In 1606 he received a gift of silver from the king of Denmark on a visit of the latter to the English court; on 29 September 1607 he was given a lease on a saltworks in Worcestershire which had come into the king's hands after the attainder of Robert Winter; and on 19 June 1608 he was knighted.

Prosperity, and relationship with Robert Carr Overbury's relationship with Robert Carr (subsequently Viscount Rochester and earl of Somerset) was the most significant of his life. It has often been seen, perhaps simplistically, as one in which Carr depended on Overbury's superior intelligence. Certainly Carr, as the king's favourite, had a great deal of business to transact, and he needed to delegate some of it. Once Carr had become the king's unofficial secretary, incoming letters of state were routinely read and abstracted by Overbury, and outgoing dispatches were apparently drafted by him. Overbury was helpful in other ways: he could deal with Carr's suitors; he could handle business with which Carr and the king did not want to be openly associated; he could help acquire works of art for Carr's collection. He was both Carr's personal assistant and his bosom friend: in Sir Roger Wilbraham's description, his 'bedfellow, minion, and inward councillor' (*Journal* in *Camden Miscellany*, 10.116). What matters in this description is its emphasis on intimacy. The relationship may or may not have included sex; it was certainly emotionally charged. Carr's relationship with other associates such as Sir Robert Killigrew did not carry the same charge.

Being the favourite of the king's favourite brought Overbury his knighthood; it also brought him influence. According to Nicholas Overbury:

> [Francis Bacon] used … to stoope & crouch to Sir Tho: Overbury, in hope of Somerset's favour to bee Master of the court of wards: for which place, hee offered much; and Sir Thomas his father might once have had 1000 li. if he would have spoken effectually to his sonne. (Oldisworth, fol. 93*v*)

Overbury was granted the reversion of the treasurership of the chamber, a position valued in 1613 at £2000. His family also received benefits: at the end of 1609, his brothers Giles and Walter were given a life grant of the office of registering assurances on ships or goods in the royal exchange.

Overbury was not, however, interested simply in office and patronage. Hugh Broughton claimed to have heard from him that the king would give £500 per year to fund the exposition of the New Testament in Hebrew and on Talmudic principles (*Petition to the King to Hasten Allowance for Ebrew Institution of Ebrewes*, 1610?, 1v). James is not very likely to have made this promise; what is likelier is that Overbury had made an encouraging response when

Broughton mentioned the project to him. It should have appealed to a man of the godly sympathies recorded by Manningham. These were of a piece with Overbury's political opposition to the pro-Spanish international interests of the Howard family. In 1613 Viscount Fenton wrote:

> all theis that Overberrye drew to him and about my Lord of Rotchester are lyke to make a pairtye to [i.e. opposed to] the Howards … Southehamptoun and Pembrouke are joyned in that syde, and thaye stand mutche to have Nevell Secreterrye. Thaye have vith them sume of the moste discontented nobill men of the younger sort, and all the Parlement mutineers. (*Mar and Kellie MSS*, 51)

Overbury's alliance with men like Sir Henry Neville and the earl of Southampton placed him in a group self-identified as patriotic and protestant, several of whom had been at least marginally involved in the Essex rebellion.

Overbury was not an entirely satisfactory ally, on account of his arrogance. This was commented on by many contemporaries, one of whom subsequently remarked that it was 'a great question who was the proudest, Sir Walter [Ralegh], or Sir Thomas Overbury, but the difference that was, was judged on Sir Thomas' side' (*Brief Lives*, 2.182). In May of 1611:

> Rochester and his dear Overbury, walking in the garden at Greenwich whither the queen's window openeth, she broke into a sudden and contemptible laughing at them. 'So', saith she, 'they did at her', which belief carried her so far that she went to the king with tears in her eyes and complained. (*Downshire MSS*, 3.83)

This account suggests that the quarrel may have been partly of the queen's making, but Overbury had overstepped the mark by laughing at her, and he was banished from court until November. On this occasion his own conceited self-confidence led him into a battle with a person stronger than himself, which damaged his political influence.

Imprisonment and death The intimacy between Robert Carr and Frances Howard, then countess of Essex, had at first been abetted by Overbury, who was to claim to Carr that 'you fell in love with that woman, as soone as you had wonne her by my letters' (BL, MS Cotton Titus B.vii, fol. 483*v*). As it progressed, and especially as it became apparent that there was a possibility of a nullification of Frances Howard's marriage to the earl of Essex which would leave her free to marry Carr, Overbury became opposed to the relationship. Any marriage would expose his patron to influence other than his own, and an alliance with the Howards would expose him to an influence which Overbury had always detested. He made his feelings on the subject clear. A number of people now wanted to see Overbury moved away from court. The queen had never been fully reconciled to him since the quarrel of 1611. The king was aware of him as a troublemaker. Carr and Frances Howard both found Overbury standing in the way of their relationship. Overbury's enmity to the Howards was well known, and Henry Howard, earl of Northampton, was particularly interested in an alliance with Carr, to be cemented by his marriage to Howard's great-niece Frances. So, Overbury was offered an ambassadorship, which would have been a nominal promotion for him but which would have broken his daily personal influence in Carr's life. It is not certain where the post would have been; contemporary rumour suggested Paris, Brussels, or Moscow. He refused it, however, even when it had been made clear to him that the king wanted him to accept. He did this with Carr's encouragement, and Carr knew what the result would be. In the afternoon of 21 April 1613, Overbury evidently supposed that he had won the argument, remarking, as he discussed his future prospects with Sir Henry Wotton, that they had never looked better. That evening he was arrested, and taken to the Tower of London, 'Forasmuch,' in the words of the warrant for his imprisonment, 'as his Ma[tie] hath conceaved a greate displeasure against [him] for a matter of high contempt' (PRO, SP 14/72/119).

Overbury remained in the Tower for more than four months. He was kept a close prisoner, permitted no communication with the outside world; when Sir Robert Killigrew, returning from a visit to Sir Walter Ralegh, spoke briefly through a window to Overbury, he was himself imprisoned briefly. The object of the imprisonment was clearly to keep Overbury well out of the way while the Essex marriage was annulled and the Carr–Howard marriage was arranged. Overbury threatened, in a letter written to Carr from the Tower, that he would disclose 'the story betwixt you and me from the first hour to this day', so that 'whether I die or live, your shame shall never die' (BL, MS Cotton Titus B.vii, fol. 483*v*); but while he was a close prisoner, he could not be as damagingly indiscreet as he threatened here. It was not in any powerful person's interests to agitate for his release, nor in the king's to order it. Overbury hoped in vain that Carr would help him. By 4 June a correspondent of William Trumbull remarked that '[n]ot a man enquires after him' (*Downshire MSS*, 4.125).

Even before his imprisonment Overbury had experienced some illness, and he had mentioned this as an excuse for refusing an ambassadorship (the reply had been, prophetically, that a foreign posting might actually be rather good for his health). By the middle of May he was described by Henry Wotton as 'much damaged in his health by close imprisonment' (*Life and Letters*, 2.23). He became feverish, and could not eat; he suffered nausea and vomiting; he was permanently thirsty; and his urine smelt unusually foul. Wotton's assumption that Overbury's uncertain health had been worsened by imprisonment is certainly plausible. The decline may, moreover, have been accelerated by any or all of three factors. First, Overbury was dosing himself with emetics, apparently concocted by Killigrew and sent him by Carr. Second, he was receiving professional medical treatment from Theodore Turquet de Mayerne and others, which may have led to iatrogenic illness; it has been suggested that the painful, stinking ulcer present on Overbury's back in his last days may have been the gangrenous result of an incision made under Mayerne's direction to drain harmful humours from the body. Third, Frances Howard was probably making attempts, the likelihood of which will be discussed below, to have him poisoned. Overbury died in the Tower, unattended, after prolonged physical and mental suffering, early on 15 September 1613. He was buried that evening in the chapel of St Peter ad Vincula, the haste of his interment being explained by the foulness of his corpse.

Two years later it was rumoured that Overbury had been poisoned. The evidence is problematic, because it largely consists of confessions made under fear of torture or as part of a series of show trials. The case for the prosecution was that Frances Howard had been anxious to have Overbury murdered, and had even tried to bribe Sir David Wood, a servant of the queen who had been angered by Overbury's handling of some patronage business, to assassinate him before his imprisonment. Thereafter she had allegedly had Sir Gervase Elwes substituted for Sir William Waad as lieutenant of the Tower of London in May 1613 so that her agents would have easier access to Overbury; she had allegedly employed her dependants Richard Weston, Anne Turner, and James Franklin to obtain poisons and introduce them into food sent to Overbury; and, after Overbury proved resistant to these poisons, she had allegedly instructed Weston to commission an apothecary's boy to give Overbury a fatally toxic enema. The plot seems pointlessly elaborate: for instance, Franklin confessed to having obtained seven different poisons, 'that is to say, aqua fortis, Mercury water, white arsenick, pouder of diamonds, lapis Cosmatis, great spiders and Cantarides' for Frances Howard (PRO, SP 14/83/38). As Edward Coke handled it in the trials, the elaboration developed, and he hinted at a widespread conspiracy to poison, of which Henry, prince of Wales, had been one victim and Overbury another.

The likeliest reading of the evidence is that Frances Howard probably did attempt to incapacitate Overbury by poison, though not necessarily to kill him, still less to employ five different persons to subject him to repeated large doses of a variety of poisons. Robert Carr probably did not know of this until after the fact, and Overbury's death cannot be ascribed with any certainty to poison. Be that as it may, Elwes, Weston, Turner, and Franklin were all executed for it, and Carr and Howard (the earl and countess of Somerset as they had then become) were spared execution but imprisoned and disgraced. Sir Nicholas Overbury believed of the earl of Northampton that he:

> knew, there was nothing to bee gotten of the king without the helpe of Somerset; and therfore hee flattered Somerset, and plotted the poysoning of Overbury. Hee had doubtlesse suffered, if hee had not dyed betweene the Murther & the Discovery of it. (Oldisworth, fol. 93*v*)

The murder trials certainly brought down the promising Carr–Howard alliance for which Northampton had worked hard.

Genuine and apocryphal writings The only poem which can certainly be ascribed to Overbury is 'A Wife', comprising forty-seven verses in the same metre as Shakespeare's 'Venus and Adonis'. It discusses the origins and benefits of marriage, and the qualities of the ideal wife, with particular regard to her usefulness and subservience to her husband. John Owen praised it in an epigram published before November 1612, which was to be translated by Joshua Sylvester. Jonson's complimentary poem to Carr on the occasion of his marriage expresses the hope that Carr's wife would 'Out-bee that *Wife*, in worth, thy freind did make' (*Ben Jonson*, 8.384). Sir Nicholas Overbury's claim that his son's poem was written to persuade Carr to choose a better wife than Frances Howard is at once made doubtful by this reference of Jonson's, and is unlikely on other grounds too: 'A Wife' is expressed in very general terms, and its tone is reflective rather than didactic. The poem was not printed in Overbury's lifetime. It was, however, circulated in manuscript, and a copy came into the hands of the publisher Lawrence Lisle late in 1613. Lisle published it as an anonymous duodecimo early in the next year. It sold well enough to justify a second edition, published as *A wife now the widdow of Sir Thomas Overburye … whereunto are added many witty characters … written by himselfe and other learned gentlemen his friends*. The so-called 'characters' were short prose descriptions of imaginary persons, imitating Joseph Hall's *Characters of Virtues and Vices* of 1608.

The prose descriptions were not by Overbury. The first three, one of which describes a good woman and the other two bad women, had a limited manuscript circulation as an appendix to 'A Wife'; in one of the manuscripts, their anonymous author claims that his purpose was to make Overbury's material more intelligible. Lisle evidently obtained a manuscript of the poem in which these characters were present, and commissioned more, from one or more unknown authors, passing them off disingenuously as by Overbury and his learned friends. The collection was a great success, and Lisle issued a series of progressively augmented editions. In 1615, as the murder trials began, new editions of the collection contained topical poems on the alleged poisoning by William Browne, Richard Corbett, and others. By 1622 an eleventh edition had appeared, with eighty-two characters occupying most of its pages. Some of these were by John Webster; others have been ascribed, less certainly, to Thomas Dekker and John Ford; and one of them was later printed with the juvenilia of John Donne, though it is not very likely to be his.

A number of other works have been ascribed to Overbury, none with certainty. The first of these, a report of the arraignment of Sir Walter Ralegh in 1603, was published as Overbury's in 1648. It is perfectly possible that in 1603 Overbury, with his background in the inns of court, witnessed the arraignment and took notes upon it which eventually came to a publisher's hands, and it is equally possible that his name was added as a publisher's ploy to a report made by an anonymous or unimportant writer. In 1609 Overbury travelled on the continent, and the unspectacular *Observations in his Travailes … in 1609*, of which at least twelve manuscript copies are extant, appear to be notes of his on the Low Countries and France made at that time. Lisle entered the work in the Stationers' Register in 1616, but it was not published until 1626. Anthony Wood noted that '[t]his goes under his name, but doubted by some, whether he wrote it' (Wood, 2.135). A translation of Ovid's *Remedium amoris* is associated with 'A Wife' in some manuscripts, and was published as by Overbury in 1620. Finally, a collection of the table talk of King James, identified in manuscript as 'Crumms fal'n from King James's table … taken by S^r. Thomas Overbury' (BL, MS Harleian 7582, fol. 42) cannot, on internal evidence, be earlier than 1622.

Historiography Interest in Overbury was particularly vigorous at two points in the seventeenth century: the years 1615–16, and the early 1650s. The most substantial writings from the earlier period are manuscript reports of the murder trials, which are sometimes associated with reports of the Essex annulment case. A great number of short pieces, mostly in verse, were circulated in manuscript at the same time; these tended to vilify Frances Howard and, to a lesser extent, Robert Carr. Some more or less ephemeral printed texts also circulated, such as the anonymous *The Bloody Downfall of Adultery, Murder, Ambition*, the poem *Sir T. Overburies Vision*, by Richard Niccols, and the broadside poem *The Poysoned Knights Complaint*, by Samuel Rowlands. John Ford's 'Sir Thomas Overburyes Ghost', entered by Lisle in the Stationers' Register in 1615, is no longer extant. One or two accounts of the trials were published in Dutch. Prints of Weston, Elwes, the Somersets, and Overbury himself were also sold at the time. Those of Overbury depict a man with a long, thin face and large, dark, slightly sunken eyes. His features are regular, but he is not strikingly handsome. He has bushy and slightly receding hair, and a closely trimmed beard and moustache. In one image, by Renold Elstrack, he wears a thoughtful, melancholy expression, and is writing a poem on his own death.

Writings on Overbury from the period just after the execution of Charles I either present his death as an example of the depravity of the Stuart court, or answer such representations. In the first category, which tends to set Overbury up as a martyr to the evil schemes of Frances Howard, are the accounts of Sir Anthony Weldon, Arthur Wilson, Francis Osborne, and Sir Edward Peyton; in the second are those of Sir William Sanderson and Godfrey Goodman. Since the seventeenth century Overbury has generally been seen as the sad poet of Elstrack's print, betrayed by his friend, victim of the deadly designs of a corrupt monarch (according to Andrew Amos and Edward Rimbault) or of a beautiful murderess. Several semi-popular books have treated his death as a sensational murder story. He has, as the supposed author of the 'characters' printed with 'A Wife', been overestimated as a prose writer, and even praised for his wide knowledge of human nature. The latter judgement is almost the reverse of the truth: Overbury's friendship with Carr might have been the foundation for a career at least as comfortable as Sir Robert Killigrew's, but his arrogance and indiscretion in dealing with other people led eventually to his imprisonment and death. John Chamberlain wrote, when he heard that Overbury had died, that 'he was a very unfortunat man, for nobody almost pities him, and his very frends speake but indifferently of him' (*The Letters of John Chamberlain*, ed. N. E. McClure, 1939, 1.478).

Sir Thomas Overbury the younger His nephew **Sir Thomas Overbury** (*b*. in or before 1627, *d*. 1684), landowner and author, was the eldest of the eight children of Sir Giles Overbury (1590–1653), landowner, who was a brother of Sir Thomas Overbury the courtier, and his wife, Anne (1603–1660), daughter of Sir John Shirley of Ifield, Sussex. Thomas Overbury inherited the manors of Bruton and Bourton on the Hill on his father's death. He and his wife, Hester Leach (*d*. 1686), had one daughter, Mary, who married William Whitelocke, a son of Bulstrode Whitelocke. In 1659 Overbury was suspected of collecting weapons to furnish a rising to restore the Stuart monarchy; in 1660 he was knighted. In 1676 his account of a supposed murder in his part of the country was published. This described the disappearance of William Harrison, steward to Viscountess Campden, in 1660; the claim by Harrison's servant John Perry that he, his mother, and his brother had conspired to murder Harrison; and the execution of all three Perrys. It then printed the claim made by Harrison on his reappearance that he had been kidnapped, taken to the coast, and put on board a ship which was then captured by Turks, by whom he was enslaved for a while, until on his master's death he returned to England. The story is, as Overbury pointed out, a puzzling one, and the book ran to three editions.

In 1671 Overbury wrote a brief argument for liberty of worship, 'Queries proposed to the serious consideration of those who … persecute … upon the account of religion', which was circulated locally in manuscript and was attacked in print by Overbury's near neighbour George Vernon of Bourton on the Water in 1677. Overbury replied to Vernon, also in print, in *Ratiocinium vernaculum* in 1678. Anthony Wood remembered him as 'a favourer of Protestant dissenters' (Wood, 2.136). Another locally circulated tract of Overbury's, on the prospects for a new parliament, was denounced to the king as a 'scurvy libel' in 1676 (*CSP dom.*, 1659–84, 18.56). In 1679 he sold the manor of Bruton to Lord Brooke, and in 1680 he sold that of Bourton on the Hill for £3050 to Alexander Popham, the son-in-law of Sir Edward Harley, who helped with the purchase. Overbury died at Admington, near Quinton, Gloucestershire (now part of Warwickshire), on 28 February 1684, and was buried at Quinton on 6 March.

John Considine

Sources A. Somerset, *Unnatural murder: poison at the court of James I* (1997) · B. White, *Cast of ravens: the strange case of Sir Thomas Overbury* (1965) · N. Oldisworth, 'A booke touching Sir Thomas Overbury', 1637, BL, Add. MS 15476 · J. P. Considine, 'The invention of the literary circle of Sir Thomas Overbury', *Literary circles and cultural communities in Renaissance England*, ed. C. J. Summers and T. L. Pebworth (2000), 59–74 · D. Lindley, *The trials of Frances Howard: fact and fiction at the court of King James* (1993) · J. P. Considine, 'The humanist antecedents of the first English character-books', DPhil diss., U. Oxf., 1994 [esp. chap. 'Sir Thomas Overburies wife'], 37–79 · C. Dunning, 'The fall of Sir Thomas Overbury and the embassy to Russia in 1613', *Sixteenth Century Journal*, 22 (1991), 695–704 · *The diary of John*

Manningham of the Middle Temple, 1602–1603, ed. R. P. Sorlien (Hanover, NH, 1976) • *Memorials of affairs of state in the reigns of Q. Elizabeth and K. James I, collected (chiefly) from the original papers of … Sir Ralph Winwood*, ed. E. Sawyer, 3 vols. (1725) • Wood, *Ath. Oxon.*, new edn • *The life and letters of Sir Henry Wotton*, ed. L. P. Smith, 2 vols. (1907) • *Ben Jonson*, ed. C. H. Herford, P. Simpson, and E. M. Simpson, 11 vols. (1925–52) • C. Roberts, 'Sir Henry Neville and the origins of parliamentary undertaking', *Schemes and undertakings: a study of British politics in the seventeenth century* (1985), 3–30 • *Brief lives, chiefly of contemporaries, set down by John Aubrey, between the years 1669 and 1696*, ed. A. Clark, 2 vols. (1898) • *VCH Warwickshire*, vol. 5 • *VCH Gloucestershire*, vol. 6 • *CSP dom., 1659–84* • *DNB* • J. B. Williamson, ed., *The Middle Temple bench book*, 2nd edn, 1 (1937), 89 • *Report on the manuscripts of the marquis of Downshire*, 6 vols. in 7, HMC, 75 (1924–95) • www.familytreemaker.com/users/s/i/g/Nancy-A-Sigerson

Archives BL, parchment volume containing 'Observations on the 17 Provinces and France, on the Arch-duke's Country, and on France under Henry IV', 26 • BL, letters, Harley MS 7002 | BL, Trumbull MSS • Bodl. Oxf., report of the trials relating to his poisoning, MS Rawl. C63 • NRA, priv. coll., report on the trials relating to his poisoning • PRO, materials on the trial of those accused of his murder, SP 14/81 onwards

Likenesses attrib. M. Gheeraerts junior, oils, *c.*1613, Bodl. Oxf. • R. Elstrack, line engraving, *c.*1615, BM • S. de Passe, line engraving, *c.*1615 (after Gheeraerts), BM, NPG

Wealth at death made some money at court

Overbury, Sir Thomas (*b.* in or before **1627**, *d.* **1684**). *See under* Overbury, Sir Thomas (*bap.* 1581, *d.* 1613).

Overd, Emma (1838–1928), folk-singer, was born on 10 October 1838 at Port Field, a hamlet near Langport, Somerset, the fourth child and third daughter of Charles Weaver (*c.*1807–1871x81), an agricultural labourer, and his wife, Elizabeth Suttiett. Her mother died in 1846 and the children were brought up by Charles Weaver's mother, Rebecca. Emma was at work on the land from an early age, but as she was able to sign her name she may have received some elementary education. She married William Overd (1835/6–1914), an agricultural labourer, on 25 February 1860, and during the next sixteen years they had nine children, six of whom survived into adult life. She supplemented her husband's earnings by 'willow peeling'—removing the bark from willow saplings—one of Somerset's cottage industries. The family lived in the hamlet of Wick and later at Langport Westover.

Against this background of poverty and unceasing hard work, Emma Overd became known in the neighbourhood for singing folk songs. In 1903 Cecil Sharp, a London music teacher, began a search for songs in collaboration with his friend Charles Marson (1859–1914), vicar of Hambridge. In the summer of 1904 Sharp began to work in Langport and sought out Emma Overd. As Sharp's biographers told the story,

> A woman who had a great reputation as a singer lived in a mean street, which was inhabited—so he was told—by 'bad people'. She was out when he first called on her, but was said to be at the public-house round the corner. As he approached the public-house he saw a group of women standing outside and chatting. 'Is Mrs. Overd here?' he asked. 'That's my name,' an elderly woman replied, 'and what do you want of me?' Sharp explained that he was hunting for old songs and hoped that she would sing him some; whereupon without any warning she flung her arms around his waist and danced him round and round with the utmost vigour, shouting 'Lor, girls, here's my beau come at last!' (Fox Strangways and Karpeles, 36)

To complete the tableau, the vicar of Langport and his daughter then appeared, gazing with horror on the scene. But Sharp was not easily put off, and over the next five years he visited Emma Overd at least eleven times. She became interested in Sharp's search and helped by introducing him to other singers, beginning with her neighbours Eliza Hutchings (1833–1914) and Ellen Trott (1870–1912).

The store of traditional music so unlocked was remarkable in its quantity, in its quality, and in the circumstances of its performance. Sharp collected about sixty items from Emma Overd. Among them were 'Our captain cried all hands', to the tune Ralph Vaughan Williams used to set Bunyan's Pilgrim's hymn; 'In Bruton Town', a localized retelling of a story first written down by Boccaccio and used by Keats in 'Isabella and the Pot of Basil'; 'The Wraggle-taggle Gipsies'; and 'The Crabfish', variants of which are known to generations of rugby club singers. Her performances were not at all in the calm, impassive mould observed by Sharp in other folk-singers: she sang 'The Crabfish' 'at breakneck speed, beating time on the kitchen table'. At the gruesome climax of 'In Bruton Town', she would rise and walk about the room. Some songs she both sang and danced with Eliza Hutchings, like a medieval carol. She also used a number of other dramatic devices including some handsome variations in her tunes. Sharp's observation of the special gifts of singers like Emma Overd led him to formulate his theory of variation, one of the three principles by which, he claimed, English folk music was transmitted and recreated.

Six of Emma Overd's songs were published in Sharp's and Marson's *Folk Songs from Somerset* (5 vols., 1904–09), and during the brief period of enthusiasm before 1914 they could even be heard on the music-hall stage. But for the Overds life went on very much as before. The introduction of old-age pensions in 1909 allowed Emma a weekly indulgence of beer at Langport's Railway Hotel. William Overd died in 1914. Emma's health began to decline in 1927 and she died on 21 June 1928 at Langport Westover, aged eighty-nine. She was buried on 26 June at Curry Rivel, but the site of the grave is not known. Emma Overd's life was one of poverty and hardship among a class of people despised and rejected when they were not ignored by respectable society. But her spirit rose triumphantly above her circumstances, and her legacy is a handful of songs and tunes known and loved wherever English-speaking people are gathered together. C. J. Bearman

Sources private information (2004) [S. Nicholas, great-granddaughter] • Mr and Mrs H. Overd, interview, 5 March 1974, Vaughan Williams Memorial Library, Cecil Sharp House, London, David Bland MSS • A. H. Fox Strangways and M. Karpeles, *Cecil Sharp* (1933) • *Langport and Somerton Herald* (23 June 1928) • *Langport and Somerton Herald* (30 June 1928) • census returns for Curry Rivel, 1851, PRO, HO 107/1926/532/2; 1881, RG 11/2382/6/5; 1891, RG 12/1890/5/3 • b. cert. • m. cert. • d. cert.

Likenesses C. Sharp, photographs, Cecil Sharp House, London, Vaughan Williams Memorial Library, Cecil Sharp photograph collection • photograph, repro. in 'Mr. Cecil Sharp', *Musical Herald* (1 Dec 1905), 355–8

Overend, Hall (1772–1831), surgeon apothecary and teacher of medicine, was born on 23 November 1772 in Settle, Yorkshire, the son of John Overend (*c.*1734–1826), variously described as woolcomber, weaver, and husbandman, and his wife, Isabel (*c.*1732–1803); they were members of the Society of Friends. Hall, with his elder brother, John, were the only two of the children to survive into adulthood; John went on to become head of the highly regarded London discount house of Overend, Gurney & Co. As boys they walked daily to a school which was probably Giggleswick School, founded in 1512.

When aged about eighteen Hall Overend was sent to Sheffield to be apprenticed to the Quaker Richard Sutcliffe, a chemist, druggist, and apothecary, who was the son of Abraham Sutcliff, apothecary. Sutcliff had been the master and mentor of John Coakley Lettsom. After achieving his freedom Overend matriculated at Edinburgh University for the 1795/6 and 1796/7 sessions, registering for courses in anatomy with surgery, medicine, and obstetrics. Ambitious young apothecaries frequently rounded off their training by attending classes at that university without intending to proceed to graduation. In 1800 Overend married Ruth Wilson (1776–1847); they had seven children. Overend ran an extensive and profitable general practice as surgeon apothecary in Sheffield, visiting his patients on a handsome, if stubborn, mule.

The Apothecaries Act of 1815 empowered the London Society of Apothecaries to run an external licentiateship examination (LSA) open to any man who fulfilled the requirements, which included a five-year apprenticeship, the examination providing for the first time an opportunity for preparatory medical teaching to take place anywhere in England. In this context Overend began to develop his own school of anatomy and medicine in Sheffield, so that it became one of the earliest of the English provincial medical schools. Its creation was Overend's most important achievement. The school succeeded in winning external recognition when its teachers were formally recognized by the Society of Apothecaries in 1828. Overend's teaching was popular; it took place in his museum, formerly a maltings at the back of his home, where he displayed examples illustrating natural history, anatomy, pathology, and chemistry, along with diagrams. He also possessed an electrifying machine using brass spheres. Overend spent much of the income from his practice on the development of his teaching museum, which was praised by visitors from the Royal College of Surgeons of London. The collection was ultimately dispersed by the family and given to local natural history and medical interests. Seven of Overend's own apprentices had passed the LSA examination between 1816 and 1826 and their successes doubtless set the pattern on which the school was developed. Overend was forced to use the resurrectionists to provide him, illegally, with the bodies needed for teaching anatomy, his pupils being asked at times to go by night and superintend a disinterment following a recent burial, and it is on record that this macabre task provided an excitement to his students which 'totally overbore the risk'.

In 1828 Overend publicly seconded a motion in favour of creating another medical school in Sheffield, which was in some ways to be like his own but was to be corporately owned and to provide facilities for doctors already in practice in the town. It has been wrongly reported that Overend then went back on his word by continuing to support his own thriving private school. Confusion arose because Overend's 24-year-old son Wilson took over ownership of his father's school at the commencement of 1829. The date is made clear in Overend's will. Hall Overend was thus the successful creator of Sheffield's first medical school, who subsequently transferred his support to the creation of a second, but corporately owned school, which opened in 1829 and survives as a faculty of Sheffield University with more than 1200 medical students.

Overend helped the painter and sculptor Francis Chantrey to finance his studies while he was still in Sheffield, Chantrey being nine years the junior. Chantrey acknowledged this generosity by sending to Overend a signed early self-portrait in chalks, now in the National Portrait Gallery, London.

Overend took a responsible part in Sheffield societies, literary, philosophical, and social, and he presented papers on scientific and other topics, although nothing was published. He did not involve himself much in public affairs but he may have been a signatory to the prayers sent in 1828 and 1829 from the physicians and surgeons of the town to both houses of parliament, as was reported in the *Sheffield Iris*, seeking 'for means of facilitating dissection'.

Overend died at his home, Bolsover Hill, Barnsley Road, Sheffield, on 28 May 1831 after a period of ill health and was interred five days later in the Quaker burial-ground in Sheffield. No trace remains even of the site. It was written in his obituary 'He merited well of the public [for] his strenuous endeavour to improve the state of medical education' (*Sheffield Independent*, 4 June 1831). H. T. Swan

Sources H. T. Swan, 'Sheffield medical school: origins and influences', *Journal of Medical Biography*, 2 (1994), 22–32 • Exchequer Probate Records, will of Hall Overend, Dec 1831, Borth. Inst. • W. S. Porter, *The medical school in Sheffield, 1828–1928* (1928) • R. E. Leader, ed., *Reminiscences of old Sheffield* (1875) • U. Edin. L., special collections division, Matriculations MS Da35 • *Sheffield Independent* (4 June 1831) • *Sheffield Iris* (13 May 1828) [letter of 3 July 1992 in Sheffield University Library Special Collections relates to this note, from Record Office, House of Lords to H. T. Swan] • W. S. Porter, *Sheffield Literary and Philosophical Society, 1822–1922* (1922) • 'Resolutions of the Court of Examiners', 1825–32, RCS Eng., 30 Nov 1832 • L. Rosner, *Medical education in the age of improvement: Edinburgh students and apprentices, 1760–1826* (1991) • Quaker register of births, marriages, and burials, RS Friends, Lond., Yorkshire

Likenesses E. Law, marble bust, *c.*1831, University of Sheffield, school of medicine • photograph (after E. Law), University of Sheffield, school of medicine

Wealth at death approx. £5000 in cash; plus several freehold and leasehold properties in Sheffield; also woodland estate at Longshaw, Derbyshire; contents of medical teaching museum: will, 1831, Borth. Inst.

Overend, Marmaduke (*d.* 1790), organist and composer, was organist of Isleworth, Middlesex, from 1760 until his death. He studied with William Boyce, and corresponded with him until Boyce's death in 1779, about ancient Greek musical doctrines and the mathematical calculation of musical intervals. Following Boyce's death, Overend purchased his manuscript treatise on music. Based on it, he published *A Brief Account of, and Introduction to, Eight Lectures in the Science of Music* (1781), containing a method of finding musical ratios; it does not appear that the lectures were ever delivered. He also wrote music, much of which remained in manuscript. His published music includes an *Epithalamium* on the marriage of George III and Queen Charlotte (1761), *Twelve Sonatas* for two violins and cello (1762), and *A Hunting Cantata* (*c.*1780). Overend was buried at Isleworth on 25 June 1790, describing himself in his will as 'Student in Music'. His library was sold in 1791, when his manuscripts and that of Boyce were acquired by J. W. Callcott. They were eventually purchased by the Bodleian Library in 1972. L. M. MIDDLETON, *rev.* K. D. REYNOLDS

Sources J. C. Kassler, 'Overend, Marmaduke', *New Grove* • 'Overend, Marmaduke', Grove, *Dict. mus.* (1927)

Archives BL, papers relating to a dictionary of music, Add. MSS 27651–27686 • Bodl. Oxf., papers relating to musical theory

Overman family (*per. c.*1800–1933), farmers, were tenants of the Holkham estate, Norfolk, by the 1790s, and remained active farmers in the county until the 1950s. The Holkham estate in north-west Norfolk was owned by the Coke family (created earls of Leicester in 1837), and consisted of about 40,000 acres of mainly light land which responded well to the 'improved' farming methods that became more widely practised during the eighteenth century. It was the promotion of these methods and the encouragement of farmers such as the Overmans which made T. W. Coke (Coke of Norfolk) famous. The Overman family was one of about a dozen well-to-do families who stayed on the estate for more than 100 years, farming progressively and on a large scale.

A Mr Overman of Burnham Deepdale is described by Arthur Young in 1793 as 'a farmer remarkable for the neatness of his husbandry in general' (Young, 457). Young described Overman's experiments in drill cultivation and his enthusiasm for marling. Three years later Nathaniel Kent commented on Overman's entrepreneurial activities, describing how he kept a sloop 'constantly employed taking corn to London and bringing rape cake and manure from Holland, or London or Hull, wherever it could be procured at the best and cheapest rate' (Kent, 144).

The first member of the family about whom there is evidence is **Robert Overman** (*d.* 1815?), who became tenant of Crab Hall Farm, Burnham Sutton, in 1801. Little is known about him; he may even have been the Mr Overman already mentioned by Young and Kent. He was certainly an enthusiastic improver. His brother, F. W. Overman (who in 1814 took on a farm belonging to the duke of Norfolk), described how he marled his land to increase its productivity (Overman, 234–6). Robert had at least two sons, John [i] Overman [*see below*] and Henry Jacob [i] Overman [*see below*] who both became tenants of Holkham farms.

The elder son, **John** [i] **Overman** (1789/90–1856), took over Crab Hall Farm in 1815, perhaps at his father's death, and the farm was described in glowing terms by the Holkham agent, Francis Blaikie, in 1816. The buildings were in perfect repair, the farm was in a '*superior* state of cultivation', the new hedges were kept clean, and claying and marling were carried out with great spirit. The stock was well selected. In conclusion, Blaikie wrote, 'Mr Overman is a very deserving, industrious, attentive and persevering good tenant and may be styled a "pattern farmer"' (Blaikie, 'Report'). John had at least two sons, John [ii], born about 1811, and Robert Wright, born in 1814 or 1815.

Henry Jacob [i] **Overman** (1793/4–1859), the younger son of Robert Overman, moved from the family farm to take over Manor Farm, Weasenham St Peter, also on the Holkham estate, in 1819. In 1843 he gave R. N. Bacon of the *Norwich Mercury* a copy of the rotation he had practised since 1820, for Bacon's book on Norfolk agriculture published in 1844. It shows that Overman was practising a typical Norfolk four-course system (Bacon, 208–10). His 700 acre farm contained a mixture of soils from light to heavy and he kept 800 southdown ewes, 30–40 store cattle, and 30 cows. He was visited by James Caird in 1850, who was surprised to find a herd of dairy cows in Norfolk. Butter and cheese were made and sent to London. The Holkham agent, William Keary, visited the farm in 1851 and described it as a 'really good occupation' in a 'high state of cultivation', and he was also surprised to find a herd of Ayrshire cows (Caird, 170). Henry's wife, Mary Ann, was born in nearby Sharrington, and they had four children surviving in 1851, including Henry Robert Overman [*see below*], their elder son.

Robert Wright Overman (1814/15–1874), younger son of John Overman, was farming the Burnham Sutton farm when it was visited by William Keary in 1851, and was obviously continuing his father's tradition of good husbandry.

> It is almost impossible to speak too highly of the excellent cultivation and good management to be seen … Much might be said in praise of Mr Overman's management, both as to stock and everything else, but it must suffice to say that as a specimen of light land farming and clean cultivation, it stands unrivalled in west Norfolk and probably the kingdom. (Keary's description, Holkham MSS)

In 1854 Robert Wright Overman left Burnham Sutton and moved to Egmere, still on the Holkham estate, where he stayed until 1872. The tenancy at Burnham was taken over in 1854 by his brother **John** [ii] **Overman** (*c.*1811–*c.*1900), who remained there until his death about 1900. Either Robert or John was the Mr Overman, 'one of our princely and enlightened sort of farmers', who was described by the Revd Benjamin Armstrong of Dereham as taking 'forty of his men to have a day at the seaside' (Lowestoft). He had shown them the oil-crushing machines and taken them for a sail. 'As he paid them their wages just the same I reckon the treat must have cost him about £20. I told him how grateful the community should be to his right conduct and told the men how grateful they should be for so excellent a master' (Armstrong, 61–2).

Henry Robert Overman (1825/6–1891) took over Manor Farm, Weasenham St Peter, from his father in 1859. By 1881 he was also farming 600 acres in the same parish rented from Viscount Townshend. In 1881 he was interviewed by the royal commission on agriculture, when he was still keeping Ayrshire cattle and producing butter. He also kept 40–50 store cattle and a flock of about 500 Oxford Down sheep. His knowledge of stock meant that he was frequently a judge at Smithfield in London as well as at local county shows. He acknowledged the problems that agriculture was facing by the 1880s and the difficulties there were in finding tenants with capital to run farms ('Royal commission', 17.735). Nationally, Henry Robert Overman was a prominent member of the Royal Agricultural Society of England. Locally, he was a supporter of Joseph Arch, Liberal MP for north-west Norfolk, and a patron of the county school set up at North Elmham, Norfolk. However, he was never persuaded to become a county councillor. He died on 2 January 1891, and was buried at Weasenham St Peter.

His elder son, **Henry Jacob** [ii] **Overman** (1862–1933), took over the farm from his father in 1891. By 1892, at a time when tenants were leaving the Holkham estates and replacements were difficult to find, he was able to add North Hall Farm and Kipton Ash Farm, both in Weasenham, to his holding, meaning that he was running an enterprise of at least 1806 acres there. His obituary in the *Eastern Daily Press* on 11 January 1933 stated that he farmed more than 3700 acres in Norfolk and 1000 in Northamptonshire in partnership with his brother. He also followed in his father's footsteps in taking a prominent role in farming affairs, giving evidence to the royal commission on agriculture in 1916. Described as the most versatile farmer in Norfolk, he was a member of the research committee of the Royal Agricultural Society of England and a protectionist, which led him to be deeply involved in the Agricultural Party set up briefly in 1931. He was nominated by the Central Association of Chambers of Agriculture to be the official representative at the Imperial Conference on wheat prices in Ottowa in 1932, but was not appointed.

Henry Jacob Overman was an active member of the Norfolk chamber of agriculture and its president in 1916. He was a member of the central wages board in 1917 and a long-serving chairman of the Norfolk farmers' union. He was on the committee of the Norfolk agricultural station in the 1920s. He died at Kipton House, Weasenham St Peter, Norfolk, on 9 January 1933.

Members of the Overman family, though tenants of the Holkham estate rather than owners, were significant agricultural innovators in Norfolk from at least the 1790s. Succeeding generations were prominent in the local or national farming community, and became renowned for their contribution to farming progress. In 1952 H. R. Overman was chairman of the Farmers' Club of London.

SUSANNA WADE MARTINS

Sources R. A. C. Parker, *Coke of Norfolk* (1975) • S. Wade Martins, *A great estate at work* (1980) • F. Blaikie, 'Report of the estates of Thomas William Coke Esq. in the county of Norfolk', 1816, Holkham Hall, Norfolk, Holkham MSS • William Keary's description of the Holkham estate, 1851, Holkham Hall, Norfolk, Holkham MSS • A. Young, 'A week in Norfolk', *Annals of Agriculture*, 19 (1793), 457 • N. Kent, *General view of the agriculture of the county of Norfolk* (1796), 144 • R. N. Bacon, *Agriculture of Norfolk* (1844) [Bacon MS 4363, Norfolk RO] • J. Caird, *English agriculture in 1850–51* (1852), 170 • 'Royal commission on the depressed condition of agricultural interests', *Parl. papers* (1881), 17.735–48, C. 3096 • *Eastern Daily Press* (11 Jan 1933) • H. B. J. Armstrong, ed., *Armstrong's Norfolk diary: further passages from the diary of the Reverend Benjamin John Armstrong* (1963), 60–61 • F. W. Overman, 'On claying or marling land', *Journal of the Royal Agricultural Society of England*, 3 (1842) • b. cert. [Henry Jacob [ii] Overman] • d. certs. [Henry Jacob [i] Overman; Henry Jacob [ii] Overman; Robert Wright Overman; Henry Robert Overman] • *CGPLA Eng. & Wales* (1860) • *CGPLA Eng. & Wales* (1933) [Henry Jacob [ii] Overman]

Likenesses watercolour, *c.*1850 (Henry [i] Overman), priv. coll. • photograph, 1912 (Henry Jacob [ii] Overman), repro. in J. Hutchinson and A. C. Owers, *Change and innovation in Norfolk farming* (Wymondham, 1980), p. 14 • photograph, 1952, Farmers' Club, London

Wealth at death £18,487 8*s*. 5*d*.—Henry Jacob [ii] Overman: probate, 14 Dec 1933, *CGPLA Eng. & Wales* • under £7000—Henry Jacob [i] Overman: probate, 8 March 1860, *CGPLA Eng. & Wales*

Overman, Henry Jacob (1793/4–1859). *See under* Overman family (*per. c.*1800–1933).

Overman, Henry Jacob (1862–1933). *See under* Overman family (*per. c.*1800–1933).

Overman, Henry Robert (1825/6–1891). *See under* Overman family (*per. c.*1800–1933).

Overman, John (1789/90–1856). *See under* Overman family (*per. c.*1800–1933).

Overman, John (*c.*1811–*c.*1900). *See under* Overman family (*per. c.*1800–1933).

Overman, Robert (*d.* 1815?). *See under* Overman family (*per. c.*1800–1933).

Overman, Robert Wright (1814/15–1874). *See under* Overman family (*per. c.*1800–1933).

Overs, John A. (1808–1844), author and cabinet-maker, was born in Birmingham, the eldest of the three sons of Richard Overs (1778–1851) and his wife, Elizabeth, *née* Mykins (or Meakins; *d. c.*1814). His father was descended from a staunchly Roman Catholic family of copyholders in the manor of Knowle, with a family home at Chesset Wood. The home that he inherited on the death of his brother Charles was heavily mortgaged, yet Richard Overs managed to pay off the debts through business interests which are now, unfortunately, unrecorded—he is described only as 'yeoman' at the Knowle Manor court. John Overs's two brothers died when he was five, and his mother died a year later. Richard Overs remarried, but there is no evidence of any further children before his second wife died.

John Overs was apprenticed to a cabinet-maker, and slowly rose through the profession. He harboured dreams of being recognized as a writer, however: a manuscript notebook of his poetry from the 1820s is extant, including some striking love poems to his fiancée. On 4 August 1828 John Overs married Amelia Horton (*d.* 1885), the eighth of the fourteen children of Daniel Horton, a gold-cutter who had lived near the centre of Birmingham, and his wife, Mary Wilkinson. This marriage caused a rift in the family, as Amelia was an Anglican; John Overs's father disowned him, and continued to remain distant from the family, even after his son's death.

By 1834 John Overs and Amelia were living in Hoxton, London. Overs was working as a cabinet-maker, but continued to educate himself and to write in his spare time. He acquired several influential friends who assisted him in his attempts to publish his poetry and short stories. Charles Dickens, in particular, provided him with feedback on his writing, with introductions to newspaper editors, and with practical and financial assistance when Overs became seriously ill. Overs first wrote to Dickens in January 1839, hoping to have some poetry placed in *Bentley's Miscellany*. Dickens, who had just resigned as editor of the publication, thought several of Overs's pieces were rather fine. He went on to recommend them to his successor, and continued to correspond with Overs, recommending his writing to editors in his circle, reading and commenting on his work, and even going so far as to meet him:

> I have … sat down to alter your story. I find it, however, almost an impossible job without having you at my elbow … If you can be with me at *12 exactly* next Sunday, I can spare an hour and a half, and I have no doubt that will be quite sufficient for our purpose. (*Letters of Charles Dickens*, 2.19)

They corresponded on other matters as well: on one occasion, Dickens sent Overs a copy of Carlyle's *Chartism*, with the aim of obtaining a working man's view of the work, and Overs wrote back, giving his opinion of its strengths and weaknesses.

Dickens also assisted Overs when he became ill. He sent him £5 on at least three occasions, arranged for his friend Dr John Elliotson to provide treatment, and in the autumn of 1841, when Overs's lung complaint became too grave for him to continue as a cabinet-maker, even found him a job as an administrator in William Macready's new Drury Lane Theatre. This latter assistance led to some friction between the two men, as Overs was dissatisfied with his working conditions and salary—the letters to him from Dickens at this time are quite heated, and interesting for their condemnation of Overs's ostensible tendency to 'vaunt [his] independence too much, and to flourish it rather unnecessarily in the eyes of a stranger' (*Letters of Charles Dickens*, 2.408). After a remonstrative letter from Overs, Dickens calmed down, and continued to offer him assistance, for instance in recommending him as a writer to Murdo Young, proprietor of the *Sun Newspaper*.

Perhaps more importantly, however, Dickens advised Overs on the publication *Evenings of a Working Man* (1844), and wrote the preface to the work. This collection was dedicated to Dr Elliotson, and contains one story, 'The carpenter', which bears signs of a response to W. H. Ainsworth's advice that Overs should write from his own experience. In his preface Dickens is careful to emphasize Overs's autonomy, stating that although he had given advice to the author on this collection of short pieces, he 'never altered them, otherwise than by recommending condensation now and then', and assuring the reader that the volume's sketches represented Overs's 'genuine work, as they have been his sober and rational amusement'. Dickens described him as 'a simple, frugal, steady, upright, honourable man' who had 'risen superior to the mere prejudices of [his] class … without losing his sympathy for all their real wrongs and grievances'. He also calls upon the reader to sympathize with Overs in his ill health and to recognize that the publication of the volume was largely motivated by the desire to make 'some temporary provision for his sick wife and very young family' (Dickens, preface, *Evenings of a Working Man*). Overs was paid £25 for the book by T. C. Newby, the publisher whom Dickens had recommended; the money went through Dickens's account, and was forwarded to Overs by him. The book ran into two editions.

John Overs died at 55 Vauxhall Street, Lambeth, London, on 28 September 1844. According to Dickens:

> When poor Overs was dying he suddenly asked for a pen and ink and some paper, and made up a little parcel for me which it was his last conscious act to direct. She [Amelia Overs] told me this and gave it me. I opened it last night. It was a copy of his little book in which he had written my name, 'With his devotion.' I thought it simple and affecting of the poor fellow. (*Letters of Charles Dickens*, 4.240)

John Overs was given a pauper's burial in a public grave, no. 576, West Norwood cemetery, London.

Dickens was out of the country at the time of Overs's death, and so it was T. C. Newby who arranged for a subscription to be taken up for the relief of Overs's destitute widow and six children (Amelia, John Richard, Harriet, Geraldine, Editha, and John). Newby himself gave £20 and, among other contributions, Amelia and her children received £25 from the Royal Literary Fund, after recommendations from Newby, Elliotson, and D. A. Mullock. Dickens interested Angela Burdett Coutts in the case of Overs's family, and she sent Amelia 'at different times, sixteen pounds … sent a doctor to her children, and … got one of the girls into the Orphan School' (*Letters of Charles Dickens*, 4.293). Help from Overs's friends enabled Amelia Overs to set up in a 'small millinery and fancy stationery business' (*The Examiner*, 24 May 1845) at 16 Carthusian Street, Charterhouse Square. In February 1846 she married Robert John King, a bookbinder and widower. They lived in London for the rest of their lives; Amelia King died in 1885. M. Clare Loughlin-Chow

Sources R. Vine and S. Smith, 'John Overs: family tradition, poetry and memorabilia', *The Dickensian*, 90 (1994), 85–94 · *IGI* · *The letters of Charles Dickens*, ed. M. House, G. Storey, and others, 2 (1969) · *GM*, 2nd ser., 22 (1844), 551 · S. Smith, 'John Overs to Charles Dickens: a working-man's letter and its implications', *Victorian Studies*, 18 (1974), 195–217 · d. cert.

Overstone. For this title name *see* Loyd, Samuel Jones, Baron Overstone (1796–1883).

Overton family (*per.* *c.*1665–*c.*1765), map and print publishers, dominated print publishing in London for a century. **John Overton** (1639/40–1713) was the son of Thomas Overton of Covent Garden, tailor. He was apprenticed to Thomas Gould for eight years on 30 June 1655 and made free of the Stationers' Company on 4 July 1663. When London's leading printseller, Peter Stent, died of the plague in 1665, Overton took over his shop: the White Horse, near Pye Corner. This burned down in the great fire of 1666, but by 1669 Overton was established at the White Horse on Snow Hill, opposite St Sepulchre's Church. He built up the most powerful wholesale printselling business in London by publishing widely saleable prints and buying up and republishing successful plates, such as John Speed's maps. He sold maps, topographical views, portraits, and sets of months or stories from scripture for display. Phrases in his will suggest that he married three times. If so, his 'second wife' was a daughter of Benjamin Dunn, and his 'last wife', married in 1677, was Sarah Garrett, sister to a John Garrett (*fl.* *c.*1665–1722) who was probably the printseller who had a shop in the Royal Exchange. He had seven children, Thomas, Henry [*see below*], Philip [*see below*], James, Anne, Margaret, and Sarah. The eldest, Thomas, had emigrated to America and had not been heard of since 1700. John Overton died in March 1713, and was buried in the church of St Sepulchre on 31 March. He named his second son, Henry, as his executor but left the lease of his house and shop to his unmarried daughter Sarah. Both his portrait (the print of which gives his age as sixty-eight in 1708) and his will give an impression of a stern patriarch but he took great care that all his children should get a share of the small fortune that he had amassed.

The business of printselling was altogether more lucrative for the next generation. **Henry** [i] **Overton** (1675/6–1751) was the second son of John Overton, whose stock he bought by indenture in 1707, having married Sarah Baker in 1706. He ran the shop at the White Horse until his death, extending the network of provincial contacts that John Overton had perhaps already established. The first auctions of prints held in country towns seem often to have consisted chiefly of prints supplied by Henry Overton. He steadily expanded his range of plates along the lines established by his father, responding rapidly to new fashions and demands—for prints of hunting and horse-racing, for instance. Although occasionally involved with prestigious publications such as the prints after Louis Laguerre of the *Battles of the Duke of Marlborough* (1717), many of Henry Overton's designs were plagiarized from fine prints published by others. Until the Copyright Act of 1735 William Hogarth was a notable victim of such piracy. His *Harlot's Progress*, for instance, was copied cheaply by their employees in a wide range of sizes at different prices, down to the crudest woodcut royal and pot sheets distributed by rural salesmen. Some of the firm's oldest plates remained valuable: Henry Overton reprinted Wenceslaus Hollar's plates in April 1743. He died at his house in Charterhouse Square on 27 June 1751; his death 'in the 76th Year of his Age' was reported next day in the *General Advertiser*, which noted that 'He was married a few Days since to a young Lady of about Thirty, to whom he has left 10,000 *l.*' The marriage to Mary Green had taken place on 8 April 1751 at St Michael Cornhill. To his 'dear wife Mary' he left his sizeable share in the New River, his freehold house in Charterhouse Square, his house and garden in Middlesex, and £500 bank stock. The lease of his house, shop, and premises and all his copperplates, wood blocks, maps, prints, paper, and other stock went to his nephew Henry [*see below*]. He left a house in Ormonde Street and two more off Fetter Lane to his niece Henrietta and further property to his niece Catherine Skynner.

Philip Overton (*c.*1681–1745) was the third son of John Overton. He was apprenticed to his father in 1695 so it is likely that he was born about 1681. He was made free of the Stationers' Company in 1702. In 1707 his father gave him £200 'toward his advancement and setting up a trade' and lent him two further amounts of £100 in August and October 1711. He had set himself up at the White Horse opposite St Dunstan's Church, Fleet Street, by May 1708 but changed his sign to the Golden Buck by January 1710. Philip Overton's shop set a higher tone than that of Henry Overton. Although the brothers often published in alliance, Philip was involved in the distribution of a number of fine modern prints and helped to publish some, such as William Hogarth's *Hudibras* set (1726). He also sold imported prints of quality. From 1738 he published a few political satires. Nevertheless, his staple was in interesting and decorative prints for the middle market. Philip Overton's will, signed on 5 February 1745 and proved on 20 February 1745, left his estate to his second wife, Mary [*see below*]. He desired to be buried in Aston, Hertfordshire, where he presumably had property. He also had a house in Kentish Town as well as his shop in Fleet Street.

Mary Overton (*fl.* 1745–1748), widow and successor of Philip Overton, briefly ran the Golden Buck in Fleet Street after her husband's death in February 1745. On 6 January 1747 she married James Sayer at Christ Church, Spitalfields. It would seem that at about this time James's younger brother Robert *Sayer became her assistant. In the art dealer Arthur Pond's account books there are a number of references to her buying prints from him. The shop was run by Mary until December 1748 when in newspaper advertisements Robert Sayer was first named as manager.

Henry [ii] **Overton** (*fl.* 1751–1764), nephew and successor of Henry [i] Overton, was presumably the son of John Overton's fourth son, James. Taking over the business in 1751 he moved vigorously into the market for engraved views, usually publishing in partnership with Robert Sayer. He maintained the White Horse at Snow Hill until at least November 1764. On 29 February 1752 an announcement appeared in the *London Evening-Post*, 'On Thursday last Mr. Overton, an eminent Printseller without Newgate, was married to Miss Dawson, of Gilt-Spur Street, an agreeable young Lady with a considerable Fortune.' Sadly, a correction appeared in the next issue to the effect that the announcement had been 'premature'. A printed catalogue of his stock of 'Common and Fine Prints', issued in

1754, extended to seventy-nine pages. At that time his latest innovation was wallpaper, designed by John Baptist Jackson, 'printed in oil' with special designs 'in chiaro oscuro and in chints colours' to have the effect of prints displayed on the wall. He advertised a new edition of George Bickham's *Universal Penman* in November 1764 but after that date he disappeared from view.

TIMOTHY CLAYTON

Sources will, PRO, PROB 11/789/216 [Henry [i] Overton] • will, PRO, PROB 11/532/86 [John Overton] • will, PRO, PROB 11/738/54 [Philip Overton] • *London Evening-Post* (April 1743) • *General Advertiser* (28 June 1751) • *London Evening-Post* (29 Feb 1752) • S. Tyacke, *London map-sellers, 1660–1720* (1978) • D. Hodson, *County atlases of the British Isles published after 1703: a bibliography*, 3 vols. (1984–97) • S. O'Connell, *The popular print in England* (1999) • A. Griffiths and R. A. Gerard, *The print in Stuart Britain, 1603–1689* (1998) [exhibition catalogue, BM, 8 May – 20 Sept 1998] • A. Globe, *Peter Stent, London printseller circa 1642–1665: being a catalogue raisonné of his engraved prints and books* (1985) • T. Clayton, *The English print, 1688–1802* (1997) • parish register, London, St Sepulchre [burial, John Overton], 31 March 1713 • parish register, London, St Sepulchre [burial, Henry [i] Overton], 5 July 1751

Likenesses mezzotint (John Overton; after unknown portrait), BM, NPG • oils (John Overton)

Wealth at death est. over £10,000—Henry [i] Overton

Overton, Benjamin [*formerly* Ebenezer] (*c.*1647–1711), politician and political pamphleteer, was a younger son of the radically inclined Cromwellian major-general Robert *Overton (1608/9–1678/9) and his wife, Ann (1615/16–1665), daughter of Jeremy Gardiner of Stratford, Middlesex.

Much of what is known of Overton's early life comes from a posthumous publication entitled *Good Advice to the Whigs, by an Old Dying Whig* (1712), which purported to be a public letter of advice written by Overton on his deathbed to his quondam political friends, prefaced by an anonymous biographical introduction. According to this brief life, he had been baptized Ebenezer, but 'changed his Christian name at confirmation into Benjamin, as being best suited to the common abridgement of it, for he was commonly called Ben' (*Good Advice to the Whigs*, 3–4). After 'a good progress in a virtuous education' he achieved a moral liberation of sorts with the restoration of the monarchy and 'the ruin of his family' (ibid., 3). He 'shook off the principles of all revealed religion, and allowed himself great liberties in many ill practices, chiefly in gaming both at cards and dice'. For the next thirty years or so 'he lived without any sense of religion' (ibid., 4). But he was not without political principles, and retained the devotion to the cause of 'liberty both in church and state' (ibid., 7) in which he had been brought up. Overton's father's will, made in June 1678, raises a question mark over details of this account, without necessarily contradicting it. While he silently ignored his eldest son and heir, John, whom he regarded as an apostate, the deeply pious Robert made Ebenezer (as he is named in the will) the executor of his estate and coheir with another younger son of the bulk of his personal estate.

Whether or not Overton 'acted a part in the Revolution' (*Good Advice to the Whigs*, 4) as his public letter claimed (and in the late 1690s he made a similar claim, grounding a request in a petition upon his having taken part in the expedition to England), he was evidently regarded as a whig. In 1689 he was made a commissioner of prizes, and the following year he became warden of the Royal Mint (a position he held until the spring of 1696). Soon, however, he attached himself to Robert Spencer, second earl of Sunderland. A pamphlet that has been attributed to Overton, *A Dialogue betwixt Whig and Tory* (1693), although partisan in tone, and heavily critical of the erstwhile whigs who had joined forces with tories to form a 'new Country party' opposition, is thought to have been inspired by Sunderland and intended to support his plans for a ministerial reconstruction to incorporate the whig junto. A year later Sunderland recommended Overton to Lord Portland as one who had been 'more serviceable by writing, talking, acting, and keeping others in order than any man whatsoever' (U. Nott. L., Portland (Bentinck) MSS, Sunderland to Portland, 13 July 1694). His eventual acquisition of a customs commissionership in 1696 should probably be put down to Sunderland's influence, though by this time he had also acquired another patron, Charles Powlett, marquess of Winchester (later second duke of Bolton), with whom he was on close enough terms to advise against the perils of drink and loose living.

After a long time on the fringes of party politics Overton was eventually returned to parliament in 1701 for St Ives in Cornwall, on the duke of Bolton's interest, but made no impact whatsoever in the House of Commons and was not proposed again. He lost his place in the customs in 1703, at about the time his anonymous biographer says that he fell seriously ill with 'a rheumatical palsy, which took from him the use of his limbs, and put him under great and constant pains' (*Good Advice to the Whigs*, 4). By 1706 he was writing to Portland that he intended henceforth to winter in Bath every year: 'though it is melancholy next to the grave, it is the more suitable to my circumstances, and the most proper ante-room to that common bedchamber of kings and clowns' (Portland (Bentinck) MSS, Overton to Portland, 17 Feb 1706). Physical suffering served 'to awaken his conscience, and … give him a sad view of his past life, his wicked principles, and bad actions' (*Good Advice to the Whigs*, 4–5). He was particularly remorseful at having cheated so many victims at the gaming tables, and made such attempts at restitution as were possible in his reduced circumstances. Evidently in his closing years he determined to recall his fellow whigs to their former principles, in both religion and politics, which was the purpose of his public letter, in which he reminded his readers that 'virtue and industry are indispensably necessary to maintain a free government', and urged them to 'show a true concern for the reformed religion' rather than simply 'an opposition to popery'.

Overton died in 1711, leaving a son and a daughter, the former still a minor. Nothing is known of his marriage (or marriages). Nor does Overton's will mention another son, alive and an adult in the late 1690s when Overton sought a place for him as chief searcher in the port of London. His will appointed former secretary of state, James Vernon, Under-Secretary Norris, and admirals Matthew Aylmer and Sir John Norris as executors and guardians of his young son, but none agreed to act, and the will was not proved until his son's death in 1738. D. W. Hayton

Sources HoP, *Commons, 1690–1715* [draft] • *Good advice to the whigs, by an old dying whig, or, Mr Overton's last letter to his friends, with an account of his sickness and death* (1712) • J. A. Downie, 'Ben Overton: an alternative author of *A dialogue betwixt whig and tory*', *Papers of the Bibliographical Society of America*, 70 (1976), 263–71 • Bolton Hall, Wensley, North Yorkshire, Bolton MSS • U. Nott. L., Portland (Bentinck) MSS • will, PRO, PROB 11/521, sig. 116 • *Letters illustrative of the reign of William III from 1696 to 1708 addressed to the duke of Shrewsbury by James Vernon*, ed. G. P. R. James, 3 vols. (1841) • B. Taft, '"They that pursue perfaction on earth": the political progress of Robert Overton', *Soldiers, writers and statesmen of the English revolution*, ed. I. Gentles and others (1998), 286–303 • J. Redington, ed., *Calendar of Treasury papers*, 1, PRO (1868), 482, 501 • will, PRO, PROB 11/359, sig. 8 [Robert Overton] • Greaves & Zaller, *BDBR*, vol. 2, 279–81

Archives Bolton Hall, Wensley, North Yorkshire, Bolton MSS • U. Nott. L., Portland (Bentinck) MSS

Wealth at death died in 'reduced circumstances': will, PRO, PROB 11/521, sig. 116

Overton, Charles (**1805–1889**), Church of England clergyman and author, the sixth son of John *Overton (1763–1838), rector of St Crux and St Margaret, York, and his wife, Elizabeth, *née* Stodart (*d*. 1827), was born in York. He was expected to become a civil engineer, and so not sent to university, but in 1829 he was ordained a deacon by the archbishop of York, Vernon Harcourt. He was for a short time assistant curate of Christ Church, Harrogate, but in the year of his ordination became curate of Romaldkirk, Yorkshire. In the same year he married Amelia Charlesworth, who died in 1885. They had four sons and three daughters. In 1837 J. B. Sumner, bishop of Chester, presented him to the vicarage of Clapham, in the West Riding of Yorkshire, and in 1841 to that of Cottingham, near Hull, where he spent the rest of his life.

Like his father Overton was a firmly convinced evangelical, but was not narrowly partisan and could sympathize with good men who belonged to other schools of thought. He was an able preacher and an active pastor in his large and scattered parish, then encompassing Skidby and Newland, which later became separate parishes. Chiefly through his own exertions funds were raised to enable the parish church to be restored and parsonages and schools to be built.

Overton wrote both in prose and in verse. His first poem, entitled *Ecclesia Anglicana* (1833), was written at Romaldkirk to celebrate the restoration of York Minster after its partial destruction by the arsonist and religious fanatic Jonathan Martin (1782–1838). A later edition appeared in 1853. It was good-humouredly satirized by Tom Moore, who began his parody:

Sweet singer of Romaldkirk, thou who art reckoned,
By critics episcopal, David the Second,
If thus, as a curate, so lofty your flight,
Only think in a Rectory how you would write!

Probably the best-known of his other works was *Cottage Lectures, or, 'The Pilgrim's Progress' Practically Explained* (1847–8). He died on 31 March 1889 at Cottingham, where he was buried in the churchyard six days later.

J. H. Overton, *rev.* Stephen Gregory

Sources *The Guardian* (17 April 1889) • Boase, *Mod. Eng. biog.* • Crockford (1889) • private information (1894)

Wealth at death £11,762 17*s*. 7*d*.: probate, 13 July 1889, *CGPLA Eng. & Wales*

Overton, Constantine [Constant] (*b*. **1626/7**, *d*. in or after **1690**), Quaker activist, was the son of Rowland Overton of Shrewsbury, carpenter. When his father became a freeman of Shrewsbury in 1639 Constantine was twelve, the youngest of four children: two sisters, Katherine and Eleanor, and a brother, Humphrey, three years his senior. Constantine became a shoemaker and was admitted freeman of Shrewsbury in 1653; a trade-token which he issued ten years later bore the arms of his occupation. The hearth tax roll of 1672 records him as living in Welsh Ward within the Walls, paying on four hearths. He married twice. His first wife, Jane, the mother of Samuel, who was baptized in January 1651, died the following year and was buried in St Chad's, Shrewsbury, on 20 November 1652. His second wife, also called Jane, was the mother of a daughter, Jane, born on 14 September 1656.

Constantine Overton was one of the first to join the Quaker movement in Shropshire, and he frequently appears as a witness to marriages in the Shrewsbury Quaker marriages from the very first entry in August 1656. In April 1657, while in Shrewsbury gaol, his name heads the list of those Quakers whose names were attached to *The Priest's Wickednesse and Cruelty, Laid Open, and Made Manifest*, which describes how he and other Quakers were attacked by people from the church in neighbouring Cressedge. The Quakers were later sent to gaol, fined for keeping their hats on in court, and imprisoned for a further three months.

Overton was to suffer further in the Quaker cause following the Restoration. In 1662 he and his brother, Humphrey, were imprisoned for non-payment of tithes. On 26 February 1663 Constantine was seized at a meeting at Shrewsbury and sent to prison; and in 1665 he was disfranchised as freeman of Shrewsbury for refusing to take the proffered oaths and for holding meetings in his house. He suffered further when he, Humphrey, and their two servants were committed to gaol for keeping their shops open on Christmas day. In May 1670 the mayor and local officers took down the names of all those present at a Quaker meeting, sending four to prison and fining the rest—Constantine, Humphrey, and Thomas Overton (whose exact relationship to the brothers is uncertain) being the heaviest sufferers. Constantine was heavily fined again, and he was to incur additional loss for the offence of keeping his shop open on Christmas day.

It would seem probable that Constantine Overton was an important Friend in his locality, for the minutes of the London yearly meeting for 1672 list Constant Overton as the recipient of five books for the county of Shropshire. There is no record of the date of his death or burial: he last appears in the Shrewsbury Quaker register as a witness to a marriage in June 1690.

Charlotte Fell-Smith, *rev.* Caroline L. Leachman

Sources J. Besse, *A collection of the sufferings of the people called Quakers*, 1 (1753) • J. Smith, ed., *A descriptive catalogue of Friends' books*, 2

(1867) • H. Owen and J. B. Blakeway, *A history of Shrewsbury*, 1 (1825) • digest registers of births, marriages, and burials, RS Friends, Lond. • yearly meeting minutes, 1668–93, RS Friends, Lond., vol. 1, p. 4 • H. E. Forest, ed., *Shrewsbury burgess roll* (1924) • G. E. Evans, ed., 'Register of Society of Friends, Shrewsbury, 1657–1834', *Shropshire parish registers: nonconformist registers*, 1, Shropshire Parish Registers (1903) • W. P. W. Phillimore and others, eds., *Diocese of Lichfield: St Chad's, Shrewsbury parish registers*, 3 vols., Shropshire Parish Registers, 29–31 (1913) • W. Watkins-Pitchford, *The Shropshire hearth-tax roll of 1672*, Shropshire Archaeological and Parish Register Society (1949) • [C. Overton and others], *The priest's wickednesse and cruelty, laid open, and made manifest* (1657)

Overton, Henry (1675/6–1751). *See under* Overton family (*per. c.*1665–*c.*1765).

Overton, Henry (*fl.* 1751–1764). *See under* Overton family (*per. c.*1665–*c.*1765).

Overton, John (1639/40–1713). *See under* Overton family (*per. c.*1665–*c.*1765).

Overton, John (1762/3–1838), theological writer, was born at Tetford in Lincolnshire, the son of a cottager. He was appointed an excise officer thanks to the influence of the rector, the Revd Mr Emmeris, in whose home he lived, and Thomas Cholmondeley (later Lord Delamere). This gave him the opportunity to pursue his interest in astronomy. Overton built the telescopes he was to use in his observations. Combining his immense knowledge of biblical writings with his expertise in astronomy he began, from 1812, to formulate anti-deistic arguments, aiming to demonstrate the compatibility of biblical chronology and genealogies with Newtonian laws of science and knowledge of the universe.

Having installed a printing press at his house in Crayford, Kent, in 1816, Overton published his first work, *The genealogy of Christ elucidated by sacred history … with a new system of sacred chronology and the true meaning of the weeks in Daniel* (2 vols., 1817). This he wrote as 'an antidote to the venomous pen' of the ideologue Comte C.-F. C. de Volney. By demonstrating the harmony of the laws of the universe with the biblical accounts 'rightly understood', Overton aimed not only to counter Volney's denial of the scientific basis of biblical accounts, but to establish the authenticity of the biblical record on the basis of its accuracy in matters astronomical. In this and other works he defends the Bible as a work of science, proved through the accuracy of its chronology and genealogies. This thesis was advanced, too, in *The books of Genesis and Daniel (in connection with modern astronomy) defended against Count Volney and Dr. Francis* (1820), supplemented by *The Sonship of Christ* which was written against J. S. Gorton and the Revd J. H. Evans. The conclusions of these two works were afterwards summarized in a pamphlet, *A View of Sacred History and its Chronology in Connexion with Modern Astronomy* (1827). Other pamphlets by Overton include *The Chronology of the Apocalypse Investigated and Defended* (1822), and *The Apocalyptic Whore of Babylon Considered not the Pope of Rome* (1830), reflecting his interest in the correct interpretation of prophetic writings. He was a contributor to the *Gentleman's Magazine*, on the subjects of astronomy and biblical history, for forty years.

Overton founded two Sunday schools, at Foot's Cray and Paul's Cray, Kent. He moved to Rose Cottage, King's Road, Chelsea, London, in 1827 and died there on 1 December 1838, aged seventy-five. He left a widow.

JOANNA HAWKE

Sources *GM*, 2nd ser., 11 (1839), 102
Likenesses pencil drawing, repro. in J. Overton, *The books of Genesis and Daniel (in connection with modern astronomy) defended against Count Volney and Dr. Francis* (1820), frontispiece

Overton, John (1763–1838), Church of England clergyman and evangelical apologist, was born at Monk Fryston in Yorkshire, where his father, George Overton, was a small landed proprietor. He belonged to an ancient Yorkshire family which early in the fourteenth century settled at Easington Hall in Holderness, and which included Major-General Robert Overton, though the estates were sold to the Milner family at the end of the seventeenth century.

Overton was educated at the village school at Monk Fryston, and in 1786 matriculated at Magdalene College, Cambridge, where he graduated BA in 1790 and MA in 1803. Overton was well thought of at Magdalene, which was just beginning to become established as an evangelical stronghold, and worked hard for exams, although he fell ill just before finals and took a pass degree. After ordination he became assistant curate to William Richardson, vicar of St Michael-le-Belfry in York and one of the leaders of the evangelical party in the north of England. He remained with Richardson until 1802, when he was appointed, through the influence of William Wilberforce, to the chancellor's livings of St Crux and St Margaret's in York. Like most early evangelicals he was a strong tory in politics and a great admirer of Pitt, and he took an active part in promoting the election of Wilberforce for the county of York.

In 1792 Overton married Elizabeth, *née* Stodart (*d.* 1827), of Reeth in the Yorkshire dales, whose father was agent to the lairds of Arkendale. They had four daughters and eight sons, four of whom—John, William, Thomas, and Charles *Overton—became clergymen, two others becoming lawyers, and two doctors.

It was Overton's *The true churchmen ascertained, or, An apology for those of the regular clergy of the establishment who are sometimes called evangelical ministers* (1801) which brought him to public notice. In this work he tried to prove from an examination of the Thirty-Nine Articles and the Book of Common Prayer that the evangelicals were the true churchmen and their opponents the real dissenters from the Church of England. This provoked a vigorous response from several churchmen, particularly Charles Daubeny—one of those criticized by Overton—in his *Vindiciae ecclesiae Anglicanae* (1803). Even the recently established evangelical periodical, the *Christian Observer*, had reservations about Overton's book, to which he replied in *Four Letters to the Editor of the Christian Observer* (1805). However, prominent evangelicals such as Charles Simeon welcomed *The True Churchmen Ascertained* as an able and manly defence of their position. Overton also published a few other works, mostly sermons, but none of these sparked controversy. He died at York on 17 July 1838, and was buried in a vault alongside his wife in the chancel of St Crux.

STEPHEN GREGORY

Sources private information (1894) • Venn, *Alum. Cant.* • *GM*, 2nd ser., 10 (1838), 224 • Allibone, *Dict.* • G. R. Balleine, *A history of the evangelical party in the Church of England* (1908) • *DNB*

Overton, John Henry (1835–1903), Church of England clergyman and ecclesiastical historian, born at Louth, Lincolnshire, on 4 January 1835, was only son of Francis Overton, surgeon, of Louth, a man of learning and of studious habits, and his wife, Helen Martha, daughter of Major John Booth of Louth. Educated at Louth grammar school (1842–5) and at a private school at Laleham, Middlesex, under the Revd John Buckland, Overton went to Rugby School in February 1849, from where he obtained an open scholarship at Lincoln College, Oxford. He gained a first class in classical moderations in 1855 and a third in the final classical school in 1857 (BA 1858, MA 1860), was captain of his college boat club, rowed stroke of its eight, was a cricketer and throughout his life retained a keen interest in the game, and in his later years was a keen golfer.

In 1858 Overton was ordained to the curacy of Quedgeley, Gloucestershire, and in 1860 was presented by J. L. Fytche, a friend of his father, to the vicarage of Legbourne, Lincolnshire. While there he took pupils and studied English church history, specially of the eighteenth century. On 17 July 1862 he married Marianne Ludlam, daughter of John Allott of Hague Hall, Yorkshire, and rector of Maltby, Lincolnshire; she survived him with one daughter.

In 1878, in conjunction with his college friend Charles John Abbey, rector of Checkendon, Oxfordshire, Overton published *The English Church in the Eighteenth Century* (2 vols.), intended as a review of 'different features in the religion and church history of England' during that period rather than as 'a regular history' (*The English Church in the Eighteenth Century*, 2nd edn, 1887). It was well received and ranked high among English church histories; an abridged one-volume edition was published in 1887.

Overton was collated to a prebend in Lincoln Cathedral by Bishop Christopher Wordsworth in 1879, and in 1883, on Gladstone's recommendation, was presented by the crown to the rectory of Epworth, Lincolnshire, the birthplace of John Wesley, in whose career he took a warm interest. While at Epworth he was rural dean of Axholme. In 1889 he was made honorary DD of Edinburgh University. From 1892 to 1898 he was proctor for the clergy in convocation, and took an active part in its proceedings, speaking with weight and judgement. In 1898 he was presented by the dean and chapter of Lincoln to the rectory of Gumley, near Market Harborough, Leicestershire, and represented the chapter in convocation. He was a frequent and popular speaker at church congresses. In 1901 he was a select preacher at Oxford, and from 1902 Birkbeck lecturer at Trinity College, Cambridge. Early in 1903 Dr Carr Glyn, the bishop of Peterborough, made him a residentiary canon of his cathedral; he was installed on 12 February and, as the canonry was of small value, retained his rectory. He kept one period of residence at Peterborough, but did not live to inhabit his prebendal house. A high-churchman and member of the English Church Union, he appreciated the views of those who differed from him. He was an excellent parish priest, and was courteous, good-tempered, and humorous.

Overton died at Gumley rectory, Leicestershire on 17 September 1903. He was buried in the churchyard of the parish church of Skidbrook, near Louth, where many of his family had been interred. As memorials, a brass tablet was placed in Epworth parish church by the parishioners, a stained-glass window and a reredos in Skidbrook church, and a window in the chapter house of Lincoln Cathedral.

As a historian and a biographer Overton specialized in the history of the Church of England from the mid-seventeenth century into the mid-nineteenth century. His most important work was *The English Church in the Eighteenth Century*, which has maintained an important place in the historical literature, and which can be read as an ecclesiastical analogue to the *History of English Thought in the Eighteenth Century* by Leslie Stephen, which appeared two years earlier in 1876. The pioneering work of Abbey and Overton retains much which is of enduring value to scholars of the eighteenth-century church.

Much of Overton's work has strong associations with his own Lincolnshire connections, including his membership of Lincoln College, Oxford. This is most apparent in his admiring biography *John Wesley*, which appeared in the Leaders of Religion series in 1891. It is also discernible in his *Life of Christopher Wordsworth, Bishop of Lincoln* (1888; 2nd rev. edn, 1890), which he was invited to write alongside the bishop's daughter, Elizabeth Wordsworth, principal of Lady Margaret Hall, Oxford. Similarly, *John Hannah, a Clerical Study* (1890), which he acknowledged to be something of a study in high-church clerical failure, has strong associations with Lincolnshire and Lincoln College. He also wrote a volume entitled *Biographical Notices of the Bishops of Lincoln, from Remigius to Wordsworth* with another canon of Lincoln, George Cresley Perry, which, although set up by the printer in 1900, did not finally appear in print until 1972. Although Overton does not directly refer to his work, it is interesting that Mark Pattison, a fellow of Lincoln when Overton and Abbey were undergraduates, should have developed his own interests in the eighteenth-century church in his contribution to *Essays and Reviews* (1860).

There is certainly an air of apologetic in much of Overton's writing, and his frequently sympathetic understanding of eighteenth-century Anglican theology acted as an implicit antidote to elements of the criticism of the evolving status of revealed religion as discussed in the writings of Pattison and Stephen. His high-churchmanship, which informed much of his work in *The English Church in the Eighteenth Century* and a great deal of his appreciation of Wesley's career, came to the fore in two of his more openly apologetic studies, *William Law: Nonjuror and Mystic* (1881) and *The Nonjurors: their Lives, Principles and Writings*

(1902). He also provided a useful edition of Law's devotional classic, *A Serious Call*, for the English Theological Library in 1898. His high-church piety was also reflected in the short character sketches which were posthumously published as *Some Post-Reformation Saints* (1905). Overton was also sympathetic to the aims and ideals of the earlier generations of evangelicals, and this appreciation informed both the whole of his useful, if too biographical, study *The Evangelical Revival in the Eighteenth Century* (1886) and his otherwise rather high-church-inclined surveys *The English Church in the Nineteenth Century* (1894) and *The Anglican Revival* (1897). Overton saw the high-church and the evangelical movements as complementary wings in the Church of England; his real suspicions were of latitudinarian and liberal churchmanship, as is demonstrated in much of the argument of *Life in the English Church, 1660–1714* (1885), a work which began life as lectures to his Wednesday evening congregation at Epworth, and which has the directness of approach one would expect of it. His strong sense of the specifically English nature of the Church of England pervades his study *The Church in England* (2 vols., 1897), which covered the inextricably linked life of the church in national life from its origin in St Augustine's mission to his own time. His strongly Anglican style of churchmanship and ecclesiology was reflected in a sermon repudiating the papal denial of Anglican orders, which was published in Lincoln at the request of his bishop as *Anglican Orders* (1896).

At his death Overton left unpublished *A history of the English church from the accession of George I to the end of the eighteenth century*, which was edited and completed by the Revd Frederic Relton in 1906. In his preface to this last work, Relton defined Overton's approach in terms which suggest the central defect of his work for other scholars: 'Canon Overton, moreover, had not, in this instance, departed from his favourite method of writing history, namely, that of dealing with the lives of the great men of the time rather than writing a consecutive narrative of events and tendencies' (F. Relton, 'Preface' to J. H. Overton, *English Church from George I*, 1906, ix–x). At times, Overton's biographical instincts tended towards the hagiographical, especially when he was writing about high-churchmen or pioneering evangelicals. He contributed many memoirs of divines to the *Dictionary of National Biography*, and wrote for the *Dictionary of Hymnology* and the *Church Quarterly Review*, and other periodicals.

B. W. Young

Sources *DNB* · *The Times* (19 Sept 1903) · *The Guardian* (23 Sept 1903) · private information (1912) · Foster, *Alum. Oxon.* · Crockford (1902) · *WWW*

Wealth at death £10,792 16*s.* 4*d.*: probate, 21 Nov 1903, *CGPLA Eng. & Wales*

Overton, Mary (*fl.* **1646–1647**). *See under* Overton, Richard (*fl.* 1640–1663).

Overton, Mary (*fl.* **1745–1748**). *See under* Overton family (*per. c.*1665–*c.*1765).

Overton, Philip (*c.***1681–1745**). *See under* Overton family (*per. c.*1665–*c.*1765).

Overton, Richard (*fl.* **1640–1663**), Leveller and pamphleteer, is of uncertain background and origins.

Early life There are two conflicting accounts of Overton's early life, both largely conjectural. In Amsterdam there exists a signed Latin confession of faith made by Overton on his conversion to General Baptism, and it was once generally assumed that this was made at the same time as other General Baptist confessions in the same archive, about 1615. If so, this would give him a probable date of birth some time before 1600. The relatively greater emphasis than other Levellers in his writings on such rural grievances as enclosure may indicate that he had rural origins, possibly in Lincolnshire, a county in which the surname Overton was common and which was the original centre of General Baptism in England. By the time he made his confession he was living in the Dutch Republic, and he returned to England some time prior to 1640. On the basis of his later printing activities and the existence of a printer called Henry Overton, it has also been widely assumed that Overton was a professional printer. This reconstruction of Overton's early life is doubtful. There is evidence that Overton's confession of faith may date from as late as 1643, and there is no known connection between Richard and Henry Overton; both the quality of works printed by Richard and his habitual use of other professional printers suggest that his own printing activities were undertaken on an amateur basis, as a by-product of his political activities.

A Richard Overton matriculated as a sizar from Queens' College, Cambridge, at Easter 1631, and this may have been the future Leveller; if so, this may indicate a date of birth about 1614 or slightly before. Overton's works do suggest a relatively high level of educational attainment, showing a competent command of Latin, traces of classical culture, and some knowledge of medicine, the law, formal rhetoric, astronomy, astrology, and alchemy.

Some conjectures have been made about Overton's life on the basis of works attributed to him, but these are made uncertain by the difficulty of establishing his *œuvre*. About 150 pamphlets and journalistic writings have been attributed to Overton, although only about a sixth were signed or subsequently acknowledged by him. In many cases there is clear evidence against Overton's authorship; conversely, there is evidence that he was the author of some later anonymous pamphlets generally attributed to John Lilburne or William Walwyn. A reference to himself in the anonymous *Old Newes Newly Revived* (June 1641) as 'the little Levite that writ Lambeth Faire' (sig. A2*v*) implies that Overton had been a clergyman, and a passage in *The Curates Conference* (April 1641), attributed to Overton on stylistic grounds, suggests that he left university to become a curate, and that he subsequently accompanied the English army during the bishops' wars in the capacity of a chaplain; a question asked by the earl of Essex in 1646 implied that Overton had at some time been a soldier, but whether during the bishops' wars or the early years of the civil war is not known. Some of Overton's early works take dialogue form and include stage directions, and he may have been involved in writing and performing anti-Laudian satirical playlets between 1640 and 1642.

Overton's first signed pamphlets were *Articles of High Treason Exhibited Against Cheap-Side Crosse* (January 1642) and *New Lambeth Fayre* (March 1642), an expanded version of the anonymous *Lambeth Faire* (June 1641). Strong stylistic evidence and internal references suggest that he was also the author of other pamphlets at this time, beginning with *Vox Borealis* (October 1640), claiming to be printed by Margery Mar-Prelate. The pseudonym had already been used by the author of several presbyterian pamphlets in 1588–9, two of which were twice reprinted in 1641–3, possibly by Overton; his use of this pseudonym foreshadows the Martin Mar-Priest persona he was later to adopt.

The works written by and attributed to Overton in 1640–42 are all primarily anti-Laudian and anti-Catholic satires, attacking church courts, the high commission, the 'etcetera oath', pluralism, the Book of Sports, surplices, bowing at the name of Jesus, and wedding rings. They are written from the point of view of a puritan within the Church of England: he criticizes the tithe system, not because tithes were wrong in themselves, but because the income they generated was used to support lazy parsons rather than industrious curates; and his criticism of episcopacy was aimed more at the conduct of particular bishops than the office itself. He also occasionally satirized separatists, suggesting that Overton had not yet converted to General Baptism. The early pamphlets often raise such secular grievances as ship money and monopolies, and they already display Overton's marked hostility to lawyers, but there is little in them that foreshadows his later radicalism. The king is not attacked as such, but is represented as being misled by his evil councillors, especially William Laud and Thomas Wentworth, first earl of Strafford. These early works are frequently written either in verse or as dialogues. Overton depended heavily on punning, employed a good deal of coarse humour, and had a tendency to use violent language, features which were to remain characteristic of his style throughout his later career. They contain no indication of the theoretical sophistication that he was later to achieve, and nothing in the way of a positive programme other than a call for triennial parliaments.

General Baptism and the Mar-Priest tracts Overton seems to have ceased writing between April 1642 and January 1644. It has been suggested that he may have married his wife **Mary Overton** (*fl.* 1646–1647), Leveller, in this period. Nothing is known of her background or parentage and she was first mentioned by her husband in 1646. There is no evidence to support the identification of Overton and his wife with the Richard and Mary who were married at St George the Martyr, Southwark, in March 1643, but the fact that the couple had three young children and a six-month-old baby in 1647 would suggest a marriage some time in the early 1640s. A pamphlet of 1643 protesting against imprisonment for debt has been attributed to Overton; the evidence for Overton's authorship is not compelling, but if this attribution is sound he himself was in prison for debt at this time.

Overton had resumed his writing career by January 1644 when he published his treatise *Mans Mortalitie*, the first edition of which was printed by himself; a second edition correcting the copious printer's errors was published shortly afterwards. The treatise argued in favour of the mortalist heresy known as thnetopsychism: Adam had originally been created to be immortal, but after the fall both his soul and body became subject to death; both, however, would be miraculously reconstituted at the last judgement. Although some historians have taken *Mans Mortalitie* to be evidence of Overton's secularism and rationalism, thnetopsychism was widespread in General Baptist circles; this, together with the anti-separatism of his earlier works, makes it probable that Overton's conversion to General Baptism occurred about 1642–3. Thnetopsychism was a doctrine which tended to be accompanied by the belief that the kingdom of God would be established on earth rather than in heaven, and it involved strong millenarian tendencies. *Mans Mortalitie*, together with Milton's *Doctrine and Discipline of Divorce*, was condemned by the Commons on 26 August 1644, and it subsequently attracted much criticism from presbyterian writers. Throughout his life thnetopsychism remained an important concern of Overton's. He was present at a General Baptist meeting in London discussing the topic in January 1646; the lord mayor ordered the meeting to be broken up, but at Overton's instigation the participants succeeded in debating both mortalism and the right of civil authorities to interfere in matters of conscience for a further five hours. Overton published a revised edition of *Mans Mortalitie* (*Man Wholly Mortal*) in 1655; unsold copies of this edition were reissued with a new title-page in 1675.

The debate on mortalism in 1646 took place in Thomas Lambe's General Baptist congregation in Bell Alley, Coleman Street, and Overton was a member of this church at least as early as January 1644. According to Overton the church was frequently harassed by presbyterian mobs, ranging from throwing stones in the street to firing musket-shots into the congregation. The London General Baptists included a number of other future Levellers, including Nicholas Tew. Overton was mentioned in connection with Tew after the latter's arrest for operating an illegal press on 17 January 1644. Tew's press was also used for printing works by Lilburne and possibly Walwyn, suggesting that the future Leveller leaders may already have been in close contact.

In April 1645 Overton published *The Araignment of Mr Persecution* under the pseudonym Martin Mar-Priest. This was the first of a series of satirical attacks on the presbyterians: *A Sacred Decretall* (May), *Martin's Eccho* (June), *The Nativity of Sir John Presbyter* (July), *The Ordinance of Tythes Dismounted* (December), and *Divine Observations upon the London Ministers Letter* (January 1646). Overton evidently regarded these tracts as the source of his celebrity, since he continued to refer to himself as 'little Martin' in several of his later Leveller pamphlets published under his own name. Richard Baxter recorded that the Mar-Priest tracts were 'abundantly dispersed' in the army (*Reliquiae Baxterianae*, ed. M. Sylvester, 1696, 53) and their popularity is witnessed by the appearance of several imitations, published mostly under the pseudonym of Sir John Presbyter; these latter tracts, however, appear to be the work of a royalist satirist.

The Mar-Priest tracts are primarily concerned with arguing for complete freedom of conscience and a rigorous separation of church and state. They also mount a vigorous attack on the system of tithes, an issue raised to prominence by an ordinance of November 1644 which attempted to enforce their payment. Overton argued that the clergy should either work for a living or be supported by voluntary contributions; tithes themselves might continue to be collected, but they should be used to create a system of poor relief. The Mar-Priest tracts repeatedly contrast the Independents and Baptists in the army, whom he believed primarily responsible for parliamentarian victories, with the presbyterians in parliament and the City, who are represented rather paradoxically as war profiteers who were eager to capitulate to the king. In *Martin's Eccho* Overton became the first of the future Levellers to raise the issue of the soldiers' arrears of pay, foreshadowing the attempt to forge a Leveller–agitator alliance in 1647. The Mar-Priest tracts mark an important stage in Overton's intellectual development. They are still primarily concerned with issues affecting Overton and his fellow sectaries, but they also introduce the basic elements of his later political theory. He repudiated any notion of rule by divine right, and he asserted that all legitimate political authority is held as a 'trust' from the people. Overton, however, did not as yet give an elaborate exposition of his political theory or detail any of the practical constitutional arrangements that would be necessary to ensure that political authorities would not betray the people's trust.

Leveller career Overton may have developed a more secular political outlook by September 1645, if he was the author of *Englands Miserie and Remedy*. There is, however, no firm evidence for Overton's authorship of this pamphlet, but it is possible that he was the author of *Englands Birth-Right Justifed* (1645), a pamphlet often attributed to John Lilburne. This tract is of some historical importance, since it gives for the first time a fairly full statement of what became the Leveller programme. The author calls for the abolition of tithes, monopolies, and the excise; all taxation should be by way of 'subsidy' (a tax on wealth). Arbitrary imprisonment is to be abolished, no one is to be forced to testify against themselves, and all laws should be written in English. Lawyers and anyone holding a paid state office were to be excluded from parliament, and parliament itself should meet and if necessary be elected on an annual basis.

Overton was probably the author of a number of anonymous pamphlets published early in 1646, beginning with *The Last Warning to All the Inhabitants of London*, a call for democratic reform of the City government. The pamphlet warns against compromise with the king, condemns the presbyterians' intolerance, and shows traces of the anti-Scottish sentiments which were prominent in Overton's later works. It was condemned by the Commons on 22 March; the printer William Larner was arrested and a number of pamphlets were seized, including *The Afflicted Christian Justified* and *Divine Light*, which show traces of Overton's style. More doubtful attributions to Overton at this time include *The Interest of England Maintained* and *A Pearle in a Dunghill* (otherwise ascribed to Henry Marten and William Walwyn respectively).

Overton was almost certainly sole or part author of *A Remonstrance of many Thousand Citizens* (1646), which is widely regarded as the founding manifesto of the Levellers. The *Remonstrance* attacks the presbyterian-dominated Commons for merely attempting to substitute their own tyranny for that of the king; more significantly, it marks a shift to republicanism in attacking kingship as such rather than Charles I's conduct of the office. Nevertheless, Overton does not seem to have been a republican on principle, and in his later works he veered from expressions of qualified support for monarchy to outright republicanism in accordance with the exigencies of the current situation. The *Remonstrance* also expounded what was to become a favourite theme in subsequent Leveller propaganda: the theory of the Norman yoke (that the English had enjoyed full constitutional liberty before the Norman conquest, and that William the Conqueror and all his successors were tyrannical usurpers). The programme suggested in the *Remonstrance* is simply an expanded version of that offered in *Englands Birth-Right Justified*; its underlying political theory is substantially the same as that of the Mar-Priest tracts, but developed at greater length.

In July 1646 Overton published *An Alarum to the House of Lords*, which was condemned by the House of Commons on 4 August. He was subsequently arrested at his Southwark home in a dawn raid on 11 August, while his wife was recovering from having given birth to their youngest child. Overton attempted to escape but was captured by a party of musketeers waiting outside and robbed of his money before being led away. A number of manuscripts were seized, including that of *The Last Warning*, 'A propheticall warning and sounding of the trumpet', and a treatise on baptism and the Lord's supper; if this last was the work of Overton himself, it clearly suggests that despite his politicization he continued to be interested in purely theological issues. After his arrest Overton was taken before a committee of the House of Lords chaired by the earl of Essex, refusing to answer any questions on the basis that no one should be forced to testify against themselves. As a consequence he was committed to Newgate for contempt.

While in Newgate, Overton may have written *Liberty Vindicated Against Slavery* (a pamphlet usually attributed to Lilburne, despite his own disclaimer). This tract calls for comprehensive prison reform, a theme which was prominent in Overton's other writings. Gaolers should be forbidden to charge fees from their prisoners, and were instead to be paid a salary by the state; prisoners were no longer to be expected to maintain themselves, but were to be provided with food and bedding at the state's expense. Imprisonment for debt was to be abolished, and prisons themselves were to be institutions purely for the remand of prisoners awaiting trial.

In September 1646 Overton published the first of his signed Leveller tracts, *A Defiance Against All Arbitrary Usurpations*, calling for the removal of all tyrants, whether 'Royall, Lordly or Clericall'. This was followed in October by *An Arrow Against All Tyrants*, a pamphlet which completed Overton's contribution to political theory. It restated his theory of political trusteeship, but it also developed one of the earliest statements of what has been called the theory of 'possessive individualism', a theory which was later to be expounded by John Locke and which became central to eighteenth-century political thought. Overton argued that everyone possesses a 'self-propriety' or right of property in their own person. This self-propriety was inalienable and it formed the basis of all other political rights.

On 3 November 1646 Overton appealed to a Commons' committee for protecting the liberties of the subject, chaired by the republican Henry Marten. The committee found him guilty of nothing, but nevertheless recommitted him to Newgate. Overton refused to co-operate, and his gaolers were forced to carry him, beating him along the way. His copy of Coke's *Institutes* was confiscated, and he was put in leg-irons.

Overton may have collaborated with Henry Marten on *Vox plebis* (1646), and later that month he published *An Unhappy Game of Scotch and English*, a savage attack on the Scottish presbyterians which the Commons condemned to be burned on 30 November. He was also the probable author of *Regall Tyrannie Discovered*, published in January 1647 (often attributed to Lilburne, despite his own disclaimer), the first Leveller pamphlet to call for the execution of the king. The Lords condemned this pamphlet as treasonous, ordering the arrest of anyone involved in its publication. On 6 January officers of the Stationers' Company raided Overton's house where they discovered his wife and his brother Thomas stitching copies of the offending pamphlet. Mary and Thomas were arrested and taken before the Lords where they refused to answer interrogatories. As a result Thomas and Mary, accompanied by her six-month-old baby, were consigned on the same day to Maiden Lane prison; Mary's three older children were left in the care of Overton's sister and brother-in-law. On the following day a second raid was mounted in search of Overton's sister and her husband, but both escaped. Overton condemned the treatment of his family in *The Commoners Complaint* (1647), describing how on 7 January the Lords ordered his wife, a 'poore little harmlesse innocent woman' with a 'tender Babe on her breast' (p. 18), to 'be cast into the most infamous Goale of *Bride-well*, that common Centre and receptacle of bauds, whores, and strumpets' (p. 17). When Mary refused to obey the order she was

> drag'd … headlong upon the stones in all the dirt and mire of the streetes, with the poore Infant still crying and mourning in her Armes … and all the way as they went, utterly to defame and render her infamous … the fellowes which dragged … her on two Cudgels, calling her *Strumpet* and vild [*sic*] *Whore* … a sufficient matter to blast her reputation for ever … and this is the honour that their Lordships are pleased to conferre on the free Commoners wives who stand for their Freedoms and Liberties. (*Commoners Complaint*, 1647, 19–20)

In March Overton drew up *The Humble Appeale and Petition of Mary Overton* on his wife's behalf, a pamphlet which was more an attack on the Lords and Commons than an appeal for clemency. Mary herself petitioned the Lords privately in April, by which time her infant child had died.

In February Overton and Lilburne collaborated on *The Out-Cryes of the Oppressed Commons*, arguing that arbitrary government had dissolved the social contract and returned the people to a state of nature, enabling them legitimately to draw up a new constitution. The Commons' refusal to hear petitions was condemned, and the right of petitioning was to be a prominent concern of Overton's subsequent writings; as presbyterian critics were to note, Overton and other Levellers tended to reduce parliament's proper role to that of ratifying mass petitions, provided they had been openly and fully debated.

In March 1647 the Levellers began their major petitioning campaign with the circulation of the large petition; a number of Levellers were subsequently arrested. In April Overton published *A New Found Stratagem*, which vigorously defended the right of petitioning parliament. This pamphlet was primarily addressed to the army, and its distribution among the soldiery led to the arrest of two officers. *A New Found Stratagem* voiced the grievances that were coalescing in the agitator movement; the presbyterian plan to disband the New Model Army should be abandoned and the soldiers should receive their arrears of pay. It also made the first tentative appeal to the army to become the arbiter of revolution.

Overton renewed his call for the army to intervene in the affairs of the nation in *An Appeale from the Degenerate Representative Body* (1647), which explicitly called for the House of Commons to be purged of its 'putrified and corrupt members'. Apart from attempting to forge closer links between the Levellers and the New Model's agitator organization, this pamphlet also demonstrates the flexibility of Overton's political strategy, since it contains a remarkable passage calling on the nation to rise up and free the king from his parliamentary captors. It also develops Overton's theory of law, the legitimacy of which derives from its conformity with 'common equity and right reason' rather than on the legislative body that enacts it. Overton's appeal to reason has been widely misinterpreted as evidence of his rationalism; his concept of reason, like that of other General Baptists, in fact has mystical overtones, virtually identifying it with the spirit of God working in the human soul.

At the end of the *Appeale* Overton appended 'Certain articles for the good of the common wealth', in effect a first draft of the series of constitutions proposed by the Levellers between November 1647 and May 1649. Legislative authority was to reside in a single elected chamber, members of which were to be supervised by county commissioners throughout their term of office. The law was to be administered in monthly or twice-monthly hundredal courts, the officers of which were to be elected. All laws were to be written in English and there was to be full equality before the law. Prisons were to be reformed along the lines already suggested in *Liberty Vindicated Against Slavery*, but with specific recommendations for alternatives to the purely punitive function of prisons. A first offence of theft was to be punished by forced labour, with thieves compensating their victims; a second offence would result in branding, and a sentence of 'perpetual servitude' was to be imposed on anyone offending for a third time. Overton also makes a number of economic and social recommendations, including the throwing open of enclosures, a rural grievance which attracted little attention among the Levellers. Monopolies were to be abolished and there was to be complete freedom of trade. There were to be no tithes and glebe lands were to be used to finance 'hospitals' (for the poor rather than the sick). A system of schools should be established throughout the country to ensure basic literacy for all 'the free men of England'.

Overton was released from prison on 16 September 1647, and from early November he and Lilburne were reported to be involved in a series of City meetings with army agitators at The Mouth in Aldersgate Street and the Windmill Tavern in Coleman Street. He also accompanied Lilburne to Ware in Hertfordshire on 15 November, in the vicinity of the Leveller-inspired mutiny at Corkbush Field. After the failure of the mutiny there is no certain information about Overton until April 1648, when the agitators were renewing their efforts to gain control of the army; on 18 April Overton consulted the astrologer William Lilly, asking for advice on whether or not to support the agitators.

Overton may have contributed to the Leveller petition of 18 January 1648 and may have written *The Mournfull Cryes of Many Thousand Poore Tradesmen* (1648), both of which express the lively sympathy for the poor which can be found in his other writings. Throughout 1648 there is an apparent decline in his literary output. This may reflect disillusionment on his part, or he may have been devoting his energies to committee work for the Leveller organization, which was acquiring a more formal structure at this time. The Levellers also established their own newspaper, *The Moderate*, in July 1648, and several of the paper's leaders between October 1648 and April 1649 have been attributed to Overton. These leaders are more radical than contemporary writings by other Leveller leaders, but are consistent with Overton's known opinions. Whereas Lilburne opposed the trial and execution of the king, for example, Overton and the editor of *The Moderate* supported it as necessary for securing English liberties. *The Moderate*'s editorials at this time are also characterized by an emphasis on the economic grievances of the people.

On 14 December 1648 Overton was at Whitehall during the debate between army grandees, Levellers, and City Independents concerning the settlement of the nation through a Leveller-inspired constitution, the *Agreement of the People*. The specific question on that day was what power, if any, the representative should have over religious matters. Overton and Lilburne withdrew after the first session, having been under the impression that the content of the *Agreement*, including a clause denying the magistrate any power in the religious sphere, had been agreed at earlier discussions. Although their Leveller colleagues Walwyn and John Wildman chose to attend the debate on 18 December, the discussions at Whitehall ended in failure for the Levellers. On 28 December Lilburne and Overton were among a Leveller deputation that delivered a petition to General Fairfax, protesting at the officers' alteration of the *Agreement*, published the same day as *A Plea for Common Right and Freedom*.

While Oliver Cromwell and his allies were overthrowing the monarchy in January 1649 the Levellers as a whole remained puzzlingly quiescent, but on 3 March Overton published a *Humble Petition* in which he commended the purging of parliament and execution of the king, while at the same time condemning the new council of state. Following the court martial of five troopers for organizing a petition critical of the new military regime, Overton mounted a more vigorous attack in *The Hunting of the Foxes* (March), warning that Cromwell was simply aspiring to replace the old monarchy with 'a new regality'.

On 24 March 1649 Lilburne published *The Second Part of Englands New-Chaines Discovered*, and the Rump Parliament declared its supposed authors to be guilty of high treason; as a consequence, Lilburne, Overton, Walwyn, and Thomas Prince were arrested on 28 March. The prisoners were taken before the council of state and, after refusing to answer any questions, dispatched to the Tower. In April Lilburne, Overton, and Prince recounted the story of their arrest and interrogation in *The Picture of the Councel of State*. In his contribution Overton states that an unfinished manuscript of a treatise called 'Gods word confirmed by his works' was seized; his account of this text suggests that it was a fairly typical specimen of natural theology, attempting to prove the truth of Christian revelation on the basis of natural phenomena.

All four Leveller prisoners subscribed a *Manifestation* on 14 April (probably written by Walwyn), calling for a third and final *Agreement of the People*; this was duly published on 1 May, again subscribed by all four men. A month later Overton and Lilburne published a joint protest against the execution of a parliamentarian soldier, Robert Lockyer, for his part in a small London mutiny on 24 April.

In May 1649 another Leveller-inspired mutiny broke out at Salisbury, and was ultimately suppressed at Burford. Among the leaders of the mutiny was Henry Denne, who had been associated with Overton throughout his career as a General Baptist and Leveller. Denne earned a reprieve by issuing a denunciation of the Levellers, prompting Overton to condemn him bitterly in *Overton's Defiance of the Act of Pardon*; he also defended himself from accusations by the Levellers based at the Whalebone Tavern that he had ceased to be politically active. The Whalebone Tavern

Levellers were offended by certain remarks in this pamphlet, especially a reference to seizing the bull of Bashan (Cromwell) by his genitals. In his last signed pamphlet, *The Baiting of the Great Bull of Bashan* (1649), Overton defended his sense of humour and condemned the Whalebone Tavern Levellers for their own cowardice and apathy.

Later life Overton and the other Leveller leaders were released from the Tower on 8 November 1649, following Lilburne's acquittal on charges of treason. A condition for their release was that they should take the oath of engagement to the new regime; according to a royalist satirist Overton agreed to take the engagement, adding the promise to be as faithful to his oath as the present council of state had been to the solemn league and covenant (i.e., not at all).

Various Leveller petitions of 1650–51 have been attributed to Overton, as has *Vox plebis* (1653), an attack on the Rump, but there is no firm evidence for these attributions. He was present at Lilburne's trial in June–August 1653. He tried unsuccessfully to secure a lawyer for Lilburne, delivered a letter to one of the judges and was part of a deputation presenting a petition to parliament on Lilburne's behalf.

In December 1653 Overton was paid £20 by Cromwell's secretary of state, John Thurloe. This may have been in connection with Edward Sexby's mission to the Huguenots in Bordeaux, but the evidence also suggests that Overton was by this time acting as a double agent. On 6 September 1654 Overton again offered his services to Thurloe in connection with a conspiracy against the government. Shortly afterwards a plot led by Wildman and Sexby was discovered; Sexby fled to Amsterdam, where he was joined by Overton in February 1655. While in Holland, Overton and Sexby entered into a conspiracy with Sir Marmaduke Langdale and other exiled royalists. The plot collapsed in November, apparently because of Sexby's republicanism; Langdale reported that Overton himself was more favourable to the king's cause.

Overton subsequently returned to England and lodged with Colonel William Wetton in Bedford Street, London, in 1655. It was at this time that he published the revised version of his mortalist treatise, *Man Wholly Mortal*. He may have taken part in the republican campaign for the good old cause in 1659, but none of the pamphlets attributed to him at that time belongs unquestionably in his *œuvre*. He was, however, imprisoned for some unspecified offence in 1659, and the restored Rump ordered an investigation of his committal on 30 December. In 1662 Overton was living in Kennington, but he had moved by the time that a new warrant for his arrest was issued on 22 October 1663. It is not known why this warrant was issued, but the simultaneous order for the arrest of the radical publisher Elizabeth Calvert suggests that it may have been on account of subversive publications; alternatively, it may simply have been as part of the general crack-down on known radicals following the Derwentside plot. No other direct evidence on Overton's life exists, but unsold copies of *Man Wholly Mortal* were reissued with a new title-page in 1674. No more is heard of Mary Overton by name after 1647, but in a letter of 13 September 1655 Overton mentioned his intention of going to Rotterdam to meet his wife.

Historical significance Overton played a decisive role in the Leveller's history although on occasions he was as much an embarrassment as an asset; both opponents and some fellow-Levellers criticized the vulgarity of his humour, and there were rumours that he led a sexually dissolute life. Accounts of the Levellers have concentrated on Lilburne's role and tended to neglect that of Overton, but it was Overton who may have been primarily responsible for publishing their first full and coherent programmes. He was also significant in giving greater emphasis than his fellow-Levellers to social and economic policy in his programmatic statements. He was particularly concerned with the abolition of imprisonment for debt, the reform of the poor relief system, and the establishment of a national education system. He was also one of the few Levellers to address such rural grievances as enclosure, calling for a redistribution of land. Overton is rightly regarded as the Levellers' principal theoretician, since his writings contain the fullest and most coherent exploration of the philosophical basis of the Leveller programme. Overton also seems to have played a leading role in devising the Levellers' strategy of attempting to make the army an instrument for implementing the Leveller programme between 1647 and 1649. B. J. Gibbons

Sources M. Gimelfarb-Brack, *Liberté, égalité, fraternité, justice: la vie et l'oeuvre de Richard Overton, niveleur* (Bern, 1979) · D. M. Wolfe, 'Unsigned pamphlets of Richard Overton, 1641–1649', *Huntington Library Quarterly*, 21 (1958), 167–201 · B. J. Gibbons, 'Richard Overton and the secularism of the interregnum radicals', *The Seventeenth Century*, 10/1 (1995), 63–75 · J. Frank, *The Levellers: a history of the writings of three seventeenth-century social democrats; John Lilburne, Richard Overton, William Walwyn* (Cambridge, MA, 1955) · D. M. Wolfe, *Leveller manifestoes of the puritan revolution* (1944) · H. N. Brailsford, *The Levellers and the English revolution*, ed. C. Hill (1961) · H. R. Plomer, 'Secret printing during the civil war', *The Library*, new ser., 5 (1904), 374–403 · C. B. Macpherson, *The political theory of possessive individualism: Hobbes to Locke* (1964) · *Old newes newly revived* (1641) · *The curates conference* (1641) · K. Lindley, *Popular politics and religion in civil war London* (1997) · Venn, *Alum. Cant.* · W. Haller, *Tracts on liberty in the puritan revolution, 1638–1647*, 3 (1933) · A. Hughes, 'Gender and politics in Leveller literature', *Political culture and cultural politics in early modern England*, ed. S. D. Amussen and M. A. Kishlansky (1995), 162–88

Overton, Robert (1608/9–1678/9), parliamentarian army officer, was the son and heir of John Overton and Joan Snawsell, daughter of Robert Snawsell of Bilton and his wife, Anne Waters. John Overton of Easington was a landed gentleman in south-east Yorkshire, where Overtons had lived for generations. During the second civil war royalists imprisoned John Overton for twenty-two weeks and seized his personal estate. Nevertheless his will, proved in 1654, indicates that he retained substantial possessions and his numerous bequests included daughter, daughter-in-law, and many grandchildren.

Robert Overton matriculated at St John's College, Cambridge, in 1627 and was admitted at Gray's Inn in 1631. In

Robert Overton (1608/9–1678/9), by unknown artist

June 1632 he married Ann Gardiner (1615/16–1665), daughter of Jeremy Gardiner of Stratford Bow, Middlesex. Overton's manuscript volume, 'Gospell observations', illuminates his enduring devotion to his wife and reveals that in 1665 four daughters and three sons, including Benjamin *Overton, were living. Ann Overton was a strong woman, deeply religious, ambitious, and protective. In a 1647 letter to Lord Fairfax she asked that Robert be advanced to colonel. On her deathbed, eighteen years later, she expressed contentment that Robert, 'soe tender a spirit', could not witness her suffering (Princeton University Library, MS C O 199, Overton MS, 87).

Civil war and governor of Hull In the first civil war Overton served with the northern army under Ferdinando, Lord Fairfax, and his son, Sir Thomas. Both Fairfaxes thought well of Overton, whose courage and skill were demonstrated during the 1643 defence of Hull where he acquitted himself 'with much honour and gallantry' (E. Ludlow, *The Memoirs of Edmund Ludlow*, ed. C. H. Firth, 2 vols., 1894, 1.65). John Milton adds that at Marston Moor, on 2 July 1644, leaders of the left wing, 'looking behind them in flight, beheld you making a stand … repelling the attacks of the enemy amid dense slaughter' (*Complete Prose Works*, 4, pt 1, 676). In August 1645 Sir Thomas Fairfax was appointed governor of Pontefract and named Overton his deputy. Within weeks of assuming his post Overton conquered Sandal Castle. In the summer of 1647 Fairfax secured Overton a commission as colonel of foot in the New Model Army, and during the political debates of the army's general council Overton was appointed to committees at Reading and Putney. By March 1648 he was in Hull as Fairfax's deputy governor. Prominent townsmen and officials who were close to his predecessor considered Overton a radical and asked that he be replaced. No specific charges were cited, and he held the post intermittently until 1660. During the second war Overton remained with the garrison in Hull. One of his royalist prisoners in 1648–9 recalled him as 'a great Independent … ane enemie to monarchie, whatever name it had … a schollar, bot a little pedantic', who treated his prisoners with notable 'civilitie' (J. Turner, *Memoirs of his Own Life and Times*, 1829, 16.78–9).

Before the defeat of the king Overton made only one known comment about his revolutionary objective. On 11 February 1648, in a letter to Fairfax's secretary, Overton expresses pleasure that the king's servants have been removed and suggests that 'it would prove a happy privation if the Father would please to dispossess him of three transitory kingdoms to infeoff him in an eternal one' (*Memorials of the Civil War*, 2.10–11). There is no reason to infer that the comment was a covert plea for regicide. Neither is there any indication that Overton opposed the execution of the king eleven months later, when he remained in Hull instead of serving as a commissioner at the trial, apparently believing that it was more important to be with his garrison at a critical time.

Overton was apprehensive about the impending settlement of the state. Three weeks before the king's execution he addressed a letter to Fairfax that accompanied an eloquent *Declaration* from the officers of the garrison. Letter and *Declaration* are distinguished by the compelling style and vivid metaphors that are found throughout Overton's writings. After a preliminary address to Fairfax that recalls the council of officers' November *Remonstrance*—'with every tittle whereof we totally comply'—the *Declaration* reviews grievances, notes the promises of the previous six years, and condemns the 'corrupted party' in the Commons (*The Declaration of the Officers of the Garrison of Hull*, 1 March 1649, 4, 15); Overton's letter is dated 9 January. The final six pages delineate a settlement similar to proposals in the *Remonstrance*: a speedy end to the present parliament; a succession of free biennial parliaments with an equitable distribution of seats; future kings elected by the people's representatives and having no negative voice; a 'universal and mutual Agreement, … enacted and decreed, *in perpetuum*', that asserts that the power of parliament is 'inferior only to that of the people' (ibid., 16). Overton's letter reflects his belief that there is little likelihood that the 'corrupt Commons' will effect these reforms. He asks that, 'in this last act of our Age', Fairfax lead the army, resolved 'rather to perish with your honest officers and souldiers, then otherwise to enjoy the Genius of a temporall happinesse'. It is Overton's only known proposal for violent action to accomplish 'remonstrated principle' (ibid., 2–3).

Five months later, in a letter appended to his regiment's *Remonstrance* denying any association with Leveller uprisings, Overton deplores 'divisions and distractions' that would have 'destroyed us' but for the goodness of God. Overton pledges obedience to parliament and the army, 'yet ever with such due Reservations as tended to the keeping sacred and inviolable my particular and private Trust, which … I purpose never to part withall' (*The Humble Remonstrance … of Col. Overton's Regiment … with Colonel Overton's Letter to the General*, 5 June 1649, 6, 7).

Scotland and imprisonment In the summer of 1650 Overton joined Cromwell's campaign in Scotland. He led his brigade in the battle at Dunbar on 3 September, and after the occupation of Edinburgh Cromwell departed, leaving Overton as governor. In July 1651 Overton led his troops across the Firth of Forth and when Perth surrendered he became governor there. He was with Lieutenant-General Monck when Dundee surrendered and in November was governor of Aberdeen. In February 1652, after marching north, Overton established a garrison in the Orkneys before returning to Fife as sheriff. By June he was in the west, and in December he was advanced to major-general and commander of all the forces in western Scotland. Overton evinced military and administrative skills throughout his thirty months in Scotland where 'Scots of the West and North' described him as 'a most humane foe, … a merciful conqueror' (Milton, *Complete Prose Works*, 4, pt, 1, 676).

When Overton returned to Yorkshire in February 1653 he possessed considerable property. He had recently succeeded to his father's Easington estate; in 1652 parliament had voted him £400 p.a. in Scottish lands; in 1651 he had paid over £7000 for the confiscated crown fee farm rent of the manor of Holderness. He resumed his post as governor of Hull, and when Cromwell forcibly dismissed the Rump Parliament, Overton and the garrison responded with a pamphlet consisting of two letters to Cromwell that were devoid of the apocalyptic prophecies that marked many addresses of the time. The second letter offered 'free and hearty Concurrence' with the dissolution, rejected any 'meddling with State matters', and urged Cromwell to employ 'religion, reason, and resolution' in settling the state (*More Hearts and Hands Appearing for the Work*, 7 June 1653, 3, 5, 6).

The collapse of Barebone's Parliament in December was followed by the establishment of the protectorate. Again Overton was apprehensive. Cromwell had approved of Overton during the first civil war and in Scotland, and in the spring of 1654 Overton met him before returning to Scotland. Overton assured the protector that he would serve him loyally unless 'I perceived his lordship did only design the setting up of himself, and not the good of these nations'. Should the latter occur, Overton promised Cromwell that 'I could not set one foot before another to serve him'. Cromwell replied: 'Thou wert a knave, if thou wouldst' (Thurloe, 3.110). Overton repeated his pledge to Monck when he arrived in Scotland.

In December officers in Overton's Aberdeen headquarters sent letters announcing a meeting in Edinburgh to consider whether the army had been faithful to its duty 'to assert the freedomes of the people in the priviledges of parliament' (Thurloe, 3.29–30). Overton's involvement in the plan was not clear, but, in addition to the doubts he had admitted to Cromwell, before leaving London Overton had met with John Wildman who was conspiring with dissident colonels to attack the foundations of the protectorate. More immediately, Overton had not informed Monck of political dissension among his officers. He was sent to London and committed to the Tower. No hard evidence of his participation in any conspiracy was ever advanced, but he was held for more than four years without trial, charge, or, after his transfer to Jersey, right of habeas corpus. It is not unlikely that respect for Overton's ability and fear of his appeal as an opposition leader played a major role in his imprisonment.

The fall of the republic In February 1659 Commonwealthsmen in Richard Cromwell's parliament responded to a petition from Overton's sister by demanding his appearance for a hearing. On 16 March Overton addressed the house, asserting that he hoped that he had 'not done anything contrary to what I at first engaged, and fought for'. He was released the same day (*Diary of Thomas Burton*, 4.150–61). Seven weeks later the protectorate fell, and in June the re-empowered Rump restored all Overton's commands and named a committee to review indemnity.

Overton supported the returned republic as the best available expedient, but as the Rump's weaknesses became increasingly apparent he again envisioned government by godly men. His name is among the twenty signatures to *An Essay toward Settlement*, a broadsheet petition published by 19 September 1659. The petition includes demands for liberty of conscience and no state church, reform of the ministry and the law in accordance with scripture, and government by 'men of courage, fearing God, and hating Covetousness'. Although twelve signers, including Overton, have been termed Fifth Monarchy Men (B. Capp, *The Fifth Monarchy Men*, 1972, 126), the appeal does not include millenarian predictions and reflects the aspirations of the many revolutionaries who believed in the efficacy of rule by godly men. In October Overton and his officers refused to support an address to parliament in which the council of officers demanded that, except for disbandment, no officer or soldier be dismissed except by court martial. The house cashiered the nine officers who promoted the address and named Overton one of the seven commissioners in charge of the army. The next day troops of the cashiered officers closed the house and took over the government.

Monck, who also had rejected the cashiered officers' address, responded to the lock-out by declaring for parliament and preparing to march south. He asked Overton and other commanders for support, and although no direct reply from Overton to Monck has been found, in early November Overton published an impassioned appeal for a peaceful settlement in accordance with God's purpose. *The Humble and Healing Advice … to Charles Lord Fleetwood and General Monck* contends that the Lord has been forced to 'overturn and overturn' governments because none has conformed with 'what we professe'. Fleetwood and Monck are urged to come together; 'otherwise … another overturne will suddenly overtake you'. Should this occur, Overton will endeavour to secure the peace of Hull and support the settlement that has the most 'superscription of Christ upon it' (*The Humble and Healing Advice*, n.d., 2, 6).

On 1 January 1660, six days after the Rump returned, Monck's forces crossed the Tweed, and within a fortnight Monck and Overton agreed that they stood together against those who would 'bring in the Common Enimie' (*Clarke Papers*, 4.244–7). Monck's readmission of the excluded members of the house on 21 February assured the return of the 'Enimie'. Reports soon reached Monck about Overton's dissemination among Yorkshire troops of an incendiary letter expressing hope that soldiers would concur in defence of the 'Good Old Cause against … a King and Single Person' (Baker, 753). Monck named a new governor of Hull and ordered Overton to London. Overton recognized defeat and reached London on 18 March.

Overton was not excluded from the restored monarch's act of pardon, but more than half of his remaining years were passed in prison. In December 1660 he was among those seized to forestall a 'damnable Plot' (*Mercurius Publicus*, 13–20 Dec 1660, 810–11) which, if it existed, was never disclosed. Overton was moved from the Tower to Chepstow in November 1661 and at some point thereafter he gained his freedom, for in May 1663 he was again arrested on suspicion of seditious practices; as before he was not tried, and in January 1664 he was again sent to Jersey. He was confined on the island until his release to his brother-in-law, Thomas Gardiner, in December 1671.

Political and religious convictions Overton spent the last years of his life with his daughter, Anne Broughton, and her husband in Seaton, Rutland. The will that Overton signed on 23 June 1678, which was proved on 29 January 1679, states that he had been well attended during 'my long sickness' (PRO, PROB/11/359, sig. 8). He was buried in New Church Yard, Moorfields in London. His apostate son and heir, John, who succeeded to the Easington property, is not mentioned in the will, and except for books, manuscripts, and other effects, Overton's personal estate was divided between two other sons. No figures are given, but if he retained the property he had in 1653, he left a substantial estate.

The manuscripts that Overton bequeathed to two daughters included a 360-page volume, 'Gospell observations & religious manifestations, &c', that is primarily prose and poetic tributes to his wife, who died in 1665. The first section of the manuscript, except for the last entry, consists of prose maxims that may have been written before Ann Overton's death. Among them are segments that clarify Overton's political convictions and religious tolerance. A deeply religious Independent, Overton believed that no profession of piety should be despised. He questions 'incongruetyes & contradictions' of the Fifth Monarchy Men but finds their essential creed 'comfortable', as he approves aspects of the papists, protestants, puritans, and Quakers (Princeton University Library, MS C O 199, Overton MS, 42). The political segment highlights Overton's persistent realism. However disappointed with successive revolutionary governments, he served them as existent obstacles to monarchy. In custody after the king's Restoration, he advised potential rebels to submit to any expedient power. There is no evidence that he had abandoned his vision; he may have concluded that a moral state governed by godly men is the province of the Lord.

Throughout the interregnum Overton's commitment to his 'particular and private Trust' (*The Declaration of the Officers of the Garrison of Hull*, Overton's letter, 1649) diminished the intensity of his support for existing polities, which aroused concern among authorities aware of his abilities and always fearful of effective opposition. Royalists approached Overton, Levellers claimed him, and after 1660 he was imprisoned amid rumours of anti-monarchical plots. In fact, while Overton sympathized with Leveller views of justice, he was a political individualist, true to his vision of an ideal state. No hard evidence involved him in the plans of any radical activists. A proficient soldier and administrator, Overton was also a learned man who inspired respect and affection. For many years he was close to Milton, linked 'with a more than fraternal harmony, by reason of the likeness of our tastes and the sweetness of your disposition' (*Complete Prose Works*, 4, pt 1, 676). Overton's gentle spirit and enduring faith protected him from bitterness as he retained confidence in the belief he professed when first imprisoned. Quoting St Peter, '"There are given to us exceeding great and pretious promises"', Overton concludes: 'If in patience we possess our spirits, we shall inherit the promises' (Thurloe, 3.112). BARBARA TAFT

Sources *DNB* • D. Norbrook, '"This blushing tribute of a borrowed muse": Robert Overton and his overturning of the poetic canon', *English Manuscript Studies, 1100–1700*, 4 (1993), 220–66 • B. Taft, '"They that pursue perfaction on earth": the political progress of Robert Overton', *Soldiers, writers and statesmen of the English revolution*, ed. I. Gentles and others (1998), 286–303 • R. Overton, 'Gospell observations & religious manifestations, &c', Princeton University, MS C O 199 • will, 1679, PRO, PROB 11/359, sig. 8 • C. H. Firth and G. Davies, *The regimental history of Cromwell's army*, 2 vols. (1940) • M. Ashley, 'The vacillations of Major-General Robert Overton', *Cromwell's generals* (1954), 137–49 • Thurloe, *State papers* • J. Rushworth, *Historical collections*, new edn, 8 vols. (1721–2) • R. Baker, *A chronicle of the kings of England*, 4th edn (1665) • *Complete prose works of John Milton*, ed. D. Wolfe, 8 vols. in 10 (1953–82), vol. 4 • *The writings and speeches of Oliver Cromwell*, ed. W. C. Abbott and C. D. Crane, 4 vols. (1937–47) • *The manuscripts of his grace the duke of Portland*, 10 vols., HMC, 29 (1891–1931) • *Report on the manuscripts of F. W. Leyborne-Popham*, HMC, 51 (1899) • *The manuscripts of the duke of Leeds*, HMC, 22 (1888) • *CSP dom.*, 1648–72 • C. H. Firth, ed., *Scotland and the Commonwealth: letters and papers relating to the military government of Scotland, from August 1651 to December 1653*, Scottish History Society, 18 (1895) • C. H. Firth, ed., *Scotland and the protectorate: letters and papers relating to the military government of Scotland from January 1654 to June 1659*, Scottish History Society, 31 (1899) • C. H. Firth, ed., 'Two letters addressed to Cromwell', *EngHR*, 22 (1907), 308–15 • *Diary of Thomas Burton*, ed. J. T. Rutt, 4 vols. (1828) • R. Bell, ed., *Memorials of the civil war … forming the concluding volumes of the Fairfax correspondence*, 2 vols. (1849) • *The Clarke papers*, ed. C. H. Firth, 4 vols., CS, new ser., 49, 54, 61–2 (1891–1901) • *JHC*, 4–8 (1642–67) • A. Overton, letter to Ferdinando, Lord Fairfax, 1647, BL, Add. MS 18979, fol. 252 • J. W. Walker, ed., *Yorkshire pedigrees*, 3 vols., Harleian Society, 94–6 (1942–4) • Venn, *Alum. Cant.* • *Dugdale's visitation of Yorkshire, with additions*, ed. J. W. Clay, 3 vols. (1899–1917) • J. W. Clay, ed., *Abstracts of Yorkshire wills in the time of the Commonwealth*, Yorkshire Archaeological Society, 9 (1890) • *Publick Intelligencer* (Jan 1660) • *Publick Intelligencer* (March 1660) • *Mercurius Publicus* (Dec 1660) • *Mercurius Politicus* (Sept 1650) • *Mercurius Politicus* (29 Oct 1659) • *Mercurius*

Politicus (3 Jan 1660) • *Mercurius Politicus* (6 March 1660) • J. L. Chester and J. Foster, eds., *London marriage licences, 1521–1869* (1887) • M. Tolmie, *The triumph of the saints: the separate churches of London, 1616–1649* (1977)

Archives Bodl. Oxf., Thurloe state papers, MSS Rawl. Class A, vols. 1–67 • PRO, crown fee farm rent, chancery close rolls, C 54/5624/26

Likenesses portrait, priv. coll. [*see illus.*]

Wealth at death property in Easington to heir; remainder of personal estate to two other sons: will, PRO, PROB 11/359, sig. 8

Overton, William (1524/5?–1609), bishop of Coventry and Lichfield, is said by Wood to have been born in London and to have been elected a demy of Magdalen College, Oxford, in 1539, aged fifteen. He is reported elsewhere to have been first educated at Glastonbury Abbey. If the identification is correct Overton had migrated to Christ Church by 1547, when he graduated BA. He became a fellow of Magdalen in 1551, and proceeded MA on 8 July 1553, BTh on 16 February 1566, and DTh two days later. In 1552 he contributed verses to the volume commemorating the second and third dukes of Suffolk, both recently dead in their teens. There is no record of his ordination, but he was preferred in 1553 to the rectory of Balcombe, Sussex, and the vicarage of Eccleshall, Staffordshire, suggesting that he absented himself from Oxford at this time. In 1555 he was made rector of Swinnerton, Staffordshire. He does not appear to have gone into exile under Mary, though no doubt he kept a low profile, but following the accession of Elizabeth he acquired a number of prestigious livings. On 13 November 1559 he was presented by the crown to the canonry of the second prebend in Winchester Cathedral, and the rectories of Upham, Nursling, and Exton, all in Hampshire, and that of Cotton, Suffolk, soon followed. On 14 July 1561 he was collated to the prebend of Hova Villa in Chichester Cathedral.

The signs are that Overton was quick to cultivate the patronage of Lord Robert Dudley, from 1564 earl of Leicester. When Queen Elizabeth visited Oxford with Dudley in 1564 Overton took a large part in her reception, and participated in disputations held before her. On 22 May 1571 he declared to Leicester that he was his 'owne chapleyne, or at least wise the Queen's Majestie's chapleyn by your only meanes put and preferred unto her' (De Lisle and Dudley papers, Baskerville transcript, 1.237). Presumably Leicester's favour not only helped Overton to become treasurer of Chichester (6 May 1567) and prebendary of Yatesbury in Salisbury Cathedral (24 May 1570), but also enabled him to build upon his existing connections with the diocese of Coventry and Lichfield, where he became rector of Stoke-on-Trent and of Hanbury.

Overton earned himself an unsavoury reputation in some quarters, partly thanks to his ambitions for himself and his family. He married twice, on both occasions forging alliances useful for an ecclesiastical career. His first wife, whom he married about 1566, was Margaret (*d.* 1601), daughter of William Barlow, bishop of Chichester, a connection which brought him increasing prominence in that diocese, both as treasurer and vicar-general. When Barlow died on 13 August 1568 Overton immediately wrote to Sir William Cecil recommending William Day, provost of Eton and another of the late bishop's sons-in-law, as Barlow's successor, as one 'noted among all for learning and piety' (BL, Add. MS 6346, fol. 45). Richard Curteys, however, was consecrated to the see on 21 May 1570. Overton then became the focus for an anti-Curteys faction within the cathedral chapter which threatened to wreck the new bishop's hopes of reform. Curteys sought to bypass Overton's opposition by packing the cathedral chapter, and a conflict developed which reached a crisis in July 1573 when the bishop's faction held an extraordinary chapter meeting and conducted business in the absence of a quorum. Overton's faction succeeded in forcing Curteys to promulgate new statutes preventing such abuses, but the victory was more apparent than real.

Overton was consecrated bishop of Coventry and Lichfield on 18 September 1580, presumably at the instigation of Leicester. He received a bad press from twentieth-century historians for grovelling to the queen, blaming the economic plight of the diocese on Thomas Bentham, his predecessor, and depleting the resources of an already impoverished see through an extravagant lifestyle. It is certainly true that he made several long leases to the crown and demised the manor of Lichfield to Elizabeth in perpetuity, while like many Elizabethan bishops he was said to have felled excessive amounts of timber on the episcopal estates. More damningly his letters suggest that he was prepared to do whatever his patron Leicester might require:

> I am your chapleyn of olde; I have been alwaies servisable at your commandment; I have been plyable to your letters and suytes; I have ben and am in case both able and ready to do you honor if you will use me. (De Lisle and Dudley papers, Baskerville transcript, 1.237)

It may have been distaste for Overton's evident dependence on Leicester which led Cecil (now Baron Burghley) to denounce him in Elizabeth's presence for ordaining unworthy men to the priesthood for personal gain.

That charge remains unproven. It would have been impossible to staff the underfunded livings of Coventry and Lichfield without ordaining non-graduates, and there is no particular evidence to suggest that Overton was indiscriminate or irresponsible in this respect. He is, moreover, credited with being genial, hospitable (an element in the episcopal equation which weighed heavily with Elizabeth), and good to the poor. There is also evidence that he kept his episcopal residences in good repair. The jibes of Martin Marprelate that he was ignorant and unlearned are in direct contravention of the known facts of Overton's university career and his frequent appearances in the pulpit. They also fly in the face of his known preference for radical preachers of whom Marprelate must have approved. He granted preaching licences to Arthur Hildersham and William Bradshaw, lent his support to clerical exercises in Burton upon Trent and Southam, and allowed preachers like William Axton of Moreton Corbett to continue their activities despite their nonconformity.

Overton also appointed the reforming civil lawyer John Becon as chancellor of Lichfield and was prepared to defend his activities to Archbishop Whitgift and others who criticized them. Becon's 'Certain advertisements' of 1584 would have associated the bishop, the chancellor, and certain selected preachers in examining ordinands and presentees to livings, and introduced an element of parish approval in the case of the latter, thus accommodating criticism of an authoritarian system in which the diocesan merely rubber-stamped presentations by ecclesiastical patrons. But Becon seems to have played little part in running the diocese and quarrelled with Overton at an early stage. By October 1583 the bishop had appointed Zachary Babington to be Becon's coadjutor as chancellor, so initiating a running battle between the two men which ended before Star Chamber, the privy council, and the archbishop of Canterbury. Matters were resolved only by Becon's death in 1587.

The fact nevertheless remains that with regard to the revenues of his see Overton appears to have been quarrelsome, aggressive, litigious, and possibly downright dishonest. He failed in his attempts to resume rights to property by legal process against Lord Paget and the city of Lichfield, among others. If that strategy had long-term beneficial consequences for the see it had immediate consequences for himself. He estimated that in the first year of his episcopate litigation had cost him £740 and appearances before most of the major courts of the land. Perhaps more significantly it has been suggested that his tactics alienated his principal patron, Leicester, prevented his further promotion, and led to his humiliation in his own diocese. His dealings with the exchequer over his first fruits for the bishopric and annual taxes thereafter are complex to the point of incomprehensibility.

Little else can be said of Overton's twenty-nine years as bishop except that in 1600 he made a personal visitation of his diocese. If in the last analysis contemporary accounts of his corruption, venality, and nepotism seem well founded—some of his grants to his son Plasted were rejected by the Lichfield chapter—he might nevertheless also be seen as a forward-looking entrepreneur who seized opportunities to supplement the revenues of his diocese. He was responsible for bringing glass-making to Staffordshire, having as a canon of Chichester become acquainted with several leading Huguenot glass-making families. They apparently followed him to Buckholt, near Salisbury, when he became a canon there in 1570, and then to Eccleshall, after his appointment to Coventry and Lichfield. He fuelled their furnaces with timber from his own estates and the industry proved highly profitable locally.

Margaret Overton died in 1601 and (although by then seventy-six) the bishop soon remarried. His second wife was Mary, daughter of Edmund and Elizabeth Bradocke of Adbaston Hall, a few miles west of Eccleshall. Mary was related to the earls of Shrewsbury through her maternal grandmother, Dorothy Talbot, and Overton was not slow to make use of the connection. He designed an elaborate, highly coloured tomb for himself in Holy Trinity Church, Eccleshall, near his country palace, bearing his effigy and with a Latin epitaph stating that he had erected it for himself in 1603 'in the hope of resurrection' (monument). Overton died on 9 April 1609 and was duly buried at Eccleshall. Nothing is known of the life of his widow or of any surviving children. ROSEMARY O'DAY

Sources R. O'Day, 'Cumulative debt: the bishops of Coventry and Lichfield and their economic problems, c.1540–1640', *Midland History* (1975), 77–115 • R. O'Day, *The English clergy* (1979) • F. Heal, *Of prelates and princes: a study of the economic and social position of the Tudor episcopate* (1980) • P. Collinson, *Godly people: essays on English protestantism and puritanism* (1983) • P. Collinson, *The Elizabethan puritan movement* (1967) • R. B. Manning, *Religion and society in Elizabethan Sussex* (1969) • Foster, *Alum. Oxon.*, 1500–1714, 3.1097 • monument, Holy Trinity Church, Eccleshall, Staffordshire • J. Nichols, *The progresses and public processions of Elizabeth I*, 3 vols. (1823), vol. 1, p. 209 • Lichfield diocesan papers • K. Bowe and T. Harvey, *Holy Trinity Church, Eccleshall* [n.d.] • J. Berlatsky, 'Marriage and family in a Tudor elite: familial patterns of Elizabethan bishops', *Journal of Family History*, 3/1 (1978), 6–22 • Wood, *Ath. Oxon.*, new edn, 2.49–50 • CKS, De Lisle and Dudley papers (Baskerville transcript), 1

Likenesses marble monument, Holy Trinity Church, Eccleshall, Staffordshire

Overtoun. For this title name *see* White, John Campbell, Baron Overtoun (1843–1908).

Owain (*d.* **1212**). *See under* Hywel ab Owain Gwynedd (*d.* 1170).

Owain ab Edwin (*d.* **1105**), ruler in Wales, was the son of Edwin ap Gronw (a descendant of Owain ap Hywel Dda, according to some late genealogies) of Tegeingl, a north-eastern cantref between the Dee and the Clwyd, and Iwerydd, daughter of Cynfyn ap Gwerystan. His father is thought to be the Edwinus who held lands in Tegeingl and south-west Cheshire, both before 1066 and at the time of the Domesday survey, and was probably the most important Welshman at this time in Tegeingl. To this position Owain probably succeeded about 1090.

In 1098, Hugh d'Avranches, earl of Chester, and Hugh de Montgomery, earl of Shrewsbury, were aided by Owain and his brother Uchdryd in their invasion of Anglesey. Following the resulting flight of Gruffudd ap Cynan and Cadwgan ap Bleddyn to Ireland, it is possible that Owain's position was strengthened. Indeed, when the men of Gwynedd rose against the Normans later in the same year, it was Owain who led the revolt against his erstwhile lord the earl of Chester. However, Gruffudd and Cadwgan returned from Ireland in 1099 and made peace with the Normans, receiving back parts of their former territories. Owain, who was probably no longer of use to the Normans, disappears from the picture, though his brother Uchdryd was still active in 1118. Owain died in 1105, after a long illness. His wife was Morwyl ferch Ednywain Bendew. Some of his sons founded families of note in Tegeingl, but were all themselves killed in inter-dynastic or intra-familial strife: Llywarch in 1118, Gronw, Rhirid, and Meilyr in 1125 by their nephew Cadwallon ap Gruffudd ap Cynan, and Cynwrig in 1139 by Madog ap Maredudd of Powys. Owain's daughter Angharad was the wife of Gruffudd ap Cynan. DAVID E. THORNTON

Sources P. C. Bartrum, ed., *Early Welsh genealogical tracts* (1966) • P. C. Bartrum, 'Pedigrees of the Welsh tribal patriarchs', *National*

Library of Wales Journal, 13 (1963–4), 93–146, esp. 113 • J. Williams ab Ithel, ed., *Annales Cambriae*, Rolls Series, 20 (1860) • T. Jones, ed. and trans., *Brenhinedd y Saesson, or, The kings of the Saxons* (1971) [another version of *Brut y tywysogyon*] • T. Jones, ed. and trans., *Brut y tywysogyon, or, The chronicle of the princes: Peniarth MS 20* (1952) • T. Jones, ed. and trans., *Brut y tywysogyon, or, The chronicle of the princes: Red Book of Hergest* (1955) • D. S. Evans, ed. and trans., *A mediaeval prince of Wales: the life of Gruffudd ap Cynan* (1990) [Eng. trans. of *Historia Gruffud vab Kenan*, with orig. Welsh text] • A. Farley, ed., *Domesday Book*, 2 vols. (1783) • J. E. Lloyd, *A history of Wales from the earliest times to the Edwardian conquest*, 3rd edn, 2 vols. (1939) • K. L. Maund, *Ireland, Wales, and England in the eleventh century* (1991) • R. R. Davies, *Conquest, coexistence, and change: Wales, 1063–1415*, History of Wales, 2 (1987)

Owain, Sir, ap Cadwgan (*d.* **1116**). *See under* Bleddyn ap Cynfyn (*d.* 1075).

Owain ap Gruffudd (*d.* **1235**). *See under* Gruffudd ap Rhys (*d.* 1201).

Owain ap Hywel (*b.* before **929**, *d.* **988**), king of Deheubarth, was the son of *Hywel Dda, descendant of *Rhodri Mawr of Gwynedd, and Elen ferch Llywarch (*d.* 929) of Dyfed. Owain ruled the kingdom of Deheubarth, in south Wales, jointly from 950 and singly from about 954 until his death in 988. His father Hywel had possibly annexed Dyfed on account of his marriage into the ruling dynasty, and, on the death of his cousin *Idwal Foel in 942, had added Gwynedd and other parts of north Wales to his kingdom. On Hywel's own death in 949 or 950 the southern portion of this kingdom fell under the collective rule of his sons, including no doubt Owain, while the northern portion was contested by the sons of Idwal Foel, *Iago and Ieuaf. The two groups fought at Nant Carno (in Arwystli) in 950, which was a victory for the sons of Idwal and perhaps thus secured their position in the north. The latter were sufficiently strong in 952 to take the fight into Dyfed twice. In 954 Owain and his brothers retaliated and the two groups met at Llanrwst (in the Conwy valley, Gwynedd). The sons of Idwal were the victors; they slew Owain's brother Edwin, and afterwards raided Ceredigion.

It is not wholly clear at what point Owain came to dominate Deheubarth as opposed to sharing power with his brothers. Indeed, he may have achieved this position through default, for the other sons of Hywel do not appear to have lived beyond the mid-950s. In 952 or 953 one Dyfnwal (or Dyfnwallon), possibly a son of Hywel, was slain by vikings (or by the sons of Idwal); Rhodri ap Hywel died in 953 or 954; and Edwin ap Hywel in 954. There may have been only two sons of Hywel left alive by the end of 954: Owain and in addition Rhain, who is never noticed at all in the chronicles. Owain was probably sole ruler of Deheubarth by this point and it was in this capacity that he witnessed the Eamont agreement of King Eadred of England in 955.

However, having thus achieved power, Owain did not make much of an impact in the chronicles, and it is his sons, Einion (*r.* 970–84) and then *Maredudd ab Owain, who are most frequently mentioned, though whether as his representatives or independently is uncertain. In 960 Owain raided the cantref of Gorfynydd in the neighbouring kingdom of Morgannwg then ruled by Morgan Hen ab Owain. This is the last notice of Owain until that of his death twenty-eight years later. Einion attacked Gower in 970 and again in 977: this region may have been under the authority of Morgannwg at this point, otherwise Einion would have been attacking lands ruled by his own father. As such he was continuing Owain's hostility to the kings of south-east Wales, and it is perhaps significant that Einion met his death in 984 at the hands of the men of Gwent. He may have held some political power independently of Owain, for the chronicles recount that in 983 Hywel ab Idwal and Ælfhere, ealdorman of Mercia, raided 'Brycheiniog and all the territory of Einion ab Owain'. Maredudd ab Owain emerged after the death of Einion, but appears to have concentrated his efforts against the traditional rivals in the north, where he achieved a considerable amount of success, again independently of his father. Other sons of Owain might include a Llywarch (blinded in 987); late unreliable genealogies add the names Gronwy and Iestyn.

Owain ap Hywel appears to have been a patron of the literary arts. Thus it was during his reign that the scriptorium at St David's in Dyfed drew up the earliest surviving recension of the *Annales Cambriae*, compiled a collection of genealogies which commences with Owain's agnatic and maternal pedigrees, and incorporated both texts into a copy of the *Historia Brittonum*. Owain's interest in these scholarly endeavours is reflected in his importance for the genealogical collection and perhaps also by the fact that the annals were drawn up *c.*954, when he achieved sole power in Deheubarth. He died in 988, after a reign spanning over three decades. There is no indication that he was slain, and he probably died of natural causes. The kingship of Deheubarth was then added to the territories of his son Maredudd. DAVID E. THORNTON

Sources J. Williams ab Ithel, ed., *Annales Cambriae*, Rolls Series, 20 (1860) • T. Jones, ed. and trans., *Brenhinedd y Saesson, or, The kings of the Saxons* (1971) [another version of *Brut y tywysogyon*] • T. Jones, ed. and trans., *Brut y tywysogyon, or, The chronicle of the princes: Peniarth MS 20* (1952) • T. Jones, ed. and trans., *Brut y tywysogyon, or, The chronicle of the princes: Red Book of Hergest* (1955) • P. C. Bartrum, ed., *Early Welsh genealogical tracts* (1966) • *AS chart.*, S 566 • J. E. Lloyd, *A history of Wales from the earliest times to the Edwardian conquest*, 3rd edn, 2 vols. (1939); repr. (1988) • H. R. Loyn, 'Wales and England in the tenth century: the context of the Athelstan charters', *Welsh History Review / Cylchgrawn Hanes Cymru*, 10 (1980–81), 283–301 • D. E. Thornton, 'Maredudd ab Owain (d.999): the most famous king of the Welsh', *Welsh History Review / Cylchgrawn Hanes Cymru*, 18 (1996–7), 567–91

Owain Brogyntyn (*fl.* **1160–1215**). *See under* Madog ap Maredudd (*d.* 1160).

Owain Cyfeiliog [Owain ap Gruffudd] (*d.* **1197**), ruler in Wales, was the son of Gruffudd ap Maredudd (brother of *Madog ap Maredudd, prince of Powys) and, according to later genealogies, Gwerful ferch Gwrgenau, said to have been a descendant of the historically shadowy ruler of Rhwng Gwy a Hafren, Elystan Glodrydd. In 1149 Owain and his brother Meurig received from their uncle Madog, then ruling over Powys, the commote of Cyfeiliog, a region including most of the middle valley of the Dyfi in western Powys. Owain's identification with Cyfeiliog accounts for his ordinary descriptive name, which distinguished him from his rival, Owain ap Gruffudd, called Owain Gwynedd. His hold on Cyfeiliog was, however, tenuous: in 1153 Rhys ap Gruffudd of south Wales wasted the commote, and by 1162 it was held by Owain Gwynedd.

Madog ap Maredudd's death in 1160 was followed by that of his son Llywelyn immediately afterwards. Owain now became the dominant figure in a fragmented Powys, establishing himself as the ruler of the southern part of the principality with his chief seat at Welshpool. Owain probably inclined towards Madog's general policy of alliance with the English against his dangerous neighbour and rival, Owain Gwynedd. In the summer of 1165, however, he joined Owain Gwynedd, Rhys ap Gruffudd, and other Welsh princes in the united resistance to Henry II's invasion of Wales. After advancing into the Berwyn Mountains, Henry had to withdraw, beaten by the elements and lack of food as much as by the enemy, and he never ventured on another Welsh campaign. The unity of the Welsh princes was, however, short-lived. In 1166 Owain and his cousin Owain Fychan expelled their uncle Iorwerth Goch from his land of Mochnant. In the division of spoils Owain Cyfeiliog obtained the western part of the territory (Mochnant Uwch Rhaeadr). In 1167 Owain himself had to face a joint attack on southern Powys by Owain Gwynedd and Rhys ap Gruffudd. Their forces took possession of Caereinion and the castle of Tafolwern, causing Owain to flee to England. He now fell back on marcher support, soon reappearing in company with a 'French' (Anglo-Norman) army. He won back the lands he had lost and destroyed the new castle which his enemies had built at Caereinion. War continued between Owain Cyfeiliog and Rhys. In 1171 Rhys again invaded Powys, forcing Owain to surrender seven hostages for his good behaviour.

Despite Owain's opposition to Henry II in 1165, payments to him recorded in the pipe rolls testify to the generally cordial relations between them. This is confirmed by Gerald of Wales, who described Henry and the Welsh prince dining together at Shrewsbury; on this occasion Owain found the means of covertly rebuking the king for his habit of keeping benefices long vacant in order to enjoy the custody of their temporalities. In May 1177 Owain attended the great council at Oxford, at which Henry made his son John lord of Ireland. Together with other Welsh princes he took an oath of fealty to Henry as his overlord.

Owain Cyfeiliog probably married twice, first certainly to Gwenllïan, daughter of Owain Gwynedd, and second perhaps to Gwenllïan, daughter of Ednywain, claimed by later genealogies to be of the line of Gollwyn ap Tangno. As Owain grew older his sons, *Gwenwynwyn and Cadwallon, probably assumed his military role. According to the Welsh chronicles they were responsible for the murder of their kinsman Owain Fychan in 1187, though Gerald of Wales ascribes the crime to their father. In 1188 Owain Cyfeiliog was the only Welsh prince who did not go out with his people to meet Archbishop Baldwin during his crusading tour of Wales. For this negligence he was excommunicated. Earlier, in 1170, Owain had founded the Cistercian monastery of Strata Marcella (Ystrad Marchell) near Welshpool. Having taken the monastic habit in old age, he died there in 1197; he was buried near the high altar, and lauded in a Latin epitaph as 'ecclesiae cultor' (a reverencer of the church). Gwenwynwyn, who succeeded to his father's dominions, completed the endowment of Strata Marcella.

Gerald of Wales includes Owain Cyfeiliog with Owain Gwynedd and Maredudd ap Gruffudd ap Rhys of south Wales as the three Welshmen who, in his days, were conspicuous for their justice, prudence, and moderation as rulers. The lavish hospitality of Owain's court—'Where there was drinking without want, without refusal'—was celebrated by the poet Cynddelw Brydydd Mawr. Cynddelw's poetry also testifies to Owain's raids against Anglo-Norman lands in the Shropshire marches, among them the territories of the Corbet lords of Caus, an aspect of his career which is ignored by the chronicles. The poet's evidence is complemented by the portrayal of Owain in the thirteenth-century Anglo-French romance 'Fouke le Fitz Waryn' (the Fitzwarines held land of the Corbets at Alberbury). Here he features as 'un chevaler hardy e fer' (a bold and fierce knight) who grievously wounds Fouke le Fitz Waryn.

Owain, whom Gerald of Wales praised for the readiness of his tongue, is renowned in Welsh literary history as a poet. Two poems, the lengthy 'Hirlas Owain', which is definitely ascribed to Owain in the Red Book of Hergest, and the shorter '*Englynion* on the circuit of Wales' have been regarded as his work. The 'Hirlas' is an unusual poem, which, in dramatic style, depicts a feast in Owain's court following a raid in Maelor in north-east Wales to free his brother Meurig from prison, an event which the Welsh chronicles show to have taken place in 1156. Owain praises his brave warriors, calling upon his cup-bearer to bring the long blue ('hirlas') drinking-horn filled with mead to each hero in turn. Recent stylistic analysis of this and the other poem, however, implies that their true author was Cynddelw Brydydd Mawr, Owain's court poet, and that the prince's role was that of a persona in the poems rather than their creator.

T. F. Tout, *rev.* Gruffydd Aled Williams

Sources T. Jones, ed. and trans., *Brut y tywysogyon, or, The chronicle of the princes: Peniarth MS 20* (1952) · T. Jones, ed. and trans., *Brut y tywysogyon, or, The chronicle of the princes: Red Book of Hergest* (1955) · *Gir. Camb. opera*, vol. 6 · G. A. Williams, ed., 'Canu Owain Cyfeiliog', in *Gwaith Llywelyn Fardd I ac eraill o feirdd y ddeuddegfed ganrif*, ed. K. A. Bramley and M. E. Owen (1994), 193–277 · G. A. Williams, 'Owain Cyfeiliog: bardd-dywysog?', *Beirdd a thywysogion*, ed. M. E. Owen and B. F. Roberts (1996), 180–201 · *Gwaith Cynddelw Brydydd Mawr*, ed. N. A. Jones and A. P. Owen, 1 (1991) · P. C. Bartrum, ed., *Welsh genealogies, AD 300–1400*, 8 vols. (1974) · *Chronica magistri Rogeri de Hovedene*, ed. W. Stubbs, 2, Rolls Series, 51 (1869) · *Pipe rolls*, 4, 6, 12 Henry II · J. C. Davies, 'Records of the abbey of Ystrad Marchell', *Montgomeryshire Collections*, 51 (1949–50), 3–22 · J. C. Davies, 'Strata Marcella documents', *Montgomeryshire Collections*, 51 (1949–50), 164–87 · H. Ellis, ed., 'Register and chronicle of the abbey of Aberconway', *Camden miscellany, I*, CS, 39 (1847) · E. J. Hathaway and others, eds., *Fouke le Fitz Waryn* (1975)

Owain Gwynedd [Owain ap Gruffudd] (*d.* **1170**), king of Gwynedd, was the second son of *Gruffudd ap Cynan, king of Gwynedd (*d.* 1137), and his wife, Angharad.

Early conquests Before his father's death in 1137 Owain had already gained considerable military experience, contributing to the expansion of Gwynedd in the 1120s and 1130s. He is first mentioned together with his elder brother, Cadwallon, as leading an expedition against Meirionydd in 1124. In 1136 Owain, together with his younger brother, Cadwaladr [*see below*], led two campaigns against the Normans in Ceredigion, on the second of which they were joined by Gruffudd ap Rhys (*d.* 1137) of Deheubarth. Since Cadwallon had been killed in 1132 in the commote of Nanheudwy, leading an attack on Powys, Owain was the eldest surviving son of Gruffudd ap Cynan on the latter's death in 1137 and succeeded to the kingdom of Gwynedd, which he ruled until his own death in 1170. In 1138 he completed the conquest of Ceredigion, which was divided between his eldest son, Hywel ab Owain, and Cadwaladr. Owain sought to continue the alliance between his dynasty and that of Deheubarth, cemented earlier by the marriage of his sister, Gwenllian, to Gruffudd ap Rhys, by arranging the betrothal of his daughter to Anarawd, Gruffudd's son and successor. However, Anarawd was murdered by Cadwaladr's men in 1143, prompting Owain to dispossess his brother of his lands, although the brothers were reconciled the following year after Cadwaladr obtained military assistance from Ireland. By 1149 Owain had resumed the policy of expansion to the north-east that had been a hallmark of the later years of his father's reign, for in that year he occupied the commote of Iâl, building a castle at Tomen y Rhodwydd. His control of Iâl, together with Tegeingl and Ystrad Alun, was reinforced the following year by his defeat, at Coleshill, of Madog ap Maredudd, king of Powys, and forces supplied by Ranulf (II), earl of Chester. Two events in 1152 underlined Owain's determination to maintain the territorial integrity of the kingdom of Gwynedd and to protect the interests of his branch of the royal dynasty: his brother Cadwaladr was driven from Anglesey, his last remaining lands in the kingdom, while Owain's nephew, Cunedda, son of the king's deceased elder brother, Cadwallon, was blinded and castrated.

Prince of Wales Owain's ambitions were checked, however, by Henry II's first campaign against Gwynedd in the summer of 1157. Although Henry suffered military reverses, particularly in the seaborne attack on Anglesey, his show of force was sufficient to persuade Owain to submit and give homage to the king, surrender his conquests in Tegeingl (where Henry built castles at Rhuddlan and Basingwerk), and restore Cadwaladr to his lands. Later in the year Owain also lost control of Iâl, following the destruction of his castle at Tomen y Rhodwydd by Madog ap Maredudd's brother, Iorwerth Goch. These setbacks proved to be only temporary, however, for the opportunity for further expansion presented itself on the death of Madog ap Maredudd in 1160. Owain seems immediately to have occupied the Powys commotes of Edeirnion and Cyfeiliog and in 1162 he led a punitive raid against Hywel ab Ieuaf, ruler of Arwystli. True, Owain continued to be circumspect in his dealings with Henry II. Thus after Einion Clud, ruler of Elfael, had been handed over to the king of Gwynedd following his capture by his brother, Cadwallon ap Madog of Maelienydd, in 1160, Owain gave his prisoner into the custody of Henry, and on 1 July 1163 he gave homage to the English king at Woodstock following the latter's second Welsh campaign. However, by 1165 Owain was at the head of a Welsh alliance including the rulers of Powys and Rhys ap Gruffudd, ruler of Deheubarth, which successfully defied Henry, whose third campaign in Wales in that year was a disaster, coming to grief in August in the rain and mud of the Berwyn Mountains. Indeed from 1165 Owain was the undisputed leader of native Wales, a supremacy placarded in his adoption of the new titles, prince of Wales (*Waliarum princeps*) or prince of the Welsh (*princeps Wallensium*), which replaced the title king of Wales (*rex Walliae* or *Walliarum rex*) used from possibly as early as 1140. He sought to strengthen his position by offering fealty to Louis VII, king of France, whom he urged to make war on Henry II following the latter's ill-fated Welsh campaign of 1165. In Wales, Owain resumed his expansion in the north-east, capturing Basingwerk Castle in 1166 and securing the whole of Tegeingl the following year after taking, together with Rhys ap Gruffudd, the castles of Rhuddlan (after a siege of three months) and Prestatyn. The fragility of the unity achieved by the Welsh leaders in 1165 was illustrated by another campaign in 1167 in which Owain and Cadwaladr joined Rhys in attacking the Powysian ruler Owain Cyfeiliog and capturing his castle of Tafolwern. Yet the prince of Gwynedd clearly realized that Henry II remained the greatest potential threat to his territorial gains, for Owain was doubtless one of the 'kings of Wales' who sent messengers to Louis VII in 1168 to forge a military alliance against Henry, thereby continuing the diplomatic contacts with the Capetian king established earlier in the 1160s.

Church policy Owain's power in the last five years of his reign is also demonstrated by his successful defiance of Archbishop Thomas Becket and Pope Alexander III with regard to the vacant bishopric of Bangor and his own marriage. Owain was later praised by Gerald of Wales for his respect for churches, and it is very likely that he patronized rebuilding work at Penmon and possibly at other churches in Gwynedd. But he also demanded, and to a great extent obtained, the loyalty of the churchmen in his kingdom. However, at his consecration at Worcester in January 1140 Meurig, or Maurice, bishop of Bangor, had given fealty to King Stephen, despite having been prohibited from so doing by Simeon, archdeacon of Bangor; this probably explains why Owain protested to Bernard, bishop of St David's, that Meurig had been unlawfully intruded into the see. Yet although he was exiled for some years at the beginning of his episcopate, and again for a period in the 1150s (prompting an appeal on his behalf by Archbishop Theobald of Canterbury to the pope), Meurig remained bishop until his death on 12 August 1161. Owain was determined that any successor should not do fealty to the king of England, and exploited Becket's exile from November 1164 by requesting permission, probably in the autumn of 1165, for his own candidate to be consecrated by another bishop and also by asserting that obedience would be given to Canterbury as a favour rather than as of right. Becket refused to countenance these proposals but the candidate, Arthur of Bardsey, may nevertheless have been sent to Ireland for consecration. Although Becket enlisted papal support in his efforts to ensure the election of a bishop acceptable to him, the bishopric remained vacant (unless held by Arthur of Bardsey, who was recognized by neither archbishop nor pope) until 1177. Attempts to resolve the dispute through the mediation of Louis VII came to nothing. Indeed, by *c.*1169 archbishop and pope had intensified their opposition to Owain by attacking his marriage to Cristin, or Christina, ferch Gronw ab Owain ab Edwin—which had already attracted criticism from Archbishop Theobald in the mid-1150s—on the grounds that she was the prince's cousin and thus related within the prohibited degrees of consanguinity. However, here too Owain defied his ecclesiastical opponents by refusing to separate from his wife and, although as a result of this he was excommunicated by Becket, the king of Gwynedd was nevertheless given an honourable burial in Bangor Cathedral. Gerald of Wales reports how he and Archbishop Baldwin ordered the body to be exhumed and buried in unconsecrated ground on their visit to Bangor while preaching the crusade in Wales in 1188, but it is extremely doubtful whether their instructions were heeded.

It seems that Owain had married Cristin by *c.*1140, for her son Dafydd was old enough to fight Henry II in 1157. Owain and Cristin had three sons and a daughter, but Owain had numerous other children with possibly as many as eight other partners, to judge by a late fifteenth-century genealogical tract. These included Iorwerth Drwyndwn, to whose mother, Gwladus ferch Llywarch ap Trahaearn, Owain appears to have been married before his marriage to Cristin, for Gerald of Wales believed Iorwerth to be Owain's only legitimate son. However, it is very likely that many of Owain's other children were the result of extramarital unions, including his eldest son, Hywel, said in the genealogical source referred to above to have been the son of an Irish woman, Ffynod (or Pyfog). Two other sons died in their father's lifetime, namely Rhun in 1146 and Llywelyn in 1165.

Assessment Owain himself died in November 1170, probably on the 23rd, and was described (retrospectively) by the author of the Welsh chronicle *Brut y tywysogyon* as 'a man of great renown and of infinite prudence and nobility, the bulwark and strength of Wales, unconquered from his youth' (*Brut: Hergest*, 151). Although Gerald of Wales condemned Owain for his incestuous marriage, he praised him for his justice, wisdom, and moderation as a ruler; Gerald also refers, as do some charters issued in favour of Haughmond Abbey, to the prince as Owain Magnus—'the Great' or, perhaps, 'the Elder'. (The appellation, like Owain Gwynedd, may have served to distinguish Owain from his younger contemporary and namesake, Owain ap Gruffudd ap Maredudd of Powys, known as Owain Cyfeiliog.) The most fulsome praises of Owain Gwynedd occur in the poems to him by the court poets Gwalchmai ap Meilyr—for whom the prince was 'the fairest of the kings of Britain and the most royal' (Gruffydd, 1/8, ll.59–60)—and Cynddelw Brydydd Mawr: both of these emphasized that Owain possessed in abundance the military virtues deemed essential to any successful Welsh ruler of this period, and proclaimed that he was an eminently worthy successor to earlier kings of Gwynedd such as Maelgwn and Rhodri Mawr. There can be no doubt that Owain considerably strengthened his kingdom, not only preserving its territorial integrity but expanding it to embrace all of north Wales from the Dee to the Dyfi, thereby paving the way for the achievements of his grandson, Llywelyn ab Iorwerth. Although details are sparse, he may well also have undertaken important territorial reorganization and commenced the policy of endowing favoured freemen with estates in order to secure their support. However, while he seems to have contained the ambitions of his sons during his lifetime, he failed to ensure a smooth unitary succession: shortly after his death his eldest son, *Hywel ab Owain Gwynedd, who may have been his chosen heir, was killed by his half-brothers Dafydd and Rhodri at the battle of Pentraeth in Anglesey. There followed almost three decades of struggle for the control of Gwynedd among Owain's sons and grandsons, a struggle finally resolved with the ascendancy of Llywelyn ab Iorwerth.

The prince's brother Cadwaladr ap Gruffudd (*d.* 1172), king in Wales, Owain's younger brother, is first mentioned in 1136. On Owain's accession in 1137 he was granted, or confirmed in possession of, Anglesey and Meirionydd, and the following year he received the northern half of Ceredigion after its conquest from the Normans. Until 1157 his relations with Owain were strained: on the one hand, he may well have nursed ambitions of supplanting his brother as king of Gwynedd, while, on the other, Owain's sons Hywel and Cynan sought to occupy their uncle's lands. In 1140 Cadwaladr joined with his brother in complaining to Bishop Bernard of St David's about the election of Meurig to the see of Bangor, but by the beginning of the following year Cadwaladr had allied himself, quite possibly to strengthen his hand against Owain, with Ranulf (II), earl of Chester (*d.* 1153), leading a contingent of Welsh troops alongside the latter at the battle of Lincoln against King Stephen on 2 February 1141. Cadwaladr greatly angered Owain in 1143 on account of his apparent complicity in the murder of Anarawd ap Gruffudd ap Rhys, to whom Owain had planned to give his daughter in marriage, and as a result he was driven out of northern Ceredigion by Hywel ab Owain and also, apparently, from Anglesey, until restored after threatening Owain with a military force hired in Ireland. However, Cadwaladr's position in Gwynedd remained precarious. In 1147 he was driven out of Meirionydd by his nephews, Hywel and Cynan; in 1149 he transferred his portion of Ceredigion to his son, Cadfan, and in the following year

Cadfan was seized, together with his land and castle of Llanrhystud, by Hywel ab Owain; and in 1152 he was expelled from his only remaining territory of Anglesey. Meanwhile the alliance with Ranulf continued, as is shown by charters of the late 1140s and early 1150s in which Cadwaladr witnesses as king of Wales (*rege Waliarum*) and king of north Wales (*rege Nortwaliarum*). These styles suggest that Ranulf encouraged his ally's regal ambitions in Gwynedd so as to make trouble for Owain, whose expansion into Tegeingl and Ystrad Alun by 1150 posed a threat to the earl's authority. By 1153 Cadwaladr had married Aliz de Clare, quite possibly to be identified with Adeliza, widow of Richard de *Clare (*d.* 1136), the former Norman lord of Ceredigion, and thus Ranulf's sister; the marriage may have been intended to strengthen Cadwaladr's claims to Ceredigion, control of which passed to the sons of Gruffudd ap Rhys of Deheubarth by 1153. This was not his first marriage, however, for his son Cadfan was already an adult by 1149; indeed, the late medieval genealogical tract referred to above states that Cadwaladr had children with four women in all. The support given by Cadwaladr to the Angevin cause in Stephen's reign stood him in good stead after his expulsion from Gwynedd in 1152, for by 1155 or 1156 he had been granted the estate of Ness in Shropshire by Henry II, who ensured that he was restored to his lands in north Wales following the campaign of 1157 (in which Cadwaladr fought on Henry's side). These Angevin connections probably explain why Cadwaladr patronized the Augustinian abbey of Haughmond in Shropshire, to which, as early as the 1140s, he granted the church of Nefyn in Llŷn, for Haughmond (situated only 10 miles away from Ness) received benefactions from Ranulf of Chester and other Angevin supporters. After 1157 Cadwaladr remained loyal to Owain Gwynedd for the rest of the latter's reign. Together with his nephews Hywel and Cynan he took part in Reginald fitz Henry's expedition against Rhys ap Gruffudd in 1159, he participated in the campaign against Henry II in 1165, and he fought alongside his brother in the campaigns which led to the occupation of Tegeingl in 1167. Famed, according to Gerald of Wales, for his outstanding generosity, Cadwaladr outlived Owain by about fifteen months, and was buried beside his brother in Bangor Cathedral in 1172. HUW PRYCE

Sources J. E. Lloyd, *A history of Wales from the earliest times to the Edwardian conquest*, 3rd edn, 2 vols. (1939); repr. (1988) • J. B. Smith, 'Owain Gwynedd', *Transactions of the Caernarvonshire Historical Society*, 32 (1971), 8–17 • H. Pryce, 'Owain Gwynedd and Louis VII: the Franco-Welsh diplomacy of the first prince of Wales', *Welsh History Review / Cylchgrawn Hanes Cymru*, 19 (1998–9), 1–28 • J. C. Davies, ed., *Episcopal acts and cognate documents relating to Welsh dioceses, 1066–1272*, 2 vols., Historical Society of the Church in Wales, 1, 3–4 (1946–8) • R. R. Davies, *Conquest, coexistence, and change: Wales, 1063–1415*, History of Wales, 2 (1987) • H. Pryce, 'The church of Trefeglwys and the end of the "Celtic" charter tradition in twelfth-century Wales', *Cambridge Medieval Celtic Studies*, 25 (1993), 15–54 • T. Jones, ed. and trans., *Brut y tywysogyon, or, The chronicle of the princes: Red Book of Hergest* (1955) • T. Jones, ed. and trans., *Brut y tywysogyon, or, The chronicle of the princes: Peniarth MS 20* (1952) • R. G. Gruffydd, ed., *Cyfres beirdd y tywysogion*, 7 vols. (1991–6), vols. 1, 2, 4 [the Poets of the Princes series] • A. W. Haddan and W. Stubbs, eds., *Councils and ecclesiastical documents relating to Great Britain and Ireland*, 1 (1869) • Giraldus Cambrensis, 'De invectionibus', ed. W. S. Davies, *Y Cymmrodor*, 30 (1920) • *The letters of John of Salisbury*, ed. and trans. H. E. Butler and W. J. Millor, rev. C. N. L. Brooke, 2 vols., OMT (1979–86) [Lat. orig. with parallel Eng. text] • *Gir. Camb. opera*, vol. 6 • *The correspondence of Thomas Becket*, ed. and trans. A. J. Duggan, 2 vols., OMT (2000)

Owain, Gutun [Gruffudd ap Huw ab Owain] (*fl. c.*1451–1498), poet, was the son of Huw ab Owain, of gentry stock. His mother's name is unknown, but some sources claim that she was a sister of Siôn ap Rhisiart, abbot of Valle Crucis. Gutun was a native of the then Welsh-speaking north Shropshire borderland, being associated with the adjoining parishes of Llandudlyst (Dudleston) and Llanfarthin (St Martin's), where he held land in the township of Ifton.

Gutun Owain's bardic teacher was the renowned Dafydd ab Edmwnd from the neighbouring parish of Hanmer in Maelor Saesneg, winner of the chair awarded to the premier poet at the Carmarthen eisteddfod held under the patronage of Gruffudd ap Nicolas, *c.*1451. Gutun attended the eisteddfod as a young bardic pupil in the company of his teacher. As well as competitions for bards and musicians, metrical practices were discussed at Carmarthen, and Dafydd ab Edmwnd imposed his authority in introducing significant changes relating to the twenty-four bardic metres and the metrical ornamentation of *cynghanedd*. It was Gutun Owain's copies of the bardic grammar, a handbook used in bardic schools, which first incorporated these changes and provided the exemplar for later versions of that work. On the death of Dafydd ab Edmwnd some four decades later, Gutun composed a poignant elegy for his old teacher, celebrating his renown as a poet and recalling his triumph at Carmarthen.

Gutun Owain was one of the ablest practitioners of Welsh poetry during the late fifteenth century. More than sixty poems by him are extant, consisting in the main of eulogies and elegies to noble patrons, poems soliciting gifts, and love poems. A high proportion of his surviving work is addressed to patrons within a 15 mile radius of his home, in Maelor Gymraeg (Bromfield), Maelor Saesneg, Chirkland, and the commote of Iâl, though a few poems show that he occasionally sought patronage further afield in north Wales. His two most important patrons, both abbots of the Cistercian abbey of Valle Crucis near Llangollen, were his probable kinsman Siôn ap Rhisiart (abbot until *c.*1480) and his successor Dafydd ab Ieuan ab Iorwerth (*c.*1480–1503). Gutun's poems addressed to the two abbots vividly evoke their generous provision of wine and food on feast days, extol their restoration of the once neglected monastic buildings, and express his aesthetic appreciation of religious worship at the abbey. The poet also frequented the abbey of Basingwerk near Holywell, composing a poem in praise of Abbot Thomas Pennant and writing a portion of the Black Book of Basingwerk (NL Wales, MS 7006D).

Gutun's eulogies to lay patrons evoke the interests and concerns of the minor nobility of late fifteenth-century Wales, their pride in their ancestry, their joy in feasting, their martial prowess, and their enlightened support of the native culture. His elegies, though conventional to a large degree, are well wrought and quietly effective. Less original and robust than that of his contemporary Guto'r Glyn (for whom he composed an elegy), Gutun's muse was refined, fastidious, and meditative. His obvious delight in mellifluence and musicality, a characteristic particularly apparent in his *awdlau* (odes), may reflect the influence of his teacher Dafydd ab Edmwnd. As a poet he excels in these majestic, metrically complex *awdlau* and in his poems of solicitation on behalf of patrons, remarkable for their imaginative and vivid descriptions of gifts such as horses, hounds, and shields. In examples of the latter, barking hounds feature as 'harmonious, heavenly musicians' and as 'bells of Durham cathedral', and the rivet heads on a buckler are described as 'powdered like the stars on the Milky Way'.

Gutun Owain was familiar with all branches of traditional bardic learning. An expert genealogist, following the accession of Henry Tudor he assisted the commission appointed by the king—which included Abbot Dafydd ab Ieuan ab Iorwerth—to enquire into the Tudors' descent 'from the ancient British kings'. Sixteenth-century genealogists frequently cited his manuscripts as sources. His activity as a scribe is exemplified in his nine surviving autograph manuscripts. They contain copies of chronicles and bruts (the most important being his texts of *Brut Tysilio* and *Brenhinedd y Saesson*, with a continuation to 1461, in the Black Book of Basingwerk), a bardic grammar, genealogies, a heraldic treatise, religious texts (including the Welsh life of St Martin), a 'Description of the island of Britain' (a translation of the first book of Ranulf Higden's *Polychronicon*), and miscellaneous lore (some of it of a pseudo-scientific nature).

Gutun Owain's latest datable surviving poem was composed in 1498. He may not have lived to witness the elevation of his patron, Abbot Dafydd ab Ieuan ab Iorwerth, to the see of St Asaph in 1500. According to traditional manuscript lists of the burial places of Welsh poets he was buried at St Martin's. GRUFFYDD ALED WILLIAMS

Sources E. Bachellery, *L'oeuvre poétique de Gutun Owain*, 2 vols. (1950–51) • J. E. C. Williams, 'Gutun Owain', *A guide to Welsh literature*, ed. A. O. H. Jarman and G. R. Hughes, 2: *1282–c.1550* (1979), 262–7 • T. Roberts, 'Llawysgrifau Gutun Owain, a thymor ei oes', *BBCS*, 15 (1952–4), 99–109 • J. Y. W. Lloyd, *The history of the princes, the lords marcher, and the ancient nobility of Powys Fadog*, 6 vols. (1881–7) • G. J. Williams, 'Gramadeg Gutun Owain', *BBCS*, 4 (1927–9), 207–21 • G. J. Williams and E. J. Jones, eds., *Gramadegau'r penceirddiaid* (1934) • T. Jones, ed. and trans., *Brenhinedd y Saesson, or, The kings of the Saxons* (1971) [another version of *Brut y tywysogyon*] • G. J. Williams, 'Eisteddfod Caerfyrddin', *Y Llenor*, 5 (1926), 94–102 • *Report on manuscripts in the Welsh language*, 2 vols. in 7, HMC, 48 (1898–1910) • NL Wales, Mostyn MS 110

Archives Bodl. Oxf., Jesus College MSS • JRL, John Rylands Welsh MSS • NL Wales, Peniarth, Mostyn, Llanstephan, and NLW MSS • NL Wales, MS 7006D

Owen. *See also* Owain.

Owen of Wales [Owain ap Thomas ap Rhodri] (*d.* **1378**), mercenary, was the last direct heir of the dynasty of Gwynedd. He was a prominent figure in the Hundred Years' War and became a symbol of continued Welsh resistance to English rule.

Origins and early career Owen was the son of Thomas ap Rhodri ap Gruffudd (Sir Thomas Retherik; *d.* 1363) and his wife, Cecilia. Thomas's father Rhodri was the youngest son of Gruffudd ap Llywelyn ab Iorwerth (*d.* 1244) and therefore the brother of Llywelyn ap Gruffudd, prince of Wales. In 1272 Rhodri had quitclaimed all his hereditary right to lands in north Wales and elsewhere to Llywelyn for 1000 marks, but the money was never paid in full. Rhodri served in Edward I's army in the Welsh wars of 1276–7 and 1282 and acquired lands in Cheshire, Gloucestershire, and Surrey; he was dead by 1315. When Thomas died in 1363 Owen was out of the country; he returned two years later to claim his inheritance, but he appears to have gone abroad again in 1366 and after the renewal of Anglo-French hostilities in 1369 he went over to the French side and all his lands were declared forfeit.

Nothing is known of Owen's career before 1365, nor is it known why he joined the French. It is likely that he became aware of his descent and his claims at a time of increasing tension and restlessness in Wales; it may be significant that both he and his father used the arms of the princes of Gwynedd on their seals. According to Froissart he had in his youth been in the service of the French crown, had fought on the French side at Poitiers in 1356, and after the treaty of Brétigny in 1360 had served in Lombardy, but there is no evidence to confirm this. Froissart also describes him as the son of a prince of Wales put to death by Edward III, which indicates that the French were aware that he had some kind of dynastic claim. By 1369 Charles V of France was certainly ready to support his bid to recover his patrimony as a means of carrying the war to British soil. A fleet sailed from Harfleur under Owen's command just before Christmas, only to be driven back by winter storms in the English Channel; the authorities in Wales had been alerted and defensive preparations ordered.

Welsh aspirations and French support In 1370 Owen was serving under Bertrand du Guesclin during Sir Robert Knolles's *chevauchée* in Maine and Anjou and was briefly in charge of the castle of Saumur on the Loire; the following summer he and his company were employed by the town of Metz in Lorraine and at the end of 1371 he was in northern Burgundy. But Charles V was still interested in a landing in Wales and on 10 May 1372 Owen issued a proclamation in which he declared his claim to the country 'which … is and should be mine by right' (Paris, Archives Nationales, JJ[c]27, fol. 55), and in which he acknowledged the support he had had from the French in men, ships, and money. The second invasion fleet, probably with between 600 and 800 men, sailed from Harfleur at the beginning of June. On the way it attacked Guernsey where the garrison, apparently warned that Owen was on the way, had been reinforced. The raid, remembered in island tradition as 'la descente des Aragousais', was commemorated in a ballad; most of the content is entirely unhistorical but it and

Froissart agree that the attack was a failure and it is difficult to understand why, when the expedition had a clear objective, the attack on Guernsey should have been undertaken at all. In fact Owen never reached Wales; while in Guernsey he appears to have been ordered to abandon the venture and to proceed to Castile to seek ships to blockade La Rochelle. The order may have been precipitated by the news that a large English fleet under the command of John Hastings, earl of Pembroke (*d.* 1375), had sailed from Southampton with money and reinforcements for the army in Guyenne. By the time Owen reached Santander the fleet had been destroyed by the Castilians off La Rochelle and it was then, according to Froissart, that Pembroke, brought ashore in chains, was challenged by him. He now sought Castilian assistance for a further expedition to Wales, but none was forthcoming.

Campaigns in France and a Swiss fiasco Owen now set out for La Rochelle with a combined Franco-Castilian fleet. In late August he defeated the Anglo-Gascon force which had just raised the French siege of Soubise at the mouth of the Charente, taking prisoner one of the leading Gascon captains, the Captal de Buch (*d.* 1377), and the seneschal of Poitou, Sir Thomas Percy (*d.* 1403); Percy was captured by a Welsh chaplain from Owen's company, Hywel Flint. Soubise surrendered and this was followed on 8 September 1372 by the fall of La Rochelle.

Charles V was planning a further expedition to Wales in 1373, this time with Castilian assistance, but nothing came of it because of the projected invasion of Brittany by John of Gaunt, duke of Lancaster, and his great *chevauchée* through France. For the greater part of the year Owen was serving in Poitou and Saintonge as town after town fell to the French; for a time he was captain of the castle of Broue in Saintonge and was also captain of Soubise, being retained with his company in the service of the king. He may subsequently have campaigned in northern France and according to one source he was involved in the siege of St Sauveur-le-Vicomte in the Cotentin, which fell on 3 July 1375.

Two days earlier a year's truce had been agreed at Bruges, but Owen and his company were not unemployed for long; on 14 October he was recruited by Enguerrand (VII) de Coucy (*d.* 1397) to join his invasion of Austria, which Coucy claimed through his mother; the contract, in which he agreed to provide 400 men, survives in the Swiss State Archives. The Austrian expedition was a complete fiasco; the army had to pass through Switzerland and it met fierce Swiss resistance. On 27 December 1375 Owen and his men were attacked by the men of Bern at Fraubrunnen to the north of the city and they suffered a crushing defeat; even Owen's contract with Coucy was left behind in the rout. The Bernese were so proud of their victory over a distinguished mercenary captain that a ballad, the 'Bear Song', was composed to commemorate it.

Assassination In 1376 Owen was back in the king of France's service and for the next two years he was fighting in the south-west of France. In 1378 the duke of Anjou ordered him to take a force of 500 men and besiege Mortagne on the Gironde estuary. During the siege a squire called John Lamb, who claimed to be a Welshman, appeared on the scene and Owen accepted him into his service. But Lamb was an English agent and one morning, when Owen had risen early and was surveying the castle, he killed him with a dagger. For this Lamb was subsequently paid the sum of £20. Owen was buried in the church of St Léger near Mortagne, but no trace remains of his tomb; the church was demolished in 1884. There is no record of his having married or had children, although the Guernsey ballad does refer to a wife called Eleanor whom he had supposedly married in Maine; this part of the ballad, however, bears little relation to historical fact.

Welsh support for Owen's claims and the reputation of Owain Lawgoch Owen of Wales was a great deal more than an exiled pretender pursuing a forlorn hope. After he joined the French he commanded a free company, most of the members of which were Welshmen who had defected to him from the English forces. When his men were mustered at Limoges on 8 August 1376 at least 85 of the 100 members of the company were Welsh, which shows that there were Welsh soldiers in France who knew who he was and what he represented. He also had supporters in Wales; in 1370 an Anglesey man was accused of being a supporter of Owain Lawgoch, 'traitor and enemy of the lord prince' (*Record of Caernarvon*, 133), and in 1372 and 1374 Rhys ap Roppert, one of the leading men in Flintshire, a former sheriff of the county and a member of the leading lineage in north Wales, was accused of sending him money and receiving treasonable letters from him. Two of Rhys's sons were in French service, one of them probably being Owen's lieutenant Ieuan Wyn, known as the Poursuivant d'Amour, who inherited his company on his death. There are other references in the Flintshire judicial records to local men who were in France with Owen. Two poems to him also survive, one of them by one of the leading poets of the time, Gruffydd ap Maredudd ap Dafydd.

The second half of the fourteenth century in Wales was a time of restlessness and discontent when the leaders of the native community, who felt that they were no longer treated with due respect, were becoming increasingly disillusioned with the house of Plantagenet. In these circumstances the presence in France of the rightful heir of the house of Gwynedd who was also a distinguished soldier could not but be significant, although there is no evidence that Owen ever visited Wales or was even able to speak the language. The authorities were well aware of the attraction he exerted and a plan for a Franco-Castilian invasion of England in 1377, involving a renegade English knight, Sir John Minsterworth, may have led to the decision to have him eliminated.

Owen's supporters in Wales were able to draw on a long tradition of prophetic poetry which looked forward to the coming of a new leader who would drive out the English and restore the ancient glory of the Britons. Much of this poetry is obscure and allusive, but some of it undoubtedly refers to him. His charisma did not die with him; there grew up a body of stories about a great hero, Owain Lawgoch, asleep in a cave awaiting the call to rise and redeem his people, but it was not until the end of the nineteenth century that this Owain was identified conclusively as Owain ap Thomas ap Rhodri, although the Flintshire sources already mentioned do actually describe him by both names. The epithet attached to his name is not easily explained. The term *llawgoch* ('red hand') was normally applied to a murderer, but it could also have referred to a birthmark or to a scar. Several fifteenth-century poets refer to him as Owain Frych (Owain the Freckled), which may suggest that his nickname derived from the fact that his hand was heavily freckled. The Guernsey ballad describes his right hand as having been severed by a blow from a halberd during the raid of 1372, but this is probably an onomastic reference; he was certainly known as Owain Lawgoch in 1370.

There can be no doubt that Owen of Wales was perceived as a serious threat to English rule in Wales. In life an eminent captain, he was to many in Wales the Mab Darogan or 'Son of Prophecy'; after his death he joined the ranks of the 'sleeping heroes', those charismatic leaders whose death it was hard to accept. The charisma existed in France as well; in the seventeenth century the family of de Galle in Dauphiné claimed incorrectly to be descended from him. But Owen of Wales or Owain ap Thomas ap Rhodri was a significant figure in the context of Welsh political attitudes in the late fourteenth century and his activities and the support they elicited helped to pave the way for the revolt of Owain Glyn Dŵr. A. D. CARR

Sources A. D. Carr, *Owen of Wales: the end of the house of Gwynedd* (1991) • E. Owen, 'Owain Lawgoch / Yeuain de Galles: some facts and suggestions', *Transactions of the Honourable Society of Cymmrodorion* (1899–1900), 6–105 • Archives Nationales, Paris, JJ[c]27, fol. 55
Archives Archives Nationales, Paris, JJ[c]27, fol. 55
Likenesses miniature (the siege of Mortagne and the death of Owain), BL, fifteenth century French manuscript of Jean de Warrin's 'Chronique d'Angleterre', Royal MS 14 E 4, fol. 23*a*

Owen the Bald (*d.* 1018). *See under* Donald (*d.* 975).

Owen, Alexander (1851–1920), brass-band trainer, was born in Swinton, near Manchester, in 1851. Details of his childhood, some of which was probably spent in an orphanage, and of his early musical training, are obscure. He was initially apprenticed as a cabinet-maker, and about 1868 he moved to Stalybridge, where he established a tobacconist's business. In August 1868 he joined the Stalybridge Old Band as soprano cornet, and soon became conductor, though in 1871 he set up the rival Stalybridge Borough Band. His outstanding ability as a cornetist, a talent undiminished by his experiencing the brass player's nightmare of losing his front teeth in an accident, led in 1875 to his recruitment to the Yorkshire-based Meltham Mills Band, then one of England's premier bands. In 1877 he began his remarkably successful career as a band trainer, beginning with the Boarshurst Band, and at about the same time he became licensee of the Bath Hotel, Stalybridge. He eventually moved to Manchester in 1896, from which point he appears to have derived his income almost solely from band work.

Although Owen was by no means the first brass-band trainer and arranger, his challenging arrangements and rigorous approach to teaching, paralleled by the work of John Gladney (1839–1911) and Edwin Swift (1843–1904), did much to raise the technical standard of the British brass band. He trained (and often worked as soloist with) many leading bands of the period. At one stage in the 1890s he taught some twenty-five bands, and in 1898 he conducted ten separate bands at the Belle Vue contest. However, he was most closely associated with Besses o' th' Barn Band, which he trained from February 1884 until his death. Under Owen, the band enjoyed great success in contests, often using his arrangements of operatic and orchestral works. Particularly successful was his *Reminiscences of Rossini* (1882), with which Besses took fourteen first prizes from nineteen contests entered between 1884 and 1886. Among Owen's other arrangements, which were noted for placing heavy technical and physical demands upon the players, were extracts from Berlioz's *The Damnation of Faust* and a thirty-five minute piece entitled *Wagner's Works*. By the early 1900s Besses was effectively a professional musical organization and abandoned the supposedly amateur contesting arena from 1903 to 1918 to concentrate on concert work. With a repertory at any one time of more than a hundred pieces, many of them arranged or composed by Owen, the band undertook a number of lengthy tours, including one of seventeen months' duration in North America, Honolulu, Fiji, New Zealand, and Australia in 1906–7, commemorated by Owen in his popular march *Around the World*.

Owen was an exacting taskmaster: oral tradition claims that he locked bands in the bandroom during rehearsals. Although in later years he had lost some of his former power, his last rehearsal with Besses days before his death involved four hours' work on his arrangement of *Tristan und Isolde*. He could also be hard on players tutored by rival trainers, and the young Harry Mortimer found himself near to tears after his first session with Owen. He was, however, universally respected in the band world and, after his death at Chorlton upon Medlock from a stroke on 29 July 1920, a memorial fund was established, leading from 1922 to the annual awarding of the prestigious Alexander Owen Memorial Scholarship, providing two years' expert tuition to the recipient. Although Owen's reputation was based almost exclusively on his band work, and he was little known outside the band movement (revealing testimony to its social status), he possessed broad musical interests, also conducting a Stalybridge choral group and playing with the Manchester Saxophone Quartette. He served as a Conservative member on Stalybridge council from 1887 to 1897. He was married (although nothing is known of his wife), and had at least one son. He was buried at Stretford on 4 August 1920. DAVE RUSSELL

Sources *British Bandsman* (7 Aug 1920) • *Wright & Round's Brass Band News* (Sept 1920) • *Ashton-under-Lyne Herald* (7 Aug 1920) • J. N. Hampson, *Origin, history, and achievements of the Besses o' th' Barn Band* [n.d., c.1893] • A. R. Taylor, *Labour and love: an oral history of the brass band movement* (1983) • Alex Owen 60th anniversary, 1980, Chandos BBT 1009 [Besses o' th' Barn Band, sleevenotes] • d. cert.

Wealth at death £18,319 16*s.* 5*d.*: probate, 27 Oct 1920, *CGPLA Eng. & Wales*

Owen [*née* Wilkes], **Alice** (**1547–1613**), philanthropist, was the third child of Thomas Wilkes, a rich landowner of Islington. Nothing is known of her childhood apart from the story of her narrow escape from death on the archery fields of Islington; this first appeared in Stow's *Survey of London* and was subsequently embellished several times. She was playing with some other children when a stray arrow pierced her hat, providentially missing her head. Stow says that the almshouses and the school which she later founded were a thank-offering for her survival. In 1570 Alice Wilkes married Henry Robinson (*d.* 1585), a member of the Brewers' Company, with whom she had six sons and five daughters. Her second husband was William Elkin (1523–1593), an alderman of the City of London, with whom she had one daughter who was baptized in 1587. Thomas *Owen (*d.* 1598), a judge of the court of common pleas, became her third husband in 1594 or 1595. Alice Owen was left sizeable sums of money in her husbands' wills.

Stow lists benefactions that Alice Owen made in her lifetime to a number of institutions, including £200 to Oxford University (in fact £100) and £60 to Christ's Hospital. The latter was recorded in 1598. However, the most significant of her charitable activities were focused on the foundation of her almshouses for ten poor women, and her free school for thirty boys from Islington and Clerkenwell. She opened discussions with the governors of Christ's Hospital in February 1607 on her proposals, but her plans changed. Having purchased 11 acres of ground where her accident took place (known as Hermitage Fields) and property in Charterhouse Closes in 1609, she reached an agreement with the Brewers' Company, which became trustees for the almshouses, using the income from the property to fund expenses. In 1610 Alice obtained a royal patent to erect a chapel and a house for a master to 'read to the widows and teach the sons and daughters of the poor' (Dare, 19), and permission to buy lands to support this foundation.

Alice Owen drew up detailed rules for the conduct of both the school and the almshouses in 1613. The schoolmaster was to be single, of good conduct, and able to teach grammar, writing, and arithmetic to prepare his pupils for apprenticeships or other honest employment. He was to be paid £5 quarterly, live rent free, and be supplied with fuel for heating, an arrangement which compares favourably with other foundations of the period. The master also had responsibilities in the almshouses where he had to read prayers to the almswomen twice a day and take any disciplinary measures necessary. The widows admitted to the almshouses were to be given money, seacoal, a new gown every two years, and additional small benefits. Strict rules of conduct had to be adhered to, and if an almswoman married she had to leave.

At the time of Alice Owen's death the purchase of the property to fund the school had not yet been made and it was left to her executor, her son-in-law Robert Rich, to buy 40 acres at Orsett in Essex in 1617. The account books of the foundation for the first half of the seventeenth century show that the balance was often negative, which gave rise to a rather tart comment in one Brewers' Company file that the company had to find the difference. This was only partly due to an underestimate on Alice Owen's part: an allowance of £1 10*s.* for an annual inspection dinner for the Brewers' Company was by the 1630s being overspent regularly by as much as £10 while the London rents remained fixed.

In addition to her charitable bequests Alice Owen's will made generous provision for her daughters, godchildren, and grandchildren. Her servants were given money and her 'worser' clothes. There were also new benefactions including £8 to poor prisoners, £20 for a stock of coals and wood for the poor of the parish of St Michael Bassishaw, and £60 for sixty poor women. She died on 26 November 1613 and was buried in St Mary's, Islington, where a magnificent tomb was erected with an effigy of her reading a book, with smaller figures of her children and grandchildren in relief. The church was pulled down in 1742 and her body reinterred in the crypt. It was removed to Finchley cemetery in 1903 when further work was undertaken on the church. After its uncertain financial start Alice Owen's foundation became profitable. A substantial rebuilding of both the school and the almshouses was carried out in 1841 on a new site in Owen Street, Islington. This was rapidly followed by a review of the school in 1865 under the Taunton commission which investigated endowed grammar schools. A scheme was finally approved in 1878 which allowed for the demolition of the almshouses and their replacement by pensions for the occupants, the construction of a new boys' school, and the opening of a school for girls. Between 1971 and 1976 the move to the present site in Potters Bar was completed, the two schools having amalgamated as Dame Alice Owen's School in 1973. CAROLINE M. K. BOWDEN

Sources GL, Brewers' Company MSS, 5480A, 6817, 18409, 5462 • R. Dare, *A history of Owen's School, 1613–1976* (1980) • J. Stow, *A survay of London*, ed. A. M. [A. Munday], rev. edn (1618); repr. (1633) • J. Stow, *The survey of London*, ed. A. M. [A. Munday] and others, rev. edn (1633) • GL, Christ's Hospital MSS, 12806; 12819, vols. 1–2; 12812, vol. 1

Archives GL, Brewers' Company deposits

Likenesses C. Cripps, oils (after contemporary portrait), Worshipful Company of Brewers, London, The Dame Alice Foundation • death mask, Dame Alice Owen's School, Hertfordshire, Potters Bar • portrait (aged sixty-three), Dame Alice Owen's School, Hertfordshire, Potters Bar • statue from tomb, Dame Alice Owen's School, Hertfordshire, Potters Bar

Owen, Aneurin (**1792–1851**), historian, was born in London on 23 July 1792, the eldest child and only son of William Owen (1759–1835) [*see* Pughe, William Owen] and his wife, Sarah Elizabeth Harper (1771–1816). In 1806 his father took the additional name of Pughe on inheriting some property at Nantglyn, Denbighshire, to which the family moved about 1800 from London. Around 1807

Owen briefly attended Friars School, Bangor, but he was mainly educated by his father, whose own interests in Welsh history and literature were reflected in the lessons he gave his son. Owen also spent some time on the Harwood estate in Norfolk, learning estate management and agriculture.

Aneurin Owen settled at Tan-y-gyrt, near Nantglyn, and in 1820 married Jane Lloyd of Nantglyn, daughter of William Lloyd, in Liverpool. His activities were mainly literary until the passing of the Tithe Commutation Act in 1836, when he was appointed one of the assistant tithe commissioners for England and Wales. Subsequently he was made an assistant poor-law commissioner, but he resigned when the heavy duties of this post damaged his health. When the work of tithe commutation grew less urgent, he was appointed, under the Enclosures Act of 1845, a commissioner for the enclosure of commonable lands.

When the government resolved in 1822 to publish a uniform edition of ancient British historians, the Welsh part of the work was entrusted to John Humphreys Parry. On Parry's death in 1825 his duties, following some active lobbying by William Owen Pughe, who was friendly with Henry Petrie, were transferred to Owen, who thus became the adviser of the record office upon all Welsh matters. His work fell into two parts: the publication of the ancient Welsh laws and the gathering of material for an edition of the chronicle of the princes. The two tasks were carried on concurrently during the period 1830–40; libraries and private collections in Wales and in England were visited, manuscripts copied, and collations made, and in 1841 the Record edition of the laws appeared in two forms, a large folio and two quarto volumes under the title *Ancient Laws and Institutes of Wales*. It was remarkable not only for the care and accuracy with which the manuscripts were reproduced and the texts translated, but also for establishing a distinction between the three versions (which Owen termed Venedotian, Dimetian, and Gwentian) of native Welsh law. His nomenclature has been revised but the threefold categorization of versions is still valid. The edition of the chronicle of the princes (*Brut y tywysogion*, a continuation of Geoffrey of Monmouth's *Historia regum Britanniae* but, unlike it, based on contemporary evidence) did not appear in Owen's lifetime. A small section of the chronicle which took the narrative up to 1066 was edited by him for the *Monumenta historica Britannica* (1848), but the bulk of his material remained unpublished, and was handed over to the Record Office on his death in 1851. A complaint appeared in *Archaeologia Cambrensis* in 1859 that Owen's papers were carelessly kept, and access to them had been granted to readers who were using them without acknowledgement; and in 1860, when the Rolls Series edition of *Brut y tywysogion* appeared, under the editorship of the Revd John Williams ab Ithel, the reviewer in *Archaeologia Cambrensis* (3rd ser., 7, 1861, 93–103) asserted that the text, the translation, and all that was valuable in the preface were the work of Owen, who was nevertheless unmentioned in the book. In 1863 Owen's transcript and translation of the so-called *Gwentian brut* (a spurious version of the chronicle), with the introduction he had prepared for the *Monumenta* and a letter on the Welsh chronicles to Henry Petrie, were printed as an extra volume by the Cambrian Archaeological Association.

Owen was an accurate and well-informed palaeographer. His *Catalogue of Welsh Manuscripts, etc., in North Wales*, which was awarded the prize at the Cymmrodorion eisteddfod at Welshpool in 1824, was published in the *Transactions of the Honourable Society of Cymmrodorion* in 1843. Though not fluent in Welsh until early adulthood, Owen became one of the best Welsh scholars of his day and an intelligent historical critic, whose work was compared by a contemporary critic with that of Edward Lhwyd. Though Owen proved himself a scholar in his own right with none of his father's eccentricities, there is little doubt that he owed much not only to his father's support and contacts with gentry, scholars, and civil servants in London, Oxford, and Wales, but also to his practical assistance in transcribing, interpreting, and translating medieval Welsh texts and in the planning of *Ancient Laws*. Without William Owen Pughe's tuition and collaboration from about 1826 it is unlikely that Aneurin Owen could have accomplished so much.

Owen took a keen interest in the Welsh cultural movements of his day and particularly in the eisteddfod; he was one of a committee of five appointed at the Abergavenny eisteddfod of 1838 to consider the reform of Welsh orthography, and in 1832 won a silver medal at the Beaumaris eisteddfod for the best Welsh essay on 'Agriculture'. The essay was published in the *Transactions* of the eisteddfod in 1839 and also in a separate volume. Owen died on 17 July 1851 at Tros-y-parc, near Denbigh.

J. E. Lloyd, *rev.* Brynley F. Roberts

Sources G. Carr, *William Owen Pughe* (1983) · *Archaeologia Cambrensis*, 3rd ser., 4 (1858), 208–12 [correspondence] · *Archaeologia Cambrensis*, 3rd ser., 6 (1860), 184–6 [correspondence] · review, *Archaeologia Cambrensis*, 3rd ser., 7 (1861), 93–103 · NL Wales, MS 13251 · *Annual Register* (1851) · *Seren Gomer* (June 1820)

Archives NL Wales, corresp. with Walter Davies · NL Wales, corresp. with A. J. Johnes · NL Wales, corresp. with Angharad Llwyd · NL Wales, corresp. with Iolo Morganwg · NL Wales, corresp. with William Owen Pughe

Likenesses W. O. Pughe, watercolour sketch (aged two), NL Wales · painting, priv. coll.; photograph, NL Wales · photograph (after drawing by W. O. Pughe), NL Wales

Owen, Cadwallader (*c.*1562–1617). *See under* Owen, Richard (1606–1683).

Owen, Charles (*d.* 1746), Presbyterian minister and nonconformist tutor, was the third son of John Owen, of Bryn, Aber-nant parish, Carmarthenshire, and younger brother of James *Owen (1654–1706). His parents were 'inviolably firm' to the Church of England (C. Owen, 2), but the nine children who reached adulthood all became nonconformists and the three sons nonconformist ministers. Owen was educated for the nonconformist ministry at the academy at Bishop's Hall, Bethnal Green, London, conducted by Thomas Brand with the assistance of John Ker. In October 1690 he was one of eleven students who sent an adulatory address in Latin to Richard Baxter, saluting him as a promoter and pattern of piety. He was supported by a grant of £20 from the Presbyterian Fund in 1691, probably for his last year of study. He was recorded about this time in the Common Fund Survey as willing to settle in Denbighshire if a maintenance might be had. He assisted his brother at Wrexham, who gave oversight to the Presbyterian congregation there. As a result he received a grant of £6 a year in 1695 and 1696 from the Presbyterian Fund. In August 1696 the Cheshire classis approved of his preaching at Warrington on trial and the congregation unanimously chose him in succession to Peter Aspinwall, who had died in June 1696. He prepared students for the ministry, though because the numbers were small and he was not supported by the Presbyterian Fund, he may have taught them privately. He quit teaching temporarily as a result of the Schism Act in 1714. Job Orton was a student for a year in 1733, but the names of only a handful of other students are known.

Owen was a vigorous though controversial defender of dissent and of the Hanoverian succession. He published anonymously a violent funeral sermon on the death of Queen Anne, *Ahabs Evil* (1714). His *Plain Dealing, or, Separation without Schism* (1715; 12th edn, 1727), in which he attacked the high-church zealots and defended dissenters and the 'moderate and genuine sons of the Church of England' (C. Owen, *Plain Dealing*, 2nd edn, 1715, 3), was even more notorious. He was answered by *Plain Dealing Proved to be Plain Lying* (1715), and replied in turn with a *Vindication of Plain Dealing, from the Base and Malicious Aspersions of Two Country Curates* (1716), a particularly rancorous work. The work was presented to the grand jury as reflecting scandalously on the Church of England and its clergy and a bill found against him. He obtained a *nolle prosequi* but suffered heavy costs. The Presbyterian Fund made him a special grant of £25 in January 1716.

Owen's most important works were in defence of dissent. In his *Donatus redivius* (1714), reprinted in 1716 as *Rebaptization Condemned*, he attacked the Church of England's practice of rebaptizing dissenters who conformed, provoking several replies. His *Amazon Disarm'd* (1714) was in answer to Jane Chorlton's reply to *Donatus redivius*. He also had an active part in the major high-church controversy over the validity of Presbyterian ordination, publishing first *Validity of the Dissenting Ministry* (1716), edited from the works of his brother, and then his own *The Dissenting Ministry Still Valid in Answer to some Scurrilous Reflections* (1717). His *Plain Reasons* (1715; 23rd edn, 1736) defended dissenters from the charge of schism. In connection with the campaign for the repeal of the Test and Corporation Acts he published *Dissenters Claim of Right to a Capacity for Civil Offices* (1717). His *Jure Divino Woe* (1717) attacked the Jacobite rebels and *Alarm to the Protestant Princes and People* (1728) condemned the cruel behaviour of continental Catholics. In contrast, *Danger of Church and State from Foreigners* (1750) was an open-minded plea to fellow Britons to recognize the contribution of foreigners. He also wrote a number of devotional works—*Hymns Sacred to the Lord's Table* (1712), *The Wonders of Redeeming Love* (1723), a work on redemption, and *Religious Gratitude* (1731), all of which disclose a warm evangelicalism. He attacked the charismatic excesses of the French prophets and their English followers in *Scene of Delusions Opened* (1712). His remarkable *Essay on Serpents* (1742), dedicated to Sir Hans Sloane, reveals an extraordinary depth of knowledge and reading. He received a DD from Edinburgh University with Isaac Watts in 1728. He published a number of funeral sermons, including one for Gilbert Burnet, bishop of Salisbury, whom he compared with Samuel.

Owen maintained a successful and popular ministry at Warrington for nearly fifty years. A meeting-house was built in 1703 which was replaced by a new building the year he died. According to the Evans List (1715–17) Owen had the largest and most important congregation in that part of Lancashire with 713 hearers and 82 county voters. He was a member of both the Cheshire and the Warrington classes, and acted as moderator for both on many occasions. He was married but nothing about his wife is known. He died in Warrington on 17 February 1746 and was buried in his meeting-house in Cairo Street, Warrington. His nephew, Josiah Owen, preached his funeral sermon. His son John (*d.* 1775) was nonconformist minister at Wharton, Lancashire. DAVID L. WYKES

Sources A. Gordon, ed., *Freedom after ejection: a review (1690–1692) of presbyterian and congregational nonconformity in England and Wales* (1917), 4, 90, 323 • Presbyterian Fund board minutes, vol. 2, 5 Feb 1695–4 June 1722, DWL, MS OD68, fols. 9, 16, 25, 35, 273, 296, 324 • W. A. Shaw, ed., 'Minutes of the United Brethren, 1693–1700', *Minutes of the Manchester presbyterian classis*, 3, Chetham Society, new ser., 24 (1891), 349–65, esp. 358 ff. • A. Gordon, ed., *Cheshire classis: minutes, 1691–1745* (1919), 196 • A. Mountfield, *Early Warrington nonconformity* (1923) • G. E. Evans, *Record of the provincial assembly of Lancashire and Cheshire* (1896), 182 • J. Owen, *The Christian's conflict and crown: a sermon preach'd at Warrington, February 23: on occasion of the death of the late Reverend and learned Charles Owen, D.D.* [1746] • [C. Owen], *Some account of the life and writings of the late pious and learned Mr James Owen* (1709) • biographical account of Charles Owen, DWL, Walter Wilson MS, A7, fols. 24–6 • H. McLachlan, *English education under the Test Acts: being the history of the nonconformist academies, 1662–1820* (1931), 15, 81–2, 90, 148 • G. F. Nuttall, '"Queen Anne's dead!" An unusual funeral sermon', *Transactions of the Congregational Historical Society*, 20 (1965–70), 200–01 • *The Church of England vindicated: and separation from her communion shew'd to be causless and schismatical: in answer to Mr Owen's Plain dealing and its vindication* (1716), v–vi • J. Evans, 'List of dissenting congregations and ministers in England and Wales, 1715–1729', DWL, MS 38.4, fol. 59 • address from the divinity students at Bethnal Green, DWL, Baxter correspondence, MS 59.5, fol. 46*r* • *DNB*

Owen, Corbet (1645/6–1671), Latin poet, was born at Hinton in Shropshire, the son of William Owen, a clergyman of Pontesbury, and his wife, Anna. He was baptized on 5 May 1646 at Pontesbury, Shropshire. He was educated at a private school in Shrewsbury, run by a royalist parson called Scofield. Owen suffered badly from scrofula, or 'the king's evil', and had to use crutches. He was sent to France to be touched by the exiled Charles II; it is not recorded whether the hand of indigent majesty alleviated his symptoms. In May 1658 he went to Westminster School (king's scholar, 1659). Westminster was a leading centre of Latin versification, at which Owen showed great facility: 'it was usual with him to speak forty or fifty smooth and elegant verses extempore, in little more than half an hour' (*DNB*). He matriculated at Christ Church, Oxford, on 3 July 1663, aged seventeen, and was elected a student (the equivalent of a fellowship elsewhere) in 1664. He studied philosophy well, and may also have spent some time in Lincoln's Inn; later he also studied medicine. He graduated BA on 21 May 1667 and MA on 23 March 1670. Owen gained a reputation, according to Wood, as 'the most forward person of his age in the university for polite learning' (Wood, *Ath. Oxon.*, 3.924).

The chief production of Corbet Owen's brief literary career was a long Latin ode, in irregular stanzas (but with each line following a recognized metrical pattern), recited at the opening of the Sheldonian Theatre, Oxford, on 9 July 1669. This poem achieved some celebrity, and was reprinted in various editions of the popular collections of British Latin known as *Musae Anglicanae* (for example *Musarum Anglicanarum analecta*, 1721, 1.89; also 1741). These anthologies began in 1692 (Joseph Addison edited an expanded version in 1699), and Owen's ode was prominent among the university pieces thus preserved and presented to a wider public. Samuel Johnson knew it, and felt that it showed the pernicious influence of Abraham Cowley's 'Pindarick' style. In fact Owen was writing in a Renaissance tradition of irregular Latin verse; a number of continental and domestic models exist, from the mid-sixteenth century onwards. Readers of university commemorative collections would have been familiar with the technique, which, while it might irritate purists, did allow for playful or rhetorical variations. Cowley certainly helped to popularize the pseudo-Pindaric genre in the vernacular: 'Cowley was probably responsible for Corbett's unclassical performance, but Owen might very easily have done the same thing if Cowley had never lived' (Bradner, 110).

Owen's *Carmen Pindaricum* has twenty-four irregular stanzas (twenty-eight pages). He celebrates Wren's design of the Sheldonian as a triumph of the modern over the Gothic; enemies will be envious. Owen praises Sheldon for allowing the university's printing press to use the new building. Dr Fell (Owen's own head of house) is second only to Sheldon. He alludes wittily, in stanza 24, to the dangers of his irregular form: Horace has warned (*Odes*, iv.2) that Icarus's watery fate awaits imitators of Pindar, and 'obsedere vias *latrones Grammaticastri*' ('bandit-scholars have infested the roads'). Critics use procrustean beds:

> Heu docti nimium versus torquere misellos,
> Nunc *tensos* immane pedes producere gaudent,
> Nunc *sauciatis* amputare syllabis.
> ('Alas, the over-learned rejoice to torture poor verses, now to stretch out feet, now to amputate, leaving wounded syllables.')

So Owen anticipates and mocks Dr Johnson's criticism.

Owen also wrote an English Pindaric ode, in twenty-one stanzas, 'Upon the Intolerable Heat in the Latter End of May and the Beginning of June, 1665', which is the last, and only signed, poem in John Bulteel's *New Collection of Poems and Songs* (1674). It starts vigorously:

> Fire, fire, fire, fire, the Bells all backwards ring:
> Haste, haste, to every Well and Spring.

But death stalks the countryside and city, in the form of the plague, while the brave fleet faces the Dutch. Owen ends by considering his own verse:

> This onely my Pindaricks do desire,
> Not for to save my house, but my own self from fire.
> *Pindar's* bright Poetick flame
> Surviv'd his ashes, blown by Fame.

Corbet Owen's flame, alas, did not have the chance to burn quite so brightly. He died about 18 January 1671, and was buried at Condover in Shropshire. D. K. MONEY

Sources L. Bradner, *Musae Anglicanae: a history of Anglo-Latin poetry, 1500–1925* (1940) · C. Owen, *Carmen Pindaricum* (1669) · Wood, *Ath. Oxon.*, new edn · J. Bulteel, ed., *New collection of poems and songs* (1674) · Wing, *STC* · Foster, *Alum. Oxon.* · *DNB* · *Hist. U. Oxf.* 4: *17th-cent. Oxf.* · J. Ijsewijn and D. Sacré, *Companion to Neo-Latin studies*, 2 (1998)

Archives BL, royal recommendation to a scholarship at Westminster School, Sloane MS 856, fol. 2b

Owen, Daniel (1836–1895), novelist, was born on 20 October 1836 at 53 Long Row, Maes-y-dref, Mold, Flintshire, the youngest of the seven children of Robert Owen (*c.*1799–1837), miner, and his wife, Sarah, *née* Edwards (1796–1881), laundress. He was only a few months old when his father and two of his brothers were killed in a pit disaster at Argoed colliery near their home, and his early years were marked by poverty which denied him a consistent formal education, although cultural and spiritual support was provided by the Calvinistic Methodist chapel in New Street, Mold, which the family frequented. In his early teens Owen was taken on as an apprentice tailor by Angel Jones, a deacon of that chapel. In his later years Owen referred to the tailor's workshop as 'a kind of college' where he experienced an intellectual and cultural awakening.

During the 1850s Owen began competing in local eisteddfods and published poems of moderate value under the *nom de plume* Glaslwyn. His first venture as a prose writer was a serialized translation of a popular American temperance novel in 1859. Under the influence of his minister and mentor, Roger Edwards, Owen began to preach, and in 1865 he entered Bala Theological College with a view to becoming a minister of religion. His domestic circumstances (he remained unmarried and felt financially responsible for his mother and sister) forced him to leave without completing his course in 1867, and he returned to his craft as a tailor. He then settled into a life of public prominence in Mold in religious, political, and cultural circles, a life which left little room for any advance in his literary development, although he did publish a couple of character sketches in 1870, including his controversial 'Darlun' ('Portrait') of a prominent Calvinistic Methodist minister. His social career was cut short by a serious illness in 1876, but as his closest colleagues saw

Daniel Owen (**1836–1895**), by F. M. Davies, 1880s

this as an opportunity to wake his dormant literary talents, this was also the year when his career as a writer began in earnest. Roger Edwards was the editor of his denomination's monthly journal, *Y Drysorfa* ('The treasury'), and Owen published a series of sermons based on biblical characters in its pages during 1877. Religious hypocrisy and self-delusion were a recurring theme, thus anticipating a major preoccupation of his later work.

Owen's first attempt at fiction appeared in the same publication the following year. *Cymeriadau ymhlith ein cynulleidfaoedd* ('Characters among our congregations') combined portraiture with a story about the election of deacons. This short work included types that recurred in all his works, including the bombastic religious hypocrite and the plain-speaking Christian of the older generation. The sermons and story were published in a well-received volume, *Offrymau neilltuaeth* ('The offerings of seclusion'), in 1879. By then Owen's next work, his first novel, was being serialized in *Y Drysorfa*. *Y dreflan* ('The town') ran for two years and was published in book form in 1881. Originally intended as a series of twelve sketches, *Y dreflan* generated a momentum of its own as Owen became increasingly aware that his medium was a powerful vehicle for satirical social commentary. But it was his next novel, *Hunangofiant Rhys Lewis, gweinidog Bethel* ('The autobiography of Rhys Lewis, minister of Bethel'), which ensured him fame and a small fortune. After its serialization in *Y Drysorfa* from 1882 to 1884, Owen published the volume at his own expense in 1885 and then sold the copyright to Hughes & Son of Wrexham. The proceeds enabled him to build a new home for himself and his sister Leah. Owen made extensive use of his own life story in *Rhys Lewis*; he had recently lost his mother and his elder brother, David. The novel's enormous popularity owed much to Owen's superb evocations of life in Victorian Wales, and some of its characters and sayings became assimilated into Welsh popular culture. The narrator's mother and brother, Mari and Bob Lewis, are two of his most famous characters, and the first half of the novel is charged by a series of debates between the conservative evangelical mother and her radical son.

A miscellaneous collection of poems and prose, *Y siswrn* ('The scissors'), appeared in 1886, by which time Owen had his own business as tailor and outfitter. *Profedigaethau Enoc Huws* ('The trials of Enoc Huws'), published in 1891, is the novelist's finest achievement, and although it is not without blemish, its status as a major novel in the realist style cannot be denied. Originally conceived as a sequel to *Hunangofiant Rhys Lewis*, it shows similarities to *Y dreflan* in terms of satirical social commentary, but Owen displays a greater authorial confidence and arrogance in *Profedigaethau Enoc Huws* than was evident in the earlier works. The opening chapter, 'Cymru lân' ('Fair Wales'), confronts the tendency in Victorian Wales to present idealized and airbrushed images of Welsh life, and proclaims the author's unwillingness to compromise artistic and moral integrity. The world portrayed in the novel is one where deceit, hypocrisy, and self-delusion, as well as their more innocent and amusing cousins, misunderstanding and speaking at cross-purposes, are endemic. The church and the world alike are riddled with hypocrisy, most memorably incorporated in the person of Captain Richard Trefor, the outwardly respectable and religious mine owner, who uses chapel membership as a means to deceive prospective investors in his mining companies. Despite what some twentieth-century critics would regard as weaknesses in plot and structure, Owen used the realist novel with conviction and imagination in interpreting his life and times and places.

Owen's final novel, *Gwen Tomos, merch y Wernddu* ('Gwen Tomos, daughter of Wern-ddu'), was written during a period of failing health. Although a popular success, it lacks the vigour and conviction of his earlier work, and the brilliant contemporary observer has settled for being an accomplished storyteller. The strong strain of reminiscence is evident also in the stories which he wrote during his final years. *Gwen Tomos* was published in 1894, and *Straeon y pentan* ('Fireside tales') the following year. Despite his indifferent health, Owen participated in local politics during his final years, becoming a member of the Mold local board of health in 1889. He was elected a member of the new urban district council in 1894 and was its first chairman. He died on 22 October 1895 at 23 New Street, Mold, and was buried in Mold two days later. After his death a fund was established to erect a memorial to Wales's foremost novelist, and Goscombe John was commissioned to create the statue which stands by the entrance to the public library in Mold. The esteem with which he has continued to be held was reflected in a number of valuable memorial lectures, published between 1976 and 1984. ROBERT RHYS

Sources R. Rhys, *Dawn dweud: Daniel Owen* (2000) • H. T. Edwards, ed., *A guide to Welsh literature*, 5: *c.*1800–1900 (2000) • I. Foulkes, *Daniel Owen y nofelydd* (1903) • B. Wynne-Woodhouse, 'Daniel Owen the novelist: family history', *Hel Achau* [Clwyd Family History Society], 12 (spring 1984) • R. K. Matthias and T. C. Williams, *Daniel Owen a'i fyd* (1991) • d. cert.
Archives Flintshire RO, Hawarden, adjudication relating to Rhosdu eisteddfod • Flintshire RO, Hawarden, memorial room committee, collection of papers and photographs
Likenesses F. M. Davies, photograph, 1880–89, NL Wales [*see illus.*] • C. Marston, oils, *c.*1890, Flintshire RO, Hawarden • photographs, Flintshire RO, Hawarden; repro. in Matthias and Williams, *Daniel Owen a'i fyd*
Wealth at death £515 19*s.* 6*d.*: probate, 28 Nov 1895, *CGPLA Eng. & Wales*

Owen, David (*d.* 1623), Church of England clergyman and religious controversialist, was born on the Isle of Anglesey. Rector of Yardley Hastings, Northamptonshire, from 3 November 1598, and vicar of neighbouring Preston Deanery from the same year, it was not until early 1599 that he graduated BA from St Catharine's College, Cambridge. He then became a fellow of Clare College, but his tenure may have been brief since on 17 June 1600, at All Saints', Northampton, he married Elizabeth Knight (*d.* 1617) of Geyding. He returned to Cambridge and proceeded MA from Clare in 1602 and BD in 1609, having been incorporated MA from Oxford on 14 June 1608. The possibility of some period of residence in the university is suggested by the fact that his two children, Mary and John, were baptized there respectively on 10 July 1608 and 31 March 1611; the latter was buried at Yardley Hastings on 6 July 1611.

At some point in the first decade of the seventeenth century Owen became part of a proto-Arminian grouping within the diocese of Peterborough, and served under Thomas Dove (bishop from 1601) and John Buckeridge (archdeacon from 1604) as a church court official. Closely identified with Dove's vigorous drive against nonconformity, Owen presented his own curate, Thomas Randleson, for preaching false doctrine, on the ground that Randleson had asserted that 'though baptism was necessary yet it was not necessary unto salvation, that they were popish preachers that taught that children were not ordinarily saved without baptism' (Fielding, 97).

On 1 May 1610 Owen completed a manuscript tract, 'The power of princes and the dutie of subjectes according to the scripture and the judgement of the auncient fathers for an antidote against the poyson of the late and lewde doctrine of papistes & puritanes' (BL, Royal MS 18 B v). At first sight this appears to be a standard contribution to the continuing debates over the oath of allegiance. Owen claimed to attack both the puritan church polity that had grown up at Geneva since 1536 and the Jesuits, whom he dated to 1537 at Rome. He roundly disputed the three presuppositions of Robert Bellarmine and the Romanists: that the pope had absolute power over all; that although the pope had no absolute power over kings directly, yet he had supreme authority to dispose of the temporalities of all Christians; and that the pope could excommunicate kings. However, the context of the tract suggests that there was more to it than met the eye. Owen was chaplain to John Ramsay, Viscount Haddington. In 1609/10 court voices (including that of Bishop Lancelot Andrewes) were raised against the manner in which the king and his agent, Haddington, had quashed the Gowrie conspiracy of 1600. Topical in its implicit endorsement of the king's right to sanction extreme measures against Roman Catholic conspirators, it is likely Owen's piece was read at court. Published later in 1610, as *Herod and Pilate Reconciled*, at Cambridge, the printed version follows the manuscript text with a few minor corrections. These are in the concluding chapter, 'Puritan-Jesuitisme', which lists the 'generall consent of the principall Puritans and Jesuits against Kings, from the year 1536 untill the year 1602' (pp. 47–53), among them John Knox, George Buchanan, Theodore Beza, Thomas Cartwright, Robert Rollock, and William Bucanus. The work retained its topicality, being republished in 1642, 1643, 1652, and 1663. A Dutch translation was published in 1660 by Johann Utenbogaert.

On 14 January 1614, in succession to Robert Catelin, 'a key figure in the local puritan campaign' (Fielding, 97), and presumably in a move to rein in the town's notorious nonconformity, Owen became vicar of All Saints', Northampton. He resigned in 1616, having in the meantime retained Yardley Hastings, where his wife was buried on 20 May 1617. Within the next three years he married another Elizabeth, whose other name is unknown; a daughter, Jane, was baptized on 13 May 1620. In 1618 he obtained his DD degree (incorporated at Oxford in July) from Cambridge; while there he is credited with having informed on Ralph Brownrigg for discussing, in his private rooms at Pembroke College, whether kings might be deposed for breaking fundamental laws. On 19 April 1619 he took part in a disputation in the Cambridge divinity schools in which he denounced the teachings on Romans 13 of the Heidelberg-based David Pareus, and defended the divine right of kings.

In July 1621 Owen sent to his patron, newly created earl of Holdernesse, a belated response to a papist tract of 1619, 'God and the king, against God and the king'. Yielding to the persuasion of friends he had produced a 'plain and full answer' over a six-week period; 'Detectio calumniarum, sophismatum, et impostuarum anonymi papistae' (BL, Royal MS 10 B xiii, fol. 2*r*) was never published, presumably because events elsewhere came to overshadow it. As a result of the furore caused at Oxford and at court by a university sermon of 14 April 1622, in which one John Knight had not only offered a thorough defence of Pareus and his sanction of resistance by an inferior magistrate to his sovereign in matters of religion, but also specifically instanced the interference of James I in supporting the French Huguenots, an Oxford disputation was staged on 25 June to denounce Pareus and uphold royal authority. On 12 August the 'Directions to preachers' were issued, and later that month Owen's 1619 Latin disputation was rushed into print. Published as *Anti-Pareus*, *sive, Determinatio de jure regio* and dedicated on 31 August to the king, it attacked both papists and 'disciplinarians' for controverting royal authority. Conventionally, Owen saw the king as father of his country, and he conceded that 'subjects ought not to obey in those cases where the Prince commands against God' (Sommerville, 34), but he spelt out more explicitly than many the extent to which royal power was subject to no human authority. The volume concluded by quoting 1 Peter 2: 17, 'Fear God, honour the king', in Welsh.

On 2 October 1622 Owen gained the vicarage of St Sepulchre, Northampton, but he died on 23 July 1623, and was buried at Yardley Hastings church on 25 July. His will, dated 21 July, divided his property between his wife and daughters, and was proved by his widow on 29 July. Twenty years later Robert Mossom, then an army chaplain and later bishop of Derry, published in York a translation of *Anti-Pareus* as a means of rallying royalists to the flag and of cautioning those who would offer resistance to the crown. In the preface to *Anti-Pareus, or, A Treatise in the Defence of the Royall Right of Kings* (1643) he saluted Owen as a 'man of so much piety as to write nothing but what his conscience told him was the Truth; and of so much Learning as to maintaine the Truth he writ' (p. A3*).

NICHOLAS W. S. CRANFIELD

Sources H. I. Longden, *Northamptonshire and Rutland clergy from 1500*, ed. P. I. King and others, 16 vols. in 6, Northamptonshire RS (1938–52), 131 • Venn, *Alum. Cant.* • J. Fielding, 'Arminianism in the localities: Peterborough diocese, 1603–1642', *The early Stuart church, 1603–1642*, ed. K. Fincham (1993), 93–113 • A. Wood, *The history … of the University of Oxford*, ed. J. Gutch, 2 vols. (1792–6) • P. White, *Predestination, policy and polemic* (1992) • D. Owen, *Anti-Paraeus, or, A treatise in the defence of the royall right of kings*, trans. R. Mossom (1643) • G. J. Vossius, *G. J. Vossii et clarorum virorum, ad eum epistolae*, ed. P. Colomesius, 2 vols. in 1 (1690) • BL, Royal MS 10 B xiii • J. P. Sommerville, *Politics and ideology in England, 1603–1640* (1986)

Owen, David [Dafydd y Garreg Wen] (**1711/12–1741**), harper, was the son of Owen Humphreys and his wife, Gwen Roberts of Isallt Fawr, Llanfihangel-y-Pennant, Caernarvonshire, a member of a family that was traditionally believed to be descended from the physicians of Myddfai. He was born at a farmhouse called Y Garreg Wen, at Ynyscynhaearn, near Porthmadog, Caernarvonshire. There he died in August 1741, and was buried in the churchyard of Ynyscynhaearn, where in 1840 a monument with a Welsh inscription and the figure of a harp was erected by subscription over his grave.

Owen is said to have been a competent harper. Tradition attributes to him the authorship of the well-known air which, in all Welsh collections of national songs, bears his own name of Dafydd y Garreg Wen as its title, though it is known in Scotland by the name of 'July Jott'. Some account for this by saying that it was sent by Dafydd to a cousin of his (or, according to others, a brother named Rhys), who was then a gardener at Roslin Castle in Scotland, where the air soon became popular under a new name; but others, who accept its Scottish origin, assert that it was simply a favourite one of Dafydd's.

According to the Welsh tradition, Dafydd when on his deathbed had fallen in a trance and was believed to be dead, but, suddenly reviving, told his mother that he had just heard one of the sweetest songs of heaven, which, on his harp being handed him, he then played; but as the last note was dying away Dafydd, too, died. The air was subsequently preserved from memory by his mother, who was herself a harper and poet. Sir Walter Scott wrote words for the air, entitled 'The Dying Bard'. Scott adds that the bard 'requested that the air might be performed at his funeral', and his instructions were carried out. At least two other airs are ascribed to Dafydd: namely, 'Codiad yr ehedydd' ('Rising of the Lark') and 'Difyrrwch gwyr Cricieth' ('The Delight of the Men of Cricieth'), which is also known as 'Roslin Castle' in Scotland, where tradition says it was popularized by Dafydd's cousin. Evan Evans (Ieuan Glan Geirionydd) wrote words (in Welsh) for this air. The tunes of 'Dafydd y Garreg Wen' and 'Codiad yr ehedydd' were first published in *Musical and Poetical Relicks of the Welsh Bards* (1784), by Edward Jones (Bardd y Brenin). Their English and Welsh words in Henry Brinley Richards's *Songs of Wales* (1873, 58, 79) are by John Oxenford and J. Ceiriog Hughes respectively.

D. L. THOMAS, *rev.* TREVOR HERBERT

Sources *DWB* • M. Stephens, ed., *The Oxford companion to the literature of Wales* (1986) • E. Jones, ed., *The Welsh harper, being an extensive collection of Welsh music*, 1 [1839]

Owen, David [*pseud.* Dewi Wyn o Eifion] (*bap.* **1784**, *d.* **1841**), poet, was the son of Owen Dafydd and Catherine, his second wife, who lived on the farm of Y Gaerwen, in the parish of Llanystumdwy, Caernarvonshire. He was baptized in that parish on 18 June 1784, and was educated in local schools and, unusually, in a boarding-school at Bangor Is-coed, Flintshire, together with Owen, his younger brother. Owen Owen later established himself as a shopkeeper in Pwllheli and became a man of some importance in the life of the town. David Owen returned to Y Gaerwen and managed the farm himself after the death of his father in 1816.

David Owen mastered the rules of *cerdd dafod*, the strict metres of Welsh poetry, at an early age. The commote of Eifionydd was noted for its rich poetic inheritance, and the ancient tradition of bardic teacher and disciple was still alive. His older friend and neighbour Robert Williams (Robert ap Gwilym Ddu), the best contemporary poet, was his main bardic instructor. He benefited, too, from a long acquaintance with David Thomas (Dafydd Ddu Eryri), the influential mentor of the nearby Arfon group of versifiers. Dewi soon became known to the Welsh public as a cantankerous competitor in the reformed eisteddfods held in the early years of the nineteenth century under the auspices of the Gwyneddigion Society of London, whose leaders required that the main competition should be a prize for the *awdl*, a long poem in selected strict metres, with competitors using a pseudonym. Dewi's eisteddfod career was marked throughout by bitter controversy. He was declared second best in 1803. In 1805 the prize was first awarded to Bardd Cwsg (Hugh Maurice), a nephew of Owain Myfyr, the authoritative leader of the Gwyneddigion, who refused to reveal his name, and Dewi was then awarded the prize by default. In the Tremadog eisteddfod of 1811 he won a silver cup offered for the best poem on agriculture, but it was withheld owing to a conspiracy among influential members of the Gwyneddigion Society. The quarrel between the poet and the society finally came to a head in 1819. In the Denbigh eisteddfod of that year the society's medal was offered for the best poem on charity (*elusengarwch*); no announcement was made at the eisteddfod itself, but some three weeks later the Revd Edward Hughes of Bodfari was declared the winner, despite an inferior composition.

These disappointments so mortified Dewi that, after several fierce onslaughts in verse and prose upon his foes, he gave up competition and wrote nothing of importance from 1823 until his death, apart from his well-known 'Stanzas to the Menai Bridge' (1832).

From 1827 on David Owen spent much of his time in Pwllheli to be with his brother, whose health was deteriorating. On Owen Owen's death in 1837 he returned to Y Gaerwen. By this time the poet was known as a man of considerable means and miserly character. Towards the end of his life he suffered from a deep religious depression; always attracted to the Baptist denomination, he did not officially join it until the year before his death. David Owen never married and died at Y Gaerwen on 17 January 1841. He was buried five days later in Llangybi churchyard. A collection of his main works appeared in 1842, and a final supplement was published in 1869.

During his lifetime Dewi Wyn was much admired by Romantic critics as a poet of soaring imagination and sublimity. His faults were not ignored, but his genius was held to transcend those weaknesses often enumerated by modern critics: vacuous verbosity, repetitiveness, incoherent imagery, and an urge to exhaust every possible aspect of the poem's subject at interminable length. Dewi Wyn, more than any other poet of the time, was responsible for making the long poem as discursive essay an unfortunate fashion which survived into the early years of the twentieth century. Paradoxically, he regarded his most popular poem, the *awdl* on charity, as an attempt at the epic genre. His early work suggests that he might have become a poet of importance, but like many others he fell a victim to the demands of eisteddfod competition.

E. G. MILLWARD

Sources W. J. Gruffydd, *Y Llenor*, 4 (1925), 9–24 · S. J. Williams, *Gwŷr llên y bedwaredd ganrif ar bymtheg*, ed. D. Morgan (1968), 18–30 · E. G. Millward, 'Eifionydd y beirdd', *Transactions of the Caernarvonshire Historical Society*, 25 (1964), 42–65 · R. G. Llwyd, 'Bywyd Dewi Wyn o Eifion (1784–1841) ac astudiaeth o'i weithiau a'i gysylltiadau llenyddol', MA diss., U. Wales, Aberystwyth, 1979
Archives NL Wales, poems and MSS · U. Wales, Bangor, Bangor collections
Likenesses engraving (after portrait by W. Roos), repro. in D. Owen, *Blodau Arfon* (1842)
Wealth at death £3177: will, Cwrt Mawr collection, NL Wales

Owen, David [*pseud.* Brutus] (**1795–1866**), journalist and writer, was born in late 1795 at Llanpumpsaint, near Carmarthen, and baptized on 25 December 1795, the son of David Benjamin Owen, a shoemaker and an Anglican parish clerk, and Rachel Owen, a Baptist. He was educated locally, and at Carmarthen grammar school, where he learned Greek and Latin. As a youth he took an interest in magic and the 'black arts', which he satirized in later life. While serving a medical apprenticeship with Dr John Thomas, at Aberdyar, near Llanybydder, he was introduced to Baptism by the doctor's brother, the Revd Timothy Thomas, and shortly thereafter joined the Baptist church. Deciding upon a career in the ministry, he spent a year at the Baptist college, Bristol. He was then for three years a schoolmaster and lay preacher at Gilfach, near Aber, Caernarvonshire, before taking charge of the Baptist churches of Tal-y-graig, Galltraeth, Tyndonnen, and Rhoshirwaun on the Llŷn peninsula, Caernarvonshire. There he was ordained, and settled in Llangïan. In 1820 he married Anne, daughter of Thomas Jones, a farmer from Rhandir and a deacon of the Independent church.

Supplementing his income by teaching and dispensing medical advice, Owen also began to write. He made an explosive impact on literature in Wales when his article 'The poverty of the Welsh language' was published in *Seren Gomer* in 1824 under the signature Brutus, Lleyn (Brutus from Llŷn). In it he accused the Welsh of being intellectually a 'nation of thieves', wholly dependent on English literary culture. The article stimulated a lively public debate, eliciting responses from, among others, Walter Davies (Gwallter Mechain; 1761–1849), Thomas Price (Carnhuanawc; 1787–1848), and Joseph Harris (Gomer; 1773–1825). He continued to play the same provocative role in Welsh religious and cultural criticism for the remainder of his life.

Owen's relations with nonconformity also became strained at this time. For reasons not entirely clear, he informed Dr Lant Carpenter of the Unitarian Association at Bristol that his congregation in Llŷn was leaning towards Unitarianism, and appealed for Unitarian funds. Carpenter found no evidence to support Owen's claim and refused financial support: shortly thereafter, he was expelled from the Baptist church. Partly thanks to his father-in-law's connections, he was accepted into the Independent church of Capel Newydd. He moved to Tyddyn Sweep, Maenaddwyn, near Llannerch-y-medd, Anglesey, and from there to Bontnewydd, near Caernarfon, where he preached and kept school.

Owen was not a popular preacher in either place, and from January 1828 he abandoned the pulpit for journalism, becoming editor of *Lleuad yr Oes*, a general, non-denominational monthly journal published by Samuel Thomas in Aberystwyth. During this period, when he lived in Llanbadarn Fawr, he wrote a pamphlet attacking child baptism (1828), which was answered by Benjamin Jones (Llanrwst) in 1831, and a ferocious attack on Catholicism, *Cwymp babilon fawr* (1829). In 1830, facing bankruptcy, Samuel Thomas sold the title to Jeffrey Jones of Llandovery. Owen remained its editor, and moved to Pentre-tŷ-gwyn. Following the death of Jones in 1830, a successor, *Yr Efangylydd*, was launched in 1831 by another Llandovery printer, the Anglican William Rees, and a group of Independent ministers. Under Owen's editorship, the journal became increasingly conservative in both politics and theology, and the Independent contributors sought to dismiss him. Backed by the Anglican printer, Owen retained his post for a time, but the Independents withdrew their support and thus brought the journal to an end in May 1835.

In August 1835 the Independents launched their own radical, anti-tory and anti-Anglican magazine *Y Diwygiwr*, in Llanelli, under the editorship of David Rees (y Cynhyrfwr; 1801–1869), while a month earlier Owen, now returned to the Anglican church, had begun to edit for William Rees a new monthly Anglican periodical, *Yr Haul*. The two journals, led by two strong editors, defined much of Welsh religious, political, and cultural life in the period between their launch and Owen's death in 1866. In *Yr Haul*, Owen satirized and vilified nonconformity in general and Independent presbyterianism (or 'Great Independia') in particular. He was the author, under the pseudonym Bleddyn, of biographies of the leading Welsh religious figures Christmas Evans (1840), John Elias (1844), John Edwards (1849), and Thomas Williams (1861). He also published bitingly satirical pamphlets, such as *Papuryn achlysurol: drych y brad, yn cynnwys yr asyn quadrupedaidd a'r asyn bipedaidd … gan rigdum funnidos* (1843), though his most enduring creations were 'Bugeiliaid Eppynt', serialized in *Yr Haul*, 1835–66, and 'Wil Brydydd y Coed; Cofiant Siencyn bach y llwywr; a chofiant Dai Hunandyb', serialized in that journal from September 1863 to December 1865 (the latter was published posthumously in Carmarthen in 1876). A selection of his articles and poems from *Yr Haul* was published in *Brutusiana, sef casgliad detholedig o'i gyfansoddiadau* (1855), which included strong attacks on slavery (p. 237) and a passionate defence of Welsh patriotism (pp. 328–35).

As early as 1824 Joseph Harris had recognized in Owen a brilliant 'advocatus diaboli', and it was said in 1883 that 'Brutus was the first Welsh writer who made politics popular'. He received a pension from the civil list in 1858. He died of gout, in great pain, on 16 January 1866, leaving a widow and several children. He was buried on 19 January 1866 in Llywel church. ALED G. JONES

Sources *DWB* • M. Williams, 'Brutus, ei waith a'i fywyd', *Yr Haul* (1914), 69–75 • J. R. K. Jones, 'Brutus', *Y Traethodydd*, 22 (1867), 213–27, 421–8 • D. M. Davies, 'Hynt a helyntion Brutus y dychanwr', *Journal of the Historical Society of the Church in Wales*, 12 (1962), 55–68; 13 (1963), 74–84 • J. Davies, *Yr Haul*, 3rd ser., 10 (1866), 63–4 • D. Owen, *Brutusiana, sef casgliad detholedig o'i gyfansoddiadau* (1855) • A. G. Jones, *Press, politics and society: a history of journalism in Wales* (1993)

Archives NL Wales, annual reports, no. 1969017

Likenesses portrait, repro. in C. Wilkins, ed., *The Red Dragon*, 3 (1883)

Owen, Sir (Arthur) David Kemp (1904–1970), international civil servant, was born at Pontypool, Monmouthshire, on 26 November 1904, the eldest son of the Revd Edward Owen, Baptist minister, of Pontypool, and his wife, Gertrude Louisa, *née* Kemp. He was educated at Leeds grammar school and the University of Leeds, from which he received an honours degree in economics (1926) and the master of commerce degree (1929), the latter for a thesis, 'The problem of juvenile unemployment'. Between his first and second degrees he was assistant lecturer in economics at Huddersfield Technical College. He was then director of the Sheffield social survey committee from 1929 to 1933, and was responsible for producing reports on unemployment, the standard of living, and housing in Sheffield. This work was followed by appointments as secretary of the civic research division of political and economic planning (PEP) (1933–6), co-director of the Pilgrim Trust unemployment inquiry (1936–7), and Stevenson lecturer in citizenship at the University of Glasgow (1937–40). In 1940 he published his survey, *The British Social Services*. Meanwhile, on 11 November 1933 he had married Elizabeth Joyce Morgan, daughter of the Revd E. H. Morgan, Methodist minister. They had one son and one daughter.

In 1941 Owen relinquished the post of general secretary of PEP, to which he had been appointed in the previous year, to become personal assistant to the lord privy seal, Sir Stafford Cripps, on his mission to India. He remained with Cripps following the latter's transfer to the Ministry of Aircraft Production, but in 1944 was transferred to the reconstruction department of the Foreign Office, where he served as officer in charge of League of Nations affairs. He was a member of the United Kingdom delegation to the conference on international organization at San Francisco in 1945, and when the preparatory commission of the United Nations was being organized in London in the summer of 1945, he joined the United Nations staff as its first recruit, in the capacity of deputy executive secretary of the preparatory commission.

When the preparatory commission gave way to the United Nations itself and the organization moved to New York in early 1946, Owen was appointed assistant secretary-general in charge of economic affairs, one of the eight top officials of the organization. In the late 1940s the organization became increasingly concerned with economic development, and in August 1951 Owen became the first executive chairman of the Technical Assistance Board, a position which he retained until in January 1966 the Expanded Programme of the Technical Assistance Board merged with the United Nations Development Fund to form the United Nations Development Programme. He became co-administrator of the programme with Paul G. Hoffman, a post which he retained until his retirement from the United Nations service in 1969. Meanwhile, his first marriage having ended in divorce, in 1950 he married Elisabeth Elsa Miller, the adopted daughter of Frieda Segelke Miller, American labour official and director of the women's bureau of the US department of labor (1944–53). They had two sons.

Throughout his career Owen was essentially a pioneer in new areas of public service, first on the national and later on the international level. He relished new challenges, and his enquiring mind and his skill as a pragmatic and informal administrator admirably equipped him to meet them. He was a non-doctrinaire socialist of the old school with a quiet faith in the capacity of humanity to improve its condition and an ardent desire to help it to do so. His work in social and economic planning in the post-depression years and his service with Sir Stafford Cripps during the war led naturally to strong convictions about the need for international co-operation, convictions upon which he acted in the most challenging circumstances when helping to build and operate the institutional structure of the United Nations. He was one of the younger architects of the new world organization from San Francisco and thenceforth, and had an almost unique record of being associated with the creation of successive new branches on the economic side—first the economic department itself and its regional economic commissions, then the Technical Assistance Board, and finally the fully fledged United Nations Development Programme, which became by far the largest and most far-flung operation of the United Nations.

Owen was an idealist and enthusiast of a practical and realistic kind. In the emergent international civil service he found a perfect setting for his convictions. He wrote:

> It is, after all, a fine thing to belong to a service which, whatever its failings and frustrations, is engaged in the practical business of trying to establish more effective forms of international co-operation in the pursuit of peace and human well-being.

His concept of the United Nations was that of an activist, although he was very much aware of the shortcomings and difficulties of the world organization. 'It remains to be seen', he wrote in 1966, 'whether we can rise to the historic occasion or whether we will find ourselves stagnating with modest usefulness in the margin of great events'.

Owen was modest, unpretentious, quick-witted, and of an enquiring turn of mind. Small in stature, with the humour and a touch of the accent of his native Wales, he was a dominant influence in the formative years of the United Nations. His kindness, consideration, and interest in the careers of his colleagues, especially the young and intelligent, greatly influenced the early stages of organization. Later, when he was responsible for setting up the worldwide network of resident representatives of the technical assistance programme, which became the basis of the development programme, his ability to find new and promising recruits had a major effect on the development of the United Nations. His method of leadership was very personal. He was a voracious reader, which prevented him from becoming stale or bureaucratic. He never lost the simplicity and natural friendliness of his youth and was a much beloved colleague.

On his retirement from the United Nations service, Owen was appointed secretary-general of the International Planned Parenthood Federation, in succession to Sir Colville Deverell. His tenure was short-lived, as he died at St Thomas's Hospital, London, on 29 June 1970, following a heart attack, very shortly after being appointed KCMG. He had also received honorary doctorates from the universities of Leeds (1954) and Wales (1969). He was survived by his second wife, Elisabeth, and his four children.

Brian Urquhart, *rev.*

Sources *The Times* (30 June 1970) • *The Times* (2 July 1970) • *The Times* (11 July 1970) • *WWW* • personal knowledge (1981) • private information (1981) • b. cert. • m. cert. • d. cert.
Archives Bodl. Oxf., corresp. with Sidney Dell • NL Wales, corresp. with Thomas Jones • Rice University, Houston, Texas, Woodson Research Center, corresp. with Sir John Huxley
Wealth at death £723—in England: administration, 14 July 1971, *CGPLA Eng. & Wales*

Owen, Edward (1728/9–1807), Church of England clergyman and translator, was the third son of David Owen of Llangurig, Montgomeryshire. He matriculated at Jesus College, Oxford, on 22 March 1746, aged seventeen, graduating BA on 1 December 1749 and MA on 1 June 1752. He was appointed headmaster of the grammar school at Warrington on 4 June 1757, incumbent of Sankey Chapel in 1763, and rector of Warrington on 14 September 1767, an office he retained until his death. He was a strong supporter of the established church, and in 1790 preached a sermon voicing his opposition to any increase in the privileges granted to dissenters. He supervised extensive repairs to both church and school, and both as master and clergyman he acquired a high local reputation. Among his pupils were George Tierney, president of the Board of Control; Dr John Wright, fellow of Brasenose College, Oxford; John Almon, Dr Thomas Barnes, and John Fitchett. He was president of the Warrington Library, which was established in 1760, and took a prominent part in the promotion of the literary and social interests of the town.

Owen published textbooks dealing with Latin grammar and metre, but his chief work was his translation of Juvenal's *Satires*, 'cleared of all the most exceptionable passages', which was published in 1785 together with Thomas Brewster's translation of Persius. A further edition, now including Owen's own translation of Persius, appeared in 1786. The translation was aimed at fellow teachers and their pupils, and he observes in the preface that 'there are but few masters, who wish not to see the beauties of the manly Juvenal separated from his impurities'. Owen aimed to surpass Juvenal's earlier translators in 'ease and spirit, (not excepting the great and masculine but slovenly Dryden himself)', but his bowdlerised version was not a great success.

Owen's high opinion of himself was singled out for satire by Thomas Seddon in his *Characteristic Strictures* (1779) where he lampoons the vicar of Warrington as the epitome of self-consequence. However Gilbert Wakefield had a better opinion of Owen, whom he describes as 'a man of most elegant learning, unimpeachable veracity, and peculiar benevolence of heart' (Wakefield, 161). Owen died unmarried in April 1807, and was buried in the chancel of Warrington parish church.

C. W. Sutton, *rev.* Sarah Annes Brown

Sources E. Owen, *The original text of Juvenal and Persius* (1786) • T. Seddon, *Characteristic strictures* (1779) • Foster, *Alum. Oxon.* • G. Wakefield, *Memoirs of the life of Gilbert Wakefield* (1792) • J. Kendrick, *Profiles of Warrington worthies*, new edn, ed. H. Wells (1996)
Archives NL Wales, letters to John Williams
Likenesses portrait, Warrington Museum • silhouette, repro. in Kendrick, *Profiles*

Owen, Sir Edward Campbell Rich (1771–1849), naval officer, was the illegitimate son of Captain William Owen RN (*d.* 1778), of Welsh extraction, elder brother of Captain William *Owen RN, and first cousin of David Owen, senior wrangler in 1777. He was entered on the books of the *Enterprize* in the Mediterranean when he was barely four years old, and in 1780–82 he was similarly entered on the books of ships in the West Indies. His actual entry into the navy seems to have been in 1786, on board the *Culloden*, guardship at Plymouth. He afterwards served on the home, Mediterranean, North American, and West Indian stations; and on 6 November 1793 was promoted lieutenant of the *Fortunée*. Afterwards, on the home station, in the summer of 1796, he was acting captain of the *Impregnable* with Rear-Admiral Sir Thomas Rich, his godfather, and of the *Queen Charlotte* with Sir John Colpoys; and on 19 September was promoted commander.

In May 1797 Owen had charge of a division of gun-brigs at the Nore, under the command of Sir Erasmus Gower. On 23 April 1798 he was posted to the *Northumberland*, from which he was moved to the *Irresistible*, in the Medway. In 1801 he commanded the *Nemesis* in the North Sea and off Dunkirk or Boulogne. In May 1802 he was appointed to the *Immortalité*, in which, on the renewal of the war, he served on the coast of France, capturing or destroying many gunboats or privateers, more especially on 20 July 1804, when, in conjunction with four brigs and a northerly gale, he ensured the destruction of many gunboats and several hundred soldiers between Boulogne and Étaples. In October 1806 he was moved to the *Clyde* and ordered to hoist a broad pennant, and successfully attacked the town and port of Boulogne with Congreve rockets. In 1809 he was attached to the Walcheren expedition. He afterwards commanded the *Inconstant* in the North Sea, and in 1813 the *Cornwall*. In 1814 he commanded the yacht *Dorset*, and on 2 January 1815 was nominated KCB. In 1816 he was appointed to the yacht *Royal Sovereign*, which he commanded for the next six years; and from 1822 to 1825 was commander-in-chief in the West Indies, with a broad pennant in the *Gloucester*.

From 1826 to 1829 Owen was MP for Sandwich, Kent. On 27 May 1825 he was promoted to be rear-admiral; in 1827 he was surveyor-general of the ordnance; in March 1828 he was appointed on the council of the lord high admiral; and from December 1828 to 1832 was commander-in-chief in the East Indies. He married, in 1829, Selina, daughter of Captain John Baker Hay RN: they had no children.

On his return from the West Indies, Owen was nominated a GCH on 24 October 1832. In 1834 he accepted a seat on the Board of Ordnance in Peel's brief ministry, and contested Sandwich in the Conservative interest, but was defeated. He became a vice-admiral on 10 January 1837, and from 1841 to 1845 was commander-in-chief in the Mediterranean, with his flag in the *Queen* and afterwards in the *Formidable*. Owen took his wife with him aboard the flagship (a practice the government wanted to end): this caused some concern during the 1844 Morocco crisis, particularly as it was widely believed that she was insane. Distinctly unfavourable comparisons were made with Owen's far younger French counterpart, the Prince de Joinville. Owen presided over the Mediterranean command at a low ebb: Anglo-French entente had reduced the size of the fleet, while his age and infirmity ensured that it was little troubled by activity. Yet in the Morocco crisis Owen displayed good sense and diplomatic skills, earning the praise of the Admiralty.

Owen was nominated a GCB on 8 May 1845 and became admiral on 11 December 1846. He died at his residence, Windlesham House, near Bagshot, Surrey, on 8 October 1849. An able officer, politically conservative and much favoured by William IV, Owen demonstrated real ability in the channel between 1802 and 1809, and later at the Ordnance board, on the lord high admiral's council, and in command afloat.

J. K. Laughton, *rev.* Andrew Lambert

Sources Peel MSS, BL • G. S. Graham, *The China station: war and diplomacy, 1830–1860* (1978) • A. D. Lambert, *The last sailing battlefleet: maintaining naval mastery, 1815–1850* (1991) • M. E. Chamberlain, *Lord Aberdeen: a political biography* (1983) • A. Aspinall, ed., *The formation of Canning's ministry, February to August 1827*, CS, 3rd ser., 59 (1937) • O'Byrne, *Naval biog. dict.* • *GM*, 2nd ser., 32 (1849) • E. H. Burrows, *Captain Owen of the African survey* (1979)

Archives NMM, papers relating to Spithead mutiny and Walcheren expedition • Queen's University, Kingston, Ontario, letter-book | BL, letters to Nelson, Add. MS 34918 • E. Sussex RO, letters to Lord Seaton • NA Scot., letters to Lord Haddington • National Archives of Malta, corresp. relating to Malta • NL Scot., corresp. with Sir Thomas Cochrane • NMM, letters to Lord Keith • PRO NIre., corresp. with Lord Castlereagh • U. Nott. L., letters to Lord William Bentinck

Likenesses H. W. Pickersgill, oils, 1849, NMM; copy, NMG Wales

Owen, Edward Pryce (1788–1863), artist and etcher, born on 3 March 1788, was the only son of Hugh *Owen (1760–1827), curate of Berwick, Shropshire, and his wife, Harriet, *née* Jeffreys. He was educated from 1806 at St John's College, Cambridge, where he graduated BA in 1810 and MA in 1816. He was ordained deacon at Lichfield in 1811, and priest in 1812, and from 1811 to 1817 was curate of St Julian's, Shrewsbury. After officiating for some time at Park Street Chapel, Grosvenor Square, London, he became vicar of Wellington and rector of Eyton upon the Wildmoors, Shropshire, which livings he held from 27 February 1823 until 1840. During this period he produced a number of impressive topographical and genre etchings, for which he acquired considerable skill under the tutelage of his father, a noted topographer. He contributed several plates to *The History of Shrewsbury* (1825), by his father and John Brickdale Blakeway, and he published *Etchings of Ancient Buildings in Shrewsbury* (1820–21). Owen produced three further volumes of etchings in 1826, 1842, and 1855, all privately printed. On 6 December 1825 he married Mary Darby, the only daughter of Samuel Darby of Colebrookdale, with whom he had two children, Hugh and Mary, and who survived him. He first took up oil painting at the age of fifty, and he completed several hundred landscapes, many taken from the numerous sketches he produced during his tours of France and Belgium, and (in 1840) of Italy, the Levant, Germany, and Switzerland. He exhibited three paintings at the Society (later Royal Society) of British Artists between 1837 and 1840—a landscape, an interior, and *A Welsh Cottage*. He also exhibited eight works at the British Institution, including *The Prodigal*. Owen lived for many years at Cheltenham, and in the latter part of his life at Betws Hall, Monmouthshire. He died at Cheltenham on 15 July 1863 and was buried at St James's, Cheltenham.

W. W. WROTH, *rev.* GREG SMITH

Sources *Art Journal*, 27 (1865), 77–80 • Venn, *Alum. Cant.* • M. H. Grant, *A dictionary of British etchers* (1952), 154 • J. Foster, ed., *Index ecclesiasticus, or, Alphabetical lists of all ecclesiastical dignitaries in England and Wales since the Reformation* (1890) • *CGPLA Eng. & Wales* (1863) • J. Johnson, ed., *Works exhibited at the Royal Society of British Artists, 1824–1893, and the New English Art Club, 1888–1917*, 2 vols. (1975) • Mallalieu, *Watercolour artists* • Wood, *Vic. painters*, 2nd edn
Archives BM, department of prints and drawings • Shrewsbury Library • Shrops. RRC, sketches • V&A, department of prints and drawings
Likenesses E. P. Owen, self-portrait, etching (after anonymous portrait), repro. in E. P. Owen, *Etchings* (privately printed, 1820), frontispiece
Wealth at death under £186,000: probate, 2 Sept 1863, *CGPLA Eng. & Wales*

Owen, Ellis (1789–1868), antiquary and Welsh-language poet, was born on 31 March 1789 in the parish of Ynyscynhaearn, Caernarvonshire, the son of Owen Ellis, farmer, and Ann Thomas, his wife, of Cefnymeysydd in the same parish. He went to school at Penmorfa, and was afterwards sent to Shrewsbury; on returning home he settled at Cefnymeysydd, and on his father's death took charge of the farm. He spent the rest of his life at Cefnymeysydd as a prosperous farmer of much local influence, holding several minor offices, such as churchwarden, inspector of weights and measures for the county, and secretary of the Bible Society for the Tremadoc district. He was chiefly remarkable as a writer of *englynion* (stanzas), as a local antiquary and genealogist, and as the friend and tutor of the young poets of the district. The Literary Society of Cefnymeysydd (Cymdeithas Lenyddol Cefnymeysydd), the precursor of many a society of the kind in Wales, met fortnightly at his house and under his presidency for eleven years (1846–57). Four days before his death at Cefnymeysydd on 27 January 1868, Owen had been elected a fellow of the Society of Antiquaries. He was buried at Ynyscynhaearn on 31 January 1868. His poetical and prose writings were collected by Robert Isaac Jones (Alltud Eifion), and published, with a biographical notice, under the title *Cell meudwy* (*The Hermit's Cell*) in 1877.

J. E. LLOYD, *rev.* M. CLARE LOUGHLIN-CHOW

Sources *Cell meudwy, sef, Gweithiau barddonol a rhyddieithol Ellis Owen*, ed. R. I. Jones (1877) • *DWB* • M. Stephens, ed., *The Oxford companion to the literature of Wales* (1986) • Boase, *Mod. Eng. biog.*
Archives NL Wales, corresp., literary MSS, and papers | NL Wales, letters to Ebenezer Thomas
Wealth at death under £1500: probate, 23 June 1868, *CGPLA Eng. & Wales*

Owen, Sir Francis Philip Cunliffe- (1828–1894), museum director and exhibition organizer, born on 8 June 1828, was third son of Captain Charles Cunliffe-Owen RN and Mary (*d.* 1841), only daughter of Sir Henry Blosset, formerly chief justice of Bengal. He entered the navy at the age of twelve but, owing to ill health, abandoned the profession after five years' service in the Mediterranean and the West Indies. In 1854 he married Jenny (*d.* 1894), daughter of Baron Fritz von Reitzenstein, of the Royal Prussian horse guards. They had six daughters and two sons, one of whom, Sir Hugo von Reitzenstein Cunliffe-*Owen, became a successful tobacco entrepreneur. Also in 1854, the influence of an elder brother, Henry Charles Cunliffe-*Owen, obtained him a post in the recently established Department of Science and Art. The department's secretary, Henry Cole, appointed him as one of the superintendents of the British section of the Universal Exhibition held at Paris in 1855, a task for which Owen's excellent knowledge of French proved to be a great advantage. The collaboration between the two men blossomed into an extremely successful partnership in the promotion of international exhibitions, and their combined efforts helped shape the course of these events during the latter half of the nineteenth century.

Owen's successful administration in Paris in 1855 led to his appointment in 1857 as deputy general superintendent of the newly established South Kensington Museum, and he was promoted to the post of assistant director in 1860, subordinate to Cole, who served as director. In 1862 the second great London Exhibition was held, and Owen acted as director of the foreign sections. Soon afterwards, in 1864, he was elected a member of the Society of Arts, which was instrumental in promoting Cole's initiatives in the fields of education and exhibition. For the Paris Universal Exhibition of 1867, Owen was again made second in command to Cole, as assistant executive commissioner. His years of labouring under Cole were rewarded when he was appointed secretary of the royal commission appointed to represent Britain at the Vienna International Exhibition in 1873, answering directly to the prince of Wales. In the same year Cole retired from both the posts he held at South Kensington, and one of them, the directorship of the museum, was conferred upon Owen.

The next international event was the Centennial Exhibition held at Philadelphia in 1876. Owen was appointed executive commissioner for Great Britain and visited America for the purpose of making the preliminary arrangements. After he resigned, the post was filled by Herbert Sandford. In 1878 Owen was once again made secretary of the royal commission to the Universal Exhibition of that year in Paris. At the close of the exhibition he was made a KCMG and CIE, having been appointed CB after Vienna. Among his many foreign decorations was that of grand officer in the French Légion d'honneur. In 1879 he was also appointed to the council of the Society of Arts.

Owen subsequently turned his great experience in organizing exhibitions to account in Britain. Taking up the somewhat unpromising scheme for a fisheries exhibition in 1883, he succeeded in transforming it into a great public success and a fashionable amusement. This was followed up by the International Health Exhibition in 1884, the Inventions and Music Exhibition in 1885, and, finally, the Indian and Colonial Exhibition of 1886. Owen controlled to a very great extent the administration of all these 1880s exhibitions, relying on the active support of the prince of Wales and the co-operation of the duke of Buckingham and Sir Frederick Bramwell. Although Owen was made a KCB after the Indian and Colonial Exhibition, he did not receive the direction of the Imperial Institute, which was founded in 1887 as a development of that event.

After some years of failing health owing to heart disease, Owen retired from his post at the South Kensington Museum in 1893. As a museum director, he was considered nothing more nor less than a capable administrator, who possessed little expert knowledge of his own and was sometimes criticized for not valuing it enough in others. He was clearly best suited to the work of organizing exhibitions and seems to have been happiest when engaged in that capacity. He died at 13 Kirkley-cliff, Lowestoft, Suffolk, on 23 March 1894.

H. T. Wood, *rev.* R. C. Denis

Sources *The Times* (24 March 1894) • *Journal of the Society of Arts*, 42 (1893–4), 406–7 • *The Athenaeum* (31 March 1894), 419
Archives BL, letters to Sir Austen Layard, Add. MSS 39009, 39035–39037 • V&A, corresp. with Sir Henry Cole
Likenesses W. & D. Downey, cabinet photograph, NPG • Lock & Whitfield, woodburytype photograph, NPG; repro. in T. Cooper, *Men of mark: a gallery of contemporary portraits* (1880) • Smeeton & Tilly, woodcut, BM; repro. in *L'Art* (1878) • Spy [L. Ward], caricature, chromolithograph, NPG; repro. in *VF* (23 Nov 1878) • Walery, photograph, NPG • lithograph, NPG; repro. in *Whitehall Review* (12 Oct 1878) • wood-engraving (after photograph by F. Luenhardt), NPG; repro. in *ILN* (8 Nov 1873) • wood-engraving, NPG; repro. in *ILN* (31 July 1886)
Wealth at death £4832 16*s*. 2*d*.: resworn probate, Aug 1895, *CGPLA Eng. & Wales*

Owen, (Humphrey) Frank (1905–1979), newspaper editor, was born on 4 November 1905 at 10 Widemarsh Street, Hereford, the only son of Thomas Humphrey Owen and his wife, Cicely Hannah Green. Marjorie Elizabeth was the only daughter; Frank retained a close friendship with her to his dying day. His father was the innkeeper of the Black Swan, and Frank never ceased to honour his father's trade. He was sent first to Monmouth School, and from that Haberdashers' foundation to Sidney Sussex College, Cambridge. He obtained a second class (division one) of part one (1926) and a first class (division two) of part two (1927) of the history tripos, a rugby blue, and a glowing reputation as a scholar, athlete, and drinking companion. During his studies he had made himself an expert on the American Civil War, and his interest in military history had become a passion. Reading in general had become a passion too.

After a sharp apprenticeship as a journalist in Geneva, in 1928 Owen joined the staff of the *South Wales Argus*, published in Newport. A few months later he was nominated as prospective Liberal candidate for his native city of Hereford, and at the general election of 1929 was elected, with a majority of 1121, as the youngest member in the new parliament. He immediately attached himself to the Lloyd George section of the Liberal Party, and thereafter never wavered, for the rest of his life, in his allegiance to Lloyd George's special brand of vibrant radicalism (apart from a comparable and excusable hero-worship of Leon Trotsky in the years when Stalinism was supposedly a respectable creed). Mostly, in that 1929 parliament, he voted to sustain the Labour government and found his most congenial associates on the left of the Labour Party, among the spokesmen of the Independent Labour Party, or with a fellow Welshman, Aneurin Bevan, the young MP for neighbouring Ebbw Vale, with whom he formed an immediate and lasting friendship. His voting record and his insistence in 1931 on following Lloyd George in rejecting the National Government appeal together ensured his defeat by a thumping 6953 votes. 'In 1929', he would later recite, 'the wise, far-seeing, independent electors of my native Hereford sent me to Westminster, and two years later, in 1931, the lousy bastards kicked me out' (private information).

For all Owen's potential gifts as a speaker after the Lloyd George pattern, journalism suited him better, and after a brief spell on the *News Chronicle* he found his real home on the Beaverbrook newspapers and with Lord Beaverbrook himself. The two men approached the task of producing the next morning's newspaper with the same relish and tingling excitement. Owen worked first as reporter and leader writer for the *Daily Express* (1931–7). He also turned his hand, partly on Beaverbrook's prompting, to pamphleteering. *His was the Kingdom* (1937) offered an anti-Baldwinite, pro-Beaverbrookish account of King Edward's abdication.

However, it was as editor of Beaverbrook's *Evening Standard*, from 1938 to 1941, that Owen showed himself an editor of genius. He had had two years' practice to get his hand in before the actual outbreak of war. He was the first popular journalist to discover how Hitler's awful name sold newspapers; in the wretched years of appeasement, and in the same Beaverbrook press which carried the headlines 'no war this year or next', be it not forgotten, he made a special feature of rewriting *Mein Kampf* week after week to sound the alarm and raise sales by the same stroke of his dashing pen. In 1939 Owen married Grace Stewart McGillivray (*d*. 1968). She was from Boston, USA, the daughter of Daniel Augustine McGillivray, decorative artist. They had no children.

When the war actually came in September 1939, Owen led the deputation of Beaverbrook editors who privately told their proprietor that he must change his mind. Then, in the months of 1939 of the phoney war, when Beaverbrook himself was still sulking in his appeaser's tent, Owen started to fashion the paper into what it truly became, a combined sword and shield for the people of London. By the time Hitler was pushing through the Ardennes, and Lloyd George was overthrowing Neville Chamberlain in the House of Commons, and Beaverbrook was re-establishing his beneficent alliance with Churchill in the war cabinet, and the people of London were roused to save themselves and the world, the *Evening Standard* had been transformed from the West End house journal which it was in the mid-1930s into the flaming herald of the embattled city.

Even the wartime *Evening Standard*, in the liberal and inspired hands of Frank Owen, could not say everything he wanted to say—after all, his still ever-vigilant proprietor was a member of the war cabinet. Something more was needed to touch the ferment of the times. So, after the retreat from Dunkirk, Owen joined with two of his fellow Beaverbrook journalists, Peter Howard and Michael Foot, to write, under the pseudonym of Cato, the pamphlet *Guilty Men* (1940). The declared purpose of the project was to drive the Chamberlainites from Churchill's cabinet. The pseudonym was designed to deceive Beaverbrook among others, and for a while it succeeded. However, exposure when it came was not fatal, since Beaverbrook and, more still, Churchill were not included on the guilty list. *Guilty Men* was a runaway success story, even though the agent who sold the manuscript to Victor Gollancz did in fact literally run away with part of the royalties.

Owen sought some other outlets too. When Hitler's armies invaded the Soviet Union in the summer of 1941, he joined the campaign for demanding British and American support for the Soviet forces and later a demand for the opening of a second front. Again, in 1941 and 1942, under another pseudonym Thomas Rainboro', the leveller captain in Cromwell's army, he contributed a series on the conduct of the war to *Tribune*, then being edited by his old ally of the 1931 parliament, Aneurin Bevan. No such criticism of Churchill himself, no comparable condemnation of the general war strategy, had been published anywhere in any wartime newspaper before. Owen drew upon his own military knowledge but also upon the special relationship he had with such figures as General Sir Archibald Wavell, Major-General J. F. C. Fuller, B. H. Liddell Hart, Orde Wingate, Lord Louis Mountbatten, and several more. Owen was a journalist of the first order, but it was his special touch as a military correspondent which found the chinks in the Churchillian armour.

Owen himself had always wanted to join the services; journalism, even in bomb-battered London, was no tolerable substitute. Even before his Rainboro' exploits were complete, he was taken off to train in the Royal Armoured Corps. He quickly became a tank enthusiast, like one of his mentors, J. F. C. Fuller. Lord Louis Mountbatten requested his services for *SEAC*, the paper which served the army in Burma. Once again, as with Beaverbrook, the kinship with Mountbatten became explosive and decisive. The two men together helped to shape the Burma campaign. Owen was rewarded with the rank of lieutenant-colonel, and appointed to the OBE (1946), and at the end of hostilities he wrote an excellent official document, *The Campaign in Burma* (1946). Mountbatten would swear by him, as all who ever served nearby him in any cause would.

Owen returned to Fleet Street after the war, first as a contributor for the *Daily Mail*, and later, from 1947 to 1950, as its editor. The relationship with the second Viscount Rothermere could never be compared with his Beaverbrook association, and when the relationship collapsed, he renewed his work with Beaverbrook, who was looking for someone to use the extensive Lloyd George papers which he had acquired. Owen seemed to be the ideal biographer. He knew Lloyd George more intimately than any other Fleet Street observer; he held Lloyd George's trust, an uneasy hold at any time, thanks to his conduct in 1931. The result was *Tempestuous Journey*, published in 1954; not by any reckoning the definitive Lloyd George biography but one which still offers flashes of perception, not to be seen elsewhere, by one Welshman on another.

The remaining years of his life were sad; the shining talents, the glittering insights, the sparkle lost their power. He still wrote for the newspapers; he stood again as an unsuccessful Liberal candidate on two occasions for Hereford (1955 and 1956). He wrote several books, but none of the same substance as his biography of Lloyd George: *The Eddie Chapman Story* in 1953; *Peron: his Rise and Fall* in 1957; *The Fall of Singapore* in 1960. All these were themes which stirred his sympathies but, especially after the death of his wife in 1968, he lost his self-confidence.

Owen was an outstanding journalist; for a short period, and a great period in British history and especially London's history, the very best of his time. In the late 1930s and the early 1940s he understood the military and political requirements of the age better than anyone else in any editorial chair in Fleet Street during a period when Fleet Street truly helped to shape Britain's history. He died on 23 January 1979 at Worthing. He was a freeman of the City of London. MICHAEL FOOT, *rev.*

Sources personal knowledge (1986) • private information (1986) • A. J. P. Taylor, *Beaverbrook* (1972) • *WWW* • *Daily Telegraph* (25 Jan 1979) • *CGPLA Eng. & Wales* (1979) • A. Chisholm and M. Davie, *Beaverbrook: a life* (1992)

Archives HLRO, corresp. with Lord Beaverbrook

Wealth at death £2343: administration, 19 Sept 1979, *CGPLA Eng. & Wales*

Owen, George (*c*.1499–1558), physician, was born about 1499 in the diocese of Worcester, and was educated at Oxford. He became probationer fellow of Merton College in 1519 and graduated MA in 1521. He was keeper of the Bourgchier chest in 1520–21, the Chichele and Audley chest also in 1521, and the Danvers chest from 1522 to 1524. At Merton he was first bursar 1524–5 and third bursar 1525–6. He seems to have been destined for the church, but on marrying Lettice, a widow from Suffolk, he took up medicine, having first attempted to trade as a white baker in Oxford without becoming a freeman of the city. He took his BM in 1525 and his DM in 1528. In 1525 Owen received a licence to practise medicine, and at first worked in Oxford, but soon after his graduation he was appointed physician to Henry VIII, and frequently visited the court. He, together with John Chambre and William Butts, attended the birth of Prince Edward in 1537, and he was a signatory to the letter to the council announcing the serious condition of the child's mother, Jane Seymour. The statement that he performed a caesarean section upon her is untrue. Through 1537 and 1538 he was often summoned to prescribe for the prince. The king proved a generous patron, and during the dissolution of the monasteries made him many grants of lands and houses in

Oxford and its neighbourhood, to which Owen added by extensive purchases. In 1537 he was given New Hall and St Alban Hall in Oxford with a fee of £100 (these buildings were subsequently sold to Merton College) and he was allowed to purchase the manor of Yarnton, Oxfordshire. In March 1540 he acquired Godstow Abbey for £558 and in 1541 he bought Walton and Wolvercote manors and the site of Rewley Abbey, which he soon passed on to Christ Church, for £1174. In 1546, together with Dr John Bridges, he acquired Cumnor Place for £1300. Godstow Abbey became Owen's main home. He was one of the subscribing witnesses to the will of Henry VIII, who left him a legacy of £100.

Edward VI kept Owen as royal physician, and treated him with as much generosity as his father. From 1547 he was seemingly able to use the duchy of Lancaster's money as his own, having been appointed a receiver-general on 30 September that year. In 1550 he bought the rectory and chapel of St Giles', Oxford, and on 4 February 1553 Edward gave him, jointly with Henry Martin of Oxford, Durham College, which they sold a year later to Sir Thomas Pope for the site of his projected Trinity College. He received a grant of arms from Edward, and, on 25 October 1552, a royal grant of land of the value of £20 a year. These acquisitions made Owen the greatest landowner to the north-west of Oxford, and brought him into conflict with Sir John Williams over rights in Wytham Woods, and with the city over Port meadow. Fortunately his eldest son, Richard, married Mary, daughter of Sir Leonard Chamberlain, Mary's leading supporter, after Williams, in the area.

Meanwhile Owen was taking a prominent place in his profession, and was held in esteem by the public. John Leland addressed an encomium 'Ad D. Audoenum medicum regium', and, according to his friend Thomas Caius, he and Queen Katherine Parr joined in inducing Caius to translate into English Erasmus's paraphrase of St Mark's gospel. He was admitted a fellow of the College of Physicians on 25 June 1545; an elect in 1552, in place of John Chambre, deceased; and on 2 October 1553 was elected president, an office to which he was reappointed the following year.

Owen was present at the death of Edward VI, being the last person to speak to him, but this did not mark the end of his royal connection: he was nominated royal physician on Mary's accession, and in the first year of the new reign he was instrumental in obtaining an act for the confirmation and enlargement of the powers of the College of Physicians. Two years later, when a difference arose between the College of Physicians and the University of Oxford concerning the admission by the latter of Simon Ludford and David Laughton to the degree of bachelor of medicine, Cardinal Pole, then chancellor of the university, directed that body to consult Owen and Dr Thomas Huys, the queen's physicians, 'de instituendis rationibus quibus Oxoniensis academia in admittendis medicis niteretur'. Owen and his colleague suggested an agreement which the chancellor approved and ratified.

Owen remained until his death on friendly terms with Queen Mary. In 1554 he testified that Princess Elizabeth was well enough to answer the queen's summons after Wyatt's rebellion, and, in the spring of 1555, Mary sent him to Woodstock to report on Elizabeth's health. At the new year of 1556 he presented the queen with 'two pottles of preserves' (Madden, 254). Owen was made a JP in Oxfordshire in 1547 and was a commissioner of relief in 1550. In 1558 he was returned to parliament for Oxfordshire. He married twice, the second time to Mary. He died of an epidemic intermittent fever on 18 October 1558, and was buried on 24 October in London at St Stephen Walbrook. He was the author of a treatise named *A Meet Diet for the New Ague, Set Forth by Mr. Dr. Owen*, published in 1558.

Owen left a son, William, and two daughters, Lettice and Elizabeth, beside the aforementioned Richard, all from his first marriage. William, the second son, and his wife, Anne, daughter of John Rawley of Billesby, Northamptonshire, were living at Cumnor Place when Amy Robsart, wife of Robert Dudley, earl of Leicester, met her mysterious death there in 1560. William Owen sold Cumnor to Anthony Forster in 1572, and in the same year was elected MP for Oxford. He seems to have retained his father's property at Godstow, and lived there.

John Owen, described in 1615 as a Roman Catholic, of Godstow, was Richard Owen's grandson, and great-grandson of George Owen. He achieved some notoriety in 1615 by being charged with using the treasonable expression that it was lawful to kill the king, since he was excommunicate. The jury brought in a verdict of guilty, and sentence of death was passed, but, after remaining in prison in the king's bench for three years, Owen was pardoned on 24 July 1618, at the request of the Spanish ambassador, on condition of his leaving the country within twenty days. SIDNEY LEE, *rev.* PATRICK WALLIS

Sources HoP, *Commons, 1509–58* • Foster, *Alum. Oxon.* • *Literary remains of King Edward the Sixth*, ed. J. G. Nichols, 2 vols., Roxburghe Club, 75 (1857) • W. H. Turner, ed., *Selections from the records of the city of Oxford* (1880) • G. C. Brodrick, *Memorials of Merton College*, OHS, 4 (1885) • H. Ellis, ed., *Original letters illustrative of English history*, 3rd ser., 4 vols. (1846) • *VCH Oxfordshire*, vol. 4 • *The diary of Henry Machyn, citizen and merchant-taylor of London, from AD 1550 to AD 1563*, ed. J. G. Nichols, CS, 42 (1848) • F. Madden, *Privy purse expenses of the Princess Mary, daughter of King Henry the Eighth* (1831) • A. Wood, *Survey of the antiquities of the city of Oxford*, ed. A. Clark, 2, OHS, 17 (1890) • J. Chambers, *Biographical illustrations of Worcestershire* (1820) • *CSP, 1611–18*, 548, 558 • *State trials*, vol. 2

Owen, George (1552–1613), antiquary, was born at Henllys, near Newport, Pembrokeshire. He was the son of the lawyer William *Owen (*c.*1488–1574) and Elizabeth (*c.*1520–1603), daughter of Sir George Herbert of Swansea and his wife, Elizabeth, daughter of Sir Thomas Berkeley, and niece of William Herbert, first earl of Pembroke of the second creation. Nothing is known of his early education although it is likely that he received tuition in the law and estate management from his father. On 4 October 1571 William Owen settled the barony of Cemais on George, with the castle of Newport and the advowson of six churches; George's father had acquired the barony from Lord Audley. George Owen was married the same year to Elizabeth (*d.* 1606), daughter and coheir of William Philipps of

Picton Castle and his wife, Janet, daughter of Thomas Perrot of Haroldston and sister of Sir John Perrot. Philipps and Perrot were the two most powerful figures in Pembrokeshire, but much at enmity, and it was at a fracas between the two adversarial factions that occurred at Haverfordwest on 9 February 1572 that Owen made his first recorded public appearance. A retaliatory assault had been proposed upon Owen's pro-Perrott neighbour, and, although the latter (Thomas ab Owen of Pentre Ifan) prudently stayed at home, Owen's men were arrested, which was regarded as a calculated rebuff to the young lord of Cemais. He was admitted at Barnard's Inn on 5 August 1573 but there is no record of the duration of his stay there.

With his wife, Elizabeth, Owen had eleven children, four of whom died in infancy. She died in 1606 and, not long afterwards, he married his mistress, Anne or Ankred (*d.* 1634), daughter of William Obiled, a Carmarthen tucker, with whom he had already had seven illegitimate children. Deeply conscious of his position as lord of Cemais, Owen spent much time in litigation over claims to the seigneurial rights pertaining to the former marcher lordship, which had been neglected by the Audleys, who had their main baronial estate at Heleigh in Staffordshire. In his efforts to reinstate feudal rights he discomfited his tenants, who were indisposed to pay lapsed rents or perform outdated services; and in 1606, as none of the burgesses was prepared to collect the rents and dues, he was unable to exercise his right to appoint the mayor of Newport. He was also unpopular with his gentry neighbours, who reported him to the privy council charged with forgery and counterfeiting deeds, and he was arrested while sitting in his own court at Newport on 27 November 1579. His house was searched, but no incriminating evidence was found. These and other charges having failed, he was accused of adultery before the ecclesiastical commissioners, which he could not well deny. In his endeavour to prove that the lordship of Cemais had come to his father by descent rather than by purchase, Owen, although he was the leading genealogist in west Wales and had produced the first armorial in Wales, extended his pedigree and gave a misleading account of his coat of arms.

Owen's main interest lay in the land, and his desire to improve agriculture and methods of husbandry led him to investigate and describe the basic geological features of Pembrokeshire. The soil needed lime, he contended, and to enable farmers to find it, he traced the outcrops of limestone and discovered that they ran in close parallel with the veins of anthracite coal that was required to fire the limekilns. His description of clay marl, which he championed as a fertiliser in his unpublished 'Treatise of marle' (NL Wales, Bronwydd MS 3, fols. 218–22), enabled it to be recognized as glacial till, though he subscribed to the common belief that it was the deposit of Noah's flood. His contribution to geological study was later acknowledged when he was dubbed 'the patriarch of English geologists' (*EdinR*, 73, 1841, 3). His condemnation of the exposure of unschooled young men and boys to the elements while herding cattle gave him reason to recommend enclosure and to establish a school at Felindre Farchog, near Henllys, for their education.

Owen's interest in cartography became apparent in his claim that Saxton's map of Pembrokeshire (1579) gave an exaggerated view of the county and led to an unfair demand for men for the musters. He carried out a survey and produced a map of the county in 1602, bordered by lists of hundreds, baronies, towns, castles, forests, and other features, and emblazoned with the arms of the leading county families. When Camden published maps of the counties in the 1607 edition of his *Britannia*, most of them by Saxton and Norden, he invited Owen to provide the map for Pembrokeshire.

Owen took his public duties and responsibilities seriously. He was placed on the commission of the peace about 1584 and, in 1587, when Henry, earl of Pembroke, was made lieutenant of Wales, he appointed Owen and Thomas Perrot his deputy lieutenants in the county of Pembroke. He served two terms as sheriff of the county, in 1587, and again in 1602, when he had the unpleasant duty of arranging the execution of two brothers, kinsmen of his first wife, who had killed a cousin in a brawl. He was one of the commissioners appointed to survey and value the estate of his lifelong enemy, Sir John Perrot, who had died attainted in the Tower of London in 1592. He was made deputy vice-admiral of the counties of Pembroke and Cardigan in 1598. The vulnerability of Milford Haven in the event of invasion by the Spaniards caused him concern and he conducted a survey with a view to providing coastal defence. In November 1595 the earl of Pembroke wrote to 'my very good cozen George Owen, esquier' stating that he had 'long expected' to receive from him a map of the Haven that he could show to the queen. Owen sent him the map, which has since been lost, together with 'a pamphelett conteigninge the description of Mylford havon' (Owen, *Description of Penbrokshire*, ed. H. Owen, pt 2, 531–2), and he made proposals for its defence.

Owen was fortunate in having lived at a time when there was an awakening of interest in Welsh antiquities and although he resided in a remote part of Wales, he had a well-stocked library at Henllys. He gathered around him a coterie of antiquaries, including George Owen Harry and George William Griffith, and maintained contact with others such as the poet–genealogist Lewys Dwnn, and with William Camden whom he visited at the College of Arms while pursuing his researches in London. He employed three permanent scriveners.

Owen's most important work, *The Description of Penbrokshire*, was begun in December 1602, soon after the appearance of Richard Carew's *Survey of Cornwall*, and it was completed on 18 May 1603. He then proceeded to write a 'Second Booke', giving a detailed history parish by parish, but only a fragment survives, which was published by B. G. Charles in the *National Library of Wales Journal*. Although Owen was a prolific writer, none of his work appeared in print during his lifetime, nor did any until Richard Fenton published a section of the 'First booke' containing an account of the ancient game of knappan in *The Cambrian Register for the Year 1795* (1796). In the *Register* for the following year, Fenton produced the remainder of the work as 'A history of Pembrokeshire, from a manuscript of George Owen, esq., of Henllys, lord of Kemes, with additions and abbreviations by John Lewis, esq., of Manarnawan'. It was indifferently edited and John Lewis's observations were so 'very largely interlarded with personal invective and private anecdotes' that they had to be expurgated. After Fenton's death in 1821 the manuscript passed to his son who sold it to Sir Thomas Phillipps and, by 1892, it was in the hands of the marquess of Bute from whose descendant it was acquired by the National Library of Wales (NL Wales, MS 13212). A later version of the manuscript was purchased from the bookseller Thomas Osborne by William Oldys in December 1738 for Edward Harley, earl of Oxford, at whose death in 1753 it was among his collection bought by parliament and placed in the British Museum (Harley MS 6250). It is now in the British Library.

George Owen's *Description of Penbrokshire* first appeared in book form in 1892 when it was published by the Honourable Society of Cymmrodorion as number 1 in its Cymmrodorion Record Series. The society published three further volumes under the same title. The second volume (1897) contained collections of papers relating to Pembrokeshire and to the barony of Cemais in particular, together with 'A cataloge and genelogie of the lordes of the baronye of Kemes seethence the conquests', accounts of suits in Star Chamber, the inquisitions post mortem of William Owen and George Owen, and 'The description of Milford Haven'. Part 3 (1906) comprised 'The dialogue of the government of Wales', which took place between Barthol, a German civil lawyer, and Demetus, recognizable as the author; 'Cruell lawes against Welshmen … made by Henrie the ffourth' following the failure of his attempts to quell the rebellion of Owain Glyn Dŵr, laws that the author considered to be malicious; and 'A treatise of lordshipps marchers in Wales', and 'The description of Wales', which listed the lordships, towns, and features of each of the counties of south Wales. The editor stated that part 4 would include the remainder of the Welsh counties, 'The fragmentes of Wales' (1606–11), containing a collection of notes on the marcher lordships and the principality of Wales, and 'The treatise of marle', but he did not live to complete the work and the volume did not appear until 1936. *The Description of Penbrokshire* was next published in 1994. A facsimile edition of Owen's commonplace book, *The Taylors Cussion*, was published in 1906, containing inventories of livestock, lists of high office-holders, *aides-mémoire* and mnemonic verses, and passing thoughts.

Owen displayed the traditional Welsh hospitality towards the itinerant Welsh bards who came to Henllys and sang his praise during his lifetime but, strangely, no elegies survive. At his death, the main part of his collection of manuscripts passed to his neighbour and assistant, George William Griffith of Penybenglog, though some went to his natural son, George *Owen, York herald, and, after passing through many hands, they were gathered together by Edward Protheroe and acquired in 1828 by the College of Arms, where they remain as the Protheroe collection.

Although a protestant and an anti-papist and patron of six churches, Owen made little reference to religion, except that he upheld the sanctity of the sabbath and welcomed the translation of the Bible into Welsh. No likeness of him exists. It is known that he was lame as the result of an infirmity suffered in his right leg when he was four years of age and, from middle age onward, he suffered from the gout in both legs; but this did not prevent his travelling long distances in pursuit of his researches, when he had to be lifted on to his horse and to his bed. His personal character is veiled behind his insistent efforts to establish himself as a feudal lord. He died on 26 August 1613 at Haverfordwest; his body was taken to Henllys and was buried at Nevern church, where a brass plaque commemorates him.

Owen left no will, and the disposal of his estate by his only legitimate son, Alban Owen (1580–1656), led to disputes, many of them arising from an insistence on maintaining the manorial customs as his father had done. He followed his father also in his public duties as justice of the peace, deputy lieutenant, and twice as sheriff of the county of Pembroke. During the civil war he was nominated by parliament to put the militia ordinance into execution in Pembrokeshire, but he was a royalist and signed royalist declarations which led to the sequestration of his estate. A collection of the arms of the London City companies with Alban Owen's signature attached is preserved in the Phillipps Library at Cheltenham (MS 13140, no. 106).

Among Owen's natural children with Anne Obiled were George *Owen (*c.*1598–1665), York herald and Evan Owen (1599–1662), who matriculated from Jesus College, Oxford, in 1622 and proceeded BA the same day, MA on 21 June 1625, BTh on 31 August 1636, and DTh on 12 April 1643. Evan was appointed to the rectories of Newport (17 February 1623), Llanychlwydog (14 July 1626), and Walwyn's Castle (22 May 1638), and was installed chancellor of St David's on 8 May 1645. He died on 30 December 1662 and was buried at Llawhaden church where a mural tablet was placed to his memory. DILLWYN MILES

Sources B. G. Charles, *George Owen of Henllys: a Welsh Elizabethan* (1973) • G. Owen, *The description of Penbrokshire*, ed. H. Owen, 4 vols., Honourable Society of Cymmrodorion, Cymmrodorion Record Series, 1 (1892–1936) • G. Owen, *Description of Pembrokeshire*, ed. D. Miles (1994) • B. G. Charles, 'The second book of George Owen's *Description of Pembrokeshire*', *National Library of Wales Journal*, 5 (1947–8), 265–85 • G. Owen, *The taylors cussion*, ed. E. M. Pritchard (1906) • *Heraldic visitations of Wales and part of the marches … by Lewys Dwnn*, ed. S. R. Meyrick, 2 vols. (1846) • 'Baronia de Kemeys from the original documents at Bronwydd', *Archaeologia Cambrensis*, 3rd ser., 7 (1861), suppl., 1–36 [Owen's 'Prooffes … that the lordshipp of Kemes is a Lordshippe marcher'] • 'Baronia de Kemeys from the original documents at Bronwydd', *Archaeologia Cambrensis*, 3rd ser., 8 (1862), suppl., 37–136 ['A register book of the barony of Kemeys'] • A. L. Leach, *The history of the civil war (1642–1649) in Pembrokeshire and on its borders* (1937) • *Cambrian Register*, 1 (1796) • *Cambrian Register*, 2 (1799) • *EdinR*, 73 (1841)

Archives BL, description of Pembrokeshire and treatise on lordship marchers, Harley MSS 141, 6250 • Cardiff Central Library, historical and genealogical MSS • Coll. Arms, Welsh pedigrees • CUL, topographical collections relating to Kemeys, Pembrokeshire • NL Wales, papers • NL Wales, notes and papers relating to Kemeys, Pembrokeshire • NL Wales, *The first book of the description of Penbrokshire in general*, MS 13212 • NL Wales, *The second book of the description of Penbrokshire*, Bronwydd 7204 • NL Wales, treatise on Welsh marcher lordships, notes relating to seignories of Pembroke and Kemeys | Coll. Arms, Protheroe MSS • NL Wales, Bronwydd collection

Owen, George [*pseud.* George Owen Harry] (*b. c.*1553, *d.* in or before 1614), Church of England clergyman and antiquary, was, according to the pedigree he himself supplied to Lewys Dwnn, the son of Owain ap Harri of Llanelli, south Wales, and Maud, daughter of Philip ap John ap Thomas of Hendre Mor, Gower. His uncle John Harris was the parson of Dinas in Pembrokeshire, to which position he had been presented by the lord of Cemais, the antiquary George Owen of Henllys. George Owen Harry followed the same path as his uncle and was presented to the rectory of Whitchurch in Cemais, Pembrokeshire, on 18 March 1584. He was also rector of nearby Llanfihangel Penbedw and held both livings from 1597 until his death, residing at the latter. He became a close friend and continual companion to George Owen of Henllys and it was in connection with him that almost all George Owen Harry's work was produced. He signed himself George Owen, clerk, and the use of the name George Owen Harry on his publications was probably an attempt to distinguish himself from his patron.

George Owen Harry's major work is known in manuscript as 'The wellspring of true nobility' and was published as *The genealogy of the high and mighty monarch James … king of Great Brittayne, etc., with his lineall descent from Noah, by divers direct lynes to Brutus* (1604). The work is in the line of those pedigrees that traced the house of Tudor's noble Welsh descent and drew about the Tudor accession of 1485 the *mab darogan* ('son of prophecy') tradition that a descendant of Cadwaladr would return to take the throne of Britain. George Owen Harry's pedigree is a reworking that celebrates the accession of the house of Stuart and represents a last and somewhat formal transformation of a lengthy tradition.

George Owen Harry was an accomplished penman and engaged both in scribal work and in engrossing deeds for his patron. One deed executed in the year of his arrival is 'neatly embellished with scroll work, coloured flowers, little birds, a fox and dogs, and an illuminated initial O in the centre of which he drew a miniature map of Pembrokeshire' (Charles, 115). His skills also extended to heraldry. He painted an armorial achievement for George Owen in 1586 and, more notably, compiled a Pembrokeshire armorial, known only from a late copy, which together with two armorials compiled by George Owen comprise the first armorials made in Wales. It is either George Owen Harry or John Browne, Owen's scribe, who produced 'Creations of the nobilytie of Englande from the first years of William the Conqueror untyll the XXVth yeere of our most drede soueraigne lady Elizabeth' to George Owen's scheme and material. George Owen Harry also copied the Black Book of Carmarthen for George Owen of Henllys. This copy is now lost but when it was transcribed by John Jones of Gellilyfdy he noted that George Owen Harry did not understand the verse and ancient script. The date of Owen Harry's death is unknown. His will was proved on 20 August 1614.

MIHAIL DAFYDD EVANS

Sources B. G. Charles, *George Owen of Henllys* (1973) • *DWB* • J. C. Davies, 'Letters of admission to the rectory of Whitechurch', *National Library of Wales Journal*, 4 (1945–6), 83–8 • F. Jones, 'An approach to Welsh genealogy', *Transactions of the Honourable Society of Cymmrodorion* (1948), 303–466, esp. 382–3 • *Heraldic visitations of Wales and part of the marches … by Lewys Dwnn*, ed. S. R. Meyrick, 1 (1846), 32–3 • D. R. Woolf, *The idea of history in early Stuart England* (1990)

Archives BL, description of Pembrokeshire and treatise on lordships marchers, Harley MSS 141, 6250 • Cardiff Central Library, historical and genealogical MSS • Coll. Arms, Welsh pedigrees • CUL, topographical collections relating to Kemeys, Pembrokeshire • NL Wales, achievement of George Owen of Henllys by him, MS 6434, fol. 2 • NL Wales, notes and papers relating to Kemeys, Pembrokeshire; papers; treatise on Welsh marcher lordships; notes relating to seignories of Pembroke and Kemeys | BL, Add. MS 6928, pos. 29–68 • NL Wales, Bronwydd MSS, deed engrossed by him, 1341–1453, esp. 1385

Wealth at death £105: Charles, *George Owen*

Owen, George (*c.*1598–1665), herald, was born at Henllys, near Newport, Pembrokeshire, the son of George *Owen (1552–1613) of Henllys and his second wife, Anne or Ankred Obiled (*d* .1634), 'gott before mariage and in the life time of his firste wife' (London). Nothing is known about his early life or education, except that he appears to have inherited an interest in genealogy from his father. He was nominated Rouge Croix pursuivant on 28 February 1625 in the place of John Bradshaw, and appointed Windsor herald, but he was not confirmed in the office, despite an order sent by the earl marshal to the officers of arms, until 26 July 1626. He was promoted York herald by signet issued in December 1633 and by patent dated 3 January following, and created the next day. Owen may have been admitted to Gray's Inn on 4 August 1633, but he does not appear to have been called to the bar. He married Rebecca, daughter of Sir Thomas Dayrell of Livingstone Dayrell, near Buckingham. The couple had two sons, both of whom died young, and a daughter.

In the course of his work Owen compiled, among other unpublished works, pedigrees of Worcestershire families (1634) and a short tract dated 1638 'touching the precedence of a baronet's daughter' (BL, Add. MSS 19816, fols. 100–124, and 14410, fol. 35). He also contributed to the 1641 Golden Grove pedigree roll, 19 feet long and 'splendidly illuminated and fully emblazoned in the most sumptuous manner', containing the pedigree of the Vaughans, earls of Carbery (College of Arms, London). In 1639 Owen and William le Neve, Clarenceux king of arms, were attached to the staff of the earl of Arundel and Surrey, earl marshal, commander of the expedition against the Scottish covenanters. In 1640 he was sent into Wales on the king's service. When the civil war broke out he was described as a commander in the royalist army and he was with the king at Oxford on 12 April 1643, when the university conferred on him the honorary degree of doctor of laws, and at Gloucester in August.

Some time after February 1645, when Clarenceux, with the king's permission, appointed Owen his deputy during his absence abroad, he deserted the king. His petition to be admitted York herald under parliament was granted on 13 August 1646. He attended the funeral of the earl of Essex on 22 October that year, and was probably in attendance at the installation of Oliver Cromwell as lord protector on 26 June 1657. In October 1657 he was nominated Clarenceux but did not find favour with the Garter king of arms, Sir Edward Bysshe. He was said to have been 'peculiarly busy in promoting the cause of Parliament' (London) for which, it was claimed, he was rewarded in February 1659 by being made Norroy king of arms. He assisted at the lying-in-state and funeral of Oliver Cromwell and was probably at the installation of Richard Cromwell as protector.

At the Restoration, Owen was allowed to resume his appointment as York herald. He walked in the procession at the coronation and on reaching Westminster Hall frustrated an attempt by the royal footmen to seize the canopy that had been carried over the king by the barons of the Cinque ports. At the banquet he proclaimed the champion's challenge. His last appearance seems to have been at the funeral of Archbishop Juxon of Canterbury at Oxford on 9 July 1663. Owen then resigned, and his son-in-law, John Wingfield, succeeded him as York herald. He retired to Pembrokeshire where he died on 23 May 1665.

DILLWYN MILES

Sources H. Stanford London, 'George Owen, York herald', *Transactions of the Honourable Society of Cymmrodorion* (1946), 78–107
Archives AM Oxf., George Owen, *York Herald*, 'A collection of all the Droyts and Fees as heretofore have beene paid to the Officers of Arms, taken out of Severall bookes of receipts and partitions; and remayning in the Office of Armes, MS 840, fol. 579 · Coll. Arms, 'The golden grove pedigree roll' | NL Wales, Bronwydd MSS

Owen, Goronwy [*pseud.* Gronwy Ddu] (**1723–1769**), poet, was born on 1 January 1723 in the parish of Llanfair Mathafarn Eithaf, Anglesey, the fifth son of Owen or Owain Gronw (*b.* 1690), a labourer, and Jane Parry (*d.* 1741). He received very little primary education but is known to have attended a school at Llanallgo, near his home, *c.*1733–1734, probably run by an itinerant or local schoolmaster. A strong tradition exists that Owen was educated between 1734 and 1737 at Pwllheli, in the Llŷn peninsula, but conclusive proof is lacking. Between 1737 and 1741, however, he was a pupil at Friars School, Bangor, where he received a rigorous education in Greek and Latin. Born into a poor family, he was probably aided in his education by an unknown benefactor, possibly Edward Wynne of Bodewryd, possibly the influential Morris family of Pentre-eiriannell in the neighbouring parish of Llanfihangel Tre'r-beirdd. He entered Jesus College, Oxford, on 3 June 1742 but left after a week, probably because he was unable to support himself financially.

Owen had expressed his ambition to pursue an ecclesiastical career in a series of *englynion* written before entering Oxford, and he was admitted to priest's orders in 1747, after working as an usher at the Pwllheli school (1742–4) which he was supposed to have attended as a pupil, and Denbigh grammar school (1745). After a brief provisional curacy at the parish church of Llanfair Mathafarn Eithaf he obtained a curacy near Oswestry, and then at Oswestry itself in 1746. Owen married Elinor or Elin Hughes (1717–1757/8), seventh child of Owen Hughes, a merchant and an alderman of Oswestry, and his wife, Margaret, on 21 August 1747. They had four children: Robert (*b.* 1749), Gronwy or Gronw (*b.* 1751), Elin (*b.* 1753), and Owen (*b.* 1757). In 1748 Owen was arrested for debt and trespass, and was taken to Shrewsbury gaol. Debts and financial difficulties were to plague him for years to come.

Released from gaol through the benevolence of a local draper, Owen left Oswestry in September 1748 and moved to Donnington, near Shrewsbury, after procuring the curacy at Uppington which also involved running the school at Donnington. It was at Donnington that his interest in poetry was revived. He began to write once more, after neglecting his craft since he was usher at Pwllheli. Two factors were responsible for this renewed interest. John Douglas, his vicar at Uppington, who had written a pamphlet in 1751 to vindicate John Milton of the charge of plagiarism brought against him by William Lauder, introduced Owen to Milton's poetry. At Donnington, Owen also re-established contact and began correspondence with the three Morris brothers of Pentre-eiriannell, Richard, Lewis, and William, antiquaries, scholars, and men of letters, who encouraged him to write. It was Douglas, however, who was responsible for stimulating Owen's ambition to write an epic in Welsh, thus emulating Milton's great contribution to English literature with his epic masterpieces, *Paradise Lost* and *Paradise Regained*.

Unhappy with his lot at Donnington, and after a dispute with one of his parishioners, Owen accepted a curacy at Walton, near Liverpool, in 1753. Ill health, overwork, and the death of his daughter Elin in April 1755 prompted him to leave Walton unexpectedly and with no future prospects. Owen's gradual decline towards alcoholism probably began at Walton.

Owen removed himself and his family to London hoping that Richard Morris would employ him as secretary and translator of the Honourable Society of Cymmrodorion, a cultural society for the protection and enhancement of the Welsh language founded by Richard Morris himself, and also secure an ecclesiastical position for him. Richard Morris, however, was unable to employ Goronwy. A curacy at Northolt, Middlesex, in 1755 rescued Owen and his family from starvation and deprivation. He eventually became an active member of the Society of Cymmrodorion, but he quarrelled with some of the society's most prominent members, and with Lewis Morris himself. He was also often in debt during his Northolt period.

Goronwy was offered a teaching post at the College of William and Mary, Williamsburg, Virginia, in 1757. He set sail for America in December 1757 on a convict ship. Both his wife and his youngest child, Owen, died during the passage, probably of gaol fever. He married Anne Clayton, housekeeper of the college, widow of James Clayton and sister of Thomas Dawson, president of the college, in

1758, a few months after arriving at the college, but she died within a year of the marriage. Her death disrupted his newly found security, and he soon reverted to his old ways. He was involved in an affray in 1760, when he and another professor of the college, Jacob Rowe, led their students in a drunken revolt against the youths of Williamsburg. Both Owen and Rowe were summoned to appear before the board of the college for causing public disruption, and were also charged with drunkenness and swearing within college bounds. Rowe was dismissed; Owen was forced to resign. Thomas Jefferson had enrolled at the college when Owen was one of the masters there, and was probably one of his students.

Owen left Williamsburg and took up the living of St Andrews, Brunswick county. In 1763 he married Jean or Iona or Janey Simmons, with whom he had four children: John Lloyd (*b.* 1763), Gronow (*b.* 1765), Robert Brown (*b.* 1767), and Jane (*b. c.*1768). He also acquired a tobacco plantation of some 400 acres. Robert was by then the only surviving child of his first family. Owen was often in trouble with the vestrymen of his parish for debt and drunkenness. He died in 1769 at Blandford, Brunswick county, Virginia, and was buried on his own plantation near Dolphin in Brunswick county.

Owen's poetry first appeared in an anthology entitled *Diddanwch teuluaidd* (1763), edited by Huw Jones, and published with the approval and the assistance of the Cymmrodorion Society. Owen, much influenced by the poetry and literary principles of the Augustan period, wrote a highly polished, sophisticated verse, classical in outlook and intellectual in tone. He did much to widen the scope of Welsh poetry thematically. Several popular editions of his work appeared in the nineteenth century and at the beginning of the twentieth century. The most complete and the most popular, in spite of numerous factual and textual errors, was *The Poetical Works of the Rev. Goronwy Owen with his Life and Correspondence*, edited by Robert Jones, published in two volumes in 1876. Owen was an enormous influence on Welsh poetry throughout the nineteenth century. ALAN LLWYD

Sources A. Llwyd, *Gronwy Ddiafael, Gronwy Ddu: cofiant Goronwy Owen, 1723–1769* (1997) • *The letters of Goronwy Owen*, ed. J. H. Davies (1924) • *The letters of Lewis, Richard, William and John Morris of Anglesey*, ed. J. H. Davies, 2 vols. (1907–9) • *Additional letters of the Morrises of Anglesey, 1735–1786*, ed. H. Owen, 1 (1947) • *Additional letters of the Morrises of Anglesey, 1735–1786*, ed. H. Owen, 2 (1949) • LPL, Fulham MSS, vol. 13, Virginia • T. Dawson and E. Jones, 'Minutes of the college faculty, 1758', *William and Mary College Quarterly*, 2nd ser., 1 (1921), 24–6 • T. Dawson, 'Journal of the meetings of the president and master of William and Mary College', *William and Mary College Quarterly*, 2 (1893–4), 256–8 • W. Stith, 'Journal of the meetings of the president and master of William and Mary College', *William and Mary College Quarterly*, 2 (1893–4), 50–57 • A. P. Gray, 'Outline of evidence concerning burial place of Gronow Owen', *William and Mary College Quarterly*, 2nd ser., 8 (1928), 213–15 • H. M. Davies, 'Goronwy Owen, the parsons' cause, and the College of William and Mary in Virginia', *Transactions of the Honourable Society of Cymmrodorion*, new ser., 1 (1995), 40–64

Archives NL Wales, corresp. and literary papers • U. Wales, Bangor, corresp. and MSS

Wealth at death £149 6*s.* 4*d.*: will, Virginia, Brunswick county, will book no. 4, 1761–1777

Owen, Griffith (*c.*1647–1717), Quaker preacher and colonial official, was the son of Robert Owen (1628–1685/6) of Dolsereau, near Dongelly, Merioneth, and his wife, Jane Vaughan (*d.* 1685/6). Nothing is known of his early years but he appears to have been granted a bishop's licence on 16 May 1674 to practise medicine. On 23 October 1678 he married Sarah (*d.* 1702), daughter of William Barnes. They had four sons and seven daughters. Owen seems to have resided in Prescot, Lancashire, and was a member of the Knowsley meeting and Hardshaw monthly meeting. In 1680 and 1681 he was distrained for a refusal to pay tithes, and in 1681 was convicted at the Lancashire assizes, presumably under the penal laws. In May 1681 he was one of a group of Welsh Quakers who met William Penn to consider the proposed creation of a Welsh barony in Pennsylvania; on 13 March 1684 the Welsh Company received a grant of 40,000 acres, of which Owen purchased 500 acres. On 27 May 1684 he received a certificate of removal from Hardshaw monthly meeting, and emigrated to Pennsylvania, together with his parents and siblings. He arrived in Philadelphia on 17 September 1684, and by 13 November he was attending the Radnor monthly meeting. He originally settled in the Welsh tract, before moving to Merion, and then into Philadelphia itself.

Owen quickly made an impact in Pennsylvania, serving as a member of the colonial assembly in 1686–9, during which time he was a noted defender of the rights of Welsh tract proprietors. He was a member of the provincial council in 1690–92. From 1692 he was at the forefront of attempts to rebut the charges of the apostate George Keith, and in 1695 he chaired the committee that produced and published in Pennsylvania *Our Ancient Testimony Renewed*. With the arrival of a new governor in 1693 he seems to have eschewed politics, declining appointment as a JP, and embarking on several religious tours encompassing Maryland and Virginia in 1694. In 1695–7 he visited England in the company of Thomas Janney, visiting London, and leaving the latter at Chester for a journey into Wales. Having returned to Philadelphia by 1699 he was instrumental in combating an outbreak of the 'Barbados distemper' which threatened to decimate the colony.

In 1700 Owen was elected to the provincial council, and when the elected council was dissolved he was appointed by Penn to its successor, serving until his death. In September 1701 he helped form the meeting of the ministers of Philadelphia, which became the meeting of ministers and elders. He attended regularly the Philadelphia yearly meeting, often acting as chairman. Just prior to Penn's departure from the colony, in October 1701, he served as a councillor and as one of four commissioners of property. Owen was normally reluctant to become heavily involved politically, but he did help to defend Penn's interests in the colony.

Owen's wife died on 22 December 1702, and he married again on 30 November 1704. His second wife was Sarah (1664–1733), daughter of John Songhurst, who originated from Sussex, and the widow of Zachariah Whitpaine and Charles Saunders (*d.* 1699), a colonial agent of the New

Pennsylvania Company, whom she had married in Philadelphia on 8 February 1698. Owen continued to attend council meetings regularly between 1701 and 1705, but rarely thereafter until he returned from a visit to New England in 1709. In March 1711 he took part in negotiations with the American Indians at Conestoga. He died in Philadelphia on 18 August 1717, three sons acting as executors. Two of his sons practised medicine, and a daughter, Rebecca, served in the Quaker ministry.

STUART HANDLEY

Sources 'J. S. Foster', *Lawmaking and legislators in Pennsylvania: a biographical dictionary*, ed. C. W. Horle and others, 1 (Philadelphia, 1991), 576–81 • *DWB* • *The papers of William Penn*, ed. M. M. Dunn, R. S. Dunn, and others, 5 vols. (1981–7) • R. M. Jones, 'Owen, Griffith', *DAB* • P. J. Wallis and R. V. Wallis, *Eighteenth century medics*, 2nd edn (1988), 445 • *IGI* • C. Morris, 'Contributions to the medical history of Pennsylvania', *Memoirs of the Historical Society of Pennsylvania* (1826), 337–50 • J. E. Griffith, *Pedigrees of Anglesey and Carnarvonshire families* (privately printed, Horncastle, 1914), 201 • T. M. Rees, *A history of the Quakers in Wales and their emigration to North America* (1925) • I. Corcoran, *Thomas Holme, 1624–1695: surveyor general of Pennsylvania* (1992), 184–7 • G. B. Nash, *Quakers and politics: Pennsylvania, 1681–1726* (1968)

Owen, Gwilym Ellis Lane (1922–1982), philosopher, was born on 18 May 1922 in Southsea, Hampshire, at the family home, 44 Bath Road, the only child of Ellis William Owen (1883–1951), company secretary to the Portsmouth and Isle of Wight Ice and Cold Storage Company, and his wife, Edith Clara Lane (1883–1965). From Portsmouth grammar school he proceeded in 1940 to Corpus Christi College, Oxford, to read for classical moderations. But after one year he was called up for military service, ending the war as a signals officer with the Special Operations Executive, with the job of giving instruction in communications to agents who were to work behind enemy lines.

Owen returned to Oxford in 1946 to pursue the traditional Greats syllabus, but no less importantly to throw himself into intense writing activity. He moved in literary and theatrical circles, and numbered Kingsley Amis, Ludovic Kennedy, and Kenneth Tynan among his friends at this time. He published criticism, poems, short stories, and drawings in *Isis*, where he was successively literary editor and editor. Although Owen's career was to be academic, not literary, the wit, pace, and economy of his philosophical style, like his predilection for the pregnant essay instead of the monograph, surely reflect something of what he learned and enjoyed in his *Isis* days.

Through *Isis* came something else that was to be fundamental for the rest of Owen's life: his marriage on 30 July 1947 to Sally Lila Ann Clothier (*b.* 1926), the daughter of Owen Clothier, schoolmaster. She was an undergraduate reading English at St Hilda's, who had been helping out in the *Isis* office. After the student penury of their early life together and a period at Durham (1950–53), where Gwil held a research fellowship, in 1953 the Owens returned to make Oxford their permanent home; from 1963 they lived at Lower Heyford in the Cherwell valley. Here they brought up two sons, and here Sally was to remain as anchor during Gwil's long absences at Harvard (1966–73) and in Cambridge (1973–82).

After Owen's first in Greats (1948), it was Gilbert Ryle, the presiding spirit of post-war Oxford philosophy, who persuaded him to stay on and take the new BPhil course (1948–50). Oxford philosophers were in iconoclastic mood, and grandiose metaphysics was out of favour. Ryle had already in 1939 published a long article demonstrating the affinities between the work of Russell and Wittgenstein in philosophical logic and the pioneering insights of Plato's later critical dialogues. Owen was to make the theory of meaning in Plato and Aristotle the core of his own work, marrying Ryle's analytical preoccupations and abilities with a mastery of the texts that was all his own.

Owen's first article appeared in the *Classical Quarterly* for 1953. It was entitled 'The place of the *Timaeus* in Plato's dialogues'. Its chief proposal—a revolutionary redating of the *Timaeus* from Plato's late to his middle period—created extraordinary interest. Owen's purpose was to remove a major obstacle to accepting the idea that in his late critical phase Plato had renounced the metaphysics of the forms, which are prominent in the *Timaeus*. Whether or not his readers were convinced by the proposal or sympathized with the objective, all but a few were dazzled by the ambition of the paper, and by Owen's resourcefulness in argument and mature command of great tracts of the Platonic corpus.

The next decade witnessed a remarkable outpouring of creative energy. Around a dozen classic papers on Plato, Aristotle, and the presocratics Parmenides and Zeno were published or first drafted during Owen's Oxford years (like all his philosophical essays they are collected in a posthumous volume: *Logic, Science and Dialectic*, 1986). Some not only changed the course of scholarship but remain the starting point from which enquiry must still begin. Most packed as much into a couple of dozen pages as whole monographs from other hands. Together they established a new way of writing about ancient philosophy, and a demonstration for a new era in contemporary philosophy of the power of Plato and Aristotle as thinkers.

At the same time Owen was immersed in teaching, particularly the teaching of graduate students (many from North America and Australasia) in his twice weekly BPhil classes. Some knew Greek and had some acquaintance with Greek philosophy, but for most it was news that Plato and Aristotle were at the cutting edge of the subject. Owen's classes became one of the biggest attractions in Oxford philosophy. He was a charismatic teacher. To start with, he did not look or behave like a don. He dressed in tweeds and bow ties, more like an actor than an academic. When not sucking on his pipe, he gave voice to a rapid Oxford gabble in a rather musical baritone. Owen was evidently fonder of his students than of his colleagues. His classes were laboratories where their ideas as well as his own could be teased out and juggled with. Above all, he conveyed a sense of the intellectual exhilaration and abiding philosophical importance of working on Plato and

Aristotle. Together with Gregory Vlastos at Princeton, Owen was a first cause of the huge expansion of teaching and research in his field in the second part of the twentieth century, and particularly of the proliferation of teaching positions in the USA.

By the early 1960s Owen was in great demand in the USA. At Oxford he was given a personal professorship in 1963, but in 1966 he accepted an invitation to take up a chair at Harvard located in the three departments of classics, philosophy, and history of science. Here too he attracted excellent graduate students, and founded a new institution: the monthly New York seminar (since much imitated), which gathered mostly young colleagues from universities on or near the eastern seaboard to read Aristotle together. Honours came his way; and in 1973 he was elected to the premier chair in his subject, the Laurence professorship at Cambridge, where he became a fellow of King's and occupied magnificent rooms in the pediment of the Gibbs Building.

On returning to England, Owen successfully replicated his New York seminar in London. In Cambridge he continued teaching but produced little new writing. In truth he was burned out. Despite his charm (particularly with the opposite sex) and his natural high spirits, he was prone to black moods. A tendency to pour himself a whisky too early in the day was observed. He died in college of a heart attack on 10 July 1982, and was buried in the churchyard at Lower Heyford on 16 July.

Malcolm Schofield

Sources *Annual Report of the Council* [King's College, Cambridge] (1983), 32–9 • G. E. L. Owen, *Logic, science, and dialectic: collected papers in Greek philosophy*, ed. M. Nussbaum (1986) • private information (2004) [Sally Owen, widow] • M. Schofield and M. C. Nussbaum, eds., *Language and logos: studies in ancient Greek philosophy presented to G. E. L. Owen* [incl. a bibliography of Owen's pubns on Greek philosophy; a few later items are recorded in *Logic, science, and dialectic*] • b. cert. • m. cert.
Archives U. Cam., faculty of classics
Likenesses B. Potter, photograph, repro. in *Logic, science and dialectic*, frontispiece • B. Potter, photograph, repro. in Schofield and Nussbaum, eds., *Language and logos*, frontispiece
Wealth at death £6290: administration, 11 Nov 1982, *CGPLA Eng. & Wales*

Owen, Henry (1716–1795), Church of England clergyman and biblical scholar, was born at the home of his father, William Owen, gentleman, at the foot of Cadair Idris, near Dolgellau, Merioneth. Nothing is known of his mother. He was educated at Ruthin School, Denbighshire, and entered Jesus College, Oxford, on 10 April 1736, and graduated BA (1739), MA (1743), MB (1746), and MD (1753). He was ordained deacon and priest in 1746, and practised medicine for three years while a curate in Gloucestershire before giving it up because 'neither his feelings nor his health would suffer him to continue the profession' (Nichols, *Lit. anecdotes*, 2.433). He served as curate to Sir Ralph Thoresby in Stoke Newington, Middlesex, both before, and then simultaneously upon, his presentation to the vicarage of Terling, Essex, in 1752, the gift of Sir Matthew Featherstonehaugh, whose chaplain he had been. He resigned Terling in 1760, when presented to the London rectory of St Olave, Hart Street, by the trustees of Sir Andrew Pickard. He married, on 3 September 1760, Mary (*d.* 1804), daughter of Robert Butts, bishop of Norwich. Shortly after he became chaplain to Shute Barrington, then bishop of Llandaff, who presented him to the vicarage of Edmonton, Middlesex, in 1775, which he held by a special dispensation along with St Olave's.

Though he began his literary career with a mathematical treatise, *Harmonica trigonometrica* (1748), and was elected to a fellowship of the Royal Society, Owen's principal publications were in the field of biblical criticism, to which he had devoted himself even when preparing for his MD. His *Observations on the Four Gospels* (1764) was a rather conservative account of the dating and nature of the gospels; more detailed and critical observations were left for *An Enquiry into the Present State of the Septuagint Version of the Old Testament* (1769), in which he was critical of the corruptions made to the texts by Jewish and Christian commentators, and called for a collation of all these variations in order to secure a reliable version that would meet the challenge otherwise made to its authority by critics of Christianity. He met the criticisms made of his approach by a Jewish scholar, Raphael Baruch, in his *Supplement to critica sacra* (1775), and produced an edition of the Cottonian manuscript of Genesis as edited by Grabe, *Collatio codicis Geneseos cum editione Romana*, in 1778. He continued this work, which he saw as a parallel to that of Benjamin Kennicott on the Old Testament, in *A Brief Account, Historical and Critical, of the Septuagint Version of the Old Testament* (1787). He also edited two works by friends as acts of piety: an edition of Xenophon's *Memorabilia* (1785), which had been left unfinished by Edward Edwards of Jesus College, Oxford, and a new, corrected edition of an antiquarian work on Anglesey by Henry Rowlands, *Mona antiqua restaurata* (1766), with notes by Lewis Morris, which Owen dedicated to Richard Fitzwilliam, sixth Viscount Fitzwilliam of Merrion.

Owen was preoccupied with defending Christianity against its enemies on the basis of two of the most favoured grounds for such apologetic in eighteenth-century England: the proofs of miracles and of prophecy, both of which drew on his biblical researches. He first defended the miracles recorded in the Old and New testaments as the rational superintendence of events overseen by the 'correcting hand of Providence' in *The Intent and Propriety of the Scripture-Miracles Considered and Explained* (1755; p. 71); he developed these arguments as Boyle lecturer, from 1769 to 1771, and published his lectures in 1773 under the same title as his earlier treatise. He was particularly concerned to refute David Hume, whose style he especially hated, denouncing 'our fastidious author … the mere arrogance of an insulting sarcarsm … this contemptuous adversary … the sophistry of his reasonings' (H. Owen, *The Intent and Propriety of the Scripture-Miracles*, 1773, 53). Owen's appeal was to testimony and history; he was indebted for his more philosophical arguments to Joseph Butler's *Analogy*. His defence of prophecy was also firmly historical in character, and appeared in 1789, with an impressive list of subscribers that included both archbishops and many heads of houses in Oxford and Cambridge, as *The Modes of Quotation used by the Evangelical Writers Explained and Vindicated*. Admitting that his argument might already appear old-fashioned, Owen made a detailed examination of the relationship between the prophecies of the Old Testament as these were fulfilled in the New Testament, thereby satisfying himself that he had undone the chief objection to the Christian religion made by its enemies. In the same treatise he made certain of his moderate position by insisting that 'as I always disliked polemical divinity; so I am now especially too old to dispute about religion; and I live only for the hope it inspires' (H. Owen, *The Modes of Quotation*, v). This position was also apparent in a work that he had written for the instruction of non-university-educated clergy, *Directions for young students in divinity, with regard to those attainments, which are necessary to qualify them for holy orders* (1766), a work that also demonstrated why he had given up medicine for the church in his claim that:

> it is as far superior to all other professions, as the soul is superior to the body. For other professions relate only to the concerns of the body for the short term of its mental state: whereas this is employed in promoting the welfare and happines of the soul through the endless ages of eternity. (p. 2)

He was close to the pious printer William Bowyer, who brought out many of his works, as did Bowyer's associate John Nichols, who praised Owen warmly in both his *Literary Anecdotes* and his *Literary Illustrations*.

Owen died on 14 October 1795 at his vicarage in Edmonton, Middlesex, where he was also buried; he was survived by his wife, who died at Bromley College on 18 June 1804, his son, Henry Butts Owen, to whom he had resigned the living of St Olave's in April 1794, and five daughters. Owen's life was dedicated to scholarship rather than to gaining preferment, as Nichols observed: 'Dr. Owen had, through his long and useful life, no other preferment … but he had a truly great and pious frame of mind' (Nichols, *Lit. anecdotes*, 2.435). It was in order to provide for his five daughters that his son brought out an edition of Owen's sermons in 1797, noting that it was not worldly prosperity that his father had sought, as he had dedicated his life instead 'to the interests of sacred learning, and the advancement of Christian virtue' (H. Owen, *Sixteen Sermons on Various Subjects*, 1797, vi). A subscription list that covers some forty-six pages and contains the names of many divines and fellows of colleges is testimony to Owen's reputation for learning; the cultivation of Christian virtue was central to the message contained in the sermons, the last of which was a notably admonitory piece originally preached on a fast day during the war with revolutionary America. B. W. Young

Sources Nichols, *Lit. anecdotes*, 2.433–5; 3.6, 81, 99 · Nichols, *Illustrations*, 5.613, 795; 6.669 · Foster, *Alum. Oxon.*, *1715–1886* · *GM*, 1st ser., 30 (1760), 203, 489 · *GM*, 1st ser., 46 (1776), 95 · *GM*, 1st ser., 64 (1794), 670 · *GM*, 1st ser., 65 (1795), 884, 1111 · *DNB*

Likenesses W. Bromley, mezzotint, 1795 (after S. Drummond), BM, NPG; repro. in *European Magazine* (1795) · J. T. Smith, line engraving, pubd 1797, BM

Owen, Henry Charles Cunliffe- (1821–1867), army officer, son of Captain Charles Cunliffe-Owen RN, from the ancient family of Cunliffe of Wycoller, and his wife, Mary (*d.* 3 May 1841), daughter of Sir Henry Blosset, kt, chief justice of Bengal, was born at Lausanne, Switzerland, on 16 October 1821. Sir Francis Philip Cunliffe-*Owen (1828–1894) was his brother. He was educated privately and at the Royal Military Academy, Woolwich, obtaining a commission as second-lieutenant, Royal Engineers, on 19 March 1839. After the usual Chatham course, he went to Devonport. In January 1841 he was sent to Mauritius. On 30 September he was promoted lieutenant. In January 1845 he was ordered to the Cape of Good Hope, where he took part in the campaign against the rebel Boers and in the Cape Frontier War of 1846–7, and was thanked for his services in general orders. On 28 October 1847 he was promoted second-captain. He returned to England in April 1848 and was stationed at Devonport, then at Chatham, until, in November 1850, he was permitted to accept an appointment under the Royal Commission for the Exhibition of 1851 as computer of space for the United Kingdom, and later as superintendent of the foreign departments, and finally, after the exhibition was opened, as its general superintendent. Cunliffe-Owen's courtesy, firmness, and business habits won him most favourable opinions. When the exhibition closed Cunliffe-Owen was appointed inspector of art schools in the department of practical art, then under the Board of Trade, with offices at Marlborough House. He was elected an associate member of the Institution of Civil Engineers on 3 February 1852.

On the outbreak of the Crimean War, Cunliffe-Owen resigned his civil appointment, and in January 1855 he joined the army before Sevastopol. Severely wounded by a musket ball, he lost his leg and was invalided home. He was mentioned in dispatches, made a CB (February 1856), given a pension of £100 per annum, appointed officer of the Légion d'honneur, and received the Mejidiye (5th class). On 17 July 1855 he was promoted brevet major.

In October 1855 Cunliffe-Owen was appointed assistant inspector-general of fortifications at the War Office, and in April 1856 deputy inspector-general of fortifications under Sir John Fox Burgoyne. The latter post he held until August 1860, when he was appointed commanding royal engineer of the western district. He had been promoted brevet lieutenant-colonel on 6 June 1856, and on 22 November 1861 he was promoted brevet colonel. On 1 April 1862 he became a regimental lieutenant-colonel. During his command in the western district were begun the important land and sea fortifications for the defence of Devonport, converting the place into a first-class fortress, as well as the defences of the Severn at Breandown and at Steep and Flat Holmes, which were also in his district. The Plymouth defences absorbed most of Cunliffe-Owen's time and attention, and it was while inspecting some of these works that he caught a chill, from the effects of which he died.

Cunliffe-Owen married in 1855, in London, Agnes, daughter of Lewis Cubitt; they had a son, Edward, born on 1 January 1857. His widow married, in 1872, the Revd

Henry Edward Willington. Cunliffe-Owen was a good man: popular, charming, a pleasant companion, a hard worker, and devoted to his profession. He was a high-churchman, a friend of Pusey, and one of the founders of the English Church Union (1860). He contributed on fortification to the *Professional Papers of the Corps of Royal Engineers*. Cunliffe-Owen died at his home, 3 Leigham Terrace, Plymouth, on 7 March 1867, and was buried in Plymouth cemetery. A memorial window was placed in St James's Church, Plymouth.

R. H. VETCH, *rev.* ROGER T. STEARN

Sources Institution of Royal Engineers, Chatham, Royal Engineers MSS · PRO, War Office MSS · private information (1894) · O'Byrne, *Naval biog. dict.* · A. D. Lambert, *The Crimean War: British grand strategy, 1853–56* (1990) · I. V. Hogg, *Coast defences of England and Wales, 1856–1956* (1974) · G. S. Clarke, *Fortification* (1907)
Likenesses F. Adams, medallion (in later life); formerly in possession of his son, 1894 · sepia drawing (as a child); formerly in possession of his son, 1894
Wealth at death under £10,000: resworn probate, June 1878, *CGPLA Eng. & Wales* (1867)

Owen, Hugh [*alias* John Hughes] (**1615–1686**), Jesuit, was born in Bodeon in Anglesey in June 1615, the son of Hugh Owen (*c.*1575–1642) of Gwernynog, Llanfflewyn, in Anglesey, and his wife, Elizabeth, daughter of Thomas Bulkeley of Groesfechan. He was educated in the Brecknockshire–Monmouthshire area, and converted to Catholicism at the age of eleven, in 1626. He later studied humanities at the college at St Omer before being admitted a student at the English College, Rome, on 25 December 1636. On 16 March 1641 he was ordained a priest in the church of St John Lateran, left Rome on 28 September 1643, and laboured as a secular priest in Wales for five years. In 1648 he entered the Society of Jesus at Watten, and returned to the mission in south Wales in 1650. In 1655 he was recorded by the society as serving in the college of St Francis Xavier at Cwm, parish of Llanrothal, Herefordshire, a district which covered north and south Wales, Herefordshire, Gloucestershire, and Somerset.

In 1666 responsibility for north Wales was devolved to the residence of St Winifred, based on Holywell in Flintshire, and Owen was subsequently stationed there. Holywell was the location of a secular mission known as the 'Cross Keys' and a Jesuit mission called 'The Star', of which he was in charge. The adoption of these veiled place names enabled priests to attend to the needs of pilgrims who visited St Winifred's Well and offered them protection during periods of acute persecution. Holywell had been a great pilgrimage centre from the fifteenth century despite protestant attempts to 'de-Christianize' such places. 'For Catholics and Protestants alike, Holywell retained an extraordinary attraction, and from the accounts of cures there it appeared to retain its extraordinary powers'. The Jesuits had an enormous part in affording continuity to the small Catholic community around Holywell from the establishment of the residence there in 1670. Their presence and the tradition of miraculous cures helped it flourish as 'a centre of Catholic devotion in an area otherwise barren of Catholicism' (Champ, 154–5, 156).

Owen is said to have been the author of a report, in Welsh, dated 6 July 1668, of the miraculous cure of Roger Whetstone, a lame and aged Quaker from Bromsgrove, who drank the water at St Winifred's Well and may well have been given protection by the priest. Owen is also recorded as the author of *Maint pechod marwol* (1668) on the grievousness of mortal sin, especially heresy, apparently incorporated in his *Allwdd neu agoriad paradwys i'r Cymry*, published at Liège in 1670, and perhaps drawing on a book of prayers in English, the *Key to Heaven*. He also edited a translation of Thomas à Kempis into Welsh undertaken by his father, also a convert, published in 1684 as *Dilyniad Christ, a elwir yn Gyffredin Thomas a Kempis*, and of a catechism in Welsh. There is no evidence to suggest that the Popish Plot of 1679 ever endangered his life, although his alias of John Hughes may well have allowed him to avoid such suffering. He died at The Star on 28 December 1686 and is said to have had 'a great character for sanctity' (Gillow, *Lit. biog. hist.*, 2.223).

RICHARD C. ALLEN

Sources H. Foley, ed., *Records of the English province of the Society of Jesus*, 7 vols. in 8 (1875–83) · Gillow, *Lit. biog. hist.* · D. A. Bellenger, ed., *English and Welsh priests, 1558–1800* (1984) · *DWB* · G. Anstruther, *The seminary priests*, 4 vols. (1969–77) · A. Kenny, ed., *The responsa scholarum of the English College, Rome*, 2, Catholic RS, 55 (1963), 452–3 · J. F. Champ, 'Bishop Milner, Holywell and the cure tradition', *The church and healing*, ed. W. J. Sheils, SCH, 19 (1982), 153–64 · T. H. Clancy, *English Catholic books, 1641–1700: a bibliography*, rev. edn (1996) · J. C. H. Aveling, *The handle and the axe* (1976) · J. M. Cleary, 'The Catholic resistance in Wales, 1568–1678', *Blackfriars*, 38/3 (1957), 111–25 · *DNB*
Archives Stonyhurst College, Lancashire, MS unpublished report

Owen, Hugh (**1639/40–1700**), Independent minister, was the son of Humphrey Owen and his wife, Susan. Humphrey Owen was the grandson of John Lewis Owen, MP for Merioneth in 1572. Hugh matriculated from Jesus College, Oxford, on 21 July 1660. According to Calamy he was 'a candidate for the ministry' in August 1662, and 'about that time he removed from Oxford to London. But not long after he fixed in his native country' (Calamy, *Abridgement*, 2.710). For some years, it seems, Owen acted as an itinerant preacher chiefly in Merioneth, travelling also into Caernarvonshire and Montgomeryshire. By 1669 or 1670 he had married Martha, whose background is unknown; they had three daughters and a son, John.

On 22 May 1672 Owen was licensed as a congregational teacher at his house in Llanegryn, Merioneth. In July that year he was issued with licences, no doubt for preaching, in Bodwenni, Cynfal, Erwgoyel, Llanegryn, and Peniarth, also in the county. Owen was ordained as a minister in the Independent church centred upon Wrexham about 1675, the year in which Henry Maurice, pastor of the Brecknockshire Independents, wrote an account of the state of the Welsh congregations which seems to indicate that the gathering of a properly constituted church within Merioneth was a recent event:

> The few professing people that were heretofore in this county were joined either to Wrexham Church, or to Vasavour Powell's, that met in Montgomeryshire … but since the change most of them turned Quakers, and so continue. Yet of their elders, one Mr Hugh Owen, of Bronclydwr … is

> settled in that county, and being ordained a teaching elder of Wrexham church, is sent to those parts to exercise his ministry; so that, of late … they are about gathering them into church order.

Of this order, Maurice could give no details but he thought the people concerned were 'of an independent judgement' (Underhill, 515).

Owen's grandson, Hugh Farmer, claimed that during a period of imprisonment in Powis Castle in the reign of James II, Owen was treated well by Lord Powis (William Herbert, first earl and marquess of Powis), a Catholic who 'on hearing him pray, said to his priest, "Surely this is a good Christian", and on his discharge, engaged him to come to Powis castle every Christmas' (*Nonconformist's Memorial*, 3.493). Owen succeeded Henry Williams about 1685 as minister of a mixed congregation of Independents and Baptists at Ysgafell, near Newtown, Montgomeryshire, and continued its open communion tradition. From 1690 until 1696 the Common Fund of Independents and Presbyterians granted him £8 a year, reduced in 1695 to £4; in April 1696 the Congregational fund board allocated £10 to the congregational churches of north Wales, and in June they earmarked an 'additional' £3 for Hugh Owen, who was in the later part of his ministry assisted for some time by James Owen, later of Oswestry and Shrewsbury. Owen died on 15 March 1700 in his sixty-first year and was buried in the churchyard at Llanegryn. He was survived by his wife, and left property valued at £187 11*s*. He bequeathed 'all my books, whether, Hebrew, Greek or Latine' to his son, John, who succeeded to his father's ministry but who died shortly afterwards, on 27 June 1700 at the age of thirty (will, NL Wales, B/1700/75).

J. E. Lloyd, *rev.* Stephen Wright

Sources A. Gordon, ed., *Freedom after ejection: a review (1690–1692) of presbyterian and congregational nonconformity in England and Wales* (1917) • T. Rees, *History of protestant nonconformity in Wales*, 2nd edn (1883) • A. N. Palmer, *A history of the town and parish of Wrexham*, 3: *A history of the older nonconformity of Wrexham* [1888] • *The nonconformist's memorial … originally written by … Edmund Calamy*, ed. S. Palmer, [3rd edn], 1 (1802) • E. Calamy, ed., *An abridgement of Mr. Baxter's history of his life and times, with an account of the ministers, &c., who were ejected after the Restauration of King Charles II*, 2nd edn, 2 vols. (1713) • T. Richards, *Wales under the indulgence, 1672–1675* (1928) • T. Richards, *Wales under the penal code, 1662–1687* (1925) • Foster, *Alum. Oxon.* • J. E. Griffith, *Pedigrees of Anglesey and Carnarvonshire families* (privately printed, Horncastle, 1914) • will, Consistory Court of Bangor, 16 July 1700, NL Wales, B/1700/75 • A. H. Dodd, 'Owen, John Lewis', HoP, *Commons, 1558–1603* • E. B. Underhill, ed., *The records of the Church of Christ, meeting in Broadmead, Bristol, 1640–1687*, Hanserd Knollys Society (1847)

Wealth at death £187 11*s*.: will and inventory, 1700, NL Wales, B/1700/75

Owen, Hugh (1760–1827), Church of England clergyman and antiquary, born in Shrewsbury and baptized on 14 June 1761, was the only son of Pryce Owen MD (*d.* 1786), a physician of Shrewsbury, and his wife, Bridget, only daughter of John Whitfield, also of Shrewsbury. He was educated at Shrewsbury School and in 1779 matriculated at St John's College, Cambridge, where he graduated BA in 1783, and proceeded MA in 1807. He was ordained deacon in 1784 and priest in 1785. He was perpetual curate at Berwick, Shropshire (1791–1800), and in 1791 was presented by the earl of Tankerville to the vicarage of St Julian, Shrewsbury; in 1803 he was collated by Bishop Douglas to the prebend of Gillingham Minor in the cathedral of Salisbury; and in 1819 he was presented by the dean and chapter of Exeter to part of the vicarage of Bampton, Oxfordshire. He was a fellow of the Society of Antiquaries, and mayor of Shrewsbury in 1819.

Owen was collated by Bishop Cornwallis on 27 December 1821 to the archdeaconry of Shropshire, and on 30 March 1822 to the prebend of Bishopshill in the church of Lichfield. In 1826 he became minister of the royal peculiar of St Mary's, Shrewsbury, and he then resigned the church of St Julian, though he continued to be portionist of the vicarage of Bampton. He lived latterly at Betws Hall, Montgomeryshire, having in or before 1788 married Harriet, daughter of Edward Jeffries of Shrewsbury. Their only son was Edward Pryce *Owen (1788–1863). They also had a daughter.

Owen is chiefly remembered as an antiquary, though he was never so well known as his collaborator, John Brickdale Blakeway (1765–1826). His principal work, published with Blakeway, was *A History of Shrewsbury* (2 vols., 1825). Owen had already published, anonymously, *Some Account of the Ancient and Present State of Shrewsbury* (2 vols., 1808–10), which contained abundant ecclesiastical information. A second edition, much altered, was prepared by Owen but never published. To Britton's *Architectural Antiquities* (vol. 4) he contributed, with Blakeway, descriptions of Wenlock Abbey, and of Ludlow and Stokesay castles. Owen died at Shrewsbury on 23 December 1827.

Thompson Cooper, *rev.* Elizabeth Baigent

Sources Venn, *Alum. Cant.* • M. L. Charlesworth, ed., *Shrewsbury School register* (1990) • Burke, *Gen. GB* • C. R. J. Currie and C. P. Lewis, eds., *English county histories: a guide* (1994)

Archives NL Wales, sermons • Shrewsbury School, annotated copy of the *History of Shrewsbury* • Shrops. RRC, account of ancient ecclesiastical architecture of England and Wales, incomplete • Shrops. RRC, *History of Shrewsbury* (3 vols.) interleaved with sketches and illustrations by his son E. P. Owen

Owen, Hugh (1784–1861), army officer, was born at Denbigh on 23 May 1784, and educated at the grammar school at Audlem, Cheshire (*c.*1795–1800). Through the influence of Sir Corbet Corbet, bt, of Adderley, a kinsman of Sir Stapleton Cotton, Owen was appointed captain in the Shropshire Volunteers on 24 November 1803. In December 1805, with the aid of a recruiting party of the 16th light dragoons stationed at Market Drayton, Owen raised thirty men, which entitled him to a cornetcy in the regiment, which was then commanded by Sir Stapleton Cotton. He became lieutenant on 9 July 1807, and embarked for Portugal in 1809. Speaking French, Spanish, and Portuguese fluently, he was frequently employed in outpost duties and scouting, and commanded the skirmishers of the cavalry brigade at Talavera. In 1810 he was appointed captain of cavalry in the Portuguese army, under Marshal Beresford, and was aide-de-camp to Sir Henry Fane, in command of the rear-guard of General Hill's division in the retreat to

Torres Vedras. He was afterwards brigade major to Sir Loftus Otway, commanding a brigade of the 1st, 4th, 7th, and 10th regiments of Portuguese cavalry, and then aide-de-camp and brigade major to Sir Benjamin D'Urban, commanding a brigade of the 1st, 6th, 11th, and 12th Portuguese cavalry. At the battle of Vitoria on 21 June 1813, when leading the brigade into action (in the temporary absence of General D'Urban, who had been sent on to reconnoitre), his name was noted by Wellington, who next morning directed him to apply for a troop in the 18th light dragoons, to which he was duly gazetted on 22 July 1813, subsequently receiving Portuguese rank as major and lieutenant-colonel.

At the peace Owen returned with the Portuguese army to Portugal, in 1815 was ordered to organize the 6th regiment of cavalry, which in the subsequent civil wars, as 'os dragones de Chaves', became famous for its high discipline and superior capability. Choosing to remain in the Portuguese army, Owen, after obtaining a majority in the 7th hussars, sold out of the British service on 4 September 1817. In 1820 he accompanied Lord Beresford to Brazil, and was sent home to Lisbon with dispatches and the brevet rank of colonel in the 4th cavalry. On arrival he found that the king's government had been superseded, and Lord Beresford and all other foreign officers summarily dismissed. Owen retired into private life, and lived on his estate at Villa Nova de Paraisa, near Oporto. During the subsequent civil wars Dom Pedro offered to appoint Owen his personal aide-de-camp, with the rank of general, but not having the permission of his own sovereign, Owen declined.

Owen was a knight commander of San Bento d'Aviz and knight of the Tower and Sword, and had the Peninsular gold cross. Sir John Rennie, who met him in Oporto in 1855, described him as over 6 feet in height, with a determined countenance. Owen published *The Civil War in Portugal and the Siege of Oporto* (1836), an English translation of his Portuguese work. He died at Garratt's Hall, Banstead, Surrey, on 16 December 1861, aged seventy-seven.

H. M. CHICHESTER, *rev.* JAMES FALKNER

Sources *Army List* • J. Rennie, *Autobiography of Sir John Rennie, FRS* (1875)

Likenesses A. Robertson, oils, *c.*1808, NPG

Owen, Sir Hugh (1804–1881), campaigner for education in Wales, was born on 14 January 1804 at Y Foel, Llangeinwen, Anglesey, the eldest of the four children of Owen Owen (*c.*1780–*c.*1860), farmer, and his wife, Mary (1780–1862), daughter of Owen Jones, a Calvinistic Methodist leader of Llangeinwen. From 1812 he was educated for about nine years at a notable private school at Caernarfon kept by Revd Evan Richardson. In 1825 he left for London where he was employed as a clerk by W. Bulkeley Hughes, a barrister, and then by R. Vaughan Williams, a solicitor. He married in 1829 Ann Wade (*d.* 1881). In 1836 he applied for a clerkship in the poor-law commission at Somerset House and his knowledge of law so impressed the secretary, Edwin Chadwick, that he was at once appointed. In 1853 he became chief clerk, a position he retained upon the reorganization of the commission, thereafter named the Local Government Board. He was in effect the permanent secretary, representing the department at all parliamentary committees relating to the poor law, including the inquiry into the Andover workhouse scandal (1846). It is said that in preparing the Reform Bill of 1867 Disraeli placed great reliance upon two men at Gwydyr House, the office of the poor-law board, one a Catholic, the secretary of the Statistical Society, and Hugh Owen, the nonconformist. Mrs Disraeli dubbed them her husband's 'guardian angels' (B. L. Davies, 'An assessment', 630).

Both before and after his retirement in November 1872 Owen attended to a wide variety of good causes, for example, the King's Cross Cabmen's Club, the London Fever Hospital, the London Welsh Charitable Aid Society, the National Thrift Society, and the National Temperance League. He was elected a member of the London school board, for Finsbury, in 1872. In 1873 he was influential in reviving the Honourable Society of Cymmrodorion, extinct since 1843. In 1880 his plea to place the eisteddfod of Wales upon a more secure foundation led to the formation of the National Eisteddfod Association. Within Wales he introduced measures for the education of deaf mutes (1847). Indeed, the creation of educational opportunities for his compatriots was his passion and it is upon these achievements that his reputation mainly rests.

Nonconformists far outnumbered Anglicans in Wales, as Owen decisively demonstrated in a census which he himself conducted (December 1846), yet, apart from Sunday schools, educational provision for their children was far inferior. Anglicans, through the National Society (1811), had established new elementary schools; the old grammar schools were firmly in their hands and they had founded St David's College, Lampeter, in 1827. The Church of England had also taken advantage of the first government grant in 1833 to be employed through the British and Foreign School Society (BFSS) and the National Society to build schools in England and Wales. In 1839 Owen was secretary to a committee for establishing British Schools at south Islington and Pentonville, near where he lived in London. In 1843 he addressed a *Letter to the Welsh People*, widely published, pressing them to establish day schools and giving clear, simple instructions in Welsh as to the most effective way of proceeding. British Schools, free from denominational affiliations, were, he said, the solution in Wales. The British Society responded to Owen's request for an agent and upon his recommendation a well-known Calvinistic Methodist minister, the Revd John Phillips, was appointed to organize schools in north Wales. In 1846 Owen became the first secretary of the Cambrian Education Society, founded as virtually the Welsh branch of the British Society. In south Wales the voluntaryist convictions of the dissenters were an obstacle, for they opposed state aid. Nevertheless, Owen succeeded in persuading the British Society to appoint in 1853 an influential Baptist minister, William Roberts (Nefydd), as its agent in the south. Gradually, in the 1850s and 1860s, the voluntaryist spirit waned and British Schools increased rapidly, in no small measure due to the unswerving support of Owen who, in 1855, was elected a member of the committee of the BFSS. When the Education Act of 1870 created a system of elementary schools which Owen had so long struggled to provide, agents of the BFSS withdrew from Wales.

It was imperative to train suitable teachers. The Borough Road College in London was a partial answer in the early days, but when the Anglican church opened two training colleges for men in Wales, Owen determined that Welsh nonconformists should not be further disadvantaged. That the Normal College, as it became known, should have been located at Bangor, and not in a populous area of south Wales, may appear strange until it is recalled that the voluntaryists in the south had failed to establish such a college, whereas the Methodists of the north were fervent supporters. Owen's dynamism in collecting funds and in organizing the campaign led to the opening of the college in 1858. Its students contributed richly to the teaching profession in Wales (and beyond). Owen was later engaged, though less actively, in establishing a college for schoolmistresses at Swansea.

The absence of a university in Wales caused deep concern. In 1854 Owen addressed a private meeting of prominent Welshmen in London upon the desirability of founding colleges in Wales similar to the Queen's colleges in Ireland. However, the outbreak of the Crimean War, followed by the Indian mutiny, discouraged direct financial appeals to the government. Constructive action was thus deferred until 1863 when Owen invited Thomas Nicholas, a zealot for university education in Wales, to address the social science section of the Swansea eisteddfod and later a meeting in London. Nicholas was appointed secretary and Owen one of the honorary secretaries of what may now be realistically termed the university movement. Solid financial support was, however, not forthcoming, but by good fortune the organizing committee was able in 1867 to purchase the bankrupt Castle Hotel, Aberystwyth, at a fraction of its original cost. Successive appeals to Disraeli and Gladstone for state aid failed. Nevertheless, it was resolved to open the university college in October 1872. Foreseeing the challenges which lay ahead, Owen retired from the Local Government Board. He soon concluded that a systematic house-to-house canvass and organized chapel collections were to be the basis of his mission. Thus the trim figure of Hugh Owen with his black travelling bag, waiting patiently on railway platforms or alighting from a cab, became familiar throughout Wales. In this sense he took upon himself the guise of a servant. The last Sunday in October in 1875, 1876, and 1877 was known as Sul y Brifysgol ('university Sunday'), an effective method of reaching ordinary people. In 1880 he analysed the various amounts the college had received, 100,000 miscellaneous sums being below half a crown. He spoke with authority, for he had counted every penny.

The college's finances remained parlous. A change of government in 1880 enabled Lord Aberdare to remind Gladstone that in the election campaign every candidate in Wales had pledged himself to press for the repair of the defective condition of Welsh intermediate and higher education. Owen had a large share in drafting Aberdare's letter, which ranks in importance with his own letter to the Welsh people in 1843. In July 1880 the Aberdare committee, as it is generally known, was appointed. Both the papers which Owen submitted to the committee and his oral testimony were valuable. For years he had wished to see a federal university in Wales patterned upon London University, with the power to grant degrees vested in an examining board appointed by the crown. The Prince of Wales' University, as he termed it, would consist of two colleges called the Prince of Wales' College. The university would examine any candidates who presented themselves.

The Aberdare report (1881) did not fully reflect Owen's views, though it recommended that there should be two university colleges in Wales, one in Glamorgan and one in north Wales. There should be a preliminary grant of £4000 to each college. A future University of Wales was to be a federal university, as Owen had hoped, but not the metropolitan model for which he had persistently canvassed. Degrees were to be awarded only to those who had pursued a formal course of instruction at one of the affiliated colleges. The University of Wales was to be a federal teaching university, as came to pass in 1893. In the meantime the Welsh colleges had received state grants a few years before their English counterparts, though never the substantial sums distributed to the universities of Scotland and Ireland.

The zest for higher education had led to the neglect of intermediate schools. Owen recognized that it was necessary to attend to the 'missing link'. In 1879 he was largely instrumental in forming the North Wales Scholarship Association, which enabled talented pupils to proceed beyond the elementary stage. The Welsh Intermediate Act of 1889, which gave Wales in time a network of state-aided secondary schools well in advance of England, owed much to the recommendation of the Aberdare committee, itself influenced by Owen's careful examination of the Irish precedent in 1878 when the government granted £30,000 for intermediate education. Having travelled to Ireland to examine the question for himself, in a second submission to the committee he outlined a system of intermediate education more appropriate for the needs of Wales.

Owen died before several of his plans bore fruit. He was not without critics. A few denounced him bitterly, mainly, it appears, because of a ruthless streak not uncommon in determined men unwilling to be thwarted by the inadequacy of others. Although he was generally respected and admired, lesser figures have been more warmly regarded in Wales. Nor was he endowed with the gift of tongues in a land which prized, and perhaps unduly prized, the arts of eloquence. Today he is sometimes seen as a philistine who saw no reason to allow his native language and culture a place in his educational schemes. The content of education did not deeply concern him. In sum, 'he was not an educator but an organizer of education' (Williams, 77).

It would, however, be wrong to judge Owen out of his own time. The Welsh language was not then in peril, whereas the failure to master English was an impediment to a successful career in the professions within Britain and in its overseas empire. After the Forster Act of 1870 he and many others believed that there was ample provision for the working class. The prime need was to create an educated middle class in Wales, and in his evidence to the Aberdare committee he reiterated that this was the purpose of the Aberystwyth college, which, nevertheless, after his days reached down the social scale so that by 1893 it was proper to speak of 'the people's university'. False pride did not deter him from undertaking endless laborious tasks, apparently at his own charge (he left only a modest estate). Like one of his countrymen, the first of the royal Tudors, what he minded he compassed. Towards the end of his days Owen remarked 'I shall never rest until the Welsh Educational Appliances are perfected.' The three tiers of education in Wales, elementary, intermediate, and higher, owed more to him than to any other single person.

Owen was never entangled in denominational disputes. Born a Calvinistic Methodist, he became a Congregationalist after marriage; at one time he attended a Baptist church. For Roman Catholics, Cardinal Manning among them, he had respect and affection. The most familiar likeness is a photograph of him in old age. The jaw and lips are resolute, the nose firm in outline, the eyes gentle, yet shrewd, his hair silvery grey. Contemporaries recalled 'a beautiful face' (W. E. Davies, 2.136). Rather belatedly he was knighted, at Gladstone's recommendation, in August 1881. On 20 November 1881 he died of acute bronchitis in Menton, France. He was buried on 26 November 1881 in Abney Park cemetery, London. Of his eight children the eldest son was Sir Hugh Owen (1835–1916), permanent secretary to the Local Government Board.

Two buildings in the University of Wales are named after him at Aberystwyth and at the former Normal College, Bangor—as was the first intermediate school under the 1889 act at Caernarfon (1894). There is a bust of him by William Davies at the Royal Institution, Swansea, and a statue in bronze by Milo Griffith, erected by public subscription, at Caernarfon. His true memorial is more enduring than bronze. J. Gwynn Williams

Sources B. L. Davies, 'An assessment of the contribution of Sir Hugh Owen to education in Wales', PhD diss., U. Wales, 1971 • W. E. Davies, *Sir Hugh Owen, his life and life-work* (1885) • B. L. Davies, *Hugh Owen, 1804–1881* (1977) • *North Wales Chronicle* (26 Nov 1881) • 'Committee to inquire into … education in Wales and Monmouthshire', *Parl. papers* (1881), vol. 33, C. 3047 • G. A. Williams, 'Hugh Owen (1804–1881)', *Pioneers of Welsh education* (1964), 57–80 • Boase, *Mod. Eng. biog.*

Archives NL Wales | NL Wales, letters to T. C. Edwards • NL Wales, Thomas Gee MSS • NL Wales, Henry Richard MSS • UCL, corresp. with Edwin Chadwick

Likenesses J. M. Griffith, bronze statue, *c.*1888, Castle Square, Caernarfon • W. Davies, bust, Royal Institution, Swansea • J. M. Griffith, plaster statue, NL Wales • attrib. Meisenbach, photograph (in old age), repro. in Davies, *Sir Hugh Owen*, frontispiece

Wealth at death £2932 1s. 2d.: probate, 24 Feb 1882, *CGPLA Eng. & Wales*

Owen, Sir Hugo von Reitzenstein Cunliffe-, first baronet (1870–1947), tobacco industrialist, was born at Kensington on 16 August 1870, the fourth and youngest son of Sir Francis Philip Cunliffe-*Owen (1828–1894), of Lowestoft, sometime secretary of the Colonial Institute and director of the Victoria and Albert Museum, and his wife, Jenny (*d.* 1894), eldest daughter of Baron Fritz von Reitzenstein, aide-de-camp to King Friedrich Wilhelm IV of Prussia. He was educated at Clifton College for a few months in 1885, and at Brighton College. He was then articled to the civil engineer John Wolfe Barry in London.

In 1886 the second of his six sisters married Henry Herbert Wills, who in the 1890s recruited Cunliffe-Owen to assist him at the Virginia Cavendish works of his family's tobacco business, W. D. and H. O. Wills. He later worked in the Wills export department, and was sent as an emissary to the USA after James Buchanan Duke initiated the American Tobacco Company's attack on British markets. The Wills family retaliated by leading the formation of the Imperial Tobacco Company, and in 1902 negotiated a truce: world tobacco markets were divided by agreement and the joint British American Tobacco (BAT) Company was formed. Cunliffe-Owen was appointed as secretary of BAT, with a seat on its board, in 1902. Thereafter, he made frequent visits to the United States. He succeeded Duke as chairman of BAT in 1923, when its world sales amounted to 50,000 million cigarettes annually. He was an autocratic, self-reliant, and bold capitalist who centralized control and inculcated a strong company culture. His strategies and risks were often vindicated by events. His decision to cut profit margins in order to secure higher sales volumes was crucially successful. So too was his insistence on entering the American market by purchasing the North Carolina based Brown and Williamson Tobacco Company in 1927. The USA accounted for 13 per cent of BAT's total sales by 1939. One of BAT's main markets was China, which Cunliffe-Owen first visited in 1904; he maintained contacts with several Chinese politicians and financiers. He retired as chairman of BAT in 1945, retaining the honorific title of president until his death.

Cunliffe-Owen was a director of the Midland Bank from 1925, and in 1928 recruited its chairman, Reginald McKenna (1863–1943), to serve as chairman of the Tobacco Securities Trust, which he formed to buy and hold shares in associated and subsidiary companies of BAT, and to act as his own investment operation. An early deal was to buy control of Boots, the retail chemist chain, from the American combine Drug Inc. in 1933; an attempt to corner the British pepper market in 1934 was, however, an expensive failure. Cunliffe-Owen's American contacts were an important component in his success. He was also a director of Eagle Star Insurance from 1941.

His knowledge of the Orient led his friend Lord Beaverbrook to appoint him as controller of eastern propaganda at the Ministry of Information in 1918; he received a baronetcy in 1920, ostensibly for his wartime services. This friendship also led him to serve as a director of Beaverbrook's Colonial Bank in 1917–19, and of Provincial

Cinematographic Theatres in 1920–21. He was later treasurer of Beaverbrook's Empire Crusade (to which he donated £5000 in 1930). His opinions on fiscal matters were summarized in his pamphlet, *Industry and the Empire Crusade: a Statement to Manufacturers* (1930).

In the late 1930s Cunliffe-Owen bought the British manufacturing rights of the American twin-engined Burnelli aircraft, and set up the Cunliffe-Owen Aircraft Company at Eastleigh, near Southampton. It undertook government contracts during the Second World War, and in peacetime developed a fourteen-seater passenger aircraft called the Concordia. Production was suspended in November 1947 after it became clear that there was no possibility of sales of the Concordia in sufficient numbers. The company was wound up after his death a month later.

Cunliffe-Owen was plutocratic in his friendships and interests. His horses won the Derby in 1928 and the One Thousand Guineas and the Oaks in 1938. He kept a yacht, and was attracted to pretty young women. There were unsubstantiated stories of an early first marriage. In Massachusetts in 1918 he married Helen Elizabeth (1896–1934), daughter of James Oliver of New York. They had two daughters and two sons, of whom the eldest (his namesake) was killed in action in 1942. He married in 1935 Mauricia Martha, daughter of Herbert Shaw of San Francisco, but was judicially separated from her in 1946. He was by then devoted to a dancer called Marjorie Daw, who changed her surname to Cunliffe-Owen in 1947; three weeks later he made a will leaving her half of his fortune. Nineteen days afterwards, on 14 December 1947, he died of heart failure at his house, Sunningdale Park, near Ascot, his estate being sworn at £1,353,744 gross. His funeral was at Sunningdale parish church on 17 December. RICHARD DAVENPORT-HINES

Sources H. Cox, *The global cigarette* (2000) • B. W. E. Alford, *W. D. & H. O. Wills and the development of the UK tobacco industry* (1973) • R. P. T. Davenport-Hines, 'Cunliffe-Owen, Sir Hugo Von Reitzenstein', *DBB* • private information • b. cert.

Archives BAT, London, archives • BAT, Staines, archives • BAT, Southampton, archives • Duke U., Perkins L., James Buchanan Duke papers • HLRO, corresp. with Lord Beaverbrook • HSBC Group Archives, London, Midland Bank archives • Shanghai Academy of Social Sciences, Centre for Chinese Business History, papers of the British American Tobacco Co. (China) Ltd

Likenesses photographs, *c.*1923–1929, repro. in Cox, *Global cigarette*, facing p. 267 • photographs, probably Hult. Arch.

Wealth at death £1,353,744 10*s.* 6*d.*: probate, 3 Feb 1948, *CGPLA Eng. & Wales*

Owen, Humphrey (1701/2–1768), librarian and college head, was the son of Humphrey Owen, gentleman, of Meifod, Montgomeryshire. The date and place of his birth are not known, but upon matriculation at Oxford University on 17 November 1718 his age was given as sixteen. He had entered Jesus College as a batteler two days previously. He graduated BA in 1722, MA in 1725, BD in 1733, and DD in 1763. He was admitted as a scholar of his college on 23 December 1723 and was elected a fellow on 22 June 1726. He fulfilled the office of senior bursar from 1732 to 1736 conscientiously—the college archives contain both rough and fair copies of his accounts. He was ordained on 5 March 1732, and in 1744 became rector of Tredington (second portion), Worcestershire, a Jesus College living. After having held it for a year he forfeited his college fellowship which was declared void on 8 November 1745. He retained the living until 1763 when, on 11 May, he was elected principal of Jesus College and was, as a consequence, presented to the rectory of Rotherfield Peppard, Oxfordshire, which was annexed to the post. For some time during the early 1760s he was also curate-in-charge of Kingston Bagpuize, Berkshire, fulfilling the duties during 1762–3 by appointing a deputy. He never married and remained as principal of his college until his death in 1768, in which year the statute forbidding principals to marry was repealed.

On 10 November 1747 Owen was unanimously elected to the post of Bodley's librarian, and held it until his death, although for at least two years after his election to the principalship of Jesus College his duties at the Bodleian were performed by his successor, John Price, one of the many members of his college whom Owen appointed successively to the post of sub-librarian. From 1756 until his death he was also a delegate of Oxford University Press, a position in which he was also succeeded by Price.

As librarian Owen was active in improving the facilities at the Bodleian which had begun to look dated alongside the new library at Christ Church, the Codrington at All Souls, and the Radcliffe Camera. He removed the Arundel marbles from the top floor of the Old Schools quadrangle (the picture gallery) to the old moral philosophy school on the ground floor, and oversaw the wainscoting and redecoration of the gallery with fine plasterwork. Fortunately he stopped short of putting a stucco ceiling in Duke Humfrey's Library as advocated by Thomas Warton, writing as 'Thomas Hearne junior' in *Jackson's Oxford Journal* on 29 November 1766. He did, however, unchain the folio volumes in Duke Humfrey's Library, replace the benches with comfortable chairs, and play a large part in the reconstruction of Selden End and the installation of the vaulted ceiling in the Convocation House below it.

Owen was also a conscientious worker on the library's collections, being responsible, among many other undertakings, for the numbering of the Tanner manuscripts which had come to the library in 1735 and were much in demand by scholars. His period in office also saw many more major acquisitions made by the Bodleian. The Clarendon and the Carte papers began to arrive at this time and the peak was reached in 1755 with the acquisition of the Ballard, Furney, and St Amand collections together with the Rawlinson bequest—the largest collection of manuscripts ever received from one donor. Owen had been corresponding with Richard Rawlinson for many years to ensure that the manuscripts joined Rawlinson's printed books in Oxford, and was responsible for devising the classification scheme for them, although they were not finally fully sorted and catalogued until 1893.

Owen shared the enthusiasms, especially on the numismatic front, of Rawlinson, Browne Willis, Francis Wise,

William Stukeley, and other leading antiquaries, and correspondence surviving at the Bodleian shows that he also shared Rawlinson's Jacobite interests. He died in Jesus College on 26 March 1768, and *Jackson's Oxford Journal* on 2 April noted the respect in which he was held for his 'extensive learning, simplicity of manners, generosity, and constant integrity'. He was buried in the chapel of Jesus College, although the small gravestone noted by John Gutch in 1786 is no longer visible.

DAVID VAISEY

Sources W. D. Macray, *Annals of the Bodleian Library, Oxford*, 2nd edn (1890) · I. Philip, *The Bodleian Library in the seventeenth and eighteenth centuries* (1983) · I. G. Philip, 'Reconstruction in the Bodleian Library and Convocation House in the eighteenth century', *Bodleian Library Record*, 6 (1957–61), 416–27 · R. W. Hunt, ed., *A summary catalogue of Western manuscripts in the Bodleian Library at Oxford*, 1 (1953), xxxvi–xlii · *Jackson's Oxford Journal* · *Hist. U. Oxf.* 5: *18th-cent. Oxf.* · Foster, *Alum. Oxon.* · A. Wood, *The history and antiquities of the colleges and halls in the University of Oxford*, ed. J. Gutch (1786)

Archives Bodl. Oxf., in-letters · Bodl. Oxf., library records · Bodl. Oxf., report on appointment as Bodley's librarian | Bodl. Oxf., letters to Rawlinson

Owen, Jacob (1778–1870), architect, was born on 28 July 1778 in Llanfihangel, Montgomeryshire, the son of Jacob Owen, civil engineer, and his wife, Margaret Ellis. After being educated at a school in Monmouth, he was apprenticed to William Underhill of Tipton, Staffordshire, a canal engineer, whose daughter Mary (1781–1858) he married in 1798. They had seventeen children, thirteen of whom survived childhood. He joined the Royal Engineers' department of the Board of Ordnance in 1805 and was promoted to full clerk of works in the following year. Most of his career in the Ordnance was spent in Portsmouth. In 1831 his commanding officer there, Colonel John Fox Burgoyne, was appointed chairman of the newly established commissioners of public works in Ireland. Owen joined him in Dublin in June 1832 as engineer and architect to the new board of works (as it was commonly known), a post which he was to hold until his retirement in 1856, at the age of seventy-seven. In Portsmouth he was assisted in his official duties by his brother John (*d.* 1867) and in private practice by his son Thomas Ellis Owen (1804–1862), who had trained as an architect in London. Thomas became a member of Portsmouth corporation in 1831 and served as mayor in 1847–8 and again in 1862; he was instrumental in the development of Southsea as a watering-place, designing terraces and villas as well as a church, St Jude's (1850–51). He also designed the French protestant church of St Martin's-le-Grand, London (1842–3; dem. 1888).

Some of Jacob's other sons remained in England, including Jeremiah (1802–1850), who became a metallurgist to the Admiralty and store receiver at Woolwich Dockyard, and Joseph Butterworth (1809–1872), who was the rector of St Jude's, Chelsea. Other sons joined their father in the board of works, where critics perceived a dynasty in the making: William Henshaw Owen (*b.* 1813) was the board's engineer in Limerick; Henry (*b.* 1815) was his father's pupil and assistant before becoming in 1841 surveyor for Queen's county; while James Higgins Owen (*b.* 1822), who was made a clerk of works in 1849, succeeded his father as architect to the board in 1856. One of Jacob Owen's pupils, Charles Lanyon, who received a county surveyorship in 1835, married his daughter Elizabeth Helen in 1837. The board's senior clerk of works, Frederick Villiers Clarendon, married Owen's granddaughter Margaret Jane Slacke in 1853.

Most of Owen's public commissions were in Dublin, where he erected extensions and new buildings at the Four Courts (1833–40), added wings to the vice-regal lodge (1842–54), and extended the record buildings at the King's Inns (1848–9). His earliest work at Dublin Castle was a block of castellated stables (1833); he subsequently remodelled the state apartments and other buildings there. He was also concerned with monitoring the construction of the new government prisons on the separate system, including Belfast (designed by Charles Lanyon, 1842–6) and Mountjoy (offered to Owen, but designed by Joshua Jebb, 1847–50). In the late 1840s Owen oversaw a number of major projects for which consultant architects had been appointed, including the three Queen's Colleges (at Belfast, Galway, and Cork), seven new district lunatic asylums, and extensions to Maynooth College (by A. W. N. Pugin). Almost all were neo-Gothic, as was his own criminal lunatic asylum at Dundrum, near Dublin (1847–50). Although eclectic, Owen's penchant was for the Greek revival style.

Owen also carried out private commissions, including work for other departments such as the Dublin Metropolitan Police and the board of national education (for whom he adapted Tyrone House in Dublin and designed the adjacent training college and model schools, 1834–42). In 1839 he won an architectural competition for a parish church (St Patrick's) at Dalkey, co. Dublin (built 1840–43). After some years of prevarication, the Treasury compelled him to relinquish his private practice (in return for an increase in allowances) in 1846. His retirement from the public service ten years later coincided with an impending expansion of the architectural activities of the board of works, with countrywide building programmes for the police, coastguard, Post Office, and education department. These were to be overseen by his son James, who died in office in 1891. James was aided from 1863 by his assistant architect Enoch Trevor Owen (1832/3–1881)—possibly a son of Jeremiah—who joined the board of works as a drawing clerk in 1860.

Owen was short (about 5 feet 3 inches), burly, and balding, with a florid complexion. His brusque manner, family favouritism, and dominance of Irish public works architecture brought him enemies. While there were several allegations of impropriety, none was proven, though it was conceded privately by one commissioner, Thomas Aiskew Larcom, that conflicts of interest had arisen in his examination of his own pupils as candidates for county surveyorships. He was an investor in his son's developments in Southsea, where he moved from Dublin in 1867 with his second wife, Elizabeth Donnet Fry, widow of Captain John Fry. In 1864 he was a founder, with his son James, of the Irish Civil Service Building Society. He was an early fellow and vice-president (1849–67) of the Royal Institute of the Architects of Ireland.

Owen died at Tipton, Staffordshire, on 29 October 1870, and was buried in Mount Jerome cemetery, Dublin. His second wife predeceased him by five months.

BERTHA PORTER, *rev.* FREDERICK O'DWYER

Sources chief secretary's office papers, NA Ire., Board of Works MSS [incl. drawings] · Treasury MSS, records of the ordnance department, PRO · minute books; miscellaneous MSS, Royal Institute of the Architects of Ireland, Dublin · minute books of the commissioners of national education, NL Ire., Larcom papers · private information (2004) · Young MSS, PRO NIre. · F. O'Dwyer, 'The architecture of the board of public works, 1831–1923', *Public works*, ed. C. O'Connor and J. O'Regan (1987), 10–33 · B. Owen, ed., *Owen's Southsea: history and conservation of a Victorian garden suburb* (1995) · Colvin, *Archs.* · *Parl. papers* · D. W. Lloyd, *Buildings of Portsmouth and its environs* (1974) · F. O'Dwyer, 'The foundation and early years of the RIAI', *150 years of architecture in Ireland*, ed. J. Graby (1989), 9–21 · Mount Jerome cemetery records · *CGPLA Eng. & Wales* (1870)

Archives NA Ire., Board of Works papers and drawings, chief secretary's papers · NL Ire., Larcom MSS, minute books of the commissioners of national education · Royal Institute of the Architects of Ireland, Dublin, minute books; uncatalogued MSS

Likenesses photograph (after oil painting), Royal Institute of the Architects of Ireland, Dublin

Wealth at death under £20,000—effects in Ireland: double probate, 6 Jan 1871, *CGPLA Ire.* · under £12,000—in England: Irish probate sealed in England, 21 Nov 1870, *CGPLA Eng. & Wales*

Owen, James (1654–1706), nonconformist minister, was born on 1 November 1654 at the farmhouse of Bryn in the parish of Aber-nant, Carmarthenshire, the second son of John Owen. His grandfather had served in the royalist forces during the civil war and his parents were strongly attached to episcopacy but their nine children all became nonconformists. His brother David (*d.* 1710) was a protestant dissenting minister in Henllan, Carmarthenshire. His younger brother, Charles *Owen, was minister to the protestant dissenters in Warrington, Lancashire, for fifty years until his death in 1746.

After passing through a county school Owen was allegedly grounded in the classics at Carmarthen Castle by James Picton, a Quaker, before progressing to Carmarthen grammar school. About 1670 he took a course of philosophy under Samuel Jones (1628–1697) of Brynllywarch, near Bridgend, Glamorgan, and presumably received instruction in languages as he was an accomplished linguist in later life, with knowledge of Latin, Greek, Hebrew, Arabic, Syriac, Saxon, and French. His first deep religious convictions had been received about 1668 from a nonconformist preacher. He looked forward to the ministry but was undecided about conforming. After acting as a tutor he spent some time with his godfather, the clergyman James Howell, who did his best to remove his scruples. Howell was the nephew of James Howell (1594?–1666), also from Aber-nant, the author of *Epistolae Ho-elianae*. However, Owen decided for nonconformity and placed himself with Stephen Hughes (*d.* 1688), ejected from Meidrim, Carmarthenshire, and afterwards congregational minister at Swansea, who had a great reputation for training preachers. Owen's preaching attracted the notice of the ecclesiastical courts and on the advice of Henry Maurice (*d.* 1682) of Merthyr Tudful, Glamorgan, he moved to north Wales, where he settled at Bodfel, near Pwllheli, Caernarvonshire. After nine months' work there his position became unsafe. Travelling by night he made his way to Hugh Owen (*d.* 1699) at Bronclydwr, Merioneth, and then preached as his assistant for some time.

In November 1676 Owen became chaplain to Mrs Baker of Sweeny, just south of Oswestry, Shropshire, and at about the same time took charge of the nonconformist congregation founded at Oswestry by Roland Nevet (*d.* 1675) the ejected vicar. He was set apart for the ministry in October 1677. On 17 November 1679 he married Sarah George (*d.* 1692); they had seven children, two of whom survived him. From Oswestry he conducted a north Wales mission, having a monthly lecture at Ruthin, Denbighshire. In 1681 William Lloyd (1627–1717), then the bishop of St Asaph, challenged Owen to a public debate on ordination, demanding an account of 'by what right he exercised the ministry, not having episcopal ordination' (Henry, *Life of Philip Henry*, 153)—'The Grand Question propos'd and discuss'd was Whether Ordination by Such Diocesans as have uninterrupted Succession of Canonical Ordination down from the Apostles, be so necessary that Churches and Ministry are null without it?' (C. Owen, 31). The defence of presbyterian ordination was to become the cause for which Owen would subsequently enter into print and engage in controversy.

After the 1689 Toleration Act, Owen removed his Ruthin lecture to Denbigh, and set up others at Llanfyllin, Montgomeryshire, and Wrexham, Denbighshire. He had great difficulty in getting his meeting-places licensed and was often disturbed. In 1690 he started an academy for training students for the ministry at Oswestry. He was supported from London by the Common Fund with £8 in 1690 for Oswestry, reduced to £5 in 1695 and continued until 1699. He educated his younger brother Charles, whose *Some Account of the Life of … James Owen* is an invaluable account of life in the academy. After the death of Sarah in 1692 Owen married in 1693 his second wife, Jane (*d.* 1699), widow of Alderman R. Edwards of Oswestry.

About 1696 Owen seems to have begun an association with the Lancashire provincial assembly and Cheshire classis. The Cheshire classis had been due to receive a sermon from Philip Henry in August 1696 but this was cut short by Henry's death. On 11 August 1696 Owen preached in Henry's stead to the thirty assembled ministers. During the sitting of the classis the protestant dissenters of Warrington sent representatives to obtain a minister. The classis recommended Charles Owen, who was ministering in Wrexham. The Wrexham congregation agreed 'adhaering there to Mr James Owen as their fixed Pastor, and looking upon his brother Mr Charles but as his assistant' (Gordon, 21–2). Charles Owen first attended the general meeting of ministers in Lancashire at Bolton on 13 April 1697 and at the next general meeting in Warrington on 10 August 1697 James and John Owen 'Out of Wales' were in attendance. In 1696 and again in 1699 James Owen was invited as assistant to John Chorlton at Cross Street Chapel, Manchester. He declined and early in 1700 he became minister of High Street Chapel, Shrewsbury, as co-pastor with Francis Tallents. After the death of Jane in 1699, on 12 August 1700 he married his third wife, Elizabeth, daughter of John Wynne, of Coparleni, Flintshire, and widow of John Hough of Chester. He continued his academy at Shrewsbury and kept up his lecturing in north Wales.

The year 1696 seems to have been a pivotal point in Owen's career. He was drawn closer to the ministerial assemblies in Lancashire and Cheshire while his publications drew him deeper into religio-political controversy, particularly with Thomas Gipps, the rector of Bury, Lancashire. The two developments are not disconnected, with John Chorlton of Manchester playing a critical role in promoting Owen as a champion of dissent against the high Anglican party in Manchester.

In the late 1680s and early 1690s Owen published works in Welsh, including a translation of the assembly's shorter catechism, and entered into controversy with the Baptist Benjamin Keach over infant baptism. In 1694 he went into print with *A Plea for Scripture Ordination*, his defence of ordination by presbyters which contained a preface by Daniel Williams. He was answered by Gipps with *Tentamen novum* (1696) which defends Timothy and Titus as diocesan rulers. Owen replied to this with *Tutamen evangelicum* (1697) in which he maintained that Gipps's arguments would unchurch all the continental Reformed churches that lacked bishops, churches that were explicitly recognized in the articles of the Church of England. Gipps responded with *A Sermon Against Corrupting the Word* (1697) in which he accused the dissenters of substituting 'ye for we, in Acts 6:3 in the year 1638' in support of the popular election of ministers (C. Owen, 106). Owen replied with *Remarks on a Sermon* (1697), a work in which Gipps perceived the hand of Chorlton assisting Owen. This bitter exchange rumbled on until 1699 with Gipps going into print a further four times on the subject and Owen twice.

Having antagonized the Manchester high Anglicans, Owen achieved national attention with the publication of his defence of occasional conformity entitled *Moderation a Virtue* (1703). In it he argued that 'Jesus Christ, the author of our Holy Religion, was also an Occasional Conformist; a Dissenter from the imposed ceremonies of the Elders: Preach'd in private Houses, and separate Congregations' (C. Owen, 108). Against a background of repeated attempts between 1702 and 1704 to pass laws against occasional conformity, its effect was incendiary and did nothing to quell high Anglican fears of the 'Church in Danger'. Daniel Defoe engaged with Owen's arguments in his *The Sincerity of the Dissenters Vindicated* (1703) and *The Dissenters Answer* (1704) and Owen was attacked by William Hogden and Charles Leslie in 1704. He provided a further anonymous defence in 1704 with *Moderation Still a Virtue*, in which he also defended ordination by presbyters, vindicated the dissenting academies and condemned Henry Sacheverell. He published other works against organ worship (1700) and the practice of consecrating buildings (1706) and published a translation of the Huguenot John Delme's *Method of Good Preaching* (1701). The account of the Welsh ejected ministers in Edmund Calamy's *Account* is by Owen. But the strain of spending a decade defending the dissenting interest proved too much. For thirty years he had suffered from gallstones and he died of the disorder on 8 April 1706. His funeral sermon was preached by Matthew Henry and he was buried at St Chad's, Shrewsbury on 11 April. His portrait is prefixed to the biography by his brother Charles, who brought out many of his works posthumously. JONATHAN H. WESTAWAY

Sources [C. Owen], *Some account of the life and writings of the late pious and learned Mr James Owen* (1709) · M. Henry, *The life of the Rev. Philip Henry, A. M. with funeral sermons for Mr and Mrs Henry*, ed. J. B. Williams (1825), 152–5, 228, 380–97 · J. B. Williams, *Memoirs of the life, character and writings of the Rev. Matthew Henry* (1828), 34, 144, 146, 195, 259 · T. Rees, *History of protestant nonconformity in Wales* (1861), 187–92, 315–23 · A. Gordon, ed., *Cheshire classis: minutes, 1691–1745* (1919), 21, 22, 36 · N. H. Keeble, *The literary culture of nonconformity in later seventeenth-century England* (1987), 35, 37, 43, 152, 292 · A. P. F. Sell, 'Robert Travers and the Lichfield-Longdon church book', *Journal of the United Reform Church History Society*, 3 (1985), 266–78 · *DNB* · H. McLachlan, *English education under the Test Acts: being the history of the nonconformist academies, 1662–1820* (1931), 12, 19, 52–3, 64, 81–4, 90, 313 · W. A. Shaw, ed., 'Minutes of the United Brethren, 1693–1700', *Minutes of the Manchester presbyterian classis*, 3, Chetham Society, new ser., 24 (1891), 349–65 · F. Nicholson and E. Axon, *The older nonconformity in Kendal* (1915), 268–9 · M. Henry, *A sermon preach'd at the funeral of the Rev. Mr James Owen, a minister of the gospel in Shrewsbury* (1706) · F. R. Raines, *The vicars of Rochdale*, ed. H. H. Howarth, Chetham Society, new ser., 1 (1883), pt 1, 129–31 · W. D. Jeremy, *The Presbyterian Fund and Dr Daniel Williams's Trust* (1885), 12, 85 · W. F. Irvine, ed., *Marriage licences granted within the archdeaconry of Chester in the diocese of Chester*, 8, Lancashire and Cheshire RS, 77 (1924), 32 · J. Owen, *Moderation a virtue* (1703) · D. Defoe, *The sincerity of the dissenters vindicated* (1703) · D. Defoe, *The dissenters answer to the high-church challenge* (1704) · [J. Hunter], ed., *Letters of eminent men, addressed to Ralph Thoresby*, 1 (1832), 335, 377–8, 379–80, 393–4 · J. Owen, *Moderation still a virtue* (1704)

Archives BL, fragment of letter, Add. MS 4385, fol. 37 | DWL, funeral sermon for Philip Henry, MS 91.17, 91.15 · JRL, Thomas Raffles collection, letter to Philip Henry, MSS 369–371

Likenesses S. Nicholls, line engraving (aged fifty-one), NPG · portrait, repro. in Owen, *Some account of the life*

Owen, John [Joannes Audoenus] (**1563/4–1622?**), Latin poet, was born at Plas-du, Llanarmon, Caernarvonshire, the third son of Thomas Owen of Plas-du (eldest son of Owen ap Gruffydd), and his wife, Jane Morris. John's uncle Hugh Owen was a leading recusant, involved in numerous treasonous plots, including support for the Spanish Armada. Thomas had some sympathy for his brother; he was himself indicted for recusancy in 1578, but thereafter conformed.

Education and early poetry Owen was admitted a scholar at Winchester College at the age of thirteen, under Thomas Bilson, in 1577. Most of the figures he later addressed as friends in his works were from Winchester. Christopher Johnson, a distinguished Latin poet, had been headmaster shortly before Owen's time, and the school had established a thriving tradition of spoken and written Latin. Owen's verse first came to public notice while he was still at school, among poems celebrating the triumphant return of Drake in 1580; it was pinned to the mainmast of the *Golden Hind*, and was recorded and translated by Camden (*Audoeni epigrammatum*, 2.39).

John Owen (1563/4–1622?), by unknown engraver, pubd 1633

Owen proceeded to New College, Oxford, where he became a probationer fellow in 1582, and full fellow in 1584. The fellowships were restricted in subject, and Owen was obliged to study civil law to fill a vacancy as legist. He took the degree of BCL on 2 May 1590. His later sharpness against lawyers suggests that he resented the experience. Owen did, though, retain a patriotic fondness for Oxford: so, to illustrate the phrase 'hysteron-proteron' ('reverse order')—'a presposterous way of speaking'—he writes, 'Exempli causa, Cant'brigia Oxonium' ('for example Cambridge before Oxford'; *Audoeni epigrammatum*, 6.3).

Owen was the Joannes Oenus who contributed to the volume issued by New College in 1587 to commemorate Philip Sidney: *Peplus, illustrissimi viri D. Philippi Sidnaei supremis honoribus dicatus*. He wrote 64 lines, in eight separate elegiac poems: 6, 4, 20, 8, 2, 10, 2, and 12 lines respectively. In his later epigrams he was to avoid such prolixity: a poem of 20 lines is remarkably long by his standards. Owen's contribution is not dissimilar to others in that book: it was conventional to provide multiple poems for such collections (sometimes of varying length and metre, but most commonly in Latin elegiacs).

Career as schoolmaster, and professional poet Owen left Oxford in 1591, and commenced his career as a schoolmaster. He first taught at a school in Trelleck, Monmouthshire. About 1594 or 1595 he was appointed headmaster of King Henry VIII's School at Warwick; this may have been on Bilson's recommendation. One of Owen's more distinguished pupils was Sir Thomas Puckering (1592–1636); another was John Ley (1583–1662), later subdean of Chester, a puritan divine, appointed president of Sion College in 1645. In a lawsuit of 1613 the headmaster (perhaps still Owen) was described as 'sufficiently painful and diligent' (Leach, 132).

At some point Owen seems to have moved to London and made a career as a professional poet, relying on the uncertain support of a number of patrons. His first three books of epigrams were printed in London by Simon Waterson in 1606. They were an immediate success at home and abroad, with two more editions of book 1 in 1607, as well as a fourth book; two further sets of three books followed in 1612, making a total of ten books. They were 'greedily bought, and taken into the hands of all ingenious scholars' (Wood, *Ath. Oxon.*, 2.321).

Owen was writing within a tradition of British epigram collections: for example, Sir John Davies's at the end of Christopher Marlowe's Ovid translations (before 1598), as well as John Davies of Hereford's *Scourge of Folly* (*c.*1612). Owen's New College friend Thomas Bastard produced *Chrestoleros* in seven books (1598). We also find Edward Guilpin's collection, *Skialetheia* (1598); John Weever's (1599); John Heath's *Two Centuries of Epigrams* (1610); and Sir John Harington's (1613). All these date from the period when Owen was composing and publishing; several of their authors also studied at Winchester. Ben Jonson set epigrams at the start of the lyric part of his poetry, arranged over the years 1612–14. John Reinolds (or Reynolds) was another New College contemporary, with ambitious plans for the Latin epigram; James Martin (or Aretius) was also active in Oxford.

The tradition of Welsh Latin writing might also have inspired Owen; it included accomplished humanists such as Sîon Dafydd Rhys. Sir John Stradling (1563–1627) was of very similar age to Owen, and was a contemporary at Oxford. Four books of Stradling's Latin epigrams appeared in 1607, just as Owen was achieving notoriety, and Stradling praises the pleasure given by reading and rereading Owen. Owen himself is often conscious of his Welshness—a well-known epigram puns on Welsh, Hebrew, and Greek words (*Audoeni epigrammatum*, 9.67); he believes in British union, but rebukes a fellow countryman who has denied his origins. It has plausibly been suggested that his Latin style is influenced by the Welsh alliterative technique of *cynghanedd*, though much of his word play is a natural feature of the neo-Latin epigram. Puns and anagrams were loved in the Renaissance: an artful example is 'De fide. Anatramma quincuplex' ('On faith: fivefold anagram'):

Recta fides certa est, arcet mala schismata, non est
Sicut Creta fides, fictilis; arte caret.
('True faith is sure, it wards off evil schisms, is not false (like that of Crete), it lacks art.' ibid., 6.12)

Some of his attacks on Roman Catholicism pleased Owen's mostly protestant audience, but infuriated the recusant portion of his own family, most notoriously an epigram of 1612 on papal simony that questioned whether St Peter was at Rome—though Simon undoubtedly was (*Audoeni epigrammatum*, 5.8). Other anti-papal poems appeared earlier. Owen was placed on the 'Index librorum prohibitorum' (list of books prohibited to Catholics), and, according to Wood, his uncle 'dashed his name out from his last will and testament; which was the chief reason, that he ever after lived in a poor condition' (Wood, *Ath. Oxon.*, 2.321). Wood discusses his appeal to readers:

an ingenious liberty of joking … was, and is now with some, especially foreigners, not a little pleasing and delightful. But that which I must farther note of him is, that being always troubled with the disease that attends poets (indigence) he was received into the patronage of his country-man and kinsman, John Williams, bishop of Lincoln and lord-keeper of the great-seal. (ibid., 2.320)

The loss of his inheritance was doubtless a shock, but Wood probably over-simplifies. It is far from certain that Owen's condition remained 'poor', though he may never have been as comfortable, or as sure of continuing patronage, as he would have wished.

A study of Owen's network of friends and patrons suggests that Owen was much involved in the London literary scene. The dedications of individual books indicate some of his chief patrons (at least those he wished to thank, or curry favour with, most publicly): the Neville sisters, daughters of the earl of Dorset; Lady Arabella Stuart; Henry, prince of Wales (in whose lifetime he received a pension); Charles, duke of York; Sir Edward Noel; Sir William Sidley (or Sedley); and Sir Roger Owen—the last he calls his 'Three Maecenases'. The learned Jane Owen of Oxford wrote a congratulatory poem to him, and received one in return.

Owen never married, and probably died in 1622, in London. He was buried in St Paul's Cathedral. John Williams placed a memorial brass there to him, with his effigy and six lines of Latin verse.

Reputation Camden links Owen's name with Sidney, Spenser, Daniel, Holland, Ben Jonson, Campion, Drayton, Chapman, Marston, Shakespeare, 'and other most pregnant wits of these our times whom succeeding ages may justly admire' (Poole-Wilson, 242). Ben Jonson disapproved, perhaps moved by professional jealousy at what he saw as Owen's undeserved success in London literary circles: 'Owen is a pure Pedantique Schoolmaster sweeping his living from the Posteriors of little children, and hath no thinge good in him, his Epigrammes being bare narration' (*Ben Jonson*, ed. C. H. Herford and P. Simpson, repr., 1965, 1.138). Archbishop William Sancroft left his commonplace book, containing hundreds of Latin epigrams, to Emmanuel College, Cambridge (MS 105): two-thirds of them are copied from Owen (compared to a few by neo-Latinists, or his contemporary James Alban Gibbes).

Within a century of his death Owen's work had been published throughout Europe, and had been translated not only into English—including a translation by Robert Hayman (1628) prepared in 'Bristols-Hope in Britaniola, anciently called New-found-land'—but also into German, French, Spanish, and Danish. It was Owen, not Shakespeare, whom seventeenth-century Europeans knew and admired. Continental editions of Owen outnumber the English by a ratio of over three to one. Poole-Wilson has identified forty-five continental editions of Owen's Latin text before 1800. Nine appeared by 1622, the first at Amberg in 1608; Owen's book dedicated to Arabella Stuart was published at Die, in France, in 1613. There were at least thirty-seven separate editions in the seventeenth century, at least twelve of them published at Amsterdam (starting in 1624), from the distinguished presses of Jansson, Blaeu, Elzevier, and Hack.

Owen's influence in Germany was particularly strong; Heine's schoolmaster read little else. Bernhard Nicaeus translated 623 epigrams into German (both Low and High), published as *Rosarium, dat is, Rosen-Garten* (1638 and 1641); Valentin Löber produced another version (1651, 1653, and 1661), and so did J. P. Titz, along with a school of Owen's German imitators. More surprisingly, perhaps, was Owen's popularity in staunchly Catholic Spain, generally hostile to British literary culture. Francisco de la Torre cooked up a rare translation in two volumes, *Agudezas de Ivan Oven* (1674, 1682): the survival of two distinct issues from 1674 may indicate that it was immediately pirated. Erich Herlov put him into Danish: *Den berømmelige engelske poetis Johannes Oveni … tre første bøgger* (1726). Ludwig Holberg observed that copies of Owen were in everyone's hands early in the eighteenth century, and were not infrequently used as school textbooks (Wood, *Ath. Oxon.*, 2.320).

Le Brun's French version of Owen was published in Paris (1709), and reprinted as *Les épigrammes d'Owen traduites en vers François* (1719), with Latin and French on facing pages. Owen satisfied the French sense of wit throughout the eighteenth century: there was a call for Owen's works both in the *ancien régime* (where they fit a world of cutting sarcasm and *liaisons dangereuses*), and in the heat of the revolution, when Renouard's scholarly edition of 1794 was published.

Modern scholarship has often been unkind, and Owen's epigrams are summarily dismissed. More recently, however, with rising interest in neo-Latin, scholars have begun to take him seriously again, and have attempted to set him fairly in context. D. K. Money

Sources J. H. Jones, 'John Owen, Cambro-Britannus', *Transactions of the Honourable Society of Cymmrodorion* (1940), 130–43 • L. Bradner, *Musae Anglicanae* (1940) • *Joannis Audoeni epigrammatum*, ed. J. R. C. Martyn, 2 vols. (1976–8) • J. R. C. Martyn, 'John Owen and Tudor patronage: a prosopographical analysis of Owen's epigrams', *Humanistica Lovaniensia*, 28 (1979), 250–57 • C. Davies, *Writers of Wales: Latin writers of the Renaissance* (1981) • D. Sacré, 'Ein übersehenes Epigramm des John Owen', *Wolfenbütteler Renaissance-*

Mitteilungen, 18 (1994), 74–6 • P. N. Poole-Wilson, 'A best-seller abroad: the continental editions of John Owen', *Theatrum orbis librorum: liber amicorum presented to Nico Israel*, ed. T. C. van Uchelen, K. van der Horst, and G. Schilder (1989), 242–9 • J. J. Enck, 'John Owen's *Epigrammata*', *Harvard Library Bulletin*, 3 (1949), 431–4 • P. Laurens, *L'abeille dans l'ambre: célébration de l'épigramme* (Paris, 1989) • A. F. Leach, *History of the Warwick School* (1906) • J. P. Sullivan and A. J. Boyle, eds., *Martial in English* (1996) • H. H. Hudson, *The epigram in the English Renaissance* (1947) • Wood, *Ath. Oxon.*, new edn • M. A. Shaaber, *Check-list of works of British authors printed abroad … to 1641* (1975) • J. H. Jones, 'John Owen, the epigrammatist', *Greece & Rome*, 10 (1941), 65–73 • H. Harflete, *Banquet of essays* (1653) • F. A. Wright, *The love poems of Joannes Secundus* (1930) • E. Urban, *Owenus und die deutschen Epigrammatiker des XVII. Jahrhunderts* (1900) • E. Schneditz-Bolfras, 'John Owen (Johannes Audoenus) als neulateinischer Epigrammatiker', diss., Vienna, 1990 • M. Stephens, ed., *The Oxford companion to the literature of Wales* (1986)
Likenesses line engraving, BM; repro. in *Epigrammatum Joannis Owen*, 6th edn (1633) [*see illus.*] • line engraving, BM, NPG; repro. in *Epigrammatum Joannis Owen*, new edn (1668) • line engraving, BM, NPG; repro. in *Epigrammatum Joannis Owen*, new edn (Amsterdam, 1669) • portrait, repro. in L. Crasso, *Elogii d'huomini letterati* (1666)

Owen, John (*bap.* **1580**, *d.* **1651**), bishop of St Asaph, was baptized at Burton Latimer, Northamptonshire, on 8 November 1580, the eldest son of Owen *Owen (1543/4–1593), rector there and a descendant of the Owens of Bodsilin, Aber, Caernarvonshire, and his second wife, Jane, daughter of Robert Griffith of Caernarfon. He graduated BA from Christ's College, Cambridge, in 1597 and subsequently became a fellow of Jesus College, Cambridge. He proceeded MA in 1600 and DD in 1618; he was also incorporated MA at Oxford on 16 July 1600, but remained at Cambridge for some years and appeared as *taxor* there in 1608. He succeeded to the rectory of Burton Latimer, Northamptonshire, in 1608 and was appointed chaplain to Prince Charles. He became rector of Carlton in 1609 and Cottingham in 1620, both in Northamptonshire. His first wife, Sarah Hodilow (*d.* 1621) of Cambridgeshire, mother of his son Robert and of his daughter, who eventually married Dr William Griffith, chancellor of Bangor and St Asaph, was buried at Burton Latimer in February 1621. His second wife was Elizabeth Gray and his third Elizabeth Wyn (*d.* 1651), daughter of Robert Wyn of Conwy.

Owen was elected bishop of St Asaph on 18 August 1629, apparently as a compromise candidate, consecrated at Croydon on 20 September, instituted on 23 September, and had his temporalities restored on 26 September. He had earlier, on 15 September, received a grant to hold *in commendam* the archdeaconry of St Asaph and other benefices in the dioceses of St Asaph and Bangor to a value not exceeding £150 per annum; he subsequently held six rectories along with his bishopric. Owen was held in much esteem in his own diocese, where he claimed to be connected by descent with every family of quality, and *cywyddau* (praise-poems) were addressed to him by Huw Machno (1635) and Siôn Cain (two, in 1641). Owen's episcopate was given an encouraging start when in 1630 Robert Llwyd, vicar of Chirk, dedicated to him his book, *Llwybr hyffordd i'r nefoedd* (a translation of Dent's *Plain Pathway to Heaven*), where he commented enthusiastically on the zeal and ability of many of the diocesan clergy.

Owen was himself active in the pastoral work of his diocese. In a return on St Asaph dispatched to Archbishop Laud in 1633 he reported all was well, except for the number and boldness of Roman Catholic recusants, especially those focused on St Winifred's well. He made provision for Welsh sermons to be preached in parish churches on the first Sunday of every month, to be funded by those who received the tithes of the parish. He superintended improvements to his cathedral, including the building of a new organ in 1635, and in that year was much exercised about the repair of Wrexham church, one of the glories of his diocese. Two sets of visitation articles issued by Owen in 1637 and 1642 are extant; those for 1637 are the earliest surviving printed articles for any Welsh diocese. In his diocesan reports to Laud of 1633, 1634, 1635, 1637, and 1638, he claimed to have carried out the king's instructions and to have found his clergy orderly and conformable. His most serious worries were the growth in the number of recusants and the persistence of 'superstition and profaneness' (*Works of … Laud*, 5.329). In 1639 he reported the discovery of an 'unlawful conventicle' (ibid., 369) within his diocese at Llanyblodwel in Shropshire, but there was no mention of the activities of Walter Cradock and other puritans in the Wrexham area.

Owen wrote a Welsh treatise on the ten commandments and petitioned the king in 1641 to authorize its printing and command every church and chapel in Wales to obtain a copy, but nothing further was heard of it in the developing political crisis. On 30 December 1641 he was one of eleven bishops who petitioned against the growth of mob violence against their order at Westminster. He was impeached of high treason and imprisoned (possibly twice) in the Tower. His bishopric was sequestered on 6 April 1642, when he was allowed £500 per annum in composition. He also lost his sinecure rectories and his episcopal palace was sacked. Owen's third wife, Elizabeth, was buried on 22 July 1651. He died three months later, on 15 October 1651, at Aberkinsey in Rhuddlan; he was buried under the bishop's throne at St Asaph Cathedral. A brass plate was installed in his memory by Lord Harlech in 1907. GLANMOR WILLIAMS

Sources Foster, *Alum. Oxon.* • Wood, *Ath. Oxon.*, new edn, 3.1099 • Cooper, *Ath. Cantab.*, vols. 1–2 • D. R. Thomas, *Esgobaeth Llanelwy: the history of the diocese of St Asaph*, rev. edn, 3 vols. (1908–13) • *Willis' survey of St Asaph, considerably enlarged and brought down to the present time*, ed. E. Edwards, 2 vols. (1801) • J. Walker, *An attempt towards recovering an account of the numbers and sufferings of the clergy of the Church of England*, 2 pts in 1 (1714) • *CSP dom.*, *1629–41* • *The works of the most reverend father in God, William Laud*, ed. J. Bliss and W. Scott, 7 vols. (1847–60), vol. 3, p. 243; vol. 5, pp. 310–11, 320–21, 329, 334, 354, 361, 369; vol. 7, p. 23 • D. R. Thomas, ed., *Y cwtta cyfarwydd* (1883) • R. F. Roberts, *Llên Cymru*, 2 (1952), 1–35, 97–110 • J. Bridges, *The history and antiquities of Northamptonshire* (1848) • K. Fincham, ed., *Visitation articles and injunctions of the early Stuart church*, 2 (1998), xxvii, 172–82 • *DNB*
Archives BL, Lansdowne MSS 982, fols. 185–6; 983, fol. 182 • BL, Add. MS 15671, fols. 40, 46, 49, 67

Owen, Sir John (**1600–1666**), royalist army officer, was the eldest son of John Owen (*d.* 1613) of Clenennau, Caernarvonshire (who was himself the fourth son of Robert Owen of Bodsilin in the same county), who had made a fortune as secretary to the Elizabethan politician Sir Francis Walsingham. The elder John married Elin Maurice (*b.* 1578), heir to the Maurice estates in Caernarvonshire and Shropshire, which included Clenennau. Outliving two husbands, she became the senior member of the family on the death of her grandfather, Sir William Maurice, in 1622. When the younger John Owen inherited Clenennau on her death in 1626, he became one of the richest gentlemen in Caernarvonshire.

The paucity of local records in that part of Wales means that the dates of birth and death for John Owen are known only from his memorial in Penmorfa church (Caernarvonshire). Likewise, nothing is known of his youth and early manhood, save that he served as high sheriff of Caernarvonshire in 1630–31 and of Merioneth the following year, and at some stage married Janet, daughter of Griffith Vaughan of Corsygedol, Merioneth. Letters suggest that it was a deeply affectionate union, and it produced several children. It is likely that the young Owen had some military experience, for otherwise it is hard to see why he should have been singled out in September 1642 to command the foot regiment to be raised in north-west Wales for the king's service at the outbreak of the civil war. The poverty of the region made the preparation of the unit slow work, and it did not join the royal army until the end of the year.

Thereafter the regiment joined all of that army's campaigns, and Owen led it with distinction, being wounded in the face at the storming of Bristol in July 1643 and serving as governor of Reading throughout the following winter. The regiment was eventually taken prisoner with most of the royal infantry at Naseby, but by then Owen had long been detached from it for more exalted duties. These commenced in the autumn of 1644, when a parliamentarian invasion of north-east Wales placed the whole principality under pressure. There was need for a tough and loyal soldier to secure the hinterland, and Owen was chosen for the job. On 10 December he was commissioned governor of Conwy and promoted to the rank of major-general with overall responsibility for forces in the three counties of north-west Wales; seven days later he was knighted to increase his social standing. On taking up his command, he set to work at once to bring in money to pay the local soldiery, and led a body of them to help repel an enemy thrust into Denbighshire in March 1645.

For the rest of that year Owen was as much concerned with local royalists as with parliamentarians, and in particular with John Williams, archbishop of York, who resided at Conwy Castle and had paid to repair it. Owen, a born zealot, felt an instinctual suspicion of Williams, an interfering and flexible politician, and tension between the two culminated when the former seized the castle on 14 May. Owen managed to repulse parliamentarian incursions into the region until April 1646, when a full-scale invasion began under Thomas Mytton, and Conwy was blockaded. On 8 August Mytton stormed the town, using information provided by Williams, but Owen hung on to the castle even after the king himself had given permission to surrender. He did not give up until 9 November, making it one of the last three royalist fortresses to capitulate.

Sir John now lived quietly on his estates, paying fines totalling £4842 to a victorious parliament in 1647 and refusing an invitation that year from the exiled royalist general Prince Rupert to serve under him in the French army. Instead he joined the widespread royalist uprising of 1648, commanding the division of it in north-west Wales. Upon 3 June, following risings in the south of the country, Owen attacked Caernarfon with 240 supporters, driving Mytton's small garrison inside the walls and capturing the parliamentarian high sheriff, William Lloyd, who died of his wounds. Immediately he had to face a counter-attack by the troops occupying north-east Wales, led by colonels Carter and Twistleton. He met them at Llandygái on 5 June, and though his men routed the main body of their enemies, they broke in turn against the reserve. Owen himself was wounded, dragged from his horse, and made prisoner.

Despite an attempt to rescue him from Denbigh Castle, Owen was escorted to that of Windsor, and charged with treason by the parliament on 26 July. In November both houses voted to banish him, but in the harsher climate following Pride's Purge he was sent for trial with other royalist leaders. On 6 March 1649 he was sentenced to beheading, a large part of the feeling against him being owed to the belief that Lloyd's death had been caused by ill treatment in Owen's hands. Sir John appealed to the purged parliament for his life, and on 8 March it voted a reprieve by 28 voices to 23, Henry Ireton and Edmond Chaloner being especially prominent in his defence. Owen sent fulsome letters of gratitude and was subsequently pardoned, although £1000 more had been exacted from his estate to compensate Lloyd's family.

After this it is hardly surprising that Owen retired into private life again for ten years, a period broken by spells of imprisonment in 1655 and 1658 as the protectorate put prominent royalists in preventive detention during times of political tension. In 1659, however, he joined Booth's rising, and attempted to raise north-west Wales again in support of that rising. He failed, and went into hiding when Booth was defeated, while his estates were seized again. He was saved this time by the fall of the republic, and the restoration of the monarchy. In November 1660 he turned the tables by petitioning the Convention Parliament for compensation for his sufferings and for punishment of those who had inflicted them. Neither request was met, but Charles II rewarded him for his many services with appointment to the office of vice-admiral for north Wales in January 1661. Owen held this throughout the uneventful remainder of his life; he died in 1666 at Clenennau and was interred at Penmorfa church.

Owen's political sympathies are hardly a matter of surprise, as north-west Wales was a solidly royalist region at the opening of the civil war, but his fidelity to them was most unusual. It is another mark of his conscientious and rigorous nature that he saved his working papers and correspondence from the war period, which today provide the single most important body of source material for events in this part of Wales during these years.

RONALD HUTTON

Sources F. M. C. Bulkeley-Owen, *History of Selattyn parish* [1898] · letters, NL Wales, Clenennau papers · 'A narrative with letters presented by Captain E. Taylor', 1648 · *The bloody murthering of Mr Lloyd* (1648) · *Conoway [Conway] taken by storme by Major-General Mitton* (1646) · *JHC*, 5 (1646–8), 592, 600, 648; 6 (1648–51), 158–9; 8 (1660–67), 180, 200 · *JHL*, 10 (1647–8), 588 · *Memoirs of Prince Rupert and the cavaliers including their private correspondence*, ed. E. Warburton, 3 vols. (1849), vol. 2, p. 249, vol. 3, pp. 60–61, 237 · I. Roy, ed., *The royalist ordnance papers, 1642–1646*, 2 vols., Oxfordshire RS, 43, 49 (1964–75), 422 · *Diary of the marches of the royal army during the great civil war, kept by Richard Symonds*, ed. C. E. Long, CS, old ser., 74 (1859), 160, 194, 247 · *The manuscripts of his grace the duke of Portland*, 10 vols., HMC, 29 (1891–1931), vol. 1, pp. 477, 479 · *DWB* · N. Tucker, *Royalist major-general: Sir John Owen* (1963) · Bodl. Oxf., MS Turner 59, fols. 575r, 580r · W. A. Shaw, *The knights of England*, 2 (1906), 219 · memorial, Penmorfa church, Caernarvonshire

Archives NL Wales, Clenennau letters

Likenesses oils, 1660–99, NL Wales · J. Caldwell, line engraving (after unknown artist), BM, NPG; repro. in T. Pennant, *A tour in Wales* (1779), 263

Owen, John (1616–1683), theologian and Independent minister, was born at Stadham (Stadhampton), Oxfordshire, the second son of Henry Owen, vicar of Stadham, and grandson of Griffith Owen of Talhenbont, Llanegryn, Merioneth. His mother was probably Hester Owen, who married the minister John Hartcliffe following Henry's death. Owen described his father as 'a non-conformist all his daies' (J. Owen, *A Review of the True Nature of Schisme*, 1657, 38).

Education and early career until 1651 With his older brother William, Owen entered the grammar school of Edward Sylvester in Oxford about 1626, and in 1628 became a student at Queen's College, Oxford, whence he matriculated on 4 November 1631. At Queen's he was tutored in logic and philosophy by William Barlow, the future bishop of Lincoln, and in music by Thomas Wilson. After graduating BA on 11 June 1632 he proceeded MA on 27 April 1635, and shortly thereafter was ordained deacon by John Bancroft, bishop of Oxford.

Owen left Oxford in 1637 to become chaplain to Sir William Dormer of Ascott, near Wing, Buckinghamshire, and shortly thereafter accepted a similar position with John Lord Lovelace of Hurley, Berkshire. When civil war erupted in 1642 Lovelace supported the royalists, but Owen moved to London, where a sermon on Matthew 8: 26 by an unidentified preacher at St Mary Aldermanbury had a profound impact on him.

On 2 March 1643 the committee on printing in the House of Commons ordered the publication of Owen's first book, *Theomachia … or, A Display of Arminianism* (1643), which was dedicated to the committee on religion in the House of Lords. In this work he refuted the Arminians by examining the doctrines of predestination, original sin, irresistible grace, and the extent of the atonement, as well as attacking the 'idol' of free will. Offered the living of the parish church at Shepway, Kent, by Sir Edward Scott,

John Owen (1616–1683), attrib. John Greenhill, *c*.1668

Owen declined, preferring to accept the sequestrated rectory of Fordham, Essex, from parliament in July 1643. Shortly thereafter he married Mary Rooke (*d*. 1676), possibly the daughter of William Rooke, a Coggeshall clothier. Their first child, John, was baptized on 20 December 1644; ten other children followed, of whom all but one died in infancy or childhood.

By 1644 Owen had adopted presbyterian views, as the preface to his second book, *The Duty of Pastors and People* (1644), indicates. Although chary of congregational polity, he had ministered to his flock in their homes as well as in the parish church since 1643. The importance he attached to nurturing his congregants is reflected in *The Principles of the Doctrine of Christ* (1645), which contains a short catechism for children and a longer one for adults that expounds on the answers in the brief version. Nominated by Sir Peter Wentworth, MP for Tamworth, and by Scott's stepson, Thomas Westrow, MP for Hythe, Owen preached a fast sermon on Acts 16: 9 to the Commons on 29 April 1646. Published as *A Vision of Unchangeable Free Mercy* (1646), it included a section entitled 'A short defensative' about polity and toleration in which he advocated liberty for the godly to gather as congregations of visible saints, with the right to celebrate communion at least monthly. He envisioned such congregations as existing alongside parish churches governed according to presbyterian polity; his ecclesiology was thus in transition, a result of his having read John Cotton's *The Keyes of the Kingdom of Heaven* (1644). Owen's evolving views on polity may explain why the patron of Fordham, Sir John Lucas, opted not to present him to the living following the death of the sequestrated incumbent, John Alsop. On 18 August 1646 the House of Lords ordered that Owen be inducted as vicar of Coggeshall, Essex, on the recommendation of Robert Rich, earl of Warwick; he had been ministering there since May. He not only served the parish church but founded a gathered congregation. His embrace of congregational polity was complete by 1648, as reflected in his exposition of it in *Eshcol: a Cluster of the Fruit of Canaan* (1648). He argued that separating from false, unwarranted ways of worship was required by the precept to avoid the sins of others—a position he defended in a meeting of ministers at Colchester on 31 March 1648.

Troubled by the spread of Arminianism, including its espousal by Thomas Moore, a Lincolnshire sectary, in *The universality of Gods free-grace* (1646), Owen wrote a major rebuttal, *Salus electorum, sanguis Jesu* (1648), dedicated to Warwick. In this erudite attack on the doctrine of universal atonement he expounded on the necessity of Christ's satisfaction in redeeming the elect. His insistence that faith was procured by Christ's death and was irresistibly bestowed on the elect prompted various ministers to suspect him of antinomianism, including the belief that justification preceded faith. Richard Baxter responded in a lengthy appendix to *Aphorismes of Justification* (1649), insisting that faith was not the only condition for justification, and John Horne criticized Owen in *Thura aneogmene* (1650). Owen replied to Baxter in *Of the Death of Christ* (1650), accusing his protagonist of misrepresenting his views; *Salus electorum*, he averred, had been written to accommodate 'vulgar capacities' rather than adhere to scholastic precision (*Works*, 10.435). Moreover, he insisted that he did not embrace the antinomian doctrine that justification preceded believing.

In summer 1648 Owen accepted an invitation to minister to the parliamentary troops besieging Colchester, on which occasion he met Henry Ireton and other senior army officers. Following Colchester's surrender he preached two sermons on Habakkuk 3: 1–9, one at Colchester and the other at Romford. Published as *Eben-ezer: a Memoriall* (1648), they held out the promise that God always had instruments to destroy his enemies and deliver his church from oppression. Owen came to view the execution of Charles I as an example of such judgment, and in his sermon to the Commons on the day after the regicide he stressed that subjects, because of 'their retained sovereignty', were accountable for their sovereign's misrule and were therefore empowered to impose restraints. The destruction of a king was justified if he commanded 'unrighteous things' (*Works*, 8.136). Published as *A Sermon Preached ... January 31* (1649) it included an epistle to the Commons affirming Owen's belief in the imminent establishment of the millennium, although he never suggested precise dates. Appended to the sermon was a brief for toleration, though he acknowledged the state's right to punish heretics and schismatics who disrupted the peace or employed violence to thwart the gospel's progress. He preached before the Commons again on 19 April, reiterating his apocalyptic message that 'in these latter days, as antichristian tyranny draws to its period' Christ would 'shake and translate the political heights, governments, and strength of the nations' in preparation for the inauguration of his kingdom (ibid., 8.260); this sermon was published as *Ouranon ourania* (1649). Again he preached before the Commons, this time on 7 June, a service of thanksgiving to mark the Levellers' defeat at Burford. Dismissing them as poor creatures who had 'dashed themselves against the rock' he spoke of the imminent Irish expedition, which he saw in the context of Christ's battle 'with all the world' for their abuse of the divine ordinances (ibid., 9.215). Entitled *Human Power Defeated* this sermon was published posthumously in 1721. On 8 June the Commons asked the committee for Oxford to consider appointing Owen head of a college.

After hearing Owen preach to the Commons, Oliver Cromwell met him at Thomas Fairfax's house and sought his services as chaplain for the Irish expeditionary force; the house approved the appointment on 2 July 1649 and provided a stipend of £100 p.a. He went to Ireland in August, but was not at the siege of Drogheda, having remained in Dublin to preach, and to examine the statutes of Trinity College for possible revision. On 8 March 1650, by which time he had left Ireland, the council of state made him a trustee to administer the property of the archbishop, dean, and chapter of Dublin for the support of Trinity College.

Owen preached to the Rump Parliament on 28 February 1650, a day of humiliation. Published as *The Stedfastness of Promises* (1650) the sermon exhorted MPs to stand firm in the face of the hydra of Catholics, prelatists, and Scottish covenanters that threatened the gospel, the propagation of which in Ireland must be supported. On 8 March the council appointed him to preach to it every Sunday afternoon during the coming year, in return for which he received lodgings at Whitehall and a stipend. Two months later the council sought his assistance to advise a committee about the appointment of ministers for regiments lacking them. On 28 June he left for Scotland with Cromwell's forces, preaching *en route* at Newcastle and Berwick. In the latter sermon, preached in part on 21 July, completed at Edinburgh in November, and published as *The Branch of the Lord* (1650), he expounded on the qualities of the gospel church. By late August he had returned to London, but in the aftermath of the battle of Dunbar the council, heeding Cromwell's request, ordered him back to Scotland. While there he helped persuade Alexander Jaffray, provost of Aberdeen, that the Scots had erred in supporting the Stuarts.

The Oxford years, 1651–1658 Following his return to London early in 1651 Owen was appointed dean of Christ Church, Oxford, on 18 March. The previous incumbent, Edward Reynolds, had refused to take the engagement, and Joseph Caryl, who had accompanied Owen to Scotland as a chaplain, declined the post. However, Caryl succeeded Owen as a preacher to the council of state on 23 June. Within two years the new dean was complaining that his academic duties intruded on his studies and professing that he had forgotten 'the portion of polite learning' that he once had (*Works*, 10.492–3). In addition to his responsibilities at

Oxford he was asked in July 1651 to review the statutes of Trinity College, Dublin. At the service of thanksgiving on 24 October 1651 for Cromwell's victory at Worcester, Owen exhorted the Rump to consider 'the constant *appearing of God* against every party that, under any colour or pretence whatever, have lifted up themselves for the reinforcement of things as in former days' (ibid., 8.336). The theme of this sermon, published as *The Advantage of the Kingdome of Christ* (1651), was God's shaking of worldly realms. Four days later parliament ordered Owen and Thomas Goodwin to preach at Oxford, and for the next five years they alternately delivered sermons from the pulpit of St Mary's. On 6 February 1652 Owen preached the funeral sermon for Henry Ireton in Westminster Abbey, likening him to Daniel in his wisdom, love for his people, and righteous administration; dedicated to Henry Cromwell the sermon was published as *The Labouring Saints Dismission to Rest* (1652).

On 10 February 1652 Owen and other ministers submitted a petition to parliament condemning the Racovian catechism and calling for the more effective propagation of the gospel. The Rump responded by appointing two committees, one of which, with Owen as a member, examined the catechism, laying the foundation for its condemnation and burning. In consultation with select ministers, including Owen, the other committee produced a report whose expanded version was published in March as *The Humble Proposals*, with Owen's name heading the list of authors. It called for a university trained clergy, the introduction of examiners and ejectors to remove unfit ministers, the retention of tithing, and the suppression of astrology. Owen and his fellow Independents wanted to add sixteen doctrinal principles that no one could legally attack in print or sermons, and these were appended to an edition of the proposals published in December (but dated 1653). The Rump had made modest progress in dealing with the proposals when Cromwell dismissed it in April 1653.

In the meantime Owen's responsibilities continued to expand. On 29 July 1652 he and eight other ministers were asked to advise Charles Fleetwood and his colleagues about the provision of clergy for Ireland; on 15 June Cromwell named him to Oxford's board of visitors; and on 26 September he became vice-chancellor of the university following Cromwell's nomination. When Cromwell put the chancellorship in commission on 16 October, Owen served as first commissioner. He was also appointed by the council of state to the committee responsible for licensing translations of the Bible. With eleven other Independent ministers he wrote a letter to parliament, printed in Henry Whitfield's *Strengthe out of Weaknesse* (1652), endorsing missionary activity among North American Indians. Once more he was invited to preach to parliament, this time on 13 October 1652, a day of humiliation. Published as *Christs Kingdom and the Magistrate's Power* (1652) his sermon reflected his concern about the need to expedite the propagation of the gospel and the role of magistrates in this endeavour. In the same year he published *The Primer*, complete with a short catechism, Bible passages, and prayers; printed with parliamentary authorization it may have been intended as an official alternative to the old *Primer and Catechisme*.

Owen reportedly proposed names for the nominated assembly, and he and Walter Cradock preached to it on 25 August 1653. On 2 September he supported Oxford's petition to the assembly to maintain the universities and support godly ministers. His name was on a list of ministers the assembly formulated to eject and settle clergy throughout the country, but nothing came of this. When Cromwell convened a conference of prominent presbyterian, Independent, and Baptist ministers in late October to promote unity Owen participated. There is no evidence that he was troubled by the dissolution of the nominated assembly on 12 December. Eleven days later he was created doctor of divinity; his diploma noted that he was 'in disputando strenuus & acutus' ('rigorous and sharp in discussion'; Wood, *Ath. Oxon.*: *Fasti*, 2.179), some indication of which is suggested in his 1653 treatise, *Diatriba de divina justitia*. The need for this work grew out of public disputations at Oxford in which Owen, castigating the Socinians, asserted that God's justice made the punishment of sin essential; without Christ's atonement, by which Owen meant the rendering of satisfaction for sin, God could not forgive sinners. When his espousal of this doctrine in Oxford disputations prompted criticism from 'many very respectable theologians' (*Works*, 10.486), he defended his views in *Diatriba*, which included a refutation of the tenets of William Twisse, Samuel Rutherford, and the Socinian Johannes Crellius. Owen was in turn attacked by Thomas Gilbert in *Vindiciae supremi Dei dominii* (1655) and briefly by Baxter in *The Unreasonableness of Infidelity* (1655).

By 1654 Owen had completed a lengthy polemical work, *The Doctrine of the Saints' Perseverance* (1654), which he had begun in 1651 in response to John Goodwin's *Apolutrosis apolutroseos* (1651). On 7 January 1652 Robert Abbott, minister of St Augustine's, London, reported to Baxter that he had told Owen 'it was expected he should doe something to satisfy the Church' about Goodwin's work, and Owen replied that he had already begun a critique (*Correspondence of Richard Baxter* 1.73). The result was a prodigious defence of the doctrine of 'the certain, infallible continuance of the love and favour of God unto the end towards his, those whom he hath once freely accepted in Jesus Christ' (*Works*, 11.120). He grounded this doctrine on God's immutable nature, the absolute purpose of God in saving the elect, the covenant of grace, and God's faithfulness in keeping his promises. In the lengthy preface Owen attacked Henry Hammond's argument, in *Dissertationes quatuor* (1651), for the authenticity of the seven Ignatian epistles, which provided evidence for the early development of episcopacy. Hammond had directed his disquisition against the Huguenot David Blondel and various English puritans, and Owen came to their defence in his preface, only to be refuted by Hammond in *An Answer to the Animadversions* (1654).

In addition to engaging in scholarly debate Owen was active on other fronts. In the aftermath of the failed nominated assembly, on 9 January 1654 he, Thomas Goodwin,

Philip Nye, and Sidrach Simpson sent a letter to the Independent churches denouncing the Fifth Monarchists because their views 'cut the sinews of all Magistracy' and endangered England's peace (Bodl. Oxf., MS Carte 81, 16*r*–17*v*). This did not dissuade the Fifth Monarchist John Tillinghast from quoting Owen in an epistle dedicatory to Cromwell in *Generation Work* (1654). Owen and Goodwin were among a group of ministers that met with Cromwell on 28 February, probably to discuss a religious settlement. Several days later the council asked Owen to refute *A Two-fold Catechism* (1654) by the Socinian John Biddle, which led to the publication of *Vindiciae evangelicae* (1655), another expansive tome, the focus of which was an exposition of the atonement and justification by imputed grace, with commentary as well on the covenant between God the father and his son. In Owen's judgement Biddle's theology was 'a composure of rotten posts and dead men's bones' (*Works*, 12.84), but he also lashed out against the 'middle way' championed by Moïse Amyraut. In an appendix to *Vindiciae evangelicae* Owen responded to the critique of his treatise *Of the Death of Christ* by Baxter in *Rich: Baxter's Confession of his Faith* (1655), and the latter thereupon replied to Owen in *Certain Disputations of Right to Sacraments* (1657).

Owen advised Cromwell on the establishment of the commission for the approbation of public preachers in March 1654, and on the 20th was named a trier. On 28 August he and his brother William were appointed assistants to the Oxford commission for the ejection of ignorant and scandalous clergy and schoolmasters. Judging from his intervention with the Berkshire commission on behalf of Edward Pococke, who had been accused of reading the Book of Common Prayer in his parsonage at Childrey, he probably undertook these duties in a spirit of moderation. This is also suggested by his connivance at John Fell's use of the Book of Common Prayer in services in the Oxford home of Dr Thomas Willis, although he opposed the awarding of an MA degree to Robert South in 1657 because the latter insisted on using the Book of Common Prayer in Christ Church. Owen was elected to represent the university in the first protectoral parliament, but as a minister he was disqualified by the Clerical Disabilities Act of 1642; Anthony Wood's assertion that he renounced his ordination in an attempt to claim his seat is implausible. Although he could not sit in parliament he advised a parliamentary committee on the fundamentals of religion—in practice, the limits of orthodoxy. The resulting document, *The Principles of Faith*, derived from the proposals of 1652, was, according to Baxter, largely the work of Owen, 'the great doer of all that worded the Articles' (*Reliquiae Baxterianae*, 1, pt 2, 198). He was also a signatory of a letter from ministers and university professors to evangelical churches on the continent endorsing John Dury's efforts to organize an evangelical protestant alliance. When Cromwell wanted to forward his religious agenda he consulted with Owen, Stephen Marshall, and three others on 31 October 1654. Owen's loyalty to the regime was manifest in March 1655 when he raised a troop to defend the university during the Penruddock uprising, and he offered to form another in Berkshire. In December he sat on a committee that discussed Menasseh ben Israel's proposal to readmit Jews to England, and the same month Major-General James Berry suggested to the secretary of state, John Thurloe, that Owen could propose means to supply ministers for Anglesey.

Early in 1656 Owen experienced assorted tribulations, including a raging fever that claimed the lives of two of his sons and made others in his household ill. Rumours circulated in April that he was troubled by John Wilkins's marriage to Cromwell's sister, fearing this would undermine his influence with the lord protector. Moreover his stipend was two years in arrears, prompting the council to decree in August that he should be paid the £200 he was owed and £100 p.a. out of undervalued delinquents' estates. During the spring he had been apprehended at Whitehall Gate, probably because of a private debt, though he was quickly released and the men responsible for his arrest were themselves apprehended.

As vice-chancellor Owen endeavoured to reform Oxford, in part by making traditional academic dress optional, but convocation rejected his plan in April 1656. He dressed in fashionable clothing, had long hair, and wore Spanish leather boots and a cocked hat. Although he enjoyed some support among Oxford visitors they refused to reduce convocation's powers, nor was he able to reform the traditional festivities and ceremonies at the end of the academic year. Unlike his friend John Wilkins he displayed little interest in curricular reform, especially the new science, although Ralph Josselin heard reports that Owen had attempted to suppress the study of philosophy and had 'become a great scorne' (*Diary of Ralph Josselin*, 374). While John Locke was at Christ Church from 1656 to 1660 he was influenced by Owen. During his Oxford years Owen may have ministered to a gathered congregation, but there is no evidence to support George Vernon's later accusation that one met in Christ Church.

In addition to his academic duties Owen continued to serve the Cromwellian regime. With Caryl and Peter Sterry he advised the council in June 1656 on which books and manuscripts in the library of the late James Ussher should be purchased by the state, and on 17 September he preached at the opening of parliament (*God's Work in Founding Zion*, 1656). He returned to preach a fast sermon on 30 October, published as *God's Presence with a People* (1656). Meanwhile, on 16 October he was appointed to a committee to advise the council on augmenting clerical stipends. He was with Cromwell when George Fox met him to discuss the suffering of Quakers, and in the aftermath of James Nayler's symbolic re-enactment of Jesus' entry into Jerusalem on Palm Sunday Sir John Reynolds wanted Owen, Caryl, or Nye to converse with Nayler in the hope that 'some good may be wrought upon him' (*Diary of Thomas Burton*, 1.79–80). Owen encountered Quakers at St Mary's, where they justified wearing their hats during prayer because he declined to remove his own while reciting the Lord's prayer. In 1657 he advised Cromwell how to reconcile the Scottish resolutioners and the remonstrants, who had the support of the English presbyterians and Independents respectively.

Amid these activities Owen continued to write. A devotional work on sanctification, *Of the Mortification of Sinne in Believers* (1656), reached a third edition in 1668. In *Vindiciae evangelicae* he had found an affinity between the teachings of Hugo Grotius and the Socinians, whereupon Hammond had come to Grotius's defence, most recently in *A Second Defence of … Hugo Grotius* (1655). To this Owen responded in *A Review of the Annotations of Hugo Grotius* (1656). In the following year he prepared some meditations for the press that had been composed about 1650; published as *Of Communion with God* (1657) they explored the believer's fellowship with each member of the Trinity. He remained firmly opposed to Arminianism; his letter endorsing George Kendall's attack on Arminian tenets in *Fur praedestinatus* (1651) was printed in Kendall's *Fur pro tribunali* (1657). Owen incited another controversy when he published *Of Schisme* (1657), in which he argued that protestants were not guilty of schism for leaving the Catholic church, nor were Independents who organized gathered congregations in accord with Christ's command, opting 'to reform themselves, by reducing the practice of worship to its original institution' (*Works*, 13.199). To this work Daniel Cawdrey retorted in *Independencie a Great Schism* (1657), accusing Owen and his colleagues of opening the door to all heresies and blasphemies by insisting on toleration for themselves; 'Causeless Separation from a true Church', he insisted, 'is Schism' (p. 64). At the urging of the Independent minister John Beverley, Owen replied in *A Review of the True Nature of Schisme* (1657 [1658]), in which he acknowledged the influence of Cotton's *Keyes* on him. When Cawdrey continued his attack in *Independency Further Proved to be a Schism* (1658) Owen responded to his criticism of Cotton in *A Defence of Mr John Cotton* (1658). Giles Firmin joined the fray with a critique of Owen in *Of Schism* (1658).

The offer of the crown to Cromwell on 23 February 1657 troubled Owen and may explain his angry departure from London in early March. Yet on the 19th of that month the journalist Marchamont Nedham jokingly told Cromwell 'that *vox populi* said Mr. Nye should be Archbishop of Canterbury, and Dr. Owen of York' (*CSP dom.*, *1656–7*, 318). Siding with the military officers opposed to monarchy Owen acceded to the request of colonels Thomas Pride and John Desborough to draft a petition to Cromwell in May urging him to reject the crown. Although a proposal for Owen to preach a fast sermon to the Commons on 27 February 1657 had sparked a two-hour debate, his supporters, led by Colonel John Jones and Dennis Bond, persuaded parliament to settle the estate of Donadea and other lands in co. Kildare on him to provide his stipend of £100 p.a., hitherto paid by the exchequer.

After Cromwell resigned the chancellorship of Oxford in July 1657 and was replaced by his son Richard, Owen suggested his own replacement as vice-chancellor; John Conant, rector of Exeter College, succeeded him on 9 October. Shortly before this Owen and Goodwin had ceased their afternoon lectures at St Mary's, although Owen remained dean of Christ Church. Cognizant of his concern about the plight of persecuted protestants, on 4 November the council appointed him to a committee dealing with those in Piedmont, Poland, and Bohemia. A correspondent of Joseph Williamson reported in December that he was giving 'opposition' lectures at St Peter's-in-the-East, Oxford, but these were almost certainly not critical of the Cromwellian regime, judging from the innocuous content of his book *Of Temptation* (1658), the substance of which had been delivered from an Oxford pulpit. He followed this work with a substantive defence of the Bible as the word of God, *Of the Divine Originall* (1659), completed in September. Appended to this were *Pro sacris scripturis*, which denounced the Quaker belief in continuing revelation, and *A Vindication of the Purity and Integrity of the Hebrew and Greek Texts*, which criticized Brian Walton's edition of the *Biblia polyglotta* on the grounds that its inclusion of variant readings would strengthen the Catholic claim that the Vulgate was the only authoritative text. He also contended that the vowel points in the Hebrew text were as old as the letters and thus part of inspired scripture. Both appendices provoked replies: Walton defended himself in *The Considerator Considered* (1659), and Samuel Fisher denounced Owen (and others) in *Rusticus ad academicos* (1660).

The experience of defeat, 1658–1663 Owen was not with Cromwell at the latter's death in September 1658, though he attended the state funeral. Shortly thereafter he played a major role at the Savoy conference, helping to draft *A Declaration of the Faith and Order*, which was presented to Richard Cromwell on 14 October. In Baxter's judgement Owen and Nye prevented old wounds from healing by insisting on more fundamentals in the declaration than he deemed necessary. Owen's ties to the military were again evident when parliament designated 4 February 1659 a day of humiliation and debated the order in which four ministers—Owen and the presbyterians Reynolds, Thomas Manton, and Edmund Calamy—would preach; John Lambert wanted Owen to be first, whereas the civilian republican Arthur Hesilrige thought he should be last; a compromise let him preach third. In his sermon *The Glory and Interest of Nations* (1659) he registered no objection to unbelievers serving as magistrates, but he expected little good from them. By mid-March he had gathered a congregation whose members included such prominent officers as Fleetwood, Desborough, William Sydenham, James Berry, William Goffe, and possibly Lambert, and they would soon be meeting in Wallingford House. It was there that the grandees, with Owen participating, decided to force Cromwell to dissolve parliament on 22 April. Arriving late Manton thought he heard Owen call for Cromwell's removal, yet as late as 3 May Owen supported the retention of a titular protector.

In the face of growing support for the Rump Parliament's recall Owen urged the grandees to summon it, and he produced a list (obtained from Edmund Ludlow) of about 160 MPs who had served at Westminster since Pride's Purge. On 8 May, one day after the Rump was reconvened, he preached to its members. As the situation deteriorated following the Rump's demand for Cromwell's resignation on 24 May Owen tried to rally Independent churches, but the key congregation at Yarmouth refused to become involved. When Sir George Booth and his royalist supporters rebelled, the council on 15 August ordered Owen to raise a troop of horse to defend Oxford University. The unsettled times prompted leading Independents, including Owen, and presbyterians to engage in discussions in September aimed at unity, but they had little success. On 24 September the council commissioned him and Thankful Owen to preach at Whitehall on Sundays until 1 December. There was presumably a moment of levity in September when Owen was duped by a London merchant claiming to be an Eastern Orthodox patriarch, but the Baptist John Tombes was in earnest the following month when he sought the assistance of Owen and others to prevent toleration for Catholics; whether Owen saw him is unknown.

In late October copies of George Monck's *Declaration of the Officers of the Army in Scotland* reached Owen and his colleagues. Alarmed by Monck's threat to intervene militarily to restore the Rump, which had been ousted anew by the army on the 13th, Owen (whose name heads the list) and eighteen others wrote to Monck on the 31st, announcing the dispatch of a delegation to convey their concerns. When Monck replied, insisting on the restoration of parliamentary government, Owen wrote on 19 November, warning that a civil war between the armies would destroy the good old cause and 'the sober godly in both Nations' (*Correspondence*, 106–8). In a letter to Owen, William Greenhill, and William Hooke dated 23 November, Monck professed hope for a peaceful resolution. Six days later he wrote to Owen insisting that England must be liberated from military rule and pressing him to urge Fleetwood to restore the Rump. On 13 December Owen and thirteen others wrote to Monck arguing that the crucial issue was not whether parliament should convene but the threat to their lives if their cause should be overthrown. Despair set in when Owen, Desborough, and Sydenham learned on the 22nd that the troops dispatched to besiege Portsmouth had changed sides. As Monck's forces began their slow march toward London, Owen and Nye were reportedly attempting to raise £100,000 to support troops committed to toleration for protestants. As Baxter assessed the events of 1659, in a passage excised from his published autobiography by its editor, he bitterly condemned Owen for doing the 'mainework' in toppling Cromwell; Owen's 'parts, & confidence, & busybodiness, & interest in those men did give him the opportunity to do his exploits' (Nuttall, *Journal of Ecclesiastical History*, 6.78).

On 13 March 1660 parliament deprived Owen of the deanery of Christ Church and restored Reynolds. About this time Owen moved his family to Stadham, where he lived quietly, notwithstanding attempts to implicate him in spurious conspiracies in April and November. The efforts of the earl of Clarendon and Roger Boyle, Lord Broghill, to persuade him to conform were unsuccessful. In the crackdown on suspected dissidents following Thomas Venner's Fifth Monarchist rebellion in January 1661, troops seized six or seven cases of pistols from his house, where he was hosting two former Oxford colleagues, Thankful Owen and Francis Johnson. Much of his time was now devoted to writing. In *Theologoumena pantodapa*, published at Oxford in 1661 and reprinted at Bremen (1684) and Franeker (1700), he surveyed the history of theology throughout biblical times and argued that it was most accurately expounded by Calvinists. His views on set prayers, particularly the implications for the Lord's prayer, had been criticized by Thomas Long in *An Exercitation Concerning the … Lords Prayer* (1658) and Meric Casaubon in *A Vindication of the Lord's Prayer* (1660), and Owen took up this and related issues in *A Discourse Concerning Liturgies* (1662). Composed while deliberations for the Act of Uniformity were underway this work repudiated liturgies as neither apostolic nor in accord with the practice of Christian churches during the first three centuries AD. In 1662 he also rebutted the work of the Franciscan John Vincent Canes, whose *Fiat lux* (1661) proclaimed the benefits of Catholicism as a faith of truth and moderation in contrast to the destructive zeal of protestant sects. Owen's anonymously published critique, *Animadversions on … Fiat lux* (1662), condemned key Catholic beliefs and practices while denouncing Canes as a modern day Celsus, the Platonist critic of apostolic Christianity. Canes replied in *An Epistle* (1663), prompting Owen to compose *A vindication of the 'Animadversions'* (1664), a more detailed critique of Catholicism in which he charged the Catholic church with idolatry, apostasy, heresy, and schism. Canes defended himself in *Diaphanta* (1665; reprinted in *Three Letters*, 1671), which Owen ignored.

The quest for toleration, 1663–1669 After the ejection of nonconforming ministers in August 1662 Owen hoped 'that God who hath now hid his face, will repent him of the evill' (*Correspondence*, 130). By 1663 he had settled in London near Moorgate, although he continued to spend time at his Stadham home. He met often with Thomas Goodwin and Henry Jessey, and was probably involved with the declaration submitted to the king on 27 February 1663 calling for liberty of conscience and affirming the theology embodied in the Thirty-Nine Articles, though differing on certain matters of discipline and polity. The delegation that presented the paper to Charles also denounced the recent Tong plot and Fifth Monarchist principles. In August and October 1663 Owen was invited to become the minister of the congregational church in Boston, Massachusetts; he considered the offer, and as late as June 1666 the people of Boston thought that he might accept, though ultimately he resolved to stay in England.

Owen enjoyed limited protection, thanks to such friends as Philip, Lord Wharton, Arthur Annesley, earl of Anglesey, and reportedly Aubrey de Vere, earl of Oxford. With other Independent ministers he participated in a lecture at the house of the alderman Henry Ashurst. He went to Oxford in January 1664 in the hope of persuading Thomas Gilbert to become president of Harvard College, and the following month he thought he was near death because of a severe 'fluxe' (Bodl. Oxf., Rawlinson MS, 53). Although he was indicted at Oxford on 27 February 1665 for holding conventicles at Stadham he was not incarcerated. He persuaded Barlow, now provost of Queen's College, Oxford, to seek assurances from Clarendon that he would henceforth be exempt from such prosecution, but they were not forthcoming. From 1664 onwards Owen's wife and children lived primarily at Stoke Newington, where his daughter Judith died in May 1664 and his son Matthew in April 1665. Their hosts were Charles Fleetwood and his new wife, Mary, widow of Sir Edward Hartopp. Here Owen gathered a small congregation that included various former Cromwellian military officers—Fleetwood, Desborough, Berry, Lieutenant-Colonel Jeffrey Ellaston, and Captain Griffith Lloyd—as well as Bridget Bendish, daughter of Henry Ireton and granddaughter of Cromwell; William Steele, former lord chancellor of Ireland; Samuel Lee, former dean of Wadham College, Oxford; Sir John Hartopp; and Anglesey's wife and daughter. Owen's circle of friends also came to embrace the fifth or sixth Baron Willoughby of Parham, Sir Trevor Roper, Sir William Morice, and Richard Hampden. Owen and his wife were occasional guests of the Whartons at Woburn, and they stayed for a time at Theobalds, Hertfordshire, with Sir Edward Abney's wife (Caryl's daughter) and preached in their London house.

Owen played a major role in the debate over freedom of conscience that began in 1667 in anticipation of the expiry of the Conventicle Act. Published anonymously Owen's powerfully argued tract, *Indulgence and Toleration Considered* (1667), proclaimed that 'God hath not Warranted or Authorized any man to *inforce* [people] to *Act contrary to their Light*, and that perswasion of his Mind and Will which he hath given them in their own Consciences' (p. 17). Physical compulsion in religion was not practised by the apostolic church, inculcated hypocritical compliance, was abhorrent to the English, and historically failed to extirpate the views that it was designed to eradicate. Owen's companion tract, *A Peace-Offering* (1667), also published anonymously, complained bitterly that conformists were ignoring the doctrinal orthodoxy of dissenters and instead insisting on 'a Precise and Determinate Judgement and Practise in things of very *Little* Concernment' (p. 13). Dissenters, he asserted, had no desire to impose civil or ecclesiastical polity on the nation, and the indulgence they sought was not conducive to sedition as their opponents alleged. He was in turn attacked by Richard Perrinchief in *Indulgence not Justified* (1668).

The tracts by Owen along with others by John Humfrey and John Corbet set the stage for the king and parliament to consider indulgence and comprehension in 1668. Wilkins, now bishop of Chester, prepared proposals for comprehension that eventually led to a bill written by Sir Matthew Hale, whereas Owen drafted a bill that would provide liberty of worship for dissenters whose theology was orthodox. Owen's draft included provisions for the registration of ministers and their congregants, the exclusion of nonconformists from public office, and the payment of 'public dues' to parishes. Supporters of Gilbert Sheldon, archbishop of Canterbury, defeated both measures. With justification Baxter blamed the prelates for the defeat of comprehension, but Manton held Owen responsible for having advocated a different proposal. Accompanied by the presbyterian Samuel Annesley, Owen thereupon called on Manton to defend the benefits of indulgence.

In the meantime Baxter was encouraged by Owen's new catechism, *A Brief Instruction* (1667). Its defence of congregational polity elicited a critique by Benjamin Camfield, *A Serious Examination* (1668), but Baxter found reason for hope in Owen's perceived rejection of two congregational principles, namely, that the entire gathered church as a society has the authority to admit or excommunicate members, and that the congregation bestows this power at ordination to church officers. Overestimating Owen's flexibility Baxter drafted a statement of religious fundamentals (later published as part two of *Church Concord*, 1691) and asked Owen to evaluate it. The latter found it too lengthy, preferring that it be limited to key points relevant to the union of presbyterians and Independents. Owen thought that Baxter was not firm enough in rejecting Socinianism, and he also disapproved of Baxter's stress on the magistrate's authority to repress errors and heresy. Fifteen months after discussions between the two men had begun, an exasperated Baxter requested the return of his papers, and Owen complied, remarking only that 'I am still a well-wisher to those Mathematicks' (*Reliquiae Baxterianae*, pt 3, 69). Although nothing came of these proceedings the reputation of the two men was probably never higher during the Restoration era, for Barlow observed in January 1669 that Owen had kissed the king's hand, adding that he had heard reports that Owen or Baxter would receive the next vacant bishopric. This would have pleased Barlow, who thought that such an appointment might ensure the continuance of episcopacy and the church's patrimony, although he acknowledged that some people would have preferred the termination of episcopacy rather than the elevation of either man to a bishopric.

A beacon of nonconformity, 1668–1678 Owen continued to write at a prodigious pace. *The Nature … of Indwelling Sin* (1668), *A Practical Exposition upon Psalm CXXX* (1668), and *A Brief Declaration … of the Doctrine of the Trinity* (1669) were intended for godly readers, whereas his massive study of Hebrews, published in four folio volumes between 1668 and 1684, was composed primarily for biblical scholars and ministers; this is especially evident in the first volume, which explores questions of authorship and language. (*A Brief Declaration* elicited a response from the Quaker George Whitehead, *The Divinity of Christ*, 1669.) Other works reflected Owen's interest in polemics. Chief among these at this point in his career was *Truth and Innocence Vindicated* (1669), composed after Baxter had declined his request to answer the attack on nonconformists by Samuel Parker in *A Discourse of Ecclesiastical Politie* (1669). Castigating Parker's profuse use of abusive language as an unacceptable means of debate Owen rebutted his core charge that nonconformists were subversives. Baxter praised Owen's reply, adding that this work enhanced his stature among dissenters, but Parker ridiculed Owen's use of Latin phrases as 'superannuated Pedantry' and dismissed his book as 'nothing but Cavil and vulgar Talk' (S. Parker, *A Defence and Continuation*, 1671, A3r, 3). When Owen defended Sunday as the Christian sabbath in *Exercitations Concerning … a Day of Sacred Rest* (1671), he was attacked by the sabbatarian William Saller in *An Examination of a Late Book* (1671). In a lengthy preface to Theophilus Gale's *The True Idea of Jansenisme* (1669), Owen asserted that Augustine's doctrine of grace had been taught by some Catholics in every age of church history. Another brief work, *The State of the Kingdom* (perhaps published only posthumously) was part of an unsuccessful endeavour by nonconformists to prevent passage of a new Conventicle Act in March 1670.

Despite the heavy writing schedule Owen performed numerous ministerial functions. Beginning in 1669 he participated in a combination lectureship at Hackney with presbyterians and other Independents, and he also preached at White's Alley, Moorfields. With eleven others he and Goodwin wrote to the governor of Massachusetts on 25 March 1669 protesting against recent legislation against Baptists, arguing that they should be free as long as they refrained from disturbing the peace. Owen's influence extended well beyond London, for in May 1669 he and George Griffith sought to resolve a dispute involving elders in the Independent church at Hitchin, Hertfordshire, and two years later he participated in the ordination of Matthew Meade at Stepney and recommended Thomas Hardcastle for the pastorship of the open membership congregation at Broadmead, Bristol. When the ministers and magistrates of Massachusetts sought advice on raising money and recruiting students and a president for Harvard College they wrote to Owen and others in August 1671, and he and his colleagues responded in February. The presbyterian Henry Oasland remarked to Baxter about this time that Owen 'hugely riseth in the esteeme … of this Country' (*Correspondence of Richard Baxter* 2.86), but he also had his critics, such as the conformist George Vernon, author of a vitriolic attack, *A Letter to a Friend* (1670). To Vernon, Owen was the former darling of Cromwell, a purveyor of falsehood and uncharitableness, and 'a Trumpet to sound an Alarum to Sedition and Rebellion' (p. 14). Owen briefly responded in *Reflections on a Slanderous Libel* (1670), and a friend anonymously came to his defence in *An Expostulatory Letter* (1671).

When the new Conventicle Act came into effect in May 1670 Owen resolved to continue his meetings and suffer the consequences, but he also reiterated the case for religious freedom for nonconformists in *An Account of the Grounds and Reasons* (1670?), a broadside, and protested against their unjust treatment in *The Present Distresses* (1671?) and *A Word of Advice* (1671?). Charles II consulted him about a possible declaration of indulgence in August and September 1671, and following its proclamation he and three other congregationalists thanked the king on 28 March 1672. Although Owen apparently did not obtain a licence for himself he assisted others to procure them. The leathersellers gave him permission to use their hall if it were licensed, but there is no record that a licence was issued. Following Caryl's death in 1673 his congregation merged with that of Owen, who ministered to them at Leadenhall Street, where he was assisted by Isaac Loeffs (1673–82), Robert Ferguson (1674–*c*.1679), and David Clarkson (1682–3; sole pastor, 1683–6). Against the background of the indulgence Owen published an eirenic work, *A Discourse Concerning Evangelical Love* (1672), recognizing the Church of England as a genuine body of Christ, but insisting anew that separation from it was not schism.

Although Owen did not shun polemics they were beginning to take their toll. About 1672 he complained to John Eliot that he had 'a dry and barren spirit' and that 'there is scarce any one alive in the world who hath more *reproaches* cast upon him than I have' (*Correspondence*, 154). This may explain why, in 1673, he reneged on a promise to write an epistle to John Bunyan's *Differences in Judgment about Water-Baptism*. As the Parker controversy raged he read the proofs of Andrew Marvell's *The Rehearsal Transpros'd*, but he was satirized and denounced as a dangerous rebel by Parker's defender, Richard Leigh, in *The Transproser Rehears'd* (1673). When the latitudinarian William Sherlock criticized Owen's older work, *Of Communion with God*, in *A Discourse Concerning … Jesus Christ* (1673), the latter responded in *A Vindication of some Passages* (1674), attributing Sherlock's errors to ignorance or prejudice; Sherlock countered in *A Defence and Continuation* (1675), castigating Owen as an antinomian. Owen was also criticized by the Wiltshire rector Thomas Hotchkis, who commended his zeal but accused him of dishonouring the Church of England while abetting Catholicism (*A Discourse Concerning the Imputation*, 1675).

To some extent Owen must have been frustrated by the perceived need to engage in polemic, for his fundamental interests lay elsewhere. In 1674 he published the first of what would eventually be a massive five-volume work on the Holy Spirit. In *Pneumatologia* he explored the nature of the Holy Spirit as part of the triune deity, its dispensations in the Old and New Testaments, and its regenerative work. The second volume, *The Reason of Faith* (1677), explained the basis for believing that the Bible was God's word, and the third, *Synesis pneumatike* (1678), discussed God's mind as revealed in scripture. *A Discourse of the Work of the Holy Spirit* (1682) explored its role in prayer, and the final volume, *Two Discourses* (1693), expounded on the Holy Spirit as comforter and source of spiritual gifts. *Pneumatologia* elicited a critique from William Clagett, a royal chaplain, in *A Discourse Concerning the Operations* (1678), but Humfrey came to Owen's defence in *Peaceable Disquisitions* (1678). Chiding Owen's critics, including Parker, for their contemptuous treatment of him, Humfrey complained that an entire generation of men was ready to attack almost anything Owen wrote, hoping to 'render that worthy person quite useless to the Church' (p. 1).

If this was the goal of Owen's critics they failed. During summer and autumn 1674 he advised congregational churches in Lancashire, Cheshire, and Yorkshire about whether to admit Oliver Heywood's presbyterian church to their association. About this time he began participating in the morning exercises against popery in Southwark (several of these sermons were published), and he was also involved in the merchants' lectures at Pinners' Hall. While convalescing at Tunbridge Wells, Kent, in 1674, he explained his position on toleration to James, duke of York, and shortly thereafter had an audience in London with the king, who gave him a thousand guineas to aid suffering dissenters. Although an informer reported in February 1676 that his meeting was dangerous he was left alone, probably because he now enjoyed the support of the duke of Buckingham as well as Anglesey and Wharton. According to John Asty, Owen's early biographer, he was later arrested by two informers and discharged by Sir Edmund Godfrey. In June 1677 he obtained an order from Heneage, Lord Finch, the chancellor, directing Bishop Barlow to release Bunyan from Bedford gaol, and the same year he reputedly recommended that Bunyan publish *The Pilgrim's Progress* with his own printer, Nathaniel Ponder.

Following the death of Owen's wife in 1676 he married (by licence dated 21 June 1677) Dorothy, the wealthy widow of Thomas D'Oyley of Chiselhampton, Oxfordshire, and daughter of a Mr Michel of Kingston Russell, Dorset. They lived at Kensington and later at Ealing.

Owen was described by Hooke as 'valetudinarious and crazy, often down' in early August 1677 (*Mather Papers*, 8.584). His depressed mood may have been triggered by his dismay at the perceived spread of Arminianism and Socinianism, a concern that led him to write *The Nature of Apostasy* (1676). With its exposition of imputed grace *The Doctrine of Justification* (1677) was a natural sequel. Doctrinal concerns also prompted him to compose *Christologia* (1677), a treatise on the person of Christ, including the hypostatical union of the divine and human in one person.

In the shadow of persecution, 1678–1683 As reflected in some of his unpublished sermons (DWL, MS L6/3, 4), the spectre of persecution disturbed Owen by early 1678, when informers were again watching his meetings. During late spring or early summer 1679 he worked with Baxter and four other ministers to organize petitions calling for a new parliament. Against the background of the alleged Popish Plot he wrote *The Church of Rome No Safe Guide* (1679), arguing that Catholicism destroyed Christianity's simplicity, glory, and power. This was a time, he told his congregation in December 1679, of great trials and dangers, a belief shared by the ministers with whom he associated. In these circumstances it seemed propitious to call for unity among protestants, but in such a manner, as he asserted in *Some Considerations about Union* (1680), that outward compulsion would not be employed. Disturbed by Edward Stillingfleet's *The Mischief of Separation* (1680), which accused nonconformists of schism, he countered in *A Brief Vindication* (1680) that unity of faith and obedience bound conformists and dissenters. This sparked replies from Stillingfleet, *The Unreasonableness of Separation* (1681), and S. R., *An Impartial Vindication* (1680). Owen responded to the former in *An Enquiry* (1681), clearly angered by Stillingfleet's contention that nonconformists promoted the Catholic threat. Owen was in turn answered by William Sherlock in *A Discourse about Church-Unity* (1681) and William Saywell in *Evangelical and Catholick Unity* (1682).

Meanwhile, in July 1680 the secretary of state, Jenkins, had summoned Owen, Baxter, and four other ministers to request their support in return for a declaration against Catholicism. That autumn Owen and others reviewed a proposal drafted by London merchants and revised by Bristol clergy for an accord between presbyterians and congregationalists. It may have provided the inspiration for Owen's exposition of ecclesiastical polity in *The True Nature of a Gospel Church* (1689), completed shortly thereafter. In a sermon preached in December 1680 while the second Exclusion Parliament was in session, *Seasonable Words for English Protestants* (1690), he denounced those who impeded the work of godly ministers as well as Church of England clergy who tried to monopolize the ministry. Subpoenaed for violating the Five-Mile Act and recusancy in November 1681 Owen and twenty-one other ministers faced anticipated fines of £9680. As the plight of dissenters worsened he may have been aware that the earl of Shaftesbury and his confidants had considered using force to compel Charles to bar James's succession after the House of Lords rejected an exclusion bill in November 1680. In *An Humble Testimony* (1681) he worried that some men were proposing desperate means to resolve the crisis, for 'the Conflict of their *Counsels* and *Designs* encreaseth our Danger, and is like to prove our Ruine' (A3*r*).

The threat of persecution did not stop Owen from preaching. His unpublished sermons from this period reflect his sense of divine judgment on the nation, but exhort the godly to 'wait quietly and patiently for what will bee the End of Gods Judgments' (DWL, MS L6/3, 10 Feb 1682). Informers reported that he did not mention the king in his prayers, but not until November 1682 was he again prosecuted, this time for having violated the Corporation and Elizabethan Conventicle Acts. The threat of Catholicism coupled with persecution led Owen to espouse a doctrine of active resistance in 1682. Like Calvin he endorsed the right to take up arms to defend religion as long as the leaders of resistance 'had a legal Right and Power to protect themselves and their subjects' (*Brief and Impartial Account*, 1682, 12). On 19 April 1683 a grand jury presented him for preaching to conventicles. Following the disclosure of the Rye House plot, he was arrested, examined at Whitehall on 27 June, and released. Although the government lacked sufficient evidence to prosecute him he apparently was aware that the duke of Monmouth and his associates had been planning an uprising to force Charles to exclude James from the succession, for Monmouth confessed to the king that Owen, Matthew Meade, and George Griffith knew about the conspiracy. This was confirmed by the Scottish conspirator William Carstares and the plotter Richard Goodenough. Moreover, the rebels' paymaster, Francis Charlton, had met Ferguson, who was associated with both the Monmouth cabal and the Rye House plotters, at Owen's house. Although Owen was not prosecuted for his alleged knowledge of the Monmouth conspiracy, on 21 July the Oxford convocation ordered that his January 1649 sermon be burned.

Owen continued to write during his final years. *Phronema tou pneumatos* (1681) captured the essence of nonconformist spiritual experience, *A Letter Concerning … Excommunications* (1683) denounced the use of excommunication as a tool to enforce conformity, and *Meditations and Discourses on the Glory of Christ* (1684), the testimony of a dying man, reflected on Christ as mediator. Of his last works the most controversial was *An Answer unto Two Questions* (1720), which included twelve arguments against the participation of dissenters in the worship of the established church. Framed in consultation with four other congregationalists the arguments circulated in manuscript, provoking an attack by Baxter in *Catholick Communion Defended* (1684). Owen was by then dead, but he was defended by the anonymous authors of *A Vindication of … John Owen* (1684) and *Bellarminus junior enervatus* (1684), to which Baxter replied in *Catholick Communion doubly Defended* (1684).

Owen's health was failing in January 1683, when he was diagnosed as having a kidney stone too large to expel. With death imminent he wrote to Fleetwood on 22 August, observing that he was 'leaving the Ship of the Church in a Storme' (DWL, MS L6/1, no. 11). Following his death at his home in Ealing on 24 August 1683 he was buried in Bunhill Fields on 4 September, with numerous nobles and gentry in attendance. He had no surviving children or grandchildren. In his will, dated 23 March 1683, he bequeathed funds to his sometime assistants Clarkson (who preached his funeral sermon), Ferguson, and Loeffs, and to his fellow congregationalist John Collins. He owned property at Stadham and Souldern, Oxfordshire, and Eaton, Berkshire. Auctioned on 26 May 1684 (*Bibliotheca Oweniana*, 1684), his library of nearly 2800 items included Latin and Greek manuscripts, the patristics, church history, poetry, geography, and philology as well as a rich collection of theological and pious works.

Reputation As early as the 1650s Owen had a substantial reputation as reflected not only by his sermons to parliament, his close association with Cromwell, and his vice-chancellorship, but also by the dedication to him of books by Lewis du Moulin (*Oratio auspicalis*, 1652) and the mathematician John Wallis (*Johanni Wallisii … elenchus geometriae Hobbianae*, 1655). During his career he contributed numerous epistles of his own to the works of other authors. On a visit to England in 1656 the Swiss protestant Johann Zollikofer befriended him. Although Anthony Wood thought Owen 'spent most of his time in continual agitation to carry on the cause, to promote his own interest, and gain the applause of the people', he acknowledged that Owen was regarded as the head of the Independents in 1658 (Wood, *Ath. Oxon.*, 4.113, 633). He was also the butt of satire: it was possibly Thomas Ireland who in 1654 likened Owen as an orator to 'an *Ass* mumbling a thistle' (T. Ireland, *Momus elencticus*, 1654, 2), and about 1660 an anonymous satirist claimed that he could 'scarce visit a Tavern, or Country Alehouse, but forth comes some of the Learned Works of *John Owen* … as if [he] were cut out to entertain all sorts of Guests' (*Correspondence*, 117). A survey of nonconformists about 1672 depicted him as still a leading Independent, and Roger Williams addressed the epistle of *George Fox Digg'd Out* (1676) to Owen and Baxter. Among his admirers the Newcastle congregationalist Ambrose Barnes referred to him as England's Calvin, and the presbyterian John Humfrey lauded him as a scholar and gentleman. By the 1680s his works were read by students at Charles Morton's nonconformist academy, and the wealthy merchant Samuel Moyer entrusted Owen and Collins with money to distribute to the indigent. Some of his critics likewise testified to his stature; the secretary of state, Jenkins, deemed him 'the Bell-weather of Independents' (PRO, SP 63/341, p. 158), Saywell described him as 'the great Advocate for the Independents' (*Evangelical and Catholick Unity*, 1682, A3v), John Fell, bishop of Oxford, thought he was a remarkable man, and one of Jenkins's correspondents referred to 'the late famous Dr Owen' (PRO, SP 29/437/65). In the 1690s opponents of the antinomians such as Daniel Williams and William Lorimer referred more often for support to Owen than Baxter.

The verdict of modern readers has been mixed. While acknowledging Owen's intellect Samuel Taylor Coleridge thought that his treatment of Baxter during their abortive exploration of presbyterian–congregationalist unity reflected 'a very chilling want of open-heartedness' as well as resentment of Baxter (*Works*, 1.347). In 1946 Geoffrey Nuttall thought that Owen had perhaps received excessive attention, and his style has justifiably been described as ponderous and comprehensive. Yet he was indisputably the leading proponent of high Calvinism in England in the late seventeenth century.

RICHARD L. GREAVES

Sources *The works of John Owen, D. D.*, ed. W. H. Goold, 24 vols. (1850–55) · *The correspondence of John Owen (1616–1683): with an account of his life and work*, ed. P. Toon (1970) · *The diary of Ralph Josselin, 1616–1683*, ed. A. Macfarlane (1976) · J. Asty, 'Memoirs of the life of John Owen, D. D.', *A complete collection of the sermons of the reverend and learned John Owen D. D.* (1721) · *Calendar of the correspondence of Richard Baxter*, ed. N. H. Keeble and G. F. Nuttall, 2 vols. (1991) · *Reliquiae Baxterianae, or, Mr Richard Baxter's narrative of the most memorable passages of his life and times*, ed. M. Sylvester, 1 vol. in 3 pts (1696) · *CSP dom.*, *1649–62; 1656–7; 1664–5; 1670–76; 1678; 1680–84* · PRO, SP 29/28/56; 29/65/9–10; 29/113/84; 29/276/14; 29/292/157; 29/335/65; 29/379/50; 29/404/253; 29/417/122, 144.1; 29/418/106, 127; 29/421/174, 176–7; 29/425/102; 29/431/108; 29/432/32; 29/437/65; 63/341, p. 158 · J. Owen, unpublished sermons, DWL, MS L6/1, 3, 4 · J. Owen and others, 'Twelve reasons', Bodl. Oxf., MS Rawl. D. 1352, fols. 131r–138v · *Diary of Thomas Burton*, ed. J. T. Rutt, 4 vols. (1828) · P. Toon, *God's statesman: the life and work of John Owen, pastor, educator, theologian* (1971) · D. D. Wallace, jun., 'The life and thought of John Owen to 1660: a study of the significance of Calvinist theology in English puritanism', PhD diss., Princeton University, 1965 · Wood, *Ath. Oxon.*, new edn, 1.xxxviii–xxxix; 3.301, 459, 540, 600, 937–8, 1150; 4.97–113, 230, 319, 633, 744 · Wood, *Ath. Oxon.: Fasti* (1815), 465, 479; (1820), 34, 71, 126, 169, 175, 179, 181, 186, 192, 198 · *JHC*, 6–7 (1648–59) · *JHL*, 8 (1645–6), 467 · G. F. Nuttall, 'The MS of *Reliquiae Baxterianae* (1696)', *Journal of Ecclesiastical History*, 6 (1955), 72–9 · Bodl. Oxf., MSS Rawl. letters 52–3 · Bodl. Oxf., MS Carte 81, fols. 16r–17v · *The Mather papers*, Collections of the Massachusetts Historical Society, 4th ser., 8 (1868), 584 · *The writings and speeches of Oliver Cromwell*, ed. W. C. Abbott and C. D. Crane, 4 vols. (1937–47) ·

G. F. Nuttall, *The Holy Spirit in puritan faith and experience* (1946) • C. H. Firth and R. S. Rait, eds., *Acts and ordinances of the interregnum, 1642–1660*, 3 vols. (1911) • Bodl. Oxf., MS Eng. lett. C 328, fol. 509r • BL, Lansdowne MS 1152, fol. 227v • *Copies of the informations and original papers relating to the proof of the horrid conspiracy* (1685) • *The collected works of Samuel Taylor Coleridge*, vol. 1: *Marginalia*, ed. G. Whalley (1980) • A. Annesley, earl of Anglesey, diary, BL, Add. MS 18730 • *Calamy rev.* • Thurloe, *State papers*, 3.281; 4.334 • BL, Add. MS 29582, fol. 59v • *The judgment and decree of the University of Oxford past in their convocation* (1683) • *Report on the manuscripts of the earl of Egmont*, 2 vols. in 3, HMC, 63 (1905–9), vol. 1, p. 576 • B. Whitelocke, *Memorials of English affairs*, new edn, 4 vols. (1853) • Foster, *Alum. Oxon.*, *1500–1714*, 3.1100 • declaration of Independent ministers, 27 Feb 1663, BL, Add. MS 4107, fols. 16r–18v • N. Luttrell, *A brief historical relation of state affairs from September 1678 to April 1714*, 6 vols. (1857) • *Report on the manuscripts of Allan George Finch*, 5 vols., HMC, 71 (1913–2003), vol. 2, p. 10 • *The manuscripts of his grace the duke of Portland*, 10 vols., HMC, 29 (1891–1931), vol. 2, p. 236 • *The presentment for the City of London*, 1683, BL, law tracts, 515/118 (16) • *A list of the conventicles*, 1683, BL, law tracts, 515/118 (22)

Archives BL, sermon notes, Sloane MS 3680 • Bodl. Oxf., J. Owen and others, 'Twelve reasons', MS Rawl. D 1352, fols. 131r–138v | BL, Add. MSS 18730, 29582, fol. 59v • BL, declaration of Independent ministers (27 Feb 1663), Add. MS 4107, fols. 16r–18v • BL, Harley MS 1040, fol. 38 • BL, Lansdowne MSS 822, fol. 178; 833, fol. 179; 1152, fol. 227v • BL, Stowe MS 745, fols. 79r–80r; MS 3680 • Bodl. Oxf., MS Carte 81, fols. 16r–17v • Bodl. Oxf., MS Eng. lett. C 29, fol. 145; C 328, fol. 509r • Bodl. Oxf., MS Rawl. letters, 51, 52, 53, 109 • Bodl. Oxf., MSS Rawl. A 24, fol. 336; A 26, fol. 413 • Bodl. Oxf., MS Tanner 52, fol. 48 • DWL, Baxter letters, 5/18 • DWL, MSS L6/1, 3–4 • DWL, R. Morrice, 'Ent'ring book', 3 vols. • PRO, SP 29/28/56; 29/65/9, 10; 29/113/84; 29/276/14; 29/292/157; 29/335/65; 29/379/50; 29/404/253; 29/417/122, 144.1; 29/418/106, 127; 29/421/174, 176–7; 29/425/102; 29/431/108; 29/432/32; 29/437/65; 63/341, p. 158 • Staatsarchiv, Zürich, Duraeana, MS E.II.457b, fol. 1

Likenesses attrib. J. Greenhill, oils, *c*.1668, NMG Wales • attrib. J. Greenhill, oils, second version, *c*.1668, NPG [*see illus.*] • R. White, line engraving, 1709, BM, NPG • line engraving, 1788, NPG; repro. in J. Thane, *British autobiography*, 3 vols. (1788) • Vertue, portrait, repro. in *The works of the late reverand and learned John Owen* (1721) • R. White, line engraving, BM, NPG • oils, Baptist College, Bristol • portrait, Mansfield College, Oxford • portrait, Manchester Congregational College

Wealth at death £1332 10*s*; plus lands in Stadham and Souldern, Oxfordshire, and Eaton, Berkshire: will, repr. in *Correspondence of John Owen*, ed. Toon, 181–5

Owen, John (1766–1822), missionary society administrator, was son of Richard Owen, a jeweller, of Old Street, London. He entered St Paul's School on 18 October 1777, from where he proceeded in 1784, as Sykes exhibitioner, to Magdalene College, Cambridge (admitted a sizar 10 May). He migrated to Corpus Christi College and was admitted a scholar on the old foundation on 17 November 1784; he graduated BA in 1788, became a fellow on 11 April 1789, and proceeded MA in 1791.

In the spring of 1791 Owen went to the continent, at first as tutor to a young gentleman. In September 1792 he left Geneva for the south of France, and arrived in Lyons to find it in the hands of a revolutionary mob. He with difficulty escaped to Switzerland. Owen published an account of his adventures in *Travels into Different Parts of Europe, in the Years 1791 and 1792* (2 vols., 1796). On 1 September 1794 he married Charlotte Green of Cambridge and settled there. On 11 March and 5 August 1794 Owen preached two assize sermons in the university church of

John Owen (1766–1822), by Edward Scriven, pubd 1823 (after Joseph Slater)

St Mary, which were published that year. In 1794 he also published *The retrospect, or, Reflections on the State of Religion and Politics in France and Great Britain*. He was ordained on 21 June 1795 and was made curate of Fulham by Beilby Porteus, bishop of London, who also made him rector of Paglesham, Essex, in 1808. Owen held the curacy until 1813, being made minister of Park Chapel, Chelsea, in 1815.

Owen published in 1804, writing as Theophilus Christian, esq., *The Fashionable World Displayed*, which went through several editions. In that year began his connection with the British and Foreign Bible Society, his chief claim to fame. From 23 April 1804—a few weeks after its foundation—until his death he was its principal secretary, although unpaid. He was successful in persuading Bishop Porteus to allow an association between the society and the Church of England: a link vital to the society's success. At the request of some of its members Owen wrote *The History of the Origin and First Ten Years of the British and Foreign Bible Society* (2 vols., 1816), still a valuable work.

After an illness in 1817, Owen went abroad in August 1818. He helped to establish a branch Bible society in Paris, and inspected the progress of the Turkish New Testament, then in course of preparation for the society by Professor Kieffer. He visited Pastor Oberlin and the branches established at Zürich, St Gallen, Constance, and other Swiss towns. He returned to England in December and published *Brief Extracts from Letters on the Object and Connexions of the British and Foreign Bible Society* (1819) and worked on the third volume of his history, published in 1820. He also wrote *Two Letters on the Subject of the French Bible* (1822). This was in reply to a charge of Socinianism brought against that translation and symptomatic of more general criticisms of the society's translations.

Owen had a reputation for being prickly and short-tempered. He died at Ramsgate on 26 September 1822, and was buried at Fulham. His wife and several children survived him. One of his daughters married the eldest son of William Wilberforce.

CHARLOTTE FELL-SMITH, *rev.* H. C. G. MATTHEW

Sources Venn, *Alum. Cant.* • W. Dealtry, *The character and happiness of them that die in the Lord: a sermon, preached October 13, 1822, in Park Chapel, Chelsea, on occasion of the death of the late Rev. John Owen* (1822) • J. Hughes, *Attachment to life: a sermon, on occasion of the death of the late Rev. John Owen* (1822) • *A tribute of gratitude to the memory of … John Owen, by one of his congregation* (1822) • W. Canton, *A history of the British and Foreign Bible Society*, 5 vols. (1904–10)

Archives Cambs. AS, letters to duke of Manchester • NL Wales, letters to E. O. Davies

Likenesses H. R. Cook, stipple, pubd 1812 (after W. Foster), NPG • E. Scriven, stipple, pubd 1823 (after J. Slater), BM, NPG [*see illus.*] • oils, CCC Cam.

Owen, John [*pseud.* Owain Alaw] (**1821–1883**), composer, was born in Crane Street, Chester, on 14 November 1821. Both his parents were natives of Llanfachraeth, Merioneth, but had settled in Chester shortly before his birth; his father was the captain of a small vessel. Owen was initially apprenticed to a firm of cutlers, Messrs Powell and Edwards, but in 1844, having shown considerable aptitude for music, he gave up business and became a professional musician. He was subsequently organist of, in succession, Lady Huntingdon's chapel, St Paul's, Broughton, St Bridget's, St Mary's, and the Welsh church (all in Chester), and at the same time gave tuition in music.

It was, however, in connection with the eisteddfod that Owen attracted the attention of his fellow countrymen. His success in winning the prize for the best anthem at the Rhuddlan eisteddfod in 1851 with 'Deborah a Barac' was the first of a series of victories which gave 'Owain Alaw' a recognized place among Welsh musicians. He devoted himself energetically to composition, and during the next few years wrote a large number of glees, songs, and anthems, published in various Welsh musical magazines of the time. His only attempts at more ambitious works were the cantatas *Tywysog Cymru* (1862), the first Welsh secular cantata, and *Gŵyl Gwalia* (1866); the oratorio *Jeremiah* (1878) has been called his 'greatest work' (*DWB*). In 1860 he edited the first number of *Gems of Welsh Melody*, a collection of Welsh airs, published in four numbers in Ruthin. *The Welsh Harp: a Selection of Welsh National Songs* appeared in 1871, and Owen also made arrangements of songs by celebrated composers, including Mendelssohn and Weber. His fluent and melodious style of composition made him one of the most popular of Welsh musicians, and he was also much in demand as a conductor and adjudicator.

In 1842 he married a Miss Williams of Chester, and their son, William Henry, was born in 1845; he was an organist in Dublin before being killed in a railway accident at Abergele on 20 August 1868. Some of his anthems were published in Welsh by his father. John Owen died in Chester during the night of 29/30 January 1883, and was buried there in the old cemetery.

J. E. LLOYD, *rev.* DAVID J. GOLBY

Sources Brown & Stratton, *Brit. mus.* • *DWB* • *CGPLA Eng. & Wales* (1883)

Archives NL Wales, compositions and corresp.

Wealth at death £469 14*s.* 2*d.*: probate, 28 May 1883, *CGPLA Eng. & Wales*

Owen, John (**1854–1926**), bishop of St David's, was born at Ysgubor Wen, in the parish of Llanengan, Caernarvonshire, on 24 August 1854. His father, Griffith Owen (*d.* 1893), a weaver who prospered and became a wool merchant, was a Calvinistic Methodist and for many years a deacon of Bwlch chapel at Llanengan. Though he never deviated from his own loyalties, he watched his son's career as an Anglican with great pride. Owen's mother, Ann Jones from Aberdaron, could not easily reconcile herself to her son joining the church, nor could she wholly accept the fact that he married an English wife. Owen and his sister grew up in an intensely religious home; as a boy, he was learned beyond his years, and showed a particular liking for mathematics. His early education at the British School at Llanengan was extended at Botwnnog grammar school (1865–9) under a sympathetic headmaster (known to the boys as Mr Jenkin) who appointed him, when he was only fifteen, as assistant master, largely so that he could prepare for entry to university. In 1872 he was awarded a mathematical scholarship at Jesus College, Oxford, where he read classics and mathematics, gaining a second class in classical moderations (1873) and in mathematical moderations (1874). To his great disappointment, he was again placed in the second class in the final school of mathematics, and he began to read for *literae humaniores*, hoping for a first, but he did not sit the examinations.

Religion and early career As a pupil at Botwnnog, Owen was impressed by the fact that his headmaster, respecting his family background, did not oblige him to attend the parish church. When he became a teacher there he decided, in gratitude, to go to church regularly with the boys. Local Welsh clerics (notably James Rowland, rector of Botwnnog) fostered his interest, and at Oxford he came under the influence of A. M. W. Christopher (1820–1913), rector of St Aldates. He was drawn towards ordination, but he decided to teach for a few years until he was sure of his vocation. He was assistant master at Appleby grammar school in Westmorland from 1877 to 1879. There he met Amelia (*b.* 1861/2), third daughter of Joseph Longstaff of Appleby; they were married on 4 January 1882. They had four sons and six daughters.

In 1879 Owen was persuaded to apply for the post of professor of Welsh at St David's College, Lampeter, and he committed himself in two respects: if appointed he 'would of course make a special study of Welsh', and he would hope to be ordained before, or soon after, joining the college. At that stage, much to his regret, Welsh was not included in the degree structure, but Owen combined his chair with some responsibility for teaching classics. He was confirmed and ordained deacon in 1879, and priest in 1880. At Lampeter he began to emerge as a publicist, engaging for the first time in controversy over the vexed question of disestablishment. After a brief tenure he was appointed warden of Llandovery in 1885, where his role was more overtly to encourage the Welsh traditions of that college. It was a comparatively small school with some eighty boys, and he made it his concern to attract more pupils and to recruit new staff on a generous scale. Before his work had had time to mature he was drawn away to new responsibilities.

Defending the Church of England In 1889 Alfred Edwards, newly appointed as bishop of St Asaph, invited him to join him as dean—the 'Controversial Dean of a Militant Bishop', as he was to be described in the *Liverpool Mercury* (quoted in Owen, *Early Life*, 88). They had to face three major crises: the problem of tithes, the difficulties arising from changes in local government, especially in education, and the threat of disestablishment. Edwards regarded Dean Owen as his indispensable aide in the battle over tithes. As the market price of some cereals fell, the ability of many tenant farmers to pay tithes was reduced; as the value of tithe charges dropped, the clergy grew more impoverished. Resentment among Welsh nonconformists obliged to pay tithes to the church, and Welsh tenant farmers obliged to pay tithes to a church they regarded as English, exacerbated the conflict, especially in north Wales. Legal action taken by individual clerics against individual tenant farmers inflamed local feelings.

The presentation of a rational case and of statistical material, and the need to conduct the controversy with diplomacy in the current atmosphere of hostility and violence, demanded skills which Owen had in abundance. Through letters to *The Times* in the summer of 1890 he sought to win over opinion in England. Through public debate with the leader of opposition to tithes, Thomas Gee of Denbigh, conducted in August and September 1890, in Gee's Welsh newspaper, *Baner ac Amserau Cymru*, he sought to divorce the vexed issue of tithes from the major political issue of disestablishment. The remedy was found in the Tithe-Rent Charge Recovery Act of 1891 which removed the necessity for open hostility between cleric and tenant farmer by placing the liability for tithe upon the landlord, not upon the tenant. Bishop Edwards was deeply involved in the political negotiations which produced this act, but he recognized the indispensable help of his dean.

At St Asaph, Owen became increasingly involved in education. Despite some reservations, he gave a warm welcome to the Welsh Intermediate Education Act of 1889. Bishop Edwards castigated it as 'saturated with rigid undenominationalism' (Edwards, 178), but Owen argued persuasively and urged his fellow Anglicans to accept it. The act established a joint education committee for each Welsh county and a central committee for Wales and Monmouthshire. Owen was appointed to the Flintshire committee and to the central body. There he played a significant part in the development of the Central Welsh Board to supervise inspection and examinations in intermediate schools. His colleagues nominated him to serve on the charter committee of the University of Wales, established in November 1891, and that gave a new emphasis to his interest in higher education, and a new platform from which to press the claims of St David's College.

Principal of Lampeter In 1892 Owen returned to Lampeter as principal, an office he was to hold until he became bishop of St David's in 1897. There his income was augmented by the rectory of Llangeler, Carmarthenshire, a sinecure in the gift of the college. Bishop Edwards ensured that the close association between himself and the new principal should not be broken by appointing him to a residentiary canonry at St Asaph. In 1893 Owen fought a sustained battle to bring St David's College into the University of Wales. The plans for the creation of that university embraced the colleges at Aberystwyth, Bangor, and Cardiff. He was anxious that Lampeter should be included. It was already a college conferring degrees under royal charter and, for him, it was unthinkable that it should be excluded from the new university. By contrast, the advocates of the university were clear that Bishop Burgess's original plan for Lampeter had been to found a seminary in which young men could be trained for the ministry, and that identified it as a theological college which must stand as any other denominational college in relation to the new university. In January he argued his case strenuously but unsuccessfully in the charter committee. In June he petitioned the privy council, and his petition was rejected. In the autumn his influence lay behind a debate in the House of Lords, where Lampeter's case was upheld. But Gladstone refused to be moved, and the University of Wales was given its royal charter, with St David's firmly excluded. Shrugging off his defeat, Owen secured in 1896 a new charter for Lampeter which established a college council with wide powers, and which re-affirmed that the college had been founded 'to receive and educate any person whatsoever, whether destined for Holy Orders or not'.

Avoiding Welsh disestablishment In the last years of the century, two threats to Welsh Anglicans were checked. In 1893 H. H. Asquith introduced a Suspensory Bill which would have prevented the creation of any new vested interests in the Welsh dioceses. In effect, on any future disestablishment, appointments made during the interim would not have counted for any compensation. Owen was responsible for briefing Lord Randolph Churchill who spoke vehemently and effectively against the bill, which failed to secure a second reading. In 1894 Asquith went further and introduced a bill to disestablish the Welsh church. In the ensuing campaign Owen faced some difficult audiences but, as he acknowledged, opposition was always a greater stimulant to him than approval. In the event, Lord Rosebery's unexpected resignation removed the immediate danger.

Bishop of St David's In January 1897 William Basil Jones, bishop of St David's, died and within six weeks John Owen had been named as his successor. The death of the dean of St David's and the appointment of a new dean delayed Owen's consecration until May. That was the beginning of a notable episcopate. The sheer size of St David's, the largest diocese in England and Wales, created problems for its diocesan. Bishop Jones, austere and aloof, had administered his diocese efficiently with the help of his suffragan,

John Lloyd, consecrated bishop of Swansea in 1890. Lloyd continued to serve under Bishop Owen, who appointed as his successor Edward Latham Bevan of Brecon. From 1915 Bevan was largely responsible as bishop for Brecknockshire and Radnorshire.

Sir John Llewellyn, one of the most active and forthright laymen in the diocese, welcoming Owen in Swansea, rejoiced that a cold withdrawn scholar should have been replaced by a man of warm sympathy. Free from controversy for a few vital years, Owen could concentrate on his diocese, getting to know his clergy and resolving a number of local problems. He renewed an earlier attempt to deal with clerical poverty, raising large sums of money, and setting (though not achieving) a target of a minimum stipend of £200.

In April 1903 the bishop's palace at Abergwili was largely destroyed by fire. Bishop Owen and his family escaped, but it was a disaster which overshadowed his later years. The cost of rebuilding left him heavily in debt, and the immediate strain contributed to a marked decline in his health. Even while he was warden of Llandovery, long hours of work and little exercise left him with recurrent nervous exhaustion, but then (as on later occasions) he recovered quickly. Late in 1903 he suffered a breakdown which made work impossible. From 1904 until 1914 a relaxed summer holiday in Switzerland became an essential part of his routine. Ill health remained a problem. He was seriously unwell in 1920, and again in 1924 and 1925.

Much of Owen's episcopate was marked by controversy. For many years he was involved in conflict over church schools and the place of religious instruction in schools. The Education Act of 1902 gave county councils the responsibility for financing elementary education. Subject to clear conditions, church schools qualified for rate-aided status, but this gave great offence to nonconformists. Lloyd George used this discontent to advantage in Wales where some county councils, including Carmarthenshire, refused to use rates to maintain church schools. A long legal and parliamentary battle ensued before the council was obliged to give way. Between 1907 and 1911 Owen was involved in another long but ultimately successful conflict with the local education authority in Swansea over the funding of church schools in the town.

From 1902 to the last years of Owen's life the question of religious education in state schools was a recurrent problem. Churchmen defended the need for doctrinal teaching, others insisted on undenominational teaching. From an early date Bishop Edwards had been convinced that a concordat was the most practical solution, and he was concerned to negotiate an agreed compromise. Owen defended a stronger line, seeking to maintain a firm doctrinal approach. He was converted to the value of a concordat in the 1920s, only to find in 1924 that he could not persuade the governing body of the Church in Wales to accept the necessary compromise.

Confrontations never frightened Owen, and he acquired the reputation of being 'a battling bishop', but he had many gifts as a negotiator. He liked always to work closely with his associates, consulting them at every stage, and adjusting the wording of formal statements and of his own speeches to meet their point of view. In negotiation he looked for common ground and respected the standpoint of his opponents. He liked to have clear in advance what was to be proposed and agreed in formal meetings. He disliked unexpected shifts in policy and the development of new lines of thought in public discussion. He believed firmly in strong political action and knew the value of giving full and accurate briefing to the politicians who were prepared to speak in defence of his case.

Welsh disestablishment All these qualities were constantly in demand in the long conflict over disestablishment. Pressure on Welsh Anglicans was maintained throughout the 1890s, with Gladstone himself speaking in favour of disestablishment in 1892 and bills introduced in 1894 and 1895. In 1906 a royal commission on the Welsh church began to collect evidence, and Welsh bishops were thrown on the defensive. Owen was a leading figure in collecting material for the church and the evidence he presented to the commission filled seventy pages of the final report (1910). In 1909 government intentions were made clear in a Disestablishment Bill which made little progress, but in 1912 a similar bill passed through the Commons but was rejected in the Lords. It had to wait for the Parliament Act of 1911 to take effect before it was reintroduced to be passed without hindrance in 1914. In this long process, Owen became the leading spokesman for the Welsh church. In the first half of 1912 he spoke at seventy public meetings in England and ten in Wales. He was constantly in demand to consult with and advise leading politicians.

Once the Welsh church had been disestablished Owen played a leading part in securing the Welsh Church Temporalities Act of 1919 which modified parliament's original financial settlement, and he contributed to dealing with the practical problems of organizing the new Welsh province. In private correspondence there was a suggestion that he should become the first archbishop, but he refused to consider it. In Easter week 1920, he presided over the election of Bishop Edwards as the first archbishop of Wales.

Final years and death Owen's last important task was to secure the division of the diocese of St David's. For more than twenty years, schemes for smaller dioceses centred on Brecon, Swansea, and possibly Aberystwyth had been canvassed. After disestablishment they had to be modified, if only because of financial pressure. The influential churchmen of Swansea were reluctant to be severed from St David's. But the plan for a diocese combining Swansea and Brecon offered the best chance of reducing the burden of the bishop's work and of creating a viable new bishopric. In 1923 it was adopted, and the province had to elect a new diocesan. Owen was convinced that his suffragan, Bishop Bevan, should be chosen; he had been an effective suffragan and he knew much of the area well. There was one major difficulty: he could not speak Welsh. For that reason Archbishop Edwards was consistently and implacably opposed to his appointment, and the electoral college was deeply divided. Owen was not to be moved. He continued firm in his support for Bevan, who was elected by the narrowest of margins.

By that time it was becoming clear that John Owen's strength was failing. He relied more heavily on younger colleagues. As late as 1924 he was asked by the Board of Education to chair a committee to examine the use of Welsh in education, but he did not live to see its report, which was published in 1927. He held his own until the summer of 1926, but in the autumn he confided to a friend 'I am taking off my armour.' He died after a short illness on 4 November in a nursing home at 19 Manchester Street, St Mary, London, and was buried on 9 November at Abergwili, Carmarthen. In his cathedral church at St David's there is a recumbent effigy in the lady chapel. Photographs capture his characteristic stance, but he was essentially a modest man and no portrait of him was painted.

DAVID WALKER

Sources E. E. Owen, *The early life of Bishop Owen* (1958) • E. E. Owen, *The later life of Bishop Owen* (1961) • A. G. Edwards, *Memories* (1927) • P. M. H. Bell, *Disestablishment in Ireland and Wales* (1969) • D. T. W. Price, *A history of Saint David's University College Lampeter*, 1: *To 1898* (1977) • *DNB* • personal knowledge (2004) • m. cert. • *CGPLA Eng. & Wales* (1926)

Archives NL Wales, diaries, corresp., and papers | BL, corresp. with Arthur James Balfour, Add. MS 49790, *passim* • HLRO, corresp. with Bonar Law • NL Wales, letters to D. S. Evans • NL Wales, letters to Sir James Hills-Johnes

Likenesses photograph, NPG • recumbent effigy, St David's Cathedral, Dyfed

Wealth at death £11,114 17*s*. 7*d*.: probate, 16 Dec 1926, *CGPLA Eng. & Wales*

Owen, Josiah (1710/11–1755), Presbyterian minister, was the grandson of John Owen of Aber-nant, Carmarthenshire. He was a nephew of James *Owen (1654–1706), dissenting minister of Shrewsbury, and of Charles *Owen (*d*. 1746), dissenting minister of Warrington. He is said to have been the son of their eldest brother, David Owen, dissenting minister of Henllan, Carmarthenshire, who died on 7 October 1710, aged fifty-nine. He may have been a posthumous son, but has probably been confused with David Owen's son Jeremiah, who was educated by James Owen, succeeded his father at Henllan, and after various pastorates in England died in America.

Josiah was educated by his uncle Charles Owen at Warrington, and then at Carmarthen from 1725 to 1730. His first ministerial settlement was at Bridgnorth, Shropshire. As minister there he received a grant from the Presbyterian Fund Board between March 1733 and December 1739. He then ministered for short periods at Stone and possibly Walsall in Staffordshire. About this time he is supposed to have entered into a controversy with the bishop of Coventry and Lichfield, Richard Smalbroke, publishing anonymously *Remarks on two charges: deliver'd by the Lord Bishop of L—d and C—y, to the clergy of his diocese* (1738). This was answered by Smalbroke in print in the same year. Described as 'young Mr. Owen of Warrington' by the diarist Richard Kay of Bury, Owen gave a sermon to the Bury protestant dissenters on 2 September 1739. He soon became minister of Blackwater Street Chapel, Rochdale, Lancashire, the earliest evidence of his settlement there being Richard Kay's diary entry concerning a conversation with 'the Revnd. Mr Owen from Rochdale' on 18 October 1739 (Kay, 29).

Owen frequently preached at Bury as well as Rochdale and, in the tradition of his uncle Charles Owen, assiduously supported the Hanoverian cause. His sermons warned of French, Catholic, and absolutist threats to England's liberties. He preached at Bury Chapel on 30 November 1740 from Amos 3: 6, 'God is blowing his Trumpet in the City, is threatening England and all Europe with War and Famine'. He gave a thanksgiving sermon at Bury Chapel on 24 July 1743 for 'the late Victory our Forces have had over the French Army at Dettingen in Germany' (Kay, 39, 65), and this sermon appeared in print in 1753. A staunch whig, he celebrated the 'glorious revolution', publishing *National gratitude just tribute for national deliverances; exemplified in the discovery of the Powder Plot and accession of the prince of Orange to the throne, a sermon preach'd to a society of protestant dissenters at Rochdale, Nov. 5, 1742* (1742), and is known to have preached another 5 November sermon in 1744. His ministry was successful, and his chapel was enlarged in 1743. By March 1745 he was preaching the weekly lecture at Bolton, where 'he is lately chose Lecturer there instead of Mr Abraham Dawson from Rivington who has lately conformed' (ibid., 94). About 1750 he is said to have prevailed with the provincial meeting of the associated ministers of Lancashire 'to discontinue the customary questions respecting the internal state of congregations' (*DNB*).

Owen is chiefly remembered for his attacks on Jacobite and nonjuring principles; these led to harsh exchanges with Thomas Deacon and John Byrom. Owen had already controverted with Thomas Cattell, the chaplain of the Rochdale corporation, a Jacobite club at which Byrom is known to have been present. Tensions were high in the area in November 1745 when Prince Charles Edward Stuart was marching south, and many Presbyterians in Manchester and the surrounding area made themselves scarce during the brief Jacobite interlude. Owen was known to be lodging with Richard Kay at Baldingstone, Bury, when the news came through on 4 January 1746 that Carlisle had surrendered to the duke of Cumberland. In October 1746 Manchester officially celebrated the Jacobite defeat, and Owen assumed the role of 'faithful Monitor' of the Jacobites in Manchester.

An anonymous letter by Owen from Manchester, dated 6 October 1746, was published in the *Whitehall Evening Post* for 11 October 1746. In it he claims 'Jacobite, non-juring, and even popish principles are now making a greater progress here than ever', and he ridicules Deacon for doffing his hat to the severed heads of the rebels on the Manchester exchange, one of whom was Deacon's son, Thomas ('Letter from Manchester', 579). Owen preached a thanksgiving sermon, subsequently published as *All is well, or, The defeat of the late rebellion … a sermon preached at Rochdale on Oct. 9th, being the day appointed for a public thanksgiving* (1746).

Byrom responded to Owen's letter with a piece in the *Gentleman's Magazine* ridiculing Owen as Don Quixote tilting at 'innocent fulling-mills, chimeras of his own distempered brain' (ibid.). Owen attacked Byrom again as a promoter of 'the good old cause of popery and slavery' and accused the Manchester nonjurors of worshipping the 'rebel skull divinities fix'd up at the Exchange' in the same way the Catholic church venerated saints, as martyrs (Philopatriae, 688, 690). Byrom replied, charging Owen with 'false reasoning, partiality, bitterness, and fury' ('Reply to Philopatriae's answer', 76–7).

Owen raised the stakes by directing at Byrom *Jacobite and non-juring principles, freely examined, in a letter to the master-tool of the faction at Manchester, with remarks on … a Christian catechism & said to be wrote by Dr. D—c—n* (1747). In this he admits to being the author of the *Gentleman's Magazine* letters. In its preface Owen says his Rochdale thanksgiving sermon and his letter to the *Gentleman's Magazine*, together with Nichol's sermon, provoked Byrom to produce his *Epistle to a Friend*, which contains the lines 'Leave to the low-bred O—ns of the Age Sense to belie, and Loyalty to rage'. Owen retorted in the preface: 'The Master-Tool was ordered to his Post, from whence he has since been preaching up Politeness with Dunghill-Breeding, and under Pretence of advocating for the true Catholic Church … been labouring to introduce the Worship of Dunghill Gods'. Owen attacked Byrom 'for his love of scribbling verses … for his devotion to mysticism and Jacob Behmen; and above all, for his personal dealings in former days with the Pretender at Avignon' (*Poems of John Byrom*, 1.2, 360). Byrom subsequently brought out a broadside against Owen entitled *Sir Lowbred O—n, or, The Hottentot Knight*. Intended to be sung in the taverns to the tune of the 'Abbot of Canterbury', Byrom ensured that the debate remained in the gutter with couplets like

> That Son of a —, and that Son of a —,
> Would never have struck me—so quite to the Core.
> (ibid., 358–77)

Deacon then sought to vindicate himself in print. A letter written from Manchester on 18 April 1748 was first printed in the *Chester Courant* (26 April 1748) and subsequently as 'Dr Deacon's vindication of himself' in the *Gentleman's Magazine* (18, 1748, 206–7). Owen demonstrated his rebarbative powers in *Dr. Deacon, try'd before his own tribunal, or, An examination of the several facts deny'd by him in the 'Gentleman's Magazine' for May last; by those very rules laid down in his catechism for the conviction of offenders, in a letter to the said gentleman* (1748).

With Byrom's move to London in early 1748, however, much of the fire went out of the exchange. On 7 April 1748 Byrom could comment on Owen's latest attack as follows: 'thank … friend O—n for his care of my fame and reputation; I am hardly at leisure to mind him, or perhaps I might thank him myself' (Hancox, 201). Owen was debilitated by a severe illness early in 1750, and the last mention of him in Kay's diary is in May 1750. His ministry at Rochdale closed on 14 June 1752. He became the minister of the Presbyterian congregation at Ellenthorpe, Aldborough parish, near Boroughbridge, Yorkshire, where he died in 1755, aged forty-four. His will records 'I always bore my living testimony (to my great temporal loss in favour of virtue and national devotion) against the wild Phrenzy of superstition'. He was buried at Aldborough on 1 October 1755, and had asked for a company of poor men to be paid to bury him on the north side of the parish church without any form of ceremony. JONATHAN H. WESTAWAY

Sources *DNB* · [J. Byrom], 'Letter from Manchester, with remarks', *GM*, 1st ser., 16 (1746), 579–80 · Philopatriae [J. Owen], 'Remarks on the Manchester letter censur'd', *GM*, 1st ser., 16 (1746), 688–91 · [J. Byrom], 'Reply to Philopatriae's answer to the Manchester remarks', *GM*, 1st ser., 17 (1747), 76–7 · T. Deacon, 'Dr Deacon's vindication of himself', *GM*, 1st ser., 18 (1748), 206–7 · *The diary of Richard Kay, 1716–51, of Baldingstone, near Bury, a Lancashire doctor*, ed. W. Brockbank and F. Kenworthy, Chetham Society, 3rd ser., 16 (1968), 29, 39–40, 57, 62, 65, 91, 94, 105, 110–11, 117, 126, 131, 147–8, 150, 153, 155 · will, proved 6 Dec 1755, Borth. Inst. · *The poems of John Byrom*, ed. A. W. Ward, 1/2, Chetham Society, new ser., 30 (1894), 358–77 · B. Nightingale, *Lancashire nonconformity*, 6 vols. [1890–93], vol. 3, p. 242 · H. Fishwick, *The history of the parish of Rochdale in the county of Lancaster* (1889), 253–4 · W. Smith, 'Some account of Presbyterianism in Rochdale', *Christian Reformer, or, Unitarian Magazine and Review*, new ser., 12 (1856), 352–9 · *The private journal and literary remains of John Byrom*, ed. R. Parkinson, vol. 1, pt 1, Chetham Society, 32 (1854) · *The private journal and literary remains of John Byrom*, ed. R. Parkinson, vol. 1, pt 2, Chetham Society, 34 (1855) · *The private journal and literary remains of John Byrom*, ed. R. Parkinson, vol. 2, pt 1, Chetham Society, 40 (1856) · J. Hancox, *The queen's chameleon: the life of John Byrom, a study in conflicting loyalties* (1994) · J. G. Miall, *Congregationalism in Yorkshire* (1868), 260 · T. Rees, *History of protestant nonconformity in Wales* (1861), 294, 323–4 · A. P. F. Sell, 'Robert Travers and the Lichfield-Longdon church book', *Journal of the United Reform Church History Society*, 3/7 (Oct 1985), 266–78 · R. Smalbroke, *The author [Josiah Owen] of the remarks on the bishop of Lichfield and Coventry's two last charges to his clergy, … convicted of false quotations, etc* (1738) · G. E. Evans, *Record of the provincial assembly of Lancashire and Cheshire* (1896), 162 · J. J., 'Sketch of the ancient dissenters' chapel at Ellinthorp', *Congregational Magazine*, 14 (1831), 709–11

Archives BL, Thomas Birch collection, transcript, Add. MS 4292, fols. 264–5

Wealth at death see will, proved 6 Dec 1775, Borth. Inst.

Owen, Sir (William) Leonard (1897–1971), atomic engineer, was born at Walton, Liverpool, on 3 May 1897, the only child of Thomas John Owen, mariner, and his wife, Levina Elizabeth Victoria Isabella Smith. He was educated at the Liverpool collegiate school. By the time he left school, in 1915, the First World War had broken out, and he joined the 6th King's Liverpool regiment, serving as a private in the trenches. At the end of the war, he returned to Liverpool as an undergraduate student in the faculty of engineering at the university. He graduated with honours in 1922 and was awarded the degree of Master of Engineering in 1924. In 1923 he married Phyllis, daughter of Martin Condliff. They had two sons.

Owen's first professional work as an engineer was at Northwich in Cheshire with Brunner, Mond & Co. This later became one of the founding companies of Imperial Chemical Industries, as ICI (Alkali) Ltd. The factory was concerned with the production of bulk chemicals on a large scale, and Owen's responsibilities in the engineering department were concerned with the design of additions to the plant and with the development of new plant.

Shortly after the outbreak of the Second World War he was 'loaned' to the Ministry of Supply as director of the royal filling factories, a post that he held between 1940 and 1945.

The end of the war marked a watershed in Owen's career, for it was in 1946 that he began his work on the industrial development of nuclear energy in the United Kingdom—on appointment as director of engineering on the production side of the Ministry of Supply. In the following year the atomic energy division was formed, with Owen as assistant controller.

For the next decade Owen worked closely with Christopher Hinton (later Lord Hinton of Bankside), with headquarters at Risley, near Warrington, in taking responsibility for the design and construction of the atomic energy factories in the north of England. Hinton held the senior post, but it is not easy to separate the contributions of the two men. Their qualities were in some measure complementary, although both combined incisive engineering judgement with driving purposefulness. They set themselves clear objectives and approached them with determination and expert professionalism. One outstanding achievement of the partnership was the construction of the atomic power station at Calder Hall on the Cumbrian coast—the first in the world to generate electrical power on a commercial scale.

Hinton has been recognized as an engineer of world stature, but throughout their association Owen maintained his influence by quiet advice, often given in private and seldom assertive, but highly regarded for its basis in shrewd judgement and long experience. However, the two men were never warm friends and when, in 1957, their work took them in different directions they separated in an atmosphere which was cool. The cool relationship persisted, although it was clear, on later occasions when they met, that they understood and respected each other.

The UK Atomic Energy Authority had been formed in 1954, Owen taking the title of director of engineering and deputy managing director. In 1957 he was appointed managing director, industrial group, and he was knighted in the same year, having been appointed CBE in 1950. He became member for production of the Atomic Energy Authority in 1959, and continued to serve in different capacities until his retirement from the authority in 1964. In 1960 the University of Manchester conferred on him the honorary degree of DSc.

Owen was an outstanding project engineer. He was a great believer in programme planning and the immutability of target dates. He believed in taking firm decisions and he vigorously resisted changes which could not be proved to be essential. His earlier career had given him a clear insight into the complexities of human relations, and he won the respect and friendship of most of the staff working under him, whether relatively academic in outlook or down-to-earth site engineers engaged in heavy construction. He had great strength of character and a gift for swift detection of the weaknesses of any new proposals or design changes which were submitted for his comment or approval. Most of the ideas and features of the early atomic energy engineering programme were subjected to his critical analysis and were usually modified accordingly before adoption.

When he left the Atomic Energy Authority, Owen continued to exercise his profession in a variety of posts. For example, he was for two years (1968–9) chairman of Cammell Laird Shipbuilders Ltd. His engineering experience was an invaluable asset during a period in which three nuclear-powered submarines were under construction.

By way of relaxation, Owen took a great pride in his garden, and he was for many years an enthusiastic member of the Liverpool Rugby Football Club. Owen died on 25 March 1971 at his home, Euarth, Rosemary Lane, Beaumaris, Anglesey, north Wales. J. F. NORBURY, *rev.*

Sources *The Times* (26 March 1971) • *The Times* (29 March 1971) • *Atom* (May 1971) • private information (1986) • personal knowledge (1986) • *CGPLA Eng. & Wales* (1971)
Archives PRO, papers, AB38/59–67 • U. Lpool L., corresp. and papers
Likenesses M. Ward, photograph, 1970, NPG
Wealth at death £17,458: probate, 19 Aug 1971, *CGPLA Eng. & Wales*

Owen, Lewis [Lewis ab Owen] (**1522?–1555**), member of parliament and administrator, of Plas-yn-dre, Dolgellau, Merioneth, was the son of Owen ap Hywel ap Llywelyn, of Llwyn, and claimed descent from Gwrgan ab Ithel, prince of Powys.

Owen was a representative of the new class of officials drawn from the ranks of the local gentry who after the Acts of Union of 1536–43 replaced absentee sinecurists in positions of authority in the shires of the northern principality. In the reign of Henry VIII he was deputy chamberlain of north Wales and baron (justice) of the exchequer at Caernarfon. His rapid advancement was eased by his marriage to Margaret, daughter of John Puleston, constable of Caernarfon Castle and the first burgess of parliament to be returned for the town after the enfranchisement of Wales in 1536. He first served as deputy to Puleston as sheriff of Merioneth between 1534 and 1540, and in 1545–6 and 1550 he was sheriff in his own right. He was an usher of the chamber by 1550, a post he may have owed to the patronage of either Edward Seymour, who as Baron Beauchamp held the chamberlainship of north Wales, or John Dudley as president of the council in the marches and chamberlain of the household. He was returned as knight of the shire for Merioneth to four of the five parliaments between 1547 and 1554.

Early in Edward VI's reign Owen acquired leases to extensive crown lands and former monastic property in Merioneth. Lands leased jointly with the Nannau family at Dolgellau, Trawsfynydd, and Nannau were later to be a bone of contention between the two families. He was twice married and his progeny was prolific: several of the later gentry families of the county, including those of Peniarth, Hengwrt, and even Nannau, were to trace their descent from 'Baron' Owen and his first wife.

In 1536 Rowland Lee had cited the instability of Merioneth and Cardiganshire ('for though they are shire ground they are as ill as the worst part of Wales') as an argument against the extension of the shire system into the marches and the appointment of Welshmen as justices of the peace. Sir John Wynn of Gwydir in his *History of the Gwydir Family* lists Mawddwy among the most notorious of the marcher lordships which acted as sanctuaries for criminals who until the Acts of Union were retained by the lords as 'very precious jewels' (Wynn, *The History of the Gwydir Family*, ed. J. G. Jones, 1990, 39–40). Owen's zeal in implementing the new legislation incurred the wrath of the inhabitants, including the settled lesser landowners who resisted the changes. On 12 October 1555 he was ambushed and assassinated by a band of 'brigands' in a mountain pass, Dugoed Mawddwy. The lordship of Mawddwy had been attached to Merioneth in the act of 1536 and had remained a haunt of thieves after the Union settlement. Owen's death was an act of revenge for the relentless campaign which he and his ally John Wyn ap Meredydd of Gwydir, the *custos* for Merioneth, had waged against the outlaws, eighty of whom had been hanged. Owen was on his way home to Dolgellau from Welshpool after attending the Michaelmas great sessions for Montgomeryshire, where he had arranged a marriage between his son and the daughter of Richard Mytton, lord of Mawddwy.

Of the records of the subsequent trials of the perpetrators, only the indictments of the accessories to the crime, who were tried at the great sessions held at Bala as late as September 1558, have been preserved. The accused are described as yeomen, not outlaws: the first named in the indictment, Gruffydd Wyn ap Dafydd, was a substantial landowner who held former monastic lands in Brithdir, and was therefore one of Lewis's neighbours. The episode testifies to the tensions among the landowners of the shire, not all of whom had benefited from the uniform introduction of English common law or the new opportunities for holding offices under the crown. They were competitors in the market for land released by the formal abolition of Welsh tenures and the dissolution of the monasteries.

The herald bard Gruffudd Hiraethog, the most distinguished of five poets who composed elegies to 'Baron' Owen, depicted him as a martyr to the cause of the rule of law imposed as a consequence of the Acts of Union (*Gwaith Gruffudd Hiraethog*, ed. D. J. Bowen, 1990, 226–8). It is difficult to disentangle the actual events from the accretions of folklore, and the later accounts of the activities of the 'Gwylliaid Cochion' (the red-haired brigands) written by the antiquary Robert Vaughan (*d.* 1667), who was descended from Owen, and by Thomas Pennant in *A Tour in Wales* (1778–81) are not entirely free from these embellishments.

The theory that the yeomanry of Mawddwy were direct descendants of landowners who had resisted incursions on their terrain by the representatives of English law and order since the rebellion of Owain Glyndŵr remains highly speculative. PETER R. ROBERTS

Sources *DWB* • T. Pennant, *A tour in Wales*, 2 vols. (1778–81) • J. E. Griffith, *Pedigrees of Anglesey and Carnarvonshire families* (privately printed, Horncastle, 1914) • *Heraldic visitations of Wales and part of the marches … by Lewys Dwnn*, ed. S. R. Meyrick, 2 vols. (1846) • J. Jones, 'Lewis Owen, sheriff of Merioneth and the "Guylliaid Cochion" of Mawddwy in 1554–55', *Journal of the Merioneth Historical and Record Society*, 12 (1994–7), 221–40 • K. Williams-Jones, 'A Mawddwy court roll, 1415–16', *BBCS*, 23 (1968–70), 329–337, esp. 335–6 • HoP, *Commons, 1509–58*

Owen, Lewis. *See* Lewis, Owen (1533–1594).

Owen, Lewis (1571/2–1633?), religious controversialist and spy, born in Merioneth, was probably the eldest son of Gruffydd Owen, the fourth son of Lewis *Owen (1522?–1555) of Caernarfon, a baron of the exchequer. On 4 December 1590 he matriculated from Christ Church, Oxford, at the age of eighteen, but later left the university without graduating. Anthony Wood learned that he had 'some petty employment bestowed on him about that time', which from his later writings seems to have been that of an observer in Spanish territories during the Anglo-Spanish war. Wood speculated mistakenly that Owen entered the Jesuit order at Valladolid and remained as 'a curious observer among them for some time' (Wood, *Ath. Oxon.*, 1.545). However, he was never a registered student at the college of St Alban in Valladolid, and his name does not appear in the catalogues of the members of the Society of Jesus. He must be distinguished from the Lewis Owen who served in 1596 at Whitehall as 'Her Majesty's servant in the Privy Larder' (*CSP dom.*, *1595–7*, 185) and as a lawyer of the rank of serjeant-at-law, was granted a wardship in 1604, and in 1607 with others was awarded a grant in fee-farm of a tithe in Alton, Staffordshire.

Owen was in London by 1605 when he published *A Key of the Spanish Tongue, or, A Plaine and Easie Introduction …* that was dedicated to three friends from Merioneth: Sir Roger Owen, Sir Thomas Myddleton, and John Lloyd of the Inner Temple. He called it 'a little pamphlet', written 'at some vacant houres in the kingdome of Castile', that taught pronunciation and grammar, and provided a list of frequent phrases and four sample dialogues in English and Spanish for practice. Owen's travels also gave him skills in French, for in 1609 he published a translation of a tract by the protestant Morton Eudes, entitled *Catholique Traditions: a Treatise of the Beliefs of Christians* …. In his dedication to Prince Henry, Owen praised his 'learned father', King James, who ended divisions 'which the overscruple of some and the too much libertie of others had brought into the church of England'. Eudes described six different Christian churches: the Eastern (or Orthodox), the Nestorian, the Coptic, the Armenian, the Latin (or Catholic), and the protestant, and then gave each church's theological position on forty-four current controversies, such as the authority of the apostle Peter and the signs of a 'true church'. Eudes gave a brief summary of the teaching of each side, and then his 'Annotation' offered the wiser teaching, which for him was rarely that of the Latin church.

After he had arranged a second printing of this book, Owen recalled later that 'In the yeare 1610 I was sent by … a privy counceller in this land to Rome to learne … what the Earle of Tyrone did intend to do' (Owen, *Running Register*, 41). In May 1614 he informed Sir Ralph Winwood, secretary of state, of his return to London, 'sick and poor after spending many years abroad for his country's service', and of his readiness for new tasks when he reached Brussels (*CSP dom., 1611–18*, 236). Little is known about his itinerary in Winwood's service after 1615, but from the contents of his writings after 1625 it is clear that Owen's religious viewpoint had changed from that of the moderate Anglican in 1609 to that of the crusading puritan who was determined to reveal to the English the menace of Catholic religious orders. His major work, *The Unmasking of All Popish Monks, Friers and Jesuits*, printed in 1628 and dedicated to Sir John Lloyd, who had been a patron for his Spanish grammar, highlighted the role of religious orders in propping up 'the tottering kingdom' of the 'Romish Anti-Christ'. He identified numerous foundations by name and then reviewed their growth and current activities on the continent. He had scurrilous anecdotes in abundance and factual errors in several instances, as well as blanket condemnations, such as that monks and nuns only sought 'the pompe, pride and glory of the world' (p. 152). He reported meeting a fellow Welshman, 'Master Floyd', who was dismissed by the Jesuits 'because he was not wicked enough' (p. 129). He warned that in London there were 'cunning Jebusites' who 'paid the gold of the King of Spaine' to 'his pensioners that lurke about the court of England' (p. 159), regardless of the Anglo-Spanish war. He was certain that Jesuits were 'the cause of all these wars, bloodshed, commotions, Dearth, Famine, Persecutions' in Europe (p. 122).

Owen's near paranoia about the Jesuits required a second book, which in its first printing of 1626 was entitled *The running register, … a true relation of the English colledges, seminaries and cloysters* …. On page 56 of this *Register* he advised those who wished to learn more about life in a Jesuit college to read his recent book *The Unmasking*, which implied that it had been completed in manuscript first. The *Register* began with a 47-page essay, 'Ignatius his progresse', which was a disparaging commentary on Pedro de Ribadeneyra's biography of Loyola printed in 1604. There followed his listing of the locations of all 'the colleges or religious houses in Europe' of the Jesuits, but he warned that they were 'so insatiable in their covetousnesse that were they never so riche yet they thinke they have never enough' (p. 58). In 1629 the *Register* was reprinted in its entirety under a new title: *Speculum Jesuiticum, or, The Jesuites looking glasse, wherein they may behold Ignatius (their patron), his progresse, their owne pilgrimage, etc. by L.O.* This was dedicated to Sir Henry Marten, a judge of the high court of admiralty, since Owen claimed that he had to have protection after he had been warned not to speak the truth, for he was well aware 'how strongly these Romish locusts are back't and countenanced … by great personages'.

In 1628 Owen had informed the privy council that he was suspicious of the conduct of a Christopher Mallory, whom he had seen studying closely the ordnance defending the Tower Wharf, possibly for the French naval forces. Furthermore, Mallory was known to be seeking funds for 'the Carthusian cloisters at Mechlin and Nieuport' (*CSP dom., 1628–9*, 255, 328). The council began further inquiries, but Owen's subsequent activities are unknown. In frustration Anthony Wood commented: 'This Lewis Owen, who had a rambling head, was living in sixteen hundred twenty nine but what became of him afterwards, I cannot find' (Wood, *Ath. Oxon.*, 1.545). It is reported that he inherited from his mother's brother, William David Lloyd, an estate at Peniarth, Merioneth, where he died in 1633, leaving two daughters. A. J. LOOMIE

Sources M. Eudes, *Catholique traditions …*, trans. L. Owen (1609) · L. Owen, *The running register* (1626) · Wood, *Ath. Oxon.*, 2nd edn, vol. 1 · *CSP dom., 1595–1629* · *Calendar of the manuscripts of the most hon. the marquess of Salisbury*, 21, HMC, 9 (1970) · T. M. McCoog, *English and Welsh Jesuits, 1555–1650*, 2 vols., Catholic RS, 74–5 (1994–5) · E. Henson, ed., *The registers of the English College at Valladolid, 1589–1862*, Catholic RS, 30 (1930) · *DNB* · *DWB*

Wealth at death Peniarth manor, Wales: *DNB*

Owen, Morfydd [*pseud.* Morfydd Llwyn-Owen] (**1891–1918**), composer, was born on 1 October 1891 at 72 Park Street, Trefforest, Glamorgan, the last of four children born to William Owen (1864–1948), an accountant, and his wife, Sarah Jane Jones (1865–1918). She was encouraged to develop her interest in music at home, and studied from 1902 at the county school, Pontypridd, before entering the music department of University College, Cardiff, in 1909 on a Caradog scholarship. At Cardiff she studied with David Evans, who gave her every opportunity of hearing her works performed. As a pianist, Owen performed the Grieg piano concerto at Cardiff and graduated MusB in 1912. In the same year she was admitted to membership of the Gorsedd of Bards at the Wrexham national eisteddfod under the name Morfydd Llwyn-Owen. From September 1912 she studied at the Royal Academy of Music in London with Frederick Corder, winning the prestigious Charles Lucas silver medal for her orchestral *Nocturne*, the Oliviera Prescott prize, the Goring Thomas scholarship for dramatic composition in 1913, and the certificate of merit in July 1916 for singing—a remarkable record, rarely equalled in the academy's history. Nor did she neglect her career as a singer and appeared many times as soloist, winning a prize at the 1913 Swansea national eisteddfod. Her contemporaries at the academy included Eva Turner, John Barbirolli, and Harriet Cohen, all of whom testified in later years to her beauty and musical ability. In 1914 she published thirteen folk-song arrangements in Ruth Lewis's *Folk Songs Collected in Flintshire and the Vale of Clwyd*. Appointed a sub-professor of composition at the academy in 1914, her desire to study folk music in Russia was thwarted by the outbreak of war. In 1916 she met the distinguished psychoanalyst and biographer of Freud (Alfred) Ernest *Jones (1879–1958). They married on 6 February 1917, but the marriage was short-lived because she died, tragically young, on 7 September 1918 from appendicitis at Craig-y-môr, while on holiday on the Gower peninsula. She was buried four days later in Oystermouth cemetery, Swansea.

Morfydd Llwyn-Owen's death was without doubt a grievous blow to the development of music in Wales. Although only twenty-seven when she died, she had already produced a significant body of work, much of it of high quality and invariably the product of a still developing (if not always fully formed) musical personality. Songs such as 'To Our Lady of Sorrows' and 'Slumber Song of the Madonna' are superbly crafted, with a coupling of intense lyricism and a melancholy element noticeable in most of her finest works. Her *Nocturne* for orchestra shows an awareness of impressionism, and although the overall structure is stylistically inconsistent it nevertheless has a very assured sense of writing for orchestra, a feature also of her orchestral *Morfa rhuddlan*. She may be at her best in short character pieces and songs, most of which are meticulously crafted and display a remarkable feeling for poetic utterance as well as a Celtic tendency towards melancholy. One of her best-known works is the song 'Gweddi y pechadur' ('The Sinner's Prayer'), where Delian descending melodic patterns capture deftly the deeply religious side of her nature.

The colourful life Morfydd led, the friendship she enjoyed with a remarkable range of individuals (from the Crawshay family, leading figures on the Welsh and British political scene, to the likes of Ezra Pound, D. H. Lawrence, and Russian émigrés such as Alexis Chodak and Prince Yusupov, who led the assassination of Rasputin), her marriage to Jones, her tragic early death, and the body of music she left come together to form a singularly beguiling portrait. Her complex character, her struggle with her creativity after marriage, and her great beauty and gifts are all aspects of one of the most important Welsh composers in the transitional period between the Victorian age and the composers of the twentieth century.

LYN DAVIES

Sources University College, Cardiff, Morfydd Owen MSS · R. Davies, *Never so pure a light: Morfydd Owen* (1994) · V. Brome, *Ernest Jones: Freud's alter ego* (1982) · E. Crawshay-Williams, 'Morfydd Owen', *Wales*, 4 (1958), 50–56 · E. Jones, *Free associations: memories of a psycho-analyst* (1959) · K. I. Jones, 'The enigma of Morfydd Owen', *Welsh Music*, 5/1 (1975), 8–21 · G. Tritschler, 'Morfydd Owen: a biography', 1962, NL Wales, MS 18247D · R. Davies, 'Morfydd Owen', *British Music*, 13 (1991), 38–58 · b. cert. · d. cert.

Archives NL Wales, photographs · Royal Academy of Music, London, photographs, official documentation · U. of Wales, Cardiff, MSS · Welsh Folk Museum, Cardiff | NL Wales, letters to Kitty Idwal Jones | SOUND BBC WAC

Likenesses photograph, Community Centre, Llanbrynmair, Montgomeryshire · photographs, NL Wales

Owen, Morgan (1584/5–1645), bishop of Llandaff, was the third son of Owen Rees, clergyman, of Y Lasallt, in the parish of Myddfai, Carmarthenshire. His family claimed descent from the celebrated dynasty of physicians of Myddfai with legendary powers of healing acquired from a ghostly lady of Llyn Y Fan, a lake in the Black Mountains, and possessed extensive holdings of land inherited from various branches of the physicians' clan. Educated first at the grammar school in Carmarthen, Owen went subsequently to Jesus College, Oxford, where he matriculated on 16 December 1608, aged twenty-three. He became chaplain of New College, Oxford, from where he graduated BA on 6 July 1613, and proceeded MA in June 1616 from Hart Hall.

It is possible that Owen 'taught school' in Carmarthen (Yardley, 250). He was rector of Port Eynon, Gower, in 1619, and later of Shirenewton, Monmouthshire. From the status of a well-to-do parochial cleric he soon broke through to the ranks of the higher clergy. On 7 April 1620 he was collated to the second cursal prebend at St David's Cathedral, and on 26 July 1622 to the prebend of Cleddau; he became canon residentiary at St David's on the same day. He owed these rapid preferments to the interest taken in him by William Laud, his bishop, who was impressed by his 'zeal and piety'. In 1624 he became deputy chancellor of Carmarthen, and two years later prebendary of Llanarthne in the same county.

Owen's career and that of Laud himself became closely linked. When Laud became chancellor of Oxford in 1630, in an election in which Jesus College fellows supported him against hostile Welsh interests elsewhere in the university, Owen could look forward to an enhanced status outside Wales, where he had resigned his position as prebendary of Llanarthne on taking the precentorship of Brecon and the prebend of Llanfynydd in July 1635. In 1636 he was awarded the degree of doctor of divinity when Charles I visited Oxford. Using his extensive landed wealth Owen enclosed the south yard of St Mary's Church at Oxford with a freestone wall, and in 1637 commissioned the building of a 'curious and beautiful porch' (Yardley, 250) leading from High Street to the church, at a cost of £230 and adorned with a statue of the Virgin and child. It was said that he built the porch instead of giving a Latin sermon. When Laud later came to trial, his prosecutors cited Owen's conspicuous Oxford building as an example of one of the archbishop's projects. It was only a matter of time before such an active supporter of Laud was rewarded, and on 28 February 1640 the king recommended Owen for the bishopric of Llandaff. On 12 March he was elected bishop, and the appointment received the royal approval a week later. He was installed on 30 June, retaining the livings of Bedwas and Rudry, on the borders of Glamorgan and Monmouthshire *in commendam* with his bishopric. On 20 January 1641 the borough of Carmarthen recognized the achievement of its son by electing him to the common council; he was present to take the oath.

It was Owen's misfortune to reach this pinnacle just before the enemies of his great patron, Laud, began to close in on the archbishop and his allies. A little over six months after his installation, on 23 February 1641, Owen was named with bishops Richard Mountague and Roger Manwaring as objects of the attention of a committee of the House of Commons. Bills were to be drawn up against these three to deprive them of their sees and to prevent them holding any ecclesiastical office, but Owen seems to have been very much an afterthought of those framing the scope of the committee. The anti-episcopalian Sir Simonds D'Ewes does not even mention Owen in his diary entry for that day's work in the house. However, any hope he might have had that he might be regarded as small fry compared with these other Laudians would have evaporated by the spring of that year, as the promoters of the root and branch petition against episcopacy made advances in parliament. None the less, it was proposed in April to fine Owen £1000—less than the £20,000 suggested for Laud, or even the £5000 for Mountague.

The bishops were eventually impeached on 4 August, for promulgating the canons of 1640. By October 1641 Owen was imprisoned in the Tower of London, but was at large again by 31 December, when he, Archbishop John Williams of York, and nine other bishops used their seats in the Lords to protest against their treatment. According to Clarendon the other signatories were overborne by Williams. They asserted their ancient right to sit in the Lords, declared their abomination of popery, protested against threats to their safety by crowds, and demanded protection. The final part of their protest was a repudiation of all orders in the House of Lords since 27 December 1641 and all orders and votes to come, in their enforced absence. There could be no going back from this position, and the same day they were all sent to the Tower following their impeachment for high treason. Owen declined repeatedly to change his plea from not guilty when brought to the bar of the House of Lords to plead. On 6 April 1642 he was voted £200 per annum subsistence by the House of Commons, and subsequently released on bail, then rearrested.

Owen was released in May 1642, and retired to Y Lasallt, as his episcopal estate and palace at Matharn, Monmouthshire, had been seized by partisans of parliament. There he renewed friendship with Rees Prichard, vicar of Llandovery and a former colleague among the cathedral clergy of St David's. Owen accompanied Prichard, no Arminian, but a strongly moralistic devotee of the Church of England in Wales, on his last visit to St David's, on 2 August 1643, and oversaw his will a year later.

In December 1644 Owen drew up his own will, leaving lands in nine Carmarthenshire parishes, and the tithes of two, with two Pembrokeshire rectories, to his nephews. He had no children from his marriage to Maud, widow of Edward Atkins of Carmarthen. He made further provision for the poor of Myddfai and the school at Carmarthen. Owen died on 5 March 1645 at Y Lasallt—it was said that on hearing the news of Laud's execution he 'sunk down in his chair and dy'd soon after' (Willis, 70). He was buried in the chancel of Myddfai church, on the north side of the altar.

Stephen K. Roberts

Sources E. Yardley, *Menevia sacra*, ed. F. Green (1927) • *Fasti Angl.* (Hardy), 2.253 • Foster, *Alum. Oxon.* • G. E. Evans, 'Will of Morgan Owen', *Transactions of the Carmarthenshire Antiquarian Society*, 27 (1937), 16–20 • J. Pughe and J. Williams ab Ithel, *The physicians of Myddvai, Meddygon Myddfai* (1861), xxx • W. Spurrell, *Carmarthen and its neighbourhood*, 2nd edn (1879), 62 • *JHC*, 2 (1640–42), 91a, 236a • diary of Simonds D'Ewes, BL, Harleian MS 162, fol. 251a • BL, Harleian MS 477, fol. 116 • Clarendon, *Hist. rebellion*, 1.471–7 • B. Willis, *A survey of the cathedral church of Llandaff* (1719), 70 • *The works of the most reverend father in God, William Laud*, ed. J. Bliss and W. Scott, 7 vols. (1847–60), vol. 3, pp. 243, 454; vol. 5, p. 174 • *DNB* • Wood, *Ath. Oxon.*, new edn, 4.803 • 'Bishop Morgan of Llandaff—Myddfai church', *Archaeologia Cambrensis*, 3rd ser., 4 (1858), 419 • W. Rees, 'Bishop Morgan Owen of Llandaff', *Archaeologia Cambrensis*, 3rd ser., 5 (1859), 71–2

Wealth at death lands in nine Carmarthenshire parishes; four rectories: Evans, 'Will of Morgan Owen'

Owen, Nicholas [St Nicholas Owen, *called* Little John, Little Michael] (*d.* **1606**), carpenter and Jesuit lay brother, was born in Oxford, probably in St Peter le Bailey. On 2 February he was apprenticed for eight years to William Conway, an Oxford joiner. He sometimes used the aliases Draper and Andrews. He had three brothers: John (*b.* 1560), a seminary priest; Walter (1568–1591), who died as a deacon at the English College in Valladolid; and Henry, who was apprenticed to the university printer Joseph Barnes and later ran secret presses in the Clink prison in London and in Northamptonshire. All four may have been sons by a previous marriage of Walter Owen (*d.* 1607), a carpenter who leased 3 Castle Street from Magdalen College from 1566 onwards and whose wife Agnes (*d.* 1609) was a recusant in 1603–4.

In 1588 Nicholas Owen became servant to the Jesuit superior Henry Garnet. From then on

> his chief employment was in making of secret places to hide priests and church stuff … in all shires and in the chiefest Catholic houses of England … of several fashions in several places, that one being taken might give no light to the discovery of another. (*Catholics under James I*, 182–4)

From documentary and architectural evidence it is possible to identify the characteristics of his work: a liking for sites away from outside walls; an ability to think in three dimensions and in curves; and the inventiveness noted by John Gerard and not shown by some other builders. Surviving examples include those at Oxburgh, Norfolk (1589?); Baddesley Clinton, Warwickshire (1588–91); Braddocks, Essex, and Sawston, Cambridgeshire (both 1592–3); Scotney Old Castle, Kent (by 1598); and Harvington, Worcestershire (about 1602).

On 23 April 1594 Owen was arrested with John Gerard at a house in London. He was tortured, but gave nothing away and was released for 'a good round sum of money' (*Catholics under James I*, 183). In October 1597 he helped Gerard to escape from the Tower of London. About 1600 he became a Jesuit lay brother and an accident with a restive horse left him with a slight limp. Both he and Henry Garnet were finally taken at Hindlip, Worcestershire, during a twelve-day search in January 1606 when 'eleven secret corners and conveyances were found in the said house' (BL, Harleian MS 360, fol. 101*r*). Owen and a companion, Ralph Ashley alias Chambers, were starved out of a hide in the long gallery on Thursday, 23 January, after four days with one apple to eat between them. Owen was imprisoned first in the Marshalsea and then in the Tower, where he was ruthlessly tortured despite suffering from a rupture. He died of the torture on the night of 1–2 March; according to Gerard, 'his bowels gushed out together with his life', and the official version was that he had 'ripped up his own belly with a knife without a point' (BL, Stowe MS 168, fol. 364r). According to Henry More he was buried within the Tower, *in ipsa arce* (*Historia provinciae Anglicanae*, 1660, 322). He was beatified by Pope Pius XI on 15 December 1929 and canonized by Paul VI on 25 October 1970.

MICHAEL HODGETTS

Sources *The condition of Catholics under James I: Father Gerard's narrative of the Gunpowder Plot*, ed. J. Morris, 2nd edn (1872) • *John Gerard: the autobiography of an Elizabethan*, trans. P. Caraman, 2nd edn (1956) • J. Morris, *Life of Fr John Gerard* (1881) • M. Hodgetts, *Secret hiding-places* (1989) • M. Hodgetts, 'The Owens of Oxford', *Recusant History*, 24 (1998–9), 415–30 • A. Hogge, 'Closing the circle: Nicholas Owen and Walter Owen of Oxford', *Recusant History*, 26 (2002–3), 291–300

Archives PRO, two brief confessions of 26 Feb and 1 March 1606, SP 14/216/ii/192, 194

Likenesses engraving, repro. in M. Tanner, *Societas Jesu usque ad sanguinis et vitae profusionem militans* (Prague, 1675), 74

Owen, Nicholas (1752–1811), Church of England clergyman and antiquary, was born on 2 January 1752 at Llandyfrydog, Anglesey, the second son of Nicholas Owen (*c.*1730–1785), rector of Llandyfrydog, with Llanfihangel Tre'r-beirdd, and Margaret (*fl.* 1735–1790), his wife (daughter of Robert Edwards, rector of Llanrug, Caernarvonshire). On 30 June 1769 he matriculated from Jesus College, Oxford, and graduated BA in 1773 and MA in 1776.

Ordained in 1773, Owen obtained a curacy, but it is not known where. He had moved to a curacy at Winslow, Buckinghamshire, by 1779, where it is believed he also kept a school. Dissatisfied with the living, he resigned it in 1789 to live for a time with his mother at Bangor. He made several appeals to a number of patrons for the livings of Llandyfrydog, Llanbeblig, and Llangynhafal, and his letters to the bishops of Bangor and of Chester, the archbishop of Canterbury, and Lord Bulkeley contain material little short of direct insults and represent him as a persistent seeker after preferment. A stubborn and cantankerous character, Owen was severely reprimanded by Lord Bulkeley and had to make a public apology to the bishop of Bangor. The dean of Bangor made him perpetual curate of Llanfihangel Ysgeifiog and Llanffinan in November 1790, and he was given the rectory of Mellteyrn with Botwnnog in October 1800. He died, unmarried, on 30 May 1811 at Bangor, Caernarvonshire, and was buried on 5 June at Llandyfrydog.

Though Owen published a sermon on the founding of a Sunday school at Winslow in 1788, he severely criticized these establishments in a letter to Dr Porteous, bishop of London, in March 1789 because their frequenters often turned Methodists. He was no friend of dissent or Methodism, whose clergy he often attacked in the press under the pseudonym Observator. Owen's own publications were mainly about local antiquities. *British Remains* (1788) covered such topics as a history of the lords-marchers, an account of the supposed discovery of America by Madog ab Owain Gwynedd, and also a biography of the naturalist Edward Lhuyd. A selection from the 'phrases' of Horace for schoolboys appeared in 1785. *Carnarvonshire: a Sketch of its History* was published in 1792, and Owen is one of several authors who have been credited with the authorship of the anonymous *A History of the Island of Anglesey, with Memoirs of Owen Glendower* (1775).

A. F. POLLARD, *rev.* HUW WALTERS

Sources pedigree of Nicholas Owen, U. Wales, Bangor, MSS 4602–4607 • N. Owen, miscellaneous letters, U. Wales, Bangor, MS 2408 • *DWB*, 717 • W. Rowlands, *Cambrian bibliography / Llyfryddiaeth y Cymry*, ed. D. S. Evans (1869), 581–2 • J. E. Griffith, *Pedigrees of Anglesey and Carnarvonshire families* (privately printed, Horncastle, 1914), 51 • A. I. Price, *The diocese of Bangor during three centuries* (1929), 46, 115 • Foster, *Alum. Oxon.* • *GM*, 1st ser., 81/1 (1811), 682 • diocese of Bangor, bishop's transcripts, parish of Llandyfrydog, NL Wales • B. F. Roberts, '"Memoirs of Edward Llwyd, antiquary", and Nicholas Owen's *British remains*, 1777', *National Library of Wales Journal*, 19 (1975–6), 67–87

Archives NL Wales, MS of 'Carnarvonshire' • U. Wales, Bangor, letters, MS 2408

Owen [Owens], **Owen** (1543/4–1593), Church of England clergyman, the son of Owen ap Robert, was born at Bodsilin, in Aber, Caernarvonshire, where the house still bears the family inscription. He matriculated at Christ's College, Cambridge, at Easter 1560. He graduated BA in 1560–61, MA in 1564, when he was identified as Ovinus Owen, and incorporated at Oxford on 21 February 1566. He was ordained deacon, in London in 1566, and priest in February 1567, when he was identified as 'scholar of Christ's, aged 23'.

Owen became rector of Burton Latimer, Northamptonshire, in 1567, which remained his permanent home. He married Margaret Matthews and, after her death, Jane, daughter of Robert Griffith of Caernarfon, with whom he had five sons and three daughters. His eldest son, John *Owen, was baptized at Burton Latimer in 1580. Despite a long sojourn in England, he maintained firm links with Wales. He was instituted to Llangeinwen, with the chapel of Llangaffo, Anglesey, by Nicholas Robinson, bishop of Bangor, on 11 August 1573. Robinson appointed him a canon and prebendary of Bangor Cathedral on 28 December 1576. He served as archdeacon of Anglesey, drawing an income of £58 10*s*. 6*d*., from 1583 until his death. His appointment was not recorded in Robinson's register, which provides very limited information about cathedral dignitaries, but his tenure was noted by Henry Rowlands in the eighteenth century and his name occurs in modern lists of archdeacons. He was the last archdeacon of Anglesey to hold the office *pleno jure* (with full legal right); after his death the bishops of Bangor held it *in commendam* (with enjoyment of revenues). The late sixteenth century was a period when very few dignitaries resided in the diocese, and it would appear that he continued to live at Burton Latimer, where he died, and was buried on 21 March 1593. His successor at Llangeinwen was appointed on 4 May 1593. His eldest son, John, the future bishop of St Asaph, was still a youth when Owen died, but he succeeded to the rectory of Burton Latimer in 1608.

DAVID WALKER

Sources A. I. Pryce, *The diocese of Bangor in the sixteenth century* (1923) • M. L. Clarke, *Bangor Cathedral* (1969) • H. Rowlands, *Mona antiqua restaurata*, 2nd edn (1766) • Venn, *Alum. Cant.*, 1/3 • J. Peile, *Biographical register of Christ's College, 1505–1905, and of the earlier foundation, God's House, 1448–1505*, ed. [J. A. Venn], 2 vols. (1910–13) • *An* *inventory of the ancient monuments in Caernarvonshire*, 1: *East*, Royal Commission on Ancient and Historical Monuments in Wales and Monmouthshire (1956) • D. R. Thomas, *Esgobaeth Llanelwy: the history of the diocese of St Asaph*, new edn (1874) • M. P. Siddons, *The development of Welsh heraldry*, vols. 1–3 (1991–3), vol. 2 • Foster, *Alum. Oxon.*

Owen, Owen (1847–1910), department store owner, was born on 13 October 1847 at Cwmrhaeadr, near Machynlleth, Montgomeryshire, Wales, the oldest child in the family of three sons and three daughters of Owen Owen (1818–1872), tenant farmer, of Cwmrhaeadr, and his second wife, Esther Elizabeth (1814–1855), daughter of William Evans, a Wesleyan Methodist minister. His father's first wife died in 1843, leaving two sons, one of whom, Thomas, was MP for Launceston from 1892 to 1898. His father married for a third time in 1857. Owen was educated at the Wesleyan college (later Queen's College), Taunton, and in 1860 went to Bath as an apprentice to his uncle, Samuel Evans, who had built up a large linen drapery business. His half-brother, Thomas, had been working there since 1853, and became his uncle's partner in 1863.

In 1868 Owen moved to Liverpool to set up his own drapery business, hoping to attract the large Welsh population in Liverpool, and leased premises in London Road. He concentrated on rapid turnover and low profit margins, and expansion was so rapid that by 1873 he had over 120 employees and a quarter of an acre of floor space. He insisted on a high standard of service, and in the early days he himself greeted the customers as they entered the store. In 1881 his youngest brother Jabez entered into a partnership with him, which lasted until the former's fatal illness in 1885. Owen soon began to acquire neighbouring properties, and in the 1880s knocked many of them down in order to build hostels for his staff, who were mostly from Wales. He saw his staff as an extended family, and later, when he bought an estate in Wales, he invited many of them there for weekends, and even paid for some of them to go abroad for the sake of their health. Owen was one of the first big shopkeepers to introduce a weekly half-holiday for his employees, and he also set up the Owen Owen Trust in 1900 to help retired members of staff.

Unlike most other early department store owners, such as David Lewis, also in Liverpool, Owen Owen was not interested in extending the range of goods sold, and although the store had many departments, it remained a drapery business, with dress and curtain materials at the centre of the business. His clientele now came from as far away as north Wales, with people prepared to travel long distances for the good quality merchandise at low prices. Owen was similarly not interested in opening new stores in other cities, and in the 1880s he began instead to invest his profits in other enterprises, notably in North American railways. He helped other members of his family to establish their own businesses, including the drapery businesses started by his brother William in the 1870s, and his brother-in-law R. O. Davies in the 1880s, in Bayswater, London, and in 1889 he became a director of Evans and Owen Ltd in Bath.

On 19 December 1891 Owen married a shop assistant at Gorringe's store in London, Ellen Maria (*b*. 1858/9), daughter of George Richards, an innkeeper, of Southsea, Hampshire. They had two sons and two daughters. Owen moved to London, but continued to supervise the Liverpool store, which had become a limited company in 1899. It continued to grow, and by 1906 shares in Owen Owen were paying a 16 per cent dividend. The store was now one of the largest in the north. In 1906 Owen went on a fact-finding visit to the United States to investigate American department stores, and he was particularly impressed by the bargain basements and by the advertising: 'Americans don't have sales, they have advertising campaigns' (*Draper's Record*, 21 June 1906), he reported.

From the 1890s onwards, however, Owen became involved mainly in property transactions in London. In 1892 he bought a building in Kensington High Street, which he developed, and sold to Derry and Tom's in 1896 at a profit of £9000. Other developments included Gwydir Chambers in High Holborn (1900–03), and the Dollis Hill housing estate in north-west London, built on 22 acres of open land which he bought in 1903. In 1909 he formed his own property company, Owen Owen estates. Owen also continued to invest in other drapery businesses and department stores. In 1892 he made a substantial investment in the Bon Marché store in Brixton, which was in financial difficulties, and in 1897 he began to buy shares in John Barnes & Co. in the Finchley Road. He became a director of both of these.

Brought up in a Wesleyan Methodist family, Owen became a Unitarian in the 1880s. He was a Liberal, a supporter of W. E. Gladstone and home rule, and a friend of D. Lloyd George, whom he first met at Grasgarth, in Acton, the home of his brother-in-law R. O. Davies. Throughout his life he supported Welsh causes, particularly education and the arts. He was an influential member of the Welsh National Society of Liverpool, and was later at the centre of London Welsh society. He made generous donations to the national eisteddfod of Wales (which was held in Liverpool in 1884), and the North Wales College, and became a governor of the University College of North Wales at Bangor. He was a member of the Honourable Society of Cymmrodorion from 1886. He also made donations to the Liverpool University fund from 1902, and took a great interest in the Warehousemen, Clerks, and Drapers' schools at Purley, Surrey. He was involved in setting up the Linen and Woollen Drapers' cottage homes at Mill Hill for retired retail trade workers in 1897. An enthusiastic cyclist, who moved from the tricycle to the bicycle after a course of lessons in 1897, and a tennis player, Owen bought his first motor car in 1907, and travelled in it to and from the estate at Tan-y-Foel, Penmaen-mawr, in Caernarvonshire, which he had bought in 1902. He also bought the Garthgwynion estate, near Machynlleth, in 1906; this included Bwlch, his ancestral home, which his father had had to sell in 1841. He was a JP for Caernarvonshire.

Owen Owen died of cancer, after an operation, on 27

March 1910, at his London home, the Manor House, 37 Fitzjohn's Avenue, Hampstead. He was cremated at Golders Green crematorium on 30 March 1910, and his ashes were scattered on the family grave in the Machynlleth nonconformist cemetery. His wife survived him. In the years following his death the Owen Owen store in Liverpool ran into difficulties, but in 1925 his son-in-law, Duncan Norman, took it over, built a new store, and revived its fortunes by appealing to a more fashionable market.

ANNE PIMLOTT BAKER

Sources D. W. Davies, *Owen Owen: Victorian draper* (c.1984) • B. Lancaster, *The department store: a social history* (1995) • E. Midwinter, *Old Liverpool* (1971) • F. Goodall, 'Owen, Owen', *DBB* • A. Adburgham, *Shops and shopping, 1800–1914: where, and in what manner the well-dressed Englishwoman bought her clothes* (1964) • *Liverpool Courier* (29 March 1910) • *Liverpool Weekly Mercury* (2 April 1910) • *CGPLA Eng. & Wales* (1910) • *The Times* (31 March 1910)
Archives NL Wales, corresp., poems • priv. coll.
Likenesses photographs, c.1889–1899, repro. in Davies, *Owen Owen*, 27, 66 • L. Connell, photograph, repro. in *Liverpool Weekly Mercury* • photograph, repro. in Davies, *Owen Owen*, frontispiece
Wealth at death £463,568 16s. 11d.: probate, 2 May 1910, *CGPLA Eng. & Wales*

Owen, Richard (1606–1683), Church of England clergyman, was the son of **Cadwallader Owen** (c.1562–1617), Church of England clergyman, who came from Maentwrog, Merioneth, and who matriculated from Jesus College, Oxford, on 24 November 1581, graduated BA in 1583, and proceeded MA in 1589. In 1585 Cadwallader was elected a fellow of Oriel College, and he proceeded BD in 1603, but he must have resigned by 1606, before his marriage to Blanche, daughter of John Roberts, the younger brother of Lewis Anwyl of Parc, Merioneth. In 1608 Owen became rector of Llanbrynmair in the same county, and two years later he also became the sinecure rector there. He was known as a great debater and used the name 'Sic doces'. He is also supposed to have written several works, but nothing is known of them. He died in 1617 and was buried on 6 April at Llanbrynmair.

Richard Owen was born on 3 October 1606 at Llanfechain, Montgomeryshire, and baptized there on 7 October. He matriculated at Oxford on 28 June 1622 and entered Oriel College as a servitor. He was a Bible clerk from October 1624 until 2 February 1627, graduated BA on 19 February 1625, was Dudley exhibitioner from 30 March to 25 October 1626, and on 21 March 1628 was elected a fellow of his college. He proceeded MA on 22 June 1630. At an unknown date he resigned his fellowship and married Anne, whose other name is unknown; they had ten children. In 1634 Owen became rector of Llanfechain, but he was 'drawn to the richer livings of the English dioceses' (Richards, *Puritan Movement*, 6). On 10 February 1636 he was installed as the vicar of Eltham, Kent, and on 2 September 1638 he was instituted to the rectory of St Swithin at London Stone. On 4 December that year he proceeded BD.

In 1643, as a consequence of his royalist sympathies, Owen was ejected from his livings, but he continued to live at Eltham, where he was on friendly terms with John Evelyn. As the diarist noted, Owen frequently preached and administered the sacrament at Evelyn's house at Sayes Court, as well as baptizing his son and churching his wife. Owen is supposed to have published in 1650, as *Elenchus motuum nuperorum in Anglia*, a free translation and amplification in Latin of George Bate's *Royal Apologie* (1648). He also translated into English, but did not publish, most, if not all, of Juvenal's satires. In 1657 he supplied 'som British proverbs' for James Howell to enter in his *Lexicon tetraglotton*.

Meanwhile, his wife, Anne, having died in March 1653, Owen married, on 6 January 1655, Amy Kidwell, with whom he had at least two sons. On 13 November 1656, with the support of the vice-chancellor of Oxford, John Owen, and Joseph Caryl, he petitioned the council of state for a licence to preach. His appeal was referred to the committee for the approbation of public preachers, and on 30 December he was approved. In the same year he was appointed minister of North Cray, Kent, while in 1658 he resigned his position at Eltham.

Following the Restoration, Owen retained North Cray, and after being given the right to choose which living to hold by act of parliament he was nominated to St Swithin's. On 1 August 1660 he was created DD at Oxford and on 16 August was appointed to the prebend of Reculverland at St Paul's, London. He was held in 'high esteem for his holy life and conversation, for his orthodoxness in judgement, conformity to the true ancient doctrine and discipline of the Church of England, and in the former revolutions, for his loyalty to his sacred majesty' (Williams, 386). His one extant sermon was delivered at St Alfege, London, on 8 May 1666, the sixth anniversary of the proclamation of the king in London, and published as *Paulus, multiformis concio ad clerum* (1666). The family friendship with the Evelyns endured: in 1680 Amy Owen wrote an amusing letter to John Evelyn and received a reply on the subject of her 'trading for tulips' (*Diary and Correspondence*, 1.41–2).

Owen made his will on 23 January 1683 and died shortly afterwards; he was buried at Eltham, as he had wished, on 27 January. He was survived by his wife, Amy (d. 1694), son, John, and daughter, Elizabeth Evans; nine sons and three daughters who had predeceased him had been commemorated by Owen on a marble inscription in Eltham church in 1679.

BERTHA PORTER, *rev.* RICHARD C. ALLEN

Sources will, PRO, PROB 11/372, fol. 187 • parish register, Llanfechain, Montgomeryshire, NL Wales • Foster, *Alum. Oxon.* • R. Williams, *Enwogion Cymru: a biographical dictionary of eminent Welshmen* (1852), 385–6 • Wood, *Ath. Oxon.*, 1st edn • *Heraldic visitations of Wales and part of the marches … by Lewys Dwnn*, ed. S. R. Meyrick, 2 (1846), 215 • T. Richards, *A history of the puritan movement in Wales* (1920), 6 • T. Richards, *Religious developments in Wales, 1654–1662* (1923), 377 • *Gweithiau Morgan Llywd o Wynedd*, 1–2, ed. T. E. Ellis and J. H. Davies (1899–1908) • *Diary and correspondence of John Evelyn*, ed. W. Bray, rev. edn, ed. [J. Forster], 4 vols. (1859–62) • J. Walker, *An attempt towards recovering an account of the numbers and sufferings of the clergy of the Church of England*, pt 2 (1714), 53, 173 • D. R. Thomas, *Esgobaeth Llanelwy: the history of the diocese of St Asaph*, rev. edn, 3 vols. (1908–13)
Wealth at death very modest estate: will, PRO, PROB 11/372, fol. 187

Owen, Sir Richard (1804–1892), comparative anatomist and palaeontologist, was born on 20 July 1804 in Lancaster, the sixth and youngest child and second son of Richard Owen (1754–1809) and Catherine Longworth, *née* Parrin (*d.* 1838), the daughter of Robert Parrin, a church organist in Lancaster. Owen's father, a merchant in the West Indies trade, was something of a self-made man who had been raised in Fulmer Place, Buckinghamshire, by his maternal grandfather, Richard Eskrigge (his own mother having died in childbirth). Owen's mother was a descendant of French Huguenot immigrants. Like her father a knowledgeable musician, she was a woman of intelligence and social sophistication with close friends as well as more distant relatives in the middle class of the town and county.

At the time of Owen's birth the family was financially well off, living in a large house in the fashionable part of the city. When his father died five years later, however, the effects of the Napoleonic war and the defalcations of a business associate had forced a financial crisis which led to a move to the less fashionable Castle Hill area. There Catherine Owen established a girls' boarding-school that her three unmarried daughters continued to run after her death in 1838.

Education: Lancaster, Edinburgh, and London In 1810 Owen entered the old-fashioned, half collegiate Lancaster grammar school as a day student. He was said to be somewhat troublesome, a small boy who grew rapidly in his adolescence, neither particularly good at, nor very much interested in, his lessons. Although prone to high jinks and practical jokes, he nevertheless learned Latin (and probably a smattering of French), the arithmetic that passed for mathematics, a bit of theologically orientated philosophy, and some history. Strangely, natural history did not feature in his school education; during the Lancaster years he seemed to have had no interest in the subject. When he was sixteen, unable to proceed to university and intending to become a surgeon-apothecary, he began an apprenticeship with a succession of three masters for the next four years. Not only did he learn the rudiments of medical practice and develop a skill in dissection with a knowledge of human anatomy, but he also discovered his vocation. Now, with the exception of free access to the local library of the Amicable Society, which provided him with scientific literature, provincial Lancaster had little to offer Owen: he left his apprenticeship and went off to the University of Edinburgh to complete his medical qualification.

Owen arrived in Edinburgh in October 1824 but remained for only two terms, during which he completed the classes designed to prepare students for formal admission to medical practice. Except for John Barclay's proprietary course in anatomy he seems not to have been impressed with what he learned at the university, nor to have established close personal associations with either his fellow students or his professors. Barclay's last course, which Owen attended, was in the still novel comparative anatomy that, supported by a large anatomical collection, placed human anatomy in the wider context of the whole of the animal kingdom. Barclay introduced Owen to a generally anti-materialist holistic philosophical approach to what was essentially a purely analytically descriptive field. It was from Barclay's 'earnest teaching', Owen later wrote, that he had first received his 'strong predilection for Zootomical pursuits'. Of more immediate value was Barclay's recommendation that Owen leave Edinburgh and go to London to complete the requirements for membership in the Royal College of Surgeons—thus qualifying to pursue a private medical practice or, as he seemed to desire, to become a naval surgeon. More valuable still was Barclay's letter strongly recommending his student to John Abernethy, then an influential member of the London medical establishment as professor of St Bartholomew's Hospital's *ad hoc* medical programme and president of the Royal College of Surgeons.

Sir Richard Owen (1804–1892), by William Holman Hunt, 1881

Persuaded by Barclay's advice and with his letter in hand, Owen moved to London soon after the completion of his second term at Edinburgh. On his arrival he still had courses to complete and was too young to qualify for membership in the college but, impressed by Barclay's recommendation, Abernethy dissuaded Owen from his plans for a naval career and took him on as the prosector for his surgical lectures. The appointment, though unpaid, was fortunate in that it relieved Owen of the financial burden entailed by the need to complete the course requirements while at the same time providing him with valuable experience as a practising anatomist. At least as useful in a social system in which 'interest' or influence was an important factor in professional success was the sponsorship of so influential a member of the medical establishment. Within a year, immediately after reaching the minimum age requirement of twenty-two, Owen passed the examination for membership of the college. Although he had already given up the idea of becoming a naval surgeon he was still determined to become a medical practitioner and to that end he began his practice close by the college, at 11 Cook's Court on Carey Street, just off Chancery Lane, hoping to draw his patients from the young lawyers in the nearby chambers of the inns of court. With so many young men with similar hopes, the prospect for success was not a particularly happy one. Abernethy's patronage continued, however, the result of which was to change both the career and the life of his protégé.

In the mid-1820s the Royal College of Surgeons was in a difficult position. It found itself one of the targets of the aggressive attacks on the medical establishment by Thomas Wakley in his recently founded medical journal *The Lancet*. Specifically it was charged with failing to produce a useful catalogue of the collection of John Hunter, which had been purchased by the government in 1800 and entrusted to its care. Without such a catalogue the collection was virtually useless as either an instructional tool or the visual representation of the ideas of the important anatomist and surgeon upon whose reputation the existence of the college rested. William *Clift, Hunter's last student-assistant, employed by the college as conservator of the collection, had been unable to produce the long-promised catalogue. With Clift's latest assistant about to leave, Abernethy engineered Owen's appointment as his successor.

Owen's entry into the Hunterian Museum on 7 March 1827 at a salary of £30 per quarter was the beginning of his long and productive career as a natural scientist. The salary, soon increased to £150 per annum, was only just sufficient to satisfy the lifestyle his position required, yet for one his age—without family background or funds—it was a fortunate appointment. The experience with the Hunterian collection, his friendship with its long-time conservator, and the acquaintance of the influential members of the medical establishment at the college exceeded anything that a young man in his early twenties could have hoped for in the way of a training in comparative anatomy and in the making of a professional career.

Hunterian Museum, 1827–1832 Owen fitted in well at the Hunterian. Clift was an easy-going master, an engaging friend, and the professional colleague of many of those who were converting natural history into natural science. His son and presumed successor, William Home *Clift, was Owen's age and, with similar interests in music, the theatre, and the bachelor life of pre-Victorian London, the two workmates became friends. In addition, Clift's daughter Caroline Emily (1801–1873), three years older, soon became Owen's fiancée.

The work of redescribing Hunter's specimens as well as those which were being continually acquired was congenial, even exciting, for one who was entering a new world of activity far removed from the practicalities of the medical profession. To pursue science alone, still primarily the avocation of gentlemen collectors of means, Owen could hardly expect to find an income sufficient to allow him to marry and to establish himself as both a gentleman and a professional. He kept his options open. He maintained a middling medical practice that hardly covered his expenses while attending to the requirements of his position and doing the odd job from which he might earn a bit beyond his museum stipend. From 1828 he gave optional lectures in comparative anatomy at St Bartholomew's while attending to an occasional patient or assisting senior members of the college, particularly in anatomy.

At the beginning of 1830 there was the possibility of change when, having rapidly passed the tests of the Society of Apothecaries, Owen rushed to Birmingham to compete for an open position of hospital surgeon-apothecary. Although it seemed certain that he would receive the appointment, the contrast between the excitement and possibilities in London and the drabness and provincialism of industrial Birmingham led him to return to the college, his friends, and especially Caroline Clift. He resolved to stay and to make his future there as comparative anatomist, a physiologist, or, in its later redefinition, a biologist.

Owen's first task at the Hunterian had been to catalogue the natural history specimens, to be followed by the soft-tissue preparations in spirit, many of which had lost their identifying labels and virtually all of which required dissection and comparison with recently acquired materials. The anonymity of the subsequent publications of the catalogues rankled and was a source of his lifelong concern that he be given appropriate credit for his work. (Indeed, there is still debate whether a number of works were by William Home Clift or by Owen.) The position, however, was much more than that of a technician; the loose definition of his role allowed him opportunities to explore the new territory of comparative anatomy and zoology whose boundaries were being expanded primarily by French savants and their continental colleagues. Occasionally Owen would substitute for William Clift in the obligatory guided tour of the collection for distinguished visitors and, because he knew French, acted as guide to Cuvier for his visit in 1830; reciprocating, Cuvier invited Owen to visit him in his own establishment at the Jardin des Plantes in Paris.

Also in 1830 Owen became the youngest and most active member of a small group, within the recently organized Zoological Society of London, whose interests in zoological research led them to establish, as the *de facto* research arm of the society, a committee on science and correspondence, to meet fortnightly at the society's museum on Bruton Street 'for the purpose of suggesting and discussing questions and experiments in animal physiology'. At its first meeting late in 1830 Owen described, in what was to be his first publication under his own name, his dissection of a rare orang-utan that had recently died soon after its arrival in the society's gardens. This paper initiated a long series of precisely described anatomical works that, his successor at both the Hunterian and British museums wrote, 'extending over a period of more than fifty years … has done so much to advance the knowledge of comparative anatomy and to give an illustrious place to their author in the annals of science' (W. H. Flower, *Essays on Museums and other Subjects Connected with Natural History*, 1898, 177). The availability of the specimens from the zoological gardens led Owen to focus on the vertebrates, the class on which most of his subsequent work would depend. The committee operated independently until two years later, when its functions were absorbed into the main Zoological Society, and in that time Owen, although still working on the Hunterian catalogues, contributed twenty-eight papers to its meetings, the largest number of any of its members.

The Royal College of Surgeons provided Owen with a view of what comparative anatomy could be—beyond the descriptions provided by the skilful use of the scalpel in the dissecting room. Since arriving there he had attended, and had been impressed by, J. H. Green's lectures on comparative anatomy in which he introduced his audiences to the transcendental and holistic views of German natural philosophy. Owen recalled thirty years later that:

> For the first time in England the Comparative Anatomy of the whole Animal Kingdom was described, and illustrated by such a series of enlarged and coloured diagrams as had never before been seen. The vast array of facts was linked by reference to the underlying Unity [of Nature]. (J. Simon, *Memoir on the Life of Joseph Henry Green*, 1865, 1.xiv)

For Owen, coming to comparative anatomy with hardly more philosophy than the easy-going vitalism of Barclay and Abernethy, Green's Anglicized German Romanticism provided a vision of what an integrative natural science could become.

At a more limited and workable level, a sense that comparative anatomy was something more than a succession of individual dissections was reinforced by Owen's visit to Cuvier's establishment in Paris. Seizing the first opportunity available to him Owen spent a month in Paris during his vacation in the summer of 1831. He met Cuvier informally and visited his working establishment and the osteological collection which served as a reference for both his comparative anatomy and the 'fossil zoology' which he had virtually invented. Cuvier's teleological functionalism, stressing the designed unity of the organism to play a particular survival role, was different from both Hunter's systemic particularism and Green's universalism. Owen also encountered the implied transformationism of Geoffroy Saint-Hilaire and the outright materialism of Lamarck's *Philosophical Zoology*, a copy of which he bought, read, and annotated. None of these different views as to the nature of 'Nature' was totally unknown to him, but to hear them argued out, in private and at public meetings of the Institut de France, was a novel experience.

Back in London, the zoological gardens were proving to be not the only source of Owen's anatomical subjects; the Hunterian Museum received specimens from travellers and members of the College of Surgeons serving in colonial outposts around the world. It was from one of them, George Bennett (subsequently a lifelong friend of Owen), that it received a rare specimen of the pearly nautilus whose shell, outwardly similar to the fossil ammonites commonly found in the Mesozoic marine deposits, was an important desideratum for every shell collector but whose living form had not previously been described. Another singular specimen was the popularly named duck-billed platypus (*Ornithorhynchus anatinus*), rare specimens of which the college had received since its first sighting in 1799. First described by Everard Home, it generated a continuing dispute as to its classificatory status in the face of reports that, despite mammalian characteristics, it laid eggs. Owen's ingenious observations on the museum's specimens supported observations of both Blainville and Meckel that, whether egg-laying or not, this strange animal possessed lactating mammae and thus was assuredly mammalian. The publication of the nautilus memoir early in 1832 and Green's presentation to the Royal Society of Owen's paper describing the mammary glands of the platypus shortly thereafter (*PTRS*, 1832, 517–38) mark the end of a strenuous five-year training period from which he emerged a professional comparative anatomist and a promising member of the scientific community.

Despite the critical success of these accomplishments, Owen's future seemed as bleak as ever. Posts for a comparative anatomist were extremely rare, and never more than a minor adjunct to a more lucrative medical practice. With the tentativeness of his position and the precariousness of financial support, it was impossible for Owen and Caroline Clift to marry, nor did there seem any hope for anything in the future. A year after the excitement of the Paris visit, he was under great stress: Cuvier was dead; the nautilus monograph was not yet in print; he was very busy with his non-curatorial activities beyond the requirements of his appointment; some members of the council were openly critical of his increasing involvement with the Zoological Society; and there was an increasing feeling of frustration at the financial obstacles to his marriage. 'The strongest mind', he wrote to Caroline after a quarrel as to their future, 'after being on the stretch for hours, loses its tone, and is readily rendered irritable and unable to turn and avert the leading steps to misunderstanding' (Owen to Clift, 11 May 1832, Hirtzell Collection, fo1. 16). None of his subsequent successes could or would cancel the difficulties and anxieties of this period when it seemed both his career and his domestic life hung in the balance.

The 'English Cuvier' Although in 1832 Owen's career remained uncertain, the five years as junior curatorial assistant at the Hunterian provided the foundation for his future career. The particular investigations he initiated and pursued during that period each opened an expanding area of research for which he was not loath to claim proprietary rights. Although primarily a vertebrate specialist, his opportunistic anatomy of the nautilus led him to the invertebrate *Cephalopoda*, in the description and classification of which he became the recognized expert. Similarly, his initial papers on monotreme and marsupial generation were the beginning of a lifetime's work on the physiology and palaeontology of those primarily Australian orders. The first of his memoirs for the Zoological Society on the orang-utan was the start of a series on the higher apes that demonstrated ever more particularly their close physical affinities with the human species.

Apart from the grounding in both the process and substance of a broadly defined physiology that his experience provided, Owen learned to be a professional. An incessant reader with an unusually retentive memory, he drew on the well-stocked college library for the published tradition; if his citations are to be believed, he was also familiar with a greater part of the extant literature. Moreover, the Hunterian Museum was internationally renowned for its collections; no naturalist would come to London without paying a visit to the museum, whose collections and conservator were more available and helpful than those at the British Museum. From these professionals, as from the active colleagues with whom he worked at the Zoological Society's museum, he acquired the trappings of professionalism; from Clift, who had grown up with the collection, who knew everyone, and who could gossip about them all, he learned something of the institution of science and the politics of its professional practitioners. In short, during the five years Owen was immersed in and became an active member of a still small community whose members were engaged in the construction of a discipline still in the process of definition.

For Owen the most important member of that community was William Buckland who, with Cuvier dead, would become his guide and his patron. When Owen first knew him, probably in 1832, Buckland was at the peak of his career with both a scientific and political influence far beyond that of his Oxford professorship. Buckland was a geologist and not an anatomist but he followed Cuvier's functionalist model in reshaping the fossil fragments into the living forms of the past worlds for which each had been designed. No one could better bring to life the inhabitants of past creations. As the closing event of the highly successful meeting of the newly established British Association for the Advancement of Science in Oxford in 1832 Buckland gave an animated, lengthy public lecture in which, through metaphors that even the least scientific of his large and mixed audience could understand, he breathed life into the giant *Megatherium* from South America which even in Cuvier's hands had been little more than a marvellous pile of bones. Owen was in the audience and he returned to London excited by the possibilities of the Cuvierian creation of a 'fossil zoology' through the use of comparative anatomy. He immediately sent Buckland proofs of the yet unpublished nautilus memoir for comment. The subsequent correspondence established a close professional and personal friendship from which Owen received counsel, support, and political patronage. Although often referred to as the English Cuvier, Owen was more properly a Buckland disciple who would continue to operate within a Bucklandian ideological framework long after Buckland's descent into the dark world of madness in 1850 and his death six years later.

Professional advancement, 1832–1855 Just when Owen's career prospects seemed bleakest, his future was assured by the death, in September 1832, of William Home Clift in a street accident. Although he was to stay on for another decade as conservator, William Clift never recovered fully from the loss of his son, both at the personal and institutional level. Thus Owen became *de facto* co-conservator of the Hunterian Museum just at the time that the college was making plans for its major restructuring and expansion. It was a project in which Owen inevitably became involved and from which emerged his interests in the establishment of a national museum of natural history.

During the next decade through his own continuing stream of publications at a time during which an avocational natural history was becoming professionalized in Britain as natural science, Owen transformed himself (under Buckland's patronage) from temporary assistant at the Hunterian to the foremost natural scientist of his generation. He was elected a fellow of the Royal Society in 1834. His career successes were reflected in the resolution of the most pressing of his domestic problems: on his thirty-first birthday in 1835, after a long and frustrating wait for both of them, he and Caroline Clift were married.

Owen was wedded as well to his work. What he produced during this initial decade of his professional career constitutes an amazing corpus of a wide range of anatomical and palaeontological publications, most of which were first presented before the Zoological Society, the Royal Society, the Geological Society, the Linnean Society, and the British Association for the Advancement of Science—in all of which he played an increasingly important role. Chief among his anatomical works in addition to the continuing production of the Hunterian catalogues were: those on the marsupials and monotremes of Australia, culminating in his survey of both for Todd's *Cyclopedia of Anatomy* in 1847; his formal description and classification of the *Trichina*, first noticed by James Paget when a student at Bart's; a survey of the *Cephalopoda* in 1836 begun with the nautilus monograph; his grand analysis and comparative survey of dentition, the initial parts of which were published in 1840; and his continuing work on the comparative anatomy of the Primates, which demonstrated the validity on anatomical grounds of the inclusion of the human species within the order and, specially, the close affinity between that species and the higher apes. In all, the more than 150 separate publications in this decade—abstracts, memoirs, monographs, articles, books, and reports—reflect an immense amount of investigative work concurrent with fulfilling regular curatorial duties.

In 1836 Owen was appointed Hunterian professor of comparative anatomy and physiology at the Royal College of Surgeons. One of his first tasks after the inauguration of the renovated and expanded museum in 1837 was to deliver the first of what was to be an annual series of twenty-four lectures. At the same time, he became an active member of the specialist societies on whose councils he served as well as the president of the newly established Microscopical Society, which he helped to found.

However, the climax of this decade of intensive activity was his two-part report on the British fossil Reptilia requested and funded by the British Association and presented in 1839 and 1841. It was the kind of work at which he was adept. As a by-product of the rapid development of the work of structural geologists and amateur collectors, a wide variety of fossil remains of large and primarily extinct reptiles were scattered unclassified among the various public and private natural history collections in Britain. It was Owen's task, brilliantly accomplished, to examine as many collections as were available, describe the fossils, and arrange them in some anatomically based classification. The result served as the basic reference for the rest of the century. In the second part of the report he defined a coherent category of large terrestrial reptiles to which he gave the ordinal name Dinosauria, and it is on this that much of his popular reputation rests. At this time too, in good Cuvierian fashion and on the basis of a single fragment of a fossilized bone, he predicted the presence of an extinct but varied terrestrial avian fauna in New Zealand, a prediction that was fully realized by subsequent discoveries. Early in 1842, only a decade after his first major publication, Owen succeeded Clift as resident conservator of the Hunterian. In the same year, through Buckland's influence, he also received a civil-list pension of £200 per annum. Thirty-eight years old, he had become Professor Owen, a major figure in the London scientific establishment. With his election three years later to membership in The Club, an exclusive literary society, he extended his relationships to the wider intellectual community. He had become a member of the intellectual élite, an active member of a new aristocracy of merit.

Later, at the height of his career, in response to a request for biographical information, Owen merely listed his major works, his professional affiliations and his honours, and concluded disingenuously:

> The peaceful career of this indefatigable cultivator of Natural Knowledge has been a continued series of labours for the promotion of scientific truth and its practical application to the well-being of mankind; & the titles of his Publications form the best illustrations of his life.

No period of his career better illustrates the evasiveness of this autobiographical fragment than his varied activities of the mid-1840s to mid-1850s, during which he extended his territory from the zoo-anatomical analyses of the living to fragmented evidences of those from a bygone past; from the position of laboratory scientist to that of theorist; and from the position of scientist to that of government consultant and spokesman for natural science to the public at large.

Although still the comparative anatomist, the focus of Owen's science was shifting from zoology to palaeontology. As with his earlier encounter with Cuvier, his discovery of the fossil past, first with Buckland and then through the analysis of Darwin's South American collections, was something of an epiphany that opened a whole new area of creative effort. More and more he was asked to report on the increasing flow of fossils from Australia, New Zealand, and South Africa—sent to the Hunterian for his description and explication. He had become a palaeontologist whose seemingly magical success in recreating the long-extinct vertebrates depended upon collaborative data from both the anatomy of the living and the fragmentary fossil evidences of the past. His publications during the 1840s comprise an almost bewildering collection of important contributions to both palaeontology and comparative anatomy, from that of the Mylodon (and the subsequent classification of the whole of the extinct and living Edentata) to a review of British fossil mammals and birds to match that of the reptiles; descriptions of the anatomy of the living monotremes and marsupials of Australia and their extinct forebears; and dissections of chimpanzee, orang-utan, and, finally, the recently available gorilla. Averaging some ten descriptive articles a year, he wandered through the extended research territory which he had cleared and not infrequently claimed as his own. In addition there were lengthier monographs and the annual lecture series for the college which, under his revision of the charter of the lectureship, became an open-ended textbook on the changing state of contemporary natural science.

Owen's most important works of the period were the longer essays *On the Archetype and Homologies of the Vertebrate Skeleton* (1848) and *On the Nature of Limbs* (1849). Coming after almost twenty years of an intense familiarity with both the extreme diversity of the organic world as well as what seemed the patterns which underlay it, he realized the need, as others had before him, to understand and to describe the forces that not only held the system together but also directed its changes through time. The rapidly increasing fund of detailed information from geology, palaeontology, biography, and anatomy was shifting the focus from detailed studies of the Cuvierian sort to the processual questions of diversity and to that 'mystery of mysteries', the origin of species. Other than the occasional biblicist on the periphery, all geologists accepted a long period of strata building in the history of the earth; and virtually all natural scientists rejected the ideas of a continuous particularized creative process to explain the novelties that palaeontology was constantly producing. By the mid-1840s most were willing to consider the possibility that, except for the origin of the human species—considered to be the special concern of a creating deity—the whole of the natural universe owed its structure to a creative plan rather than a continuing process of *ad hoc* creative intrusions. In response, there was a re-emergence of Geoffroyan holism, of German Romanticism, and Lamarckian transformationism. As the foremost palaeontologist and comparative anatomist of his generation, Owen felt the need to enter the field. As with much of his work, his response, the concept of the archetype, was an eclectic one to which he added his own positive mark.

Owen's development of archetypes Owen's invention of the admittedly idealist archetype was based empirically on his valuable clarification of the commonly used but vaguely defined term, analogy, to describe cross-species comparisons. Analogy, important in Cuvierian teleology, was to be restricted to similarities of use or function, such as the wings of a fly and those of a bird; Owen's verbal invention, 'homology', was to note similarities of structure or form, such as the wings of a bird and the forelimbs of a horse. Analogical similarities reflected *ad hoc* adaptations to changing conditions and needs, functional in the Cuvierian sense; homological similarities, on the other hand, had their origins in an idealized simple form which gave rise to more particularized 'descendent' forms through a variety of 'secondary laws' or processes according to changing functional demands, but always in a progressive direction described graphically by a natural classificatory system with the human species at its apex. Owen's explication of the archetype, its origins, and its generative power was never very clear. It was, however, a fail-safe position, as yet inexplicable and perhaps unknowable, but both the idealization and heuristic reification of a 'primary cause' (and the presumably divinely inspired creative design that activated it). Owen, and some of his advocates, thought he had solved the problem of both diversity and progress; his critics knew, however, that he had only verbalized it. There were those who, like Owen himself, saw in the controlled process of change from an inchoate beginning through continuing progress by means of a variety of secondary causes (of which adaptive selection was one) an anticipation of Darwin's theory of the origin of species through natural selection. Superficially the two touch each other here and there, but the essential idealism of the archetype model, theological in spirit and in fact, mark it as distinct from and in opposition to the materialism of Darwin's more restricted view. Owen's attempt to resolve the problem of diversity, change, and progress through the construction of the ideal archetype as universal ancestor with some invested 'power' demonstrates, both in its eclecticism and in its philosophical confusion, his limitations as a philosopher or grand theorist.

The utility of the homology–analogy distinction and the divinely inspired progressionism of his archetype confirmed for an admiring constituency Owen's professional eminence. That, however, did not sit well with his employers at the college, who were concerned that the servant was becoming the master—something of a possibility when Owen sought, though unsuccessfully, to become a member of its council. From the beginning of his appointment as curator in 1842, a continuing series of frustrating controls was imposed on his activities by the council, not least of which was its refusal to sanction a broadening role and increased independence for the museum. Increasingly Owen found his position becoming too restrictive. He wanted out. He was virtually certain in 1851 that he would be appointed head of the important mineral and geology department at the British Museum, but he was passed over; he toyed with the idea of succeeding to the chair of natural history at the University of Edinburgh but the conditions were too restrictive; and he talked of accepting an invitation to the United States with its enthusiastic and welcoming audiences for visiting British lecturers. He was, however, too deeply rooted in London to move and, despite difficulties with his employers, the museum served as an important base for the continuation of his research. As a sign of royal favour for his accomplishments, in 1852 he was awarded lifetime occupation of Sheen Lodge in Richmond Park where he lived as something of a country gentleman, enjoying the garden he cultivated. Finally, in 1856, at the urging of influential friends, Owen was appointed superintendent of the natural history departments of the British Museum, a position newly created for him (but with duties poorly defined).

During the years leading up to this appointment—those of his greatest reputation—Owen's difficulties were not only institutional. Increasingly both he and his science were coming under attack from a younger group of professional natural scientists, building their careers upon different conceptual foundations. They drew their inspiration from German developmental anatomy and the new morphology that was replacing the increasingly outmoded French tradition, so important a part of Owen's practice. T. H. *Huxley, who was to become Owen's most vocal opponent and the leader of this new generation, was quick to pick up on the personal and ideological conflicts on his return in 1851 from his own exploratory voyage to the south Pacific. 'Owen is both feared and hated', he wrote in an unusually perceptive comment:

> It is astonishing with what an intense feeling of hatred [he] is regarded by the majority of his contemporaries … The truth is, he is the superior of most, and does not conceal that he knows it, and it must be confessed that he does some very ill-natured tricks now and then … Owen is an able man, but to my mind not so great as he thinks himself. (L. Huxley, *Life and Letters of Thomas Huxley*, 1900, 1.93–4)

There were bitter conflicts over matters of fact and priority and Owen damaged his own reputation by what were considered ill-natured attacks on Gideon Mantell and the perceived unfairness of his anonymous review of Lyell's anti-progressionism. Huxley's open criticisms of Owen's science and his barely veiled attacks on his professional character in a series of trenchant papers opened a rift between the two men which was to last for the rest of their lives.

British Museum and opposition to Darwin, 1856–1881 Owen's career as a natural scientist reached its climax at the end of the 1850s. His move to the British Museum provided him with a recognized position of eminence within the scientific community and a platform for the diffusion of his views both to a lay and professional audience. Relieved from the frustrations of the college's control of his outside activities, as well as curatorial responsibilities for which he was not temperamentally fitted, he was free to construct his own programme. He accepted a long-postponed three-year appointment as Fullerian professor of physiology at the Royal Institution and, at the same time, initiated a palaeontological lecture series at the School of Mines. For the next decade he was also a popular lecturer to provincial audiences eager to learn the latest truths from the foremost expert in natural science. With his diagrams and his drawings hung on the wall behind him, he was equally eager to satisfy their demands, to earn the fees they offered, and to educate the public in the particular value of science in the search for the ultimate truth which underlay and would explain the whole of organized nature.

In 1858 both Owen's scientific merits and the political role he had come to play in the scientific institution were recognized by his election to the presidency of the British Association. The following year he was invited to give the first of the renewed Reade lectures at Cambridge. Taking advantage of the opportunity, he laid out his new classification of the mammals, the first since that of Cuvier, in which he used neural distinctions in conjunction with the traditional classificatory criteria to provide a more natural classification of the class. Through such a classification he sought to demonstrate that the presumed distinction of human mind possessed a physical correlate in the brain that justified a distinct subclass of which the human species would be the only occupant. In general his new classification was respectfully received even by his opponents, although the elevation of human singularity provided the springboard for the violent attacks against his anatomy a year later.

Owen had become a statesman of science, one whose demonstrated excellence recommended him as a consultant to government as it became increasingly obvious that the complexity of problems within the control of government required the knowledge and competence that specialist scientists alone could provide. It was a relationship which he was willing to exploit in his effort to seek a greater—and separate—role for the natural history department of the British Museum.

These years of Owen's success were a period of significant changes in both concept and method for the analysis and understanding of the increasingly complex problems raised by the rapidly accumulating data from the natural world. A process of continuing change was replacing the stasis of designed creation as an essential assumption in the construction of a natural philosophy. The new physiology from Germany was redirecting, if not indeed replacing, the functional comparative anatomy of the French. The vast expansion of knowledge of the living world as well as that of the repopulation of eons past by palaeontology raised questions that traditional views seemed unable to answer. Ideas of the essential unity of organic nature and, in one form or another, transformationism threatened the accepted view of what was at its basis the fixity of the Cuvierian world. Owen was caught in the middle. Not unsympathetic to the new physiology and having himself created a limited transformationist model in his vertebrate archetype, he considered himself still a Cuvierian for whom the species itself was an unchanging reality. His inability, during the critical decade of the 1850s, to accommodate fully to the changes that were occurring and the controversies to which they led dislodged him from the position of leadership and prestige which he had finally attained.

The most serious confrontation arising from Owen's position—and that which unfairly later defined his place in history—was that initiated with the publication of Darwin's *Origin of Species*. The hastily arranged reading in mid-1858 of the brief reports of Darwin and A. R. Wallace on the importance of natural selection as the means by which new species arise alerted Owen to the serious threat posed to his ideological position. As shocking as the doctrine itself was the fact that so important a solution to what was essentially a zoological problem was the product of neither a professional anatomist nor a zoologist but of two naturalists with limited training or experience as either. His irritation is clear in his intemperate review, in the *Edinburgh Review* (111, 1860, 487–532), of the more detailed *Origin* a few months after its publication, in which unfairly—almost insultingly—he questioned Darwin's professional competence to discuss the species question. Darwin might have been the field naturalist *extraordinaire*, but for Owen both the definition of the problem of organic diversity and the search for its solution lay in the laboratory, his laboratory in particular. There precise anatomical dissections could (and could alone) provide the lines of division between species, the only real units of classification. A career in the laboratory, 'going from bone to bone', had not prepared him for the shift to the living population as the unit of species definition and change upon which Darwin had based his theory. In preparing his review Owen was blinded by Darwin's humility in the discussion of species through which he concluded that like the other increasingly inclusive classificatory units the species too was the product of the classifier rather than of nature.

Ignoring most of the remainder of Darwin's carefully arranged argument, Owen attacked the heresy of species indeterminance with a bitterness that many thought was the result of personal pique at being upstaged. The use of his own works in the same review as the basis for his attack merely supported such a view. Beyond the personal, however, was Owen's inability to abandon the concept of fixed species; to do so would have meant the crumbling of the whole essentially static system of organic creation to the demonstration of which he had devoted so much of his scientific activity and thought. 'That classification is the task of science, but species the work of nature', with which he concluded his long review, is a statement of his scientific faith that was impossible for him to abandon.

As important and disagreeable as the materialism of the theory itself were its implications for the equally important 'man question', the nature of the species and the place it occupied in a nature from whose workings divine concern had been excluded. Owen was caught between two positions: attempting to find a middle way between the proofs, many of which he had himself provided, of the physical affinities between the human species and the rest of the primates on the one hand, and its divinely inspired nature on the other, he was attacked by both the biblicists for the one and the scientists for the other. Huxley publicly attacked Owen's attempted anatomical demonstration of the physical locus for uniqueness of the human brain. Owen's subsequent maintenance of that position in the face of repeated proofs of his error merely emphasized his fallibility as an anatomist. Huxley's attacks on Owen's science and ideology (as well as Owen's own behaviour in continuing to defend the indefensible) alienated a new generation with whom he had little in common socially or scientifically. Not all were so open in their dislike as one distinguished scholar who even a decade after Owen's death was still sufficiently bitter to write that 'Owen was a [damned] liar. He lied for God and for malice. A bad case' (E. Clodd, *Memories*, 1926). Nevertheless, many other young scientists felt much the same. Moreover, Owen's friends, colleagues, and sympathizers of his own generation were dying, their work, like his, challenged and superseded by their successors.

Owen recognized his estrangement from the new biology and its leaders. For the rest of his life, with only an occasional return to anatomy, he restricted his scientific work to the continuing description and classification of the accumulated and accumulating fossil material from England and the colonies. He had become irrelevant to the new biology. In these later years, he was honoured more by the medical establishment than by the scientific.

With the publication of his *Palaeontology* in 1860 and his three-volume *Anatomy of the Vertebrates* (1866–8), however, Owen began to bring his separate works together to serve as visible and useful monuments of his career. *Anatomy* was followed by compilations of his long-continued series of works on the extinct mammals of Australia (1877–8), on the extinct avian fauna of New Zealand (1879), and on British fossil reptiles (1884). He saw these not only nor so much as monuments to his own industry but also as sometimes faltering steps in the progress of science from which his successors might learn.

The Natural History Museum Owen's retreat into palaeontology was made easier by his continuing efforts, initially against the almost unanimous opposition of his scientific colleagues, to establish a separate and independent natural history museum. Although he had long considered the need for such an institution it was only in 1859, after he had become familiar with the unsatisfied needs of natural science within the structure of the British Museum, that he formally proposed a plan for a new museum to be erected in South Kensington. Although initially blocked by partisan political rivalries, his plan was approved and work begun in the early 1870s. The museum's official opening in 1881 was Owen's last, and most important, contribution to natural science. It was the realization of a vision that he had pursued for almost the whole of his career. Brock's welcoming statue, now, after some controversy, standing on the landing of the great staircase facing the entrance of Waterhouse's impressive neo-Gothic structure, is symbolic of the public role he sought for professional science.

With all the collections finally transferred from the cramped Bloomsbury quarters to their new galleries in South Kensington, and with a knighthood conferred on 5 January 1884, Owen retired to Sheen Lodge but still continued his work of a lifetime in the new museum. Embittered by the incomprehensible suicide of his only son in 1886, he grew old among his grandchildren, none of whom was to understand or appreciate his accomplishments. He died on 18 December 1892 at Sheen Lodge. On 23 December his body, followed by a small but distinguished delegation representing both science and the public, was carried to the cemetery in Ham churchyard where he was buried alongside Caroline, who had died in 1873.

Lasting impressions History has served Owen poorly. Although his death was recorded in the popular press it caused little excitement. It was Darwinian theory which framed natural science, and he had been its most serious opponent. 'Owen must have been a wonderful manipulator & anatomist as well as acute observer; but I think', commented a contemporary at his death, 'his life shows that it is brain which tells in the long run. It is not the no. or weight of a man's papers but the point in them by which he is ultimately estimated' (J. W. Gregory to C. D. Sherborn, 3 March 1893, BL, Add. MS 42580, fols. 69–70). Further, the manner of his opposition—the most public of the controversies which punctuated his career—has obscured his role as the most important and most influential natural scientist of his generation. Even in a period when controversy was an acceptable part of intellectual discourse he handled it poorly. Too often he considered a personal attack and invested too much of his ego in the demonstration of error. Whether in a letter to the public press, an anonymous review, or personal encounter, his response went too often beyond the limits of gentlemanly behaviour and was considered to be hurtful rather than helpful.

Owen's accomplishments, however, were many and important, his role only recently being reassessed in a fuller understanding of the history of natural science. It was indeed by standing on his shoulders that his successors were able to see further. As significant as any of his more particular contributions which the extensive record of publications describes was his ability to bring order out of the accumulating chaos of the collectors' cabinets and the conflicting methodologies used to account for them. His annual series of Hunterian lectures at the College of Surgeons, his review of the whole of comparative anatomy, his compilations of his works in palaeontology and, in particular, the initial ordering of the fossil reptiles and mammals of Britain, the virtual creation of a comparative vertebrate osteology and odontology, and his design for the Natural History Museum—all laid the groundwork for others who, as intended in the assumption of a progressing science, would alter their shape and challenge their substance.

An essential aspect of Owen's personality was the sense of himself as a performer and as such he was never unaware of his audience, whether on the lecture platform, amid controversy, or in the many carefully composed and written letters he sent to family, friends, and colleagues. From his early years he had a deep and continuing interest in music and the theatre: he had an acceptable baritone voice and enjoyed harmony singing; he played well both the flute and the cello, either or both of which he would carry along with him when visiting friends whom he could join in an informal concert; and when in London he attended concerts and plays and was in awe of the talents exhibited by professionals in both, some of whom became friends. Except for music, however, his tastes in the theatre and in popular literature, which he read almost compulsively, were commonplace. Nevertheless, he was also a great teller of stories, recalling and sometimes embellishing anecdotes of his own history in which he would take on the characters of the participants.

Physically Owen was an imposing figure. Six feet tall, his thinness made him seem taller. Handsome in his younger years, he seemed to grow more gaunt as he aged, but until his last years he never lost the romantic flair of his public presence. William Flower, who knew him well, noted specially his 'massive head, lofty forehead, curiously round, prominent and expressive eyes, high cheek bones, large mouth and projecting chin, long, lank, dark hair, and during the greater part of his life, smooth-shaven face and very florid complexion' (Plarr). His eyes were particularly remarkable in their intensity, a character which Holman Hunt caught in his portrait of 1881.

Late in life, after the appearance of the characteristic *Vanity Fair* caricature, Owen scribbled a brief note on a scrap of paper:

> *Vanity Fair* says that I am a 'bit of a dandy;' Mr. W. K. Parker calls me a 'parlour anatomist' and 'Lotus Eater'. … How difficult it is to know oneself & how much one ought to be obliged to those who are so kind as to help us to that hardest of all knowledge. (private information)

It is just such a difficulty in defining who he was that makes it difficult to understand some of the contradictions in his own behaviour. He kept his own counsel and, as he wrote to his fiancée early in his courtship, 'I have from early life been thrown among strangers and have had greater control over my actions than is usual' (Owen to Caroline Clift, 3 May 1832, Temple University, Hirtzell Collection, fol. 15). In his work he was essentially a 'loner', acrimoniously protective of his interests and the proprietary rights to the research territory he laid out for himself but genial in the company of others where there could be no threat to that which he possessed.

Late in life Owen doubted even what he had earlier gratefully accepted as his single-minded divinely granted dedication as a 'cultivator of Natural Knowledge [through] a continued series of labours for the promotion of scientific truth and its practical application to the welfare of mankind'. Having only recently retired from the museum, and with his own research winding down, he wrote to an old student and faithful friend who had become a very successful ophthalmologist, wondering which of them had chosen the better career path:

> We can both look back, now to much life-work in our respective walks; but yours must have left many grateful memories of direct reliefs, of gifts, indeed, of the most precious of our bodily senses. My labours, when successful, bear but remotely on the needs of our fellow mortals. (Owen to W. W. Cooper, 12 Dec 1884, London, Wellcome L., Owen MS 64)

Notwithstanding doubts he may have had about his own choice of career, Owen welcomed the many honours he attracted throughout his life, from the Geological Society's Wollaston medal in 1838 for his work on Darwin's fossils to the first of the Linnean medals, jointly with Joseph Hooker, of the Linnean Society in 1888 for the corpus of his work through his career of more than half a century. Among the most satisfying were both the royal and Copley medals of the Royal Society in 1846 and 1851; membership in the Légion d'honneur in 1855 and the Prix Cuvier of the Institut de France in 1856; the Baly medal of the Royal College of Physicians in 1869, and the new honorary medal of the Royal College of Surgeons in 1883; honorary degrees from the universities of Edinburgh (1847), Oxford (1852), and Cambridge (1859); and from Queen Victoria, creation as commander of the Bath in 1873 and knight commander of the Bath in 1884.

Jacob W. Gruber

Sources N. A. Rupke, *Richard Owen: Victorian naturalist* (1994) [incl. full bibliography] · R. Owen, *The life of Richard Owen*, 2 vols. (1894) [incl. full bibliography of Owen's pubns] · J. W. Gruber and J. C. Thackray, *Owen Centenary* (1992) · R. Owen, *The Hunterian lectures in comparative anatomy, May–June, 1837*, ed. P. R. Sloan (1992) · *DNB* · A. Desmond, *The politics of evolution: morphology, medicine and reform in radical London* (1989) · Temple University, Philadelphia, Hirtzell Collection, fols. 15, 16 · L. Wilson, 'The gorilla and the question of human origins: the brain controversy', *Journal of the History of Medicine and Allied Sciences*, 51 (1996), 184–207 · V. G. Plarr, *Plarr's Lives of the fellows of the Royal College of Surgeons of England*, rev. D'A. Power, 2 vols. (1930) · private information (2004)

Archives American Philosophical Society, Philadelphia, corresp. and papers · BL, Add. MSS 33348, 34406–34407, 39954–39955, 42579–42582, 49978 · CUL, corresp. · GS Lond., corresp. and papers · Linn. Soc., corresp. and papers · NHM, corresp. and papers · NL Scot., corresp. · RCS Eng., corresp. and papers · RCS Eng., family corresp. · Shrewsbury School, annotated copy of *Origin of species* · Temple University, Philadelphia, corresp. and papers · U. St Andr. L., corresp. · Wellcome L., letters | BL, corresp. with Benjamin Dockray, Add. MS 33348 · BL, corresp. with W. E. Gladstone, Add. MSS 44397–44501, *passim* · BL, corresp. with Sir Robert Peel, Add. MSS 40518–40600, *passim* · Bodl. Oxf., corresp. with Sir Henry Acland · CUL, letters to Sir George Stokes · GS Lond., letters to Roderick Murchison · Maison d'Auguste Comte, Paris, letters to Henri Ducrotay de Blainville · NA Scot., corresp. with Sir Charles Murray · NHM, letters to Albert Gunther and R. W. T. Gunther · NL NZ, letters to Gideon Algernon Mantell · NL Scot., corresp. with Blackwoods · NL Wales, letters to Sir Henry De la Beche · NL Wales, letters to Sir George Cornewall Lewis · NRA, priv. coll., letters to Sir Norman Moore · Oxf. U. Mus. NH, letters to John Phillips [copies] · RBG Kew, letters to Sir William Hooker · RS, letters to William Buckland · RS, corresp. with Sir John Herschel · Trinity Cam., letters to William Whewell · UCL, corresp. with Sir Edwin Chadwick · Wellcome L., letters to Henry Lee

Likenesses H. W. Pickersgill, oils, *c*.1845, NPG · W. Brockedon, black and red chalk drawing, 1847, NPG · W. Brockedon, chalk drawing, 1847, NPG · H. W. Pickersgill, oils, *c*.1852, St Bartholomew's Hospital, London · W. Walker, mezzotint, 1852 (after H. W. Pickersgill), BM, NPG · Maull & Polyblank, photograph, *c*.1855, NPG · C. Hopley, pastel drawing, exh. RA 1869, RCS Eng. · E. Griset, caricature, pen and watercolour drawing, *c*.1873 (with Mr. Bryce-Wright), V&A · W. H. Thornycroft, plaster bust, 1880, RCS Eng. · W. H. Hunt, oils, 1881, NHM [*see illus.*] · R. Lehmann, drawing, 1890, BM · T. Brock, bronze statue, *c*.1895, BM · A. Gilbert, bronze bust, 1895, RCS Eng. · Barraud, photograph, NPG; repro. in *Men and Women of the Day* (1888) · E. Edwards, carte-de-visite, NPG · E. Edwards, photograph, NPG; repro. in L. Reeve, ed., *Portraits of* *men of eminence*, 1 (1863) • Elliott & Fry, carte-de-visite, NPG • attrib. W. Etty, watercolour drawing (after Pickersgill), RCS Eng. • W. H. Gilbert, oils (as an old man), Lancaster Museum and Art Gallery • Lock & Whitfield, woodburytype photograph, NPG; repro. in T. Cooper, *Men of mark: a gallery of contemporary portraits* (1878) • T. H. Maguire, lithograph, BM; repro. in T. H. Maguire, *Portraits of honorary members of the Ipswich Museum* (1852) • Mason & Co., carte-de-visite, NPG • H. J. Thaddeus, mezzotint (aged eighty-five), BM, NPG • H. J. Thaddeus, oils (as an old man), Lancaster Town Hall • J. & C. Watkins, carte-de-visite, NPG • chromolithograph caricature, NPG; repro. in *VF* (1 March 1873) • engravings (after photographs), BM, NPG • oils, Lancaster Museum and Art Gallery • stone bust, Lancaster Museum and Art Gallery

Wealth at death £33,201 9*s*. 4*d*.: probate, 26 Jan 1893, *CGPLA Eng. & Wales*

Owen, Robert (1771–1858), socialist and philanthropist, was born on 14 May 1771 at Newtown, Montgomeryshire, the son of Robert Owen (1741–1804), a saddler and ironmonger as well as the local postmaster, and his wife, Anne Williams (*c*.1735–1803), a farmer's daughter. He was the youngest, but one, of seven children, and his childhood seems to have been a happy one. Intellectually precocious, he devoured a book per day, including novels, histories, and travel books, and became the schoolmaster's assistant. As a producer of pious sermons, he was known as 'the little parson' (*Selected Works*, 4.54). At the age of ten, however, as he later claimed in his somewhat teleological autobiography, *The Life of Robert Owen*, he underwent a religious crisis, concluding that 'there must be something fundamentally wrong in all religions, as they had been taught up to that period' (*Selected Works*, 4.54). Religious scepticism was to become a dominant theme in his later life.

Anxious to leave home, Owen was permitted in 1781 to become apprenticed to James McGuffog, a cloth merchant in Stamford, Lincolnshire, who specialized in well-to-do ladies' wear. Having learned much about fabric and the trade, in 1784 Owen joined a London retailer, working twelve hours daily for £25 p.a., and then moved to a similar position at £40 p.a. under John Satterfield in Manchester. Here Owen soon became curious about the new machinery being applied to cotton spinning. Borrowing £100 from his brother William, he entered into a partnership with a machine-maker named Jones constructing 'mules' for making thread, and soon the firm of Jones and Owen had forty employees. When he was bought out in 1789–90, his old master, McGuffog, offered him half the profits in his shop. Owen chose instead in April 1792—not in 1790, as the *Life* states (*Life*, 1.32)—to manage a mill with 500 employees owned by Peter Drinkwater, who had first applied the Boulton and Watt engine to cotton spinning in Manchester. Despite his inexperience, Owen applied himself rigorously, spending six weeks studying the factory, and proposing many refinements to the manufacturing process. Soon the quality of his thread was renowned.

New Lanark It was at this time that Owen, who as yet had few political opinions to speak of (though he signed a loyalist address with other Manchester manufacturers in 1795, during the war with France), became concerned

Robert Owen (1771–1858), by Frederick Cruikshank, 1839

with the moral and physical condition of his workforce. He began to apply the principle which was to dominate most of his life, the environmentalist dogma that character was derived from 'circumstances' rather than created by the will. This did not at this stage inhibit his success as it was later to do. He accepted a partnership with Drinkwater's sons, but then characteristically renounced it, without complaint, in order to allow Drinkwater's son-in-law, the manufacturer Samuel Oldknow, greater control in the firm. He joined the Manchester Literary and Philosophical Society on 1 November 1793, and here met philanthropically inclined physicians like Samuel Bardsley. Here, too, he read at least two papers, now lost: 'On the origin of opinions with a view to the improvement of the social virtues' and 'Thoughts on the connection between universal happiness and practical mechanics'. Shy and sensitive among strangers, speaking a kind of Welsh English, Owen here began to acquire social grace.

On a business visit to Glasgow, Owen met Ann Caroline Dale (1779–1831), the daughter of a prominent cotton spinner, David Dale (1739–1806), who had started as a Paisley weaver, and in 1785 with Richard Arkwright had built a mill at New Lanark south of Glasgow. Owen first visited the site on 15 June 1798, and was impressed both with its delightful location and with Dale's pioneering efforts to improve his labourers' working and living conditions. He married Caroline Dale on 30 September 1799 at Dale's palatial house on Charlotte Street, Glasgow. In the same year Owen acquired the New Lanark mills with several partners for £60,000, and he moved there on 1 January 1800 to take the post of manager of the New Lanark Twist Company, with a ninth share in the profits. When Dale died in 1806, Owen formed a new partnership (another would follow in 1810, following resistance to his experiments) which returned him about 40 per cent of the profits, averaging 12½ per cent p.a. Eventually he was to share in approximately £300,000 from the mill. He had tremendous drive and energy, was adept at handling both his partners and business associates, and was scrupulously honest in his dealings. Skilled as both manager and entrepreneur, he typified the early self-made capitalists of the era.

Owen evidently set out to make New Lanark an experiment in philanthropic management from the outset. He was not yet a 'socialist' (the term was not coined until the mid-1820s) and advocated neither profit-sharing nor the elimination of 'competition' at the mills. Instead, he sought to reduce both vice and punishment while improving living and working conditions, expecting in return an increase in output from the workforce.

Philanthropic management Despite initial resistance from his workers and continuing suspicion from his partners, especially from the pious Quaker philanthropist William Allen, Owen was remarkably successful in all these areas. Some 1800 people were employed at the mill, including about 500 pauper children sent by various parishes. Their working day was reduced by Owen in 1816 from eleven and three-quarter hours to ten and three-quarter hours. Shoddy and expensive goods in the company store were replaced with better ones at wholesale prices. Owen aimed to reduce living costs still further with plans (never realized) to introduce communal cooking and eating arrangements. His efforts at infant education—of which he is rightly regarded as among the founders—culminated in the opening of the Institute for the Formation of Character in 1816, where dancing, singing, and other lessons were taught. At the institute Owen, who taught military tactics himself, sought in particular to exclude punishment from education, to make learning interesting to young minds, and to encourage children to believe their own happiness to be dependent on that of others. In the workplace he installed 'silent monitors'—multi-coloured blocks of wood which rotated above each labourer's workplace; the different coloured sides reflected the achievements of each worker, from black denoting poor performance to white denoting excellence. Employees with illegitimate children were fined. Pilfering and absenteeism were reduced. One-sixtieth of wages was set aside for sickness, injury, and old age. In the village surrounding the factory, groups of houses were organized as 'neighbourhood divisions', of which heads of households annually chose a 'principal'. These elected twelve 'jurors' to sit monthly for one year, hearing and judging cases respecting the internal order of the community.

All resistance to these schemes was finally broken when, in 1806, Owen continued to pay full wages during an American cotton embargo. By 1816 New Lanark, often termed 'the happy valley', was renowned throughout Europe, and was deluged with visitors (over 20,000 between 1815 and 1825) curious to see how Owen had combined high profits with philanthropy. Owen, however, could not rest satisfied, and moreover met increasing resistance from his partners. In 1813, avoiding a hostile take-over effort on their part, Owen secretly raised enough capital to outbid his partners at a public auction of New Lanark. Now he formed a new partnership composed of the Baptist physician and philanthropist Joseph Fox, a former fishmonger and future lord mayor of London, Michael Gibbs, William Allen, two other Quakers, Joseph Foster and John Walker, and the philosopher Jeremy Bentham, for whom it was a rare profitable venture. Owen found Allen's objections to his own views on religion irksome, as they clearly had a bearing on the educational ideas he first presented in *A New View of Society, or, Essays on the Principle of the Formation of the Human Character* (1813–14). Here, in what remains his best-known work, Owen demanded a system of national education to prevent idleness, poverty, and crime among the 'lower orders' (*Selected Works*, vol. 1), and recommended restricting 'gin shops and pot houses', the state lottery and gambling, as well as penal reform, ending the monopolistic position of the Church of England, and collecting statistics on the value and demand for labour throughout the country. Owen denied proposing 'that the British government should now give direct employment to all its working population'. Instead, education should lead the poor 'to find employment sufficient to support themselves, except in cases of great sudden depression in the demand for, and consequent depreciation in the value of, labour' (*Selected Works*, 1.97). To ensure the primacy of private enterprise, public labour on roads, docks, and shipbuilding would be paid less than the average local wage. There was nothing socialistic in these proposals, and it is hardly the case, as Leslie Stephen erroneously assumed (*DNB*), that Owen's 'essential views' were encapsulated here.

Instead Owen attracted widespread support from philanthropists and even, despite his growing reputation for anti-clericalism, from church officials. His ideas might have been swallowed up in the plethora of poor-law reform proposals of the immediate post-war period. But Owen possessed the supreme confidence of the self-made man. Animated by opposition, especially when his early efforts to pass a factory reform bill faltered, his views became more extreme. Between 1813 and 1818 Owen made about fifty visits to the philosophical anarchist and religious sceptic William Godwin, whose *Enquiry Concerning Political Justice* (1793) had caused a great stir during the revolutionary debates a generation earlier, and who shared Owen's environmentalist faith in the principles of 'necessity'.

Solving national poverty From 1814 Owen had a relatively free hand to pursue his ideals at New Lanark. But his eye was already on the growing problem of national poverty. In 1816 Owen announced that 'the chief object' of his existence would be to make 'universal' the results of his experiments with the character of the labouring classes. Crucially, he now also insisted that the new manufacturing process be 'gradually diminished', and that Britain aim for greater self-sufficiency in food (*Selected Works*,

1.126). In *Observations on the Effects of the Manufacturing System* (1815) he identified for the first time: 'immediate pecuniary gain, to which on the great scale every other [principle] is made to give way' as the 'governing principle of trade, manufactures, and commerce'. 'Buying cheap and selling dear', and the 'spirit of competition', which had made Owen rich, were now vilified as the moral cause of the excesses of industrialization. The factory system, moreover, bred 'a new character in its inhabitants … formed upon a principle quite unfavourable to individual or general happiness' (*Selected Works*, 1.112–13). Machinery should be introduced 'only in aid of, and not in competition with, human labour', in order to reduce the hours of work required to secure a decent living (ibid., 1.154). But technical innovation, as Owen later stressed, was possible 'in every department', so that each community might have 'a full supply of the best machinery' (Owen, *The Revolution in the Mind and Practice of the Human Race*, 1849, 45). (This contradicts David Ricardo's charge that Owen opposed all machinery, which was obviously calculated to bracket him with the Luddites.)

The experiment at New Lanark was to be the germ from which would spring model industrial townships to combat both the growing immorality fostered by industry as well as the more immediately pressing issues of unemployment and hunger. Moreover, Owen was persuaded increasingly that labour, rather than capital, essentially created wealth. In these communities, therefore, economic justice could also be attained. Moreover, not only the poor, but 'every class in society' who wished to join would soon be able to escape 'intemperance, disease, and suffering' (*Selected Works*, 1.219). These 'villages of union' of 500 to 1500 people united by 'mutual and combined interest' would be situated in the countryside, but would have some machinery of their own (shown steaming away in the background in early illustrations). Thus they could be largely self-sufficient. Ideally, he thought, communities should be constructed in the form of a large quadrangle, with public buildings in the centre. Persons of a particular political or religious persuasion might want to associate with others of their kind, and Owen designed a table showing 140 combinations of such views. Each community could start with as little as £60,000, which the government would, he hoped, provide, though if private capital were necessary a 5 per cent return was thought likely.

Owen as socialist The year 1817 was the turning point in the conversion of Owen the philanthropic 'prince of the cotton-spinners' to Owen the socialist. Much of his time was now spent in London attempting, with the assistance of the elder Sir Robert Peel, himself a cotton lord, to get a bill regulating the employment of children approved by a select committee of parliament. This sought to prohibit employment before the age of ten; to reduce hours of labour to ten and a half per day (in 1818, he proposed ten hours); and to require a minimal education to begin work. These regulations he wished to apply to all manufactories. Owen met the committee five times, first embarking on a tour of the factory districts with his eldest son. Conditions were worse than he had feared. As many as a quarter of the children he saw suffered from work-related injuries or deformities, which were well documented by some of the physicians Owen had first met at the Manchester Literary and Philosophical Society. His first substantial economic tract, *Observations on the Cotton Trade and on the Late Duties on the Importation of Cotton Wool* (1803), had argued against new duties on raw cotton imports passed by parliament, holding that these would undermine Britain's advantage over growing foreign competition. But Owen, outraged, now declared, 'perish the cotton trade, perish even the political superiority of our country (if it depend on the cotton trade), rather than they shall be upheld by the sacrifice of everything valuable in life by those who are the means of supporting them' (*Selected Works*, 1.105–6). Most of Owen's fellow manufacturers disagreed strenuously with any restriction beyond the twelve hours per day limit for workhouse apprentices established by Peel's 1802 act. When another parliamentary select committee met to consider poor law reform, it refused to his deep disappointment even to take his evidence. Increasingly frustrated, Owen suspected that the clergy were at the root of opposition to his plan.

During the summer of 1817 Owen bombarded the newspapers with letters about his proposals, and bought thousands of copies when they printed his appeals, spending some £4000 in two months and on one occasion delaying the departure of the London mail coaches by twenty minutes. His ideas about how to solve the problem of poverty had clearly shifted quite dramatically. In July he discussed 'the principle of united labour and expenditure' as applied to a 'community of mutual and combined interests', which by implication included a community of goods. Still, he claimed that communities might produce only 'to the amount of their own immediate wants; and constituted as they will be, they can have no motives to produce an unnecessary surplus'. In the long run, however, when the 'true interests' of society were clarified, they would be permitted 'gradually to supersede the others' (*Selected Works*, 1.160–65).

Owen's determination to publicize these conclusions to the entire nation reached a peak in two remarkable public meetings in 1817. On 14 August he addressed an audience of many hundreds at the City of London tavern. Prominent members of the clergy and government were present, as well as political economists and many of the leaders of London plebeian radicalism. The radicals attended chiefly to assail what they saw as a paternalistic plot to 'turn the country into a workhouse' or 'pauper barracks' and 'rear up a community of slaves' (in the words of Robert Wedderburn, himself the son of a slave; *Black Dwarf*, 20 Aug 1817, 469). Owen's plans omitted any demand for parliamentary reform and reduced taxation. Rumours abounded that the government was manipulating him in order to deflect working-class attention from political reform, and that Owen himself actually wished, as W. T. Sherwin had suggested in the spring, to deprive the working classes of their political rights. At the 14 August meeting, the radical leader Henry Hunt thus moved to amend Owen's proposals so as to portray excessive taxation as the root of pauperism. The whig political economists present also desired to see Owen defeated, since he was increasingly reputed to oppose both free trade and machinery. (Ricardo was later to state that he was 'completely at war with Mr. Owen'; *Wooler's British Gazette*, 19 Dec 1819, 412.) Their representative, Major Robert Torrens (1780–1864), thus complained at length that Malthus's population doctrines had long since invalidated all but the harshest regimes of poor relief. At the second meeting, on 21 August, Owen insisted against his radical critics that lowering taxes would only add those who lived from public spending to the ranks of the unemployed. Instead, he sought to persuade them that increasing mechanization was a far more fundamental source of distress. Most astonishingly, however, Owen for a few minutes then rounded on all teachers of religion as having made man 'a weak, imbecile animal; a furious bigot and fanatic; or a miserable hypocrite' (*Selected Works*, 1.207). His audience, Owen later recalled, was 'thunderstruck' (ibid., vol. 4, 216). A few clergymen hissed. But 'the loudest cheers' then erupted in praise of what *The Observer* politely described as Owen's condemnation of the 'vices of existing religious establishments' (*The Observer*, 24 Aug 1817, 4). None the less this support was insufficient to win over his audience, and Owen's proposals were dismissed as impracticable at the end of the meeting 'by a great majority' present, on a vote introduced by the London radical Robert Waithman.

The value of labour In 1817 Owen began to speak the language of the millennium, and to cast himself in the role of a prophet both of a secular apocalypse, 'the crisis', and, in his mind's eye, of the 'new moral world' or 'millennial world' which would succeed it, where laws, commerce, religion, war, and self-interest would disappear. He had already suggested in 1813, but now began loudly to proclaim, closely following Paul's letter to the Corinthians, that charity was the core of all religion, and the highest good any individual could attain. Owen's object, thus, was no longer solely 'the relief of the poor', but now, far more importantly, 'the emancipation of mankind'. Unfortunately his reputation in respectable circles was greatly damaged by the events of August 1817. Clerics aimed broadsides at him, and in a new edition of Malthus's *Essay on Population*, first published in 1798, he became a key target, supplanting Godwin and Condorcet.

Yet Owen still continued to court the famous and influential. Stopping at the post-war congress of the great powers at Aix-la-Chapelle in 1818, he distributed a pamphlet written for the occasion to many European leaders (failing, however, to press one into the hands of the tsar, who had no pocket large enough for the bulky octavo, and dismissed Owen so gruffly that he did not try again). At dinner, he sat next to Metternich's associate Friedrich Gentz, who complained, in response to Owen's remonstrances, that 'we do not want the mass to become wealthy and independent of us. How could we govern them if they were?' (*Selected Works*, 4.238). Much of the period 1818–20 he spent in London, chiefly at the house of John Walker at 49 Bedford Square, meeting, among others, his principal patron, the duke of Kent, father of the future Queen Victoria, who chaired meetings in 1819 of a newly formed society to further his plans, but then died suddenly in 1820.

At the invitation of a group of Lanarkshire notables, Owen in 1820 also composed one of his most important works, the *Report to the County of Lanark* (1821). Partly in reaction to a great commercial crisis in 1819, this suggested that in order to avoid fluctuations in the money supply as well as the payment of unjust wages, labour notes representing hours of work might become a superior form of exchange medium. Here Owen first proclaimed at length his belief that labour was the foundation of all value, a principle of immense importance to later socialist thought. The *Report* also offered a novel account of the relationship between money and the expansion and contraction of the market. Previously Owen had argued that mechanization at a time of reduced demand depressed wages in many industries. Now, denying the market's ability to find a natural equilibrium, Owen stressed the under-consumptionist aspects of productive capacity, and the failure to find 'a market, or means of exchange, co-extensive with the means of production'. The use of gold and silver created 'a mere artificial standard' of value which 'retarded the general improvement of society' because it was too dependent on the value and supply of metals. Hence after the gold standard had been reintroduced amid fierce debate in 1819, the resulting deflation and depression had 'plunged the country into poverty, discontent, and danger'. The *Report* also first explicitly stated Owen's intention of beginning upon 'the principle of united labour, expenditure, and property, and equal privileges' (*Selected Works*, 1.289–90, 305). For this reason, in particular, it is sometimes regarded as marking the origins of modern socialism. Owen explicitly condemned the 'principle of individual interest', or the idea:

> that man can provide better for himself, and more advantageously for the public, when left to his own individual exertions, opposed to and in competition with his fellows, than when aided by any social arrangement which shall unite his interests individually and generally with society.

The existing divisions within society, he asserted, were 'the most anti-social, impolitic, and irrational, that can be devised'. Against Adam Smith, Owen particularly insisted that further specialization within production would only harm the working classes. Private interests were 'placed perpetually at variance with the public good; and in every nation men are purposely trained from infancy to suppose that their well-being is incompatible with the progress and prosperity of other nations'. The new system, however, would combine 'extensive mental and manual powers in the individuals of the working classes [and] a complete identity of private and public interest' (*Selected Works*, 1.308–9).

In May 1822 Owen formed the British and Foreign Philanthropic Society to raise funds for a community, but soon discovered that many of its illustrious members (who included MPs, generals, and bankers) had more limited aims in mind. He journeyed to Ireland in 1822–3 to examine conditions there, speaking for three hours in Dublin to a large meeting which included the lord mayor and several nobles. At this time, his emphasis was somewhat more upon the agricultural basis of communities (as elsewhere pastoral imagery occasionally loomed large in Owenism).

New Harmony In the second half of the 1820s Owen's energies focused on the prospect of building a community in America. In 1825 he purchased from a Pietist German émigré sect, the Rappites, a ready-built township set on 20,000 acres at New Harmony in southern Indiana. Unfortunately the establishment soon became an enormous drain on his resources. In a short time Owen spent about £40,000, or four-fifths of his New Lanark fortune (his interest in the mills was finally sold in 1828), in a fruitless effort to organize the disparate group of 800 radicals, freethinkers, backwoodsmen, and scientists who had no desire to be 'governed' like mill hands. In early 1825 he addressed the president, senate, and supreme court at the house of representatives in Washington, DC.

New Harmony was briefly the most vibrant and sophisticated cultural outpost on the American frontier. But centrifugal tendencies tore at the community from the beginning, and by late 1827 the experiment was in the final stages of dissolution, with its half-dozen projected imitators elsewhere following close behind. In 1828 the opportunity arose of securing a very substantial land grant from the Mexican government to settle the Texan frontier with the United States. Owen first paused at Cincinnati for an eight-day public debate about religion to an audience of a thousand. Then he sailed to Vera Cruz via Jamaica, but failed ultimately to secure a grant of land.

On his return to Britain, Owen found that a consumer co-operative society indebted to his ideas had been started in Edinburgh by an inspired tanner named Abram Combe (1785–1827), who had also begun plans for a community modelled on Owen's ideals, at Orbiston, south of Glasgow. By 1830, moreover, some 300 co-operative societies had sprung up across the country. Owen found his ideas developed by economists like William Thompson (1775–1833) and John Gray (1799–1883). Cast once again into relative obscurity when he began to lecture in London in 1830, Owen found that his secularism was the main appeal to his small audiences. In 1830–32 he continued to oppose radical political reform, as insufficient to meet the economic evils of society. By 1832–3, however, he had emerged as the leader of several 'labour exchanges', notably at Gray's Inn Road, London, and at Birmingham, where artisans could exchange goods directly without the intercession of middlemen. The culmination of his efforts in the early 1830s came with the formation of the first attempt to create a general union of all trades, the Grand National Consolidated Trades Union, which Owen helped to lead in 1833–4, with the chief aim of achieving the eight-hour working day.

The Rational Society With the collapse of the union, however, ended Owen's always reluctant involvement with large-scale working-class organizations. In 1835, beginning what is usually termed the 'sectarian' phase of the Owenite movement, he formed the Association of All Classes of All Nations, later renamed the Universal Community Society of Rational Religionists, or Rational Society for short. As a propaganda machine the association was remarkably effective: by 1839, the *Westminster Review* observed, Owen's antipathy to competition was seemingly 'the actual creed of a great portion of the working classes' (see *New Moral World*, 20 April 1839, 404). By 1840 the Rational Society boasted over 60 branches of self-styled 'socialists' concentrated in the manufacturing districts, with perhaps 50,000 flocking to weekly lectures, among them the young German merchant Friedrich Engels, who first was instructed in the tenets of socialist political economy by the Manchester lecturer John Watts. The society's regular paper, the *New Moral World*, ran for nearly eleven years (1834–45), and achieved a circulation of about 40,000 weekly at its peak (*c.*1839–1841). In this period Owen composed his most extensive work, *The Book of the New Moral World* (7 pts, 1836–44). Intellectual stature was lent to the movement by writers like Charles Bray and John Minter Morgan. The prime minister, Lord Melbourne, even presented Owen to the queen in 1839.

Queenwood As 'Rational Social Father' of his new organization, which was intended to bear some resemblance to a dissenting sect despite his earlier dismissal of the idea, Owen retained virtually complete control over its activities until late 1844. Of the considerable sums raised by the branches, much—at least £22,000 in 1839–40 alone—went towards constructing local 'halls of science' where members attended lectures and held soirées. In the meantime, however, the Rational Society had acquired land in Hampshire, erected buildings, and in late 1839 commenced a new community called Queenwood on a 533-acre site designed for 700 members. Owen's own vision of its creation as a symbol of his ideas also became steadily more grandiose and impractical. Much of the money collected for the community was spent on constructing, in 1842, an impressively large building with lavish fittings. Especially noteworthy was a model kitchen with a conveyor to carry food and dishes to and from the dining room which, its architect exulted, rivalled the amenities of any London hotel. This would have been a great achievement had Owen been a hotelier. Owen's defence was that the community was intended to be the standard for a superior socialist future where all would enjoy privileges the wealthy monopolized at present, nay even more, for all apartments were eventually to have central heating and cooling, hot and cold water, and artificial light. Its main building thus ought to be superior to any palace. By 1844, after over £40,000 had been spent, Queenwood bankrupted the society.

Final years Organized Owenism now ground to a halt. The branches broke up, with some emigrating *en masse* to the United States. Owen himself returned to America several times over the next few years. Although he failed in 1845 to address the senate again, he bombarded the government with addresses. In 1846 he helped (having met many of the principal negotiators in Mexico nearly twenty years earlier) to ease tensions between Britain and the USA over a border dispute in Oregon, crossing the Atlantic four times in fewer than six months in the effort. In 1848 Owen spent four months in revolutionary France to popularize his views, placarding the walls of Paris with broadsheets. The last decade of his life was dominated by his conversion to spiritualism in 1853. He died at the Bear's Head Hotel in Newtown on 17 November 1858, and was buried with his parents, next to, appropriately, the abandoned church of St Mary's, Newtown.

Robert Owen was survived by three sons: Robert Dale *Owen (1801–1877), David Dale Owen (1807–1860), a prominent geologist, and Richard Owen (1810–1890), also a geologist. His other children were William Dale Owen (1802–1842), who became a merchant and bank director; Anne Caroline Owen (1805–1830), who remained in Scotland and never married; Jane Dale Owen (1805–1890), who married a civil engineer, Robert Fauntleroy, and settled at New Harmony; and Mary Owen (1810–1832).

Physically, Owen was of athletic build, of middling height, with brown hair, later white and, in the later 1850s, accompanied by a full white beard (a specimen cutting of which is preserved in the Goldsmiths' Library, University of London). His boyish looks were preserved long in life. A benevolent demeanour, with kindly eyes and compelling smile, were often recorded by contemporaries.

The reputation of Robert Owen Though he was recognized as one of the greatest philanthropists of his day, Robert Owen was marginalized after the decline of Queenwood. Communitarian socialism was disregarded during the prosperous years from 1850 to 1875, and, overshadowed by the revolutionary Marxian socialism of the 1880s and later, never again became a serious alternative socialist vision. None the less Owen's reputation revived considerably between 1880 and 1900. Leading Marxists like William Morris and H. M. Hyndman (who referred to Owen in many of his works) acknowledged his seminal role in founding British socialism (for example, Hyndman, *The Evolution of Revolution*, 1920, 270), and praised him as the 'noble and unselfish' producer of 'some of the most luminous thoughts on political economy ever met on paper' (Hyndman, *The Historical Basis of Socialism in England*, 1883, 198, 85) and the originator of labour laws. This influence was also acknowledged by ideological enemies like W. H. Mallock (for example, *The Limits of Pure Democracy*, 1918, 207–10). Practically, Owen's impact was most substantial upon the theory of the growing co-operative movement. Following J. S. Mill's conversion to co-operation in the *Principles of Political Economy* (3rd edn, 1852), many Liberals acknowledged Owen's role in their foundation; Henry Fawcett, for instance, both doubted that the failure of Queenwood had greatly undermined the popularity of Owen's principles, and noted that many subsequent co-operatives had been managed by former Owenites (Fawcett, *Essays and Lectures on Political and Social Subjects*, 1872, 11–12). Despite their distaste for his secularism, Christian socialists also took up some of his views of the poor.

Owen's biographers all underestimated the importance and vitality of the Owenite movement of 1836–45, which was first examined at length in J. F. C. Harrison's *Robert Owen and the Owenites* (1969). The claim is occasionally still heard that Owen was principally a 'scientific manager', but this view requires treating Owen's experiments at the New Lanark mills (now largely reconstructed) in isolation from his later life. More persuasively, it was argued already in Owen's lifetime (first by William Hazlitt, in *Political Essays*, 1816, 97–104) that Owen was a man of 'one idea', New Lanark, and his role in it. But the idea that character was formed by the environment and not the will—perhaps the core assumption of the Enlightenment—was in fact a fundamental one for modern thought, and was developed by Owen in many ways, though contemporaries found its endless repetition tedious. Owen's complete works comprise at least 160 titles, many of which are brief addresses. He also edited and contributed to many periodicals (a relatively complete bibliography is given in J. F. C. Harrison's *Robert Owen* (1969)).

Gregory Claeys

Sources R. Owen, *The life of Robert Owen written by himself*, 2 vols. (1857–8) • G. Claeys, *Citizens and saints: politics and antipolitics in early British socialism* (1989) • G. Claeys, *Machinery, money and the millennium: from moral economy to socialism, 1815–60* (1987) • *Selected works of Robert Owen*, ed. G. Claeys, 4 vols. (1993) • J. F. C. Harrison, *Robert Owen and the Owenites in Britain and America: the quest for the new moral world* (1969) • F. Podmore, *Robert Owen: a biography*, 2 vols. (1906) • L. Jones, *Life, times and labours of Robert Owen* (1889) • W. L. Sargant, *Robert Owen and his philosophy* (1860) • A. J. Booth, *Robert Owen: the founder of socialism in England* (1869) • G. D. H. Cole, *The life of Robert Owen*, 3rd edn (1965) • R. H. Harvey, *Robert Owen: social idealist*, ed. J. W. Caughey (1949) • d. cert. • S. Goto, *Robert Owen, 1771–1858: a new bibliographical study*, 2 vols. (1932–4) • N. Thompson, *The people's science: the popular political economy of exploitation and crisis, 1816–34* (1984) • B. Taylor, *Eve and the new Jerusalem: socialism and feminism in the nineteenth century* (1983) • C. Kolmerton, *Women in Utopia: the ideology of gender in the American Owenite communities* (1990) • E. Royle, *Victorian infidels: the origins of the British secularist movement, 1791–1866* (1974) • E. Royle, *Radicals, secularists and republicans: popular freethought in Britain, 1866–1915* (1980) • J. F. C. Harrison, *The second coming: popular millenarianism, 1780–1850* (1979) • W. H. Oliver, *Prophets and millennialists: the uses of biblical prophecy in England from the 1790s to the 1840s* (1978) • A. E. Bestor, *Backwoods Utopias: the sectarian and Owenite phases of communitarian socialism in America, 1663–1829* (1950) • G. Lockwood, *The New Harmony movement* (1920) • A. Taylor, *Visions of harmony: a study in nineteenth-century millenarianism* (1987) • J. Butt, ed., *Robert Owen, prince of cotton spinners: a symposium* (1971) • S. Pollard and J. Salt, eds., *Robert Owen, prophet of the poor: essays in honour of the two hundredth anniversary of his birth* (1971) • C. Tsuzuki, ed., *Robert Owen and the world of co-operation* (1992) • G. Claeys, ed., *The pamphlets of Owenite socialism*, 11 vols. [forthcoming], vols. 10–11 • I. Donnachie, *Robert Owen: Owen of New Lanark and New Harmony* (2000)

Archives Co-operative Union, Holyoake House, Manchester, corresp. and papers • Internationaal Instituut voor Sociale Geschiedenis, Amsterdam, corresp. and papers, incl. minutes of international societies • LUL, corresp. and MS of report to county of Lanark • NL Wales, corresp. • Nuffield Oxf., papers • Robert Owen Memorial Museum, Newtown, Montgomeryshire, corresp. and papers • U. Glas., Archives and Business Records Centre, diary · Workingman's Institute, New Harmony, Indiana, corresp. | BL, letters to Thomas Allsop, Add. MS 46344 · Burgerbibliothek, Bern, letters to Philipp von Fellenburg · UCL, letters to Lord Brougham

Likenesses W. H. Brooke, oils, 1834, NPG · F. Cruikshank, watercolour, 1839, Man. City Gall. [*see illus.*] · W. H. Brooke, oils, NMG Wales · A. Hervieu, watercolour, NPG · M. A. Knight, watercolour, Scot. NPG · J. Leverotti, bronze medallion (after life-mask), NPG · E. Morley, watercolour, NPG · SB, chalk drawing, NPG · watercolour, Fabian Society, London

Owen, Robert (1820–1902), theologian and antiquary, born at Dolgellau, Merioneth, on 13 May 1820, was the third son of David Owen, surgeon, and Ann, youngest daughter of Hugh Evans of Fronfelen and Esgairgeiliog, near Machynlleth. Educated at Ruthin grammar school, he matriculated from Jesus College, Oxford, on 22 November 1838, graduating BA in 1842 with a third class in classical finals, and proceeding MA in 1845 and BD in 1852. He was fellow of his college from 1845 until 1864, and public examiner in law and modern history in 1859–60.

Although he was ordained by Christopher Bethell, bishop of Bangor, in 1843, and served a curacy until 1845 at Tremeirchion, Owen held no preferment. Coming under the influence of the Tractarians, he maintained an occasional correspondence with Newman, even after the latter seceded to Rome. In 1847 he edited, for the Anglo-Catholic Library, John Johnson's work *The Unbloody Sacrifice*, first published in 1714. He came to believe that establishment and endowment were destructive of the catholic character of the Church of England, and gave his support to Welsh disestablishment.

Owen has a claim to be considered the most erudite of the nineteenth-century fellows of his college. His principal theological works were *An Introduction to the Study of Dogmatic Theology* (1858), which displays his patristic learning, and *Institutes of Canon Law* (1884), written at the instance of Walter Kerr Hamilton, bishop of Salisbury. His *Sanctorale Catholicum, or, Book of Saints* (1880) is notable for its record of Welsh saints, and was the first such work to include 'just men' of the Anglican church. *The Kymry: their Origin, History and International Relations* draws on a lifelong study of Welsh philology and ecclesiastical history, while his *Pilgrimage to Rome* (1883) is a curious annotated record in verse of a long vacation *voyage littéraire*.

In 1864, owing to an allegation of immorality, Owen was obliged to resign his fellowship, and shortly afterwards retired to Vron-y-graig, Barmouth, where he owned a small estate. There he died unmarried on 6 April 1902, and was buried at Llanaber.

D. L. THOMAS, *rev.* G. MARTIN MURPHY

Sources *DWB* · *The Times* (10 April 1902) · J. W. Browne, *Father and son* (1898), 60 · *CGPLA Eng. & Wales* (1902)

Wealth at death £11,525 16*s.* 1*d.*: probate, 20 June 1902, *CGPLA Eng. & Wales*

Owen, (Paul) Robert (1920–1990), engineer, was born on 24 January 1920 in Dalston, London, the elder son (there were no daughters) of Joseph Owen, estate manager, and his wife, Deborah Grossmith. His secondary education was at the Central Foundation School (1933–8), a grammar school in the City of London. He then entered Queen Mary College, London University, to read engineering, specializing in aeronautics. On the outbreak of war in 1939 the college was evacuated to Cambridge. He graduated there in 1940 with first-class honours and won the Allen Low prize for the best student in engineering.

Owen started work at the aircraft firm Boulton Paul in Norwich, but his potential for research soon became evident and in 1941 he joined the aerodynamics department of the Royal Aircraft Establishment (RAE), Farnborough. The work there was varied and challenging, ranging from problems of immediate urgency for the RAF to matters of great importance for future aircraft designs. It was evident that high speeds, extending into supersonic flight, would in due course become a reality, calling for new experimental and theoretical research tools. Owen's progress with such problems was remarkable. He quickly matured from his initial junior status to become a creative leader, and his promotion was rapid. Topics he successfully addressed included the development of low-drag wings and bodies, the stability and control of high-speed aircraft, the aerodynamic problems of guided weapons, and supersonic flight. When the war ended in 1945 he expanded his interests to include other applications of fluid mechanics.

In 1953 Owen accepted an invitation to become reader and director of the Manchester University fluid motion laboratory, and three years later he was appointed professor and head of the newly formed mechanics of fluids department. In spite of his heavy administrative load, he became interested in meteorology and was also involved with local industrial problems—for example, cotton spinning, ventilation, and the dangers of coal dust in mines. He became a member of the Safety in Mines Research Advisory Board in 1956. This led him to investigate the transport of dust particles by air flows, including saltation (the lifting of particles from a surface and their subsequent trajectories). This became a major activity, with important applications to soil erosion and desertification. In 1958 he married Margaret Ann, a law graduate of Oxford, daughter of Herbert Baron, solicitor. They had two sons and two daughters, in whom he took great pride and pleasure.

In 1963 Owen moved to the Zaharoff chair of aviation at Imperial College, London. He there extended his interests even further, to the aerodynamics of buildings, heat exchangers, blood flow, and respiration. In 1966 a physiological flows unit was founded in his department. Meanwhile, however, he was an active member of the Aeronautical Research Council and in 1971 was appointed its chairman, a position he retained for a record eight years. Since this was a time of major new developments in aeronautics, the work of the council was of first importance and he took great pride in it.

In 1984 Owen retired early, but he continued teaching and vigorously pursued his research, particularly in saltation. He developed fruitful contacts with workers elsewhere with similar interests, particularly in the Middle East, Africa, the USA, Denmark, and France, and he contributed key papers to international symposia. In 1985 he developed heart trouble and had a bypass operation. Nevertheless, he soon resumed his research, travelling and lecturing extensively, and seemed to recover well.

Owen was passionately interested in music, drama, and the arts. His good looks and musical voice made him a natural choice in his youth for leading parts in the RAE dramatic society productions. He wrote and spoke with grace, wit, and a wry, kindly, self-deprecating humour. His sympathies were with the underprivileged and he constantly sought to apply himself to the problems of the developing world. He was accorded various honours, including election as FRS in 1971, appointment as CBE in 1974, and election as FEng in 1976.

In 1988 Owen fell ill again with what was thought to be a viral infection. He continued writing and collaborating with his international colleagues, but recovery eluded him. He died of cancer in St Mary's Hospital, London, on 11 November 1990. ALEC YOUNG, *rev.*

Sources A. D. Young and J. Lighthill, *Memoirs FRS*, 38 (1992), 269–85 · *The Independent* (21 Nov 1990) · personal knowledge (1996) · *CGPLA Eng. & Wales* (1991)

Likenesses photograph, repro. in Young and Lighthill, *Memoirs FRS*, 269

Wealth at death £170,782: probate, 30 Jan 1991, *CGPLA Eng. & Wales*

Owen, Robert Dale (1801–1877), social reformer and emancipationist, was born at Glasgow on 7 November 1801, eldest son of Robert *Owen (1771–1858), entrepreneur and social reformer, and his wife, Ann Caroline (1779–1831), daughter of David Dale, a successful Glasgow merchant and philanthropist who in 1785 built the cotton-spinning community of New Lanark. It was acquired by an English partnership and managed from 1800 by Owen's father, who subsequently used it to test his social and economic ideas. Although Owen became a prominent American citizen and spent most of his life there he also followed in his father's footsteps, making an important contribution to social and educational reform in both Britain and the United States. His earliest memories were of his grandfather's funeral (1806) and being led round New Lanark mills by his father, who explained to him the importance of order, thrift, and sobriety among the workers. Like the rest of the family he was initially educated privately, being taught French by an officer prisoner of war billeted in nearby Lanark. In his early teens he had a serious illness, but after recovery accompanied his father on a tour of factories gathering evidence for a parliamentary select committee on the employment of children (1816).

Owen's father was by that time rich and successful, able to afford the lifestyle of a Scottish laird and pursue an expensive propaganda campaign designed to advance the ideas he had articulated in *A New View of Society* (1813–16). Owen was seen by his father as his successor in his plans to reform society, and was educated accordingly. In 1818, having learned German, Owen and his brother William went to Switzerland to a school at Hofwyl, near Bern, run by Phillip Emanuel von Fellenberg. Fellenberg's educational theories had been partly influenced by Pestalozzi,

Robert Dale Owen (1801–1877), by Bobbett & Edmonds (after S. Wallin)

whose ideas were becoming known in Britain. Indeed Owen's father modified them for use in the school at New Lanark. The curriculum in Fellenberg's school aimed to inculcate philanthropic and humanitarian values in its élite students and at the same time expose them to the agricultural labour those attending a parallel school for the poor were expected to undertake. As with Pestalozzi, environmental and social awareness figured prominently in the curriculum. Owen and his brother responded positively, looked upon Fellenberg as a father figure, and corresponded with him for years after.

On his return to Scotland in 1821 Owen found his father prospering in business, but as a radical reformer having lost much ground. Owen then became a teacher in the schools and institute at New Lanark, publishing in 1824 a detailed account of the facilities and curricula, emphasizing the work of the pioneering infant school (called the 'baby school' by American visitors) and the teaching of subjects such as history, geography, environmental studies, music, and dancing. While his father was in the United States during 1824–5, Owen deputized as manager of the mills. During 1825 he went to the Netherlands, where he pursued his interest in social reform by visiting Frederiksoord, Veenhuizen, and other agricultural communities for the poor resembling those proposed by his father in 1817.

In 1825 Owen left for New Harmony, Indiana, a village his father had purchased after temporarily abandoning his community experiments in Britain. Owen accompanied his father on a propaganda tour of the eastern United States before sailing down the Ohio from Pittsburgh to

Mount Vernon on a keel-boat nicknamed the Boatload of Knowledge. Its passengers included the scientists William Maclure, Thomas Say, and Charles Alexandre Lesueur, the teachers Marie Fretageot and William Phiquepal d'Arusmont, and other notables going to join the community in Indiana. Owen's diary records his experiences on the journey, noting (in German) an increasing scepticism about his father's views. On arriving at New Harmony he became one of the élite group which drew up a series of constitutions, rules, and regulations for the community, but within a short time it was in disarray. While the equality his father wanted was gradually abandoned Owen, physically unfit for the manual work for which he had volunteered, threw himself into teaching, and from September 1826 edited the *New Harmony Gazette*. The periodical soon reflected his thought on social reform issues.

When the community collapsed Owen had to decide what to do next. Rejecting his father as mentor, he went his own way. He became a trustee of Nashoba, a farming community Frances Wright, the reformer, had started near Memphis, Tennessee, to educate and emancipate slaves. He joined her in May 1827, but when she became ill accompanied her in June that year to Europe. After visiting France he returned to Scotland, hoping to marry his childhood sweetheart, a spinner at New Lanark, but later claimed that his mother prevented him doing so. During this visit he renewed his acquaintance with Jeremy Bentham, one of his father's partners, and met William Godwin, who had greatly influenced his father's thinking, Henry Leigh Hunt, and Godwin's daughter, Mary Shelley, whom he found attractive physically and intellectually.

Back in the United States, Owen continued his editing at New Harmony and co-operated with Frances Wright and others promoting liberal views on religion, divorce law, popular education, and greater equality of wealth. He moved to New York in June 1829, where for several years, periodically assisted by Wright, he edited the *Free Enquirer*, successor to the *New Harmony Gazette*. In New York he became one of the leaders of the movement for public education, which achieved some success during 1829–30. The *Free Enquirer* campaigned vigorously on behalf of the Working Men's Party, which was active on educational issues. Any thought that he might marry Frances Wright was dashed when in 1831 she revealed a liaison with Phiquepal d'Arusmont. Owen then married Mary Jane Robinson, daughter of a supporter of the Working Men's Party, on 12 April 1832. Accompanied by his bride Owen returned to Britain to assist his father in his propaganda, and from November helped edit *Crisis*, the organ of Owenism. The movement rejected political action in favour of social reform. Owen felt this was out of step with the mood of the times and, becoming even more disillusioned with his father's approach, returned to New Harmony in April 1833 after only six months as joint editor. His younger brothers, David and Richard, had also emigrated to the United States and became successful geologists.

Owen played an active part in maintaining and developing New Harmony's reputation as a centre of educational and social reform. He pursued these aims as a democratic member of the Indiana legislature (1836–8) and as a member of the United States Congress (1843–7). In 1844 he helped solve the Oregon boundary dispute with Britain and in 1845 saw through the bill that set up the Smithsonian Institution. He subsequently had a distinguished role in its design and development as a centre of research and education. His diplomatic career began in 1853 when President Franklin Pierce appointed him chargé d'affaires in Naples, making him minister in 1855. Possibly this was to remove him, for Pierce, a prominent pro-slaver, must have been aware that Owen was an emancipationist. While in Italy, Owen came to Britain on several occasions to visit his then ailing father. He was present at his death and funeral at Newtown, Montgomeryshire, in 1858.

On his return to the United States, Owen became an active emancipationist, publishing a pamphlet, *The Policy of Emancipation* (1863), which greatly influenced Lincoln, and a more detailed study, *The Wrong of Slavery* (1864). However, his views did not extend to immediate suffrage as he thought former slaves should not be given the vote until a decade had elapsed. He held liberal views on divorce law, on which he published pamphlets, he wrote about birth control (to which his father often alluded, though never directly), and from his stay in Italy was interested in spiritualism (to which his father had also been attracted). He published a series of autobiographical essays covering his early life in a book, *Threading my Way* (1874). His first wife died in 1871 and he married secondly Lottie Walton Kellogg on 23 June 1876. Following a period of mental derangement Owen died at his summer home on Lake George, New York, on 24 June 1877. Although Owen's major contributions to social reform (overshadowed to some degree by his notoriety as an exponent of liberal divorce laws and birth control) occurred in the United States, his description of the schools at New Lanark earned him a reputation as an educational pioneer in Britain. IAN DONNACHIE

Sources I. Donnachie and G. Hewitt, *Historic New Lanark: the Dale and Owen industrial community since 1785* (1993) • I. Donnachie, *Robert Owen: Owen of New Lanark and New Harmony* (2000) • *To Holland and to New Harmony: Robert Dale Owen's travel journal, 1825–1826*, ed. J. M. Elliott (1969) • H. Greeley, *Recollections of a busy life* (1868) • J. F. C. Harrison, *Robert Owen and the Owenites in Britain and America: the quest for the new moral world* (1969) • R. Leopold, *Robert Dale Owen: a biography* (1940) • R. D. Owen, *An outline of the system of education at New Lanark* (1824) • R. D. Owen, *Threading my way: twenty seven years of autobiography* (1874) • A. Taylor, *Visions of harmony: a study in nineteenth-century millenarianism* (1987) • M. F. Bednarowski, 'Owen, Robert Dale', *ANB* • OPR Lanark, Glasgow

Archives Indiana State Library • Purdue University, West Lafayette, Indiana, journal • Workingman's Institute, New Harmony, Indiana • Workingman's Institute, New Harmony, Indiana, Bramigin-Owen MSS | Burgerbibliothek, Bern, Owen–Fellenberg corresp. • Co-operative Union, Holyoake House, Manchester, letters to G. J. Holyoake • Col. U., Francis Wright collection • L. Cong., Trist MSS • NRA, priv. coll., Kenneth Dale Owen MSS

Likenesses Bobbett and Edmonds, engraving (after S. Wallin), Wisconsin Historical Society [*see illus.*] • D. D. Owen, drawing (aged about nineteen), repro. in Elliott, ed., *To Holland and to New Harmony* • photograph (in old age), Indiana Historical Society Library, Indianapolis • photograph (in old age), State Historical Society of

Wisconsin, Madison; repro. in Harrison, *Robert Owen and the Owenites* • photograph (in old age), L. Cong.

Owen, Sir Roger (1572/3–1617). *See under* Owen, Thomas (*d.* 1598).

Owen, Samuel (1768/9–1857), marine painter, exhibited eight watercolours at the Royal Academy between 1794 and 1807, including *A View of the British and Spanish Fleets* (1797) and three drawings of the engagement between the *Director* and the *Vryheid* in the action off Camperdown (South Africa) on 11 October 1797 (1799). In 1808 he joined the Associated Artists in Water-Colours and sent eleven drawings of shipping and marine subjects to its first exhibition, exhibiting twenty-nine pictures in all before he resigned his membership in 1810. Painting more as a landscape artist, concerned with atmosphere and composition, he had a more Romantic approach than the eighteenth-century marine artists, with their faithful attention to detail. He supplied a series of eighty-four drawings which were engraved by William Bernard Cooke for his work *The Thames* (1811), and seven others for the *Picturesque Tour on the River Thames*, published by Owen himself and William Westall in 1828.

Owen gave up painting many years before his death. He died on 8 December 1857 at Sunbury, Middlesex. Eleven of his paintings are in the Victoria and Albert Museum, London, including *Shipping in a Calm with Fishermen on the Beach* (1800), and two coastal scenes in sepia are in the museum's department of prints and drawings. Many prints of his works are in the collections of the National Maritime Museum, Greenwich.

R. E. Graves, *rev.* Anne Pimlott Baker

Sources *Art Journal*, 20 (1858), 62 • I. O. Williams, *Early English watercolours and some cognate drawings by artists born not later than 1785* (1952), 202–3 • Mallalieu, *Watercolour artists*, vols. 1–2 • Redgrave, *Artists* • L. Lambourne and J. Hamilton, eds., *British watercolours in the Victoria and Albert Museum* (1980) • Boase, *Mod. Eng. biog.* • 'Catalogue of prints and drawings', www.nmm.ac.uk, 7 Dec 1998 • Graves, *RA exhibitors*

Likenesses T. Montague, watercolour, 1794–5, NPG

Owen, Samuel (1774–1854), engineer, was born on 12 May 1774 at Norton in Hales, Shropshire, the son of George Owen, a farmer, and Catherine Madeley. From the age of ten, having had barely nine months' schooling and scarcely able to read, Owen had to make his own living. He was variously a farmhand, boathand, and carpenter before being taken on in 1796 as a journeyman to help build Boulton and Watt's Soho foundry in Birmingham. When the foundry was complete Owen was kept on as a pattern maker and later founder, after Abraham Storey had taken him under his wing, teaching him iron-working skills and allowing him to use his library.

Owen left Boulton and Watt in 1800 to become machine assembler at Fenton, Murray, and Wood in Leeds, making his first visit to Sweden in 1804–5 to set up three steam engines bought from the Leeds firm by a Swedish customer. One, in use by 1804, was the first steam engine to drive machinery in a Swedish factory. In 1806, after a brief spell as mechanic at the engineering firm of Arthur Woolf in London, Owen accepted the invitation to become chief mechanic at the Bergsund foundry, Södermalm, Stockholm, a firm established by the Scot Thomas Lewis in 1769. There he constructed a rolling mill, widely regarded as without equal in either England or Sweden. In 1809 he bought a site at Kungsholm, Stockholm, where he set up an iron foundry, despite attempts by his erstwhile employer from Bergsund to stop him. Under Owen's direction from 1809 to 1843, Kungsholm became the leading engineering works in Sweden. With around one hundred employees in the 1830s, Owen built sixty steam engines, seven steamships, and five rolling mills, as well as countless other items of machinery so advanced that his factory became a school for engineers and factory owners.

Owen improved the iron-founding methods introduced to Sweden by Lewis, experimenting with new methods and new sources of supply of pig iron, even buying into foundries to ensure a steady supply of pig iron. He overcame capital shortage in the early years by concentrating on traditional products, such as mobile threshing machines, for which there was steady demand. Having amassed a fortune, he used it to equip his factory with advanced heavy machinery which produced Sweden's first iron bridge in 1815 and her first steamboat in 1816. His plans for jet-powered vehicles and steam-powered cars were never realized, but he built and operated a technically impressive, if only marginally profitable, fleet of steamships working out of Stockholm. However, the establishment of competing firms, his insatiable desire to experiment and gratify his customers' technical wants, and perhaps even his lack of knowledge of metallurgy led to his bankruptcy in 1843. In 1844 his plant was auctioned, but, despite this and the fact that he was sixty-nine years old, Owen did not retire. From 1844 to 1845 he was employed setting up steam-powered machinery on a farm near Västervik and from 1847 to 1851 by an old friend as master mechanic at the Åker works, Södermanland.

Owen was deeply religious: in the 1820s and 1830s, with Joseph Stephens and George Scott, he introduced Methodism to Sweden and from 1835 to 1845 he was an important figure in Svenska Missionssällskapet, an evangelical sect critical of the established Lutheran church. He also pioneered the total abstinence movement, which was to be extremely influential. In 1831 he was the co-founder of the Kungsholm abstinence society, from 1832 the Stockholm abstinence society, whose newspaper, *Stockholms Nykterhets-Härold*, he published. He was married three times: first, on 5 September 1796, to Ann Tuft; second, on 30 November 1817, to Brita Carolina Swedell, daughter of Samuel Swedell and Brita Magdalena Gullberg; and third, on 21 April 1822, to Johanna Magdalena Elisabeth Strindberg, daughter of Zacharias Strindberg and Anna Johanna Neijber. Owen died on 15 February 1854 in Klara parish, Stockholm, survived by his third wife and thirteen of his seventeen children. He was one of the most important of the many Britons who helped to establish the Swedish engineering industry.

Elizabeth Baigent

Sources J. E. Pettersson, 'Owen, Samuel', *Svenskt biografiskt lexikon*, ed. G. Nilzén and others, 28 (1992–4), 458–62

Archives Gothenburg University, Sweden, autobiography • Kungliga Biblioteket, Stockholm, MSS • Nordiska Museet, Stockholm, MSS, etc. • Riksarkivet, Stockholm, Krigsarkivet, MSS • Tekniska Museet, Stockholm, MSS, drawings, and steam engines • Uppsala University, MSS
Likenesses photograph, repro. in *Svenskt biografiskt lexikon*

Owen, Thankful (1620–1681), Independent divine, was born in the City of London, the son of Philip Owen of Taplow, Buckinghamshire, gentleman, a member of the common council of the City of London, and Joane Smith. Owen attended St Paul's School, which granted him an exhibition to Oxford University. He matriculated from Exeter College on 1 June 1636, aged sixteen, and it was perhaps about this time that 'he was remarkably preserved in his youth as he was swimming near Oxford, after he had twice sunk under water' (Calamy, 1.181). He graduated BA on 16 January 1640 and was elected a fellow of Lincoln College in 1642. According to Wood, he then 'left the university, and so consequently did not bear arms for his majesty, as other scholars did, within the garrison of Oxford' (Wood, *Ath. Oxon.: Fasti*, 2.90). At the end of the civil war, on 1 July 1646, he proceeded MA. At a meeting of the court of assistants of St Paul's School on 5 November, Owen was 'restored to his Exhibition of £10 per annum from Midsummer last and 20 nobles (£6/13/4d) was granted to him towards the incouragement in his studies and his taking his degree' (McDonnell).

In 1647 Owen co-operated with the parliamentary commission set up to reform and regulate the university and on 30 September was appointed one of the Lincoln College delegates to the visitors. On 11 May 1648 he formally submitted to the authority of parliament vested in them and eight days later was appointed by the proctors one of the twenty delegates to be answerable for the affairs of the university. On 5 July Owen became one of the examiners of candidates for fellowships and scholarships. On 13 March 1649, in an irregular appointment, for it was not the turn of his college, he was named senior proctor for the university: 'Queen's seems to have had no one who could be trusted' and Owen was 'more in the confidence of the Visitors than even Cheynell' (Burrows, 287). The moderate presbyterian Francis Cheynell was coming to the end of his reign at St John's. Following his resignation, on 6 September 1650, Thankful Owen, a 'pious man, of an unblameable conversation, and in regard of his good parts, learning and public spirit' (Costin, 111), was appointed president of St John's College by the committee for the reformation of the universities. The senior fellows of the college consented to the new appointment, but did not let Owen get all his own way. The following year the attempts of the college to fill only one vacancy were rejected by the fellows who elected three new members; in the conflict over this, Owen found it prudent to retreat. But, also in 1651, he was added to the list of preachers before the university, a move which reflected the shift towards the Independents.

On 3 August 1652 at St Andrew's, Plymouth, Owen married Loveday, daughter of Sir Francis Vivian of Trelowarren, Cornwall, but otherwise he remained in Oxford. On 15 June 1652 a new parliamentary committee was appointed, of which Owen was a member. Its first known meeting was on 20 June 1653, and Owen was a regular attender. He was one of the commission of triers or approvers under the ordinance of 20 March 1654. There is no doubt of Owen's puritan outlook or his religious independency, and many ministers sent their sons to St John's during the protectorate. Yet the pace of reform there was slow and there were complaints that the president assigned college property on favourable leases to friends and relations. In the university Owen became a member of the third interregnum body of visitors, appointed by Cromwell on 2 September 1654, and attended its meetings until 1657. On 24 September 1659, with John Owen (1616–1683), he was ordered to preach at Whitehall during October and November or to provide another 'person of eminent Godliness and gifts for the work', and was ordered to be paid £20 for his pains (*CSP dom.*, 1659–60, 221).

Owen signed the college register for the last time on 19 July 1660, before his ejection by the commissioners. Not long after he was discovered by the militia at Stadhampton, the estate of his namesake, the extruded vice-chancellor and dean of Christ Church. He then moved to London, and before October 1665 was living in Tree Alley, Bunhill. He published *A true and lively representation of popery, showing that popery is only new modell'd paganism and perfectly destructive of the great ends and purposes of God in the gospel* (1679), but gained greater fame as the joint editor, with John Barron, of the works of Thomas Goodwin. Following the death of Goodwin in February 1680, Owen was chosen to succeed him as pastor of the Independent congregation in Fetter Lane, London, but he died suddenly, on Good Friday, 1 April 1681, at his house in Hatton Garden. He was buried near Goodwin in Bunhill Fields. In his will Owen left freehold property at Llangofen in Monmouthshire, the county of his father's father, 'granted me by the bishop, archdeacon and chapter of Llandaff' (will, PRO, PROB 11/368, fol. 21*v*). He was reportedly a man 'of genteel learning and an excellent temper; admired for an uncommon fluency and easiness in his composures and for the peculiar purity of his Latin style' (Calamy, *Abridgement*, 2.181). STEPHEN WRIGHT

Sources *Calamy rev.* • E. Calamy, ed., *An abridgement of Mr. Baxter's history of his life and times, with an account of the ministers, &c., who were ejected after the Restauration of King Charles II*, 2nd edn, 2 vols. (1713) • M. McDonnell, ed., *The registers of St Paul's School, 1509–1748* (privately printed, London, 1977) • W. C. Costin, *The history of St John's College, Oxford, 1598–1860*, OHS, new ser., 12 (1958) • *Hist. U. Oxf.* 4: *17th-cent. Oxf.*, 744–5, 763–5 • Wood, *Ath. Oxon.: Fasti* (1820), 90–91 • will, PRO, PROB 11/368, sig. 144 • *CSP dom.*, 1659–60 • M. Burrows, ed., *The register of the visitors of the University of Oxford, from AD 1647 to AD 1658*, CS, new ser., 29 (1881)
Wealth at death freehold property at Llangofen, Monmouthshire: will, PRO, PROB 11/368, sig. 144

Owen, Thomas (*d.* 1598), judge, was born at Condover, Shropshire, the eldest son of Richard Owen, a merchant and alderman of Shrewsbury, and his wife, Mary (*d.* 1562), daughter of Thomas Ottley of Shrewsbury. He graduated BA from the University of Oxford on 17 April 1559, as a member of either Broadgates Hall or Christ Church. He was admitted in 1562 to Lincoln's Inn, where he was called to the bar in 1570 and made a bencher in 1579.

By 1572 Owen married Sarah (*d.* in or before 1594), daughter of Humphrey Baskerville. The couple had five sons, including Sir Roger Owen [*see below*], and five daughters. Owen was JP for Shropshire from about 1583 and for most other counties from about 1595. He was Lent reader in 1583, and served Lincoln's Inn as treasurer between 1588 and 1589. In 1589 he was created serjeant-at-law, and he was made queen's serjeant on 25 January 1593. On 21 January 1594 he was made a judge of the court of common pleas. He was rumoured to be a candidate for the vacant mastership of the court of wards in 1598, but died before any steps could be taken to fill the position. Owen married for a second time in 1594 or 1595, becoming third husband to Alice, *née* Wilkes (1547–1613) [*see* Owen, Alice], the third child of Thomas Wilkes of London and widow of William Elkin (1523–1593) of London. They had no children. Owen was a man of wide culture, his library at his death containing books in French, Italian, and Spanish as well as the more technical works of common law. Owen was without doubt a capable technical lawyer, but he was above all a man of very sound and reliable judgement, 'a noted counsellor, and much resorted to for advice' (Wood, *Ath. Oxon.*, 1.673). From a relatively early stage of his career he was frequently called upon by the privy council to carry out a variety of commissions, and he was employed by William Cecil, Baron Burghley, in the attempts to arrange a marriage between his granddaughter and William Somerset, Baron Herbert. He attempted, perhaps for a time successfully, to defuse a serious contretemps between the courts of king's bench and common pleas; and as recorder of Shrewsbury (1588–92) he permitted the continued observance of popular customs opposed by the more puritanical faction in the town.

Owen maintained strong connections with Shrewsbury throughout his life, serving the borough in various ways and representing it in 1584 in parliament, where he was active on a range of committees, including those concerning common informers (9 December 1584) and delays of executions (5 March 1585). He purchased land in the vicinity, and was responsible for the building of Condover Hall, described as the finest Elizabethan stone manor house in Shropshire. Although his professional life required him to live in London, it was Condover that he regarded as his main residence at the end of his life. He was a member of the queen's council in the marches of Wales from 1590, though he does not appear to have taken an especially active part in its business. Owen made his will on 9 December 1598, leaving the bulk of his property to his heir, but with substantial provision for his other children. He also made bequests to the poor of Shrewsbury, Condover, and Westminster, while his wife got much of his household goods. He died on 21 December 1598 and, despite his direction that his funeral be simple, was buried in Westminster Abbey. His widow later founded a school in Islington, Middlesex, and was a notably charitable benefactress.

Owen's son **Sir Roger Owen** (1572/3–1617), landowner and lawyer, was seventeen at the time of his matriculation at Christ Church on 30 October 1590. He was educated at Shrewsbury School from 1583, entered Lincoln's Inn in 1589, and graduated BA from Christ Church on 5 February 1592. He was called to the bar in 1597. Owen's local consequence was reflected in his appointment to the quorum of the peace from 1601 to 1614. He was returned as MP for Shrewsbury in 1601, 1605, 1610, and 1614, was a member of the council in the marches of Wales from 1602 to 1607, was sheriff of Shropshire from 1603 to 1604, and was knighted on 30 May 1604. He was a notable parliamentarian, who spoke against the Pluralities Bill on 16 November 1601 and opposed James VI and I's efforts to levy impositions by his own will, being one of the MPs deputed on 21 May 1610 to confer with the House of Lords on the issue. This led to his loss of royal favour, and he was removed from the commission of the peace when the 1614 parliament was prorogued. Owen continued his association with Lincoln's Inn, becoming a bencher in 1611, treasurer in 1612 (to 1613), and barrister in 1613. He married Ursula (*bap.* 1587), only child of William Elkin, of London, and his wife, Alice (Owen's stepmother). They had two daughters. Owen died intestate in London on 29 May 1617 and was buried at Condover on 5 June, being succeeded by his brother Sir William Owen. DAVID IBBETSON

Sources HoP, *Commons, 1558–1603*, 3.162–4 · will, PRO, PROB 11/93/15 · Wood, *Ath. Oxon.*, 1.672 · admissions registers, vol. 1; Black Books, vol. 1, Lincoln's Inn, London · *VCH Shropshire* · R. Tresswell and A. Vincent, *The visitation of Shropshire, taken in the year 1623*, ed. G. Grazebrook and J. P. Rylands, 2 vols., Harleian Society, 28–9 (1889) · Baker, *Serjeants* · Sainty, *Judges* · R. A. Dare, *A history of Owen's school, 1613–1976*, rev. edn (1980) · H. Owen and J. B. Blakeway, *A history of Shrewsbury*, 2 vols. (1825) · *CSP dom.*, 1598–1601 · *DNB*

Archives Gloucester Cathedral, law reports

Likenesses marble tomb effigy, Westminster Abbey

Wealth at death had already settled most of property: will, PRO, PROB 11/93/15 · chattels at Condover: inventory, *Transactions of the Shropshire Archaeological Society*

Owen [Owens], **Thomas** (*c.*1556–1618), Jesuit, was born in Winchester 'of an ancient Catholic family', according to contemporaries (Foley, 7.562). He studied at Winchester and Douai, then read civil and canon law, 1575–8, at Paris. He entered the Society of Jesus at Lyons in 1579. He taught humanities and philosophy at Avignon, 1584–6, and at Tournai, 1586–95, where, despite frail health, he was appointed dean of the language curriculum and professor of logic. He read theology at the Collegio Bradensi, Milan, in 1596–7 prior to taking up his post at the English College in Rome. From 1597 he served at the college as confessor, consultor, and minister under the rectorship of Robert Persons, who urged that he be named his successor. Owen was duly appointed rector on 23 April 1610.

Within two years of his appointment Owen published three English versions of works by two leading French controversialists. Two were by a Jesuit friend, Pierre Coton: *A Letter of a Catholike Man … [on] the Imputation of the Death of Henry IIII* in 1610, then in 1611 *The Copie of a Letter … an Answere to … the Anti-Coton*, an abridged version of his reply. His last effort was Cardinal Du Perron's initial confrontation with James I. In 1612 appeared his *Letter Written from Paris … to Monsr. Casaubon in England.*

In 1598 Claudio Acquaviva established an administrative structure for the English Jesuits that was unique in the society; this was based upon the document 'The office and rules of a prefect'. His actions were unpopular with provincials in Spain and the Spanish Netherlands because the document created a type of ecclesiastical peculiar outside their jurisdiction yet within their geographical provinces. Their protests were rejected by Acquaviva and Owen was named prefect on 27 January 1612. However, at the general congregation convened on Acquaviva's death in 1615 they secured a decree which reduced Owen's powers as specified in 'The office and rules'. For three years Owen challenged the legality of the change, citing the authority of Clement VIII and of the previous general, who had established the unique status of the mission and its separate houses to prepare properly a clergy for the unusual problems in England. After Owen's death at the English College, Rome, on 6 December 1618 his views were vindicated since the mission was preserved in a new rank of a vice-province. At his burial in the vault of the church of the English College, Pope Paul V paid tribute to him as a 'man of distinguished prudence and a solid religious' (Foley, 6.224, 531). A. J. LOOMIE

Sources T. M. McCoog, ed., *Monumenta Angliae*, 1: *English and Welsh Jesuits, catalogues, 1555–1629* (1992) • H. Foley, ed., *Records of the English province of the Society of Jesus*, 7 vols. in 8 (1875–83) • T. M. McCoog, 'The establishment of the English province of the Society of Jesus', *Recusant History*, 17 (1984–5), 121–39 • A. F. Allison and D. M. Rogers, eds., *The contemporary printed literature of the English Counter-Reformation between 1558 and 1640*, 2 vols. (1989–94) • T. M. McCoog, *English and Welsh Jesuits, 1555–1650*, 2 vols., Catholic RS, 74–5 (1994–5) • P. Milward, *Religious controversies of the Jacobean age* (1978) • *The Elizabethan Jesuits: Historia missionis Anglicanae Societatis Jesu (1660) of Henry More*, ed. and trans. F. Edwards (1981) • T. Clancy, 'Papal power and royal supremacy', *Papist pamphleteers* (1964), 79–106
Archives Archivum Romanum Societatis Iesu, Rome, letters as rector and prefect, Anglia

Owen, Thomas (1749–1812), Church of England clergyman and translator, was born in Anglesey, the son of Thomas Owen. He matriculated from Jesus College, Oxford, on 20 March 1767, graduating BA in 1770, and proceeding MA from Queen's College in 1773. In 1779 he was presented to the living of Upton Scudamore, Wiltshire. Owen's translations included *The Three Books of M. Terentius Varro Concerning Agriculture* (1800), *Geōponika, Agricultural Pursuits* (2 vols., 1805–6), and a translation of *The Fourteen Books of Palladius on Agriculture* (1807). Owen died in Anglesey in May 1812.

A. F. POLLARD, *rev.* ANNE PIMLOTT BAKER

Sources Foster, *Alum. Oxon.* • J. Donaldson, *Agricultural biography* (1854) • *GM*, 1st ser., 72 (1802), 523–6 • *GM*, 1st ser., 76 (1806), 830–33 • *GM*, 1st ser., 82/1 (1812), 497 • *GM*, 1st ser., 85/1 (1815), 91 • R. C. Hoare, *The history of modern Wiltshire*, 6 vols. (1822–44)
Archives NL Wales, diaries and sermon notes

Owen, Thomas Ellis (1764–1814), Church of England clergyman and religious controversialist, born at Conwy on 5 December 1764, was the son of William Owen, draper, and his wife, Elizabeth Ellis of Mochdre, daughter of John Ellis, a lawyer. He was admitted to Westminster School in 1780, and matriculated at Christ Church, Oxford, on 26 May 1785. The bishop of Oxford ordained him deacon on 7 June 1789, the year of his graduation, and priest on 8 March 1790. On 25 November 1790, while yet a student at Christ Church, he was instituted to the vicarage of South Stoke, Oxfordshire. Four years later, on 10 December 1794, he returned to Wales when he was instituted rector of Llandyfrydog in Anglesey, on the presentation of the bishop of Bangor. From the end of 1812 he was also perpetual curate of Penmynydd, Anglesey. He resided at Beaumaris.

Owen is best known as the author of two anti-Methodist pamphlets, *Hints to Heads of Families* (1801) and *Methodism Unmasked* (1802). Owen was one of a number of clerics in north Wales to defend the Anglican establishment by attacking the Methodists. In his *Hints* (which ran into a third edition after one year of publication) he denounced the Methodists as sectaries, the blind instruments or wilful tools of anarchists or atheists, who were conspiring to achieve a revolution similar to the French, which had 'deluged the Continent with blood' (Owen, 23). In the course of his diatribe he accused the Welsh Methodist preachers who accompanied the Welsh militia to Ireland of fomenting disloyalty among the troops. This statement aroused the anger of the Methodist leaders in north Wales, who considered taking a libel action against him. Thomas Charles and Thomas Jones, the leading Welsh Methodists, answered the charge of disloyalty levelled by Owen and others in *The Welsh Methodists Vindicated* (1802).

Owen's last published work (1809) was an obituary on the death of William Pitt, *The Tears of Britannia*, addressed to the Menai Pitt Club, which published it. His own obituarist in the *North Wales Gazette* (8 December 1814) wrote that he was a 'man eminently endowed with talents both natural and acquired, and his abilities were strenuously and successfully exerted, in defence of the Established Religion of his country'. He died at The Green, Beaumaris, on 1 December 1814, and was buried at Llanfair-is-gaer, in Caernarvonshire, where there is a tablet in his memory.

HYWEL MEILYR DAVIES

Sources T. E. Owen, *Hints to heads of families*, ed. D. E. Jenkins (1905) • F. P. Jones, 'Gair yn ei amser: Thomas Jones o Ddinbych', *Trafodion Cymdeithas Hanes Sir Ddinbych*, 5 (1956) • J. J. Evans, *Dylanwad y chwyldro Ffrengig ar lenyddiaeth Cymru* (1928) • D. E. Jenkins, *The life of the Rev. Thomas Charles of Bala* (1908) • *North Wales Gazette* (8 Dec 1814) • *DWB* • T. R. Roberts, *Eminent Welshmen: a short biographical dictionary* (1908)
Archives U. Wales, Bangor, Bangor MS 6455

Owen, Walter Edwin (1879–1945), missionary, was born on 7 June 1879 at 144 Phillips Street, Aston, Birmingham, the son of John Simpson Owen, a British army warrant officer, and his wife, Caroline Isabella Blair. He was brought up in Belfast. He trained in England as a Church Missionary Society missionary and was ordained deacon in 1904 and priest in 1905, embarking on his life's work as a missionary in east Africa. On 8 October 1907 he married Isabel Barnes (*d.* 1910), a fellow missionary, and, on 27

December 1911, Lucy Olive Walton of Wolverhampton (1876–1953), also a missionary.

From 1904 to 1918 Owen worked on a succession of mission stations in Uganda: Bunyoro, Kabaro, and Kako, before, in 1918, becoming archdeacon of Kavirondo, in Kenya. Kavirondo had been evangelized from Uganda and had developed a vigorous church life as part of the Ugandan Native Anglican church. But in 1921 the archdeaconry was transferred to the diocese of Mombasa, a move which, in sharp contrast to Uganda, brought the African Christian community into a church structure increasingly driven by the needs and aspirations of the British settlers of Kenya colony. Owen attempted to mitigate the regressive effects of this for the Luo and Luyia peoples, immersing himself in the social and political life of Kenya. While appreciative of what, potentially, settlers could do for the development of the country, he was above all conscious of the duty of advocacy on behalf of the indigenous peoples:

> I believe that, just as in slavery many good Christian people had to be brought to see that Christianity and Slavery were incompatible so, today, many good Christian people have to be brought to see that certain features of British Administration in Kenya are but the modern expression of the desire for profit which gave rise to slavery. (Owen MSS, deposited in the CMS archives in the University of Birmingham: File 011, Owen to H. D. Hooper, 18 Sept 1939)

Owen's vigorous campaigning, in particular his doggedly persistent correspondence to the *Manchester Guardian*, brought him into conflict with settlers (who nicknamed him the Archdemon), colonial officials, and missionary colleagues. He was critical of settler attempts to dominate the political process in Kenya at the expense of the native African population, and was supportive of Indian rights to immigration and political participation, which was popular with neither settlers nor missionaries. He was outspoken in his condemnation of forced labour—whether by colonial diktat or the authoritarianism of local chiefs—not only in Kenya but in Uganda where in 1926 he denounced the use of conscripted labour in the extension of the railway. He spoke out against the brutal methods used by the British authorities in the collection of the hut tax, involving the burning of the homes of defaulters. He defended African interests in the Kakamega gold rush of the early 1930s. His advocacy was unambiguously paternalistic, and has been criticized for stifling the development of an articulate African political consciousness: in 1921 he founded and was president of the Kavirondo Taxpayers' Welfare Association, effectively keeping local politics under mission aegis for much longer than in Kikuyuland.

Owen was strongly supportive of local culture—he stressed, for example, that 'native' marriage be recognized as valid. But at times this affirmation collided with his strongly developed sense of fair play and justice. He was fiercely protective of the rights of women, and mounted a long campaign against forced marriages. He had earlier, in Uganda, insisted on a strict interpretation of the marriage ordinance, even if this went against local custom, invoking it to protect the rights of Christian women against husbands who subsequently became polygamous. Owen was interested in rural development and education to undergird the rural economy. Theologically liberal, both in biblical teaching and social attitudes, he was impatient with attempts to censure church members who supplemented their income by local brewing, noting that although personally he was almost a teetotaller, he could not agree to a rule which would have meant Christ being disciplined for turning the water into wine at Cana of Galilee 'for public consumption'. Owen was an enthusiastic amateur palaeontologist, and felt it important for the African church to be exposed to Darwinian accounts of creation. On retirement in 1945 he was made archdeacon emeritus and honorary canon of Mombasa Cathedral. He died on 18 September 1945 at Limuru, Kenya, and was buried in the churchyard of the settler church there. His second wife survived him. Max Warren, general secretary of the Church Missionary Society from 1942 to 1963, wrote of Owen: 'from him I caught the passionate conviction that the Gospel has to do with politics as well as souls. I learned about ecology from him long before anyone had thought of inventing the word' (M. Warren, *Crowded Canvas*, 1974, 41). KEVIN WARD

Sources C. R. Richards, *Archdeacon Owen of Kavirondo* (1947) · U. Birm. L., special collections department, Church Missionary Society archive, Owen MSS, Accession 83 · Kenya National Archives, Nairobi, Kenya, Anglican Church of Kenya archives · Kavirondo, Maseno, Kenya, Church Archives of the Diocese of Maseno South · b. cert.

Archives U. Birm. L., Church Missionary Society archive, papers | JRL, letters to *Manchester Guardian* · Kavirondo Church Archives of the Diocese of Maseno South, Maseno, Kenya, church documents · Kenya National Archives, Nairobi, Kenya, Anglican Church of Kenya archives

Likenesses photograph, repro. in Richards, *Archdeacon Owen*

Owen, Wilfred Edward Salter (1893–1918), poet, was born at Plas Wilmot, near Oswestry, Shropshire, on 18 March 1893, the eldest of the three sons and one daughter of Thomas (Tom) Owen (1862–1931), railway clerk, of Plas Wilmot, and his wife, (Harriett) Susan (1867–1942), daughter of Edward Shaw JP, ironmonger and former mayor of Oswestry. His father was transferred to Birkenhead in 1898, and between 1899 and 1907 Owen was educated at the Birkenhead Institute. In 1907 the family moved to Shrewsbury, where Tom Owen had been appointed assistant superintendent of the Joint Railways and Wilfred attended Shrewsbury Technical School. His enthusiasm for poetry—seemingly kindled in 1903 or 1904—was growing, but was for some time exceeded by a preoccupation with religion. Under the strong influence of his devout mother he read a passage from the Bible every day and, on Sundays, would rearrange her sitting-room to represent a church. Then, wearing a linen surplice and cardboard mitre she had made, he would summon the family and conduct a complete evening service with a carefully prepared sermon.

With his cousins Vera and Leslie Gunston, Owen formed an Astronomical, Geological and Botanical Society (of three members). As an early enthusiasm for botany had

Wilfred Edward Salter Owen (1893–1918), by John Gunston, 1916

led him to the study of geology, this in turn led him to archaeology and, in 1909, he made the first of many expeditions to the site of the Roman city of Uriconium at Wroxeter, east of Shrewsbury. He left school in 1911, eager to go to university, and passed the University of London matriculation exam, though not with the first-class honours necessary to win him the scholarship he needed. Disappointed, he accepted the offer of an unpaid position as lay assistant to the Revd Herbert Wigan, vicar of Dunsden, a village outside Reading. In return for help with his parish duties, Wigan gave Owen free board and lodging and some tuition to prepare him for the university entrance exam. The arrangement was not a success. Wigan had no interest in literature, and Owen soon lost interest in theology, the only topic offered for tuition. Over the coming months, however, he attended botany classes at University College, Reading, and was encouraged both in his writing and in his literary studies by the head of the English department. Meanwhile, he gave practical help to the poor of the parish, his early reading of the gospels having been supplemented by his reading of Shelley, atheist and revolutionary (whom he was happy to learn had lived near by).

Owen's poems of this period show him moving beyond imitations of his admired Keats, and in 1912 the compassion that would characterize his writings from the western front makes itself heard in his response to a village tragedy, the lines beginning:

> Deep under turfy grass and heavy clay
> They laid her bruisèd body and the child.

He gazes into the open grave of mother and daughter with something of the same awed fascination which prompted a more ambitious poem some months later. 'Uriconium/An Ode' is, in an important sense, his first 'war poem'. Contemplating the excavated ruins of the Roman city which, with its inhabitants (his guidebook told him) 'perished by fire and sword', his awareness of the victims' bodies—so prominent a feature of his later and greater poems—enables him to feel

> Plasters with Roman finger-marks impressed;
> Bracelets, that from the warm Italian arm
> Might seem to be scarce cold;

and it sharpens his perceptions of the weapons that killed them—'spears … unblunted yet'.

Early in 1913 a religious revival swept the parish like a springtide, carrying converts into church, but leaving Owen stranded on the recognition that literature meant more to him than evangelical religion, and that he could no longer reconcile the conservative cant of the vicarage with the godless poverty of the parish. He left Dunsden on the verge of a nervous breakdown and with congestion of the lungs which kept him in bed for more than a month. In July he sat a scholarship exam for University College, Reading, but failed, and in mid-September crossed the channel to take up a part-time post teaching English at the Berlitz School in Bordeaux. Over the next two years he grew to love France and had reached perhaps the highest point of happiness that life would offer him, tutoring an eleven-year-old French girl in her parents' villa, in the Pyrenees, when, on 4 August 1914, war was declared.

The Owen who left for France in 1913 was a late-Romantic descendant of Keats and Shelley, but the Owen who left France to enlist in 1915 was equipped to become a modern poet. The metamorphosis was largely the result of his friendship with Laurent Tailhade, a poet of the so-called 'decadent' school, who introduced him to the work of Verlaine, Flaubert, and many other nineteenth-century writers who challenged the beliefs and sensibilities of bourgeois society. Tailhade had written two pacifist pamphlets, but was also a duellist and by the end of 1914 had joined the French army. Over the next year Owen's thinking showed similar conflicts and confusion. He too considered joining the French army. His delayed decision indicates an understandable reluctance to go to war, but at no point do his letters speak of any principled aversion to fighting. 'Do you know what would hold me together on a battlefield?' he asked his mother. 'The sense that I was perpetuating the language in which Keats and the rest of them wrote!' (*Wilfred Owen: Collected Letters*, 300). Finally, he returned to England, said goodbye to his family, and, on 21 October 1915, enlisted in the Artists' Rifles.

For the next seven and a half months Owen was in training, mainly at Hare Hall camp in Essex. There were two brief but important interludes in London, spent largely at the Poetry Bookshop in Devonshire Street. Its proprietor, Harold Monro, himself a poet and the editor of the *Poetry Review*, read his poems and gave him encouraging advice. On 4 June Owen was commissioned into the Manchester regiment and underwent further training with its 5th (reserve) battalion in various parts of England, before crossing to France on 29 December. He joined the 2nd Manchesters on the Somme and, in the second week of January 1917 (one of the coldest on record), led his platoon into the trenches.

In mid-March 1917 Owen fell through a shell-hole into a cellar and was trapped there for three days with only a candle for company. He emerged with concussion and was involved in fierce fighting—at one point being blown out of the trench in which he was taking cover from an artillery bombardment—but on 1 May was diagnosed as suffering from neurasthenia (shell-shock) and sent to Craiglockhart War Hospital, near Edinburgh, to recuperate. He was put under the care of a perceptive doctor, Captain Arthur Brock RAMC, who believed shell-shock to result from broken contact with real life, and sought to re-establish that vital connection by means of 'work-cure' (or, as he termed it, 'ergotherapy'). Owen joined the field club Brock had started and became editor of the hospital magazine, *The Hydra*, which would shortly print two of his poems and four by another inmate, Siegfried Sassoon.

Sassoon's book, *The Old Huntsman and Other Poems*, had just been published. Its 'trench life sketches' (*Wilfred Owen: Collected Letters*, 484), with their dynamic use of direct speech (learned from Thomas Hardy), had an overwhelming effect on Owen. He introduced himself, and so began one of the most productive of literary friendships. The older poet's advice and encouragement, showing the younger how to channel memories of battle—recurring in obsessive nightmares which were a symptom of shell-shock—into a poem such as 'Dulce et decorum est', complemented Dr Brock's 'work-cure'. The final manuscript of 'Anthem for Doomed Youth' carries suggestions (including that of the title) in Sassoon's handwriting. Owen's confidence grew, his health returned, and in October a medical board decided that he was fit for light duties. On leave in London, he met Robert Ross who in turn introduced him to some of his literary friends: Arnold Bennett, H. G. Wells, and a number of less well known figures, several of whom were homosexual, as were Ross and Sassoon themselves. It is clear from Owen's writings that he shared their sexual orientation; but it is debatable whether he ever entered into a physical relationship that, if detected, could have resulted in a prison sentence like that imposed on Oscar Wilde, a relationship that would have horrified his mother, whose good opinion he valued above all others. There is no evidence that he did. What is certain, however, is that Owen and Sassoon wrote more eloquently than other poets of the tragedy of boys killed in battle because they felt that tragedy more acutely, more personally.

In November 1917 Owen rejoined the 5th Manchesters in Scarborough. There he read *Under Fire* (the English translation of Henri Barbusse's book *Le feu*), the last significant text to filter into his poems: one sentence, for example, being transformed into the lines beginning 'Cramped in that funnelled hole'. This vision of 'one of the many mouths of Hell' would be more fully elaborated in 'Miners' and 'Strange Meeting' and can be traced back, by way of 'Uriconium', to the hell of which he heard at his mother's knee.

The following March Owen was transferred to Ripon where, over the next three months, he either wrote or revised and completed many of his most celebrated poems, including 'Insensibility', 'Strange Meeting', 'Exposure', and 'Futility'. Part of the power of these derives from his pioneering use of 'pararhymes': escaped/scooped, groined/groaned. In 'Strange Meeting', from which these examples are taken, the second rhyme is usually lower in pitch than the first, giving the couplet a dying fall which musically reinforces the poem's tragic theme.

Owen was graded GS (fit for general service) in June and rejoined the 5th Manchesters at Scarborough. He was recommended for a home posting but the recommendation was rejected, and when in July he heard that Sassoon was back in England with a head wound, he seems to have accepted that it was his duty as a poet to take his place. He had come to share his friend's sense of mission, a word with appropriately religious overtones. Although both poets were, by this time, fiercely critical of the role of the church that had forgotten the biblical commandment 'Thou shalt not kill', both had a fundamentally religious outlook. Owen never lost his belief in the person and teachings of Christ, and his mother's evangelical influence no doubt contributed to his conviction that he must go out again, as he told her, 'to help these boys—directly by leading them as well as an officer can; indirectly, by watching their sufferings that I may speak of them as well as a pleader can' (*Wilfred Owen: Collected Letters*, 580). He returned to the front in September 1918 during the final advance on the German lines. His courage in the ensuing conflict won him the MC, but he was killed while crossing the Sambre and Oise Canal near Ors in the early morning of 4 November—one week before the armistice, and two years before the first collection of his poems was published. He was buried in the Ors village cemetery.

In Owen's famous draft preface for that book, he wrote: 'All a poet can do today is warn. That is why the true Poets must be truthful' (autograph poems, BL, Add. MS 43720–43721). This document came to have the force of a manifesto for the socially concerned poets of the 1930s, who accorded him the status of saint and martyr. Dying at twenty-five, he came to represent a generation of innocent young men sacrificed—as it seemed to a generation in unprecedented rebellion against its fathers—by guilty old men: generals, politicians, war profiteers. Owen has now taken his place in literary history as perhaps the first, certainly the quintessential, war poet. He would have preferred another title. On new year's eve 1917 he had told his mother: 'I am a poet's poet.' This proved to be true. The four successive editions of his work have all been edited by poets, and it was only with Benjamin Britten's sensitive setting of Owen's poems in his *War Requiem* (1961) that he became known to a national and an international audience as the Orpheus of the trenches.

JON STALLWORTHY

Sources J. Stallworthy, *Wilfred Owen* (1974) • *Wilfred Owen: the war poems*, ed. J. Stallworthy (1994) • *Wilfred Owen: the complete poems and fragments*, ed. J. Stallworthy, 2 vols. (1983) • *Wilfred Owen: collected letters*, ed. H. Owen and J. Bell (1967) • H. Owen, *Journey from obscurity*, 3 vols. (1963–5) • D. Hibberd, *Owen the poet* (1968) • D. Hibberd, *Wilfred Owen: the last year* (1992) • b. cert. • *CGPLA Eng. & Wales* (1919) • J. E. Edmonds, ed., *Military operations, France and Belgium, 1914*, 3rd edn, 2 vols., History of the Great War (1933)

Archives Ransom HRC, letters | Col. U., letters to Siegfried Sassoon and poems • U. Oxf., faculty of English language and literature, letters to Vera Gunston and Leslie Gunston • U. Oxf., faculty of English language and literature, multimedia digital archive

Likenesses J. Gunston, bromide print, 1916, NPG [*see illus.*] • double portrait, photograph, *c.*1917 (with Arthur Newboult), Hult. Arch. • photographs, U. Oxf., faculty of English language and literature

Wealth at death £162 13*s.*: administration, 16 April 1919, *CGPLA Eng. & Wales*

Owen, William (*c.*1488–1574), lawyer, was the son of Rhys ab Owen (*d.* *c.*1544), a freeholder, of Henllys, near Newport, Pembrokeshire, and Jane, daughter of Phillip Elliot of Earwere, near Amroth, and his wife, Janet, daughter of Sir Thomas Perrot of Eastington; his mother had previously been married to Philip ap Gwilym of Stone Hall in the Pembrokeshire parish of St Lawrence. On 28 November 1514 he was admitted at the Middle Temple where he had such travail in copying Sir Anthony Fitzherbert's abridgement of the laws, *La graunde abridgement*, that he produced his own version 'in soe small a volume as the price thereof was but 12d.' (Owen, *Description*, ed. Owen, 238) under the title *Le breggement de touz les estatutz … par Guillame Owein de Medill' Temple*. This was printed by Richard Pynson in London in 1521, and a second edition followed in 1528. His son, George *Owen, claimed that he 'also wrote other works'; one of these was an unsigned edition of the *Natura brevium*.

William Owen was settled at Pembroke by 1521 and, in 1527, he was mayor of that town. In 1521 he married Margaret Swyllyngton of St Clement Danes. He was afterwards clerk of the court of Pembroke, and was controller of the ports of Pembroke, Haverfordwest, and Tenby. He shared in the duties of steward and receiver of the county of Pembroke with Sir Rhys ap Gruffydd until the latter was executed for treason. He was a member of the commission for the division of Wales into shire ground under the Act of Union, 1536, and held the office of escheator for the county of Pembroke from 1545 to 1560. In 1535 he acquired the estate of Maesgwenith in the county of Monmouth, conveniently situated between Pembrokeshire and London and Bristol, for the pursuit of his legal activities. Owen still had chambers in the Middle Temple in 1521, and was described as of the Temple in 1540 and in 1552, when Middle Temple sued him for dues.

Owen had no children with his first wife. However, he had already had nine natural children, five by his mistress, Jane Lee, and four by other mistresses, by the time he was married again, to Elizabeth (*c.*1520–1603) in 1551. She was the daughter of Sir George Herbert of Swansea and his wife, Elizabeth, daughter of Sir Thomas Berkeley, and niece of the earl of Pembroke; they had a son, George, and a daughter, Katherine.

While he was in London Owen met John Touchet, Lord Audley, who had been restored to the barony of Cemais, in north Pembrokeshire, that had become forfeit to the crown on the attainder and execution of his father; and Audley appointed him clerk of the courts of Cemais. Being impoverished following the sequestration of his father's property, Audley obtained a loan of £600 from Owen in November 1523 for which he made him 'a bargain and sale of the barony … with a condition of redemption upon payment of £300' (Owen, *Description*, ed. Owen, viii, n. 1). Twenty years later, he conveyed the barony to Owen and commanded his tenantry to 'obbey the said William Owen as theire very lord and right owner of the barony.' On 4 October 1571 Owen settled the barony, with the castle of Newport and the advowson of six churches on his son, George.

Although George Owen claimed that his father 'was accounted to have lyved 105 yeares', he could not have been more than eighty-six years when he died at his home, Henllys on 29 March 1574, and was buried the next day at St Brynach's Church, Nevern. A number of bards sang elegies at his passing.

DILLWYN MILES

Sources B. G. Charles, *George Owen of Henllys: a Welsh Elizabethan* (1973) • G. Owen, *The description of Penbrokshire*, ed. H. Owen, 4 vols., Honourable Society of Cymmrodorion, Cymmrodorion Record Series, 1 (1892–1936) • G. Owen, *Description of Pembrokeshire*, ed. D. Miles (1994) • G. Owen, *The taylors cussion*, ed. E. M. Pritchard (1906)

Archives NL Wales, Bronwydd MSS

Owen, William. *See* Wiliam Llŷn (1534/5–1580).

Owen, William (1769–1825), painter, was born at 13 Broad Street, Ludlow, Shropshire, and baptized in Ludlow parish church on 3 November 1769, the eldest of the six children of Jeremiah Owen, hairdresser and bookseller, and his wife, Mary (*d.* 1785). His father had trained for the church but failed to obtain a living and so returned to Ludlow to assist his father, William Owen (*d.* 1783), who had a barber's shop at 13 Broad Street. By 1779 Jeremiah Owen had enlarged the shop to include a bookselling and stationery business, but in 1800 he went bankrupt. Owen was educated at Ludlow grammar school. His uncle was butler to Richard Payne Knight and it was through his recommendation that Owen moved to London in 1786 and was apprenticed for seven years to the coach-painter Charles Catton RA (1728–1798). Owen, however, wished to develop further and was encouraged by Sir Joshua Reynolds after he saw Owen's copy of his own painting, *Perdita* (Bryan, *Painters*). On 14 October 1791 he entered the Royal Academy Schools. His first work was exhibited at the Royal Academy in the following year and he continued to exhibit every year, with the exception of 1823, until his death. His portrait of the dowager Lady Clive (exh. RA, 1793; priv. coll.) and other members of her family, together with Ludlow landscapes by Owen in her possession, indicate that she was an early patron of Owen's work.

Owen married the daughter of a London shoemaker who lived in the Haymarket. According to Farington (17 December 1803) the shoemaker was supposedly wealthy, but at his death was found to be insolvent, which resulted in Owen being declared bankrupt and carried to gaol in Dover. Farington (12 November 1803) also reported that Owen's supposed neglect of his wife was one of the reasons he was not elected a member of the Royal Academy earlier. However, he was elected ARA in 1804 and RA in 1806. Owen and his wife had one son, the Revd William Owen.

Owen's work comprised mainly portraits. His output was prodigious and he had a distinguished list of sitters including William Pitt, Lord Grenville, William Howley, Sir John Soane, and John Wilson Croker. Although his portraits were admired as truthful representations, contemporaries felt he 'did not succeed in displaying the graces of the female form' (*GM*, 571), and that they lacked the fluency and sparkle of contemporaries such as Sir Thomas Lawrence. He painted and exhibited many rustic scenes and fancy subjects such as *Boy and Kitten* (1807; RA) and *Horatia Nelson Kneeling before her Father's Tomb* (NMM). Many of these became popular engravings. His work shows a strong sense of composition but his anatomical knowledge of the human figure and his drawing are sometimes weak. Owen was made portrait painter to the prince of Wales in 1810 and was commissioned to paint *Sir David Dundas* (1812; Royal Collection), which was well received. The prince of Wales promised to sit for Owen but never did, and he was left to copy John Hoppner's portrait of the prince.

Owen was a dark-haired, full-lipped, handsome man who, according to contemporaries, diligently carried out his duties at the academy, winning the students' respect. He became severely disabled by an infection of the spine and after 1820 was unable to paint. He died of poisoning on 11 February 1825 at his home, 33 Bruton Street, Berkeley Square, London, because a chemist's assistant mistakenly gave him a bottle of opium instead of a harmless draught. His funeral was held on 19 March 1825. Many of Owen's unfinished portraits were completed by Edward Daniel Leahy. R. E. GRAVES, *rev.* HELEN VALENTINE

Sources *GM*, 1st ser., 95/1 (1825), 570–71 • Farington, *Diary* • artist's file, archive material, Courtauld Inst., Witt Library • *The Times* (15 March 1825) • *The Times* (17 March 1825) • Bryan, *Painters* (1903–5) • Graves, *RA exhibitors* • O. Millar, *The later Georgian pictures in the collection of her majesty the queen*, 2 vols. (1969) • S. C. Hutchison, 'The Royal Academy Schools, 1768–1830', *Walpole Society*, 38 (1960–62), 123–91 • private information (2004) [Jennifer Davies]

Archives Ches. & Chester ALSS, corresp. with Sir John Leicester

Likenesses W. Owen, self-portrait, oils, *c.*1785–1790, RA • H. Meyer, stipple, 1809 (after J. Wright), BM, NPG; repro. in *The Cabinet* (1809)

Owen, William Fitzwilliam (1774–1857), naval officer and hydrographer, was the second illegitimate son of Captain William Owen RN, of the Glansevern Owens of Montgomeryshire and of Passamaquoddy Bay, New Brunswick. His mother, and that of his brother, was either Sarah Haslam or Jane Johnson, both of whom were in Captain Owen's household. Owen was born near Warrington, Lancashire, on 17 September 1774. Abandoned in Madras on his father's death in 1778, he was taken aboard the frigate *Cormorant* as the captain's servant by Captain Sir Thomas Rich. He went with his benefactor to the *Enterprize*, in which he was present at the moonlight battle off Cape St Vincent in 1780, before being sent to schools in north Wales and near Liverpool.

Owen went back to sea in 1788 as a midshipman, joining the *Culloden* (74 guns) under Sir Thomas Rich again. He was present in her at the battle of the Glorious First of June in 1794. After service in the *Ruby* (64 guns) in the expedition to capture the Cape of Good Hope, Owen was appointed to the *London* (98 guns), flagship of Vice-Admiral Sir John Colpoys. In May 1797, when the crew of the *London* joined the mutiny at Spithead, Owen was among the officers put ashore.

Later that year Owen was promoted lieutenant in command of the gun-vessel *Flamer*, in which after the battle of Camperdown he salvaged the Dutch prize *Overijssel*. His next command was the fireship *Nancy*, where he came under the orders of Nelson for a planned attempt to fire the invasion fleet mustering in Boulogne. In 1803 Owen was given command of the brig *Seaflower*, employed first off Brest and later in eastern seas. It was here that he first began the hydrographic work for which he is best-known, discovering and charting deep-water channels through the Maldives and in the islands off Sumatra. In September 1808 the *Seaflower* was taken by the French frigate *La Manche*, and Owen was imprisoned on Mauritius until January 1810. Meanwhile he had been promoted commander and appointed to the sloop *Barracouta*. Before taking up his command he was involved in the planning for the capture of Mauritius. After its fall he returned to the East Indies, where he helped Sir Stamford Raffles impose British rule over Java and Sumatra. He was promoted captain in May 1811 and appointed to the frigate *Cornelia*, where, as senior officer of the Batavia squadron, he suppressed piracy in the Indies.

In 1815 Owen was ordered to Kingston, Ontario, to survey the Great Lakes of Canada. In the next two years Owen and his team of four assistants charted most of the Canadian shores of the Great Lakes and the upper St Lawrence River, as well as delineating the border between the United States and Canada from Lake Champlain to the St Lawrence. In 1818 he married Martha Evans; they had two daughters. After her death in 1852 he married later the same year Amy Nicholson, a widow, of Saint John, New Brunswick.

After a period on half pay Owen was appointed in 1821 to the sloop *Leven*, in which, with the brig *Barracouta* also under his command, he was instructed to survey the east coast of Africa from the boundary of Cape Colony to Cape Gardafui. The squadron arrived at Simonstown in July 1822, and returned there from their last surveying season in September 1825, having surveyed some 20,000 miles of coast, depicted in almost 300 charts. Fever ravaged the ships' companies, and it was not until they began treating it with the native remedy of chinchona bark infusion, instead of bleeding, that mortality was brought within bounds, though it was never eliminated.

Already disgusted by the slave trade from his experiences in the East Indies, Owen was determined to stamp it out. Finding the Mazrui rulers of Mombasa under siege by their suzerain, Sayyid Said, sultan of Oman, Owen in February 1824 on his own initiative raised the siege and took the town under British protection in return for a promise by the Mazrui to abolish slavery. Though disowned by the home government, the protectorate lasted over two years.

After leaving Simonstown in October 1825, the two ships carried out extensive surveys on the west coast of Africa on their way home, before reaching Deptford in August 1826. Owen published *A Narrative of a Voyage to Explore the Shores of Africa, Arabia and Madagascar* in 1833, but the similar work by Thomas Boteler, a lieutenant on the survey, is generally considered the better record.

At the end of 1826 Owen was appointed to the frigate *Eden* and as superintendent of Fernando Po, where it was intended that he should establish a colony for freed slaves. Despite a promising start, hopes that the island was free from fever proved false, and Owen left at the end of 1829. He remained in the *Eden* until August 1831, when he came ashore for the last time.

In 1835 Owen and his family moved to the estate on Campobello Island in Passamaquoddy Bay, New Brunswick, colonized by his father, where, apart from short trips away, he remained for the rest of his life. In 1842 the surveying ship *Columbia* was sent out to chart the coast of the Bay of Fundy, and Owen was placed in charge of her operations for five years. He was promoted rear-admiral in 1847, and vice-admiral in 1854. He died in St John on 3 November 1857, and was buried at St Anne's churchyard, Welshpool, Campobello Island. R. O. MORRIS

Sources E. H. Burrows, *Captain Owen of the African survey* (1979) • G. S. Ritchie, *The Admiralty chart: British naval hydrography in the nineteenth century*, new edn (1995) • L. S. Dawson, *Memoirs of hydrography* (1885); repr. (1969) • R. Oliver and G. Mathew, *History of East Africa*, 1 (1963)

Archives Hydrographic Office, Taunton • New Brunswick Museum, Saint John, New Brunswick • NMM, papers; narrative • Owen Sound Library, Owen Sound, Ontario

Likenesses oils, *c*.1855, repro. in Burrows, *Captain Owen of the African survey* • stipple and line print, BM

Wealth at death Campobello Island estate and property of his second wife in Saint John, New Brunswick: Burrows, *Captain Owen*

Owens, John (1790–1846), merchant and philanthropist, was born in Manchester, the eldest son of Owen Owens (1764–1844) and his wife, Sarah (*née* Humphreys). Two other sons died in infancy. His parents were Welsh, his father being a native of Holywell, Flintshire; they married in 1788 and moved to Manchester shortly after. Owens was educated at a private school in Manchester owned by John Huthersal, author of textbooks on English grammar, arithmetic, geography, and Latin, but by 1808 he was helping in his father's business of hat-lining cutter and hat maker. Until 1812 the firm confined itself to the home trade, but from then on began to seek markets overseas.

In 1815, at the age of twenty-five, Owens became a partner in the firm, which by then also made a variety of cotton goods on the putting-out system, manufactured umbrellas, and exported all these and other goods to North and South America. The firm's home trade was neglected after about 1820 and soon ceased to have any importance. In and after 1825 the Owenses invested £10,000 in a cotton mill owned by Samuel Faulkner & Co., in which George Faulkner was a partner. The investment proved satisfactory, giving a return of nearly 10 per cent per annum over eighteen years, after which Owens withdrew his capital. About 1830 Owen Owens retired from business, leaving his son in sole charge at their dingy warehouse in Carpenters Lane off Tib Street. There was an immediate widening of the firm's range of export markets to include the Middle East, India, and China. At the same time the manufacture of cheap cotton goods for export was abandoned. The profits of foreign trade were by no means derisory if a merchant had the patience to wait for his returns, but by 1840 Owens was turning, in a familiar transition, from trade to finance. Speculating in corn, cotton, and railway shares, and moneylending on the security of such shares, occupied most of his business mind in the remaining years of his life. He died at his home, 10 Nelson Street, Rusholme, Manchester, on 29 July 1846, at the age of fifty-six, and was buried in the churchyard of St John's, Byrom Street, Manchester. In the forty years during which he was associated with the business he had seen its capital grow from perhaps £5000 to more than thirty times as much.

Accounts of Owens's appearance agree in describing him as unprepossessing, and in little else: he has been called above and below middle height, broadly built, and sharp featured. Like his father, he disliked borrowing, spent little of his income, worked long hours, and had few holidays, none of them further from home than London. In his lifetime he subscribed moderately to local medical and educational charities, supported the Anti-Corn Law League, bought the *Edinburgh Review*, read some at least of Scott's novels, and worshipped at his local Anglican church, St Saviour's. At his death his personal effects were valued at £400, which did not allow for much plate or for a large library. Although variously described as morose or a recluse, he belonged to a glee club, and entertained modestly at his house in Rusholme, then a pleasant Manchester suburb. He died a bachelor, with no relatives closer than cousins.

Nothing in his life suggested that Owens would in death found a university college, but it does not follow that the idea was put into his head by George Faulkner or Samuel Fletcher; there is no evidence one way or the other. Talk of a university college in Manchester had been in the air since the mid-1830s. The idea, whatever its origin, was already in Owens's mind in 1844, because he was instructing his solicitor about a will embodying large charitable bequests within five weeks of his father's death. He finally signed the will on 31 May 1845. After substantial bequests to relatives, friends, and servants, and small bequests to local charities, he left the residue (nearly £100,000) to found a college for the instruction of young men not less than fourteen years old, 'in such branches of learning and science as are now or may be taught in the English universities'. Apart from the restriction to men, which was to be expected at the time, no stipulations were to be imposed on staff or students, whether as to religion, condition in life, or place of birth.

Owens's trustees lost no time in liquidating the remaining stock of textiles and other often ancient reminders of businesses long since abandoned. They sold all but the soundest of his railway shares, and invested the proceeds in safe securities. In view of the subsequent fall in share prices the trustees acted wisely, for Owens would probably have died a poorer man had he lived a few years longer. Owens College opened in 1851 in Quay Street, Deansgate, Manchester, and remained there until 1873 when it moved to new and much larger premises in the Oxford Road. The University of Manchester traces a direct line of descent from this foundation, and until recently was affectionately and fittingly known to its students as 'Owens'. B. W. CLAPP

Sources *Manchester Guardian* (5 Aug 1846) • J. C. Lockhart, 'John Owens', *Papers of the Manchester Literary Club*, 4 (1878), 136–7 • E. Swanwick, *The founder of Owens College* (1878) • J. Thompson, *The Owens College: its foundation and growth* (1886) • B. W. Clapp, *John Owens, Manchester merchant* (1965) • *DNB* • d. cert.
Archives JRL
Likenesses T. Woolner, medallion, after 1846, University of Manchester
Wealth at death approx. £160,000

Owens, John Lennergan (*fl. c.*1780), actor, was born in Ireland, where apparently he confined his performances. He acted at the Smock Alley Theatre in Dublin, where his Zanga in Edward Young's tragedy *The Revenge* was considered the best that ever succeeded that of Henry Mossop. He was known for his persistent inebriety and once, coming onstage as Polydore in Thomas Otway's *The Orphan*, he was hissed by the audience for obvious intoxication. Placing himself in a fighting position at the front of the stage he delivered the soliloquy 'Here I'm alone and fit for mischief' with a scowl. The audience's resentment was subdued by the rage of the actor; they joined in laughter and he was permitted to finish his performance. Unfortunately, Owens's alcoholism reduced him to extreme poverty and he eventually became a beggar in the streets. On seeing John Kemble announced to play Zanga, his favourite character, six years after playing it himself Owens begged money from a person of decent appearance. When asked his name he replied with tragic solemnity 'Has six years' cruel absence extinguished majesty so far that nought shines here to tell you I'm the real Zanga? Yes, sir, John Lennergan Owens, successor to Henry Mossop'. The gentleman was moved with compassion and gave him a shilling. On his way to get some dinner Owens was stopped by another mendicant, who implored his assistance; he stepped into a public house, changed his shilling, and gave half to the other beggar. Though the foreword to *The Thespian Dictionary* claims to list only important actors of the period Owens does not seem to be noted in other contemporary theatrical memoirs or records. ROBERTA MOCK

Sources *The thespian dictionary, or, Dramatic biography of the present age*, 2nd edn (1805)

Owenson [*formerly* MacOwen], **Robert Nugent** (1744–1812), actor and theatre manager, was born in the barony of Tyrawley, co. Mayo, Ireland, the son Walter MacOwen and his wife, Sydney Bell. His parents were poor, and he was principally educated in a hedge-school. He converted to protestantism, Anglicized his name, and travelled to London about 1765, under the patronage of an Irish absentee landlord who had recently returned from the West Indies and had been impressed by hearing Owenson sing. With the assistance of Thomas Augustine Arne, who declared him to have one of the finest baritone voices he had ever heard, particularly in falsetto, Owenson took singing lessons from John Worgan.

Owenson's earliest known appearance as a singer was in 1770 at Vauxhall Gardens, and he made his anonymous acting début with Younger's provincial company in Southampton in July 1771. On 4 November that year he made his first appearance in London, at Covent Garden (in the title role of Nicholas Rowe's *Tamerlane*) and was engaged for a further two seasons, during which he added considerably to his repertory of comic stage Irishmen, including Sir Lucius O'Trigger in Sheridan's *The Rivals*, Major O'Flaherty in Richard Cumberland's *The West Indian*, Teague in Robert Howard's *The Committee*, and Foigard in Farquhar's *The Beaux' Stratagem*. Cumberland and Sheridan thanked Owenson for redeeming their creations from caricature.

On 15 December 1772 Owenson married Jane Hill (*d.* 1789). Jane's family were prosperous, evangelical Methodists from Shropshire (her father was at one time lord mayor of Shrewsbury); deeply opposed to the theatre, they were shocked by her marriage to an actor, but did not cut her off, and she was left a significant legacy by her father. The Owensons had four children, of whom two daughters survived infancy. They were the novelist Sydney [*see* Morgan, Sydney, Lady Morgan] and Olivia, who married the physician Sir Arthur Clarke. Owenson left Covent Garden at the end of the 1773–4 season and performed in 1774 with Samuel Foote's summer company at the Haymarket and in 1776 with Tate Wilkinson's company, where he was noticed by Dublin's Crow Street Theatre manager, Thomas Ryder, and offered a small share in that theatre and the post of deputy manager.

Owenson's twenty-year association with the Irish theatre began at Crow Street on 21 October 1776, when he appeared in his most famous role, Major O'Flaherty in *The West Indian*. A Dublin critic found his brogue 'characteristic, and not too vulgar' (*Freeman's Journal*, 22 Oct 1776). Owenson quickly established himself as Crow Street's Irishman, playing a wide variety of Irish roles and singing Irish songs in the Irish language, both in Dublin and on his frequent visits to provincial theatres. He also became known for his comic monologues, such as 'Larry

O'Shaughnessy's Tour thro' Dublin' and 'The Black Cart, or, A Peep at Channel Row'. In the next nine seasons he acted regularly in nearly a hundred roles, about half of which were Irish parts, and he became very popular, especially during the period after 1779 when the Irish Volunteers, to which Owenson belonged, constituted a significant part of Irish theatre audiences. Owenson was the only entertainer of any stature in his day to sing songs in the Irish language in the professional theatre. In addition to at least one prologue in Irish, Owenson is credited with writing a popular comic piece called *The Prelude* (1777), at least two songs, 'Rory O'More' and 'Love's the Fairest Creature', and a long poem entitled 'Theatrical Fears' (1804).

Owenson led a company of actors to Sligo and Galway in October 1782 and was so successful that, with the encouragement of the local gentry, he built a small but elegant new theatre in Kirwan's Lane, the first structure to be built in Galway specifically for theatrical performances. Whether his experiences in Galway ignited in him the desire to manage in Dublin, or whether he quarrelled with Daly, is not known with certainty, but on 20 December 1784 Owenson opened a rival new City Theatre in the refurbished playhouse in Fishamble Street. Lady Morgan's largely inaccurate account of the life of this theatre must be corrected. Owenson had long been associated with the nascent nationalist movement in Ireland, and, although this point is largely conjectural, he had almost certainly hoped to capitalize on these connections in his new venture. But Lady Morgan's claim that her father had founded the first Irish 'national' theatre at Fishamble Street is not reflected in the repertory, which contained little that was original, or even particularly Irish. After a strong start the Fishamble Street theatre operated with increasing irregularity until early June 1785. There is, however, some evidence to support Lady Morgan's insinuation that the Fishamble Street venture was discouraged, if not suppressed, by the Irish government in order to grant a patent and theatrical monopoly to Daly.

By August 1785 Owenson was to be found again with Daly's Crow Street company, where he remained for the next ten seasons. During a part of the 1793–4 season, and again in the following season, he was at Kilkenny at the head of a company, probably as Daly's deputy. He spent the summer of the 1796–7 season at Crow Street and made a visit to Cork in October 1797. Thereafter he retired from the stage, and perhaps became the landlord of a Dublin public house. As early as the time of the closing of the Fishamble Street theatre he had taken up the importation of French wines as a sideline, and he met with considerable success in the business. His wife, Jane, died in late May or early June 1789 in Drumcondra. She had never deviated from her evangelical piety and opposition to the stage, nor had she settled easily into Irish society. Her daughter observed that she was forced to live in 'her penal settlement … hating both potatoes and papists with Christian inveteracy, and culinary prejudice' (Campbell, 22–3).

Owenson came out of retirement briefly in 1807, when he acted the part of O'Driscoll several times in his daughter's comic opera *The First Attempt*. On 27 May 1807 at Crow Street he took what was almost certainly his farewell benefit. He died, at the age of sixty-eight, at the Dublin home of his younger daughter shortly before 28 May 1812, and was buried in the graveyard in Irishtown.

JOHN C. GREENE

Sources Highfill, Burnim & Langhans, *BDA* • W. S. Clark, *The Irish stage in the county towns, 1720–1800* (1965) • *Lady Morgan's memoirs: autobiography, diaries, and correspondence*, ed. W. H. Dixon, 2 vols. (1862) • W. J. Fitzpatrick, *Lady Morgan: her career, literary and personal, with a glimpse of her friends, and a word to her calumniators* (1860) • *DNB* • M. Campbell, *Lady Morgan* (1988) • *IGI*

Likenesses J. R. Maguire?, miniature, exh. 1809 (of Owenson?)

Owtram [Outram], **William** (*bap.* **1626**, *d.* **1679**), Church of England clergyman, was the son of Robert Owtram and was baptized in Derbyshire either at Barlow, near Chesterfield, on 17 March 1626, or at the adjacent parish of Dronfield six weeks earlier on 5 February. In May 1642 he was admitted to Trinity College, Cambridge, whence he graduated BA in 1645 and proceeded MA in 1649. From 1648 to 1657 he was a fellow of Christ's College, Cambridge; in 1655 he was junior proctor of the university. In 1660 he was created DD.

In May 1656 Owtram was presented to the living of Navenby in Lincolnshire, which he held until 1659 when he was appointed to the rectory of St Mary Woolnoth, London. It is likely that he received episcopal ordination during this time, as others like Simon Patrick did, for he continued to hold the living at the Restoration and retained it until 1666. In 1664 he was appointed rector of St Margaret's, Westminster, and in 1670 a prebendary of Westminster Abbey. In July 1669 he was also installed as archdeacon of Leicester. He died on 23 August 1679, and was buried two days later in Westminster Abbey, where a monument was erected to him.

Owtram was a respected churchman, and the nonconformist Richard Baxter had a high regard for him, considering him 'understanding, Conscionable & peaceable' (Keeble and Nuttall, 2.105). He gained a reputation as a scholar, especially knowledgeable in rabbinic literature. This was demonstrated in his work *De sacrificiis libri duo* (1677), which he dedicated to Thomas Osborne, earl of Danby. The book was written to defend the doctrine of atonement against the Socinians, and to refute the idea that Christ's death was merely an example of piety. It is a discussion of Hebrew sacrifices and their meanings, buttressed with patristic and rabbinical references, and concludes with a discussion of Christ's heavenly intercession. An English translation by John Allen was published in 1817.

After Owtram's death Joseph Hindmarsh published six sermons which he alleged were shorthand versions of Owtram's sermons. His friends repudiated their authenticity, claiming that they were 'thrust out into the world' only to serve the ends of profit (*Twenty Sermons*, sig. A5r). James Gardiner, later bishop of Lincoln, published some of Owtram's genuine sermons under the title *Twenty Sermons Preached upon Several Occasions* in 1682, with a revised edition in 1697. The introduction portrayed Owtram as identifying the danger of three enemies—papists, libertines, and dissenters—and the sermons were commended as 'an Antidote very seasonable for the malignity of the Age' (*Twenty Sermons*, 380). The sermons bear out the description. They advocated stability in the nation and obedience to the magistrate, and several took issue with the Roman Catholic church on the use of scripture and on its teaching on the eucharistic presence. Against the dissenters who repudiated the use of a set form of prayers Owtram noted: 'All the Protestant Churches of other Nations, and all the Christian Churches in the World, have set forms for their publick Offices, and so hath the whole Church had for fourteen hundred years at least' (*Twenty Sermons*, 137–8). Preaching on 1 John 3: 7 Owtram launched an attack on John Saltmarsh and other antinomians who 'own no covenant between God and us, but only between God and Christ. This, say they, Christ hath performed, and so reconciled us unto God without the performance of any condition on our parts' (*Twenty Sermons*, 380).

In his will Owtram bequeathed lands in Derbyshire and Lincolnshire to his widow, Jane, and left legacies to his nephews and nieces. Surviving him by forty-two years, his widow died on 4 October 1721 and was buried in Westminster Abbey eight days later. A catalogue of Owtram's library was compiled by William Cooper in 1681.

BRYAN D. SPINKS

Sources Venn, *Alum. Cant.* • J. L. Chester, ed., *The marriage, baptismal, and burial registers of the collegiate church or abbey of St Peter, Westminster*, Harleian Society, 10 (1876), 197, 304 • *Twenty sermons preached upon several occasions by William Owtram, DD*, 2nd edn (1697) • *IGI* • *Calendar of the correspondence of Richard Baxter*, ed. N. H. Keeble and G. F. Nuttall, 2 (1991), 91–2, 105 • *Reliquiae Baxterianae, or, Mr Richard Baxter's narrative of the most memorable passages of his life and times*, ed. M. Sylvester, 1 vol. in 3 pts (1696) • *N&Q*, 7th ser., 11 (1891), 205 • *Fasti Angl., 1541–1857*, [Lincoln] • *Fasti Angl., 1541–1857*, [Ely] • J. Nichols, *The history and antiquities of the county of Leicester*, 2/2 (1798)

Likenesses R. White, line engraving, BM; repro. in *Twenty sermons*

Oxberry, William (1784–1824), actor and printer, was born in Moorfields, London, on 18 December 1784, the son of an auctioneer. At the age of fourteen he was made a pupil of the artist George Stubbs, but having developed at school a fascination for the stage he quickly abandoned painting, first for bookselling and then for indentures with a Tottenham Court Road printer named Seale, who fortuitously was equally obsessed with the theatre. Oxberry appeared in amateur theatricals (in nearby Queen Ann Street and Berwick Street), where he performed in *Macbeth* and *The Castle Spectre*. In the intervals between acting he learned the printing trade, but in 1802 made a bid for the professional stage, and made his first appearance at Watford as Antonio in *The Merchant of Venice*. Later, at Godalming, he was noticed by Trotter, manager of the Worthing and Hythe circuit, and given a renewable engagement as low comedian. While thus employed, he married at Southend in 1806 sixteen-year-old Catherine Elizabeth Hewitt, 'a lady of most respectable connexions' ('Memoir', 235).

At Worthing, Oxberry impressed Henry Siddons, who

William Oxberry (1784–1824), by George Clint, in or before 1822 [as Master Stephen in *Every Man in his Humour* by Ben Jonson]

recommended him to Covent Garden, where he was offered by John Kemble a three-year contract, beginning at £5 per week. On his début as Robin Roughhead in Allingham's farce *Fortune's Frolic* (7 November 1807) reviewers were divided: the hostile *Monthly Mirror* refused to 'consider him as a desirable acquisition to the London stage', yet *The Times* liked his 'perfect boyish simplicity' and compared his rustic characterization with that of experienced players such as Edward Knight, John Emery, and John Liston. Oxberry played Lord Duberly in Colman's *The Heir-at-Law* (14 November), but did not settle at Covent Garden and, before the season was over, negotiated release from his contract. Thereafter at Glasgow and Aberdeen he performed with reasonable success in tragedy. George Raymond, on tour in Scotland, induced him to return to London to play in Siddons's *The Russian Imposter* (Lyceum, 22 July 1809), when Samuel Arnold was impressed enough to offer him a three-year rising contract, beginning at £7 a week. He later obtained similar terms at Drury Lane, and a handsome follow-on four-year contract rising from a £9 base to £12 in the last two years. From 1807 to 1811 he also contributed occasional journalism to *The Cabinet* and the *Monthly Mirror*, which, as well as the *Theatrical Inquisitor*, he seems to have edited for a short while.

Oxberry was a regular member of the Drury Lane company between 1812 and 1820, when his roles included Dan in Colman's *John Bull*, Justice Greedy in Massinger's *A New*

Way to Pay Old Debts, Mawworm in Bickerstaffe's *The Hypocrite*, and Leo Luminati in Kenney's *Oh! This Love*. But when Robert Elliston reduced salaries in 1820, Oxberry left to star at the Sadler's Wells, east London, and Surrey theatres. He also played at the Haymarket in the summer of 1821.

The last years of Oxberry's short life were bound up with Elliston, who took on the Olympic in 1818 and Drury Lane in 1819. At the former, where he is said to have been stage-manager and partly responsible for the theatre's straightened finances, Oxberry made a successful début in 1819 as a playwright with the one-act afterpiece *The Actress of All Work* (28 January), usually erroneously attributed to his son. In this essentially single-actor piece, the heroine is in love with a theatrical manager's son. Desperate to join the company, she auditions in six disguises, ranging from 'country gawky', through Parisian opera singer, to amorous eighty-year-old, before convincing the father of her talent. Refused by Frances Kelly, for whom it was written, the part went to Elizabeth Edwin, who 'made it a sterling favourite' ('Memoir of Mrs Edwin', 208). Later performers, including Mrs Tayleure and Clara Fisher, gave the play an extended life in the repertory. Oxberry altered Pilon's comedy *He Would be a Soldier* (1786) into *The High Road to Marriage* (9 November 1820), in which he starred himself. It had some success but was never published. Winston credits Oxberry with authorship of *How to Pay your Taxes*, which when read in the green room was discovered to be 'so bad it had to be given up' (*Drury Lane Journal*, 6). It was licensed for the Olympic in November 1820, but apparently not performed. Another piece, described as 'taken from the poem of *Marmion*, [was] performed at the West London Theatre' ('Memoir', 240). Oxberry was also a leading actor at the Olympic from 1820 onwards (notably as Jerry Hawthorn in Moncrieff's *Tom and Jerry*). He gave the address on the opening night of the 1821 season (3 November); but in January 1822 he led an actors' strike when Elliston fell behind with the wages. The theatre remained closed for a month. In the year of his death, Oxberry agreed a new three-year contract with Elliston for the ensuing season at Drury Lane.

Oxberry utilized his skills as a printer throughout his life. From his press at 8 White Hart Yard, Drury Lane (moved to 1 St George's Place, Camberwell, in 1824), he issued playbills and several lightweight collections of anecdotes and miscellaneous material under his own editorship, including *The Theatrical Budget* (2 vols., 1809) and *Flowers of Literature, or, The Encyclopaedia of Anecdote* (*c*.1821–2; 2nd edn, 4 vols., 1824), published in shilling numbers, and designed for 'amusement without toil'. Considerably more substantial was *Oxberry's [Edition of the] New English Drama*, issued as separate plays (from 1818) and collected into twenty (sometimes twenty-two) volumes from 1819 to 1825 or 1826. It featured 'the peculiar business of the Performers, and the general directions of the Stage, as practised at the *London Theatres Royal* … [with] costumes, acting times for each act, & "Original Remarks" on the merit of every Drama'. Some commentaries were Oxberry's, some were by unknown writers, and eighteen were by William Hazlitt (later reprinted by him elsewhere). Also noteworthy is *Oxberry's Dramatic Biography, and Histrionic Anecdotes*, a series of 'chiefly original' memoirs of contemporary actors and actresses, edited after Oxberry's death by his widow, Catherine, who claimed her husband delayed publication because of the sensitivity of some of the material: he 'could not review as a critic the man that he met as a brother' ('Advertisement'). Between 1 January 1825 and 15 April 1826, when Mrs Oxberry's responsibility ended, sixty-four memoirs were issued (4 vols.), some written by Oxberry himself. Later that year a fifth volume, usually ascribed to Catherine Oxberry's second husband, Leman Thomas Rede, whom she married in 1824, concluded the original series.

Oxberry's strength as an actor was in dialect and rustic parts, though he was never a great performer, partly perhaps because, unlike rivals such as Liston, 'he bestowed too little study on his profession' ('Memoir', 239). However, Hazlitt gave a superbly evocative description of his role as Justice Greedy, in whom 'apparitions of fat turkeys, chines of bacon, and pheasants dressed in toast and butter, evidently floated in rapturous confusion before his senses' (*The Examiner*, 14 Jan 1816). Art seemed to imitate life, for Oxberry had a reputation as a 'free liver' and was never happier than feasting and drinking in company with like-minded friends. It was no surprise when in December 1821 he acquired the Craven's Head chop-house in Drury Lane, a popular venue for theatrical people, where 'we *vocalize* on a Friday, *conversationize* on a Sunday, and *chopize* every day' ('Memoir', 239). Although he tried latterly to moderate his habits, he simply lived life too hard. Following two attacks, from which he appeared to recover, he died of an apoplectic fit at the Craven's Head on 9 June 1824. As the *Gentleman's Magazine* put it, an addiction to tavern life 'shortened the days of a very shrewd, pleasant, good-humoured man'. Winston was blunter: 'this is another instance of early death from drinking' (*Drury Lane Journal*, 89). Oxberry was buried in a vault at St Clement Danes, Strand.

Dark in complexion, with curly dark hair, Oxberry was just under 5 feet 10 inches tall and, in later years, rather plump. A distinctive feature was the piercing and expressive nature of his eyes. Of Oxberry's three children two survived infancy and aspired to theatrical careers: a daughter, who made her début in 1826 at the Olympic, and, much more successfully, a son, William Henry *Oxberry. JOHN RUSSELL STEPHENS

Sources 'Memoir of William Oxberry', *Oxberry's Dramatic Biography*, 1/14 (1825), 233–41 • *The Times* (10 June 1824), 3 • *GM*, 1st ser., 94/2 (1824), 186 • *Monthly Mirror* (Nov 1807), 360 [review] • *The Times* (9 Nov 1807), 3 [review] • *The Times* (19 Nov 1821), 2 [review] • *The complete works of William Hazlitt*, ed. P. P. Howe, 21 vols. (1930–34) • *Drury Lane journal: selections from James Winston's diaries, 1819–1827*, ed. A. L. Nelson and G. B. Cross (1974) • 'A prospectus of *Oxberry's new English drama*', 1818 • *Oxberry's Dramatic Biography*, 1/14 (1825), 234–41 • C. Murray, *Robert William Elliston: manager* (1974) • Hall, *Dramatic ports*. • 'Memoir of Mrs Edwin', *Oxberry's Dramatic Biography*, 4/60 (1826)

Likenesses S. De Wilde, watercolour drawing, 1811, Garr. Club • G. Clint, group portrait, oils, 1820, Garr. Club • G. Clint, portrait, in or before 1822; Christies, 15 Oct 1976, lot 74 [*see illus.*] • E. Blake, engraving • H. R. Cook, engraving (after S. De Wilde; as Leo Luminati in *Oh! This love*), repro. in *Theatrical inquisitor* (1812) • H. R. Cook, engraving (after T. Wageman; as Mawworm in *The hypocrite*), repro. in *Oxberry's new English drama*, 1 (1819) • G. Cruikshank, engraving (as Justice Greedy in *A new way to pay old debts*), repro. in *British Stage* (April 1817) • I. R. Cruikshank, engraving (as Humphrey Gull in *The dwarf of Naples*), repro. in *The theatre* (1819) • I. R. Cruikshank, engraving (as Jerry Hawthorn in *Tom and Jerry*) • S. De Wilde, portrait (as Petro in *Petro's bridge*), Garr. Club • S. Drummond, portrait, possibly NPG • R. Page, engraving (as Leo Luminati), repro. in *The drama* (1821) • J. Rogers, engraving (after S. Drummond), repro. in 'Memoir of William Oxberry' • T. Woolnoth, engraving (after G. Clin; as Master Stephen in *Every man in his humour*), repro. in *Oxberry's new English drama*, 16 (1823) • T. Woolnoth, engraving (after vignette by R. Sherwin) • engraving (as Dan in *John Bull*) • engraving (as Tom Baggs in *St Mary's eve*) • prints, BM, NPG • prints, Harvard TC

Oxberry, William Henry (1808–1852), actor, the son of the actor and theatrical writer William *Oxberry (1784–1824) and his wife, Catherine, *née* Hewitt, was born on 21 April 1808, probably in London. He received his preliminary education at Merchant Taylors' School, London, which he entered in September 1816. At a school in Kentish Town, kept by a Mr Patterson, he received some training in acting. On leaving there his education was continued under John Clarke, the author of *Ravenna*, and Revd R. Nixon. First placed in his father's printing office, he became afterwards, like him, 'the pupil of an eminent artist'. He was then apprenticed to Septimus Wray, a surgeon of Salisbury Square, Fleet Street, where he remained until his father's death in 1824.

About the beginning of 1825 Oxberry appeared at a private theatre in Rawstorne Street, London, as Abel Day to the Captain Careless of Frank Matthews. After playing Tommy in *All at Coventry*, he made his first professional appearance at the Olympic at a benefit for his stepfather, Leman Thomas *Rede, on 17 March 1825, as Sam Swipes in *Exchange No Robbery*. He was then employed by Leigh Hunt of *The Examiner*, but soon returned to the stage, and played in Chelmsford, Hythe, Manchester, and Sheffield before joining Hammond's company at York and Hull. In the autumn of 1832 he acted at the Strand in Rede's *Loves of the Angels*. At the close of the season he went with Harriet Smithson to Paris and played low-comedy parts at the Italian Opera.

After returning to England, Oxberry accepted a four-year engagement at the English Opera House (Lyceum), of which, with disastrous effect upon his fortunes, he became manager. He was then at the Princess's. In autumn 1841 he succeeded Robert Keeley at Covent Garden and played Flute in *A Midsummer Night's Dream*. In 1842 he was again at the Lyceum, where he appeared principally in burlesque and won a reputation as a comic dancer. The occasional parts he took in farce included his repeatedly revived Victim in John Oxenford's *My Fellow Clerk* and Mizzle in the same author's *A Day Well Spent*. In January 1843 he was at the Princess's playing the hero, a jealous husband, of *A Lost Letter*. In June he was a ridiculous old schoolmaster in John Poole's drama *The Swedish Ferryman*, and in September, with Edward Wright and Paul Bedford, was at the Strand playing in *Bombastes furioso* and *The Three Graces*. On returning to the Princess's Oxberry appeared with the Keeleys and Walter Lacy in W. T. Moncrieff's farce *Borrowing a Husband*, and in 1844 was Wamba in the opera of *The Maid of Judah*, a version of *Ivanhoe*. In February 1845 he was Sir Harry in James Townley's *High Life below Stairs*, and in April, Verges to Miss Cushman's Beatrice. In July he was the original Mrs Caudle to the Mr Caudle of Henry Compton in *Mr and Mrs Caudle*. He was also at Covent Garden under the management of Madame Vestris. There were few theatres at which he was not seen, and for a time he managed the Windsor theatre.

A very little man, with a quaint, peculiar manner and a thin voice, Oxberry was a lively actor and dancer in burlesque, but was said rarely to know his part on first nights. He was a member of the Dramatic Authors' Society, and a somewhat voluminous dramatist. His plays have never been collected, and many of them were never printed. Nicoll lists twenty-two, of which the melodrama *Matteo Falcone* (performed at the Lyceum in June 1836) and the farce *The Pacha's Pets* (Royal Victoria, September 1838) are perhaps the most noteworthy. Oxberry himself claimed to have left behind thirty unacted plays, which he trusted would be given after his death for the benefit of his second wife (his first wife, Ellen Lancaster, had died in 1842) and three children, otherwise unprovided for. He was responsible for *Oxberry's Weekly Budget of Plays* (1843–4), consisting of thirty-nine plays edited by him, and *Oxberry's Dramatic Chronology* (1850). Up to his death he was, with Charles Mathews and Madame Vestris, playing in *The Game of Speculation* and *The Prince of Happy Land*. His death, through lung disease, augmented by somewhat festive habits, took place on 29 February 1852. By a curious and painful will, printed in *The Era* for 21 March 1852, and written four days before he died, he left such property as he possessed to Charles Melville, a tragic actor better known outside London, in trust for his children. He expressed many wishes concerning his funeral which were not observed; asked that his heart might be preserved in some medical museum as a specimen of a broken one; hoped that a benefit might be given him to pay his debts, which were moderate; and left messages of farewell to many well-known actors.

JOSEPH KNIGHT, *rev.* KLAUS STIERSTORFER

Sources *Dramatic and Musical Review* (1842) [et seq.] • A. Nicoll, *Early nineteenth century drama, 1800–1850*, 2nd edn (1955), vol. 4 of *A history of English drama, 1660–1900* (1952–9) • *The Era* (21 March 1852) • *N&Q*, 8th ser., 5 (1894), 16, 79 • G. B. Bryan, ed., *Stage deaths: a biographical guide to international theatrical obituaries, 1850–1990*, 2 vols. (1991) • C. J. Robinson, ed., *A register of the scholars admitted into Merchant Taylors' School, from AD 1562 to 1874*, 2 (1883), 203 • Hall, *Dramatic ports*.

Likenesses G. Cruikshank, coloured etching (after his earlier work; as Justice Greedy in *A new way to pay old debts*), repro. in *British Stage* (April 1817) • I. R. Cruikshank, coloured etching (as Jerry Hawthorn in *Tom and Jerry*), Harvard TC • I. R. Cruikshank, coloured etching (after his earlier work; as Humphrey Gull in *The dwarf of Naples*), repro. in *The theatre* (1819) • J. Rogers, stipple and line engraving (after S. Drummond), repro. in *Oxberry's Dramatic Biography* (1825) • plate (after unknown portrait; as Peter White), repro. in *Theatrical Times* (20 Feb 1847)

Oxburgh, Henry (*d.* 1716), Jacobite insurgent, was a member of a Roman Catholic family of Bovin, King's county, Ireland, a cadet branch of the Oxburghs of Emneth, Norfolk. A Hewer Oxburgh (a name common to both English and Irish branches of the family) had almost 1000 acres in King's county in 1655–6. The family were staunch supporters of James II, with a Hewer Oxburgh serving as sheriff in 1687 and as an MP in 1689. Both a Colonel Francis Oxburgh and Henry Oxburgh were named as assessors for tax in King's county in April 1690, and a Henry Oxburgh served as a captain in Sir Hewer Oxburgh's infantry regiment. No fewer than six Oxburghs were attainted in 1691. A Colonel Oxburgh (probably Sir Hewer) was killed at Aughrim in July 1691, as his widow, Clare, filed a claim for her jointure out of his estate, and a Henry Oxburgh filed a claim for a remainder in tail.

In December 1692 Colonel Henry Oxburgh was arrested in Dublin as a precaution against a French descent. He may have been the Colonel Oxburgh who it was suggested might be secured from doing any mischief at home by serving in the army of the emperor or the duke of Bavaria in 1695. Henry served in the army of Louis XIV, and he may have returned home about 1700 and settled in Lancashire. However, in May 1705 and March 1714, Colonel Henry Oxburgh of Bovin, King's county, was licensed to carry arms. According to his own account, Oxburgh was in London when the oaths to George I were tendered 'and having truly a scrupulous conscience' (Boyer, 533–5) he left London for the north. His claim to have been persuaded into the rising lacks credibility, and it seems that he was sent to foment rebellion in the guise of a tourist. He was present at the first gathering of the Jacobites in Northumberland, and was an important commander of the English forces during the rising.

Oxburgh led a party of soldiers to Lowther Hall, home of Viscount Lonsdale, and also to Hornby Hall, the residence of Colonel Francis Charteris. He was 'frequently at the head of the English horse' (Boyer, 522) during the march into Lancashire, and a key adviser of the commanders, Thomas Forster and Lord Widdrington. Having reached Preston and being confronted by Hanoverian troops under the command of General Charles Wills, Forster decided to treat for terms. Oxburgh was subsequently blamed for this decision, some Jacobites opining that 'he was better at his beads and prayers, than at his business as a soldier, and we all thought him fitter for a priest than a field-officer' (Patten, 121). Oxburgh was sent into the English camp on the grounds that he had an acquaintance with some English officers, but he met an intransigent Wills who would only offer surrender 'at discretion'. Some dispute remains about whether Wills implied that he would intervene with the king by saying 'you cannot better entitle yourselves to clemency than by surrendering yourselves prisoners at discretion' (Ware, 140). In the event the Jacobites surrendered and Oxburgh was sent to London.

Oxburgh was tried on 7 May 1716. His defence counsel argued that the indictment was invalid as it referred to 'Colonel Oxborough', and that he had only ever worn a sword (the normal attire of a gentleman), had not committed any overt act of hostility, and that his being sent by the rebels to treat was not manifest treason. Lord Chief Justice Parker dismissed these arguments and Oxburgh was sentenced to death on the 9th. Oxburgh petitioned for clemency, but there is no evidence that his petition reached the king and on 14 May he was hanged, drawn, and quartered at Tyburn. In his speech from the scaffold he denied that the rebellion was designed to re-establish Roman Catholicism in England, 'for I never could find, that either by the laws of God, or the ancient constitution of this nation, difference of religion in the prince made any change in the allegiance of the subject' (Szechi, 66). His head was placed on Temple Bar which, according to reports reaching the Jacobite court, occasioned some resentment among the populace. It appears that Oxburgh was married, for following his execution Queen Mary evinced some concern for his children. His estate was confiscated and sold.

STUART HANDLEY

Sources A. Boyer, *The political state of Great Britain*, 11 (1716), 521–5, 533–5 • R. Patten, *The history of the late rebellion* (1717), 112–40 • S. Hibbert Ware, *Lancashire memorials of the rebellion*, 2 pts in 1, Chetham Society, 5 (1845), 21, 77, 87, 139–40, 168 • J. D'Alton, *Illustrations historical and genealogical of King James's Irish army list, 1689* (1855), 30, 851–3, 957 • *The manuscripts of the marquis of Ormonde*, [old ser.], 3 vols., HMC, 36 (1895–1909), vol. 2, pp. 156, 476, 480 • Gillow, *Lit. biog. hist.*, 5.225 • D. Barlow, ed., *The records of the forfeited estates commission*, Public Record Office Handbooks, 12 (1968), 59, 65, 77 • *Calendar of the Stuart papers belonging to his majesty the king, preserved at Windsor Castle*, 7 vols., HMC, 56 (1902–23), vol. 2, pp. 209, 241, 298 • L. Gooch, *The desperate faction? The Jacobites of north-east England, 1688–1745* (1995), 34, 62, 84 • *CSP dom.*, *1693*, p. 16 • *Report on the manuscripts of the marquis of Downshire*, 6 vols. in 7, HMC, 75 (1924–95), vol. 1, p. 599 • D. Szechi, 'The Jacobite theatre of death', *The Jacobite challenge*, ed. E. Cruickshanks and J. Black (1988), 57–73

Likenesses engraving, repro. in J. Caulfield, *Portraits, memoirs and characters of remarkable persons, from … 1688 to the end of the reign of George II*, 4 vols. (1819–20)

Oxenbridge, Daniel (1571–1642), physician, the only son of the Revd John Oxenbridge (*d.* 1618) and his wife, Mary, was born in Surrey. In the following year his father was presented to the living of Southam in Warwickshire by the Throgmorton family, who were both puritan and well-connected. He was later expelled from his rectory at Southam because of his involvement with the presbyterian movement of Thomas Cartwright, and was one of a number of Warwickshire ministers who subscribed the presbyterian Book of Discipline in 1588.

Daniel Oxenbridge's early years were spent in Warwickshire; he was first educated at St Peter's College, Westminster, from where he was elected to Christ Church, Oxford. He entered the university in 1590 and took his BA in 1593, and MA in 1596. Any thought of following his father into the ministry vanished with the violent suppression of the presbyterian movement in the 1590s. Medicine remained a realistic alternative for many puritans, and Oxenbridge practised medicine for many years in Daventry, Northamptonshire. About 1601 he married Katherine Harby, a member of a local gentry family. They had four daughters, Mary (*b.* 1602), Dorcas, Katherine, who married the parliamentarian commander Philip

Skippon, and Elizabeth, who married the prominent parliamentarian leader Oliver St John; and three sons, John *Oxenbridge, Daniel, and Clement. The Restoration poet Katherine Philips was Oxenbridge's granddaughter.

After many years in practice in Daventry, in 1620 Oxenbridge rather suddenly accumulated his MB and MD degrees at Christ Church. Soon after he moved his practice and his family to London. The need to increase his income to support his large family may have prompted the move, or it may have been due to increasing pressure from bishops on the practice of medicine by puritans. A university medical degree obviated an episcopal medical licence, while an MD from Oxford or Cambridge was also a primary qualification for a fellowship of the College of Physicians in London.

Oxenbridge first appeared before the college on 23 May 1623, asking for preferential treatment based on the currency of his degree, and his many years of practice before its award. Oxenbridge's advanced age was somewhat unusual in a prospective fellow, as was his extensive medical experience. However, he did not become a candidate in the college until August 1626, and was not formally elected a fellow until 22 November 1627. His tenure in the college was uneventful: he held no office, but regularly attended meetings, at which he, like all the fellows, complained about the medical malpractice observed in the City. Oxenbridge's financial contributions to the college were average; modest, too, was the house in which he and his wife lived in St Benet Sherehog parish. A tithing survey of 1638 rated the house the ninth most valuable out of the twenty-eight houses noted in the parish. A circumspect life did not, however, preclude his coming to the aid of his puritan co-religionists, which he did in 1639, when he stood surety for Peter Smart, canon of Durham, in his struggle with Durham's Laudian canon Dr John Cosin. Oxenbridge died at his London house in St Sythe Lane, St Benet Sherehog, on 24 August 1642, the eve of the puritan revolution. He was buried in St Benet Sherehog churchyard.

Oxenbridge's will of 1641 revealed that, as well as his house, he owned a number of landholdings, which he passed on to his wife, children, and grandchildren. These included lands and tenements in the most radical puritan parish in the City, St Stephen's, Coleman Street; lands in Northumberland and Bermuda; and a property called the Tynne Farm. Among the physician's other bequests were £10 to his daughter Katherine Fowler, then the wife of a London merchant, and £10 more to the Fowlers' daughter, Oxenbridge's granddaughter, Katherine. The anonymous *General Observations and Prescriptions in the Practice of Physick*, published in 1715, is said to have been based on Oxenbridge's casebook. WILLIAM BIRKEN

Sources *Brief lives, chiefly of contemporaries, set down by John Aubrey, between the years 1669 and 1696*, ed. A. Clark, 2 (1898), 152–4 • H. F. Waters, 'Genealogical gleanings in England', *New England Historical and Genealogical Register*, 44 (1890), 83–8 • *CSP dom.*, 1638–9 • G. E. Aylmer, *The state's servants: the civil service of the English republic, 1649–1660* (1973) • Munk, *Roll* • B. Hamey, 'Bustorum aliquot reliquiae …', RCP Lond. • annals, RCP Lond. • *The visitation of London, anno Domini 1633, 1634, and 1635, made by Sir Henry St George*, 2, ed. J. J. Howard, Harleian Society, 17 (1883) • A. F. S. Pearson, *Thomas Cartwright and Elizabethan puritanism, 1535–1603* (1925) • J. T. Cliffe, *The puritan gentry: the great puritan families of early Stuart England* (1984) • Tai Liu, *Discord in Zion: the puritan divines and the puritan revolution, 1640–1660* (1973) • Foster, *Alum. Oxon.* • I. Macalpine and R. A. Hunter, 'Daniel Oxenbridge, John Twysden and William Harvey', *Journal of the Royal College of Physicians of London*, 4 (1970), 169–76

Wealth at death wealthy; left property and cash

Oxenbridge, John (1608–1674), preacher and pastor in the West Indies and America, eldest son of Daniel *Oxenbridge (1571–1642), physician, and of his wife, Katherine Harby (*d.* 1651), and grandson to the Northamptonshire puritan radical divine John Oxenbridge (*d.* 1618), was born at Daventry on 30 January 1608. Admitted a pensioner of Emmanuel College, Cambridge, on 8 April 1626, he matriculated the same year but received his BA from Magdalen Hall, Oxford, on 13 November 1628 and his MA on 18 June 1631, subsequently becoming a tutor of the college, where the future Unitarian John Biddle was among his students. Laud deprived Oxenbridge in May 1634, after he had required his scholars to sign an oath that regulated their lives and deportment towards him more strictly than required by university statutes.

Oxenbridge left Oxford and about 1635 married his first wife, Jane Butler (*c.*1621–1658). She was said to be 'a scholar beyond what is usual in her sex, and of a masculine judgment in the profound points of religion' and Oxenbridge 'loved commonly to have her opinion upon a text of scripture before he preacht from it' (*Ambrose Barnes*, 64). The Oxenbridges left England in 1635 for Bermuda, where Oxenbridge provoked controversy with his conventicles and his vigorous catechizing. He and his wife were later said to have planted the seeds of congregationalism on the island.

Oxenbridge returned (in 1641) to England, where he preached in various towns. Having served in 1643 as an assistant to William Bridge at the congregationalist church in Norwich, he proceeded to Beverley, Yorkshire, where he was filling the perpetual curacy of the minister in 1644. In 1648 he was appointed a joint preacher at St Mary's, Beverley, and served as a minister in Beverley and Berwick upon Tweed. On 25 October 1652 he was appointed a fellow of Eton College (perhaps because his sister Elizabeth had married Oliver St John) and on 25 June the next year Cromwell appointed Oxenbridge a member of a new company charged with governing Bermuda. Andrew Marvell boarded with the Oxenbridges in Eton, and it was probably they who inspired him to write his poem 'Bermudas'. Marvell wrote a tender epitaph for a memorial slab for Jane Oxenbridge, who died on 25 April 1658 and was buried in Eton chapel, describing her as 'with primitive modesty plying the same successful pursuit for souls at home as he abroad'. Anthony Wood, the Oxford antiquary, regarded Oxenbridge as displaying the height of nonconformist hypocrisy in that, although Oxenbridge had vowed eternal love to his first wife, within a year of her death he married a 'religious virgin', Frances Woodward (Wood, *Ath. Oxon.*, 3rd edn, 3.468). Frances died within the year in childbirth and was also buried at Eton.

At the Restoration, Oxenbridge was ejected from his

Eton fellowship. He published a set of sermons in 1661 to discourage Fifth-Monarchy sentiments, and, having returned to Berwick upon Tweed, preached there until silenced by his refusal to comply with the Act of Uniformity in 1662. That year he moved to Surinam in order to propagate the gospel. A letter from him (superscribed Comaween, 29 October 1662) to his wife's brother-in-law, the Newcastle merchant Ambrose Barnes, trying to round up money and settlers, reports that 'having many English servants is not good; but some negros, cattle, and Indian trade will bring an ordinary English estate to a comfortable subsistence and use in these parts'. The Indians were more peaceful than elsewhere in the Americas and their language was easily learned, he reported (*Ambrose Barnes*, 45–6). He published a brief prospectus for propagating the gospel in Surinam, part of a larger manuscript.

Oxenbridge left for Barbados in 1667, perhaps because of the turmoil undergone by Surinam in the Anglo-Dutch War and his own financial and personal losses there. In Barbados his affairs did not prosper either, and in 1669 he moved to Massachusetts. While in Barbados he married his third wife, a widow, Susanna Abbot (*d.* 1696). Oxenbridge's friend, Thomas Parris, introduced the couple, and it was probably Oxenbridge's presence in Massachusetts that induced Parris to send his son Samuel, later best known for setting off the Salem witchcraft hysteria in 1692, to Harvard.

In Massachusetts, Oxenbridge first preached at the Charlestown church, but he turned down a call there on 25 October 1669 because he had already accepted a call from the First Church of Boston; on 20 January 1670 he and Susanna were made members there. The elderly teacher of the church, John Davenport, having died on 13 March 1670, Oxenbridge was ordained as his replacement on 4 May, and was made a freeman a week later. The First Church was currently at the storm centre of a major controversy over the half-way covenant. This reconceptualization of New England congregationalist church membership allowed members' children who had become parents but who had not testified to a work of grace in their souls to have partial church membership in order to have their own children baptized. The synod of 1662 had endorsed the half-way covenant, with a vocal minority protesting against it as a betrayal of the New England church order. The First Church had sided with the minority, and Oxenbridge continued that alignment. He and his church encouraged like-minded dissidents to resist the installation of a new minister at Newbury and to form their own church at Salem; he preached an election sermon in 1671 denouncing the half-way covenant and advocating tolerance for Baptists, who were admired by his minority of congregationalists because, whatever their errors about baptism, they preserved the purity of church membership; he harassed dissenters who had split from the First Church to form their own church. In 1672 Oxenbridge was appointed one of the licensers of the press. He died on 28 December 1674 of an apoplexy with which he was seized while delivering a sermon.

MICHAEL P. WINSHIP

Sources J. Oxenbridge, *A double watchword* (1661) · J. Oxenbridge, *New England freeman warmed and warned* (1673) · W. D. Cooper, *The Oxenbridges of Brede Place, Sussex, and Boston, Massachusetts* (1860) · J. H. Lefroy, *Memorials of the discovery and early settlement of the Bermudas or Somers Islands*, 2 vols. (1878–9), vol. 1, pp. 556, 570–75, 583, 594, 617, 687, 688, 705, 706 · *The complete works in verse and prose of Andrew Marvell*, ed. A. B. Grosart, 4 vols. (1872–5), vol. 2, pp. 3–7 · L. D. Gragg, 'The Barbados connection: John Parris and the early New England trade with the West Indies', *New England Historical and Genealogical Register*, 140 (1986), 99–113 · H. A. Hill, *History of the Old South Church (Third Church) Boston, 1669–1884* (1890), 1.80, 95, 165, 168, 169, 173, 190, 199, 210 · J. F. Hunnwell, 'The first record-book of the First Church in Charlestown, Massachusetts', *New England Historical and Genealogical Register*, 24 (1870), 131–6 · H. F. Waters, 'Genealogical gleanings in England', *New England Historical and Genealogical Register*, 44 (1890), 83–8 · W. Prynne, *A fresh discovery of some prodigies and new wandering-blazing stars, and firebrands, stiling themselves new lights* (1646), 4 · N. B. Shurtleff, ed., *Records of the governor and company of the Massachusetts Bay in New England*, 5 vols. in 6 (1853–4), vol. 4/2, p. 509, 584 · J. Hull, 'Diary', *Proceedings of the American Antiquarian Society*, 3 (1857), 234, 239 · J. Duncan, 'William Bridge, puritan divine, 1600–1670', 1960, DWL, 8 · BL, Add. MS 5831, fols. 60v, 61v · S. Foster, *The long argument: English puritanism and the shaping of New England culture, 1570–1700* (1991), chap. 5 · *DNB* · *The poems and letters of Andrew Marvell*, ed. H. M. Margoliouth, 2nd edn, 1 (1952), 262 · *Memoirs of the life of Mr Ambrose Barnes*, ed. [W. H. D. Longstaffe], SurtS, 50 (1867)

Wealth at death £1715 14*s.* 8*d.*: will, reprinted in Waters, 'Genealogical gleanings', 87

Oxenden, Ashton (1808–1892), bishop of Montreal, sixth son of Sir Henry Oxenden, seventh baronet (1756–1838), and Mary, daughter of Colonel Graham of St Lawrence, near Canterbury, was born at Barham, Broome Park, Canterbury, on 20 September 1808. He had six brothers and five sisters.

Educated at Ramsgate School and at Harrow School (with H. E. Manning and Christopher Wordsworth), Oxenden matriculated from University College, Oxford, on 9 June 1826, graduated BA in 1831, MA in 1859, and was created DD 10 July 1869. At university he neglected his work to hunt and play cricket. In December 1833 he was ordained to the curacy of Barham, Kent, where he introduced weekly cottage lectures and tried to enliven the services. His parish work ruined his health and he spent much of the decade from 1838 travelling on the continent. From 1849 to 1869 he was rector of Pluckley with Pevington, Kent, and in 1864 was made an honorary canon of Canterbury Cathedral. On 14 June 1864 he married Sarah (*d.* 1903), daughter of Joseph Hoare Bradshaw, a London banker; they had a daughter, Mary. At Pluckley he first began extemporaneous preaching. He published his cottage lectures as the popular *Barham Tracts*, followed by the *Pluckley Tracts*, 116 pamphlets in all.

In May 1869 Oxenden was elected—as a compromise candidate between the evangelicals and the Tractarians—bishop of Montreal and metropolitan of Canada by the Canadian provincial synod. He was consecrated in Westminster Abbey on 1 August, and installed in Montreal Cathedral on 5 September. Three-quarters of the population of the city were Roman Catholics, but the Church of England possessed twelve churches there besides the

Ashton Oxenden (1808–1892), by William Notman

cathedral. Oxenden presided over nine dioceses. He assiduously attended to his episcopal duties, generally living in Montreal during the winter and visiting the country districts in the summer. *My First Year in Canada* (1871) was written to raise funds for the diocese. He considerably increased the number of clergy, but found his time much taken up by rows about ritualism. Ill health caused his resignation of the bishopric in 1878.

On his return to England Oxenden attended the Pan-Anglican synod and then moved to southern France, acting as chaplain at Cannes, 1878–9. From 30 May 1879 to 1884 he was vicar of St Stephen's, near Canterbury, and from 1879 to 1884 he officiated as rural dean of Canterbury. In 1891 he wrote *The History of my Life*, the last of his many works which had made him one of the best-selling clerical authors of his time. He was a master of the plain but lively exposition of Christian principles. Oxenden died at Chalet Esperance, Biarritz, France, on 22 February 1892. G. C. Boase, *rev.* H. C. G. Matthew

Sources A. Oxenden, *The history of my life* (1891) • *The Times* (23 Feb 1892) • *The Guardian* (24 Feb 1892) • J. I. Cooper, *The blessed communion: the origins and history of the diocese of Montreal, 1760–1960* (1960) • J. P. Francis, 'Oxenden, Ashton', *DCB*, vol. 12 • *CGPLA Eng. & Wales* (1892)

Likenesses W. Notman, photograph, NA Canada [*see illus.*] • portrait, repro. in O. R. Rowley, *The Anglican episcopate of Canada and Newfoundland*, 2 vols. (1928–61) • portrait, repro. in F. D. Adams, *A history of Christ Church Cathedral, Montreal* (1941) • portrait, repro. in Oxenden, *History* • portrait, repro. in *The Graphic* (5 March 1892), 298

Wealth at death £2354 3*s*. 6*d*.: probate, 10 May 1892, *CGPLA Eng. & Wales*

Oxenden, Sir George (1620–1669), administrator in India, was the third son of Sir James Oxenden of Dene, Kent, and Margaret, daughter of Thomas Nevinson of Eastry, Kent. He was baptized at Wingham, Kent, on 6 April 1620. His older brother was Sir Henry Oxenden, first baronet (1614–1686), and his nephew, George *Oxenden (*bap.* 1651, *d.* 1703), was a notable lawyer and politician. In 1632 he went to India in attendance upon the Revd Arthur Hatch of Wingham. During the following six years he became fluent in the languages used in north-western India and made himself invaluable, mostly at Ahmadabad, to the East India Company's factors. In their letter to the company (4 January 1639) the president and council at Surat praised the young man's activities and his character and recommended him to the directors for more formal and better-paid employment in the company.

In 1639 Oxenden returned to England, where the Surat council's recommendation for 'his civil carriage and expert knowledge of the Industan language' resulted in his formal employment by the company as a factor for Surat on a salary of £25 per year (29 Jan 1641, Sainsbury and Foster, 2.137). Back in India between October 1641 and January 1653, he continued to demonstrate the linguistic and commercial skills which had so impressed his colleagues. He was entrusted with ventures to Goa, Cape Comorin, and Macao, but mostly to Mocha (Yemen). He also demonstrated a willingness to advocate strong measures against local rulers who attempted to expropriate the company's property, and a constant loyalty for the company's senior officers. These aspects of his character gained him a continuing respect and affection from indigenous merchants and governors and Englishmen alike, throughout his career in India.

In 1653 Oxenden returned to England. Between 1656 and January 1659 he pursued private stock ventures to the East, taking advantage of the East India Company's loss of its old monopoly (1654–7). The ventures do not appear to have been very successful, and when offered the post of president at Surat, Oxenden accepted (25 October 1661). On 24 November 1661 he was knighted at Whitehall. His commission of employment (19 March 1662) described him as 'President and Cheife Director of all our affaires at Suratt and all other our factories in the north parts of India from Zeilon to the Redd Sea'. Excluded from his control were Madras, Bengal, and Bantam, areas of which he had little experience. It was also thought that his responsibilities in north-western India would take all his time. His salary, £300 plus a gratuity of £200 per year, reflected his great experience and value to the company.

At the end of March 1662 Oxenden sailed for India, accompanied by the third earl of Marlborough and royal troops intending to take over the old Portuguese possession of Bombay, ceded to Charles II in his marriage settlement with Catherine of Braganza. He arrived at Surat on 18 September. At this time he focused his attention on re-establishing amicable relationships with local powers; trying to secure the release of Englishmen held captive by the Maratha chieftain Sivaji at Rairi; reorganizing the company's trade following the royal charter given to the

East India Company; and suppressing private trading activities. Affairs at Bombay were in the hands of the crown's forces. When the Portuguese refused to surrender Bombay, causing great difficulties for the English personnel, Oxenden was forced to take a greater role, especially in supplying the dwindling numbers of men with provisions and shelter. This was made more difficult by the Mughal fears that Bombay would take trade from Surat, and their concern about armed foreigners landing in their dominions. Oxenden skilfully balanced the different contending demands and responsibilities.

Sivaji raided Surat on 6–13 January 1664 and only the English and Dutch factories held out against him. The town itself was severely damaged and looted. The English actions gained the Mughal governor's gratitude and friendship, and the more tangible benefit of a reduction in the customs duties to which English trade had been liable at Surat. For the employees' heroism in protecting the company's substantial possessions the directors expressed their gratitude through a reward of £200 and a gold medal worth £20 for Oxenden, and various much smaller sums of money for other employees at Surat. These were not sent to India until 1668.

In 1665 Oxenden's attention was taken by consequences in India of the Second Anglo-Dutch War (March 1665–July 1667); the transfer of Bombay to the English, and the reprehensible activities of the crown's personnel at Bombay in seizing Indian ships, causing retaliation by the Mughal governor at Surat; and the problems created by Sir Edward Winter's usurpation of the English settlement at Madras. He was also increasingly disturbed personally by the company's willingness to listen to accusations against him of trading privately outside the company's indulgence to him. In 1666 he asked the company to nominate his successor, so that he could return to England according to his contract (1 January 1666). His increasingly poor health, the difficulties in India, and the death of his sister Elizabeth (Dallison), who was also his agent in England, caused him to renew his request on 26 March 1667 to return to England.

This request caused the directors to state their appreciation of, and total support for, Oxenden's administration. The directors realized that they needed Oxenden's experience, abilities, and skills more than ever. The grant of letters patent making Bombay over to the East India Company (27 March 1668) removed the basis for the conflict between the two sets of English authorities in western India, and the directors asked Oxenden to stay in India to secure the company's authority at Bombay (dispatch to Surat, 27 March 1668).

Oxenden made his only visit to Bombay on 2–29 January 1669, where he made clear his hopes for an orderly and efficient settlement under the company's administration. The commission appointing him 'Governor and Comander in Cheife of our port and island of Bombay' was sent to India on 10 March 1669; it arrived at Bombay on 4 October 1669, after Oxenden had died. His long struggle with various debilitating illnesses succumbed to a consumptive disease at Surat on 14 July 1669. He was buried the following day in the English cemetery alongside his brother Christopher, who had died at Surat in February 1659. A large mausoleum was erected over their remains, probably by their nephews Streynsham Master and Henry Oxenden.

Reports of his death and funeral demonstrate clearly the high regard in which Oxenden was held among all the communities in Surat. The letter from the council at Surat to the company (26 November 1669) records that he

> departed this life the 14 July last, to your and our unvalluable loss and the unspeakable greife of the Governor and all the officers and merchants in Surat, among whome his language, wisdome, and obliging deportment hath rendered him highly honnoured. The next day he was enterred with all possible solemnity; the French Director and Dutch Comandore attending the corps on foot, with an incredible number of people, so universally was his loss apprehended by all. (Foster, 13.182)

In England, despite all its protestations of appreciation, the company scrambled to audit Oxenden's accounts and liabilities for permitted trade, and only allowed Oxenden's estate to be finalized in July 1675. I. B. WATSON

Sources BL OIOC · E. B. Sainsbury, ed., *A calendar of the court minutes … of the East India Company*, 11 vols. (1907–38), vols. 3–10 · W. Foster, ed., *The English factories in India*, 4–13 (1910–27) · C. Fawcett, ed., *The English factories in India*, new ser., 1 (1936) · G. W. Forrest, ed., *Selections from the letters, despatches and other state papers preserved in the Bombay secretariat*, 2 vols. (1885–7) · *The diaries of Streynsham Master*, ed. R. C. Temple, 1 (1911), 190–92 · *DNB*

Archives BL, corresp., letter-books, and papers, Add. MSS 40696–40713, 54332–54334 · BL OIOC, letters, papers, corresp., E/3 | BL OIOC, factory records Bombay, G/3 · BL OIOC, factory records misc., G/40 · BL OIOC, factory records Surat, G/36 · BL OIOC, Home misc. series, H

Likenesses portrait, Broome Park, Kent; repro. in W. Foster, *The English factories in India, 1618–1669*, 13 vols (1906–27)

Wealth at death owed £22,222 salary in arrears; rumoured to be worth £37,500 at death: will, PRO, PROB 11/342, sig. 42; Foster, ed., *English factories, 1668–1669*, pp. 35, 353 and no. 2

Oxenden, George (*bap.* **1651**, *d.* **1703**), lawyer and politician, was baptized at Wingham, Kent, on 31 October 1651, the fourth (but third surviving) son of Sir Henry Oxenden, first baronet (1614–1686), of Dene, Wingham, and his second wife, Elizabeth (*d.* 1659), daughter of Sir William Meredith, first baronet, of Leeds Castle, Kent. His uncle was Sir George *Oxenden, governor of Bombay, and the poet Henry Oxenden was a distant cousin. Oxenden was entered at Trinity Hall, Cambridge, as a scholar on 8 July 1667, and he graduated LLB in 1673, MA *per literas regias* in 1675, and LLD in 1679. On 14 July 1674 he was incorporated at Oxford. He was admitted to the court of arches on 10 July 1679, and on 12 July 1679 registered at Doctors' Commons.

A fellow of Trinity from 1671, Oxenden regularly contributed to the compilations of Latin verse composed by members of the university to commemorate public events; the first of his seven offerings was on the occasion of Princess Anne's marriage in 1683, and the last following the death of William III and accession of Queen Anne in 1702. They included some congratulatory verses on the birth of the prince of Wales in 1688, which were to prove somewhat embarrassing in future years. Oxenden was elected regius professor of civil law in 1684, an appointment which prompted John Dolben, the archbishop of York, to say that he was 'as well read in Galen and Hippocrates as he is in Corpus J[uris] C[ivilis]' (*Downshire MSS*, 1.25). He became master of Trinity on 11 November 1688 and remained so until his death. By 23 October 1689 he was president of Doctors' Commons. In that year he was also made vicar-general to the archbishop of Canterbury, dean of arches, and a judge of Admiralty; he retained all of these offices until his death. He served as vice-chancellor of Cambridge University in 1692–3.

In 1693 Oxenden married Elizabeth (*d.* 1704), daughter of Sir Basil Dixwell, first baronet, of Broome House, Kent, a maid of honour to Queen Mary, who ordered £2000 to be given as a marriage portion in May 1693. Oxenden had first attempted to enter parliament for the university at a by-election in 1692, but he had withdrawn his candidature. He was successful at the 1695 general election. Evidence from division lists indicates that he was a court whig in politics, and he spoke and voted on the prosecution side in the debates on the attainder bill against the Jacobite plotter Sir John Fenwick. He did not stand in 1698 and was subsequently rebuffed by Sandwich and the university in later years.

Oxenden's most controversial case as a judge concerned the deprivation for simony of the high-flying bishop of St David's, Thomas Watson. His conduct on that occasion was described as more akin to that of an advocate than that of a judge. With less controversy he presided over the trial for piracy in May 1701 of Captain Kidd.

Oxenden died on 21 February 1703 at his house in Doctors' Commons, and was buried in Wingham church. His will referred to his estate 'great part out upon funds in the Exchequer and Bank of England'. His wife died at Bath on 18 September 1704. His son Henry succeeded his uncle Sir Henry as fourth baronet in February 1709, and he in turn was succeeded in April 1720 as fifth baronet by Oxenden's second son, **Sir George Oxenden** (1694–1775), who was born on 26 October 1694 and educated at Trinity Hall, Cambridge, where he was a fellow from 1716 to 1720. Sir George was 'an extremely handsome' but profligate man, who served as MP for Sandwich (1720–54) and, successively, as a lord of the Admiralty (1725–7) and a Treasury lord (1727–37). In May 1720 he married Elizabeth, the eldest daughter and coheir of Edmund *Dunch, seduced his sister-in-law, Bell Dunch, and was thought to be the father of the third earl of Orford. He died on 20 January 1775.

STUART HANDLEY

Sources HoP, *Commons, 1690–1715* [draft] • K. W. Murray, 'Extracts from a seventeenth century note-book [pt 1]', *The Genealogist*, new ser., 8 (1891–2), 38–41, esp. 40 • J. Philipott, 'The visitation of the county of Kent, taken in the year 1619 [pt 3]', *Archaeologia Cantiana*, 6 (1866), 251–301, esp. 278–9 • will, PRO, PROB 11/469, sig. 55 • will, PRO, PROB 11/477, sig. 173 [Elizabeth Oxenden] • G. D. Squibb, *Doctors' Commons: a history of the College of Advocates and Doctors of Law* (1977), 117, 183 • Venn, *Alum. Cant.* • J. Le Neve, *Monumenta Anglicana*, 5: *1700–15* (1719), 54, 91 • P. Le Neve, 'Memoranda in heraldry [1]', *The topographer and genealogist*, ed. J. G. Nichols, 3 (1858), 25–48, esp. 44 • A. Boyer, *The history of the reign of Queen Anne, digested into annals*, 1 (1703); 2 (1704), appx, 19 • *Report on the manuscripts of the marquis of Downshire*, 6 vols. in 7, HMC, 75 (1924–95), vol. 1, p. 25 • R. R. Sedgwick, 'Oxenden, Sir George', HoP, *Commons, 1715–54* • *DNB*

Archives BL, corresp. with Lord Holland, Add. MS 51408 [Sir George Oxenden] • BL, corresp. with duke of Newcastle, Add. MSS 32706–32974, *passim* [Sir George Oxenden] • Cambs. AS, letters to duke and duchess of Manchester [Sir George Oxenden]

Oxenden, Sir George, fifth baronet (1694–1775). *See under* Oxenden, George (*bap.* 1651, *d.* 1703).

Oxenden, Henry. *See* Oxinden, Henry (1609–1670).

Oxenedes, John de. *See* Oxnead, John of (*d.* in or after 1293).

Oxenford, John (1812–1877), playwright and translator, was born on 12 August 1812 at Camberwell, Surrey, the son of William Oxenford (1783–1867), merchant, and his wife, sister of Thomas Massa Alsager. Acquiring most of his compendious knowledge as an autodidact, he was also privately educated for some two years under the tutorship of S. T. Friend. The latter probably tried to dissuade Oxenford from his dramatic career, considering that he had the 'highest philosophical faculties, together with a versatility of powers which pointed to another sphere', but was powerless, since Oxenford's 'dramatic taste … was developed so early that his heart was not to be given to other pursuits' (*The Times*). Urged by his family, however, Oxenford began his working life as an articled clerk with Willis & Co. of Tokenhouse Yard, and was admitted to practise as a solicitor in 1833.

Apparently Oxenford did not much enjoy his profession, finding relief, like many of his colleagues, in the theatre. His first play, entitled *My Fellow Clerk* (Lyceum, 20 April 1835), is set in a lawyer's office and displays this autobiographical background. It was followed by a rapid succession of all types of drama which ended only two years before Oxenford's death. Out of his total of well over a hundred plays it is perhaps his farces that retain the greatest freshness today. They include such memorable successes as *A Day Well Spent* (Lyceum, 4 April 1836), which was adapted by J. Nestroy as *Einen Jux will er sich machen* (Vienna, 1845), and via Nestroy's adaptation formed the basis of such well-known pieces as Thornton Wilder's *The Merchant of Yonkers* (Boston, Massachusetts, 1936)—later reworked, adapted, and turned into David Merrick's hit musical *Hello Dolly!*—and Tom Stoppard's *On the Razzle* (Edinburgh, 1981). His numerous melodramas, most of which are adaptations or translations from the French, were equally applauded, particularly *The Two Orphans* (Olympic Theatre, 14 September 1874), based on Dennery and Cormon, but also *East Lynne* (Surrey Theatre, 5 February 1866), which was the most successful of the many adaptations of Mrs Henry Wood's novel.

Like many of his poorly paid fellow playwrights at the time, Oxenford also had to find other ways to make a living. About 1840 he became theatre critic for *The Times* through the influence of his uncle, Thomas Massa Alsager (1779–1846), who managed the City department of *The Times* from 1817 to 1846. Although today his theatrical reviews would be considered of slight value as works of criticism, their concise plot summaries and often minute documentation of the productions render them a precious source to the theatre historian. Oxenford's greatest contribution to theatre criticism must, however, be seen in the respectability with which he endowed the profession. As the acclaimed 'doyen of critics', he was deferentially allowed a private box in all theatres (Fitzgerald, 77f.).

Beyond his work connected with the theatre, the variety of Oxenford's interests is reflected in the many review articles he contributed to a long list of periodicals. His mature and independent critical judgement can best be exemplified by his article on Rabelais in the 1843 *Foreign Quarterly Review*, and by 'Iconoclasm in German philosophy' in the *Westminster Review* for 1853. The latter essay, an assessment of Schopenhauer's style and philosophical system, played a significant role in bringing about the German philosopher's final breakthrough to public recognition: not only in Great Britain, but, in its German translation in the *Vossische Zeitung* (May 1853), also in his own country.

Oxenford's work as a translator was equally fruitful. From the French he rendered a number of plays, including Molière's *Tartuffe*; from the Spanish, Calderón's *La vida es sueño* (*Monthly Magazine*, 1843) and several ballads (*New Monthly Magazine*, 1846). However, the foreign language in which he felt most at home was clearly German. His major translations of Goethe were that of *Aus meinem Leben: Dichtung und Wahrheit* as *The Autobiography* (1848), and of *Die Wahlverwandschaften* as *Affinities*, first serialized in the *Musical World* (1846–7); together with *Conversations with Eckermann and Soret* (1850), translated from *Gespräche mit Goethe* they set a high standard and were frequently re-edited, *The Autobiography* as recently as 1971. To this must be added a host of other serialized and minor translations of German legends, stories, and poems by such diverse authors as Gottfried August Bürger, Hermann Ferdinand Freiligrath, Heinrich Heine, Heinrich von Kleist, Lenau, Jean Paul and Friedrich Rückert, to mention only a few.

Oxenford's original writings are more scarce. They, too, range from the musingly philosophical and romantic, such as the 173 sonnets included in the *Musical World* (1846–50), to the witty and broadly humorous, such as his contributions to the early numbers of *Punch*, *Bentley's Miscellany*, or Dickens's *Household Words*. Nevertheless they cannot be credited with the same merits as his other literary activities. Here, as with his manifold critical output, it appears that the focusing of the gleanings from his most diverse and wide reading, reliable judgement, and acquired literary taste into unified concepts and original textual structures ultimately eluded him.

Later in life Oxenford began to suffer from some form of pneumonial disease, which more or less disabled him during the last two years before his death. 'Long a deist', as Hawkins reports (Hawkins, 89), he was received into the Roman Catholic church in September 1875. He died on 21 February 1877 at his home at 28 Trinity Square, Southwark, London. After a requiem mass at St George's Cathedral, Southwark, he was buried at Kensal Green cemetery on 28 February. He had been married, albeit none too happily (*Life and Reminiscences of E. L. Blanchard*, 1.134), and was survived by his wife, Alice, a son, John, and a daughter, Caroline.

KLAUS STIERSTORFER

Sources *Musical World* (7 April 1877), 249 • P. Fitzgerald, *The Garrick club* (1904) • Gillow, *Lit. biog. hist.* • F. Hawkins, 'John Oxenford', *The Theatre*, 4th ser., 30 (1897), 80–90 • *The life and reminiscences of E. L. Blanchard, with notes from the diary of Wm. Blanchard*, ed. C. W. Scott and C. Howard, 2 vols. (1891) • K. Stierstorfer, *John Oxenford (1812–1877) as farceur and critic of comedy* (1996) • W. J. I., letter, *The Times* (26 Feb 1877), 4f • *DNB* • Oxenford's testament

Archives News Int. RO, *The Times* archive, letters to Francis Goodlake

Likenesses London Stereoscopic Co., photograph, NPG • caricature, repro. in Scott and Howard, eds., *Life and reminiscences*, vol. 2, facing p. 465 • photograph, repro. in *Harper's Magazine*, 63 (1881), 845 • photograph, repro. in C. Scott, *The drama of yesterday and today*, 2 vols. (1899), vol. 1, p. 87 • wood-engraving (after photograph by London Stereoscopic Co.), NPG; repro. in *ILN* (10 March 1877), 229 • woodburytype, NPG

Wealth at death under £12,000: probate, 30 Aug 1877, *CGPLA Eng. & Wales*

Oxenham, Elsie. *See* Dunkerley, Elsie Jeanette (1880–1960).

Oxenham, Henry Nutcombe (1829–1888), Roman Catholic convert and ecumenist, was the son of William Oxenham, an Anglican clergyman and second master of Harrow School. He was born on 15 November 1829 at Harrow and was educated at Harrow School and at Balliol College, Oxford, where he won a classical scholarship. He graduated in 1850 with a BA second-class honours (MA, 1854), and was president of the Oxford Union in 1852. He was ordained in the Church of England in 1854 and served as a curate at Worminghall, Buckinghamshire, and then at St Bartholomew's, Cripplegate, London. As an Anglican curate, he began to write and publish religious works which testified to his Tractarian views and practice. His slim volume of poetry, *The Sentences of Kaires and other Poems*, first published in 1854, eventually ran to three editions. In the same year *Simple Tracts on Great Truths by Clergymen of the Church of England* and a *Manual of Devotions for the Blessed Sacrament* were published under his editorship.

Oxenham was at the inaugural meeting of the Association for the Promotion of the Unity of Christendom (APUC) in September 1857 with the Anglican, F. G. Lee and the Roman Catholic Ambrose Phillipps De Lisle. The APUC promoted a reunion of the Roman Catholic, Anglican and Orthodox churches, which would allow each to retain its distinctive patterns of worship and customs. Less than two months after joining the APUC, however, Oxenham was received into the Roman Catholic church by his fellow convert H. E. Manning. As he explained in *The Tractarian Party and the Catholic Revival* (1858), he had lost confidence in Anglicanism which he saw as Erastian and ununified. He retained a strong attachment to the Church of England, however, and disliked what he considered to be the excesses of ultramontanism. He became a member of the Brompton Oratory and received minor orders but did not proceed to the priesthood. He could not be convinced that his Anglican orders were invalid and clashed with members of the Roman Catholic hierarchy. In the 1860s he vigorously defended the liberal Catholic periodical *Rambler* to Bishop Ullathorne of Birmingham, who regarded it as the mouthpiece of the restless unorthodox. Oxenham also publicly drew attention to the deficiencies of English Catholic seminaries. He took up a teaching position at St Edmund's College, Ware, and then at the Oratory School, Birmingham. He increasingly came under the influence of J. J. I. von Döllinger, the Bavarian church historian and liberal, later translating his major works as *First Age of Christianity and the Church* (1866) and *Lectures on the Reunion of the Churches* (1872). In 1865 Oxenham published his own *The Catholic Doctrine of the Atonement.*

Oxenham remained a passionate supporter of reunion even after the APUC was criticized in a papal rescript in 1864 for encouraging the idea that churches other than the Roman Catholic were truly 'catholic', and after the English bishops had pressed for a condemnation of the society. Oxenham contributed essays to F. G. Lee's two series of *Sermons on the Reunion of Christendom* (1864, 1865) in which he advocated reunion as a response to rationalism, and argued for theological discussion between churches and for a distinction to be drawn between the essentials and non-essentials of faith. In terms that anticipated the twentieth-century ecumenical movement, he argued that Christians would naturally begin to understand one another as they worked side by side on social questions. In 1866 his *Dr Pusey's Eirenicon Considered in Relation to Catholic Unity: a Letter to Revd Fr Lockhart* included a plea for an official Roman Catholic investigation into the validity of Anglican orders. In response to rigorous criticisms by the ultramontane *Dublin Review* he returned to the subject in another collection edited by Lee, *Essays on the Reunion of Christendom* (1867), which dismissed 'the bluster of a little coterie of amateur theologians [and] the idiosyncrasies of a crotchety journalist' with disdain (Oxenham, 189). Like his mentor, Döllinger, Oxenham was appalled by the definition of papal infallibility pronounced at the First Vatican Council in 1870, although he came to disapprove of the Old Catholic church. He continued to write on reunion and to criticize ultramontanism in the pages of the *Saturday Review*. He edited and translated the second volume of Bishop Hefele's *The History of the Christian Church* (1876) in the same year that he brought out *Catholic Eschatology and Universalism*. In 1879 Oxenham published *Eirenicon of the Eighteenth Century* and an edition of *Essay towards a Proposal for Catholic Communion* which was first published anonymously in 1704 and is usually ascribed to Joshua Basset. In 1884–5 he published *Short Studies in Ecclesiastical History and Biography* and *Short Studies, Ethical and Religious*, and in 1886 a *Memoir of Lieutenant Rudolf de Lisle RN*. Oxenham's tall, thin, and dark appearance, as well as his manner, may have suggested a recluse, but he was passionate, and his theology and approach to reunion were to be officially adopted by the Roman Catholic church less than a hundred years after his death. He died in full communion with the Roman Catholic church at 42 Addison Road, Kensington, on 23 March 1888, and was buried in Chislehurst, Kent. ELIZABETH STUART

Sources W. G. Gorman, *A biographical list of the more notable converts to the Catholic church in the UK during the last 60 years* (1910) • *The Tablet* (3 March 1888), 534 • *Church Times* (29 March 1888) • H. R. T. Brandreth, *Dr Lee of Lambeth* (1951) • *The letters and diaries of John Henry Newman*, ed. C. S. Dessain and others, [31 vols.] (1961–) • *DNB* • H. N. Oxenham, 'Postscript on Catholic unity', *Essays on the reunion of Christendom*, ed. F. G. Lee (1867)

Archives BL, letters to W. E. Gladstone, Add. MSS 4433–4478 • CUL, letters to Lord Acton • Pusey Oxf., APUC MSS • Quenby Hall, Leicestershire, Ambrose Phillipps De Lisle MSS

Wealth at death £11,778 1s. 5d.: probate, 29 May 1888, *CGPLA Eng. & Wales*

Oxenham, John (*c*.1536–1580), sea captain, was by his own account a native of Plymouth. He accompanied Sir Francis Drake's 1572 raid upon Nombre de Dios, on the Caribbean coast of the Panama isthmus; of him and Thomas Sherwell, the English mariners were said to have 'conceived greatest hope of them next our Captaine' (Wright, 169, 322). At Nombre de Dios, Oxenham and John Drake were appointed by their now injured leader to lead an attack upon the treasure-house there, but were obliged to withdraw when Francis Drake collapsed. The success of Drake's expedition inclined Oxenham to make his own attempt on the isthmus in 1576. With fifty-seven men and a ship of 100 tons' burden, he departed from England on 9 April. According to his later testimony, he intended to trade with the *cimarrones*—escaped black slaves who preyed upon Spanish possessions in the isthmus—but his subsequent actions indicate that any trade he undertook was only to acquire allies in plunder. In his ship he carried two dismantled pinnaces; these he assembled and, leaving his ship in a bay to the west of Cartagena, took them to range the isthmus coast. At Veragua his pinnaces assaulted a Spanish ship but were repulsed with some loss. At Acla, some 45 miles from Nombre de Dios, he struck inland and made contact with a group of *cimarrones*. In the meantime, Spanish forces found and took Oxenham's ship with most of his trading goods and artillery, and destroyed a small fortified camp he had built at Acla. Between September 1576 and February 1577 the Englishmen remained inland with the *cimarrones* at or near the Pacific watershed. There they built a new boat, and in spring descended the Piñas River to the Pacific shore: the first Englishmen to enter the ocean. For several weeks they raided the Pearl Islands, freeing slaves (whom they handed over to the *cimarrones*) and, according to Spanish eyewitnesses, desecrating Catholic churches. Finally, at Quayaquil, they captured a bark laden with Peruvian treasure. Following this hugely profitable seizure, they returned to the Piñas to begin their passage back to the Atlantic Ocean.

The Spanish authorities reacted swiftly to these new depredations. A small flotilla sailed north from Lima; at the mouth of the Piñas some 200 soldiers under Juan de Ortega disembarked to pursue the Englishmen. In May

1577 Ortega caught up with and fell upon a group of them, killing several, though Oxenham was elsewhere at the time. A ship's boy who surrendered to the Spaniards disclosed the nearby hiding place of his compatriots' hard-won treasure. The Spaniards thereafter attacked and destroyed the *cimarrone* village where Oxenham planned to replenish his supplies. Half of his remaining men left the expedition to make for the Atlantic and attempt to steal a boat in which to return home; the *cimarrones* themselves, apparently angered by Oxenham's refusal to kill every Spaniard he captured, would give no further assistance. When Ortega's men advanced upon them, they fled without warning their English ally. Oxenham and his remaining men were captured on 7 September 1577 in a banana grove near Villano.

The Englishmen were taken to Panama, where, after a brief trial, most were hanged. Oxenham and seven others were taken to Lima. For more than three years the authorities there hesitated to impose the death penalty; but news of Drake's depredations in the Pacific probably inclined them to make an example. Oxenham, his master, and pilot were hanged at Lima, several days after an *auto-da-fé* of 29 October 1580; the remaining five captives, all ship's boys, were alive still in 1586. During his interrogation at Panama, Oxenham had given his age as forty-two. Undoubtedly courageous and bold, he wantonly underestimated his enemies and paid the price. He was reported by his interrogators to have been 'thick of speech … of grave demeanour, much feared and respected and obeyed by his soldiers' (Wright, 112–3, 234). Drake appears to have liked and respected him; while at the port of Calloa de Lima in February 1579, during his circumnavigation, he heard of Oxenham's incarceration and sent a Spanish prisoner to plead for his release and to threaten reprisals if he were executed. JAMES MCDERMOTT

Sources I. A. Wright, ed., *Documents concerning English voyages to the Spanish main, 1569–1580*, Hakluyt Society, 2nd ser., 71 (1932) • Z. Nuttall, *New light on Drake*, Hakluyt Society (1914) • R. Hakluyt, *The principal navigations, voyages, traffiques and discoveries of the English nation*, 10, Hakluyt Society, extra ser., 10 (1904) • K. R. Andrews, *Drake's voyages: a re-assessment of their place in Elizabethan maritime expansion* (1967) • J. S. Corbett, *Drake and the Tudor navy*, 2 vols. (1898) • E. S. Morgan, *American slavery, American freedom: the ordeal of colonial Virginia* (1975)

Oxford. For this title name *see* Vere, Aubrey (III) de, count of Guînes and earl of Oxford (*d.* 1194); Essex, Agnes of, countess of Oxford (*b.* 1151, *d.* in or after 1206); Vere, Robert de, third earl of Oxford (*d.* 1221); Bolebec, Isabel de, countess of Oxford (*c.*1164–1245); Vere, John de, seventh earl of Oxford (1312–1360); Vere, Robert de, ninth earl of Oxford, marquess of Dublin, and duke of Ireland (1362–1392); Vere, Aubrey de, tenth earl of Oxford (1338x40–1400); Vere, John de, twelfth earl of Oxford (1408–1462); Vere, John de, thirteenth earl of Oxford (1442–1513); Vere, John de, fifteenth earl of Oxford (1482–1540) [*see under* Vere, John de, sixteenth earl of Oxford (1516–1562)]; Vere, John de, sixteenth earl of Oxford (1516–1562); Vere, Edward de, seventeenth earl of Oxford (1550–1604); Vere, Anne de, countess of Oxford (1556–1588); Vere, Henry de, eighteenth earl of Oxford (1593–1625); Vere, Aubrey de, twentieth earl of Oxford (1627–1703); Davenport, Hester, styled countess of Oxford (1642–1717).

Oxford, John of (*d.* 1200), administrator and bishop of Norwich, was the son of Henry of Oxford, sheriff of Oxfordshire (*d.* 1164). He had become rector of St Peter's-in-the-East and of St Mary's, and also rural dean of Oxford, by *c.*1160, when he was already active in royal administration, frequently attesting charters of Henry II both in England and on the continent. It was, however, the king's dispute with Thomas Becket that propelled him to the front rank of royal councillors. He was probably one of a group charged with drawing up the constitutions of Clarendon, and in February 1164 he was dispatched on the first of several missions to the papal curia and other European courts to argue the royal case. In May 1165, during an embassy to negotiate the marriage of the king's daughter Matilda to Henry the Lion, duke of Bavaria and Saxony, he was present with Richard of Ilchester at the imperial Council of Würzburg, and here he allegedly swore that Henry II and his dominions would renounce obedience to Alexander III (*r.* 1159–81) and would recognize the emperor Frederick Barbarossa's rival pope, Paschal III. Although John strongly denied this, Becket's circle henceforth contemptuously dubbed him *iurator* ('the oath-taker'). Also early in 1165 John received the deanery of Salisbury, and Becket argued that this was against papal prohibition and effected by royal coercion. John headed the list of those excommunicated by the archbishop at Vézelay on Whitsunday (12 June) 1166, a sentence confirmed by the pope. This did not, however, disrupt his diplomatic career, and in November 1166 he obtained papal absolution, to the fury of Becket's supporters, who were alarmed by the apparent success of his latest mission to the papal court. He returned to England early in 1167, and convened a council to transmit to the higher clergy of England the instructions of king and pope.

The anticipated settlement was, however, delayed, and for the next three years John was still involved in negotiations relating to the dispute. In August 1169 he was present at discussions between Henry II and the papal legates at Domfront, and subsequently went once more to the papal curia, now at Benevento. When peace was eventually made between archbishop and king at Fréteval, it was John who escorted Becket back to England at the end of November 1169, and he who averted an ugly incident when royal officers attempted to intercept the archbishop at Sandwich. He had left Becket before the martyrdom a month later, which ended an episode in his own life. His role is difficult to assess. At times he appears to be an agent, even the instigator, of royal malevolence; occasionally, however, he seems to have been a moderator, attempting to restore peace on reasonable terms. The abuse heaped on him by Becket's adherents is, however, certainly a recognition of his influence in these years of conflict.

After a period of silence John's diplomatic career resumed following his elevation to the bishopric of Norwich in December 1175. The next year he was dispatched to Sicily to finalize negotiations for the marriage of another of the king's daughters. Ralph de Diceto preserves a vivid account of his tribulations on this mission, presumably from John's own mouth. In 1185 he was sent to mediate between the king of France and the count of Flanders. In England he was present at important councils, such as Henry II's arbitration between the kings of Castile and Navarre in March 1177, and at Geddington two months later when the king reached an agreement with the Welsh princes. Between 1176 and 1189 he attested some sixty royal charters, although now these were all issued in England. Most notably, he served Henry II in a judicial capacity. In April 1179 he was appointed with the bishops of Ely and Winchester as one of three chief justices who were to superintend a general eyre of the realm. This fusion of ecclesiastical and secular office, condemned by Becket, was now vigorously defended by Richard of Dover (*d.* 1184), Becket's successor as archbishop of Canterbury. Thereafter John frequently delivered judgments at Westminster, and as late as 1189 was on eyre in the eastern and south-eastern counties. He was one of the most active justices in the later years of Henry II's reign. He appeared frequently in the company of the new king, Richard I, in late 1189, and in February 1190 was one of the group that crossed to Normandy to discuss the problems arising from the conflict of the two justiciars. In October 1191 he attended the council convened to protest at William de Longchamp's treatment of Archbishop Geoffrey of York. He also acted as justice on eyre at York in 1192 and on the eastern circuit in 1194–5. He was, however, no longer at the centre of policy making, and it is very possible that his relationship with Richard I had become strained after John, who had set out on the third crusade, obtained absolution from his vow from Pope Clement III (*r.* 1187–91) and returned home from Italy—he was subsequently amerced by the king. His last appearance on the national stage was at the coronation of King John, just a year before his own death on 2 June 1200.

John's elevation to the episcopate in December 1175, at the king's behest, may in one sense be seen, with the promotion of other leading opponents of Becket to Ely and Winchester two years earlier, as a triumph for Henry II's interpretation of the correct relationship between the crown and the English church. In fact, however, John as bishop was far from subservient to the king's government, and was rebuked very publicly by Henry II for his excommunication of the earl of Arundel during a dispute over their respective rights in Lynn. Several times before 1170 John had met Pope Alexander III, one of the great legislators of the medieval church, and after 1175 he participated actively in the expansion and definition of Roman canon law instigated by that pope and his successors. He attended the Third Lateran Council of 1179, and although not one of the most prominent of those employed by the papacy to judge cases in England, he was commissioned as papal judge-delegate by Alexander III on at least five occasions between 1176 and 1181, and in at least three cases thereafter. Three of his letters to the pope requesting the elucidation of doubtful points of canon law were incorporated into the universal law of the church in the *Decretals*, or *Liber Extra*, of 1234.

The evidence for John of Oxford's administration of his diocese is provided by over 160 surviving *acta*—this is as many as for the previous three bishops over eighty-three years, and many more have certainly been lost. Their content, as is usual with such collections, is extremely varied—confirmations, institutions, to benefices, institutions and judgments. A large number, however, relate to the regulation of the parochial ministry in East Anglia, and it is notable that, although on fifty-seven recorded occasions he granted the revenues of parish churches to monastic houses, in forty-five of these, in marked contrast to his predecessor, he made specific provision for the service of the church. There is strong circumstantial evidence that, after his retirement from court in the early 1190s, he devoted himself in person to the regulation of his large diocese along lines advocated by more prominent reformers.

John of Oxford's episcopate was, however, marred by a long-running dispute with his monastic cathedral chapter at Norwich. Like many of his contemporaries, including the primate, he was hostile to such institutions, not least because they deprived bishops of lucrative prebends with which they might reward their own clerks. The monks of Norwich complained that Bishop John had inflicted serious financial losses on them, had usurped their patronage of parish churches, had interfered capriciously in the internal administration of their community, and had forbidden them to appeal against his unilateral actions. Pope Celestine III in 1194 and Pope Innocent III in 1200 ruled in favour of the convent, and the bishop's successor, John de Gray (1200–14) made a determined effort to reach an agreement with the monks of Norwich.

John of Oxford was, during the middle years of his career, the object of much abuse from Becket's circle, and, as a bishop, from his own cathedral chapter. The records reveal that he was one of the most active of Henry II's administrators throughout his long reign, employed indifferently in diplomatic, judicial, and financial tasks. It may point to a parallel breadth of intellectual interests that he had links with the astronomer Daniel of Morley, whose *Philosophia* was written at John's request. After 1175 John experienced no dramatic conversion, but the evidence of his own *acta* and of papal decretals addressed to him suggests that he did attempt to apply reforming principles in his own diocese and that he did not shrink, on the rare occasions when he felt it necessary, from confrontation with the secular government. In general, however, he was one of those who believed, like Gilbert Foliot and Hubert Walter, that the interests of the church in England were best served by co-operation with the crown. His criticism of Thomas Becket, expressed to the aged Empress Matilda in 1164, that the archbishop was striving to extend the privileges of the clergy for the sake of ambition and worldly gain, may have been more than propaganda, and a genuine statement of his personal view.

CHRISTOPHER HARPER-BILL

Sources C. Harper-Bill, ed., *Norwich, 1070–1214*, English Episcopal Acta, 6 (1990) • J. C. Robertson and J. B. Sheppard, eds., *Materials for the history of Thomas Becket, archbishop of Canterbury*, 7 vols., Rolls Series, 67 (1875–85) • *The letters of John of Salisbury*, ed. and trans. H. E. Butler and W. J. Millor, rev. C. N. L. Brooke, OMT, 2: *The later letters, 1163–1180* (1979) [Lat. orig. with parallel Eng. text] • H. W. Saunders, ed., *The first register of Norwich Cathedral priory*, Norfolk RS, 11 (1939) • R. W. Eyton, *Court, household, and itinerary of King Henry II* (1878) • *Radulfi de Diceto … opera historica*, ed. W. Stubbs, 2 vols., Rolls Series, 68 (1876) • *Pipe rolls* • C. Harper-Bill, 'John of Oxford, diplomat and bishop', *Medieval ecclesiastical studies in honour of D. M. Owen*, ed. M. J. Franklin and C. Harper-Bill (1995), 83–105 • J. Boussard, *Le gouvernement d'Henri II Plantegenêt* (1956) • C. Duggan, *Twelfth century decretal collections and their importance in English history* (1963) • Emden, *Oxf.*

Likenesses seal, BL, MS Add. ch. 47955 (EEA vi, pl. 4)

Oxford, Sir Kenneth Gordon (1924–1998), police officer, was born on 25 June 1924 at 44 Bengeworth Road, Camberwell, London, the son of Ernest George Oxford, at that time a stoker in a hospital and later an interior decorator, and his wife, Gladys Violet Seaman. His mother died when he was seven, and he was brought up by an elder brother and his father. He left the Caldecott School, Lambeth, at fifteen, and joined the RAF at eighteen, spending five years with Bomber Command in south-east Asia (1942–7). Returning to civilian life he joined the Metropolitan Police. Within six months he was a detective, and from his earliest days with the force he thoroughly embraced the ethos of the CID. On 6 March 1954 he married Muriel Panton (*b.* 1926/7), a copy typist in an advertising agency. They had no children.

In 1963 Oxford was involved at a relatively junior level with the Profumo investigation, arresting the secretary of state for war's mistress, Christine Keeler, for perjury and conspiring to pervert the course of justice. His most famous (indeed notorious) case however was that of the A6 murder, which resulted in the execution of James Hanratty in 1962. Oxford, then a detective sergeant, arrested Hanratty. The suspicion of miscarriage of justice hung over the case for forty years, and the controversy continues to reverberate, although according to at least one authority on the case Oxford himself emerged untainted.

In 1969 Kenneth Oxford joined the Northumbria police as assistant chief constable (crime). By this time the CID in London had acquired a reputation for corruption, and the arrival of any Met man seeking promotion in the provinces was greeted with both hostility and suspicion. Oxford had developed an abrasive and forthright style, but despite clashing with HM inspector for the region, was appointed deputy chairman of the Association of Chief Police Officers (ACPO) crime committee. Five years later he was appointed deputy chief constable of Merseyside, and in the following year was appointed chief constable. Oxford set about improving facilities and restructuring the force. Indeed, in his early years he appears to have succeeded in melding some of the more benign characteristics of traditional police work with the concerns of the

Sir Kenneth Gordon Oxford (1924–1998), by Jack Manwaring, 1962 [on his way to court during the A6 murder trial]

community. For instance he was applauded by the Merseyside Community Relations Council for scrapping the heavy-handed task force, and he favoured beat policing at the expense of motorized patrols as a means of improving relations between the police and the public. But Oxford resented and resisted demands from the Merseyside county council police committee (later authority) to be accountable for his actions, interpreting any criticism from the elected councillors and their appointees about himself or his force as a political assault upon the police service, and a personal attack upon himself.

The death in police custody of Jimmy Kelly in June 1979 after he had been arrested for being drunk and disorderly prompted claims that he had been assaulted by the police, and further allegations of police violence followed; one local MP called for a public enquiry. Oxford's refusal to discuss the case enraged Merseyside, including both Conservative and Labour groups on Merseyside council. Margaret Simey, who led the Labour group on the police committee, demanded an inquiry, and Oxford responded aggressively in his annual report. The inquest into Kelly's death returned a verdict of death by misadventure, but the Home Office rejected demands for a public inquiry. The dispute over Kelly's death was a foretaste of things to come, as Oxford railed against anyone who questioned his authority.

By the time rioting swept Britain in summer 1981 Oxford had implemented vast improvements to his command and control facilities, and had achieved the highest ratio of police to population outside London. But tensions between his police force and the multiracial community in Toxteth fuelled the riots there: they were among the most severe of the century on the British mainland. One policeman was speared in the head with a 6-foot railing, and a police vehicle killed a disabled man uninvolved in the riots. Another man was severely injured when a police Land-Rover was driven into a crowd. Oxford's stance merely hardened: 'They can see the vehicles coming and they know what will happen if they get in the way', he said (*The Independent*). He was responsible for the first use of CS gas on the mainland during the riots, and serious injuries resulted from the use of inappropriate canisters designed to penetrate buildings during armed sieges. Oxford responded to his critics by blaming the riots on 'black hooligans' (ibid.) and a failure of proper parental control over children, and refused to justify his tactics, despite the casualties inflicted on the police. He continued to resist what he regarded as political interference in operational policing, and chose instead to repeat his long-held belief that Liverpool's multiracial culture required his particular policing style.

Oxford became the focal point for the debate over police accountability that raged throughout the 1980s and remains unresolved. As chairman of ACPO (1982–3) he remained in the spotlight, branding his critics extremists. Ironically, while he railed against political interference in policing he was regarded by his opponents as a tool of the Conservative government, especially during the miners' strike of 1984–5, when he successfully opposed an attempt by the police committee to obtain an injunction preventing Merseyside officers from assisting other forces. He vehemently opposed the Police and Criminal Evidence Act of 1984, which imposed controls over the behaviour of the police. Uncharacteristically he appointed Britain's first woman assistant chief constable, Alison Halford, but their relationship became acrimonious and in 1992 (after his retirement) she took Merseyside police to an industrial tribunal claiming that he had discriminated against her on grounds of her sex. The case was settled outside the tribunal. Less controversially Oxford had served as chairman of ACPO's crime committee (1977–83), its joint standing committee on the police use of firearms (1979–89), and its anti-terrorism committee (1982–9). He was awarded the queen's police medal in 1976, appointed CB in 1981, and knighted in 1988. After his retirement in 1989 he became a regional director of Lloyds Bank (1989–91), served as deputy lieutenant of Merseyside, and was active in charity work. He died at Walton Centre, Fazakerley, Liverpool, on 23 November 1998; he was survived by his wife.

Oxford was a police officer of 'the old school'. He was anathema to the new breed of graduate police officer that began to emerge in the 1980s, and the feeling was reciprocated. He maintained a starkly traditional view of police work and its management, and a conservative view of the society that he policed. His management style was feudal, his personality authoritarian. 'If I am arrogant then the spice of arrogance is a necessary constituent of command' he claimed (*The Independent*). RICHARD HOBBS

Sources *The Independent* (26 Nov 1998) · *The Guardian* (26 Nov 1998) · R. Reiner, *The politics of the police* (1985) · M. Kettle and L. Hodges, *Uprising* (1982) · B. Loveday, *The role and effectiveness of the Merseyside police committee* (1985) · *Daily Telegraph* (25 Nov 1998) · *The Times* (25 Nov 1998) · b. cert. · m. cert. · d. cert.

Likenesses J. Manwaring, photograph, 1962, News International Syndication, London [*see illus.*] · photograph, repro. in *The Independent* · photograph, repro. in *The Guardian*

Wealth at death under £200,000—gross; under £ 70,000—net: administration, 27 Jan 1999, *CGPLA Eng. & Wales*

Oxford, Thomas. *See* Glazier, Thomas (*d.* in or before 1427).

Oxford, Walter of (*d.* in or before **1151**?), ecclesiastic and supposed historian, occupied a strategic position in the ecclesiastical politics of Oxford as archdeacon of that town for over forty years. Nothing is known of his birth and family, and little about his education except that his contemporaries Henry of Huntingdon and Geoffrey of Monmouth credited him with exceptional rhetorical skills and a taste for abstruse histories. To judge from his length of tenure, Walter may have gained the rank of archdeacon at a young age. By *c.*1130, as a canon of the chapel of St George in the castle of Oxford, he held the prebend of Walton. By at least 1146 he was provost of the college. Before 1150 he is recorded as a canon of St Mary's, Warwick, a secular college under the patronage of the Beaumont family. He died probably before 1 October 1151 when his successor as archdeacon, Robert Foliot, is first recorded in office.

During his career as archdeacon Walter heard important suits concerning ecclesiastical property, frequently in the vicinity—at Abingdon *c.*1111, and at Reading and St Denis *c.*1145–8. He witnessed many transactions involving various neighbouring religious communities, including the foundation charters of Osney Priory in 1129 and of the Benedictine nunnery of Godstow ten years later. At least one local house benefited from his patronage. At its foundation he granted Godstow various immunities from dues, and later added tithes from his estate at Cutteslowe and, more intriguingly, land at Shillingford bequeathed to him by one Brityn, *amica*, presumably his mistress. After 1149, when St George's was absorbed into the priory of Osney, Walter built a chapel in the parish of St Mary Magdalen, inside his prebend, and supposedly gave it to the priory of St Frideswide in Oxford. This chapel became the centre of a feud between Osney and St Frideswide's which ran until 1200 and required papal arbitration.

Much of Walter's later reputation rests on false assumptions. He can no longer be regarded as the recipient of Henry of Huntingdon's *De contemptu mundi* (*c.*1135), nor as the author of a British history. This latter claim derives from Walter's association with a fellow canon of St

George's, Geoffrey of Monmouth, author of the famous *Historia regum Britanniae* ('History of the kings of Britain'), written before 1139, which traced the early history of the crown of Britain from Brutus the Trojan, via King Arthur, to King Cædwalla under whom dominion was lost to the Saxons. For this novel version of events Geoffrey claimed the authority of an ancient book in the British language which he had translated into Latin and which, he alleged, had been brought over from Brittany by Walter, archdeacon of Oxford. No such book is known, despite the claim of Gaimar, Geoffrey's Anglo-Norman translator, to have it in his possession. Ranulf Higden, in his fourteenth-century *Polychronicon*, listed Walter not as importer but author of the book, a misapprehension perpetuated by John Bale in the sixteenth century. It is very likely that Bale was also responsible for the sobriquet Calenius formerly assigned to Walter, a name derived from a misrepresentation of Oxford as the Roman settlement of 'Calena', which was itself a misreading of Calleva, or Silchester.

J. C. CRICK

Sources *Fasti Angl., 1066–1300*, [Lincoln] · Emden, *Oxf.*, 3.1971–2 · H. L. D. Ward and J. A. Herbert, *Catalogue of romances in the department of manuscripts in the British Museum*, 1 (1883), 218–20 · *VCH Oxfordshire*, 2.5–6, 160 · M. Brett, *The English church under Henry I* (1975), 126, 170, 171 n.1, 203, 209–10 · H. E. Salter, 'Geoffrey of Monmouth and Oxford', *EngHR*, 34 (1919), 382–5 · H. E. Salter, *Medieval Oxford*, OHS, 100 (1936), 114–16 · H. E. Salter, *Facsimiles of early charters in Oxford muniment rooms* (1929), nos. 60, 80–81, 96, 101 · Bale, *Cat.*, 1.180–81 · J. Pits, *Relationum historicarum de rebus Anglicis*, ed. [W. Bishop] (Paris, 1619), 198, no. 1120/183 · Godstow cartulary, exchequer, queen's remembrancer, miscellaneous books, ser. 1, PRO, E 164/20, fols. 1*r*, 5*r*, 99*r*, 145*r* · cartulary of Warwick College, PRO, E 164/22, fol. 16*v*

Oxford and Asquith. For this title name *see* Asquith, Herbert Henry, first earl of Oxford and Asquith (1852–1928); Asquith, Margaret Emma Alice, countess of Oxford and Asquith (1864–1945); Asquith, Anne Mary Celestine, countess of Oxford and Asquith (1916–1998) [*see under* Palairet, Sir (Charles) Michael (1882–1956)].

Oxford and Mortimer. For this title name *see* Harley, Robert, first earl of Oxford and Mortimer (1661–1724); Harley, Edward, second earl of Oxford and Mortimer (1689–1741); Harley, Henrietta Cavendish, countess of Oxford and Mortimer (1694–1755); Harley, Edward, third earl of Oxford and Mortimer (*bap.* 1699, *d.* 1755).

Oxfurd. For this title name *see* MacGill, James, of Cranstoun Riddel, first viscount of Oxfurd (*d.* 1663).

Oxinden [Oxenden], **Henry** (1609–1670), gentleman and letter-writer, was born on 18 January 1609 at the house of Sir Adam Sprakeling in the parish of St Paul, Canterbury, the eldest son of Richard Oxinden (*bap.* 1588, *d.* 1629), gentleman, of Great Maydekin in the village of Barham in Kent, and his wife, Katherine Sprakeling (1587–1642) and grandson of Sir Henry Oxinden, knight, of Deane, near Wingham, Kent. He had three younger brothers and two younger sisters. Most of the information about Oxinden's life comes from his surviving correspondence, held in the British Library, the Centre for Kentish Studies in Maidstone, Canterbury Cathedral Archives, and the Folger Shakespeare Library, Washington, DC. In addition over 200 titles from Oxinden's library survive as the core of the Elham parish library, now housed in Canterbury Cathedral Library. This material provides a rich source for the life of a country squire in seventeenth-century Kent, in particular during the civil war.

Henry Oxinden attended Wye grammar school in Kent. He went to Oxford in 1624, aged fifteen, matriculated at Corpus Christi College on 10 November 1626, and was awarded the BA on 1 February 1627. His studies at Oxford were cut short by the death of his father in 1629, and he returned to Barham to administer the family estates. In June 1632 he was admitted to Gray's Inn. On 28 December of that year he married Anne Peyton (1613–1640), daughter of Sir Samuel Peyton (1590–1623) of Knowlton in Kent; they had a son, Thomas (1633–1668), and two daughters, Margaret (*b.* 1635) and Elizabeth (*b.* 1636). After Oxinden returned from Oxford he had to settle his brothers and sisters in life. For James (1612–1660), the second eldest, he obtained the living of Goodnestone, near Faversham in Kent. Both Richard (*b.* 1613) and Adam (1622–1643) were apprenticed to London merchants but neither was happy in trade. In 1641 Richard joined the army, in which he prospered. Both Oxinden sisters were successfully married: Katherine to Thomas Barrow, a London merchant, in 1636, and Elizabeth to James Love of Faversham in 1645.

Oxinden took no part in the stirring events of the 1640s except to serve on the parliamentary side in the siege of Arundel in 1643. The ties of kinship and friendship can clearly be seen to override political differences in his correspondence. He helped both Sir Thomas Peyton and Sir Anthony Percivall, imprisoned as royalists. His uncle Sir James Oxinden and his cousin Henry were prominent in the parliamentary committees running Kent, and with these he kept in close touch throughout the 1640s and 1650s; he also counted as friends Captain John Dixwell, the regicide, and Robert Hales of Howletts. However, his correspondence shows a desire to be left out of the political and military conflict of the time. In June 1642 Oxinden's friend Vincent Denne of Wenderton, near Wingham in Kent, died, leaving his nephew Thomas Denne the younger his main heir, and Oxinden his executor. This was the start of a troublesome and ultimately ruinous relationship between Oxinden and the Denne family. Thomas Denne the elder, father of the heir and recorder of Canterbury, angered by his late brother's dispositions, disowned his son and began a series of legal suits against Oxinden, which were to drain Oxinden's financial resources.

Following the death of his first wife in 1640, Oxinden married, on 15 September 1642, his young ward, Katherine Culling (1624–1698); they had two daughters, Katherine (1644–1716) and Mary (1648–1674). Two of Oxinden's older children caused him grief in the 1650s. The marriage of his daughter Margaret to John Hobart, in August 1649, involved him in yet more lawsuits, on his new son-in-law's behalf. Thomas, Oxinden's only son, caused him anxiety all through his life, from his poor performance as a scholar to his shameful death. Thomas married Elizabeth Edwards, heir of Nowds in Lynsted, in 1652, when he was nineteen years old and she was fourteen. Elizabeth was sent to live with Oxinden's wife, Katherine, at Barham, and here she formed close relationships with her mother-in-law and with Thomas's two half-sisters, Katherine and Mary. By the time that she reached her majority, in November 1660, the marriage was in difficulties, despite the birth of a son, Richard, in 1655. Thomas seems to have lived a life of dissipation on the fringes of the Restoration court after bouts of soldiering in the 1650s. He fell in with some notorious criminals by the late 1660s, was arrested in June 1668, and was incarcerated in king's bench prison, where he died in December 1668.

In 1647 Oxinden had published the first of his four volumes of verse, all of which were produced at his own expense. *Religionis funus et hypocritae finis* included an engraved portrait by Glover and was in two parts: a criticism of contemporary attitudes towards what Oxinden called true religion, and an attack on puritan ministers. It ended with support for Charles I, surprising from one who claimed to be neutral in his views. His *Jobus triumphans* (1651) applied Job's story and stoicism to the current troubles, and in 1660 he published both *Eikon basilike*, a celebration of Sir Basil Dixwell's marriage, and *Charls Triumphant*, in praise of the Restoration. From 1647 Oxinden kept a list in his commonplace book of all the plays in his library. There were 123 in total and they included a remarkable number of early plays, probably not collected by Oxinden himself.

The sale of Great Maydekin in December 1662, for £800 to Edward Ady of Greenwich, and Oxinden's attempts to obtain a living in the church shows the increasingly desperate state of his finances. He was ordained, probably in 1661, by the bishop of Winchester, and in 1663 he was presented to the living of Radnage, near High Wycombe in Buckinghamshire. He preached there twice in 1664 but never took up residence, citing ill health as the reason. He died of an unknown cause, at the age of sixty-one, and was buried in Denton church on 17 June 1670. Oxinden having died intestate, his library and papers, reflecting his literary and antiquarian interests, were handed down through his daughter Katherine's family. She married the Revd John Warly (1640–1673); their son, John (1673–1732), a physician in Canterbury, and their grandson, Lee Warly (1714–1807), attorney of Canterbury, inherited her estate. Warly died, unmarried, and left the library, which he had greatly augmented, to the parish of Elham in Kent.

SHEILA HINGLEY

Sources D. Gardiner, ed., *The Oxinden letters, 1607–1642* (1933) • D. Gardiner, ed., *The Oxinden and Peyton letters, 1642–1670* (1937) • D. Gardiner, 'Henry Oxinden's authorship', *Archaeologia Cantiana*, 57 (1944), 13–20 • K. W. Murray, 'Extracts from a seventeenth century note-book [pt 1]', *The Genealogist*, new ser., 8 (1891–2), 38–41 • K. W. Murray, 'Extracts from a seventeenth century note-book', *The Genealogist*, new ser., 31 (1914–15), 125–32, 189–95, 269–73; 32 (1915–16), 54–60, 121–5, 196–201, 273–8; 33 (1916–17), 59–64, 129–33, 184–8, 266–70; 34 (1917–18), 80–86, 166–9, 207–9; 36 (1919–20), 153–7; 37 (1920–21), 146–51, 191–5 • D. Gardiner, background material for editions of Henry Oxinden's letters, Canterbury Cathedral, archives, MS U96 • H. Oxinden, annotations in books in Elham parish library, Canterbury Cathedral Library • S. Hingley, 'Elham parish library', in P. Isaac and B. McKay, *The reach of print* (1998), 175–90 • G. E. Dawson, 'An early list of Elizabethan plays', *The Library*, 4th ser., 15 (1934–5), 445–56 • parish register, Canterbury, St Paul, Canterbury Cathedral, archives, MS U3/81/1/1 [baptism] • parish register, Barham, Kent, Canterbury Cathedral, archives, DCb/BT1/11 [bishop's transcript]

Archives BL, corresp. and commonplace books, Add. MSS 27999–28013; 44846–44848; 54332–54334 • BL, MSS, Add. charters 66129–66239 • Canterbury Cathedral, archives, MSS, U96, U137 • Canterbury Cathedral, archives, DCC Stebbing collection, MSS, U102/6–14 • CKS, MSS • Folger, commonplace book | BL, corresp. with Charles Nicholls, Add. MS 44847

Likenesses G. Glover, line engraving, BM; repro. in H. Oxinden, *Religionis funus* (1647) • portraits, repro. in Gardiner, ed., *Oxinden letters* • portraits, repro. in Gardiner, ed., *Oxinden and Peyton letters*

Wealth at death £104 in goods; approx. £70 debts: inventory, accounts, Canterbury archdeaconry court, PRC 11/36/188, PRC 2/36/103

Oxlee, John (1779–1854), philologist and writer on theology, son of a well-to-do farmer in Yorkshire, was born at Guisborough in Cleveland, Yorkshire, on 25 September 1779, and educated at Sunderland. After working as a tailor for a short time he studied mathematics and Latin, taught classics at a school near Greta Bridge, and made such rapid progress in Latin that in 1802 Dr Vicesimus Knox appointed him second master at Tonbridge School. There he lost, through inflammation, the use of an eye, yet began studying Hebrew, Chaldee, and Syriac. In 1805 he was ordained to the curacy of Egton, near Whitby, where he married a daughter of John R. A. Worsop of Howden Hall, Yorkshire, and took in pupils. In 1811 he moved to the curacy of Stonegrave, from 1816 to 1826 he held the rectory of Scawton for the master of Downing College, and in 1836 the archbishop of York presented him to the rectory of Molesworth in Huntingdonshire.

Oxlee's power of acquiring languages, considering that he was self-educated, has rarely been excelled. He is said to have obtained a knowledge more or less extensive of 120 languages and dialects. In pursuing his studies he often had to form his own grammar and dictionary. He left among his numerous unpublished writings a work entitled 'One hundred and more vocabularies of such words as form the stamina of human speech, commencing with the Hungarian and terminating with the Yoruba' (1837–40). He spent much time on mastering the Hebrew law and in studying the Talmud. His only recreation was walking, and he at times walked 50 miles to York or Hull to obtain a book in Hebrew or some other oriental language. He was a contributor to the *Anti-Jacobin Review*, *Valpy's Classical Journal*, the *Christian Remembrancer*, the *Voice of Jacob*, the *Voice of Israel*, the *Jewish Chronicle*, the *Jewish Repository*, *The Yorkshireman*, and *Sermons for Sundays and Festivals*.

Oxlee's minute study of the Hebrew writings led him to differ on many important points both from the Jewish and Christian interpreters. His most important work is *The Christian doctrine of the Trinity and incarnation considered and maintained on the principles of Judaism* (3 vols., 1815–50). During the thirty-four years which elapsed between the publication of the first and third volumes he was busy collecting materials. The work contains a mass of abstruse learning. He held that the Jewish rabbis were well aware of the doctrine of the Trinity, and that in the Talmuds the three persons of the Godhead are clearly mentioned and often referred to. In his *Three Letters to the Archbishop of Canterbury* (1842) and *Three More Letters* (1845) he stated his reasons for declining to take any part in the London Society for the Promotion of Christianity among the Jews, and his grounds for not believing in the personality of the devil. From 1842 to 1854 he corresponded with a Jewish scholar, Mr Peynado, respecting the differences between Judaism and Christianity. Seven previous letters, addressed to J. M., a Jew, are printed in the *Jewish Repository* (1815–16). An article in the *Jewish Chronicle* welcomed his stance on Judaism, calling him 'a believing priest of the Church Tolerant' (11 July 1845).

Oxlee's many controversial pamphlets, letters, and sermons included his *Three letters to the Archbishop Lawrence of Cashel on the apocryphal publications of his grace (Enoch, Ezra, and Isaiah) on the age of the Sepher Zoar and on the two genealogies of Christ as given in the gospels of St. Matthew and St. Luke* (1854). This publication amazed Dr Nicholl, regius professor of divinity at Oxford, by its immense number of correct extracts from early and late Jewish writers. Oxlee's taste for controversy is exemplified in *Three letters to Mr. C. Wellbeloved, tutor of the Unitarian College, York, on the folly of separating from the mother church*.

Oxlee died at Molesworth rectory on 30 January 1854, leaving two children: an unmarried daughter, Marianna, and a son, John Oxlee (*d.* 1892), vicar of Over Silton in 1848 and rector of Cowesby in 1863 (both in Yorkshire). The latter's intention of publishing a memoir of his father does not seem to have been fulfilled. Oxlee himself left many unpublished works, including an Armenian and an Arabic lexicon. G. C. BOASE, *rev.* JOHN D. HAIGH

Sources private information (1895) [J. A. O. Oxlee] • *GM*, 2nd ser., 41 (1854), 437 • *GM*, 2nd ser., 43 (1855), 203–4 • T. Whelland & Co., *History and topography of the city of York, and the North Riding of Yorkshire*, 2 (1859), 204–6 • G. Smales, *Whitby authors and their publications* (1867), 105–11 • G. Bartle, *A synopsis of English history*, 2nd edn (1866), 296 • *N&Q*, 8th ser., 8 (1895), 203 • T. H. Horne, *Manual of biblical bibliography* (1839), 183, 184 • d. cert.

Likenesses portrait, repro. in W. Smith, ed., *Old Yorkshire*, 2 (1882), 55–6

Oxley, John Joseph William Molesworth (*c.*1785–1828), surveyor and explorer in Australia, born at Kirkham Abbey, Yorkshire, was the son of John Oxley, a man of landed stock, and his wife, Isabella, said to have been a daughter of the fourth Viscount Molesworth in the peerage of Ireland. He joined the navy in 1799 and arrived in Australia on the *Buffalo* in 1802. His ship was involved in survey work, and his enthusiasm and efficiency impressed Governor King. After returning to England in 1807 Oxley obtained a lieutenancy, and in 1808 he was back in Sydney as first lieutenant on HMS *Porpoise*. However, the business opportunities in the colony had not escaped him; he brought £800-worth of goods to sell and an order for a grant of 600 acres, which Lieutenant-Colonel Paterson, the acting governor, increased to 1000 acres.

Oxley began a life which mixed surveying, exploration, and business. Back in England in 1810 he twice sought the surveyor-generalship of New South Wales, allegedly paying the incumbent to resign before obtaining the position in February 1812, through the interest of the Farquhar family, patrons of John Macarthur, his one-time friend. Oxley reached Sydney in November, and during Macquarie's administration was more involved in exploration than in the technicalities of his profession. In March 1817, with the botanist Alan Cunningham, he led an expedition to follow the Lachlan River and to search for the fabled inland sea; after nineteen weeks he was stopped by impenetrable marshes on the Lachlan and returned to Bathurst, the praise of his governor, and a gift of £200.

Convinced that the inland sea did exist, Oxley set out again in May 1818 and followed the Macquarie River from Bathurst until he met the reeds of the Macquarie marshes. Then he turned north-east and came across the Castlereagh River; to the east he traversed the rich Liverpool plains and the Peel River, and followed the Hastings River to its mouth at Port Macquarie. The six months' expedition had found valuable grazing land, and Oxley thought (wrongly) he was close to 'an inland sea, most probably a shoal one' (Oxley, entry for 3 July 1818). He explored Jervis Bay and the five islands in 1819 but was unimpressed, though in December 1820 he recommended Port Macquarie as the site of a new penal settlement. In 1823 he sailed up the Queensland coast as far as Port Curtis, and on his return surveyed Moreton Bay and the Brisbane River, recommending that a penal colony be established there—as it was, at Redcliffe, in August 1824. The administration of his department came to occupy more of Oxley's time. He advised Commissioner Bigge on land sales, drew up regulations on the matter for Governor Brisbane (1824, 1825), and was involved in the first attempt to survey the colony on the orders of London, constantly complaining about the inadequacies of his staff and his fees.

Oxley failed as a merchant and businessman. He was constantly in debt, and in 1812 this cost him his hoped-for marriage to Elizabeth Macarthur; her father, John Macarthur, refused Oxley's offer for her hand, declaring, correctly, that Oxley would never survive among the 'sharks' of the colony. Even his illegal deals to sell cattle to the government stores failed; his only success was as a grazier, although even here he was accused of selling crossbred sheep as pure merinos. He antagonized both Macquarie and Macarthur; indeed, many thought him unprincipled and factious, but he was a member of the legislative council in 1824–5, a generous patron to the churches and to charity, and active in all aspects of public life in New South Wales.

Denied Elizabeth Macarthur's hand in 1812, on 31 October 1821 Oxley married an educated English gentlewoman, Emma (1798–1885), the daughter of John Norton, a landowner of Mulgoa, New South Wales, with whom he had two sons, John and Henry. He already had three illegitimate daughters, two with Charlotte Thorpe and another with Elizabeth Marnon. He lived well, dividing his time between his town house in Sydney and his property at

Kirkham, near Camden, where he had moved in 1817. He died on 26 May 1828, at Kirkham, from a kidney disease probably caused by the privations of exploring, and was buried in the Devonshire Street cemetery in Sydney. He was virtually penniless, but the British government awarded his sons 5000 acres in recognition of their father's explorations.

A brave, diligent explorer, Oxley was a complex man who craved social acceptance and economic success. The latter eluded him, but his travels through New South Wales were crucial to the great pastoral 'break-out' of the 1830s. Australians remember him as a man who tried—and failed—to solve the problems of the western rivers, but his book, *Journals of Two Expeditions into the Interior of New South Wales* (1820), was the first detailed account of Australian exploration by land.

H. M. CHICHESTER, *rev.* GEORGE PARSONS

Sources *AusDB*, 2.305–7 • [F. Watson], ed., *Historical records of Australia*, 1st ser., 5–15 (1915–22) • E. C. Rowland, 'Life and work of Lieutenant John Oxley, RN', *Royal Australian Historical Society Journal and Proceedings*, 28 (1942), 249–72 • J. Oxley, *Journals of two expeditions into the interior of New South Wales, 1817–18* (1820) • K. Fitzpatrick, ed., *Australian explorers: a selection from their writings* (1958)

Archives CUL, university medical library, Library of the Royal Commonwealth Society, journal • Mitchell L., NSW, corresp., journals, notebooks, papers | Mitchell L., NSW, Blake MSS • Mitchell L., NSW, Macarthur MSS • Mitchell L., NSW, Riggall MSS • PRO, CO papers

Wealth at death died in debt: *AusDB*; proceedings of executive council, New South Wales, 1828

Oxley, Joseph (1715–1775), Quaker minister, the eldest son of John Oxley (1682/3–1724), corn factor, and Ann, *née* Peckover (1685/6–1720) of Fakenham, Norfolk, was born at Brigg in Lincolnshire on 4 November 1715. His mother, who was a Quaker minister, died in 1720, aged thirty-four; four years later, in January 1724, his father died, and thereafter he was raised by his Quaker uncle Edmund Peckover. After five years at Gilbert Thompson's school at Sankey in Lancashire he was apprenticed to Robert Henderson, a Quaker clockmaker, at Scarborough. It has been suggested that as a youth Oxley was 'led away by the influence of evil associates to an indifference towards religion, a neglect to attend meetings for worship and other unprofitable and disorderly practices. He became a source of great trouble to his relations and friends' ('Oxley, Joseph', Dictionary of Quaker biography). In 1738, aged twenty-three, he moved to London to find employment. Soon afterwards he attended a large meeting on Kennington Common, held by the Calvinistic Methodist George Whitefield, and on account of his small stature was almost crushed to death. A gentlewoman who witnessed his predicament helped rescue him from danger, and this event led to his conversion to Quakerism. In 1742 he became a minister of the Society of Friends and travelled on missionary visits to Scotland, Ireland, and all parts of England.

In 1741 Oxley moved to Fakenham in Norfolk and opened a shop. On 28 June 1744 he married Elizabeth Fenn (1719?–1753), a Quaker from Norwich, and formed a partnership in a prosperous woollen mill. On 22 March 1745 Ann, the first of his five children, was born; his wife died in 1753, when his children were still in their infancy. On 5 January 1757, at Huntingdon in Cambridgeshire, Oxley married Mary Burr (1716–1794), a Quaker minister originally from Royston in Hertfordshire; they had no children.

During the summer of 1762 Oxley conducted a missionary visit to Friends in Cork, where on 15 July it was recorded that he was 'a sound Minister, a worthy Friend and a most agreeable companion' ('Travelling in Ireland', 261). In July 1770 he sailed for America, and in September arrived at New York and proceeded to visit many Quaker meetings. At the yearly meeting in Philadelphia later that month Oxley recorded that it was a solemn meeting 'such as he had not seen before; so consistent in appearance of dress and uniformity throughout, agreeably to our holy profession' (Janney, 3.392). His letters and details of his life were later published by John Barclay under the title *Joseph's offering to his children: being Joseph Oxley's journal of his life, travels, and labours of love in the faith and fellowship of our Lord Jesus Christ* (1837) and provide interesting information about the colonies of Virginia, Maryland, and New England.

Oxley returned to Norwich in April 1772, having travelled 13,755 miles, and died there suddenly on 22 October 1775; he was interred in the Quaker burial-ground at Norwich four days later. On 26 April 1776 Norwich Friends composed the following testimony:

> This our dear Friend was exemplary in conduct and agreeable in conversation, honest in advice, charitable in sentiment, and unwearied in Benevolence. He was therefore deservedly esteemed by his neighbours and beloved by his Friends … The love of God being shed abroad in his heart, he preferred the Lord's business to his own and when he felt divine drawings to visit the Churches he resigned himself fully. (*Testimonies*, 3.87)

RICHARD C. ALLEN

Sources 'Dictionary of Quaker biography', RS Friends, Lond. [card index] [see also 'Burr, Mary' and 'Peckover, Edmund'] • 'Testimonies concerning ministers deceased', RS Friends, Lond., 3.82–7 • *Some account of the life of Joseph Pike … also, A journal of the life and gospel labours of Joseph Oxley*, ed. J. Barclay (1837) • 'An account of ministering Friends from Europe who visited America, 1656 to 1793', *Journal of the Friends' Historical Society*, 10 (1913), 117–32, esp. 120, 130–31 • 'Record of Friends travelling in Ireland, 1656–1765 [pt 2]', *Journal of the Friends' Historical Society*, 10 (1913), 212–62, esp. 261–2 • J. Tomkins, *Piety promoted*, new edn, 2 (1812), pt 9, 445–7 • S. M. Janney, *History of the Religious Society of Friends from its rise to the year 1828*, 4 vols. (1870), 3.392 • R. M. Jones, *The later periods of Quakerism*, 1 (1921), 205 • *DNB*

Oxlie, Mary (*fl.* 1616), poet, is known for a single commendatory poem addressed to the Scottish poet William Drummond of Hawthornden. Her fifty-two-line poem, a striking apologia for female creativity as well as a panegyric, 'To William Drummond of Hawthornden', appeared in the 1656 edition of Drummond's *Poems*. It is signed by 'Mary Oxlie of Morpet' but her identity is subsequently confused in the next reprinting of her poem. Edward Phillips, in the section of his *Theatrum poetarum* (London, 1675) entitled 'Women among the moderns eminent for poetry', declares her a 'Scotch Poetess' but names her 'Mary Morpeth'. Oxlie is the only ostensibly Scottish female writer to be named in Phillips's collection. Phillips alludes to 'many other things in Poetry' by Oxlie (Phillips, 259) but nothing else can be securely attributed to her. David Laing in his *Various Pieces of Fugitive Scottish Poetry* (1825) attributed to Oxlie two political broadsides but later retracted the ascription, first assumed on the evidence of the initials 'M. M.' (the spurious 'Mary Morpeth').

The original 1656 ascription identifies Oxlie as a Northumbrian writer; one inference may be that she either directly moved to Scotland or became indirectly associated with literary circles around Drummond at Hawthornden, south of Edinburgh. David Masson's biography of Drummond (1873) suggests that Phillips obtained this and other dedicatory poems from Drummond's brother-in-law, Sir John Scot of Scotstarvet. Although Oxlie's poem cannot be dated, its presumed existence among Drummond's manuscripts, partly exchanged between Phillips and Scot, implies that it predated the 1656 posthumous edition. The poem contains allusions to Drummond's *Tears on the Death of Moeliades* (1613) and the amatory sonnet sequence of *Poems* (1616). It may have been presented to Drummond shortly after the 1616 edition, and was possibly not intended for publication. This remains conjectural, but there is evidence to suggest that the literary milieu cultivated by Drummond included women writers such as Anna Hume.

Oxlie's poem opens disingenuously with a plea that her 'worke' should not be compared to Drummond's, claiming in her defence, and on behalf of women artists, that creativity is frustrated by social and material concerns and by psychological anxiety:

From an untroubled mind should Verses flow;
My discontents makes mine too muddy show;
And hoarse encumbrances of household care
Where these remaine, the muses ne're repaire.

This humility is superseded by Oxlie's skilful 'recreation' of Drummond's pastoral mode. Ironically, Oxlie's poetic identity has been constituted through imitation. The poem's proposition that 'the Tree-turn'd *Daphne*' will crown the poet with the laurel 'garland' is possibly a reply to the commendatory sonnet of William Alexander published in the 1616 edition, as if to consciously 'feminize' the original dedication signifying male patronage. Oxlie's extant poem offers an insight into post-1603 Scottish literary culture and the coterie environment which cultivated women writers. Its proto-feminist justification of 'limited' female creativity was observed by the American writer and critic Tillie Olsen (*b.* 1913) in her pioneering work *Silences* (1978). S. M. DUNNIGAN

Sources *Poems by that most famous wit William Drummond of Hawthornden* (1656) • D. Laing, ed., *Various pieces of fugitive Scottish poetry; principally of the seventeenth century* (1825) • D. Laing, ed., *Various pieces of fugitive Scottish poetry; principally of the seventeenth century* (1853) • E. Phillips, *Theatrum poetarum, or, A compleat collection of the poets, especially the most eminent of all ages* (1675) • S. M. Dunnigan, 'Scottish women writers, c.1560–c.1650', *A history of Scottish women's writing*, ed. D. Gifford and D. McMillan (1997), 15–43 • G. Greer and others, eds., *Kissing the rod: an anthology of seventeenth-century women's verse* (1988), 79–82 • F. Rowton, *The female poets of Great Britain chronologically arranged with copious selections and critical remarks* (1848) • B. Travitsky, ed., *The paradise of women: writings by Englishwomen of the Renaissance* (1981), 139–41 • M. Bell, G. Parfitt, and S. Shepherd, *A biographical dictionary of English women writers, 1580–1720* (1990), 148 • D. Masson, *Drummond of Hawthornden: the story of his life and writings* (1873) • *The poetical works of William Drummond of Hawthornden*, 1, ed. L. E. Kastner, STS, 2nd ser., 3 (1913), 1.157

Oxnead, John of [John de Oxenedes] (*d.* in or after **1293**), Benedictine monk and chronicler, was presumably born at Oxnead, Norfolk. He became a monk of the abbey of St Benet of Hulme, 9 miles east-north-east of Norwich. A chronicle of the world, from the creation to 1293, which was composed at Hulme at about the latter date, has been attributed to him. However, the only evidence for his authorship and, indeed, for his existence, is an inscription in the late thirteenth-century copy of the chronicle in BL, Cotton MS Nero D.ii, folios 217–37, in which Sir Robert Cotton himself, in an inscription at the top of the first page, attributes it to John of Oxnead, monk of St Benet's of Hulme. This attribution has generally been accepted and, since the chronicle itself has no reference to John of Oxnead, Cotton must have had some other evidence, possibly a medieval inscription. However, in 1888 Liebermann stated that he found nothing to substantiate such a possibility and no John of Oxnead has been found in the abbey's records.

The chronicle is mainly a compilation from standard authorities, for example William of Malmesbury, Henry of Huntingdon, John of Wallingford, and the chronicle of Bury St Edmunds formerly attributed to John of Everden, interspersed with additional matter concerning the history of Norfolk, but more especially that of St Benet's Abbey: although of little value for general history it is an indispensable source for local affairs. Oxnead's chronicle also has historiographic value because it is one of the East Anglian chronicles that throws light on the composition of the Everden chronicle, from which it borrows for the annals for 1020–1169 and 1258–92. Bartholomew Cotton (*d.* 1321/2), another borrower from 'Everden', uses Oxnead's chronicle for his annals for 1279–84. From the mid-1270s, however, the variants in Oxnead's chronicle from that of Everden become increasingly important and by *c.*1290 the Oxnead chronicle was indebted to a collection of Bury material rather than to a written-up text. For example, although the letter of Edward I of 1291, enclosing the letters of submission of the competitors for the Scottish throne to Edward's judgment, is addressed to the abbot and convent of St Edmunds, the competitors' letters are in Latin, not French as in Everden's chronicle.

Two copies, both late thirteenth-century, are known of Oxnead's chronicle. Neither is copied from the other, but they descend from a common exemplar. One, the already mentioned Nero D.ii, folios 217–37, is a codicological curiosity. The chronicle is on quarto-sized leaves. Each page has six, eight, ten, or twelve blocks of text copied onto it in three columns. Originally the leaves were folded, once horizontally and twice vertically, down each column. Presumably they were once kept in a pouch. Such folded manuscripts are extremely rare. Henry Ellis edited the chronicle in Nero D.ii in 1859 for the Rolls Series. After he had completed his edition another copy was discovered in a historical miscellany of the thirteenth and fourteenth centuries in the duke of Newcastle's possession. It is now BL, Egerton MS 3142. This volume had belonged to St Benet's of Hulme until *c.*1294 when it was acquired by the Augustinian priory of Hickling (about 6 miles north-east of Hulme). It has many additions relating to the priory's history. A collation of the Oxnead text (fols. 105–200v) was appended to Ellis's edition. ANTONIA GRANSDEN

Sources *Chronica Johannis de Oxenedes*, ed. H. Ellis, Rolls Series, 13 (1859) • R. Pauli and F. Liebermann, eds., [*Ex rerum Anglicarum scriptoribus*], MGH Scriptores [folio], 28 (Stuttgart, 1888), 598–9 • [H. Wharton], ed., *Anglia sacra*, 1 (1691), 405 • T. Smith, ed., *Catalogus librorum manuscriptorum bibliothecae Cottonianae* (1696) • Tanner, *Bibl. Brit.-Hib.*, 567 • *Catalogue of additions to the manuscripts, 1936–1945*, British Museum, Department of Manuscripts, 1 (1970), 335–6 • A. Gransden, ed. and trans., *The chronicle of Bury St Edmunds, 1212–1301* [1964], xxvii–xxviii and n. 1 • A. Gransden, *Historical writing in England*, 1 (1974), 402–3, 422, 432 (n.281), 443 • J. R. West, ed., *St Benet of Holme, 1020–1210: the eleventh and twelfth century sections of Cott. MS Galba E ii, the register of the abbey of St Benet of Holme*, 2 vols., Norfolk RS, 2–3 (1932), vol. 2, pp. 191–7 • A. Gransden, 'The chronicles of medieval England and Scotland', *Legends, traditions, and history in medieval England* (1992), 228, 234–7, pl. 26 • *Bartholomaei de Cotton … Historia Anglicana*, ed. H. R. Luard, Rolls Series, 16 (1859), lvii–lviii
Archives BL, Egerton MS 3142 [copy] • BL, Cotton MS Nero D.ii, fols. 217–37 [copy]

Ozell, John (*d.* 1743), translator, was the son of John Ozell. Little is known about his parents. His father was said to be from a Leicestershire family, of French origin. Ozell was educated at the free school in Ashby-de-la-Zouch, and then at Christ's Hospital, after which it was expected that he would go to Cambridge, and become a clergyman. However, he decided instead to enter business and he moved to London where he joined an accountant's office. He was successful in this, and managed several important accounts, including those of the City of London, St Paul's Church, and St Thomas's Hospital.

While Ozell was working as an accountant he taught himself a number of foreign languages, which, together with the classical languages he had learned at school, enabled him to undertake the series of translations of foreign classics for which he is chiefly known. Some of the most significant translations that he produced were his versions of Boileau. In 1708 he translated his *Le Lutrin*, and between 1711 and 1713 he published an edition, *The Works of Monsieur Boileau* (translated by Ozell and others), both of which were influential in introducing the French author's works to an English-speaking public at this time. Like many translators of this period, Ozell's treatment of the texts that he was working on was a free one, in which he continually expanded upon the original. Thus he used Boileau's account of the 'battle of the books' in the *Lutrin* to comment upon contemporary English writers.

The attack on William Wycherley's poetry included in this translation brought Ozell into conflict with the influential group of Scriblerian writers. Alexander Pope was a friend of Wycherley's, and at this time he was engaged in editing and revising the older writer's *Miscellaneous Poems*. He immediately responded to Ozell in his 'Epigram, Occasion'd by Ozell's Translation of Boileau's Lutrin', written in 1708, in which he claimed that 'those were slander'd most whom Ozell prais'd' (*Minor Poems*, 6.37). Ozell continued to be lampooned as the epitome of the hack translator in both Pope's *Dunciad* and Jonathan Swift's 'Introduction to Polite Conversation'. Yet although he was mocked for his literary incompetence, his translations were not only good by the standards of the time, but also useful to Pope for his own work on the classics. In 1712 Ozell produced a blank-verse translation of Anne Dacier's French version of Homer's *Iliad*, and Pope borrowed from this heavily when he began to publish his own famous *Iliad* translation three years later.

Part of the tory Scriblerians' hostility to Ozell may have been due to his political affiliations. He seems to have been associated with the group of whig writers such as Eustace Budgell and Ambrose Philips, who centred around Joseph Addison, and 'Button's' club, held at Daniel Button's coffee house in Covent Garden. Ozell's translations certainly suggest that his political views were whiggish. His violent anti-Catholicism is demonstrated in his 1716 translation of the life of the 'saint' Veronica of Milan, and in 1717 he published a translation of Rapin de Thoyras's very whiggish *Dissertation sur les Whigs et les Torys* of that year (*An Historical Dissertation upon Whig and Tory*). Ozell's literary career continued to be marked by literary controversy: in 1728 the Anglican churchman Richard Bundy began to publish a version of F. Catrou's and P. J. Rouillé's *Histoire romaine, depuis la fondation de Rome* (1725–35), as *Roman History*, upstaging Ozell, who had also been planning to release a translation of the text. Ozell responded by publishing a lengthy commentary on the various mistakes and omissions in Bundy's translation. He also issued an advertisement in the newspaper the *Weekly Medley*, in which he attacked both Bundy, and his old enemy Pope, whose *Dunciad variorum* had appeared that year. In the advertisement he vindicated the reputation of his own scholarship, and claimed that Pope was 'that second Cain, whose Hand is against every Body, and every Body's Hand against him' (*Weekly Medley*, 20 Sept 1729).

Ozell never married. At the time of his death he was financially secure, due to his accountancy work and an inheritance that he was left by an old family friend from Leicestershire. He died at his house in Arundel Street in Westminster on 15 October 1743, and was buried in the church of St Mary Aldermanbury, Westminster. He left his estate to his brother, Austin Ozell.

ABIGAIL WILLIAMS

Sources R. Shiels, *The lives of the poets of Great Britain and Ireland*, ed. T. Cibber, 5 vols. (1753) • A. F. B. Clark, *Boileau and the French classical critics in England, 1660–1830* (1925) • A. Chalmers, ed., *The general biographical dictionary*, new edn, 32 vols. (1812–17) • *Minor poems*, ed. N. Ault (1954), vol. 6 of *The Twickenham edition of the poems of Alexander Pope*, ed. J. Butt (1939–69) • [G. Jacob], *The poetical register, or, The lives and characters of the English dramatick poets*, 2 vols. (1719–20) • *GM*, 1st ser., 13 (1743) • *Weekly Medley* (20 Sept 1729)

Pabo [*called* Pabo Post Prydain] (*supp. fl. c.*500), chieftain, is named by the earliest Welsh genealogies (BL, Harley MS 3859) as a son of Cenau ap Coel Hen and thus placed at the beginning of the sixth century. Later genealogical sources make him the son of Arthwys ap Mar ap Cenau ap Coel, but internal chronology supports the earlier versions. In the genealogies Pabo is chiefly named as the father of Dunod Fwr, Sawyl Benuchel, and Ardun Benasgell, and as the grandfather of three Welsh saints, Deiniol, Asaf and Tysilio. In medieval Welsh literature he is styled 'Post Prydain' ('the Pillar of Britain'), an epithet also applied to Urien Rheged. Pabo is alleged by tradition to have been buried at Llanbabo in Anglesey and to have given his name to the church there. The earliest written reference to this tradition appears in the work of the eighteenth-century antiquary Henry Rowlands, but Pabo Post Prydain is also linked to Llanbabo by a fourteenth-century monument discovered, according to Lewis Morris, in the churchyard during the reign of Charles II. The slab is carved in low relief with the figure of a king and an inscription, which can be read in part and has been interpreted as: 'Hic iacet Pa[bo] Post Priid Co[nf Gr] … [t]el [i]ma[ginem obtulit]' ('Here lies Pabo the Upholder of Britain, Confessor, Gruffudd ab Ithel offered (this) image'). However, as there is no earlier evidence that the north British Pabo became an ecclesiastic or that he died in Anglesey, it is likely that it is some other Pabo who is commemorated in the name of the church. NERYS ANN JONES

Sources P. C. Bartrum, ed., *Early Welsh genealogical tracts* (1966) · R. Bromwich, ed. and trans., *Trioedd ynys Prydein: the Welsh triads* (1961), 483–4 · S. Baring-Gould and J. Fisher, *The lives of the British saints*, Honourable Society of Cymmrodorion, Cymmrodorion Record Series, 4 (1913), 38–9 · H. Rowlands, *Mona antiqua restaurata* (1723); repr. (New York, 1979), 157 · H. Owen, *The life and work of Lewis Morris (Llewelyn Ddu o Fôn), 1701–1765* (1951), 14 · *An inventory of the ancient monuments in Anglesey*, Royal Commission on Ancient and Historical Monuments in Wales and Monmouthshire (1937) · L. Morris, *Celtic remains*, ed. [D. S. Evans] (1878), 339

Paca, William (1740–1799), lawyer and revolutionary politician in America, was born on 31 October 1740 at his father's plantation on the Bush River near Abingdon in Baltimore (later Harford) county, Maryland, the third child and second son of John Paca (*c.*1712–1785), planter, and his wife, Elizabeth Smith (*d.* *c.*1766). Both of his parents were natives of Maryland and of English descent. In addition to his older brother, Aquila, Paca had five sisters.

William, at age eleven, and Aquila were sent to the Academy and Charity School of Philadelphia in 1752. Beginning in 1756 William Paca continued his education at the College of Philadelphia, from which he received a BA degree in May 1759. Three years later he collected an MA degree, available upon request to graduates in good standing without requirement of further study. In the late spring or early summer of 1759 Paca took up residence in Annapolis, capital of Maryland, where he studied law with Stephen Bordley, one of the pre-eminent lawyers of the day. Records of the Inner Temple (where Bordley had also studied) indicate that Paca was admitted to commons, but the timing and duration of his stay in London remain unclear.

Paca began his legal career in 1761, qualifying as an attorney both in several county courts and in the more prestigious provincial courts. In addition to a successful law practice, he solidified his position among the Maryland gentry by his marriage on 26 May 1763 to heiress Mary (*c.*1736–1774), daughter of Samuel Chew (*c.*1704–1737) and his wife, Henrietta Maria Lloyd (*d.* 1765). Immediately after the marriage, they built an elegant Georgian mansion with a 2 acre pleasure garden, which still stands. Before Mary's death on 15 January 1774 the couple had three children, of whom only John Philemon (1771–1840) survived to adulthood. During the 1760s Paca also took an active role in the political life of Maryland. With fellow attorney Samuel Chase he was one of the leaders of the Annapolis protests in 1765 against the Stamp Act, by which parliament attempted to tax internal American trade, and an organizer of the Anne Arundel chapter of the American patriot organization the Sons of Liberty. In May 1766 Paca was elected as a common councilman for the city of Annapolis and the following year local voters chose him as one of their representatives in the Maryland house of delegates. He remained a representative for Annapolis through the final provincial assembly of 1774.

Paca continued to play an active political role as protests against Maryland's proprietary actions evolved into protests against British rule. Both in court and in print Paca argued against the proprietary position on determination of officials' fees and against the Church of England clergy's position on the poll tax levied for their support—despite being himself a member of the vestry. As Maryland moved towards independence Paca represented Annapolis in the extra-legal Maryland conventions that ruled the province beginning in 1774, and was chosen as one of Maryland's delegates to the first continental congress in 1774. Paca served longer as a delegate than any other Marylander, and was one of the two who both voted for and signed the Declaration of Independence. He also served in the Maryland senate from 1777 until his resignation in 1780. Paca held no military commission during the war but did serve as one of three commissioners responsible for organizing the defence of the eastern shore.

In late 1774, Paca developed a relationship in Philadelphia with a woman known only as Levina. Their relationship produced Hester (1775–1793?), to whom Paca referred as his 'natural daughter'. Levina had probably died by 1781 when Paca, prior to his return to Maryland, made arrangements for Hester's education and medical care. By 1775 or 1776 Paca had become involved with Sarah Joice (*d.* 1803), a relationship that produced at least one child, Henrietta Maria (*c.*1777–1850). The affair was not secretive, as Paca bought Joice a house in Annapolis and in 1798 she was living on one of his plantations, property that Paca later devised to Henrietta Maria.

While in Philadelphia as a congressional delegate, on 28 February 1777 Paca married Anne (1757–1780), daughter of Henry Harrison (*c.*1713–1766), merchant and former mayor, and his wife, Mary Aspden. The couple had one child before Anne's death in February 1780; their son, Henry, died in 1781.

Paca resigned as a delegate to congress when appointed a judge of the court of appeals for admiralty and prize cases in 1780, and resigned that position when elected governor of Maryland in November 1782. He served three one-year terms as governor (the statutory limit) and was in office when congress met in Annapolis in 1783–4, where it ratified the treaty of Paris on 15 January 1784. Following the expiration of his third term as governor, Paca was elected to both the senate and house of delegates; he chose to sit in the house as the body more responsive to the interests of the people.

Paca refused election to the constitutional convention in 1787, but did represent Harford county (a recently created county that included his birthplace) as an anti-federalist in the ratification convention held in April 1788. He proposed twenty-eight amendments to the constitution designed to ensure personal freedoms and limitations on federal powers similar to safeguards written into the Maryland constitution. Although his efforts were thwarted by the federalists who controlled the convention, a number of Paca's ideas were later incorporated in the Bill of Rights. Despite Paca's opposition to the new form of government, George Washington appointed him a judge for the federal district court of Maryland in December 1789, recognizing that without men like Paca there would have been no American government, federal or otherwise.

After selling his grand Annapolis home in 1780, Paca made his primary residence on Wye Island in Queen Anne's county on Maryland's eastern shore (property inherited by Mary from her brother and held in trust for their son John), where he built an even more grand house, Wye Hall, in the 1790s. Paca died at Wye Hall on 13 October 1799 and was most likely buried in the grounds, although the location of his grave is unknown. JEAN B. RUSSO

Sources E. C. Papenfuse and others, eds., *A biographical dictionary of the Maryland legislature, 1635–1789*, 2 (1985) [pt of the Maryland state archives biography project] · G. A. Stiverson and P. R. Jacobsen, *William Paca: a biography* (Baltimore, Maryland, 1976) · R. Hoffman, *A spirit of dissension: economics, politics, and the revolution in Maryland* (1973) · William Paca research files, Historic Annapolis Foundation, Annapolis, Maryland · register, Christ Church, Philadelphia

Archives Maryland Historical Society, Baltimore, corresp.

Likenesses C. W. Peale, oils, 1772, Maryland Historical Society, Baltimore · J. B. Bordley, oils, 1836, State House, Annapolis, Maryland · etching, Maryland Historical Society, Baltimore, Hayden collection

Wealth at death approx. 4500 acres of land and probably at least 100 slaves: Papenfuse and others, eds., *A biographical dictionary*, 2.635

Pace, John (*b. c.*1523, *d.* in or before 1592), scholar and court jester, was probably the son of John Pace, a brother of Richard *Pace (1483?–1536), secretary to Henry VIII, diplomat, and humanist. In 1522 the elder John Pace received 'license to exercise by deputy the office of customer … in the port of Lynne' and 'to keep, buy and sell ships, and negociate as to the freightage of ships'. He was then a London resident, and owned 'lands and offices' estimated at the yearly value of £40, 100 marks (*LP Henry VIII*, 3.2, 889, 1052). Richard Pace informs us that, in 1527, his brother John had a 'wife and children' (ibid., 4.2, 1472), but their names are unknown.

John Pace the younger studied at Eton College and was afterwards elected to King's College, Cambridge. In 1539 he is described as a 'went away Fellow' at the latter institution (Harwood, 157), although John Heywood, a contemporary satirist, credits him with a master of arts degree (Camden, 266). However, Pace, who was known for his caustic wit, abandoned his scholarly career to become a court jester, in which capacity he was 'appointed' to Henry VIII (Harwood, 157) and then to the duke of Norfolk. To those contemporaries who were outraged 'that Pace being a maister of Arte had disgraced himselfe with wearing a fooles coate', John Heywood presumably indicated that 'it is lesse hurtfull to the common-weale, when wise men goe in fooles coates, than when fooles goe in wise mens gownes' (Camden, 266).

Pace's religious affiliation has been subject to debate. Cole believes that he 'retained his integrity' as a Roman Catholic (Cole, fols. 26*v*–27). To this attests an anecdote included in Cardinal Allen's *Apologie* for the English colleges, an anti-protestant pamphlet written and published in exile in 1581, as a response to Queen Elizabeth's two recent proclamations issued against the English Catholics studying in foreign seminaries. After blaming his adversaries for their attempts to 'forbid the entering, having, or reading' Catholic books, Allen relates that 'madde Pace meeting one day with M. Juel [John Jewel, bishop of Salisbury] … saluted his L. courtly, and said, Now my Lord, quoth he, you may be at rest with these felowes [the Catholics], for you are quit by Proclamation' (Allen, 58*v*). Pace's anachronistic remark (Jewel had died in 1571) served to voice Allen's disapproval of the queen's legal ban on Catholic books. Doran maintains that Pace was, on the contrary, a supporter of the protestant movement, although he himself questions the reliability of the story which supports his view (Doran, 164–6).

Whatever his religious credo might have been, Pace remained hostile to Queen Elizabeth. Francis Bacon, who coined the name Bitter Fool for Pace, relates in his *Apophthegmes New and Old* (1625) that Pace, who had been kept away from the queen because of his acerbity, was admitted one day before her, at the insistence of her courtiers, 'undertaking for him that he should keep compass'. But when the queen said: 'Come on, Pace: now we shall hear of our faults', Pace uninhibitedly replied: 'I do not use to talk of that that all the town talks of' (*Rogeri Bacon opera*, 330). His witty sayings earned Pace the reputation of an authority in satirical literature. In his pamphlet *Pierce Penilesse* (1592) Thomas Nashe includes Pace among famous 'Orators and Poets', such as 'Machevill', 'Tully' (Cicero), Ovid, Roscius, and Robert Greene (Nashe, 1). In the prologue to the tragedy *Thorney Abbey, or, The London Maid*, by 'T. W.' (1662), the Fool nostalgically calls 'Pacy' one of his 'venerable predecessors' (Welsford, 249). Pace is mentioned again in a nineteenth-century historical account of anecdotal literature (*GM*, 410).

Pace had died by 1592, for Nashe, in *Pierce Penilesse*, includes the 'Ghost of … Pace, the Duke of Norfolks Jester' among those to whom he claims to have dedicated 'epistles' (Nashe, 1). OLGA ANNA DUHL

Sources *DNB* · T. Harwood, *Alumni Etonenses, or, A catalogue of the provosts and fellows of Eton College and King's College, Cambridge, from*

the foundation in 1443 to the year 1797 (1797) • M. Davies, *Athenae Britannicae*, 6 vols. (1716–19), vol. 1, pt 1 • *LP Henry VIII*, vols. 3/2, 4/2, 13/2 • Wood, *Ath. Oxon.*, new edn, vol. 1 • Cooper, *Ath. Cantab.*, vol. 1 • T. Nashe, *Pierce Penilesse, his supplication to the divell*, ed. G. B. Harrison (1924) • W. Allen, *An apologie and true declaration of the institution and endevours of two English colleges, the one in Rome, the other now resident in Rhemes* (1581); repr. (1971) • W. Camden, *Remains concerning Britain*, ed. R. D. Dunn (1984) • *The works of Francis Bacon*, ed. J. Spedding, R. L. Ellis, and D. D. Heath, 14 vols. (1857–74), vol. 13 • E. Welsford, *The fool: his social and literary history* (1966) • J. Doran, *The history of court fools* (1858); repr. (1966) • W. Cole, 'King's College historiettes', BL, Add. MS 5815, fols. 26*v*–27 • *GM*, 1st ser., 90/2 (1820), 406–10

Pace, Richard (1483?–1536), diplomat, humanist, and administrator, was probably born in Winchester, Hampshire, in 1483, of parents whose identity is unknown. The Pace family were probably members of the minor gentry. Few details of Pace's early life are known, apart from those revealed in his *De fructu qui ex doctrina percipitur* (written in 1517). He had a brother, John Pace, who became customer of King's Lynn, Norfolk.

Early years and education, *c*.1483–1509 Pace joined the household of Thomas Langton, bishop of Winchester from 1493 to 1501, and became his amanuensis. He was educated in Langton's *domestica schola* at his Winchester palace of Wolvesey. Langton sent the musically gifted and academically promising Pace to study *bonae literae* at the University of Padua about 1498. Pace was not, as traditionally believed, a student at Queen's College, Oxford, before leaving for Italy. Langton provided for his expenses in Italy from about 1498, and his will of 1501 bequeathed £10 a year for seven years further. Abbot de Bere, much interested in the study of Greek, also assisted Pace financially.

Pace was educated by Niccolò Leonico Tomeo of Padua, Paolo Bombace of Bologna, and Leoniceno of Ferrara in rhetoric, Greek, medicine, Platonic and Aristotelian philosophy, and the natural sciences. He may not have studied in Padua for more than a few years, because by 1501 he was studying at Bologna. He was definitely in Ferrara some time before the end of 1508, when Desiderius Erasmus was his guest. Pace there introduced Erasmus to his good friend Celio Calcagnini, a scholar of Hebrew and of Roman law. Calcagnini would later offer his services to Henry VIII on the divorce issue on Pace's encouragement. Pace, William Latimer, and Cuthbert Tunstall belonged to the second generation of English scholars gathered around the Anglophile Tomeo in Padua. Thomas Lupset, Thomas Starkey, and Reginald Pole constituted the younger generation, and Tomeo's correspondence reveals that Pace acted as their patron in the years 1522 to 1525 when he was in Rome and the Veneto on diplomatic business. Lupset for a time was Pace's secretary.

Pace struck up an enduring friendship with Erasmus, and the latter wrote to him more than to any other correspondent during the period until 1536. Pace said that they spent much time together in study at various places, including Bologna. In 1508 Erasmus praised his expertise in Greek and Latin literature. Pace collected notable classical metaphors and allegories into a companion volume to Erasmus's adages, although it was never published. While in Ferrara, Pace translated the preface to Simplicius's commentary on the Aristotelian *Categories*, and at some point was preparing a treatise on arithmetic along Pythagorean and Neoplatonic lines.

Pace's other humanist and, later, diplomatic friendships which were forged in Italy during this time included those with Gasparo Contarini, Pietro Bembo, Marco Musurus, Gianmatteo Giberti, Alberto Pio, Francesco Maria Molza, Niccolò Guideco, Polydore Vergil, Alexander Alexandrini, Cornelius Agrippa, and Ulrich von Hutten. Through a network of associations he very probably had contact with the Roman Academy of John Goritz and the Aldine circle.

Royal service, 1509–1525 Erasmus's efforts to find Pace patronage in the English court in return for kindnesses rendered in Italy bore fruit. Pace entered the service of Christopher Bainbridge, archbishop of York and Henry's newly appointed agent at Rome from the end of 1509. Bainbridge was Langton's nephew. Firmly pro-Venetian and vehemently anti-French in his policies, the bellicose Bainbridge was given the brief to assist in forming a league around Julius II which would drive the French out of Italy (the Holy League). Pace shared his views. For its part the Venetian republic regarded Pace as a learned and virtuous advocate for its interests, who was to be received as a native Venetian rather than a foreign diplomat.

Bainbridge was made a cardinal in March 1511, by which time Pace was his Latin and Italian secretary. Pace's long series of lively and colourful diplomatic dispatches to Henry and Thomas Wolsey dates from September 1513. From 1512 Bainbridge was patron of the important humanist satiric and poetic *festa* of Pasquino celebrated on 25 April each year. (The statue in the Piazza Navona was dressed as a pagan deity and scurrilous—and frequently obscene—pasquinades attacking the prominent were attached to carpets at its feet.) Pace was among Bainbridge's senior servants who probably assisted the various printers in selecting and editing the Latin and Italian epigrams for the printed collections, and contributed pasquinades of their own. Bainbridge called him his Master Pasquyll. In the spring of 1514 Pace visited England, where he was made archdeacon of Dorset, having taken holy orders before 1 May 1510, when he was made prebendary of North Muskham in Southwell, Nottinghamshire. His friendship with Thomas More probably dates from this time.

Pace attended Bainbridge at the 1513 conclave which elected Leo X, and his experience of this was subsequently used by Henry and Wolsey. The Holy League began to disintegrate as early as October 1513 with Leo's reconciliation with France, and in March 1514 Ferdinand II of Aragon and Sicily and Louis XII signed a truce. Bainbridge's ascendancy in Rome had in fact began to decline from 1512 as a result of double-dealing in the Tudor court, but Pace served him loyally until his death from suspected poisoning in July 1514. Pace, then in Zürich, hurried back to Rome to act as Bainbridge's executor; he suspected that Wolsey's agent, Silvestro Gigli, bishop of Worcester, had instigated the crime and strenuously pursued the cause but without result. When Gigli was absolved by a papal consistory Pace acted prudently, and upon the recommendations of the pope and the cardinals accepted the patronage of Wolsey and entered his service. Pace returned to England in April 1515.

Pace had begun researching a history of music in the Vatican library on the urgings of Latimer, but as Bainbridge's sudden death ended his life in Italy it was left unfinished. He did complete and publish a collection of Latin translations of Plutarch and Lucian, *Plutarchi Cheronaei opuscula … Ex Luciano*, with the press of Jacopo Mazzochi in 1514 or 1515, dedicating it to Bainbridge and addressing it to students. It was only the third book by an Englishman ever to be printed at Rome, and the second translation of Lucian by an Englishman (after More). It was both a tribute to Tomeo's interests in teaching Greek, ethics, and rhetoric through the vehicle of Plutarch and Lucian, and a testament of loyalty to Bainbridge. Pace pointedly drew attention to the appropriateness of the essay 'How to derive benefit from enemies' for the diplomatist cardinal and described a careworn and anxious Bainbridge denied rest by the demands of serving curia and country. If Pace's diplomatic career had begun auspiciously under Bainbridge it was to become an arduous, frustrating, and health-denying one also. Vergil and Shakespeare (and Fletcher) attributed his final insanity and impoverishment to a jealous Wolsey's desire to keep him away from England and the king's favour on continuous and gruelling ambassadorial duties from 1515 to 1525. He was often adequately provided neither with the necessary salary for conducting negotiations (especially with Maximilian I) nor with full and unambiguous instructions, and so it is not surprising that his missions usually achieved little success. This was especially true of his mission to Switzerland from October 1515 to late 1517. In the wake of François I's victory at the battle of Marignano against the Swiss, Henry hoped to work with Maximilian and to buy Swiss soldiers in order to counteract the intrigues of the papal and French emissaries. The *De fructu* was composed, in an inn in Constance, as a Stoic consolation amid the dangers of diplomatic life, and published hurriedly about January 1518 because, as Pace explained, 'I am free by nature but not by choice. For I have bound myself to serve my invincible King as the servant of the wise Cardinal of York. To serve one's country exceeds all freedom' (Pace, *De fructu*, 13). His fears for his life and health were not exaggerated. The French apparently tried to poison him, the Swiss imprisoned him twice as security for the emperor's debts to their soldiers, and he suffered many attacks of fever before his return to London.

Pace had also alternated between periods of elation and depression in 1516, the year in which he became Henry's 'primarius secretarius' or principal secretary (J. S. Brewer, *The Reign of Henry VIII from his Accession to the Death of Wolsey*, 2 vols., 1884, 2.64). He was the king's personal secretary and owed his appointment to his energy, connections, ability, fluency in several languages, and experience of foreign travel. As secretary he was in close proximity to the king and wrote almost all his personal correspondence. This relationship gave him great influence over royal patronage and he built a strong rapport with Henry. His appointment did not please all, and several prominent people thought him an odd choice. For his part Maximilian expressed his wonder to Sir Robert Wingfield that the king should use 'such a proterve and dyssymulyng persone; for whatsoever he saith now, within an hour he turneth it of another, or rather into twenty divers fashions' (*LP Henry VIII*, 2/1, 2104).

Pace's writing came under criticism too. Erasmus criticized the *De fructu* for its stylistic transgressions and lack of judgement while praising Pace and his scholarship. However, he wrote to Pace in October 1518 saying that the book was read avidly by the Germans, although some in Constance had been offended by being characterized as bereft of learning and fond of drinking. Guillaume Budé, Beatus Rhenanus (a likely editor), and Martin Bucer were also initially appreciative. By 1520 at least an *Apologia ad Pacaeum* was circulating in Germany and Switzerland. Accepting Erasmus's judgement, twentieth-century commentators were critical of the apparent incoherence and disconcerting shifts in tone and diction of the *De fructu*, even attributing this to Pace's mental illness. More recently, however, the work has been re-evaluated. It is a pedagogical miscellany and Menippean satire commissioned for use in the study of Greek and Latin at St Paul's School by Erasmus on behalf of John Colet, to whom it is dedicated. Its literary form accounts for its hybrid and anecdotal presentation, and it has much in common with More's *Utopia*, published only months earlier. The *De fructu* is one of the earliest statements by an Englishman of humanist methods and theories of education and is the earliest English rhetorical textbook.

For Pace the vital fruit of a humanist education was the provision of counsel to the secular and spiritual realms of Christendom. The *De fructu* is highly critical of attempts made to stifle counsel offered in the appropriate courtly, ecclesiastical, or conciliar context. The declamation of each of the liberal arts introduces satire of the papacy, clergy, and courts of Europe of a type even more pointed and specific than that of Erasmus's *Praise of Folly* (1511), and this alarmed the ever cautious Erasmus. Pace insinuated a theory of conciliarism against the background of European war and peace, and the failures of the Pisa–Milan and the Fifth Lateran councils to effect reform in the years 1511–17.

Erasmus suppressed Pace's unpublished letter to Martin Dorp, composed while staying with More in Bruges in December 1517. This was not the only occasion on which More and Pace collaborated to defend humanist and Greek studies, and the scriptural methods of Erasmus. Letters of More and Pace to Edward Lee in support of Erasmus were published in the *Epistolae aliquot eruditorum virorum* of 1520. In March 1521 More and Pace both attended the court at Abingdon. With the apparent approval of Henry and Wolsey they attacked the Trojans at Oxford. In April 1520 the king offered Pace £10 per annum for a certain lecture in Greek to be read and taught at the University of Cambridge.

Early in 1518 Pace was reported as occupying the third

seat in the secret council and in February was made a gentleman by a grant of arms. He remained in England until May 1519, attending the king at court and travelling from one royal palace to another. On the occasion of the proclamation of the treaty of universal peace of 1518 at St Paul's Cathedral on 3 October, which he had helped to negotiate, Pace delivered a much admired Latin oration before Henry, the two papal legates Wolsey and Lorenzo Campeggi (who was also bishop of Salisbury), and foreign ambassadors, praising peace as the highest good. On 25 October 1518 Pace succeeded Colet as dean of St Paul's. After the death of Maximilian on 12 January 1519 he was sent to Germany on the delicate task of discovering the intentions of the electors while appearing neutral—there were several likely imperial candidates including Henry, François I, Charles, king of Spain, and Frederick Weftra III, duke of Saxony. If support for election of Henry proved impossible to garner Pace was to press for Charles rather than François. He arrived on the continent in May 1519 and travelled to the meeting of the Frankfurt diet, where the imperial election was to be held. Pace and Erasmus travelled on together to Brussels, for the former's interview with Margaret of Austria. Charles was elected on 28 June; Pace returned to England at the end of July and was rewarded with many benefices. In 1519 he was made archdeacon of Colchester, Essex, rector of Barwick in Elmet, West Riding of Yorkshire, prebendary of Exeter, vicar of St Dunstan's, Stepney, Middlesex, and prebendary of Finsbury, Middlesex. He was made dean of Exeter in 1522 and later of Salisbury (*c.*1529–31).

Henry apparently did not perceive, or was not averse to, the strong undercurrents of warning and correction in Pace's 1518 peace oration. He again chose him to deliver a 'goodly speech' in Latin to the royal congregation on the manifest benefits of peace at the Field of Cloth of Gold in June 1520, although the text does not survive. In the following year Wolsey had Pace make a copy of Martin Luther's *De captivitate Babylonica* for the king. John Fisher, bishop of Rochester, preached in support of the papal bull against Luther, promulgated in London on 12 May amid much ceremony, and Pace produced a Latin translation to be sent to the pope. Nicolas Wilson's preface describes Pace as possessing superlative eloquence and facility in languages, as of much and varied learning, and as a man of candour and integrity (J. Fisher, *Joannis Fischerii Opera omnia*, 1967, 1374). As dean Pace attended the burning of Luther's books at Paul's Cross.

Leo X died on 2 December 1521 and Pace was dispatched to Italy for the first time since 1515 to promote Wolsey's candidature for the papacy. Adrian VI was elected, however, before Pace reached Rome. Pace's *Plutarchi* was reprinted in January 1522 in Venice by Bernard dei Vitali, and Plutarch's *De garrulitate* and *De avaritia* added, the first dedicated to Tunstall and the second to his friend Campeggi. The *De avaritia* was issued in a second and corrected edition later the same year. In his preface to Campeggi, Pace explained that it was translated when the pestilence at Rome and his own illness impeded *negotium*. In 1523 Pace obtained permission from the Venetian senate for the publication of Tomeo's famous translation of and commentaries on Aristotle's *Parva naturalia*; its dedication to Pace praises his learning fulsomely. After spending some months in Venice and Switzerland, Pace and his colleague John Clerk were again sent to Rome to support Wolsey's bid for papal election upon the death of Adrian on 14 September 1523. But Clement VII, well known to Pace, was elected. Pace was welcomed back to England with an encomium from John Leland, but was soon ordered to Lombardy to take part in negotiations with Charles Bourbon III, duke of Bourbon, François's rebellious subject. He remained with Bourbon's army when it invaded France, retreating to Italy after the failure of the siege of Marseilles in September. Once more attempting to persuade the Venetians to fight against the French, Pace shuttled between Brescia, Mantua, and Venice. His dispatches reveal his suspicions that Wolsey had come to a secret understanding with François and was hence to blame for Henry's failure to send sufficient troops and funds to support Bourbon, and describe the cardinal as having a base nature. Pace himself seems to have supplied credit so that the soldiers were paid and could therefore fight for Bourbon.

The defeat of the French at Pavia on 24 February 1525 may have given Pace much satisfaction, but from 1522 onwards he was frequently seriously ill, attended by the finest Italian physicians, and nursed in Venice and Padua by Tomeo and Pole. In reply to Lupset's description of Pace's unrelieved fever and insomnia Erasmus wrote that he feared that it was his love affairs that were the source of his illness rather than his burdensome diplomatic duties. Pace made few references to women, apart from those to Katherine of Aragon, Margaret of Austria, Lady Darcy, and his sister-in-law, suggesting that he may have been socially awkward in their company. The doge himself urged Pace's recall in October 1525, after Wolsey failed to heed Pace's similar request in March. Pace may have taken some comfort from the birth of his nephew John *Pace about 1523.

Final years, 1525–1536 Pace arrived in London in November 1525. After some months William Knight became secretary and coadjutors were appointed to administer his deaneries of St Paul's, Exeter, and Salisbury. Pace retired to the Brigettine cloister of Syon at Isleworth, Middlesex, and recovered sufficiently to move back to the deanery of St Paul's only in the autumn. He found solace in a continuation of the scriptural and language studies which had recently occupied him in Italy, such as the translation of the Psalms. In 1527 he became involved in a dispute with his friend Fisher over the doctrine of the inspiration of the Septuagint, and Richard Rex argued that Pace's neglected *Praefatio in Ecclesiasten recognitum ad Hebraicam veritatem* was the first sally. It is extant in only two copies, one of which belonged to Pace's friend Thomas Elyot. Pace claimed to have learned Hebrew in one month, and Richard Wakefield said that he taught him Hebrew, Chaldean, and Aramaic in three months while at Syon. Pace's revised

Ecclesiastes is not extant. This intensity of work, study, and debate was central to his character but affected his physical and mental health.

In August Pace presented the *Praefatio* to Henry, and during an interview was apparently called upon to give his opinion on the legality of the king's marriage to Katherine. The following day he sent Henry a letter and book written by Robert Wakefield, reader in Hebrew at Oxford, which answered some of the king's counsel, who maintained that Deuteronomy 25: 5–10 annulled Leviticus 22: 21. Thus was Wakefield drawn into the controversy. Enclosed in the letter Pace sent a Hebrew alphabet to be delivered to Edward Foxe, believing that within the space of one month he would have sufficient knowledge to compare the Hebrew, Greek, and Latin translations of the Bible to assist Henry to his great advantage. However, for his part Pace appears to have become convinced of the validity of the marriage after discussions with Fisher.

By 1527 Wolsey was actively hostile to one who now seemed a rival for the king's confidences and who was poised for a return to courtly service if his health allowed. A dispatch of 26 October sent by the imperial ambassador, Inigo de Mendoza, bishop of Burgos, reported rumours that Pace had made prejudicial disclosures regarding Wolsey's government to Henry in his absence, and had spoken out in support of Katherine. These reports must be handled with care because Henry's councillors were putting misinformation out at this time. Pace need not have been overtly critical of the divorce to Henry's face. Wolsey may have been behind his fall. He knew that Pace's extensive library of humanist works gathered over many years in Italy was dangerous. Pace had been offended by Julius's behaviour as pope and collected an extraordinary library on conciliarism and anti-papal critique. He made his library readily available to others who supported the divorce, giving them the necessary material to attack Wolsey's careful diplomacy and putting the cardinal in a difficult position. Therefore Wolsey was keener than ever at this critical time, when the momentum for divorce was growing, to remove Pace from power. On Wolsey's return in September he ordered a legal inquiry into Pace's conduct, with the outcome that Pace and some of his servants were committed to the Tower of London. His papers and books were seized although nothing incriminating was found except one which Pace had written on the irregularities of the pope and cardinals. An inventory of Pace's plate was carried out by his own brother at the end of the month. Wealthy from 1519, Pace had a substantial household, with plate and furniture, and was described as taking many servants and goods with him on his embassies.

Anthony Wood claimed that Pace made charges against Wolsey which the king asked him to refute. Instead Pace was tried by Wolsey and Thomas Howard, third duke of Norfolk. Pace was reported to have been deeply critical of the divorce. People felt the charges against him were dubious, and it is difficult to reconstruct what really happened from the available sources. Fisher himself later seems to have pleaded when he defended himself against Thomas Cromwell for not having revealed the supposed prophecies of Elizabeth Barton, the nun of Kent, that the treasonable sayings of Pace had not been reported by others but were hearsay. Erasmus wrote in August 1528 that Pace had written indiscreetly to Wolsey. This delighted many of Pace's critics at court when it became known, and he was subsequently imprisoned. Anybody too forthright might have been both unwelcome and dangerous in the atmosphere at court in the late 1520s.

On 25 October 1529 Eustace Chapuys, Mendoza's successor as imperial ambassador, wrote to Charles V that Pace was at liberty after two years' imprisonment. Pace probably spent only a short time in the Tower before being entrusted to the care of Thomas Skevington, bishop of Bangor and abbot of Beaulieu, who presumed him incurably insane. Part of the reason for keeping him in custody may have been to monitor his condition during his bouts of illness. He probably spent much of his time at Syon Abbey. He was not always cared for well. Wakefield complained at some point after 1532 to Thomas Boleyn, earl of Wiltshire, about Pace's ill treatment at the hands of 'an enemy of his and mine, or rather a common enemy of all' (H. H. Milman, *Annals of St. Paul's Cathedral*, ed. A. Milman, 1869, 185). It has been suggested that this was Stephen Gardiner, bishop of Winchester. Wolsey's treatment of Pace was one of the charges brought against him in 1529. It is poignant to recall that in 1517 Pace had referred to Wolsey as *quasi alter deus*, almost another God to him, who had preserved his life two or three times and modelled him as a tool to be turned to whatever uses he desired. This ambiguously poised encomium had even then implied that Wolsey was usurping the king's temporal jurisdiction—it was Pace who first described the cardinal as *alter rex*. Erasmus wrote to Pace to tell him he was delighted by the news that he was safe and restored to his former dignity. He observed that the deity who rescued the innocent and cast down the proud was not asleep.

Pace was recalled to court but retired ill to St Dunstan's, Stepney, in 1530 and remained there until his death in 1536. In Pace's last years John Foxe reported that his condition was 'no perpetual frenzy, but came by fits; and the fit was past, he could look on his book, and reason and talk handsomely' (*The Acts and Monuments of John Foxe*, ed. G. Townsend and S. R. Cattley, 8 vols., 1837–41, 4.599). There was a false rumour of Pace's death in 1532. He died on 28 June 1536 and was buried in the church of St Dunstan, near the great altar. Originally a monument and epitaph (preserved by John Weever and incorrectly stating that he died in 1532) marked his burial place.

There is no authenticated image of Pace. However, it is known that he presented himself to the doge of Venice wearing a long gown of satin trimmed with sable and this was said to be his usual attire. Accomplished, witty, and musical, with a great capacity for arousing affection from princes and scholars alike, Pace could also provoke enmity and mistrust. His forthrightness and impulsiveness sometimes impaired his abilities as a diplomat, but the imperial ambassadors considered him the most able and best-informed of Henry's envoys and a possible successor to Wolsey as chief counsellor, if the cardinal became pope. Erasmus and Tomeo regarded him as an outstanding scholar whose time and strength were wasted in public service. In his role as dean of St Paul's School, Pace's *De fructu*, oratory, and scriptural studies reveal a principled and reforming spirit, much concerned with education. His periodic and increasingly severe bouts of mental illness (possibly bipolar disorder, despite Erasmus's suspicion that it was syphilis), combined with recurrent attacks of 'fever' and gastritis, were eventually to cut short his active political and literary life. His importance as a Tudor diplomat, humanist, and cleric have all been contested by twentieth-century scholars, but he is now re-emerging as a substantial figure worthy of the attention bestowed on him by his contemporaries.

CATHY CURTIS

Sources R. Pace, *De fructu qui ex doctrina percipitur*, ed. and trans. F. Manley and R. S. Sylvester (1967) • J. Wegg, *Richard Pace: a Tudor diplomatist* (1932) • C. Curtis, 'Richard Pace on pedagogy, counsel and satire', PhD diss., U. Cam., 1996 • J. Woolfson, *Padua and the Tudors: English students in Italy, 1485–1603* (1998) • *CSP Spain* • *CSP Venice* • *The correspondence of Erasmus*, ed. and trans. R. A. B. Mynors and others, 22 vols. (1974–94), vols. 5, 7, 11 • *LP Henry VIII* • *DNB* • *The Anglica historia of Polydore Vergil, AD 1485–1537*, ed. and trans. D. Hay, CS, 3rd ser., 74 (1950) • *Opus epistolarum Des. Erasmi Roterodami*, ed. P. S. Allen and H. M. Allen, 7: 1527–1528 (1928) • S. Giustinson, *Four years at the court of Henry VIII*, trans. R. Brown, 2 vols. (1854), vol. 1 • R. Pace, *Plutarchi Cheronaei opuscula: De garrulitate. De avaritia. Quomodo poterit quis ab inimicius aliquid commodi reportare. De modo audiendi. Ex Luciano: Demonactis philosophi vita. Per R. Paceum … versa* (1522) • D. S. Chambers, *Cardinal Bainbridge in the court of Rome, 1509 to 1514* (1965) • D. De Bellis, 'La vita e l'ambiente di Niccolò Leonico Tomeo', *Quaderni per la Storia dell'Università di Padova*, 13 (1980), 37–75 • A. Wood, *The history and antiquities of the colleges and halls in the University of Oxford*, ed. J. Gutch (1786) • J. Weever, *Antient funeral monuments*, ed. W. Tooke (1767), 308–9 • R. Rex, *The theology of John Fisher* (1991) • A. Reynolds, 'Cardinal Oliviero Carafa and the early cinquecento tradition of the feast of Pasquino', *Humanistica Lovaniensia*, 34 (1985), 178–208 • A. E. Surtz, 'Richard Pace's sketch of Thomas More', *Journal of English and Germanic Philology*, 57 (1958), 36–50 • V. Murphy, 'The literature and propaganda of Henry VIII's first divorce', *The reign of Henry VIII: politics, policy and piety*, ed. D. MacCulloch (1995), 135–58 • C. Curtis, 'Richard Pace's *De fructu* and early Tudor pedagogy', *Reassessing Tudor humanism*, ed. J. Woolfson (2002)

Archives BL, diplomatic corresp., Add. MS 40676; Add. MS 29549; Cotton MSS Vitelli B.5, B.19; Royal MS 5.C.111; Stow MS 147 • BL, papers, Harley MSS • BL, letters to Thomas Wolsey, Henry VIII, etc., Cotton MSS

Pächt, Otto Ernst (1902–1988), art historian, was born in Vienna, Austria, on 7 September 1902, the elder son (there were no daughters) of David Pächt, a Jewish businessman, and his wife, Josephine Freundlich. He attended the Volkschule and Stadtgymnasium in Vienna and in 1920 proceeded to Vienna University where, with a brief interlude in Berlin, he studied art history and archaeology. He achieved his doctorate in 1925. His first book, devoted to Austrian Gothic panel painting, appeared in 1929. In 1933 he was appointed *Privatdozent* at the University of Heidelberg, but the Nazi embargo on Jews holding posts in Germany prevented him from taking up the position.

Frustrated and alarmed by the political situation, Pächt paid his first visit to London at the end of 1935 and settled there in 1938. He was invited to undertake a catalogue of illuminated manuscripts (a field new to him) at the British Museum, liaising with Francis Wormald, then assistant keeper in the manuscripts department, who rapidly became a close personal friend. The evacuation of the manuscripts in 1939 ended this scheme and in 1941 he moved to Oxford to begin a similar project at the Bodleian Library. The resulting three-volume catalogue, completed by his pupil Jonathan Alexander, appeared between 1966 and 1973. Specialists in the study of manuscript illumination were rare and the scope of this undertaking left Pächt with a virtually unrivalled expertise. During his two decades in Oxford he published on a wide variety of topics, paying particular attention to English work of the twelfth century, which he viewed within its wider European context. His contribution to the collaborative monograph on the St Albans psalter (1960) is especially significant. During the same period he turned once more to his original fascination with northern painting of the fifteenth century, publishing *The Master of Mary of Burgundy* in 1948.

In March 1945 Pächt had been made fellow and lecturer in the history of medieval art at Oriel College, Oxford. In May 1947 he took British citizenship, which he retained for the remainder of his life. He became senior lecturer in the history faculty in 1952 and was advanced to reader in 1962. His subject was not, however, part of the formal syllabus and opportunities for direct teaching even at postgraduate level were disappointingly meagre. In 1963 he decided to accept an invitation to return to Vienna to fill the chair of art history in succession to K. M. Swoboda, thus becoming one of the few refugee scholars from Austria to return to his roots after the war. His work in England was acknowledged by election to the fellowship of the British Academy in 1956 and by the award of the honorary degree of DLitt at Oxford in 1971.

In the 1960s Pächt's energies were directed almost entirely to his university commitments. His students welcomed him as an outstanding teacher and lecturer and he, in turn, was greatly stimulated by their enthusiasm. Fortunately for posterity, his carefully prepared lectures were all preserved in typescript and a series of publications, including *Buchmalerei des Mittelalters* in 1984, made their content and his methodology accessible to a wider audience. After his retirement in 1972 he returned to his own research and published extensively up to the time of his death, paying particular attention once more to the problems of northern painting in the fifteenth century. At the same time he was responsible, in collaboration with Dagmar Thoss and Ulrike Jenni, for the appearance of five volumes in the ambitious catalogue of illuminated manuscripts in the Österreichische Nationalbibliothek in Vienna (French in 1974 and 1977, Dutch in 1975, and Flemish in 1983 and 1990). A fellow of the Austrian Academy since 1967, he was awarded the Order of Merit by France in 1982 and became a commander of the order of Arts and Letters in 1984.

Throughout his long career Pächt's circle of scholarly

acquaintance was very wide. His attachment to the Bodleian Library brought him readily into contact with the international fraternity of manuscript specialists drawn there by their individual work. He maintained friendships with other members of the academic refugee community, notably colleagues from the Warburg Institute in London. Back in Vienna his many students found his approach inspiring. Pächt was stockily built and bespectacled, with thick dark eyebrows recalling the original colour of his sparse hair. Twenty-five years' residence in England did not entirely rob his speech of the evidence of his German origins.

Pächt married, on 11 January 1940, Jeanne Thalia (*d.* 1971), the daughter of Constantine A. Michalopulo, import–export merchant; she was an art historical researcher whom he met when she was working as assistant librarian at the Courtauld Institute, London. They had one son, Michael. Otto Pächt died in hospital in Vienna on 17 April 1988. He bequeathed his important personal working library to the Kunsthistorischen Gesellschaft in Vienna. JANET BACKHOUSE, *rev.*

Sources J. J. G. Alexander, 'Otto Pächt, 1902–1988', *PBA*, 80 (1993), 453–7 • O. Demus, 'Otto Pächt', *Almanach der Österreichischen Akademie der Wissenschaften*, 138 (1988) • *The Independent* (11 May 1988) • personal knowledge (1996) • private information (1996) [Michael Pächt, son] • *CGPLA Eng. & Wales* (1989)

Likenesses photograph, repro. in Alexander, 'Otto Pächt, 1902–1988', 455

Wealth at death £74,476: probate, 5 Jan 1989, *CGPLA Eng. & Wales*

Pacifico, David [*known as* Don Pacifico] **(1784?–1854)**, merchant, was a Sephardic Jew of Italian descent. Accounts of his early life, founded on his own conflicting statements, vary considerably. The child of parents married at the Bevis Marks Synagogue, London, in 1761, he variously gave his birthplace as Oran or Gibraltar, and once claimed Spanish nationality. While resident in Portugal, he allegedly suffered for his liberal sympathies at the hands of the legitimists. As compensation, the victorious liberals made him consul in Morocco and Portuguese by naturalization (1835). In 1837 he moved to Athens as consul-general, an appointment he lost in 1842. His duties, light in Greece, were combined with trade.

Pacifico achieved international notoriety in April 1847. To avoid offence to a visiting financier, a Paris Rothschild, the authorities banned the burning of Judas Iscariot in effigy from the Orthodox Easter celebrations. Popular resentment was visited on Pacifico, prominent in the small Jewish community. Police allowed the mob to sack his house. As a British subject, with the legation's support, he sought some £32,000 compensation from an unresponsive Greek government. On instructions from Lord Palmerston interest at 10 per cent was added, with £500 for physical violence and distress inflicted. While another claim of Pacifico's for land acquired by the state was accepted, Greek ministers ignored or evaded representations about his losses in the riot.

Britain eventually deployed her fleet in January 1850, giving Greece twenty-four hours to meet the demands in this and other outstanding cases. Underlying the Anglo-Greek dispute and Palmerston's high-handed action was the resistance of the Bavarian King Otto of Greece to the constitutionalism Palmerston preached. The ensuing blockade elicited protests from France and Russia; co-founders with Britain of the Greek kingdom, they objected to the British attitude. France, backed by the tsar, negotiated a settlement, but not before British tactics provoked the recall of her ambassador in London (May 1850). The British minister in Athens, Thomas Wyse, used force to compel acceptance on terms less favourable to Greece (28 April) than those agreed a few days earlier between Britain and France in London (19 April). Wyse pleaded the absence of instructions from Palmerston, who placated France by adhering, substantially, to the London convention (20 June). Under its provisions, the figure put on Pacifico's compensation, based on claims which Palmerston conceded were inflated, was drastically reduced.

The combined forces of the parliamentary opposition at Westminster attacked Palmerston's handling of the whole question. In a celebrated speech (25 June), he asserted Britain's right to ensure that her subjects everywhere enjoyed the security of Roman citizens in their day. Even such a man as Pacifico might say, as it were, 'Civis Romanus sum', and receive armed assistance (*Hansard* 3, 112, 1850, 444). Unenforceable against powerful countries, the declaration was one of equality with nations strong enough to overawe weaker states. It won a majority of forty-six in a full house, and delighted the public. Gladstone, who deplored British methods in Greece, thought the defence 'extraordinary and masterly' (Gladstone, *Diaries*, 4.221). Palmerston condemned the racial prejudice evident in references to Pacifico, 'as if … because a man is of the Jewish persuasion, he is fair game for any outrage' (*Hansard* 3, 112, 1850, 387). In more senses than one, he gained a famous victory for contemporary liberalism. Nevertheless, Pacifico embarrassed his co-religionists. When he died at 15 Bury Street, London, on 12 April 1854 and was buried on 14 April at the Spanish and Portuguese Jews' burial-ground at Mile End Road, London, the *Jewish Chronicle* (21 April) merely noted the demise of 'this individual who … caused so much sensation in the political world'. DAVID STEELE

Sources 'Correspondence respecting demands on the Greek government', *Parl. papers* (1850), 56.43, no. 1157; 'Further correspondence' (1850), 56.407, no. 1179; 56.419, no. 1209; 56.811, no. 1211; 56.839, no. 1226; 56.845, no. 1230 • 'Convention … for the settlement of British claims on the Greek government', *Parl. papers* (1851), 57.17–22, no. 1297 • 'Correspondence on the mixed commission to investigate the claims of M. Pacifico', *Parl. papers* (1851), 57.105–28, no. 1415 • *Annual Register* (1850), 57–88, 244–8, 277–94 • G. Finlay, *A history of Greece*, ed. H. F. Tozer, new edn, 7 (1877), 208–15 • A. E. M. Ashley, *The life and correspondence of Henry John Temple, Viscount Palmerston*, 2 vols. (1879), 126–63 • *Jewish Chronicle* (14 April 1854) • *Jewish Chronicle* (21 April 1854) • *Jewish Chronicle* (6 Nov 1903) • *Jewish Chronicle* (13 Nov 1903) • A. W. Ward, *The Cambridge history of British foreign policy, 1783–1919*, ed. A. W. Ward and G. P. Gooch, 3 vols. (1922–3), 330–31, 586–99 • A. M. Hyamson, 'Don Pacifico', *Transactions of the Jewish Historical Society of England*, 18 (1953–5), 1–39 • T. A. Couloumbis and others, *Foreign interference in Greek politics: an historical perspective* (1976), chap. 5 • d. cert.

Wealth at death houses in London: *Jewish Chronicle* (6 Nov 1903, 13 Nov 1903)

Pack, Sir Denis (*c.*1772–1823), army officer, was probably born in Kilkenny, Ireland, the son of Thomas Pack DD, dean of Kilkenny, and his wife; he was the grandson of Thomas Pack of Ballinakill, Queen's county. He was described as a descendant of Christopher *Packe (*c.*1599–1682), lord mayor of London, whose younger son, Simon, settled in co. Westmeath, Ireland.

Pack was appointed cornet in the 14th light dragoons on 30 November 1791 and served with a squadron that formed the advance guard of Lord Moira's force in Flanders in 1794. Pack volunteered to carry an important dispatch into Nieuwpoort and had much difficulty in escaping when the French invested it. Later he was engaged at Boxtel and in the winter retreat to Bremen. Following that retreat the 14th squadron was transferred to the 8th light dragoons after being attached to it. When Pack came home he obtained his lieutenancy in the 14th on 12 March 1795. He commanded a small party of dragoons in the Quiberon expedition, and in this period did duty for some months as a field-officer on Isle Dieu. He received his troop in the 5th dragoon guards on 27 February 1796, and while serving with them in Ireland in 1798 he led a patrol near Prosperous against a party of rebels, who lost twenty men and eight horses.

Pack commanded the escort which conducted General Humbert and other French officers to Dublin after their surrender at Ballinamuck. On 25 August 1798 he was promoted major in the 4th Royal Irish dragoon guards and on 6 December 1800 he was appointed lieutenant-colonel in the 71st highlanders. He commanded the 71st at the recapture of the Cape of Good Hope in 1806, where he was wounded at the landing in Lospard's Bay. During the ill-fated operation in South America in 1806–7 he was taken prisoner, but he managed to escape. He then commanded the light troops of the army in two successful actions against the enemy and in Whitelocke's disastrous attack on Buenos Aires, in which he received three wounds.

In 1808 the 71st was ordered to Portugal, and he commanded it at the battles of Roliça and Vimeiro. He marched with Sir John Moore's army into Spain and in the retreat to Corunna. After returning to England he took part in the Walcheren expedition in 1809, in which he bravely stormed one of the enemy's batteries during the siege of Flushing. He became aide-de-camp to the king with the rank of colonel on 25 July 1810. He was then appointed with local rank to a Portuguese brigade under Marshal Beresford and commanded it at Busaco in 1810, and in front of Almeida in May 1811. When the French garrison escaped Pack pursued them to Barba del Puerco, and upon orders of Sir Brent Spencer blew up the defences of Almeida. At the capture of Ciudad Rodrigo, Pack, who had been appointed a British brigadier-general, led his Portuguese brigade to make a feint attack on the outwork of the Santiago gate, which was converted into a real attack.

Pack distinguished himself at the battle of Salamanca and was honourably mentioned for his services in the operations against Burgos. He became a major-general on 4 June 1813 and was present with his brigade at Vitoria. Wellington placed him in temporary command of the 6th division in the Pyrenées, and he was wounded again at Soraven. He commanded a division at the battles of Nivelle, the Nive, Orthez, and Toulouse, where he received yet another wound and was honourably mentioned. For his Peninsular services, in which he was eight times wounded, he received the Peninsular gold cross and seven clasps. He was offered a brigade in the expedition to America but instead was appointed to command at Ramsgate. He was made KCB on 2 January 1815.

In June 1815 Pack commanded a brigade of Picton's division at Quatre-Bras and Waterloo, where he was again wounded. That was his last foreign service. He married, on 10 July 1816, Lady Elizabeth Louisa Beresford (*d.* Jan 1856), fourth daughter of the second earl of Waterford, and sister of the first marquess. Pack held the orders of the Tower and Sword in Portugal, Maria Theresa in Austria, and St Vladimir in Russia. He was appointed colonel of the York chasseurs in 1816, lieutenant-governor of Plymouth on 12 August 1819, and colonel of the 84th foot on 9 September 1822. Pack died at Lord Beresford's house in Upper Wimpole Street, London, on 24 July 1823. In 1828 his widow erected a monument to him, surmounted by a marble bust by Chantrey, in the cathedral church of St Canice, Kilkenny, of which his father had been dean. After his death Lady Pack married, in 1831, Lieutenant-General Sir Thomas Reynell KCB (*d.* 1848), who had been one of Pack's majors in the 71st.

H. M. CHICHESTER, *rev.* GORDON L. TEFFETELLER

Sources *The dispatches of … the duke of Wellington … from 1799 to 1818*, ed. J. Gurwood, 13 vols. in 12 (1834–9) • *Supplementary despatches (correspondence) and memoranda of Field Marshal Arthur, duke of Wellington*, ed. A. R. Wellesley, second duke of Wellington, 15 vols. (1858–72) • Fortescue, *Brit. army*, vols. 4–10 • W. F. P. Napier, *History of the war in the Peninsula and in the south of France*, new edn, 6 vols. (1886) • *Army List* • *GM*, 1st ser., 93/2 (1823), 372–3 • *GM*, 1st ser., 98/2 (1828), 478 • C. W. C. Oman, *A history of the Peninsular War*, 7 vols. (1902–30) • J. Philippart, ed., *The royal military calendar*, 3rd edn, 4 (1820)

Archives U. Southampton L., papers

Likenesses C. Turner, mezzotint, pubd 1834 (after G. L. Saunders), BM, NPG • F. Chantrey, marble bust, AM Oxf. • W. Theed junior, bust, Royal Military Academy, Sandhurst, Camberley, Surrey

Pack, Faithful Christopher (1760–1840), painter, was born on 12 August 1760 in Norwich, the son of a Quaker merchant whose family claimed a connection with that of Sir Christopher Packe, lord mayor of London. Though employed by his father in early adulthood Pack showed a strong aptitude for painting. With the failure of the family business he took up painting as a profession, and moved to London in 1781. He made friends with the painter John Hamilton Mortimer, and studied under Sir Joshua Reynolds, making copies after his portraits. After a brief spell in Norwich,Pack spent four years (1783–7) in Liverpool, exhibiting at the Society for Promoting Painting and Design in 1784. Returning to London, he showed at the Royal Academy in 1786 and 1787.

With a recommendation from Reynolds to the duke of Rutland, then lord lieutenant of Ireland, Pack departed for his first period in Dublin about 1789. He had some success as a portrait painter, reputedly meeting Gilbert Stuart at an artists' dinner on St Luke's day in 1789. In 1790 he contributed two pictures to an exhibition at the Lyceum in College Green. Again in London, he exhibited four pictures at the Royal Academy in 1796 (the same year that he stood as a candidate for associate there) including *One of the Society of Quakers, Aged 83*. He then taught drawing for a number of years in Bath, living at 19 Green Park Street.

Returning to Dublin once more in 1802, Pack continued as a teacher of drawing and painting. From that time until 1821 he exhibited widely, including pictures of horses, portraits, and landscapes. He was president of the Society of Arts in 1812, showing thirty-seven works there, and was vice-president of the Royal Hibernian Society in 1814. By 1820, however, he seemed to experience harder times. His offer to lecture at the Dublin Society was declined, and in the following year, on 21 March 1821, a sale of his pictures was conducted from his residence, 33 Dawson Street. He finally left Dublin for London, contributing to the Royal Academy in 1822 and 1840, but mainly to the British Institution (1825–39), works in oil and watercolour. He also made landscapes in pastels, and reproduced some of his Irish views in aquatint, of which proofs were signed 'F. Chris Pack'. In exhibition catalogues his name appears under the names 'C.' 'F. C.' or 'F. Christopher' Pack. He died aged eighty-one at 20 Sandwich Street, Gray's Inn Lane, London, on 25 October 1840, a few months after his wife, who had died in August that year.

L. H. Cust, *rev.* Tina Fiske

Sources W. G. Strickland, *A dictionary of Irish artists*, 2 vols. (1913) • D. Foskett, *A dictionary of British miniature painters*, 2 vols. (1972) • A. M. Steward, ed., *Irish art loan exhibitions, 1765–1927*, 4 vols. (1995) • B. Stewart and M. Cutten, *The dictionary of portrait painters in Britain up to 1920* (1997) • Farington, *Diary* • Graves, *RA exhibitors* • [J. Gere], *Portrait drawings, XV–XX centuries* (1974), 93 [exhibition catalogue, BM, 2 Aug – 31 Dec 1974] • Redgrave, *Artists* • A. Pasquin [J. Williams], *An authentic history of the professors of painting, sculpture, and architecture who have practiced in Ireland … to which are added, Memoirs of the royal academicians* [1796] • Waterhouse, *18c painters* • Bryan, *Painters*

Likenesses F. C. Pack, self-portrait, 1787; exh. RA 1840 • J. Jackson, portrait; exh. RA 1829 • J. Reynolds, portrait; Christies, 24 May 1902, lot 3 • J. T. Smith, drawing, pen and ink with wash, BM

Pack, George (*fl.* **1700–1724**), actor and singer, had a light voice, bordering on the contralto. According to William Chetwood he pleased audiences by taking the female part in sung dialogues with Richard Leveridge. Nothing is known of his birth or upbringing, but he made his acting début as Westmoreland in Betterton's revival of *1 Henry IV* at Lincoln's Inn Fields on 9 January 1700. He made regular appearances in that theatre from 1700 to October 1705, always in supporting roles such as Roderigo in *Othello*. He was probably at his best in playing social misfits, losers, and eccentrics, and managers tried to provide him with songs when the text allowed it. As Ogle in Susannah Centlivre's *The Beau's Duel* on 21 October 1702, for example, he was applauded for his whimsical song. It was Centlivre's later play *The Busy Body* that provided Pack, as Marplot, with his most famous original part. That was at Drury Lane on 12 May 1709, at a time when London's actors were still in search of a settled theatrical home.

Pack had already learned something of the perils of his craft when, in 1701–2, he was one of the group of actors brought to trial for 'using indecent expressions in some late plays' in the wake of Collier's *Short View of the Immorality and Profaneness of the English Stage* (1698). The actors were acquitted, and Pack was part of the company that struggled with the acoustics of the new Queen's Theatre in the Haymarket from 1705 to 1707 before settling at Drury Lane in 1708. He remained at Drury Lane until the end of 1714, relishing in particular the chance to play the title role in *Marplot* (30 December 1710), Centlivre's opportunistic sequel to *The Busy Body*. The lightness of his voice served him in occasional transvestite roles, and these became more frequent after his move to John Rich's company at Lincoln's Inn Fields in 1715. Pack's singing was useful to Rich, who rated high art below entertainment, and Pack remained at Lincoln's Inn Fields for the rest of his active theatrical life, singing between the acts when he was unable to sing during them, and often enough wearing women's dress when doing so.

When the playhouses closed Pack entertained at London's summer fairs. In 1717 he and Pinkethman operated a booth at Southwark fair, and in the summer of 1718 he performed at Pinkethman's playhouse in Richmond, where he sang one of his best-loved songs, 'London is a Fine Town'. That autumn he was again at Southwark fair, and in 1720 he operated a booth in Hounslow. On 10 March 1722 he announced his farewell performance at Lincoln's Inn Fields. The part he chose was Marplot, and a portrait sign of Pack in that role hung outside the tavern he opened in August 1722. According to Chetwood the tavern was called The Globe and situated near Charing Cross, but the likelier alternative is that it was called the Busy Body and situated at the corner of Haymarket and Pall Mall. It may be that his business did not flourish. Certainly he returned to Lincoln's Inn Fields in the spring of 1724 to play in his own benefit performance and in that of Mrs Knight. Nothing is known of his later career, but he had evidently been dead for some time by 1749, when Chetwood published his *General History*. According to Chetwood, Pack was unmarried, but an otherwise unknown Mrs Pack was awarded a benefit at Lincoln's Inn Fields on 28 May 1719; she may have been his wife.

Peter Thomson

Sources Highfill, Burnim & Langhans, *BDA* • W. R. Chetwood, *A general history of the stage, from its origin in Greece to the present time* (1749) • E. L. Avery, ed., *The London stage, 1660–1800*, pt 2: *1700–1729* (1960) • J. W. Bowyer, *The celebrated Mrs Centlivre* (1952)

Pack, Richardson (1682–1728), army officer and writer, born on 29 November 1682, was the son of John Pack (1652–1723) of London, gentleman, who settled at Wickham Skeith and then Stoke Ash in Suffolk, serving as high sheriff there in 1697, and his wife, Hannah (*d.* 1713), the daughter and coheir of Robert Richardson of Tudhoe, co. Durham. From Merchant Taylors' School, which he entered in 1693, Pack matriculated as a fellow-commoner at St John's College, Oxford, in June 1697, but left in 1698 to study law at the Middle Temple. After eight terms he was called to the bar but, preferring the active life, joined the army, and by March 1705 had obtained command of a company of foot under Colonel Nicholas Lepel. He was still a bachelor when on 5 October 1707 he and Audrey Gibson (later Mrs White) baptized their daughter, Rebecca, at St Giles Cripplegate; the child was given Pack's name and he remembered her in his will of 1729, recalling that 'on other occasions' he had 'encouraged her good behaviour'.

Pack next served in the War of the Spanish Succession; he wrote from Mombris in Catalonia in October 1709 to John Creed at Oundle. His regiment served with Marshal Stahrenberg at the battle of Villaviciosa in December 1710. The day after General Stanhope and his troops were taken at Brihuega, Pack's major was killed, and his bravery, as senior captain, won him immediate promotion and the lifelong friendship of his general, John Campbell, duke of Argyll. More of Pack's movements and friends are revealed by addresses on his published pieces, the first collection of which he dedicated to Colonel William Stanhope, ambassador in Madrid. The notorious Edmund Curll was his faithful London publisher, but others produced Dublin editions. In 1713 he was writing to his friend Captain David Campbell from Minorca, presumably while on the staff of Argyll, governor there at the time.

Back in Ipswich in June 1714, Pack complained of the hardships of a half-pay officer; later that summer he was at Stoke Ash with his widowed father. At the time of the Jacobite rebellion he was recalled as major in Colonel Lucas's regiment of foot, in which he served for three years. About then Captain Campbell died, and Pack married Mary, a Campbell heiress (perhaps the daughter David and Mary Campbell, baptized at St Martin-in-the-Fields, London, on 30 November 1688); whether she was related to the captain cannot now be established. Some time in 1719 Mary gave birth to a son, John, at their house in Jermyn Street, St James's, but the next year they were living at Bury St Edmunds in Suffolk, where Pack had acquired the ruins of the great abbey. Probably for the materials, he dismantled the 400 foot east range of the Great Court, the former abbot's palace, and obliterated all traces of the abbey's formal gardens. Pack's poems, headed 'Bury Toasts', show how much he enjoyed the society of young ladies of good family there; he wrote and dedicated verses to, *inter alia*, a Bunbury, a Paston, a Hervey, a D'Ewes, even the countess of Rochford.

It was during the last nine years of his life that Pack's work began to be published. He admired the Roman elegiac poets, translating their poems, and three of their lives from the Latin of Cornelius Nepos: T. P. Atticus, Miltiades, and Cimon; he was too indolent to do more as he intended. The three lives appeared in his *Miscellanies in Prose and Verse* (1719); for the second set the same year he added two 'essays on study and conversation' in letters to David Campbell. Both were printed at Dublin in 1726, and the year after his death his complete works appeared in one volume. Pack wrote a prologue to George Sewell's *Tragedy of Sir Walter Raleigh* and an epilogue to Thomas Southerne's *Spartan Dame*; Sewell responded with lines written on reading Pack's poems. He exchanged poems with Matthew Prior, and asked Prior to sit for his picture for him, and to ask Pope and Congreve to do the same.

In 1722 Pack bought Northgate House in the street of that name in Bury St Edmunds; and when in spring 1724 he became dangerously ill, it was the celebrated Richard Mead who saved his life. Early in 1725 he was again in service at Exeter as a major in Colonel Montagu's regiment of the Devonshires, the 11th foot. In October 1727 he wrote an ode in praise of George II, addressed to the new monarch through the earl of Scarbrough. Expecting an invitation to court to be thanked, he was instead ordered to march with his regiment from Exeter to Aberdeen. In December 1728 Scotland, that 'country, which was his aversion when living, proved to be the scene of his death' (Pack, 'Memoir'). His wish to be buried at Stoke Ash was not carried out, and he was buried on 3 January 1729 in St Nicholas churchyard, Aberdeen.

Pack's will was locked in a desk at Northgate House, as one of his executors, Sir Edmund Bacon, bt, of Garboldisham, deposed: 'about the middle of December … a messenger came express from one Mr ACourt in Scotland' bearing a letter with the key. Pack's widow, Mary, was left an annuity of £50 without further comment; that and the episode of the key imply that they were estranged. Rebecca Pack and Edmund Bacon both received £50 legacies, but the other executor, George Read, esquire, of Golden Square, was left a 'gold watch that was the glorious King William's'. Pack's estates near Birmingham and at Hepworth in Suffolk, as well as property in Bury St Edmunds, were to provide for his 'dear and entirely beloved and only son John', not yet ten years old. John went up to Pembroke College, Cambridge, where in 1744 he became LLB and a fellow, and was ordained. From 1752 to his death eleven years later he was rector of Little Whelnetham, where he was buried. J. M. Blatchly

Sources R. Pack, *The whole works of Major Richardson Pack* (1729) [with memoir, 1–viii] • R. Yates, *History of the Abbey of Bury St Edmunds* (1843) • PRO, PROB 11/629, sig. 114, Abbott 1729 • armorial bookplate with Campbell in pretence, priv. coll. • monument, Stoke Ash, Suffolk [John Pack and Hannah Pack] • monument, Great Whelnetham, Suffolk [John Pack] • R. D. Cain, 'Richardson Pack (1682–1728)', *N&Q*, 170 (1936), 344–6 • *Calendar of the manuscripts of the marquis of Bath preserved at Longleat, Wiltshire*, 5 vols., HMC, 58 (1904–80), vol. 3

Wealth at death property in Bury St Edmunds, and estates near Birmingham and at Hepworth, Suffolk: will, PRO, PROB 11/629, sig. 114

Packard, Sir Edward (1843–1932), fertilizer manufacturer, was born on 28 September 1843 at Saxmundham, Suffolk, one of at least two sons of Edward Packard, druggist, and his wife, Mary Woods. His father had begun making superphosphate at the outset of the industry in the 1840s. Trained in chemistry at King's College, London, and in agriculture at the Royal Agricultural College, Cirencester, Packard joined his father in business in 1863 at Bramford, near Ipswich. With his brother Henry he became a partner in August 1866 and immediately opened a London office. On 23 May 1867 he married Ellen (1846/7–1927), daughter of Walton Turner, a merchant; they had four sons and six daughters. In his early years he was an enthusiastic yachtsman and played a part in improving racing rules.

In 1872 Packard patented a method for making highly concentrated superphosphate for the export market and the following year set up a new works at Wetzlar, near Koblenz, in Germany. At the end of the decade he helped to promote the *Irish Farmers' Gazette*, to provide publicity for the firm's products, and began building a phosphoric acid plant to make fertilizer for sugar plantations. By 1881 the firm was in difficulties because of the decline in demand, as British agriculture suffered in the face of foreign competition. Packard became senior partner and in 1888 was appointed the eastern counties' representative on a subcommittee of the Chemical Manure Manufacturers' Association, set up to investigate ways of improving trading conditions. The committee recommended a quota scheme for production by each member. The scheme failed and some businesses collapsed, including Henry Chapman & Co. of Ipswich, whose goodwill Packard acquired.

By the late 1880s Packard was totally committed to rationalizing production by joint action through the association. In 1888 he had also spearheaded the industry's response to a Board of Trade inquiry into the proposed increases in railway freight charges. Two years later Packard was the association's leading witness in negotiations with the Board of Agriculture over proposed legislation to impose stiff standards of quality on fertilizers. His advice was adopted in the Fertiliser and Feeding Stuffs Act of 1893. In an effort to reduce costs he also financed exploration for sources of mineral phosphate in various parts of the world and invested in several abortive ventures in North America and west Africa. When the association's price agreement collapsed in 1897, he developed overseas markets in Russia, Japan, and the West Indies. By 1902 his firm was again in difficulties because of price cutting by competitors. After very fraught negotiations the Eastern Counties' Chemical Manure Manufacturers' Centre came to a price fixing arrangement. This proved difficult to sustain and Packard's problems were magnified by the eruption of a volcano on Martinique which devastated the properties of many customers.

Despite these set-backs Packard remained committed to industry action, representing the association in a review of the working of the Fertiliser and Feeding Stuffs Act, in 1903. He wrote a pamphlet on the benefits of fertilizing autumn crops, of which the association distributed 60,000 copies. In 1906 he was elected president of the association, which shortly before had been renamed the Fertiliser Manufacturers' Association; and the following year he led the eastern counties' centre in buying and closing the works of John Evison at Ramsey in Huntingdonshire. However, his hopes that the association could form a national cartel failed. It was only possible with difficulty to maintain local understandings. Even Packard himself began to take unilateral action to close competing firms by acquiring their goodwill. During the First World War, all the firm's plant was controlled by the Ministry of Munitions. In 1917 Packard was appointed to the phosphate and potash distribution committee as the industry's representative, and he joined the executive committee of the newly formed National Sulphuric Acid Association.

All these duties told on Packard's health. He became seriously ill in the autumn of 1917 and his place was taken by his son Walter. However, he was fit enough to take part in the negotiations in early 1919 which led to the merger of Edward Packard & Co. and James Fison (Thetford) Ltd, of which he became chairman. He was knighted in 1922 for his services to the industry. Sir Edward Packard died on 11 April 1932 at his home, The Grove, Bramford, Suffolk. He was mourned for his public service in a galaxy of activities, ranging from those arranged by Ipswich town council and the town's fine art club, to those of the local Conservative Party, the Bramford school management committee, and the Harwich Harbour Board.

MICHAEL S. MOSS

Sources M. S. Moss, 'From fertilisers to pharmaceuticals — history of Fisons plc', Suffolk RO, Ipswich, Fisons plc company papers • private information (2004) [interviews with family members and Sir George Burton] • Suffolk RO, Ipswich, Fisons plc company archives • International Fertiliser Manufacturers' Association, Paris, Fertiliser Manufacturers' Association records • E. Gaskell, *Suffolk leaders* (1910) • *Cox's county who's who series: Norfolk, Suffolk, and Cambridgeshire* (1912) • *WWW* • b. cert. • m. cert. • d. cert. • *CGPLA Eng. & Wales* (1932)

Archives International Fertiliser Manufacturers' Association, Paris, Fertiliser Manufacturers' Association records • Suffolk RO, Ipswich, Fison MSS

Wealth at death £28,252 3*s.* 3*d.*: resworn probate, 11 July 1932, *CGPLA Eng. & Wales*

Packe, Christopher, appointed Lord Packe under the protectorate (*c.***1599–1682**), politician, was the son of Thomas Packe of Kettering, Northamptonshire, and his wife, Catherine. He was bound apprentice in the Drapers' Company of London to John Kendrick, a merchant adventurer, who died in 1624 leaving Packe a legacy of £100 and a £300 loan to set up in business in the woollen trade. After gaining his freedom in the Drapers in 1633, Packe was admitted to the livery in 1639; he served on its governing body in 1647–77 and 1679–81 and was master in 1648–9 and 1654–5. He married three times. His first wife was his late master's granddaughter, Jane Newman (*d.* 1638), daughter of Thomas Newman of Newbury, Berkshire, a merchant and fellow draper. Anne Edmonds (*d.* 1658), daughter of Simon Edmonds, a London merchant and future alderman, was his second wife. On 13 July 1669 Packe married his third wife, Elizabeth (*b. c.*1609, *d.* in or before 1681), daughter of one Richards of Berkshire and widow of Alderman Michael Herring, another prosperous London merchant. With his second wife Packe had two sons and five daughters, two of whom died in infancy; his two other marriages were childless.

Packe acquired considerable wealth in the 1630s by trading in cloth in English and European markets and investing in the Company of Merchant Adventurers and the East India Company. He lived close by Blackwell Hall, the headquarters for the woollen trade, in one of the substantial merchants' houses on Basinghall Street, in St Michael Bassishaw, one of the parishes nestling under the Guildhall. In the 1638 tithe assessment Packe had the fourth highest rating in the parish and he was one of the wealthy merchants in his ward listed in 1640 for a possible forced loan.

By 1640, therefore, Packe was an experienced and successful merchant comfortably established in the heart of the City. He played no noticeable part in London's reaction to the developing political tensions between king and parliament prior to August 1642, when he was appointed by parliament as a collector for money and plate in the ward of Bassishaw. The following December he became a ward assessor for parliamentary levies and in the summer of 1643 contributed £100 towards defending the City. Once his political sympathies were known his financial expertise was soon being drawn upon by parliament. In 1643 he was called upon to advise the committee for the advance of money on raising money to supply the army in the west and he also acted as an intermediary between parliament and the City about raising money to pay the Scots. By 1643 Packe had also become a common councillor for Bassishaw, followed by promotion to ward deputy in 1645–7. He served on more than a dozen common-council committees in 1643–7, including the influential City lands committee in 1646–7. But it was membership of more senior financial committees that increasingly drew on his energy in the 1640s, including committees for the accounts of the whole kingdom, for assessment, for customs, for bishops' lands, and for compounding.

A cautious pragmatism refined on the road to mercantile success may have been the key to Packe's ambiguous reactions to the divisions of presbyterians versus Independents that opened up in the mid-1640s. He would appear to have been a religious presbyterian; he acted as a lay trier for elders in the seventh London classis, was twice delegated to the London provincial assembly, and served on all the common-council committees concerned with setting up a presbyterian church. Furthermore, a leading London presbyterian divine, Dr Thomas Jacombe, was a close friend and was to be a beneficiary under Packe's 1681 will. Yet Packe's political stance was more complex for, although he was appointed to the presbyterian-dominated London militia committee of May 1647, he subsequently adopted a role as mediator between the City, parliament, and the army during the tense summer months and was one of three City representatives sent to reside with the army until the parties reached agreement. As a result, after the army's march on London he was trusted enough to be appointed to the September militia committee with its strong Independent bias. Shortly afterwards Packe joined the aldermanic bench; he was elected for Cripplegate in 1647–53 and for Bassishaw in 1653–60.

Packe was an active supporter of both the Commonwealth and the protectorate and during these years his influence and wealth grew. He attended the special session of the court of aldermen in April 1649 when the pro-royalist Mayor Reynardson was deposed from office, and was one of the fifteen aldermen who attended the formal proclamation of the abolition of monarchy on the following 30 May. The same year saw him elected as one of the London sheriffs and appointed president of the Bridewell and Bethlem hospitals; he also became a member of the indemnity committee. At the beginning of 1649 he had paid over £8000 for the Huntingdonshire manor of Buckden, part of the estates of the bishop of Lincoln, and in March 1650 he was able to add the Leicestershire manors of Prestwold and Cotes. However, there was a big setback too for Packe in 1649 when he and two fellow merchants were removed from the customs committee and ordered to present their accounts. The matter of the accounts was to drag on, and surface acrimoniously on occasion, until the late 1650s.

Although unsuccessful in the City elections of July 1654 for the first protectorate parliament, Packe was shortly afterwards elected lord mayor and subsequently established close relations with Oliver Cromwell as they purged government opponents from City offices. Packe also helped deal with the threat of royalist plots in early 1655 as a member of a new militia committee charged with the task of raising fresh regiments. Among the actions he was responsible for as lord mayor were the arrest and commitment for trial of the Socinian John Biddle in July 1655. Following the end of his mayoralty, Packe was knighted by a grateful Cromwell. Packe's known financial and commercial expertise earned him further responsibilities in 1655 as one of the treasurers for contributions for the relief of Piedmont protestants and as a member both of the admiralty and of the trade committees. He was also appointed to a committee to consider the arguments for the readmission of the Jews, an initiative he was said to have most vehemently opposed. A proposal in January 1656 that he accompany Bulstrode Whitelocke on a mission to Sweden to further a protestant alliance was aborted shortly afterwards.

Packe was finally returned as a City MP in the August 1656 elections to the second protectorate parliament. He was to prove an active member, being nominated to seventy-one committees, with trade, religion, and City affairs being his principal concerns. He developed a particular animosity towards the Quakers at this stage. In the December 1656 debate over what kind of punishment should be inflicted on James Naylor, Packe initially favoured clemency, only to move in support of the motion that the house consider the death sentence when Naylor proved recalcitrant, and in the following May he was to speak out strongly in favour of a bill against Quakers. Packe became governor of the Company of Merchant Adventurers in 1656 and vociferously defended the company's monopoly of the woollen trade at the committee of trade when it later came under attack. Completing his ascension of the mercantile heights, he also joined the governing body of the East India Company in 1657. His greatest claim to fame in 1657, however, was his part in the presentation to the house on 23 February of a new constitution, the 'Humble petition and advice', which provided for a second chamber and held out the possibility of

Cromwell's becoming king. Packe was not one of the constitution's authors, only agreeing to act for them in presenting it after Whitelocke had declined to do so, yet during the subsequent constitutional debate he voted in favour of inviting Cromwell to accept the crown. On 10 December 1657 Packe was called to the new second chamber as Lord Packe.

The end of the protectorate, however, was the signal for Packe's enemies to rally against him. The restored Rump considered excluding him from the Act of Indemnity and initiated an inquiry into any public funds still in his hands. As a result he was forced to return over £10,000 of the money collected for the Piedmont protestants and later a further £22,000 of customs money owed by him and a fellow commissioner was ordered to be repaid. In both cases allegations of corruption were vehemently denied and the blame placed on parliament.

At the Restoration, Packe formally attended the proclamation of the king in London and signed a senior City declaration on 5 June 1660 accepting the royal pardon and pledging obedience. He faced the lesser penalty of exclusion from holding public office for life and accordingly in August 1660 he was removed from the aldermanry and the presidency of the hospitals. Nevertheless, while necessarily maintaining a low profile, he continued to prosper and became one of the creditors of Charles II's government. An attempt in 1666 to procure a baronetcy for his elder son, Christopher *Packe (*b.* in or before 1657, *d.* in or after 1708), mysteriously failed after the grant had been issued. After his third marriage in 1669 Packe retired to his manor at Cotes, where he died after a long illness on 27 May 1682. He was buried in the parish church at Prestwold, where his heir erected an impressive monument. His will, made on 10 November 1681 and proved on 26 June 1682, was that of a prosperous merchant who had diversified into land and other properties. The bulk of his estate had already been settled upon his elder son, his three surviving daughters had each received a dowry of £3500 on their marriage, and his younger son, Simon, had been given £1150. Packe's remaining property in London, Huntingdonshire, Leicestershire, and Devon was divided among his children and heading his numerous charitable bequests was £100 for ejected godly ministers and their widows.

KEITH LINDLEY

Sources 'Packe, Christopher', HoP, *Commons, 1640–60* [draft] • journals, CLRO, court of common council, vol. 40, fols. 52, 62, 81, 134, 148, 186, 215 • C. H. Firth and R. S. Rait, eds., *Acts and ordinances of the interregnum, 1642–1660*, 3 vols. (1911), 1.388, 667, 795, 880, 914, 928, 1007–8, 1261–2; 2.149 • will, PRO, PROB 11/370/74 • will of John Kendrick, PRO, PROB 11/144/116 • J. R. Woodhead, *The rulers of London, 1660–1689* (1965), 124 • A. B. Beaven, ed., *The aldermen of the City of London, temp. Henry III–[1912]*, 2 (1913), 68 • *The visitation of London, anno Domini 1633, 1634, and 1635, made by Sir Henry St George*, 2, ed. J. J. Howard, Harleian Society, 17 (1883), 136 • J. L. Chester and J. Foster, eds., *London marriage licences, 1521–1869* (1887), 1006 • 'Boyd's Inhabitants of London', Society of Genealogists, London, 10,001 • R. Brenner, *Merchants and revolution: commercial change, political conflict, and London's overseas traders, 1550–1653* (1993), 81, 384, 386, 434, 455, 482, 483, 489 • PRO, SP19/79/86; SP19/1/38; SP16/491/47 • *DNB* • T. C. Dale, ed., *The inhabitants of London in 1638*, 1 (1931), 141 • W. J. Harvey, ed., *List of the principal inhabitants of the City of London, 1640* (1886), 2 • *IGI*

Likenesses J. Basire, line engraving, BM, NPG; repro. in J. Nichols, *History of Leicestershire* (1795) • C. Jansen, oils; in possession of family, 1895

Packe, Christopher (*b.* in or before **1657**, *d.* in or after **1708**), chemical physician, was the son of Sir Christopher *Packe (*c.*1599–1682), a woollen merchant, who was lord mayor of London during part of the Commonwealth, and his wife, Anne (*d.* 1658), eldest daughter of Simon Edmonds, alderman of London. Packe set up his laboratory in 1670 at the sign of the Globe and Chemical Furnaces in Little Moorfields, London, and styled himself a professor of chemical medicine. He supposedly practised as a quack under powerful patronage, including that of Robert Boyle and the king's physician, Edmund Dickinson, though there is little to confirm this; in 1684 he circulated a list of his specifics.

In 1689 Packe brought out in folio his translation of Glauber's writings, which he published as *Works of the Highly Experienced and Famous Chymist, John Rudolph Glauber*, accompanied by the original copperplates, which he had purchased at Amsterdam. This task occupied him for three years, and he secured a large number of subscribers. He must have been an able Latin scholar as the translation reads very well. Packe also included a great deal of scarce German material by Glauber, but for the translation of this, he says, he relied upon a friend. His other publications were chiefly designed to promote the sale of his specifics. They include *One Hundred and Fifty Three Chymical Aphorisms* (1688); *Mineralogia, or, An account of the preparation, manifold vertues, and uses of a mineral salt, both in physick and chyrurgery* (1693); and *Medela chymica, or, An account of the vertues and uses of a select number of chymical medicines* (1708), at the end of which is a catalogue of his medicines, with their prices.

Little is known of Packe's private life. He appears to have been married, as he had at least one son—Edmund Packe [*see below*] who inherited the business; the physician Christopher *Packe (1686–1749) was probably also his son. The details of his death and burial are obscure.

His son **Edmund Packe** (*fl.* 1735) carried on the business at the Golden Head in Southampton Street, Covent Garden, calling himself 'M.D. and chemist'. He published an edition of his father's *Mineralogia* (n.d. [1730?]) and *An answer to Dr Turner's letter to Dr Jurin on the subject of Mr Ward's drop and pill, wherein his ignorance of chymical pharmacy is fairly exposed* (1735).

GORDON GOODWIN, *rev.* MALCOLM OSTER

Sources L. G. Matthews, 'Medical men as mapmakers', *Pharmaceutical Historian*, 5/2 (1975), 1–4

Packe, Christopher (**1686–1749**), physician and cartographer, was born in St Albans, Hertfordshire, on 6 March 1686 and was probably the son of Christopher *Packe (*b.* in or before 1657, *d.* in or after 1708), chemist. Little is known of his life, but he was educated at Merchant Taylors' School, London, from 11 September 1695; received the degree of doctor of medicine at Cambridge in 1717, *comitiis regiis*; and was admitted as a candidate of the Royal

College of Physicians on 25 June 1723. In January 1726 he presented an organ to St Peter's Church, St Albans. On 30 July of that year he married Mary Randolph of the precincts, Canterbury, in Canterbury Cathedral and from about that date settled with her in Canterbury, where he practised medicine until his death.

In 1726 and 1727 Packe was embroiled in a heated controversy and pamphlet war with Dr John Gray of Canterbury. The dispute concerned the treatment of one Robert Worger of Hinxhill, Kent, who died of 'concussion of the brain' after falling from his horse. Worger had at first been treated by Packe, but his relatives, not satisfied with Packe's methods, called in Gray and two surgeons, who, Packe argued, caused Worger's death by excessive bleeding and trepanning.

As well as contributing several papers to *Philosophical Transactions*, Packe published two cartographical works: *A dissertation upon the surface of the earth, as delineated in a specimen of a philosophical-chorographical chart of East Kent* (1737) and *Ankographia* (1743, by subscription), an expanded version of the former. Cartography occupied Packe's thoughts during 'many otherwise tedious journeys' around his Kent practice (Jarcho, 52), and both works endeavoured to describe and explain the topography around Canterbury by using charts which Packe had made by taking bearings from the tower of Canterbury Cathedral. They also indicate that Packe considered the structure of the human body to be a microcosm of the natural world, for when writing of the River Stour he claimed that its

> minute Division and Graphic Portrait of the Vallies and their Waters … differ[s] but little, if at all, from the Anatomical Descriptions of the several Systems of the Arteries, Veins, or Nerves, that are with such exquisite Art distributed all through our bodies. (Jarcho, 50)

Packe died on 15 November 1749. He was buried in St Mary Magdalene, Canterbury, and left a son, Christopher, who also became a physician (graduating bachelor of medicine from Peterhouse, Cambridge, in 1751); who also practised in Canterbury; and who, after his death on 21 October 1800, aged seventy-two, was buried in St Mary Magdalene, alongside his father.

GORDON GOODWIN, *rev.* GILES HUDSON

Sources Munk, *Roll* • Venn, *Alum. Cant.* • S. Jarcho, 'Christopher Packe (1686–1749): physician-cartographer of Kent', *Journal of the History of Medicine and Allied Sciences*, 33 (1978), 47–52 • *GM*, 1st ser., 19 (1749), 542

Archives BL, Sloane MSS, Add. MS 4055

Packe, Christopher. *See* Pack, Faithful Christopher (1760–1840).

Packe, Edmund (*fl.* 1735). *See under* Packe, Christopher (*b.* in or before 1657, *d.* in or after 1708).

Packer, Sir (Douglas) Frank Hewson (1906–1974), media proprietor, was born on 3 December 1906 at 8 Craigend Street, Kings Cross, Sydney, Australia, the first child of Robert Clyde Packer (1879–1934), a journalist and newspaper proprietor, and his wife, Ethel Maude (1878–1947), daughter of the Revd Frank Hewson of Ireland and his wife, Frances. He attended Abbotsholme College, Turramurra College, Eltham College, and the Sydney Church of England grammar school. The mischievous youngster struggled academically but excelled at sport.

In 1923 Frank Packer became a cadet at Smith's Newspapers Ltd, which published the lively *Smith's Weekly* and the Sydney *Daily Guardian* and was co-owned by his father. Though he lacked his father's literary flair, Packer participated in a number of journalistic exposés and served a diverse newspaper apprenticeship. After a spell as a jackaroo in central New South Wales, he returned to Smith's Newspapers in 1926, first as assistant business manager and then as advertising director. His financial acumen now became apparent.

In 1930 the company's principal assets were sold to a greedy newspaper chain, Associated Newspapers Ltd, in somewhat controversial circumstances. R. C. Packer, his health in decline, moved to Associated Newspapers as managing editor to protect his family's shareholding. Frank Packer joined his father a few months later, but a suspicion that he was acting as a 'detective' led to a quick departure.

In October 1932 Packer and E. G. Theodore, a former Labor premier and federal treasurer, announced a plan to take over an ailing Sydney newspaper and publish it at a discounted price. Alarmed by the threat, Associated Newspapers authorized R. C. Packer to 'fix up the matter' (John Fairfax Group archives). When R. C. Packer agreed to pay his son's nascent company, Sydney Newspapers Ltd, £86,500 in return for an agreement not to publish a daily or Sunday newspaper for three years, business, political, and trade union observers were aghast. Having executed a masterly coup, Frank Packer followed Theodore into a profitable gold-mining venture in Fiji.

Meanwhile a journalistic associate of the Packers, G. W. Warnecke, was developing a pilot for a national women's journal. In 1933 Sydney Newspapers agreed to launch the *Australian Women's Weekly*. Edited by Warnecke, vigorously promoted, and containing a mixture of news and traditional magazine features, this inexpensive publication was an instant success. It became Australia's best-selling magazine and a lucrative source of advertising revenue.

In January 1934 Frank Packer rushed to England to join his father, who died of a heart condition a few months later. On 24 July that year, at All Saints' Church, Woollahra, Sydney, Packer married with Anglican rites Gretel Joyce Bullmore (1907–1960). He had pursued this elegant society beauty for some years with typical zeal. He was 6 feet 1 inch tall and thickset, with blue eyes, dark brown wavy hair, a jutting jaw, and a husky voice. Packer took his bride to live at Cairnton, a mansion in Bellevue Hill in Sydney's exclusive eastern suburbs. They had two sons, (Robert) Clyde (1935–2000) and Kerry (*b.* 1937).

In 1936 Packer became managing director and Theodore became chairman of a new company, Consolidated Press Ltd, which took over the publication of a moribund morning newspaper, the Sydney *Telegraph*. The *Sunday Telegraph* appeared three years later. Champions of progressive and modernist ideas, the newspapers became tabloids during the war.

Packer volunteered for the militia in April 1939. Despite his family and business commitments, he transferred to the Australian Imperial Force as a lieutenant in February 1941. The following year the prime minister, John Curtin, appointed Theodore director-general of the Allied Works Council (AWC), which was responsible for wartime civil works. Theodore, who was like a father figure to Packer, seconded his partner to serve as director of personnel. After resigning from the AWC in 1944, Packer served in New Guinea before transferring to the reserve of officers in July 1945.

The *Telegraphs* turned sharply to the right during the cold war. Afraid that Australia would be left alone, 'a tiny white population on the perimeter of Asia' (*Daily Telegraph*, 20 Oct 1945), Packer was in 1950–51 New South Wales president of the Australian–American Association and from 1954 a founding councillor of the nuclear research foundation at the University of Sydney. His editorial interventions were spectacular; in 1953 he had the *Telegraph* mark Joseph Stalin's death with a sketch of a crocodile crying. He made generous donations to charities on the understanding that they were not to be publicized, bestowed largesse on employees who were down on their luck, and adopted stray dogs, while counting petty cash receipts, fighting against increases in award wages, and indulging in ritual sackings.

In 1955 Packer established Television Corporation Ltd in Sydney, which broadcast Australia's first television programmes. In 1960 his group moved into television in Melbourne and acquired the legendary weekly *Bulletin* magazine. But Packer sometimes overplayed his hand. Most notably, his bid in 1953 to obtain a majority shareholding in an afternoon newspaper failed, which meant that he was unable to utilize his company's idle printing capacity. Despite impressive sales the *Telegraph* appealed most to readers in lower socio-economic groups and did not attract lucrative retail or classified advertising.

Packer was appointed CBE in 1951 and a knight bachelor in 1959. But even though he joined the boards of several charities and supported the conservative Liberal Party, he was always regarded as representing 'new money'. His success was due largely to two exceptional mentors, financial cunning, bravado, prodigious energy, an ability to identify and nurture the talents of others, and a determination to prove his mettle to his father's contemporaries. The 'young master's' blustering manner and robust sense of humour hid a shyness and self-consciousness about his limited journalistic credentials.

In August 1960 Packer was by Gretel's side when she died at a clinic in New York. Their marriage had endured his roving eye and more than one affair. By this time their sons were working at Consolidated Press, where they were subjected to their father's bullying. On 15 June 1964 at Westminster register office in London, Packer married the socialite Florence Adeline Vincent, *née* Porges, a half-Russian, half-French divorcee with two previous husbands.

Sport was always Packer's passion. He had won the New South Wales amateur heavyweight boxing championship in 1929, and was an accomplished polo player and yachtsman before the Second World War. He bred champion thoroughbreds, held Sunday golf parties, and commissioned Australia's first 12-metre sloop, *Gretel*. He spearheaded two vigorous but unsuccessful challenges for the America's Cup in 1962 and 1970, and was appointed KBE in 1971.

By this time Packer had developed elaborate measures to hide the *Telegraphs'* losses. In June 1972 he finally yielded to pressure from his sons to sell the mastheads to Rupert Murdoch's News Ltd for A$15 million. Packer was devastated by the loss of his papers, which he candidly admitted were political bludgeons: 'he cried when he spoke of it; his face was pinched and his gaze distracted' (Horne, 55). In August 1972 Clyde resigned from the magazine and television empire in protest at his father's decree that an interview with a union leader should not be broadcast on television.

A heavy drinker and smoker, Packer took risks and lived fast. He was plagued by chest complaints and fitted with a pacemaker, and glaucoma forced him to wear thick dark glasses. Survived by his wife and the sons of his first marriage, he died of pneumonia and cancer on 1 May 1974 in Royal Prince Alfred Hospital, Sydney. Though Packer had not been a regular churchgoer, he had liked talking to religious ministers and trying to shock them, and death held an awesome fascination for him. After an Anglican service at St Andrew's Cathedral, Sydney, his body was cremated and his ashes interred in the family vault at South Head cemetery, Vaucluse, Sydney.

Packer's estate was sworn for probate at A$1.3 million; complex tax minimization schemes meant that the assets under his control were worth much more. Clyde had been reconciled with his father, but it was Kerry who took charge of the empire. A veteran Consolidated Press foreign correspondent recorded in his diary: 'The King is dead. I was fond of that strange buccaneer' (Emery Barcs papers). BRIDGET GRIFFEN-FOLEY

Sources R. S. Whitington, *Sir Frank: the Frank Packer story* (1971) • B. Griffen-Foley, *Sir Frank Packer: the young master* (2000) • D. McNicoll, *Luck's a fortune* (1979) • D. Horne, *Money made us* (1976) • private information (2004) • *Sydney Morning Herald* (2 May 1974) • *The Times* (2 May 1974) • *Sunday Telegraph* [Sydney] (5 May 1974) • *The Bulletin* [Sydney] (11 May 1974) • *Australian Women's Weekly* (15 May 1974) • Mitchell L., NSW, Emery Barcs papers, MS 5770 • NL Aus., Sir Robert Menzies papers, MS 4936 • NL Aus., Sir Ernest K. White papers, MS 6455 • NL Aus., Sir Lloyd Dumas papers, MS 4849 • John Fairfax Group archives, Sydney, Australia • University of Sydney archives, Sydney, Australia

Archives priv. coll., family papers | John Fairfax Group, Sydney, archives • Mitchell L., NSW, Emery Barcs papers • NL Aus., Sir Robert Menzies papers • NL Aus., Sir Lloyd Dumas papers • NL Aus., Sir Ernest K. White papers • University of Sydney, Nuclear Research Foundation and Postgraduate Medical Foundation records, archives | FILM Australian Broadcasting Corporation archives, Sydney | SOUND Australian Broadcasting Corporation archives, Sydney

Likenesses J. Cassab, oils, 1956, Australian Consolidated Press Ltd, Sydney • G. Finey, drawing, Mitchell L., NSW

Wealth at death A$1,340,256: *Sydney Morning Herald* (6 Feb 1975)

Packer, John (1572–1649), politician and landowner, was born at Twickenham, Middlesex, on 12 November 1572, the son of William Packer (*d.* 1600), clerk of the privy seal, and Elizabeth Borwell (*d.* 1611). He was educated at Westminster School and then matriculated from Trinity College, Oxford, on 13 March 1590; during the same year he was admitted a scholar at Trinity College, Cambridge, and he took a BA degree in 1593–4. He dedicated to Lord Burghley, addressed as Maecenas, a manuscript book of Greek and Latin verses which he composed while at Cambridge, entitled 'Elizabetha, sive, Augustissimae Anglorum principis encomium'. After university Packer travelled in France and became secretary to Sir Henry Neville, English ambassador there from February 1599. After Neville's departure in August 1600 he acted as agent in France for a time. In July 1604 Packer was granted the reversion of a clerkship of the privy seal, and in March 1614, with Francis Godolphin, was made a protonotary of the chancery, for life. According to his son-in-law, he was also made French secretary. He enjoyed the patronage of the Sackville earls of Dorset, and in January 1610 reported that Thomas, Lord Dorset, had invited him to be his travelling companion in France. In the autumn of that year Packer was sent to Denmark as a special ambassador. His instructions concerned relations between Denmark and Sweden, and giving the Swedish delegates James I's response to the Swedish proposal for a marriage between Gustavus Adolphus, Charles IX's heir, and Princess Elizabeth. He returned in 1611.

On 13 July 1613, at the church of St Katharine Cree, London, Packer married Philippa (*bap.* 1590, *d.* 1665), daughter of Francis Mills of Westminster and Alice Jones. Four of their sons, Robert, George, Philip, and John, were educated at Oxford. Robert Packer (1616–1687) was MP for Wallingford and married Temperance, daughter of Colonel Edward Stephens of Sodbury. George Packer (1617–1641) was a fellow of All Souls College, Oxford. Philip Packer (1618–1686) married Isabella, daughter of Sir Robert and Elizabeth Berkeley. Isabella died in 1664, and he then married, in 1666, Sarah Isgar of West Lavington, Wiltshire. He was paymaster of the king's works, usher of the exchequer, and an original fellow of the Royal Society. John Packer (1626–1708) married Jane Fettiplace of Fernham, Berkshire, and was a fellow of the Royal College of Physicians. William Packer (1627–1655), fifth son of John and Philippa, married Jane Saunders of Woolston. Of his sisters, Elizabeth (*b.* 1616) married in 1636 John Browne, clerk of the parliaments from 1638 until his death in 1691 (but not during the interregnum), and Katherine (1623–1721) married John Gell of Kopton, Derbyshire. Frances was born in 1619 and died in 1633.

In 1612 Packer became secretary to Robert Carr, later earl of Somerset. After Somerset's fall, in 1615 Packer was appointed secretary to George Villiers, who was created successively earl, marquess, and duke of Buckingham, and held the post until Buckingham's assassination in 1628. According to John Browne he often acted as secretary to the king and declined offers to be made a secretary of state. Yet when, in February 1619, the king decided to appoint a new secretary of state he preferred Sir George Calvert to Packer and Dudley Carleton, both of whom were being promoted by Buckingham. When the king's preference became clear Buckingham dropped his support for Packer. His influence as Buckingham's secretary was considerable. In 1623 Isaac Barrow wrote from Cambridge seeking Packer's support for his, ultimately successful, efforts to obtain the post of regius professor of physic for John Gostlin, master of Gonville and Caius College. Packer enjoyed an appreciable income from fees and gratuities, as well as from other sources. In May 1614 he was one of four men granted a licence for thirty-one years for the manufacture of indigo neale; in March 1617 he was awarded an annual pension of £115 from the court of wards on the surrender of a similar annuity from the exchequer and treasury of the chamber; and by 1635 he was receiving payments of £292 per annum out of the duchy of Lancaster.

Packer acquired a considerable estate. He bought from Lord Dorset the manor of Groombridge in Kent and Sussex, and in 1620 the manor of Shellingford in Berkshire from Sir Henry Neville's son, also Sir Henry. In 1632 he acquired the manor of Shaw-cum-Donnington in the same county, and Charles I, on his coronation, gave him other lands in Berkshire, in recognition of his loyalty. His property included Chilton Foliat in Wiltshire and Berkshire, and land at Kingston Lisle, Fawler, and Baulking in Berkshire, and at Hams and Spencers in Sussex, which he held on lease from the earl of Dorset. He also owned a share of the New River Company. In 1625 Packer spent over £500 on a new church at Groombridge, in thanksgiving for the king's safe return from Spain, as recorded in a Latin inscription on a tablet on the porch. He allowed a minister there £30 per annum, and in his will provided an endowment of £20 per annum for the minister's stipend. Also in 1625 he spent at least £200 in work on St Faith's Church at Shellingford, which included the raising of a new spire and the erection of a new south porch. In 1629 he paid most of the cost of rebuilding St Mary's, Chilton Foliat, where the body of the church was rebuilt and re-roofed, and a new chancel screen was installed. John Browne's account mentions that at his own expense Packer sent ministers to preach in Lancashire, Staffordshire, Westmorland, south Wales, and 'other remote parts of the kingdom' (*Abergavenny MSS*, 174); he allowed them at least £30 and in some cases £50 per annum. He was a regular frequenter of sermons and an assiduous reader of the Bible, knowing by heart the New Testament, the Psalms, and Proverbs.

Packer sat as an MP for West Looe, Cornwall, in the parliament of 1628–9. He made a number of brief interventions in debates and was appointed to several committees, some of which were to draft petitions to the king. His influence, and presumably fees and perquisites, fell after Buckingham's assassination, but in 1635 he served on a commission that enquired into the abuses of the Fleet prison in London, and on 1 May 1647 he was appointed a visitor of Oxford University. When the king asked for loans of money in March 1640, Packer refused. In November 1641 he donated £100 for the affairs in Ireland. He was a supporter of parliament during the first civil war. The royalists sequestered his lands within their control and garrisoned Donnington Castle, which was largely ruined by the time that it was surrendered on 1 April 1646. Packer made his will in July 1645, directing that there should not be any feasting at his funeral, which would be 'very unfitting and unseasonable at such a time' (will, PRO, PROB 11/209/153). This stipulation was not changed in the codicil he added in May 1648. Packer died at his house in the college at Westminster, and was buried at St Margaret's Church on 15 February 1649.

Browne praised Packer's behaviour to all who knew him, his lack of pride at his success and his charity, mentioning his donations to the poor clergy banished from the Palatinate and La Rochelle, and to the poor protestants of Ireland, and his bequest providing for the bringing up of Irish children as protestants. His other bequests included provision for medicines and surgery for the poor, £100 for the poor at an almshouse, £200 to young divinity students at Oxford and Cambridge, and sums for his servants. His wife, who acted as his executor, was buried at Shaw in Berkshire on 21 November 1665.

A collection of letters and state papers formed by Packer passed to G. H. Fortescue of Dropmore, Buckinghamshire, and in 1872 was deposited in the Bodleian Library. It was calendared by the Historical Manuscripts Commission, and in 1871 the Camden Society published a selection, edited by S. R. Gardiner. STEPHEN PORTER

Sources *The manuscripts of the marquess of Abergavenny, Lord Braye, G. F. Luttrell*, HMC, 15 (1887), 123, 174 • G. E. Aylmer, *The king's servants: the civil service of Charles I, 1625–1642* (1961), 157–8, 358 • *CSP dom., 1603–10*, 131, 199; *1611–18*, 228, 232, 440; *1619–23*, 357, 605; *1629–31*, 355, 357; *1635*, 56, 80–81; *1639–40*, 511, 521–2 • will, PRO, PROB 11/209/153 • R. C. Johnson and others, eds., *Commons debates, 1628*, 6 vols. (1977–83), vol. 2, pp. 42, 211, 383, 564; 3.22, 208, 215, 221, 301, 328, 331, 355, 367, 446, 465, 477, 593; vol. 4, pp. 40, 127, 180, 184, 187, 332 • PRO, SP 75/4, fols. 191–206 • G. M. Bell, *A handlist of British diplomatic representatives, 1509–1688*, Royal Historical Society Guides and Handbooks, 16 (1990), 32 • R. Lockyer, *Buckingham: the life and political career of George Villiers, first duke of Buckingham, 1592–1628* (1981), 69, 114 • *JHC*, 2 (1640–42), 320 • *VCH Berkshire*, 4.92, 476–7 • A. M. Burke, ed., *Memorials of St Margaret's Church, Westminster* (1914), 621 • Foster, *Alum. Oxon., 1500–1714*, 3.1104 • Venn, *Alum. Cant.*, 1/3.293

Archives Berks. RO, letters and papers | Berks. RO, Harley MSS • Berks. RO, Winchcombe MSS • Bodl. Oxf., Fortescue MSS

Packer, John Hayman (1730–1806), actor, was born on 21 March 1730 in the Strand, London, the son of John Packer, a Glass House Street saddler, and his wife, Anne Partridge. He was baptized at St Martin-in-the-Fields on 16 March 1731. His mother was a widow when she died in 1763, leaving John a freehold house in Kensington Square. It is unknown whether he ever married. One sister, a widow named Elizabeth Foster, survived him. After being apprenticed to his father Packer followed the saddler's trade, but went on the stage at Newcastle upon Tyne in 1754. His London début at Covent Garden on 24 January 1758 led to an engagement with Garrick at Drury Lane, where he first appeared on 19 September 1758 as Selim in Congreve's *The Mourning Bride*. In forty-seven seasons at Drury Lane he played supporting parts, creating such roles as Patent in Garrick's *A Peep behind the Curtain* (23 October 1767), Snake in Sheridan's *The School for Scandal* (8 May 1777), and Allan in Lewis's *The Castle Spectre* (14 December 1797). His parts in the Shakespeare repertory chart an undistinguished career. Assigned at first to young, supporting roles—Rosencrantz in *Hamlet* (1758), Benvolio in *Romeo and Juliet* (1759), Malcolm in *Macbeth* (1761)—he later assumed maturer, but still secondary, parts, such as Horatio and Banquo (1758). Finally he was relegated to the old men he would play for the rest of his career: Friar Lawrence (1772), Claudius (1777), Duncan (1780), Gloster (1788). He seems to have been a useful actor who, if he ever possessed 'animation and fire', had lost those qualities by the time Waldron mentioned their absence in 1795. He retired from the stage in 1805. A fall downstairs on 31 January 1806 hastened his death, which occurred on 16 September of that year. He may have been buried on 21 September at St Paul's, Covent Garden. He left an estate of less than £200. ALAN HUGHES

Sources Highfill, Burnim & Langhans, *BDA* • G. W. Stone, ed., *The London stage, 1660–1800*, pt 4: *1747–1776* (1962) • C. B. Hogan, ed., *The London stage, 1660–1800*, pt 5: *1776–1800* (1968) • B. R. Schneider, *Index to 'The London stage, 1660–1800'* (1979) • *GM*, 1st ser., 77 (1807), 371 • *GM*, 1st ser., 76 (1806), 984 • [F. G. Waldron], *Candid and impartial strictures on the performers belonging to Drury-Lane, Covent-Garden, and the Haymarket theatres* (1795) • *IGI*

Likenesses B. Vandergucht, double portrait, oils, *c.*1761 (with J. Moody), Leicester Museum and Art Gallery • G. J. Caldwell and S. Smith, line engraving, pubd 1783 (after G. Carter), BM • G. Carter, oils (as Friar Lawrence in *The Apotheosis of Garrick*), Gallery of the Royal Shakespeare Company • W. Loftis, watercolour (as Claudius), Folger • oils, Garr. Club

Wealth at death under £200: Highfill, Burnim & Langhans, *BDA*

Packer, William (*fl.* 1644–1662), army officer and deputy major-general, entered the parliamentary army early in the civil war, and was a lieutenant in Cromwell's 'Ironsides' in 1644. In the spring of that year he was put under arrest by Major-General Crawford for disobedience to orders, although the incident may have arisen from the presbyterian Crawford's known distaste for Packer's Particular Baptist views. Cromwell, however, strongly defended Packer as a 'Godly man' and secured his release. Following Marston Moor, he held the rank of captain from 29 July 1644 to 29 April 1645. Originally named to the 9th regiment of horse in the New Model he was objected to by the Lords. He later exchanged places with Robert Swallow and became senior captain of the 1st regiment of horse, Fairfax's own regiment. He sided with the army in its quarrel with the parliament, but helped to quash Leveller agitation within the army in April 1648. During the second civil war he was present at the siege of Colchester. In November 1648 he was one of the officers selected for a committee charged with drafting a compromise version of the *Agreement of the People* but took a prominent part in suppressing the Leveller-inspired mutinies of May 1649. At the battle of Dunbar he seems to have commanded Cromwell's own regiment of horse in the absence of its major, and took part in that flank attack on the Scottish army which decided the issue of the battle. In 1652 he became major of the regiment, and, as such, was colonel in all but name, receiving the salary and exercising all the functions of the office on behalf of Cromwell. Noted for his godliness, on 7 July 1653 he received a licence from the council of state authorizing him to preach in any pulpit in England, if it was not required at the time by its legal possessor. By 1652 he was allied with the London Fifth Monarchy preachers, but he broke with them when he failed to oppose the protectorate. He was on the commission to promote the gospel in Wales, became a trier, and served on a number of 1650s committees, including the Hale commission on law reform. In 1656 he acted as deputy major-general for Buckinghamshire, Oxfordshire, and Hertfordshire, and proceeded against Edmund Waller until the protector interfered on behalf of the poet.

By this time Packer had become a man of property, and bought, in conjunction with some other officers, the royal manor of Theobalds, Hertfordshire. George Fox mentions him as a great enemy to the Quakers, and describes an interview between himself and Packer. In Cromwell's second parliament he represented Woodstock; but he had become discontented with the policy of the protector, and joined the opposition in the parliament and the army. Cromwell, after failing to convince him of the error of his ways by argument, deprived him of his command. According to Packer's own account, his opposition to the revival of the House of Lords was the cause of his dismissal.

> I thought it was not 'a lord's house', but another house. But for my undertaking to judge this, I was sent for, accused of perjury, and outed of a place of 600l. per annum. … without any trial or appeal, with the breath of his nostrils I was outed, and lost not only my place, but a dear friend to boot. (*Diary of Thomas Burton*, 3.165)

Packer was returned to Richard Cromwell's parliament for Hertford, but on a petition he was unseated. On the restoration of the purged 'rump' of the Long Parliament in 1659, that assembly made Packer colonel of his old regiment, regarding him as a sufferer for republican principles; but having taken part in the promotion of a petition which the house considered dangerous, he was cashiered by vote of 12 October 1659. He consequently assisted Lambert to expel the parliament, and was one of the leaders of the army during the two months of military rule which followed. But the restoration of the Rump Parliament at the end of December put an end to his power; the command of his regiment was given to Sir Arthur Hesilrige, and Packer was ordered to leave London on pain of imprisonment. When Lambert escaped from the Tower, Packer was immediately seized and committed to prison (15 April 1660). The Restoration entailed upon him the loss of the lands he had purchased, and, though he escaped punishment, the government of Charles II considered him dangerous, and more than once arrested him on suspicion of plots. His wife, Elizabeth, petitioned for her husband's release in August 1661, stating that he had been for three months closely confined without being brought to trial. In May 1662 Packer was transferred from the Fleet prison to the Gatehouse. In September 1662 he was taken from king's bench prison and put on board the *Colchester* for Dublin Castle, where he arrived in October. His subsequent history and the date of his death are unknown.

C. H. Firth, *rev.* D. N. Farr

Sources C. H. Firth and G. Davies, *The regimental history of Cromwell's army*, 2 vols. (1940) • *Diary of Thomas Burton*, ed. J. T. Rutt, 4 vols. (1828) • Thurloe, *State papers* • [W. T. Whitley], 'Theobalds and Colonel Packer', *Transactions of the Baptist Historical Society*, 4 (1914–15), 57–63 • J. Bruce and D. Masson, eds., *The quarrel between the earl of Manchester and Oliver Cromwell*, CS, new ser., 12 (1875) • *CSP dom.* • *The journal of George Fox*, ed. N. Penney, 2 vols. (1911) • D. Underdown, 'Cromwell and the officers, February 1658', *EngHR*, 83 (1968), 101–7 • I. Gentles, 'The management of the crown lands', *Agricultural History Review*, 19 (1971), 25–41 • I. Gentles, 'The choosing of the officers for the New Model Army', *Historical Research*, 67 (1994), 264–85 • R. K. G. Temple, ed., 'The original officer list of the New Model Army', *BIHR*, 59 (1986), 50–77 • B. S. Capp, *The Fifth Monarchy Men: a study in seventeenth-century English millenarianism* (1972) • R. L. Greaves, *Deliver us from evil: the radical underground in Britain, 1660–1663* (1986) • *Original memoirs written during the great civil war: being the life of Sir Henry Slingsby and memoirs of Capt. Hodgson*, ed. W. Scott (1806) • M. Tolmie, *The triumph of the saints: the separate churches of London, 1616–1649* (1977) • BL, Egerton MS 2538, fol. 105 • I. Gentles, *The New Model Army in England, Ireland, and Scotland, 1645–1653* (1992) • *JHC* • *The Clarke Papers*, ed. C. H. Firth, 2, CS, new ser., 54 (1894) • W. Erbury, *The bishop of London* (1652) • G. Davies, 'The army of the eastern association, 1644–5', *EngHR*, 46 (1931), 88–96 • PRO, C5/27/33; C5/30/31; C5/30/34 • J. Rushworth, *Historical collections*, new edn, 8 vols. (1721–2) • S. R. Gardiner, *History of the Commonwealth and protectorate, 1649–1656*, new edn, 4 vols. (1903), vol. 1

Archives Bodl. Oxf., Thurloe state papers

Packington [Pakington]**, William** (*d.* **1390**), administrator and supposed chronicler, probably came from the Leicestershire village of Packington near Ashby-de-la-Zouch; he later held the living of Burton Overy in the same county. His will refers to a brother named John and two sisters named Lucy and Reyne. Packington was in the service of Edward, prince of Wales, the Black Prince, from at least 1364. His brother, too, was apparently a servant of the prince. On the death of Edward in 1376 Packington became the receiver-general of his widow, Joan, and, following the succession to the throne of Richard II, was appointed keeper of the wardrobe on 1 July 1377. On 6 January 1381 he was appointed chancellor of the exchequer, and continued to hold both offices until his death on 25 July 1390. Although wardrobe expenditure was fairly low during Packington's keepership, he was unable to obtain sufficient funds from the exchequer to cover the wardrobe's outgoings, and at the time of his death the wardrobe had accumulated debts of approximately £6000–7000.

Packington held at various times livings at Burton Overy, Ivinghoe in Buckinghamshire, Wearmouth in co. Durham, and elsewhere. He exchanged Ivinghoe for a canonry at Windsor in October 1381. On 20 September 1381 he was appointed archdeacon of Canterbury, an office that he retained until his death. On 28 December 1381 he became dean of Lichfield. He also held prebends in York, Lincoln, Chichester, and London. Shortly before his death he resigned as dean of Lichfield and became dean of St Martin's-le-Grand, London. A street in Islington, London, built on what was once prebendal land of St Paul's, is named after him.

John Leland claimed that Packington 'did write a Cronique yn Frenche from the IX Yere of King John of Englande on to his tyme, and dedicatid it to his Lord Prince Edwarde' (*De rebus Britannicis*, 2.455). The extracts given by Leland show that he was referring to BL, Cotton MS Tiberius A.vi, folios 121–9, a fourteenth-century chronicle based on the French *Brut*, the *Flores historiarum*, and the long continuation of the French *Brut*. However, the manuscript contains no contemporary evidence indicating that Packington was the author of this chronicle, and Leland's attribution must remain doubtful. Given that Leland's comment is the only evidence that Packington ever wrote a chronicle, it is difficult to accept without further supporting evidence Galbraith's suggestion that Packington wrote the account of the rising of 1381 in the Anonimalle chronicle. ANDREW PRESCOTT

Sources *Joannis Lelandi antiquarii de rebus Britannicis collectanea*, ed. T. Hearne, [3rd edn], 6 vols. (1774), vol. 2, pp. 455–70 • Tout, *Admin. hist.*, vols. 2, 4 • *Fasti Angl., 1300–1541*, [Lincoln] • *Fasti Angl., 1300–1541*, [Coventry] • *Fasti Angl., 1300–1541*, [Chichester] • *Fasti Angl., 1300–1541*, [St Paul's, London] • *Fasti Angl., 1066–1300*, [York] • J. C. Sainty, ed., *Officers of the exchequer: a list* (1983) • J. Taylor, *English historical literature in the fourteenth century* (1987) • V. Galbraith, 'Thoughts about the peasants' revolt', *The reign of Richard II: essays in honour of May McKisack*, ed. F. R. H. Du Boulay and C. M. Barron (1971), 46–51 • C. Given-Wilson, *The royal household and the king's affinity: service, politics and finance in England, 1360–1413* (1986) • register of William Courtenay, LPL, fols. 234*v*–235*v*

Padarn [St Padarn] (*fl.* **6th cent.**), founder of churches, is traditionally thought to belong to the sixth century. Along with David and Teilo he was regarded in medieval times as one of the principal saints of south-west Wales. He is the subject of a life, *Vita Paterni* (BL, Cotton MS Vespasian A.xiv), probably originally written *c.*1120 at Llanbadarn Fawr near Aberystwyth. Unfortunately the *Vita Paterni* cannot be depended upon for a single historical fact since it is, in the words of G. H. Doble, 'a collection of traditions and legends, mostly late and untrustworthy, arranged by a writer who used the Lives of two different saints and corrupted them to suit his own ideas'. It has been shown that the text is a combination of a Welsh life, now lost, and a life of Paternus, bishop of Vannes, in the fifth century, which had already been combined with the life of Paternus, bishop of Avranches, who lived in the sixth century. The identification of the Welsh Padarn with the Breton saint was probably facilitated by the fact that Padarn in his original life was, like many other Welsh saints, possibly associated with Letavia (Llydaw), a district in south-east Wales often mistakenly identified with Armorica.

There are numerous scattered references to Padarn in medieval texts, the earliest of which occurs in the life of St David written about 1097. None of these appears to contain information about the original historical saint however, although it has been thought by some historians that the pedigree that appears in *Bonedd y saint*, a genealogical table of the Welsh saints compiled in the thirteenth century, may contain ancient traditions about him. The churches dedicated to Padarn are Llanbadarn Fawr, Llanbadarn Odwyn, and Llanbadarn Fach (or Trefeglwys) in Cardiganshire, Llanbadarn Fawr, Llanbadarn Fynydd, and Llanbadarn Garreg in Radnorshire, and Pencarreg in Carmarthenshire. Views as to what extent these sites reflect the movements of the historical Padarn and his cult vary, but it is generally agreed that his headquarters and the mother church of his cult was at Llanbadarn near Aberystwyth where a *clas* (the church of a hereditary clerical community) existed until Norman times. In the eleventh and twelfth centuries it included the family of the scholar Sulien, including his son Rhigyfarch ap Sulien. His feast day is 15 April. NERYS ANN JONES

Sources G. H. Doble, *Saint Patern*, Cornish Saints Series, 43 (1940) • E. G. Bowen, *A history of Llanbadarn Fawr* (1979) • E. G. Bowen, *The settlements of the Celtic saints in Wales* (1954), 50–55 • A. W. Wade-Evans, ed. and trans., *Vitae sanctorum Britanniae et genealogiae* (1944) • S. Baring-Gould and J. Fisher, *The lives of the British saints*, Honourable Society of Cymmrodorion, Cymmrodorion Record Series, 4 (1913), 39–51 • BL, Cotton MSS, MS Vespasian A.XIV

Paddock [Padock], **Tom** (**1822–1863**), pugilist, was born near Redditch, Worcestershire, and baptized at St Stephen's Church, Redditch, on 25 August 1822, the son of George Padock, a labourer, and his wife, Elizabeth. His place of origin earned him the sobriquet of the Redditch Needle-pointer. A burly, pugnacious farm boy, he developed a taste for boxing and became a strong, enduring, and resolute fighter, but never attained to the first rank as a scientific boxer. When his professional career commenced in 1844 his height was 5 feet 10½ inches, and his fighting weight was 12 stone. His career progressed steadily, if unspectacularly, interrupted by ten months' hard labour at Derby in 1852, when police intervention at his fight with Harry Poulson was riotously opposed.

In 1850 Paddock was defeated by William Thompson (Bendigo), a very shifty performer, who was declared winner in consequence of a foul blow which his conduct had invited. Five years later Paddock arguably became champion of England through default of Harry Broome, but he was not generally recognized and forfeited the position next year (1856) to Bill Perry (the Tipton Slasher). He made two unsuccessful attempts to regain the title. Paddock had for a long time been ambitious to fight Tom Sayers, but before the arrangements for the meeting had been finalized Paddock fell ill. Sayers visited him in the hospital and, on learning that he was poor, generously gave him £5. On his recovery Paddock renewed his application to fight Sayers for the championship; but as he was unable to raise the usual stake of £200 he appealed to his opponent to waive £50, a request that was at once granted. The fight took place on 16 June 1858, and Paddock was defeated in twenty-one rounds, which occupied an hour and twenty minutes. In the last round Sayers delivered a crushing blow with his left and drew back his right hand to complete the victory; but seeing his adversary staggering forward at his mercy, instead of hitting he offered his right hand in friendship, and led him to his seconds, who accepted defeat.

Paddock's last fight took place in 1860 (when he was

unfortunately suffering from a knife wound). His opponent was the gigantic Sam Hurst, who gained the victory by a chance blow. Paddock died of heart disease on 30 June 1863 at 22 Upper Rathbone Place, London, and was buried at Finchley on 5 July. His widow died four days later.

WILLIAM BROADFOOT, *rev.* JULIAN LOCK

Sources *Bell's Life* (5 July 1863), 6 • *Bell's Life* (12 July 1863), 7 • H. D. Miles, *Pugilistica: being one hundred and forty-four years of the history of British boxing*, 3 vols. (1880–81), vol. 3, pp. 271–307 • Boase, *Mod. Eng. biog.* • D. Johnson, *Bare fist fighters of the 18th and 19th century: 1704–1861* (1987) • B. Lynch, *Knuckles and gloves* (1922) • [F. Dowling], *Fights for the championship; and celebrated prize battles* (1855) • [F. Dowling], *Fistiana* (1868) • d. cert. • parish register, Redditch, Worcs. RO

Likenesses portrait (after photograph by Watkins), repro. in Miles, *Pugilistica*, vol. 3, facing p. 272

Paddon, George (*bap.* 1670, *d.* 1719), naval officer in the British and Russian service, though frequently, and erroneously, described as a colonial American, was in fact born and baptized in the Devon parish of Seaton and Beer. There is no record of his schooling, though it is likely that he came from a seafaring family with roots in Plymouth and Stepney, Middlesex. His lieutenant's passing certificate (December 1692) records that he had spent twelve years in merchant ships before he was pressed aboard the *Duke* in 1690, and that he was immediately advanced from able seaman to master's mate aboard the *Archangel*. After two brief Caribbean voyages aboard the *Vanguard* he gained a commission, having met the minimum requirement for a lieutenant of three years' sea service, including one in the Royal Navy.

After ten years of service, Paddon had the good fortune to serve on the *Lennox* with Captain William Jumper, who recommended him to Sir George Rooke. As Rooke's first lieutenant on the *Royal Sovereign* he gained his first commands, on the fireship *Vesuvius*, at Vigo Bay and on the 24-gun *Newport* at the battle of Malaga. He was promoted to captain on the *Vesuvius* in 1703, but lost her at Spithead during the great storm (November 1703) and was assigned another fireship, before taking command of the 32-gun frigate *Swallow's Prize*. He saw considerable action in the War of the Spanish Succession under admirals Shovell and Byng and he took part in actions at Barcelona, Tarragona, and Gibraltar. On convoy duty, he took prizes in the North Sea, in the channel, and on the New England station.

Commanding the 62-gun *Windsor* in 1711, Paddon built his combat reputation in one of the most dramatic single-ship engagements of the war, when he captured four prizes, including the 50-gun *Thetis*, in the West Indies. Yielding a rich cargo and the governor of St Domingue, Count Choiseul de Beaupré, Paddon took the ships to Boston where he encountered a fleet commanded by Admiral Hovenden Walker. Walker was transporting an expeditionary force commanded by Brigadier-General Jack Hill to the St Lawrence on a secretive expedition to seize Quebec before the close of the war. Immediately acknowledging Paddon's change in fortune and reputation, Walker made him his flag captain aboard the *Edgar*. The invasion proved a fiasco when over 900 men, several ships, and many supplies were lost in the St Lawrence. The misfortune was compounded, after the fleet returned to England, when the *Edgar* blew up in harbour, killing most of the crew while Walker and Paddon were ashore. Two years later Walker was called to account and dismissed from service.

Despite John Charnock's argument that Paddon suffered the same fate as Walker, he never faced a judicial inquiry. Indeed, he was given a combat assignment in 1713, when he took command of the *Ruby* and a squadron of six ships to deal with an incident in Morocco. He successfully disciplined Mulay Isma'il at Tetuan Bay and forced a new treaty. Charnock described his performance as a combination of 'the wariness of a politician happily united with the true gallant spirit of a British commander' (Charnock, 2.312–14). After his return the *Ruby* was laid up, her crew were paid off, and Paddon was placed on half pay. In 1715 he returned to Morocco on a mission for the southern department to supervise the fulfilment of the treaty, but at the same time he began to receive distressing signals of disfavour from the Admiralty, possibly because of tory sympathies. Charged with financial mismanagement on the *Vesuvius*, Paddon gave good account of himself, but chose to accept an offer to enter Russian service in 1717 as a rear-admiral.

Paddon's appointment was enmeshed in the diplomacy of the 'northern crisis' and was the subject of patents issued by George I and Peter the Great. The tsar desperately wanted a senior combat officer to command his fledgeling Baltic fleet, and he interviewed Paddon in the Netherlands.

Having met the tsar's approval, Paddon entered Russian service with a contract more generous than any other line officer of foreign origin. He took command of the fleet, during the summer of 1717, but died of influenza at St Petersburg on 1 January 1719, before he could employ the skills for which he had been hired. During his sojourn in Russia, he played a role in the formulation of the Russian naval regulation and offered proposals for other naval improvements. His candid evaluation of Russian naval developments is contained in a letter of 17 January 1718 to Josiah Burchette, in which he praised Russian shipbuilding but criticized Russian methods of manning their ships with officers and crew. He also observed the unpopularity of the navy and the foreigners it employed, writing that 'the great men of Russia, to a man, wish to see the fleet burnt' (PRO, ADM 1/2882). As the highest ranking officer of English origin Paddon was a spokesman for the national interest and was instrumental in the tsar's programme to replace the older Dutch-Scandinavian leadership with a newer English one. He actively recruited British officers, including William Cooper, keeper of naval stores at Plymouth, as a replacement for Vice-Admiral Cruys.

Admiral Paddon was interred with great ceremony in the cathedral of St Samson in St Petersburg, with the tsar marching over a mile in the procession. He was survived by his wife, Elizabeth, *née* Brown (*d.* 1726), who remained in St Petersburg and was granted 1000 roubles and a pension until her death on 14 February 1726. Their son, also George Paddon, a volunteer in the British navy and then a midshipman in the Russian navy, was commissioned as lieutenant in 1720, reached the rank of captain-commodore, and served as commandant of the Kronstadt naval base. A daughter married Captain John Little, who had served as Paddon's lieutenant on the *Ruby* and as a captain in Russia. They returned to England, where Little resumed service in the Royal Navy.

RICHARD H. WARNER

Sources R. H. Warner, 'Peter the Great's combat admiral: George Paddon', *Mariner's Mirror*, 75 (1989), 7–20 • V. N. Berkh, *Zhizneopisaniia pervikh rosisskikh admiralov* [Descriptions of the lives of the first Russian admirals], 1 (St Petersburg, 1831), 252–7 [descriptions of the lives of the first Russ. admirals] • J. Charnock, ed., *Biographia navalis*, 2 (1795), 312–14 • 'Paddon, Georg, kntr. admiral', *Russkii biograficheskii slovar'* [Russian biographical dictionary], ed. A. A. Polovtsov, 13 (1902), 110 • S. I. Elagin, ed., *Materialy dlia istoriia Russkago flota*, vols. 2 and 3 (1866) [materials for the study of the Russ. fleet] • captains' letters, PRO, ADM 1/2882 • lieutenants' passing certificates, PRO, ADM 107/1–267 • patent to George Paddon, PRO, SP 44/354/257 • *IGI* • *Arkhiv Kniazia F. A. Kurakina*, 2 (1892), 20–22 [The archive of Count F. A. Kurakin] • G. S. Graham, ed., *The Walker expedition to Quebec, 1711* (1953) • *Boston Newsletter* (May–June 1711)

Archives PRO, ADM 1/2882, 107/1–267; SP 44/354/257 • Russian Naval Archives, St Petersburg, Apraksin papers

Paddy the Cope. *See* Gallagher, Patrick (1870/71–1966).

Paddy, Sir William (1554–1634), physician, was born in Middlesex, the first of the two children of Roger and Margery Paddy, merchants. His brother, Nicholas, died in 1602. William was educated at the Merchant Taylors' School, London, from 15 January 1568 to 1570, then at St John's College, Oxford. After receiving his BA in July 1573, he travelled to the University of Leiden to study medicine and was awarded his MD on 21 July 1589. This was incorporated at Oxford on 22 October 1591. Shortly after receiving his MD Paddy returned to London and applied to the College of Physicians for a licence to practise physic. He was examined at the college on 23 December 1589 and unanimously approved for admission as a licentiate, and was sworn in on 8 May 1590. He became a fellow on 25 September 1591 and was a censor in 1595 and between 1597 and 1600; he became an elect in 1606, and was president of the college in 1609, 1610, 1611, and 1618. He became a consiliarius in 1624. Between 1596 and 1609 he was 'desector of Anathomies' to the Barber-Surgeons' Company.

From 1594 to 1602 Paddy was physician to William Cecil, Lord Burghley. In 1603 he wrote verses lamenting Queen Elizabeth's death, and praising her successor. James I knighted Paddy on 9 July 1603, and appointed him his personal physician. Paddy was summoned in March 1625, when James I became acutely ill. James died two days later, and Paddy recorded the king's last solemn profession of faith in his copy of the Book of Common Prayer, which is preserved in St John's College, Oxford. Paddy was MP for Thetford, Norfolk, from 1604 to 1611, and was a member of the privy council from 1609 to 1610. On 7 April 1620, with

Sir William Paddy (1554–1634), by Marcus Gheeraerts the younger, *c.*1600

his colleague and friend Thomas Gwinne and several merchants, grocers, and apothecaries, he was commissioned to set down ordinances, orders, and directions to regulate the quality and sale of tobacco.

As one of the most prominent physicians of his time, Paddy was a vocal proponent of learned medicine and firmly defended the privileges of the College of Physicians. In 1614 he was appointed to plead the immunity of the members of the college from bearing arms before the lord mayor, Sir Thomas Middleton, and the recorder, Sir Henry Montagu. He spoke before the court on 4 October, and pointed out the nature of the acts 14 and 32 Henry VIII, which set out the privileges of physicians. The recorder decided in favour of the claim of the college. Later that year Paddy and Edward Lister were sent to the bishop of London, John King, to plead for the suppression of Helkiah Crooke's treatise on anatomy. The physicians argued that parts of it were obscene and that no such work should be printed in English. Paddy and Lister succeeded in ensuring that the final two sections of the book were corrected by members of the college, and the work was published, as *Mikrokosmographia: a description of the body of man*, in 1615. In February of that year Paddy spoke against the proposals of Henry Atkins for the separation of the apothecaries' professional association from that of the grocers. When the midwives of London petitioned the king in 1615 for a charter for incorporation, regulation, and education, the College of Physicians was consulted, and Paddy proposed an alternative scheme. In May 1624 he again opposed innovations, this time by the surgeons, which potentially infringed the territory of the physicians. Though Paddy's medical ideas were thoroughly Galenic, his 1592 communications with Joannes Heurnius in Leiden show signs of a less rigid adherence to classical medical ideas.

Although Paddy did not publish anything in the field of medical politics, many of his friends and colleagues did. He supported Matthew Gwinne's attack on the chemical physician Francis Anthony, and contributed commendatory verses to Gwinne's *In assertorem chymicae, sed verae medicinae desertorem, Fra. Anthonium, Mattaei Gwynn adversaria* (1611), as he had earlier done for his play, *Vertumnus sive annus recurrens Oxonii …* (1607). Paddy also contributed verses to another work aimed against Anthony, Thomas Rawlin's *Admonitio pseudo-chymicis* (1610?). Many years before, Paddy had written in support of the *Sphaera civitatis* (1588) of the Aristotelian scholar John Case. In 1619, as president of the College of Physicians, Paddy drafted a preface for its pharmacopoeia. Paddy's power and prestige are signalled by the fact that Michael Maier's *Arcana arcanissima* (1614?), Robert Fludd's *Medicina catholica* (1629), and Raphael Thorius's *Hymnus tabaci* (1626) were all dedicated to him. Sir Theodore Turquet de Mayerne praised Paddy in the preface to his edition of Thomas Moffett's *Insectorum … theatrum* (1634). Paddy was also a friend of William Laud, and on one occasion defended him when he was ostracized after delivering an offensive sermon at Oxford.

Little is known about Paddy aside from his contributions to St John's College, Oxford, and the College of Physicians. However, it is recounted that at the age of fifty-five the eminent physician and one of his female patients were caught with their clothes off (Pady, 74). Paddy had a son, William (1600–1658), perhaps the product of a brief marriage. Paddy died in London on 3 December 1634, and was buried in the chapel of St John's College, Oxford. He left nearly everything to St John's College; this was in addition to his gift in 1602 of 1123 works in 682 volumes. His bequest included an organ, £1800 for the improvement of the choir, and £1000 towards the commons. After his father's death William Paddy travelled to America, where he became a prominent citizen in Plymouth and Boston.

LAUREN KASSELL

Sources annals, RCP Lond. • D. S. Pady, 'Sir William Paddy (1554–1634)', *Medical History*, 18 (1974), 68–82 • J. F. Fuggles, 'A history of the library of St John's College, Oxford', BLitt diss., U. Oxf., 1975 • Rymer, *Foedera*, 1st edn, vol. 17 • R. W. Innes Smith, *English-speaking students of medicine at the University of Leyden* (1932) • Foster, *Alum. Oxon.* • H. B. Wilson, *The history of Merchant-Taylors' School*, 2 (1814) [incl. Paddy's poem of 1603] • P. C. Molhuysen, ed., *Bronnen tot de geschiedenis der Leidsche Universiteit*, 1 (The Hague, 1913), 465 • court minute books of the Barber–Surgeons' Company, MSS 5257/2, fol. 60v, 5274/4, p.87 • *Correspondence of King James VI of Scotland with Sir Robert Cecil and others in England during the reign of Elizabeth*, ed. J. Bruce, CS, old ser., 78 (1861) • W. C. Costin, *The history of St John's College, Oxford, 1598–1860*, OHS, new ser., 12 (1958) • C. L. Clark, *History and genealogy of the Mayflower planters and first comers to ye olde colonies* (1941) • private information (2004) • *DNB* • will, proved, 10 Dec 1634, PRO, PROB 11/166, sig. 109

Likenesses M. Gheeraerts the younger, oils, *c.*1600, St John's College, Oxford [*see illus.*] • marble bust on monument, St John's College, Oxford • oils, St John's College, Oxford

Wealth at death exact sum unknown: administration, 1634, Pady, 'Sir William Paddy'

Padmore, George. *See* Nurse, Malcolm Ivan Meredith (1902–1959).

Padmore, Sir Thomas (1909–1996), civil servant, was born on 23 April 1909 at 193 Shirebrook Road, Sheffield, the elder son of Thomas William Padmore, steel merchant, and his wife, Emily, *née* Handley. Educated at the central secondary school, Sheffield, he won a scholarship to Queens' College, Cambridge, in 1928, graduating with first-class honours in French and German. After entering the civil service in the Inland Revenue in 1931 he was transferred to the Treasury in 1934 as having potential for high office. In the same year, on 22 December, he married Alice (*d.* 1963), daughter of Robert Alcock, of Ormskirk, Lancashire. They had three children—a son, John (*b.* 1937), and two daughters, Margaret (*b.* 1939) and Katharine (*b.* 1944).

In the Treasury, Padmore's advancement was rapid; an able administrator, and a powerful advocate in both speech and writing (though on his own admission less of an originator of policies), he was principal private secretary to the chancellor of the exchequer, Sir John Anderson, from 1943 to 1945. Very much the protégé of Sir Edward Bridges, then permanent secretary to the Treasury and head of the home civil service, Padmore was selected to succeed Sir Norman Brook as cabinet secretary when the latter moved to the Treasury on Bridges' expected retirement in 1952. But the change of government after the October 1951 general election led to the new prime minister, Winston Churchill, countermanding these moves, and Padmore (who had already moved to the Cabinet Office as deputy cabinet secretary) returned to the Treasury. He took this major check to his career philosophically, and was promoted second secretary (equal in rank to permanent secretary in other departments) in 1952. In 1953 he was made a KCB. Until 1962 he was for the most part in charge of personnel and management matters for the civil service. Though he was considered for the top posts of permanent secretary to the Treasury and head of the civil service, in the event these went elsewhere. During this period the death of his son in 1956 at the age of eighteen from a long-drawn-out cancer was a great grief to him and his wife.

In 1962 Padmore went to the Ministry of Transport as permanent secretary, doubtless glad to have his own department after ten years as no. 2 at the Treasury. The ministry had been substantially changed in the previous three years under Sir James Dunnett; the main lines of the motorway programme had been set in hand, and new policies for inland transport, particularly the railways, had also been developed and were the subject of legislation just enacted. While this had certainly raised the profile of the ministry it had created a good deal of turmoil among the senior staff, some of whose hopes had been set back in the new conditions. Padmore, with his long experience in staffing matters in the civil service, made it a main objective to try to assuage this; and he was the more able to devote himself to this as the principal lines of policy had already been laid down. This period of his career was beset by another personal loss in the death of his first wife, like their son from a lingering cancer, on 30 September 1963. On 1 May 1964 he married Rosalind Culhane (*d.* 1995), a former colleague as chief welfare adviser at the Treasury, and for some years a close friend.

The advent of the Labour government in 1964, with its not thoroughly worked out aspirations for co-ordination of the country's transport system, required a firm policy input from the top. Unfortunately Tom Fraser, the first minister of transport in Wilson's government, was a somewhat weak minister, unable to give the necessary lead. It is certainly a criticism of Padmore's leadership that he did not organize in the department the development of policies in line with the new government's aspirations, so as to allow the minister to put before his colleagues proposals with some prospect of cabinet approval. It was no surprise that in the first government reshuffle Fraser was replaced as minister by the much more dynamic Barbara Castle; and it is clear that, from the outset, she intended to replace Padmore as permanent secretary. There is contradictory evidence as to whether this was because he was thought to have opposed the government's co-ordination objectives, or because he was thought to have been more in favour of the motorway programme than of the development of public transport—neither of which opinions was well-founded—or because he was thought to have run out of steam, which might have had some justification. The minister's intention to dispose of Padmore was leaked to the press. His reaction was instant—he told her he would fight to stay, believing that it was hardly proper for ministers to try to change their permanent secretary in such a manner when they came into a department. Stay he did (though other posts were mooted for him they came to nothing) until after Castle had herself left the department, when he retired some months before he was due to go. It is fair to say, however, that in the last three years of his career in the Ministry of Transport he played a distinctly muted role as a formulator of policy.

Padmore had been promoted GCB in 1965. In retirement he took a number of directorships; he also continued his long-standing interest in music as chairman of the Handel Opera Society from 1963 until 1986. His second wife died on 4 March 1995; he himself died at his home, 39 Cholmeley Crescent, Highgate, London, on 8 February 1996. He was survived by the two daughters of his first marriage.

GEOFFREY WARDALE

Sources personal knowledge (2004) • private information (2004) • *The Castle diaries, 1964–1970* (1984) • P. Hennessy, *Whitehall* (1989) • *WWW* • Burke, *Peerage* • *The Times* (10 Feb 1996) • *The Independent* (17 Feb 1996) • b. cert. • d. cert.

Likenesses photograph, repro. in *The Times* • photograph, repro. in *The Independent*

Wealth at death £759,484: probate, 7 June 1996, *CGPLA Eng. & Wales*

Padua, John of (*fl.* **1543–1557**), architect and musician, was one of a number of foreign architects and craftsmen employed at the court of Henry VIII. He is first recorded in the exchequer accounts on 30 January 1544, when a fee of 2*s.* a day was paid 'in consideration of the good and faithful service which [he] has done and intends to do us in architecture and in other inventions in music' (Rymer, *Foedera*, 34). This grant ran from Easter 1543 and was renewed in 1549 and 1554. Although the exchequer invariably refers to him as an 'architect', John is described variously elsewhere as 'artificer', 'deviser', and 'engineer'. No work can be ascribed to him, although he must have been engaged in some form of architectural design, possibly ephemeral, and possibly in a number of mediums. The only evidence of his life outside the royal works is as executor of the will of a London-based Murano glassworker in 1551, where he was described as 'architect and servant of the king's majesty' (Colvin, 3.44). In 1557 he was provided with mourning cloth for the funeral of Henry, and his last annuity was paid in Michaelmas that year. His movements after this date are not known; however, the cancellation of his annuity in the early years of Elizabeth's reign, when he is described as a musician, was not recorded as due to his death.

DEBORAH GRAHAM-VERNON

Sources H. M. Colvin and others, eds., *The history of the king's works*, 3–4 (1975–82) • *DNB* • Rymer, *Foedera*, 1st edn, 15.34

Pagan, Isobel (**1741/2–1821**), poet, was a native of New Cumnock, Ayrshire, and passed her life mainly in the neighbourhood of Muirkirk in that county. Born with a deformed foot, she was abandoned early by her parents. In one of her poems she describes her education as 'ten weeks when I was seven years old'. However, she read in her spare time, especially the Bible.

A charitable landlord allowed Pagan to live rent-free in an old brick store in Muirkirk. In what was essentially a hovel, she sold whisky to both peasants and gentry and entertained them with her dramatic monologues and bawdy songs. Pagan reputedly had a beautiful singing voice, but she was habitually drunk and unashamedly sexually promiscuous. Her sarcasm was formidable. A clergyman once said she was 'the most perfect realisation of a witch or hag that I ever saw' (Blain, Clements & Grundy, *Feminist comp.*).

Since Pagan could not write, her poems were transcribed by her friend William Gemmell, a tailor. In 1805 her *Collection of Songs and Poems on Several Occasions* was published in Glasgow. Two songs attributed to her but not included in the *Collection*, 'Ca' the Yowes to the Knowes' and 'Crook and Plaid', demonstrate her lyrical abilities. Having heard 'Ca' the Yowes to the Knowes', Robert Burns created his own version by adding a verse of his own, but he did not acknowledge Pagan as the original source. Isobel Pagan died on 3 November 1821 in Muirkirk and was buried in Muirkirk churchyard.

T. W. BAYNE, *rev.* JANE POTTER

Sources Blain, Clements & Grundy, *Feminist comp.* • C. Kerrigan, ed., *An anthology of Scottish women poets* (1991) • C. Rogers, *The modern Scottish minstrel, or, The songs of Scotland of the past half-century*, 4 (1857) • I. Pagan, *Collection of songs and poems on several occasions* (1805) • J. Paterson, *The contemporaries of Burns and the more recent poets of Ayrshire* (1840) • R. Burns and others, *The Scots musical museum*, ed. J. Johnson, 6 vols. (1787–1803) • D. Gifford and D. McMillan, eds., *A history of Scottish women's writing* (1997) • K. A. Stewart, *Scottish women writers to 1987: a select guide and bibliography* (1987)

Pagan, James (1811–1870), newspaper editor and antiquary, the son of James Pagan and Elizabeth Blackstock, was born on 18 October 1811 at Trailflat, in the parish of Tinwald, near Dumfries, where his father was a bleacher. The family removed to Dumfries shortly after James's birth, and he received a sound education at Dumfries Academy. On leaving school he was apprenticed as a compositor in the office of the *Dumfries Courier*, and afterwards became a reporter for the paper. He soon left to become partner in a printing firm in London; but in 1839 he settled in Glasgow on the staff of the *Glasgow Herald*, and also edited a little broadsheet, the *Prospective Observer*. In 1841 Pagan married Ann, *née* McNight-Kerr, a native of Dumfries and a friend of Robert Burns's widow, Jean. They had three sons (two of whom died in infancy) and two daughters.

In 1856 Pagan was appointed successor to George Outram as editor of the *Glasgow Herald*, which he converted in January 1859 from a tri-weekly into a daily paper. He was also, from 1857, the correspondent of *The Times* in Glasgow. Under his editorship the *Herald* became one of the first provincial daily papers. Pagan greatly expanded coverage of local news, verbatim reporting of political and religious speeches, and news by telegraph. He was a shrewd, genial man, and a keen snuff taker (he used his snuff-box also as a store for shorthand notes).

Pagan was a devoted student of Glasgow's history and antiquities, and published *Sketches of the History of Glasgow* (1847), *History of the Cathedral and See of Glasgow* (1851), *Glasgow Past and Present; Illustrated in Dean of Guild Reports* (2 vols., 1851), *Old Glasgow and its Environs* (1864), and *Relics of Ancient Architecture and other Picturesque Scenes in Glasgow* (1885). Pagan died in Glasgow on 11 February 1870.

GEORGE STRONACH, *rev.* H. C. G. MATTHEW

Sources *In memoriam: Mr James Pagan, editor of the Glasgow Herald* (privately printed, Glasgow, 1870) • Boase, *Mod. Eng. biog.* • A. Phillips, *Glasgow's Herald, 1783–1983* (1982)

Wealth at death £5480 7*s.* 8*d.*: confirmation, 15 March 1870, NA Scot., SC 36/48/63/349–352

Paganell, Gervase. *See* Paynel, Gervase (*d.* 1194).

Page, Sir Archibald (1875–1949), engineer and electricity supply manager, was born at Alloa, Scotland, on 5 September 1875, the only son of John Page, wool merchant, and his second wife, Helen Ann McKillop. His general education was gained at Alloa School and Dollar Academy. After two years of technical training at the Heriot-Watt College, Edinburgh, he served a full apprenticeship in mechanical engineering and supplemented it by a period of electrical engineering with Mavor and Coulson, of Glasgow, who were among the British pioneers in the construction of electrical plant. Meanwhile he added to his theoretical knowledge by studies at the Glasgow and West of Scotland (later Royal) Technical College.

Recognizing the potentialities of electricity supply, he obtained, in 1899, a position as a mechanic in the Port Dundas generating station of the Glasgow corporation electricity department, and ultimately became deputy city electrical engineer. This early progress was due entirely to his sterling qualities as a man and as a practical engineer. He improved the efficiency of the existing generating stations and interconnected them; he installed new plant of, for those times, great capacity; and he planned the first major municipal power station at Dalmarnock. At about this time he became fully imbued with the principles of electricity supply development advocated by C. H. Merz, and he was thereafter invariably guided by them. He examined with meticulous care every plan for which he became responsible, and almost invariably suggested improvements. This faculty for constructive criticism had been developed in his purely engineering days, when he had to discuss details of plant with the most eminent manufacturing designers. In 1906 Page married Anne, daughter of John Forsyth, a merchant, of Clackmannan; they had one son and three daughters.

In 1917 Page joined the Clyde Valley Electric Power Company as deputy manager. Subsequently he became general manager. In that capacity he continued his policy of development on the basis of interconnection, and acquired a wider experience, in a more difficult territory, of the problems of transmission and distribution. When the Electricity (Supply) Act, 1919, was passed, he was an obvious choice as an electricity commissioner, but in 1925 he was called from this administrative appointment to the more specifically constructive post of director and general manager of the County of London Electric Supply Corporation. His period of office was marked by the construction of the Barking generating station (to become one of the largest thermo-electric stations in Europe) and of the associated high-voltage transmission system.

The formation of the Central Electricity Board in 1927 brought Page the final opportunity of his career. With Sir Andrew Rae Duncan as chairman, Page, as chief engineer and general manager, directed the construction of the 'grid' and the standardization of frequency of the national system. The enterprise was conducted with promptness and efficiency and Spartan economy, both in construction and in operation. The first scheme being that for central Scotland, Page's earlier experience was particularly valuable. The efficiency of the project was largely due to the personal example of Page, who was knighted in 1930 for his share in the work. In 1935 he succeeded Duncan as chairman of the board.

Page's career was planned from first to last, and he accomplished, so far as any individual can, all that he set out to do. He read omnivorously documents and publications essential to his duties and relating to electrical engineering; but his general reading was largely in the book of life. International and foreign electrical developments interested him to a minor degree, mainly enabling him to assess the relative efficiency of Britain and other countries. He was very British in his outlook, and his main business characteristics were objectivity, reliability, thoroughness, and an untiring energy. He was kind and helpful, and had an ironical sense of humour, which he exercised on rare occasions to great effect. Almost his only recreations were gardening and an occasional visit to a Rugby international. He loved Scotland, and spent each of his annual holidays in the Highlands.

In 1943 Page was awarded the Faraday medal of the Institution of Electrical Engineers, of which he became a member in 1909, and an honorary member in 1939, serving as president in 1927. He retired from the Central Electricity Board in 1944, although he continued to take a close interest in the industry and its personnel, until he died, worn out by excessive toil, on 7 March 1949, at his home, Haworth, 1 West Hill, Sanderstead, Surrey. His wife survived him. C. W. Marshall, *rev.*

Sources L. Hannah, *Electricity before nationalisation: a study in the development of the electricity supply industry in Britain to 1948* (1979) • private information (1959) • personal knowledge (1959)
Likenesses W. Stoneman, photograph, 1940, NPG • J. Gunn, portrait; in family possession, 1959
Wealth at death £32,614 1s. 8d.: confirmation, 18 May 1949, *CCI*

Page, Benjamin William (1765–1845), naval officer, was born at Ipswich, Suffolk, on 7 February 1765. He entered the navy in November 1778 under the patronage of Sir Edward Hughes, with whom he went out to the East Indies in the *Superb*, and in her was present in the first four actions with Suffren, the French commander. In December 1782 he was appointed acting lieutenant of the *Exeter*, and in her took part in the fifth action, on 20 June 1783. In August he was moved into the *Worcester*, in the following February to the sloop *Lizard*, and in September to the frigate *Eurydice*, in which he returned to England in July 1785. His commission as lieutenant was then confirmed, dating from 20 November 1784. From 1786 to 1790 he was on the Jamaica station in the frigate *Astraea*, commanded by Captain Peter Rainier, whom he followed to the *Monarch* in the channel for a few months during the Spanish armament. In December 1790 he was appointed to the *Minerva*, in which he went out to the East Indies; in August he was transferred to the *Crown*, and in her returned to England in July 1792. In January 1793 he was appointed to the *Suffolk*, again with Rainier, and in the spring of 1794 went out in her to the East Indies. In September Rainier promoted him to command the sloop *Hobart*, a promotion afterwards confirmed, but to date only from 12 April 1796.

In consequence of Page's long acquaintance with eastern seas, he was ordered, in January 1796, to pilot the squadron through the intricate passages leading to the Moluccas, which were taken possession of without resistance, and proved a very rich prize, each of the captains present receiving, it was said, £15,000. Unfortunately for Page, some important dispatches were found on a Dutch brig which was taken on the way, and the *Hobart* was sent with them to Calcutta. Page was thus absent when Amboyna, in the Dutch East Indies, was captured, and did not share in the prize money. In December 1796 he convoyed the China trade from Penang to Bombay City with success, for which he was specially thanked by the government, and by the merchants, who presented him with 500 guineas. In February 1797 he was appointed acting captain of the frigate *Orpheus* (32 guns), but a few months later he received his post rank from the Admiralty, dated 22 December 1796, and was ordered to return to England. In January 1800 he was appointed to the *Inflexible* (64 guns), which, without her lower-deck guns, was employed during the next two years on transport service in the Mediterranean. She was paid off in March 1802, and in November Page commissioned the frigate *Caroline* (36 guns), in which, in the following summer, he went to the East Indies, where he captured several privateers, and especially two in the Bay of Bengal, for which the merchants of Bombay and Madras each voted him a present of 500 guineas. In February 1805 he was transferred to the *Trident*, as flag captain to Vice-Admiral Rainier, with whom he returned to England in October. In 1809 to 1810 Page commanded the sea-fencibles of the Harwich district, and from 1812 to 1815 the *Puissant* (74 guns), guardship at Spithead.

Page had no further service afloat, but became, in course of seniority, rear-admiral on 12 August 1819, vice-admiral on 22 July 1830, and admiral on 23 August 1841. He had married Elizabeth (*d.* 1834), only child of John Herbert of Totnes in Devon; they had no children. During his retirement he lived principally at Ipswich, and he died there on 3 October 1845. He left the Ipswich corporation a collection of marine paintings.

J. K. Laughton, *rev.* Andrew Lambert

Sources C. N. Parkinson, *War in the eastern seas, 1793–1815* (1954) • O'Byrne, *Naval biog. dict.* • J. Marshall, *Royal naval biography*, 1/2 (1823), 767–9 • J. Ralfe, *The naval biography of Great Britain*, 4 (1828) • *GM*, 2nd ser., 24 (1845), 533
Archives NMM, papers, incl. relating to courts martial • Suffolk RO, Ipswich, travel journal | BL, Merrick Shawe corresp., Add. MS 13753 • BL, letters to Earl Spencer • NMM, Spencer MSS

Page [*née* Aderson, Addersell; *married name* Dry], **Damaris** (*c.*1610–1669), bawd and brothel keeper, was the daughter of one John Aderson (Addersell). Little is known about her private life. She was from an early date publicly known as Damaris Page, but how she acquired that surname is obscure. She was married on 18 April 1653 at St Mary Magdalen, Bermondsey, to James Dry. Two years later, when she was indicted and tried for bigamy, it was alleged that since 1640 she had also been married to one William Baker of Stepney. But it is probable that this was a trumped-up charge, for there is no record of the marriage in the relevant parish register, and she was found not guilty by a jury at Middlesex quarter sessions. James Dry predeceased her and she did not marry again. Towards the end of her life she remained close to her sister Margaret, a widow, to whom she bequeathed an annuity of £10.

Damaris Page made her fortune as one of the most successful bawds in the east end of London, catering especially to its large seafaring population. By the 1650s she was able to diversify into property speculation, building several houses on Ratcliffe Highway which provided her with a steady income for the remainder of her life. Page herself never learned to write, but at the Restoration in 1660 her public notoriety was reflected and fuelled by a series of Grub Street pamphlets that used her name to peddle fictitious accounts of metropolitan prostitution, beginning with John Garfield's serialized *The Wandring Whore*, in each episode of which she was made to head the list of 'Crafty Bawds'.

The restored monarchy's massive expansion of the navy in the mid-1660s brought Page further success and a new association with the highest circles of government. The naval high command was desperate for sailors, and she proved adept at recruiting them through her trade. But the connection was unpopular as well as profitable. On Easter Monday 1668 hers was the first house to be targeted in the great bawdy house riots that swept across the capital in protest at the government's repressive religious policies. The tradition of Shrove Tuesday apprentice riots against brothels was appropriated to contrast the regime's laxness in policing morals with its severity in persecuting dissenters. 'Some blood hath been spilt', reported Samuel Pepys a few days later, 'but a great many houses pulled down; and among others, the Duke of York was mighty merry at that of Damaris Page's, the great bawd of the seamen' (Pepys, *Diary*, 9.132). In the propaganda war that accompanied and followed the demonstrations Page's name was again used to attract publicity to scurrilous writings, this time in a satirical 'petition' on behalf of all the whores and bawds of London to their supposed leader, the king's own whore, the countess of Castlemaine, and in the supposed replies by Lady Castlemaine to this. But the riots did not interrupt business for long, and her bawdy house, the Three Tuns in Stepney, was soon resurrected. Barely a year later, in June 1669, the duke of York, the lord high admiral, was no doubt delighted to learn that Sir Edward Spragge, who was about to sail to the Mediterranean,

> was the day before at Damaris Page's, the most famous bawd in town, and there had made so much of her that she had already furnished him with about forty seamen to man his ship the *Revenge*, and that she would do more.

'As long as Damaris Page lived', Spragge told Pepys publicly, 'he was sure he should not lack men' (*Samuel Pepys and the Second Dutch War*, 216–17). A few months later, while in the Marshalsea prison, she fell ill and died on 9 October. She was buried the following day at St George the Martyr, Southwark. FARAMERZ DABHOIWALA

Sources will, PRO, PROB 11/331, sig. 139 · Middlesex Sessions Roll, Oct 1655, LMA, MJ/SR/1142, membrane 19 · parish register, St George, Southwark, 10 Oct 1669, LMA, P92/GEO/141, fol. 86v · *The life and death of Damaris Page* (1669) · Pepys, *Diary* · *Samuel Pepys and the Second Dutch War: Pepys's navy white book and Brooke House papers*, ed. R. Latham, Navy RS, 133 (1995) [transcribed by W. Matthews and C. Knighton] · *The poor-whores petition: to the most splendid, illustrious, serene and eminent lady of pleasure, the countess of Castlemayne* (1668) · 'The most gracious answer of dame Barbara countesse of C. to the peticon of undone, poore, & distressed company of whoores. &c.', 1668, BL, Don MS b. 8, 190–193 · *The gracious answer of the most illustrious lady of pleasure, the countess of Castlem— to the poor-whores petition* (1668) · [J. Garfield?], *The wandring whore*, 5 pts (1660–61) · *A strange and true conference between two notorious bawds, Damarose Page and Pris. Fotheringham, during their imprisonment and lying together in Newgate* (1660) · E. Theodidactus [J. Heydon], *The ladies champion confounding the author of 'The Wandring Whore'* (1660) · T. Harris, *London crowds in the reign of Charles II* (1987)

Page, David (1814–1879), geologist and author, was born on 24 August 1814 at Plantation Street, Lochgelly, Fife, the son of a mason, builder, and contractor. Educated at the parish school, he entered the University of St Andrews in 1828 to study for the ministry in the Church of Scotland. He pursued a literary career upon leaving St Andrews in 1834, although he remained a lifelong adherent of the moderate party in the church. He lectured, edited, and wrote for the newspapers, publishing a geological essay on Fife and Kinross in 1834 and a volume of poems in 1838. His switch of allegiance from the liberal whig *Fife Herald* to the tory *Fifeshire Journal* led to Page's being known as the 'Judas' editor and 'a literary prostitute' (Campbell, chap. 6). In 1843, on 16 October, he married Annzella Maria Wetier, daughter of Thomas Snooks, a captain in the Fifeshire militia.

From 1843 until 1851 the Edinburgh publisher W. and R. Chambers employed Page to contribute to its ambitious programme of popular education. The anonymous *Rudiments of Geology* (1844) was the first of Page's hugely successful series of geological primers. In the course of his work for the firm, he was told the great secret of Robert Chambers' authorship of the anonymous *Vestiges of the Natural History of Creation* (1844), and he corrected scientific mistakes in early editions of this evolutionary best-seller. Page was willing to consider creation through secondary causes, as long as this was subsidiary to the divine plan. Enraged by 'the moral cowardice that shrinks from avowing its paternity' (Page, 209), he exposed Chambers as the *Vestiges* author in 1854, although many continued to attribute the work to others.

By this time Page had left his position after a bitter disagreement about terms of employment. He returned to journalism and rewrote his textbooks, which henceforth appeared under his own name as *Introductory Text-Book of Geology* (1854, 11th edn, 1877) and *Advanced Text-Book of Geology* (1856, 5th edn, 1872). From the late 1850s a torrent of geological titles appeared from his pen, usually brief and often repetitive: among the most important were a *Handbook of Geological Terms* (2nd edn, 1865); *The Earth's Crust* (1864, 6th edn, 1872); and *Geology for General Readers* (1866, 12th edn, 1888). His books on physical geography were equally successful.

Although Page presented over a dozen research papers to scientific societies, his reputation as a prolific writer led to accusations of book-making. As the *Athenaeum* (12 June 1869, 801) said in reviewing *Chips and Chapters*, 'It is the business of working geologists to make Chips, as it seems to be that of Dr. Page to make Chapters'. Readers, however, appreciated Page's flair for clarity and logical organization, and his writings introduced a generation to the fundamentals of a rapidly developing and controversial science. He also became a popular lecturer, and in 1871 moved from Edinburgh to Newcastle upon Tyne to take up an appointment as professor of geology and mineralogy at the Durham University College of Physical Science.

Page had two sons and a daughter. He died on 9 March 1879 at his home, 6 Pleasant Row, Newcastle, from a paralysis which had been in progress for several years. His widow was granted a civil-list pension of £100 in 1890.

J. A. Secord

Sources *Nature*, 19 (1878–9), 444 • H. C. Sorby, *Quarterly Journal of the Geological Society*, 36 (1880), 39–40 • *Transactions of the Geological Society of Glasgow*, 6 (1876–80), 182–5 • D. Page, *The past and present life of the globe* (1861) • J. A. Secord, *Victorian sensation: the extraordinary publication, reception, and secret authorship of 'Vestiges of the natural history of creation'* (2000) • *Transactions of the Geological Society of Edinburgh*, 3 (1880), 220–21 • [J. R. Leifchild], review of Page's *Chips and chapters*, *The Athenaeum* (12 June 1869), 801 • A. J. Campbell, 'Cupar: the years of controversy: a study of the newspaper press, 1822–1872', U. St Andr. L., chap. 6 • m. reg. Scot. • d. cert.
Archives NL Scot., corresp. with *Blackwood's* and receipts
Likenesses photograph, *c.*1845, Royal Scottish Museum, Edinburgh
Wealth at death under £1500: probate, 2 Aug 1879, *CGPLA Eng. & Wales*

Page, Sir Denys Lionel (1908–1978), classical scholar, was born in Reading on 11 May 1908, the third in the family of five children (three boys and two girls) of Frederick Harold Dunn Page, a chartered civil engineer in the Great Western Railway, and his wife, Elsie Daniels. He was educated at Newbury grammar school, and in 1926 won a scholarship to Christ Church, Oxford. He benefited much from the teaching of Gilbert Murray, and received special coaching from J. D. Denniston, who became a close friend. In 1928 Page was Craven and De Paravicini scholar, and won the Chancellor's prize for Latin verse and the Gaisford prize for Greek verse. He obtained first classes both in classical moderations (1928) and *literae humaniores* (1930). One of his closest Christ Church friends was Quintin Hogg, later Lord Hailsham of St Marylebone. Page did not confine himself to the classics but earned his place in the Christ Church cricket team as a terrifying fast bowler. Next he went as Derby scholar to the University of Vienna, where he spent a year working under Ludwig Radermacher. In 1931 he became a lecturer at Christ Church, and the next year student and tutor of the House. He quickly made his mark as tutor and lecturer, and was highly congenial to his pupils and his colleagues. In 1937 he became junior censor, but a year later resigned the office to marry Katharine Elizabeth (*d.* 1978), daughter of Joseph Michael Dohan, of Philadelphia, Pennsylvania. Their married life was singularly happy, and they had four daughters.

In 1934 Page published a study of *Actors' interpolations in Greek tragedy, with special reference to Euripides' 'Iphigeneia in Aulis'*. His close acquaintance with the texts and keen critical intelligence were immediately apparent, and the book received high praise. In 1938 he brought out a text of Euripides' *Medea* with introduction and commentary, which made a striking contribution to the understanding of the play, not seriously marred by youthful dogmatism. At this time Page was making a close study of the early Greek lyric poets, whose remains had been notably increased by new papyrus discoveries. Most current texts of them were disfigured by rash supplements and conjectures, but Edgar Lobel in his editions of Sappho (1925) and Alcaeus (1927) had set new standards of accuracy and learning, and Page followed in his tracks. The Loeb Classical Library asked him to edit and translate all the fragments of Greek poetry on papyrus not included in the volumes devoted to individual authors, and the resulting volume of *Greek Literary Papyri* (1942) was a masterly performance which proved Page to be a scholar of the first order.

During the Second World War Page served in the Government Code and Cypher School located at Bletchley Park which dealt with the branch of intelligence known as Ultra. He was assigned to the section which under the direction of Oliver Strachey dealt with the various hand ciphers used by Britain's enemies, and was so successful that when Strachey retired in 1942 he was chosen to succeed him. After the war he headed for a year a special command mission to the headquarters of Viscount Mountbatten of Burma, first at Kandy and then at Singapore.

Page resumed his teaching and research with all his usual vigour, serving as senior proctor in 1948–9. But in 1950 he was elected to the regius chair of Greek in Cambridge, and to a professorial fellowship at Trinity College. Classical studies in Cambridge at that time were by no means as lively as in Oxford, where the presence of learned refugees from Germany, the work of Sir John Beazley and other distinguished scholars, and the publication of the papyri were having an exhilarating effect. But Page by his outstanding lecturing and his influence upon colleagues and pupils had from the first a powerful effect. He was also highly congenial to his Trinity colleagues, and was soon elected to the college council.

Page's long and intensive study of early Greek lyric now bore fruit in a series of important publications. In 1951 appeared a book on Alcman's 'Louvre Partheneion', in 1953 an edition of Corinna, with commentary, and in 1955 *Lesbiorum poetarum fragmenta*, in which Page added the texts published since Lobel's editions of the twenties to Lobel's work, and a book called *Sappho and Alcaeus*, which included commentaries on the more substantial fragments and discussions of various problems which the poems raised. Page took over from Lobel a somewhat austere editorial technique, but the texts are edited in masterly fashion; the commentaries are no less admirable, though the treatment of purely literary questions leaves something to be desired.

Page's book *The Homeric Odyssey* (1955) was based on Flexner lectures given at Bryn Mawr (1954) and his *History and the Homeric Iliad* (1959) on Sather lectures given at Berkeley

(1957–8). Both books show mastery of the relevant material, including archaeological data, the newly deciphered Linear B tablets, and oriental evidence thought to be relevant to the poems, and both are written with great clarity and elegance. But they are marked by a displeasing dogmatism, accentuated by the rhetorical manner in which the argument is presented, and the assumption of multiple authorship is too readily used to account for features of the poems which might be explained by other considerations.

Denniston had prepared a small-scale edition of the *Agamemnon* of Aeschylus, with commentary, which he had intended to revise in the light of the long-awaited *Agamemnon* of Eduard Fraenkel. But he died in 1949, a year before Fraenkel's edition appeared, and it was left to Page to prepare the work for publication (1957). Perhaps Page was too eager to differ from Fraenkel, but the work has great value and did good service in showing that the vastly learned editor was not infallible. The weakest part was the introduction, whose confident assumption that the poet's outlook and technique were crude and primitive has not gone unchallenged.

During the late fifties Page's life was complicated by his wife's serious illness; but in 1959 his domestic difficulties were alleviated by his election to be master of Jesus College, Cambridge. His wife's health improved, and his great energy enabled him to discharge the duties of his new office without reducing his production of learned work. In 1962 he published *Poetae melici Graeci*, a critical edition of the Greek lyric poets other than the Lesbians, in 1968 a minor edition of these poets called *Lyrica Graeca selecta*, and in 1974 a supplement including newly published material with the title *Supplementum lyricis Graecis*. All these works are of a high order.

In 1965 Page contributed the edition of Meleager to the two-volume work *The Greek Anthology: Hellenistic Epigrams* which was otherwise the work of his Trinity colleague A. S. F. Gow, and when in 1968 the same two editors brought out the two volumes of *The Greek Anthology: the Garland of Philip, and some Contemporary Epigrams* Gow was responsible for Antipater of Thessalonica, but Page for all the other poets; in 1975 Page published a minor edition of many of the poems contained in these collections with the title *Epigrammata Graeca*. His last book, *The Epigrams of Rufinus*, appeared in 1978, just before his death, and a further volume containing all epigrams not included in the other volumes down to the year AD 50 was published posthumously. These books constitute a major contribution to the study of Hellenistic poetry.

In 1972 Page published a new Oxford Text of Aeschylus, using and supplementing the work on the manuscripts of his former pupil R. D. Dawe; it is undoubtedly an improvement on all previous editions of this author. A full bibliography of his writings may be found in the volume *Dionysiaca: nine studies in Greek poetry by former pupils, presented to Sir Denys Page on his seventieth birthday* (1978).

Many people regretted that Page was denied, almost certainly on grounds of his political Conservatism, the office of vice-chancellor, which he would certainly have filled with great distinction; he was an effective president of the British Academy from 1971 to 1974. In 1973 his wife's ill health obliged him to resign the offices of master and professor and to retire to his house, Thorneyburn Lodge, Tarset, near Hexham in Northumberland, where he continued to work without remission. He died at home on 6 July 1978, and his wife survived him by only a few weeks.

In the work of editing and explaining the Greek poets Page's achievement is very great; he combined intimate knowledge of the texts, mastery of grammar, syntax, and metre, and much skill in the reading of papyri with keen critical acumen. He was weaker in literary appreciation, and his tendency to see things and people in strong black and white made it hard for him to do justice to the complexity of life. He was for several years not on speaking terms with E. R. Dodds, of whose appointment to the regius chair in Oxford he deeply disapproved, and, after early friendship, he became estranged from Sir Maurice Bowra, for whose scholarship he had little regard. But he was always ready to help pupils or colleagues, and his charm and gaiety delighted most of those who met him. His place in the history of Greek scholarship is assured.

Page was knighted in 1971. He was elected fellow of the British Academy in 1952, and received its Kenyon medal in 1969; he was a corresponding member of the Academy of Athens, the American Academy of Arts and Sciences, the American Philosophical Society, and the Greek Humanistic Society. He was a doctor of letters of Cambridge (1960), and held honorary doctorates from Oxford (1972), Trinity College, Dublin, and the universities of Newcastle, Hull, and Bristol. He was an honorary fellow of Trinity and Jesus colleges and an honorary student of Christ Church.

HUGH LLOYD-JONES, *rev.*

Sources H. Lloyd-Jones, 'Denys Lionel Page, 1908–1978', *PBA*, 65 (1979), 759–69 [repr. in H. Lloyd-Jones, *Blood for the ghosts: classical influences in the nineteenth and twentieth centuries* (1982), 295–304] • personal knowledge (1986) • private information (1986)

Likenesses P. Gaskell, photograph, repro. in Lloyd-Jones, 'Denys Lionel Page', facing p. 759

Wealth at death £88,711: probate, 24 Aug 1978, *CGPLA Eng. & Wales*

Page, Sir Francis (1660/61?–1741), judge, probably was born at the end of 1660 or in 1661, the second son of Nicholas Page (*d.* 1696), a country parson whose parish was Bloxham in Oxfordshire. He was admitted to the Inner Temple in June 1685 and called to the bar in June 1690. On 18 December of that year he married Isabella White of Greenwich, Kent; after her death he married, on 11 October 1705, Frances (*c.*1689–1730), the daughter of Sir Thomas Wheate, first baronet, of Glympton, Oxfordshire. By neither marriage were there any children.

Having begun his legal training somewhat later than was customary Page's career at the bar was slow to develop. Although his whiggish views were said to have prompted him to pen several political pamphlets in his early days as a barrister he came to wider public notice in 1705 as one of four lawyers engaged by Thomas Wharton,

Sir Francis Page (1660/61?–1741), by George Vertue, 1733 (after Jonathan Richardson)

fifth Baron Wharton, on behalf of the 'men of Aylesbury' in the celebrated case of *Ashby* v. *White*, which bore upon the crucial question of whether the House of Commons or the courts of law (and ultimately the House of Lords as the highest appellate authority) had the power to determine the right to vote. The Commons had committed the Aylesbury men to Newgate for having brought proceedings against the local returning officer who had refused their votes, and in February 1705 Page and the other counsel presented their plea in queen's bench for a grant of habeas corpus. The Commons responded by declaring him and his colleagues guilty of a breach of privilege and immediately ordered them into the custody of the serjeant-at-arms. Though granted protection by the House of Lords, Page went into hiding until parliament was prorogued in April.

Page was himself elected to parliament, for Huntingdon in 1708, through the offices of one of his clients, Edward Montagu, third earl of Sandwich, who controlled the borough seat, and he remained an MP until 1713. He featured moderately in proceedings but was not an active spokesman for the whigs, his professional obligations sometimes requiring absences from parliament. In May 1713 he was elected a bencher at the Inner Temple. Having failed to make any headway in his career during the tory administration of Robert Harley, first earl of Oxford, he received rapid promotion from the whigs in the early years of George I's reign. By 28 November 1714 he had been made a serjeant-at-law, he was knighted on 21 January 1715, and a week later he was appointed king's serjeant, a rare distinction which gave him superiority over barristers who were king's counsel. During 1715–16 he served on a special commission for the trial of Jacobite rebels in Lancashire, and on another for investigating the outbreaks of rebellious behaviour in Oxfordshire.

In May 1718 Page was raised to the judicial bench as a baron of the exchequer. His integrity as a judge came under the scrutiny of the House of Commons in 1722, when it was complained that he had acted with corrupt intent in the political affairs of Banbury. The profits of his law practice had enabled him in 1714 to purchase the manor of Middle Aston, in Oxfordshire, which he had consolidated with further acquisitions of land. The borough of Banbury lying nearby, he became involved with the corporation's whig faction, so much so that in 1722, with a general election rapidly approaching, he offered to fund improvements in the town to the tune of £1200 if the corporation would elect a whig of his choosing, Sir William Codrington. A hearing in the Commons on 13 and 14 February ended with a division in which Page was exonerated by a mere four votes.

The following year, however, 'Baron Page' had the opportunity of showing himself a true pillar of the whig establishment when it found itself under attack. With deer-stealers at large in Berkshire and Hampshire he took the opportunity, at Winchester assizes in January 1723, to supplement the reading of a proclamation against the 'blacks' with his own strict charge against them; and in June he presided over the special commission of oyer and terminer at Reading, a showcase event at which four death sentences and six transportation sentences were meted out over three days to men who had caused menace in Windsor Forest.

In November 1726 Page was promoted judge in the court of common pleas, and in September 1727 was transferred to king's bench. He has often been branded one of the most brutal judges of the Walpolean era, who with a reputation as 'the hanging judge' exemplified the worst excesses of the eighteenth-century judiciary. These verdicts must be treated with a degree of caution, however, and Page may have been no worse or no better than any other occupant of the bench. A nineteenth-century authority on the lives of the judges, Edward Foss, observed that the few reported trials over which Page presided did not appear to warrant his ill fame but concluded that it was unlikely that he would have been so reviled by leading eighteenth-century men of letters had there been no justification. It was Page's misfortune, however, to have made a particular enemy of the literati of his time through his treatment of the poet Richard Savage, who was tried before him for murder in 1727. Two of Savage's literary friends, Alexander Pope and Samuel Johnson, in addition to Savage himself, subsequently denounced Page in their work in a way destined to ensure his distinctive notoriety. The account of the trial by Johnson in his *Life of Savage* (1744) reports verbatim the roaring manner in which Page was supposed to have blatantly misrepresented Savage's defence and incited the jury against him.

Pope's *Imitations of Horace* (satire 1), published in 1733, contained the couplet:

Slander or poison dread from Delia's rage,
Hard words or hanging if your judge be Page
(ll. 81–2)

which was said to have provoked Page to fury. After Page's death Pope's fourth book of *The Dunciad* (1742) included an allusion to him that was damningly footnoted with a declaration that 'there was a judge of this name, always ready to hang any man that came his way, of which he was suffered to give a hundred miserable examples during a long life' (Thompson, 211). There is at least one occasion on record, however, when Page and Pope dined together amicably. Henry Fielding had had the opportunity of seeing Page presiding at the summer assizes at Salisbury in 1739, and in his novel *Tom Jones* (1749) described the trial of a horse-stealer that he had witnessed on that occasion (book 8, chap. 11). Fielding drew on and embellished Page's 'literary' persona to epitomize the workings of judicial terror, and the judge is seen coarsely haranguing the defendant, denying his counsel a hearing, and condemning the man to death. At the original trial that Fielding had seen Page had in fact acquitted the prisoner.

Page continued to sit as a judge in king's bench until his death, apparently at the age of eighty. There is a story, the provenance of which is uncertain, but quoted by the *Dictionary of National Biography*, that towards the end of his life, as he shuffled unsteadily one day away from court, an acquaintance enquired after his health. 'My dear sir,' came the reply, 'you see, I keep *hanging* on, *hanging* on'. He died at Middle Aston on 19 December 1741 and was buried on 29 December at Steeple Aston church, near his country seat close to a huge and ornate monument with full-length reclining figures of himself and his second wife that he had commissioned during his lifetime from the Flemish sculptor Peter Scheemakers. A. A. Hanham

Sources 'Page, Francis', HoP, *Commons*, 1690–1715 [draft] · C. C. Brookes, *History of Steeple Aston and Middle Aston* (1929), 216–31 · Foss, *Judges*, 8.143–6 · Baker, *Serjeants* · Sainty, *King's counsel*, 24 · Sainty, *Judges*, 36, 80, 128 · E. P. Thompson, *Whigs and hunters* (1975), 146, 211, 233 · J. H. Plumb, *Sir Robert Walpole*, 1 (1956), 371–3

Likenesses G. Vertue, line engraving, pubd 1720 (after J. D'Agar), BM, NPG · P. Scheemakers, double portrait, tomb effigy, *c*.1730–1741 (with his wife), St Peter's Church, Steeple Aston, Oxfordshire · G. Vertue, line engraving, 1733 (after J. Richardson), BM, NPG [*see illus.*] · oils, Inner Temple, London

Page, Frederick (1769–1834), writer on the poor laws, was born in Newbury, Berkshire, the son of Francis Page. He matriculated at Oriel College, Oxford, on 14 July 1786 but left the university without taking a degree. Called to the bar at the Inner Temple in 1792, he became a bencher in 1826. A substantial landowner, he was also interested in the development of the navigation of the River Thames and a major shareholder in the Kennet and Avon Canal Company.

Page's attention was first drawn to the poor laws by the manner in which the poor rate affected his own property. Having been assessed to the value of the whole amount of the tolls for the navigation of the Kennet between Reading and Newbury, which were collected by his agent, he appealed to the Berkshire quarter sessions, where the rate was confirmed. The case was later tried in the court of the king's bench in 1792, where the result was upheld.

Between 1794 and 1818 Page served as an overseer in three separate parishes of Berkshire and later he became a magistrate and then deputy lieutenant for the county of Berkshire. His practical experience of administering relief in the difficult year of 1795 was communicated to his friend Sir F. M. Eden, who included it in his *The State of the Poor*, of 1797 (Eden, 1.576–87). This account highlighted the difficulties which arose from the practice of subsidizing the wages of labourers in line with the price of bread adopted by the famous meeting of Berkshire magistrates at Speenhamland that year. This mode of relief, Page argued, encouraged idleness in the labourer by removing the necessity of finding additional sources of income and also produced a perverse effect upon the labour market by allowing farmers to retain labourers at less than the market rate, passing their costs on to the community as a whole.

Page continued to study the influence of the poor laws and became an active participant in the debates leading up to their eventual reform in 1834. He favoured an improved organization of the existing model of the poor law through such means as the Select Vestries Act which facilitated a growing professionalism in pauper management, and retained the belief that local administration provided the most effective model for judicious and economical relief. In opposition to the more radical critics of the poor law, including Malthus, Page defended its moral basis and its practical efficacy in comparison to other systems. To this end he engaged in historical and comparative researches into the principles of relief, travelling to Ireland and more widely in continental Europe, and published two works which set out his comprehensive views on the subject: *The Principles of the English Poor Laws Illustrated and Defended* (1822), and *Observations on the State of the Indigent Poor in Ireland* (1830). Page died at Newbury on 8 April 1834. In his will he named among the beneficiaries his wife, Sarah. R. D. Sheldon

Sources F. Page, *The principles of the English poor laws illustrated and defended* (1822) · F. Page, *Observations on the state of the indigent poor in Ireland* (1830) · Foster, *Alum. Oxon.* · F. M. Eden, *The state of the poor*, 3 vols. (1797) · M. Neuman, *The Speenhamland county: poverty and the poor laws in Berkshire, 1782–1834* (1982) · *GM*, 2nd ser., 1 (1834) · will, PRO, PROB 11/1830

Wealth at death over £10,000 assets; plus large landholdings in Berkshire and shares in the Kennet and Avon Canal Company: will, PRO, PROB 11/1830

Page, Sir Frederick Handley (1885–1962), aircraft designer and manufacturer, was born on 15 November 1885 at 141 Cranham Villa, Cheltenham, the second child in a family of four sons and one daughter of Frederick Joseph Page, master upholsterer and an active member of the Plymouth Brethren sect, and his wife, Eliza Ann Handley. He was educated at Cheltenham grammar school until 1902 and at Finsbury Technical College for a three-year course in electrical engineering under Professor Silvanus Thompson. In 1906 he was appointed chief electrical designer at the engineering firm of Johnson and Phillips Ltd at Charlton. He joined the Aeronautical Society in 1907, and helped José Weiss to construct an automatically stable aeroplane.

In 1908 Handley Page was dismissed by his employers, who were displeased with his aviation experiments on their premises. He set up in business himself, determined to construct aeroplanes. He was not a wealthy man or a skilful pilot but in 1909 he moved to Barking, where he established Handley Page Ltd, the first British company registered specifically to manufacture aeroplanes. To earn extra money he did some evening teaching at Finsbury Technical College and then, in 1911, joined the Northampton Polytechnic Institute (later Northampton Engineering College and then the City University) at Clerkenwell as lecturer in aeronautics under Dr Mullineux Walmsley. He installed there a wind tunnel, thereby combining practical course work with investigation of design problems at Barking. His first passenger-carrying monoplane flew across London in July 1911, and the following year another two-seater competed in military trials on Salisbury Plain. In 1913 he moved to Cricklewood and his first biplane was demonstrated at Hendon during the following year. When Murray Sueter at the Admiralty demanded a 'bloody paralyser' to halt the German advance into Belgium, Handley Page produced a large twin-engined bomber for the Royal Naval Air Service, followed in 1918 by a still larger four-engined machine to bomb Berlin, one of each type being the first aeroplanes to fly from England to India. By the end of the war the name Handley Page had become identified with big bombers. Handley Page was appointed CBE in 1918, and in May of that year he married Una Helen (*d.* 1957), daughter of John Robert Thynne at St George's, Hanover Square, London; they had three daughters.

In 1919 Handley Page Transport Ltd was founded to promote a civil air service to the continent. This company, with three others, formed Imperial Airways in 1924. The aircraft manufacturing side of the business incurred massive losses and for a while Handley Page lost control of his company which was run, until 1924, by a chairman appointed by his creditors. From 1924 until rearmament began in 1936 Handley Page Ltd was not very profitable. Graceful airliners were produced for Imperial Airways, but orders were too few to guarantee large profits. It was fortunate that Handley Page had, in 1919, patented the slotted wing which, when fitted to the leading edge of a wing, reduced the danger of stalling. When the patent expired in 1938 the company had earned £750,000 from worldwide sales. Frederick Handley Page himself also gained financially from his invention, receiving £100,000 from the Royal Commission on Awards to Inventors. Handley Page employed an excellent design staff which included George Volkert and Gustav Lachmann, who had independently discovered the slot principle in 1918. Before the war the company moved its headquarters to Radlett, Hertfordshire, where the Halifax bomber was produced. Handley Page was knighted in 1942 for his contribution to the war effort. He produced the first post-war civil airliner, the Hermes, and later the Victor bomber but by the 1950s the viability of the small independent aircraft producer was under serious threat. Handley Page refused to yield to government pressure to merge with other firms in the industry, and at his death in 1962 his company was the only remaining major independent aircraft manufacturer.

A pioneer of technological education, Handley Page initiated sandwich courses for his apprentices in 1923, in conjunction with Northampton Engineering College. He was elected a fellow of the City and Guilds of London Institute in 1939, and became chairman of its council and executive committee ten years later. In 1946 he was instrumental, with Sir Roy Fedden, in setting up the College of Aeronautics at Cranfield at the behest of Sir Stafford Cripps, and remained chairman of its governing body until his death. An autocrat intolerant of governmental interference, he refused to merge his company with other groups under the plan proposed by the minister of defence, Duncan Sandys, because he insisted on protecting his dedicated team of employees, whose loyalty he had earned and esteemed highly. He was a founding member of the Society of British Aircraft Constructors in 1916, was twice its chairman and, in 1938–9, its first president, and was also vice-chairman of the Air Registration Board, president of the Institute of Transport (1945–6) and of the Royal Aeronautical Society (1945–7), master of the Worshipful Company of Coachmakers and Coach Harness Makers (1943–4), and deputy lieutenant (1954–6) and lieutenant (1956–60) of Middlesex. In debate a master of repartee, well spiced with quotations from the Bible and Gibbon, he was always abreast of current technology and objective in criticism.

The Royal Aeronautical Society awarded Handley Page its gold medal in 1960, and in the same year he received the Royal Society of Arts Albert gold medal and the German Scientific Society for Aviation's Ludwig Prandtl ring. He was an officer of the Légion d'honneur and of the order of the Crown (Belgium). This latter honour he received personally from King Albert for saving two bathers at Blankenberge from drowning. The annual Handley Page memorial lecture, first given in May 1963 by Prince Philip, duke of Edinburgh, is sponsored jointly by the Cranfield Society and the Royal Aeronautical Society. Handley Page died at his home, 18 Grosvenor Square, London, on 21 April 1962. C. H. BARNES, *rev.* PETER FEARON

Sources P. Fearon, 'Page, Sir Frederick Handley', *DBB* • C. H. Barnes, *Handley page aircraft since 1907* (1976) • P. Fearon, 'The vicissitudes of a British aircraft company: Handley Page Ltd. between the wars', *Business History*, 20 (1978), 63–86 • *The Times* (23 April 1962) • d. cert.

Archives Royal Air Force Museum, Hendon, MSS

Likenesses photograph, 1909, Hult. Arch. • F. May, pen and wash drawing, 1936, Royal Air Force Museum, Hendon • oils, after 1962 (after set of photographic studies by D. Glass, 1955), Royal Aeronautical Society, London • D. Glass, photograph, NPG • C. Pibworth, bronze bust, Royal Aeronautical Society, London • oils, Royal Aero club; on loan to Royal Air Force Museum, Hendon

Wealth at death £140,959 16*s.* 10*d.*: probate, 23 May 1962, *CGPLA Eng. & Wales*

Page, Sir Gregory, second baronet (1689–1775), art collector, was born in Greenwich, the elder son of Sir Gregory Page, first baronet (1668–1720), and his wife, Mary, daughter of Thomas Trotman, citizen of London. Both his father and his grandfather had been directors of the East India Company. The first baronet was MP for New Shoreham in 1708–13 and 1715–20: on his death in 1720 his executors sold his large shareholding in the South Sea Company, and his son was left about £600,000. Page himself was also a director of the East India Company (1719–20), and a large stockholder. In 1717 he began buying land in Kent and the City of London, which eventually placed the family among the largest landowners in the county; it was said to be possible to walk for a day in north-west Kent without leaving Page property.

In 1721 Page married Martha, third daughter of Robert Kenward of Yalding, Kent; they had no children. In 1723 he bought the freehold of Wricklemarsh on Blackheath from the executors of the widow of Sir John Morden, the founder of Morden College, Blackheath. Almost at once the construction of a new house was begun, Page's ample fortune ensuring an astonishing rate of progress. He chose as his architect John James of Greenwich, who had succeeded Nicholas Hawksmoor as clerk of the works at Greenwich, and who designed a restrained Palladian house: a ground plan and cross-section through the rooms were included in the fourth volume of *Vitruvius Britannicus*, (1739). According to a contemporary description, Wricklemarsh was one of the finest mansions in England, resembling 'a royal palace rather than a residence of a gentleman' (Sutton, 364). The viewer goes on to describe elegantly laid out gardens, rooms hung with green or crimson silk damask, cornices, doorcases and chair frames carved in gilt, and chimney-pieces of polished marble.

A complete list of Page's collection of pictures was printed in the first volume of *London and its Environs Described*, published in 1761 by R. and J. D. Dodsley. It comprised 118 pictures, with paintings by Claude, Poussin, Veronese, Van Dyck, Rubens, Salvator Rosa, Nicolaes Berchem, and a group of ten pictures by Adriaen van der Werff, a contemporary Dutch classicist painter much admired in the eighteenth century. Page presumably had links with the Dutch East India Company: six Dutch East India wood chairs inlaid with the Page/Kenward arms in mother-of-pearl are now in Sir John Soane's Museum. Page was the founder and patron of the dining club the Free and Easy Society, for which a number of Qianlong Chinese armorial punchbowls were made about 1755.

Page died at Wricklemarsh on 4 August 1775 and was buried alongside his wife in the family vault at St Alfege, Greenwich. He left Wricklemarsh and its collections to his great-nephew Sir Gregory Turner, baronet, of Ambrosden in Oxfordshire, who took the name and arms of Page in compliance with his great-uncle's request. Turner did not live at Wricklemarsh, but let it to a succession of tenants. Horace Walpole (later fourth earl of Orford), wrote in 1779 that 'half the van der Werffs, which cost an immense sum … are spoiled since Sir Gregory Page's death by servants neglecting to shut out the sun' (*Horace Walpole's Correspondence*, ed. W. S. Lewis, 33, 1965, p. 137). The picture collection was sold in parts in 1775, 1783, and 1787. Wricklemarsh was sold in 1784 to John Cator, who instructed Christies to auction the materials of the house in 1787; its shell was finally demolished in 1800.

CHARLES SEBAG-MONTEFIORE, *rev.*

Sources D. Sutton, 'Aspects of British collecting [pt II]', *Apollo*, 116 (1982), 358–420 · J. Brushe, 'Wricklemarsh and the collections of Sir Gregory Page', *Apollo*, 122 (1985), 364–71 · HoP, *Commons, 1715–54*, 2.319

Wealth at death left house and collection of pictures

Page, John (*c*.1760–1812), singer and music editor, was from 1790 until 1795 lay clerk of St George's Chapel, Windsor, and he also deputized in the Chapel Royal and St Paul's Cathedral, as a tenor. In 1801 he was appointed vicar-choral at the cathedral. He was a professional member of the Catch Club between 1792 and 1797. In 1800 Page completed the three volumes of *Harmonia sacra*, a collection of anthems by English composers of the sixteenth to eighteenth centuries, including previously unpublished works by contemporary composers such as his friend Jonathan Battishill, Samuel Wesley, and Thomas Attwood. This was intended as a supplement to the collections of *Cathedral Music* of William Boyce (1760–73) and Samuel Arnold (1843). Among other collections of religious music made by Page were *The Anthems and Psalms as Performed in St Paul's Cathedral* (1795) and *Divine Harmony* (1798). In 1804 a collection of four volumes of madrigals, glees, and elegies, *Festive Harmony*, appeared. Page edited the music from Lord Nelson's burial service in 1806, and he composed a little himself, notably the Christmas hymn 'See the morning star appear'. He died on 16 August 1812, at 19 Warwick Square, Newgate Street, London.

L. M. MIDDLETON, *rev.* ANNE PIMLOTT BAKER

Sources *New Grove* · J. S. Bumpus, *A history of English cathedral music, 1549–1889*, 2 vols. [1908], 360–62 · Grove, *Dict. mus.* · *GM*, 1st ser., 82/2 (1812), 196

Page, Sir Leo Francis (1890–1951), magistrate, was born on 2 April 1890 at Hobart, Tasmania, the youngest of six sons, only two of whom survived childhood, of William Humphrey Page, of the Indian Civil Service, and his wife, Alice, daughter of Richard Pope. His father had become a Roman Catholic in early manhood and Leo was educated at Beaumont College, Berkshire. At the wish of his father he entered the Royal Military Academy, Woolwich, and after a year transferred to the 16th lancers. But he was not suited to the army and withdrew. He entered University College, Oxford, where he obtained a second in jurisprudence in 1914. On the outbreak of war he joined the Royal Flying Corps, but after a serious accident while bringing home a plane from France he was invalided out in 1916, having attained the rank of flight commander. In that year he married Edith Violet, daughter of Captain Frederick Cleave Loder-Symonds RA, of Hinton Manor, Faringdon, Berkshire, with whom he had two sons and a daughter.

Page became a member of the Inner Temple and was called to the bar in 1918. He practised for several years and had reason to anticipate success, but he was never robust and tuberculosis developed. Enjoying a secure private income, he abandoned practice and settled with his family at Faringdon. There in 1925 he became a justice of the peace for Berkshire and a member of the bench at Faringdon where his father-in-law had earlier been chairman for many years. In 1946 he himself was elected chairman, an office which he held until his death. He also served as chairman of the local juvenile court and for a period as chairman of the appeals committee at the Berkshire quarter sessions.

In all this work Page took more than the ordinary interest. While doing his full share of the court work, he made a deep study of the problems of local justice. Not content with his limited experience in a rural court, he visited many other courts in different parts of the country. This qualified him to write several books about the work of magistrates, on which he became a leading authority. The most influential were *Justice of the Peace* (1936) and *Crime and the Community* (1937). In court, while always merciful, Page was a realist and more open to appeals to reason than to sentiment.

Although he was known primarily as a leading justice of the peace, Page also gave much time and enthusiasm to helping prisoners and former prisoners, and prisons and borstals became his main interest in his later years. From 1939 for many years afterwards he was chairman of the visiting magistrates at Oxford prison; he also became chairman of its Discharged Prisoners' Aid Society. He took a keen interest in many individual cases and kept in touch with some of them after their release. No case which Page considered deserving was too much trouble for him, although he had a quick eye for those who sought to impose on him without adequate effort to make good. He favoured probation while also recognizing the need for deterrence.

From 1940 to 1945 Page served in the Lord Chancellor's Department as secretary of commissions of the peace. He had a freer hand than was usual since Lord Simon was much occupied with wartime problems outside his office. Page was considerably shocked by much of what he saw. Many of those recommended for appointment as justices of the peace in local areas were, in his own words, 'older than was desirable', and selected in recognition of some other form of public service. It was 'rare to find anyone wholly without political connection'. Page did all he could to improve matters. The reforms which took place after the war were not yet being planned, but Page's influence on them was apparent when they came. It was he who influenced the lord chancellor to secure the passing into law of the Justices (Supplemental List) Act in 1941, which empowered the lord chancellor to prevent elderly and infirm lay justices from sitting in court.

Page was essentially a conservative reformer. Keen and successful though he was in bringing about many reforms within the existing system, he was apparently not aware that demands were being made for radical changes in the system itself. To some extent his mind widened as his experience increased. In 1937 Page was nominated by his bench as its representative on the council of the Magistrates' Association, many of whose members, without being in any way extremists, had ideas for reform beyond what Page then considered reasonable. To such members Page seemed unwilling to pursue his ideas to their logical conclusion. For instance, while he profoundly believed that criminal courts should be better informed about the offenders whom they convicted, he was at first satisfied with the existing method whereby such social inquiries as were made about offenders took place before trial and thus before guilt was established. A substantial majority took the view that most serious cases should be adjourned after conviction for full inquiries to be made before sentence was passed. Page resigned in protest in 1940 and took no further part in the association's work. This was mainly due to the claims of his official work, but when this ceased he did not return to the association, although he later came to accept the idea that serious cases should be adjourned for inquiries only after conviction.

In 1946 a strong royal commission was set up under Lord du Parcq to inquire into the work of justices of the peace. Page's evidence was printed as an appendix to its minutes of evidence. The report of this commission (1948) greatly influenced the preparation of the post-war reforms and reflected many of the ideas which Page had laid before it. Valuable as the new code was, the reforms were all within the existing system and on some points were less drastic than Page himself had hoped.

The usefulness of psychiatry was gradually realized by Page, who wrote that 'medical men who have specialised in this branch of research have a very definite and valuable contribution to make to the treatment of delinquency' (*Quarterly Review*, April 1940). However, in his view the help of such experts applied only to abnormal cases and should be limited to examining and reporting on offenders. He did not sympathize with the idea that psychiatrists should share the responsibility of selecting appropriate sentences, a task which Page considered only those on the bench were competent to perform, although he urged that they should be better informed about the various methods of dealing with offenders. Thus in 1948 he wrote in his book *The Sentence of the Court* that all those on the bench, including professional lawyers, should receive instruction which would fit them to pass sentence. But he put forward no plan whereby lawyers appointed in mid-life to the criminal bench could receive such instruction. His last book, *The Young Lag* (1950), reviewed the treatment of young offenders.

Page was high sheriff for his county in 1937, and in 1948 he received a knighthood. Although afflicted by severe ill health he continued bravely with as much work as he could undertake. His consistent love, sympathy, and understanding for suffering humanity and his humility were the qualities most valued by his friends; to the end his sense of humour never left him. He died at his home at

Faringdon, Berkshire, on 31 August 1951. A contemporary tribute described his life as one 'of service and self-sacrifice. Few men have done more for those who are, by the standard of many, the least hopeful material and the least deserving' (*Justice of the Peace*, 559).

CLAUD MULLINS, *rev.* ALEC SAMUELS

Sources private information (1971) • personal knowledge (1971) • *The Times* (1 Sept 1951) • *Justice of the Peace*, 115 (8 Sept 1951), 559
Likenesses W. Stoneman, photograph, 1948, NPG
Wealth at death £15,389 3*s.* 6*d.*: probate, 21 Jan 1952, *CGPLA Eng. & Wales*

Page, Sir Richard (*d.* 1548), courtier, probably came from Surrey or Middlesex, and began his career in the service of Cardinal Wolsey, whose chamberlain he became. His parentage is unknown. By 1516 he was a knight and a gentleman of the king's privy chamber. As such he served the crown in the localities, both in the home counties (he was a JP for Surrey in 1522–6 and 1528, and for Middlesex in 1524) and in the north. In 1525 he accompanied Henry VIII's illegitimate son, the young duke of Richmond, to Yorkshire, where he helped to administer his household and was a member of the council of the north. Probably his offices as chief steward of the lordship of Beverley and recorder of Hull date from this time. In 1527 he accompanied Wolsey to Calais, dignified by a great chain made for the occasion which weighed 200 pounds. Other rewards included the comptrollership of customs for the port of London in 1522, granted 'in consideration of his services to the King and Cardinal Wolsey' (*LP Henry VIII*, 3/2, no. 2016, 8), and the joint surveyorship of kerseys for London and Southampton, which he received in March 1528. By 1530 he also had two annuities of £100, and after Wolsey's fall was given the Essex manor of Thoby which had belonged to Cardinal College, Oxford.

In 1532 the terms of Page's service in the privy chamber were revised, and he became a member of one of the two groups of gentlemen each of which was to attend for six weeks at a time. His colleagues included Sir Nicholas Carew and Sir John Russell, and it may have been the rivalries generated by this milieu which lay behind the most striking event in Page's career, his arrest and imprisonment in the Tower in 1536 on suspicion of treason, arising from his (unidentifiable) connection with Queen Anne Boleyn—he had earlier sided with Sir Thomas Cheyne in a dispute with Russell over a wardship, and later sat on the jury which convicted Carew of treason. By 8 May 1536 Page was a state prisoner, but by 18 July he had been freed, perhaps because of his friendship with Thomas Cromwell. Even so, the episode had clearly shaken his nerve, and in reporting his release to Lady Lisle he reported that 'he has not greatly assayed to be a daily courtier again' (*LP Henry VIII*, 11, no. 107). He wrote to her from West Molesey in Surrey, from a house he described as 'my poor cabin'. None the less in October that year he accompanied the king to Welbeck in his proposed campaign against the Pilgrimage of Grace, and by November he was sheriff of Surrey and Sussex. Two years later, however, he received another lesson in the perils of royal service, when the king confiscated Page's 'cabin' and instead gave him the former nunnery of St Giles-in-the-Wood at Flamstead, Hertfordshire. Perhaps as a reward for his acquiescence, Page received other grants of former monastic property: the manor of Woodhall, Hertfordshire, in 1539; the manor of Northall, Buckinghamshire, in 1542; and the manor of Flamstead in 1544, in exchange for his northern offices. In 1541 he had a life-grant of the London house of the Carmelite provincial.

By the beginning of 1540 Page was lieutenant of the gentlemen pensioners. Later that year he accompanied the king to the north, and in 1542 he oversaw the fortification of Hull. He retained his position at court, for on 7 July 1544 the regency arrangements made to cover the king's absence in France included Page's appointment as chamberlain to head Prince Edward's new household at Hampton Court. He died in 1548, at either Flamstead or St Mary-at-Hill, London, to all appearances a model of discretion and good service. The image is belied, however, by a last reference to Page from the year after his death, when Sir William Sharington, during the trial for treason of Thomas, Baron Seymour of Sudeley, alleged that Seymour had resented his brother the protector's entrusting the governance of the young king to 'so drunken a soul as Sir Richard Page' (*CSP dom.*, 1547–53, 188).

His letters show Page to have been hospitable, willing to intercede for friends, and anxious to protect his servants. In earlier days he evidently had access to Wolsey and then Cromwell. His links to Anne Boleyn remain obscure, though Wolsey entrusted him with a letter to her pleading his cause, and he reported that she and Henry were merry after the birth of Elizabeth. In the 1540s his most important links were with the Seymours, which doubtless explains his apparently controversial position in the young King Edward's household. Some time before 1534 he married Elizabeth Stanhope (*née* Bourchier), the mother of Anne Stanhope, who married Sir Edward Seymour, the future Protector Somerset, as his second wife. Page himself had one daughter, another Elizabeth, who married Sir William Skipwith. CATHARINE DAVIES

Sources *LP Henry VIII*, vols. 2–21 • M. St C. Byrne, ed., *The Lisle letters*, 6 vols. (1981) • R. M. Warnicke, *The rise and fall of Anne Boleyn* (1989) • S. J. Gunn and P. G. Lindley, eds., *Cardinal Wolsey: church, state and art* (1991) • E. W. Ives, *Anne Boleyn* (1986) • *VCH Hertfordshire*, 2.104–6.224 • *VCH Surrey*, 2.88; 3.455 • *VCH Essex*, 2.163 • *CSP dom.*, rev. edn, *1547–53* • will, PRO, PROB 11/34, sig. 10 • J. K. McConica, *English humanists and Reformation politics* (1965) • HoP, *Commons, 1509–58*, 3.326 • D. Starkey, *The reign of Henry VIII* (1991)
Archives PRO, state papers, domestic, Henry VIII
Wealth at death see will, PRO, PROB 11/34, sig. 10

Page, Samuel (1574–1630), poet and naval chaplain, was the son of a Bedfordshire clergy family. He matriculated as a scholar of Corpus Christi College, Oxford, on 1 July 1587, aged thirteen; he graduated BA on 5 February 1591 and became a fellow on 16 April. He proceeded MA on 15 March 1594. Before 1595 he took holy orders and became chaplain to the earl of Nottingham, Charles Howard, admiral of the fleet. He accompanied Howard on the Cadiz expedition of 1595 and, as he says in his funeral sermon for Sir Richard Leveson, Howard's son-in-law:

> It pleased him [Leveson] in this expedition, to take knowledge of mee, and often to vouchsafe me his conference, he received at my hands the Sacrament of the body and blood of Christ … in one of the harboroughs of that land [Spain]. (Page, *Sermon*, 2.234)

By 1597 he had obtained the living of St Nicholas, Deptford (or West Greenwich).

Before this appointment, which he retained for the rest of his life, Page had had a reputation as a poet and Francis Meres, in *Palladis tamia* (1598), ranked him among the very greatest when describing 'the most passionate among us to bewaile and bemoane the perplexities of love … Spencer, Daniel, Drayton, Shakespeare, Wetstone, Gasgoyne, Samuall Page sometime fellowe of Corpus Christi College in Oxford' (p. 284). His surviving poems are slight: a short commendatory poem to *Coryats Crudities* (1611) and 'The Love of Amos and Laura', published in a miscellany called *Alcilia* (1613); in the second edition of 1619 it has a dedication to 'my approved and much respected friend Iz[aak] Wa[lton]', but in the third edition of 1628, this dedication becomes merely an address by 'the author to his book'. This 'heroic poem' was his 'maiden muse'.

Page proceeded doctor of divinity on 6 June 1611. His naval experience led to patronage by the brethren of Trinity House 'by whose unexpected and undeserved bounty, my labours and Studies have been comforted and encouraged' (Page, *Cape of Good Hope*, dedication). He was also commissioned to preach *God be thanked: a sermon of thanksgiving for the happy successe of the Englishe fleetes sent forth by the … Company of Adventurers to the East Indies, preached to … the whole company of their good ship the Hope Merchant, happily returned to Deptford on Maunday Thursday, 29 March 1616*. This is addressed to Sir Thomas Smith, governor of the company, and Page declares that he is 'no stranger to your free Charity'. His church in Deptford seems to have had a special relationship with the burgeoning merchant marine for, 'we the people of this Congregation, … have ever ioyned in Common supplications before the Throne of Grace, for the good successe of your voyages' (*God be Thanked*, 30). He compiled a 'Divine Sea Service containing sundry and necessary and useful formes of prayer and thanksgiving for the helpe of such as travaile by sea' (*God be Thanked*, added at end).

Page died in 1630 and was buried in St Nicholas's on 8 August. His personality is characterized by his friend Nathaniel Snape of Gray's Inn: 'the Clergy thought him a reverend, learned, and orthodoxe Divine; and … the laytie found him alwaies painfully zealous in his Ministry, upright, and conscionable in his life and conversations' (Page, *A Godly and Learned Exposition*, dedication).

Reavley Gair

Sources S. Page, *A godly and learned exposition on the Lord's prayer*, ed. N. Snape (1631) • S. Page, *The Cape of Good Hope: five sermons for the use of mariners* (1616) • S. Page, 'A sermon preached at the funerall of … S. Richard Leveson', in E. Brydges, *Restituta, or, Titles, extracts, and characters of old books in English literature*, 2 (1815), 226–37 • Wood, *Ath. Oxon.*, new edn, 2.486–7 • F. Meres, *Palladis tamia: wits treasury, being the second part of wits common-wealth* (1598) • P. W. Miller, ed., *Scholars' facsimiles and reprints: seven minor epics of the English Renaissance* (1967)

Page, Thomas (*bap.* 1680?, *d.* 1733). *See under* Mount, Richard (*bap.* 1654, *d.* 1722).

Page, Thomas (1803–1877), civil engineer, was born in London on 26 October 1803, the eldest son of Robert Page of Nags Head Court. His father was a solicitor, first in Gracechurch Street and later in Mark Lane, London. Page grew up at Romaldkirk on the banks of the Tees and was educated for a career at sea, but, at the suggestion of Thomas Tredgold, he took up civil engineering instead. After working as a draughtsman in an engineering works at Leeds he subsequently moved to the London office of the architect Edward Blore. While making a measured survey at Westminster Abbey he discovered a previously unknown passage connecting the transept to the crypt under the chapter house.

In 1835 Page became an assistant engineer under I. K. Brunel on the Thames Tunnel, progressing to acting engineer in 1836 when Richard Beamish retired. He was responsible for the completion of the tunnel and of the shaft on the north bank. In 1842, in competition with Walker and Burges, Charles Barry, Colonel French and others, his design for the embankment of the Thames from Westminster to Blackfriars was recommended for adoption by the commissioners for metropolis improvements. Under Page's control the Thames Embankment office was set up within the Office of Woods and Forests to consider the various schemes and he became its consulting engineer. A dispute between the crown and the City of London corporation over rights to the bed and soil of the river, and difficulties over the coal dues, resulted in the project's being abandoned. His position as engineer to woods and forests meant that any railway scheme affecting crown property had to receive his approval, often only after incorporating revisions he had suggested. This happened on lines through the New Forest, the Old Deer Park at Richmond, and in the Home Park at Windsor.

In January 1844 Page made a survey of the Thames from Battersea to Woolwich and the tidal action of the river between Sheerness and St Katharine's Dock. In 1845 he prepared plans for a central railway terminus to be constructed on reclaimed land in the Thames between Hungerford and Waterloo bridges. Connections were to be made with the Great Western Railway at Hanwell, the Eastern Counties Railway at Blackwall, and the south coast railways by a river crossing on the site of the present Blackfriars Bridge. In the same year he designed, in conjunction with Joseph D'Aguilar Samuda, a railway, to be worked by the atmospheric system, connecting the Brighton lines with the Eastern Counties Railway via a tunnel under London docks. He also prepared and deposited plans for a railway from Lincoln via Horncastle to Wainfleet, with a branch to Boston.

In 1846 Page reported on the relative merits of Holyhead

and Porth Dinllaen as harbours for the Irish mail service and prepared plans for the construction of docks at each. In 1847 he prepared plans for docks at Swansea. In 1848–9 he designed and constructed new roads between Windsor and Frogmore, the Albert Bridge over the Thames at Datchet, and the Victoria Bridge near Old Windsor. These works included opening out a considerable area of the Home Park for public use. At the request of the government he prepared plans for the south side of the Thames between Vauxhall and Battersea bridges, involving an embankment and road (opened in 1869) along the river, the Chelsea suspension bridge across it (opened in 1858, replaced in 1936–8), and the road leading to Sloane Square.

In May 1854, after lengthy examination by a select committee, work started on Page's design for the Westminster new bridge. The bridge was divided longitudinally into two halves, the first half being demolished and reconstructed before the demolition and reconstruction of the second half, so that traffic on the river and across it was not interrupted. It was built without the use of coffer dams or centering and opened on 24 May, 1862. His scheme for Blackfriars Bridge was accepted by the bridge house lands committee of the City corporation, but a vote in common council selected the design by Joseph Cubitt. Page designed and constructed bridges at Lendale, York, and Thornton and produced designs for many others, including a single span across the Thames at the Tower, across the Golden Horn at Constantinople, the Rhine at Cologne (which was displayed at the 1851 exhibition), and the Danube at Budapest. He was consulted on the reclamation of land on the River Tagus at Lisbon and on the railway between Lisbon and Cintra, and in 1860 reported on the improvement of the River Nene at Wisborough, recommending widening from Peterborough to the sea. As engineering surveying officer he held courts and reported on proposed improvements for Cheltenham, Taunton, Liverpool, Falmouth, Folkestone, and Penzance. With Sir John Rennie he advised the City of London on the widening of London Bridge and the treatment of the Thames as a navigable river.

Page was interested in naval matters and in 1859 investigated and published a report on the suitability of Milford Haven as a port for ocean-going steamships and as a naval arsenal. He invented a system for firing guns under water. In 1870 he read a paper to the Society of Arts proposing a tunnel in the form of a submerged tube between England and France.

Described by contemporaries as a man with a large circle of friends, Page was seen as one of the last links that connected the rising generation of engineers with the heroic figures from the early years of the nineteenth century. His early architectural training was considered responsible for his ability to combine architectural beauty with engineering utility. Both his Chelsea suspension bridge and Westminster Bridge were admired for their architectural elegance, even if the latter was sometimes criticized for a lack of rigidity in the bridge deck. He died suddenly in Paris on 8 January 1877. Nothing is known of his wife, but his eldest son, G. G. Page, and his youngest son were both present at his funeral.

Stanley Smith

Sources memoir, *PICE*, 49 (1876–7), 262–5 · *Engineering* (26 Jan 1877), 75 · *The Engineer* (12 Jan 1877), 31 · *The Builder*, 35 (1877), 70, 78 · *The Times* (20 Jan 1877), 10 · Boase, *Mod. Eng. biog.* · *DNB*

Page, Thomas Ethelbert (1850–1936), classical scholar and schoolmaster, was born at Lincoln on 27 March 1850, the second son of William Tomlinson Page, general manager of the Lincoln and Lindsey Banking Company, and his wife, Ann Watson. He attended Lincoln grammar school and Shrewsbury School before entering St John's College, Cambridge, in 1869. After a brilliant career as an undergraduate (he was ranked second classic in 1873), he became a sixth-form master at Charterhouse, where he managed a house and participated fully in school life. He held a fellowship of his college which he relinquished on his marriage, on 16 October 1875, to Delamotte Caroline Eugenie, only daughter of Edward Toynbee of Lincoln, a half-brother of Joseph Toynbee.

Page was the most prominent figure in the Association of Assistant Masters, and worked for fifty years to improve the conditions of teachers. In Godalming he served for thirty years on the town council, brought about the founding of Godalming grammar school, and was made an honorary freeman of the town in 1924. In addition, he edited Horace's *Odes* (1883), the Acts of the Apostles (1886), and the whole of Virgil (1894). Thanks to their economy, humanity, and good sense, his editions remained in use for almost a hundred years. Page's scholarship was recognized in 1904, when Jebb asked him whether he would be willing to succeed Mayor as professor of Latin at Cambridge (Page had to say no, because his wife refused to leave Godalming), and again in 1913, when he received the degree of LittD from Manchester University. In his time at Charterhouse, Page was offered at least two headships (Harrow and Shrewsbury) on condition that he took holy orders. But although he was a devout Christian who prayed and read a chapter of his Greek Testament every morning, Page objected to this stipulation; hence in spite of his fame as a teacher he was never promoted.

After his retirement in 1910, Page was appointed first editor of the Loeb Classical Library. He selected (and rejected) translators from both sides of the Atlantic, and corrected their copy with a precision which was not always welcome. By 1935, along with his two colleagues (E. Capps and W. H. D. Rouse), he had supervised the preparation of some 200 volumes. As Loeb editor Page was paid £800 a year in addition to his paltry pension of £150 from Charterhouse. He also received a legacy of £2000 from his father, had shares in Eastman Kodak, was a director of the Brentford Gas Company, and had interests in a hotel at Hindhead. In the end all this amounted to an estate of £68,000—a substantial sum in 1936. This financial comfort enabled him in later life to indulge the tastes of a man of the world. He enjoyed good food and drink, he attended race meetings at Ascot and Longchamp, and he was a welcome guest in the country houses and on the yachts of the well-to-do.

As an independently minded Liberal, who believed in the two great principles of individual freedom and individual responsibility, Page joined the Reform Club in 1890. There he became a familiar figure, with his tall stature (6 foot 2 inches), his deep voice with its short Lincolnshire 'a', his long hair and closely-clipped beard, and his unvarying dress (black boots, off-white trousers of St Kilda tweed, white shirt with navy blue poplin tie, black tailcoat and waistcoat). More important, his combination of knowledge, courtesy, and wit won him respect and affection among all the members. A special seat was reserved for him at luncheon, and his portrait, by Clive Gardiner, was hung there in 1927. Among his friends were Conan Doyle, Hilaire Belloc, Arnold Bennett, and also H. G. Wells, who called him 'King of the Reform Club'. A wider reputation still resulted from his public speeches (especially during the First World War), his reviews in *The Bookman* and *The Spectator*, and his long series of letters to *The Times*. In those letters he directed his powerful rhetorical satire against the Headmasters' Conference (for insisting that heads should be in holy orders), bishops (for upholding outmoded doctrines in the Thirty-Nine Articles and the Athanasian creed), and professors (for presuming to pronounce on teaching—a craft of which they knew nothing). Nevertheless, on his eightieth birthday Page was presented with an amazing tribute, which included over 500 signatures from every part of the establishment—British and American. In 1931 he became an honorary fellow of his old college; finally, in 1934, he was made a Companion of Honour. Owing to the dominant position of classics before 1918 and to his own outstanding qualities, Page reached an exceptional eminence in his profession. He died at his home at Woodcote, Godalming, Surrey, on 1 April 1936. He had two daughters. NIALL RUDD

Sources N. Rudd, *T. E. Page: schoolmaster extraordinary* (1981) • *The Times* (2 April 1936) • personal knowledge (2004)
Archives Charterhouse School, Surrey, material • St John Cam., papers
Likenesses L. Dickinson, portrait, 1883, St John Cam. • J. Collier, oils, 1911, Charterhouse School, Surrey • C. Gardiner, oils, 1927, Reform Club, London • M. Beerbohm, caricature, drawing, 1928, Charterhouse School, Surrey • W. Stoneman, photograph, 1934, NPG
Wealth at death £68,065 12s. 11d.: probate, 8 July 1936, *CGPLA Eng. & Wales*

Page, Sir Thomas Hyde (1746–1821), military engineer, was born in Harley Street, Westminster, the son of Robert Hyde Page (*d.* 1764), military engineer, and Elizabeth, daughter of Francis Morewood. He attended the Royal Military Academy, Woolwich, and as the first cadet received a gold medal from George III. Appointed practitioner engineer and second lieutenant in the corps of Royal Engineers on 28 July 1769, Page was promoted sub-lieutenant and engineer in 1774. The following year Lord Townshend, then master-general of the ordnance, requested Page 'to take a view of the Bedford Level', with the purpose of improving the general drainage in the county. This he did, and his manuscript report to Lord Townshend, dated 31 March 1775, is in the library of the Institution of Civil Engineers. He also constructed a ferry at Chatham and was awarded a gold medal of the Society of Arts, 1775.

Page went with his corps to North America and distinguished himself in his capacity as aide-de-camp to General Pigott at Bunker Hill (17 June 1775), when he was severely wounded, losing his leg below the knee. His disability earned him a pension of 10 shillings per day. In 1777 he married Susanna, widow of Edmund Bastard of Kitley, Devon, and sister of Sir Thomas Crawley-Boevey, baronet. Appointed commanding royal engineer of the eastern coastal district, for the next few years Page supervised the refurbishment of defences at Dover, Chatham, Tilbury, Gravesend, Sheerness, and Landguard Fort. He also organized, in 1780, the Dover Volunteers. In 1782 the Board of Ordnance, anxious about the lack of pure water in its garrisons and dockyards, asked Page to bore a well at Sheerness garrison. He determined to try to sink through the quicksands by means of two cylindrical frames of wood of different diameters, excavating within the small circle first, and lowering it progressively as the large circle was formed above it. The experiment failed, and Page was much blamed. In the House of Commons the experiment was said to be 'not a well for fresh water, but a sink for the money of the public'. A second attempt was made, this time in Fort Townshend at Sheerness, and was successful. Page's report upon the Sheerness well is dated 12 May 1783. Plans and sections were published in the *Philosophical Transactions of the Royal Society*, 74, together with an account of similar treacherous soils at Harwich and Landguard Fort.

Page's certificate of candidature of the Royal Society was read on 3 April 1783 and supported by Charles Hutton and others. On 10 July 1783 he was elected a fellow, being described as 'a gentleman well versed in mechanics and many other branches of experimental philosophy'. He was knighted on 23 August 1783, but states in his *Account of the Commencement and Progress in Sinking Wells at Sheerness* (1797), p. 10, that he 'considered the knighthood to have reference to his military services, and not to the well at Sheerness'. In 1783 he married Mary Albinia (*d.* 1794), daughter of John Woodward (formerly captain in the 70th regiment) of Ringwould, Kent, and they had five children. His third marriage, to Mary, widow of Captain Everett RN, was childless.

Page was promoted captain-lieutenant in 1784 and captain on 20 April 1787, before being moved to the invalid engineers four months later. His expertise remained in demand none the less. He was chief consulting engineer in the improvement of the port of Dublin, of Wicklow harbour, of the inland navigation of Ireland, and of the Royal Shannon and Newry canals. He directed the repairing of the disastrous breach in the dock canal at Dublin in 1792, and was chief engineer for forming the new cut from Eau Brinck to King's Lynn, a problem of navigation and drainage that had puzzled engineers since the time of Charles I.

Page lived for many years at Betshanger Park, Kent, but latterly retired, for reasons of health, to France. He died at Boulogne on 30 June 1821, and was buried there.

HERBERT RIX, *rev.* W. JOHNSON

Sources 'Notitia historica', 1860, Royal Engineers' Library, Chatham, Kent, Connolly MSS, 4.25–35, 40–48 • Burke, *Gen. GB* [Page of Holbrook] • W. Y. Carman, 'Sir Thomas Hyde Page, engineer', *Journal of the Society for Army Historical Research*, 33 (1955), 61–2 • R. F. Edwards, ed., *Roll of officers of the corps of royal engineers from 1660 to 1898* (1898) • *The Times* (5 July 1821)
Archives priv. coll., MSS | Inst. CE, archives • Royal Engineers' Library, Chatham, Kent, Connolly MSS, 'Notitia historica', 4.25–35, 40–48 • RS, book catalogue
Likenesses J. Northcote, portrait; known to be in priv. coll. *c.*1970

Page, William (1590–1664), Church of England clergyman, was born at Harrow on the Hill, Middlesex, and probably baptized there on 20 December 1590, one of at least two sons of Richard Page, and his wife, possibly Frances Mudge. His father's profession is unknown, but several members of the family were barristers of the Inner and Middle temples; a brother, John, was a master in chancery. Page entered Balliol College, Oxford, on 7 November 1606, graduated BA in 1610, and proceeded MA in 1614 (incorporated at Cambridge in 1615). In 1618 he became a fellow of All Souls, becoming bachelor of divinity in 1621 and attaining the doctorate in 1634. He was known within the university as a preacher and polemicist, tending towards the Arminian side in the then current disputes within the Anglican church.

His first published work, *A Treatise Justifying Bowing* (1631), was a 266 page treatise defending, against the attacks of William Prynne, the Arminian practice of bowing at the name of Jesus during prayer. Archbishop Abbot attempted to prevent its printing as unnecessarily provocative, but was overruled by his nominal subordinate, William Laud, then bishop of London; the Calvinist professor of divinity, John Prideaux, was obliged to issue an imprimatur. From 1634 Page was rector of Hannington, Hampshire, and at some point he became chaplain to Walter Curll, bishop of Winchester from late 1632, whose ecclesiological outlook he evidently shared. Page's translation in 1639 of Thomas à Kempis's *De imitatio Christi* was noteworthy mainly for its introduction, which followed the fashionable eirenic line that the different churches ought to practise charity towards one another, and chided the Catholics for their insistence that salvation was impossible outside their version of the faith. A suggestion that all Christians, from papists to Socinians, should find unity in a crusade against the Turks says little for his sense of political reality. While ready to admit that all sides of the current religious disputes were sincere in their beliefs, he saw this as an argument for settled authority within the church, and was unable to accept the conclusions of John Hales and William Chillingworth that reason could be a valid criterion. In his 1642 *Animadversions* to Hales's *Tract Concerning Schism* he was concerned to register his dissent from Hales's attack on hierarchical authority; this, he argued, was dangerous, and there was no knowing where it might lead.

In addition to his published works Page left a number of manuscripts, preserved in the Bodleian and various Oxford college libraries. Two are on the special merits of women and of widows, a genre popular in the 1620s; others deal with more esoteric themes—the existence of paradise, and the state of the soul when separated from the body. In 1635 he wrote an opinion for the warden and fellows of All Souls that praying for the soul of their founder, Henry V, did not necessarily imply a papistical belief in purgatory.

Sequestered from his rectory at Hannington in 1646 by the committee for plundered ministers, apparently more for absence than for any doctrinal reasons, Page was appointed in January 1647 by All Souls to the vacant rectory of East Lockinge, then in Berkshire. His name does not appear as a fellow at the time of the parliamentary visitation in 1648, but is mentioned in connection with a college election in 1657. Anthony Wood and various later writers have erroneously conflated him with another William Page MA and later BM of St John's College, Oxford, sometime schoolmaster at Reading. Page does not seem to have married. He died in 1664 and was buried at East Lockinge on 19 February, leaving goods to an inventory value of £67 14*s*. and, in a will dated 20 November 1661, naming a nephew, Nathaniel Page, as residual legatee.

MANFRED BROD

Sources Wood, *Ath. Oxon.*, new edn, 3.653 • Committee for plundered ministers, BL, Add. MS 15670, fols. 234, 238 • Page's will, Berks. RO, D/A1/107/54 • parish registers, East Lockinge, Berks. RO • *Walker rev.*, 188 • M. Burrows, ed., *The register of the visitors of the University of Oxford, from AD 1647 to AD 1658*, CS, new ser., 29 (1881), 447, 473–7 • C. P. Martin, ed., *Archives of All Souls College* (1877), 356 • H. O. Coxe, ed., *Catalogus codicum MSS qui in collegiis aulisque Oxoniensibus hodie adservantur*, 2 vols. (1852); facs. edn under title *Catalogue of the manuscripts in the Oxford colleges* (1972), vol. 1, pp. 31, 126; vol. 2, pp. 53, 58 • W. H. Hallam, *History of the parish of East Lockinge, Berks.* (1900), 82–90 • Bodl. Oxf., MS Barlow 54, fols. 29–35*v* • A. Milton, *Catholic and Reformed: the Roman and protestant churches in English protestant thought, 1600–1640* (1995) • *Hist. U. Oxf.* 4: *17th-cent. Oxf.*, 588 • *IGI* • *DNB*
Archives All Souls Oxf. • CCC Oxf. • Queen's College, Oxford
Wealth at death £67 14*s*.

Page, William (*bap.* **1729**, *d.* **1758**), highwayman, was baptized on 22 October 1729 at the church of St Mary the Virgin, Hampton, Middlesex, the son of William Page (*d.* 1740) and his wife, Mary. His father is said to have been a bargeman in the coal trade who drowned in the Thames above Putney Bridge in 1740. Page received a rudimentary education, apparently at a charity school in Hampton, and it was there that he met his future confederate William Darwell. Giving evidence at Page's trial at the Old Bailey in 1758, one who had known Page and Darwell as children at Hampton remembered that they were 'acquainted like brothers' (*Old Bailey Sessions Papers*). Page entered domestic service. According to his contemporary biographer, however, he was of too 'proud and haughty' a spirit to submit to orders and eventually resolved to become a highwayman in order to throw off 'that badge of slavery, a livery', and set himself 'on a level with gentlemen' (*A Genuine Narrative*, 4).

Page pursued his new trade with businesslike efficiency.

He made a careful study of the roads around London and took pains to disguise and alter his appearance. It is said that he frequently drove out from London in a phaeton and pair, parking the carriage in a secluded spot, changing clothes, and saddling one of the horses in order to commit robberies. Afterwards he would return to the phaeton, resume his former disguise, and drive back to London. Page never drew attention to himself by speaking of his activities as a highwayman, and for many years he levied a toll upon travellers approaching or leaving the capital. Before his last arrest in 1757 he was brought to trial only once. This occurred at Hertford at the Lent assizes of 1753. Page was indicted for robbing a Mr Savile Cockayne Cust of his purse on the highway on 10 January 1753. An impressive array of witnesses was marshalled against him but Page was able to produce evidence that he was elsewhere at the time of the offence and he was acquitted.

In 1755 Page teamed up with his old schoolfriend Darwell and, on and off, the two robbed together for the next two years. Strenuous efforts to hunt them down were made by the Bow Street magistrate John Fielding after their robbery of Laurence Shirley, fourth Earl Ferrers, on the Northern Road, Hertfordshire, on 16 February 1757. Typical of the many entries in Fielding's accounts is one dated 9 March 1757: ‘Paid Phillipson & Jones for watching one week at the Red Lyon near Westminster Bridge … to apprehend Page, £3 10s. 6d.’ The hunt became so intense that Page visited Scotland. In July he was back, working the Tonbridge Road in Kent with Darwell and robbing the post-chaise of the bishop of Bath and Wells in Maidenhead Thicket. It was his last major success. Darwell was taken near Sevenoaks and in order to save his own life divulged Page's regular haunts and agreed to give evidence against him. Page was arrested at the Golden Lion, near Grosvenor Square Gate, London, and committed to Newgate on 8 August 1757. In his possession were three loaded pistols, a wig, a cockade, and ‘a curious plan of the roads round London in his own handwriting’ (*Public Advertiser*, 10 Aug 1757). Fielding was largely responsible for assembling the evidence against Page, and the importance he attached to the task is indicated by such entries in his accounts as: ‘Paid to the Lord Provost of Edinburgh to bring an evidence against Page to town from thence, £8 8s. 0d.’ (30 Sept 1757).

In February 1758 Page was brought to trial at the Old Bailey for robbing John Webb in Bedfont Lane, Middlesex, in March 1757 of two pistols, a purse containing 9 guineas, and a gold watch. The only material evidence adduced against him was Darwell's and Page did much to undermine it by reminding the court that ‘he [Darwell] would have given testimony against any person that he should happen to fix upon to save his own life’ (*Old Bailey Sessions Papers*). Page was acquitted but detained in custody pending indictment in four other counties. The acquittal damaged Darwell's credibility as a witness, and when Page was next tried, at the Lent assizes at Hertford for the robbery of Earl Ferrers, he was again acquitted. He was then indicted at the Lent assizes for Kent at Rochester for robbing Thomas Farrington of a gold watch and 20 guineas in January 1757. On this occasion Darwell's testimony was supported by that of a witness who identified Page as the man who had pawned the watch, and he was convicted and sentenced to death.

Page was about 5 feet 11 inches tall and of gentlemanly appearance and manner. He was hanged on Pennenden Heath, near Maidstone, on 6 April 1758, and was survived by his wife, about whom no details are known. With Darwell alone Page is said to have committed more than 300 robberies. Such claims are now impossible to substantiate or refute. He was, nevertheless, one of the most able and successful of all eighteenth-century highwaymen, and his success is the more remarkable in that it occurred at a time when improved communications and the police reforms of John and Henry Fielding were beginning to make the roads around London unsafe for highwaymen.

PHILIP SUGDEN

Sources *A genuine narrative of the life and surprising robberies and adventures of William Page* (1758) • Hertfordshire (Lent 1753, Lent 1758) and Kent (Lent 1758) assize records, PRO, ASSI 94/822, ASSI 94/892, and ASSI 94/894 • Sir John Fielding's accounts, 1756–9, PRO, T 38/671 • *The proceedings on the king's commission of the peace* (1757–8) [Old Bailey sessions papers, 22–5 Feb 1758] • W. Jackson, *The new and complete Newgate calendar*, new edn, 4 (1818) • *Public Advertiser* (5 Aug 1757) • *Public Advertiser* (10 Aug 1757) • *Public Advertiser* (1 Sept 1757) • *Public Advertiser* (8 Sept 1757) • Middlesex gaol delivery roll, 22 Feb 1758, LMA, OB/SR. 18 • parish register (baptisms), 22 Oct 1729, St Mary the Virgin, Hampton, Middlesex • *GM*, 1st ser., 27 (1757), 382 • *GM*, 1st ser., 28 (1758), 92, 143, 192
Archives LMA, OB/SR. 18 • PRO, ASSI 94/822; ASSI 94/892; ASSI 94/894; ASSI 31/3; T38/671
Likenesses line engraving, repro. in *Genuine narrative*

Page, William (1861–1934), historian and antiquary, was born on 4 September 1861 at 26 Norfolk Square, Paddington, London, the third son and fifth and last child of Henry Page (1811–1874), merchant, and his wife, Georgiana (Georgina) Forrester (*b. c.*1823). He was baptized on 16 October 1861 at St James's, Sussex Gardens. After a short time at Dr Westmacott's local private school, and despite his father's death, he attended Westminster School from January to May 1875. After being articled to a civil engineer, and following his brother to Australia, he was assistant executive engineer to the Queensland government from 1880 to 1884.

In 1885 Page returned to England and joined his brother-in-law William John Hardy, son of Sir William Hardy, the deputy keeper of public records, as partner in the firm of Hardy and Page, record agents. He married on 8 June 1886, apparently at Penzance, Kate Marion (Marianne; 1863–1947), youngest daughter of Charles William Roe of Chiswick, London; they had a son and daughter. He was elected a fellow of the Society of Antiquaries before he was twenty-six and his first paper, ‘Some remarks on Northumbrian palatinates and regalities’, appeared in *Archaeologia* in 1888. Hardy's residence at St Albans encouraged Page to research Hertfordshire history and archaeology, and to move to St Albans from 1896 to 1902.

Page's output of articles and editions was already voluminous when he came to the attention of Herbert Arthur

Doubleday, co-founder of the *Victoria History of the Counties of England* (*VCH*), begun in 1899. Doubleday had realized that the records on which his contributors depended to produce topographical chapters and manorial descents needed centrally organized searching in London by specially trained researchers and writers. For that he turned to Hardy and Page, who in 1902 became joint, and from 1904 to 1934 was sole, editor of the *History*.

Page returned to London, living at Battersea from 1904 to 1906 and at Frognal Cottage, Hampstead, from then until 1922. His impact on the *VCH* was dramatic. By 1902 only one volume had appeared; by the end of 1910 there were forty-six. A *Guide* published about 1903 was largely Page's work. It underlay *VCH* practice until 1950 and indirectly later. He was probably responsible for encouraging the marked architectural content of the early *VCH*, served on the Royal Commission on Historical Monuments (England) from 1909 to 1934, and was also an inspector under the Historical Manuscripts Commission.

Failure of funds and the First World War disrupted the *VCH*. Page occupied himself with his works *Commerce and Industry* (1919) and *London* (1923), on the city's early history. After the war he worked, largely without assistance, to bring to publication twenty-one more volumes. In 1922, despite obtaining an office at the University of London's new Institute of Historical Research, he moved to Middleton-on-Sea, Sussex, taking all the *VCH*'s materials with him, and became its proprietor in 1928. In 1932 Oxford University awarded him the honorary degree of DLitt, the sole recognition of his service to local history. In order to ensure the *VCH*'s continuance he conveyed all the rights in 1933 to the University of London, which set up a management committee of which he remained chairman until he died at Middleton on 3 February 1934.

Page's last edited work, *VCH Rutland*, volume 2, appeared posthumously in 1935 prefaced by a full bibliography of his publications, which combined archaeological investigation with a deep knowledge of historical sources and an interest in innovative methodology. His editorial work for the *VCH* displays both immense energy and productivity and great tact in dealing with contributors.

C. R. J. CURRIE

Sources *DNB* · *VCH Rutland*, 2.ix–x · *WWW*, *1929–40* · *VCH General introduction* · census returns, 1861, PRO, RG 9/10, fol. 67*v*; 1871, RG 10/23, fol. 62 · parish registers, LMA, P 87/JS/010 · VCH records, U. Lond., Institute of Historical Research, corresp. A and B · H. A. Doubleday and W. Page, *A guide to the Victoria history of the counties of England* [n.d., *c*.1903]

Archives Essex RO, Colchester, corresp. as executor of J. H. Round · Institute of Historical Research, London, Victoria County History records · Man. CL, Manchester Archives and Local Studies, letters to John Brownbill and William Farrer · Man. CL, Manchester Archives and Local Studies, letters to R. D. Radcliffe · W. Yorks. AS, Leeds, Yorkshire Archaeological Society, calendar of Yorkshire deeds, notes on sources for history of Scarborough

Likenesses H. J. Stock, oils, 1926, Institute of Historical Research, London · photograph, 1932, Institute of Historical Research, London, VCH records; repro. in *VCH Rutland*, facing p. ix

Wealth at death £7542 6*s*. 1*d*.: probate, 14 May 1934, *CGPLA Eng. & Wales*

Pageham, John de. *See* Pagham, John of (*d*. 1157).

Pagel, Walter Traugott Ulrich (1898–1983), medical historian and pathologist, was born on 12 November 1898 in Berlin, the youngest son of five children of Julius Leopold Pagel (1851–1912), an eminent medical historian and physician, and his wife, Marie, *née* Labaschin (*d*. 1909). After attending the Volksschule, Berlin (1904–8), and the Humanistisches Friedrichs Gymnasium, Berlin (1908–16), Pagel graduated in medicine in Berlin in 1922. After university posts at Tübingen and Berlin he gained a higher doctorate in 1930 at Heidelberg University, habilitating himself with a paper on R. C. Virchow. In 1923 at Hohegaife, he married Dr Magdalene M. E. Koll (*d*. 1980). Tall and handsome, she dedicated her whole life to caring for her husband. They had one son, Bernard Ephraim Julius (*b*. 1930), who became an astronomer and a fellow of the Royal Society.

In the field of medicine Pagel researched and applied K. E. Ranke's new theories on the immunology of pulmonary tuberculosis and became particularly expert in the histopathology of tuberculosis. His *Pulmonary Tuberculosis* (1939), written with G. G. Keyne and L. O'Shaughnessy, went into several editions.

In 1933 Pagel and his family emigrated, first to France, where he worked at the Calmette Laboratory at the Pasteur Institute, Paris, and then to England, where Pagel became pathologist to the Papworth Village settlement, near Cambridge. In the same year he became one of the founders of the Cambridge history of science lectures committee. With Joseph Needham he published a selection from these lectures entitled *Background to Modern Science* (1938), with contributions from Lord Rutherford, Sir Arthur Eddington, and J. B. S. Haldane. From 1939 to 1956 he was consultant pathologist to the Central Middlesex Hospital, Harlesden, London, and from 1956 to 1967 to the Clare Hall Hospital, Barnet, Hertfordshire.

More important than Pagel's contribution to the study of the pathology of tuberculosis was his work in the history of medicine. Pagel's view that medical ideas and practices could only be understood by placing them in their proper historical context and should not be judged according to contemporary criteria has since, partially as a result of his influence, become a commonplace in the history of medicine. Pagel's first book on Jan Baptista Van Helmont (1579–1644) was published in 1930. A book about Helmont's biological ideas, their sources and background, *J. B. Van Helmont, Reformer of Science and Medicine*, edited by Margaret Pelling, was published in 1982. A third large work on Van Helmont remains unpublished. Pagel's 'Religious motives in medical biology of the seventeenth century', originally published in 1935, may be found, together with many of his other articles on medical history, in *Religion and Neoplatonism in Renaissance Medicine* (1985) and *From Paracelsus to Van Helmont* (1986). In 1958 Pagel's English book on Paracelsus, *Paracelsus, an Introduction to Philosophical Medicine in the Era of the Renaissance*, was published. Another aspect was treated in his German work, *Das medizinische Weltbild des Paracelsus: seine Zusammenhänge mit Neuplatonismus und Gnosis* (1962). In 1967 Pagel published

William Harvey's Biological Ideas, which examined the background to Harvey's ideas and avoided presenting him solely as the discoverer of the circulation of the blood who was of interest because of his role in the development of modern medicine. 'William Harvey revisited' in the journal *History of Science* (1969–70) and his *New Light on Harvey* of 1976 dealt with Harvey's Aristotelianism and controversies regarding Harvey's discoveries. A collection of essays called *The Smiling Spleen* was published posthumously in 1984. A two volume Festschrift, *Science, Medicine and Society in the Renaissance*, appeared in 1972, edited by Allen Debus.

Pagel was awarded honorary MD degrees by Basel University in 1961 and Heidelberg University in 1966, a DLitt by Leeds University, the Dexter award in the history of chemistry by the American History of Chemistry Society in 1969, and the fellowship of the British Academy in 1976. He was awarded the Sarton medal in 1970, the Julius Pagel medal in 1971, the Robert Koch medal in 1973, the William H. Welch medal in 1976, and the Paracelsus ring of the city of Villach.

Physically, Pagel was of small stature and was in delicate health as a result of having suffered from tuberculosis and, later in life, asthma. However, Pagel's all-pervasive intellect, exuberant sense of humour, and sparkling wit, together with his compassion for, and empathy with, scholars from all over the world, whether young research students or famous professors, all of whom he encouraged and helped, rendered these impediments unimportant. Tea at his home, 58 Millway, Mill Hill, London, remained unforgettable. Pagel was Jewish, but his knowledge and interest in the mystical component of religion determining the philosophy of life and consequently the work of savants of the past was universal. Pagel died in the Royal Free Hospital, Camden, London, of kidney failure on 25 March 1983 and was cremated at Golders Green on the 31st. A Walter Pagel memorial symposium was held in December 1983, at the Wellcome Institute for the History of Medicine, London. MARIANNE WINDER

Sources W. T. U. Pagel, 'Erinnerungen und Forschungen', *Wege zur Wissenschaftsgeschichte II: Beiträge zur Geschichte der Wissenschaft und Technik*, 17 (1982), 45–56 • M. Winder and R. Burgess, *Medical History*, 27 (1983), 310–11 • *The Times* (4 April 1983) • *The Lancet* (16 April 1983) • J. Gromer, *Julius Leopold Pagel, 1851–1912* (1985) • private information (2004) • personal knowledge (2004) • M. Winder, 'A bibliography of the writings of Walter Pagel', *Science, medicine and society in the Renaissance*, ed. A. G. Debus (1972), 2.289–326 • M. Winder, 'Die Spezialbibliographie Walter Pagel: sein Medizin- und Wissenschaftsgeschichtliches Oeuvre', *Pharmaziegeschichtliche Rundschau* [Beilage zur Pharmazeutischen Zeitung] (June 1985), 15/2421–16/2422 • M. Winder, 'Die Spezialbibliographie Walter Pagel: sein Medizin- und Wissenschaftsgeschichtliches Oeuvre', *Pharmaziegeschichtliche Rundschau* [Beilage zur Pharmazeutischen Zeitung] (Dec 1985), 30/308–31/309 • M. Winder, 'Die Spezialbibliographie Walter Pagel: sein Medizin- und Wissenschaftsgeschichtliches Oeuvre', *Pharmaziegeschichtliche Rundschau* [Beilage zur Pharmazeutischen Zeitung] (June 1986), 46/2126–47/2127 • *WW* (1996) • d. cert.

Archives Wellcome L.

Likenesses group portrait, photograph, 1926 (with Berlin-Sommerfeld hospital staff), Wellcome L. • group portrait, photograph, *c.*1930 (with Tübingen staff), Wellcome L. • group portrait, photograph, 1930 (with Berlin TB hospital staff), Wellcome L. • group portrait, photograph, *c.*1930, Wellcome L. • group portrait, photograph, 1936 (with his wife and son), Wellcome L. • group portrait, photograph, 1940 (with Middlesex Hospital staff), Wellcome L. • photographs, *c.*1954–1980, Wellcome L. • A. Debus, photographs, 1978, Wellcome L. • photographs, Wellcome L.

Wealth at death £196,919: probate, 16 Aug 1983, *CGPLA Eng. & Wales*

Paget, Lord Alfred Henry (1816–1888), official in the royal household, was the second son of Henry William *Paget, first marquess of Anglesey (1768–1854) from his second marriage, to Lady Charlotte, *née* Cadogan (*d.* 1853), the divorced wife of Sir Henry Wellesley. He was born on 29 June 1816, and educated at Westminster School. He became a lieutenant in the Blues in 1834, purchased an unattached company in 1840, and exchanged into his father's regiment, the 7th hussars, in which he served for several years, rising to the rank of general on the retired list in 1881. On 8 April 1847 he married Cecilia (*d.* 1914), second daughter and coheir of George Thomas Wyndham of Cromer Hall, Norfolk, and had six sons and six daughters.

Paget was MP for Lichfield from 1837 to 1865, and held court office under all the whig ministries during that period. He was equerry to the queen in 1837–41 and chief equerry and clerk marshall in 1846–52 and 1852–8, and again held those positions in 1859–74 (the clerk marshall having ceased to change with the ministry in 1866). In 1874 he resigned as chief equerry, remaining clerk marshall until his death (on 24 August 1888, on his yacht off Inverness), after which the post was abolished.

K. D. REYNOLDS

Sources W. A. Lindsay, *The royal household* (1898) • Burke, *Peerage*

Archives BL, papers, Add. MSS 51245–51250

Likenesses R. B. Davis, group portrait, oils, 1837, Plas Newydd, Anglesey • Ape [C. Pellegrini], chromolithograph caricature, NPG; repro. in *VF* (3 July 1875) • R. J. Lane, lithograph (after Count D'Orsay), BM, NPG • photograph, NPG

Wealth at death £134,697 3*s.* 7*d.*: resworn probate, April 1890, *CGPLA Eng. & Wales* (1889)

Paget, Sir Arthur (1771–1840), diplomatist, third and most distinguished of the six sons of Henry Bayly Paget, first earl of Uxbridge of the second creation, and his wife, Jane, eldest daughter of the Very Revd Arthur Champagne, dean of Clonmacnoise, was born on 15 January 1771. He was brother of Henry William *Paget and Edward *Paget. He entered Westminster School on 10 April 1780 and was elected to the foundation in 1783. From there he went to Christ Church, Oxford, matriculating on 8 June 1787; he took no degree but established a close relationship with Dean Cyril Jackson. In 1791 he entered the diplomatic service, and on 22 November 1794 he was returned to parliament for Anglesey, which he continued nominally to represent until 1807. Paget was a man of easy charm who made his way with little difficulty up the diplomatic ladder, assisted by his moderate whiggery. On the abandonment by Prussia of the defence of Holland, in July 1794, he was dispatched to Berlin as envoy-extraordinary to remind King Frederick William of his obligations. His conduct of this delicate mission was commended by Lord Malmesbury. Obtaining no satisfactory assurances from the king, he withdrew to Pyrmont about Christmas, and,

Sir Arthur Paget (1771–1840), by John Hoppner, c.1804

when the French crossed the Waal, he returned to England by way of Brunswick and Holland. Some letters from him to the countess of Lichtenau written during this dangerous journey, in which, as a last resort, he implores her to use her influence with the king on behalf of the Dutch, are printed in *Apologie der Gräfin von Lichtenau* (2 vols., 1808).

Paget was accredited envoy-extraordinary to the elector palatine and minister to the Diet of Regensburg on 22 May 1798. He was appointed envoy-extraordinary and minister-plenipotentiary to the court of Naples on 17 January 1800, and to that of Vienna on 21 August 1801, where his extravagance gained him the nickname 'The Emperor' (*Paget Papers*, 1.xiii). His dispatches from Vienna in July 1802, after Napoleon's reorganization of the smaller German states, contained a remarkable prediction of the eventual acquisition by Prussia of the hegemony of Germany. In 1805 he contributed materially to the formation of the third coalition against France, and reported its total discomfiture by the battle of Austerlitz, on 2 December 1805. His gloomy dispatch on the day after the battle is said to have contributed to the death of Pitt. Recalled in February 1806, he was accredited, on 15 May 1807, ambassador to the Ottoman Porte. On the signature of the peace of Tilsit on 7 July following, he told the sultan of the secret article by which the provisions in favour of Turkey were rendered nugatory, and exhausted the resources of persuasion and threat, even bringing the British fleet into the Dardanelles, in an attempt to detach the Porte from the French alliance. In this, however, he failed. In May 1809 he was recalled, and retired on a pension of £2000.

Paget was sworn of the privy council on 4 January 1804, and was nominated KB on 21 May following. On 18 May 1808 he eloped with Augusta Jane Parker, Lady Boringdon (*née* Fane), second daughter of John, tenth earl of Westmorland, causing considerable scandal. He married her on 16 February 1809, two days after her divorce from John, second Baron Boringdon, afterwards earl of Morley. With her he had several children who survived him, one of whom was the diplomatist Sir Augustus Berkeley *Paget. He spent his retirement years as an agriculturalist and yachtsman. He was made GCB in January 1815. Paget died at his house in Grosvenor Street, London, on 26 July 1840 and was buried on 1 August in Kensal Green cemetery.

J. M. Rigg, *rev.* H. C. G. Matthew

Sources *The Paget papers: diplomatic and other correspondence of the Right Hon. Sir Arthur Paget, G. C. B., 1794–1807*, ed. A. B. Paget, 2 vols. (1896) • *The Paget brothers, 1790–1840*, ed. Lord Hylton [H. G. H. Jolliffe] (1918) • HoP, *Commons* • *Diaries and correspondence of James Harris, first earl of Malmesbury*, ed. third earl of Malmesbury [J. H. Harris], 4 vols. (1844)

Archives Bedford estate office, London • BL, corresp. and papers, Add. MSS 48383–48416 • PRO, letter-book and corresp., FO 353 • Woburn Abbey, Bedfordshire, dispatches and papers | BL, letters to Lord Grenville, Add. MS 59019 • Hants. RO, corresp. with first earl of Malmesbury • NL Scot., letters to Sir Thomas Graham • NL Scot., corresp. with first earl of Minto • NRA Scotland, Fraser MSS • Suffolk RO, Ipswich, letters to Alexander Straton • U. Aberdeen L., corresp. with A. M. Fraser • W. Sussex RO, letters to duke of Richmond

Likenesses J. Hoppner, oils, c.1804, Plas Newydd, Gwynedd [*see illus.*] • Count D'Orsay, pen and chalk drawing, 1840, NPG • G. Hayter, drawing, repro. in Hylton, ed., *The Paget brothers* • S. Percy, wax model, V&A

Paget, Sir Augustus Berkeley (1823–1896), diplomatist, the fourth son of Sir Arthur *Paget (1771–1840), diplomatist, and his wife, Augusta Jane, *née* Fane, was born on 16 April 1823. The father was the third son of the first earl of Uxbridge, and a brother of Henry William *Paget, first marquess of Anglesey, and of Sir Edward *Paget. Augustus Paget was privately educated, and in 1840 entered the service of the crown as clerk in the secretary's department of the General Post Office, soon transferring to the Audit Office, and again on 21 August 1841 to the Foreign Office.

Paget then decided to enter the diplomatic service, and on 2 December 1843 was appointed temporary attaché at Madrid, where he remained until 1846. On 6 February 1846 he was appointed précis writer to the foreign secretary, Lord Aberdeen, but on 26 June became second paid attaché to the British embassy at Paris. Here he witnessed the *coup d'état* of 1848, and the establishment of the Second Empire; on 18 December 1851 he became first paid attaché. On 12 February 1852 he was promoted to be secretary of legation at Athens at a time when diplomatic relations with Greece were more or less in abeyance, so that his position was peculiar and required much tact. From the end of the same year, Paget succeeded to a number of important diplomatic posts: in Egypt (1852–3); The Hague (1854–7); Lisbon (1857–8); Berlin (1858–9); and Copenhagen (1859–66). He was created CB on 10 February and KCB on 16 March 1863.

As minister at Copenhagen, Paget saw the accession of Christian IX at the close of 1863, and had to play a leading part with respect to the Schleswig-Holstein difficulty in 1864; nor was his position much less difficult when in 1866 Prussia meditated war against Austria. On 9 June 1866 he was sent to Portugal as envoy-extraordinary. Appointed on 6 July 1867 to Italy as envoy-extraordinary and minister-plenipotentiary to Victor Emmanuel, he represented Great Britain in Italy during one of the most critical periods of Italian history; he saw the entry of the Italian troops into Rome and the beginning of a new era of national life there. In that trying period his tact was conspicuous. He remained in Italy for a long time, becoming ambassador-extraordinary on 24 March 1876, the same year in which he was sworn of the privy council in London. On 12 September 1883 he relinquished his post in Rome and, after a short period of leave, became ambassador at Vienna on 1 January 1884. From that post he retired on 1 July 1893. He devoted much of the leisure which now came to him to the preparation of his father's memoirs, *The Paget Papers* (2 vols., 1898).

On 20 October 1860, Paget married the **Countess Walpurga Ehrengarde Helena de Hohenthal** (*d.* 1929), eldest daughter of Charles Frederick Anthony de Hohenthal, count of the Austrian empire. They had two sons and a daughter. Lady Paget was maid of honour to Queen Victoria's eldest daughter, Princess Victoria, crown princess of Prussia, who called her 'Wally', finding her, at least in 1869, 'prettier than ever … but I regret that she is a little affected and grand sometimes' (*Your dear letter*, 248). The princess thought Lady Paget and her husband unsuited for Vienna, where 'she is not likely to be well or cordially received' and regretted the '36 naked little boys and girls' with which she decorated the embassy (*Beloved mama*, 157). Lady Paget entertainingly recorded embassy life in *Embassies of other Days* (2 vols., 1923) and other books. A woman of progressive views, she was a vegetarian and an anti-vivisectionist; she also wrote an introduction for *Talks about Girls* (1905) in the Kirk Sex Series.

Augustus Paget died suddenly on 11 July 1896 while visiting Lord Salisbury at Hatfield House. He was buried at Tardebigge, Bromsgrove.

C. A. Harris, *rev.* H. C. G. Matthew

Sources *The Paget brothers, 1790–1840*, ed. Lord Hylton [H. G. H. Jolliffe] (1918) • *FO List* (1895) • *The Times* (13 July 1896) • *The Times* (17 July 1896) • *Annual Register* (1896) • *Your dear letter: private correspondence of Queen Victoria and the crown princess of Prussia, 1865–1871*, ed. R. Fulford (1971) • *Beloved mama: private correspondence of Queen Victoria and the German crown princess, 1878–1885*, ed. R. Fulford (1981) • J. Abdy and C. Gere, *The Souls* (1984) • Burke, *Peerage*

Archives BL, corresp. and papers, Add. MSS 51205–51236 | BL, letters to W. E. Gladstone, Add. MSS 44420–44478 • BL, letters to Sir Austen Layard, Add. MSS 38988–39116 • Bodl. Oxf., letters to fourth earl of Clarendon • CUL, corresp. with Lord Hardinge • Lpool RO, corresp. with fifteenth earl of Derby • PRO, Ampthill MSS • PRO, letters to Lord Hammond, FO 391 • PRO, corresp. with Lord John Russell, PRO 30/22 • PRO, letters to Lord Odo Russell, FO 918

Wealth at death £26,566 8*s*. 0*d*.: probate, 24 Sept 1896, *CGPLA Eng. & Wales*

Paget, Sir Bernard Charles Tolver (1887–1961), army officer, was born on 15 September 1887 at Oxford, the third son and fourth of the six children of Francis *Paget (1851–1911), regius professor of pastoral theology and canon of Christ Church, Oxford, 1885–92, and bishop of Oxford from 1901, and his wife, Helen Beatrice (*d.* 1900), daughter of Richard William *Church (1815–1890), dean of St Paul's. He was educated at Shrewsbury School, and the Royal Military College, Sandhurst (1905–7), and was commissioned into the Oxfordshire and Buckinghamshire light infantry on 13 November 1907.

After a winter with the 2nd battalion at Tidworth, Paget joined the 1st battalion in India in February 1908, and was promoted lieutenant in 1910. He returned to England on leave in 1914, and on the outbreak of war was appointed adjutant of the new 5th (service) battalion, which he helped form, and with which he went to France in May 1915 and remained until November 1915 when he became brigade-major 42nd infantry brigade, 14th light division (MC November 1915.) In October 1917 he was employed as a general staff officer, grade 2 (GSO 2), first with the 62nd division, and then on the general headquarters staff of Sir Douglas Haig.

During the German advance in March 1918 Paget was wounded for the third time, severely in the elbow, which rendered his left arm virtually useless for the rest of his life. He had been appointed DSO in January 1918 and was four times mentioned in dispatches.

There followed a series of staff appointments, graduation at the Staff College, Camberley, in 1920, and promotion to major in 1924 and brevet lieutenant-colonel in 1925. In April 1925 he rejoined the 1st battalion of his regiment as a company commander in Cologne; he left in January 1926 to become an instructor at the Staff College, and in January 1929 he became a student at the Imperial Defence College. He was promoted colonel in 1929. Paget's last regimental appointment was commander of the depot at Cowley barracks, Oxford, in 1930, where he instituted many improvements. One achievement then, which he always recalled with pride, was the dedication of the regimental chapel in Christ Church Cathedral, Oxford.

The normal three-year tenure of his command was reduced to two, with Paget's return to India as chief instructor (GSO 1) at the Staff College, Quetta (1932–4); he won distinction for his role following a disastrous earthquake. At the War Office, 1934–6, he commanded the 4th Quetta infantry brigade, was promoted major-general in December 1937, and returned to England to become commandant of the Staff College, Camberley (1938–9).

In November 1939 he took over command of the 18th division, then in East Anglia, from which he was summoned 'literally at a moment's notice' in April 1940 to take part in the ill-fated Norwegian campaign. German

Sir Bernard Charles Tolver Paget (1887–1961), by Henry Lamb, 1941

superiority, both on the ground and in the air, was overwhelming, the ship carrying the British troops' artillery and transport had been sunk, and the prospects were hopeless. When the cabinet, unwilling to face further losses of ships, and unable to provide the reinforcements for which Paget asked, decided on evacuation, he fought a series of skilful rearguard actions, worthy of his distinguished predecessor, Sir John Moore, and succeeded not only in extricating his troops but also in inflicting heavy losses on the enemy. His achievement brought not only the public praise of the prime minister, but also promotion, though he never again had a fighting command.

After Dunkirk, Paget was for a short time chief of staff, home forces (1940), and when a German invasion seemed imminent, would never permit the airing of pessimistic views or contemplate the possibility of defeat.

When South-Eastern command was formed in 1941 Paget was appointed general officer commanding-in-chief and promoted lieutenant-general. At the end of 1941 he succeeded Sir Alan Brooke as commander-in-chief, home forces, a command he held until July 1943, when, having been promoted general, he was assigned to form Twenty-First Army group of fifteen divisions, in preparation for the Normandy invasion. However, he never commanded in the field the force he trained; the appointment went to General Sir Bernard Montgomery, fresh from his campaigns in north Africa and Italy. Montgomery, who had been at Sandhurst with Paget and become his friend, had a high regard for Paget and praised his training of the force.

Paget was very disappointed but he may go down in history as the greatest trainer of British soldiers since Sir John Moore, teaching them how to overcome the difficulties of attacking against modern firepower—'to bridge', as he described it, 'the gap between the barrage and the bayonet'. To further this he established a school of infantry, with divisional battle schools, in which he aimed at creating 'a true offensive spirit, combined with the will-power which will not recognize defeat', as well as battle inoculation using live ammunition.

Shortly after Paget's death, papers which he had refused to allow to be published disclosed details of operation 'skyscraper', prepared by him in the spring of 1943 as a detailed study of the proposed invasion of north-western Europe. It was described as 'a blueprint for the D-day operations of 1944; there were the same beaches, and the same objectives, while the problems of an opposed landing had all been fully assessed … the first key plan of the invasion'.

In January 1944 Paget became general officer commanding-in-chief Middle East forces in succession to Sir Henry Wilson, where he remained until October 1946, when he retired from the army at his own request. During this command, while no active service was involved, there were many difficulties, and in dealing with these he enhanced his reputation. Again he was successful in a tough assignment, and few could have handled so adroitly such varied problems as the administration of the Polish base and the April 1944 Greek mutiny in Egypt. He was 'the only man who really understood the problem', observed a prominent Greek official afterwards. Paget was appointed CB in 1940, KCB in 1942, and GCB in 1946. In the Second World War he received honours from Greece, Belgium, the United States of America, Czechoslovakia, and Norway—the last the grand cross of the order of St Olaf. He was also an honorary MA (Oxon), Christ Church, Oxford.

Paget married, on 7 February 1918, Winifred Nora (*b*. 13 Aug 1896), his cousin, daughter of Sir John Rahere Paget, second baronet, and they had two sons, both of whom served with distinction in the Second World War. The younger, Lieutenant Anthony Francis Macleod Paget (*b*. 5 Nov 1924), Oxfordshire and Buckinghamshire light infantry, died on 5 March 1945 of wounds received in a gallant action in the Reichswald, Germany, for which he was awarded a posthumous DSO and recommended for the VC.

Paget's retirement was far from idle. Already colonel commandant of the Reconnaissance Corps and the intelligence corps (1943–52), he became in October 1946 colonel of his regiment (1946–55), which gave him pride and pleasure. He was principal of Ashridge College (1946–9), then devoted to adult education in citizenship, until he became, to his delight, governor of the Royal Hospital, Chelsea (October 1949–1957).

There were other activities as well, all of which reflected his care for the soldier, to whom, despite crippling arthritis, the legacy of his wounds, he devoted his last years. Among these were his work for the Forces Help Society, of which he was national chairman, the Lord Roberts Workshops, and not least the Royal Commonwealth Society for the Blind, his efforts for which raised nearly £400,000. He was also governor of the corps of commissionaires.

Shortly before going into complete retirement, in 1956, he took his last parade, a passing out of national servicemen at Cowley barracks, to whom he paid a moving tribute. Afterwards, to the officers in the mess, he said retirement would mean that, for the first time in his life, he would be living in his own house and have to clean his own shoes; nevertheless, he was looking forward to it.

To those who served with him in the regiment, he was its greatest soldier of the century. To many, especially the junior officers, he was rather a frightening person to meet: 'his eyes seemed to bore holes in you' and he made no secret of his dislike of things which he considered to be 'sloppy'. Innately shy, and so apparently not entirely at his ease when talking to men, he was a champion of private soldiers, and, if their conditions were not as good as he thought they should be, 'the fur flew'. He was reportedly without fear, either physical or moral, deeply religious, selfless, and devoted to his country.

Paget died suddenly at his home, the Old Orchard, Heath Road, Petersfield, Hampshire, on 16 February 1961.

ROGER OWEN, *rev.*

Sources *The Times* (18 Feb 1961) • *The Guardian* (22 Feb 1961) • *Oxford Times* (24 Feb 1961) • *Chronicle of the 1st green jackets 43rd and 52nd and the Oxfordshire and Buckinghamshire light infantry* (1960) • private information (1981) • *WWW* • Burke, *Peerage* (1959) • B. Bond, *British military policy between the two world wars* (1980) • B. L. Montgomery, *The memoirs of field-marshal the Viscount Montgomery of Alamein* (1958) • *CGPLA Eng. & Wales* (1961)

Archives NRA, priv. coll., MSS | Berks. RO, letters to Lord Glyn • JRL, corresp. with E. E. Dorman O'Gowan • King's Lond., Liddell Hart C., corresp. with Sir B. H. Liddell Hart | FILM BFI NFTVA, news footage • IWM FVA, actuality footage • IWM FVA, news footage

Likenesses K. Green, oils, 1939, Staff College, Camberley, Surrey • H. Lamb, charcoal and coloured chalk, 1941, NPG [*see illus.*] • H. Lamb, pencil and chalk drawing, 1941, IWM

Wealth at death £15,836 13*s.* 8*d.*: probate, 14 April 1961, *CGPLA Eng. & Wales*

Paget [*née* Masterson], **Briget** (*b.* **1570**, *d.* in or after **1647**), literary editor, was born in Nantwich, Cheshire, the daughter of Richard Masterson and Elizabeth Grosvenor. There is no record of her education but her preface to *Meditations of Death* shows her as literate and engaged in political and theological ideas. Its author, her husband, John *Paget (*d.* 1638), was rector of Nantwich from 1598 to 1604, and their marriage must have taken place during this time. He was ejected for nonconformity, and the couple moved to the Netherlands, where he worked as an army pastor. They had no children of their own, but adopted John Paget's nephew Robert, who later became an English minister in the Netherlands. In 1607 John Paget was offered the pastorship of the newly opened Begynhof Church, Amsterdam, an English Reformed church under the aegis of the Dutch church. He retained this post until 1637, when he retired, owing to ill health, and died in 1638.

Most of what is known about Briget Paget is contained in her preface to her publication of her husband's posthumous work, *Meditations of death, wherein a Christian is taught how to remember and prepare for his latter end* (Dort, 1639). John Paget was active in the politics of the English church abroad, many of his publications being directed against Separatists, but he remained a strict Calvinist. Briget's support for his views is borne out by the contents of her preface; she speaks, for example, of 'those large lessons which by Divine providence have been dispensed to teach and affect with what may be helpful to mortification' (sig. A1). The Pagets actively supported the protestant and political cause of Elizabeth of Bohemia and her husband, both of whom attended services at Paget's church and remarked on his sermons. Briget dedicates her preface and edition of her husband's work 'To the most illustrious and most excellent lady, Elizabeth queene of Bohemia, Countess Palatine of the Rhine etc' and suggests that they had a more intimate relationship when she speaks of 'the gentle and propitious respects your Majesty hath at sundry times manifested unto the author and sometimes also unto myselfe' (sig. A1). She makes an explicit and overt political prayer for their restoration to the Bohemian crown:

> The most high who ruleth in the kingdomes of men and giveth them to whomsoever he will, [may] he rayse and establish your throne and confirm it unto your princely progeny, that with his blessing the house of your Majesty may be blessed forever. (sig. A1)

Briget Paget's preface to *Meditations of Death* shows that she was responsible for editing her husband's sermons for the purposes of publication, suggesting her active, intellectual engagement with his life and work. She frames her boldness in publishing within the conventional feminine modesty topos: the publication is primarily to salve her own loss, and is directly addressed to Elizabeth of Bohemia, rather than to a public audience.

After her husband's death in 1638 Briget Paget moved to live with her adopted son, Robert Paget, in Dordrecht, where he was minister. She managed her own money, since her name is on the sale, in 1647, of two properties previously owned by her husband in Amsterdam. In or after that year she died in Dordrecht. Her will echoed that of her husband's, leaving legacies to nephews and nieces, and to Robert Paget.

KATE AUGHTERSON

Sources *Heralds' visitations of Cheshire*, Harleian Society, 18, 176–7 • A. C. Carter, *The English Reformed church in Amsterdam in the seventeenth century* (1964) • C. A. Burrage, *The early English dissenters in the light of recent research* (1912) • W. Steven, *The history of the Scottish church, Rotterdam* (1832, 1833) • will, Notarial Archives, Amsterdam, 709, fol. 687

Wealth at death exact sum unknown: will, Notarial Archives, Amsterdam, 709, fol. 687

Paget, Charles (*c.*1546–1612), Roman Catholic conspirator, was a younger son of the Tudor statesman William *Paget, first Baron Paget (1505/6–1563), and Anne (*d.* 1587), daughter and heir of Henry Preston. He matriculated on 27 May 1559 as a fellow-commoner of Gonville and Caius College, Cambridge, and was a member of Trinity Hall in August 1564, being present there when Elizabeth I visited the college. Like many other students of his rank he left without taking a degree. He was also admitted to the Middle Temple on 9 October 1560, but never practised the law. Following his father's death in 1563 he inherited, among other property, the lordship of Weston upon Trent, Derbyshire, which he claimed in 1598 was worth £200 a year.

Agent in France of Mary, queen of Scots, 1581–1587 Various members of Paget's family were overt or covert Roman Catholics, and it was to enjoy religious freedom that about 1581 he began his exile. He went to Paris and was to make his base in France for the next seven years. He lived largely in Paris, but also in Rouen, where he first went in late 1582 to recover his health by drinking English beer, which was more readily available there. Paget quickly associated himself with Thomas Morgan, who was a representative of Mary, queen of Scots, in Paris. Within a short time he was also a correspondent of Mary's and enjoyed her confidence, as well as a pension from her. Paget was possibly already known to Mary, since his family had their estates not far from her main place of imprisonment; his noble blood would also have recommended him to her. Even before he went into exile Paget had defended Mary in conversations he had with Henry, Lord Howard. Paget and Morgan worked but also quarrelled with James Beaton, archbishop of Glasgow, who was official ambassador of Mary at the court of the king of France. They kept Mary informed, as far as they could, of events in France and in the Catholic world generally, corresponding by way of Claude Nau and Gilbert Curle, Mary's resident secretaries in her English prison. Paget certainly deferred to Morgan as representative of Mary in Paris, and according to Morgan until 1585 Paget led a rather private life. In 1585, however, Morgan was placed in the Bastille at the insistence of Elizabeth I, and Paget was forced to take a more prominent role.

Paget and Morgan also helped Beaton administer Mary's income from her dower lands in France, which were considerable, and which provided them with their pensions. The degree of control which they were able to exercise over Mary's finances was probably quite slight, although Morgan and to a lesser extent Paget were accused by their enemies of fraud. However, it seems unlikely that they could cheat Beaton and also the French officials who were in charge of her funds. Indeed it is possible that Paget himself was deceived, since in 1586 Mary wrote to Beaton asking him to conceal from Paget the fact that Beaton had received a sum of money from Philip II of Spain; this, she explained, was so that Paget did not ask for repayment of a loan of 4000 crowns which Paget had previously made to Mary's estate.

Paget's mysterious journey to England in 1583 Paget and Morgan were, like their mistress, involved in a number of plots against the government of England. The first plot with which Paget was associated was hatched by Robert Persons and William Allen, and discussed with Beaton in 1582. The plan was to involve the duke of Guise, Philip II of Spain, the pope, and Scottish and English Catholics in a concerted effort to invade England, release Mary, and depose Elizabeth. According to Persons's later account of this plot, Paget and Morgan did not give it their full support, although they pretended to do so. Paget should have been an influential figure in all this since he could give the foreign plotters contact with the alienated Catholic aristocracy in England. Persons alleges that out of personal rivalry and spite Paget refused to co-operate sincerely with the plans. Another less hostile interpretation of the very scattered evidence might be that Paget was cautious and not keen to involve himself and his English friends in plans which would not be successful, but which threatened their lives.

Whatever the case, in the summer of 1583 Paget went from Rouen secretly into England, using the pseudonym Mope. He stayed first with William Davies at Patching in Sussex, and then at Conigar Lodge in the grounds of Petworth House, the residence of the earl of Northumberland. He met the earl, and also his own brother Thomas *Paget, third Lord Paget, who came to the lodge to meet him. Charles Paget was known to the earl and had been looking after Northumberland's sons, who had recently been staying in Paris. He also had a meeting in Patching Wood with a gentleman called William Shelley. He probably also met Henry, Lord Howard, who had come to Sussex from Norfolk at that time. Paget then returned to France.

It is difficult to interpret Paget's visit to England. Clearly there may have been both some Paget and Northumberland family business to transact. An interpretation which is consistent both with Persons's account and that given later in a letter to Mary, queen of Scots, by Paget himself is that Paget met his friends in Sussex and told them what was being discussed, but advised them that it was unlikely to succeed and that they should keep out of it. The impracticality of these plots is perhaps illustrated by the fact that Persons was also at this time attempting to get Paget to agree that Northumberland's sons should be sent into Italy expressly to be arrested by the Inquisition, so that they might be weaned away from protestantism. Paget rejected this scheme, which he may have broached with the earl at Petworth. After Paget returned to France things unravelled quite quickly because the government got wind of the meetings. Lord Paget fled abroad and the Throckmorton plot, which was linked to these projects, was revealed. Shelley and Northumberland were arrested eventually, and the former was executed for treason, while the latter was found shot dead in the Tower of London, apparently a suicide. These deaths were blamed on Paget by his enemies, but unless he actually revealed what he had done to the English government, for which there is no evidence, this accusation is unfair.

That Paget was not a double agent at this time is demonstrated by the response of the English government to his journey to England. In June 1584 Sir Edward Stafford, the

English ambassador in Paris, asked the French authorities, unsuccessfully, for the extradition of the two Paget brothers and various of their associates. They were attainted of treason by act of parliament in 1587.

Paget and the Babington plot, 1585–1587 In 1586 Mary, queen of Scots, was revealed by the English government to have received and written treasonable letters as part of what became known as the Babington plot. She was tried and executed early in 1587. Charles Paget was named in Mary's trial as one of the correspondents who had plotted with her, and her letter to him of 17 July 1586, which the government intercepted, formed part of the evidence against her. Elizabeth I demanded Paget's extradition from the French ambassador, and in her interview with the ambassador threatened that she could easily have Paget assassinated if he remained in Paris. Paget and Morgan have also been accused by Catholic historians of helping lure Mary into a trap set by Walsingham to convict her. Thus Paget discussed invasion schemes and plans for insurrections with Ballard, a misguided adventurer priest who was travelling the continent in 1585, and who then plotted with Babington and his associates in England early in 1586. Ballard was executed along with the other plotters a little before Mary's own death. In a letter to Mary of late 1585 Paget had recommended Ballard to her. Similarly, Morgan had written to Mary advising her to write to Babington. Were they, therefore, culpable of Mary's death? The notion that they deliberately co-operated with the English authorities and that Paget was, as Lady Antonia Fraser puts it, following the Jesuit Leo Hicks, an 'outright spy' in 'Walsingham's service' (Fraser, 553), is not supported by any real evidence. It is difficult to see, in any case, what their motive was for such an action, since it led Morgan to the Bastille, and led to Paget being threatened with assassination by the queen of England. Furthermore, to have Mary killed was to remove their chief financial support. It is worth emphasizing also that Mary retained to the end her affection for Paget and Morgan, but condemned her own secretaries, Nau and Curle, who definitely did betray her.

Had Paget and Morgan innocently led Mary to her death by themselves being duped by Walsingham and his agents? Clearly there is some truth in this, but an air of caution is at times present in their letters written to Mary at this time. In 1585, after the Throckmorton plot, Paget had written to Mary advising her to avoid further plotting, but also saying that if she had the physical strength to escape she should do so. But by early 1586 it is possible that Mary's only hope was a plot of some sort since, as the armada campaign developed, the chances of her surviving a Spanish invasion were very slight indeed. If anyone could help Mary escape it was Babington, whose family estate was only a few miles from Mary's prison, and who was furthermore one of the midland gentry known to Paget.

Exile and faction, 1588–1603 In March 1588 Paget moved from Paris to Brussels, where he lived for the next eleven years. France was no longer safe owing to its descent into civil war. He had already while in Paris been granted, like many other English Catholic exiles, a pension from Philip II; he received, intermittently, the comparatively large sum of 70 escudos a month. He was, not unreasonably, an enthusiastic supporter of the Spanish armada. However, the defeat of the Spanish efforts to conquer England gradually exposed the tensions within the English Catholic movement. Paget was involved at a number of levels in these faction struggles, which had first surfaced in 1582 in disagreements between himself and Morgan on the one hand and Robert Persons and William Allen on the other hand over policies to help Mary, queen of Scots. These quarrels rumbled on even after Mary's death, and in 1590 the rival group was able to get Morgan imprisoned in the Low Countries by the Spanish authorities on a series of charges which questioned his integrity in the service of Mary, queen of Scots. There was clearly a personal element in this, and also rivalry between Paget and Morgan as laymen and Allen and Persons as clergymen, although both factions had supporters from both groups. In addition, anti-Jesuit feeling was growing among the secular clergy and laity all over Europe at this time, but especially in France, and this sharpened hostility to Persons, and to Jesuit control over the English College, Rome. There were fundamental issues of strategy at stake, and these can be traced back to the quarrels of the 1580s too. Although an enthusiastic supporter of the Spanish armada and a recipient of a Spanish pension, Paget became in the 1590s again a committed supporter of a Scottish solution to the English succession question, while Persons adopted the Spanish alternative.

Paget was also willing, as he had been from the beginning of his time in exile, to countenance some sort of accommodation with the English government in return for a degree of religious toleration in England. He had written to both the queen and Walsingham when he first went into exile in respectful terms, and like other exiles was in occasional contact with the various English ambassadors in Paris. After the armada he tried to make contact again with the English government, and was reported as early as 1591 as hoping to discuss the question of toleration for Catholics with them. During the reign of Elizabeth, however, he never recovered his credit in England, and in 1594 when Sir Thomas Wilkes was sent to the Netherlands on an embassy he was instructed to seek the extradition of Paget and other exiles.

Specific events sharpened the faction fighting among Catholic exiles. The death of Allen in 1594 led Paget and his group to oppose the promotion of Persons to the vacant position of cardinal, and to support the candidature of Owen Lewis instead. In 1595 disputes began in the English College at Rome, and one of the dissidents, Robert Fisher, received Paget's strong support when he travelled to Brussels on his way to canvass for support among the secular clergy at Wisbech Castle in England, with whom Paget also had contacts. In 1598 fresh quarrels arose, due to the appointment of George Blackwell as archpriest. Paget supported Blackwell's opponents, the appellants, enthusiastically, and contributed a short written memoir to the controversial publications which were generated by the dispute. By late 1598 he had returned to Paris, now at peace, and a more congenial base from which to maintain an anti-Jesuit and anti-Spanish campaign.

Return to England From Paris, Paget worked hard to curry favour with the English statesmen already preparing for a Scottish succession. The accession of James VI, whose mother Paget had served for six years, enabled him to return to England. His attainder was reversed, and on 13 July 1603 he recovered his lands. The king also granted him a pension of £200 per annum. He died, probably on his estate at Weston upon Trent, at the beginning of February 1612. He was unmarried and left his estate of six manors, a park, and the advowson of three benefices to his niece, Mary Gerard.

Paget has suffered considerably at the hands of later writers. He has been accused of dishonesty and betrayal, or, at the very least, of hopeless incompetence as adviser to Mary Stewart. These assessments are very harsh, and not supported by evidence. What Paget's career illustrates is the difficulties faced by the dissident Catholic aristocracy in the reign of Elizabeth. The clerical Counter-Reformation proclaimed by Persons and Allen was a reasonable course to follow, but only if it worked; otherwise, a more pliable, co-operative policy, rather on the lines of the politique programme developed in France in the years of Paget's exile there was to be preferred. Paget's approach triumphed personally and James I allowed him to return. In the longer term the strategy of Catholic accommodation with the protestant authorities also won through. Unfortunately for Paget's reputation, the history books have tended to be based on the researches of those who have regarded themselves as descendants of his opponents. PETER HOLMES

Sources *DNB* • GEC, *Peerage* • L. Hicks, *An Elizabethan problem: some aspects of the careers of two exile-adventurers* (1964) • C. Nau, *The history of Mary Stewart*, ed. J. Stevenson (1883) • *Lettres, instructions et mémoires de Marie Stuart, reine d'Écosse*, ed. A. Labanoff, 7 vols. (1852) • A. Fraser, *Mary, queen of Scots* (1972), 552–3, 555–6, 561, 566, 586 • *CSP Scot.*, 1581–6 • 'The memoirs of Father Robert Persons', ed. J. H. Pollen, *Miscellanea, II*, Catholic RS, 2 (1906), 12–218, esp. 12, 31–6, 183–5, 253–72 • J. H. Pollen, ed., 'Official lists of Catholic prisoners during the reign of Queen Elizabeth', *Miscellanea, II*, Catholic RS, 2 (1906), 219–88, esp. 253, 255–6, 258, 263, 265, 272 • A. J. Loomie, *The Spanish Elizabethans* (1963), 35, 37–8, 42, 58, 95, 113, 255–6 • *The letters and despatches of Richard Verstegan, c. 1550–1640*, ed. A. G. Petti, Catholic RS, 52 (1959), 136, 140, 166, 205–7, 231 • P. Renold, ed., *The Wisbech stirs, 1595–1598*, Catholic RS, 51 (1958) • *Miscellanea, IV*, Catholic RS, 4 (1907), 97–9 • L. Hicks, ed., *Letters and memorials of Father Robert Persons*, Catholic RS, 39 (1942) • *Letters of William Allen and Richard Barret, 1572–1598*, ed. P. Renold, Catholic RS, 58 (1967) • 'Correspondence of Cardinal Allen', ed. P. Ryan, *Miscellanea, VII*, Catholic RS, 9 (1911), 12–105, esp. 42–3 • T. G. Law, ed., *The archpriest controversy: documents relating to the dissensions of the Roman Catholic clergy, 1597–1602*, 1, CS, new ser., 56 (1896), 7ff., 207, 237; 2, CS, new ser., 58 (1898), 205 • H. A. C. Sturgess, ed., *Register of admissions to the Honourable Society of the Middle Temple, from the fifteenth century to the year 1944*, 3 vols. (1949) • Cooper, *Ath. Cantab.*, 3.53–7 • PRO, PROB 11/119

Likenesses oils, *c.*1595, Parham Park, West Sussex

Wealth at death £40 p.a. rental income; plus six manors, three advowsons, and a park: will, PRO, PROB 11/119

Paget, Sir Charles (1778–1839), naval officer, born on 7 October 1778, was fifth son of Henry Bayly Paget, ninth Baron Paget, first earl of Uxbridge of the second creation (1744–1812), and his wife, Jane (1746–1817), daughter of the Revd Arthur Champagne, dean of Clonmacnoise. Henry William *Paget, first marquess of Anglesey, Sir Arthur *Paget, and Sir Edward *Paget were elder brothers. Paget entered the navy in 1790 under the patronage of Sir Andrew Snape Douglas, and, having served in the North Sea and the channel, was, on 12 December 1796, promoted lieutenant of the guardship *Centaur* in the Thames. On 27 June 1797 he was promoted to command the sloop *Martin* in the North Sea, and on 17 October 1797 was posted to the *Penelope* in the channel. From October 1798 to April 1801 he commanded the *Brilliant* in the channel, and afterwards the *Hydra* in the channel and the Mediterranean until November 1802. On 30 March 1803 he commissioned the large frigate *Endymion*, and commanded her for the next two years, cruising in the channel, the Bay of Biscay, and on the coast of Spain or Portugal. In 1804 he captured four Spanish treasure ships from South America, gaining £26,000 prize money, much of which he spent on a country seat and a wife. He married, on 7 March 1805, Elizabeth Araminta (*d.* 1843), daughter of Henry Monck of Foure, co. Westmeath; they had four sons and six daughters.

Paget was superseded in April 1805. He afterwards commanded various frigates or ships of the line in the channel, and from 1812 to 1814 the *Superb* (74 guns), in the Bay of Biscay and on the coast of North America. From 1817 to 1819 he was in command of one of the royal yachts in attendance on the prince regent; on 19 October 1819 he was made a KCH; on 30 January 1822 he was appointed groom of the bedchamber; and on 9 April 1823 was promoted rear-admiral. From 1828 to 1831 he was commander-in-chief at Cork, and was made a GCH on 3 March 1832. On 10 January 1837 he was made vice-admiral, and commanded on the North America and West Indies station until his death. Paget sat as tory MP for the family boroughs of Milborne Port (1804–6) and Caernarfon Boroughs (1806–26, 1831–3, and 1833–4). He died of yellow fever at St Thomas, Jamaica, on 27 January 1839.

J. K. LAUGHTON, *rev.* ANDREW LAMBERT

Sources Marquess of Anglesey [G. C. H. V. Paget], *One-leg: the life and letters of Henry William Paget, first marquess of Anglesey* (1961) • D. Syrett and R. L. DiNardo, *The commissioned sea officers of the Royal Navy, 1660–1815*, rev. edn, Occasional Publications of the Navy RS, 1 (1994) • Burke, *Peerage* • J. Marshall, *Royal naval biography*, 1/2 (1823), 854–6 • HoP, *Commons* • *GM*, 2nd ser., 11 (1839), 657

Archives NMM, letter-book • NRA, priv. coll., corresp. and papers | BL, letters to Sir Arthur Paget, Add. MS 48405 • NL Scot., letters to Sir Alexander Cochrane • NMM, corresp. with Lord Minto • NRA, priv. coll., corresp. with Sir Charles Adam • Plas Newydd, Anglesey, marquess of Anglesey papers • W. Sussex RO, letters to duke of Richmond

Likenesses T. C. Thompson, double portrait, exh. RA 1823 (with the first marquess of Anglesey), Army and Navy Club, London

Paget, Lord Clarence Edward (1811–1895), naval officer and politician, was born on 17 June 1811, the first son of Henry William *Paget, first marquess of Anglesey (1768–1854), and his second wife, Charlotte Cadogan (1781–1853), previously married to Henry Wellesley. His half-brothers included Henry *Wellesley, first Earl Cowley. After attending Westminster School Paget entered the navy on 29 May 1823. As a midshipman he served on board the *Asia* at the battle of Navarino on 20 October 1827. He passed his examination in 1830 and was promoted lieutenant on 14 May 1831; after a number of flagship appointments he was promoted commander on 25 September 1834, through the intervention of the prime minister, prompted by his father. In 1835 his father took him to Germany to cure venereal disease, and in 1836 he was seriously ill with abscesses on the liver. The former illness permanently damaged his eyesight.

In 1837 Paget commanded the sloop *Pearl* on the North American station; he paid her off after being promoted captain on 26 March 1839. That summer he accompanied his father to Russia, where he visited the tsar and observed naval and military manoeuvres. The following year he served as flag captain to Admiral Otway at Sheerness. He commanded the *Aigle* in the Mediterranean between 1841 and 1845. In 1846 he was appointed secretary to the Board of Ordnance by his father, then the master-general, and in 1847 was elected a Liberal MP for the government borough of Sandwich, which he held until 1852. On 7 April 1852 he married Martha Stuart (*d.* 1895), daughter of Admiral Sir Robert Waller *Otway. They had one son and two daughters. In 1852 he left the Board of Ordnance on the retirement of his father. He was not considered to have been a success in this post, giving little indication of his real ability.

In February 1854 Sir James Graham appointed Paget to command the steam battleship *Princess Royal*. He served in the Baltic during 1854 and, with other aristocratic officers, was openly and unjustifiably critical of the admiral, Sir Charles Napier. Paget's letters to his brother-in-law Lord Sydney were used to discredit Napier in cabinet and at court. Paget had incurred Napier's wrath by poor station keeping and running his ship aground. He was transferred to the Black Sea for the 1855 campaign, during which he developed a system of lights to permit night attacks on Sevastopol from the sea. In July he had to be invalided home with a recurrence of severe eye problems and general ill health. On 4 February 1857 he became a rear admiral. In March 1857 he regained the seat at Sandwich, this time supported by his business colleague Richard Green, a leading London shipbuilder and shipowner with local influence.

Paget used his seat in the Commons to attack the administration of the navy, and quickly secured an offer of a seat at the Board of Admiralty, which he turned down, as acceptance would have required him to end his links with Green. In this period Paget co-operated with the economic radicals, especially William Schaw Lindsay and Richard Cobden, speaking effectively against the conservative navy estimates of 1859. The combination of radical links, parliamentary talent, and aristocratic origins persuaded Lord Palmerston to appoint him first or political secretary to the Admiralty under Edward Adolphus Seymour, twelfth duke of Somerset, first lord of the Admiralty. He held this post from June 1859 until April 1866, acting as departmental spokesman in the House of Commons. Gradually the members realized that his apparently frank and honest statements were artfully constructed smokescreens. He was an early advocate of the ironclad warship, encouraging and advising Gladstone in his attempt to circumvent the declared policy of the government and the Admiralty that it was necessary to build further wooden warships until the ironclad was proven. His support for smaller ironclads led the controller of the navy, Admiral Sir Baldwin Walker, to leave office. Paget joined Gladstone's attempt to secure a naval arms limitation treaty with France, using Lindsay and Cobden as emissaries, once again in clear opposition to the stated policy of the Admiralty and Palmerston. Having accepted office he was never again trusted by the radicals, a fact that had some influence over his decision to take a seagoing command rather than face a new election.

On 24 April 1865 Paget reached the rank of vice-admiral and resigned from the Admiralty; he accepted the post of commander-in-chief of the Mediterranean Fleet on the 28th, took the Chiltern Hundreds on the 30th, and was sworn of the privy council. After a largely uneventful three-year term in the Mediterranean Paget returned home and actively canvassed for the post of first lord under his friend Gladstone, with the proviso that he was to be promoted to the peerage. In this he was unsuccessful. He reached the rank of admiral on 1 April 1870, but had no further employment and retired in 1876. In retirement he devoted his time to the arts, being an accomplished sculptor. He modelled and erected a colossal statue of Nelson on the coast of Anglesey, close to his home. He was made GCB in May 1886. Paget died at 65 Regency Square, Brighton, on 22 March 1895, and his wife died the next day. They were buried at Patcham, near Brighton, on 28 March.

After an early career made by his father's whig connections Paget matured into an ambitious political admiral. Keenly aware of his limited opportunities as a younger son, albeit his father's favourite, Paget exploited his profession for personal advancement. Although an unimpressive sea officer, and an unscrupulous politician, he was, as first secretary, the most effective naval officer in the House of Commons in the nineteenth century.

ANDREW LAMBERT

Sources *Autobiography and journals of Admiral Lord Clarence E. Paget*, ed. A. Otway (1896) • BL, Gladstone MSS • NMM, Lindsay MSS • BL, Wood MSS • O'Byrne, *Naval biog. dict.* • Marquess of Anglesey [G. C. H. V. Paget], *One-leg: the life and letters of Henry William Paget, first marquess of Anglesey* (1961) • A. D. Lambert, *The Crimean War: British grand strategy, 1853–56* (1990) • J. H. Briggs, *Naval administrations, 1827 to 1892: the experience of 65 years*, ed. Lady Briggs (1897) • *Annual Register* (1895) • J. Vincent, *The formation of the British liberal party, 1857–1866* (1966) • F. W. G. Andrews, 'An analysis of the poll-books of Sandwich, 1831–1868', MPhil diss., U. Lond., 1987 • Boase, *Mod. Eng. biog.* • Burke, *Peerage* (1959) • *WWBMP* • *CGPLA Eng. & Wales* (1895)

Archives NRA, priv. coll., bills | BL, memoranda and corresp. with W. E. Gladstone, Add. MSS 44393–44752, *passim* • Bucks. RLSS, letters to Lord Cottesloe

Likenesses oils, 1866, Gov. Art Coll. • D. J. Pound, stipple and line engraving (after photograph by J. Watkins), BM; repro. in *Illustrated News of the World* [supplement] • portrait, repro. in Otway, ed., *Autobiography and journals* • portrait, repro. in *VF* (July 1875), pl. 120
Wealth at death £26,780 3*s*. 4*d*.: resworn administration with will, Jan 1896, *CGPLA Eng. & Wales*

Paget, Dorothy Wyndham (1905–1960), racehorse owner and eccentric, was born on 21 February 1905, at 32 Green Street, Mayfair, London, the second daughter and youngest child of Almeric Hugh Paget, first Baron Queenborough (1861–1949), politician and yachtsman, and Pauline Payne (*d*. 1916), daughter of a wealthy American politician, William C. Whitney. She was a spoilt child and her bad behaviour, accentuated perhaps by her mother's death when she was ten or eleven, led to expulsion from six schools, beginning with Heathfield School at Ascot. She finished her formal education in Paris at an establishment run by Princess Meshchersky, a Russian émigrée.

Dorothy Paget's wealth, inherited from her maternal grandfather, allowed her to indulge in expensive leisure pursuits. In 1931 she supported the motor-racing team of the 1929 Le Mans winner Tim Birken to the tune of £32,000. The involvement led to a lifelong passion for fast driving. She also invested heavily in show-jumping. As a girl she had been an accomplished rider in the show-ring and she returned to this pursuit as an owner in the 1950s with a number of successful horses.

It was as a racehorse owner that Dorothy Paget gained sporting and public fame. Statistically her career in racing was a successful one, bringing her 1532 winners, securing among them seven Cheltenham Gold Cups (five in succession with Golden Miller), two Champion Hurdles, a Grand National (also with Golden Miller), and a wartime Derby in 1943 with Straight Deal. In 1940/41 and again in 1951/2 she was leading National Hunt owner. Financially her sojourn on the turf was a disaster, costing her over £3 million. This was in addition to her vast gambling losses. She bet huge sums daily. Her largest recorded bet was £160,000 to win £20,000 and although this was successful others were not.

Dorothy Paget paid little attention to her appearance and on the racecourse invariably clad her 20 stone bulk in a substantial speckled blue tweed coat. Not easily approachable, she was domineering, often abominably rude; she described herself as 'desperately fussy' (Gilbey, 138), but had a sense of humour, often at her own expense. She cared nothing for public esteem, declaring that 'the public don't pay my training bills' (ibid., 44). She knew little about politics but declared herself an ardent Conservative 'because I dislike being ruled by the lower classes' (ibid., 134). Like many gamblers she was superstitious and had a particular aversion to the colour green. Her behaviour in other areas bordered on the obsessive. She referred to her staff by a colour code rather than name and often communicated with them by memoranda. She would hire a railway compartment to ensure her privacy and always took two seats at the theatre or Wimbledon, one for her handbag.

With a few exceptions in racing circles, Dorothy Paget found male company distasteful and claimed she was sometimes physically sick in the presence of men. When she congratulated Golden Miller it was remarked that this was the first male she had ever kissed, though it was noted that he was a gelding! Not surprisingly she never married, though she lavished affection on Olga (Olili) de Mumm, niece of Princess Meshchersky. Her charity was not for the bookmakers alone. When at schools in Paris, she became a benefactor to a home for elderly Russian refugees in Ste Geneviève-des-Bois and her financial assistance continued until the German invasion of France in 1940.

Dorothy Wyndham Paget (1905–1960), by unknown photographer, 1934 [centre, leading in Golden Miller, ridden by Gerry Wilson, after winning the Grand National in 1934]

At 4.30 a.m. on 9 February 1960, twelve days before her fifty-fifth birthday, Dorothy Paget was poring over her racing calendar at her home, Hermits Wood, Chalfont St Giles, sorting out her entries for racing at Wetherby. An hour later she was found dead from heart failure, no doubt influenced by her weight and the smoking of 100 cigarettes a day. Although she professed no religious beliefs, she was buried on 12 February at St Mary's, Hertingfordbury, Buckinghamshire. An honest but acerbic obituary in the *Sporting Life* led to a spirited response from Olili. Despite her gambling, Dorothy's estate was valued at £3,803,380 (reduced by duties to £736,000); as she died intestate, the beneficiary was her sister, Lady Baillie, to whom in later years she had rarely spoken.

WRAY VAMPLEW

Sources Q. Gilbey, *Queen of the turf: the Dorothy Paget story* (1973) • C. Ramsden, *Ladies in racing: sixteenth century to the present day* (1973) • R. Mortimer, R. Onslow, and P. Willett, *Biographical encyclopedia of British flat racing* (1978) • *The Times* (10 Feb 1960) • *Sporting Life* (10 Feb 1960) • *Sporting Life* (13 Feb 1960) • J. Fairfax-Blakeborough, ed., *The turf who's who* (1932) • R. Green, *A race apart: the history of the Grand National* (1989) • *WWBMP* • b. cert. • d. cert.
Archives FILM 'History of the Cheltenham Festival', BBC video

Likenesses W. W. Rouch and Co., photograph, 1920–29, repro. in Gilbey, *Queen of the turf* • Press Association, photograph, 1929–30, repro. in Gilbey, *Queen of the turf* • photograph, 1934, Empics Sports Photo Agency, Nottingham [*see illus.*] • photograph, 1938, Hult. Arch.; repro. in Gilbey, *Queen of the turf* • photograph, 1941, Hult. Arch. • Press Association, group portrait, photograph, 1954, repro. in Gilbey, *Queen of the turf*

Wealth at death £3,803,380 6*s*. 9*d*.: administration, 19 Feb 1960, *CGPLA Eng. & Wales*

Paget, Sir Edward (1775–1849), army officer and colonial governor, born on 3 November 1775, was fourth son of Henry Paget, first earl of Uxbridge of the second creation (1744–1812), and his wife, Jane (*d.* 1817), eldest daughter of Arthur Champagne, dean of Clanmacnoise, Ireland. Edward entered the army on 23 March 1792 as cornet in the 1st lifeguards and through skill, connections, and family fortunes, he advanced rapidly up the ranks. On 1 December 1792 he became captain in the 54th foot, on 14 November 1793 major, and on 30 April 1794 lieutenant-colonel of the 28th foot at the age of eighteen. He served in Flanders and Holland until March 1795, when he was ordered with his regiment to Quiberon, recalled, and then ordered to the West Indies under Sir Ralph Abercromby. Twice driven back by storms, he finally landed at Portsmouth in January 1796, and in July went to Gibraltar, and, remaining on the Mediterranean station, was present on 14 February 1797 at the action off Cape St Vincent. On 1 January 1798 he was made colonel in the army and aide-de-camp to the king; the same year he was at the capture of Minorca, and in 1801 served through the Egyptian campaign, his regiment being in the reserve under Sir John Moore. He was in the actions of 8, 13, and 21 March 1801, and was severely wounded in the last; was present at the investment of Cairo and Alexandria, and was given as a hostage to the French army at Cairo until they embarked in July 1801. Having returned to England late in 1801, he was in October 1803 appointed brigadier-general on the staff at Fermoy in Ireland; on 2 July 1804 he returned to England, and was made major-general on 1 January 1805. He stayed at Eastbourne until October when he went with his regiment to Cuxhaven and Bremen, returning in February 1806. In June he was sent to the Mediterranean, and placed in command of the reserve in Sicily, returning in January 1808 with the part of the army which was under Sir John Moore. On 23 February he became colonel of the 80th foot, and in April accompanied Sir John Moore to Sweden in command of the reserve. On his return to England in June he was immediately ordered to Portugal, and placed by Sir Hugh Dalrymple in command of the advanced corps of his army. He soon rejoined Sir John Moore in Spain, where he was credited with commanding the reserves at Corunna in such a way as to ensure victory; for this he received a medal, and was appointed to the staff of the Peninsular army under Wellesley, with the local rank of lieutenant-general, and command of the left wing of the army. It was in the Peninsula that Paget earned a reputation for energy and decisiveness, as well as for being a strict disciplinarian. He conducted the advance from Coimbra to Oporto, and on 12 May 1809, in the action before Oporto, lost his right arm. After recuperating in

Sir Edward Paget (1775–1849), by Robert Home, 1823

Britain, during which time he was promoted to lieutenant-general (4 June 1811), Paget rejoined Wellesley as his second-in-command. In November 1812 Paget, accompanied only by his Spanish orderly, rode out from his headquarters to try to restore some order to British troops who were then retreating from Burgos. Paget was captured by a French cavalry patrol and held prisoner until 1814.

On 26 December 1815 Paget rejoined his old regiment, the 28th foot. On 31 October 1818 he was made captain of Cowes Castle, and in 1819 he readied himself for the office of commander-in-chief of Ireland, only to be informed at the last moment that the position had been given to Sir David Baird. On 4 November 1820 he received a commission as governor of Ceylon, and administered the colony uneventfully from August 1821 to March 1823. Meanwhile, on 3 January 1822, he had been appointed commander-in-chief of the forces in the East Indies, and took up his new duties as soon as he was relieved in Ceylon. Paget initially welcomed the posting to India on account of the very generous salaries paid by the East India Company. However, his tenure there gave him little pleasure as he soon became embroiled in several controversies. Ill health and a deep aversion to bureaucracy drove him out of Calcutta and he chose to spend much of his time touring cantonments in upper India. His presence was really needed in Calcutta where the British administration was coping with the demands of a difficult frontier war with Burma. His reputation was further battered by the controversy surrounding his brutal suppression of a mutiny in the Bengal army in 1824. Efforts by the East India Company to have him recalled were blocked by Wellington who, while publicly defending Paget's handling of the Barrackpore mutiny, privately criticized him for his cavalier attitude to his office. Paget became full general on 27 May 1825. He returned to England in 1825, and made Cowes Castle, on the Isle of Wight, his principal residence. Paget received the Portuguese order of the Tower and Sword on 29 April 1812, and was made a GCB on 12 June of that year. He was governor of the Royal Military College from 25 March 1826 to 1837 and then a governor of Chelsea Hospital until 1849.

On 1 May 1805 Paget married Frances Bagot, fourth daughter of William, first Lord Bagot, who died in 1806 at the birth of her child Francis Edward *Paget. In 1815 he married Harriet Legge, (*d.* 1855), fourth daughter of the third earl of Dartmouth. They had eight children: Henry William, Patrick, Edward, Heneage, Frances Jane, Harriet, Charlotte-Louisa, and Mary Georgiana. Paget died on 13 May 1849 at Cowes Castle; after a private funeral he was buried on 21 May in the cemetery of Chelsea Hospital.

C. A. HARRIS, *rev.* DOUGLAS M. PEERS

Sources *Letters and memorials of General the Honourable Sir Edward Paget*, ed. H. M. Paget and E. Paget (1898) • *The Paget brothers, 1790–1840*, ed. Lord Hylton [H. G. H. Jolliffe] (1918) • *GM*, 2nd ser., 32 (1849) • Burke, *Peerage* • GEC, *Peerage* • Fortescue, *Brit. army*, vols. 6–9 • D. M. Peers, *Between Mars and Mammon: colonial armies and the garrison state in India, 1819–1835* (1995) • *Supplementary despatches (correspondence) and memoranda of Field Marshal Arthur, duke of Wellington*, ed. A. R. Wellesley, second duke of Wellington, 15 vols. (1858–72), vols. 6–15 • [A. Wellesley, duke of Wellington], *Despatches, correspondence, and memoranda of Field Marshal Arthur, duke of Wellington*, ed. A. R. Wellesley, second duke of Wellington, 2–3 (1867–8) • C. Oman, *Sir John Moore* (1953) • W. F. P. Napier, *History of the war in the Peninsula and in the south of France*, 6 vols. (1828–40)

Archives NRA, priv. coll., corresp. and papers | BL, Moore MSS • BL, letters to Sir Arthur Paget, Add. MS 48405 • BL OIOC, letters to Lord Amherst, MS Eur. F 140 • NAM, letters to Sir George Wetherall • U. Southampton L., Wellington MSS

Likenesses H. Edridge, watercolour, 1810, V&A • A. C. Lovett, watercolour, 1810 (after H. Edridge), NAM • R. Home, miniature, 1823, NPG [*see illus.*] • R. Home, oils, 1823, Asiatic Society, Calcutta • J. P. Knight, oils, 1844 • H. Weekes, marble bust, 1846 • M. Dubourg, coloured lithograph (*Capture of General Paget 1812*; after portrait by J. A. Atkinson), NAM; repro. in R. Nevill, *British military prints* (1909) • oils, Plas Newydd, Gwynedd

Paget, Edward Francis (1886–1971), archbishop of central Africa, was born on 8 July 1886 in the canon's house, Christ Church, Oxford, the third child and second son of the six children of Francis *Paget (1851–1911), canon, and from 1892 dean, of Christ Church, and bishop of Oxford from 1901, and Beatrice (the daughter of Richard William *Church, dean of St Paul's). He was educated at Shrewsbury School and at Christ Church, Oxford, where he obtained in 1908 a pass degree. He trained at Cuddesdon College and was ordained by his father in 1911, to work in the East End of London. In 1914 he was invited by Archbishop Cosmo Gordon Lang of York to become his chaplain, but had already accepted Bishop Michael Furse's call to become vicar of Benoni in Pretoria, South Africa. After a period as chaplain to the South African forces serving in east Africa (for which he was awarded the MC), he returned to parish work in Transvaal, where he was noted for his vigour and enthusiasm, and for his concern for moral and social questions. In 1922 he played a valuable part as a go-between in the labour disputes on the Reef. In 1925 he was elected as bishop of Southern Rhodesia, within the ecclesiastical province of South Africa. He married Rosemary Allin on 20 October 1932; they had no children.

Paget, whose experience had been overwhelmingly with white congregations, took very seriously the dual nature of the Anglican church in Rhodesia, as the church both for English settlers and for black Africans, evangelized under the auspices of the Society for the Propagation of the Gospel. He began his episcopate with ambitious plans for expansion. These were sometimes seen as unrealistic and overly sanguine by the priests and missionaries who worked under him. The depression of the 1930s further exacerbated the severe financial crisis under which the church operated. But Paget did much to foster the institutional life of the African church: St Augustine's and St Monica's at Penhalonga, the farm of St Faith's, Rusape, and the Cyrene School, near Bulawayo, with its emphasis on African arts and crafts. He also encouraged institutions for Europeans: the boys' school near Marandellas, homes for orphans, and work for people of mixed race. Paget expected his (European) priests to have responsibilities for all Christians in their area, in keeping with his vision of the catholicity and multiracial nature of the church. His overall political philosophy was that enshrined in Cecil Rhodes's dictum of 'equal rights for every civilized man'; the criteria were unambiguously those of English culture. He was proud to claim that he had 'consistently refused to consecrate any church building which has any colour clause attached to its title deeds' (annual report, 1943). In 1929 he had opposed government plans to enshrine racial difference in marriage legislation. It offended his ideas of justice and equality for 'people of culture', it was a slur on the African Christian community, and was an interference in the independence of the church. These attitudes often made him unpopular with his white congregations, who were both more discriminatory in race and less catholic in ecclesiology than their bishop. On the other hand he was paternalist in his attitudes to African initiative, encouraging African vocations as priests (there was one in 1925; twenty-five by the early 1950s), while stressing the need for a long period of European supervision, both in church administration and synodical government, and in educational work. He was ambiguous in his attitude to the Land Apportionment Act, which increasingly affected Africans, since so many missions had been established on land rescheduled as 'European'. In 1940 he agreed to move the African church in Salisbury to the Harare township, feeling it better to accept generous compensation rather than resist and await expropriation.

In the Second World War Paget was chaplain-general of the Rhodesian forces, and visited the troops in the Middle East, where his eldest brother, Sir Bernard Charles Tolver *Paget, was general officer commanding-in-chief. He optimistically saw signs of important changes in the attitudes of Europeans to Africans as a result of their close collaboration during the war, but was realistic about the difficulties:

> It will be the duty of the Church in these parts of Africa … to do all that can be done with great courage and frankness and boldness to safeguard them [Africans] from disillusionment and also from the sense of frustration upon their return … Any colour bar in the Christian Church must go before we can impress this need and this justice upon Governments. (Temple MSS, vol. 53)

The aftermath of the war was to dash these hopes, not least because of a vast influx of settlers into Southern Rhodesia, which more than doubled the white population.

In 1950, to celebrate Paget's twenty-five years as a bishop, the archbishop of Canterbury awarded Paget the Lambeth DD. Paget had little sympathy for close co-operation with protestant missions in Rhodesia. He felt that protestants were 'dying societies, lacking clear and firm convictions on matters of faith and order' (annual report, 1943), a prejudice which spoke more of his persistent English perspective on things and the constraints of the Anglo-Catholicism in which he was reared, than of the realities of a vigorous African protestant Christianity.

Paget had long urged the division of the diocese, and this took place in 1952 with the creation of the dioceses of Mashonaland (which Paget retained) and Matabeleland. This in turn paved the way for an ecclesiastical province of central Africa, encompassing Southern and Northern Rhodesia, Nyasaland, and Bechuanaland. Paget had been anxious that these developments should not be mixed up with the creation of the Central African Federation, an event regarded with deep suspicion by Africans. In fact the new province came into being in 1955, when criticism of the federation was mounting. Paget was chosen as first archbishop, and he served in this position until his retirement in 1957.

Paget retired to Kloof in Natal, but had little sympathy for the South African National government and apartheid. Always an admirer of what he saw as the liberalism of the administrations of Sir Godfrey Huggins and Sir Edgar Whitehead in Rhodesia, he was distressed by the increasingly illiberal trends of the 1960s. He died on 21 April 1971 at St Mary's Hospital, Mariannhill, South Africa, after a flight in an unpressurized aeroplane. His ashes were placed in the cathedral at Salisbury, which he had played such an important part in building. KEVIN WARD

Sources annual report to the Missionary Council of the Church of England, 1943, LPL, MS 3121 • LPL, Lang MSS • LPL, Fisher MSS • LPL, Temple MSS • *DNB*
Archives LPL, MSS
Wealth at death £3978 in England: probate, 8 Sept 1971, *CGPLA Eng. & Wales*

Paget, Francis (1851–1911), bishop of Oxford, second son of Sir James *Paget, first baronet (1814–1899), surgeon, was born on 20 March 1851 at St Bartholomew's Hospital, London, in his father's official residence as warden. His mother was Lydia (1815–1895), youngest daughter of the Revd Henry North, and his brothers were Sir John Rahere Paget KC, Dr Henry Luke Paget, bishop-suffragan of Stepney, and Stephen *Paget FRCS. He was educated first at a private day school near Regent's Park, and then (1864–9) at Shrewsbury School under Benjamin Hall Kennedy and Henry Whitehead Moss. He was elected to a junior studentship at Christ Church, Oxford, in 1869. In 1871 he won the Hertford scholarship, the chancellor's prize for Latin verse, and a first class in classical moderations. He graduated BA with a first class in the final classical school in 1873, proceeding MA in 1876 and DD in 1885. He was elected senior student in 1873, tutor in 1876, and honorary student in 1901. Ordained deacon in 1875 and priest in 1877, he became a devoted follower of the great tractarian Edward Bouverie Pusey, who allowed him to read in the university pulpit a sermon of his which ill health prevented him from delivering himself. Other tractarian mentors included Henry Parry Liddon, Richard William Church, dean of St Paul's, and James Russell Woodford, bishop of Ely, whom Paget served as examining chaplain (1878–85). Paget married Helen Beatrice Church (1858–1900), Church's daughter, on 28 March 1883 at St Paul's Cathedral; Liddon officiated. Paget's eulogy of Pusey in his Bodleian Oration of 1882 earned him the foolish description of a 'round-collared idiot' from Mark Pattison, the rector of Lincoln College. Being a witty and stimulating companion, Paget established warm friendships with younger and less conservative men of the same school, particularly during reading parties at home and abroad. Paget enjoyed his years as a tutor, and his influence over undergraduates grew as they became accustomed to a certain reserve in his manner for which he had been notable even at Shrewsbury. In 1881 Paget was appointed Oxford preacher at the Chapel Royal, Whitehall. His tutorial career ended in inauspicious circumstances. In a division in the Christ Church governing body on 26 June 1882 he voted in the minority with Pusey (who was making his last appearance in that forum) and others for the re-election of R. W. Macan, tutor in ancient history, whose views in *The Resurrection of Jesus Christ* (a publication sponsored by the nonconformist Hibbert Trust, 1877) had caused grave disquiet. There might have been dissension as to whether Paget should be elected junior censor at the last governing body of Michaelmas term, but an offer of the living of Bromsgrove (a nail making town) arrived apropos, and Paget accepted it.

Paget returned to Oxford in 1885, having been nominated by Gladstone to succeed Edward King, bishop of Lincoln, as regius professor of pastoral theology and canon of Christ Church. Bromsgrove had given Paget a brief insight into parochial activities and had considerably widened the range of his sympathy. Liddon's influence was counteracted by close association with younger men, and in the autumn of 1889 Paget joined Charles Gore, his successor in the see of Oxford, Henry Scott Holland, and others, in publishing the volume of essays *Lux mundi*. The authors had a common programme, to make clear that high Anglicanism was open to new knowledge. Paget, as on other issues during his life, sought to avoid open dissension: Liddon discussed Gore's own essay (by which Liddon was deeply distressed) with Paget in Christ Church, and asked Paget not to communicate on the matter with Gore. But he did, and exchanges ensued. However, Liddon regarded Paget's own essay 'Sacraments' as 'a real contribution to Christian Theology' (Johnston, 362, 367).

In 1892, on the resignation of Henry George Liddell, Paget was promoted by Lord Salisbury to the deanery of Christ Church. His task was difficult not least because of Liddell's success, and a certain tendency to extravagant rowdiness among the undergraduates had to be dealt with firmly. In his sixth term as dean Paget was faced by a notorious case of indiscipline: in 1893 the censors (E. F. Sampson and T. B. Strong) refused permission for undergraduates to attend a ball in November at Blenheim Palace. On the night the rope of Great Tom was cut, the dean's door painted red, and opprobrious legends ('Damn Sampson', 'Damn the Dons') marked in the snow. One man was sent down, the 'funeral' for his departure and other incidents being shown in a series of prints. Some acrimonious correspondence ensued in *The Times*. But Paget was not to blame for the Blenheim row, and ultimately suffered little harm from it. Estimates of his popularity vary, for 'he could only open out to a few', and his 'elaborate courtesy' was apt 'to keep people back behind barriers of civility' (Holland, 277). But he was an anxious and capable administrator (cf. letter from 'Ex Aede Christi', *The Times*, 7 Aug 1911). The deanery was more accessible than heretofore.

As a tutor Paget was among the early supporters of Lady Margaret Hall. As dean he took a great interest in the foundation of Reading University College, which he formally opened in 1892 and of which he was appointed visitor; Christ Church made a considerable gift of books to the new college's library and its influence was important in the early days of the new foundation. Paget was chaplain to William Stubbs, bishop of Oxford, from 1889 until the bishop's death. Thus in 1901 the cathedral and the diocese were drawn closely together, and Paget learned much of local episcopal problems. Paget's career was permanently saddened by his wife's death from meningitis at the deanery on 22 November 1900, aged forty-two.

In 1901, on the death of Stubbs, Dean Paget was promoted by Lord Salisbury to the bishopric of Oxford, and was consecrated on 29 June following. To the bishopric is attached the chancellorship of the Order of the Garter; Paget's most notable function in that capacity was the admission of Edward, prince of Wales, to the order at Windsor on 10 June 1911. He was also chosen as 'supporter' bishop at their coronations by both Queen Alexandra in 1902 and Queen Mary in 1911. His administration of the diocese of Oxford was marked by the same anxious care which he had devoted to his college. He was eager to do everything himself; much of the episcopal correspondence was written in his own clear but characteristic handwriting. It took some time for the people to feel that they knew him intimately, although his pastoral earnestness was keenly appreciated by the inhabitants of the rural villages, which, from 1907, he was able to visit in the episcopal automobile. Early in 1903 he declined Arthur Balfour's offer of the see of Winchester. In April 1904 he became a member of the royal commission on ecclesiastical discipline, and signed its report on 21 June 1906. He was one of the three out of fourteen members who attended each of the 118 sittings, and he exhibited 'a genius for fairness towards hostile witnesses' (*The Times*, 3 July 1906) and a remarkable gift for fusing opinions in the drafting of the report; Archbishop Davidson thought he was 'at his best' on this commission. His attitude to prevailing excesses in ritual was shown in the charge which he began to deliver to his diocese on 8 October 1906, and by the action which he took against the Revd Oliver Partridge Henly, vicar of Wolverton St Mary, in respect of 'reservation' and 'benediction'. The case was taken to the court of arches (*The Times*, 20 and 21 July 1909); the vicar, who was deprived, obtained employment in another diocese, and afterwards joined the Roman Catholic church.

Paget sought to provide for a subdivision of the diocese, a difficult objective not achieved nearly a century later. For this purpose he made a vain endeavour to dispose of Cuddesdon Palace. In July 1910 he showed his active zeal for the wider work of the church by becoming chairman of the Archbishops' Western Canada Fund. He was the author of the prayer 'That in tranquillity Thy kingdom may go forward', which found a place in the 1928 prayer book.

During the first half of Paget's episcopate a group in north Oxford, under the formidable leadership of a Second South African War veteran, Colonel Le Mesurier, pressed him to allow the establishment of an evangelical church there. Paget was uncertain, again anxious to avoid open dissension, and laid himself open to charges of evasion and indecision, but eventually he came out in favour, and in 1906 attended the laying of the foundation stone of St Andrew's, Linton Road.

As a theological scholar Paget is remembered chiefly for his *Introduction to the Fifth Book of Hooker's Treatise of the Laws of Ecclesiastical Polity* (1899; 2nd edn 1907), for his *Lux mundi* essay already mentioned, and for a masterly essay on *acedia*, or accidie, written at Christ Church in 1890 (reprinted separately in 1912), and published with a collection of sermons entitled *The Spirit of Discipline* in 1891 (7th edn 1896); the undergraduates called accidie 'the Dean's new sin'. He also published *Faculties and Difficulties for Belief and Disbelief* (1887; 3rd edn 1894) and two other collections of sermons entitled respectively *Studies in Christian Character* (1895) and *The Redemption of War* (1900). Some sermons were published separately, including *The Virtue of Simplicity*, a gift surely erroneously applied to C. L. Dodgson (Lewis Carroll) and H. G. Liddell, whom it fell to Paget to commemorate together in March 1898.

To his intimate friends, and in particular to Archbishop Davidson, Paget was not only a wise counsellor but a delightful companion. He had a cultivated sense of beauty in nature, in music, and in words; he had been head of the new choir at Shrewsbury, and Dante and Ruskin were among his interests. His tall, willowy figure and impressive, courtly bearing made him a notable figure in any assembly. Paget was attacked by a serious illness (volvulus) in the summer of 1910, and seemed to recover, but he died of a sudden recurrence of the malady, in a London nursing home at Welbeck House, Welbeck Street, on 2 August 1911. He was interred three days later in his wife's grave in the little burying-ground to the south of Christ Church Cathedral, Oxford.

The Pagets' four sons all at some time held commissions in the army; they included Archbishop Edward Francis *Paget (1886–1971) and General Sir Bernard *Paget (1887–1961). The Pagets' two daughters both married clergymen; the younger predeceased her father. Her husband jointly with her uncle, Stephen Paget, wrote a biography of the bishop (1912) which contains much detail on the Pagets' domestic life. E. H. PEARCE, *rev.* J. F. A. MASON

Sources S. Paget and J. M. C. Crum, *Francis Paget, bishop of Oxford … and sometime dean of Christ Church* (1912) • H. S. Holland, *Commonwealth* (Sept 1911) • *The Times* (3 Aug 1911) • *The Guardian* (Aug 1911) • *Church Times* (4 Aug 1911), 139 • Crockford (1911) • *Oxford Diocesan Magazine* (Sept 1911) • E. B. Moser, *The Salopian*, 31 (1911), 4–5 • private information (1912, 2004) [E. H. Pearce; Shrewsbury School; bishop of Oxford; Dr Henry Chadwick] • P. Clifford, *Living stones* (1990) • H. P. Liddon, *The life of Edward Bouverie Pusey*, ed. J. O. Johnston and others, 4 vols. (1893–7)
Archives Christ Church Oxf. | BLPES, corresp. with E. D. Morel • Glos. RO, corresp. with Sir Michael Hicks Beach • Pusey Oxf., corresp. with R. Eden
Likenesses W. Q. Orchardson, oils, 1904, Christ Church Oxf. • Spy [L. Ward], caricature, watercolour study, NPG; repro. in *VF* (22 Nov 1894) • carved head, Christ Church Cathedral, Oxford • group portrait, photograph (with praepostors at Shrewsbury School), NPG
Wealth at death £15,225 15*s.* 2*d.*: probate, 13 Dec 1911, *CGPLA Eng. & Wales*

Paget, Francis Edward (1806–1882), Church of England clergyman and author, was born on 24 May 1806, the eldest son of General Sir Edward *Paget (1775–1849) and his first wife, Frances (*d.* 1806), daughter of William, first Baron Bagot. He was educated at Westminster School, where he was admitted on 16 September 1817; he proceeded to Christ Church, Oxford, matriculating on 3 June 1824. From 1825 to 1836 he held a studentship, and graduated BA in 1828 and MA in 1830. He became rector of Elford, near Lichfield, in 1835, and for some years was chaplain to Richard Bagot, bishop of Bath and Wells. On 2 June 1840 he married Fanny (*d.* 1890), daughter of William Chester, rector of Denton, Norfolk, with whom he had six daughters and one son.

Paget was an early and consistent supporter of the Oxford Movement, and in common with other Tractarian clergy he exploited the contemporary popularity of the novel to disseminate the ideas of the movement to a wider audience. In 1840 he began to contribute to The Englishman's Library (vols. 9, 16, and 18) with his *Tales of the Village* (3 vols., 1840–41), short stories designed to show how the parochial life of the Church of England could be revived. In 1841 followed *St Antholin's, or, Old Churches and New: a Tale for the Times*, which dealt with the problems of raising funds for church restoration. In 1842 came *Milford Malvoisin, or, Pews and Pewholders*, significant for its early criticism of the social fractures resulting from pewed churches, and in which Paget argued that, as a consequence, 'the wealthy few have driven, in many places, the Poor from our Churches'.

In his own parish of Elford, Paget implemented in a practical way the ideas advocated in his fiction. As with other Tractarian clergy he introduced the practice of daily morning and evening prayer in the church, and began to increase the frequency with which holy communion was celebrated. He raised funds to restore the building, including the collection of pennies from the children for a new font. The reopening of the restored church was celebrated on 2 August 1849, during which Paget preached a sermon published as *The Destinies of God's Temples* (1849). The annual dedication festival became, in subsequent years, an important meeting place for Staffordshire clergy. Further restoration work in 1869 was followed by his published account of the church in 1870.

Paget's literary output was also notable for the variety of its subject matter. In 1840 he edited Bishop Simon Patrick's *Discourse Concerning Prayer* and *Treatise of Repentance and Fasting*, similar to Newman's reprints from the writings of English bishops. He wrote for children in The Juvenile Englishman's Library from 1845, including two series of *Tales of Village Children*, and for some while was editor of this collection. Under the pseudonym William Churne of Staffordshire he wrote the fairy tale *The Hope of the Katzekopfs* in 1844. In 1859 his novel *The Curate of Cumberworth and the Vicar of Roost* was published as a warning to his fellow clergy not to be too enthusiastic or to move too quickly in matters of parochial reform. *Lucretia, or, The Heroine of the Nineteenth Century* (1868) was a satire on the sensationalist novel. *The Pageant*, a novel deploring the employment conditions of milliners' apprentices, led to Paget's appearance as defendant in a successful libel case in 1844. He also published other novels, and volumes of sermons, prayers, and religious treatises.

Paget's final works continued this note of variety. In 1873 he privately printed *Some records of the Ashtead estate and of its Howard possessors: with notices of Elford, Castle Rising, Levens, and Charlton*, an uncritical compilation from family papers and other private sources. *A Student Penitent of 1695*, based on seventeenth-century letters between an Oxford undergraduate and his tutor, followed in 1875. *Homeward Bound* in 1876 was a series of meditative essays about preparation for death, in a style typical of the period. Paget died at his rectory in Elford on 4 August 1882, and was buried there on 8 August. GEORGE HERRING

Sources *Guardian* (16 Aug 1882) • Burke, *Gen. GB* • Allibone, *Dict.* • S. Halkett and J. Laing, *A dictionary of anonymous and pseudonymous publications in the English language*, ed. J. Horden, 3rd edn (1980–) • Foster, *Alum. Oxon.* • G. W. Herring, 'Tractarianism to ritualism: a study of some aspects of tractarianism outside Oxford, from the time of Newman's conversion in 1845 until the first Ritual Commission in 1867', DPhil diss., U. Oxf., 1984 • *The Times* (17 June 1844)
Archives Pusey Oxf., letters to William Gresley

Wealth at death £2873 0s. 6d.: probate, 14 Sept 1882, *CGPLA Eng. & Wales*

Paget, Lord George Augustus Frederick (1818–1880), army officer, sixth son (third of the second marriage) of Henry William *Paget, first marquess of Anglesey (1768–1854), and his second wife, Charlotte (1781–1853), daughter of the first Earl Cadogan, was born at Burlington Street, London, on 16 March 1818. He was educated at Westminster School (1829) and on 25 July 1834 was appointed cornet and sub-lieutenant in the 1st lifeguards, in which he became lieutenant on 1 December 1837. On 17 August 1840 he purchased an unattached company and exchanged to a troop in the 4th light dragoons (later hussars); he was promoted major on 30 January 1846 and lieutenant-colonel on 29 December the same year. After becoming a brevet colonel on 20 June 1854, he went out in command of the 4th light dragoons to the East, landed with them in the Crimea, and at the Alma and Balaklava was next senior officer of the light cavalry brigade to Lord Cardigan. He was privately critical of both Cardigan and Lucan, 'two spoilt children' (Hibbert, 158), and of Nolan. In the famous charge of the light brigade Paget's regiment at first formed the third line, and he appears to have done his utmost to fulfil Lord Cardigan's desire that he should give him 'his best support'. With the remnants of his own regiment and the 11th hussars (from the second line of the brigade), which he held together after the first line had disintegrated at the guns, he was enabled to check the Russian pursuit, and was one of the last to leave the 'Valley of Death'. He commanded the remains of the light brigade at Inkerman, and immediately afterwards he went home with a view to retirement from the service, an arrangement he had contemplated at the time of his marriage before the outbreak of the war. Although his bravery was not questioned, his return at this critical period exposed him to much press criticism, and he was reportedly 'greatly snubbed at home' (Hibbert, 236), which probably induced him to reconsider.

Paget went back to the Crimea on 23 February 1855 accompanied by his wife—whom Roger Fenton called 'the belle of the Crimea' (Hibbert, 329); he was reappointed to the command of the light brigade, and was in temporary command of the cavalry division during the absence of Sir James Yorke Scarlett, Lord Lucan's successor. Together with his wife, Paget was one of the small group of personal friends who gathered round Raglan's deathbed. Paget commanded the light cavalry brigade at Eupatoria and in the operations under General d'Allonville, and until a month before the evacuation of the Crimea; he received the CB (July 1855), Légion d'honneur, Mejidiye (third class), and Sardinian and Turkish medals. He became major-general on 11 November 1861, commanded the cavalry at Aldershot in 1860–62 and the Sirhind division of the Bengal army from 1862 to 1865, when he came home, and was appointed inspector-general of cavalry. He was made lieutenant-general and KCB in June 1871 and general in 1877; he was appointed colonel 7th dragoon guards in 1868, and succeeded Lord de Ros as colonel of the 4th hussars in 1874. Paget was whig MP for Beaumaris from 1847 to 1857, voting for the ballot in 1853.

Paget married, first, on 27 February 1854, shortly before he left for the war, his beautiful young cousin Agnes Charlotte, youngest daughter of Sir Arthur *Paget; she died on 10 March 1858, leaving two children. He married on 6 February 1861 Louisa, youngest daughter of Charles Fieschi Heneage and granddaughter on her mother's side of Thomas North, second Lord Graves; she survived Paget, married Arthur Algernon Capell, sixth earl of Essex, in 1881, and died on 25 January 1914.

Paget in May 1852 addressed a letter to Lord John Russell on the establishment of an army reserve, which was printed for private circulation. He proposed that, instead of the revival of the militia, a bill for which was before the house, a reserve force should be established by compelling all soldiers who left the service at the end of ten years, under the act of 1847, without re-engaging, to serve five years after discharge in a reserve, which was to undergo six days' local military training in each year. Paget's Crimean journals were printed for private circulation in 1875; but after the publication of A. W. Kinglake's *The Invasion of the Crimea* he appears to have revised them, and, in accordance with a wish expressed in a memorandum found among his papers, they were published by his son in 1881. Paget died very unexpectedly at his residence, 1 Farm Street, Mayfair, London, on 30 June 1880.

H. M. CHICHESTER, *rev.* ROGER T. STEARN

Sources *Army and Navy Gazette* (July 1880) • G. A. F. Paget, *The light cavalry brigade in the Crimea*, ed. C. S. Paget (1881) • A. W. Kinglake, *The invasion of the Crimea*, [new edn], 9 vols. (1877–88), vols. 5–7, 9 • C. Hibbert, *The destruction of Lord Raglan* [1961] • J. Sweetman, *Raglan: from the Peninsula to the Crimea* (1993) • A. D. Lambert, *The Crimean War: British grand strategy, 1853–56* (1990) • Boase, *Mod. Eng. biog.* • Burke, *Peerage* • GEC, *Peerage* • *WWBMP*

Likenesses Spy [L. Ward], chromolithograph caricature, NPG; repro. in *VF* (13 Oct 1877) • wood-engraving (after photograph by J. Watkins), NPG; repro. in *ILN* (8 May 1858)

Wealth at death under £25,000: probate, 23 Aug 1880, *CGPLA Eng. & Wales*

Paget, Sir George Edward (1809–1892), university professor, was born at Great Yarmouth, Norfolk, on 22 December 1809, the seventh son of Samuel Paget and his wife, Sarah Elizabeth Tolver. After private tutoring in Yarmouth he followed his elder brothers to Charterhouse School in 1824. He matriculated at Gonville and Caius College, Cambridge, in 1827, won a college prize in mathematics in his second year, and graduated in 1831 as eighth wrangler. His success delighted his family; such were their celebrations that his brothers Charles and James *Paget commented that it was worth a lifetime's reading to have such an hour of rejoicing. In 1832 he was elected to a medical fellowship of his college and began to study medicine. He walked the wards at St Bartholomew's Hospital, London, and visited Paris with his brother James. He graduated MB at Cambridge in 1833, ML in 1836, and MD in 1838.

The annual income of £300 from Paget's fellowship proved vital in supporting his family, whose brewing business had fallen on hard times. His loans kept the business going through the 1830s, and in 1841 he raised £1500 on

Sir George Edward Paget (1809–1892), by unknown photographer

his own credit and security to save it from bankruptcy. He paid for the surgical education of his brother James, and the clerical education of his brother Alfred. He looked after his brothers Frank and Charles who suffered from physical and mental illness respectively—results of their efforts to keep the family business afloat. Paget himself was a lifelong sufferer from rheumatism and hay fever.

Paget was a leading figure within Caius College, and from his earliest days in the fellowship was earmarked to rise to the very top. In 1837 he passed over the chance to stand for the Downing professorship of medicine in the expectation that he would be able to stand for the mastership of Caius when Martin Davy, the incumbent, died. Unfortunately for Paget, Davy died in May 1839, when Paget was considered too young to become a candidate for the mastership. He did, however, become bursar of the college. In 1852, when Davy's successor Edward Chapman died, Paget's Norfolk origins made him unelectable following the university commissioners' attack of 1851 on closed fellowships. Paget took consolation in his election to the Linacre lectureship of physic at St John's College, and in his marriage, on 11 December 1851, to Clara, youngest daughter of Thomas Fardell, vicar of Sutton in the Isle of Ely; they had ten children.

Paget was elected physician to Addenbrooke's Hospital, Cambridge, on the resignation of John Haviland, in 1839. He held this post for forty-five years. He was responsible for innovative uses of the hospital in the education of Cambridge medical students: in 1842 he created a practical examination in clinical medicine, the first of its kind in the country, in which the candidate was required to examine a patient, and discuss the diagnosis, prognosis, and best course of treatment. The following year, in collaboration with the recently elected surgeon George Humphry, he inaugurated a system of clinical lectures at the hospital. Paget and Humphry also collaborated in cataloguing the physiological and pathological series of the anatomical museum in the 1840s.

Paget believed, as did most leading doctors of the time, that individual judgement was the physician's most important skill. He taught his students that for most diseases there was no one method of treatment, and that they should therefore treat each case individually. Nevertheless, Paget recognized the potential of scientific investigation for medicine. As he pointed out in his Harveian oration delivered at the Royal College of Physicians in 1866, he believed that physiological and pathological discoveries would ultimately advance medicine; until then scientific knowledge guarded the clinician against making errors, and was a 'trustworthy guide' in the prevention of disease. Paget was an ardent advocate for science within the university and the medical profession. In his presidential address to the 1864 meeting of the British Medical Association, held in Cambridge, he called for a broader public understanding of science among the classes of influence in the country and the empire, as well as among the medical profession, for whom, he argued, science was becoming the measure of its social influence, and its strength in maintaining truth in medicine against the errors of alternative practices such as phrenology or homoeopathy. He reiterated these views in his medico-political dealings in London, where he served as president of the General Medical Council from 1869 to 1874. His support of science was rewarded with the presidency of the Cambridge Philosophical Society, in 1855–6, and his election as FRS in 1873. He was knighted in 1887.

Paget succeeded Henry Bond as regius professor of physic in 1872. By this time he was beginning to feel that the development of medical subjects such as sanitary science, medical jurisprudence, and midwifery were being neglected because most of the university's resources were being diverted towards the rapidly expanding departments of natural science. Paget's campaign on behalf of medicine brought him into direct conflict with scientists such as Michael Foster, to whose departments he had previously given his wholehearted support. He had some early successes: in 1875, at his instigation, the university created a diploma in public health, and in the early 1880s a programme of clinical teaching was created which allowed students to complete their medical education at Cambridge. Paget was unable, however, to procure resources to expand the range of subjects offered at the clinical school, and students continued to leave Cambridge for the majority of their clinical training. This process accelerated after Paget's death when Clifford Allbutt, who did not believe that Cambridge should have a clinical school, was appointed as his successor.

Paget was one of the leaders of the conservative faction within the university, representing their interests on the council of the senate for many years from its inception in 1856. He was strongly against the abolition of university tests and the admission of women, and particularly disapproved of the redistribution of wealth away from the colleges in the late 1870s. Yet even when the university changed in ways of which he did not approve, Paget continued to be passionate in its defence, never letting an attack on Cambridge, medicine, or William Harvey go unanswered.

Paget died of influenza at his home, 2 St Peter's Terrace, Cambridge, on 29 January 1892. His obituary in *The Times* suggested that the 'remarkable confidence reposed by the governing body of the University' in Paget's judgement was 'a potent factor in effecting the various reforms which resulted in the proper recognition of the study of natural and medical science' (*The Times*, 30 Jan 1892, 7a). It was a just comment. Paget presided over a remarkable transformation of the Cambridge medical school, and even if it did not become exactly what Paget had intended, the emergence of Cambridge as a leading centre in the natural and medical sciences owes much to his efforts.

MARK W. WEATHERALL

Sources C. E. Paget, ed., *Some lectures by the late Sir George E. Paget, KCB, MD, FRS, with a memoir* (1893) • A. Paget, 'Paget & Sons', CUL, department of manuscripts and university archives, MS Add. 8568/1 • R. M. Acheson, 'Sir George Paget and postgraduate medical education; state medicine, the MD degree, and the diploma in public health', Cambridge, 21 • *The Lancet* (13 Feb 1892), 392 • S. Paget, *Memoirs and letters of Sir James Paget* (1902) • *The Times* (30 Jan 1892), 7a • H. D. Rolleston, *The Cambridge medical school: a biographical history* (1932) • A. Rook, M. Carlton, and W. G. Cannon, *The history of Addenbrooke's Hospital, Cambridge* (1991) • d. cert.

Archives CUL, letters to George Stokes • NRA, priv. coll., letters to Sir Norman Moore • Wellcome L., corresp., mainly with his brother, James Paget

Likenesses H. Wiles, marble bust, 1885, Addenbrooke's Hospital, Cambridge • bust, U. Cam., Medical Library • oils, Gon. & Caius Cam. • photograph, priv. coll. [*see illus.*]

Wealth at death £21,939 11*s*. 3*d*.: probate, 22 March 1892, *CGPLA Eng. & Wales*

Paget, Henry, first earl of Uxbridge (*c*.**1663–1743**), politician and official in the royal household, was the son of William *Paget, sixth Baron Paget (1637–1713), and his wife, Frances, the daughter of the Hon. Francis Pierrepont. He was admitted to the Middle Temple in 1683 and was married on 2 January 1686 to Mary (*d*. 1734), the eldest daughter of Thomas Catesby of Whiston, Yorkshire; the couple had one son. Paget served as MP for Staffordshire from 1695 to January 1712, taking an active part in parliamentary affairs. Although from a Presbyterian, whig background, Paget was at first considered to be a member of the 'country' party, and then a moderate tory and supporter of Robert Harley (later earl of Oxford). From the start of his parliamentary career he was involved in the preparation and management of legislation. In 1699 his interest in the house was described as 'considerable'. In 1701 he was appointed to several committees, including the one formed to draw up the impeachments of four whig lords, and he was involved with the Militia Bill of the following year. In April 1704, when Prince George of Denmark became lord high admiral, Paget was appointed one of his council, a post he held until 1708. He voted against the tories in 1704 when they attempted to tack the Occasional Conformity Bill on to the Land Tax Bill, supported the court on the Regency Bill in 1706, and voted against the impeachment of Dr Sacheverall in 1710. From 10 August 1710 to 30 May 1711 he was a lord of the Treasury in Harley's administration, then, from June 1713 to September 1715, captain of the yeomen of the guard. On 14 June 1711 he became a member of the privy council.

Paget was created Baron Burton of Burton, Staffordshire, on 1 January 1712, being one of twelve peers created to obtain a tory majority in the Lords for Oxford's ministry. Towards the end of Anne's reign he opposed the government on a number of issues, but did not lose his household offices. He succeeded his father as seventh Baron Paget on 26 February 1713, and was lord lieutenant of Staffordshire from March 1713 until 30 September 1715. On 13 April 1714 he was appointed envoy-extraordinary to Hanover. He was created earl of Uxbridge on 19 October of that year and made a privy councillor on 16 November.

In September 1715 Uxbridge resigned all his court employments and acted as part of the tory opposition in the Lords. As one of Oxford's 'dozen' he voted for the latter's acquittal in 1717. He became recorder of Litchfield in 1715, a post he kept until his death. His second marriage, on 7 June 1739, was to Elizabeth (1674–1749), the daughter of Sir Walter Bagot of Blithefield, Staffordshire. He died on 30 August 1743 at West Drayton, Middlesex, and was buried in Hillingdon church.

His only son, **Thomas Catesby Paget**, Lord Paget (1689–1742), politician, was educated at Trinity College, Oxford. He was one of the gentlemen of the bedchamber to the prince of Wales. On the latter's accession as George II he continued in the same post, which he held until 1736, when ill health forced him to resign. He was elected MP for Staffordshire on 3 February 1715 and on 22 March 1722. He also stood for Middlesex in 1727, but was defeated. He generally voted with the opposition. He married Elizabeth (*d*. 1736), the second daughter of John Egerton, third earl of Bridgewater, on 6 May 1718 at Gray's Inn Chapel; they had two sons, Henry and George (1721–1737). Paget was a writer of minor repute, and his work, which was mildly praised by Horace Walpole, was collected as *Miscellanies in Prose and Verse* (1741). He died at West Drayton on 4 February 1742, and was buried in Westminster Abbey.

He was survived by his son **Henry Paget**, second earl of Uxbridge (*bap*. 1719, *d*. 1769), miser, who was baptized at Isleworth, Middlesex, on 22 January 1719. Following his education at St John's College, Oxford, he succeeded his grandfather in 1743 as earl of Uxbridge. He was chiefly remarkable for an inordinate love of money. Peter Walter, the well-known usurer, who had been the first earl's steward, bequeathed to him in 1746 the principal part of his immense wealth. Uxbridge is said, however, to have continued to pay Walter's daughter, Mrs Bullock, a sizeable annuity during her life, although her father's will did not require it. He died, unmarried, on 16 November 1769, and on this date the earldom became extinct. The barony-in-fee of Paget passed to Henry, the great-great-grandson of William, fifth Baron Paget. M. E. CLAYTON

Sources HoP, *Commons* [draft] • E. Cruickshanks, 'Paget, Thomas Catesby', HoP, *Commons* • C. Jones, ed., *Party and management in parliament, 1660–1784* (1984) • G. S. Holmes, *British politics in the age of Anne* (1967) • R. O. Bucholz, *The Augustan court: Queen Anne and the decline of court culture* (1993) • *DNB* • GEC, *Peerage*, new edn • Foster, *Alum. Oxon.*

Archives BL, corresp., Add. MS 61830

Likenesses E. Harding, portrait (Paget, Thomas Catesby), BM, NPG; repro. in J. Adolphus, *British cabinet* (1799)

Wealth at death over £42,000—value of unentailed estates and bequests: HoP, *Commons*

Paget, Henry, second earl of Uxbridge (*bap.* **1719**, *d.* **1769**). *See under* Paget, Henry, first earl of Uxbridge (*c.*1663–1743).

Paget [*formerly* Bayly], **Henry William, first marquess of Anglesey** (**1768–1854**), army officer and politician, was born on 17 May 1768 in London, probably at Uxbridge House, Burlington Gardens, the eldest of the twelve children of Henry Bayly (1744–1812) and his wife, Jane (*d.* 1817), daughter of Arthur Champagne, dean of Clonmacnoise, Ireland, and his wife, Marianne. By a tortuous line of descent from William, first Baron Paget (1505–1563), Henry Bayly became in 1770 the ninth Baron Paget (taking by royal licence the name Paget in place of Bayly) and, in 1784, the second earl of Uxbridge of the second creation.

Education and early military career Henry William Bayly, as he then was, attended Westminster School, London, in 1777 and, as Lord Paget, Christ Church, Oxford, in 1784. After a two-year grand tour in Europe, he was elected unopposed for Caernarfon boroughs in 1790 and for Milborne Port, Somerset, in 1796. These he represented silently until succeeding to the earldom in 1812. Soon after the outbreak of war with France he raised, at the age of twenty-four, the 80th foot, largely from his father's tenantry. In June 1794 the regiment went to Flanders, joining the duke of York's army there. At Meteren on 30 December he had his baptism of fire, leading his regiment in a successful charge. During the army's disastrous retreat he found himself commanding an infantry brigade after only one year's service. On 25 July 1795 he married Lady Caroline Elizabeth Villiers (1774–1835), known as Car, daughter of George Bussy *Villiers, fourth earl of Jersey; they had three sons and five daughters.

In 1795 Paget, so as to achieve permanent rank without purchasing it, ran speedily (on paper) through all the ranks from lieutenant to colonel-in-the-army. In 1797 he obtained 'the height of his ambition'—command of the 7th (Queen's Own) light dragoons. He became full colonel of the regiment in 1801, remaining thus for forty-five years.

Henry William Paget, first marquess of Anglesey (1768–1854), by Sir Thomas Lawrence, *c.*1816–17

Paget commanded the cavalry brigade in the ill-fated Anglo-Russian Helder campaign in the Netherlands in 1799. Near Egmont-op-Zee on 2 October he first made his name as an enterprising cavalryman; through a speedy reaction he destroyed a French formation led by General Vandamme. On 6 October at Castricum he ambushed a superior body of enemy cavalry, which resulted in a complete rout and hundreds of soldiers taken prisoner. Over the next eight years he turned his regiment into one of the most efficient in the army. In 1802 he was promoted major-general and in 1808 lieutenant-general. At about this time he was gaining the reputation of a dandy: in the 7th light dragoons he set a famously high sartorial standard, and up to his death, seventeen years into the Victorian era, he still wore his unfashionable Regency 'Paget blue coat'.

Commanding the cavalry in the Peninsular War In 1808, on Sir John Moore's being given command of a 20,000-strong expeditionary force to Spain, Paget obtained command of the cavalry of Sir David Baird's 19,000-strong force sent to Corunna to join Moore's marching up from Lisbon. Napoleon's rapid advance and his complete overthrow of the

Spanish armies that Moore was to have succoured, led to the necessity for an immediate retreat, of Baird to Corunna and of Moore to Lisbon. Moore desired Baird to send him a regiment of cavalry. Instead, Paget persuaded Baird to let him have three cavalry regiments and six horse artillery guns to make 'a rapid march over an immense plain … overrun by the enemy's cavalry' (Paget and Paget, 113–14).

Meanwhile, it was learned that Napoleon, believing that Moore and Baird were in full flight, had decided to march on Madrid, leaving only Marshal Soult's 18,000 men in the north-west. Moore's and Baird's armies met at Mayorga on 20 December 1808. So successful was Paget in masking the junction that Soult was quite unaware that it had taken place. Next morning there followed what Charles Oman described as 'perhaps the most brilliant exploit of the British cavalry during the whole six years of the [Peninsular] war' (Oman, 536). At Sahagún Paget totally surprised a French cavalry brigade, charging with only the 15th hussars and killing or capturing 500 French soldiers.

On 22 December Moore learned that, on the capitulation of Madrid, Napoleon's 200,000 men were marching to attack him. The retreat was instantly resumed. It now fell to Paget's five regiments, facing thirteen of the French on a 30 mile front, to keep the retreat secret and the advance guard at bay. Nearly every troop was constantly in action, leading Napoleon himself to set down the cavalry at double its actual strength.

At Benavente, on 29 December, the bridge over the Esla having been blown up, General Lefebres-Desnouettes, commanding the élite of Napoleon's cavalry, took time to find a ford. While Paget's pickets kept the French occupied, he concealed the 10th hussars until the enemy were in the act of charging down upon the pickets. The regiment then crashed into the French flank. Utterly surprised, the enemy horsemen broke and did not again attempt a crossing that day; Moore's army had gained a vital day's march. Although the retreat started on 24 December, it was not guessed at by Soult until late on the 27th. 'By this time', wrote Fortescue, 'the contempt of the British for the French horse was such that they cheerfully engaged greatly superior numbers' (Fortescue, *Brit. army*, 352). Moore found it impossible 'to say too much' (ibid.) in praise of the cavalry.

As the plains were replaced by the Galician Mountains, the infantry commanded by Paget's brother, Edward *Paget, took over the rearguard. Paget himself, meanwhile, had succumbed to the prevalent ophthalmia, being practically blinded by it. From this resulted the *tic douloureux* (facial neuralgia), from which he suffered untold agonies during the last thirty-five years of his life. He was already aboard ship when he heard of Moore's death on 16 January 1809 at the battle of Corunna.

Elopement, divorce, duel, and second marriage Back home, Paget, fêted as a hero, became the centre of a famous scandal. Earlier he and Lady Charlotte Wellesley (1781–1853) had fallen in love. A daughter of Earl Cadogan and the wife of Henry Wellesley (Sir Arthur Wellesley's youngest brother and later Lord Cowley), Char, as she was known, was the mother of five children. Paget deserted his wife Caroline and eloped with her. Henry Wellesley offered to take Char back conditionally but she replied that, not being 'lost to all Sense of Honor' (Plas Newydd MSS), she could not return to a husband whom she had left or to children she had abandoned. Paget's family, while condemning him and, more forcefully, Char ('that *maudite sorcière*'), befriended 'poor Car' (ibid.). Paget's brothers failed to persuade him to return to his wife.

Char's brother, meanwhile, required her to give Paget up. On her refusing to do so, he challenged Paget to a duel. This he refused, writing that, as Char had 'lost the world' upon his account, the only atonement he could make was to devote himself to alleviating 'her suffering', adding that: 'my motive for acting thus is good' (Plas Newydd MSS). Since Paget failed to contest Wellesley's action for 'criminal conversation' (6 May 1809), his damages were assessed at £20,000 with costs. The final decree was granted on 7 July and a private act passed on 22 February 1810.

Nine months earlier, Paget's brother had persuaded him to be temporarily reconciled to Car. It seems that she agreed to his returning 'without any stipulations whatever' (Plas Newydd MSS), but the transaction is shrouded in mystery. All that is certain is that Paget returned to Car on 17 May 1809 and that Char was financially looked after. Thus, Paget now felt able to accept Cadogan's further challenge to a duel, which took place on 30 May. Cadogan fired his pistol and missed, but Paget aimed off, saying that nothing would induce him to add to the injuries he had already inflicted on the family 'by firing at the brother of Lady Charlotte Wellesley' (ibid.). On 4 March 1810 Char gave birth to a baby girl whose father was Paget.

Paget's conduct was markedly unlike the typical military libertine of a generation earlier and the actions of all concerned were illustrative of the growing decencies of life of that period. Though both families involved were tory, the comments of the whig press, eschewing past practice, were irreproachable.

Car now set in motion divorce proceedings. Only in Scotland did the law provide a wife with the same remedy as a husband; and to Scotland, therefore, she and Paget resorted. As soon as all was settled, Paget married Char, while Car married the duke of Argyll, to whom she had for some time been engaged. Car and her husband had no children, while Char and Paget had ten. It was many years before Char was accepted in society. The whole business had cost Paget £55,000.

The death of Paget's father in 1812 revealed large debts. Yet extensive estates, and copper-, lead-, and coalmines, still produced income between 1819 and 1835 averaging £76,200 p.a., while overspending averaged £1600 p.a. In the meantime, Paget had commanded an infantry division in the ill-starred, short-lived Walcheren expedition of 1809. He saw little action but escaped the miasmatic fever which decimated the army.

For the next five years, besides commanding the London district troops in the corn law riots early in 1815, Uxbridge (as he now was) saw no active service. This was partly because the duke of Wellington disliked 'clever' cavalry officers. Uxbridge's view that a cavalry general should 'inspire his men … with the most perfect confidence in his personal gallantry', with his added comment of 'let him but lead, they are sure to follow … hardly anything will stop them' (Le Marchant, 157–8), would have alarmed the duke. For the Waterloo campaign Wellington would have preferred the more experienced, but plodding Lord Combermere. Yet Uxbridge was thrust on him by the prince regent and the duke of York.

Commanding allied cavalry in the Waterloo campaign On 15 April 1815 Uxbridge assumed command of some 13,000 allied cavalry and forty-four horse artillery guns, the duke of Wellington giving him *carte blanche*. (The Dutch/Belgian horse, until the eve of Waterloo, remained under the prince of Orange.) Chiefly for forage supply reasons, the cavalry was distributed over a wide area. This meant that at Quatre-Bras (16 June) it failed to concentrate in time to assist the infantry. On the 17th Uxbridge was left by Wellington to cover the infantry's retirement from Quatre-Bras to Mont-St Jean. He was enjoined to avoid a serious engagement and remain in position as long as possible, and he did both admirably. In the course of the operation, described by Uxbridge as 'the prettiest Field Day of Cavalry and Horse Artillery that I ever witnessed' (Siborne, 7), the 7th hussars, through no fault of their own, were repulsed by the French *lanciers* at Genappe. Consequently, as soon as the *lanciers* had debouched from the narrow village street, Uxbridge ordered the heavy horsemen of the 1st Life Guards to charge, thus retrieving the situation.

On 18 June, at perhaps the most critical moment of the great battle, when Lieutenant-General Thomas Picton's infantry of 3000 were facing some 10,000 enemy infantry about to pour through a gap left by the flight of Rijlandt's Netherlanders, Uxbridge 'galloped up to the Heavy Cavalry', as he later wrote, 'and ordered the Household Brigade to prepare to form line, passed on to [the Union Brigade]', told its commander 'to wheel into line when the other Brigade did, instantly returned to the Household Brigade, and put the whole in motion' (Siborne, 8, 238). He put himself at the head of the two brigades as they poured over the ridge and crashed headlong into the enemy's serried ranks. Thus, 2000 'heavies' swept 15,000 French soldiers in wild disorder before them, destroying two field batteries and taking more than 2000 prisoners and two eagles. The enemy's casualties numbered about 4500, but the cavalry lost 700 men and 900 horses.

These high casualties are accounted for, in part, by Uxbridge placing himself at the head of the first line instead of the second: 'a great mistake', as he put it. 'The *carrière* once begun, the leader is no better than any other man.' When he sounded the rally, 'neither voice nor trumpet availed. The pursuit continued without order and too far' (Siborne, 9–10). It penetrated even to Napoleon's 'great battery'. As they retired, the exhausted survivors were badly cut up by fresh French cavalry.

For the rest of the battle Uxbridge galloped from regiment to regiment of his light brigades, leading numerous counter-attacks against the massed cavalry which again and again assaulted the British 'squares'. He had eight or nine horses shot under him. At a moment of maximum crisis he saw an infantry regiment wavering. 'Galloping to the rally, he reminded this regiment of its distinguished name … told them who he was, and led them to the charge. They followed him to a man, drove back the Enemy, and maintained their post' (Siborne, 17, 20).

As the battle was ending, a grapeshot passed over the neck of Wellington's horse and smashed into Uxbridge's right knee as he rode beside the duke. 'By God, sir, I've lost my leg!' he is supposed to have exclaimed. The duke momentarily removes the telescope from his eye, considers the mangled limb, says 'By God, sir, so you have!' (marquess of Anglesey, 149), and resumes his scrutiny of the victorious field. The leg had to be amputated that night and was buried in a Waterloo garden under an elaborately inscribed 'tombstone'. For its loss Uxbridge was offered and refused an annual pension of £1200, thus saving the nation £47,000.

Within three weeks Uxbridge was back in London. Later, the first articulated artificial limb ever devised—the 'Anglesey leg'—was fitted to his stump. On 4 July he was created marquess of Anglesey. Baron Stockmar described him at this time as 'a tall, well-made man, wild martial face, high forehead, with a large hawk's nose, which makes a small, deep angle where it joins the forehead. A great deal of ease in his manners' (*Memoirs*, 53). In 1816 a 100-foot grey marble column by Thomas Harrison was erected in Anglesey, paid for chiefly by local subscriptions, commemorating Anglesey's 'heroic conduct'. In 1859 a bronze statue by Matthew Noble was placed on top of it.

Anglesey was made a knight of the Garter in 1818 and promoted general in 1819. At the time of Queen Caroline's trial in 1820 he is said to have been surrounded by an angry crowd insisting that he should give the cry 'The Queen!' He complied and said: 'God save the Queen—and may all your wives be like her!' (marquess of Anglesey, 163–4). At George IV's coronation in 1821, he acted as lord high steward.

First Irish administration On 30 April 1827 Anglesey succeeded Wellington as master-general of the ordnance in Canning's cabinet. In midsummer, before Canning's death, he was designated to succeed Marquess Richard Colley Wellesley as lord lieutenant of Ireland at the end of the year. Being more of a Canningite than an ultra, he had scruples—which he soon overcame—about serving under Wellington when he became prime minister in January 1828. His views on Catholic emancipation, the great Irish question of the day, had long been equivocal. To the king, fussed about breaking his coronation oath, he protested that he was neither protestant nor Catholic and would act impartially.

Daniel O'Connell's Catholic Association was already a potent nationwide organization. When—though as a Roman Catholic unable to sit or vote—O'Connell was returned at the County Clare by-election, £14,000 in 'Catholic Rent' was subscribed in a week to his election fund. Anglesey, faced (he believed) by 'open rebellion' from both Catholics and Orangemen, made it known that 'the first moment of tranquillity should be seized' to adjust the question (Anglesey to F. L. Gower, 2–3 July 1828, Plas Newydd MSS). This gained him much popularity but angered Wellington, who refused to discuss the subject until he had won the king round. Meanwhile, he made massive military force available to Anglesey.

Anglesey and Wellington now engaged in an acrimonious correspondence. Wellington wrote privately that he thought Anglesey had been bitten by 'a mad Papist or instigated by the love of popularity' (*Despatches, Correspondence*, 5.280). On 30 December he was recalled.

Anglesey's departure was hastened, but not caused, by his letter to Dr Patrick Curtis, the Catholic primate, who had drawn from Wellington a letter stating that he was anxious for a settlement and advising that the question should be buried 'in oblivion' for a time. This Curtis sent on to Anglesey. Since Wellington had thus gone behind his back, Anglesey decided to 'follow His Grace's example'. He wrote to Curtis saying that allowance should be made for the difficulties of the prime minister's situation, but disagreeing with the 'burying in oblivion' and adding that all constitutional means should be used 'to forward the cause' and recommending 'patient forbearance' (Anglesey to Curtis, 23 Dec 1828, Plas Newydd MSS). The letter's publication led to Anglesey being ordered home immediately, but not before the Catholic Association had resolved that all Catholics should be guided by so enlightened a lord lieutenant.

On 19 January 1829, a day of mourning in Dublin, hundreds of thousands of silent, sober people lined the route to Kingstown as Anglesey departed. Hearing of the recall, the French politician Talleyrand told Palmerston that 'he saw at once that the Duke had determined on conceding the Irish Catholic claims, and that he did not mean anyone else to have the credit' (Ashley, 185). Thus it was, for, five days after Anglesey's departure, the Relief Bill was announced from the throne, and on 13 April 1829 it became law.

Second Irish administration Declaring that he was 'attached and bound to no party' (memorandum, 1 Nov 1830, Plas Newydd MSS), Anglesey had no hesitation in accepting the lord lieutenancy again when Earl Grey's whig administration succeeded Wellington's in December 1830. O'Connell's campaign for repeal of the union (home rule) had now made that the great issue of the day. Anglesey, like virtually everyone in England, was unequivocally against it. O'Connell's prodigious power by the time of Anglesey's arrival had so inflamed the people that the first of numerous, mostly fruitless, proclamations had to be issued. On 14 January 1831 'the Liberator' (as O'Connell was called) publicly recommended a run on the banks. Anglesey decided to arrest him, declaring that 'things are now come to that pass that the question is whether he or I shall govern Ireland' (*Greville Memoirs*, 2.109). However, O'Connell was never brought to court, for the political situation had suddenly undergone a radical change.

When on 1 March 1831 the government outlined its scheme for parliamentary reform (of which Anglesey was an ardent advocate), O'Connell gave it his fullest support and temporarily ceased to agitate for repeal. Instead he pressed for the abolition of the compulsory payment of tithes by the Catholic population to the protestant clergy. Anglesey urged the cabinet to remove this and other intolerable imposts and corrupt practices—with only partial success, the Irish Church Act of 1833 achieving only a few of the desired reforms. At the same time a stringent Coercion Act was thought necessary, but Anglesey, finding that the threat of it was enough, never put it in force. When an unaccustomed period of calm followed, Anglesey took advantage of it and in September 1833 he resigned, leaving behind him his greatest achievement, the national education system. In 1830 the mass of the Irish population received no education whatsoever, but by 1843 400,000 children were attending state-aided schools.

In 1842 Anglesey exchanged the colonelcy of the 7th hussars for that of the Royal Horse Guards, thus becoming gold stick-in-waiting. In 1846 he was made field marshal.

Master-general of the ordnance again In July 1846 Anglesey became for the second time master-general of the ordnance, under the prime minister, Lord John Russell—but without a seat in the cabinet. He presided over 'this charming department', as he called it, until the government's fall in 1852, at which time he was then nearly eighty-four.

Together with Sir John Burgoyne, whom he had appointed inspector-general of fortifications, Anglesey and Wellington (the latter as commander-in-chief) fought hard to bring government and public opinion to realization of the defenceless state of the country when steamships were beginning to make, as Anglesey put it, 'all parts of the coasts of this Empire' (Wellington to Anglesey, 3 April 1847, Plas Newydd MSS) vulnerable to attacks in all weathers. Both men made numerous visits to coastal defensive works, on horseback and by steamer, Anglesey in his yacht on one occasion looking into the French port of Cherbourg and finding it 'amply protected' (ibid.). He and Wellington became in their last years the closest of old cronies, being often seen together in public and private—two deaf old noblemen shouting at each other. Anglesey was the only senior commander present at Waterloo to outlive his chief.

Death and state funeral Anglesey also outlived Char by nine months, dying of a stroke at Uxbridge House, Burlington Gardens, London, on 29 April 1854. At Queen Victoria's wish, he was given a state funeral and was buried in Lichfield Cathedral on 6 May.

The lord lieutenancies of Anglesey and Staffordshire (in which were his principal residences, Plas Newydd and Beaudesert Hall) were among the many posts Anglesey held. He was also constable of Caernarfon Castle, ranger of Snowdon forest, and captain of Cowes Castle. Of his eighteen children, Lord Clarence *Paget became an admiral and Lord Alfred *Paget clerk-marshal of the royal household, and Lord George *Paget served as second in command to Lord Cardigan in the charge of the light brigade at Balaklava during the Crimean War.

ANGLESEY

Sources Marquess of Anglesey [G. C. H. V. Paget], *One-leg: the life and letters of Henry William Paget, first marquess of Anglesey* (1961) • *The Paget brothers, 1790–1840*, ed. Lord Hylton [H. G. H. Jolliffe] (1918) • *Letters and memorials of General the Honourable Sir Edward Paget*, ed. H. M. Paget and E. Paget (1898) • *The Capel letters, being the correspondence of Lady Caroline Capel and her daughters with the dowager countess of Uxbridge from Brussels and Switzerland, 1814–1817*, ed. Marquess of Anglesey [G. C. H. V. P. Paget] (1955) • Marquess of Anglesey [G. C. H. V. P. Paget], 'Two brothers in the Netherlands, 1794–1795', *Journal of the Society for Army Historical Research*, 32 (1954), 74–82, 96–106 • H. T. Siborne, ed., *Waterloo letters* (1891) • *Despatches, correspondence, and memoranda of Field Marshal Arthur, duke of Wellington*, ed. A. R. Wellesley, second duke of Wellington, 8 vols. (1867–80) • C. W. C. Oman, *A history of the Peninsular War*, 1 (1902) • G. Alexander, *A cavalry officer in the Corunna campaign, 1808–1809: the journal of Captain Gordon of the 15th hussars*, ed. H. C. Wylly (1913) • C. R. B. Barrett, *The 7th, queen's own, hussars*, 2 vols. (1914) • Fortescue, *Brit. army*, vol. 6 • *The letters of King George IV, 1812–1830*, ed. A. Aspinall, 3 vols. (1938) • *The journal of Mrs Arbuthnot, 1820–1832*, ed. F. Bamford and the duke of Wellington [G. Wellesley], 2 vols. (1950) • D. Le Marchant, *Memoirs of the late Major-General Le Marchant* (1841) • *N&Q*, 3rd ser., 2 (1862), 249, 320, 339 • *The Greville memoirs, 1814–1860*, ed. L. Strachey and R. Fulford, 8 vols. (1938) • *Memoirs of Baron Stockmar by his son Baron E. von Stockmar*, ed. F. M. Müller (1872), vol. 1 • A. E. M. Ashley, *The life and correspondence of Henry John Temple, Viscount Palmerston*, 2 vols. (1879) • Boase, *Mod. Eng. biog.* • U. Wales, Plas Newydd MSS [Plas Newydd, Anglesey, and Bangor] • GEC, *Peerage*

Archives BL • Duke U., Perkins L., corresp. relating to Ireland • NAM, military corresp. and papers • NRA, priv. coll., corresp. and papers • PRO NIre., corresp. and papers as lord-lieutenant of Ireland • Staffs. RO, corresp. relating to Staffordshire affairs • U. Wales, Bangor, corresp. relating to patronage, etc. | BL, corresp. with Lord Holland, Add. MSS 51567–51568 • BL, corresp. with William Huskisson, Add. MSS 38753–38758 • BL, corresp. with Prince Lieven, Add. MSS 47289–47296 • BL, corresp. with Sir Arthur Paget, Add. MS 48404A • BL, corresp. with Sir Robert Peel, Add. MSS 40325–40326 • BL, corresp. with Lord Wellesley, Add. MSS 37298–37313, *passim* • Borth. Inst., letters to Sir Charles Wood • Durham RO, letters to Lord Londonderry • Lpool RO, letters to Lord Stanley • NRA, priv. coll., letters to Lady Sydney • PRO, corresp. with Lord John Russell, PRO 30/22 • PRO NIre., letters to E. G. (afterwards Lord) Stanley • Staffs. RO, letters to Dyott • U. Durham L., corresp. with second Earl Grey • U. Durham L., corresp. with third Earl Grey • U. Southampton L., corresp. with Lord Palmerston • U. Southampton L., letters to first duke of Wellington • W. Sussex RO, letters to duke of Richmond

Likenesses J. Hoppner and S. Gilpin, oils, 1798, Plas Newydd, Gwynedd; repro. in Anglesey, *One-leg* • R. Dighton junior, watercolour, 1806, Royal Collection; repro. in Anglesey, *One-leg* • R. Dighton junior, portrait, 1808 (*A scene at Ipswich barracks*), Plas Newydd, Gwynedd; repro. in Anglesey, *One-leg* • H. Edridge, watercolour, 1808, NPG; repro. in Anglesey, *One-leg* • F. Chantrey, marble bust, 1816, AM Oxf. • C. F. Coene, portrait, 1816 (*An apocryphal meeting between Wellington and Uxbridge after the battle of Waterloo*), Plas Newydd, Gwynedd; repro. in Anglesey, *One-leg* • T. Lawrence, oils, *c.*1816–1817, Plas Newydd, Gwynedd [*see illus.*] • F. Chantrey, two pencil drawings, 1818, V&A • F. Chantrey, marble bust, 1819, Plas Newydd, Gwynedd • Mrs D. Turner, etching, 1819 (after sketch by F. Chantrey), BM; repro. in Anglesey, *One-leg* • W. Hackwood, Wedgwood medallion, 1821 (after W. Beechey, 1815), City Museum and Art Gallery, Stoke-on-Trent • J. W. Pieneman, oil sketch for *The Battle of Waterloo*, 1821, Wellington Museum, London • J. W. Pieneman, oils, 1821, Plas Newydd, Gwynedd; repro. in Anglesey, *One-leg* • J. Stephanoff, drawing, 1821, priv. coll., V&A; repro. in Anglesey, *One-leg* • J. W. Pieneman, group portrait, oils, 1824 (*The Battle of Waterloo*), Rijksmuseum, Amsterdam • attrib. P. E. Ströhling, oils, 1826, NAM • G. Cruikshank, etching, 1827 (*The ordnance going off and relieving guard*; after cartoon by W. H. Merle), BM; repro. in Anglesey, *One-leg* • J. Dickinson?, lithograph, pubd 1828 (after unknown artist), NPG • P. Turnerell, marble bust, 1828, Royal Collection • G. Cruikshank, double portrait, caricature sketch, *c.*1829, BM; repro. in Anglesey, *One-leg* • G. Jones, group portrait, oils, 1829 (*The Catholic Emancipation Act*); on loan to House of Lords • coloured impression, 1829, BM; repro. in Anglesey, *One-leg* • R. B. Davis, oils, 1830, Plas Newydd, Gwynedd; repro. in Anglesey, *One-leg* • R. Seymour, lithograph, 1830 (*An in and an out*), BM; repro. in Anglesey, *One-leg* • W. Theed junior, bronze statuette, *c.*1830, Plas Newydd, Gwynedd; repro. in Anglesey, *One-leg* • R. Seymour, lithograph, 1831 (*The retort courtious*), BM; repro. in Anglesey, *One-leg* • R. Seymour, lithograph, 1831 (*The tinker*), BM; repro. in Anglesey, *One-leg* • coloured impression, 1831 (*Good morning to you, Daniel—will I not get lave to spake?*), BM; repro. in Anglesey, *One-leg* • W. Salter, oils, 1836, NPG • M. A. Shee, oils, 1836, Royal Collection • D. Wilkie, group portrait, oils, 1837 (*The First Council of Queen Victoria*), Royal Collection • C. Paget, double portrait, watercolour, 1840, Plas Newydd, Gwynedd • F. X. Winterhalter, oils, *c.*1840, Plas Newydd, Gwynedd; repro. in Anglesey, *One-leg* • W. Salter, group portrait, oils, 1841 (*The Waterloo banquet at Apsley House*), Apsley House, London; oil study, *c.*1835, NPG • Count D'Orsay, pencil drawing, 1843, Plas Newydd, Gwynedd; repro. in Anglesey, *One-leg* • Count D'Orsay, pencil drawing, 1843, Plas Newydd, Gwynedd • J. R. Jackson, mezzotint, pubd 1845 (after T. Lawrence), BM, NPG • H. Graves, pencil drawing, 1848, NPG • coloured print, *c.*1850, Plas Newydd, Gwynedd; repro. in Anglesey, *One-leg* • H. Graves, watercolour, 1851, priv. coll.; repro. in Anglesey, *One-leg* • H. Graves, watercolour, 1851, Plas Newydd, Gwynedd; repro. in Anglesey, *One-leg* • R. C. Lucas, wax medallion, 1851, NMG Wales, NPG; repro. in Anglesey, *One-leg* • M. Noble, marble bust, 1854, Royal Collection • M. Noble, bronze statue on top of column, 1859–60, Llanfair Pwyllgwyngyll, Anglesey • W. Beechey, chalk drawing, Goodwood, West Sussex • formerly attrib. W. Beechey, oils, NPG • H. Graves, coloured engraving, Plas Newydd, Gwynedd • G. Hayter, group portrait, oils (*The trial of Queen Caroline, 1820*), NPG • G. Hayter, group portrait, oils (*The House of Commons, 1833*), NPG • T. Lawrence, oils, second version, Apsley House, London

Paget, Sir James, first baronet (1814–1899), surgeon, was born on 11 January 1814 at Great Yarmouth, Norfolk, the eighth of seventeen children of Samuel Paget (1774–1857), brewer and shipowner, and his wife, Sarah Elizabeth (Betsey; 1778–1843), daughter of Thomas Tolver and Sarah Elizabeth Applewhite (only nine of the children survived to adulthood). His oldest brother, Frederick, migrated to Vienna and established himself in business there. Another brother entered the medical profession: Sir George *Paget became regius professor of physic in Cambridge. His brother Arthur, a student at the inns of court and a friend of W. M. Thackeray, died of consumption at the age of twenty-five. Another brother, the Revd Alfred Paget, was a schoolmaster at Shrewsbury and later rector of Kirstead. Two brothers worked in their father's brewery. These last two, Alfred, and his sisters Martha and Katherine never married.

After attending a local private school James Paget served an apprenticeship in Great Yarmouth with Charles Costerton, who had trained at St Bartholomew's Hospital, London. With introductions from Costerton and his brother George, Paget moved to London in 1834, where he

Sir James Paget, first baronet (1814–1899), by Sir John Everett Millais, 1872

enrolled at St Bartholomew's to continue his medical education. There he met Henry Wentworth Acland, who became a very close friend. Acland later became regius professor of medicine at Oxford. After a prize-winning student career, Paget qualified as a member of the Royal College of Surgeons on 13 May 1836, and he was elected one of the original group of fellows when that rank was created in 1843. After qualifying he visited Paris on a short medical tour and then returned to London to establish himself in his profession.

Even before qualifying Paget began publishing scientific and medical letters. While living in Great Yarmouth, he and his brother Charles studied the local flora and fauna and produced *A Sketch of the Natural History of Yarmouth and its Neighbourhood* (1834). Paget contributed a number of biographies of famous medical practitioners to Knight's *Penny Cyclopedia* between 1833 and 1844, and from 1837 to 1842 he was sub-editor of, and contributor to, the *London Medical Gazette*. He also contributed articles to the *British and Foreign Medical Quarterly* and the *Biographical Dictionary*.

Remaining in London was a clear sign that Paget meant to make a career for himself in the metropolis, and the first rung of the ladder was his appointment in 1837 as curator of the museum at St Bartholomew's Hospital. A second step was his teaching appointment from 1839, as demonstrator of morbid anatomy at Bart's, a post he held for four years. His excellence as a teacher led to his promotion to lecturer on general anatomy and physiology in May 1843. This, together with his appointment as the first warden of the college for students of St Bartholomew's Hospital medical school in August of the same year led Paget to believe that 'all was changed' (Paget MS 236), for it signalled the possibility of a bright professional future. The students admired and respected him, and he stayed on as warden until October 1851. Writing, teaching, and administration were essential sources of livelihood in these early years, for Paget's practice brought in £8 a year in the first two years and had not reached £50 even a decade later; he lived on meagre earnings and money borrowed from his brother George.

In 1836 Paget had engaged himself to Lydia North (1815–1895), daughter of the Revd Henry North, domestic chaplain to the duke of Kent, despite the limited prospects he then had. She was a pious and talented young woman. As a girl she studied at the Royal Academy of Music, where she won prizes. Her musical talents included both composition and playing the piano. But the collapse of Paget's father's businesses, and James and George Paget's commitment to pay their father's debts and those of their brother Arthur, meant that family life had to be postponed. James and Lydia finally married on 23 May 1844; they had two daughters and four sons, including Francis *Paget, and enjoyed a tender and affectionate relationship for more than fifty years of married life.

In 1841 Paget had been appointed surgeon to the Finsbury Dispensary, but real professional opportunities came only with an appointment to one of the teaching hospitals, and in 1847 the chance for a post at Bart's arose. In a hotly contested election Paget won appointment as assistant surgeon—contested perhaps because of his lack of experience as a surgical dresser and houseman, and perhaps because of the opposition of one senior member of the hospital staff. He became a full surgeon at Bart's in July 1861, a position he resigned in May 1871 to become consulting surgeon to the hospital. He continued his teaching at the medical school, as lecturer in physiology from 1859 to 1861 and as lecturer in surgery from 1865 to 1869.

Benefiting from his links with St Bartholomew's, Paget's practice as a surgeon blossomed. At the height of his career he travelled two, three, or even four thousand miles within Britain each year to confer with other medical practitioners and to operate. Among his patients were many medical and public figures, as well as ordinary sufferers. His most famous patients were members of the royal family. In 1858 he became surgeon-extraordinary to Queen Victoria, and at various times he treated members of the royal family, including Princess Alexandra. He was named serjeant-surgeon-extraordinary in 1867 and a decade later was appointed serjeant-surgeon to Queen Victoria. He left the poverty of his early professional days behind and was able to afford excellent education for his sons; he estimated that it cost some £19,000 to establish them in life (Paget MS 223). At his death his personal estate was valued at almost £75,000.

In the emerging environment of medico-scientific

inquiry in the 1840s and 1850s Paget found a place congenial to his scientific interests, his fine abilities as an observer, and his desire to launch a successful professional career. His acute observational powers were applied to medical pathology throughout his working life. Early in his London studies in the hospital dissecting room, he noticed that what others were seeing as specks in the muscle tissue of a cadaver were, in fact, spiral worms enclosed in cysts. He presented a paper before the Abernethian Society on *Trichina spiralis* in February of 1835, though with his agreement the first publication credit went to his senior, the anatomist Richard Owen.

The opportunity to make his name in pathology was not lost, however. Indeed, Paget made the most of his early appointments at St Bartholomew's. In 1846 he published *A Descriptive Catalogue of the Anatomical Museum of St Bartholomew's Hospital* (2 vols.); a third volume was edited by W. S. Savory. This, together with his *Descriptive catalogue of the pathological specimens contained in the museum of the Royal College of Surgeons of England* (5 vols., 1846–9), established, some believe, the basis for his reputation in medical science.

Appointed Arris and Gale lecturer at the Royal College of Surgeons from 1847 to 1852, Paget carried out research in the Hunterian museum of the college and then delivered a series of lectures in pathology. He published these as *Lectures on Surgical Pathology* (2 vols., 1853), and the next generation credited Paget with reviving, thereby, the neglected study of pathology.

Paget was an indefatigable writer, publishing nearly two hundred books and papers. He researched, delivered speeches, and wrote articles on a range of topics in addition to medicine, surgery, and pathology—on alcohol, science and religion, medical education, and medical history—many of which remain documents of the medical, moral, and social life of his times. A few of his papers have become medical classics.

In 1874 Paget published 'On disease of the mammary areola producing cancer of the mammary gland' (*St Bartholomew's Hospital Reports*, 10, 1874, 87–90). This classic paper described a skin eruption associated with breast cancer which was subsequently called Paget's disease of the mammary nipple and areola. Paget's most famous paper, a description of a long-known disease, was 'On a form of chronic inflammation of bones (osteitis deformans)' (*Medico-Chirurgical Transactions*, 60, 1877, 37–63), in which he identified an inflammatory disease characterized by thickened bones and lesions in the neck and skull. This disease came to be known as Paget's disease of the bone.

Paget's name has been attached to other medical processes and syndromes, among them Paget's cell, Paget-von Schroetter syndrome (a form of thrombosis), Paget's abscess (a residual abscess), Paget's test (to differentiate between solid and cystic tumours), and Paget's quiet necrosis (bone disease without signs of inflammation). In the twentieth century he was credited by B. V. Shenoy and W. B. Scheithauer with original observations regarding dermatofibrosarcoma protuberans in Paget's article 'Recurring fibroid and fibro-nucleated tumors' (*Lectures in Surgical Pathology*, 1853).

Paget's wardenship of Bart's was only the first of his long series of positions of influence and leadership in the medical profession. He also served on the council of the Royal College of Surgeons from 1865 to 1889 and was vice-president in 1873 and 1874, examiner on the midwifery board in 1874, and president in 1875. He went on to serve as the college's representative on the General Medical Council from 1876 to 1881. At the college he delivered the Hunterian oration in 1877, the Bradshaw lecture in 1882, and the Morton lecture in 1887. He held many other professional positions, including chairmanship of the Clinical Society (1869), the Royal Medical and Chirurgical Society (1875), and the Pathological Society of London (1887), and the presidency of the International Medical Congress in 1881. Honours were many, among them election as fellow of the Royal Society (1851) and honorary degrees at Oxford, Cambridge, Edinburgh, Dublin, Bonn, and Würzburg. Paget was created a baronet in 1871.

The relationship between the hospital medical schools and the University of London was a complex and vexed one for most of the century. In 1860 Paget was elected to the senate of the university, where he served until 1895. He served as vice-chancellor of the University of London from 1884 to 1895. During this period tensions between the university (in its examining role) and the teaching faculty led to proposals for changes in the university or, alternatively, to the creation of other degree-granting institutions in London. Paget's governance of the university senate in these years was 'gentle and considerate' but might have been more effective if he had been more forceful (Harte, 142). Two royal commissions (Selborne, 1888–9, and Gresham, 1892–4) examined the situation of university education in London.

Paget was known for the clarity and eloquence of his speech and for his courteous but reserved manner. At the end of his life colleagues remembered his 'self-restraint, self-judgment, reserve, self-discipline'. To some 'he seemed an austere man … rather hard on soft people. … But to all men who were strong enough to feel his strength, and good enough to see his goodness, he was guide and master and friend' (*BMJ*, 6 Jan 1900). His lack of a classical and Oxbridge education and his family's financial collapse may have contributed to his reserve, seriousness, and caution. But he rarely took absolute moral positions (for instance, on the use of alcohol), and he did not use medical arguments to sustain moral positions (for example, on masturbation). He supported the entrance of women into the medical profession.

Paget was a devoted and perhaps demanding father. The Pagets' eldest child, Catherine Paget, married the Revd H. L. Thompson, schoolmaster and later vicar of St Mary the Virgin, Oxford. Their eldest son and heir to the baronetcy, John Rahere Paget, was a barrister and the author of *The Law of Banking* (1904; 10th edn, 1989). Their second and third sons, Francis and Henry Luke, were churchmen: one was dean of Christ Church and later bishop of Oxford and the other was bishop of Chester. Their fourth son,

Stephen *Paget, became a surgeon but then turned to writing and to campaigning for medical research. The Pagets' youngest child, Mary Maud, lived with her parents throughout their lives. She was a musician, wrote articles on music history, and engaged in philanthropic activity. Lady Paget died on 7 January 1895.

Paget died of pneumonia on 30 December 1899 at his home, 5 Park Square West, Regent's Park, London. He was buried in Finchley cemetery after a funeral service on 4 January 1900 in Westminster Abbey.

M. JEANNE PETERSON

Sources *Memoir and letters of Sir James Paget*, ed. S. Paget (1901) • B. V. Shenoy and W. B. Scheithauer, 'Paget's perspectives on pathology', *Mayo Clinic Proceedings*, 63 (1988), 184–92 • Wellcome L., Paget MSS • *BMJ* (6 Jan 1900), 49–55 • N. B. Harte, *The University of London, 1836–1986: an illustrated history* (1986) • J. Paget, bt, *Paget family tree* (1963) • H. C. Putnam, *Sir James Paget in his writings: bibliography* (1903) • W. C. Campbell, 'History of trichinosis: Paget, Owen and the discovery of *Trichinella spiralis*', *Bulletin of the History of Medicine*, 53 (1979), 520–52 • S. Paget, unpublished memoir, priv. coll. • H. Paget, 'The Pagets of Great Yarmouth, 1800 to 1850, from the memoirs of the Rev. Alfred Tolver Paget, rector of Kirstead, Norfolk', unpublished typescript, 1933, priv. coll. • M. J. Peterson, *The medical profession in mid-Victorian London* (1978) • m. cert. • d. cert. • *DNB*

Archives American Philosophical Society Library, Philadelphia, corresp. and papers • RCS Eng., archives • RCS Eng., corresp. and papers • St Bartholomew's Hospital, London, archives • Wellcome L., corresp. and papers | BL, letters to W. E. Gladstone, Add. MSS 44431–44789 • BL, corresp. with Florence Nightingale, Add. MSS 45797–45808 • BL, letters to Richard Owen, Add. MS 39954 • Bodl. Oxf., letters to Sir Henry Acland • ICL, letters to Thomas Huxley • NRA, priv. coll., letters to Sir Norman Moore • RCP Lond., index to references for his medical biographies • UCL, letters to Society for the Diffusion of Useful Knowledge • Wellcome L., corresp. with Sir Edward Sharpey-Schafer

Likenesses W. H. N., pencil drawing, 1838, RCS Eng. • T. H. Maguire, lithograph, 1849, NPG; repro. in Paget, ed., *Memoir*, facing p. 120 • G. Richmond, chalk drawing, 1867, NPG • J. E. Millais, oils, 1872, St Bartholomew's Hospital, London [*see illus.*] • Spy [L. Ward], cartoon, pubd 1876, NPG; repro. in *St Bart's Hospital Journal*, 33 (1925), frontispiece • G. Jerrard, photograph, 1881, Wellcome L. • J. E. Boehm, marble bust, exh. RA 1886, RCS Eng.; repro. in Paget, ed., *Memoir*, facing p. 326; replica, 1887, St Bartholomew's Hospital, London • T. O. Barlow, mixed-method engraving (after J. E. Millais), BM, NPG • H. J. Brooks, group portrait, oils (*Council of the Royal College of Surgeons of England, 1884–85*), RCS Eng. • Maull & Polyblank, photograph, Wellcome L. • A. J. Meluish, photograph (late in life), repro. in Paget, *Memoir*, ed. Paget, facing p. 378 • drawing (after G. Richmond), repro. in Paget, *Memoir*, ed. Paget, frontispiece • engraving, repro. in *ILN*, 59, 369 • group portrait, repro. in *The Graphic* (23 May 1891) • oils (in his late years), Wellcome L. • portrait, repro. in *Pictorial World* (25 July 1874), 353

Wealth at death £74,861 15*s*. 5*d*.: resworn probate, Aug 1900, *CGPLA Eng. & Wales*

Paget, John (*d*. 1638), Reformed minister in the Netherlands, was apparently descended from the Paget family of Rothley, Leicestershire; his parents' names are unknown. He was educated at Trinity College, Cambridge, graduating BA in 1595 and proceeding MA in 1598. From earliest years he sensed an inner call and 'ardent affection' to be a preacher (J. Paget, *An Answer to the Unjust Complaints*, 1635, 16). He served as rector of Nantwich from 1598 to 1604, but was ejected for nonconformity. In 1605 he went into exile in the Netherlands and for two years was a chaplain with English troops, under the commands of Sir John Ogle and Sir Horace Vere.

In 1607 Paget moved to Amsterdam to become founding pastor of the English Reformed church, which ministered to English and Scottish residents of the city. Supported by the city magistrates, the church was the English-language wing of the Dutch Reformed church. Paget's inaugural sermon, on 5 February 1607, was on the text 'Create in me a clean heart, O God' (Psalm 51: 10); these words are to this day inscribed on the walls of the church sanctuary. He was formally established in office on 29 April 1607. Paget held this position for thirty years, often with a co-pastor, and became emeritus in 1637.

Under Paget's leadership, the English church took a strong puritan, presbyterian stand. He refused any use of the English prayer book or Anglican ceremonialism; rather, he joined the Amsterdam classis of the Dutch church and thoroughly approved of the Dutch Reformed way of religion, which he considered compatible with his own presbyterian sentiments. The presbyterian system, he said, is 'appointed by God' (J. Paget, *A Defence of Church Government*, 1641, 2.29). Under Paget's leadership, the church grew in membership. Amsterdam had several other English churches composed of separatists and Anabaptists, but Paget always opposed these sectarian factions. He preached and wrote against them and had success in winning a few of the dissidents to his own church. His was the respectable, 'English Orthodoxicall church' (membership registers, nos. 85, 86) in comparison to the separatist, schismatic groups.

In the 1630s, having somewhat quieted the separatists and Anabaptists, Paget had trouble within his own flock, from members who wanted more lively, powerful preaching and discipline. The agitators favoured a newer kind of puritanism, the emerging non-separatist congregationalism (based on teachings of William Ames and Henry Jacob), and they tried to bring in as co-pastors of the church first Thomas Hooker (1631) and then John Davenport (1634), who had gone to the Netherlands as exiles. Paget labelled this new puritanism as a dangerous semi-separatism. Although he finally withstood Hooker and Davenport and sent them on elsewhere, Paget was troubled for several years with controversy with fellow puritans about the role of baptism, the authority of synods, and the degree of congregational autonomy. These troubles spilled over into the English synod of the Netherlands, headed by John Forbes of Delft. Paget refused to join, fearing its radical tendencies.

Through his well-publicized debates and books, Paget became famous as a champion of the Reformed, presbyterian religion. He was author of five books. Most important were *An Arrow Against the Separation* (1618), in opposition to Henry Ainsworth, *An Answer to the Unjust Complaints* (1635), against William Best and John Davenport, and finally, *A defence of church-government, exercised in presbyteriall, classical, & synodall assemblies* (posthumously published in 1641). Through his books and church work, from his Amsterdam location, he became one of the chief defenders of the presbyterian version of puritanism.

In addition to his dogmatic writings, Paget was active in the intellectual life of Amsterdam, being a part of a learned circle of puritans in exile (composed of Paget, Henry Ainsworth, Hugh Broughton, and Matthew Slade), who studied languages and Jewish history. He worked at Hebrew and Arabic and, according to his nephew Robert Paget, he could use the 'Chaldean, Syriack, Rabbinicall, Thalmadicall, Arabick, and Persian' versions and commentaries 'with much ease'. However, he was hesitant to allow such knowledge into his religious faith. He had a debate with Henry Ainsworth in 1618 about how far to go in appreciation of Hebrew language and learning, with Paget on the conservative, cautious side.

John Paget married Briget Masterson [*see* Paget, Briget (*b.* 1570, *d.* in or after 1647)] of Nantwich at an unknown date. They were prosperous; they had investments in the West India Company and owned two houses. They had no children, but they took in their nephew, Robert Paget (*d.* 1683), supporting his education at Leiden University and making him a beneficiary in their will. He became pastor of the English church at Dort. John Paget died on 18 August 1638 from weakness, colic, and catarrh. His wife lived until at least 1647, when she sold their two houses.

Thomas Paget (*d.* 1660), John's younger brother, was also educated at Trinity College, Cambridge, becoming a sizar in 1605, graduating BA in 1608, and proceeding MA in 1612. After being driven from his position at Blackley, Lancashire, because of nonconformity, he too, from 1639 to 1646, served the English church at Amsterdam. On returning to England in 1646, he served at Shrewsbury until 1656, and then was rector of Stockport, Cheshire, until his death in 1660. All the Pagets, John, Thomas, and Robert, were strong presbyterians.

KEITH L. SPRUNGER

Sources A. C. Carter, *The English Reformed church in Amsterdam in the seventeenth century* (1964) • A. C. Carter, 'John Paget and the English Reformed church in Amsterdam', *Tijdschrift voor geschiedenis*, 70 (1957), 349–58 • K. L. Sprunger, *Trumpets from the tower: English puritan printing in the Netherlands, 1600–1640* (1994) • K. L. Sprunger, *Dutch puritanism: a history of English and Scottish churches of the Netherlands in the sixteenth and seventeenth centuries* (1982) • W. Steven, *The history of the Scottish church, Rotterdam* (1832, 1833) • H. F. Wijnman, 'De geleerdenkring van Mathaeus Sladus', *Zeven eeuwen Amsterdam*, ed. A. E. D'Ailly, 6 vols. [n.d., 1943–1950?], vol. 2, pp. 437–53 • R. Paget, 'Preface', in J. Paget, *Meditations of death* (1639) • Venn, *Alum. Cant.* • B. Brook, *The lives of the puritans*, 2 (1813), 291–4 • R. C. Richardson, *Puritanism in north-west England: a regional study of the diocese of Chester to 1642* (1972) • J. S. Morrill, *Cheshire, 1630–1660: county government and society during the English revolution* (1974) • membership registers, nos. 85, 86, Archive of the English Reformed Church of Amsterdam, Amsterdam, Gemeente Archief, P. A. 318

Archives Gemeente Archief, Amsterdam, archive of the English Reformed Church of Amsterdam, P. A. 318 • Gemeentelijke Archiefdienst, Leiden, Goodyear MSS, corresp. • NL Scot., Wodrow MSS, corresp.

Wealth at death see Carter, *English Reformed church*, 25; will, 1627, Notary archives 709, p. 49

Paget, John (1808–1892), agriculturist and writer on Hungary, was born on 18 April 1808 at Loughborough, Leicestershire, the eldest of the three children of John Paget (1773–1833), manufacturer, and his wife, Anne (1789–1811), daughter of John Hunt, surgeon. His father, a pillar of the Unitarian church in the midlands, retired to the estates at Thorpe Satchville, which he bought about 1821. Paget completed his early education at Revd Charles Berry's academy, a Unitarian private academy in Leicester, and in 1823 was sent to Manchester College, York. He matriculated at Trinity College, Dublin, in 1827 as a medical student, but received his degree of MD from Edinburgh University in 1831. He never used the title or practised, although he successfully pursued further medical studies in Paris and maintained a lifelong interest in medicine. Between 1833 and 1837 he travelled extensively on the continent. During the winter season in Rome in 1835 he met the Baroness Polyxena Wesselényi (1801–1878), the estranged wife of a Hungarian magnate, Baron László Bánffy, a highly cultivated woman and society belle. They married on 15 November 1836, on Paget's second visit to Hungary (the first had been in 1835). As a result of these visits, Paget gained an intimate knowledge of Hungarian society including the protagonists of the liberal opposition.

Out of his rich experience Paget produced a well-written travelogue in two volumes: *Hungary and Transylvania; with Remarks on their Condition, Social, Political, Economical* (1839), illustrated by George Hering, who had accompanied him to Hungary. The book was well received and soon translated into German. It was, however, on account of the Hungarian war of independence in 1848–9 that the work achieved the prominence it deserved. In the general search for reliable background information on Hungary it was 'ransacked' (*The Times*, 3 April 1850) by editors, and new issues followed in quick succession (1849, 1850, 1855), including an American edition (1850). Many of Paget's observations found their way into reference books.

Before the war of independence Paget purchased an estate in Transylvania at Gyéres where he settled with his family and was granted Hungarian citizenship by an act of the Diet of Transylvania in 1847. There he devoted his energies to introducing the latest farming techniques, modern machinery, improved animal husbandry, and selective horse breeding. However, all his efforts were ruined in late 1849 or early January 1850, when marauding Romanian peasants burnt down his English-style manor house and destroyed his possessions; he fled with his family to England. After periods in Loughborough (and subsequently Dresden and Nizza) the family was able to return to Gyéres in 1855 having finally (with the assistance of the British authorities) managed to obtain safe conduct. Paget spent the rest of his life there in high-standard farming and viniculture.

During his time in Transylvania Paget had been a staunch supporter of the Unitarian church there, and had forged strong links with British Unitarians. As a result, he came to the rescue of the independent Unitarian schooling when it was threatened by measures of the Austrian government (1857).

Paget also published scientific treatises and was a contributor to *Erdélyi Gazda* on agricultural matters. A regular visitor to, and adjudicator at, international agricultural fairs, in 1878 he was awarded the Légion d'honneur at the World Exhibition in Paris. His wife died in the same year. Paget himself died on 10 April 1892 at Gyéres; he was buried on 12 April in the Házsongárd cemetery at Kolozsvár. Both of his sons predeceased him—the elder, Walter, in childhood, and the younger, Oliver (1841–1863), who fought in the Hungarian legion of Garibaldi, at the age of twenty-two. LÓRÁNT CZIGÁNY

Sources D. L. Wykes, 'John Paget M.D., of Transylvania (1808–1892)', *Transactions of the Unitarian Historical Society*, 17/2 (1979–82), 54–72 • S. Maller, 'John Paget János', in J. Paget, *Magyarország és Erdély*, ed. S. Maller (1987), 329–48 • J. Balogh, 'John Paget (1808–1892)', *Hungarian Quarterly*, 5/4 (1939), 610–32 • J. Balogh, 'John Paget (1808–1892)', *Hungarian Quarterly*, 6/1 (1940), 65–81 • I. Gál, 'Paget János angol asszimiláns', *Magyarország, Anglia és Amerika* (1945), 121–31 • 'The diary of John Paget', ed. H. M. Madden, *Slavonic Yearbook*, 19 (1940), 237–64 • S. Tonelli, 'A reformkorszak Magyarországa angol megvilágításban', *Magyar Figyelő*, 3/2 (1913), 278–90 • S. Fest, *'Angolok Magyarországon a Reformkorszakban, 1825–48* (1920), 56–60 • J. Kovács, *Paget János, Esq. életírata* (1893) • *DNB* • *GM*, 2nd ser., 7 (1837), 201
Archives National Széchenyi Library, Budapest, diary [fragment] | NA Scot., letters to Sir John McNeill
Likenesses Morelli, portrait, repro. in J. Kovács, *An oration in memory of the late John Paget* (1893) • photograph, repro. in Paget, *Magyarország és Erdély* • photographs, repro. in I. Gál, *Magyarország*
Wealth at death considerable wealth; estates in Transylvania and England

Paget, John (1811–1898), police magistrate and author, was born in Humberstone, Leicestershire, on 14 May 1811, the second son of Thomas Paget, a Leicester banker and a man of some wealth. John Paget was involved in a bitter feud with his brother, Thomas Tertius Paget, over their father's substantial estate. The family was of Huguenot origin, descended from Valerian Paget who fled to England after the massacre of St Bartholomew. John Paget was educated entirely at home and for some years he was an assistant in his father's bank. He entered the Middle Temple on 16 October 1835, and was called to the bar on 2 November 1838.

On 1 March 1839 Paget married Elizabeth, eldest daughter of William *Rathbone (1787–1868) [*see under* Rathbone, William (1757–1809)] of Greenbank, Liverpool, and his wife, Elizabeth, *née* Greg (*d.* 1882). Her Unitarian family had long been associated with social reform. Her brother William Rathbone (1819–1902) was an MP and philanthropist, as was his daughter, Eleanor Florence Rathbone (1872–1946). They had a son and two daughters, one of whom, Mary Rosalind *Paget (1855–1948), became an influential nurse and reformer of midwifery.

From 1850 until 1855 Paget was secretary first to Lord Chancellor Truro and secondly to Lord Chancellor Cranworth. In 1864 he was appointed a magistrate at the Thames police court; he was transferred from this to the Hammersmith and Wandsworth courts, and on their separation he presided over the court at west London until his resignation in 1889.

Paget gave his leisure to writing. He was a contributor to *Blackwood's Edinburgh Magazine* between 1860 and 1888. His papers criticizing Macaulay's views of Marlborough, the massacre of Glencoe, the highlands of Scotland, Claverhouse, and William Penn, were reprinted in 1861 as *The New Examen*. Other articles on a wide range of topics, including Nelson, Byron, well-known legal cases, and art, were published in 1874 as *Paradoxes and Puzzles: Historical, Judicial, and Literary.*

Paget was also a skilful draughtsman, and his illustrations to *Bits and Bearing-Reins* (1875) by Edward Fordham Flower helped to make the reader understand the cruelty caused to horses by the method of harnessing against which Flower protested. In early days Paget was an ardent whig, and enrolled himself among those who were prepared to fight for the Reform Bill. He joined the Reform Club when it was founded in 1836, and was a member of its library committee for twenty-four years and chairman from 1861 to 1865. He died on 28 May 1898 at his residence, 28 The Boltons, West Brompton, London. He was survived by his wife and two daughters.

W. F. RAE, *rev.* ERIC METCALFE

Sources J. Foster, *Men-at-the-bar: a biographical hand-list of the members of the various inns of court*, 2nd edn (1885), 349 • private information (1901) • *Wellesley index*
Archives Leics. RO, personal and legal papers • NL Scot., corresp. with Blackwoods
Wealth at death £97,632 13*s.* 6*d.*: resworn probate, Feb 1899, *CGPLA Eng. & Wales* (1898)

Paget, Sir John Starr, third baronet (1914–1992). *See under* Paget, Sir Richard Arthur Surtees, second baronet (1869–1955).

Paget, Dame (Louise Margaret) Leila Wemyss (1881–1958), hospital administrator, was born at 3 Halkin Street West, Belgravia, London on 9 October 1881, the only daughter and second of four children of Sir Arthur Henry FitzRoy Paget (1851–1928), army officer, and his wife, Mary Fiske (Minnie) Stevens (*d.* 1919). Her father, a grandson of the first marquess of Anglesey, rose to be general-officer-commanding the forces in Ireland (1911–17); as such, he sparked the Curragh 'mutiny' of 1914. Her American mother cut a figure in London society. They were friends of King Edward VII.

Educated by governesses, Leila became a débutante, yet an air of diffidence seemed to preclude her absorption into the smart set. On 28 October 1907 she wed her third cousin once removed, Ralph Spencer Paget (1864–1940), a diplomat who was then British minister in Bangkok. His KCMG in 1909 made her Lady Paget. She delighted in Siam, found Bavaria dull (1909–10), and encouraged her husband to accept a transfer to Serbia in July 1910.

Befriended by Mabel Grujić, American wife of the Serbian under-secretary for foreign affairs, Lady Paget volunteered to assist in the management of a military hospital in Belgrade during the First Balkan War (October 1912–May 1913). This experience had a profound effect on her; she worked so hard that her health gave way (temporarily) when the crisis was over. The Pagets returned to London, where Sir Ralph became an assistant under-secretary for foreign affairs in August 1913. Artists and musicians were often invited to their home at 32 York Terrace, Regent's Park.

The outbreak of the First World War found Lady Paget

on holiday in California, but she hastily came back and immersed herself in the lord mayor's Serbian Relief Fund (SRF), which took premises in Cromwell Road, South Kensington, and purchased equipment for a war hospital. On 29 October 1914, the first SRF unit (of four doctors and sixteen nurses) sailed from Southampton, with Leila Paget in charge. They were making for northern Serbia, near the front line, but, on reaching Skoplje (modern Skopje, then still known to some by its Turkish name of Uskub) on 17 November, the SRF was invited by the Serbian Red Cross to take over the third reserve hospital in the town (a converted secondary school with 330 beds). When the first 180 casualties arrived on 22 November, nurses perceived that Serbian standards of care resembled those found by Florence Nightingale in Turkey six decades before. Lady Paget as 'head SRF Skoplje' displayed dedication and leadership of a similar order. A slender, elegant young woman, she took on the most unpleasant tasks and never asked anyone to do what she would not do herself. Dysentery, sepsis, and gangrene were rife; the water supply proved unreliable; half the staff were usually off sick. Nevertheless the SRF hospital looked after not only Serbian wounded but also Austro-Hungarian prisoners.

In February 1915 a typhus epidemic hit Skoplje. As the Serbian authorities did not seem to realize its seriousness Lady Paget took the initiative in setting up an isolation hospital outside the town. She contracted typhus herself on 8 March and appeared near to death when Ralph Paget arrived as chief commissioner of British relief units in Serbia (which included the Red Cross and Scottish Women's Hospitals as well as the SRF). She recovered, however, and the advent of a second SRF unit at Skoplje allowed her to go to England in May 1915 for recuperation. Hailed as a heroine, she received the grand cordon of the order of St Sava from King Peter I of Serbia and a street in Belgrade was named Ledi Pažet ulica.

When Lady Paget resumed her duties in Macedonia in July 1915 the Balkan front was quiet, but all that changed when Austria-Hungary relaunched its invasion of Serbia in October and Bulgaria joined the central powers. Skoplje lay open to Bulgarian attack and Lady Paget appealed in vain for Anglo-French intervention. Instructed by her husband to evacuate the town, she judged the transport to be hopelessly inadequate for hundreds of gravely wounded men, so the SRF units decided to remain with their patients and be taken prisoner. The Bulgarians captured Skoplje on 22 October. Having nursed Bulgarians in the First Balkan War (and been received by Queen Eleanore of Bulgaria), Lady Paget seemed unafraid. Though shortages of food and fuel caused severe privation, she managed to keep the hospital open and to administer relief to thousands of refugees, while evading Bulgarian attempts to pressurize her into attesting to alleged Serbian atrocities. Her determination to supply humanitarian aid to all in need, wholly regardless of nationality, impressed the Bulgarians so much that they helped her ward off German plans to commandeer the hospital and intern the British staff, who did not leave until 17 February 1916, by which time Serbia had been overrun. The International Red Cross arranged their repatriation via Sofia, Bucharest, and Petrograd.

Lady Paget reached England on 3 April 1916. Despite disapproval in 'jingo' circles of her co-operation with the Bulgarians, the king appointed her GBE in August 1917. Dame Leila Paget resided in Copenhagen (1916–18) and Rio de Janeiro (1919–20) during her husband's final postings. The couple, who had no children, then retired to Sittingbourne, Kent, before moving in 1929 to Warren House, her late father's mansion at Kingston Hill, Surrey. She had it turned into a convalescent home during the Second World War. She died at her final home, Soames House, Coombe Hill Road, Kingston upon Thames, Surrey, on 24 September 1958. JASON TOMES

Sources M. Krippner, *The quality of mercy: women at war, Serbia, 1915–18* (1980) · W. Mead, 'With a British hospital in Serbia—the experiences of Lady Paget's unit at Skoplje', *World's Work*, 26 (1915), 243–58 · *The Times* (25 Sept 1958) · 'Men and women of today: Lady Paget', *World's Work*, 26 (1915), 204–5 · Burke, *Peerage* · *WWW* · b. cert.

Archives BL, papers, Add. MSS 51242–51262 | IWM, first and second Serbian relief fund reports

Likenesses photograph, repro. in Krippner, *Quality of mercy*, 45 · photograph, repro. in Mead, 'With a British hospital', 193

Wealth at death £114,640 2*s*. 6*d*.: probate, 27 Nov 1958, *CGPLA Eng. & Wales*

Paget [*née* Finch-Hatton], **Lady Muriel Evelyn Vernon (1876–1938)**, humanitarian relief worker, was born in London on 19 August 1876, the only daughter and elder child of Murray Edward Gordon Finch-Hatton, twelfth earl of Winchilsea and seventh earl of Nottingham (1851–1898), and his wife, Edith (1855–1939?), only daughter of Edward William Harcourt, of Stanton Harcourt and Nuneham Park, Oxfordshire. She was educated at home. On 31 May 1897 she married the inventor Sir Richard Arthur Surtees *Paget, second baronet (1869–1955), of Cranmore Hall, Shepton Mallet. They had five children.

Muriel Paget's only brother had died in March 1892, when she was fifteen, and her own eldest child, born in March 1898, died in the following October, when she was just twenty-two. She collapsed into invalidism. But in 1905 she rallied to respond to the wretchedness of others when her aunt, Lady Templetown, suggested she become honorary secretary of a charity organizing soup kitchens in Southwark. Very soon Muriel Paget discovered that all the poor districts of London housed hungry people needing soup kitchens, and she founded a new association, the Invalid Kitchens of London, for which she remained honorary secretary until her death. By 1913 there were soup kitchens for mothers, children, and old people in Stepney, Victoria Docks, and St Pancras as well as in Southwark—for which Muriel Paget had raised immense sums, principally via charity balls in high society.

Although pregnant with her fifth child in August 1914, Muriel Paget extended her invalid kitchens to help the Belgian refugees evacuated to London after the German invasion. In November 1914 her baby, John Starr *Paget [*see under* Paget, Sir Richard Arthur Surtees], was born, but 1915 found her organizing the funding and staffing of an Anglo-Russian base hospital in Petrograd—she having been deeply moved by the account by her friend Bernard Pares of the suffering of the Russian army. In 1916 she left her family to begin a life of almost continuous humanitarian intervention abroad, returning home only for Christmas, Easter, and birthdays. She had no doubt that her own privileged children needed her less than did the millions of people in remediable pain. First she organized field hospitals, including 100 British-funded ambulances, in Galician Ukraine in 1916, for the thousands of untended Russian casualties who lay bleeding, unbandaged, and without morphine among the flyblown corpses on the battlefield. When, in 1917, the first Russian Revolution hit Petrograd, she found herself 'looking into the mouth of a revolver with a fierce Russian behind it. I pushed the revolver away and laughed at the soldier, who let me pass' (Blunt, 109). The British and French authorities then asked her to organize civil relief in the south that had not yet fallen to the Bolsheviks, so she went to Odessa. On learning that the situation in Kiev was still worse, she left for Kiev to find her food kitchens for 6000 people there under bombardment. The Bolshevik siege was victorious, and she and other British subjects had to be evacuated from Russia in February 1918, via Siberia, Japan, and America.

'[Lady Muriel] never distinguished … between Imperial and Socialist Russia' (R. Byron, *The Times*, 21 June 1938). Being politically colour-blind, she was immune to the twentieth century's terrible selective indignation and selective compassion. In December 1919 she founded a Women and Children of Russia Relief Fund to support a hospital in the Crimea—until Wrangel's White Russian campaign was defeated in November 1920. Then, during the Russian famine, she was permitted to return to the Soviet Union to try to set up child welfare centres and a training school for Russian nurses. That project was less successful than was her amazing relief work elsewhere in eastern Europe—in Slovakia, the Baltic states, Romania, and Poland, often in conjunction with the recently established Save the Children Fund. As Harold Nicolson had reported during the Versailles conference of 1919: '"Her energy is terrifying. She sends Prime Ministers scuttling at her behests" … [and] "Protégez-moi, protégez-moi de cette dame!" cried Beneš, the Czechoslovak foreign minister' (Blunt, 136–7). For while the male leaders were debating the political frontiers of Europe, Muriel Paget was travelling indefatigably, telephoning, writing letters, and lobbying day and night for Europe's sick, starving children. 'Collect all the milk you can up to 60 tons or more. Clear all the stores and get permission for export … Try to get *fats* at all price' (Blunt, 137). And her relief train duly left Paris for Prague. One very important part of the Paget Mission was the training of local paediatric nurses in Czechoslovakia and elsewhere so that sanitation, isolation, and inoculation procedures could be carried out in the war against typhus and tuberculosis.

In the new Baltic states of Latvia, Lithuania, and Estonia the chaotic civil wars of revolution and counter-revolution continued into the 1920s. When Muriel Paget found herself on one of these battlefields she tied a white jersey to a stick and was waved through. The people of Riga, Taunus, Vilna, and Dvinsk owed their earliest food kitchens, feeding centres, infant clinics, and travelling first aid units to the Paget Mission nurses and volunteer social workers she had recruited on one of her lightning fund-raising visits to London. By 1922 all these countries' governments had taken over the work she had inaugurated. Nevertheless she had been subjected to criticism at home in *John Bull* and the Northcliffe press for not putting British needs first.

In 1924 Muriel Paget began work on her last rescue operation, on behalf of the destitute, stranded Britons in Russia—elderly governesses, nurses, former employees of former British firms. Her organization on their behalf became known as the British Subjects in Russia Relief Association. At first she sent them money and food parcels, but by 1930 she realized she had to intervene in person and, accompanied by a social worker Dorothea Daunt, made frequent visits to Leningrad to keep up morale. 'When someone tried to dissuade her, saying that her protégés were "mere riff-raff", she said, "I know. That's why I want to save them. No one else will."' (Blunt, 243). Despite the bogus charge of espionage rustled up against her in the Rakovsky show trial, she succeeded in evacuating 'her' stranded Britons to Estonia in 1938—so they escaped being deported to the gulag.

Lady Muriel's work brought her into frequent contact with the British consul-general in Moscow and then Leningrad, Reader Bullard, whose diaries, in which she is variously described as 'mad' and a 'kind of steam-roller', record his reactions to her interventions, and leave the impression that she was 'a classic do-gooding pest' (Pryce-Jones). 'When Lady M. is about all you can do is walk about and wait until she has gone', he wrote of one meeting with her (*Stalin's Russia*, 19–20). Yet he acknowledged that 'when one is exasperated by her incompetence and dishonesty one forgets her courage' (ibid., 174). Those whom she saved between 1905 and 1938 would have more than reinforced this verdict. She died at her London home, 1 Devonshire Terrace, of cancer and exhaustion on 16 June 1938, having been appointed OBE in 1918 and CBE in 1938 as well as having received decorations from Belgium, Japan, imperial Russia, Romania, Czechoslovakia, Lithuania, and Latvia. The hundreds of condolence letters came from people of every social class from all over the world. She was buried at Cranmore, Shepton Mallet, Somerset.

SYBIL OLDFIELD

Sources W. Blunt, *Lady Muriel: Lady Muriel Paget, her husband, and her philanthropic work in central and eastern Europe* (1962) · *DNB* · *The Times* (17–18 June 1938) · *The Times* (21–3 June 1938) · Burke, *Peerage* (1939) · *Inside Stalin's Russia: the diaries of Reader Bullard, 1930–1934*, ed. J. Bullard and M. Bullard (2000) · D. Pryce-Jones, review of *Inside Stalin's Russia*, ed. J. Bullard and M. Bullard, *TLS* (25 Aug 2000), 6 · *CGPLA Eng. & Wales* (1938)

Archives U. Leeds, Brotherton L., Russian archive, Paget collection, MS 1405

Likenesses photographs, 1880–1935, repro. in Blunt, *Lady Muriel* · Bassano, photograph, 1912, repro. in Bullard and Bullard, eds., *Inside Stalin's Russia* · B. Hatton, pencil sketch, 1912, priv. coll. · photograph, c.1920, repro. in Blunt, *Lady Muriel*, frontispiece

Wealth at death £593 14*s*. 6*d*.: probate, 21 Sept 1938, *CGPLA Eng. & Wales*

Paget, Nathan (*bap.* **1615**, *d.* **1679**), physician, was born in Manchester and baptized on 31 March 1615, the son of the puritan divine, Thomas *Paget (*d.* 1660) [*see under* Paget, John (*d.* 1638)], rector of Stockport, Cheshire, and St Chad's, Shrewsbury, and his wife, Margery Goldsmith (1588–1628). His uncle, John Paget (*d.* 1638), was minister of the Amsterdam Presbyterian church from 1607 to 1637. His early education was under the tutelage of Richard Pigot at Northwich grammar school, Cheshire. He subsequently graduated MA at Edinburgh University in 1635, and on 25 November 1638 he entered Leiden University as a student of medicine, and graduated MD there on 3 August 1639. Paget's thesis, 'De peste' (1639), was dedicated to his father and various puritan ministers and laymen in Cheshire and Shropshire. On his return to England he practised at first outside London and was admitted an extra licentiate of the College of Physicians on 4 April 1640. He was incorporated MD at Cambridge on 3 June 1642, and was elected a fellow of the College of Physicians on 4 November 1646. Almost certainly sympathetic to the new regime, Paget was nominated physician to the Tower by the council of state of the Commonwealth on 31 December 1649. Best known, perhaps, as the friend of John Milton, to whom he introduced his cousin who became Milton's third wife, Paget probably shared his reformist religious inclinations. In 1662, for example, through his friendship with the Quaker Isaac Penington, he secured the services of the young Quaker Thomas Ellwood to act as a reader to the near-blind poet. Moreover, his residence in Coleman Street, London, was certainly well known as a haunt of radical puritans; and his extensive library of over 2000 works, which was dispersed after his death, contained a large number of heterodox works dating from the 1640s and 1650s. Further evidence of Paget's parliamentarian and puritan sympathies is provided by the evidence of his subscription to the solemn league and covenant in his parish of St Stephen's, Coleman Street, in 1643, as well as his marriage to Elizabeth (*b.* 1614), the daughter of Sir Philip Cromwell of Ramsey, Huntingdonshire, a first cousin of the lord protector. Paget's attendance on the miraculous Baptist maid, Sarah Wight, in London in 1647 is also suggestive of a man with radical puritan interests and connections.

Little is known of Paget's medical practice, though the evidence which survives would appear to point to a man sympathetic toward the contemporary movement in favour of medical reform and innovation. In 1647, just six months after his election as fellow of the College of Physicians, he presented the college with a three-volume edition of the works of Francis Bacon. He also contributed, along with seven other physicians, to Francis Glisson's pioneering work on the rickets, first published in 1650. Interest in therapies other than Galenism is also suggested by Paget's ownership of large numbers of chemical and alchemical treatises, as well as by the fact that in 1651 he was lending rare chemical manuscripts to Elias Ashmole. Further evidence of his radical inclinations in this respect are suggested by his acquaintance with Samuel Hartlib, with whom he communicated in 1651. None the less, he remained an active figure within the tradition-bound College of Physicians, acting as censor in 1657, 1659, 1669, and 1678, and serving as an elect from 1667 until 1677. On 20 September 1663 he was designated Harveian orator for the following year. Paget died at his home in Coleman Street in January 1679 and was buried in the same month. The main beneficiary of his will, dated 7 January 1679, and proved eight days later, was his brother Thomas Paget, clerk, to whom he bequeathed property in Shropshire and London. He also gave £20 a year for thirty years to the president and fellows of the College of Physicians, as well as £20 to his cousin Elizabeth Milton.

PETER ELMER

Sources Munk, *Roll* · annals, RCP Lond., 3.205b, 461, 482, 570; 4.83a · R. W. Innes Smith, *English-speaking students of medicine at the University of Leyden* (1932), 176 · C. Hill, *Milton and the English revolution* (1977), 492–5 · *Elias Ashmole (1617–1692): his autobiographical and historical notes*, ed. C. H. Josten, 5 vols. (1966 [i.e. 1967]), vol. 2, p. 595 · H. Jessey, *The exceeding riches of grace advanced by the spirit of grace, in an empty nothing creature, viz. Mris Sarah Wight* (1647), 8–9 · *Bibliotheca medica Nathanis Paget, MD* (1681) · will of Nathan Paget, PRO, PROB 11/359/9 · Venn, *Alum. Cant.* · *CSP dom.*, 1649–50, 460, 506 · F. Glisson, *De rachitide* (1650), sig. A5v. · Ephemerides of Samuel Hartlib, 1651, Sheffield University Library, Hartlib MSS, 28/2/5B, 9A, 14A · *VCH Huntingdonshire*, vol. 2

Wealth at death see will, PRO, PROB 11/359/9

Paget, Reginald Thomas Guy Des Voeux, Baron Paget of Northampton (**1908–1990**), politician, barrister, and master of foxhounds, was born on 2 September 1908 at Sulby Hall, Northamptonshire, the younger son and second of three children of Major Thomas Guy Frederick Paget, sometime independent tory MP for the Bosworth division of Leicestershire, and his wife, (Emma) Bettine, daughter of Sir (George) William *Des Voeux, colonial governor. He was educated at Eton College and at Trinity College, Cambridge, where he read law, receiving a third class in part one of the tripos in 1928. He then decided to read for an ordinary degree and passed parts one and two of military studies, which would have enabled him to achieve an ordinary BA, for which, however, he never presented himself. It was while an undergraduate at Cambridge that he joined the Labour Party, a decision not unusual in the political climate of the time but made perhaps more striking in his case by the fact that the previous five generations of his family had all been tory MPs. During the 1930s he practised as a barrister, having been called to the bar in 1934.

Within the Labour Party, for which Paget fought his first (unsuccessful) parliamentary election at Northampton in 1935, he was always something of an anomaly. Once he reached Westminster in 1945, winning Northampton at his second attempt, he contrived to represent the voice of the squirearchy far more convincingly than anyone on the Conservative benches. His socialism was essentially paternalistic, and it was typical of him that he should have thought nothing of receiving a delegation of trade unionists while still dressed in his full hunting kit. He took silk in 1947.

Before becoming a life peer in 1974, Paget sat in the House of Commons for twenty-nine years. In all that time he was only briefly the recipient of preferment from his party. From 1960 to 1964 he was a junior opposition spokesman first for the Royal Navy (during the Second World War he had served in the Royal Naval Volunteer Reserve before being invalided out in 1943) and then for the army; but the death of Hugh Gaitskell in 1963 put paid to any hopes he may have held of progressing to government office. An outspoken critic of Harold Wilson during the leadership election which followed Gaitskell's death, he never relented in his belief that Wilson was quite the wrong man to lead the Labour Party or, indeed, to be prime minister.

In appearance and diction more like a whig grandee from an earlier age, Paget was nevertheless a man of parts. Said to be the slowest speaker in the house, Paget had a long chin and beetling brows. An intrepid yachtsman, a fearless rider to hounds (he must have been the only Labour MP ever to become master of the Pytchley, a position he held from 1968 to 1971), he was also a competent amateur painter (he held his first exhibition at the Fine Arts Gallery at Ebury Street, London, in 1988), as well as being the author of three books. The first, *Manstein, his Campaigns and his Trial* (1951), commemorated his spirited defence of Field Marshal Fritz Erich von Manstein, for which he waived his normal barrister's fees, before one of the last war crimes tribunals in 1949; the second, co-authored with his fellow Labour MP Sydney Silverman, arose in part out of the Christopher Craig and Derek Bentley murder case of 1953 and conveyed its message in its title *Hanged—and Innocent?* (1953); while the third, and far the most ambitious, *The Human Journey*, published in 1979 well after his retirement from the Commons, represented an attempt to tell the whole story of the human race.

Courage, sometimes leading to recklessness, was in fact the hallmark of Paget's career. In 1963, after a row in the Commons over the extradition of Chief Enahoro of Nigeria who, he argued, should properly have been regarded as a political refugee, he insisted on reporting the attorney-general of the day, Sir John Hobson, to the inn (the Inner Temple) to which they both belonged, almost certainly the first time a queen's counsel (and fellow bencher) had taken such action against a law officer of the crown. But then no one was ever less a respecter of rank, station, or person, and it was this total lack of deference in his otherwise patrician character which clinched Paget's claim to be considered a genuine radical.

In 1931 Paget married Sybil Helen (Nancy), daughter of Sills Clifford Gibbons, of Scaynes Hill, Sussex, widow of Sir John Bridger Shiffner, sixth baronet, and former wife of Sir Victor Basil John Seely, fourth baronet. They had no children of their own. In London Paget tended to lead a faintly eighteenth-century bachelor life. But his roots were in the country and in particular at his family home, Lubenham Lodge, Market Harborough, where he and his wife brought up four adopted children, two boys and two girls. They were the offspring of an RAF pilot, whose wife died when the children were young. Paget adopted them because the father did not want them split up, and, when the father retired from the RAF, gave him a job and took him into the household too. He separated from his wife before his death and entered into a relationship with Diana Spearman (formerly of the Conservative Research Department), the widow of Sir Alexander (Alec) Spearman, Conservative MP for Scarborough and Whitby, which caused some embarrassment to his country friends. He died on 2 January 1990, at his London home, 9 Grosvenor Cottages. ANTHONY HOWARD, *rev.*

Sources *The Times* (4 Jan 1990) · *The Independent* (6 Jan 1990) · private information (1996) · personal knowledge (1996) · *CGPLA Eng. & Wales* (1990)

Archives CAC Cam., corresp. with M. P. A. Hankey · CAC Cam., corresp. with Monty Belgion · King's Lond., Liddell Hart C., corresp. with Sir B. H. Liddell Hart · Northants. RO, corresp. with his election agent W. J. Lewis

Wealth at death £2,297,509: probate, 14 Aug 1990, *CGPLA Eng. & Wales*

Paget, Sir Richard Arthur Surtees, second baronet (1869–1955), barrister and scientific investigator, was born at Cranmore Hall, Somerset, on 13 January 1869, the eldest son of Sir Richard Horner Paget, first baronet (1832–1908), of Cranmore, MP, and his wife, Caroline Isabel (*d.* 1946), daughter of Henry Edward Surtees, of Redworth Hall, co. Durham. He was educated at Eton College and at Magdalen College, Oxford, where he obtained a third class in chemistry in 1891; he was called to the bar by the Inner Temple in 1895, and succeeded his father in 1908.

Paget's legal and scientific background, together with his engaging personal qualities, fitted him admirably for such tasks as secretary to several boards and committees, including the patent law committee (1900) and the submarine and electrical section of the Admiralty board of invention and research (1915–18). He contributed to both scientific and artistic departments of knowledge, such as acoustics, music, architecture, town planning, agriculture, anthropology, and human speech, besides cultivating practical music and artistic crafts such as pottery and drawing. His penetrating foresight made him appear ahead of his time. This was certainly true with regard to the streamlined car he designed in 1910, and to some aspects of speech: his book, *Human Speech*, first published in 1930, was reissued in 1964 because of its connection with developments in communication engineering.

Paget's most important original investigations were those connected with language, not only in regard to phonetics and the technique of vocalization, or linguistics and vocabulary—to all of which he added new conceptions—but in the most fundamental processes and means through which individuals can transfer ideas from one to another. His famous theory of pantomimic action of the tongue and lips explained lucidly how language arises at all and related it directly to the senses and affections. From this followed naturally his special interest in the communication problems of deaf mute people. He laid down the principles for an entirely new approach in communication with deaf and deaf mute people by means of a systematic sign language, the further development of which was continued after his death.

Paget was well equipped for work in language and

speech as he possessed a remarkable musical aural sensitivity which enabled him to give widely known improvisatory musical performances; he was also genial, deeply sympathetic, and capable of great affection for young and old alike—hence his efforts on behalf of those deprived of the powers of speech and hearing. From 1953 he was president of the British Deaf and Dumb Association. Esteemed as a lecturer and research worker, Paget was an active member of several learned societies: fellow of the Institute of Physics, the Physical Society, and the Royal Anthropological Institute, honorary associate of the Royal Institute of British Architects, honorary associate member of the Town Planning Institute, and member and sometime manager of the Royal Institution.

Paget married, on 31 May 1897, Lady Muriel Evelyn Vernon Finch-Hatton (1876–1938) [*see* Paget, Lady Muriel Evelyn Vernon], only daughter of the twelfth earl of Winchilsea; they had two sons (one of whom died in infancy) and three daughters. His second wife, whom he married on 22 July 1939, was Grace Hartley Glover, only daughter of Walter Herbert Glover, of Birkdale and Grasmere. Paget died at his home, 9 Alexandra Court, Queens Gate, London, on 23 October 1955. He was survived by his second wife and four children.

Paget's youngest child and only surviving son, **Sir John Starr Paget**, third baronet (1914–1992), aeronautical engineer and company director, was born on 24 November 1914 in Somerset, and in the absence of his eccentric parents was brought up largely by his nanny, Nurse Evans. As a boy he contracted jaundice, so his schooling at Oundle was curtailed and he was sent to Château d'Oex in the Swiss Alps. He read engineering at Trinity College, Cambridge, and gained firsts in all parts of the tripos (BA 1936, MA 1939). In 1936 he began a graduate apprenticeship with the English Electric Co. Ltd at Stafford, later working for them at Preston and contributing innovative ideas to aircraft manufacture. In 1943 he moved to D. Napier & Son, Liverpool, where he worked on the Sabre aero-engine (used in the Hawker Typhoon and the Tempest fighter). On 11 November 1944 he married Nancy Mary, elder daughter of Lieutenant-Colonel Francis Woodbine Parish, army officer, and a great-granddaughter of W. E. Gladstone; they had two sons and five daughters. Paget then moved to Napier's London works, first as manager (1946) and later as director and general manager. From 1949 he was connected with Acton Technical College (later Brunel University), where he promoted the sandwich course. After retiring from Napier in 1962 he moved to Taunton, Somerset, and became a successful bespoke cabinet-maker and cider-apple grower. He founded Somerset Fruit Machinery, which manufactured fruit-picking machines that he had designed (these were also used in Japan to pick up golf balls). Paget died on 7 February 1992 at his home, Haygrass House, Taunton, survived by his wife and seven children.

Harry Lowery, *rev.* John Bosnell

Sources *Year Book of the Physical Society* (1956) • *Nature*, 176 (1955), 1246–7 • *Science*, 123 (1956), 215 • *The Times* (24 Oct 1955) • *The Times* (28 Oct 1955) • *Motor* (29 Aug 1956) • personal knowledge (1971) • *WWW* • Burke, *Peerage* (1959) • *CGPLA Eng. & Wales* (1955) • *Daily Telegraph* (13 Feb 1992) • *The Independent* (13 Feb 1992) • *CGPLA Eng. & Wales* (1992)

Archives RBG Kew, corresp. • UCL, corresp. and papers | BL, letters to Lord Gladstone, Add. MSS 46062–46065

Likenesses P. Scott, portrait, repro. in P. Scott, *Portrait drawings* (1949); in family possession, 1971

Wealth at death £56,055—limited to settled land: probate, 23 Nov 1955, *CGPLA Eng. & Wales* [Sir Richard Paget] • £4484 18*s*. 10*d*.—save and except settled land: probate, 6 Dec 1955, *CGPLA Eng. & Wales* [Sir Richard Paget] • £600,613—Sir John Paget: probate, 27 July 1992, *CGPLA Eng. & Wales*

Paget, Dame (Mary) Rosalind (1855–1948), nurse and midwife, was born on 4 January 1855 at Greenbank, Liverpool, in the home of her grandfather, William *Rathbone (1787–1868) [*see under* Rathbone, William (1757–1809)], whose daughter Elizabeth married John *Paget (1811–1898), a London police magistrate, author, and an ardent whig, who had joined the Reform Club on its foundation. On her maternal side she came from a long line of social reformers, including her uncle William Rathbone (1819–1902), MP for Liverpool, who had a lifelong interest in nursing reform and played a leading role in the formation of the Queen Victoria's Jubilee Institute for Nurses (QVJIN). His daughter Eleanor Rathbone, who maintained close contact with her cousin Rosalind, took an interest in social questions and women's suffrage.

As a young woman Rosalind Paget was influenced by this family commitment to social reform and public service and, like many educated, middle-class women of her day, she sought to lead a 'purposeful' life. When her desire to study as an artist was opposed by her family, she entered the Westminster Hospital at the age of twenty, to train as a nurse, and there, under the Nightingale disciple Miss Luckes, she obtained her nursing certificate. She went later to the London Hospital (1882–4), before training as a midwife at Endell Street Lying-in Hospital, gaining the diploma of the London Obstetrical Society in January 1885. Although Rosalind Paget returned to the London Hospital, where she worked for some years, her main interest lay in the reform of midwifery. In 1886 she was taken by Miss Freeman, matron at the British Lying-in Hospital, to her first meeting of the Matron's Aid Society, soon to be renamed the Midwives' Institute (later the Royal College of Midwives). She recalled that 'There were only about ten persons present and it was very dull'. She agreed to join only if there was a 'Midwives Club and lectures and a library … Next day I was asked to help them organise one' (Cowell and Wainwright, 17).

From then on Rosalind Paget's energetic leadership helped to turn a small society with limited aims into a centre of midwifery reform. At that time the word midwife was hardly mentioned in polite society and the majority of midwives received little or no training. Rosalind, and the other middle-class leaders of the institute, helped to give respectability to midwifery and sought to obtain better education and training for midwives. They hoped to raise the status of midwifery as an area of women's work, to instil a sense of professionalism and public service into midwives, and at the same time to improve the conditions

Dame (Mary) Rosalind Paget (1855–1948), by Elliott & Fry

under which working class women gave birth. Rosalind Paget held the post of treasurer from 1890 to 1930 and used her wide circle of social and professional connections to push forward the cause of midwifery reform and to give financial support to the institute. She also took rooms so that the institute would have a permanent headquarters for meetings, a club, and a library, and she organized lectures on midwifery by some of the most prestigious medical names of the day. In 1887 she founded the institute's journal, *Nursing Notes* (later *Midwives' Chronicle*), and, with Emma Brierly, edited it for many decades. She was also one of the founders of what later became the Chartered Society of Physiotherapy.

During the 1890s Rosalind Paget played an active role in the campaign for midwife registration, giving evidence in 1892 to the select committee on midwifery. A bill for the registration of midwives was introduced into the House of Commons in 1890, but although England in this respect lagged behind most other European countries, the measure was continually rejected, mainly because it was considered an unnecessary restriction of individual liberty. In some quarters the advent of trained midwives was felt to be an encroachment not only upon the friendly services of neighbours but also upon the medical profession. Rosalind Paget knew that poor women could not in any case afford medical attention and insisted that it was wholly advantageous for the midwife to be trained and supervised. Finally in 1902 the Midwives Act provided for the registration of midwives, made it an offence for anyone not properly certificated to describe herself, or practise, as a midwife, and established the Central Midwives' Board. Rosalind Paget was a member of the board from 1902 to 1924 as a representative of the QVJIN, which had been established to promote district nursing and midwifery services throughout the country. She had a long association with the QVJIN; in 1890 she was appointed as its first chief officer and, although she resigned from this position in 1891, she continued as a member of the council, with special responsibility for midwifery.

The Midwives Act, coupled with a growing interest by policy makers in the health and welfare of babies, meant an increased workload for Rosalind Paget. She frequently represented the institute at official enquiries and conferences and acted as an effective lobbyist on behalf of midwives whenever proposals for legislation—such as the 1911 National Insurance Act—appeared to affect their position. She also sought to maintain the importance of the independent midwife, although this became increasingly difficult in the inter-war years, when midwives' earnings were too low to attract well-qualified recruits.

Rosalind Paget always had a close personal and intellectual relationship with the contemporary women's movement and helped to maintain links between the institute and groups such as the Women's Liberal Federation and the National Union of Women Workers, often giving papers at their conferences. She was a strong supporter of women's suffrage and urged all members of the institute to take part in suffrage demonstrations; in July 1908 she led twenty members in a suffrage procession under the banner of Florence Nightingale. Rosalind Paget believed that women's lack of a vote meant that they were unable to influence policy making and saw the suffrage as the first step in enabling women to 'help forward social, moral and economic reforms', in particular those relating to 'the healthy upbringing and proper education of the children whose care is admittedly their special sphere' (*Nursing Notes*, July 1908).

Rosalind Paget's effectiveness in a variety of activities, and the respect that she gained from members of the institute, was not simply the result of her political acumen, it was also helped by her wit and sense of humour; she even managed to present the annual budget in a lively and humorous way.

Rosalind Paget never married and throughout her professional life she devoted herself entirely to the work she took in hand; no detail of a midwife's life or work was too trivial for her interest and she was seen as the friend of all. She refused all recognition of her services until in 1935 she was appointed DBE. She found relaxation in music and art, tastes inherited from her father, and died at the age of ninety-three, on 19 August 1948, at her home, Colwood Park, Bolney, Sussex. JUNE HANNAM

Sources E. Brierley, 'In the beginning: a retrospect', *Nursing Notes* (1923) • J. Rivers, *Dame Rosalind Paget: a short account of her life and work* (1981) • B. Cowell and D. Wainwright, *Behind the blue door: the history of the Royal College of Midwives, 1881–1981* (1981) • B. V. Heagerty, 'Class, gender and professionalization: the struggle for British midwifery, 1900–1936', PhD diss., Michigan State University • J. Hannam, 'Rosalind Paget: class, gender and the Midwives

Act, *c.*1886–1914', *History of Nursing Society Journal*, 5 (1994–5), 133–49 · *DNB*

Archives Wellcome L., personalia and records relating to her management of the journal *Nursing Notes* | Queen's Nursing Institute, London · Royal College of Midwives, London

Likenesses E. Canzini, oils, Royal College of Midwives, London · Elliott & Fry, photograph, NPG [*see illus.*]

Wealth at death £57,303 15*s.* 3*d.*: probate, 24 Feb 1949, *CGPLA Eng. & Wales*

Paget, Sidney Edward (1860–1908), painter and illustrator, was born on 4 October 1860 at 60 Pentonville Road, London, the fourth son of Robert Paget, a vestry clerk from 1856 to 1892 of Clerkenwell and his wife, Martha Clarke. He received his early education at the Cowper Street School in London and afterwards attended the Heatherley School of Fine Art. In 1881 he entered the Royal Academy Schools, where he was preceded by his brothers Henry Marriott and Walter Stanley, both well-known artists and illustrators. At the Academy Schools he won, among other prizes, second place in 1885 in the Armitage competition and first place and medal in 1886 for his *Balaam Blessing the Children of Israel.* Between 1879 and 1905 Paget contributed to the Royal Academy exhibitions eighteen miscellaneous paintings, of which nine were portraits. The best known of his pictures, *Lancelot and Elaine*, exhibited in 1891, was presented to the Bristol Art Gallery by Lord Winterstoke. Among the portraits painted by Paget were *Dr Weymouth* (exh. RA, 1887), headmaster of Mill Hill School, depicted in a three-quarter-length painting dressed in scarlet robes as DLitt; his father, and his brother Robert Ernest (his father's successor as vestry clerk), both displayed in the town hall, Finsbury; Sir John Aird, as mayor, which hung in Paddington town hall; and the journalist Sir William Henry Wills (exh. RA, 1901).

It was as an illustrator that Paget won a wide reputation. His vigorous work as a black and white artist became well known not only in the United Kingdom but also in America and the colonies through his drawings for the *Pictorial World* (1882), for *The Sphere*, and for many of Cassell's publications. He also drew occasionally for *The Graphic*, the *Illustrated London News*, and the *Pall Mall Magazine*. Paget's spirited illustrations for Sir Arthur Conan Doyle's *Sherlock Holmes* and *Rodney Stone* in the *Strand Magazine* greatly assisted in popularizing those stories. The assertion that the artist's brother Walter, or any other person, served as model for the portrait of Sherlock Holmes is incorrect.

On 1 June 1893 Paget married Edith (*b.* 1865/6), daughter of William Hounsfield, a farmer; they had six children. During the last few years of his life he suffered from a painful chest complaint, to which he succumbed at 16 Surrey Road, Margate, on 28 January 1908. He was buried at Marylebone cemetery, Finchley.

J. D. Milner, *rev.* Mark Pottle

Sources *The Times* (1 Feb 1908) · *Daily Telegraph* (1 Feb 1908) · *Morning Post* (1 Feb 1908) · *Daily Chronicle* [London] (1 Feb 1908) · *The Sphere* (8 Feb 1908) · *WW* (1908) · Graves, *RA exhibitors* · private information (1912) · G. M. Waters, *Dictionary of British artists, working 1900–1950* (1975) · Wood, *Vic. painters*, 2nd edn · B. Stewart and M. Cutten, *The dictionary of portrait painters in Britain up to 1920* (1997) · J. Johnson and A. Greutzner, *The dictionary of British artists, 1880–1940* (1976), vol. 5 of *Dictionary of British art* · *CGPLA Eng. & Wales* (1908) · m. cert.

Wealth at death £2650: probate, 17 Feb 1908, *CGPLA Eng. & Wales*

Paget, Stephen (1855–1926), writer and pro-vivisection campaigner, was born on 17 July 1855 at 24 Henrietta Street, Cavendish Square, London, the fifth child and fourth son of Sir James *Paget, first baronet (1814–1899), surgeon, and his wife, Lydia (1815–1895), daughter of the Revd Henry North, domestic chaplain to the duke of Kent. He attended Marylebone and All Souls' Grammar School, Regent's Park, London, before enrolling at Shrewsbury School, where his paternal uncle Alfred had been mathematics master. Paget remained there from 1870 to 1874. He entered Christ Church, Oxford, on 16 October 1874: he was Fell exhibitioner from 1876 to 1880, and in 1878 took second-class honours in classical moderations and Greats. While in Oxford he studied basic medical sciences, but did not seek a university medical degree. On 1 October 1878 he entered St Bartholomew's Hospital medical school (where his father was no longer on the active staff). He served as house surgeon to Thomas Smith, once a student, now a friend of his father. He qualified FRCS in 1885 and took up medical practice.

Paget married, on 17 September 1885, Eleanor Mary (Nell) Burd (1853/4–1933), second daughter of Edward Burd, a Shrewsbury physician. A talented painter, she studied at the Slade School before their marriage, and Paget had a studio built for her at their home, 57 Wimpole Street. The couple had two daughters, Eleanor (*b.* 1888) and Dorothea (*b.* 1890).

Paget's medical career did not prove to be as successful as his father's. He had a brief sojourn at the Western General Dispensary, gained full surgical appointments at the Metropolitan and West London hospitals, and served as assistant in the surgical out-patients' department at the children's hospital, Great Ormond Street. However, to his great disappointment, in seven years there he failed to win a post on the surgical staff. Furthermore, none of these institutions had the prestige of the teaching hospitals. His only appointment of this sort came late; in 1897 he was named aural surgeon to the Middlesex Hospital, becoming consulting surgeon in 1917. Paget abandoned general surgery in 1897 at the age of forty-two, and in 1910 he ceased practising medicine until 1917, during the First World War.

Contemporaries said he was unsuited to a surgical career. He himself later recalled that he never made an adequate living from his practice, earning 'only a few hundred pounds a year' ('Oct 5th, 1925, etc.', 10, in S. Paget, 'Memoir'). His medical career was always carried out in the shadow of his father's success. In *Confessio medici* (1908) Paget warned young men of the dangers of following in a distinguished father's profession. He likened the outcome to that of Icarus trying to fly on wings his father had made, and falling instead into the sea. Two decades later he expressed this view more personally: 'I know that I achieved some good … saved some lives …. But the cloud of regrets and mistakes is over the whole thing, and if I could start again, I could not be a surgeon' ('Memoir', 117).

While his surgical career disappointed him, Paget found gratification in other spheres: particularly in the arena of medical politics and propaganda and in the world of letters. His activities as a propagandist resulted from his commitment to vivisection for medical research. The 1877 legislation to prevent cruelty to animals had led to the creation of the Association for the Advancement of Medical Research (AAMR), and Paget was named its secretary in 1888. By 1908 the AAMR was defunct, and Paget took the leadership in establishing a new body, the Research Defence Society (RDS), to support vivisection in medical research. He became honorary secretary, and served as editor of the society's journal, *The Fight Against Disease*. Between 1891 and his death Paget published a number of reports and essays on vivisection. He organized, lectured, and campaigned endlessly in support of the benefits that could come from the use of animals in medical research.

Paget's third (and perhaps most successful) career was that of biographer and essayist. Between 1897 and 1919 he published biographies of Ambroise Paré, John Hunter, Louis Pasteur, his father James, his brother-in-law H. L. Thompson (with his sister Catharine Paget Thompson), his brother Francis *Paget (with J. M. C. Crum), his friend Henry Scott Holland, and the surgeon Sir Victor Horsley. Beginning with *The Young People* 'by one of the old people' (1906), he established himself as an eloquent and accessible writer for young people (and often the elders as well). His self-deprecating humour, his classical learning, and his lack of self-righteousness made him a popular writer in his generation. His prose had a delicacy of touch that allowed him to take up potentially controversial subjects such as sex education and venereal disease without giving offence. Perhaps because he was the father of daughters, his writings always reflected his recognition that young people were both 'he' and 'she'.

With the outbreak of war in 1914 Paget gave of his expertise and time to the health of soldiers. He lectured at military camps on hygiene and vaccination, and in 1916–17 went to Russia, where he served on the staff of the Anglo-Russian Hospital in Petrograd. His health, never robust, deteriorated during his stay there, and he returned to England.

To some, Stephen Paget seemed shy, even diffident. Others found in him a warm friend. One contemporary said he was 'a delightful and lovable companion, one who drank the wine of life as a gentleman, thankful if the vintage were sound, tolerant of other men's tastes, and holding to conviction without intruding a strong religious feeling' (*The Times*, 20 May 1926). He retired, in ill health, in 1917, and died at his home, Furzedown, in Limpsfield, Surrey, on 8 May 1926.

C. S. Sherrington, *rev.* M. Jeanne Peterson

Sources S. Paget, 'Memoir', typescript, priv. coll. • Wellcome L., Paget MSS • *The Times* (20 May 1926) • V. G. Plarr, *Plarr's Lives of the fellows of the Royal College of Surgeons of England*, rev. D'A. Power, 2 (1930) • J. Paget, *Paget family tree* (1963) • S. Paget, *Confessio medici* (1908) • b. cert.

Archives Wellcome L., MSS | BL, corresp. with Macmillans, Add. MS 55043

Likenesses J. Russell & Sons, photograph, NPG • photograph (after drawing), priv. coll. • portrait, repro. in G. Grey Turner, 'What research owes to the Paget tradition', *The Fight Against Disease*, 25/3 (1937) • portrait, repro. in W. Pickles, 'Meditationes medicorum', *Rhode Island Medical Journal*, 24 (Oct 1941), 181–9

Wealth at death £6587 18*s*. 8*d*.: resworn probate, 3 July 1927, *CGPLA Eng. & Wales*

Paget, Thomas, third Baron Paget (*c*.1544–1590), Roman Catholic layman and exile, was the second son of William *Paget, first Baron Paget, the noted Tudor statesman (1505/6–1563), and Anne, Lady Paget (*d*. 1587), the daughter of Henry Preston. He matriculated as a fellow-commoner of Gonville and Caius College, Cambridge, on 27 May 1559, and was admitted to the Middle Temple two years later. He succeeded to his title and family estates on the death of his elder brother in 1568, and accordingly received a summons to parliament in 1571. He is mentioned in Ridolfi's memoranda about this time as having Catholic sympathies. Nevertheless, throughout the 1570s he was used by the privy council for various local government purposes in Staffordshire, where he principally resided, partly rebuilding Beaudesert House. He married, about 1570, Nazareth, daughter of Sir John Newton, and widow of Thomas Southwell of Woodrising, Norfolk (whose family was noted for its Catholicism). Their eldest son was the politician William *Paget.

By 1580 Paget's own religious views seem to have hardened. In July, when the Jesuit Edmund Campion landed in England, Paget arranged for him to preach a sermon to a gathering of London notables. In August he was summoned before the privy council and confined to a house in Windsor for fourteen weeks, where he was instructed in the doctrine of the Church of England by the dean. Early in 1581 he is to be found writing to Walsingham, asking to be excused attendance at St Paul's. The following year the bishop of Lichfield and Coventry wrote to complain of his conduct in providing 'singing cakes' rather than bread for use by the parishioners of Burton upon Trent, and of the behaviour of his servants in disrupting Easter Sunday service in Colwich parish church. Paget's life was in turmoil at this point: in 1582 he separated from his wife, telling Burghley that this was 'less ill than … living together with continual jars'. His wife died a year later. When the Throckmorton plot was uncovered in 1583 he fled abroad to join his brother, Charles *Paget, who was in Paris, acting as agent there for Mary, queen of Scots. He presumably feared that his brother's connection with Mary and perhaps other links of his own with the plotters, who came like himself from the midlands, placed his life in England in danger. He wrote to Burghley from France that he had long had it in mind to travel, partly to find a cure for his gout, but also because for the past three years he had been much troubled in conscience.

Paget's time in exile seems to have been a miserable one. The English ambassador in Paris, Stafford, described him a few weeks after his arrival there as 'toungue-tied … cold and patient … [he] governs himself either wisely or extremely cunningly'. A proclamation was issued in England commanding him to return, and there was a formal—and unsuccessful—request to the French authorities for his extradition. His estates in England were quickly seized by the government and in 1587 he was convicted of treason by the act of attainder which also condemned the Babington plotters. When he arrived on the continent he found himself in the middle of disagreements between the exiled English, with his brother in one camp and the leading Catholic exile clergymen, Robert Persons and William Allen, in another. He travelled from Paris to Milan and then to Rome, where he stayed in the spring of 1585 at the English College, along with his two servants. He was rather coolly received there, on account of the strength in Rome of the faction opposed to his brother. He then went to Spain where Philip II gave him a pension of 180 crowns a month. He next moved to the Spanish Netherlands in the hope of being restored by the Armada, and was consulted by Parma over the invasion plans. It was at Brussels that he died, some time in 1590.

PETER HOLMES

Sources *DNB* • GEC, *Peerage* • Cooper, *Ath. Cantab.*, 3.4–5 • J. Hutchinson, ed., *A catalogue of notable Middle Templars: with brief biographical notices* (1902) • *The letters and memorials of William, Cardinal Allen (1532–1594)*, ed. T. F. Knox (1882), vol. 2 of *Records of the English Catholics under the penal laws* (1878–82), 228–9, 233, 315–16, 387, 393, 420 • *CSP dom.*, *1581–90*, 134 • A. G. Petti, ed., *Recusant documents from the Ellesmere manuscripts*, *1577–1715*, Catholic RS, 60 (1968), 34 • *CSP Scot.*, *1563–9*, 946, 951–2, 988 • J. H. Pollen, *Mary queen of Scots and the Babington plot*, Scottish History Society, 3rd ser., 3 (1922), 43, 65, 74, 92, 127, 147 • L. Hicks, ed., *Letters and memorials of Father Robert Persons*, Catholic RS, 39 (1942), xvii, 50, 58, 189, 192, 194–6, 226 • 'The memoirs of Father Robert Persons', *Miscellanea, II*, Catholic RS, 2 (1906), 12–218, esp. 27, 33, 35–6, 178–9, 181, 183 • *Miscellanea, IV*, Catholic RS, 4 (1907), 4–5, 62–3, 120–23

Archives Bucks. RLSS, papers concerning title to lands • Staffs. RO, corresp.

Wealth at death property confiscated

Paget, Thomas (*d.* 1660). *See under* Paget, John (*d.* 1638).

Paget, Thomas Catesby, Lord Paget (1689–1742). *See under* Paget, Henry, first earl of Uxbridge (*c.*1663–1743).

Paget, Violet [*pseud.* Vernon Lee] (1856–1935), art historian and writer, was born on 14 October 1856 at Château St Léonard, near Boulogne, France. Her mother, Matilda (1815–1896), was the daughter of Edward Hamlin Adams (1777–1842), who came from a wealthy planter's family in Kingston, Jamaica, but made his own fortune from a variety of West Indies business ventures, some of a questionable nature, and eventually purchased Middleton Hall, Carmarthenshire. Despite his strongly voiced opinions against conventional religion and education, he became a member for the county in the reform parliament of 1832. On his death, his sons carried on only their father's contentiousness, not his ability in business, with one brother challenging the legitimacy of the other's children; the resulting litigation blocked all of Edward's children from their inheritance for several years.

Vernon Lee's father, Henry Ferguson Paget (1820–1894), was reputedly the son of a French émigré nobleman who, after settling his family in Warsaw, founded a college for the nobility. Henry, after attending his father's college, undertook various soldiering missions until his involvement in the Warsaw uprising of 1848 forced him to flee to Paris. Meanwhile, Matilda Adams, facing limited financial resources on the death of her first husband, a Captain Lee-Hamilton, also moved to Paris in 1852 with her son from that marriage, Eugene Lee-Hamilton (1845–1907). At that time, Henry Paget was engaged as Eugene's tutor, a position he held until 1855, when he and Matilda were married. Vernon Lee was the much beloved only child of their marriage.

Violet Paget [Vernon Lee] (1856–1935), by John Singer Sargent, 1881

Intellectual development The Paget household moved at least twice yearly from one place on the continent to another, through France, Germany, Switzerland, and Italy, with the result that Vernon Lee gained fluency in four languages as well as an instinctive internationalist perspective. While she was still very young, both her mother and her half-brother, Eugene, determined that she was to be another Madame de Staël, so that Vernon Lee was raised 'in an atmosphere of fantastic prodigy-worship', as Ethel Smyth later described it (Smyth, 51). In a portrait of her mother in *The Handling of Words* Vernon Lee commented that her mother had taught her to write with 'common sense and good manners' (*The Handling of Words*, 1923, repr. 1968, 297). While Eugene was studying at Oxford and later serving at a Foreign Office post in Paris, his letters to his mother and sister make clear his preoccupation with 'Baby's intellectual development'. In return, Vernon Lee would dutifully send him essay-like letters in her most careful French, which he would then correct. As a writer, Vernon Lee would pay tribute to Eugene's role in her education when she took on part of his surname as hers in her pseudonym. She also acknowledged his influence in her writings in her dedication to him of *Baldwin: being Dialogues on Views and Aspirations* (1886). From 1875 until 1894 an almost complete paralysis confined Eugene to an invalid's existence at home, but Vernon Lee became her half-brother's representative to the London literary establishment and sought to interest publishers in his poetry.

Another important influence on Vernon Lee's intellectual development was her childhood friend the American painter John Singer Sargent, whom she first met in Nice when they were ten. During the winter of 1868–9, when they were with their families in Rome, their shared interests, especially in music, and their similar precocity led them to spend so much time together that when John later wrote to Vernon Lee, he described himself as her twin. At this time too, the young friends determined that in their future lives he was to be a painter, she a writer. John's mother, Mary Newbold Sargent, was also an early muse for the young writer. It was during her frequent excursions with the Sargent family in Rome that Vernon Lee acquired from Mrs Sargent what was to be a lifelong appreciation of antiquities and of the true spirit of place. In 1881, on meeting Vernon Lee after a separation of many years, John Singer Sargent painted the portrait of his childhood friend now in the Tate collection. It was clear from the result that he had not forgotten his knowledge of her. Vernon Lee would write to her mother that everyone thought the portrait characteristic of her, and she agreed with them, describing herself in it as appropriately 'fierce and cantankerous' (*Vernon Lee's Letters*, 65).

Early literary career As her literary mentor during the earliest stages of her career and as her guide to the London literary establishment, Vernon Lee was to choose Camilla Jenkin, a successful popular novelist and family friend. Vernon Lee's letters to her from 1871 to 1878 are a detailed record of the emotional and intellectual development of a gifted young woman of letters. In one of the most memorable of these, dated 28 June 1871, the fifteen-year-old Vernon Lee describes her visit to Rome's Bosco Parrasio on the Janiculum, the site of the long-forgotten eighteenth-century Arcadian Academy and the meeting-place of the leading Italian men of letters. Together with her special attachment to the music of this period, this visit was to confirm eighteenth-century Italy as the focus of her scholarship. She tells Mrs Jenkin how, having recently read Metastasio's works and now having recognized his portrait as a member of the Arcadian Academy, she has decided on her first major literary project:

> I now think that Metastasio having lived from one end of his century to the other, having known all the celebrated writers of the 18th century, amongst whom indeed he is perhaps the most admirable and at the same time the most vilified by the modern Italian school, he might with propriety be taken as a specimen of Italian thought of that period, and his life, his friends, his works and his times form an interesting work. (*Vernon Lee's Letters*, 26)

In addition, she writes, the current custodian of the academy, impressed by Vernon Lee's knowledge, has offered to lend her all the volumes from the archives that she might require for her work. This letter to Mrs Jenkin records a highlight of Vernon Lee's research into the culture of the Italian eighteenth century, begun at the age of thirteen, when, as she described it, she had done so still under the inspiration of 'an unconscious play instinct', but it was Mrs Jenkin who would give Vernon Lee the practical guidance she needed to transform into the pioneering scholarship of her first book, *Studies of the Eighteenth Century in Italy* (1880), her 'lumber room full of discarded mysteries and of lurking ghosts' (*Studies*, 2nd edn, 1907, xvi). Published when she was twenty-four, it was the culmination of ten years of arduous study, much of it of manuscripts of original materials. Often cited as responsible for reviving interest in eighteenth-century Italian drama and music, *Studies of the Eighteenth Century in Italy* in addition pays special attention in individual chapters to the comedy of masks, the work of Goldoni, and 'Carlo Gozzi and the Venetian fairy comedy'. It was greeted with critical and scholarly acclaim and was to remain a classic reference work for scholars until the early 1960s. Above all, it demonstrates the young Vernon Lee beginning to carve out a unique domain for herself as a woman writer, as she defines herself as 'neither a literary historian nor a musical critic, but an aesthetician' whose role encompasses both fields (*Studies*, 1880, 1).

In 1881, on the first of her almost annual visits to England from her family's new permanent residence in Florence, Vernon Lee found that her literary success brought her numerous invitations to the most notable literary and artistic circles of the time. Robert Browning and Walter Pater, it was said, were among her admirers. She soon became known for her tailored dress, with high Gladstone collar and starched shirtfront, her clever conversation, and her piercingly intelligent eyes behind her spectacles. From this first visit until 1894 Vernon Lee recorded all that she observed and all that she experienced of literary London in detailed 'letters home', intended to entertain her family in Florence.

An established reputation questioned Throughout the 1880s and the 1890s Vernon Lee's reputation was enhanced, as she published supernatural and historical short fiction, travel impressions, and personal recollections, as well as essays on religious belief, aesthetics, and literary criticism. In 1884 alone she published three books: *Euphorion, being Studies of the Antique and the Mediaeval in the Renaissance*; *The Countess of Albany*, a biography of the Princess Louise of Stolberg; and *Miss Brown*, a three-decker novel about a beautiful servant–governess who is 'discovered' and subsequently educated by a wealthy aesthetic painter–poet. While the first two works were well received in literary circles, and are still considered among Vernon Lee's finest, *Miss Brown* was 'a deplorable mistake' (Gunn, 104) in the words of Henry James, to whom it was dedicated 'for good luck'. She had seriously misjudged the response of those she had come to know among London's writers and artists. She had intended her first novel to be a thought-provoking satire of a 'fleshly school' of poetry and painting resembling the Pre-Raphaelites. Instead, many readers were shocked by her impropriety in presenting what appeared to be only thinly disguised caricatures of well-known people in an embarrassingly overwritten novel. From the *succès de scandale* of *Miss Brown*, Vernon Lee's reputation was never fully to recover.

Aesthetic theory Vernon Lee would also misjudge the popular response to her pioneering work in the field of psychological aesthetics, a development of the new 'scientific' school that had begun to dominate German aesthetic thought in the late 1870s. Her interest in the field grew out of the most significant love relationship of her life, her romantic friendship with Clementina (Kit) Anstruther-Thomson, a painter who was concerned with 'what art *does with us*', that is, with exploring the connection between the perception of artistic form and the human response. Beginning in the early 1890s, the two women, living together at least six months of every year in Florence and working as collaborators, undertook practical experiments to document physiological responses to art and studied psychology and physiology in order to learn the new methodology of experimentation and analysis. Their work would eventually lead them to discover 'in an entirely empirical way … the general principle of an aesthetics of *empathy*' (Wellek, 169). Through their major publication together, *Beauty and Ugliness and other Studies in Psychological Aesthetics* (1912), they were to introduce this new aesthetics into an English aesthetic tradition that had long been dominated by Walter Pater's theories. But it is *The Beautiful: an Introduction to Psychological Aesthetics* (1913), commissioned as part of the Cambridge Manuals of Science and Literature series and written by Vernon Lee alone, that represents a more significant contribution to the advance of English aesthetics. It offers a brilliant synthesis of Vernon Lee's and Kit Anstruther-Thomson's principles of empathy with the latest theories of the German aestheticians. Yet this contribution has never been fully appreciated, except in histories of modern aesthetics, because its serious consideration demanded a difficult technical presentation. Even close friends such as Ethel Smyth and Irene Cooper Willis doubted the seriousness of the two collaborators' intentions and in later recollections of the two women's aesthetic experiments ridiculed them. Vernon Lee's immersion in psychological aesthetics would influence two other works by her—*The Handling of Words and other Studies in Literary Psychology* (1923), which, in adapting her methodology in the study of artistic form to the analysis of literary texts looks ahead to 'New Criticism', and *Music and its Lovers: an Empirical Study of Emotional and Imaginative Responses to Music* (1932), which introduced terminology and perspectives from the aesthetics of artistic form into the aesthetics of music.

Travel and political writings While originally defining herself as a cross between the bluestocking and the nineteenth-century man of letters, Vernon Lee's broadening interests in contemporary literary and social theory and in international politics gave her a new role as a twentieth-century intellectual. Her curiosity had led to her fascination with new developments in psychology, which, in turn, not only enriched her fiction but deepened her analysis of social and moral issues as her collections of essays, *Gospels of Anarchy and other Contemporary Studies* (1908) and *Proteus, or, The Future of Intelligence* (1925), demonstrate. To the role of woman of letters she added the dimension of travel writer, becoming one of the finest, most original of all time. She published seven collections of travel essays in her lifetime, from *Limbo and other Essays* in 1897 to *The Golden Keys and other Essays on the Genius Loci* in 1925. In each she transforms the conventional *genius loci* genre of travel writing through a unique sensitivity to place and a particularly graceful style. Vernon Lee's gift in these essays for easily combining imagination with great learning would later be admired by Aldous Huxley and Desmond MacCarthy, while Edith Wharton would pay tribute to what she had learned from her in her dedication of *Italian Villas and their Gardens* to 'Vernon Lee, who, better than any one else, has understood and interpreted the garden-magic of Italy' (1904, v). It is also significant that Irene Cooper Willis, one of Lee's closest friends, would recall Vernon Lee most clearly in the light of this special gift: 'I see her best in my mind's eye, standing by some old building, wrapped in her homespun cloak … waiting, entranced, for the spirit of place to take possession of her' ('Vernon Lee', *Colby Library Quarterly*, June 1960, 115–16).

In the years just before the First World War, Vernon Lee added a political dimension to the role of woman of letters. Closely observing the death of Liberal England and the rise of the labour and suffrage movements, she used her pen in defence of women's equality, economic justice, international co-operation, and anti-militarism in a wide range of publications. During the war, she became a member of the anti-war Union of Democratic Control and a supporter of the women's peace crusade that would culminate in an International Congress of Women at The Hague. In 1915 she would write one of her most moving works, the anti-war morality play *The Ballet of the Nations*, and in 1920, setting it within a philosophical commentary, she republished it as *Satan the Waster*. In 'Out of the limelight' (1941), Desmond MacCarthy wrote of the work that it is 'an anti-war classic', 'the most thorough literary analysis of war neurosis' (*Humanities*, 1853, 192). Yet appearing when it did, so soon after the war, when few people were ready for self-examination, it fell into literary oblivion.

Death and reputation Throughout the 1920s and early 1930s, Vernon Lee was painfully aware of her isolation and lack of power as a writer. She died on 13 February 1935 at her home, Villa Il Palmerino, Maiano, San Gervasio, Florence; after cremation her ashes were buried in the Allori cemetery in Florence in the grave of her half-brother, Eugene. Her rich and complex legacy still remains largely untouched. Desmond MacCarthy gives the best sense of it: 'Mr Birrell once said that a man could live like a gentleman for a year on the ideas that he would find in Hazlitt; and the remark applies also to her. Her essays swarm with ideas' ('Out of the limelight', 189). Still to be rediscovered are her individual masterly achievements such as the play *Ariadne in Mantua* and *The Handling of Words*, and the full range of her influence on other writers and artists is, as yet, unappreciated. Vernon Lee deserves to be recognized for the exceptional life she led as a woman of letters.

PHYLLIS F. MANNOCCHI

Sources P. Gunn, *Vernon Lee: Violet Paget, 1856–1935* (1964) • *Vernon Lee's letters*, ed. I. C. Willis (privately printed, London, 1937) [incl. preface by her executor [I. C. Willis]] • Colby College, Waterville, Maine, USA, Special Collections, Vernon Lee Collection • *DNB* • P. F. Mannocchi, '"Vernon Lee": a reintroduction and primary bibliography', *English Literature in Transition, 1880–1920*, 26 (1983), 231–67 • C. Markgraf, '"Vernon Lee": a commentary and annotated bibliography of writings about her', *English Literature in Transition, 1880–1920*, 26 (1983), 268–312 • W. V. Harris, 'Eneas Sweetland Dallas (1829–79) and Vernon Lee (1856–1935)', *Victorian prose: a guide to research*, ed. D. J. DeLaura (1973), 444–6 • V. Colby, 'The puritan aesthete: Vernon Lee', *The singular anomaly: women novelists of the nineteenth century* (1970), 235–304 • A. Fremantle, 'Vernon Lee, a lonely lady', *Commonweal*, 44 (1950), 297–9 • R. Wellek, 'Vernon Lee, Bernard Berenson and aesthetics', *Discriminations: further concepts of criticism* (1970), 164–86 • E. Smyth, *What happened next* (1940) • P. F. Mannocchi, 'Vernon Lee and Kit Anstruther-Thomson: a study of love and collaboration between romantic friends', *Women's Studies*, 12 (1986), 129–48

Archives Colby College, Waterville, Maine, corresp., literary MSS, and papers • Somerville College, Oxford, corresp. and papers | Bodl. Oxf., letters to various members of the Lewis family together with two MS articles • FM Cam., letters to E. J. Dent • Harvard U., Centre for Italian Renaissance Studies, letters to B. Berenson and M. Berenson • Hove Central Library, Sussex, letters to Lady Wolseley • NL Scot., corresp. with Blackwoods • Ransom HRC, corresp. with John Lane

Likenesses J. S. Sargent, oils, 1881, Tate Collection [*see illus.*] • J. S. Sargent, pencil sketch, 1889, AM Oxf. • M. Cassatt, watercolour sketch, 1895; formerly priv. coll. • B. Noufflard, oils, 1934

Wealth at death £5216 17*s.* 2*d.*: probate, 25 June 1935, *CGPLA Eng. & Wales*

Paget, William, first Baron Paget (1505/6–1563), diplomat and administrator, was born probably in Colman Street near the Guildhall, London, the son of John Pachett or Paget of London, a citizen of small fortune variously employed as a shearman and sergeant-at-mace to the sheriff of London—William's enemies later reviled him as the son of a catchpole.

Education and early career Paget was educated at St Paul's School, under William Lily, where his contemporaries and friends included Thomas Wriothesley, Edward North and Anthony Denny, and also John Leland whose Latin encomium, written in the mid-1540s, is the main source for Paget's youth. He went from there to Trinity Hall, Cambridge, during the mastership of Stephen Gardiner, who refers to Paget, Wriothesley, and himself as acting together in a performance of Plautus' *Miles gloriosus*—Paget played Meliphidippa and Wriothesley Palestrio. Strype reports Paget as having been a scholar supported by Thomas Boleyn, and as reading books by Luther and Melanchthon, but there is no independent corroboration for this. John Foxe even states that Paget was an 'earnest protestant' at Cambridge, but it is improbable that an overt radical would have been acceptable to Gardiner. The latter once wrote to Paget, 'ye told me once ye love noe

William Paget, first Baron Paget (1505/6–1563), by unknown artist

extremites and the meane is best' (*Letters*, ed. Muller, 74), and it was widely accepted in his later life that he was a man who abhorred extremes. In Mary's reign Foxe and Ponet saw him as a Catholic. That Richard Cox became godfather to his eldest son, Henry, along with Paget's acceptability to the German protestants, suggests that he always held a moderate course in religion.

It is usually assumed that Paget read civil law, but although a later hand wrote in the margin of one of the Cambridge grace books that he was the 'dominus Pachett' admitted *in utroque jure* in 1525–6 after two years of philosophy and four years in civil law, this man is more likely to have been Robert of Gonville Hall, who was probably William's brother. Although Gray's Inn admitted William Paget as an honorary member in 1537, and knowledge of civil law was certainly an asset in diplomatic posts, it is certain only that Paget was thoroughly trained in the literary, rhetorical, and linguistic skills which made him an excellent humanist, one to whom reforming rhetoricians, like Ramus, later dedicated their works. Probably about 1526–7 he went to Paris for at least a year, and on his return he joined Stephen Gardiner's household.

In June 1528 Paget suffered an attack of sweating sickness, but recovered to take up his first appointment as one of the four clerks of the signet, and in 1529 he was elected to parliament for an unidentified seat; he is thought to have sat in every parliament thereafter until he became a peer. In June 1530 he was ordered to assist Edward Foxe, Reginald Pole, and Sir Francis Bryan, who were going to the University of Paris to solicit opinions on Henry VIII's marriage, and was credited with persuading the University of Orléans to condemn the pope's summons to the king. He evidently overcame his handicap of humble birth, for between 1531 and 1534 he was sent on a series of diplomatic missions to France and to the German princes, chiefly in connection with the king's divorce. He was already a master of the commonplaces of Renaissance rhetoric through which diplomacy was mediated, on more than one occasion, for instance, offering the platitude that 'society in a realm doth consist and is maintained by means of religion and laws. And these two or one wanting, farewel al just society' (Strype, 2/2.431).

Paget's associate in these early missions was Christopher Mount, who at first had to act as interpreter, but Paget seems to have learned languages quickly and gained the confidence of German princes, especially the landgrave of Hesse and the elector of Saxony. His social insignificance made him a suitable envoy for conferences with Melanchthon and other protestant divines, with the added advantage that in a crisis he was easily disavowed. Hence, perhaps, his first surviving letter, thanking Thomas Cromwell for restoring him to the king's good graces. In 1534 he was sent back to Prussia and Poland with an impressive train, for negotiations with princes who had been sweetened by a gift of 50,000 crowns. His own reward was a licence to import 400 tons of Gascon wines at reduced customs. Shortly after Paget had made another secret trip to an undisclosed destination in 1535, Henry VIII was told by Edward Foxe that Paget should be sent back to the protestant princes as the best man for the job. During these comings and goings Paget married Anne (*d.* 1587), daughter of Henry Preston of 'Prestcon', Lancashire. The exact date of their marriage is uncertain, but if he is the Mr Pachett noted in Cambridge University sources in 1532–3 then he was already married by then. The arrival of a family may be indicated by Paget's having leased a substantial house in Aldersgate in 1534. Their eldest surviving son Henry was born in 1536–7, and in March 1555 they had nine children living, six of them daughters. That the eldest of the latter, Etheldreda, was herself married by 1550, is a further pointer to her father's having married in or by the early 1530s. Paget was devoted to Anne, writing in 1545, when she was reported to have died, of 'my most obedient, wise, gentle and chaste wife, the remembrance of whom sitteth so deep in my heart that it maketh the same well near to burst for pain and anguish' (*LP Henry VIII*, 20/1, no. 496). She recovered and outlived her husband, dying in February 1587.

Upward mobility By 1536 Paget was well established and starting to accumulate a gentleman's estate, initially in West Drayton, Middlesex, where he was soon appointed a JP. He was appointed secretary successively to queens Jane Seymour, Anne of Cleves, and Katherine Howard, served on the grand jury which indicted Sir Geoffrey Pole for treason in 1539, and in autumn 1539 was sent to Ireland with £2600 and nearly 1000 soldiers, greatly to the satisfaction of the Irish establishment.

On 10 August 1540, following Cromwell's execution, Paget was appointed clerk of the privy council, with the duties of maintaining its journal and engrossing bills. On 15 July 1541 he was also appointed clerk of the parliament. He attempted to reorganize government record keeping, but in September 1541 had to leave this to a deputy when he was sent as ambassador to the French court. To make him acceptable there in June 1541 he was granted a coat of arms, evidently an unsatisfactory one as the design was changed when he was knighted in 1544. As Henry was keeping Paget in ignorance of royal dealings with the emperor he lacked specific instructions, but nevertheless felt able to assure the king that 'I trust I have holden the balance so upright, as Your Majestie may put your fote in which syde You will, nothwithstanding anything that I have saide' (*State Papers, Henry VIII*, 9.180). He was also learning to manage a network of spies, maintaining informants as far afield as Rome. His long-drawn-out negotiations for the marriage of Henry's daughter Mary to the duc d'Orléans foundered, however, after the defeat of the Scots at Solway Moss on 24 November 1542. François I now roundly told Paget that no alliance would be made with England unless Scotland was an equal partner, and he sent 2000 German troops to Scotland, permitted Scottish privateers to take English shipping in Le Havre, and refused Paget permission to leave the country until his successor arrived. These actions confirmed Paget in his preference for an alliance with the emperor.

Paget's exchange having been effected on 18 April 1543 he was appointed on the 23rd as one of the two principal secretaries of state and admitted to the privy council, rapidly becoming the senior when his old friend Wriothesley was created lord chancellor. In January 1544 he was knighted. In 1546 he bought eleven former episcopal manors in Staffordshire, Derbyshire, and Worcestershire, centred on Beaudesert, Staffordshire, thereby becoming a prominent landowner. He actively developed his landed interests, establishing ironworks and exploiting his woods.

Meanwhile Paget had become one of the most powerful office-holders in the kingdom. He spoke for the monarch, controlled considerable patronage, and was the linchpin both of Henry's diplomatic correspondence and the national intelligence network. It was Paget's job to sift out from the intercepted mail and oral communications real plots from imaginary or invented ones, to distinguish reliable from double agents. To ensure the speed and secrecy of royal letters he became joint master of the posts on 29 September 1545. From 1544 he was involved in the desperate expedients employed to raise money for Henry's war with France—land sales, benevolences, foreign loans, and above all currency debasement. He also became particularly concerned with the Anglo-Scottish borders, paying mercenaries and ensuring military supplies. As Henry became increasingly reclusive, Paget, who was always at the king's side except when absent on short diplomatic missions, became the essential conduit for information and direction for the resident ambassadors and for the king's other servants, while at the same time offering the advice of experience, on the principle that 'Men may better speke or do, beying present then absent' (Haynes, 7). He was drafting Henry's devices—his personal correspondence and policy documents—although the king did not always accept them. In his dealings with the imperial ambassador Vanderdelft, Paget's persuasiveness was critical to the deceptions that concealed England's weakness from her enemies.

During this time Paget went on five short special embassies. In May 1544 he went to the emperor, for negotiations over a proposed Anglo-imperial attack upon France. He was largely unsuccessful and had come home by 12 June, after which he was plunged into the preparations for Henry's departure for France, along with negotiations for the marriage of the fourth earl of Lennox to the king's niece, Margaret Douglas, intended to bind the earl to English interests. Paget himself led 100 foot to Boulogne but was principally absorbed in negotiations with François and Charles V in an abortive attempt to prevent them making a separate peace. Although Henry held Boulogne he was diplomatically isolated and therefore permitted Paget to make approaches to the German protestant princes. In February 1545, although his wife was seriously ill, he was sent back to the emperor, with whom he had a difficult interview, reporting afterwards that 'dissimulation, vanity, flattery, unshamefastness reign most here' (*LP Henry VIII*, 20/1, no. 426). In November he was again sent to treat with the French, who still would not yield enough, but further negotiations in 1546 finally led on 7 June to a treaty whereby for 2 million crowns over eight years England would return Boulogne to France. Paget saw this peace as essential to his country's interests. His memoranda had made his attitude clear—as long as they perceived England as disaffected in religion, the emperor and France would both be potentially hostile, and England's security required that they be kept at odds.

Paget and Seymour When Henry was in his last illness Paget conversed with him night after night, and he became a key figure in the politics surrounding Henry's death. The king looked to him to secure the condemnation of the earl of Surrey for high treason. He sat as one of the commissioners, and went to Henry VIII for secret instructions when the jurymen showed signs of doubt, returning to ensure that they convicted. It was Paget who made an agreement with Edward Seymour, earl of Hertford, in the gallery outside the death chamber, that the provisions in Henry's will for a council of state should be amended to admit the earl as protector to his nephew, the new king, and that in return he would be Hertford's principal adviser. It was Paget also who kept the notes of the promotions and grants that Henry was alleged to have planned and which were implemented within days of the king's death, with Hertford becoming duke of Somerset and Paget receiving lands worth a nominal 400 marks (£266 6*s*. 8*d*.) per annum. In adhering to Somerset Paget became involved in the downfall of his old friend Wriothesley, and also of his old master Gardiner.

Somerset did for a time honour his part of the bargain. In 1547 Paget was made both a knight of the Garter and high steward of Cambridge University, and though the imperial ambassador's report that Paget was to be made Wriothesley's successor as lord chancellor proved false, on 29 June, as Somerset went north against the Scots, he was appointed comptroller of the household, giving him authority to protect the king's interests, and also chancellor of the duchy of Lancaster. In 1548 he acquired the bishop of Exeter's former London house, just outside Temple Bar, a suitable residence for a leading government official. He was concerned to reform the crown's finances, though he was aware that there were powerful vested interests in the *status quo*—he later observed that Gardiner had once shown that more beer was consumed in a day at court than could run from a series of barrels, each one opened as the previous one ran dry, and 'proved it to be trewe in the presence of some whiche liked him ever after the worse for it' ('Letters', 118).

Over time, however, Paget found the protector heeding him less and less, until he could describe himself as 'a Cassandra', fated to tell the truth and not be believed. By 1548 he was increasingly concerned for England's position both abroad and at home. He warned that Somerset's policies were giving rise to disturbances, and though he loyally followed the protector's instructions over both Sir Thomas Seymour's interrogation and Princess Elizabeth's household, his distrust of Somerset's advisers, men like Sir John Thynne, was growing, and by spring 1549, moreover, he was out of favour with Somerset's wife. He was also increasingly nervous of Somerset's sharpness and his neglect of the council, whose advice he had expected Somerset to take. He felt that in England's present financial straits, her peril from foreign foes could only be allayed by pretending to the emperor that her current religious changes were matters of little substance. Too much the realist to rely on divine intervention, he quoted on old proverb 'Youe maie lye longe ynough in the dytche or God will helpe youe yf youe helpe not your selfe' ('Letters', 24). May 1549 saw the first of a series of risings, but Paget, who in April had been devising papers on foreign policy for the council, was in early June sent to the emperor on a vain mission to revive the treaty of alliance and extend it to comprehend Boulogne.

When Paget returned on 1 August the western rebellion in which his brother Robert had been a leader, had been subdued; despite a letter from Somerset saying that Robert Paget should not be spared because of his relationship to William, there is no firm evidence of his fate. The earl of Warwick, leading German mercenaries, was crushing the Norfolk risings, while France had declared war and was besieging Boulogne. Somerset's leadership, as Paget had warned, was largely discredited and Warwick gathered a majority of the lords around him. Paget avoided publicly defecting to Warwick, but although he was at Windsor with Somerset, the king, Archbishop Cranmer, and Sir Thomas Smith on 6 October, he was already preparing to mediate and was principally responsible for the conciliatory wording of the letter sent by the protector to the London lords. Somerset's surrender without a fight on 10 October, if Smith can be believed, caused Paget to fall weeping on his knees, clasping the duke about the knees and exclaiming, 'O my Lord, my lord, ye see now what my lords be' (BL, Harley MS 353, fol. 77). It still fell to Paget to arrest Somerset.

Ruin and recovery Following his coup, Warwick had still to deal with the conservative group that had supported Somerset, and for this required that Paget should at least remain neutral. He also needed to put the comptrollership in the hands of a reliable subordinate in order to secure his own hold on the royal household. Following negotiations Paget surrendered the comptrollership without obtaining an alternative office, but on 3 December 1549 was summoned to the lords as Baron Paget of Beaudesert. His elevation required him to surrender his clerkship of the parliament, and he also resigned his clerkship of the signet. In January 1550 Warwick ensured Paget was out of the country when he staged his mini-coup against Wriothesley, Arundel, and others, sending him to negotiate peace with France, which kept him abroad until April. Paget was so certain that England should be rid of Boulogne, that he missed at least one concession that the French would have made over two English fortresses in Scotland. After his return Warwick acted quite contrary to Paget's advice on England's best strategy in foreign affairs, and failed to reward him with any lucrative or influential office.

Paget hoped that Warwick would pay more heed to the council than Somerset had done, and pressed upon him a proposal for restructuring it. Warwick certainly did restore the council to a central place in government, and the rules about the signing of warrants which had been established at the end of Henry VIII's reign were reinstituted, but Paget's crucial suggestions, including secret voting, were rejected. Indeed Warwick sidelined him, although he still required him to testify at Gardiner's trial in January 1551, when Paget alleged that Henry had thought of trying Gardiner for treason. By the summer Paget was being kept away from court under virtual house arrest, and rumours circulated that he had plotted with Arundel and Somerset to arrest his enemies at a banquet to be held in his house. When he was arrested on 21 October, however, it was for the scandal of contradicting the emperor, who claimed Paget had promised religious freedom for Mary, an embarrassment for Warwick who was pressing conformity on her. On 8 November he was in the Tower, where he stayed until more serious charges could be prepared. Although Warwick was unable to tie Paget to the plots of which Somerset was accused, he was none the less degraded, being stripped of the Garter on 22 April 1552. Edward noted in his diary that it was because Paget was no gentleman on either his father's or his mother's side. Accused of corruption as chancellor of the duchy, on 31 May 1552 he signed a submission of guilt, and two weeks later made a public confession in Star Chamber, according to John Ponet 'on his knes of his bribery, extortion, dissimulacion, ambicion, robbing of the king, and suche like vertues, wherby he became noble' (Ponet, sig I 1*v*). He lost his chancellorship and was then released from the Tower. His £8000 fine was later reduced to £4000 for which he gave lands worth £125 per annum and £2000 in cash, paying the latter in February 1553. In December 1552 he received a full pardon, in February following he was restored to the privy council, and in March he kissed the king's hand. Nevertheless, he remained in retirement and may not have attended the March parliament. As Edward VI neared death, it was said that 10,000 men led by the earl of Huntingdon's brother were gathering at Paget's West Drayton house. As Jane's situation became desperate Paget was summoned back to the council and signed a letter to the lord lieutenant of Essex on her behalf, but then he and the earl of Arundel almost immediately led the councillors in London in declaring for Mary and himself informed her of their decision.

Queen Mary's minister Mary appointed Paget to her privy council, restored him to the Garter, made him a commissioner to hear coronation claims, and honoured him with the role of carrying the sword of state before her at the coronation, but she did not fully trust him. She had restored Gardiner, whom Paget had so spectacularly betrayed, to his ecclesiastical offices and also appointed him lord chancellor while Paget received no immediate office in reward. The two men have generally been seen as antagonists whose rivalry tended to divide the privy council over such contentious issues as the programme for the restoration of religious ties to Rome, with Paget heading a group predominantly 'secular' in outlook. In fact there seems to have been no fixed factional divide as groups coalesced and split up over particular issues, while Gardiner and Paget were not as far apart as has been suggested. Although Paget took a minimal interest in theology he none the less saw religion as the glue that held society together, and merely sought, as ever, to see necessary changes made with as little disruption as possible.

To outward appearances Paget was the principal negotiator of Mary's marriage to Philip of Spain in the latter months of 1553, while Gardiner promoted Edward Courtenay. Ponet, however, implies that such appearances were deceptive, and that the cunning Gardiner, whom he describes in this context as the 'doctour of practices', had merely left Paget, as 'his scholar', to do the necessary work and bear any odium arising from the queen's Spanish match (Ponet, sig. I iiii *r–v*). Certainly although he was one of those officially appointed to treat for the marriage on 1 January 1554 Paget received no obvious reward. And although he appeared on horseback in arms at the muster in St James' Field during Sir Thomas Wyatt's rebellion and later brought Wyatt as a prisoner to court, mistrust of his advice continued. The emperor had disliked his earlier suggestion that Courtenay and Princess Elizabeth be married. He and Gardiner disagreed over the treatment of Elizabeth in the aftermath of the rebellions, and suspicions that Paget was a covert heretic, fanned by his wish to see only a few rebel leaders executed, undermined his authority, although it was said that he and some other councillors did obtain a pardon for eight conspirators by cornering Mary in her oratory. He was one of the councillors appointed to consider the laws to be put to parliament and decide who should draft them, but his preference for a step-by-step approach was ignored by Gardiner and his overt opposition in the April 1554 parliament to the detailed programme that Gardiner put forward for the restoration of the church as it had been before ties to Rome were severed, and particularly for a revival of the heresy laws, exasperated Mary who condemned him for inconstancy. Paget then avoided the council for four months.

Philip, however, found Paget's temperate advice essential, gave him a pension of 1500 crowns, and returned him to power. Paget argued that the distribution of monastic lands to numberless secular owners could not now be undone, and that the pope must acknowledge the *fait accompli* if Cardinal Pole's return to England and the country's reconciliation to Rome were to be made acceptable. This was reluctantly agreed and on 7 November 1554 Paget and Sir Edward Hastings went to the Low Countries and escorted Pole home. Paget took the opportunity for a private interview with the emperor, where he urged that a small inner council be set up and sought to persuade him that those born after England's breach with Rome should be treated more leniently than heretics of long-standing commitment.

By this time Paget's health, which had been poor for some time, was seriously deteriorating and he spent long periods either in his bed 'like a beast' or seeking amelioration in the baths. He was absent from the council in March and April 1555, but by May was organizing a fruitless conference to arbitrate a peace between the empire and the French at Marck. He returned to England on 12 June and when it was plain that Mary's apparent pregnancy was false, again advised Philip on managing the kingdom. He was one of the inner council whose establishment Philip recommended in August before his departure for the continent. Gardiner's death on 11 November, after a reconciliation with Paget, saw the latter's formal return to the council, but although his influence was needed to counter growing anti-Spanish sentiment the queen rejected Philip's advice that Paget should be made lord chancellor on the grounds that a layman was inappropriate, appointing him lord privy seal instead on 29 January 1556. Shortly afterwards he was among those blamed for the truce of Vaucelles made on 5 February between France and the empire, which took no account of English interests.

Paget was now once again the main supervisor of the country's failing finances, which were further stretched in March thanks to the French-backed Dudley conspiracy. He went to Brussels in April to attempt to bring Philip back to England but though he had intended to wait and return with Philip, on 12 May he was on his way back to England. It was at this point that there occurred the event that earned him condemnation by Ponet and others. He met Sir John Cheke and Sir Peter Carew *en route* near Brussels, and although he greeted them kindly, they were suddenly arrested by the provost-marshal, carried aboard a ship, and taken to the Tower. As well as this apparent breach of faith, Ponet also accused him of seeking to betray the fervently protestant duchess of Suffolk and claimed that for this he had the queen's thanks. Always primarily concerned for peace and order, Paget may in fact have felt that a moderate Catholicism would be its best bastion, but his relations with the queen did not improve for Philip did not appear. In October and November he was away from court, but though confined to his bed he corresponded through the queen's Latin secretary James Basset about the problems of the proposed recoinage and the reduction of household expenditure. He also, uncharacteristically, led the minority of advisers who supported Philip's desire to persuade England to fight alongside the empire under the treaty of 1542. Philip's coming to England and Thomas Stafford's apparently French-backed attack on Scarborough in April 1557 put further pressure on the English government to support the Habsburgs, and in May Paget was heading a small war council as well as financing his own privateer. As war resources were virtually non-existent he also concerned himself with raising the customs rates. In January 1558 Calais fell, and Paget was virtually alone in continuing to plan for its recovery. In September he was again ill.

Retirement, death, and assessment Despite general expectations that Elizabeth would give him a post, the new queen set Paget aside. His illness was a convenient excuse and he remained undisgraced, offering advice from his sickbed to Sir William Cecil and Sir Thomas Parry about peace negotiations and arguing the need for at least the appearance of a position of strength. He also provided a long analysis of the problems attendant upon the recoinage. In November 1559 he was back at court and closetted with Elizabeth who thought of sending him as ambassador to Spain, but he declined on grounds of health. In November 1560 he was again sick and made his will on the 4th, providing for his wife, children, kinswomen, and servants in conventional style. He recovered and attended the St George's day Garter feast in 1561. He died on 9 or 10 June 1563, probably at West Drayton, and was buried there on the 18th. On the evidence of his portrait dated 1549, which records him as then aged forty-three, he was about fifty-seven years old when he died. A cenotaph bearing his effigy was erected in Lichfield Cathedral by his eldest son, Henry. His second son Thomas *Paget died in exile as a committed Catholic.

William Paget's subsequent reputation has always been that of a 'politique', albeit one endowed with considerable ability and presence. In the words of one seventeenth-century assessment, 'His addresse was with state, yet insinuating, his discours free but weighed, his apprehension quick but stayed, his ready and present mind keeping its pauses of thoughts and expression even with ye occasion and ye emergency' (BL, Sloane MS 1523, fol. 29*v*). Recent scholarship has generally doubted the sincerity of his convictions, while disagreeing about whether he should be seen as a statesman or merely as a pragmatist. But his political and administrative skills have been usually, though not invariably, acknowledged. Yet although the enigmatic mask that shrouded his personal feelings and beliefs reinforced his diplomatic skills, it did not prevent his being accepted as a wise and honest counsellor by the princes of Europe. It is hard to doubt the fundamental sincerity of his concern for good governance and the maintenance of law and order. His appreciation of the realities and the limitations that the existing structure of society in Europe imposed on rulers made him essentially conservative, concerned above all to avoid actions that would destabilize the realm. His invariable preference for caution and moderation enabled him to avoid the numerous traps implicit in involvement in high matters of state, but his scheming was directed more towards the benefit of the realm than of himself, and although he amassed a considerable fortune, there is no convincing evidence that he did so dishonestly. SYBIL M. JACK

Sources 'The letters of William Lord Paget of Beaudesert, 1547–1563', ed. B. L. Beer and S. M. Jack, *Camden miscellany, XXV*, CS, 4th ser., 13 (1974) • HoP, *Commons, 1509–58*, 3.42–6 • *LP Henry VIII*, vols. 5–21 • *APC, 1542–70* • *CSP dom., 1547–80; addenda, 1547–65* • *CPR, 1547–63* • *CSP for., 1547–63* • *CSP Ire., 1509–73* • *CSP Spain, 1509–67* • *CSP Venice, 1509–80* • Baron Kervyn de Lettenhove [J. M. B. C. Kervyn de Lettenhove] and L. Gilliodts-van Severen, eds., *Relations politiques des Pays-Bas et de l'Angleterre sous le règne de Philippe II*, 11 vols. (Brussels, 1882–1900) • S. Haynes, ed., *A collection of state papers … left by W. Cecill Lord Burghley* (1740) • wills, PRO, PROB 11/46, fols. 210r–211v • BL, Harley MS 353 • BL, Sloane MS 1523 • M. Bateson, ed., *Grace book B*, 2 vols. (1903–5) • J. Ponet, *A short treatise of politic power*, 1556, facs. edn (1970) • *The letters of Stephen Gardiner*, ed. J. A. Muller (1933) • J. Strype, *Ecclesiastical memorials*, 3 vols. (1822) • C. Wriothesley, *A chronicle of England during the reigns of the Tudors from AD 1485 to 1559*, ed. W. D. Hamilton, 2 vols., CS, new ser., 11, 20 (1875–7) • *Literary remains of King Edward the Sixth*, ed. J. G. Nichols, 2 vols., Roxburghe Club, 75 (1857) • *The diary of Henry Machyn, citizen and merchant-taylor of London, from AD 1550 to AD 1563*, ed. J. G. Nichols, CS, 42 (1848) • J. G. Nichols, ed., *The chronicle of Queen Jane, and of two years of Queen Mary*, CS, old ser., 48 (1850) • N. Pocock, ed., *Troubles connected with the prayer book of 1549: documents … in the record office*, CS, new ser., 37 (1884) • P. F. Tytler, ed., *England under the reigns of Edward VI and Mary*, 2 vols. (1839) • S. Shaw, *The history and antiquities of Staffordshire*, 2 vols. (1798) • GEC, *Peerage*, new edn, 10.276–80 • E. H. Harbison, *Rival ambassadors at the court of Queen Mary* (1940) • S. R. Gammon, *Statesman and schemer: William, first Lord Paget, Tudor minister* (1973) • M. A. R. Graves, *The House of Lords in the parliaments of Edward VI and Mary I* (1981) • D. M. Loades, *Two Tudor conspiracies* (1965) • D. R. Starkey, *The reign of Henry VIII* (1985) • *The acts and monuments of John Foxe*, ed. J. Pratt, [new edn], 8 vols. (1877) • J. Leland, *Collectanea*, ed. T. Hearne, 6 vols. (1725) • D. E. Hoak, *The king's council in the reign of Edward VI* (1976) • J. Loach and R. Tittler, eds., *The mid-Tudor polity, c.1540–1560* (1980) • M. L. Bush, *The government policy of Protector Somerset* (1975) • J. Loach, *Parliament and the crown in the reign of Mary Tudor* (1986) • G. Lefèvre-Pontalis, *Correspondence politique de Odet de Selve* (1888) • R. A. de Vertot d'Aubeuf, ed., *Ambassades de Messieurs de Noailles en Angleterre*, 5 vols. (1763) • C. Weiss, ed., *Papiers d'état du Cardinal de Granvelle*, 9 vols. (1841–52) • *State papers published under … Henry VIII*, 11 vols. (1830–52)

Archives BL, Cotton MSS, instructions as ambassador • BL, Harley MSS, corresp. and papers • Northants. RO • Staffs. RO, corresp. and papers • William Salt Library, Stafford, MSS | Northants. RO, Newydd Anglesey MSS • Northants. RO, Finch Hatton MSS

Likenesses attrib. master of the Statthalterin Madonna, oils, *c.*1549 (with Garter George), NPG; repro. in Starkey, *Reign of Henry VIII*, 155 • group portrait, oil on panel, *c.*1570 (*Edward VI and the pope*), NPG • probably by Holbein, portrait; formerly at Beaudesert, Warwickshire • oils, Plas Newydd, Gwynedd [*see illus.*]

Wealth at death £300 but underestimate • £1500 p.a., plus iron furnaces: Gammon, *Statesman and schemer*

Paget, William, fourth Baron Paget (1572–1629), politician, was son and heir of Thomas *Paget, third Baron Paget (*c.*1544–1590), and Nazareth, widow of Sir Thomas Southwell of Norfolk and youngest daughter of Sir John Newton of East Harptree, Somerset, and Barre's Court, Gloucestershire, and his wife, Margaret, daughter of Sir Anthony Poyntz. His father was attainted for treason in 1586 and in 1587 the conviction was confirmed by statute, whereby the barony and family estates were forfeited. On 27 April 1587 Elizabeth I, 'of her gracious favor and princely care for the good educacion of yonge William Pagett', made him a ward of Sir George Carey, her kinsman (*APC, 1586–7*, 352). In 1587 he matriculated at Oxford, where he attended Christ Church; he graduated BA on 25 February 1590. He was admitted to the Middle Temple on 20 February 1611. Paget married, before 19 June 1602, Lettice Knollys (*d.* 1655) of Kingsbury, Warwickshire. They had three sons—William *Paget (who was to succeed his father as fifth Baron Paget), Henry, and Thomas—and four daughters, one of whom was called Anne [*see* Waller, Anne].

During the 1590s Paget was knighted, saw active military service on the earl of Essex's Cadiz expedition of 1596, and was one of the gentlemen who accompanied Sir Robert Cecil on his embassy to Paris in 1598. When Cecil returned to England, Paget travelled to Italy, which troubled his uncle Charles *Paget because it 'may prejudice him' (*CSP dom., 1598–1601*, 43). In 1597 William Paget petitioned to rent his attainted father's forfeited lands, and in July he and his heirs were granted lordships and manors in Middlesex and Buckinghamshire and other lands in Staffordshire, all of which had belonged to Thomas Paget and which had a rental value of £1053 19*s.* 10¼*d.* Paget and other Staffordshire gentlemen, 'frequenters to the earl of Essex', were suspected of complicity or at least sympathy with his rebellion in February 1601 (*Salisbury MSS*, 11.34). No action, however, seems to have been taken against them.

Paget was restored in blood and honours by James I and this was confirmed by statute in 1604. Not everyone approved. Ralph Fetherstonhalgh wrote, in November 1603, 'What! say they, hath not the King restored Arundel, Westmoreland and Paget, all of them known favourers, if not professors of the Romish religion'. Lord Saye and Sele wrote, 'I gave no consent to Mr. Pagett's bill', because of 'my duty to God' and his remembrance of the late queen (*Salisbury MSS*, 15.283; 16.63). From 5 November 1605 to 1628 Paget was summoned to parliament as Baron Paget. He was one of those peers who protested against the creation of a large number of baronets (1618) and of Scottish and Irish nobles (1621). In May 1628 he also spoke at length in the House of Lords against a proposed saving clause to be added to the petition of right.

Paget was widely involved in the promotion of colonial trade, through the East India Company, and in colonial projects: as a councillor of the Virginia Company (1612)

and of the Amazon River Company until the surrender of its charter (1620), and as a commissioner of the new board for Virginia in June 1624. He was also a founder member of the Bermudas Company (1614) to colonize the Somers Islands, where his name was given to a fort and a people. Despite these endeavours he appears to have been in a permanent state of indebtedness. In 1620 he called himself 'the poorest man of his rank … endeavouring to pay off great debts to the King' (*CSP dom.*, *1619–23*, 196). He died at West Drayton, Middlesex, on 29 August 1629 and was buried there the next day. His will required that his younger children 'be instructed to serve God after the rule of the Religion professed at this daie in the Church of England and in no otherwise' (PRO, PROB 11/154, sig. 110).

MICHAEL A. R. GRAVES

Sources GEC, *Peerage*, new edn, vol. 10 • *CSP dom.*, *1595–1601*; *1603–10*; *1619–23* • *Calendar of the manuscripts of the most hon. the marquis of Salisbury*, 24 vols., HMC, 9 (1883–1976) • *JHL*, 2 (1578–1614) • *DNB* • Foster, *Alum. Oxon.* • *APC*, 1586 7, 1619–21, 1623–5, 1627 • F. H. Relf, ed., *Notes of the debates in the House of Lords … AD 1621, 1625, 1628*, CS, 3rd ser., 42 (1929) • H. A. C. Sturgess, ed., *Register of admissions to the Honourable Society of the Middle Temple, from the fifteenth century to the year 1944*, 1 (1949), 96 • will, PRO, PROB 11/154, sig. 110

Archives Folger, estate and household account book • Staffs. RO, corresp. and papers

Wealth at death exact sum unknown: will, PRO, PROB 11/154, sig. 110

Paget, William, fifth Baron Paget (**1609–1678**), politician, was born on 13 September 1609, the eldest son of William *Paget, fourth Baron Paget, Staffordshire (1572–1629), and his wife, Lettice (*d.* 1655), daughter and coheir of Henry Knollys of Kingsbury, Warwickshire. Anne *Waller, Lady Waller, was his sister. After a 'strict' (E. E. Harcourt, ed., *The Harcourt Papers*, 14 vols., 1880–1905, 1.171) religious upbringing in West Drayton, Middlesex, Paget attended Christ Church, Oxford, from where he matriculated on 18 December 1627.

Made a knight of the Bath at Charles I's coronation, Paget inherited the title of Baron Paget on his father's death. However, he was an unsuccessful courtier, being confined to purely ceremonial roles such as waiting on ambassadors and appearing in court masques. Even Paget's marriage in 1632 to Lady Frances Rich (*d.* 1672), the eldest daughter of the royal favourite, Henry *Rich, first earl of Holland (*bap.* 1590, *d.* 1649), failed to secure him a major court office, although thanks to his father-in-law's influence he was appointed keeper of New Lodge Walk in Windsor Forest on 9 February 1642.

By the end of the personal rule Paget had become increasingly alienated with royal policies, as shown by his refusal to serve in the first bishops' war in March 1639 and by his vote against granting the king supplies to renew hostilities with the Scots in the Short Parliament of 1640. His opposition to Charles I had become even more overt by August 1640 when he supported the twelve peers' petition urging the king to summon another parliament. On 28 September 1640 Paget was one of the sixteen peers appointed by the king to negotiate an Anglo-Scottish treaty following his disastrous defeat in the second bishops' war. During the first session of the Long Parliament 'honest Paget' as he was later termed by the earl of Manchester (*CSP dom.*, *1644–5*, 160), played a key role in the impeachment of Strafford and Laud, the passage of major constitutional measures like the abolition of Star Chamber, and, above all, the promotion of religious reforms. His 'violence' (J. Rochester, 'Diary of a bishop', BL, Harley MS 6424, fol. 39) against the bishops and the Book of Common Prayer was what one might have expected of a man who was an unalloyed presbyterian and who showed a keen 'desire' (*JHL*, 7, 1644–5, 19) to take the national covenant in October 1644.

Paget's anti-court stance continued in the second session of the Long Parliament and is best epitomized by his support for the militia ordinance, which he implemented as lord lieutenant of Buckinghamshire in mid-May 1642. However, he now experienced a crisis of conscience and defected to the king, joining him at York on 14 June. There he signed a declaration to defend Charles's 'just rights and prerogatives' (*CSP dom.*, *1641–3*, 340, 342) and undertook to raise a 1200-strong infantry regiment. After seeing his regiment badly mauled at the battle of Edgehill in late October 1642, Paget joined the king in Oxford, residing at Wadham College. In January 1644 he served in the Oxford parliament and subscribed to the letter addressed to the earl of Essex calling for peace negotiations. By the following autumn his growing disillusionment with the royalist cause prompted his return to the parliamentarian fold. He surrendered at Plymouth in late September 1644 and, following a brief period of imprisonment, was fined £1500, of which he paid only a third. For all his efforts, Paget never secured readmission to the House of Lords, and this perhaps explains why he lent covert support to his father-in-law's pro-royalist uprising in June 1648.

Paget was clearly horrified by Charles I's execution and viewed the Rump as a 'usurped authority' (PRO, SP 29/20/21); however, in Lord Lisle's telling phrase, he learned to be 'a good Commonswealthman' (*De L'Isle and Dudley MSS*, 6.482), which was just as well, since in October 1651 his estates again fell forfeit after the committee for compounding was informed of his former complicity in the earl of Holland's rebellion. The case dragged on until March 1653 when Paget was finally discharged by the Act of Pardon. During the rule of the major-generals, however, Paget was threatened with decimation, but after an appeal to the protector he secured his exemption from the hated tax as well as obtaining a licence to reside within the cavalier exclusion zone around London.

The meeting of the Convention Parliament marked Paget's return to public life, although he had to be commanded 'to give [his] attendance' (*JHL*, 11, 1660–66, 27) by formal letter on 14 May 1660. He gave his full support to Charles II's restoration, but for the next decade concentrated on restoring his family's financial fortunes which were now in an 'ill-condition' (BL, Add. MS 29910, fol. 20). With debts amounting to over £3000, and living on an income of little more than £23, Paget was forced to petition the king for relief, but to no avail. This rebuff may partly account for Paget's opposition to the crown in the later stages of the Cavalier Parliament. In April 1675 he was one of the 'Country' (Swatland, 270, appx 1, col. 11) peers who expressed their dissent at government moves to tamper with the freedom of debate and the voting rights of members of the upper chamber.

In the last eight years of his life Paget's health began to deteriorate: in November 1670 he was excused attendance in the Lords for being 'sick' (*JHL*, 13, 1675–81, 16), and again in November 1675 his absence was condoned because he was 'not well' (ibid., 364). He died, intestate, at his house in Old Palace Yard, Westminster, on 19 October 1678 and was buried in the family mausoleum at West Drayton, Middlesex, on 7 November and succeeded by his son William *Paget. He was said by a post-Restoration commentator to have been of 'Noe parts … except a good stomack' (Kidson, 40); and significantly in the funeral sermon preached by his chaplain, John Heynes, there is a deafening silence about his personal attributes.

GORDON GOODWIN, *rev.* JOHN SUTTON

Sources *DNB* • GEC, *Peerage*, new edn, 10.283–5 • Clarendon, *Hist. rebellion*, 1.244, 263; 2.181–2 • *Remarkable passages from York* (1642) • *JHL*, 4–10 (1628–48); 11 (1660–66), 27; 12 (1666–75), 364; 13 (1675–81), 16 • R. M. Kidson, 'The gentry of Staffordshire, 1662–1663', *Collections for a history of Staffordshire*, Staffordshire RS, 4th ser., 2 (1958), 1–41, 40 • J. Finet, *Ceremonies of Charles I: the note books of John Finet, 1628–1641*, ed. A. J. Loomie (1987), 135, 157, 209 • W. Dugdale, *The baronage of England*, 2 vols. (1675–6), vol. 2, p. 342 • B. Whitelocke, 'Bulstrode Whitelocke's annals, 1645–9', BL, Add. MS 37344, fols. 248, 341 • D. R. Lacey, *Dissent and parliamentary politics in England, 1661–1689* (1969), 469 • A. Swatland, *The House of Lords in the reign of Charles II* (1996), 270, appx 1, col. 11 • J. Sutton, '"Loyalty" and a "good conscience": the defection of William, fifth Baron Paget, June 1642', *Staffordshire histories: essays presented in honour of Michael Greenslade*, ed. P. Morgan and A. D. M. Phillips, Staffordshire RS (1999), 127–56 • *CSP dom.*, 1644–5, 160 • W. A. Shaw, *The knights of England*, 1 (1906), 161 • Foster, *Alum. Oxon.*, 1500–1714, 3.167 • J. Jenny, *A sermon [on Matt. xxiv. 46] preached at the funeral of … Lady F. Paget* (1673)

Archives Bucks. RLSS, autograph account book • NA Scot., letters • NRA, priv. coll. • Staffs. RO, corresp. and papers • Staffs. RO, letters | U. Wales, Bangor, corresp. of the fifth Baron Paget, 1640–60

Paget, William, sixth Baron Paget (1637–1713), politician and diplomat, was born at Beaudesert, Staffordshire, on 10 February 1637, the oldest surviving son of William *Paget, fifth Baron Paget (1609–1678), and his wife, Lady Frances Rich (*d.* 1672), daughter of Henry *Rich, first earl of Holland, and his wife, Isabel, daughter of Sir Walter Cope of Kensington. Nothing is known of his education and early life, except that in January 1656 he was given a pass to travel abroad. By licence dated 20 July 1661 he married Frances (*c.*1644–1681), daughter of Francis Pierrepoint, younger son of Robert Pierrepoint, first earl of Kingston. Following the death of his father on 19 October 1678 Paget took his seat in the House of Lords (25 November 1678). There was a strong puritan element in the Pagets: his father had adhered first and last to the parliamentarians in the civil war, despite a short-lived attachment to the king in 1642–4; his father's sister Anna had two notable puritan husbands, and his mother belonged to one of the most famous puritan magnate families in England. Paget himself, by temperament and conviction, clearly remained throughout his life in the puritan/radical whig interest. In 1681 he was a signatory to the petition against the convening of parliament at Oxford, where he opposed the Lords' rejection of the impeachment of Edward Fitzharris as a conspirator in the Popish Plot. In the same year, after the death of his first wife, Paget married his cousin Isabella (*d.* 1685), daughter of Sir Thomas Irby of Boston, and of his father's sister Katherine.

Paget's own whig sympathies prevented his political advancement under the later Stuarts. In 1688 he was present at the trial in the Lords of the seven bishops, and on the landing of the prince of Orange Paget was one of the peers who unsuccessfully petitioned James II to call a free parliament and to negotiate with William; subsequently he voted for the vacancy of the throne and for settling the crown on the prince and princess of Orange. On 24 December 1688 he moved in the Lords that the princess of Orange should be declared queen. Following the accession of William and Mary, Paget was appointed lord lieutenant of Staffordshire (patent 24 March 1689; sworn 15 May). A few months later, on 4 September 1689, he was appointed English envoy to Vienna. At fifty-two Paget embarked on what was to be a lengthy diplomatic career in the king's service. At this point in his life he was twice a widower, and had lost both his elder son by his first marriage, William (*d.* 1684), and his only son by his second wife, also William (*d.* 1687). He never remarried; it is not clear how far the tragedies of his private life precipitated or magnified in diplomatic exile his known austerity of manner and almost Roman stoicism, as well as his conspicuous patience and on occasion notoriously short temper. With only one short break in London, in summer 1692, Paget remained abroad from September 1689 until April 1703, living first at the court of the Habsburg emperor, Leopold I, in Vienna and then, from 1693 to 1703, at the Ottoman court, living either at the English embassy at Constantinople or in uncomfortable circumstances at Adrianople, now Edirne, the principal residence of successive Ottoman sultans in the latter part of the seventeenth century.

William III's aim, in appointing Paget to Vienna in 1689, was not only to cement his alliance with the emperor, but to add weight to his existing policies, carried on by Dutch diplomats in the field, of extracting the emperor by mediation from the conflict in Hungary with the Ottomans, which had been going on since 1683 and which was becoming increasingly successful, in order to free the best imperial generals and the emperor's most seasoned troops for the conflict against the armies of Louis XIV on the Rhine and in the Low Countries. In the event William's attempts at mediation were less than successful. Early in autumn 1692, following the successive deaths of two English ambassadors to the Porte (Sir William Hussey, who had died at Adrianople in summer 1691, and William Harbord, who had died at Belgrade a year later), the king transferred both Paget and his Dutch colleague Coenraad van Heemskerck from Vienna to the Porte in an effort to force the pace of the mediation diplomacy. At Vienna Paget was succeeded by George Stepney; at the Porte,

Paget's strenuous but cautious advocacy of William's policies met with little immediate success, partly as a result of deep-seated personal animosities between Paget and van Heemskerck, partly because of the continuing primacy of pro-French grand viziers in the counsels of successive sultans, and the insurmountable difficulties of long-distance diplomatic communication between the Porte, Vienna, The Hague, and London. It was not until late in 1697, after the conclusion at Ryswick of peace in the west between William III and Louis XIV on 11 September and of the destruction at the battle of Zenta on 12 September of the Ottoman army and the main military leaders of the pro-French war party, that Paget was able to induce a new Ottoman regime to agree to a mediated peace with Austria and its Sacra Liga allies. Paget's subsequent roles, as chief intermediary in the year-long preliminary negotiations, as co-mediator with his Dutch colleague Jacobus Colyer, and as joint chairman at the congress of Carlowitz (Karlofça; Karlofci) from 2 November 1698 to the conclusion of peace on 26 January 1699, mark the culmination of his diplomatic career. Paget remained at the Porte for almost four more years, returning home loaded with honours from both the Ottoman and Habsburg rulers, some months after the death of William III.

Paget arrived in London in April 1703. On 24 June, after an interval of nearly fourteen years, he was reappointed lord lieutenant of Staffordshire. His later years were uneventful. Having professed his personal faith in his will of 14 April 1711, he died at his London house in Bloomsbury Square on 26 February 1713 and was buried in the church of St Giles-in-the-Fields on 20 March. His sole surviving son, Henry *Paget (*c.*1663–1743), later created earl of Uxbridge, the younger son of his first marriage, succeeded to the title. COLIN HEYWOOD

Sources C. J. Heywood, 'English diplomacy between Austria and the Ottoman empire in the war of the Sacra Liga … 1689–1699', PhD diss., U. Lond., 1970 · C. J. Heywood, 'English diplomatic relations with Turkey, 1689–1698', *Four centuries of Turco-British relations*, ed. W. Hale and A. T. Bağiş (1984), 26–39 · C. Heywood, 'An undiplomatic Anglo-Dutch dispute at the Porte: the quarrel at Edirne between Coenraad van Heemskerck and Lord Paget (1693)', *Friends and rivals in the East: studies in Anglo-Dutch relations in the Levant*, ed. A. Hamilton, A. H. de Groot, and M. H. van Boogert (Leiden, 2000), 59–94 · C. J. Heywood, 'The Kapudan pasha, the English ambassador, and the *Blackham Galley*: an episode in Anglo-Ottoman maritime relations (1697)', *Papers from a conference on the Ottoman Kapudan pasha and his office*, ed. E. Zachariadou (Crete, [forthcoming]) · GEC, *Peerage* · D. Lysons, *An historical account of those parishes in the county of Middlesex which are not described in 'The environs of London'* (1800), 32–43 · will, PRO, PROB 11/532, sig. 66 · *VCH Staffordshire*

Archives BL, corresp. and papers, Add. MS 61830 · BL, diplomatic MSS, Add. MSS 8880, 28939, 28942; Egerton MS 918 · SOAS, corresp. and papers · Staffs. RO, corresp. and notebook · Staffs. RO, personal and estate corresp. and papers | BL, letters to W. D. Colt, Add. MSS 34095, 36662 · BL, corresp. with Lord Lexington, Add. MS 46540 · PRO, corresp. with George Stepney, SP105/58–60 · PRO, SP 97/20–21; 80/17 · U. Wales, Lligwy MSS · Yale U., Beinecke L., letters to W. Blathwayt and others

Likenesses miniature, 1665; in possession of Lieutenant-Colonel Leopold Paget, 1895

Wealth at death property in Staffordshire, West Drayton, Middlesex, London, and elsewhere; mining interests in Staffordshire: will, PRO, PROB 11/532, fols. 165*v*–167*r*; *VCH Staffordshire*, 2.73, 110 ff., 217n.

Pagett [Pagit], **Ephraim** (1574–1646), heresiologist, was baptized at Wold (Old), Northamptonshire, on 28 May 1574, the second of three children of Eusebius *Pagit (1546/7–1617), vicar of Lamport in the same county, and his wife, Anne Gyles, about whom nothing else is known. Pagett's sister, Katherine (*b.* 1573), and brother, Nathaniel (*b.* 1589), died shortly after birth. At the age of eleven, Pagett translated from Latin twenty-eight of Ludwig Lavater's sermons on the book of Ruth. On 25 May 1593 he matriculated at Christ Church, Oxford, aged eighteen. Though no record remains of his graduation, he was a great linguist, speaking fifteen or sixteen languages. On 19 August 1601 he was admitted rector of St Edmund the King, Lombard Street, London. On 29 June 1602 he married Jane Rogers (*b.* 1584), with whom he had two children, Ephraim and Elizabeth. At some point, Jane died; a second wife, Anne, was buried at St Nicholas's, Deptford, in 1621. On 16 April 1632 Pagett married Mary, widow of Sir Stephen Bord.

Pagett's *Christianographie, or, The description of the multitude and sundry sorts of Christians in the world not subject to the pope* (1635) was an attack upon Roman Catholicism and appeared in subsequently enlarged editions (1636, 1640; reissued 1674). Pagett described protestantism's international solidarity and accepted as protestants many exotic kinds of Christian around the world. His increasing episcopalianism in later editions has caused him to be identified as a 'Laudian' writer, but such Laudianism was probably contrived by Pagett himself since he was trying to secure Laud's support in exporting *Christianographie* to the continent. About 1635 Pagett commended *Christianographie* to the patriarchs of Constantinople, Alexandria, Antioch, and Jerusalem, the Maronites, Prince Radziwill of Poland, and John Tolnai of Transylvania, along with Elias Petley's Greek translation of the English prayer book and Laud's account of his conference with the Jesuit John Fisher. In 1638 Pagett produced an abbreviated version of *Christianographie* and, in 1640, two Latin versions, all of which were dedicated to Laud.

Despite the wide definition of reformed opinion in *Christianographie*, Pagett's religious beliefs were Calvinist and unequivocally rooted in the reformed traditions of the English church: the monarch, the prayer book, and the Thirty-Nine Articles. By the 1640s his stance began to appear anachronistic, and his conception of orthodoxy narrowed as he turned away from international protestant Christianity towards describing the heterodoxies immediately around him.

His *Heresiography, or, A Description of the Heretickes and Sectaries of these Latter Times* (1645) grew out of a sermon he delivered against heresy, first published as *The Mysticall Wolfe* (1645) and reissued as *The Tryall of Trueth* (1645). Pagett claimed that he knew several heretics personally, but *Heresiography* is principally a compilation of heresies from the period's radical literature and earlier continental and patristic heresy lists. As a heresy list *Heresiography* is heresiological rather than heresiographical; it is only modern scholarship which has come to use Pagett's coinage, 'heresiography', to refer to all anti-sectarian writing, thereby underlining his historical and literary importance. Indeed, *Heresiography* went through six successively enlarged editions (1645 (again), 1646, 1647, 1654, 1661) and three issues (1647, 1648, 1662); more than any similar text. It remains perhaps the most systematically copious, if excessive, account of the sects during the period.

Circumstances forced Pagett to take the covenant in 1645, but he was soon silenced; an interim was introduced into the parish the same year. He left his ministry and retired to Deptford. He wrote his will on 6 August 1646 and died within a few months. He was buried on 27 October 1646 at St Nicholas's Church, Deptford, aged seventy-two. His bookseller, however, who oversaw *Heresiography*'s editions after 1646, claimed he was eighty-four, in accordance with Pagett's nicknames, Old Ephraim Pagitt and Old Father Ephraim. Pagett's cause of death is unknown. His will instructed that most of his land and property be sold to settle his debts, though he provided for his wife and children. S. C. DYTON

Sources H. I. Longden, *Northamptonshire and Rutland clergy from 1500*, ed. P. I. King and others, 16 vols. in 6, Northamptonshire RS (1938–52), vol. 10, pp. 141–3 • Wood, *Ath. Oxon.*, new edn, 3.210–11 • B. Brook, *The lives of the puritans*, 3 (1813), 62–3 • Foster, *Alum. Oxon., 1500–1714* • S. Dyton, 'Fabricating radicalism: Ephraim Pagitt and seventeenth-century heresiology', PhD diss., U. Cam., 2002 • A. Milton, *Catholic and Reformed: the Roman and protestant churches in English protestant thought, 1600–1640* (1995) • *Walker rev.*, 55 • parish register, Deptford, St Nicholas, 27/10/1646 [burial] • will, PRO, PROB 11/200, fol. 227r

Archives BL, Harley MSS 823–825

Wealth at death in debt; sold most of his land probably 16½ acres: will, PRO, PROB 11/200 fol. 227r; N. Dews, *The history of Deptford* (1971), 289–90

Pagham, John of (*d.* 1157), bishop of Worcester, took his name from Pagham, Sussex, where the archbishops of Canterbury held property. He joined Archbishop Theobald's staff about 1145, witnessing his charters, sometimes with the title *magister*, which suggests that he was educated at one of the nascent universities. His studies probably included law. A letter of John of Salisbury shows that he was consulted by the archbishop on a legal problem, along with known legal experts; he also acted as a papal judge-delegate, and a report from him about a lawsuit involving the abbey of St Victor, Le Mans, shows evidence of the influence of Roman law on ecclesiastical procedure in England.

Pagham was consecrated bishop of Worcester on 4 March 1151. He gave to the abbey of Osney the rich church on his episcopal manor at Bibury, Gloucestershire, in spite of the protests of his monks; the grant was challenged later, and Worcester won substantial compensation. He was also an early benefactor to his former colleague in Theobald's household, Thomas Becket, giving him the church of St Mary-le-Strand in London. Pagham died at Rome in December 1157. He may have been out of England for a year or more, for John of Salisbury noted in 1156 that the bishop was about to leave the island, and Becket, writing in 1166, mentions the expulsion of Bishop Pagham by the king. The incident is otherwise unrecorded. The continuation made at Bec of Robert de Torigni's chronicle, noting the bishop's death in Rome in December, describes him as a godly man, and outstandingly learned. His obit was commemorated at Osney on 22 December. Copies survive of some thirty of his charters, dealing with episcopal and judicial business. In some of these instruments he employs a style—*Wigorn' ecclesie servus devotus*—reminiscent of the papal *servus servorum Dei*. M. G. CHENEY

Sources A. Saltman, *Theobald, archbishop of Canterbury* (1956) • *The letters of John of Salisbury*, ed. and trans. H. E. Butler and W. J. Millor, rev. C. N. L. Brooke, OMT, 1: *The early years, 1153–1161* (1986), 15, 56 [Lat. orig. with parallel Eng. text] • *Materials for the history of Thomas Becket, archbishop of Canterbury*, 5, ed. J. C. Robertson, Rolls Series, 67 (1881), 289 • A. Chédeville, ed., *Liber controversiarum S. Vincentii Cenomanensis* (1968), no. 251 • H. E. Salter, ed., *Cartulary of Oseney Abbey*, 1, OHS, 89 (1929), xxvii • H. E. Salter, ed., *Cartulary of Oseney Abbey*, 5, OHS, 98 (1935), 511–12, 515 • R. Howlett, ed., *Chronicles of the reigns of Stephen, Henry II, and Richard I*, 4, Rolls Series, 82 (1889), 317 • M. G. Cheney, ed., *Worcester, 1066–1212*, English Episcopal Acta [forthcoming] • F. Barlow, *Thomas Becket* (1986) • C. R. Cheney, *English bishops' chanceries, 1100–1250* (1950)

Pagit, Ephraim. *See* Pagett, Ephraim (1574–1646).

Pagit, Eusebius (1546/7–1617), Church of England clergyman, was born at Cranford, Northamptonshire, the third son of Richard Pagit, gentleman, and his wife, Katherine, daughter of Euseby Isham of Pitchley, Northamptonshire. In 1559, at the age of twelve Pagit was admitted to Christ Church, Oxford, as a chorister. According to his son, he injured his right arm while carrying the pax in a religious service, an accident that may have prompted him to question aspects of the traditional ceremony. The arm failed to heal properly, and he later subscribed documents as 'lame Eusebius Pagit'. Admitted to Christ's College, Cambridge, on 22 February 1564, Pagit graduated BA in early 1568, having earned repute as 'the golden sophister'. He was ordained deacon in London in June 1569, aged twenty-two, and priest three months later. In either 1569 or 1570 he became rector of Old, Northamptonshire, where his uncle, John Isham, was patron. At Old, Pagit became a popular preacher of funeral sermons. For refusing to subscribe the articles, he was suspended in 1571. He became rector of nearby Lamport, which was also in John Isham's patronage, on 21 April 1572. On 12 June of that year, in a sermon preached less than a mile from Greenwich Palace, he likened the English bishops to Pharisees and to Catholic abbots and cardinals. Edmund Scambler, bishop of Peterborough, suspended Pagit on 29 January 1574 for nonconformity, depriving him of Lamport three weeks later. However, Pagit was appointed rector of Barnwell St Andrew, also in Northamptonshire, on 19 June 1575. By the following year he and John Oxenbridge were serving as moderators of the prophesyings at Southam, Warwickshire. With the support of such gentry as Sir Richard Knightley and, probably, Anthony Cope of Hanwell, he travelled throughout the midlands, visiting exercises, organizing classes (clerical conferences), and acting as what John Aylmer, later to be bishop of London, called a 'posting apostle'. For these activities Pagit and Oxenbridge were arrested and taken to London. Although no record of his fate at the hands of the ecclesiastical commission survives, his deprivation must be assumed.

Pagit found refuge with his uncle, John Isham, in whose Northamptonshire household he used a catechism, published in 1579 as *Short Questions and Answeares*, intended to benefit both householders and outsiders in worship and instruction. Appearing in thirty-one known editions by 1641, it contained brief answers averaging just over twenty words apiece. Pagit and Robert Openshaw later revised it, doubling the number of questions and halving the length of answers (other than biblical quotations). A Latin version appeared in 1585. Every day for twenty-six years, Pagit had a question-and-answer session on the Bible in his household, reading an Old Testament chapter at dinner and a New Testament one at supper.

Although Pagit refused to conform, John Woolton, bishop of Exeter, instituted him as rector of Kilkhampton, Cornwall, in 1580. The living, which was in Sir Richard Grenville's gift, had been obtained with the help of Sir Francis Hastings of Leicestershire. During Pagit's tenure he published two of his sermons, *A Verie Fruitful Sermon* (1583) on predestination, and *A Godlie and Fruitefull Sermon* (1583) on Genesis 14: 20–21, in which he defended tithing, outlined acceptable social behaviour, and criticized bishops who granted leases of benefices to relatives. In March 1584 Woolton insisted that Pagit conform, but he refused to do so. Later that year, the curate of Barnstaple, Devon, brought charges against Pagit before the high commission. He was cited before the court on 11 January 1585 for declining to observe all the provisions of the Book of Common Prayer. He denied the charge, admitting only that he had varied from some of its provisions. Such practice, he argued, was followed by Archbishop Whitgift, Woolton, and other clergy. Although the commissioners suspended him, he continued to preach, possibly having received a royal pardon, but was eventually deprived for refusing to wear the surplice, use the sign of the cross when baptizing, and read the prayers in full. Grenville took possession of the parsonage, prompting allegations that he had terrorized Pagit's wife and committed unlawful violence. Pagit in turn charged Woolton with failing to undertake diocesan visitations, not attending sermons, and refusing to punish two members of his household who had impregnated harlots.

With the Scot David Black, Pagit established a 'reformed College' at Kilkhampton, but this, too, he was forced to relinquish for refusing to subscribe the articles. He subsequently taught for a time at Heston, Middlesex, and then at Deptford, Kent. A homily preached at Deptford was published in 1586 under the title *A Godly Sermon*. Wrongly suspected of having written the Marprelate tracts, Pagit was cruelly satirized by the anonymous author of *The Returne of the Renowned Cavaliero Pasquill* (1589) as a man with two clubs, 'one in his foote, another in his head', and by the author of *An Almond for a Parrat* (1590) as a schismatic, whoremaster, and 'poltfoote Paget' (Carlson, 66–7, 70).

Weary of being harried for his beliefs, Pagit wrote to the lord admiral, Charles, Lord Howard of Effingham, on 3 June 1591, after Sir John Hawkins had approached Howard on his behalf. For twenty years, Pagit averred, separatists had urged him to join them, and in the past six months he had devoted considerable time to conferences with them, and with learned men opposed to them. Professing loyalty to the established church notwithstanding its blemishes, he insisted that the essence of a true church was gospel preaching. Calling attention to his children and orphans entrusted to his care, he appealed not to be evicted from his house and forced to beg. He appears to have continued to live and to teach at Deptford until 1598, when he was appointed lecturer at St Botolph, Aldgate, in London, succeeding William Hubbock, who obtained the post for him. For failing to obtain a proper licence he was temporarily suspended, but by 1599 he was attracting so many people from neighbouring parishes to his lectures that the vestry complained. He explored biblical passages in depth, lecturing on John 19: 1–33 from 17 June to 30 September 1599. In 1603 he published another best-seller, *The History of the Bible*, which used the question-and-answer format. Having now made his peace with the ecclesiastical authorities, Pagit left his lectureship to become rector of St Anne and St Agnes, Aldersgate, on 21 September 1604, a position he held until his death in May or June 1617. He was interred in his church. His son, the heresiographer Ephraim *Pagett, was granted letters of administration for his estate on 16 June that year. RICHARD L. GREAVES

Sources Venn, *Alum. Cant.* • J. Strype, *The life and acts of … John Whitgift* (1718) • P. Collinson, *The Elizabethan puritan movement* (1967) • I. Green, *The Christian's ABC: catechisms and catechising in England, c.1530–1740* (1996) • *CSP dom.*, 1581–90, 228 • L. H. Carlson, *Martin Marprelate, gentleman: Master Job Throkmorton laid open in his colors* (1981) • P. S. Seaver, *The puritan lectureships: the politics of religious dissent, 1560–1662* (1970) • LPL, carte misc. XII/15 • *DNB* • Wood, *Ath. Oxon.*, new edn, 2.204–6 • Fuller, *Worthies* (1840) • W. J. Sheils, *The puritans in the diocese of Peterborough, 1558–1610*, Northamptonshire RS, 30 (1979) • G. Hennessy, *Novum repertorium ecclesiasticum parochiale Londinense, or, London diocesan clergy succession from the earliest time to the year 1898* (1898)

Archives LPL, carte misc. XII/15

Wealth at death see admon, PRO, PROB 6/9, fol. 121r

Pagitt, Justinian (1611/12–1668), lawyer and diarist, was the eldest son of James Pagitt (*c*.1581–1638), controller of the pipe and baron cursitor of the exchequer, and his first wife, Catherine, a daughter of the civil lawyer William *Lewin. Born at Monkton Hadley, near Barnet, Middlesex, Justinian was privately educated, spending two years in Bramley, Staffordshire, under Mr Dudson, followed by seven years in total with Mr Ball and then Mr Rawlett in London. He entered Christ's College, Cambridge, aged fifteen, as a pensioner pupil of Joseph Mead on 12 January 1627, remaining in residence for nearly two years without taking a degree. Admitted to membership of the Middle Temple on 11 October 1628, Justinian was in commons by the autumn of 1633, and gained formal admission to a house chamber in Elm Court with his brother Thomas in June 1634. On 8 May 1635 he was called to the bar, and two months later, on 7 July, married Dorcas (*d.* 1669), the daughter of Richard Wilcox, a London haberdasher.

Besides the lands which he inherited at his father's death, from at least November 1634 Pagitt enjoyed a half share in the lucrative office of clerk of the treasury and custos brevium (keeper of writs and records) in the court of king's bench. Following the death in 1645 of his wealthy partner and brother-in-law, Robert Dewhurst of Gray's Inn and Cheshunt, Hertfordshire, Pagitt paid £2500 to acquire sole possession of the office. This he eventually passed on to his own eldest son and namesake, despite a legal challenge mounted at the Restoration by two sons of the former chief justice, Sir Robert Heath, who had been granted the place in 1644 following the failure of Dewhurst and Pagitt to attend Charles I in Oxford. Pagitt served as justice of the peace for Middlesex from 1642 to 1648, and again from 1655 to 1660; his name also appears as a parliamentary assessment commissioner and on other local committees for Hertford and Middlesex from 1643 onwards. In 1656 he successfully sought the lord protector's permission to transfer the upper bench records in his care to a more accessible and spacious location in Westminster Hall. Two years later he became a member of Gray's Inn, paying only half the usual entry fine 'in respect of his office' (Fletcher, 424). Having survived the Restoration unscathed 'Pagett the counsellor, an old lover of Musique', so termed by his friend Samuel Pepys (Pepys, 3.281), died at his home in High Holborn on 29 December 1668 and was buried at St Giles-in-the-Fields parish church on 2 January 1669. His widow, Dorcas, mother of their three sons and two daughters, died less than a year later on 14 September 1669.

Some evidence of Pagitt's early musical interests appears in note form, in the entries of the occasional journal he began to keep in 1633, as well as in his characteristically anxious question: 'Whether is not playing on the viol immediately after meales hurtfull, by reason that it stirrs the fancy & bringeth a heate into my face at that time?' (BL, Harley MS 1026, fol. 6). The manuscript includes a good deal of such self-catechizing, as well as copies of personal letters, notes of books read and sermons heard, and memoranda on astrology, dancing, domestic and family conflicts, etiquette and personal advancement, law suits, political events, theological issues, and the current state of his body, mind, and soul. Read in conjunction with the brief yet revealingly detailed daily record of Pagitt's doings over several months, this volume provides a uniquely informative source on the cultural, intellectual, and social milieu of the pre-civil war inns of court. WILFRID PREST

Sources J. Peile, *Biographical register of Christ's College, 1505–1905, and of the earlier foundation, God's House, 1448–1505*, ed. [J. A. Venn], 1 (1910), 378 • R. L. Hine, *The cream of curiosity* (1920), 181–212 • R. L. Hine, 'A seventeenth century pacifist', *Blackwood*, 204 (1918), 358–73 • W. R. Prest, *The inns of court under Elizabeth I and the early Stuarts, 1590–1640* (1972) • C. H. Hopwood, ed., *Middle Temple records*, 1–2 (1904) • *Elias Ashmole (1617–1692): his autobiographical and historical notes*, ed. C. H. Josten, 5 vols. (1966 [i.e. 1967]), vols. 2–3 • BL, Harley MS 1026 • F. C. Cass, *Monkton Hadley* (1880) • C. H. Firth and R. S. Rait, eds., *Acts and ordinances of the interregnum, 1642–1660*, 3 vols. (1911) • *CSP dom.*, *1655–6* • M. A. E. Green, ed., *Calendar of the proceedings of the committee for advance of money, 1642–1656*, 3 vols., PRO (1888) • Pepys, *Diary*, vols. 1–3 • BL, Sloane MS 1039, fol. 98 • R. J. Fletcher, ed., *The pension book of Gray's Inn*, 1 (1901) • Venn, *Alum. Cant.* • admon, PRO, PROB 6/44, fol. 1 • will, PRO, PROB 11/330, sig. 107 [Dorcas Pagitt, widow] • W. R. Prest, *The rise of the barristers: a social history of the English bar, 1590–1640* (1986)

Archives BL, commonplace book, Harley MS 1026 | University of Illinois, Urbana-Champaign, Heath papers

Wealth at death see administration, PRO, PROB 6/44, fol. 1; will, PRO, PROB 11/330, sig. 107 [Dorcas Pagitt]

Pagula [Paull]**, William** (*d.* 1332?), canon lawyer and theologian, probably came from Paull, near Hull, Yorkshire. Granted letters dimissory by Archbishop Greenfield of York on 24 November 1313, he was instituted as perpetual vicar of the church of Winkfield, near Windsor Forest, Berkshire, just inside the boundary of Salisbury diocese, on 5 March 1314, during the episcopate of Simon Ghent (*d.* 1315). He was ordained into the priesthood by Archbishop Walter Reynolds (*d.* 1327) in Canterbury Cathedral on 1 June 1314.

Pagula seems to have been intermittently in residence at Winkfield during the early years of his vicariate. Perhaps already a master in 1314, he received a doctorate in canon law at Oxford, possibly as late as 1323 but probably by 1319–20. Thereafter Pagula devoted himself primarily to his parish. The subject matter of his chief writings, as well as specific references within them, indicate considerable familiarity with the conditions of rural parishioners and clergy, especially in the Windsor Forest region.

Pagula was licensed as penitentiary for Reading deanery on 8 March 1322, an appointment possibly later extended to the whole of Berkshire. But although he was made a canon of St Paul's, London, about 1323, there is no evidence that he sought or was granted further ecclesiastical preferment. He was still vicar of Winkfield in 1326, but seems to have been succeeded in that post by Master John Lavyngham in November 1332. Since records make no mention of Pagula after the latter date, he probably died in the summer or autumn of 1332.

Pagula's literary productions encompassed a broad range of topics. His *Oculus sacerdotis*, a manual of pastoral theology, deals comprehensively with the matters that ought to fall within the 'view' of the parochial clergy. The *Oculus sacerdotis* represents an elaboration of the programme of pastoral instruction imposed by the Council of Lambeth in 1281 for the Canterbury province. The work is composed of three parts: the *Pars oculi*, dealing with confessional practice; the *Dextra pars oculi*, concerned with the teaching of morals; and the *Sinistra pars oculi*, which addresses matters of dogma. The *Dextra pars* and *Sinistra pars* have been dated on internal and external evidence to 1320–23, while the *Pars oculi* was written after 1326 but probably before 1328.

The readership and influence of the *Oculus sacerdotis* were extensive. Fifty manuscripts of it survive, and it is often mentioned in church registers and in the wills of priests. Later in the fourteenth century an abbreviated version was produced under the title *Pupilla oculi* by John

Burgh (*fl.* 1370–1386), chancellor of Cambridge University, and in that form it was printed at least three times between 1510 and 1518.

In addition to the *Oculus sacerdotis* Pagula compiled a substantial tract on the responsibilities and station of the clergy entitled the *Summa summarum*, which was also probably completed between 1320 and 1323. Comprising five books and about 350,000 words, the *Summa summarum*, cast in question and answer form, was designed to enumerate the duties pertaining to each office in the ecclesiastical hierarchy, ranging from the parochial clergy to the upper echelons. The *Summa summarum* enjoyed a wide readership, attested by the eleven manuscripts presently known.

Even more ambitious than the *Summa summarum*, however, was Pagula's *Summa praelatorum*, a treatise approaching 700,000 words written as a definitive source book for parish priests. The *Summa praelatorum* contains, among other features, a large collection of church statutes relevant to parish affairs, and an extensive set of sermon themes for every Sunday, feast day, and special occasion within the liturgical year. Dated to 1320–23, the *Summa praelatorum* clearly did not enjoy the popularity of Pagula's other theological writings, as only a single (and incomplete) manuscript has been identified.

Pagula later formed excerpts from the *Summa praelatorum* into the much briefer *Speculum religiosorum*, a handbook that concentrates on the rudiments of canon law necessary for pastoral care. Although the *Speculum religiosorum* incorporates some new material, it demonstrates no awareness of important developments in ecclesiastical legislation from the mid-1320s. Thus, it was most likely compiled soon after the *Summa praelatorum* and the *Dextra pars oculi*, to which it also refers, and certainly before 1325–6. The *Speculum religiosorum* is known to exist in ten manuscripts, suggesting a broader audience than was achieved by the *Summa praelatorum*.

Near the end of his career at Winkfield (and possibly of his life) Pagula turned his pen to political affairs. He has been conclusively identified as the author of two recensions of a *speculum regis* treatise, addressed to Edward III, which defends the right of the king's subjects, especially the peasantry, to refuse royal prises and purveyance. The first version, sometimes known as the *Epistola ad regem Edwardi III*, has been dated on internal evidence to 1331, while the second was evidently completed the following year. Both tracts warn Edward III that his soul is endangered by permitting the theft of his subjects' goods, and foretell the loss of his kingdom if he does not reform his administration. Pagula advises the king to curtail his expenditures, pay his debts, and care for the churches and poor of the realm.

The origins of Pagula's complaints against Edward are obscure. He claims to have witnessed personally the exploitative practices of royal officials in the Windsor Forest area, and to be among those who fear the coming of Edward's entourage. But purveyance records do not indicate any exactions in the region during or immediately before 1331–2. Moreover, the language and grievances of the *Speculum regis* closely resemble a document dating to 1316 which is quoted in the *Vita Edwardi secundi*. It is possible that Pagula adapted and revised an earlier work (either by himself or another) directed against Edward II, in order to express renewed dissatisfaction about royal conduct. CARY J. NEDERMAN

Sources L. E. Boyle, 'A study of the works attributed to William of Pagula', DPhil diss., U. Oxf., 1956 • L. E. Boyle, 'The *Oculus sacerdotis* and some other works of William of Pagula', *TRHS*, 5th ser., 5 (1955), 81–110 • Emden, *Oxf.* • Tanner, *Bibl. Brit.-Hib.* • Bale, *Index* • L. E. Boyle, 'William of Pagula and the *Speculum regis Edwardi III*', *Mediaeval Studies*, 32 (1970), 329–36 • L. E. Boyle, 'The *Summa summarum* and some other English works of canon law', *Second International Congress of Medieval Canon Law* [Boston 1963], ed. S. Kuttner and J. J. Ryan (1965), 415–56 • C. J. Nederman and C. J. Neville, 'The origins of the *Speculum regis Edwardi III* of William of Pagula', *Studi Medievali*, 3rd ser., 38 (1997), 317–29

Pagula, William. *See* Paul, William (*d.* 1349).

Pain fitz John (*d.* 1137), baron and administrator, was perhaps the eldest son of John, nephew of Waleram, also known as John fitz Richard, and the grandson of a moneyer who held a mill in the Avranchin. He shared two characteristics with several other of the 'new men' who served Henry I: a link with western Normandy and the status of an inferior tenant-in-chief—in 1086 his father held only a few estates in Norfolk and Essex. His brother *Eustace fitz John (*d.* 1157) was drawn by marriage to northern England; for the same reason Pain was attracted to the west midlands.

The sources are not precise about dates and offices in Pain's career. He was too young to serve William Rufus, but according to a story retailed by Walter Map, he was (perhaps briefly) a royal *cubicularius*, or chamberlain, to Henry I; but no attestations survive styling him thus, and the story suggests that Pain's duty was body service for the king (in this case the nocturnal supply of wine), rather than any concern with the royal finances. Gerald of Wales, another late source, describes Pain fitz John and his colleague Miles of Gloucester as *secretarii et praecipui consiliari* (*Gir. Camb. opera*, 6.34), a phrase helpfully glossed as 'personal confidants' (*VCH Shropshire*, 3.11). Such services notwithstanding, when Pain was allowed, about 1115, to marry Sybil Talbot, niece of Hugh (I) de *Lacy, his personal ambitions turned firmly to the southern Welsh march, though he continued to attest royal *acta* quite frequently, if seldom in Normandy. Pain's interest in the marches is evidenced by a mandate from Pope Calixtus II of as early as 1119, ordering Pain and others to return to the churches of the diocese of Llandaff all lands and other rights which they had 'wickedly withdrawn and retained' (Davies, 2.616). Between 1123 and 1127 he became sheriff of Herefordshire, and in the latter year he was also made sheriff of Shropshire, succeeding Richard de Belmeis as the king's vicegerent. In both shires Pain was almost certainly justice as well as sheriff, and in the pipe roll for 1130 he appears as an itinerant justice in Staffordshire, Gloucestershire, and Pembroke.

The *Gesta Stephani* couples Pain with Miles of Gloucester,

attributing to Miles the lordship (*dominatum*) of Gloucestershire and to Pain that of Herefordshire and Shropshire, and asserting that between the Severn and the sea (that is, the Bristol Channel) they ran a highly acquisitive regime by means of litigation and forced services (*placitis … et angariis*). This may have meant that Pain dealt with the Welsh (his external problem) by impressing men to serve against them. According to the *Gesta*, Pain and Miles were among those who at the beginning of Stephen's reign sought safe conducts when summoned to court, as a precaution against the compulsory surrender of ill-gotten gains. An order of Pope Honorius II in 1128 shows that Pain had continued depredations against the church, in which Miles had joined him. However, at about this time the two men jointly lobbied Henry I to appoint the prior of Llanthony to the vacant see of Hereford.

There are indications that under Pain the centre of royal power in Shropshire, perhaps even in the marches as a whole, might have moved from Shrewsbury to Bridgnorth. Not only does a writ of the 1120s by Belmeis to the barons of Shropshire show that Pain held his first plea at Bridgnorth with Walter the constable, the father and in this context the forerunner of Miles of Gloucester, but in 1128, soon after Pain had succeeded Belmeis, Mareddud ap Bleddyn, the ruler of Powys, characteristically handed his nephew Llywelyn ab Owain over to Pain, who imprisoned him in Bridgnorth Castle; the king had already confined a noble Norman rebel there in 1126.

For some years Pain devoted much effort to consolidating his position in and around Ludlow by improving its financial and military resources. Apart perhaps from William fitz Osbern he was the first to see the strategic potential of Ludlow, half-way between Shrewsbury and Hereford and a nodal point for routes into Powys, the Welsh province whose southern portions contained Elfael (part of the Tosny lands, of which Pain had custody) and Ismynydd, which took Pain's name to become Painscastle (just as a former Lacy estate in Gloucestershire became Painswick).

According to William of Malmesbury, in 1128 Henry I granted the *comitatus Salopesberie* to Queen Adeliza, perhaps implying a wish to exercise more control over Pain's activities. The latter included conflict with the Welsh, who triumphed at least once; late in Henry I's reign, according to Orderic, they attacked and burnt Caus Castle, west of Shrewsbury, and slew the garrison. Orderic states that the castle was Pain's, but he was probably only its custodian.

Following King Henry's death Pain was present at his funeral: he declared early for Stephen and witnessed the royal charter of concessions given at Oxford in April 1136. But the Welsh—perhaps those who had moved on Caus—drew him back to the border and to his death. On 10 July 1137 he was killed in an ambush while pursuing a raiding party: a missile split his head open and he was buried in Gloucester Abbey. Pain left no son but he had two daughters, Cecily and Agnes, who between them had five husbands. Cecily was married first (in 1137) to Roger, the son of Miles of *Gloucester, but Pain's acquisitions did not descend as an entity. In Shropshire his role as a border administrator and guardian was assumed by the Fitzalans and then the Lestranges. J. F. A. MASON

Sources GEC, *Peerage*, 12/2.268–74; appx B • B. Coplestone-Crow, 'Payn Fitz John and Ludlow Castle', *Shropshire History and Archaeology*, 70 (1995), 171–83 • Ordericus Vitalis, *Eccl. hist.*, vol. 6 • William of Malmesbury, *The Historia novella*, ed. and trans. K. R. Potter (1955) • K. R. Potter and R. H. C. Davis, eds., *Gesta Stephani*, OMT (1976) • John of Worcester, *Chron.* • *Gir. Camb. opera*, vol. 6 • W. Map, *De nugis curialium / Courtiers' trifles*, ed. and trans. M. R. James, rev. C. N. L. Brooke and R. A. B. Mynors, OMT (1983); repr. with corrections (1994) • U. Rees, ed., *The Shrewsbury cartulary*, 2 vols. (1975) • J. C. Davies, *Episcopal acts … relating to Welsh dioceses*, 2, Historical Society of the Church in Wales, 3–4 (1948) • *VCH Shropshire*, vol. 3 • J. Green, *The government of Henry I* (1986) • F. C. Suppe, *Military institutions on the Welsh marches: Shropshire, 1066–1300* (1994) • W. E. Wightman, *The Lacy family in England and Normandy, 1066–1194* (1966) • J. A. Green, *English sheriffs to 1154*, Public Record Office Handbooks, 24 (1990) • private information (2004) [B. Coplestone-Crow]

Wealth at death see *Reg. RAN*, 3, no. 312

Pain, Barry Eric Odell (1864–1928), writer, was born at 3 Sidney Street, Cambridge, on 28 September 1864, one of the four children of John Odell Pain, linen draper of Cambridge, and his wife, Maria, *née* Pain. After attending Sedbergh School from 1879 to 1883, he went up to Corpus Christi College, Cambridge. Awarded a scholarship in 1884, he graduated in 1886, obtaining a third class in part one of the classical tripos. He then spent four years as an army coach at Guildford before moving to London in 1890 to devote himself to writing.

Pain had contributed to *Granta* at Cambridge with much success and soon obtained regular work from the *Daily Chronicle* and *Black and White*. In 1891 he published his first book, *In a Canadian Canoe*, compiled from his *Granta* pieces. Shortly afterwards he was invited by James Payn, editor of the *Cornhill Magazine*, to become a contributor. He soon made his name as a novelist and writer of short stories, mainly of a humorous nature, publishing books at yearly intervals.

Pain's dislike of banality led him to satirize the stock characters and accepted formulas of Victorian fiction. His parodies of the best-selling novels of the time displayed an iconoclastic approach to well-worn literary conventions, and made him and other apostles of the 'new humour' popular, although in their day they aroused as much criticism as they did enthusiasm.

On 2 June 1892 at Emmanuel Church, Maida Vale, London, Pain married Amelia Nina Anna (1865/6–1920), daughter of the portrait painter Rudolf *Lehmann (1819–1905) and sister of Liza Lehmann, the composer. They had two daughters. A burly, bearded figure who enjoyed family life and foreign travel, Pain was a man of many interests including Georgian literature, occult lore, and precious stones. It is typical that he gave up writing for a year to learn to draw.

In 1897 Pain succeeded Jerome K. Jerome as editor of *To-Day* and, three years later, published the first of the Eliza books for which he is now best remembered. Although *Eliza* (1900) was rejected by many publishers including those who were publishing his other books, it proved to be an instant success. A series of domestic sketches narrated by a despotic and fussy London clerk, it reflected an aspect of the everyday life of his readers. Pain had success with other sketches of working-class life—the charwoman Mrs Murphy and the scrounging gardener Edwards are good examples—but his public wanted more of Eliza, and he produced four sequels in the next twelve years.

At the outbreak of the First World War, Pain was touring the United States. Although well over age, he returned to join the anti-aircraft section of the Royal Naval Volunteer Reserve in April 1915. Posted to a searchlight station on Parliament Hill, north London, he attained the rank of chief petty officer but the eye-strain caused by this work eventually forced him to abandon it. In 1917 he became a member of the London Appeal Tribunal, adjudicating on claims for exemption from military service.

Although Pain is best-known today for his humorous working-class sketches, it was his serious writing that earned critical acclaim during his lifetime. He was admired for his narrative ability and economy in a range of books that included novels, fantasies, a theological study, a detective story, and a series of parodies that were widely admired. In all, he wrote over sixty books and a mass of uncollected articles and short stories in every conceivable vein, and it is possible that the diversity of his writing meant that he never developed the reputation he deserved. If it is ironic that Pain is now best remembered for *Eliza* and the sequels he produced in response to popular demand, it is also true that their wit and detailed description of suburban life and snobbery stand up very well today and led to a television series and reissue of the stories in the 1980s. Barry Pain died of heart disease on 5 May 1928 at his home, 69 Bushey Grove Road, Bushey, Watford, Hertfordshire, and was buried in the Bushey parish churchyard. N. T. P. MURPHY

Sources private information (1937) • J. H. Bowen, introduction, in B. Pain, *More stories* (1930), v–ix • A. Noyes, introduction, in B. Pain, *Humorous stories* (1930) • *The Times* (7 May 1928) • *Daily Telegraph* (7 May 1928) • A. Noyes, 'Barry Pain', *The Bookman*, 73 (1927–8), 166–7 • *Truth* (9 May 1928) • *London Mercury*, 18 (1928), 123 • T. Jones, introduction, in B. Pain, *The Eliza stories* (1984), [7]–[10] • *West Herts and Watford Observer* (12 May 1928) • P. G. Wodehouse, 'Preface', *A century of humour* (1934) • b. cert. • m. cert. • d. cert.
Archives King's Cam., letters to Nathaniel Wedd • U. Leeds, letters to Clement Shorter
Likenesses portrait, repro. in B. Pain, *Humorous stories* (1930), frontispiece
Wealth at death £1623 11s. 8d.: probate, 27 June 1928, *CGPLA Eng. & Wales*

Pain, George Richard (1792/3–1838). *See under* Pain, James (1779/80–1877).

Pain, James (1779/80–1877), architect and builder, was born at Isleworth in Middlesex, the eldest son of James Pain, builder and surveyor, and a grandson of William *Pain. He was apprenticed to John Nash, as was his younger brother **George Richard Pain** (1792/3–1838), who was born in London. After Nash had designed Lough Cutra Castle, co. Galway, for Charles Vereker in 1811, he recommended that the two brothers should be given charge of carrying out the work. James, who was already in his early thirties, had arrived in Ireland by the summer of 1813 and soon established himself in Limerick. George Richard, who exhibited architectural designs at the Royal Academy from the London address of 1 Diana Place, Fitzroy Square, between 1810 and 1814, may possibly have gone to Ireland a little later; he settled in Cork but worked in close partnership with James until his death.

Between them the two brothers were responsible as architects or contractors for a large number of churches, country houses, court houses, prisons, and bridges in the south and west of Ireland. It was said that, of the two, James was better at running the business and planning buildings, while George Richard, the more skilful draughtsman, designed the elevations. The brothers tended to take an orthodox, academic approach towards their classical buildings, but they were generally more fanciful in their Gothic and Tudor Gothic designs. Their country houses, usually castellated or Tudor Gothic in Nash's picturesque manner, include Dromoland Castle, co. Clare (from 1819), Mitchelstown Castle, co. Cork (1823), Strancally Castle, co. Waterford (*c*.1830), and Castle Bernard, King's county (*c*.1833). At Blackrock, on the outskirts of Cork, they remodelled the existing riverside castle in 1828–9 for the use of Cork corporation. Within the city they designed the house of correction (1818–19), the Cork county club (1829–31) and the county and city court house (1830–35), all classical buildings. Works in Limerick included the county gaol (1817–22), Bael's Bridge (1831), Athlunkard Bridge (1833), and Thomond Bridge (1837).

In 1823 James Pain was appointed architect to the board of first fruits for the ecclesiastical province of Cashel, responsible for all the churches and glebe houses within the jurisdiction. He continued to work for the board, which was replaced by the ecclesiastical commissioners in 1833, until at least 1843. Assisted by George Richard he built many new churches, some—such as St John's, Buttevant, co. Cork (1826)—on a cruciform plan but most of them simple rectangular halls with a tall tower at the west end and ornamented with needle-sharp pinnacles. Between the 1820s and the 1840s he surveyed all the existing churches in the province of Cashel, some of which had been built to his own designs; these survey plans and elevations, bound into six volumes, are preserved in the library of the Representative Church Body, Dublin. George Richard designed several Catholic churches, including the Gothic Holy Trinity Capuchin Church, Cork (begun 1832) and the classical St Patrick's, Cork (1836). For the Church of Ireland in Cork he made classical alterations to Christ Church (1828) and designed St Luke's, Summerhill (1837), in a Tudor Gothic style.

George Richard Pain died in Cork, where he lived, on 26 December 1838 at the age of forty-five and was buried at the church of St Mary Shandon in Cork. James lived on for many years in Limerick, where he died at his home, 17

Upper Glentworth Street, on 13 December 1877, aged ninety-seven. He was buried four days later at St Mary's Cathedral, Limerick.

W. A. van S. Papworth, *rev.* A. M. Rowan

Sources [W. Papworth], ed., *The dictionary of architecture*, 11 vols. (1853–92) • D. Scott Richardson, *Gothic revival architecture in Ireland* (1983), 126–48, 202–8, 224–5 • *The Builder*, 35 (1877), 1303–4 • *The Builder*, 100 (1911), 769–73 • *CGPLA Eng. & Wales* (1878)
Archives Representative Church Body Library, Dublin, church drawings
Wealth at death under £8000: probate, 23 Jan 1878, *CGPLA Ire.*

Pain, James Charles (*bap.* **1836**, *d.* **1923**), fireworks manufacturer, was baptized on 20 November 1836 at St Mary's parish church, Lambeth, the son of William Pain, pyrotechnist, and his wife Eliza, who were then living at Walnut Tree Walk, Lambeth. Although James Pain was the founder of the business named after him, he was seventh in descent from a Pain mentioned in the *London Gazette* in 1670 as a gunpowder seller.

Pain was probably apprenticed to his father, who would have trained him in the increasingly sophisticated science of pyrotechnics. Although fireworks themselves are of ancient Chinese origin, and were used in crude form in medieval times in Europe to celebrate military victories, more specialized kinds of fireworks, such as the Catherine wheel, are first recorded only in the eighteenth century, and it was not until the nineteenth century that new ingredients, such as magnesium and aluminium, could be added to the staple gunpowder base to achieve a colourful and brilliant display.

On 26 November 1855, at the church where he was baptized, Pain married his first wife, Mary Ann Craig, a musician's daughter, also of Lambeth. They had six sons and three daughters.

About 1860 Pain set up his own fireworks business at 20 Albion Place (later Heygate Street), off Walworth Road, south-east London. Following a fire at the premises in 1864, however, he moved to no. 10 in the same street, and later to no. 15. On 29 September 1873 Pain took a lease on 121 Walworth Road, and at about the same time opened a factory at Brixton, subsequently transferring the works to a new factory in Mitcham about 1878. It was at this stage that he added the manufacture of marine distress flares to the production of conventional fireworks.

Pain made many visits abroad in the course of his business, travelling to New York, Australia, and Portugal, among other places. In Portugal he was awarded the order of knight of the order of Christ for services to the Portuguese royal family. While on his travels he married his second wife, Elizabeth Ramsay, *née* May, a Scot, his first wife having died on 12 September 1884. Pain subsequently moved to Argyll Lodge, Atkins Road, Balham, and Elizabeth Pain died there in 1902, leaving her estate to her daughter from her first marriage.

By the early 1920s Pain had seen his firm grow into manufacturers of, and contractors for, illuminations and decorations at several towns and sites, while the chief company works at Mitcham covered over 200 acres, with branches at Manchester, Liverpool, and Gravesend. He died of cystitis and acute orchitis on 12 October 1923 at his home, 56 Moyser Road, Streatham, leaving the business in the hands of his sons Philip, in England, and Henry, in the United States. He was buried at Mitcham parish church.

Adrian Room

Sources private information (2004) • history of Pain family, Pains-Wessex Schermuly Ltd [unreferenced] • m. cert. • d. cert. • A. St Hill Brock, *A history of fireworks* (1949) • A. St Hill Brock, *Pyrotechnics: the history & art of firework making* (1922) • parish records (baptism), St Mary's, Lambeth, 20 Nov 1836
Wealth at death £13,492: administration with will, 3 Dec 1923, *CGPLA Eng. & Wales*

Pain [*née* Taylor], **(Florence) Nesta Kathleen** (**1905–1995**), broadcaster and author, was born on 27 July 1905 at 6 Normanton Avenue, Toxteth Park, Liverpool, the daughter of Harold Taylor, shipbroker, and his wife, Frances Jane Williams. Her family had long been prominent in Liverpool: her grandfather had been an archdeacon, and her uncle, Sir Francis Kyffin Taylor, later Lord Maenan, was presiding judge of the court of passage. She was educated at West Heath School, Liverpool, and at Liverpool University, where she took a first-class honours degree in classics and played lacrosse at county level. She then went to Somerville College, Oxford, to study for a doctorate in comparative philology. On 25 March 1926 she married Coard Henry Pain, a 39-year-old surveyor and valuer, in the Wirral Register Office in Cheshire. Shortly afterwards, having given birth to a daughter, she abandoned academe to look after their child in Liverpool.

Nesta Pain's creative work really started at this stage. Although she gave private coaching in classics, her main interest was in the theatre. She became closely involved with the Liverpool Playhouse and wrote two plays: *The Jews of York*, produced in 1938 by the Sunday Theatre Society at the Duchess Theatre in London, and *Services Club*, produced in 1941 by a repertory company in Llandrindod Wells. In the following year (having separated from her husband) she left Liverpool and travelled with her fifteen-year-old daughter to London, a city much in danger of air raids. It must have seemed a reckless move. On 9 February 1942, however, Pain joined the BBC and began writing and producing programmes both for the external services and for domestic audiences. Two programmes in particular—*Insect Invader* on illness caused by tsetse flies, and *War Against Disease* on sleeping sickness—led her to become extremely interested in scientific matters. She wrote and produced a range of programmes in collaboration with many leading scientists, including, for example, Sir Alexander Fleming, who advanced the discovery of penicillin, Professor F. G. Donnan, the discoverer of Donnan's equilibrium, and Sir Archibald McIndoe, the plastic surgeon, who allowed her to attend some of his operations on badly burned airmen.

In 1947 Pain was given a permanent staff contract at the BBC and for the next twelve years played a major role in the features department. Under the distinguished leadership of Laurence Gilliam, who maintained proudly that the feature 'was the one unique form that radio has achieved in its short history' (Briggs, 702), Pain variously wrote, produced, and directed an enormous range of talks, features, and plays, mainly for the Home Service but also many for the Third Programme and some for the Light Programme. In 1957, after many attempts, she persuaded John Mortimer to write his first play for radio: *The Dock Brief*. In *Clinging to the Wreckage* (1982), the first volume of his autobiography, he described how, to his lasting benefit, he met Pain and how 'she turned out to be a remarkable woman' who 'talked precisely, but with a slight stammer, and seemed like an enlightened, extremely intelligent headmistress' (Mortimer, 127). *The Dock Brief* won that year's Italia prize. In 1956 Pain was seconded to the television service where she wrote, produced, or directed several programmes, including two documentaries—*Result of an Accident* and *Portrait of Man*—and Simon Raven's military drama-documentary *A Move up Country*.

In the early 1960s, Sound Broadcasting (as BBC Radio was called) was undergoing major changes, and the features department was closed in 1965. In the previous year Pain had resigned from her post as producer with the department and had taken a part-time post as scriptwriter–producer with the programme contracts department. In her new role she continued to produce an impressive range of programmes. These included serialized versions of the life of Queen Victoria, with Dame Peggy Ashcroft as the queen, *War and Peace* (a star production of the 1960s), and plays on the love lives of Byron and Nelson. She also wrote three books: two on English royalty, and one on insects.

In her seventies Pain had severe problems with her sight and found reading almost impossible, but after an operation partly restored her vision she started work on a book entitled *The Price of Freedom*, seeking to explain why England had never suffered from tyranny. In her final years, when confined to bed after a fall, she kept her mind active by learning English and Latin poetry and reading the newspapers every morning. She died of bronchial pneumonia at the Chelsea and Westminster Hospital, London, on 23 July 1995, and was later cremated. She was survived by her daughter. RICHARD HEWLETT

Sources A. Briggs, *The history of broadcasting in the United Kingdom*, 4 (1979), 686–720; 5 (1995), 341–350 • D. G. Bridson, *Prospero and Ariel: the rise and fall of radio* (1971), chap. 10 • J. Mortimer, *Clinging to the wreckage: a part of life* (1982), 227–30 • *The Times* (25 July 1995) • *The Independent* (27 July 1995) • b. cert. • m. cert. • d. cert. • staff records, BBC WAC

Archives BBC WAC, MSS | SOUND BBC Sound Archives Library?

Likenesses photograph, *c*.1939, repro. in *The Times* • photograph, repro. in *The Independent*

Wealth at death £80,103: probate, 18 Dec 1995, *CGPLA Eng. & Wales*

Pain, William (*fl.* 1743–1794), writer on architecture, described himself variously as an architect, carpenter, and joiner. Almost nothing of his professional or private life is known, but it is safe to assume that his great success as an author of pattern books made him an influential figure in eighteenth-century building practice, both in Britain and North America. His first book, *The Builder's Companion, and Workman's General Assistant* (1758), was co-published by the London printseller and publisher Robert Sayer. Like most of Pain's subsequent output, this substantial folio was intended to instruct builders and craftsmen who wished to work in one or other of the prevailing styles (Palladian, rococo, or Gothic). A minimum of text accompanies a large number of technical illustrations. *The Builder's Pocket-Treasure* (1763), containing the first known architectural engravings by Pain's future publisher Isaac Taylor, was a smaller book of the same kind. In its preface Pain claims more than twenty years of professional experience and states that in his course of work he had 'executed almost every Part of the Book himself'.

A decade later, when Taylor's firm began marketing a series of new books by Pain, he was sufficiently abreast of fashion to be of significant help in diffusing the so-called Adam style (named after the architect brothers Robert and James Adam). In *The Practical Builder* (1774), *The Carpenter's and Joiner's Repository* (1778), and *The Carpenter's Pocket Directory* (1781) Pain concentrated on his principal area of expertise, that of wood construction. His reputation established, he then published independently *The Builder's Golden Rule* (issued in parts, 1780–81; with a supplement, 1782), *The Practical Measurer* (1783), *Pain's British Palladio* (1786), *The Practical House Carpenter* ('second edition', 1788; 1st edn untraced), and *The Builder's Sketch Book* (1793). The title-pages of these books indicate that Pain lived in London at 3 Little Red Lion Court, Charter House Lane, near West Smithfield, from 1782 to 1786; at 12 Fisher Street, Red Lion Square, Holborn, from 1787 to 1793; and at 1 Diana Place, New Road, opposite the west end of Fitzroy Square, in 1794.

Most of Pain's books were published in several editions, often improved with an unusual degree of care by the author for at least the first few years after their initial appearance. *Pain's British Palladio*, his most ambitious work, included designs by his son James Pain, described as a builder and surveyor. It may have been this family partnership that allowed the father to advertise his willingness to build the houses he featured at the listed prices.

It was undoubtedly the number and clarity of Pain's illustrations for all kinds of structural and decorative woodwork that made these pattern books popular in America, where the existence of numerous copies can be traced from 1760 onwards, and where four of Pain's titles were reprinted before 1800. *The Practical House Carpenter*, his most successful work, had the rare distinction of being reprinted both in Boston (1796) and Philadelphia (1797). Unlike its predecessors it shows roof trusses complete with purlins and wall plates rather than as isolated frames, and it was this kind of advance in technical illustration, rather than any great innovation in building techniques, that made Pain's books useful in New England even as they were being superseded in Britain by the works of the architect Peter Nicholson. Pain was last noticed in 1794, and his date and place of death are unknown. GERALD BEASLEY

Sources Colvin, *Archs.* • E. Harris and N. Savage, *British architectural books and writers, 1556–1785* (1990) • P. W. Nash and others, eds.,

Early printed books, 1478–1840: catalogue of the British Architectural Library early imprints collection, 3 (1999) • W. Pain, *The builder's pocket treasure* (1763) • D. T. Yeomans, 'Early carpenters' manuals, 1592–1820', *Construction History*, 2 (1986), 13–33 • J. G. Schimmelman, *Architectural books in early America* (1999)

Paine, Charles Hubert Scott- (1891–1954), designer of aircraft and motor boats, was born at New Shoreham, Sussex, on 11 March 1891, one of three sons of Henry Paine, an ironmonger, and his wife, Roseanna Scott. He and his brothers later added their mother's family name to their own. From his earliest youth Paine had a passion for the sea and ships and he is said to have run away to sea from school in the best tradition. In 1910 he had a short flight in an aeroplane and this was the start of an equal enthusiasm for the air. In 1912 he met Noel Pemberton Billing, who was already active in aviation, and in the following year Scott-Paine joined Pemberton Billing Ltd on its formation to manufacture seaplanes at Woolston, Southampton. This company, which later became Supermarine, concentrated from the beginning on flying boats—seaplanes with hulls which performed the dual functions of accommodation and flotation. The first Supermarine product, an advanced but unsuccessful flying boat with circular-section hull, was displayed at the fifth Aero Show held at Olympia in 1914. Following the outbreak of war the prototype of a landplane scout was designed and built in the remarkably short time of eight days. This was followed by a number of other experimental aircraft of unusual design.

When Pemberton Billing joined the Royal Naval Air Service in 1914 Scott-Paine became the firm's general manager. In 1916 Pemberton Billing entered parliament and sold his interest in Supermarine, transferring some of his shares to Scott-Paine, who became managing director. For the rest of the war, under government control, Supermarine manufactured in quantity a successful series of flying boats. It also produced several experimental seaplanes to Admiralty designs. In 1919, 1922, and 1923 Scott-Paine entered Supermarine seaplanes for the international Schneider Trophy races. Victory in 1922 and three successive Supermarine victories some years later were finally to win the contest outright for Britain in 1931 with John Boothman as pilot.

In 1919 Scott-Paine opened a flying boat airline service to the Isle of Wight, and, in the following year, one between Southampton and Le Havre. These experimental services did not long survive but in 1923 Scott-Paine and James Bird, who had joined Supermarine in 1919, founded the British Marine Air Navigation Company Ltd. This pioneer airline operated regular services from Southampton to the Channel Islands with Supermarine flying boats and became one of the four constituent companies in the national airline, Imperial Airways Ltd, formed in 1924. Scott-Paine remained on the board of Imperial Airways until it was itself absorbed into British Overseas Airways Corporation after the latter's formation in 1939.

Scott-Paine left Supermarine in 1923, when it passed into the control of outside interests. He and a colleague then bought the boatyard of May, Harden, and May at Hythe near Southampton, and there in 1927 founded the British Power Boat Company Ltd, of which he remained chairman for the rest of his life. His enthusiasm for the sea was given greater scope in the new company, and he was able to concentrate entirely on the fascinations of producing and racing high-speed motor boats. A skilful boat driver, he won many races and made records himself.

The most famous of Scott-Paine's boats, *Miss Britain III* (preserved in the National Maritime Museum), was the first really successful all-metal motor boat and the first to be powered with an aero-engine. From this boat were developed the Royal Navy's motor torpedo boats and motor gunboats and the RAF's rescue launches which rendered notable service during the Second World War. Shortly before the war started Scott-Paine took one of his boats to the United States and the Electric Boat Company of Bayonne, New York, undertook the manufacture of similar craft for the US Navy. Scott-Paine then settled in Greenwich, Connecticut, and formed the Marine Design and Engineering Development Corporation and the Canadian Power Boat Company Ltd. After the war he was associated with the Sea Beaver Corporation at Greenwich which successfully marketed fast pleasure boats and later became a supplier of patrol torpedo boats to the US Navy.

Scott-Paine was a burly, good-natured, exceptionally energetic man, with a will to get things done. His farsightedness stimulated the early development of marine aircraft and their later application to air transport. He made a significant contribution to the inauguration of the airline industry and was one of the most important figures in the development of the modern high-speed motor boat, by initiating the hard-chine boat of high power-to-weight ratio which owed much to aircraft design and construction techniques. His sound engineering common sense and, particularly, his practical eye for good hull design contributed to the success of the early Supermarine aircraft and later to that of his motor boats. It also helped him to make full use of engineers like R. J. Mitchell, who joined Supermarine as Scott-Paine's personal assistant in 1916, became chief engineer in 1919, and later designed the Spitfire and other outstanding aircraft. Scott-Paine was a born salesman and this quality almost as much as their intrinsic merits was perhaps responsible for the success of his boats.

Scott-Paine was first married between the wars but was later separated from his wife. He married a second time in 1946, to Margaret Dinkeldein; they had a son and three daughters. He died on 14 April 1954 at his home, Smythe House, Shore Road, Greenwich, Connecticut.

P. W. Brooks, *rev.*

Sources *The Aeroplane* (9 Oct 1953) • *The Aeroplane* (30 April 1954) • *Flight* (18 April 1940) • *Flight* (2 Oct 1953) • *Flight* (29 Jan 1954) • *Flight* (30 April 1954) • C. G. Grey, *British fighter planes* (1941) • C. G. Grey, *Seaflyers* (1942) • J. F. T. Jane, ed., *Jane's all the world's aircraft* (1913–23) • private information (1971) • *The Times* (17 April 1954), 9a • *DNB*

Wealth at death £89,263 15*s*. 9*d*.—in England: administration with will, 17 March 1955, *CGPLA Eng. & Wales*

Paine [Payne], **James** (*bap.* **1717?**, *d.* **1789**), architect, can probably be identified with the infant of that name baptized on 9 October 1717 at Andover, Hampshire, the youngest in the family of three sons and two daughters of John Paine (*d.* 1727), carpenter, of Andover, and his wife, Jane Head (*bap.* 1684). The date is compatible with the statement in his obituary of November 1789 that he died 'in his 73rd year' (*GM*, 1153), and the location with his remark in a letter to Sir William Chambers that, on his journeys to Wardour Castle in Wiltshire, he passed through the town where he was born. However, little is known of Paine's early life. In the preface to the first volume of his collected designs he stated that 'he began the study of architecture in the early part of his life, under the tuition of a man of genius ... the late Mr. Thomas Jersey' (Paine, 1.i); but Jersey (*d.* 1751) is an obscure figure, a builder or surveyor who is known only as having later acted as clerk of works for the building of the Radcliffe Camera in Oxford. More significantly, Paine appears to have studied in London at the St Martin's Lane Academy, an institution founded by William Hogarth in 1735 to enable artists to practise life drawing—and Paine was later said to have attained considerable skill in drawing the human figure. Here he would have come into contact with a number of the period's most innovative designers, and more particularly with the architect Isaac Ware, who was in charge of the academy a few years later, in 1739. He then appears to have become known to the circle of the third earl of Burlington, an introduction which was presumably due to Ware, and to have started on his career from this point. His first professional task, which he received at the age of nineteen, was to supervise the erection of Nostell Priory, Yorkshire (*c.*1737–1750), a large country house designed by Colonel James Moyser, a friend and follower of Lord Burlington.

Career While Paine was still engaged on this project, and living in the nearby town of Pontefract, he was commissioned to design a prominent public building in the area, the Mansion House at Doncaster, Yorkshire (1745–8); from these beginnings he developed during the 1750s a large country-house practice in the north and north midlands, which he appears to have extended from Yorkshire to the north-east by taking over the north-country practice of Daniel Garrett, another associate of Lord Burlington, who died in 1753. His patrons in the region included the first duke of Northumberland at Alnwick Castle, Northumberland (*c.*1754–1768), Lord Burlington's son-in-law the fourth duke of Devonshire at Chatsworth, Derbyshire (1756–66), the ninth duke of Norfolk at Worksop Manor, Nottinghamshire (*c.*1758–1767), and the fourth earl of Scarbrough at Sandbeck Park, Yorkshire (*c.*1763–1768). As early as 1746, however, he returned to live in London, and his practice was never wholly confined to the north. From the mid-1750s onwards he also established a significant presence in London, beginning with a large town house in Whitehall, for Sir Matthew Featherstonhaugh (1754–8). From the end of the decade, following his contact with the duke of Norfolk, he received further major commissions from Roman Catholic patrons, notably at the ninth Lord

James Paine (*bap.* 1717?, *d.* 1789), by Sir Joshua Reynolds, 1764 [seated, with his son, James]

Petre's Thorndon Hall, Essex (1764–70), and the eighth Lord Arundell's Wardour Castle, Wiltshire (1770–76). In the final phase of his career during the 1770s and 1780s he erected a number of bridges in the Thames valley, the finest being that over the Thames at Richmond, Surrey (1774–7). It was this extensive and varied output which prompted Thomas Hardwick's well-known observation of 1825, that Paine and Sir Robert Taylor 'nearly divided the practice of the profession between them, for they had few competitors till Mr. Robert Adam entered the lists' (Chambers, xlviii–xlix). Hardwick's comment does also raise the question of the extent to which Robert Adam's rise to fame in the 1760s had an adverse impact on Paine's career; and it was in the north that the effect was most marked, with Adam supplanting him at Kedleston Hall, Derbyshire, early in the decade and at Alnwick Castle in 1768. But the atrophying of his northern practice was compensated for by developments elsewhere and Paine's personal prosperity appears to have been on the increase throughout this period; by the later 1770s he was able to move towards an affluent semi-retirement and the life of a country gentleman.

Alongside his private practice Paine also pursued a career in the office of works; but this aspect of his professional life can hardly be regarded as having been a success, as promotion to a senior position, commensurate with his standing in the profession, proved elusive. His first appointment, in January 1745, was as clerk of the works at the Queen's House at Greenwich—a post he is said to have owed to the patronage of a former surveyor-general, the Hon. Richard Arundell, another close associate of Lord

Burlington. In December 1746 he was promoted to the clerkship at the Royal Mews at Charing Cross, but in August 1750 he exchanged posts with Kenton Couse for the almost sinecure clerkship at Newmarket and in March 1758 he also became clerk of the works at Richmond New Park Lodge. At that time, however, he had hopes, with the support of Richard Arundell, of succeeding Thomas Ripley as comptroller of the works, but the post went to the older and longer-established Henry Flitcroft; and an even more serious disappointment came two years later, when, in spite of the support of the earl of Northumberland and Sir Rowland Winn of Nostell, he failed to secure one of the two newly created posts of architect to the works. It was only in December 1780 that he was belatedly appointed to one of these positions, and in a final stroke of irony the posts were abolished two years later under Burke's reform of the civil service.

Works In 1755–6 Paine made a tour of Italy, visiting Rome and apparently the Veneto, but the visit does not seem to have played a very significant part in his artistic development. In the preface to his *Plans, Elevations and Sections of Noblemen and Gentlemen's Houses* (1767) he criticized the fashion for foreign travel among architects and the age's developing obsession with archaeological precedent, emphasizing the importance of practical convenience rather than the pursuit of 'inconsistent antiquated modes' and dismissing the architecture of the Greeks as 'despicable ruins' (Paine, 1.ii). He nevertheless valued highly the 'new and striking' in architecture, but his own considerable originality was achieved almost entirely within the framework of English Palladianism. He was a pioneer of the compact, centrally planned Palladian villa as a country-house form, in particular exploiting the practical and visual potential of the central top-lit staircase and the practical advantages of the 'villa with wings'. At the same time he developed a lively and individual elevational style, based on the 'staccato' isolation of architectural components found in the work of Lord Burlington and William Kent. For a number of his villas he adopted a hallmark formula in which coupled pilasters at the angles were combined with a subsidiary cornice linking the heads of the piano nobile windows, while early experiments with interlocking pediments on the model of Palladio's Venetian church façades were succeeded by striking tripartite compositions derived from Kent's triple-pedimented wings at Holkham Hall, Norfolk. His distinctive repertory of smaller-scale details—mainly derived from a single source, Kent's *Designs of Inigo Jones* of 1727—included empty niches, splayed window surrounds, open pediments, and vestigial cornice-strips. These characteristics are or were to be found in a sequence of works including Heath House, near Wakefield, Yorkshire (1744–5)—his first independent commission as an architect—Kirkstall Grange, Yorkshire (1752), Serlby Hall, Nottinghamshire (1754–73; remodelled 1812), Belford Hall (*c*.1755–1756), and Gosforth Hall (1755–64; altered 1880 onwards), Northumberland, Stockeld Park, Yorkshire (1758–63), Bywell Hall, Northumberland (*c*.1760), and Hare Hall, Romford, Essex (1768–70).

Paine's greater houses of a more traditional non-villa type were by contrast relatively few in number, the principal examples being the uncompleted Worksop Manor (1761–7; demolished 1843), where he combined a palatially expanded version of the main block of Holkham Hall with a central 'Egyptian hall' on the model of Lord Burlington's at the York assembly rooms; and Sandbeck Park, Yorkshire (*c*.1763–1768), and Thorndon Hall, Essex (1764–70), which are both variants on Colen Campbell's Houghton Hall, Norfolk. In two designs, however—his proposals for Kedleston Hall, Derbyshire (1759), and Wardour Castle, Wiltshire (1770–76)—he used the Palladian villa form for a house of the largest size, the logical consequence of the progressive development of the villa idea. At Kedleston, as one of several different architects involved in the project, his part in the finished building was not extensive, but Wardour represents the real climax of his career, the juxtaposition of its great circular staircase hall and the quadrant form of the wings suggesting a creative revision of Palladio's unexecuted circular-salooned villa design for the Trissino brothers in the light of the practical requirements of English country-house design. His individual manner was also displayed in some of his urban buildings, notably the Middlesex Hospital, London (1755–78; dem. 1925), his second major public building, and his redevelopment of Salisbury Street, off the Strand, London (1765–73; dem. *c*.1923), a speculative venture where in the riverward frontage he ingeniously combined a tripartite grouping with the quadrant form. On a small number of occasions he appears to have absorbed influences from beyond his normal range of sources, notably at the Gibside Chapel, co. Durham (1760–66), his only free-standing ecclesiastical structure, and in the staircase at Brocket Hall, Hertfordshire (*c*.1770). The former appears to represent a fusion of Palladio's Pantheon-inspired Tempietto at Masèr and the Greek-cross-in-square form used by Christopher Wren in a number of the City churches; while the latter, with its free-standing columns carrying isolated blocks of entablature, is reminiscent of the interior of James Gibbs's church of St Martin-in-the-Fields, London.

Paine also made a contribution to mid-eighteenth-century Gothic. His most substantial projects in this manner were reconstructions and modernizations of actual medieval buildings, at Raby Castle, co. Durham (*c*.1753–1760; altered *c*.1870), and Alnwick Castle, Northumberland (*c*.1754–1768; reconstructed 1854–8), where practical convenience rather than either antiquarian scholarship or an appreciation of the style's pictorial or emotive qualities was evidently the prime consideration; but even so some of his details appear to be the fruit of a close observation of authentic Gothic design. For his interior decoration Paine adopted in his early years the rococo style which had been pioneered in England in circles close to the St Martin's Lane Academy; but he combined such enrichment with elements of Palladian detail, and in his chimneypieces in particular (a speciality of his, for which from the 1760s he maintained his own craftsmen and workshop) he endowed conventional Palladian formulae with a new lightness and delicacy. Examples of this manner are at Nostell Priory, the Doncaster Mansion House, Wadworth Hall, Yorkshire (*c*.1749–1750), and Felbrigg Hall, Norfolk (1751–6). Later, however, conceding only that 'Palmyra and Baalbec' were 'valuable for the ornaments' (Paine, 1.i–ii), he devised a variant on the type of neo-classical decoration popularized by Robert Adam, examples of which are in the ballroom at Sandbeck Park and the Temple of Diana at Weston Park, Staffordshire (*c*.1770). He also favoured the Kentian combination of plasterwork and decorative painting, the most notable instance being the saloon at Brocket Hall (1771–3).

Other professional activities For a number of years Paine was a leading member of the Society of Artists of Great Britain, showing many of his designs at the society's annual exhibitions between 1761 and 1772, as well as serving as a director from the same year and as its president in 1770–72; and during his presidency he designed its Exhibition Room in the Strand, London (1771–2; dem. 1815), a project which was undertaken on his initiative. The circumstances surrounding this undertaking, however, were controversial. In 1768 the society had split and the Royal Academy had been founded by the defecting group led by William Chambers, and the Exhibition Room quickly proved to be an ill-affordable luxury; at the end of his presidency, with the society still losing ground to the new body, Paine himself abandoned it. However, the story that the original schism was the result of rivalry between Paine and Chambers is without foundation, and although he was to exhibit at the Royal Academy only once, in 1783, Paine's relations with Chambers were always a model of professional propriety—as was his attitude to his principal successor in the north, John Carr of York. Paine was also one of the first English architects to take articled pupils on a regular basis, among whom were Christopher Ebdon, John Eveleigh, John Kendall, and Charles Middleton; while John Woolfe served as his assistant during the 1750s. In 1751 he published his *Plans, elevations, sections and other ornaments of the mansion-house, belonging to the corporation of Doncaster* and subsequently two volumes of his collected designs, *Plans, Elevations and Sections of Noblemen and Gentlemen's Houses*, the first in 1767 and the second in 1783, when a second edition of the first volume was also issued; but perhaps because of the unfashionable opinions which were trenchantly expressed in the preface of the 1767 volume, they were not in general directly influential among the architects of the following generation.

Residences, family, and death On becoming based in London Paine lived at the Royal Mews and then from 1750 in Holles Street. In 1754 he remodelled a large house in St Martin's Lane as his residence, then in 1768 he moved into one of the new houses of the redeveloped Salisbury Street. In 1773 he bought the lease on a country estate, Sayes Court, near Chertsey, Surrey, where he is said to have made additions to the house 'in the Elizabethan style' (Papworth, 6.8) and to have formed a fine collection of architectural drawings. In his role of country gentleman he then became a justice of the peace for Middlesex in December 1776 and for Surrey in June 1777, and served as high sheriff of Surrey in 1785. He was married twice, first in March 1741 to Sarah Jennings, daughter and coheir of George Jennings of Pontefract, and second, by June 1748, to Charlotte Beaumont (1722–1766), youngest daughter of Richard Beaumont of Whitley Beaumont, near Huddersfield. With his first wife he had a son, the architect, sculptor, and topographical watercolourist James *Paine (1745–1829), and with the second two daughters, the younger of whom married the painter Tilly Kettle. In 1789, 'finding the infirmities of age steal fast upon him, and a family occurrence of a singular nature preying upon his spirits' (*GM*, 1153), Paine retired to France, where he died a few months later in the autumn of that year. The nature of the 'family occurrence' is not recorded.

PETER LEACH

Sources P. Leach, *James Paine* (1988) • Colvin, *Archs.* • E. Harris and N. Savage, *British architectural books and writers, 1556–1785* (1990) • J. Paine, *Plans, elevations, and sections of noblemen and gentlemen's houses*, 2 vols. (1767–83) • *GM*, 1st ser., 59 (1789), 1153 • M. Binney, 'The villas of James Paine', *Country Life*, 145 (1969), 406–10, 466–70, 522–6 • W. Chambers, *A treatise on the decorative part of civil architecture*, ed. J. Gwilt (1825) • office of works minute books, PRO, Works 4/11 • [W. Papworth], ed., *The dictionary of architecture*, 11 vols. (1853–92), vol. 6 • parish register, Andover, 9 Oct 1717 [baptism]

Archives BL, Add. MSS • Nostel Priory, Yorkshire, Nostel Priory MSS • RA, papers relating to Society of Artists • RA, corresp. with Ozias Humphry • Raby Castle, co. Durham, Raby Castle MSS • Sandbeck Park, Yorkshire, corresp. and accounts with Lord Scarbrough for alterations at Sandbeck Park, Lumley Castle, and Downing Street • W. Yorks. AS, Leeds, letters to Sir Roland Winn • Wilts. & Swindon RO, Arundell of Wardour MSS

Likenesses J. Reynolds, double portrait, oils, 1764 (with his son, James), AM Oxf. [*see illus.*] • D. P. Pariset, engraving, 1769 (after P. Falconet) • D. P. Pariset, stipple, pubd 1795 (after P. Falconet, 1769), BM, NPG • C. Grignion, engraving (after F. Hayman), repro. in J. Paine, *Plans, elevations, sections and other ornaments of the mansion house, belonging to the corporation of Doncaster* (1751)

Wealth at death wealthy; £5000 each to daughters as marriage settlements; remainder in trust for son's children: will, PRO, PROB 11/1192, sig. 260

Paine, James (1745–1829), architect, sculptor, and artist, was baptized at Pontefract, Yorkshire, on 28 August 1745, the only child of James *Paine (*bap.* 1717?, *d.* 1789), architect, then of Pontefract, subsequently of London, and his first wife, Sarah Jennings. Like his father before him, he studied at the St Martin's Lane Academy and as early as 1761 started exhibiting watercolours at the Society of Artists of Great Britain; and he trained as an architect with his father, assisting the latter in supervising the erection of Thorndon Hall, Essex, which was begun in 1764. He visited Rome on two occasions, the first in 1766–9, when he also spent some time sketching in the Campagna, and in Venice, where he made the acquaintance of the celebrated connoisseur Consul Joseph Smith; the second, with his wife in 1773–5, when he made a number of measured drawings and other studies of buildings in and around the city (J. Paine sketchbooks, V&A). In 1771 he was elected a fellow of the Society of Antiquaries, and he was one of the original members of the Architects' Club, founded in 1791. On 16 August 1773 he married Elizabeth Crow; they had four children, a son who died young and three daughters. Before his marriage, after leaving his father's house in 1772, he had lived in King Street, Covent Garden; and by 1776 he was living in Charlotte Street, Marylebone. By 1788 he had moved to North End, Hammersmith, and by 1809 to a 'model cottage' at Sunninghill, Berkshire.

In relation to two of the three media which he essayed, however, Paine's career was essentially a failure. Regarding his work as a sculptor, his friend the artist Joshua Green commented in 1776 that 'he cannot now flatter himself of ever getting anything but Chips in the Phidian Art' (Green to Humphrey, 10 Dec 1776, Royal Academy, Ozias Humphrey MS HU 2/47), and it never amounted to much more than a small group of chimney-pieces and funerary monuments, mainly executed in the 1770s. As an architect, even more starkly, he has only a single executed commission credited unambiguously to his name, a villa called Belmont at Mill Hill, Middlesex, of *c*.1770, which was evidently deputed to him by his father; and the main reason for this state of affairs was a serious and prolonged estrangement from the latter, which began shortly after the Mill Hill commission. There followed only a sequence of rejected or otherwise abortive proposals and optimistic exhibition projects, and at the most mere scraps of executed work; and by the time the breach was healed, in 1783, his father was virtually in retirement and no longer had an active practice to pass on. So in the 1790s he appears to have abandoned his attempts to establish himself in this field also and turned instead to the third string in his bow, that of topographical painting, in which he seems to have achieved a modest success. A sketchbook inscribed 'J. Paine Rome 1776' containing Italian views is in the Victoria and Albert Museum.

Paine's Belmont is nevertheless a building of some interest, a creative variation on his father's manner, notable features of which include a virtuoso sequence of varied room shapes. In his subsequent projects he adopted a rather different idiom, examples being the designs for a stable block and a pavilion at Ugbrooke, Devon (1779), in a visionary neo-classical style, and an ambitious scheme for residential development on the marquess of Salisbury's Thames-side estate at Millbank, Westminster (1787–9). Of his works of sculpture the most substantial are the monument to the actor William Powell in Bristol Cathedral (1771) and an elaborate chimney-piece embellished with caryatids for Brocket Hall, Hertfordshire (*c*.1773), designed and executed in conjunction with his father's reconstruction of the house. Of his achievement as a topographical artist it is not possible to form a just estimate owing to the dearth of identified examples, but in 1809 Joseph Farington recorded a comment on 'Payne's best manner', that he 'has a little too much manner, and does too much' (Farington, *Diary*, 10.3564). A 'worthy little man' in Joshua Green's estimation (Green to Humphrey, 10 Dec 1776, Royal Academy, Ozias Humphrey MS HU 2/47), he died at Sunninghill in May 1829, aged eighty-three, and was buried there on 12 May. W. A. VAN S. PAPWORTH, *rev.* PETER LEACH

Sources P. Leach, 'James Paine, junior: an unbuilt architect', *Architectural History*, 27 (1984), 392–400 • P. Leach, *James Paine* (1988) • RA, Ozias Humphry MSS • Farington, *Diary*, 6.2083, 2406–7; 7.2741; 9.3449, 3490–91; 10.3564; 11.3864–5; 13.4657, 4679 • Colvin, *Archs.* • *The exhibition of the Royal Academy* [exhibition catalogues] • will, PRO, PROB 11/1758, sig. 438 • J. Paine, sketchbooks (1766, 1774), V&A • Graves, *RA exhibitors* • Graves, *Soc. Artists* • R. Gunnis, *Dictionary of British sculptors, 1660–1851*, new edn (1968) • J. Ingamells, ed., *A dictionary of British and Irish travellers in Italy, 1701–1800* (1997)

Archives BL, Add. MSS • V&A, sketchbooks | Hatfield House, Hertfordshire, Salisbury MSS

Likenesses J. Reynolds, double portrait, oils, 1764 (with his father), AM Oxf.; *see illus. in* Paine, James (*bap.* 1717?, *d.* 1789) • D. Berger, line print, 1773 (after J. Reynolds), NPG • G. Romney, portrait

Wealth at death property in Yorkshire, Surrey, and Middlesex; leasehold properties in west London; also shares in Sun Life Assurance and other funds: will, PRO, PROB 11/1758, sig. 438

Paine, Robert Treat (1731–1814), lawyer and revolutionary politician in America, was born on 11 March 1731 in Boston, Massachusetts, the son of Thomas Paine (*d.* 1757), merchant and clergyman, and his wife, Eunice Treat, a member of the established and prominent New England family. Paine, whose father became a successful merchant after leaving his church at Weymouth, Massachusetts, in 1730, enjoyed the privileges of the Boston élite. He spent seven years at the élite Latin school in School Street, which was next to his family's mansion, and when he entered Harvard College in 1745, the institution ranked him socially higher than the majority of his classmates. Paine excelled at his studies, voluntarily attending upperclassmen lectures in divinity and mathematics.

Paine's social security was threatened about the time of his graduation from Harvard in 1749, when his father's business failed. Left to make his own way in the world, he pursued a variety of careers which included positions as a teacher and as a chaplain to a militia regiment. He tried his hand at salvaging his father's mercantile interests in the 1750s, trading in North Carolina, the Azores, and Spain. He even gathered a shipment of whale blubber from Greenland. Paine ultimately decided on the law, studying with Benjamin Prat. He was called to the Suffolk county, Massachusetts, bar on 6 May 1757; this marked the beginning of a long and distinguished career. He first tried to establish himself in Boston but, sensing too much competition, left for Taunton, Massachusetts; it was the seat of Bristol county and had only one other practising lawyer. In 1763 he became justice of the peace for that county. On 15 March 1770 he married Sally (*b. c*.1754), daughter of Colonel Thomas Cobb, with whom he had eight children. Paine, who always preferred the pleasures and company in Boston to that of the smaller Massachusetts towns, first entered the arena of radical politics as one of the lawyers hired by the town to prosecute the British soldiers involved in the Boston massacre, in which troops fired on a riotous crowd on 5 March 1770. The case brought marked the first confrontation in what proved to be a lifelong rivalry between Paine and John Adams. Adams, who, although a future revolutionary, successfully defended the soldiers, thought little of Paine, whose conceit and impolite competitiveness were notorious. Adams observed:

> He is an impudent, ill bred, conceited fellow; yet he has wit, sense, and learning, and a great deal of humor; and has virtue, and piety, except his fretful, peevish, childish complaints against the disposition of things. … This character is drawn with resentment of his ungenerous treatment of me, and allowances must therefore be made; but these are unexaggerated facts. (Shipton, 467–8)

In 1773 Taunton elected Paine as its delegate to Massachusetts's lower house, where he excelled and grew in political importance. In 1774 he was chosen, along with John Adams, as one of the Massachusetts delegates to the first continental congress. He was a delegate to the second session, where after war erupted he became involved with committees that organized the supply of the army. Tensions with fellow Massachusetts delegates flared in the winter of 1775–6 when Paine was appointed to a commission to visit Canada in hopes of bringing some of its inhabitants to the side of the thirteen rebelling colonies. The commission was turned by poor weather, and Paine was called back to Philadelphia, where he assumed some of the duties of John Adams, who was on leave. He set about opening what appeared to be Adams's official mail and found a letter from James Warren questioning Paine's abilities. Furious, Paine lashed out. Despite his fury, Paine remained one of Massachusetts's representatives and was a signatory to the Declaration of Independence. He was elected again to the continental congress in 1777, but declined the position and remained in Boston, where he served as a member of the revolutionary legislature. That June he became the state's attorney-general, with the unsavoury task of confiscating loyalists' property. Informing on friends and acquaintances must have been as palatable as his appointment at Harvard to turn in fellow students who used profanity. In neither case did he make many prosecutions. In 1780 he moved his family permanently to Boston, purchasing the former mansion of Governor William Shirley. That year he also became a founding member of the American Academy of Arts and Sciences. After the war he sought a federal judgeship, and even wrote a letter in 1789 to John Adams, then vice-president, requesting his favour. The request was denied, and Paine satisfied himself with accepting an appointment from his old friend and governor John Hancock as an associate judge of the Massachusetts supreme court in January 1790. He served on the court until his retirement in 1804. He died ten years later at his home, Shirley Mansion, on the corner of Mill Street and Federal Street, Boston, on 11 June 1814, and was buried in the town's Granary burying-ground. TROY O. BICKHAM

Sources C. K. Shipton, *Sibley's Harvard graduates: biographical sketches of those who attended Harvard College*, 12 (1962), 462–82 • S. Patterson, *Political parties in revolutionary Massachusetts* (1973) • W. Pencak, *War, politics and revolution in provincial Massachusetts* (1981) • E. W. Hanson, 'Paine, Robert Treat', *ANB*

Archives Mass. Hist. Soc., papers

Paine, Thomas (1737–1809), author and revolutionary, was born in Thetford, Norfolk, on 29 January 1737, the first of two children of Joseph Pain (1708–1787), stay-maker and tenant farmer, and Frances Cocke (1697–*c.*1790), daughter of Thomas Cocke, attorney and town clerk of Thetford. Paine's only sibling, Elizabeth, born a year later, died aged seven months. Paine's father was a Quaker and his mother an Anglican, and it is likely that Paine was baptized into the Anglican church, as was his sister.

Thomas Paine (1737–1809), by John Wesley Jarvis, *c.*1806–7

Early life Paine's father retained his Quaker principles and, though Thomas was confirmed, his father forbade him to learn Latin when he attended the local grammar school at the age of seven. He received a basic education, in which he showed some signs of mathematical ability and a bent for poetry; a short poem to a crow, supposedly written when Paine was eight, shows a certain prescience: 'Here lies the body of John Crow / Who once was high but now is low / Ye brother crows take warning all / For as you rise, so must you fall'. When he was twelve his father removed him from school and took him on as an apprentice.

Paine recounts, in *Rights of Man*, how, as a youth of little more than sixteen, influenced by the maritime stories of the Revd William Knowles, a master of Thetford grammar school, he enlisted on the *Terrible*, a privateer commanded by Captain Death (fitted out at execution dock and carrying on board Lieutenant Devil and Mr Ghost, the ship's surgeon). It is likely he was nearer twenty, but he was fortunate in yielding to his father's pleas to stay ashore, since the ship lost all but 26 of her crew of 200 in an engagement. Within six months he enlisted again, this time on the *King of Prussia*, also a privateer, but one which enjoyed considerably greater success. The exact movements of Paine at this time are uncertain. Either between his privateering bouts, or subsequently, he worked in London for John Morris, a stay-maker on Hanover Street, Long

Acre, in Covent Garden. Some biographers suggest that Paine's later account in *Age of Reason*, that he attended the scientific lectures of Benjamin Martin and James Ferguson, refers to this period, but he may equally refer to other times spent in London, especially in 1773, which fit more exactly with the little evidence available and with his memory. In the spring of 1758 he worked for the staymaker Benjamin Grace in Dover, and the following year established his own business in Sandwich, where he is reputed to have taken up as an occasional Methodist preacher. On 27 September 1759 he married Mary Lambert (*d.* 1760), who died in childbirth the following year after the couple moved to Margate following business difficulties.

After his wife's death Paine resolved to abandon the stay-making business and sought a career in the excise, the occupation of his wife's father. He returned home to live with his parents while he learned the skills of the trade at the hands of Henry Cocksedge, recorder of Thetford. He was accepted into the service and received a first appointment to Grantham in December 1762, moving subsequently to Alford, also in Lincolnshire, in August 1764. His career was cut short in August 1765 when he was dismissed from his post for 'stamping'—certifying examinations not actually made. He was forced to resume staymaking, finding work at Diss under a Mr Gudgeon, from where he wrote apologizing to the excise board. He was reinstated on 4 July 1766 but had to await a new posting. In the interim he taught first at a school run by Daniel Noble in Mill Yard, Leman Street, Goodman's Field, London, and then from January 1767 in a school in Kensington run by a Mr Gardiner. His teaching seems to have kept him adequately provided for, since he was able to turn down an excise post in Grampound, Cornwall, in May 1767 in the hope of finding something closer to London. This is the longest period Paine spent in the capital, and it may have been at this time that he developed his scientific interests. On 19 February 1768 he accepted the post of excise officer in Lewes, where he took up lodgings with Samuel Ollive, an innkeeper, and his family, eventually sharing with them in the setting up of a tobacco mill to supplement his income. Paine settled comfortably in Lewes. His name appears alongside Ollive's in records of the town's governing body and he was a vocal member of the local debating club, known as the Headstrong Club, where he developed a reputation as an obstinate haranguer. He was also known as a player of bowls and as a skater, with his skills earning him the nickname the Commodore. His friend from this period, Thomas 'Clio' Rickman, described him as of about 5 feet 10 inches, rather athletic, and broad-shouldered. His eye 'was full, brilliant and singularly piercing', and had in it the 'muse of fire'. He was cleanly dressed, 'wore his hair cued with side curls and powdered and looked altogether like a gentleman of the old French school' (Rickman, xv). In manners he was easy and gracious, his knowledge was universal and boundless, and while in private company he was fascinating, in mixed company he was reticent and was no public speaker. Paine's political views were whig: he was 'tenacious of his opinions which were bold, acute, and independent, and which he maintained with ardour, elegance, and argument' (ibid., 38). Although he subsequently claimed that America had made him an author, biographers agree that he wrote several poems, a mock drama, *The Trial of Farmer Carter's Dog Porter*, and some prose pieces, several of which he published a few years later in America. In one of the most stable periods of his life he lived for 'several years in habits of intimacy with a very respectable, sensible, and convivial set of acquaintance, who were entertained with his witty sallies and informed by his more serious conversations' (ibid.).

Samuel Ollive died in July 1769, leaving his widow, Esther, and daughter, Elizabeth, in poor circumstances. For propriety's sake, Paine took up lodgings elsewhere, but the following year he joined the Ollives in opening a shop, and on 26 March 1771 he married Elizabeth (*c.*1749–1808) who was at least ten years his junior. The following year he was nominated to press the excisemen's case for improved pay and conditions in London. He wrote his first political pamphlet, *The Case of the Officers of Excise*, and late in 1772 travelled to London. He corresponded with Oliver Goldsmith and developed (or expanded) his acquaintance with members of scientific circles, including John Bevis and George Lewis Scott. It is also possible that his acquaintance with Benjamin Franklin dates from this visit. In the cause of the excisemen he was unsuccessful. He failed to have the matter brought before parliament, and the petition he carried with the signatures of some 3000 excisemen was ignored. He returned to Lewes in mid-April 1773 to face the collapse of his business affairs. Little or nothing is known of Paine in the year subsequent to his return, but the following April he received a double blow, being dismissed from the excise on 8 April 1774 for 'having quitted his business, without obtaining the Board's Leave for so doing, and being gone off on account of the Debts which he hath contracted', and being forced to sell off by auction on 14 April 'all the household furniture, stock in trade and other effects … also a horse tobacco and snuff mill, with all the utensils for cutting tobacco and grinding off snuff' (Conway, *Life*, 1.29–30). Moreover, in May 1774 Paine and his wife separated, with a formal document being signed on 4 June 1774. Twenty years later the separation generated extensive prurient speculation, with reports that the marriage was not consummated, but Paine remained characteristically reticent: 'It is nobody's business but my own: I had cause for it, but I will name it to no one' (Rickman, 47). The settlement gave Elizabeth her full inheritance from her father and left her free to trade. The April sale must have left Paine with some money, since we have no record of him working between April and October, when, carrying a letter of introduction from Benjamin Franklin, he paid for a berth on a ship to America. Early biographies of Paine, especially the deeply hostile lives by Francis Oldys (George Chalmers) and James Cheetham, were often maliciously inventive in their reconstruction of Paine's first thirty-seven years, ascribing his first wife's death to his cruelty and accusing him of a variety of fraudulent practices. Despite his friendship with Paine, Rickman is no more informed about the early years. Subsequent biographers devoting space to this period of Paine's life have compensated for the paucity of evidence by literary licence and speculation. What is clear is that Paine's early life was not a success and that he was probably heartily glad to leave England behind him and to embark on a new set of challenges in the new world.

The writing of *Common Sense* (1776) When his ship docked in Philadelphia on 30 November 1774 Paine had to be carried off on a stretcher. He was so weakened by acute seasickness and putrid fever that it took him several weeks to recover. Franklin's letter introduced him to his son-in-law, Richard Bache, who sought pupils for him to teach, and he also became acquainted with Robert Aitkin, in whose Front Street bookshop he frequently browsed. Aitkin offered to employ him as the editor of a new journal he was planning, the *Pennsylvania Magazine*, for an annual salary of £50. Aitkin proposed to leave the detailed editorial work to Paine while retaining the right to control the policy and content of the magazine. Paine's contributions have been much disputed as none appears under his name and various pen names were used, but he wrote between seventeen and twenty-six pieces for it over the following eighteen months, including an essay against slavery which brought him an introduction to Benjamin Rush, and pieces on the deaths of Wolfe and Clive which raised issues of British colonial policy that were highly pertinent given the growing tensions between Britain and her American colonies. Paine's developing literary reputation introduced him into political circles in Philadelphia, through which he became acquainted with the issues of the day and many of the leading activists. As he later commented, he 'thought it very hard to have the country set on fire about my ears almost the moment I got into it' (Conway, *Life*, 1.55–6). After growing tension between Britain and the Americans, active conflict broke out in April 1775 with skirmishes between British troops and American militiamen at Lexington and Concord. A second continental congress was called in May, at which further moves towards reconciliation with Britain were made. However, these too failed, and by December the colonies were openly denying parliament's right to rule them directly, while continuing to look to George III as their protector and king.

In the autumn of 1775, encouraged by Rush, Paine began work on a pamphlet putting the case for independence. Although he read aloud drafts to Rush and showed a completed draft to David Rittenhouse, Benjamin Franklin, and Samuel Adams, the work was wholly Paine's—except for the title, for which Rush claimed credit. The result, *Common Sense*, 'written by an Englishman', was the most widely distributed pamphlet of the American War of Independence, and has the strongest claim to have made independence seem both desirable and attainable to the wavering colonists. Paine's ability to write in accessible prose, and to convey his beliefs as simply the promptings of common sense, was coupled with his insistence that the issues between Britain and America were of universal import. This was not a little local difficulty. Rather,

> the cause of America is in a great measure the cause of all mankind … 'Tis not the concern of a day, a year, or an age; posterity are virtually involved in the contest, and will be more or less affected, even to the end of time, by the proceedings now. (*Complete Writings*, 1.3, 17)

It is a universal cause because America remains the providentially chosen asylum for liberty while Europe crumbles into despotism. Society, Paine announces in the opening paragraphs of the pamphlet, 'in every state is a blessing, but government even in its best state is but a necessary evil; in its worst state [it is] an intolerable one' (ibid., 1.4). People are driven into society by the multiple benefits it brings; government only becomes necessary as vice develops, and it best serves the end of protecting freedom and security by taking a representative and republican form. The much vaunted constitution of England is an amalgam of pure republican elements with the remains of monarchical and aristocratic tyrannies, which are wholly incompatible with the preservation of freedom. Government by kings runs contrary to the natural equality of man, ''Tis a form of government which the word of God bears testimony against, and blood will attend it' (ibid., 1.16). This is what has happened in America: following the commencement of hostilities in April, all plans for reconciliation must be jettisoned and Americans must recognize that they are dealing not with a 'mother country' but with a tyrannical oppressor. Moreover, America cannot reap a single advantage from reconciliation which could not be had from independence, while 'the injuries and disadvantages we sustain by that connection, are without number' (ibid., 1.20). 'Reconciliation is *now* a fallacious dream', since, citing Milton: 'never can true reconcilement grow where wounds of deadly hate have pierced so deep' (ibid., 1.23). Having shown that the obvious and necessary step is independence, Paine sketches a plan of self-government for the country, which is to begin from a continental conference to frame a continental charter and a government 'securing freedom and property to all men, and above all the free exercise of religion'. In contrast to Europe, 'in America THE LAW IS KING' (ibid., 1.29).

The pamphlet appeared on the same day as news of the king's intransigent response to the colonists' petitions arrived in Philadelphia and was able to turn widespread dismay at the king's failure into a recognition that monarchical government was simply not to be trusted. The success of the pamphlet was unparalleled. Rival second editions appeared within a matter of three weeks, and Paine turned against his publisher, Robert Bell, whom he accused of pirating a second edition. Seven editions appeared in Philadelphia alone, with other cities also producing editions from the beginning of February. Despite this, Paine made no money by the pamphlet, and probably financed an edition from his own resources to promote circulation. His objective was to ensure that the argument for independence should be spread throughout America. By April 1776 he was claiming that 120,000 copies had been sold, and he later gave a figure of 150,000 for America alone. It is unlikely that he greatly exaggerated: Rush, in July 1776, recalled:'Its effects were sudden and extensive upon the American mind. It was read by public men, repeated in clubs, spouted in Schools, and in one instance, delivered from the pulpit instead of a sermon by a clergyman in Connecticut' (*Autobiography of Benjamin Rush*, 114–15). The pamphlet also produced a flood of criticism, beginning with James Chalmers's *Plain Truth*, some resisting independence while others, such as John Adams's highly influential *Thoughts on Government*, offered more nuanced and subtle criticism of his enthusiasm for simple, democratically elected and centralized government. Overnight Paine became a controversialist, embarking on a series of essays (signed The Forester), engaging with some of the criticisms raised against his arguments for independence, and becoming embroiled in both local Philadelphia politics and those around the continental congress based there. On 2 July congress declared independence, and on 4 July it approved Thomas Jefferson's declaration (in which some have thought Paine had a hand).

American patriot A few days later Paine joined a body of Pennsylvania volunteers who marched towards New York. The anticipated British attack never materialized, and Paine spent the summer as secretary to Daniel Roberdeau, the commander of the flying camp. When it was disbanded he travelled to Fort Lee and served as aide-de-camp to General Nathanael Greene, who became a close friend. He also served as a field correspondent, puffing American successes in small skirmishes and supporting the decisions of Greene and Washington despite their frequent military blunders. The retreat of Washington's army towards Trenton and Philadelphia at the end of 1776 produced despondency in those who six months before had been enthusiastic for independence. When Paine visited Philadelphia he found the people in a 'deplorable and melancholy condition … afraid to speak and almost to think, the public presses stopped, and nothing in circulation but fears and falsehoods' (*Complete Writings*, 2.1164). To rouse their spirits he produced *The American Crisis*, the first of thirteen letters designed to muster the American people to the cause and to set straight the record of military affairs. It is a resounding piece of political rhetoric, with as powerful an opening as any political pamphlet published:

> These are the times that try men's souls. The summer soldier and the sun-shine patriot will, in this crisis, shrink from the service of his country: but he that stands it *now*, deserves the thanks of man and woman. Tyranny, like hell, is not easily conquered: yet we have this consolation with us, that the harder the conflict, the more glorious the triumph. What we obtain too cheap, we esteem too lightly; it is dearness only that gives everything its value. (ibid., 1.50)

Tradition has it that Washington ordered the pamphlet to be read aloud to the troops on the evening of Christmas day before the battle of Trenton.

With the American War of Independence Paine had found a cause and an apposite voice with which to advocate it. In reinventing himself as an American patriot, Paine discovered a gift for articulating the hopes and fears of ordinary men and women in ways which revealed to them their higher purpose as Americans. John Quincy Adams later described Paine as having 'no country, no affections that constitute the pillars of patriotism' (Hawke, 33). Some of Paine's comments encourage such a view—in his *Crisis No. 7* he insisted 'my principle is universal. My attachment is to all the world, and not to any particular part' (*Complete Writings*, 2.146), and his concern for America was a concern for the principles it represented—liberty, security, and republican government (which he understood as representative democracy and the sovereignty of the people). He never wavered in his commitment to these principles, but nor did he ever doubt that America offered the greatest hope for their realization. His writings during the War of Independence, including *The American Crisis* and subsequent *Crisis* essays, were often directed at particular events and matters of local importance, but he rarely failed to lift the issue onto the larger stage of the cause of freedom against the despotism of England and its corrupt monarchy.

Paine also became still more practically involved in the struggle, coupling his need to make some money with his commitment to the cause by accepting a job as secretary to a congressional commission to treat with Native American peoples on the Susquhanna. In March 1777, when congress returned to Philadelphia, he was appointed secretary of a new committee for foreign affairs. This relatively undemanding post left him time to work on a projected history of the American War of Independence for which he was collecting materials. Late in the summer, when the British landed in Delaware Bay and marched towards Philadelphia, defeating the Americans at Brandywine Creek on 11 September, Paine was forced to pack his papers and quit the city. After a brief stay with his friend Colonel Joseph Kirkbride in Bordentown, New Jersey, he set off to find Washington's army, arriving during the battle of Germantown. He stayed only a few days, but returned in October after Timothy Matlack, secretary of Pennsylvania's executive council, suggested he act as an observer to ensure a more constant intelligence of Washington's army. Over the next six months Paine divided his time between visits to Valley Forge, where the army waited out the winter, the hospitality of Kirkbride's house, and, after January 1778, William Henry's home in Lancaster, where his reported indolence caused considerable resentment among those more active in the cause.

In the spring of 1778, following British proposals for peace and the prospect of a political treaty with France, Paine's optimism grew. With French support, he believed, the Americans could bring the war to a close. Although the British proposals were inadequate they vacated Philadelphia, and in June congress returned to take up its business there. Paine's energies also revived: *The American Crisis*, number 6, in October 1778, attacked the British peace proposals, and was followed in November by number 7, explaining why the British would never conquer the

Americans and inciting the British to overthrow their government. In December he also wrote a series of letters defending the unicameral form of the Pennsylvanian constitution, something which he had first commented on over a year previously in his *Candid and Critical Remarks on a Letter signed Ludlow* (1777).

Paine's responsibilities as secretary had not been onerous, and it may well have been intended as a sinecure, but he was encouraged by friends to see it in a larger light, leading his detractors to accuse him of styling himself 'secretary of foreign affairs'. His sense of the importance of his office led to the first major set-back in his American career. Silas Deane was one of three commissioners (with Franklin and Arthur Lee) with responsibility for securing financial support under cover of a commercial treaty with France. The covert nature of the gift of arms and supplies enabled Beaumarchais, who headed the company which acted as a front for the arrangement, to demand payment from congress. When Deane wrote from Paris supporting Beaumarchais's claim against congress for 4.5 million livres he was ordered home to report. On his arrival in Philadelphia in the summer of 1778 opinion rapidly polarized between those who accepted his claim to have been a loyal servant of American interests and those who saw him as profiteering. With his knowledge of the secret arrangements with France, Paine felt obliged to attack Deane, but his veiled accusations were perplexing for observers and infuriated Deane's supporters, who physically attacked Paine on the street on two occasions. None the less, he maintained a stream of letters attacking both Deane and mercantile interests in congress for profiteering. Broadening his attack increased his enemies and blunted the force of his main claim. Moreover, in claiming that the supplies from France were a gift, Paine betrayed a secret which was extremely embarrassing to France. The French minister, Conrad Gérard, flatly denied the gift and demanded that congress repudiate Paine's allegations. When congress complied Paine offered his resignation, but refused to apologize. After several days of intense debate congress, by the narrowest margin, accepted his resignation, sparing him the indignity of dismissal. Gérard, rather surprisingly, then offered Paine a large sum (Paine claimed it was in excess of £700) to write supporting French interests and the alliance with America. Paine refused, but seemed mollified until he discovered that Gérard had thanked congress for their repudiation of Paine's 'false and dangerous insinuations' (Hawke, 92). He sought a retraction from Gérard and, on failing, secluded himself in his rooms, shunning all company and writing eight further pieces to vindicate his conduct in the affair and establish Deane's culpability. The affair gradually subsided, but it was not until two years later, when Deane wrote a series of letters encouraging American union with Britain, that his supporters finally questioned Deane's integrity.

Paine's seclusion ended when financial difficulties led him to accept a job as clerk in Owen Brindle's merchant office. He also accepted appointment to two committees to scrutinize Robert Morris's business affairs. He returned to print in the summer of 1779 with a series of letters defending America's Newfoundland fishing rights. The rights were a source of contention in negotiations with Britain, and Gérard and others believed that insisting on them would only prolong the war. During the controversy Whitehead Humphreys, a local merchant, penned a series of vicious attacks on Paine until he was lectured firmly on the freedoms and duties of the press by Paine's supporters. In November he was fully rehabilitated when he was appointed as clerk to the Pennsylvania assembly, and in the following year he was awarded an honorary MA from the University of Pennsylvania.

Military financier Paine was convinced that a principal obstacle to American success was inadequate federal finance. A few days before the dramatic surrender of General Lincoln and some 5000 American troops at Charleston in May 1780, he drew out the salary he was owed as clerk and sent half of the sum, $500, to Blair M'Clenaghan as a priming contribution for a voluntary subscription fund to support the recruiting system. As a result a permanent securities subscription was established, which developed into the Bank of North America and supplied the army throughout the rest of the war. The bank, and the subscription initiative, exemplify Paine's conviction that the interests of the poorer and wealthier classes were essentially identical and that each could be prevailed upon to contribute their due to the war effort. The same conviction informed his *Crisis Extraordinary* in October 1780, in which he argued for the acceptance of higher rates of taxation to support the war. The land claims of Virginia to the western territories also drew him into controversy, partly because Maryland (a small state with no adjacent territories) refused to ratify the articles of confederation without limitations being placed on territorial claims, thereby leaving America without a constitution, and partly because it opened the possibility of raising federal income. Drawing heavily on information supplied by the Indiana Company, Paine's *Public Good* (1780) argued that the western territories should be recognized as the property of the federal government, and might accordingly be sold to support the war effort. The pamphlet turned many Virginians against Paine, and his acceptance of shares and cash from the Indiana Company led to allegations of his being a company hireling.

Paine also sought more practical involvement in the conflict. He asked congress to support him on a secret mission to England to write encouraging efforts for peace and recognition of American independence, thereby following up suggestions in *Crisis No. 8* that the conflict be somehow brought onto British soil. Late in the day he was dissuaded by friends who feared that, if caught, the British would use him as a reprisal for the American execution of the spy Major André. However, he welcomed the suggestion of Colonel John Laurens, the son of Paine's friend Henry Laurens, the former president of congress, that he act as his secretary while special envoy to France. When objections were raised in congress to Paine acting in an official capacity, he agreed to go as Laurens's companion, paying his own expenses. They sailed in February 1781, with an eventful voyage encompassing icebergs and the liberation of a Venetian merchantman from a Scottish cutter. In France Paine made a number of new acquaintances. Franklin's grandnephew, Jonathan Williams, found him 'a pleasant as well as sensible man' (Aldridge, *Man of Reason*, 87). Elkanah Wilson, on the other hand, described him as 'coarse and uncouth in his manners, loathsome in his appearance, and a disgusting egoist, rejoicing most in talking of himself and reading the effusions of his mind' (Hawke, 116). Moreover, Wilson claimed he was filthy of appearance, awkward and unseemly in address, and that he stank from being treated for scabies—a fault Wilson cured by insisting Paine took a bath. In Paris, Paine had little social life, being received only at Franklin's (then American ambassador) and at Laurens's hotel. Laurens's trip was successful (although credit for this seems best placed with Franklin) and they returned to America in August with substantial funding.

Paine returned penniless: he had no income and claimed to have spent all his savings. Because of his financial plight and his sense that he was unappreciated, he talked of quitting America for Europe, where he hoped to live by his pen. However, Robert Morris wrote to him in September 1781 encouraging him to write in support of taxation for funding the war, and over the next six months Paine and Morris reached an agreement whereby congress paid him $800 per annum to urge state legislatures to allow the federal government sufficient tax income and to press for the extension of federal powers (the first fruits of which were his *Six Letters to Rhode Island*, 1782–3). Paine needed the money, but he was advocating a cause to which he was already publicly committed. He also regarded the payment as part compensation from congress for the fact that he had neglected his own interests by publishing without thought of personal profit. On several occasions he pressed both Morris and Washington for official financial recognition of his services to the revolution. It also seems likely that he received some payment from the French ministry. Barbé de Marbois, the French chargé d'affaires, reported in April 1782 that Paine had published nothing since his return from France without previously consulting La Luzerne (Gérard's successor as French minister to America), and it is likely that *Crisis No. 11* was a result of French encouragement, repudiating as it did the possibility of America making a peace with Britain independently of her allies France and Spain.

Paine's projected history of American Revolution never materialized. La Luzerne claimed he was too indolent for such a task and it is true that his forte lay elsewhere. However, the work he had done doubtless contributed to his decision to write a refutation of the Abbé Raynal's *A Philosophical … History of the … Indies*, the last volume of which was published in translation in 1781 and dealt with the American War of Independence. Paine objected to Raynal's claims that the war arose entirely from a dispute over taxation and that peace efforts had been hampered by the Americans' alliance with France. His *Letter to the Abbé Raynal, on the Affairs of North America* (1782) is an exemplary piece of diplomacy, carefully establishing the self-driven character of the American War of Independence and implicitly denying a special significance to France's involvement. It is also an immensely optimistic work, which insists that the American cause cannot be understood wholly in pragmatic terms, but is evidence of a progressive enlightenment which is bringing man from barbarism to civilization. Commerce is central to this process: just as it once formed men into societies to furnish their wants and harmonize their interests, so too will it operate between nations, when guided by reason rather than the interests of despotic regimes, to end war through the emergence of universal society of mutual benefit. The *Letter* did much to secure Paine's European reputation; it also earned him both gratitude and financial reward from the French minister.

Post-war years, 1783–1790 When the war finally ended Paine required a means of subsistence. On Robert Morris's advice, he drew up a letter to congress outlining his services and suggesting that if congress were to make him financially independent he could undertake a history of the war. A committee was appointed to consider his suggestion and recommended he be appointed official historian, but congress took no action. In June 1784 the New York assembly presented him with a farm in New Rochelle confiscated from a tory, but similar initiatives in the Virginia assembly failed because of local opposition. Following further letters from Paine, congress agreed in October to pay him $3000 for his services, and the following March Pennsylvania set aside £500 as a temporary recompense for Paine, while referring to congress the matter of any further grant. Paine bought a farm in Bordentown, near his friend Colonel Kirkbride, having decided to rent out the New Rochelle property. Hope of further support from Pennsylvania was ended by conflicts over the Bank of North America and the issue of paper currency in the aftermath of the war. The assembly sought to repeal the bank's charter following its opposition to issuing paper currency. Paine remained a staunch defender of the bank and its charter, and in February 1786 published *Dissertation on Government: the Affairs of the Bank: and Paper Money*, followed by a number of letters amplifying his position. Many of his contemporaries saw Paine's defence of the bank as a reactionary and élitist move, and assumed he had been paid to champion the interests of property against those of the people, but his position is consistent with his belief in the independence of financial institutions and the dangers of paper currency. In the course of his defence Paine insisted both that sovereignty could not bind successive generations (a key principle in his *Rights of Man*) and that contracts between the state and particular individuals (such as charters) could not subsequently be revised without the consent of both parties. On Paine's account the assembly was acting unconstitutionally in attempting to repeal the charter.

Once established at Bordentown, Paine's interests turned towards scientific experiments. He was invited by Washington to stay near Princeton, where they spent a day investigating marsh gas in a local creek, and he experimented on a smokeless candle with Franklin. His energies were increasingly absorbed, however, on his plans for a single-span bridge, constructed in sections from iron and designed to span large distances without the use of piers. Late in 1785 he hired John Hall, a carpenter and mechanic recently emigrated from England, to work with him on a model of the bridge which he hoped to persuade the Pennsylvania assembly to build across the Schuylkill river. He may well have drawn his ideas from models he had seen on his trip to France, where proposals for single-arched iron bridges had recently been discussed at the Royal Academy of Sciences. Paine's design was distinctive in constructing the arch on the model of a spider's web, on the grounds that 'when Nature enabled this insect to make a web, she taught it the best means of putting it together' (Aldridge, *Man of Reason*, 109). Hall and Paine began with models made from wood, and in May 1786 set to work on a model in iron. In December he took a single-arched model of wrought iron to Franklin's house and demonstrated it first to Franklin and subsequently to the Pennsylvania assembly. The cost of building a bridge of iron was high, American foundries being small, and although the assembly discussed the project no action was taken. This discouraging response, combined with a long-standing sense on Paine's part that he was inadequately appreciated in his adopted land and had little role to play in the newly constituted republic, determined him to take his model to France to solicit expert opinion and find financial backing to build the bridge. He sought letters of introduction to members of the French court from Franklin and embarked for France in April 1787.

Paine landed in Le Havre in May 1787 and set off for Paris. His letters of introduction brought him into contact with French scientific circles, and he renewed his acquaintance with Thomas Jefferson (now American minister in Paris). He presented his model to the Academy of Sciences in July, which reported favourably at the end of August. Paine then left France to visit his parents, while Jefferson and Lafayette continued to encourage the government to use his design for a bridge across the Seine. He returned to Paris briefly in December and, once back in England, sent Jefferson a proposal for financing the bridge in France, asking him to read it and, if appropriate, have it translated and communicated to the ministry. The search for finance for the bridge continued until the summer of 1788, when Paine decided to concentrate on securing support in Britain. He applied for and received letters patent and engaged the Walker brothers' ironworks in Rotherham to construct an arch of 90 feet, this being a more practical proposition than his original aspiration for a 250 foot span (and one which could be accomplished indoors). He remained in Rotherham until November 1788, when the first half was completed, and returned to London. In April 1789 he was present when the arch was assembled, to his great satisfaction. He entered an agreement with the Walkers that they should manufacture a complete bridge of 110 feet, to be erected over the Thames and then put up for sale, with proceeds being divided equally. The bridge was cast in Rotherham and shipped down to London, arriving in May 1790. It was assembled on a field halfway between Paddington and Marylebone near a public house, the Yorkshire Stingo, where Paine and his mechanic, a Mr Buel, took up residence. The bridge was completed in September 1790 and attracted public interest, along with a fair amount of criticism—not least from Gouverneur Morris, who found himself living uncomfortably close to Paine and noted that 'it is not so handsome as he [Paine] thinks it is. Qu. also whether it be as strong. It has a very light appearance however' (*Diary of the French Revolution*, 1.589). By October the wood abutments on which the bridge rested began to yield beneath the load and the metal began to rust in the poorer weather. The Walkers repossessed the ironwork and transported it back to Rotherham, and by the end of November Paine had become wholly engaged in political affairs.

When he had arrived in France in 1787, Paine had formed a friendship with the secretary of the archbishop of Toulouse, the Abbé André Morellet, to whom he had written at length on the prospects for peaceable relations between France and Britain, suggesting that there was no interest in war in either court, but that France had an enemy in the vulgar prejudices of the British. He accordingly planned a pamphlet to rectify the misunderstanding between the two peoples. Assured by Morellet of French support, Paine brought out his *Prospects on the Rubicon*, in which the British are offered a stark sense of their choice between war and its many costs, and peace and its benefits. The pamphlet is striking for its support of the French monarchy and its assertion of the common interest between the king and the people. Paine also canvassed his view that France was committed to peace with leading members of the whig opposition, including Edmund Burke, the marquess of Lansdowne, Charles James Fox, and the duke of Portland, claiming that he was 'in pretty close intimacy with the heads of the opposition' (*Complete Writings*, 2.1276). He hoped for the fall of the Pitt government, believing he would be well placed to act in the capacity of American ambassador to England should the opposition attain power, and he watched closely the unfolding of the regency crisis during the illness of George III in early 1789. Through visits and correspondence he remained well informed about developments in France, and his membership of Lafayette's circle led to him being entrusted with conveying the key of the Bastille to President Washington—a symbol of the common view that America's revolution had provided the spark for change in Europe.

***Rights of Man*, 1791–1792** In January 1790 (before Burke's February speech on the army estimates which publicly signalled his abhorrence of the revolution) Paine was engaged in writing an account of the French Revolution. He also corresponded extensively with his English contacts (including Burke), informing them of French affairs. On both counts he drew heavily on letters from Jefferson. When Burke declared his intention of publishing an attack on the French Revolution Paine committed himself to answering it, and the material he had been preparing was put to this purpose (although there is some indication that he also tried to publish something in French to influence events through Lafayette in the summer of 1790). Burke's *Reflections on the Revolution in France* appeared in November 1790; Paine's response, *Rights of Man*, was printed by Joseph Johnson for publication on 21 February 1791, then withdrawn for fear of prosecution. J. S. Jordan stepped in and published it on 16 March.

Rights of Man opens by taking issue with Burke's understanding of the settlement following the revolution of 1688. Paine counters Burke's insistence that the British people had submitted themselves and their posterity forever to the crown with the claim (broached in his *Dissertations on Government* of 1786) that

> There never did, there never will, and there never can exist a parliament, or any description of men, or any generation of men, in any country, possessed of the right or the power of binding and controuling posterity to the *end of time*, or of commanding for ever how the world shall be governed, or who shall govern it. … Every age and generation must be as free to act for itself, *in all* cases, as the ages and generations which preceded it. (*Complete Writings*, 1.251)

Government is by the living for the living, and each age must be sovereign over its own concerns. Paine then turns to the details of the French case. Continuing to canvass his views from *Prospects*, that the interests of the monarch and his people were united, he insists that the revolution should be understood as one which attacks the despotic principles of the French monarchy, not the king himself, and he takes the Bastille to symbolize the despotism that had been overthrown, giving a detailed account of destruction of the prison and countering Burke's account of the march on Versailles by the Parisian mob. Returning to his claims about the sufficiency of the rights of each generation, he distinguishes between the natural rights man has by virtue of his existence and his equality before his creator, and the civil rights we create by which we attempt to secure those natural rights which we lack the power perfectly to enjoy. Some natural rights, such as intellectual rights, or rights of the mind, or of religious belief, are rights we have the power to enjoy without needing society's support, but where our power is defective, as in the right to redress, we deposit the natural right in the common stock of society and use society as the means to enforce the right.

Although there are intimations of this view as early as Paine's *Candid and Critical Remarks … Ludlow*, the fuller development of this position seems to have been worked out one night in France after an evening spent with Jefferson, and possibly Lafayette, discussing a pamphlet by the Philadelphia conservative James Wilson on the proposed federal constitution. On this view, and against Burke, natural rights are the ground and justification for civil rights, they are not simply given up on entering society. Moreover, against Burke's veneration of the English constitution, Paine insists that Britain has no constitution: that its government has arisen out of conquest and has never been generated by a sovereign act of the people. In contrast, the meeting of the estates general provided a convention of the people to form a constitution—which can be compared item by item with its pretended British alternative, as he does. Turning subsequently to give an account of the development of pressure for reform in France leading to the declaration of the rights of man, he suggests that a major role was played by France's involvement in the American War of Independence, though the promulgation of its principles and from the return of those Frenchmen, like Lafayette, who had fought for the Americans. In his final miscellaneous comments he develops an attack on monarchy which reiterates the critique advanced in *Common Sense*, but now emphasizes its significance for the European states of which he had earlier despaired. Quoting Lafayette, he insists that 'For a Nation to be free, it is sufficient that she wills it' (*Complete Writings*, 2.322): 'hereditary governments are verging to their decline, and … Revolutions on the broad basis of national sovereignty, and government by representation are making their way in Europe' (ibid., 1.344).

In many respects *Rights of Man* is a disordered mix of narrative, principled argument, and rhetorical appeal—betraying the composite materials Paine used and the speed with which it was composed. But the vigorous and trenchant style in which it was written accounts for its huge success. It was quickly reprinted and widely circulated, with copies being read aloud in inns and coffee houses, so that by May some 50,000 copies were said to be in circulation. Of the 300 or more pamphlets which the revolution controversy spawned, *Rights of Man* was the first seriously to damage Burke's case and to restore credit to the French both in Britain and America.

When Paine returned to France in April 1791, those who encountered him found him intoxicated by his success. Étienne Dumont recorded that: 'his egregious conceit and presumptuous self-sufficiency quite disgusted me. He was drunk with vanity. If you believed him, it was he who had done everything in America. He was an absolute caricature of the vainest of Frenchmen' (Keane, 311). Nor was his conviction in the pace of progress dimmed when he was nearly lynched by a Parisian mob for failing to wear a cockade. Indeed, recognizing the increasingly republican spirit animating the French and parting company with Lafayette's circle, especially after the royal family's flight to Varennes, he joined Brissot, Etiènne Chauvière, François du Châtelet, and Condorcet, and, with the help of Nicholas de Bonneville and François Lathenas, established a newspaper. Paine produced a republican manifesto which was translated by Châtelet printed by Bonneville, and stuck up in the streets of Paris on 1 July. Paine's sense of the common interest between the king and the people had vanished; instead, the flight to Varennes was seen as tantamount to abdication, and he insisted throughout on referring to the king as Louis Capet. Although few supported the declaration, and the Abbé Sieyès engaged Paine in debate in the *Gazette Nationale* on the virtues of elective monarchies, Paine rightly sensed that the tide was turning fast in a republican direction. Following a 4 July dinner in Paris, where Morris thought Paine 'inflated to the Eyes and big with a Litter of revolutions' (*Diary of the French Revolution*, 2.212–13), he returned to England to follow events there and in Ireland more closely, and to work on a book, *Kingship*, which he later changed to a second part of *Rights of Man*.

In England, Paine lived a relatively retired life. He stayed with Thomas 'Clio' Rickman, an old acquaintance from Lewes, and now a London bookseller, visited John Horne Tooke, who held open house for radicals at his Wimbledon home, and in August attended a meeting chaired by Tooke at the Thatched House tavern, where a manifesto written by him for Tooke, celebrating events in France and calling for reforms in England, was read and warmly received. His circles of acquaintance also spread to literary radicals such as Mary Wollstonecraft, William Godwin, John 'Walking' Stewart, and William Blake. He also searched for a publisher, since neither Jordan nor Johnson was prepared to accept the risk. Through Thomas Christie he found a Thomas Chapman who was willing to proceed but who, late in the day, sought to persuade Paine to sell him the copyright, and when he was unsuccessful claimed to have had cold feet over the content of the work and refused to proceed. Paine inferred government intervention. He was able to persuade Jordan to take up the printing, indemnifying him by writing a disclaimer in which he claimed to be the sole author and publisher of the work. With a minimum of delay, *Rights of Man: Part the Second, Combining Principle and Practice* was published on 16 February 1792.

The controversy over the French Revolution is still signalled in Paine's dedication to Lafayette and in some perfunctory comments on Burke and his *Appeal from the New to the Old Whigs* (1791) in the preface. But the introduction changes the focus dramatically by arguing that it is the American War of Independence which has inaugurated the changes which are bringing down the whole order of European despotism. In the first four chapters of the pamphlet it is America, rather than France, which is offered as exemplifying a society united by interest and ruled by a properly constituted representative government. Where in *Common Sense* government was the badge of lost innocence, Paine now treats society as so united by instinct and reciprocal benefits that it needs very little from government. 'The more perfect civilisation is, the less occasion has it for government, because the more does it regulate its own affairs, and govern itself' (*Complete Writings*, 1.358–9). Paine's attack on monarchy and aristocracy, his insistence that constitutions must arise from conventions of the people and cannot be amended by the governments which they order, and his defence of representative government as taking 'society and civilisation for its basis; nature, reason and experience, for its guide' (ibid., 1.367) are all familiar themes from his earlier writings, but they are brought together with an unequalled consistency of argument and clarity of presentation and are couched in a thoroughly trenchant, almost insouciant, language. Throughout, the American experience provides a touchstone for the practicality of republican government and the ease with which it can be established. The most innovatory arguments appear in the final chapter, when he turns to a detailed examination of the obstacles to commerce and progress in Britain, and in particular to the amount of taxation being raised. Assuming the abolition of the court and its extravagances and the pooling of military expenditure with France and America, Paine argues that government spending could be reduced from £7.5 million to £1.5 million. Rather than cutting tax rates, he proposes a reform of the taxation system together with a whole range of welfare measures. A national system of poor relief financed by taxation would replace local poor rates. Benefits would include child benefit, conditional on attendance at school; supplementary benefits for those over fifty, with a full pension at sixty; a system of maternity and death grants; education for all those in need; a fund for the accommodation and employment of the casual poor of London; and compensation for disbanded soldiers and sailors and their families. Moreover, direct taxation would be replaced by progressive taxation, to be directed against inherited wealth rather than wealth from labour.

Reactions Writing to John Hall in November 1791 Paine indicated that he was to bring out a new work which he hoped would

> produce something one way or another. I see the tide is yet the wrong way, but there is a change of sentiment beginning. I have so far got the ear of John Bull that he will read what I write—which is more than ever was done before to the same extent. (*Complete Writings*, 2.1321–2)

Paine's confidence was undiminished when he met Gouverneur Morris shortly after publication of part two of *Rights of Man*, when Morris was on his way to Paris to take up his new post as American ambassador—an appointment Paine regarded as '*a most unfortunate one*' (ibid., 2.1323). Morris recorded: 'He seems Cock Sure of bringing about a Revolution in Great Britain, and I think it quite as likely that he will be promoted to the Pilory' (*Diary of the French Revolution*, 2.368). Over the next six months, while parliamentary whigs sought to distance themselves from Paine's radicalism, the extra-parliamentary movement seized on the pamphlet as a means for mobilizing popular feeling for reform. Cheap editions combining the two parts of *Rights of Man* were published throughout the country, and societies established among members of the artisan classes, such as Thomas Hardy's London Corresponding Society, provided new means for circulating and discussing Paine's work. At the same time, government newspapers attempted to stir up feeling against Paine, and friends persuaded him to decamp to Bromley, where he stayed incognito with William Sharp, the engraver. A visit to London to attend a meeting of the Society for Constitutional Information resulted in his being arrested for a debt of Peter Whiteside an associate in his bridge scheme. He was rescued by Johnson, but the rapid appearance of the story in the press was taken by all as indicating government plotting in the episode. At the end of May, Jordan was indicated for sedition as the publisher of *Rights of Man*. Paine tried to persuade him to fight the case but Jordan chose to plead guilty and pay the fine. Two weeks later Paine was summoned to answer a charge of seditious libel, and a royal proclamation was issued ordering magistrates to seek out and prosecute those involved in writing or printing wicked and seditious writings. When asked in parliament why the government had delayed so long a prosecution against Paine, Henry Dundas (Tooke's next door neighbour) stressed the subversive character of the second part of *Rights of Man* and the determination with which it was being disseminated throughout the kingdom. However Paine refused to be cowed. He wrote an address to the Jacobin Society in Paris claiming that reform societies dedicated to freedom, peace, and the rights of man were springing up throughout the country. In June he published a series of letters, to Dundas and Onslow Cranley, reiterating his scorn for hereditary government and the need for reform, and taunting the government on its decision to postpone his trial until December. He also produced his *Letter Addressed to the Addressers of the Late Proclamation* (1792), effectively a third part to *Rights of Man*, in which he insisted that representative government relies upon a prior right of manhood suffrage—a principle he had not previously clarified (partly, it seems, to avoid drawing attention to the limits on the franchise within the French constitution). The *Letter* also set out a plan for a British convention to provide for a reform of parliament, a proposal which issued the following year in reform societies taking an increasingly confrontational attitude to the government, and subsequently in draconian sentences being handed down to delegates of the British Convention held in Scotland at the end of 1793 by Lord Justice Clerk and Judge Braxfield and in the arrest and indictment for treason of leading English radicals in the summer of 1794. Paine's only concession was to remove the paragraphs upon which his indictment for sedition was based from the six-penny edition published at the beginning of August 1792. Finally, on 13 September, only days after the September massacres, Paine left London with Achille Audibert and John Frost, took a circuitous route to Dover, where he was detained by a customs officer and searched before eventually being allowed to leave, and, seen off by a hostile crowd, caught the boat for a dramatically changed revolutionary France. He was accorded a contrastingly warm welcome when he landed in Calais.

The National Convention and imprisonment, 1792–1794 Paine had been one of seventeen foreigners accorded honorary French citizenship in August 1792, and four of the departmental electoral assemblies which met at the beginning of September had elected him as deputy to the new National Convention. Audibert had been in London to urge Paine to accept the seat for Calais and play a part in the new order, and he now conducted Paine through the obligatory ceremonies in Calais before seeing him off to attend the opening session of the convention on 21 September. It must quickly have been clear to Paine that he was out of his depth. He spoke little or no French and had to rely on a fellow deputy translating for him, and he had not grasped how dramatically the course of the revolution had changed with the elimination of the monarchy, the eruption of the sans-culottes onto the political scene, and the growing prominence of the Jacobin Club. Only days after the convention opened he sought to challenge Danton's proposal for a purge of the judiciary, only to be swept aside by the convention. Moreover, while he tried his hand at stirring addresses to the French people, it cannot be said that he showed the political nous which he had demonstrated in America or England. Above all he failed to see that the orderly constitutional process which he had believed to be central to revolution was being swept aside by forces that could no longer be controlled. Some of the forms of order remained: the convention elected him to sit on one of these, a committee of nine (including Sieyès, Condorcet, Brissot, Petion, Barère, and Danton) to design a republican constitution. But, although Paine did not recognize it, it was mainly a form. The committee was dominated by the Brissotins, and its recommendations would stand or fall according to their ability to dominate the Mountain: they failed, and of the nine members of the committee, only three survived the subsequent eighteen months. However, French success against the Prussians augured well, and the victory at Jemappes led the Brissotins to internationalize the revolution and offer aid to all oppressed people in November, and gave some grounds for Paine's continuing optimism. Sharing the Brissotin mood, Paine now saw no alternative to a revolution in England, and he said as much in an open letter to Archibald MacDonald, the prosecutor in his trial *in absentia* in December 1792, at which he was outlawed.

The Brissotins had resisted bringing the king to trial, but the discovery of incriminating documents in his former apartments in the Tuileries made this position untenable. Paine acknowledged this in his moderate discussion of the issues in *On the Propriety of Bringing Louis XVI to Trial*, but he also sought to save the king's life. After a bare majority had voted for execution, Paine sought to press for detention not execution (with Bancal reading a translation of his speech). Marat shouted him down on the grounds that he was a Quaker, and further interruptions by Marat and Thuriot challenged the accuracy of the translation being read and wrecked any chance of his plea finding support.

The king's execution opened the French Revolutionary War, and the Brissotins' power began to crumble. The draft constitution, whose 368 articles and 85 pages ran against Paine's preference for simple structures, was shelved, and Paine's increasing distance from affairs was physically signalled by his move to a house in St Denis, a remote and quiet section of Paris, from which he watched the revolution begin to consume its own leadership. He sought to help the Brissotins when Marat was impeached by reporting a comment Marat made to him when they had first met belittling Paine's belief in republican government, but the initiative failed, and then became dangerously compromising when a fellow boarder, William Johnson, attempted suicide, leaving a note accusing Marat of seeking to extinguish the very liberty he had come to France to enjoy. Although Brissot reported Johnson's dying words, Johnson erred by surviving, and Marat turned the trial into a powerful endorsement. Paine was also involved in the trial of General Miranda, whom he had known in America and who was charged with failing to rally troops at the battle of Neerwinden—on this occasion the charge was being prosecuted by the Jacobins in the hope of discrediting the Brissotins who championed Miranda. Paine was involved solely as a character witness, Miranda was acquitted, but Paine had again come to the attention of the increasingly powerful Jacobins.

On approaching the National Convention on 31 May 1793 Paine was advised by Hanriott, the captain of the guard, to use his deputy's card for hair curlers, and Danton warned him not to go in. Three days later the convention voted to suspend and imprison twenty-two Brissotin members, but these did not include Paine. A few days later a deputation from Arras congratulated the convention on its decision, denounced Paine for his association with the Brissotins, and announced that he no longer represented the interests of the department of Calais. Although he seldom attended the convention, he remained willing to try to use his influence where he could, supporting on one occasion a number of American seamen detained in Bordeaux. Indeed, in the summer of 1793 Barère consulted him on the advisability of sending commissioners to America to seek an alliance in the war with Britain. Paine supported the proposal, warning Barère against trusting Gouverneur Morris, who was neither favourable to the French nor well liked in America. A memorandum from Barère's office proposed Paine as one of the commissioners to be sent to America, and Paine worked hard to bring the two nations closer, with Barère crediting him with responsibility for shipments of rice and grain which came from America in 1794. But the proposal came to nothing, and much as Paine wished to return to America (despite news in April that his New Rochelle house had burnt down) he took no active steps to do so. Within three months Barère had denounced Paine in the National Convention. On 27 December the committee of public safety ordered Paine's arrest; a memorandum among Robespierre's papers noted that it was 'for the interests of America as well as of France' (Aldridge, *Man of Reason*, 205), which has encouraged some commentators to think that both Morris and Robespierre wanted Paine out of the way. He was arrested at the Hotel Philadelphia and was required to deliver up his papers. This took all day, and involved Audibert as translator and Joel Barlow as an independent witness, but the soldiers found nothing suspicious. Indeed, they allowed him to hand over to Barlow the manuscript in English of *The Age of Reason* before escorting him to the Luxembourg prison. Three weeks later a group of American citizens led by Barlow petitioned the convention for Paine's release, but found no support. The issue of Paine's citizenship seemed to become pivotal. As a French or British citizen he would be wholly at the mercy of the convention; if American, his government would have a legitimate interest in his case and would have some weight with the French. After representation from Paine, Gouverneur Morris wrote to Defourges, the minister for foreign affairs, stating that Paine had taken American citizenship during the American War of Independence, although admitting that he had subsequently been accorded French citizenship and had been elected as a member of the National Convention. Deforges treated Paine's election as overriding any claims he might have had as an American. Conway's biography of Paine was deeply critical of Morris for his inactivity, but without real cause. Morris's conduct, which Conway attributes to his deep dislike of Paine, derived from his view that if Paine kept his head down while in prison, he might contrive to keep it on.

In prison Paine managed to produce (and to convey to Daniel Isaac Eaton, the radical London publisher) a dedication for *The Age of Reason* and a new edition of the *Rights of Man* with a new preface. Other essays written in prison, including one on Robespierre, did not survive, but he successfully maintained a poetic correspondence with an anonymous lady (whom he subsequently learned was the wife of his friend the banker Sir Robert Smyth), who signed herself 'a little corner of the world' to complement his 'the castle in the air'. Conditions in the prison deteriorated during the terror, and after six months Paine contracted a severe fever which rendered him semi-conscious for several weeks. He was cared for by the prison doctor, Markoshi, and two British inmates, Dr Graham, a physician, and Mr Bond, a surgeon, who successfully brought him through to give him the news of Robespierre's overthrow and execution. Within two weeks Paine was writing to the convention and to the committee of public safety, as were his friends, and when he learned that Morris had been replaced by James Monroe he immediately urged him to take up his case, producing a forty-three page memorial to Monroe insisting on his citizenship. Monroe reassured Paine that he was regarded as an American and entitled to his services, and after he wrote to the convention asking them either to bring Paine to trial or release him the papers were signed for his release. He was delivered from custody on 4 November 1794 and brought to Monroe's house to stay as long as he wished. A month later Antoine-Claire Thibaudeau rose in the convention and successfully proposed that Paine be restored to his seat.

Although Paine played little role in the remaining days of the convention he did adapt a pamphlet written two years earlier in support of his case for eliminating the property qualification for voting from the new constitution. He attended the convention for the first time since his imprisonment in June to have his speech read to his fellow deputies. *Dissertation on the First Principles of Government* (1795) is essentially an epitome of his case in *Rights of Man* and provides an extremely clear and uncluttered statement of his mature views on government. The case for universal manhood suffrage was not, however, obvious to a convention which had been driven by the fury of the Parisian mob over much of the preceding two years, and the new constitution survived Paine's prose to be inaugurated in October 1795. Paine was not elected to it and his official role in France now ended.

***The Age of Reason*, 1793** It is unclear exactly when Paine wrote *The Age of Reason* (Conway, *Life*, 2.100; Hawke, 293, 446). Paine made conflicting statements, but it seems likely that he began early in 1793 and in March was able to turn over a number of completed chapters to Lanthenas for translation and setting. Events in the summer then caused a break in activity, but he returned to the work in the autumn, with Lanthenas translating as he wrote, ensuring that the first edition was published in French, possibly within days of his arrest. In his introduction to part 2 he claimed that he had written the book without either a New or Old Testament to hand, and that he had seen the likelihood of his arrest and had hurriedly drawn the work to a close. Neither circumstance harmed the text. *The Age of Reason* is a trenchant and uncompromising attack on Christianity and all formal religions together with a brief statement of Paine's religious beliefs. More than anything else he wrote it was responsible for the hostility with which he was subsequently treated. Although denounced as epitomizing atheism and infidelity, the work was written with the express design of combating atheism, and it begins with a frank statement of Paine's faith: 'I believe in one God, and no more; and I hope for happiness beyond this life' (*Complete Writings*, 1.464). He disavows both religious institutions, 'All national institutions of churches, whether Jewish, Christian or Turkish, appear to me no other than human inventions, set up to terrify and enslave mankind, and monopolize power and profit' (ibid.), and all revelation, 'A thing which everyone is required to believe requires that the proof and evidence of it should be equal to all, and universal' (ibid., 1.468). The only text which can claim this status is the text of nature: 'THE WORD OF GOD IS THE CREATION WE BEHOLD and it is in *this word*, which no human invention can counterfeit or alter, that God speaketh universally to man' (ibid., 1.482). Appealing again to the touchstone of common sense, Paine can find nothing to warrant belief in Christianity, and a great many grounds for suspecting imposture. His arguments follow the pattern of criticism developed in the deist controversy in England in the first quarter of the eighteenth century, but he makes his points in inimitably earthy fashion:

> Whenever we read the obscene stories, the voluptuous debaucheries, the cruel and torturous executions, the unrelenting vindictiveness, with which more than half the bible is filled, it would be more consistent that we called it the word of a demon than the Word of God. (ibid., 1.474)

His deism and the associated account of the order of nature draws heavily on his understanding of celestial mechanics which he learned at the lectures of Benjamin Martin and James Ferguson and provides an alternative vision of the true religion. Soon after his release from prison he began working on part 2 of *The Age of Reason*. With Old and New Testament now to hand he develops a line of biblical exegesis which shows the conflicting evidence and claims which the Bible contains. Part 2 lacks the power and vision of the first part, but it offers instead a careful, often pedantic, critique, book by book, of the Bible's claim to authority—although some books are given lighter treatment, such as Ruth: 'an idle, bungling story, foolishly told, nobody knows by whom, about a strolling country-girl, creeping slyly to bed with her cousin Boaz. Pretty stuff indeed, to be called the Word of God!' (ibid., 1.535). Paine's case is that the Bible must rest its claim to validity on the testimony it contains, but this testimony must itself be unimpeachable, especially given the improbability of the claims made, and that authority evaporates when the testimony is founded to be anonymous and contradictory.

Paine completed part 2 of *The Age of Reason* in August 1795 and left the Monroes for a brief holiday. Within a week he was back with a recurrence of the fever he had in prison and an abscess in his side. He remained seriously ill and bed-ridden, and recovered fully only by the beginning of 1796. During his illness, his long-standing sense of grievance towards America for having forsaken him in the Luxembourg prison finally spilt over, crystallizing into certainty that Washington had served him treacherously. He wrote a long, acerbic letter to James Madison complaining of Washington's treatment of him. Monroe sought to dissuade Paine, or at least to persuade him that he should not attack the president when he was a guest of his ambassador, but Paine sent at least one angry letter that reached Washington. Moreover, Washington's appointment of John Jay as minister to Britain resulted in a treaty which, to Paine, sacrificed American and French interests to Britain. Paine, and Monroe, feared that the treaty would provoke a breakdown in good relations with France and realign America with her former rulers.

***Agrarian Justice* and American polemic** As he recovered from his illness Paine wrote *Agrarian Justice* (1796), the most egalitarian of his writings, in which he identified a tendency for civilization to make one part of society more affluent, and the other more wretched, than would have been the case in a natural state. Developing a justification for the redistribution of property which had been absent from *Rights of Man*, the pamphlet argues that owners of property owe a ground rent for what they have acquired to the rest of mankind, and that the aim should be to ensure that increased wealth has, and is seen to have, reciprocal benefits for the general mass of society. To achieve this he advocated the creation of a national fund, out of which every person arriving at the age of twenty-one would be paid £15 in compensation for the loss of his or her natural inheritance by the introduction of the system of landed property. In addition, each person over the age of fifty would be paid £10 per annum. In both cases this would be a matter of justice, not charity. The English agrarian radical Thomas Spence criticized Paine for not advocating common ownership, but Paine was advancing a doctrine which he believed would be compatible with individual freedom and commercial activity, and which he saw as a necessary bedrock for the political equality that was required to ensure stability within modern states.

Within two months of *Agrarian Justice* Paine published *Decline and Fall of the English System of Finance* (1796), an analysis of the financing of the British national debt and its exponential growth which predicted the collapse of the fiscal system as the government sought to fund the current war. The Council of Five Hundred voted for it to be officially printed and distributed, and it served to reintroduce Paine into the political circles of the Directory, which increasingly turned to him for advice on France's relations with America. This, in turn, raised further problems for Monroe, who suspected that Paine was indiscreet with information he obtained by residing with him. Moreover, Paine's anger at Washington resurfaced in public outbursts, and Monroe was finally forced to ask him to find alternative lodgings. Once he had done so—in the spring of 1796 he moved to rooms in Suresnes, a suburb of Paris—there was little to stop him from venting his anger in print. His *Letter to Washington* (1796) is a long, rambling piece, prefaced by an attack on Jay's treaty and sideswiping at many of America's elder statesmen. The portrait of Washington is unmitigatedly critical, and extends back to accusations of a lacklustre performance as leader of the army during the war. Paine arranged to have it published in America, where it tarnished his reputation still further with the federalists and embarrassed most republicans. It is probably Paine's least likeable publication, even if many found *The Age of Reason* more deeply offensive. Relations between France and America deteriorated further when Monroe was recalled in November—a decision Paine saw as typical of 'the ingratitude and clandestine manoeuvring of the Government of Washington' (*Complete Writings*, 2.614). Paine, now deeply despondent, decided to return with Monroe, until Monroe pointed out that this might not help him, and so instead Paine left for Havre-de-Grâce in March 1797 to find a ship. However, his fears for his safety, with English warships stopping and searching American shipping, led to successive delays until, three months later, he gave up and returned to Paris. Bonneville invited him to stay for a week; he was still in residence five years later. Paine's reluctance to risk the journey, and the lack of any corroborating evidence, suggests that the Hambledon Cricket Club's minute for August 1796, which reports Paine's attendance at a club dinner in July 1796, is false!

Opinions of French government Paine returned to Paris as the newly elected Council of Five Hundred moved in an increasingly anti-republican direction and sought to reinstate some of the privileges of the Catholic church. In June, Paine criticized proposals to allow the ringing of church bells on the grounds that a stable republican polity required, in addition to equal political rights and a basic level of social and economic equality, a public culture free from the superstitions of Christianity and the power of its religious institutions. Some members of the Directory clearly shared this view. In January 1797 Paine, the Director La Révellière-Lépaux, and an assorted group of intellectuals and leftists had organized the first meeting of the Théophilanthropy sect, which espoused a broadly rationalist deism, held services revolving around edifying readings, sentimental music, and meditation, and was thought to have the potential to become a state religion.

Paine's sympathies with the Directory were also in evidence in September 1797 when the *coup d'état* of Fructidor purged the council, accorded emergency powers to the Directory, and halted the counter-revolutionary moves. His *Letter of Thomas Paine to the people of France, and the French armies, on the event of the 18th Fructidor, and its consequences* accepts that the revolution had faced a crisis, owing to the 'darksome manoeuvres of a faction' (*Complete Writings*, 2.605), and that the Directory had acted swiftly and without bloodshed to restore public tranquillity. None the less, he insisted that the 1795 constitution remained the best yet devised by human wisdom, and he regretted the necessity of overturning the results of the republic's first free elections. (When, in May 1798, the Directory acted again, in the *coup* of 22 Floreal, against the newly elected left-republicans, Paine said nothing.) Also in his assumed role of adviser, encouraged by Irish republican exiles in Paris, he wrote to the Directory encouraging it to send troops to assist an Irish rebellion. The resulting rising and invasion attempt in August 1798 was a disaster, and the consequent repression destroyed Irish radicalism for a generation. Paine was also sought out by Bonaparte, who claimed he slept with a copy of *Rights of Man* under his pillow, with whom he discussed the prospects for an invasion of England. In December 1797 he wrote two essays canvassing the design and financing of a fleet of 1000 gunboats to carry an invasion force across the channel, but Bonaparte abandoned the idea of attacking England in favour of Egypt in the first part of 1798. His sense of the increasing betrayal of France by the American administration, now under his long-standing enemy John Adams, may have driven him to the ultimate form of sedition—an article appeared in Bonneville's newspaper *Le Bien Informé* in September 1798 advising the government on the best means to conquer America.

Paine became increasingly absorbed in non-political matters. He became close friends with the inventor Robert Fulton, revived his interests in matters scientific, and spent much of his time at Bonneville's residence working on bridge models which he cast himself. He visited Dieppe and went on to Bruges to spend several months with Joseph Vanhuele, a fellow inmate of the Luxembourg prison. His finances were in a disastrous state and his bills in Dieppe seem to have been paid by Captain Nathan Haley from Connecticut, a casual friend. The overthrow of the Directory by Bonaparte and the establishment of the Consulate in November 1799 slipped by without comment from Paine. When he returned to Paris and tried to involve himself in the newly arrived commission from America, he was warned by the Foreign Office that they considered his behaviour irregular and that he would be sent back to America at the first complaint against him. He revived thoughts of returning to America when he heard that Jefferson was likely to be elected president as Adams's successor, and he wrote a spate of letters to Jefferson in October 1800, including an essay entitled *Compact Maritime* on the desirability of an international association of nations dedicated to protect the rights of commerce. These went unanswered until March, when Jefferson's reply offered him a place on a public ship due to return soon and informed him that an old friend of Paine's, Robert Livingston, would be the next minister to France. Paine deferred acceptance, saying he would await Livingston's arrival, imagining that if he delayed he might be offered a public post. To Jefferson's embarrassment, he published a copy of the letter. The peace of Amiens, signed in March 1802, gave him the opportunity to return safely. Six months later, having arranged for Bonneville's family to follow him, and with his financial problems largely solved by a gift of about £500 (from Francis Burdett and William Bosville), he set off again for Havre-de-Grâce, accompanied by Rickman, who came to bid him farewell.

Return to America, 1802–1809 Paine arrived in Baltimore on 18 October 1802 to a seemingly friendly reception. But the impression was fleeting. He was temporarily arrested on a dubious charge of indebtedness, and the federalists immediately sought to make capital of Paine's irreligion and Jefferson's offer of a public vessel. When he arrived in Washington only Jefferson and the most ardent republicans welcomed him. Even old colleagues, such as Benjamin Rush and Samuel Adams, turned against him because of his religious heterodoxy. And when he wielded his pen against the federalists in a series of seven letters, *To the Citizens of the United States*, written between November 1802 and April 1803, he often provided his enemies with ammunition against himself and his friends. He supported Jefferson both publicly and privately over the Louisiana purchase in 1803, and gave copious advice to Monroe, who was sent as minister extraordinary to negotiate over the purchase with the French government. When he suspected Jefferson of a certain coolness toward him and wrote in protest, the president's reply was warm and gracious, and satisfied Paine of his continuing affection. He left Washington in February and visited Bordentown. When he tried to catch the coach on to New York he was refused admittance by the coachman on account of his infidelity, and a crowd hissed and booed him as he left on horseback. His reception in New York was friendlier, with a testimonial dinner being held in his honour. He spent much of the next few months visiting friends and arranging for a cottage on his New Rochelle estate to be enlarged, although he also talked of returning to France should Napoleon's campaign against England be successful (and in 1804 wrote an epistle *To the People of England on the Invasion of England* to assist that end). Although received warmly by friends and fellow republicans his proposal to publish a third part of *The Age of Reason* was the cause of trepidation, and Nicolli Fosdick wrote to Jefferson, warning him that Paine was in the habit of reading out aloud letters from Jefferson which were best kept confidential, and encouraging the president to dissuade Paine from further publications on religious matters.

In the summer of 1804 Paine settled again in New Rochelle. He arranged for Marguerite de Bonneville, the wife of a Parisian friend who had arrived in the summer of 1803, and whom he had lodged in his house at Bordentown, to move to New York and secured her employment as a French teacher, but financial difficulties quickly developed. They agreed that he should take her three sons into his care and see to their education at New Rochelle, but their mother seemed both to want them with her without being willing either to live at New Rochelle (because it was too quiet) or to have the children with her in New York. Her husband remained in France. On Christmas eve, 1805, Christopher Derrick, whom Paine had employed to look after the farm while in New York the previous year, combined an overindulgence in drink with bottled-up resentment against Paine and fired a musket at him while he was reading in his living room. Paine escaped without harm. Characteristically, he refused to press charges.

Paine continued to write—an eighth and final letter *To the Citizens of the United States* in June 1805, against the federalists; *Constitutions, Governments, and Charters* (also in June), in which he argued that the legislature proposing charters should not have the power to make them law; a brief *Remarks on English Affairs* in July 1805, which contained such positive comments on Napoleon that Rickman, who had heard Paine's private views, declined to believe Paine was the author; and the essays *The Origin of Freemasonry* and *Constitutional Reform*. The following year he produced the speculative *The Cause of Yellow Fever* and returned briefly to the federalists and affairs in Europe, and in 1807 wrote several essays on the use of gun boats and on the likelihood of war with Britain. But his health and powers were gradually fading, and he kept sliding into financial difficulties, from which he extracted himself by selling, reluctantly, parts of his farm. He tried to interest Jefferson and George Clinton in asking congress to take up the issue of financial acknowledgement for his services to the War of Independence, but although efforts were made nothing came of them, and Jefferson turned down Paine's offer to act as a special envoy to Napoleon. In the spring of 1806 Paine left the farm to lodge in a local inn, where his friend William Carver found him weeks later, dishevelled, unshaven, drunk, and a good deal the worse for wear. Carver brought him to live with him in New York, but in June Paine had a fit of apoplexy and was so badly injured he was bed-ridden for weeks, nursed by Mrs Palmer, the widow of Paine's deist friend Elihu. On doctor's advice he moved from Carver's to lodge with John Wesley Jarvis, a portrait painter, in November. Carver then sent him a bill for his lodgings, and for the services of Mrs Palmer. His health improved and Jarvis reported him 'one of the pleasantest companions I have met with for an old man' (Aldridge, *Man of Reason*, 296). In November 1806 he visited New Rochelle to vote in the congressional elections, but the election inspector, Elisha Ward, refused to register his vote, insisting that he was not an American citizen—a charge Paine sought to challenge in the courts. When Jarvis moved in April 1807, Paine found lodgings with Zakarias Hitt—a disciple of Paine's—who lived on the outskirts of New York. When Hitt raised his rent the following January Paine insisted he could not afford to pay, despite his continued ownership of property at both New Rochelle and Bordentown. He also insisted on writing to congress to ask for the reimbursement of his expenses for the trip he had taken to France with Laurens twenty-five years earlier. Congress demurred and an offer on the farm fell through, and he moved to a cheap tavern in February, where he remained until removed by friends in July. The Bordentown farm was sold for $800 and a new lodging was found in Greenwich Village. Paine had lost the use of his legs and he grew increasingly weaker. By January 1809 he needed constant care and he set out his will, in which the bulk of the estate went to Madame Bonneville for the education of her children. He asked the Quakers to allow him to be buried in their burial-ground, but was refused, and he made Madame Bonneville promise that he would be buried on his New Rochelle farm. In May, overwhelmed by his isolation, he persuaded Madame Bonneville to rent a house in which to care for him. He moved in with her on 4 May to 59 Grove Street in Greenwich Village and died at 8 o'clock in the morning of 8 June 1809. He was buried at New Rochelle, mourned by his negro servant, Madame Bonneville, her son Benjamin, and a handful of local people. In 1819 the former tory turned radical William Cobbett had his bones dug up and brought back to England, where they subsequently disappeared.

Reputation The first biography of Paine was published in the summer of 1791, with government encouragement, by George Chalmers (under the pseudonym Francis Oldys), a government clerk in the Board of Trade and an accomplished and serious writer. The work is the sole source for a great many of the stories about Paine's life prior to his departure for America, but its thirst for information is coupled with an evident antipathy to its subject. However, it is only in the second edition of 1793 that any reference is made to Paine's drinking. Thereafter, accusations of drunkenness and associated slovenly habits become commonplace in reports of Paine. These reached new heights in the biography produced by James Cheetham, published shortly after Paine's death. Cheetham, a former radical and newspaper editor, had fallen out with Paine in 1806 and presented him as a hopeless drunkard and atheist, portraying the symptoms and side effects of Paine's stroke and deteriorating health as evidence of his alcoholism. Subsequent favourable biographies of Paine, notably Rickman's in 1819 and the first scholarly biography by Conway in 1892, tend to the opposite extreme, and tend also to underplay Paine's increasing egoism and vanity. From a wide variety of sources it seems clear that Paine drank to excess, especially when under strain; that he could be extremely lazy and self-indulgent; that he was prone to exaggerate his contribution to the world of politics, theology, and philosophy; that he lacked restraint in expounding his principles in company; that he bragged of disinterestedness in publishing as he did, then clamoured for compensation; that he was a hopeless manager of money and was not particular about repaying his debts; that in matters of dress and appearance he fell short of the standards of many of his contemporaries; and that his once rather handsome appearance was ravaged by his indulgence in alcohol. Moreover, after his imprisonment and illness these faults were exacerbated and his bitterness over his fate frequently clouded his judgement. But, alongside these faults, which contemporaries assiduously recorded and relayed, and which most biographers have subsequently either ignored or magnified, there are many other reports, often from unlikely quarters, of an entertaining conversationalist, with considerable charm and an engaging manner—even if he was capable of reciting the most part of his major works by heart, while insisting that there was nothing to be gained by going back to earlier writers. If there is a balanced picture to be had, it is that he was a man from a poor background in an aristocratic age, whose capacity to offend was increasingly enhanced by his lack of deference and his sense of his own importance. That sense may have irritated his contemporaries, but it was not misplaced: he was an extremely effective pamphleteer, with a capacity to capture and relay ideas and principles of which his audience had hitherto only an inchoate appreciation. His originality is frequently disparaged, but he offers a powerful and distinctive account of the principles of democratic politics in which political and civil equality are supported by a degree of social and economic equality. Although commentators often stress the similarities of his account to John Locke's *Second Treatise of Civil Government*, despite Paine's claim never to have read it, there is nothing in Locke to match Paine's redistributive policies, his sense of his intimate connection between equal citizenship and political stability, or his insistence on the universalism of his political ideas and citizenship. And although his religious writings did most to stir up hostility against him for 100 years or more—with Teddy Roosevelt describing him in 1888 as 'a filthy little atheist' (Roosevelt, 289)—many working-class readers found in them the resources with which to rethink their religious commitments, just as the other writings allowed them to rework their politics.

Although his precise intellectual and historical importance remains disputed, Paine is now accepted as a leading figure in the age of revolutions. Collections of his work have appeared regularly since his death, with M. D. Conway making the most important contribution at the end of the nineteenth century with a four-volume collection. A two-volume collection, edited by Philip Foner in 1945, remains the most comprehensive, but is far from complete and is flawed in some parts. No comprehensive bibliography has yet appeared. Statues of him have been erected in Paris, in the Parc Montsouris, and in Thetford, and one is mooted for Washington; active Tom Paine societies exist in both Britain and America, with regular meetings and newsletters, and the United States postal service issued a commemorative stamp with Paine's head in January 1968. He has also been the subject of a novel by Howard Fast, *Citizen Tom Paine* (1945), and several plays, notably Paul Foster's *Tom Paine* (1967) and Jack Shepherd's *In Lambeth* (1990). MARK PHILP

Sources *The complete writings of Thomas Paine*, ed. P. S. Foner, 2 vols. (Secaucus, NJ, 1945) • F. Oldys [G. Chalmers], *The life of Thomas Paine* (1791/3) • J. Cheetham, *The life of Thomas Paine* (1809) • C. Rickman, *Life of Thomas Paine* (1819) • M. D. Conway, *The life of Thomas Paine, with a history of his literary, political, and religious career in America, France, and England*, 2 vols. (1892) • M. D. Conway, *Thomas Paine (1737–1809) et la révolution dans les deux mondes* (Paris, 1900) • A. O. Aldridge, *Man of reason: the life of Thomas Paine* (1960) • A. O. Aldridge, *Thomas Paine's American ideology* (Cranbury, NJ, 1984) • D. F. Hawke, *Paine* (1974) • *A diary of the French Revolution by Gouverneur Morris*, ed. B. C. Davenport, 2 vols. (1939) • H. R. Yorke, *Letters from France in 1802*, 2 vols. (1804) • J. Keane, *Tom Paine: a political life* (1995) • J. Fruchtman, *Thomas Paine: apostle of freedom* (New York, 1994) • J. Fruchtman, *Thomas Paine and the religion of nature* (Baltimore, 1993) • G. Claeys, *Thomas Paine: social and political thought* (1989) • E. Foner, *Tom Paine and revolutionary America* (New York, 1976) • E. Foner, *Tom Paine: collected writings* (1995) • D. A. Wilson, *Paine and Cobbett: the transatlantic connection* (Montreal, 1988) • B. Bailyn, *Faces of revolution: personalities and themes in the struggle for American independence* (New York, 1990) • R. R. Fennesey, *Burke, Paine, and the 'Rights of man'* (The Hague, 1963) • R. Gimbel, *Thomas Paine: a bibliographical checklist of 'Common sense'* (New Haven, 1956) • W. H. G. Armytage, 'Thomas Paine and the Walkers: an early episode in Anglo-American cooperation', *Pennsylvania History*, 18 (1951), 16–30 • H. H. Clark, 'An historical interpretation of Thomas Paine's religion', *University of California Chronicle*, 35 (1933), 56–87 • H. H. Clark, 'Introduction', *Thomas Paine: representative selections, with introduction, bibliography and notes* (1944) • J. G. James, 'Thomas Paine's iron bridge work, 1785–1803', *Newcomen Society Transactions*, 57 (1987–8), 189–221 • 'Paine and science', *Enlightenment and dissent*, 16 (1998) • D. Abel, 'The significance of the letter to the Abbé Raynal in the progress of Thomas Paine's thought', *Pennsylvania Magazine of History and Biography*, 66 (1942), 176–90 • I. Kramnick, 'Tom Paine: radical liberal', *Republicanism and bourgeois radicalism: political ideology in late-eighteenth century England and America* (Ithaca, 1990) • I. Dyck, ed., *Citizen of the world: essays on Thomas Paine* (New York, 1988) • I. Dyck, 'Local attachments, national identities and world citizenship in the thought of Thomas Paine', *History Workshop Journal*, 35 (1993), 117–35 • G. Kates, 'From liberalism to radicalism: Tom Paine's *Rights of man*', *Journal of the History of Ideas*, 50 (1989), 569–87 • *The autobiography of Benjamin Rush*, ed. G. W. Corner (1948) • C. Robbins, 'The lifelong education of Thomas Paine (1737–1809): some reflections on his acquaintance among books', *Proceedings of the American Philosophical Society*, 127 (1983), 135–42 • J. Turner, 'Burke, Paine, and the nature of language', *Yearbook of English studies: the French Revolution in English literature and art*, ed. J. R. Watson, special number, 19 (1989), 75–92 • E. A. Payne, 'Tom Paine: preacher', *TLS* (31 May 1947), 267 • T. Roosevelt, *Gouverneur Morris* (Boston, 1888) • T. Copeland, 'Burke, Paine, and Jefferson', *Edmund Burke: six essays* (1950), 146–89 • F. K. Prochaska, 'Thomas Paine's "The age of reason revisited"', *Journal of the History of Ideas*, 33 (1972), 561–76 • A. Williamson, *Thomas Paine: his life, work and times* (1973) • A. J. Ayer, *Thomas Paine* (1988) • W. E. Woodward, *Tom Paine: America's godfather, 1737–1809* (1945) • A. Thomson, 'Thomas Paine and the United Irishmen', *Études Irlandaises*, 16 (1991), 109–19 • B. Vincent, *Thomas Paine, ou la religion de la liberté* (Paris, 1987) • B. Vincent, ed., *Thomas Paine, ou la république sans frontières* (Nancy, 1993)

Archives American Philosophical Society, Philadelphia, Richard Gimbel collection of Thomas Paine manuscripts • Indiana University, Bloomington, Lilly Library, Paine collection • Norwich Central Library, Thomas Paine collection at Thetford: an analytical catalogue • Thomas Paine National Historical Association, New York • Thomas Paine Society, Nottingham | Bodl. Oxf., Petty MSS, letters to Lord Lansdowne • NRA, priv. coll., letters to Lord Lansdowne

Likenesses J. Watson, oils, 1783 (after C. W. Peale), American Philosophical Society Library, Philadelphia • W. Angus, line engraving, pubd 1791 (after C. W. Peale), BM, NPG • H. Scratch, oils, 1791, American Philosophical Society Library, Philadelphia • Barlow, line engraving, pubd 1792 (after S. Collings), BM • G. Romney, engraving, 1792 • J. Sayers, etching, pubd 1792, BM, NPG • W. Sharp, line engraving, pubd 1793 (after G. Romney), BM, NPG • J. Godby, engraving, 1805 (after drawing by E. Stacey), American Philosophical Society Library, Philadelphia • S. Godby, stipple, pubd 1805, BM, NPG • J. W. Jarvis, portrait, 1806, New York Historical Society • J. W. Jarvis, portrait, *c.*1806/7, National Gallery of Art, Washington [*see illus.*] • J. W. Jarvis, bust, *c.*1807, New York Historical Society • J. W. Jarvis, death mask, 1809, New York Historical Society • portrait, 1860–69 • A. Mollière, oils (after G. Romney), NPG • prints, BM, NPG

Wealth at death shares in New York Phoenix Insurance to value of $1500; farm at New Rochelle, plus sundry monies and personal effects; $200 to each of his executors, Walter Morton and Thomas Addis Emmet; $100 to Mrs Elihu Palmer; land of New Rochelle farm to be sold and split between Nicholas Bonneville and Clio Rickman; rest to be used by Mrs Bonneville for the education and support of her children: last will and testament, T. C. Rickman's *Life of Paine*, pp. 273–7

Paine, Sir Thomas (1822–1908), lawyer, was born in Yarmouth, the only child of a retired naval officer and his wife. His education, at a private school in Yarmouth, was minimal, for his father's income at that time had been much reduced by unfortunate investment, but he was, by his own account, a voracious and omnivorous reader.

In 1837, at the age of fifteen, Paine was articled to Harry Verelst Worship, senior partner of a well-known Yarmouth firm of solicitors. His professional education was the responsibility of Worship's partner, his younger son, William, who was ten years Paine's senior and became the boy's mentor and his lifelong friend. Paine completed his articles and was admitted in 1843. He then spent a year in the chambers of the eminent conveyancing barrister Francis Turner before finding a position as a managing clerk with Timothy Tyrrell's practice in Guildhall Yard, London. Tyrrell had a large number of private clients and Paine recalled that as soon as he arrived he was placed in charge of the firm's railway business and conducted it largely unsupervised.

In August 1847 Paine married Anna Neave (*d.* 1893), to whom he had been engaged for a year. She was a Norfolk girl, sister of a friend of his at home. There were seven children of the marriage, five of whom survived to adulthood, three boys and two girls. In 1849 Tyrrell offered Paine a partnership in the firm and until 1857 they practised together, accompanied from 1852 by Thomas Layton. In 1857 Tyrrell was obliged to retire when it emerged that he had, in what Paine described as 'a serious breach of duty', shared the profit made by a property speculator on the sale of a building in Threadneedle Street to the newly established Bank of London, a client of the firm. Paine became, therefore, senior partner of the firm at a much younger age than he might ever have anticipated. His ability and probity ensured the continuation of the firm without loss of clients, even the Bank of London.

The firm, now Paine and Layton, moved to Gresham House in Old Broad Street and developed a considerable City practice, with clients among the railway companies (the North London Railway Company was one of the most significant), the breweries—in both the UK and the USA—and, in the 1880s, investment trusts and the London and Lancashire Life Assurance Company, of which Paine himself became a director. Well respected in the City, Paine was a member of the select dining club, the City Law Club, from 1863. Despite his increasing professional duties, Paine always found time for his holidays, usually spent walking and climbing in the Alps. He was a member of the Law Society's council from 1871 to 1889, serving in 1882–3 as the society's president. In December 1882, following the opening by Queen Victoria of the new Law Courts in the Strand, Paine was knighted, the first president to be so honoured. Of Paine's three sons (educated at Rugby School), the eldest, Tyrrell (*b.* 1849), went to the bar while the two younger sons, Edgar (*b.* 1851) and William (*b.* 1861), were articled at the firm and became their father's partners. Edgar left the firm in 1893 and practised alone so that it was William who succeeded his father as senior partner when he retired in 1898, five years after the death of his wife. Paine enjoyed ten years of retirement, spent mainly at Broomfield, Westcott, near Dorking in Surrey, the house he had had built in 1868. He died on 12 February 1908. Ten years later his son, William, left the firm to become legal adviser to Lloyds Bank; he was instrumental in arranging for the firm to merge with another City practice, Linklater & Co., to create Linklaters and Paines, making it then and ever since one of the largest City firms of solicitors. JUDY SLINN

Sources T. Paine, *Recollections of past years* (privately printed, 1901) • *Solicitors' Journal*, 52 (1907–8), 700 • J. Slinn, *Linklaters and Paines: the first one hundred and fifty years* (1987)

Wealth at death £153,500 15*s.* 1*d.*: resworn probate, 28 Feb 1908, *CGPLA Eng. & Wales*

Painter, Edward [Ned] **(1784–1852)**, pugilist, was born at Stretford, 4 miles from Manchester, in 1784, and as a young man worked as a brewer. He may have been the infant baptized at St Mary's Church, Stretford, on 15 February 1784, the son of John and Mary Painter. A quarrel with a fellow employee in the brewery called Wilkins—a man of heavy build—led to a formal fight in the yard of The Swan inn, Manchester, where Painter quickly defeated his opponent and showed unusual power as a boxer. After receiving some training under his fellow countryman Bob Gregson, he was matched to fight J. Coyne, an Irish boxer from Kilkenny, 6 feet tall and weighing 14 stone. Painter weighed 13 stone; his height was 5 feet 9¾ inches. The men met at St Nicholas, near Margate, on 23 August 1813, when, after a fight of forty minutes, the Irishman was beaten. J. Alexander, known as the Gamekeeper, was Painter's next opponent, at Moulsey Hurst, Surrey, on 20 November 1813. In the twentieth round the victory seemed to be going to the challenger, but Painter, with a straight, well-directed hit, stunned the Gamekeeper, and became the victor. He was now reckoned a match for Tom Oliver, but in the fight, which took place on 17 May 1814, his luck for the first time deserted him. For a purse of 50 guineas he next took on John Shaw, the lifeguardsman, at Hounslow Heath, Middlesex, on 18 April 1815, when the height and weight of Shaw prevailed after twenty-eight minutes.

On 23 July 1817 Painter met Harry Sutton, the black fighter, at Moulsey Hurst, and after forty-eight minutes found himself unable to continue the encounter. Not satisfied with the result, he again challenged Sutton to meet him at Bungay in Suffolk on 16 December 1817. The event excited great interest, and, despite rainy weather, 15,000 people assembled. There was a quadrangle of 24 feet for the combatants to engage in, with an outer roped ring for the officials. Outside this stood the spectators, several rows deep, and three circles of wagons surrounded the whole, giving the ring the appearance of an amphitheatre. This time Sutton, although he fought with great spirit, conceded defeat at the close of the fifteenth round. At Stepney, on 21 March 1817, Painter undertook for a wager to throw half a hundredweight against Mr Donovan, a man of great size, and beat him by 18½ inches. He was equally good at running. On 7 November 1817, on the Essex Road, in a 5 mile race against an athlete named Spring, he ran the distance in thirty-five and a half minutes.

The well-known Thomas Winter, alias Spring, was the next to engage with Painter, in a fight on Mickleham Downs, Surrey, on 1 April 1818. After thirty-one rounds, occupying eighty-nine minutes, Spring was victorious. The two men fought again on 7 August 1818, at Russia Farm, 5 miles from Kingston. In the first round Spring was floored by a blow over the eye, from which, although he continued fighting to the forty-second round, he never completely recovered. Painter now became landlord of The Anchor, Lobster Lane, Norwich, and intended to give up fighting, but on 17 July 1820 he again met his old opponent Tom Oliver, at North Walsham, and on this occasion was the victor. It is remarkable that Painter was defeated at the first attempt by Oliver, Sutton, and Spring, but in each case won the rematch. For many years he lived at The Anchor, then removed to the White Hart inn, Market Place, Norwich. He occasionally played a role in the arrangement of fights and was instrumental in founding a Norwich pugilistic club. Painter died at the home of his son, near The Ram, Lakenham, Norwich, on 18 September 1852, and was buried in St Peter's churchyard, Lakenham, on 22 September. G. C. BOASE, *rev.* JULIAN LOCK

Sources *Bell's Life in London* (26 Sept 1852), 7 • H. D. Miles, *Pugilistica: being one hundred and forty-four years of the history of British boxing*, 3 vols. (1880–81), vol. 2, pp. 74–88 • [F. Dowling], *Fights for the championship; and celebrated prize battles* (1855) • [F. Dowling], *Fistiana* (1868) • J. Ford, *Prizefighting: the age of Regency boximania* (1971) • 'An operator', *The Fancy* (1826), 1.393–400 • D. Brailsford, *Bareknuckles: a social history of prize fighting* (1988)

Likenesses W. M. Fellows, aquatint (after G. Sharples), NPG • portrait, repro. in 'An operator', *The Fancy* • portrait (after drawing by G. Sharples), repro. in Miles, *Pugilistica*, vol. 2, facing p. 74

Painter, William (1540?–1594), translator and administrator, may have come from a Kentish family. The *Dictionary of National Biography* suggests his father may have been William Painter, a woolcomber who applied for the freedom of London about 1543; Ashley states that Painter's father was headmaster of Sevenoaks School. There is no record of the name of his mother. Painter matriculated from St John's College, Cambridge, in November 1554. On 30 November he was admitted clock-keeper of the college and named Lady Margaret scholar. In 1556 he was awarded a Beresford scholarship. The next year he left Cambridge without a degree, and joined the Tower of London as a gunner and clerk of the armoury.

Painter began his translation career in 1558 with 'Horrible and Cruell Murder of Sultan Solyman', translated from the work of Nicolas Moffan, which appears as novel 34 in volume 2 of *The Palace of Pleasure*. About 1560 Painter was appointed headmaster of Sevenoaks School, even though the school statutes required the headmaster to hold a BA degree. A house and a salary of £50 per annum went with the post. On 25 April 1560 Painter was ordained deacon by Edmund Grindal, bishop of London, and appointed vicar of Grain in Kent. His translation of William Fulkes's attack on astrology, *Antiprognosticon*, 'written from Sevenoke', followed almost immediately. Even though he did not give up his parish until 1563, he became clerk of her majesty's ordnance at the Tower of London on a wage of 8*d*. a day in February 1561, and moved to an address near the Tower. As he was in charge of the day-to-day administration of the ordnance, Painter had considerable scope to increase his somewhat inadequate salary by creative management of the funds under his control. About 1565 he married Dorothy Bonham (1537?–1617) of Cowling. They had one son, Anthony, and four daughters. At about this time Painter bought the manors of Twedale and East Court at Gillingham, near Chatham. His official income was handsomely supplemented on 24 July 1566 by Edward Randolph, lieutenant-general of the ordnance, who assigned to 'William Painter, Clerk of the Ordnance, Richard Webb, Master Gunner of England, and Edward Partridge, Keeper of the Queen's Harquebutts, certain annuities and pensions' (Painter, 1890, 1.lvi).

The printer William Jones entered Painter's 'Cytie of civelitie' on the Stationers' register in 1652 but it was never published. In 1566 Jones published the first volume of Painter's *Palace of Pleasure*, whose title-page promises readers a book 'beautified, adorned and well-furnished with Pleasant Histories and excellent Novels'. It was followed the next year by the second volume. The complete work was republished in two volumes in 1575 with a dedication to Ambrose Dudley, earl of Warwick, master of the ordnance. It is a collection of anecdotes and stories translated from ancient and humanist writers for recreational reading and some moral instruction. Painter's sources range from the Greek historian Herodotus through Romans, mainly Livy and Aulus Gellius, to Italians like Matteo Bandello and Frenchmen like François de Belleforest. The book was widely read, imitated, and plagiarized. Roger Ascham has a long passage in *The Scholemaster* on the moral dangers such importations from Italy posed the more innocent English. Stephen Gosson, having abandoned the theatre, complains it 'was ransacked to furnish the playhouses of London' (Painter, 1929, 1.xviii).

Painter seems to have left traces in every notable Tudor playwright, who dramatized popular literature with the zeal of the modern film producer. John Webster, for instance, takes all but minor details of the plot of *The Duchess of Malfi* from Painter's version of Belleforest (*Palace of Pleasure*, 2.23). Though there are some verbal echoes of Painter in his text, in general Webster's language is influenced by Philip Sidney's *Arcadia*. Painter was hardly ever the sole or even the main source. The primary source of Shakespeare's *Rape of Lucrece* was the Marsus edition of Ovid, *Fasti*, 2.725ff. (1550), but he coloured Ovid with Livy, 1.57–8, keeping an eye on the *Palace of Pleasure* (1.2), Painter's version of the Livy story. The argument of the poem has strong echoes of Painter. Painter's 'Whereuppon they rode to Rome in Post' is echoed by Shakespeare's 'They all posted to Rome'; Shakespeare has Lucretia 'late in the night, spinning amongst her maids', where Painter writes 'late in the night, occupied and busie amonges her maids in the middes of her house spinning', a close translation of the Livy. The poem itself follows Ovid, with narrative touches taken from Painter (Baldwin, 113–31). There are touches of the Painter version of Livy in *Titus Andronicus*, IV.i. He is also supposed to be the Guil. P. G. who wrote *A Moorning Diti upon the Deceas of the High and Mighti Prins Henri, Earl of Arundel* in 1579.

The assiduous and skilled corruption endemic in the Elizabethan civil service exacerbated office rivalries. In 1586 John Powell, surveyor of the ordnance, formally accused Geoffrey Turville, Richard Bowland (who by now were dead), and Painter of embezzling £7075. Painter falsified his accounts either by billing the treasury for full shipments but taking delivery of only a part of them, or by charging the treasury the market price for equipment he issued to other military units from his stores in the Tower. Turville was held responsible for £2715 2*s*. 8*d*., Bowland for £2418 2*s*. 8*d*., and Painter for £1949 2*s*. 8*d*. Painter admitted to £1079 17*s*. 3*d*., gave an accounting for £795 13*s*. 10*d*., and ignored the shortfall of £73 11*s*. 7*d*. He 'humbly beseeched Her Majesty to have pitifull regard for his wife and marriageable children', and promised to repay 'in a reasonable time'. But he was overstretched. According to the charge-sheet the value of his lands at Gillingham was £413 10*s*. 0*d*., their gross annual revenue £94 10*s*. 0*d*., and annual profit £61 6*s*. 10*d*. But Painter was in debt for about £1200 for mortgages and the like. No action was taken against Painter and he never repaid the whole amount. This did not prevent him from laying counter-charges of corruption against Powell, who was just as vulnerable.

In September 1587 Powell replied by charging Painter with false accounting and Dudley with 'great oppressions' (Painter, 1890, 1.lv). In answer to these charges Painter's son, Anthony, whom Painter employed as his assistant, acknowledged irregularities on the part of both himself and his father and Painter admitted on 23 June 1589 that equipment recently moved from store had been sold to its end-users rather than issued to them. No action was taken against the Painters or the earl. And finally in 1591 George Hogge, clerk of deliveries, laid detailed charges relating to July and August 1575. All of them relate to goods, mainly gunpowder and bowstaves charged for but not delivered. But Painter's accusers were no more innocent than he was. He could therefore present himself as the careful steward slandered by others whom he had found out and who were jealous of his administrative abilities. Apart from saving £40 a year by small economies, 'he yearly increases HM stores to the value of £2000 by taking returns of such munitions as return from the seas unspent in HM ships, which formerly were concealed and converted to private use' (BL, Lansdowne MS 75, no. 55; Painter, 1890, 1.lx–lxi). Painter claimed to have saved his employers £11,000 by careful accounting. Again no action was taken against him.

Painter died on 14 February 1594 and was buried in London. Soon after his death the clerk of the Tower estimated that the Painters, father and son, had defrauded the crown of £27,000. Little wonder that William's nuncupative will of 14 February 1594 is singularly uninformative about his property and the manner of dividing it among his heirs (Painter, 1890, 1.xiii). On 11 May 1622 James I granted Painter's grandson discharge of the residue of his grandfather's debt to the crown which by then amounted to £7800. L. G. Kelly

Sources W. Painter, *The palace of pleasure*, ed. J. Jacobs (1890) [incl. documents relating to the hearing against him] • W. Painter, *The palace of pleasure*, ed. H. Miles (1929) • R. Ashley, 'Getting and spending: corruption in the Elizabethan ordnance', *History Today*, 40/11 (1990), 47–53 • T. W. Baldwin, *On the literary genetics of Shakespeare's poems and sonnets* (Urbana, 1950) • G. Boklund, *'The duchess of Malfi': sources, themes, characters* (1962) • G. Bullough, ed., *Narrative and dramatic sources of Shakespeare*, 8 vols. (1957–75) • Venn, *Alum. Cant.* • *DNB* • BL, Lansdowne MSS 51, 73, 75, 78

Wealth at death his lands were worth £413 10s. 6d. at time of first inquiry against him; value of estate £25,000–£30,000 (possibly incl. £27,000 previously embezzled): BL, Lansdowne MS 51 no. 25

Paish, Frank Walter (1898–1988), economist, was born in Croydon on 15 January 1898, the eldest of five sons (there were no daughters) of Sir George *Paish (1867–1957), joint editor of *The Statist* (1900–16) and author of many publications on economic and social problems, and his wife, Emily Mary, daughter of Thomas Whitehead, of Liverpool. He was educated at Winchester College before being commissioned into the Royal Field Artillery in 1916. He served in France in 1917–18 with the rank of lieutenant and was awarded the MC (1918) during the German offensive of March 1918, when he was wounded by shrapnel. From 1919 to 1921 he was a student at Trinity College, Cambridge, where he obtained a second class (division one) in both part one of the history tripos (1920) and part two of the economics tripos (1921).

On leaving university Paish joined the Standard Bank of South Africa, first in London in 1921 and then, from 1922 to 1932, in South Africa, at Aliwal North, where he was manager of a country branch, and finally in Cape Town, where his responsibility became that of economic intelligence and analysis. In 1927 he married Beatrice Mary (*d.* 1992), sister of Rachel, who married Sir Bryan Matthews, and daughter of Gustav Conrad Eckhard, shipping agent, of Manchester. They had two sons and a daughter.

In 1932 Paish left the bank and was appointed a lecturer at the London School of Economics (LSE). His work for the Standard Bank led him to throw new light on the working of the gold standard and he was one of the first economists to emphasize the role of changes in national income and expenditure, in addition to the quantity of money, in bringing about balance of payments adjustments. Paish was made a reader at the University of London in 1938 and Sir Ernest Cassel professor of economics (with special reference to business finance) in 1949. During this period his publications included *Insurance Funds and their Investment* (1934, with George Schwartz) and a study of the cheap money policy of 1932. From 1941 to 1945 he was deputy director of programmes in the Ministry of Aircraft Production. During the war he was also commissioned into the Home Guard, reaching the rank of captain.

Paish was elected president of section F of the British Association in 1953. He held his professorship until retirement in 1965, when he was appointed professor emeritus; and in 1970 he was made an honorary fellow of LSE. Between 1965 and 1970 he acted as consultant to Lloyds Bank on economic affairs. He had neither the training nor the taste for the mathematical theorizing and complex econometric testing which became prevalent in his profession. Instead, he had an unusually shrewd eye for applied economic problems and for the basic statistics needed to throw light on them. He always saw the formulation of economic theory as an art, and he was content to make contributions to the solution of difficult questions by means of a first approximation; econometric refinements he was content to leave to others. He had a rare understanding of the cyclical behaviour of the British economy and had a better forecasting record than most. He was one of the first economists to emphasize the need for a margin of spare capacity ('unused productive potential') to prevent inflation and the dangers of an ambitious policy of stimulating demand in the hope of stimulating long-term economic growth. In the conditions of the 1960s he argued that the spare capacity needed to prevent inflation would involve a level of unemployment of 2½ per cent, a view which was the subject of hostility on the part of those who believed that economic policy should be less restrained, including trade unionists; although he held policy makers rather than trade unions responsible for inflation and did not believe in the efficacy of 'incomes policy'.

Changes in the characteristics of the British economy in the 1970s and 1980s, like those in most other countries, rendered Paish's original estimate of the level of unemployment implied by anti-inflationary policy much too low; and later all economists accepted the need for some margin of spare capacity, even though they might disagree on its precise level and on the role of different instruments of economic policy. In the 1960s Paish's views were unpopular in Whitehall, where his prescriptions were neither sought nor taken. The tension between the supporters of his approach, who included colleagues at LSE, and advocates of more ambitious demand policies, broadly identified with the Keynesian school in general and with economists in Cambridge in particular, made difficult his task as editor of the London and Cambridge Economic Service, which produced regular assessments of economic conditions by economists from LSE and Cambridge. He was its secretary from 1932 to 1941 and again between 1945 and 1949, and editor from 1947 to 1949.

Paish's publications included *The Post-War Financial Problem, and other Essays* (1950), *Business Finance* (1953), *Studies in an Inflationary Economy* (1962), *Long-Term and Short-Term Interest Rates in the United Kingdom* (1966), (ed.) *Benham's Economics*, fifth to eighth editions (1962–7), and, with A. J. Culyer, the ninth edition (1973), *Rise and Fall of Incomes Policy* (1969), and *How the Economy Works, and other Essays* (1970).

Paish was of medium height and fair-haired, with strikingly blue eyes. His war wound left him with a limited degree of movement in his right shoulder, which necessitated some unusual but spectacular shots at the table tennis which was an off-duty diversion of the senior common room at LSE. His writing and his teaching had a directness, clarity, and lack of pretentiousness which were characteristic of the man. He had a boyish sense of humour and would reach the heart of a subject by means of brief and pithy comment. He was always ready to help his students and was an amiable colleague; but behind his friendliness and humour there was a robustness and even a hint of steel, which owed something, perhaps, to his experience in the First World War. Paish died at his home, the Old Rectory Cottage, Kentchurch, Hereford, on 23 May 1988.

HAROLD ROSE, *rev.*

Sources private information (1996) · personal knowledge (1996) · *CGPLA Eng. & Wales* (1988) · *WWW* · *The Independent* (1 June 1988) · *The Times* (26 May 1988)
Archives BLPES, papers
Wealth at death £96,053: probate, 17 Aug 1988, *CGPLA Eng. & Wales*

Paish, Sir George (1867–1957), financial journalist and economist, was born at Morths Gardens, Horsham, Sussex, on 7 November 1867, the tenth son of Robert Paish, a coachman, and his wife, Jane Smith, a domestic servant. After attending the United Westminster schools he began his career in 1881 as an office boy at the weekly *Statist* magazine, which had been founded in 1878 by Robert Giffen and others, and was fast becoming a rival to *The Economist*. Paish rose through sheer ability and energy from secretary to *The Statist*'s editor to become a financial journalist in his own right, being sub-editor from 1888 to 1894, assistant editor from 1894 to 1900, and joint editor from 1900 to 1916. On 24 March 1894 he married Emily Mary (1866/7–1933), daughter of Thomas Whitehead, auctioneer, with whom he had five sons.

The Statist, together with *The Economist*, was at this time in the vanguard of the movement to formulate a more analytical approach to contemporary social and economic debates. Paish's special gifts for compiling and analysing quantitative information made him one of the foremost practitioners of the new statistical journalism. He quickly established himself as an expert on British and later United States railway statistics, publishing a number of books: *The British Railway Position* (1902), *Railways of Great Britain* (1904), and *Railways of the United States* (1913). He was a pioneer in the use of ton-mile freight figures to assess a railway company's efficiency. This led to his first appointment as an official economic adviser, when he became a member between 1906 and 1908 of the departmental committee of the Board of Trade on railway accounts and statistics.

Paish's knowledge of railway statistics led also to his developing an expertise in the compilation and interpretation of the data for Britain's overseas investments. In two papers published in the *Journal of the Royal Statistical Society* ('Great Britain's capital investments in other lands', 1909; 'Great Britain's capital investments in individual colonies and foreign countries', 1911), and a *Statist* supplement ('The export of capital and the cost of living', 1914), Paish laid the statistical and interpretative groundwork for all future research in this area. Described by one contemporary as 'an heroic effort to solve an insoluble problem' (W. R. Lawson, cited in Platt, 14), Paish's estimates of the stock and distribution of UK portfolio investment overseas on the eve of the First World War have since been subjected to detailed criticism and significant downward revision by Platt. None the less, the basics of his direct estimation procedures have endured.

The third strand to Paish's career was as a special adviser to David Lloyd George when chancellor of the exchequer. Paish recorded in his *Who's Who* entry that he served in this capacity between 1914 and 1916, but from Paish's unpublished memoirs and other sources Offer has shown that he was acting as an unofficial adviser from 1909 to 1910 and that he acquired this position, at least in part, through his association with Sir Edgar Speyer, a financier who moved in Liberal Party high circles. Paish, who was knighted in 1912, quickly became an important independent source of advice both on the City and on the prospects for the national economy. Such forecasts became an essential component of the chancellor's budgetary deliberations at a time when, economically and constitutionally, the budget was unusually politicized. Offer's researches reveal that 'in George Paish, Lloyd George had found an economist close to his own heart, an analyst whose explanations were congenial and successful and who gave him the confidence to defy his critics' (Offer, 126). This meeting of minds continued until the outbreak of war and indeed a little beyond. At the beginning of hostilities he was fully involved in decisions directed at quelling City anxieties; in November 1914 he and the Treasury's Sir Basil Blackett were members of the official mission to the American government charged with securing supplies and financing for the war. But already ill health—probably mental exhaustion—was taking its toll. By the time J. M. Keynes entered the Treasury in January 1915 as his assistant, Paish's influence was in eclipse and shortly afterwards he resigned. Thereafter he continued his association with *The Statist* and frequently published on international and economic issues (*The Road to Prosperity*, 1927; *The Way out*, 1937), but he was never again close to the centre of British government or the policy debate. On three occasions he stood unsuccessfully for parliament as a Liberal: at Glasgow Central (1922), Edinburgh West (by-election 1935), and Manchester Exchange (1935). His wife died in 1933 and on 30 September 1936 he married Anita Carolyn Rouse (*b*. 1895/6), formerly the wife of Ludwig Otto Rettig and daughter of Charles James von Hartmann, landed proprietor. Paish died on 1 May 1957 at Fulmer Grange Nursing Home, Wexham, Buckinghamshire. The economist Frank Walter *Paish was his eldest son. ROGER MIDDLETON

Sources *The Times* (3 May 1957) • A. Offer, 'Empire and social reform: British overseas investment and domestic politics, 1908–1914', *HJ*, 26 (1983), 119–38 • D. C. M. Platt, *Britain's investments overseas on the eve of the First World War: the use and abuse of numbers* (1986) • D. W. Parsons, *The power of the financial press* (1989) • R. J. A. Skidelsky, *Hopes betrayed, 1883–1920* (1983), vol. 1 of *John Maynard Keynes* (1983–2000) • b. cert. • m. certs. [1 and 2] • d. cert. • *Debrett's Peerage* (1924) • *CGPLA Eng. & Wales* (1957)

Archives BLPES, memoirs and papers | Bodl. Oxf., corresp. with Gilbert Murray • JRL, *Guardian* archives, letters to *Manchester Guardian*

Wealth at death £1412 18s. 9d.: probate, 26 Sept 1957, *CGPLA Eng. & Wales*

Paisible, James [Jacques] (*c*.**1656–1721**), composer and recorder player, was born in France, probably in or near Paris. He was related to Guillaume Paisible (*c*.1659–1728), a page in the *chambre du roy* at Louis XIV's court, and probably to Louis Paisible, a wind musician there. Paisible presumably grew up learning wind and stringed instruments from one of the *joueurs de violons, hautbois, sacquebouttes et cornets* in the *grande écurie*. Paisible apparently came to England in September 1673 with the composer Robert Cambert, whose plan to produce French-style operas failed. Paisible was among the French oboe and recorder players in John Crowne's masque *Calisto* (Whitehall, February 1675). In 1677 he composed an unsuccessful *comédie-ballet*, *Rare en tout*, performed at Whitehall for Charles II's birthday. That October, the poet Rochester wrote to Henry Savile at court, sending Paisible, 'the best present I can make at this time', as the bearer, 'whom I beg you to take care of, so that the King may hear his tunes when he is easy and private, because I am sure they will divert him extremely' (*Letters of John Wilmot*, 160). Savile replied that Charles had heard Paisible's compositions 'with very great delight' (ibid., 165) but failed to acknowledge the implied sexual present. That same year Paisible and three other French recorder players received a court appointment that was concealed, perhaps because of anti-Catholic sentiment. To the French ambassador, Honoré Courtin, they played 'perfectly' (Buttrey, 200). Upon James II's accession in 1685 Paisible was openly appointed as a court musician, and on Christmas day 1686 he was given another post as an instrumentalist in James's new Roman Catholic chapel.

About 1676–86 the French *philosophe* Saint-Evremond organized musical activities at the duchesse de Mazarin's Chelsea home. His biographer, Desmaizeaux, wrote that he 'himself wrote the Idylls, Prologues and other pieces. … The *symphonie* he charged with Monsieur Paisible, or some other capable musician' (Desmaizeaux, 231). *Les noces d'Isabelle* features 'an old poet', presumably Saint-Evremond, and 'a young musician', once addressed as Paisible (*Œuvres meslées*, 3.155–9). Saint-Evremond described Paisible as a 'great and slothful musician … with manners that savoured of a well-bred man, and expressions which he must have learnt in his little library' (*Lettres*, 2.223). A later assessment of Paisible's character, that he was 'likely to forget in the morning what he promised the day before' (Nagel, 585–6), is due to the German viola da gamba player Ernst Christian Hesse (1711).

On 4 December 1686 Paisible obtained a licence to marry Mary (Moll) *Davis (*d*. 1708), a former singer, actress, and mistress of Charles II. Their marriage attracted ribald comments from court wits. Sir George Etherege wrote: 'Mrs Davies has given proof of the great passion she always had for music, and Monsieur Peasible has another bass to thrum than that he played so well upon' (*Letters*, ed. Bracher, 118). On 16 December 1687 Paisible became a denizen. The following year he was living in St James's Place. When James II fled England about Christmas time, Paisible, being a Catholic, left to serve him in exile at St Germain-en-Laye, near Paris. In 1693 the Paisibles returned to England. Paisible was appointed composer to Prince George of Denmark, the consort of Princess Anne, and after Anne's accession (1702) wrote her annual birthday dance. Upon George's death (1708) he received a court annuity. For the London theatre he wrote act tunes (consisting of an overture and dances played between the acts) for Dorset Garden in 1693, then frequently for Drury Lane from 1694 to 1702. He also performed in public concerts and taught.

By 1702 Paisible belonged to the Drury Lane 'band' (a small orchestra). He normally played the bass violin (almost obsolete in England), but for the interval 'entertainments' switched to the recorder. He and other members of the band often took part in concerts at York Buildings. In January 1708 he became a cellist at the new opera house, the Queen's Theatre in the Haymarket. The anonymous translator of François Raguenet's *Paralèle des italiens et des françois* (1709) attested that 'the famous Mr Paisible' on the recorder 'need not give place to any [Masters] at Paris' (*Comparison*, 9). In 1710 the German traveller Zacharias Conrad von Uffenbach, hearing Paisible play the recorder in a concert, claimed that his 'equal is not to be found' (Quarrell and Mare, 66–7). In 1713 Paisible moved to White Hart Yard, off Castle Street, in the parish of St Martin-in-the-Fields, Westminster, and he remained there until his death. By 1715 he was playing again at Drury Lane, appearing in interval entertainments in competition with the recorder player John Baston from the Lincoln's Inn Fields Theatre. Both there and in concerts Paisible played the recorder and the echo flute or small echo flute (apparently two slightly different recorders fastened together to allow for soft and loud playing).

Paisible died in the first half of August 1721 and was buried in the churchyard of St Martin-in-the-Fields on the 17th. Although he had been known in England as James, his French will preserved the original form of his forename, Jacques. His possessions were valued at £26 2*s*. 0*d*. plus 60 guineas in gold.

Paisible's attractive theatrical music, consisting largely of French-style dances, was good enough to have been mistaken for Henry Purcell's. During the 1690s Paisible was one of the leading composers in England integrating elements of the French and Italian styles—in his case, in a rather quixotic manner. His thirteen mixed-style recorder sonatas were probably the most virtuosic music written for the instrument up to that date, giving some idea of the impact he clearly made as a performer. His best-known work is the sombre *The Queen's Farewell* (1695) for Mary's funeral, apparently for six-piece oboe band.

DAVID LASOCKI

Sources A. Ashbee and D. Lasocki, eds., *A biographical dictionary of English court musicians, 1485–1714*, 2 vols. (1998) · D. Lasocki, 'Professional recorder players in England, 1540–1740', PhD diss., University of Iowa, 1983 · *The letters of John Wilmot, earl of Rochester*, ed. J. Treglown (1980) · J. Buttrey, 'New light on Robert Cambert in London, and his *Ballet et musique*', *Early Music*, 23 (1995), 199–220 · P. Desmaizeaux, *La vie de M. de Saint-Evremond* [n.d.] · *Œuvres meslées de Mr. de Saint-Evremond*, 2nd edn, 3 vols. (1709) · *Lettres [de] Saint-Évremond*, ed. R. Ternois, 2 vols. (Paris, 1967–8) · *Letters of Sir George Etherege*, ed. F. Bracher (1974) · W. Nagel, 'Das Leben Christoph Graupner's', *Sammelbände der Internationalen Musikgesellschaft*, 10 (1908–9), 568–612 · *A comparison between the French and Italian musick and opera's* (1709) · *London in 1710: from the travels of Zacharias Conrad von Uffenbach*, ed. and trans. W. H. Quarrell and M. Mare (1934)

Wealth at death possessions valued at £26 2*s*. plus 60 gold guineas; bequests of £100, plus unspecified 'effects' in London and France: Ashbee and Lasocki, eds., *Biographical dictionary*, vol. 2, p. 865

Paisley. For this title name *see* Hamilton, Claud, first Lord Paisley (1546?–1621).

Paisley, Robert [Bob] (**1919–1996**), football manager, was born on 23 January 1919 at 7 Avenue, Hetton-le-Hole, co. Durham, the second of four sons of Samuel Paisley (1894/5–1978), coal hewer, and his wife, Emily, *née* Bunker. His soccer talent was brought on at Barrington junior and Eppleton senior schools, but it began on the streets with him booting pigs' bladders donated by his uncle, a Co-op slaughterman. Though sturdy—the physique was part inherited and part developed by pushing coal barrows uphill to his grandmother's—Paisley was short; and he was rejected, after leaving school at fourteen, by Sunderland (of which he was a fan), Tottenham, and Wolves. He joined his elder brother at the mine as a surface worker; shortly afterwards he was shocked to see his father borne past with arm injuries so severe that he was unfit to work for five years. Like most pitmen, Sam Paisley wanted his sons to avoid mining and Bob became an apprentice bricklayer while continuing with his football. In 1937 he signed for Bishop Auckland, the top amateur club, to play for 3*s*. 6*d*. per match, the maximum expenses rules permitted;

Robert [Bob] **Paisley** (**1919–1996**), by unknown photographer, *c*.1981

and he was in the team that won the amateur cup. Liverpool Football Club scouted him; he joined it on 8 May 1939 for a £10 fee and £5 per week.

Paisley's formal first-team début was deferred until 1946 because he was drafted into the 73rd Royal Artillery as a gunner in October 1939. For four years overseas from 1941, in the north African and Italian campaigns, Paisley spent his leaves playing football for his regiment and the combined services. A left half, he was noted for resoluteness, an aggressive tackler, defensively solid; but his distribution was generally uninspired. He was conscious of this, and also that even the best players of his generation appeared trapped within what he called 'their own skill bracket' (Keith, 29). 'There hasn't been a player yet without a weakness', he said (ibid., 336). This perception of what players lacked was the platform of his shrewd planning in building teams of complementary parts which disguised their individuals' lopsidedness and exploited opponents' frailties.

Paisley made 253 league and 25 FA cup appearances for Liverpool, and scored thirteen goals. He earned a league championship medal in 1947 but he was mortified in 1950 when omitted from the FA cup final side, in spite of having played in every previous round. His reaction to his disappointment cannot be overestimated in the history of the club. Wembley appearances were pinnacles in every player's career. Liverpool lost in 1950, and Paisley was left pondering might-have-beens. At his nadir in spirit he considered quitting Liverpool; but he neither did that nor succumbed to press inducements to sell his story. The test of character was telling. When, as trainer and manager, he too dropped players from crucial games, they knew that he knew their feelings. He never shirked hard decisions. No player was allowed to believe himself bigger than the club. Ironically, an FA cup win also eluded Paisley as manager.

Paisley was appointed captain in the 1950–51 season but a succession of struggling sides saw Liverpool relegated in 1954, the first time since 1904. Retirement beckoned. To re-start bricklaying at the age of thirty-five was unappealing, and a newsagency or greengrocery appeared no better. It was a director, later chairman of Liverpool Football Club, cotton broker Tom Williams, who invited Paisley to become reserve team trainer. Paid less than he had been as a player, Paisley was more importantly kept in the game. His wage was supplemented by his wife's as a primary school teacher. They had married on 17 July 1946, when he was twenty-seven and she, Jessie, daughter of Arthur Chandler, an organ builder, was aged thirty. They had two sons, Robert and Graham, and a daughter, Christine.

Few football trainers in the 1950s were themselves trained. Having taken a correspondence course in physiotherapy, Paisley was more qualified than most. He proved to have uncanny diagnostic skills and magic hands, a practical grasp of psychology as well as of physiotherapy. The rejuvenation of Liverpool in the 1960s under Bill Shankly involved Paisley's promotion to first-team trainer, then to manager's assistant; a perfect partnership, according to those who played for them, with Paisley supplying steadiness and tactical subtlety to Shankly's messianic passion.

Shankly's retirement in July 1974 was sudden, though not surprising in a man who lived on the edge. Paisley succeeded as manager of Liverpool F. C. without the job being advertised. Liverpool's boardroom knew their man, perhaps better than Paisley then knew himself. His reluctance to step out of the shadows was genuine and, at fifty-five, he did not expect to remain long. He was underestimated outside Liverpool. People saw an avuncular, even grandfatherly, figure, quietly spoken but generally lost for words. The image was not entirely false. There was no flashiness about Paisley. Normally a half of lager and lime was his tipple; and a meal out was to his local Chinese or chippy. Swanky clothes were not his style either. Relaxation at home involved looking—nothing more—at the garden and tinkering at an electric organ, on which he could pick out 'Amazing Grace'. His principal escape was to friends in the horse-racing world such as Frank Carr and Frankie Durr. He placed a bet daily but it was rationed, never more than £3 even when he was earning over £50,000 p.a. as the most successful manager in the country. And it appeared related to football: Paisley studied the training at stables and temperament and form in horses just as he did with players. His love of boxing was similar. His office under Anfield's main stand was, to put it mildly, modest. Brian Clough, manager of Nottingham Forest, compared it to 'a foreman's hut on a Wimpey site' (Keith, 212).

Counting the trophies that Paisley's teams accumulated, it is easy to forget the problems and pressures. His first trial was dealing with the aftermath of an ill-tempered charity shield match against champions Leeds. The next months saw Shankly's reappearances at the training ground, where some players addressed him still as 'boss'; and a spell of eight games without a win caused Liverpool's slide down the league table, exit from the cup winners' cup, and a clamour for Shankly's reinstatement or promotion to director. The board stood firm; so did Paisley. What followed was an unprecedented record of nineteen trophies in eight years: three European cups, one UEFA cup, one European super cup, six league championships, three league / milk cups, and five charity shields. Liverpool was regarded as the world's best team at this period. Between January 1978 and January 1981 the team established a record of eighty-five consecutive matches unbeaten at 'Fortress Anfield'. Paisley was appointed OBE in 1977. Some suspected that the climate of soccer hooliganism cost him a knighthood. In popular estimation he was 'manager of the millennium'.

Paisley's judgement of players was unrivalled. From his first signing, full back Phil Neal, a succession of talent was brought to Liverpool: Terry McDermott, Joey Jones, Kenny Dalglish, Alan Hansen, Graeme Souness, Alan Kennedy, Ronnie Whelan, Ian Rush, Bruce Grobbelaar, Craig Johnston, Mark Lawrenson, and Steve Nicol. Equally, local ability was nurtured, such as Phil Thompson, Sammy Lee, Jimmy Case, and David Fairclough. Paisley's teams, like Shankly's, were famed for durability. No first division club used fewer first-team players in the 1960s, 1970s, and 1980s—some fifty-two per decade—yet this continuity masked a readiness to remove players who had peaked. Paisley did not spare even the captains Emlyn Hughes and Phil Thompson, and attention was always paid to grooming reserves so that seniors battled for places. 'Nobody has the right to win anything they haven't earned', was Paisley's philosophy; and players chorused the credo that 'First is first, and second's nowhere' (Hansen, 22).

Paisley was not just a driver of men. As Alex Ferguson reflected after his team of Scottish champions, Aberdeen, suffered 'annihilation' by Liverpool in the European cup in 1980, Paisley was 'full of cunning'. Sometimes this involved flattering the opposition before difficult games: what Paisley called 'giving them a bit of toffee' (Keith, 280–01). Dealing with the media was inescapable, though unloved by Paisley, whose preferred profile was low. He could show irritation and on occasion banned players from talking to reporters before matches, though he progressively cultivated a few such as John Keith of the *Daily Express*, who became his biographer. It was his understanding of players and tactics that mattered most, blending the best of continental European and British styles. 'Hold on to the ball, keep passing it, and let other teams do the chasing' (Keith, 282) was the strategy. At training players were schooled to operate as a unit, with an emphasis on positional intelligence.

There was no rigidity in the Paisley method: 'It's not about the long ball, and it's not about the short ball; it's about the right ball', Alan Hansen remembered him saying (BBC1, 22 Feb 2001). Mental as well as physical fitness was what Paisley looked for in a player: not just wholeheartedness but those vital ingredients vision and anticipation. He impressed on them that, 'at the highest level, the first two yards are in the head' (Hansen, 77). Emlyn Hughes identified Paisley's 'greatest attribute as a manager … [as] dealing with strengths and weaknesses, the opposition's and your own … in plain and simple language' (Keith, 136). The gentle Geordie dialect helped keep spirits high. Players enjoyed mimicking Paisleyisms, especially his all-purpose deployment of 'doin's'. Tommy Smith recalled: 'He often left us doubled up laughing. But only because of his delivery. He always got his message over and you didn't cross him. He demanded that everyone played to their maximum and gave their best. He was uncompromising in that' (ibid., 115).

Paisley preannounced his retirement during the 1982–3 season, to be succeeded by Joe Fagan, the next senior member of the bootroom staff, whose tradition of analysing play and players had been nourished by Paisley. Paisley now joined the board as a director. His dependability was again proved in a crisis. In 1985, in a crush at Heysel Stadium in Brussels before the European cup final, Liverpool fans precipitated the deaths of thirty-nine Juventus fans. The club was banned from European competitions and, his decade's work practically negated overnight, Paisley unobtrusively served as counsellor for two years to the novice player–manager Kenny Dalglish. Alzheimer's disease thereafter crept up on him. He resigned from the board in 1992, though the club made him honorary life vice-president. He died at Arncliffe Court Nursing Home, Arncliffe Road, Halewood, Lancashire, on 14 February 1996, from bronchopneumonia and dementia, and was buried at St Peter's Church, Woolton, Liverpool. He was survived by his wife and their three children. He was commemorated by the Paisley Gateway to the Kop entrance at Anfield, opened by his widow in April 1999.

PHILIP WALLER

Sources R. Paisley, *Bob Paisley: an autobiography* (1983) · J. Keith, *Bob Paisley: manager of the millennium* (1999) · S. F. Kelly, *Bill Shankly* (1996) · A. Hansen and J. Tomas, *A matter of opinion* (1999) · K. Dalglish and H. Winter, *Dalglish: my autobiography* (1996) · *The Times* (15 Feb 1996) · *The Guardian* (15 Feb 1996) · *The Independent* (15 Feb 1996) · *Daily Telegraph* (15 Feb 1996) · *WWW* · b. cert. · m. cert. · d. cert.

Likenesses photograph, 1981, repro. in Keith, *Bob Paisley* · photograph, *c.*1981, Hult. Arch. [*see illus.*] · photograph, repro. in *The Times* · photograph, repro. in *The Guardian* · photograph, repro. in *The Independent* · photographs, repro. in Keith, *Bob Paisley* · photographs, Hult. Arch.

Wealth at death £205,005: probate, 10 June 1996, *CGPLA Eng. & Wales*

Pakeman, Thomas (*c.*1614–1691), clergyman and ejected minister, matriculated from Trinity College, Cambridge, at Easter 1631, later migrating to Clare College, where he was admitted on 1 June 1633; he graduated BA in 1634 and proceeded MA in 1637. He was then employed for some years as a proofreader in the king's print house, and with three others presented a petition protesting against deteriorating conditions of work and a reduction in pay, imposed by the customs farmers.

On 28 January 1643 Pakeman began his ministry at Little Hadham, Hertfordshire. He was one of sixty-three Hertfordshire ministers who petitioned the Lords on 24 July 1646, in protest against the growth of sects and of anti-Scottish sentiment, urging the establishment of presbyterian church government. On 13 August that year the county committee of Hertford was ordered to investigate the estates at Hadham of its sequestered minister, Thomas Paske, and Pakeman was named as a minister there. On 4 November 1646 Pakeman was nominated vicar of Harrow on the Hill, Middlesex; he was officiating there by September 1648. He had already married Mary (*d.* 1690), daughter of Andrew Studeley of Shrewsbury, for they had baptized seven children at Harrow by 1659 and a son, Thomas, matriculated at St Edmund Hall, Oxford, on 18 October 1662, aged seventeen.

After his ejection under the Act of Uniformity in 1662 Pakeman seems at first to have remained at Harrow, and there 'had the instruction and boarding of several children of persons of quality' (Calamy, *Abridgement*, 2.468). Soon, however, he moved to Brentford, where he continued to preach and to teach, with the assistance of Ralph Button, the former professor of geometry at Gresham College, who lived next door. Button was imprisoned under the Five Mile Act but Pakeman escaped, finding shelter at the house of a Mrs Methwold in Brompton, near Knightsbridge. Here he continued as a preacher until finding more permanent accommodation in the household of Erasmus Smith, where, Calamy reports, he continued some years. Philip Henry recorded on 25 June 1672 a dinner at Stanwardine Hall, Shropshire, at which Pakeman and other ministers were present, and this may suggest he was sheltering with relations of his wife. In 1685 the family settled in London, where Pakeman attended the parish church of St Martin Outwich under its then minister, Richard Kidder, and sometimes received communion. Also in that year, when he was preaching at the house of his son Thomas both men were seized by the city marshal and fined by the lord mayor, Sir Henry Tulse. Pakeman moved in 1687 to Stratford, Essex, where he employed a schoolmaster at his own expense to teach poor children to read. He died in June 1691 aged seventy-seven, and was buried at St Martin Outwich on 8 July. His funeral sermon was preached by Kidder, who was soon to be instituted as bishop of Bath and Wells. In his will, dated 18 March 1691, Pakeman left land in and around Shrewsbury to his son, Timothy, and small sums to his daughters, Elizabeth Brise, Johanne Paulfreman, Anne Scadding, and Mary Abbott.

CHARLOTTE FELL-SMITH, *rev.* STEPHEN WRIGHT

Sources *Calamy rev.*, 379 · Venn, *Alum. Cant.* · E. Calamy, ed., *An abridgement of Mr. Baxter's history of his life and times, with an account of* *the ministers, &c., who were ejected after the Restauration of King Charles II*, 2nd edn, 2 vols. (1713) · W. Urwick, *Nonconformity in Hertfordshire* (1884) · W. T. Gun, *The Harrow School register, 1571–1800* (1934) · A. Gordon, ed., *Freedom after ejection: a review (1690–1692) of presbyterian and congregational nonconformity in England and Wales* (1917) · W. A. Shaw, *A history of the English church during the civil wars and under the Commonwealth, 1640–1660*, 2 vols. (1900) · will, PRO, PROB 11/405, sig. 119 · *Diaries and letters of Philip Henry*, ed. M. H. Lee (1882)

Pakenham, Sir Edward Michael (1778–1815), army officer, second son of Edward Michael Pakenham, second Baron Longford (1743–1792), and his wife, Catherine (1748–1816), second daughter of Hercules Longford Rowley, was born at Longford Castle, co. Westmeath, on 19 April 1778. His younger brother was Sir Hercules Robert *Pakenham (1781–1850). After a perfunctory education he became, on 28 May 1794, aged sixteen, lieutenant in the 92nd foot (an Irish unit afterwards drafted); a few days later he was made captain, and on 6 December, though still not seventeen, he became major in the 33rd or Ulster light dragoons.

On 1 June 1798 Pakenham became major in the old 23rd light dragoons (disbanded in 1802), with which he served in Ireland during the uprising; and on 17 October 1799 he was appointed lieutenant-colonel, 64th foot, which he commanded at the capture of the Danish and Swedish West India islands in 1801. Socially Pakenham appears to have been a general favourite. The inhabitants of Sainte-Croix, one of the captured islands, presented some silver cups in token of their esteem for him and his officers. He commanded the 64th at the capture of St Lucia on 22 June 1803, when he was wounded. In 1805, after returning home, he became a brevet colonel. He was then appointed to a lieutenant-colonelcy in the 7th Royal Fusiliers, whose 1st battalion he joined at Weymouth in 1806, and commanded at Copenhagen in 1807 and at the capture of Martinique in 1809; afterwards he returned with the battalion to Nova Scotia. Pakenham joined Wellington, who in 1806 had married his sister Catherine (Kitty), in the Peninsula after the battle of Talavera (27–8 July 1809). He liked, admired, and worked well with Wellington. He was employed as an assistant adjutant-general to the fusiliers; the officers of the battalion placed his portrait in the mess, and presented him with a sword valued at 200 guineas. He was appointed deputy adjutant-general in the Peninsula on 7 March 1810; no desk soldier, he disliked what he called 'this insignificant clerking business' (Ward, 59).

Pakenham commanded a brigade of the two battalions 7th fusiliers and the Cameron Highlanders, in Sir Brent Spencer's division at Busaco and Fuentes d'Oñoro in 1810, and in 1811 he received the local rank of major-general in the Peninsula, and served with the headquarters staff. At the battle of Salamanca, on 22 July 1812, described by Wellington as the best manoeuvred battle in the whole war, Pakenham commanded the 3rd division, which broke the French centre. The two armies faced each other, and had been moving on parallel lines for three days. They saw each other clearly, from opposite rising grounds, as the valley between was not more than half a mile wide. Marmont's design was to interpose between Wellington and Badajoz; Wellington's object was to prevent this. In their eagerness to gain their point the French leading divisions outmarched those following, and thus left a vacant space in the centre, which Wellington saw, and at once exploited. 'Now's your time, Ned', he said to Pakenham, who was standing near him; Pakenham gave the order to his division, and began the movement which won the battle. Wellington wrote to the Horse Guards on 7 September 1812:

> I put Pakenham to the third division, by General Picton's desire when he was ill; and I am very glad I did so, as I must say he made the movement which led to our success in the battle of 22 July last with a celerity and accuracy of which I doubt if there are very many capable, and without both it would not have answered its end. Pakenham may not be the brightest genius, but my partiality for him does not lead me astray when I tell you that he is one of the best we have. (*Dispatches*, 6.434)

Pakenham commanded the division at the capture of Madrid. He became major-general on 4 June 1812, and was appointed adjutant-general on 10 May 1813. He commanded the 6th division at Sauroren (battle of the Pyrenees), was made KB on 11 September 1813, was appointed colonel of the 6th West India regiment the same year, and was present as adjutant-general in the succeeding campaigns. He received the gold cross and clasps for Martinique, Busaco, Fuentes d'Oñoro, Salamanca, Pyrenees, Nivelle, Nive, Orthez, and Toulouse. On the reconstitution of the Order of the Bath (4 January 1815), he was made GCB. Agreeable and widely liked, he was called by Sir George Napier, 'that most delightful of all characters' (Longford, 357). In 1812 he had proposed to Annabella Milbanke but she rejected him, alleging 'all the Pakenham family have a strong tendency to insanity' (ibid., 117). Instead she married Byron.

Pakenham did not want to fight in the Anglo-American War, but the death of General Ross (of Bladensburg) before Washington (in 1814) led to his selection to command the British force that had operated on the Chesapeake, and which was to be used against New Orleans. Pakenham ought to have joined it in Jamaica, but adverse winds detained him, and he did not reach his command until after a landing had been made at New Orleans, and an action had taken place, in which each side had lost more than 200 men. He found the army on a narrow neck of land flanked on one side by the Mississippi River and on the other by impassable swamp, and unwisely he accepted this unfavourable position. Though brave, he failed in independent command. Against him was one of the ablest United States generals—Andrew Jackson.

After a costly reconnaissance Pakenham erected bastions of hogsheads of sugar, and mounted on them thirty guns; but on 1 January 1815 these were destroyed by American fire. In the following week both sides were reinforced. It is just possible that, if Pakenham had been patient enough to wait the development of his plans, he might have carried the American lines and entered New Orleans. He intended to attack on both sides of the river before dawn on 8 January 1815, but there was delay in crossing, and he sent up the signal rocket before his men on the west side of the river were ready. He was killed, shot through the spine, in the unsuccessful assault that followed. Also killed was his second in command, Sir Samuel Gibbs. Over 3000 officers and men were killed or wounded. Pakenham's body was brought back to Ireland and buried there.

H. M. Chichester, *rev.* Roger T. Stearn

Sources J. Foster, *The peerage, baronetage, and knightage of the British Empire for 1883*, 1 [1883] • *LondG* • *Army List* • R. Cannon, ed., *Historical records of the British army*, 70 vols. (1835–53) • R. Cannon, ed., *Historical record of the seventh regiment, or the royal fusiliers* (1847) • *The dispatches of … the duke of Wellington … from 1799 to 1818*, ed. J. Gurwood, new edn, 3–7 (1837–8) • W. F. P. Napier, *History of the war in the Peninsula and in the south of France*, new edn, 6 vols. (1886) • J. G. Wilson and J. Fiske, eds., *Appleton's cyclopaedia of American biography*, 7 vols. (1887–1900) • G. R. Gleig, *A narrative of the campaigns of the British army at Washington and New Orleans* (1821) • E. Longford [E. H. Pakenham, countess of Longford], *Wellington*, 1: *The years of the sword* (1969) • R. Muir, *Britain and the defeat of Napoleon, 1807–1815* (1996) • S. G. P. Ward, *Wellington's headquarters: a study of the administrative problems in the Peninsula, 1809–14* (1957) • GEC, *Peerage*
Likenesses R. Westmacott, sculpture, 1823 (with General Walsh), St Paul's Cathedral, London • T. Heaphy, watercolour, NPG

Pakenham, Sir Francis John (1832–1905), diplomatist, born on 29 February 1832 in London, was the fourth son of Thomas Pakenham, second earl of Longford, and his wife, Emma Charlotte, daughter of William *Lygon, first Earl Beauchamp [*see under* Lygon, Frederick (1830–1891)]. After private education he matriculated from Christ Church, Oxford, on 17 October 1849. On leaving the university he was appointed attaché at Lisbon in 1852, and was promoted paid attaché at Mexico two years later. He was transferred in 1858 to Copenhagen, and in 1863 to Vienna. In June 1864 he was promoted to secretary of legation at Buenos Aires. During April, May, and June of the following year he was employed on special service in Paraguay on board HMS *Dotterel*, which had been sent up the River Plate and its tributaries for the protection of British subjects during the war between Paraguay, Argentina, and Brazil. He acquitted himself of this duty to the entire satisfaction of his superiors. In August 1865 he was transferred to Rio de Janeiro, but remained in charge of the legation at Buenos Aires until December. In December 1866 he was employed on special service at Rio Grande do Sul in connection with an attempt that had been made on the life of the British consul, R. de Courcy Perry, from motives of personal revenge.

Pakenham was transferred to Stockholm in March 1868, and later in the same year to Brussels. From there he went to Washington, DC, in 1870, and to Copenhagen in 1874. In March 1878 he was promoted to minister-resident and consul-general at Santiago, where he remained until 1885, serving in 1883 as British commissioner for claims arising out of the war between Chile and Bolivia and Peru. In February 1885 he was appointed British envoy at Buenos Aires, with the additional office of minister-plenipotentiary to Paraguay. In February 1896 he was transferred to Stockholm, where he remained until his retirement from the service in 1902. He was made KCMG in 1898. In retirement he lived at Bernhurst House, Hurst Green, Sussex, which he inherited in 1858 by the will of Count Pierre Coquet de Tresseilles. Pakenham married on 29 July 1879 Caroline Matilda (*d.* 25 June 1938), seventh daughter of Henry Ward, rector of Killinchy, co. Down. They had no children. Travelling for reasons of health, Pakenham died in Alameda, California, on 26 January 1905.

T. H. Sanderson, *rev.* H. C. G. Matthew

Sources *The Times* (27 Jan 1905) • *FO List* (1905) • personal knowledge (1912)
Archives Bodl. Oxf., corresp. with Lord Kimberley
Likenesses G. de Rosen, portrait, 1900
Wealth at death £65,281 13*s.* 7*d.*: probate, 28 April 1905, *CGPLA Eng. & Wales*

Pakenham, Sir Hercules Robert (1781–1850), army officer, third son of Edward Michael, second Baron Longford (1743–1792), and his wife, Catherine (*d.* 12 March 1816), second daughter of Hercules Langford Rowley, was born on 29 September 1781. He was brother of Sir Edward Michael *Pakenham, and brother-in-law of the first duke of Wellington. He was appointed ensign 40th regiment on 23 July 1803, became lieutenant on 3 February 1804, was transferred to the 95th rifles in April the same year, and obtained his company there on 2 August 1805. He served in the expedition to Copenhagen and in Portugal, where he was wounded at Obidos on 16–17 August 1808. 'He is really one of the best officers of riflemen I have seen,' wrote Sir Arthur Wellesley, recommending him for promotion (Gurwood, 3.129). He was promoted to a majority in the 7th West India regiment on 30 August 1810, but remained with the Peninsular army, and was assistant adjutant-general of Picton's division up to the storming of Badajos, where he was wounded.

After being repeatedly recommended for promotion, Pakenham was made a brevet lieutenant-colonel on 27 April 1812, was appointed lieutenant-colonel 26th Cameronians on 3 September 1812, and transferred as captain and lieutenant-colonel to the Coldstream Guards on 25 July 1814, from which he retired on half pay in 1817. He was made brevet colonel and aide-de-camp to the king on 27 May 1825, became a major-general on 10 January 1837, was appointed colonel 43rd light infantry on 9 September 1844, commanded the Portsmouth district from 1843 to 1846, and became a lieutenant-general on 9 November 1846. He was made CB on 4 June 1815 and KCB on 19 July 1838.

Pakenham married, in November 1817, Emily (*d.* 26 Jan 1875), fourth daughter of Thomas Stapylton, Lord Le Despenser; they had six sons (one of whom was killed at Inkerman and another at the relief of Lucknow) and three daughters. He died suddenly at his residence, Langford Lodge, co. Antrim, on 7 March 1850.

H. M. Chichester, *rev.* James Falkner

Sources *Army List* • *Naval and Military Gazette* (16 March 1850) • Burke, *Peerage* • *Hart's Army List* • *The dispatches of … the duke of Wellington … from 1799 to 1818*, ed. J. Gurwood, 3–5 (1837–8)
Archives Hants. RO, corresp.
Likenesses A. Plunier, oils, *c.*1815, Stratfield Saye House, Basingstoke • wood-engraving, NPG; repro. in *ILN* (1846–7)

Pakenham, Sir Richard (1797–1868), diplomatist, was born on 19 May 1797 at Pakenham Hall, Castle Pollard, co.

Westmeath, Ireland, the fifth son of Admiral Sir Thomas *Pakenham (1757–1836) and his wife, Louisa, daughter of the Rt Hon. John Staples. He was a cousin of General Sir Edward Pakenham (1778–1815), who was killed at the battle of New Orleans in 1815. After attending Trinity College, Dublin, Pakenham began his diplomatic career on 15 October 1817, as attaché to his uncle the earl of Clancarty, at The Hague. On 26 January 1824 he was assigned to Switzerland as secretary of legation. He was promoted and transferred on 29 December 1826 to Mexico, where he spent the next sixteen years of his life, first as secretary of legation and then from 12 March 1835 as minister-plenipotentiary. He was a friend of Sir Charles Vaughan (1774–1849), minister to the United States from 1827 to 1835, with whom he corresponded while in Mexico. Pakenham never married, although it was said he had been engaged intermittently to Luz Escandón, sister of Manuel Escandón, a prominent Mexican businessman.

Pakenham was a very astute and effective diplomat, dealing mainly with the commercial and financial questions that formed the basis of Britain's connection with Mexico at a time of great political instability caused by years of revolutionary upheaval. He spoke perfect Spanish, often wore Mexican dress, and by contemporary accounts was well liked and respected by government, diplomatic, and commercial élites in Mexico. He was instrumental behind the scenes in effecting a settlement between France and Mexico in 1839 after the French attack on Vera Cruz (1838) over claims against the Mexican government. Less successful was the attempt to mediate a settlement between Mexico and Texas, who were at war after 1836, when Texas overthrew Mexican rule and established an independent republic. The Texas question preoccupied Pakenham for the remainder of his stay in Mexico, which lasted until 1842, when he took a leave of absence in England. On 13 December 1843 he was sworn of the privy council, and the next day he was appointed envoy-extraordinary and minister-plenipotentiary to the United States.

Two important issues were pending upon Pakenham's arrival in Washington on 13 February 1844: the annexation of Texas and the Oregon boundary dispute. The former question was especially delicate, as the American secretary of state, John C. Calhoun, accused Britain of having promoted the abolition of slavery in Texas to undermine the institution in the United States. The two exchanged diplomatic notes on the subject, later known as the Calhoun–Pakenham correspondence. Although the correspondence is better known for Calhoun's defence of slavery, Pakenham's deliberate avoidance of a continuing debate on Britain's official anti-slavery position enabled him to defuse the attacks against Britain during the annexation crisis.

More threatening to the Anglo-American peace, however, was the Oregon boundary crisis resolved in 1846, during which Pakenham suffered a profound crisis of confidence in his diplomatic abilities. He received a reprimand from Lord Aberdeen, the foreign secretary, for having rejected outright an American counterproposal and thereby precipitated a temporary suspension of the negotiations. Pakenham asked to be recalled over the incident since 'the little confidence that I ever possessed in my own judgment is now so completely shattered that I shall no longer be able to proceed' (Pakenham to Aberdeen, 28 Oct 1845, BL, Add. MS 43123). Aberdeen reassured him and the crisis ended peacefully, but Pakenham felt that the American government mistreated him. He wrote of James Buchanan, Calhoun's successor, 'if you knew what it was to be pitied by such a man as Mr. Buchanan, you would understand that I could not but take the thing [the Oregon negotiations] a little to heart' (Pakenham to Aberdeen, 29 Dec 1845, BL, Add. MS 43123).

Pakenham returned to Britain on leave in May 1847 and, rather than return to his post in the United States, took an early retirement. He was made KCB in 1848. The Foreign Office asked him to resume his career however, and on 28 April 1851 he was assigned to Lisbon as envoy-extraordinary and minister-plenipotentiary. In May 1855 he returned to Britain on leave and on 28 June he retired on pension. His last assignment was a brief special mission to Lisbon from August to October 1855. He was awarded a diplomatic pension of the second class and retired to his family home at Castle Pollard, co. Westmeath. He died at Coolure, near Castle Pollard, during the last week of October 1868; there is uncertainty over the precise date, but 28 October seems most likely.

LELIA M. ROECKELL

Sources J. J. Barnes and P. P. Barnes, *Private and confidential: letters from British ministers in Washington to the foreign secretaries in London, 1844–1867* (1993) • D. Pletcher, *The diplomacy of annexation: Texas, Oregon and the Mexican war* [1973] • *Life in Mexico: the letters of Fanny Calderón de la Barca*, ed. H. T. Fisher and M. H. Fisher (1966) • Pakenham to Aberdeen, BL, Aberdeen MSS, Add. MS 43123 • Foreign office papers, series 50 (Mexico), 1835–42, PRO • Foreign office papers, series 5 (United States), 1843–7, PRO • *The Times* (31 Oct 1868) • L. M. Roekell, 'British interests in Texas, 1825–1846', DPhil diss., U. Oxf., 1993 • All Souls Oxf., Sir Charles Vaughan MSS

Archives PRO NIre., corresp. and papers | All Souls Oxf., corresp. with Sir Charles Richard Vaughan • BL, corresp. with Lord Aberdeen, Add. MSS 43104–43105, 43154–43155 • Bodl. Oxf., corresp. with Sir John Fiennes Crampton • Hants. RO, corresp. with third earl of Malmesbury • PRO, FO papers, series 50 (Mexico) • PRO, FO papers, series 5 (United States)

Likenesses photograph, National Archives, Washington DC

Wealth at death under £35,000 in Ireland: probate, 25 Nov 1868, *CGPLA Ire.* • under £18,000 in England: further action, 19 Dec 1868, *CGPLA Ire.*

Pakenham, Sir Thomas (1757–1836), naval officer and politician, fourth son of Thomas Pakenham, first Baron Longford (1713–1766), and Elizabeth Cuffe (1719–1794), was born on 29 September 1757, possibly at Pakenham Hall, co. Westmeath. Owing to the modest circumstances of his father, Pakenham was destined early on for a military career. Following the example of his eldest brother, Edward Michael Pakenham (later second Baron Longford), he entered the Royal Navy. In 1771 he joined the *Southampton*, under the command of a fellow Irishman, Captain John Macbride, with whom he moved to the *Orpheus* in 1773. In the following year he was on the coast of Guinea with Captain William Cornwallis in the *Pallas*, and in 1775 he was appointed acting lieutenant of the *Sphinx* on the coast of North America. Following the arrival of reinforcements under Lord Charles Cornwallis off the American coast in May 1776 he was sent to deliver urgent dispatches to General Sir William Howe in Halifax. After successfully evading pursuit by an American squadron he completed his mission, and was consequently promoted by Vice-Admiral Molyneux Shuldham, commander-in-chief of the North American station, to the rank of lieutenant in the frigate *Greyhound*.

While assigned to this ship Pakenham was engaged in several actions both ashore and afloat, in the course of which he was severely wounded. On the return of the *Greyhound* to England in 1778 he transferred to the *Courageux* (74 guns), commanded by Lord Mulgrave, as second lieutenant. In the following spring he was moved into the *Europe* (64 guns) as first lieutenant, going to North America with the flag of Rear-Admiral Marriot Arbuthnot, and on 21 September 1779 he was promoted to the command of the sloop *Victor*, newly captured from the enemy. He was then sent to the Jamaica station where, on 2 March 1780, he was appointed by Sir Peter Parker the elder to command the *San Carlos* (32 guns), a ship captured from the Spanish. However, Pakenham's poor health compelled him to return to England in the autumn. In December 1780 he was appointed to command the *Crescent* (28 guns), attached to the fleet under Vice-Admiral George Darby, which relieved Gibraltar in April 1781, and was sent to Minorca in company with the *Flora*.

On their way back, in passing through the strait of Gibraltar on 30 May, the British ships encountered two Dutch frigates, one of which, the *Castor*, eventually surrendered to the *Flora*, while the other, the *Brill*, overpowered and captured the *Crescent*. However, the *Crescent* was immediately recaptured by the *Flora*, the *Brill* making her escape; but both *Crescent* and *Castor* had received so much damage in the action that they fell into the hands of two French frigates on the way home, only the *Flora*, with Pakenham aboard, escaping. He had refused to resume the command of the *Crescent*, maintaining that by his surrender to the *Brill* his commission was cancelled, and that when recaptured by the *Flora*, the *Crescent* was on the same footing as any other prize. For the loss of his ship he was tried by court martial and honourably acquitted, it being proved that he did not strike the flag until through heavy casualties, the fall of her masts, and the disabling of her guns further resistance was impossible. In recognition of his exemplary conduct he was at once appointed to the new frigate *Minerva* (38 guns), which he commanded in 1782 at the relief of Gibraltar by Admiral Lord Howe.

In 1785 Pakenham married Louisa (*c.*1765–1833), daughter of the Rt Hon John Staples of co. Tyrone, and niece of the prominent Irish politician and landowner Thomas Conolly. As a consequence of this marriage he came into wealth and property, and assumed a prominent place in Irish polite society. His eldest son, Edward Michael, born in 1786, later inherited the major part of the estates belonging to Conolly, and took this surname in lieu of Pakenham. In 1793 Pakenham commissioned the *Invincible* (74 guns), and in her took part in the battle of 1 June 1794, when his conduct was described as particularly brilliant. Afterwards he was recommended by Lord Howe for the gold medal. Late in 1794 he seems to have been involved in negotiations at Spithead with striking Irish sailors and marines aboard the *Culloden*, then commanded by Captain Thomas Troubridge. In the following year he was made colonel of marines, and assumed command of the *Juste* (84 guns), in the capture of which, on 1 June 1794, he had played a crucial role. In December 1796 he may have sensed the mood of dissatisfaction in the fleet that eventually led to the Nore and Spithead mutinies, warning the first lord of the Admiralty that seamen were 'increasingly discontented' at the substantial arrears in the payment of their wages (Dugan, 33).

A flamboyant and popular officer, Pakenham was described by one contemporary as a 'regular character', who maintained a large following of Irishmen under his command at sea (Dillon, 1.137). He was promoted rear-admiral on 14 February 1799, became vice-admiral on 23 April 1804, and admiral on 31 July 1810, but despite his proven merit he never hoisted his flag on active service. He was for some time master-general of the ordnance in Ireland, and was active in this capacity during the uprising of 1798, serving under Lord Cornwallis and General Lake. He was an MP in the Irish House of Commons from 1783 to 1800, was knighted on 16 May 1820, and died in Dublin on 2 February 1836. His fifth son, Sir Richard *Pakenham, achieved prominence in the diplomatic service.

ROBERT MCGREGOR

Sources *DNB* • *GM*, 2nd ser., 5 (1836), 660–61 • Burke, *Peerage* (1963) • GEC, *Peerage* • J. Ralfe, *The naval biography of Great Britain*, 4 (1828) • W. H. Dillon, *A narrative of my professional adventures, 1790–1839*, ed. M. A. Lewis, 1, Navy RS, 93 (1953) • R. Beatson, *Naval and military memoirs of Great Britain*, 2nd edn, 5 (1804) • W. James, *The naval history of Great Britain, from the declaration of war by France in 1793, to the accession of George IV*, [3rd edn], 6 vols. (1837), vol. 1 • J. Dugan, *The great mutiny* (New York, 1965); repr. (1966) • N. A. M. Rodger, *The wooden world: an anatomy of the Georgian navy* (1986) • T. Pakenham, *The year of liberty: the story of the great Irish rebellion of 1798* (1969) • B. FitzGerald, *Lady Louisa Conolly, 1743–1821: an Anglo-Irish biography* (1950)

Archives BL, log of HMS *Invincible*, Add. MS 23207, fol. 81 • Castlepollard, Tullynally, papers • NMM, logbook as lieutenant of HMS *Europe*, ADM/L/E/178 • NMM, logbook as lieutenant of HMS *Greyhound*, ADM/L/G/192 • PRO NIre., MSS | BL, corresp. with Sir Robert Peel, Add. MS 40236, fol. 5; 40261, fols. 20, 96; 40270, fol. 237 • PRO NIre., D/1398 • PRO NIre., MIC/537 • PRO NIre., T/1063, 3763 • PRO NIre., letters in the collection of Thomas Pelham, first earl of Chichester, T/755/3

Likenesses G. Stuart, portrait, *c.*1787–1792 (*Captain Thomas Pakenham*), Sterling and Francine Clark Art Institute, Williamstown, Massachusetts • Bartolozzi, Landseer, Ryder, and Stow, group portrait, line engraving, pubd 1803 (*Commemoration of the victory of June 1st 1794*; after R. Smirke), BM, NPG • R. Smirke and J. Stow, engraved medallion, 1803 (*Commemoration of the victory of June 1st 1794*) • H. Hone, miniature; Christies, 10–11 July 1984, lot 136

Wealth at death over £50,000; three estates in Ireland, one in England; also house in Grosvenor Place, London: will, 1836, court of prerogative, Ireland

Pakenham, Sir William Christopher (1861–1933), naval officer, was born in London on 10 July 1861, the second son of Rear-Admiral Thomas Alexander Pakenham (1820–

Sir William Christopher Pakenham (1861–1933), by Francis Dodd, 1917

1889), the third son of the second earl of Longford, and his wife, Sophia Frances (*d.* 1898), the third daughter of Sir Tatton Sykes, fourth baronet, of Sledmere. He entered the training ship HMS *Britannia* as a naval cadet in 1874 and, having passed out two years later, went to sea in the *Monarch* in the Mediterranean, being promoted midshipman in 1876. The following year he was transferred to the frigate *Raleigh*. Together with an able seaman he was highly commended for gallantry in plunging into the sea and rescuing a coxswain who had fallen overboard as the ship was leaving Larnaka, Cyprus, in August 1878. In September 1879 he joined the *Alexandra*, the flagship of Sir Geoffrey Hornby, and remained in her when Sir F. B. P. Seymour succeeded to the command until he was promoted sub-lieutenant in October 1880. Having undergone the usual gunnery course in the *Excellent* at Portsmouth he was in December 1882 again appointed to the *Alexandra* (still the flagship of Lord Alcester); but soon after Lord John Hay had assumed the command he was transferred in April 1883 to the corvette *Canada*, destined to join the North America squadron. In this ship he was a strict though benevolent autocrat of the gun-room mess in which Prince George (afterwards George V) was serving as midshipman. He was promoted lieutenant in October 1883, and was soon brought home again, having been chosen as flag-lieutenant by Rear-Admiral George Tryon (flag in the *Nelson*) during the three years (1884–7) of his command of the new Australia station.

Pakenham's remaining nine years as lieutenant were spent mainly as gunnery officer of the small cruisers *Calypso*, *Garnet*, and *Sybille* in the training squadron, and on the Pacific and Mediterranean stations. While in the *Calypso* he again distinguished himself by a brave attempt to save the life of a petty officer who had fallen into the sea from the foreyard during drill in Kiel harbour.

After being promoted commander in June 1896, Pakenham served for nine months in the old *Galatea* (a coastguard ship at Hull) and for eighteen months in the *Venus* under Sir Berkeley Milne in the Mediterranean. He had qualified as an interpreter in French while on half pay in 1884, and was selected for duty in the naval intelligence department from August 1899 until March 1901. He then commanded the sloop *Daphne* on the China station, and, after being lent to Rear-Admiral Harry Tremenheere Grenfell's flagship *Albion* as acting captain early in 1902, returned home in June of that year. He was promoted captain in June 1903.

The outbreak of war between Russia and Japan was imminent, and Pakenham's experience in intelligence work and his linguistic abilities (although he never learned the difficult Japanese language) marked him out as the officer to succeed Captain Troubridge, who was due for relief in 1904 as naval attaché in Japan. War broke out on 6 February 1904 and Pakenham relieved Troubridge in March, taking his place on board the battleship *Asahi*, in which he remained continuously until after the final Japanese victory at Tsushima on 27 May 1905. His reports to the Admiralty throughout the war were brilliantly written and revealed a thorough appreciation of the strategic, tactical, and technical implications of the events and situations which he described. His cool daring in exposing himself to danger in order more completely to observe the proceedings of the great battle much impressed the Japanese, and led the emperor of Japan, on Admiral Togo's recommendation, to confer on him the second class of the order of the Rising Sun. He was specially appointed CB (military division) soon after the battle.

After returning to England in 1906 Pakenham commanded the cruiser *Antrim* for two years in the Atlantic Fleet, and then the *Glory* and the *Triumph* (a battleship bought from Chile in 1904) in the Mediterranean until January 1910, when he came home to take command of the new battleship *Collingwood* in the Home Fleet, until December 1911. Winston Churchill, in reconstituting his board soon after taking office as first lord of the Admiralty, selected Pakenham to be fourth sea lord, being impressed by his reputation as an officer of strong character and his unique experience of modern naval warfare. Before Pakenham left the board two years later he had in June 1913 reached flag rank, and in December he took command of the 3rd cruiser squadron of the Home Fleet, with his flag in his old ship *Antrim*. In March 1915, with his flag in the *Australia*, he took charge of one of the two battle-cruiser squadrons which belonged to the Australian commonwealth and had been willingly lent for service in the Grand Fleet after the victory of the Falkland Islands (8 December 1914) had disposed of German danger in the Pacific. He thus had the titular appointment of rear-admiral commanding the Australian fleet. In the battle of Jutland (31 May 1916) Pakenham's flag was flown in the *New Zealand*, the *Australia* being under repair at Devonport after a collision with the *New Zealand* in fog on 22 April. His remaining ship, the *Indefatigable*, was blown up and lost early in the battle. Pakenham distinguished himself by able support of Vice-Admiral Sir David Beatty and was rewarded by appointment as KCB (1916); he was personally decorated with that order and also as KCVO by the king on the occasion of his visit to the fleet at Rosyth in 1917. In November 1916 Beatty became commander-in-chief in succession to Sir John Jellicoe, and on his insistent recommendation Pakenham was appointed to succeed him in the command of the battle-cruiser force (there were many officers with strong claims senior to him but who had seen less service with battle cruisers). He transferred his flag from the *Australia* to the *Lion* in January 1917 and retained the command until April 1919, having been promoted acting vice-admiral in June 1917 and been confirmed in that rank in September 1918, and having been present at the surrender of the German fleet in the Forth at the end of the war.

After a well-deserved rest on half pay Pakenham was appointed president of the Royal Naval College, Greenwich, in August 1919, but at his own request was given another command afloat as commander-in-chief of the North America and West Indies station in October 1920. After two and a half years he returned home. He had been promoted admiral in April 1922 and retired at his own request in March 1926. He long maintained correspondence with his Japanese friends and made a great impression at Geneva in 1927 by travelling from England for the sole purpose of calling upon Admiral Viscount Saito, who had been minister of marine in 1905. He was appointed GCB in 1925 and succeeded Sir C. C. Monro as Bath king of arms in 1930. He resigned from this post only a few days before his death, which took place at San Sebastian, Spain, on 28 July 1933. He was unmarried.

Pakenham was appointed KCMG (1919), made chevalier of the Légion d'honneur, and given the Croix de Guerre (bronze palms), the first class of the Japanese order of the Rising Sun, the grand cordon of the Chinese order of the Excellent Crop, and the DSM of the United States of America in the post-war award of honours.

Pakenham was a strong-minded, somewhat austere, able, and well-read officer, wholeheartedly devoted to the service. He was also something of a character, with his faultless care of his personal appearance and dress, his quiet sense of caustic humour, and his studiously polite, if somewhat elaborate, manners. Churchill paid him a notable tribute in *The World Crisis* (1923).

Numerous stories are told of Pakenham, as that during the battle of Tsushima the casemate on which he was stationed was struck by a shell, with resulting casualties, and his white uniform was splashed with blood. He quietly left the deck and returned in a few minutes with spotless attire and resumed his notes of the battle. It is also related that while in the Grand Fleet he always slept fully dressed as in daytime, and that he had all the furniture of the admiral's quarters burnt, together with all inflammable articles in the ship, including the deck corticine and the companion ladder, in order to minimize the danger of fire during an action; and he kept only a chair in his bridge cabin. V. W. BADDELEY, *rev.*

Sources *The Times* (31 July 1933) • S. W. Roskill, *Admiral of the fleet Earl Beatty: the last naval hero, an intimate biography* (1980) • *WWW* • A. J. Marder, *From the Dreadnought to Scapa Flow: the Royal Navy in the Fisher era, 1904–1919*, 5 vols. (1961–70) • private information (1981) • Burke, *Peerage* (1980) • *CGPLA Eng. & Wales* (1933)
Archives East Riding of Yorkshire Archives Service, Beverley, papers • NMM, letters, diaries, and papers | FILM IWM FVA, actuality footage
Likenesses F. Dodd, charcoal and watercolour drawing, 1917, IWM [*see illus.*] • W. Stoneman, photograph, 1919, NPG • W. Nicholson, oils, 1920, IWM • A. S. Cope, group portrait, oils, 1921 (*Naval officers of World War I, 1914–18*), NPG
Wealth at death £65,979 9s. 10d.: probate, 24 Oct 1933, *CGPLA Eng. & Wales*

Pakington. For this title name *see* individual entries under Pakington; *see also* Tasburgh, Dorothy [Dorothy Pakington, Lady Pakington] (1531–1577).

Pakington, Dorothy. *See* Tasburgh, Dorothy (1531–1577).

Pakington [*née* Coventry], **Dorothy, Lady Pakington** (*bap.* **1623**, *d.* **1679**), friend of learned clergy, was baptized on 17 December 1623 at St Bride's, Fleet Street, London, the daughter of Sir Thomas *Coventry (1578–1640), lord keeper from 1625 to 1639 and first Baron Coventry from 1628, and his second wife, Elizabeth (1583–1653), daughter of John Aldersey of Spurstow, Cheshire, and widow of William Pitchford. Dorothy Coventry married Sir John *Pakington, second baronet (1621–1680), of Westwood, Worcestershire. The marriage probably took place in the early 1640s. Sir John Pakington had been Lord Coventry's ward since his father's death in 1624, and the match may have been arranged by Dorothy's parents, but however it was initiated it appears to have been a loving and companionate marriage. It is not known how many children Lady Pakington bore. In 1660 the couple had three children living, all of whom survived her: a son, John *Pakington (*c*.1649–1688) [*see under* Pakington, Sir John], who succeeded as third baronet, and two daughters. Her daughter Elizabeth, who married Anthony Eyre about 1660, was given possession of Lady Pakington's manuscript prayers and other papers.

Like her husband, Lady Pakington was a zealous royalist. Many of her prayers composed during the civil war and interregnum express strong partisanship for the royalist cause, with fervent appeals to God during the trial and execution of Charles I. In early 1649 Lady Pakington begged God to 'suffer not the effusion of his [Charles's] blood to be added to the many provocations of a rebellious people … shew thyself a Lord of power … in averting this horrible fact' (Bodl. Oxf., MS Add. B.58, fols. 4*v*–5). Once the king's death was a *fait accompli*, she drew parallels between Charles's execution and Christ's crucifixion (ibid., fols. 5–5*v*). She also beseeched God to give political guidance to the youthful Charles Stuart, whom she considered an unsophisticated player in the game of factional politics: 'he is a young unexperienced Pilot to steer to turne a vessel in so impetuous a storme' (ibid., fol. 2). Lady Pakington pleaded for his restoration to the throne, but not by the 'unchristian complyances' Charles had offered to the Scots:

> Let thy mercy pardon whatever hath already of this kind past from him, and let the unsuccessfullnes of these sinister expedients but most principally the sinn of them, be a perpetuall document to him, to rely no more on such broken reeds … let not that treacherous party within our own bosomes [those royalists who promoted a Scottish alliance], continue to blast all his Enterprises. (ibid., fols. 2–3)

Meanwhile Sir John Pakington had compounded for his estates, which had been sequestered in 1646. In 1649 the lands were conveyed to the regicide Thomas Scott, although the Pakington family continued to live at Westwood throughout the interregnum. At this time Lady Pakington and her husband invited the king's chaplain, Dr Henry Hammond, to stay with them at Westwood, where Dr Hammond remained as an honoured guest until his death in 1660. Lady Pakington's exceptional intellect and her deep interest in theology led to a close friendship with Hammond. She was welcomed into the circle of Hammond's clerical colleagues, including such eminent divines as John Fell (dean of Christ Church and later bishop of Oxford), Richard Allestree, John Dolben (later archbishop of York), Humphrey Henchman (later bishop of London), George Morley (later bishop of Winchester), and other prominent churchmen, many of whom became her personal friends. As well as participating in theological and philosophical discussions Lady Pakington shared in the circulation of manuscripts (some of which were found in her possession at her death) written by Hammond and his coterie. Lady Pakington's friendship with Anglican divines and her scholarly interests were later continued by her son, John. Like his mother, John led a quiet studious life at Westwood, and under the tutelage of the non-juror George Hickes he became an outstanding Anglo-Saxon scholar.

It may have been the close ties between Lady Pakington and the group of learned divines centring on Henry Hammond that led contemporaries to conjecture that she was the anonymous author of *The Whole Duty of Man* and other works presumably composed by the same writer. The hypothesis of Pakington's authorship appeared to be supported by a range of contemporary evidence, including her daughter Mary Eyre's alleged possession of a copy of *The Whole Duty* in Lady Pakington's autograph, and the statement of Dr Hickes in the dedication of his *Linguarum septentrionalium thesaurus* to Lady Pakington's grandson (1697) that Lady Pakington's piety and intellectual talents entitled her to be called author of *The Whole Duty*. Citing these and other 'witnesses', George Ballard argued the claim vigorously in his biography of Lady Pakington (Ballard, 290–300). In 1864, however, the Revd Francis Barham suggested that the author of *The Whole Duty* was Hammond's friend Richard Allestree, a theory supported in 1884 in three articles by C. E. Doble, and now accepted virtually unanimously by modern scholarship. Nevertheless, the fact that her scholarly acquaintance were willing to assign authorship of such celebrated works to Lady Pakington gives some idea of her impressive intellectual gifts, and of the general esteem in which she was held during her lifetime.

Lady Pakington died of a stroke at Westwood Manor on 10 May 1679. The cause of death was confirmed by autopsy, whose results are summarized in 'An account of the appearances upon dissection in the body of the honorable the Ladie Pakington' (BL, Sloane MS 4034, fol. 363). She was buried in the family vault in the church at Hampton Lovett, near Westwood, on 13 May. A memorial inscribed on the monument erected for her husband declared Lady Pakington 'Justly reputed, the Authoress of the Whole duty of Man; Who was Exemplary for her great Piety and Goodness' (Ballard, 303). SARA H. MENDELSON

Sources *DNB* • G. Ballard, *Memoirs of several ladies of Great Britain* (1752) • Lady Pakington's prayers, Bodl. Oxf., MS Add. B. 58 • BL, 'An account of the appearances upon dissection in the body of the honorable the Ladie Pakington', Sloane MS 4034, fol. 363 • BL, prayers by Lady Pakington, with portrait at fol. 26, Add. MS 28659, fols. 21, 26 • GEC, *Peerage* • J. Fell, preface, in H. Hammond, *A practical catechism … to which is prefixed the life of the author, by John Fell, D.D.*, 16th edn (1847), xvii–cxxv • T. Cox, 'Description of Aylesbury Manor', *Magna Britannia et Hibernia* (1806) • *IGI*

Likenesses V. Green, mezzotint, 1781, BM, NPG • portrait, BL, Add. MS 28659, fol. 26

Pakington, Sir John (*b.* in or before **1477**, *d.* **1551**), judge, was the eldest son of John Pakington and Elizabeth, daughter of Thomas Washbourne of Stamford-le-Teme, Worcestershire. He began his professional career as an attorney of the common pleas, appearing for a Shropshire client in 1498, and acting as deputy for the sheriff of that county in 1500; his signature is also found on a bill in chancery as early as 1500. This may explain how he came to be chirographer of the common pleas in 1508, a valuable clerical office which he held until his death, though since the office was in the gift of the crown Pakington must have acquired a significant patron. Shortly before 1505 he became a member of the Inner Temple, but he did not immediately abandon attorneyship and in 1506 represented the inn itself in a debt action. In 1512 he was appointed solicitor to the Mercers' Company. However, by 1507 he was described as 'counsel' in the court of requests, in 1513 he became a justice of the peace for Gloucestershire, and in 1515 member of parliament for the same shire, while in 1517 he was sufficiently advanced at the bar to become a bencher of his inn without having read.

In 1519 Pakington is mentioned as 'legis peritus de consilio' in a case in the London Guildhall (PRO, CP 40/1026, m. 101d). He delivered readings in the Inner Temple in 1520 and 1528, serving as treasurer from 1528 to 1533. Some new chambers erected in the inn at this time, doubtless at his expense, were named Pakington's Rents. In 1529 he received a very remarkable patent allowing him to wear a hat in the king's presence (and on all other occasions), and exempting him from being made a knight, a baron of the exchequer, or a serjeant-at-law. Perhaps a call of serjeants was already in the offing. Pakington was indeed offered the coif in 1531, but, presumably relying on his privilege, was never created. The reason may have been that his principal activities were keeping him away from London.

By his marriage in the 1520s to Anne (*d.* 1563), daughter of Henry Dacres, sheriff of London, and widow of Robert Fairthwaite (*d.* 1521), Pakington acquired valuable city connections; but most of his land purchases were in his native county of Worcestershire, where in 1528 he settled at Hampton Lovett. He was a steward of estates in Worcestershire for Worcester Cathedral and Fotheringhay College; and he was active in the council in the marches in the 1530s, becoming a justice for north Wales (1532), recorder of Worcester (by 1539, when he was elected member for the shire), a Welsh judge on the Brecon circuit (1541), and recorder of Ludlow (1542). Waiving his patent of 1529, he accepted knighthood in 1545. He died on 21 August 1551 and was buried at Hampton Lovett, where there is a tomb chest. His sons having predeceased him, his daughters Bridget Littleton and Ursula Scudamore were his heirs-at-law, and his entailed estates passed to his nephew Thomas Pakington. Among various charitable bequests he left money for the marriage of between forty and sixty poor maidens, for making highways and bridges around Hampton Lovett, and for the poor-boxes of the Inner Temple and various parishes. The household servants remembered in his will included two minstrels. Dame Anne founded almshouses in Fleet Street and a charity for the poor of St Botolph, Aldersgate.

J. H. BAKER

Sources HoP, *Commons, 1509–58*, 3.47–8 • F. A. Inderwick and R. A. Roberts, eds., *A calendar of the Inner Temple records*, 1 (1896) • *CPR, 1494–1509*, 607 • Rolls of warrants of attorney, PRO, CP 40 • PRO, CP 40/1026, 1034 • PRO, C1/264/23 • PRO, REQ 1/3. fol. 299 • L. Lyell and F. D. Watney, eds., *Acts of court of the Mercers' Company, 1453–1527* (1936), 402 • Baker, *Serjeants*, 168 • W. R. Williams, *The history of the great sessions in Wales, 1542–1830* (privately printed, Brecon, 1899), 124–5 • J. Caley and J. Hunter, eds., *Valor ecclesiasticus temp. Henrici VIII*, 6 vols., RC (1810–34), vol. 3, p. 226; vol. 4, p. 289 • PRO, C 142/93/102 [writ of diem clausit extremum, 3 Oct. 1551] • will, PRO, PROB 11/34, sig. 30 • PRO, PROB 11/47, sig. 10 [widow's will] • J. Stow, *A survey of the cities of London and Westminster and the borough of Southwark*, new edn, ed. J. Strype, 1/3 (1720), 113–14, 118 [Anne Pakington's charities]

Pakington, Sir John (1549–1625), courtier, was the son of Sir Thomas Pakington (*d.* 1571), sheriff of Worcester, and Dorothy Kytson (1531–1577) [*see* Tasburgh, Dorothy]. His grandfather Robert Pakington was a London mercer and MP for the city, murdered in 1537. Robert was brother to the judge Sir John *Pakington (*b.* in or before 1477, *d.* 1551). From his uncle Sir John, Sir Thomas inherited estates near Droitwich in Worcestershire, including the manors of Hampton Lovett and Westwood; and from his mother, lands in and around the town of Aylesbury, Buckinghamshire. The main Worcestershire estates passed in turn to John, but John's mother, Dorothy, exercised what she evidently considered to be regalian rights at Aylesbury. On 4 May 1571, as 'lord and owner of the town', she nominated its burgesses without reference to any of the inhabitants. Dorothy's second husband, Thomas Tasburgh, sat more than once for the town and during the reign of Elizabeth,

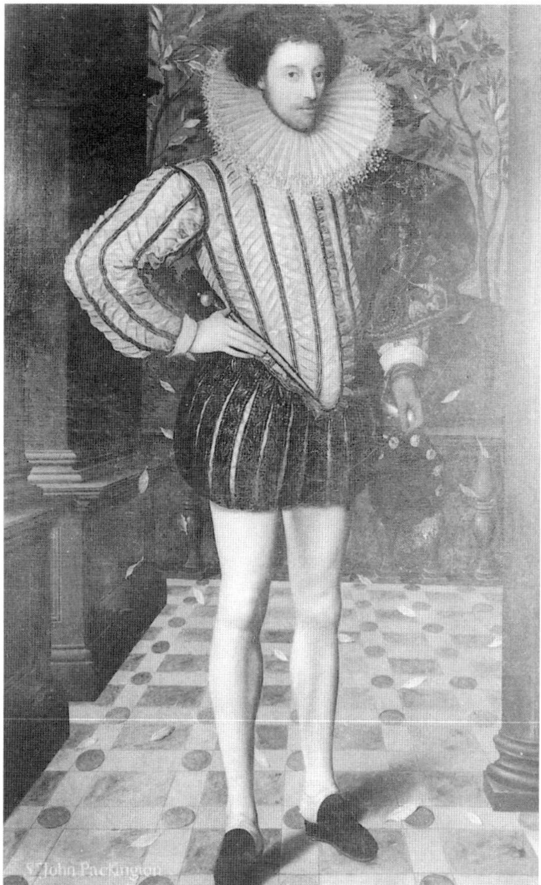

Sir John Pakington (1549–1625), by unknown artist, *c.*1580–90

Aylesbury seems to have almost always sent Pakington nominees to parliament and has been justly described as an Elizabethan pocket borough.

Pakington was enrolled as a student by special admission at Lincoln's Inn on 22 November 1570. He was presented to the queen during her visit to Worcester in 1572, and was invited to court. It was reported that Elizabeth admired his athletic achievements, but that when he challenged other courtiers to swim against him from Westminster to London Bridge, she vetoed the competition. Naunton described him as 'a brave gentleman and a very fine courtier', but 'an ill husband of opportunity'; for while at Elizabeth's court he 'stood very high in her grace, but he came in and went out, through disassiduity, drew the curtain between himself and the light of her grace' (Naunton, 32). However, Pakington remained sufficiently in the queen's favour to win a knighthood, conferred in November 1587.

Pakington found other routes to fortune. In November 1598 he married Dorothy, daughter of Humphrey Smith and widow of Alderman Benedict Barnham, a liveryman of the Drapers' Company; one son, John, was born to them. On 20 May of the same year Pakington was granted the lucrative starch patent, which he assigned to the grocer George Berisford and three others, who in turn issued licences to five London retailers. Another monopoly, of salt, appears to have borne heavily on the burgesses and bailiffs of Droitwich, where salt was extracted, and to have led to their refusal later that year to pay taxes. As their local lord, John Pakington was one of the justices to whom the privy council looked to enforce obedience. Probably in early 1601, a Nicholas Scott lodged a complaint to the effect 'that Sir John Pakington the starch patentee, and his assigns, have farmed the counties of England for yearly rents, to the impoverishment of the retail grocers of London' (*Salisbury MSS*, 14.169). In the same year resentment at such patents was vented in parliament. The starch monopoly was later acquired by Robert Cecil and Lord Buckhurst.

In June 1603 Pakington demonstrated his loyalty to the new king, providing James with lavish hospitality at his Aylesbury mansion. In the latter part of 1607 he became involved in his only recorded subversive act. He had been a member of the council of the marches in 1597, when he was in receipt of a sugar loaf for his pains. However, the council's continuing exercise of jurisdiction in four English marcher counties was said to involve many abuses and aroused growing opposition. In 1607 legal resistance began, led by the bishop of Hereford and twenty-six leading gentry. These included Pakington himself, a member of the commission of the peace and in that year the sheriff of Worcester, who refused to obey the precepts of the council in its role as a court. The dispute engaged the attention of the privy council and the lords chief justices.

Pakington's family was not a happy one. In February 1607 it was reported that 'Sir John Pakington and his little violent lady are parted on foul terms' (*Letters of John Chamberlain*, 1.243). The scandal caused concern at the highest levels, King James even writing to Archbishop Bancroft urging that the couple be pressed to compose their differences. At about the same time, Dorothy Pakington was involved in an acrimonious dispute with Sir Francis Bacon, into which she drew Robert Cecil. Bacon had married Alice Barnham, Lady Pakington's daughter from her previous marriage, and she charged him with forcing into marriage another of her daughters, aged twelve. Relations between husband and wife did not improve. On 21 June 1617 there were reported to have broken out 'great warres between Sir John and his lady' (*Letters of John Chamberlain*, 2.86), and hostilities continued in the court of high commission. The issue finally fell to the arbitration of the lord keeper, who, unluckily for Dorothy, was then her old enemy, Francis Bacon. His verdict went against her.

Sir John had fine properties with which to console himself for his familial strife. His main residence, which he erected early in the reign of Queen Elizabeth, still stands on high ground in the middle of Westwood Park. It was a substantial house in his time, and four distinctively designed wings were added after his death. In 1618 Sir John Pakington received a licence to enclose 1000 acres at Westwood, Hampton Lovett, and surrounding parishes, and here he impaled two great parks, stocking one with red deer and the other with fallow. His enclosure met with some opposition from the burgesses of Droitwich, on account of rights of way which they had enjoyed over the manor of Westwood. Sir John Pakington died in January 1625 and was buried at Aylesbury.

Sir John Pakington, first baronet (1600–1624), was the only son of Sir John Pakington and his wife, Dorothy. He was created a baronet in 1620 and sat in parliament for Aylesbury in 1623–4. His marriage to Frances, daughter of Sir John Ferrers of Tamworth, brought them one son, the politician Sir John *Pakington (1621–1680), and one daughter, Elizabeth, who married first Colonel Henry Washington and second Samuel Sandys of Ombersley in Worcestershire. Pakington died in October 1624 and was buried on 29 October at St Mary's, Aylesbury. His widow married Robert Leasly on 29 December 1626.

STEPHEN WRIGHT

Sources *The works of Francis Bacon*, ed. J. Spedding, R. L. Ellis, and D. D. Heath, 14 vols. (1857–74), vols. 7, 10, 11 • R. Naunton, *Fragmenta regalia* (1641) • *VCH Worcestershire*, vols. 2–4 • *The letters of John Chamberlain*, ed. N. E. McClure, 2 vols. (1939) • J. E. Neale, *The Elizabethan House of Commons*, rev. edn (1963) • R. Gibbs, *A history of Aylesbury* (1885) • *Calendar of the manuscripts of the most hon. the marquis of Salisbury*, 8, HMC, 9 (1899); 11 (1906); 14 (1923); 20 (1968) • *APC*, 1597–8 • HoP, *Commons*, 1558–1603 • *Seventh report*, HMC, 6 (1879), 520a • J. Nichols, *The progresses, processions, and magnificent festivities of King James I, his royal consort, family and court*, 1 (1828) • *DNB* • W. P. Baildon, ed., *The records of the Honorable Society of Lincoln's Inn: admissions*, 2 vols. (1896)

Likenesses portrait, *c*.1580–1590, Kentchurch Court, Hereford [*see illus.*] • T. Shutle, oils, *c*.1723–1724, Guildhall, Worcester • J. Rose, tomb effigy on monument, 1727, Hampton Lovett church, Worcestershire • R. Clamp, stipple, 1794 (after painting), BM, NPG; repro. in S. Harding, *Biographical mirror*

Wealth at death substantial landowner: *VCH Worcestershire*

Pakington, Sir John, first baronet (1600–1624). *See under* Pakington, Sir John (1549–1625).

Pakington, Sir John, second baronet (1621–1680), politician, was born on 13 August 1621 and was baptized the next day at Hampton Lovett, Worcestershire. He was the only son of Sir John *Pakington, first baronet (1600–1624) [*see under* Pakington, Sir John (1549–1625)], and Frances, daughter of Sir John Ferrers of Tamworth, Staffordshire. He succeeded to the baronetcy on the death of his father in October 1624, and to Westwood Park, Worcestershire, on the death of his grandfather, also Sir John *Pakington (1549–1625), in January 1625. He was the ward of Thomas *Coventry, the lord keeper. He would later (*c*.1648) marry Coventry's daughter, Dorothy [*see* Pakington, Dorothy, Lady Pakington (*bap.* 1623, *d.* 1679)]. He took the oath of allegiance in May 1638, when he was granted permission to travel abroad for three years with the proviso that he should not visit Rome. Returned to parliament in March 1640 for Worcestershire and for the borough of Aylesbury, where he had property, he chose to sit for the county. In the Long Parliament he sat for Aylesbury. In November 1640 he participated in an attack in the House of Commons on Sir Francis Windebank, secretary of state, for remarks he was alleged to have made regarding those who had refused to pay ship money. Although he apparently acquiesced in the attainder of Strafford, by 1642 Pakington's sympathies lay with the court, and he received the king's commission of array for Worcestershire. He was then, in August 1642, disabled from sitting in parliament.

With the other commissioners of array for Worcestershire, in August 1642 he raised a cavalry force to serve in the county. He fought at the battle of Edge Hill and was a member of the royalist committee of safety during the first civil war. In June 1643 he was admitted a freeman of Worcester on condition that he took no advantage from the privilege, and was serving as a justice of the peace for Worcestershire by 1644.

In March 1646 he obtained a pass to travel to London, where he presented himself to the speaker of the Commons with the intention of compounding for his support of the royalist cause. He was imprisoned, and was held for two months. His own figure for the annual value of his estates was £1520, but the sequestrators assessed them as worth £1947 per annum. Pakington put his losses during the civil war at £12,000 in rents sequestered and damage to his woods and houses. He was fined £7670, a third of the value of his estates, with £3000 accepted as first payment. This was paid and in May 1649 he was restored to his estates, with the balance paid in May 1650. But his tenants at Aylesbury refused him possession, petitioning for restoration of their common rights at Heydon Hill, which they claimed had been unjustly taken away, and he was compelled to grant his property there to the inhabitants of the town.

Pakington was arrested as the Scottish army under Charles II approached Worcester in August 1651, but was released when they entered the city. He attended the muster of the army on 26 August and was taken prisoner at the battle of Worcester on 3 September. He was tried in 1653 for appearing at the muster, but was acquitted. Nevertheless he was again fined, paying £1000, and undertook to pay £1000 more. In December 1654 he was one of the recipients of crates, said to contain bottles of wine, sent by the royalist agent Henry Norwood to Sir Henry Littleton. These aroused suspicion and in the following January he was arrested and charged with receiving arms in those crates. He was released in September 1655, but was again taken into custody in 1659, suspected of being involved in Sir George Booth's rising. During the 1650s his Westwood Park residence provided a congenial centre for Anglican and royalist sympathizers, and was the home of Henry Hammond, canon of Christ Church and archdeacon of Chichester, who died there in 1660.

Following the Restoration Pakington was again appointed justice of the peace for Worcestershire, in June 1660, and served as deputy lieutenant for the county. He was returned to parliament unopposed in 1661 as member for Worcestershire. In 1661 a bill was introduced to cancel the conveyance of his property at Aylesbury, but it failed to make progress and was not reintroduced until 1664, when it passed.

In November 1661 two letters dropped in a country lane in Worcestershire were taken to Pakington. Alarmed that they implied the existence of a plot for a 'suddaine riseing of the Presbiterian and factious party' (Greaves, 72), he forwarded them to Sir Edward Nicholas, secretary of state, and informed the lord lieutenant. A number of people were taken into custody, including the entrepreneur Andrew Yarrenton, and Ambrose Sparry, rector of Martley, the addressees of the letters. Richard Baxter was among the ministers implicated in what was referred to as the Pakington Plot or the Yarrenton Plot. He accused Pakington of intercepting a letter from him to his mother-in-law and sending it to George Morley, bishop of Worcester and Pakington's close friend. Impressed by Pakington's testimony, which was supported by that of other members, the Commons requested the king to issue a proclamation ordering all 'suspicious and loose persons' to leave London (Greaves, 76). The proclamation duly appeared and required all cashiered soldiers of the Commonwealth regime to leave the capital by 4 December and not return before 14 June 1662. Writing in 1681, in the context of the exclusion crisis, Yarrenton accused Pakington of having written the letters, and although this was not refuted, it seems possible that they were by another hand, perhaps that of a neighbour of Sparry's who had been rebuked by him for adultery.

Dorothy, Lady Pakington, died on 10 May 1679; Sir John Pakington was buried at Hampton Lovett on 3 January 1680. Their only son, **Sir John Pakington**, third baronet (*c.*1649–1688), matriculated at Christ Church, Oxford, on 3 May 1662. In May 1665 he was granted a licence to travel for three years with his tutor, and visited Italy, Switzerland, Germany, and the Low Countries. He became a notable Anglo-Saxon scholar, tutored by George Hickes, appointed dean of Worcester in 1683. In 1668 Pakington married Margaret (*d.* 1690), daughter of Sir John Keyt of Ebrington, Gloucestershire. Pakington was made a freeman of the borough of Droitwich in 1683 and an alderman of Bewdley in 1685. He was returned as member for Worcestershire in 1685 as a tory. He was buried at Hampton Lovett on 28 March 1688. His son, also Sir John *Pakington (1671–1727), was a prominent tory politician.

STEPHEN PORTER

Sources Keeler, *Long Parliament*, 292–3 · E. Rowlands and G. Jagger, 'Pakington, Sir John, 2nd bt', HoP, *Commons, 1660–90* · E. Rowlands, J. P. Ferris, and G. Jagger, 'Pakington, Sir John, 3rd bt', HoP, *Commons, 1660–90* · M. A. E. Green, ed., *Calendar of the proceedings of the committee for compounding … 1643–1660*, 1, PRO (1889), 1194–6 · R. L. Greaves, *Deliver us from evil: the radical underground in Britain, 1660–1663* (1986), 72–7 · M. Atkin, *Cromwell's crowning mercy: the battle of Worcester, 1651* (1998), 36, 49, 51, 53 · D. Underdown, *Royalist conspiracy in England, 1649–1660* (1960), 130, 143, 254 · GEC, *Baronetage* · *DNB* · *The journal of Sir Simonds D'Ewes from the beginning of the Long Parliament to the opening of the trial of the earl of Strafford*, ed. W. Notestein (1923), 26–7 · G. Lipscomb, *The history and antiquities of the county of Buckingham*, 4 vols. (1831–47), vol. 2, pp. 9–11 · *Calendar of the correspondence of Richard Baxter*, ed. N. H. Keeble and G. F. Nuttall, 2 vols. (1991), 51

Archives Worcs. RO, MSS

Pakington, Sir John, third baronet (*c.***1649–1688**). *See under* Pakington, Sir John, second baronet (1621–1680).

Pakington, Sir John, fourth baronet (**1671–1727**), politician, was born on 16 March 1671, the only son of Sir John *Pakington, third baronet (*c.*1649–1688), politician, of Westwood, Worcestershire [*see under* Pakington, Sir John, second baronet], and his wife, Margaret (*c.*1647–1690), the second daughter of Sir John Keyt, first baronet (1616–1662), of Ebrington, Gloucestershire. Pakington's father prepared for his early demise by appointing Viscount Weymouth and his two brothers, James and Henry Frederick Thynne, as the guardians of his son. No doubt under their guidance Pakington matriculated at St John's College, Oxford, in October 1688. However, his stay there was short and he left without taking a degree in order to enter politics. When parliament was dissolved in February 1690 Pakington was still a minor, but he sought a seat at Droitwich, where he had inherited some fee farm rents and a small stake in the local salt industry. His pretensions were challenged by Philip Foley, and in defeat Pakington determined to stand for the county seat against the head of that family, Thomas Foley of Witley. He duly won a seat, defeating Foley's partner, Sir Francis Winnington.

Early political career, 1690–1700 Pakington's minority may explain the low-key beginning of his parliamentary career. However, it was assumed by observers that he would follow in the footsteps of his father and grandfather, taking his cue from their strongly royalist and Anglican opinions. In June 1690 he caught smallpox, but having recovered he was named in November to the Worcestershire lieutenancy, the first step towards asserting his family's power in local society. The next step was a favourable marriage, and on 28 August 1691 he was licensed to marry Frances (*c.*1672–1697), the daughter of Henry Parker of Honington, Warwickshire, with a portion of £4000. This marriage produced four sons and three daughters, though all but one daughter predeceased him. At this stage of his career Pakington was already being noted as sympathetic to the 'country' reform programme, which was becoming increasingly attractive to the tory party, and he supported an attempt to enact triennial legislation in January 1693. Pakington's decision not to contest the 1695 election is difficult to explain, especially as he was involved in the Worcestershire campaign and also at Aylesbury, where he was lord of the manor. Out of parliament, he then lost his local offices in 1696 for refusing to sign the Association. Early in 1697 his wife died, bringing forth in Pakington, according to Sir Charles Lyttelton in a letter of March 1697, a desire 'to break up house and go abroad' (BL, Add. MS 29578, fol. 615), in order to improve his education. However, by June 1697 he had abandoned any such plans.

Pakington re-entered parliament for Worcestershire in 1698, an election notable for a backlash against the court. Such a mood was much in keeping with Pakington's own views, and on 18 January 1699 he delivered an amusing speech in support of the Disbanding Bill, in which he singled out for criticism those who sought to justify a larger force by reference to the threat posed by the exiled James II. Pakington saw this as an empty threat unless King William's title was precarious, and he knew of only one man who had questioned it publicly. This was a sharp dig at Gilbert Burnet, bishop of Salisbury, whose *Pastoral Letter* (1693) had argued that William's right to the throne was founded on conquest. Pakington's dislike of whig latitudinarian bishops resurfaced in the next session, when on 12 December 1699 he attacked Burnet as an inappropriate choice as preceptor to the duke of Gloucester, since the bishop was 'a republican in principle' (Bodl. Oxf., MS Carte 130, fol. 406). A motion for Burnet's removal supported by Pakington was lost on the following day.

On 16 November 1700 Pakington married for the second time; his new wife was Hester (*c.*1672–1715), the daughter and heir of Sir Herbert Perrott, of Haroldston, Pembrokeshire. By this match he acquired 'a good £1,100 a year' (BL, Add. MS 29579, fol. 242) and a small role in Welsh politics. The 1701 parliament saw him again preoccupied with the sins of whig bishops. Perhaps irked by rumours of Burnet's translation to the wealthy see of Winchester, on 8 March, after 'a very eloquent fine oration, long but admirably witty' (*Diary of Sir Richard Cocks*, 81), Pakington moved successfully for a bill preventing the translation of bishops. This bill, which also contained a clause against the practice of occasional conformity, never emerged from committee.

Defence of the Church of England, 1701–1710 The second election of 1701 saw Pakington retain his seat by a mere fifteen votes in the face of concerted opposition from bishops Lloyd of Worcester and Talbot of Oxford. Indeed, his quarrel with Lloyd provoked Pakington into a defence of his views as a member of the Church of England and a believer in toleration. This battle with Lloyd was to grow more virulent during the 1702 election, when both sides entered into print to disparage their opponents. Lloyd used his episcopal visitation to campaign against Pakington, whom he criticized in private for debauchery and Jacobitism. *The True Character of a Churchman* was erroneously believed to be written by Lloyd, but it was distributed about the diocese by the bishop's allies. It was answered by *The Character of a Low Churchman*, a panegyric to Pakington penned by Henry Sacheverell. Pakington complained to the newly assembled House of Commons on 2 November 1702 of a breach of privilege, and on 18 November Lloyd and his son were voted 'malicious, unchristian and arbitrary', and the queen addressed to remove Lloyd from his post as lord almoner.

Pakington returned to the issue of occasional conformity in the 1703–4 session. In a speech being distributed in tory circles in February 1704, he attacked those who remained neutral in matters pertaining to the church, a thinly veiled criticism of the leading ministers lords Godolphin and Marlborough, before referring to the role of dissenters in the civil wars and execution of Charles I: the whigs and their dissenting allies were 'a party of men that are against the church and government; whose principle of hatred and malice to the family of the Stuarts descends to them by inheritance' (Cobbett, *Parl. hist.*, 153–4). He saw a bill against the practice of occasional conformity as designed to prevent hypocrisy (the taking of Anglican communion in order to qualify for political office) and to protect the Anglican monopoly of power. Without it, he prophesied the rise of dissent to a majority in parliament and an end to the Church of England. Such was his apocalyptic vision, born out of the experiences of his own family earlier in the century. Following the bill's defeat in the Lords, in the next session Pakington was a proponent of attaching the measure to a supply bill, an act dubbed 'the tack', in order to force it through the upper house.

At the 1705 election Pakington was more involved than ever in the campaign. He did not limit his activities to Worcestershire, but stood also at Aylesbury (where he had been elected in 1702, though chose to sit for Worcestershire) to protect his interest. The previous parliament had seen the culmination of the celebrated *Ashby* v. *White* case, which had begun as an attempt to undermine Pakington's interest and ended as a dispute between the two houses concerning the determination of the right to vote. Although narrowly defeated at Aylesbury, Pakington was re-elected for Worcestershire, his supporters carrying a banner proclaiming 'For the Queen and Church, Pakington'. 'The tack' and the supposed threat to the church played a large role in the election, with Bishop Lloyd again attacking his old adversary and even threatening to prosecute Pakington's supporters in the ecclesiastical courts. On this occasion the dispute between bishop and MP petered out, and there was even a reconciliation between the two men in September 1706 when Lloyd confirmed Pakington's daughter.

Three of Pakington's speeches survive for the 1705–6 session. His principles refused to allow him to support the tories' cynical attempt on 4 December 1705 to embarrass the ministry by proposing an address to the queen that the electress of Hanover should be invited to reside in England. However, he was stirred into action on 8 December when it was proposed that the Commons endorse a resolution passed by the House of Lords that the Church of England was in a flourishing condition. He responded by listing four dangers to the church: the freedom to publish pamphlets against the church; the increase in the number of dissenting academies; the increase in the number of conventicles; and the influence of the kirk in Scotland, which could again be used in conjunction with English dissent to threaten the church (as in the civil wars). In this Pakington could be seen as putting in coherent form the inchoate fears of his high Anglican brethren. He also felt it necessary to criticize the Regency Bill on 19 December, which he saw as putting the armed forces and the revenue into the hands of a group of regents who might endanger the succession. He preferred the traditional authority of parliament and privy council. Pakington viewed the impending union with Scotland with trepidation. He was particularly concerned for the fate of episcopalianism north of the border and the attendant threat to the Church of England posed by state-sponsored Presbyterianism in Scotland. Thus on 4 February 1707 he attacked the union as being carried by bribery and force and reflected so severely on the ministry that he risked being sent to the Tower of London.

In the 1707–8 session Pakington was relatively quiet, and it is possible that Robert Harley had promised him office in a revamped Board of Trade as part of a scheme to reconstruct the ministry. In the event Harley lost office in a power struggle in February 1708. At the general election in May of that year Pakington was returned unopposed. In the new parliament he was soon involved in yet another tory *cause célèbre*—the battle to prevent a new charter being foisted upon Bewdley in order to facilitate whig control of the borough. His 'flaming speech' (*Wentworth Papers*, 70) when the election was decided at the bar of the house on 8 February 1709 was eventually published in the more propitious circumstances of 1710–11. Most startlingly he compared the silent surrender of Bewdley's charter unfavourably to the arbitrary surrenders of James II's reign. In the following session he voted against the impeachment of his erstwhile champion from 1702, Dr Sacheverell.

The Harley ministry, 1710–1714 With the return of the tories to power under Robert Harley in 1710, Pakington may again have harboured hopes of office. Certainly Lord Weymouth was pressing for his inclusion in the new Board of Trade, but Harley's predilection for moderates no doubt precluded Pakington. Instead Pakington concentrated his parliamentary energies on bringing the defeated whig ministry to account for their mismanagement. Thus, on 31 May 1711, as part of a long representation to the queen, the surrender of Bewdley's charter was voted illegal and destructive of the constitution. Pakington was also a member of the tory back-bench pressure group the October Club, which was dedicated to forcing a more complete tory policy upon the ministry. In order to buy off some of this opposition, in the summer of 1711 Harley (by then Lord Oxford) decided to take more tories into office, and Pakington accepted a secret pension of £800 per annum on the Irish establishment (paid under the name of Edwards). Possibly because of his pension, in the 1711–12 session Pakington was noticeably more restrained in his attacks on the ministry, although he still deemed the misdeeds of the previous administration and the duke of Marlborough as legitimate targets, speaking against the latter in January 1712. In June 1712 Pakington was rebuffed when he approached Lord Oxford for a public mark of the queen's favour, rather than his pension, which was technically in breach of the place legislation then in force.

By 1713 Pakington was a keen advocate of a more active strategy in support of the Pretender, which sought to make public the regents named by the elector of Hanover under the Regency Act (and widely reputed to be whigs) and then have them voted enemies of the constitution. In this scenario, the ensuing crisis would destroy the ministry and the Act of Settlement could then be overturned. This aggressive strategy was vetoed by the Pretender, who preferred to rely on the assurances of the Oxford ministry. Returned in the 1713 election, Pakington was one of those tories who hoped for a lead from Henry St John, Viscount Bolingbroke. Bolingbroke, locked into a power struggle with Oxford, was keen for Jacobite support. Indeed, in late July 1714 rumours circulated of Pakington's imminent appointment to a new Treasury board. The queen's death on 1 August was thus a huge blow to Pakington's hopes. Indeed, he was so upset that on 6 August he sought to have the eminent physician Dr John Radcliffe expelled from the Commons for not attending the queen's sickbed.

Later political career, 1715–1727 Despite unpropitious circumstances, Pakington topped the poll for Worcestershire in the 1715 election, once again falling out with Bishop Lloyd. The outbreak of the Jacobite rising later in the year saw Pakington arrested at Westwood. Forewarned of the event, he was able to arrange a comfortable trip to London in a stagecoach and upon his arrival convinced the privy council of his innocence. Although the exiled Stuarts continued to regard him as a potential supporter, it would seem that he was unwilling to countenance an armed insurrection backed by foreign troops to secure a restoration.

In the 1715 parliament Pakington was an active opponent of the whig ministry, speaking against the Peerage Bill in December 1719. Having been returned again in 1722 he opposed the re-election of Spencer Compton as speaker, although he could not find a seconder. However, he remained a popular figure with the opposition, even being elected recorder of Worcester in 1726.

Pakington died on 13 August 1727, shortly after the dissolution, thereby allowing the only surviving son of his second marriage, Sir Herbert Perrott Pakington, fifth baronet, an easy accession to his seat in parliament. His will, written three days before his death, ordered that his body be interred in the parish church of Hampton Lovett, Worcestershire. A monument in the church referred to his parliamentary service in 'speaking his mind there without reserve, neither fearing nor flattering those in power, but despising all their offers of title and preferment upon base and dishonourable terms of compliance' (Nash, 1.539). This outspokenness, at once vituperative and partisan, makes it unlikely that Pakington was the model for Joseph Addison's amiable tory squire Sir Roger de Coverley in *The Spectator*, as used sometimes to be thought.

STUART HANDLEY

Sources 'Pakington, Sir John', HoP, *Commons, 1690–1715* [draft] · HoP, *Commons* · T. Nash, *Collections for the history of Worcestershire*, 1 (1781), 539 · PRO, PROB 11/394, sig. 44 [father's will] · will, PRO, PROB 11/617, sig. 240 · *The parliamentary diary of Sir Richard Cocks, 1698–1702*, ed. D. W. Hayton (1996) · BL, Add. MSS 29578, fol. 130, 29579, fol. 242 · Bodl. Oxf., MS Carte 130, fol. 406 · Cobbett, *Parl. hist.*, 6.153–4 · *The Wentworth papers, 1705–1739*, ed. J. J. Cartwright (1883)

Archives Worcs. RO, letters and papers

Likenesses T. Shuter, portrait, *c.*1723–1724, Guildhall, Worcester · J. Rose sen., tomb effigy on monument, 1727, Hampton Lovett parish church, Worcestershire

Pakington [*formerly* Russell], **John Somerset, first Baron Hampton** (1799–1880), politician, was born at Slaughter's Court, Powick, Worcestershire, on 20 February 1799, the second son of William Russell (*d.* 1812) and his wife, Elizabeth (*d.* 1813), daughter of Sir Herbert Perrott Pakington, seventh baronet. Orphaned in his early teens, after attending Eton College Russell was admitted at Oriel College, Oxford, in 1818. On the death of his elder brother, William Herbert Russell, in 1819, however, he became heir to the family estates and left the university without a degree to

John Somerset Pakington, first Baron Hampton (1799–1880), by Herbert Watkins, 1858

take up the life of a country gentleman. In his young manhood he adopted the style of a dandy and was nicknamed Mr Brummell. On 14 August 1822 he married Mary (*d.* 1843), only child of Moreton Aglionby Slaney of Shifnal, Shropshire, with whom he had a son (born in 1826). He fought a duel in 1827, reputedly the last such event in Worcestershire. On 14 March 1831 he assumed the name of Pakington in lieu of Russell, having inherited in the previous year, jointly with his maternal aunt, the estates of his uncle, Sir John Pakington, eighth baronet. These included Westwood Park, near Droitwich, Worcestershire, which became his seat.

Into parliament After three failed attempts to enter parliament—for East Worcestershire in December 1832 and for West Worcestershire in May 1833 and January 1835—at the general election in July 1837 Pakington was elected Conservative MP for Droitwich, the seat he was to hold until 1874. He made his first Commons speech the following January (1838). Its subject, Canada, marked the beginning of a long interest in colonial issues: in 1841 he secured a select committee to inquire into the state of Newfoundland; the following year he chaired the select committee appointed to investigate the depression in the sugar plantations of the West Indies; and in 1848 he sat on Lord George Bentinck's select committee which examined the grievances of the colonial planters.

Following the death of his first wife, on 4 June 1844 Pakington married Augusta Anne (1817–1848), daughter of George *Murray, bishop of Rochester. During their short marriage they had a son and daughter. On 5 June 1851 he married his third wife, Augusta (1799–1892), daughter of

Thomas Champion-de-Crespigny and widow of Thomas Henry Hastings Davies of Elmley Park, Worcester. On 3 July 1846, shortly after the fall of Robert Peel's ministry, he was created a baronet.

Pakington began his parliamentary career as a supporter of Peel, though he was never quite a consistent one. Although he voted with Peel on the second reading of the Maynooth Bill in April 1845, he voted against corn law repeal in 1846, and opposed reductions in sugar duties in 1848. 'All his liaisons are with Peel's party, whilst all his votes have been with yours', Disraeli was told (Stewart, 138). Nevertheless, he did not become clearly identified with protectionist Conservatism until he joined Lord Derby's government in February 1852, as secretary of state for war and the colonies. He had expected only a minor post, but such was the paucity of administrative talent on the protectionist side that he was 'pitchforked into the vacant place'. His appointment was the occasion of the duke of Wellington's famous remark, applicable to the ministry as a whole, 'Who is he? I never heard of him' (Vincent, 71–2); he had no experience of office, and spoke only occasionally in parliamentary debates. Pakington himself thought the 1852 government 'not strong enough numerically to be quite comfortable and independent' (Pakington to Disraeli, 9 Aug 1852, MS Hughenden B/XX/P/6). He was also perhaps somewhat hostile to Disraeli personally.

Pakington's only major legislative act during the 1852 administration was successfully to carry through a bill, which he had inherited from his predecessor Sir George Grey, granting New Zealand a representative constitution. The New Zealand Act (1852) 'was not unjustifiably claimed to be the most liberal colonial measure since the American Revolution' (Morrell, *Policy in the mid-Victorian Age*, 338). Other concessions which he made to colonial reformers included granting the Australian colonies control of lands and land revenues, and an undertaking to abolish the transportation of convicts.

Educational reform It was in the following six years, when the Conservatives were in opposition, that Pakington developed the most distinctive side of his political identity with a very public espousal of radical reform of working-class education. This was not a completely new departure, for it drew on his long experience of county government. From 1834 to 1858 he was chairman of the Worcestershire quarter sessions, where he formed an interest in penal policy and the roots of crime. He was one of the Conservatives who campaigned against beerhouses, introducing a Sale of Beer Act in 1840. The link between ignorance and crime particularly impressed him. His Juvenile Offenders Act (1847) reflected a longstanding concern about young offenders, which led him to support Mary Carpenter and Matthew Davenport Hill in their proposals for industrial schools. He was a member of the Worcester diocesan board of education, and helped to found in 1852 the teacher training college at Saltley.

Although Pakington stressed the importance of religion in education, he took a less rigid denominational line than the leaders of the National Society, the body which ran most Anglican schools. He was the only member of Derby's cabinet in 1852 to voice disapproval of the proposed management clauses for elementary schools receiving government grants, on the decidedly unorthodox grounds (for a tory) that it would give too much power to the local clergy. In religious matters generally he was more liberal than the rest of his party, voting in favour of a bill (1857) to permit Jews to take their seats in parliament, and proposing (1858) a settlement of the contested issue of church rates by exempting dissenters from payment. He supported the work of the Church of England Education Society, founded in 1853 on a broader basis than the National Society, in that it did not restrict instruction to members of the established church, or require every pupil to be taught the catechism.

Pakington's knowledge of the state of elementary schooling convinced him that schools supported by rates were needed to supplement the existing schools run by the churches. James Prince Lee, the Birmingham headmaster and subsequently bishop of Manchester, was an important influence. In October 1853 Pakington was approached by Manchester educational reformers, led by Lee, and asked to take charge of their Local Rating Bill during the 1854 parliamentary session. Having consulted Lord Derby, Pakington refused, partly for political reasons and partly through doubts about some of the bill's religious provisions. But he made it clear that had time allowed he would have brought forward his own bill in 1854, and in 1855 he did so.

In January 1855 Pakington gave notice of a bill which foreshadowed many of the features of the 1870 Education Act, and which was indeed in some respects more radical. He believed he could promote educational reform in an independent and private capacity while, if the bill were successful, political advantage could accrue to the Conservative Party. His proposal was to allow ratepayers to elect school committees which could both build new schools and aid existing ones. New schools would be free. Existing ones would be aided only if they granted all pupils a conscience clause (that is, a declaration allowing parents to withdraw their children from denominational religious instruction), and gave up any power to refuse attendance on religious grounds. Religious instruction would be Anglican unless a majority of inhabitants were dissenters, in which case the privy council would decide. Undoubtedly Pakington expected some support from his front bench colleagues, if not official endorsement. Instead Derby and Disraeli believed they had been placed in 'an inconvenient and embarrassing position' (Disraeli to Pakington, 5 Jan 1855, Hampton MSS, 3835/7). The bill threatened the unity of the Conservative front bench—Lord Stanley, a crucial figure, supported it, though with reservations—at a time when the leadership anticipated the disintegration of the Aberdeen government. They urged Pakington to abandon the bill.

Ignoring the pleas of Derby and Disraeli, Pakington introduced his bill on 16 March 1855. He depended on the Liberal government for parliamentary time, however, and Palmerston would only give him enough to keep the issue alive as an embarrassment for Derby, not to pass the bill. It was eventually abandoned in June. In the meantime Pakington had on 23 February 1855 been appointed to the committee of inquiry into the condition of the army before Sevastopol.

In 1857 Pakington introduced another, slightly less radical, education bill. This time he had the support even of the Cobdenite radicals, represented by the National Public School Association, who were willing to back a measure aimed at satisfying both moderate Anglicans and dissenters. In 1856 he delivered an address on national education to the members of the Manchester Athenaeum; it was one of his few publications. As in 1855 he unsuccessfully tried to get party support for his bill, and after resisting strenuous efforts by Derby and Disraeli, the party leaders, to 'stave off the measure' (Vincent, 149), he introduced his bill in February 1857. It was lost in the dissolution, however, and never got a second reading. Nevertheless his espousal of educational reform, acknowledged by his appointment as president of the education department at the first congress of the National Association for the Promotion of Social Science, held in 1857, was not without result. It was his resolution of 11 February 1858 which secured the appointment of the Newcastle royal commission on elementary education which he later referred to as 'my child' (Pakington to Disraeli, 10 April 1862, MS Hughenden B/XX/P/67).

First lord of the Admiralty In March 1858 Palmerston's government fell and Pakington became first lord of the Admiralty in Lord Derby's second administration, having turned down the Home Office. Like that of his colleagues, much of Pakington's energy was taken up with the parliamentary reform issue, which it was widely recognized would make or break the administration. That aside, perhaps his most significant act was the announcement in February 1859 that the navy was to build its first two ironclad battleships, the *Warrior* and the *Black Prince*. Pakington was later president of the Institution of Naval Architects, and took part in establishing the Royal College of Naval Architecture. He left office on the government's fall in June 1859, and was created GCB.

In 1862 Pakington's involvement in educational reform resumed when he stepped into the controversy surrounding the Liberal government's revised education code, which was their response to the report of the Newcastle commission. He attempted to move resolutions widening the narrow political debate about the technicalities of the code to the principles upon which state support for education should be based. He particularly advocated giving power to local agencies—the county and borough boards of education proposed by the royal commission—as opposed to the centralizing authority of the committee of the privy council. But although he secured support from educationists such as Kay-Shuttleworth, and for once from other leading Conservatives such as Henley Walpole and Manners, Disraeli and Derby again acted to suppress the initiative.

In February 1865 Pakington did secure the appointment of a select committee, which he chaired, into the structure of the education department. His motion attracted the support of many tories hostile to the general approach of the department, with its strong emphasis on securing access for children of all denominations to state-aided schools. But the committee's approach disappointed these tories. Pakington was perceived to have packed the committee 'with his own friends to the prejudice of genuine Tory principles' (Lygon to Disraeli, 9 Feb 1866, MS Hughenden B/XX/L/43); and the committee's draft conclusions were liberal in tone and noticeably wider in scope than originally envisaged. However, before the committee finalized its report the Russell government fell, and while the committee's draft report was published, no final recommendations were made.

Embarrassment on the education issue having been duly avoided, in June 1866 Pakington was appointed first lord of the Admiralty for the second time, in Derby's third government. However, his second spell at the Admiralty was brief. In March 1867 resignations over the Conservative Reform Bill forced Lord Derby to reshuffle his cabinet, and Pakington moved to the War Office. His speech on re-election at Droitwich (13 March 1867) was to become famous for revealing the hastily constructed nature of the cabinet's initial reform proposals, which as a consequence became known as the Ten Minutes Bill. Pakington left office for the last time following the Conservative defeat at the general election of 1868.

Pakington remained in the Commons throughout the 1868 parliament. He was generally supportive of the 1870 Education Act, although he disliked the compromise Cowper-Temple clause which introduced broadly undenominational religious education in board schools. In the summer of 1871 he embarked on a brief flirtation with the new social movement—an alliance of working-class leaders and aristocratic Conservatives designed by John Scott Russell, the naval architect with whom Pakington had a previous association, to find common ground on social issues. Pakington, Derby noted on 26 July 1871, was 'intoxicated with the prospect of being one of the regenerators of society, and reconciling the people with the aristocracy' (*Diaries*, 86). His address later that year as president of the Social Science Association congress at Leeds was similarly criticized for 'giving encouragement to wild theories' of a socialist tendency (ibid., 90–1). In the general election of February 1874 he suffered the humiliation of losing his Droitwich seat to a Liberal, a result which may have come as a relief to the Conservative leadership. Disraeli related to the queen Pakington's self-deprecatory remark that 'Providence had disposed of him' (*Letters of Queen Victoria*, ed. A. C. Benson and Lord Esher, and G. E. Buckle, 2nd ser., 1926–8, 2.321).

Death and assessment On 6 March 1874 Pakington entered the Lords as Baron Hampton. In his first speech in the upper house he moved a resolution in favour of appointing a minister of education, something he had long favoured and for which he pressed strongly when in 1868 the Conservatives sought, unsuccessfully, to construct a passable Education Bill. In November 1875 he was appointed first civil service commissioner, with a salary of £2000 a year, which he needed to alleviate his financial problems. But in view of his age the appointment was regarded as inappropriate in some quarters, and it was said to have contributed to the Conservative government's defeat on a vote on patronage in July 1877. Hampton died at his London home, 9 Eaton Square, on 9 April 1880. He was buried in the family mausoleum at Hampton-Lovett church, Worcestershire, on 15 April.

Pakington was described as being 'of the middle size, with a pale face, and rather a hooked nose'. His dress and bearing gave 'indications of correctness and finish, rather than of greatness or genius' (J. E. Ritchie, *British Senators*, 1869, 40). Although never a serious candidate to lead his party—and regarded by his colleagues as prone to muddled thinking—Pakington was a front-bench political figure for almost twenty years. Known as a competent and an orthodox administrator when at the colonial, naval, and War offices—and disapproving of Liberal policy in those areas—he was in many respects representative of orthodox squirearchical Conservatism. However, he had a definite eccentric streak. A Peelite who nevertheless voted against corn law repeal, he was later attracted to the idea of fusion with Palmerstonian Liberalism. Above all he persistently promoted Liberal, indeed radical, educational reform. In retrospect that was the most distinctive aspect of his political identity. PAUL CHILCOTT

Sources R. Aldrich, *Sir John Pakington and national education* (1979) • P. J. Chilcott, 'British politics and the elementary education question, 1850–70', DPhil diss., U. Oxf., 1990 • GEC, *Peerage* • *DNB* • Bodl. Oxf., Dep. Hughenden • Worcs. RO, Hampton papers • P. Smith, *Disraelian Conservatism and social reform* (1967) • *Disraeli, Derby and the conservative party: journals and memoirs of Edward Henry, Lord Stanley, 1849–1869*, ed. J. R. Vincent (1978) • *The diaries of E. H. Stanley, 15th earl of Derby, 1869–1878*, CS, 5th series, 4 (1994) • R. Stewart, *The politics of protection: Lord Derby and the protectionist party, 1841–1852* (1971) • D. I. Allsobrook, *Schools for the shires: the reform of middle-class education in mid-Victorian England* (1986) • W. P. Morrell, *British colonial policy in the age of Peel and Russell* (1930) • W. P. Morrell, *British colonial policy in the mid-Victorian age* (1969) • G. I. T. Machin, *Politics and the churches in Great Britain, 1832 to 1868* (1977) • A. Hawkins, *Parliament, party and the art of politics in Britain, 1855–1859* (1987) • J. B. Conacher, *The Peelites and the party system* (1972) • S. E. Maltby, *Manchester and the movement for national elementary education* (1918) • B. Coleman, *Conservatism and the conservative party in nineteenth-century Britain* (1988)

Archives Worcs. RO, corresp. and papers • Worcs. RO, letter and candidate books | BL, corresp. with Richard Cobden, Add. MS 43669 • BL, corresp. with W. E. Gladstone, Add. MSS 44356–44386, *passim* • BL, corresp. with Sir William Martin, Add. MS 41409 • BL, corresp. with Sir Stafford Northcote, Add. MS 50022 • BL, corresp. with Sir Robert Peel, Add. MSS 40417–40612, *passim* • Bodl. Oxf., corresp. with Benjamin Disraeli • Bodl. Oxf., corresp. with Sir Thomas Phillipps • Borth. Inst., letters to Sir Charles Wood • Hunt. L., letters to Grenville family • Lpool RO, letters to fourteenth earl of Derby • NMM, corresp. with Sir Alexander Milne • NRA, priv. coll., letters to Sir George Cathcart • PRO, letters to Lord John Russell, PRO 30/22 • Representative Church Body Library, Dublin, letters to E. A. Stopford • Som. ARS, letters to Sir William Jolliffe

Likenesses J. Doyle, pen-and-ink caricature, 1851, BM • H. Watkins, photograph, 1858, NPG [*see illus.*] • C. Marochetti, marble bust, *c*.1860, Haslar Hospital, Portsmouth • D. J. Bond, engraving (after photograph), repro. in D. J. Pound, *Drawing room portrait gallery of eminent personages*, 2nd ser., 2 (1859), pl. 20 • E. Burton, mezzotint (after J. W. Gordon), BM • Faustin, coloured lithograph, NPG • H. Gales, group portrait, watercolour (*The Derby cabinet of 1867*), NPG • J. Phillip, group portrait, oils (*The House of Commons, 1860*), Houses of Parliament, London • A. Thompson, watercolour, NPG; repro. in *VF* (12 Feb 1870), pl. 40 • photograph, NPG • portrait, repro. in D. J. Pound, *The statesmen of England* (1862) • portrait, repro. in *ILN*, 20 (1852), 321 • portrait, repro. in *ILN*, 21 (1852), 237 • woodcut, repro. in *Harper's Weekly*, 11 (1867), 168

Wealth at death under £14,000: probate, 25 June 1880, *CGPLA Eng. & Wales*

Pakington, William. *See* Packington, William (*d.* 1390).

Palairet, Elias (1713–1765), classical and biblical philologist, was born in Rotterdam, of a French family which had taken refuge in the Netherlands following the revocation of the edict of Nantes in 1685. He studied at Leiden, where his first published work, the *Histoire du patriarche Joseph mise en vers héroïques*, appeared in 1738. After ordination he became in turn preacher at Aardenburg (1741), Doornik (1749), and Tournai (by 1752), before moving to England where he became pastor of the French church at Greenwich (1755) and later of St John's Church, Spitalfields. His first philological work, *Observationes philologico-criticae in sacros Novi Foederis libros*, was published in 1752, with the addition of a four-part index for ease of reference, first to the location of scriptural passages, and then in Hebrew, Greek, and Latin. Its advertisement hailed the author as a man of rare industry and judgement as well as erudition. Palairet followed this, in 1754, with an eight-page specimen of critical thesaurus of the Greek language and, in 1755, a twenty-four-page pamphlet of philological exercises based on the books of the New Testament, intended to precede a revised edition of his *Observationes*. In 1756 his *Notes on the New Testament* appeared, while his correction of the *Ajax* and *Electra* of Sophocles, prepared in the same year, was published in 1758. On 8 April 1756 Palairet married Margaret Lefebure at Christ Church, Spitalfields.

Palairet's work rapidly entered mainstream philological debate; several of his arguments from 1752 were refuted in the 1757 *Acta eruditorum Lipsiensium*, 451–8, and by Charles-Louis Bauer in his *Stricturarum Periculum* (1760), but Palairet returned to the task in 1760 with a study of Latin ellipses based on clear principles of linguistic structure, *Thesaurus ellipsium Latinarum*, a work accompanied by a dual index of authors and phrases and regarded as his most useful publication (*Nouvelle biographie générale*). In his preface Palairet promised a second edition, corrected and augmented, of Lambert Bos's *Ellipses Graecae* to complement his own work, but this was never completed.

Palairet dedicated the *Thesaurus* to John Egerton, bishop of Bangor and, subsequently, of Durham, whose chaplain he had become after attracting notice with his preaching and pastoral work in London; this is said latterly to have included serving as preacher to the Dutch Chapel at St James's Palace, but there is no formal record of such an appointment in the memorials or admissions entries for the St James's Chapels Royal (PRO, RG4-4574 and 4575). None the less it is not unlikely that, given his ancestry, linguistic background, and continental experience, which remained defining influences throughout his career in England, he may have preached at the Dutch Chapel or had some connection with it.

Palairet died at Marylebone on 2 January 1765; his philological reputation subsequently declined although Edmund Henry Barker, in the preface to his 1829 new edition of the *Thesaurus*, claimed that Palairet's work, as meritorious and useful as that of other philologists, deserved rescue from scholarly oblivion—an aspiration never wholly fulfilled. T. P. J. EDLIN

Sources L. G. Michaud and E. E. Desplaces, eds., *Biographie universelle, ancienne et moderne*, new edn, 45 vols. (Paris, 1843–65), vol. 32, p. 4 • *Nouvelle biographie générale* (1862), vol. 39, p. 70 • E. H. Barker, preface, in E. Palairet, *Thesaurus ellipsium Latinarum*, new edn (1829) • private information (2004) • *DNB* • *IGI*

Palairet, John (1697–1774), tutor and educational writer, was born in Montauban, France, the fifth of six children of Dominique Palairet (*b.* 1654) and Marie (*b.* 1658), daughter of Blaise Lacaze and Isabeau Treissedre. He became agent of the states general of the United Provinces and went to London, where he married Elizabeth Dorsan (*d.* 1734x8) in 1727. He had acted as tutor to the young prince of Orange, William IV (1711–1751), in the Netherlands; his royal pupil married Anne, the daughter of George II, in London in March 1734. From the 1730s Palairet was French tutor to three of George II's children: William Augustus, duke of Cumberland, Mary, and Louise. His second wife, Marthé Dorrée (1712–1766), was born in Amsterdam, and the first two of their eight children were born in Rotterdam, in 1738 and 1739.

Palairet wrote the first of several educational works, *Nouvelle méthode pour apprendre à bien lire et à bien orthographier*, in 1721; it reached a twelfth edition in 1755 and continued to be reprinted until the mid-nineteenth century. He followed this in 1731 with a short treatise in French and English on the arts and sciences, and a French grammar that he wrote for the prince of Orange; both works ran to numerous editions. The most significant of his later works were a comprehensive atlas, dedicated to the prince of Orange, and an introduction to modern geography, both of which were published in the 1750s. Palairet died in the parish of St James, Piccadilly, in 1774. GORDON GOODWIN, *rev.* S. J. SKEDD

Sources *The family of Palairet, formerly Palayret* (1917) • will, PRO, PROB 11/1004, sig. 26 • Nichols, *Illustrations*, 4.634

Palairet, Sir (Charles) Michael (1882–1956), diplomatist, was born on 29 September 1882 at Berkeley, Gloucestershire, the second of three sons of Charles Harvey Palairet, army officer, of Westhill, Ledbury, Herefordshire, and his wife, Emily, *née* Henry. He was descended from a French family called Palayret who had fled initially to the Netherlands when Louis XIV revoked the edict of Nantes in 1689. Subsequently the family lived in England. In Palairet's lifetime the family name was best known for the cricketing ability of his older cousins, L. C. H. and R. C. N. Palairet. On his mother's side he was a great-grandson of Thomas Allan, the mineralogist.

Palairet was educated at Eton College, and then went to

Sir (Charles) Michael Palairet (1882–1956), by unknown photographer, *c*.1907

Touraine to improve his French and to Weimar to improve his German. He joined the diplomatic service in 1905, and after serving the usual probationary period in the Foreign Office was posted to Rome in 1906. In 1907 he was promoted from attaché to third secretary, and in 1908 he was transferred to Vienna, a posting which provided useful experience for his later time there. On 29 June 1915 he married Mary de Vere, daughter of Brigadier-General Herbert William Studd, commanding officer of the Coldstream Guards. They had one son and one daughter. In 1916, while posted to Paris, Palairet and his wife were received into the Roman Catholic church. They were to remain staunch Catholics for the rest of their lives.

Soon after arriving in Paris in 1913 Palairet had been promoted to second secretary, and in 1917 he was sent to Athens (where he was later to be ambassador). A second period in Paris followed during the peace conference (1918–19), and later in the embassy, after which Palairet was briefly transferred to the Foreign Office, which in those days was quite distinct from the diplomatic service. Palairet's progression through the ranks of the diplomatic service resumed with his posting to Paris as first secretary, as a replacement for Nevile Henderson. He then served variously in Tokyo, during the catastrophic earthquake of 1923 which destroyed the embassy, and in Peking (Beijing) and Rome. As an experienced middle-rank diplomatist, Palairet then became minister to Romania in December 1929. Here their charm and hospitality and keen interest in Romanian culture won the Palairets a wide circle of friends. Prince Carol, who returned from exile and became king in 1930, showed no grudge at having been requested to leave England in 1928 because of his alleged involvement in a plot to place him on the Romanian throne. Good Anglo-Romanian relations, both political and commercial, were established, but German economic and political penetration had become menacing before Palairet left for Stockholm in 1935.

All this was preparation for the most important posting of Palairet's career, which was to Vienna in December 1937. He spent only a few months there, but this period coincided with the overthrow of the independent Austrian republic in March 1938. Palairet's reporting to the Foreign Office was robust. He told of how Hitler had 'raved like a madman' at the unfortunate Chancellor Schuschnigg in their notorious interview in February 1938 (*Documents on British Foreign Policy*, 2/19, no. 50), and admired the chancellor's courage in calling a plebiscite over the issue of Austrian independence. He advised the foreign secretary, Lord Halifax, that it was pointless to send a message to Schuschnigg disclaiming any British responsibility for encouraging a plebiscite. In Palairet's opinion it would 'not have done any good', even though he was sympathetic to the plight of the Austrian government, because Austria was doomed (Palairet to Halifax, 11 March 1938, PRO, R2478/137/3-22315). Palairet reported that Austrians constantly told him that Britain was their last hope, but there was never any possibility of British intervention to prevent the *Anschluss*. Subsequently, however, he believed that Schuschnigg's decision to hold the plebiscite was mistaken. Following the *Anschluss* the British legation in Vienna was closed, and Palairet was recalled to London. In June 1938 Palairet's work in Vienna was recognized by his appointment as KCMG and in September–December he took charge of the British legation in Bucharest during the illness of Sir Reginald Hoare.

In June 1939 Palairet went as minister to Athens, a welcome appointment. Yet again his period of service was to coincide with a Nazi invasion, in April 1941, following the unsuccessful Italian attack in October 1940. But his diplomacy did not impress his American colleague MacVeagh, who found him intellectually limited, lackadaisical, and in comparison with his predecessor Sir Sydney Waterlow 'as a .22 calibre target pistol to a bell-mouthed blunderbuss' (*Ambassador MacVeagh Reports*, 163). The Foreign Office did not share this perception of Palairet, and he retained his accreditation to the Greek government in exile, being promoted ambassador in 1942. He retired in April 1943, but returned to the Foreign Office as a temporary assistant under-secretary, dealing with matters concerning prisoners of war. He remained in this post until July 1948.

Palairet never secured an embassy in the diplomatic 'magic circle' of Paris, Berlin, Washington, and Moscow. In his retirement he indulged an interest in the translation of German religious books. He died at his home, Lynch Mead, Allerford, Minehead, Somerset, on 5 August 1956.

Palairet's only daughter, **Anne Mary Celestine Asquith**, countess of Oxford and Asquith (1916–1998), was born on 14 November 1916 in Paris and educated in Bucharest, Paris, and elsewhere, and at St Anne's College, Oxford (1936–9), though she did not take her final examinations. During the Second World War she worked at Bletchley Park, then joined the WAAF and tracked German air raids. In 1945 she was posted to Palestine and narrowly escaped death when the King David Hotel in Jerusalem was blown up. She married on 28 August 1947 Julian Edward George Asquith, second earl of Oxford and Asquith (*b.* 1916), colonial official, the eldest son of Raymond Asquith (1878–1916); they had two sons and three daughters. She accompanied her husband on postings to Libya, Zanzibar, St Lucia, and finally the Seychelles, where Asquith was governor (1962–7), before they retired to the Manor House, Mells, Frome, Somerset. Lady Oxford was described by contemporaries as beautiful, intelligent, enthusiastic, and interested in the arts. She died on 19 August 1998 at Frome, Somerset, survived by her husband and their five children. PETER NEVILLE

Sources *DNB* • *The Times* (6 Aug 1956) • PRO, Halifax MSS • E. L. Woodward and R. Butler, eds., *Documents on British foreign policy, 1919–1939*, 3rd ser., 1 (1949) • W. N. Medlicott and others, eds., *Documents on British foreign policy, 1919–1939*, 2nd ser., 19: *European affairs, July 1 1937 – August 4 1938* (1981) • *Ambassador MacVeagh reports*, ed. J. O. Iatrides (1980) • PRO, Henderson MSS, FO 800/269 • G. L. Weinberg, *The foreign policy of Hitler's Germany: starting World War II, 1937–9* (1980) • K. von Schuschnigg, *Brutal takeover* (1971) • G. B. Shepherd, *Anschluss* (1977) • A. J. Crozier, *The causes of the Second World War* (1997) • *CGPLA Eng. & Wales* (1956) • *The Independent* (7 Sept 1998) • Burke, *Peerage* (1999) • *WWW*

Archives PRO, Halifax MSS, FO 800 • PRO, Henderson MSS, FO 800

Likenesses photograph, *c.*1907, NPG [*see illus.*]

Wealth at death £63,266 2*s.* 1*d.*: probate, 12 Nov 1956, *CGPLA Eng. & Wales*

Palavicino, Sir Horatio (*c.*1540–1600), merchant and diplomat, was born in Genoa, Italy, the second son of Tobias Palavicino (*d. c.*1580), a well-connected merchant aristocrat, and his wife, Battina (1522–1607), the daughter of Andrea Spinola. The family firm handled the papal monopoly of alum, an essential ingredient in the dyeing process, from the mines at Tolfa from 1566, and Horatio seems to have acted as their agent in Antwerp. When their monopoly expired in 1578 the family sought to undermine the new grantees by buying up alum stocks and negotiating monopoly agreements with the major consumers in England and the Low Countries. The plan backfired in England because of Burghley's anxieties about the consumer and because of attempts by the customs official Thomas Smythe to manipulate the markets himself. In the Low Countries the Palavicini were more successful. In return for a six-year monopoly of alum imports, they loaned stocks of alum worth about £30,000 to the states general, who could sell it to the clothiers for cash to support the war effort. Palavicino was sucked into England's orbit because this loan was underwritten by Queen Elizabeth and the city of London, and in 1581 he took over the share of his Spinola partners. Although the loan was never repaid, the interest payments proved lucrative, and by 1593 (when Elizabeth stopped the interest payments) Palavicino had received £45,479 11*s*. 11*d*. During the early 1580s he was based for much of the time in France, where he conducted the family's alum business, but his contacts among the international merchant community made him an invaluable source of intelligence to the English government, and he was used to transmit funds by bills of exchange to prop up the duke of Anjou's campaigns in the Low Countries. Like many in his position, his business interests were very diverse. He undertook the purchase of *objets d'art* for the great; in 1591 he secured a portion of Sir Edward Stafford's licence for the export of undressed cloths which was sold to merchant adventurers; he had a reputation for speculating in corn in times of dearth; he lent money on a large scale, and in 1585 negotiated the earl of Leicester's loan from city merchants; and in 1592 he handled £24,000-worth of goods from the captured carrack the *Madre de Dios*.

Palavicino's allegiance to the Roman Catholic church was strained by the pope's arrest and torture of his brother Fabritio, and in 1584 Horatio was himself condemned by the Inquisition in absentia and his goods seized. Although he adopted the language of the godly in his correspondence with Walsingham, describing the pope as the Antichrist, he mixed more easily with the more conservative members of the protestant establishment, such as William Cecil, Lord Burghley, Robert Cecil, Lord Buckhurst, Gilbert Talbot, seventh earl of Shrewsbury (who acted as godfather to his first son), and Sir William Cornwallis. He was granted letters of denization in November 1585 and was knighted by the queen in November 1587. In 1588, in a demonstration of *l'ardore dell'animo mio*, he volunteered for service against the armada and wrote a propagandist pamphlet on the campaign. It is probably his talent for self-promotion which accounts for his otherwise inexplicable appearance among the naval commanders commemorated in the armada tapestry presented to the lord admiral by the Dutch government. His close relations with the queen are clear from the fact that in 1589 he was among the sixteen knights to receive new year's gifts of gilt plate from Elizabeth, and the exchange of presents continued through the 1590s.

Palavicino's Anglophilia, his wide contacts in the commercial world, and his possession of courtly graces sufficient to commend him to the snobbish Queen Elizabeth made him an ideal candidate for diplomatic missions. He felt that the key to the neutralization of the Spanish threat lay in France rather than in the Netherlands. From March 1586 until April 1587 he was employed on an embassy to the German princes to persuade them to levy troops to assist Henri of Navarre and to free Henri III from the domination of the Guise and the Catholic league. It was not an easy mission. Elizabeth expected the Germans to pay for an army of 23,000 men in France for an indefinite period for the miserly sum of 50,000 écus (then worth £15,468 15*s*. 0*d*.); she underestimated the reluctance of Brandenburg and Saxony to get involved, and she was banking on John Casimir of the Palatinate, whose reliability was in doubt, to act as her cat's-paw. In June 1586 Elizabeth agreed to supply an extra 50,000 écus, enabling Palavicino to negotiate the treaty of Fridelsheim in January 1587, by which Casimir agreed to support an army of 9000 in France for three months. However, the expedition was undermined by Elizabeth's claim that she had intended that the extra 50,000 écus should be paid only if the Germans provided their share. Palavicino was convinced of the need for a negotiated peace. He put out feelers to Philip II through his brother Fabritio and the Genoese authorities in 1586 and, hoping to exploit the tensions between Philip and his general, wrote to Parma to encourage him to take on the sovereignty of the Netherlands in 1588. But he also recognized the need to negotiate from strength and therefore pressed strongly on the queen the need for intervention in France in 1587–8. Elizabeth rejected his counsel until the dire position of Henri of Navarre after the assassination of Henri III necessitated a rethink. In March 1590 he was sent to negotiate joint action by the German princes in France, but his efforts were undermined by Elizabeth's diversion of her interests to Brittany. Palavicino's diplomatic efforts on a further embassy to Germany beginning in December 1590 bore fruit in the peace of Torgau (February 1591), by which Elizabeth was pledged to pay £15,000 to support the princes' campaign in France. Unfortunately Elizabeth claimed that he had exceeded his instructions by granting £5000 more than she had intended, even though his instructions had left him with discretion to agree to that amount if necessary. Although Robert Cecil turned to him for help in constructing his spy network in 1596, Elizabeth's fury over the German embassy of 1590–91 ensured that his diplomatic career was over.

Palavicino did not marry until late in life, but it is clear that his sexual energies had found other outlets. In 1578 the governors of Bridewell Hospital in London interviewed one of his servants, who explained how his master had required him to find him some maiden who had not been 'meddled with' before. Unable to find one in London, the hapless servant was dispatched with a horse and 10*s*. to Guildford. It was at about this time that Palavicino's illegitimate son Edward (*c*.1578–1630) was born. His quest for the hand of Anne, the daughter of the Huguenot leader François de la Noue, was rebuffed in 1588. Three years later, on 27 April 1591, he was married at Frankfurt to Anna Hooftman, the daughter of the Antwerp banker Gieles van Eychelberg, alias Hooftman. The marriage was not entirely happy, as Anna was inclined to melancholy, doubtless not helped by the dull Cambridgeshire society to which she was condemned, but there were three children, Henry (1592–1615), Toby (1593–*c*.1644), and Baptina (1594–1618).

In London Palavicino resided in the parish of St Dunstan-in-the-East (1578–84) and thereafter in a large house outside Bishopsgate. From 1585, however, he began to acquire property in the countryside, and purchased the manors of Cranbrook and Rayhouse in Essex from the earl of Leicester in 1585, Westacre in Norfolk from Sir Thomas

Cecil in 1588, and Babraham and Mompillers in Cambridgeshire from Robert Taylor, the recently ruined teller of the exchequer, in 1589. His total investment in land has been estimated at £20,000. From the early 1590s he regularly resided in the house built by Taylor at Babraham in 1576, but he was never accepted by the Cambridgeshire gentry. His tax assessments in the county became a major cause of friction, as Lord North and his allies sought to make him pay a disproportionate share. Palavicino declared that they acted 'upon conceit of riches which are not in substance but in men's talk' (*Salisbury MSS*, 8.282). His subsidy assessment was the highest in the city of London in both 1582 and 1598, and his fortune at his death was estimated to be £100,000.

Palavicino died on 5 July 1600 at Babraham, where he was buried. By his will he left his daughter an annuity of £150 until her marriage, when she was to be given a portion of £5000. Apart from a number of other legacies, the bulk of the estate was to be held in trust to be divided equally between the two sons at marriage. Unfortunately Palavicino decided on his deathbed to remove his hitherto trusted agents, Giovanni Battista Giustiniano and Francisco Rizzo, from the position of executor, and died before he could appoint replacements, leaving his wife as sole executor. She remarried on 7 July 1601, taking as her second husband the heavily indebted Sir Oliver Cromwell of Hinchinbrook, possibly with the encouragement of the overseers of the will, Sir Robert Cecil and Gilbert, earl of Shrewsbury, who did nothing to remove the Lady Anne from the executorship on her remarriage as Palavicino had instructed. Cromwell managed the extraordinary feat of marrying his two daughters Catherine and Jane to Henry and Toby Palavicino on 24 April 1606, and later marrying his eldest son, Henry, to Baptina, so that there was no way in which the Palavicino fortune could not fall into the Cromwell family's hands. Sir Oliver's reckless extravagance was matched by that of his son-in-law Toby, who succeeded to the estates on his elder brother's death in 1615. A prodigious builder and gambler, he wasted his assets, fell into the toils of the London moneylenders, disentailed his estates by private act in 1624, and in the years which followed sold them off. IAN W. ARCHER

Sources L. Stone, *An Elizabethan: Sir Horatio Palavicino* (1956) • *Calendar of the manuscripts of the most hon. the marquis of Salisbury*, 24 vols., HMC, 9 (1883–1976) • *CSP for.*, *1558–1603* • will, PRO, PROB 11/96, sig. 64 • BL, Cotton MSS • BL, Lansdowne MSS • minutes of the governors of Bridewell Hospital, GL • list and analysis of state papers, foreign series: Elizabeth I, 5 vols., 1964, PRO • *CSP dom.*
Archives Essex RO, Chelmsford, accounts • Hatfield House, Hertfordshire, letters and papers | BL, Cotton MSS, letters to Sir Thomas Bodley, Walsingham, etc.
Likenesses miniature, 1584 (of Palavicino?), priv. coll.
Wealth at death est. at approx. £100,000: Stone, *Palavicino*, 298

Paleotti, Massimo [Max William] **Salvadori-** (1908–1992), anti-fascist activist, was born Max William Salvadori-Paleotti on 16 June 1908 at 75 Harvard Court, Honeybourne Road, London, the only son and second of the three children of Count Guglielmo Giacomo Vittorio Salvadori-Paleotti (1879–1953), philosopher, and his wife, Giacinta (1875–1960), daughter of Colonel Arturo Galletti di Cadilhac and his wife, Margaret. Massimo or Max could trace his forebears back to an Albanian prince who, settling in the Papal States in the later fifteenth century, commissioned from the Venetian Carlo Crivelli a polyptych, of which part is now in the National Gallery, London. The Salvadori intermarried with the local nobility, becoming substantial landowners on the Italian Adriatic coast. Max's parents were both of protestant Italian and English descent. His mother, expecting a son, came back to England, where she had been partly brought up, so that he would be born on English soil and have dual British and Italian nationality. His father, professor of philosophy at Pisa and Rome universities, wrote articles on the Italian political scene for English periodicals. One in 1924 for the *New Statesman* criticized the fascist regime, an English admirer of which drew it to the attention of Mussolini. He sent an order to Florence, where Count Guglielmo was living, that he should be silenced. On 1 April 1924 Max Salvadori, aged fifteen, witnessed his father being beaten up by fascist thugs and left with cuts across his face and forehead. The family fled to Switzerland.

There Salvadori continued his education, gaining a degree at Geneva University, and in 1929 he started on an active anti-fascist role. The opposition to Mussolini had been reduced to exiles and their tacit sympathizers in Italy, together welded into the Giustizia e Libertà movement. It needed a link between its two parts, somebody who could be both liaison officer and recruiting agent. Salvadori volunteered to return to Italy, where he used study at Rome University followed by work for the institute of foreign trade as his cover occupations while travelling all over the country to meet and encourage supporters of the underground opposition. They ranged from miners and factory workers to the most prestigious liberal intellectuals, Einaudi and Croce. It took three years for Mussolini's agents in their campaign of suppression to catch up with him on 21 July 1932. Sent to the notorious Regina Coeli prison in Rome, Salvadori was among the last of his group of friends to be interrogated. The authorities had enough captives to feel that the network in Rome was broken and he was spared the excruciating tortures regularly inflicted on prisoners to force confessions. There were by then 600 political prisoners at Regina Coeli, an embarrassing number for a government pretending it no longer faced substantial opposition within Italy. Hence, of the 600 none was publicly tried and the police were empowered to hand out prison sentences of no more than five years. Salvadori, given the full five, was sent to the island prison of Ponza.

Here dual nationality proved invaluable. Salvadori's friend and cousin Laurence Collier at the Foreign Office asked the British ambassador in Rome to remind the Italian government that Salvadori was a British subject. He was released on 20 July 1933 on condition that he went to live at his father's country home. Kept under police supervision and forbidden to travel, he determined to escape abroad. Rather than adopt elaborate subterfuges, he sent a message by a local peasant to the police station in September 1933, saying that he was going to Switzerland. The superintendent, thinking he would never do so without permission from the ministry of the interior, failed to alert the frontier guards. Using the British passport of a cousin whom he closely resembled, Salvadori crossed the border unhindered. He moved to England, and married Joyce Woodforde Pawle (1908–1999), descended from Parson Woodforde, the diarist, on 7 May 1934. On their way to Njoro, Kenya, he learned of Italian preparations to invade Ethiopia and told Giustizia e Libertà to give an early warning of the impending aggression. Farm management kept them in Kenya (where they had a son and daughter) until 1937, when he started university lecturing, first at Geneva, then from 1939 at St Lawrence, USA. Recruited by British intelligence in 1941, he served in Mexico and central America, where he swam across cayman-infested rivers to disrupt radio transmissions to German submarines. In January 1943 he became a British army officer. Joining Special Operations Executive, he participated in the Sicily, Salerno, and Anzio landings, earning a Military Cross at the Garigliano. Consulted by the Allied Control Commission as an expert on anti-fascism, he was offered a post in the Badoglio government by Harold Macmillan. His refusal to serve a prime minister and king who had collaborated with Mussolini may have influenced the commission in sidelining them soon afterwards. Macmillan was brought to realize the strength of public antagonism.

Salvadori had many friends among the mass of released political prisoners and returning exiles, including Emilio Lussu, head of Giustizia e Libertà, who came to Rome and married Salvadori's sister, Joyce. To arrange communications between the Rome committee of national liberation and the allied command, she crossed the front line, met her brother and crossed back with detailed plans.

As partisan activities spread and gained in importance, Salvadori's contacts and knowledge were increasingly valued. Promoted major in June 1944, he acquired administrative experience at allied commission headquarters but soon saw that remote control hampered decision making. He welcomed a change to decentralization. The commission sent him behind enemy lines as a lieutenant-colonel, heading a mission to the national liberation committee (or underground government) of northern Italy. During winter 1944–5 he and other liaison officers to subordinate committees helped co-ordinate and keep supplied partisans whose numbers rose from some 100,000 in the autumn to about 150,000 in the spring. Constantly dodging enemy patrols and informers, Salvadori was contriving by April to meet forty to fifty people a week. He had to save Milan from a German 'scorched earth' retreat. Its archbishop, Cardinal Montini (later Pope Paul VI), and Salvadori together persuaded the German commander to leave the city unharmed. In gratitude the municipality made Salvadori an honorary citizen. The British army awarded him a DSO.

Post-war domination of Italian politics by a Catholic Christian Democrat party left little room for a protestant uneasy at clerical influence. Apart from spells at UNESCO (1948–9), and NATO (1952–3), Salvadori lectured as professor of social science at Bennington College, Vermont, between 1945 and 1962, and of history at Smith College, Massachusetts, between 1947 and 1975. He wrote over twenty books, many on the United States in a historical context, championing its democratic institutions and competitive economy. His principal works in English were *American Capitalism* (1957), *Liberal Democracy* (1958), *The Economics of Freedom* (1959), and *Free Market Economics: the Liberal Heresy* (1977). They were widely read, notably by President Eisenhower. As closely reasoned statements of strong convictions, they are typical of a man of intelligence, courage, and tenacity. His social ease and courtesy went with good looks and a tall, athletic build.

Salvadori died at his home, 36 Ward Avenue, Northampton, Massachusetts, USA, on 6 August 1992. He was cremated at Springfield, Massachusetts.

William Collier

Sources M. Salvadori, *Resistenza ed azione (Ricordi di un liberale)* (1951) · priv. coll., Archivio Salvadori-Paleotti di Fermo · priv. coll., Collier family archive · R. Battaglia, *The story of the Italian resistance* (1957) · M. Munthe, *Sweet is war* (1954) · M. Salvadori, *Liberal democracy* (1958) · C. Baker and T. Henry, *The National Gallery complete illustrated catalogue* (1995) · J. Lussu, *Fronti e frontiere* (1945) · PRO, HS 6/775–776 · b. cert.
Archives priv. coll. | priv. coll., Collier family archive
Likenesses photograph, 1943–5

Paley, Frederick Apthorp (1815–1888), classical scholar and writer, was the eldest son of Edmund Paley (1782–1850), rector of Easingwold, York, where he was born on 14 January 1815. He was the grandson of Archdeacon William *Paley, whose works his father edited, and elder brother of E. G. Paley (1823–1895), who was active as an architect and builder in the north of England. His mother was Sarah, daughter of the Revd Dr Apthorp. Educated under Samuel Butler at Shrewsbury School and at St John's College, Cambridge, he graduated BA in 1838 but, owing to his dislike of mathematics, did not attempt the mathematical tripos and was therefore ineligible for the classical tripos. He was devoted to classical studies from early youth, although his interests were always wide; as a boy he was good with mechanical things and fond of natural science. He published his first book as early as 1838, a translation of G. F. Schömann's *De comitiis Atheniensium* (1819). He proceeded MA in 1842, and received the honorary degree of LLD from Aberdeen in 1883.

From 1838 to 1846 Paley was in residence at Cambridge; in addition to reading with pupils, he studied classics and ecclesiastical architecture, and published in both. He was an original member of the Cambridge Camden Society, became honorary secretary and member of committee, and contributed largely to *The Ecclesiologist* while that paper was the organ of the society. He eagerly supported the restoration of the Round Church at Cambridge. During the progress of the Oxford Movement, by which he was greatly influenced, he identified himself with the high-church party in the university. In 1846 he was suspected of having encouraged one of his pupils, John Morris, to join the Roman Catholic church, and he was ordered by the master of St John's to give up his rooms in college. The affair created a brief scandal in both local and national press, and it cost Paley any chance of conventional advance at Cambridge, then or later. Some of his letters reveal a certain bitterness, and he was caustic in print about the indolence of many who enjoyed college fellowships.

Paley accordingly left Cambridge, but not before he had himself converted to Catholicism. From 1847 to 1856 he was employed as private tutor in Catholic families, successively those of the Talbots (earls of Shrewsbury), Throckmortons, and Kenelm Digbys. On 31 July 1854 he married Ruth, sixth daughter of G. M. Burchell of Bramley, Surrey; they had two sons and a daughter. After a brief period at Peterborough, where he also took pupils, he returned to Cambridge University in 1860, on the partial removal of religious disability, and became a private tutor to undergraduates.

During the 1840s Paley began issuing an edition of Aeschylus in separate parts, with Latin notes, which, though coldly received abroad, met with success at home. Throughout his absence from Cambridge from 1846 to 1860 he studied and wrote incessantly, publishing in particular editions of Aeschylus and Euripides with English notes, Propertius and Ovid's *Fasti*, and works on architecture. His growing reputation as a scholar, as well as teacher, led to his being considered in 1854 by J. H. Newman for the chair of Greek at the new University College of Dublin; but a rival successfully thwarted the appointment. He also studied botany, geology, and zoology, publishing pamphlets and numerous articles on these and other scientific, religious, and educational matters. Among his studies were the habits of earthworms; he published on the subject both before and after the appearance of Charles Darwin's book on it (1881), which he reviewed.

At Cambridge from 1860 to 1874 Paley was a thorough and well regarded tutor, who never consented to teach solely for the examinations (he published opinions on reform of the classical tripos, and examined in it in 1874). Among his pupils T. Field, W. Leaf, and S. S. Lewis wrote recollections of him. In 1872 he applied unsuccessfully for the chair of Latin at Cambridge, when J. E. B. Mayor was appointed; then in 1874 his probably unique qualifications and experience led to his selection by Cardinal Manning as professor of classical literature at the new Catholic University College at Kensington, London; this was the only professional post Paley ever held. The college quickly failed, and Paley ceased to be professor in 1877. The year before, he had been briefly considered for election as fellow of Peterhouse, Cambridge, expressly to complete the edition of Thucydides begun by the college's recently dead R. Shilleto; in fact Paley completed Shilleto's book ii privately, in 1880, and insisted on anonymity. While in London, he was classical examiner to the university (1875–80), a prestigious appointment, and to the civil service commission.

Paley's first wife was killed in a carriage accident in 1870 near Peterborough and buried there. On 3 October 1871 he married his second wife, Selena Frances, youngest daughter of Revd T. Broadhurst of Bath. In 1881, owing to lifelong weakness of the chest (this, and his lean build, gave some the impression of desiccation), he removed to Bournemouth, delighting in the house he bought at Boscombe Spa and calling it Apthorp, his mother's family name. There he died on 9 December 1888 and was buried in the Catholic churchyard. His second wife survived him until 1908. She allowed his personal library to be purchased by his friend and former pupil S. S. Lewis, who presented it to Cavendish College, Cambridge; part survives still at Fitzwilliam College.

The range, quantity, and quality of Paley's published work were determined by various factors: he was without reliable and salaried employment for much of his life; the flow of private pupils at Cambridge lessened in the 1860s; and most of his classical articles and reviews, as well as the papers on general subjects, were written to earn money, especially in his retirement (such investments as he had in lieu of a pension were largely in land which lost value or income in the agricultural depression of the 1880s). Great changes in the educational market from the 1850s, with a new demand for classical commentaries in English, gave Paley's unquestionable talent and facility its chance; he published about thirty such commentaries, some of them going into conscientiously revised editions. Many of these were the first of their kind and became for a time standard works, for scholars as well as students, like his *Propertius* (1853; 2nd edn, 1872) and *Select Private Orations of Demosthenes* (with J. E. Sandys, 1874), and above all his *Aeschylus* (1855; 4th edn, 1879) and *Euripides* (3 vols., 1857; 2nd edn, 1872); the latter, almost 150 years later, was still the most recent complete commentary on Euripides to have been undertaken. These two works were his best, singular in their day for the breadth and approachability of their introductions; the commentaries were workmanlike and honest, founded on knowledgeable sensitivity to tragic diction which led Paley to textual conjectures, and to suspicion of interpolation, judged rather more favourably nowadays than then. Paley seldom had leisure or patience for true research, and he could not read important German scholarship at first hand. He nevertheless studied accessible manuscripts for his editions and published scholarly papers on many topics, especially in the *Journal of Philology* after its foundation in 1868. Homer was a particular interest. He wrote a commentary on the *Iliad* (1866; 2nd edn, 1884), soon superseded by that written by his Cambridge pupil W. Leaf; he early formed, and constantly re-argued, his own 'Homeric theory', that the discrepant mythical and linguistic phenomena of the poems were only to be explained if they had been assembled 'anonymously' in the fifth century BC from a variety of older and newer sources. The theory won indifference or scorn in Britain, but appealed temporarily to German analysts of Homer. One pure work of scholarship stands out, his *Commentarius* on the important Medicean scholia of Aeschylus (1878; reprinted 1978). The best appreciation of his scholarship by a near contemporary was that of E. C. Marchant in the *Dictionary of National Biography*, where a very great number of his publications is listed; judgements made one century later appeared in C. Collard, Liverpool Classical Papers, no. 5 (1995).

CHRISTOPHER COLLARD

Sources [F. A. Paley], 'The adventures of a school-boy: by a convert', *Dolman's Magazine*, 6 (1847) • [F. A. Paley], 'The adventures of a school-boy: by a convert', *Dolman's Magazine*, 7 (1848) • C. Collard, 'A Victorian classical "outsider": F. A. Paley (1816–88)', *Tria lustra: essays and notes presented to John Pinsent*, ed. H. D. Jocelyn (1993), 329–39 • C. Collard, 'F. A. Paley', *Aspects of nineteenth-century classical scholarship*, Liverpool Classical Papers, 5 (1995) • T. Field, *The Eagle*, 15 (1889), 442–7 • S. S. Lewis, 'Frederick Apthorp Paley', *Biographisches Jahrbuch für Alterthumskunde*, ed. I. von Müller and C. Bursian, 12 (Leipzig, 1890), 15–17 • *DNB* • M. N. L. Couve de Murville and P. Jenkins, *Catholic Cambridge* (1983), 107–8 • C. D. Scott, *Classical Review*, 3 (1889), 80–82 • *The Athenaeum* (15 Dec 1888), 813–14 • Venn, *Alum. Cant.* • Boase, *Mod. Eng. biog.*

Archives CUL, letters to Lord Acton • DWL, letters to H. Y. Allon • U. Reading L., letters to George Bell, Publisher

Wealth at death £2676 3*s.* 8*d.*: resworn probate, Dec 1889, *CGPLA Eng. & Wales*

Paley, Mary. *See* Marshall, Mary (1850–1944).

Paley, Richard (*bap.* **1746**, *d.* **1808**), industrialist and entrepreneur, was born in Langcliffe, Giggleswick, and baptized on 10 August 1746 at Giggleswick parish church in the West Riding of Yorkshire, the second of the four children of George Paley (1721–1765), a freeholder, of Langcliffe Scar Farm, and his wife, Mary Lawson. The Paley family can be traced in Langcliffe for the two previous centuries. William Paley, the theologian, was Richard's cousin, and his uncle William (*d.* 1799) the incumbent of Giggleswick and sometime master of Giggleswick School. Nothing is known of his education or of an apprenticeship. He was already established as a soap-boiler in Leeds when the *Leeds Intelligencer* of 25 June 1771 announced his marriage on 15 June at Otley to Mary Preston of Merebeck Hall, Giggleswick, 'an agreeable lady with a fortune of £1000'. In April 1775 the daughter of the squire of Langcliffe Hall, his 'cousin' Mrs Margaret Cookson (*née* Dawson), provided him with further economic support by a forty-year lease of domestic and industrial buildings in open wharfside ground at Kirk Ing, next to the parish church of Leeds, part of the extensive Cookson estate. In February 1776 these, improved and valued for fire insurance at £1700, were the basis of a mortgage from his elder brother Thomas, who remained a source of further loans by mortgages throughout Richard's lifetime. From October 1777 Middleton colliery began to supply coal for Paley's malthouse and soap works on this site.

The Paleys' first child, Mary, was born on 3 September 1772, when they were still living in Meadow Lane, Hunslet, but from October 1776 Paley began to attend as a juror at the manor court of Leeds Kirkgate. Nine other children were born between 1777 and 1788 at a house at Kirk Ing, 'next the Old Church Yard', though five died in infancy. From November 1778 Paley owned seats in a new gallery at the church.

In November 1780 Paley made his first purchases of land alongside the Aire Navigation at Knostrop (Knowesthorp), east of Leeds, where he later transferred the soap works and his own residence to new premises which he named Gibraltar. Even more significant for his future activities as a property developer was a contract of October 1786 to pay £255 for Coneyshaws, a close of 3 acres adjoining the York turnpike at Marsh Lane, on the eastern fringe of the town. There, and in other fields nearby, Paley became the town's largest landlord of working-class houses. By 1803 he owned 275 houses, generally back-to-backs of two storeys with separate cellar dwellings beneath, arranged in terraces with courtyards behind.

'Mr Paley and Mr Dade [a raff merchant of Otley] purchased the above Estates with the sole View of parcelling them out in Building Lots', began a note (W. Yorks. AS, Leeds, DB 233) prepared after Dade's death early in May 1803 and Paley's bankruptcy on 21 May. At that time 56 of the 67 acres acquired by the partners between 1787 and 1803 still remained in lots unsold; a measure of their over-optimism was the twenty years that the assignees in bankruptcy then took to market these lots.

Paley's bankruptcy was not due solely to failed building speculation. His mortgages, of £8170, from banks in Malton, Huddersfield, and Pontefract had been obtained on the security of other property ventures in Leeds and beyond. He had brought cotton spinning to Leeds by building two cotton mills at Bank Top as early as 1790, that is, before the flax mill of John Marshall and the woollen mill of Benjamin Gott. One mill was intended for letting, and in the other the partnership of Holdforth, Wilkinson, Paley & Co. installed steam engines for spinning cotton. In 1795 James Watt jun. was sent to spy on these for infringement of patent, and under duress a 36 hp Soho-made engine machine was ordered the following year (but seems not to have been delivered). In November 1798 Paley contracted to build a flax mill in Marsh Lane, Leeds, to be tenanted by G. and J. Wright, and another, complete with steam engine, in 1801; nearby he built premises for the ironsmith Cawood, another for the whitesmith Farmery, and a nail works for Liddle & Co. In 1793 he became landlord of a water-powered frizzing mill at Mill Garth and nearby, at Lady Bridge, the workshops that became Brumfitt's carpet factory. He also built smaller premises to be leased, including cloth-dressing shops, and at Skinner Lane he built a fine pair of three-storey bay-fronted houses, with workshops behind, as residences for cloth merchants still dependent on handicraftsmen. In addition he built riverside warehouses to rent to corn merchants and others.

Paley became a partner in enterprises further afield: in ironworks at Fall Ings, Wakefield (1787–92); in the cotton mill of King, Turner, Varden, Paley & Co. at Mytholmroyd, near Halifax (by 1790); in the new Bowling ironworks at Bradford (1787), in which he had a quarter share; in three cotton mills at Colne, Lancashire (1797); and in a potash works at Bristol, which supplied the Paley soap works. He also made overtures for a soap works at Oban in Scotland and the supply of kelp from there to Leeds.

Paley was elected a member of the closed tory Leeds corporation on 29 September 1789; he was a shareholder in the new private subscription library from 1770 and in the

Leeds waterworks, and a subscriber to the Leeds General Infirmary from 1785. His name frequently appeared in the press at the head of charity subscription lists for Kirkgate ward, where in November 1803, six months after his bankruptcy, he subscribed 10 guineas for the relief of the poor. In the currency shortage of small coins in 1791 he placed orders with Boulton and Watt for copper coins bearing his name to be put into circulation in Leeds, and in March 1797 he publicly guaranteed his acceptance of Bank of England notes. He more than once took over property as claimant against local bankrupts indebted to him in the course of trade or to whom he had lent money on mortgage.

After his bankruptcy Paley resigned from the borough council, leaving no other record until his death at Knostrop, 'from inflamation', on 24 November 1808; he was buried on the 26th in St Peter's churchyard, Leeds. He was intestate, the Gibraltar works being already in trust for his eldest son, George (1779–1828). At first the trustees expected to raise £50,000 as well as a dividend of 20s. in the pound for all creditors, but the first dividend of 1804 was only 2s. in the pound. A further small dividend was paid in 1809, with an additional contribution from his nephew John Green Paley. A settlement was made with Dade's heir in March 1807. The original trustees in bankruptcy were stormily replaced in December 1814, and intermittent land sales continued until 1823.

No street or mill perpetuated Paley's name in the town where he had built its first textile mills, although, until they disappeared under railway sidings, Paley's Galleries in Marsh Lane were a reminder that he also pioneered a style of high-density, low-cost housing that, together with the mill smoke, gave the town a classic east end. His bankruptcy showed an aspect of entrepreneurial fortunes that were as characteristic of the industrial revolution as its successes. MAURICE BERESFORD

Sources W. Yorks. AS, Leeds, DB 176, 233; DB maps 119, 233, 419 · M. W. Beresford, 'Richard Paley in the East End of Leeds', in C. W. Chalkin and M. A. Havenden, *Rural change and urban growth, 1500–1800* (1974), 281–320 · registry of deeds, W. Yorks. AS, Wakefield, esp. BX 71/111 and HX 510/507 [incl. wills] · Leeds poor rate assessments, 1774–1805, W. Yorks. AS, Leeds, LORB 32, 34–7 · *Leeds Intelligencer* (1771–1823) [esp. property advertisements and bankruptcy assignments] · *Leeds Mercury* (1771–1823), esp. property advertisements and bankruptcy assignments · parish register, St Peter's, Leeds, 1772–1809, W. Yorks. AS, Leeds · R. W. Hoyle, ed., *Giggleswick Parish Register*, 2 (1986) · Sun Fire Insurance register, GL, MSS 11935–11936; OS 299/452883–452884; 391/607866, 608040 and 609136; CS 86/837252 · Royal Exchange registers, GL, MS M 72521/32A/156289 · PRO, C 12/1760/20; C 13/57(ii)/50; E 112/1539/506 · Leeds corporation property deeds, esp. LCD 359 · Langcliffe enclosure award and map, 1789, W. Yorks. AS, Leeds · Argyll and Bute District Archives, Inveraray, TD 40/295
Archives W. Yorks. AS, Leeds, bankruptcy and other documents
Wealth at death under £3500 in chattels: wills, administration books, 27 Dec 1808, Borth. Inst.

Paley, William (1743–1805), theologian and moralist, was born in July 1743 in Peterborough and baptized on 30 August in Peterborough Cathedral, the only son and eldest of four children of William Paley (1711–1799) and Elizabeth Clapham (1713?–1796), both of Giggleswick in the West Riding of Yorkshire. The elder Paley was a sizar at Christ's College, Cambridge, the traditional place of learning for Paley men since the early seventeenth century, where he graduated BA in 1733. In 1735 he became vicar of Helpston, Northamptonshire, and went to live in nearby Peterborough where he was a minor canon of the cathedral. In 1745 he was appointed headmaster of the free grammar school in Giggleswick, a post he held until his death, and it was here that his son received his early schooling. Paley was a studious boy, who displayed an early interest in mechanical ingenuity and whose principal amusement was angling. On 16 November 1758 he was admitted as a sizar to Christ's, with the benefit of a scholarship from Giggleswick. Before beginning his residence at Christ's in October 1759, he studied geometry and algebra with William Howarth at Topcliffe, near Ripon. Paley's father commented to one of his pupils that he expected his son to 'turn out a great man—very great indeed—I'm certain of it; for he has by far the *clearest* head I ever met with in my life' (Meadley, 4).

William Paley (1743–1805), by George Romney, 1789–91

Cambridge years Paley's interest in mathematics continued at Cambridge. In classics he was not so well trained, but his training was sufficient for his needs. To the Giggleswick scholarship he added a foundation scholarship and a Mildmay exhibition. At Cambridge he enjoyed a certain celebrity; his powers of conversation and good humour, just as often directed against himself as others, made him an easy companion. On his own admission he spent the first two years at Cambridge 'happily, but unprofitably', frequently in society 'where we were not immoral, but idle and rather expensive' (Lynan, 1.5).

His provincial dress and manners were a source of fun to his fellow students, but the superiority of his mind was soon discovered. At the commencement of his third year Paley was rescued by the intervention of a friend, who chided him that he was a fool for wasting his talents and threatened to cut him off if he did not change his ways. The admonishment seems to have had some effect. On 26 May 1761 Paley was awarded the Bunting scholarship, the highest mathematical prize offered at Cambridge.

Paley's formal studies at Cambridge were conducted under the Plumian professor Anthony Shepherd (algebra, geometry, and natural philosophy) and William Backhouse (logic, metaphysics, and moral philosophy). To compete for honours an undergraduate was required to engage in a number of 'acts' and 'opponencies'. For one of these public disputations in Latin his opponent was John Frere, who was second to Paley in the mathematical tripos of 1763. Paley discussed whether eternal punishment was contradictory to the divine attributes. The fluent delivery of his thesis and strength of conception were the ingredients of his success, and in June 1763 he graduated as senior wrangler.

From 1763 to 1765 Paley was a schoolmaster's assistant and then a Latin tutor at Bracken's academy in Greenwich, specializing in preparing boys for the military. For recreation he attended trials at the Old Bailey and visited the theatre, particularly when Garrick was on stage, an entertainment he enjoyed throughout his life. In 1765 he won one of the Cambridge members' prizes offered for the best dissertations in Latin prose by senior bachelors. His subject was 'A comparison between the Stoic and Epicurean philosophy, with respect to the influence of each on the morals of the people'; he argued that the Epicurean philosophy was more favourable to virtue and happiness, and characterized the Stoics as 'Pharisees in philosophy' ('Account of the life', 1.50). The dissertation concluded with a eulogy of Christian faith, including an imitation of a sentence from Locke with respect to the New Testament: 'It has God for its author; salvation for its end: and truth, without any mixture of error, for its matter' (Lynan, 1.11). Paley nearly lost the prize because he added notes in English, raising a suspicion that the essay was plagiarized. It is often said that this critique of the ancient moralists revealed an emerging utilitarianism. In the same year Paley left Bracken's academy after being ordained deacon and appointed assistant curate to John Hinchliffe, vicar of Greenwich and afterwards bishop of Peterborough. In Paley's lexicon curates were 'rats', and he referred to himself as a 'rat of rats' suffering from 'rat sickness' ('Account of the life', 1.63). For a time he continued working as a private tutor in Greenwich; one of his favourite pupils, John Ord, remembered him as his 'much loved friend and as it were a second father' (*GM*, 1809, 103).

On 24 June 1766 Paley became a fellow of Christ's, where Shepherd was now master, returned to Cambridge to take his MA, and remained there for the next ten years, during which time he earned a reputation as one of the university's most popular teachers. Among his closest friends at Cambridge were John Law, John Jebb, and Edward Waring. Law was the son of the theologian Edmund Law, then master of Peterhouse, and Knightbridge professor of moral philosophy; Jebb was a fellow of Peterhouse and the chief voice of reform at Cambridge; and Waring was the Lucasian professor, whose *Miscellanae analytica* Paley later helped correct for the press. In 1767 Paley became praelector at Christ's (a position he held until 1779), junior dean, and catechist, and Bunting, Walhampton, and Knapwell preacher. He was ordained priest by the bishop of London on 21 December 1767, and the following year he and John Law were appointed assistant tutors under Shepherd, with Paley as senior Greek lecturer teaching Backhouse's old courses in ethics, metaphysics, and the Greek Testament. Soon after, he was appointed steward, Mildmay preacher, and Hebrew lecturer. The last position, which Paley held from 1768 to 1770, was probably a sinecure, since he appears to have known little of the Hebrew language. In 1769 he was appointed chaplain to Edmund Law, newly elevated to the bishopric of Carlisle, and in 1771 was nominated one of the preachers at the Royal Chapel, Whitehall, a position he retained until 1776. He held the university post of taxor for the year 1770–71. The most senior post held by Paley at Christ's was senior dean, to which he was appointed in 1775.

For his lectures on ethics Paley compiled his own material, later revised and reorganized for *The Principles of Moral and Political Philosophy* (1785). For first-year metaphysics he used Locke's *Essay Concerning Human Understanding*, then went on to Clarke's *On the Being and Attributes of God* and Butler's *Analogy of Religion*. All undergraduates at Christ's were required to attend Paley's Greek Testament lectures twice a week, for which he drew substantially on Locke's *Reasonableness of Christianity*. The main point on which he insisted, a student later recalled, was 'that we should listen to God, not to man; that we should exert our faculties in understanding the language of holy men of old … and we should not call any our master in religion but Jesus Christ'. The same student recalled that as a lecturer 'the driest subjects were made interesting' by Paley, and notes from his lectures were highly sought after ('Anecdotes of Dr Paley', 414–17).

While a fellow at Cambridge, Paley joined the Hyson Club, established by the wranglers of 1757, where he 'contributed to the general stock of brilliancy and merriment' ('Account of the life', 1.68). The members of the club met to drink hyson (green tea) and engage in 'rational conversation', and were mainly reform-minded latitudinarian Cambridge men, including Edmund and John Law, Jebb, and Richard Watson, the moderator who examined Paley's dispute with John Frere. The Hyson was at the centre of the controversy over subscription to the Thirty-Nine Articles, which began in 1766 with the publication of Francis Blackburne's *The Confessional*. Five years of continued public debate culminated in the subscription meetings held at the Feathers tavern in London. The subsequent petition called for the liberty of every man to judge for himself to subscribe without penalty. Signed by almost all the members of the Hyson, it was presented to parliament in January 1772 by a group of Anglican clergy led by Jebb. Although Paley did not sign the petition on the regrettably flippant grounds that he 'could not afford to keep a conscience' (Meadley, 89), his general disposition on toleration was commonly known through his university lectures. In 1774 he defended Edmund Law against the criticisms of Thomas Randolph, Lady Margaret professor of divinity and president of Corpus Christi College, in an anonymous pamphlet, *A defence of the 'Considerations on the propriety of requiring a subscription to articles of faith'* (1774). An early biographer dismissed it as 'written with a spirit of contemptuous superiority, and in the boldest tone of latitudinarian inquiry', the arguments of which 'will satisfy none but lax consciences' (Lynan, 1.16, 27). The arguments for toleration and free enquiry contained in this pamphlet stand as a summary of the position of the reformers, and were repeated later in a brief chapter in the *Principles*, criticized by the radical Gilbert Wakefield as a 'shuffling chapter on subscription' ('Account of the life', 1.75). In 1776 Paley's 'Observations upon the character and example of Christ, with an appendix on the morality of the gospel' was printed privately and bound together with Edmund Law's 'Reflections on the life and character of Christ', and distributed among the students at Cambridge.

Clerical career Paley's connection with the Law family greatly advanced his clerical career. He regularly spent vacations with John Law while they were Cambridge fellows, and they once met John Wilkes on one of their excursions to Bath and enjoyed an evening with him. Paley's 'long and faithful friendship' with Law was acknowledged in the dedication to *Horae Paulinae* (1790). In 1777 Paley was invited to preach the visitation sermon in Carlisle Cathedral for Edmund Law, and in 1782 he preached the sermon at John Law's consecration as bishop of Clonfert and Kilmacduagh. Both John and Edmund Law encouraged Paley to revise his lectures on ethics for publication, and the *Principles* was dedicated to the bishop of Carlisle. When the bishop died at Rose Castle in Carlisle in 1787 Paley wrote a short memoir of his life, which afterward appeared in the *Encyclopaedia Britannica*. The Law connection extended to the prelate's third son, Edward, later Lord Ellenborough and lord chief justice of the king's bench, whom Paley is said to have aided in his study of the law.

It was at John Law's Carlisle residence that Paley met Jane Hewitt (1751?–1791), the daughter of a local spirit merchant, and they were married by Law on 6 June 1776. Initially they settled in Appleby, Westmorland, near Great Musgrave where Paley had been appointed to his first benefice by Bishop Law on 8 May 1775. The marriage produced a family of four sons and four daughters, including Edmund (1782–1850), his father's biographer. Paley once remarked: 'though I am a pluralist in preferment, I am a much greater pluralist in children' (Meadley, 161). Edmund later wrote of his mother, who died in May 1791, 'Sensible, but mild and unassuming, of retired habits, of a sweet and negative disposition, but inactive from ill health, and, as she used to call herself, a mere thread-paper wife' ('Account of the life', 1.91).

In Paley pluralism was coupled with indifference to elevation in the church. Though he gained much in his career through patronage, he coined the term 'rooting' for 'that baseness and servility which like swine rooting in a dunghill will perform the basest acts for a rich patron, to gain his protection and good benefice' ('Anecdotes of Dr Paley', 511). Towards the end of 1776 Bishop Law presented Paley with the vicarage of Dalston, Cumberland, and the following year he was favoured by the dean and chapter of Carlisle with a more substantial benefice, the vicarage of St Lawrence, Appleby. Paley resigned Musgrave, which he attended only rarely to preach, and thereafter divided his time equally between Dalston and Appleby, until he resigned the latter in 1785. He often declared that he had passed some of the happiest days of his life in Appleby.

In June 1780 Paley was appointed to a prebendary stall in Carlisle Cathedral, and on 29 July 1781 preached a general ordination sermon there. It was published in 1783, and was afterwards recommended to those preparing for holy orders 'as a correct standard by which they may examine their resolutions' (Lynan, 1.19). In August 1782 he succeeded his friend John Law as archdeacon of Carlisle, after the latter's elevation to the Irish bench, and with it acquired the vicarage of Great Salkeld, Cumberland. About this time he published anonymously a help manual for the clergy of Carlisle, perhaps originating from his own pastoral experience, *The Clergyman's Companion in Visiting the Sick*, a selection from the Book of Common Prayer with extracts from the works of eminent divines. Paley held the archdeaconry until 1805. At the end of 1785 he was appointed chancellor of the diocese of Carlisle, succeeding Richard Burn, author of *The Justice of the Peace*.

Residing mainly in Carlisle, Paley enjoyed a diverse and agreeable society of friends and neighbours, paid close attention to the well-being of the local clergy, and was noted for the liberality with which he treated his curates. As chancellor Paley was responsible for the ecclesiastical courts, involving cases of clergy discipline and matrimonial and testamentary cases. He worked to establish a dispensary in the town, and promoted Sunday schools. The latter initiative led to a charge of plagiarism over a cheap compendium of materials for the schools which Paley compiled from the writings of various authors. He did not accept any money from the sales of this volume, and apologised to the Revd J. Robertson, one of the original authors, for unknowingly offending him, although the lessons in spelling he borrowed hardly constituted the plagiarism of which he was charged. From Carlisle, Paley frequently rode to Dalston, but he was a poor horseman and took little pleasure in the journey, save that he thought it good exercise. Summers were spent in the vicarage at Dalston, where he fished, farmed, and worked in the garden.

In 1789 Bishop Yorke of Ely offered Paley the mastership of Jesus College, Cambridge. He declined because he was satisfied with his situation at Carlisle, commenting that the bishop was 'a man I know no more of than I do the pope' ('Account of the life', 1.95). John Law thought the decision hasty, on the grounds that this might be Paley's last chance for preferment. The offer is acknowledged in Paley's dedication of *A View of the Evidences of Christianity* (1794), a work generally praised as a masterpiece of Christian apologetics, and which confirmed his reputation as one of England's most respected theologians. In May 1791 Paley was presented to the vicarage of Addingham, near Great Salkeld, by the dean and chapter of Carlisle, and in 1793 he vacated Dalston for the vicarage of Stanwix, near Carlisle, to which he was presented by the new bishop, Vernon. Paley's annual income was about £900 at this time, a princely sum by the standards of the day. In August 1794 Bishop Porteus of London, a fellow with Paley at Christ's College and an admirer of *Evidences of Christianity*, gave him the prebend of St Pancras in St Paul's Cathedral. Also in recognition of this book, in January 1795 Bishop Pretyman presented Paley to the subdeanery of Lincoln, the additional income from which permitted him to resign his prebend and the chancellorship at Carlisle. *Evidences of Christianity* led to a doctorate of divinity from Cambridge in 1795, and the honour of preaching the commencement sermon before the university. On 14 March Paley acquired one of the most valuable livings in England, the rectory of Bishopwearmouth in the gift of Bishop Barrington of Durham, at which time he resigned from Stanwix and Addingham. The gift was repaid in the dedication of *Natural Theology* (1802). In Bishopwearmouth Paley met the good friend of his final years, George Wilson Meadley, a banker and merchant of liberal views who later wrote his life. On 14 December 1795 Paley married Catherine Dobinson (1748?–1819) of Carlisle, and thereafter divided the year between Bishopwearmouth and Lincoln.

In Lincoln, Paley was an active member of the local literary society and served as a magistrate. In the latter capacity his assertive manner served him well, although his main effort appears to have been directed unsuccessfully against the indiscriminate licensing of public houses, the consequences of which he often witnessed from the bench. In 1799 he assisted in measures to help the poor deal with food scarcities. Paley's value to the intellectual life of Lincoln was not doubted, but some thought him lacking in the dignity appropriate to a man of his station: 'The familiarity of his manners, his almost perpetual jests, his approximations to coarseness of language, weakened the splendour of his literary reputation' (Best, 182). Others appreciated his bluntness and self-deprecatory manner.

Writings Paley is best known as an orthodox theologian and utilitarian moralist, who tended to support established institutions but was progressive on questions of toleration and humanity. The popularity of his writings was due in part to his natural and easy style, but also to the fact that his philosophy expressed the leading scientific, theological, and ethical ideas of the day. He was a master at making complex philosophical positions accessible to a wider audience. As his son remarked: 'Christianity is treated as it would offer itself to the illiterate fisherman, or the ignorant natural man. Moral Philosophy is brought to the level of common sense' ('Account of the life', 1.73). A contemporary commented that the *Principles* 'presents a subject which has always been considered as harsh and difficult, in the most agreeable and intelligible form … we sit down to be informed of our duty, and are surprised to meet with amusement' (*Public Characters*, 118).

Paley pointed out that his books should be read in the reverse order from that in which they were written. Thus the moral and political philosophy of the *Principles* is grounded in the revelation of the scriptures, the subject matter of *Horae Paulinae* and *Evidences of Christianity*. In turn, this revealed theology is underpinned by the natural philosophy of the *Natural Theology*, in which knowledge of the attributes of the deity is derived from an empirical study of nature. In these works Paley posited a rationally ordered, purposeful, and divinely legitimated universe, assumptions later restated in a selection of the Bridgewater treatises of the 1830s.

The *Principles* was written in a forceful and clear style, which readily suited it for adoption as a textbook at Cambridge, with the consequence that the principle of utility penetrated the teaching of morality at the university. 'Whatever is expedient, is right', taught Paley. 'It is the utility of any moral rule alone, which constitutes the obligation of it' (W. Paley, *The Principles of Moral and Political Philosophy*, 1785, 161). The practice of virtue was supported by the expectations of a futurity in which there would be a proportionable accession of happiness. In developing this theory Paley owned that he drew upon many different sources and acknowledged a particular debt to Abraham Tucker. He also borrowed material from Thomas Rutherforth's *Institutes of Natural Law* and was influenced by Locke, Gay, Hartley, and his patron Bishop Law. From Law he took his definition of virtue: 'the doing good to mankind, in obedience to the will of God, and for the sake of everlasting happiness' (ibid., 35; quoting Law, lii). His arguments underpinning moral and political obligation were thrown into question by the provocative and often misunderstood pigeon analogy in the Cambridge lectures of 1773–4. The depiction of ninety-nine pigeons gathering food for 'the weakest perhaps and worst pigeon of the flock' (ibid., 91), which he used to justify the inequality of property, was understood by some to be a criticism of monarchy, and caused John Law to warn Paley that it might cost him a bishopric. 'Bishop or no bishop', replied the author, 'it shall stand' ('Account of the life', 1.341). Paley was paid handsomely for the copyright to this popular text, and exulted: 'Little did I think that I should ever make a thousand pounds by any book of mine' (Lynan, 1.21). The appearance of the *Principles*, with its religious and conservative utilitarian moral and political philosophy, prompted Jeremy Bentham to issue his own secular utilitarian and reformist *Introduction to the Principles of Morals and Legislation* in 1789.

Horae Paulinae and *Evidences of Christianity* were concerted attempts to prove the credibility of the New Testament as a historical record of revelation. In *Horae Paulinae* Paley showed he was thoroughly versed in St Paul's teachings, to which he applied a good deal of original criticism. He mounted a detailed comparison between Paul's epistles and the Acts of the Apostles, concluding that the similarities between the two reinforced the authenticity of the testimony they contained. In so doing he demonstrated that Paul's letters were not the contrived product of a personal or political agenda but rather were an authentic source of early Christian history. *Horae Paulinae* was translated into German in 1797, by 1810 had gone through ten editions, and appeared in numerous editions throughout the nineteenth century. The arguments of this work were later challenged by Bentham in *Not Paul, but Jesus* (1823).

Evidences of Christianity was principally directed against Hume's scepticism concerning the grounds for belief in miracles, arguing for the reliability of the apostles' testimony. Paley's general approach was based on the four rules of biblical criticism laid down by the nonjuror Charles Leslie, and he also drew upon Bishop Lardner's *Credibility of the Gospel History*, Bishop Douglas's *Criterion of Miracles*, and Soame Jenyns's *A View of the Internal Evidence of the Christian Religion*. His defence of the established religion in *Evidences of Christianity* and the *Principles* was based on its utility in the preservation and communication of religious knowledge. Though Paley later expressed surprise at the popularity of his writings, he thought *Evidences of Christianity* would become a standard book at the universities and for persons entering into orders, and on this score was effective in getting better terms from the bookseller for its publication.

Natural Theology was not based on lectures, and is the most original and entertaining of Paley's works. He wrote it, he says in the book's dedication, 'to make up my works into system'. Between 1802 and his death in 1805 it passed through nine editions. The centrepiece of the work is the argument from design, introduced in the famous opening pages. From the existence of a watch and observance of its mechanism we infer the existence of a watchmaker; so, from the existence of the world and its constituent elements we infer the existence of an intelligent creator. The conformity of empirical evidence to this central analogy between the watchmaker and the divine creator constituted a compelling probability argument. However, Paley thought it amounted to more than this and claimed invincibility for his proof, based on the intuitive certainty that any contrivance, natural or artificial, must be the product of an intelligent author. He dismissed evolutionary theory as a conjecture lacking empirical evidence, a weakness in the evolutionist position which persisted down to Darwin's *Origin of Species*. In writing the book Paley received assistance from John Law and from Law's friend John Brinkley, the Andrews professor of astronomy at Trinity College, Dublin. He also drew substantial hints from many other authors, as his manuscripts make clear, including Boyle, Gregory, Cheselden, Derham, Ray, Monro, Adams, Wilkes, Tucker, Sturm, Goldsmith, Lesser, Smellie, Seed, Hervey, Addison, Keill, Watson, St Pierre, Cappe, Priestley, Maclaurin, and the *Memoirs of Natural History* produced by the Académie Royale, Paris. Paley also seems to have borrowed from Cleanthes' side of the debate in Hume's *Dialogues Concerning Natural Religion*, while the essentials of the watch analogy were a commonplace of the day and can be found in Locke, Nieuwentyt, Rousseau, and Tucker, among others. Another vital ingredient, however, was the material Paley compiled from his own investigations of nature, bringing home stones and plants from his walks and analysing the bone structures of the hare, fish, or fowl he consumed at table. The principal arguments of *Natural Theology* were countered by Bentham and George Grote in *An Analysis of the Influence of Natural Religion on the Temporal Happiness of Mankind* (1822), which resurrected the chief elements of Hume's scepticism stated in the *Dialogues*.

Paley's theological publications placed him at the forefront of Anglican apologetics during this period and guaranteed his writings a place in the Cambridge curriculum for several generations. However, his religious commitments were not confined to the study and the lecture hall. Though a noted pluralist, he was assiduous and devout in the performance of clerical duties. Toward the end of his life he took up a study of clerical residence and he drew up proposals to tax non-residence in order to augment small livings for 'An act for the better promoting the residence of the parochial clergy'. When at Cambridge, Paley recommended that his pupils compose one sermon and steal five. However, he always took great pleasure in the composition of sermons and, even when he was no longer able to preach, continued to jot down hints for use in sermons. His sermons were popular, written in a style that was plain and unrhetorical and modelled on Sherlock, Clarke, and Hoadley. He never completed the project to publish a volume of his sermons. Knowing he was near to death in May 1805 he put his sermons in order, left directions for their publication in a codicil to his will, and expressed himself satisfied 'that now he had left that ready' ('Account of the life', 1.371). An edition of five hundred copies was to be produced, but not for sale; in the 'Advertisement' to the *Sermons* Paley indicated they were to be 'distributed in the neighbourhood, first to those who frequented church, then to farmers' families in the country, then to such as had a person in the family who could read, and were likely to read them'. The task of editing was assigned to his curate, George Stephenson. The sermons, many of which covered themes familiar from his books, appeared in 1806 and went through seven editions by 1825. Another expanded volume was published in 1817, and Edmund Paley edited a two-volume collection in 1825. Certain omissions in the sermons raised doubts about Paley's trinitarian orthodoxy, a charge supported by the circumstantial evidence of his association with Edmund Law and others inclined to Socinianism. However Meadley, himself a convert to Unitarianism, was unconvinced. He found in Paley's works (including the sermons) sufficient evidence that he believed in 'the common notions, about the pre-existence, the propitiation, the present agency, and the intercession of Christ' (Meadley, 165).

Paley's politics Paley never considered himself a party man. Though he enjoyed the daily paper, *The Sun*, and frequently commented on passing political events, in his writings he attempted to strike a balance between opinions on particular subjects. Above all a man of common sense, he had an instinctive distrust of the innovative and untested. Edmund Paley thought his father would have looked with amusement on those who sought to find political bias in his writings. He was not 'a secret advocate for ecclesiastical reform, or a political dabbler' ('Account of the life', 1.72), but rather an 'advocate of liberal principles' who never went 'beyond the bounds of fair and candid conclusions, or of established order' ('Account of the life', 1.71).

Paley's liberal principles are evident in his opposition to the slave trade and his discussions of subscription. He also took a keen interest in prison reform and, in 1801, the plight of the Irish Catholics. In 1789 his views opposing compensation for slave traders were discussed in the newspapers of the day, and in 1792 he aired his criticisms of the 'diabolical traffic' at a public meeting in Carlisle convened to petition parliament and at which he occupied the chair. In general, however, Paley adopted a cautious attitude towards established institutions. Worried by events in France and by the popularity of Paine's *Rights of Man*, he published two tracts in defence of England's political institutions in 1792. The first, *Archdeacon Paley's 'Essay upon the British Constitution'*, was a reprint of chapter 7 of book 6 of the *Principles* in which he extolled the virtues of the existing political arrangements. The second, originally a sermon given in Dalston in 1790, was *Reasons for Contentment, Addressed to the Labouring Part of the British Public*, in which he disingenuously argued that the labouring man should look on his lot as a happier one than that of the wealthy and pointed out the risks to every man of violent disturbance. This pamphlet elicited a good number of responses from the ranks of the radical reformers, and its arguments were contemptuously dismissed by the then radical Coleridge as 'Themes to debauch Boy's minds on the miseries of rich men & comforts of poverty' (S. T. Coleridge, *Note Books*, ed. K. Coburn, 1957, 1.75). Even moderate reformers, such as Samuel Parr, who respected Paley for his stand on the slave trade, were horrified by his apparent reversal, but Paley did not see anything inconsistent in it. Similar criticisms of Paley were later voiced by William Hazlitt and John Austin.

A good number of Paley's manuscripts and notebooks survive, although often written 'in one of the worst and most illegible hands that ever adorned genius, mixed up in a confused and unconnected heap with penmanship of a fair and seemly quality' ('Account of the life', 1.133). It was his habit suddenly to snatch a pen and scribble down his ideas as and when they occurred to him, and in later life he used an impenetrable sort of shorthand. When reviewing his notes he was often heard to exclaim: 'What could I have been thinking or speaking about!' (ibid., 1.135).

Final years The general caution and orthodoxy of Paley's principal works were counterbalanced by the easiness of his conversation, the tendency of which was to undermine subordination and question the appropriateness of existing rules and practices. On the basis of his conversation Isaac Milner, the evangelical president of Queens' College, found him 'as loose in politics as he is in religion' (M. Milner, *Life of Isaac Milner*, 1842, 83). Paley was by no means lacking in courtesy or a proper deference to superiors, and his blunt manner of expression rarely rankled with his friends. In the company of young men engaged in a philosophical discussion of the *summum bonum*, he once remarked: 'I differ from you all; the true *summum bonum* of human life consists in reading *Tristram Shandy*; or in blowing with a pair of bellows into your shoes in hot weather, and in roasting potatoes in the ashes under the grate in the cold' (Meadley, 18–19). Thrifty, humorous, and down to earth, in old age he shocked an intellectual visitor, Henry Digby Best, by complaining about the discomfort of a small rush-seated chair: 'I hate these nasty little chairs, they sink in the middle and *throost one's goots* up into one's *brains*' (Best, 182). When Best first met Paley in the 1790s he found him 'a thick, short, square-built man' with 'bushy brows, a snub nose, and projecting teeth', in short 'ugly' (Best, 162–4). Other contemporaries remembered him as a man of considerable integrity and generosity. His buoyant optimism remained with him to the end. It is said that he was never grave but upon grave occasions, and it was one of his apophthegms that 'a man who is not sometimes a fool, is always one' (Lynan, 1.49). His son Edmund remembered him with great affection as a cheerful and witty man, who was fond of field sports, though it seems his dedication to angling was an excuse for quiet contemplation.

For long Paley suffered from an intestinal complaint which he nicknamed 'the scorpion'. In later life he paid regular visits to the spas of Bath, Harrogate, and Buxton, and to Harwich for the balm of its sea water. In December 1800 the illness was exacerbated by what was probably a kidney stone, described by Meadley as 'a violent nephralgic complaint accompanied with a species of melaena' (Meadley, 197). A recurrence in the winter of 1801–2 curtailed his public appearances. Paley's physician, John Clark of Newcastle, spoke highly of his courage while he dedicated himself to the completion of *Natural Theology*. During these years Paley still amused himself with reading. In particular, he admired Malthus's *Essay on Population*, certain arguments of which had much in common with the sections of the *Principles* devoted to economic issues. Never a brilliant classicist, he continued his lifelong engagement with the works of Horace, Virgil, and Cicero. There was some talk of a bishopric and rumours that George III had vetoed William Pitt's recommendation that Paley should be made bishop of Gloucester—purportedly stating: 'I can have no notion of the man who, in the direction of his conduct, would look for what is expedient, if he knows what is right' ('Account of the life', 1.340). His son thought there was little truth in the rumour, and quoted a letter from a friend stating that the king had enjoyed reading Paley's *Principles*.

Shortly after visiting his residence in Lincoln in the spring of 1805 Paley suffered from painful complications arising from his illness and died at Bishopwearmouth on

25 May. On 4 June he was buried in the north aisle of Carlisle Cathedral, beside his first wife.

Influence In the last twenty years of his life Paley became an intellectual colossus at Cambridge, and he long remained a significant influence through the use of his works by generations of university students. Keynes, who thought the *Principles* 'an immortal book' (Keynes, 108), placed Paley high among the intellectual influences shaping Malthus's political economy and pointed out that his influence at Cambridge for a generation or more was second only to Newton's. From 1787 into the early nineteenth century the *Principles* was mandatory for Cambridge examinations, and from 1822 to 1920 the *Evidences of Christianity* was on the required list for the Previous, or Little-go, examination for all second-year undergraduates. By 1814 twenty English editions of the *Principles* had appeared and by 1821 ten editions were published in the United States, where it is said to have been the most popular text on moral philosophy from the 1790s to the civil war. There were also French, Spanish, and German editions. The text remained on the Cambridge syllabus until 1920, providing an education in ethics and political economy for many generations of university graduates and leading to many abridgements and analyses. Darwin, who entered Christ's College in 1828, wrote of the *Evidences of Christianity* and *Natural Theology*: 'The careful study of these works … was the only part of the Academical Course which … was of the least use to me in the education of my mind' (*The Autobiography of Charles Darwin*, ed. N. Barlow, 1958, 59). In the second half of the century Paley's influence waned, falling victim to Darwin's evolutionary theory, which served to destroy the idea of nature as the product of design and with it the essential theological basis of his whole system.

Early critics of Paley's utilitarian theory included Thomas Gisborne, Richard Whately, Dugald Stewart, Edward Pearson, and Thomas Brown, against whom Paley was ably defended by Latham Wainewright in *A Vindication of Dr. Paley's Theory of Morals*. Whether they supported or refuted him, nineteenth-century thinkers had to take Paley's moral philosophy into account. John Austin followed Paley in adumbrating a religious form of utilitarianism and in explicating the necessity of rules in practical morality in *The Province of Jurisprudence Determined* (1832), and William Whewell gave considerable weight to Paley's moral thought in his critical *Lectures on Morality* (1852). As a mark of the popularity of the *Principles*, Brown denounced the 'Paleyans' not the Benthamites. And when Coleridge penned his anti-utilitarian barbs it was Paley rather than Bentham who was uppermost in his mind. On the other hand, Leslie Stephen, though he recognized the clarity of expression in Paley's work, thought him 'a condenser and a compiler' in moral philosophy who merely followed Locke, Waterland, and Law (Stephen, 2.121, 131).

Twentieth-century commentators pointed to Paley as marking a philosophical era. Norman Sykes believed that Paley's importance 'lay in the exactitude with which he represented the *zeitgeist*' of the utilitarianism of the eighteenth-century English establishment (N. Sykes, *Church and State in England in the Eighteenth Century*, 1962, 326). Gerald Cragg held that Paley 'represented the Indian summer of eighteenth-century assumptions' (G. Cragg, *Reason and Authority in the Eighteenth Century*, 1964, 215). In LeMahieu's account, the coherence of Paley's philosophy reflects 'an ideological consensus among British intellectuals in the eighteenth century'; he 'distilled and crystallized the strategic ideas of his predecessors into a philosophy whose very comprehensiveness justified its modest claims to originality' (LeMahieu, *The Mind of William Paley*, 152).

JAMES E. CRIMMINS

Sources [E. Paley], 'An account of the life and writings of W. Paley, DD', in *The works of William Paley, DD*, new edn, ed. E. Paley, 7 vols. (1825) · R. Lynan, 'Memoirs of the author', in *The complete works of William Paley, DD*, ed. R. Lynan, 4 vols. (1825) · G. W. Meadley, *Memoirs of William Paley, DD*, 2nd edn (1810) · D. L. LeMahieu, *The mind of William Paley: a philosopher and his age* (1976) · M. L. Clarke, *Paley: evidences for the man* (1974) · E. Barker, *Traditions of civility* (1948) · *DNB* · V. Nuovo, introduction, in *The works of William Paley*, 6 vols. (1998) · will, PRO, PROB 11/1429 · *GM*, 1st ser., 75 (1805), 675 · *GM*, 1st ser., 79 (1809), 103 · review, *QR*, 9 (1813), 388–400 · 'Anecdotes of Dr Paley', *Universal Magazine*, new ser., 4 (1805), 414–17, 509–13 · *Public characters of 1802–1803* (1803) · J. R. Fenwick, *Sketch of the professional life of John Clark, M.D.* (1806), 25–8 · L. Stephen, *History of English thought in the eighteenth century*, 3rd edn, 2 vols. (1902); repr. (1949) · E. Albee, *A history of English utilitarianism* (1902) · E. Halévy, *The growth of philosophic radicalism*, trans. M. Morris, new edn (1972) [Fr. orig., *La formation du radicalisme philosophique*, 3 vols. (1901–4)] · J. M. Keynes, *Essays in biography* (1933) · G. A. Cole, 'Doctrine, dissent and the decline of Paley's reputation, 1805–1825', *Enlightenment and Dissent*, 6 (1987), 19–30 · T. P. Schofield, 'A comparison of the moral theories of William Paley and Jeremy Bentham', *Bentham Newsletter*, 11 (1987), 4–22 · J. E. Crimmins, 'Religion, utility and politics: Bentham versus Paley', *Religion, secularization and political thought: Thomas Hobbes to J. S. Mill*, ed. J. E. Crimmins (1990), 130–52 · A. M. C. Waterman, *Revolution, economics and religion: Christian political economy, 1798–1833* (1991) · A. M. C. Waterman, 'A Cambridge "via media" in late Georgian Anglicanism', *Journal of Ecclesiastical History*, 42 (1991), 419–36 · A. M. C. Waterman, 'Why Paley was "the first of the Cambridge economists"', *Cambridge Journal of Economics*, 20 (1996), 673–86 · Venn, *Alum. Cant.* · E. Law, 'On morality and religion', in W. King, *An essay on the origin of evil*, trans. E. Law, 4th edn (1758) · H. D. Best, *Literary and personal memorials* (1829) · N. Hitchin, 'The life and thought of William Paley (1743–1805)', PhD diss., U. Cam., 2001 · D. L. LeMahieu, foreword, in W. Paley, *The principles of moral and political philosophy* (Indianapolis, IN, 2002)

Archives BL, notes on moral philosophy, Add. MSS 12078–12080 · Christ's College, Cambridge, lecture notes · CUL, letters · Giggleswick grammar school, Yorkshire, sermons · PRO, letters from and relating to him, 630/12/17/4 | Bodl. Oxf., Montague MSS · Boston PL, English Literature MSS · CKS, letters to bishop of Lincoln · King's Cam., Keynes MSS · U. Edin., Laing MSS

Likenesses G. Romney, oils, 1789–91, NPG [*see illus.*] · W. Beechey, oils (after G. Romney), NPG · W. Beechey, oils (after G. Romney), Christ's College, Cambridge · W. Ridley, stipple (after S. Drummond), BM, NPG; repro. in *European Magazine* (1805) · stained glass, St Alfege's, Greenwich, London

Wealth at death approx. £5000—in cash bequests; rents of lands and houses (not named) to wife; rents from Giggleswick shared between Paley children; house (with furniture), garden and orchard in Giggleswick to William and John Chapman in trust for Paley's sisters Mary and Elizabeth: will, PRO, PROB 11/1429

Palfreyman, Thomas (*d.* 1589?), author, was a gentleman of the Chapel Royal under Edward VI and Elizabeth I. In Edward's reign he was paid 7½*d.* a day along with the thirty-one other members of the lay choir, who included the well-known musicians William Hunnis, Richard Farrant, and Thomas Tallis; they were joined in 1569 by Tallis's pupil, William Byrd. He seems to have lived in the parish of St Peter Cornhill in the city of London. In 1589 Palfreyman, presumably on his death, was replaced by Robert Allison. John Pankhurst, bishop of Norwich, addressed a Latin epigram to Palfreyman and Robert Couch, praising their knowledge of both music and the Bible, as well as the piety of their lives:

Vos non queo non dicere
Doctos viros, viros pios.
('I cannot but say that
You are learned men, pious men.')
(Pankhurst, 156)

Palfreyman's most popular works were his various revisions and enlargements of William Baldwin's *A Treatise of Morall Phylosophie, Contaynyng the Sayinges of the Wyse* (1547), a collection of moral apophthegms attributed to ancient thinkers. In the first of Palfreyman's revised editions, issued *c.*1555 and dedicated to Lord Henry Hastings, he rearranged the adages in Baldwin's treatise, wrote summaries of each chapter, and added three new books to the original four, but omitted much of the material on the history of ancient philosophy 'that therby the treatise should seme the lesse to be enlarged, and the more handsome of the reader to be caried' (sig. A4*r*). This omission led Baldwin to complain, when reissuing his own treatise in 1556, that 'mayster Palfreyman … hath lefte that out, whiche many most desyer' (sig. A2*v*). A further augmented edition, still in seven books, was brought out by Palfreyman in 1557, followed in 1564 by a ten-book version, bearing both authors' names on the title-page and printing both their letters of dedication. The treatise reached its final twelve-book form in 1579, with Palfreyman not only adding several new chapters but also restoring the previously omitted ones. This version was reprinted seven times from 1584 to 1610. Five further editions, published between *c.*1620 and *c.*1640, state on the title-page: 'Now the sixt time inlarged by T. Palfreyman'; in reality, however, they simply reprint his 1579 letter 'To the Reader', with the number of the edition altered, almost certainly by another hand.

Apparently attempting to produce a Christian counterpart to Baldwin's work, Palfreyman published *The Treatise of Heavenly Philosophie* (1578), dedicated to Thomas Radcliffe, third earl of Sussex. He drew on the Bible and Christian writings in place of pagan works, which, though 'not utterly to be contemned', were 'not altogether to be tarried upon … or in any one jot to be compared to the Scriptures' (sig. *5*v*). Unsurprisingly, perhaps, this 900-page patchwork of biblical and patristic quotations, interspersed with devout prayers and hectoring exhortations, and prefaced by lives of Moses and David, failed to capture the popular market exploited by Baldwin and was never reprinted.

Palfreyman's earliest work in print, *A Myrrour Conteinyng the True Knowledge and Love of God* (1560), sets out in detail the Christian duties of different estates of the realm, from lords to rich farmers and merchants. Another devotional work, *Divine Meditations* (1572), was dedicated to Isabel Harington, a gentlewoman of the queen's privy chamber. He also edited *A Paraphrase uppon the Epistle of … S. Paule to the Romanes* (1572?), an anonymous work 'voide of good stile' and 'evell Englished' (sig. *3*r*), along with letters by Ulrich Zwingli, and tracts by Martin Borrhaus. These works, he explained, had been given to him by a friend during the 'dolefull dayes' of Queen Mary's reign, 'fastened in their bandes' in preparation for burning, 'although by Gods providence prevented to the contrary' (sig. *2*v*).

Palfreyman's descendants may include the three Thomases surnamed Palfreman, Palfryman, and Palfreyman, recorded in the registers of the University of Oxford for the years 1586, 1633–6, and 1662–5 respectively.

Jill Kraye

Sources *DNB* · J. Hunter, 'Chorus vatum Anglicanorum', BL, Add. MS 24490, p. 498 · E. F. Rimbault, ed., *The old cheque-book, or book of remembrance, of the Chapel Royal, from 1561 to 1744*, CS, new ser., 3 (1872) · J. Pankhurst, *Ludicra, sive, Epigrammata juvenilia* (1573) · Foster, *Alum. Oxon.* · W. Baldwin, *A treatise of morall philosophie*, ed. R. H. Brown (1620), facs. edn (Gainesville, FLA, 1967) · C. F. Bühler, 'A survival from the middle ages: William Baldwin's use of the *Dictes and sayings*', *Speculum*, 23 (1948), 76–80

Palgrave [*formerly* Cohen], **Sir Francis** (**1788–1861**), archivist and historian, was born in July 1788 at Green Street, Kentish Town, London, the only son of Meyer Cohen (*c.*1760–1831), a stockbroker, and his wife, Rachel, *née* Levien (*d.* 1815). In 1797 Meyer Cohen published a volume of his son's verses, an innocent gesture which ultimately became a source of painful embarrassment. Francis changed his religion and his surname upon his marriage in 1823, an act that his detractors treasured zestfully far beyond his death.

Francis Cohen was educated at home, where he mastered modern languages as well as Latin and Greek, but he was constrained to make his own way when his father lost his fortune on the resumption of war in 1802. He was then articled with a firm of solicitors, Loggen and Smith, of Basinghall Street. From 1808 he was their managing clerk, but by 1822, when he left the firm, he was also a frequent contributor on historical and literary subjects to the *Edinburgh Review* and the *Quarterly Review*, and an editor and historian of whom Scott and Byron spoke with admiration. He was elected to the fellowship of the Royal Society in 1821.

In 1822 Palgrave was appointed a sub-commissioner of the record commission, and also began to read for the bar. He had been intent on antiquarian studies since his youth, and his interest in Anglo-Norman, and in the Anglo-Norman period, may have provided his first common ground with Dawson *Turner, the Norfolk antiquary. On 13 October 1823 he married Dawson Turner's daughter Elizabeth (1799–1852). Before his marriage he converted from Judaism to the Church of England, and changed his name by royal licence to Palgrave, the family name of Elizabeth's mother, Mary. There were four children of the marriage, all notably talented: Francis Turner *Palgrave, William Gifford *Palgrave, Sir Robert Harry Inglis *Palgrave, and Sir Reginald Francis Douce *Palgrave.

Sir Francis Palgrave (1788–1861), by Thomas Woolner, 1861

Palgrave was called to the bar by the Middle Temple in 1827, and found a successful practice in peerage cases, but his interest was increasingly engaged by the business of archives. His *Parliamentary Writs and Writs of Military Summons* was published by the record commission in two volumes in 1827 and 1834, and *Rotuli curiae regis: rolls and records of the court held before the king's justiciars or justices* in 1831.

Palgrave's marriage was a source of strength to him, as well as an obvious social advantage. It brought him no accession of wealth, however, for his wife had five sisters with claims upon their father's fortune, and until 1831 Palgrave had to maintain his own father, who had no other resource. He had useful political connections, including access to Holland House, and enjoyed manifest professional success, but his early history made him anxious about the security of his income.

In his extensive editorial work Palgrave employed transcribers, both for the publications which he undertook for the record commission and on his own account. The brothers Thomas Duffus Hardy and William Hardy were among them, and his association with them bred largely trivial but long-enduring animosities. The troubles seem to have begun with disputes over the terms of their employment, and to have flared into intrigue in and out of the office, and on one occasion into a brawl. The Hardys despised Palgrave for his birth and resented his undeniable accomplishments; he on his side was proud and, beneath his remarkable outward composure, irritably sensitive to slights. The record commission was itself a notable focus of scholarly contention and much ill feeling, and after its demise in 1837 several of its feuds echoed through the century.

Palgrave was made a KH in 1832. In 1833 he was appointed to the municipal corporations commission, but though he took part in its investigations he did not sign its final report, and submitted a memorandum of his own which the Webbs subsequently praised. In 1834 he succeeded John Caley as the keeper of the records in the chapter house at Westminster. The building was leased to the crown as a repository for the ancient records of the exchequer, including Domesday Book, and a mass of parliamentary material. One of the most original and valuable of Palgrave's editorial works, *The Ancient Kalendars and Inventories of the Treasury of H. M. Exchequer*, appeared in 1836. The chapter house and its great archival hoard had narrowly escaped destruction in the fire of 1834, an event which spurred on public discussion of a secure general record office. When the Public Record Office Act (1 & 2 Vict. c. 94) was passed in 1838 Palgrave was, in point both of his administrative and political experience, and of his scholarship, the obvious choice for its executive head.

There was, however, a delay of some months, from September to December 1838, in confirming the appointment, caused by Palgrave's own sensitivities and financial concerns, Treasury intransigence over the salary to be offered, and some reservations which the master of the rolls, Lord Langdale, had over the quasi-ministerial role which the act had visited upon him. The hiatus led Thomas Duffus Hardy to suppose, quite erroneously, that he had himself been denied the post by some political machination. It was an ominous beginning to what was essentially a felicitous appointment, for though Langdale appreciated Palgrave's merits, his relations with Palgrave were never entirely easy, while Hardy was a watchful colleague and, like his brother, an unforgiving enemy.

Palgrave's first care was to assemble the public records on the Rolls estate, in Chancery Lane, which became the designated site of the projected office, and to obtain funds to build a secure repository for them. In both endeavours he was strongly though not always harmoniously supported by Henry Cole, a senior assistant keeper. The records, ranging from the ponderous but generally well-ordered series of the great rolls of the exchequer to mouldering and congealed masses of loose parchment, came from more than fifty places in London and Westminster, principally the chapter house and the Tower, but including Carlton Ride, Somerset House, Lincoln's Inn, and the Temple. They rapidly filled what space remained in Rolls House and the Rolls chapel, where divine service was regularly conducted over and among them, and they packed the ramshackle tenements which stood in the grounds and along Chancery Lane. The foundation-stone of the new building, which was designed by Sir James Pennethorne, was not laid until 1851, and the repository then took nine years to build and occupy. By the time it was complete the records, which now included the contents of the state paper office, far outran its capacity, and an extension was begun in 1863.

Palgrave would not move Domesday Book from Westminster until its new quarters were secure, but he then allowed it to be taken to Southampton to be photographed by the Ordnance Survey and published in facsimile in 1861–3. He was deeply anxious for its safety, but it was a characteristically imaginative decision. So, ten years earlier, was his resolve to save the enumerators' returns for the decennial census, when the registrar-general proposed to destroy them.

Palgrave had a genuine feeling for archives and a clear view of the historical potential of modern records, which was rare at the time. His professional sense was essentially self-inculcated, like the librarianship of Anthony Panizzi (of the British Museum), with whom he bears some comparison. Hypersensitive himself, he was not always a tactful manager, but he worked in difficult circumstances, and his accomplishments were formidable. The first twenty-two of the deputy keeper's reports show Palgrave and his colleagues collecting and gradually ordering the public records. The chief problems lay in the sheer profusion and the very various physical condition of the documents, which comprised both comparatively lucid series such as the chancery rolls and innumerable sacks of loose parchments and papers. Palgrave's achievement was to direct their assembly and secure accommodation, to supervise their arrangement and begin their listing for the first time as a single holding, and to enable the public to refer to them as a matter of right, and without the payment of fees for literary searches. He also constantly looked ahead to the acquisition and management of modern administrative records. He sought from the beginning to maintain the historical coherence of the records of all periods, but sanctioned the creation of some special categories, such as royal letters, ministers' accounts, and rentals and surveys, which despite their specious interest are in the long run a hindrance rather than an aid to research. They have to be seen, however, against an oppressive mass of material and the concomitant problems of conservation which it posed. Palgrave's annual reports are a monument to his understanding of fundamentals, and the office has developed ever since upon the general lines which he established.

Palgrave's historical works are of less consequence than his editions of documents, though some, such as *The Rise and Progress of the English Commonwealth* (1832), contain matter still of interest. In his medieval studies he emphasized the legacy of Rome in thought and institutions, but later English scholars dwelt rather upon the influence of Germanic traditions. Both approaches had their value, but each distorted the issues when deployed in isolation. Medieval scholarship was still inchoate in England, and Palgrave's works bear comparison well with others of their time; he was certainly on firm ground in seeking to consider England and Normandy together. Palgrave's scholarship was genuinely cosmopolitan, and his interests were wide: his publications include the first edition of the *Handbook for Travellers in Northern Italy*, produced by John Murray in 1842. Palgrave continued in post until the end of his life, though his health was evidently failing in the last months. He died on 6 July 1861 at The Green, Hampstead, where he had lived since 1846, and was buried at Irstead, Norfolk, beside his wife, who had died in August 1852. G. H. MARTIN

Sources *DNB* · *GM*, 3rd ser., 11 (1861) · J. D. Cantwell, *The Public Record Office, 1838–1958* (1991) · L. Edwards, 'A remarkable family: the Palgraves', *Remember the days: essays on Anglo-Jewish history presented to Cecil Roth*, ed. J. M. Shaftesley (1966), 303–22 · John Murray, London, archives

Archives BL, corresp. and papers, Add. MSS 24700, 26083–26091, 34794–34797, 45738–45739, 45741 · Harvard U., Houghton L., fragments of a history of Anglo-Saxon England (1 vol.) · NL Wales, transcripts of MSS in PRO and BM · NRA, priv. coll., corresp. and papers · S. Antiquaries, Lond., historical notes | BL, corresp. with John Allen, Add. MSS 52187–52188 · BL, corresp. with W. E. Gladstone, Add. MSS 44356–44527 · BL, letters to Lord Spencer · Bodl. Oxf., corresp. with Sir Thomas Phillips · PRO, letters to John Allen, 30/26/109

Likenesses Mrs D. Turner, etching, 1823 (after T. Phillips), NPG · G. Richmond, portrait, 1844, priv. coll. · T. Woolner, plaster cast of medallion, 1861, NPG [*see illus.*] · portrait, repro. in Cantwell, *Public Record Office*, pl. 7

Wealth at death £4000: probate, 12 Oct 1861, *CGPLA Eng. & Wales*

Palgrave, Francis Turner [Frank] (1824–1897), anthologist and art critic, was born on 28 September 1824 in Great Yarmouth, Norfolk, in the house of his maternal grandparents, Dawson Turner, a banker, and Mary Turner, *née* Palgrave. He was the eldest of the four sons of Sir Francis *Palgrave (1788–1861), the medieval historian, and Elizabeth Turner (1799–1852). Elizabeth's parents had permitted her to marry Francis Cohen only if he converted to Christianity and took his wife's mother's maiden name. As a child, Palgrave was not told of his Jewish heritage, but in later life he had to endure Swinburne sneering at his 'Cohenisms' (*Swinburne Letters*, 16).

As an outsider, Sir Francis struggled to support his family: until he became keeper of the public records, he could not afford to send his sons to school. Instead, he and his wife taught them at home in Hampstead, in what the *Dictionary of National Biography* called an atmosphere of 'fervid anglo-catholicism' and 'strenuous thought', and his parents gave Palgrave a passion for classical Italy and Greece. When he finally went to school at fourteen as a day boy at Charterhouse School, Surrey, his early intellectual training did not, as he later told his daughter, compensate for his priggishness and lack of social skills. His early education did enable him to become head boy at Charterhouse and to win a Balliol College scholarship. In 1843 he went up to Oxford, where he joined a short-lived Balliol secret society called the Decade Club. He met Matthew Arnold and Arthur Hugh Clough there, and came under the influence of the master of Balliol, Benjamin Jowett. Jowett turned him (briefly) into an ardent republican, and together they went to Paris in 1848 to witness the revolution.

Palgrave's university years were interrupted in 1846 because his father had arranged for him to take a university term off to act as private secretary to W. E. Gladstone, then colonial secretary in Sir Robert Peel's government. He did not enjoy the experience (though he retained links with Gladstone for the rest of his life) and returned to Oxford, where his first-class honours degree in classics was rewarded with a fellowship at Exeter College, though he stayed there only a year and in 1849 left Oxford. His first choice of career had been architecture, but his father had insisted that he join the civil service instead. Palgrave followed other Balliol men into the newly created education committee of the privy council. His first job, in 1849, was as a teacher at Kneller Hall in Twickenham, Middlesex, an experimental training college for teachers in the workhouses. After it closed in 1855, he returned to the ministry, where he stayed until his retirement in 1884. His job, first as an examiner and then as an assistant secretary, allowed

Francis Turner Palgrave (1824–1897), by Samuel Laurence, 1872

him enough spare time to publish art and literary criticism, to write novels and lyric poems, and to cultivate his passion for artistic and literary celebrities.

Palgrave's friendships with artists, particularly the Pre-Raphaelites, led him to produce articles and reviews on art (and literature) for, among other publications, the *Saturday Review* and the *Quarterly Review*. His criticism is recognizable for its intemperate language: he had difficulty balancing his loyalty to his friends with his critical objectivity, while his sometimes bitter jealousy of other more talented poets and artists often comes through. In fact, his violently expressed opinions got him into trouble early in his career. He was commissioned to write the *Official Catalogue of the Fine Art Department of the International Exhibition of 1862*, but instead of simply describing the works on exhibit, he praised the work of the Pre-Raphaelite sculptor Thomas Woolner at the expense of other, better-known exhibitors. One of those insulted, Matthew Higgins, writing under the pseudonym Jacob Omnium, pointed out in the letter column of *The Times* that Palgrave and Woolner were housemates. The guide was immediately withdrawn, but on the strength of his notoriety Palgrave became the art critic of the equally outspoken *Saturday Review* for three years, a period which produced a toned-down selection of his articles published as *Essays on Art* (1866).

In London in 1849 Palgrave had also been introduced to Tennyson, who had yet not achieved the fame that *In Memoriam* (1850) would bring. His time as Tennyson's disciple was one of the highlights of his life, but Tennyson's need for admiring followers was eventually overcome by his dislike of being harried by the devoted Palgrave. On a walking tour of Cornwall in 1860, for example, while hunting for Arthurian sites for the *Idylls of the King*, Tennyson complained to William Holman Hunt that:

> all day long I am trying to get a quiet moment for reflection … but before I have finished a couplet I hear Palgrave's voice like a bee in a bottle, making the neighbourhood resound with my name, and I have to give myself up to escape the consequences. (Hunt, 2.213)

It was, therefore, little wonder that Tennyson 'dismissed' Palgrave in 1868, though Palgrave continued to regard himself as a lifelong friend. In fact, when Tennyson died in 1892, Palgrave immediately offered to help his widow, Emily, and their son, Hallam, to 'edit' Tennyson's papers. Appointing himself one of the guardians of Tennyson's reputation, he helped burn nearly 30,000 letters, including all those to Tennyson from Arthur Hallam.

The friendship between Palgrave and Tennyson was responsible for producing Palgrave's only lasting claim to fame: *The Golden Treasury of the Best Songs and Lyrical Poems in the English Language* (1861), an anthology so successful that, as J. W. Mackail wrote in the *Dictionary of National Biography*, 'it remains one of those rare instances in which a critical work has substantive imaginative value, and entitles its author to rank among creative artists'. On the walking tour of Cornwall which they had made together in 1860, Palgrave had suggested to Tennyson the idea of an anthology which would differ from all previous ones by being a collection of *all* the best lyrics and songs in English. As Palgrave had had little success with his own lyric poetry and literary criticism, he hoped that this project would bring him fame, and that it would also be a project on which he could work with Tennyson. As he used Tennyson's name to help get the *Golden Treasury* published, most critics have assumed that Tennyson must also have chosen the poems. The manuscript in the British Library reveals that although Tennyson was consulted on the manuscript, Palgrave himself made the initial and final selections, and that he often disregarded Tennyson's suggestions. The idiosyncratic editing principles, including the thematic arrangement of 'books' and the removal or rearrangement of lines, words, and whole stanzas, were Palgrave's alone.

Tennyson did influence the *Golden Treasury* in two important ways. First, he encouraged Palgrave to pursue the project, probably as a way of giving what he called Palgrave's 'pertinacious devotion' (Tennyson, 327) another outlet. He also refused to be included, causing Palgrave to omit all living poets, in whose work his taste was much shakier: his *Golden Treasury* 'second series' of living poets, which appeared just a few days after his death in 1897, was a failure with critics and the public because his loyalty to his contemporaries had overruled his critical judgement. He also attempted to replicate the original anthology's remarkable popular success with *Treasuries* of children's verse and sacred song. He wrote lyrics of his own, producing five volumes of original lyrics, from *Idyls and Songs* in 1854 to *Visions of England*, based on his father's historical theories, in 1881. Like the lyrics he chose for the

Golden Treasury, most of his own lyrics deal with love, mutability, and nature, modelled on those of his favourite poet, William Wordsworth. As his reputation as an editor grew after the *Golden Treasury* appeared, he also edited selections of lyric poetry by others, including Shakespeare, Herrick, Keats, Wordsworth, and, of course, Tennyson.

Although Palgrave's friendship with Tennyson was a great source of joy to him, his adult emotional life was initially very unhappy as a result of the unrequited love he felt for a childhood friend, Georgina Alderson, the subject of his two autobiographical novels, *Preciosa* (1852) and *The Passionate Pilgrim* (1858). After she married Sir Robert Cecil in 1857, he became suicidal, according to William Holman Hunt, but recovered eventually, though he was prone to depression throughout his life. Cecil Greville Milnes (1834–1890), whom he married on 30 December 1862, provided him with a happy and stable married life. They had four daughters and two sons. (One son died in infancy.)

Upon his retirement from the education ministry, Palgrave stood (successfully) for election as professor of poetry at Oxford University in 1885, and served two consecutive five-year terms. While at Oxford he wrote a semi-official *Ode* for Queen Victoria's jubilee (1887) and lectured on Chaucer, the influence of the Renaissance on English poetry, and the relationship between art and poetry, the last published as *Landscape in Poetry from Homer to Tennyson* (1897). After his wife's death in 1890, Palgrave suffered a number of small strokes before the one which killed him on 24 October 1897, at the age of seventy-three, at his home, 15 Cranley Place, South Kensington, London. He was buried alongside his wife and infant son in the cemetery at Barnes Common, Barnes, Surrey.

MEGAN NELSON OTTON

Sources *DNB* • M. J. Nelson, 'Francis Turner Palgrave and *The golden treasury*', PhD diss., University of British Columbia, Vancouver, Canada, 1985 [including comprehensive bibliography] • *Francis Turner Palgrave: his journals and memories of his life*, ed. G. F. Palgrave (1899) • *The Swinburne letters*, ed. C. Y. Lang, 6 vols. (1959–62), vol. 6, p. 16 [letter, 1570, 10/8/1891] • W. H. Hunt, *Pre-Raphaelitism and the Pre-Raphaelite Brotherhood*, 2 (1905), 213 • R. Martin, *Tennyson: the unquiet heart* (1980), 583 • C. Tennyson, *Alfred Tennyson* (1949), 327 • D. Holman-Hunt, *My grandfather, his wives and loves* (1969), 211–12 • Gladstone, *Diaries*

Archives BL, corresp., literary MSS, and papers, Add. MSS 42126, 45734–45741 • BL, family corresp., Add. MS 45741 • Bodl. Oxf., journal of visit to Paris • Dorset RO, literary agreements • Lincoln Central Library, Tennyson Research Centre, journal of tours made with Tennyson • NYPL, Berg collection, library MSS • Ransom HRC, papers • University of Virginia, Charlottesville, papers • Yale U., corresp. | BL, corresp. with W. E. Gladstone, Add. MS 44270 • BL, corresp. with Macmillans, Add. MS 54977 • Bodl. Oxf., letters to Mr and Mrs A. H. Clough • Bodl. Oxf., letters to W. M. Rossetti • Bodl. Oxf., letters to F. G. Stephens • CUL, letters to Lord Acton • E. Sussex RO, letters to Frederick Locker-Lampson, Eleanor Locker-Lampson, and Lady Augusta Stanley • JRL, letters to J. L. Warren • Lincoln Central Library, Tennyson Research Centre, letters to Lord Tennyson and Hallam Tennyson • NL Scot., letters to Blackwoods • NRA, priv. coll., letters to the ninth earl of Carlisle • Trinity Cam., letters to Dawson Turner • Trinity Cam., letters to Lord Houghton • Trinity Cam., letters to C. W. King • University of British Columbia, Angeli MSS, letters to William Michael Rossetti • Yale U., Beinecke L., letters to Frederick Locker-Lampson, Eleanor Locker-Lampson, and Lady Augusta Stanley

Likenesses S. D. Laurence, chalk drawing, 1872, NPG [*see illus.*] • R. T., wood-engraving, NPG; repro. in *ILN* (26 Dec 1885) • photograph, repro. in Palgrave, ed., *Francis Turner Palgrave*, frontispiece

Wealth at death £26,701 19*s*. 7*d*.: probate, 23 Feb 1898, *CGPLA Eng. & Wales*

Palgrave, Sir (Robert Harry) Inglis (1827–1919), banker and economist, was born on 11 June 1827 at 22 Parliament Street, Westminster, the third of the four sons of Sir Francis *Palgrave (1788–1861), historian, and his wife, Elizabeth (1799–1852), daughter of Dawson Turner, banker, of Great Yarmouth. Named after his father's high-tory friend, Palgrave acquired an early and deep love of learning. A day boy at Charterhouse School (1838–43), unlike his elder brothers Francis Turner *Palgrave and William Gifford *Palgrave, he did not proceed to university but in 1845 joined the maternal family bank, an offshoot of Gurney & Co. in Great Yarmouth, where he had already spent his summer vacations. Country banking left him much time for self-education and travel, including several trips to the continent in the 1840s. Above all, with an early initiation into the writings of Adam Smith he trained himself as a political economist, specializing in his own occupation of banking and finance. Having settled among a group of unusually cultivated provincial bankers, in 1859 he married Sarah Maria (*d*. 1898), the daughter of George Brightwen and his wife, Sarah.

Palgrave's interest in banking led in the early 1870s to his publishing several books, one of which earned him a Swedish knighthood. He became a prominent member of the banking profession, representing the country bankers in parliamentary evidence and in helping to form the Bankers' Institute. By this time the great age of banking debate was over, and most of his works were statistical in inspiration and form. Even so he was a critic of the Bank Charter Act's failure in 1844 to regulate properly the banking reserve of the Bank of England and was a stalwart defender of note issue by the country banks. His knowledge of the theory of finance, as well as the practice of country banking, recommended him as successor to Walter Bagehot at *The Economist*, at first jointly with D. C. Lathbury, from 1877 to 1881, and then alone, from 1881. He wisely decided not to leave banking for journalism, because he was too much of a money market specialist for the proprietors of *The Economist*, and he resigned in 1883. Before this, in 1882 he achieved a childhood ambition in following his father and maternal grandfather in becoming a fellow of the Royal Society.

In the 1880s Palgrave was one of a group of economists who were developing ambitious plans for their discipline. His presidency of section F of the British Association, in 1883, launched the idea of an economic association, which led eventually to the foundation of the British Economic Association (later the Royal Economic Society) in 1890. The publication of classic texts, a review, and a dictionary of economics were mooted, but it was the last that Palgrave took up with single-minded enthusiasm, perhaps inspired by his brother's *Golden Treasury* (1861).

Equally he took as his models contemporary French and German economic dictionaries, as well as the *Dictionary of National Biography* and Grove's *Dictionary of Music*. In 1888 he signed a contract with Macmillan to publish a work in two volumes, a plan then abandoned in favour of publication in 12–14 parts (the first of which appeared in 1891), before that plan was abandoned in favour of three volumes.

Palgrave sought to create a compendium of contemporary economic thought, although with a bias to history and institutions. The professional academic Alfred Marshall distrusted the enthusiasm of the gifted amateur, but through his persistence, pestering, and sustained drive Palgrave brought together most of the country's leading economists (Marshall was conspicuous by his absence), many of whom were invited for working visits to his country home in East Anglia: Henstead Hall, Wrentham, Suffolk. Painstakingly, with much advice from men such as John Neville Keynes, Langford Lovell Price, James Bonar, and Francis Ysidro Edgeworth, he put together his *Dictionary of Political Economy*. The volumes eventually appeared in 1894, 1896, and 1899, with several appendices, the last in 1908. In 1909 Palgrave was knighted, the first 'modern' economist so honoured. The dictionary met a mixed critical reception but few could doubt that it was a reference tool of immense value, fulfilling Palgrave's wish for a work of scholarly distinction and of practical usefulness to the burgeoning number of students of economics. The eponymous edition by Henry Higgs appeared between 1923 and 1926.

Palgrave's dictionary took him the best part of twenty years, during which time he continued his banking activities while reviewing widely, writing copiously for the *Bankers' Magazine* (which he had briefly edited early in his career), and editing the *Banking Almanack*, from 1875 until his death. In 1885–6 he served on the royal commission on the depression in trade and industry, contributing a valuable appendix on currency; he was inclined to accept more readily than many the reality of depression. In 1888 and 1891 he aspired to the Drummond chair of political economy in Oxford ('I should have liked the quiet time in a University', he wrote to Neville Keynes on 21 April 1891; Keynes papers). But he was destined to remain a man of affairs, physically vigorous, fresh in complexion, bearded, and large of feature. As a practitioner of finance and statistics he continued to publish a series of works whose value was widely appreciated. He was an early critic of Gladstonian finance and later proved sympathetic to the movement for tariff reform.

Palgrave continued as a director of the Yarmouth bank on its amalgamation with Barclays in 1896, while also serving on the boards of several local companies, chairing the Yarmouth gas and water companies and Grout & Co., silk manufacturers. He played a prominent part in local schools, cultural societies, and the bench, and was patron of his local church, to which he appointed the Revd Rowland Barker, the husband of his only child, Elizabeth. In 1910 he was granted the freedom of Great Yarmouth. During the First World War he remained a concerned observer of the monetary front but he largely devoted his later years to preparing the posthumously published edition of his father's works. He died on 25 January 1919 at 1 Westcliff Road, Bournemouth, and was buried at Fritton church, Great Yarmouth, on 7 February.

Palgrave's life was well mirrored in his review (*Quarterly Review*, January 1886) of George Rae's *The Country Banker* (1885), whose business was not exhausting and whose mind, when unbent from business, lent itself to engrossing occupations. The best testimony to his scholarly achievement came in the publication of *The New Palgrave: a Dictionary of Economics* (1987), in four volumes, a summa of modern scholarship on economics, essentially along the lines that Palgrave had set out a century earlier. More recently, in 2000 the imprint Palgrave was adopted by Macmillan for their global academic publishing division, an unusual tribute to the formidable contribution to Victorian culture and learning made by Palgrave and his brother Francis. A. C. HOWE

Sources Palgrave papers, priv. coll. • R. H. I. Palgrave, *Dictionary of political economy*, 1st edn, 3 vols. (1894–9); [2nd] edn (1915) • J. Eatwell, M. Milgate, and P. Newman, eds., *The new Palgrave: a dictionary of economics*, 4 vols. (1987) • 'The late Sir Inglis Palgrave', *Bankers' Magazine* (1919), 306–13 • Palgrave reviews and essays, BLPES, Coll. misc. 0448 • *Yarmouth and Gorleston Times* (1 Feb 1919) • *Yarmouth and Gorleston Times* (8 Feb 1919) • W. H. Bidwell, *Annals of an East Anglian bank* (1900) • R. D. Edwards, *The pursuit of reason: The Economist, 1843–1993* (1993) • BLPES, Cannan MSS • L. Edwards, 'A remarkable family: the Palgraves', *Remember the days: essays on Anglo-Jewish history presented to Cecil Roth*, ed. J. M. Shaftesley (1966), 303–22 • *WWW* • John Neville Keynes papers, Marshall Library, Cambridge

Archives Barclays Bank archives, London • BL, journal in France, Add. MS 45738 • BLPES, collected writings • King's AC Cam., corresp. • NRA, priv. coll., corresp. and papers | BLPES, letters to E. Cannan • Col. U., letters to E. Seligman • King's Cam., Jevons papers • Norfolk RO, Grout & Co., silk manufacturers • PRO NIre., letters to J. K. Ingram • U. Cam., Marshall Library of Economics, letters to J. N. Keynes • U. Reading, Macmillan archives

Likenesses S. Lucas, chalk and charcoal, 1913, priv. coll. • photograph, repro. in *Bankers' Magazine*, facing p. 306

Wealth at death £47,456 11*s*. 9*d*.: probate, 22 May 1919, *CGPLA Eng. & Wales*

Palgrave, Sir Reginald Francis Douce (1829–1904), clerk of the House of Commons, was born at 26 Duke Street, Westminster, on 28 June 1829, the fourth son of the historian Sir Francis *Palgrave (1788–1861) and his wife, Elizabeth Turner (1799–1852). William Gifford *Palgrave and Francis Turner *Palgrave were his elder brothers. He entered Charterhouse School in 1841 and left in 1845. He was articled to Messrs Bailey, Janson and Richardson, solicitors, of Basinghall Street, London, was admitted solicitor in May 1851, and entered the office of Messrs Sharpe and Field. On 1 August 1857 he married Grace (1832–1905), daughter of Richard *Battley, the apothecary. They had a son and five daughters.

Through the influence of Sir Robert Harry Inglis and other friends of his father Palgrave was appointed to a clerkship in the House of Commons in 1853. From 1866 to 1868 he was examiner of petitions for private bills; he became second clerk assistant in 1868, clerk assistant in 1870, and from 1886 until his retirement in 1900 was clerk of the House of Commons. In 1887 he was made CB, and in 1892 KCB.

Palgrave's appointment as clerk of the house represented a further advance in the professional status of the clerkship, the foundations for which had been laid by his predecessor Sir Thomas Erskine May, Lord Farnborough. Even in 1886, however, it was still possible to contemplate the appointment to the most senior official post in the Commons of men with no professional experience there. Palgrave became clerk only after the post had been declined by Sir Henry Maine and Charles Lennox Peel. Though personally a strong Conservative, he did not simply reverse his predecessor's notorious readiness to give junior clerkships to the sons of Liberal fathers. Limited competition for posts was introduced, giving for the first time a preference to ability over connection.

In some respects Palgrave's clerkship was overshadowed by that of his remarkable predecessor. Yet although he lacked May's instinct for procedural development, there is no doubt of the sureness of his grasp of the practice of the house, particularly in the development of questions to ministers. The breadth of his capability was fully displayed in his editorial work (with Alfred Bonham Carter) on the tenth (1893) edition of May's *Parliamentary Practice*, when he undertook structural revision and expansion as well as updating of much of the text, both of which May in his later years had lacked the energy to tackle.

Most of Palgrave's other published works—apart from a little guidebook to Reigate (1860; repr. in facsimile, 1973), where he lived until 1870—had a parliamentary or historical connection. There were two editions (1869 and 1873) of illustrations of the history and practice of the house, and no fewer than thirteen of *The Chairman's Handbook* (1877), a guide to the conduct of public meetings. Palgrave was a particular admirer of Cromwell, whose life he wrote (1890; new edn, 1900). He contributed to *The Athenaeum*, the *Edinburgh Review*, *Macmillan's Magazine*, the *North American Review*, and the *Quarterly Review* on historical subjects.

From 1870 to 1900 Palgrave lived at an official residence in the Palace of Westminster. For many years after 1870 he spent his summer vacations at a house built for him at Swanage, Dorset. He had much artistic taste, inherited probably from his maternal grandfather, Dawson *Turner, and to the end of his life practised watercolour sketching, at which he was fairly proficient, and he was for an amateur an exceptionally skilful modeller in low relief. He was a high-churchman and was churchwarden of St Martin's, Salisbury, where he lived in retirement. Palgrave died at his home East Mount, Milford Without, Salisbury, on 13 July 1904, and was buried in the cemetery there. A village cross at Swanage was erected to the memory of Sir Reginald and Lady Palgrave by members of their family.

WILLIAM MCKAY

Sources W. R. McKay and J. C. Sainty, eds., *Clerks in the House of Commons, 1363–1989* (1989) • *Men and women of the time* (1899) • D. A. Palgrave and P. T. R. Palgrave-Moore, *History and lineage of the Palgraves* (1978) • C. J. Palmer and S. Tucker, eds., *Palgrave family memorials* (1878) • M. Allan, *Palgrave of Arabia: the life of William Gifford Palgrave, 1826–88* (1972) • *Francis Turner Palgrave: his journals and memories of his life*, ed. G. F. Palgrave (1899) • *Wellesley index* • Mr Speaker Peel to Sir T. E. May, 18 April 1886, HLRO, Erskine May MSS, 5/17 • J. M. Carmichael to Sir T. E. May, 20 April 1886, HLRO, Erskine May MSS, 8/270 • private information (1912) • d. cert.

Archives CAC Cam., corresp. with Lord Randolph Churchill

Likenesses B. Stone, photograph, 1897, Birm. CL • Bassano, photographs, *c.*1898, NPG • photographs, Palace of Westminster, London • portrait, Palace of Westminster, London

Wealth at death £19,027 2*s.* 3*d.*: resworn probate, 20 Aug 1904, *CGPLA Eng. & Wales*

Palgrave, William Gifford (1826–1888), traveller and diplomatist, was born at 22 Parliament Street, Westminster, London, on 24 January 1826. He was the second son of Sir Francis *Palgrave (1788–1861), founder of the Public Record Office, whose name had been Francis Cohen until in 1823 he converted to the Church of England before marrying and entering the legal profession. Palgrave's mother, formerly Elizabeth Turner, was the daughter of Dawson Turner, banker, of Great Yarmouth. Palgrave's three brothers, Francis Turner *Palgrave, Robert Harry Inglis *Palgrave, and Sir Reginald *Palgrave, all achieved scholarly distinction.

Palgrave attended Charterhouse School (1838–1844), where he won the gold medal for classical verse and became the school captain. He then went as a scholar to Trinity College, Oxford, gained a first in *literae humaniores* and a second in mathematics, and graduated in 1846. He went to India and in 1847 received a lieutenant's commission in the 8th Bombay regiment of native infantry. His prospects as an officer were reportedly good, but after two years he converted formally to Roman Catholicism and entered the Jesuit college, Madras. He was employed in its missionary work in southern India until the summer of 1853, when he went to Rome. Following his conversion, Palgrave changed his name to Cohen, a possible indication of the deep concern about identity—whether racial, national, or religious—that runs through much of his writing. He was also known by other names, including Michael Sohail, before he resumed the name Palgrave.

After studying in Rome, Palgrave went to Syria, in 1855, drawn to the Arab world by early impressions from reading the Arab romance *Antar*. For some years he was a successful missionary, particularly in the town of Zahlah, making many converts and founding numerous schools. He became so accustomed to Arab society that he could pass as a native of the Middle East without difficulty. In the Druse attacks on Christians in 1860–61, Palgrave was nearly killed at the Damascus massacre; later he is reported to have organized the Christian defence of Zahlah. The Syrian mission being for the time disrupted, he returned to western Europe where Napoleon III obtained from him a report on the causes of the persecution of the Syrian Christians. He also visited England and Ireland, where he delivered fund-raising lectures on the Syrian massacres which were afterwards republished from newspaper reports, under the title *Four Lectures on the Massacres of the Christians in Syria* (1861).

With Vatican permission, Palgrave became a French

William Gifford Palgrave (1826–1888), by Ernest Edwards

agent. His first mission was to sound Halim Pasha about becoming viceroy of Egypt under French suzerainty; although that project failed, Palgrave used the opportunity to prepare plans for a French invasion of Syria from Egypt. His next mission was to report on the Arabian kingdoms of Ha'il and Riyadh. For many years Arabia had remained closed to Europeans. Ha'il had been penetrated by Europeans only once; Riyadh, never. Disguised as a Syrian Christian physician named Selim Abu Mahmoud al-'Eis, Palgrave now undertook an adventurous journey across central Arabia, which he accomplished in 1862 and 1863, thereby becoming the first westerner to cross Arabia by an approximately diagonal route (from the north-west to the south-east). Travelling among the Wahabbis, he was in considerable danger, should he be detected as a European. Once, at Ha'il, he was recognized as having been seen at Damascus, and at Riyadh he was suspected and accused of being an English spy, but his skill at disguise, coupled with his presence of mind and good fortune, secured his safety. Palgrave returned to Europe in late 1863 and wrote *Personal Narrative of a Year's Journey through Central and Eastern Arabia* (2 vols., 1865), a classic of Arabian travel literature, though its veracity has been attacked by several distinguished orientalists.

Shortly after writing *Personal Narrative* Palgrave renounced both Catholicism and Napoleon III and began his final career with the British foreign service. In July 1865 he was sent to Abyssinia on a mission to obtain from King Theodore the release of Consul Cameron and his fellow captives. Falsely informed that the captives had been released, the Foreign Office halted Palgrave as he was passing through Egypt on his way out. There he remained until June 1866, when he returned home and was at once appointed British consul at Soukhoum-Kalé. In 1867 he was transferred to Trebizond, where he made extensive journeys in northern Asia Minor.

In 1868 Palgrave married Katharine Simpson, daughter of G. E. Simpson of Norwich; they had three sons. He was appointed consul at St Thomas in the West Indies in 1873, and in 1876 he was transferred to Manila; two years later he was appointed consul-general in Bulgaria, but Disraeli soon dismissed him for his conduct towards the Austrians. In 1879 he was sent to Bangkok. While travelling in the Far East, he came under the influence of various Eastern religious systems, especially Shintoism.

Palgrave's diplomatic career disappointed many who expected him to rise higher and in different postings. General Gordon forcefully proposed him as British minister to Cairo, but to no avail. Palgrave himself yearned to serve in the Arab world, but his tendency to disregard instructions and to act on his own, which caused repeated conflicts with the Foreign Office, cannot have enhanced his prospects.

In 1884 Palgrave was appointed minister-resident in Uruguay, where he became reconciled to the Roman Catholic church. His health, which had been impaired by hardships on his return journey from Arabia and by the Siamese climate, did not improve in Uruguay, and he died of bronchitis at Montevideo on 30 September 1888. His body was brought to England and buried in St Thomas's cemetery, Fulham, London.

Palgrave's published writings were, in addition to those already mentioned: *Hermann Agha* (1872), *Essays on Eastern Questions* (1872), *Dutch Guiana* (1876), *Ulysses, or, Scenes and Studies in many Lands* (1887), and a mystical religious poem entitled *A Vision of Life: Semblance and Reality* (1891), with which he had been occupied almost until the time of his death. He wrote a number of notable articles for various periodicals, especially the *Cornhill Magazine*, *Macmillan's Magazine*, *Fraser's Magazine*, and the *Quarterly Review*. He was a notable linguist, and acquired languages with extreme ease—Japanese, for example, he learned colloquially in two months—but his interest was not that of a philologist. He learned languages only for practical use; when he no longer required them he ceased to speak them. He was an accomplished student of Dante, a good Latin scholar, and something of a botanist; wherever he went, as his writings show, he was a keen observer. He became a fellow of the Royal Geographical Society, a medallist of the French Geographical Society, and a member of the Royal Asiatic Society.

Many who have written about Palgrave have assessed his accomplishments with reservations, sensing some measure of failure. He may indeed have dispersed his efforts while leaving his potential unrealized, but expectations for him were always unusually high. He earned a permanent place as a leading British explorer and scholar of the Middle East. JASON THOMPSON

Sources M. Allan, *Palgrave of Arabia: the life of William Gifford Palgrave, 1826–88* (1972) • K. Tidrick, *Heart-beguiling Araby* (1981), 84–106 • R. Trench, *Arabian travellers* (1986), 98–117 • B. M. Broude, 'The spiritual quest of William Gifford Palgrave', undergraduate diss., Harvard U., 1967 • Boase, *Mod. Eng. biog.* • *The historical register of the University of Oxford … to the end of Trinity term 1900* (1900) • Foster, *Alum. Oxon.*

Archives NRA, priv. coll., letters to family • St Ant. Oxf., Middle East Centre, letters • Yale U., Beinecke L., travel journal | BL, corresp. with Sir Austen Layard, Add. MSS 39011–39133, *passim* • Bodl. Oxf., letters to Benjamin Disraeli • Lpool RO, corresp. with Lord Derby • U. Reading L., letters to Macmillans

Likenesses T. Woolner, medallion, 1864, NPG • J. M. Cameron, albumen print, 1868, NPG, U. Texas, Gernsheim collection • Abdullah Frères, carte-de-visite, NPG • E. Edwards, carte-de-visite, NPG [*see illus.*] • C. H. Jeens, line engraving (after T. Woolner), BM, NPG; repro. in W. G. Palgrave, *Narrative of a year's journey through central and eastern Arabia*, 2 vols. (1865) • Lock & Whitfield, woodburytype, NPG; repro. in T. Cooper, *Men of mark: a gallery of contemporary portraits* (1880) • carte-de-visite, NPG

Wealth at death £920 18*s*. 3*d*.: resworn probate, July 1891, *CGPLA Eng. & Wales* (1889)

Palin, William (1803–1882), Church of England clergyman and author, youngest son of Richard Palin and his wife, Sarah Durden, was born at Mortlake, Surrey, on 10 November 1803. He was educated at Mortlake School, Lewes, in Sussex. While a private tutor he published in June 1829, when living at Southampton, *The Persians of Aeschylus*. On 17 December 1829 he matriculated from St Alban's Hall, Oxford, but soon migrated to Trinity College, Cambridge, where he graduated BA in 1833 and MA in 1851. He was admitted *ad eundem* at Oxford on 21 June 1861. He married Emily Isabella Slaughter (1813–1878), daughter of Stephen Long, a solicitor; they had three daughters and one son.

Palin was ordained deacon by the bishop of London on Trinity Sunday, 1833, and was curate-in-charge of Stifford in Essex for twelve months. He was ordained priest in May 1834. From July 1834 until his death he was rector of Stifford. Between 1861 and 1863 the parish church was restored through his efforts. With one of his daughters he compiled *Stifford and its Neighbourhood, Past and Present*, a description of twenty parishes in south Essex (privately printed, 1871), and *More about Stifford and its Neighbourhood* (1872); both volumes contained extracts from parish registers, and were full of information on local social life.

Palin also published many religious works, including *Village Lectures on the Litany* (1837), *Bellingham: a Narrative of a Christian in Search of the Church* (1839), several papers on the weekly offertory, and *The Christian Month: Original Hymns for each Day of the Month*. He wrote two hymns for Orby Shipley's *Lyra messianica* (1864), to which his daughter Emily Isabella Jane also contributed. From 1853 to 1857 he edited the *Churchman's Magazine*, and he contributed frequently to various church periodicals. In 1851 he published a *History of the Church of England, 1688–1717*. He planned to write a continuation, but the work involved more research than his clerical duties allowed. Palin died at the rectory, Stifford, Essex, on 16 October 1882, and was buried in the churchyard there.

W. P. COURTNEY, *rev.* MARI G. ELLIS

Sources Venn, *Alum. Cant.* • Foster, *Alum. Oxon.* • *Men of the time* (1868) • *The Guardian* (25 Oct 1882), 1485 • J. Julian, ed., *A dictionary of hymnology* (1892) • *CGPLA Eng. & Wales* (1882) • Crockford (1865) • W. Palin, *Stifford and its neighbourhood* (privately printed, 1871), 72, 179–80

Archives BL, index to epitaphs and arms in History of Stifford, Add. MS 33526

Wealth at death £4522 8*s*. 6*d*.: probate, 28 Dec 1882, *CGPLA Eng. & Wales*

Palk, Sir Robert, first baronet (1717–1798), Church of England clergyman and administrator in India, was born in December 1717, apparently at Ambrooke, Ashburton, Devon, and was baptized on 16 December 1717 at the Old Mission House, Ashburton. He was the second son of Walter Palk (*b.* 1686), yeoman farmer, and his wife, Frances Abraham. He was educated at Ashburton grammar school and at Wadham College, Oxford, from where he graduated in 1739. Having taken deacon's orders, on 27 April 1746 he entered the Royal Navy as chaplain to the *Namur*, Edward Boscawen's flagship. After seeing action against the French fleet off Cape Finisterre (3 May 1747), the *Namur* proceeded to the Coromandel coast (4 November 1747).

In July 1748 Palk arrived at Fort St David, at that time the chief British settlement while Fort St George at Madras was under French control (1746–9). Early in 1749 the company's chaplain at Fort St David, Francis Fordyce, was dismissed after publicly insulting Robert Clive. Palk, 'this very worthy and able divine' (Love, *Report*, v), was invited to replace Fordyce, which he did on 1 April 1749. This created confusion over the seniority and placement of the other chaplains. As a consequence, in October 1750 Palk sailed with the fleet to Bombay to resign his service and to seek formal employment with the East India Company. In March 1751 Palk returned to Fort St David, where he was reinstated.

When Fort St George was restored by the French to the East India Company, Palk accompanied the government back to Madras (April 1752). Once again there was confusion over the numbers and seniority of the chaplains, so the Revd Robert Palk was appointed 'Paymaster and Commissary in the Field' (August 1752). In this position Palk associated with Major Stringer Lawrence, with whom he formed a lifelong friendship. In April 1753 and May 1754, during the contest for the Carnatic between Chanda Sahib (favoured by the French) and Muhammad Ali (supported by the British), Palk was deputed envoy to the raja of Tanjore, and prevailed on that prince to give assistance to the British candidate. In January 1754 Palk and Henry Vansittart were the two delegates appointed to discuss terms of settlement with the French agents, Father Lavaur, M. de Kerjean, and M. Bausset, at Sadras, a Dutch settlement between Pondicherry and Madras. No agreement could be reached. At the end of 1754 Palk and Vansittart arranged a provisional peace treaty at Pondicherry. Peace was eventually signed on 11 January 1755.

During these years Palk developed a taste for matters political and commercial rather than religious. From a letter written on 26 October 1755 by the historian Robert Orme, a colleague of Palk's at Madras, a glimpse can be gained of some of the characteristics that identified the man. According to Orme, Palk had 'long since' given up studies of history and theology, and had thrown himself into active engagement with the contemporary affairs of the British at Madras. Palk enjoyed a reputation at this time for decency and a desire to conciliate everybody, even at the risk of being seen as all things to all men. Palk's early support for Thomas Saunders (governor from 1750 to 1755) changed to indifference when Palk became friends with Stringer Lawrence, whose relations with Saunders were acrimonious. Palk also received substantial financial benefits from activities put his way by Lawrence, making 'at least £10,000 from two he came with into India' (Love, *Vestiges*, 2.485–6). Palk's influence in the community as chaplain, paymaster, and commissary was such that his opinions of Saunders and Lawrence swayed public opinion against the former and in favour of the latter. When in 1758 the directors of the company instructed Palk to confine himself to his religious duties and to go to Fort St David, he decided to return instead to England. While there he married, on 7 February 1761, Anne (1738–1788), daughter of Arthur Vansittart and sister of his friend Henry Vansittart, now governor of Fort William, Bengal. They had three daughters, two of whom died in adolescence, and a son.

Palk renounced his holy orders, and on 2 October 1761 entered the East India Company's civil service, and in company with Stringer Lawrence returned to Madras (16 October 1761), where he was appointed to council. When George Pigot resigned on 14 November 1763 Palk succeeded him as governor of Madras. In 1765 Lord Clive obtained a grant from the Mughal emperor Shah Alam of the five districts known as the Northern Circars, for the Madras presidency. In 1766 Colonel John Caillaud was sent from Madras to take possession of them. But Nizam Ali, *subahdar* of the Deccan, to whom the territories had previously belonged, resented the transfer, and threatened to invade the Carnatic with a large army. Palk, alarmed for Madras, and with his usual desire to placate antagonists, hurriedly directed Caillaud to come to terms with the nizam. On 12 November 1766 a treaty was signed at Hyderabad, by which the company agreed to leave the Guntur Circar in the hands of the nizam's brother Basalat Jang, and to pay a tribute of eight lakhs of rupees a year for the remaining territory. The worst article in the treaty, however, was the second, by which the British promised to give the nizam military assistance 'to settle the affairs of his Highness's government in everything that is right and proper', a vague expression which, after Palk's departure in January 1767, involved the Madras government in the nizam's attack on, and the resulting war with Haidar Ali, the sultan of Mysore.

On his return to England in 1767 Palk was 'well received by both the King and the Court of Directors' (Love, *Report*, viii). He had accumulated a large fortune in India, from his various salaries, gifts from local dignitaries, and army contracts, and from his own commercial activities. In 1769 he purchased and greatly enlarged and improved Haldon House, near Exeter. His old friend General Lawrence resided with him, and on his death in 1775 left all his property to Palk's children. In return, Palk set up a large monument to Lawrence's memory within his estate, on the summit of Haldon Hill.

Palk was never a director of the East India Company, but his friendships with Laurence Sulivan and others kept him in constant contact with Indian affairs. He took a great interest in political matters, and was MP for Ashburton in 1767–8 and 1774–87. He generally supported the government, but took an independent line on Indian matters. On 19 June 1772 he was created a baronet. Palk Strait, which separates Sri Lanka from India, was named after him. Palk died at Haldon House on 29 April 1798, and was buried at Dunchideock churchyard. He was succeeded in the baronetcy by his son, Lawrence (1766–1813).

G. P. Moriarty, *rev.* I. B. Watson

Sources BL OIOC · *Report on the Palk manuscripts*, HMC, 74 (1922) · H. D. Love, *Vestiges of old Madras, 1640–1800*, 4 vols. (1913) · C. U. Aitchison, *Hyderabad, Mysore and Coorg* (1929), vol. 9 of *A collection of treaties, engagements and sanads relating to India and neighbouring countries* · *GM*, 1st ser., 68 (1798), 445 · Burke, *Peerage* (1939) · R. Polwhele, *The history of Devonshire*, 3 vols. (1793–1806)

Archives BL, corresp. and papers, Add. MSS 34685–34688 · Devon RO, corresp. | BL, letters to Warren Hastings, Add. MSS 29132–29193, *passim* · Bodl. Oxf., corresp. with Laurence Sulivan

Wealth at death see Love, introduction, *Palk manuscripts*

Páll inn Ómálgi. *See* Paul the Silent (*d. c.*1137) *under* Magnús Erlendsson, earl of Orkney (1075/6–1116?).

Palladius (*fl.* 429–*c.*433), missionary and bishop, was the first bishop of the Irish. There are three direct references to him in the contemporary writings of Prosper of Aquitaine. First, in his chronicle under the year 429, the deacon Palladius is said to have been responsible for inducing Pope Celestine to send Germanus, bishop of Auxerre, as papal representative to Britain to combat Pelagianism. In the second, also in the chronicle (s.a. 431), it is written that Celestine sent Palladius as the first bishop for the Irish who believed in Christ. In the third, in Prosper's *Contra collatorem* (against Cassian, author of the Conferences), written a year or two later, Celestine is praised for two achievements in the far north-west: he has saved 'the Roman island' for Catholicism and has made 'the barbarian island' Christian (chap. 21). The pope, therefore, was being praised for having saved Britain from Pelagianism and for having initiated the conversion of Ireland.

Palladius, unfortunately, was a common name in the late Roman empire, especially in the east. There was a family of Palladii in Gaul whose number included, according to Sidonius Apollinaris, both bishops and rhetoricians; they are likely to have belonged to Berry. The first bishop of the Irish has been linked with these Palladii but on no good evidence. Palladius has usually been seen as deacon of Auxerre rather than of Rome; in other words, it has been thought that Germanus sent him to Rome to obtain papal authority for his anti-Pelagian expedition to

Britain. There is no positive evidence for or against this theory.

What remains very likely is that the mission to the Irish arose from Germanus's journey to Britain. Explicit papal policy at this period was that missions should be mounted only when those who were to be evangelized had already expressed an interest in Christianity. The Irish Christians to whom Palladius was sent must therefore have been considered a credible base from which to work; they may have requested a bishop when Germanus was in Britain. Since Germanus was then acting as papal representative, their request went to the pope; he responded by sending the same Palladius who had recommended Germanus. This small group thus brought about, in the eyes of Prosper, two notable achievements on behalf of the papacy: Celestine had saved one island from heresy and another from paganism. He had intervened in a former province where the Roman empire was now powerless, and also beyond the furthest bounds of the empire, even at its strongest. Prosper, having become the friend of Pope Leo I (*r.* 440–61), lived in Rome for part of the 430s and probably for most or all of the period from 440 to 455. Leo preached a sermon to the people of Rome on the feast of Peter and Paul in 441, in which he declared that Rome, 'a royal and a priestly city, having been made the head of the whole world through the holy see of the blessed Peter … came to rule over a wider territory through the worship of God than by earthly domination' (Leo, ed. Chavasse, *Sermo* 82). The sermon is textually linked with Prosper's *De vocatione omnium gentium*, a work which considers both the theology and some of the practical details of missionary work. The mission of Palladius to the Irish was the clearest and most recent example which could be used to justify Leo's claim. The latter's friendship with Prosper makes it likely that he indeed had Ireland and therefore Palladius in mind.

Leo's sermon casts doubt, therefore, on the late seventh-century Irish account by Muirchú which makes Palladius die shortly after 431. Muirchú was manifestly making such claims in order to exalt the reputation of St Patrick as the true missionary to all the Irish, whereas the contemporary Prosper expressed, and Pope Leo's sermon implied, a continued optimism about Palladius's mission. On the other hand, Muirchú may be approximately correct in so far as he is supported by place-name evidence in associating both Palladius and the other likely early missionaries, Iserninus, Secundinus, and Auxilius, with Leinster. Those three early bishops are more likely to have been disciples of Palladius than, as Muirchú, Tírechán, and the early annals claim, of Patrick. In the first half of the fifth century Leinster probably extended as far north as the River Boyne. This greater Leinster was the part of Ireland which has yielded most evidence of Roman influence, but it was to be reduced in size by Uí Néill conquests in the midlands, probably in the late fifth and early sixth centuries. Serious progress in the conversion of Leinster would be an achievement sufficient to give some justification to Prosper's optimistic claim that Celestine had made Ireland Christian.

Palladius's relationship to Patrick can only be conjectured. It was already the subject of different ideas in the late seventh century. To judge by Patrick's own writings, especially his *Confessio*, his main area of activity was in the western part of Ireland: his proudest claim was to have taken the Christian faith to the furthest western extremity of the inhabited world; and the only part of Ireland with which he is securely connected is Mayo. Palladius and Patrick may, therefore, be seen as exemplifying two stages in the geographical expansion of Christianity in Ireland: Palladius, in the 430s, found a Christian community already established, but without a bishop; he was their first bishop and probably worked in Leinster; Patrick on the other hand took Christianity to the furthest west of the island; his activity as a missionary probably belongs to the second half of the fifth century.

T. M. Charles-Edwards

Sources 'Prosperi Tironis epitoma chronicon', *Chronica minora saec. IV. V. VI. VII.*, ed. T. Mommsen, 1, MGH Auctores Antiquissimi, 9 (Berlin, 1892), 341–499, esp. 385–485 • Prosper of Aquitaine, 'De gratia Dei et Libero arbitrio contra Collatorem', *Patrologia Latina*, 51 (1846), 213–76, esp. 271 • *Sancti Leonis magni Romani pontificis tractatus septem et nonaginta*, ed. A. Chavasse (1973), 82 • *Libri epistolarum sancti Patricii episcopi*, ed. L. Bieler, [2nd edn] (1993) • Muirchú, 'Vita S. Patricii', *The Patrician texts in the Book of Armagh*, ed. and trans. L. Bieler, Scriptores Latini Hiberniae, 10 (1979), 62–122 • Tírechán, 'Collectanea de Sancto Patricio', *The Patrician texts in the Book of Armagh*, ed. and trans. L. Bieler, Scriptores Latini Hiberniae, 10 (1979), 122–67, esp. 164–6 • T. M. Charles-Edwards, 'Palladius, Prosper, and Leo the Great: mission and primatial authority', in D. N. Dumville and others, *Saint Patrick, AD 493–1993* (1993), 1–12 • D. N. Dumville, 'Auxilius, Iserninus, Secundinus, and Benignus', in D. N. Dumville and others, *Saint Patrick, AD 493–1993* (1993), 89–105 • J. R. Martindale, *The prosopography of the later Roman empire*, 2: *AD 395–527* (1980), 821 • E. A. Thompson, *Who was Saint Patrick?* (1985), chap. 4 and 169–74

Pallady, Richard (*b.* **1515/16**, *d.* in or before **1563**), household official and member of parliament, was born of a yeoman family at Irthlingborough, Northamptonshire. He was educated as a king's scholar at Eton College from about 1529 and admitted to King's College, Cambridge, on 18 August 1533 at the age of seventeen; he was a fellow of the college in 1536–7. From 1540 to 1548 he was an attorney in the sheriff's court of London; at some time during the same period he entered the service of the duke of Somerset, almost certainly under the patronage of his steward, Sir John Thynne, who had previously been a member of the household of Lord Vaux of Harrowden, lord of the manor of Irthlingborough, where Pallady was born. There is no evidence that he had any particular expertise in architectural matters and the attribution to him of the precocious design of Somerset House in the Strand, London (begun 1546), considered to be 'the most serious attempt to compose a classical facade yet seen in England' (*History of the King's Works*, 4.252), cannot be substantiated. It is based on an unattributed description of Pallady as 'overseer of the works of the Duke of Somerset in the Strand' (*DNB*) but he is not named among the 'cheiff and principall officers' (Pikarell) in the account roll drawn up after Somerset's execution, although he did account for over £500 of ready money in his hands. The earlier description of him as 'clerk of the works to the said Duke' (Tytler, 272) in the list of prisoners lately committed to the Tower with Somerset in October 1549 would explain his possession of such substantial sums and suggests a more humble administrative role without design responsibility. He was released three months later without any formal charges being brought against him. In 1552 he was responsible for settling a number of Somerset's outstanding debts in Reading and elsewhere in Berkshire. His rehabilitation was completed later in the year when he resumed his seat in the House of Commons, to which he had been elected in 1547 for Peterborough. He was elected to the parliament of 1559 to represent Heytesbury, Wiltshire, where Thynne had an interest. By this date he had moved from Ruscombe, Berkshire, where he had been living for most of the decade, to the Thynne manor of Buckland in Gloucestershire. He was married before 1544 to Catherine, daughter of Guy Armston of Armston, Northamptonshire, and then to Anne, daughter of William Kirkby of Upper Rawcliffe, Lancashire. He died intestate before 27 March 1563, when letters of administration were granted to his widow. MALCOLM AIRS

Sources HoP, *Commons* • Venn, *Alum. Cant.* • Cooper, *Ath. Cantab.*, 1.125, 546 • W. Sterry, ed., *The Eton College register, 1441–1698* (1943), 255 • P. F. Tytler, *England under the reigns of Edward VI and Mary*, 1 (1839), 272 • H. M. Colvin and others, eds., *The history of the king's works*, 4 (1982), vol. 4, p. 252 • J. Pikarell, account roll, 1548–51, BL, Egerton MS 2815 ['cofferer of housholde' of late duke of Somerset and 'paye mr of all his buildinges woorkes and reparacons at his saide late severall houses'] • 'Disbursements of Rich[d] Palady esquier on the duke of Somersett's account', Bodl. Oxf., MS Top. gen. 481, fols. 5–27

Archives Bodl. Oxf., MSS. Top.gen.

Palles, Christopher (1831–1920), judge, was born at 5 Lower Gardiner Street, Dublin, on 25 December 1831, the third son of Andrew Christopher Palles, a Dublin solicitor, and his wife, Eleanor Plunkett. Both were members of Roman Catholic families which had adhered to that religion throughout the period of the penal laws. Those laws, which imposed severe disabilities on Catholics, had been significantly relaxed by the time Palles was born. He was educated at Clongowes Wood College, near Dublin, which had been founded by the Jesuits for the education of Catholic boys in 1814. From there he went to Trinity College, Dublin, from which he graduated in 1851 as a senior moderator in mathematics. The school of mathematics in Trinity at that time had a considerable reputation: one of its most famous graduates, Sir William Rowan Hamilton, was internationally known for his work on quaternions. Palles might well have chosen to pursue an academic career in mathematics or philosophy, but at this point, not for the only time, his career was affected by the state of Irish university education, which was to be a controversial political and religious issue until the early years of the twentieth century. Fellowships in Trinity were not open to Catholics, and Palles, who had been admitted as a student in the King's Inns in Dublin in 1849 and had in 1851 started to keep terms in Gray's Inn, London, decided to make the law, rather than mathematics, his career.

The relaxation of the penal laws had enabled Catholics

Christopher Palles (1831–1920), by Sir Hubert von Herkomer, 1903

to be called to the Irish bar since 1793, among them such celebrated advocates as Daniel O'Connell. The King's Inns in Dublin began to provide a course of education for prospective barristers for the first time in 1851, and Palles was among the first Irish barristers to sit the new examinations as a preliminary to being called to the bar in the Hilary term of 1853. He rapidly built up a good practice on the old home circuit, in the counties near Dublin, and he took silk in 1865 at the unusually early age of thirty-three, specializing in chancery law. He was highly regarded by his peers at the bar and played a part in the reforms of the King's Inns which were implemented by the benchers towards the end of the 1860s. He also at this stage became increasingly involved in politics.

Palles was a Liberal but had no sympathy with the developing movement for Irish home rule led by his great contemporary at the bar, Isaac Butt, and later by Charles Stewart Parnell. The Liberal administration led by W. E. Gladstone, who had yet to declare his support for home rule, appointed him to the post of solicitor-general for Ireland in 1872. A few months later he was promoted to the office of attorney-general for Ireland and almost immediately contested a by-election in Londonderry on behalf of the Liberals. He was opposed, not only by a Conservative, but by a home-rule candidate.

It was not only his opposition to home rule which involved the Catholic Palles in controversy during the by-election; he was also noticeably reluctant to express support for the Liberal administration's proposals for the establishment of non-denominational university colleges in Ireland. That scheme, which was designed to placate

Irish Catholic opinion by providing alternatives to Trinity College, was strenuously opposed by Cardinal Cullen and other members of the Irish hierarchy, who wanted a professedly Catholic university to be established. Palles's views on religion tended to be of the ultramontane variety, supporting as he did the Vatican in its struggle with the new Italian monarchy and, in private at least, he espoused Cardinal Cullen's opposition to the government's university proposals. But his unwillingness to make his views publicly known during the campaign drew down on him the wrath of many of his co-religionists, and the supporters of the home-rule candidate were also unsparing in their invective. One poster read: 'Who is likely to attain the judgeship which will probably be vacant in four months? Palles, of course, for defeating the cause of Ireland in Derry!'

As a result of the split in the Catholic vote, the Conservative candidate was elected. Palles's defeat in the by-election was a critical event in his career; had he been elected, he would probably have spent the rest of his life involved in politics at Westminster. As it was, just over a year later, in February 1874, at the age of forty-two, he was appointed the chief baron of the Exchequer Division, one of the senior judicial posts in Ireland. He was the youngest Irish judge to be appointed since Tudor times. The vacancy arose just in time for Palles, before Gladstone made way for Disraeli. The story, long current at the Irish bar, that he was appointed by the outgoing prime minister on the platform at Paddington Station as he was about to board the train for Windsor to tender his resignation, is undoubtedly apocryphal (Gladstone does not record a conversation with him that day).

Palles's brief excursion into politics was darkened by the ferocity of the attacks on him as an unscrupulous careerist. In contrast, his reputation as a judge has always been remarkably high. Several factors contributed to this, one of them undoubtedly being the length of his tenure: his forty-two years on the bench is without parallel in Irish judicial history. He had thus ample time to develop the qualities which equipped him to be an outstanding judge: a powerful intellect, a deep and comprehensive knowledge of the law, and a strong and independent personality. Nor does he seem to have suffered from the mental infirmity, deafness, remoteness from ordinary life, and increasing rigidity of views which marred other lengthy judicial careers. In his case, there were only harmless eccentricities, such as his habit of kicking the bench and twisting his head around as though he were trying to bite his ear off, when he was carried away by the intellectual excitement of a complex legal debate.

Palles's experience at the Chancery bar was reflected in his judgments in that area of the law, but he was also acknowledged to be a master of the common law. His decisions in both branches of jurisprudence demonstrated his reverence for precedent: he was a passionate believer in the virtues of the system of common law and equity which had developed in Ireland since the twelfth century, but he was also well known for his open-minded approach to novel arguments. His insistence on going out on assize regularly every year almost until his retirement ensured that his knowledge of Irish conditions was not confined to Dublin.

The reputation of Irish judges in the nineteenth century was not uniformly high. They were seen in some instances as being unduly eager to win favour with the executive. Palles was one of a generation in the later part of the century which did much to redeem the reputation of the judiciary: his robust assertion of the independence of the judges in a *cause célèbre* with a strongly political background at the Connaught winter assizes of 1886 was characteristic. A riot broke out during the course of an eviction and there was evidence that the police had not intervened, apparently on instructions from the executive. Palles caustically observed that the execution of the decrees of the court in a civilized country did not depend on the will of the executive which happened to be in office.

Two of Palles's reported judgments illustrate his qualities as a judge. In *Ussher* v. *Ussher* (1912), his lucid and magisterial survey of the English and Irish law of marriage demonstrated his erudition, his understanding of legal principle, and his capacity for closely knit reasoning. The same qualities were evident in *O'Hanlon* v. *Logue* (1906), in which Irish law diverged sharply from English in treating bequests for the celebration of masses, even when said in private, as valid charitable gifts. A remarkable feature of that case is that Palles, having carefully weighed the arguments, had no compunction in reversing a decision he had arrived at to contrary effect at the outset of his judicial career some thirty years earlier.

In 1877 a unified Irish High Court and Court of Appeal was established for the first time and this involved the abolition of the old Exchequer Division over which Palles presided. That change was not fully implemented, however, until 1897, and it was agreed that even thereafter Palles should retain his title of lord chief baron, which he did until his retirement. It is a measure of the esteem in which he was held that long after his death Irish lawyers continued to refer to him simply by his title: 'I believe there is a decision of the chief baron on the point.'

Towards the end of his career Palles was again concerned with the contentious topic of Irish university education. He was largely responsible for the drafting of the instrument which led to the establishment of the National University of Ireland, including the new Dublin college, in 1909, thus ending the virtual monopoly of Trinity College in higher education in the capital, which had lasted since the sixteenth century.

Palles's private life was clouded by tragedy. He married Ellen, the only daughter of Denis Doyle of Dublin, in 1862, while he was still a junior. She was frequently ill and died in 1885. Their only child was mentally handicapped. Palles retired from the bench in June 1916 in his eighty-fifth year, after suffering a slight stroke; he died at his home, Mount Anville House, Dundrum, co. Dublin, on 14 February 1920, and was buried in Glasnevin cemetery, Dublin. He remained a devout Roman Catholic throughout his life. His son, Christopher, died without issue at the age of ninety. RONAN KEANE

Sources V. T. H. Delany, *Christopher Palles* (1960) • F. E. Ball, *The judges in Ireland, 1221–1921*, 2 (1926) • *The Irish reports* (1874–1916) • C. Palles, correspondence with Lord Chancellor O'Hagan, PRO NIre., O'Hagan MSS

Archives priv. coll. | NL Ire., corresp. with Alice Stopford Green • NL Ire., corresp. with Lord Chancellor O'Hagan • PRO NIre., letters to Lord O'Hagan • TCD, corresp. with W. J. M. Starkie

Likenesses H. von Herkomer, oils, 1903, TCD [*see illus.*] • J. B. Yeats, pencil sketch, 1906 • J. B. Yeats, chalk drawing, King's Inns, Dublin • portrait (after H. von Herkomer), King's Inns, Dublin

Wealth at death £59,234: Delany, *Christopher Palles* • £1525 5s.—in England: Irish probate sealed in England, 16 April 1920, *CGPLA Eng. & Wales*

Pallis, Marietta (1882–1963), ecologist, painter, and author, was born on 26 October 1882 in Bombay, the first of the five children of Julia Ralli (1857–1940) and her scholar-poet husband, Alexandros Pallis (1850–1935), a member of the Greek trading firm Ralli Brothers. The family left India in 1892 and settled in Liverpool in 1894. Pallis was educated at Summerfield School, Liverpool, and Maywood School, Camberley, attended the University of Liverpool (1904–8), and studied natural sciences independently of a tripos at Newnham College, Cambridge (1910–12). Her father tolerated rather than encouraged her scientific ambition, and unlike her siblings she did not come into her £30,000 inheritance until his death.

At Liverpool, tutored by F. J. Lewis, Pallis studied the Dee estuary flora, and with fellow student Jean Shaw began a survey of the Norfolk broads. In April 1909 Lewis introduced their work to the Central Committee for the Survey and Study of British Vegetation (from 1913 the British Ecological Society). In December Pallis addressed the committee, and she and Shaw were elected the first associate members in April 1910. In December 1910 Pallis addressed a paper to the Royal Geographical Society called 'Salinity in the Norfolk broads', later published in the *Geographical Journal* (March 1911). In August 1911, during the first International Phytogeographical Excursion, based at Cambridge, she guided ecologists around the broads, and contributed 'The river-valleys of east Norfolk: their aquatic and fen formations' to A. G. Tansley's edited volume *Types of British Vegetation* (1911).

In September–October of 1912 and 1913 Pallis studied 'plav' in the Danube delta. Her paper 'The structure and history of plav: the floating fen of the delta of the Danube' was presented to the Linnean Society by Professor A. C. Seward in December 1915 and was published in the *Journal of the Linnean Society: Botany* (July 1916). Pallis engaged with vitalistic ideas, a 'philosophical biology' later developed in *An attempt at a statement concerning a vital unit as shown by the reed in the delta of the Danube* (1958), *The Species Unit, and Archetypal, Primeval and Primitive Vegetation* (1960), and *The Species Unit: Unit III* (1963). While in the delta she collected a species of hairy-leaved ash named *Fraxinus pallisae* in her honour, in 1916, by A. J. Wilmott of the British Museum natural history department.

Pallis's Danube fieldwork in 1913 formed part of a journey through Greece and south-eastern Europe from July to November 1913. From January to April of that year she had travelled in Greece, nursing refugees from the Balkan wars; Ioannina, her father's birthplace, was liberated in March. Fluent in Greek, Pallis sat on the ladies' committee of the Anglo-Hellenic League from its inauguration in December 1913, and was a life member and a member of its council in the 1920s. She engaged in Greek cultural activity in London, including folk dancing and theatre, and expounded her Greekness in the extraordinary *Tableaux in Greek History*, issued in preliminary form in 1949 and in 160 copies in 1952, which contained ten hand-coloured illustrations. Pallis damned 'modernist civilization' as a force of cultural homogenization, misguided progress, and environmental degradation, eulogizing Orthodox Christian Byzantium as a civilization of spirituality, rootedness, and order. Her theocratic maverick conservative social philosophy was expressed through a bizarrely alliterative prose. *Times Literary Supplement* reviewer C. M. Woodhouse noted (6 February 1953) that 'the book can evidently not be summed up in the words of the author'; other scholars privately praised it.

After 1916, forbidden by her father to undertake ecological research in the Amazon, Pallis turned to painting, producing portraiture and self-portraiture, still life and landscape throughout her life. She took drawing classes at the Slade School of Fine Art in 1924 and 1925, exhibited with the London Group in 1926 and 1929, and held a solo exhibition at the Bloomsbury Gallery in May–June 1938. Her painting, in a broadly post-impressionist style, was never commercially successful and received no critical attention. A portrait of A. J. Wilmott was presented to the natural history department of the British Museum in December 1958. She also wrote unpublished poems and stories and drafted a novel.

From 1918 Pallis usually spent the winter in London and the summer in Norfolk. From 1921 she owned property on Cheyne Walk, Chelsea, and led a gregarious life; a passionate swimmer, she had a swimming bath installed (illegally) indoors. At Long Gores, Hickling, Norfolk, she rented a marsh cottage from 1918, purchased cottages and marshland in 1935, and constructed a large, thatched studio in 1937; she recited the Orthodox liturgy beneath a corona hung from the ceiling.

Pallis's circle of independent female scholarly friends included historian Joan Wake, who described her as 'this erratic genius' (letter to Allen, *c.*1955, Joan Wake collection, Northampton, box 17), and Hope Emily Allen, an American scholar of medieval English mysticism from Oneida, New York state, who accompanied Pallis on travels in the USA from May to October 1914 and co-owned the Chelsea property until 1948. From 1928 to 1946 Pallis corresponded with Joan (Pernel) Strachey, principal of Newnham College (1923–41), whose judgement she valued enormously. From about 1926 she shared her life with Phillis Ursula Clark, *née* Riddle (1885?–1955), separated wife of Andrew Clark of Hickling. The couple travelled in

Greece in 1936, and in the eastern Mediterranean and the Middle East in 1954–5. Clark died in Cyprus on 6 July 1955, and was buried in Kyrenia. Pallis published *Four Stories* by Phillis Riddle in 1957.

On her travels in 1936 Pallis collected material for *The General Aspects of the Vegetation of Europe*, published in 1939, after rejection in 1938 by the Linnean Society, and sympathetically reviewed in *Nature*. The book decried the 'Interference' in nature of 'Man and his herds'. Viewing woodland as the 'global dominant', Pallis sought its re-emergence on her Norfolk marshes, and abandoned grazing in 1935. In 1953, on the 500th anniversary of the fall of Byzantium, she performed perhaps the most curious act of a curious life, cutting a three-quarter-acre symbolic bathing pool in the peat at Long Gores around islands shaped as a double-headed Byzantine eagle with papal and patriarchal crosses and crown, and the Greek initials MP. Phillis Clark was reburied on the island in spring 1959. Pallis believed that her pool, dug with traditional tools by local men, supported Dr Joyce Lambert's theory, first published in 1953, of the Broads as medieval peat diggings. She corresponded with Lambert and published *The impermeability of peat and the origin of the Norfolk broads* [and] *A note on acorn-distributing birds* (1956) and *The Status of Fen and the Origin of the Norfolk Broads* (1961). She was never active in Norfolk naturalist societies but was friendly with individual naturalists E. A. Ellis, Catherine Gurney, and Emma Turner.

The only study of Pallis is by W. T. Stearn, who commented: 'Neither Greece nor Britain noted the passing of this colourful strongly individualistic forceful woman' (Stearn). Pallis's early work, particularly on plav, remains respected by ecologists, but the later work is seen as tainted by metaphysics. Described by some as bird-like, photographs and self-portraits of Pallis show her in masculine attire, whether opulent clothing or naturalist's field dress of jacket and trousers. The eagle pool, overgrown after her death but cleared in the early 1980s, has been periodically sighted from the air and publicized, with its creator, as a curiosity. Pallis died at St Helen's Nursing Home, Bishopsgate, Norwich, on 30 August 1963 and was buried on 5 September, with Orthodox rites, alongside Phillis Clark on the island at Long Gores.

LAURA CAMERON and DAVID MATLESS

Sources W. T. Stearn, 'Marietta Pallis (1882–1963): ecologist and author', *Annales Musei Goulandris*, 7 (1985); (1986), 157–73 [*recte* 1986] • J. C. Hirsch, *Hope Emily Allen: medieval scholarship and feminism* (Norman, OK, 1989) • D. Nicholls, *Quite a lot: a memoir* (2001) • gravestone, Norfolk, Hickling, Long Gores [P. U. Clark]

Archives priv. coll., Vlasto/Pallis archive | Bodl. Oxf., letters and papers of H. Allen • Northants. RO, J. Wake collection • Norwich Castle Museum, E. A. Ellis collection • Oneida Community Archives, Kenwood, Oneida, New York State, H. Allen papers • U. Cam., H. Godwin collection; A. G. Tansley collection | FILM priv. coll., the Vlasto/Pallis archive

Likenesses group portraits, photographs, 1910, Newnham College, Cambridge • photographs, 1911, British Ecological Society, Tansley collection • W. Wulff, two photographs, 1913, priv. coll. • M. Pallis, about twelve self-portraits, oil or charcoal, priv. coll. • Pallis and others, about forty photographs, priv. coll.

Wealth at death property at Long Gores to nephew; property in Chelsea to niece: will, 15 Jan 1957 • £103,471 10*s*. 6*d*.: probate, 1963, *CGPLA Eng. & Wales*

Palliser, Fanny Bury [*née* Fanny Marryat] (1805–1878), writer on art, was born on 23 September 1805, the daughter of Joseph Marryat (1757–1824) of Wimbledon House, Surrey, and Sydenham House, Kent—a businessman and later MP for Horsham and Sandwich—and his wife, Charlotte, daughter of Frederic Geyer of Boston, New England. She was one of fifteen children, many of whom later published; her siblings included Frederick *Marryat (1792–1848), the novelist, and Joseph Marryat (1790–1878), the ceramics expert. On 8 August 1832 she married Captain Richard Bury Palliser (1796/7–1852), the third son of John Palliser of Derrybuskan, co. Tipperary; they had four sons and two daughters.

Mrs Bury Palliser approached her career as a writer on artistic subjects in the oblique fashion common to nineteenth-century women art critics and art historians. In 1845 she published *The Modern Poetical Speaker*, a collection of modern verse suitable for recitation, and in 1855 *Handbook of the Arts in the Middle Ages*, a translation from the French of Jules Labarte. She also assisted her brother Joseph—with whom she shared a long-standing interest in the history of ceramics—to revise the second edition (1857) of his *History of Pottery and Porcelain*, and was a significant figure among the growing number of women collectors of ceramics led by Lady Charlotte Shreiber and Lady Dorothy Nevill. She showed an interest—unusual among women collectors—in Italian maiolica, and in July 1857 was proposed for membership of the newly founded Collectors' Club (soon the Fine Arts Club) by J. C. Robinson. In later life, she published *The China Collector's Pocket Companion* (1874), and *History of the Ceramic Art* (1878), a translation from the French work by Albert Jacquemart.

Fanny Bury Palliser's most significant publication dealt with an area of art history which, like ceramics, was considered eminently suitable for women writers. *The History of Lace*, published in 1865, established her as an expert on this subject; it reached a second edition in 1869 and a third in 1875. Her obituarist in *The Academy* rightly described it as 'a complete and valuable work, abounding in illustrations' (p. 73): if not a model of style, it is a comprehensive classification of varieties of lacework and a mine of information on its history. Its durability was confirmed by a full revision in 1902, by Margaret Jourdain and Alice Dryden: in the preface, they described it as 'still the classic work on the subject'. It still features frequently in the footnotes of contemporary studies of lace and its history. Palliser was chosen to produce *A Descriptive Catalogue of the Lace and Embroidery in the South Kensington Museum* (1871); she produced a revised edition in 1873 and at the time of her death was preparing another revision (later completed and published by her fellow lace expert, Alan Summerley Cole, in 1881). She took a leading part in the organization of the International Lace Exhibition of 1874 at South Kensington, arranging and cataloguing the materials, and donated many examples of lacework to the museum. Thus she assisted in the formation of what is now one of the largest lace collections in the world; she may also have contributed indirectly to the revival of the lace industry which took place after her death, with the philanthropic foundation of lace associations in the 1870s and 1880s.

A contributor to the *Art Journal* and *The Academy*, Palliser also published *Historic Devices, Badges, and War Cries* (1870)—a collection of papers which had earlier appeared in the *Art Journal*—and *Mottoes for Monuments, or, Epitaphs Selected for Study and Application* (1872). An engaging travelogue, *Brittany and its Byways*, appeared in 1869. She died at her home, 33 Russell Road, Kensington, on 16 January 1878, and was buried in Brompton cemetery on 21 January. Her memorialist in *The Reliquary*, L. F. W. Jewitt, praised her as 'a discriminating, clear-headed and just critic', who was nevertheless 'a true woman in every thought, feeling, and impulse and action' (Jewitt, 227–8). His opinion may not have been uninfluenced by her extremely favourable review of his *Ceramic Art in Great Britain* (1878) in the *Art Journal* for January 1878—probably the last piece she wrote. ROSEMARY MITCHELL

Sources L. F. W. Jewitt, *The Reliquary*, 18 (1877), 227–8 • *The Academy* (26 Jan 1878), 73–4 • *Art Journal*, 40 (1878), 108 • A. Eatwell, 'Private pleasure, public beneficence: Lady Charlotte Schreiber and ceramic collecting', *Women in the Victorian art world*, ed. C. C. Orr (1995), 124–45 • A. S. Cocks, *The Victoria and Albert Museum: the making of the collection* (1980), 104 • F. B. Palliser, *A descriptive catalogue of the lace and embroidery in the South Kensington Museum*, rev. A. S. Cole, 3rd edn (1881) • *Life and letters of Captain Marryat*, ed. F. Marryat, 2 vols. (1872) • HoP, *Commons*, 1790–1820, vol. 4 • *CGPLA Eng. & Wales* (1878)

Wealth at death under £2000: probate, 11 Feb 1878, *CGPLA Eng. & Wales*

Palliser, Sir Hugh, first baronet (1723–1796), naval officer and politician, was born on 26 February 1723 at Kirk Deighton in the West Riding of Yorkshire. He was the son of Captain Hugh Palliser, army officer, of North Deighton and Mary, daughter of Humphrey Robinson of Thicket Hall, Cottingworth, Yorkshire. In 1735 he was entered as a midshipman on the *Aldborough*, commanded by his uncle, Nicholas Robinson. Two years later he moved, with Robinson, to the *Kennington*, in which he remained for three years. He was for a few months in 1740 in the *Deptford* storeship and in the *Tiger*, and early in 1741 he joined his uncle in the *Essex*. He passed his examination for lieutenant on 12 May 1741, and, continuing in the *Essex*, was promoted to that rank on 18 September 1741. At the beginning of the winter Robinson was superseded in the command by Richard Norris, son of Sir John Norris, and Palliser, continuing with him, was first lieutenant of the *Essex* in the action off Toulon on 11 February 1744. Amid the charges and counter-charges that followed, Palliser, with some of the other lieutenants of the *Essex*, preferred a charge of cowardice and misconduct against Norris, whose career was subsequently terminated.

On 3 July 1746 Palliser was promoted commander of the *Weasel*, and on 25 November captain of the *Captain*, going out to the West Indies with the broad pennant of Commodore Edward Legge. On Legge's death (19 September 1747) Palliser was moved into the *Sutherland* (50 guns), and in the following March he was severely wounded by an explosion and was obliged to return to England. By December

Sir Hugh Palliser, first baronet (1723–1796), by Nathaniel Dance, *c.*1770

he had recovered sufficiently to be appointed to the frigate *Sheerness*, in which he was sent out to the East Indies with news of the peace. He joined Edward Boscawen on the Coromandel coast in July 1749, and returned to England in the following April, when the ship was paid off.

In January 1753 Palliser was appointed to the *Yarmouth*, guardship at Chatham, from which in March he was moved to the *Seahorse*, a small frigate employed during that and the next year on the coast of Scotland to prevent smuggling. At the end of September 1754 the *Seahorse* was ordered to refit at Sheerness. From there she went to co. Cork, and sailed in January 1755, in charge of a convoy of transports, for Virginia, from where Palliser returned to England on 26 July, Commodore Augustus Keppel taking a passage with him; they arrived at Spithead on 22 August 1755.

A month later Palliser was appointed to the *Eagle* at Plymouth, and early in October he was sent to cruise off Ushant, where he captured several vessels coming home from Newfoundland. During 1756 the *Eagle* was one of the fleet cruising off Ushant and in the Bay of Biscay under Admirals Edward Hawke, Edward Boscawen, or Sir Charles Knowles, and in 1757 she was with Rear-Admiral Francis Holburne off Louisbourg. During the summer of 1758 Palliser commanded the *Shrewsbury* in the fleet off Ushant under Lord Anson; and in 1759 he took part in the operations in the St Lawrence leading up to the reduction of Quebec. In 1760 he was with Sir Charles Saunders in the Mediterranean, and for some time had command of a detached squadron in the Levant. In 1762 he was sent out to Newfoundland with a small squadron to retake St

John's; but that service having already been accomplished, he returned to England.

In April 1764 Palliser was appointed governor and commander-in-chief at Newfoundland, with his broad pennant in the *Guernsey*. This was at that time a summer appointment, the ships coming home for the winter; but in Palliser's case it was twice renewed, in 1765 and 1766, during which time he acted as a commissioner for adjusting the French claims to fishing rights, and directed a survey of the coasts, which was carried out by the circumnavigator James Cook. In 1770 Palliser was appointed comptroller of the navy, and on 6 August 1773 he was created a baronet. In the following year he was elected MP for Scarborough. He took his seat as a supporter of Lord North's ministry and spoke on naval affairs during the American War of Independence. On 31 March 1775 Palliser was promoted rear-admiral, and shortly afterwards he was appointed one of the lords of the Admiralty, under the earl of Sandwich. In the same year, by the will of his old chief Sir Charles Saunders, he came into a legacy of £5000, and was appointed lieutenant-general of marines in succession to Saunders. On 29 January 1778 he was promoted vice-admiral of the blue; and in March, when Vice-Admiral Keppel was appointed to the command of the Channel Fleet, Palliser, while still retaining his seat at the Admiralty, was appointed third in command under him.

Off Ushant for three days (24–7 July 1778), the English and French fleets were in each other's presence, Keppel vainly trying to bring the enemy to action. On the morning of 27 July a shift of wind enabled Keppel in the *Formidable* to bring the enemy to a brief, indecisive but damaging action. After the two fleets drew clear of each other Keppel signalled to reform the line, hoping to renew the battle. However, Palliser's rear squadron had been damaged and was unable to get into its station until after nightfall. Next day the French fleet was not in sight and Keppel returned to Plymouth. This indecisive engagement created great disappointment at home. The 'opposition' press, led by the *General Advertiser*, blamed Keppel's failure to defeat the French on Palliser's tardiness in supporting him for a renewed attack. Furious at this, Palliser in November desired Keppel to write to the press to contradict their accusation. Keppel refused, whereupon Palliser issued his own explanation of events in the *Morning Post*. The two men clashed in the House of Commons on 2 December, when Keppel implied Palliser had been negligent if not disobedient in failing to answer his signals. Impulsively Palliser demanded a court martial on Keppel for misconduct and neglect of duty. In a court packed with Keppel's friends he was honourably acquitted in February 1779. The London mob celebrated his acquittal by gutting Palliser's house in Pall Mall, and by burning Palliser in effigy. In York they are said to have demolished the house of Palliser's sister.

The court martial on Keppel had pronounced the charges 'malicious and ill-founded' (Drummond, 3.247). Palliser consequently resigned his appointments, including his Admiralty seat, withdrew from parliament, and applied for a court martial on himself in February 1779. Keppel declined to prepare the charge for the trial which began at Portsmouth on 12 April. Because of Keppel's decision there was accordingly no prosecutor and no charges; proceedings were rather in the nature of an inquiry. Even so they lasted twenty-one days. Palliser's 'conduct was considered in many respects highly exemplary and meritorious' (ibid.); however, he was criticized for failing to inform his commander-in-chief of the state of his ship, and, though he was acquitted of any misconduct, his acquittal was neither unanimous nor with honour.

Although he requested to be reinstated in the offices which he had resigned Palliser was appointed, only through the efforts of Sandwich, to the governorship of Greenwich Hospital in 1780. He did not stand at the 1780 general election but did contest, and win, the vacant seat of Huntingdon in October of that year. He became an admiral on 24 September 1787 and died, unmarried, at his country seat of Vach in Buckinghamshire, on 19 March 1796, allegedly 'of a disorder induced by the wounds received on board the *Sutherland*'. He was buried in the parish church of Chalfont St Giles. At his death the bulk of his estate passed to his illegitimate son. The baronetcy descended to his grandnephew Hugh Palliser Walters, who took the name Palliser, and from him to his son, on whose death it became extinct.

J. K. LAUGHTON, *rev.* ROGER MORRISS

Sources J. Charnock, ed., *Biographia navalis*, 5 (1797), 483 • 'Biographical memoir of the late Sir Hugh Palliser', *Naval Chronicle*, 39 (1818), 89–112 • *European Magazine and London Review*, 29 (1796), 219–20 • R. M. Hunt, *The life of Sir Hugh Palliser, bart* (1844) • *Minutes of the proceedings at a court-martial assembled for the trial of the Honourable Admiral Augustus Keppel* (1779) • T. R. Keppel, *The life of Augustus, Viscount Keppel*, 2 vols. (1842) • *Considerations on the principles of naval discipline* (1781) • Cobbett, *Parl. hist.*, vols. 20–21 • R. Beatson, *Naval and military memoirs of Great Britain*, 3 vols. (1790) • J. H. Broomfield, 'The Keppel–Palliser affair, 1778–1779', *Mariner's Mirror*, 47 (1961), 195–207 • M. M. Drummond, 'Palliser, Hugh', HoP, *Commons*, 1754–90

Archives BL, corresp. with first earl of Liverpool, Add. MSS 38214–38227, 38308–38310 • NMM, corresp. with Lord Sandwich

Likenesses N. Dance, oils, *c*.1770, Los Angeles County Museum of Art, Los Angeles, California [*see illus.*] • J. R. Smith, mezzotint, pubd 1787, BM • attrib. G. Dance, oils (after N. Dance), NMM • E. Orme, stipple (after D. Orme), BM; repro. in *European Magazine* (1796)

Palliser, John (1817–1887), geographer and explorer, was born on 29 January 1817, the eldest of five sons born to Wray Palliser (*d.* 1862) of Comragh, co. Waterford, sometime lieutenant-colonel of the Waterford militia, and Anne, daughter of John Gledstanes of Annesfift, co. Tipperary; Sir William *Palliser was his younger brother. John Palliser was sheriff of Waterford in 1844 and served in the Waterford militia. In 1847 he went on a hunting expedition among the native people of western and north-western America and his *Adventures of a Hunter in the Prairies* (1853) sold at least eight thousand copies. In 1856 he proposed to the Royal Geographical Society that he explore the Canadian prairies and continental divide. The society's expedition committee refined his aims to comprise tracing the course of the Southern Saskatchewan, evaluating the region for settlement, and exploring the

Rockies for a southerly pass to British Columbia. They estimated that this would take two years and cost £5000. Roderick Murchison, president of the society, stressed in his submission of the plan to the Colonial Office that there was a possibility that coal would be discovered and that a British expedition would be timely given the United States' railway surveys in the far west. In 1857 Henry Labouchere, secretary of state for the colonies, agreed to support the expedition. The Treasury subscribed £5000 and the Royal Society advised on the scientific aspects of the journey; but more important than science were the strategic desires to counteract American infiltration of the British prairies, to develop transport routes to stop the Red River colony looking south rather than east for links to the outside world, and to review the activities of the Hudson's Bay Company which was widely criticized for maintaining the isolation of the Pacific west and understating its resource endowment in order to protect its own trading privileges. It was in part Palliser's aloofness from the political controversy surrounding the venture that led, on 31 March 1857, to his appointment as leader of the expedition, supported by Thomas Blakiston as astronomer and James Hector as geologist and zoologist.

The expedition had assumed a far more scientific and political character than Palliser had originally envisaged, and became even more highly charged politically after gold was discovered on the Fraser River in 1858. In 1857 Palliser explored the White Fish and Kaminstikwia rivers and the land between the Southern Saskatchewan and the border with the United States, and confirmed the feasibility of establishing communication, particularly a railway line, between the rocky regions of lakes Superior and Winnipeg and the prairies. In 1858 he approached the Rockies from the Buffalo prairie between the Northern and Southern Saskatchewan and explored the passes through the mountains lying in British territory. For the results of this journey he was awarded the patron's gold medal of the Royal Geographical Society in 1859. In 1860 he headed for the Southern Saskatchewan River following the course of the Red Deer River. He went westwards to the Rocky Mountains from the point where he had turned in his first season's explorations and thus completed the survey of the hitherto unknown prairie region. He also examined the country to the west of the Columbia River, establishing the fact that there was a route connecting the Saskatchewan plains east of the Rockies with the gold mining regions of British Columbia—information which was vital in the struggle to establish British control over areas which were attracting more American than Canadian prospectors. Palliser considered that western North America should form a series of British colonies independent of Canada—an idea which proved unworkable; and that the Hudson's Bay Company should have its privileges curtailed—a view which prevailed soon afterwards.

As the government sponsors of the expedition feared, its actual cost of £13,000 was nearly three times the original estimate; yet much had been achieved for costs far more modest than those spent on the United States' side in surveying western lands. The general topography of a huge swathe of territory had been established, the first accurate map of the British Rocky Mountains drawn, several passes discovered, and substantial knowledge gained about the geology and natural history of the area. On 30 May 1877 Palliser was awarded the companionship of St Michael and St George. He died, unmarried, at Comragh, co. Waterford, on 18 August 1887.

ELIZABETH BAIGENT

Sources R. A. Stafford, *Scientist of empire: Sir Roderick Murchison, scientific exploration and Victorian imperialism* (1989) • J. Palliser, 'Progress of the British North American expedition under the command of Capt. John Palliser', *Proceedings* [Royal Geographical Society], 2 (1857–8), 38–47 • J. Palliser, 'Progress of the British North America exploring expedition', *Proceedings* [Royal Geographical Society], 2 (1857–8), 146–52 • E. Bulwer Lytton, 'Discovery by Captain John Palliser, and Dr Hector of practicable passes through the Rocky Mountains within the British possessions', *Proceedings* [Royal Geographical Society], 3 (1858–9), 122–7 • J. Palliser, 'On the Rocky Mountains', *Proceedings* [Royal Geographical Society], 4 (1859–60), 73–6 • *The Times* (29 Aug 1887) • Boase, *Mod. Eng. biog.* • *DNB*

Archives PRO, papers relating to exploration in North America, CO66 • University of Toronto, reports on North American journeys [copies]

Likenesses photograph, 1860–69, Glenbow Archives, Calgary, Canada; *see illus. in* Hector, Sir James (1834–1907) • watercolour, RGS

Palliser, William (1646–1727), Church of Ireland archbishop of Cashel, was born at Kirby Wiske in Yorkshire, the son of John Palliser. He received his early education at Northallerton, probably under Thomas Smelt. Having entered Trinity College, Dublin, as a pensioner on 13 January 1661, he became a fellow in 1668 and graduated BD in 1674 and DD in 1679. He married Mary Wheeler, a granddaughter of Jonah Wheeler, bishop of Ossory and son-in-law of Sir Philip Perceval, at an unknown date.

Palliser received deacon's orders at Wexford in November 1669, and priest's orders on the 28th of the following January in St Patrick's Cathedral, Dublin. He was elected *medicus* in Trinity College in October 1670, and appointed professor of divinity there in 1678. In the same year he delivered a Latin oration at the funeral of James Margetson, archbishop of Armagh. In October 1681 Palliser resigned his fellowship in Trinity College for the rectory of Clonfeacle, co. Tyrone. However, four days after his resignation he was readmitted as a fellow to Trinity College by dispensation, on his resigning Clonfeacle.

By patent dated 14 February 1693 Palliser was appointed bishop of Cloyne, and was consecrated in the chapel of Trinity College on 5th March. In 1694, on the orders of the government, he prepared an account of the diocese of Cloyne in 1693–4, and supplied with it a plan for union of parishes. He was translated to the archbishopric of Cashel on 26 June 1694, and continued to occupy it until his death at Rathfarnham, Dublin, on 1 January 1727. He was buried in St Andrew's Church, Dublin, later that month. The great wealth which he accumulated was inherited by his only son, William. Archbishop Palliser made a gift of communion plate to the cathedral of Cashel. He donated £1500 to Trinity College, to which he also bequeathed a selection of 4000 of his books, on condition that they should be always kept together as a collection in the college library and designated Bibliotheca Palliseriana.

J. T. GILBERT, *rev.* J. FALVEY

Sources T. W. Moody and others, eds., *A new history of Ireland*, 9: *Maps, genealogies, lists* (1984), 392–438 · Burtchaell & Sadleir, *Alum. Dubl.* · H. Cotton, *Fasti ecclesiae Hibernicae*, 6 vols. (1845–78) · W. M. Brady, *Clerical and parochial records of Cork, Cloyne, and Ross*, 3 vols. (1863–4) · W. A. Phillips, ed., *History of the Church of Ireland*, 3 vols. (1933–4) · T. C. Barnard, 'Improving clergymen', *As by law established: the Church of Ireland since the Reformation*, ed. A. Ford, J. I. McGuire, and K. Milne (1995), 136–51 · J. Falvey, 'The Church of Ireland episcopate in the eighteenth century', MA diss., University College, Cork, 1995

Archives PRO NIre., letters to Arthur Pomeroy · TCD, corresp. with William King

Sir William Palliser (1830–1882), by R. & E. Taylor, pubd 1873 (after Bassano)

Palliser, Sir William (1830–1882), army officer and engineer, was the fifth and youngest son of Lieutenant-Colonel Wray Palliser (*d.* 1862) of the Waterford militia and Anne Gledstanes of co. Tipperary. He was born in Dublin on 18 June 1830, and was educated at Rugby School (1845–9), Trinity College, Dublin, from 1849, and Trinity Hall, Cambridge, from 1851. He was admitted to the Inner Temple in 1854, after which he went on to the Royal Military College, Sandhurst, obtaining a commission as ensign in the rifle brigade on 22 April 1855. In the same year he became lieutenant and joined the 1st battalion in the Crimea, but saw no active service, returning to England in June 1856. In 1858 he exchanged into the 18th hussars, and on 5 August 1859 was promoted to the rank of captain. He then served as aide-de-camp to Sir William Knollys at Aldershot for a time, before going to Dublin as brigade major of cavalry on 6 July 1860. He remained there until 4 October 1864, when he accepted an unattached majority, finally retiring from the army in December 1871.

Palliser is chiefly remembered for his innovations in ordnance, and it was while still an undergraduate at Cambridge that he first turned his mind in that direction. Some shot of his design was tested at Shoeburyness in 1853, followed by a rifled mortar in 1855, and he took out a patent for projectiles as early as 20 July 1854. However, it was in 1862 and 1863 that he developed the three inventions that proved most fruitful, and with which his name is chiefly identified. The first of these, entitled 'Improvements in the construction of ordnance and in the projectiles to be used therewith', was granted a patent on 11 November 1862. The essential problem that this patent attempted to address was the propensity of cannon and other artillery to explode unexpectedly when placed under the severe stress produced when they were fired. The solution Palliser offered was to form the barrels of such cannon from concentric tubes of metal of different elasticities, so that, as he explained in the patent, 'owing to their respective ranges of elasticity, when one tube is on the point of yielding, all the tubes may be on the point of yielding'. One application of this principle was to insert tubes of coiled wrought iron into cast-iron guns that had been suitably bored out. Guns so treated were found, when tested, to give excellent results, and the method provided an efficient means of utilizing the large stockpile of cast-iron smooth-bore ordnance. It became possible to convert 68-pounder smooth-bore guns into 80-pounder rifled guns, and 8 inch and 32-pounder smooth-bores into rifled 64-pounders, at one-third of the cost of new guns. Some thousands were altered in this way, and became known as 'Palliser converted guns'.

On 6 December 1862, Palliser took out a patent for screw-bolts, the second invention for which he was known. The stem or shank of these bolts was designed so as to be slightly smaller in diameter than the bottom of the thread of the screw in order to cause any extension in the shank to be confined to the screwed part, resulting in an increase in the strain they could take before breaking. This was especially intended for the bolts used in securing armour-plates, and the principle proved so effective that Palliser bolts, even without elastic washers, were found to be better than ordinary bolts with them. Supplemented afterwards by Captain English's spherical nuts and coiled washers, the 'plus thread', as it was called, satisfactorily solved the very difficult problem of armour bolts.

Palliser's third main invention was granted a patent on 27 May 1863, and was for what were called 'chill-cast projectiles'; these subsequently became known as 'Palliser projectiles', despite the claim of James Nasmyth to have invented them first, some months earlier. When tested in November 1863 these projectiles were found to be a marked improvement on ordinary cast iron, but it was not until 1866 that chill-cast shot was actually recognized as superior to steel for attack on wrought-iron armour, and introduced into service at a cost of one-fifth that of steel projectiles. However, owing to the introduction of steel-faced armour, steel shot subsequently superseded them. Between 1867 and 1871 Palliser was awarded £15,000 for his chilled projectiles.

Palliser's inventions were further developed in subsequent patents, of which he took out fourteen dealing with guns, bolts, and projectiles, between 1867 and 1881. He also patented improvements in fastenings for railway lines, in powder magazines, and in boots and shoes, between 1869 and 1873. In 1868 he married Anne, daughter of George Perham. During the siege of Paris he wrote several letters to *The Times* and some leading articles in it, which were afterwards embodied in a pamphlet of 1871 entitled *The Use of Earthen Fortresses for the Defence of London, and as a Preventive Against Invasion*. In these, he proposed to surround London with a chain of unrevetted earthworks, about 5 miles apart, extending from Chatham to Reading, and to occupy the most important strategical points between this chain and the coast by similar works, or clusters of works.

In acknowledgement of his services, Palliser was made CB (civil) in 1868, and was knighted on 16 January 1873. In March 1875 he received the cross of a commander of the Crown of Italy. After unsuccessfully contesting Devonport and Dungarvan, he was elected in 1880 for Taunton, as a Conservative, heading the poll.

Palliser died suddenly from 'angina pectoris' (heart disease) at 21 Earl's Court Square, London, on 4 February 1882, and was buried in Brompton cemetery five days later. Before his death he complained that he was 'persecuted to the bitter end' by officials in the War Office, a complaint that was repeated by others, who said that the treatment he received hastened his death. The basis of the complaint was that the War Office had deliberately blocked Palliser's application for an extension on his patent for chill-cast shot. A valuable account of the controversy that resulted can be found in the report of the royal commission on warlike stores, published in 1887.

Wray Richard Gledstanes Palliser (1821/2–1891), one of Sir William's elder brothers, became sub-lieutenant RN on 13 May 1845, and lieutenant on 28 February 1847. He distinguished himself in 1854 in expeditions against Chinese pirates, being in command of the boats of the frigate *Spartan*, of which he was first lieutenant. He stormed three forts, mounting seventeen guns, and he boarded the chief vessel of a pirate fleet and rescued a French woman who was a prisoner in it. In the act of boarding he himself fell between his own boat and the other, and broke several ribs. For his gallantry in these actions, which were colourfully related in his obituary in *The Times*, he was made commander on 6 January 1855. In 1857 he married Elizabeth, daughter of Richard Fitzgerald of Muckridge House, co. Cork. He was placed on the retired list as a captain on 21 April 1870, and died of bronchitis at the Queen's Hotel, Chester, on 6 June 1891.

E. M. LLOYD, *rev.* GILES HUDSON

Sources Boase, *Mod. Eng. biog.* • Venn, *Alum. Cant.* • 'Royal commission appointed to inquire into … warlike stores: minutes of guidance', *Parl. papers* (1887), 15.89, 161, 255–6, 352, C. 5062-I • *ILN* (22 Feb 1893), 177–8 • *The Times* (6 Feb 1882) • *PICE*, 69 (1881–2), 418–21 • Ward, *Men of the reign* • *Men of the time* (1875) • *James Nasmyth, engineer: an autobiography*, ed. S. Smiles (1883) • *Papers on subjects connected with the duties of the corps of royal engineers*, new ser., 13 (1864), 128 • *Papers on subjects connected with the duties of the corps of royal engineers*, new ser., 14 (1865), 163 • *Papers on subjects connected with the duties of the corps of royal engineers*, new ser., 16 (1868), 125 • 'Return showing the amount expended on experiments', *Parl. papers* (1878), 47.495, no. 233 [awards to inventors; ships of war and weapons] • d. cert. • d. cert. [Wray Palliser] • A. T. Mitchell, ed., *Rugby School register*, 2: *From August 1842 to January 1874* (1902) • *The Times* (16 June 1891)

Archives Tyne and Wear Archives Service, Newcastle upon Tyne, letters to Lord Rendel

Likenesses R. & E. Taylor, engraving, pubd 1873 (after photograph by Bassano), NPG [*see illus.*]

Wealth at death £89,689 16*s.* 2*d.*: administration, 25 Feb 1882, *CGPLA Eng. & Wales* • £5946 17*s.* 7*d.*—Wray Richard Gledstanes Palliser: probate, 21 July 1891, *CGPLA Eng. & Wales*

Palliser, Wray Richard Gledstanes (1821/2–1891). *See under* Palliser, Sir William (1830–1882).

Palmer, (Charles) Alan Salier (1913–1990), intelligence officer and businessman, was born on 23 October 1913 at Shinfield Grange, Shinfield, Berkshire, the only son of Sir (Charles) Eric Palmer (1883–1948), a former chairman of Huntley and Palmers, and his wife, Gwenllian Salier, second daughter of David Jones of Melbourne, Australia. Great-grandson of George *Palmer, the founder of the famous biscuit dynasty, he was educated at Harrow School and Exeter College, Oxford, where he read modern languages (French and German), before entering the family business in 1934. In 1938 he joined the firm's board. In the following year he married Auriol Mary, only daughter of Brigadier-General Cyril R. Harbord.

In August 1939, having served as a Territorial Army officer since May 1935, Palmer received an immediate commission into the Royal Berkshire yeomanry. He was adjutant from 1939 until late 1941, when he was posted to the headquarters staff of the 61st division. In June 1942 he moved onto the headquarters staff of 3rd corps. In the summer of 1943, after his promotion to major, Palmer volunteered for service with Britain's secret sabotage organization, the Special Operations Executive (SOE). After taking part in an operation in the Dodecanese he was earmarked to join Brigadier E. F. ('Trotsky') Davies's SOE mission to the Albanian resistance. Palmer parachuted into enemy-occupied Albania in early October 1943.

Shortly after the drop, made to the Biza plateau in central Albania, Palmer was sent south by Davies to join and act as liaison officer to the Albanian 1st partisan brigade. It was a fortunate move for Palmer, as Davies was soon encircled and captured along with many of his headquarters mission. Lieutenant-Colonel Norman Wheeler succeeded Davies as senior British liaison officer to the partisans. When Wheeler was withdrawn from Albania late in May 1944, Palmer was promoted lieutenant-colonel and assumed Wheeler's role. He retained command until the Germans left Albania in November 1944.

Palmer took over when British relations with the partisans were on a knife-edge. The communist-led partisans were deeply suspicious of the motives behind Britain's vain attempts at making nationalist Albanians come out to fight the Germans. Palmer, like most SOE personnel in Albania, saw clearly that the partisans were the only Albanians committed to fighting the Germans and with the potential to continue to do so. As widespread civil war loomed between right and left, Palmer, on military grounds, strongly recommended the withdrawal of British support for the nationalists and all-out assistance to the partisans. After much prevarication by the allied high command, the break was finally made in the early autumn of 1944. Palmer's intelligent and careful handling of Enver Hoxha, the partisan leader and future communist dictator, did much to maintain co-operation between SOE and the partisans until the end of the campaign.

Palmer subsequently became political adviser to Brigadier D. E. P. Hodgson's British military mission to Albania in 1945. His efforts in the country since 1943 were recognized by the award of the DSO, an addition to the earlier mention in dispatches he received for a hair-raising attempt to rescue three American nurses after their transport plane had crash-landed in Albania. A confidential SOE report on him in 1944 read: 'Personality strong, amiable and impressive … quick and skilful at sizing up an intricate political or military situation. An extremely capable leader of men both in and out of action' (private information).

After the war Palmer returned to Reading and the family firm, where he was appointed production director and oversaw a rapid expansion of the business. He became deputy chairman of Huntley and Palmers in 1955 and chairman in 1963. He was also responsible for the firm's French subsidiary. Continued improvements, combined with excellent industrial relations encouraged through Palmer's introduction of many joint management and employer groups, saw steady growth in production. He became chairman of the Cake and Biscuit Alliance in 1967, and received the CBE two years later.

Throughout the 1960s Palmer's vision and sound business sense saw him lead Huntley and Palmers towards the successful merger with the other independent family companies, Peak Frean and W. & R. Jacobs, to form Associated Biscuit Manufacturers and counter the challenge of United Biscuits. The merger was completed in 1969 and Palmer, appointed vice-chairman in 1963, chaired the group for the next three years. He retired in 1972.

A warm, thoughtful, and creative man with a generous nature and a ready smile, Palmer had many friends and appreciated and liked the good things in life. Retirement allowed him to indulge his love of racing and he owned and bred several horses. He also spent time on his estate in St Lucia. Devoted to jazz, he was a member of the Cotton Club in New York and a friend of Duke Ellington. Shooting, fishing, and politics were among his other interests: he was president of the Reading Conservative Association from 1946 to 1986.

Palmer died from a cerebral haemorrhage at his home, Forest Edge, Farley Hill, Berkshire, on 13 September 1990.

RODERICK BAILEY

Sources *Daily Telegraph* (17 Sept 1990) • *The Independent* (19 Sept 1990) • R. Hibbert, *Albania's national liberation struggle: the bitter victory* (1991) • private information (2004) [SOE adviser] • b. cert. • d. cert. • T. A. B. Corley, *Quaker enterprise in biscuits: Huntley and Palmers of Reading, 1822–1972* (1972)

Palmer, Alicia Tindal (1763–1822), writer of historical fiction and biography, was born in Bath, the daughter of the actor John *Palmer (1728–1768), called Gentleman John to distinguish him from another of the several actor John Palmers, who was known as Plausible Jack, and of Hannah Mary Pritchard (1739–1781), who had been an actress since the age of six. The more famous tragedienne Hannah *Pritchard was grandmother to Alicia and her brother, William Vaughan Palmer, army officer (1762–1822). Alicia probably spent her early years in Bath and in London, where her father died on 23 May 1768. Her mother then retired from the stage, inherited property in London and Twickenham from Hannah Pritchard in the same year, and in the next year married Maurice or Morris Lloyd, wealthy businessman and close friend of Lord North. Hannah Mary died in August 1781 at Dillington House, Whitelackington, near Ilminster, Somerset, a house rented for her by her husband.

Palmer was thus comfortably off in her early years. It was 1809 before she published her first book, *The Husband and Lover*, which she subtitled 'An Historical Moral Romance'. It was well reviewed. Next year came *The Daughters of Isenberg: a Bavarian Romance*, designed to inculcate in young female readers a proper filial obedience and respect for the proprieties. Her heroine shows 'bewitching timidity' and 'sweet deprecation'. The plot has Gothic and stereotypical elements—wicked barons, idyllic landscape gardens, a coquette being punished, and a learned lady being mocked—but also shows evidence of some shrewd observation of human behaviour. It hardly deserves the attack it received in the *Quarterly Review*, from John Gifford, who ridiculed Palmer's ideas on history and geography, indulged in sideswipes at other women writers, and ended with a circumstantial tale of how Palmer had offered him £3 (disguised as a charitable contribution) for a favourable review. His final insult was to say he would pass on the money to either the Lying-In or the Foundling Hospital, thus equating Palmer with the mother of an illegitimate child.

Undeterred, Palmer issued her next book, *The Sons of Altringham* (1811), as a venture to raise money for a boy who was deaf and mute. *Altringham* is not a novel but a collection of three tales. Her last publication was a historical biography, *Authentic Memoirs of the Life of John Sobieski, King of Poland* (1815), published with a distinguished subscribers' list. The nobility and clergy are well represented, as well as the literary world (Byron and others), the theatrical world (Edmund Kean), women, and book clubs. Sobieski, who lived in the seventeenth century, was a national military hero as well as a ruler; his name had recently been mentioned in parliament in connection with the current fate of Poland. Palmer emphasizes the value of liberty, and the responsibility of those countries, such as Britain, which enjoy liberty, to work to make it more widespread in the world. Palmer died in 1822.

ISOBEL GRUNDY

Sources Highfill, Burnim & Langhans, *BDA* • *Critical Review*, 3rd ser., 19 (1810), 448 • *QR*, 4 (1810), 61–7

Palmer, Anna (*fl.* 1393–1394). *See under* Lollard women (*act. c.*1390–*c.*1520).

Palmer, Anthony (*bap.* 1613, *d.* 1693). *See under* Palmer, Anthony (*bap.* 1616, *d.* 1679).

Palmer, Anthony (*bap.* 1616, *d.* 1679), ejected minister, was baptized at Great Comberton, Worcestershire, on 27 October 1616, the only son of Anthony Palmer. Although the younger Anthony Palmer was married with at least two children, nothing is known of his mother, his wife, or his family life, although one of his works mentioned 'many dear Relations and Kindred' in Gloucestershire (Palmer, *Gospel New Creature*, sig. A2). He matriculated at Balliol College, Oxford, in 1634, graduated BA on 7 April 1638, was admitted fellow on 29 November 1640, and graduated MA on 7 December 1641, taking orders shortly afterwards. He took the solemn league and covenant in 1643 and signed the rigidly presbyterian 'Gloucester-shire ministers testimony' in 1648, but was always a committed Independent. He was presented to the rectory of Bourton on the Water, Gloucestershire, on 4 July 1646, resigning his fellowship and taking the engagement in 1649.

Palmer was an influential figure in Cromwellian Gloucestershire, as part of a closely knit group of Independent pastors, notably Carnslew Helme at Winchcombe, William Tray at Oddington, and John Wells at Tewkesbury. They were connected to several radical JPs who had risen through military service and membership of gathered churches. With these men, their congregations, and others, Palmer signed four petitions between 1653 and 1657. They successfully nominated the Gloucestershire members of the Barebone's Parliament, urged Cromwell to reject the crown in 1656, and generally upheld the cause of the gathered churches. As part of this group, Palmer was involved in two significant local controversies: a disputation in Winchcombe church against the Anglican Clement Barksdale in November 1653, and the attempted prosecution of the itinerant Ranter Richard Coppin for the doctrines he preached at Stow on the Wold in March 1654. He was also an assistant commissioner to the Gloucestershire expurgators in 1654 and attended the Savoy House conference in 1658. Of Palmer's six published works, *A Scripture-Rale to the Lord's Table* (1654) and *The Gospel New Creature* (1658) were the most important. The former expounded his belief in the need for the godly to separate voluntarily from the profane masses and preserve unmixed communion under the discipline of the minister, as in the primitive church. This, to Palmer, transcended differences of emphasis between presbyterian and Independent over matters such as appeals. After much prayer, his group agreed that attempting to enforce purity through the magistrate was derogatory to Christ; only mutual agreed subjection to him could bring people together in holy fellowship. In practice they depended on sympathetic JPs to enforce their views, which caused much discontent in their parishes.

Palmer was ill-treated by the cavalier-dominated militia in the spring of 1660. Like Helme, he abandoned his living and moved to London, where he lived at Little Moorfields and headed a mixed Baptist–Congregationalist church at Pinners' Hall. Both men remained committed opponents of the Restoration regime, which regarded them as Fifth Monarchists and kept them under sporadic surveillance. Palmer preached to the large gathering in Glovers' Hall on 10 March 1661, soon after Venner's rising, and was one of five main preachers at the large conventicle of All Hallows-the-Great in late 1661, where he prayed for the final fall of Babylon and urged the faithful to have no dealings with the restored Anglican clergy or with superstition of any kind. In November 1661 he and Helme were reportedly travelling around to 'blow up the Coales of rebellion' (PRO, SP 29/44/135) and he was named by some informers as one of the 'council of six' which masterminded the Tong Plot of late 1662. This—and, indeed, the existence of the plot—is uncertain, but Palmer did have connections with known plotters at various times. He was licensed as a Congregationalist at a house on London Bridge on 19 April 1672, died in London on 26 January 1679, and was buried in the New Bethlehem graveyard, Moorfields, London.

Another **Anthony Palmer** (*bap.* 1613, *d.* 1693), also an ejected minister, was baptized in Barnstaple, Devon, on 23 January 1613, the son of William Palmer of Barnstaple. He matriculated at Exeter College, Oxford, in 1631, graduated BA in 1635, and proceeded MA in 1637. He was presented to the sequestered rectory of Bratton Fleming, Devon, in 1645. He was a member of the Devon Association in 1655 and was ejected by October 1662, despite having previously protested his fidelity to the Thirty-Nine Articles; Edward Walker noted that he had administered communion only once in fourteen years in Bratton. He then returned to Barnstaple, where he was licensed as a presbyterian in April 1672. In 1690 he was recorded as having no fixed ministry. He was buried on 12 September 1693 in Barnstaple. ANDREW WARMINGTON

Sources *Calamy rev.* • A. Palmer, *A scripture-rale to the Lord's table* (1654) • W. Lamont, *Godly rule* (1969) • R. L. Greaves, *Deliver us from evil: the radical underground in Britain, 1660–1663* (1986) • J. Nicholls, *Originall letters and papers of state* (1743) • A. Palmer, *The gospel new creature* (1658) • [C. Barksdale], *The Winchcomb papers revived* (1675) • R. Coppin, *Truths testimony* (1655) • Bodl. Oxf., MS Rawl. A. 39, fol. 28 • B. S. Capp, *The Fifth Monarchy Men: a study in seventeenth-century English millenarianism* (1972) • H. J. [H. Jessey], *A relation of the imprisonings, plunderings* (1660) • A. Gordon, ed., *Freedom after ejection: a review (1690–1692) of presbyterian and congregational nonconformity in England and Wales* (1917)

Palmer, Anthony (*c.*1675–1749), colonial governor, was probably born in England but went at an early age to Barbados, where he made a considerable fortune as a merchant at Bridgetown. In 1707 he invested in land in Philadelphia and, after moving there, continued to prosper through his mercantile ventures.

In 1708 Palmer was summoned to the provincial council of Pennsylvania, a position that he held for the rest of his life. He became in 1718 a justice of the peace, and soon after a judge of the court of common pleas, and in 1720 one of the first masters in chancery. In 1747 he was president of the council, and in May, when Governor George Thomas resigned, he assumed the administration of the colony, which he governed for eighteen months through a period of great anxiety. Britain was then at war with France and Spain, whose privateers were making constant attacks along the Delaware coast. The provincial council, which was controlled by Quakers, declined to take measures of defence. Palmer induced his government to act independently, and was remarkably successful. About the same time he made treaties of friendship with several

American Indian peoples, especially those of the Six Nations.

In 1730 Palmer purchased Fairman Mansion at Philadelphia: he cut up part of the grounds into building plots, and became the founder of what is now the city's Kensington district. He lived here in some comfort until his death, in Philadelphia, in May 1749. His daughter Thomasine married the son and heir of Sir William Keith, a later governor of Pennsylvania.

C. A. HARRIS, *rev.* PHILIP CARTER

Sources Mass. Hist. Soc.
Wealth at death presumed wealthy

Palmer, Arthur (1841–1897), classical scholar and critic, was born at Guelph, Ontario, Canada, on 14 September 1841, the sixth child of the Ven. Arthur Palmer, archdeacon of Toronto, and his first wife, Hester Madeline Crawford. He was educated first by his father, then at the grammar school, Guelph, under the Revd Edward Stewart, leaving there after about four years in 1856. In 1858 he went to Cheltenham College, where he remained less than a year and had, as he used to say, 'just a sweet taste of English public school life'. He entered Trinity College, Dublin, in 1859, obtained a university scholarship in 1861, and in 1863 he graduated with senior moderatorship and gold medal in classics, as well as a junior moderatorship and silver medal in experimental and natural science. In 1867 he was elected a fellow, and in 1880 succeeded Professor Tyrrell in the chair of Latin. In 1888 he succeeded Judge Webb as public orator. He was MA (1867) and LittD of his own university, and honorary LLD of Glasgow (1890) and DCL of Oxford (1894). From 1867 to 1880 he was a college tutor, and as such exercised a marked influence on a large number of pupils. On 4 October 1879 he married Miss Frances Greene of Clevedon. They had two sons: Arthur (*b.* 1881) and Uther (*b.* 1892).

Palmer's contributions to classical scholarship were mainly emendations of Latin and Greek texts. He was most successful in his corrections of the works of Plautus, Catullus, Propertius, Horace, and Ovid, while he aided largely in constituting the text of the *editio princeps* of Bacchylides (1897), and made many excellent suggestions in the first edition of Herondas (1891). Specimens of some of his cleverest and most convincing emendations will be found in an obituary notice in *Hermathena*, 10 (1899). A. E. Housman gave a brief and characteristically two-edged assessment of his critical ability in a review in the *Classical Review* of Palmer's *Heroides*.

Palmer had special qualifications for the emendation of poetry. He had a wide knowledge of ancient and modern literature and a sensitive appreciation of style. His versions in *Kottabos* and *Dublin Translations* exhibit his skill in reproducing the idiom and spirit of Latin poetry. His most important editions were of Ovid's *Heroides* (1874; revised and enlarged 1898), Propertius (1880), Horace's *Satires* (1883), and Catullus (1896). He also contributed articles, chiefly critical, to *Hermathena*, the *Journal of Philology*, the *Classical Review*, and other periodicals.

Palmer was very attractive as a youth. He was a fair cricketer, and for some seasons he successfully captained a team of old university cricketers who assumed the name of Stoics. He was a good racket-player and golfer. As a conversationalist he was delightful, and he greatly enjoyed society until failing health forced him largely to forgo it. His health until middle age was excellent, but during the last ten years of his life he suffered much from disease of the bladder, and died of a cancerous growth in that region on 14 December 1897 at his home, Noel Lodge, Kingstown, co. Dublin.

R. Y. TYRRELL, *rev.* RICHARD SMAIL

Sources *The Times* (15 Dec 1897) · *Hermathena*, 10 (1899) · R. B. McDowell and D. A. Webb, *Trinity College, Dublin, 1592–1952: an academic history* (1982) · A. E. Housman, review of Arthur Palmer's *P. Ovidi Nasonis Heroides, with the Greek translation of Planudes*, *Classical Review*, 13 (1899), 172–8 · E. S. Skirving, ed., *Cheltenham College register, 1841–1927* (1928)
Wealth at death £4153 9*s.* 0*d.*: probate, 1 Feb 1898, *CGPLA Ire.*

Palmer, Sir Arthur Hunter (1819–1898), politician and pastoralist in Australia, was born on 28 December 1819 in Armagh, Ireland, the elder son of Lieutenant Arthur Palmer RN (*d.* 1836), and his second wife, Emily (1797–1826), the daughter of Robert Hunter of Dublin and Downpatrick. He was educated at Youghal grammar school and by private tutor in Dublin. In 1838 he sailed in the *City of Edinburgh* for Sydney, Australia, and, after a pastoral apprenticeship in the Illawarra district, in 1840 he became manager of the properties of Henry Dangar. He expanded the latter's interests and became general manager in 1856.

Backed by savings and experience, Palmer was ready to become a squatter in his own right. Queensland was opening up to European settlement, having in 1859 become a self-governing colony. In 1863 Palmer leased Beaufort run; later he acquired Cambridge Downs and shared ownership of Gin Gin station with the McIlwraith brothers. Through the 1890s he relinquished these interests, partly through resumptions, but especially because of foreclosures. On 8 June 1865 he married Cecilia Jessie (*d.* 31 Aug 1885), the daughter of Archibald Mosman, a merchant and pastoralist. They had three sons and two daughters.

Palmer's interest in political and civic matters began in 1865 when, in squatter tradition, he acted as magistrate. The next year he was elected to the legislative assembly as member for Port Curtis, and in 1867–8 he was colonial secretary and secretary for public works in the 'Pure Merino' administration of Robert Mackenzie. His political interests were mainly pastoral and regional.

In 1870 Palmer was surprised to be asked by Governor Blackall to form an administration, and in April that year, taking the offices of colonial secretary and premier, he put together a cohesive ministry. With colonial finances shaky, he initially pursued retrenchment and consolidation. By 1872, however, despite his squatter background, he was often proving as liberal as his opponents, and embarking upon progressive policies, notably manhood suffrage after six months' residence and single-member electorates. Palmer's political interests were broadening, and he sought to govern in the interests of all sectors and parts of the colony. In 1873, while premier, he introduced a private bill on state education, propounding the principles of free (through to university), compulsory, and secular education, with state funding going only to state schools. Thereby he lost the support of most conservatives, and he failed to regain the premiership after the subsequent election.

Palmer's political principles were described by a contemporary as those of 'a radical of the Old Cobbett school' (W. Coote). Between 1874 and 1878 Palmer led the opposition, but his role as conservative leader was increasingly being assumed by Thomas McIlwraith. Palmer was elected for North Brisbane in 1878, and served in McIlwraith's ministry as colonial secretary and secretary for public instruction (1879–81). Appointed KCMG in 1881, he transferred to the legislative council that year and became president; twice he was administrator in the absence of the governor, and in 1893 he was appointed the first lieutenant-governor of Queensland.

The interests of Palmer and McIlwraith were intermeshed—through marriage, when McIlwraith married Palmer's wife's sister in 1879, and through land-holding and financial matters. In 1879 McIlwraith transferred his directorship of the Queensland National Bank to Palmer. Both were also involved in two land finance companies. This association implicated Palmer in financial scandals in the 1880s and 1890s, but he was cleared of any impropriety. Nevertheless, the financial collapse that settled upon Queensland (and the Queensland National Bank) in the early 1890s took its toll on him.

Palmer appeared to his contemporaries as bluff, brusque, arrogant—'the great Mogul'; often the bully, he displayed a violent temper. Seen as a capable administrator, he behaved as the tory patrician. He died at his home, Easton Gray, Toowong, Brisbane, on 20 March 1898, and was buried quietly in the Toowong cemetery on the following day. W. Ross Johnston

Sources J. X. Jobson, 'A biography of Sir Arthur Hunter Palmer', BA diss., University of Queensland, 1960 • *AusDB* • *Queensland parliamentary debates* (1866–98) • *Votes and proceedings*, Queensland Legislative Assembly (1866–81) • W. Coote, *The Week* (26 May 1877) • *Brisbane Courier* (19 March 1898) • *Brisbane Courier* (21 March 1898) • *Brisbane Courier* (22 March 1898) • C. A. Bernays, *Queensland politics during sixty years, 1859–1919* [1919] • D. B. Waterson, *A biographical register of the Queensland parliament, 1860–1929* (1972) • H. Holthouse, *Looking back: the first 150 years of Queensland schools* (1975) • *DNB*

Archives State Library of Queensland, South Brisbane, John Oxley Library, McIlwraith MSS

Likenesses photographs, State Library of Queensland, Brisbane, John Oxley Library

Wealth at death A$23,900—in Australia: *AusDB*

Palmer, Sir Arthur Power (1840–1904), army officer, was born on 25 June 1840 at Kurubul, India, the son of Captain Nicholas Power Palmer of the 54th Bengal native infantry, and his wife, Rebecca Carter, daughter of Charles Barrett of Dungarvan, co. Waterford. His father was killed on the retreat from Kabul in 1841, and in 1849 his mother married as her second husband Morgan Crofton, son of Captain Morgan Crofton RN, of co. Roscommon. Educated at Cheltenham College (1852–6), Palmer entered the Indian army on 20 February 1857 as ensign in the 5th Bengal native infantry. He served throughout the uprisings of 1857–9, raising a regiment of Sikhs 600 strong for service in Oudh in March 1858. He received his commission as lieutenant on 30 April 1858, and joined Hodson's horse at Lucknow in the following June. At the actions of Nawabganj and Bara Banki his horse was killed under him, and he was present at minor actions (during one of which he was wounded) in the Oudh campaign until its conclusion on the Nepal frontier, and was mentioned in dispatches.

In 1861 Palmer was transferred to the Bengal staff corps, and served in the campaign on the north-west frontier in 1863–4, being present in the action with the Mohmands near Shabkadar. He served as adjutant to the 10th Bengal lancers in the Abyssinian expedition of 1868, and his services were favourably noticed by Napier. He had married, in 1867, Helen Aylmer (*d.* 1896), daughter of Aylmer Harris; his second wife, whom he married in 1898, was Constance Gabrielle Richardson (*d.* 1912), daughter of Godfrey Shaw and widow of Walter Milton Roberts.

Palmer acted as aide-de-camp to General Stafford in the Duffla expedition of 1874–5, and was mentioned in dispatches. In 1876–7 he was on special duty with the Dutch troops in Achin, and fought in several actions in the Dutch war against native forces. He was mentioned in dispatches and received the Dutch cross with two clasps from the Netherlands government. He had been promoted captain in 1869, and served in the Second Anglo-Afghan War (1878–80), when he acted as assistant adjutant and quartermaster-general to the Kurram field force. In the attack on the Paiwar Pass (2 December 1878) Palmer rendered good service by making a feint on the right of the Afghan position, and in January 1879 he accompanied the expedition into the Khost valley. He was mentioned in dispatches, and was given the brevet of lieutenant-colonel on 12 November 1879. From 1880 to 1885 he was assistant adjutant-general in Bengal, becoming colonel in 1883. Two years later he took part as commander of the 9th Bengal cavalry in the expedition to Suakin, and showed great dash and energy throughout the campaign. For his share in the raid on Thakul (6 May 1885) he was mentioned in dispatches. He was made a CB on 25 August 1885.

During the campaign in Burma in 1892–3 Palmer commanded the force operating in the northern Chin hills. He received the thanks of the government of India, was mentioned in dispatches and government orders, and on 8 May 1894 was made KCB. He became major-general in 1893 and lieutenant-general in 1897. In 1897–8 he served in the Tirah campaign as general officer on the line of communications, and subsequently commanded the 2nd division at the action of Chagru Kotal. He commanded the Punjab frontier force from 1898 to 1900, being promoted general in 1899. On the death of Sir William Lockhart, he was appointed provisional commander-in-chief in India, and member of the executive council (19 March 1900).

In selecting regiments and commanders for service in South Africa and China in 1900 Palmer showed high administrative capacity, but the provisional nature of his appointment, and a somewhat accommodating character, hardly equipped him to deal with as masterful a viceroy as Curzon. According to his adjutant-general, Smith-Dorrien, Curzon 'snubbed him on every possible occasion', and 'the tone of the minutes on his recommendations was hurtful and trying' (Mason, 395). Palmer was succeeded by Kitchener in 1902. He was made GCIE in 1901, and GCB in 1903. He died at his home, 15 Buckingham Palace Gardens, Westminster, on 28 February 1904, after an operation for appendicitis, and was buried in Brompton cemetery. He was survived by his second wife and two daughters.

H. M. VIBART, *rev.* JAMES LUNT

Sources *The Times* (29 Feb 1904) • A. A. Hunter, ed., *Cheltenham College register, 1841–1910* (1911) • *The Cheltonian*, 2nd ser., 30 (1904), 52–3 • Lord Roberts [F. S. Roberts], *Forty-one years in India*, 2 vols. (1897) • [S. P. Oliver], *The Second Afghan War, 1878–80; abridged official account*, rev. F. G. Cardew (1908) • R. H. Vetch, *Life of Sir Gerald Graham* (1901) • H. D. Hutchinson, *The campaign in Tirah, 1897–1898: an account of the expedition against the Orakzais and Afridis* (1898), 62 • *Hart's Army List* • P. Mason, *A matter of honour: an account of the Indian army, its officers and men* (1974) • H. Smith-Dorrien, *Memoirs of fifty-eight years service* (1925) • *WWW, 1897–1915*

Wealth at death £2492 2*s*. 3*d*.: probate, 7 May 1904, *CGPLA Eng. & Wales*

Palmer [*née* Villiers], **Barbara, countess of Castlemaine and *suo jure* duchess of Cleveland** (*bap.* **1640**, *d.* **1709**), royal mistress, was baptized at St Margaret's, Westminster, on 27 November 1640, the only child of William Villiers, second Viscount Grandison (1614–1643), and his wife, Mary (*c*.1623–1672), daughter and coheir of Paul Bayning, first Viscount Bayning, a wealthy merchant. Grandison was one of the influential Villiers family, his father being half-brother to George *Villiers, first duke of Buckingham. He himself was a royalist colonel who was seriously wounded at the siege of Bristol in July 1643 and died some two months later, on 30 September 1643. His daughter later put up a monument to him in Christ Church Cathedral, Oxford. Mary Bayning was twice married again: in 1648 to Grandison's cousin, Charles Villiers, second earl of Anglesey, who died in 1661; and then to Arthur Gorges of Chelsea, Middlesex.

Early life, 1640–1660 Barbara Villiers was living in London when she became the mistress of Philip *Stanhope, second earl of Chesterfield (1633–1714) in 1656 or 1657. In 1657 she wrote him arch, lively letters arranging several assignations:

> My freind [Lady Ann Hamilton] and I are just now abed together a contriving how to have your company this afternoune. If you deserve this favour, you will come and seek us at Ludgate Hill, about three a clock, at Butler's shop

and 'the joy I have of being with you the last night, has made me doe nothing but dream of you' (Steinman, 11–13). It was an affair which she continued after marrying, on 14 April 1659, Roger *Palmer (1634–1705), royalist and lawyer, second son of Sir James Palmer of Dorney Court, Buckinghamshire, at St Gregory by Paul, London. Palmer seems to have soon become aware of the situation as Barbara wrote again to Chesterfield after her marriage, 'Since

Barbara Palmer, countess of Castlemaine and *suo jure* duchess of Cleveland (*bap.* **1640**, *d.* **1709**), studio of Sir Peter Lely, *c*.1665–75 [as the Madonna]

I saw you, I have been at home, and I find the mounser [monsieur, Roger Palmer] in a very ill humer, for he sayes that he is resolved never to bring mee to town again and that nobody shall see me when I am in the country' (Steinman, 16). She advised Chesterfield to put off visiting her that day but the affair probably continued until January 1660 when Chesterfield, having killed a man in a duel, went to France. Little trace remains of Barbara's whereabouts immediately before the Restoration and it is unclear how or where she met *Charles II (1630–1685): the king acknowledged her first daughter, Anne, born on 25 February 1661, a birth date which suggests that their affair must have begun within two or three weeks of his arrival in London on 29 May 1660, but leaves open the question of whether they had in fact met before Charles's return to England.

The king's mistress, 1660–1670 By July 1660 the Palmers were living in King Street, just across from the privy garden of Whitehall Palace, when one evening the diarist Samuel Pepys stood listening to the music he could hear from the house, an entertainment put on for the king and his brothers James, duke of York, and Henry, duke of Gloucester, by 'Madam Palmer'. According to Pepys's information the royal brothers had 'a fancy to make her husband a cuckold' (Pepys, 1.199), but in fact Barbara was already the king's mistress, something Pepys certainly knew by October 1661 when Charles determined to give

Barbara a title. The king instructed a grant to be prepared making Roger Palmer Baron Limerick and earl of Castlemaine with a remainder limited to his heirs male by Barbara, 'the reason whereof everybody knows' commented Pepys (ibid., 2.229). Barbara thus became countess of Castlemaine on 11 December 1661. She was then pregnant with her first son with the king, baptized Charles on 18 June 1662 in a ceremony attended by the king [*see* Fitzroy, Charles, second duke of Cleveland and first duke of Southampton]. In July, Pepys heard that the earl of Castlemaine had had the boy baptized in a Catholic ceremony, causing a furious row with his wife, who left the house and went to her uncle Colonel Villiers at Richmond Palace. Although she soon returned, thenceforward they lived separate lives. A bond indemnifying the earl of Castlemaine for any debts, up to £10,000, contracted by Barbara was signed by her uncle George Villiers, third Viscount Grandison, and James *Howard, earl of Suffolk, her uncle by marriage, in 1662 and effectively signals the couple's separation. Charles II's new queen, Catherine of Braganza, arrived in England in May 1662, and Castlemaine appeared determined to maintain her position as the king's acknowledged mistress and to gain an ascendancy over Catherine. Her proposed appointment as a lady of the bedchamber to Catherine (which had first been reported in March 1662), caused great conflict in the court, Catherine initially refusing to accept Castlemaine and the courtiers dividing over the issue. However, Charles did not waver in supporting his mistress, writing to his chancellor, the earl of Clarendon, that 'whosoever I finde to be my Lady Castlemaine's enemy in this matter, I do promise upon my word, to be his enemy as long as I live' (Wynne, 32). Catherine's resistance was eventually overcome and Castlemaine was victorious, being appointed along with the rest of the ladies of the bedchamber on 1 June 1663. Castlemaine often appeared at court events, sometimes taking a leading part, as at a ball held on 31 December 1662, when she appeared in the first dance partnered by the duke of Monmouth, and was placed third in line after the king and queen and the duke and duchess of York. Castlemaine also formed a mutually beneficial alliance with the court artist Sir Peter Lely: in the 1660s he painted a series of portraits of her in the guise of Magdalen, Madonna, a 'Sultana', and St Catherine, which allude to her relationship with the king and may be seen as part of her challenge to the queen. It was in part through Lely's many and influential portraits of her that she established her image as a great court beauty and the king's accepted mistress, and the great number of copies of Castlemaine's portraits attest to her success in this programme of self-promotion. The portraits suggest that she had dark, almost black, hair and blue eyes, confirming the description of her in Mme d'Aulnoy's *Memoirs of the Court of England* (p. 150).

As early as January 1663 there were rumours that Castlemaine was having an affair with the courtier Henry *Jermyn (*bap.* 1636, *d.* 1708). However, she did not lose her position as royal mistress and indeed by May 1663 had moved into apartments in Whitehall situated over Holbein's Gatehouse, where Charles frequently dined and where courtiers sought an invitation. Castlemaine's main rival for the king's affections in the 1660s was not the queen but a maid of honour, Frances Stuart, later duchess of Richmond. Early in 1663 Charles began to show an interest in Frances: his insistence that she be allowed entry to Castlemaine's apartments when he was there caused Castlemaine to withdraw from court in July. She was soon persuaded to return, and it was reported that she 'commands the King as much as ever, and hath and doth what she will' (Pepys, 4.238). Her second son, Henry *Fitzroy, first duke of Grafton, was born on 20 September 1663. There may have been some doubt over his parentage as he was not at first acknowledged by the king when further titles were given to Castlemaine in 1670.

In December 1663 Castlemaine's conversion to Roman Catholicism was made public. Contemporaries speculated that her motives were not genuine, but some years later Lorenzo Magalotti was told that it was prompted by a fear of death brought on by a dangerous illness, and indeed Castlemaine remained a Catholic for the rest of her life. The contradictory rumours concerning Castlemaine's credit with the king continued. In February 1664 she made her presence felt at the theatre by moving from her box to go and sit between the king and the duke of York; at least one observer thought that 'she did it only to show the world that she is not out of favour yet as was believed' (Pepys, 5.33). Indeed, Charles dined frequently with Barbara, and in September she gave a magnificent dinner for the French ambassador and his wife, where it was remarked that Charles behaved more as a host than a guest (Comminges to Lionne, 15 Sept 1664, PRO, PRO 31/3/113, fol. 300). Barbara's daughter Charlotte was born on 5 September 1664, and her last child with the king, a son, George *Fitzroy, duke of Northumberland, on 28 December 1665 at Oxford. Her children with the king were one of her great advantages over the childless queen: Charles was said to be 'mighty kind to his bastard children' visiting them often in her apartments (Pepys, 5.164). Castlemaine's favour with the king was often used on behalf of others: she influenced the appointment of her great-uncle, Henry Glenham, as bishop of St Asaph in February 1667, and in the same year Sir Robert Paston wrote to Castlemaine thanking her for interceding with the king over a grant to himself and 'that I must with silence and admiration consider a bounty in you beyond all things of example' (Wynne, 85). Paston's praise of Barbara may have been more than usually extravagant as it seems he owed her money for her intercession but was unable (or unwilling) to pay.

From 1667 Castlemaine's pre-eminence gradually diminished. Her name was again associated with Henry Jermyn in 1667, and in July that year a report circulated that she was pregnant and insisting that the king own the child 'or she will bring it into Whitehall gallery and dash the brains of it out before the King's face' (Pepys, 7.355). The king's refusal led to another tactical withdrawal from court by Castlemaine, whereupon Charles soon felt compelled to visit her and a reconciliation was effected; nothing more is heard of the pregnancy. On the other hand the king's attraction for Frances Stuart survived her marriage with the duke of Richmond and by the end of 1667 her imminent return to Whitehall was thought likely to cause conflict between the factions of the two women.

Then in January 1668 the king's affair with the actress Mary Davis was public knowledge and said to be discomforting Castlemaine. In May that year Castlemaine moved into Berkshire House, opposite St James's Palace and purchased for her by the king for £4000, but she confounded expectations that she would fade into the background. In February 1668 she acted in a court production of Corneille's *Horace*, and wore some of the crown jewels, 'far outshining the queen' (Evelyn, 3.505). Later that year she made an appearance at the queen's birthday ball 'so glorious in jewells that she was the wonder of all who saw her' (newsletter, 18 Nov 1668, BL, Add. MS 36916, fol. 119). In 1668–9 the king continued to make frequent visits and was especially assiduous when she fell ill in October 1669. Castlemaine had apparently made the transition from royal mistress to close friend. Her lovers were said to include the rope-dancer Jacob *Hall (*fl.* 1662–1681) about 1667, the actor Charles *Hart (*bap.* 1625, *d.* 1683) the next year, the playwright William *Wycherley (*bap.* 1641, *d.* 1716) in 1671, and John *Churchill, later duke of Marlborough (1650–1722)—apparently giving the last a substantial sum of money—in 1671–5.

During the first decade of the Restoration, Castlemaine was involved in the factions which formed around the king's ministers. Those she helped into high office included Henry Bennet, earl of Arlington, and Charles Berkeley, earl of Falmouth, who were appointed secretary of state and keeper of the privy purse respectively in 1662. Berkeley paid Castlemaine money from the king's privy purse and when he was killed in 1665 in the Second Anglo-Dutch War she was anxious to promote Baptist May to the post. Although the king favoured another for the position Castlemaine used her usual tactic of withdrawing from court and eventually prevailed. On the other hand, the earls of Clarendon and Southampton, the king's lord chancellor and lord treasurer, disapproved of Castlemaine and obstructed all official grants to her. The hostility was reciprocated: on one occasion in September 1662 Castlemaine denounced Clarendon in public and hoped she would see his head on a stake outside Westminster. Her apartments came to be frequented by Clarendon's enemies and his downfall in 1667 was widely reported to have been 'certainly designed in my Lady Castlemaine's chamber' (Pepys, 8.404). In Bishop Burnet's assessment 'the mistress [Castlemaine] and the whole bedchamber were perpetually railing at him [Clarendon]. This by a sort of infection possessed the King' (*Burnet's History*, 1.369–71). The king clearly resented Clarendon's hostility towards Castlemaine and on one occasion rebuked him for his wife's lack of courtesy in refusing to visit Castlemaine, whereupon Clarendon seized the opportunity to expostulate on 'the lady' and those who courted her favour. Castlemaine did not hide her satisfaction when the end came: Clarendon wrote that as he was leaving Whitehall on 25 August he saw Castlemaine, Arlington, and Bab May looking 'out of her open window with great gaiety and triumph, which all people observed' (*Life of … Clarendon*, 2.304–7).

Castlemaine had a changeable relationship with her kinsman, George *Villiers, duke of Buckingham. In 1666 they had a falling out (of unknown motivation), which greatly displeased the king. In July 1667, however, when Buckingham was in the Tower for his behaviour during the last parliamentary session, Castlemaine was reported to have:

> so far solicited for him, that the King and she are quite fallen out; he comes not to her nor hath for some three or four days, and parted with very foul words, the King calling her a whore, and a jade. (Pepys, 8.331, 334)

It seemed doubtful that Buckingham would be freed but, in fact, a few days later he was at liberty. Pepys speculated that Castlemaine 'hath at last overcome the King' (Pepys, 8.342), and it was Castlemaine who brought Buckingham to the king in her apartments where they were formally reconciled. This temporary alliance may have been prompted because both Castlemaine and Buckingham desired Clarendon's ruin. The situation altered during the course of 1668, however, when James, duke of York, returned to favour. Previously relations between Castlemaine and the duke and duchess of York had been distant but in 1666 there were rumours that Castlemaine was attempting a rapprochement with James by encouraging the affair of the duke and Margaret, Lady Denham. Certainly by April 1668 Castlemaine had joined the rush to court James, beginning by ingratiating herself with Anne, duchess of York, whom she had not seen for six months. At the same time Pepys wrote that 'the King and the Duke of York and Duchess and my Lady Castlemaine are now all agreed in a strict league' (Pepys, 9.153).

This new alliance may have contributed to Buckingham's and Castlemaine's next disagreement. Late in 1668 Castlemaine, in alliance with the duchess of York, used her influence to block an attempt by Buckingham and Lord Arlington to replace the duchess's brother, Henry Hyde, Lord Cornbury, as the queen's lord chamberlain with another man. Buckingham and Arlington consequently engaged Elizabeth, Lady Harvey, in an attempt to destroy Castlemaine's credit with the king. Lady Harvey, who was well known for her wit and involved in many court intrigues, took every opportunity to ridicule Castlemaine's conduct in the king's hearing. Castlemaine retaliated and eventually the campaign was carried to the stage in January 1669 when it appears that Castlemaine arranged for an actress to caricature Lady Harvey during a performance of Ben Jonson's *Cataline*, whereupon the actress was imprisoned but soon released by Castlemaine's influence. The episode culminated in victory for Castlemaine: Lady Harvey retired from the fray while Buckingham presented himself at Castlemaine's house and a reconciliation was effected. Castlemaine's friendship with the duke and duchess of York continued: she was seen enjoying herself at a party arranged by the royal couple in March 1669 and in May she told the French ambassador's wife that it was she who had achieved the recent reconciliation between the duke and the king. Other courtiers agreed that it was her influence. Castlemaine also found a new ally in Roger Boyle, earl of Orrery, whom she hoped would be useful against Arlington, and her feud with Buckingham soon recommenced.

Castlemaine was also courted by foreign ambassadors. At first she favoured the Spanish, and gave a dinner in honour of the Spanish ambassador in June 1665 in return for one given for her. However, in 1667 the intrigues of the Spanish in attempting to interest Charles in another woman turned Castlemaine towards the French, and she indicated to the French ambassador her willingness to work for the French interest. In 1669 when negotiations for an Anglo-French treaty were under way this offer was taken up, and Castlemaine began to pass information to Ambassador de Croissy concerning the attitudes of the king and his ministers, in particular denouncing Buckingham and Arlington as ill-intentioned. She and the ambassador gave dinners in honour of each other and a substantial gift was presented to Castlemaine from Louis XIV. De Croissy reported that Castlemaine was sincere in wishing to do everything in her power to contribute to the success of Anglo-French negotiations; however, in the event the French drew back from further involving her in their negotiations for fear of annoying Arlington, and how much, if anything, she knew of the secret treaty of Dover with the French is unclear. Castlemaine attended the state visit of the king's sister Henriette-Anne at Dover in 1670, when the treaty was secretly signed, a newsletter writer specifically noting the jewel worth £2500 given by Castlemaine to Henriette-Anne (newsletters, 7 May, 25 June, BL, Add. MS 36916, fols. 180, 185).

Declining influence, 1670–1676 In 1670 Castlemaine was given a series of grants by the king. In January she was granted the reversion of the office of keeper of Hampton Court, which seems to have come into her possession almost immediately. On 3 August she was created duchess of Cleveland, countess of Southampton, and Baroness Nonsuch, with remainders to her sons Charles and George (the latter being described as her second son, no mention being made of Henry). She was also granted substantial interests in land including Nonsuch Palace and its surrounding grounds of 1701 acres in July 1670. In 1673 a grant of Phoenix Park in Dublin, a place traditionally used for the benefit of the lord lieutenant of Ireland, was resisted by the then lord lieutenant, Arthur Capel, earl of Essex, who enlisted several senior courtiers on his side and eventually persuaded her to accept other lands of equivalent value. His subsequent delays in finding such lands make it uncertain whether she ever enjoyed the benefit of this grant. In addition to her palace apartments and Berkshire House (renamed Cleveland House), Castlemaine was given several substantial pensions for life by the king, usually paid to her trustees, her uncles George, Viscount Grandison, and Colonel Edward Villiers. Beginning with £1000 per annum from the Post Office revenues granted in May 1667, which was increased to £4700 per annum from January 1669, the pensions gradually increased until they reached, in theory, some £12,000 per annum from July 1674. However, Castlemaine's declining status at court after 1670 undoubtedly affected her ability to collect her pensions and by 1684 she was owed some £23,000. Such financial difficulties as this caused were, however, relieved on occasion by supplementary gifts of money.

The arrival in 1670 of Louise de Kéroualle, duchess of Portsmouth, and her establishment as the leading royal mistress in 1671–2 marked the end of Cleveland's 'reign', although she did not entirely lose her influence. She was present at the court masque of February 1671 and in spring that year it was reported that 'the great duchess of Cleveland goes about the streets with eight horses in her coach, the streets and balconies and windows full of people to admire her' (*CSP dom., 1671*, 271). In February 1672 there was a disturbance at court to do with Cleveland, perhaps the revelation of her pregnancy, probably to John Churchill, and the king's visits decreased. The child, Barbara, was born on 16 July 1672, and was never acknowledged by the king. However, Cleveland retained some semblance of cordial relations with the king and her children with him helped maintain her importance at court. In July 1672 Cleveland's son Henry was acknowledged, being given the title of earl of Euston and the surname Fitzroy. (Cleveland's other children also took this surname at the same time.) The title was in anticipation of the marriage of Henry and Arlington's daughter, Isabella, which took place on 1 August 1672 with much magnificence. A few days later Cleveland invited many courtiers to a dance where one of the guests was Sir Robert Southwell, who wrote that, 'as her grace is very obliging, so the whole company are very forward in their respects' (*CSP dom., 1672*, 429, 463). Cleveland's children were then granted arms signifying their royal connection: her sons in December 1672, and her first two daughters the following February.

Cleveland's daughter Charlotte was much sought after by courtiers and in May 1674 the successful suitor was Edward Lee, created earl of Lichfield in honour of the marriage, and a connection by marriage of the earl of Danby, whom Cleveland wished to court due to his influential position as lord treasurer. At the same time Cleveland's first daughter, Anne, was married to her relative Thomas Lennard, created earl of Sussex. The French ambassador noticed that Cleveland appeared much in favour with Charles at Newmarket in October 1672, and in September 1674 it was reported that when Cleveland had been at Oxford to arrange for the education of her son Charles, on the morning she left, 'she sate at least one hour in her coach that everybody might see her' (Wynne, 44–5). On 10 September 1675 her eldest son, Charles, was created duke of Southampton; the following day his brother Henry was made duke of Grafton, while Cleveland's third son, George, was created earl of Northumberland on 1 October 1674, his title being elevated to duke of Northumberland on 6 April 1683.

Cleveland also continued to be active in managing the king's patronage. This could be for straightforward financial benefit, as in the case of Benjamin Mildmay, who was said to have paid both Cleveland and the duke of Buckingham to promote his claim to a barony. In a more complex case, in 1671 Cleveland intervened to help Thomas Wood become bishop of Lichfield in return for Wood's help in the marriage of his niece to Cleveland's eldest son. Wood was the brother of the extremely wealthy Sir Henry Wood, who died on 25 May 1671 having signed a contract arranging for the marriage of his seven-year-old daughter and sole heir, Mary, to Charles Fitzroy. Mary at first went to live with her aunt Lady Chester but before long was living with Cleveland who, when challenged, apparently returned the haughty reply that 'The Dutchess hath her and will keep her, and that the Dutchess wonder that so inconsiderable a person as the Lady Chester will contend with a person of her Quality' ('The case of Mrs Mary Wood', BL, Harley MS 5277, fols. 22–3). In the subsequent lawsuits over the marriage and control of the Wood estates it was distinctly to Cleveland's advantage to have one of that family obliged to her.

Another who benefited from Cleveland's patronage was Sir John Trevor, whom she employed to advise her on her land interests, and who was with her help returned as an MP in 1673. It was clear, however, that Cleveland's credit was slowly fading: by 1673 she had resigned her place in the queen's bedchamber, in 1674 she was fined for recusancy, in 1675 the duchess of Portsmouth's son was created a duke before her own sons, and then, finding herself in some financial difficulties, she decided to go to France for two years in order to economize. She left in March 1676, and did not return permanently until 1682.

Parisian intrigues, 1678–1682 Cleveland took her daughters with her to be educated in the English convent of the Order of the Conception in Paris, to which she donated £1000 for new buildings. In 1678 she made a brief but dramatic re-entry into court politics, two long letters by her to the king giving an unusual insight into her life at this time. In France she had established an amicable relationship with the English ambassador there, Ralph Montagu (1638?–1709), later duke of Montagu, and may even have had an affair with him. She also apparently had an affair with Alexis-Henri de Châtillon (1652 NS – 1737 NS) which Montagu betrayed to the king, intercepting some of her love letters and sending them to Charles. Moreover while Cleveland was visiting England in April–June 1678, Montagu evidently began an affair with her daughter Lady Sussex. Cleveland became aware of this double betrayal and some days after her return to Paris she wrote a letter to Charles which exposed the ambassador to certain ruin. Without actually admitting an affair with Châtillon, she wrote:

> Now all I have to say for myself is that you know, as to love, one is not mistress of one's self, and that you ought not to be offended with me, since all things of this nature is at an end with you and I; so that I could do you no prejudice.

She then launched into details of Montagu's conversations with her when he had

> several times told me that in his heart he despised you and your brother; and that for his part he wished with all his heart that the Parliament would send you both to travel; for you were a dull governable fool and the Duke a wilful fool.

She reported that Montagu planned to ensnare the king with a certain fortune-teller whom he would control and in whom, he claimed, Charles set great store. Montagu was confident he could soon rise to be lord treasurer and had said, 'and for the King, I will find a way to furnish him so easily with money for his pocket and his wenches that we will quickly out Bab May and lead the King by the nose'. Cleveland had turned down the invitation to join with Montagu in ruining the current lord treasurer and the duchess of Portsmouth, and told him, 'the Devil was not more designing than he was'. Cleveland swore to the king that this was all true and that she was not motivated to write by malice, indeed, 'I would not have been so base as to have informed against him for what he said before me had he not provoked me to it'. She begged for the king's commands on the situation with their daughter and after yet more revelations of Montagu's appalling behaviour, promised that her conduct would be 'such as that you nor nobody shall have occasion to blame me', while also reminding Charles that the last time he had seen her, he had said, 'Madam, all that I ask of you … is live so for the future as to make the least noise you can, and I care not who you love'. Charles's reply to this letter was evidently all that Cleveland hoped for, but she was forced to tell him that his commands had had little effect on Lady Sussex, who was still being manipulated by the shameless Montagu (Andrews, 201–6). The result was that Montagu, afraid of what Cleveland might have revealed, returned to England without leave and attempted to see the king but Cleveland having 'done his errand', Charles cut off his explanations, removed him from his posts and banished him from court (*Ormonde MSS*, new ser., 4.441).

Both her finances and her religion kept Cleveland in France, proclamations against Catholics during the Popish Plot crisis giving rise to fears that she would be prevented from going near Whitehall and indeed would be pressured to reconvert to protestantism. Evidently Cleveland received reassurances that she would be protected as she did in fact make another visit to England in 1679 for some four months, undoubtedly to request some money, but also to try and break off the match between her son Henry and Isabella Bennet in favour of a match with the heiress Elizabeth Percy, countess of Northumberland, and to ask for a promise of her aunt's place as first lady of the bedchamber and groomess of the stole, the last two projects being unsuccessful.

Declining years, 1682–1709 After returning to England in 1682 Cleveland was little regarded by the court in the face of Portsmouth's ascendancy, and it was reported that the king delayed for some time in seeing her. About 1684 she began an affair with the actor Cardell *Goodman (*b.* 1653), but, in what may have been a conspiracy by Cleveland's sons to remove him from her presence, he was convicted of conspiring to poison the dukes of Grafton and Northumberland and fined £1000 in September 1684. Cleveland however, continued to see Goodman for some time: it was rumoured that she had a son by him in 1686 (although this cannot be confirmed as nothing more is heard of the child), and he witnessed a deed involving some of her property in 1687. Their affair probably finished about 1690 and had certainly ended by 1696 when he was exposed as a Jacobite conspirator and went into exile. Little more is heard of Cleveland until 25 November 1705 when Robert, or Beau, *Feilding (1650/51–1712), a former army captain, involved her in a bigamous marriage. Feilding had recently married one Mary Wadsworth thinking she was a rich widow named Mrs Deleau. Unaware that he had been tricked he went on to marry the duchess of Cleveland who was then living in Bond Street. Living with her was her granddaughter Charlotte Calvert (*née* Lee) who had taken refuge from an unhappy marriage, and who soon began an affair with Feilding and consequently moved out of Cleveland's house in March 1706. The bigamy was eventually discovered in June 1706 when Mary Wadsworth and her accomplice Mrs Villars went to Cleveland and told her the story. On being confronted Feilding attacked the duchess and threatened her with a gun until she managed to call for help out of a window, whereupon the watch arrived and Feilding was arrested. Cleveland exacted revenge by suing Feilding for adultery at the Old Bailey where she had his obscene love letters to Mary Wadsworth read out in court and subsequently published. The marriage was annulled in May 1707. Cleveland lived her last years in Chiswick and died there of a dropsy on 9 October 1709; she was buried in Chiswick parish church four days later. Her will, written on 11 August 1709 and proved the day after her death, constituted her grandson Charles, duke of Grafton, as her principal heir and sole executor.

As the first acknowledged royal mistress in Britain for some centuries, Cleveland's potential influence over the king was of prime concern to Restoration courtiers, and her great beauty, forceful personality, and genius for self-promotion made her both admired and feared. Contemporary comment concentrated on condemning her flagrant affairs and extravagant expenditure: in Bishop Burnet's disapproving opinion she was a 'woman of great beauty but most enormously vicious and ravenous; foolish but imperious' (*Burnet's History*, 1.132), while another observer wrote, 'the prodigious amount of money dissipated by this woman, who has no moderation or limit in her desires, passes all bounds and exceeds all belief' (*Lorenzo Magalotti*, 72). The author Mary Delariviere Manley, who had lived with Cleveland for a short time in the 1690s, characterized her in a scandal novel, *The New Atalantis*, as 'querilous, fierce, loquacious, excessively fond, or infamously rude … The extreames of prodigality and covetousness; of love and hatred; of dotage and aversion were joyn'd together in Hilaria's [Cleveland's] soul' (Steinman, 192). Indeed, Cleveland's relationship with Charles II often threatened to dissolve under the strain of their respective infidelities, yet she maintained her position for some ten years, in the process establishing the position of royal mistress as one of political significance and acquiring great wealth and high honours for her children.

S. M. Wynne

Sources G. Steinman, *A memoir of Barbara, duchess of Cleveland* (privately printed, Oxford, 1871); addenda (1874); 2nd addenda (1878) • E. Hamilton, *The illustrious lady: a biography of Barbara Villiers, countess of Castlemaine and duchess of Cleveland* (1980) • S. Wynne, 'The mistresses of Charles II and Restoration court politics, 1660–1685', PhD diss., U. Cam., 1997 • Pepys, *Diary* • A. M. Burke, ed., *Memorials of St Margaret's Church, Westminster* (1914) • L. Stone, *Uncertain unions and broken lives: marriage and divorce in England, 1660–1857* (1995) • J. M. Marciari-Alexander, 'Self-fashioning and portraits of women at the Restoration court: the case of Peter Lely and Barbara Villiers, countess of Castlemaine, 1660–1668', PhD diss., Yale U., 1999 • GEC, *Peerage* • Highfill, Burnim & Langhans, *BDA*, vols. 6–7 • *DNB* • F.-A. A. de La Chenaye-Desbois, *Dictionnaire de la noblesse: contenant les généalogies, l'histoire et la chronologie de familles nobles de la France*, 3rd edn, 5 (Paris, 1864) • A. Andrews, *The royal whore: Barbara Villiers, countess of Castlemaine* (1971) • A. Hamilton, *Memoirs of the comte de Gramont*, trans. P. Quennell (1930) • *Bishop Burnet's History of his own time*, another edn, 1 (1753) • *Lorenzo Magalotti at the court of Charles II: his Relazione d'Inghilterra of 1668*, ed. and trans. W. E. K. Middleton (1980) • Evelyn, *Diary*, vol. 3 • *The life of Edward, earl of Clarendon … written by himself*, 2 vols. (1857) • newsletters, 18 Nov 1668, 7 May, 25 June 1670, BL, Add. MS 36916, fols. 119, 180, 185 • *CSP dom.*, 1671–2 • W. S. Churchill, *Marlborough: his life and times*, 1 (1947), vol. 1 • M. C. La Mothe, *Memoirs of the court of England in 1675*, ed. G. D. Gilbert, trans. Mrs W. K. Arthur (1913)

Likenesses S. Cooper, miniature, 1660–1669?, Althorp, Northamptonshire • P. Lely, oils, *c.*1660–1675, Knole, Kent • P. Lely and studio, oils, *c.*1660–1675, Euston Hall, Suffolk • P. Lely and studio, oils, *c.*1660–1675, Euston Hall, Suffolk • P. Lely and studio, oils, *c.*1660–1675, Uffizi, Florence, Italy • P. Lely and studio, oils, *c.*1660–1675, Althorp, Northamptonshire • P. Lely and studio, oils, *c.*1660–1675, Goodwood, West Sussex • S. Cooper, miniature, *c.*1662, Royal Collection • studio of P. Lely, oils, *c.*1665–1675, NPG [*see illus.*] • P. Lely, oils, *c.*1667–1668 (as St Catherine), priv. coll. • J. M. Wright, oils, 1670, NPG • oils, *c.*1705 (after G. Kneller), NPG • I. Beckett, mezzotint (after oils by G. Kneller), BM, NPG • S. Cooper, miniature, priv. coll. • N. Dixon, double portrait, miniature (with her child), Althorp, Northamptonshire • G. Kneller, oils, Bank of England, London • P. Lely, oils, Royal Collection • P. Lely, oils, Lydiard Park, Swindon • P. Lely and studio, oils, National Gallery of Art, Washington, DC • R. Williams, mezzotint (after W. Wissing), BM, NPG • portraits (after P. Lely), NPG

Palmer, Charles (1777–1851). *See under* Palmer, John (1742–1818).

Palmer, Charles Ferrars (1819–1900). *See under* Palmer, Shirley (1786–1852).

Palmer, Charles John (1805–1882), antiquary, only son of John Danby Palmer (1769–1841), a merchant, and Anne (*d.* 1819), daughter of Charles Beart, of Gorleston, Suffolk, was born on 1 January 1805 at Great Yarmouth, where the family had lived since the early sixteenth century. Palmer was educated at a private school at Yarmouth, and in 1822 was articled to Robert Cory, an attorney, under whom he had previously served for two years, in order to qualify to become a notary public. He was admitted an attorney in June 1827, and practised at Yarmouth until he was forced to retire owing to ill health.

Palmer's father had served as mayor in 1821 and 1833 and he followed the family tradition of civic service. He was elected to the common council in 1827 and was mayor-elect in 1835, but the passing of the Municipal Corporations Act prevented him from taking office. He held a seat in the reformed corporation as a representative of the south ward. In 1854 he was installed as mayor, and was re-elected the following year. He also served as deputy lieutenant for the county of Norfolk. He was anxious to promote Yarmouth as a watering-place and instigated the Victoria Building Company and the Wellington pier, acting as solicitor to both schemes. He also took a prominent part in the establishment of the assembly- and reading-rooms and the Yarmouth Public Library, and was on the restoration committee for the parish church. In 1830 he was elected a fellow of the Society of Antiquaries. Palmer married Amelia Graham, daughter of John Mortlock Lacon, on 11 February 1840, but they had no children.

Palmer's antiquarian interests centred upon the town and people of Great Yarmouth, stimulated by the presence there of other antiquarian scholars, such as Dawson Turner and his employer Robert Cory (who had himself compiled notes towards a history of the town), and by his own civic loyalty. His earliest work, a study of the house in which his family had lived since 1809, *The history and illustrations of a house in the Elizabethan style, the property of John Danby esq.* (privately printed, 1838) was followed in 1847 by an edition of a sixteenth-century manuscript history of Great Yarmouth, *A Booke of the Foundacion and Antiquitye of the Towne of Greate Yermouthe*; Palmer attributed the manuscript to Henry Manship the elder but it has since been shown to have been the work of Thomas Damet, the town clerk. Palmer was a moving force behind the record committee, which was established by the corporation to bring some order to that body's archives; this involvement no doubt contributed to his subsequent publications for which he is best remembered: *The History of Great Yarmouth, by Henry Manship* (1854), which he edited; *The History of Great Yarmouth, Designed as a Continuation of Manship's History of that Town* (1856); and *The Perlustration of Great Yarmouth, with Gorleston and Southtown* (3 vols., 1872–5), which he rightly regarded as his most important achievement. Palmer took the reader through every street of the town, recounting the history of the buildings and the family history of all who lived there. A mine of anecdotal detail and information for the local historian, the *Perlustration* is a testament to Palmer's deep affection for the town.

Palmer's other works were considerably briefer and included *Remarks on the Monastery of Dominican Friars at Great Yarmouth* (1852), *Memorials of the Family of Hurry, of Great Yarmouth, Norfolk, and of New York, United States* (privately printed, 1873), and *Palgrave Family Memorials* (privately printed, 1878). He also published a number of pamphlets relating to local affairs in which he was involved, such as the construction of the railway between Norwich and Yarmouth. Palmer died at his home, Villa Graham, Great Yarmouth, on 24 September 1882. His wife survived him. R. H. SWEET

Sources *Yarmouth Mercury* (30 Sept 1882), 5 • F. D. Palmer, ed., *Leaves from the diary and journal of Charles John Palmer* (1892) • *The Times* (28 Sept 1882), 9 • *Solicitors' Journal*, 26 (1881–2), 731 • *Law Times* (7 Oct 1882), 388 • P. Rutledge, 'Thomas Damet and the historiography of Great Yarmouth [pt 1]', *Norfolk Archaeology*, 33 (1962–5), 119–30 • W. Rye, *Norfolk families*, 2 (1913), 638 • m. cert. • *CGPLA Eng. & Wales* (1882)

Archives CUL, autograph collection of peers and MPs • Great Yarmouth Library, literary collections and press cuttings • Mannington Hall, Norfolk, corresp. and collected papers | Maritime Museum for East Anglia, Great Yarmouth, letters to Sir J. P. Boileau

Likenesses W. Holl, stipple, in or before 1838, BM; repro. in Palmer, ed., *Leaves from the diary* • oils, Tolhouse Museum, Great Yarmouth

Wealth at death £2292 13*s.* 9*d.*: probate, 13 Dec 1882, *CGPLA Eng. & Wales*

Palmer, Sir Charles Mark, first baronet (1822–1907), coal-owner, ironmaster and shipbuilder, was born on 3 November 1822 at King Street, South Shields, the fourth child of seven sons and one daughter of George Palmer (1789–1866), a Tyneside merchant and shipowner, and his wife, Maria, daughter of Thomas Taylor of Hill House, Monkwearmouth. Palmer was educated first in South Shields, then at the renowned Bruce's academy in Percy Street, where Robert Stephenson, railway engineer, was formerly a pupil, and at Dr Lockart's, both in Newcastle upon Tyne. A commercial training with Newcastle shipbrokers, followed by a period in a merchant house in Marseilles, prepared Palmer to join his father's business, but instead, aged twenty-two, and regarded as 'an exceedingly active and pushing young man' (Hardy, 76), he became a partner with John Bowes and others in the newly formed Marley Hill Coking Company.

Bowes, and his partners in the 1839 Marley Hill Coal Company, had secured excellent coking coals at Marley Hill, but the concern languished as none of the partners was willing to dedicate himself to it; taking Palmer into the concerns in 1844–5 proved an astute move. Palmer was managing partner of the two businesses by 1846, rapidly increasing outputs and finding sales in Britain and France, where his earlier contacts helped greatly. In the same year he married Jane Robson (*d.* 1865), daughter of a Newcastle draper, and the couple had four sons. Re-named John Bowes & Partners in 1847, the concern owned fourteen collieries by the 1850s, producing about 1 million tons of coal each year, a twenty-fold increase on the outputs of the early 1840s.

This astonishing performance was achieved by the purchase of neighbouring collieries, and the rationalization of their railways to provide a direct link to staiths at Jarrow-on-Tyne. But Palmer did not stop there, and seeking to control the company's coal, and coke, shipments, he and his brother, George, leased a shipyard near the staiths in 1851. In 1852 they launched the *John Bowes*, the first successful iron-built, steam-powered, screw-propelled, water-ballasted collier. A revolutionary vessel, it could carry 650 tons of coal to London, and return, inside five days. On the stocks at its launch was the *James Dixon*, capable of carrying 1200 tons and crewed by twenty-one men; it could perform the work of sixteen collier brigs with a combined crew of 144 men. Palmer's yard soon produced 'colliers by the mile', and the coastal coal trade could now compete with the rail-hauled coal suppliers to London, who had threatened it.

In 1856, Palmer branched into warship-building with the *Terror*, and soon the Jarrow yard was supplying vessels

Sir Charles Mark Palmer, first baronet (1822–1907), by Sir Benjamin Stone, 1899

to navies across the world, while another yard, acquired in 1860 at Howden-on-Tyne, built cargo vessels, oil tankers (probably the first yard to do so), and passenger ships. Palmer further diversified into shipping lines, to secure orders for his yards, and became first chairman of the Tyne Shipping Company, established in 1864 by an amalgamation of Tyneside lines.

Leases on ironstone mines in north Yorkshire, purchases of limestone quarries, and the establishment of iron, boiler, and engine works at Jarrow, gave Palmer total industrial integration, manufacturing ships from their basic raw materials; later, haematite ores were shipped from Spain for steel manufacture. In 1865, perhaps to gain additional capital for further expansion, the Jarrow works was re-formed as Palmer's Iron and Shipbuilding Company Ltd, and although now largely owned by Manchester interests, Palmer remained as its head. By the 1880s it was the largest such concern in the country. When Palmer finally relinquished his position with the company in 1893, the works occupied some three-quarters of a mile of river frontage, had fifteen building slips, and employed 7600 hands; Jarrow's population had increased from 3835 in 1851 to 35,000 in 1891.

Palmer's industrial success story was somewhat marred by an unfortunate speculation in plate glass manufacture, a venture which caused considerable difficulties for John Bowes & Partners, but his standing as a great Victorian industrialist, a pillar of Tyneside commerce, a benefactor to his adopted town of Jarrow, and a thoughtful and responsible employer, remained assured. He became chairman or president of a number of local, and national, institutions and trade associations; he supported the mechanics' institute, schools, churches, chapels, and hospitals in Jarrow. Through his works' building society nearly half the town's houses came to be owner-occupied; he was the first mayor of Jarrow, and an alderman of the town until his death.

Palmer's first wife died in 1865 and in 1867 he married Augusta Mary (1844–1875), daughter of Albert Lambert of Paris; they had two sons. Two years after Augusta died he married Gertrude (1845–1918), daughter of James Montgomery of Cranford, Middlesex, and they had a son and daughter.

After losing as a Liberal at the 1868 election, Palmer became Liberal MP for North Durham in 1874, and then for Jarrow in 1885, holding that seat until his death. He spoke in the House of Commons with authority on matters of shipping and labour, and was a member of the 1884–6 royal commission on the depression of trade and industry. He purchased the Grinkle estate, North Riding of Yorkshire, in 1876, was created baronet in 1886, and finally withdrew from involvement in the Bowes Company in 1895. Ten years earlier, Noble had described him as an 'earnest, clear-headed, practical, and decided' man (Noble, 51); and his achievements were truly formidable. He died on 4 June 1907 at his London home, 37 Curzon Street, Mayfair. He was buried at Easington church, Loftus, North Riding of Yorkshire.

STAFFORD M. LINSLEY

Sources D. J. Rowe, 'Palmer, Sir Charles Mark', *DBB* • C. E. Mountford, *The Bowes railway* (1976), 9–29 • *DNB* • M. Noble, *Short sketches of eminent men of the north of England* (1885), 51 • *History, topography, and directory of the county palatine of Durham*, F. Whellan & Co., 2nd edn (1894) • J. Jamieson, *Durham at the opening of the twentieth century: contemporary biographies*, ed. W. T. Pike (1906) • C. E. Hardy, *John Bowes and the Bowes Museum* (1970) • 'Palmer's Shipbuilding and Iron Company Ltd', *Tyneside industries* (c.1887) • private information (2004) • *CGPLA Eng. & Wales* (1907) • d. cert. • *DNB*

Archives Gateshead Central Library, letter-book; draft speech, articles • Tyne and Wear Archives Service, Newcastle upon Tyne, corresp. and business MSS | Durham RO, Strathmore MSS

Likenesses Sprague & Co., ink photograph, c.1890, Newcastle upon Tyne Central Library • B. Stone, photograph, 1899, NPG [*see illus.*] • A. Toft, bronze statue, 1903, near Tyne Street, Jarrow • Ape [C. Pellegrini], caricature, watercolour study, repro. in *VF* (18 Oct 1884) • A. Toft, marble bust; formerly in the Newcastle upon Tyne Commercial Exchange • portrait, Newcastle upon Tyne Central Library • wood-engraving (after photograph by W. & D. Downey), NPG; repro. in *ILN* (7 March 1874)

Wealth at death £15,226: Rowe, 'Palmer, Sir Charles Mark' • £3423 15*s*. 8*d*.: probate, 22 July 1907, *CGPLA Eng. & Wales*

Palmer, Charlotte (*b*. *c*.**1762**, *d*. in or after **1834**), writer and schoolmistress, lived most of her life in Hendon, Middlesex. Little is known of her life, although much of her writing was instructive, springing from her teaching experience, as she stated she had 'taught Writing to young Ladies above nine years' (Lantz, 239). Her first published work, however, was an epistolary novel in five volumes, *Female Stability, or, The History of Miss Belville* (1780). In the preface she claimed it had been written by a sister who had died, and was published unrevised. On the title-page the author is called the late Miss Palmer, perhaps referring to this sister. Certainly there is evidence that Charlotte Palmer was still living after this date. In 1791, for instance, appeared *Letters on several subjects from a preceptress to her pupils who have left school addressed chiefly to real characters*. More characteristically didactic, it treats such subjects as dress, choice of books, and clandestine marriage. This book, and *A Newly-Invented Copybook* (1797), were intended for use by male tutors, and the latter work was prefaced by a carefully worded and politic apology: 'I hope I shall not be considered as having encroached on an Employment belonging to the opposite sex, nor as endeavouring to diminish their superiority' (Lantz, 240).

Charlotte Palmer's other works are *Integrity and Content: an Allegory* (1792) and *It is and it is not: a Novel* (1792). Another work attributed to Charlotte Palmer, which appeared in Newberry's 1800 catalogue list, was *Three instructive tales for little folk: simple and careful, industry and sloth, and the cousins*.

With another sister, Charlotte Palmer ran schools near London, teaching writing and grammar. In 1805, however, one school was in debt for over £200, and she was imprisoned. Her application for assistance to the Royal Literary Fund was successful, and it made her small payments for some years. When released she ran a day school and also had a private stall in a bonnet shop. Her last communication with the Royal Literary Fund is dated 12 March 1834. ELIZABETH LEE, *rev.* REBECCA MILLS

Sources Blain, Clements & Grundy, *Feminist comp.* • D. L. Lantz, 'Palmer, Charlotte', *A dictionary of British and American women writers, 1660–1800*, ed. J. Todd (1984), 239–40 • *GM*, 1st ser., 68 (1798), 699 • Watt, *Bibl. Brit.*, vol. 2 • Allibone, *Dict.* • *IGI* • Archives of the Royal Literary Fund, 1790–1918, microfilms, 1982, reels A1, A14 and I

Palmer, Edward (*c.*1555–1624), antiquary, was born in Upper Lemington, Todenham, Gloucestershire, one of the three children of Giles Palmer, esquire, and his wife, Muriel Field. In the 1540s Leland described the 'Four Shire' stone sited on land belonging to Edward's grandfather; the latter's son acted as Leland's informant, suggesting a family tradition of antiquarian interest. Edward appeared in the list of students of Magdalen Hall, Oxford, in 1572. He was admitted to the Middle Temple in 1575 where his fellow students included the antiquaries Henry Ferrers of Baddesley Clinton, Warwickshire, and Richard Carew of Antony, Cornwall. He married a kinswoman, Muriel, the daughter of Richard Palmer of Compton Scorpin, Ilmington, Warwickshire. Three sons and four daughters of the marriage were alive in 1624. The Palmers were closely linked to the Overburys, Edward being Sir Thomas Overbury's uncle.

Edward Palmer's interests were predominantly numismatic. Upper Lemington and Compton Scorpin lay either side of the Fosse Way, and Roman coins were often ploughed up in the surrounding fields. Some of these coins Palmer bestowed on Camden, who calls him 'an industrious Antiquary' (*Britannia*, ed. Gibson, 240). Fuller writes that 'Great [was] his store of Coins, Greek and Roman, in Gold, Silver, and Brasse; and greater his skill in them' (Fuller, *Worthies*, 387). As so often with antiquaries drawn from among the county gentry in this period, Palmer published nothing and his collections were dispersed after his death. When Wood included an account of Palmer in his *Athenae Oxonienses*, the latter's collections were already lost. A wider interest in scholarship is evidenced by his purchase of an island in Virginia for the purpose of setting up an academy; he died before the scheme was accomplished. At the time of his death Palmer was living in London. His will, which shows him to have been a wealthy man (able to make bequests totalling more than £1000 and owning property in New England as well as Virginia), was written on 22 November 1624 and proved on 15 December. His wife had predeceased him.

JAN BROADWAY

Sources Fuller, *Worthies* (1811), 387–8 • *Camden's Britannia*, ed. and trans. E. Gibson (1695); facs. edn (1971), 240 • W. Dugdale, *The antiquities of Warwickshire illustrated*, rev. W. Thomas, 2nd edn, 2 vols. (1730), 633 • will, PRO, PROB 11/144/114 • H. A. C. Sturgess, ed., *Register of admissions to the Honourable Society of the Middle Temple, from the fifteenth century to the year 1944*, 1 (1949) • Foster, *Alum. Oxon.* • *John Leland's itinerary: travels in Tudor England*, ed. J. Chandler (1993); repr. (1998), 374 • Wood, *Ath. Oxon.*, new edn, 2.28 • J. Maclean and W. C. Heane, eds., *The visitation of the county of Gloucester taken in the year 1623*, Harleian Society, 21 (1885)

Wealth at death plentiful estate: Fuller, *Worthies* • £1024 plus £40 annuity to daughter; ring of gold of four angels each to six overseers; bulk of estate to eldest son, incl. property in Virginia and New England; provided for monument to grandfather: will, PRO, PROB 11/144/114

Palmer, Edward Henry (1840–1882), orientalist, was born on 7 August 1840 in Green Street, Cambridge, the only son of William Henry and Mary Palmer. His father kept a private school in Cambridge. Left an orphan in infancy, Palmer was brought up by an aunt at Cambridge, where he attended the Perse School. As a boy he spent much time with Gypsies, and acquired a fluency in Romani and a knowledge of Gypsy life and ways. On leaving school, at the age of sixteen, he became a junior clerk to Hill and Underwood, wine merchants, of Eastcheap, London. He learned to speak French and several Italian dialects fluently by mixing with native speakers living in London and his success made him a firm upholder of this informal, conversational method of learning languages. His evenings were often spent at the theatre, where he formed a lifelong friendship with Henry Irving; or else in mesmeric experiments, in which he exhibited extraordinary powers.

In 1859 Palmer developed grave symptoms of pulmonary tuberculosis and returned to Cambridge prepared to die, but suddenly recovered. While convalescing he published poetry and wrote a farce which was performed at the Cambridge Theatre in 1860. Towards the end of 1860 he met Saiyid Abdullah, teacher of Hindustani at Cambridge. The two became friends and Palmer began to study oriental languages. His progress in Persian, Arabic, and Hindustani was phenomenally rapid.

Some fellows of St John's College discovered Palmer's gift for languages and by their influence he was admitted as a sizar there in October 1863. He matriculated in

November 1864 and in 1865 was awarded a foundation scholarship. He graduated BA in 1867, with only a third class in the classical tripos, and proceeded MA in 1870; but his main energies as an undergraduate were given to oriental studies. During this period he catalogued the Persian, Arabic, and Turkish manuscripts of King's College and Trinity College (1870), and also of the university library. His catalogues were considered by Arberry (*Oriental Essays*, 1960) still to be useful to scholars, although their method was antiquated. Palmer also wrote in Persian and Urdu for the *Oudh Akhbâr* and other Indian newspapers, also becoming a recognized expert in Hindustani. He published *Oriental Mysticism: a Treatise on the Sufiistic and Unitarian Theosophy of the Persians* (1867), founded on the 'Maksad-i Aksâ' of ʿAziz ibn Mohammad Nafasi, preserved in manuscript at Trinity College; and translated (1865) Thomas Moore's *Paradise and the Peri* into Persian verse. He was a member of the French Société Asiatique and of the Royal Asiatic Society.

Palmer was elected to a fellowship at St John's College on 5 November 1867. The fellowship gave him time to pursue his studies and visit the East. He had in 1867 unsuccessfully sought the post of oriental secretary to the British legation in Persia and in 1869 he was chosen to join the survey of Sinai, for the Palestine Exploration Fund. His principal duty was to collect from the Bedouin the correct names of places on the Sinai peninsula. He thus came for the first time into contact with Arabs, learned to speak their dialects, and obtained an insight into their modes of thought and life. In the summer of 1869 he returned to England, but left again on 16 December for another expedition. This time he and Charles Frederick Tyrwhitt-Drake walked alone the 600 miles from Sinai to Jerusalem, identifying sites and searching vainly for inscriptions. They explored for the first time the Desert of the Wanderings (Tih), and many unknown parts of Edom and Moab, and accomplished much useful geographical work. En route Palmer made many friends among the Arab sheikhs, among whom he went by the name of ʿAbdallah Efendi. The travellers went on to Lebanon and to Damascus, where they met Captain Richard Burton, who was then consul there, and with whom Palmer struck up a friendship. They returned home in the autumn of 1870 by way of Constantinople and Vienna.

A popular account of these two expeditions was written by Palmer in *The Desert of the Exodus: Journeys on Foot in the Wilderness of the Forty Years' Wanderings* (2 vols., 1871, illustrated with maps and engravings; reprinted, 1977); he also published an article in the *British Quarterly Review* (1873) on the secret sects of Syria, while the scientific results of the second expedition were detailed in the Palestine Exploration Fund's *Journal* of 1871, and included in *Special Papers Relating to the Survey of Western Palestine* (1881). Although he took no further part in the expeditions of the Palestine Fund, he devoted much time and interest to the work of the society. In 1881 he transliterated and edited the *Arabic and English Name-Lists of the Survey of Western Palestine*—some 10,000 place names—and assisted in editing the *Memoirs* of the survey (1881–3). He also wrote, with Walter Besant, a close friend and later his biographer, a short history of Jerusalem, *Jerusalem, the City of Herod and of Saladin* (1871; new edn, 1888), a book which Arberry considered still of value.

Palmer returned to Cambridge, where he studied, wrote, and lectured for the next ten years. In 1871 he failed in his bid for the Adams professorship of Arabic, but was appointed the lord almoner's professor of Arabic. The post was worth only £40 10*s*. a year, but it enabled him to retain his fellowship though married, and on the day after his appointment, 11 November 1871, he married Laura Hanbury Davis (*d*. 1878), to whom he had been engaged for several years, daughter of Thomas H. Davis of Grantchester. They had two daughters, and a son who died in infancy. In 1873, in consequence of the creation of the triposes of oriental languages, Palmer's salary and his workload increased considerably. In addition he was one of the interpreters to the shah of Persia during his visit to London in 1873, and wrote an account of it in Urdu for a Lucknow paper. He published a *Concise Dictionary of the Persian Language* (1876; 2nd edn, 1884), of which the English–Persian counterpart was edited from his notes after his death by Guy Le Strange (1883). It was a useful work for beginners although by 1960 largely superseded.

Palmer's verse translation of *Poetical Works of Behá-ed-din Zoheir of Egypt* appeared in two volumes (1876–7) but the third volume, of notes, was never published. The work was admired by contemporaries, not least as it was the first translation of the entire works of any Arabic poet. It was Palmer's most serious work but he laid himself open to charges of unscholarliness, as he chose to make free with the verse in an attempt to catch its spirit. His Koran (1880) was the best-known of his works, being reprinted numerous times throughout the nineteenth and twentieth centuries. It is immature and hastily written, and has the opposite fault from that of his other, too free, translations in its literal, often word-for-word rendering although it, too, had its admirers. His *Arabic Grammar* (1874), like everything he did, broke new ground in Europe, by explaining and illustrating Arabic inflexion, syntax, and prosody in a method used by the Arabs themselves. Among his other writings were a *Simplified Grammar of Hindustani, Persian, and Arabic* (1882; 2nd edn, 1885) and two little books on Jewish history and geography, written for the Society for Promoting Christian Knowledge (1874).

Besides these, Palmer revised a Persian New Testament for the Bible Society; examined, in 1881–2, in Hindustani for the civil service commission; assisted Eirikr Magnússon in translating Johan Ludvig Runeberg's *Lyrical Songs* from the Finnish (1878); edited Pierce Butler's translation of A. G. Oehlenschläger's *Axel og Valborg* from the Danish (1874); joined Charles Godfrey Leland and Janet Tuckey in producing *English Gipsy Songs in Romany, with Metrical English Translations* (1875); edited the first six volumes of Trübner's *Simplified Grammars*; wrote the articles 'Hafiz' and 'Legerdemain' for the *Encyclopaedia Britannica*; and developed a marvellous talent in conjuring. Originally with a view (soon abandoned) to Indian practice, he was called to the bar in 1874 at the Middle Temple, and even went on the eastern circuit for two or three years, taking briefs occasionally.

With his eclectic talents and interests Palmer found himself out of sympathy with university life. The death of his wife, after a long illness, in 1878, unsettled him although he married again on 26 June 1879. His second wife was Augusta Marghereta Elisabeth, daughter of Count von Langa of Poland. Palmer grew tired of college life and lectures and in 1881 abandoned his lectures; retaining only the professorship, with its nominal salary, he began life as a journalist on the staff of *The Standard*, where he acted as leader writer on social and general topics, until his departure for Egypt on a secret service mission on 30 June 1882.

Palmer was sent by Gladstone's government to attempt to detach the Arab tribes from the side of Arabi Pasha, the nationalist leader, and to use his influence, backed by English gold, with the sheikhs of the Bedouin, to secure the immunity of the Suez Canal from Arab attack, and provide for its repair after possible damage by Arabi's men. On his arrival at Alexandria, on 5 July 1882, he received instructions to proceed to Jaffa, thence to enter the desert and make his way to Suez, talking to the principal sheikhs en route. As ʿAbdallah Efendi, Palmer rode his camel through the desert, armed and dressed in the richest Syrian style, giving handsome presents to his old acquaintances among the Tiyâha, and securing their loyalty to the khedive rather than to Arabi. Palmer reported that he had:

> got hold of some of the very men whom Arâbi Pasha has been trying to get over to his side; and when they are wanted I can have every Bedawi at my call, from Suez to Gaza … I am certain of success. (journal to his wife, in Besant, 270ff.)

After three weeks' disappearance in the desert Palmer joined the British fleet at Suez on 1 August. The next day he was in the first boat that landed for the occupation of Suez, and was engaged in reassuring the non-combatant inhabitants. He was appointed interpreter-in-chief to her majesty's forces in Egypt. His work among the Bedouin was approved by Admiral W. Hewett in Egypt and by the first lord of the Admiralty (Lord Northbrook), and Palmer himself was convinced that, with £20,000 or £30,000 to buy their allegiance, he could raise a force of 50,000 Bedouin to guard or unblock the Suez Canal. On 6 August £20,000 was placed at his disposal by the admiral; but Lord Northbrook instructed that Palmer was initially to spend only 'a reasonable amount'. In fact on the night of 19–20 August the British troops occupied the canal zone, which had always been their primary objective, so promptly and effectively, that the Bedouin were largely irrelevant: but they gave the invaders no trouble, and this may have been due to Palmer's presents and influence. The bulk of the money which was to have secured their more active support never reached them, owing to the tragic fate which overtook Palmer. On 8 August he set out to meet the leading sheikhs to arrange the final terms of their allegiance. In accordance with Lord Northbrook's instructions, he took with him only £3000 in English gold for this purpose, to begin with. He took a naval officer, Flag-Lieutenant Harold Charrington, as a guarantee of his official status. Captain William John Gill RE, the traveller, also accompanied him, with the intention of turning aside and cutting the telegraph wire which crossed the desert and connected Cairo with Constantinople. Two servants attended them, besides camel-drivers; and 'Meter Abu Sofieh', who claimed to be a prominent sheikh, joined the party, as a guide and protector. Heading for Nakhl, Abu Sofieh led them into an ambush on the night of 10–11 August. They were made prisoners and their baggage was plundered. There was at the time an order out from Cairo for Palmer's arrest, dead or alive; but it is probable that the original motive of the attack was robbery. On the following morning, 11 August, the prisoners were driven about a mile to the Wadi Sudr, between al-ʿArish and Nakhl, and shot, Palmer being the first to die. The facts were ascertained only after an inquiry by Colonel Charles Warren RE, who was sent out by the government on a mission, which ended in the conviction of the murderers. The fragmentary remains of Palmer, Gill, and Charrington, identifiable only by their clothes, were brought home and buried in the crypt of St Paul's Cathedral on 6 April 1883. Richard Burton wrote a long account of his journey to investigate Palmer's murder, but it was never published.

Palmer was by all accounts light-hearted and good company, a fine linguist but ill-suited to the academic life or careful sustained scholarship. His journals to his wife suggest that he was thoroughly enjoying his new role as a secret agent and he appears to have revealed the details of his mission to his friend and biographer Besant before setting out: the seriousness of the task in which he had become embroiled is shown not by his excited accounts of his exploits but by the sordid brutality of his death. His end attracted both widespread sympathy but also controversy in Britain and Egypt. ELIZABETH BAIGENT

Sources W. Besant, *Life and achievements of Edward Henry Palmer* (1883) • A. J. Arberry, *Oriental essays: portraits of seven scholars* (1960) • A. E. Haynes, *Man-hunting in the desert, being a narrative of the Palmer search expedition* (1894) • Venn, *Alum. Cant.* • G. F. Nicholl, *Palmer's work as an oriental scholar* (1882) • J. W. Clark, *Old friends at Cambridge and elsewhere* (1900) • A. Schölch, *Egypt for the Egyptians: the socio-political crisis in Egypt, 1878–1882* (1981); trans. of *Ägypten den Ägyptern! Die politische und gesellschaftliche Krise der Jahre 1878–1882 in Ägypten* (1972) • private information (1895) [R. F. Scott, master, St John Cam.; librarian, King's Cam.; registrary, U. Cam] • H. Bradshaw, letter, *Journal of the Royal Asiatic Society of Great Britain and Ireland*, new ser., 3 (1868), 106–31 [appended to E. H. Palmer's 'Catalogue of the oriental manuscripts in the library of King's College, Cambridge'] • W. S. Blunt, *Secret history of the English occupation of Egypt: being a personal narrative of events* (1922); repr. (1967) • *CGPLA Eng. & Wales* (1883) • *DNB*

Archives FM Cam., MS notebook kept in Palestine • NRA, priv. coll., MSS relating to Palestine survey work • St John Cam., Sinai notebooks and scrapbook

Likenesses J. Collier, oils, 1884, St John Cam. • wood-engraving, NPG; repro. in *ILN* (4 Nov 1882)

Wealth at death £2431 2s. 1d.: probate, 29 Jan 1883, *CGPLA Eng. & Wales*

Palmer, Edwin James (1869–1954), bishop of Bombay, was born in Oxford on 10 January 1869, the only son of the Ven. Edwin Palmer (1824–1895), successively fellow of Balliol,

Edwin James Palmer (1869–1954), by Lafayette, 1930

Corpus professor of Latin, and archdeacon of Oxford, and his wife, Henrietta (*d.* 1915), daughter of another Tractarian cleric, James Riddell. There were two daughters. Jimmy was moulded by tightly interwoven agencies: an intensely devout high-church family, Winchester College, and Balliol.

Palmer's uncle Roundell Palmer, first earl of Selborne, was a leading ecclesiastical lawyer and lord chancellor, whose son William became both an ecclesiastical and an imperial statesman. Both went to Winchester, which admitted Palmer from the Dragon School, Oxford, with the outstanding scholarship of 1882. W. A. Fearon, his second Winchester headmaster, informed his parents that he had never known a clever boy more docile. It was a tensely competitive docility: teachers observed that his stammer, a lifelong affliction, deteriorated as exams approached.

Palmer's cousin William's sister, Laura (Lolly), was the second wife of Fearon's reforming predecessor, 'the strong, reliable, strange and original Ridding', of a colleague's description. Palmer himself was to celebrate 'Dr Ridding's Mind and Thought' in chapter 17 of Lady Laura's *George Ridding: Schoolmaster and Bishop* (1908). George Ridding aimed to produce an intellectually independent moral élite, within the foundation's guiding assumptions. Jimmy's identification with this ideal emerges in precocious critiques of Sunday sermons, interspersed with severe appraisals of his own prize and class-work, with which he regaled his mother in letters home.

Craven scholar at Balliol, Palmer took firsts in classical moderations (1889) and *literae humaniores* (1891), winning a prize fellowship in 1891. Jowett's Balliol was already displaying the supposedly 'effortless superiority' of Asquith's notorious gratulation (Jones, chap. 16). As a fellow Palmer contributed fully to the heavy labour sustaining it, teaching intensively—Plato for honour moderations and also theology—engaging in the reading parties and time-consuming cultivation of individual students, to which his Roman Catholic friend Sligger Urquhart and others devoted their bachelor existence. He was assistant bursar under Sir William Markby. Appointed chaplain, following ordination in 1896, he increased chapel attendance, while serving as examining chaplain to Ridding, now bishop of Southwell (1899–1904), Rochester (1904–5), and Southwark (1905–8). Photographs hint at his reputed brusqueness; spectacles and trim beard mask an intent scrutiny. Following his kin, and Oxford lawyers such as A. V. Dicey, he abandoned Gladstone over home rule for Ireland and joined the Liberal Unionists in 1893.

About 1900 Palmer grew restless. He was unsettled by the suggestion that he pursue the headmastership of Winchester. He contemplated matrimony, a lamentable deviation in the eyes of senior fellows, but was disappointed. However, from 1904 he chaired the Junior Clergy Missionary Association. A visit in 1907 to South Africa, where Willie Palmer, now Lord Selborne, was high commissioner, provided his only first-hand experience of imperial practice before Bombay in 1908.

Pressure for church union in south India was, Palmer knew, indigenous and 'pastoral', an impulse to consolidate communities scattered across a hostile heathendom. But he was shaken by the gulf dividing the pragmatic, 'undogmatic' ecumenism, towards which a historically fortuitous assortment of denominations was drifting in Bombay diocese, from his own vision, of an unbroken descent of apostolic authority, from the church of the early fathers to the Church of England.

Palmer attacked immediately, initiating a long series of charges, letters, sermons, *Diocesan Record* articles, and books, by roasting the confused congregationalism of the American Marathi Mission in Ahmednagar for inviting a 'horrible absorption of Christianity by Hinduism' (Palmer, *Reunion*, 40). But he also pursued a process of accommodation towards the milestone of the Indian church measure (1927), exploiting common ground in debates with the Pentecostalist V. Bartlet, and a champion of the Reformation, J. H. Maclean. Foss Westcott, the metropolitan, promoted union, but Palmer devised its constitutional structures and rules, diocesan and synodical. Thus he protected the canonical rule of episcopal authority with a functional argument for the authority of bishops in India: India had evolved hierarchical social systems, dominated by rajahs but resting on horizontal strata of communal *panchayats*, so something analogous was only natural for church union, as it had been, for corresponding reasons, for the early church. His protagonists could accept the practical implications, without sharing his reading of history or acknowledging apostolic succession.

He supported the appointment of the first Indian bishop, V. S. Azariah of Dornakal, in 1912.

Sacraments and creeds were sensitively confronted. To break a deadlock over ordination Palmer successfully proposed, as an 'exception', a thirty-year transition to a ministry ordained by bishops. In 1912 he entered a supportive marriage with Hazel (*d.* 1931), daughter of Colonel E. H. Hanning-Lee of the 2nd Life Guards.

Consistently a liberal whig imperialist, Palmer kept his head down over Indian nationalism, remaining silent over the Jallianwalla Bagh massacre, and wishing privately that the die-hard 'Christian statesman' George Lloyd, governor of Bombay, could be given 'carte blanche' to deal with 'bolshevik' Gandhian agitation (Palmer MSS, LPL, MS 3005, fol. 34).

'Retirement', from 1928, was unobtrusively active, as assistant to the bishop of Gloucester, A. C. Headlam, also at Lambeth conferences, and as consultant to his Balliol friend Archbishop William Temple over Indian church union. This Palmer sustained against hostility from other Anglo-Catholics, with self-critical lucidity and a passionate belief in the promised awakening of the 'Great Church' into which all others must die in order to be born again (Palmer, *The Great Church Awakes*). He died in Oxford on 28 March 1954. GERALD STUDDERT-KENNEDY

Sources LPL, Palmer MSS • B. Sundkler, *Church of South India: the movement towards union, 1900–1947* (1954) • Balliol Oxf., Palmer MSS • E. J. Palmer, *The great church awakes* (1920) • E. J. Palmer, *Reunion in western India: papers and articles by the bishop of Birmingham* (1910) • J. Jones, *Balliol College: a history, 1263–1939* (1988) • L. Ridding, *George Ridding: schoolmaster and bishop* (1908) • G. Studdert-Kennedy, *British Christians, Indian nationalists and the raj* (1991) • J. D'E. Firth, *Winchester College* (1949)
Archives Balliol Oxf., corresp., diary, and papers • LPL, corresp. and papers
Likenesses Lafayette, photograph, 1930, NPG [*see illus.*] • group portrait, photograph (with fellows), Balliol Oxf. • photograph, Balliol Oxf., Palmer MSS
Wealth at death £31,987 2*s.* 3*d.*: probate, 19 July 1954, *CGPLA Eng. & Wales*

Palmer [*née* Ambrose], **Eleanor**, **Lady Palmer** (**1718x20–1818**), society beauty, was probably born at Ambrose Hall, co. Dublin, the second daughter and coheir of Michael Ambrose, a wealthy brewer of co. Dublin, and his wife, the daughter of Richard Archbold. Little is known of her early life. It was recorded that she was 'gifted with exquisite beauty, and possessed of considerable mental acquirements' (Webb, 4). Philip Dormer Stanhope, fourth earl of Chesterfield, during the period of his viceroyalty in Ireland (1745–7), was a great admirer of hers and was said to have called her 'the most dangerous papist in Ireland' (GEC, *Baronetage*, 5.390). It was observed she was 'constantly in the viceroy's company and attended all state ceremonies' (Gerard, 21). Despite her constant appearance with Chesterfield it was noted that she 'guarded her reputation, keeping well within the limits of platonic friendship' (ibid., 22). It is difficult to know exactly how influential Palmer was on the politics of the period. Her beauty and wealth provided her with an entrée into society and political contacts were made in this context.

On 10 October 1750, at St George's, Mayfair, Westminster, Eleanor married Roger Palmer (*d.* 1790?) of Castle Lackin, co. Mayo, and Kenure Park, co. Dublin. He was a member of parliament for Jamestown from 1761 to 1768, and for Portarlington from 1769 to 1783. The couple had three sons: Francis, who died in his father's lifetime; John Roger (*d.* 6 Feb 1819); and William Henry (*d.* 29 May 1840). Palmer was created a baronet on 29 May 1777, and died probably in 1790. In the later years of her life Lady Palmer lived in lodgings in Henry Street, Dublin. She was acquainted with many of the leading figures of the day. She knew the poets Byron and Thomas Moore. Richard Lalor Sheil visited her in her old age and noted:

> after the ordinary formulas of civility, she placed herself in a huge chair, and entered at once into politics. She was a most vehement Catholic … Lord Fingall and the Catholic question were the only subjects in which she seemed to take any interest. Upon the wrongs to her country she spoke not only with energy, but with eloquence; and with every pinch of snuff, poured out a sentence of sedition. (Sheil, 1.137–8)

Lady Palmer died in Dublin either on 10 February 1818, 'in the full possession of all her faculties, aged 98' (*GM*, 1st ser., 88/1, 1818, 379), or on 3 February 1818 in Abbey Street, Dublin, in her hundredth year, according to sources used by G. E. Cockayne when compiling his *Baronetage*. A pastel portrait that revealed 'seductive eyes, a dazzling complexion, and an arch expression' (*DNB*) was exhibited at the Dublin National Portrait Exhibition in 1872, but had been destroyed in a fire by 1895. MARIA LUDDY

Sources F. Gerard, *Some celebrated Irish beauties of the last century* (1895), 14–28 • R. L. Sheil, *Sketches, legal and political*, ed. M. W. Savage, 1 (1855), 136–8 • A. J. Webb, *A compendium of Irish biography* (1878) • GEC, *Baronetage*, 5.390–91 • *DNB*

Palmer, Sir Elwin Mitford (**1852–1906**), colonial official, was born in London on 3 March 1852, the second son of Edward Palmer and Caroline, daughter of Colonel Gunthorpe. After education at Lancing College, he entered the finance department of the government of India in 1870, becoming assistant comptroller-general in November 1871. In 1881 he married Mary Augusta Lynch, daughter of Major Herbert Clogstoun VC, with whom he had a son and two daughters. Palmer was seconded briefly to Egypt between 31 December 1878 and 30 April 1879, during the period when the Egyptian khedive sought to reassure the European powers that he would carry through an extensive programme of financial reconstruction. Subsequently, on 16 August 1885, three years after the British occupation, Palmer succeeded Sir Gerald Fitzgerald as director-general of accounts in Egypt. Fitzgerald and Palmer were largely responsible for creating a modern system of public accounts in Egypt. Palmer was created CMG in 1888. In the following year he succeeded Sir Edgar Vincent as financial adviser to the Egyptian government, a key position in the 'veiled protectorate' which Evelyn Baring had created after 1883. As financial adviser, Palmer played a major role in the conversion of parts of Egypt's public debt (the Daira and domains loans) and was closely concerned with the contract for the construction of the Aswan Reservoir. When the National Bank of Egypt was set up in 1898, Palmer resigned as financial adviser to become its first governor. In the same year he became the chairman of the Cairo committee of the Daira Sanieh Company, which had taken over from the government the management of the *daira* or private estates of Isma'il Pasha. In 1902, he was appointed president of the Agricultural Bank of Egypt, an offshoot of the National Bank.

Palmer was a shrewd, hard-working man, with long financial training and wide knowledge of accounts; his expertise lay more in public finance than in general administration. The later part of his career was occupied in the commercial development stimulated by Egypt's return to solvency, its buoyant cotton exports and the irrigation and drainage works promoted by British officials. Palmer was made KCMG in 1892, KCB in 1897, and held the grand cordons of the orders of Osmanieh and Mejidiye (conferred formally by the Ottoman sultan). He died in Cairo on 28 January 1906.

C. P. LUCAS, *rev.* J. G. DARWIN

Sources E. R. J. Owen, *The Middle East in the world economy, 1800–1914* (1981) • A. Colvin, *The making of modern Egypt* (1906) • A. Milner, *England in Egypt* (1892) • earl of Cromer [E. Baring], *Modern Egypt*, 2 vols. (1908) • *WWW*

Palmer, Sir Geoffrey, first baronet (1598–1670), lawyer and politician, was born in Carlton, Northamptonshire, the eldest son of Thomas Palmer of Carlton and Catherine, daughter of Sir Edward Watson of Rockingham in the same county. He matriculated as a pensioner from Christ's College, Cambridge, in December 1612, graduated BA in 1616, and proceeded MA in 1619. Admitted 'specially' to the Middle Temple on 14 June 1616, he was called to the bar on 23 May 1623. Palmer declined to serve as a reader in the spring and summer terms of 1626, and was fined. At an unknown date he married Margaret, daughter of Sir Francis Moore, serjeant-at-law, of Fawley, Berkshire. They had four sons: Thomas, who died young, Lewis (1630–1713), Geoffrey (1642–1661), and Edward, and two daughters, Elizabeth and Frances.

Elected to the Long Parliament in 1640 for Stamford, Lincolnshire (when he was a junior member of the queen's counsel), Palmer left a career in conveyancing for high law and politics. He joined the committee to hear the petitions of the ministers of London on church government on 23 January 1641, and the committee for ecclesiastical affairs on 9 February. As a manager of Strafford's impeachment in April he gave legal opinions on points of law and made interventions on behalf of the accused's procedural rights. He advocated moderation on the articles concerning arbitrary government, and signed the protestation of 3 May in defence of the protestant religion. After an act was passed perpetuating the life of the parliament he joined Edward Hyde and Viscount Falkland in supporting the king against his new council. In July he negotiated the queen's terms for settling the banishment of priests and retaining her Roman Catholic chaplains.

Palmer's political views changed during the debates on the grand remonstrance on 22–3 November 1641. After the remonstrance was passed in the early hours of 23 November and John Hampden moved to print it, he rose and shouted 'I do protest!' (Bruce, 128). The commotion that followed nearly caused bloodshed in the excited atmosphere of the Commons. Palmer was threatened with expulsion, but the vote against him failed. Speaking after midnight on 24 November he called the majority 'A Rabble of inconsiderable persons, set on by a juggling Junto' (*Journal*, ed. Coates, 187), and was committed to the Tower, from where he was released on 8 December. After the vote authorizing the militia ordinance on 30 April 1642 he withdrew from the house and became commissioner of array for his county.

Palmer was awarded the degree of DCL by Oxford University in 1643 and was a member of the royalist parliament which met in the city on 22 January 1644. He was one of Charles's commissioners for the negotiation of the abortive treaty of Uxbridge in January–February 1645 and a later negotiation in December of that year that was stillborn. Appointed solicitor-general on 3 November 1645, he remained in Oxford during the siege of the city. Upon its fall he had letters of composition for compounding his estates when he surrendered them on 22 June 1646; his fine was eventually set at £500 in September 1648. During the 1650s Palmer was able to practise law in London, obtaining licences to move cases and appear as a witness. He seems to have given legal advice to various peers. Committed to the Tower on 9 June 1655 on suspicion of raising forces against Cromwell's government, he was probably released in the following September.

At the Restoration Palmer was made attorney-general on 31 May 1660, was elected bencher of the Middle Temple in the following month, and later served as its treasurer. He was knighted on 1 June, conferred with a baronetcy on 7 June 1660, was appointed serjeant in October of that year, and was active as crown legal counsel and in the preparation of prosecutions. In 1662 he was prominent in the trial of the regicides, taking depositions and handling the maintenance and discharge of the prisoners. Although Palmer was quite favourable to Lambert, Ludlow characterized him as one 'of the tyrant's bloodhounds, at the bar', thirsting for the blood of innocent lambs (*A Voyce from the Watch Tower*, ed. A. B. Worden, CS, 4th. ser., 21, 1978, 315).

Palmer became an intimate part of a circle of friends recruited by Hyde, now earl of Clarendon, from his former inn, the Middle Temple, who collaborated on enacting parliamentary legislation. In parliament he was a strong supporter of the royal prerogative and argued against compromise with opponents. He had his son Geoffrey elected MP for Ludgershall, Wiltshire, in March 1661 by forcing the sheriff to deliver the election writ to his agent there. His son Lewis was elected MP for Higham Ferrers. Palmer was briefly appointed chief justice of Chester in late 1661. An active attorney-general, he held the office until his death. He was also recorder of Boston in 1662–70, and chief justice of the common pleas temporarily in 1666.

In 1663 Palmer edited the law reports of his father-in-law, Sir Francis Moore, which he gave to the Middle Temple Library. A volume of cases partly drawn from his own manuscript reports appeared under his judicial imprimatur as *Les reports de Sir Gefrey Palmer, chevalier et baronet* in 1678. They consist of cases chiefly in the king's bench between 1619 and 1629, which he collected and edited as a young attorney and barrister. Published posthumously, this work set a new standard for law reports as it named the barristers and judges for each statement made. Whether Palmer did more than edit them is doubtful.

Palmer died on 5 May 1670 at his house in Hampstead Fields, Middlesex, where his hospitality was famous among contemporaries. He lay in state at the Middle Temple and his funeral had a great train of nobles and judges to Carlton, where his remains were buried alongside those of his wife (who had predeceased him) in the parish church. Lewis, his eldest surviving son, succeeded him in the baronetcy. His rich collection of political and legal manuscripts and printed books went to his grandson Geoffrey. Palmer gave generously to the poor of Northamptonshire, Middlesex, and Rutland, and to the Hospital of the Blessed Jesus in Rutland, for which he established a charitable trust. LOUIS A. KNAFLA

Sources T. Wotton, *The baronetage of England*, 3 (1741), pt 1, pp. 10–12 • Baker, *Serjeants*, 443–4 • P. Seaward, *The Cavalier Parliament and the reconstruction of the old regime, 1661–1667* (1988) • R. Hutton, *The Restoration: a political and religious history of England and Wales, 1658–1667* (1985) • *The journal of Sir Simonds D'Ewes from the first recess of the Long Parliament to the withdrawal of King Charles from London*, ed. W. H. Coates (1942) • M. Jansson, ed., *Two diaries of the Long Parliament* (1984) • C. Russell, *The fall of the British monarchies, 1637–1642* (1991), 224–7, 427–9, 501 • J. Bruce, ed., *Verney papers: notes of proceedings in the Long Parliament*, CS, 31 (1845), 4, 125–8 • *DNB* • E. Hyde, earl of Clarendon, *The history of the rebellion and civil wars in England*, 7 vols. (1849), vol. 3, p. 106; vol. 4, pp. 52–8, 77; vol. 8, pp. 211, 233; vol. 9, p. 164 • J. Rushworth, *Historical collections*, new edn, 8 vols. (1721–2), vol. 4, p. 573; vol. 8, pp. 426–705 • *CSP dom.*, *1645–51* • will, PRO, PROB 11/333, fols. 119–20 • C. H. Hopwood, ed., *A calendar of the Middle Temple records* (1903) • A. R. Ingpen, ed., *The Middle Temple bench books* (1912) • Pepys, *Diary*, vols. 1, 5, 8–9 • John, Lord Campbell, *The lives of the chief justices of England*, 1 (1849), 493 • *JHC*, 2 (1640–42), 81, 324, 335 • Thurloe, *State papers*, 1.56; 3.537 • J. Peile, *Biographical register of Christ's College, 1505–1905, and of the earlier foundation, God's House, 1448–1505*, ed. [J. A. Venn], 1 (1910), 288 • *VCH Northamptonshire*, vol. 4 • 'Palmer family pedigree', BL, Lansdowne MS 1023, fols. 45–53

Likenesses P. Lely, oils, *c.*1660–1663, Rockingham Castle, Northamptonshire; version, NPG • studio of P. Lely, oils, *c.*1660–1663, Clarendon collection; on loan to Plymouth City Museum and Art Gallery • R. White, line engraving, BM, NPG • engraving, repro. in *Les reports de Sir Gefrey Palmer* (1688)

Wealth at death see will, PRO, PROB 11/333, fols. 119–20

Palmer, George (1740–1795), glass merchant and colour scientist, was born on 18 November 1740 in London, the son of Thomas Palmer and his wife, Elizabeth. The prosperous family firm, established at 118 St Martin's Lane, Westminster, was prominent in the supply and fitting of window glass. Its speciality was coloured glass, and Thomas Palmer supplied stained glass to Horace Walpole, fourth earl of Orford, for Strawberry Hill.

Palmer was a freeman of the Drapers' Company by patrimony and served as a member of the court (1792–5). He and his wife, Sarah, had four sons. Practical experience with stained glass must have led Palmer to consider the nature of colour, and he was the first to put forward the modern theory of colour vision and colour blindness. In his *Theory of Light and Colour* (1777) he suggested that the retina of the eye contains three different kinds of particle (elsewhere he speaks of 'molecules' or 'fibres'), each of which is excited by a different kind of light. 'The complete and uniform motion of these particles produces the sensation of white.' Colour blindness, he correctly supposed, arose when either one or two of the three types of molecules were non-functional. He also introduced the idea that different sensory fibres within the normal retina could be selectively fatigued, so as to yield coloured afterimages. He suggested that a residual motion of the fibres was present in the dark, so that true blacks could be seen only in daylight, by comparison with surrounding objects. He conceived the idea of artificial daylight and gave it practical reality by filtering the light of an Argand oil lamp through blue glass.

Although Palmer's theory of the physics of colour was mistaken (he held there were three discrete forms of light), it is remarkable that this entrepreneur and tradesman came so close to a modern account of the physiology of colour vision. It remained for an establishment scientist, Thomas Young, to suggest in 1802 that the physical variable underlying colour is a continuous one, whereas Palmer's idea of three discrete receptors is correct at the retinal level.

Young may have been exposed to Palmer's ideas while a student of G. C. Lichtenberg in Göttingen. Although largely unrecognized by the scientific establishment in England, Palmer enjoyed some contemporary recognition on the continent: his explanation of colour blindness first appeared in a secondary account in L. C. Lichtenberg's *Magazin für das Neuste aus der Physik* in 1781 and was then cited in texts such as J. S. T. Gehler's *Physikalisches Wörterbuch*, while his first monograph of 1777 (which he issued in translation in Paris in the same year) was extravagantly reviewed in the *Journal Encyclopédique*. Perhaps because his ideas were well received in France, but more probably for reasons of business, Palmer lived in Paris, at 18 rue Meslée, in the period 1785–7. *Watin's Directory* gives his business there as the supply of 'verres colorés adaptés aux verres ordinaires'. And it was during this period that he published, in fair French, his monograph on artificial daylight (*Lettre sur les moyens de produire, la nuit, une lumière pareille à celle du jour*, 1785) and his second essay on light and vision (*Théorie de la lumière, applicable aux arts, et principalement à la peinture*, 1786). The date of Palmer's death is unknown. He was buried on 8 August 1795 in the parish church of Hendon. JOHN MOLLON, *rev.*

Sources G. Walls, 'The G. Palmer story', *Journal of the History of Medicine and Allied Sciences*, 11 (1956) • J. Mollon, *Actes du 5ème Congrès de l'Association Internationale de la Couleur*, 1 (1985) • *The letters of Horace Walpole, earl of Orford*, ed. P. Cunningham, 9 vols. (1857–9) [letter to H. Mann, 6 Oct 1753] • parish records, City Westm. AC • Drapers' Company Records

Wealth at death see will, PRO, PROB 11/1110

Palmer, George (1772–1853), merchant and philanthropist, born on 11 February 1772, was the eldest son of William Palmer (1748?–1821), a London merchant descended from the Palmers of Wanlip, an old Leicestershire family, and his wife, Mary (*b.* 1747), only daughter of John Horsley, rector of Thorley, Hertfordshire. After schooling at Charterhouse, he served in the navy of the East India Company (1786–99). He married Anna Maria, daughter of William Bund of Wick, Worcestershire, in 1795, and they had three sons, including the legal scholar William *Palmer, and two daughters, one of whom died young.

In 1802 Palmer entered into partnership with his father, his brother, John Horsley *Palmer, and Captain John(?) Wilson as East India merchants and shipowners at 28 Throgmorton Street in the City of London. This firm was a branch of one of the first and most successful private agencies in India. Founded by Sir John Palmer in the 1770s, it had a large sailing fleet and was greatly respected. As was the custom at that time, the house of Palmer in India had associate partnerships: Palmer and Horsley (later Palmer, Mackillop & Co.) in London, and William Dent & Co. in China. In the late 1820s Palmers suffered an unprecedented bankruptcy brought about by speculation in indigo; debts were well over £400,000. Many houses went down with Palmers, but the London branch was not seriously affected.

George Palmer appeared in public life in London in 1831, when he combined with other shipowners to set up a lobby for the shipping interest. With his experience in naval and merchant shipping, he was well suited to chair the provisional committee. After two years of negotiation with owners in London and the outports, the foundation was laid, and Palmer was chosen to be the first chairman of the General London Ship Owners' Society when it was launched in 1833. It soon became an influential and lasting national institution.

At the same time Palmer was engaged in two matters of global importance. He chaired the provisional committee set up to form and establish rules for a new Lloyd's register of shipping. Under his guidance, the new register emerged in 1834 as a model for shipping all over the world. The next task was to find a standard mode of measuring the capacity of vessels. Some of the principles proposed by Palmer were incorporated by the Admiralty in the Tonnage and Measuring Act in 1835.

Having unsuccessfully contested South Shields in December 1832, Palmer entered parliament for South Essex in 1836 on the death of the incumbent and held the seat until 1847. As befitted an MP of the Conservative tendency, he fought against what he saw as power being taken from the parishes to the centre, the 'cloven hoof' that would deprive individuals of their liberty; but he could not bring himself to take Peel's side when the abolition of the corn laws was debated. His main concern, however, was safety at sea. He chaired two parliamentary inquiries on shipwrecks, and in 1845, against strong opposition, pushed an amendment through that finally settled the law prohibiting timber-laden ships from carrying deck cargoes.

Palmer never forgot the narrow escape he and his crew had from drowning in 1788 in eastern waters; he took a keen interest in the Royal National Lifeboat Institution and in his later life was its vice-chairman for twenty-five years. His own design of a lifeboat was in use until 1858. The institution honoured him with its gold medal a few weeks before his death. He died on 12 May 1853 at Nazing (later Nazeing) Hall, the family home near Epping.

FREDA HARCOURT

Sources *ILN* (21 May 1853), 402 • *GM*, 2nd ser., 39 (1853), 656–7 • 'The late Mr Palmer, of Nazing-Park', *The Times* (24 Oct 1872), 3d • 'Messrs Palmer and Co., of Calcutta', *The Times* (1 May 1830), 5d • London General Ship Owners' Society minutes, 1831–45, Chamber of Shipping, London • minutes, 1833–4, Lloyd's register of shipping • 'A brief outline of the origin, constitution and history of Lloyd's register of British and foreign shipping, together with an account of early registers', Lloyd's register of shipping archives • M. Greenberg, *British trade and the opening of China, 1800–42* (1951) • 'Select committee to inquire into shipwrecks', *Parl. papers* (1839), 9.335, no. 333 • 'Select committee on shipwrecks', *Parl. papers* (1843), 9.1, no. 549; 9.669, no. 581 • S. Palmer, *Politics, shipping and the repeal of navigation laws* (1990) • *Hansard 3* (1838), 44.722–6; (1839), 49.420–22, 1386 • J. Phipps, *A series of treatises on the principal products of Bengal: indigo* (1832) • J. Phipps, *A guide to the commerce of Bengal* (1823) • *DNB* • d. cert. • will, PRO, PROB 11/2174, sig. 488

Archives Chamber of Shipping, London • Lloyd's, London, register of shipping archives

Palmer, George (1818–1897), biscuit manufacturer, was born at Upton Farm, Long Sutton, Somerset, on 18 January 1818, the eldest of three sons and a daughter (another son died young) of William Palmer, a farmer, and his wife, Mary, daughter of William Isaac, a Dorset tanner. Both families were Quakers of long standing, Mary Isaac being the first cousin of Cyrus and James Clark, founders of C. and J. Clark, shoemakers at Street, Somerset.

After William Palmer died prematurely in 1826, his energetic widow gave up farming in order to train her sons for various trades or professions. George received his education at Sidcot School, near Weston-super-Mare, leaving at the age of fourteen to be apprenticed to an uncle as a miller and confectioner. His ambition was to mechanize the production of biscuits, then made by hand. In 1841 he therefore went into partnership with his cousin by marriage, Thomas Huntley (1802–1857), owner of a Reading firm, founded in 1822, which sold high-quality biscuits over much of southern England; the firm then became Huntley and Palmers. With the technical help of a Reading engineer, William Exall (1808–1881), Palmer in 1846 invented the first continuously running biscuit machinery in the world, which was set up at a factory in Kings Road, Reading. On 17 January 1850 he married Elizabeth Sarah Meteyard (1825–1894), daughter of Robert Meteyard, a Quaker druggist at Basingstoke; they had six sons and four daughters, of whom two sons and a daughter did not survive infancy.

When Thomas Huntley died in 1857, annual turnover of the company was £125,000, as against £2700 in 1841, profits having risen from nil to £18,000 over the same period. George Palmer bought out Huntley's son and took into partnership his own brothers, Samuel and William Isaac Palmer, the former managing the London office and the latter running the factory. Despite all his business commitments, George Palmer took an active part in public affairs. From 1850 onwards he was a Liberal councillor in Reading; he served as mayor in 1857–8, and later became an alderman. In 1878 his Quaker friend, John Bright, persuaded him to stand for parliament, and he was elected MP for Reading, serving until 1885. After a maiden speech which supported the granting to women of the vote, he remained very largely a silent member, but his advice on industrial matters was widely sought. In 1885 he stood as a Liberal for Newbury and was defeated; he did not seek election again.

As early as 1873 Palmer owned 2000 acres of land in Berkshire and neighbouring counties, and subsequently added 2800 acres, including Marlston House near Newbury, which became his country retreat. In 1874–5 the second generation of Palmers—three sons of George, including George William *Palmer (1851–1913), and four of Samuel—became partners in the business, which justifiably claimed to be the largest biscuit firm in the world. About a quarter of its output went overseas, its global reputation being enhanced by successive medals won at international exhibitions, most notably those at Paris in 1867, 1878, and 1900. At home the firm became a kind of national institution after a local bishop had praised its biscuits for conveying ‘a savour of the quiet fireside and of the social board’, *The Times* responding with a bland leader (3 October 1883) and *Punch* with a gentle cartoon (13 October 1883).

Palmer was of medium height, and rather rugged in appearance, with a bushy beard, and a tight-lipped expression, perhaps inherited from his formidable mother. He occasionally indulged in devastating outbursts of temper, as when two employees approached him for a rise in wages. Yet he willingly accepted his responsibilities as a paternalistic businessman. Until the firm grew too large in the 1860s, he knew every operative by name; he maintained a sick club with a part-time doctor, a library, and a schoolmaster for the boy employees. He and his bachelor brother, William Isaac Palmer, helped factory hands in need, paying for the funerals of those who died in their service, and providing cash or coal tickets as necessary. To the town of Reading he was generous, presenting to its citizens the 49 acre Palmer Park and the Thames-side Kings Meadow. He also made donations to Reading University College, Reading School, the Royal Berkshire Hospital and, less predictably, several Anglican churches. It was said that his practice of handing out half-crowns to all and sundry turned Reading in his lifetime into a magnet for beggars from all over the kingdom.

In 1891, the golden jubilee of his partnership, he was given the freedom of Reading, a statue of him being erected in the town's main shopping street. That year he refused a baronetcy, and with typical candour made it clear that such an honour would yield him neither comfort nor satisfaction. His last years were darkened by bereavement: he never recovered from his wife's death in 1894, and he suffered from increasing debility. He died of a stroke, at The Acacias, his house in Reading, on 19 August 1897, and was buried at the Quaker burial-ground, Church Street, Reading. That year, the turnover of the company was more than £1.25 million, representing 23,000 tons of biscuits, and profits were £165,000. T. A. B. Corley

Sources T. A. B. Corley, *Quaker enterprise in biscuits: Huntley and Palmer of Reading, 1822–1972* (1972) • *Reading Mercury* (21 Aug 1897) • *Reading Observer* (21 Aug 1897) • *The Times* (20 Aug 1897) • *Christian World* (26 Aug 1897) • *Reading Mercury* (7 Nov 1891) • *Reading Observer* (7 Nov 1891) • T. A. B. Corley, ‘Palmer, George’, *DBB* • *The Times* (3 Oct 1883) • *Punch*, 85 (1883), 178 • *DNB* • personal knowledge (1901) [*DNB*]

Archives U. Reading, Huntley and Palmer MSS

Likenesses statue, 1891, Palmer Park, Reading, Berkshire • portrait, U. Reading, Palmer Building • two photographs, U. Reading • wood-engraving, NPG; repro. in *ILN* (1 June 1878)

Wealth at death £967,554 6*s*. 6*d*.: probate, 2 Nov 1897, *CGPLA Eng. & Wales*

Palmer, George Herbert (1846–1926), church musician and music scholar, was born at Grantchester on 9 August 1846, the eldest son of Jonathan Palmer, a master printer, of Cambridge, and his wife, Elizabeth, the daughter of Thomas Stevenson, of Rainton, Yorkshire. He was a cousin of the printer and bibliographer William Blades and also of the music critic and historian George Grove.

Brought up in Cambridge, Palmer was greatly influenced by a friend of his father, the liturgiologist John Mason Neale, and after graduating BA at Trinity College, Cambridge, in 1869 was ordained deacon in 1869 and priest in 1871 at Chester. His first curacy was at St Margaret's, Toxteth Park, Liverpool, where he also played the organ and attracted the attention of William Thomas Best, one of the greatest organ virtuosos of the nineteenth century.

As priest and organist at St Barnabas's Church, Pimlico, from 1876 to 1883, Palmer made the acquaintance of Thomas Helmore, precentor of St Mark's College, Chelsea (1846–77), and one of the pioneers of the revival of Gregorian chant. With G. R. Woodward, the curate of St Barnabas, he began his work on the rediscovery of the authentic plainchant tradition and the adaptation of the chants to English texts. Despite his adaptations being somewhat free, his work in this area was valuable and he was able to keep in touch with the researches of the Benedictine community at Solesmes, near Le Mans, where his music scholarship was greatly respected. Several examples, including *Sarum Hymn Melodies* and *Plain Song Manes*, were published in the early 1880s by the London Gregorian Choral Association.

In 1888 Palmer co-operated in the foundation of the Plainsong and Medieval Music Society, to which he later made several contributions. He also actively promoted the training of English religious communities in the liturgical music of the church. He produced *The Antiphoner and Grail* (1881) and *Harmonies to the Office Hymn Book* (1891), and issued, through St Mary's Press, Wantage, *The Sarum Psalter* (1894; 6th edn 1920), *The Order of Vespers from the Sarum Breviary* (1899), *The Offices, or Introits* (1904; 3rd edn 1927), and *A Selection of Grails, Alleluyas and Tracts … from the Sarum Gradale* (1908), as well as many other adaptations of the music of the mass and divine office.

In 1917 the archbishop of Canterbury, Randall Davidson, acting on a petition from a number of influential musicians, conferred on Palmer a Lambeth degree of Doctor of Music. He was presented for the degree by Richard Runciman Terry, organist and director of music at Westminster Cathedral, demonstrating further the esteem with which Palmer's learning was held outside the Anglican communion. During the same year he went to Oxford, and took over for a time the direction of the music at the church of the Society of St John the Evangelist, Cowley, where he had founded a plainchant tradition many years before. He now had the opportunity to concentrate on perhaps his most important work, *The Diurnal Noted*, the text of which appeared in 1921 under the title *The Diurnal after the Use of the Illustrious Church of Salisbury*. The manuscript of the music was completed just before his death, part 1 being published in 1926 and part 2 in 1929.

An apparently single-minded but generous man, Palmer died at his home, 18 Fairacres Road, Oxford, on 20 June 1926, and was buried in the churchyard of St Mary and St John. J. M. Close, *rev.* David J. Golby

Sources *WWW* • *Church Times* (25 June 1926) • private information (1937) • personal knowledge (1937) • Venn, *Alum. Cant.*
Wealth at death £5300 12*s.* 1*d.*: probate, 23 Oct 1926, *CGPLA Eng. & Wales*

Palmer, George Josiah (1828–1892), newspaper founder and editor, was born in Clapham, Surrey, on 30 June 1828, the eldest son and second child in the family of four sons and a daughter of George Josiah Palmer, printer, of Savoy Street, Strand, and his wife, Charlotte, daughter of John Hatchard, the evangelical publisher and bookseller, founder of Hatchards in Piccadilly. He was educated at Clapham grammar school and King's College School, London, and entered his father's printing firm as a compositor, later becoming manager. He married Marianne, daughter of James Beall, upholsterer, of Cheshunt, Hertfordshire, on 15 May 1851. They had six sons and a daughter.

In 1852 Palmer purchased a small bookselling and printing business in Bloomsbury, London. Trade did not prosper, however, and in 1860 he was forced to sell out and take humbler premises at 32 Little Queen Street, Lincoln's Inn Fields, later to be the home of the *Church Times*. The turning point in his fortunes came in October 1861, when he was asked to take on the printing and publishing of *The Union* newspaper, which was trying to bring Tractarian Anglicans into touch with Roman Catholics. The connection soon snapped, however, as by mid-1862 internal squabbles among the paper's managers led to its demise. But Palmer's connection with *The Union* enabled him to build up a link with leaders of the advanced wing of the high-church party.

Palmer then decided to enter journalism on his own account and launch a popular church paper. On 7 February 1863 the first number of the *Church Times* appeared. Like *The Union* it was founded to forward the work and views of the Tractarians, who were then fighting an uphill battle against fierce opposition in the church. (Such practices as having candles on the altar were then considered popish.) The paper soon attracted readers, outshining all its Anglican rivals, and its sales rose steadily throughout Palmer's lifetime.

Palmer himself edited the *Church Times* from its foundation until his retirement in 1887, besides being responsible for its general direction and management. He was a realist, having little faith in committees. His experience of the committee-managed *Union* convinced him that personal guidance was the safest way to run any enterprise. Three of his sons also spent all or most of their working lives in the service of the *Church Times*. (The paper remained in the ownership and under the control of the Palmer family until its sale to Hymns Ancient and Modern Ltd in 1989.) Palmer's paper was certainly outspoken: and, as his *Church Times* obituary remarked, 'our friend was no respecter of persons, however high in official standing, if he deemed it necessary, in support of God's truth or the Church's laws, to condemn their conduct'. Like so many Victorians, he looked the part, his face possessing an authority worthy of a minor prophet. Palmer was also closely concerned with the work of the Church of England Working Men's Society and was for many years its honorary treasurer. He died at 3 Victoria Crescent, Ramsgate, on 27 January 1892. Bernard Palmer, *rev.*

Sources *Church Times* (8 Feb 1963) • archives of *Church Times* • m. cert. • MSS, priv. coll. • *CGPLA Eng. & Wales* (1892)
Archives priv. coll.
Wealth at death £25,639 16*s.* 4*d.*: probate, 10 March 1892, *CGPLA Eng. & Wales*

Palmer, George William (1851–1913), biscuit manufacturer and benefactor, was born in Reading on 23 May 1851, the eldest of the six sons and four daughters of George *Palmer (1818–1897), co-founder of Huntley and Palmers of Reading, and his wife, Elizabeth Sarah (1825–1894), daughter of Robert Meteyard, Quaker druggist of Basingstoke. He was educated at the Quaker school of Grove House, Tottenham, and joined his father's firm in 1867, becoming a partner seven years later. He specialized in the production side, two of his brothers and four sons of George Palmer's brother Samuel in due course respectively managing the firm's two departments. In 1879 he married Eleanor, the eldest daughter of Henry Barrett, of Surbiton. They had no children. Soon after their marriage, they ceased to be Quakers and joined the Church of England.

Despite being a full-time partner in Huntley and Palmers, George William Palmer devoted much time to public affairs. In 1882 he was elected to Reading borough council, serving as mayor in 1888–9 and later becoming alderman. He was Liberal member of parliament for Reading from 1892 to 1895, and again from 1898 to 1904, espousing Gladstonian free-trade views that were at variance with those of his conservatively minded brothers. He believed in the payment of MPs, a step not taken until 1912, and pressed for the Church of England to be freed from all state patronage and control. In addition, he served as justice of the peace both for Reading and for Berkshire. In

1902 he was made freeman of the borough of Reading, his father having been the only other person so honoured.

In 1898, after the death of George Palmer senior, Huntley and Palmers became a private limited company. There was no chairman until 1904, when George William Palmer was appointed after resigning his parliamentary seat owing to deafness. For the same reason he resigned the company chairmanship in 1906, the year in which he was given the rare honour, as a former back-bencher, of appointment to the privy council. Often absent on lengthy trips abroad, he scarcely provided the lead to the company that might have been expected of its senior family member. Huntley and Palmers' national and international supremacy in biscuit manufacture was being eroded at this time by Peek Frean, and a number of Scottish biscuit makers, some of which, during Palmer's lifetime, established manufacturing plants in England. Huntley and Palmers only reluctantly began heavy advertising in the popular press, and, although turnover in 1912/13 exceeded £1.5 million for the first time, compared with £1.25 million in 1897/8, net profit had increased only from £165,000 to £193,000.

Palmer's reputation is therefore likely to rest on his benefactions, most notably to Reading University College, on whose council he served from 1902 onwards; he was vice-president from 1905 until his death. He gave £50,000 in memory of his father in 1905, and a recreation ground in 1909. Two years later he and his wife subscribed £100,000 towards an endowment fund of £200,000, intended to enable the college to achieve university status, which it did, in 1926. He founded a scholarship to allow former pupils of Reading School to attend the college. In his will he bequeathed to the college a further £10,000. Over and above *ad hoc* gifts for building, and other funds of the college, he anonymously contributed large sums in order to wipe out its accumulated debt.

Like many other sons of formidable entrepreneurial pioneers, he was highly strung, peppery, and obstinate when he judged himself to be in the right. Yet he exercised a strong unifying influence throughout the extended Palmer family. A childless couple, he and his wife loved to entertain children, their parents, and other relatives and friends in the over-large mansion into which he had converted his father's modest Newbury residence of Marlston House. Since he detested the new-fangled motor car, he drove himself regularly in his carriage with a fine pair of horses to Newbury Station *en route* for Reading or London. His recreations included hunting and shooting. He adopted as his heir a nephew, Ronald, younger son of Sir Edward Bagnall Poulton, and a celebrated rugby football blue and international. Ronald Poulton-Palmer, as he became, was killed in 1915 during the First World War. George William Palmer did not live to see that distressing conflict, dying suddenly of a heart attack at Marlston House, on 8 October 1913. He was buried at Marlston, and was survived by his wife. T. A. B. Corley

Sources T. A. B. Corley, *Quaker enterprise in biscuits: Huntley and Palmer of Reading, 1822–1972* (1972) • *Reading Mercury* (11 Oct 1913) • *Reading Standard* (11 Oct 1913) • *Berkshire Chronicle* (11 Oct 1913) • *The Times* (10 Oct 1913) • W. M. Childs, *Making a university: an account of the university movement at Reading* (1933) • T. A. B. Corley, 'The Palmer family and the University of Reading', *Staff Journal, University of Reading*, 6 (1968), 6–12 • *WWW*, *1897–1915* • Huntley and Palmers MSS • *DNB* • personal knowledge (1927) [*DNB*]

Archives U. Reading, Huntley and Palmer MSS

Likenesses oils, U. Reading • photographs, U. Reading, Huntley and Palmer MSS

Wealth at death £765,676 18*s*. 6*d*.: probate, 14 Nov 1913, *CGPLA Eng. & Wales*

Palmer, Harold Edward (1877–1949), linguist and teacher of languages, was born on 6 March 1877 at 63 Wornington Road, North Kensington, London, the elder child of Edward Palmer (*b*. 1853), schoolmaster and (from 1890) newspaper proprietor, and his wife, Minnie, *née* Frostick (*b*. 1857). In the early 1880s his father moved the family back to his home town of Hythe in Kent, where he set up a school. Later he opened a stationery shop and in 1890 launched a local newspaper, the *Hythe Reporter*, a venture that provided his son with his first publishing opportunities.

Harold Palmer's education began at local elementary schools, but he was withdrawn at the age of ten and tutored at home for three years. He spent two further years at a small private secondary school in Hythe before leaving for good in 1892 at the age of fifteen. His later adolescent years included a six-month exchange visit with a family in Boulogne (1892–3), but his time was largely spent pursuing personal interests like cycling, collecting fossils, playing the piano, and writing (mostly humorous) pieces for the *Reporter*. In 1899 he took over the paper's editorship for two years but then left Hythe to pursue a teaching career abroad.

By February 1902 Palmer was teaching English in a language school run on Berlitz (direct method) lines in Verviers, Belgium. The following year he established his own school, later known as the Institut Palmer, which flourished and in time came to occupy two separate sites in the town. On 19 November 1904 he married a local woman named Elisabeth Purnode (*b*. 1885), and a daughter, Dorotheé, was born on 28 April 1905.

During his time in Verviers, Palmer (who had no university training) set out on a determined course of self-education. He became a member of the local *société polyglotte* and started writing language teaching materials (his first book, *Méthode Palmer*, an English course for French speakers, appeared in 1906). He deepened his linguistic studies by joining the International Phonetic Association and had the first of many contributions accepted by its journal *Le Maître Phonétique* in 1910, work that attracted the attention of Britain's leading twentieth-century phonetician, Daniel Jones of University College, London.

Palmer and Jones met by chance on a cross-channel ferry in 1912, an encounter that proved helpful two years later when Palmer and his family, after being forced to escape hurriedly from German-occupied eastern Belgium, returned to England in straitened circumstances. After an attempt to start a school in Folkestone, Palmer took up a post teaching French in a London grammar school. He contacted Jones, who invited him to deliver a series of (extra-mural) lectures at University College on methods of language teaching, the success of which, plus Palmer's evident skill as a phonetician, encouraged Jones to employ him in the department. His duties included teaching spoken English and organizing a year-long course in language teaching methodology, the first of its kind at university level in Britain. Palmer's time at the college was unusually fruitful, and resulted in three substantial works that won him a lasting reputation as a leading thinker in the theory and practice of language teaching: *The Scientific Study and Teaching of Languages* (1917), *The Principles of Language-Study* (1921), and *The Oral Method of Teaching Languages* (1921).

Having established himself at home, Palmer moved on. He accepted a post as linguistic adviser to the Japanese ministry of education and in February 1922 left for Tokyo, where an Institute for Research in English Teaching (IRET) was set up with Palmer as its director. The decision to focus on research was unique for its time, and made imaginative use of Palmer's academic and practical expertise. After opening in May 1923, the institute attracted a substantial membership and started a monthly journal, the *Bulletin*. IRET's basic aims were well summarized later by Palmer's Tokyo colleague A. S. Hornby: '(1) the compilation of English language courses; (2) the encouragement of reformed methods of language teaching; (3) the starting of research and experimental work in linguistic subjects, and (4) the training of teachers of English' (Hornby, 88). All IRET's work was underpinned by a strong theoretical framework derived from modern linguistics and psychology, in particular the ideas of Saussure and Bloomfield with their emphasis on spoken language, reflected in the titles of Palmer's major publications in the 1920s: *English Intonation* (1922), *A Grammar of Spoken English* (1924), *English through Actions* (classroom oral exercises devised with his daughter Dorotheé, 1925), *A Dictionary of English Pronunciation* (1926), and *The Five Speech-Learning Habits* (1927).

From the late 1920s onwards Palmer became increasingly interested in text simplification and vocabulary control. Dissatisfied with the educational limitations of word-frequency statistics, he conducted a series of lexicological studies with broader pedagogical relevance, laying the groundwork for an innovative learner's dictionary combining both grammatical and lexical information. To extend his linguistic expertise (and publicize the institute), he undertook a lengthy lecturing tour in 1931–2 which took him to the United States, where he met Sapir and Bloomfield, both of whom became public supporters of his work in Tokyo. The culmination of these efforts came in 1935 with his participation in a working party (established in New York in 1934) to determine a definitive basic ('general service') word-list for English language teaching. The provisional list appeared in the *Interim Report* (1936), but full publication was delayed until 1953.

Now approaching sixty and with the international situation deteriorating, Palmer decided to return to England and he left Japan with a DLitt from Tokyo Imperial University in the spring of 1936. On their return the Palmers settled at Felbridge, on the Surrey–Sussex border, where Harold continued writing English language teaching materials, including *The New Method Grammar* (1938) for young learners, which used railways as a metaphor for grammar (he even constructed a working model in his garden), and *A Grammar of English Words* (1938). His last major work was his innovative *International English Course* (1943 onwards), which unexpectedly adopted a bilingual approach to make it suitable for self-instruction purposes. Various versions appeared in the mid-1940s, but it became enmeshed in London publishing politics and was discontinued.

In July 1942 Tristram, the Palmers' twenty-one-year-old son, was killed in action over the Netherlands while on a bombing mission. Harold Palmer never fully recovered from the shock, falling victim to serious depression and ill health (he had to return early from a lecturing tour of South America in 1944, for instance). He was also disappointed that his ideas for a British IRET fell on deaf ears.

With the end of the Second World War, however, the influence of IRET began to emerge. The British Council founded *English Language Teaching* using the IRET *Bulletin* as its model, with Hornby as editor. Hornby also took responsibility for the dictionary Palmer had initiated in the 1930s (now the world-famous *Oxford Advanced Learner's Dictionary of Current English*). In fact English language teaching in the 1950s and beyond reflected many of Palmer's pedagogical values: the emphasis on spoken language, for instance, the importance of ordered progression, and the need for effective classroom procedures. He died at his home, Coopers Wood, Felbridge, from acute heart failure on 16 November 1949, and was buried at Folkestone cemetery. His wife survived him. His death removed the man himself and with him the personality and charisma that had attracted so many people to him and to his ideas throughout his life.

A. P. R. Howatt

Sources *Bulletin of the Institute for Research in English Teaching*, 7 vols. (1985) • *The selected writings of Harold E. Palmer*, 10 vols. (1995–9) • R. C. Smith, *The writings of Harold E. Palmer: an overview* (1999) • A. S. Hornby, 'H. E. Palmer', *English Language Teaching* (Jan 1950) • R. C. Smith, 'Harold E. Palmer's formative years (1877–1901)', *Area and Culture Studies*, 57 (1998), 1–37 • H. Bongers, *The history and principles of vocabulary control* (1947) • D. Anderson, 'Harold E. Palmer: a biographical essay', in H. E. Palmer and H. V. Redman, *This language-learning business*, ed. R. Mackin (1969), appendix, 135–66 • A. P. R. Howatt, *A history of English language teaching* (1984) • R. C. Smith, 'The Palmer–Hornby contribution to English teaching in Japan', *International Journal of Lexicography*, 11/4 (1998), 269–91 • M. Tanaka, 'Harold E. Palmer after he left Japan', *Annual Review of English Language Education in Japan*, 2 (1991), 181–6 • D. Jones, 'Harold Palmer', *Le Maître Phonétique* (Jan–June 1950), 4–7 • B. Collins and I. M. Mees, *The real Professor Higgins: the life and career of Daniel Jones* (1999)

Likenesses photograph, repro. in Howatt, *History*

Wealth at death £6758 12*s*. 6*d*.: administration, 10 March 1950, *CGPLA Eng. & Wales*

Palmer, Sir Henry (*d*. 1559), soldier, was the second son of Edward Palmer of Angmering, Sussex, and Alice, daughter of John Clement of Ightham Mote, Kent. Palmer was one of those younger sons to whom a successful career in royal service offered substantial rewards. Palmer's chosen path was military: by 1528 he was serving as a spear in the Calais garrison. In the late 1530s he successfully sought the patronage of Thomas Cromwell, receiving the keeping of Guînes Forest near Calais and the bailiffship of Guînes in 1540. Palmer's association with Cromwell and Archbishop Cranmer's commissary in Calais, Sir Thomas Butler, attracted accusations of evangelical sympathies. Palmer survived the fall of Cromwell in 1540, and the capture of Boulogne four years later offered him further opportunities. After the town's fall Palmer was knighted by Henry VIII on 30 September 1544. The following year he was master of the ordnance and a member of the town's governing council. Palmer, however, was critical of the defence of Boulogne and was dismissed from his post at the Old Man bulwark amid unfounded accusations of cowardice.

By 1536 Palmer had married Jane, daughter of Sir Richard Windebank of Guînes, with whom he had three sons. In the early 1550s he acquired lands in east Kent, including Wingham College near Canterbury, and in 1554 sat in parliament for the borough of Bramber in Sussex. Given his possible evangelical links and his family's association with John Dudley, duke of Northumberland (he was arrested on the duke's fall but pardoned in October 1553), it seems unlikely that his election was due to the influence of Bramber's overlord, the third duke of Norfolk.

Palmer's military exploits continued under Mary I and by 1556, now aged '60 years and above' (PRO, SP 69/8/510), he was back in Calais. He was captured at the fall of Guînes in 1558 and held ransom by the seigneur de Cipierre, governor of Orléans. Although pledges to redeem him were forthcoming, he died apparently intestate in captivity on 15 January 1559; in the fighting he had suffered a severe leg wound which necessitated amputation. His place of death is unknown. His property passed to his son, Thomas *Palmer. DAVID GRUMMITT

Sources HoP, *Commons*, 1509–58, 2.140, 3.26–7 • D. I. Grummitt, 'Calais, 1485–1547: a study in early Tudor politics and government', PhD diss., U. Lond., 1997 • *CSP for.*, 1547–53 • *CSP dom.*, 1553–8 • Lord Grey of Wilton, *A commentary of the services and charges of William Lord Grey of Wilton, K.G.*, ed. P. De Malpas Grey Egerton, CS, 1st ser., 40 (1847) • T. Churchyard, *A generall rehearsall of warres* (1579), sigs. Iir–Iiiv • *LP Henry VIII*, 12/2.1278; 13/2.863; 14/2.808; 19/1.846; 21/1.33, 364, 481, 1487; 21/2.232

Archives PRO, signature appended to letters of Boulogne Council to Privy Council, SP 1/213, fol. 47 • PRO, signature appended to letters of Boulogne Council to Privy Council, SP 1/215, fol. 50 • PRO, signature appended to letters of Boulogne Council to Privy Council, SP 1/216, fol. 21 • PRO, signature appended to letters of Boulogne Council to Privy Council, SP 1/223, fol. 139 • PRO, report to the Privy Council on his meeting with monsieur Deuras, SP 1/189, fol. 202 • PRO, answer to complaints levelled against Henry Palmer as bailiff of Guînes, SP 1/156, fols. 80–90 • PRO, Lord Edmund Howard, Thomas Fowler, and Henry Palmer to Thomas Cromwell, SP 1/127, fol. 156 • PRO, deposition relating to Sandingfield Abbey, Calais, SP 69/8/510 • PRO, to duke of Somerset, SP 68/15/138 • PRO, William, Lord Grey, Sir Thomas and Sir Henry Palmer to duke of Somerset, SP 68/14/121

Likenesses portrait; known to be at Wingham, Kent, in 1672

Palmer, Sir Henry (*c*.1550–1611), naval commander, first appears in the queen's service at sea off the coast of Flanders in 1576, which indicates that he was probably born about 1550. He was literate, but there are few other indications of his upbringing; he may, like Francis Drake, have been apprenticed to the sea. From 1580 he was a commissioner for the maintenance of Dover harbour, and was probably the Henry Palmer, esquire, who was a commissioner for concealed lands in Kent in 1581. He served under the earl of Leicester in the Netherlands, and was knighted by him in 1586, an honour that was followed by a grant of arms in the same year. In 1587 he was commanding a squadron in the narrow seas, and in 1588 was captain of the *Antelope* (300 tons) against the Armada, when he is described as the third in command under Lord Henry Seymour. It was he who obtained and organized the fireships that caused such consternation to the Spaniards off Calais, and he played a conspicuous and gallant part in the battle of Gravelines which followed. When most of the fleet was stood down on 27 August, Palmer remained in service and commanded the winter guard over the following months.

In July 1589 Palmer was again commanding in the channel, and in September was given the responsibility of escorting the troops that Elizabeth sent to the aid of Henri IV against the Catholic league. Further sea service is recorded twice in 1591, and he was still involved with harbour works at Dover in that year. By this time he had purchased an estate at Howletts, Bekesbourne, Kent; he first appears as a justice of the peace for Kent in 1589. His main service, however, continued to be at sea, and he took part in the blockade of Calais in 1596. This appears to have led to rumours in Spain that his head was cut off for refusing to serve against the Spaniards there; but there is no indication in the English records that he was out of favour. He appeared again upon the commission of the peace in 1593, 1594, and 1601. In July 1598 he acted as an executor for the controller of the navy, William Borough—described as his cousin—and he succeeded to Borough's post on 3 January 1599. He retained this position until his death, although his last recorded command at sea was in 1601.

Palmer married twice. His first wife was Joan, daughter and coheir of Edward Isaac, and widow of Nicholas Sidley. They had at least two sons, although only Henry *Palmer is known to have survived his father. His second wife was Dorothy (*née* Scott), widow of Thomas Hernden. He died at Bekesbourne on 20 November 1611 and was buried in the parish church, leaving modest bequests to the poor of Bekesbourne and a number of neighbouring parishes. The younger Henry was granted the reversion of his father's controllership on 17 August 1611, but did not secure the position until 1632. DAVID LOADES

Sources PRO, SP 12 • *Hasted's history of Kent: corrected, enlarged, and continued to the present time*, ed. H. H. Drake (1886) • N. A. M. Rodger, *The safeguard of the sea: a naval history of Britain*, 1: 660–1649 (1997) • D. M. Loades, *The Tudor navy* (1992) • M. Zell, 'Kent's Elizabethan JPs at work', *Archaeologia Cantiana*, 119 (1999), 1–43 • H. F. Waters, *Genealogical gleanings in England*, 2 vols (1901) • J. K. Laughton, ed., *State papers relating to the defeat of the Spanish Armada, anno 1588*, 2 vols., Navy RS, 1–2 (1894) • BL, Stowe MS 670, fol. 13 [grant of arms]

Likenesses M. Gheeraerts junior, oils; in possession of David Laing, 1895

Palmer, Sir Henry (*bap.* **1582**, *d.* **1644**), naval officer, was the son of Sir Henry *Palmer (*d.* 1611) of Howletts, Bekesbourne, in Kent, a distinguished naval officer and controller of the navy, and his first wife, Joan (or Jane) Isaac. He married Phoebe Fotherbye, daughter of Charles Fotherbye, archdeacon of Canterbury, in 1606. In 1611 he was given a grant in reversion of the office of controller of the navy following his father and Sir Guildford Slingsby. Palmer senior died the same year and was succeeded by Slingsby, but the position was then placed in commission from 1618 to 1628. Palmer was knighted in 1618. His earliest recorded naval experience was as commander of the *Antelope* on the Algiers expedition of 1620–21. In 1623 he was captain of the *Rainbow* in the narrow seas.

By 1626, following the Cadiz expedition, Palmer was in command in the Downs at a time when the fleet was close to collapse, with desertions rife owing to lack of funds and material. He managed to resupply the Île de Ré with provisions in September 1627 and was appointed vice-admiral of the proposed La Rochelle expedition of 1628. This year saw the culmination of a series of accusations of inactivity, notably from the duke of Buckingham, lord high admiral. Palmer argued, with some validity, that the poor state of the fleet precluded an offensive policy. His career in this period, however, is marked by a lack of effectiveness and vigour that continually earned the irritation of Buckingham. As a result he was unable to obtain a patent letter for his appointment as vice-admiral. Attempts to persuade Buckingham to stand godfather to his expected child proved fruitless and his position continued to decline despite Buckingham's death. By 1630 he had effectively been demoted to the rank of captain.

With his old rank of vice-admiral having been declared void in 1631, Palmer finally succeeded Sir Guildford Slingsby as controller in 1632. He was quickly implicated in a scandal involving the sale of old cordage ('brown paper stuff') from state shipyards for personal gain, his initial defence to the charge being 'because his predecessors had done the like' (*Naval Tracts of Sir William Monson*, 3.282). He subsequently tried to claim that he had actually spent the profits on supplies for the fleet, but he, Phineas Pett, and several others were briefly suspended in 1634 when the charges were proved against them. In 1636, along with the other principal officers, he defended the state of the fleet in response to a statement of abuses presented to the king by the earl of Northumberland following his first summer guard as admiral of the ship money fleet. Measures were taken in March 1637 to address the issues, but Northumberland's statement prompted a number of similar criticisms, notably that of John Hollond, aimed at reforming naval administration.

Palmer's health had broken down by the late 1630s, and in 1638–9 he was arranging for a younger man to share his office. As the prospect of hostilities increased in the spring and early summer of 1642 parliament refused to accept the king's nominee (Sir John Pennington) for command of the fleet in the Downs. Charles ignored parliament's opposition and ordered Pennington to take command regardless of opposition. Pennington wrote to Palmer at his home in Bekesbourne near the Downs (via Edward Villiers) ordering him to board the fleet, assume command, and if necessary transfer the fleet to Scarborough. Palmer, however, was too old and frail to perform the task or indeed to understand fully the implications of what was being asked of him. This, combined with his natural lack of energy, turned the coup into a fiasco. Villiers and Pennington arrived with separate and differing orders while Palmer was refused permission by the earl of Warwick even to approach the fleet, leaving parliament in undisputed control. Palmer played no further part in public affairs until his death in 1644. He had at least one son, Henry (1611–1659), who succeeded him.

ROY MCCAUGHEY

Sources *CSP dom.* • *The naval tracts of Sir William Monson*, ed. M. Oppenheim, 5 vols., Navy RS, 22–3, 43, 45, 47 (1902–14) • *The autobiography of Phineas Pett*, ed. W. G. Perrin, Navy RS, 51 (1918) • G. E. Aylmer, *The king's servants: the civil service of Charles I, 1625–1642*, rev. edn (1974) • *IGI* • E. Hasted, *The history and topographical survey of the county of Kent*, 2nd edn, 12 vols. (1797–1801) • A. P. McGowan, 'The Royal Navy under the first duke of Buckingham', PhD diss., U. Lond., 1971 • Venn, *Alum. Cant.*, 1/3 • *Boteler's dialogues*, ed. W. G. Perrin, Navy RS, 65 (1929) • M. Oppenheim, *A history of the administration of the Royal Navy* (1896) • C. E. Fayle, 'The ship-money fleets', *EdinR*, 234 (1921), 375–89 • *DNB* • J. M. Cowper, ed., *Canterbury marriage licences*, 6 vols. (1892–1906) • Clarendon, *Hist. rebellion*

Palmer, Henry. *See* FitzRoy, Henry, first duke of Grafton (1663–1690).

Palmer, Henry Robinson (**1795–1844**), civil engineer, was born in Hackney in 1795, one of the many children of the Revd Samuel *Palmer, nonconformist minister, and his wife, Elizabeth, *née* Walker. He was educated at the academy run by his father. From 1811 to 1816 he was apprenticed to Bryan Donkin and he early displayed the keen interest in education and the formation of scientific societies that he pursued throughout his life. About 1813–14 he organized in Bermondsey a society of workmen which virtually constituted a mechanics' institute, almost ten years before those established by Leonard Horner in Edinburgh and George Birkbeck in Glasgow and London.

On completing his apprenticeship Palmer was engaged by Thomas Telford and worked for him for ten years on a large number of road and canal surveys and associated designs. About 1817 he suggested to Joshua Field the idea of founding a society of engineers which would be more accessible to the younger members of the profession than the rather élitist Society of Civil Engineers founded by John Smeaton in 1771. The first meeting of the Institution of Civil Engineers was held on 2 January 1818 with eight founder members present and Palmer gave the opening address, outlining the objectives of the institution. The institution, however, made slow progress until in 1820 Telford, who never joined the Smeatonians, agreed to become the first president and the rules restricting membership to younger engineers were relaxed. Palmer subsequently became a member of the council of the institution and in 1835 was elected one of the vice-presidents; he was always very attached to the body, contributing several interesting papers and seldom failing to take part in the discussions, which he considered to be the most valuable part of its meetings.

On 30 March 1827 Palmer married Mary Ann Emma Osmond at St Margaret's, Westminster. The previous year he had been appointed resident engineer to the London docks where, over the next nine years, he designed and executed the Eastern Dock, with the associated warehousing, entrance locks, bridges, and other works. He then moved to Westminster as a consulting engineer and was involved in numerous surveys for projected railways, and the design and construction of several docks and harbours, including those at Port Talbot, Ipswich, Penzance, and Neath. He carried out the original surveys for the South Eastern Railway, assisted by P. W. Barlow, and would have executed the scheme but ill health intervened. His original surveys for a Kentish railway dated from the time he was associated with Telford, and he gave parliamentary evidence in favour of navigation interests and against the Liverpool and Manchester Railway in 1825. Between 1821 and 1842 he took out five patents, one of them for a 'suspension railway' which was tried out unsuccessfully in Cheshunt and Deptford Dockyard. Of more importance were those relating to a system of constructing roofs and bridge decks in corrugated wrought or cast iron. The roofs were used extensively in London docks and the patent rights sold to Richard Walker of Rotherhithe, who marketed the system widely. Palmer was elected FRS in 1831; he published two papers on tides and the movement of shingle, in the *Philosophical Transactions* of 1831 and 1834.

Palmer died of dropsy on 12 September 1844 at 2 Great George Street, Westminster. A memorial window to him was installed in the main hall of the Institution of Civil Engineers in 1954.

RONALD M. BIRSE, *rev.* MIKE CHRIMES

Sources *PICE*, 4 (1845), 6–8 · G. Watson, *The civils: the story of the Institution of Civil Engineers* (1988) · A. W. Skempton, *British civil engineering, 1640–1840: a bibliography of contemporary printed reports, plans, and books* (1987) · A. W. Skempton and others, eds., *A biographical dictionary of civil engineers in Great Britain and Ireland*, 1 (2002)
Archives Inst. CE [almost all the papers had been lost by 1906] | CKS, survey of Looe Road
Wealth at death left enough to endow scholarship at Institution of Civil Engineers, London

Palmer, Henry Spencer (1838–1893), soldier and surveyor, third and youngest son of Colonel John Freke Palmer of the Madras staff corps of the East India Company's army, and his wife, Jane (*d.* 1838), daughter of John James of Truro and sister of Sir Henry *James, superintendent of the Ordnance Survey, was born at Bangalore, India, on 30 April 1838. He was educated at private schools at Bath, and by private tutors at Woolwich and Plumstead, and in January 1856 was admitted to the Royal Military Academy, Woolwich. He was gazetted lieutenant in the Royal Engineers on 20 December 1857, and studied in the School of Military Engineering at Chatham (1857–8), and between January and October 1858 served at Portsmouth and then on the Isle of Wight.

In October 1858 Palmer was appointed to the expedition to British Columbia under Colonel Richard Clement Moody RE. The expedition was originated by Sir Edward Bulwer Lytton, then secretary of state for the colonies, and consisted of six officers and 150 men from the Royal Engineers, who were to preserve order, which was rapidly deteriorating as gold prospectors rushed into the newly created colony, and carry out engineering works and surveys there. In British Columbia Palmer undertook a reconnaissance survey of the Cariboo gold fields in 1862, accomplished under great difficulties, and in that year it was largely due to his judgement that his party escaped massacre by the Bella Coola Indians at North Bentinck arm. The reports and maps prepared by him in connection with these surveys were published in parliamentary and colonial blue books. He also superintended the construction of roads, bridges, and other public works, including the wagon road through the canyon of the Fraser River, between Lytton and Yale. He married, on 7 October 1863, at New Westminster, British Columbia, Mary Jane Pearson, daughter of Archdeacon Henry Press Wright; they had nine children, of whom six survived to adulthood.

At the end of December 1863 Palmer arrived back in England and the following March joined the Ordnance Survey. He went first to Southampton and then to Tonbridge, Kent, from where he surveyed the greater part of Kent and east Sussex, and parts of Berkshire and Buckinghamshire. He was promoted second captain on 4 March 1866. Under the 1867 Reform Act he was appointed assistant commissioner in the parliamentary boundaries commission: with a colleague, Joseph Kay, he designated parliamentary boroughs in Kent and east Sussex, and subdivided county boroughs of west Kent and east Surrey.

At this time Palmer and a friend, the Revd Pierce Butler, of Ulcombe, Kent—an Arabic scholar—were planning a survey of the Sinai peninsula. Palmer persuaded his uncle, Henry James, head of the Ordnance Survey, to support the scheme and James persuaded the Royal Geographical Society and Royal Society to give financial support to a survey of the topography and a study of the geology, botany, and zoology of the region. Butler's death in 1868 did not stop the expedition, which set off in October 1868 under Palmer and C. W. Wilson. They completed their work by April 1869, despite the extremes of terrain and climate that they encountered. The two leaders edited the *Ordnance Survey of the Peninsula of Sinai* (5 vols.), officially dated 1869 though published in 1872. Palmer returned to England in May 1869 and resumed work at Tonbridge.

On 11 December 1873 Palmer was promoted major and in the same year he was appointed head of the expedition to observe the transit of Venus in New Zealand, for which he underwent a course of practical preparation at the Royal Observatory, Greenwich. He left England in June

1874, accompanied by Lieutenant L. Darwin RE, and Lieutenant Crawford RN, as his assistants. His work in observing the transit was highly praised by the astronomer royal in his *Report to the Board of Visitors* (1875). Before leaving New Zealand, Palmer, at the request of the governor, George Phipps, second marquess of Normanby, undertook an investigation of provincial surveys throughout the colony, to advise how to make them more systematic and scientifically sound. His recommendations earned him the thanks of the government, and were adopted as a guide for future reforms. He helped the French to determine the longitude of Campbell Island, for which he received the medal of the Institut de France.

Palmer returned to England in June 1875 and against his inclination, which was to continue with survey and engineering work, resumed military duty, going to Barbados in November 1875, where he was appointed aide-de-camp to the governor, Sir John Pope-Hennessy; he remained in this post through the riots of 1876 and until the governor's departure from the colony. In January 1878 he went to Hong Kong, where, in addition to his ordinary duties, he was appointed engineer of the Admiralty works and aide-de-camp to the governor, again John Pope-Hennessy. On 1 July 1881 he was promoted brevet lieutenant-colonel. In the same year he designed an observatory for Hong Kong to facilitate astronomical, magnetical, meteorological, and tidal observations. The design and report were approved by the Kew committee of the Royal Society and though the scheme was adapted to reduce its cost, the observatory was built largely to his design, which became a standard guide for similar observatories. In 1882 Palmer declined to take charge of another expedition to observe the transit of Venus, but he made in that year an exact determination of the Hong Kong observatory station at Mount Elgin, Kowloon, with instruments lent to him from the American surveying ship *Palos*.

On 1 October 1882 Palmer was promoted regimental lieutenant-colonel, and was ordered home. On his way he stayed at the British legation in Tokyo and was asked by the Japanese government to design waterworks for Yokohama. He completed two alternative schemes of water supply, one from Tamagawa and the other from Sagamigawa. On his arrival in England in July 1883 he was appointed commanding royal engineer of the Manchester district. In the autumn of 1884 the Japanese government applied to the British government for his services to superintend the construction of waterworks in accordance with his design. Permission was given, Palmer reached Japan in April 1885, and the works were started at once. On 1 July Palmer was promoted brevet colonel, and on 1 October 1887 he retired on a pension with the honorary rank of major-general. The same date saw the successful completion of the waterworks, for which in November he received from the emperor of Japan the third class of the order of the Rising Sun; he obtained the queen's permission to wear the order. After his retirement he remained in Japan and undertook numerous important engineering works. These included water supply works for Osaka and Hakodate, harbour works for the Yokohama Harbour Company, and water supplies for Misakamura in Hiogo Ken and for Tokyo; he supervised the building of many of his works. With Uta Saito, whom he may have married about 1890, he had a daughter. He died of apoplexy at 41 Imaicho Azabu, Tokyo, on 10 February 1893, while working on a project there. He was buried in the Aoyama cemetery in Tokyo.

A contemporary obituarist wrote that Palmer was a man of exceptionally clear, vigorous intellect, and remarkable breadth and liberality of view. His faculty of rapid calculation was of a high order, and he possessed a 'rare power of assimilating and marshalling facts' (Captain F. Brinkley, *Japan Weekly Mail*, 18 Feb 1898, cited in Higuchi, iv). He had a keen sense of humour and power of anecdote. His books *The Ordnance Survey of the Kingdom* (1873) and *Ancient History from the Monuments: Sinai from the Fourth Egyptian Dynasty to the Present Day* (1878) are memorable but he was perhaps most important as a journalist writing in English on Japan (his fifty-five newspaper articles are listed in Higuchi, 107–10) and those forty-eight which were published in *The Times* did much to increase understanding of Japan among the British.

A bust to his memory was erected in the Nogeyama public garden, Yokohama, in 1987. A full length biographical memoir by his grandson J. Higuchi was published in 2002. He also published, in 1982, a Japanese translation of his grandfather's *Letters from the land of the rising sun* (1894). An exhibition catalogue, *Henry Spencer Palmer—a special exhibition of his work and designs for the water works and harbour works of Yokohama* (Yokohama, 1987) marked the centenary of one of his most important engineering projects.

ELIZABETH BAIGENT

Sources J. Higuchi, *The biography of Major-General Henry Spencer Palmer RE FRAS (1838–1893)*, 2nd edn (privately printed, Japan, 2002) · *Royal Engineers Journal* (1 May 1893) · *DNB* · F. M. Woodward, 'Palmer, Henry Spencer', *DCB* · A. Kershaw, *The North Bentinck arm route* (1981) · *CGPLA Eng. & Wales* (1893) · W. A. Seymour, ed., *A history of the Ordnance Survey* (1980)

Archives priv. coll. | Provincial Archives, Victoria, British Columbia, Canada

Likenesses portrait, repro. in Higuchi, *Biography* · portrait, repro. in *Henry Spencer Palmer* (Yokohama, 1987)

Wealth at death £5528 1s. 3d. in England: probate, 19 April 1893, *CGPLA Eng. & Wales*

Palmer, Herbert (1601–1647), Church of England clergyman and college head, was born at Wingham, Kent, in 1601 and baptized on 29 March, the younger son of Sir Thomas Palmer (*d.* 1625) of Wingham, and Margaret, daughter of Herbert Pelham, esquire, of Crawley, Sussex; Sir Thomas *Palmer (1540/41–1626) was his grandfather. From an early age he demonstrated an aptitude for study and a religious disposition, maintaining the ambition to become a clergyman. In 1616 he was admitted as a fellow-commoner to St John's College, Cambridge, from where he graduated BA in 1619 and proceeded MA in 1622. On 17 July 1623 he was elected a fellow of Queens'. He was ordained in 1624 and proceeded BD in 1631.

In 1626, during a visit to his brother Sir Thomas Palmer (*d.* 1666), Palmer preached at Canterbury Cathedral and was subsequently persuaded by Philip Delmé, the minister of the French church in Canterbury, to take up a lectureship there at St Alphege's Church. Here Palmer found himself troubled by both separatists and the cathedral clergy. His lectureship was briefly suspended by the dean and archdeacon, but was reinstated by Archbishop George Abbot upon receiving a petition from the prominent citizens of Canterbury and members of the local gentry. Palmer's contemporary biographer records that he was not at this time persuaded of the 'unlawfulnesse' of either episcopal church government or some of the ceremonies then in use, but he opposed the 'innovations and corruptions, both in doctrine and worship, which in those days were creeping on apace' and was instrumental in preventing the spread of 'formality' in the city ('Life', 420). In Canterbury Palmer preached every sabbath afternoon at St Alphege and he also preached to the French congregation in their native tongue, which he had learned almost as soon as he could speak English.

Palmer was instituted to the rectory of Ashwell, Hertfordshire, in February 1632 and about the same time he was appointed as a university preacher in Cambridge, which gave him licence to preach anywhere in England. At Ashwell Palmer perfected his system of catechism, which was greatly admired. It was intended to help those with weak understanding or poor memories and to these ends Palmer broke up the answer into short questions, to which the simple response of 'yes' or 'no' was sufficient. This was followed by the main answer, which formed a coherent statement and did not require the memorization of the question. Palmer's catechism was first published in 1640 under the title *An Endeavour of Making the Principles of Christian Religion … Plain and Easie*. He was later involved in the drafting of the Westminster assembly's *Shorter Catechism* (1647), which was also published according to Palmer's own method after his death as *A Brief and Easie Explanation of the Shorter Catechisme* (1648) by John Wallis. Many of Palmer's publications were aimed at making the principles of the Christian faith clear and easy to understand. In 1644, for example, he published a brief spiritual guide to fasting based on the book of Nehemiah, chapters 9 and 10, with the intention of helping the 'weak' and the 'willing' to avoid 'the greate Evill of Formalitie in our solemne Humiliations' (*The Soule of Fasting, or, Affections Requisite in a Day of Solemne Fasting and Humiliation*, 1644, foreword).

Palmer never married but he had a large household at Ashwell, where he took the sons of noblemen and gentry as pupils and employed an assistant to help him to teach them. His pupils and servants were expected to adhere to a strict regime of religious observance, which involved regular attendance at church services with daily household prayers and readings from the Bible. Palmer catechized his household twice a week and also required a regular account of sermons and of chapters of the Bible from his pupils. He found time to follow a strict regime of private devotion, which included the daily maintenance of a spiritual diary and the personal observation of days of fasting and prayer. He also encouraged his parishioners to pledge themselves against drunkenness, swearing, whoredom, and fighting, among other things. In a visitation sermon at Hitchin in 1638 Palmer preached against the church 'innovations' of the time. He not only opposed bowing to the altar and reading the prayer book from the altar, he also opposed the Book of Sports in 1633 and the 'et cetera' oath enjoined by the church canons of 1640. In the 1640s he collaborated with Daniel Cawdrey on a work in defence of sabbatarianism, *Sabbatum redivivum*, part 1 of which was published in 1645 and parts 2 to 4 in 1652 (after Palmer's death).

In 1640 Palmer was chosen as one of the clerks of convocation for Lincoln diocese with Anthony Tuckney and on 19 July 1642 he was appointed by the House of Commons as one of fifteen Tuesday lecturers at Hitchin, Hertfordshire. In 1643 he was appointed to the Westminster assembly and moved to London, leaving Ashwell in the charge of his half-brother, John Crow. In 1643 Palmer collaborated with a number of other divines in writing *Scripture and Reason Pleaded for Defensive Armes* (1643), a tract justifying parliament's 'defensive' war against the king, in which they argued that 'an open and publike resistance by armes, is the last Refuge under Heaven, of an oppressed, and endangered Nation' (p. 80). Palmer also preached to both the House of Lords and the House of Commons on several occasions between 1643 and 1646. The central thrust of sermons such as *The Necessity and Encouragement of Utmost Venturing for the Churches Help* (1643), *The Glasse of Gods Providence* (1644), *The Soule of Fasting* (1644), and *The Duty and Honour of Church Restorers* (1646) was the need for further spiritual and church reforms. On 28 June 1643 he addressed the Commons on their fast day and urged them to undertake further reforms of the church especially in the matters of idolatry and the abuse of the sabbath. He also called for laws against clandestine marriages and drunkenness, and the suppression of stage plays. In a sermon to both houses of parliament on 13 August 1644 he urged caution in the matter of religious toleration, and support for the recommendations of the Westminster assembly. In the assembly Palmer supported a presbyterian church settlement, although at first he had doubts about the divine right of ruling elders and about the abolition of a clerical hierarchy. The debates that took place in the assembly fully persuaded him to accept both points. In London Palmer became lecturer at St James's, Duke Place, and later at the 'new church' in the parish of St Margaret's, Westminster. He was also one of the seven morning lecturers appointed by parliament at Westminster Abbey. On 11 April 1644 he was appointed master of Queens' College, Cambridge, by the earl of Manchester. As master Palmer encouraged the students in their religious observances and in their studies. He also donated money to the college library for books and helped to maintain poor scholars and refugee students from Germany and Hungary.

Palmer died in September 1647; John Crow was his sole executor and the main beneficiary of his will. Palmer also left all his history books in English, French, and Italian to his brother Sir Thomas Palmer, except for those already in the possession of Philip Delmé. He ordered that his papers, apart from those that had been 'transcribed', should be burnt (PRO, PROB 11/203, fol. 340r). Several manuscript volumes of his sermons preached between 1626 and 1644 do survive (LUL, MS 302; CUL, Add. MSS 3860–3861). Palmer had a reputation as a biblical scholar; in a letter written in 1643 Robert Baillie described him as 'gracious and learned little Palmer' (on account of his small stature) and in a letter of 1644 as 'the best Catechist in England' (R. Baillie, quoted in Shaw, 1.342). Palmer's biographer commented that it was almost a miracle that a man with 'so weak a body as his' should be able to achieve so much, including speaking publicly for six to eight hours on the sabbath ('Life', 431). So small was Palmer's frame that when he first preached to the French congregation at Canterbury an elderly Frenchwoman cried out 'What will this child say to us?'. She was overjoyed when she heard him pray and preach 'with so much spiritual strength and vigour' (ibid., 421). JACQUELINE EALES

Sources S. Clarke, 'The life of Master Herbert Palmer, B.D. late master of Queens-Colledge in Cambridge, who died Anno Christi, 1647', *A generall martyrologie … whereunto are added, The lives of sundry modern divines* (1651), 416–40 • will, PRO, PROB 11/203, fols. 339–40 • J. Wallis, *A brief and easie explanation of the shorter catechisme* (1648) • W. A. Shaw, *A history of the English church during the civil wars and under the Commonwealth, 1640–1660*, 1 (1900), 342 • Venn, *Alum. Cant.* • J. Rippon, ed., *The Baptist annual register* (1798–1801) • *DNB*

Archives CUL, sermons, Add. MSS 3860–3861 • LUL, sermons, MS 302

Likenesses line engraving, repro. in *Life of Master Herbert Palmer*, facing p. 417

Wealth at death see will, PRO, PROB 11/203, fols. 339–40

Palmer, (John) Horsley (1779–1858), merchant banker, was born at Nazeing Park, Essex, on 7 July 1779, the fourth son of the nine children of William Palmer (1737–1821), merchant, of Nazeing Park, and his wife, Mary, daughter of the Revd John Horsley and his wife, Mary. He was born into a well-established group of London mercantile families, among whom were the Lyalls and the Cottons, united by high Anglicanism, economic interests in India, and by service in the East India Company or the Bank of England.

Palmer was educated at Charterhouse, and in 1802 joined his brother George *Palmer and Captain Wilson as East India merchants. In November 1810 he married Elizabeth (*d.* 1839), daughter of John Belli of the East India Company and sister-in-law of Archbishop William Howley. The couple had three sons and three daughters. In 1811 he became a director of the Bank of England, having previously acted as a director of the London Assurance Company (1808–11). The family firm, Palmer, Wilson & Co., appears to have operated as the London house for the Indian agency Palmer & Co., Calcutta, one of the Indian trading giants that crashed in 1830. Palmer, by that date governor of the bank, had, however, tied his own fortunes to the mercantile house of Palmer, Dent, MacKillop & Co., a firm which developed into a major accepting-house financing trade with China and the United States as well as later floating loans on the London market. On his retirement from this firm in 1857, its partnership capital of £500,000 placed it in the front rank of London merchant banks.

Palmer's transition from gentlemanly capitalist of the *ancien régime* to powerful merchant banker was paralleled by the highly important part he played in shaping the Bank of England as it faced the challenges both of political reform and of its emergence as a pivot of the world's international monetary and trading system. Elected deputy governor of the bank in 1828, he had succeeded Jeremiah Harman as the bank's most influential director. In 1827 he had successfully resisted William Huskisson's scheme for a limited bimetallic standard, and in 1830 he frustrated attempts by Henry Goulburn, chancellor of the exchequer, to limit the bank's privileges, especially with regard to joint-stock banks, which he regarded as unnecessary and potentially destabilizing competitors for the English country banks and the bank's own branches. However, after the Reform Act of 1832 it became impossible to resist some reduction of the bank's monopoly. But as governor (1830–33) Palmer deflected the attempt to create a rival national bank, and through his negotiations with Lord Althorp to some extent held back whig recognition of English joint-stock banks. The bank therefore, in its new charter of 1833, emerged with greater security for its privileges than had at one point seemed likely but also came away with a greater recognition of its utility to the state.

Palmer's conception of the bank as a national institution rather than a private corporation was accompanied by a rigorous rethinking of its position in the monetary system of the British empire (and the world), a task to which he brought a growing theoretical understanding, honed by membership of the Political Economy Club (1829–46). His vision now embraced the goal, however, distant, of the Bank of England as the country's single bank of issue, offering a solution to the chronic over-issue of notes which had jeopardized the currency in the 1820s. He also set out clearly its role as the lender of last resort, retaining its discounting facilities as a buffer in times of crisis. Most controversially, he articulated, in his evidence to the banking inquiry of 1831–2, what became known as the 'Palmer rule'. His explanation of the bank's management principles emphasized their aim of retaining high-reserve ratios, a one-third reserve of bullion against its combined note and deposit liabilities. When the circulation was 'full'—that is, when the exchanges were on the point of becoming unfavourable—securities, forming two-thirds of its assets, were to be kept fixed, while bullion and notes and deposits should vary together. This was a policy which regulated currency according to the state of the exchanges but which left discretion in the hands of the bank.

In the complex financial crises of 1837 and 1839, the exercise of that discretion, it seemed to some, had brought the system to the brink of disaster. In the former crisis especially, Palmer's 'firmness … and … practical knowledge … in ascendancy over the doctrinaires' (Ledward, 189) had supported credit for failing firms in the American trade, but his actions were considered 'indefensible on any sound view of banking' (Norman, fol. 478) by his critics. Against the Palmer rule, the views of George Warde Norman and especially of Palmer's friend, the banker Samuel Jones Loyd, Lord Overstone, now took shape as the 'currency school'. They provided, in the eyes of Robert Peel and others, a damning indictment of the bank's failure to follow its own rules in the 1830s, preparing the way for the more rigid management of money enshrined in the Bank Charter Act of 1844.

Palmer himself orchestrated the opposition to this bill and remained its strong critic, particularly regretting the absence of a relaxing power in the act; he attributed the commercial crisis of 1847 to the act's underlying defects, and again urged repeal in 1856. In the event therefore, his policies—clearly, and for the most part consistently, defended in a series of pamphlets and in evidence before parliamentary committees—proved most influential as the foil against which the rigid monetary policy of the 1840s emerged as a dominant orthodoxy, with his ideas too readily dismissed as the mere rationalization of the bank's existing practices. Palmer was also a close observer of Irish, Indian, and American banking, and in 1842 he offered lucid advice to the American treasury (following a visit there, partly to restore his firm's affairs). He remained an influential voice within the bank until his retirement in 1857, widely respected as a man of vision, ability, and force of will.

Outside the bank, Palmer was a leading figure in the City of London, being signatory of the Merchants' free trade petition in 1820, advocate of a moderate settlement in the reform crisis of 1831, and consulted by the duke of Wellington on the formation of the minority tory government in 1834. His parliamentary ambitions were, however, unfulfilled, for he was narrowly defeated in 1837 as the tory candidate for the City constituency, and in 1843 he lost at Ashburton, Devon, a seat he had first contested in 1835 but which had now fallen under the sway of the Jardine and Matheson families, the leading commercial rivals of Palmer, Dent & Co. in the Eastern trade.

Following the death of his first wife in 1839, Palmer married, on 8 July 1841, Jane Louise (*d.* 1865), fifth daughter of the architect Samuel Pepys Cockerell and sister of John Cockerell, another long-serving director of the bank. There were no children of this marriage. He died on 7 February 1858 at Hurlingham House, Fulham, London, a home whose warm hospitality had been appreciated by his nephew, the future earl of Selborne. He was succeeded in the bank directorate by the eldest of his three sons, Edward Howley Palmer (1811–1901), at the time of his father's death the partner of Thomas Dent (1796–1872), and later governor of the bank (1877–9). A. C. Howe

Sources J. Clapham, *The Bank of England: a history*, 2 (1944) · F. W. Fetter, *Development of British monetary orthodoxy, 1797–1875* (1965) · E. V. Morgan, *The theory and practice of central banking, 1797–1913* (1943) · *The correspondence of Lord Overstone*, ed. D. P. O'Brien, 1 (1971) · J. K. Horsefield, 'The opinions of Horsley Palmer', *Economica*, new ser., 16 (1949), 143–58 · W. P. Ledward, 'Monetary policy, 1833–9, with special reference to the Anglo-American crisis of 1837', DPhil diss., U. Oxf., 1983 · B. Hilton, *Corn, cash, commerce: the economic policies of the tory governments, 1815–1830* (1977) · D. Kynaston, *The City of London*, 1 (1994) · A. C. Howe, 'From old corruption to new probity: the Bank of England and its directors in the age of reform', *Government and institutions of the post-1832 United Kingdom*, ed. A. O'Day (1995), 269–304 · M. Greenberg, *British trade and the opening of China, 1800–42* (1951) · R. Palmer, first earl of Selborne, *Memorials. Part I: family and personal, 1766–1865*, ed. S. M. Palmer, 2 vols. (1896) · G. W. Norman, 'Autobiography', CKS, MS fol. 478 · Bank of England Archives, London · *The Times* (11 Feb 1858), 7b · Burke, *Peerage* [Selborne]

Archives Bank of England Archive, London · Bodl. Oxf., Palmer & Co. archives | BL, Huskisson MSS · BL, Peel MSS · CKS, Norman MSS · Duke U., Perkins L., Ince MSS

Likenesses J. R. Swinton, coloured chalks, Bank of England coll.

Wealth at death £60,000: probate, 13 March 1858, *CGPLA Eng. & Wales*

Palmer, James (*bap.* 1581, *d.* 1660), Church of England clergyman and benefactor, was born in the parish of St Margaret's Westminster, and baptized there in July 1581, the son of Henry Palmer. He graduated BA of Magdalene College, Cambridge, early in 1602 and proceeded MA in 1605; while there he received an exhibition from the Worshipful Company of Carpenters. On 26 May 1605 he was ordained deacon and priest in the diocese of Peterborough. It may be that he was a kinsman of John Palmer (*d.* 1607), who was both master of Magdalene and dean of Peterborough. On 9 July 1611 James Palmer incorporated his MA at Oxford, and in 1613 he proceeded BD at Cambridge.

On 6 December 1615 the dean and chapter of Westminster agreed to appoint Palmer to their vicarage of St Bride, Fleet Street, but it was not until 18 April 1616 that they made their presentation; he was instituted on the following day. He spent his entire professional life serving this parish. It therefore fell to him, on 3 March 1633, to baptize Samuel Pepys, the fifth child of John Pepys of Salisbury Court, a boy destined to become the most famous alumnus of Palmer's old college. Palmer was among a number of London clergy reported in 1637 for irregular performance of the liturgy; it was said that at matins he 'often omits the prayer for the bishops and the rest of the clergy, and reads divine service sometimes in his gown and sometimes without either surplice or gown, in his cloak' (*CSP dom.*, *1637*, 519). This in itself does not mean that he was a radical, but he was undoubtedly disposed to the more austere churchmanship which the parliamentary regime imposed on London in the 1640s.

In March 1642 Palmer was required to allow a lecturer, Simeon Ashe, to share his pulpit. Palmer himself was a regular preacher before parliament on the days of public penitence which were frequently decreed. In 1645 he voluntarily resigned his living; on 18 October the committee for plundered ministers accepted a petition from Palmer and his parishioners that 'in regard of his old age and the palsey wherewith he is visited and the greate decay of his voice he is disabled to discharge the dutie of pastor to soe grete a congregation' (BL, Add. MS 15669, fol. 193*v*). A successor was appointed on 15 November. The royalist newspaper *Mercurius Rusticus* reported that Palmer had been ejected, and in consequence he was mistaken for a sufferer in the king's cause.

Palmer devoted the rest of his life to good works. It was

his kindly habit to leave gifts of money lying about the houses of those he found to be in need. While at St Bride's Palmer was said to have lodged in his own steeple; by these and more conventional frugalities he had acquired 'a pretty good estate', from which he was able to support his charitable activities (Walker). Specifically, he had in November 1637 conveyed to trustees some property at Upper Holloway in Clerkenwell, from which £5 a year was to be given to each of twenty widows of 'orthodox' divines. The original trustees included Ralph Brownrigg and Richard Holdsworth (both opponents of Archbishop William Laud, but committed to the established church and so churchmen with whom Palmer was in sympathy). He also built an almshouse in Westminster for twelve inmates, with a chapel and school attached. Despite the debilities which had obliged him to surrender his benefice, he regularly conducted services and preached in the almshouse chapel. The almshouses were re-erected in Rochester Row in the 1880s, and the school was eventually absorbed into the City of Westminster School, where his name is commemorated in that of a house.

Palmer made his will on 20 December 1659, leaving all his books to his old college and making many small benefactions to apparently humble Londoners; a codicil of 31 December revoked some provisions. He died in Westminster on 5 January 1660, and was buried in St Margaret's, Westminster, on 9 January. A fine memorial was erected there by Sir William Playter, bt, incorporating a portrait bust and a blazon of azure, a chevron between three crescents, or. The monument was once thought to be of the school of Inigo Jones, but is now attributed to Joshua Marshall. It was severely damaged by enemy action on 23 September 1940; a partial restoration was undertaken by Janet Becker in 1947. C. S. KNIGHTON

Sources Venn, *Alum. Cant.*, 1/3.300 • Westminster Abbey muniments, Chapter Act Book II, fol. 16*v*; Register XI, fol. 316 • Pepys, *Diary* • *CSP dom.*, 1637, 519 • *JHC*, 2 (1640–42), 479 • A. M. Burke, ed., *Memorials of St Margaret's Church, Westminster* (1914), 659, n. 3 • P. W. Holland, *St Margaret's, Westminster* (1993), 52, 82 • 'St Margaret's Church, Westminster: Rev. James Palmer, 1659', *N&Q*, 6th ser., 6 (1882), 83–4 • BL, Add. MS 15669, fols. 193*v*, 206 (old fols. 379*v*, 405) • J. Walker, *An attempt towards recovering an account of the numbers and sufferings of the clergy of the Church of England*, pt 2 (1714), 174 • T. Fuller, *The worthies of England*, ed. J. Freeman, abridged edn (1952), 383–4 • will, PRO, PROB 11/298, sig. 61

Likenesses T. Trotter, line engraving, pubd 1794, BM, NPG • attrib. J. Marshall, bust on monument, St Margaret's, Westminster

Wealth at death significant disposable wealth: will, PRO, PROB 11/298, sig. 61

Palmer, Sir James (*bap.* **1585**, *d.* **1658**), herald and miniature painter, was baptized on 29 January 1585, the third and youngest son of Sir Thomas *Palmer (1540/41–1626), author, of Wingham in Kent, known as the Travailer, created baronet on 29 June 1621, and his wife, Margaret (1540–1625), the daughter of John Pooley of Badley, Suffolk. All three sons were knighted. Thomas, the eldest, was a lawyer, educated at St John's College, Cambridge (matriculated 1586), and admitted to Gray's Inn in 1590; he was knighted on 11 May 1603 and died in September 1608; his eldest son, Thomas (*d.* 1656), succeeded his grandfather, the Travailer, as second baronet, and his second son, Herbert (1601–1647), was a fiery puritan divine during the years of his uncles' ascendancy at court. Roger Palmer (1577–1657), the second son of the Travailer, was a courtier and became master of the household to Charles I. James, having a handsome face, also became a courtier, securing an appointment in the king's household at an early age and becoming a close friend of Prince Charles. A portrait of him was seen at Cornbury House, Oxfordshire, by George Vertue, and a miniature by Nicholas Hilliard, identified as of him in family tradition, shows him as a young courtier (*c.*1605–8; priv. coll.).

Soon after his father was raised to the baronetcy, James Palmer was appointed a gentleman of the bedchamber, with an initial salary of £200 (27 April 1622; his salary was later raised to £400). He retained his position at court after the accession of Charles I and was appointed gentleman usher of the privy chamber and subsequently keeper of the privy closet; he was knighted in 1629. His main expertise was in heraldry, particularly in relation to the Order of the Garter, which enjoyed special prominence under the early Stuarts. In February 1638 he served for the first of three times as deputy to the absent Sir Thomas Roe, chancellor of the order, and he ultimately succeeded him in the office on 2 March 1645.

He married, firstly, Martha (*d.* 1617), the daughter and heir of Sir William Garrard of Dorney Court. With her he had a son, Philip, who became the ancestor of the Palmers of Dorney. Secondly, he married Catherine, the daughter of Sir William Herbert (later Baron Powis) and the widow of Sir Robert Vaughan of Llydiarth in Montgomeryshire. Their son was Roger *Palmer (1634–1705) (created 11 December 1661 earl of Castlemaine), a scholar, mathematician, diplomat, and conspicuous cuckold: he was the husband of Barbara, the daughter and heir of William Villiers, second Viscount Grandison, who was the mistress of Charles II.

Palmer's long-standing friendship with Prince Charles was probably secured through their shared interest in art, and Palmer was active in assisting the expansion of the Royal Collection. He also became a governor of the Mortlake tapestry works. He is referred to frequently by Abraham van der Doort as the source of acquisition for paintings in the king's collection, as borrowing pictures for use at Mortlake, and as copying the Titianesque *Tarquin and Lucretia*. He was present when Charles famously astonished the company of connoisseurs by correctly distinguishing separate hands in a painting brought up for his inspection by Palmer (Vertue, *Note books*, 4.153). His own collection, which was dispersed at auction on 20 April 1689, was distinguished, having benefited latterly from purchases which he made at the Whitehall sale of 1651. Dalloway (in his edition of Walpole's *Anecdotes*) alleges that he somehow rigged the market in his own favour, but his purchases probably seemed at the time more like 'buying in' than dishonesty or disloyalty to the collection he had done much to create.

Like Balthasar Gerbier and Alexander Marshal, Palmer

was outside the main succession of professional miniature painters at the early Stuart court. As a courtier and well-connected gentleman, however, he was one of those whose practice of the art secured its enormous prestige in the ordering of the arts in early seventeenth-century England. His surviving works are: *James I* (signed and dated 1623; V&A); *Unknown Man* (signed and dated 1623; formerly Glenconner collection); *Sir Robert Carr, Earl of Somerset* (signed and dated 1619; Fitzwilliam Museum, Cambridge); *Elizabeth, Lady Garrard, Wife of Sir William Garrard* (signed and dated 1614; priv. coll.); and *Martha, Lady Palmer, Wife of Sir James* (priv. coll.). Two further works may be his: *Duke of Buckingham* (signed, apparently with a variant monogram, and dated 1627; ex Sothebys 1 March 1965); and *Lord Compton, First Earl of Northampton* (Royal Collection), attributed to Palmer 'or Norgate' (Reynolds, *Miniatures*, 83). The so-called *3rd Earl of Southampton* (Foskett, 82) is not an addition, but the Glenconner miniature mentioned above with a new title.

As a painter, Palmer had an excellent sense of the structure of the human face and a clarity of focus, which come across in the crisp outlines and minute detail of the surviving miniatures. The enlarged and somewhat sunken eye sockets appear to be characteristic of the way he saw his sitters. Graham Reynolds pointed also to 'the drawing of shadow under the chin, which is heavily underscored many times' and 'the pronounced shadow of the upper eyelid' (Reynolds, 'Newly identified miniaturist', 197) as recognizable markers of his hand. Technically, he worked with a short, repetitive hatching stroke, not confident but certainly competent. As a herald, skill in the design and execution of coats of arms would have been a useful accomplishment, but Palmer's ability goes beyond that level. He was evidently fully aware of the 'secrets of enluminure', which he would possibly have learned directly from Hilliard, or at any rate from the detailed accounts of technique in the latter's *A Treatise Concerning the Arte of Limning*. He must also, however, have known the Olivers, and, from studying Isaac's work, have learned the lessons in facial chiaroscuro which characterize the developments in the English school in the age of the elder Hoskins. Palmer died at Dorney, Buckinghamshire, on 15 March 1658.

JOHN MURDOCH

Sources A. G. Reynolds, 'A newly identified miniaturist of the early seventeenth century, probably Sir James Palmer', *Burlington Magazine*, 91 (July 1949), 196–7 • A. G. Reynolds, *The sixteenth and seventeenth century miniatures in the collection of her majesty the queen* (1999) • Vertue, *Note books*, esp. 2.64 • H. Walpole, *Anecdotes of painting in England: with some account of the principal artists*, ed. R. N. Wornum, new edn, 3 vols. (1849) • D. Foskett, *Collecting miniatures* (1979) • Burke, *Peerage* • J. Murdoch, *Seventeenth-century English miniatures in the collection of the Victoria and Albert Museum* (1997)

Likenesses N. Hilliard, miniature, 1605–8, repro. in Reynolds, 'A newly identified miniaturist', fig. 18; priv. coll. • miniature; formerly at Cornbury House, Oxfordshire

Palmer, Sir James Frederick (1803–1871), businessman and politician in Australia, was born on 7 June 1803 at Great Torrington, Devon, the fourth son of John Palmer, rector of Great Torrington, and his wife, Jane, the daughter of William Johnson. He received a medical education under John Gunning, surgeon-in-chief of the army, and practised as a surgeon as St George's Hospital and St James's Dispensary, London. He also edited a four-volume collected edition of the works of the anatomist John Hunter (1835–7) and was a member of the Royal Medical and Chirurgical Society. On 21 November 1831 he married Isabella, the third daughter of Dr *Gunning, who was by then inspector-general of hospitals.

After suffering rejection in trying to advance his career, Palmer and his wife emigrated to Australia in 1840. He registered as a medical practitioner but never 'seriously' took to the profession in Australia, setting up instead in Melbourne in 1841 a business for 'the manufacture of sodawater, effervescing lemonade and ginger beer' (Garryowen, 2.886). Later he became a wine and spirit merchant and invested in pastoral properties, and he also established a very successful and well-known punt service across the Yarra River, mainly for the cartage of wood from the nearby bush.

Palmer was a churchwarden of St James's Anglican Church and gained election to Melbourne city council, representing the Lonsdale ward. In 1845 he became mayor of the city. He strongly supported the cause of separation of the Port Phillip district from New South Wales, and in March 1846 wrote a paper proposing this, and critical of the financial arrangements for Port Phillip, to the governor, George Gipps. This drew an angry response, with the governor attacking Palmer's 'impudence' in preparing a document 'studiously offensive and abounding in misrepresentations' (*Gipps–La Trobe Correspondence*, 384–5). In 1848 Palmer was elected to the New South Wales legislative council, but he resigned the following year. Following the creation of the new colony in 1851, he was elected to the legislative council of Victoria for the Normandy, Dundas, and Follett constituency in the western district and was elected first speaker of the council. He helped prepare a new constitution for Victoria, allowing for two chambers of parliament, was elected to the seat of Western Province in the new council, and was chosen as its first president in 1856. He served in this role until 1870, when he resigned on account of ill health. He was knighted in 1857.

Palmer was respected as 'clever and incisive' (Garryowen, 2.686) and was well regarded for his 'character and reliability' (Gross). His past medical experience was evident in the leading role he took in the foundation of the Melbourne Hospital. He was also chairman of the board of national education from 1851. He died at his home, Burwood, in Hawthorn, Melbourne, on 23 April 1871, and was buried at Melbourne general cemetery on 26 April. It appears that his wife predeceased him.

MARC BRODIE

Sources Garryowen [E. Finn], *The chronicles of early Melbourne, 1835 to 1852: historical, anecdotal and personal*, 2 vols. (1888); repr. 1976 • *The Argus* [Melbourne] (24 April 1871) • *The Argus* [Melbourne] (27 April 1871) • A. Gross, 'Palmer, James Frederick', *AusDB*, vol. 5 • *Gipps–La Trobe correspondence, 1839–1846*, ed. A. G. L. Shaw (1989) • K. Thomson and G. Serle, *A biographical register of the Victorian legislature,*

1851–1900 (1972) • G. Serle, *The golden age: a history of the colony of Victoria, 1851–1861* (1963) • *DNB*

Palmer, John (*d.* 1607), dean of Peterborough, was a native of Kent. He matriculated as a pensioner of St John's College, Cambridge, on 25 October 1567 and became a scholar on 9 November 1568. Having graduated BA in early 1572 he was admitted a fellow of his college on 12 March 1573. On 26 July 1578, when Queen Elizabeth paid a visit to Audley End, Palmer was among the opponents in a philosophy disputation which members of the university conducted before her. In 1580 he took the part of Richard when Thomas Legge's play 'Richardus tertius' was acted before the queen in the hall of St John's; theatrical success had unfortunate consequences, according to Fuller, for Palmer thereafter 'had his head so possest with a princelike humour that ever after he did, what then he acted, in his prodigal expences' (Fuller, *Worthies*, 2.491).

Through the influence of William Cecil, Lord Burghley, Palmer (who had been incorporated MA at Oxford on 12 July 1580) was able to turn from the study of civil law to that of divinity. He was made junior dean of St John's on 21 January 1585, principal lecturer on 10 July following, senior bursar on 9 February 1587, a proctor of the university in 1587, and senior dean of St John's on 24 September 1589. During the 1580s Palmer's was one of the names mentioned among the fellowship of St John's as a possible successor to the outgoing master, Richard Howland, elevated to the bishopric of Peterborough in 1585. However Burghley, chancellor of the university and himself an alumnus of the college, was steadily determined to impose an outsider, William Whitaker, and he got his way. Perhaps as a form of compensation Burghley recommended Palmer about this time for the post of public orator, but he was not elected.

Relations between Whitaker and a conservative coterie among the fellows, including Palmer, were never easy. The two apparently worked harmoniously together in matters of finance, for during Palmer's term as bursar the college's affairs were considerably better managed than in the recent past. During 1587 and 1588, moreover, they co-operated over Whitaker's bid to smash opposition to his authority by the expulsion of the 'popish' Everard Digby, a fellow since 1573. On this issue Palmer had personal reasons for supporting the new master, for he had been publicly insulted by Digby in the hearing of a group of undergraduates. But the affair incurred the wrath of Archbishop John Whitgift, who declared that the pair had acted contrary to their own statutes, to all rules of charity 'and I might say of honesty also' (BL, Lansdowne MS 57, fol. 160).

In 1589, however, Palmer dropped a bombshell that could well have wrecked Whitaker's career, hinting in various quarters that he had been conducting a secret 'presbytery' in the college. Whitaker's vigorous and successful defence of his conduct drove Palmer into a corner: evidently unnerved, he eventually assured Burghley on 5 November 1590 that it had never been his intention to discredit Whitaker. He ended by requesting Burghley's 'good favour and protection' (BL, Lansdowne MS 63, fol. 229). He may have received it, for in 1595 Palmer was elected master of Magdalene College, proceeding DTh the same year. On 30 November 1597 on the recommendation of Robert Devereux, earl of Essex, he was presented by the queen to the deanery of Peterborough. Essex described him as a man 'whom I do especially respect and love and hold worthy of preferment' (*Salisbury MSS*, 7.256). Since Palmer thereafter necessarily divided his time between Cambridge and Peterborough, Magdalene's governing body ordered on 26 April that the president of the college must be resident during the master's absence. Failing that, a deputy president was to be appointed.

Palmer's career, like Essex's, came to an abrupt and ignominious end. As Fuller's remarks suggest, he was apparently a noted spendthrift, and is said to have sold the lead from the roof of Peterborough Cathedral to meet his liabilities. Evidently this emergency measure was not enough to save him. He resigned his mastership in 1604 and died in a debtors' prison about July 1607—still, apparently, in possession of his deanery.

The dean of Peterborough may have been the John Palmer who in 1587 published memorial verses on the death of Sir Philip Sidney. Alternatively their author was the **John Palmer** (*d.* 1614) who became archdeacon of Ely. Educated at Westminster School, Palmer matriculated as a pensioner at Trinity College, Cambridge, on 26 May 1576 and graduated BA in 1580. In 1581 and 1582 he wrote two finely crafted letters to Burghley, asking for his interest in procuring him a fellowship. He was elected to one in the latter year, and proceeded MA in 1583. He became a chaplain to the queen, while in 1591 the master and fellows of Trinity presented him to the vicarage of Normanton, Yorkshire. He proceeded BTh in 1592. On 5 June that year, at the queen's presentation during the vacancy of the see, Palmer became archdeacon of Ely and prebendary of the first stall in Ely Cathedral. Some time before March 1593 he made a clandestine marriage to Katherine, daughter of William Knyvet of Vastern, Wiltshire, in Lord Thomas Howard's chapel in Chesterford, Essex.

Palmer is not mentioned as archdeacon in the Ely records after June 1594, though a successor was collated by Bishop Martin Heton only in June or July 1600. Trinity presented him to another of its livings, Trumpington, just outside Cambridge, in 1596, and he also seems to have held two other Cambridgeshire benefices, Wilburton and Haddenham. To these were added the vicarage of South Somercotes, Lincolnshire, on 14 March 1597, and that of Alwalton, Huntingdonshire, on 13 February 1602. He had died by 6 November 1614, when a successor was collated to his Ely prebend.

LEONARD W. COWIE

Sources Venn, *Alum. Cant.*, 1/3.300 • Foster, *Alum. Oxon.* • T. Baker, *History of the college of St John the Evangelist, Cambridge*, ed. J. E. B. Mayor, 2 vols. (1869) • Fuller, *Worthies* (1840), vol. 2 • E. K. Purnell, *Magdalene College, Cambridge* (1904) • J. Nichols, *The progresses and public processions of Queen Elizabeth*, 3 vols. (1788–1805), vol. 2 • J. Bentham, *History of Ely Cathedral* (1771) • J. Strype, *The life and acts of … John Whitgift* (1718) • A. Gibbons, ed., *Ely episcopal records: a calendar and concise view of the episcopal records preserved in the muniment room of the palace of Ely* (privately printed, Lincoln, 1891) • J. Heywood and T. Wright, eds., *Cambridge University transactions during the puritan* *controversies of the 16th and 17th centuries*, 2 vols. (1854) • J. L. Chester and G. J. Armytage, eds., *Allegations for marriage licences issued by the bishop of London*, 1, Harleian Society, 25 (1887) • B. Willis, *A survey of the cathedrals*, 3 vols. (1742) • *Fasti Angl.*, 1541–1857, [Ely] • *Fasti Angl.*, 1541–1857, [Bristol] • *Fasti Angl.*, 1541–1857, [Lincoln] • H. C. Porter, *Reformation and reaction in Tudor Cambridge* (1958) • P. Lake, *Moderate puritans and the Elizabethan church* (1982) • BL, Lansdowne MSS 57, 63 • *Calendar of the manuscripts of the most hon. the marquis of Salisbury*, 7, HMC, 9 (1899)

Palmer, John (*d.* 1614). *See under* Palmer, John (*d.* 1607).

Palmer, John (*c.*1650–1700?), lawyer and colonial administrator, began his professional career in the military. He served as an ensign under Colonel William Burt, in the Barbados regiment of foot, where he met Major Edmund Andros. Palmer participated in a successful expedition sent by Sir William Stapleton in 1672 to capture the island of Tortola. In 1675 Palmer, now retired from military service and trained as a lawyer, went to New York, where he became a trusted friend and ally of New York's governor, Edmund Andros, and his successor, Thomas Dongan. He was named to the governor's council, was a ranger, or head of a mounted military force, responsible for the defence of Staten Island, and a supreme court judge.

Dongan thought highly of Palmer, and in 1687 sent him as an envoy to England to inform James II of French incursions into New York. Dongan also sent Palmer to Maine, then under New York's jurisdiction, to serve as commissioner. Palmer and his partner John West used the opportunity to acquire land for themselves. The men called into question the titles of colonists and then denied them grants to their own lands, which they then appropriated for themselves. They leased it back to about 140 former owners, who each paid a fee of £2 10s. Palmer's actions alienated colonists and led to charges of improper behaviour. Maine colonists in the spring of 1688 complained to the now knighted Sir Edmund Andros, governor-general of the dominion of New England. Andros was appalled by Palmer's behaviour, but appointed him to the council when New York and New Jersey became part of the dominion in the summer of 1688. Palmer incurred further enmity from New Englanders as a trusted adviser to Andros, strongly supporting the governor's determination to impose taxation on New Englanders without a representative assembly.

As a result of the 1688 revolution in England, Boston crowds rebelled against the dominion of New England government of Andros, James II's appointee. On 18 April 1689 the governor and twenty-six of his most trusted aides, including Palmer, were seized by colonists and imprisoned, while the rebels reinstituted their old charter government. Palmer was held in a below ground-level cell in a fort on Castle Island in Boston harbour. The cell, which flooded every time it rained, was damp, small, and mouldy. It housed Palmer, along with the governor and another aide, James Graham. The provincial government that superseded the dominion government refused to release Palmer on bail, despite the pleas of his wife, Sarah, who claimed that her husband suffered from gout and other ailments.

The officials were held until William III, on being informed of the arrests, ordered that Andros and the other imprisoned men be returned speedily to England. After a nine-month imprisonment, the prisoners sailed on the *Mehitabel*, arriving in England on 7 April 1690. The New England leaders charged that Andros had published a broadside warning of a possible invasion of North America by William and his Dutch forces and made laws that were destructive of liberty. His assistants were accused of extortion and aiding Andros. The New England colonists who were in England to represent their American brethren refused to sign the charges, and the privy council committee on trade subsequently dismissed the complaint.

While in the Boston prison Palmer wrote a defence of the Andros regime, 'An impartial account of the state of New England, or the late government there vindicated'. He argued that Andros's commission as governor of the dominion of New England was entirely legal. He observed that all colonies were directly subject to the monarch and the crown could impose any government it saw fit on them. He argued that representative government was not a colonial right but instead a privilege bestowed by the crown that could be withdrawn at any time. Colonial privileges had never been confirmed by parliament, he argued, and in fact colonial rights and liberties were not the same as those enjoyed by Englishmen at home.

Palmer, exonerated of all charges of ill behaviour, resumed his colonial career on the Leeward Islands, where on 17 March 1693 he was sworn in as councillor and secretary and named attorney-general by Governor Christopher Codrington. He held these posts until 1698, when, despite his friendship with Codrington, he was removed from office for having spoken defamatory words against the late Queen Mary. His indiscretion led to charges of Jacobitism. Under political attack, he left the Leeward Islands to settle in Jamaica until his death, probably in 1700.

Palmer was typical of many English appointees who served in the American colonies. He came to America primarily to make money. Colonists recognized the fact that most colonial appointees were similarly motivated but Palmer was particularly resented because of his excessive greed and his open defence of the royal prerogative. Colonists believed they had the same rights and liberties as Englishmen at home, that their charters, or constitutions, were inviolable, that representative government was an inherent right that could not be withdrawn, and that taxation could be imposed only by an elected government. Royal officers did not agree with these views either in 1689 or 1776. The two positions were irreconcilable and eventually led to the American War of Independence.

MARY LOU LUSTIG

Sources W. H. Whitmore, ed., *The Andros tracts*, 3 vols. (1868–74) • T. B. Lewis, ed., 'Sir Edmund Andros's hearing before the lords of trade and plantations, April 17, 1690: two unpublished accounts', *Proceedings of the American Antiquarian Society* (1913), 241–50 • *CSP col.*, vols. 1, 5, 7, 9–42 • *Narratives of the insurrections, 1675–1690*, ed. C. M. Andrews (1915) • *The Glorious Revolution in America*, ed. M. G. Hall, L. H. Leder, and M. Kammen (1964) • *Edward Randolph: including his letters and official papers*, ed. R. N. Toppan and A. T. Goodrick, 7 vols.

(1898–1909) • V. F. Barnes, *The dominion of New England: a study in British colonial policy* (1923) • S. S. Webb, *Lord Churchill's coup: the Anglo-American empire and the Glorious Revolution reconsidered* (1995) • B. Bailyn, *The New England merchants in the seventeenth century* (1955) • M. G. Hall, *Edward Randolph and the American colonies, 1676–1703* (1960) • T. Hutchinson, *The history of the colony of Massachusetts-bay*, 2nd edn, 3 vols. (1764–1828); repr. (New York, 1972) • D. Lovejoy, *The glorious revolution in America* (1972) • *DNB*

Palmer, John (1728–1768), actor, was possibly born in Devon of a theatrical family. A sister, Mary Palmer (Mrs Adcock), is known of as an actress, but nothing is recorded of Palmer himself until he was engaged by David Garrick at Drury Lane in 1748. He had obviously acted before that season, but no trace of his early career remains. However, that he continued to play in booths at both Bartholomew and Southwark fairs after his introduction to Drury Lane audiences may give some clues as to his theatrical origins. His first role for Garrick was as Townley in Edward Ravenscroft's *The London Cuckolds*, and he followed this with Gratiano in *The Merchant of Venice* and a series of largely second male leads, including the part of Young Worthy in Colley Cibber's *Love's Last Shift* and Plume in George Farquhar's *The Recruiting Officer*. By 1757 *The Theatrical Review* described him as:

> an easy and judicious actor … [whose] performance of the parts of Gentlemen, might be proposed as a model, if he was not a little given to mouthing; and if he would give his body and gait a little more steadiness, then, these two faults excepted, he is very good in his kind, and has beauties that are entirely his own. (*BDA*)

Indeed, he became popularly known as 'Gentleman John'.

A jobbing actor who evidently relied on the constant reiteration of essentially the same performance, Palmer worked at Drury Lane for twenty years, never offering anything less than a properly professional performance. According to *The Theatrical Review* of 1758, he was particularly adept at ad-libbing his way smoothly out of trouble whenever potential problems loomed on stage. However, that he should have played Farquhar's Plume as well as Horner in William Wycherley's *The Country Wife*, both parts that require rather more than a bland presentation of gentlemanly qualities, may well mean that he was possessed of a greater versatility than is realized, although the author of *The Present State of the Stage* (1753) complained of a 'sameness in every thing he does' (*BDA*). He certainly had a strong physical appearance, and was evidently a charmer. Six years after joining the Drury Lane company, the then leading lady of the company, Hannah Pritchard, had encouraged her daughter, Hannah Mary (1739–1781), to become an actress. The daughter frequently performed with Palmer, both at Drury Lane and at Bristol, where he played the summer seasons from 1759 to 1763. Romance seems to have flourished quite quickly, and on 20 April 1761 the pair were married at St Giles-in-the-Fields. Hannah Pritchard's biographer records (in *Born to Please*) that the couple had two children; the son, William Vaughan Palmer (1762–1822), took a commission in the army, and the daughter, Alicia Tindal *Palmer (1763–1822), became a novelist.

In *The Dramatic Censor* (1770), Francis Gentleman has qualified praise for Palmer's depiction of Mercutio in *Romeo and Juliet*, a part that, with its call for lively acting and wit, would have been perfect for him. In 1767 he was due to play the part of Harcourt in *The Country Girl*, Garrick's adaptation of Wycherley's *The Country Wife*. Incapacitated with illness, he was forced to withdraw and, ironically, the part was given to a younger actor of the same name, though unrelated, a John Palmer who would soon eclipse what small theatrical achievements had accrued to Gentleman John. The older actor never really recovered his health and watched the younger man take over from him at Drury Lane. His final appearance was at Drury Lane on 5 May 1768 as Cassio. He died on 23 May at his home in Great Queen Street, London, the victim of an erroneous medical prescription, according to Thomas Davies in *The Dramatic Miscellanies*. His wife's acting career did not last beyond his death. JOHN BULL

Sources Highfill, Burnim & Langhans, *BDA* • Genest, *Eng. stage* • J. Doran and R. W. Lowe, *'Their majesties' servants': annals of the English stage*, rev. edn, 3 vols. (1888) • T. Gilliland, *The dramatic mirror, containing the history of the stage from the earliest period, to the present time*, 2 vols. (1808) • W. C. Russell, *Representative actors* [1888] • *The private correspondence of David Garrick*, ed. J. Boaden, 2nd edn, 2 vols. (1835) • *The letters of Horace Walpole, earl of Orford*, ed. P. Cunningham, 9 vols. (1857–9) • J. Bernard, *Retrospections of the stage*, ed. W. B. Bernard, 2 vols. (1830) • R. Cumberland, *Memoirs of Richard Cumberland written by himself* (1806) • *Dramatic Magazine* (1829–31) • *The theatrical review, or, Annals of the drama*, 1 (1763) • A. Vaughan, *Born to please: Hannah Pritchard, actress, 1711–1768* (1979) • T. Davies, *Dramatic miscellanies*, 3 vols. (1784)

Palmer, John (1729–1790), Presbyterian minister, was born in Southwark, the son of an undertaker, and his wife, Sarah. He was brought up in the Independent church and received his ministerial training under David Jennings at Wellclose Square Academy, which he entered in 1746. Although educated in Calvinistic principles he gradually relinquished them and adopted Socinian views.

In 1755 Palmer became assistant to John Allen, Presbyterian minister at New Broad Street, London. On Allen's move (1759) to Worcester, Palmer became pastor. He was a member of the Presbyterian board from 1759 to 1772 and a trustee of Dr Williams's foundation from 1768 to 1790. The congregation at New Broad Street declined, and on the expiry of the lease of the meeting-house in 1780 was dissolved. Palmer left the ministry and lived in retirement at Islington.

Palmer was a man of considerable talents and learning, as is illustrated in his spirited defence of free will against Joseph Priestley in a series of letters published in 1779 and 1780. He published also some occasional funeral sermons, of which his first was *A Sermon Occasioned by the Death of King George II, Preached at New Broad Street, Nov. 2 1760*. His *Prayers for the Use of Families and Persons in Private* (1773) was much admired by rational dissenters, while his passionate belief in religious liberty was demonstrated in *Free thoughts on the inconsistency of conforming to any religious test, as a condition of toleration, with the true principle of protestant dissent* (1779).

Palmer, who was married to 'a lady of considerable wealth', Mary, whose maiden name was probably Corbyn, died in Islington on 26 June 1790, aged sixty-one (Wilson, 2.227). ALEXANDER GORDON, *rev.* M. J. MERCER

Sources W. Wilson, *The history and antiquities of the dissenting churches and meeting houses in London, Westminster and Southwark*, 4 vols. (1808–14) • C. Surman, index, DWL • W. D. Jeremy, *The Presbyterian Fund and Dr Daniel Williams's Trust* (1885) • A. Chalmers, ed., *The general biographical dictionary*, new edn, 32 vols. (1812–17) • PRO, PROB 11/1194, fol. 150*r–v*

Wealth at death probably rich; married a wealthy lady: will, PRO, PROB 11/1194, fol. 150*r–v*

Palmer, John (1742–1786), Unitarian minister, son of John Palmer, wig maker, was born at Norwich. He was a protégé and pupil of John Taylor, the Hebraist and Presbyterian minister of the Octagon Chapel, Norwich, who, on becoming principal and divinity tutor at Warrington Academy, placed Palmer in 1757 at school in Congleton under Edward Harwood. He entered Warrington Academy in 1759 and remained a student there until 1764. From 1761 Joseph Priestley was one of his tutors. In his last year he regularly supplied the pulpit from 14 May 1763 to 15 August 1764 at Allostock, Cheshire.

In July 1764, while still a student-supply, Palmer accepted an invitation to become minister at Back Street Chapel, Macclesfield (from 1825, King Edward Street Chapel). He probably commenced his duties in late August but was not ordained until 23 July 1765. Palmer belonged to the rational wing of dissent and embraced Unitarian opinions. As a consequence it was not long (1768) before there was a secession from his congregation, with the orthodox members seceding to found Townley Street Congregational Chapel and Back Street becoming Unitarian. Palmer incurred the wrath of orthodox dissenters within the town and eventually, in 1779, as a result of this unpopularity, resigned.

Palmer moved to Birmingham where, as a result of his two financially beneficial marriages, he was able to live without a regular ministerial income, for both his wives were the principal beneficiaries from their fathers' wills. He married firstly, on 27 October 1767 at Prestbury, Cheshire, Mary Heald, daughter of George Heald, a Macclesfield landowner. Following her death, on 25 November 1777 he married Sarah White, eldest daughter of Thomas White, Unitarian minister of Friar Gate Chapel, Derby. At Birmingham Palmer renewed his acquaintance with Priestley, and was a member of a fortnightly clerical club which decided and edited the contributions to the *Theological Repository*. Priestley thought highly of Palmer and recommended him in glowing terms to pulpit vacancies at George's Meeting, Exeter, and Walthamstow, Essex, but nothing came of these recommendations.

Palmer wrote several religious tracts, which were mainly concerned with outlining and defending unitarian opinions, such as *Free remarks on a sermon entitled 'The requisition of subscription not inconsistent with Christian liberty'*, published in 1772, and a *Letter to Dr. Balgvy* (1773), in which he defended himself against the charge of being responsible for the schism within the ranks of dissenters in Macclesfield. He wrote also numerous contributions to the *Theological Repository*. His literary efforts, however, were not confined exclusively to religious issues. In 1774 he published *A New System of Shorthand: being an Improvement upon Byrom*.

Palmer died from a stroke at Birmingham on either 26 or 28 December 1786, and was buried in the Old Meeting graveyard there on 2 January 1787. He was survived by his daughter from his second marriage. Priestley preached his funeral sermon on 8 January. Palmer was reputed to be gifted but eccentric. Priestley wrote of him, 'You will never find any man perfect, or without some disagreeable peculiarities', but immediately followed this with huge praise for his abilities as a scholar and preacher (Rutt, 1.362). ALEXANDER GORDON, *rev.* M. J. MERCER

Sources C. Surman, index, DWL • H. L. Short, 'Macclesfield's first Unitarian minister', *Transactions of Unitarian Historical Society*, 10/3 (1951–4) • G. Malmgreen, *Industry and culture in Macclesfield, 1750–1835* (1985) • G. E. Evans, *Vestiges of protestant dissent* (1897) • [W. Turner], 'Historical account of students educated in the Warrington Academy', *Monthly Repository*, 9 (1814), 201–5, esp. 203–4 • *Life and correspondence of Joseph Priestley*, ed. J. T. Rutt, 1 (1831) • *IGI*

Palmer, John (1742–1818), theatre proprietor and postal reformer, was born in Bath, probably at 1 Gallaway's Buildings, the third child and only son of John Palmer (1702/3–1788) and his wife, Jane Long (1714/15–1783). His family were prosperous tradesmen in Bath, to which town his grandfather had moved, probably from Faringdon, then in Berkshire. His father ran a tallow chandlery, a brewery and maltings, and a theatre there. Palmer was educated locally at the Revd Needham's academy at Colerne and then at Marlborough Free Grammar School. In a quarrel which presaged his later disputes with authority, he opposed his family's wishes that he should enter the church and worked for a time in the brewery, before investing his energies in their theatrical concerns. On 24 August 1769 he married Sarah Mason, a widow of Clifton, establishing their family of six children in West Hall, Weston, Bath. After her death he married on 2 November 1786 a Miss Pratt, probably a relative of the Hon. J. J. Pratt, MP for Bath.

Palmer's association with the theatre in Bath sharpened his entrepreneurial skills. With the support of Bath corporation he promoted in London an act (8 Geo. III c. 10, 1768), which secured the position of the Orchard Street Theatre by royal patent, the only one outside the capital to be thus protected. The prologue delivered by Palmer in celebration of this victory is included in a collection he edited about 1770, *The New Spouter's Companion*. On the retirement of his father in 1776 the patent was renewed in his name (patent rolls, 16 Geo. III pt iv). In 1779 a Bristol theatre was taken in hand on similar terms and the programmes of the two theatres Royal were dovetailed, with actors such as Mrs Siddons travelling sometimes daily between the two for rehearsal and performance. This

John Palmer (1742–1818), by George Dance, 1793

experience, and Palmer's own travels and correspondence in search of talent, convinced him of the need for improved communications. The success of Bathonian Ralph Allen in the introduction of the cross-post, bypassing London, had already shown that a provincial base was no bar to great financial rewards for national endeavour.

The essence of the scheme devised by Palmer was that the unarmed post boy with a 'worn-out hack' or small cart, should be replaced by mailcoaches, similar to the stagecoaches on the improved turnpike roads that were already completing journeys with speed and security, which meant they were sometimes the preferred but unofficial way of sending letters and packages. The mailcoaches would be equipped with a strongbox, watched over by an armed guard. Mail was to be dispatched promptly—that from London no longer held back by government letters. The coaches contracted from private firms would travel overnight, stopping only to change horses, deal with mail bags, and meet the needs of passengers. Momentum would be maintained by an exemption from tolls and by the granting of priority over other vehicles.

In 1782 the plan was brought to the attention of William Pitt, chancellor of the exchequer, by the Hon. J. J. Pratt. Pitt showed interest, not least because of the promise of an increased revenue, but the plan's acceptance was held up by changes in government and by the opposition of the Post Office, which feared a loss of its authority. However, in June 1784 Pitt ordered a trial run on the Bristol–Bath–London road, which was so successful that a minute was sent from the Treasury to the Post Office, requiring that every assistance be given to the introduction of the service on all major routes in England and Wales. On Palmer's initiative most of this was accomplished by the end of 1785, and he then visited Scotland in 1786, France in 1787, and Ireland in 1788, to explore the extension of the service by land and sea.

The reforms were welcomed by the public but the fact that Palmer had greater support from the Treasury than the Post Office led to problems, especially as the tasks arising from his appointment as surveyor and comptroller-general, which included arranging contracts with innkeepers and training staff in new duties, were undertaken on the basis of a verbal agreement with Pitt. Palmer had understood he would receive 2½ per cent of the increase of the Post Office revenue and an annual salary of £1500, but instead found himself making a personal investment in the reform of a government institution with respect to which his powers and rewards had not been properly defined. Not until August 1786 was Palmer's dire financial position relieved when the Post Office agreed to appoint him on the terms noted, and to employ the guards, sorters, and others he had been financing, though the measures were not fully retrospective. His position was confirmed in July 1789, but to his dismay he remained under the jurisdiction of the postmasters-general, then lords Walsingham and Chesterfield, whose authority he continued to flout. They referred to him in private correspondence as 'the Dictator' (Clear, 100). A dispute early in 1792, in which his previously trusted assistant, Charles Bonnor, gave evidence of manoeuvres against the postmasters-general, led to Palmer's suspension. However, his departure was eased by the pension of £3000 per annum from April 1793, granted by William Pitt in recognition of the importance of his work.

Despite these battles, Palmer had managed not only to reform the national system for the collection and delivery of mail, but also to improve some antiquated procedures within the Post Office. His stay was short but some of his appointees, such as Francis Freeling, became influential figures there. Palmer's claim for recompense was not met fully, but in 1813 (53 Geo. III, c. 157) an award of some £50,000 was made. The approval of the people had meanwhile been shown by the striking of tokens and medals, the presentation of silverware, and the granting of the freedom of eighteen towns and cities.

Palmer continued to be notably active in the civic life of Bath. He had been elected a common councilman in 1775 and he became a Bath improvement commissioner in 1789. In 1791 he promoted a silver cup for horse racing. After the ending of his postal activities, Palmer increased his local responsibilities, becoming a Bath turnpike trustee in 1793, an alderman in 1795, and mayor of Bath in 1796 and 1809. He gave silver cups to the Bath Volunteers in 1805. In addition, he served as Bath's member of parliament from 1801 to 1807, in the whig interest. He lived in Bath at 25 Circus and 9 Laura Place and in London at Upper Gower Street; his wife died in Weymouth in 1807. He took the Chiltern Hundreds in 1808 and his son Charles was elected in his place. He died in Brighton on 16 August 1818 and was buried in the abbey church of Bath, with civic honours but without the expected public monument.

His eldest son, **Charles Palmer** (1777–1851), army officer and politician, was born on 6 May 1777 at Weston, Bath. He was educated at Eton College and at Oriel College, Oxford, and then served in the army, being appointed an aide-de-camp to the prince regent in 1811 and promoted major-general in 1825. He married Mary Elizabeth, daughter of John Thomas Atkyns of Hunterscombe House, Buckinghamshire, and niece and coheir of John Atkyns Wright, MP for Oxford. He represented Bath as MP in the whig interest from 1808 to 1826 and from 1830 to 1837. A radical reformer, he gave strong support to the Reform Bill, attending rallies in Bath and publishing a *Speech on the State of the Nation* (1832) on the occasion of the bill's third reading. His brothers John and Edmund served in the navy. He succeeded his father as proprietor of the Bath theatre, and was a large vine-grower in the Gironde. He died on 17 April 1851. BRENDA J. BUCHANAN

Sources C. R. Clear, *John Palmer (of Bath) mail coach pioneer* (1955) · J. Palmer, *Papers relative to the agreement made by government … for the reform and improvement of the posts* (1797) · C. Bonnor, *Mr. Palmer's case explained* (1797) · S. Davis, *John Palmer and the mailcoach era* (1984) · H. Robinson, *The British Post Office: a history*, another edn (1970) · R. S. Neale, *Bath, 1680–1850: a social history, or, A valley of pleasure, yet a sink of iniquity* (1981) · H. Joyce, *The history of the Post Office from its establishment down to 1836* (1893) · *Public characters of 1802–1803* (1803) · 'Memoir of the late John Palmer', *GM*, 1st ser., 88/2 (1818), 276–80 · B. S. Penley, *The Bath stage: a history of dramatic representations in Bath* (1892) · J. Palmer, *The new spouter's companion, or, A choice collection of prologues and epilogues*, new edn (c.1770) · C. G. Harper, *Stage-coach and mail in days of yore*, 2 vols. (1903) · W. T. Jackman, *The development of transportation in modern England*, 2 vols. (1916) · parish register (burials), 28 Aug 1818, Bath Abbey, Bath, Somerset, Bath RO · parish register (baptism), 5 Dec 1742, St James's Church, Bath, Somerset, Bath RO · parish register (marriage), 24 Aug 1769, All Saints, Weston, Bath, Somerset, Bath RO · *WWBMP*, vol. 1 · Boase, *Mod. Eng. biog.* · *GM*, 1st ser., 56 (1786), 995

Archives NRA, priv. coll.

Likenesses T. Worlidge, oils, c.1759, Victoria Art Gallery, Bath · T. Gainsborough, oils, c.1775, Pennsylvania Museum, Philadelphia · G. Dance, pencil drawing, 1793, NPG [*see illus.*] · J. Fittler, engraving, 1803 (after G. Robertson) · M. Jervis, etching, 1817 · G. Robertson, portrait

Wealth at death £3000 p.a. pension from 1793; capital sum of £50,000 received in 1813

Palmer, John (1744–1798), actor, was born in the parish of St Luke's, Old Street, London. Nothing is known of his mother, but his father, Robert Palmer (1699–1787), had served in the army and was employed as a doorman at the Drury Lane Theatre. He is unusual among his contemporaries in that a detailed account of his career was published five years before he died. Unfortunately, however, the 'Memoirs of John Palmer, esq.' (which appeared in the *Thespian Magazine and Literary Repository*, November, December 1793 and January, February 1794) was almost certainly written by the man himself and, given that he had come to be known as Plausible Jack, it is perhaps more

John Palmer (1744–1798), by John Russell, 1786

reliable on the details of roles played than on the estimations of his talent or, indeed, the financial rate at which those talents were rewarded.

Early struggles Palmer's family intended him for the army but he declined both that and a potential career as an artist, determined from his early years on becoming an actor. At the age of sixteen he was unsuccessful in attempting to sell his services to David Garrick, but was taken up by Samuel Foote at the Haymarket Theatre and made his first stage appearance, as Harry Scamper in Foote's *The Orators*, on 28 April 1762. It was not a momentous début and, after a short period touring, he returned to Foote and to the same part, only to learn his services were no longer required, probably because he was engaged to play Buck in Foote's *An Englishman in Paris* in a benefit night for his father and three of his colleagues at Drury Lane on the same night as he should have been reprising his Scamper in a performance of *The Orators*.

By 1762 Palmer's efforts to interest Garrick had briefly succeeded and he played at Drury Lane in the 1762–3 and 1763–4 seasons, mostly in smallish parts, but including the role of George Barnwell in George Lillo's *The London Merchant*. He parted with Garrick's company in 1764, apparently over a disagreement about a rise in salary, and joined the Norwich Company on tour in eastern England. One benefit of this move was that he was given more substantial parts and he began to establish a small reputation with his depictions of Young Wilding in Foote's *The Liar* and Aimwell in Isaac Bickerstaff's *The Maid of the Mill*. In Norwich he successfully courted and married, in 1764 or 1765, Mrs Frances Berroughs (*d.* 1798), whose chief attraction appears to have been her wealth since Palmer soon abandoned her in favour of a mistress from Yarmouth whom he had acquired while touring with the Norwich Company. Reconciliation with his wife followed shortly, but the couple, shunned by her family, took refuge back in London. However, as a result of his previous record there, Palmer found it impossible to find work and eked out an existence giving performances of George Alexander Stevens's 'A lecture on heads', travelling as far afield as Nottingham, Northampton, and Derby (where he briefly joined a touring company) to do so. He returned to London in April 1766 but an anticipated season with Foote at the Haymarket Theatre was thwarted by a serious horse-riding accident incurred by Foote. Things got little better as Palmer jumped from one brief engagement to another; hired by Spranger Barry to play Iago alongside the famous man's Othello, he soon dropped to the minor role of Montano, unable to cope with Barry's stage presence; he rejected the chance to return to Dublin with Barry for the 1766/7 season and was offered work by John Beard at the Covent Garden Theatre. Instead he threw in his lot with Garrick once more and, in return for a very small remuneration, was rewarded with walk-on parts. In the summer of 1767 he appeared at the Haymarket Theatre, where his roles included Ben Budge in John Gay's *The Beggar's Opera*.

Success Just when it appeared that Palmer's career was never going to take off, fate—in the shape of a peculiar coincidence—stepped in. One of his problems had been that he was cursed with exactly the same name as another, far more established actor. The other John Palmer (1728–1768), also known as Gentleman John, a stalwart of the Drury Lane company, was not related to his younger namesake, who was distinguished from him on the playbills by appearing merely as J. Palmer. Gentleman John was due to take on once more the part of Harcourt in *The Country Girl*, Garrick's adaptation of William Wycherley's *The Country Wife*, but was taken ill (he never really recovered and died two years later in 1768). Plausible Jack was offered the part and acquitted himself sufficiently well as to be offered a longer-term, though still low-paid, contract. Garrick thought enough of him that he also briefly employed Palmer's wife as an actress. Gradually Palmer began to stretch his theatrical muscles, a process that was greatly aided not only by Gentleman John's death and that of another Drury Lane dependable, Charles Holland, in December 1769 but by the defection of William Powell to the Covent Garden company at the end of the 1766–7 season. Given the opportunity to widen his repertoire, Palmer flourished, in both tragic and comic roles. In the 1767–8 season he played a wide variety of parts, including Edmund in *King Lear*, Kastrel and Wellbred in Ben Jonson's *The Alchemist* and *Every Man in his Humour* respectively, and Jenkins in a pantomime, *Harlequin's Invasion*. Undoubtedly Palmer was intent on demonstrating his worth to Garrick, but for a young actor only in his mid-twenties it was not only a rapid about-turn in fortunes but an invaluable apprenticeship. There suddenly seemed almost no kind of role that he could not take on, though he had yet to be entrusted with any of the really major roles at Drury Lane. He became increasingly impatient. In 1769 Palmer had started doing the summer season at Liverpool, which he continued to do until 1775 when he summered in Dublin and in Birmingham. Money was tight in the Palmer household, his wife having apparently been disinherited after the fuss over the marriage. By 1776 they had moved to Bow Street in Bloomsbury (where they lived until 1782), and from that point Palmer established a pattern of working at Drury Lane in the winter season and at the Haymarket—where he was joined by his younger brother, Robert [*see below*]—in the summer. That same year Garrick had given over the management of Drury Lane to R. B. Sheridan, and Palmer became the first actor to take on the part of Joseph Surface in Sheridan's *The School for Scandal* when it premièred in 1777.

Palmer's career continued to flourish, and in 1782 the family moved to Goodge Street and then, in 1785, to Kentish Town. His wife's brief theatrical career had ended; she was doubtless too busy giving birth to and raising their eight children. Stories circulated of the actor's ill treatment of her, and generally he seems to have been something of a philanderer, his nickname Plausible deriving from that of the coxcomb in Wycherley's *The Plain Dealer*. However, despite his continually increasing popularity, and a considerable rise in salary, John Palmer thought that there were better ways of earning money in the theatre than as an actor and determined to run his own company.

Actor-manager With a friend, the Revd William Jackson, Palmer planned to open a new theatre in the East End of London, thereby avoiding the monopoly granted to Drury Lane and Covent Garden for the summer season and the Haymarket for the winter season in the West End. Palmer was successful in raising money at first but, although he was granted a slightly problematic licence, the project was crippled from the outset by under-funding, and more than a year elapsed after the announced opening of 1 May 1786 before the new theatre, the Royalty, finally opened on 20 June 1787. Progress had also been slowed by a publicly advertised threat of prosecution of any actors who performed at the Royalty by the patentees of the other three theatres. When the theatre finally opened, it did so with Palmer playing Jaques in *As You Like It*. The evening also contained an afterpiece, which was somewhat cheekily Garrick's *Miss in her Teens*, and a defence of the new theatre's activities delivered by Palmer. However, fear of prosecution caused the theatre to close briefly before reopening on 3 July with a night of varieties, the kind of entertainment with which it was to be exclusively concerned in the rest of its short life. Several of the performers were arrested and charged, and some were even imprisoned, but all were soon released on bail. The Royalty staggered on but by April 1788 it had closed, never to reopen. The pamphlet war over its activities, which had started in 1787 and continued after Palmer's death, receives an account in James Boaden's *Memoirs of Kemble* (359–68), and the various pamphlets are listed in Robert Lowe's *Bibliographical Account of English Theatrical Literature*. Having sworn that he would never return to the Drury Lane management that had hounded his enterprise, Palmer—ever the opportunist—was re-engaged there for the 1788–9 season, as well he needed to be, since he was now chronically in debt and threatened with financial ruin.

Ever the man of all parts, Palmer, hiding from the law for a period in his dressing-room at Drury Lane, next turned to the Royal Circus, where he produced a series of spectacles, including a long-running and extremely popular 'Demotion of the Bastille'. He was briefly imprisoned following the closure of the Drury Lane Theatre in 1789 (prior to its demolition), as a rogue and a vagabond, but by 1790 he had assumed control of productions at the Circus, and on 14 May of that year appeared as Ranger in Benjamin Hoadly's *The Suspicious Husband*, on a benefit night for his brother, Robert. He made regular appearances at the Haymarket in the summer season, and was engaged for the 1790–91 season at Drury Lane. His stock, like his salary, had fallen, however, and by 1793 Palmer was trying his luck in Scotland. In April 1794 he set up home in London again (at 12 New Lisle Street, Leicester Square) and, surprisingly, was taken on by the acting manager of Drury Lane, John Philip Kemble, in the new building, a third Drury Lane. He continued to appear there until his death, fulfilling his accustomed summer engagements at the Haymarket with occasional visits to the provinces. Towards the end of his career, he finally played Hamlet in a London production (at Drury Lane in 1796, the same year that he played Shylock at the Haymarket). Throughout his adult life he had been dogged by accidents. In his 'Memoirs' he tells of the occasion in 1776 or 1777 when, playing Dionysius opposite Mrs Barry's Euphrasia in *The Grecian Daughter* (by Arthur Murphy), he was badly wounded 'owing to failure in the spring of the dagger'. Having himself drawn the blood of the actor playing Iachimo to his Posthumus in Shakespeare's *Cymbeline* in 1771, he was the victim of a reverse mishap in 1776, and again when appearing in James Cobb's *The Siege of Belgrade* in 1791; and in September 1778 he suffered a near fatal accident when the stage trap of the Haymarket, on which he was set to sink slowly down as the ghost of Banquo, was released too quickly. In 1796 he was badly wounded in a public assault, and his health began to fail him. In February 1798 his long-suffering wife died, and Palmer was soon to follow. He played Drury Lane for the last time, taking the part of Father Philips in Matthew Lewis's *The Castle Spectre* and the title part in John Dalton's adaptation of John Milton's *Comus*. Palmer then embarked on a strenuous summer season at Liverpool. The death of a young son, Robert (in July), coupled with the loss of his wife and continuing financial worries, was too much for his ailing physique to bear. On 2 August 1798 John Palmer gave his last performance, taking on at very short notice the lead role in Benjamin Thompson's *The Stranger* (adapted from Kotzebue's *Menschenhass und Reue*). Clearly struggling, he collapsed and died on stage during the fourth act, a professional to the last. Benefit nights were given at the Liverpool as well as at the Drury Lane and Haymarket theatres, producing substantial sums of money for his surviving children, in itself a testimony to his popularity. At least four, and possibly six, of the eight children performed as professional actors.

Assessment Palmer's theatrical career was uneven, but he remained highly popular until the end. His most successful, and most acclaimed, parts were in comedies and included Joseph Surface, Sir Toby Belch in *Twelfth Night*, Captain Absolute in Sheridan's *The Rivals*, and Falstaff, as well as young likely-lad roles such as Young Wilding in Foote's *The Liar* and Dick Amlet in Vanbrugh's *The Confederacy*. The sheer number and variety of the parts he took, his willingness to play both major and minor roles throughout his life, and his evident versatility, must have contributed to this popularity. The *Biographical Dictionary of Actors* estimates that he may have performed more than 375 different parts. He did not always find favour with contemporary critics—but there were many more to praise than to damn him. He was clearly more at home in comedy than in tragedy, although he played a number of tragic roles, and was thought better than the 'late Mr Palmer as Edmund in *King Lear* by Francis Gentleman' (Gentleman, 1.374), who also acquitted him well in a comparison of the same two actors' portrayal of Cassio in *Othello*: he did 'not fall much behind in execution; to which is added the advantage of a much more soldier-like appearance, a person much better framed to make women fall' (ibid., 1.153). Charles Lamb remembered him with affection as Surface in Sheridan's *The School for Scandal*, and wrote of his:

> gay boldness, the graceful, solemn plausibility, the measured step, the insinuating voice … the downright *acted* villainy of the part, so different from the pressure of conscious, actual wickedness, the hypocritical assumption of hypocrisy,—which made Jack so deservedly a favourite in that character. (Lamb, 155)

Of his Sir Toby Belch, Lamb claimed that 'for sock or buskin there was an air of swaggering gentility about Jack Palmer. He was a gentleman with a slight infusion of the footman' (ibid., 60); which helps to explain the warmth with which his frequent pieces of extempore stage-business were greeted by audiences. This mixture of the airs of a 'gentleman' and a 'footman' was thought to be 'vulgar' by Dibdin (Dibdin, 10.349), and William Hawkins found him, in 1775, limited in his potential:

> a promising actor, and what we may call a handsome and portly figure, save an unpardonable stoop and awkward gait; his voice is loud and commanding, but neither pleasing nor distinct … he is respectable in several parts of tragedy and comedy; and would he endeavour to give his body a little more steadiness he cannot fail (when placed in his proper sphere of acting) to meet applause. (Hawkins, 19)

By the end of his career such grudging recognition had fallen more in line with the evident acclaim of audiences. James Boaden celebrated his talents: 'Mr Palmer was the most general actor that lived … In the long list of tyrants in tragedy, and fine gentlemen in comedy, he was better, oh, how much better, than all other men!' (Boaden, 2.221).

It was perhaps appropriate that this 'most unrivalled' and almost certainly most travelled actor of his times should not have died or been buried in the London to which he kept returning. He was interred at Woolton, near Liverpool, on 6 August 1798; in the fifty-fourth year of his life the frequently troubled body of this remarkable man was at last at rest.

Robert Palmer (*bap.* 1756?, *d.* 1817), actor, the younger brother (possibly a half-brother) of John Palmer, was probably born at Banbury Court, Long Acre, London and was probably the Robert, son of Robert and Mary Palmer, baptized at St Martin-in-the-Fields on 6 October 1756, and educated at Brook Green in Hammersmith. His first known stage appearance was made on 23 November 1763 at the age of six, as Mustardseed in a Drury Lane performance of *A Midsummer Night's Dream*, in which his other brother, William (*d.* 1787), played Demetrius. After a limited juvenile career, he trained as a dancer under Grimaldi at Hart Street, Covent Garden, and was employed as such in the 1774–5 Drury Lane season. In 1776 he was contracted to Samuel Foote at the Haymarket Theatre, and played a number of minor roles in Foote's own plays, *The Commissary*, *The Liar*, *The Capuchin*, and *The Bankrupt*, as well as in Thomas Francklin's *The Contract*, Nahum Tate's *A Duke and No Duke* and Shakespeare's *1 Henry IV*.

On 24 June 1780, at St Mary-le-Strand, he married Jane Cooper of whom nothing more is known, and in the 1782–3 season he acted at the Capel Street and Smock Alley theatres in Dublin. In 1784 he was living at 23 Cecil Street, Bloomsbury, but was unable to perform as he had broken his arm. He spent the summer of 1786 acting at the Stourbridge fair with both John and William Palmer; indeed, generally where John was to be found until his death in 1798, Robert was not far behind; in the summer of 1793 they were together in Edinburgh and Dundee. On his return to London he moved to Eaton Street, Pimlico, having previously abandoned his Bloomsbury address for lodgings in Kennington. He was as unable to manage his finances as John, and in 1797 he was briefly imprisoned for debt. From the 1790–91 season Robert was regularly employed at Drury Lane, but continued to suffer money problems. Contemporary critics were frequently hostile to his acting, comparing it unfavourably with that of John, under whose wing he appeared constantly; although Charles Lamb found some things to praise in Robert when making such a comparison.

The problem was solved when John died in 1798. The relationship between the brothers was a close one and at the Haymarket benefit for John's orphaned children (given at the King's Theatre, so that more people could be squeezed in) Robert attempted to speak of his brother, but was so overcome by emotion that he could neither give the speech nor take a part in the performance. He inherited the part of Joseph Surface in Sheridan's *School for Scandal*, a part that John had played from the very first performance and made very much his own. He continued at Drury Lane, quarrelling fiercely with Sheridan on two occasions over pay, and at the Haymarket Theatre, alternating the winter and summer seasons at the two theatres from 1776 until 1817. His was a long career, fifty-two years if counted from the Mustardseed début, and, towards its end, and free of the inevitable comparisons with his brother, he began to find a wider acceptance. His particular talents came to the fore with over-the-top characters such as Sir Lucius O'Trigger in Sheridan's *The Rivals*, any comic role that demanded a foreign accent, and the kind of swaggering young men that John had also done so well—Tybalt in *Romeo and Juliet* and Gratiano in *The Merchant of Venice*, for instance.

He died on Christmas day 1817 at 12 King's Row, Pimlico, where he had lived since 1798, and was buried at St Martin-in-the-Fields. He had evidently been in severe ill health for some time and had made elaborate arrangements about his funeral. He left a will in which Elizabeth Willett was given the power of executor and all benefits from his personal effects; no further details are known of their relationship. He was not remembered as his brother John had been after his death, but his career, which included about forty newly created roles, had not been without its high points.

JOHN BULL

Sources Highfill, Burnim & Langhans, *BDA* • 'Memoirs of John Palmer, esq.', *Thespian Magazine and Literary Repository* (Nov 1793–Feb 1794) • J. Fullarton and J. Robinson, eds., *English theatrical literature, 1559–1900* (1970) [incl. R. Lowe's *A bibliographical account of English theatrical literature* (1888)] • *The thespian dictionary, or, Dramatic biography of the eighteenth century* (1802) • J. Boaden, *Memoirs of Kemble, including a history of the stage*, 2 vols. (1825) • C. Dibdin, *A complete history of the English stage*, 10 vols. (1797–1800) • F. Gentleman, *The dramatic censor, or, Critical companion*, 2 vols. (1770) • C. Lamb, 'On some of the old actors', *The dramatic essays*, ed. B. Matthews (1981) • C. Lamb, 'The artificial comedy of the last century', *The dramatic essays*, ed. B. Matthews (1981) • W. Hawkins, *Miscellanies in prose and verse, containing candid and impartial observations on the principal performers belonging to the two Theatres-Royal, from January 1773 to May 1775* (1775) • Genest, *Eng. stage* • M. Banham, *The Cambridge guide to theatre*, new edn (1995) • *GM*, 1st ser., 68 (1798), 725–8 • *GM*, 1st ser., 87/2 (1817), 632 • J. De Castro, *The memoirs of J. De Castro, comedian*, ed. R. Humphreys (1824) • *IGI*

Likenesses Walker, line engraving, pubd 1776 (after Barralet), NPG • T. Parkinson, group portrait, oils, 1778, Garr. Club • J. Roberts, group portrait, oils, exh. RA 1779, Garr. Club • J. Russell, pastel drawing, 1786, Garr. Club [*see illus.*] • Arrowsmith, oils (as Colonel Cohenberg in *The siege of Belgrade*), Garr. Club • T. Hull, miniature, NPG • J. Roberts, drawing, BM • H. Walton, oils, NPG • J. Zoffany, group portrait, oils, Castle Howard, North Yorkshire • oils, Garr. Club • prints, BM, NPG

Wealth at death very little; benefits organized for orphaned children • Robert Palmer: Highfill, Burnim & Langhans, *BDA*

Palmer, John (**1767–1836**). *See under* Palmer, William (1740–1816).

Palmer, John [*name in religion* Bernard] (**1782–1852**), abbot of Mount St Bernard, born on 15 October 1782, was the son of William Palmer, a small farmer in the parish of Charmouth, Dorset, and his wife, Anne; he was brought up a low-churchman. In 1806 he went to London to seek employment, and was prompted to attend the divine services at the Roman Catholic chapel in Warwick Street, off Regent Street. He obtained a copy of Richard Challoner's manual of devotion, *The Garden of the Soul*, which he read with great delight, and which led him to convert to Roman Catholicism in 1807. He had entered the service of

Thomas Weld of Lulworth Castle, Dorset, and in 1808 became a novice in the Cistercian monastery of St Susan, Lulworth, where he was professed by the name of Bernard on 21 November 1810. Harassed by the government in 1817, the Lulworth community found refuge in the abbey of La Meilleraie, near Nantes, France, where Bernard Palmer received minor orders. In 1831 the abbey of La Meilleraie was suppressed and dissolved by Louis-Philippe's government, and, though a few of the monks were permitted to remain, the majority emigrated to Ireland, where they founded the abbey of Mount Melleray, co. Waterford. A little community of about seven brothers was established in Charnwood Forest, Leicestershire, in 1835, some of them coming from Mount Melleray. At first they resided in a cottage, where they were joined in March 1837 by Bernard Palmer, who had been living at Nantes under the protection of the British consul since the suppression of the abbey.

In 1837 the monks moved from their cottage to a little monastery which had been built for them in the immediate vicinity from funds contributed by, among others, Ambrose Phillipps De Lisle. On 31 July 1838 Father Bernard was ordained to the priesthood, and in January 1841 was appointed prior, which was then the position of first superior of the house. The community rapidly grew in numbers and an extensive building programme was undertaken. During 1844 a new and much larger structure, built in Pugin's severest lancet style, near a prominent outcrop of granite, was sufficiently advanced for the community to inhabit it; it was given the name Mount St Bernard. The major portion of the building funds was contributed by the earl of Shrewsbury, the rest being raised by public subscription.

Three decrees were issued by the Congregatio de Propaganda Fide, and ratified by Pope Pius IX on 9 May 1848, by which the monastery was constituted an abbey with independent jurisdiction, in union with the general chapter of the Cistercian Congregation of the Strict Observance (the Trappists) in France. In the same year Father Bernard was elected abbot by the unanimous votes of the community. Bishop Ullathorne of Birmingham consecrated him on 18 February 1849, and invested him with mitre, crozier, and ring. As abbot, the teaching which he gave to his brethren was simple and unadorned, but felt to be full of religious fervour.

As the first English mitred abbot since the Reformation, Father Bernard Palmer occupies a conspicuous position in the history of the Catholic revival of the nineteenth century. He was notable for his profound humility, selfless charity, and for the resolute austerity of his lifestyle. After a long and painful illness, borne with great patience, he died of dropsy on 10 November 1852. On the 13th his remains were interred in a vault beneath the chapter-house, later the sacristy, of the abbey.

J. M. RIGG, *rev.* HILARY COSTELLO

Sources *The Tablet* (20 Nov 1852) • *Catholic Directory* (1853), 181 • R. Smith, *Concise history of the Cistercian order* (1852) • *A brief sketch of the life of the Right Rev. John Bernard Palmer* (1855) • M. Pawley, *Faith and family: the life and circle of Ambrose Phillipps de Lisle* (1993)

Archives Mount St Bernard Abbey, Leicestershire, corresp. and papers

Palmer, John (*fl.* 1818), traveller in North America, of King's Lynn, Norfolk, sailed from Liverpool on 28 March 1817 on a visit to the United States and Canada. During the voyage he had for companions William Cobbett and his two sons. Soon after his return to England on 28 February 1818, he published his *Journal of Travels in the United States of North America and in Lower Canada* (1818). It contains details of the prices of land and provisions, descriptions of the principal towns of the eastern seaboard, of the mid-western states, and of the old south, and a description of a pair of sea serpents that were said to have been seen off Marblehead and Cape Ann in 1817. A Dutch translation of the book appeared at Haarlem in 1820. Sydney Smith, in reviewing the *Journal* in the *Edinburgh Review* (December 1818, 133), described it as having been written by a 'plain man, of good sense and slow judgment'.

Nothing more is known of Palmer. Microfilm and -fiche reprints of both the English and the Dutch versions of his book (1959, 1980, 1984, and n.d.) show that it still has some value as a historical source in the absence of many competitors.

GORDON GOODWIN, *rev.* ELIZABETH BAIGENT

Sources Allibone, *Dict.* • J. G. Wilson and J. Fiske, eds., *Appleton's cyclopaedia of American biography*, 10 vols. (1924)

Palmer [*formerly* Budworth], **Joseph** (*bap.* 1756, *d.* 1815), writer, was baptized on 3 June 1756 at Manchester Cathedral, the son of Joseph Budworth of Coventry, and the nephew of the Revd William Budworth, master of Brewood School, Staffordshire. At an early age he joined the 72nd regiment, or Royal Manchester volunteers. He was promoted to the rank of lieutenant, and proceeded with the regiment to Gibraltar, where he was wounded during the course of the siege of that fortress by the combined forces of France and Spain. He returned home with his regiment in 1783, and accepted a cadetship in the Bengal artillery, though he did not long remain in India. Subsequently he retired from the service; but in the war occasioned by the French revolution, he volunteered as a captain in the North Hampshire militia. Shortly after leaving the army he married Elizabeth, sister of Roger Palmer of Rush, near Dublin, and of Palmerstown, co. Mayo, and succeeded, in her right, on the death of her brother in 1811, to the estates and name of Palmer.

Palmer wrote much in the *Gentleman's Magazine*, under the signature Rambler. His works include *A Fortnight's Ramble to the Lakes in Westmoreland, Lancashire, and Cumberland* (1792; 2nd edn, 1795; 3rd edn, 1810) which also contains many interesting anecdotes of the siege of Gibraltar, including particulars of his own military services. He also wrote 'The Lancashire collier-girl: a true story', which first appeared in the *Gentleman's Magazine* (1st ser., 65, 1795, 197), and was subsequently reprinted and widely disseminated by the Society for Circulating Serious Tracts among the Poor, but with some alterations not approved by the author. His other works include *The Siege of Gibraltar: a Poem* (1795) and *Windermere: a Poem* (1798).

Palmer was elected a fellow of the Society of Antiquaries on 4 June 1795. He died of apoplexy at Eastbourne, Sussex, on 4 September 1815, and was buried on 14 September in the churchyard of West Moulsey, Surrey, to which parish he had been a liberal benefactor. His only daughter and sole heir, Emma Mary, in 1812 became the wife of W. A. Mackinnon, of Newtown Park, MP for Lymington. She died on 15 November 1835, aged forty-three (*GM*, 2nd ser., 4. 663).

THOMPSON COOPER, *rev.* M. CLARE LOUGHLIN-CHOW

Sources *IGI* • [J. Watkins and F. Shoberl], *A biographical dictionary of the living authors of Great Britain and Ireland* (1816) • P. J. Budworth, *Memorials of the parishes of Greensted-Budworth, Chipping Ongar, and High Laver, Ongar* (1876) • *GM*, 1st ser., 81/2 (1811), 403–4 • *GM*, 1st ser., 85/2 (1815), 285, 388–91 • *GM*, 2nd ser., 4 (1835), 663 • Watt, *Bibl. Brit.* [see Budworth]

Archives BL, letters to G. Cumberland, Add. MSS 36500–36515 *passim*

Palmer, Julia (*fl.* 1664–1673), poet, was the author of an autograph manuscript of devotional verse. Nothing is known of her parentage, though her maiden name may have been Hungerford. Based on the evidence of her poem entitled 'Some few perticular mercy (amongst many) taken notice of throug the whole course of life' it is possible she was an orphan: she thanks God for being 'most kinnd / unto the fatherlese' (William Andrews Clark Memorial Library, MS P1745 M1 P744 1671–3 Bound, the 'First Century', poem 70, lines 11–12, p. 112). She was probably the Julia Hungerford who married Nicholas Palmer on 12 May 1664 at All Hallows, London Wall; a Nicholas and a Julia Palmer had a son called Samuel baptized at St Margaret's, Westminster, on 17 June 1667. Julia Palmer's absence from later Anglican records suggests that she became a nonconformist, and her husband may be the 'Mr Palmer of London' who preached at New Windsor in 1669 (*Calamy rev.*, 380): a licence was requested on 24 May 1672 for 'Nicholas Palmer, Presbyterian, at Mrs. Jane Price's new house, Frogmore, New Windsor, Berkshire' (*CSP dom.*, *1672*, 55) which was granted on 10 June. Nicholas Palmer was buried at New Windsor on 28 February 1681. The evidence of her poetry supports the case that Julia Palmer was presbyterian; her emphasis on the necessities of ordinances and duties (set services such as holy communion ordained by authority) suggest that she was presbyterian rather than a member of a more radical sect. The main dedicatee of Palmer's manuscript of 200 devotional poems (written 1671–3) was Joseph Biscoe, a nonconformist and prominent apothecary, who became master of the Society of Apothecaries in 1711–12. Samuel Palmer appears in the court minutes of the society on 7 July 1682; he is listed as the son of the deceased Nicholas Palmer of New Windsor, Berkshire, and was bound as an apprentice to the apothecary Edward Baker for eight years.

In her manuscript, comprising entirely devotional verse, Palmer meditates upon her personal salvation. She alternates between fear that she is unworthy of God's grace and thankfulness for his mercy; for example, poems 44 and 45 in the 'First Century' are headed, 'The soull greatly clouded novem 20 71' and 'upon Christs return november 22'. Drawing on the erotic poetry of the Song of Solomon, Julia Palmer's poems speak of a passionate desire for a mystical marriage with Christ. A longing for death pervades the manuscript, the logical result of the nonconformist belief that only with death comes the full consummation of union with Christ. Palmer's favoured verse form is a simple quatrain rhyming in alternate lines, but she experiments with complex stanzaic forms, particularly in the 'Second Century'. The poems were composed during the period 28 September 1671 to 21 July 1673, as dates in many of their titles indicate. Palmer evidently compiled this manuscript at a later date, however, since the chronological arrangement of the poems is disrupted once: poem 48 in the 'Second Century' is dated 26 September 1672 and thus should follow poem 52, dated 25 September 1672. Whether Palmer's poetry circulated among a circle of apothecaries and nonconformists is uncertain, but we can be sure that she desired to reach an audience: the first poem of the manuscript begins:

Blessed spirit, doe thou endite
Help me to speak thy praise
That soe I may others envite
To love thee, all there days
(fol. ivr)

VICTORIA E. BURKE and ELIZABETH R. CLARKE

Sources U. Cal., Los Angeles, William Andrews Clark Memorial Library, MS P1745 M1 P744 1671–3 Bound • H. F. Westlake and L. E. Tanner, eds., *The registers of St Margaret's, Westminster, London, 1660–1675*, 1, Harleian Society, 64 (1935) • *IGI* • parish register, London, All Hallows, London Wall, 12 May 1664, GL • Society of Apothecaries, court minutes, 1651–80, GL, MS 8200/2; 1680–94, MS 8200/3, fols. 6, 64, 160 • parish register, New Windsor, Berkshire, 28 Feb 1681, Berks. RO [burial] • *CSP dom.*, *1672*, 55, 216 • *Calamy rev.*, 380 • P. Hunting, *A history of the Society of Apothecaries of London* (1998), 302 • C. R. B. Barrett, *The history of the Society of Apothecaries of London* (1905), 122–31 • *DNB*

Archives U. Cal., Los Angeles, William Andrews Clark Memorial Library, MS P1745 M1 P744 1671–3 Bound

Palmer, Julins (1531/2–1556), protestant martyr, was the son of Roger Palmer, mercer or upholsterer, who was sheriff of Coventry in 1525 and mayor in 1533. His name Julins was apparently a form of Joscelin, and has been generally misspelt Julius. He was born at Coventry, but at an early age entered Magdalen College School, Oxford, where he was for some time a pupil of John Harley, afterwards bishop of Hereford. He then became a clerk at Magdalen College, and graduated BA in 1547; in 1549 he was elected a fellow and in 1550 was appointed reader in logic. He soon attracted notice by his uncompromising Catholic opinions, and in 1552 was accused of having written libellous verses against Walter Haddon, the president of Magdalen College. Palmer denied the charge, but soon afterwards he left the college on a leave of absence. He then became a tutor in the household of Sir Francis Knollys.

On the accession of Mary, Palmer returned to his fellowship at Magdalen, but a perusal of Calvin's *Institutes* began to unsettle his religious opinions. His orthodoxy was further undermined by the persecution of leading protestants in Mary's reign. Palmer sent, at his own expense, one of his scholars and a bachelor of the college to Gloucester to report the details of John Hooper's execution to him. Palmer also witnessed the examinations and executions of Nicholas Ridley and Hugh Latimer at Oxford and vehemently denounced the proceedings. This inspired him to the study of protestant theological works, particularly Peter Martyr's commentary on 1 Corinthians. He now became as vehement a protestant as he had before been Roman Catholic, absented himself from mass, and made a point of walking out whenever Roman Catholic ceremonies occurred in the church service. He avoided expulsion from his fellowship by voluntarily leaving Oxford, and obtained the grant of a mastership in Reading grammar school.

Palmer was not long left in peace at Reading, for his study was searched by rivals who wanted his post, and various anti-Catholic manuscripts were discovered, including a poem called *Epicedium*, written in answer to an epitaph on Gardiner by Peter Morwen. His rivals threatened to inform against him unless he at once left Reading. Palmer then sought a legacy bequeathed by his late father from his mother, who, after her husband's death, had retired to Eynsham, but she refused it on account of his heretical opinions. He now, through the intervention of Alan Cope, obtained letters from the president of Magdalen recommending him for a mastership in a school in Gloucestershire, but an incautious visit to Reading to secure his manuscripts and arrears of pay led to his arrest. He was brought before the mayor, Robert Bowyer, and then taken to Newbury. There he was examined before the consistory of Dr Jeffrey on 16 July 1556, and, after an examination marked by acerbic exchanges, Palmer was condemned to be burnt. The sentence was carried out the next day about 5 p.m. Palmer was burnt along with two other protestant martyrs, John Gwin and Thomas Askin, at a spot Foxe only identifies as the sand-pits. During his interrogation Palmer stated that he was twenty-four years old. Besides his answer to Morwen, Strype attributes to Palmer various fugitive pieces, which were never printed and are not known to be extant.

A. F. POLLARD, *rev.* THOMAS S. FREEMAN

Sources J. Foxe, *Actes and monuments* (1563), 1539–41 • J. Foxe, *The second volume of the ecclesiasticall history, conteyning the acts and monuments of martyrs*, 2nd edn (1570), 2117–24 • W. D. Macray, *A register of the members of St Mary Magdalen College, Oxford*, 8 vols. (1894–1915), vol. 2, pp. 119–20 • J. G. Nichols, ed., *Narratives of the days of the Reformation*, CS, old ser., 77 (1859), 87–130

Palmer [*née* Reynolds], **Mary** (**1716–1794**), writer, was born on 9 February 1716, the eldest daughter and third child of Theophila Potter and Samuel Reynolds, the master of the grammar school at Plympton Earl, Devon. She was married on 18 July 1740 to John Palmer of Torrington, Devon, a wealthy gentleman and non-practising solicitor. She had two sons, John and Joseph, who both became clergymen; and three daughters, Mary, Theophila (named for Palmer's mother and sister), and Elizabeth (named for Palmer's sister). Her husband's wealth allowed the building, in 1752, of a large house in Great Torrington, Devon, later called Palmer House, at which she entertained Dr Johnson, among other luminaries of the time. The *Dictionary of National Biography* relates that Palmer, upon learning of Johnson's love for pancakes, 'had a good supply served up, and the doctor ate thirteen'. In 1770 Palmer's husband died.

Mary Palmer (**1716–1794**), by Sir Joshua Reynolds, *c.*1746–7

Palmer is the author of *A Devonshire Dialogue*, which was privately circulated during her lifetime; some extracts were printed without acknowledgement in periodicals. It was never published in full while she lived: in 1837 a portion appeared with a glossary by J. F. Palmer (probably one of her sons), and in 1839 a full version was published, edited by her daughter Theophila. There was another edition in 1869; it was still being sold in Devon in 1895. Considered by the *Dictionary of National Biography* as the 'best piece of literature in the vernacular of Devon', it 'gives some account of customs and characters peculiar to the west of England' in the mid-eighteenth century. It tells the story of Betty (Bet) and Robin (Rab), her 'Measter' Hogg and his mistreated wife, the Dame. Unusually, Bet is allowed to love reading despite her class position. As a serious study of dialect form rather than a novelistic rendering of a regional accent, *A Devonshire Dialogue* anticipates the vernacular poetry of John Clare.

Palmer apparently wrote nothing else, and is primarily discussed in relation to her brother, Sir Joshua *Reynolds, seven years her junior. Her love of drawing apparently influenced him at a young age, and later she had a more material affect on his art: in 1740 (the year of her marriage) she paid half his premium to Thomas Hudson the portrait painter, and nine years later paid his expenses in Italy. In addition Reynolds made her daughter Mary his heir, often had Mary and her sister Theophila to stay with him in London, and painted Theophila frequently, the most famous portrait of her being *Strawberry Girl*. He also painted Palmer twice, once about 1747, and again when she was in late middle age.

Despite the greater prominence of her famous younger brother, Palmer's *Dialogue* indicates an individual take on portrait painting in words, and a concern to preserve the character of the Devon countryside. In the preface to his 1837 edition of the *Dialogue*, her son praised her work in terms of her life: 'the Author's conduct through life is perhaps the best guarantee for the excellent moral which pervades the whole'; and she has been remembered most often as the sister of a great painter, rather than the author of an invaluable work on dialect. At her death she was wealthy enough to leave about £1000 to her children and sisters, as well as a 'dwelling-house and garden' to her son John. She died on 27 May 1794 in Great Torrington.

JACQUELINE M. LABBE

Sources *DNB* • J. Todd, ed., *A dictionary of British and American women writers, 1660–1800* (1984) • Blain, Clements & Grundy, *Feminist comp.*, 826–7

Likenesses J. Reynolds, portrait, *c.*1746–1747, priv. coll. [*see illus.*] • J. Reynolds, portrait, *c.*1776

Wealth at death over £1000: will, 14 July 1794, PRO, PROB 11/1248

Palmer, (Beatrix) Maud [*née* Lady (Beatrix) Maud Gascoyne-Cecil], **countess of Selborne (1858–1950)**, suffragist and political wife, was born on 11 April 1858 at 9 Park Crescent, Marylebone, London, the eldest of the five sons and three daughters of Lord Robert Arthur Talbot Gascoyne-*Cecil, later third marquess of Salisbury (1830–1903), prime minister, and his wife, Georgina Caroline (1826/7–1899), daughter of Sir Edward Hall *Alderson. Maud Cecil grew up in a household steeped in public affairs. During her youth, her father served in Disraeli's cabinet (1874–80), and the family home at Hatfield was a centre of political discussion. The Cecils also involved themselves in the popular side of Conservative politics, through local Primrose League habitations which provided female election workers for the party. This activity, strengthened by Lord Salisbury's sympathy for female enfranchisement, led Maud Cecil, despite her lack of a formal education, to accept as natural her own involvement in public affairs, and, by extension, to support a wider role for women generally.

On 27 October 1883 Lady Maud Cecil married William Waldegrave *Palmer, Viscount Wolmer (1859–1942), who succeeded as second earl of Selborne in 1895. They had three sons, Roundell Cecil *Palmer, later third earl of Selborne, Robert, and William, and a daughter, Mabel, later Countess Grey. Lady Wolmer, who had developed strong political opinions of her own before marriage, and assured her fiancé that her conversion to his Liberalism was 'of all the most improbable eventualities … one of the most unlikely' (Jalland, 237), rapidly became Wolmer's 'best and most trusted counsellor' (*The Times*, 6 May 1950). Although in some ways very conventional, establishment-minded figures, the couple shared a certain detachment from party politics, and in fact it was William whose allegiances changed. He began as a Liberal MP in 1885, but became a Liberal Unionist in 1886 and had moved to the far right by 1910. At that stage he professed to deplore the Conservative Party's shallow convictions and lack of moral courage, but Maud argued that it had been much the same in the early 1880s when she knew it intimately. Their political partnership developed further when Selborne, as he then was, left the Admiralty in 1905 to serve as high commissioner in South Africa and governor of the Transvaal and the Orange River Colony until 1910. In this role Lady Selborne's unfailing sense of humour, unconventionality, and readiness to throw herself into good causes surprised and pleased South Africans.

(Beatrix) Maud Palmer, countess of Selborne (1858–1950), by Philip A. de Laszlo, 1923

On the Selbornes' return to Britain they became absorbed by the controversy over the enfranchisement of women. In order to persuade the Conservative Party to adopt the women's cause a Conservative and Unionist Women's Franchise Association had been established in 1908, and in August 1910 Lady Selborne became its president. In this capacity she undertook extensive speaking tours and played a key role in promoting the suffragist cause in the party in which it had, traditionally, been weak. When the leading female anti-suffragist, Mrs Humphry Ward, charged Conservative women's suffragists with being false to their party and creating divisions within it, Lady Selborne countered by pointing to the list of leading tories, including Disraeli, Northcote, W. H. Smith, and Salisbury, who had advocated the vote for women before the National League for Opposing Women's Suffrage had been thought of. As Salisbury's daughter, she was perfectly placed to lend respectability to the female cause within Conservatism.

Like most Conservatives the Selbornes favoured no more than a limited measure of female enfranchisement and opposed complete suffrage. However, by 1912 Lady Selborne had concluded that a wider measure of reform to incorporate married, not just single, women was acceptable since wives constituted an essentially conservative element in society. Her husband backed her up, publishing 'Surely the family is the foundation of conservatism?' (*Conservative and Unionist Women's Franchise Review*, January–March 1913, 258). He argued that the party would reap the benefits of enfranchising wives because they would extend the influence of married men at the polls. In this way the Selbornes helped to prepare Conservatism for a major readjustment to modern democracy during the First World War. While their formal campaign for suffragism gave way to patriotic work in August 1914, both continued to exercise influence behind the scenes for a generous extension of the vote to both men and women, and for the retention of female workers in their new jobs after the war ended.

Although by 1918 the Selbornes' political influence and activity had greatly diminished, Maud Selborne enjoyed some of the fruits of the sudden enhancement in women's status by becoming a justice of the peace for Hampshire. She died from pneumonia at the age of ninety-two on 27 April 1950 and was buried on 1 May at St Matthew's, at the family seat at Blackmoor near Liss in Hampshire. MARTIN PUGH

Sources *Conservative and Unionist Women's Franchise Review* (1908–14) • *The Times* (6 May 1950) • Bodl. Oxf., MSS Maud Palmer, countess of Selborne • *The crisis of British unionism: the domestic political papers of the second earl of Selborne, 1885–1922*, ed. D. G. Boyce (1987) • P. Jalland, *Women, marriage and politics, 1860–1914* (1986) • b. cert. • m. cert. • d. cert. • Burke, *Peerage* (1939) • GEC, *Peerage*

Archives Bodl. Oxf., corresp. and papers • Hants. RO, family MSS | Bodl. Oxf., William Waldegrave Palmer, second earl of Selborne MSS • Hants. RO, letters to Mabel, Lady Harwick • University of Cape Town, corresp. with Patrick Duncan

Likenesses P. A. de Laszlo, portrait, 1923, Courtauld Inst., Witt Library [*see illus.*] • photograph, Bodl. Oxf., MS Selborne 196 no. 5; repro. in Jalland, *Women* • portrait, repro. in *ILN* (3 Nov 1883)

Wealth at death £7261 9*s*. 10*d*.: probate, 4 July 1950, *CGPLA Eng. & Wales*

Palmer [*née* Worrall], **Phoebe** (1807–1874), Methodist Episcopal evangelist and exponent of holiness, was born on 18 December 1807 in New York, USA, the fourth of nine surviving children of Henry Worrall (1771–1847), engine manufacturer, and his wife, Dorothea, *née* Wade (*d*. 1856). As a youth in his native Yorkshire, Henry Worrall had received his membership ticket from the hand of John Wesley, and emigrated in the late 1770s to New York, where he and his American-born wife became active members of the Methodist Episcopal church. Their children were raised in an atmosphere of middle-class gentility. Their fourth child, Phoebe, on 28 September 1827 married Walter Clarke Palmer (1804–1883), a recent graduate of the Rutgers Medical College of Physicians and Surgeons in New York. The Palmers were both ardent Methodists and financially comfortable, and they quickly assumed a leading role in church and benevolent work. Strongly influenced by the loss in infancy of three of their six children, and by the teaching and example of her elder sister, Sarah Lankford, Phoebe Palmer in 1837 experienced a dramatic Wesleyan 'second blessing', or 'entire sanctification'.

First under the leadership of Sarah, who with her husband, the architect Thomas A. Lankford, shared her home until 1840, and thereafter on her own, Palmer opened her residence to a weekly prayer meeting, which evolved into the well-known Tuesday Meeting for the Promotion of Holiness. This gathering attracted 50 to 150 participants, in particular clergymen; it played a major role in sparking a revival of holiness among Methodists and other evangelical protestants during the mid-nineteenth century, and continued after her death.

Seen as an integral factor in the surge of benevolent and reform activity in the ante-bellum United States, holiness found its practical expression in Palmer's establishment in 1847 of the Five Points mission, located in one of New York's most poverty-stricken districts. A wider field for holiness teaching opened during the 1840s and 1850s as she received invitations to speak at camp meetings in the northern United States and central and maritime Canada. Modifying somewhat Wesley's doctrine of entire sanctification by stressing its instantaneous rather than gradual nature, Palmer's 'altar theology' called on Christians to follow a simple three-step process consisting of entire consecration (placing 'all on the altar'), faith in the biblical promises, and a life of testimony. Although it encountered some opposition within the Methodist ministry, her thought met the needs of a devout and increasingly middle-class laity concerned to find a practical, less emotional expression for piety.

At a time when the religious presses were beginning to tap a growing market, Palmer encountered a receptive readership for her writings, most notably *The Way of Holiness* (1843), *Entire Devotion to God* (1845), *Faith and its Effects* (1848), and *The Promise of the Father* (1859), a lengthy defence of women's ministry. As a result, and thanks to her influential role in the well-publicized 'businessmen's revival' which swept urban centres in the United States in 1857–8, she and her husband were invited to Britain in 1859. During an extended campaign, described in *Four Years in the Old World* (1865), and including major revivals in Belfast, Newcastle, Glasgow, south Wales, and the midlands, over 17,300 people were reported to claim justification and several thousand more professed entire sanctification. In attendance were the co-founders of the Salvation Army, William and Catherine Booth, the latter so influenced as to take up a preaching career of her own. Palmer's teaching would become the characteristic form of the army's doctrine of holiness, as well as having a profound influence on the Keswick movement in the 1880s. Her role as a female revivalist, her insistence upon teetotalism as a mark of sanctification, and her outspoken criticism of non-evangelical lifestyles, did, however, meet with resistance in Britain, and in 1862 the Wesleyans and the Primitive Methodists closed their chapels to 'irregular' itinerant preachers.

After her return to the United States in 1863, Palmer resumed her preaching at camp meetings, as well as editing, with her husband, the religious periodical the *Guide to Holiness*, which reached a circulation of nearly 40,000. Troubled by a perceived move towards 'worldliness' among Methodists, and battling ill health in her final years, she succumbed to Bright's disease at her home, 316 East 15th Street, New York, on 2 November 1874, mourned by her many devoted admirers. She was buried at Greenway cemetery in New York. After her death, through such institutions as the National Camp Meeting Association for the Promotion of Holiness, Palmer's teachings on entire sanctification and 'the higher life' continued to shape the theology of the holiness movement and early twentieth-century Pentecostalism. MARGUERITE VAN DIE

Sources R. Wheatley, *The life and letters of Mrs Phoebe Palmer* (1881); repr. (1984) · C. E. White, *The beauty of holiness: Phoebe Palmer as theologian, revivalist feminist, and humanitarian* (1986) · H. E. Raser, *Phoebe Palmer: her life and thought* (1987) · J. Kent, *Holding the fort: studies in Victorian revivalism* (1978) · K. T. Long, *The revival of 1857–58: interpreting an American religious awakening* (1998) · *Four years in the old world: comprising the travels, incidents, and evangelistic labors of Dr. and Mrs. Palmer in England, Ireland, Scotland and Wales*, 3rd edn (1886) · G. Hughes, *The beloved physician: Walter C. Palmer, M.D.* (1884) · T. L. Smith, *Revivalism and social reform in mid-nineteenth-century America* [1957]; repr. as *Revivalism and social reform: American protestantism on the eve of the civil war* (1980) · N. A. Hardesty, 'Minister as prophet? or as mother?: two nineteenth-century models', *Women in new worlds: historical perspectives on the Wesleyan tradition*, ed. H. F. Thomas and R. S. Keller (1981), 88–101 · R. Carwardine, *Transatlantic revivalism: popular evangelicalism in Britain and America, 1790–1865* (1978) · D. W. Dayton and L. S. Dayton, 'Your daughters shall prophesy: feminism in the holiness movement', *Methodist History*, 14 (Jan 1976), 67–92 · M. E. Dieter, *The holiness revival of the nineteenth century* (1980)

Archives New England Methodist Historical Society Collection, Boston, letter to Gersham F. Cox · Wesleyan University, Middletown, Connecticut, Olin manuscript collection, letters to Stephen M. Olin

Likenesses engravings, repro. in Wheatley, *Life and letters* · engravings, repro. in P. Palmer, *Incidental illustrations of the economy of salvation* (1857) · engravings, repro. in *Four years in the old world*

Wealth at death financially comfortable; lived in expensive residential area: Wheatley, *Life and letters*, 150–52

Palmer, Richard. *See* Richard (*d.* 1195).

Palmer, Richard (*d.* **1625**), physician, son of Andrew Palmer, of St Peter-le-Poer, London, matriculated as a pensioner from Christ's College, Cambridge, in December 1576 and there graduated BA in 1580. He migrated to Peterhouse, where he gained his MA in 1583; he was a fellow of Peterhouse from 1582 to 1586. He received a licence to practise in London from the College of Physicians on 9 April 1593, and was elected a fellow in February 1597. He was nine times censor between 1599 and 1619, was treasurer from 1621 to 1624, and president in 1620. On 20 November 1586 he married Alice Bradley at Little St Mary's, Cambridge; they had three children: Andrew, John, and Elizabeth.

On 5 November 1612 Palmer attended with John Giffard at the bedside of Henry, prince of Wales. In October, several long consultations had been held with Sir Theodore Mayerne, John Hammond, Henry Atkins, and Dr Butler, and in the presence of Sir Thomas Challoner and Sir David Murray (1567–1629), and as a result of these discussions, a medicine made of the dried leaves of *Teucrium scordium* and other herbs was administered to the prince. It was unsuccessful, for he died the next day. Palmer was present at the post-mortem examination, and in the original report his signature is fourth out of the six physicians. In the report as printed by Mayerne, his name is last.

Palmer died early in 1625, leaving a will which gives his residence as St Olave, Silver Street, London.

NORMAN MOORE, *rev.* SARAH BAKEWELL

Sources Venn, *Alum. Cant.* · Munk, *Roll* · will, PRO, PROB 11/145, fol. 375*r–v*

Palmer, Robert (*bap.* **1756**?, *d.* **1817**). *See under* Palmer, John (1744–1798).

Palmer, Roger, earl of Castlemaine (**1634–1705**), diplomatist and Roman Catholic apologist, was born on 3 September 1634, the second son of Sir James Palmer (*d.* 1657), of Dorney Court, Buckinghamshire, being the son of Sir James's second marriage, to Catherine, daughter of Sir William Herbert, later first Baron Powis, of Powis Castle, Montgomeryshire. He was educated at Eton College from 1648, and then at King's College, Cambridge, which he entered as a fellow-commoner on 25 March 1652. On 29 October he was admitted to the Inner Temple. He was intelligent, highly literate, and good at languages. He inherited his lifelong loyalty to the house of Stuart from his father, on which the exiled Charles II congratulated him. Palmer married at St Gregory's, London, the beautiful Barbara Villiers (*bap.* 1640, *d.* 1709) [*see* Palmer, Barbara, countess of Castlemaine and *suo jure* duchess of Cleveland], daughter of William Villiers, second Viscount Grandison, on 14 April 1659. In marrying above himself he espoused a woman whose beauty was as famous as her conduct was already scandalous.

The Restoration At the general election of 1660 Palmer, like his father in the 1620s, stood for parliament. Despite the ordinance forbidding the sons of royalists from standing he was returned for the borough of New Windsor on 27 March. In the convention his words and activities were those of a high spirited cavalier 'younker'. He favoured the re-establishment of the Church of England, drove on the Indemnity Bill, and backed the reinstatement of the ejected royalist dons at Oxford. In the spring of 1661 he did not stand for election to the Cavalier Parliament, probably because of an increasingly stormy marriage and growing dissatisfaction with the protestant religion.

At the Restoration Palmer's wife became Charles II's mistress. On 25 February 1661 she bore a daughter, Anne, whose paternity was disputed between her husband and the king. On 11 December Charles created Palmer Baron Limerick and earl of Castlemaine in the Irish peerage merely to give his wife a title and rank to her children. The patent added insult to injury by confining the remainder to the heirs of her, not his, body. The recipient showed his contempt by never taking his seat in the Irish parliament. The arrival of the king's Portuguese bride, Catherine of

Roger Palmer, earl of Castlemaine (1634–1705), attrib. Sebastiano Bombelli, 1664 [left, with his secretary]

Braganza, in May 1662, did not terminate the liaison. Barbara's first son, named Charles after his true father, was born in June. Castlemaine, who in the interval had declared himself a Catholic (the faith of his mother), had the child baptized by a priest, only to be defied by the countess, who had him re-baptized by the protestant minister at St Margaret's, Westminster, on 18 June; the king, the earl of Oxford, and Lady Suffolk standing as godparents. After a violent quarrel the countess deserted her husband.

Humiliated beyond endurance Castlemaine left the country, unable to bear the reproach of being thought a complaisant husband. He travelled in France and Italy, mastering their languages and deepening his faith. In 1664 he took service with the Venetian republic, joined its fleet, and sailed to the Levant under Admiral Andrea Cornaro. Returning to England towards the end of 1664 he was embarrassed to find his family increased by a boy and a girl, of whom he knew nothing. The marriage—but not the affair with Charles—foundered on the countess's interminable infidelities. The couple were formally separated. Castlemaine did not attempt to remarry. In 1665 he returned to sea, serving under the command of James, duke of York, against the Dutch.

The year 1666 marked Castlemaine's début as an author. Responding to the upsurge of anti-Catholic feeling which sought to blame his co-religionists for the great fire of London he published *The Catholique Apology*, an eloquent vindication of Catholic loyalty to the Stuarts. Its persuasive force was such that it involved him in recurrent bouts of controversy with protestant writers, including William Lloyd and Edward Stillingfleet, who laboured to fix the threadbare charge of treachery on all papists. His loyalty to the state was demonstrated by his seeking action at sea in the Second Anglo-Dutch War of 1665–7. In 1666 he also published, in the form of a letter written to the king from Venice, *An Account of the Present War between the Venetians and Turks*, with a supplement on conditions in the island of Candia (Crete). Dutch and German translations were printed in Amsterdam and Frankfurt-am-Main in 1668. Much later, in 1671, his patriotic memoir of the Anglo-Dutch War, originally written in French and translated by Thomas Price, was published as *A Short and True Account of … the Late War between the English and Dutch*. It went into a second edition in 1672.

In 1668 Castlemaine resumed his travels. He accompanied the king's ambassador, Sir Daniel Harvey, on his mission to the Sublime Porte. From Constantinople he journeyed into Syria, and then to Jerusalem. Following the northern coast of Africa he returned to Europe by way of Tangier. He spent time in the Netherlands, France, Spain, and Italy, including Rome, obviously preferring to live in Catholic countries.

The Popish Plot By the autumn of 1677 Castlemaine was back in England, where he was soon caught up in the hysteria of the so-called Popish Plot, becoming one of its earliest victims. Having made no secret of his profession of the Catholic faith, and having newly returned from a long period living abroad he was ideally qualified to attract the hostility of the ultra-protestant faction.

On 25 October 1678 Titus Oates, the fabricator in chief of the alleged Catholic conspiracy, denounced Castlemaine as a Jesuit. Improving on the facts supplied by common fame, he swore that he had seen in the hands of Richard Strange, provincial of the English Jesuits, a decree granting him a divorce. For good measure Oates added that he had heard Castlemaine state his approval of the plot to murder the king. It was, of course, a pack of lies, but in the atmosphere of panic engendered by the Plot, it sufficed to ensnare Castlemaine. After examination before justices of the peace he was placed under arrest and committed to the Tower on 31 October. He was admitted to bail on 23 January 1679.

While awaiting trial Castlemaine published a narrative of the sufferings of Oates's earlier victims, entitled *The compendium, or, A short view of the late tryals in relation to the present plot against his majesty and government*. The work, besides manifesting courage, showed that he was not to be overawed by one whom he knew to be a liar. His fearlessness prompted him to defray the expense of lodging the students who had been brought over from St Omer to aid the defence of the five Jesuits tried at the Old Bailey in June 1679. When they reappeared to testify at Langhorn's trial and were mobbed he protested at the treatment of the witnesses.

Oates struck back by fabricating fresh evidence on the basis of which Castlemaine was examined by the king and council and sent back to the Tower on 2 November. There he remained a close prisoner until his trial in the court of king's bench before Lord Chief Justice Scroggs on 23 June 1680. The crown prosecution fielded a formidable team: solicitor-general Heneage Finch; York's solicitor, George Jeffreys; and Francis Wythens. Unperturbed Castlemaine elected to defend himself, no easy undertaking in an age in which court and counsel were permitted wide powers of intimidation. With persistence and skill he discredited the evidence of his accusers, Oates and Thomas Dangerfield, to the extent that Scroggs in his summing up disparaged the testimony of the convicted felon, Dangerfield. As the proof of treason required two witnesses, the charge fell. Castlemaine was acquitted by the jury after the briefest of recesses.

The verdict, together with Sir George Wakeman's acquittal, prepared the ground not only for Oates's downfall, but also for throwing the whole edifice of the plot into doubt. Flushed with his triumph Castlemaine ventured on further moves to destroy the sham conspiracy altogether, with a view to freeing the 'Popish Lords' from the Tower, including his cousin William Herbert, earl of Powis. The design did not succeed. In 1681 he published *The Earl of Castlemaine's Manifesto*, a defiant résumé of his trial and a vindication of the Catholics.

Royal service The accession of James II in 1685 transformed Castlemaine's fortunes. No longer an outcast, he was welcomed into royal favour. Accounted by the Jesuits 'a noble and cordial friend of all the Society, even in the height of our greatest troubles' (Foley, 5.23), and a sufferer for the faith, he was bound to be taken up by the king. His linguistic prowess and knowledge of the continent suggested a diplomatic posting.

James wished to proclaim to the world the return of England's king to the fold of the Catholic church by re-establishing relations with the papacy. By November 1685 he had appointed Castlemaine his ambassador-extraordinary, with Sir John Lidcott as his secretary. He gave him a grant of £3000 for his equipage, £100 a week for his ordinary expenses, and generous allowances. James intended his embassy to impress Rome with the might of the British monarchy. Castlemaine undertook the mission despite Jeffreys's warning that he would, in law, be committing high treason. He left the royal presence on 4 January 1686, embarked at Greenwich on 15 February, and proceeded to Rome via Paris. He reached Rome on Easter eve, 13 April (NS). Though received privately by Pope Innocent XI he postponed his public entry for another nine months, which he spent making elaborate preparations.

In furnishing himself with the trappings of grandeur Castlemaine drew on the services of the Roman artist, Ciro Ferri, and his own majordomo, the Scottish portraitist John Michael Wright. The magnificence of his state entry on 8 January 1687 astounded the curia and corps diplomatique. Castlemaine showed an acute appreciation of the propaganda value of the occasion by publishing an illustrated account of it, first in Italian in 1687 and in 1688 in English. The frontispiece showed him bowing low to kiss the foot of the enthroned pope.

Castlemaine's negotiations achieved only a partial success. They did induce Innocent XI to raise Queen Mary Beatrice's uncle, Prince Rinaldo d'Este, to the sacred purple, but they failed to persuade the pope to do the same for the king's Jesuit favourite, Edward Petre. Anxious to fulfil his instructions Castlemaine made the serious mistake of pressing his suit too hard, to the open annoyance of the pope. He was no more successful in advocating reconciliation between the Holy See and the absolutist Louis XIV. To the pope, an inveterate enemy of Gallicanism, his conduct smacked of the defiance he had encountered in the French. At Innocent's insistence Castlemaine was recalled. He returned to the royal presence on 12 August 1687.

Back in England Castlemaine retained James's favour. The expenses of his embassy were reimbursed in full. On 25 September he was sworn a privy councillor, and served on the committee that regulated municipal corporations with an eye to calling a general election. On 4 May 1688 he signed the order for reading the second declaration of indulgence in favour of religious toleration, and on 8 June the order committing the disobedient protestant bishops to the Tower. Two days later he was present at the announcement of the birth of James Francis Edward, prince of Wales. He attended the extraordinary council called on 22 October for clarifying the circumstances of the prince's birth, and on 17 November received notice of the king's going to his army at Salisbury to oppose William of Orange's invasion. His last recorded attendance in council was on 27 November, when warrants were issued for a parliament to assemble at Westminster on 15 January 1689. It never met, for the king, having been ejected from Whitehall on William's order, had fled to France.

Revolution and retribution Castlemaine quitted Whitehall for his country seat in Montgomeryshire, carrying with him, under a privy seal, plate from the royal household for James's future use (damages of £2500 were recovered from him in May 1691 on the invalidation of the 'abdicated' monarch's privy seal). He was arrested at Oswestry in Shropshire, returned to London, and committed to the Tower in February 1689 on suspicion of treason. Brought before the Commons on 28 October he was examined regarding his embassy. His plea that he had obeyed James's express command was rejected, and he was recommitted to the Tower on the capital charge of 'endeavouring to reconcile this Kingdom to the See of Rome' (*JHC*, 10.276) and other matters. On 10 February 1690 he was released on recognizances amounting to £30,000, of which he provided £10,000. He was excepted from the Act of Indemnity.

In August he was recommitted to the Tower, suspected of Jacobite plotting, but was bailed on 28 November. In 1695 he again fell under suspicion, having spent some years abroad in France and Flanders. He was summoned to attend the Irish parliament on 12 September, and, on failing to comply, was indicted for high treason. To avoid outlawry he returned to England, surrendered himself on 28 February 1696, and was sent back to the Tower. He was released, without trial, on 18 July on condition of going overseas.

Castlemaine died at Oswestry on 21 July 1705, and was buried in the Herbert vault at Welshpool, Montgomeryshire. His will, dated 30 November 1696, bequeathed the substance of his property to his nephew, Charles Palmer. A devout Catholic, he remained staunchly loyal to James II and his son. Though much maligned in his day, and persistently underrated by historians, the scholar Elias Ashmole thought him both learned and honourable. His writings reveal an alert mind, unafraid to express itself in the defence of an unpopular cause. R. A. P. J. BEDDARD

Sources Marquise Campana de Cavelli, ed., *Les derniers Stuarts à Saint-Germain en Laye*, 2 vols. (Paris, 1871) • [J. M. Wright], *Ragguaglio della solenne comparsa dell' illustrissimo conte di Castelmaine* (Rome, 1687) • *LondG* (7–10 Feb 1687) • GEC, *Peerage*, new edn, vol. 3 • Evelyn, *Diary* • *Elias Ashmole (1617–1692): his autobiographical and historical notes*, ed. C. H. Josten, 5 vols. (1966 [i.e. 1967]) • S. Halkett and J. Laing, *Dictionary of anonymous and pseudonymous English literature*, ed. J. Kennedy and others, new edn, 9 vols. (1926–62) • G. M. Bell, *A handlist of British diplomatic representatives, 1509–1688*, Royal Historical Society Guides and Handbooks, 16 (1990) • J. Y. Akerman, ed., *Moneys received and paid for secret services of Charles II and James II from 30th March 1679 to 25th December 1688*, CS, 52 (1851) • Pepys, *Diary* • H. Foley, ed., *Records of the English province of the Society of Jesus*, 7 vols. in 8 (1875–83) • *JHC*, 10 (1688–93) • Venn, *Alum. Cant.*

Archives BL, Add. MSS 9341, 15396 • Bodl. Oxf., Ashmole MS 1131 • Bodl. Oxf., MSS Clarendon, 69, 71 • Bodl. Oxf., MSS Rawl. • NRA, priv. coll., letters to Sir Philip Baxter • PRO, SP 29, SP 31, SP 44

Likenesses attrib. S. Bombelli, oils, 1664, Powis Castle, Powys [*see illus.*] • W. Faithorne, line engraving, 1666, BM, NPG • A. van Westerhaut, line engraving, *c*.1687 (after G. B. Lenardi), NPG • G. Kneller, portrait • J. M. Wright, portrait, repro. in Wright, *Ragguaglio*, frontispiece • engraving (after G. Kneller), repro. in H. Walpole, *A catalogue of the royal and noble authors of England, Scotland, and Ireland*, ed. T. Park, 5 (1806), 212 • portrait, priv. coll.

Wealth at death land and other properties: will, 30 Nov 1696

Palmer, Roundell, first earl of Selborne (1812–1895), lord chancellor, second son of William Jocelyn Palmer (1778–1853), rector of Mixbury and of Finmere, Oxfordshire, and his wife, Dorothea Richardson (*d.* 1867), youngest daughter of the Revd William Roundell of Gledstone, Yorkshire, was born at Mixbury rectory on 27 November 1812. Both parents belonged to landed families. The Palmers were also East India merchants in the City; George Palmer (1772–1853), philanthropist and tory MP, was Roundell's uncle; and William Palmer (1802–1858), the legal writer, was his cousin.

Parsonage, school, and Tractarian Oxford, 1812–1835 The elder Palmer, who enjoyed a private income, was an exemplary country clergyman, ruling his two parishes in paternal fashion. His ten children grew up in an atmosphere of unaffected piety and deep respect for classical and theological learning. Three sons became clergymen, including William *Palmer (1811–1879), the advocate of intercommunion with the Eastern Orthodox, and an eventual convert to Roman Catholicism. Well taught by his father, Roundell proceeded to Rugby School (1823–5), where he was bullied, and Winchester College (1825–30), where he made lasting friendships with W. G. Ward, Robert Lowe, and, especially, Edward Cardwell.

Roundell Palmer, first earl of Selborne (1812–1895), by Bassano, 1883

The academic promise of Palmer's school career was spectacularly fulfilled at Oxford, where he matriculated from Christ Church (3 May 1830) before winning an open scholarship at Trinity. He went on to gain the chancellor's prize for Latin verse (1831), the Ireland scholarship (Greek), and the Newdigate prize for poetry (1832), a first class in the classical schools (BA 1834, MA 1836) and the Eldon law scholarship. Elected to a fellowship at Magdalen (1834–48), he added the chancellor's Latin essay prize (1835) to his trophies. President of the union in the politically exciting year of 1832, he led a not entirely serious secession—the Rambler Club—from the society. His undergraduate politics resembled those of his near contemporary W. E. Gladstone: a deeply religious toryism intensified by the transition from an older high-churchmanship to the new Tractarianism.

Some of his Oxford friends were bound to Palmer by shared tastes in religion. None was closer to him than F. W. Faber; together they explored the poet whose influence Palmer acknowledged as second only to that of scripture: 'From Wordsworth I learnt, in Frederic Faber's company, large human sympathies' (Palmer, 1/1.136). Neither Wordsworth nor scripture saved him from years of struggle with what was evidently his strong sexuality, mastered with difficulty. When he eventually overcame 'Terror and Despair' (ibid., 233, 393), it was from the Psalms and the poet's 'Ode to Duty' that he drew strength, likening himself to Christian in Bunyan's *Pilgrim's Progress*. In common with so many of the Tractarians, he was turned away from Rome by Newman's secession, unable to follow him in rejecting the established church: 'neither antiquity, nor beauty, nor symbolism could reconcile me to what was not lawful' (Palmer, 2/1.340). The increasing preoccupation of the Oxford Movement's Anglican heirs with ceremonial did not attract him, and his judgment in the Folkestone ritual case many years afterwards (1877) reflected his personal convictions as well as a careful interpretation of the law. Evangelical contacts, subsequently strengthened by his marriage (1848), led him into Sunday school teaching until late in life. He disciplined intellect and emotions by the prayer life described in his autobiography. Not everyone cared for his consciously Christian bearing, even in moments of relaxation; a fellow judge, Lord Bowen, once called him 'a pious cricket on the hearth' (Atlay, 2.420).

The bar and politics: Peelite and Gladstonian, 1835–1872 Palmer chose to follow the law, aided by an uncle's generosity, and was called at Lincoln's Inn (9 June 1837), where he became a bencher (1849) and treasurer (1864). The quasi-academic character of pleading at the equity bar suited him best. He felt out of his element before a jury, and, until made a law officer, tried to avoid appearing in cases that involved one. His powers of work and qualities of mind, which suggested that his generation had lost a formidable theologian in him, ensured a rapid rise. The gift of impressing and pleasing judges and the authority which his opinions acquired brought him an extremely lucrative practice. Some of his wealth was invested in the purchase (1865) of 1800 acres at Blackmoor, close to Selborne and near Petersfield in Hampshire. The great satisfaction he derived from playing the squire, in all seriousness, was reflected in his later emergence as an eloquent defender of the landed interest.

Palmer married into the aristocracy. His wife, Laura (*d.* 1885), was the second daughter of the eighth Earl Waldegrave, and sister of her husband's close friend, Samuel Waldegrave, afterwards bishop of Carlisle. Hers was an evangelical family, but before their marriage on 2 February 1848 her future husband satisfied himself that the difference was 'not … an insuperable objection … she had been brought up by good parents … *within the Church*' (Palmer, 1/1.468). For her sake he made All Souls, Langham Place—a centre of evangelicalism—the family's parish church, and changed his working habits to keep the evenings for her, rising very early indeed to compensate. They both subscribed to the high Victorian ideal of marriage, shot through with a profound humility which in others might have been pharisaical: 'Think of me, darling', he told her, 'as a part of yourself—only more lazy and unwilling … and therefore surely deserving no praise' (24 June 1849, Selborne MS 1880). She was fulfilled by her dedication to a husband whom she relieved of 'all private business and cares' (Palmer, 1/1.163). They had a son and four daughters, one of whom became a notable suffragist [*see* Ridding, Lady Laura Elizabeth].

Like ambitious and successful lawyers in every age, Palmer pursued the political career that was the surest road to high judicial office. Experience as a leader writer on *The Times* (1840–43) gave him a taste for the arena which he entered on his return as MP for Plymouth in 1847. A Peelite, he lost the seat at the next general election in 1852, but recaptured it at a by-election a year later. He stood by the dwindling band of Peelites, and espoused its losing causes. Defeat in 1852 was his reward for defying popular anti-Catholicism and voting against the Ecclesiastical Titles Bill. In 1857 he fell victim to the electoral backlash against those identified with an unpatriotic opposition to the Crimean War and the Second Opium War. He was above all a Gladstonian, before the man he so much admired had a real following. In a house that contained several lawyer–politicians of great ability, Palmer had shown his quality and clear liberal tendencies, as on the admission of Jews to parliament.

Nevertheless, beaten again at Plymouth in 1859, Palmer made no move to re-enter the Commons until his eminence at the bar and the Gladstone connection brought him (28 June 1861) the solicitor-generalship in Palmerston's second government, and with it a safe seat at Richmond in Yorkshire. Knighted on 5 August 1861 and promoted attorney-general on 2 October 1863, he, with his fellow law officers, had to handle the delicate questions of international law that strained relations between London and Washington during the American Civil War. It was fortunate for his country that Palmer's advice had an in-built bias in favour of the north on political and constitutional grounds (Palmer, 2/2.384–5). He distinguished between the invasion of Britain's neutral rights in the *Trent* and other cases, and the claim, advanced by the Confederacy's British friends, that neutrals might legitimately use force to break the North's blockade of southern ports: 'An armed neutrality … is a species of war, and not the most honourable, because it is not avowed', he successfully maintained (*Hansard* 3, 165, 7 March 1862, 1223).

In opposition from July 1866, Palmer was one of the first, if not the first, of conservatives, to argue for household suffrage as the natural outcome of the demand for a wider franchise which both parties endeavoured to meet in 1866–7. The Irish church question, however, evoked his profound dislike of really radical change. He could not go with Gladstone and most Liberals of all shades in adopting a policy of substantial disendowment as well as disestablishment, but refrained from speaking or voting on Gladstone's Irish church resolutions of April 1868, carried against tory ministers. Nor did he take part in the protests organized outside parliament by opponents of the policy. At the general election in the autumn, he stood for Oxford University and Richmond, but retired from the university contest after declaring that, if elected, he must be free to decide for himself on legislation affecting the church, an attitude too high-minded for worried clerical electors. Having done everything in his power to avoid hurting the Liberals by his objections to their Irish church policy, on which the general election largely turned, he declined Gladstone's successive offers of the great seal and a lord justiceship with a peerage in order to fight the church bill from his seat in the Commons and the Liberal side. This act of self-abnegation made a deep impression, and added considerably to his political stature. He voted against the bill's second reading (22 March 1869), but acted as an intermediary between government and the leadership of the Irish establishment.

When Gladstone followed his attack on corporate property with the act of 1870 invading the rights of Irish landlords, he accused Palmer of being 'nearly the death of the … Bill' (Steele, 305). It was the latter's contention that statutory intervention on behalf of tenants—the leaders of their class—who were capable of driving a commercial bargain with the landowner amounted to 'confiscation and communism' (ibid.). Gladstone overcame his formidable opposition at the committee stage by mingling threats of a stronger measure next session, if the bill were unacceptably limited to the small occupiers, with an appeal to Palmer's sense of responsibility: the conciliation of Ireland was an imperial question. The government eased his submission by narrowing the eligibility of larger tenants for compensation for disturbance in their holdings.

'Tired and dispirited' (Palmer, 2/1.131) by these setbacks, Palmer nevertheless persisted in his usually constructive opposition to a reforming administration with which he sympathized. On the University Tests Bill, finally enacted in 1871, and the Elementary Education Bill of 1870, he was prominent in the intelligent defence of the church's interests. When ministers were strongly criticized for their use of prerogative in abolishing purchase in the army, they sought the help of his legal authority: the secretary for war, his old friend Cardwell, read out Palmer's private letter in the Commons. He was frequently consulted in the course of the Anglo-American negotiations leading up to the treaty of Washington (1871), and the subsequent reference of the *Alabama* claims, a dangerous legacy of the civil war, to international arbitration. He then argued the unsuccessful British case before the tribunal sitting at Geneva in the knowledge that its proceedings did not conceal their essentially political nature.

Lord chancellor, 1872–1874, 1880–1885 These assorted services to the Gladstone government were eventually rewarded. Palmer was contemplating retirement to Blackmoor within a few years when, as he put it, 'providence … brought again within my reach the … prize of my profession' (Palmer, 2/1.13). He succeeded Lord Hatherley on the woolsack (15 October 1872) when he was sworn of the privy council, and was created Baron Selborne (18 October). As chancellor, Selborne set himself to revive an office which had lost some of its political significance in the last generation. For all their differences over the Irish church and land questions, he was devoted to his leader: 'to co-operate at length officially with Gladstone', he wrote of his entry into the cabinet, 'was … a pleasure in itself so great as to overpower for the time almost all other considerations' (Palmer, 2/1.282–3). It was in a Gladstonian spirit—no legal reformer was less of a Benthamite—that he carried through the overdue reform of the administration of justice embodied in the 1873 Judicature Act, 'the work of my own hand' (ibid., 298). The creation of a unified supreme court reduced the old courts of common law, of chancery, and of admiralty, probate, and divorce to divisions of the new structure. Appeals were to be concentrated in one court of final appeal, ending the appellate jurisdiction of the House of Lords. He thought he had contrived to reconcile 'policy and sentiment' (ibid., 300); but the phased abolition of appeals to the Lords was so unpopular with lawyers and peers that the next government restored and strengthened this function of the upper house in 1876.

With a major reform as his 'monument' (Palmer, 2/1.300) Selborne spent six years out of office. He tried, and failed, to amend the contentious Public Worship Regulation Bill of 1874 by substituting the bishops for a lay judge in ritual cases. Liberal leanings, both whig and radical, to disestablishment increasingly troubled him; his loyalty to the party, he told a close friend in 1874 (ibid., 336), was conditional upon its continued acceptance of a state church. As chairman of the statutory commission for his old university, appointed under the Oxford and Cambridge Act of 1877, he reluctantly agreed to changes which diminished the clerical presence in the colleges. But he was uneasy at the pronounced clericalism of militant high-churchmen and their tendency to entertain the thought of disestablishment. His fidelity to the church, like his attachment to the landed interest, made him a slightly dated figure to many Liberals when he returned to the woolsack in the second Gladstone cabinet (28 April 1880).

His devotion to the premier did not blind Selborne to the unpredictable element of radicalism in his make-up. He was, for instance, disturbed by Gladstone's flirtation with English land reform in the early 1880s, believing that if he embraced it in earnest, his emotional nature would be seized by 'the idea of breaking down aristocratic and territorial interests' (Palmer, 2/1.471). Selborne was uncomfortable with the new government's ground game and employers' liability bills: 'very unacceptable … to landowners … and … large capitalists' (ibid., 489), he feared. He disliked but took charge of the Burials Bill (1880), giving dissenters the right of sepulture in parish churchyards with their own service; and he squared ministerial consciences, including his own, in the Bradlaugh affair. Admitting a member to the Commons who rejected the customary oath was, he advised his numerous religious correspondents, a predestined trial: 'It is … part of our probation here, to determine … how … to deal with unbelievers … Scripture [has] … no rule on which to found any exclusive or theocratic constitution of civil society' (ibid., 491–2).

This capacity to adjust principle to political realities smoothed the passage of the Irish land legislation that tested the party in 1880–2. Selborne did not resign with the great landlords who left the government. The new measures flowed from the 1870 Land Act, 'really a much greater … change of law, to accommodate it to the habits, customs and, therefore, moral rights of the people' (*Hansard* 3, 264, 2 Aug 1881, 516). It was the Gladstonian line of argument, stressing the antagonism between English and Irish notions of tenure. In private, he added that ministers had yielded 'to what we thought an overwhelming necessity' (Palmer, 2/2.60). Gladstone and Gladstonian conservatives like himself shared with Fenians and ribbonmen the responsibility for a social revolution. The coercion bills that accompanied the land legislation had his fullest support; he was devoid of his leader's latent sympathy with Irish nationalism, as distinct from the agrarian grievance. Promotion to an earldom (29 December 1882) on the opening of the Royal Courts of Justice in the Strand recognized his political assistance as much as his legal eminence.

A critic of Disraelian imperialism in the 1870s, Selborne tended in this cabinet to side with those who favoured the continuing expansion of empire. He did not relish the withdrawal from the Transvaal and made much of British suzerainty over the restored republic. The occupation of Egypt in 1882 he saw as unavoidable to safeguard British interests, although he granted that '"Egypt for the Egyptians" … had a good sound' (Palmer, 2/2.65). The readiness of Gladstone and his foreign secretary, Lord Granville, to indulge Germany's colonial ambitions aroused his concern: 'I would rather have risked a quarrel with Bismarck' (ibid., 132). Strongly for intervention in the Sudan, and for standing up to Russia in the Panjdeh crises, he viewed both episodes in a characteristic light: 'It is duty … not vainglory or selfishness which requires a great nation to maintain its power' (ibid., 147). His divergence from Gladstone was also evident in domestic politics, where he inclined to the position of Lord Hartington on a further instalment of parliamentary reform. The main beneficiaries, it was widely assumed, would be radicals bent on subverting the church, the landed interest, and the empire. These, in retrospect, exaggerated fears took hold of Gladstone's once devoted follower. It was as a frightened conservative that he used his influence behind the scenes to avert a dissolution on the Lords' obstruction of the third reform bill; his last service to a statesman who had been too radical for him.

Liberal Unionism and the church militant, 1885–1895 After the fall of the ministry in June 1885, Selborne openly expressed his alarm at the radical trends in Liberalism. He found proof of their advance in Gladstone's Midlothian address of September 1885 with its 'vague, misty, facing-both-ways' (Palmer, 2/2.180) references to Lords reform, to the future of the established church and her schools, and its hints at home rule for Ireland. Selborne was the most important signatory of a remonstrance by Liberal churchmen against the radical attempt to make disestablishment party policy. Gladstone protested that while divisions over the church probably would be fatal to Liberal unity sooner rather than later, his colleague was wrong to bring the day forward (Gladstone, *Diaries*, 11. 430–31). In the event, it was not disestablishment that split the Liberals and led Selborne to refuse a third term as chancellor in July 1886. He considered the Home Rule Bill a surrender to 'the Revolutionary party, here and in Ireland' (Palmer, 2/2.213). His last ten years of active life were spent in defending the union and the church against Gladstone's real or imagined intentions: 'If he lived long enough there is nothing … he would not destroy' (ibid., 226). Though Hartington was his leader as a Liberal Unionist, he transferred his true allegiance to Lord Salisbury, who, he rightly forecast, would pursue policies congenial to his Liberal allies, even to Joseph Chamberlain. With other conservatives, Selborne accepted from Salisbury what he would have deplored had it come from Gladstone. He never forgave his old hero, now identified with '*moral* as well as political evil' (ibid., 261), so strong was the sense of personal betrayal.

It would be facile to depict Selborne as reverting to the pious toryism of his youth. In politics as in the law he remained a believer in evolutionary change, which he thought incompatible with home rule and disestablishment. Lawyers remembered his astonishing industry—he admitted to sixty hours at a stretch—and the surgical skill with which he dissected a case: 'I have seen him', wrote Lord Hobhouse, 'all trembling and quivering with overstrain, and yet apparently as quick and alert … as ever' (Palmer, 2/2.438). His style of advocacy was quiet, and relatively free from technicalities; his language in court, another eminent judge recorded, was that of any 'cultivated gentleman' (ibid., 439). While he seldom had time to suffer fools gladly, he observed the legal courtesies punctiliously, and treated young barristers with discriminating kindness. As a judge, the subtlety in exposition and command of case law that distinguished him at the bar tended to produce unnecessarily involved judgments. The political partisanship of his later years did not materially lessen the respect in which his profession held him. He had strengthened the chancellorship by giving it the support of a department organized like others; the ancient clerkship of the crown in chancery was united with the new post of permanent secretary to the chancellor (1884). The same modernizing Conservatism was apparent in the Judicature Bill of 1883 which renewed the circuit system and in a reform of chancery cut short by the Liberal government's untimely end in 1885.

Death, honours, and religious publications Selborne died at Blackmoor, his Hampshire seat, on 4 May 1895 and was buried on 8 May in St Matthew's, Blackmoor, a church of his foundation. FRS (1860), DCL (Oxford), and an honorary fellow of Magdalen (1862), and honorary student of Christ Church (1867), high steward of Oxford University (1892), he was also lord rector of St Andrews (1877), an honorary LLD, Cambridge, and master of the Mercers' Company (1876). His literary activity was mainly an extension of the zealous churchmanship that made him, in retirement, the first chairman of the new house of laymen that met with convocation in the province of Canterbury (1866), and sent him all over the country '*stumping* … an odious necessity' (Palmer, 2/2.276) in the unending fight with radicals and liberationists. He published extensively on the hymnody, liturgy, and historic rights of his church. The hymnal he edited in 1862, *The Book of Praise*, went through several editions, as did his substantial pamphlet of 1886 against disestablishment. His posthumous *Letters to his Son on Religion* (1898), reissued as *The Catholic and Apostolic Church* (1899), were a final affirmation of his church's claims to catholicity. The four volumes of his autobiographical *Memorials*, edited by his daughter Sophia, comtesse de Franqueville, elicited from Gladstone the comment that 'The padding … is something fearful' (J. B. Atlay, *Henry Acland, Bart: a Memoir*, 1903, 495). They are nevertheless an important, and at times moving, source for the Tractarians and for the law and politics of half a century. The author's strengths and weaknesses emerge in an almost artless fashion. Selborne was succeeded by his son, William Waldegrave *Palmer, who as Lord Wolmer was the first Liberal Unionist whip in the Commons and later a cabinet minister. DAVID STEELE

Sources R. Palmer, first earl of Selborne, *Memorials. Part I: family and personal, 1766–1865*, ed. S. M. Palmer, 2 vols. (1896) • R. Palmer, first earl of Selborne, *Memorials. Part II: personal and political, 1865–1895*, ed. S. M. Palmer, 2 vols. (1898) • J. B. Atlay, *The Victorian chancellors*, 2 vols. (1906–8) • LPL, Selborne MSS • BL, Gladstone MSS • D. Southgate, *The passing of the whigs, 1832–1886* (1962) • Gladstone, *Diaries* • J. P. Parry, *Democracy and religion* (1986) • E. D. Steele, *Irish land and British politics: tenant-right and nationality, 1865–1870* (1974) • T. A. Jenkins, *Gladstone, whiggery and the liberal party, 1874–1886* (1988) • A. B. Cooke and J. Vincent, *The governing passion: cabinet government and party politics in Britain, 1885–86* (1974) • Burke, *Peerage*

Archives Bodl. Oxf., family corresp.; corresp. • LPL, corresp. and papers | BL, corresp. with W. E. Gladstone, Add. MSS 44296–44298 • BL, letters to Sir A. H. Layard, Add. MSS 38989–39116 • BL, corresp. with Lord Stanmore, Add. MSS 49217–49220 • Bodl. Oxf., corresp. with Sir William Harcourt • Bodl. Oxf., letters to Lord Kimberley • Bodl. Oxf., corresp. with Wilberforce family • Chatsworth House, Derbyshire, letters to Lord Hartington • Hants. RO, letters to William Wickham • LPL, corresp. with E. W. Benson • LPL, letters to A. C. Tait • LPL, letters to Charles Wordsworth • NL Scot., corresp., mainly with Lord Rosebery • NRA, priv. coll., letters to Lady Chewton and memoir of Lord Chewton • PRO, letters to Lord Cairns, 30/51 • PRO, corresp. with Lord Cardwell, 30/48 • PRO, corresp. with Lord Granville, 30/29 • PRO, corresp. with Lord John Russell, 30/22 • PRO NIre., corresp. with Herbert Asquith • U. Birm. L., corresp. with Joseph Chamberlain

Likenesses N. Sanders, mezzotint, pubd 1864 (after F. Grant), NPG • H. T. Wells, oils, exh. RA 1874, Mercers' Hall, London • Bassano, carte-de-visite, 1883, NPG [*see illus.*] • H. W. Petherick, pencil drawing, 1884, NPG • E. M. Busk, oils, exh. RA 1889, Trinity College, Oxford • H. A. Olivier, double portrait, oils, exh. RA 1892 (with Bishop Gore-Browne), Athenaeum, London • G. F. Watts, oils, 1893, Lincoln's Inn, London • Elliott & Fry, photogravure photograph, NPG • W. Holl, stipple (after G. Richmond), BM • Lock & Whitfield, woodburytype photograph, NPG; repro. in T. Cooper, *Men of mark: a gallery of contemporary portraits* (1876) • W. W. Ouless, oils, Magd. Oxf. • J. Phillip, group portrait, oils (*The House of Commons, 1860*), Palace of Westminster, London • J. M. Stewart, portrait (after E. M. Busk), NPG • T [T. Chartran], chromolithograph caricature, NPG; repro. in *VF* (5 July 1882) • cartes-de-visite, NPG • chromolithograph caricature, NPG; repro. in *VF* (16 March 1872)

Wealth at death £69,030 16s. 0d.: probate, 18 June 1895, *CGPLA Eng. & Wales*

Palmer, Roundell Cecil, third earl of Selborne (1887–1971), politician, was born on 15 April 1887 at his mother's parents' house, 20 Arlington Street, Mayfair, London. He was the eldest of three sons (one of whom was killed in action in the First World War) and second of four children of William Waldegrave *Palmer (1859–1942), the future second earl of Selborne, politician, and his wife, Lady (Beatrix) Maud Gascoyne-Cecil (1858–1950) [*see* Palmer, (Beatrix) Maud], elder daughter of Robert Arthur Talbot Gascoyne-Cecil, third marquess of Salisbury, then prime minister. After the first earl's death in 1895 he was styled Viscount Wolmer. He was educated at Winchester College, of which his father became a fellow, and at University College, Oxford, where he founded and ran a vigorous New Tory Club and took a third class in modern history (1909). His friends called him Top. He married on 9 June 1910 Grace (*d.* 1959), youngest daughter of Matthew White *Ridley, first Viscount Ridley; they had four sons (one of whom died in infancy) and three daughters.

Palmer's Liberal-Conservative ancestry settled his career. He contested the Newtown division of south-west Lancashire in January 1910, and narrowly carried it, in the Conservative interest, in the following December. He sat in the Commons for all but thirty years, representing the safer seat of Aldershot from December 1918 until in October 1940 he was called up to the House of Lords in his father's subsidiary title, Baron Selborne. He left Winchester in July 1905 and in 1906 was commissioned into the third (militia) battalion of the Hampshire regiment, of which his father was honorary colonel. He was promoted captain on 19 September 1914, early in the First World War, and served with his training unit in the Isle of Wight and at Gosport for nearly two years. In 1916 his brother-in-law Lord Robert Cecil, who was organizing the blockade, made him his parliamentary private secretary, and when David Lloyd George formed his government that December, Wolmer became assistant director of the war trade department, under Lord Emmott. He was still in constant official touch with Lord Robert Cecil, now minister of blockade.

Wolmer returned to the back benches at the end of the war, and resigned from the army with the rank of major in 1922. That October he again took minor office, and served for fourteen months as parliamentary secretary to the Board of Trade. From 1924 to 1929, as assistant postmaster-general, he developed technical ideas rather ahead of his time. He was sworn of the privy council on 5 July 1929, just after he resigned. That autumn he wrote several articles, in *The Times* and elsewhere, which he developed into his only book, *Post Office Reform* (1932).

Wolmer became known as the embodiment in the house of the Conservative Party's conscience. There was no room for him in the coalition governments of 1931–40, though he sat on the Sea-Fish Commission in 1934–6. He aligned himself with his friend Winston Churchill in the struggle against the India Act of 1935. He was a shrewd and capable administrator, and began to develop some business interests, which led him to the chairmanship of the Cement Makers' Federation (1934–42, 1945–51) and to a directorship of Boots drug company (from 1936, deputy chairman from 1951 to 1963). Under Churchill's wartime coalition he served in 1940–42 as director of cement in the Ministry of Works: anti-invasion pillboxes in concrete, still scattered all over southern England, thus provide mementoes of him.

On 23 February 1942, three days before his father's death, Wolmer succeeded Hugh Dalton as minister of economic warfare. The title was little more than a cover: economic war took up, in his own estimate, about a fifth of his time. The rest went on managing the Special Operations Executive (SOE), the secret service devoted to fostering subversion in enemy-occupied territory, of which he now became the politically responsible head.

Under-informed men thought that Selborne's slight and stooping figure indicated an insignificant character: they were soon undeceived. He early showed himself a minister of principle. Within a week of taking office he had written a commentary on a cabinet paper on the Indian question by Sir Stafford Cripps so sharp that his staff supposed it would cost him his new post. He dealt resolutely with those in the high command of SOE whom he thought unfit for their tasks, sending them briskly into retirement or back to the departments that had seconded them to his. In 1942 he replaced Sir Frank Nelson with Sir Charles Hambro as SOE's executive head; even Hambro, within eighteen months, had to bow before the storm of Selborne's displeasure. With Hambro and his successor Colin Gubbins, Selborne had a daily meeting at noon, whenever both were in London. This enabled him to keep his finger on the pulse of SOE's principal activities; he never wished nor sought to interfere in technical detail. In spite of all the work that Dalton and Nelson had already done, Selborne had to fight incessantly to maintain for SOE the position that he was sure it deserved to hold in the British strategic machine, and was several times able to appeal to his friendship with Churchill to rescue SOE from its worst domestic enemies.

Selborne bore ultimate responsibility for numerous important clandestine coups and, much more, for helping to restore self-respect to the populations of the axis-occupied countries. In recognition of his wartime work he was appointed CH on the conclusion of the war in Europe in 1945. A proposal of his to use SOE's world-wide friendships and signals facilities as a base for a permanent peacetime intelligence network was brusquely rejected by C. R. Attlee.

Selborne then gave his main attention to his significant parallel career in the Church of England. He strove ardently for self-government in it. His pamphlet entitled *The Freedom of the Kirk* (1928) argued that the Church of England would do well to cut itself off, as the Scottish kirk had done by the act of 1921 (11 & 12 Geo. V c. 29), from any doctrinal interference by the state. He was president of the Church Army (1949–61) and chairman of the house of laity of the church assembly from 1955 until increasing deafness compelled him to resign in 1959. He also did much to improve the church's financial position; as chairman of the National Provincial Bank (1951–4) he could speak with authority.

On the family estates—something under 2000 acres round Blackmoor on the Hampshire–Surrey border—Selborne diversified from hops as a main crop into dairy farming and fruit growing; he initiated the use of concrete posts for training soft fruit bushes. Even during the war he tried to visit Blackmoor once a week at least, to advise and supervise, and he greatly increased productivity over the years. Following the death of his first wife he married in 1966 Valerie Irene Josephine Margaret de Thomka (*d.* 1968), formerly wife of Bryan Henry Bevan and daughter of J. A. N. de Thomka de Tomkahaza, secretary of state for Hungary. He died at Blackmoor House, Selborne, Alton, Hampshire, on 3 September 1971 and was succeeded in the earldom by his grandson John Roundell Palmer (*b.* 1940), the eldest son of his eldest son, who had been killed on active service in the Hampshire regiment in 1942. M. R. D. Foot, *rev.*

Sources *The Times* (6 Sept 1971) · *The Times* (9 Sept 1971) · *The Times* (11 Sept 1971) · private information (1986) · Burke, *Peerage* · d. cert.

Archives Bodl. Oxf., corresp. and papers · Hants. RO, personal and family papers · LPL, corresp. | Bodl. Oxf., corresp. with Sir W. L Worthington-Evans · Bodl. RH, corresp. with Sir R. R. Welensky · CAC Cam., corresp. with Sir H. Page Croft · LPL, corresp. with Edwin James Palmer · Nuffield Oxf., letters to Lord Cherwell

Likenesses W. Stoneman, two photographs, *c.*1917–1942, NPG · C. White, oils, *c.*1945, Special Forces Club, London · pencil drawing, Church House, London

Palmer, Samuel (*d.* 1724), dissenting minister and pamphleteer, is of unknown origins. He was educated for the dissenting ministry at Bethnal Green, and afterwards at Highgate, under Dr John Ker, who was noted as a nonconformist teacher of philosophy. On the death of Henry Read about 1698 Palmer succeeded him as minister of the Presbyterian congregation in Gravel Lane, Southwark. According to John Dunton, Palmer continued his studies, both theological and classical, reading for seventeen hours a day.

In the midst of the controversy surrounding the issue of occasional conformity, then being debated in parliament, the quality of education provided by dissenting academies was attacked by Samuel Wesley, who addressed to parliament a publication entitled *A letter from a country divine to his friend in London* (1703). Wesley cited his own deficient education at two dissenting academies—Morton and Veal—as evidence that the academies neglected learning, religious instruction, and moral education. Palmer swiftly responded by publishing anonymously his spirited pamphlet *Defence of the Dissenters' Education in their Private Academies* (1703). Wesley parried with another pamphlet in 1704, and in the following year Palmer issued *A vindication of the learning, loyalty, morals, and most Christian behaviour of the dissenters toward the Church of England*, this time with his name on the title-page. Much praised by Matthew Henry, Palmer's pamphlets offer a valuable description of the subjects and texts he studied at Ker's academy. Ker's course ran over four years and taught in turn logic, metaphysics, ethics, and natural philosophy.

Between October 1706 and October 1709 Palmer took orders in the Church of England. His motives for abandoning dissent in favour of the established church are unclear, although Job Orton suggested that he thought himself neglected by the dissenting hierarchy. On 20 April 1710 he became vicar of All Saints' and St Peter's Church in Maldon, Essex, and he held this living until 1724, the year of his death, which occurred in Maldon. Described as an excellent extempore preacher by Dunton, Palmer published only two of the sermons he preached as a nonconformist and one of those he preached as a Church of England clergyman. A volume entitled *Moral Essays on some of the most Curious and Significant English, Scotch, and Foreign Proverbs* appeared in 1710.

ALEXANDER GORDON, *rev.* S. J. SKEDD

Sources *The life and errors of John Dunton*, [rev. edn], ed. J. B. Nichols, 2 vols. (1818) • *Protestant Dissenter's Magazine*, 6 (1799), 13 • W. Wilson, *The history and antiquities of the dissenting churches and meeting houses in London, Westminster and Southwark*, 4 vols. (1808–14) • P. Morant, *The history and antiquities of the county of Essex*, 1 (1768), 334 • D. Wykes, 'The dissenting academy and rational dissent', *Enlightenment and religion*, ed. K. Haakonssen (1996), 99–139 • G. B. Williams, *Memoirs of the life, character, and writings of the Rev. Matthew Henry* (1828), 184 • E. Calamy, *An historical account of my own life, with some reflections on the times I have lived in, 1671–1731*, ed. J. T. Rutt, 2 vols. (1829), vol. 1, p. 459, vol. 2, p. 505

Palmer, Samuel (*bap.* **1692**, *d.* **1732**), printer and historian of printing, was baptized on 31 August 1692 at St Giles-in-the-Fields, London, the second and only surviving son of John Palmer (*d.* 1697), perfumer, and his wife, Dorothy, *née* Provost (*d.* 1694). On 7 June 1708 he was apprenticed to Benjamin Motte (*c.*1653–1710), printer, of Aldersgate Street, and on 8 August 1715 made free by Benjamin's widow, Anne. Palmer set up as a master printer himself, likewise in Aldersgate Street, prior to 1 April 1717, when he bound the first of his own apprentices.

Within a career spanning only sixteen years, Palmer became one of the most aesthetically ambitious and prestigious English printers of his time, and he gave his name to a *General History of Printing*, which, despite its deficiencies, brought together much valuable information, and helped to stimulate interest in the subject in Britain. Palmer married Elizabeth Clarke on 24 March 1717 in the church of St Mary Magdalen, Old Fish Street, London; they had one child, also called Samuel (*b.* 1723). The line engraver John Pine was Palmer's brother-in-law.

By 1719 Palmer moved his printing business to Swan Alley, off St John Street in Clerkenwell; at Christmas 1723–4 he shifted it again, to occupy part of the converted lady chapel of the church of St Bartholomew-the-Great, West Smithfield, where it remained until his death. In 1729 Palmer took a younger man, John Huggonson, into a loose partnership. At least five of his twelve apprentices became master printers.

However, Palmer's best-known employee was Benjamin Franklin, who took up work as a compositor in what was 'then a famous printing-house' just after Christmas 1724, and stayed there 'near a year' before moving on to the 'still greater printing-house' of John Watts, where a greater volume of work meant he could earn more money. While with Palmer he wrote and printed on his own account *A Dissertation on Liberty and Necessity, Pleasure and Pain* (1725). Franklin recalled that, 'It occasion'd my being more consider'd by Mr Palmer as a young man of some ingenuity, tho' he seriously expostulated with me upon the principles of my pamphlet, which to him appear'd abominable' (*Autobiographical Writings*, 246–8).

Of the books Palmer is known to have printed, relatively few were literary; many were sermons or theological discourses; and many were learned works, in English, French, or Latin, some involving the use of Greek, Hebrew, Syriac, Chaldean, or Arabic. His contributions to several prestigious collaborative printing projects included the second of three volumes of John Selden's *Opera omnia* (1725–6), and part of the second of four volumes of Sir Francis Bacon's *Opera omnia* (1730). Palmer printed the weekly periodicals the *Free Briton*, heavily subsidized by Sir Robert Walpole (from December 1729), and the *Grub-Street Journal* (from January 1730), in which he and Huggonson owned one-twelfth shares.

A distinguished, yet financially calamitous, printing job that Palmer carried out was the production of the Psalms and the New Testament in Arabic, for the Society for Promoting Christian Knowledge. Begun in January 1721, the project dragged on until 1727, plagued by delays due to the SPCK's financial constraints and the project's own inherent difficulties. William Caslon, at an early stage in his career as a type-designer, punch-cutter, and founder, and in the midst of producing more straightforward and profitable fonts, created a new font of Arabic, which took him nearly two and a half years (Ross, 'A progress report', 119–23).

On 15 February 1731, 'a printing press and cases for composition were put up at St James's House for their Majesties to see the noble art of printing'. Under Palmer's 'direction' the duke of York set the type for 'a little book of his own writing, called "The Laws of Dodge Hare". The two youngest princesses likewise composed their names, &c.' (*GM*, 1731).

Palmer's *General History of Printing* (1732) was another of his unlucky projects. He had wanted to publish a book about the 'Practical part' of printing, based upon the works of Fertel and Endters, yet incorporating his own 'observations and improvements'. He was deterred, however, by the unexpected hostility of his fellow stationers to the supposed cheapening of their 'mystery'; accordingly his 'friends and patrons' induced him to undertake the 'Historical' part first (preface). It was launched by subscription in 1729, to be issued in instalments; but Palmer was too busy to undertake the whole task himself, and the first third of the book was compiled by George Psalmanazar ('almost blind' at that time), who admitted that the result was 'a horrid performance'. Palmer completed the second third before he died, but the remainder of the book had to be cobbled together from his 'materials' and drafts by Psalmanazar and Thomas Birch (*Memoirs*, 284–9).

Psalmanazar recalled that, by about 1731:

> [Palmer's] circumstances were by this time so unaccountably low and unfortunate, considering the largeness and success of his business, and that he was himself a sober, industrious man, and free from all extravagance, that he could not extract himself by any other way, but by a statute of bankrupt … Notwithstanding all the care and kind assistance of his good friend Dr Mead, a stubborn distemper, which his misfortunes brought upon him, carried him off

before the third part of [the *General History*] was finished. (*Memoirs*, 288)

Palmer died on 9 May 1732, intestate. His wife, Elizabeth, was awarded the administration of his estate on 8 June 1732, but had accomplished little before she herself died, about March 1734, also intestate. The administration, and the guardianship of their son Samuel, were awarded on 2 August 1734 to Thomas Rutty, a vintner, one of Palmer's creditors. The boy had none the less been admitted in April 1733 to Christ's Hospital, and remained there as an inmate and pupil until 8 February 1739, when he was discharged to begin his apprenticeship to the printer Charles Ackers.

A listing of what purported to be Palmer's manuscript for the 'practical part of Printing' among Joseph Ames's books was evidently misleading, relating simply to an unmodified translation of Martin-Dominique Fertel's *La science pratique de l'imprimerie*, now extant within the Birch papers (Nichols, *Lit. anecdotes*, 5.264; Ross, 'Martin-Dominique Fertel').

As the ostensible author of the *General History of Printing*, Palmer was to be excoriated by John Lewis as 'a good Printer but a bad Historian, ignorant, careless and inaccurate' (Lewis to Ames, 10 Dec 1740, in Nichols, *Illustrations*, 4.173–4), and by Thomas Frognall Dibdin as 'that wretched pilferer and driveller' (Dibdin, 2.379). He can, however, fairly be judged only for that central third of the book for which he was directly responsible.

JOHN C. ROSS

Sources J. C. Ross, 'A progress report upon a study of Samuel Palmer', *An index of civilisation: studies of printing and publishing history in honour of Keith Maslen*, ed. R. Harvey, W. Kirsop, and B. J. McMullin (1993), 113–28 · D. F. McKenzie, ed., *Stationers' Company apprentices*, [3]: *1701–1800* (1978) · parish register, St Giles-in-the-Fields, London [baptism; burial of parents] · *Benjamin Franklin's autobiographical writings*, ed. C. Van Doren (1945) · Nichols, *Lit. anecdotes* · *Memoirs of ****, commonly known by the name of George Psalmanazar* (1764) · Society for Promoting Christian Knowledge, London, archives · archdeaconry court of London bonds administrations, GL, MS 9053 · Stationers' Company archives, Stationers' Hall, London · GL, Christ's Hospital MS 1218/8 · Nichols, *Illustrations* · T. F. Dibdin, *The bibliographical decameron*, 3 vols. (1817) · J. C. Ross, 'Martin-Dominique Fertel', *The Library*, 6th ser., 9 (1987), 384–6 [letter] · *GM*, 1st ser., 1 (1731), 79 · *GM*, 1st ser., 2 (1732), 775 · parish register, St Mary Magdalen, Old Fish Street, London [marriage]

Archives CUL, university medical library, Society for Promoting Christian Knowledge archives · Stationers' Company, Stationers' Hall, London, Stationers' Company archives | BL, Add. MS 4386 · CLRO, City freedom records, CF1, Bundle 333 · GL, archdeaconry court of London bonds administrations, MS 9053 · GL, Christ's Hospital MS 1218/8

Wealth at death almost bankrupt; printing house equipment: *Memoirs of *****; archdeaconry court of London bonds administrations, GL, MS 9053

Palmer, Samuel (1741–1813), Independent minister and memorialist, was born on 26 March 1741 at Bedford and baptized on 5 April at St Paul's in the town, the son of John and Anna Palmer. He was educated at Bedford grammar school and studied for the ministry from 1756 to 1762 at Daventry dissenting academy under Caleb Ashworth. In 1762 he became afternoon preacher to the Independent (originally Presbyterian) congregation at Mare Street, Hackney, assisting William Hunt; he was ordained on 21 November 1763. From 10 June 1763 he occasionally assisted William Langford at the Weigh-House chapel, Little Eastcheap, and he was the regular morning preacher there from 20 June 1765 to 28 December 1766. He succeeded Hunt as morning preacher at Mare Street and remained in charge of the congregation, which moved to St Thomas's Square, Hackney, in 1771, until his death.

In or soon after 1766 Palmer married Elizabeth Walker. Of their large family, Samuel was baptized on 13 November 1768, entered the Daventry academy in 1786, and became a schoolmaster at Chigwell; Thomas was baptized on 2 November 1774; and Elizabeth married Stephen Charles Hope, barrister. From 1780 Palmer kept a boarding-school for several years, and he was quick to establish a Sunday school in connection with his church.

Palmer's reputation rests on two works: *The Protestant Dissenter's Catechism* (1772) and *The Nonconformist's Memorial* (2 vols., 1775). At the request of several ministers he undertook to add a supplement to the Westminster assembly's shorter catechism to expound the history and principles of nonconformity. His manuscript was revised by Philip Furneaux and Job Orton, and on publication *The Protestant Dissenter's Catechism* proved an immediate success. Immediately reprinted, it was translated into Welsh in 1775, was adapted for Irish Presbyterians in 1824, and reached its twenty-ninth edition in 1890. Palmer was encouraged by Orton to publish an abridged version of Edmund Calamy's *Account of many of those Worthy Ministers Ejected*, incorporating Calamy's *Continuation of the Account*. Orton was convinced that 'Nothing can be more striking and awakening than the Lives of such men' (letter to S. Palmer, 24 February 1772; Orton, 132) but underestimated the amount of work involved in such a project. *The Nonconformist's Memorial* appeared in parts, and a revised version followed in 1777–8, but it proved an inadequate work and was dismissed by the nonconformist historian Walter Wilson as 'a slovenly performance' (letter to J. Wilson, 15 February 1822, DWL, II c.12). Palmer's projected additional volumes on the lives of the earlier puritans and 'an account of the principal dissenting ministers since the ejectment' were never executed.

Palmer was a quiet, instructive preacher who emphasized practical religion in his sermons. He preached funeral sermons for several fellow ministers, including his old tutor, Caleb Ashworth, and published numerous other sermons separately. In theology he was close to the views of his friend Job Orton, and in his theological writings as much as his historical works he took pains to uphold the dissenting tradition, as evidenced in *The Calvinism of the Protestant Dissenters Asserted* (1786). He defended the dissenting cause against attacks made by the Anglican William Hawkins and wrote in favour of Sunday observance. In keeping with his biographical interests he published memoirs of Matthew Henry and Job Orton, wrote memoirs of Samuel Clark and Caleb Ashworth for the *Monthly Repository*, and edited Samuel Johnson's life of Isaac Watts. He was a frequent contributor to both the *Protestant Dissenter's Magazine* and the *Monthly Repository*.

From October 1811 Henry Foster Burder assisted Palmer in his ministry but Palmer remained active to the last, preaching with vigour on the Sunday before his death. He died on 28 November 1813, after a few days' illness, and was buried on 6 December in the burial-ground at St Thomas's Square, Hackney. His interment was attended by many of his former pupils, and the sermon was preached by his good friend Thomas Toller, of Kettering. He was survived by his wife.

ALEXANDER GORDON, *rev.* S. J. SKEDD

Sources T. N. Toller, *A sermon occasioned by the death of the Rev. S. Palmer* (1814) • 'Memoir of the Rev. Samuel Palmer', *Congregational Magazine*, 2 (1819), 577–83, 649, 641–8 [sic], 705–13 • *Monthly Repository* (1814), 65 • *Monthly Repository* (1822), 164, 286 • *Letters to dissenting ministers and to students for the ministry from the Rev. Job Orton*, ed. S. Palmer, 2 vols. (1806) • W. Wilson, *The history and antiquities of the dissenting churches and meeting houses in London, Westminster and Southwark*, 4 vols. (1808–14) • *IGI*

Likenesses H. Meyer, mezzotint, pubd 1814 (after A. W. Devis), BM, NPG • Hopwood, engraving (after H. W. Pickersgill), repro. in Wilson, *History*, facing 1.187

Palmer, Samuel (1805–1881), landscape painter and etcher, was born on 27 January 1805, at Surrey Square, Newington, London, the eldest child of Samuel Palmer (1775–1848) and Martha Giles (1778–1818), who were married on 12 October 1803. The Palmers were an upper-middle-class family, who had in the eighteenth century been prosperous feltmakers in the City of London. Palmer's father, the youngest of three brothers among five siblings, was scholarly but improvident. Before his son was born he had set up as a stationer and bookseller in London.

Boyhood and education Palmer was a delicate child: during his first months of life he suffered from a persistent cough, which may have been a precursor of the asthma that plagued his adult life. But he prospered after an unusually intelligent nurse, Mary Ward (*d.* 1837), was given charge of him, and subjected him to a sensible regimen. A Baptist, she had—like many of that persuasion—an intimate knowledge of the Bible, much of which she passed to Palmer; later she drew his attention also to the work of Milton, Edward Young, and other poets.

From his earliest years Palmer was also much influenced by his father. A wayward eccentric, but widely read, the elder Samuel encouraged his son to read too, allowing him unlimited access to his stock of books. Under his father's guidance Palmer memorized long extracts from *The Pilgrim's Progress* and from John Ray's *English Proverbs* (1680), including the aphorism, which he was made to repeat every day: 'Custom is the plague of wise men, and the idol of fools!' It was a sentiment he endorsed throughout his life. Father and son took pleasant country walks together, sometimes walking as far afield as Dulwich, which in later life Palmer and his friends called 'The Gate into the World of Vision' because of the idyllic countryside beyond. Martha Palmer admired her eccentric husband, despite his improvidence and indecisiveness, and together they encouraged boyish attempts by Samuel to express divine ideas in his drawings, thinking these indicated an eventual religious calling. Unfortunately, none of these early efforts survives. Palmer was encouraged also to copy prints in books from his father's stock.

Samuel Palmer (1805–1881), self-portrait, *c.*1824–8

In 1810 Martha Palmer gave birth to another son, William; a daughter, Martha, followed in 1817. Palmer's mother died in January 1818, when he was thirteen and staying with his grandfather at Margate, and he later said the news 'was like a sharp sword sent through the length of me' (*Letters*, 2.676). Nevertheless it was time a decision was made about his future. He had earlier attended the Merchant Taylors' School, but such was his reaction—he later said the big boys resembled baboons (ibid., 2.921)—that he was withdrawn after two terms. Finally his father decided to place him with a teacher of painting, William Wate (*d.* 1832). Palmer's artistic education was further extended by Thomas Stroud, a friend of his grandfather William Giles, who gave him tickets for the wide-ranging Royal Academy lectures of John Flaxman.

Early artistic career and influence of Finch and Linnell Immediately after his wife's death, Palmer's father moved to 126 Houndsditch, and in 1820 he moved to 10 Broad Street, Bloomsbury. For a time Palmer's health deteriorated in this noisy, insalubrious quarter; yet he had already, during the previous year at the British Institution, made his first sale, a landscape (now untraced) at 7 guineas. In 1819 also three of his works were hung at the Royal Academy. At this time he saw and was greatly impressed by J. M. W. Turner's *Orange Merchant at the Bar* (Tate collection). George Cooke, engraver of many plates after Turner, regularly visited the Palmer home, and doubtless discussed Turner's art with young Palmer, whose future work sometimes bore its impress. But Palmer was not yet giving undivided attention to art, and he dissipated valuable time in soul-searching and religious speculation; he also joined an amateur musical society, which met in the daytime, when he should have been practising his art. In addition, he suffered from attacks of hypochondria, which kept him brooding indoors.

At this time—probably at the music society—Palmer met the watercolour painter Francis Oliver Finch, who helped him towards what he believed were the proper pathways of art, philosophy, and belief, as reflected in one of his notebooks. Here Palmer wrote:

> Now it is twenty months since you began to draw. Your second trial begins. Make a new experiment. Draw near to Christ, and see what is to be done with him to back you. Your indolent moments rise up, each as a devil and a thorn at the quick … Lay up, silently and patiently, materials … in your sketch-book, and copy the prints to learn such nicety in pen sketching, or rather making careful studies as may enable you to give the expressions. But smaller subjects of separate glories of Heaven might be tried—hymns sung among the hills of Paradise at eventide … (Palmer, *Life and Letters*, 12–13)

Such spiritual insistence and self-doubt affected Palmer throughout his life. He struggled, too, to overcome difficulties in painting, caused partly by the limitations of his training, but this had a positive side, enabling him to take an uncluttered view of his work: 'Excess is the essential vivifying spirit, vital spark, embalming spice … of the finest art. Be ever saying to yourself, "Labour after the excess of excellence"' (ibid., 16).

Palmer was excessive not only in his art, but in all he did. As a young adult he was dandified, but he soon became more homespun, wearing clothes home-made by Mary Ward. They included an enormous greatcoat with pockets large enough to contain two quarter-imperial palettes with drawing paper between them, plus quantities of books and art materials. In bad weather he threw over this a capacious cloak; because his legs were short, such clothing gave the impression that he had none. In short, he was a sight to elicit jeers from street boys.

In September 1822 Palmer was introduced by Finch to the artist John Linnell, who for a time provided some of the strongest tutelage in his practice of art. 'It pleased God', wrote Palmer, 'to send Mr. Linnell as a good angel from Heaven to pluck me from the pit of modern art' (Palmer, *Life and Letters*, 14). He urged Palmer to study the works of Dürer, Michelangelo, the Bolognese engraver Guilio Bonasone (1498–1580), and antique sculptures. On the evidence of the sketchbook, begun in 1824 and now held in the British Museum, London, Linnell's impact on Palmer's work was immense: the comparison of its contents with those of an earlier sketchbook (1819; British Museum) shows a startling transformation.

Most of the designs in the 1824 sketchbook, and in Palmer's finished work of the period, depict English landscape sublimated into spiritual prospects of valleys and little rounded hills, illuminated by vast suns or by full or crescent moons and bright stars, inhabited by ploughmen, gleaners, and shepherds and their flocks, and dotted here and there with little thatched cottages. Real English country life was not portrayed; it was rather a rural world imagined by Palmer, with strong overtones derived from biblical sources and from Virgil's pastoral poetry.

At this period much of Palmer's work was realized in brown watercolour, mixed with gum and richly textured, the amassed detail reminiscent of engravings by Wenzel Hollar (1607–77) and Bonasone; examples include *Early Morning* (1825; Ashmolean Museum, Oxford). Some are inscribed with quotations gleaned from Palmer's reading: John Lydgate, Shakespeare, Virgil, and the book of Psalms. A few subjects were painted in oil such as the numinous *The Rest on the Flight into Egypt* (*c.*1824–5; Ashmolean Museum), the subject of which is derived from chapter two of Matthew's gospel.

The Ancients It was Linnell who introduced Palmer to William Blake, on 9 October 1824. Palmer became almost ecstatic at meeting the poet-artist, later recalling, 'In him you saw at once the Maker, the Inventor; one of the few in any age' (*Letters*, 1.506). At this time Blake had indifferent health, but three years before he had completed a work which was to have a tremendous impact on Palmer: his wood-engravings for Ambrose Philips's 'imitation' of the first eclogue in the *School Virgil* (1821), published by Linnell's family doctor, Robert John Thornton. 'They are', wrote Palmer, 'visions of little dells, and nooks, and corners of Paradise; models of the exquisitest pitch of intense poetry' (Palmer, *Life and Letters*, 15). His fervent young mind was then at its most receptive and responded with intensity to Blake's stimulus.

Palmer soon became the leading member of a group of young artists and enthusiasts who gathered around Blake during the last three years of his life; to this circle Blake was a prophet, a seer, and his Virgil illustrations were central to their admiration. Their homage extended to Blake's poetry, especially *Songs of Innocence and of Experience*, but his recondite poetry they comprehended only mistily. Their extravagant affection was coyly expressed by their kissing the bell-handle on the door of his shabby lodging in Fountain Court, Strand, before entering. Calling themselves the Ancients, because they believed ancient man superior to modern man, they numbered, in addition to Palmer, the watercolour painter Francis Oliver Finch; George Richmond, painter and son of the miniaturist Thomas Richmond; two sons of the architect Charles Heathcote Tatham, Frederick (1805–1878), a sculptor and miniaturist, and Arthur (1809–1874), then an undergraduate at Magdalene College, Cambridge, and later prebendary of Exeter; Welby Sherman (*fl.* 1827–1834), an engraver; Edward Calvert, an engraver and painter; the painter Henry Walter (1799–1849); and Palmer's cousin John Giles (1810–1880), later a stockbroker. Linnell was never an Ancient, but he knew them all, and some of them benefited from his advice.

Life and work at Shoreham During the 1820s Palmer's ill health, which included attacks of asthma and bronchitis, made him consider settling in the countryside. He and Frederick Tatham pooled their resources, and in spring 1826 they settled in the Kent village of Shoreham. At first they lodged with Arthur Tooth, a local farmer. However Palmer soon inherited a modest legacy from his grandfather William Giles, which allowed him to buy an old cottage, so dilapidated and vermin-infested that he dubbed it Rat Abbey. Here the young men, joined at times by other Ancients (and once by William and Catherine Blake), lived simply on a diet of bread and butter, eggs, milk, and wild nuts, supplemented with fruit and vegetables grown locally for the London market, and local cider costing 9*d.* a gallon. On rare occasions this was supplemented by the luxury of green tea. They bathed each morning in the River Darent. There was little spare cash, but when it was available it went on books, postage, and art materials.

To Palmer Shoreham was an ideal *locus amoenus*. While not oblivious of the ever-present rural realities of grinding labour and poverty, he preferred to imagine and portray the countryside as a world of God-given abundance and spiritual light, its inhabitants living a life of rewarding toil in a state of happy humility and grace. Yet they were not what Palmer called 'the Strephons and Chloes of the coffee-home poets' (*An English Version of the 'Eclogues' of Virgil*, 1883, 1). They were somewhat closer to Virgil's Corydons and Damons set in a utopian world of love and yearning, but Palmer's portrayals went beyond, attempting to show the divine vitality of nature, and man's spiritual place amid landscapes of sacramental golden corn.

Palmer's ideas were developed further in a few tempera and watercolour paintings, such as *Coming from Evening Church* (1830; Tate collection) and *The Magic Apple Tree* (1830; Fitzwilliam Museum, Cambridge). The former seems to have been influenced by miniatures in fifteenth-century illuminated manuscripts, with foreshortened perspective, trees forming a rustic arch, steep hills in the distance, and a train of grave villagers wending homewards under a full moon. *The Magic Apple Tree* is an impressive portrayal of colourful, even hallucinatory abundance in a landscape enriched by both Ceres and Pomona. Not all of Palmer's Shoreham work has such intensity of vision; some of it portrays actual landscapes and buildings—for instance the drawing of *Sepham Barn* (1828; Ashmolean Museum)—but they all are conceived with visionary accentuation, expressed in a myopic intensity of detail: this Palmer described as 'a thousand pretty eyes and buds and spires and blossoms, gemm'd with dew … the leafy lightness, the thousand repetitions of little forms' (*Letters*, 1.47).

Life at Shoreham was emphatically devotional. In his cottage Palmer arranged a private chapel, in which he planned to hang prints of the sixteenth-century English Catholic martyrs John Fisher and Sir Thomas More. Much of his reading had a distinctly religious theme: it included Isaac Barrow's *Exposition of the Creed* (1669), William Law's *A Serious Call to a Devout and Holy Life* (1728), Joseph Butler's *Analogy of Religion* (1736), and John Flavel's *Husbandry Spiritualized* (1669). This serious existence was relieved, however by light-hearted walks over the countryside in all weathers, especially during thunderstorms. The Ancients carried sketching stools, which the villagers thought were some kind of scientific or astrological device: they dubbed their bearers Extollagers.

Palmer's father, persuaded and financed by his prosperous brother Nathaniel, gave up his bookshop, sold his Broad Street house, and moved to Shoreham with his son William and Mary Ward. They settled for a time in Waterhouse, a Queen Anne house; overflow guests from the incommodious Rat Abbey were often put up there. There was another reason for old Palmer's move: he had become an enthusiastic Particular Baptist, and felt urged to preach his beliefs; fortuitously, a vacancy had occurred at a chapel at Otford, near Shoreham, which he was invited to fill. He accepted and for a time settled down, until his instability obtruded, and he considered returning to bookselling or starting a school. Later still he remarried, but by then his brother had decided to help him no more.

Palmer's rural tranquillity was disturbed during the early 1830s by agricultural unrest and rick-burning, and he turned his attention to politics. In 1832 he wrote, had printed, and circulated an unsigned pamphlet *An Address to the Electors of West Kent*. It has a distinctly tory tone, and demonstrates the void between his views and those of his friend John Linnell, an extreme nonconformist and a whig, a void which was to lead to much animosity. Palmer's calm was further ruffled in September 1836, when John Giles informed him that his fellow Ancient Welby Sherman had relieved his brother William of much of his savings by betting on billiards; William had married only a year before, and his wife was pregnant. Giles devised a deed of trust to secure the remnants of his money. Palmer was also perplexed by Edward Calvert, who had continual backslidings into paganism; Calvert was a strong character who successfully withstood his blandishments.

Marriage During the early and mid-1830s the intensity of Palmer's vision began to diminish, but he was portraying figures more convincingly, especially in movement. This is demonstrated in the oil and tempera painting *The Shearers* (*c.*1833–4; priv. coll.). In this, a vista of corn is seen from within a barn, and, just outside, men and women shear sheep and collect the fleeces in sacks; the almost dancing figures recall groups in Blake's *Songs of Innocence and of Experience*. At this time Palmer sought a new *genius loci*, visiting Devon, the Wye valley, and north Wales. Although they lack the exaltation of his earlier work, he painted some major landscapes in these districts, such as the watercolour *Snowdon from Moel Siabod* (1835/1836; Art Gallery of Greater Victoria, British Columbia), an inspired portrayal of the immensity of Snowdonia.

Meanwhile Linnell's children were growing up: the eldest, Hannah (1818–1893), his favourite, was nearly fifteen. She was lively and sturdy, small and pretty, and Palmer became strongly attracted to her. On 6 July 1833 Linnell noted in his diary: 'Palmer's first hint about Hannah' (Linnell Trust). Influenced by Palmer, Hannah, to her parents' displeasure, joined the Church of England, and they became betrothed. Just before his engagement Palmer had moved into a London house, 4 Grove Street, Lisson Grove, Marylebone, where he attempted to establish a teaching practice. The other Ancients were also dispersing: Calvert, Walter, Finch, Frederick Tatham, and Richmond were married, but continued to practise their art;

Arthur Tatham followed his calling in the church; John Giles his profession. But they continued to gather at monthly meetings in each others' homes, to discuss art, to sup, and to enjoy music, poetry, and conversation.

In January 1837 Palmer's beloved old nurse, Mary Ward, died. She had guided his early years with sympathy and understanding, and had for long thereafter attended to almost every detail of his personal life. Within months of Mary's death, on 30 September 1837, Palmer married Hannah Linnell; he was thirty-two, she was nineteen. On Linnell's insistence they were married, not in church, but at a civil ceremony at the court house, Marylebone, a move which burdened Palmer throughout his life with what he considered to be an act of apostasy.

Italy Soon after their marriage Palmer and Hannah left for Italy. In summer 1837 Richmond and his wife had planned such a visit, and Palmer was determined to accompany them. The Palmers and Richmonds sailed for Calais on 3 October 1837; they arrived in Paris a few days later, by 6 November were in Florence, and on 14 November they arrived in Rome. Here Hannah at once began work on a commission from her father, to colour after the originals a set of outline lithographs he had made of Michelangelo's frescoes on the ceiling of the Sistine Chapel; he had also asked her to make small coloured copies of Raphael's frescoes in the Vatican loggia. The Palmers' happiness in Italy and each other was soon overcast by letters from Linnell, scolding them—Palmer especially—for not writing more often. For the time being Palmer dismissed this from his mind, remembering Linnell's earlier kindness and encouragement.

On the road from Florence, Palmer had already begun to make sketches of scenery, buildings, and weather effects. But it was in Rome that he began to react strongly to the Italian landscape, and started to create work on a far grander scale than he had so far attempted. Some of this work was unsuccessful—such as the watercolour *Rome from the Borghese Gardens* (1837; V&A), his earliest attempt to paint such a broad and complex subject. The surrounding landscape and its details are convincing, but the perspective of the architecture is shaky. In contrast the watercolour *The Forum, Rome* (1837; priv. coll.), a more compact subject, is fully convincing. Within a few months Palmer had succeeded in controlling his portrayals of complicated townscapes, as in *A View of Modern Rome during the Carnival* (1838; City Museums and Art Gallery, Birmingham), a copy of which was commissioned by John Baring, of the banking family, who was then in Rome; the fee was 40 guineas. It was the only work Palmer sold in Italy. One cogent reason for this was that—unlike Richmond, who had little difficulty in obtaining commissions in Italy—Palmer had few social accomplishments, and did not move among potential buyers. As he lamented to Linnell, 'I think I could sell, if I could once come in contact with the buyers; but *that* is the difficulty … I have not been introduced to a single person but Mr Baring' (*Letters*, 1.130).

Palmer was further disturbed by a barrage of uncomprehending, usually disapproving, often scolding letters from Linnell, covering all kinds of subjects, including religious matters. Linnell, conscious of the close proximity of the Vatican, and feeling assured that Roman Catholicism was but a step from the Church of England, continually and sarcastically upbraided Samuel for his convictions. Palmer replied gently, doing his best to placate his father-in-law. Later he wrote back with spirit, but it was too late to retrieve their previous good relationship; Linnell continued to pursue his arguments with overbearing sarcasm, and Palmer withdrew within himself.

From Rome the Palmers travelled to Naples and Tivoli, where Palmer painted some of his best Italian watercolours: for example, *The Cypresses at the Villa d'Este, Tivoli* (1838/1839; Paul Mellon Center for British Art, New Haven), in which the foliage and bark of the great trees are drawn with the minute observation of some of his later Shoreham watercolours. Back in Rome, Hannah Palmer became ill, affected by the climate and overwork; Palmer had to finish her father's commissions. From others, there were similar commissions for copies by Hannah of various works, but the labour was becoming too much for her, and Palmer feared that she might be permanently affected if they did not leave Rome immediately. So, when Linnell's commissions were completed, they travelled northwards by way of Civitella, Subiaco, and Papignia to Florence, where Palmer made some drawings, including the unfinished watercolour *Florence, Drawn on the Spot* (1839; V&A). They visited the Uffizi Gallery, noting particularly works by Giorgione and Titian, and making slight copies for future reference.

Domestic life and children The Palmers left Italy on 29 October 1839 and returned home by way of Paris, and then by ship from Calais to London. Trouble awaited Palmer: in addition to strained relations with the Linnells, he found that his brother William had pawned his pictures, left in his care; he had disappeared, ashamed to face Palmer, leaving an apologetic note in which he promised to pay back the money with interest. There is no record that he ever did, and Palmer had to redeem his work himself.

Married life at home began pleasantly, despite Hannah's inexperience as a housekeeper (until she married, her mother had limited her domestic duties to sewing). She knew nothing of cooking, and had no experience of household management; however, with Palmer's help, matters were brought to some kind of order. Despite bounty from Linnell, Palmer's real problem was to earn enough to support his wife in comfort. With some success, he set up again as a teacher of watercolour; one of his early pupils was Louisa Twining, of the family of tea and coffee merchants, and he was also engaged as drawing master to the children of James William Freshfield MP, solicitor to the Bank of England.

The couple's first child, Thomas More Walter George, was born on Palmer's own birthday, 27 January 1842. Responsibility for the boy's upbringing was, from the beginning, undertaken by Palmer with great earnestness: he intended his son to be a paragon of virtue, morality, devotion, and learning, and allowed little leeway for the high spirits of childhood. Thomas More could read when he was three, and by the same age was subjected to moral blandishments. When he was two and a half, and holidaying with his mother at Margate, Palmer wrote to him, urging him to keep his father's letters safely:

> for when you grow up … I shall die and my body will be put into a hole and you will never see me again while you live in this world—and perhaps then you will like to look at some of the letters I have written to you. (*Letters*, 1.432)

In 1844 Hannah gave birth to a daughter, Mary Elizabeth. The little girl gave her parents only a brief happiness, for she died in December 1847, aged only three. Hannah Palmer was weakened by a series of miscarriages in the 1850s, but one pregnancy was successful, and their third child, Alfred Herbert, was born on 25 September 1853. He became a somewhat neglected and unhappy child, but he lived until 1931, long enough to write a biography of his father, to publish some of his letters, and to help to perpetuate his memory in other ways. After Mary Elizabeth's death, the Palmers felt unable to continue living at Grove Street, and looked for another abode, which they found in the form of a picturesque cottage, 1A Love Lane (later renamed Victoria Road), Kensington, then separated from London by open country. In 1851 they moved again, to nearby 6 Douro Place.

Work in the 1840s and 1850s; etching Palmer continued to paint landscapes, many of them influenced by his Italian studies; indeed, some portrayed Italian subjects. He exploited his gift for transforming a conventional subject into a visionary concept, as in the Turneresque watercolour *Tintagel Castle, Approaching Rain* (1848; Ashmolean Museum). He sought subjects in many areas, especially Berkshire, Buckinghamshire, Surrey, Somerset, Devon, Cornwall, the Isle of Wight, the Lake District, and Wales. In 1854 he was elected to full membership of the Society of Painters in Water Colours, having been an associate for eleven years.

About 1850 Palmer began to practise etching: his first essay was a small plate entitled *The Willow*. On the strength of this he was, on 19 February 1850, elected a member of the Etching Club. Etching was a demanding taskmaster: 'If this kind of needlework could be made fairly remunerative', he wrote in 1871, 'I should be content to do nothing else, so curiously attractive is the teazing, tempertrying, yet fascinating copper. But my etchings consume much time' (*Letters*, 2.819). In thirty-one years he etched thirteen plates and began four more (illustrations for Virgil's *Eclogues*) which were finished posthumously by his son Alfred Herbert. Although his output was small, his etchings are among his best later work.

Domestic problems and the death of Palmer's son In the meantime Palmer suffered many misfortunes. His relationship with Hannah deteriorated as she came increasingly under her father's influence, especially in her religious views, which drew ever closer to Linnell's brand of puritanism. She also became more house-proud, refusing to have Samuel's plaster casts and relics in the main rooms. Palmer's own health deteriorated: in 1856 he complained to Richmond that he found breathing difficult, and in 1859 he wrote to Hannah, then staying at Redstone Wood, Linnell's home, that he dreaded the dust of town; in despair he turned to homoeopathy, which apparently brought relief.

As Thomas More Palmer grew up, he became priggish and wayward, despite Palmer's efforts to mould him into a perfect character—or perhaps because of them. One day he persuaded Richmond's son Willy (later the painter Sir William Blake Richmond) to run away from home with him; they were found at Staines and marched home by a policeman. Each was subjected to hours of admonition from their parents and family friends and they were forbidden to communicate with one another. Thomas More aspired to a career at sea, but his father was determined he should enter the clergy, which led to endless dispute and heart-searching. He was doing so well at his school, Charterhouse, that Palmer pushed him unremittingly into redoubled effort. This affected his health and in November 1859 he suffered a bad attack of scarlet fever, following which he was sent on a recuperative holiday. Even here, Palmer continually nagged him, for he expected him to work for an Oxford scholarship on his return.

For summer holidays in 1861, Palmer sought a location where the family could rest, and he could paint: he found what he was looking for at High Ashes Farm, near Leith Hill, Surrey. Here he persisted in driving Thomas More, despite the boy's obvious decline. Too late he realized the truth, when his son died on 11 July 1861, aged nineteen, probably from severe heart disease. Palmer rushed from the house in hysterical grief: he never visited his son's grave, and never ceased blaming himself for Thomas More's early death.

The Palmers felt unable to return to Douro Place, with its poignant memories; accordingly they moved into a cottage in Park Lane, Reigate, near Redstone Wood. Park Lane was not a success, and they soon moved into a Gothic villa, Furze Hill House, Mead Vale, in Redhill. It was too remote for Palmer to continue with much teaching, but it was near Redstone Wood, and it was peaceful enough to allow the Palmers to remake their lives in their different ways: Palmer working in his study and indulging in his other interests, Hannah enjoying her preferred bourgeois lifestyle. Over the coming years the house's melancholy atmosphere diminished, and although he still grieved inwardly, Palmer concealed his feelings behind a cheerful, even jovial exterior. There was no indication of tragedy in his paintings, some are even tranquil, but he was for some time less productive. As Hannah's domestic customs became more entrenched, Palmer, living mainly in his study, became more eccentric. He turned to his surviving son, Alfred Herbert, for companionship and assistance in his lesser pursuits, typical of which were the repair of slippers with cobbler's wax and the discharge of a gun up the chimney to dislodge soot.

Palmer's later life and works Palmer's later years were dominated by two important undertakings. The first was a group of six large subjects (each approximately 504 mm x 718 mm) from Milton's *L'allegro* and *Il Penseroso*, commissioned by John Ruskin's solicitor, Leonard Rowe Valpy. In these Palmer brought together a lifetime's experience of imagination and technique. They occupied him for over fifteen years: examples are in the Victoria and Albert Museum; the Rijksmuseum, Amsterdam; the Cincinnati Art Museum, Ohio; and the Yale Center for British Art, New Haven. The second large project arose from his own translation of Virgil's *Eclogues*, begun about 1856. He planned to illustrate this with etchings, but only one, *Opening the Fold*, for the fourth eclogue, was completed. Four further subjects were finished by A. H. Palmer after his father's death. Drawings for the other passages were made, but never transferred to plates; they were, however, reproduced in his translation, *An English Version of the 'Eclogues' of Virgil*, published posthumously in 1883.

In old age Palmer maintained what were left of his old friendships and made more, many among younger people. But his friendship with Linnell faded, probably because Palmer was over-sensitive about Linnell's continuing financial support. His last letter to his father-in-law was written on 8 July 1878, on the subject of oil lamps. Of the Ancients he was outlived only by Calvert and Richmond. But the tensions between Palmer and Hannah lessened, being replaced by new tenderness and understanding. Samuel Palmer died at Furze Hill House on 24 May 1881, while George Richmond knelt in prayer and wept beside his bed. He was buried in Reigate churchyard; Hannah Palmer, who became senile, died in 1893 and was laid beside him.

Assessment and reputation Initially Palmer's work was conventional; it showed little promise of its later, more imaginative, development in the early 1820s. But by 1824 it had a poetic intensity, derived in part from medieval drawings and engravings, and was encouraged by Finch and Linnell, and had improved in both conception and technique. During his years at Shoreham its intensity increased, becoming almost hallucinatory. A few years later, its visionary content abated. With marriage and children to support, Palmer needed a steady income, and worked more on conventional landscapes and topographical studies. Yet even such subjects were often given imaginative emphasis. Such work places Palmer in the mainstream tradition in the English school of watercolours; it is the content derived from his early work added to the construction of such watercolours that sets him apart. Palmer's labours between 1850 and 1880 were largely devoted to his etchings: *tours de force* of technique, they mark a peak among his later poetic conceptions.

Palmer received little critical attention during his lifetime, but he and his work were known to many leading artists and to some critics, such as Philip Gilbert Hamerton, who admired his work and wrote about it in his book *Etching and Etchers* (1868) and in the periodical *The Portfolio*. But there is otherwise little critical commentary of note and it was not until the publication of his son's posthumous *Memoir* (1882) and *The Life and Letters of Samuel Palmer* (1892) that there was any serious study of him or his work. Since then, his reputation has varied. Initially his more conventional watercolours and etchings, and his few oil paintings, were esteemed more than his early imaginative work. In 1926 a major exhibition of his work and that of his fellow Ancients was held at the Victoria and Albert Museum, south Kensington; here his early visionary work could be seen and its importance realized. It again came into prominence during and after the Second World War, its pastoral overtones providing an artistic antidote to the anxious war years. Later, after new exhibitions and studies, it became obvious that Palmer's early visionary studies are only a part (though an important one) of his best work, in which his etchings and the best of his later watercolours have their place. Palmer's influence on many neo-romantic artists working during the second half of the twentieth century may be clearly discerned in the conceptions of, among others, Paul Nash, Paul Drury, Graham Sutherland, David Jones, and Robin Tanner.

RAYMOND LISTER

Sources *The letters of Samuel Palmer*, ed. R. Lister, 2 vols. (1974) • R. Lister, *Catalogue raisonné of the works of Samuel Palmer* (1988) • A. H. Palmer, *The life and letters of Samuel Palmer* (1892); repr. (1972) • R. Lister, *Samuel Palmer: his life and art* (1987) • E. Malins, *Samuel Palmer's Italian honeymoon* (1968) • G. Grigson, *Samuel Palmer: the visionary years* (1947) • R. Lister, *Samuel Palmer and his etchings* (1969) • R. Lister, *Samuel Palmer and 'the ancients'* (1984) [exhibition catalogue, FM Cam., 9 Oct–16 Dec 1984] • G. E. Bentley jun., M. D. Paley, and R. R. Wark, *Essays on the Blake followers* (1983) • R. Lister and A. K. Astbury, *Samuel Palmer in Palmer country* (1980) • L. Binyon, *The followers of William Blake* (1925) • *Catalogue of an exhibition of drawings, etchings and woodcuts by Samuel Palmer and other disciples of William Blake* (1926) [exhibition catalogue, V&A] • A. H. Palmer, *Samuel Palmer: a memoir* (1882) • A. Gilchrist, *Life of William Blake, 'Pictor ignotus'*, 2 vols. (1863) • C. Harrison, *Samuel Palmer* (1997) • D. B. Brown, *Samuel Palmer, 1805–1881: loan exhibition from the Ashmolean Museum, Oxford* (1982) • G. Barton and M. Tong, *Underriver: Samuel Palmer's Golden Valley* (1995) • R. Lister, *Samuel Palmer: a biography* (1974) • G. Keynes and others, eds., *Samuel Palmer, a vision recaptured: the complete etchings and the paintings for Milton and for Virgil* (1978) • S. Palmer, *The parting light: selected writings*, ed. M. Abbey (1985) • priv. coll., Ivimy MSS • D. Linnell, *Blake, Palmer, Linnell and Co: the life of John Linnell* (1994) • m. cert. • d. cert.

Archives AM Oxf., MSS • BM, MSS • V&A, MSS | Birmingham Museums and Art Gallery • Bodl. Oxf., letters to F. G. Stephens • FM Cam. • L'Institut Néerlandais, Paris • Man. City Gall. • priv. coll., Richmond family MSS • priv. coll., Linnell Trust MSS • priv. coll., Ivimy MSS • Yale U. • Yale U. CBA

Likenesses H. Walter, pencil and wash drawing, 1819, BM • S. Palmer, self-portrait, chalk, *c*.1824–1828, AM Oxf. [*see illus.*] • G. Richmond, pencil caricature, 1825, V&A • G. Richmond, ink drawing, *c*.1828, V&A • G. Richmond, pen-and-ink, and chalk drawing, 1828, Yale U. CBA • G. Richmond, ink drawing, *c*.1829, V&A • G. Richmond, miniature, watercolour and body colour, 1829, NPG • G. Richmond, pen-and-ink, and watercolour drawing, 1829, AM Oxf. • G. Richmond, pencil, pen, and wash drawing, *c*.1829, NPG • G. Richmond, drawings, 1830, Graves Art Gallery, Sheffield • H. Walter, watercolour and ink caricature, 1835, BM • C. W. Cope, pencil drawing, NPG • Cundall, carte-de-visite (in middle age), NPG • J. Linnell, drawing (in old age), FM Cam. • G. Richmond, two pen-and-ink sketches, Walsall Museum and Art Gallery • photograph, V&A • woodcut (after carte-de-visite by Cundall, Downes & Co.), NPG

Palmer, Shirley (1786–1852), physician and medical writer, was born on 27 August 1786 at Coleshill, Warwickshire, the son of Edward Palmer, solicitor, and his second wife, Benedicta Mears. Educated at Coleshill grammar school and Harrow School, Palmer was by 1804 a pupil of Thomas Salt, surgeon, of Lichfield in Staffordshire. He subsequently studied under the eminent surgeon John Abernethy at St Bartholomew's Hospital, London, became a member of the Royal College of Surgeons in 1807, and graduated MD at Glasgow in 1814. He married on 29 September 1813 Marie Josephine Minette Breheault (*d.* 1868), who had come from France as a child refugee and had been adopted by the Revd Michael Ward of Tamworth, Staffordshire; Charles Ferrars Palmer [*see below*] was their son.

By 1818 Palmer had settled at Tamworth, where he was twice elected high bailiff of the town. In 1831 he also established a practice at Birmingham, though he still lived and practised at Tamworth. As a popularizer of medicine and science, he wrote for and edited the *New Medical and Physical Journal* from 1815 to 1819, and the *London Medical Repository*, from 1819 to 1821, and between 1834 and 1836 he contributed to the London monthly, *The Analyst*. He contributed to his local newspaper, the *Lichfield Mercury*, and published *Popular Illustrations of Medicine* (1829) and *Popular Lectures on the Vertebrated Animals of the British Islands* (1832), as well as the *Pentaglot* [French, English, Latin, Greek, German] *dictionary of the terms employed in anatomy, physiology, pathology, practical medicine …* (1845).

Palmer died on 11 November 1852 at Church Street, Tamworth, and was buried on 16 November in the new churchyard at St Editha's Church, which had once formed part of his garden. Marie died at Kingswood, Warwickshire, on 5 February 1868 and was buried at Water Orton, Warwickshire.

Charles Ferrars Palmer (1819–1900), physician and historian, was born at Tamworth on 9 September 1819. He was educated at Tamworth grammar school and studied medicine at Queen's College, Birmingham, where in 1842 he became a Roman Catholic. He was admitted MRCS in 1846 and practised at Tamworth. In 1845 he published the first history of that town. He joined the Dominican order in 1855, taking the name Raymund, and in 1859 he was ordained priest. He spent the years 1853–66 at Woodchester, Gloucestershire; thereafter he lived at St Dominic's Priory, Maitland Park, St Pancras, London. Most of his prolific publications concerned the history of the Dominican order in England, but in 1871 and 1875 he published two further books on the history of Tamworth, and in 1895 he contributed the article on his father to the *Dictionary of National Biography*. He died at the priory on 27 October 1900. C. F. R. PALMER, *rev.* D. A. JOHNSON

Sources R. Simms, ed., *Bibliotheca Staffordiensis* (1894) · M. W. Greenslade, *The Staffordshire historians*, Staffordshire RS, 4th ser., 11 (1982), 132 · S. Palmer, *The Swiss exile* (1804) · parish register, Tamworth, St Editha, Staffs. RO · W. Parson and T. Bradshaw, eds., *Staffordshire general and commercial directory, for 1818* [1818] · W. I. Addison, *A roll of graduates of the University of Glasgow from 31st December 1727 to 31st December 1897* (1898), 482 · d. cert. · d. cert. [Charles Ferrars Palmer]

Archives BL, corresp. with Sir Robert Peel, Add. MSS 40426–40590

Palmer, Thomas (*fl.* 1371–1415), prior of the Dominican convent, London, and theologian, was an inmate of the Winchester convent when ordained acolyte and subdeacon in 1371 and 1375, but of the Guildford convent when ordained priest in September 1376. The general chapter of the Dominican order in 1378 appointed him to read the *Sentences* in Cambridge; by 1393 he was a doctor of theology (though whether of Oxford or Cambridge is unclear). He was elected prior provincial of the order in England in 1393, but his tenure was ended on 28 June 1396 by decision of Raymond of Capua, minister-general, following inquiry into complaints concerning Palmer's excessive severity and assertion of unjustified powers. He became prior of the London convent in 1397. Palmer preached before Richard II at least four times between 1384 and 1393, and before Henry IV in 1403; he received royal alms for the London convent in 1401 and 1402 and for the provincial chapter in 1400.

Palmer is several times recorded as a spokesman for orthodoxy. About 1393 he answered a Lollard letter upbraiding Master Nicholas Hereford for his apostasy; later he was present at the trial of Sir John Oldcastle in 1413, and was one of Chichele's officials in the investigation of the London heretic John Claydon in 1415. A determination on the worship of images, with a colophon stating that Thomas Palmer had delivered it in the schools at St Paul's, London, in 1398, survives both complete (Assisi, Biblioteca Comunale, MS 192, fols. 133–46), and without either a beginning or an attribution (BL, Harley MS 31, fols. 182–194*v*). Another determination, without date or location, on the unacceptability of vernacular translations of scripture, is ascribed by an annotator's hand to Palmer in the single surviving copy. If this attribution is correct, the date of its origin is likely to have been earlier than 1407, since no mention is made of Archbishop Arundel's *Constitutions* (in which new biblical translation was prohibited, and earlier versions had retrospectively to be approved). Palmer, unlike Richard Ullerston and William Butler who had argued the question in Oxford in 1401, identified the proponents of translation as the Lollards; his contribution may well be dated later than this. Bale lists six works, the four with incipits deriving from Merton College, Oxford, MS 68, where two texts are wrongly ascribed to Palmer. Leland includes a determination by Palmer in a sequence of five on the schism that he saw at Westminster Abbey Library; the date of all five seems likely to be 1395–6, when Richard II consulted the University of Oxford on the issue. ANNE HUDSON

Sources T. Kaeppeli, ed., *Registrum litterarum Fr. Raymundi de Vineis Capuani, magistri ordinis, 1380–1399* (1937), vol. 19 of *Monumenta ordinis fratrum praedicatorum historica* · R. P. Mortier, *Histoire des maîtres généraux de l'ordre des frères prêcheurs*, 3 (Paris, 1907), 648–72 · T. F. Kirby, ed., *Wykeham's register*, 1, Hampshire RS, 11 (1896), 263, 278, 280 · London, BL, Add. MS 35115, fols. 33, 33*v*, 34 · PRO, E101/401/2, fol. 38 · PRO, E101/402/5, fol. 26 · PRO, E101/402/10, fol. 33*r–v* · PRO, E101/404/21, fol. 35*v* · PRO, E101/403/573, mem. 26 · PRO, E101/403/564 · W. W. Capes, ed., *Registrum Johannis Trefnant*, CYS, 20 (1916), 396–401 · M. Deanesly, *The Lollard Bible* (1920), 418–37 · D. Wilkins, ed., *Concilia Magnae Britanniae et Hiberniae*, 3 (1737), 355 · E. F. Jacob, ed., *The register of Henry Chichele, archbishop of Canterbury, 1414–1443*, 4, CYS, 47 (1947), 136 · Bale, *Cat.*, 1.540–41 · Bale, *Index*, 449 · A. Hudson, 'The debate on Bible translation, Oxford 1401', *EngHR*, 90 (1975), 1–18 · *Joannis Lelandi antiquarii de rebus Britannicis collectanea*, ed. T. Hearne, [3rd edn], 6 vols. (1774), vol. 3, p. 49

Archives Biblioteca Comunale, Assisi, MS 192, fols. 133–146 • BL, Harley MS 31, fols. 182–194*v* • Trinity Cam., MS B.15.11, fols. 42–47*v*

Palmer, Sir Thomas (*b*. after **1496**, *d*. **1553**), soldier and conspirator, was the youngest of three sons and a daughter of Edward Palmer of Angmering, Sussex (*d*. 1516), landowner, and his wife, Alice, daughter and coheir of John Clement of Ightham Mote, near Sevenoaks, Kent, and his wife. Nothing is known of his education. His elder brothers were John Palmer (*b*. in or before 1495, *d*. 1563) and Sir Henry *Palmer (*d*. 1559). As a younger son of modest means, a military career seemed an obvious choice for him.

Palmer, who never married, was nicknamed 'Buskyne Palmer' and 'Long Palmer'. The former nickname suggested his impatience and energy and the latter, apparently in reference to his height, distinguished him from a namesake, who had the sobriquet of 'Little Palmer' (J. G. Nichols, ed., *Narratives of the Days of the Reformation*, CS, 77, 1859, 158, 324). He was probably one of Henry VIII's young companions during the opening years of the reign and appears in the revels accounts at this time. He is often confused with another namesake, Sir Thomas Palmer of Pollicot, Buckinghamshire, who was probably his uncle, and was also a courtier. He became one of the king's spears in 1513 and served at Tournai in 1514. In 1519 he was appointed a gentleman usher to the king. He probably joined Charles Brandon, first duke of Suffolk on his expedition to France in 1523. Henry began to promote him for good service and in June 1526 Palmer became chief porter of Calais and in 1528 received the captaincy of Newneham Bridge. He was knighted at Calais on 10 November 1532 and captured by the French in 1534, subsequently paying the ransom himself. In 1535 he was commissioned to collect tenths of spiritualities at Calais. He was granted an annuity of £50 in 1538, but the following year he was temporarily imprisoned for assaulting his brother Henry Palmer.

Palmer was a good gambler and diced with the king, whom he frequently beat. His brother John Palmer was incorrectly ascribed this role by the historian John Strype. Palmer was involved in the hostilities at the bridge of Ardres in 1540 and was in attendance in December as Anne of Cleves passed through Calais on her way to England. He was imprisoned in the Tower of London in 1540 along with Arthur Plantagenet, sixth Viscount Lisle, deputy of Calais, though Palmer was released early in 1541. His arrest was either the result of a close association with Thomas Cromwell, earl of Essex and principal secretary, or, more likely, because he was a known protestant and among the circle in Calais that the latter was accused of protecting. It appears that Palmer was a gentleman pensioner soon after, though his goods were not restored until 1543, in which year he was appointed treasurer of Guînes. In 1544 he became muster master to the mercenary captain, Clayn von Buren, Count Buren, and lieutenant of the cavalry under Sir Francis Bryan. In January 1545 he was appointed captain of 'the Old Man', an outlying fort of Boulogne, which office he then resigned to Henry Palmer.

Palmer received lands in Sussex in 1547, in reward for service to Henry. He retained his offices in Calais but in early 1548, because of his expertise in fortifications, especially of the most modern design (*trace Italienne*), he was sent to Scotland, where he fortified Broughty Craig and Dundee Law. These skills were particularly useful because of the policy of building fortifications in Scotland adopted between 1547 and 1549 by Edward Seymour, duke of Somerset and lord protector to Edward VI. In mid-1548 Palmer was involved in daring missions to keep Haddington supplied and worked on strengthening the site during the siege by the French and Scottish forces. He recklessly disobeyed orders during a diversionary action on 16 July and was captured after the loss of about 200 men. The king noted dryly of his efforts: 'sellfwyll and glorie in that journey did cast awaye the whoale power, for they were all over-throwen' (*Literary Remains*, ed. Jordan, 222). Palmer held a grudge against Somerset, even after his release. He served under John Dudley, earl of Warwick, against Kett's rebellion in the summer of 1549. He then became one of Warwick's clients. In November 1550 he was granted an annuity of £100.

On 7 October 1551 Palmer was the first to reveal Somerset's alleged treason. He was arrested himself and sent to the Tower as an associate. In reality, he was probably working for the duke of Northumberland (Warwick). His disclosures were vital and the case against Somerset followed them closely. True to his reckless nature, Palmer's accusations tended to the lurid and extreme, claiming, among other things, that Northumberland and his supporters were to be invited to a banquet in order to 'cutte of there heades' (BL, Cotton MS Nero C.x, fol. 44*r*). In February 1552 he was released and granted a pardon. He was appointed to the commission to investigate the debatable land later that month and in June he received further grants of land worth £113 14*s*. 0*d*. per annum in exchange for Standingfeld, Guînes. Although assessed at £105 per annum in lands for the subsidy of 1527, he had money and goods to the value of £897 4*s*. 5*d*. and an income of £309 2*s*. 10*d*. in August 1553—not bad for the youngest son of a minor gentleman. He joined Northumberland's ill-fated uprising against Princess Mary in support of Lady Jane Grey in July 1553, and returned to the Tower on the 25th at its collapse. Palmer was convicted of treason with Northumberland and Sir John Gates on 19 August. During the trial he accused the judges of being worse traitors than he. On the 22nd the prisoners heard mass and took communion before being brought to the scaffold on Tower Hill. The charismatic Palmer, last to be executed, leapt onto the scaffold that was covered with the blood of his comrades. Beginning with a smile he spoke passionately of a common Christian faith and of a personal conversion but affirmed his protestantism. He said that in the Tower he 'saw God omnipotent, his power infinite, his mercy incomprehensible; and when I saw this, I most humbly submitted' (Froude, 6.74). He was then beheaded.

M. M. Norris

Sources A. Bryson, '"The speciall men in every shere": the Edwardian regime, 1547–1553', PhD diss., U. St Andr., 2001 • *CSP Scot. ser.*, *1509–89* • HoP, *Commons*, *1509–58*, 3.51–6 • *LP Henry VIII* •

DNB • *APC*, *1540–54* • *CPR*, *1547–53* • *Literary remains of King Edward the Sixth*, ed. J. G. Nichols, 2 vols., Roxburghe Club, 75 (1857); repr. [1963] • J. A. Froude, *History of England*, 2nd edn, 12 vols. (1858–66), vol. 6 • M. Merriman, *The rough wooings: Mary queen of Scots, 1542–1551* (2000)

Archives PRO, Hamilton papers • PRO, State papers

Wealth at death approx. £500 p.a. in annuities from offices held and rents received from land

Palmer, Sir Thomas (**1540/41–1626**), author, was the son of Sir Henry *Palmer (*d.* 1559) of Wingham, Kent, his mother being Jane, a daughter of Sir Richard Windebank of Guînes. He was later known as the Travailer from the fact that he published (in 1606) *An Essay of the Meanes how to Make our Travailes More Profitable*. There is no evidence, however, that he was a traveller in any practical sense, because his book was a straight imitation of T. Zwinger's *Methodus apodemica* of 1577, and seems to reflect a literary pretension rather than a career in trade or seafaring. His father died in 1559, at which point Thomas, being under age, was placed in the wardship of one John Muschamp. As he inherited Wingham on coming of age in 1562, it may be deduced that he was born in 1540 or 1541. There were several Thomas Palmers active at about that time, including his cousin of Angmering and the scholar of St John's College, Oxford, who in 1563 became principal of Gloucester Hall. The latter was a strong Catholic, who was forced to resign in 1564. It may (or may not) have been Thomas of Wingham who was enrolled as a student at Gray's Inn in 1562; but it was certainly he who in the same year married Margaret (1539/40–1625), the daughter of John Poley of Badley, Suffolk, with whom he had six sons and five daughters; two sons, including James *Palmer, and an unknown number of daughters survived him.

Palmer became a justice of the peace in 1577, at the mature age of about thirty-six, and was continuously active in that capacity until shortly before his death. He was member of parliament for Arundel in 1586 and 1601, and sheriff of Kent in 1595–6, all of which suggests a prominent rather than a distinguished career. He also enjoyed a great reputation for generous hospitality over more than sixty years. He was knighted by James I in 1603, became a gentleman of the privy chamber to the king, and a baronet in 1621. Probably he was wealthy and well established, but if he had any previous court connections, it is not known what they were. It is unlikely that the Thomas Palmer who served with the army at St Jean de Luz in 1590 was the same man, because another person of that name was also knighted during the Cadiz expedition of 1596, and was clearly a soldier. Sir Thomas died at Wingham on 2 January 1626, his wife having predeceased him by about four months; they were both aged eighty-five. He appears to have been buried in the parish church of Wingham, but no monument survives. His second son, Sir Roger, became master of the household to Charles I. DAVID LOADES

Sources *CSP dom.*, *1558–1603* • HoP, *Commons*, *1558–1603* • GEC, *Peerage* • M. Zell, 'Kent's Elizabethan JPs at work', *Archaeologia Cantiana*, 119 (1999), 1–43 • E. Hasted, *The history and topographical survey of the county of Kent*, 4 vols. (1778–99)

Palmer, Thomas (*b.* **1611/12**, *d.* in or after **1667**), Fifth Monarchist preacher and conspirator, was an elder son of Robert Palmer, clergyman, of Shepshed, Leicestershire. On 1 July 1631, aged nineteen, he and his younger brother Robert matriculated from St Edmund Hall, Oxford; Thomas graduated BA in 1635. He is said to have served in the parliamentarian army during the early years of the civil war as a major in John Lambert's regiment. By July 1644 he was chaplain to Serjeant-Major-General Philip Skippon's regiment of foot in the earl of Essex's army, having succeeded William Erbury. The following November he was appointed curate of the London parish of St Laurence Pountney, where he remained until April 1646, when he was installed as rector of Aston-on-Trent, Derbyshire. By 1646 he had married Joyce Powell of St Albans, who gave birth to their daughter Martha on 7 September that year.

Palmer's publication in 1644 of *The Saints Support in these Sad Times* revealed that millenarian views had become central to his theological outlook. His preface dedicated to the earl of Essex, the parliamentarian general, remarked how 'God hath graced you with his Name, Lord of Hosts, Generall of Armies' and 'hath called forth your Excellency as a choise worthy to be his Generall, and the Champion of Jesus Christ to fight the great and last Battle with Antichrist in this your Native Kingdom' (sig. A2*r*). Palmer's religious enthusiasm became more extreme as a consequence of the civil chaos of the late 1640s and during the 1650s he became a Fifth Monarchist, functioning as an itinerant evangelist throughout the east midlands and London. In 1658 he communicated to congregations in Derbyshire and Nottinghamshire the articles agreed upon by Independent ministers at Oxford. In July of that year he was prosecuted at Lincoln assizes for refusing the sacrament to a number of his Aston parishioners. His 1659 publication *A Little View of this Old World* stated that he was serving as a 'Pastor of a church of Christ in Nottingham' during the latter 1650s alongside his duties at Aston. This was almost certainly the Independent congregation that met in the town. His Nottinghamshire connections also allowed him to develop close links with, and to attain considerable influence upon, a Fifth Monarchist group at Skegby in the county.

At the Restoration Palmer was ejected from his living at Aston and his radical views and increasing involvement in Fifth Monarchist activities meant that the nervous authorities had him closely monitored. In November 1661 he was said to be holding meetings at the home of a rich brewer in Limehouse. A Colonel Colepepper, who threatened to hang Palmer on the spot because of his radical views, arrested him at Egerton, Kent, in 1662. Though spared this summary execution, he was incarcerated at Canterbury for a time. Early in 1663 he was living in Rope Alley in Little Moorfields, London, being identified by the authorities as a person of dangerous opinions. Palmer was imprisoned at Nottingham in June 1663 for preaching illegally at a conventicle. More seriously he was implicated in the Farnley Wood plot of that year, having undertaken to raise a troop of horse to meet at Nottingham on 12 October. He managed to avoid arrest and escaped back to London, and was described as ‘a tall man, flaxen hair'd and to be between 40 and 50 years of age’ in the king's proclamation for his apprehension (Wood, *Ath. Oxon.*, 3.1194). In 1666 he travelled to Ireland with Thomas Blood to organize Fifth Monarchist activities. In the following year he published *The Saints Freedom from Tyranny Vindicated* in which he examined ‘The Power of Pagan *Caesars*, and Antichristian Kings’ and demonstrated that they were ‘Condemned by the Prophets and Apostles, as no Magistrates of God to be obeyed by Saints for the Lords sake’ (title-page). Palmer subsequently disappears from surviving records and the place and date of his death are unknown.

STUART B. JENNINGS

Sources *Calamy rev.* • *CSP dom.*, 1663–4, 635, 663 • B. S. Capp, *The Fifth Monarchy Men: a study in seventeenth-century English millenarianism* (1972) • M. B. Endy, ‘Palmer, Thomas’, Greaves & Zaller, *BDBR*, 3.4 • *DNB* • A. R. Henderson, *The history of Castle Gate Congregational Church, Nottingham, 1655–1905* (1905) • Wood, *Ath. Oxon.*, new edn, 3.1194 • Foster, *Alum. Oxon.* • A. Laurence, *Parliamentary army chaplains, 1642–1651* (1990)

Palmer, Thomas Fyshe (1747–1802), Unitarian minister and radical, was born at Ickwell, Bedfordshire, in July 1747, the son of Henry Fyshe and his wife, Elizabeth Ingram. His mother belonged to the Palmer family of Nazeing Park, Essex. His father, who was the representative of the family of Fyshe of Essex, assumed the additional name of Palmer in order to ensure an inheritance.

Having received his elementary education under the Revd Henry Gunning at Ely, Palmer was sent to Eton College (1762), and thence to Cambridge, entering Queens' College in 1765 with the purpose of taking orders in the Church of England. He graduated BA in 1769, MA in 1772, and BD in 1781. He obtained a fellowship of Queens' in 1781, and officiated for a year as curate of Leatherhead, Surrey. While at Leatherhead he was introduced to Dr Johnson, and dined with him in London; according to Boswell they discussed the inadequate remuneration of the poorer clergy. About this time the writings of Joseph Priestley of Birmingham, advocating progressive Unitarianism, so powerfully influenced Palmer that he decided to abandon the Church of England and to renounce the brilliant prospects of preferment that were open to him.

A Unitarian society had been founded by William Christie, merchant, at Montrose, and Palmer offered his services as a preacher (14 July 1783). In November 1783 Palmer reached Montrose, and remained as Christie's colleague until May 1785. At that date he moved to Dundee to become pastor of a new Unitarian congregation there. At the same time he preached frequently in Edinburgh, Glasgow, Arbroath, and Forfar, and formed Unitarian societies in all these places. In 1789 Palmer took temporary charge of the society at Newcastle. He contributed regularly to the *Theological Repository* (1789–90) under the signature of Anglo-Scotus. In 1792 his sermons in Edinburgh attracted the attention of literary circles, and several pamphlets were published in refutation of his doctrines, such as Alexander Pirie's *An attempt to expose the weakness … of the Unitarian … arguments … a reply to a pamphlet … by T. F. Palmer* (1792).

When the agitation for political reform began in 1792, Dundee became one of its chief centres in Scotland. A society called the Friends of Liberty was formed in 1793, and met in the Berean meeting-house in the Methodist Close, beside the house where Palmer lived in the Overgait. The society was composed mainly of artisans. One evening in June 1793 Palmer was induced to attend a meeting, at which George Mealmaker, a Dundee weaver, brought up the draft of an address to the public which he purposed circulating as a handbill. Mealmaker's grammar was defective and Palmer revised it, modifying some strong expressions. When it left his hands it was no more than a complaint against the government for the extravagant war taxation in which the country had been involved, and a claim for universal suffrage and short parliaments. The address was sent to be printed in Edinburgh in July 1793.

The authorities were unduly alarmed, however, and, worried by events in France, interpreted the dissemination of this and similar documents as the beginning of a new campaign of subversion. They determined to meet the anticipated revolution in time, and, in the belief that they were attacking a revolutionary leader, Palmer was arrested in Edinburgh on 2 August on a charge of sedition as the author of the document. At the preliminary legal inquiry he refused to answer the questions put to him, pleading his ignorance of Scots law. He was confined in Edinburgh gaol, but afterwards liberated on bail. An indictment was served upon him directing him to appear at the circuit court, Perth, on 12 September to answer to the charge of treason. The presiding judges were Lord Eskgrove (Rae) and Alexander, Lord Abercromby; the prosecutor was John Burnett, advocate-depute, assisted by Allan Maconochie (afterwards Lord Meadowbank), and Palmer was defended by John Clerk (afterwards Lord Eldin) and John Haggart. A number of preliminary objections to the indictment were offered, one of these being founded on the spelling of his name ‘Fische’ instead of ‘Fyshe’, but these were all rejected.

One of the first witnesses was George Mealmaker, who admitted that he was the author of the address, and stated that Palmer was opposed to its publication. Other officials of the Friends of Liberty corroborated this testimony, and the evidence proved nothing relevant to the charge beyond the fact that Palmer had ordered 1000 copies to be printed, but had given no instructions as to distribution. Both the judges summed up adversely, and, when the jury found the accused guilty, he was sentenced to seven years' transportation. The conviction of Palmer, following so close upon that of Thomas *Muir, raised a storm of indignation among whigs and other reformers throughout the kingdom. During February and March 1794 repeated attempts were made by the earl of Lauderdale and Earl Stanhope in the House of Lords, and by Charles James Fox and R. B. Sheridan in the House of Commons, to obtain the reversal of the sentence; but these efforts were unavailing.

Palmer was detained in Perth Tolbooth for three months, and was thence taken to London and placed on the hulk *Stanislaus* at Woolwich, where he was put in irons and forced to labour for three months with convicted felons. On 11 February 1794 he, William Skirving and Thomas Muir—all three numbered among the reformers known as the 'Scottish martyrs'—were sent on board the *Surprise* with a gang of convicts to Botany Bay. Their embarkation took place at this date in order to forestall the debate on their case in the House of Commons, though the vessel did not leave Britain until the end of April. The sufferings they endured on the passage and the indignities put upon them were fully detailed in the account which Palmer wrote after landing and published in 1797 (*A Narrative of the Sufferings of T. F. Palmer and W. Skirving*). Their difficulties were exacerbated by divisions among the prisoners themselves and by allegations of incitement to mutiny levelled against Palmer.

The vessel arrived at Port Jackson, New South Wales, on 25 October, and as Palmer and his companions had letters of introduction to the governor, they were well treated, and had contiguous houses assigned to them. In two letters dated June 1795 and August 1797 Palmer wrote enthusiastically of the climate and natural advantages of the infant colony, which had been founded in 1788.

> I have no scruple in saying it is the finest country I ever saw. An honest and active governor might soon make it a region of plenty. In spite of all possible rapacity and robbery (on the part of the officials), I am clear that it will thrive against every obstacle. (Palmer to John Disney, 14 Aug 1797, *Monthly Repository*, 12.264)

Besides cultivating the land, the exiled reformers constructed a small vessel and traded to Norfolk Island, establishing a dangerous but lucrative business. At the close of 1799 Palmer and his friend James Ellis—who had followed him from Dundee as a colonist and who became his legatee—combined with others to purchase a vessel in which they might return home, as Palmer's sentence expired in September 1800. They intended to trade on the homeward way, and provisioned the vessel for six months; but their hopes of securing cargo in New Zealand were disappointed, and they were detained off that coast for twenty-six weeks. They sailed to Tongatabu and then to the Fiji Islands, where they were well received.

Having refitted their ship, they started for Macao, then almost the only Chinese port open to foreign traffic. Adverse storms drove them about the Pacific until their provisions were exhausted, and they were compelled to put in to Guguan, one of the Ladrone Islands, then under Spanish rule, though they knew that Spain and Britain were at war. The Spanish governor treated them as prisoners of war. At length Palmer was attacked with dysentery, a disease that had first afflicted him during his confinement in the hulks, and, as he had no medicines with him, his condition rapidly deteriorated. He died on 2 June 1802 at Guguan and was buried by the seashore. Two years afterwards an American captain touched at Guguan and, having ascertained where Palmer had been buried, he caused the body to be exhumed and conveyed on board his vessel, with the governor's permission. The remains were taken to Boston, Massachusetts, where Palmer was reinterred. A monument was erected in the Calton burying-ground, Edinburgh, in 1844 to commemorate Palmer, Muir, and their fellow martyrs in the cause of reform. Palmer himself became a symbolic embodiment of the campaign for religious and political 'liberty', although his cause was very much a minority one.

A. H. MILLAR, *rev.* G. M. DITCHFIELD

Sources T. F. Palmer, *A narrative of the sufferings of T. F. Palmer and W. Skirving, during a voyage to New South Wales, 1794* (1797) • G. S. Veitch, *The genesis of parliamentary reform*, new edn (1965) • C. Bewley, *Muir of Huntershill* (1981) • W. Turner, *Lives of eminent Unitarians*, 1 (1840), 214–38 • G. Thompson, *Slavery and famine … and a sketch of the character of Thomas Fyshe Palmer, by George Dyer*, 2nd edn (1794) • *The trial of the Revd. Thomas Fyshe Palmer, before the circuit court of judiciary held at Perth, on the 12th and 13th September, on an indictment for seditious treatment* (1793) • *State trials*, vol. 23 • H. Cockburn, *An examination of the trials for sedition … in Scotland*, 2 vols. (1888) • M. Masson, 'Thomas Fyshe Palmer, a political exile, 1793', *SHR*, 13 (1915–16), 159–67 • W. L. Mathieson, *The awakening of Scotland: a history from 1747 to 1797* (1910) • H. W. Meikle, *Scotland and the French Revolution* (1912) • J. A. Hone, *For the cause of truth: radicalism in London, 1796–1821* (1982) • W. Christie, 'Account of Mr William Christie, written by himself [pt 1]', *Monthly Repository*, 6 (1811), 129–38, esp. 135–6 • 'Letters from Thomas Muir and the Rev. Thomas Fyshe Palmer', *Monthly Repository*, 12 (1817), 261–7 • *AusDB* • PRO, PROB 11/1403, fols. 424–5

Archives BL, Add. MS 37873 • Harris Man. Oxf. | DWL, letters to J. Johnson • DWL, corresp. with Robert Millar • DWL, corresp. with James Purves • DWL, letters to J. T. Rutt • Harris Man. Oxf., letters to William Shepherd

Likenesses J. Kay, caricature, etching, BM; repro. in Bewley, *Muir of Huntershill*

Wealth at death approx. £200; plus personal effects: will, 2 Jan 1804, PRO, PROB 11/1403, fols. 424–5

Palmer, William (1538/9–1605), Church of England clergyman, was born in Nottinghamshire and educated at Cambridge University, graduating BA in 1560 from Pembroke College and MA from St John's College in 1563, subsequently proceeding to the degrees of BTh in 1571 and DTh in 1598. Very briefly a fellow of Pembroke in 1560 and then of St John's, he served as university preacher in 1565, and after his ordination in 1560 was vicar of Trumpington from 1564 to 1567. He owed his advancement in the church largely to Edmund Grindal, who as bishop of London made him one of his chaplains in 1563, and in 1565 gave him the prebend of Mora in St Paul's Cathedral, which he held until 1574. In December 1566 he acquired the city living of St Lawrence Jewry, which he resigned in 1570, having been preferred to that of St Michael Bassishaw the previous year by the dean and chapter of St Paul's. It seems likely that he married Anna Taylor, the daughter of the Marian martyr Dr Rowland Taylor, during his London ministry: they had seven children.

Palmer's career took a new direction on Grindal's elevation to the see of York in 1570. On 17 June of that year the new archbishop appointed him to the prebend of Riccall, which he resigned in 1573 after his promotion in 1571 to chancellor of York Minster. In 1570 he obtained the Yorkshire rectory of Kirk Deighton, which he exchanged for that of Wheldrake in 1577. Lastly in 1575 he secured the prebend of Norwell Palishall in Southwell Minster.

By attracting highly educated ministers to the north,

Grindal intended both to promote protestantism and combat Catholicism. Palmer soon gained a reputation for his evangelical sermons, relished by protestants like the countess of Huntingdon (who in 1575 invited him to preach at a cousin's wedding), but resented by Catholics and Catholic sympathizers like the mayor of York, Robert Cripling, who in 1579 caused a disturbance in the minster by railing against the chancellor's teachings.

The council in the north and the northern high commission repeatedly called upon Palmer to confer with Catholic prisoners. In 1572 he attended the earl of Northumberland before his execution but failed to convert him to the protestant faith, and he suffered a similar rebuff in a disputation in March 1583 with the Jesuit William Hart. From his arrival in York he regularly participated in sessions of the high commission.

Palmer also assiduously attended chapter meetings, in 1576 deputizing for Sandys at his installation as archbishop, and in 1586 reporting on the actions of the northern convocation jointly with the dean, Matthew Hutton. Together with the bishops and many other cathedral clergy he was named on the commission to suppress schism in 1599. In the spring of 1605 the York chancery court required clergy unwilling to subscribe the canons of 1604 to resort to Palmer, 'a great, ancient and learned preacher', to resolve their scruples (Borthwick Institute Chanc. AB 14, fol. 373*v*).

Active in the chapter until a week before his death, Palmer died at York on 23 October 1605, aged sixty-six, and was buried in the south choir aisle of the minster, where there is a mural tablet to his memory. Notes survive of a sermon preached by Palmer on 1 Corinthians 10: 1–2 at Paul's Cross on 11 August 1566 (Bodl. Oxf., MS Tanner 50).

CLAIRE CROSS

Sources York Minster Library, H 4, fols. 81*r*–390*r* • Borth. Inst., HC AB 7, HC AB 8, HC AB 9, HC AB 10, HC AB 11, HC AB 12, HC AB 13, HC AB 14, Chanc. AB 14 • Borth. Inst., PR Whel. 1, p. 30 • Venn, *Alum. Cant.*, 1/3.302 • F. Drake, *Eboracum, or, The history and antiquities of the city of York* (1736), 508 • *The correspondence of Dr Matthew Hutton, archbishop of York*, ed. [J. Raine], SurtS, 17 (1843), 56, 57, 65–6 • [J. Gibbons and J. Fenn], *Concertatio ecclesiae catholicae in Anglia adversus Calvinopapistas et puritanos*, 2nd edn (1588), 45–9, 106*v* • J. Morris, ed., *The troubles of our Catholic forefathers related by themselves*, 3 (1877), 214–5 • *Diary of Lady Margaret Hoby*, ed. D. M. Meads (1930), 73 • J. Strype, *Ecclesiastical memorials*, 3 vols. (1822), 279 • J. Strype, *The life and acts of John Whitgift*, new edn, 3 vols. (1822), vol. 1, p. 499 • J. Strype, *Annals of the Reformation and establishment of religion … during Queen Elizabeth's happy reign*, new edn, 2/2 (1824), 42 • Rymer, *Foedera*, 2nd edn, 16.386–94 • R. Marchant, *The puritans and the church courts in the diocese of York, 1560–1642* (1960), 149 • C. Cross, *The puritan earl: the life of Henry Hastings, third earl of Huntingdon* (1966), 228, 232 • G. E. Aylmer and R. Cant, eds., *A history of York Minster* (1977), 218, 229 • J. C. H. Aveling, *Catholic recusancy in the city of York, 1558–1791*, Catholic RS, monograph ser., 2 (1970), 49 • P. Collinson, *Archbishop Grindal, 1519–1583: the struggle for a reformed church* (1979) • *Fasti Angl., 1541–1857*, [York], 8, 53

Archives Borth. Inst., evidence for Palmer's activity in the High Commission 1573–1603 (and doubtless till his death in 1605, but there is a break in the High Commission act books March 1603–1607), HC AB 7, HC AB 8, HC AB 9, HC AB 10, HC AB 11, HC AB 12, HC AB 13, HC AB 14; chanc. AB 14, fol. 373*v* • Borth. Inst., PR Whel. 1, p. 30 • York Minster Library, evidence for Palmer's activity in the York Chapter 1571–1605, H 4, fols. 81*r*–390*r*

Wealth at death over £200 p.a., incl. £85 as chancellor, *c.*£100 as residentiary canon, plus stipend as rector of Kirk Deighton, then of Wheldrake: Aylmer and Cant, eds., *History of York Minster*, 229

Palmer, William (1740–1816), army officer in the East India Company and diplomatist, was the son of Samuel Palmer of Holborn Yard, London, and his wife, Frances. He joined the British army, serving in the West Indies where in St Kitts in 1761 he married Sarah Hazell. In 1765 he left the army for the East India Company service, being posted to Bengal as a cadet. In 1774 he became aide-de-camp to the governor-general, Warren Hastings, who made him his military secretary in 1776. Hastings came to have great confidence in Palmer's ability to act as his agent with Indian rulers, and Palmer in return became a devoted admirer of the governor-general. As he put it, 'I love, I revere Mr Hastings' (Palmer to D. Anderson, 12 Feb 1782, BL, Add. MS 45427, fol. 86). Hastings sent him on missions to the court of the wazir of Oudh at Lucknow.

When Hastings left India in 1785 Palmer's career became more chequered. He spent ten years (1787–97) as the company's agent with the Maratha leader Sindhia, and in 1798 took up his most important diplomatic post, as resident at Poona with the peshwa, the titular head of the Maratha confederacy. He despised the peshwa's politics but refused to deviate from a policy of 'argument, persuasion and conciliation' with him (Palmer to W. Hastings, 10 July 1801, BL, Add. MS 29178, fol. 63), which he knew was unacceptable to the forceful governor-general, the Marquess Wellesley, who recalled Palmer from Poona in 1801.

Palmer's wife had borne three sons, Samuel (1762–1814), William George (1764–1814), and John [*see below*], and two daughters, before he went to India. She remained at home, never to see her husband again, but after their schooling the boys were sent to join their father in India, where he had started a new family with a Muslim lady of distinguished lineage, Faizh Baksh (*d.* 1828), granted the title of begam in 1796. In his will Palmer was to describe her as 'my affectionate friend and companion during a period of more than 35 years' (BL OIOC, L/AG/34/29/28). With Faizh Baksh he had four illegitimate sons, William [*see below*], Hastings (1785–1860), Charles and John (both born in 1791), and two daughters, Mary (*b.* 1783) and Frances (*b.* 1792). Palmer and the begam and three of the children were strikingly depicted by Johan Zoffany in a group portrait of 1785. Palmer seems to have made no distinction between his legitimate and his illegitimate children, sending the sons to be educated in Britain.

The Poona residency was the last of Palmer's diplomatic postings. He stayed in India in the army, rising to the rank of lieutenant-general by the time of his death at Berhampore in Bengal on 20 May 1816. He was buried at Berhampore.

John Palmer (1767–1836), merchant, was born in Britain on 8 October 1767, just before his father left for India. He joined the navy, fighting in Indian waters in the American War of Independence. In 1784 he went to Bengal and was employed in one of the new private concerns called agency houses. With the decline of the East India

Company's commercial activities, these businesses enjoyed a spectacular if febrile prosperity, managing funds entrusted to them by British and Indian clients and investing them in shipping and new export crops, above all in indigo. Palmer entered the house of Burgh and Barber, becoming a partner in 1793. In 1803 he became a partner in the well-established business of Cockerell, Trail, which was known as Palmer & Co. from 1810. For nearly twenty years the Palmer house was to hold a dominant position in the Calcutta business world.

In the years of his prosperity John Palmer had an honoured place in Calcutta society. He married Mary, daughter of Colonel Samuel Hampton, in 1791; they had five sons and seven daughters. As befitted a man dubbed 'the prince of merchants', he lived in a great house, where he dispensed extravagant hospitality and a range of charitable giving which contemporaries feared went beyond even his extensive means. He was public-spirited and liberal in his opinions, supporting the freedom of the press and the rights of people of mixed race as well as forming close friendships with Indian businessmen.

In the late 1820s the house of Palmer was beset with difficulties that were to force it into insolvency on 4 January 1830, inflicting losses on a large body of investors and starting the slide that was to drag down the rest of the great agency houses. Palmer later reflected that his 'Hopes of Utility and Distinction' had 'seduced me into Gigantic Engagements, I wanted moral, phisical [*sic*] and financial Force to sustain' (J. Palmer to M. Palmer, 5 April 1833, Bodl. Oxf., MS Eng. lett. d 107, fol. 52). In particular, the house was over-committed to indigo on a falling market. Palmer resumed a limited agency business in 1833, dying of 'quinzy' on 21 January 1836. 'The Friend of the Poor' was inscribed on his tomb in North Park Street cemetery, Calcutta.

William Palmer (1780–1867), banker, was John Palmer's half-brother. He was born in Calcutta, and baptized there on 20 March 1780. Although as a person of mixed race he was officially classified as a 'native of India', he insisted that his 'feelings, his education, his habits, his descent from his father are all peculiarly English' (*Memorial of William Palmer*, 32). He sought his fortune in Hyderabad, the largest of all the nominally independent Indian states tied to the East India Company by treaty. In the early nineteenth century, states where the British exercised influence without formal control were happy hunting grounds for enterprising individuals. In 1799 William Palmer became an officer in the nizam's army, fought in several campaigns, and was ultimately granted the rank of brigadier. In 1810 he established a trading and banking business. To meet his commitments, including heavy obligations to the British, the nizam was obliged to borrow extensively. With the encouragement of his half-brother John in Calcutta, William Palmer's company advanced money to the nizam, sometimes at 25 per cent or more, in return for assignments on the Hyderabad revenues. To protect these transactions Palmer made the resident at Hyderabad a beneficiary of them, and even succeeded in involving the governor-general, the marquess of Hastings, through making a protégé of his a partner. In 1820, however, a new resident, Charles Metcalfe, began a campaign to reform the nizam's government, which, in his view, required an end to William Palmer's profiteering and to his influence at Hyderabad.

The Palmer Company's outstanding loans were paid off by the East India Company, but interest was reduced and

William Palmer (1740–1816), by Johan Zoffany, 1785 [centre, with: (left) Faizh Baksh and their children Mary, Hastings (on his mother's knee), and William Palmer; (right) a figure thought to be the sister of Faizh Baksh; and three attendants]

various claims were disallowed. As a result the business was declared bankrupt in 1824. Some money was recovered through pressure on the nizam's government and this, together with a pension from the nizam, enabled William Palmer to continue to live in Hyderabad in some prosperity. He had a number of children, apparently by more than one Muslim lady, most of the sons being commissioned into the company's army. One of his sons-in-law described him as having 'a fascination about him quite irresistible to me, his knowledge was so varied, classical, historical and political' (Taylor, 1.97). Even Metcalfe paid tribute to his amiability. In 1848 he married Hester Desormeaux (1811–1877), widow of a surgeon at Hyderabad, who supported him in the 'difficulties and distress' that afflicted his old age (Crofton, 18–19). He died on 20 May 1867 at Hyderabad, where he had lived for some seventy years, and was buried in St George's cemetery, Chandraghat, Hyderabad. P. J. MARSHALL

Sources 'Pedigree of General Palmer', BL OIOC, MS Eur. G 0124 · William Prinsep's memoir, BL OIOC, MS Eur. D 1160 · *The Bengal obituary, or, A record to perpetuate the memory of departed worth*, Holmes & Co. (1848) · will and inventory of General William Palmer, BL OIOC, L/AG/34/29/28, L/AG/34/27/59 · P. Wood, 'A vassal state in the shadow of empire: William Palmer's bank in Hyderabad, 1799–1867', PhD diss., University of Wisconsin, 1981 · *The memorial of William Palmer of Hyderabad* (c.1824) · BL, Warren Hastings MSS, Add. MSS 28973–29236 · BL, David Anderson MSS, Add. MS 45427 · J. Sarkar, ed., *English records of Maratha history: Poona residency correspondence*, 6: *Poona affairs, 1797–1801: Palmer's embassy*, ed. G. S. Sardesai (1939) · John Palmer MSS, Bodl. Oxf., MS Eng lett. d. 107 · V. C. P. Hodson, *List of officers of the Bengal army, 1758–1834*, 4 vols. (1927–47) · S. B. Singh, *European agency houses in Bengal* (1966) · M. Archer, *India and British portraiture, 1770–1825* (1979) · Z. Yazdani, *Hyderabad during the residency of Henry Russell, 1811–20* (1976) · M. Taylor, *The story of my life*, ed. A. M. Taylor, 2 vols. (1877) · O. S. Crofton, *List of inscriptions on tombs or monuments in HEH the nizam's dominions* (1941) · BL OIOC, N/1/2, fol. 439 [William Palmer (1780–1867)] · private information (2004) [W. Dalrymple]

Archives BL, David Anderson MSS, Add. MS 45427 · BL, Warren Hastings MSS · Bodl. Oxf., John Palmer MSS, MSS Eng Letts c. 67–127, d. 105–107; Eng hist c. 301–302 · Bodl. Oxf., Russell MSS, MS Eng Letts c. 148–180, d. 149–164

Likenesses J. Zoffany, group portrait, 1785, BL OIOC [*see illus.*]

Wealth at death Rs 5000 left to his son as executor; house left to the begam: inventory, BL OIOC, L/AG/34/27/59 · any assets likely to have been owed to creditors of Palmer Company - John Palmer: BL OIOC · died in distressed circumstances - William Palmer: Crofton, *List of inscriptions*, 18–19

Palmer, William (1780–1867). *See under* Palmer, William (1740–1816).

Palmer, William (1802–1858), lawyer and jurist, was born on 9 October 1802, the second son of George *Palmer (1772–1853) of Nazeing Park, Essex, MP for the southern division of that county from 1836 to 1847, and Anna Maria, daughter of William Bund of Wick Episcopi, Worcestershire. He matriculated at St Mary Hall, Oxford, on 16 February 1822, graduated BA in 1825, and proceeded MA in 1828. On 14 May 1830 he was called to the bar at the Inner Temple, where he gained a large practice as a conveyancer. In 1836 he was appointed to the professorship of civil law at Gresham College, which he held for the rest of his life. He was the author of four works, two of which dealt with navigation law. His publication of *Principles of the Legal Provision for the Relief of the Poor* (1844) no doubt gave rise to his contemporary reputation for philanthropy. Palmer never married; he died in London, at his home, 56 Eaton Place, on 24 April 1858.

J. M. RIGG, *rev.* JOANNE POTIER

Sources *GM*, 3rd ser., 4 (1858), 679 · *GM*, 2nd ser., 20 (1843), 181 · *The Guardian* (28 April 1858) · Foster, *Alum. Oxon.* · Boase, *Mod. Eng. biog.* · Allibone, *Dict.*

Wealth at death under £12,000: resworn probate, Feb 1861, *CGPLA Eng. & Wales* (1858)

Palmer, William (1811–1879), theologian and ecumenist, was born on 12 July 1811, at the rectory, Mixbury, Oxfordshire, the eldest son of William Jocelyn Palmer (1778–1853), rector of Mixbury, and Dorothea Richardson (*d.* 1867), daughter of the Revd William Roundell of Gledstone, Yorkshire. Initially he was educated at home, then sent to Rugby School in 1823, together with his younger brother Roundell *Palmer, later first earl of Selborne (1812–1895). William Palmer matriculated at Oxford on 27 July 1826, and was soon elected to a demyship at Magdalen College (a post he held until 1832). His proficiency in Latin gained him the chancellor's prize in 1830 for his poem 'Tyrus', and the university essay prize in 1833 for his 'Oratio de comoedia Atticorum'. He obtained first-class honours in classics, and graduated BA on 17 February 1831; in 1832 he was elected to a fellowship at Magdalen, a position he held until 1855. From 1834 (when he proceeded MA) until 1836 Palmer served as the first classical tutor at the newly founded University of Durham, after which he returned to Oxford where, on 8 December 1836, he was ordained deacon. He was also appointed bursar of his college in 1836, and served as a university examiner in *literae humaniores* from 1837 to 1839. From 1838 to 1843 he was a tutor at Magdalen, and held the offices of prelector of moral philosophy (1842) and vice-president (1844). He is not to be confused with his contemporary William Palmer (1803–1885), theologian, of Worcester College, Oxford.

Palmer was best known for the controversial visits he made to Russia in the 1840s and 1850s, and for the contacts he made there with both ecclesiastical and lay officials. As an adherent of the Oxford Movement, to which he was drawn by the personality of John Henry Newman, he came to appreciate and advocate high-Anglican claims for the catholicity of the Church of England; this theological stance aroused in him an intense desire for intercommunion, particularly with the Orthodox church. He was also inspired by meeting various Orthodox Christians, both in Oxford and on the continent, including the Russian tsarevich (later Alexander II) in 1839. Finally he initiated plans for a visit to Russia, lasting from August 1840 to July 1841; the expedition was sanctioned by the president of Magdalen, Martin Routh (1755–1854), but it did not have the official approval of the archbishop of Canterbury. Undaunted, and carrying letters of introduction from both Routh and Lord Clanricarde, the British ambassador to the Russian court, Palmer embarked on his journey.

Palmer arrived in St Petersburg with the intention of studying Orthodox theology and ritual, and thereafter being admitted to communion in the Russian church. He quickly realized, however, that his hosts did not sympathize with his views; indeed they met his claim to be a member of the Catholic (that is, universal) church with astonishment. In response to his desire for communicant status, he was told that he must submit absolutely to Orthodox doctrine and practice. In addition, the Russians were unsure whether Palmer could be regarded as an authentic representative and interpreter of Anglican teaching. Confronted with such an absolute rejection of all he had proposed, Palmer had no choice but to return to England, with his visit being judged—on an official level—as an utter failure.

On a personal level, however, Palmer did promote Anglican–Orthodox relations. He had the opportunity to converse with some of the major Russian ecclesiastics of the time (initially through the medium of French or Latin, and later in Russian), and introduced them to current theological debates in England. Some, like Count Protasov, chief procurator of the Holy Governing Synod, were unsympathetic; others listened more intently, but could still not concur with his theological stance. Among them was the under-procurator, Andrey Nikolayevich Muravyov (1806–1874), whose *History of the Church in Russia* Palmer edited and published in 1842; while Muravyov understood Palmer's motivations, he nevertheless believed that Anglo-Catholicism would find a better ally in Rome than in the East. Another enlightened contact was Metropolitan Filaret of Moscow (1782–1867), an influential, independently minded churchman who was deeply interested in Orthodox relations with the West. While Filaret treated Palmer with seriousness and respect, he too could not accede to his requests, because of doubts about his official status.

Palmer's most fruitful contact was with Aleksey Stepanovich Khomyakov (1804–1860), founder of the Slavophil school, whose members were openly critical of what they saw as the overly institutionalized nature of the Russian Orthodox church. Khomyakov approved of Palmer's desire for intercommunion, but, as a layman, could offer little practical assistance. Nevertheless he proved a willing correspondent over many years (1844–54), and instigated a widened range of contacts between the Church of England and the Orthodox. For his part Palmer assisted Khomyakov by publishing a number of Slavophil tracts in Britain. Their correspondence was eventually published by W. J. Birkbeck in 1895 as *Russia and the English Church during the Last Fifty Years*.

Palmer returned to Russia in 1842 with better credentials and a strengthened desire for intercommunion. The Russian synod again refused to negotiate on his terms, but welcomed his desire to take Orthodox communion, should his faith be considered acceptable. With a view to achieving this goal, he entered into a prolonged attempt to demonstrate Anglican–Orthodox doctrinal agreement, the conclusions of which were eventually published anonymously as *A harmony of Anglican doctrine with the doctrine of the Catholic and Apostolic church of the East* (English edn, 1846; Greek edn, 1851). Palmer feared that his ideas would not be accepted by the Church of England hierarchy, and he therefore made overtures to the Scottish Episcopal church, in the hope that its synod might officially sanction his doctrinal assertions; he outlined these meticulously in *An Appeal to the Scottish Bishops and Clergy, and Generally to the Church of their Communion* (1849). When the synod met in September 1849 the appeal was dismissed, leaving Palmer in a state of disbelief.

In 1853, after several years of indecision, Palmer decided to seek admission to the Orthodox church—this time to its Greek branch; however he again experienced resistance, on account of his refusal to undergo an unconditional rebaptism (a requirement not imposed earlier by the Russians). Feeling exasperated with what he considered the failings of both Anglicanism and Orthodoxy, Palmer finally made the decision to convert to Roman Catholicism. After a period of retreat in Rome during January and February 1855 he was received into the Roman church on 28 February of that year. For the rest of his life he remained a devout Catholic, dividing his time between England and Italy, with occasional trips to Russia. When in Rome (where he usually spent the winter) he resided in the piazza Campitelli, undertaking extensive research in ecclesiastical history and archaeology, and publishing such works as *An Introduction to Early Christian Symbolism* (1859), *Egyptian Chronicles* (1861), and *The Patriarch and the Tsar* (1871–6). After succumbing to a violent cold in the spring of 1879 he contracted a lung infection, and died on 5 April 1879 at piazza Campitelli 3. He was buried in the cemetery of San Lorenzo in campo Verano on 8 April.

Throughout his life Palmer was renowned as a trenchant controversialist. To many of his contemporaries his theological views, private ventures, and overpowering desire for intercommunion might have seemed singular, even misdirected; but his sustained contacts with the Orthodox church—particularly his lengthy correspondence with Khomyakov—provided a firm basis for subsequent ecumenical advances. The significance of his endeavours was confirmed posthumously by his literary executor, John Henry Newman, who edited and published Palmer's *Notes of a Visit to the Russian Church in the Years 1840, 1841*, in 1882. LEON LITVACK

Sources W. Palmer, *Notes of a visit to the Russian church in the years 1840, 1841*, ed. J. H. Newman (1882) · W. J. Birkbeck, ed., *Russia and the English church during the last fifty years*, 1 (1895) · R. D. Middleton, 'William Palmer', *Magdalen Studies* (1936), 99–124 · P. E. Shaw, *The early Tractarians and the Eastern church* (1930) · L. Litvack, *John Mason Neale and the quest for Sobornost* (1994) · E. C. Miller jr, *Towards a fuller vision: Orthodoxy and the Anglican experience* (1984) · R. Rouse and S. C. Neill, eds., *A history of the ecumenical movement, 1517–1948* (1954) · G. Florovsky, *Aspects of church history* (1975) · Foster, *Alum. Oxon.* · R. Palmer, first earl of Selborne, *Memorials. Part I: family and personal, 1766–1865*, ed. S. M. Palmer, 2 vols. (1896) · *The Times* (12 April 1879) · J. R. Bloxam, *A register of the presidents, fellows … of Saint Mary Magdalen College*, 8 vols. (1853–85), vol. 7, pp. 297–318

Archives Birmingham Oratory, diaries, corresp., notes, and papers · Bodl. Oxf., prize verses and essay · LPL, corresp., journals, and papers | BL, corresp. with W. E. Gladstone, Add. MSS 44359–44527, *passim* · Bodl. Oxf., letters to Edwin Palmer and corresp.

Likenesses J. Brown, lithograph, repro. in Palmer, *Notes*

Wealth at death under £12,000: probate, 12 May 1879, *CGPLA Eng. & Wales*

Palmer, William [*called* the Rugeley Poisoner] (**1824–1856**), poisoner and physician, was born in August or September 1824, at The Yard, Rugeley, Staffordshire, the fourth of five sons and two daughters of Joseph Palmer (1777–1836), a rich timber merchant, and his wife, Sarah Bentley (1793–1861). After attending Rugeley grammar school he was apprenticed to a Liverpool firm of wholesale druggists, from which he was discharged for embezzlement. He was then apprenticed to a surgeon near Rugeley, to whom his sexual and financial irregularities soon became intolerable. Palmer absconded, and next became a pupil at Stafford Infirmary before completing his medical studies at St Bartholomew's Hospital, London. He was admitted a member of the Royal College of Surgeons (1846), and then worked briefly as a house surgeon at St Bartholomew's before entering general practice at Rugeley.

On 7 October 1847 Palmer married Ann (1827–1854), daughter of William Brookes of Stafford, late colonel in the Indian army (who shot himself in 1834), and his housekeeper, Mary Thornton. His bride was a ward in chancery whose guardians opposed the marriage. Palmer and his wife had four sons and one daughter, but Palmer often complained of the expense of raising children, and all except the eldest, William, died of convulsions in infancy between 1851 and 1854, as did two of his illegitimate children, who both perished after visiting him. Palmer's mother-in-law died in 1849 within a fortnight of coming to live at his house, he acquiring property by her demise; Leonard Bladen, to whom Palmer owed £800 for bets, died in 1850 while staying with him. Dark conjectures were raised about these and other deaths at Rugeley.

About 1852 Palmer abandoned his medical practice to devote himself to the turf. He owned and bred racehorses, but was soon obliged to borrow money at punitive rates. Shortly after he had insured his wife's life for £13,000, though he possessed only a life interest in her property worth £3000, she died of 'bilious cholera' on 29 September 1854. Most of the insurance money was promptly used to discharge his most pressing liabilities to moneylenders. At the time of Annie Palmer's death a family maidservant, Eliza Tharm, conceived a child by Palmer. He was also involved in 1855 with a Stafford woman, Jane Burgess, for whom he procured an abortion and by whom he was blackmailed for the return of compromising letters.

Following his wife's death Palmer raised £13,500 from moneylenders by forging the name of his mother as acceptor of new bills. A policy was assigned to Palmer worth £13,000 on the life of his brother Walter, who died in his presence on 16 August 1855. The insurers refused to pay and instituted inquiries into the death (undertaken by the policeman who inspired the character of Inspector Bucket in *Bleak House*). Palmer, who was thus unable to cover the forged bills, in October 1855 tried to insure for £10,000 the life of George Bate, who was his groom at £1 a week. Before this could be settled his needs became more urgent when, on 6 November, a moneylender issued two writs for £4000 against Palmer and his mother, but withheld them from service pending arrangements that Palmer might make. Palmer's problem was to keep meeting portions of the forged bills until his brother's life policy was paid.

On 13 November Palmer attended Shrewsbury races with another betting man, John Parsons Cook, who won heavily. It was later proved that Palmer obtained payment of many of Cook's bets, and applied the money to meeting instalments on the bills. Next evening Cook was taken ill with retching and vomiting while staying at a Shrewsbury hotel with Palmer. Although Cook accused Palmer of putting something in his glass, he nevertheless returned with him to Rugeley, where he took a room in the Talbot Arms opposite Palmer's house (15 November). Palmer is supposed to have tampered with Cook's food and drink, and to have substituted his own concoctions for pills which a local physician prescribed for the continuing illness of Cook, who died after five days of violent tetanic spasms. Cook's stepfather was made suspicious by the corpse's appearance, the disappearance of Cook's betting book, Palmer's conversations on money matters and haste to order a coffin, and by local suspicion of Palmer as a mass murderer. The stepfather insisted on a post mortem, which Palmer tried to sabotage. Its results led to the arrest for murder on 14 December of Palmer, who was already in sheriff's custody for the bills.

A bill was hastily enacted in 1856 enabling offenders to be tried at the central criminal court. This innovation in English criminal procedure was ostensibly because local excitement was so great that it was judged inexpedient to try Palmer in the provinces, but it also facilitated a show trial in London where official resources and public opinion could be more effectively mustered against him. The prosecution's pharmacological argument was weak, the motives attributed for killing Cook were flimsy, and on the evidence Palmer should have been acquitted. The case was won by the overpowering accumulation of circumstantial details brilliantly expounded by an implacable prosecution team aided by a ruthlessly tendentious judge, Lord Chief Justice Campbell. After twelve days' trial Palmer was found guilty on 27 May. He was hanged outside Stafford gaol on 14 June 1856, dying bravely in the presence of 20,000 people, his naked body being buried in unslaked lime within the prison precincts. His horse, the Chicken, on which he had hitherto lost heavily, was renamed Vengeance by new owners and later won the Cesarewitch.

The Rugeley Poisoner, as Palmer came to be known, was confident and persuasive, getting his way with his women, victims, and neighbours, including the coroner and the postmaster whom he persuaded to intercept letters. He was florid and bull-necked, with the good-humoured, fleshy appearance of a sporting man, but looked older than his age. His sensational trial inspired pictures, doggerels, and books; the structure of Wilkie Collins's *The Woman in White* has been attributed to it. The drinker's salutation, 'What's your poison?', was coined at this time. Many commentators admired Palmer's equanimity at the Old Bailey, but Charles Dickens argued that his behaviour indicated 'miserable restlessness' (Dickens, 505). Sir James Stephen, who attended the trial, thought

Palmer 'courageous, determined and energetic ... yet he was as cruel, as treacherous, as greedy of money and pleasure, as brutally hard-hearted and sensual a wretch as it is possible ever to imagine' (Stephen, 272).

RICHARD DAVENPORT-HINES

Sources *Illustrated life, career, and trial of William Palmer of Rugeley, containing an unabridged edition of the Times report of his trial for poisoning John Parsons Cook* (1856) • G. Fletcher, *The life and career of Dr William Palmer of Rugeley* (1925) • R. Graves, *They hanged my saintly Billy* (1957) • E. R. Watson, *The trial of William Palmer* (1952) • G. H. Knott, ed., *Trial of William Palmer* (1912) • J. F. Stephen, *A general view of the criminal law of England* (1890), 231–72 • C. Dickens, 'The demeanour of murderers', *Household Words* (14 June 1856), 504–7 • 'The Rugeley poisoning cases', *ILN* (24 May 1856), 554–5, 560–64, 566–7 • 'The Rugeley poisoning cases', *ILN* (31 May 1856), 598 • *Reynold's miscellany*, 16 (1856), 377–9, 391–2 • J. Sutherland, *Victorian fiction: writers, publishers, readers* (1995) • *DNB*

Archives Staffs. RO, letters and relics

Likenesses sketch, 1854, repro. in Fletcher, *Life and career of Dr William Palmer*, frontispiece • lithograph, c.1855, repro. in Graves, *They hanged my saintly Billy*, 3 • portrait, c.1856, repro. in Fletcher, *Life and career of Dr William Palmer*, facing p. 196 • J. Simpson, sketch, c.1910 (after waxwork at Madame Tussaud's; based on casts of his head and face taken after execution), repro. in Knott, ed., *Trial of William Palmer*, frontispiece

Palmer, William Patrick (1803–1885), Church of England clergyman and theologian, was born on 14 February 1803, only son of William Palmer (*d.* 1865), officer in the 53rd foot, of St Mary's, Dublin, and originally of Streamstown, co. Meath, and Invermore, co. Mayo, and his wife, Helen (*d.* 1836), daughter of J. Gratrix Hill of Fieldtown, co. Westmeath. On 5 July 1819 he was admitted as a pensioner at Trinity College, Dublin, where he was tutored by George Miller before graduating in 1824. After studying for ordination in the diocese of Limerick under a newly improved course introduced by the Irish high-churchman John Jebb (1775–1833), bishop of Limerick, Palmer migrated to Oxford, where he was incorporated at Magdalen Hall on 20–23 October 1828, proceeding MA on 28 January 1829. In 1831 he transferred to Worcester College, living with his mother in a house in Beaumont Street (he is not to be confused with William Palmer of Magdalen College, 1811–1879). After his mother's death Palmer married, in October 1839, Sophia Mary Bonne (*d.* 1872), first daughter of Admiral Sir Francis *Beaufort, originator of the Beaufort scale of wind speed. They had one daughter, who died in infancy, and one son, Francis.

Towards the *Origines liturgicae* Palmer settled in Oxford in order to pursue his scholarly studies into the primitive origins of the English liturgy, which he had commenced in 1826 under the inspiration of his mentor, Bishop Jebb. He abandoned his aim of writing a commentary on the English liturgy when he found Charles Lloyd, bishop of Oxford, apparently working on the same topic. Lloyd's premature death in 1829 revived Palmer's interest, particularly when Edward Burton, Lloyd's successor as regius professor of divinity, turned over Lloyd's notes to him. Palmer's scholarly labours bore fruit in the publication in 1832 of his widely acclaimed two-volume *Origines liturgicae, or, Antiquities of the English ritual and a dissertation on primitive liturgies* (4th edn, 1845). Against a background of latitudinarian threats to remodel the liturgy, Palmer aimed to demonstrate that the Book of Common Prayer was a product of 1500 years' development. By far the best book in the English language on the neglected theme of the history and significance of Anglican liturgical offices, the partly derivative nature of Palmer's work—he drew heavily on earlier Anglican liturgists as well as Lloyd—and its dry and technical character did not lessen its impact. Palmer's historical account of the Roman breviary, his analysis of the English ritual, and his illustrated appendix on vestments came as a revelation to many of his contemporaries, and encouraged a rising demand for missals and breviaries.

The timely appearance of the *Origines* brought Palmer to the attention of Hugh James Rose, who, impressed by his learning and orthodoxy, sought Palmer's aid as a contributor to the newly founded *British Magazine*. Palmer contributed a series of important articles on the subject of protestant dissent in 1832. Palmer's strictures on dissent in these articles and his assault on latitudinarianism in his *Remarks on Dr Arnold's 'Principles of Church Reform'* (1833) firmly established his high-church credentials.

Collaboration with the Oxford Movement By 1831–2 Palmer's liturgical scholarship had brought him into contact with the future leaders of the Oxford Movement, John Henry Newman, Hurrell Froude, and John Keble. Palmer's relations with the Oxford Movement formed the crucial component of the next two decades of his life: his important role and collaboration with Newman in the movement's early phase have been largely neglected. Palmer seems to have had a direct hand in Newman's own education in high-churchmanship, in that Newman consulted Palmer when preparing his *Arians of the Fourth Century* (1833). By the summer of 1833, when the Oxford Movement was launched, Palmer and Newman were close friends, with a mutual respect for each other's learning and abilities. Palmer's alliance with the movement's leaders was forged by a shared alarm at the crisis which appeared to be about to engulf the Church of England. As an Irish high-churchman Palmer particularly was troubled by the Erastian challenge to the Church of Ireland represented by the whig ministry's suppression of ten episcopal sees and confiscation of revenues. Palmer's initial enthusiasm for the movement can be explained by the apparent readiness of his Oxford friends to take up the cause of the embattled Irish church. One response to the crisis was the formation of an Association of Friends of the Church in 1833, in which Palmer was deeply involved. The inauguration of the series of Tracts for the Times, in the same year, represented another response. Palmer contributed number 15, *On the Apostolical Succession* (dated 13 December 1833), to the series, though his contribution was revised and completed by Newman.

One reason for Palmer's later neglect in Tractarian historiography was the early emergence of a temperamental as well as a doctrinal gulf between the Tractarian leaders and their disciples, and those more conservative high-churchmen with whom they had formed a temporary alliance in 1833. In his *Apologia pro vita sua* (1864) Newman paid tribute to Palmer's learning and integrity, but also portrayed him as a conservative churchman with establishment connections whose '*beau ideal* in ecclesiastical action was a board of safe, sound, sensible men' (Newman, 109), and who did not understand the principle of 'personality' which guided Newman. Palmer shared the anxieties of his friends among the Hackney Phalanx over the contents of the tracts and direction of the movement, believing that the tract writers deferred too much to the views of the later nonjurors in their advocacy of primitive doctrines and practices such as prayers for the dead. Whereas Palmer's approach was conservative, Newman's was restorative, even innovative. Newman's early alliance with Palmer was essentially tactical. After a clash with Newman over a committee for the revision of the tracts, Palmer was deprived of direct influence over the course of the movement. In Tractarian Oxford eyes, Palmer's Irish background meant, according to Newman, that he 'had never really grown into an Oxford man, nor was he generally received as such' (ibid., 108). When in the summer of 1838 Newman learned of Palmer's engagement to be married, Newman consoled himself with the reflection that 'good fellow as he is, he has never been one of our own' (Newman to J. W. Bowden, 6 Nov 1838, *The Letters and Diaries of John Henry Newman*, ed. C. S. Dessain and others, 31 vols., 1–10, 2nd edn, 1978–, 6.337).

Major writings and controversies Palmer's magisterial two-volume *Treatise on the Church of Christ* (1838; 3rd edn, 1842) represented his most significant contribution to theological scholarship. In it, he sought to prove that the Church of England was a branch of the church catholic co-ordinate with the Roman and Greek churches (the so-called 'branch theory'), earning Newman's critical admiration and, later, commendation from Gladstone. Palmer's conclusions were anti-Romanist, and his Irish birth and education come out in his history and denunciation of the Roman Catholic church in Ireland under the description of the 'Irish schism'. The *Treatise*, however, was much more akin than Newman's *Lectures on the Prophetical Office* (1837) to the 'static' logical methodology of the Roman schools, but Palmer's dry and technical approach may not have appealed to the more general reader: Newman feared that the *Treatise* might be merely regarded as 'a useful reference book for facts and nothing more' ([J. H. Newman], 'Palmer's *Treatise on the Church of Christ*', *British Critic*, 24, Oct 1838). In 1840 Newman recommended, as superior to his own *Arians*, Palmer's *Compendious Ecclesiastical History* (1840), published in The Englishman's Library, edited by William Gresley and Edward Churton.

Although Palmer did not believe that the Roman church was the Antichrist, as some other high-churchmen and evangelicals still asserted, the anti-Roman basis of his apologetic was marked. He was alarmed by the publication of Hurrell Froude's *Remains* (1838). According to J. W. Burgon, Palmer had the advantage of having studied the claims to catholicity of the churches of England and Rome more carefully than had the Tractarian leaders. When Newman's first doubts about Anglicanism were raised by Wiseman's article in the *Dublin Review* (1839), in which the position of the Church of England was compared to that of the Donatists, Palmer was untroubled by the analogy. He met Wiseman's challenge head-on in a series of publications which included *Apostolical jurisdiction and succession of the English episcopacy vindicated against the objections of Dr Wiseman in the 'Dublin Review'* (1840), *A Letter to N. Wiseman, DD* (1841), and seven subsequent letters in reply to Wiseman's rejoinder (1842 and 1851). Palmer also engaged in controversy with an Anglican convert to Roman Catholicism, R. W. Sibthorp (1792–1879), in his *Examination of the Rev. W. Sibthorp's Reason for his Secession* (1842). Palmer argued that Roman Catholics in England and Ireland had forfeited the apostolical succession and that the Roman church as a whole was guilty of adding to 'the Faith once delivered to the Saints'. His repudiation of Roman doctrines and practices such as transubstantiation, invocation of saints, and purgatory rested on a high-church appeal to the antiquity. Palmer's method, however, was criticized, not without justice, as selective and unscrupulous by the Roman Catholic convert Peter Le Page Renouf (1822–1897), in a damaging pamphlet entitled *The Character of the Rev. William Palmer as a Controversialist* (1843).

Palmer was portrayed by some Oxford contemporaries as sedate, shy, and cold in manner, traits which hindered his acceptance at Oxford. There was a feeling among the inner Tractarian coterie that he lacked any sense of humour, though Henry Wilberforce purported to find a latent humour in the very gravity of some of Palmer's more ponderous pronouncements. Palmer's character was marked by humility, gentleness, and generosity of spirit. The claims of friendship blinded him to the extent of his own theological differences with Newman and other Tractarian leaders. Although among his conservative high-church associates Palmer was critical of Tract 90, he publicly defended it and even assured Newman that he regarded it as 'the most valuable' in the series. He delayed the inevitable public breach with his Oxford friends as long as possible, but after Newman's withdrawal of earlier anti-Roman statements and resignation as vicar of St Mary's in 1843, and the emergence of a 'romanizing' party led by W. G. Ward, he could keep silent no longer. In his *Narrative of Events Connected with the Publication of the Tracts for the Times* (1843) he sought to draw a clear 'line between sound church principles and Ultra and Romanising views' (Palmer to W. Gresley, 15 Sept 1843, Gresley MSS, Gres 3/40/6). But to the dismay of other old high-churchmen Palmer still refused to pass censure on the Tracts for the Times or to include Newman and Pusey in his denunciation of 'Ultra' views. Palmer even initially refused to allow the *English Review*, a conservative high-church journal which he helped establish in 1844, to take sides against Newman. He adopted a more strident tone against Newman only after his friend's secession to Rome. But, shocked by Newman's theory of development of Christian doctrine, which he regarded as an abandonment of the patristic basis on which Tractarianism had rested and as rationalistic in tendency, Palmer responded to both Newman's *Development of Christian Doctrine* (1845) and Ward's *Ideal of a Christian Church* (1844) with his *Doctrine of development and conscience considered in relation to the evidences of Christianity and of the catholic system* (1846).

Palmer's hopes that the Tractarian movement would return to a more moderate course after Newman's departure were not fulfilled. He remained outspoken in defence of church principles and deplored the Gorham judgment in 1850. Fearing the threat to the Church of England from latitudinarian and Erastian pressures, in 1850–51 he even privately contemplated a radical separation of church and state on the lines advanced by Hurrell Froude in 1833. Palmer, however, increasingly tried to disavow his own earlier Tractarian associations, and by the early 1850s found himself in conflict with advanced high-churchmen who dominated the newly founded church unions. Palmer became disillusioned with ecclesiastical affairs. Apart from a controversy with a Roman Catholic neighbour in Dorset, Joseph Weld of Lulworth, in 1854–5, and offering support for protestant missionaries in Ireland in the 1850s, he effectively withdrew from public controversy for over two decades.

The country clergyman In 1846 Bishop Richard Bagot of Bath and Wells presented Palmer to the vicarage of Whitchurch Canonicorum, Dorset, which he held until 1869, along with that of the vicarage of Monckton-Wyld, from 1864. From 1849 until 1858 he was prebend of Highchurch in Salisbury Cathedral. There is little evidence for Palmer's life as a country pastor, but he always remained concerned with the church's spiritual efficiency as well as her theological orthodoxy. In 1841 he had submitted an ambitious scheme for over 100 new bishops, and in 1842 was the author of an *Enquiry into the possibility of obtaining means for church extension without parliamentary grants*. In the early part of his incumbency at Whitchurch Canonicorum, Palmer opened the coffin of St Wite, in which there were reputed to be relics. A small box containing a few bones was found, but Palmer was persuaded that the bones were those of the De Mandevilles, one-time lords of the vale. Palmer's mistake—the bones were later identified as those of St Wite—was surprising given that he had enquired very deeply into the subject of St Wite.

On grounds of ill health Palmer moved from Dorset about 1869, and thereafter resided at Montagu Square, Marylebone, London. He reappeared in public debate in 1875 by entering the controversy between Newman and Gladstone over 'Vaticanism', but his contribution, *Results of the 'Expostulation' of the Rt. Hon W. E. Gladstone in their relation to the unity of Roman Catholicism* (1875), was made under the cover of the pseudonym Umbra Oxoniensis. It was only the premature valediction of Thomas Mozley in the first edition of his *Reminiscences of Oriel College and the Oxford Movement* (1882) which metaphorically brought Palmer back to life. In the early 1880s Gladstone urged him, unsuccessfully, to issue a new edition of the *Treatise*. However, in 1883 he republished his *Narrative* verbatim, with the addition of an eighty-page historical introduction and a sixty-page supplement, while in an article in the *Contemporary Review* Palmer gave a condensed version of his account in the *Narrative*. This final literary flowering came too late to prevent him from becoming the 'forgotten man' in the history of the Oxford Movement. No memoir or biography for Palmer exists. In his *Lives of Twelve Good Men* (1888) J. W. Burgon refers so frequently and with so much affection to Palmer that it is surprising that he did not include him among the men whose lives he had written. As Thomas Mozley concluded, reward 'he wanted not, but he had not even recognition' (*Reminiscences*, 2 vols., 1882, 1.322).

Palmer, in later life, claimed the disputed baronetcy of Wingham, Kent, created in 1621 and dormant after the death of Sir Charles Harcourt Palmer in 1838. William Palmer's father claimed to inherit the title from his brother Thomas, who purportedly succeeded in 1838 as seventh baronet; Palmer himself assumed the baronetcy in 1865, as ninth baronet, after his father's death. Although Palmer's claim was not challenged in the courts, it was not recognized, mainly on the grounds that the title to a baronetcy descends by the patent of creation, not by heirship. Palmer died in London in October 1885, leaving one son who, it is believed, discontinued the assumption of the baronetcy. He was buried in the churchyard at Sandford-on-Thames, near Oxford, alongside his mother and wife; the latter had died in 1872.

PETER B. NOCKLES

Sources P. B. Nockles, *The Oxford Movement in context: Anglican high churchmanship, 1760–1857* (1994) · Pusey Oxf., Palmer papers · Pusey Oxf., Gresley papers · BL, Gladstone MSS · M. O'Connell, *The Oxford conspirators: a history of the Oxford Movement* (1969) · W. Palmer, *A narrative of events connected with the publication of the Tracts for the Times*, [new edn] (1883) · J. W. Burgon, 'Hugh James Rose: the restorer of the old paths', *Lives of twelve good men*, 4th edn, 1 (1889), 116–283 · W. S. Adams, 'William Palmer's *Narrative of events*: the first history of the Tracts for the Times', *The divine drama in history and liturgy: essays presented to Horton Davies*, ed. J. E. Booty (1984), 81–106 · R. H. Grenfield, 'The attitude of the Tractarians to the Roman Catholic church', DPhil diss., U. Oxf., 1957 · A. C. Mead, 'A critical investigation of the controversy between Newman and the Tractarians over the development of doctrine', BLitt. diss., 1973 · J. H. Newman, *Apologia pro vita sua* (1864) · J. R. Griffin, 'Newman and William Palmer: a note on the *Apologia*', *English Language Notes*, 24/2 (1986), 33–6 · G. T. Botle, *Recollections of the Very Rev. G. D. Botle, dean of Salisbury* (1895) · *N&Q*, 4th ser., 1 (1868), 460, 520–21 · *N&Q*, 4th ser., 2 (1868), 47 · *N&Q*, 7th ser., 1 (1886), 474 · *N&Q*, 7th ser., 7 (1889), 369, 511 · *N&Q*, 8th ser., 5 (1894), 132 · Burtchaell & Sadleir, *Alum. Dubl.* · Foster, *Alum. Oxon.* · Gladstone, *Diaries* · S. Creed, *Dorset's western vale* (1987), 58–9 [St Wite] · *DNB*

Archives BL, Gladstone MSS, corresp. · LPL, letters to Charles Wordsworth · LPL, letters to Christopher Wordsworth · Pusey Oxf., letters to William Gresley

Palmer, William Waldegrave, second earl of Selborne (1859–1942), politician, was born at 30 Portland Place, London, on 17 October 1859, the only son and the youngest of five children of Roundell *Palmer (1812–1895), politician, who was created earl of Selborne in 1882, and his wife, Lady Laura Waldegrave (*d.* 1885), second daughter of the eighth Earl Waldegrave. He was educated at Temple Grove, East Sheen, and at Winchester College and he entered University College, Oxford, in 1878, graduating with a first in modern history in 1881. When he was only ten his mother urged him not to forget the family motto 'to do my duty in that state of life into which it shall please God to call me', but although he performed ably enough at

William Waldegrave Palmer, second earl of Selborne (1859–1942), by James Russell & Sons

school and university, he himself recollected that, while at Oxford, 'I hunted and played cards and cricket and tennis and ragged—I took no part in politics'. He was a JP in Hampshire and joined the county militia. He considered a career in the army, but was persuaded by his father to enter politics, gaining administrative experience as private secretary to his father in the Lord Chancellor's Office, and then to H. C. E. Childers, first at the War Office and then at the exchequer, between 1882 and 1884. On 27 October 1883 he married Lady (Beatrix) Maud Cecil [*see* Palmer, (Beatrix) Maud (1858–1950)], eldest daughter of Robert Arthur Talbot Gascoyne-*Cecil, the third marquess of Salisbury; at the wedding, Salisbury gave the bride away, and Gladstone proposed the toast to the bride and groom.

Entering politics When his father was made an earl in 1882 Palmer gained the courtesy title of Viscount Wolmer. He began his political career as a Liberal, standing for the second seat at Coventry and then, in December 1885, winning the Eastern or Petersfield division of Hampshire. Gladstone's conversion to Irish home rule was made public in January 1886, and Wolmer followed his father in opposing it, though not without some misgivings. He decided to vote for the motion by Jesse Collings which turned out Lord Salisbury's administration on 27 January 1886, because in his election speeches he had called on the Liberals to take steps to 'multiply the owners of the land'. When he stood as a Liberal Unionist in June 1886 he was supported by Gladstonian Liberals and opposed by Conservatives.

Wolmer joined the newly organized Liberal Unionist Party which sought to play an independent political role. The union was the main issue; but Wolmer warned that it would 'rest with the Government [the Salisbury administration] whether we should continue to support them. We cannot entirely abandon our Liberal principles, and support them in reactionary legislation.' From 1886 until his father's death in 1895, Wolmer sat in the Commons. He served as chief whip for the Liberal Unionists, predicting exactly the home-rule majority of forty in 1892. He contested that election in the Edinburgh constituency, mainly because he did not like to compete for his Hampshire seat against Gladstonian Liberals who had been loyal to him in 1885 and 1886. His father's death in 1895 provoked a constitutional issue of whether or not the succession to the peerage necessarily involved forfeiting a seat in the Commons. Selborne and his close friend Lord Midleton had agreed that whoever lost his father first would fight a test case—a select committee found against him. On 3 June 1895 Lord Rosebery's Liberal government fell and the Liberal Unionists ended their independence, taking office in Lord Salisbury's administration. Selborne was offered the post of under-secretary of state for the colonies under Joseph Chamberlain.

Colonial and naval affairs For the next fifteen years Selborne's career centred on imperial and international affairs: five years in the Colonial Office were followed by a decade divided equally between the Admiralty and the post of governor of the Transvaal and the Orange River Colony, and high commissioner for South Africa. He held these key positions at a time when the British empire confronted some of its most dangerous crises: the Second South African War, the naval race with Germany and other great powers, the making of the South African Union. This was a period whose mood was fairly caught by Rudyard Kipling's poem, 'Recessional'; and no one was more aware of the vulnerability of the empire than Selborne. His years at the Colonial Office witnessed a series of vexatious disputes, with the United States of America over Venezuela, Portugal over her African possessions, France over Siam and the upper Nile, and the war with the Boer republics in 1899. This assisted Selborne's rise, for the Colonial Office, formerly a backwater, became central to the assertion of British power. He played a difficult role in the Colonial Office, acting as an intermediary between Lord Milner (who became high commissioner in 1897) and the cabinet, supporting Milner in his defence of British interests, but moderating his impatient desire to bring matters to a head. When war broke out, Selborne was appalled at the catalogue of British military disasters, but he took comfort in the reflection that 'we were getting a bit too self-exalted and self-reliant, and therefore … in this temporary anxiety and humiliation is a merciful discipline'. He prepared a memorandum in November 1899, elaborating his views on the future of South Africa; but his attention was soon focused on another, even more important aspect of Britain's international role. On 27

October 1900 he was offered the post of first lord of the Admiralty, which he described as 'the most delectable … for a British subject after that of prime minister'.

The choice of Selborne as first lord aroused suspicions of nepotism, since he was Lord Salisbury's son-in-law; but he had the administrative and personal gifts essential for the post. He was methodical, and possessed great powers of concentration—indispensable qualities for the large administrative burden. He had the capacity to get the best out of those responsible to him. He overcame the caution of his first sea lord, Lord Walter Kerr, controlled the exuberance of his House of Commons spokesman, H. O. Arnold-Forster, and released, yet disciplined, the ferocious reforming zeal of Sir John Fisher, who became his second sea lord in 1902 and first sea lord in 1904, reflecting that it was 'wholesome for services like the Navy and Army to have occasionally Radicals among their senior officers'.

Selborne first met Fisher in April 1901, when on a trip to the Mediterranean. He was impressed by Fisher's intelligence and quickness of mind, and believed that with careful management he would 'run straight'. Under Selborne's supervision, Fisher pushed through the great naval reforms: the planning of the 'dreadnought' battleship, the scrapping of obsolete warships, the redistribution of the fleet. Selborne also recognized the need to improve the quality of officer training, and to reduce the social distinction between executive and engineer officers (though this was a less successful reform). He set up a committee on naval reserves, and modernized the navy's technological equipment. The burden of defending the empire was great; and it was increasing at a time, Selborne noted, when Britain's 'two-power standard'—committing her to maintain a navy the equal to beating the combined strength of the next two strongest naval powers—was under strain. After 1900 the naval race was joined by Japan and Germany, and this placed an intolerable pressure on British resources. Selborne was among those who believed that the United Kingdom must seek an ally, and, after considering Germany, he supported an agreement with Japan.

Selborne's initial consideration of Germany appears at odds with one of his major policy decisions—the redistribution of the fleet, and its concentration against a potential threat in the North Sea. But as early as 1902 he admitted to A. J. Balfour that he had not realized 'the intensity of the hatred of the German nation to this country'. If Britain was to retain her naval pre-eminence, then she must deploy her resources according to the German threat. Moreover, she must not remain a great power, but become a greater one: this meant placing the empire at the centre of her foreign policy, seeking to strengthen its bonds, perhaps even moving towards imperial federation.

South Africa In February 1905 Selborne was finally persuaded to leave the Admiralty and replace Lord Milner in South Africa. He went out of a sense of duty, for the Unionist government was moving towards its inglorious close, and defeat in the next general election was anticipated. Balfour resigned in December 1905, and Selborne found himself serving under Lord Elgin and then Lord Crewe, Liberal colonial secretaries who were not always in sympathy with his aims. He was obliged to defend Lord Milner's policy of employing Chinese labour in the Transvaal, and he opposed the government's decision to grant full responsible government to the former Boer republics, seeking to mitigate the impact of this (as he saw it) rash policy by influencing the West Ridgeway committee's decision on the distribution of seats. This earned him the cabinet's censure, and he considered resigning; but Selborne's greatest quality was his resilience. No sooner did the Transvaal and Orange River Colony gain responsible government than he was planning his next move, which was to lend his carefully concealed support to a group of young imperialists, led by Lionel Curtis, who were planning to federate all the South African states. This, they believed, would attract enough British immigration to secure South Africa for the British empire. Selborne presided over the production of 'the egg': the 'Selborne memorandum', which was published in July 1907 ostensibly as a result of an initiative from South African politicians. In October 1908 a National Convention assembled to settle the economic and political future of South Africa.

Selborne intervened on several key issues: the future of the protectorates of Bechuanaland, Basutoland, and Swaziland; the native franchise; and the voting formula for the new state. His overriding concern was to reconcile the first two of these interests with the need for South African unity; and to ensure that a united South Africa would be dominated by the British. He hoped to place the protectorates under the new state, but with trusted administrators appointed to run them, thus eliminating the British House of Commons from interference. He struggled to keep an 'open door' for a native franchise; but neither he, nor the Liberal government, was prepared to jeopardize union on this question. Selborne *was* prepared to jeopardize union on the question of the white franchise, defending a voting system based on each MP representing roughly the same number of voters (which gave the British the advantage) rather than the same number of people (which worked to the advantage of the Afrikaners). Eventually a compromise was reached, by which proportional representation (which Selborne favoured) was abandoned, but the voters' basis retained, and the constitution amended to require that all bills intended to change the electoral system should be submitted to the crown for approval.

Selborne left South Africa in April 1910, convinced that he had saved it for the empire. But he and his young federalists, and indeed the Liberal government, hardly realized the deeper levels of the politics of that country. The union was agreed because each side thought they would gain the upper hand. The Afrikaners saw it as the chance to work for a position of domination, albeit most of them accepted that this domination could be reconciled with membership of the British empire.

British politics again When Selborne returned to England in 1910 he did so convinced that the House of Commons was no fit body to run a great empire. He saw all domestic questions from an imperialist perspective. This explains his apparently contradictory behaviour between 1910 and 1914, when he fought bitterly to defend the House of Lords against the Liberal government's determination to remove its veto, while advocating the use of the referendum on constitutional matters, and a federal Ireland to reconcile the competing claims of Ulster Unionists, Irish nationalists, and the British empire. Overall, an imperial government was needed 'responsible to all the electors of the Empire and with power to act directly on individual citizens'. This would help maintain Britain as an imperial nation for it would, combined with Joseph Chamberlain's policy of imperial preference, pay for social reform, which Selborne acknowledged was naturally a priority for the working man.

Selborne's cordial relations with certain Liberals were strained to breaking point before 1914. He greeted the declaration of war in August 1914 with grim resignation; but his mood soon turned to further disillusionment with Asquith's government over its conduct of the war. In May 1915 the Liberals offered a coalition which the Unionists, whatever their misgivings, could hardly refuse. Selborne became president of the Board of Agriculture and Fisheries. He displayed his usual vigour and organizational skills, and within a few months of his appointment he had persuaded Lord Milner to chair a subcommittee to examine the possibility of stimulating an increase of foodstuffs. By July 1915 an interim report (recommending a guaranteed minimum price for wheat) was ready, but was shelved. Selborne's concern over the failure to establish an effective co-ordinating body to wage war increased his frustration; in October 1915 he nearly resigned. In June 1916 he finally left the cabinet over Lloyd George's conduct of negotiations between Sir Edward Carson and John Redmond following the Easter rising in Dublin in April 1916. But, again, Selborne's position was more complex than it first appeared. He was concerned that any Irish settlement should only be made in the context of the future constitution of the United Kingdom and the empire. To this end he co-operated with F. S. Oliver in advocating a federal solution, seeking to achieve for Ireland what he believed he had given to South Africa, and using similar methods of persuasion. Selborne and Oliver worked hard to influence the Irish Convention of 1917–18, but this came to nothing because of poor chairmanship by Sir Horace Plunkett, the stern opposition of the Ulster Unionists, and the indifference of the British government, especially of Lloyd George.

Selborne's administrative gifts were given further scope, however, on his appointment as chairman of the agricultural policy subcommittee of the reconstruction committee which in 1917 supported his advocacy of state interventionist policies, including a minimum wage for farm labourers, guaranteed wheat prices, and powers to enforce good cultivation—measures embodied in the Corn Production Act of 1917. In 1919 he was elected chairman of the joint committee of both houses of parliament on the bill to carry out the recommendations of the Montagu–Chelmsford report on the government of India, but he entertained grave doubts about the efficacy of seeking to impose Western style government on an Asian nation. His deep interest in ecclesiastical matters was given scope in a report by the archbishops' committee on church–state relations which Selborne chaired from 1913, and which in 1917 recommended the introduction of what became the church assembly. The Enabling Act of 1919, based on this report, still left final power in the hands of the crown and parliament. But Selborne's dislike of a political world dominated by Lloyd George was increasing. He refused the offer of the viceroyalty of India, and of Ireland, and the offer of a marquessate. He watched with growing concern the rise of trade union power, and he was appalled at the Anglo-Irish treaty of 1921. In 1924 he caused a sensation when he broke his silence on the question of what had been promised to the Ulster Unionists when the Lloyd George cabinet was drawing up the Government of Ireland Act of 1920, revealing that Walter Long had pledged that the boundaries of Northern Ireland would remain inviolate, except for very slight adjustments which might prove desirable. Selborne wrote frequently to the press on public issues. He advocated women's suffrage, which he had supported since 1910, and reform of the House of Lords.

Other activities In these years also Selborne filled a number of congenial posts, including the office of lord high steward of Winchester from 1929 until his death, and warden of Winchester College from 1920 to 1925. He was chairman of the house of laity in the church assembly from 1924. In 1905 he was made a GCMG, and he was given the Order of the Garter in July 1909 in recognition of his South African work. He was an elder brother of Trinity House from 1904. He received the honorary degree of LLD from Cambridge in 1910 and DCL from Oxford in 1911.

Selborne's home life was a particularly happy one. He relied heavily on the support of his wife, corresponding freely with her on important issues in South African politics between 1905 and 1910. They had three sons and one daughter; their second son, Robert, was killed in action in Mesopotamia in 1916. Selborne died at his home, 14 Buckingham Palace Gardens, London, on 26 February 1942, and was buried in the family grave at Blackmoor churchyard, near Liss, in Hampshire. He was succeeded by his son, Roundell Cecil *Palmer (1887–1971), who had just been appointed minister of economic warfare in Winston Churchill's government. D. GEORGE BOYCE

Sources *The crisis of British unionism: the domestic political papers of the second earl of Selborne, 1885–1922*, ed. D. G. Boyce (1987) · *The crisis of British power: the imperial and naval papers of the second earl of Selborne, 1895–1910*, ed. D. G. Boyce (1990) · D. G. Boyce and J. O. Stubbs, 'F. S. Oliver, Lord Selborne and federalism', *Journal of Imperial and Commonwealth History*, 5 (1976–7), 53–81 · GEC, *Peerage* · *The Times* (27 Feb 1942) · *DNB*

Archives Admiralty Library, London, naval papers · BL, corresp. and papers relating to South Africa, Add. MS 46003 · Bodl. Oxf., corresp. and papers · CUL, university medical library, Library of the Royal Commonwealth Society · Hants. RO, corresp. and papers · LPL, corresp. · LPL, papers relating to his chambers in

Serles Court, Lincoln's Inn | BL, corresp. with Arthur James Balfour, Add. MSS 49707–49708 • BL, corresp. with Lord Cecil of Chelwood, Add. MS 51157 • BL, corresp. with Herbert, Viscount Gladstone, Add. MS 46003 • BL OIOC, letters to Lord Curzon, MSS Eur. F 111–112 • Bodl. Oxf., corresp. with Lewis Harcourt • Bodl. Oxf., letters to Lady Milner • Bodl. Oxf., corresp. with Lord Milner • Bodl. Oxf., corresp. with John Sanders, etc. • Bodl. RH, corresp. with Lord Lugard • CKS, letters to Aretas Akers-Douglas • CKS, letters to Lord Edward Cecil • Derbys. RO, corresp. with Philip Gell • Durham RO, letters to Lady Londonderry • Glos. RO, corresp. with Sir Michael Hicks Beach • Hatfield House, Hertfordshire, Salisbury MSS • HLRO, corresp. with Andrew Bonar Law • LPL, letters to Edward Benson • LPL, corresp. with Athelstan Riley • LPL, Selborne MSS • LPL, corresp. with Frederick Temple • Lpool RO, corresp. with Lord Derby • NA Scot., corresp. with A. J. Balfour and G. W. Balfour • NA Scot., corresp. with Philip Kerr • NRA, priv. coll., corresp. with Brinsley Fitzgerald • Plunkett Foundation for Cooperative Studies, corresp. with Sir Horace Plunkett • PRO, corresp. with Lord Kitchener, PRO 30/57; WO 159 • PRO NIre., corresp. with Edward Carson • PRO NIre., letters to A. E. Skeen • U. Birm., corresp. with Joseph Chamberlain • U. Newcastle, Robinson L., corresp. with Walter Runciman

Likenesses Spy [L. Ward], lithograph, 1895, repro. in *ILN*, 106, 570 • Spy [L. Ward], lithograph, 1900, repro. in *Harper's Magazine*, 110, 298 • P. A. de Laszlo, oils, 1911, Mercers' Hall, London • W. Stoneman, photographs, 1917–39, NPG • P. A. de Laszlo, portrait, 1920, Blackmoor House, Liss, Hampshire • P. A. de Laszlo, oils, 1931, Church House, Westminster • Bassano, photograph, NPG; repro. in *Our Conservative and Unionist Statesmen*, 2 vols. (1896–7), vol. 2 • London Stereoscopic Co., photograph, NPG • J. Russell & Sons, photograph, NPG [*see illus.*] • Spy [L. Ward], caricature, chromolithograph, NPG; repro. in *VF* (3 Oct 1901) • Spy [L. Ward], lithograph, repro. in *VF* (15 July 1882) • Spy [L. Ward], lithograph, repro. in *VF* (27 Nov 1883) • photographs, priv. coll.

Wealth at death £18,649 12s. 2d.: probate, 5 Aug 1942, *CGPLA Eng. & Wales*

Palmerston. For this title name *see* Temple, Henry, first Viscount Palmerston (1672/3–1757); Temple, Henry, second Viscount Palmerston (1739–1802); Temple, Henry John, third Viscount Palmerston (1784–1865); Temple, Emily Mary, Viscountess Palmerston (1787–1869).

Palmes, Sir Brian (*c*.1599–1654), politician, was the eldest son of Sir Guy *Palmes (1580–1653) of Ashwell, Rutland, and Lindley in Otley parish, West Riding of Yorkshire, and his wife, Anne (*d*. before 1626?), daughter of Sir Edward Stafford. His father had been MP for Rutland in every parliament from 1614 to 1643 and had served three times as high sheriff of that county. Palmes matriculated at Trinity College, Oxford, on 17 March 1615 and was MP for Stamford, Lincolnshire, in 1625–6. A close friend of the poet William Browne (1591–1645), he toured France with him. Browne addressed to Palmes, who was then staying at Saumur, his humorous poem, written at Thouars, on the 'most intolerable jangling of the Papists' bells on All Saints' Night' (W. Browne, *Poetic Works*, ed. G. Goodwin, 2 vols., 1894, 2.229). About 1628 Palmes married Mary, daughter of Gervase Teverey, esquire, of Stapleford, Nottinghamshire; they had three sons and four daughters. At the time of his marriage, his father settled on him the manor of Ashwell. He briefly served as a JP at Knaresborough, Yorkshire, in October 1637 and he may have fought against the Scots during the bishops' wars as there are records of a Captain Palmes's troop among the state papers. He was MP for Aldborough, Yorkshire, during the Short Parliament of 1640.

On 21 April 1642 Palmes was knighted; he was created a DCL at Oxford in November that year. Along with his father he supported the royalists during the civil war. While it remains doubtful whether they were in arms, Brian Palmes signed royalist orders to Yorkshire parish constables in August 1642 and also served as a commissioner of array, while his father was ejected from the House of Commons for his prolonged absence. Palmes is erroneously reported as the governor of Belvoir Castle (A. C. Wood, 220), but he was among the commission of array that sat there. On 14 October 1646 he applied to compound for his estates, pleading illness to explain his delays, and on 20 October his fine was set at £681. On 1 September 1651 he was assessed at £200 but no proceedings were taken. Palmes died in 1654 at Ripon in the West Riding of Yorkshire and was buried in Otley church on 25 May. His wife had predeceased him.

GORDON GOODWIN, *rev*. ANDREW J. HOPPER

Sources Foster, *Alum. Oxon.*, *1500–1714*, vol. 3 • J. Foster, ed., *Pedigrees of the county families of Yorkshire*, 3 (1874) • Keeler, *Long Parliament* • *VCH Rutland*, vol. 2 • W. Brigg, ed., *The parish registers of Otley, co. York*, 1, Yorkshire Parish Register Society, 33 (1908) • J. Lister, ed., *West Riding sessions records*, 2, Yorkshire Archaeological Society, 54 (1915) • *JHC*, 3 (1642–4) • E. Peacock, 'On some civil war documents relating to Yorkshire', *Yorkshire Archaeological and Topographical Journal*, 1 (1869–70), 89–106 • *CSP dom.*, 1640–41 • M. A. E. Green, ed., *Calendar of the proceedings of the committee for compounding … 1643–1660*, 5 vols., PRO (1889–92) • M. A. E. Green, ed., *Calendar of the proceedings of the committee for advance of money, 1642–1656*, 3 vols., PRO (1888) • PRO, PROB 6/29, fol. 647r • A. C. Wood, *Nottinghamshire in the civil war* (1937) • Wood, *Ath. Oxon.*, 1st edn

Archives BL, Add. MSS 5531, 39795 zz (c.f. 39806, fols. 1, 2), 37998 fol. 59b • BL, Egerton MS 2986 fols. 133, 143, 144

Wealth at death no value given: Keeler, *The Long Parliament*; will, PRO, PROB 6/29, fol. 647*r*

Palmes, Sir Guy (1580–1653), politician, was the eldest son of Sir Francis Palmes (*c*.1554–1613), landowner, of Ashwell, Rutland, and Lindley, Yorkshire, and Mary (*d*. 1595), daughter of Stephen Hadnall of Lancelevy, Hampshire, and Marsh, Shropshire. Guy Palmes was admitted to the Inner Temple in 1597 but was never called to the bar. By 1599 he had married Anne (*d*. before 1626?), daughter of Sir Edward Stafford, whose grandmother, Lady Dorothy Stafford, Queen Elizabeth's mistress of the robes, had been guardian to Palmes's father in his youth. They had four sons, including the politician Sir Brian *Palmes, and four daughters.

Palmes spent most of his adult life in Rutland, where he was one of the supporters of the Harington faction at a hotly contested by-election in November 1601. John, first Baron Harington, returned the favour by nominating Palmes to the deputy lieutenantcy in 1607, while in 1614, following the deaths of the senior members of the Harington family, Palmes was returned as one of the knights of the shire. Palmes, who had been knighted on 11 May 1603, played little part in the Commons' proceedings until the day before the dissolution, when he moved that the lawyer John Hoskins, whose professional services he had used in the previous year, should be cleared of any charges the king might bring against him for dark threats of a massacre of Scottish courtiers. On the following day Palmes opposed last-minute attempts to avert dissolution by a grant of supply, but Hoskins's subsequent arrest may have sobered him, as he gave the relatively generous sum of £20 to the benevolence the crown collected in lieu of parliamentary taxation after the end of the session.

Palmes continued to be returned to parliament for Rutland during the remainder of his active life. He is known to have received the support of the shire's lord lieutenant, Henry, fifth earl of Huntingdon, at the election of 1624, but his standing as a local landowner made him a natural candidate, and if he relied on any outside influence for his seat it was probably the earl's mother, a Harington by birth, who also interceded with her third husband Edward, Lord Zouche, to secure Palmes a nomination at Hythe in 1621.

During the 1621 session Palmes pandered to one of the king's best-known prejudices in calling for a complete ban on sales of tobacco, which he claimed 'undoes men in their bodies and estates, draws them to drink and to continue at it' (Notestein, Relf, and Simpson, 5.77–8). The government must have come to regard him as a minor irritant during the session: he took part in the impeachment of Sir John Bennett on corruption charges, and when abuses of monopolies were considered it was he who moved to widen the investigation to include the crown lawyers who had drafted the offending patents. As was undoubtedly his intention, this shed light upon the murky patronage dealings of the royal favourite, George Villiers, marquess of Buckingham.

When the session resumed in the autumn Palmes opposed the crown's unusual request for a second grant of supply on the grounds that 'the country saith that we have already given subsidies, but have brought them nothing' ([E. Nicholas], *Proceedings and Debates of the House of Commons*, 2 vols., 1766, 2.226). He went on to support complaints about government harassment of one of the Commons' most outspoken members, Sir Edwin Sandys, and when the king picked a fight over this issue Palmes endorsed the decision to suspend all business, a confrontation which led to the dismissal of the parliament. His refusal to contribute to the benevolence collected after the dissolution earned him a summons before the privy council and there may have been some truth in the later allegation that his appointment to the 'burthensome' office of sheriff of Yorkshire in 1622 was intended as a punishment for his behaviour (Scott, 2.436). During this year he married one of his daughters to the heir of William Mallory, one of the three MPs who had been arrested at the end of the 1621 parliament, and it seems likely that the two men occasionally acted in concert during subsequent parliaments. His first wife having died, Palmes married, on 23 December 1624, Elizabeth (*d.* 1634), daughter of John Doyley of Chiselhampton, Oxfordshire, and widow of Francis Harby of Adston, Northamptonshire, and of Sir Robert Browne, first baronet, of London and Walcot, Northamptonshire. There were no children of this marriage.

The 1624 parliament was dominated by the efforts of a loose coalition of self-styled 'patriots' to secure the consent of both king and Commons to a war with Spain. Palmes was among those repeatedly wooed by Prince Charles and Buckingham at conferences with the House of Lords, but even after a month of such persuasion he was not inclined to vote funds for mobilization. In the key debate of 20 March he argued that 'time never brought forth repentance' (Harvard U., Houghton L., Eng. MS 980, p. 150) and suggested the question should be further delayed by referring it to a committee, while on 7 April he called for a proclamation to enforce the recusancy laws (suspended during the previous year) as a demonstration of the crown's intentions. With the king reluctant to commit himself to war without clear signs of the Commons' support, Palmes's behaviour suggests that he should be ranked among the covert opponents of war within the house. He was more concerned to ensure the passage of legislation which had been lost owing to the abrupt dissolution of the previous parliament, and even moved that bills which had not completed their passage through both houses at the prorogation should be revived at the same stage in the next session.

Preparations for war began in earnest almost immediately after Charles's accession in March 1625, but Palmes returned to parliament more obdurately opposed to a belligerent foreign policy than in the previous year. On 10 August, despite heavy government pressure, he flatly refused to consider any increase in the modest sum offered for the war effort early in the session, and reminded the house that 'for the disorders in H[enry] VII time, Empson and Dudley were hanged in H[enry] VIII time' (Jansson and Bidwell, 451). The implication that Buckingham might share the same fate under his new master would have been obvious to both his audience and the duke, who ensured Palmes's absence from the next parliament by having him pricked as sheriff of Rutland.

Although his shrievalty passed without incident, Palmes was one of the duke's critics who were removed from the commission of the peace in June 1626. Following this snub it is hardly surprising that he was listed as a refuser of the forced loan in Northamptonshire, where his second wife's estates lay. However, he was not involved in the public opposition to the loan organized by gentry from the western end of the shire, and the local lords lieutenant allowed him to continue his service as deputy lieutenant in Rutland and Northamptonshire. His resentment at his treatment surfaced in the Commons in 1628, when he insisted that a hopelessly inadequate grant of four subsidies would suffice for maintenance of the war with France and Spain. He played very little part in the key debates on the petition of right, busying himself with the question of militia charges and the billeting of troops on civilian households, with which he was rather better acquainted:

> I am sorry and ashamed to speak what I know, what misery these billetings have brought us to. For my part, I think Deputy Lieutenants have been too slack, but I pray you let us

be the more speedy in framing of a bill to remedy this disorder. (Johnson and others, 2.365)

Palmes was virtually invisible during the 1629 session, during which he was distracted by a lawsuit brought before the Lords by one of his sons-in-law.

Active as JP, deputy lieutenant, and commissioner of knighthood fines in Rutland during the 1630s, Palmes was an intermittent critic of the crown's policies during the opening months of the Long Parliament, moving for a vote to condemn lord keeper John Finch but standing up for the earl of Huntingdon over his controversial Star Chamber prosecution of Sir William Faunt. One of Palmes's sons was implicated in the first army plot of May 1641, but his own loyalties were divided, and both king and parliament named him as a militia commissioner in the months before the outbreak of the civil war. He remained at Westminster, supporting the peace party's proposals for a negotiated peace after the battle of Edgehill, but in May 1643 he retired to his Yorkshire estates. Although he later claimed to have acted under a warrant from the speaker, his willingness to remain in the north after the rout of local parliamentarian forces led the Commons to vote for his ejection from the house and sequestration of his estates on 28 September 1643. Captured at Newark in May 1646, he had his claims to have remained neutral discounted, and he and his son Brian, a royalist colonel, were fined £3905 for their delinquency. He retired to his Rutland estates where he died; he was buried at Ashwell on 25 March 1653. SIMON HEALY

Sources S. H., 'Palmes, Sir Guy', HoP, *Commons, 1604–29* [draft] · C. Russell, 'Sir Thomas Wentworth and the anti-Spanish sentiment, 1621–1624', *The political world of Thomas Wentworth, earl of Strafford, 1621–1641*, ed. J. F. Merritt (1996), 47–62 · R. Cust, 'Wentworth's "change of sides" in the 1620s', *The political world of Thomas Wentworth, earl of Strafford, 1621–1641*, ed. J. F. Merritt (1996), 63–80 · R. P. Cust, *The forced loan and English politics, 1626–1628* (1987) · T. Cogswell, *The blessed revolution* (1989) · C. Russell, *Parliaments and English politics, 1621–1629* (1979) · W. Notestein, F. H. Relf, and H. Simpson, eds., *Commons debates, 1621*, 7 vols. (1935) · M. Jansson and W. B. Bidwell, eds., *Proceedings in parliament, 1625* (1987) · R. C. Johnson and others, eds., *Commons debates, 1628*, 6 vols. (1977–83) · W. Scott, ed., *Secret history of the court of James the First*, 2 vols. (1811), vol. 2, p. 436 · parish register, Ashwell, St Mary, 25 March 1653 [burial]

Archives Hunt. L., Hastings corresp.

Palsgrave, John (*d.* 1554), teacher and scholar of languages, was born in London. The identity of his parents is unknown, though Palsgrave was evidently close to his mother, his provision for her being mentioned in the state papers in 1529. He is first recorded at the end of 1503 as a student at Cambridge, where he graduated BA in 1504. He then went to Paris, where he gained a thorough knowledge of French and acquired the degree of MA. With these qualifications he had by January 1513 been appointed schoolmaster to Henry VIII's sister, Princess Mary, who in the following year married King Louis XII of France. The wedding took place on 9 October, and the princess must have had a high regard for her teacher, since he accompanied her to France as her secretary and she commended him warmly to Wolsey in letters of 13 November 1514 and 3 April 1515. Mary's English attendants were all dismissed on the day after her wedding, however, and by late 1516 Palsgrave was in Louvain, studying law as well as reinforcing his knowledge of Latin and Greek. He had come to enjoy a high reputation among contemporary scholars, and in a letter of 4 December 1516 Thomas More notified Erasmus, who was himself then resident in Louvain, of Palsgrave's imminent arrival there and asked him to favour the visiting Englishman:

> he has heard that you will be living there, and in view of his old acquaintance with you reckons that he can count on you for anything; but all the same … he has asked me … to add my own recommendation to the good will he thinks he already enjoys with you on his own account; he wants to be allowed to enjoy your advice and help in his pursuit of a liberal education. I know, my dear Erasmus, I need waste few words in asking you to assist the studies of a man who is devoted to good literature, full of promise, known to be a hard worker, and his progress hitherto is already familiar to you; one moreover who is both my friend and yours, which means yours twice over. (*Correspondence of Erasmus*, 162–3)

By the summer of 1517 Palsgrave was back in England. In 1514 he had been collated to the prebend of Portpool in St Paul's Cathedral, though only an acolyte, and in 1518 he was presented to the rectory of Asfordby, Leicestershire, which he held until 1525. He continued to enjoy the favour of Thomas More, who secured for him two Suffolk rectories, Alderton in 1520 (resigned 1525) and Holbrook near Ipswich in 1523 (resigned 1533), and in 1524 the living of Keyston in Huntingdonshire, which he held until his death. And he also entered the service of Henry VIII. He formed part of the royal entourage when Henry met the emperor Charles V at Calais on 10 July 1520, while in 1525 he was appointed schoolmaster to the king's illegitimate son Henry Fitzroy, created duke of Richmond that year, and was made a member of his council. His letters to More and to Lady Tailboys, Richmond's mother, show that he was committed to the boy's intellectual and moral education, and assiduously carried out the king's brief to bring up his son 'in vertu and learnyng' (Childe-Pemberton, 167). But he complained to More that his efforts to instil his charge with humanist learning were being thwarted by the duke's attendants, and he seems to have left his position before the end of 1526.

Palsgrave was far from rich, and it would not have helped him that he seems to have fallen foul of Wolsey. He continued to earn his living principally as a teacher, and in the late 1520s was tutoring a group of young gentlemen and nobles who included Lord Thomas Howard, a son of the third duke of Norfolk, Thomas Cromwell's son Gregory, and Charles Blount, later Lord Mountjoy and a notable patron of humanist studies. In 1529 he was ordained deacon, and in 1532 took the degree of BTh at Oxford. On 23 September 1533 he was ordained priest, a step doubtless associated with his being collated just ten days later by Archbishop Cranmer to the valuable London living of St Dunstan-in-the-East. Once freed from financial anxiety Palsgrave largely disappears from the records. Nothing is known of his position on current religious issues, but from the fact that by 1540 he had become a royal chaplain it may be deduced that he did not step out of line with the progress of the English Reformation. In 1545 his former pupil Charles Blount presented him to the Northamptonshire living of Wadenhoe. He died in 1554, some time before 3 August, when his successor was instituted to that benefice.

Palsgrave was very much a 'schoolmaster' in the vein of Roger Ascham, or even a 'governor' in the manner of his contemporary Sir Thomas Elyot. In his greatest work, *Lesclarcissement de la langue francoyse*, he shows his concern with moral instruction, for instance in dealing with the expression 'to make cowardish' or 'faint-hearted': 'Some thynke that lernynge dothe but make one cowardysshe ["doctrine ne fait que accouardyr ung home"] … but Alexanders and Cesars actes prove the contrarye' (Palsgrave, *Lesclarcissement*, Book 3, fol. ccxc). But he was even more concerned with the intellectual training of the youth of the realm, as he shows in his dedication to Henry VIII of *The Comedy of Acolastus*, his translation of William Fullonius's Latin original of 1529, published as a double-text edition in 1540. Stressing the need for an education in the mother tongue to accompany all academic study, he describes the purpose of his bilingual edition of *The Comedy of Acolastus* on its title-page as:

> translated into oure englysshe tongue, after suche maner as chylderne are taught in the grammar schole, fyrst worde for worde, as the latyne lyeth, and afterwarde accordynge to the sence and meanyng of the latin sentences: by shewing what they do value and counteruayle in our tongue, with admonitions set forth in the margyn.

The chief task of the teacher, in his view, is 'to open the diuersities of phrases betwene our tonge and the latyn' (A [iiii]).

This was the task that Palsgrave had fulfilled in an unparalleled way in his *magnum opus* of 1530, *Lesclarcissement de la langue francoyse*. In a work of over 1000 pages he discloses to his English learners the French idiom, writing the first French grammar and the first English–French dictionary. The novelty of his approach can be seen in his close study both of the French language as it was spoken at the time in its regional and social variation, and of the French writers held in high literary esteem, for instance Jean Lemaire de Belges and Octavien de Saint-Gelais. Equally pioneering were the observational descriptive detail and the depth of the linguistic analyses of a vernacular in the first decades of the sixteenth century. The comprehensiveness of the volume—both the grammar and the lexicon of French are meticulously described—makes it a unique treasure trove for the beginnings of French lexicology, lexicography, and grammar writing. As his endeavours were meant to help speakers of English to acquire a vernacular they could use in speech as well as writing, Palsgrave also provides an outline of French pronunciation, even attempting pioneering 'phonetic' transcriptions for poetry and prose texts.

But Palsgrave's achievement is more remarkable yet. His conviction that a foreign language had to be made understandable in the pupils' mother tongue led him to a thorough study not just of French but also of English, again with reference to regional and social variation, and again with attention to literary use. In applying this, his basic precept, and demonstrating the differences between French and English, he came in fact to be comparing in meticulous detail two vernacular languages, an achievement never previously attempted at a time when language comparison involved the ancient languages of learning, Latin, Greek, and Hebrew, or a comparison of one of these with a contemporary vernacular.

Palsgrave's determination to base his linguistic descriptions on how the two vernaculars were actually used led him to offer literary examples, including some from Chaucer and many from John Lydgate, a widely read writer at the time. His interest in English also had a historical dimension, albeit not as prominent or extensive as he showed for French, with its references to Jean Froissart, Alain Chartier, and even to the *Roman de la rose* of 300 years earlier.

Among Palsgrave's many achievements are his perceptive generalizations drawn from his linguistic analyses and their explicit formulation. He thus brought rules into two sixteenth-century vernaculars and their functioning, including even word-formation patterns. Such writing called for a linguistic terminology couched in English, his learners' mother tongue. The only such terminology in scholarly use was of course Latin: Palsgrave proceeded to adapt this to the vernacular. A good number of present-day grammatical terms, for example 'article', 'adverb', 'interjection', and 'phrase', were in fact introduced by him.

The most extensive part of *Lesclarcissement de la langue francoyse* is the bilingual English–French dictionary. Palsgrave's close observation of English used in daily communication as well as in more specialized contexts caused him to record many lexical items and colloquial idioms for which the *Oxford English Dictionary* credits him with first attestations. Many of these neologisms, listed as headwords by Palsgrave, are first explained in English before the French equivalent is given. The same lexicographical practice is used when an English word has several senses. By paraphrasing a particular meaning first in English and then providing the corresponding French word or phrase, his dictionary really becomes a double dictionary: learners are first supplied with a monolingual segment, expanding their command of the mother tongue, and then with a bilingual one to address their needs in the French they are learning. In order to offer his learners more practical language use, he introduces illustrative examples: everyday utterances in English, mostly contrived out of his creative imagination, which are then rendered into idiomatic French. This he achieves notably in that most difficult area of foreign language learning and teaching, the handling of verbs and their complementation. These are features long taken for granted in language learning materials; but they could not be taken for granted in Palsgrave's time or until long thereafter. GABRIELE STEIN

Sources J. Palsgrave, *Lesclarcissement de la langue francoyse* (1530) • J. Palsgrave, *The comedy of Acolastus* (1540) • G. Stein, *John Palsgrave as*

Renaissance linguist (1997) • P. M. Reidenbaugh, 'Elements of language variation in Palsgrave's "Lesclarcissement de la langue francoyse" (1530)', PhD diss., University of Illinois, Urbana, 1997 • G. Gnaphaeus, *'The comedy of Acolastus': translated from the Latin of Fullonius by John Palsgrave*, ed. P. L. Carver, trans. J. Palsgrave, EETS, 202 (1937) • J. Palsgrave, *L'éclaircissement de la langue Française … suivi de la grammaire de Giles du Guez*, ed. F. Génin (Paris, 1852) • *The correspondence of Erasmus*, ed. and trans. R. A. B. Mynors and others, 22 vols. (1974–94) [letters 446–593, 1516–1517] • *LP Henry VIII*, vol. 1/2 • W. S. Childe-Pemberton, *Elizabeth Blount and Henry VIII: with some account of her surroundings* (1913)

Paltock, Robert (1697–1767), romance writer, was both born and baptized on 16 October 1697 at Little Hadham, Hertfordshire; he was the only son of Thomas Paltock (*bap.* 1664, *d.* 1701), gentleman, and his wife, Anne (*d.* 1712). Thomas was Anne's third husband: she was previously married to a Mr Johnson of Woodford, Essex, and to Edward Curll, jeweller, of Red Lion Square, Holborn. She was widowed for a third time when Thomas Paltock died in April 1701. She died in January 1712, leaving Robert, aged fourteen, in the guardianship of Robert Nightingale and John Green of Enfield.

Robert Paltock was then at Charterhouse School, where he was admitted on 1 July 1709. On 20 October 1714, with John Green's consent, he was bound apprentice to William Ballett of Enfield, a member of Clement's Inn and clerk to George Clerk, head prothonotary of the common pleas. He found brighter prospects when he came of age in October 1718 and inherited £150 and a house at Enfield, left to him by his paternal grandmother, Elizabeth Paltock, *née* Steward (1631–1707). On 13 January 1719 he was admitted to the Middle Temple and in 1722 to Clement's Inn, where he now acquired chambers and practised as an attorney. On 13 June 1729 he married Anna Skinner (*bap.* 1705, *d.* 1767), eldest daughter of John Skinner (*d.* 1737) of Austin Friars, London, and Enfield, a merchant trading with Italy, and his wife, Ellienor. The Paltocks' first child was probably John, baptized at St Andrew's, Enfield, on 6 November 1733; by 1746 they had produced three more sons, Robert, Thomas, and Garbrand, and three daughters, Elizabeth, Anna, and Eleanor. It seems that all but John, Robert, and Anna died early. By 1748 Paltock was in financial difficulties of some kind: this may have been his reason for turning author.

Paltock is not known to have written anything for publication before 11 January 1749, when (giving his address as Clement's Inn) he assigned copyright of his prose romance, *The Life and Adventures of Peter Wilkins*, to Jacob Robinson and Robert Dodsley for a consideration of £21, twelve copies of the book in sheets, and proof copies of the engravings by Louis Peter Boitard with which it would be illustrated. Though dated 1751 on the title-page, the book was published in November 1750. The author was not named, but a fulsome dedication to Elizabeth, countess of Northumberland (1716–1776), thanking her for some unspecified kindness, was signed 'R. P.'. The romance itself, telling the story of a castaway in a fantastic land where men and women can fly, owes much to *Robinson Crusoe* and something to the *Arabian Nights' Entertainments* and the non-satirical elements of *Gulliver's Travels*, but is highly inventive on its own terms. The surname of Paltock's hero perhaps recalls John Wilkins (1614–1672), who, in *Mathematical Magick* (1648), argued that man might master the art of flying.

Peter Wilkins was very little noticed in Paltock's lifetime: it received one review (unfavourable, in the *Monthly Review*, December 1750) and only one contemporary reference to Paltock's authorship has been traced. It was not reissued in England until 1783, though there was a cheap Dublin reprint (1751), a French translation (1763), and a German abridgement (1767), from none of which Paltock would have profited. After the book became popular and its author's name well known in the nineteenth century, other works of fantasy or novels with 'R. P.' on the title-page were attributed to Paltock. The only such attribution that is not highly improbable is *Memoirs of the life of Parnese, a Spanish lady: interspersed with the story of Beaumont and Sarpeta*, 'translated from the Spanish manuscript by R. P., Gent.' (1751). This dull work has nothing in common with *Peter Wilkins* but it was dedicated to Paltock's second cousin, Frances (1723–1810), wife of Commodore Matthew Mitchell (1706–1752).

By 1759 the Paltocks were living in Back Lane, Lambeth, perhaps in straitened circumstances. In 1764 Anna inherited property under the will of her brother, Brinley Skinner of Ryme Intrinsica, Dorset, formerly consul at Leghorn and resident at Venice, but it is doubtful if her husband was allowed to administer it. A notice in the *London Gazette*, 10–13 November 1764, invites creditors of Robert Paltock 'on or before 21 June 1748 … to come in and prove their Debts' by 20 December next, 'in order to receive their distribution of the Trust Estate and Effects of the said Robert Paltock' according to a 'Decree and General Order of Transfer of the High Court of Chancery'.

The couple continued to live in Back Lane. Anna died first and was buried at St Mary, Lambeth, on 14 January 1767. Her husband soon followed: he died on 20 March 1767 and was buried at Ryme Intrinsica, Dorset, where his son Robert (1737–1814) was a surgeon and apothecary. He made no will; letters of administration were granted on 15 April to his son John (1733–1789), formerly a merchant in Bengal.

Peter Wilkins had to wait over forty years for widespread recognition. It was admired by Coleridge, Southey, Shelley, Leigh Hunt, Charles Lamb, and others of their generation; it provided material for pantomimes and melodramas from 1800 to the 1870s, and was frequently reprinted, entire or abridged, during the nineteenth century. Though less admired today, it is usually given some attention in scholarly discussions of imaginary voyages and early science fiction. JAMES SAMBROOK

Sources R. Paltock, *The life and adventures of Peter Wilkins*, ed. C. Bentley (1973) • J. Crossley, *N&Q*, 10 (1854), 212–13 • W. E. A. Axon, *N&Q*, 10th ser., 12 (1909), 286 • B. Marsh and F. A. Crisp, eds., *Alumni Carthusiani: a record of the foundation scholars of Charterhouse, 1614–1872* (1913) • J. Hutchins, *The history and antiquities of the county of Dorset*, 3rd edn, ed. W. Shipp and J. W. Hodson, 2 (1863), 609; 4 (1874), 493–4 • C. Carr, ed., *The pension book of Clement's Inn*, SeldS, 78 (1960) • H. A. C. Sturgess, ed., *Register of admissions to the Honourable*

Society of the Middle Temple, from the fifteenth century to the year 1944, 3 vols. (1949) • *IGI* • *DNB* • index of the bishop of London's marriage licences, typescript, Society of Genealogists • A. J. P. Skinner, 'The author of *Peter Wilkins*', *TLS* (14 May 1925), 335 • E. P. Poole, 'Peter Wilkins', *TLS* (4 Oct 1928), 711

Pam, Albert Samuel (1875–1955), natural historian and financier, was born on 26 June 1875 at Clapham, London, eldest of three sons of Leopold Pam (1838–1909), merchant and rentier, and his wife, Philippine (1851–1938), who had Anglicized her Austrian maiden name of Fürth (or Fuerth) to Firth. He was educated at the City of London School (1889–92) and then spent two years at a *Gymnasium* at Frankfurt am Main and a year at Ouchy near Lausanne perfecting his languages. He began his career working for a sugar merchant in Mincing Lane, London; shortly afterwards he joined a voluntary brigade of the Royal Fusiliers, which he commanded both at the diamond jubilee and at the funeral of Queen Victoria. In 1907 he married Maude le Clerc (1872–1960), divorced wife of Walter Fowle and daughter of Surgeon Major-General John George Faught. They had one daughter.

From an early age Pam was interested in ornithology, zoology, and horticulture. He first visited South America in 1900 with his maternal uncle, who had business interests in the Amazon basin. Thereafter he returned frequently on visits which combined capitalism with natural history, and he became possibly the leading English authority on the plants, birds, and animals of South America. He was a member of the council of the Zoological Society of London from 1907; he received its silver medal in 1914 and served as treasurer from 1932 to 1945. In 1912 he bought the Wormley Bury estate at Broxbourne, Hertfordshire, including its derelict gardens, which contained rare specimens planted by Sir Abraham Hume. Pam cultivated a large collection of South American flora and fauna, especially bulbous plants, in the grounds and glasshouses at Wormley Bury; he also had a menagerie and an aviary there. An unknown genus of Amaryllidaceae discovered by him in Peru in 1926 was named *Pamianthe Peruviana*, or the flower of Pam. He was a fellow of the Linnean Society from 1939 and was awarded a medal of honour by the Royal Horticultural Society in 1944. He often contributed to the *Journal of the Royal Horticultural Society*, and he wrote on aviculture, botany, and zoology in scientific periodicals. His achievements as a natural historian were recognized in 1944 by an honorary MA from Oxford University, with special rights at Wadham College.

Pam became a stockbroker with Vivian Gray and specialized in South American securities. During the Edwardian period he was the most active member of the Ethelburga syndicate, a group of rich men including Arthur Stanley, which speculated in risky overseas ventures carrying the possibility of large profits. After visiting Venezuela in 1905, Pam was granted a monopoly on salt in that country, and he transferred his rights to the Ethelburga syndicate. Through Pam's contacts, the syndicate also obtained match monopolies in Venezuela (1905) and Bolivia (1907) which it sold in 1927 to the Swedish Match Company. Pam also represented a syndicate led by Lord Howard de Walden, which in 1910 secured a contract to build the Chilean Longitudinal Railway.

Few men in the City of London knew South America more intimately than Pam. Sir Vincent Corbett described him as 'a keen businessman, used to fishing in troubled waters', who 'does not hesitate to push his own interests by any means that may come to hand' but who 'acted quite frankly in his dealings' (Corbett to Hardinge, 2 May 1908, PRO, FO 368/241). In December 1914 Pam was sent to Chile by the director of naval intelligence, and later he undertook espionage on the German community in Bolivia. He served at army headquarters in France in 1916–18, reaching the rank of major, which title he thereafter bore in business life. He became an OBE, was decorated with the Belgian Croix de Guerre, and was made a member of the French Légion d'honneur. From November 1918 until April 1919 he was a British member of the International Armistice Commission at Spa, negotiating Germany's surrender.

In 1919 Pam was recruited as an associate partner in the merchant banking firm of J. Henry Schroder and was thereafter instrumental in several advances in British institutional finance. Schroders was the first major London issuing house to handle domestic industrial issues, and Pam was critical in this innovation. From its inception in 1926 he had charge of Schroders' investment department, which by the 1930s was providing one-fifth of the firm's revenues. His expertise in industrial finance was recognized by the Bank of England, which consulted him on the rationalization of declining staple industries. Most notably the Lancashire Steel Corporation was formed in 1930 with a substantial Bank of England holding as a result of his plans and negotiations. The co-operation among financial institutions obtained by Pam on this occasion was perpetuated, at his suggestion, by the formation of the Bankers' Industrial Development Corporation to support industrial rationalization. Pam also supervised the work of Leadenhall Securities Corporation, formed by Schroders in 1935, to finance medium and small industrial companies. Leadenhall's usual method was to invest in redeemable preference shares and to take some ordinary shares for a fixed term.

As a result of his position at Schroders, Pam was instrumental, with William Morris (Viscount Nuffield), in forming the Pressed Steel Company of Great Britain, whose products were chiefly used in the motor-car industry. He was a director of this company from 1926, and chairman from 1930 until his death in 1955. Pam was also active in Schroders' eastern European interests. He was managing director (1924–40) and then chairman of the Continental and Industrial Trust, which was formed to specialize in advances to German companies and in underwriting their securities. This trust also held extensive investments in Europe and the Americas. As members of the Schröder family became ill or died in the 1930s, Pam's importance in their merchant bank increased. It reached its apogee during the Second World War.

Pam had interests outside Schroders. As a young man he joined the board of the Marmite Food Extract Company, and he served briefly as managing director and became chairman after the armistice. He also had a long connection with Sena Sugar estates, which controlled extensive properties in Portuguese East Africa.

Pam was energetic, crisp, and observant, with fierce, sharp features and a small, dark moustache. Piercing eyes indicated his acuity both as a natural historian and as a financier. He combined physical fortitude with analytical intelligence. His nickname Pamski was an allusion to his foreign antecedents, and the prejudice which he encountered may have aggravated his well-attested prickliness. He was an inveterate traveller for pleasure and a gastronome, whose personal motto was *Labor ipse voluptas*. His memoirs, entitled *Adventures and Recollections*, which were privately printed by Oxford University Press in 1945, mainly describe his South American travels.

Pam died on 2 September 1955 at Wormley Bury. He left bequests to Wadham College and to the Oxford Botanic Garden. RICHARD DAVENPORT-HINES

Sources A. Pam, *Adventures and recollections* (1945) · R. Roberts, *Schroders: merchants and bankers* (1992) · letter of Sir Vincent Corbett to Sir Arthur Hardinge, 2 May 1908, PRO, FO 368/241 · PRO, FO 368/444 · PRO, FO 368/580 · PRO, FO 368/66 · PRO, FO 368/140 · M. Allan, *E. A. Bowles and his garden at Myddelton House (1865–1954)* [1973] · W. Norris, *The man who fell from the sky* (1987) · R. C. Whiting, *The view from Cowley* (1983) · S. E. Katzenellenbogen, *Railways and the copper mines of Katanga* (1973) · R. S. Sayers, *The Bank of England, 1891–1944*, 3 vols. (1976) · register of births, marriages and deaths, St Catherine's House, London · *The Times* (5 Sept 1955) · *The Times* (16 Sept 1955)

Archives Schroders plc, London, autobiographical typescript | Nuffield Oxf., corresp. with Lord Cherwell

Likenesses photograph, *c.*1920, repro. in Roberts, *Schroders*, pl. 55 · photograph, *c.*1925, Royal Horticultural Society, London · photograph, *c.*1945, repro. in Allan, *E. A. Bowler and his garden*

Wealth at death £217,318 9*s.* 8*d.*: probate, 30 Dec 1955, *CGPLA Eng. & Wales*

Paman, Henry (*bap.* **1623**, *d.* **1695**), physician, son of Robert Paman, was born at his father's estate of Chevington, Suffolk, and baptized there on 10 April 1623. He entered on 22 June 1643 as a sizar at Emmanuel College, Cambridge, where William Sancroft was his tutor. They became friends for life. Paman migrated to St John's College on 22 July 1646, graduated BA the same year, and was elected a fellow of that college. He became MA in 1650, and was incorporated MA at Oxford on 11 July 1655. On 20 June 1656 he kept an act for a medical degree before Francis Glisson, maintaining the thesis: 'Morbis acutis convenit dieta tenuissima' (note in Glisson's handwriting, vol. 3 of his papers). In the same year Paman was senior proctor, and in 1658 he graduated MD, being incorporated MD at Oxford on 13 July 1669. He was elected public orator at Cambridge on 5 March 1674, and held office until 9 July 1681. Eight Latin letters written by him in this capacity were printed under the title *Literae academiae Cantabrigiensis ab Henrico Paman cum esset orator publicus scriptae* (Ward, appendix, xvi). They are addressed to the astronomer John Hevel on 12 May 1674; to James, duke of Monmouth, on 12 June 1674, and twice without date; to Charles II on 11 September 1674; to Chief Justice Sir Francis North; to William, duke of Newcastle, on 7 August 1676; and to Sancroft, archbishop of Canterbury, on 8 January 1677.

In 1677 Paman went to reside in Lambeth Palace, with Archbishop Sancroft. On 21 June 1679 he was appointed professor of physic at Gresham College, and on 1 December 1679 he was elected FRS. In 1683 he was admitted a candidate at the Royal College of Physicians, and elected a fellow on 12 April 1687. He graduated LLD at Cambridge in 1684, and was thereupon appointed master of the faculties by Sancroft. He resigned his professorship on 21 June 1689. When Sancroft declined the oaths to William III and left Lambeth Palace, Paman also declined, and gave up his mastership of the faculties. He went to live in the parish of St Paul, Covent Garden, where he died in June 1695; he was buried in the parish church. Paman was rich, and after providing for his relations, left considerable sums of money and books to St John's College, to Emmanuel College, to the Royal College of Physicians, and to his native parish. Although he published nothing himself, he is known because of a Latin letter by him to Thomas Sydenham, published in Sydenham's works as a preface to the treatise, *De luis veneriae historia et curatione*. It praises Sydenham's method, and urges him to write on this subject. Sydenham says that Paman had long been his friend, and adds, 'I always valued your friendship as a most precious thing' (*Whole Works*, 244).

NORMAN MOORE, *rev.* MICHAEL BEVAN

Sources Venn, *Alum. Cant.* · Munk, *Roll* · BL, Sloane MSS, 3309 vol. iv and 4162 vol. iii · *The whole works of … Thomas Sydenham*, ed. and trans. J. Pechey, 9th edn (1729), 244 · J. Ward, *The lives of the professors of Gresham College* (1740), appx, xvi

Archives Bodl. Oxf., corresp. with Sancroft, etc.

Pandit, Vijayalakshmi [*née* Sarup Kumari Nehru] (**1900–1990**), diplomatist, was born on 18 August 1900 at Anand Bhavan, Allahabad, India, the second of the three children and elder daughter of Motilal *Nehru (1861–1931), lawyer and nationalist leader, and his wife, Swarup Rani. Her father, one of the most successful lawyers of his day, ensured that she received a good education from an English governess. Eleven years younger than her brother, the statesman Jawaharlal *Nehru, she was nevertheless close to him both as a child and throughout their lives. As a young woman Sarup Kumari Nehru formed a close attachment to a Muslim journalist, Saiyid Hossain, who was working on a newspaper owned by her father. However, he was not acceptable to her family, let alone to conservative Allahabad society, and the relationship was brought to an end. Shortly thereafter her family sent her to stay for a short while with Mahatma Gandhi in his *ashram*; she remained unconvinced of the value of a wholly ascetic life. On 10 May 1921 she married Ranjit Sitaram Pandit (*d.* 1944), a lawyer and scholar from Kathiawar, and took the name by which she became known throughout the world. They had three daughters, one of whom, Nayantara Saghal, became a well-known novelist.

As a young bride Vijayalakshmi Pandit lived in Calcutta, where her husband practised law. From 1930, however, she joined the other members of her family in Gandhi's civil disobedience campaign against British rule. Her first arrest came in 1932, and she served several terms of imprisonment, totalling thirty-six months. She also held a series of elected offices, including that of minister of local government and health in the pre-independence Congress governments in the United Provinces in 1937–9 and 1946–7. From 1944 to 1945 and again in 1946 she was in the United States, where her daughters were attending college, and where, at Gandhi's request, she spoke for the Indian nationalist cause in the critical period leading up to independence. Her rapport with Americans, statesmen and public alike, played a major role in sustaining American support for India's cause. In the same period, in 1945 she attended the San Francisco United Nations preliminary conference as an unofficial delegate, and in 1946 headed the Indian delegation to the first United Nations general assembly at Lake Success. She headed India's delegation on four further occasions. In 1947 she became India's first ambassador to the USSR, although here she was unable to establish a close rapport with the Soviet leadership. She was transferred to Washington in 1949, where her earlier popularity with the American public grew. On her return to India in 1951 she stood successfully for the Lok Sabha (lower house of the Indian parliament), where she sat until 1954.

In 1953 Vijayalakshmi Pandit became president of the United Nations general assembly, a significant first for a country in the developing world (she was also the first woman to occupy the post). She was then sent to London as high commissioner, where she served from 1954 to 1961, as well as being accredited as India's first ambassador to Ireland and Spain. She was also to be governor of Maharashtra state from 1962 to 1964. It was a notable achievement at this time for a woman to hold such a range of distinguished political and diplomatic positions.

After her brother's death in May 1964 Mrs Pandit's political star dimmed and she held no further public offices, although she took over Nehru's Phulpur constituency in the Lok Sabha from 1964 until she resigned in 1969. She did not hide her disagreements with her niece, Indira Gandhi, and she was strongly critical of the declaration of an internal emergency in 1975. In the 1977 election campaign she campaigned vigorously for the opposition. Mrs Pandit spent her retirement in the foothills of the Himalayas, near Dehra Dun, where she died on 1 December 1990. She had published a memoir of her time in gaol, *Prison Days* (1945), and an autobiographical volume, *The Scope of Happiness* (1979). DAVID TAYLOR

Sources V. L. Pandit, *The scope of happiness* (1979) • R. H. Andrews, *A lamp for India* (1967) • V. Brittain, *Envoy extraordinary* (1965) • *Selected works of Jawaharlal Nehru*, ed. S. Gopal and others, 15 vols. (1972–82) • V. L. Pandit, *Prison days* (1945) • *WWW, 1981–90* • *The Times* (2 Dec 1990)

Archives Nehru Memorial Library, New Delhi, Nehru MSS | FILM BFI NFTVA, current affairs footage • BFI NFTVA, documentary footage • BFI NFTVA, news footage

Likenesses photographs, repro. in Pandit, *Scope of happiness* • photographs, repro. in Andrews, *A lamp for India*

Pandulf [Pandulph, Pandulph Verraccio] (*d.* **1226**), bishop of Norwich and papal legate, was a member of the family of Verraccio native to San Germano close to the monastery of Monte Cassino in southern Italy. His father and mother, his brothers Odo (*d.* 1220) and Master Giles, archdeacon of Ely (*d.* before 1241), and his nephew Master Pandulf, treasurer of Chichester (*d.* before 1231), were all commemorated in obit celebrations at Monte Cassino.

Envoy to England: dealings with King John Nothing is known of Pandulf's early training, although a later connection with the bishop and see of Bologna might suggest that he had studied in the Bolognese schools. He first appears in April 1211, with title as papal subdeacon, appointed as an envoy of Pope Innocent III (*r.* 1198–1216) to the court of the excommunicate King John. In July 1211 he crossed to England and met the king at Northampton, to discuss the interdict then in force, and to attempt to obtain restitution of damages to the exiled clergy. A detailed account of this meeting, preserved in the Burton annals, claims that king and envoys quarrelled violently and that Pandulf attempted to depose the king, but since no such sentence was ever passed, the Burton account must be rejected as apocryphal.

None the less Pandulf clearly played a leading role in the negotiations between Rome, the court of King John, and the exiled English bishops. In February 1213 he was reappointed as papal envoy to England, charged with communicating the pope's conditions for the ending of the interdict, and on 15 May, at Ewell near Dover, it was to Pandulf that John surrendered his realm, doing homage for England to the papacy as for a papal fief. In the aftermath Pandulf was involved in the collection of 'Peter's pence' and of the annual subsidy promised to the pope by John. In 1213 he was sent to negotiate with the king's enemies in Wales and France, and as the pope's agent he secured the promotion of various papal clerks to English benefices. In the following year he followed John to Poitou, and travelled on to Rome as an envoy of the papal legate Nicolò, cardinal-bishop of Tusculum. By 1215 he had been promoted to unspecified benefices in the dioceses of Salisbury and Chichester. As a papal judge-delegate he was appointed to a long-standing dispute between the churches of Bath and Glastonbury.

In June 1215 Pandulf attended the meeting between King John and the barons at Runnymede, and, as a result, his name appears in the preamble to Magna Carta. At least one contemporary writer claims that it was the activities of Pandulf and of the papal legate Nicolò that helped bring about civil war between king and barons, in particular through their financial extravagance and the favouritism that they displayed in the promotion of royal candidates to vacant abbeys and bishoprics. On 15 July 1215 Pandulf was sent to negotiate with the barons at Oxford. A few days later, on 25 July, through the intervention of proctors appointed by the pope, he was elected bishop of Norwich. There is no evidence that he attended these election proceedings. Indeed, he appears to have paid only the briefest of visits to his new see before his consecration as bishop in 1222. In all probability he deliberately avoided consecration to Norwich in order to retain his independence from the authority of the archbishop of Canterbury, Stephen

Langton (*d.* 1228). In September 1215, acting together with Peter des Roches, bishop of Winchester (*d.* 1238), he pronounced a papal sentence of excommunication against the rebel barons, and a few days later, suspended Archbishop Langton from office. Thereafter he set out for Rome, where he attended the Fourth Lateran Council as a representative of King John.

Papal legate: the minority of Henry III Following the death of Pope Innocent in July 1216 and the election of the latter's chamberlain to succeed him as Honorius III (*r.* 1216–27), Pandulf was appointed chamberlain in Honorius's place. He occurs with title as chamberlain between January 1217 and 1222, and until the summer of 1218 remained at the papal court, active in the financial and diplomatic affairs of the see of Rome. He returned to England in 1218 after a three-year absence, and was present at the dedication of Worcester Cathedral on 7 June 1218. By papal letters dated 1 September 1218 he was appointed legate to England, in place of Cardinal Guala Bicchieri, who had asked leave to retire. Guala relinquished his legation at Reading on about 17 November, and Pandulf entered London, as Guala's successor, on 3 December. There he is said to have obtained the release of various clerks, condemned to imprisonment by Guala for their support of the rebels during the late civil war. As legate, Pandulf served as the chief mediator between the government of the boy king, Henry III, and the papacy. On 9 April 1219 he attended the deathbed of William (I) Marshal, earl of Pembroke, late regent of England, and was nominated by the Marshal as his successor in the keeping of the young king.

For the next three years England was effectively governed by a triumvirate comprising the legate (who in consequence of John's surrender of his kingdom to the papacy was in the unusual position of being also the agent of a superior lord), the justiciar, Hubert de Burgh (*d.* 1243), and the bishop of Winchester, Peter des Roches. The relations between these three men were by no means entirely harmonious. In April 1219, for example, it appears that des Roches and de Burgh attempted to limit Pandulf's access to the royal treasury, fearing that Pandulf intended to appropriate the king's revenues for the uses of the church and the papacy. The resulting crisis, in which Pandulf stepped in to demand control of the king's seal, was settled at a council held at Gloucester in June 1219. Thereafter, it is evident that Pandulf inclined more and more to support de Burgh at the expense of des Roches within the minority council. For much of his legation he appears to have travelled the country, at a considerable distance from the king and his court, maintaining contact only by letter. During the summer and autumn of 1219 he was active in negotiations with the Welsh, and with Alexander II, king of Scots. He later intervened in disputes among the English baronage over the custody of various castles, including those of Tickhill (Yorkshire), Bristol, and Bytham (Lincolnshire).

On papal instruction Pandulf played a crucial role in the resumption by the crown of castles and custodies alienated since the late civil war. As the pope's agent he was engaged in the hearing of ecclesiastical suits, the assessment of papal taxation for the fifth crusade, the commutation of crusader vows, and the collection of procurations intended to fund his own legatine mission. At Ely he was instrumental in the appointment of Abbot John of Fountains (*d.* 1225) as bishop, and at Carlisle he presided over a division of property between the bishop and chapter. He was also commissioned by the pope to investigate a series of episcopal elections in Ireland and Scotland. Much of his time as legate was spent in the west country and in at least one letter, he complained that the climate of London was injurious to his health. In 1220 he helped negotiate a prolongation of the truce with France, attended the second coronation of Henry III at Westminster, and, in July, the translation of the relics of St Thomas at Canterbury. In April 1221 he attended the foundation of the new cathedral church of Salisbury, laying the first stone as the pope's representative. He was instrumental in the resignation of William de Ste Mère-Église (*d.* 1224) as bishop of London in January 1221, and in arranging for the consecration as bishop of William's successor, Eustace de Fauconberg (*d.* 1228), on 25 April.

Bishop of Norwich However, the return to England of the archbishop of Canterbury, Stephen Langton, combined with Langton's insistence that the pope appoint no further legate during his own lifetime, effectively put an end to Pandulf's mission. Pandulf resigned as legate at Westminster on 26 July 1221, and soon afterwards set out for Poitou charged with an embassy of the count of La Marche. From there he travelled on to Rome where, having resigned his office as papal chamberlain, he was consecrated bishop of Norwich on 29 May 1222. In 1223 he attended the funeral of the French king, Philip Augustus, in Paris, and unsuccessfully pressed Philip's successor, Louis VIII (*r.* 1223–6), for the restoration of Normandy to the English crown. In the following year he was involved in the collection of the census due from England to the papacy, but he again retired to Italy in the winter of 1224, arriving in Rome on 17 February 1225. During the last eighteen months of his life he is to be found at Rome, Reati, and Tivoli. He died at Rome on 16 or 17 September 1226.

For most of his time as bishop and bishop-elect Pandulf was an absentee from his diocese. Although his body is said to have been carried back to Norwich for burial, during his lifetime the diocese was administered by a series of officials. As bishop he appropriated various churches to the religious, including a moiety of the church of Holkham, Norfolk, granted in 1219 to the convent of San Martino al Cimino at Viterbo. His episcopal and legatine household included numerous Italian clerks, many of them provided to churches in England. The late thirteenth-century Norwich chronicler, Bartholomew Cotton, claims that Pandulf granted the monks of Norwich a chest containing relics, and, according to another local source, he introduced the payment of first fruits from all the clergy of his diocese. His will bequeathed considerable sums of money to the crusade, administered by his Italian executors. A collection of the sermons of Pope

Honorius III, once in Pandulf's possession, passed afterwards to the Cistercian abbey of Santa Croce in Gerusalemme in Rome. As bishop of Norwich he made only a negligible impression upon the history of his see. However, as the pope's chamberlain and as papal legate, he played a crucial part in papal administration, and in the restoration of royal government in England after the civil war of 1215–17. NICHOLAS VINCENT

Sources *Chancery records* • *Pipe rolls* • W. W. Shirley, ed., *Royal and other historical letters illustrative of the reign of Henry III*, 2 vols., Rolls Series, 27 (1862–6) • P. Chaplais, ed., *Diplomatic documents preserved in the Public Record Office*, 1 (1964) • N. Vincent, The election of Pandulph Verracclo [*sic*] as bishop of Norwich (1215), *Historical Research*, 68 (1995), 143–60 • P. Pressutti, ed., *Regesta Honorii Papae III*, 2 vols. (Vatican City, 1888–95) • *The letters of Pope Innocent III (1198–1216) concerning England and Wales*, ed. C. R. Cheney and M. G. Cheney (1967) • *The letters and charters of Cardinal Guala Bicchieri, papal legate in England, 1216–1218*, ed. N. Vincent, CYS, 83 (1996) • J. Sayers, *Papal judges delegate in the province of Canterbury, 1198–1254* (1971) • D. A. Carpenter, *The minority of Henry III* (1990) • *Ann. mon.*, vol. 1 • *Fasti Angl., 1066–1300*, [Monastic cathedrals], 56

Paneth, Friedrich Adolf (1887–1958), chemist, was born on 31 August 1887 in Vienna, the second of the three sons of Joseph Paneth, a distinguished physiologist, and his wife, Sophie Schwab, the daughter of a leading industrialist. His mother was unusually well educated, and had a strong interest in the natural sciences and philosophy. Both his parents were of Jewish descent but he and his two brothers were brought up as protestants. He was educated at the Schotten Gymnasium and the University of Vienna. He then studied for a year under Adolph von Baeyer (1835–1917) in Munich before returning to Vienna to obtain his PhD in 1910.

As a research student Paneth worked on organic chemistry, but his interests changed when in 1912 he became assistant to Stefan Meyer in the recently established Radium Research Institute attached to the Vienna Academy of Science. The institute rapidly became a leading international centre for the study of radioactivity; after his five years there Paneth remained an inorganic chemist for the rest of his life. On 6 December 1913 he married Else Hartmann, daughter of the distinguished medieval historian Ludo Moritz Hartmann (1865–1924), who served as Austrian ambassador in Berlin after the First World War. She was a doctor of medicine and practised in Vienna and later in Edinburgh. They had two children, Eva and Heinrich Rudolf, the latter of whom, known generally under the name Heinz Post, became a distinguished philosopher of science. In 1917 Paneth joined the Deutsche Technische Hochschule at Prague, and two years later he went as assistant professor to the University of Hamburg. In 1922 he became head of the inorganic department of the Chemical Institute of the University of Berlin. In 1929 he received a call to become a full professor at the University of Königsberg and was also made head of the chemical institute there, an unusual distinction for an inorganic chemist.

When Hitler came to power in 1933 Paneth was on a lecture tour in Britain and decided to remain as a guest lecturer at the Imperial College of Science and Technology. In 1938 he was appointed reader in atomic chemistry at the University of London. In 1939 he was invited to the chair of chemistry at Durham. In 1943–5 he was in charge of the chemistry division of the joint British–Canadian atomic energy team in Montreal. In addition to his long experience in radioactivity studies, staff at Montreal also appreciated his efforts to inject 'an element of old world courtesy and culture' (Emeléus, 229) into the often tense atmosphere of wartime research. After the war he returned to Durham where he established the Londonderry Laboratory for Radiochemistry and resumed his former researches. When he reached the age of retirement in 1953 he accepted an invitation to become director of the Max Planck Institute of Chemistry in Mainz where the last five years of his life were spent in building up an active research school.

One of Paneth's first pieces of research was an unsuccessful attempt to separate radium *D* from radiolead. George Hevesy was engaged in a similar attempt in Manchester and the results of their investigations, which proved negative, were published in a joint paper in 1913. The consequent probability that radium *D* was inseparable from lead was immediately put to use. Early in January 1913 the first joint investigation with radioactive tracers was carried out in the study of the solubility of lead sulphide and lead chromate; labelled lead and bismuth were also used in electrochemical studies. In the ensuing years Paneth carried out several important studies applying radium *D* and *E* and thorium *B* as tracers. One of these was the study of adsorption of Th*B*, Th*C*, and Ra on such compounds as titanium, chromium and manganese oxides, barium sulphate and chromate, and the silver halides. Adsorption was strong when the radio-elements formed an insoluble compound with the electronegative component of the adsorbing material. This work was embodied in *Radioelements as Indicators and other Selected Topics in Inorganic Chemistry* (1928).

Before he left the Radium Research Institute Paneth discovered the existence of a volatile polonium hydride, which led to the discovery of volatile bismuth and lead hydrides. After he left Vienna he discovered a volatile hydride of tin and much enlarged the knowledge of an already known germanium hydride. These studies led to the recognition that all elements with atomic numbers which have one to four units less than a rare gas are capable of forming gaseous hydrides. Through these investigations Paneth became the greatest authority of his time on volatile hydrides.

At Hamburg Paneth continued his important studies on surface adsorption and worked out a method which enabled him to determine the surface area of powders by using radioactive indicators.

Possibly Paneth's most important work, the demonstration of the existence of free radicals, was to a large extent carried out while he was at Königsberg. The preparation of free methyl had been attempted by Kolbe in 1849 and the concept of an organic radical had since been prominent in many theories of organic reactions, although direct proof was lacking. Paneth and his co-workers succeeded in showing that free methyl radicals produced in the gas phase could persist for a small but measurable time before recombining to form methane. Free ethyl was similarly produced from lead tetraethyl and shown to react with zinc, cadmium, antimony, and lead. He also succeeded in estimating the mean half-life of radicals.

In the spring of 1913 Paneth spent a few months with Frederick Soddy at Glasgow where he became interested in gas analytical methods which he later developed extensively and applied to the study of the isolation and measurement of minute amounts of helium and other atmospheric gases. He then applied these methods of helium analysis to the determination of the age of meteorites, and published *The Origin of Meteorites* (1940). He arrived at very high values for the age of some meteorites but the discovery of the production of helium by cosmic rays led him in 1952 to re-examine some of his conclusions. He arrived at the result that a substantial part of the helium present in iron meteorites was composed of ^{3}He and the age of the meteorites was correspondingly less. According to his paper published in 1954 the age of most meteorites is between 100 and 200 million years and some very much less. He investigated numerous meteorites and bequeathed to the Radium Research Institute in Vienna his collection of over a hundred specimens together with literature on the subject. His studies of meteorites led him on to the problem of the formation of the elements and the universe. He also made numerous contributions to the study of the stratosphere. Always a most fascinating lecturer, he was especially stimulating on these topics.

The methods of separating and measuring very small quantities of helium and other rare gases were used in other ways by Paneth. The first recorded measurement of a microscopic product in a nuclear reaction involving neutrons was made by him when he succeeded in measuring the helium formed in the neutron irradiation of methyl borate. Excited by this result, he presented it with characteristic flair. Describing the experiment to produce helium from methyl borate in such a way as to echo the alchemical pursuit of transmutation, he called it the 'Chemical detection of artificial transmutation of elements', and announced: 'for the first time, so far as we are aware—an artificially produced element has been separated, spectroscopically observed, and measured. We presume that the old alchemistical goal can be achieved today in other cases too' (*Nature*, 136, July–Dec 1935, 950).

An urbane man, Paneth—in his various posts in Britain, Germany, and Canada—was skilled in establishing an academic climate in which national differences among his staff were irrelevant, and in which values and opinions were freely exchanged. He encouraged chemistry students to take an interest in the history of science, a subject on which he lectured periodically from his earliest days as a university teacher, and on which he wrote many papers for journals such as *Nature*, *Discovery*, and *Endeavour*. These interests were reflected in his own way of life as a scientist. In a tribute to Frederick Soddy (*Nature*, 180, July–Dec 1957, 1086) he attributed Soddy's 'tragic isolation' in part to his inability as a chemist to come to terms with the increasing influence of physicists on the study of radioactivity. Paneth, for his part, while expressing understanding of Soddy's predicament, promoted a historical understanding of the nature of chemistry as the antidote to such disciplinary resentments. Specifically, in an article entitled 'The role of chemistry in the study of atomic transmutation' (*Nature*, 137, Jan–June 1936, 560–62), he urged that his parallel between the alchemical pursuit of transmutation and the modern field of radioactivity provided the kind of historical context that could assist chemists to carve out a specifically chemical role for themselves at the same time as working co-operatively with physicists.

Some of Paneth's general writings were published posthumously in 1964 under the title *Chemistry and beyond*, edited by H. Dingle and G. R. Martin. At Durham he energetically championed the reputation of the forgotten Durham cosmologist Thomas Wright (1711–1786), whose work had influenced Immanuel Kant. Few knew that the round stone tower at Westerton near Durham had been Wright's observatory. Paneth succeeded in arousing public interest with the result that a memorial plaque was affixed to the tower and the two hundredth anniversary of the publication of Wright's *Original Theory* duly celebrated in 1950. Paneth was naturalized in 1939. He was a member of the Athenaeum and was elected FRS in 1947. He died at 78 Billrothstrasse, Vienna, on 17 September 1958 and was buried in the suburban churchyard of Döbling, where by his wish the inscription on his grave bears no more than his name followed by the letters FRS.

GEORGE HEVESY, *rev.* JOSEPH GROSS

Sources H. J. Emeléus, *Memoirs FRS*, 6 (1960), 227–46 · *DSB* · *The Times* (19 Sept 1958), 13d · *The Times* (25 Sept 1958), 15d · *Nature*, 182 (1958), 1274–5, 1773 · E. Glueckauf, *Proceedings of the Chemical Society* (1959), 103–5 · *CGPLA Eng. & Wales* (1959)
Archives Nuffield Oxf., corresp. with Lord Cherwell
Likenesses W. Stoneman, photograph, 1953, NPG · L. Meitner-Graf, photograph, RS · W. Stoneman, photograph, RS
Wealth at death £15,307 9*s*. 6*d*. in England: administration with will, 25 June 1959, *CGPLA Eng. & Wales*

Panizzi, Sir Anthony [*formerly* Antonio Genesio Maria] (**1797–1879**), librarian, was born on 16 September 1797 at Brescello in the duchy of Modena (then part of the Cisalpine Republic). He was the first child and only son of Luigi Panizzi (1764–1845) and Caterina Gruppi (who were married in 1796) and was baptized Antonio Genesio Maria. His sister Margherita was born in 1802 and lived until 1851. His father was a pharmacist, but several of his ancestors on both his father's and his mother's side were lawyers.

Early years, 1797–1823 After his initial education in Brescello, Panizzi went in 1810 to the grammar school at Reggio nell'Emilia, and from there in 1814 to the University of Parma, where he took his degree in jurisprudence in August 1818. It was probably while he was in Parma that he joined one of the secret societies which had been established to advance the cause of Italian unity. He always denied that he had belonged to the Carbonari, and it is possible that he became a member of a similar body called the Sublimi Maestri Perfetti.

Sir Anthony Panizzi (1797–1879), by George Frederic Watts, *c.*1847

He returned home to Brescello and, after recovering from a severe attack of typhoid, he was in 1819 appointed Amministratore del Commune e della Congregazione di Carità, and also Giudice dell'Annona (roughly the equivalent of town clerk and inspector of weights and measures). He also practised as a lawyer, and in 1821 became inspector of the public schools of Brescello.

Panizzi became deeply involved in the activities of the secret societies which were campaigning for the liberty and unification of Italy. Alarmed by a revolt in Naples which for a time placed that kingdom under the control of the Carbonari, Duke Francis IV of Modena in September 1820 issued a decree that membership of the Carbonari or similar bodies constituted the offence of *lèse-majesté*, for which the death penalty could be awarded. Arrests of suspects began on the orders of Giulio Besini, Francis's feared chief of police, and friends of Panizzi were among those sent to prison. On 14 May 1822 Besini was murdered, and Francis reacted by setting up a court at Rubiera (a small town between Reggio and Modena) to demonstrate how determined he was to crush the revolutionaries. Forty-seven persons were convicted and one of these, a young priest named Giuseppe Andreoli, was executed on 17 October. The others were sentenced to imprisonment or to the galleys.

Panizzi's name had been mentioned during the court proceedings, and although they lacked sufficient evidence to prosecute him, the authorities were well aware by this time of his opposition to the regime. He began to make arrangements to flee the country and, having been warned by a friend that his arrest was imminent, he set out for Switzerland on 22 October 1822. He was not to revisit Brescello until 1857, eleven years after the death of Duke Francis IV. He was in Switzerland (first at Lugano and then at Geneva) from the late autumn of 1822 until the spring of 1823. During this time he wrote a book of 247 pages on the Rubiera trials with the title *Dei processi e delle sentenze contra gli imputati di lesa-maestà e di adherenza alle sette proscitte negli stati di Modena*; this was published in Switzerland in 1823 with the false imprint of Madrid; only two copies are known to survive.

Panizzi's authorship was not in doubt since he printed his name on the title-page, and the bitterness of his attacks on the conduct of the trials must have infuriated the Modena government. In February 1823 they began proceedings against him, despite the fact that he was safely outside their jurisdiction. A trial was held in September and on 6 October, in his absence, he was condemned to death in effigy, to the confiscation of his goods, and to the payment of costs. The execution in effigy probably never took place, and the attempt by the inspector of finances to obtain from Panizzi the costs of the trial was predictably unsuccessful.

First years in England, 1823–1837 Panizzi arrived in London in May 1823, after he and other Italian exiles had been ordered by the authorities in Geneva to leave, as a result of pressure from the Austrian, French, and Sardinian governments. Being short of money, he had to live very cheaply. He became acquainted with other Italian exiles, especially Santorre Santa Rosa, a Piedmontese noble, and Ugo Foscolo, the poet, and was advised by them to try his fortune in Liverpool, since London was over-provided with teachers of Italian. Foscolo gave him a letter of introduction to William Roscoe, the Liverpool banker and biographer of Lorenzo de' Medici, and after three months in London Panizzi travelled north, having borrowed the money for his fare. He was kindly received by Roscoe and by the Revd William Shepherd, another enthusiast for Italy, and soon acquired a number of pupils. He made friends, including Francis Haywood, the translator of Kant, with whom he remained on very close terms until Haywood's death in 1858. In 1824 he contributed an article to the *Edinburgh Review*, and the next year he gave two series of lectures at the Royal Institution of Liverpool. He visited Oxford to study manuscripts of Dante in the Bodleian Library, and began to prepare his editions of Boiardo and Ariosto.

By 1826 Panizzi had become acquainted with the lawyer and politician Henry Brougham, who was on friendly terms with Roscoe and other Liverpool figures. He accompanied Brougham to the Lancaster assizes in 1827, when Brougham was one of the counsel for the prosecution of Edward Gibbon Wakefield for the abduction of an heiress, and is said to have found Panizzi's knowledge of continental marriage law of considerable help. So when the University of London (later University College) was founded in 1828 by a group among whom Brougham was prominent, he supported Panizzi's application for the professorship of Italian, and in February 1828 Panizzi was appointed to the post. He settled at 2 Gower Street North, where he lived until he moved into a residence in the British Museum in 1837.

The professorship proved a great disappointment because Panizzi had very few pupils, and his financial prospects were worse than they had been in Liverpool. This troubled Brougham, who had largely been responsible for Panizzi's return to London, so when he became lord chancellor in November 1830 (and so one of the three principal trustees of the British Museum, who were responsible for appointing all the staff) he strongly favoured the proposal that Panizzi should be appointed an extra assistant librarian in the department of printed books. Brougham was supported by another trustee of the museum, Thomas Grenville, the wealthy book collector, who had assisted Panizzi's studies of Boiardo by allowing him to consult the early editions in his library. So on 27 April 1831 Panizzi became a member of the staff of the British Museum at a salary of £200 per annum for a five-day week, with an extra £75 if he worked a sixth day. He remained professor of Italian at the university until December 1837, and he continued his work on his editions of Boiardo's *Orlando innamorato* and Ariosto's *Orlando Furioso*, which were published in nine volumes between 1830 and 1834.

When he joined the staff of the museum Panizzi at first spent much of his time cataloguing the French Revolution tracts that had been bought from J. W. Croker in 1831. Then in 1834, when the museum trustees decided to suspend the classified catalogue of the library which had been begun in 1824, and to concentrate on the production of a revised version of the alphabetical author catalogue, H. H. Baber, the keeper of printed books, recommended that Panizzi should supervise this work. Unfortunately the trustees rejected this advice, and Panizzi became one of a team of four working on the revision—he dealt with books in the Romance languages. He produced so many more catalogue entries than his colleagues that a subcommittee of the trustees recommended that his salary should be increased by £75 per annum. When the matter came before the full body of the trustees, however, they refused to grant this increase, while paying tribute to Panizzi's zeal and ability.

From 1832 onwards Panizzi worked in his spare time on a catalogue of the books in the library of the Royal Society. Relations between him and the society became very strained because the council interfered with his work and delayed payments to him. The catalogue eventually appeared in 1839 and 1841, after Panizzi had protested about the whole transaction in a pamphlet addressed to the duke of Sussex, president of the Royal Society. Panizzi was left with a permanent dislike of scientists, whom he described as 'crotchety'.

In the 1830s there was a good deal of criticism of the British Museum. From its foundation in 1753 to the end of the eighteenth century it had been a very torpid institution, but after the appointment of Joseph Planta as principal librarian in 1799 matters had begun to improve. The collections increased, more attention was paid to service to the public, and the number of staff began to grow. Despite this, public opinion demanded more, and select committees of the House of Commons met in 1835 and 1836 to investigate the museum. With his usual energy Panizzi gathered information to be laid before the committees, by sending questionnaires to continental libraries and visiting many of them during the winter of 1835–6. Thus, when he appeared before the select committee in June 1836 he spoke confidently on the basis of a sound knowledge of the problems involved. His emphatic statements about the need for a first-class catalogue and for considerably increased purchase funds to enable poor students to have access to as good collections as rich men did, created a considerable impression.

Keeper of printed books, 1837–1856 It was not surprising, therefore, that when Baber retired from the keepership of printed books in 1837 he was succeeded on 15 July by Panizzi rather than Henry Cary, who was senior to Panizzi and well known as the translator of Dante, but whose health was poor and whose vigour was not comparable with that of the man who overtook him. Energy was certainly a prerequisite for the new keeper, who was faced with formidable problems. He was short of staff and of money for acquisitions, and he had to cope with the enormous task of compiling a new general catalogue. The problem requiring most immediate attention, however, was that of moving the 163 thousand volumes of the old library from the decaying Montagu House to the north wing of the new museum designed by Robert Smirke. This building had begun with the east wing, which was constructed between 1823 and 1827, and from 1828 held the library of George III (presented by George IV). Panizzi organized the move of the remainder of the collections of printed books to the new museum between June 1838 and May 1840, and ensured that on average only 8000 volumes (five per cent of the whole) were unavailable at any one time. In September 1838 he moved the reading-rooms from the south-east corner of the museum to larger rooms at the east end of the north wing, and improved the methods of supplying books to readers.

In October 1837 Panizzi submitted his first report on the catalogue to the trustees, and a month later he argued against printing the catalogue until the whole work had been prepared in manuscript. This began a battle that lasted for eight years. The trustees demanded that the catalogue should be printed letter by letter and that the whole work should be complete by the end of 1844. Much against his will, Panizzi produced the first volume, containing the entries for the letter A, in 1841, but he was so dismayed by the number of errors that it contained as a result of the excessive speed of production that he determined to print no more volumes. Despite the trustees' attempts to force him to do so, he adhered to this resolution, and at last in 1846 the trustees admitted defeat and agreed to the suspension of printing. The catalogue was finally printed between 1880 and 1900, after Panizzi's death, when it was complete in manuscript form.

Attention was then focused on the need for an increased purchase grant. Between 1837 and 1845 the average parliamentary grant for the normal purchase of printed books was about £3600 per annum. Panizzi produced a preliminary report on the state of the collections in 1842, and then a much fuller one in 1843 and 1844. This sketched the history of the growth of the collections, and then reported the result of checking the library's holdings against various bibliographies and standard works. This conclusively showed that many gaps needed to be filled, and Panizzi argued for regular parliamentary grants on a liberal scale to make good the neglect of the past: 'The expense … will no doubt be great; but so is the nation which is to bear it.' (*On the Collection of Printed Books at the British Museum*, 1845, 74). The trustees forwarded Panizzi's report to the Treasury with a request for a much larger grant. With unusual speed and generosity the Treasury, in January 1846, agreed that £10,000 per annum should be granted for some years to come. This increased grant continued for much of the remainder of the century.

Panizzi's friendship with Thomas Grenville caused the latter to bequeath to the museum his 20,000 volume library—one of the most valuable collections of the department of printed books. This arrived in 1847, which was the year in which a royal commission was set up to investigate the museum. This had been asked for by scientists who were dissatisfied with the state of the natural history department, but in fact the commission spent much of its time dealing with the affairs of the department of printed books. Panizzi fought for his department with his usual energy and was entirely successful. The report of the commission, which appeared in 1850, supported his stand on the catalogue, and spoke highly of the service provided for those who used the reading-rooms. The abolition of the post of secretary to the trustees was recommended; this was an important victory for Panizzi, who had fought a long battle with Josiah Forshall, secretary since 1827. Forshall had been the most powerful official of the museum since the changes that followed the report of the 1836 select committee.

The decision to abolish Forshall's post led to the control of the intake of copyright deposit books being transferred to Panizzi, and he set about enforcing the museum's right to a copy of every work published in Great Britain and Ireland. He made himself very unpopular with the publishers by doing so, and the attacks on him grew so fierce that he asked the trustees to relieve him of the task. They refused to do so, but awarded him extra pay for his success in increasing the intake by over fifty per cent.

This increase, added to the great number of additional purchased items as a result of the extra grant, caused an accommodation crisis in the early 1850s. So Panizzi produced his scheme to build, mainly of iron, a new circular reading-room surrounded by bookstacks in the interior quadrangle of the museum. This was constructed between 1854 and 1857, to the plans of Sydney Smirke, which were drawn up in close collaboration with Panizzi and which created great public interest. The new building—one of the noblest of the Victorian age—held 302 readers and up to 1.5 million volumes.

Part of Panizzi's success was the result of his good relations with many influential people. It is remarkable that a person who arrived in this country as a penniless refugee, and who always spoke English with a strong accent, became such an accepted figure in high political and social circles. He was a very sociable man, and by the 1840s was a regular visitor to Holland House, the great whig meeting-place. He was highly regarded by Lord Clarendon, and was a friend of Lord Lansdowne, Lord Palmerston, Lord Rutherfurd, and Lord Langdale. He was for many years on close terms with W. E. Gladstone, who last visited him four days before his death.

Panizzi's long hours of labour at the museum and his busy social life did not prevent him from retaining a keen interest in the affairs of Italy, even though he had become a naturalized British subject in 1832. This change of allegiance had annoyed Mazzini, who arrived in England in 1837; he and Panizzi were acquainted, but the latter was suspicious of Mazzini's constant intrigues. Nevertheless, when Mazzini's letters were opened at the Post Office by order of the home secretary, and the contents communicated to the Austrian embassy, Panizzi wrote an article in the *North British Review* in 1844 criticizing the government for acting as a spy for foreign despots.

After Gladstone visited southern Italy in 1850 and publicized the disgraceful treatment by the Neapolitan government of such liberals as Carlo Poerio and Luigi Settembrini, Panizzi went to Naples the next year, visited the prisons, and lectured King Ferdinand (Bomba) on the sufferings of the political prisoners. By 1855 there had been no improvement, and so Panizzi raised money to buy a ship to be used to rescue Settembrini and others from the prison on the island of San Stefano. His hopes were dashed when the ship bought was wrecked in a storm off Yarmouth. Eventually in 1859 Settembrini and other prisoners were rescued by his son when they were being deported to the USA, and arrived in England, where Panizzi arranged a fund for their support.

Principal librarian, 1856–1866 In March 1856 Panizzi became head of the British Museum when he was promoted principal librarian to succeed Sir Henry Ellis, to the fury of Sir Frederic Madden, the keeper of manuscripts, with whom Panizzi had fought a series of battles, nearly all of which he had won. During his twenty years as keeper of printed books, the number of volumes had increased from 235,000 to 540,000, the number of staff from thirty-four to eighty-nine, considerable progress had been made with the revision of the catalogue, the purchase grant had been increased, the Grenville Library had been received by bequest, the intake of copyright deposit material had been enlarged, and the bulk of the new reading-room and bookstacks had been constructed.

By the time that he became principal librarian Panizzi's greatest work for the museum had been completed, and as the 1860s progressed his health grew steadily worse. He concerned himself with the need for more space for the antiquities and natural history departments, and campaigned for the transfer of the latter collections to a new building elsewhere—a move that did not in fact take place until after his death. Plans for extra accommodation involving new buildings adjoining the existing museum also failed to materialize until the 1880s. He did, however, succeed in having the unwieldy department of antiquities divided into three separate departments.

Panizzi was also successful in obtaining the agreement of the Treasury to improvements in the pay of the staff of the museum. He had long argued that the staff should be granted the right of superannuation, and in 1860 he successfully negotiated this. A condition was that normally no future entrants would be entitled to pensions unless they had been examined and certificated by the civil service commissioners. This led to disputes between the commissioners and Panizzi, who complained that unsatisfactory candidates were granted certificates, while satisfactory ones were rejected by the commissioners.

Such disputes appealed to Panizzi's combative instincts. He battled with colleagues such as Sir Frederic Madden, the Revd Josiah Forshall, Edward Hawkins, and Edward Edwards, with the authorities of the Royal Society, with users of the reading-room, such as Sir Nicholas Harris Nicolas, and with trustees who disagreed with him. One of his successors commented on his quickness in taking offence, his acerbity in argument, and his firm belief that he was always right (A. H. Chaplin, *150 Years of the General Catalogue of Printed Books in the British Museum*, 1987, 6). Against this must be set his generous spirit, his concern for the well-being of his staff (from whom he expected in return dedicated and obedient service), and the great number of friends who were devoted to him.

In 1863 Panizzi had to take four months' leave in the hope that a period of residence abroad would improve his health. By 1865 he felt that he could bear the burden of office no longer, and he asked permission to resign. The trustees reluctantly agreed, but asked him to stay on until his successor was appointed. A year later he had to insist that he must be relieved, and on 26 June John Winter Jones succeeded him.

Despite his official duties and his poor health Panizzi continued in the 1850s and 1860s to play an important part in the affairs of Italy; he has been described as his native country's unofficial ambassador in his adopted country. He was in close touch with Cavour, and through his friend Prosper Merimée he influenced Napoleon III (who had a high opinion of Panizzi, as did his wife, the Empress Eugénie) in the period leading up to the creation of the kingdom of Italy. His contacts with such British politicians as Palmerston, Russell, and Gladstone enabled him to put to them the views of the Italians who were working for the unification of their country. When Garibaldi paid his triumphant visit to England in April 1864, Panizzi played a prominent part in the arrangements, organized a dinner for him with leading whigs and Liberals, and accompanied him on a visit to the tomb of Foscolo at Chiswick.

Last years and reputation During his retirement Panizzi maintained his interest in the affairs of Italy and the British Museum until the final breakdown of his health. In 1868 he became a senator of Italy (although illness prevented him from ever taking his seat), and in 1869 he reluctantly accepted a KCB (having refused a knighthood in 1861). In 1859 he had been awarded a DCL by Oxford University, and he had also been given the Légion d'honneur in 1851, the Sardinian order of Saints Maurice and Lazarus in 1855, and he was made a commander of the order of the Crown of Italy in 1868. He attached little importance to such honours, and was probably more pleased by the fact that in 1856 the staff of the department of printed books subscribed for a bust of him by Baron Marochetti which was placed above the door of the new reading-room.

In 1868 Panizzi nearly died as a result of a serious illness, and was very angry when he discovered that a Roman Catholic priest had tried to gain access to him. Born and brought up as a Catholic, Panizzi developed into a typical continental anti-clerical, but although he ceased to practise he never renounced his faith. When the subject of religion arose he avoided controversy, and simply said, 'I am a Roman Catholic'. Gladstone tried to ensure that he died in a state of grace. Panizzi died unmarried at 31 Bloomsbury Square (where he had lived since leaving his residence in the British Museum in 1865) on 8 April, after a period when he was blind and paralysed. A Catholic priest officiated at his funeral, which took place at Kensal Green Roman Catholic cemetery, London, on 12 April 1879.

The pressures of his political life and of his political activities prevented Panizzi from continuing the literary work that he had begun with his editions of Boiardo and Ariosto. He did produce an edition of Boiardo's *Sonetti e canzone* in 1835, but his only other scholarly works (both of which were published in 1858) were *Chi era Francesco da Bologna?*, in which he attempted to identify the goldsmith and typecutter of this name with the painter Francesco Raibolini, and *Le prime quattro edizioni della 'Divina Commedia' letteralmente ristampate*, edited by Panizzi and printed at the expense of the fifth Lord Vernon. Apart from about twenty articles which he published in various reviews between 1824 and 1850 his only other writings concerned his official work. *On the Supply of Printed Books from the Library to the Reading Room* (1846) was a robust attack on the critics of his department, and *Passages in my Official Life* (1871) was a defence of his achievements which was not weakened by any false modesty.

Panizzi was rightly aware of his own worth. A big man in every sense, tall and broad, and full of self-confidence, he was in the words of *The Times* obituary 'free-spoken, almost to bluntness; the most genial companion when pleased; decidedly a rough customer if ruffled' (*The Times*, 9 April 1879). He is the outstanding figure in the history of the British Museum Library. He transformed the department of printed books into the leading library of the world, a position it retained for many years after his death. More than a century later the methods that he introduced were still in operation in the library. P. R. Harris

Sources E. Miller, *Prince of librarians: the life and times of Antonio Panizzi of the British Museum* (1967) · C. Brooks, *Antonio Panizzi* (1931) · L. Fagan, *The life of Sir Anthony Panizzi*, 2 vols. (1880) · L. Fagan, ed., *Lettere ad Antonio Panizzi* (1880) · [W. C. Cartwright], review, *QR*, 151 (1881), 463–501 · *The Times* (9 April 1879) · *The Athenaeum* (19 April 1879), 503–5 · Gladstone, *Diaries* · d. cert.

Archives BL, corresp., etc. · BL, corresp. and papers, Add. MSS 30999, 31124, 36714–36729, 49596, 59778; Egerton MS 3677 · BM, corresp., etc. · UCL, letters | BL, corresp. with Count Cavour, Add. MS 39757 · BL, letters to Sir H. Ellis, Add. MS 48340 · BL, corresp. with W. E. Gladstone, Add. MS 44274 · BL, corresp. with Lord Holland, Add. MSS 52008–52009 · BL, letters to Sir J. P. Lacaita, Add. MS 42177 · BL, corresp. Sir A. H. Layard, Add. MSS 38986–39116, *passim* · BL, corresp. with Sir F. Madden, Egerton MSS 2842–2848, *passim* • Bodl. Oxf., corresp. with Sir Thomas Phillipps • NHM, corresp. with Sir Richard Owen and William Clift • NL Scot., letters to Lord Rutherfurd • NL Wales, letters to Sir George Cornewall Lewis • PRO, corresp. with Lord John Russell, PRO 30/22 • U. Southampton L., letters mainly to Lord Palmerston and Lady Palmerston

Likenesses G. F. Watts, oils, *c*.1847, NPG [*see illus.*] • R. C. Lucas, wax medallion, 1850, BM, NPG • C. Marochetti, marble bust, 1856, BL • E. Edwards, photograph, 1864, repro. in L. A. Reeve, *Portraits of men of eminence*, 2 (1864), 17 • G. F. Watts, portrait, *c*.1866, BM • Ape [C. Pellegrini], watercolour caricature, NPG; repro. in *VF* (17 Jan 1874) • photographs, BM, NPG

Wealth at death under £3000: probate, 21 April 1879, *CGPLA Eng. & Wales*

Panke, John (*fl*. 1604–1618), Church of England clergyman and author, was 'a very frequent and noted preacher of his time, and well read in theological authors, but withal a very zealous enemy … against the papists' and, Anthony Wood also affirms, attended Oxford University (Wood, *Ath. Oxon.*, 2.274). The report is plausible for although there is no record of his college or of any degree all but one of Panke's extant works were printed at Oxford. Before 25 March 1604 he had been instituted on presentation of the crown to the rectory of Broad Hinton, Wiltshire, for on that date he signed from there the preface to his book *A Short Admonition by Way of Dialogue*, dedicated to his patron, Lady Katherine Wroughton 'daughter to the last Marquess deceased' (William Paulet, third marquess of Winchester; *d*. 1598) and wife of Giles Wroughton, the lord of the manor. Panke's *The Fall of Babel, by the Confusion of Tongues*, was signed on 1 November 1607 from Tidworth, that is North Tidworth, Wiltshire, where he had become rector. Wood reports that Panke 'at length had some cure in the church of Salisbury'. Again, he seems to have been well informed for, while John Mompesson was rector at Tidworth from 1617, Panke's *Collectanea out of St Gregory the Great* prefaced 'to my friend Mr George Churchowse, mayor of Salisbury', and 'to the justices and aldermen, his assistants, and the whole incorporation there' was signed from 'the close at Sarum' on 24 June 1618 (misprinted in *Romanism Condemned*, 1635 as '24th January 1618'). Of his further activities, or his death, nothing is known.

STEPHEN WRIGHT

Sources Wood, *Ath. Oxon.*, new edn, 2.274 • *VCH Wiltshire*, 12.109, 116; 15.161 • G. D. Squibb, ed., *Wiltshire visitation pedigrees, 1623*, Harleian Society, 105–6 (1954), 219–20 • Foster, *Alum. Oxon.* • J. Panke, *The fall of Babel, by the confusion of tongues* (1607), preface • J. Panke, *A short admonition by way of dialogue* (1604), preface

Pankhurst, Dame Christabel Harriette (1880–1958), suffragette, was born on 22 September 1880 at 1 Drayton Terrace, Old Trafford, Manchester, the daughter of Richard Marsden Pankhurst (1835/6–1898), a radical barrister, and his wife, Emmeline Goulden (1858–1928) [*see* Pankhurst, Emmeline]. The eldest of their five children, Christabel was her mother's favourite. In 1886 the family moved to London where their home in Russell Square became a centre for gatherings of socialists, leading reformers, Fabians, suffragists, and freethinkers. The young Pankhursts were encouraged at an early age to attend such meetings and to make themselves useful by arranging chairs, giving out leaflets, and collecting contributions. Dr

Dame Christabel Harriette Pankhurst (1880–1958), by Kate Simmons, 1910

Pankhurst, an ardent campaigner for the advanced cause of women's suffrage, would often exclaim, 'Why are women so patient? Why don't you force us to give you the vote?' (E. S. Pankhurst, 97). Such experiences had a decisive effect on Christabel. Nothing she learned from the inadequate education offered by governesses or, when the family moved back to the north in 1893, at the high schools she attended—first in Southport and then in Manchester—compared with the political education she received at home. One day, when the family were discussing women's suffrage, Christabel startled her mother with the remark, 'How long you women have been trying for the vote. For my part, I mean to get it' (E. Pankhurst, 35–6).

In summer 1898, accompanied by her mother, Christabel went to Geneva to perfect her French; while she was there, news arrived unexpectedly of her father's death. Since Dr Pankhurst left nothing but debts, his wife had to sell their home and move to a humbler residence at 62 Nelson Street, Manchester. She gratefully accepted the post of registrar of births and deaths and also opened a shop in the hope that it might provide some income as well as employment for Christabel, who intensely disliked the work. Seeing her unhappiness, Emmeline suggested that her eldest daughter attend some classes at Manchester University, and it was there that Christabel met Esther Roper, who, with Eva Gore-Booth, was active in encouraging working women to campaign for the parliamentary vote. By the end of 1902 Christabel, who, like her mother, was already a member of the Independent Labour Party (ILP), was lecturing in Cheshire, Lancashire, Yorkshire, and Scotland for the North of England Society for Women's Suffrage, of which Esther Roper was secretary. Becoming increasingly critical of the ILP's lukewarm attitude on the women question, Christabel warned that working men could be as unjust to women as men of other classes. On 10 October 1903 Emmeline and a few other socialist women founded the Women's Social and Political Union (WSPU) to campaign for votes for women on the same terms as they were, or might be, granted to men. Taking the motto 'Deeds, not words', the WSPU restricted its membership to women only, and aimed to be free of class and party political affiliation. That same autumn, Christabel enrolled for a law degree at Manchester University.

The militant campaign of the WSPU begins Despite the demands of her university studies, Christabel became an energetic speaker in the early years of peaceful campaigning, but soon decided that a more confrontational approach was necessary if women's suffrage was to be won. Furthermore, she believed that government support was essential if women's enfranchisement was to be granted. Thus on 13 October 1905 she and Annie Kenney, a working-class factory worker recently recruited to the WSPU, attended a Liberal Party meeting in the Free Trade Hall, Manchester, where at question time Annie asked, 'Will the Liberal government give votes to women?' When no answer was given, Christabel repeated the question. The meeting broke into uproar as the women were dragged outside where Christabel deliberately committed the technical offence of spitting at a policeman in order to court arrest. Charged with causing an obstruction, both chose prison rather than pay a fine, an action that brought the desired effect of media attention to the women's cause. From now on, heckling politicians became a key WSPU tactic, along with other minor acts of civil disobedience, including demonstrations to parliament.

In July 1906 Christabel graduated with a first-class honours degree in law and then moved to WSPU headquarters, now in London, where she became chief organizer on a salary of £2 10*s.* per week. Emmeline Pethick-Lawrence, married to a wealthy barrister, Frederick, was treasurer of the WSPU and, inspired by Christabel's faith in militant tactics as well as enchanted by her personality, the Pethick-Lawrences took her into their own home where she lived for the next six years. Surveying the London scene, Christabel decided that it was too dependent for its demonstrations on ILP women from the East End, and reaffirmed the policy of no affiliation to any political grouping or any particular class. At the Cockermouth by-election the following month, she announced that in the future the WSPU would oppose all Labour parliamentary candidates in addition to Liberals and Conservatives, a move strongly supported by her mother but not by her sisters (Estelle) Sylvia *Pankhurst and Adela [*see* Walsh, Adela]. In September 1907 both Christabel and Emmeline resigned their membership of the ILP, since the Labour Party, fearing that votes for women on the same terms as men would only enfranchise middle-class women who would vote Conservative, now opposed the extension of the franchise on a property qualification to a section of the population. Through all the long years of campaigning ahead, the uncompromising and determined Christabel never wavered in her conviction that the breaking of the sex barrier against women was the key barrier to be broken, a view that had been undoubtedly strengthened by the fact that she had been refused admission to the bar because of her sex.

Christabel as a WSPU leader Christabel's insistence on an independent policy for the WSPU and her increasingly autocratic style of leadership caused tensions among the membership, so that by the autumn of 1907 a splinter group had left to form another militant organization later called the Women's Freedom League. As Emmeline Pankhurst, the leader of the WSPU, spent most of her time speaking in the provinces, the daily administration of business fell to Christabel and the Pethick-Lawrences. Although Emmeline was consulted on major issues, she had the greatest faith in the political flair of her eldest daughter. It was Christabel who played the key role in policy making, emerging as a confident, fearless, and imaginative strategist.

Christabel helped to plan spectacular events that attracted widespread attention, such as the 'Trojan horse' raid on the House of Commons in February 1908 when between twenty and thirty women jumped out of a pantechnicon van in an attempt to gain entrance. When Emmeline, Christabel, and Flora Drummond appeared at Bow Street court in October 1908, charged with conduct likely to provoke a breach of the peace, she acted as lawyer for the trio and, in a brilliant move, subpoenaed as witnesses two cabinet ministers, Herbert Gladstone and Lloyd George. Called 'Suffragette Portia' by the press, Christabel's name became a household word. Her youth, charm, vitality, accomplished oratory, and wit as a speaker captivated her audiences. Furthermore, she outlined WSPU policy in regular articles published in *Votes for Women*, edited by the Pethick-Lawrences, and in a series of pamphlets.

In July 1909, the imprisoned suffragette Marion Wallace Dunlop refused to eat food until her demand to be treated as a political prisoner and placed in the privileged first division was granted. After fasting for ninety-one hours, she was released. The hunger strike was soon adopted by other imprisoned suffragettes, but two months later the government responded not by releasing the women but by forcible feeding, an act that was condemned with burning indignation by Christabel and the other WSPU leaders.

When the Liberals were returned to government but with no overall majority in the general election of January 1910, Christabel attributed their declining electoral fortunes to WSPU tactics. Realizing that a political situation where the government depended on the support of

Labour and Irish nationalists could be helpful to the women's cause, Henry Brailsford, a journalist, formed a Conciliation Committee for Women's Suffrage which the WSPU leaders ultimately supported. Christabel, although full of doubts that Prime Minister Asquith would ever grant votes to women, nevertheless hoped that a settlement could be reached by peaceful means, since she believed that 'mild' militancy was played out. The suspension of militancy, announced at the end of January, remained in force until 21 November 1911, apart from one week during 1910. When Asquith stated on 7 November 1911 that the government would introduce next session a Manhood Suffrage Bill that could be amended to include women, Christabel denounced his scheme as disreputable, and appealed for one thousand women to march to Westminster two weeks later. While the demonstration was taking place, however, a smaller group armed with bags of stones and hammers broke windows of government offices and businesses. Convinced that the government would not concede women's suffrage until they were forced to do so, the WSPU engaged in further window breaking, this time on a mass scale, in early March 1912; the policy had been jointly agreed by Christabel, her mother, and Emmeline Pethick-Lawrence. On 5 March, the police rushed to Clement's Inn with a warrant for the arrest of the leaders. Christabel, however, now lived in a flat nearby. Warned of what was happening, and fearful that the movement would collapse if all the leaders were in prison, she fled to France where a political offender was not liable to extradition.

Emmeline urged WSPU members to trust Christabel and those she put in command under her at Clement's Inn and, between imprisonments, travelled regularly between England and France to consult her daughter, as did the trusted couriers Annie and Jessie Kenney. At one such meeting, in the summer of 1912, Christabel and Emmeline decided that a more aggressive militant campaign should be conducted, involving widespread attacks on public and private property, a direction with which the Pethick-Lawrences disagreed. In October, Christabel risked detection and arrest by travelling in disguise to London, in order to tell the Pethick-Lawrences that she was in complete agreement with her mother that their connection with the WSPU should be severed and that, contrary to their wishes, she would not return to England but continue to direct affairs from Paris. Such plans must have been well prepared, since on 17 October a new official WSPU newspaper appeared, *The Suffragette*, of which Christabel was editor. From now on, militancy was driven further underground as widespread destruction of letters in mailboxes became common as well as arson, window breaking, and other acts of vandalism. The government responded by prohibiting WSPU meetings and raiding its central offices.

From April 1913 Christabel published a series of articles in *The Suffragette* on the double sexual standard, prostitution, and venereal disease, probably with the aim of heightening consciousness among her followers that they were fighting a just sex war. She outlined how, in a male-dominated society, where women were kept in a state of subservience and economic dependence, the social evil of prostitution was the fruit of women's slavery. The cure for the social evil, she explained, was to have stronger women and purer men, a situation that would come with and through the vote. By the end of the year, when the series was published collectively as *The Great Scourge and How to End It*, subscriptions to the WSPU had declined dramatically.

Despite criticisms of her policy and residence in Paris, Christabel remained convinced that escalating violence would eventually win the parliamentary vote for women since it would create, she believed, an intolerable situation for politicians. Furthermore, she would brook no opposition to the WSPU's independent political stance, even by a member of her family. Thus in early January 1914, she asked Sylvia to travel to Paris where she told her, in Emmeline's presence, that her East London Federation must be separate from the WSPU since it was allied to the socialist movement. Her distrust of socialism deepened when the Labour Party supported the government's Plural Voting Bill in the belief that it would bring in some electoral advantage, despite the fact that the sex disqualification against women would not be removed. Indeed, she warned:

> For Suffragists to put their faith in any men's party, whatever it may call itself, is recklessly to disregard the lessons of the past forty years … The truth is that women must work out their own salvation. Men will not do it for them. (*The Suffragette*, 17 April 1914, 10)

The WSPU and the First World War On the outbreak of the First World War in August 1914, all suffragette prisoners were released unconditionally, and on 12 August Emmeline Pankhurst sent a circular to all WSPU members announcing a temporary suspension of activities. The following month Christabel returned to London and at a meeting at the London Opera House announced that the WSPU would abandon the votes for women campaign and support the government in its hour of need. In October she began a six-month tour of the USA, with financial backing from Mrs Belmont, a wealthy American suffragist, and the blessing of the British government, her role being primarily to persuade the Americans to support the allies by entering the war. In *Britannia* (the new name for *The Suffragette*, with 'For King, For Country, For Freedom' as its motto) she expounded her views, including attacks on the war policy of Asquith. The offices of the WSPU were again raided, and *Britannia* was forced to be produced wherever it was considered safe. However, the government decided to utilize the skills of the WSPU leaders in a women's 'Right to Serve' demonstration, to help overcome trade union opposition to widespread use of women's labour, and a successful march, financed by the government, took place in July 1915. Further verbal attacks by Christabel on government figures led to further raids and increasing difficulties for WSPU office staff. When Annie Kenney wrote to her in early 1917 explaining the problems, Christabel returned immediately from France to England.

Initially, Christabel stayed with her mother at 50 Clarendon Road, Holland Park, the new home that Emmeline had created for her four adopted war babies—Kathleen, Mary, Joan, and Elizabeth (Betty). Then she moved to a flat on the top floor of the new WSPU headquarters at 4 William Street. Since it was becoming clear that, in the near future, women would be granted the parliamentary vote, a decision was made to remould the WSPU into a different organization that could serve the interests of women voters. Thus later that year the WSPU became the Women's Party, whose policies included a mixture of feminist concerns—equal opportunity of employment, equal pay, equal marriage laws, and equality of parental rights—as well as some anti-socialist measures such as the abolition of trade unions. Emmeline Pankhurst was the honorary treasurer, Annie Kenney the honorary secretary, Flora Drummond chief organizer, while Christabel continued as editor of *Britannia*, its official newspaper. The four women campaigned throughout the country, especially in industrial areas, warning against Bolshevism and arguing for industrial peace.

Neither Christabel nor Emmeline took an extensive part in the negotiations that granted a partial enfranchisement to women in 1918 if they were over thirty years of age and householders or wives of householders, occupiers of property with an annual rent of £5 or more, or graduates of British universities. Instead they concentrated on a scheme dear to Emmeline's heart, that Christabel should be the first woman MP. In the general election of December 1918 she stood as a Women's Party candidate for the constituency of Smethwick, with the support of the coalition government, but lost by 775 votes. In early 1919, she announced her intention of standing again as a Women's Party candidate, this time for the Westminster Abbey division. However, the plan did not materialize since there was lack of support for the Women's Party, which ceased to exist by the autumn.

Post-suffrage career For some years Christabel had been drawn to Christianity and she now became a Second Adventist. In 1921 she joined her mother in Canada and then went to California, preaching the second coming. She became both a popular speaker and author, publishing books such as *'The Lord Cometh', the World Crisis Explained* (1923) and *Pressing Problems of the Closing Age* (1924). In 1925 Emmeline decided that the running of a tea-shop in the French riviera could provide a home, an income, and also an answer to her failing health in the cold Canadian winters. Christabel accompanied her mother and Mabel Tuke, a former WSPU colleague, to France, but the venture was unsuccessful and she returned to England in the spring of 1926. When the unmarried Sylvia Pankhurst became pregnant the following year and gave birth to a son in December 1927, Christabel was among those who kept the news hidden from Emmeline, who discovered the truth only the following April when reading an article written by Sylvia in the *News of the World*. The old rivalries between the two sisters hardened as Christabel refused her sister's requests to see their ailing mother who was deeply distressed by the news. Both sisters, however, attended their mother's funeral, witnessed by huge crowds, on 17 June 1928, just a few weeks before women over the age of twenty-one were granted the vote on equal terms with men.

During the years immediately following Emmeline's death, Christabel thought about rewriting her mother's autobiography *My Own Story* but eventually decided against it. She did, however, have a contract to publish her own memoirs but, after the manuscript had been delivered to the publisher, decided it should be withdrawn since she did not want to engage in a family literary duel with Sylvia, whose book *The Suffragette Movement* appeared in 1931; neither did she want to provide for the enemies of Britain a picture of the brutal way the British government had treated WSPU campaigners. She did, however, launch a new adventist monthly journal, *Present and Future*, but it ran only from May to November 1934. Christabel then spent all her free time ministering to the sick and the dying. Recognition of her services to the enfranchisement of women was not forgotten, however, and in the 1936 new year honours list she was created DBE.

In 1939 Christabel returned to the USA where she continued her career as an author and lecturer on religion. She was followed there by her adopted daughter, Aurea Elizabeth Clifford, but the relationship between the two, always strained, ended well before Aurea's early death, at a date unknown. On 5 May 1953, Sylvia's birthday, Christabel renewed contact with her sister, writing her a warm letter and wishing her well after her recent heart attack. The correspondence between the two sisters continued intermittently until Christabel's death at her home, 943 Ocean Avenue, Santa Monica, California, on 13 February 1958 from a heart attack. She was buried at Woodlawn cemetery, Los Angeles, on 17 February. At a memorial service held in March at St Martin-in-the-Fields, Frederick Pethick-Lawrence spoke of how Christabel had changed the course of history by undertaking the formidable task of rousing women to a sense of their own worth and dignity in order to break down the walls of prejudice and opposition. The following year the manuscript of her memoirs, discovered by Grace Roe, was published as *Unshackled: the Story of how we Won the Vote*. On 13 July 1959 a bronze medallion of Christabel was added to a low circular wall at the base of her mother's statue in Victoria Tower Gardens. It was a fitting tribute to the close relationship between daughter and mother who jointly had fought courageously for women's right to the parliamentary vote.

Historiographical interpretations of Christabel Pankhurst's life have changed over time, from the 'great woman' style, through David Mitchell's critical approach, to more sympathetic interpretations by those who see her emphasis on male power and the sisterhood of women as anticipating many of the separatist concerns of radical feminism in western Europe in the 1970s and 1980s.

JUNE PURVIS

Sources D. Mitchell, *Queen Christabel: a biography of Christabel Pankhurst* (1977) · Museum of London, London, David Mitchell Collection · E. Sarah, 'Christabel Pankhurst: reclaiming her power', *Feminist theorists: three centuries of women's intellectual traditions*, ed. D. Spender (1983), 256–85 · J. Purvis, 'Christabel Pankhurst and the Women's Social and Political Union', *The women's suffrage movement, new feminist perspectives*, ed. M. Joannou and J. Purvis (1998), 157–72 · priv. coll., Suffrage MSS Collection [privately owned by Jill Craigie] · C. Pankhurst, *Unshackled: the story of how we won the vote* (1959) · E. S. Pankhurst, *The suffragette movement: an intimate account of persons and ideals* (1931) · E. Pankhurst, *My own story* (1914) · E. Crawford, *The women's suffrage movement: a reference guide, 1866–1928* (1999) · T. Larsen, *Christabel Pankhurst: fundamentalism and feminism in coalition* (2002) · b. cert. · d. cert. (English) · d. cert. (American)

Archives BL, corresp. with Arthur James Balfour, Add. MS 49793, *passim* · GL, autograph letter collection · JRL, letters to C. P. Scott · New York University, Fales Library, Elmer Holmes Bobst Library, letters to Elizabeth Robins · priv. coll. · Ransom HRC, letters to Elizabeth Robins · Trinity Cam., corresp. with F. W. Pethick-Lawrence | FILM BFI NFTVA, *Shoulder to shoulder*, BBC2, 24 April 1974 · BFI NFTVA, documentary footage

Likenesses photographs, *c.*1900–1913, Hult. Arch. · Mrs. A. Broom, group photograph, 1910, NPG; *see illus. in* Davison, Emily Wilding (1872–1913) · K. Simmons, photograph, 1910, NPG [*see illus.*] · P. Hills, bronze medallion, 1959, Victoria Tower Gardens, London · O. Edis, photographs, NPG · J. Holliday, pencil drawing, NPG · Spy [L. Ward], Hentschel-colourtype print, NPG; repro. in *VF* (15 June 1910) · photographs, London, Women's Library

Pankhurst [*née* Goulden], **Emmeline** (1858–1928), suffragette leader, was born on 15 July 1858 in Sloan Street, Moss Side, Hulme, Lancashire, to Robert Goulden, a cashier (later the owner of a calico printing and bleach works), and his Manx-born wife, Sophia Jane Craine.

Childhood and youth The eldest daughter in a family of ten children, Emmeline had maturity forced upon her early as she looked after her younger brothers and sisters. A precocious child, she learned to read at an early age and was set the task of reading the daily newspaper to her father as he breakfasted, an activity that led to the development of an interest in politics. Although her brothers called her 'the dictionary' (E. S. Pankhurst, 7) for her command of language and accurate spelling, she soon learned that the education of girls was considered of less importance than that of the boys when she and her sister were sent to a middle-class girls' school where the prime aim was learning how to make a home comfortable for men, a situation Emmeline found difficult to understand. One evening, feigning sleep in her bed, she heard her father say 'What a pity she wasn't born a lad' (E. Pankhurst, 6). Although her first impulse was to protest that she did not want to be a boy, she lay still, pondering on the remark for many days to come. 'It was made quite clear', she later recollected in her ghost-written autobiography, *My Own Story* (1914), 'that men considered themselves superior to women, and that women apparently acquiesced in that belief' (ibid.). The rebellious streak in her nature was further enhanced by stories about how her paternal grandfather had narrowly escaped death at the Peterloo franchise demonstration in Manchester in 1819 and, with his wife, had taken part in demonstrations in the 1840s against the corn laws

Emmeline Pankhurst (1858–1928), by Olive Edis

which imposed duties on imported foodstuffs to protect producers.

Reform was a frequent topic of conversation in the Goulden household. Indeed, one of Emmeline's earliest memories related to when she was about five years old and entrusted to collect pennies in a 'lucky bag' for the newly emancipated slaves in the United States. 'Young as I was', she remembered, 'I knew perfectly well the meaning of the words slavery and emancipation' (E. Pankhurst, 1). Both parents too were advocates of equal suffrage for men and women, her mother taking the monthly *Woman's Suffrage Journal* edited by Lydia Becker, a Manchester woman who was a well-known figure in the women's rights movement in England. When fourteen years old, Emmeline begged her mother to be allowed to accompany her to a woman suffrage meeting where Miss Becker was speaking. 'I left the meeting', she later recorded, 'a conscious and confirmed suffragist' (ibid., 9). Later in 1872 she attended an academic girls' school in Paris, a city that was still bearing the scars of the recently ended Franco-Prussian War. From this time onwards, Emmeline developed a deep affection for all things French and a lifelong prejudice against Germany. Released from her lessons on the grounds of ill health, Emmeline explored Paris with a motherless schoolfriend, Noemie, whose father was the famous republican Henri Rochefort, imprisoned in New

Caledonia for the part he had played in the Paris commune. Noemie's stories of her father's duels, imprisonments, and escapes fired the imagination of the adolescent Emmeline who at the age of nine had read Carlyle's *French Revolution*, a book which she claimed remained all her life a source of inspiration (ibid., 3). On her return home between the age of eighteen and nineteen, Emmeline was expected to take her place as a young lady and was frequently in conflict with her mother. On one occasion when Mrs Goulden ordered her daughter to fetch her brothers' slippers, the spirited Emmeline replied that if she was in favour of women's rights, she did not show it at home. Eager to be useful in the world, she began to work for the woman suffrage movement and met Dr Richard Marsden Pankhurst (1835/6–1898), a well-known radical lawyer and advocate for the women's cause. Despite the fact that he was more than twenty years her senior, they fell in love and married on 18 December 1879.

Early radical campaigns and family life The birth of four children in the first six years of her marriage—Christabel Harriette *Pankhurst in 1880, Sylvia *Pankhurst in 1882, Henry Francis Robert (Frank) in 1884, and Adela Constantia in 1885 [*see* Walsh, Adela Pankhurst]—restricted but did not stop Emmeline's involvement in public affairs. In 1880 she was elected onto the executive committee of the influential Manchester National Society for Women's Suffrage of which Richard had been an elected member for a number of years. She was also co-opted onto the married women's property committee. She campaigned on her husband's behalf in 1883 when, unsuccessfully, he stood as an independent parliamentary candidate advocating, among other things, the abolition of the House of Lords and the monarchy, adult suffrage on equal terms for both sexes, the disestablishment of the Church of England, nationalization of the land, and home rule for Ireland, an issue on which no other contender had yet made a stand. In the general election of 1885 Emmeline Pankhurst again campaigned unsuccessfully on her husband's behalf when, at the invitation of the local Liberal and Radical Association, he was asked to contest Rotherhithe. His defeat was mainly attributed to the opposition of the Irish vote, Charles Parnell, leader of the Irish nationalists, having instructed his followers to vote against all government candidates, irrespective of whether they supported home rule or not. Although Emmeline felt indignant about the way her husband had been treated, he defended Parnell's policy, pointing out that tactics of constant obstruction could eventually wring from a hostile Liberal government surrender on the home rule issue. 'That was a valuable political lesson', Emmeline recalled, 'one that years later I was destined to put into practice' (E. Pankhurst, 18).

The following year the Pankhurst family moved to a new home in Hampstead Road, London. Emmeline, eager for financial independence and keen to make enough money so that her husband could concentrate on his political work, opened a fancy goods shop. She often accompanied Richard on his frequent trips to Manchester and during one such absence, their four-year-old son Frank became ill. Emmeline returned home to find the boy in a critical condition. Diphtheria was wrongly diagnosed as croup, and he died in September 1888. Distraught in her grief, Emmeline took little comfort in the knowledge that defective drainage was found at the rear of the house. The shop was closed and her family hurried away to a new rented home, at 8 Russell Square. It was there that her fifth and last child was born in 1889, another son, also called Henry Francis (Harry) as a reminder of little Frank. Her involvement in political life continued through membership of the Fabian Society, the Women's Liberal Association, and the Women's Franchise League, and 8 Russell Square became a centre for political gatherings, especially of socialists, Fabians, anarchists, suffragists, freethinkers, and radicals. In particular, a warm friendship developed between the Pankhursts and Keir Hardie who was elected as a Labour MP in 1892. The following year, the family returned to Manchester, to 4 Buckingham Crescent, where Emmeline resigned from the Women's Liberal Association and joined the Independent Labour Party (ILP). In 1894 she was elected as an ILP candidate for the Chorlton board of guardians. The conditions she found in the workhouses, and especially those for girls and single mothers with babies, appalled her. A compassionate and fearless reformer, with a passion for the oppressed, she helped to introduce many improvements.

Both Emmeline and her husband now became dedicated to socialism. When members of the ILP were sent to prison in May 1896 for speaking in the open space of Boggart Hole Clough, recently acquired by Manchester city council, the Pankhursts and their children were actively involved in defending the right of free speech. Emmeline, in her pink straw bonnet, became a familiar figure in the Clough, declaring she would rather go to prison than pay a fine. Although she did appear in the dock, the case against her was dismissed. The following year she was elected to the national administrative council (NAC) of the ILP.

The unexpected death of her beloved husband on 5 July 1898 was a devastating blow. Richard had championed unprofitable causes and the close connection with the ILP had lost him many legal clients so that he had little money to leave. Robert Blatchford appealed to *Clarion* readers for subscriptions to help the struggling family but Emmeline replied firmly that she did not wish working people to contribute towards the education of her children when they could not provide for their own; instead she suggested that money be collected to build a hall in her husband's memory. In straitened circumstances, the family moved to 62 Nelson Street, Manchester, where Emmeline opened another shop which eventually had to be abandoned too. She also accepted the salaried post of registrar of births and deaths for the district of Chorlton. In this work she heard many sad stories from the working-class women who came to register the birth of their babies, some of them young girls who had been seduced by male relatives. Her conviction grew that if society was to progress, then women must lift themselves out of their subordinate position and campaign for the parliamentary vote. When the hall in memory of Dr Pankhurst was eventually opened in Salford, five years after his death, his family were astonished to hear that women were not permitted to join the branch of the ILP that would use it as its headquarters. Emmeline declared that her time in the socialist movement had been wasted and decided to form a new women's organization that would run in parallel to the ILP. Thus on 10 October 1903 she called to her home some wives of ILP men and formed the Women's Social and Political Union (WSPU), an organization that was to campaign for votes for women on the same terms they were, or might be, granted to men. Membership was to be limited to women only, and free from affiliation to any particular social class. 'Deeds, not words' was the WSPU's motto.

The WSPU's first campaigns During its early years the WSPU engaged in a range of peaceful activities such as campaigning at trade union meetings, parks, and fairgrounds, as well as street demonstrations and petitions to parliament. Emmeline threw herself with zeal into this work, believing that the vote would soon be won. In the autumn of 1905, on the eve of a general election, when it looked as though the Liberal Party would form the new government, a new strategy was decided on. Christabel Pankhurst and Annie Kenney, a working-class woman recently recruited to the WSPU, interrupted a Liberal Party meeting in Manchester on 13 October by asking the question 'Will the Liberal Government, if returned, give votes to women?' When the question was not answered and repeated, the two women were roughly ejected from the hall. Both were charged with obstruction and sentenced to pay fines or face imprisonment. An anxious Emmeline offered to pay the fines, a gesture that was refused by Christabel. Extensive newspaper coverage of the event made women's suffrage a live issue in an unprecedented way and increased Emmeline's admiration for her brilliant daughter. Under Emmeline's leadership, the policy of heckling politicians became a strategy in which innumerable suffragettes engaged.

The following year, the WSPU moved its headquarters to London and in March 1907 Emmeline resigned her post as registrar of births and deaths, thus forfeiting a government pension. The Manchester home was given up and Emmeline's sister Mary, who had stayed there and acted as deputy registrar while Emmeline was away, became a WSPU organizer. From now on, until the end of the militant campaign, Emmeline had no settled home but stayed in a number of rented flats, hotels, or homes of friends. Her main source of income was her £200 fee per annum as a union speaker which came out of WSPU funds, which were managed by Emmeline Pethick-Lawrence, who was appointed treasurer in February 1906. Together with her husband, Frederick, the wealthy Emmeline Pethick-Lawrence brought organizational and business skills to the WSPU, occasionally donating money for particular events. Funds were raised too at the meetings where Emmeline Pankhurst spoke; indeed, sometimes as much as £14,000 would be collected in one evening as money, jewels, and other valuables were thrown onto the platform where the beloved leader was speaking.

Internal disputes in the WSPU During 1907, differences of view between Emmeline and her daughters began to widen over the WSPU's links with the Labour Party. Christabel, the organizing secretary of the WSPU, its key strategist, and main policy maker, had already declared that in future the WSPU would oppose not only all Liberal and tory parliamentary candidates, but also be independent of Labour men. While Emmeline shared this view, her two youngest daughters, Sylvia and Adela, did not. The disillusionment that Emmeline and Christabel felt about the lukewarm attitude of socialists towards women's suffrage came to a head in April 1907 when both resigned from the ILP: the Labour Party now opposed extending the franchise to women if the ownership of property remained a qualification for voting. Although links between the WSPU and the socialist movement were never completely severed, especially at the individual level, the independent policy plus an autocratic style of leadership caused tensions within the union so that rumours of a coup surfaced during the summer of 1907. Emmeline, who had been travelling in the provinces, returned to headquarters, and at the request of the Pethick-Lawrences, declared the democratic constitution of the union abolished, the annual conference cancelled, and invited members to support her; the majority agreed. A group of dissenters, including Teresa Billington Greig and Charlotte Despard, formed another militant organization, later called the Women's Freedom League. Although Emmeline Pankhurst was now regarded as the autocrat of the WSPU, its leader and inspirational figurehead, in the years immediately following this split she chose to travel up and down the country speaking for the cause, rather than exercise direct personal control over the organization. Although she was consulted on major developments and, when in London, led various demonstrations, the day-to-day running of the union was left to Christabel and the Pethick-Lawrences—the latter also being joint editors of the WSPU's paper, *Votes for Women*, founded in October 1907.

A charismatic person, whose personal qualities drew people to her, Emmeline Pankhurst was a gifted speaker whose power of oratory could sway an audience. She spoke from the heart, without notes and with few gestures, drawing on her own experience of life as she used clear arguments of persuasion to convert her listeners. The important part she took in the non-militant side of the campaign must not be forgotten. However, it is chiefly in connection with her defiance of the law and her participation in militancy, which she readily embraced, that she will be remembered.

The militant campaign Mrs Pankhurst's first imprisonment occurred on 13 February 1908 when, still lame from an injury to her ankle, she had led a deputation to the House of Commons and was arrested, along with her companions, for obstruction. She served a month in the second division, alongside common criminal offenders, and not in the first division where political offenders were placed. On 14 October in the same year she stood in the dock at Bow Street, together with Flora Drummond and Christabel, charged with incitement to disorder, based on a handbill that had been published encouraging the public to 'rush' the House of Commons. The three accused did not employ counsel, but spoke for themselves. In a poignant speech that moved many to tears, Emmeline spoke of her life experiences and of her conviction of the burning necessity for making women self-governing citizens. No mercy was shown, however, and she was sentenced to three months' imprisonment.

Events took a different turn from July to the end of September 1909 when WSPU members, on their own initiative, began to hunger strike, in a bid to be granted political offender status, and the government responded with forcible feeding. Fiercely protective of her followers, Emmeline responded with disbelief and anger, condemning the government for violating and torturing the exhausted and starved bodies of women. In addition to such public worries, private troubles also weighed heavily on her since her surviving son, Harry, had developed inflammation of the spinal cord and was paralysed from the waist down. Needing money for his medical treatment, she felt she could not cancel her already planned American and Canadian tour and so set sail on 13 October. Wherever she went, enthusiastic crowds greeted her, especially at New York's Carnegie Hall; a hush fell when the small, well-dressed leader rose to spoke, but at her first words, 'I am what you call a hooligan' (E. Pankhurst, 160), a wave of laughter erupted. On arrival back in England, she found that Harry's condition had worsened. When he died in January 1910, Sylvia commented that their mother was broken as she had never seen her (E. S. Pankhurst, *The Suffragette Movement*, 1931, 324). Work ever being her refuge in times of sorrow, she threw herself into election campaigning, since a general election had been called, and followed WSPU policy of opposing all Liberal candidates, whether or not they were pledged, if elected, to support women's enfranchisement.

The Liberal government and the Conciliation Bill To what extent the heavy losses sustained by the Liberals were due to WSPU policy is debatable, but they were returned with no overall majority in the Commons holding only 275 seats while the Conservatives held 273, the Irish nationalists 82, and Labour 40. Believing that a women's suffrage measure might have more chance of success under such conditions, Henry Brailsford, a journalist, formed a Conciliation Committee for Women's Suffrage which had the support of fifty-four MPs across the political spectrum. After some initial reluctance, the WSPU leaders supported the initiative and on 31 January Emmeline declared a truce on militancy.

The conciliation committee's Women's Franchise Bill was drafted along narrow lines, in order to win the support of the Conservatives. It sought to extend the vote to independent women occupiers but not to enfranchise married women whose husbands met the property qualifications. Since relatively few women (especially working-class women) would be enfranchised under these terms, Emmeline was among its critics, although she voiced her concerns only in private. The bill passed its second reading on 12 July; however, the home secretary, Lloyd George, declared that it was anti-democratic while Prime Minister Asquith claimed that it was better to maintain the distinction of sex. Warning that if the bill was killed by the government the truce was at an end, Emmeline decided to lead a deputation on 18 November. When parliament reassembled and no reference was made to the bill, the women's deputation set forth and was treated with exceptional brutality by the police who, rather than arrest them prolonged the struggle in the streets by trying to force them to move away from the houses of parliament. Four days after 'black Friday', as it became known, Emmeline led another deputation to Downing Street. This time she was among the 156 arrested but was discharged since no evidence was offered against her. Also arrested was her sister Mary Clark, who died that Christmas as a result of the injuries she suffered. As before, the leader of the WSPU attempted to cope with another personal tragedy by channelling her efforts into the cause so dear to her heart.

A second 1910 election saw Asquith returned to power with the distribution of seats in the Commons being little changed. The WSPU renewed their truce in the hope that the revised Conciliation Bill (now titled 'A Bill to confer the parliamentary franchise on women') would win greater support since it now included all women householders. In high hopes, Emmeline marched in the women's coronation procession on 17 June 1911, a spectacular event in which at least twenty-eight other women's suffrage organizations accepted the WSPU's invitation to participate. In poor health and in need of a rest, she decided later that year to undertake another tour in the USA and Canada. On 7 November she was cabled the news that Asquith had announced that a manhood suffrage bill would be introduced next session which would allow amendment for the enfranchisement of women. Knowing that such an amendment would be doomed, since it could not be carried without government support, she cabled back to Christabel that protest was imperative. She returned to England on 18 January 1912 with the words 'Sedition!' and 'The Women's Revolution' on her lips (E. S. Pankhurst, 103).

Militancy resumed At a meeting the following month to welcome released prisoners, Emmeline announced that the weapon and argument they were going to use at the next demonstration would be the stone, a policy which was jointly agreed with Christabel and the Pethick-Lawrences. Although Emmeline expected to be arrested after this speech, she was not, and shortly afterwards spent some time being taught how to throw stones by Ethel Smyth, the composer and recent union recruit. On 1 March, for the first time, the WSPU struck without warning, smashing shop windows in London's West End. Late in the afternoon, Emmeline and two other women broke four of the prime minister's windows. In court the next day, where she was sentenced to two months' imprisonment, she reminded the magistrate that women had failed to get the vote because they had failed to use the methods of agitation used by men. After two more days of window smashing, the police swooped on WSPU headquarters with a warrant for the arrest of Christabel Pankhurst, who was in hiding and later escaped to Paris, and the Pethick-Lawrences. Emmeline was now released from prison in order to attend a new trial at which she and the Pethick-Lawrences were charged with conspiracy.

At the conspiracy trial, which began on 15 May, Emmeline made another poignant speech, explaining how women had been driven to greater militancy by the stubborn opposition of the government. When all three defendants were found guilty and sentenced to nine months in the second division, they threatened to hunger strike unless given political status and placed in the first division. Although the plea was granted, it was not extended to other suffrage prisoners and so the three leaders joined their members in a mass hunger strike that began on 19 June. Three days later forcible feeding began. When the doctors and wardresses came to Emmeline's cell, she picked up a heavy earthenware jug and warned that if any of them dared to come near her, she would defend herself. They retreated. Two days later, she was released on medical grounds and no attempt was ever made to force feed her again.

Travelling under the name of Mrs Richards, she made the first of many visits to Christabel in France. Emmeline now spent less time as an itinerant speaker and more time at the London headquarters. Differences of view in regard to the form and direction of militancy had already begun to emerge between the union leader and the Pethick-Lawrences. Shortly after the Pethick-Lawrences returned from Canada in early October, Emmeline and Christabel told them that their connection to the WSPU was severed. Most WSPU members seem to have been shocked by this action; while some of Emmeline Pankhurst's followers accepted the situation, agreeing with their leader that it was the cause rather than the individual that was important, the WSPU lost many of its most influential supporters. The task of fundraising now fell on Emmeline's shoulders as she replaced Mrs Pethick-Lawrence as treasurer of the union. At a Royal Albert Hall meeting on 17 October, she reiterated the policy of opposition to all political parties and outlined a new policy of attacks on public and private property but never on human life.

The escalation of militancy When Asquith announced early in 1913 that the Manhood Suffrage Bill was dropped for that session, Emmeline immediately declared war on the government. Over the next eighteen months, the WSPU was increasingly driven underground as it engaged in destruction of property, including setting fire to pillar boxes, raising false fire alarms, arson and bombing, attacking art treasures, large-scale window smashing campaigns, the cutting of telegraph and telephone wires, and damaging golf courses. At a meeting in late January 1913, Emmeline emphasized that she took full responsibility for all acts of militancy, a theme that was to recur in many subsequent speeches. Now regarded as a dangerous subversive, she was watched by the police who appeared in plain clothes at her meetings and transcribed her speeches. On 24 February she was arrested for procuring and inciting persons to commit offences contrary to the Malicious Injuries to Property Act 1861, and on 2 April was sentenced to three years' penal servitude. However, she served less than six weeks of her sentence between the time of her conviction and August 1914 when militancy ended. Exploiting the Prisoners' Temporary Discharge for Ill-health Act, known as the Cat and Mouse Act, passed in April 1913, which allowed prisoners who had damaged their health to be released on licence in order to recover so that they would be fit enough to be readmitted, she was repeatedly in and out of prison. On many occasions she engaged in hunger, thirst, and sleep strikes and was released in a state of physical collapse but never once did she hesitate to share with her followers that which they too experienced. Always in the thick of the action, her defiance, determination, and courage won her admiration, even from many who considered WSPU tactics ill-conceived. In the autumn of 1913, while still under sentence, Emmeline paid another trip to the USA where she was detained as an undesirable alien, a ruling that was overturned by President Wilson. 'Nothing ever has been got out of the British Parliament without something very nearly approaching a revolution', she told an enthusiastic audience in New York. On arrival back in England she was re-arrested, released after a hunger strike, and then travelled openly to Paris where she spent all of January 1914.

Family concerns which had been pressing for some time were now confronted when Sylvia and Adela visited their mother in Paris. Sylvia was told by Christabel, with her mother's support, that her East London Federation must be separate from the WSPU since it was allied with the Labour Party, contrary to union policy. Adela, who had suffered a breakdown in 1912 and then not found a steady job when she graduated from Studley Horticultural College, had been a worry to her mother for some time. Anxious that her youngest daughter should have a new start in life, Emmeline gave Adela the fare to Australia, a letter to Australian suffragist Vida Goldstein, and £20. Adela never saw her mother or England again.

Still subject to her three-year sentence, Emmeline managed to evade detectives and travel back to England where her recently formed bodyguard was waiting to protect her, not always successfully, from re-arrest. When she spoke at St Andrew's Hall, Glasgow, on 9 March 1914, she looked pale and fragile, her hair now a silvery white. The day after her arrest in Glasgow, Mary Richardson slashed Velázquez's *Rokeby Venus* in the National Gallery in protest at the treatment of the union leader. On 21 May, Emmeline led the last major WSPU deputation, this time to the king. She was among those arrested as Inspector Rolfe, crushing her in his arms, lifted her to a car waiting behind police lines, an incident captured in a famous photograph. Further raids by the police took place on WSPU headquarters and private dwellings in an attempt to crush the militant suffrage movement and to prevent the printing and sale of *The Suffragette*, a newspaper edited by

Christabel and founded in October 1912, after the ousting of the Pethick-Lawrences.

The First World War and militancy suspended With the outbreak of the First World War in early August 1914, all the imprisoned suffragettes were released unconditionally. Emmeline called a temporary suspension of militant activities and asked her followers to support the war effort, arguing that it would be pointless to fight for the vote without a country to vote in. *The Suffragette* was renamed *Britannia* with 'For King, For Country, For Freedom' as its motto. Emmeline supported conscription and campaigned for the opening of women's war work. In 1915 she and others involved in the WSPU, such as Annie Kenney and Flora Drummond, accepted the request of Lloyd George, minister of munitions, to organize a Women's Right to Serve demonstration to help overcome trade union opposition to the employment of female labour. In 1916 she travelled to the USA to help raise money for Serbia and in 1917 visited Russia where she advised Kerensky, the head of the provisional government, to be firm with the Bolsheviks. In 1918 she again toured the USA and Canada, supporting women's war work and condemning Bolshevism.

During these years, the distance between Emmeline and her two youngest daughters, Sylvia and Adela, widened as she denounced their anti-war views. Although she still remained close to Christabel, Emmeline now acquired a second family. In the summer of 1915 she announced that the WSPU would help the 'war babies' problem by adopting fifty baby girls and appealed for financial support from WSPU members. The response was lukewarm. Nevertheless, she herself adopted four babies (Betty, Kathleen, Mary, and Joan) and had the worry of finding enough money to support them, as well as raising enough funds to support the union of which she was still honorary treasurer. In the autumn of 1916 she made a home for herself, her second family, and the faithful Nurse Pine, who had cared for her after so many hunger strikes, at 50 Clarendon Road, Holland Park, London. She managed to maintain this home for about three years.

Emmeline was now becoming increasingly preoccupied with what women should do when granted the vote since it was becoming clear that this would happen in the near future. In November 1917, in preparation for the event, the WSPU was renamed the Women's Party. Emmeline became the new party's treasurer, Annie Kenney the secretary, and Flora Drummond the chief organizer; *Britannia* became its official newspaper and continued to be edited by Christabel. On 6 February 1918 royal assent was given to the Representation of the People Act which gave women over thirty years of age the vote if they were householders, the wives of householders, occupiers of property with an annual rent of £5 or more, or graduates of British universities. Although this bill enfranchised only about eight and a half million women, Emmeline Pankhurst, like all the women's suffrage campaigners, knew that at last the sex barrier had been broken and that full citizenship for all women could not be delayed indefinitely.

After the vote was won Emmeline greatly desired that Christabel, rather than she, should be the first woman member of parliament. Christabel fought the Smethwick constituency on a Women's Party ticket in the autumn general election and narrowly lost. Emmeline was bitterly disappointed. Seeking a steady income, she accepted the Canadian government's offer to lecture on social hygiene, such was the concern about the spread of venereal disease among the returning soldiers, and settled in Toronto. The following year some former suffragettes raised about £3000 in a testimonial fund for her and spent more than half of this amount on a country house which she could not afford to maintain and which was eventually sold. The strain of her life now began to tell on Emmeline and in the spring of 1924, when she was almost sixty-six years old, her health began to fail. She took her second family and Christabel to Bermuda, for a six months' rest. As money was scarce, she reluctantly agreed for two of the young girls to be sent to England and adopted by more prosperous people. Christabel had already adopted her favourite child, Betty, while Mary stayed with Emmeline.

The following year Emmeline decided to escape the Canadian winters by settling in the French Riviera and running a tea-shop, with the help of Christabel and a trusted old WSPU friend, Mabel Tuke. But the venture was not a success and before Christmas 1925 she had returned to London. She was invited to become a parliamentary candidate for the Conservative Party and, as was typical of her, accepted the offer of a socialist working-class district, Whitechapel and St George's, that she could not win. While campaigning in the spring of 1928, she was deeply shocked and distressed to read in the *News of the World*, a newspaper not then read in respectable homes, that Sylvia had given birth to a son, out of wedlock, some four months previously. Forewarned that she would be heckled about this during her election campaign, she curtly replied that she would not discuss private matters in public (Smyth, 266). Feeling that the Pankhurst name had been disgraced, Emmeline was never reconciled with her daughter.

Emmeline resolved to live in her constituency, a move that necessitated parting with Mary. Once settled in her new lodgings, she became ill again and worried about her finances. In late May she was taken by her sister Mrs Goulden Bach and Christabel to a nursing home at 43 Wimpole Street, where she died on 14 June 1928 from septicaemia due to influenza, a month before her seventieth birthday. She was buried in Brompton cemetery, London. Although a second Representation of the People Act, which would give women voting rights over the age of twenty-one on equal terms with men, had passed all its stages, the new bill did not become law until 2 July 1928. On 6 March 1930 the prime minister, Stanley Baldwin, unveiled a bronze statue of Emmeline Pankhurst in Victoria Tower Gardens, close to the houses of parliament, the opening of which to women she had fought for so bravely all her life.

JUNE PURVIS

Sources P. Bartley, *Emmeline Pankhurst* (2002) • E. S. Pankhurst, *The life of Emmeline Pankhurst: the suffragette struggle for women's citizenship*

(1935) • E. Pankhurst, *My own story* (1914) • C. Pankhurst, *Unshackled: the story of how we won the vote* (1959) • J. Purvis, 'Emmeline Pankhurst and votes for women', *Votes for women*, ed. J. Purvis and S. S. Holton (2000) • J. Purvis, 'Emmeline Pankhurst (1858–1928): suffragette, militant feminist and champion of womanhood', *Representing lives: women and autobiography* [Nottingham 1997], ed. A. Donnell and P. Polkey (2000) • J. Purvis, *Emmeline Pankhurst: a biography* (2002) • E. Smyth, *Female pipings in Eden* (1934) • R. West, 'Mrs Pankhurst, 1858–1928', *The post Victorians*, ed. [W. R. Inge] (1933), 477–500 • S. S. Holton, '"In sorrowful wrath": suffrage militancy and the romantic feminism of Emmeline Pankhurst', *British feminism in the twentieth century*, ed. H. L. Smith (1990) • private information (2004) [J. Craigie] • b. cert. • m. cert. • d. cert.

Archives Internationaal Instituut voor Sociale Geschiedenis, Amsterdam, letters and papers • Museum of London, Suffragette Fellowship collection, MSS • Women's Library, London, autograph letter collection | BLPES, corresp. with the Independent Labour Party • JRL, letters to C. P. Scott • L. Cong., corresp. with Adelaide Johnson • New York University, Fales Library, Elizabeth Robins MSS • Smith College, Northampton, Massachusetts, Sophia Smith collection | FILM BFI NFTVA, documentary footage; news footage | SOUND BL NSA

Likenesses G. Brackenbury, oils, 1927, NPG; version, Museum of London • A. G. Walker, statue, 1929, Victoria Tower Gardens, London • Mrs A. Broom, photograph, NPG • O. Edis, photographs, NPG [*see illus.*] • photographs, Women's Library, London • photographs, Museum of London

Wealth at death £86 5*s*. 6*d*.: probate, 25 July 1928, *CGPLA Eng. & Wales*

Pankhurst, (Estelle) Sylvia (1882–1960), political activist, writer, and artist, was born at 1 Drayton Gardens, Old Trafford, Manchester, on 5 May 1882, the second of five children of Dr Richard Marsden Pankhurst (1835/6–1898), a barrister, and his wife, Emmeline *Pankhurst (1858–1928), the daughter of Robert Goulden, a prosperous Manchester cotton manufacturer. Sylvia spent her childhood in a household immersed in radical politics and women's rights campaigns. When the family moved to London in 1885 Emmeline and Richard, who had joined the Fabian Society, became involved in a circle of radical and socialist friends and in 1889 helped to form the Women's Franchise League which emphasized the rights of married women. After their return to Manchester in 1893 they joined the recently formed Independent Labour Party (ILP) in 1894. Richard Pankhurst stood unsuccessfully as an ILP parliamentary candidate, but Emmeline had greater success in being elected to the Chorlton board of guardians.

Childhood and education Sylvia's own interest in socialist and feminist politics was influenced by her parents' activities and also by the many well-known speakers and writers who visited the family. In her early years in London she was mainly educated at home, although there was often no governess, and both she and her elder sister Christabel *Pankhurst were frequently left to their own devices to develop their literary and artistic talents. Sylvia was later sent to a school in Southport and also attended the Manchester high school. In 1898, at the age of sixteen, she suffered a devastating emotional blow when her father died suddenly from a perforated ulcer. Of all the children she was closest to him and it is likely that his death had a long-lasting effect, in particular in encouraging her steadfast commitment to socialist politics. A more immediate consequence of his death was her mother's need to clear the debts that he had left and to support her family; Emmeline secured a position as registrar for births and deaths and also kept a small shop.

(Estelle) Sylvia Pankhurst (1882–1960), by Bassano, 1927

Financial problems did not prevent Sylvia, however, from pursuing her aspirations to become an artist. She won a scholarship to the Manchester Art School, where she studied from 1898 to 1903, and then gained a travel award to the Accademia in Venice. After this she was awarded a scholarship to study for two years at the Royal College of Art in Kensington, where she lived in lodgings in Chelsea. She was frequently lonely but managed to spend alternate Sundays with her brother Harry who was at school in Hampstead. It was also at this point that she became a frequent visitor to the home of Keir Hardie MP, one of the leaders of the ILP whom she had first met as a schoolgirl when he stayed with her parents. They developed a close and intimate relationship which was to last until his death in 1915. During this period Hardie was the most important person in Sylvia's life and he helped her to deal with the emotional turmoil that she felt when she became increasingly estranged from her mother and sister just before the First World War.

The Women's Social and Political Union Sylvia shared Hardie's socialist beliefs. At the turn of the century she had been involved, along with her mother and Christabel, in the Manchester branch of the ILP. In this same period there was a renewed interest in women's suffrage, in particular among Lancashire textile workers, and the failure of the newly formed Labour Representation Committee (later the Labour Party) to give a commitment to votes for women on the same terms as men led Emmeline and

Christabel Pankhurst to establish the Women's Social and Political Union (WSPU) in 1903 to campaign for women's suffrage. At first members of the WSPU were drawn largely from the ILP and carried out propaganda for both socialism and women's suffrage in the north of England. Sylvia became increasingly involved in the affairs of the WSPU from her base in London where she attempted to combine training as an artist with paid work and political agitation. In 1906, however, she gave up her studies so that she could devote most of her time to the suffrage campaign. In that year she suffered her first imprisonment after protesting in court at a trial in which women had not been allowed to speak in their own defence.

From then onwards Sylvia was always in the thick of the fight. She was arrested and imprisoned on numerous occasions and also suffered hunger and thirst strikes as well as forcible feeding. She gained notoriety at the time for her suffrage militancy and it is for this that she tends to be best remembered in subsequent histories. However, she never saw women's emancipation in isolation from her broader socialist politics and this was to cause tension between herself and Emmeline and Christabel Pankhurst who became increasingly hostile to the labour movement. Sylvia's relationship with her mother was made even more strained when Emmeline embarked on an American speaking tour in 1909, leaving her daughters to care for their brother Harry (Henry Francis), born 7 July 1889, who had contracted polio and subsequently died on 5 January 1910.

The East London Federation of Suffragettes Sylvia remained loyal to the WSPU and its militant methods, but was determined to emphasize the needs of working women and to develop links with broader labour struggles. She was supported in this by her younger sister Adela [*see* Walsh, Adela Pankhurst], who was also active in the affairs of the WSPU but never felt comfortable in the organization which she left in 1911. In the following year Sylvia tried to involve more working women in the suffrage movement by campaigning in the East End of London. She supported George Lansbury, the Labour MP for Bow and Bromley, who resigned his seat in 1912 so that he could run again on the single issue of women's suffrage. Although he lost, the excitement generated by the campaign encouraged Sylvia to establish a new organization in 1913, the East London Federation of Suffragettes (ELF), which was successful in gaining support from working women and also from dock workers. The ELF organized suffrage demonstrations and its members carried out acts of militancy. Between February 1913 and August 1914 Sylvia was arrested eight times. After the passing of the Prisoners' Temporary Discharge for Ill Health Act of 1913 (known as the Cat and Mouse Act) she was frequently released for short periods to recuperate from hunger striking and was carried on a stretcher by supporters in the East End so that she could attend meetings and processions. When the police came to re-arrest her this usually led to fights with members of the community which encouraged Sylvia to organize a people's army to defend suffragettes and dock workers. She also drew on East End traditions by calling for rent strikes to support the demand for the vote.

The ELF took an interest in trade union struggles and in 1913 supported the men and women involved in the Dublin lock-out. Sylvia Pankhurst was one of the main speakers alongside George Lansbury and the Irish socialist James Connolly at a rally organized to demand the release of Jim Larkin, a leader of the Dublin strikers. This was the immediate cause of a split between Sylvia and her mother and sister, although Sylvia was already disillusioned with the way in which militancy had come to focus on individual attacks on property rather than on building a mass struggle. By 1914 the ELF was no longer part of the WSPU; Sylvia established and edited her own newspaper, the *Woman's Dreadnought*, and also led a deputation of working women from the East End which was received by the prime minister, Asquith. She remained close, however, to Emmeline and Frederick Pethick-Lawrence, who also left the WSPU at this time. They provided Sylvia with financial support for her personal and political endeavours throughout the inter-war years.

War, socialism, and pacifism The outbreak of war in August of 1914 made Sylvia's break with her mother and Christabel, who were fervent supporters of the war effort, even more complete. Sylvia had strong pacifist convictions and through the ELF initiated anti-war activities in London. She worked with other socialist men and women in opposing conscription and, despite being critical of its timidity and political moderation, she also joined in peace work with the Women's International League. The *Dreadnought* became one of the best sources for information on peace campaigning at home and abroad and helped to establish Sylvia's reputation as a leading anti-war activist. Sylvia was pulled simultaneously in many different directions as she became involved in social welfare questions as well as peace agitation. She worked closely with Norah Smythe, the daughter of a wealthy Liverpool merchant, who had joined her in the East End before the war, to build up social welfare agencies in the area, including nurseries, baby clinics, and communal restaurants, and tried to draw government attention to the sweated conditions of women workers. The broader aims of the ELF were reflected in its change of name to the Workers' Suffrage Federation in March 1916 as a reaction to the narrow provisions of the Franchise Bill.

As the war went on, however, Sylvia's political outlook became more revolutionary and she began to put less emphasis on the importance of the vote. The Easter rising in Ireland, the Russian Revolution, and the industrial unrest of 1917–19 all helped to develop her revolutionary ideas. In July 1917 she renamed her newspaper the *Workers' Dreadnought* and in 1918 the Workers' Suffrage Federation became the Workers' Socialist Federation. Sylvia worked on behalf of the Hands Off Russia campaign and visited Russia at the end of the war where she met Lenin. In 1920 she published an article in the *Dreadnought*, based on information from an English sailor, which discussed growing unrest on an unnamed battleship and which urged sailors to support the red navy. This led to her arrest and imprisonment for refusing to name her sources or to reveal who wrote the article. She spent all but one week of her five-month sentence in the infirmary cell of Holloway prison. She was centrally involved with other revolutionary socialists in the activities which led to the formation of the British Communist Party, but her determination to express her own views as freely as possible led to her expulsion in 1921.

Artist and journalist During all of these years of campaigning for socialist and women's causes, Sylvia Pankhurst continued to express her ideas in her art and in her writings. One of her first commissions was to decorate the Pankhurst Hall in Manchester, built in memory of her father by the Hightown ILP. She designed the membership card of the WSPU which depicted working-class women, and her 'trumpeting angel' was used as a design on banners and letter heads. Her paintings were based on socialist realism or on Pre-Raphaelite allegory derived from Walter Crane and as far as possible she used working women as her subjects. It was difficult for her to combine art and political agitation, however, and she soon gave up her painting, but she remained prolific as a writer. Her journalism and a lecture tour to the United States before the First World War helped to finance her political work. She wrote a series of articles on women's work, including potato-picking and pit-brow employment, for the WSPU newspaper *Votes for Women* which were based on a year-long journey, starting in the summer of 1907, to the north of England and Scotland. She also contributed numerous articles to the suffrage and the socialist press about the importance of the vote for working women and during the First World War used her journalism to develop ideas about revolutionary communism.

Sylvia Pankhurst wrote books about the movements in which she had been active which were partly historical and partly autobiographical. As one of the earliest chroniclers of the suffrage movement she published *The Suffragette* (1911) which depicted Christabel as an inspiring leader and legitimated the militant suffrage woman. Her best-known histories were written several years later. *The Suffragette Movement* (1931) is a lively and vivid account of the militant movement which has been used extensively by historians. Sylvia's judgements on people and events, however, were influenced by her growing commitment to revolutionary politics and by her split with her mother and sister. Christabel was now demonized as an autocratic leader and Sylvia emphasized that the suffrage campaign grew from, and was closely allied to, socialist politics. The same argument is used in the biography of her mother, *The Life of Emmeline Pankhurst*, written in 1935.

At the end of the First World War Sylvia met Silvio Erasmus Corio (1875–1954), an exile from Italy whose libertarian socialist views and concern with the rise of fascism in his country accorded with her own. They worked together on journalistic projects and in 1924, when Sylvia gave up the *Dreadnought*, they opened a café. They then moved to Woodford Green in Essex where Sylvia concentrated on her writing and where, in 1927 at the age of forty-five, she gave birth to her only child, Richard Keir Pethick, named after Keir Hardie and the Pethick-Lawrences, who were among the most important people in her life. She had long believed in sexual freedom and, despite pressure from Christabel, lived out her ideas in practice by refusing to marry. During this period she also wrote extensively, commenting on events in India in *India and the Earthly Paradise* (1926) and arguing for better maternity care in *Save the Mothers* (1930). Alongside her suffrage histories she also published an account of her wartime experiences in the East End, *The Home Front* (1932).

Anti-fascism and Ethiopia During the 1920s Sylvia had helped to assist Italian refugees, but it was in the 1930s that she became more politically active in fighting for peace and against fascism. She joined several women's peace groups and was treasurer of the Women's World Committee against War and Fascism. She also helped Jewish refugees and supported the republican cause in Spain. The issue which was to become central to her political work for the rest of her life, however, was the cause of Ethiopian independence. When Italian fascists invaded Ethiopia in 1935–6 she began a weekly journal, *New Times and Ethiopian News*, which she edited for twenty years. This publicized the efforts made by Emperor Haile Selassie to persuade the League of Nations to prevent colonization and led to her being dubbed in Ethiopia the Sword of the Press. After the liberation of Addis Ababa by General Orde Wingate she sent the BBC a record of the Ethiopian national anthem. She helped to raise funds to build and equip a hospital, opposed plans to turn Ethiopia into a British protectorate, and supported proposals for unity between Eritrea and Ethiopia. In the early summer of 1936 she was responsible for the creation of an 'anti-air war memorial' on land next to her Essex home. This stone edifice (designed and carved by Eric Benfield) was unveiled on 21 June by a group including the secretary of the imperial Ethiopian legation. It was accompanied by a plaque condemning 'those who in 1932 upheld the right to use bombing planes' (P. W., *London Review of Books*, 23 Aug 2001). This 'stone bomb' still stands at Woodford Green, and in the 1980s it became a grade II listed edifice. After Corio died in 1954 Sylvia accepted an earlier invitation from the emperor and moved with her son to live permanently in Ethiopia in 1956. There she helped to found the Social Service Society and edited a monthly periodical, the *Ethiopia Observer*. She was honoured with the decoration of the queen of Sheba, first class.

Towards the end of her life Sylvia Pankhurst re-established contact with friends from the early suffrage days, including Teresa Billington-Greig, a founder member of the WSPU, who sent a copy of her autobiography to Sylvia for her comments. She had maintained a relationship with her sister Adela, who shared her socialist views, and in the 1950s Sylvia even corresponded once more with Christabel. In 1959 an exhibition of her art was held at the French Institute in London and she willingly contributed material to the organizers. Sylvia died the following year in Addis Ababa, on 27 September 1960. She was regarded so highly in Ethiopia that the emperor ordered that she should receive a state funeral, which was attended by himself and other members of the royal family. She was buried outside Trinity Cathedral in a special plot reserved for the country's heroes. A memorial service was held in London in the Caxton Hall on 19 January 1961.

Assessment Although the focus of her activities changed over time, Sylvia Pankhurst supported socialist and revolutionary politics and campaigns for women's political and sexual freedom throughout her life. She was a serious and dedicated campaigner who lacked the glamour of her sister and mother, insisting on wearing unstylish clothes and no cosmetics since she thought that lipstick 'reveals the slave mentality' (Romero, 266). None the less, with her thick sandy hair, heavy lidded eyes, and slender build she was an attractive figure. She could be warm and compassionate, but Jessie Stephen, one of her co-workers in the East End, claimed that she could 'charm when she liked, but at the core was inclined to be as autocratic as her mother and elder sister Christabel' (Winslow, 82).

Sylvia is usually best remembered for her activities as a militant suffragette and for her history of the movement. Her contribution to socialist and revolutionary politics has been taken less seriously, perhaps because she never settled in one particular organization and always expressed independent views. Her arrogance, impatience, and reluctance to compromise also limited her political influence at a personal level. In many biographies emphasis has been placed on the difficulties she faced because her mother always favoured Christabel and because of her father's early death, leading one biographer to claim that her life was driven by 'a succession of dependencies on men' (Romero, 287). Yet recent studies of her politics and re-evaluation of her writings have shown that as an anti-fascist, a socialist, a communist, a peace campaigner, an internationalist, and a feminist Sylvia Pankhurst made an important contribution in her own right to radical politics during the twentieth century. The way in which she put together the different strands of her interests meant that at various times she could be politically isolated, but her lengthy involvement in political life deserves serious consideration. June Hannam

Sources O. Banks, *The biographical dictionary of British feminists*, 1 (1985) • S. Pankhurst, 'Sylvia Pankhurst', *Myself when young, by famous women of to-day*, ed. Countess of Oxford and Asquith (1938), 259–312 • P. Romero, *E. Sylvia Pankhurst: portrait of a radical* (1987) • B. Winslow, *Sylvia Pankhurst: sexual politics and political activism* (1996) • K. Dodd, ed., *A Sylvia Pankhurst reader* (1993) • L. Tickner, *The spectacle of women: imagery of the suffrage campaign, 1907–14* (1987) • R. Pankhurst, *Sylvia Pankhurst: artist and crusader* (1979) • I. Bullock and R. Pankhurst, eds., *Sylvia Pankhurst: from artist to anti-fascist* (1992) • P. W., 'The stone bomb', *London Review of Books* (23 Aug 2001) • G. Alem-Ayehu, 'Reflections on the life and work of Sylvia Pankhurst: the Ethiopian dimension', priv. coll. • private information (2004) [S. Ayling]

Archives Internationaal Instituut voor Sociale Geschiedenis, Amsterdam, corresp. and papers • Women's Library, London, corresp. | BL, corresp. with Society of Authors, Add. MSS 56769–56771 • BLPES, corresp. with the independent labour party • Bodl. Oxf., letters to David Lloyd George • JRL, letters to the *Manchester Guardian* • Labour History Archive and Study Centre, Manchester, corresp. with William Gillies • State Historical Society of Wisconsin, Madison, corresp. with Ada Lois James • Trinity Cam., corresp. with F. W. Pethick-Lawrence | FILM BFI NFTVA, *Shoulder to shoulder*, BBC2, 8 May 1974 • BFI NFTVA, *Cracking up*, Channel 4, 18 Dec 1989 • BFI NFTVA, news footage

Likenesses Mrs. A. Broom, group photograph, 1910, NPG; *see illus. in* Davison, Emily Wilding (1872–1913) • photographs, 1913–43, Hult. Arch. • H. Cole, chalk drawing, *c.*1925, NPG • Bassano, photograph, 1927, NPG [*see illus.*] • photograph, 1935, NPG; repro. in *Daily Herald* • H. Coster, photographs, 1938, NPG • I. Walters, two bronze maquettes/sculptures, *c.*2002 • S. Pankhurst, self-portrait, chalk drawing, NPG • photographs, repro. in Romero, *E. Sylvia Pankhurst* • photographs, Women's Library, London

Wealth at death £3627 8*s.* 3*d.*: administration with will, 22 March 1961, *CGPLA Eng. & Wales*

Panmure. For this title name *see* Maule, Patrick, first earl of Panmure (1585–1661); Maule, James, fourth earl of Panmure (1658/9–1723); Maule, Harry, styled fifth earl of Panmure (1659–1734); Maule, William, earl of Panmure of Forth (1699/1700–1782); Maule, William Ramsay, first Baron Panmure (1771–1852); Maule, Fox, second Baron Panmure and eleventh earl of Dalhousie (1801–1874).

Panter, David (*d.* 1558), administrator and bishop of Ross, was the illegitimate son of Patrick *Panter (*c.*1470–1519), secretary to James IV, and Margaret Crichton, the illegitimate daughter of William, third Lord Crichton, and Margaret Stewart, a younger daughter of James II. Having attended university (probably St Andrews), where he acquired the degree of MA, he was legitimized under the great seal, along with his sister Katherine, on 12 August 1513. His career was facilitated by a number of useful family connections (they included Gavin Dunbar, bishop of Glasgow), and also by royal favour. He became a trusted agent of James V, who appointed him a judge in the college of justice, and after the king's death in 1542 was employed by Mary of Guise, the king's widow, and the earl of Arran, who had become governor of Scotland; in 1543 he was appointed their secretary. He also served for seven years as an ambassador on the continent, dealing with the German emperor, the kings of England and France, and Mary of Hungary, the governor of Flanders. He sought to sow divisions between England and the empire while attempting to secure military aid for Scotland from France, and to that end tried to secure a French bride for Arran, and he was present at the Anglo-French treaty of Boulogne in 1550. It was doubtless his activities overseas which brought him the abbacy of Absie-en-Gâtine in Poitou.

His long sojourn abroad did not prevent Panter from acquiring ecclesiastical benefices in Scotland. In 1534 the king had petitioned the papacy for a dispensation for him to become coadjutor to Alexander Mylne, abbot of Cambuskenneth, and in 1536 he was provided to the priory of St Mary's, Isle of Trail, *in commendam*. While he was in Paris in 1542 he petitioned for the vicarage of Carstairs. He was also a canon of St Salvator's, St Andrews, parson of Kinnell, vicar of Aberlady, and a canon of Dunkeld Cathedral. On 23 December 1545, following the death of Robert Cairncross, Panter was granted the temporalities of the see of Ross, and also those of the Premonstratensian abbey of Fearn. Papal provision to Ross followed on 28 November 1547, and Panter resigned Trail in that year, but consecration to his see only took place (at Jedburgh) in 1552, after his return to Scotland. Mylne died in July 1548, whereupon the pope granted Panter the *commendam* of Cambuskenneth, and he was admitted to the abbey's temporalities in 1549. In spite of his ecclesiastical eminence, Panter was alleged to have been contaminated with the new opinions in religion circulating in Scotland, and to have favoured the men who in 1546 assassinated Cardinal Beaton. In his last years he was regular in attending sessions of the privy council and of parliament. He died in Stirling on 1 October 1558. J. A. Gould

Sources W. Fraser, ed., *Registrum monasterii S. Marie de Cambuskenneth*, Grampian Club, 4 (1872), xcviii–civ • J. M. Thomson and others, eds., *Registrum magni sigilli regum Scotorum / The register of the great seal of Scotland*, 11 vols. (1882–1914), vol. 3, nos. 2072, 113, 138, 338, 2262, 2375, 3086; vol. 4, nos. 886, 1225 • M. Livingstone, D. Hay Fleming, and others, eds., *Registrum secreti sigilli regum Scotorum / The register of the privy seal of Scotland*, 2 (1921), 497 • *Reg. PCS*, 1st ser., 1.107, 111, 114, 116–17, 119, 139–40 • R. K. Hannay, ed., *Acts of the lords of council in public affairs, 1501–1554* (1932), 433, 441, 451, 466, 535, 553–4, 588 • *LP Henry VIII*, vols. 20–21 • J. Lesley, *The history of Scotland*, ed. T. Thomson, Bannatyne Club, 38 (1830), 188, 232, 244, 267 • *Foreign correspondence with Marie de Lorraine, queen of Scotland: from the originals in the Balcarres papers*, ed. M. Wood, 1: *1537–1548*, Scottish History Society, 3rd ser., 4 (1923), 93, n.1 • *Foreign correspondence with Marie de Lorraine, queen of Scotland: from the originals in the Balcarres papers*, ed. M. Wood, 2: *1548–1557*, Scottish History Society, 3rd ser., 7 (1925), 47, 66, 189, 245–7, 256–8, 283, 301 • J. B. Paul, ed., *Compota thesaurariorum regum Scotorum / Accounts of the lord high treasurer of Scotland*, 8 (1908), 194, 278, 485, 489 • *The Scottish correspondence of Mary of Lorraine*, ed. A. I. Cameron, Scottish History Society, 3rd ser., 10 (1927), 32, 153, 169, 171, 173–5, 177, 179 • J. Dowden, *The bishops of Scotland … prior to the Reformation*, ed. J. M. Thomson (1912), 226–8 • R. S. Rait, introduction, in *The Warrander papers*, ed. A. I. Cameron, 1, Scottish History Society, 3rd ser., 18 (1931), 15–16; 2, Scottish History Society, 3rd ser., 19 (1932) • D. E. R. Watt, ed., *Fasti ecclesiae Scoticanae medii aevi ad annum 1638*, [2nd edn], Scottish RS, new ser., 1 (1969), 270 • J. Watkins, trans., *Buchanan's history of Scotland* (1840), 359, 387, 392 • R. J. Adam, ed., *The calendar of Fearn: text and additions, 1471–1667*, Scottish History Society, 5th ser., 4 (1991) • *The letters of James V*, ed. R. K. Hannay and D. Hay (1954)

Panter, Patrick (*c.*1470–1519), ecclesiastic and administrator, was born at Newmanswells, Montrose, the son of David Panter, a burgess of that town. Having attended the Collège de Montaigu in Paris, he entered the University of Louvain in 1498 and remained in the Low Countries until January 1503. Described as a clerk of Brechin diocese, he never became a priest—on no fewer than seven occasions he received papal dispensations from taking holy orders—and his accumulation of church benefices was essentially the reward for his services to the crown. In 1505 he became secretary to James IV, and he also acted as tutor to two of the king's illegitimate sons, Alexander Stewart, later archbishop of St Andrews, and James Stewart, earl of Moray. By 1507 he was vicar of Cathcart, parson of Fetteresso, and preceptor of the hospital of St Mary near Montrose. In 1508 he was appointed archdeacon of Dunkeld, and by 1509 he had become parson of Tannadice. He became archdeacon of Moray in 1510 but resigned that office a year later, and in 1513 he was provided to the abbacy of Cambuskenneth for a payment of 400 florins. Able as well as ambitious, in 1513 Panter was described by the English ambassador as the man who 'doothe all with his maister' (Macdougall, 209); in 1511 he had embroiled his king in a dispute with the papacy by persuading James to secure papal provision for him to the wealthy hospitaller preceptory of Torphichen, ignoring the rights of another candidate who had secured the right of expectation several years earlier.

Panter was among the king's councillors who in 1513 supported his policy of war with England, and he was present at Flodden on 9 September. One of the relatively few Scots to survive the battle, he subsequently sought papal absolution for his involvement, which had been as one of the managers of the (largely ineffective) Scottish artillery. He retained his secretaryship in the immediate aftermath of Flodden, but was discharged in 1514. He continued to attend the court and maintained his claim to Torphichen, but by 10 September 1515 his opposition to the duke of Albany, now governor of the realm, had led to his being imprisoned at Inchgarvie, on the Firth of Forth. In the following year, however, Panter returned to favour; he received the subdiaconate, but was dispensed from proceeding to a deacon's orders. In 1517 he was sent as an ambassador to France, where he helped to negotiate the Franco-Scottish treaty of Rouen. He remained in France, in 1518 writing from Paris to the authorities at Middelburg about trading agreements. A year later he was reported to have been immobilized by ill health, and he died, still in Paris, in 1519, perhaps on 18 November.

In spite of having apparently been consistently non-resident in his various benefices, Panter was not entirely negligent of their interests. He approached the abbot of St Victor at Paris for assistance in raising educational and religious standards at Cambuskenneth, and he effectively refounded the hospital at Montrose. Having recovered its endowment from local landowners, he restored the church and other buildings, and in 1517, with Albany's support, he obtained papal licence to grant the hospital and its estates to the Dominicans of Montrose. At an unknown date he formed a liaison with Margaret Crichton, whose mother, Margaret Stewart, was a younger daughter of James II. They had at least two children, a son, David *Panter, who became bishop of Ross, and a daughter, Katherine. J. A. Gould

Sources W. Fraser, ed., *Registrum monasterii S. Marie de Cambuskenneth*, Grampian Club, 4 (1872), lxxii–lxxxvii • J. M. Thomson and others, eds., *Registrum magni sigilli regum Scotorum / The register of the great seal of Scotland*, 11 vols. (1882–1914), vol. 2, nos. 3765, 3293, 3430, 3366, 3453, 3446; vol. 3, nos. 22, 133, 138, 139 • R. K. Hannay, ed., *Acts of the lords of council in public affairs, 1501–1554* (1932), lxii, lxiv–lxv, 1, 6, 7, 14, 15, 17, 18, 19, 20, 21, 23, 24, 33, 35, 36, 37, 41, 51, 56, 64, 65, 73, 78 • *The letters of James the Fourth, 1503–1513*, ed. R. K. Hannay, R. L. Mackie, and A. Spilman (1953), xxvii–xxxiv, 40, 42–3, 62–3, 153–4, 234–6, 314 • *The letters of James V*, ed. R. K. Hannay and D. Hay (1954), 8–9, 12–13, 15, 17, 23, 32, 37–8, 45, 58–9, 63, 70–71, 90 • C. M. MacDonald, 'The struggle of George Dundas and his rivals Patrick Panter, James Cortesius and Alexander Stewart for the preceptory of Torphichen', *SHR*, 14 (1916–17), 19–48, esp. 27–8 • M. Livingstone, D. Hay Fleming, and others, eds., *Registrum secreti sigilli regum Scotorum / The register of the privy seal of Scotland*, 1 (1908), nos. 1365, 2186, 2435; 1771, 1772 • G. Burnett and others, eds., *The exchequer rolls of Scotland*, 13 (1891), 366, 371 • E. B. Fryde and others, eds., *Handbook of British chronology*, 3rd edn, Royal Historical Society

Guides and Handbooks, 2 (1986), 193 • J. Dowden, *The bishops of Scotland … prior to the Reformation*, ed. J. M. Thomson (1912), 227–8, 343 • N. Macdougall, *James IV* (1989) • I. B. Cowan and D. E. Easson, *Medieval religious houses: Scotland*, 2nd edn (1976)

Pantin, Carl Frederick Abel (1899–1967), zoologist, was born on 30 March 1899 at Blackheath, London, the second child and elder son of Herbert Pantin, head of a family manufacturing company, and his wife, Emilie Juanita Abel. She was a descendant of the distinguished Abel family which included Pantin's great-uncle, Sir Frederick A. Abel (1827–1902), the inventor of cordite, and Karl Friedrich Abel (1723–1787), the celebrated viola da gamba player. Pantin's brother W. A. Pantin FBA became keeper of the university archives at Oxford.

From childhood Pantin was fascinated by natural history; at Tonbridge School, Kent (1913–17) he was recognized as having outstanding scientific ability, and in the words of his headmaster, a 'nobility of character'. After brief service with the Royal Engineers he went up in 1919 to Christ's College, Cambridge, as a scholar. He graduated with distinction, obtaining first classes in parts one (1921) and two (1922, zoology and comparative anatomy) of the natural sciences tripos, and was awarded the Frank Smart prize in 1922.

Later that year Pantin joined the staff of the Marine Biological Laboratory at Plymouth, embarking on a series of elegant and fundamental investigations into the functioning of the lower animals. His work on amoeboid movement contained the elements of the later biophysical approach to the structure of cytoplasm; he investigated the effect of ions on and in tissues and made similarly fundamental discoveries about osmoregulation in flatworms. Pantin believed that physiological mechanism is only meaningful when understood in the context of the biology of the animal in nature; he was one of the first zoologists to employ an ecological, rather than morphological, approach. To this end he would call on his encyclopaedic knowledge of the animal kingdom, backed by a sound knowledge of palaeontology and geology.

While working at the Marine Biological Laboratory Pantin married in 1923 Amy, second daughter of Dr James Cruickshank Smith CBE LittD LLD, a senior chief inspector of schools in Scotland. She was also a zoologist, who qualified in medicine. They had two sons.

In 1929 Pantin became a fellow of Trinity College, Cambridge, directing studies and lecturing in the department of zoology of the university, but returning regularly to Plymouth to research and run the renowned 'Easter' courses, where his colleagues and pupils included many distinguished zoologists. Pantin took his Cambridge ScD in 1933.

Following a period at the Stazione Zoologica in Naples in 1933, Pantin published a series of papers on the functioning of the nervous system of the sea anemone: this was his most influential work. He demonstrated how the organization of the nerve net, and its very low frequency impulses, could produce the response of different muscles each to its appropriate range of impulse rate, and also create integrated movement and behaviour of a comparatively complex kind in seemingly the simplest of nervous organizations. His work formed a foundation from which much of later neurophysiology and the interpretation of behaviour in neural terms originated. Despite contracting tuberculosis, Pantin continued his work, and was elected a fellow of the Royal Society in 1937, the year in which he organized the now classic discussion of that body on the transmission of excitation in living material.

Pantin researched the lower animals for the rest of his life, especially the coelenterates and nemertine worms, though with his increasing involvement with the national bodies of his science, this research was increasingly done through associates and assistants. Yet for thirty-five years his lectures to undergraduates communicated an enthusiasm and excitement of a remarkable kind. He became reader in invertebrate zoology in 1937 and succeeded Sir James Gray as professor in 1959. Despite failing health, as head of the zoology department Pantin succeeded in obtaining new buildings for the Museum of Zoology, and a modern research wing which today bears his name. In 1964 he was diagnosed as having leukaemia and he died in the Hope Nursing Home, Cambridge, on 14 January 1967, only a few months after he retired.

Pantin was president of the Linnean Society of London from 1958 to 1960, president of the Marine Biological Association of the United Kingdom (1960–66), and from 1963 until his death, chairman of the board of trustees of the Natural History Museum. He received the royal medal of the Royal Society in 1950, and the gold medal of the Linnean Society in 1964. He became an honorary member of the Royal Society of New Zealand in 1955 and was given honorary doctorates of the universities of São Paulo and Durham. He became an honorary fellow of his old Cambridge college, Christ's. Despite this, those closest to him felt that he did not receive the public recognition he deserved, for he lacked any vestige of ruthlessness or selfishness; he was a man of transparent sincerity and personal charm, who communicated a radiant enjoyment of life and its study. JAMES BEAMENT, *rev.*

Sources F. A. Russell, *Memoirs FRS*, 14 (1968), 417–34 • *Journal of the Marine Biological Association of the United Kingdom*, 47 (1967) • W. T. Stearn, *The Natural History Museum at South Kensington: a history of the British Museum (Natural History), 1753–1980* (1981)

Archives Bodl. Oxf., corresp. with G. E. Blackman • CAC Cam., corresp. with A. V. Hill • Rice University, Houston, Texas, Woodson Research Center, corresp. with Sir Julian Huxley

Likenesses W. Stoneman, two photographs, 1937–53, NPG • C. Rogers, drawing, 1959, Trinity Cam. • H. A. Freeth, portrait (near death), U. Cam., department of zoology • photograph, repro. in Russell, *Memoirs FRS*, p. 417

Wealth at death £46,469: probate, 5 May 1967, *CGPLA Eng. & Wales*

Pantin, Thomas Pindar (1792–1866), theologian, was the son of Thomas Pantin of St Sepulchre's, London. He matriculated from Queen's College, Oxford, on 24 June 1817, and graduated BA in 1821 and MA in 1827. He was instituted rector of Westcote, Gloucestershire, in 1828, and remained there until his death, apparently unmarried, on 2 September 1866. He was succeeded at Westcote by his kinsman, John Wicliffe Pantin.

Pantin wrote several small polemical works directed against Roman Catholic claims, including *Observations on certain passages in Dr Arnold's Christian duty of granting the Roman Catholic claims* (1829), *The Novelty of Popery in Matters of Faith and Practice* (1837), and *The Church of England, apostolical in its origin, episcopal in its government, and scriptural in its belief* (1849). He also edited, with additional notes, Bishop Stillingfleet's *Origines Britannicae* (2 vols., 1842), and Bishop Bull's *Corruptions of the Church of Rome* with a preface and notes (1836).

THOMAS SECCOMBE, *rev.* H. C. G. MATTHEW

Sources *GM*, 4th ser., 2 (1866), 553 • Foster, *Alum. Oxon.*
Wealth at death under £300: probate, 26 Oct 1866, *CGPLA Eng. & Wales*

Panton [*née* Frith], **Jane Ellen** (1847–1923), writer, was born on 18 October 1847 at 13 Park Village West, Regent's Park, London, the second daughter and third of the twelve children of the painter William Powell *Frith (1819–1909) and his first wife, Isabelle Jane (1823–1880), daughter of George Baker. Except for three days at a boarding-school in Bath, from which she ran away, she was educated at home by governesses, one of whom was a sister of the insane painter Richard Dadd (1817–1886). In 1852 or 1853 the family moved to a large house, 10 Pembridge Villas, Notting Hill, London, where she grew up, during a period in which her father's paintings sold for immense sums; she lived to see the eclipse of his reputation. The several autobiographical volumes she published describe a happy childhood in a circle of artists and writers, but have an undercurrent of antagonism towards her father, who 'got rid of us one after the other as soon as he could, and never troubled about us for one moment directly we had left the nest' (Panton, *More Leaves*, 26). No doubt their relationship was embittered by the revelation after her mother's death that he had been keeping a mistress (whom he then married) and had several illegitimate children. The fact that the memoirs give a child's view of what it was like at the heart of the Victorian art world has made them of much use to historians. Jane Frith modelled frequently for her father and other painter friends: she appears as one of the little girls building a house of cards while her mother confesses adultery to her father in the 1858 *Past and Present* by Augustus Egg (1816–1863), in a pink print dress in her father's *The Railway Station* (1861), and as Katherina in *The Taming of the Shrew* (1869) by Alfred Elmore (1815–1881).

On 10 August 1869 at All Saints' Church, Kensington, Jane Frith married James Albert Panton (1841–1921), son of James Panton, brewer, and his wife, Mary Sarah Gillingham. James Panton was in partnership with his brother as a brewer at Wareham in Dorset; he and Jane were to have three sons and two daughters, of whom one son predeceased her. Victorian Wareham is described in her memoir *Fresh Leaves and Green Pastures* (1909). After the brother's death his widow bought out James Panton's share of the brewery, and in 1882 he and Jane left Wareham. After a short time in Bournemouth they went to live for four years at Shortlands, Bromley, Kent, where Dinah Maria Craik (1826–1887) was a neighbour and friend. In 1883, anxious to earn money, Jane Panton proposed a series of articles on furnishing a house to the editor of the *Lady's Pictorial* magazine. These articles were published as *From Kitchen to Garret* (1887) and were a success, as well as pioneering a whole school of women's domestic journalism. She was encouraged by this to start a scheme for selling needlework done by indigent gentlewomen, but gave it up when they proved troublesome. She also earned money advising people how to decorate their homes: 'the most amusing and lucrative branch of my work' (Panton, *Fresh Leaves*, 361). Later she worked on the magazine *The Gentlewoman* and she was a fellow of the Zoological Society. She published between 1882 and 1916 ten undistinguished volumes of fiction, including *The Cannibal Crusader: an Allegory for the Times* (1908), in which a noble savage exposes the folly of modern society. Her other publications include a book of verse for children and a large number of advice books. According to an obituary in *The Times* she had 'a vivid and brilliant personality' and was 'a witty and outspoken conversationalist' (21 May 1923). She and her husband celebrated their golden wedding anniversary, and two years later she lined his coffin with her wedding dress. Her brother Walter Frith (*d.* 1941) was a playwright and novelist. She died of diarrhoea and heart failure at her home, 1 Taviton Street, Bloomsbury, London, on 13 May 1923. CHARLOTTE MITCHELL

Sources [J. E. Panton], *Fresh leaves and green pastures* (1909) • [J. E. Panton], *Leaves from a life* (1908) • [J. E. Panton], *More leaves from a life* (1911) • W. P. Frith, *My autobiography and reminiscences*, 2 vols. (1887) • private information (2004) [Christopher Wood] • *The Times* (14 May 1923) • *The Times* (21 May 1923) • *The Times* (19 Sept 1921) • b. cert. • m. cert. • d. cert. • *CGPLA Eng. & Wales* (1923)
Likenesses A. Egg, triptych, 1858 (*Past and present*), Tate collection • J. Phillip, portrait, 1858 • W. P. Frith, portrait, 1861 (*The railway station*), Leicester Art Gallery • A. Elmore, portrait, 1869 (*The taming of the shrew*)
Wealth at death £938 9s. 5d.: probate, 27 June 1923, *CGPLA Eng. & Wales*

Panton, Paul (1727–1797), literary patron and antiquary, was born on 4 May 1727 in Bagillt, Flintshire, the eldest son of Paul Patton or Panton (*d.* 1752) and his wife, Margaret, the daughter and heir of Edward Griffith of Bagillt. Despite their English-sounding surname, the Pantons were an old Welsh family who could trace their ancestry back to Marchweithan, the supposed founder of one of the so-called fifteen tribes of Gwynedd. Through his mother, Paul Panton was a descendant of John Jones (*c.*1585–1657/8) of Gellilyfdy, the celebrated copier and collector of Welsh manuscripts. He was educated from 1740 at Westminster School and from June 1744 at Trinity Hall, Cambridge. He was elected a scholar in 1745, but he did not matriculate until 1746. He went to Lincoln's Inn in December 1744, was called to the bar in November 1749, and was for a period a practising barrister. On 1 March 1756 he married Jane (1725–1764), the daughter and heir of William Jones (1688–1755), of Plas Gwyn, Pentraeth, Anglesey, the former recorder of Beaumaris. This marriage brought him a fine estate in Anglesey whose focal point was the newly built red-brick Georgian house of Plas Gwyn, of which Thomas Pennant stated that it 'may be reckoned among the best on the island' (Pennant, 2.264).

Panton made a significant contribution to public life both in Flintshire, where he was lord of the manor of Coleshill, and in Anglesey, and was sheriff of the former in 1770 and the latter in 1771. He was appointed a justice of the peace in Anglesey and took seriously his responsibilities as squire of Plas Gwyn, to the evident satisfaction of the Morris brothers of Anglesey. He also proposed to stand for parliament in the 1761 election, but eventually withdrew and lent his support to the successful campaign of the Treasury-supported candidate Owen Meyrick of Bodorgan. He was also associated with the Druidical Society of Anglesey (founded in 1772), a charitable and benevolent society which also undertook to promote agricultural improvements, and was himself one of the Anglesey landowners who was most conspicuous as an agricultural reformer. George Kay, in his *General View of the Agriculture of Anglesey* (1794), noted that 'enclosures are growing in every part of Anglesey. Paul Panton of Plas Gwin Esq. has enclosed more than any gentleman in the island' (Kay, 10). In a similar vein, William Morris, on a visit to Plas Gwyn in 1758, noted playfully how a horse-ride from the estate enabled him to view both 'rhyfeddodau'r greadigaeth ac imprwfments y Bantwn' ('the wonders of the creation and Panton's improvements'; *The Letters of Lewis, Richard, William, and John Morris*, 2.83). The wider infrastructure of the island also concerned Panton, and he was involved both in the Turnpike Trust for Anglesey in the 1760s (an act was passed to facilitate the building of a turnpike road to Holyhead in 1765) and in the unsuccessful attempts in the 1780s to have a bridge built over the Menai Strait. He also took a practical interest in the growing metal industries in Flintshire, and was described by William Morris in 1761 as being 'mine mad' (ibid., 2.321).

Panton had a wide circle of friends which included the antiquaries Thomas Pennant and Daines Barrington. He also travelled extensively in Wales, England, and Scotland. He shared many of Pennant's antiquarian interests and although he could not speak much Welsh himself, Panton took a keen, knowledgeable, and practical interest in Welsh literature and history. A large portion of the historically important papers of the Wynn family of Gwydir came into his possession, probably through family connections. He befriended Evan Evans (Ieuan Fardd; 1731–1788), the greatest Welsh scholar of his day, and eventually gave him an annuity of £20 on the understanding that Evans's papers would go to Plas Gwyn on his death. These, and other important papers which he collected, are now lodged at the National Library of Wales. Along with his son Paul, he encouraged Owen Jones (Owain Myfyr), William Owen Pughe, and Edward Williams (Iolo Morganwg) to consult his literary manuscripts at Plas Gwyn and so aided the publication of the important *Myvyrian Archaiology* (1801–7), the first volume of which was dedicated to Paul Panton junior. He and his son also provided patronage for the Caernarvonshire poet David Thomas (Dafydd Ddu Eryri; 1759–1822), who also dedicated his volume of poetry *Corph y gaingc* (1810) to Paul Panton junior.

Panton had four children with his first wife, Jane—Jane (*b.* 1757), Paul (*b.* 1758), Jones (*b.* 1761), and Elisabeth Maria (*b.* 1763)—and the family at Bagillt were the subject of two short series of *englynion* (preserved in NL Wales, MS 2068) by the poet and publisher Huw Jones (*d.* 1782) of Llangwm. Jane died on 21 June 1764 and on 6 June 1770 Panton married Martha Kirk, a widow from Chester, who died in Holywell, Flintshire, on 27 July 1814, aged eighty-two. They had two sons, Thomas (*b.* 1771) and Bulkeley (*b.* 1772). Panton died on 24 May 1797 and was buried in St James's Church, Holywell, where a memorial to him by John Flaxman was erected. His estates were inherited by his eldest son Paul, who died unmarried on 24 August 1822, after which they passed on to his sisters and his brother Jones Panton, who died in 1837. Although his papers show that his interests were many and varied, Paul Panton senior is primarily noted as a literary patron and antiquary whose collections of manuscripts have, from his own day onwards, proved to be an invaluable source for different aspects of the history and literature of Wales. DYLAN FOSTER EVANS

Sources *DWB* · NL Wales, Panton papers · *The letters of Lewis, Richard, William and John Morris of Anglesey*, ed. J. H. Davies, 2 vols. (1907–9) · *Additional letters of the Morrises of Anglesey, 1735–1786*, ed. H. Owen, 2 vols. (1947–9) · H. Ramage, *Portraits of an island* (1987) · 'The Panton papers, including the Wynn of Gwydir papers', *Anglesey manuscripts in the National Library of Wales* (c.1927), 3–10 · T. Pennant, *A tour in Wales*, 2 vols. (1778–83) · G. Roberts, 'The county representation of Anglesey in the eighteenth century', *Transactions of the Anglesey Antiquarian Society and Field Club* (1930), 60–78 · J. Steegman, *A survey of portraits in Welsh houses*, 2 vols. (1957–62) · G. Kay, *General view of the agriculture of Anglesey* (1794) · [J. Thomas?], *A history of Anglesey* (1775) · *Old Westminsters*, 2.723 · Venn, *Alum. Cant.*

Archives NL Wales, corresp. and MSS, MSS 1970–2068, 9051–9107 · NL Wales, collection of papers · NL Wales, itineraries | NL Wales, Plas Gwyn collection; volume of legal reports

Likenesses portrait, c.1760; last known at Trefan, Llanystumdwy, Gwynedd, in 1957

Wealth at death presumed wealthy; owned land in Flintshire and Anglesey

Panton, Thomas (*d.* 1685), gambler and rake, was the youngest son of John Panton, a Leicestershire gentleman living at Ashby-de-la-Zouch. When the nucleus of a regular army was formed by Charles II in 1661 Panton, who may have attended the king abroad and already enjoyed a titular colonelcy, obtained a commission in his majesty's Life Guards, and also held a captaincy in the foot guards. He drew his pay from both regiments until 1667 when, having become a Roman Catholic, he resigned his commissions into the king's hands during a review in St James's Park.

Panton lived in extravagant splendour in lodgings near the court, and made his reputation through his skill at gambling and his relentless pursuit of amorous intrigues with other citizens' wives. One such affair was with the wife of a goldsmith, in which he spent 100 guineas in pursuit of her favours; it became the subject of street ballads and barber-shop gossip for many years afterwards. The story of this affair was finally printed years after his death in Lucas's *Memoirs of the lives, intrigues, and comical adventures of the most famous gamesters and celebrated sharpers*, and contributed to the construction of the myth of a libertine Restoration court after the revolution of 1688. Panton really excelled, however, as a card player. 'There was no game', says Lucas, 'but what he was an absolute artist at it, either upon the Square or Foul Play … His chief game was hazard, and in one night at this play he won as many thousand pounds as purchased him an estate of above £1,500 a year' (Lucas, 67).

After this coup Panton married Dorothy Stacy (1640/41–1725), the daughter of John Stacy of London and his wife, Elinor Blake of Easton, Hampshire; bought the manor of Cuxhall in Bucknall and other estates in Herefordshire; and entirely abjured all games of chance. He speculated, however, in property about London, and about 1670 he bought from Mrs Baker the well-known seventeenth-century gaming house known as Piccadilly Hall. He improved this property and in 1671 began building a 'fair street of good houses' (Wheatley, 26) between the Haymarket and Whitcomb Street near Leicester Fields. The street retains Panton's name to the present day. He died in 1685 and was buried on 26 October of that year in Westminster Abbey. His widow, Dorothy, lived in 'a capital mansion on the east side of the Haymarket' (*DNB*) until her death on 1 April 1725 at the age of eighty-four. She was buried by the side of her husband on 5 April. Her will, dated 1 June 1722, was proved on 8 April 1725 by her eldest son, Brigadier-General Thomas Panton, who fought with distinction in the War of the Spanish Succession and who died on 20 July 1753, the oldest general in the army. Their eldest daughter, Elizabeth (*d.* 1700), married Henry, fifth Lord Arundell of Wardour, about 1679, while another daughter, Dorothy, married William Stanley of Chelsea in 1675. THOMAS SECCOMBE, *rev.* BRIAN COWAN

Sources *Analytical index, to the series of records known as Remembrancia, preserved among the archives of the City of London*, Corporation of London, ed. [W. H. Overall and H. C. Overall] (1878), 19–20 • R. Beatson, *A political index to the histories of Great Britain and Ireland*, 3rd edn, 2 (1806), 130 • J. L. Chester, ed., *The marriage, baptismal, and burial registers of the collegiate church or abbey of St Peter, Westminster*, Harleian Society, 10 (1876), 214–15, 313 • C. Dalton, ed., *English army lists and commission registers, 1661–1714*, 1 (1892), 1, 7, 37 • *GM*, 1st ser., 23 (1753), 344 • *The manuscripts of the House of Lords*, 4 vols., HMC, 17 (1887–94), vol. 3, p. 347 • *Letter-books of John Hervey, first earl of Bristol*, ed. S. H. A. H. [S. H. A. Hervey], 3 vols. (1894) • T. Lucas, *Memoirs of the lives, intrigues, and comical adventures of the most famous gamesters and celebrated sharpers in the reigns of Charles II, James II, William III and Queen Anne* (1714), 59–67 • H. B. Wheatley and P. Cunningham, *London past and present*, 3 vols. (1891), vol. 3, pp. 25–7 • GEC, *Peerage*, new edn, 1.265

Likenesses etching, pubd 1813, BM, NPG

Panton, Thomas (1731/2–1808), racehorse owner, was born after 29 November 1731 at Newmarket, the son of Thomas Panton (1697–1782). The elder Panton was master of the king's running horses at Newmarket and was described by Horace Walpole as 'a disreputable horse jockey' (Walpole to Mann, 7 July 1779, *Correspondence*, 24.499). Details of the younger Panton's education and upbringing are not known. On 27 November 1750 his sister, Mary, married Peregrine Bertie, third duke of Ancaster; the marriage produced seven children. Three years later Panton was elected a member of the Jockey Club and in time became a significant figure in the horse-racing world, subscribing to the Jockey Club Cup in 1768. A resident of Fen Ditton, Cambridgeshire, he offered himself, unsuccessfully, as parliamentary candidate for the county seat following the death of John Manners, marquess of Granby, in 1770; he later served as high sheriff for Cambridgeshire in 1789. In 1777 he was depicted as the 'Sporting rover' in the *Town and Country Magazine*'s tête à tête series and appeared in Charles Pigott's satire, *The Jockey Club* (1792), in which he was described as a 'truly well-bred, agreeable, good-humoured man … [who] is extremely popular amongst his acquaintances'. Pigott also referred to Panton's lengthy relationship with the 'celebrated Mrs M—y' (the couple were alleged to have a son serving in the Horse Guards), and a later association with an unknown woman with whom 'he has lived many years very domestically'. Panton's greatest sporting achievement came in 1786 when his horse Noble won the Derby. He died at Newmarket on 29 November 1808 in his seventy-seventh year. The obituary in the *Gentleman's Magazine* records that he had married a Miss Gubbins 'a few years ago', but no further details are known. In his will she was bequeathed an annual income of £1200. The remainder of his estate, worth £40,000, was divided between his two nieces, Lady Priscilla Barbara Elizabeth Burrell, Baroness Willoughby of Eresby (1761–1828), and Georgina, third countess of Cholmondeley (1764–1838), who both also received £3000 a year. PHILIP CARTER

Thomas Panton (1731/2–1808), by unknown engraver, pubd 1777 [*The Sporting Rover*]

Sources *DNB* • *GM*, 1st ser., 78 (1808), 1131 • C. Pigott, *The Jockey Club* (1792) • R. Black, *The Jockey Club and its founders* (1891) • *Annual Register* (1808) • *GM*, 1st ser., 52 (1782), 21–2, 559 • *Town and Country Magazine*, 9 (1777) • Walpole, *Corr.*, 24.499

Likenesses engraving, NPG; repro. in *Town and Country Magazine*, facing p. 570 [*see illus.*]

Wealth at death over £40,000, incl. £1200 p.a. to wife; £3000 p.a. to nieces: *GM*, 1131

Pantulf, Hugh (*d.* **1224**), baron, was the eldest son of Ivo *Pantulf (*b.* before 1114, *d.* in or before 1176) [*see under* Pantulf, William], lord of Wem in Shropshire, whom he succeeded *c.*1175. The family had held of the Montgomerys, but in 1212, as a result of the forfeiture of Robert de Bellême in 1102, Hugh was said to be a tenant-in-chief of the crown, owing the service of five knights. He also had close links with the Fitzalans, resulting from his marriage in 1170 to Christiana, daughter of William fitz Alan, the lord of Oswestry and Clun. The marriage brought him Badminton in Gloucestershire; Pantulf later gave its church to Lilleshall Abbey. From Michaelmas 1179 to Michaelmas 1189 Pantulf was sheriff of Shropshire, an office wellnigh hereditary to the Fitzalans. Christiana's brother William held it until Easter 1201, and on being called on to answer for the lack of stock in the royal castles in Shropshire, gave 20 marks so that Pantulf should be compelled to give up to the king the stock and provisions which he had received with the castles. In 1208/9 Pantulf was charged with £360 1*s.* 10*d.*, of which he paid £100 and was pardoned the rest. William fitz Alan, charged with £174 14*s.* 10*d.*, received no pardon. Between 1186 and 1189 Pantulf served as a justice itinerant in a number of counties in the midlands and Welsh marches, including Shropshire; in June 1188 he appeared alongside the king in a final concord made at Geddington, Northamptonshire. He witnessed charters for Henry II, Richard I, and John. Henry granted him lands in Stanford, Herefordshire, to be held 'by the service of one brachet hound'; when Pantulf was sued in the bench for them by Ralph de Planez in 1223, he proffered a charter of confirmation from King John, who also gave him pardons for scutages and sent him under safe conducts to the Welsh princes. A benefactor of the Shropshire abbeys of Haughmond, Shrewsbury, and Lilleshall, Hugh Pantulf was dead by 28 December 1224, when the king took the homage of William, the eldest of his five sons.

William Pantulf (*d.* 1233), baron, claimed to hold his father's lands of the escheated Bellême fee rather than in chief, and in consequence was pardoned £75 of the usual relief of £100 payable for a barony. He served King John in Ireland in 1210, and, like his father, retained that king's favour. He is therefore unlikely to have been the William Pantulf who made peace with John at Belvoir in December 1215, or who paid a ransom in 1217/18 following his capture in Carrickfergus Castle. Under Henry III he assessed and collected the fifteenth of 1225 in Shropshire and Staffordshire; in the following year it was ordered that peace be made between him and Madog ap Gruffudd, the ruler of northern Powys. In 1231 he was one of the lords instructed to give counsel and aid to the king's brother, Richard, earl of Cornwall (*d.* 1272), lately appointed to guard the Welsh marches. William Pantulf married Hawise, daughter of Fulk Fitzwarine, lord of Whittington in Shropshire. He died in January 1233, leaving two daughters, Elizabeth, who died without heirs, and Matilda, who married Ralph Butler. JULIA BOORMAN

Sources *Pipe rolls* • R. W. Eyton, *Antiquities of Shropshire*, 12 vols. (1854–60), vol. 9, esp. pp. 162–9; vol. 7, p. 239; vol. 11 • I. J. Sanders, *English baronies: a study of their origin and descent, 1086–1327* (1960) • J. Meisel, *Barons of the Welsh frontier … 1066–1272* (1980) • U. Rees, ed., *The cartulary of Shrewsbury Abbey*, 2 vols. (1975) • D. M. Stenton, ed., *Pleas before the king or his justices, 1198–1212*, 3, SeldS, 83 (1967), appx 1 • H. Hall, ed., *The Red Book of the Exchequer*, 3 vols., Rolls Series, 99 (1896), vol. 1, p. 273 • *Chancery records* • R. W. Eyton, *Court, household, and itinerary of King Henry II* (1878) • H. C. M. Lyte and others, eds., *Liber feodorum: the book of fees*, 3 vols. (1920–31), 100, 142, 144, 147, 1337 • *Curia regis rolls preserved in the Public Record Office* (1922–), vol. 11, pp. 199–200 • T. D. Hardy, ed., *Rotuli de liberate ac de misis et praestitis, regnante Johanne*, RC (1844), 189, 204, 212, 223 • C. Roberts, ed., *Excerpta è rotulis finium in Turri Londinensi asservatis, Henrico Tertio rege, AD 1216–1272*, 1, RC, 32 (1835), 123, 237 • J. M. Boorman, 'The sheriffs of Henry II and their role in civil litigation, 1154–89', PhD diss., U. Reading, 1989

Pantulf, Ivo (*b.* before **1114**, *d.* **1176**). *See under* Pantulf, William (*d.* 1112?).

Pantulf, Robert (*fl.* **1130**). *See under* Pantulf, William (*d.* 1112?).

Pantulf, William (*d.* **1112?**), baron, was one of Roger de Montgomery's tenants in the district of Hièmes in the diocese of Sées. The tenurial relationship between these two families existed as early as 1027–35. His mother's name was Beatrice, and she held lands 'apud Fossas' (not identified). Pantulf received large grants of land, and held authority in Roger's earldom of Shrewsbury, founded after 1071, but his lands were worth considerably less than those of the earl's other major tenants: the sheriff, Picot, and the Corbet family. He held eleven manors in Hodnet hundred, and Wem was their head.

In 1073–4 Pantulf was in Normandy, and gave the two churches of Noron, near Falaise, to the abbey of St Evroult, with 40 marks to establish a priory at Noron, and tithes of all the churches which belonged to him. The monks of St Evroult contributed £16 to a pilgrimage to the shrine of St Giles, near Nîmes, which he was about to make. On 23 October 1077 he was present with William I at the consecration of the church at Bec, and then went with Robert, a former abbot of St Evroult, to serve Robert Guiscard in Apulia. He was treated with honour, and was offered a gift of three cities if he would stay, but he returned to Normandy.

In 1077 Earl Roger suspected Pantulf of complicity in the murder of the Countess Mabel, Roger's wife, who had deprived Pantulf of his castle of 'Piretum' (Peray en Saonnais). Pantulf had had dealings with the murderer, Hugh d'Iglé, and took refuge with his family in the monastery at St Evroult. He submitted to the ordeal of hot iron before the king's court at Rouen, was acquitted, and gave four silk altar cloths from Apulia to St Evroult as a thank-offering. After the murder his estates had been confiscated by Earl Roger, but in 1086 he was in possession of twenty-nine manors in Shropshire, and others in Staffordshire and Warwickshire. After the death of William I, in 1087, Pantulf revisited Apulia, and in June 1092 gave the relics of St Nicholas to Noron. After becoming earl of Shrewsbury in 1098 Robert de Bellême deprived him of his lands, but when Bellême rebelled in 1102, Pantulf offered him his services. They were rejected, and he turned to Henry I, who put Stafford Castle in his custody with 200 soldiers. Pantulf detached Bellême's Welsh ally,

Iorwerth ap Bleddyn, by negotiation, and he persuaded the garrison of Bridgnorth to surrender to the king. The king restored Pantulf's lands and gave him the fief of Roger de Courcelles as his reward for these services.

In 1112 Pantulf and his wife, Lescelina, and sons Philip, Ivo, and Arnulf confirmed their gifts to St Evroult, and granted 60 marks in silver to the new church, which Pantulf did not live to see completed. He died on 16 April, probably in 1112, and was buried in the cloister at Noron, together with his wife, who died on 21 September. His eldest son, Philip, succeeded to his Norman estates, and his second son, Robert, to his English ones.

Robert Pantulf (*fl.* 1130), according to the cartulary of the nunnery of Caen, robbed the nuns of 6 pounds of silver. In the Bedfordshire pipe roll for 1130 an entry is found concerning a trial by combat between him and Hugh Malbanc, whose estates were contiguous to Robert's.

Ivo Pantulf (*b.* before 1114, *d.* in or before 1176), probably Robert's son, succeeded him as baron of Wem. He attested a charter of Stone, Staffordshire, between 1130 and 1135 and a royal charter in December 1137 or 1138, and made grants to Shrewsbury and Combermere abbeys between 1141 and 1155. He appears in 1165 in the Black Book of the Exchequer and in the Staffordshire pipe rolls of 1167 and 1168/9. He made a grant to Haughmond Abbey in 1175/6. He had three sons with a first wife—Hugh, Hameline, and Brice—and two with Alice de Verdon—William and Norman. He was dead by 1176.

MARY BATESON, *rev.* FREDERICK SUPPE

Sources J. Meisel, *Barons of the Welsh frontier … 1066–1272* (1980) • R. W. Eyton, *Antiquities of Shropshire*, 12 vols. (1854–60) • Ordericus Vitalis, *Eccl. hist.*, 4.72–3 • C. P. Lewis, 'English and Norman government and lordship in the Welsh borders, 1039–1087', DPhil diss., U. Oxf., 1985 • J. Morris, ed., *Domesday Book: a survey of the counties of England*, 38 vols. (1983–92), vol. 25 [Shropshire] • J. Tait, 'Introduction to the Shropshire Domesday', *VCH Shropshire*, 1.279–308 • D. C. Douglas, *The Norman achievement, 1050–1100* (1969) • I. J. Sanders, *English baronies: a study of their origin and descent, 1086–1327* (1960) • D. Bates, *Normandy before 1066* (1982) • *Reg. RAN*, 3.312 • L. C. Loyd, *The origins of some Anglo-Norman families*, ed. C. T. Clay and D. C. Douglas, Harleian Society, 103 (1951) • J. E. Lloyd, *A history of Wales from the earliest times to the Edwardian conquest*, 2 vols. (1911) • *Black Book of the Exchequer, or, Liber niger scaccarii*, ed. T. Hearne, 2 vols. (1774)

Pantulf, William (*d.* 1233). *See under* Pantulf, Hugh (*d.* 1224).

Panufnik, Sir Andrzej (1914–1991), composer and conductor, was born on 24 September 1914 in Warsaw, the younger son of Tomasz Aleksander Panufnik (1865–1953), who had trained as an engineer but who became Poland's finest stringed instrument maker, and his wife, Matylda Maria Thonnes (1883–1945), daughter of Jan Thonnes and his wife, Henryka Szuster. Both parents were Polish; however, Jan Thonnes's father was of part English and half Polish descent. Andrzej's elder brother, Mirosław (Mirek; 1910–1944), was reading mathematics at the University of Warsaw when his studies were interrupted by the Second World War; he served valiantly in the underground and was killed during the Warsaw uprising.

Poland A frail child, Panufnik experienced the generally benevolent neglect of his parents and formed a close attachment to his maternal grandmother, Henryka, who became his first piano teacher. Following kindergarten he attended a succession of secondary schools in Warsaw: the Lorentz Gimnazjum (1924–5), the Szkoła Mazowiecka (1925–7, interrupted by typhoid), and the Municipal Gimnazjum (1927–9). He was enrolled as a junior student at the Warsaw conservatory in 1925 but, through a bout of nerves, failed his public performance examination at the end of the academic year and was advised to abandon any hope of a career in music. He reluctantly chose engineering as a profession and attended the State Engineering School, Warsaw, from 1929 to 1930; but after increasing disillusionment and depression he finally acknowledged that music was his true vocation. His parents agreed to support his decision provided that he first return to the Municipal Gimnazjum to complete his *matura* (1930–32). Dividing his time between academic studies and preparation for the entrance examinations at the conservatory, he also began to compose jazz pieces influenced by Gershwin and Ellington. One of these, 'Ach pardon', a foxtrot with lyrics by Marian Hemar, became a hit for Adolf Dymsza; his next song with Hemar, 'I want no more', was also a success, but Panufnik's love of serious music soon ended the collaboration.

Owing to his lack of formal musical training and technique, Panufnik managed to secure a place at the Warsaw conservatory only as a part-time percussion student in February 1932. Nevertheless he had advanced enough to enter the conservatory as a part-time student in the autumn, studying in the faculty of theory and composition. By 1936 he graduated in half the usual time as both composer and conductor, and he was awarded by unanimous decision the highest honour of a diploma with distinction. As a laureate of the conservatory, he conducted the Warsaw Philharmonic Orchestra in the première of his *Symphonic Variations*. He then obtained a grant from the state-run Foundation for National Culture to study conducting with Felix von Weingartner in Vienna. Called up for national service, he was forced to postpone his plans until 1937. Weingartner proved to be an inspirational teacher, but the Anschluss brought his studies to an end.

After returning to Warsaw, Panufnik secured a commission to compose and direct the music for a film by Stanisław Wohl and Eugeniusz Cękalski, *Ghosts*; the fee enabled him to travel to Paris to study conducting with Philippe Gaubert. After six months he travelled to London in March 1939; unimpressed by the 'dull and conservative' programmes of music (Panufnik, *Composing Myself*, 91), he turned to studying the works of eighteenth-century English composers at the British Library—an experience that later proved of great value during his career as a conductor.

Although urged to remain in England with war impending, Panufnik returned to Poland. Following the surrender to Germany on 1 October, the dreadful economic conditions forced him to abandon all thoughts of serious composition. He entered into a three-year partnership with

Witold Lutosławski as a piano duo in artistic cafés, and was active in the underground, composing (under a pseudonym) patriotic songs, notably 'Warszawskie dzieci' ('Warsaw children'). His *Tragic Overture*, the first of his compositions to explore the small-cell method that later became characteristic of his music, was composed during the destruction of the Warsaw ghetto in 1943. By moving his mother to a safe place outside Warsaw, he inadvertently escaped the worst effects of the 1944 uprising. In May 1945 he returned to Warsaw to arrange a proper interment for his brother. During his stay he discovered that all his manuscripts had been mistaken for rubbish and had been burnt by the new occupants of his apartment.

Having secured accommodation for his family in Cracow in 1945, Panufnik took up the position of musical director of the Polish army film unit based at Łódź. At the request of the ministry of culture he also became musical director and conductor of the Cracow Philharmonic Orchestra. He helped to found Polskie Wydawnictwo Myzyczne (PWM), the state music publishing house, and his method of substituting blank spaces for staves with rests in music printing was adopted in the interest of musical clarity; this innovation found favour with many modern composers and became a standard feature of musical notation. He returned to composition and reconstructed from memory the *Tragic Overture*, *Five Polish Peasant Songs*, and the piano trio.

In the spring of 1946 Panufnik was appointed director of the newly reconstituted Warsaw Philharmonic Orchestra; he also represented Poland at the International Festival of Contemporary Music, and conducted concerts in Paris and Zürich. He resigned his post with the Warsaw Philharmonic and returned to Cracow in 1947 in protest at reneged promises of accommodation for musicians from outside the capital and the failure to provide a permanent venue. His first major post-war composition, *Nocturne*, won the Karol Szymanowski competition in 1947. In 1948 he was appointed to the governing body of the Composers' Union and elected vice-president; his vocalise *Hommage à Chopin* of the same year was commissioned by UNESCO in Paris for the centenary of Chopin's birth.

Tragically, the blossoming of Polish art was to be short-lived, as Stalinist doctrine was imposed across eastern Europe. Panufnik was forced to accept an appointment to the bogus Polish committee of the defence of peace, and soon afterwards the general assembly of Polish composers was forced to embrace Stalinist cultural doctrine by which all artistic endeavours were expected to serve an ideological purpose; modernism was condemned and socialist realism became the only official means of expression. Initially, confusion over the definition of socialist realism allowed composers a certain latitude, and Panufnik's first major post-war symphonic work, the *Sinfonia rustica*, gained the first prize at the Chopin competition in Warsaw in 1949. Nevertheless, in a complete reversal of official policy, it was judged 'formalistic' and was expunged from the state-approved repertory. After moving back to Warsaw in 1950, Panufnik met Marie Elizabeth (Scarlett) Rudnicka (*née* O'Mahoney), and he married her the following year. They had one daughter, Oonagh.

With the banning of the *Sinfonia rustica*, Panufnik's musical focus shifted largely to the reconstruction and adaptation of early Polish music, although he was still seen by the authorities as Poland's foremost composer and conductor; he was awarded state laureates in 1951 and 1952 even though he steadfastly refused to join the Communist Party. With the combination of conducting and administrative duties, and the increasingly repressive regime, he found little time or inclination to compose works other than those for his continuing job with the film unit. In 1953 he was coerced into being named leader of the cultural delegation to China and conducted a series of concerts of approved music, including two in the presence of Mao Zedong. However, the death of his daughter forced him to return prematurely to Warsaw.

England With personal despair added to his concern at the plight of Polish artists, Panufnik concluded that he could best serve the cause of Polish artistic freedom by defecting. With help from colleagues in the West he was invited to Zürich; after successfully slipping his minders, he arrived in London on 14 July 1954 and sought asylum. This was granted, and he was naturalized in 1961.

Panufnik's publishing contract (1955) with Boosey and Hawkes Ltd marked the beginning of a lifelong association with the firm. In 1956 he received a BBC commission for the tenth anniversary of the Third Programme: *Rhapsody* (performed in January 1957) included an invented hybrid rhythm based on Polish dances—the *Krakowiak* (binary) superimposed on the *Mazurek* (ternary). Financial considerations led to his accepting the post of musical director and conductor of the City of Birmingham Symphony Orchestra for the seasons 1957–8 and 1958–9; during his fruitful tenure he raised the orchestra to international standards. Living in Birmingham, however, led to irreparable strains on his marriage, which ended in divorce in 1958.

In 1959 Panufnik received the Feeney Trust commission for his piano concerto and conducted the première of the BBC commission *Polonia* at the Promenade Concerts. However, with the almost exclusive emphasis on serialism instituted by the new BBC controller, William Glock, Panufnik's music disappeared from programming for almost a decade; the irony of this happening in the country in which he had sought asylum was not lost to him. The next three years proved an unsettled time, during which he composed only *Autumn Music*. He gave up his flat in London and undertook conducting engagements abroad in 1960; on his return to England he lived in a series of small villages as well as spending time in France and Spain.

Early in 1961 Panufnik received a fellowship of the (Polish–American) Kościuszko Foundation to compose a symphony for Poland's millennium in 1966 and began work on *Sinfonia sacra*, destined to be one of his most popular and enduring works. In 1963 the symphony, inspired by the earliest known Polish hymn, 'Bogurodzica', was awarded the prix de composition Prince Rainier de Monaco, and was placed first of 133 entries from thirty-eight countries. On 27 November that year Panufnik married the author and photographer Camilla Ruth Jessel (*b.* 1937), daughter of Commander Richard Frederick Jessel, a much decorated Royal Navy officer. They had a son and a daughter.

With his second marriage, and a settled life near the Thames in Twickenham, Panufnik felt that he could no longer draw on his Polish roots and withdrew from composition for almost four years in the search for a new, original means of expression. It was only in 1968 that he fully devised the small-cell method of composition, out of which all his later works were derived; a limited number of intervals with their permutations and transpositions were employed as the basic building blocks from which large-scale compositions could be created. Pope's *Universal Prayer* provided the inspiration for his first full-scale use of small-cell composition; the violin concerto, commissioned by Yehudi Menuhin, followed in 1972. The chance encounter with tantric philosophy not only provided the inspiration of a BBC television commission (*Triangles*) but also led to a fully integrated system of composition combining the small-cell method with the perfection of geometric form. From this point each work would draw on a pre-prepared structure—an 'unseen skeleton' from which the music, 'unfrozen architecture', would grow.

The first half of the 1970s saw the composition of the *Sinfonia concertante* (1973) and the *Sinfonia di sfere* (1975). Through recordings, leading choreographers too began to discover and make use of Panufnik's music. His growing confidence with his almost structuralist method of composition was almost certainly spurred on by the fortuitous, although unrelated, relaxations of restrictions on broadcasting his works by the BBC and of censorship in Poland where, at the insistence of the Polish Composers' Union, the *Universal Prayer* was performed at the Warsaw Autumn Festival in 1976. From that year, major works appeared annually, including the *Sinfonia mistica* (1976), *Metasinfonia* (1978), and *Concerto festivo* (1979). The growing recognition of his works in Poland encouraged him once again to draw inspiration from his native land, albeit transformed through his personal musical language. In 1980 the *Sinfonia votiva*, dedicated to the Black Madonna of Częstochowa, was commissioned for the Boston Symphony Orchestra's centennial in 1982. During the period of composition Panufnik also produced chamber works including the string quartet no. 2 ('Messages') of 1980, based on childhood memories of the sounds of wooden telegraph poles vibrating in the wind.

In 1983 Panufnik was selected as the first laureate of the prix Prince Pierre de Monaco in recognition of his entire œuvre. He continued to conduct, primarily premières of his own works and the works of Mozart. For his seventieth birthday celebrations in 1984 he conducted the London Symphony Orchestra; in that same year he was made an honorary member of the Royal Academy of Music, London. The crowning achievement of the year was the New York première of *Arbor cosmica*; commissioned in 1982 by the Koussevitsky Foundation, this piece—with its underlying structure reflecting both Panufnik's lifelong love of trees and the metaphoric 'cosmic tree'—remains one of his most popular works.

The second half of the 1980s marked the final flowering of Panufnik's genius, beginning with the bassoon concerto (1986), the ninth symphony (*Sinfonia della speranza*, 1987), and *Harmony* (1989). The symphony no. 10 marked Panufnik's decision no longer to title his works; a joint centennial commission by the Chicago Symphony Orchestra and Sir Georg Solti, the work was premièred in 1990, with the composer conducting. Later that year, following the collapse of communism, Panufnik made a triumphal return to Warsaw after thirty-six years of exile, conducting the Warsaw Philharmonic in an all-Panufnik programme which opened the Warsaw Autumn Festival.

In 1991 Panufnik was knighted in the new year honours, and later in that year he received an honorary PhD from the Fryderik Chopin Academy of Music, Warsaw. Struggling with cancer, he continued to draw inspiration and comfort from both his music and his family. He made his final conducting appearance recording the symphony no. 9 and the piano concerto with the London Symphony Orchestra, and completed the cello concerto, commissioned by the same orchestra for Mstislav Rostropovich, a month before his death. He died at his home, Riverside House, Riverside, Twickenham, on 27 October, and was buried at Richmond cemetery on 5 November. He was survived by his second wife, Camilla, and their two children. He was posthumously awarded the knight's cross of the order of Polonia restituta by President Lech Wałęsa.

Assessment Panufnik's compositions include a number of fine chamber works as well as short orchestral pieces. He published a short pamphlet, *Impulse and Design in my Music*, in 1974, documenting the underlying theoretical structures of several major works. His autobiography, *Composing Myself* (1987), presented a vivid account of his eventful life; written from memory because Polish documents were inaccessible, it is remarkably accurate.

Many younger American composers came to regard Panufnik as one of the originators of minimalism; however, this arose from an erroneous perception of the small cell as a compositional tool. Unlike the minimalists, Panufnik constructed large and complex structures from small phrases; moreover, the small cell represented an inspirational point of departure rather than rigidly dominating his compositional method. He was firm in his refusal to attach himself to any school of composition, developing a unique musical language. His works helped to revitalize the symphony and advanced it at a time when its very validity was being called into question. Much of his sensitivity to orchestral forms stemmed from his broad experience as conductor; by all accounts he could have enjoyed an international career at the highest level in the latter profession, but he was firm in his conviction that composition was his calling. He remained true to this conviction throughout his life, declining several important commissions for operas, ballets, and films because he did not feel comfortable with that genre.

Despite enjoying a wide social life, Panufnik was a very private person when it came to his music and never took on any students of composition. He eschewed all forms of self-promotion, preferring his works to stand or fall on their own merits. Despite his feeling uncomfortable posing for photographs, many fine examples, primarily taken by Lady Panufnik, exist. These show a handsome, classically Slavonic face, and great sensitivity tempered by a hearty sense of humour. Despite the vicissitudes of his life before settling in England, the child of early surviving photographs is easily recognizable in those of his maturity. JON A. GILLASPIE

Sources A. Panufnik, *Composing myself* (1987) · A. Panufnik, *Impulse and design in my music* (1974) · A. Panufnik, 'About my "Autumn music" and "Universal prayer"', *Tempo* (1996), 11–15 · private information (2004) [Lady Panufnik; others] · Boosey and Hawkes Ltd, London, archives · A. Panufnik, 'Andrzej Panufnik', pre-concert talk, 27 July 1989, Royal College of Music, London, Boosey and Hawkes Ltd archive, London · C. MacDonald, *Andrzej Panufnik* (1994) · R. Maycock, 'Lines of approach', *Classical Music* (23 Sept 1989), 24–5 · *The Guardian* (28 Oct 1991) · *The Independent* (28 Oct 1991) · *The Times* (28 Oct 1991) · *Daily Telegraph* (28 Oct 1991) · B. Jacobson, *A Polish renaissance* (1995) · naturalization cert., PRO, HO334.849; BNA 69336 · m. cert. [Camilla Ruth Jessel] · d. cert.
Archives Boosey and Hawkes Ltd, London · priv. coll. | FILM Polish Film Archive, Warsaw | SOUND BBC WAC · BL NSA, 'Sir Andrej Panufnik (1914–1991)', BBC Radio 3, 22 Dec 1991, B8926/2 · BL NSA, oral history interview
Likenesses photograph, 1957, Hult. Arch. · photograph, repro. in *The Times* · photograph, repro. in *The Independent* · photographs, priv. coll. · portrait, priv. coll.
Wealth at death £121,886: probate, 7 May 1992, *CGPLA Eng. & Wales*

Paoli, (Filippo Antonio) Pasquale (1725–1807), politician in Corsica, was born on 6 April 1725 in the hamlet of Stretta di Morosaglia in the *pieve* (canton) of Rostino, Corsica. He was the younger son of Giacinto Paoli and Dionisia Valentini, and had one brother, Clemente, and two sisters, Maria Francesca and Maria Chiara.

Insurrection and first exile, 1729–1755 Paoli was not yet five when, on 27 December 1729, an insurrection broke out at Bustanico, a village in the *pieve* of Bozio, marking the start of the forty-four-year struggle against the oppression of the Republic of Genoa. By 1733, as the insurrection spread to the part of the island known as *Di quà da monti* ('the country on this side of the mountains'), Paoli's father had become head of the Corsican resistance in the *pieve* of Rostino. On 30 January 1735 a *consulta* or assembly held at the inland town of Corte confirmed Giacinto Paoli, along with Luigi Giafferi and Andrea Ceccaldi, as the three *primati del regno* (chiefs or generals of the kingdom). Earlier that month Genoa's sovereignty of the kingdom of Corsica had been repudiated. A *consulta* at Orezza had adopted the fifteen articles of what proved to be, in conjunction with the twenty articles established during the Corte assembly, a fledgeling form of the constitution drafted by Pasquale Paoli in 1755. However, with the onset of dearth from Genoese blockades, and with the Corsican throne declared vacant, these resolutions could not be implemented. In 1736 the throne was occupied, albeit briefly, by an adventurer, Theodore, Baron von Neuhoff (1694–1756),

(Filippo Antonio) Pasquale Paoli (1725–1807), by Sir Thomas Lawrence, *c.*1798

who was welcomed by the insurrectionists and crowned Theodore I in April. Theodore's departure from the island in November (for want of funds and foreign national support) prompted from 1738 a series of French military interventions, including that of the marquis de Maillebois, which eventually led to Paoli's father, then regent of the northern part of the island, being exiled to Naples in July 1739. He was accompanied by Pasquale, then aged fourteen. His experiences as a child born, as he later wrote, 'when the tyrants [of his homeland] contemplated its downfall' (Cristiani, 8), convinced him of the importance of never forgetting his father's determination 'per non lasciare ai nostri posteri altra eredità che quella del servaggio' ('not to leave our descendants no other heritage than serfdom'; Yvia-Croce, 75).

In 1741 Paoli entered the Royal regiment of Corsica stationed at Naples. The period he spent at the Royal Military Academy of Artillery between 1745 and 1749, coinciding with a period of considerable Neapolitan intellectual activity—principally through the work of the political economist Antonio Genovesi—was to have a significant impact on Paoli's outlook in adulthood. These were also years of personal academic improvement based on his reading of the histories of Tacitus, Polybius, Livy, and Thucydides, the lives of Plutarch, the literature of Virgil, and the political economy of his tutor Genovesi. His culture in this period was both sacred and profane. In letters to his father in 1754, a year before his return to Corsica, Paoli referred to the Maccabees 'whose lot could be compared to the Corsicans' (Letteron, 31–2). However, religion would prove only one means to serve his homeland. In contrast to his father, who wished him to enter the church, Paoli preferred a military career in the royal Farnese, garrisoned first at Sicily and then Elba.

On Corsica the assassination in October 1753 of the current general, Gian Pietro Gaffori, strengthened patriot resistance, contrary to Genoese expectations. At the time it was suggested by some that Corsica would fare better as a Maltese protectorate, a plan Paoli described on 30 August 1754 as 'solennissima minchioneria' ('unmitigated stupidity'; Letteron, 16). For two years of his exile Paoli served with his regiment at Longone near the port of Leghorn. At Leghorn, a prominent point of contact for members of the anti-Genoese resistance, he kept himself informed of events in Corsica and impressed remaining patriot leaders, including his brother Clemente, of his military and political qualities and as a potential leader of the struggle for an independent Corsica.

General of the nation, 1755–1769 Invited by Clemente and his followers, Paoli returned to Corsica on 16 April 1755. On 15 July he was elected to the generalship (*capo generale politico e economico*) during the *consulta* of Sant' Antonio della Casabianca. Paoli's first responsibility was to draft a founding constitutional text to ensure the 'felicita della Nazione' ('happiness of the nation') and to make the Corsican people 'patrone di se medesimo' ('their own masters'; Oberti, 2.48). The *consulta*, which was held at Corte between 16 and 18 November 1755, adopted, in theory at least, Montesquieu's principles of the separation of executive and legislative powers. At the same assembly Paoli was also appointed general and president of the executive for life. His leading champion, James Boswell, later spoke admiringly of what he considered Corsica's 'compleat and well ordered democracy' comprising its legislative assembly (*dieta generale*) and its *procuratori* elected by villagers. Yet Paoli's reputation as a pragmatic and realistic politician also convinced him of the need at times to transcend the restrictions of the Montesquean political model and to co-opt to government any loyal Corsican he deemed useful to the regime, among them clergy and relatives of patriots killed in the struggle against Genoa. Paoli's quest to establish a solid and respected Corsican nationhood also led him to confront the deep-rooted clan conflicts which the Genoese had exploited for their own ends. Largely through the force of personality he abolished the feudal lordships and the practice of vendetta. To these improvements he added the formation of a merchant navy (agreed at a *consulta* at Casinca on 20 May 1760), a mint (*zecca*), and an official press (*stamperia*), whose paper, the *Ragguagli dell' Isola di Corsica*, was distributed from his capital at Corte. In January 1765 came one of the principal achievements of his generalship, the foundation of a university at Corte at which one of the first students was Carlo Buonaparte, Paoli's one-time secretary and later father of Napoleon.

Throughout this period Paoli's efforts to secure national unity and independence were hindered by internal and external resistance. On his return to Corsica he had not found the level of support he had hoped for. Only sixteen of a total of more than sixty *pieves* had been represented at the July assembly, and Paoli's victory was quickly disputed by a rival, Mario Emanuele Matra, who was declared general by his own partisans. The contest produced an eight-year internecine struggle which was maintained, after Mario Emanuele Matra's death in March 1757, by his brother Alerio and by support from Genoa until its final defeat at Furiani in 1763.

From the mid-1750s the Genoese presence on Corsica had been reduced to possession of a series of fortified coastal towns. In August 1764, in a policy confirming arrangements established during the Seven Years' War, the French and Genoese signed the second treaty of Compiègne, which confirmed additional French military support and their defence, over a four-year period, of the towns of Bastia, Calvi, Algajola, St Florent, and Ajaccio. Faithful to the policy that had been implemented since 1738, Louis XV and his foreign minister, the duc de Choiseul, resumed their tactics of negotiation, mediation, and repression. French assurances of neutrality were dismissed by Paoli, who was further encouraged to pursue independence following the Genoese abandonment of the neighbouring island of Capraja in 1767, after local and Corsican resistance. However, with the treaty of Versailles, signed in May of the following year, the French ceded control of Corsica in return for their recapture of the strategically important Capraja. On 22 May 1768 the *consulta* decreed the mobilization of the Corsican army to confront the expected French attack against Paoli's administration. Though heavily outnumbered, Paoli's forces put up a determined resistance, convinced in February 1769 of the imminent arrival of British reinforcements. However, at Westminster the duke of Grafton's ministry finally decided that the French invasion should not be halted, and on 8 May Paoli's army was defeated by a 34,000-strong French force at Ponte Nuovo. The defeat, which Paoli blamed on the *banditaglia* (bandits bribed by French gold) ended the Corsican state and Paoli's generalship. On 13 June he left the island on a British frigate bound for Leghorn, and arrived three days later. According to the *London Chronicle* (8–11 July) Paoli was greeted by the cannonades of British warships in the Tuscan port, and was met by the British consul, Sir John Dick. Paoli now began a journey through northern Italy and central Europe *en route* for England, the location for his second political exile.

Paoli's British exile, 1769–1790 Paoli landed at Harwich on 18 September 1769, where he was met by supporters of the radical John Wilkes and by members of the Society of Supporters of the Bill of Rights. He reached London two days later. To many educated Britons, Paoli arrived as a hero and a celebrity. His stand against the Genoese and latterly the French had won him the praise of Rousseau, who, in *The Social Contract* (1762) and elsewhere, had done much to promote the Corsican struggle as a case study of the Enlightenment contest between liberty and tyranny, or noble primitiveness against civilized corruption. Similar compliments had come from Voltaire, Frederick II of Prussia, and successive European dignitaries who met Paoli in the summer and autumn of 1769.

In Britain no one had done more to publicize Paoli's achievements and Corsica's plight than the young James Boswell. Boswell, having received a letter of introduction from Rousseau, had visited the island in October–November 1765 as part of his Italian tour, and spent a week in Paoli's company. It was this encounter, one of the most significant in the Scottish writer's life, which dominated Boswell's immensely popular *An Account of Corsica, the Journal of a Tour to that Island, and Memoirs of Pascal Paoli*, published in February 1768. Keen to evoke the struggles of classical history and the nobility of the Corsican people, Boswell characterized their leader in impressive terms: 'tall, strong, and well made; of a fair complexion, a sensible, free, and open countenance, and a manly and noble carriage' (Boswell, *Account*, 171). Initially reserved, Paoli had gradually warmed to his unknown guest (whom he had first suspected of being a spy), revealing himself to be considerate, polite, and, to Boswell's surprise, well read in British politics. However, the prevailing and intended image of Boswell's account was that of Paoli as classical hero: a contained, selfless leader, dedicated to establishing justice for his people. Via the press, fund-raising, the commission of a portrait (1767), stunts including his appearance on 6 September 1769 at Stratford in Corsican national costume, and finally his very successful book, Boswell raised Paoli's profile prior to his British exile. His, moreover, was a view shared by many other influential commentators. Reviewing Boswell's account, the poet Thomas Gray spoke of Paoli as 'a man born two thousand years after his time!' (Gray to H. Walpole, 25 February 1768, Walpole, *Corr.*, 14.174). For William Pitt he was a hero out of Plutarch, and for John Wesley 'as great a lover of his country as Epaminond', while a selection of *British Essays in Favour of the Brave Corsicans*, edited by Boswell, appeared in December 1768.

Paoli and Boswell met again at the general's London home in Old Bond Street on 22 September 1769. They quickly resumed a friendship which saw Paoli, though only fifteen years Boswell's senior, take on a role akin to a surrogate father, providing advice and support during Boswell's many personal dilemmas. In the following weeks the London press carried numerous reports of sightings of Paoli, invariably with his friend, while in the streets 'a crowd followed … He graciously smiled and bowed, while they paid him what honours they could' (James Boswell papers, Beinecke Rare Book and Manuscript Library, Yale University, MS J19). The government, though reluctant to become involved in the affairs of Corsica, was equally eager to acknowledge its leader. Paoli had met Grafton on 21 September, and the prime minister returned the visit a week later. He was received by George III at St James's Palace on 27 September and was thereafter granted a pension from the civil list. The earl of Pembroke estimated this to be £1500 p.a., a considerable sum, though one which he still thought insufficient to provide adequately for his 'poor Countrymen, who attend him in shoals, [and] eat him out of house and home' (Paoli to Boswell, 12 March 1772, ibid., MS C.2196).

Despite the publication of the occasional condemnatory pamphlet by opposition and Wilkite supporters, critical of what they saw as his treacherous association with the ministry, Paoli remained free of the wranglings of British domestic politics and retained strong public support throughout his exile. In preference to political associations he developed a series of friendships with writers and enlightened thinkers. He met Samuel Johnson on 31 October 1769 and David Garrick soon after. His circle later expanded to include Edmund Burke, Horace Walpole, Lord Lyttleton, General James Oglethorpe, Lord Bute, Fanny Burney, and Maria Cosway, who succumbed to this modern day Lycurgus and named her only child, to whom the general was godfather, Louisa Paolina Angelica. Though never elected to Johnson's Literary Club, Paoli was initiated into the Lodge of the Nine Muses (15 June 1778) and, during his second British exile, the Prince of Wales's Lodge on 21 February 1800. Paoli's first residence in England ended with the French Revolution of which he took a pragmatic, sometimes optimistic, view as a route to establish Corsican rights if not outright independence. To his friend Joseph-Octave Nobili-Savelli he wrote that Corsica's union with the free French nation was no servitude but a rightful participation (Vergé-Franceschi, 2.435–6). The comte de Mirabeau, who felt his youth had been tainted by involvement in the Corsican invasion of 1769, secured the adoption of an amnesty for expatriates, including Paoli, from the French constituent assembly. On 22 March 1790 Boswell hosted a farewell dinner for his friend, whom he would never see again. Initially sceptical of Paoli's motives for returning to Corsica, Boswell was gradually convinced of the decision and in November provided the *London Magazine* with a translation of Paoli's address to the island's assembly.

Revolution, counter-revolution, and the Anglo-Corsican kingdom, 1790–1795 Paoli left England on 29 March 1790. In Paris in April he was received as a hero by the French National Assembly, was welcomed by Robespierre at the club of the Friends of the Constitution, and was presented to Louis XVI. On 14 July he landed on Corsica where he was greeted by a jubilant population. The first signs of the island's new freedom were displayed during the Orezza assembly which opened on 9 September, when Paoli was elected president of the general council and commander of the national guard. But Corsica's co-existence with revolutionary France proved short-lived. Paoli advocated a constitutional monarchy and relations quickly deteriorated following the Jacobins' execution of the French king and members of the royal family in January 1793. Paoli himself became a target for extremist members of the National Convention whom the general regarded as anarchists. Of these the most severe on the island were Barthelemy Arena, the Bonapartes, and Philippe Buonarotti, who accused Paoli of forty-six crimes, including his attachment to Sardinia (a long-standing ally of Corsica) and to George III and the British government, with whom the French were now at war. On 2 April 1793 Paoli was denounced in the convention, which accused him of conspiring with the British and ordered his arrest. At its next meeting the Corsican *consulta* elected Paoli its *generalissimo* and he in turn declared his continuing loyalty to the French republic. Paoli's Corsican critics were then forced to leave the island, and there began a brief period (May 1793 to May 1794) of genuine separation and independent government by Corsica. On 17 July Paoli was declared a traitor to the republic, a claim he denied in a letter to Boswell (12 October), and his followers were vilified as counter-revolutionaries.

Paoli now sought protection from the British. Admiral Samuel Hood entrusted Sir Gilbert Elliot, fourth baronet, to negotiate with the general for the cession of Corsica to Britain in January 1794 and for the formation of an Anglo-Corsican kingdom. Positive thinking by Hood provided British marines and Paoli's patriot resistance with sufficient support to ensure the surrender of the French garrison in May. On 19 June 1794 an assembly led by Paoli voted for its own constitution and in the same month Elliot arrived as the island's provisional viceroy, gaining his commission on 1 October. However, relations between Paoli and Elliot were poor throughout this brief constitutional experiment. The viceroy proved distrustful of, and had difficulty asserting his authority over, Paoli, who had by then been proclaimed 'padre della patria, fondatore e restauratore della nazionale liberta' ('father of his country, founder and restorer of its national freedom'; Oberti, 2.376). Elliot was further troubled by division among leading British officers on the island who either sided with Paoli or with the Corsican president of the council of state, Carlo Andrea Pozzo di Borgo. In October 1795, as mistrust became outright hostility, the viceroy secured Paoli's departure from the island on the orders of the British government. Britain's involvement with Corsica ended in October 1796 when, following Spain's entry into the French Revolutionary Wars, the navy withdrew from the Mediterranean and, once more, the island passed into French control.

Return to Britain, 1796–1807 Paoli's closest ally, Boswell, had died in May 1795, and many of his former literary acquaintances were also dead. The once enjoyable London scene now offered few charms for the ageing general, who spent his last twelve years corresponding assiduously with friends in Corsica, Italy, and the United States of America. A series of letters recently published by Paul-Michel Villa sheds a new light on Paoli's final years. Though now reconciled with France and its first consul, he was not prepared to apologize for any of his past actions. Paoli remained committed to the idea that freedom for Corsica, his one and only political and personal concern, depended on a proper education for all islanders. In his final will, completed on 23 November 1804, he bequeathed a yearly allowance of £50 sterling to maintain a school in Morosaglia, one of £200 to reopen a school in Corte and to maintain four professors, and, if possible, an allowance of £250 to maintain five students in any of the best French universities. Paoli had suffered ill health since 1801 and died, unmarried, on 5 February 1807 at his London house. He was buried, in accordance with his wishes, at an unostentatious ceremony at the Roman Catholic church in St Pancras, on 13 February. His contribution to Corsican independence was commemorated with a bust by John Flaxman honouring his 'patriotic and public zeal'; the general had himself criticized the sculpture, which he thought lacked solemnity (Villa, 200).

Paoli had requested that he be buried in a vault in St Pancras church, fearful that his corpse would be stolen for surgical experiment. It was spared this indignity, and on 31 August 1889 his remains were exhumed and transferred to Corsica, where he was reinterred at Morosaglia on 7 September. The move was commemorated once more in 1989.

Eighteenth-century observers, drawing on the descriptions of Voltaire, Rousseau, and Boswell, viewed Paoli as a virtuous and enlightened statesman who dedicated his life to freeing his people from oppression. Dignified, respected, and civic-minded, in Boswell's journals he also appears as a man of considerable intelligence, charisma, and loyalty. His return to Corsica in 1790 likewise displays a political pragmatism at a time when supporters, like Boswell, questioned whether his decision to leave England was consistent with his earlier statements on Corsican liberty. This pragmatism is also evident in his efforts during the 1760s to reduce the factionalism which had previously hindered Corsican attempts at independence, and made possible the later struggle for national identity for which he is now best known across Europe. Paoli's reputation was later revived during the Risorgimento through the work of writers Niccolo Tommaseo and Francesco Domenico Guerrazzi, who cast this *uomo di bronzo* ('man of bronze') as an exemplary precursor of the Italian fight for freedom.

MARIE-JEANNE COLOMBANI

Sources P. Paoli, correspondence to the *supremo consiglio di stato*, 1769, Archives of the Department of Northern Corsica, 2MI 76 Bastia · Yale U., Beinecke L., Boswell papers, GEN MS 89 · T. de Neuhoff, 'Manifesto di Teodoro primo ré di Corsica', 1736, Yale U., Beinecke L., MS 11080, fol. 389 · L. A. Letteron, 'Pascál Paoli avant son élévation au généralat (1749–1755)', *Bulletin de la Société des Sciences Historiques et Naturelles de la Corse*, 358–60 (1913), 1–47 · M. T. Avon-Soletti, *La Corse et Pascal Paoli: essai sur la constitution de la Corse* (Ajaccio, 1999) · P.-M. Villa, *L'autre vie de Pascal Paoli* (Ajaccio, 1999) · G. Oberti, *Pasquale de' Paoli*, 2 vols. (1990) · J. Boswell, 'An account of Corsica, the journal of a tour to that island, and memoirs of Pascal Paoli', in *Boswell on the grand tour: Italy, Corsica and France, 1765–1766*, ed. F. Brady and F. A. Pottle (1955), vol. 5 of *The Yale editions of the private papers of James Boswell*, trade edn (1950–89) · P. Paoli, 'Valorosa Gioventù di Corsica', *Ragguagli dell' Isola di Corsica* (1768) · H. Yvia-Croce, *Quarante ans de gloire et de misère: la révolution corse (1729–1769)* (1996) · N. Peyre, 'L'établissement des Français en Corse, 1768–1789: le traité et la conquête', *Revue des Questions Historiques*, 3rd ser., 3 (1923), 52–61 · P. Buonarroti, *La conjuration de Corse entièrement dévoilée* (1794) · M. Vergé-Franceschi, *Histoire de Corse du XVIIe siècle à nos jours*, 2 vols. (1996) · C. L. Cristiani, Pascal Paoli, sa vie, son œuvre, [n.d.] · *Lettere di Pasquale de Paoli*, ed. N. Tommaseo (1846) · P. Paoli, Discours prononcé le 9 septembre 1790 à l'ouverture de l'assemblée du département de Corse, 1790 · M. Cini, ed., *La nascita di un mito: Pasquale Paoli tra '700 é '800* (1998) · G. Livi, 'Lettere inedite di Pasquale de Paoli', *Archivio Storico Italiano*, 5/5 (1890) · Walpole, *Corr.* · A. Costa, 'Le testament du Général Paoli', *Bulletin de la Société des Sciences Historiques et Naturelles de la Corse*, pt 2 (1930) · F. Pomponi, ed., *Le mémorial des Corses* (1982) · A.-M. Graziani, *Pascal Paoli: père de la patrie corse* (Paris, 2002)

Archives Archives of the Department of Northern Corsica, Bastia, fonds du Gouvernement Corse de Pascal Paoli · Archives of the Department of Southern Corsica, Ajaccio, fonds Paoli · Musée Pascal Paoli, Morosaglia | ministry of defence, Vincennes, Corsica and Corsican corresp. · ministry of foreign affairs, Paris, Corsican political corresp. · PRO, Foreign Office, 20 Corsica · Yale U., Beinecke L., Boswell papers

Likenesses H. Benbridge, oils, 1769, Pascal Paoli Museum, Morosaglia · P. Gherardi, oils, 1769 · R. Houston, mezzotint, pubd 1769 (after P. Gherardi), BM · mezzotint, pubd 1769 (after H. Bembridge), BM, NPG · R. Cosway, oils, 1784, Uffizi, Florence · G. Dance, pencil drawing, 1797, BM · T. Lawrence, portrait, *c.*1798; Sothebys, 6 April 1993, lot 59 [*see illus.*] · R. Brookshaw, mezzotint (after Gambalini), BM, NPG · J. Flaxman, bust, Westminster Abbey · H. J. Hesse, drawing, repro. in Delpech, *L'iconographie des contemporains depuis 1789 jusqu'en 1820* (1832) · J. Lodge, engraving (after H. Benbridge), repro. in Boswell, *An account of Corsica* · G. Macpherson, miniature, Burghley House, Northamptonshire · R. Purcell, mezzotint (after Constantinus), NPG · group portrait, Wilton House, Wiltshire

Wealth at death at least £1450; personal bequests of £500, £250, and four of £50; also annual bequests of £50 for school at Morosaglia; £200 to another school: A. Costa, 'Le testament du Général Paoli', *Bulletin de la Société des Sciences Historiques et Naturelles de la Corse*, 2me semestré (1930), [101]–12

Papas, William Elias [Bill] **(1927–2000)**, cartoonist and illustrator, was born Elias Papas on 15 July 1927 in Ermelo, Transvaal, between Johannesburg and South Africa's border with Swaziland, the third son and the fourth of the six children of Constantine Nickolas (Kostas) Papas (1883–1943), and his wife, Laura, *née* Vollmer (1900–1976). His father was a Greek immigrant who had arrived in Ermelo in 1894 and opened a tea-room. Within a few years he had become one of the town's leading citizens, owning a bakery, a restaurant, blocks of flats, and a cinema. His mother was half Greek and half German. His older siblings were Theodore, Anastasios (Tasso), and Irene, and his younger ones Athena and Vassilis (Bobby). Educated privately until the age of seven, he then attended Ermelo primary school (1934–40) and Pretoria Boys' High School (1940–42). After his father died he ran away from home and, lying about his age, joined the South African Air Force in Durban as a rear-gunner flying coastal missions during the Second World War (1943–5).

After demobilization Papas received an ex-servicemen's grant to study at Johannesburg Art School (1945–6) but left before graduating to set up a fabric design studio in the city. When this failed he moved to England in 1946 and continued his art studies part-time at Beckenham Art School, Kent (1946), and at St Martin's School of Art in London (1947–9), while working as a waiter and freelance illustrator. He then travelled around Europe for two years, sketching as he went (and studying art briefly at Cité Université, Paris), and earning his keep by taking on odd jobs: washing dishes in Sweden, advertising schnapps as a sandwich-board man in Germany, and working as a riveter's assistant, a waiter, and a bricklayer. In 1951 he returned to South Africa and found a job as a staff artist and reporter on the *Cape Times*, which published his first cartoon the same year. He produced his first book, *Under the Tablecloth: Papas Looks at the Peninsula* in 1952. In 1953 he married Aroon Jessica Mary McConnell (*b.* 1932), a nurse. They had two sons, Warren (Aziz) and Vollmer, and a daughter, Peta.

In 1954 Papas left the *Cape Times* and decided to travel overland back to England, but he had to abandon his journey when his jeep broke down only 30 miles from Cape Town. He then joined up with his younger brother, Bobby, a farmer, but after a timber trucking business they had set up together in Plaston, Transvaal, failed he took a job drawing mines for an Anglo-American company in Johannesburg. Having tired of this, he then worked as a freelance for the *Johannesburg Star*, *Drum Magazine*, and other publications as artist and reporter. His coverage of Nelson Mandela's treason trials for *The Star* in 1958 was syndicated to *The Observer* in London and to other European newspapers.

In 1959 Papas returned with his family to Britain and joined *The Guardian* in its old offices in London's Gray's Inn Road as artist and reporter. He succeeded David Low as political cartoonist in April 1963 and also produced a satirical strip, 'Theodore', about a mouse. In addition he worked as a pictorial reporter, covering the conflict in Cyprus in 1964–5 and the Six Days' War in Israel in 1967, among others. In 1964 he became political cartoonist for the *Sunday Times* (1964–9), for which he also drew a strip ('Bella and Lujah'). His contributions to *Punch* (1965–72) included some memorable full-colour covers. In 1964 the publication of his book *The Press* marked the beginning of a long association with Oxford University Press, notably of children's books (Charles Causley later described him as 'a born children's writer'). He was runner-up in the prestigious Kate Greenaway medal awards for children's book illustration in 1967 and 1968. He also illustrated a children's story by his brother Theodore, *Mr Nero* (1966), and adult titles such as Malcolm Muggeridge's *In a Valley of this Restless Mind* (1977), Pope John Paul I's *Illustrimi* (1978), C. S. Lewis's *The Screwtape Letters* (1979), and Amos Oz's *Soumchi* (1980).

Papas was divorced from his first wife in 1967, and early in 1969 he was granted a year's sabbatical from *The Guardian* and moved to Ermioni, his father's village in Argolis, Greece. He returned to *The Guardian* briefly in May that year but then, disillusioned by the Wilson government, left the paper for good. In 1970 he married Theresa Judith (Tessa) Pares (*b.* 1946), the daughter of the English writer Marion Pares (alias Judith Campbell and Anthony Grant), whom he had met in London in 1965. He remained in Greece for thirteen years (1970–83), sailing the Mediterranean in his 60 foot yacht, painting and exhibiting watercolours (including a major exhibition in Jerusalem in 1978), and writing and illustrating books. An attempt to return to his homeland in 1980 ended in failure (he had been banned from South Africa since 1965 for his anti-apartheid cartoons) and in 1983 he moved to Geneva. In the following year he travelled around the USA and eventually settled in Portland, Oregon. There he drew illustrations, designed posters, ran his own art gallery, and produced books (with texts by Tessa), such as *Papas' America* (1987) and *Papas' Portland* (1994). In 1992 he set up his own self-syndication service, supplying political cartoons and caricatures to the *Los Angeles Times*, *Newsday*, *Kansas City Star*, and other US and Canadian papers.

Papas's political cartoons were usually drawn in a loose, flowing style with an old-fashioned scratchy dip pen. Interviewed in the mid-1960s, he said: 'I don't caricature too much. I don't see the point of dwelling on deformities to bring over the point … It's their policies, not the politicians, that count' (Bateman, 18). He cited his influences as Daumier and Toulouse-Lautrec. Cartoons by Papas were among those chosen for the 1970 National Portrait Gallery exhibition 'Drawn and Quartered: the World of the British Newspaper Cartoon, 1720–1970', and examples of his work are held in the permanent collections of the Victoria and Albert Museum, the Centre for the Study of Cartoons and Caricature, University of Kent at Canterbury, the Vorres Museum (Athens), the Old City Museum (Jerusalem), and elsewhere.

A greatly respected artist and a much-loved character around Fleet Street, at the Savage Club, and the British Cartoonists' Association (of which he was a founder member in 1966), Bill Papas was a flamboyant, good-humoured, handsome man, over 6 feet tall, with brown eyes and black hair and eyebrows, and usually sporting a neat Zapata-style moustache. Indefatigable, he was still working at the age of seventy-two when he was drowned in Hotnarko Lake, British Columbia, Canada, on 19 June 2000, as a result of a flying accident while on a fishing trip. He was cremated in Prince George, British Columbia, on 24 June and his ashes were scattered at the mouth of the Nestucca River on the coast of Oregon. MARK BRYANT

Sources *The Independent* (12 July 2000) · *The Guardian* (26 June 2000) · *New York Times* (28 June 2000) · *Cape Times* (29 June 2000) · *The Oregonian* (22 June 2000) · M. Bryant, *Dictionary of twentieth-century British cartoonists and caricaturists* (2000) · M. Bryant and S. Heneage, eds., *Dictionary of British cartoonists and caricaturists, 1730–1980* (1994) · M. Bateman, *Funny way to earn a living* (1966) · A. Horne, *The dictionary of 20th century British book illustrators* (1994) · A. Gaster, ed., *The international authors and writers who's who*, 9th edn (1982) · *Contemporary Authors* · private information (2004) [Tessa Papas]

Archives priv. coll., family archives

Likenesses A. Mischan, oils, 1992, priv. coll. · W. Papas, self-portrait, caricature, repro. in Bateman, *Funny way to earn a living*, 10 · photograph, repro. in *The Guardian*, 20

Papillon, David (1581–1659), architect and military engineer, was born on 14 April 1581 in Dijon, France, the younger son of Thomas Papillon (*d.* 1608), captain of the guard and valet de chambre to Henri IV, and his wife, Jeanne Vieue de la Pierre. His mother drowned in a shipwreck off the coast of Kent in 1588 while fleeing with her children from the persecution of the protestants in her native country and David was brought up in the French Huguenot community in London. He became a deacon of the church and in 1611 he married the daughter of the pastor, Marie Castol, with whom he had two children. She died on 3 May 1614 and on 4 July 1615 he married Anna-Maria Calandrini (1591–1675), from a distinguished Italian family, who had also fled to Britain via France. His second marriage produced five children.

In 1629 Papillon accompanied Philippo Burlamachi, the brother-in-law of his second wife and a dealer in precious stones, on an expedition to the Netherlands to sell the king's jewels on commission, but it was in the world of building that he made his reputation. He was involved in housing developments in the city and suburbs of London and prospered sufficiently to settle at Roehampton House, Putney, by the early 1620s. At the same time he acquired a country estate at Lubenham, Leicestershire, where in 1622 he built a curious octagonal house which he named after himself, with a roof in the form of a Greek cross separated by four viewing platforms between the arms. Papillon Hall was considered in the eighteenth century to have been built 'with a view to military defence' (Nichols, 708) but this comment probably reflects his later career as a designer of fortifications rather than his original intention. During the civil war he fortified Leicester and Gloucester and offered advice about the defences of Northampton for the parliamentary forces, having published *A Practicall Abstract of the Arts of Fortification and Assailing* in 1645. In 1653 he prepared designs for a new house at Lamport, Northamptonshire, for Sir Justinian Isham but his proposal was not adopted.

No other architectural works are known but Papillon was the author of several political and religious tracts. In 1635 he translated into French three essays by the puritan divine Robert Bolton, and in 1647–8 he prepared in manuscript a discussion on government which he called 'Several political and military observations'. His 'rather abstruse' (*Memoirs of Thomas Papillon*, 7) religious essay on *The Vanity of the Lives and Passions of Men* was published in 1651. He took an active role in county life and was treasurer of Leicestershire from 1642 to 1646. Although usually described as gentleman of Lubenham, he seems to have maintained his London connections and his youngest son, Thomas *Papillon (1623–1702), who was born at Roehampton, became a prosperous City merchant and member of parliament for Dover. David Papillon died in March 1659 at either Lubenham or Roehampton and was commemorated by a monument in the chancel of St Katharine Coleman, London. MALCOLM AIRS

Sources *Memoirs of Thomas Papillon, of London, merchant*, ed. A. F. W. Papillon (1887), 1–11 · J. Nichols, *The history and antiquities of the county of Leicester*, 2/2 (1798), 708–9 · G. Isham, 'The architectural history of Lamport', *Reports and Papers of the Northamptonshire Architectural and Archaeological Society*, 57 (1953), 13–28 · J. Bold, *John Webb* (1989), 81 · A. Oswald, 'Acrise Place, Kent II', *Country Life*, 122 (1957), 300–03 · plans for Lamport, Northants., Northants. RO, 11.3079/A47, A49 and C.3 · letter to J. Isham, 12 May 1652, Northants. RO, IC 312 · D. Gerhold, *Villas and mansions of Roehampton and Putney Heath* (1997), 11–12, 14, 26

Archives CKS, corresp. and family papers | Northants. RO, plans of work at Lamport Hall

Likenesses T. Cross, line engraving, BM, NPG; repro. in D. Papillon, *A practicall abstract of the arts of fortification and assailing* (1645), title page · engraving, repro. in Papillon, *Memoirs*, facing p. 1

Papillon [*née* Broadnax], **Jane** (1627–1698), letter writer, was born on 16 March 1627 at Godmersham, Kent, the daughter of Thomas and Jane Broadnax. Against the wishes of her parents she married her cousin Thomas *Papillon (1623–1702) on 30 October 1651. She is now known for the detailed records of her life as the mistress of a household and mother, and observer of the community, preserved in her letters to her husband from 1667 to 1668, when he was maintaining the interests of the East India Company at Breda, in the Netherlands, and she was running the household in Fenchurch Street, London, and the estate at Acrise Place, Kent.

In her letters Papillon requests household necessities, relays news of tenants and workers on the estate, and discusses local happenings. She also writes of the English perception of the Dutch on 5 July 1667:

> They say for certain that 1,200 Dutch are landed amongst us, and that they have taken Mersey Island and the Block-house, being six miles from Colchester, and that they are in the attempt to take Landguard Fort. We have little expectation of peace. (*Memoirs of Thomas Papillon*, 395)

She writes of the children on 31 May 1667:

> Betty retains her wildness still and Philly does not much advance for want of pronunciation; Sarah, I fear, will be a dull girl, like the Mother; but yet I will not doubt but however God shall deal with me, thou wilt find some reason to continue they tender live [*sic*] to every one of them; and 'Does Father remember me?' 'and me', they all say. Ann Mary is well. (*Memoirs of Thomas Papillon*, 387)

The Papillons had eight children, four of whom survived.

Jane Papillon died in London on 12 July 1698 and was buried at Acrise Place. Thomas Papillon's nephew John Shower (1657–1715) published a funeral sermon for her entitled *Of Long Life and Old Age* (1698). In the 'epistle dedicatory' he praises her as 'Wife, Mother, Mistress, Friend, Neighbor, &c. in that manner, as perhaps there have been few such Examples of Piety and Prudence, in our Age'.

PATRICIA J. NEBRIDA

Sources *Memoirs of Thomas Papillon, of London, merchant*, ed. A. F. W. Papillon (1887) · J. Shower, *Of long life and old age a funeral sermon, occasion'd by the death of the much honour'd Mrs. Jane Papillon* (1698) · *DNB*

Likenesses portrait, repro. in *Memoirs of Thomas Papillon*

Papillon, Philip (1620–1641). *See under* Papillon, Thomas (1623–1702).

Papillon, Thomas (1623–1702), merchant and politician, was born on 6 September 1623, the fifth son of David *Papillon (1581–1659) of Roehampton, Surrey, and Lubenham, Leicestershire, and his second wife, Anna-Maria (1591–1675), daughter of Jean Calandrini of Sedan, France, and Putney, Surrey. Papillon boasted a tempestuous Huguenot ancestry, his great-grandfather having fallen victim to the St Bartholomew's day massacre of 1572. Brought to England as a child, Papillon's father became one of the leaders of the Huguenot congregation in Threadneedle Street, London, as well as a respected military engineer and builder. Papillon faithfully reflected this heritage, maintaining a fierce hatred of Catholic intolerance, as well as a true Calvinist piety.

After schooling at Drayton, Northamptonshire, Papillon was apprenticed in 1637 to Thomas Chamberlain, a London merchant. He became a freeman in 1646 and later joined the Mercers' Company, the mastership of which he held in 1673/4, 1682/3, 1692/3, and 1698/9. He first came to public notice at the height of the 'counter-revolution' of the summer of 1647, when he supported the Presbyterian rioters who stormed parliament. After the army had regained control of the capital, he spent a brief exile in France, but returned, confident of his immunity, and was arrested. He was in Newgate from 1648, and only with difficulty obtained release. Thereafter he was content to live quietly under the interregnum regimes, only seeking to advance himself in the French church, where he emulated his father by becoming deacon. On 30 October 1651 he married his cousin Jane Broadnax (1627–1698) [*see* Papillon, Jane], daughter of Thomas Broadnax of Godmersham, Kent, a match which yielded three sons and five daughters. In 1666 he strengthened his Kentish links by buying an estate at Acrise, which the following year accounted for a third of his personal fortune of some £18,000.

After the Restoration Papillon became a respected figure in the City, joining the Eastland Company in 1661, and serving as a committee man in the East India Company in 1663–71, 1675–6, and 1677–83. Moreover, he attended the treaty of Breda on the company's behalf in 1667, and was elected its deputy governor in 1680 and 1681. The king also recognized Papillon's mercantile status, appointing him in 1668 a commissioner for trade. Accustomed to taking the sacrament of the Anglican church (he was a communicant of St Katharine Coleman), he was able to progress up the civic ladder, serving as common councilman in 1672–3, 1675–7, and 1681, bridgemaster in 1675–6, and auditor in 1672–4, 1675–7, and 1680–82.

In February 1673 Papillon stood as a parliamentary candidate at Dover, which lay only 10 miles east of Acrise. He was defeated at the poll, but petitioned the Commons, and on 16 January 1674 the result was overturned in his favour. Although always professing support for the monarchy, at Westminster Papillon proved a steady opponent of the court, contributing to the attack on Lord Treasurer Danby in 1675, and on the Navy Office in 1677. Charles II intervened in 1676 to block his election as deputy governor of the East India Company, but Papillon stuck to his principles, attacking the secretary of state, Sir Joseph Williamson, in November 1678 for having issued military commissions to papists. He stood successfully for Dover at each of the three parliaments of 1679–81, and continued to be a thorn in the court's side, voting for the Exclusion Bill in 1679, and condemning the presentation of abhorrences. In May 1681 he warned London leaders that the protestant religion and the king were still imperilled, and was a prominent member of the grand jury which in November returned an *ignoramus* verdict in the trial of Lord Shaftesbury. He was even prepared to sever links with the East India Company rather than bow to the wishes of the court. Most controversially, following his failed candidacy at the London shrievalty contest of June 1682, when he was beaten by the tories Dudley North and Peter Rich, he started legal proceedings against the City, causing the arrest of the mayor, Sir William Prichard, and several aldermen in April 1683. Prichard counter-sued and won enormous damages of £10,000 against Papillon, who, in fear of his life, fled abroad in January 1685, and settled at Utrecht. Although James II influenced Prichard to waive the damages in 1688, Papillon remained in exile until after the revolution. He did not abet the invasion of 1688, 'not hasting to meddle in what I understand not, nor to act by an implicit faith', but he subsequently supported the canopy at the coronations of William and Mary (*Memoirs*, 343).

Papillon's political career prospered under the Williamite regime, for he secured his Dover seat at the elections of 1689 and 1690, and, despite declining an aldermanship in 1689, became a member for London in the parliaments of 1695 and 1698. He confessed distaste for party politics, but naturally inclined towards the whigs, whom he saw as supportive of public morality, and as defenders of European protestantism against 'the common enemy' of France and Rome (*Memoirs*, 374–6). Although active at Westminster, most of his energies were consumed by the victualling commission, on which he served from 1690 until his death. Such responsibilities demanded close attention to parliamentary debate during the War of the League of Augsburg and caused him much heartache, for the commission was often accused of maladministration. He also had frequent opportunity to speak on the East India trade, and in 1696 there appeared *A treatise concerning the East India trade: being a most profitable trade to the kingdom, and best secured and improved by a company and joint stock*, a tract which he had first published in 1680. However, although actively promoting mediation between the old and new companies in 1698–9, he did not live to see an accommodation.

In the latter half of the 1690s Papillon did not enjoy good health, suffering from gout and the palsy, and it was probably such illness that brought an end to his parliamentary career in 1700. He died in London on 5 May 1702, and was buried at Acrise on 21 May, leaving considerable bequests to various good causes, including Christ's Hospital and the French church. Shortly after his death, his heir, Philip, became member for Dover, and held the seat until August 1720.

Philip Papillon (1620–1641), elder brother of Thomas, was born on 1 January 1620. He showed an early aptitude for the classics, and at fourteen matriculated at Exeter College, Oxford, where he gained a BA on 7 April 1638, and an MA in February 1641. Although he showed a keen interest in theology, he remains best-known for his promotion of secular works, publishing in 1640 *Sicily and Naples*, a tragedy written by a fellow student, Samuel Harding, and composing verses in praise of William Browne. However, his premature death in 1641 pre-empted any further contribution; he died and was buried at Lubenham.

PERRY GAUCI

Sources *Memoirs of Thomas Papillon, of London, merchant*, ed. A. F. W. Papillon (1887) • D. Ormrod, 'Puritanism and patriarchy: the career and spiritual writings of Thomas Papillon, 1623–1702', *Studies in modern Kentish history*, ed. A. Detsicas and N. Yates (1983), 123–37 • M. Priestley, 'London merchants and opposition politics in Charles II's reign', *BIHR*, 29 (1956), 205–19 • I. Scouloudi, 'Thomas Papillon, merchant and whig, 1623–1702', *Proceedings of the Huguenot Society*, 18 (1947–52), 49–72 • J. R. Woodhead, *The rulers of London, 1660–1689* (1965) • A. B. Beaven, ed., *The aldermen of the City of London, temp. Henry III–[1912]*, 1 (1908), 185; 2 (1913), 117 • A. Grey, ed., *Debates of the House of Commons, from the year 1667 to the year 1694*, new edn, 6 (1769), 224–5, 235; 7 (1769), 388; 9 (1769), 442–3; 10 (1769), 321, 357 • *The parliamentary diary of Narcissus Luttrell, 1691–1693*, ed. H. Horwitz (1972), 10, 25, 43–4, 56, 73–4, 88, 175, 224, 230, 268, 328, 358 • *CSP dom., 1672–3; 1676–7; 1680–81* • *The diaries and papers of Sir Edward Dering, second baronet, 1644 to 1684*, ed. M. F. Bond (1976), 78–9 • *State trials*, 8.759–820 • G. de F. Lord and others, eds., *Poems on affairs of state: Augustan satirical verse, 1660–1714*, 7 vols. (1963–75), vol. 3, pp. 235, 348, 432–4, 520 • will, PRO, PROB 11/465, sig. 101

Archives CKS, corresp. and papers • Northants. RO, account book, corresp.

Likenesses G. Kneller, oils, 1698, NPG • J. Closterman, portrait, 1701–2 (after unknown portrait), repro. in Papillon, *Memoirs*; priv. coll. • portrait, repro. in *Proceedings of the Huguenot Society of London*, 18 (1947–52), facing p. 49; priv. coll.

Wealth at death in 1667 £8600 trading capital, £500 East India stock, £8060 in lands, £600 in household goods: Ormrod, 'Puritanism and patriarchy', 126

Papilon, Ralph. *See* Arundel, Ralph (*d.* 1223).

Papin, Denis (1647–1712?), natural philosopher, was born in August 1647 in Blois, France, and baptized there on 22 August at the temple of Haut-Bourg St Jean, the fourth of the thirteen children of Denis Papin and his wife, Marie, *née* Pineau. His father was a royal counsellor and district revenue collector, his mother's forebears were medical practitioners, and both his parents held property. The extended family was staunchly protestant, a religion which was tolerated during Papin's early years. At the age of six he was put in the care of his uncle Nicholas, a medical practitioner at Saumur, and educated at the protestant academy in that town. From there he entered the medical faculty of the University of Angers: he came away with a low opinion both of the teaching and of his fellow students but considered it worthwhile to obtain the degree of MD in 1669. The following year he arrived in Paris intending to practise medicine, but soon became disillusioned and, having developed a taste and talent for mathematics and machinery, sought the patronage of the wife of the minister Colbert, herself from Blois. She arranged for him to lodge in the Louvre and to assist the Dutch physicist Christiaan Huygens, who had been invited to develop his many scientific interests under French protection.

At the time that Papin joined him in 1673, Huygens was investigating the force of gunpowder as a means of creating a vacuum under a piston in order to drive machinery, in particular to operate a pump to raise water from the Seine to the palace of Versailles. Papin, who was continuing the investigations into the preservation of foodstuffs under vacuum that he had begun at university, was led to consider the vacuum as a possible motive force. During this period Leibniz, then in Paris, became a regular visitor to Huygens's laboratory. Papin learnt a great deal from Leibniz and the friendship thus engendered lasted for many years. The pumps that Papin developed, together with his vacuum experiments, were described in his first treatise, *Nouvelles expériences du vuide* (1674); favourably received by the Académie des Sciences, it was republished in the *Journal des Savants* in 1765.

Huygens's invention of the coiled watch spring caught public attention on both sides of the English Channel, and when Lord Brouncker, president of the Royal Society, asked Huygens for an example, Papin was instructed to deliver it in person to Henry Oldenburg, the society's secretary. Papin arrived in London in July 1675, bearing the watch and a letter from Huygens testifying to his abilities. He swiftly made the acquaintance of Robert Boyle, whose friendship and patronage he enjoyed, and polished his English by translating Boyle's *Physico-Theological Considerations* into French. He joined fellow Huguenots of the Threadneedle Street congregation, and was found lodging and employment as a tutor by Oldenburg. He translated further works for Boyle and improved the latter's air-pump, before building one to his own superior design. From July 1676 to February 1679 he worked closely with Boyle on experiments connected with respiration, magnetism, air, and the chemistry of blood and various medicaments, which he described in his *Continuation of New Experiments* (1680).

To this fruitful period belongs the invention forever linked to Papin's name—his digester—though he had left Boyle's service before it was made public. From his experiments with air-pumps Papin realized that the boiling point of water would be raised if it was heated under pressure. He constructed a strong cylindrical vessel to hold water and a container for various foodstuffs, and sealed the vessel's lid to prevent the escape of steam. He also devised a safety valve, which proved to be a technically important feature in the later development of steam power. In this primitive pressure cooker, Papin found that food cooked rapidly, requiring less fuel, and that even old meat became tender, with much nourishment extracted from the softened bones, advantages which he considered would be of considerable value to poor families. He demonstrated his invention to the Royal Society in May 1679, and was permitted to publish *A New Digester or Engine for Softening Bones* in 1681 and his further developments as *A continuation of the new digester of bones, together with some improvements and new uses of the air pump* in 1687.

Papin remained in London and was for a while employed by Robert Hooke to write letters for the society at 2*s*. each. At a date probably between 1680 and 1682 he was elected to the Royal Society, he was briefly in Paris with Huygens in 1680, and the following year, equipped with pneumatic apparatus and a digester, went to Venice, where he was employed by Ambrose Sarotti as director of experiments to the academy whose members gathered weekly in Sarotti's palace. But this was unprofitable business, and early in 1684 Papin returned to London, where the Royal Society appointed him temporary curator of experiments at a small salary.

Prospects of a better life opened up in 1687 with Papin's appointment as professor of mathematics at the University of Marburg, in Germany. There he was reunited with other Huguenots who had fled France, among them his cousin Marie Papin and her husband, Jacques Maliverne, likewise a professor at the university, who shortly died, leaving his widow to support their small daughter, Charlotte. Papin's desire to marry Marie was opposed by the local pastor on the grounds of consanguinity and only achieved, on 1 January 1691, by special dispensation from the landgrave of Hesse.

In 1690 Papin designed a simple one-cylinder atmospheric steam engine, an account of which he published in the *Acta Eruditorum* of Leipzig. A modified version of this engine figured among the diverse machines published as *Fasciculus dissertationum de novis quibusdam machinis atque alliis argumentis philosophicis* (1695), but Papin seems to have been ignorant of the significance of his invention. Disappointed by the Marburg students' lack of interest in mathematics, he moved in 1696 to the landgrave's court at Kassel, where his principal occupation was to design a pumping machine to raise water from mines. In 1705 Leibniz sent him a diagram of Thomas Savery's high-pressure steam pump, which Papin modified, though without improving it. His design was published as *Ars nova ad aquam ignis adminiculo efficacissime elevandam* (1707). He then turned to steam propulsion for boats, in which he seems to have had only limited success.

Papin was back in London in 1707, lodging in the parish of St Ann, Westminster, where he remained, apart from a few months in Kassel during 1708 and 1709; his wife and stepdaughter apparently stayed in Germany. His old friends were now dead, and Isaac Newton proffered no welcome at the Royal Society, of which he was now president. However, Papin was paid for any experiments to which they had agreed beforehand. Bad feeling may have been caused by arguments over the priority of the invention of the steam engine. Papin's engine of 1690, in which the vacuum under the piston was created by condensation of steam, demonstrated the concept from which the Newcomen and all cylinder and piston engines descend. The arguments turn on whether Newcomen was aware of Papin's invention. It is unlikely that Newcomen knew of Papin's article in the *Acta Eruditorum*, but, as a fellow of the Royal Society, he could have read the brief review of Papin's *Fasciculus* in the *Philosophical Transactions* in 1697.

Papin continued to send papers to the society, many of which were read but not thought worthy of publication. Some of these are now seen to contain innovative ideas, notably that on the Hessian bellows, demonstrated on 26 April 1711, which created a blast sufficient to melt or refine ores. This was the first suggestion for the creation of blast furnaces. The last that is heard of Papin is a letter of 23 January 1712 to Sir Hans Sloane: it is assumed that he died shortly afterwards, and was buried without being identified. ANITA MCCONNELL

Sources C. A. Klein, *Denis Papin, illustre savant blaisois* (1987) • E. Gerland, *Leibnizens und Huygens' Briefwechsel mit Papin* (1881) • *DSB* • J. L. Heilbron, *Physics at the Royal Society during Newton's presidency* (1983) • M. E. Rowbottom, 'Some Huguenot friends and acquaintances of Robert Boyle, 1627–1691', *Proceedings of the Huguenot Society*, 20 (1958–64), 177–94 • R. Jenkins, 'The heat engine …: a

contribution to the history of the steam engine', *Transactions* [Newcomen Society], 17 (1936–7), 1–11
Likenesses portrait, probably Marburg, Germany

Papin, Isaac (1657–1709), theologian, was born in Blois on 27 March 1657, the only son of Isaac Papin, receiver-general of the domains of Blois, and Madelaine Pajon, sister of the pastor and theologian Claude Pajon. Destined to be a Huguenot pastor but by all accounts a frail child, Isaac appears to have been educated at home before going in 1676 to the academy in Geneva, where he was inscribed as a student of philosophy and theology. Geneva was at that time the scene of bitter quarrels between universalists, who held that salvation was open to all and that all could play an active part in securing it, and particularists, who held that the elect represented only a small minority of the faithful chosen by God, and it was there that he was first exposed to the particularist intransigence that would have so much influence over his life and career. In 1679, having finished his studies in Geneva, Papin moved to Orléans, to study under his universalist uncle, Claude Pajon. In 1683 he proceeded to Saumur to complete his theological studies but was unable to do so because of his refusal to subscribe to a condemnation of Pajonism. Barred from his calling he went to Bordeaux, where he took up residence as a tutor in the home of William Popple, a merchant and translator of John Locke's *Letter Concerning Toleration*. It is said that Popple offered him his daughter's hand as well as a part in his business but that Papin declined. Following the revocation of the edict of Nantes in 1685 Papin sought refuge in England and, in 1686, was ordained by the bishop of Ely, Francis Turner.

In 1687 Papin went to the Netherlands in search of a living among refugee congregations. Unfortunately two works he had probably written during his time in Bordeaux were published in the same year: his *Essais de théologie*, attacking Pierre Jurieu and the particularists, as well as his *Foy réduite à son veritable principe*. This second work, a plea for toleration of differing scriptural interpretations and freedom of conscience for Catholics and Jews, caused a sensation. Although it was published anonymously the identity of its author was never in doubt. It was condemned, at Jurieu's instigation, by the synod of Bois-le-Duc of September 1687. Convinced that Jurieu's influence would prevent him from practising his ministry in the Netherlands, Papin moved to Hamburg in December of the same year, preaching in Altona for six months before Jurieu forced him out. While in Hamburg in 1688 he married a Mademoiselle Viard, originally from Châlons-sur-Marne.

On the suggestion of the bishop of Salisbury, Gilbert Burnet, Papin moved to Danzig in 1688, but was no more fortunate and, having been condemned by the synod of The Hague, was barred from practising. In his autobiographical sketch, contained in *Les deux voies opposées en matière de religion* (1713), Papin claimed that he had wanted to convert to Roman Catholicism from the time he lived in Bordeaux but had demurred out of duty to his family. This jars with his outspoken defence of universalism after Bordeaux and it is more likely that, in later years, he invented an early commitment to Catholicism in order to secure a pension and that his decision to convert was taken in Danzig, the fruit of an intellectual evolution combined with relentless persecution. Whatever the truth, from Danzig Papin entered into contact with Jacques-Bénigne Bossuet, the bishop of Meaux, and negotiated his return to France. Obliged to dissimulate his intentions he left Danzig in 1689 for London where, he later asserted, he was offered the post of chaplain to the crown's envoy to Switzerland but turned this down and instead travelled to Dover where he was issued with a passport for France stating, equivocally, that he intended to preach. His wife joined him before the end of the year and, together, they were received into the Roman Catholic church by Bossuet, in Paris, on 15 January 1690.

Such a high-profile conversion was bound to cause tremors and Jurieu duly published a pastoral letter accusing Papin of hypocrisy. Papin replied with his self-justificatory *Traité de tolerance* (1692, republished as *Les deux voies opposées en matière de religion* in 1713) in which he argued that the freedom of interpretation championed by reformed religion must inevitably lead to universal tolerance and, ultimately, impiety. The Catholic church, by contrast, was a church of authority and faith in authority. Papin's writings probably earned him a pension from the French crown, enabling him to carry on with his work. He died in Paris on 19 June 1709. His complete works were published in 1723. A slight man, he was said to be possessed of a remarkable, thunderous voice and appears to have been a popular preacher. There is no evidence, as has sometimes been suggested, that he was directly related to the scientist Denis Papin. R. W. J. Michaelis

Sources E. Haag and E. Haag, *La France protestante*, 10 vols. (Paris, 1846–59), vol. 8 • P. A. Dormoy, *Isaac Papin, étude historique et dogmatique* (1883) • *Le Journal des Sçavans* (16 April 1714) • L. Thomassin, *Traité dogmatique et historique des édits*, 3 vols. (1703), vol. 3 • I. Papin, *Les deux voies opposées en matière de religion, l'examen particulier et l'autorité* (1713), 274–9 • *Le livre du recteur de l'Académie de Genève* (1559–1878), 6 vols. (1959–80), vol. 5 • C. Robbins, 'Absolute liberty: the life and thought of William Popple, 1638–1708', *William and Mary Quarterly*, 24/2 (1967), 190–223 • *DNB*
Archives BL, corresp. with J. Leclerc, Add. MS 4297

Papineau, Louis-Joseph (1786–1871), politician in Canada, was born on 7 October 1786 in Montreal, Lower Canada, the eldest of the ten children of Joseph Papineau (1752–1841), a surveyor and notary, and his wife, Rosalie Cherrier. Papineau's great-grandfather settled in New France in the late seventeenth century, but the family remained comparatively humble until his father married into the influential Cherrier family and acquired the seigneury of Petite-Nation, which he sold to his son in 1817. Since Papineau had an intellectual bent, he was sent to the Sulpician college in Montreal to study for the priesthood, but he rebelled against the discipline and completed his education at the Petit Séminaire de Québec. Like his father, Papineau eventually abandoned the Catholic church. In 1804 he left the seminary to study law, but though he qualified in 1810 he never seriously practised, and devoted his time instead to politics after his election to the assembly in 1809. He supported the *parti Canadien* and in 1815 became speaker of the assembly and head of the party. On 29 April 1818 he married Julie Bruneau, the daughter of a Quebec merchant; they had three sons and two daughters.

During the 1820s the *parti Canadien* sought to gain control over the substantial revenues placed at the disposal of the government in 1774 and thus antagonized the Colonial Office, which introduced but then withdrew a bill reuniting Upper and Lower Canada. In 1823 Papineau went to London to oppose its reintroduction. His success confirmed his leadership of the Reform Party in Lower Canada, which after 1826 called itself the *parti patriote*. Although the party had widespread support among all ethnic groups and in all regions of the colony, its leadership was based in Montreal and was dominated by the interrelated Papineau, Viger, and Cherrier families. Initially the goals of the party were moderate: Papineau himself was a constitutional monarchist who much admired British institutions (he served as a militia captain during the Anglo-American War). He blamed the problems of the colony on bad governors such as Lord Dalhousie, who provoked a crisis in 1827 by refusing to accept Papineau's election as speaker. In 1828 Dalhousie was replaced by the more conciliatory Sir James Kempt, whose successor in 1830, Lord Aylmer, even offered Papineau a seat on the executive council—an invitation which he declined.

By this time Papineau was becoming increasingly influenced by radicals in England, by the Paris revolution of 1830, and by Jacksonian democracy in the United States, and was moving gradually towards republicanism. After the British government surrendered control over the disputed revenues in 1831, he persuaded the *patriotes* to follow a policy of systematic obstruction to force the colonial government to surrender all remaining revenues, to make the appointed legislative council an elective body, and to render the members of the executive council responsible to the assembly. After a sweeping victory in 1834 the *patriotes* embodied their demands in ninety-two resolutions, but the British government refused to agree to changes which would place all effective power in the hands of the French-Canadian majority. The assembly responded by refusing to vote any supplies, even for essential services. When the British government announced that the local government would be given emergency authority to take funds from the colonial treasury, Papineau called for a boycott of British imports, and at a series of huge rallies advocated civil disobedience.

As the *patriotes* became more radical, the party lost most of its support among the substantial British minority, and gradually became estranged from the hierarchy of the Roman Catholic church and virtually all of the French-Canadian seigneurs. By 1837 Papineau could no longer control the popular movement which he had helped to create. In the countryside the movement took on the appearance of a peasant revolt against the power of the church and the imposition of seigneurial dues, and the radical middle-class leadership of the party began to prepare for an armed insurrection. At a huge public meeting at St Charles in October 1837 Papineau issued what was effectively a declaration of independence and, when the government decided to arrest the leading *patriotes*, the rebellion began. Despite an initial victory at St Denis, the *patriotes* lacked the resources and organization to defeat the British regular troops under the command of Sir John Colborne. Papineau was theoretically supreme commander of the rebel forces, but he effectively surrendered military control to younger *patriotes* and, after a defeat at St Charles, fled to the United States. The rebellion shortly collapsed. Later his flight would be attributed to cowardice, but he had hoped to achieve his goals by civil resistance and was ambivalent from the outset about the revolutionary direction the *patriote* movement had taken. In exile in the United States he found himself unable to control the radicals, who adopted a thoroughly republican platform, including universal manhood suffrage and the abolition of seigneurial tenure. He played no role in the second rebellion of 1838, even though his name was used as a rallying cry by the rebels. After that rebellion was crushed, in 1839 he sailed for Paris, where he spent the next few years frequenting republican salons and copying documents in the archives about the history of French rule in Canada.

Papineau was granted an amnesty in 1844, and in 1845 he returned to the united province of Canada, which had been created by the union of Upper and Lower Canada in 1841. He profited handsomely from his seigneury. He even petitioned for and received the arrears he had been owed as speaker of the assembly of Lower Canada and built a large and handsome manor house at Montebello. In 1848 he was elected to the assembly and attacked the moderate French-Canadian reformers for defending the union and being content with the power they had achieved under responsible government. He gathered around him a group of younger French-Canadian professionals who formed the nucleus of the future *parti rouge*, or Liberal Party. They continued to advocate republican principles, an end to the union, and the creation of a separate political unit with a French-Canadian majority, even if this meant becoming a state in the American union. Papineau supported the annexation movement of 1849, but he did not stand for election in 1854. He retired to his manor house, where he died on 25 September 1871, holding true to the end to his deist convictions and refusing absolution from his parish priest. He was survived by his wife.

Papineau has always been a controversial figure. Clearly the principal French-Canadian nationalist of his generation, he was ultimately responsible for leading a rebellion which he did not want and which had radical goals that he did not share. He was pleased to be called the Daniel O'Connell of Lower Canada and, like O'Connell, he hoped to achieve his nationalist objectives through constitutional agitation. Many of his radical supporters were dismayed by his social conservatism. His family had risen from relative obscurity to comparative affluence, and Papineau defended the rights of landed proprietors, including seigneurs like himself. Although he supported the separation of church and state and was critical of the Catholic church's control over education, he refused to attack the endowments of the church. He believed that the Catholic church and the seigneurial system had ensured the survival of the French-Canadian nation and were essential components of the French-Canadian identity. Fernand Ouellet, Papineau's twentieth-century biographer, described him as 'A Divided Soul', torn between his liberalism and his traditionalism, and denounced him—and by implication modern-day separatists—for seeking to establish an independent French-Canadian republic. Even historians more sympathetic to the rebellion, such as Alan Greer, see Papineau as a conservative figure holding back the democratic forces in Lower Canada. Ironically it was the rebellion which Papineau did not want, but could not prevent, that ensured his place in Canadian history. Although the rebellion failed, it did lead to the appointment of Lord Durham, the Act of Union, and ultimately the introduction of responsible government. Thus Papineau came to be seen by Canadian liberal-nationalists, of both English and French origin, as a hero in the struggle for responsible government, even though Lower Canada would have become an independent republic had the rebellion succeeded, and despite the fact that Papineau denounced both the union and responsible government after he returned from exile. More secure is Papineau's popularity among those Quebec nationalists who have not abandoned his dream of creating a separate state for the French-Canadian nation.

PHILLIP BUCKNER

Sources F. Ouellet, 'Papineau, Louis-Joseph', *DCB*, vol. 10 • F. Ouellet, *Louis-Joseph Papineau: a divided soul* (1972) • A. Greer, *The patriots and the people: the rebellion of 1837 in rural Lower Canada* (*c.*1993) • P. A. Buckner, *The transition to responsible government: British policy in British North America, 1815–1850* (1985) • F. Ouellet, *Lower Canada, 1791–1840: social changes and nationalism*, ed. and trans. P. Claxon (Toronto, 1980) • F. Ouellet, *Papineau: textes choisis* (1964) • R. Chabot, 'Papineau, Joseph', *DCB*, vol. 7
Archives Archives Nationales du Québec, Québec, Canada • NA Canada, corresp. • National Library of Canada, Ottawa, corresp. | Archives du Séminaire de Québec, Verrean Collection, Viger MSS • Archives Nationales du Québec, Québec, Canada, Ludoper Davernay MSS • Archives Nationales du Québec, Québec, Canada, Edouard-Raymond Fabre MSS
Likenesses photogravure, NPG

Pappworth [*formerly* Papperovitch], **Maurice Henry** **(1910–1994)**, medical ethicist and educationist, was born on 9 January 1910 at 27 Pleasant Street, Liverpool, the second child in the family of three sons and six daughters of (Isaac) Jacob Papperovitch (*d.* 1960), master tailor, who changed his name to Pappworth in the 1930s, and his wife, Mary (Miriam), *née* Poplavitch (*d.* 1935). He was educated at Birkenhead Institute and Liverpool University, where he graduated from the medical school with honours in 1932. After obtaining both the MD and the MRCP in 1936 he held various junior appointments in Liverpool hospitals, mostly as a registrar in the medical professorial unit under Henry Cohen. From 1941 to 1946 he served as a medical specialist in the Royal Army Medical Corps in the UK, north Africa, Italy, Greece, and India, where he was officer in charge of a British general hospital with the rank of lieutenant-colonel. This was as far, however, as Pappworth's ascent of the clinical medical ladder was to go. He had encountered antisemitism before the war in Liverpool, when, turned down for a consultant appointment, he had been told that 'no Jew could ever be a gentleman' (*Medical News*, 21 Aug 1970), a sentiment to be repeated after the war when he applied for prestigious posts in London, where he moved in 1946. Rejecting offers of lacklustre appointments in peripheral hospitals, he decided instead to become a freelance consultant physician, and crucially also a medical tutor. On 4 October 1953 he married Jean Goldberg (*b.* 1922/3), artist and textile designer, and daughter of Philip Goldberg, company director; they had three daughters.

In the early post-war years the Royal College of Physicians was a stuffy, élitist, and inward-looking institution. From its cramped headquarters in Pall Mall (known to taxi drivers as the 'dirty end of Canada House') it controlled entry to the consultant physician establishment through the higher diploma of its membership examination (MRCP). In the late 1940s and 1950s the pass rate was little more than 15 per cent, occasionally, it was said, dipping to 10 per cent. The resultant frustration, anger, and expense forced many talented candidates into non-clinical posts, general practice, or emigration—a retreat likened in 1958 by one former college president, Lord Moran, to falling off the ladder that led to the élite of the profession, the consultants, especially the consultant physicians. Nevertheless, though part of the problem resulted from such an attitude and the arbitrarily set standards of the college, the examination also disclosed the dreadfully poor standards of teaching in British medical schools. In particular, there was virtually no formal teaching of postgraduates, and housemen and registrars were expected to prepare for the MRCP examination on their own. Pappworth determined to remedy this, especially to give already qualified doctors a grounding in the elements of medicine and the logical sequence of examining patients. He started to give tutorials for the MRCP, at first in his consulting rooms, and then in a nearby public hall in the West End of London. The cost was not small—a pound note (then a twentieth of a houseman's monthly salary) dropped into a bowl as the student left the two-hour class—but the results were outstandingly good. On occasion half the successful candidates had been to his classes (and often to his, more expensive, mock clinical examinations, held in peripheral mental hospitals, as well). Over the years he coached more than 1600 young doctors, many from the old dominions. He could claim that 75 per cent of the doctors from New Zealand and Australia who passed the MRCP during the post-war period had done so because of him. At this time he was acknowledged as the best medical teacher not only in London but probably throughout Britain as well. He did not mince his words about the medical establishment, while the Royal College of Physicians was (behind closed doors) equally forthright about what it saw as unfair trespassing on its domain.

It was through his contact with junior doctors that Pappworth became aware of their growing concern for human experimentation. Often they had to participate for the sake of their careers but found it ethically distasteful and taking little heed of guidelines such as the Nuremberg code produced after the trial of the Nazi doctors. He wrote letters to the editors of medical journals that had published work that he found ethically doubtful, but these were often rejected for publication. Hence he collected together fourteen such examples, publishing them in 1962 in a special issue of the influential quarterly *Twentieth Century*. Planning to produce an expanded version as a book Pappworth encountered considerable legal objections from the first few publishers he approached, but eventually his book, entitled *Human Guinea Pigs*, appeared in 1967. This included many more, fully referenced, examples than the article—including experiments on children, the mentally defective, and prison inmates, as well as seventy-eight examples from National Health Service hospitals. One notable example was cardiac catheterization, performed on patients who had been admitted for routine surgery and had lightly given permission for blood specimens to be taken while they were under the anaesthetic.

Pappworth's book was an immediate sensation, with newspaper and television features devoted to the subject, and questions raised in the houses of parliament. Moreover, it complemented similar findings across the Atlantic by Henry Beecher, a Harvard professor of anaesthesiology, who published them in the *New England Journal of Medicine*, though without naming the experimenters concerned. Pappworth's and Beecher's publications led eventually to strict codes for human experimentation—not merely a revision of the declaration of Helsinki but the establishment of research ethics committees (institutional review boards in the USA) to scrutinize all projects (and subsequently those for animal experimentation as well). In this way Pappworth did more by his vehement campaigning for patients' interests than anyone of his time in Britain. Certainly, without his (and Beecher's) persistence in the face of professional obloquy and stonewalling and official lack of interest, the implementation of proper ethical standards for research would have been considerably delayed.

Perhaps part of Pappworth's problem was his acerbity—not merely about the Royal College of Physicians as an institution, but also about the personal proclivities of its grandees and other fellows. Invited to address the residents of Hammersmith Hospital, whose associated postgraduate medical school was frequently named in his book for its unethical behaviour, within a few minutes he had alienated most of his audience by his personal comments. His brusque treatment of students who answered a question wrongly left them feeling ignorant, foolish, and humiliated. Yet it was this quality that enabled him to persist with pressing a case that was so evidently morally right, and in a society traumatized by the thalidomide affair and the anti-science book *Silent Spring* by Rachel Carson it eventually sparked enough pressure for determined action. Finally, moreover, a new team at the college recognized his contribution and in 1993 elected him to its fellowship—an honour normally granted only ten to fifteen years after obtaining the MRCP but in this case denied him for fifty-seven years. He had the grace to accept this with dignity, and the spontaneous applause at the ceremony, led by a former director of the Royal Postgraduate Medical School, testified to the recognition of his achievement.

Pappworth's main interests were intellectual, in fine art, classical music, photography, and especially in reading about philosophy, religion, and politics. He died of coronary heart disease at his home, Vale Lodge, Vale of Health, Hampstead, London, on 12 October 1994, and was survived by his wife and three daughters.

STEPHEN LOCK

Sources *The Independent* (12 Nov 1994) · 'The David among medical Goliaths', *Medical News* (21 Aug 1970) · C. Booth, 'M. H. Pappworth', *BMJ* (10 Dec 1994), 1577 · Munk, *Roll* · b. cert. · m. cert. · d. cert. · personal knowledge (2004) · private information (2004)
Archives Wellcome L., corresp. and notes
Wealth at death £785,707: probate, 22 May 1995, *CGPLA Eng. & Wales*

Papworth, Edgar George (1809–1866), sculptor, was born probably at 30 Portland Place, Cavendish Square, London, on 20 or 21 August 1809. A member of a family of artists, he was baptized on 9 January 1810 at St Marylebone, Marylebone Road, Middlesex, the only son of Thomas Papworth (1773–1814), who ran a large stucco and plastering business, and his wife, Sarah. Following his father's death, Edgar George lived with his uncle, the architect John Buonarotti *Papworth, and received sculptural training from Edward Hodges Baily. Papworth married Baily's daughter, Caroline (*d.* 1867), at the Old Church, St Pancras, on 10 February 1831. At the Royal Academy Schools (1826–34) Papworth won a gold and two silver medals and a travelling scholarship to Italy in 1834. Although illness forced his return to London in 1837, his Italian visit was highly productive. He worked on watercolour panoramas of Rome and Naples; the former was exhibited in London in 1844, but is now lost. The 540 cm wide view of Naples (1835; priv. coll.) provides an invaluable architectural record of the city at the time and received attention from Cesare De Seta in *Vedutisti e viaggiatori in Italia tra settecento e ottocento* (1999). Papworth also began work in Italy on his *Original Sculptural Designs*, which was published as a volume of engravings in 1840.

Papworth exhibited at the Royal Academy from 1832 to 1866. Few of his sculptures survive but to judge from their titles and surviving illustrations it is clear that his repertoire was wide. It ranged from designs for monuments and portrait busts to precious metalwork and ideal sculpture. Like his contemporary, Joseph Durham, Papworth explored historical, literary, and genre themes in such works as *Poor Little Nell* (1841), *The Bird's Nester* (1857), and *An Incident in the Siege of Lucknow* (1858). Papworth unsuccessfully competed for the national memorials to Horatio Nelson (1838) and William Wordsworth (1851); his design for the Wellington monument for St Paul's Cathedral, London (1857), was placed third in the competition. Reproduced in the *Illustrated London News*, Papworth's entry was praised by the *Art Journal* for its 'eminently solemn and sepulchral' character and 'great poetic beauty' and was declared the popular favourite (Sept 1857, 292). Despite this, the commission went to the sixth-placed Alfred Stevens.

Papworth's sculpture is characterized by its careful carving and marks a transition from neoclassical idealism to Victorian realism. The former is evident in his Wellington monument design, which was strongly influenced by Antonio Canova. His portraiture, such as the posthumously executed bust of William Dyce (1864; RA), tends towards greater realism. The *Bust of an Unknown Man* (1856; Leeds Museums and Galleries) has been gently mocked for its swathes of carved drapery, apparently indicating Victorian prudery (Hall). This image is contradicted, however, by Papworth's undraped bust *Ruth* (1856). One of his few public sculptures is the tomb of John Bunyan (1862; Bunhill Fields, London), which involved reconstructing an existing effigy and the addition of bas-relief carvings. For understandable if unfortunate reasons, Papworth is frequently confused with his eldest son and namesake, Edgar George Papworth (1832–1884), whose sculpture represents a close continuation of the father's style.

Papworth died at his home, 36 Milton Street, Dorset Square, London, on 26 September 1866. He was buried in Highgate cemetery and was survived by his wife and children. According to the *Dictionary of National Biography* 'his circumstances were embarrassed owing to his extravagant and careless habits'. These habits were not identified but were probably less squalid than those of his alcoholic contemporary William Behnes. Although Papworth failed to fulfil his early promise, he nevertheless continued to exhibit at the Royal Academy until the year of his death.

MARK STOCKER

Sources *DNB* • R. Gunnis, *Dictionary of British sculptors, 1660–1851* (1953); new edn (1968) • J. Physick, *The Wellington monument* (1970) • E. G. Papworth, *Original sculptural designs* (1840) • C. De Seta, *Vedutisti e viaggiatori in Italia tra settecento e ottocento* (Turin, 1999) • C. De Seta, 'Parthenopean panopticon: Edgar George Papworth', *FMR*, 68 (1994), 97–126 • Graves, *RA exhibitors* • *ILN* (15 March 1862), 266 • *ILN* (7 June 1862), 570 • B. Read, *Victorian sculpture* (1982) • N. Penny, *Church monuments in Romantic England* (1977) • J. Hall, 'Head and shoulders above the rest', *The Independent* (17 Oct 2000) • P. Curtis and others, *Return to life: a new look at the portrait bust* (2000) [exhibition catalogue, Henry Moore Institute, Leeds, 27 Sept 2000 – 7 Jan 2001, NPG, 7 Feb – 20 May 2001, Scot. NPG] • *CGPLA Eng. & Wales* (1866) • *IGI*

Wealth at death under £100: probate, 27 Nov 1866, *CGPLA Eng. & Wales*

Papworth, George (1781–1855), architect, third son of the stuccoist John Papworth (1750–1799) and his wife, Charlotte Searle, and uncle of the sculptor Edgar George Papworth, was born in London on 9 May 1781. He was educated at Dr Thwacken's academy, Hammersmith, and at the age of fifteen exhibited a 'design for a bath' at the Royal Academy. On his father's death in 1799 he became a pupil and clerk in the office of his elder brother the architect John Buonarotti *Papworth, after which he spent two years in the office of a Northampton architect, Luke Kershaw. Through his brother's connection with Sir George Wright, holder of a patent for circular stonecutting, he was appointed manager of a new stone pipe manufactory on the North Strand in Dublin in 1806. He also dabbled in architectural practice, which he entered full-time in 1812 after the failure of the company. Lords Westmeath and Gormanston were among his early patrons. In 1808 he married Margaret Davis, daughter of a solicitor. He was admitted a freeman of Dublin in 1810. Papworth is credited with introducing the London fashion for stucco façades to Dublin, such as the Nash-type terrace on Gloucester Street which bankrupted his father-in-law, John James Davis, in 1831. From 1833 until his death Papworth had a town house in Marlborough Street and a suburban residence at Raheny, co. Dublin (on the estate of his client the hotelier Thomas Gresham).

Papworth's early works in Dublin included the Dublin Library Society premises in D'Olier Street (1818–20; refaced in the art deco style in 1932) and the Carmelite church on Whitefriar Street (1825–7). He had a particular interest in structural ironwork, which he used for the estate bridge at Oak Park, co. Carlow (1815), for Henry Bruen; the 100 foot span King's Bridge in Dublin (1822–7); the portico of Castlebar court house (1822); and the British and Irish Steampacket Company warehouse on the North Wall (1839). He designed a number of country houses, including Seafield, co. Sligo (1842; dem.), for William Phibbs, and Middleton Park, co. Westmeath (1850), for George Augustus Boyd, and reconstructed others, including Portumna Castle, co. Galway (1824–6; burnt down in the latter year), for the marquess of Clanricarde; Hollymount, co. Mayo (1834), for Thomas Spencer Lindsey; Kilcornan House, co. Galway (1836), for Sir Thomas N. Redington; and Kenure Park, Rush, co. Dublin (1842; dem. except for the portico), for Sir Roger Palmer, bt. His work in the Dublin suburbs included the remodelling of Brennanstown House, Cabinteely, for George Pim (1842; rebuilt in the 1950s), the Richmond Hill development in Monkstown (1826–9), and Gresham Terrace in Kingstown (completed by William Murray, 1832; dem.). In 1832 he was lampooned in a pseudonymous poem by Nicholson Numskull (reputedly Henry Kelly, a Dublin architect). His public and institutional buildings included the neo-Gothic district lunatic asylum at Kilkenny (1847–53), and, in Dublin, the reconstruction of 51 St Stephen's Green as the Museum of Irish Industry (1850–52) and the Freemasons' Orphan School, Burlington Place (1852; dem.). From 1837 to 1842 he acted as architect to the ecclesiastical commissioners for the province of Connaught. He later held the appointment of architect to the Dublin and Drogheda Railway, and to the Royal Bank in Foster Place, Dublin.

In 1826 Papworth was made an associate of the Royal Hibernian Academy, at which he regularly exhibited (a total of over eighty designs) up to 1853. He was elected a member in 1831 and appointed treasurer in 1849. In 1839 he was one of the founders of the Institute of the Architects of Ireland, but he resigned in 1841 after a dispute with its president, Richard Morrison. He rejoined after Morrison's death in 1849.

Papworth died on 14 March 1855, aged nearly seventy-four, and was buried at Mount Jerome cemetery, Dublin.

The National Museum of Ireland has a piece of Carrickmacross lace designed by him and made by his daughter, as well as a relief portrait of him in wax by Christopher Moore. His numerous children included Collins Edgar Papworth (1824–1862), who worked in the colonial engineers' office in Melbourne, and Charles William Papworth (*d.* 1892), who succeeded to his father's practice. His eldest son, **John Thomas Papworth** (1809–1841), architect, was born in Dublin on 17 December 1809. He was an associate of the Royal Hibernian Academy of Painting, Sculpture, and Architecture (1836), master of the school of architectural drawing and architect to the Royal Dublin Society (1838), and first honorary secretary of the Institute of the Architects of Ireland (1839). He assisted his father before joining him in partnership in 1835, but designed on his own account the monument to John Philpot Curran in Glasnevin cemetery (1840) as well as alterations to Leinster House, Kildare Street, for the Royal Dublin Society, which were completed under the superintendence of his father. He married Anais Muzard in Dublin in 1838. He died in Paris on 6 October 1841 and was buried in Montmartre cemetery.

W. A. VAN S. PAPWORTH, *rev.* FREDERICK O'DWYER

Sources [W. Papworth], ed., *The dictionary of architecture*, 11 vols. (1853–92) • *The Builder*, 13 (1855), 150 • A. M. Stewart, *Royal Hibernian Academy of Arts: index of exhibitors and their works, 1826–1979*, 3 (1987) • A. M. Stewart, ed., *Irish art loan exhibitions, 1765–1927*, 2 (1995) • N. Numskull [H. Kelly (?)], *An essay on the rise and progress of architectural taste in Dublin* (1832) • G. N. Wright, *Ireland illustrated* (1829) • Graves, *RA exhibitors* • F. O'Dwyer, 'The foundation and early years of the RIAI', *150 years of architecture in Ireland*, ed. J. Graby (1989), 9–21

Archives RIBA BAL, signed specifs of New Library, Dublin

Likenesses C. Moore, wax relief, National Museum of Ireland, Dublin

Wealth at death under £1500: British inland revenue board, administrations in the prerogative court, NA Ire., 1852–5 • approx. £646—John Thomas Papworth: British inland revenue board, administrations in the prerogative court, NA Ire. 1839–42

Papworth, John Buonarotti (1775–1847), architect and designer, was born in Marylebone, Middlesex, on 24 January 1775, the second son and one of twelve children of John Papworth (1750–1799), a leading stuccoist, and his wife, Charlotte, *née* Searle. It was originally intended that Papworth would follow a medical career, but his artistic abilities attracted the attention of Sir William Chambers, who encouraged an architectural one instead. He was taught drawing by his father, perspective by Thomas Malton, and modelling by the sculptor John Deare. He spent two years in the office of John Plaw before, in 1789, becoming apprenticed to the builder Thomas Wapshott, under whose direction he became involved with executing the designs of John Plaw, Thomas Hardwick, and Michael Novosielski. He later worked for a time in the office of Michael Novosielski. He also spent a year studying internal decoration with Sherringham, the upholsterer of Great Marlborough Street, who was working at Carlton House, before becoming involved with the erection of Ray Lodge at Woodford for Sir James Wright (1796–7; dem.), where he was appointed clerk of works and

John Buonarotti Papworth (1775–1847), by William Brockedon

executant architect on behalf of Philip Norris. He entered the Royal Academy Schools in 1798, was noted for his mastery of perspective and classical ornament, and became a regular exhibitor, contributing to nineteen of the Royal Academy exhibitions which were held between 1794 and 1841.

In 1801 Papworth married Jane Harrison Wapshott, for whose father he had worked, though she died in 1809. Then, in 1817, he married Mary Anne Say (*b.* 1794), the daughter of the mezzotint engraver William Say, and they had three children: two sons, John Woody *Papworth and Wyatt Angelicus van Sandau *Papworth, and one daughter, Julia Mary Ann. His brother, George *Papworth (1781–1855), architect, and nephews Edgar George *Papworth (1809–1866), sculptor, and John Thomas *Papworth (1809–1841) [*see under* Papworth, George] are noticed separately.

Papworth's contribution to the evolution of design is particularly important, spanning, as it does, the changes in taste and fashion that mark the transition from the late Georgian to the early Victorian periods. This was a time which saw the emergence of a new group of patrons—bankers, industrialists, and businessmen—who were to constitute Papworth's main clients, and for whom he not only designed estates, villas, and business premises, but also handled the internal furnishing and decorations of these buildings, as well as landscaping of the gardens. Furthermore, the end of the Napoleonic wars heralded a boom in trade, and a desire by shopkeepers to improve the display of goods they had on offer. Papworth was responsible for designing a new style of shop front, one which used large panes of plate glass in preference to the smaller panes of Newcastle Crown glass which had previously been popular.

Papworth's design activities became widely known because of his long-term association with Rudolph Ackermann's *Repository of Arts* (1809–28), where he was a contributor of prose, verse, and drawings. For Ackermann he designed a showroom at 101 Strand (1812), and then an extensive new building at 96 Strand (1826; dem.). He was also associated with three of London's leading artistic firms, W. and E. Snell, cabinetmakers, of Albemarle Street; George Morant, decorator, of New Bond Street; and John Blades, glass manufacturer, of Ludgate Hill. He was responsible for designing the first gin palace to be built in England (for Thompson and Fearon at 94 Holborn Hill in 1829–32; dem.), for inventing the severed column which was used as a sepulchral monument and erected at Waterloo to commemorate Colonel Gordon of the Highland regiment, who fell in the battle there in 1815, and for using cast iron as a roof support for the first time (at Galloway's engineering factory in Smithfield, 1821–2; dem.).

As a town planner Papworth was responsible for much of the development which took place in Cheltenham during the second part of the 1820s, and especially the building of the Montpellier and Lansdowne estates. He designed the Montpellier pump room (the Rotunda), Montpellier Gardens (both 1825–6), Lansdowne Place and Crescent (1825–9); numerous terraces (*c.*1824–1828); St James's Church, Suffolk Square (1826–32); and St John's Church (1827–9; dem. 1967). He was also responsible for designing the Brockwell estate at Dulwich (1825–30), the Maison Dieu estate in Dover, and St Bride's Avenue, off Fleet Street in London (1825–30), a redevelopment which enabled the steeple of St Bride's Church to be seen from Fleet Street. Beyond these, he also designed a model town planned for construction near Cincinnati (*c.*1827), and a number of new roads in the City of London (1825–30): neither of these designs were executed, though the concepts behind his London works were incorporated in later redevelopment plans.

Papworth's furniture designs were chiefly in the French empire and Grecian styles, and were usually produced and sold through W. and E. Snell. He furnished Boodle's Club (1821, and 1833–4) and Cranbury Park, Hampshire (*c.*1830). His designs were also reproduced in a number of publications, including Peter Cox's *The Social Day* (1823), and J. C. Loudon's *Encyclopaedia* (1833). As a landscape gardener he was employed at Claremont by Prince Leopold, king of the Belgians, and Princess Charlotte (1816); at Alton Towers by the earl of Shrewsbury (1818–22); at Holly Lodge, Highgate (1825), and Kirkby Hall, Yorkshire (1833). He was also responsible for the decoration of a paddle steamer which plied the Thames (the *London Engineer* of *c.*1820), for directing the manufacture of a glass throne for the shah of Persia, and designing an elaborate sherbet service for Mohammed Ali, pasha of Egypt (1838). His designs for cut-glass chandeliers and candelabra were very popular in London, Egypt, and Persia, and he also helped to revive the use of decorative floor tiles. He designed the covers of the *Forget-me-Not* annual (1825–30), three blinds with Greek ornamentation for the Phoenix Bank in New York (1827), and a Gothic lantern for Eaton Hall, Cheshire.

Apart from the buildings he designed in Cheltenham, his most notable architectural works were connected with country houses, and include the design of Laleham Park, Middlesex (1803–6), and its subsequent extension (1827–30, and 1839) for the second earl of Lucan; alterations to Haresfoot, near Berkhamsted, for Thomas Dorrien (1817–19; dem. *c.*1965); the design of Leigham Court, Streatham, for J. G. Fuller (1820–22), and then the addition of a second house (1823–44; both dem. 1908); the design of lodges, entrance gateways, and other works at Fonthill Abbey, Wiltshire (1829–42; dem. 1921); restoration of Orleans House, Twickenham, for Alexander Murray (1837–9; dem. 1927); much works at Basildon Park, near Reading (1839–44), and the redecoration of 57 Harley Street (1831–2), both for James Morrison.

Between 1817 and 1820 Papworth was engaged on three designs for a palace which Wilhelm I, king of Württemberg, intended to build at Cannstatt. His drawings for the entrance front and south front were exhibited at the Royal Academy in 1823, and the west front and east front in 1827. The works were not completed, though his designs for laying out the parks were partly executed, and in 1820 he was granted the title 'architect to the king of Wurtemberg'.

Papworth was one of the original members of the Associated Artists in Watercolours (founded 1807), where he was the honorary secretary (1808–10) and a regular exhibitor. He was also a member of the Society of Arts, and one of the original members of the Graphic Society (founded 1833). In 1835 he gave evidence to the House of Commons select committee on arts and manufacturers; in 1836 he was consulted by the government on the formation of a school of design, and in that same year was appointed director of the Government School of Design which was to occupy rooms in Somerset House; he resigned in 1838. He was also involved with the formation of the Institute of British Architects in 1834, and was its vice-president eight times. He adopted the additional name of Buonarotti in 1815 (it was Michelangelo's name) after his friends praised a painting he had produced to commemorate the battle of Waterloo.

Papworth was a prolific writer, publishing, among other works, an *Essay on the Causes of Dry Rot in Timber* (1803); *Select views of London, with historical and descriptive sketches of some of the most interesting public buildings* (1816); *Rural residences, consisting of a series of designs for cottages, small villas, and other buildings, with observations on landscape gardening* (1818 and 1832); and *Hints on ornamental gardening, consisting of a series of designs for garden buildings, useful and decorative gates, fences, railings, &c., accompanied by observations on the principles and theory of rural improvements* (1823). He also contributed to Sir William Chambers's *Treatise on the Decorative Part of Civil Architecture* (1826). Papworth retired at the end of 1846 because of ill health, and moved to Little Paxton, near St Neots, Huntingdonshire, early the next year. He died there on 16 June 1847 and was buried in the churchyard. ARTHUR CATES, *rev.* JOHN ELLIOTT

Sources Colvin, *Archs.* • R. P. R. Williamson, 'John Buonarotti Papworth', *ArchR*, 79 (1936), 279–81 • *Country Life*, 147 (1970), 130–31 • *Country Life*, 147 (1970), 245 • G. McHardy, ed., *Catalogue of the drawings collection of the Royal Institute of British Architects: Office of J. B. Papworth* (1977) • *The Builder*, 5 (1847), 300 • W. Papworth, *John B. Papworth: a brief record of his life and works* (1879) • will, PRO, PROB 11/2059, fol. 385
Archives RIBA BAL, papers
Likenesses W. Brockedon, chalk drawing, BM, NPG [*see illus.*] • J. Green, mezzotint (after W. Say), BM • J. Green, portrait • F. Say, portrait • J. Wood, portrait • portrait, repro. in Papworth, *John B. Papworth*
Wealth at death see will, PRO, PROB 11/2059, fol. 385

Papworth, John Thomas (1809–1841). *See under* Papworth, George (1781–1855).

Papworth, John Woody (1820–1870), architect and antiquary, was born on 4 March 1820 in Bath Place, New Road, in Marylebone, Middlesex, the eldest son of John Buonarotti *Papworth (1775–1847), architect, and his second wife, Mary Anne, daughter of the mezzotint engraver William *Say. His brother was Wyatt Angelicus van Sandau *Papworth. From the age of sixteen he trained in his father's office, and remained there until 1846, when his father retired. In 1837 he became, on its formation, secretary to the council of the Government School of Design, Somerset House, and assisted his father, the director, in the school's organization. In 1839 he entered the Royal Academy Schools, and between that date and 1851 he exhibited many architectural designs at the academy, including a design for the façade of the cathedral of Santa Maria at Florence. In 1838 he received from the Society of Arts the silver Isis medal, in 1840 the gold Isis medal, and in 1845 the Stock medallion; and in 1842 he was awarded the Soane medallion, in 1843 the medal of merit, and in 1847 the silver medal of the Institute of British Architects. In 1841 he was elected an associate, and in 1846 a fellow, of the Institute of British Architects, and he took an active part in the institute's proceedings.

Papworth's most important work was *An Alphabetical Dictionary of Coats of Arms Belonging to Families in Great Britain and Ireland* (ed. A. W. Morant, 1874), which, by arranging the coats of arms on a new plan, made them easy to reference. He made numerous designs for glass, pottery, terracotta, paper hangings, and other art manufactures. He designed the carpet which was presented to Queen Victoria by 150 ladies and which was exhibited by her at the Great Exhibition of 1851. He designed the tomb of the radical politician Thomas Hardy (1752–1832) in Bunhill Fields cemetery and the Albert Institution, Gravel Lane. He was involved with the formation of the Architectural Publication Society in 1848, and contributed a number of important articles to its publications. He helped during the first years of the production of the society's *Dictionary of Architecture*, of which his brother Wyatt was the editor from its commencement in 1852 until its completion in 1892.

In conjunction with his brother Wyatt, Papworth published, with plates engraved by the authors, *Specimens of decoration in the Italian style selected from the designs of Raffaello in the Vatican* (1844) and *Museums, libraries, and picture galleries, public and private: their establishment, formation, arrangement, and architectural construction, to which is appended the Public Libraries Act, 1850, and remarks on its adoption by mechanics and other scientific institutions, with illustrations* (1853). He also published *The ladies' carpet, designed by J. W. P., presented to, and exhibited by, her majesty in the Great Exhibition, 1851* (1852); and he was a frequent contributor to *The Builder*, the *Proceedings of the Institute of British Architects*, and also the *Transactions* of the institute. Overwork and inattention to health brought on an attack of gangrene in his right foot, which after a confinement to the house for about six years, resulted in his death at his home, 13 Hart Street, Bloomsbury Square, on 6 July 1870, unmarried, aged fifty. He was buried in Highgate cemetery.

ARTHUR CATES, *rev.* JOHN ELLIOTT

Sources *The Builder*, 28 (1870), 559–60 • R. Kerr, 'The late John W. Papworth', *The Architect*, 4 (1870), 30–31 • Redgrave, *Artists* • [W. Papworth], ed., *The dictionary of architecture*, 11 vols. (1853–92) • *IGI* • *CGPLA Eng. & Wales* (1870)
Archives RIBA
Wealth at death under £1000: resworn probate, Jan 1871, *CGPLA Eng. & Wales* (1870)

Papworth, Wyatt Angelicus van Sandau (1822–1894), architect and antiquary, was born in Highgate, Middlesex, on 23 January 1822, one of three children and the younger son of the architect John Buonarroti *Papworth (1775–1847) and his second wife, Mary Anne Say, eldest daughter of William *Say, mezzotint engraver. He was educated at University College School and then received his professional education in his father's office, and was for a few years employed in the office of the commissioners of sewers for Westminster, one of the predecessors of the London county council. After a short period in the office of Sir John Rennie, he was appointed joint surveyor, with a Mr Allason, and later sole surveyor to the Alliance Assurance Company from 1866 until his retirement, aged sixty-five, in 1887. In addition to supervising numerous rebuildings and restorations he designed and erected the company's branch office at Ipswich in Suffolk, and published notes on fire risks. Papworth married in London on 5 February 1873 Marian Baker, with whom he had two sons and a daughter.

His father was a member of the Clothworkers' Company of the City of London, and Papworth in due course became a liveryman of that company. After his election to the court he served as junior and senior warden in 1879–81 and was master of the company in 1889. During his year of office he represented the company at the opening of two new technical schools at Bingley and Dewsbury in Yorkshire. On each occasion he delivered an address on the importance of drawing and design in connection with technical instruction and the textile industries. Papworth was always deeply interested in technical education. He was a governor of the City and Guilds of London Institute, and represented his company on the governing body of the Northern (Islington) Polytechnic.

Papworth's interest in the history of building began early in his career and he had already collected a large

Wyatt Angelicus van Sandau Papworth (1822–1894), by unknown photographer, 1890

quantity of material when he issued, in 1848, a circular letter proposing a 'Society for the Promotion of Architectural Information intended for the Revival and Restoration, Investigation and Publication, of Knowledge in Architecture and the Arts connected therewith'. This led to the formation of the Architectural Publication Society for the production of 'Detached Essays and Illustrations', with the idea that these might subsequently be incorporated into an encyclopaedia of architecture. Papworth prepared a list of 12,127 terms or headings for this proposed work, which was in 1852 redefined as a 'Dictionary of Explanation and Reference'. The work on the dictionary then commenced under the guidance of a committee of architects, with Papworth as secretary and editor, assisted by his brother, John Woody *Papworth. The first part of the *Dictionary of Architecture* was published in 1853 and the last in 1892; the publication ran to eight folio volumes of text and three volumes of illustrations. The final work contained 18,456 articles, and remains a valuable work of reference today. The whole conception and successful production of the dictionary were in Papworth's hands and he also compiled most of the biographical and topographical articles. His own grangerized copy, extending to seventeen volumes, was acquired by Sir John Soane's Museum, London, in 1860.

Papworth's contribution to architectural history was not limited to the dictionary. In 1849 he was awarded the silver medal of the Institute of British Architects for an essay on 'The peculiar characteristics of the Palladian school of architecture' (published in the *Journal of the Institute of British Architects*, 1, 3rd ser., 631). Papworth's other historical investigations covered a variety of topics associated with his profession. In one series of enquiries he sought to define the periods when fir, deal, and house painting were introduced into England (*Transactions of the Royal Institute of British Architects*, 8, 1857), and to determine the extent of the use of chestnut timber in old buildings (ibid., 14 June 1858). He researched the architects of medieval buildings and their connections with freemasonry, although he was not himself a freemason (see his papers in the publications of the Lodge Quatuor Coronati between 1888 and 1894). He endeavoured to identify those entitled to the credit of designing the buildings erected in England during the middle ages and published a number of papers relating to this work in the *Journal of the Royal Institute of British Architects* (1860–90).

In 1867 Papworth revised and edited Joseph Gwilt's *Encyclopaedia of Architecture*, first published in 1842. Papworth's edition included a vast amount of new information which was greatly increased in two further revisions in 1876 and 1889. He was also the author of many papers for the *Transactions of the Royal Institute of British Architects*, including memoirs of Professor Donaldson (1886), Joseph Bonomi (1869), and Arthur Ashpitel FSA (1869), as well as articles on 'The fall of the dome of the Koltovskoie Church, St Petersburg' (1872) and 'On the fall of the iron dome of the Anthaeum at Brighton' (1872). He also contributed many memoirs of architects to the *Dictionary of National Biography*, and produced a number of books with his brother, John Woody Papworth, including *Specimens of Decoration in the Italian Style* (1844), *Museums, Libraries and Picture Galleries* (1853), *Memoirs of A. W. Morant* (1881), and *The Renaissance and Italian styles of architecture in Great Britain: their introduction and development shown by a series of dated examples* (1883). Together they also published two works on the causes of fires in buildings in 1853 and 1855 and a memoir of their father, *John B. Papworth: architect to the king of Würtemburg, a brief record of his life and works* (privately printed, 1879).

Sir John Summerson described Papworth as 'the father of modern architectural scholarship' (unpublished notes on past curators, curatorial papers, Sir John Soane's Museum). Arthur Cates, author of the *Dictionary of National Biography* entry on Papworth, observed from personal knowledge that 'few men were closer students of the subjects connected with the history of architecture, possessed more special knowledge, or imparted it with truer modesty'.

Papworth played a leading role in the affairs of the Royal Institute of British Architects (RIBA). The unattributed obituary of Papworth in the institute's journal (*RIBA Journal*, 1, 3rd ser., 1894, 618) referred to him as one of the institute's 'staunchest supporters, a firm and constant friend of sixty years'. It recalled that he was 'present, a boy of twelve years, at the First General Meeting, held 2nd July

1834, when his father with eleven others subscribed their names to the First Address' (ibid.). He was elected a fellow in 1860, and sat for many years on the council. An article in *Building News* (6 June 1890, 793–4) recalled that when the institute moved to Conduit Street in 1860 Papworth undertook the arrangement of the books in the library along with the entire revision of the catalogue and its publication in 1864. His research notes for the 'History of the king's artificers', 'The clerk of works of the City of London', and 'The district surveyors of London', are deposited in the library along with his (unpublished) abstract of his father's diaries.

Papworth exhibited various drawings at the Royal Academy between 1836 and 1851, including a design for an arch of peace and plenty in Kensington Gardens (1845) and 'A suggestion for an improvement in Westminster adapted to the 19th century' (1850), inspired by a passage in John Evelyn's diary of 27 February 1695, referring to the proposal by King Charles II to buy up the whole of King Street, Westminster, and 'build it nobly'. Although he won a number of architectural competitions, only three or four of Papworth's designs were executed. His obituary in the *Journal of the Royal Institute of British Architects* refers to his rearrangement of the large corner building in King Street, St James's, London, for the Junior Army and Navy Club and he is also known to have been the architect of Prince's Park Terrace at the junction of Croxteth and Sefton Park roads in Liverpool—won in a competition of 1843—which survives. On the death of James Wild in 1892, he was appointed curator of Sir John Soane's Museum in Lincoln's Inn Fields, pro tem on 14 November 1892, and formally on 9 January 1893. During his time as curator he produced a new and revised edition (the sixth) of the museum's guidebook, the 'General description'. He carried out alterations to the rear kitchen of the museum in 1893. At that time it remained largely as it had been at the time of Soane's death in 1837, and the removal of internal walls and the remnants of the original kitchen fittings is regarded in the twenty-first century as highly regrettable. Although his curatorship was brief, his association with the museum extended over many years as a result of his work on the *Dictionary of Architecture*. Wyatt Papworth died at Sir John Soane's Museum on 19 August 1894, succumbing to paralysis after six weeks' illness. He was buried on 23 August in Highgate cemetery. Mrs Papworth survived her husband, and remained in residence at the museum for several months after his death. Their younger son, Alfred Wyatt Papworth (1879–1917), followed Papworth into the architectural profession: he won the medal of merit in the RIBA measured drawings competition (1901) and with Gilbert H. Lovegrove (1878–1951) formed the architectural practice of Lovegrove and Papworth. Papworth's only daughter, Lucy Wyatt Papworth, was general secretary of the Women's Industrial Council for thirteen years from 1903 and died in 1921, aged forty-seven.

ARTHUR CATES, *rev.* HELEN DOREY

Sources *RIBA Journal*, 1 (1893–4), 618 • *Journal of the Clerks of Works Association*, 11/136 (1894), 95 • biographical file, RIBA BAL • *Dir. Brit. archs.* • Graves, *RA exhibitors* • *Building News*, 58 (6 June 1890), 793 • personal knowledge (1895) • J. Summerson, unpublished notes on past curators and other unpublished MS material, Sir John Soane's Museum, London, archive • *RIBA Journal*, 24 (1916–17), 172 [obit. of A. W. Papworth] • *South Lancashire*, Pevsner (1969) • G. McHardy, ed., *Catalogue of the drawings collection of the Royal Institute of British Architects: Office of J. B. Papworth* (1977) • *CGPLA Eng. & Wales* (1894) • [W. Papworth], ed., *The dictionary of architecture*, 11 vols. (1853–92) • m. cert.

Archives Clothworkers' Company, London, papers • RIBA, corresp. and working papers • RIBA BAL, papers • Sir John Soane's Museum, London, papers

Likenesses C. Haag, oils, *c.*1889–1890 • photograph, 1890, RIBA BAL [*see illus.*] • group portrait, photograph, Clothworkers' Hall, London • photograph (after C. Haag), repro. in *The Graphic* (2 Aug 1890), supplement • photograph, Sir John Soane's Museum, London • photograph, repro. in *Building News*, p. 578 • wood-engraving (after photograph by Elliott & Fry), NPG; repro. in *ILN* (25 Aug 1894)

Wealth at death £9199 2*s.* 10*d.*: probate, 15 Sept 1894, *CGPLA Eng. & Wales*

Paradise, John (1743–1795), linguist, was born at Salonika in Macedonia in April 1743, the only son of Peter Paradise (1704–1779), British consul in that town since 1741, and his wife, the half-Greek daughter of Philip *Lodvill (*d.* 1767). John was educated at the University of Padua, and in the 1760s moved with his parents to London. His talent for learning languages was remarkable. He knew ancient and modern Greek, Latin, Turkish, French, Italian, Arabic, and English, though, according to Bennet Langton in 1775, his command of English was imperfect. John continued his education at Oxford University and on 14 April 1769 gained his MA degree (the degree of DCL was conferred on him on 3 July 1776).

In London, Paradise and his father met Colonel Philip Ludwell 'the third' (1716–1767), a wealthy Virginian plantation owner, and perhaps a kinsman. Ludwell had three daughters—Hannah, Frances, and Lucy (1751–1814)—to whom, on their future marriages, he willed equal parts of his estate, Peter and John Paradise being among his executors. Ludwell died on 25 March 1767, Frances died in 1768, and in March 1769 Hannah married an American cousin, William Lee. On 18 May 1769 Lucy Ludwell married John Paradise.

The marriage soon faced problems over the division of Frances's inheritance, but there was also a basic incompatibility of temperament and interests. Lucy was a lively beauty with an uncertain temper, a socialite with an interest in public affairs, whereas Paradise was a quiet scholar with a genius for friendship. On 2 May 1771 he was elected FRS 'for his skill in geometry, philosophy and ancient literature'; he was later a founder member of Johnson's Essex Head Club (1783). Their house in London's fashionable Cavendish Square was always open to literary men and they entertained a distinguished circle, which included Sir William Jones, Hester Lynch Thrale (later Piozzi), Sir Joseph Banks, Edmund Burke, William Goldsmith, Sir Joshua Reynolds, David Garrick, James Boswell, and Samuel Johnson himself. Johnson frequently dined with Paradise, despite the latter's whig and pro-American convictions.

Lucy was no bluestocking, and her temper sometimes

overcame her good sense. She once called the short-sighted artist Mary Moser 'a mole' (Smith). Fanny Burney records how Lucy was once so irritated by Baretti that she turned the boiling water of her tea urn over him (*Early Diary*, 1.198n.). Once when a servant brought her a dirty plate she audibly threatened him: 'If you bring me a dirty plate again I will break your head with it' (Hawkins, 1.72).

John Paradise, no businessman, was troubled by Virginian legislation seeking to disinherit non-residents. He travelled to Paris in 1779 with his friend the linguist William Jones and there met Benjamin Franklin, then the rage of Parisian society; Franklin gave him much valuable advice and assistance, and in October 1780 Paradise obtained American citizenship. In 1786 he met Thomas Jefferson, who also took an interest in the Paradises' problems, which Lucy later followed up in a stream of letters. In the end, however, Paradise refused to move to America, and there were attempts at living apart. The couple's elder daughter, Lucy (*b.* 1771), was unwisely 'brought out' by her mother at the age of fourteen. She was widely courted, and two years later wished to marry Count Antonio Barziza of Venice. When her father refused his consent she eloped, with her mother's active connivance, and married Barziza on 4 April 1787. Friends sought to reconcile Paradise and his wife, and in September they at last visited their estate in Virginia, where they met George Washington. At Green Spring, in February 1788, they were shocked by news of the sudden death in London of their younger daughter, Philippa (aged thirteen), and shortly returned to London.

Paradise shared his health and drink problems with his fellow hypochondriac Boswell, who admired his 'amiable disposition' and 'gentleness of manner' (*Boswell's Life of Johnson*, 4.364). During Johnson's protracted illness Paradise was his most devoted friend. A letter from Johnson to Hester Lynch Thrale, dated 21 June 1783, states that 'no one has shown more affection than Paradise' (*Letters of Samuel Johnson*, 4.156), while another to Paradise himself, dated 20 October 1784, acknowledges his great and constant kindness (ibid., 424–5). He was a mourner at Johnson's funeral. Paradise himself died at his home in Great Titchfield Street, London, on 12 December 1795, and is thought to have been buried at the church of St Mary-le-Bow, Cheapside.

A. B. Shepperson, in his *John Paradise and Lucy Ludwell* (1942), stresses the paradoxes of John Paradise's life, describing him as:

> a scholar who never wrote a book, a Fellow of the Royal Society who never recorded an experiment, a widely reputed linguist who spoke imperfectly the language of the country in which he lived, a Doctor of Civil Laws of Oxford who knew but little of the law, [and] a philosopher whose domestic life was a tragic failure. (Shepperson, 5)

In August 1805 Lucy returned to America. She re-entered society, where her growing eccentricities made her notorious. In 1812 she was declared insane and entered an asylum. She died two years later. JOHN D. HAIGH

Sources A. B. Shepperson, *John Paradise and Lucy Ludwell of London and Williamsburg, Richmond, Virginia* (1942), 1–450 • *The letters of Samuel Johnson*, ed. B. Redford, 2–4 (1992–4) • *GM*, 1st ser., 49 (1779), 103 • *GM*, 1st ser., 57 (1787), 1030 • *GM*, 1st ser., 65 (1795), 1059 • *Boswell's Life of Johnson*, ed. G. B. Hill, 6 vols. (1887), vol. 1, p. 64; vol. 3, p. 386; vol. 4, pp. 225, 254, 272, 364, 434 • L.-M. Hawkins, *Memoirs, anecdotes, facts and opinions*, 2 vols. (1824) • *The correspondence of James Boswell with certain members of the Club*, ed. C. N. Fifer (1976), vol. 3 of *The Yale editions of the private papers of James Boswell*, research edn (1966–) • J. T. Smith, *Nollekens and his times*, 1 (1828), 1.347–9 • *The early diary of Frances Burney, 1768–1778*, ed. A. R. Ellis, rev. edn, 2 vols. (1907)
Archives Virginia Historical Society, Richmond, Ludwell MSS

Pardoe, Julia (*bap.* **1804**, *d.* **1862**), writer, the younger daughter of Thomas Pardoe (1777/8–1849), an army officer, and his wife, Elizabeth, was born at Beverley, Yorkshire, and baptized there on 4 December 1804. While in her teens, Julia Pardoe published, anonymously, *The Nun: a Poetical Romance, and Two Others*; an anonymous novel, *Lord Morcar of Hereward*, followed in 1829. Fear of consumption necessitated a fifteen-month journey abroad, and this produced the first of Pardoe's popular travel books, *Traits and Traditions of Portugal*. Published in 1833, it was dedicated to the Princess Augusta, who took a warm interest in the writer. In 1835 Pardoe accompanied her father to Constantinople, and at the time it was felt that no woman apart from Lady Mary Wortley Montagu had acquired so intimate a knowledge of Turkey. In 1837 Pardoe published *The City of the Sultan and Domestic Manners of the Turks*. The book was very successful, and was reprinted in three volumes in 1838, 1845, and 1854. Aiming to disabuse Europeans of their 'ideal of Oriental mysteriousness, mysticism, and magnificence' (vol. 1, p. 89), it offered what was hitherto 'probably the most detailed, most sympathetic description of the Turkish élite' (Melman, 50). There followed in rapid succession *The Beauties of the Bosphorus* (1838, new editions in 1854 and 1874), *The River and the Desart, or, Recollections of the Rhône and the Chartreuse* (1838), and *The City of the Magyar, or, Hungary and her Institutions in 1839–40* (1840). The latter was remarkable for its comprehensive research into Hungarian economic and political life; less florid in style than its predecessors, it also induced Elizabeth Barrett to praise Pardoe's 'word-painting' (*Letters of Elizabeth Barrett Browning*, 328).

About 1842, when suffering from overwork, and possibly also from the failure to propose to her of the journalist H. F. Chorley, Pardoe retired from London, and lived with her parents first at Perry Street, near Gravesend, and afterwards at Northfleet, Kent. She continued to write novels and short stories; of very uneven quality, they are at their best in their sharp observation of the greed and affectations of both fashionable and middle-class circles. She contributed to *Fraser's Magazine* and the *Illuminated Magazine*, as well as to several annuals; she also edited Anita George's *Memoirs of the Queens of Spain* (1850) and wrote an introduction to *A Thousand and One Days: a Companion to the Arabian Nights* (1857). Most enduring were her historical works on French sixteenth- and seventeenth-century court life—*Louis the Fourteenth and the Court of France in the Seventeenth Century* (1847), *The Court and Reign of Francis the First, King of France* (1849), and *The Life of Marie de Médicis, Queen and Regent of France* (1852)—all of which were reprinted into the twentieth century. The book on Francis I, which covers his private and public life in detail, was for

Julia Pardoe (*bap.* 1804, *d.* 1862), by Samuel Freeman, pubd 1849 (after John Lilley)

many years the most comprehensive work on his reign, but the study of Marie de Médicis was justifiably criticized by reviewers for being diffuse and unfocused. Pardoe was granted a civil-list pension in January 1860, 'in consideration of thirty years' toil in the field of literature, by which she has contributed both to cultivate the public taste and to support a number of helpless relations' (Colles, 39).

Pardoe struck contemporaries as warm-hearted, bright, and animated, though some also commented unsympathetically on her constant wish to appear younger than she was (Hall, 376; *Letters of Elizabeth Barrett Browning*). Leigh Hunt mentions her among the women authors, in the 'Feast of the Violets', as 'Pardoe all spirits', to whom Apollo, when dancing with the learned ladies, 'showed Spain's impassioned velocity'. Julia Pardoe died, unmarried, on 26 November 1862, at 24 Upper Montagu Street, London, after suffering from insomnia and a long-standing chronic disease of the liver. Her death certificate records her age as fifty-six, when baptismal records reveal that she was actually fifty-eight.

ELIZABETH LEE, *rev.* JOANNE WILKES

Sources 'Preface', J. Pardoe, *The court and reign of Francis the First, king of France* (1887), 1.xiii–xvi • *BL cat.* • *National union catalog*, Library of Congress • B. Melman, *Women's orients: English women and the Middle East, 1718–1918*, 2nd edn (1995) • *The letters of Elizabeth Barrett Browning to Mary Russell Mitford, 1836–1854*, ed. M. B. Raymond and M. R. Sullivan, 1 (1983) • *Letters of Mary Russell Mitford*, ed. H. Chorley, [2nd edn], 1 (1872) • private information (1895) • W. M. Colles, *Literature and the pension list* (1889) • S. C. Hall, *A book of memories of great men and women of the age* (1871), 374–6 • *Fraser's Magazine*, 23 (1841), 316–27 [review of J. Pardoe, *City of the Magyar*] • review of J. Pardoe, *Life of Marie de Médicis*, *EdinR*, 96 (1852), 435–52 • review of J. Pardoe, *Life of Marie de Médicis*, *Blackwood*, 78 (1855), 449–51 • *IGI*

Archives Brown University Library, Providence, Rhode Island, letters to Royal Literary Fund, BL in loan no. 96 | BL, agreements with publisher R. Bentley, Add. MSS 46614, fol. 308; Add. MSS 46615, fols. 172–5 • Bodl. Oxf., Hughenden Dep. 245/1, fols. 94–8

Likenesses S. Freeman, engraving, pubd 1849 (after portrait by J. Lilley), NPG [*see illus.*] • J. Thomson, stipple (after H. Room), BM, NPG

Pardoe, William (1630/31–1692), General Baptist minister, was originally from Tenbury, Worcestershire. Nothing is known of his parents or of his early life, but it seems he began evangelizing about 1660, after joining Mr Richard Stead's Baptist society some time before 1658. His career as a General Baptist messenger carried him extensively around Worcestershire and beyond, and he travelled as far as Bristol, Leicestershire, Staffordshire, and possibly even Yorkshire to preach. He became chiefly responsible, though, for the General Baptist communities of Worcester, Leominster, and Lichfield, and was pastor for the latter by 1688.

From the early 1660s Pardoe suffered persecution for nonconformity. Excommunicated from the Church of England in 1662 (and subject to imprisonment by writ *de excommunicato capiendo*), he subsequently faced many years of captivity. For his conscience, he endured seven years in Worcester gaol 'from *June* 1664, to *April* 1671' (according to Calamy, *Abridgement*, 2.776), between three and four years in Hereford, one year in Lichfield, and (during 1675) nine months in Leicester prison.

It was in Worcester gaol that Pardoe began writing *Antient Christianity revived: being a description of the doctrine, discipline and practice, of the little city Bethania* (1688). This treatise (eventually completed in Leicester prison) describes 'the estate of the true Church of *Christ*', figured here as the city of Bethania (Pardoe, A5*v*). Divided into three sections, the book accounts for Pardoe's doctrine of salvation (including his belief in 'Universal Redemption' (Pardoe, a2*v*)) and argues for personal and congregational discipline: the final part (entitled 'Bethania's Walks with God') presents a series of devotional meditations on Christian wisdom.

In Leicester prison, Pardoe also composed *The Mariner's Compass* (apparently dated 6 March 1675), a short paper of divinity which has been described as 'a little piece designed for a frame' ('Baptist church at Leominster', 137). No copy appears extant. However, some of Pardoe's letters, offering spiritual advice to one of his converts (Lawrence Spooner of Curborough, Worcestershire), have survived, being reprinted in early volumes of the *Baptist Magazine* (2, 1810, 56–7, 289–90, 413–14, 503; 3, 1811, 12–13). Pardoe's crucial role in Spooner's conversion is, moreover, recounted in the latter's spiritual autobiography, collected by Samuel James in *An Abstract of the Gracious Dealings of God* (10th edn, 1842, 68–100).

It seems that Pardoe married, the body of his wife having been discovered interred with his own by builders digging in a private garden in Lowesmore, Worcester, in the early nineteenth century. Pardoe was buried there following his death in August 1692, aged sixty-one. The identity of his spouse and the exact place of his burial are no longer known.

William Pardoe the General Baptist preacher must be

distinguished from other contemporaries sharing the same name. A William Pardoe appears in records for the county committee of Worcester (on 26 May 1650 and 13 August 1652), but it is not certain that this person was the General Baptist. Similarly, a William Pardoe ('a clothworker of Christ-Church parish') was arrested in January 1663, possibly in connection with political conspiracy. A Worcestershire Quaker named William Pardoe is also recorded as having been imprisoned and fined during the early 1680s, and must obviously be kept distinct from the General Baptist divine. MICHAEL DAVIES

Sources *DNB* • 'Original letters of the Rev. W. Pardoe', *Baptist Magazine*, 2 (1810), 56–7, 289–90, 413–14, 503; 3 (1811), 12–13 • 'The Baptist church at Leominster', *Baptist Magazine*, 12 (1820), 136–8, 182–4 • J. Chambers, *Biographical illustrations of Worcestershire* (1820), 237–8 • E. Calamy, ed., *An abridgement of Mr. Baxter's history of his life and times, with an account of the ministers, &c., who were ejected after the Restauration of King Charles II*, 2nd edn, 2 vols. (1713), vol. 2, p. 776 • W. T. Whitley, *Baptist association life in Worcestershire, 1655–1926* (1926), 5–6 • W. Pardoe, *Antient Christianity revived: being a description of the doctrine, discipline, and practice, of the little city Bethania* (1688) • J. Noake, *Worcester sects, or, A history of the Roman Catholics & dissenters of Worcester* (1861), 158, 164–5, 168, 233–5, 259, 261 • W. Stevens, 'Dissent in the city of Worcester, 1660–1740', MA diss., U. Birm., 1984, 153–8 • J. Besse, *A collection of the sufferings of the people called Quakers*, 2 (1753), 69, 77, 83–4, 88–9 • S. James, *An abstract of the gracious dealings of God with several eminent Christians*, 10th edn (1842), 68–100 • R. L. Greaves, *Deliver us from evil: the radical underground in Britain, 1660–1663* (1986), 127, 252 (n. 70) • T. Crosby, *The history of the English Baptists, from the Reformation to the beginning of the reign of King George I*, 4 vols. (1738–40), vol. 3, p. 114 • J. Ivimey, *A history of the English Baptists*, 4 vols. (1811–30), vol. 2, pp. 208, 580 • W. T. Whitley, ed., *A Baptist bibliography*, 2 vols. (1916–22) • W. T. Whitley, ed., *Minutes of the general assembly of the General Baptist churches in England, 1: 1654–1728* (1909), xxxiii • M. A. E. Green, ed., *Calendar of the proceedings of the committee for compounding … 1643–1660*, 1, PRO (1889), 236–7 • M. A. E. Green, ed., *Calendar of the proceedings of the committee for advance of money, 1642–1656*, 1, PRO (1888), 106 • *CSP dom.*, 1663–4, 13, 19, 21

Archives DWL, *Antient Christianity revived* • Regent's Park College, Oxford, Angus Library, *Antient Christianity revived*

Pardon, George Frederick [*pseud.* Rawdon Crawley] (**1824–1884**), compiler of books on games and journalist, of Cornish descent, was born in London, the son of Benjamin Pardon, a customs official. After education at a private school, at the age of fifteen he entered the printing office of Stevens and Pardon in Bell Yard, Temple Bar, London. Soon afterwards he contributed articles to the *Old Monthly* and the *Sunbeam*, periodicals edited by John Abraham Heraud. In 1841–2 he sub-edited the *Evening Star*, and became close to most of the radical leaders.

On 3 July 1847 at St Philip's Church, Stepney, London, Pardon married Eliza Rosina Wade (*d.* 1889), daughter of Charles Henry Wade, auctioneer. They had three sons, Charles Frederick, Sydney Herbert, and Edgar Searles, all writers and journalists. The eldest, Charles Frederick Pardon (*d.* 18 April 1890), edited *Wisden's Cricketer's Almanack* (1887–90), and wrote, with A. S. Wilks, *How to Play Solo Whist*.

From 1847 to 1850 Pardon edited the *People's and Howitt's Journal*, and in summer 1850 he joined the staff of John Cassell as editor of the *Working Man's Friend*. In 1851 he initiated the *Illustrated Exhibitor*, a weekly description of the Great Exhibition, which was revived in 1862, and afterwards merged in the *Magazine of Art*. In 1851 he also initiated and edited for Cassell the *Popular Educator* and other Cassell educational publications. In 1854–5 he was editor of the *Family Friend* and the *Home Companion*; and he assisted in launching *Orr's Circle of Sciences*. In 1861–2 he wrote for Routledge a *Guide to the Exhibition* and the *Popular Guide to London*, besides numerous handbooks to chess, draughts, and card games. Under the pseudonyms Captain Crawley and Rawdon Crawley he compiled *The Billiard Book*, *Games for Gentlemen*, and about twenty other volumes—many of them similar to those published under his own name—on games, sports, and pastimes. For the ninth edition of the *Encyclopaedia Britannica* he wrote articles 'Billiards' and 'Bagatelle'. His other works included fiction for adults and for boys. While visiting Canterbury, Pardon died suddenly on 5 August 1884, at the Fleur de Lis Hotel. THOMPSON COOPER, *rev.* ROGER T. STEARN

Sources *The Times* (6 Aug 1884), 8 • Boase, *Mod. Eng. biog.* • private information (1895) • *Men of the time* (1884) • m. cert. • *CGPLA Eng. & Wales* (1884)

Likenesses engraving, repro. in *Illustrated Sporting News*, 5 (1886), 381

Wealth at death £613 3*s.* 11*d.*: probate, 13 Dec 1884, *CGPLA Eng. & Wales*

Pardon, Walter William (**1914–1996**), carpenter and folk-singer, was born on 4 March 1914 at Hall Lane, Knapton, Norfolk, the only child of Thomas Pardon (1877–1957), farmworker, and his wife, Emily, *née* Gee (1874–1953). He was educated at the local elementary school. After an apprenticeship, begun at the age of fourteen, in the neighbouring village of Paston, he became a carpenter, and was so employed (even during his four years' army service in the Second World War) until his retirement at the age of sixty-five. He lived in Knapton throughout his life, except during his army service.

Pardon's life would have been unremarkable but for his emergence in 1975 as an outstanding traditional singer with the issue of a solo unaccompanied long-playing record, *A Proper Sort*. This came about after a cousin, Roger Dixon, persuaded him to record some of his songs on a tape and then forwarded it to a young revival folk-singer, Peter Bellamy. From Bellamy it went to Bill Leader, then running a small record company specializing in traditional song, who immediately recognized the quality of Pardon's singing and the interest of his repertory.

Pardon's style and songs came from various members of his family, and especially from his uncle, Billy Gee (*b.* 1867), who had in turn learned a good deal from his father, Pardon's maternal grandfather, Thomas Gee (*b.* 1827). Billy Gee sang in public houses, but family singing became gradually restricted to occasions such as church and harvest suppers and Christmas parties. When these ended, so did the singing. In Pardon's view, people of his generation turned away from traditional songs: 'They didn't want anything to do with them. Thought they were old-fashioned. They wanted modern things, didn't like the old-fashioned ways' (Yates, disc notes, 3). He set out to keep them alive in his memory by playing through the tunes on a melodeon during his solitary Saturday nights, seated on the stairs of his house, so that the sound did not travel too far. When his repertory came to be fully recorded, some 180 items emerged: traditional ballads, music-hall compositions, Victorian tear-jerkers, bawdy pieces, broadside romances, and songs of the sea and countryside, the latter including anthems from the agricultural workers' union struggles of the early twentieth century: as a boy, Pardon heard the campaigner (later MP) George Edwards speak from the back of a farm wagon.

Such riches led to further LPs, *Our Side of the Baulk* (1977), *A Country Life* (1982), and *Bright Golden Store* (1983). Some of Pardon's songs were transcribed, and printed in anthologies; he appeared in folk clubs and at folk festivals. In 1976 he performed in America with other British singers for the bicentennial celebrations, and in 1983 he received the English Folk Dance and Song Society's coveted gold badge.

As a singer Pardon was quiet, even slightly introspective. He would begin a song in a gentle, thoughtful way, and draw in listeners, almost as if by enchantment. He allied sure musical instinct with excellent diction and first-class memory. A quiet, modest, and intelligent man, he read avidly—Dickens and Hardy for preference. When at the age of seventy-five he decided that his powers were on the wane, he gave up singing in public. He died at the Norfolk and Norwich Hospital, Norwich, on 9 June 1996, and was buried in St Nicholas's churchyard at Swafield, Norfolk, on 17 June. He was unmarried.

Interest in Pardon's singing continued after his death. In 2000 further recordings were issued in the form of a double and a single CD, respectively entitled *Put a Bit of Powder on it, Father* and *A World without Horses*. These confirmed A. L. Lloyd's earlier assessment of Pardon's qualities as 'a fine feeling for the sense of the words, a deep musicality, and that delicate balance of style between the solid traditional and the personal fanciful that is the mark of the true folk singer'. For Lloyd, he was 'the pick of the bunch' (Lloyd, 'Walter Pardon'). ROY PALMER

Sources *The Guardian* (21 June 1996) • W. Pardon, disc notes, *Put a bit of powder on it, father* (2000) [CD-ROM] • A. L. Lloyd, 'Walter Pardon — an appreciation', in W. Pardon, *A country life* (1982) [Topic Records 12TS392, disc notes] • P. Mackenzie and J. Carroll, 'Walter Pardon, 1914–1996', *Folk Music Journal*, 7 (1995–9), 264–5 • M. Yates, '"Stand up ye men of labour": the socio-political songs of Walter Pardon', *Musical Traditions*, 1 (April–Sept 1983), 22–7 • P. Bellamy, 'Walter Pardon', *Folk Review*, 3/10 (Aug 1974), 10–15 • D. Schofield, 'Walter Pardon', *English Dance and Song*, 58/3 (1996), 27 • K. Dallas, 'The Walter Pardon tapes', *Folk News* (Aug 1977), 14–15 • M. Yates, disc notes, in W. Pardon, *A world without horses* (2000) [Topic Records TSCD 514] • d. cert.

Likenesses portrait, repro. in *The Guardian* • portrait, repro. in Pardon, *Put a bit of powder on it, Father* • portrait, repro. in Lloyd, 'Walter Pardon' • portrait, repro. in Mackenzie and Carroll, 'Walter Pardon' • portrait, repro. in Yates, 'Stand up' • portrait, repro. in Bellamy, 'Walter Pardon' • portrait, repro. in Schofield, 'Walter Pardon' • portrait, repro. in Dallas, 'The Walter Pardon tapes' • portrait, repro. in Pardon, *A world without horses*

Wealth at death under £180,000: probate, 5 Aug 1996, *CGPLA Eng. & Wales*

Pare, William (1805–1873), co-operative movement activist, son of John Pare, cabinet-maker and upholsterer, of Birmingham, was born in Birmingham on 11 August 1805. Educated at a grammar school in Birmingham, he was apprenticed to his father, but became a reporter. He subsequently established a business as a tobacco and cigar retailer in the town's New Street. In 1826 he helped to found the Birmingham Mechanics' Institute and became active in the movement for parliamentary reform. He also took part in the movement for the repeal of the Test and Corporation Acts, and for Roman Catholic emancipation. A member of the council of the Birmingham Political Union (established in 1829), he advocated extension of the suffrage, shorter parliaments, and vote by ballot. On 7 August 1832 he drafted and moved in the parish church three resolutions against the payment of church rates. The petition, then adopted and sent by him to Joseph Hume, was the last presented to the unreformed House of Commons; this refusal of the Birmingham vestry to levy a church rate convinced Thomas Arnold and others that the days of the established church were numbered. When the Reformers' Registration Society was established in 1835, Pare became secretary. He was the first registrar of births, marriages, and deaths for Birmingham in 1837. He became a member of the first town council in 1838, having promoted Birmingham's incorporation.

Pare was widely known as an able disciple of Robert Owen. Converted to Owen's teaching by William Thompson's *Inquiry into Principles of Distribution of Wealth*, which he later edited (2nd edn, 1850), Pare was one of the founders in 1828 of the first Birmingham Co-operative Society. From April 1829 to October 1830 he edited the society's newspaper, the *Birmingham Co-operative Herald*, and lectured throughout the north-west in support of co-operation. From May 1830, when the first Co-operative Congress was held at Manchester, until 1838, he constantly attended the congresses as one of the secretaries. From 1832 he advocated the establishment of labour exchanges, and mainly through his efforts, including the distribution of 10,000 leaflets explaining their operation, the one at Birmingham had some success. He was one of the trustees of the property bequeathed for co-operative purposes by Thompson in 1833; and when the heirs-at-law instituted an action in the Irish court of chancery, he went to Ireland to watch over the interests of the trustees, lecturing at various co-operative centres on the way. He was vice-president of the Owenite Association of all Classes of all Nations when the central board was located at Birmingham. He continued an active member of the board until its move to London in November 1840. Forced to resign his registrarship because of his socialist opinions, he left Birmingham in November 1842, when he was presented with a public testimonial. From 1842 to 1844 he was acting governor of the Owenite community at Queenwood, Hampshire. He moved to London in 1844, and as a railway statistician he was frequently employed to prepare reports for presentation to parliament for some of the principal lines projected in Britain, on the continent, in India, Algeria, and elsewhere. He was elected a fellow of the Statistical Society in 1855.

From 1846 to 1865 Pare lived near Dublin, and was engaged in the management of ironworks at Clontarf, Liverpool, and Chepstow. In 1868 he helped to establish a co-operative ironworks in Norway. On Owen's death in 1858 he became his literary executor. He was honorary secretary to the committee by which the Co-operative Congress was called in 1869, and afterwards to the central board, from which position he advocated co-operative banking, insurance, newspapers, and a co-operative college for education. He presided at the Owen centenary in 1871, and gave an address on the life of Owen. Pare hardly changed his social philosophy from his early Owenism, and lectured constantly on equitable commerce and labour exchanges. He was a prolific contributor in the 1860s to Henry Pitman's *The Co-operator*, where he argued that co-operators should return to Owenism and away from store-keeping. His visit in the 1830s to William Thompson's Ralahine community bred a lifelong faith in co-operative agriculture as the solution to the land question.

Pare married Ann Oakes (*d.* 1886) of Market Drayton, Shropshire, and they had one son and two daughters. He died, after a long illness, on 18 June 1873, at the house of his son, Ruby Lodge, Park Hill, Croydon, and he was buried on 23 June in Shirley churchyard, near Croydon.

W. A. S. HEWINS, *rev.* MATTHEW LEE

Sources R. G. Garnett, *William Pare, 1805–1873: co-operator and socialist* (1973) • R. G. Garnett, 'William Pare: a non-Rochdale pioneer', *Co-operative Review*, 38 (1964), 145–9 • J. Saville, 'Pare, William', *DLB*, vol. 1 • J. F. C. Harrison, *Robert Owen and the Owenites in Britain and America: the quest for the new moral world* (1969) • private information (1895)

Archives Co-operative Union, Holyoake House, Manchester, letters to G. J. Holyoake • Co-operative Union, Holyoake House, Manchester, letters to Robert Owen

Wealth at death under £14,000: probate, 19 Aug 1873, *CGPLA Eng. & Wales*

Parent, Étienne (1802–1874), journalist and politician in Canada, was born at Beauport, near Quebec, on 2 May 1802, the eldest of fifteen children, nine boys and six girls, born to Étienne-François Parent, a farmer, and Josephte Clouet. He was descended from Pierre Parant, who had gone to New France in 1634 from Mortagne, Perche, France. Étienne attended primary school in Quebec, then from 1814 to 1819 the college of Nicolet, and finally the seminary in Quebec. For unknown reasons he left the seminary abruptly in 1821 and worked briefly in his uncle's shop in Quebec before returning to the family farm. That same year he was offered and accepted the editorship of *Le Canadien*, whose views were broadly those of the Parti Canadien. He immediately took a leading role in the controversy surrounding the proposed union of the Canadas, and his articles helped bring about the withdrawal of the plan. However, when another paper became the official organ of the Parti Canadien in 1823, Parent's readers deserted him and his paper was forced to close.

Parent turned to law, studying from 1825 to 1829; during the same period he became editor of the French section of *La Gazette de Québec* (1825) and translator and law officer of the assembly of Lower Canada (1827). In 1829 he was called to the bar of Lower Canada. On 30 June that year he married Marie-Mathilde-Henriette (*d.* 1890), the daughter of Gabriel Grenier, a Beauport cooper. They had five daughters and one son.

As dissatisfaction with *La Gazette* grew, Parent revived *Le Canadien* in 1831 and through it became the hub of *patriote* activity and the intellectual inspiration of the party. Lack of money obliged him to seek other work and, in addition to his posts as translator and law officer of the assembly, he became its librarian in 1833. He was industrious in this office, but gave it up in 1835 and shortly afterwards was appointed clerk of the assembly. As the political situation deteriorated he argued through his paper for reform and against abuse, but never supported either the radical ends or the violent means advocated by the more extreme *patriotes*. This led to a rift with Papineau after 1835 and to his denunciation by the more radical *patriote* press. The British authorities, too, regarded him with disfavour, and on 26 December 1838 he was arrested. He remained in prison until April 1839, accused of 'seditious schemings'. Receiving and sending messages concealed inside tarts, he continued to direct his paper from gaol, and on his release gave up his other posts to concentrate solely on journalism. Initially he campaigned actively against the union of the Canadas as a device to force the assimilation of French Canadians. In 1840, for example, he gathered signatures for a petition against the union, but he later resigned himself to it, and determined to help French Canadians get the most they could out of it.

In 1841 Parent was elected to the assembly of the united Canadas as representative of Saguenay county, but the deafness from which he had suffered since his imprisonment hampered him. In October 1842 he relinquished the editorship of *Le Canadien* to become clerk to the executive council. In his new office he moved with the government, which was based in Kingston (until 1843), Montreal (1844–9), Toronto (1849–52, 1855–9), Quebec (1852–5, 1859–66), and finally Ottawa (from 1866). He was appointed assistant secretary of the province of Canada in 1847 and under-secretary of state in the federal government in 1868. He retired in 1872 and, increasingly blind as well as deaf, died on 22 December 1874 at Ottawa. Through his journalism and other writings, his lectures, and his wide personal contacts he was for many years a spokesman and intellectual leader of the French-Canadian people, as well as a staunch defender of their constitutional liberties and of their right to maintain their identity as a separate nation within Canada.

ELIZABETH BAIGENT

Sources *DCB*, vol. 10 • *Étienne Parent, 1802–1874*, ed. P.-E. Gosselin (Montreal and Paris, 1964)

Parepa, Euphrosyne. *See* Rosa, Euphrosyne Parepa- (1836–1874).

Pares, Sir Bernard (1867–1949), historian, was born at Albury, Surrey, on 1 March 1867, the third son and seventh child of John Pares (1833–1915), of independent means, and Katharine (*née* Back). From Harrow School—to which

Sir Bernard Pares (1867–1949), by Bassano, 1935

he remained devoted throughout his life (along with cricket)—Pares took a foundation scholarship at Trinity College, Cambridge (1885), where he read classics, which never held his interest: as a consequence he was placed in the second class of part one of the tripos (1887) and in the third class of part two in 1889. After graduating he spent some years as a schoolmaster. His first visit to Russia was undertaken in 1898, after studying on his private income in France, Italy, and Germany, apparently in rapt pursuit of Napoleon's fields of battle. Finally his interest was sparked by the exotic that Russia represented in contrast to Britain; the challenge presented itself of reconciling two societies that had, for the better part of the previous century, found themselves in contention.

After marriage on 27 August 1901 to Margaret Ellis, daughter of Edward Austin Dixon, dental surgeon, of Colchester, Pares became a university extension lecturer at Cambridge. In 1906 he moved to firmer ground as reader in Russian history at Liverpool. Always very young for his age, at Liverpool he made his mark with his youthful exuberance, including composition of the university song book; he also unselfishly held open house, now graced with a growing family, to the undergraduates. It was typical of his impish humour that the first initials of his children spelt the family name: Peter (who became a diplomatist), Andrew (the army), Richard *Pares (a historian), and two daughters: Elizabeth and Susan.

The year 1906 also saw the formation of the first Russian parliament—the Duma—albeit on a highly restricted franchise. Pares visited St Petersburg, rapidly befriended the more liberal representatives, wrote about it all for the British press, and came away utterly convinced that the constitutional experiment would succeed. This resulted in his first work, *Russia and Reform*, published in 1907, and in active work as secretary for the Anglo-Russian Committee in London, which arranged parliamentary exchanges between the two capitals. The strength of the book derived from his personal contacts; the weakness, here as elsewhere in his historiography, was the almost complete neglect of the economic and social undercurrents ultimately determining events. But Russian studies was still in its infancy and Pares its most dynamic pioneer. He was promoted to a chair in Russian history, language, and literature in the following year, a post he formally held until 1917. He also edited the *Russian Review* from 1912 to 1914. Meanwhile he spent as much time as practicable in Russia, and when war broke out in 1914 he was a natural choice as official observer to the Russian army. This too resulted in a publication—*Day by Day with the Russian Army* (1915)—and decorations: the Russian red cross, the soldier's cross, and the medal of St George, of which he was indubitably proud.

Early in 1917, as the old regime tottered into collapse, Pares was seconded to the staff of Sir George Buchanan, British ambassador in Petrograd. On Pares's view, as later published, 'the dynasty fell by its own insufficiency' (B. Pares, *History of Russia*, 1926, 471). He 'knew all the Ministers' of the provisional government. Exciting possibilities thus opened up for realizing the dreams of 1906. However, as he later confessed: 'It was the most absurd time, for a country inexperienced in liberty, to make its first attempt at democratic government while the world war was still in progress, that is, while the world was ruled by force' (B. Pares, *The New Russia*, 1931, 38–9). The seizure of power by the Bolsheviks and their dismissal of the constitutional assembly early in 1918 (after they lost the elections to that body) spelt disaster for Pares's dreams for the triumph of liberalism in Russia. At the request of the diplomatist Robert Hodgson, Pares went to Siberia, which was dominated by the less-than-liberal Admiral Kolchak, whom the British were backing blindly in a fruitless war against the Bolsheviks. Here Pares entertained the counter-revolutionary forces to lectures twice a week on the duty of Russia to others and the duty of others to Russia. As Hodgson recalled, even though the former was less popular than the latter, Pares none the less held his audience.

Russia, though a cruel disappointment, was, however, too much a part of Pares to be forsaken. In 1919 he was appointed KBE for his service, and from then until 1936 he held the key chair in Russian language, literature, and history at London University. His boundless energies and enthusiasm for things Russian saw him become editor of the *Slavonic Review* and simultaneously director of the fledgeling School of Slavonic and East European Studies at King's College, London, a position which he held until his retirement in 1939. Such distractions, not yet relieved by the emergence of the omnicompetent Dorothy Galton as his indispensable assistant, and the trauma of the changes in Russia inevitably slowed publication. But the stream of thought and work was blocked only briefly: in 1924 he issued an English translation of *Letters of the Tsaritsa to the Tsar*, followed in 1925 by a translation of Griboedov's *Gore ot uma* ('The misfortune of being clever'), and in 1926 by a delightful rendition into English of Krylov's political *Fables*. Although *The Fall of the Russian Monarchy* (1939) was well regarded, his most significant work was the popular *History of Russia* (1926). For all its neglect of diplomacy and economic change, it ran through several editions, and changes from one to the other edition illustrated Pares's shifting state of mind about the country, which for long he was prohibited from visiting, at least until 1935. Having abandoned the expectation that the regime would soon collapse, he resembled many Russians in exile and not a few British liberals in hoping very much that Stalin represented a return to old Russia in its symbolic reacquisition of the title Motherland in 1934, and in its new focus on industrialization—though he was consistently firm in condemning the use of terror by the Bolsheviks. As with others of the left and centre, his concern at the rise of Hitler's Germany helped to divert criticism from the Soviet Union while Litvinov was charting the 'indivisibility of peace' at the League of Nations in Geneva.

The revised edition of Pares's *History of Russia* (1937) thus naïvely saw something positive in the new constitution and in the execution of Zinoviev and Kamenev as spelling an end to advocates of world revolution. The edition of 1944 (which found him lecturing in the United States on behalf of the Ministry of Information) now acknowledged the Webbs' 'fundamental misapprehensions' in lauding the Stalinist regime as a new civilization, but it also evinced signs of Pares's irrepressible Romanticism—for example, in his passing comment: 'to know and love the people of Russia—the two go together almost automatically for an Anglo-Saxon' (*History of Russia*, 4th edn, 1944, 11). The hopes that accompanied these sentiments reawakened by the common struggle against fascism had by no means been extinguished three years later, as the world drifted into the cold war.

The title of Pares's final and autobiographical work, entitled *A Wandering Student* (1948), inadvertently captures two significant features evident throughout his long life: a rootlessness and a youthful spirit which both, perhaps, explained an unhappy emotional life but which also account for the bursts of creativity from which many greatly benefited. Pares died of pneumonia at the Midtown Hospital on East 49th Street in New York on 17 April 1949, having lived in the United States for the previous seven years. His wife survived him.

JONATHAN HASLAM

Sources *DNB* • B. Pares, *My Russian memoirs* (1931) • B. Pares, *A wandering student* (1948) • *Slavonic and East European Review*, 28/70 (Nov 1949) • R. Pares, preface, in B. Pares, *History of Russia* (1959) • *The Times* (18 April 1949) • *New York Times* (18 April 1949) • letters, *The Times* (4 May 1949) • *WWW*, *1941–50* • Burke, *Gen. GB* (1937) • Venn, *Alum. Cant.*

Archives UCL, school of Slavonic and east European studies, papers | JRL, letters to the *Manchester Guardian* • NA Scot., letters and memoranda to Philip Kerr • NL Wales, letters to John Glyn Davies

Likenesses A. Lipczinski, group portrait, oils, 1915 (with staff), U. Lpool, faculty of arts • W. Stoneman, photograph, 1920, NPG • Bassano, photograph, 1935, NPG [*see illus.*] • P. Vincze, bronze plaque, *c.*1942, UCL, school of Slavonic and east European studies

Wealth at death £10,225 11*s.* 2*d.*: probate, 21 March 1950, *CGPLA Eng. & Wales*

Pares, Richard (1902–1958), historian, was born on 25 August 1902 in Colchester, Essex, the eldest in the family of three sons and two daughters of Sir Bernard *Pares (1867–1949), historian, and his wife, Margaret Ellis, daughter of Edward Austin Dixon, dental surgeon, of Colchester. After winning scholarships at Winchester College and at Balliol College, Oxford, he took a first class in *literae humaniores* in 1924 and was elected to a fellowship of All Souls which he held until 1945. A one-year stint as assistant lecturer at University College, London, was followed in 1928 by a year of research in the United States and the West Indies, financed by a Laura Spelman Rockefeller memorial studentship.

In 1929 Pares was appointed lecturer at New College, Oxford. In 1937 he married Janet Lindsay, daughter of F. Maurice *Powicke (1879–1963), historian. They had four daughters. War interrupted the early stages of a brilliant academic career: from 1940 to 1945 Pares served with distinction as an administrative-class civil servant in the Board of Trade, being appointed CBE in 1945. He was joint editor of the *English Historical Review* from 1939 to 1958; professor of history in the University of Edinburgh from 1945 until his resignation on health grounds in 1954; and in 1951–2 Ford's lecturer in Oxford, delivering the lectures which became probably the most widely known of his books, *King George III and the Politicians* (1953). He was elected FBA in 1948.

Pares published extensively in a series of monographs illuminating various aspects of his chosen field, the role of the West Indies in the development of the British empire, and the determination of British international policy during the eighteenth century: his pioneering investigations ranged widely over questions of war and trade and international law. From the start his scholarship, like his wartime work in the civil service, was characterized by indefatigable industry, commanding intellectual powers, personal detachment, and complete integrity. His first book, *War and Trade in the West Indies, 1739–1763* (1936), a *tour de force* based on immense research, was infused throughout by his pursuit of what he once declared to be his prime interest in history—'to find out how things worked'. In these earlier years he eschewed biography as a path to understanding. But he had revised his view by the time he wrote *A West-India Fortune* (1950): there, and in *King George III and the Politicians*, the two approaches were fruitfully combined. In the last-named work he opened up lines of interpretation which, even if somewhat modified since, set firm foundations on which other scholars might build: the exuberant vigour and almost Niagara-like outpouring of scholarship gave it a memorable quality. Much of his later work, achieved under the shadow of inexorably crippling and ultimately fatal illness, which he faced

Richard Pares (1902–1958), by unknown photographer

with the utmost fortitude, was latterly facilitated by the research fellowship conferred on him by All Souls in 1954. Pares died in the Churchill Hospital, Oxford, on 3 May 1958; his wife survived him. He was considered to be among the outstanding British historians of his time.

IAN CHRISTIE, *rev.*

Sources *The Times* (5 May 1958) • L. S. Sutherland, Introduction, in R. Pares, *The historian's business, and other essays*, ed. R. A. Humphreys and E. Humphreys (1961) • A. L. Rowse, 'Richard Pares, 1902–1958', *PBA*, 48 (1962), 345–56 • I. Berlin, *Personal impressions* (1981), 91–5 • personal knowledge (1993) • *CGPLA Eng. & Wales* (1958)
Archives NL Scot., corresp., lecture notes, and papers | NL Wales, corresp. with Goronwy Edwards
Likenesses photograph, British Academy, London [*see illus.*]
Wealth at death £6103 19*s.* 6*d.*: probate, 29 July 1958, *CGPLA Eng. & Wales*

Parfitt, Edward (1820–1893), gardener and natural historian, born at East Tuddenham, Norfolk, on 17 October 1820, was the son of Edward Parfitt (1800–1875), head gardener to Lord Hastings, and his wife, Violet Howlet (1800–1836). He was educated at East Tuddenham and Honingham, and studied gardening under his father. He worked for some years as a gardener to Anthony Gwyn of Sennow Lodge, Norfolk (and subsequently to John Hay Hill of Gressinghall House, near East Dereham). Some time in or before 1848, he went on a voyage for scientific purposes. He was wrecked near the Cape of Good Hope, and an enforced stay in the Cape Colony intensified his taste for botany and entomology. He returned to England in 1848, and became gardener to John Milford at Coaver House, Exeter. On 23 December 1850, at Exeter, he married Mary (Elizabeth?), the eldest daughter of Thomas and Elizabeth Cooper of Exeter, and widow of James Sanders.

In 1859 Parfitt was appointed curator to the Archaeological and Natural History Society of Somerset, a post which on 26 January 1861 he exchanged for that of librarian to the Devon and Exeter Institute and Library at Exeter. He died at his home in the close, Exeter, on 15 January 1893, leaving a manuscript work on the fungi of Devon, in twelve volumes, illustrated by 1530 plates, drawn and painted by himself. He had also contributed numerous papers to the *Transactions of the Devonshire Association for the Advancement of Science*, *Annals and Magazine of Natural History*, *Entomological Magazine*, *Naturalist*, and *Transactions of the Royal Microscopical Society*.

A. F. POLLARD, *rev.* ALEXANDER GOLDBLOOM

Sources Desmond, *Botanists*, rev. edn, 539 • G. C. Boase, *Collectanea Cornubiensia: a collection of biographical and topographical notes relating to the county of Cornwall* (1890), 651 • *Natural Science*, 2 (1893), 320
Archives Oxf. U. Mus. NH, notes and MSS relating to Devon fauna
Wealth at death £1697 18*s.* 11*d.*: probate, 4 Feb 1893, *CGPLA Eng. & Wales*

Parfre, Jhon (*fl.* 1512), writer, may have some claim to be described as the author of a medieval biblical play entitled *Candlemas Day, or, The Killing of the Children*. The play, which was occasionally quoted as 'Parfre's Candlemas day', was written in English verse in the fifteenth century, and was probably composed in East Anglia, to judge from its dialect. It deals mainly with Herod and the massacre of the innocents. From the unique manuscript which is in the Bodleian Library, it was printed for the first time in 1773 in Thomas Hawkins's *Origin of the English Drama*. The definitive modern edition was published by the Early English Text Society in 1982.

At the end of the manuscript appear the words 'Jhon Parfre ded wryte thys booke anno d'ni mill'mo CCCCCXIJ', in a hand different from that of the scribe of the play. Whoever wrote this may have intended to convey that either a John Parfrey was the author of the play, or that a person of that name had compiled the collection of texts in which the Candlemas play is found. Parfrey is a name that was widespread in late medieval Norfolk and Suffolk, and none of the various John Parfreys mentioned in local records is otherwise known to have been connected with the drama.

RICHARD BEADLE

Sources Bodl. Oxf., MS Digby 133 • D. C. Baker, J. L. Murphy, and L. B. Hall, eds., *The late medieval religious plays of Bodleian MSS Digby 133 and E Museo 160*, EETS, 283 (1982), lv–lvi • T. Sharpe, ed., *Ancient mysteries from the Digby manuscripts* (1835)

Pargeter, Edith Mary [*pseud.* Ellis Peters] (1913–1995), novelist and translator, was born on 28 September 1913 in the Shropshire hamlet of Horsehay, the youngest of three children of Edmund Valentine Pargeter (*d.* 1940), head clerk at Horsehay ironworks, and his wife, Edith, *née* Hordley (*d.* 1954). The household also included Edith's Welsh maternal grandmother, Emma Ellis. While the Pargeters had little money, living in a two-bedroom cottage with no gas, water, or electricity, the house was, as Edith noted 'full of books and music' (Peters and Morgan, 10). Edith's mother had antiquarian and artistic interests, and introduced her children at an early age to the historical and natural features of the surrounding countryside. For Edith this was the beginning of her notable engagement with the Welsh-English borderland which would inform her fiction so deeply. Her attachment to Shropshire was permanent: she would live within 3 miles of her birthplace throughout her life.

Education and early life Edith attended the local Church of England elementary school at Dawley, a mile away from Horsehay, and then the Coalbrooke County High School for Girls as a scholarship pupil. Particularly interested in English, Latin, and history, she successfully gained her Oxford school certificate and left school in 1930 determined to become a writer. From 1933 to 1940 she lived at home and worked at a chemist's shop in Dawley, where she accumulated a knowledge of drugs and poisons which would feature later in her detective fiction.

Pargeter's evenings were spent writing. She had every reason to be encouraged in her apprenticeship for her profession as a writer. In 1936 her stories appeared in *Good Housekeeping* magazine and she sent her first book manuscript to the publisher William Heinemann who, while rejecting it, asked to see any further work she might produce. Her first novel, *Hortensius, Friend of Nero*, was published by Lovat Dickson in the same year and, while this did not make a great impact, *The City Lies Four-Square* (1939), published by Heinemann, established her reputation. By 1939 she had published six novels, including two crime novels published under the pseudonym of Jolyon Carr, and one romance, under the pen-name of Peter Benedict.

The war and after During the Second World War Pargeter continued to write prolifically while she served in the Women's Royal Naval Service (WRNS) from 1940 to 1945. Her first posting, to Devonport in Plymouth where she worked for the western approaches command, involved tracking allied convoy routes across the Atlantic. This was her first extended period away from home. The command then moved to Liverpool, where Edith spent the rest of the war, working as a teleprinter operator in the signals office. For her 'meritorious service', she was presented with the British Empire Medal by George VI on VE-day, 8 May 1944, in London where she joined the vast crowds celebrating the end of the conflict. She was demobilized in July 1944, leaving the WRNS with the rank of petty officer. Pargeter published *The Victim Needs a Nurse* as John Redfern in 1940, and her first best-seller, *She Goes to War*, based on her war service, in 1942. The war, she believed, proved the case for the equality of men and women, and she hoped that work and pay in the post-war period would recognize this principle. In the trilogy comprising *Lame Crusade* (1945), *Reluctant Odyssey* (1946), and *Warfare Accomplished* (1947) Pargeter again put her time in the service to use and chronicled the progress of a young private with a much-praised eye for detail.

Pargeter's father died in 1940 and after the war Edith returned to Shropshire to live with her mother, a happy arrangement which continued until her mother's death in 1954. At this time Edith and her brother Ellis, neither of whom ever married, jointly bought Parkville, an eighteenth-century house in Madeley, which they shared for the next thirty-five years. The siblings were very close and shared many interests, including a devotion to adult education. Both were members of the Workers' Education Association and helped to found the short-lived Shropshire Adult College at Attingham Hall near Shrewsbury.

The Pargeters' passion for education also led them to attend an international summer school in Czechoslovakia in 1947. This was an important moment for Edith. She had felt deeply humiliated by Neville Chamberlain's strategy of appeasement in the Munich agreement of 1938, which allowed Germany to annex part of Czechoslovakia. The 1947 Czech summer school not only marked the beginning of friendships with many Czech readers and writers, it also sparked a permanent interest in their language. Pargeter taught herself Czech and put her expertise to work by translating major Czech poetry and prose into English. After 1947 Edith and her brother went to Czechoslovakia every year they could.

Ellis Peters Following her return to Shropshire after the war Pargeter lived by her writing. In the 1940s, publishing with Heinemann, she produced mainly historical and romantic novels, many of which drew on her own experiences, but she returned to crime fiction in 1951 with *Fallen into the Pit*, which was the first of her successful series of novels to feature Inspector George Felse. *Death Mask* (1959) was the first crime novel Pargeter published under the pseudonym of Ellis Peters, a name she constructed from her brother's and grandmother's name, Ellis, and from Petra, the name of the daughter of her close Czech friends whom she loved for forty years 'without in the least wanting to get married' (*The Times*). Ellis Peters became Pargeter's most successful literary incarnation and the name by which she is best known as a writer.

In the 1960s and 1970s Pargeter, as Peters, produced seventeen crime novels, most of them featuring Felse, first with the publishing house of Collins and then with Macmillan. During the same period she continued to publish historical and romantic fiction for Heinemann and later Macmillan, which included the *Heaven Tree* trilogy of novels in the early 1960s. She always regarded this trio of books, *The Heaven Tree* (1960), *The Green Branch* (1962), and *The Scarlet Seed* (1963), set in the twelfth century, as her finest work. Her non-crime fiction, notable for its historical depth and accuracy, and often drawing skilfully on the history of Shropshire and the Welsh borders, was widely admired. However, she attracted the greatest accolades for her crime writing. To her enormous pleasure, she was awarded the Edgar Allan Poe award by the Mystery Writers of America in 1963 for *Death and the Joyful Woman* (1962) which featured Inspector Felse.

In 1968 Pargeter's sixteen volumes of translations of Czech poetry and prose by distinguished authors, such as Jan Neruda, were gratefully recognized by the Czechoslovak Society for International Relations with the award of their gold medal and ribbon at the Prague Writers' Club in the spring. A period of the Czech communist government restrictions in the early 1950s had prevented her visits to Czechoslovakia, but after 1956 she and her brother returned each year for long summer holidays. They made many friends and delighted in the increasing liberalization of the country in the 1960s. A week after Pargeter returned home to England after her Czech summer holiday in 1968, however, Soviet tanks moved into the country. By 1969 the Union of Czechoslovak Writers which had honoured her was outlawed and censorship imposed. Pargeter published no more translations from Czech after 1970, though she maintained her Czech friendships and her compassionate interest in developments in the country. Her Prague connections also led to her invitation to travel in India in 1961, an experience which stood behind her two novels set in the subcontinent: *Mourning Raga* (1969) and *Death to the Landlords!* (1972).

Brother Cadfael Successful as Pargeter's writing career had been for nearly five decades, it was lifted to new heights with the publication in 1977 of her first Brother Cadfael crime novel, *A Morbid Taste for Bones*. With Cadfael, a former crusader and herbalist turned Benedictine monk at Shrewsbury Abbey in the twelfth century, Pargeter created one of the most memorable and greatly loved of fictional detectives. Although *A Morbid Taste for Bones* was not initially intended to launch a series, Pargeter was so intrigued by the character that she wrote twenty further Cadfael novels. In these books she helped to develop the highly popular subgenre of historical detective fiction, which only attracted wholehearted publishers' support after the international success of Umberto Eco's post-modern medieval detective novel *The Name of the Rose* (1981). Slightly annoyed by the comparison, Pargeter pointed out that by the time Eco's best-seller appeared, she had already published seven Cadfael novels.

Nevertheless, the fashion for medieval mysteries drew a large and faithful international readership to Pargeter's work. Cadfael attracted attention and affection not only for the character but for his author. An Ellis Peters Appreciation Society was founded in the United States in 1989, and there are official leaflets for Cadfael walks in Shrewsbury. Cadfael needlework kits, goblets, pot-pourri, notepaper, and mystery weekends, over which Pargeter had right of veto during her life, have all proved popular. A variety of rose called the 'Cadfael' was introduced at the Chelsea Flower Show in 1990.

Pargeter's Cadfael novels were not only a popular success. Producing them, she said, gave her the greatest pleasure of her writing life. In addition, her 'medieval whodunnits' attracted high praise and recognition. In 1981 she was honoured by her fellow crime writers in Britain by the award of the Crime Writers' Association's silver dagger for *Monk's Hood* (1980), and in 1993 by the award of the Cartier diamond dagger for her lifetime's achievement in crime writing, an accolade shared since its inception in 1986 with only a small group of other writers such as Eric Ambler, P. D. James, Ruth Rendell, and John le Carré. The latter award was presented in a ceremony in the House of Lords. Pargeter was further honoured with an OBE in 1994 and an honorary MA from Birmingham University.

Later life and reputation Pargeter's latter years, after her beloved brother's death in 1984, and in spite of increasing frailty, were contented ones. She moved from the house she shared with her brother to a convenient modern house next door to her cousins Mavis and Roy Morgan. Pargeter and Roy Morgan, a retired architect with interests in photography, collaborated on two illustrated volumes on the local area: *Shropshire* (1992) and *Strongholds and Sanctuaries* (1993). Her first book-signing tour took place in 1991, when she visited five cities in the United States. During the 1990s, in old age but at the height of her fame, Pargeter took pleasure in the broadcasting of several of her novels on BBC Radio 4 in 1991 and 1993, and was pleased with the filming of Cadfael mysteries by Central TV on a set she visited near Budapest in Hungary. Pargeter produced nearly eighty books as well as many short stories and articles during her life and was working on a Cadfael novel at her death.

Pargeter, who had her right leg amputated at the knee at the age of eighty-two, died a few weeks after a stroke at home at Troya, 3 Lee Dingle, Madeley, Shropshire, on 14 October 1995. Her funeral was held at the Coalbrookdale church and her body was cremated at the Emstry crematorium near Shrewsbury, where her ashes were scattered in the garden. Her family and friends held a further memorial service to celebrate her life at Shrewsbury Abbey on 18 February 1996. A window in the abbey, depicting St Benedict, is dedicated to her.

Pargeter was a private, humane, modest, loyal, intelligent, and scholarly woman. A Christian believer but not a regular churchgoer, a woman of generous left-wing convictions who declared herself uninterested in common party politics, she had a great affection for every aspect of her locality, for her family and friends, and for her terriers. As a writer she was a realist, immersed in history and attuned to moral questions. She said that she did not find 'vice and evil more interesting than virtue', and she hoped her books would 'go some way to defy that too-easily accepted judgment' ('Pargeter, Edith Mary', 2279). 'The thriller', she insisted:

> must be a morality. If it strays from the side of the angels … takes pleasure in evil, that is the unforgiveable sin … It is probably true that I am not very good at villains. The good interest me so much more. (Gottschalk, 848)

This serious ethical intent always informed Pargeter's pioneering work in medieval historical crime fiction, whose popularity she did so much to consolidate. In 1999 the Crime Writers' Association honoured her further with the institution and award of its first annual Ellis Peters historical dagger, sponsored by Pargeter's estate, for the best novel in the genre in which she so excelled.

KATE FULLBROOK

Sources M. Lewis, *Edith Pargeter: Ellis Peters* (1994) · *The Times* (16 Oct 1995) · *The Independent* (16 Oct 1995) · 'Pargeter, Edith Mary', *Major twentieth-century writers*, ed. B. Ryan, 3 (1991), 2277–80 · P. Altner, 'Pargeter, Edith (Mary)', *Twentieth-century romance and historical writers*, ed. L. Henderson, 2nd edn (1990), 506–8 · J. Gottschalk, 'Peters, Ellis', *Twentieth-century crime and mystery writers*, ed.

J. M. Reilly, 2nd edn (1985), 707–10 · S. Feder, 'Peters, Ellis', *Twentieth-century crime and mystery writers*, ed. L. Henderson, 3rd edn (1991), 846–9 · D. Wynter, 'The green detective', *The Guardian* (22 Nov 1989) · S. Pile, 'Murder is her habit', *Telegraph Magazine* (12 Oct 1991) · S. B. Conroy, 'The prime crimes of Ellis Peters', *Washington Post* (28 Sept 1991) · R. Herbert, 'Ellis Peters', *Publishers' Weekly* (9 Aug 1991) · A. M. Coreeley, 'Ellis Peters: another Umberto Eco?', *Armchair Detective*, 18/3 (1985) · www.twbooks.co.uk [Crime Writers' Association website], 24 June 2000 · E. Peters and R. Morgan, *Ellis Peters' Shropshire* (1992) · *CGPLA Eng. & Wales* (1996) · d. cert.

Likenesses photograph, repro. in *The Times* · photograph, repro. in *The Independent*

Wealth at death £7,960,790: probate, 18 April 1996, *CGPLA Eng. & Wales*

Paris, Sir Archibald (1861–1937), Royal Marine officer, was born at Lansdown, Bath, on 9 November 1861, the youngest son of the Revd Archibald Paris (1816–1861), of Ludgvan, Cornwall, and his wife, Caroline, second daughter of the Revd Sir Henry Delves Broughton, eighth baronet. Having been educated at Eton College and the Royal Naval College, Greenwich, he joined the Royal Marine Artillery in 1879. On 3 September 1885 he married Lilian Jean (*b.* 1861/2), youngest daughter of Colonel Henry Melvill of the 7th Bengal cavalry.

Paris graduated from the Staff College, Camberley, in 1888, and, after a period afloat and five years as adjutant of the 1st Antrim artillery militia (1894–9), he was appointed to serve in the Second South African War in South Africa in 1900. Initially he was employed in training field batteries in Rhodesia, and he finally commanded, under Lord Methuen, the 'Kimberley column', a mixed force, mostly mounted irregulars, which was attacked and forced to surrender near Tweebosch in March 1902 owing to the flight of most of the mounted troops. Paris was exonerated from blame and later commended for organizing the gallant resistance. Thrice mentioned in dispatches, he was promoted brevet lieutenant-colonel in June 1902 for distinguished service in the field. From 1903 to 1906 he was chief instructor in military history and tactics at the Royal Military Academy, Woolwich.

In September 1914 Paris relieved Sir G. G. Aston in command of the Royal Marine brigade, and in October he was promoted temporary major-general and appointed to command the Royal Naval division, which he led with distinction at Antwerp, throughout the Gallipoli campaign, and in France. Paris had limited opportunities to display his abilities as a divisional commander in action: at Antwerp his forces were dispersed and communications with them were difficult, in many cases non-existent; on Gallipoli the Royal Naval division only came together as an entity under his command three weeks after the initial landings. Further severe casualties in their early actions and lack of reinforcements so depleted the division that, for the latter stages of the campaign, they were used primarily for trench-holding duties. He was severely wounded in October 1916, with the eventual loss of a leg, shortly before his division took part in its first major action in France. His greatest contribution to the RND was in establishing the organization and *esprit de corps* to enable it to develop into an efficient fighting formation—one which eventually came to be regarded as an élite unit of the British expeditionary force. In addition Paris was instrumental in ensuring the continued existence of the division and the retention of its peculiarly naval identity, in particular after the Dardanelles campaign, when it looked certain that the RND would be disbanded or converted into a 'normal' army unit. In June 1917 he was placed on the retired list as 'unfit for further service owing to wounds'.

Paris was five times mentioned in dispatches, and promoted major-general in 1915. He was appointed CB in 1907 and KCB in 1916. He also received many foreign decorations. He was honorary colonel commandant of the Portsmouth division, Royal Marines (1923–33), and was awarded a good-service pension in 1925.

Tall and spare, with a cast in one eye caused by an accident, Paris had a thorough grasp of his profession; he was popular with his men, and a highly regarded commander. His only son, Brigadier Archibald Charles Melvill, was killed on active service in Malaya in 1942. Archibald Paris died at Chatelard, Montreux, Switzerland, on 30 October 1937, and was survived by his wife.

R. C. Temple, *rev.* C. L. W. Page

Sources J. F. Maurice and M. H. Grant, eds., *History of the war in South Africa, 1899–1902*, 4 (1910) · C. Field, *Britain's sea soldiers: a history of the royal marines and their predecessors*, 2 vols. (1924) · H. E. Blumberg, *Britain's sea soldiers: a record of the royal marines during the war, 1914–1919* (1927) · E. Fraser and L. G. Carr-Laughton, *The royal marine artillery, 1804–1923*, 2 vols. (1930) · D. Bittner, *A ghost of a general and the royal marine officer corps of 1914* (1984) · *The Royal Navy list, or, Who's who in the navy* (1917); repr. as *The naval who's who, 1917* (1981) · D. Jerrold, *The royal naval division* (1923) · L. Sellers, *Hood battalion* (1993) · m. cert. · Venn, *Alum. Cant.* · *CGPLA Eng. & Wales* (1937) · C. Page, *Command in the royal naval division* (1999)

Archives IWM, letters

Likenesses W. Stoneman, photograph, 1917, NPG · H. D. Smith, oils, 1920, Royal Marines Museum, Eastney barracks, Southsea, Hampshire · F. A. Swaine, photograph, repro. in Jerrold, *The Royal Naval division*

Wealth at death £12,925 15*s.* 9*d.*: probate, 9 Dec 1937, *CGPLA Eng. & Wales*

Paris, John Ayrton (*bap.* 1785, *d.* 1856), physician and author, was baptized on 7 August 1785 at St Benedict's, Cambridge. He was the son of Thomas Paris and his wife, Elizabeth (1762/3–1847), eldest daughter of Edward Ayrton, doctor of music at Trinity College, Cambridge. Paris was well educated, being taught first by Mr Barker of Trinity Hall, Cambridge, and later by Dr Curteis at the grammar school, Linton, Cambridgeshire. He then received private tuition from Dr Bradley, a physician of the Westminster Hospital in London, before matriculating at Cambridge in 1803. He gained a Tancred studentship at Gonville and Caius College, Cambridge, and graduated as a bachelor of medicine in 1808. At some time during his studentship he was also at Edinburgh. In 1808 he was elected a physician at the Westminster Hospital, where his duties included lecturing in pharmaceutical medicine. He married Mary Catherine (*d.* 1855), daughter of Francis Noble of Fordham Abbey, on 11 December 1809, and the couple had one son.

Seeking further experience, in July 1813 Paris accepted

an appointment as physician to the Penzance Dispensary on the recommendation of W. G. Maton of the Westminster Hospital. Before leaving to take up his post in Cornwall (in September 1813) he was created a doctor of medicine at Cambridge on 6 July. In Penzance, Paris played a leading role in founding a geological society; he was elected its first secretary, a post to which he devoted much time and enthusiasm. He remained in Penzance until 1817, when he returned to London to set up in practice in Dover Street, having found that the income from his private practice in Cornwall was insufficient for his needs, for the dispensary post had been unpaid. His patients in London included some families from Cornwall whom he had come to know while working in the county. He also began a series of lectures in materia medica at Great Windmill Street school of medicine, which attracted a considerable class, and between 1819 and 1826 he gave lectures on the same subject for the Royal College of Physicians. Paris had become a member of the Linnean Society in 1810, and after returning to London joined the Royal Institution, where he attended lectures by Sir Humphry Davy. He became president of the Royal College of Physicians in 1844 and served in this role until his death.

Paris was noted for his many books, most of them on medical subjects. The first edition of his *Pharmacologia on the History of Medical Substances* was published in 1812, and the final and ninth edition in 1843. MacMichael and Munk suggest that he made over £5000 profit from this book alone. Other books included *Medical Jurisprudence* (1823), co-authored with J. S. M. Fonblanque, and *A Treatise on Diet* (1826). His interests ranged beyond medicine, and he was particularly noted for his chemistry, having studied with William Farish at Cambridge and T. C. Hope in Edinburgh. He gave several lectures on chemistry to the Royal Geological Society of Cornwall, including one on a new method of detecting the presence of arsenic in poisoning cases, and in 1825 published his *Elements of Medical Chemistry*.

Geology was also among Paris's interests, for he had followed this subject at Cambridge under E. D. Clarke, and at Edinburgh with John Playfair, and had used his knowledge while involved with the Royal Geological Society of Cornwall. After leaving Penzance he ceased from active participation in this discipline. His university tutors had encouraged him to adhere to a modified version of the Wernerian system of geology, as made clear by the details on a 'geological pillar', devised by him and presented to the Royal Geological Society of Cornwall before he left Penzance, and in his description of an imaginary geological temple, dedicated to Werner and described in *Philosophy in Sport Made Science in Earnest* (1827), a book of science for children. In the same book he described a simple toy, the thaumatrope, which could demonstrate the compound nature of white light and was marketed to make him a large profit. Paris also wrote a number of biographies; these included a life of his mentor, W. G. Maton, and most controversially *The Life of Sir Humphry Davy* (1831), which prompted John Davy to write a revised version of the life of his elder brother. While in Penzance, Paris had written, under the pseudonym 'A Physician', *A Guide to the Mount's Bay* (1816) which included much information on the geology of the Land's End peninsula.

As a medical man Paris became concerned when he learned of the number of deaths and serious injuries which occurred in accidents with explosives in the mines of Cornwall. He actively promoted the use of a safety tamping bar, devised by a member of the Royal Geological Society of Cornwall, which would prevent accidental explosions of gunpowder, and wrote a pamphlet, *On the Accidents which Occur in the Mines of Cornwall* (1815), describing the injuries he had seen and the methods of preventing them. He was later particularly noted for the care with which he prescribed for his patients.

In his later years Paris endured ill health from a malignant disease of the bladder and died 'under circumstances of lengthened and excruciating suffering' as described in the annual report of the Royal Geological Society of Cornwall for 1857. His death took place at his home, 27 Dover Street, Piccadilly, London, on 24 December 1856. He was buried at Brookwood cemetery, Woking.

DENISE CROOK

Sources Munk, *Roll* • W. MacMichael, *The gold-headed cane*, 3rd edn, ed. W. Munk (1884) • Boase & Courtney, *Bibl. Corn.*, vol. 3 • *Annual report of the Royal Geological Society of Cornwall* (1857), 5–8 • D. A. Crook, 'The early history of the Royal Geological Society of Cornwall: 1814–1850', PhD diss., Open University, 1990 • Venn, *Alum. Cant.* • d. cert.

Archives Archives of the Royal Geological Society of Cornwall • Cornwall Geological Museum, Penzance, Cornwall, geological pillar, presented to the Royal Geological Society of Cornwall by Paris in 1817, and bearing the inscription: *HOC STUDIUM GEOLOGICUM J A Paris invenit ac posuit MDCCCXVI* • RCP Lond., author's annotated copy of 'A memoir on the physiology of the egg'

Likenesses C. Skottowe, oils, *c.*1838, RCP Lond. • Bellin, engraving (after portrait by Skottowe), RCP Lond. • W. Drummond, lithograph (after E. U. Eddis), BM, NPG; repro. in *Athenaeum portraits* (1836) • attrib. I. Jackson, plaster bust, RCP Lond. • portrait, Royal Institution of Great Britain, London • portrait, Royal Geological Society of Cornwall

Paris, Matthew (*c.*1200–1259), historian, Benedictine monk, and polymath, reveals very little about his own life and personal circumstances. This is disappointing as well as ironical, considering his compulsive concern to collect and record information relating to the events and affairs of his own time, and his acute inquisitiveness concerning times past. Even his parentage, nationality, and social origins remain uncertain.

The monk of St Albans His surname, which Matthew Paris usually wrote as Parisiensis, occasionally as de Parisius, might suggest French origins, but Parisiensis was by no means an uncommon patronymic in thirteenth-century England, and there is nothing in his many works, or elsewhere, to indicate that he was anything other than English, especially in view of his characteristically Anglocentric attitude towards the events of his day. Nevertheless, it is quite possible that he studied in the schools of Paris early on in his career. If so, this might account for his surname, his knowledge of French sources for many of his chronicle illustrations, his keen interest in the affairs of the University of Paris and of French affairs generally, and

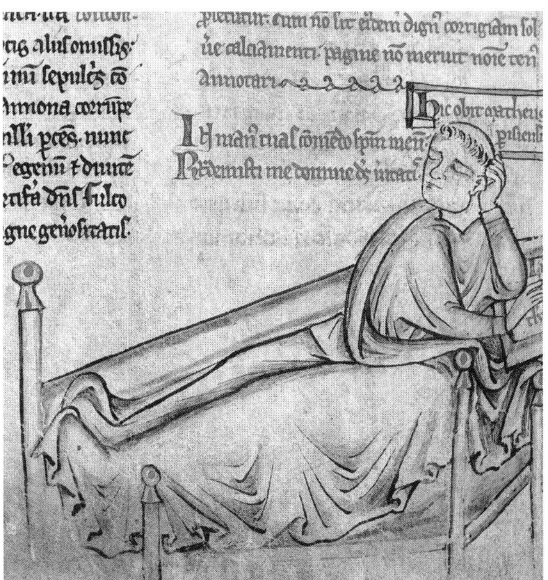

Matthew Paris (*c.*1200–1259), manuscript drawing

the number of French correspondents and contacts revealed in his works. But Paris himself says only that he became a monk of St Albans, Hertfordshire, on St Agnes's day (21 January) 1217, which suggests that he was born *c.*1200. The house remained the focus of his life and activities until his death, almost certainly in late May or June 1259. He describes very little about that life, but plainly he was soon attached to the scriptorium, where he worked in some undefined capacity with the first great historian of the abbey, Roger of Wendover, many of whose attitudes profoundly informed those of Paris himself. Upon his mentor's death in 1236 Paris took up the mantle, be it as official historiographer of the house or not, but necessarily with the abbot's licence, and devoted himself largely to his various writings until his own death.

Despite his seclusion, Matthew Paris was by no means isolated from the world. He had access to papal bulls, imperial *acta*, royal writs and charters, news reports and correspondence from a wide range of sources, English and continental, secular and ecclesiastical; his closest informants, many of whom knew him personally, included Richard, earl of Cornwall (*d.* 1272), a number of Henry III's councillors and *curiales*, and a variety of clerics and nobles, apart from the king himself. Some of these are known to have visited St Albans in this period, a direct and personal means for the transmission of documentary material, as well as gossip and news, which Paris then worked upon for inclusion in his various historical works. Indeed, there are a number of clear indications that it became known to many who mattered that Paris was compiling a vast, universal, contemporary history, the *Chronica majora*, and they fed his voracious appetite for information, some naturally hoping that he would repay his debt in appropriate fashion by means of his pen. This expectation certainly lies behind his presence at Westminster for the celebration of the feast of St Edward the Confessor on 13 October 1247, when Henry III presented to his beloved abbey his recent, precious, acquisition of a vase of the holy blood. According to Paris, Henry required him to write an accurate and full account of what had transpired for the enlightenment of posterity. He then invited Paris and his companions to dinner. The event was supremely worthy of record in Henry's mind, and Paris surely attended the ceremony, doubtless at royal command, precisely because the king was already well aware of his abilities as a historical writer and wished to press them into service.

The two men certainly came to know each other well. Henry is known to have visited St Albans on at least nine occasions between 1220 and 1259, and these provided opportunities for discussion between monarch and monk in which Paris, or so he would have his readers believe, was frank in his views. In 1250, for example, he remonstrated with Henry for granting rights contrary to the privileges of St Albans, and for allowing others to do the same. During what was probably their last meeting, in March 1257, the two appear to have spent much time together, at table and in the king's private chamber, discussing current affairs, notably the election of Richard of Cornwall as king of the Romans, and Paris records that he took the opportunity to argue with the king on behalf of the masters of the University of Oxford in their dispute with the bishop of Lincoln. Paris was no sycophant. Indeed, he was highly opinionated, and Henry, in particular among his various informants, would not have been happy if he ever knew of the charges that Paris brought against him on various grounds, even though some were later tempered, toned down, or erased.

Travels in England and abroad Paris's monastic routine was interrupted on other occasions, when he travelled beyond St Albans. He records that he attended the king at Winchester in July 1251, and he was most probably present at the dedication of the abbey church of Hailes, Gloucestershire, in November; the founder, Richard of Cornwall, urged him to give a correct account of the event in his chronicle. At Christmas that year he was at York, for the marriage of Henry III's daughter Margaret to Alexander III of Scotland. But the detail and vividness of his descriptions of some other events, along with the long list of contacts and informants that he acknowledges, suggest strongly that he was more frequently absent from St Albans, meeting members of the English social élite and attending ceremonial gatherings of the court, than he himself reveals. He was undoubtedly well known to many of the great and the good and respected by them. A precious confirmation of some of his contacts, and the relationships engendered, is provided by the list of the various gifts that he had received and then left to his house, including silks and copes from Henry III, Eleanor of Provence, and Hákon IV, king of Norway.

King Hákon had a part to play in Paris's greatest adventure when, in 1248, he was sent by Pope Innocent IV to reform the monastery of St Benet Holm, on the island of Nidarholm in western Norway. Paris had already been involved in the house's affairs in 1246–7 when, for reasons that remain unclear, he was requested by Hákon to mediate between the monks and their creditors, merchants of Cahors resident in London. He was successful, and this prior contact probably explains why it was Paris who was chosen to go to Norway himself in 1248. He describes himself as visitor to the entire Benedictine order in Norway, but the papal mandate, which he reproduces, indicates that his remit was altogether more modest, for only the abbot and monks of St Benet Holm are mentioned. His arrival in Bergen in early June 1248 occurred at a dramatic time: a great fire was raging through the city, followed by a severe thunderstorm, the lightning shattering the mast of the ship in which he had sailed. He was unharmed and visited King Hákon, who was in Bergen at the time, and delivered letters to him from Louis IX of France, requesting Hákon's participation in Louis's projected crusade and granting him victualling rights in France. Why Paris should have acted as letter-bearer and probably as a fully accredited envoy of the French king is a mystery, but if he was previously known to Louis this would strengthen any surmise that he had spent time in the schools of Paris. On completing his mission to Norway he returned home, presumably in 1249.

Illustrator and artist The paucity of detail concerning Matthew Paris's life contrasts sharply with the astonishing volume of information and material that he provides in relation to the events and issues of his contemporary world, and which renders him such an important historian. He will always be known chiefly for his historical writings, but his cultural significance extends far beyond them. As a cartographer, his contribution was considerable. He produced one world map, four versions of an itinerary from London to central or southern Italy, four maps of the Holy Land, a diagram showing the principal Roman roads of Britain, another showing the kingdoms of the Anglo-Saxon heptarchy, and four versions of a map of Britain. The maps, in particular, are of the greatest significance, not because they were influential at the time, but because of their originality, since Paris was experimenting with cartographic concepts virtually unknown in his time and when the idea of a map was not generally understood. His interest here is closely linked to his general interest in collecting and recording information of every kind, and the same may be said of his common practice of illustrating his historical texts with paintings of the shields of individuals mentioned in them. His own observations make it plain that he had a keen interest in heraldry, leading him to reproduce nearly 300 devices, coloured and uncoloured, continental as well as English. At a critical moment in the development of heraldry these representations are precious to the historian of heraldry, and Paris was certainly one of the first to perceive the value of systematic collection of coats of arms. His interest, however, stemmed from his artist's eye and the sense of the illustrator, as well as from his awareness of the historical value of heraldry. Most of his representations occur as marginal illustrations to his historical works, the shields of the persons involved in a battle or other event described being painted in the margins of the text, or at the point when the text mentions the individual's death.

This urge to illustrate and extend the text pictorially also underlies the inclusion of the scores of drawings that adorn Paris's works, some 130 in the *Chronica majora* alone. Their attribution was once highly controversial, but on the basis of palaeographical, codicological, and stylistic analysis it is now generally agreed that, with a few exceptions, Paris was solely responsible for these drawings. Comparison between his first tentative efforts, and those more mature and polished drawings executed later in his life, strongly suggests that he was not trained as an artist but was self-taught, taking ideas from models available to him. These included the products of the goldsmiths, led by Walter of Colchester, who are known to have flourished at St Albans in Paris's time, and the illuminated manuscripts then extant in the abbey library. On the basis of these and other influences, some external to his house, Paris came to evolve a highly distinctive and personal style, eclectic, experimental, and innovative, which developed over about twenty-five years. The drawings that resulted are almost all of the same type, either line alone or tinted line. Whether he knew it or not, Paris was following an old Anglo-Saxon tradition which had been revived in England in the first decades of the thirteenth century. But as a result, in particular, of his distinctive use of tints, his extension of the range of colours applied, and his interesting blend of elements of late Romanesque and early Gothic styles, Paris contributed to a notable advance within the genre.

Finally, it is probable that metalworking should be included among his accomplishments, if credence is given to the words of Thomas Walsingham when he wrote his renowned eulogy and summing-up of Paris 150 years later:

> Matthew Paris, monk of St Albans and an eloquent and famous man full of immeasurable virtues, a magnificent historian and chronicler, an excellent author … Diligently compiling his chronicle from the earliest times up to the end of his life, he fully recorded the deeds of magnates, both lay and ecclesiastical, as well as various and wonderful events; and left for the notice of posterity a marvellous record of the past. He had such skill in the working of gold and silver and other metal, and in painting pictures, that it is thought that there has been no equal to him since in the Latin world. (*Gesta abbatum*, 1.395)

Chronica majora During his forty-two years at the monastery of St Albans, Matthew Paris wrote or supervised five chronicles, six hagiographies, two domestic histories, a cartulary, and a collection of fortune-telling tracts. They amount to well over a million words, most of them penned by Paris himself. Eighteen St Albans manuscripts containing his hand testify to a staggering diligence in the scriptorium. The *Chronica majora* fuelled Paris's later historical reputation. A universal chronicle, it is the longest of his annalistic works, spanning two and a half manuscript volumes. Cambridge, Corpus Christi College, MSS 26 and 16 (conventionally termed A and B), contain the annals from the creation to 1253, with the volume division occurring at the end of the annal for 1188. The remainder of the *Chronica* (1254–9) is to be found in BL, Royal MS 14 C.vii (R). These volumes comprise the original, complete manuscript of the *Chronica*, much of which, after the annal for 1213, is autograph. The *Chronica*'s entries up until the mid-1230s are culled in the main from Roger of Wendover's *Flores historiarum*. Yet there is some debate as to the precise point at which Wendover's *Flores* ended and Paris's original contribution in the *Chronica* began. The argument for July 1235 rests in part on a marginal note occurring in B after the account of Frederick II's marriage on 20 July 1235. The note, written in a hand of *c*.1300, states that 'Master Roger of Wendover, once prior of Belvoir, arranged his chronicle up until this point. Here begins Brother Matthew Paris' (text B, fol. 95*r*). The earliest extant manuscripts of Wendover's *Flores* (BL, Cotton MS Otho B.v, and Bodl. Oxf., MS Douce 207) close after July 1235 with a colophon indicating that Roger of Wendover was author up to this point. However, in a copy of the *Chronica* supervised by Paris (see below, C), a note similar to that in B occurs in the hand of the original rubricator at the foot of folio 252*r*, on which events of April–May 1234 are described, and a heading in the Otho manuscript of Wendover's *Flores* suggests that the work ends in 1234.

The authorship of the final eight folios of the annal for 1259, which are not in Paris's hand, has been disputed, yet the closing colophon is generally considered supportive of Paris's claims: 'Be it known that up to this point wrote the venerable brother Matthew Paris; and although the hand may vary in style, the manner of composition being retained however, the whole shall be ascribed to him' (text R, fol. 218*v*). Paris can therefore be credited with the *Chronica*'s annals for the period from either May 1234 or July 1235 to May 1259. His sources for the period 1235–59 included royal letters, exchequer records, and papal documents as well as a host of informative personal acquaintances, Bishop Robert Grosseteste (*d*. 1253), Henry III, and Hákon IV of Norway among them. The *Chronica* was produced over a period of two decades, 1240–59. It was completed as far as the annal for 1250 by February 1251, and the continuation from 1251 through to 1259 was not begun before 1252. Although continued into the fifteenth century, the *Chronica* was not a popular work, failing to gain wide circulation. Two copies of the section up to 1188 (A), made after Paris's death, are extant as BL, Cotton MS Nero D.v, part 1 and BL, Harley MS 1620. Paris himself supervised the copying of the section from 1189 to 1250 into BL, Cotton MS Nero D.v (termed C). This was made in or shortly after 1250, before Paris decided to continue the work beyond this year. Partial expurgation of the *Chronica* in C resulted in the omission of all matters that Paris had considered, in hindsight, to be 'offensive' to Henry III. The *Chronica* was edited for the Rolls Series by H. R. Luard between 1872 and 1883, and was translated by J. A. Giles from an inferior edition under the title *Matthew Paris's English History* in 1852–4.

Other chronicles The *Chronica* was the prime source for Matthew Paris's *Flores historiarum*, a selective abridgement of the text, intermingled with additional material derived from the monastic annals of Reading and Southwark. The earliest extant manuscripts of the *Flores* are Manchester, Chetham's Library, MS 6712 (Ch) (datable to the mid-thirteenth century) and Eton College, MS 123 (E) (datable to *c*.1300). A common exemplar is believed to underlie these two manuscripts. Only the annals for 1241–9 in Ch (fols. 173*v*–202*v*) are in Paris's hand, yet he is credited with authorship of book 1 (ending at 1066 and datable to *c*.1240–45) and book 2 up until the annal for 1249 (datable to *c*.1250–55). The *Flores* was previously ascribed to the mythical **Matthew of Westminster** (*supp. fl.* 1300). The provenance of the Chetham manuscript is disputed. It has been argued that Ch was produced by Paris at St Albans for a Westminster audience and that it did not reach Westminster until after 1265. But a more recent view is that Ch up to folio 170*r* was compiled at Westminster from an adapted text by Paris. It was returned to St Albans, probably in 1256, so that Paris could insert his revised version of the annals for 1241–9, and then it was sent back to Westminster. The *Flores* was edited by Luard for the Rolls Series in 1890.

There is no doubt as to the provenance of the *Historia Anglorum*. Bound with the third part of the *Chronica* in BL, Royal MS 14 C.vii, it is written almost exclusively in Paris's hand. Apart from abridging the autograph manuscript of *Chronica*, it draws upon Wendover's *Flores* and the epitome of the *Chronica* in C. It omits matter that Paris had pronounced 'impertinent' to English history in the margins of the *Chronica*, and it tones down passages critical of king and pope. On the first folio of the *Historia* Paris declares that 1250 is his time of writing. By 1255 the work was complete as far as the annal for 1253 with which the work ends. Sir Frederick Madden edited the *Historia* for the Rolls Series in the years 1886–9.

Two further abridgements of the *Chronica* resulted in the *Abbreviatio chronicorum* (included in volume 3 of Madden's edition of the *Historia*, 159–348) and the *Chronica excerpta a magnis cronicis*. The former, covering the years 1000–1255, made additional use of the *Historia*, Wendover's *Flores*, and Henry of Huntingdon's *Historia Anglorum*. It probably dates from 1255, and remains unfinished. The *Chronica excerpta* is the shortest of Paris's abridged editions of the *Chronica majora*, extending from 1066 to 1246. It is difficult to prove Paris's authorship of the work, but it was certainly written under his supervision, for he wrote some of the text himself in the unique manuscript BL, Cotton MS Vitellius A.xx (fols. 77*r*–108*v*). Datable to approximately 1246–59, it draws upon the *Abbreviatio*, Wendover's *Flores*, and the 'new material' that Paris added in the margins of his *Chronica* (from the annals of Southwark and Reading). Several charters, Henry III's forest charter of 1225 for example, are to be found in the *Chronica excerpta*, in a less corrupt and more complete form than in any other of Paris's manuscripts.

Local histories The universal history of the *Chronica* and its abridgements found its domestic counterpart in Matthew Paris's *Gesta abbatum monasterii sancti Albani*, a work of local history which was edited by H. T. Riley for the Rolls Series in the years 1867–9. The *Gesta* is a history of the abbey of St Albans from 793 to 1255, arranged according to the twenty-three abbacies that spanned the period, beginning with Willegod and ending with John of Hertford. The autograph manuscript is extant as BL, Cotton MS Nero D.i, folios 30*r*–62*r*, and 63*v*–68*v*. How great a debt Paris owed to a twelfth-century cellarer Adam in his writing of the first eighteen lives of the *Gesta* has yet to be determined. Opinion has commonly supposed that Paris made considerable use of a lost chronicle roll of Adam the Cellarer for the early section of the *Gesta* ending in 1166. This belief was spawned by an ambivalent note that Paris wrote at the beginning of the autograph copy of the *Gesta*: 'According to the ancient roll of Bartholomew the Clerk, who was for a long while with Adam the Cellarer, serving him, and he retained for himself this roll from among his writings, choosing this one alone' (BL, Cotton MS Nero D.i, fol. 30*r*). Yet the grounds for considering Adam the abbey's first domestic chronicler are not altogether firm. While the *Gesta* chronicles in some detail Adam's role in the abbey's quest for royal confirmation of its papal privileges, and his acquisition of land for the monks' kitchen, it makes no reference to his historical endeavours. It even terms him 'illiterate'. Adam is praised in later sources for his sanctity and the healing powers of dust from his tomb. Again, there is no mention of a domestic history. Walsingham praised Wendover and Paris for their historical writings but all he could say of Adam was that he was 'a Martha in worldly affairs and a Mary in contemplation' (*Annales … Amundesham*, 2.304).

It is significant, too, that Wendover betrays no sign in the *Flores* that he had used or even knew of a history of St Albans. With the early lives of the *Gesta* bearing Matthew Paris's stylistic imprint, it seems reasonable to conclude that Paris was responsible for their literary reconstruction of Anglo-Saxon and Anglo-Norman St Albans. The dating of the *Gesta* is less contentious. The portion of the text that ends with the death of Abbot William of Trumpington (1214–35) was penned some time before 1250, since the *Historia*, which was begun in this year, refers to it on five occasions. Paris resumed the *Gesta* in 1255 for, at the end of this short section, he proclaims the year in which he is writing to be the twentieth year of the abbacy of John of Hertford (1235–63). Although the *Gesta* did not pass into general circulation, it was abridged in Paris's lifetime by **John of Wallingford** (*d.* 1258), infirmarer of St Albans some time between *c.*1246–7 and his death in 1258. John's historical miscellany (BL, Cotton MS Julius D.vii) was culled chiefly from the works of Paris, whose friend he was; Paris himself executed the portrait of John on folio 42*v*. The *Gesta* was continued at the end of the fourteenth century by Thomas Walsingham.

The *Vitae duorum Offarum* shares the *Gesta*'s interest in the early history of St Albans, although it might also be termed a work of hagiography. While ostensibly chronicling the reigns of Offa, a fourth-century king of the Angles, and Offa, king of Mercia (*r.* 757–96), the *Vitae*'s narrative pivots on Offa of Mercia's foundation of the abbey of St Albans in fulfilment of a promise made by his earlier namesake. The antiquity of the abbey is stressed and the character of its royal founder whitewashed. Authorship of the work was once accredited to John de Cella, abbot of St Albans (1195–1214), yet the discovery that it made use of Wendover's *Flores* as copied into the *Chronica majora* resulted in its reattribution to Paris. The work is littered with stylisms characteristic of his prose. Although it precedes the *Gesta* in BL, Cotton MS Nero D.i, the *Vitae*'s later date of composition is betrayed by its closing words: 'The deeds of all the abbots who presided over the church of St Albans from the time of its founder, King Offa, up until the year 1250, are also described in this volume' (Paris, *Historia duorum Offarum*, 31). The *Vitae* thus dates to *c.*1250. It was last edited by William Wats in 1639.

Hagiographies: St Edmund and St Thomas Matthew Paris's literary talents also found an outlet in hagiography. Two Latin saints' lives occupied some of his time in the 1240s and 1250s. The *Vita Stephani archiepiscopi Cantuariensis* has survived in three fragments, all written in Paris's hand (BL, Cotton MSS Vespasian B.xiii, fol. 133*v*, Nero D.i, fols. 196*r*, and a leaf attached to 196*v*). They describe the journey to Rome in 1216 of Stephen Langton, archbishop of Canterbury (1207–28), whom Paris charitably declared the equal in theology of Augustine, Gregory, and Ambrose. The fragments also contain accounts of Stephen's meeting with Innocent III, his preaching on the return journey, and the translation of Thomas Becket in 1220. They were edited by F. Liebermann in *Ungedruckte anglo-normannische Geschichtsquellen* in 1879. Paris's *Vita beati Edmundi* documents the life and sanctity of a later archbishop of Canterbury, Edmund Rich (1234–40). It is extant only as a fourteenth-century copy, in BL, Cotton MS Julius D.vi, folios 123–156*v*. Although initially attributed to Eustace, a monk of Canterbury, the work has lain firmly at Paris's feet since the late 1890s. It was written some time after 1247, for it contains a letter of Richard of Wyche recounting the translation of St Edmund in June 1247, and it must have been completed before 1253 for it refers to the French queen Blanche of Castile as still living. A date nearer 1247 than 1253 would explain the apparent use made of this work by the *Historia Anglorum*. The *Vita* is based on a collection of materials made at Pontigny, but it depends also on information supplied by Richard of Wyche, Robert Bacon, and Edmund's brother, Robert of Abingdon. It was published in 1996 in an English translation by C. H. Lawrence.

Paris translated his Latin life of Edmund into Anglo-Norman octosyllabic verse for the *Vie de Seint Edmond*, one of his four vernacular saints' lives. A late thirteenth- or early fourteenth-century copy of the work was discovered at Welbeck Abbey, Nottinghamshire, at the beginning of the twentieth century, compensating in part for the loss of another copy of the work (BL, Cotton MS Vitellius D.viii) in the Cottonian fire of 1731. Paris's claim to the authorship of *Edmond* rests on three pieces of evidence. First, it is dedicated to Isabel de Warenne, countess of Arundel (*d.* 1282), who had also borrowed Paris's lives of Thomas Becket and Edward the Confessor. Second, the author says that he has written the life of Edmund in two languages and the source for *Edmond* is, as stated above, Paris's Latin life of the saint. Third, the author discloses his name—Maheu

(Matthew) (Paris, *Vie de Seint Edmond*, 1.1692). A recent suggestion that *Edmond* is the work of an anonymous translator has yet to gain acceptance. It was written some time after 1253, for the reference to a living Queen Blanche in the Latin life is lent a posthumous feel in *Edmond*. *Edmond* was probably the latest of Paris's Anglo-Norman hagiographies. It was edited by A. T. Baker in *Romania* in 1929.

The *Vie de Seint Thomas de Cantorbéry* drew its inspiration from the twelfth-century *Quadrilogus*. P. Meyer edited the *Vie* for the Société des Anciens Textes Français in 1885. While there is general agreement that the four extant leaves (BL, Loans MS 88, not in Paris's hand) date from *c*.1220–30 to 1240, opinion is divided as to their provenance and their author. Some consider them a close, 'first' copy of Paris's lost autograph manuscript, executed in the scriptorium of St Albans during Paris's lifetime. Others argue for their production in London by an unknown poet; it is suggested that Paris was not the creator of the first Anglo-Norman version of the *Vie*, and that the leaves have nothing to do with him. The evidence for the former position is twofold. In a note on the flyleaf of his *Vie de Seint Auban* in TCD, MS 177, Paris mentions 'a book about St Thomas the Martyr and St Edward which I translated and illustrated [*transtuli et protraxi*]'. Over a century later Thomas Walsingham stated that Paris had 'written and most elegantly illustrated' (*conscripsit et depinxit elegantissime*) lives of saints Alban, Amphibalus, and the archbishops Thomas and Edmund (BL, Cotton MS Claudius E.iv, fol. 331*v*). Textual and stylistic similarities between *Thomas* and these other lives appear to confirm common authorship. The evidence for the view that Paris did not write *Thomas* hangs on an interpretation of the word *transtuli*. It is suggested that Paris may have meant simply that he had 'transferred' an existing saint's life into his own manuscript.

Hagiographies: St Edward and St Alban If, as seems probable, Matthew Paris was the author of *Thomas*, then the implication of Paris's Dublin note is that he wrote it about the same time as his *Estoire de Seint Aedward le Rei*, for they were originally in the same book. The *Estoire*'s most recent editor, K. Y. Wallace, who edited the text for the Anglo-Norman Text Society in 1983, confines it to the period 1236–45. Attempts to date it to the 1250s have failed to gain support. The *Estoire* is a verse hagiography of King Edward the Confessor. He was staunch in his repulsion of foreigners, wise in his dependence on baronial counsel, and his reign was a paradigm of conciliatory kingship—the Edward of the *Estoire* was everything Paris wished for in Henry III. Paris's dedication of the work to Henry's queen, Eleanor of Provence, possibly sought to communicate these wishes. The provenance of the earliest extant manuscript of the *Estoire*, CUL, MS Ee.iii.59, is debated. It has generally been labelled a close copy and adaptation of the prototype by Paris, executed at St Albans during the 1250s. More recent assessments favour London as its place of origin. The Cambridge manuscript, it is suggested, was a metropolitan copy of between *c*.1250–55 and 1260, produced perhaps for Eleanor of Castile, daughter-in-law of Henry III, about the time of her marriage to Prince Edward in 1254.

Attitudes regarding the authorship of the text it contains are similarly shifting. A monk of Westminster initially received credit for the work. He was ousted by Matthew Paris in 1920. Paris's authorship of *Edward* rests on the documentary foundations shared by *Thomas*, namely the Dublin note and the statement by Walsingham. Although the *Estoire*'s latest editor has fought Paris's corner, an attempt has also been made to credit the work to an anonymous poet. This poet, it is suggested, may be identified with the poet to whom is dubiously attributed the authorship of *Edmond*. A recent resurrection of a theory that Henry d'Avranches (*d*. 1262/3) was author of the *Estoire* rests on a statement in the exchequer liberate rolls of 1244–5 that a certain Henry the Versifier was paid £10 for his writing of the lives of saints Edward and George. Yet the majority rally round Paris, while acknowledging that the extant copy hails from Westminster. For the most part the *Estoire* constitutes a free translation of Ailred of Rievaulx's *Vita Edwardi Confessoris*, with an introductory section derived from Ailred's *Genealogia regum Anglorum*. Yet it also made use of Paris's *Flores*, and this may explain the Westminster angle that led earlier commentators to ascribe the *Estoire* to a Westminster monk. In addition, Paris sprinkled the text with original material; his detailed description of Edward's church at Westminster probably sprang from firsthand observation of the abbey before it began to be rebuilt in the 1240s.

Paris's *Vie de Seint Auban* is his only vernacular saint's life extant in the autograph. Both the text and illustrations of the *Vie* in TCD, MS 177 (fols. 29*v*–50) were executed by Paris himself, at a date that has yet to be firmly established. Scholarship in the 1950s and 1960s settled on the decade 1230–40 for production of *Alban* and this was a dating with which the work's only editor, A. R. Harden, concurred (Paris, *Vie de Seint Auban*, xv–xvii). It was argued that *Alban* was probably the first of Paris's Anglo-Norman saints' lives, for its handwriting and illustrations were tidy and controlled and it was written in archaic alexandrine *laisses* instead of the octosyllabic couplets of the other three lives. Recent studies, however, have placed the work a decade or so later, in the 1240s and early 1250s. It is suggested that Paris began *Alban* in the 1240s, temporarily suspended work on it when he visited Norway in 1248–9, and finished it on his return. *Alban* is a verse hagiography of England's first Christian martyr, who died in the third century. The central theme of conflict between Christian and pagan dictates its epic form. William of St Albans's twelfth-century Latin life of Alban, of which *Alban* is a literal, vernacular translation, was written out by Paris himself in the Dublin manuscript. *Alban* was produced for a monastic audience and the Dublin manuscript is probably that to which Thomas Walsingham refers when he tells of Paris's Lives of saints Alban and Amphibalus.

Subsidiary works A short genealogical chronicle, a collection of fortune-telling tracts, and a cartulary comprise the remainder of Matthew Paris's written legacy. His genealogical chronicle, *Cronica sub conpendio abreviata a fratre*

M. Parisiensi, appears in three different versions on the opening and closing leaves of his manuscripts of the *Chronica* and *Abbreviatio* (text A, fols. ivv and 285, text B, fol. iii*r–v*, and BL, Cotton MS Claudius D.vi, fols. 6*v*–8*r*). Sketching the reigns of the kings of England from Alfred onwards, this work proved to be popular outside St Albans, for two contemporary copies are known to exist. Paris's collection of fortune-telling tracts is extant in a single autograph manuscript. Decorative portraits of Socrates, Plato, Euclid, and Pythagorus adorn the pages of Bodl. Oxf., MS Ashmole 304, which is datable to 1240–50. Prognostic works, including the *Experimentarius* of Bernard of Chartres, constitute the bulk of this volume.

The *Liber additamentorum* (BL, Cotton MS Nero D.i) was the name by which Paris himself referred to his cartulary. The documents contained therein are those mentioned by Paris in his historical chronicles, and they span the years 1242–59. A number of earlier St Albans charters and papal privileges complete the collection. The *Liber* began as a small appendix of documents at the end of the *Chronica*'s annal for 1250; after the annal for 1247 Paris no longer wished to clutter his text with documentary transcripts. This appendix, which survives as folios 85–100, was detached *c.*1251–3 when Paris decided to continue the *Chronica* beyond 1250. It became part of a separate volume of miscellaneous material (BL, Cotton MS Nero D.i), which also contains the *Gesta abbatum* and the *Vitae Offarum*. Most of the *Liber* was pieced together in the last ten years of Paris's life. B's documentary appendix, however, was produced before 1250, and the series of St Albans charters and privileges which occupy folios 149–61 had an even earlier genesis. Instead of compiling this series himself, as was previously thought, Paris copied it from a twelfth-century St Albans cartulary which is preserved, in a seventeenth-century hand, in the Bollandist manuscript Brussels, Bibliothèque Royale, MS 7965–7973 (3723), folios 151*r*–216*v*. The order of charters relating to the abbey's early endowment in the Brussels manuscript is the same as that found in the *Liber*. Paris's alterations comprised the omission of vernacular boundary clauses, which suggests that he felt uncomfortable with Old English. Thus the *Liber*, which was once considered the abbey's first cartulary, reproduces and extends a cartulary compiled a century earlier.

Later influence Beyond St Albans, where his chronicles at any rate were known to Thomas Walsingham, a great admirer, Matthew Paris's works were largely unknown in the later middle ages. Only the *Flores historiarum*, of which there were a number of continuations, enjoyed some popularity. His reputation began to revive with Polydore Vergil (*d.* 1555), who set Paris and William of Malmesbury (*d.* 1142) on a pedestal apart from other medieval chroniclers, but it was the Reformation that led to a notable renewal of interest in his work largely because his acid-sharp anti-papal streak inevitably appealed to protestant scholars. As John Bale (*d.* 1563) commented to Archbishop Matthew Parker (*d.* 1575), 'no chronycle paynteth out the byshopp of Rome in more lively colours, nor more lyvely declareth hys execrable procedynges' (Levy, 96). It was Parker himself who produced the first printed editions of *Flores historiarum* in 1567, and of the *Chronica majora* (from 1066 onwards), in 1571, drawing attention in the process to Paris's exposure of the pride, greed, and tyranny of the pope. A similar position was taken up by such other historians as Edward Hall (*d.* 1547), John Stow (*d.* 1605), and John Hayward (*d.* 1627). The learned puritan controversialist William Prynne (*d.* 1669), too, clearly knew Matthew Paris's chronicles well, and drew upon them for anti-Roman ammunition. Paris was also important, moreover, for the growing opposition to the Stuart monarchy, as the source for the received text of Magna Carta, even though he presents a conflation, inherited from Roger of Wendover, of the version of 1215 and the reissues of 1217 and 1225. Only the exceptionally learned John Selden (*d.* 1654) appears to have noticed this. Against this background of controversy the edition of the *Chronica majora* (also from 1066 onwards) which was published in 1640 by William Wats (*d.* 1649), appears as the epitome of moderation, despite anti-papal invective in the introduction.

Wats's edition was reprinted in 1644 and 1684, and no doubt this was the text used by Sir William Dugdale (*d.* 1686) and other historians and antiquarians in late seventeenth- and early eighteenth-century England. However, Paris fell from sight in the later eighteenth century as medieval scholarship gave way to the Gothicizing antiquarianism of Horace Walpole (*d.* 1797) and his contemporaries, although a copy of the *Chronica majora* in the edition of 1684 was one of the very few medieval English narrative sources recorded in the library of Edward Gibbon at the time of the historian's death in 1791. Another change in literary and historical fashion, identifiable with the influence of Romanticism, seems to have been needed to bring about a renewed interest in Matthew Paris in the nineteenth century. That this was a development led by fashion rather than scholarship, at least initially, is suggested by the fact that English translations of the *Chronica majora* and *Flores historiarum* were published in 1852–4 and 1853 respectively, although, remarkably, they were preceded by a French translation published in 1840–41. These works were published before the scholarly editions of Paris's chief historical works appeared in the Rolls Series. Sir Frederick Madden's edition of the *Historia Anglorum* (1866–9), and H. R. Luard's editions of the *Chronica majora* (1872–84) and *Flores historiarum* (1890), provided texts altogether more reliable than those of Wats and Parker, and they remain the standard editions of these works. They also furthered significantly the understanding of Paris and his works through their accompanying editorial apparatuses, and thus helped to make further advances possible, notably in the work of V. H. Galbraith, who elucidated such issues as the transmission of Paris's texts and the relationship of his work to that of Roger of Wendover, and in the comprehensive monograph study of Richard Vaughan (1958), the first to consider Paris's talents, interests, and productions as a whole.

Style and method Despite a well-provisioned library, as evidenced by the twelfth-century catalogue of Walter the Chanter, the historiographical flowering of St Albans postdated that of other monastic institutions by several decades. Its successful propagation required a well-equipped scriptorium and creative personalities. St Albans possessed wealth for the former. Roger of Wendover and Matthew Paris contributed the latter. For a man who disclosed so few autobiographical details, Paris found intrusion of private thoughts and prejudices upon his works remarkably easy. Monastic humility battled with historical subjectivity. Foreigners riled him. The Savoyards and the Poitevins, he felt, greedily fattened themselves on English revenues and deprived native Englishmen of wealth and rank. The French as a whole he denounced as proud and effeminate. Yet Paris's xenophobia did not feed upon rife patriotism. Although the persistent incursions of the devious Welsh into English territory irritated him, he could admire their bravery, which he considered infinitely preferable to the imbecility and gullibility of the English. The English displayed these characteristics, said Paris, in the face of papal avarice.

Paris's hatred of the papacy spawned many a torrid passage in the *Chronica*. He considered its draining of ecclesiastical revenues, and its intrusion of Italians into positions of prominence within the English church, to be evidence of loose morals. Its morals, he said, were those of a prostitute. It practised usury and simony in an endeavour to satisfy its insatiable greed. The secular arm of divine authority fared no better in Paris's hands. Henry III suffered a barrage of criticisms, ranging from poor financial management to cowardice and self-indulgence. He preferred foreign over native counsel, he obstructed abbatial and episcopal elections, and he violated his coronation oaths. He was indecisive, bending one way and another like a reed in the wind. Together, king and papacy comprised the 'two millstones' between which England was metaphorically crushed. Paris was fond of such imagery; commenting upon the detrimental effect of pope and foreigner on the material wealth of England, he likened his country to a vineyard without a wall, open to plunder by all.

Matthew Paris's irreverent attitude to authority has been lavishly termed 'constitutionalism', and his *Chronica majora* labelled an *apologia pro baronibus*. That constitutional matters held some fascination for Paris is certain. Frenzied assaults on taxation, royal extortion, forest inquisitions, and itinerant justices constitute some of the most vibrant passages in the *Chronica*. His constitutional sensitivities also operated in the domestic arena. His support for the convent in the question of an abbot's right to banish monks to distant cells is evidenced by the *Gesta abbatum*. The latter text, in addition, maps out the procedures of abbatial elections, such as that of John of Hertford in 1235, with painstaking attention to detail. Yet Paris's constitutional interests appear amateur. They give no impression of having coagulated into coherent political theory. He no more conceived of the *communitas regni* wielding complete power over a monarch than he conceived of monks ruling abbots. Even his thoughts on the events of 1258 and the implications of baronial reform lack complexity. As a Benedictine monk he lived within the constraints of a traditional hierarchy. This, in itself, may serve to explain why his constitutional leanings lack the definition and impetus that characterize his other attitudes and prejudices.

Ardent though Paris's prejudices may have been, they never choked his narratives. Documentary evidence comprised the backbone of his historical methodology. 350 documents are preserved in the *Chronica* and *Liber additamentorum*. He knew that it was his duty to adhere to the facts. 'The lot of historians', he said, 'is hard indeed, for, if they speak the truth, they provoke man, and if they record falsehoods, they offend God' (Paris, *Chron.*, 5.469–70). Divine displeasure did not prevent him from tampering with documents. Noble intentions floundered beneath his burning desire to communicate a personal vision of the world. He lent an anti-papal slant to a letter of Patriarch Germanos of Constantinople to Pope Gregory IX written in 1232 but included in the *Chronica*'s annal for 1237. Germanos laments the tyranny of the papacy, holding it responsible for the disharmony between the Greek and Roman churches. Interpolations provided literary release for Paris's staunch convictions. In describing a dispute over three knights' fees in Horncastle between Hugh Fitzralph and Silvester of Everdon, bishop of Carlisle (*d.* 1254), he relished attacking the royal absolutism that he felt stamped the actions of the king's agents in the affair, misrepresenting the facts in the process. Furthermore, Paris's ahistorical acquittal of King Offa of Mercia of the murder of Æthelberht of East Anglia in 794, undertaken in the *Vitae Offarum*, stemmed from little more than loyalty to the founder of St Albans. On occasion, Paris can be charged with plain carelessness rather than wilful adulteration. His pastiche of the Magna Carta originated in a thoughtless conflation of the version of 1215 with the reissues of 1217 and 1225, inherited from Roger of Wendover. He had failed to question whether the charters of John and Henry were significantly different.

The historian and his outlook The scholarly liberties Matthew Paris claimed render his works unreliable in places. Yet he was not consistently inept. Neither was he an obsessive trickster. The accurate transmission of documents was not beyond his technical mastery. His account of Henry III's speech at the exchequer in October 1256 can be checked against the exchequer memoranda rolls and it fares well. Many of the writs and charters that he copied into the *Liber additamentorum* from the twelfth-century cartulary of the abbey remain faithful to their originals. He alternated fraudulence with precision, prejudice with impartiality. A recent description of him as 'tolerably accurate' captures the duality of his approach. He battled to control his material, shaping and tailoring hundreds of documents and endless amounts of detail into a narrative style. Success could never be unqualified. His historical works as a whole were shifting entities, undergoing endless stages of revision and censorship. They were flighty works, diverse in content. In his sprightly if crude Latin, Paris told of a thunderbolt which struck the queen's bedroom in 1251, crushing her bed to a powder, and a disease that drove cows mad in the autumn of 1252. He wondered sometimes like a child. The sparkling disintegration of a comet in 1239 seemed to him the fiery trail of a dragon.

Paris's fascination with the world probably fed on his uneasy conviction that human history was drawing to a close. For most of his life he laboured under the notion that time would end in 1250. Apocalyptic verses conclude the *Chronica* in this year, although Paris had later to resume the work when the last judgement failed to occur. Within Paris's closed historical chronology the wheel, or die, of fortune played havoc with men's lives and tempered human joys with human woes. In maudlin moments he lamented the deceptive and transitory nature of earthly events. Yet melancholia was not his favourite state. His works bear the hallmark of an effervescent imagination partially constrained by scholarly purpose and historical integrity. Together they comprise a spirited and evocative portrayal of political and intellectual life in England and Europe in the first half of the thirteenth century. SIMON LLOYD and REBECCA READER

Sources Paris, *Chron.* • *Matthaei Parisiensis, monachi Sancti Albani, Historia Anglorum, sive … Historia minor*, ed. F. Madden, 3 vols., Rolls Series, 44 (1886–9) • H. R. Luard, ed., *Flores historiarum*, 3 vols., Rolls Series, 95 (1890) • *Gesta abbatum monasterii Sancti Albani, a Thoma Walsingham*, ed. H. T. Riley, 3 vols., pt 4 of *Chronica monasterii S. Albani*, Rolls Series, 28 (1867–9) • *Annales monasterii S. Albani a Johanne Amundesham*, ed. H. T. Riley, 2 vols., pt 5 of *Chronica monasterii S. Albani*, Rolls Series, 28 (1870–71) • M. Paris, *Historia duorum Offarum*, ed. W. Wats (1639) • M. Paris, *The life of St Edmund*, trans. C. H. Lawrence (1996) • F. Liebermann, ed., *Ungedruckte anglo-normannische Geschichtsquellen* (1879) [incl. fragments of Matthew Paris's life of Stephen Langton] • M. Paris, *Vie de Seint Edmond*, ed. A. T. Baker, *Romania*, 55 (1929) • M. Paris, *Vie de Seint Thomas de Cantorbéry*, ed. P. Meyer, Société des Anciens Textes Français (1885) • M. Paris, *Estoire de Seint Aedward le Rei*, ed. K. Y. Wallace, Anglo-Norman Text Society, 41 (1983) • M. Paris, *La Vie de Seint Auban: an Anglo-Norman poem of the thirteenth century*, ed. A. R. Harden, Anglo-Norman Text Society, 19 (1968) • *Matthew Paris's English history*, trans. J. A. Giles, 3 vols. (1852–4) • R. Vaughan, *Matthew Paris*, Cambridge Studies in Medieval Life and Thought, new ser., 6 (1958); repr. (1979) • S. Lewis, *The art of Matthew Paris in the 'Chronica maiora'* (1987) [incl. comprehensive bibliography] • A. Gransden, *Historical writing in England*, 1 (1974) • R. Vaughan, 'The handwriting of Matthew Paris', *Transactions of the Cambridge Bibliographical Society*, 1 (1953), 376–94 • P. Binski, 'Reflections on *Le estoire de Seint Aedward le rei*: hagiography and kingship in thirteenth-century England', *Journal of Medieval History*, 16 (1990), 333–49 • P. Binski, 'Abbot Berkyng's tapestries and Matthew Paris's *Life of St Edward the Confessor*', *Archaeologia*, 109 (1991), 85–100 • N. Morgan, 'Matthew Paris, St Albans, London and the leaves of the life of Thomas Becket', *Burlington Magazine*, 130/1019 (1988), 85–96 • N. Morgan, *A survey of manuscripts illuminated in the British Isles 4: early Gothic manuscripts* (1988) • R. Kay, 'Wendover's last annal', *EngHR*, 84 (1969), 779–85 • H.-E. Hilpert, *Kaiser- und Papstbriefe in den 'Chronica majora' des Matthaeus Paris* (1981) • F. M. Powicke, 'The compilation of the *Chronica majora* of Matthew Paris', *PBA*, 30 (1944), 147–60 • R. Reader, 'Matthew Paris and the Norman conquest', *The cloister and the world: essays in medieval history in honour of Barbara Harvey*, ed. J. Blair and B. Golding (1996), 118–47 • J. Backhouse and C. de Hamel, *The Becket leaves* (1988) • S. Keynes, 'A lost cartulary of St Albans Abbey', *Anglo-Saxon England*, 22 (1993), 253–79 • R. Vaughan, ed., 'The chronicle attributed to John of Wallingford', *Camden miscellany, XXI*, CS, 3rd ser., 90 (1958) • N. Denholm-Young, *Handwriting in England and Wales* (1954) • M. R. James, ed., *'Estoire de Seint Aedward le Rei': facsimile* (1920) • H. R. Luard, ed., *Lives of Edward the Confessor*, Rolls Series, 3 (1858) • V. H. Galbraith, *Roger Wendover and Matthew Paris* (1944) • *The illustrated chronicles of Matthew Paris*, trans. R. Vaughan (1993) • P. D. A. Harvey, 'Matthew Paris's maps of Britain', *Thirteenth century England: proceedings of the Newcastle upon Tyne conference* [Newcastle upon Tyne 1991], ed. P. R. Coss and S. D. Lloyd, 4 (1992), 109–21 • R. W. Hunt, 'The library of the abbey of St Albans', *Scribes, manuscripts and libraries: essays presented to N. R. Ker*, ed. M. B. Parkes and A. G. Watson (1978), 251–77 • R. M. Thomson, *Manuscripts from St Albans Abbey, 1066–1235*, 2 vols. (1982) • F. McCulloch, 'Saints Alban and Amphibalus in the works of Matthew Paris: Dublin Trinity College MS 177', *Speculum*, 56 (1981), 761–85 • R. Bérard, 'Grapes of the cask: a triptych of medieval English monastic historiography. Bede, Jocelin of Brakelond and Matthew Paris', *Studia Monastica*, 24/1 (1982), 75–103 • M. McKisack, *Medieval history in the Tudor age* (1971) • C. L. Kingsford, *English historical literature in the fifteenth century* (1913) • F. J. Levy, *Tudor historical thought* (1967) • D. C. Douglas, *English scholars, 1660–1730*, 2nd edn (1951) • G. Keynes, ed., *The library of Edward Gibbon*, 2nd edn (1980) • D. A. Carpenter, *The reign of Henry III* (1996), 137–50

Archives BL, Royal MS 14 C.vii • BL, Cotton MS Nero D.i • CCC Cam., MSS 26 and 16 • TCD, MS 177

Likenesses M. Paris, self-portrait, BL, Royal MS 14 C.vii, fol. 6r • manuscript drawing (on his deathbed), BL, Royal MS 14 C.vii, fol. 218v [*see illus.*]

Parish, William Douglas (1833–1904), writer on dialect, was born on 16 December 1833 at 5 Gloucester Place, Portman Square, St Marylebone, London, the fifth son of Sir Woodbine *Parish (1796–1882), diplomatist, and his first wife, Amelia Jane (*d.* 1835), daughter of Leonard Becher Morse. Of his seven brothers and five sisters, the eldest, Major-General Henry Woodbine Parish CB (1821–1890), served with distinction in South Africa under Sir Harry Smith, and later in Abyssinia; the second, John Edward (1822–1894), became an admiral; and the third, Francis (1824–1906), was sometime consul at Buenos Aires, and later consul-general and state commissioner at Havana. His half-sister, Blanche Marion Parish, married in 1871 Ughtred James Kay-Shuttleworth, first Baron Shuttleworth (the biography of Sir Woodbine is by their daughter).

William Douglas Parish was at Charterhouse School from 1848 to 1853. He matriculated at Trinity College, Oxford, in the latter year, and graduated BCL in 1858. In 1859 he was ordained to the curacy of Firle and Beddingham in Sussex, and in 1863 became vicar of the adjoining parishes of Selmeston and Alciston, a benefice he held until his death. He was for a time diocesan inspector of schools. He endeared himself not only to his parishioners but also to Gypsies and vagrants, and his sense of humour was proverbial. From 1877 to 1900 he was chancellor of Chichester Cathedral.

Parish's principal work, *A Dictionary of the Sussex Dialect and Collection of Provincialisms in use in the County of Sussex* (1875, 2 editions), is both a contribution to etymology and a classic example of what a country parson with antiquarian tastes, a sense of humour, and a sympathetic affection for his rural parishioners could do to record for posterity the dialect and the domestic habits of the people of his time and place. He also produced, with the Revd W. F. Shaw, *A Dictionary of the Kentish Dialect* (1887).

Parish's other publications included *The Telegraphist's Easy Guide* (1874), an explanation of the Morse system written primarily for the boys of his parish, to whom he taught signalling as a pastime. He also produced an educational work, *School Attendance Secured without Compulsion* (1875, 5 editions), a pamphlet describing his successful system of giving back to parents their children's school payments as a reward for good attendances. His *Domesday Book in Relation to the County of Sussex* (1886, fol.) was written for the Sussex Archaeological Society, on the council of which Parish served for many years, and he edited a useful alphabetical *List of Carthusians* [*Charterhouse schoolboys*], *1800–79* (1879).

Parish died unmarried in Selmeston vicarage on 23 September 1904, and was buried in Selmeston churchyard. A window and two brasses were erected to his memory in the church. PERCEVAL LUCAS, *rev.* JOHN D. HAIGH

Sources N. L. K. Shuttleworth, *A life of Sir Woodbine Parish (1796–1882)* (1910), 419–25 · *The Times* (26 Sept 1904) · *The Times* (28 Sept 1904) · W. D. Parish, *A dictionary of the Sussex dialect* (1875), i–ii · private information (1912) · Crockford (1880) · Foster, *Alum. Oxon.* · 'Parish, Sir Woodbine', *DNB*
Wealth at death £6365 9*s*.: probate, 25 Oct 1904, *CGPLA Eng. & Wales*

Parish, Sir Woodbine (**1796–1882**), diplomatist, born in London on 14 September 1796, was the eldest son of Woodbine Parish (1768–1848) and Elizabeth, daughter of the Revd H. Headley. His father was a well-connected London merchant who traded with the Netherlands and Italy, and was chairman of the board of excise for Scotland, 1815–23. After attending a school in Essex and a year at Eton College, Parish received in 1812 his first appointment in the public service from John Charles Herries, the commissary-in-chief, who sent him to Sicily in 1814. In 1815 Parish accompanied the expedition to Naples that restored the Bourbon dynasty after the fall of Murat and, travelling home with dispatches, crossed the field of Waterloo a month after the battle. He was then ordered to Paris, where he was attached as junior secretary to Lord Castlereagh's extraordinary embassy for the settlement of the general peace of Europe upon the overthrow of Napoleon; he was proud of having written out the final text of the treaty of peace, signed on the part of Great Britain on 20 November 1815. Upon the return of Lord Castlereagh to Britain he was employed as assistant to his private secretary, Joseph Planta, an old family friend. In 1816 he was sent to the Ionian Islands, and was employed by Sir Thomas Maitland, the lord high commissioner, with Thomas Cartwright (afterwards consul-general at Constantinople and minister to Sweden), in arranging with Ali Pasha of Yanina in Albania the cession of Parga and the indemnities for the Parganots.

Recalled to England in 1818, Parish then accompanied Lord Castlereagh to the Congress of Aix-la-Chapelle, when the treaty arrangements of 1815 were modified, and the allied armies of occupation withdrawn from France. In 1819 Parish married Amelia Jane, daughter of Leonard Becker Morse; they had five sons, including the writer William Douglas *Parish, and three daughters. She died in 1835. On 7 May 1844 he married Louisa Ann Hubbard (*d.* 1887), with whom he had three more sons and two more daughters. In 1821, when Castlereagh attended George IV on a visit to Hanover, Parish went too. He was, as the 'devoted servant' of 'never a kinder chief' (Shuttleworth, 226), much affected by Castlereagh's suicide in August 1822, but Planta remained under-secretary at the Foreign Office under Canning, and Parish with him.

Sir Woodbine Parish (**1796–1882**), by Isaac W. Slater (after Thomas Phillips, *c.*1824–7)

In 1823 the government determined to send out political agents to the Spanish American states, and Parish was appointed commissioner and consul-general to Buenos Aires. He sailed in HMS *Cambridge*. After he had sent home a report upon the state of the people and their newly constituted government, full powers were sent to him in 1824 to negotiate with them a treaty of amity and commerce. This was concluded on 2 February 1825 at Buenos Aires, and was the first treaty made with any of the new states of America, and the first recognition by any European power of their national existence. Parish was subsequently appointed chargé d'affaires to the new republic. In 1825, by a timely representation to Dr Gaspar Rodríguez de Francia, dictator of Paraguay, he obtained the release of a number of British subjects, and other foreigners, who had been detained in that country, and received the thanks of the governments of France and Switzerland. About the same time war broke out between Brazil and Buenos Aires for the possession of Montevideo and the Banda Oriental. From September 1826 until July 1828 Parish continued to serve in Buenos Aires under the brief mission of Lord Ponsonby. In part through Ponsonby's mediation, in 1828 the Banda Oriental, the bone of contention, was recognized as the independent state of Uruguay. Ponsonby thereupon became minister to Brazil, and Parish resumed his duties as chargé d'affaires.

During nearly nine years' residence in Argentina, Parish worked energetically on behalf of the interests of the British community, which grew to some five thousand by the time of his departure. By the treaty of 1825 he obtained full security for their persons and property, exemption from forced loans and military service, and the free and public exercise of their religion; he laid the foundation stone of the British protestant church in Buenos Aires. He brought the importance of the Falkland Islands to the notice of his government, and in consequence was instructed to revive the claim to them as a British possession. His reports reveal him as a discerning, forceful, and straightforward diplomat, who was able to establish a good rapport with many prominent Argentines of the time. His collection of historical documents, fossils, and minerals shows a more than professional interest in the new country. In 1837 William IV conferred upon him the rank of knight commander of the Royal Guelphic Order. In 1839 Juan Manuel de Rosas's government conferred on him honorary citizenship of the Argentine confederation, the rank of colonel of cavalry, and the right to him and his descendants to incorporate the symbols of the republic in their coat of arms.

In 1840 Parish was sent as chief commissioner to Naples to settle the British claims on the Neapolitan government over the sulphur monopoly. By a treaty of 1816 Naples had agreed not to grant to any other state mercantile privileges disadvantageous to the interests of England. Nevertheless, in June 1838 the king had granted to a company of French and other Europeans a monopoly of all the sulphur produced in Sicily. The British government protested; the king of Naples refused its demands, and orders were sent to Sir Robert Stopford to commence hostilities. After the capture of some Neapolitan vessels the king gave way. Parish succeeded in obtaining full indemnities for the claimants, and Sir Robert Peel in the House of Commons paid tribute to his 'great ability and zeal' (Shuttleworth, 394). On the conclusion of the sulphur commission in 1842, Parish received full powers as plenipotentiary separately or jointly with William Temple, minister at Naples, to make a new commercial treaty with the king of Naples; it was a difficult negotiation, and was complicated by the jealousy of other powers, but it was eventually signed in 1845.

Parish combined with his diplomatic work much historical and scientific research, chiefly in geology and palaeontology. In 1839 he published *Buenos Ayres and the Provinces of the Rio de la Plata*, which achieved a second edition in 1852. He describes the history and geography of the provinces, and gives an account of their geology and of his fossil finds and investigations, the megatherium, mylodon, and glyptodon. From the remains of the megatherium that Parish presented to the Royal College of Surgeons, Sir Richard Owen built up a skeleton exhibited in the Natural History Museum in London. Parish was elected a fellow of the Royal Society in 1824. He was also a fellow of the Geological and Geographical societies, and served as vice-president of the latter for many years; he also contributed various papers to the Royal Geographical Society, mainly on South American subjects. He died on 16 August 1882, in his eighty-sixth year, at his residence, Quarry House, St Leonards, Sussex, and was buried at Fairlight churchyard, on the cliffs above Hastings.

CHARLES PARISH, *rev.* MALCOLM DEAS

Sources N. L. K. Shuttleworth, *A life of Sir Woodbine Parish (1796–1882)* (1910) • H. S. Ferns, *Britain and Argentina in the nineteenth century* (1960) • R. A. Humphreys, ed., *British consular reports on the trade and politics of Latin America, 1824–1826*, CS, 3rd ser., 63 (1940) • W. Parish, *Buenos Ayres and the provinces of the Rio de la Plata* (1839) • J. Goebel, *The struggle for the Falkland Islands* (1927) • *Morning Post* (21 Aug 1882) • *Proceedings* [Royal Geographical Society], new ser., 4 (1882), 612–13 • m. cert.

Archives BL, corresp. and papers relating to Buenos Aires, Add. MSS 19571–19576, 32603–32609 • PRO, corresp. and papers, FO 354 • RGS, corresp. and papers relating to South America | BL, corresp. with Lord Aberdeen and Sir Roderick Murchison, Add. MSS 43151, 46127 • NHM, corresp. with Sir Richard Owen and William Clift • NL NZ, Turnbull L., letters to Gideon Algernon Mantell • U. Durham L., letters to Viscount Ponsonby • University of British Columbia Library, corresp. with Frank Parish

Likenesses Thompson, miniature, 1818, repro. in Shuttleworth, *Life of Sir Woodbine Parish*; priv. coll. • T. Phillips, oils, *c.*1832, repro. in Shuttleworth, *Life of Sir Woodbine Parish*; priv. coll. • I. W. Slater, lithograph (after T. Phillips, *c.*1824–1827), BM, NPG [*see illus.*]

Wealth at death £16,376 2*s*. 4*d*.: resworn probate, May 1883, *CGPLA Eng. & Wales* (1882)

Park, Andrew (1807–1863), poet, was born at 23 Manse Street, Renfrew, on 7 March 1807, the son of James Park, and his wife, Bridget, *née* Campbell. Following his parents' early deaths he was cared for by an aged aunt. Having been educated in the parish school and at Glasgow University, at the age of fifteen he entered a commission warehouse in Paisley. Aged about twenty he was made salesman in a hat manufactory in Glasgow, and there he shortly afterwards started in business for himself. Having proved unsuccessful in this venture he attempted for a time to live by his pen in London but he returned to Glasgow in 1841 and, having bought the book stock of Dugald Moore (1805–1841), he made another fruitless experiment in business. Thenceforth he devoted himself mainly to literature.

Park published several volumes of poetry, which were appreciated by contemporary critics. They include *The Bridegroom and the Bride, and other Poems* (1834); *Silent Love* (1845), a graceful poem published under the pseudonym James Wilson, druggist, Paisley; and the autobiographical *Veritas* (1849). A collected edition of his works, including both tragical and operatic material, was published in 1854. In 1856 he made an oriental tour and the following year he published *Egypt and the East*. Park was popular with the general public as a writer of over 250 patriotic and sentimental songs, with titles such as 'Old Scotland, I love thee!'. His lyrics were set to music by Auber, Donizetti, and others. However, he became increasingly impoverished and ended his days as a barfly at the Whitebait Inn—a haunt of singers and composers—in St Enoch's Wynd, Glasgow. He was known there for his only partly humorous antipathy to Tennyson. Park died, unmarried, at 66

South Portland Street, Glasgow, on 27 December 1863 and was buried in Paisley cemetery, where a monument was erected to his memory in 1867.

T. W. Bayne, *rev.* James How

Sources *Andrew Park: a biographical sketch*, Renfrew District Libraries (1978) · J. Kilpatrick, *Literary landmarks of Glasgow* (1898), 269 · A. Park, *Egypt and the east, or, Travels on sea and land* (1857) · Allibone, *Dict.* · Boase, *Mod. Eng. biog.* · D. Baptie, ed., *Musical Scotland, past and present: being a dictionary of Scottish musicians from about 1400 till the present time* (1894) · R. Inglis, *The dramatic writers of Scotland* (1868) · W. D. Adams, *Dictionary of English literature*, 2nd edn [1878] · R. Brown, *Paisley poets: with brief memoirs of them and selections from their poetry*, 2 vols. (1889–90) · C. Rogers, *The modern Scottish minstrel, or, The songs of Scotland of the past half-century*, 6 vols. (1855–7) · bap. reg. Scot. · d. cert.

Likenesses bronze bust on monument, 1867, Paisley cemetery · daguerreotype or photograph, repro. in *Andrew Park* · drawing, repro. in Park, *Egypt and the east*

Park, Henry (1745–1831), surgeon, was born on 2 March 1745 at Water Street, Liverpool, the son of Henry Park, surgeon, of Water Street. He received his early education under the Revd Henry Wolstenholme. At fourteen he was placed with a surgeon at the Liverpool Infirmary, and when only seventeen had the care of a large number of French prisoners of war. Park then went to London to begin an apprenticeship with Percivall Pott and subsequently completed his studies at Paris and Rouen, where he studied under C. N. Le Cat. In 1766, when he was about twenty-one, Park returned to Liverpool, and in the following year he was appointed surgeon to the infirmary, a post which he held for thirty-one years. He married, in 1776, the eldest daughter of Mr Ranicar of West Leigh Hall, Leigh, Lancashire, with whom he had eight daughters and a son, John Ranicar *Park (1779–1847). Edward Lyon Berthon (1813–1899) was his grandson.

In 1777 Park entered into a partnership with Edward Alanson, who was also a surgeon at the infirmary. For many years Park vaccinated infants at his house in Basnett Street. He also kept a record of all his midwifery cases in what he called his 'Book of Genesis'; W. E. Gladstone was perhaps the best-known of the infants whom Park delivered. He was also a member of the board which licensed the surgeons who served on the slave ships leaving from Liverpool, and he was on the medical committee of the school for blind children. Park took part in Matthew Dobson's experiments on the effects of heat on the body which were performed in the 'sweating-room' at Liverpool Infirmary. On one occasion Park entered the room when the temperature had reached 202 °F and 'remained in the room long enough for three eggs to be cooked by the heat of the chamber. These he consumed and on coming out walked to Everton in a hard frost and felt no ill effects' (Bickerton, 43).

Park is best remembered for his *Account of a New Method of Treating Diseases of the Joints of the Knee and Elbow* (1783), which was translated into French in 1784 and into Italian in 1792. It was afterwards published with P. F. Moreau's *Cases of Excision of Carious Joints, with Observations by James Jeffray* (1806). The operation which led to the writing of this book is described by the *Edinburgh Review* (October 1872) as one of the greatest surgical triumphs of the time. Park's 'short, round figure, and his bright good-natured face' were familiar to many in Liverpool. 'His good spirits were unfailing; fatigue, cold and wet made no impression on him' (Bickerton, 40). Park died near Liverpool on 28 January 1831.

C. W. Sutton, *rev.* Michael Bevan

Sources P. J. Wallis and R. V. Wallis, *Eighteenth century medics*, 2nd edn (1988) · T. H. Bickerton and R. M. B. MacKenna, *A medical history of Liverpool from the earliest days to the year 1920*, ed. H. R. Bickerton (1936) · *Transactions of the Provincial Medical and Surgical Association*, 7 (1839), 459 · J. A. Picton, *Memorials of Liverpool*, rev. edn, 2 (1875), 237

Likenesses G. T. Doo, line engraving, 1832 (after T. Hargreaves), Wellcome L.

Park, Sir James Alan (1763–1838), judge, the son of James Park, an Edinburgh surgeon, was born in Edinburgh on 6 April 1763. He was brought up in England, his father having taken up a practice at Newington, Surrey. He was educated at Northampton grammar school, and eventually he became a student at Lincoln's Inn, where he read with a conveyancer. He was called to the bar on 18 June 1784. With the encouragement of his friend, fellow countryman, and patron, William Murray, Lord Mansfield, he published a *Treatise on the Law of Marine Insurance* in 1787, which was largely based on Mansfield's opinions and decisions. This work proved useful and successful; it passed through six editions in Park's lifetime, and quickly brought him into practice, especially in mercantile causes. It reached its eighth edition in 1842. Although Park was not an eloquent advocate, he was a lucid, earnest, and persuasive one, and his habit of constantly discussing cases with Mansfield gave him considerable experience in the application of principle.

On 1 January 1791, Park married Lucy, daughter of Richard Atherton, a woollen draper of Preston and one of the original partners of Preston Old Bank. In the same year he was appointed vice-chancellor of the duchy of Lancaster, in 1795 recorder of Preston, in Trinity vacation 1799 a king's counsel, in 1802 recorder of Durham, and in 1811 attorney-general of Lancaster. When Edward Law, later Lord Ellenborough, left the northern circuit in 1802, to become attorney-general, Park obtained the lead of the circuit; in London practice his only equals for many years were Sir Vicary Gibbs and Sir William Garrow.

Park played a small role in politics. With his friend, William Stevens, treasurer of Queen Anne's bounty, he brought about the repeal of penal statutes against Scottish episcopalian clergy. He was one of the original members of Nobody's Club, founded in honour of William Stevens, and published a memoir of him on his death (privately printed in 1812; republished in 1815). An active upholder of the established church, he published in 1804 *A Layman's Earnest Exhortation to a Frequent Reception of the Lord's Supper*. In 1823 he publicly criticized the Quakers for their refusal to take judicial oaths. On 22 January 1816, he was promoted to the bench of the common pleas, and was knighted. He sat in that court until the time of his death, which took place at his house in Bedford Row, Bloomsbury, on 8 December 1838. He was buried in the family vault at Elwick, co. Durham.

As a judge, though not eminent, he was fair and sensible, a little irascible, but highly thought of. Some stories of his bad temper are to be found in the memoir of him in the *Gentleman's Magazine*. He was a fellow of the Society of Antiquaries, and received the degree of DCL at Oxford on 10 June 1834. He was a benefactor to the poor of the village of Merton, Surrey, where he had a country residence. He left two sons, James Allan Park of Balliol College, Oxford, who was collated to the rectory of Elwick, co. Durham, by Bishop Van Mildert in 1829, and Alexander Atherton Park, who was called to the bar at Lincoln's Inn in 1827.

J. A. HAMILTON, *rev.* JONATHAN HARRIS

Sources *GM*, 2nd ser., 11 (1839), 210–11, 226 • H. Brougham, *EdinR*, 69 (1839), 7–14 • Foss, *Judges*, 9.229–31 • Allibone, *Dict.* • J. S. Mill, *Newspaper writings*, ed. A. P. Robson and J. M. Robson (1986), vol. 22 of *The collected works of John Stuart Mill*, ed. J. M. Robson and others (1963–91), 33
Archives CKS, letters to W. Cowburn
Likenesses W. J. Ward, mezzotint, pubd 1833 (after W. J. Newton), BM

Park, John (1804–1865), Church of Scotland minister and composer, was born in Greenock, Renfrewshire, on 14 January 1804, the son of John Park of the White Hart inn and Old Tontine Hotel, and his wife, Mary Weir. He attended school in Greenock and Paisley before entering Glasgow University, where he was friendly with Alexander John Scott (1805–1866), theological dissident and educationist. He also spent a session at university in Aberdeen in 1826. Park was licensed by the presbytery of Greenock in 1829 before serving as assistant in the West Church, Greenock, and later at Bonhill, Dunbartonshire.

On 27 June 1831 Park was ordained to St Andrew's Church, Rodney Street, Liverpool. This fortunately distanced him from the turmoil that engulfed the Church of Scotland in the following years, for he rarely attended the church courts and had no taste for controversy. During this period (1842) Park visited Wordsworth at Rydal Mount, his account of which, entitled *A Greenockian's Visit to Wordsworth*, was later published by his nephew. The Disruption in the Church of Scotland and the consequent loss of ministers to the Free Church worked to his advantage as it resulted in numerous vacancies. Park was translated to the parish of Glencairn, Dumfriesshire, on the presentation of the duke of Buccleuch, on 24 August 1843. He remained in these tranquil surroundings until translated and admitted to the first charge of the collegiate parish church (Holy Trinity), St Andrews, on 7 September 1854, at which time St Andrews University awarded him the degree of DD. He remained at Holy Trinity until his death.

Park's portrait suggests a thoughtful, intelligent man, clean-shaven and with a high forehead emphasized by dark, receding hair. He never married, a fact that perhaps emphasized the solitary aspect of a gentle and retiring nature. His tastes were cultured and included poetry, painting, and, above all, music. He played several instruments and was a talented composer. He wrote for piano, chamber ensemble, and dance, but was best known as a composer of songs. Admirers called him 'the Scottish Schubert' (*New Grove*). He refused to publish any of his works during his lifetime, but a selection of his songs was published posthumously (1876). While his work was not, in the main, Scottish, a version of the air 'Where gadie rins' was composed by him, apparently after hearing it whistled by a fellow student at Aberdeen. Though not a regular visitor of his parishioners, he was said to have visited all the cathedrals of England. As a preacher Park was considered eloquent, but he apparently felt the strain of meeting the expectations of a congregation in a university town. His *Lectures and Sermons* (1865) appeared shortly after his death. Park was seized with paralysis at a concert of the St Andrews Amateur Choral Union, of which he was the honorary president, and was taken to his home in Hope Street where he died the next day, on 8 April 1865. He was buried in the grounds of the ruined cathedral.

LIONEL ALEXANDER RITCHIE

Sources *Songs composed and in part written by the late Rev John Park DD St Andrews with introductory notice by Principal Shairp LL D* (1876) • *Fasti Scot.*, new edn, 5.236 • *The Scotsman* (10 April 1865) • D. H. Edwards, *Modern Scottish poets, with biographical and critical notices*, 9 (1886), 73–9 • C. Rogers, *The Scottish minstrel*, 2nd edn (1870), 338–40 • J. Park, *A Greenockian's visit to Wordsworth* (1887) • *DNB* • J. M. Allan, 'Park, John', *New Grove*
Archives U. Edin., MS songs, pianoforte works, music sketchbooks
Likenesses portrait, repro. in *Songs*, frontispiece

Park, John James (1793–1833), jurist, born on 6 June 1793, was the only son of the antiquary Thomas *Park (1758/9–1834) and his wife, Maria Hester Reynolds (1760–1813) [*see* Park, Maria Hester], composer and keyboard player. His health being delicate, he was educated at home, but he read widely in his father's library and before he was twenty published his *Topography and Natural History of Hampstead* (1814; 2nd edn, 1818).

In 1813 Park entered the office of Mr Seymour, a solicitor in Brighton. In 1815 he was admitted a student at Lincoln's Inn, and he was called to the bar on 6 February 1822, having practised for some years below it. He was initiated into the mysteries of conveyancing by Richard Preston, and, while still a student, published *A Treatise on the Law of Dower* (1819), which long remained a standard work. He drafted the bill on tithes introduced into the House of Commons by R. W. Newman in 1817, and published a treatise on the subject in 1823.

As a jurist, Park belonged to the historical school, and in regard to law reform he was strongly opposed to codification. Two works concerning this were his *Contre-project to the Humphreysian code, and to the project of redaction of Messrs Hammond, Uniacke, and Twiss* (1828) and (under the pseudonym Eunomus) *Three juridical letters: addressed to the Right Hon. Sir Robert Peel in reference to the present crisis of law reform* (1830); in these he argued that the particular historical development of English law left it unsuited for such a reform. Of his remaining works, the most important was *The Dogmas of the Constitution: Four Lectures Delivered at King's*

College, London (1832), in which he insisted that real governmental power resided in the House of Commons.

Park was a doctor of laws of the University of Göttingen, and in January 1831 he was appointed to the chair of English law and jurisprudence at King's College, London. His health, however, was by now failing and he died at Brighton on 23 June 1833.

J. M. RIGG, *rev.* JONATHAN HARRIS

Sources *GM*, 1st ser., 103/2 (1833), 84–6, 541–2 • Holdsworth, *Eng. law*, 13.295, 444–5, 474 • J. R. Dinwiddy, 'Early nineteenth-century reactions to Benthamism', *Radicalism and reform in Britain, 1780–1850* (1992), 349–50

Archives King's Lond., college archives, legal papers

Park, John Ranicar (1779–1847), physiologist and theological writer, was born in Liverpool on 11 May 1779, the son of the eminent surgeon Henry *Park (1745–1831) and his wife, the eldest daughter of Mr Ranicar of West Leigh Hall, Leigh, Lancashire; he had eight sisters and no brothers. Park was educated at Warrington Academy, where Joseph Priestley had once taught, and then under a private tutor whose name is unknown. He attended medical lectures at the University of Edinburgh from 1807 to 1810 and was president of the student-led Royal Medical Society from 1809 to 1810, but, as was common, did not graduate from Edinburgh. As president he presented two dissertations that are still in the university library. He is also recorded as joining Jesus College, Cambridge, on 1 July 1807 as a sizar (a student who worked in the college in exchange for tuition) and as becoming a fellow-commoner (one who holds an honorary, non-teaching post) in 1810. How he combined studying at both universities simultaneously is a mystery. Munk claims that Park spent time on the continent before joining Jesus College on his return. This is puzzling, since if Park entered Jesus in 1807 his visit would have coincided with hostilities between France and Britain. Although it is not known where, why, or for how long he visited the continent, judging by his subsequent enthusiasm for the latest French medical science, it is possible he went to Paris to study.

Having matriculated in 1810 Park graduated MB from Jesus in 1813, the year his first book, *An Inquiry into the Laws of Animal Life*, was issued (a year after the publication date on the title-page); it is possible that around this time he gave lectures based on this work. The basic principles of *An Inquiry* were reworked, in 1817, in the *Quarterly Journal of Science and the Arts*; Park was elected fellow of the Linnean Society on 1 June 1813 and not in 1812, as the title-page of *An Inquiry* suggests. He was licensed to practise, by his university, on 18 November 1815 and became MD in 1818. He was proposed member of the Royal Institution on 3 June 1816, when he gave his address as Southampton Street, Bloomsbury, and in the same year published an article in the *Quarterly Journal* on the physiology of sleep, dreams, nightmares, and sleepwalking. On 30 September 1819 he was made fellow of the Royal College of Physicians, and in 1821 delivered the Goulstonian lectures, which provided the basis for his *Pathology of Fever* (1822). After 1822 Park concentrated exclusively on theological subjects. His first theological book, *A New Exposition of the Apocalypse* (1823), was a minor success; it went into two further editions (1826 and 1834) and was published in a shorter format as *The Apocalypse Explained in the same Compass as the Prophecy* (1833). He also published *An Amicable Controversy with a Jewish Rabbi on the Messiah's Coming* (1832) and *An Answer to Anti-Supernaturalism* (1844). No information on his medical practice has been found. He is said to have married but nothing is known of his wife or of any family. Park died on 14 December 1847 at Downshire Hill, Hampstead, Middlesex.

Since Park was an enthusiast of Xavier Bichat, his physiological writings are perhaps best appreciated as part of the incorporation, by British medical men, of French medical science in the years during and after the defeat of Napoleon. As a theologian Park argued three main principles. First, he believed in the primacy of the prophetic works over the gospel as proof of God's intervention in the world, and he focused exclusively on them in his writings. Second, in a position first decisively enunciated by Calvin, he rejected literalism in the interpretation of sacred writings and emphasized the centrality of metaphor. Third, he rejected attempts to fit the prophecies with political events, such as the fate of Rome or the career of Napoleon (a common tactic in the early 1800s), and instead saw them as referring to the state of Christ's immanence in the world and the establishment of Christ's kingdom on earth. While thoughtfully executed, none of these positions was especially original and, like his physiological work, his theology did not attain any appreciable influence on subsequent debate; he was no polemicist and his name cannot be found in current histories of nineteenth-century theology. Park's tone is lucid, unfussy, respectful, and pragmatic, but his interest in prophecies has perhaps sealed his historical anonymity for good; although popular while he was writing, theological interest in the prophecies did not last the century and has not been revived.

L. A. F. DAVIDSON

Sources Munk, *Roll*, 3.202–3 • Venn, *Alum. Cant.* • *DNB* • medical matriculation registers, U. Edin. L., special collections division • private information (2004) [Royal Medical Society of Edinburgh, Royal Institution of Great Britain, London, and Linn. Soc.] • J. Hunt, *Religious thought in England in the nineteenth century* (1896) • R. C. Manlitz, *Morbid appearances* (1987) • A. E. McGrath, *Christian theology: an introduction* (1994) • H. Davies, *Worship and theology in England*, 4 (1962) • *GM*, 2nd ser., 29 (1848), 106 • d. cert. • *IGI*

Park, Sir Keith Rodney (1892–1975), air force officer, born in Thames, a small town south-east of Auckland, New Zealand, on 15 June 1892, was the third son and ninth of the ten children of James Livingstone Park (1857–1946), of Aberdeen, who earned in New Zealand an international reputation as a geologist, and his first wife, Frances Rogers (*d.* 1916), of Wellington. He was educated until 1906 at King's College, Auckland, and then at Otago Boys' High School, Dunedin (after his father's appointment as professor of mining at Otago University), and in June 1911 joined the Union Steam Ship Company. By December 1914, when granted war leave, he was a purser aboard passenger vessels and had visited most Australian ports, several Pacific islands, and North America's west coast.

Sir Keith Rodney Park (1892–1975), by Bassano, 1946

In 1914 Park joined the New Zealand expeditionary force as a volunteer and in January 1915 sailed to Egypt as a lance bombardier with the 3rd reinforcements. He served with a howitzer battery at Anzac Cove, Gallipoli, from 25 April. Commissioned as a second lieutenant in July, he took part in the Suvla Bay landings in August and then transferred to the British army as a regular officer, serving with the Royal Field Artillery until 2 January 1916, when his battery was evacuated to Suez. In March it was sent to the Somme front in France, where Park narrowly survived a campaign even more ineptly managed than that at Gallipoli. By June, acutely aware that aircraft posed a serious threat to gunners by accurately identifying their positions, he advocated careful camouflage, but nothing effective was done. He was wounded in October and shipped to England, where he 'managed to effect' (his words) in December a long-sought transfer to the Royal Flying Corps.

Early postings Park was taught to fly at Netheravon, on Salisbury Plain, early in 1917, then spent four months teaching others (and greatly improving his own flying skills) before joining 48 squadron, equipped with the excellent two-seater Bristol Fighter, on the western front in July. He commanded that squadron from April 1918 until the armistice. Park and his various rear-gunners probably destroyed eleven enemy aircraft, damaged (perhaps fatally) at least a further thirteen, and drove away scores; they protected artillery observation aircraft and gathered valuable information from flights behind enemy lines. These feats earned Park four medals (two MCs, a DFC, and a Croix de Guerre).

On 25 November 1918, at Christ Church in Paddington, London, Park married Dorothy (Dol) Margarita (1893–1971), the daughter of Lieutenant-Colonel Woodbine Parish—a genuine cockney whose family had strong links with Argentina, her father being director of Buenos Aires Great Southern Railway. They had two sons. Park was one of twenty officers selected to attend the first course at the world's first air force staff college at Andover, Hampshire, in April 1922: seven of those men would occupy vital posts during the Second World War.

In August 1926, after three years in Egypt, Park went to the headquarters of air defence of Great Britain at Uxbridge, west London. During the next fifteen months ideas about air defence were discussed that had become matters of urgent concern by July 1938, when he was promoted to air commodore and became Sir Hugh Dowding's deputy at Fighter Command headquarters, Bentley Priory, a few miles north-east of Uxbridge.

That appointment followed a succession of prestigious postings: command of 111 (fighter) squadron (1927–9), a staff appointment at fighting area headquarters (1929–31), command of Northolt (1931–2) and then of Oxford University air squadron (1932–4, for which he received the unusual distinction of an honorary MA), service as air attaché to all independent South American states (1934–6), and appointment as air aide-de-camp to King George VI for 1937, coronation year. In that year Park attended the Imperial Defence College, near Buckingham Palace, where senior officers of all three services in company with a few civil servants improved their minds and made useful contacts. That 'ardent spirit', recalled a civilian member of the course, was their star questioner: no lecturer got away without going through a veritable barrage of searching questions.

Under Dowding's direction at Bentley Priory, Park found his chief concern was to employ newly introduced, high-speed, heavily armed monoplanes (Hurricanes and Spitfires) in combination with equally new radar and radio equipment to frame an effective defence of vital British targets against a growing danger of aerial attack. This daunting task was complicated by peacetime restrictions on realistic training—restrictions which delayed an accurate appreciation by Park, other senior commanders, and pilots of the most effective means of employing modern fighters in combat.

The battle of Britain In April 1940 Park was promoted again—to air vice-marshal—and appointed to command 11 group, Fighter Command's principal subdivision, charged with the defence of London and south-east England. His first operational test was to improvise, in partnership with the Royal Navy, the Dunkirk evacuation. By 4 June some 340,000 allied troops had been rescued: a figure to compare with 'up to 45,000' hoped for when evacuation began on 27 May. But some 450 experienced aircrew were lost in the French campaign, and their absence gravely handicapped Park's conduct of operations during the battle of Britain.

That battle was actually a year-long campaign, fought at first in daylight (June–September 1940), then mainly in darkness (September 1940–May 1941). By mid-September it was clear that, although Britain's daylight defences had held, the German switch to a night offensive was causing heavy casualties and serious damage. That offensive was expected to intensify during the long dark hours of the next six months, and when long light hours returned Britain would face a better organized and more destructive resumption of the daylight offensive. So grim a prospect provoked anxious debate in Air Ministry and government circles. The debate was sharpened by ignorance of fighter, bomber, and radar capabilities, fear of German conquest, and resentment of Dowding's irascibility and Park's assertiveness, exacerbated by fierce ambition among those officers who believed they could do better.

Throughout the battle Park was short of experienced combat pilots (as opposed to young men who could, after a fashion, handle high-performance modern fighters), and by October 1940 many of those who had survived were very tired. They had not defeated the Luftwaffe, but they had bought Britain time. There could be no seaborne invasion until good weather returned—in March 1941 at the earliest. During those five months Britain would build more fighters; radar and other ground defences would be improved and operated by more skilful personnel. Novice pilots would have time for combat practice, veterans for rest, and neutral countries, particularly the United States, would observe that the Nazis were not invincible and might see in Britain a rallying-ground.

Park's tactics were therefore defensive. If bombers could be destroyed, so much the better, but his main aim was to break up their formations (and so reduce the concentration of their bombing) and force them to turn back. Combat against German fighters, he insisted, should be avoided unless they were escorting bombers approaching British targets. He favoured employing the squadrons of 11 group singly or in pairs, in order to achieve maximum disruption of as many raids as possible, and wanted the squadrons of 12 group (under Leigh-Mallory's command) to be regarded as in reserve, with the protection of 11 group airfields as their primary task.

The 'big wings' idea was, by contrast, offensive. Conceived by one of Leigh-Mallory's squadron commanders, Douglas Bader, it was taken up with enthusiasm by Leigh-Mallory, in part at least because he resented his position in the rear when he was in fact senior to Park. A wing of three or more squadrons should take off from 12 group airfields as soon as news was received that a raid was building up over France. Having had time to gain vital height, the wing should intercept the enemy formation in force as it crossed the English coast. Park's squadrons should then join in and harry the departing raiders. The big wing could not operate from 11 group airfields, as Bader recognized, because the time needed to assemble and climb to a safe height was too short. The primary intention was not to prevent bombers from reaching their targets—which were, supposedly, protected by anti-aircraft guns—but to punish raiders so severely that they would be reluctant to return.

Unfortunately, radar in 1940 could not give accurate information about the number and height of approaching aircraft; German aircraft did not select one target for each raid and head straight for it; Park's squadrons would have been in even greater danger of being caught on the ground and less able to gain combat altitude once German aircraft were actually overhead; and, above all, it was far from certain that an all-out fighter-to-fighter contest resulting from such tactics would end in British favour.

Big wings took a long time to assemble and used up fuel while doing so that was especially precious to short-range fighters. Once assembled, it proved virtually impossible in cloudy conditions to keep thirty to fifty fighters together *en route* for an interception. Bader and his supporters made extravagant victory claims, unsubstantiated at the time or by post-war research. The presence of many fighters in one place left others vulnerable. Worse still, as a result of the poor personal relations between Park and Leigh-Mallory (and Dowding's failure to control them), the unexpected appearance of big wings in the 11 group area confused the defensive system.

At the time, however, the conclusion of the debate was that more aggressive tactics might have achieved victory—as opposed to avoiding defeat—in the day battle and that Dowding was mishandling the night battle. Dowding was therefore replaced on 25 November 1940 and Park, deeply grieved and angered, left 11 group on 18 December.

A year later the danger to Britain had receded as a result of Hitler's failure to conquer the Soviet Union quickly, his consequent commitment to a long campaign there, and his decision to declare war on the United States following the Japanese attack on Pearl Harbor. Also, Fighter Command's attacks across the English Channel, strongly urged by its new masters, had been severely rebuffed by a Luftwaffe now enjoying the advantage of fighting over home territory with early radar warning. These and subsequent events leading to allied victory helped an overwhelming majority of airmen who fought in the battle, as well as historians who have studied it, to look back on the events of 1940 and recognize that Dowding's defensive strategy and Park's tactics had in fact been correct.

In February 1947, at the New Zealand Society's annual London dinner, Lord Tedder (chief of the air staff) said of Park:

> If ever any one man won the Battle of Britain, he did. I don't believe it is realized how much that one man, with his leadership, his calm judgment and his skill, did to save not only this country, but the world. (*The Dominion*, 11 Feb 1947)

This was high praise from a man ideally placed to know the facts, and who also knew—most people then did not—that Park's immediate reward was the sack, with only appointment as a CB to console him.

Air chief marshal Meanwhile, Park spent 1941 as head of a flying training group in Gloucestershire, followed by six months organizing an air defence system in Egypt. In July 1942 he became RAF commander of the strategically vital base of Malta. There he displayed an ability both to handle fighters offensively (rarely possible at 11 group in 1940, when facing superior Luftwaffe numbers) and to co-operate with other services and Americans in a succession of campaigns that gave the allies control of the Mediterranean. He was knighted (KBE) in November 1942.

In January 1944 Park was promoted to air marshal and appointed air officer commander-in-chief, Middle East, in Cairo. His immense area of responsibility was one in which training and preserving good relations with a host of allies, as well as with Egyptian authorities, mattered far more than actual fighting.

Knighted again (KCB) in January 1945, Park became air commander-in-chief, south-east Asia command, in February. His outstanding achievement there, under Mountbatten as supreme allied commander, was joint direction with Americans (who made him a commander in their Legion of Merit) of a huge air supply operation to support Burma's liberation by General Slim's Fourteenth Army. Together with Mountbatten and his army and naval commanders, Park had the satisfaction on 12 September 1945 of formally accepting Japan's surrender in south-east Asia. His last months of RAF service were spent winding down a vast military machine, extending from Karachi to Hong Kong, as painlessly as possible and creating its peacetime successor.

Park was told in February 1946 that he would be retired in December. The award of yet another decoration (GCB) and permission to make an official visit to New Zealand in May and June, accompanied by his wife, sweetened his departure. The visit escalated into a triumphal progress. Park left the RAF as an air chief marshal: the highest rank, equivalent to full general or admiral, attained at that date by a New Zealander in British service.

Retirement Park spent the first five months of 1947 in Argentina on Hawker Siddeley's behalf, successfully negotiating a sale of aircraft with the help of an old acquaintance, Juan Peron, now president. In June 1947 he was awarded the honorary degree of doctor of civil law by Oxford University. From 1948 to 1960 he acted as Hawker Siddeley's Pacific representative, based in Auckland. In 1951 he became chairman of the Auckland international airport committee and worked to persuade a reluctant government to purchase a site at Mangere in 1955. Construction began in 1960 and the airport opened in 1966. Although several attempts to attach his name to it failed, an airfield at Auckland's Museum of Transport and Technology honours his achievements in war and peace.

Park served three terms (1962–71) as an Auckland city councillor, polling very highly on all three occasions, even though (or perhaps because) he was no politician. For many years he was active in the New Zealand Foundation for the Blind, the Epilepsy Association, and the Pakuranga children's health camp, and he helped to raise money to save the church of St Matthew-in-the-City, Auckland. His wife, Dol, died at their home in Remuera, Auckland, on 9 August 1971, her last years clouded by chronic bronchitis and grief for her second son, Colin: an officer in the Perak aboriginal areas constabulary, he was murdered in Malaya on 3 September 1951.

Park was a tall, handsome man (despite prominent ears) with a full head of hair and a neat moustache, both turning silver in later years. He retained a slim figure, upright carriage, and brisk walk so well that, at the age of eighty, when seen from behind wearing his customary smart suit and trilby, he easily passed for forty. His gaze was disconcertingly direct, but offset by a pleasant voice and good manners, neither of which prevented him from expressing blunt opinions. A competent amateur seaman and navigator from his earliest days, he remained a willing, efficient crew member until the end.

Park was admitted to Mater Hospital, Auckland, suffering from carcinoma of the prostate, on 2 February 1975 and died peacefully in his sleep there on the 6th. He received a massive military funeral at Holy Trinity Cathedral, Parnell. Following cremation at Purewa on 12 February 1975 his ashes were scattered by an aircraft into the Waitemata harbour on 20 February. A memorial service was held on 12 September at the RAF's own church, St Clement Danes, in the Strand, London. Sir Douglas Bader, an eloquent critic in 1940, there put an end to whatever bitter feelings remained. The battle of Britain, he declared, 'was controlled, directed and brought to a successful conclusion by the man whose memory we honour today'. VINCENT ORANGE

Sources V. Orange, *Sir Keith Park* (1984) · J. Terraine, *The right of the line: the Royal Air Force in the European war, 1939–1945* (1985) · H. L. Thompson, *European theatre, September 1939–December 1942* (1953), vol. 1 of *New Zealanders with the Royal Air Force* · H. L. Thompson, *Mediterranean and Middle East: south-east Asia* (1959), vol. 3 of *New Zealanders with the Royal Air Force* · H. Probert, *The forgotten air force: the Royal Air Force in the war against Japan, 1941–1945* (1995) · R. A. Hough and D. Richards, *The battle of Britain* (1989) · J. P. Ray, *The Battle of Britain: new perspectives* (1994) · C. Shores and others, *Above the trenches: a complete record of the fighter aces and units of the British empire air forces, 1915–1920* (1990)

Archives Archives New Zealand, Wellington · Museum of Transport and Technology, Auckland · PRO · Royal New Zealand Air Force, Wigram, New Zealand, museum, papers | FILM BFI NFTVA, news footage · IWM FVA, actuality footage · IWM FVA, news footage | SOUND BL NSA, documentary recording · IWM SA, oral history interview · IWM SA, recorded talk · Radio New Zealand Sound Archives, Timaru · U. Leeds, Liddle Archive

Likenesses C. Orde, portrait, 1940, probably IWM · W. Rothenstein, portrait, 1941, repro. in W. Rothenstein, *Men of the RAF* (1942), pl. 17 · L. Cole, portrait, 1943, IWM · B. Hailstone, portrait, 1945–6, IWM · Bassano, photograph, 1946, NPG [*see illus.*] · group photograph, 1947, Hult. Arch. · Sandy, caricature, repro. in *New Zealand Flying*, 33 (15 May 1950), 34 · print, RNZAF, Wigram, New Zealand, Museum

Wealth at death £9946 in England and Wales: New Zealand probate sealed in England, 18 May 1976, *CGPLA Eng. & Wales*

Park [*née* Reynolds], **Maria Hester** (**1760–1813**), composer and keyboard player, was born on 29 September 1760. She was almost certainly the Miss Reynolds who on 5 November 1772 sang and played a harpsichord concerto in a concert at the Oxford Music Room. She was a vocal and harpsichord soloist at concerts there in 1773, and then appeared regularly as a harpsichordist. For her benefit concert on 11 February 1779 tickets were available from Miss Reynolds in Holywell, Oxford. In spring 1783 she was one of the principal instrumental soloists for the series of Wednesday concerts at the Hanover Square Rooms, London. Jane

Guest was the other harpsichordist for these concerts, and 'Miss Reynolds, Oxford' subscribed to Miss Guest's *Six Sonatas*, for which subscriptions closed in April 1783. At the benefit concert of the oboist John Parke at the Tottenham Street Rooms she joined his daughter, the ten-year-old Maria Frances Parke (with whom she has often been confused), in a Clementi piano duet, and 'displayed great ability on the instrument' (*Morning Herald*, 1 May 1783). In March 1784 she organized her own London benefit at Willis's Rooms, when tickets were to be had of Miss Reynolds at 102 Pall Mall.

Maria Hester Reynolds's first publication, a set of six *Sonatas for the Harpsichord or Piano forte* (1785), was dedicated to the countess of Uxbridge, with the word 'Gratitude' prominent on the illustrated title-page. The impressively long list of subscribers included a large Oxford contingent. She became a sought-after music teacher of the aristocracy, and later dedicatees were to include the duchess of Ancaster, the duchess of Devonshire, Lady Charlotte Greville, Lady Mary Bentinck, and Lady Harriet Montagu. At times she stayed with her pupils at their country houses, for Anna Seward later remembered Miss Reynolds as 'resident near Lichfield, in the unintellectual house of pride' (*Letters of Anna Seward*, 4.187). She published her op. 2, *Three Sonatas for Harpsichord or Piano forte*, before her marriage on 21 April 1787 to Thomas *Park (1758/9–1834), engraver and future man of letters. 'Mr Park, engraver and wife' visited Horace Walpole's Strawberry Hill that September (Walpole, *Corr.*, 229). Her compositions from op. 3, *A Set of Glees with the Dirge in 'Cymbeline'*, appeared under the name Maria Hester Park or M. H. Park. She was a very capable, professional composer, whose published works reached op. 13. Keyboard sonatas predominate, several with a violin accompaniment; they are varied and show rhythmic vitality. Her most striking work is her op. 6, the concerto for piano or harpsichord and string orchestra.

During his visits to England, Joseph Haydn became acquainted with Maria Hester, and a letter of October 1794 survives in which he thanked Thomas Park for 'the two so charming Prints' and continued 'I tack me the liberty to Send for the Mistris Park a little Sonat, and to come to Her next Friday or Saturday' (Landon, *Haydn in England*, 275). Three prints engraved by Thomas Park were in Haydn's possession at the time of his death. The Parks' fifth daughter was born in August 1796, and there was also a son, John James *Park (1793–1833). Maria Hester continued to teach and so was able 'to contribute very materially to the comfort of that happy and united home' (Jenkins, 11). Thomas Park was a devoted husband, and his wife figures in many of his published poems:

> By skill and science highly was she grac'd
> In Music's melting art, and with such taste
> And touch of feeling did she sounds convey,
> Her heart appear'd more than her hands to play.
> (Park, *Morning Thoughts*, 112)

She continued teaching in London until at least 1807, but suffered increasingly from rheumatism. Various cures were tried, but the mineral water and salubrious air of Hampstead proved most helpful, and the Parks spent the summers there from 1801. A house in Church Row, Hampstead, became their home, and Maria Hester died there, aged fifty-two, on 7 June 1813. She was buried at St Mary's, Acton, on 12 June.

OLIVE BALDWIN and THELMA WILSON

Sources *Jackson's Oxford Journal* (31 Oct 1772) • *Jackson's Oxford Journal* (6 Nov 1773) • *Jackson's Oxford Journal* (4 Dec 1773) • *Jackson's Oxford Journal* (5 Nov 1774) • *Jackson's Oxford Journal* (9 March 1776) • *Jackson's Oxford Journal* (8 Nov 1777) • *Jackson's Oxford Journal* (14 Nov 1778) • *Jackson's Oxford Journal* (6 Feb 1779) • *Morning Chronicle* (15 Feb 1783) • *Morning Chronicle* (10 March 1783) • *Morning Chronicle* (26 March 1783) • *Morning Chronicle* (30 April 1783) • *Morning Chronicle* (9 May 1791) • *Morning Herald* (1 May 1783) • *Public Advertiser* (13 March 1783) • *Public Advertiser* (27 March 1784) • L. Baillie and R. Balchin, eds., *The catalogue of printed music in the British Library to 1980*, 62 vols. (1981–7), vols. 44, 47 • O. Baldwin and T. Wilson, 'Park, Maria Hester', *New Grove*, 2nd edn • H. C. Robbins Landon, *Haydn in England: 1791–1795* (1976), vol. 3 of *Haydn: chronicle and works* • H. C. Robbins Landon, *Haydn: the late years, 1801–9* (1977), vol. 5 of *Haydn: chronicle and works* • T. Park, *Morning thoughts and midnight musings* (1818) • R. C. Jenkins, *The last gleanings of a Christian life: an outline of the life of Thomas Park, F.S.A.* (1885) • T. Park, letters, BL, Add. MSS 18916, 20083, 34567 • *Letters of Anna Seward: written between the years 1784 and 1807*, ed. A. Constable, 6 vols. (1811) • Walpole, *Corr.*, vol. 12 • *GM*, 1st ser., 83/1 (1813), 596 • *Annual Biography and Obituary*, 20 (1836), 257–63 • parish register, Piccadilly, St James, 21 April 1787 [marriage] • will, J. Park, proved, 4 Oct 1786, Family Records Centre, London • will, T. Park, proved, 20 March 1835, Family Records Centre, London • parish register, St Margaret's, Westminster, 9 June 1790 [baptism] • parish register, Richmond, St Mary Magdalene, 30 Oct 1791 [baptism] • parish register, Hanover Square, St George, 3 Aug 1793 and 9 March 1795 [baptism] • parish register, London, St Marylebone, 10 Oct 1797 [baptism] • parish register, Acton, St Mary's, 12 June 1813 [burial]

Park, Mungo (1771–1806), traveller in Africa, was born on 11 September 1771 at Foulshiels (sometimes misspelt Fowlshiels), near Selkirk, the seventh of the thirteen children of Mungo Park (1714?–1793), a prosperous tenant farmer on the estate of the duke of Buccleuch, and Elspeth Hislop (1742–1817). The dates of his birth and other events in his life, persistently misattributed by successive authors, have been authoritatively corrected by Kenneth Lupton in *Mungo Park, the African Traveler* (1979).

Education and early exploration Park was brought up in the Church of Scotland, and was educated at home by a hired tutor, and then at Selkirk grammar school. In 1785, aged fourteen, he was apprenticed to Thomas Anderson, a surgeon in Selkirk, and in 1788 entered Edinburgh University to study medicine. He took more interest in botany than medicine, and in 1792 went to London where his brother-in-law, James Dickson, a seedsman, had made himself a well-known botanist. Through him he met Sir Joseph Banks, a wealthy patron of botanical research, who arranged for him to go, in 1793, as surgeon's mate on an East India ship to Bencoolen, Sumatra, then under British rule. During his stay there he collected botanical specimens for Banks.

Banks was a member of the African Association, founded in 1788 'for promoting the discovery of the inland parts' of Africa. In 1790 it had sent Daniel Houghton, a retired army officer, to go up the Gambia River and make for Timbuktu, but he had died within a year. On

Mungo Park (1771–1806), by Thomas Rowlandson, *c.*1805

Park's return to London in 1794 Banks suggested him as a successor. He agreed, and the association appointed him, his instructions including 'to ascertain the course, and if possible, the rise and termination' of the Niger. He left on 22 May 1795 for the Gambia, and on 5 July reached Pisania, 200 miles up the river. There he stayed five months in the house of Dr John Laidley, a long-established slave-trader, learning Mandinka, and recovering from his first attack of malaria.

On 2 December Park set out on horseback, accompanied by two Mandinka servants on donkeys—Johnson who, having been shipped as a slave to Jamaica, gained freedom there, and had spent seven years in England, and Demba, one of Laidley's young household slaves. They were joined from time to time by other travellers who could act as guides. Park wore ordinary European clothes, including a beaver hat in which he kept his daily journal (it was the only article of his original clothing he was to return with), and took with him a small supply of trade goods to pay his expenses. 'And although the African mode of living was at first unpleasant to me, yet I found, at length, that custom surmounted trifling inconveniences, and made everything palatable and easy' (*Travels*, 45). His route was eastwards, making for Segou, a city known to be on the Niger.

Park faced potential hostility. Here, as elsewhere in coastal west Africa, local rulers refused to let European traders venture inland. They had to stay in their trading posts and trade through local middlemen. When he explained he was not a trader, he was allowed to go on, but still had to give the customary presents, and pay transit duties, out of his small supply of trade goods, or with any articles of his personal property, including clothing, that were fancied. This he resented, but could not avoid. There were a few small hold-ups, but by the end of the year he had covered over 300 miles, and reached the Bambara states of Khasso and Kaarta where he was well received by the respective rulers.

At this period militant Islam was spreading through the west African interior. North of Kaarta, the desert-edge Muslim rulers (called 'Moors', though a thousand miles from Morocco) were threatening their Bambara neighbours, who were themselves in rivalry with one another. Park, fearing war, diverted his route north through Ludamar where he was captured by Moors, and held prisoner by their ruler, Ali. Here, as a Christian, and believed to be a spy, he was deliberately tormented and humiliated (he was made to share his hut with a pig) and deprived of almost all his belongings, even sometimes of food and drink. After three months in almost intolerable heat, he was allowed to go on, but was forced to leave Demba behind as a slave, while Johnson went back to the Gambia with his papers. He subsequently tried to have Demba redeemed but never knew if he had succeeded.

In constant fear of being recaptured and ill used by Moors, Park had to avoid villages at first, and struggled on through barren savannah, tormented by thirst. When he could safely emerge he was sometimes refused food, having nothing to pay for it—though more than once he was fed by village women whom he found 'uniformly kind and compassionate' (*Travels*, 263). Then, at last, 'I saw with infinite pleasure the great object of my mission; the long sought for majestic Niger, glittering to the morning sun, as broad as the Thames at Westminster, and flowing slowly *to the eastward*' (ibid., 194). But when he reached Segou the ruler denied him entry to his city (though sent some cowries to help him pay his way). He went on to Sansanding, another substantial town, then to Silla where 'worn down by sickness, exhausted by hunger and fatigue, half naked, and without any article of value' (ibid., 211), he decided to turn back. He followed the Niger upstream, making for Bamako, under the heavy rains that had now begun. Three times he had to swim swollen streams, pushing his horse ahead of him (his journal notes safe in his hat). At Bamako he turned west. During the rains food was scarce, so he had little to eat. Then he was set upon by robbers who stole his horse and most of his clothes. Yet he refused to despair. Conscious that 'I was still under the protecting eye' of Providence, comforted and inspired by seeing 'the extraordinary beauty of a small moss in fructification' (ibid., 244), he went on. At the next town his patience was rewarded for the ruler recovered his clothes and his long-suffering, now almost skeletonic, horse (which Park gave him as a present, with the saddle and bridle). Severely ill with fever, he struggled on to Kamalia where he found a kindly Muslim trader, Karfa Taura, who agreed to look after him and eventually to take him to the Gambia.

Park waited at Kamalia for seven months, recovering his

health, and, as always, informing himself about the country and its peoples: a print of a sketch he drew of Kamalia was included in his published *Travels*, depicting him in one corner, bearded and barefoot, though still hatted. When the rains ceased, his host went round the country collecting debts most of which were paid in slaves. At last a large caravan set out, including thirty-five slaves, chained together and forced to travel at a speedy pace when they crossed country where there was either no food, or there was danger from robbers, covering the 500 mile journey in just under two months. On 10 June 1797 they reached Pisania where Park met his friends (who had supposed him dead), shaved off the 'venerable encumbrance' of his beard, and arranged to have Karfa paid twice what he had been promised. He then embarked on an American slave ship, where, the surgeon having died, he acted as surgeon to the slaves, returning eventually to England, via Antigua, after an absence of two years, seven months.

Park's *Travels* (1799) Together with Bryan Edwards, the secretary of the African Association, Park drew up a draft account of his travels for the members of the association. James Rennell added a map which showed the Niger flowing eastward (as Park had seen it) and petering out into a vast swamp. Park then returned to Selkirk and wrote up the draft for publication. His *Travels*, published in 1799, was a best-seller. Three editions were printed during the first year, and it was immediately translated into French and German, and eventually other languages. Written in a straightforward, unpretentious, narrative style, it gave readers their first realistic description of everyday life in west Africa, depicted without the censorious, patronizing contempt which so often has disfigured European accounts of Africa. For though Park disliked what he perceived as the superstitions of paganism and the bigotry of Islam, and regretted that 200 years of acquaintance with Europeans had left them totally ignorant of Christianity, he presented the people he met as people basically like himself. Having shared their activities, he recorded their joys and sorrows sympathetically, admiring what he thought admirable, and deploring what he thought deplorable. In it he comes over personally as an attractively modest figure, anxious to impart information but without making it boring or pedantic, and making light of his recollected adventures. The volume included as appendices a Mandinka vocabulary, Rennell's comments on the apparent implications of his geographical discoveries, and a women's song he had recorded, turned into verse by the duchess of Devonshire, and printed with accompanying music by G. G. Ferrari.

What was to disconcert (and still disconcerts) some readers was the detached way in which Park wrote not only on slavery but on the slave trade (in which indeed he had been a participant), presenting them without condemnation as established social institutions. Of the proposed abolition of the trade, then an active political issue, his only comment was, 'my opinion is, the effect would neither be so extensive or beneficial as many wise and worthy persons fondly expect' (*Travels*, 298).

Marriage, and the last expedition On 2 August 1799 Park married Allison Anderson, daughter of his former employer, qualified as an MRCS, and rather unwillingly practised as a doctor in Peebles, hoping for some more attractive employment. War with France gave the government ideas of a military expedition into the west African interior, and in 1803 he was approached as a possible leader. But the government fell, and the scheme lapsed. Meanwhile he invited a Moroccan from the Egyptian embassy in London to Selkirk to teach him Arabic. He also came round to feeling that the Niger must eventually turn south, and would perhaps emerge as the Congo.

At last, in 1804, another invitation came. With £5000 expenses allowed, Park was to go out to the former French island colony Goree, recently captured, recruit up to forty-five soldiers from the garrison, make for the Niger, and then follow its course 'to the utmost possible distance to which it can be traced'. He was commissioned as a captain (as he was to command soldiers), with a salary of £5000, and £1000 for his brother-in-law and close friend, Alexander Anderson, who went with him. Another Selkirk man, George Scott, went as draughtsman. For reasons beyond Park's control, their departure was delayed until the end of January 1805, and it was the end of March before they reached Goree, where thirty-five soldiers and one officer, Lieutenant John Martyn, with two sailors and four carpenters, volunteered to go with him. On 6 April they left for the Gambia, where Park recruited a Serahuli trader, Isaaco, as their guide, and then set off for the interior. The rulers whose territories they passed through made no objection, but, as always, demanded the customary payments.

They followed Park's former homeward route, making for the Niger at Bamako and hoping to reach it within a couple of months. But travelling with so large a party, their baggage loaded on donkey-back, was slow work. The earlier delays to his proposed timetable now proved disastrous, for early in June the heavy rains began. The soldiers fell sick, and one after another they died. But, having gone so far, Park felt he could not turn back. By the time they reached Bamako, and 'I *once more saw the Niger* rolling its immense stream along the plain!' (*Journal*, 140), thirty-one of the party were dead, including George Scott. Park managed to cure himself of severe dysentery by taking mercury, an agonizing form of treatment. The ruler of Segou let them go on to Sansanding where Park sold off his surplus goods in the market to raise money to construct a boat to take them down the river. He and one of the remaining soldiers, Abraham Bolton, put together and decked two large canoes, making a 40 foot, flat-bottomed sailing boat, rigged to sail with any wind, which he named his majesty's schooner *Joliba* (a local name for the Niger). Meanwhile, after four months' illness, despite Park's devoted care, Alexander Anderson died—a cruel blow. Isaaco was sent back with Park's journal and correspondence, and a much-travelled trader, Amadi Fatouma, agreed to accompany them as far as the Hausa country. By late November only Martyn and three soldiers (one deranged in his mind) survived to accompany Park, with Amadi and three slaves, down the river with (as Park wrote in his last dispatch to London) 'the fixed resolution to discover the termination of the Niger or perish in the attempt' (*Journal*, lxxx).

They had food supplies on board, and Park determined to press on without stopping at the towns they passed, or seeking permission from the riverine rulers. As he wrote in his last letter to his wife, 'I do not intend to stop or land anywhere, till we reach the coast' (*Journal*, lxxxii). This hazardous decision (which raises the conjecture that his own emotional sufferings from the deaths of so many companions had impaired his judgement) meant shooting at those who approached them, provoking retaliatory fire, and inflicting casualties. In one engagement Amadi had great difficulty in restraining the trigger-happy Martyn from more needless slaughter. Eventually the river ran south, and early in the new year (1806) they reached Yelwa in the Hausa country (modern Nigeria), some 1500 miles from Sansanding (and, had they known it, not much more than 500 miles from the mouth). Here, as agreed, Amadi left them. Then, a few miles on, at Bussa, where they were slowed by rapids, they were apparently attacked from the shore. They retaliated, and in the subsequent conflict Park, Martyn, and the soldiers perished, probably by drowning.

The details of their deaths had to be pieced together from contradictory statements, and have never been fully resolved. When rumours of Park's death reached the coast Isaaco was sent, in 1810, to gather evidence. He contacted Amadi who gave him, in journal form, in Arabic, an account of his experiences on the expedition. Isaaco too wrote a journal of his experiences in Arabic. Both were translated into English and published in London in 1815 with Park's journal, and a memoir of Park by John Whishaw. Added to these published accounts were stories picked up by subsequent European travellers, notably Hugh Clapperton and Richard and John Lander.

Park's death put a stop to the quest for the Niger until after the Napoleonic wars, and it was 1830 before the Landers finally reached its mouth. But his story caught popular imagination, particularly in Scotland. Tall and handsome, practical, adventurous and aspiring, but at the same time unassuming and rather reserved in manner, he seemed an exemplar of Scottish virtues. An imposing statue by a local sculptor, Andrew Currie, was put up in Selkirk in 1859. Bronze figures were added to the pedestal in 1906 by Thomas Clapperton, and there are commemorative plaques on houses he was connected with in Selkirk and Peebles. Monuments were also put up by the colonial government of the Gambia at Pisania, and by the colonial government of Nigeria on Jebba Island, near Bussa. And at the bi-centenary of his birth, 1971, money was raised to install two memorial chairs in St Giles' Cathedral, Edinburgh.

Park's wife, three sons, and a daughter survived him. His wife was paid the £4000 contracted in case he failed to return. His son Thomas, a naval officer, set out in 1827 from the Gold Coast to try to discover any news of his father's fate, but died on the way. His line and name continued through his youngest son, Archibald, an officer in the Indian army. CHRISTOPHER FYFE

Sources K. Lupton, *Mungo Park, the African traveler* (1979) • M. Park, *Travels in the interior districts of Africa* (1799) • *The journal of a mission to the interior of Africa in the year 1805 by Mungo Park* (1815) • B. H., *The life of Mungo Park* (1835)
Archives NL Scot., family corresp. and papers • NL Scot., personal and family corresp. | NHM, corresp. with Sir Joseph Banks [copies] • Selkirk Library, letters to Sir Joseph Banks
Likenesses T. Rowlandson, watercolour drawing, *c*.1805, NPG [*see illus.*] • A. Currie, statue, 1859, Selkirk, Scotland • R. Bell, engraving (after miniature by H. Edridge), repro. in B. H., *Life of Mungo Park* • T. Dickinson, engraving (after miniature by H. Edridge), repro. in Park, *Travels*, frontispiece • miniature (after H. Edridge), NPG
Wealth at death £2079 15*s*. 7*d*.: Lupton, *Mungo Park*

Park, Patric (1811–1855), sculptor, was born on 12 February 1811 in Glasgow, the third of six children of Matthew Park (1769–1820), mason and builder, and his wife, Catherine (1785–1876), daughter of Robert Lang, a Hamilton wood merchant. After attending school at Duntocher, Old Kilpatrick, and then Glasgow grammar school, Park was apprenticed at fourteen, on the advice of the architect David Hamilton, to John Connell who was building Hamilton Palace. During his three years there he developed considerable skill as an architectural mason. A carving of the Hamilton coat of arms he made from an engraving so impressed the tenth duke of Hamilton that the sixteen-year-old was entrusted with carving the armorial bearings above the palace main entrance. There followed two years' similar work with the architect Graham Gillespie at Murthly Castle.

Park left for Rome in October 1831, supported by patronage and a letter of introduction to the sculptor Bertel Thorvaldsen by the duke of Hamilton. Park's two years of study under Thorvaldsen imbued him with an admiration for the heroic nude which was later to disconcert a conservative Scottish audience. Returning late in 1833, he settled in Edinburgh. His most important large works are the marble funerary relief to the solicitor-general of Scotland Andrew Skene (*d*. 1835), with four lifesize figures—*Misfortune Soothed by Wisdom* flanked by two nude mourning youths (new Calton cemetery, Edinburgh); the statue of the educationist Michael Sadler for Leeds (exh. RA, 1837; formerly Leeds parish church, moved to the university cemetery in 1958); and the over-lifesize statue of the industrialist Charles Tennant (1838) in the Glasgow necropolis.

In 1835 Park moved to London, establishing a studio at 8 George Street, Euston Square. By the time of his marriage to Robina Roberts, daughter of the proprietor of the *Inverness Courier*, Robert Carruthers, on 15 October 1844, Park had moved to 13 Bruton Street, Berkeley Square.

Park was best known as a portrait sculptor. The *Illustrated London News* (17 August 1855) considered him the best in Scotland and equal in stature to Sir Francis Chantrey. His sitters included many famous names, among them Macaulay (exh. RA, 1836; marble, 1843; Wallington, Northumberland), the dukes of Hamilton and Newcastle (latter exh. RA, 1836), Lord Jeffrey (exh. Royal Scottish Academy, 1840; NPG), Charles Dickens (exh. Royal Scottish Academy, 1842), Sir Charles Napier (exh. Royal Scottish Academy, 1842), and Lord Dundonald (exh. Royal Scottish Academy, 1848; Scot. NPG). Generous and impulsive, he sometimes gifted busts—for example, to the poet Thomas Campbell (1839), and one of Robert Burns (1845) to the Burns monument in Ayr. His busts characteristically employ drapery in bold folds surrounding an energetically rendered dignified likeness. Later portraits include *Charles Barry* for the duke of Sutherland (1849), *Sheriff William Fraser-Tytler* (1851; Inverness Sheriff Court), *Lord Chief-Justice Boyle* (exh. Royal Scottish Academy, 1854; Society of Solicitors, Edinburgh), and the *Duke of Cambridge* (exh. Royal Scottish Academy, 1856). Contemporary reviewers particularly praised a colossal head of Oliver Cromwell (exh. Royal Scottish Academy, 1850), derived from a deathmask, and *Napoleon III* (1854; V&A) for the eleventh duke of Hamilton. Park's busts are represented in the Scottish National Portrait Gallery, the National Gallery of Scotland, and the Royal Scottish Academy, Edinburgh; the National Portrait Gallery, the Victoria and Albert Museum, the Royal Society, and the Geological Museum, London, and in the Glasgow Museums.

Most of Park's mythological and other figurative works are now lost including the *Sphaerobolos* (exh. RA, 1837); *Hector* (exh. RA, 1843); *The Descent of Mercury with the Cestus of Venus*, and the *Greek Huntsman* group sent to Westminster Hall in 1844 and 1845, respectively; and the statue for Culloden battlefield of a wounded highlander (1867; Exhibition of Art and Industry, Inverness).

Enthusiastic and headstrong, Park frequently flouted convention in his life and his art. Although vigorous and expressive, his style was sometimes criticized as exaggerated or 'eccentric'. *Modesty Unveiled* was refused for the 1846 Art Union competition as too sensual. He competed unsuccessfully for major memorials including the Edinburgh Scott monument (a fountain design, exh. RA, 1838); five designs for the Nelson monument, London, 1839 (his 1844 offer to complete it at his own expense with four reliefs was declined); and an impressive design for the Wellington testimonial, Manchester, 1854.

A major commission in 1846 to carve twenty lifesize characters from the writings of Sir Walter Scott for the Scott monument, Edinburgh, ended in disaster. Fourteen models were exhibited at the third Edinburgh Waverley ball in March 1846. Although paid for, the twenty models and thirteen lifesize statues, at least seven of them finished, were sold to prevent their being seized for rent arrears and soon decorated a merchant's garden at Clapham Common. Park had considered departing for India but fled to Scotland in the winter of 1848/9 in serious financial difficulties.

From 23 York Place, Edinburgh, Park submitted no fewer than thirteen busts to the 1849 Royal Scottish Academy exhibition. Early in 1850 he was working without commission on a colossal statue of William Wallace with the lion of Scotland, 15 feet high and using up to 10 tons of clay. After exhibition in a specially built pavilion at Bellevue Crescent, Edinburgh, in 1851, the statue was abandoned, despite critical support. A nude hero without even the customary figleaf did not accord with Scottish public taste. This typically ambitious undertaking contributed towards Park's sequestration, with no assets, in August 1851. Following this embarrassment, he moved in 1852 to 104 King Street, Manchester.

Elected associate of the Royal Scottish Academy in 1849 and full academician in 1851, Park exhibited fifty-four works at the Royal Academy, 1836–55, and eighty-two at the Royal Scottish Academy, 1839–55. He also showed work at the West of Scotland Academy, the British Institution, the Society of British Artists, and the Royal Manchester Institution. He wrote well on art, expounding his views at length in *The Scotsman*, the *Art Union*, and in pamphlets. His letter to Sheriff Alison, *On the Use of Drapery in Portrait Sculpture*, 1846, was circulated privately and his *Observations upon D.R. Hay's 'Theory of Proportion'* were included in Hay's published reply in 1851. In 1850 he gave two well-received lectures in Edinburgh entitled *On the Application of High Art to Public Sculpture*.

Park's promising career ended abruptly after a professional visit to Speke Hall, Lancashire, when he characteristically helped an old man staggering under a large hamper of ice at Warrington Station and haemorrhaged with the strain, dying four days later on 16 August 1855 in a local hotel. He left a widow and five children. He was buried at Ardwick Green, Manchester. The *Gentleman's Magazine* later described Park as 'one of the great but unappreciated geniuses of his time; a man of powerful intellect as well as powerful frame, a true artist of heroic mould and thought' but whose 'conceptions [were] too grand to find a market' (*GM*, 257, 1884, 451–8).

J. M. GRAY, *rev.* DIANNE KING

Sources P. Park, letters, 1832–55, NL Scot., Acc. no. 10098 [incl. cuttings (2 vols.)] • History of Scott monument, NL Scot., MS 23.3.15 [incl. copies of Park correspondence] • *GM*, 257 (1884), 451–8 [tribute by Charles Mackay] • R. L. Woodward, 'Nineteenth century Scottish sculpture', PhD diss., U. Edin., 1979 • *Building Chronicle* (1855), 236 • *The Builder* (1850), 190, 357 • *The Builder* (1851), 126, 144 • *The Builder* (1855), 408 • *The Builder* (1866), 733 • *Scottish Notes and Queries*, 3rd ser., 1 (1923), 72–4 • P. J. M. McEwan, *Dictionary of Scottish art and architecture* (1994) • *The Scotsman* (18 Jan 1845), 3 • *The Scotsman* (13 Sept 1845), 3 • *The Scotsman* (11 March 1846), 3 • *The Scotsman* (21 Oct 1846), 3 • *The Scotsman* (29 April 1848), 3 • *The Scotsman* (17 Feb 1849), 2 • *The Scotsman* (17 March 1849), 2 • *The Scotsman* (24 March 1849), 3 • *The Scotsman* (28 July 1849), 3 • *The Scotsman* (18 Aug 1849), 3 • *The Scotsman* (21 Nov 1849), 3 • *The Scotsman* (27 Feb 1850), 3 • *The Scotsman* (2 March 1850), 3 • *The Scotsman* (30 March 1850), 2 • *The Scotsman* (17 July 1850), 2 • *The Scotsman* (20 July 1850), 2 • *The Scotsman* (31 July 1850), 2 • *The Scotsman* (3 Aug 1850), 2 • *The Scotsman* (28 Aug 1850), 2 • *The Scotsman* (7 Sept 1850), 2 • *The Scotsman* (19 Oct 1850), 3 • *The Scotsman* (2 Nov 1850), 4 • *The Scotsman* (1 Feb 1851), 2 • *The Scotsman* (12 Feb 1851), 2 • *The Scotsman* (15 Feb 1851), 2 • *The Scotsman* (19 Feb 1851), 2 • *The Scotsman* (29 March 1851), 2 • *The Scotsman* (12 Nov 1851), 2 • *The Scotsman* (31 Dec 1851), 3 • *The Scotsman* (24 Jan 1852), 4 • *The Scotsman* (2 June 1852), 2 • *The Scotsman* (16 June 1852), 3 • *The Scotsman* (25 Sept 1852), 2 • *The Scotsman* (30 Aug 1854), 3 • *The Scotsman* (23 June 1855), 3 • *The Scotsman* (18 Aug 1855), 2 • *The Scotsman* (22 Aug 1855), 3 • W. Simpson, 'Inverness artists', *Inverness Courier* (2 Jan 1925), 4 [source for 'Highlander' information] • *Literary Gazette and Journal of Belles Lettres* (1846), 722 • sequestration document, NA Scot., CS 280/37/54 • *Art Union [Art Journal]* (1850), 102, 178 • *Art Union [Art Journal]* (1851), 95, 162 • *Art Union [Art Journal]* (1852), 80 • *Art Union [Art Journal]* (1854), 24, 55–6 • *Art Union [Art Journal]* (1855), 156 • *Art Union [Art Journal]* (1846), 18, 263 • *Art Union [Art Journal]* (1845), 258 • *Art Union [Art Journal]* (1844), 171, 214 • *Art Union [Art Journal]* (1842), 128 • *Art Union [Art Journal]* (1841), 103 • Graves, *RA exhibitors* • W. D. McKay and F. Rinder, *The Royal Scottish Academy, 1826–1916* (1917) • D. R. Hay, *A letter to Patric Park* (1851)

Archives NL Scot., corresp., acc. no. 10098 | NA Scot., sequestration, CS 280/37/54 • NL Scot., incl. copies of corresp. relating to Scott figures, MS 23.3.15 • NL Scot., letters and cuttings, 1832–55, 2 vols., acc. no. 10098 • NL Scot., MSS 590 (nos. 1545 and 1546), 3217, fols. 29, 3447, fols. 88, 3449, fols. 191, 4080, 4085, 4090, 6294, fols. 77, 9716, fol. 163 • NRA, priv. coll., corresp. with Robert Brown • Royal Scot. Acad., letters mainly to D. O. Hill

Likenesses K. MacLeay, watercolour drawing, 1859 (after photograph), Scot. NPG • P. Park, self-portrait, chalk drawing, NL Scot., acc. no. 10098, following fol. 4 • marble bust, Wallington, Northumberland • photograph, NL Scot., acc. no. 10098 (at end)

Park, Thomas (1758/9–1834), antiquary and bibliographer, was the son of parents who lived at East Acton, Middlesex, and were both buried in Acton churchyard; Park erected a tombstone there with a poetical epitaph to his father's memory. His mother's maiden name was Reynolds. When he was ten Park was sent to a grammar school at Heighington in Lincolnshire, where he lodged for more than five years with a Dame Morris. He was brought up as an engraver, and in the late 1780s produced several mezzotint portraits, including John Thomas, bishop of Rochester, and Penelope Boothby, after Sir Joshua Reynolds; Mrs Dora Jordan as the Comic Muse, after Hoppner; and a Magdalen after Gandolfi.

In the 1790s Park turned increasingly to literature. In 1792 he met William Cowper, corresponded with him, and submitted for comment poems which Cowper encouraged him to publish. Writing to Samuel Rose in March 1792 Cowper says, 'He [Park] has genius and delicate taste; and if he were not an engraver might be one of the first hands in poetry' (Southey, 7.99). He later corresponded on literary topics with Anna Seward who 'corrected' some of his verses. His *Sonnets and other Small Poems* (1797) pay graceful tributes to Cowper and Seward, depict scenes in Kent, Sussex, and Hertford, and show a devotion to the English poets. From this date Park abandoned his engraving and turned entirely to literature and the study of antiquities. For about ten years before this date he had been a collector, especially of English poetry and of the portraits of poets, and his possessions, though few in number, soon became famous. He followed his 1797 volume with *Cupid turned volunteer. A series of prints designed by the Princess Elizabeth and engraved by W. N. Gardiner. With poetic illustrations by Thomas Park* (1804).

Park now embarked on an editorial career, which led Southey to state that his 'knowledge of English bibliography, and English poetry in particular, have never been surpassed' (Southey, 7.322). His generosity and kindness led him to help Robert Bloomfield (1766–1823), author of *The Farmer's Boy*, in publishing and correcting various editions of his poems, and he was reputed to have helped the posthumous fame of Henry Kirke White. He lived first in Piccadilly, where Richard Heber used to drink tea two or three times a week and discuss the acquisition of ancient literature; then at Durweston Street, Portman Square; and from 1804 at Church Row, Hampstead. On 11 March 1802 he was admitted as FSA, but his financial means were limited, and in order to economize he resigned on 24 April 1815.

Park's family life was marked by misfortune. His wife, whom he married on 21 April 1787, the composer Maria Hester *Park, *née* Reynolds (1760–1813), who must be distinguished from Maria Frances *Parke, afterwards Beardmore (*bap.* 1772, *d.* 1822) [*see under* Parke, John], had suffered for many years from a form of rheumatism, and died at Hampstead on 7 June 1813. One of his daughters, who was noted for her piety, became mentally ill, and later his son, John James *Park (*b.* 1793), whose education for the law had been a heavy expense, died in 1833, a sad blow to his father.

Southey praised Park to Longmans as the best editor for the *Bibliotheca Britannica* which they projected. Among the earlier works which he edited were several books for the 'mental culture and moral guidance of youth', printed by a bookseller called Sael, who died in 1799 (Nichols, *Lit. anecdotes*, 3.663), and *Nugae antiquae: a miscellaneous collection of papers by Sir John Harington, selected by the late Henry Harington, and newly arranged, with illustrative notes*, 2 vols. (1804); his own copy of this work, with many manuscript additions for a new issue, is in the Dyce Library.

Park's editions of poetry included Sharpe's *Works of the British Poets* (1805–8), published in forty-two volumes, with a supplement in six more volumes; Dryden's *Fables from Boccaccio and Chaucer*, collated with the best editions (2 vols., 1806); and Horace Walpole's *Royal and Noble Authors, Enlarged and Continued* (5 vols., 1806), with many portraits. He also edited *Harleian Miscellany* (1808–13), in ten volumes, two of which were supplementary, and *Reliques of Ancient English Poetry. By Bishop Percy*, 5th edn, 3 vols. (1812).

Later editions included Cooke's *Translation of Hesiod* for the *Greek and Roman Poets* (1813); Ritson's *Select Collections of English Songs, with their Original Airs* (2nd edn, with additional songs and occasional notes, 3 vols., 1813); and *Heliconia: a Selection of English Poetry between 1575 and 1604* (3 vols., 1815). Park perhaps assisted Edward Dubois in editing, in 1817, the works in two volumes of Sir John Mennes and Dr James Smith; and the Lee Priory Press reprinted under his editorship *The Trumpet of Fame, Written by H. R. 1595* (1818).

Park's assistance was acknowledged by Sir Egerton Brydges in the *Restituta* (4.xi), and in almost every preface to the volumes of the *Censura literaria*. He helped George Ellis in his various collections of poetry and romance; he aided Ritson in the *Bibliographia poetica* and the unpublished *Bibliographia Scotica*, though their friendly relations were broken off before Ritson's death; and George Steevens, when editing Shakespeare, called on him for advice and information daily. At one time he meditated completing and editing Warton's *History of English Poetry*, but this plan was abandoned. His notes were added to the 1824 edition of that work, and incorporated under their legitimate headings in the 1840 edition. Several poetical articles were supplied by him for Nichols's *Progresses of Queen Elizabeth*; a few of his notes and illustrations were added to W. C. Hazlitt's edition of *Diana, Sonnets and other Poems, by Henry Constable* (1859); and he was a contributor to the *Gentleman's Magazine* and the *Monthly Mirror*.

In his later life at Church Row, Hampstead, Park was respected for his Christian piety and good works. He was devoted to 'parochial and church affairs, and to the education and comforts of the poor of the neighbourhood' (*Annual Biography and Obituary*, 261). The title-page of his volume of miscellanies, *Nugae modernae: Morning Thoughts and Midnight Musings* (1818), refers to him as 'Depository of an auxiliary Bible Society, Treasurer of the Sunday and National Schools, Secretary of a benevolent institution, Manager of a Bank of Savings, and one of the Guardians of the Poor in the parish of Hampstead'. His later publications include the religious *Advantages of Early Rising* (1824), *Solacing Verses for Serious Times* (1832), and cards of 'Christian remembrance: a plain clue to the gospel of peace'. His hymn 'My soul praise the Lord; speak good of His name' is discussed by Josiah Miller (*Our Hymns: their Authors and Origin*, 1866, 285). At some unspecified point he sold many of his precious books to Thomas Hill (1760–1840) on condition that he could consult them whenever he liked, which for a long time he did. Ultimately they passed with many others to Longmans, were catalogued by A. F. Griffiths in his *Bibliotheca Anglo-poetica*, and then dispersed by sale. Park annotated his own volumes profusely, and the British Library has copies of many antiquarian and poetical works containing his manuscript notes. Park died at Church Row, Hampstead, on 26 November 1834, aged seventy-five, survived by four of his five daughters.

W. P. Courtney, *rev.* John D. Haigh

Sources *GM*, 2nd ser., 3 (1835), 663–4 • *GM*, 1st ser., 103/2 (1833), 84–6 • *GM*, 1st ser., 83/1 (1813), 596 • *Annual Biography and Obituary*, 20/22 (1836), 257–63 • R. C. Jenkins, *The last gleanings of a Christian life: an outline of the life of Thomas Park* (1885), 7–23 • Bryan, *Painters* (1886–9) • R. Southey, *Life and works of William Cowper* (1836), 7.90, 99–100, 322–33 • *Letters of Anna Seward: written between the years 1784 and 1807*, ed. A. Constable, 6 vols. (1811), vols. 4–5 • *N&Q*, 3rd ser., 6 (1864), 283 • *N&Q*, 11 (1855), 217 • *N&Q*, 2nd ser., 12 (1861), 221–2 • Nichols, *Illustrations*, 8.376 • J. Miller, *Our hymns: their authors and origin* (1866), 285 • *The literary correspondence of John Pinkerton*, 2 vols. (1794), 1.349–50

Archives BL, corresp., Add. MS 18916 • University of Toronto, papers | BL, letters to Thomas Hill, Add. MS 20083 • BL, letters to Royal Literary Fund, loan 96 • Bodl. Oxf., letters to Francis Douce

Likenesses I. T. Wedgwood, stipple, pubd 1820, NPG

Park, William (1844–1925), minister of the Presbyterian Church in Ireland, was born in Stewartstown, co. Tyrone, on 29 March 1844, the son of William Park, merchant, whose brother the Revd Robert Park was clerk of the General Synod of Ulster from 1830 to 1840 and clerk of the general assembly of the Presbyterian Church in Ireland from 1840 to 1876.

William Park was educated at Armagh Royal School and had a distinguished academic record in classics at Queen's College, Belfast, winning scholarships in his second and third years and graduating BA with second-class honours in 1864 and MA with first-class honours in 1865. After theological studies in Edinburgh and Belfast he was licensed as a probationer for the Irish Presbyterian ministry by the Armagh presbytery on 8 May 1866. On 25 September of the same year he was ordained and installed in the First Ballymena Congregation in succession to the Revd S. M. Dill, who had been appointed professor of theology in the Magee Presbyterian College in Londonderry. This was a heavy responsibility for a young man of twenty-two years but Park was clearly equal to it and in 1873 he was called to the historic Rosemary Street congregation in Belfast where he was to minister for fifty years.

The following year, on 21 January 1874, Park married Susan (*d.* 1911), the youngest daughter of the late Dr John *Edgar, formerly professor of theology in the Presbyterian college, Belfast, and the father of the temperance movement in Irish Presbyterianism. Park established a considerable reputation as a preacher, pastor, and church leader. He was convener of the foreign mission of the Irish Presbyterian church from 1886 until 1902 and in 1890 he was elected moderator of the jubilee general assembly of the Presbyterian Church in Ireland at the early age of forty-six—the youngest ever moderator of the general assembly.

J. E. Davey, in his history of the first hundred years of the Irish general assembly, has described Park as contributing 'three splendid and able addresses, at the beginning of the Assembly, at the end of the Assembly and in a survey of the missionary work of the half century under review' (Davey, 62). From his experience of the foreign missionary movement he foresaw the rise of the modern ecumenical movement and, prophetically, he warned that secularization and agnosticism would prove more formidable challenges to Irish Presbyterianism in the future than Roman Catholicism which was so much feared in the late nineteenth century.

Although never a political parson like Henry Cooke, nor sharing his high public profile, like most Irish Presbyterians of his generation Park was a determined opponent of the Irish home rule movement. His obituarist in the Presbyterian weekly newspaper *The Witness* described him as 'a Strong Unionist' and claimed that 'when the Home Rule danger became really acute no one was more prominent to defend with voice and pen the Unionist cause' (9 June 1925). Some words of his at the 1890 assembly have often been quoted as articulating the Irish Presbyterian sense of their British identity: 'It is something to be an Englishman in the widest sense of the word, a citizen of that great Empire on which the sun never sets, and whose flag, wherever it waves, brings justice, liberty and peace' (Davey, 62; *Jubilee of the General Assembly of the Presbyterian Church in Ireland*, 1890, 27–8).

Park was president of the World Presbyterian Alliance—later the World Alliance of Reformed Churches—from 1913 until 1921, covering the period of the First World War. It was only then that he consented to accept honorary degrees—a DD from the Presbyterian Theological Faculty, Ireland, in 1914 and an LLD from the Queen's University, Belfast, in 1921.

For half a century Park was unrivalled in debate in the general assembly and it was after a characteristic speech in the assembly that he died suddenly on 5 June 1925 at the age of eighty-one. He was buried three days later in Belfast's city cemetery. He had retired from his pastorate in the Rosemary Street congregation in 1923. His wife had died in 1911 and of their two sons and three daughters, one son, John Edgar Park, had a distinguished career as a churchman and a scholar in the United States where he became president of Wheaton College, Massachusetts.

FINLAY HOLMES

Sources Archives of the Presbyterian Historical Society, Church House, Belfast • J. W. Kernohan, *Rosemary Street Presbyterian Church, Belfast, 1723–1923* (1923), 61–94 • J. E. Davey, *The story of a hundred years* (1940), 62–5 • *The Witness* (24 Jan 1874) • *The Witness* (16 Feb 1923) • *The Witness* (16 March 1923) • *The Witness* (6 April 1923) • *The Witness* (7 Sept 1923) • *The Witness* (4 June 1924) • *The Witness* (9 June 1925) • *Irish Presbyterian Missionary Herald*, new ser., 5 (1 May 1914), 110 • *Jubilee of the general assembly of the Presbyterian Church in Ireland*, 21–34; 123–50; 193–206 • Album of the Presbyterian College, Belfast • baptismal records, First Stewartstown Presbyterian Church, Belfast

Likenesses W. G. Mackenzie, portrait, 1924, Rosemary Church, Belfast • photograph, repro. in Kernohan, *Rosemary Street Presbyterian Church*, facing p. 61 • photograph, repro. in Davey, *Story of a hundred years*, facing p. 62

Wealth at death £3373 16*s*. 11*d*.: probate, 4 Sept 1925, *CGPLA NIre* • £17,324 13*s*. 2*d*.—in England: Northern Irish probate sealed in England, 2 Oct 1925, *CGPLA Eng. & Wales*

Park, William [Willie], **junior** (**1864–1925**), golfer and golf course architect, was born at 52 High Street, Musselburgh, on 4 February 1864, the second son of William (Willie) Park senior (1834–1903), golf professional and maker of golf balls and clubs, and his wife, Susannah Law, who had a family of five sons and five daughters. The Park family of Musselburgh was one of several eminent Scottish golfing families of the nineteenth century. Willie Park senior won the first ever open championship, at Prestwick in 1860, and subsequently won three further open titles, all at Prestwick, in 1863, 1866, and 1875. His brother Mungo Park (1839–1904) also won an open championship, at Musselburgh in 1874. From as early as his seventh year Willie junior learned both the game of golf and the art of making golf clubs from his father and elder brother, and honed his putting skills playing for marbles with anyone who would agree to play with him. When not at school he would surreptitiously creep into his father's workshop and borrow the tools of one of the workers to practise making club heads.

Park played in the open championship for the first time in 1880, at the age of sixteen: he won the title twice, at Prestwick in 1887 and at Musselburgh in 1889, and finished second to Harry Vardon at Prestwick in 1898. His last appearance in the championship was in 1910. During this period, with few recognized competitions, professional golfers frequently played challenge matches against other professionals for substantial money stakes: Park had a standing challenge, as did his father before him, to play anyone in the world for a wager of £100. The normal practice was to play such matches over two nominated courses, home and away, and several notable golfers picked up the gauntlet, including Willie Fernie, Ben Sayers, and John Henry Taylor, all of whom Park defeated. In 1894, however, he lost to Douglas Rolland at Sandwich over thirty-six holes, and five years later was heavily beaten by Harry Vardon in a celebrated 72-hole challenge match sparked by Park's near miss in the open the previous year. A crowd of 10,000 watched Park hold Vardon to a lead of two holes over North Berwick, but on his home course at Ganton the Englishman pulled away to win by eleven up with ten to play.

Through his experience as a professional golfer and the knowledge he had gained at his father's workshop Park became an excellent designer and maker of golf clubs. Among a number of patented designs was a 'bulger' made with a convex face to reduce the spin on the ball as a result of a mishit. He also brought out a 'lofter', of which over 17,000 were sold at 7*s*. 6*d*. each, and, in 1891, a patented wry-necked putter. Park himself was generally recognized as the best putter of his day, and would practise this aspect of his game for many hours at a time. His celebrated dictum, that 'a man who can putt is a match for anyone', reflected the confidence of a golfer seldom known to miss from within 6 feet. In the early days of golf-ball design, the patterns on gutta-percha ('gutty') balls were many and varied, and Park experimented first with a diamond-mesh pattern in 1890 and then, in 1894, a hexagonal pattern entitled The Royal, designed to slow down the roll of the ball on the putting greens.

None the less, Park's most lasting fame has been his reputation as a golf-course designer. He first laid out courses with his father and uncle, before branching out on his own. His personal tally is at least 160 different course designs worldwide, including over forty in the USA (Park himself claimed seventy, many of which have not survived), around twenty in Canada, over ninety in Great Britain and Ireland, and three on the continent of Europe. Royal Antwerp in Belgium and Royal Quebec, Royal Montreal, and Mount Bruno in Canada were among his major designs overseas, and in Britain his major work was at Carnoustie, Huntercombe, the Nottinghamshire club at Hollinwell, and (perhaps most famously of all) at Sunningdale in Berkshire. The Huntercombe course, near Henley-on-Thames, was one of the first golf courses planned to include a housing development, now standard practice worldwide. While working at Sunningdale in 1900 Park became aware of the Huntercombe project and when Chiltern Estates Ltd was formed to buy the land and develop the property, he invested £5000 of the £25,000 authorized capital, of which £11,200 was issued. Park was appointed managing director of the company, as well as the promoter, but the housing scheme never came to fruition, and the project almost ruined him financially.

In 1896 Park wrote *The Game of Golf*, the first golfing book written by a professional golfer, and he followed this in 1920 with *The Art of Putting*, part of which is autobiographical. He also wrote occasionally for *Golf Illustrated* and *Golf Monthly*, and judged the entries at the golf exhibition of 1910.

Around 1892 Park married, but his wife died in 1893,

after the birth of a daughter, Rebecca. He subsequently married Margaret Sinclair Inglis (*d.* 1943) on 15 October 1895; she was the daughter of John Inglis, spirit merchant. They had one son, who died at eight years of age of diphtheria, and four daughters, one of whom, Meta, died of peritonitis aged seven. Park himself was taken fatally ill while working in Canada in December 1924 and was taken home to Musselburgh. He died at Craighouse, Edinburgh, on 22 May 1925. Warmly praised by contemporaries for his courage, temperance, hard work, and devotion to his family, Park gained a brilliant reputation as a course designer which remains intact. Sir Guy Campbell thought him the doyen of all golf course designers, and believed that Park set the standard for all who followed him.

R. A. DURRAN

Sources J. Adams, *The Parks of Musselburgh* (1991) • G. S. Cornish and R. E. Whitten, *The golf course* (1982) • W. Park, *The art of putting* (1920) • *Golfer's Handbook* (1924); (1927) • A. F. Jackson, *The British professional golfers, 1887–1930: a register* (1994) • J. Adams, *Huntercombe golf club, 1900–1983* (1984) • b. cert. • m. cert. • d. cert. • *CGPLA Eng. & Wales* (1927)

Archives FILM BFI NFTVA, sports footage

Likenesses photographs, *c.*1887–*c.*1915, Hobbs Golf Collection, 5 Winston Way, New Ridley, Stockfield, Northumberland

Wealth at death £1409 6*s.* 1*d.*: probate, 1927, *CGPLA Eng. & Wales*

Parke, Daniel (1664/5–1710), colonial governor and army officer, was born probably at Queen's Creek, Virginia, the third but only surviving son of Daniel Parke (*d.* 1679), London merchant, plantation owner, and member of the governor's council in Virginia, and his wife, Rebecca Knipe, *née* Evelyn (*d.* 1672/3), a cousin of the diarist John Evelyn.

Parke was educated in England under the care of his mother's family at Wotton House in Surrey, returning to the family estates in Virginia in 1674. He married Jane Ludwell about 1685. They had two surviving daughters, Frances (Fanny) and Lucy; a third daughter, Evelin, died as an infant in November 1696. Fanny Parke, who died in 1715, married John Custis of Arlington in Virginia, and their son, Daniel Parke Custis, was the husband of Martha Dandridge, who, when widowed, became the wife of the first president of the United States, George Washington.

In 1690 Parke travelled to London with his father-in-law, Philip Ludwell, bearing complaints about the conduct of the governor of Virginia over the matter of oppressive taxation. He returned to Virginia in 1692 taking with him his mistress, a Mrs Barry or 'Cousin Brown', who gave birth to their illegitimate son, Julius Caesar Parke, shortly after their arrival. The boy was brought up in the same nursery as his half-sisters.

Elected to the house of burgesses in Virginia in 1693, and a member of the governor's council in 1695, Parke proved to be a troublesome colleague, engaging in numerous petty quarrels and feuds with his neighbours. He returned to England with Cousin Brown in 1701 and bought property in Whitchurch in north Hampshire, intending to get a seat in parliament. The irregularities evident in his attempt to secure the seat of Malmesbury in Wiltshire attracted wide notoriety. At the opening of the War of the Spanish Succession in 1702, Parke attached himself to the suite of John Churchill, first duke of Marlborough, in the Low Countries. Although he claimed the title of colonel there is no reference to him in the English army commission lists and registers, and if his colonelcy had any standing, it related to a colonial militia appointment in Virginia. On 2 July 1704 Parke took part in the storming of Schellenberg Hill at Donauworth in southern Germany, and was shot through both ankles. He recovered sufficiently to be at Marlborough's side during the battle of Blenheim on 13 August 1704, and it was to him that the duke handed the scribbled Blenheim dispatch. After an extraordinary ride of eight days Parke handed the same note to Queen Anne in Windsor Castle. Among the rewards he received for the exploit was a jewelled miniature portrait of the queen, which Parke always wore thereafter and, after some delay during which he hoped to get the governorship of Virginia, he was appointed as governor of the Leeward Islands in the Caribbean.

Daniel Parke (1664/5–1710), by John Closterman, *c.*1705

Parke arrived in Antigua on 14 July 1706 and promptly took robust measures both to improve the flimsy defence of the islands against French raiders and privateers, and to limit the smuggling activities of many of the leading sugar plantation owners. His commendable vigour was unmatched by any sense of tact. Parke became increasingly unpopular and isolated as governor, and he was rumoured to be philandering with the wives of certain planters. A daughter, Lucy, was born to Catherine Chester in the summer of 1710, and was acknowledged by Parke. The notoriety of the affair added to Parke's unpopularity, and he survived an assassination attempt in November 1710. He refused a demand from prominent planters to stand down as governor and, during a riot at Government House, Antigua, on 7 December 1710, Parke shot dead one of the ringleaders, John Piggott. He was then himself shot in the thigh and dragged into the street where he died soon afterwards. A general awareness in London of the ill effects of Parke's autocratic manner resulted in no firm action being taken against those involved in the affair, although one, Henry Smith, was arraigned at the king's bench in London in 1715. The case against him failed for lack of evidence.

Parke's will gave rise to lengthy dissent, as his considerable estates in England and Virginia were heavily entailed and mortgaged. His generous bequests to his illegitimate son gave great offence to his, now married, legitimate daughters and their families.

Daniel Parke was an energetic, colourful, and contentious character, wilful and headstrong to an astonishing degree. He was self-seeking and sublimely indifferent to the opinion of others. His family in Virginia were often short of money and his estates suffered from lack of management. His long-suffering wife, Jane, died in 1708, in straitened circumstances owing to his neglect. However, Parke's letters to his daughters, when he was resident in London, are affectionate and laced with paternal good sense. Despite his intemperate and bullying ways, Parke lacked nothing in courage; Marlborough found him valuable on campaign, and he showed considerable bravery when faced with a mob on the day of his mean and unwarranted murder on the steps of Government House, Antigua. JAMES FALKNER

Sources H. H. Miller, *Colonel Parke of Virginia* (1989) • *DNB* • *Journal of the Society for Army Historical Research*, 24 (1946) • *The letters and dispatches of John Churchill, first duke of Marlborough, from 1702 to 1712*, ed. G. Murray, 5 vols. (1845) • *Some instances of the oppression and male administration of Col. Parke, late governor of the Leeward Islands* (1713) [Ogilby Trust archives]

Likenesses J. Closterman, oils, *c.*1705, Virginia Historical Society, Richmond [*see illus.*] • G. Vertue, line engraving, 1717 (after G. Kneller), BM • G. Vertue, engraving (after G. Kneller), Virginia Historical Society, Richmond

Parke, Edward (*fl.* **1792–1844**). *See under* Parke, Robert (*d.* 1792).

Parke, Ernest (**1860–1944**), newspaper editor and local politician, was born at Stratford upon Avon, the youngest of the four sons of Fenning Plowman Parke. He was educated at the local grammar school. A career in banking was abandoned in 1882 when he became a reporter on the *Birmingham Gazette*. He rapidly graduated via the *Midland Echo* to Fleet Street and *The Echo*, an evening newspaper. In 1884 he married Sarah Elizabeth (*d.* 1937), the daughter of Joseph Blain of Manchester; the couple had one son.

John Robinson, editor manager of the *Daily News*, recommended the tyro journalist and businessman to T. P. O'Connor, editor of the recently founded *Star*. Parke was appointed chief sub-editor, and soon impressed O'Connor by his 'keenness, tremendous flair for news, and the capacity to work twenty four hours a day if necessary' (O'Connor, 2.256–7). Although 'few could be persuaded to take [*The Star*] seriously … for it did not take itself seriously' (Fyfe, 68), it is some measure of Parke's amazing energy and capacity that within three years he was appointed *The Star's* editor. Simultaneously he edited the *Morning Leader*, running both newspapers in tandem and working 'harder than any editor had done before or has done since' (ibid.). In 1912 the Cadbury-Rowntree agreement amalgamated several Liberal newspapers. Parke was appointed to the reconstructed board of the *Daily News*. A. G. Gardiner was appointed editor, but as C. P. Scott correctly surmised, Parke was really in command. As a reporter, Parke is best remembered for his account of the Jack the Ripper murders; as an editor, he was among the first to use stop-press news—racing results printed with a rubber stamp. He had a fondness for supporting 'anti' movements: anti-vaccination, anti-vivisection, anti-protection, and anti the Second South African War. This last earned him the supreme radical accolade of having his newspaper burned on the stock exchange. For all his radicalism, he was an important and trusted adviser to the Liberal Party on all aspects of the press.

As his editorial duties lessened, so Parke increased his many business commitments, serving on the boards of national and local newspaper companies, including the Daily News and Star, the Northern Newspaper Company, and the Sheffield Independent Press. He was a successful farmer, an experience that informed his membership of the agricultural small holdings and the land cultivation committees of Warwickshire county council. He was first elected to the county council in 1917, serving for a quarter of a century as councillor and then alderman, the last six years as vice-chairman. In local politics he retained the radical spirit of his youth, and his 'damn the consequences' approach, which led him to speak his mind plainly on social issues, found him frequently in a minority of one. He assiduously performed his duties as a magistrate, was chairman of several local councils, and made a significant contribution to the work of such bodies as the National Farmers Union, the Severn catchment board, and the Newspaper Proprietors' Association, of which he had been a founder member.

Until his eighty-third year Parke remained physically robust and mentally alert. He died at Warneford Hospital, Leamington Spa, on 21 June 1944, the consequence of a fall at his home, Moorlands, Kineton, Warwickshire. He was cremated, and his ashes were buried on 25 June in his wife's grave at the parish church of St Peter and St Paul in Butlers Marston.

Parke was 'an important Liberal editor … a founder of modern journalism who conceived his calling to be a public trust in the first place and a commercial enterprise only in the second' (Koss, *Fleet Street Radical*, 9, 12). J. L. Garvin, reviewing Parke's career, described him as 'A master of the news … who found the time and space to help … the underdog, to conduct crusades, more disinterested than profitable, in favour of social reforms about which he felt so deeply' (*Warwick Advertiser*, 30 June 1944). There was in Parke's character a rare mixture of kindliness, idealism, and shrewdness; a fervent radical, a thoroughly practical journalist, and a very successful businessman, he was loved by many and respected by all. A. J. A. Morris

Sources *Warwick Advertiser* (30 June 1944), 1 • *The Times* (23 June 1944), 7 • S. E. Koss, *The rise and fall of the political press in Britain*, 2 vols. (1981–4) • S. Koss, *Fleet Street radical: A. G. Gardiner and the Daily News* (1973) • H. Fyfe, *Sixty years of Fleet Street* (1949) • T. P. O'Connor, *Memoirs of an old parliamentarian*, 2 vols. (1929) • *WW*

Wealth at death £34,625 8*s*. 1*d*.: probate, 18 Sept 1944, *CGPLA Eng. & Wales*

Parke, Henry (*bap.* 1790, *d.* 1835), painter and architect, was baptized on 25 December 1790 at St Martin-in-the-Fields, London, the son of the celebrated oboist John *Parke (1745–1829) and his wife, Hannah Maria. He was intended for the bar, but owing to an indistinct utterance abandoned law. He tried several other professions and first showed ability as a painter of marine views, winning the Society of Arts gold medal in 1812 and exhibiting at the Royal Academy from 1815.

In November 1814 Parke became a pupil of the architect John Soane at 13 Lincoln's Inn Fields, London. Parke's principal role in the office was as a draughtsman; next to Joseph Gandy he was the finest to pass through the office. Parke worked up Soane's designs into finished drawings for presentation to clients, and he produced the finest of the large watercolour perspectives which illustrated the lectures Soane gave as professor of architecture at the Royal Academy. He depicted contemporary buildings such as Soane's Bank of England, drawn during construction, and visited Stonehenge to make topographical views, but the majority of his illustrations were buildings of Europe rendered from engravings in Soane's library. In 1819 Soane took Parke to Paris to draw the city's new monuments for the lectures, including panoramic views of the cemetery of Père Lachaise. Parke had visited Paris in the autumn of 1815, after Waterloo, and was also there in 1833.

Parke left Soane's office in May 1820 and travelled abroad until 1824, assisted by a grant of £100 a year from Soane; for Fanny Parke, a sister, Soane arranged a ticket to the coronation of George IV in 1821, and a visit behind the scenes of the Drury Lane Theatre with their mother. In Italy Parke joined up with several young British architects. With Charles Tyrrell, a fellow former pupil from Soane's office, he visited Sicily in the winter of 1821–2. In the winter of 1823–4 he went to Egypt with J. J. Scoles and Frederick Catherwood and travelled extensively in Nubia, where he made measured drawings of the temples and rock-cut tombs on the banks of the Nile. In 1829 Parke and Scoles published *A Map of Nubia Comprising the Country between the First and Second Cataracts of the Nile*, recording the position of these temples and tombs and giving a plan of the island of Philae. This important survey is now very rare, and was the most significant achievement of Parke's career.

Parke does not seem to have practised as an architect on his return, although he designed a house for himself in Queen Square, Westminster, and exhibited several imaginary designs for monumental urban improvements at the Royal Academy. He made designs for two instruments to facilitate architectural draughtsmanship; one was an architectural sextant which could take angles of up to 180°, a wider arc than a naval sextant; the other was for an instrument to measure angles internal and external for the purpose of making architectural plans. He continued to work as a painter and over 100 of his works were sold posthumously at Sothebys on 20 May 1836. The majority were topographical views of buildings and landscapes in Italy and Egypt in pencil, sepia, and watercolour, but some were marine views in oil. The introduction to the sale catalogue claims that Parke was 'justly esteemed one of the most eminent Marine Painters this Country ever produced'. Several hundred of Parke's drawings of France, Italy, and Egypt were given to the Royal Institute of British Architects by his widow in 1837.

Parke was a member of the committee of the newly formed Institute of British Architects, which presented its first gold medal to Sir John Soane in a ceremony on 24 March 1835. Parke is credited with designing the reverse of the Soane medallion. Soane lived until 1837 but Parke died less than two months after the ceremony, on 5 May 1835. He had failed to establish an identity outside his master's shadow. He suffered from ill health and was remembered in the *Gentleman's Magazine* as 'Diffident and retiring … ill fitted for the jarring warfare of life, and consequently … little known beyond the immediate circle of his friends' (*GM*, 1835, 325).

Christopher Woodward

Sources *GM*, 2nd ser., 4 (1835), 325, 670 • *GM*, 2nd ser., 9 (1838), 528 • A. T. Bolton, ed., *The portrait of Sir John Soane* (1927), 289–93 • J. Lever, ed., *Catalogue of the drawings collection of the Royal Institute of British Architects: O–R* (1976), 20–28 • D. Watkin, *Sir John Soane: enlightenment thought and the Royal Academy lectures* (1996) • day books, 1814–20, Sir John Soane's Museum • Parke sale (1836) [Sothebys, 20 May 1836] • *IGI*

Archives RIBA, drawings collection, architectural sketches and travel drawings • Sir John Soane's Museum, London, lecture drawings

Likenesses J. Gibson, bust, exh. RA 1816 • bust, presented 1838, RIBA

Parke, James (1636–1696), Quaker preacher and writer, was possibly born in Lancashire. In the 1650s he was living in or near Wrexham, Denbighshire, where he was almost certainly a member of Morgan Llwyd's Independent congregation. By 1663 he had become a Quaker, possibly before he returned to northern England. He went back to the Wrexham area in 1663 to visit some of his former Independent friends who had embraced Quakerism. To those who had not converted he left an admonition, dated 9 March, entitled 'A lamentation and warning from the Lord God' with Richard Davies. A year later Parke debated with the Baptist and Fifth Monarchist John Wigan, who had been incarcerated in Lancaster Castle for plotting; Wigan recounted their dispute in *Antichrists Strongest Hold Overturned* (1665). An indefatigable traveller on behalf of the Friends, Parke visited Ireland, Surrey, Middlesex, Berkshire, Buckinghamshire, Oxfordshire, and Bristol in 1664–5. From London he exhorted his fellow Friends on 12 August 1664 to withstand fiery trials and tribulations, be vigilant, and remember they were a city on a hill. In 1666–7 he travelled in the eastern counties, suffering imprisonment at Harwich, Essex, for attending a conventicle. This was probably the occasion for his tract *Another Trumpet Sounded in the Ears of the Inhabitants of England* (1667), in which he warned persecutors they would 'drink of their Plagues, Woes, and Misery' (p. 8). The same year he married Frances Ceele (*c*.1634–1696), a widow of Horsleydown, Southwark, where he had probably settled before this time and where he lived the rest of his life.

About this time Parke travelled to the Netherlands; his tract *Christus Jesus Verhooght* (Amsterdam, 1670) attacked Jan Korneliszoon Knoll. Parke was preaching at Quaker meetings in Cornwall in 1670 or 1671, and he was in Cheshire in 1673, thwarting an attempt by the quarterly women's meeting that probably involved the management of money. He returned in 1673 to Ireland, where he refuted a work by the presbyterian Daniel Burgess, *The Cheat of the Quakers Chaff*. In *The Way of God* (1673) Parke repudiated Burgess's allegations that the Friends rejected the doctrines of the Trinity and predestination, worshipped in a manner contrary to scripture, and gloried in their wealth. Parke dismissed Burgess as a malicious cheat, a blind guide, and a ravenous wolf. Ireland's six-months' meeting ordered 500 copies of Parke's book in May 1674. Although critics such as Burgess condemned the Quaker doctrine of perfection, Parke reiterated it in *A General Epistle to All the Called and Chosen* (1676), which urged Friends to go 'on to Perfection' (p. 16). Parke revisited Ireland in the spring of 1677, going from Dublin, where he visited his friend Anthony Sharp, to Rosenallis, Cavan, Armagh, Lurgan, and Drogheda.

Following the suspicions of Quaker conspiracy which surfaced during the Popish Plot, Parke composed *A General Epistle to Friends* (1678), entreating Quakers to eschew carnal weapons and rely on God for their safety. Most of Parke's numerous works have a markedly prophetic tone, as reflected in two tracts of 1679, *A Warning to England* and *A Warning to London*. The same year he joined William Penn and ten other Friends in witnessing John Story's apology for questioning the submission he and John Wilkinson had made in 1676. Parke wrote a testimony to Isaac Penington, published with the latter's *Works* in 1681. In the crackdown on nonconformists following disclosure of the Rye House plotting, parish officials at St Olave's, Southwark, seized £12 worth of Parke's goods in August 1683 for recusancy; he was fined on other occasions. When the Baptist Benjamin Keach likened Quakers to Catholics in *The Progress of Sin* (1684) Parke rebutted the charge in *False Fictions and Romances Rebuked* (1684). In *The Hour of God's Judgments Come and Coming* (1690) he warned that God would inflict the harshest punishments on nations to which he had shown the most love. The same prophetic tone pervades *A Call, in the Universal Spirit* (1692), written in the aftermath of the great earthquake: 'Howle, howle, lament, lament with great Lamentation and Weeping' (p. 3).

In addition to preaching and writing Parke served the Quaker movement by examining manuscripts for the morning meeting. He was close to George Fox, who sometimes stayed at his house. Parke spoke at Fox's funeral in January 1691. Parke's stature is reflected in his role as a signatory to such Quaker documents as the epistle 'Against loose spirits denying ministry' (1666), the 1689 general epistle on marriage, George Whitehead's 'Christian doctrine' (1693), and Richard Farnsworth's epistle on the need to subordinate individual interpretations of truth to that of the society (1696). Parke died at Southwark on 11 or 12 November 1696, several weeks after his wife's death. His two children, James and Frances, also predeceased him.

RICHARD L. GREAVES

Sources *The short journal and itinerary journals of George Fox*, ed. N. Penney (1925) · R. Davies, *An account of the convincement, exercises, services and travels, of that ancient servant of the lord, Richard Davies*, 2nd edn (1752) · *DNB* · Religious Society of Friends, Dublin, Sharp MSS, S2, fols. 139, 142–3; S4, fols. 93–4, 98–100 · R. L. Greaves, *God's other children: protestant nonconformists and the emergence of denominational churches in Ireland, 1660–1700* (1997) · J. Besse, *A collection of the sufferings of the people called Quakers*, 2 vols. (1753), 1.119, 705; 2.202 · W. C. Braithwaite, *The second period of Quakerism*, ed. H. J. Cadbury, 2nd edn (1961) · 'Record of Friends travelling in Ireland, 1656–1765 [pt 1]', *Journal of the Friends' Historical Society*, 10 (1913), 157–80 · *The papers of William Penn*, ed. M. M. Dunn, R. S. Dunn, and others, 1 (1981), 556–7 · H. Barbour and A. O. Roberts, *Early Quaker writings, 1650–1700* (1973) · H. L. Ingle, *First among Friends: George Fox and the creation of Quakerism* (1994)

Archives Religious Society of Friends, Dublin, Sharp MSS · RS Friends, Lond., Swarthmore MSS · RS Friends, Lond., Barclay MSS

Parke, James, Baron Wensleydale (1782–1868), judge, was born on 22 March 1782 at Highfield near Liverpool, the ninth son and thirteenth child of Thomas Parke (*d*. 1819), merchant of Liverpool, and Anne, daughter of William Preston. From Macclesfield grammar school, he went up to Trinity College, Cambridge. A brilliant academic career followed: he won a Craven scholarship and Browne's gold medal, was senior chancellor's medallist in classics and fifth wrangler, and was elected to a Trinity fellowship in 1804, a year after his graduation. Parke was called to the bar at the Inner Temple in 1813, after practising, as was not uncommon, as a special pleader. His career at the bar was a successful one, although he was neither a great advocate nor skilful in the examination and cross-examination of witnesses. But he 'talked common sense to average minds, in simple language, and won them by his intelligibility and fairness' (Manson, 18). These qualities and his mastery of the common law explain why he was retained by the crown to support the bill of pains and penalties against Queen Caroline in 1820. His public role was a muted one, in comparison with that of the attorney-general and solicitor-general who led him (*Hansard* 2, 2, 1820, 612 ff.; 3, 1820, 11 ff.).

On 28 November 1828, even though he was not a KC, Parke was appointed a judge of the king's bench on the nomination of Lord Lyndhurst, the lord chancellor, in succession to Sir George Sowley Holroyd. He was knighted on 1 December of the same year. In 1833 he became a member of the judicial committee of the privy council. His king's bench tenure was short-lived, as on 29 April 1834 he was transferred to the court of exchequer, and became 'the dominant personality in that court', until his resignation in 1855 (Holdsworth, *Eng. law*, 15.487).

Sir John Byles dedicated his treatise on *Bills* to Parke, and Sir James Shaw Willes, a most distinguished Victorian judge, said that 'to him the law was under a greater obligation than to any judge within living memory' (*Select Essays in Anglo-American Legal History*, 1.747). Parke's judgments, usually written, were 'models of lucid statement and cogent reasoning' (*DNB*), and 'more frequently than any of the barons he gave the judgment of the court' (Holdsworth, *Eng. law*, 15.488). His judgments in the exchequer are to be found in the reports of Meeson and Welsby. An early and important decision was *Langridge* v. *Levy* (1837), where the seller had fraudulently represented to the plaintiff's father that a gun was safe; it burst injuring the plaintiff. The court held that the seller was liable even though the contract was made with the father and not with the plaintiff.

As a trial judge Parke was grave but not pompous, patient, and courteous. He had a passion for fresh air, insisting that windows should be open even on the coldest day; so at one assize 'the jury, each member with a different colour handkerchief over his head, a shivering sheriff, and despairing Ordinary, presented a sufficiently comical scene to those not too frozen to be amused at it' (Ballantine, 1.157–8). His great defect was said to be his 'superstitious reverence for the dark technicalities of special pleading' (*DNB*) which led to much delay and on occasions to injustice and the exclusion of the merits of the particular case. The Common Law Procedure Acts of 1852 and 1854 recast this system of pleading. Parke, who disapproved of their enactment, resigned in 1855.

As early as 1850 Sir Richard Bethell, as attorney-general, voiced concern that 'judicial business was conducted before the Supreme Court of Appeal [the House of Lords] in a manner which would disgrace the lowest court of justice in the kingdom' (Campbell, 582). There were very few law lords, and their composition was constantly changing. Palmerston, on Bethell's advice, decided that life peerages for eminent lawyers would solve that problem; he therefore nominated Parke. In January 1856 letters patent were granted. Parke was created Baron Wensleydale of Wensleydale in the North Riding of Yorkshire for life. Because of a severe attack of gout he was unable to take his seat when the house met on 31 January, which gave the Conservative opposition in the House of Lords, joined by the lawyers who were hereditary peers, an opportunity to object to the creation of life peerages. Lyndhurst, then eighty-four, in a speech of great vigour, claimed that the creation of life peers was a 'flagrant violation of the principles of the Constitution', and asked rhetorically, what 'has the profession of the law done to merit this indignity?' Derby objected that the creation of life peers would enable the government to swamp the house. In a lively debate on 7 February (*Hansard* 3, 140, 1856, 263–379), Lyndhurst successfully moved that the matter be referred to the committee of privileges which reported that there was no prerogative power to create life peers, a conclusion which was 'shakily based on the argument of long desuetude' (Thompson, 52). Consequently, Parke was given a hereditary peerage in tail male, as Baron Wensleydale of Walton in the county of Lancaster, finally taking his seat on 25 July 1856. Wensleydale was 'never a politician or the adherent of any political party', though 'he kept in touch with movements of the day' (Lowther, 1.117). He was now seventy-four, and, except on legal matters, he rarely spoke in the house. Wensleydale's legal opinions in the House of Lords have been less influential than his judgments in the exchequer. They include *Whicker* v. *Hume* (1858, defining 'domicile') and *Cox* v. *Hickman* (1860, defining a 'partnership').

Parke married on 8 April 1817 Cecilia Arabella Francis (*d.* 1879), youngest daughter of Samuel Francis Barlow of Middlethorpe, Yorkshire, and they had three sons and three daughters. Of these only Charlotte Alice survived her father. She married the Hon. William Lowther of Campsea House, Suffolk, in 1853. Their son, later Viscount Ullswater, remembered his grandfather 'in his last years' as

> short in stature, with very keen, piercing, brown eyes, a fine head of white hair standing erect, dark eyebrows, a large but well shaped nose and a rather underhung mouth. I never remember him wearing anything but a top hat, a black cloth coat, a double-breasted waistcoat and dark trousers fastened with straps under his boots for riding. He carried himself very well, and was very fond of riding exercises. (Lowther, 1.116–17)

Among Wensleydale's friends were literary, as well as legal, celebrities, including Palgrave; he had a 'passion for poetry' (ibid., 1.117). The peerage became extinct on Wensleydale's death which occurred at his home, Ampthill Park, Bedfordshire, on 25 February 1868. He was buried in Ampthill church on 29 February. GARETH H. JONES

Sources Holdsworth, *Eng. law*, vol. 15 • *Hansard 2* • *Hansard 3* • J. W. Lowther, Viscount Ullswater, *A speaker's commentaries*, 1 (1925) • W. Ballantine, *Some experiences of a barrister's life*, 2nd–5th edns (1882) • A. W. B. Simpson, ed., *Biographical dictionary of the common law* (1984) • *Select essays in Anglo-American legal history*, 3 vols. (1907–9) • E. Manson, *Builders of our law during the reign of Queen Victoria*, 2nd edn (1904) • *The Times* (28 Feb 1868) • J. Campbell, *Lives of Lord Lyndhurst and Lord Brougham* (1869) • F. M. L. Thompson, *English landed society in the nineteenth century* (1963) • E. Foss, *Biographia juridica: a biographical dictionary of the judges of England … 1066–1870* (1870) • Boase, *Mod. Eng. biog.* • *DNB*

Archives BL, letters • Northumbd RO, corresp. and papers, with those of his wife

Likenesses G. Hayter, group portrait, oils, 1820 (*The trial of Queen Caroline*), NPG; study, NPG • George, Lord Carlisle, pencil drawing, *c.*1863, NPG; repro. in Lowther, *Speaker's commentaries* • T. Phillips, oils, Inner Temple, London • Walter & Sons, photograph, NPG • G. F. Watts, oils, Castle Howard, North Yorkshire • portrait, repro. in *ILN* (22 March 1845)

Wealth at death under £120,000: administration, 8 April 1868, *CGPLA Eng. & Wales*

Parke, John (1745–1829), oboist, was born in London and studied the oboe with Simpson and music theory with Baumgarten. William Thomas *Parke was his younger brother and pupil for a time. In 1768 John was appointed principal oboe at the King's Theatre, and in the same year he played at the first Birmingham festival and also at the

Three Choirs festival at Hereford. He continued to perform at the Three Choirs festivals for thirty-five years.

In 1768 the Dresden oboist J. C. Fischer first went to London and he replaced Parke at the opera in 1769. His performances and 'soft sweet tone' (*New Grove*) inspired Parke. He improved his style and two years later succeeded Fischer as concerto player at Vauxhall Gardens. About 1771 he accepted an offer from Garrick, always a good friend, to become first oboe at Drury Lane Theatre, a post he retained for most of his career. This did not prevent Smith and Stanley from engaging him as a principal at the Lenten oratorios, and summer performances at Ranelagh and Vauxhall gardens.

In 1783 the duke of Cumberland took Parke into his band, which was led by Baumgarten, and the prince of Wales employed him as a chamber musician at Carlton House with a salary of £100. He was also a member of the king's band and a prominent performer as principal oboe at the Concert of Ancient Music, the Professional, and other concerts, including, with his brother, the Haydn concerts in Hanover Square. He retired in 1815 at the age of seventy, and he died in London on 2 August 1829. He composed some unpublished oboe concertos, which he often played in oratorio intervals and at the pleasure gardens. Parke and his wife, Hannah Maria, had at least seven children between 1772 and 1790, of whom the youngest was the architect Henry *Parke.

Parke's eldest child, **Maria Frances Parke** (*bap.* 1772, *d.* 1822), musician, baptized at St Anne's, Soho, on 24 September 1772, was trained by her father. Many reference works have confused her with the musician and composer Maria Hester Park. Her first public appearance as a vocalist and pianist was at her father's benefit concert in April 1782. She sang at the Handel commemoration concerts in 1784, and on 11 February 1785 played in a concerto during the interval of a performance of *Messiah* at Drury Lane. Her performance was highly praised and warmly received. Her earliest known published work, a vocal piece called 'I have often been told', dates from 1787. In 1790 she performed at the Three Choirs festival in Gloucester as second soloist, and in 1794–7 and 1807 appeared as principal soprano. She was heard at many London concerts, oratorios, and provincial festivals, but not in opera. The family's associations with Haydn led to the composer directing 'one of his new symphonies at her benefit concert in Hanover Square Rooms on 19 May 1794' (*New Grove*). Other published works included three grand sonatas in 1799, two further grand sonatas in 1800, and a divertimento, probably in 1807, and two duets. A fine musician, scientific and accurate in her singing, she retired from the profession on her marriage to John Beardmore of Queen Street, Mayfair, in 1815. She died in London on 31 July 1822.

L. M. MIDDLETON, *rev.* DAVID J. GOLBY

Sources R. Fiske, 'Parke', *New Grove* • S. McVeigh, *Concert life in London from Mozart to Haydn* (1993) • Brown & Stratton, *Brit. mus.*, 308 • O. Baldwin and T. Wilson, 'Parke, Maria F.', *The new Grove dictionary of women composers*, ed. J. A. Sadie and R. Samuel (1994) • *IGI*

Likenesses G. H. Harlow, group portrait, oils, *c.*1817 (*Court for the trial of Queen Catherine (Henry VIII)*), Royal Shakespeare Memorial Theatre Museum, Stratford upon Avon

Parke, Maria Frances (*bap.* **1772**, *d.* **1822**). *See under* Parke, John (1745–1829).

Parke, Mary Winifred (**1908–1989**), marine botanist, was born on 23 March 1908 in Bootle, Liverpool, second of the six children of William Aloysius Parke (1873–1925), partner in a company operating barges, and his wife, Mary Magdalene (1879–1968). She was educated at the Notre Dame Convent, Everton Valley, Liverpool, where, although showing promise as a pianist, she made biology her main interest, in spite of discouragement from her headmistress. Subsequently she entered Liverpool University, gaining its BSc with honours in botany and the Isaac Roberts Research Scholarship in 1929. A PhD followed in 1932 and a DSc in 1950. Her postgraduate research was supervised by Margery Knight. In 1930 she transferred to the University Marine Station at Port Erin, Isle of Man, where she was appointed as algologist.

Mary Parke's first publication, *Manx Algae* (1931), written in collaboration with Knight, served for long as a standard reference work. At the suggestion of the director of the station, she undertook investigation of the minute planktonic organisms on which oyster larvae were believed to feed. Her work eventually focused on hitherto undescribed micro-organisms, one of which proved spectacularly successful for rearing oyster larvae and came to be used worldwide in mariculture. However, the Second World War forced her to turn her attention to seaweeds: Britain was cut off from its wonted supplies of agar and alginate, needed in medicine and industry, and it became urgent to assess the British marine flora as a source of these materials. In 1941 Parke was seconded to Plymouth, where this work was organized by the Marine Biological Association. Her study of the growth and regeneration of the larger brown algae was a rigorous quantitative approach, setting a new standard in seaweed ecology. In 1947 she was appointed as botanist with the association and was to remain at Plymouth for the rest of her life. Resuming the work on minute plankton initiated at Port Erin, she described many new species and assembled an important culture collection. She established the ecological importance of these forms and in collaboration with Irene Manton, an accomplished electron microscopist, elucidated their fine structure, shedding light on the classification and phylogeny of the algae. Her *Check-List of Marine Algae* (1953), the third revision of which (1976) she published with P. S. Dixon, was used worldwide as a working document and model of taxonomic judgement. Altogether, she produced fifty-nine scientific papers, mostly in the *Journal of the Marine Biological Association*.

Mary Parke was always a rotund figure, but nevertheless agile on rocky shores. She was a Roman Catholic of deep convictions which were manifest in her friendly manner, high standards, and willingness to help those in distress or to undertake menial tasks. As the senior female member of staff, she had extra duties in organizing the common room and supervising the general cleanliness of the laboratory. Outside Plymouth her greatest contribution was in the British Phycological Society: she was a founder

Mary Winifred Parke (1908–1989), by Godfrey Argent

member, a council member and editor of its journal for many years, and president from 1959 to 1960. She was commemorated by the Mary Parke bursary, set up by this society and the Marine Biological Association to assist young students to work at marine laboratories. Her honours included corresponding membership of the Royal Botanical Society of the Netherlands (1970), membership of the Norwegian Academy of Sciences and Letters (1971), and the fellowship of the Royal Society (1972). Her own university conferred on her an honorary DSc in 1986, the ceremony taking place in the Plymouth laboratory, deemed for the occasion an outstation of the University of Liverpool, on account of her ill health. She never married. After retirement in 1973 she continued to live in Plymouth and, for some years, still worked in the laboratory. She died, after a short illness, from septicaemia on 17 July 1989 at her home, 6 Alfred Street, The Hoe. Her body was cremated and her ashes scattered at sea. G. E. Fogg

Sources G. T. Boalch and G. E. Fogg, *Memoirs FRS*, 37 (1991), 383–97 · J. C. Green, 'Mary Parke, FRS, 1908–1989', *British Phycological Journal*, 25 (1990), 211–16 · G. Boalch, 'Mary Parke', *Prominent phycologists of the 20th century*, ed. D. J. Garbary and M. J. Wynne (1996) · RS · private information (2004)

Archives Marine Biological Association, Plymouth

Likenesses G. Argent, photograph, RS [*see illus.*] · D. Nicholson, photograph, repro. in Green, 'Mary Parke', 211

Wealth at death £117,544: probate, 28 Nov 1989, *CGPLA Eng. & Wales*

Parke, Robert (*fl.* **1588–1589**), translator, is an obscure figure, known only for his *Historie of the great and mightie kingdome of China, and the situation thereof, togither with the great riches, huge citties, politike governement, and rare inventions in the same* published in 1588. It is a translation of Gonzales de Mendoza's account of China first published at Rome in 1585. Mendoza's work proved immediately popular, with several more editions, and translations into Italian, French, German, and Latin, in addition to Parke's translation. Parke dedicated the work to Thomas Cavendish, the explorer, on 1 January 1589. He stated that the translation had been undertaken 'at the earnest request and encouragement of my worshipfull friend Master Richard Hakluit late of Oxford'. With a familiar mixture of providential and economic language, Parke encouraged Cavendish, who had just returned from his first voyage to the Philippines and China, to attempt to reach the China seas by a north-west passage, an action 'so highly importing the generall state of this lande'. Parke's translation was edited for the Hakluyt Society by Sir George T. Staunton, with an introduction by R. H. Major, in 2 volumes, in 1853. It has been suggested that Parke was the R. P. who translated various parts of Diego Ortúrez de Calahorra's *Espejo de principes y cavalleros* into English from 1585 to 1601. Another possible candidate is the author Robert Parry.

Ronald Bayne, *rev.* Eleri Larkum

Sources R. Parke, *The history of the great and mighty kingdom of China*, ed. G. T. Staunton, Hakluyt Society (1853) · *ESTC*

Parke, Robert (*bap.* **1600**, *d.* **1668**), clergyman and ejected minister, was baptized on 17 August 1600 in Bolton, Lancashire, the son of John Parke and his wife, Elizabeth. He was educated locally and admitted pensioner to Emmanuel College, Cambridge, on 20 June 1615. While at Cambridge he acquired the puritan values that directed his life. He graduated BA in 1619 and proceeded MA in 1622.

By this time Parke had apparently already returned to Bolton as curate and married his wife, Margery: their first child, Lidia, was baptized there on 8 July 1622 and at least two other daughters followed, Anne, baptized on 29 April 1627, and Mary, buried there on 8 May 1631. On 16 December 1625 Parke was instituted vicar of Bolton, serving until 1631. He then emigrated to the Netherlands, where he became a fractious and controversial pastor at Delft (1636–41) and Rotterdam (1641–9). Nevertheless, he maintained close links with the Lancashire godly and returned to preach at Gorton, near Manchester, in April 1639. In 1644, following the death of William Gregg, his successor at Bolton, he was persuaded by a former parishioner to return to Lancashire. However, a new vicar had been appointed, and so Parke elected to go back to Rotterdam.

After 1649 Parke did settle again in Bolton, where he lectured locally during the 1650s and was Gosnall lecturer between 1660 and 1662, paying the clerical subsidy in 1661. In 1662 he was ejected for refusing to conform, but maintained links with local nonconformists. He became friends with the Manchester divine Henry Newcome and, having paid hearth tax in Bolton in 1664, retired about 1665 to Broughton, near Manchester, with his large library. He died in 1668 and was buried in Bolton on 25 December. His friend Oliver Heywood preached the funeral sermon. S. J. Guscott

Sources Venn, *Alum. Cant.* • *The nonconformist's memorial … originally written by … Edmund Calamy*, ed. S. Palmer, [3rd edn], 2 (1802), 355 • R. C. Richardson, *Puritanism in north-west England: a regional study of the diocese of Chester to 1642* (1972), 61, 133, 188 • K. L. Sprunger, *Dutch puritanism: a history of English and Scottish churches of the Netherlands in the sixteenth and seventeenth centuries* (1982) • *DNB* • A. Sparke, ed., *The registers of the parish church of Bolton* (1913), 13 • *The Rev. Oliver Heywood … his autobiography, diaries, anecdote and event books*, ed. J. H. Turner, 1 (1881), 83–4, 263, 273, 276 • *The diary of the Rev. Henry Newcome, from September 30, 1661, to September 29, 1663*, ed. T. Heywood, Chetham Society, 18 (1849), 107 • *Calamy rev.*, 381
Archives Man. CL, Worsley MSS

Parke [Park, Parks], **Robert** (*d.* **1792**), architect, may be the 'Mr Parke' who in 1772 entered the competition for designing the Blue Coat School in Dublin which was won by Thomas Ivory. Of his parents nothing is known. He was clerk of works to Thomas Cooley in the first stages of the construction of the Four Courts complex in Dublin, which was started in 1776 and interrupted by Cooley's death in 1784. He was also employed by the Dublin Society from at least 1784 and had dealings with the Dublin wide streets commissioners between 1784 and 1787. He was probably also architect to the linen board. At the time of his death at his home, 31 William Street, Dublin, in 1792 he was superintending additions to the Irish House of Commons to designs claimed by the amateur architect Samuel Hayes but largely attributable to James Gandon.

Parke was succeeded in this work by his son **Edward Parke** (*fl.* 1792–1844), with whom he has been confused. Edward Parke enjoyed the patronage of John Foster, who was speaker of the Irish House of Commons when the additions were being made to the building. Foster commissioned Parke to design farm offices at his house at Collon, co. Louth, *c.*1812 and must have been influential in the choice of Parke as architect of Dundalk court house at about the same time. Parke and Foster subsequently quarrelled, with the result that the court house commission was handed over in 1813 to John Bowden. Like his father, Edward Parke was architect to the Dublin Society. He was also architect to the linen board and to the trustees of the royal exchange. His principal works in Dublin were the Commercial Buildings, Dame Street (1796–9; dem. 1970, when the shell was rebuilt and reorientated), and the Royal College of Surgeons (1806–10; enlarged by William Murray, 1825–7). Parke's known works show him to have been a competent classical architect, but the extent of his contribution, if any, to the impressive Greek-revival design of Dundalk court house has not been established. He appears to have continued as architect to the Commercial Buildings Company until as late as 1844.

W. A. van S. Papworth, *rev.* A. M. Rowan

Sources *The journals of the House of Commons of the kingdom of Ireland*, 19 vols. (1796–1800), vol. 12, p. 45; vol. 15, p. 409; vol. 16, p. 89ff • E. McParland, *James Gandon: Vitruvius Hibernicus* (1985), 84–5, 204 • J. Warburton, J. Whitelaw, and R. Walsh, *History of the city of Dublin*, 2 vols. (1818), 234, 987 • J. D. H. Widdess, *An account of the schools of surgery, Royal College of Surgeons, Dublin, 1789–1948* (1949), 56 • *North-west Ulster: the counties of Londonderry, Donegal, Fermanagh and Tyrone*, Pevsner (1979), 268–9 • *Public Register, or, Freeman's Journal* (9–12 Jan 1773) • *The Post Office directory* (1844), 596 • Dublin City Archives, Wide streets commissioners MSS • J. Turpin, *A school of art in Dublin since the eighteenth century: a history of the National College of Art and Design* (1995), 62, 123 • A. P. W. Malcomson, *John Foster: the politics of the Anglo-Irish ascendancy* (1978), 17 • PRO NIre., Foster / Massereene MSS

Parke, Thomas Heazle (**1857–1893**), army medical officer and explorer in Africa, was the second son of William Parke JP, of Clogher House, Drumsna, co. Roscommon, and Henrietta, daughter of Henry Holmes of Newport House, Isle of Wight. The family, said to be of Kentish origin, settled in Ireland in the seventeenth century. Born at the family residence on 27 November 1857, Parke spent his early days in the neighbourhood of Carrick-on-Shannon, co. Leitrim. He was privately educated from 1869 in Dublin, and in 1875 he moved to the school of the Royal College of Surgeons in Ireland, and attended the City of Dublin Hospital; at a later date he studied at the Richmond, Whitworth, and Hardwicke hospitals as an intern surgical pupil for six months. He became a licentiate of the Royal College of Surgeons in Ireland in 1878, and of the King and Queen's College of Physicians in Ireland, and a licentiate in midwifery in 1879. For a time he acted as dispensary medical officer at Ballybay in co. Monaghan, and as surgeon to the Eastern Dispensary at Bath. In February 1881 he was gazetted as surgeon in the army medical department and saw service in the Tell al-Kebir campaign of 1882. During the cholera epidemic in Egypt in 1883, when two-fifths of the English soldiers were prostrated by the disease, he acted as senior medical officer at the Helwan cholera camp near Cairo; his report on this epidemic won approbation. He accompanied the desert column sent to rescue Gordon in 1884–5, marching with the convoy for Gakdul under Colonel Stanley-Clarke, and taking part in all the engagements which occurred in crossing the Bayuda Desert. He was present at Abu Klea on 17 January, at the action of Gubat on the 19th, and at the reconnaissance at Metemmah on the 21st. Decorated for these services, he was subsequently employed at Cairo and elsewhere in Egypt.

Towards the end of January 1887, when stationed at Alexandria, Parke offered to accompany the Emin Pasha relief expedition formed under the leadership of Henry Morton Stanley who badly needed the services of a medical officer. Duly commissioned by the khedive, on 4 February he set sail with his new commander for Zanzibar, where the main body of the expeditionary force was collected. To oblige Stanley's employer, the Belgian king Leopold II, they went from Zanzibar by sea round the Cape of Good Hope, and thence to the mouth of the Congo. They ascended the lower river to the head of its navigation in steamers, and thence marched overland for 200 miles to Stanley Pool. From that place there was a long river voyage up the Congo, and its affluent, the Aruwimi—nearly 1000 miles in all—to the point on the latter selected by Stanley as his base. Here an entrenched camp was formed, and the famous march into the Congo Forest was commenced. Parke was always with the advance column and so close to Stanley for most of the time. Although not afraid to remonstrate with this violent and ruthless man, Parke remained loyal to Stanley, recognizing his remarkable

Thomas Heazle Parke (1857–1893), by unknown photographer

qualities. Parke himself was quiet, mature, and sensible and not without humour even in the gravest difficulties.

Throughout the expedition, in addition to all his medical and sanitary responsibilities, Parke commanded his own company, and proved himself as efficient as any in the management of men. On several occasions, the complicated manoeuvres necessary to get all the large, unhealthy, and semi-mutinous expedition together in Emin's domain near Lake Albert meant that Parke was in independent command of sections of the company for long periods. He attracted the devotion of a pygmy girl servant. Stanley asserted that without Parke the expedition would have been a failure. He ministered to the wants of the Zanzibari porters and locally recruited Africans, as well as to the eleven Europeans who accompanied the expedition, with all the patience and skill possible. He attended Stanley in two bouts of severe illness, almost certainly saving his life in April 1889.

On 20 April 1888 Parke and A. J. Mounteney Jephson became the first explorers to see the snow-covered peaks of the Ruwenzori massif. Stanley unfairly glossed over this fact and implied that he himself was the discoverer. On the return of the expedition to the coast Parke successfully treated Emin Pasha, who had fallen off a balcony during a welcoming banquet at Bagamoyo and fractured his skull. On 16 January 1890 Parke returned to Cairo; he was then recovering from fever, and was hardly able to walk upstairs. He landed in England at the beginning of May, when he was warmly welcomed, and received many tokens of cordial recognition from the medical profession and from various scientific bodies. The Royal College of Surgeons in Ireland awarded him an honorary fellowship, the University of Durham conferred on him the honorary degree of DCL, and he was presented at Birmingham with the gold medal of the British Medical Association 'for distinguished merit'. He received the gold medals of the Royal Geographical societies of London and Antwerp, and was elected an honorary fellow of those and many similar societies. The only consideration he received from the government was permission to count his time in Africa as full-pay service. After his return he was attached to the 2nd lifeguards in London, and was subsequently employed at the Royal Victoria Hospital, Netley, near Southampton. He was promoted to surgeon-major on 5 February 1893.

The hardships which Parke had undergone during the near disastrous expedition had ruined his health, and during the latter years of his life he had several seizures of an epileptiform nature. He died suddenly on 10 September 1893, at Alt na Craig, while on a visit to Argyll. He was interred in the private burying-ground of the Parke family at Kilmessan, co. Leitrim. A fund was opened to erect a statue of Parke in Dublin.

Parke's account of the Emin Pasha expedition was based on a 'sanitized' version of his diary with unkind comments on Stanley removed. The book was actually written by Parke's old friend and tutor, John Knott. J. B. Lyons has established that Knott wrote *all* the medical and imperial works which appeared in Parke's name after 1890, although this was never publicly acknowledged. Most important were *Guide to Health in Africa* (1893) and an article in the *Nineteenth Century* giving Parke's view that Gordon could have been saved in 1885 if Sir Charles Wilson had acted with greater promptness. The medical works were not pathbreaking and the imperial propaganda said nothing new. These publications were a desperate attempt to make some money for Parke and Knott.

W. W. Webb, *rev.* Roy Bridges

Sources T. Heazle Parke, *My personal experiences in equatorial Africa* (1891) · J. B. Lyons, *Surgeon-Major Parke's African journey, 1887–89* (1994) · H. M. Stanley, *In darkest Africa*, 2 vols. (1890) · *The diary of A. J. Mounteney Jephson: Emin Pasha relief expedition, 1887–1889*, ed. D. Middleton, Hakluyt Society, extra ser., 40 (1969) · I. R. Smith, *The Emin Pasha relief expedition, 1886–1890* (1972) · A. J. Mounteney-Jephson, *Emin Pasha and the rebellion at the equator* (1890) · *Times atlas of world exploration* (1991), chap. 40 · *CGPLA Eng. & Wales* (1894)

Archives BL · Royal College of Surgeons in Ireland, Dublin, Mercer Library, diary kept during 1887–9 expedition, 4 vols. · Royal College of Surgeons in Ireland, Dublin, letters to J. Knott · Wellcome L. | SOAS, Mackinnon MSS

Likenesses H. Barnes, marble bust, Royal College of Surgeons of Ireland, Dublin · Barraud, photograph, NPG; repro. in *Men and women of the day*, 3 (1890) · Miss Ffolliott, oils; Parke Memorial Hall, Carrick-on-Shannon, in 1895 · P. Wood, statue, Dublin Natural History Museum · engraving (after photograph), repro. in Stanley, *In*

darkest Africa, vol. 1, p. 50 • memorial window, Ballybay, co. Monaghan • photograph, repro. in D. Middleton, ed., *The diary of A. J. Mounteney-Jephson*, pl. 2b • photograph, repro. in Parke, *My personal experiences in equatorial Africa*, frontispiece • photograph, Royal College of Surgeons of Ireland, Dublin • photograph, NPG [*see illus.*] • plaque, Kilmore church, Down • plaque, Victoria Hospital, Netley
Wealth at death £38 in England: Irish administration sealed in England, 27 Feb 1894, *CGPLA Eng. & Wales*

Parke, William Thomas (1762–1847), oboist, was born in London. He studied the flute from the age of ten and the oboe from the age of eleven with his elder brother, John *Parke, and the violin with William Dance. When he was thirteen he took piano lessons with Charles Rousseau Burney. In 1773 or 1774 he sang in the chorus at Drury Lane, and in 1776 he played the viola there and at Vauxhall. However, he began to concentrate on the oboe, playing second at Drury Lane and Vauxhall in 1777 and performing double concertos with his brother. In 1783 he became principal oboe at Covent Garden, a post he retained for forty years. William Shield, who had recommended him, wrote arias with important oboe obbligatos for him in several works, and Shield, James Hook, and Joseph Mazzinghi included concertante oboe parts for him in their overtures. Having studied theory with Karl Friedrich Baumgarten, Parke played a concerto of his own composition in an oratorio concert at Drury Lane in 1786. He also published two sets of duets for flutes or oboes (1791–2) and wrote overtures and other instrumental music for several of Shield's works. He adapted N.-M. Dalayrac's *Nina* for the benefit concert of the soprano Elizabeth Martyr, who became his mistress. They had two sons. On Elizabeth's death in 1806 she bequeathed him her farm at Yalding in Kent. She also sang many of the light songs on which he latterly concentrated. Apart from these (some 150 written for Vauxhall), Parke later composed elegies, odes, and further concertos. His performances at the Noblemen's Subscription Concerts won him the patronage of the duke of Cumberland, and the prince of Wales made him a member of his band at Carlton House, where he met Haydn. He was one of the original members of a glee club founded in 1793, and belonged to the Anacreontic Society. He made many provincial tours, visiting such towns as Birmingham (1794), Dublin (1796), and Cheltenham (1800), as well as Portsmouth and Worcester.

Parke's tone on the oboe was sweet and his technique brilliant. He extended the range of the instrument by a third, first demonstrating his top G in a concerto at the Hanover Square Rooms in 1796, and, by his own account, exciting great admiration with his abilities in the high register. He retired in 1825, and in 1830 published his *Musical Memoirs*, a valuable if gossipy record of the period between 1784 and 1830. His judgement of other artists is sometimes warmly appreciative though occasionally spiced with malice. He died in London on 24 August 1847.

L. M. Middleton, *rev.* John Warrack

Sources *New Grove* • W. T. Parke, *Musical memoirs*, 2 vols. (1830) • P. Bate, *The oboe* (1956)

Parker, Agnes Miller (1895–1980), painter and printmaker, was born on 25 March 1895 in Irvine, Ayrshire, the eldest of eight children of William Parker, an industrial chemist, and his wife, Harriet Miller. She was educated at Glasgow's Whitehill Higher Grade School, before entering the Glasgow School of Art in 1911, receiving her diploma in 1917. An art school contemporary was the painter and critic William *McCance (1894–1970), always known as Mac. He was imprisoned for conscientious objection in 1917; they married at Bucklow in 1918. That year Agnes began to teach art at the Glasgow school; both exhibited with the Glasgow Society of Painters and Sculptors, before moving to London in 1920. Contemporary portraits and photographs show Agnes as a small handsome woman with distinctively large and piercingly blue eyes in an open face under a fringe.

Agnes Miller Parker (1895–1980), by William McCance, 1925

The vorticist artist William Roberts lodged at their Earls' Court home; his influence upon Agnes Miller Parker's painting was significant throughout the decade, and in inverse proportion to his ability to pay rent. She taught in Gerrards Cross and Clapham, 1920–30; Mac painted, lectured, and was art critic for *The Spectator*, 1923–6. By November 1925 they were part of the Chiswick group: 'that clever couple from Scotland who believe in cubist methods' (*Daily Chronicle*, 30 Nov 1925). Other clever Chiswick couples were the Mitchisons, socialist patrons, and Blair Hughes-Stanton (1902–1981) and his wife, Gertrude Hermes (1901–1983). While Agnes had taught herself the rudiments of wood-engraving, it was Hughes-Stanton and Hermes who encouraged and refined her talent. Agnes was the source for the engraver Phoebe Fraser in Naomi Mitchison's 1935 novel *We Have Been Warned*.

In 1928 Agnes Miller Parker, William McCance, Gertrude Hermes, and Blair Hughes-Stanton had a major joint exhibition of their painting and sculpture at St George's Gallery, London. Their modernism unsettled one uncomprehending critic who observed that 'eccentricity ran riot with rather lamentable results!' (*Studio*, 95, 1928, 344). In 1929 Agnes's large engraving *Sheep Dipping in Wales* won the Brewster prize at the first International Exhibition of Engraving and Lithography, in Chicago. In 1930 both couples moved to Wales, Mac to become the controller and the other three to be artist-illustrators of the Gregynog Press, dedicated to producing fine books in limited editions. *The Fables of Esope* (1932) and *XXI Welsh Gypsy Folk-Tales* (1933) illustrated by Agnes's engravings are rightly celebrated as among the finest of the period: her silvery and exquisitely stylized representations are reproduced by superb press work. An influential but not a happy time; all four had left by 1933.

Agnes Miller Parker also illustrated for the Golden Cockerel Press and the commercial firm of Gollancz, collaborating with H. E. Bates on *Through the Woods* (1936) and *Down the River* (1937). These were excellently printed popular triumphs and published in a format uniform with Clare Leighton's (1898–1989) own *Four Hedges* (1935) and *Country Matters* (1937); as a whole the four probably had a far greater impact on the general reading public in the television-less 1930s than all Leighton and Parker's work for the fine presses.

Post-war commissions included illustrations for Richard Jefferies's novels for the Lutterworth Press, 1946–8, and works by Shakespeare and Thomas Hardy for the Limited Editions Club of New York, 1956–69; paradoxically Agnes felt Hardy's work hardly needed 'decoration': 'so many of the jobs that I get to do I feel ought not to have been illustrated. Hardy describes so well that illustrations seem to be superfluous' (Rogerson, *Agnes Miller Parker: Wood Engraver*, 46). Finances after the successes of the 1930s were usually precarious, though in 1944 McCance became lecturer in book production at Reading University. The couple separated in 1955, and Agnes returned to Glasgow; they were divorced in 1963, after which she moved to the Isle of Arran. Agnes Miller Parker died in Ravenscraig Hospital, Greenock, on 15 November 1980. She was buried at Lamlash on the Isle of Arran on 17 November.

Trained as a painter who developed a modernist and vorticist idiom (in tempera!), Agnes Miller Parker was married to an equally talented man of conflicting personality. Her extraordinary talent as a wood-engraver came to fruition only in her mid-thirties. Her achievement as a book illustrator was rarely equalled; she produced extremely fine work with an inimitable silvery sheen, never devoid of character or content, which technical perfection can produce. Agnes illustrated nearly fifty books, exhibited prints with the English Wood Engraving Society, 1926–31, and after election in 1932 with the Society of Wood Engravers until 1956; she was elected an associate of the Royal Society of Painter-Etchers and Engravers in 1939.

HAL BISHOP

Sources I. Rogerson and J. Dreyfus, *Agnes Miller Parker: wood-engraver and book illustrator* (1990) • P. Elliot, *William McCance, 1894–1970*, Scottish Masters Series, 14 (1990) • private information (2004) [Judith Russell, Margaret McCance] • R. Addison, 'Fine lines: Agnes Miller Parker', *Scottish Book Collector*, 6/2 (1998), 16–19 • I. Rogerson, *Agnes Miller Parker: wood engravings from 'The fables of Esope': the story of a remarkable book* (1995) • D. Harrop, *The Gregynog Press* (1980) • A. Horne, *The dictionary of 20th century British book illustrators* (1994) • D. Buckman, *Dictionary of artists in Britain since 1945* (1998) • J. Selborne, *British wood-engraved book illustration, 1900–1940* (1998) • J. Hamilton, *Wood engraving and the woodcut in Britain, c.1890–1990* (1994) • P. Jaffé, *Women engravers* (1988) • W. Hardie, *Scottish painting, 1837–1939* (1976)

Archives Manchester Metropolitan University, archive • NL Scot., corresp. and papers | V&A, corresp. with Phillip Gibbons

Likenesses W. McCance, pencil drawing, 1918, priv. coll. • W. McCance, oils, 1919, priv. coll. • W. McCance, pencil drawing, 1919, Scot. NPG • W. McCance, black crayon drawing, 1925, Scottish National Gallery of Modern Art [*see illus.*]

Parker, Albert Edmund, third earl of Morley (1843–1905), politician, was born at Kent House, Knightsbridge, London, on 11 June 1843. He was the only son of Edmund *Parker, second earl of Morley (1810–1864) [*see under* Parker, John, first earl of Morley (1772–1840)], and his wife, Harriet Sophia (*d.* 1897), the only daughter of Montagu Edmund Parker of Whiteway, Devon, and Harriet Newcombe of Starcross, and the widow of William Coryton of Pentillie Castle, Cornwall; Prince Albert was his godfather. He was educated at Eton College, where he subsequently became a fellow and governor, and at Balliol College, Oxford, where he took a first class in *literae humaniores* and graduated BA in 1865. He succeeded his father in the peerage in 1864 and in 1876 married Margaret (*d.* 1908), daughter of Robert Stayner Holford of Westonbirt and his wife, Mary Anne, *née* Lindsay. They had a daughter and three sons, the eldest, Edmund Robert, succeeding to the title.

In the House of Lords, Morley figured as a polished speaker of Liberal principles. From 1868 to 1874 he was a lord-in-waiting to Queen Victoria during Gladstone's first administration. When Gladstone returned to office in 1880 he became under-secretary for war, serving first under H. C. E. Childers and then under Lord Hartington. He proved an efficient minister, notably in speeches on recruiting and army organization, and he displayed a grasp of affairs during the debates on the occupation of Egypt and the expedition to Khartoum. He left office in 1885.

When the home-rule question arose to divide the Liberal Party, Morley at first followed Gladstone, and from February to April 1886 was first commissioner of public works in Gladstone's third government. On 12 April he resigned, together with Edward Heneage, chancellor of the duchy of Lancaster, after Gladstone had divulged the scope of his measure. He was elected chairman of committees and deputy speaker of the Lords on 4 April 1889, defeating Balfour of Burleigh, the tory candidate. Morley's pronounced unionism meant this was no real defeat for Salisbury. 'My majority', Morley noted, 'was made up of 20 Gladstonians, 44 Liberal Unionists, 30 Conservatives and one bishop.' Morley considerably extended the powers of the chairman, exercising an often decisive influence on the success or failure of private members' legislation. For the guidance of promoters, 'a model bill' was annually devised by his standing counsel and himself, and by the beginning of every session the proposed measures, however numerous, had been passed under thorough review. As '"Lord Chairman"', *The Times* concluded, 'Lord Morley was an autocrat.'

Attacked by a lingering illness, Morley sent in his temporary resignation in February 1904; his departure was generally regretted. Lord Balfour of Burleigh took his place. On 12 February 1905 he finally resigned and he died fourteen days later, on 26 February 1905, at his home, Saltram, Plympton St Mary; he was buried on 2 March in the parish churchyard.

Morley took an active interest in Devon affairs. He was a chairman of quarter sessions, and vice-chairman of the Devon county council from 1889 to 1901, then chairman from 1901 to 1904. His speeches displayed a wide knowledge of local finance and requirements. In succession to his father and grandfather he involved himself in the Plymouth chamber of commerce, became its president in 1864, and made its annual dinner the occasion for a speech on public affairs. He took pride in the fine collection of pictures at Saltram, and was an enthusiastic gardener. L. C. SANDERS, *rev.* H. C. G. MATTHEW

Sources GEC, *Peerage* • A. Adonis, *Making aristocracy work: the peerage and the political system in Britain, 1884–1914* (1993) • *The Times* (27 Feb 1905) • *Western Morning News* (27 Feb 1905)

Archives BL, corresp., papers, and journals, Add. MSS 48265–48300 • Plymouth and West Devon RO, Plymouth, corresp. | BL, corresp. with W. E. Gladstone, Add. MSS 44417–44788 • Bodl. Oxf., letters to Lord Kimberley • Glos. RO, letters to Sir Michael Hicks Beach

Likenesses E. Roberts, oils (copy), Saltram, Devon; copy, Devon county hall • wood-engraving (after photograph by Elliott & Fry), NPG; repro. in *ILN* (20 April 1889) • wood-engraving, NPG; repro. in *ILN* (10 Feb 1866)

Wealth at death £127,650 0s. 4d.: probate, 20 March 1905, *CGPLA Eng. & Wales*

Parker, Alexander (1628–1689), Quaker preacher and author, was born on 21 June 1628 at Chipping, Lancashire, north-east of Preston, the son of Robert Parker (*d.* in or after 1661). He was probably a scion of the Parkers of Browsholme, the principal family in the Bowland district. Although the early historian of the Friends, Gerard Croese, described him as a butcher, he was well-educated and had a gentlemanly demeanour.

The young Friend, 1653–1658 Convinced at Lancaster in 1653, Parker was with George Fox the following year when the latter was arrested at Whetstone, Leicestershire, and accompanied him when he was sent under guard to London. One of Parker's first contributions to the Quaker cause was the publication of *Several Papers* (1654) by Fox and James Nayler. An indefatigable traveller in fulfilling his responsibilities as a public Friend (minister) which he faithfully reported to Margaret Fell, in 1655 he toured the midlands as well as Kent and Sussex, staying for a time with the JP John Crook in Bedfordshire and Thomas and Ann Curtis in Berkshire. At Canterbury in June he was apprehended after speaking to a group of Independents, but the mayor freed him when he expressed agreement with the contents of the oath of abjuration. When he preached in a church near Horsham, Sussex, the minister had the bells rung to drown him out and then used dogs to chase him from the building.

In 1656 Parker journeyed through the north, going from Cheshire into Lancashire where in March he, John Audland, Thomas Lawson, and others participated in a debate with ministers at Preston over which Major-General Charles Worsley presided. From there he went to Westmorland, Yorkshire, and Northumberland. By May he was at Old Radnor, where he engaged in a disputation with the Independent minister Vavasor Powell, which he recounted in *A Testimony of God* (1656). The same month he visited Leominster, Herefordshire, and debated there with the erudite Baptist minister John Tombes. As he travelled in Devon and Cornwall during the summer, Parker evaded soldiers with orders to arrest Friends, and on 19 August he reported to Fell that he knew of no public Friend at liberty but himself. 'This is the day of the lords batle', he wrote on 13 September, 'and the warre is strong betweene the Beast and the Lamb but the lamb shall gett the victory' (Swarthmore MSS, 1.167). Responding to attacks by ministers in Cornwall he wrote *A Testimony of the Light Within* (1657), which prompted a refutation from the Banbury minister Samuel Grevill, who in turn was attacked in William Penn's *Urim and Thummim* (1674). In February 1657 Parker returned to London from the south-west, stopping *en route* at Reading, where he met Isaac Penington, and the same year he urged Baptists to forsake their 'fading and carnal Ordinances' in the tract *To All ye who be called Baptists* (p. 8).

With Fox and others, Parker went to Scotland in September 1657. Despite the conversion of Lady Margaret Hamilton, the Scots were generally antagonistic to their message. The party made its way across Scotland, visiting Stirling, where soldiers briefly detained them, and Burtisland in Fife before going to Perth. There they disputed with Baptists, whose complaint to the governor resulted in their deportation to Dundee where Parker and Fox preached in the market place. At Leith in November, Parker completed *A Discovery of Satans Wiles* (1657), in which he defended Friends from reproaches by such adversaries as the Baptist James Brown, who lumped them with Ranters in *Antichrist in Spirit Unmasked*. After visiting Edinburgh, where warrants for their arrest had been issued, Parker and Fox returned to Perth, and the former continued alone to Dundee. He apparently made another swing through the west, for on 13 January 1658 he reported to Fox that he had been imprisoned for ten or eleven hours after preaching in Glasgow Cathedral and being manhandled by a crowd. On 18 February General Monck ordered the commander at Leith to arrest Parker and Fox, but the latter had already returned to England. Parker's Scottish experiences are reflected in *A Testimony of the Appearance of God* (1658), in which he discussed Hamilton's conversion and denounced presbyterian clergy as false prophets and hirelings.

By spring 1658 Parker was in London, where he visited Nayler in prison on several occasions, finding him willing to recant publicly his Bristol re-enactment of Jesus's entry into Jerusalem the previous year. In tears Parker implored Fox to adopt a conciliatory approach toward Nayler, and on 15 June he wrote to Fell, warning that those who circulated papers castigating Nayler, as Fox urged, would 'kindle as great A fire if not greater then ever, which would be to all our sorrow' (Caton MS, 3.313–17). After another trip to Buckinghamshire and Bedfordshire, Parker visited

Nayler again, this time with Edward Burrough, before leaving on 14 July for the south-west. He later contributed a preface to Nayler's works. Parker's tract, *A Tryall of a Christian*, in which he stressed the importance of a believer's inner life and articulated the Quaker view of the church and ministry, was published in 1658. So, too, was an attack on him and his fellow Friend, John Moon, in *The Sun Outshining the Moon*, by John Price, minister at Maesygelli, Nantmel, Radnorshire.

The middle years, 1659–1667 After a successful preaching tour in the south-west that took him as far as Land's End, in part with Thomas Salthouse, Parker returned to London in late March 1659. On 6 April he signed a declaration to the speaker of parliament offering to take the place of incarcerated Friends, and in *A Call out of Egypt* (1659) he offered hope to persecuted saints and castigated parish clergy as ministers of Antichrist. During the spring he travelled to Buckinghamshire, Cambridgeshire, and Bedfordshire, where members of John Bunyan's congregation opposed him. At Reading in late June he completed *A Testimony of Truth*, refuting an attack on Quaker tenets by the Cheshire minister James Livesey. On 7 August, *en route* for the south-west, Parker wrote to Fox expressing concern about whether Friends should serve as militia commissioners: 'I have had a great weight upon my spirit about it' (Swarthmore MSS, 3.143). From London on 8 October 1659 he sent an epistle to Friends exhorting them to make certain of their calling and election, and a month later he was with Fox and Burrough at Penington's house in Chalfont St Peter, Buckinghamshire.

As Monck's army advanced towards London, Parker wrote an epistle to Friends on 14 January counselling them not to be troubled because the secret hand of God was guiding events. Friends, he advised, should not take sides but use spiritual weapons to wage war against fleshly lusts. (This letter was subsequently published in *A Manifestation of Divine Love*, 1660, with an epistle of Salthouse's.) In *An Epistle to Friends* (1660) Parker urged his coreligionists to 'be valiant in the spiritual Combat, untill all your Enemies be made your Footstool' (p. 1). Parker was with Fox and Curtis at Plymouth in February, and it was probably shortly thereafter that he wrote an epistle averring that Friends obeyed the just commands of magistrates and honoured those who ruled for God, executed justice, and were a terror to evil-doers; it was published with Burrough's *A Declaration to All the World* (1660). Arrested at Northwich and imprisoned at Nantwich, Cheshire, in May, Parker soon asserted that Friends should not have assisted John Lambert's capture of Sir George Booth's men after Booth's uprising failed in 1659. Parker told Fell on 22 August that he had given the magistrates a statement professing his intention to live peacefully under the king's rule, and by 10 September he had been discharged after providing recognizances. By 12 October he was again in prison, this time at Chester, from where he wrote an epistle of spiritual counsel to Friends advising them not to be confused by fickle human doctrine. Another letter followed on 14 November: *To All who are Lovers of, and Believers in the True Light*.

Released by royal proclamation on 20 May 1661, Parker went to Yorkshire to see his ailing father, but by August he was in Cornwall. Although he had recently held numerous peaceful meetings in Bristol, he was arrested there in July 1662. He reported large, mostly peaceful meetings in London in July 1663 and April 1664, but on 17 July 1664 he was apprehended at a meeting in Mile End Green and incarcerated in Newgate on charges of violating the Conventicle Act. He was still there on 30 August, when he wrote an epistle to Friends, published with Francis Howgill's *A Visitation of Love* (1664), exhorting them to remain faithful in the face of persecution and denouncing 'mens invented Customary formes and worship' (p. 13). By 20 October Parker had apparently been discharged. In 1665 he published his broadside *To the Mayor and Aldermen* (of London). He remained in the capital to minister to plague victims, though by December he was again in Bristol. He met with other Quaker leaders, in London in May 1666, to deal with the schism instigated by John Perrot; in 'A testimony from the brethren' they called on Friends to submit to the judgment of meetings and banned separatists from holding office in the society or serving as public Friends. After spending a week in prison at Kingston, Parker travelled to Buckinghamshire, Berkshire, Wiltshire, and Bristol, where he remained until he returned to London with Fox in 1667.

Marriage and later years, 1669–1689 On 8 April 1669 Parker married Prudence (*d.* 1688), daughter of William Goodson and widow of Charles Wager, a naval commander. They lived in London, where Parker worked as a haberdasher, and had four sons and four daughters, three of whom married clergymen (one of whom was George Stanhope, dean of Canterbury). Prudence's son from her first marriage was Admiral Sir Charles Wager.

While preaching in London to the Gracechurch Street meeting on 18 May 1670, Parker was arrested and subsequently fined £20 for having violated the second Conventicle Act. The same year he was in Kent with Fox and George Whitehead, and in 1671 all three contributed testimonies to *The Books and Divers Epistles of … Josiah Coale*. Parker was one of eighty-four Friends who founded the six-weeks' meeting for the management of Quaker affairs, in October 1671. A friend and correspondent of Penn, he signed the certificate when Penn married Gulielma Springett on 4 April 1672. Parker subsequently bought 1000 acres of land in Pennsylvania, though he never emigrated. In May 1672 he helped to draft an epistle admonishing Friends to avoid controversy and the young to keep their place. When John Story and John Wilkinson challenged the growing centralization of the Friends and the role of women's meetings, Fox welcomed the mediatory efforts of Parker and Whitehead, but these were unsuccessful, and in April 1675 the quarterly meeting read statements about the controversy from Parker, Fox, Whitehead, and Penn. In the following month Parker signed an epistle addressing contentious issues among Friends. On 5 October he wrote to Fox, urging him to seek a reconciliation of the Story–Wilkinson dispute, but on the 18th the society asked Parker, George and John Whitehead, and three others to meet with Story and Wilkinson. Although Parker detested strife, he participated in the ensuing meeting at Draw-well, Yorkshire, in April 1676, but this failed to heal the breach. In the meantime he and twelve others affixed their names on 25 May 1675 to *A Treatise of Oaths*, a defence of the Quakers' position which they submitted to parliament; Parker's name appeared first, suggesting he may have been the principal author.

Parker continued to travel on behalf of the Friends, visiting Kent and Sussex in 1672, and Surrey, Hampshire, Dorset, Devon, Cornwall, Somerset, Bristol, and Buckinghamshire in 1676. With Fox he drafted an address to the king on 9 January 1678 concerning the condition of Friends, and on 8 August 1683 he, Whitehead, and Gilbert Latey presented an address to Charles at Windsor on behalf of persecuted Friends. Parker accompanied Fox to the Netherlands, leaving London on 31 May 1684; he returned on 21 July after visiting Rotterdam, Amsterdam, Leeuwarden, and Friesland. In the following winter he and Whitehead presented another petition to the king on behalf of imprisoned Friends. In March 1686 he was himself briefly detained in king's bench prison, but thereafter he attended meetings in the London area and at Waltham Abbey without apparent difficulty. Fox had intended that Parker be one of the Friends responsible for the publication of his journal and papers, but Parker died in London on 8 March 1689 following a fever; he was buried the next day in the Quaker burial-ground in the capital, at Bunhill Fields. His wife predeceased him, on 9 July 1688. His will, dated 6 March 1689, left nearly all his estate to five of his children.

Fox wrote a testimony to Parker that has apparently not survived. A trusted travelling companion and confidant of Fox, the mild-mannered Parker, with his commitment to conformity with the spirit as manifested through Quaker meetings, played an important role in developing the society's organizational structure. In an undated epistle to Margaret Fell he modestly described himself as a lover of truth and simplicity, and this was a key to his success in befriending both the rustic Fox and the aristocratic Penn.

RICHARD L. GREAVES

Sources RS Friends, Lond., Swarthmore MSS 1.97, 161–9, 356; 3.136–7, 139–40; 142–9, 170–72 • RS Friends, Lond., Caton MS 3.258–310, 318–25 • RS Friends, Lond., Penington MS 4.4–6, 103–5 • *The journal of George Fox*, ed. N. Penney, 2 vols. (1911) • *Narrative papers of George Fox*, ed. H. J. Cadbury (1972) • A. R. Barclay, ed., *Letters, &c. of early Friends* (1841) • J. Besse, *A collection of the sufferings of the people called Quakers*, 1 (1753), 394, 408, 480 • N. Penney, ed., *'The first publishers of truth': being early records, now first printed, of the introduction of Quakerism into the counties of England and Wales* (1907) • *The papers of William Penn*, ed. M. M. Dunn, R. S. Dunn, and others, 5 vols. (1981–7) • *The short journal and itinerary journals of George Fox*, ed. N. Penney (1925) • will, PRO, PROB 11/395, sig. 53 • G. Croese, *The general history of the Quakers* (1696) • 'Dictionary of Quaker biography', RS Friends, Lond. [card index] • W. C. Braithwaite, *The beginnings of Quakerism*, ed. H. J. Cadbury, 2nd edn (1955) • H. L. Ingle, *First among Friends: George Fox and the creation of Quakerism* (1994) • *DNB*

Archives RS Friends, Lond., corresp. | RS Friends, Lond., Caton MSS; Penington MSS; Swarthmore MSS

Parker, Alice (*d.* 1692). *See under* Salem witches and their accusers (*act.* 1692).

Parker, (Richard) Barry (1867–1947), architect and town planner, the eldest son of Robert Parker (1826–1901), a bank manager, and his wife, Frances (Fanny) Booth (1835–1922), was born at Chesterfield, Derbyshire, on 18 November 1867. He was educated at schools in Ashover and Buxton and at Wesley College, probably in Sheffield, and attended T. C. Simmonds's atelier of art, Derby, from 1886 to 1889, taking external examinations at South Kensington School of Art, London. From 1889 to 1892 he was articled to G. Faulkner Armitage (1849–1937), architect, of Altrincham, Cheshire, whose studio included craft workshops and a smithy. Parker also acted as Armitage's clerk of works at Brockhampton Court, Herefordshire. He returned to Buxton in 1894, to design three houses for his father in the Park Ring, including the family home Moorlands, following which he commenced independent practice.

In 1893 Parker's elder sister Ethel (1865–1949) married her half-cousin Raymond *Unwin (1863–1940); distrustful of Unwin's Socialist League activities, Robert Parker long disapproved of the match. Unwin had grown up in Oxford, deeply influenced by Ruskin, Morris, and the socialist philosopher Edward Carpenter. After serving an engineering apprenticeship at Chesterfield, he had worked for two years in Manchester, and then for the Staveley Coal and Iron Company at Barrow Hill, near Chesterfield. In 1894 Barry Parker, who responded to Morris's reforms in decorative design rather than his politics, collaborated with Unwin over the design of St Andrew's Church, Barrow Hill, a prelude to the formation of a partnership in 1896, with offices in Buxton.

Parker's commissions included individual middle-class houses, often complete with fittings and furniture. Unwin brought his engineering and costing skills to the practice, but wished to design working-class housing: Parker assisted with the visualization of this ideal, designing 'an artisan's living room' and a housing quadrangle (unbuilt) for a Bradford site. Both designs appeared in their joint book *The Art of Building a Home* (1901), which incorporated Parker's earlier manifesto *Our Homes* (1895). The influence of C. F. A. Voysey and M. H. Baillie Scott was evident in Parker's houses, which included The Shanty, Marple, Cheshire (1895–6), Chetwynd, Northwood, Staffordshire (1899–1902), The Homestead, Chesterfield (1903–5), and Whirriestone, Rochdale, Lancashire (1907–9). These works showed progressive simplification of form, growing confidence of spatial design, and integration of furniture into a total ensemble.

In September 1901 Unwin attended the Garden City Association conference at Bournville; his appearance here led to a commission from Joseph Rowntree for the model village of New Earswick, north of York. Parker and Unwin collaborated on the cottage designs, which became a staple of the practice from 1902. In 1903 Unwin took part in the limited competition for the layout for Letchworth, the first garden city; Parker was asked to give reference as to his partner's experience. In 1904, after approval of the plan, the main office moved to Baldock, Hertfordshire, 2 miles from Letchworth, and in 1907 it moved to a thatched office block at 296 Norton Way South, Letchworth (later the First Garden City Heritage Museum). Unwin moved to Hampstead Garden Suburb in 1906, and opened a separate office at Wyldes, which became his home.

The extensive cottage estates at Letchworth and Hampstead Garden Suburb set standards for the new century. Parker continued to be involved with individual houses: at Letchworth these included Laneside and Crabby Corner, a semi-detached pair built in 1904 in Letchworth Lane, where he and Unwin were neighbours for a short while. Parker married (Constance) Mabel Burton (1882–1974) on 25 July 1906; the birth of their two sons, Geoffrey Barry (1909–1979) and Robert (*b.* 1914) necessitated the extension of Crabby Corner, so a three-storey tower was added, with an open-air sleeping porch on its top floor. Other individual Letchworth houses by Parker included Glaed Haem (1906) and 102 Wilbury Road (1909, for his brother Stanley). He also designed the earliest community buildings, the Mrs Howard Memorial Hall, Norton Way South (1906) and The Skittles inn (The Settlement), Nevells Road (1907).

With the dissolution of the partnership in 1914, and Unwin's recruitment to the Local Government Board, Parker pursued an independent career. In 1915 he spent six months in Oporto, Portugal, redesigning the civic centre, and from 1917 to 1919 he worked in São Paulo, Brazil, on the Jardim America Garden suburb. In 1919 he took the consultancy for New Earswick, and designed its inter-war housing. Council housing schemes for Newark, Nottinghamshire, St Neots, Huntingdonshire, Bridport, Dorset, and Loughborough, Leicestershire, were followed by a planning consultancy for Wythenshawe, the garden satellite of Manchester (1927–41). Influenced by American practice, its innovative master plan incorporated parkways and defined neighbourhood units, which Parker had seen in New York in 1925. Although building was not begun until Wythenshawe was brought within the Manchester city boundary, by 1934 its population of 25,000 was greater than Letchworth and Welwyn Garden City combined.

Barry Parker's extensive writing includes twenty-nine articles on house design, published between 1910 and 1912 in the American arts and crafts periodical *The Craftsman*. Papers in the *Town Planning Institute Journal* and *Town Planning Review* described his work at Wythenshawe and New Earswick. In 1929 Parker served as president of the Town Planning Institute. He had been elected fellow of the Royal Institute of British Architects in 1913, and he was awarded the Howard medal for services to town planning in 1941 by the Town and Country Planning Association, on whose council he served for many years. In 1943 he retired from his consultancy to First Garden City Ltd, developers of Letchworth. In July 1946, a few months before his death on 21 February 1947 at his home at 296 Norton Way South, Letchworth, Barry Parker was visited by the great American cultural sociologist Lewis Mumford, who admired him as a consummate social artist and a lovable personality. He was cremated at Golders Green crematorium on 24 February 1947. The Letchworth Garden City corporation acquired Parker's studio from his widow in 1973: it was opened and extended as the First Garden City Heritage Museum, featuring the development of Letchworth and the contribution of Parker and Unwin to its built environment. MERVYN MILLER

Sources C. M. Parker, 'Material available for a memoir of R. B. Parker at 296 Norton Way South, Letchworth', First Garden City Heritage Museum, Letchworth, Hertfordshire · M. K. Miller, *Raymond Unwin: garden cities and town planning* (1992) · M. Miller, *Letchworth: the first garden city* (1989) · D. Hawkes, ed., *Modern country homes in England: the arts and crafts architecture of Barry Parker* (1986) · *The Builder*, 172 (1947), 217 · *The Friend* (March 1947) · *Letchworth Citizen* (28 Feb 1947) · *Manchester Guardian* (22 Feb 1947) · H. V. Lanchester, *RIBA Journal*, 54 (1946–7), 286 · *Journal of the Town Planning Institute*, 33 (1947), 88 · *The Times* (26 Feb 1947) · *Town and Country Planning*, 15/57 (spring 1947), 32 · *Town Planning Review*, 20/3–4 (summer 1947), 117 · m. cert.
Archives First Garden City Heritage Museum, Letchworth, papers and architectural drawings · RIBA | Welwyn Garden City Library, Hertfordshire, corresp. with Frederic Osborn | SOUND BL NSA, oral history interview
Likenesses family photographs, *c.*1890–1899, First Garden City Heritage Museum, Letchworth, Hertfordshire · oils, *c.*1895, First Garden City Heritage Museum, Letchworth, Hertfordshire · F. Dodd, pastel drawing, 1909, First Garden City Heritage Museum, Letchworth, Hertfordshire · Elliott & Fry, photograph, 1929, First Garden City Heritage Museum, Letchworth, Hertfordshire
Wealth at death £11,473 16*s.* 8*d.*: probate, 3 May 1947, *CGPLA Eng. & Wales*

Parker, Benjamin (*d.* 1747), author, was born at Derby; further details of his parents and upbringing are unknown. He was originally a stocking maker who, having failed in business, took to manufacturing books. In 1731 he was living at Horsley, near Derby, when his first work, *Parker's Projection of the Longitude at Sea*, was submitted to the 'great Edmund Halley' and published in Nottingham. Three years later he was living at Mary Bridge, Derby, when he published *Philosophical Meditations with Divine Inferences*, followed by a second volume in 1735 and by *Philosophical Dissertations* two years later. In 1739 he moved to London and established himself at Sir Isaac Newton's Head on the corner of Lincoln's Inn Fields, next to Great Turnstile. Here he sold 'restorative jelly' for chest complaints and a 'cordial cholick water'. In these years Parker maintained his writing career with *Money: a Poem* (1740), dismissed by the *Dictionary of National Biography* as 'sad stuff'. Not meeting with success as a quack physician, Parker moved in the early 1740s to Fulwood's Rents, Holborn. Here he lectured and later published on the philosophical proof of the divine authority of scripture (1742), together with a survey of the first six days of creation (1745) and *A Review of the State of the Antediluvian World* (1745). Though he failed to attract the notice of George II, Parker could count among his patrons the duke of Devonshire, the earl of Chesterfield, and Sir William Lee, chief justice of the king's bench. None the less, he died 'very poor' in Marylebone on 17 September 1747 and was buried at Paddington on the following day.
PHILIP CARTER

Sources W. Hutton, *The history of Derby*, 2nd edn (1817) • *GM*, 1st ser., 17 (1747), 448 • D. Lysons, *The environs of London*, 4 vols. (1792–6) • D. Lysons and S. Lysons, *Magna Britannia: being a concise topographical account of the several counties of Great Britain*, 6 vols. (1806–22)
Wealth at death very poor: *GM*, 448

Parker, Charles (1799–1881), architect, was a pupil of Sir Jeffry Wyatville and studied drawing with George Maddox (1760–1843). He subsequently spent several years travelling in Italy. He began a successful architectural practice in London in around 1826. On 5 November 1834 he was elected one of the original fellows of the Institute of British Architects, and he was a regular contributor of papers to its sessional meetings until his retirement on 15 November 1869. He became a fellow of the Society of Antiquaries on 9 January 1834, but withdrew in 1844. He was steward and surveyor to the duke of Bedford's London property from 1859 to 1869.

Parker designed Hoare's Bank, 37 Fleet Street (*c*.1829–1833), and in 1840 added a portico to Stourhead for Sir Hugh Hoare. He designed the tower of Kimpton church, Hampshire, in a lancet style (1837–8), and the Italianate Roman Catholic church of St Raphael, Kingston upon Thames, Surrey, in 1846–7. He altered the Spanish Chapel, Manchester Square, in 1846, heightening the campanile. Perhaps more importantly, he published in monthly parts his *Villa rustica selected from the buildings and scenes in the vicinity of Rome and Florence, and arranged for rural and domestic dwellings; with plans and details* (1832; 2nd edn, 1848), in which the descriptions accompany a series of ninety-three carefully detailed plates. *Villa rustica* was influential in the continued development of Italianate domestic architecture in nineteenth-century England, in offering illustration of and practical guidance on the adaptation of Italian villa forms to contemporary use and the English climate.

Towards the end of his life Parker's sight failed and he became totally blind. He died on 9 February 1881 at home at 48 Park Road, Haverstock Hill, aged eighty-one, leaving four daughters. He was buried at St Thomas's Church, Fulham. M. A. Goodall

Sources Colvin, *Archs.* • *Dir. Brit. archs.* • A. K. Placzek, ed., *Macmillan encyclopedia of architects*, 4 vols. (1982) • Boase, *Mod. Eng. biog.* • Allibone, *Dict.* • D. Ware, *A short dictionary of British architects* (1967) • R. Dixon and S. Muthesius, *Victorian architecture* (1985), 48 • *GM*, 2nd ser., 1 (1834), 212 • *The Builder*, 5 (1847), 602–3 • C. Parker, *Villa rustica* (1832) • H. B. Wheatley and P. Cunningham, *London past and present*, 3 vols. (1891), vol. 3, p. 290 • *A compendium of Pevsner's Buildings of England*, ed. M. Good (1995) [CD-ROM] • *CGPLA Eng. & Wales* (1881)
Wealth at death under £16,000: probate, 12 March 1881, *CGPLA Eng. & Wales*

Parker, (Hubert) Charles (1919–1980), radio producer and documentary maker, was born on 5 April 1919 at 47 Richmond Park Road, Bournemouth, Hampshire, the second child of Percy Bond Parker, a general dealer, and his wife, Sarah Stretton. He later recalled that his father, although disabled, sold paraffin from a barrow. Educated at Bournemouth grammar school, and later at the National Physical Laboratory at Teddington in Middlesex, where he received a BSc degree in 1939, he enlisted in the Royal Naval Volunteer Reserve. When war came he became a 'snottie' (midshipman), briefly scooping up soldiers from the Dunkirk jetty before being posted to HM submarine *Sceptre*. Being long and thin he was nicknamed Dip Rod Parker after the folding rod used to check oil levels in the fuel tanks. He kept a guitar aboard and was in demand for the singing of American railway songs. As first lieutenant his efficiency and vigour earned him a DSC in 1944 and he rose to command HMS *Umba*. On 16 December 1944 he married Phyllis Rosemary Norman and they had two children: a daughter, Sarah, and a son, Matthew. After demobilization Parker went to Queens' College, Cambridge, graduating in 1948 with honours in English literature. He then joined the BBC North American service. Parker was mainly interested in drama and the dramatic rather than the documentary handling of material; his war service and contact with America had moved him to the international, but above all he was attracted by the human voice, folksong, and the oral tradition. In 1953 he was appointed senior features producer in Birmingham. He and his family moved to Harborne and Parker, a devout Anglican, joined the choir of St Peter's Church there. The EMI Midget portable tape recorder became generally available in the BBC regions at that time, giving fresh momentum to the new folk music movement and in particular to Ewan MacColl and A. L. (Bert) Lloyd. Parker's involvement with their work and beliefs was a source of serious prejudice against him in the BBC management, and together with his costly method of making programmes, eventually led to his premature termination of his employment in 1972.

Parker's approach to programme making involved spending many hours recording the voices of ordinary local people reliving their experiences. This was followed by meticulous editing in the studio, which was carried out by his assistant, Mary Baker, and eventually by Parker himself, in order to reduce the amount of channel time involved. His first programme was on local politics. His next, *Bridge Across the Silence*, on 16 May 1954, was an innovative studio documentary for television about deafness centred around a church service. In 1956 Parker's attention had been caught by an item in the *Manchester Guardian*. This described a train driver who had stayed at his post in a cloud of blinding and scalding steam and had given his life in an attempt to avert a crash; he was posthumously awarded the George Cross. Parker worked with MacColl to write a radio programme about the event. *The Ballad of John Axon*, broadcast on 2 July 1958, was very unusual. The form and techniques of the folk ballad were the model of the programme; there was no narrator—the listener was carried along by an exciting blend of music and speech, using the voices of the people themselves, who spoke from the heart 'talking themselves into song', as Parker himself described it. Unknown friends and workmates of John Axon revealed an ability to express themselves with flashes of extraordinary poetry—'Railways went through the back of your spine like Blackpool went through rock' (*The Ballad of John Axon*). Paul Ferris writing in *The Observer* commented 'Last week a technique and subject got married. And nothing in radio kaleidoscopy or whatever you like to call it will ever be the same again' (*Melody Maker*, 3 Jan 1981). The team went on to make seven more radio ballads between 1960 and 1964: *Singing the Fishing* (1961) won the Italia prize; *The Big Hewer* (August 1961) introduced Parker to the community of pitmen; *The Body Blow* (March 1962) dealt with the world of polio victims; *On the Edge* (February 1963) with teenagers; and *The Fight Game* (July 1963) with boxers. The last was *The Travelling People* (April 1964) about Gypsies. In a broadcast on BBC Radio 3 on 11 September 1971 Parker argued that vernacular speech was the key to good communication, and that the development of industry and technology was in danger of destroying the social and historical roots needed to stabilize personal and collective identity. As the space for his type of radio, which involved so much preparation, increasingly closed down in the late 1960s he was driven more and more towards his other great love, documentary theatre.

At the same time as Parker maintained a devout Christian humanism he associated with communists such as Lloyd and MacColl. It was integral to his ideas that he spent as much time with workers as with intellectuals, supporting the setting up of the West Midlands Gypsy Liaison Group. Whatever the exact nature of Parker's humanism, whether Christian or socialist or a mixture of both, it was not a generalized liberal humanism but one committed to the cause of the underdog. Parker was now working towards a distinctive theatre form with tape-recorded speech, newspaper quotes, or historical material interwoven with traditional or contemporary folk song. He contributed documentary dramas to six festivals for Arnold Wesker's Centre 42 project.

After Parker had left the BBC, in the autumn of 1973 came a new group out of the Grey Cock Folk Club that he had founded in 1965. This was the future Banner Theatre Company in embryo, and it produced a version of *The Big Hewer*. The first completely original Banner show was in 1975, *The Saltley Gate Show* by Arnold Wesker, which retold an incident in the 1972 miners' strike. Parker played a policeman. In due course, however, the strain became too much. In the second week of rehearsal for a show about the steel industry on the night of 9 December 1980 Parker suffered a severe stroke. He died the following morning at Dudley Road Hospital, Birmingham. He was buried in the churchyard at Eye, Herefordshire, a week later. Charles Parker was a man of two worlds. When he died both *The Times* and the *Daily Worker* carried tributes. They reflected his move from the safe conventional career of a Cambridge-educated, officer-class BBC producer to the radical fringe of community theatre. As Peter Cheeseman, first director of the New Victoria Theatre, Stoke-on-Trent, has written, 'The most important thing that Charles Parker ever said to me was "Listen! Listen to the people around you. And you will find great richness"' (Charles Parker archive, Birmingham Central Library).

PHILIP A. DONNELLAN

Sources personal knowledge (2004) · private information (2004) [M. Baker] · Birm. CL · interview with Carol Dixon, *The Guardian* (6 July 1973) · *The Times* (20 Dec 1980) · *CGPLA Eng. & Wales* (1981) · b. cert. · m. cert. · d. cert.

Archives BBC WAC · Birm. CA, corresp. and papers | NL Wales, letters to G. E. Evans, with related items | SOUND BBC WAC · Birm. CL

Wealth at death £5189: administration, 28 Jan 1981, *CGPLA Eng. & Wales*

Parker, Sir Charles Christopher, **fifth baronet** (1792–1869), naval officer, was born at Harley Street, London, on 16 June 1792. He was the youngest son of Vice-Admiral Christopher *Parker (1761–1804) [*see under* Parker, Sir Peter (1721–1811)] and his wife, Augusta, daughter of Admiral John *Byron; and grandson of admiral of the fleet Sir Peter *Parker (1721–1811). Sir Peter *Parker (1785–1814) was his eldest brother and George Byron, the poet, was his first cousin. He entered the navy in June 1804 on the *Glory*, with Captain George Martin, whom he followed to the *Barfleur*. In June 1805 he was moved to the sloop *Weasel* with his brother Peter, and in March 1806 to the *Eagle*, in which, under Captain Charles Rowley, he saw much active service on the coast of Italy. In 1809 he was in the Baltic, in the *St George*, flagship of Rear-Admiral Pickmore; afterwards he was in the *San Josef* in the Mediterranean, and from May 1810 in the frigate *Unité* with Captain Patrick Campbell. He was promoted lieutenant on 17 June 1811. Shortly afterwards he was seriously hurt by a fall from the *Unité*'s quarterdeck into the gun-room, and in August 1811 was invalided to recover his health.

Early in 1812 Parker joined the *Menelaus*, commanded by his brother Peter, in the Mediterranean. In May he moved into the *Malta* with Rear-Admiral Hallowell, and continued in her until promoted commander on 5 April 1815. In the same year he married Georgiana Ellis Pallmer; they had no children, and she survived him. He spent the three years from 1819 to 1822 in the *Harlequin*, on the coast of Ireland, and was posted on 23 April 1822. He had no further service. On the death of his brother, John Edmond George Parker, on 18 November 1835, he succeeded to the baronetcy. Parker became rear-admiral on the retired list on 7 October 1852, vice-admiral on 28 November 1857, and admiral on 27 April 1863. He died at 12 West Mall, Clifton, near Bristol, on 13 March 1869, when the title became extinct.

J. K. LAUGHTON, *rev.* ANDREW LAMBERT

Sources D. Syrett and R. L. DiNardo, *The commissioned sea officers of the Royal Navy, 1660–1815*, rev. edn, Occasional Publications of the Navy RS, 1 (1994) · O'Byrne, *Naval biog. dict.* · P. Mackesy, *The war in the Mediterranean, 1803–1810* (1957) · Boase, *Mod. Eng. biog.* · *Dod's Peerage* (1858) · *CGPLA Eng. & Wales* (1869)

Likenesses T. Unwins, oils, 1826, NMM

Wealth at death under £9000 0s. 0d.: probate, 12 April 1869, *CGPLA Eng. & Wales*

Parker, Charles Stuart (1829–1910), politician and biographer, born at Aigburth, Liverpool, on 1 June 1829, was the eldest son of Charles Stewart Parker of Fairlie, Ayrshire, a partner in the prosperous Liverpool firm of Sandbach, Tinne & Co., merchants for the West Indies. His mother was Anne, eldest daughter of Samuel Sandbach of Hafodunnos, Denbighshire. Thomas Chalmers, a friend of his paternal grandparents, was one of Parker's godfathers, and he was throughout life influenced by the

Charles Stuart Parker (1829–1910), by James Russell & Sons, 1887

evangelical temper of his home training. On 13 August 1838 his father's sister Annie married Edward (afterwards Viscount) Cardwell, whose political views he came to share. Parker was at Eton College from 1842 to 1847, and in 1846 won the prince consort's prize for German. On 10 June 1847 he matriculated from Brasenose College, Oxford, but the next year migrated to University College where he had won a scholarship. There he began a long and close association with the college and formed friendships with A. P. Stanley, Goldwin Smith, John Conington, Arthur Gray Butler, William Bright, and T. W. Jex-Blake. Friends at other colleges included A. W. Peel (afterwards speaker of the House of Commons), G. C. Brodrick, T. H. Green, G. J. Goschen, W. H. Fremantle, Frederic Harrison, and Grant Duff. In 1852 he joined Goschen, Brodrick, and others in starting the Oxford Essay Club, and he frequently attended the club dinners in later life, at Goschen's house and elsewhere.

In Easter term 1852 Parker was placed in the first class in *literae humaniores*, and in the second class of the mathematical school, graduating BA and proceeding to MA in 1855. He was a fellow of his college from 1854 until 1868, and lived in Oxford until 1864, throwing himself with vigour into the work of both college and university. He was college tutor from 1858 to 1865, and was one of the first lecturers in modern history. He was examiner in *literae humaniores* in 1859, 1860, 1863, and 1868. He won the confidence of undergraduates, and introduced them to men of note from the outer world, whom from an early date he entertained at Oxford. He organized the university volunteer corps and did much while major of the battalion (1865–8) to improve its efficiency, especially in shooting. The main recreation of his university days was mountaineering. He preferred climbing without guides, and it was without guides that he, with his brothers Sandbach and Alfred, made the second and fourth attempts on the Matterhorn in 1860 and 1861 respectively. Subsequently Parker's climbing companions included W. H. Gladstone and Stephen Gladstone, sons of the statesman, who was a friend of Parker and his family.

Like Brodrick, Goldwin Smith, and other Oxford men, Parker was a contributor to the early issues of the *Saturday Review* in 1855, but he soon withdrew owing to his dislike of the cynical tone of the paper, and a characteristic impatience of its partisan, tory spirit. He gradually concentrated his interest on liberal reform of the university. He especially urged a prudent recognition of the claims of science, modern history, and modern languages in the academic curriculum, and the throwing open of scholarships to competition. He was an early supporter of a national system of elementary education which should be efficient and compulsory, rather than voluntary. In 1867 he published two essays, one on 'Popular education', in *Questions for a Reformed Parliament*, arguing that only a reformed parliament would pass an adequate elementary education measure, and the other on 'Classical education', in F. W. Farrar's *Essays on a Liberal Education*.

In 1864 Parker, who inherited ample means, diversified his academic duties by becoming private secretary to his uncle, Edward Cardwell, who was then colonial secretary, working for him until he went out of office in 1866. At the wish of Gladstone, with whom his relations steadily became closer, Parker stood for Perthshire in 1868 as a Liberal. He gained a startling victory over the former Conservative member, Sir William Stirling Maxwell, who regained the seat from him at the general election of 1874. Parker was however elected for the city of Perth in 1878, and retained the seat until 1892, when he was defeated in a three-cornered contest. He failed to win a seat in West Perthshire in 1900. He was a competent back-bencher but a poor speaker. He never held ministerial office, nor appears to have been offered it. But he was quite close to the Peelites among the Liberal leadership, and prepared for publication Gladstone's Midlothian speeches of 1879–80.

It was on educational policy that Parker exerted his chief influence. Joining the public schools commission (1868–74), he proved one of its most active members, urging that the public school curriculum should be modernized in sympathy with a progressive policy at the universities. He also sat on the commission for military education in 1869, and advocated the linking up of the public schools with Sandhurst and Woolwich, so as to ensure a broad general culture before technical and professional training. Again, as a member of the Scottish educational endowments commission in 1872, he argued persistently that the benefits of endowments should go 'not to the most necessitous of those fairly fitted intellectually, but to the most fit among those who were fairly necessitous'. His views greatly stimulated the development of secondary education in Scotland: he wished the Scottish elementary schools to form a 'ladder' to the university, and he sought to protect them from the evil system of 'payment by results'. He was in 1887 chairman of a departmental committee on higher education in the elementary schools of Scotland, and wrote its report with Sir Henry Craik.

Parker, whose wide interests embraced a precise study

of scientific hypotheses, in his later years became an important historian of the Peelites. His *Sir Robert Peel from his Private Papers* (3 vols., 1891–9), for which he was given special access by Gladstone and others, remains an important source, as does his *Life and Letters of Sir James Graham* (2 vols., 1907). He was elected honorary fellow of University College in 1899, and was made honorary LLD of Glasgow and honorary DCL of Oxford in 1908. In 1907 he was sworn of the privy council.

Parker died unmarried at his London house, 32 Old Queen Street, Westminster, on 18 June 1910, and was buried at Fairlie. He bequeathed £5000 to University College, Oxford, where two Parker scholarships for modern history were established but later discontinued.

[ANON.], *rev.* H. C. G. MATTHEW

Sources *The Times* (19 June 1910) • C. Harvie, *The lights of liberalism* (1976) • J. P. Parry, *Democracy and religion* (1986) • Gladstone, *Diaries* • H. C. G. Matthew, *Gladstone, 1809–1874* (1986)
Archives Lpool RO, corresp. • Mitchell L., Glas., Glasgow City Archives, family corresp. • Strathclyde Regional Archives, Parker family MSS | BL, corresp. with W. E. Gladstone, Add. MSS 44411–44500 • BL, corresp. with David Stanmore, Add. MS 49272 • CAC Cam., corresp. with David Saunders
Likenesses J. Russell & Sons, photograph, 1887, NPG [*see illus.*] • H. von Herkomer, oils • plaster medallion, Scot. NPG
Wealth at death £104,400 18*s.* 5*d.*: confirmation, 22 Aug 1910, *CCI* • £2667 0*s.* 9*d.*: additional estate, 15 March 1911, *CCI*

Parker, Christopher (1761–1804). *See under* Parker, Sir Peter, first baronet (1721–1811).

Parker, Christopher Comyns (1774–1843), land agent and landowner, was born at The Friars, Moulsham, near Chelmsford, Essex, the second of the three sons and one daughter of John Oxley Parker (*d.* 1826), a successful solicitor in Chelmsford, and his wife, Sarah Griffinhoofe. His two brothers, John Oxley (II) Parker (1773–1798) and Charles George Parker (1780–1847), followed their father in the Chelmsford law firm, which prospered greatly, so that by the 1840s Charles had been able to acquire an estate of 2500 acres in Essex.

Parker had the chance of joining his brothers but preferred a more active outdoor life, and after a short attachment to a local farmer his father helped him, in 1796, to take a lease of Woodham Mortimer Place, near Maldon, Essex, a farm of several hundred acres. The substantial seventeenth-century house became the family home, and his success in farming what he claimed was land of naturally very bad quality established his reputation as an agriculturist conversant from practical experience with the latest techniques and with their economic viability. In July 1797 Parker married Emma Gepp (*d.* 1829), daughter of his father's friend Edward Gepp, also a solicitor in Chelmsford, and he was enlisted to look after his father-in-law's small estate. On the twin foundations of his own reputation and the connections furnished by family legal business, he established a practice as a land agent, which before long became his main occupation. At first his work concentrated on specific functions, such as valuing timber and marking trees for felling, and especially on tithe matters—surveying, valuing, collecting, and handling disputes. This led to extensive involvement in the business of tithe commutation after 1836; it also led, as in the case of Oriel College, Oxford, to progression from looking after the college's tithe interests in Essex to the full management of its Essex estates. From the mid-1820s onwards Parker acquired the agency for many estates, of middling to small size, so that by 1836 he could tell the select committee on the state of agriculture that he farmed 2000 acres himself and had the management of another 20,000 acres.

Parker's first wife, Emma, died in 1829, leaving three daughters and a son; a year later he married Frances Sutton (*d.* 1870), then aged forty-five. In his later years he was successful, prosperous, well established in county society, and well regarded in his profession. He was a large man, over 6 feet tall and weighing 21 stone. He owned an estate of some 1500 acres (besides renting more land), the purchases partly financed by inheritance on his father's death in 1826 and partly by the profits of his own business. This presence on the land was overtaken by the 2500 acres funded by the Chelmsford law business and owned after 1826 by his brother Charles. Parker drew on family experience in answering a complaint from Dr Shuttleworth, warden of New College, Oxford, over the size of his bill for surveying Writtle parish for tithe in 1829:

> I am not surprised at the observation you state my brother to have made—he is like all other legal men who although they do not forget to charge for their own exertions do not appear aware of the time, trouble and responsibility that attaches to the duties of those who value landed property, also that it takes them generally far from home at considerable expense instead of being transacted in the office where the greater part of the business of legal Men is performed by their Clerks and from precedents. (Parker, 123)

Parker was a keen huntsman and built kennels for the Essex Union hunt at Hyde Farm, Danbury, at his own expense. He was a JP and deputy lieutenant, and he was elected to the Land Surveyors Club in 1837, a mark of considerable professional standing. He was also chairman of the Maldon board of guardians from 1835, and an alderman of Maldon borough until unseated after the Municipal Reform Act, celebrated in doggerel by the victorious Liberals:

> The magic dreams of Tory times, alas, are waning fast,
> The stout and lofty Alderman is put to bed at last …
> But paralyz'd poor Comyns dies, not Alderman nor Mayor,
> Lord Melbourne's Municipal Bill has eas'd him of this care.
> (Parker, 270)

Parker died on 1 August 1843 at Woodham Mortimer Place, survived by his wife.

Parker's only son, **John Oxley Parker** (1812–1887), was sent at the age of five to a private boarding-school in Chelmsford run by the Revd James Hutchinson; then, from 1824 to 1829, he attended Dr J. C. Burney's fashionable school in Greenwich (a plan of sending him to Winchester College was abandoned because of its reputation for bullying). Finally he went to Oriel College, Oxford, from 1829 to 1833, where he was tutored by John Henry Newman. John Oxley probably then trained with an Essex farmer before becoming his father's assistant in 1836. By

1841 he was a fully independent land agent, acting as his father's partner and able to carry on the practice on his father's death in 1843, in which year he was elected to the Land Surveyors Club. He managed the estates of several old Essex families, including the Tufnells of Langleys, the Rounds of Birch Hall, the Bramstons of Skreens, and the Mildmays of Moulsham (and Dogmersfield, Hampshire), as well as several Oxford college estates—New College, Oriel, and University College—and he was heavily involved with railway land purchases in the 1840s and 1850s. In 1856 he became entangled with Sir Morton Peto in the (unsuccessful) scheme for a railway from Tilbury to Colchester, and in 1876 he joined the project for manufacturing the Darby pedestrian steam digger, a gigantic steam-powered spade which, at its trials, proved to be too feeble to turn a spit of earth. He was, however, sufficiently canny to turn down the offer of the agency for Lord Rayleigh's estate at Terling in 1873, apparently because he foresaw bad times ahead for Essex farming. In 1883 he served as sheriff of Essex.

A tall, handsome man of 16 stone, Parker was to be seen in white buckskin breeches and long wellington boots, and was very fond of dancing. He met Louisa (*d.* 1893), the sister of his schoolfriend Richard Durant, while valuing a country estate at Sharpham, near Totnes, Devon, which her father, a wealthy London silk merchant, was purchasing. He married Louisa in May 1847 after a long courtship, which elicited a friend's comment: 'I consider the 1*d* post the greatest boon to lovers' (Parker, 57). They had four sons (one of whom died young), and three daughters. One son made his career in the Essex bank of Sparrow, Tufnell & Co., in which his father had become a partner in 1859; and another joined Edward Gerald Strutt in 1877 in founding the aristocratic firm of estate agents, Strutt and Parker. Parker himself died on 8 October 1887 at Woodham Mortimer Place, and the Essex land agency business came to an end. F. M. L. THOMPSON

Sources J. O. Parker, ed., *The Oxley Parker papers* (1964) • Essex RO, Oxley Parker MSS • *VCH Essex*, vols. 2–3 • 'Select committee on the state of agriculture: third report', *Parl. papers* (1836), vol. 8/2, no. 465 • d. cert.

Archives Essex RO

Likenesses portraits, repro. in Parker, ed., *Oxley Parker papers* • portraits (Parker, John Oxley), repro. in Parker, ed., *Oxley Parker papers*

Wealth at death £58,940 0*s*. 6*d*.—John Parker: probate, 1888

Parker, Daniel (*fl.* 1700–1730), violin maker, worked in London during the early eighteenth century. The little that can be discovered about his life has to be inferred from studying his thirty or so known violins and violas and the labels and dates that some of them bear. No record can be found of any apprenticeship, but his most likely mentor was Barak Norman. Parker made mainly for the trade, apparently having no retail establishment of his own. He became particularly associated with the shop and music publishing business of John and Joseph Hare, which operated from various addresses at Cornhill and the important violin-making district of St Paul's Churchyard, London. A fine, certified Parker violin was auctioned at Phillips, London, in November 1994; its original label was that of Joseph Hare's establishment and dated 1727, towards the end of Parker's working life.

Historically, Parker is respected as probably the first non-Italian maker to copy Stradivari's model. This was at a time when the model of the Austro-German school of Jacob Stainer, with its highly arched features, was starting to carry all before it, and it undoubtedly took courage to realize the tonal advantages of Stradivari's much flatter design. It is believed that Parker must have seen an early Stradivari of the type he copied belonging to the violinist and composer Gaspari Visconti of Cremona, a friend of Stradivari, during Visconti's sojourn in London, where in 1703 he published works for solo violin under the joint imprint of J. Walsh and J. Hare.

Parker's international reputation was greatly enhanced when the Hill family, London's most eminent dealers and restorers, sold a Parker violin to the great virtuoso Fritz Kreisler in 1911 (for £50). Kreisler pronounced its tone better than that of his Joseph Guarnerius and used it enthusiastically for some of his concerts, having first asked the Hills to remove the label as he intended to attribute it to the Italian maker Balestrieri. Worldwide recognition of the merits of the old English makers has been slow, and Parker has been a victim of these regrettable false labelling practices. To the expert, though, his style is recognizably English in character and distinct from the best contemporary Italian work in many technical and aesthetic details. An outstanding but self-effacing craftsman, Parker continues to be much revered by players and connoisseurs. BRIAN W. HARVEY

Sources B. W. Harvey, *The violin family and its makers in the British Isles: an illustrated history and directory* (1995) • T. Baker and others, *The British violin*, ed. J. Milnes (2000) [exhibition catalogue, Royal Academy of Music, London, 31 March – 11 April 1988] • J. Dilworth, 'Pioneer spirit', *The Strad*, 97 (1986), 571–5

Parker [*née* Kerr-Fisher; *other married name* Chichester], **Dame Dehra** (1882–1963), politician, was born on 13 August 1882 in the military hospital at Dehra Dun, north of Delhi, India, the only child of James Kerr-Fisher (1827–1891) of Kilrea, co. Londonderry, and Annie Kerr-Forsythe. Educated in the United States, where her father had extensive property holdings, and Germany, she was twice married: first, on 11 December 1901, to Lieutenant-Colonel Robert Peel Dawson Spencer Chichester, a Unionist MP, who died in 1921, with whom she had a son and daughter. On 4 June 1928 she married Henry Wise Parker (1875–1940). Before entering parliament her first husband, a native of co. Londonderry, served with the Central African Rifles 1897–9 and in South Africa in 1899 and 1900. He commanded the 6th battalion (the duke of Cambridge's own) Middlesex regiment from 1904 to 1913, in which capacity he commanded combined escorts to the Anglo-German boundary commission, Nyasa, and Tanganyika in 1908. Latterly, he commanded the 14th service battalion, Royal Irish Rifles, and served as a captain in the Irish Guards. Her second husband, Parker (CB 1916, CMG 1924), spent his career in the Royal Navy, becoming an admiral in 1933. In 1916 he commanded HMS *Benbow* at the battle of Jutland

Bank. Shortly after their marriage he was rear-admiral commanding 1st cruiser squadron, Mediterranean Fleet (1928–30). He retired the list in 1934.

Throughout her life Dehra Parker was a staunch and unapologetic unionist. This stance was signalled early in her political career by her involvement in the formation of the Ulster Women's Unionist Council in 1911, and in 1912 when she acted as an organizer of the nursing units for the Ulster Volunteer Force created by Sir Edward Carson to resist the introduction of home rule. During the First World War she worked under the aegis of the Soldiers' and Sailors' Families Association, for which services she was to become an OBE in 1918. In 1949 she was created DBE and in 1957 GBE.

Chichester was one of only two women to be elected to the first Northern Ireland parliament in 1921, and in 1924 moved the loyal address to the king's speech, the first woman to do so in the empire. She remained in parliament as the Ulster Unionist member for Londonderry until 1929, when she resigned her seat shortly after her second marriage. In 1933 she returned to the Northern Ireland parliament as Ulster Unionist member for South Londonderry, a seat she held continuously until her retirement in 1960, when she was succeeded by her grandson, Major James Chichester-Clark (Lord Moyola), who was to serve as Northern Ireland's penultimate prime minister between 1969 and 1971. Her loyalty to Ulster and to successive administrations in Northern Ireland was unflinching. Never to vote against any Unionist government throughout her parliamentary career, she found some reward when in 1937 she was appointed to the junior ministerial post of parliamentary secretary to the Ministry of Education. In 1944 she resigned from the post for 'personal reasons' (Northern Ireland parliament, *Official Report and Debates*, vol. 27, col. 321, 29 Feb 1944), although her relationship with the minister for education, Professor William Corkey—who was himself sacked for neglecting his duties—had been acrimonious, a fact widely acknowledged in parliamentary circles. Passed over as Corkey's successor, she returned to the back benches until 1949, when she was appointed minister for health and local government by the Northern Ireland prime minister, Sir Basil Brooke. Her appointment represented a triple achievement: not only was she one of the first women elected to the Northern Ireland parliament, but she was the first to hold a junior ministerial post in the province, and she was also the only woman appointed to the Northern Ireland cabinet and thus its sole female privy councillor.

During her tenure as minister Parker oversaw the implementation of the National Health Service in Northern Ireland and piloted a number of housing bills through parliament, including one that decontrolled rents in the private rented sector and as such was at variance with housing legislation in Great Britain. The bill, which she described in characteristically egotistical terms as 'a monument to me' (Paisley, 80), aroused enormous controversy, occasioning the resignation of the attorney-general, Edmund Warnock, who considered it 'unjust' (Northern Ireland parliament, *Official Report and Debates*, vol. 35, col. 733, 18 April 1956). Parker was forced to concede a number of critical amendments and, following a stroke, stood down as minister in 1957 and returned to the back benches until her retirement from parliament in 1960.

In parliament Parker was a controversial figure, seldom missing an opportunity to chide Irish nationalists and her particular *bêtes noires*, independent unionists, for 'disloyalty' to Ulster, and fundamentalist protestants, for whom she had a withering disregard. As a minister she was described by one of her senior officials as 'capricious, an adroit politician and a most formidable operator' (Oliver, 224) and acquired a reputation as a 'kingmaker' in Unionist political circles (Paisley). Beyond parliament Parker was a long-serving local councillor on Magherafelt rural district council, president of both the Northern Ireland Physical Training Association and the Girls' Training Corps, chairman of the ancient monuments advisory committee and chairman and later president of the Council for the Encouragement of Music and the Arts in the province. She died at her home, Shanemullagh House, Castledawson, co. Londonderry, on 28 November 1963 and was buried two days later in the grounds of Christ Church, Castledawson. R. A. WILFORD

Sources Northern Ireland parliament, *Official report and debates*, 80 vols. (1922–71) • I. Paisley Jnr, 'The political career of Dame Dehra Parker', MSc thesis, Queen's University, Belfast, 1994 • J. Oliver, *Working at Stormont: memoirs* (1978) • Burke, *Peerage* (1959) • d. cert. • *WWW* • L. McRedmond, ed., *Modern Irish lives* (1996) • A. Byrne and S. McMahon, *Great northerners* (1991) • priv. coll, MSS • parish register (burial), co. Londonderry, Castledawson, Christ Church, 30 Nov 1963

Archives NRA, priv. coll., MSS

Wealth at death £12,561 8*s*. 0*d*.: probate, 9 Aug 1965, *CGPLA NIre.*

Parker, Edmund, second earl of Morley (**1810–1864**). *See under* Parker, John, first earl of Morley (1772–1840).

Parker, Elizabeth. *See* Shackleton, Elizabeth (1726–1781).

Parker [*née* Masgreave], **Ellen** [Helen] (*bap.* **1790**, *d.* **1828**), pauper and letter writer, was baptized on 7 June 1790 at Alton in Staffordshire, sixth of the eight children of John Masgreave (1749–1817), farmer, and his wife, Ann Jenkinson (*bap.* 1755, *d.* 1829/30). Ellen was married on 23 April 1810 to Stephen Parker (*bap.* 1789, *d.* 1818), a surgeon apothecary of relatively low status from Doveridge, Derbyshire, who practised medicine in the parish of Colwich, Staffordshire. They had four children, of whom the fourth, their only daughter, was born posthumously. After Parker's death in February 1818 Ellen travelled to Bramshall, apparently in order to be near her eldest sister, Lydia Warner, but she was effectively destitute by April when she applied to Colwich, her parish of settlement, for poor relief. By the close of 1818 Ellen had been awarded a regular cash payment and she remained a pauper until her death. In the period December 1818 to March 1828 she lived in Uttoxeter and therefore was compelled to communicate by letter with Colwich, approximately 10 miles south-west of Uttoxeter. She wrote over thirty letters, of which twenty survive, wherein she queried the relief she was receiving and urged that more might be paid. During

1824 she entered a sexual relationship with John Smith (*fl.* 1824–1828) of Uttoxeter, and in 1825 she gave birth to an illegitimate, fifth child. She fell ill in 1827, died in March 1828, and was buried in Bramshall, 2 miles west of Uttoxeter, on 31 March 1828.

Ellen's significance is threefold. First, in comparison to other pauper letter writers, she was able to command rare eloquence. She wrote in a legible hand with fluency and a sense of drama, which made her communications more effective than many pauper letters. She demonstrated an unusual awareness of her likely impact on any readers. She wrote in the first instance to the overseer of the poor for Colwich, John Wetton, with whom she claimed a measure of friendship, but she knew that her correspondence would also be read at vestry meetings. On one occasion she wrote her letter in two parts, with a private portion for Wetton and a public portion for the benefit of the vestry, on the pretext of making a personal apology to Wetton.

Second, Ellen represents two of the stereotypes into which pauper women fell under the old poor law. When she first applied for parish relief in 1818 she enjoyed a good reputation as the widow of a semi-professional parishioner, who had three children under ten and was pregnant with a fourth. Consequently she was almost certainly classed as one of the deserving poor. None the less when her fifth, illegitimate pregnancy became obvious early in 1825 she lost status and became one of the undeserving poor, a 'bastard-bearer' who was technically punishable by law. Characteristically Ellen made every effort to regain some of this lost respect. In April 1825 she took the very unusual step of writing to John Wetton's wife, Elizabeth. Ellen probably judged that a woman would read her letter apologizing for a sexual indiscretion with more sympathy than a male parish officer. Ellen effectively used her claim of friendship with the Wettons to force Elizabeth to act as her intermediary at a time when Ellen's relationship with the parish was subject to particular strain.

Third, Ellen illustrates the crucial relationship between gender and poverty. Her father and at least three of her siblings were wealthy, yet she died a pauper and her children were made pauper apprentices. During Ellen's life her family granted her some assistance, but this mainly took the form of advancement given to her two eldest sons. After their apprenticeship the two boys received help from Ellen's brothers to become successful tradesmen in Birmingham. Her second son, John, married the eldest daughter of a wealthy manufacturer and when he died in 1865 his estate was valued at a little under £3000. Ellen remained poor because she was a woman, the widow of a poor surgeon apothecary, whose young family and relatively late fifth pregnancy condemned her to poverty and an early death. By contrast her parents, siblings, and two eldest sons benefited from inheritances, advantageous marriages, and kinship support. ALANNAH TOMKINS

Sources Colwich overseers' correspondence, Staffs. RO, D24/A/PO/2939, *passim* • Colwich overseers' accounts, Staffs. RO, D24/A/PO/66–75 • Colwich constables' accounts, Staffs. RO, D24/A/PK/109, 118 • Colwich vestry minutes, Staffs. RO, D24/A/PV/1 • Colwich overseers' vouchers, Staffs. RO, D24/A/PO/1034, *passim* • will of John Parker proved 10 Aug 1865, Birmingham Probate Registry • will of John Masgreave, 1817, Lichfield RO, B/C/11 • parish registers, Alton, Staffs. RO, D1343/1/3, 5, 7 • parish registers, Colwich, Staffs. RO, D874/1/7, 8 • parish registers, Uttoxeter, Staffs. RO, D3891/1/9 • parish registers, Stone, Staffs. RO, F/Stone/4 • parish registers, Aldridge, Staffs. RO, D4093/1/10 • parish registers, Bramshall, Staffs. RO, D3892/1/2, 3, 11 • N. W. Tildesley, ed., *Chebsey parish register* (privately printed, Willenhall, [1965]) • Handsworth parish registers, Birm. CA • parish registers, Doveridge, Derbys. RO, PI 1/2, 5/1 • *Pigot's Commercial Directory* (1835) • *White's Directory of Birmingham* (1849)

Archives Staffs. RO, letters, Colwich parish records, D24/A/PO/2939, 2941, 2952, 2978, 2981, 2999, 3003, 3007–3012, 3014, 3017, 3021, 3040, 3048, 3061, 3244

Parker, Emma [*pseud.* Emma de Lisle] (*fl.* **1809–1817**), novelist, of whom very little is known, belonged to the gentry class, though her family was short of money, and lived (in solitude, she says) at Fairfield House in Denbighshire, the name of which she borrowed for the family central to her first novel. She was an Anglican. She had several sisters, of whom the eldest died before 1817, and a close male relation in the army.

In 1809 Parker published her first novel, *A Soldier's Offspring, or, The Sisters*, saying she had written it without confiding in anybody, and submitted it to the Minerva Press, hoping to earn some much needed cash. (It was out by October 1809, when it was reviewed; but the title-page says 1810.) She dedicated it to her mother, and took pains to display her learning in chapter headings from Lucan and Ariosto in the original languages. The plot is a well-worn one about a pair of sisters, one good and sensible, one flighty though teachable. Each suffers before winning through to a happy ending. In an introduction and a conclusion Parker addresses her readers in a tone of raillery, hoping, she says, to pique them to read on.

In 1810 and 1811 Minerva published two novels which are often mistakenly attributed to Parker: *Eva of Cambria, or, The Fugitive Daughter* and *Ora and Juliet, or, Influence of First Principles*. The first appeared under her pseudonym, Emma de Lisle, and the second as 'by the Author of Eva of Cambria'. This was a misunderstanding based on similarity of title: a manuscript by Parker was confused with one by the equally obscure Amelia de Beauclerc, the author of both the disputed texts.

Parker was, however, productive enough. She wrote six more novels and a volume of essays: *Elfrida, Heiress of Belgrove* (December 1810, though the title-page says 1811), *Fitz-Edward, or, The Cambrians*, 1811 (which was the novel confused with Amelia Beauclerc's *Eva of Cambria*, and was the last which Parker published with the Minerva Press), *Virginia*, 1811, *Aretas*, 1813, *The Guerrilla Chief*, 1815, the epistolary *Self-Deception*, 1816, and *Important Trifles: Chiefly Appropriate to Females on their Entrance into Society*, 1817. In *Elfrida* (published with Crosby), the author defends the value of novels in a manner reminiscent of Jane Austen in *Northanger Abbey*. She pronounces it 'ridiculous and injudicious' for novelists to abuse their own craft by attributing female bad behaviour to the baneful influence of the Minerva Press (*Elfrida*, 1.22).

> Now, if such are the woeful consequences of Novel reading, why, in the name of common sense and prudence, my learned contemporaries! do you continue to write them? Let me entreat ye not to be so blind to our common interest … but let us firmly enter into a league to support their rights with all the powers of our pens, and fight their cause to the very last drop of our ink. (ibid., 1.23)

Parker's work, always intelligent, became more interesting as her career progressed. Her conduct book demonstrates learning and advocates religious belief and strong-mindedness. Her novels often touch on political and military matters, on the hardships of soldiers and the difficulties of readjusting to civilian life. *Self-Deception* (a novel set after the marriage of the hero and heroine) explores the cultural and religious differences between English and French life. It attracted the first carping reviews for Parker, whose work had generally been praised. The date of her death is unknown.

ISOBEL GRUNDY

Sources *Critical Review*, 5th ser., 4 (1816), 511 • D. McLeod, 'The Minerva Press', PhD diss., University of Alberta, 1997 • D. Blakey, *The Minerva Press, 1790–1820* (1939) • M. Summers, *A Gothic bibliography* (1940) • A. Block, *The English novel, 1740–1850: a catalogue including prose romances, short stories and translations of foreign fiction*, new edn (1961) • *Critical Review*, 3rd ser., 18 (1809), 223 • *Critical Review*, 3rd ser., 21 (1811), 488 • *Critical Review*, 5th ser., 1 (1815), 211

Parker, Frances Mary [Fanny; *alias* Janet Arthur] (**1875–1924**), militant suffragette, was born in Little Roderick, Kurow, Otago, New Zealand, on 24 December 1875, one of the five children of Harry Rainy Parker (1837–1912), JP, of Rotheley Temple, Leicestershire, and his wife, Frances Emily Jane Kitchener (*d.* 1925). Her mother (always known as Millie) was the sister of Horatio Herbert Kitchener, first Earl Kitchener, and he paid for his niece's education at Newnham College, Cambridge. Fanny Parker entered Newnham in 1896 and obtained an ordinary degree in 1899. She was a *répétrice* at a French school from 1899 to 1902 and thereafter for several years a visiting teacher in Auckland, New Zealand.

Fanny Parker became involved in the women's suffrage movement in 1908. She took part in a demonstration, was arrested for obstruction, and endured six weeks' imprisonment in Holloway. In 1909 she was a speaker for the Scottish Universities Women's Suffrage Union; in 1910 she organized their caravan tour; and in 1911 she was their delegate to the International Suffrage Convention at Stockholm. In January 1912 she became an organizer for the Pankhurst-led militant suffrage organization, the Women's Social and Political Union (WSPU), for Glasgow and the west of Scotland. The WSPU initiated a window-smashing raid in London in March of that year, and Fanny Parker took part. She was sentenced to four months in Holloway, went on hunger strike, and was forcibly fed.

In October 1912 Fanny Parker became WSPU organizer for Dundee, where she was an indefatigable worker; scarcely a week went by without her writing letters to the press and addressing meetings of all kinds. In November she was arrested for breaking a window; she was released from prison after a three-day hunger strike. In December she was one of several suffragettes who smuggled themselves into the Music Hall, Aberdeen, with the intention of causing a disturbance at Lloyd George's meeting; on that occasion she was on hunger strike for five days before release. Lord Kitchener was 'disgusted' when he learned of his niece's involvement in the movement. 'Whatever her feelings on the subject may be,' he wrote to his sister, 'I cannot help thinking she might have some consideration for her family' (Royle, 248). Ethel Moorhead, who became a close friend of hers at this time, said that she was 'small and looked innocent and disarming with her charming looks, brown eyes, and silky hair. But she had an exquisite *madness*,—daring, joyous, vivid, strategic' (Moorhead, 264).

By 1914 militancy had escalated into violence, and suffragettes all over Britain were burning down and blowing up buildings. Buildings of national or symbolic importance were obvious targets, and therefore a watchman was on duty at Robert Burns's cottage in Alloway when Fanny Parker and another suffragette attempted to set fire to it in July of that year. She 'allowed herself to be taken that her comrade [Ethel Moorhead] might escape' (*This Quarter*, no. 1) and was arrested, giving her name as Janet Arthur. She created a fuss when charged at Ayr sheriff court, denying that the court had any jurisdiction over her, yet while there she also showed her sympathy for a woman who had been sentenced to pay a fine of £1 or undergo ten days' imprisonment for receiving stolen goods, eventually paying her fine.

Janet Arthur immediately put the prison commissioners and Scottish Office in a quandary by going on hunger and thirst strike. She was a prisoner on remand, but if she were to be released the chances of recapturing her were slight. The authorities wanted to send her to a nursing home, but she refused to go. After six days of hunger and thirst strike she was transferred to Perth prison where forcible feeding of suffragettes was taking place. Her family heard rumours about her condition, and her brother Captain Parker went up from London and favourably impressed the Scottish Office ministers, particularly as the captain had 'no sympathy with his sister's views' (NA Scot., HH16/43). Nevertheless, Fanny Parker was forcibly fed and, when she was unable to retain food, an attempt was made to feed her by the rectum, resulting in bruising of the genital area as well. She was released to a nursing home in a state of collapse but still managed to escape before her trial. However, war broke out on 4 August, militancy was suspended, and there was an amnesty for suffragettes.

After the outbreak of war Fanny Parker was recruited by the other militant suffrage society, the Women's Freedom League, to head their new organization which found suitable jobs for women and made sure those women were not exploited. Subsequently she followed the family's military tradition, being appointed deputy controller in the Women's Army Auxiliary Corps (subsequently Queen Mary's Army Auxiliary Corps) in June 1917. She was twice mentioned in dispatches and was appointed a military

OBE. Fanny Parker died on 19 January 1924 in Arcachon, near Bordeaux, France, where Ethel Moorhead and her protégé, Ernest Walsh, were living. By her will, of which Janie Allan was executor, apart from a small bequest to her sister, Fanny Parker left all her property to Ethel Moorhead 'in grateful remembrance for her care and love'. The first issue of *This Quarter*, funded by the bequest, contains a poem and the reproduction of two paintings by Fanny Parker.

Fanny Parker epitomized the articulate, well-educated, wholly committed suffragette, who at the beginning of the campaign in Edwardian Britain believed that reasoned argument would win women the vote, but subsequently became convinced that only violent methods would prevail. As a consequence she suffered the horrors of forcible feeding of a particularly brutal nature, but she also formed a close friendship which was apparently the most important thing to her at the end of her life.

LEAH LENEMAN

Sources L. Leneman, *A guid cause: the women's suffrage movement in Scotland* (1995) • L. Leneman, *Martyrs in our midst: Dundee, Perth and the forcible feeding of suffragettes*, Abertay Historical Society Publication, 33 (1993) • [A. B. White], ed., *Newnham College register*, 1: *1871–1923* (1964) • records of students, Old Hall, 1888–1909, Newnham Archives, M2 • T. Royle, *The Kitchener enigma* (1985), 248 • *Army List* (1917–18) • prison records, Scottish home and health department, NA Scot., HH2/22, HH16/41, HH16/42, HH16/43 • A. J. R., ed., *The suffrage annual and women's who's who* (1913) • *Votes for Women* (27 Jan 1911) • *Votes for Women* (15 Dec 1911) • *Votes for Women* (8 March 1912) • *Votes for Women* (6 Dec 1912) • *Votes for Women* (13 Dec 1912) • *Votes for Women* (7 Aug 1914) • *The Vote* (18 June 1915) • *Common Cause* (23 Sept 1909) • *Common Cause* (5 Oct 1911) • *Dundee Advertiser* (11 Dec 1912) • *Dundee Advertiser* (18 Dec 1912) • *Dundee Advertiser* (24 Jan 1913) • Burke, *Gen. GB* (1939) • *CCI* (1924) • E. Moorhead, 'Incendiaries (work in progress)', *This Quarter*, 2 (1925) • *This Quarter*, 1 (1920x29?) [biographical note] • E. Crawford, *The women's suffrage movement: a reference guide, 1866–1928* (1999)

Likenesses photograph, NA Scot.; repro. in Leneman, *A guid cause*

Wealth at death £3177 15*s*. 3*d*.: confirmation, 15 Oct 1924, *CCI*

Parker, Frederick Moore Searle [Eric] (1870–1955), author and journalist, was born at The Grange, East Barnet, Hertfordshire, on 9 October 1870, the eldest son of Frederick Searle Parker, a solicitor of Bedford Row, and his wife, Elisabeth, daughter of William Wilkieson, of Woodbury Hall, Bedfordshire. As a King's scholar at Eton College, fishing was already his passion and, with no encouragement, he was a keen naturalist. He went as a postmaster to Merton College, Oxford, where he obtained a second class in classical moderations (1891) and a fourth in *literae humaniores* (1893). Then came a few years of schoolmastering until in 1900, at the age of thirty, he entered journalism as a junior assistant editor on the *St James's Gazette*, under Theodore Cook. He soon started to write also for St Loe Strachey in *The Spectator*, to which he was a regular contributor for twelve years. In 1902 Strachey bought the *County Gentleman*, a sporting weekly devoted mainly to horses, and, with Parker as editor, set about widening its appeal.

Meanwhile *Macmillan's Magazine* had serialized Parker's first novel, *The Sinner and the Problem*, published as a book in October 1901 and twice reprinted within three months. Parker married in 1902 Ruth Margaret (*d.* 1933), daughter of Ludwig Messel, of Nymans, Handcross, Sussex. They had four sons, two of whom were killed in the Second World War, and two daughters.

When Strachey's ownership and his editorship of the *County Gentleman* came to an end in 1907, Parker devoted himself with his customary thoroughness to the Surrey volume (1908) in Macmillan's Highways and Byways series, exploring on foot every nook and cranny of the county where much of his life was to be spent; few came to know it better or loved it more. For two years (1908–10) he edited the monthly *Gamekeeper*; it was then, in *A Book of the Zoo* (1909), that he foresaw that the grey squirrel might 'become a country problem', a couple of decades before it was officially recognized as such. In 1910 Parker was in the running for the post of editor-in-chief of *The Field*; but the trustees regarded him as 'too much of a poet' and appointed the same Theodore Cook with whom he had started his journalistic career. Cook invited Parker to help him and a year later appointed him shooting editor, a post he was to fill with distinction for over twenty years (1911–32). At this time he was writing regularly for *The Field*, *The Spectator*, and *Cornhill Magazine*, but he found time to finish a novel of child life, *Promise of Arden* (1912), to prepare with William Hyde *A West Surrey Sketch-Book* (1913), and to undertake at the request of Reginald J. Smith a book of reminiscences, *Eton in the 'Eighties* (1914).

In November 1914 Parker was gazetted to a captaincy in the 5th battalion of the Queen's Royal West Surrey regiment, in which he served until June 1918, when he was attached to the intelligence department at the War Office. During the war years, which he spent in England, he wrote *Shooting Days* (1918) and began *Playing Fields* (1922), the story of life at a preparatory school and at Eton as seen through the eyes of a schoolboy; it has been described as the best school story ever written. Between the wars not a year passed without the appearance of at least one book written, compiled, or edited by him. A selection of titles indicates their range: *Elements of Shooting* (1924), *Between the Wickets* (1926), *Field, River and Hill* (1927), *English Wild Life* (1929), *Ethics of Egg-Collecting* (1935), *The Gardener's England* (1936), and the autobiographical *Memory Looks Forward* (1937).

In 1927 Parker gave the first in what became a series of talks to schools for the BBC. In the following year he became editor of the Lonsdale Library of Sports, Games and Pastimes. Then, in December 1929, came Sir Leicester Harmsworth's offer of the post of editor-in-chief of *The Field*. In the eight years that followed Parker put new life into the weekly, widening its interest and appeal. His most noteworthy achievement was the devastating exposure of the trapping and caging of linnets, goldfinches, and other small birds, which was largely responsible for the passage of the Protection of Birds Act, 1933. Parker also gave a talk on the subject for the BBC. The broadcasting of 'Birds in Paper Bags' did much to alert public opinion to the cruel conditions in which wild birds were kept and sold at London markets. He also campaigned in *The Field* against the docking of horses, which was later made illegal. At the end of 1937 Parker gave up his post with the journal so that he might have more time for writing and broadcasting, and accepted a seat on the board. His literary output was maintained, although with less emphasis on field sports and more on cricket, dogs, natural history, and gardens. He contributed the volume on Surrey (1947) to Hale's County Books series and added to the Lonsdale Library *The History of Cricket* (1950). The last of his fifty-odd books, *Surrey Gardens* (1954), was published shortly before his death at his home, Feathercombe, Hambledon, Surrey, on 13 February 1955.

In his bearing, talk, kindness, honesty of mind and purpose, outlook on life, and general character Parker was outstandingly an English country gentleman. He had a fund of humour, was a keen observer, and wrote with ease and sureness. He enabled readers to see about them things which they had not noticed before, and shared with them delightfully his appreciation of beauty in the countryside. JOHN CRIPPS, *rev.* MARK POTTLE

Sources E. Parker, *Memory looks forward* (1937) · *The Times* (14 Feb 1955) · personal knowledge (1971) · private information (1971)
Wealth at death £564: probate, 29 April 1955, *CGPLA Eng. & Wales*

Parker, George (1654–1743), astrologer, was born on 9 August 1654 at Shipston-on-Stour, Worcestershire, and brought up among the Quakers, though he denied having ever been a full member of the Friends. He moved to London to become an apprentice cutler, probably when he was about fifteen. In 1697 he remarked that he had been a freeman for twenty-two years and a householder in the parish of Christ Church Greyfriars for eighteen. Initially he kept a cutler's shop in Newgate Market, but on marrying his wife Elizabeth, a Quaker widow, about 1678, he moved at her insistence to Newgate Street, and then to a larger shop and house (The Leopard) close by.

Parker learned astronomy and astrology from his friend Thomas Streete, and in 1690 launched an annual almanac, *Mercurius Anglicanus*. It included unusually elaborate astronomical data (adapted from Streete's tables), and the first edition printed a letter from Edmond Halley commending them as the best available. In preparing his edition for 1692 Parker acknowledged the assistance of Halley and John Flamsteed. The tables pushed up the price and depressed sales, however, and from 1695 he issued his almanacs (published by the Stationers' Company) and ephemerides as separate titles, a practice continued until 1699. By then he had established his name, and he claimed in 1699 that a group of wealthy gentlemen with scientific interests had retained his services for a 'generous Sallary' of £300 and later £400. Parker needed this support, for his marriage had ended in personal and financial disaster. By 1693 he was bankrupt and estranged from his wife.

Parker's failed marriage featured prominently in the ferocious pamphlet war between him and his neighbour John Partridge in the late 1690s. They differed over astronomy, astrology, and politics, but the quarrel quickly descended to personal abuse which was scurrilous even by the standards of the age. It began when Parker interpreted an attack on 'pretenders' in Partridge's almanac for 1696 as aimed at him, and hit back. Partridge renewed his assault in 'Flagitiosus Mercurius flagellatus, or, The whipper whipp'd', an appendix to his *Defectio geniturarum* (1697), and in his almanacs for 1698–9. He accused Parker of having turned Quaker merely to secure his wife's £300 estate, and then systematically abusing and whipping her, locking her in a garret for a week, trying to poison her, and eventually turning her out and living with another woman. He mocked Parker's bankruptcy and dismissed him as a dangerous charlatan in both medicine and astrology. Partridge obtained many of these personal details from Mrs Parker, and her husband vehemently denied them. He admitted, however, that his marriage had been disastrous, complaining that his wife suffered delusions, stole money and goods from the shop, had run up debts in his name, deliberately engineered his bankruptcy, and then abandoned him and the children.

Parker lost his house, goods, and shop, and later acknowledged that he had been forced to turn his hand to many things to support his family. Besides taking up medicine he worked for a time as a 'calculator' (accountant), and as a 'Devil to a Glass-house'. He also sold stationery, beginning with blank astrological schemes and adding tradesmen's bills, tax receipts, tide tables and logarithm tables. From 1694 he lived at the Blue Ball, and later the Ball and Star, in Salisbury Court, off Fleet Street, where he was to remain for the rest of his life. For some time he ran an alehouse or tavern there which, according to his friend Thomas Hearne, the antiquary, was frequented by 'many honest and ingenious men' (*Reliquiae*, 1.499). These were no doubt the patrons who settled a 'salary' on him in the late 1690s. One of them was Edward Thwaites, professor of Greek and moral philosophy at Oxford; he lodged with Parker in London and invited him back to stay in his rooms in Oxford to teach him astrology. Parker's bankruptcy was eventually discharged under the act of 1696.

Despite his Quaker background Parker became a staunch tory and high-churchman. He conformed to the Church of England from the end of 1687, and had his three children baptized together on 23 January 1688, at Christ Church Greyfriars. In 1699 Partridge called him a Jacobite, though this cannot be proved from his publications. Parker's first almanac (completed in August 1689) employed the neutral formula that 'William and Mary now enjoy the Crown', but he later accepted the revolution, at least in public. The 1692 edition noted that James II had abdicated after being led astray by the Jesuits, and the 1693 edition was even dedicated to William and Mary. He warmly supported the stand of the seven bishops, gaoled for defying James's declaration of indulgence. Under Queen Anne, Parker adopted a more aggressively high-church–tory position, at odds with most other almanac makers. He engaged in fierce disputes with whig rivals such as John Wing and Francis Moore, pursued further in the *Gardiners Almanack* (1702–3) which he published under the pseudonym Gregory Kepar. He quickly turned against the war with France, and his edition for 1710 gave a rapturous welcome to the new tory, anti-war ministry. He praised Sacheverell's campaign against occasional conformity.

Most of Parker's publications during Anne's reign were not published by the Company of Stationers, with which he became embroiled in a political row in 1704. He wished to commemorate not only saints but traitors, including the Rye House plotters; the company refused. His edition for 1706 ran into serious trouble when Partridge pointed out that it listed the Pretender as prince of Wales. Partridge denounced Parker as an 'Impudent Jacobite Conjuror', and dared him to come out openly for 'James the T..rd'. According to Hearne's slightly different account, Parker listed the Pretender among the sovereign princes of Europe (as the 'Chevalier de St George'), and was fined £50. From 1707 Parker published his annual ephemeris without an almanac section, using his freedom to denounce the company's greed, corruption, and whiggish politics. The breach lasted until 1715.

Parker always remained intensely loyal to Queen Anne, despite the taunts of Jacobitism, but he viewed the Hanoverian succession with some dismay. His 1715 edition noted without comment that George was now king, while heaping praise on the late queen, though his strong Anglicanism kept his Jacobite sympathies in check. The later almanacs were uncontroversial. He never lost his faith in judicial astrology, which he defended vigorously in 1741 against attacks by the almanac maker Edward Smith. In a long career Parker published nothing apart from almanacs and ephemerides, except a revised edition of William Eland's *Tutor to Astrology* (1704). Despite his lowly origins, he aimed at a more sophisticated readership than most compilers. From Anne's reign his editions included lists of peers, MPs, bishops, judges, and London mayors or aldermen. His *Ephemerides* were recommended by the mathematician and natural philosopher William Whiston, who explained their use in his public lectures. After the death of his wife, perhaps about 1709, Parker married again, and in July 1723 Hearne notes a visit by Parker and his second wife, on their way back from visiting relatives in Worcestershire. Parker died in London on 16 July 1743.

BERNARD CAPP

Sources B. S. Capp, *Astrology and the popular press: English almanacs, 1500–1800* (1979) • E. G. R. Taylor, *The mathematical practitioners of Tudor and Stuart England* (1954) • J. Partridge, *Defectio geniturarum* (1697) • *Reliquiae Hearnianae: the remains of Thomas Hearne*, ed. P. Bliss, 2 vols. (1857) • *GM*, 1st ser., 13 (1743), 390 • W. A. Littledale, ed., *The registers of Christ Church, Newgate, 1538 to 1754*, Harleian Society, 21 (1895)

Likenesses W. Elder, line engraving, BM, NPG; repro. in G. Parker, *Mercurius Anglicanus, or, The English Mercury* (1694) • J. Nutting, line engraving, BM, NPG

Parker, George, second earl of Macclesfield (*c.*1697–1764), astronomer and politician, was the only son of Thomas *Parker, first earl of Macclesfield (1667–1732), and his wife and cousin Janet Carrier (*c.*1666–1733). He was instructed in mathematics by Abraham De Moivre and William Jones (1675–1749). His father procured for him in 1719 an appointment for life as one of the tellers of the exchequer, and he took the title of Viscount Parker from 1721 until 1732, when he succeeded his father in the earldom. In March 1720 he set out for Italy in company with Edward Wright, who published in 1730, in two quarto volumes, an account of their travels. On their return Parker married, on 18 September 1722, Mary (*d.* 1753), the eldest daughter of Ralph Lane, of Woodbury, Cambridge, an eminent merchant in Middle Eastern goods; they had two sons: Thomas, Lord Parker (*d.* 1795), MP for Rochester, who succeeded as third earl of Macclesfield, and George Lane Parker [*see below*].

Parker was MP for Wallingford from 1722 to 1727, and was elected a fellow of the Royal Society on 23 October 1722. His residence at this time was in Soho Square, London, but he spent much time also at Shirburn Castle, Oxfordshire, where he pursued his studies under Jones's guidance. With Jones's assistance he formed what is today one of the most important collections of seventeenth-century English mathematical manuscripts, including letters of Isaac Newton. At Shirburn, aided by James Bradley, with whom he had early formed a friendship, Macclesfield erected about 1739 an astronomical observatory. Its instrumental equipment, perhaps the finest then existing, consisted of a 5 foot transit and a quadrant (both by Sisson), clocks by Tompion and Graham, and a 14 foot refractor fitted with a micrometer. The series of Macclesfield's personal observations, begun on 4 June 1740, was continued nearly to his death. Among the subjects studied was the great comet of December 1743. The castle observing records extend, for the transit, from 1740 to 1787, for the quadrant, from 1743 to 1793. In 1742 Macclesfield succeeded by untiring exertions in procuring for Bradley, his frequent guest and occasional assistant, the post of astronomer royal; he then trained a stable-boy and a shepherd, named Thomas Phelps and Bartlett respectively, to work under him. In 1748 he obtained from the Royal Society the loan of two object-glasses by Huygens, of 120 and 210 feet focus, and had one, or both, mounted at Shirburn.

In parliament Macclesfield was a principal proponent in 1752 (with Lord Chesterfield) for the adoption of the Gregorian calendar and the change in the new year from 26 March to 1 January. He communicated to the Royal Society on 10 May 1750 a preparatory paper entitled 'Remarks upon the solar and the lunar years' and made most of the necessary calculations, and his speech in the House of Lords on 18 March 1751, on the second reading of the Bill for Regulating the Commencement of the Year, was printed by general request. Lord Chesterfield wrote of him as the virtual author of the bill, and as 'one of the greatest mathematicians and astronomers in Europe', adding that he

> spoke with infinite knowledge and all the clearness that so intricate a matter could admit of; but as his words, his periods, and his utterance, were not near so good as mine, the preference was most unanimously, though most unjustly, given to me. (*Letters … Chesterfield*, 2.76)

Macclesfield's action in the matter was in some quarters unpopular. When his eldest son, Lord Parker, contested Oxfordshire in 1754, one of the cries of the crowd was,

'Give us back the eleven days we have been robbed of', and a ballad of the day commences:

In seventeen hundred and fifty-three
The style it was changed to Popery.
(Wilkins, 2.211)

Macclesfield was elected president of the Royal Society in 1752, and for twelve years discharged the duties of the office with great assiduity. An account of his observations while at Shirburn of the earthquake in 1755 was published in the *Philosophical Transactions*. The University of Oxford conferred an honorary degree of DCL on him on 3 July 1759. He was a member of the French Academy, a vice-president of the Foundling Hospital, and high steward of Henley-on-Thames. At the funeral of Frederick, prince of Wales, on 13 April 1751, he was one of the pallbearers. He married, secondly, on 20 November 1757, Dorothy Nesbit (*d*. 1779); they had no children. He died at Shirburn Castle on 17 March 1764, and was buried there.

George Lane Parker (1724–1791), his second son, served for many years in the 1st foot guards (lieutenant and captain 1749; captain and lieutenant-colonel 1755; second major 1770). He attained the rank of major-general and in 1773 was appointed colonel of the 20th foot. In 1777 he became a lieutenant-general and in 1782 was transferred to the colonelcy of the 12th dragoons. He was for many years MP for Tregony, and he died at his country seat, Woodbury Hall, Cambridge, on 14 September 1791, leaving a fortune of £130,000, said to be 'derived from industrious exertions in India' (*GM*, 1791, 877).

A. M. Clerke, *rev*. Owen Gingerich

Sources S. P. Rigaud, 'Memoirs of Bradley', in *Miscellaneous works and correspondence of the Rev. James Bradley*, ed. [S. P. Rigaud] (1832) · E. Wright, *Some observations made in travelling through France, Italy &c. in the years 1720, 1721, and 1722* (1730) · S. P. Rigaud and S. J. Rigaud, eds., *Correspondence of scientific men of the seventeenth century*, 2 vols. (1841) · *Letters written by the late Right Honourable Philip Dormer Stanhope, earl of Chesterfield, to his son*, ed. E. Stanhope (1774) · C. R. Weld, *A history of the Royal Society*, 2 vols. (1848) · *Debrett's Peerage* · Foster, *Alum. Oxon.* · J. H. Jesse, *George Selwyn and his contemporaries, with memoirs and notes*, 4 vols. (1843–4), vol. 1, p. 277 · M. Maty, *Memoirs of Lord Chesterfield* (1777), 320 · *GM*, 1st ser., 34 (1764), 147 · *GM*, 1st ser., 61 (1791), 877 · Nichols, *Lit. anecdotes*, 1.464 · W. W. Wilkins, ed., *Political ballads of the seventeenth and eighteenth centuries*, 2 vols. (1860), vol. 2, p. 311 · M. F. Parker, *Scattered notices of Shirburn Castle, Oxfordshire* (1887) · *Parliamentary history of England*, 15, 136 · G. Parker, second earl of Macclesfield, 'Remarks upon the solar and the lunar years', *PTRS*, 46 (1749–50), 417–34 · GEC, *Peerage*

Archives BL, corresp. with T. Birch, Add. MSS 4313, 4443 · BL, letters to his father describing his travels, Stowe MS 750 · Hants. RO, letters to Lady Elizabeth Heathcote, his sister

Likenesses T. Hudson, oils, *c*.1753, RS · J. Faber junior, engraving, 1754 (after T. Hudson), BM · B. Wilson, oils, 1760, Thomas Coram Foundation for Children, London · Hogarth, portrait, Shirburn Castle, Oxfordshire

Wealth at death £130,000—George Lane Parker

Parker, George (1732–1800), actor and public lecturer, was born at Green Street, Kent, the son of a tradesman. Little is known of his life apart from the account given in his memoirs, *A View of Society and Manners in High and Low Life, being the Adventures of Mr G. Parker* (1781), which though highly entertaining is not the most reliable of sources. Parker was educated at the King's School, Canterbury, and at an early age became a midshipman on the *Falmouth* and the *Guernsey*. His misbehaviour on leave in London caused him to leave the navy, and in 1754 he enlisted as a soldier in the 20th foot, the 2nd battalion of which became the 67th regiment in 1758, under the command of James Wolfe. He served for seven years, in Portugal, Gibraltar, and Minorca, and rose to the rank of sergeant. He returned home as a supernumerary exciseman but attempted a new career when he was made innkeeper of the King's Head in Canterbury. He soon failed, and then failed again in a London inn.

Parker decided to try his luck on the stage; he may have been the George Parker who acted with the Norwich company in 1765 or in Belfast in January 1769. In his memoirs Parker tells how he travelled through Ireland with a clergyman named Brownlow Ford and played at the Haymarket Theatre on his return to London. He was engaged for one season at the Canongate Theatre, Edinburgh, by the actor manager West Digges. There he married Miss Heydon, an actress who had appeared at the Haymarket, Sadler's Wells, and Bartholomew fair; their marriage was reported in the *Evening Courant* (16 November 1771). It proved unhappy, and Parker soon left his wife to return to London, apparently because of her drinking and promiscuity.

Parker's next known engagement was as Launcelot in *The Merchant of Venice* at the Smock Alley Theatre, Dublin, in September 1772. About this time he tried to make a living by touring through England giving lectures on elocution in an entertainment called *The World, Scientific, Theoretic, and Practical*, which was interspersed with recitations from popular authors. He occasionally lectured on freemasonry, for he was an active member of the brotherhood. In November 1776 he travelled to Paris, where he remained for eight months, financed by his father, yet met with little success. He lectured at Boulogne for a while, this time in the character of the 'universal traveller', and embarked on another lecturing tour after he had returned to England. During the 1770s several influential acquaintances in Samuel Johnson's circle tried to help him, and Oliver Goldsmith secured him an interview with George Colman, who refused to cast him in any of his productions because he was too fat. Parker's last known role was at the Haymarket in the anonymous *A School for Ladies*, on 5 April 1780. In 1782 he was connected with the school of eloquence at the Lyceum, in the Strand.

A genial and witty man, Parker was able to secure enough subscribers to publish not only his memoirs but also *Humorous Sketches, Satyrical Strokes and Attic Observations* (1782) and *Life's Painter of Variegated Characters in Public and Private Life* (1789). He spent his final years selling gingerbread at fairs and race meetings, to make a meagre living, and died in Coventry poorhouse in April 1800.

Gordon Goodwin, *rev*. S. J. Skedd

Sources *A view of society and manners in high and low life, being the adventures of Mr G. Parker*, 2 vols. (1781) · *GM*, 1st ser., 70 (1800), 901 · *European Magazine and London Review*, 38 (1800), 237 · *N&Q*, 2nd ser., 4 (1857), 168 · J. Forster, *The life and times of Oliver Goldsmith*, [new edn], 2 (1888), 109 · Highfill, Burnim & Langhans, *BDA*

Likenesses engraving (as Mr Hardcastle in *She stoops to conquer*), Harvard TC; repro. in Highfill, Burnim & Langhans, *BDA*, vol. 11, p. 206 • stipple and line engraving, BM, NPG; repro. in G. Parker, *Life's painter of variegated characters* (1789)

Parker, George, fourth earl of Macclesfield (1755–1842), courtier, was born on 24 February 1755, second child and eldest son of Thomas Parker, third earl of Macclesfield (1723–1795), politician, of Shirburn Castle, Oxfordshire, and his wife and cousin, Mary (1726–1812), daughter of Sir Thomas Heathcote, first baronet, of Hursley, Hampshire. Styled Viscount Parker from 1764, he was educated at Eton College (1765–9), and at Exeter College, Oxford (1773–6), to which he presented his portrait on leaving. He was returned to parliament for Woodstock, on 1 December 1777, on the Blenheim interest. He seconded the address on 25 November 1779. He married on 25 May 1780 Mary Frances (1761–1823), daughter of the Revd Dr Thomas Drake of Amersham, Buckinghamshire, and his wife, Elizabeth Whittington; in December he became a gentleman of the bedchamber to George, prince of Wales. He attended Westminster in February 1783, speaking on the 14th and voting for peace on the 18th. He found no seat at the general election in 1784, as he was haplessly associated with the prince's opposition to Pitt. The prince dismissed his household in 1786–7, and Parker was dismissed again in 1789 after his father's support of Pitt over the regency. This martyrdom prompted him to write to Pitt, on 18 May 1790, requesting a Treasury board vacancy, preferably before he contested Sandwich at the general election in 1790. Defeated at Sandwich, he procured Minehead on the Luttrell interest, armed for the contest with a secret service subsidy.

Adhering to Pitt's ministry, Parker became comptroller of George III's household, and privy councillor, in April 1791. At Westminster he delivered royal messages. Succeeding his father as earl, and as high steward of Henley, on 9 February 1795, he took his seat in the Lords on 11 March, having informed Pitt of his wish to remain comptroller unless offered a better position. He was created DCL at Oxford, but demoted to lord of the bedchamber in April 1797, despite a plea to Pitt. He was appointed captain of Watlington yeoman cavalry in 1798, and on Pitt's return to power he became, from 1804 to 1830, captain of the yeomen of the guard. His general support for successive governments was silent. In June 1827 he offered the king his resignation when unable to support the Corn Bill, but was dissuaded. He also served as president of the board of agriculture (1816–18), and his wife was lady of the bedchamber to Queen Charlotte (1811–18). He later eschewed publicity, and died at 9 Conduit Street, Hanover Square, London, on 20 March 1842, 'a good Conservative', lord lieutenant of Oxfordshire since 1817, FRS, and the second oldest privy councillor (*GM*, 548). He was buried at Shirburn on 29 March 1842. A son having died in infancy, he left one daughter, and his brother, Thomas, succeeded as earl.

ROLAND THORNE

Sources J. Brooke, 'Parker, George', HoP, *Commons, 1754–90* • L. Taylor, 'Parker, George', HoP, *Commons, 1790–1820* • *The later correspondence of George III*, ed. A. Aspinall, 5 vols. (1962–70) • *The letters of King George IV, 1812–1830*, ed. A. Aspinall, 3 (1938) • *The correspondence of George, prince of Wales, 1770–1812*, ed. A. Aspinall, 1: *1770–1789* (1963) • *GM*, 2nd ser., 17 (1842), 547–8 • J. Stockdale, ed., *The debates and proceedings of the House of Commons: during the sixteenth parliament of Great Britain*, 19 vols. (1785–90) • Cobbett, *Parl. hist.* • GEC, *Peerage* • Foster, *Alum. Oxon.*

Archives NRA, priv. coll. • Royal Library, Windsor, Berkshire | BL, corresp. with first and second earls of Liverpool, Add. MSS 38215–38321, 38458, 38474, 38571, *passim*

Likenesses oils, 1776, Exeter College, Oxford

Wealth at death under £140,000: *Complete peerage*, vol. 8, p. 335

Parker, Sir George (1767–1847), naval officer, was the son of George Parker, the elder brother of Sir Peter Parker (1721–1811). He was on the books of the *Barfleur*, at Portsmouth, under his uncle's command, from 21 December 1773 to 31 October 1775, and on the books of the *Bristol*, on the coast of North America and at Jamaica, from December 1777 to April 1780; but whether he was on the *Bristol* or, if he was, for how long, is doubtful. He probably went out to Jamaica at the end of 1779 or the beginning of 1780. On 13 April 1780 he was entered on board the *Lowestoft* with his first cousin, Christopher Parker, son of the admiral, and in November followed him to the *Diamond*. On 13 March 1782 he was promoted lieutenant of the *Nestor* (Captain James Macnamara), and went home in her in the summer of 1783. In 1787 he was appointed to the *Wasp* on the home station, and in October 1788 was moved into the *Phoenix*, going out to the East Indies under the command of Captain George Anson Byron. He continued in her with Sir Richard John Strachan, and after the action with the *Résolue* on 19 November 1791 was sent home with the dispatches from the commodore, William Cornwallis.

In October 1792 Parker joined the frigate *Crescent*, with Captain James Saumarez, afterwards Lord de Saumarez, and was first lieutenant of her when she captured the French frigate *Réunion* on 20 October 1793. On 4 November Parker was promoted to command the sloop *Albacore* in the North Sea, and on 7 April 1795 he was posted to the *Squirrel* (20 guns), also in the North Sea. From December 1796 to February 1802 he commanded the *Santa Margarita* (36 guns) in the channel, West Indies, and Mediterranean. In 1804 he was captain of the *Argo* (44 guns) in the North Sea, and from April 1805 to May 1808 of the *Stately* (64 guns) in the North Sea and Baltic. In company with the *Nassau*, on 22 March 1808, he captured the Danish 74-gun ship *Prince Christian Frederick*, off the island of Zealand, Denmark, which surrendered only after a most obstinate defence and a loss of 143 killed and wounded, the killed and wounded in the British ships amounting to fifty. A few minutes after the Danish ship struck her colours she ran aground, and, as she could not be got off, was set on fire and blown up. In May 1808 Parker was moved into the *Aboukir* (74 guns), which he commanded in the North Sea, in the expedition to the Scheldt in 1809, and afterwards in the Mediterranean, until September 1813, when he was transferred to the *Bombay*. He returned to England in the *Bombay* in May 1814.

On 4 June 1814 Parker became rear-admiral. He never hoisted his flag, but became, in due course, vice-admiral, on 27 May 1825. He was nominated a KCB on 12 June 1833, and became admiral on 10 January 1837. He died at his home at Great Yarmouth, Norfolk, of influenza on 24 December 1847. Parker had married a daughter of Peter Butt, but they had no children.

J. K. LAUGHTON, *rev.* ANDREW LAMBERT

Sources *The Saumarez papers: selections from the Baltic correspondence of Vice-Admiral Sir James Saumarez, 1808–1812*, ed. A. N. Ryan, Navy RS, 110 (1968) • D. Syrett and R. L. DiNardo, *The commissioned sea officers of the Royal Navy, 1660–1815*, rev. edn, Occasional Publications of the Navy RS, 1 (1994) • O'Byrne, *Naval biog. dict.* • *GM*, 2nd ser., 29 (1848), 305 • service book, PRO, Naval Records • J. Marshall, *Royal naval biography*, 1/2 (1823), 639–40

Parker, Sir George, fourth baronet (1813–1857), army officer in the East India Company and administrator in India, was born in London on 3 February 1813, the second son of Vice-Admiral Sir William George Parker, second baronet (*d.* 1848), of Harburn, Warwickshire, and his wife, Elizabeth, daughter of James Charles Still of East Knoyle, Wiltshire. Vice-Admiral Sir William *Parker, first baronet (1743–1802), was his grandfather.

Parker was educated at Addiscombe College, and went to India as an infantry cadet in 1833, but was not posted until 30 January 1837. He was then appointed lieutenant in the 74th Bengal native infantry, in which he became captain on 3 October 1845. After serving as second in command of the Bundelkhand military police battalion, he was successively commandant of the Ambala and Meerut police battalions. He was appointed superintendent of Akbara and joint cantonment magistrate at Meerut on 10 June 1847. Parker married, first, on 24 January 1838, Eliza Cecilia, *née* Marshall, by whom he had a son, George Law Marshall (1838–1866), who succeeded to the baronetcy, and two daughters. His first wife died at Calcutta on 5 August 1843. He married, second, on 10 December 1846, Gertrude, the youngest daughter of Lieutenant-Colonel C. A. Elderton; she died at Meerut in April 1850, leaving one daughter.

In June 1852 Parker went home sick, and succeeded to the baronetcy on the death of his elder brother, Sir William James Parker, third baronet, in the same year. After his return to India in December 1854, he was reappointed superintendent of Akbara and made magistrate at Cawnpore on 5 May 1856. During the siege, Parker, Wiggins, the judge advocate-general, and Brigadier Alexander Jack were the only residents who courageously remained in their houses. Parker died of sunstroke on 8 June 1857, before the massacre. He had been promoted major a few days earlier.

H. M. CHICHESTER, *rev.* JAMES LUNT

Sources J. Foster, *The peerage, baronetage, and knightage of the British empire for 1883*, 2 [1883] • J. W. Kaye and G. B. Malleson, *Kaye's and Malleson's History of the Indian mutiny of 1857–8*, 2 (1888) • *GM*, 3rd ser., 2 (1857), 467 • G. O. Trevelyan, *Cawnpore* (1865) • C. E. Buckland, *Dictionary of Indian biography* (1906) • NAM, Hodson papers

Wealth at death see NAM, Hodson papers

Parker, George Lane (1724–1791). *See under* Parker, George, second earl of Macclesfield (*c.*1697–1764).

Parker, Sir (Horatio) Gilbert George, baronet (1860–1932), novelist and politician, was born on 23 November 1860 at Camden East, Addington, Ontario, Canada, the fourth surviving child and eldest son of Joseph Parker (1807–1900), former soldier, justice of the peace, militiaman, and shopkeeper, and his second wife, Samantha Jane (1834?–1908), daughter of George and Mary (*née* Gardineer) Simmons, a family of United Empire loyalist extraction. His father emigrated to Canada from Ireland about 1834 and pursued a variety of occupations before settling as a shopkeeper. Parker attended various schools, including one in Frankford when the family moved there in 1877. He spent six weeks at Belleville model school training as a teacher and started his teaching career at Marsh Hill, near Frankford, where he stayed for three years until 1880. He continued his teacher training at Ottawa normal school from late 1880 to early 1881. He then taught at Bayside School before teaching at the Ontario Institute for the Deaf at Belleville in January 1882. In April 1881 he was ordained an Anglican deacon and a curate at St George's Church, Trenton. In 1883 Parker began a divinity course at Trinity College, Toronto, where he was also professor of elocution. In 1884 he became lecturer in elocution at Queen's College, Kingston, and he finally abandoned any thoughts of the ministry. Early in 1886 Parker left on a trip to Australia where he joined the staff of the *Sydney Morning Herald*, eventually becoming associate editor. While in Australia, Parker began his literary career by publishing stories and articles in the newspapers and he wrote the plays *Faust* (1888) and *The Vendetta* (1889), both of which were failures.

Parker left Australia in 1889 and settled in Britain as his home for the rest of his life. He contributed to some of the major journals and papers and began his stories of the Canadian north. His first book, *Pierre and his People: Tales of the Far North* (1892), was well received in Britain but not in Canada, where it was felt that it lacked realism, a criticism that was applied to many of his later works. Throughout the 1890s he was a prolific writer in both article and novel form. He published his first full-length novel, *The Chief Factor*, in 1892 and then followed with his first modern novel, *Mrs Falchion* (1893), which received mixed reviews, and *The Trespasser* (1893). The year 1894 saw his first historical romance, *The Trail of the Sword*, his only novel to be translated into French. His greatest success was *The Seats of the Mighty* (1896), a story based on the British capture of Quebec, which Beerbohm Tree persuaded him to adapt for the stage, though without much success.

On 5 December 1895 Parker married Amy Eliza Vantine (*d.* 1925), a wealthy young New York heiress, and they settled into a fairly hectic social life where he endeavoured to seek influence both literary and political. Parker's love for Canada and his belief in the imperial destiny led him to have political ambitions both in Canada and Britain, and in 1900 he was elected Conservative MP for Gravesend, a seat he held until ill health forced him to resign in 1918.

After a stay in the Channel Islands, Parker wrote *The Battle of the Strong* (1898), a story of the French Revolution, and this was followed by *The Right of Way* (1901), a psychological study of mental illness and marital disharmony which became a best-seller in the USA. Despite his parliamentary work, he still managed to write both fiction and non-fiction, and in 1902 he published *Donovan Pasha*, a story set in Egypt. He used his vast experience of travels abroad in his novels and this is a mark of his style and art. However, a criticism often made was that his characters were too extreme in their make-up and actions to be believable. Despite this, Parker was recognized as a major Canadian writer with the award of a knighthood in 1902. His literary position was recognized in 1912 with the start of the publication of the Imperial edition of his works, a rare honour for a living novelist.

Parker's staunch support of the empire led him to organize the first colonial universities' conference in 1903 and in the following year he became chairman of the Imperial South African Association. In parliament he promoted colonial interests, a concern reflected in his novels and contributions to periodicals. His ambitions for high political office were slow to be fulfilled (he failed to become high commissioner for Canada) until the First World War provided an opening for his talents. From November 1914 to late 1916 he was in charge of British propaganda in the USA and he 'built up an organisation of 13,000 influential people in the USA who were distributing British propaganda' (Buitenhuis, 17–18). He published *The World in a Crucible: an Account of the Origins and Conduct of the Great War* in 1915, and in the same year was rewarded for his political and war work with a baronetcy and the following year was sworn of the privy council. His contribution to the war effort was recognized with the offer of an earldom in 1921, but it was refused as being too late to be of value (Adams, 186). His wife died in 1925 and Parker never recovered from the loss. His novels no longer satisfied the public, though sixteen of them were filmed.

Photographs show Parker as of medium height, bearded, and with rather intense eyes. He was somewhat of a dandy in his dress. He died of a heart attack on 6 September 1932 at his home, 2 Whitehall Court, Westminster, London, and was buried in Belleville, Ontario, on 27 September; his title became extinct. DAMIAN ATKINSON

Sources J. C. Adams, *Seated with the mighty: a biography of Sir Gilbert Parker* (1979) • E. Waterston, *Gilbert Parker and his works* (1989) • DLitB • *The Times* (7 Sept 1932) • *WWBMP* • *DNB* • E. Kilmurray, *Dictionary of British portraiture*, 3 (1981) • P. Buitenhuis, *The great war of words: British, American, and Canadian propaganda and fiction, 1914–1933* (1987) • *CGPLA Eng. & Wales* (1932)

Archives Bodl. Oxf. • McGill University, Montreal • NA Canada • NRA, corresp. and literary papers • Princeton University Library, New Jersey • Queen's University, Kingston, Ontario, Douglas Library, Queen's archives, corresp. and papers • Ransom HRC, corresp. • Stanford University Library, California | BL, corresp. with Society of Authors, Add. MS 56722 • BLPES, corresp. with E. D. Morel • Col. U., William Barclay Parsons MSS • Col. U., A. P. Watt & Son corresp. • Harvard U., Harvard College Library, Alice Kauser MSS • Harvard U., Houghton L., Horace Elisha Scudder corresp. • HLRO, corresp. with Lord Beaverbrook • HLRO, letter to Ralph Blumenfeld • HLRO, Bonar Law collection • HLRO, Lloyd George MSS • HLRO, Samuel MSS • NA Canada, George Taylor Denison III MSS • NA Canada, Sir Stamford Fleming MSS • NA Canada, George Monro Grant MSS • NA Canada, Martin Griffin MSS • NA Canada, Sir Wilfrid Laurier MSS • NA Canada, Sir George Parkin MSS • NA Canada, Sir Joseph Pope MSS • NYPL, Berg collection • Ohio State University, Columbus, Creelman MSS • Public Archives of Ontario, Toronto, corresp. with William Kirby • Queen's University, Kingston, Ontario, Douglas Library, Hale–Garvin collection • Queen's University, Kingston, Ontario, Douglas Library, Edith and Lorne Pierce collection • Richmond Local Studies Library, London, corresp. with Douglas Sladen • Royal Society of Literature, London, letters to the Royal Society of Literature • Syracuse University, New York, Robert H. Davis MSS • U. Leeds, Brotherton L., letters to Clement Shorter • U. Leeds, Brotherton L., letters, mainly to Bram Stoker • University of Toronto, Thomas Fisher Rare Book Library, Arthur S. Bourinot collection • Fredericton, New Brunswick, Carmen Bliss MSS | FILM BFI NFTVA, *It is for England*, 1916

Likenesses photograph, *c*.1888, repro. in *Sydney Morning Herald* • photograph, *c*.1894, Metropolitan Toronto Library • photograph, Aug 1902, Archives of Ontario, Toronto • H. von Herkomer, oils, 1910, National Portrait Gallery of Canada, Ottawa • M. Beerbohm, caricature, *c*.1914, repro. in Adams, *Seated with the mighty* • J. Russell & Sons, photograph, *c*.1915, NPG • W. Stoneman, photograph, 1919, NPG • A. P. F. Ritchie, watercolour, 1932, NPG • H. Furniss, pen and ink caricature, NPG • Spy [L. Ward], caricature, Hentschel-colourtype, NPG; repro. in *VF* (27 June 1909) • photographs, repro. in Adams, *Seated with the mighty*

Wealth at death £11,327 11*s*. 6*d*.: probate, 23 July 1933, *CGPLA Eng. & Wales*

Parker, Henry (*d*. after **1504**), Carmelite friar and theologian, was born in Fleet Street, London, the son of a skinner, and joined the order in London. He studied at Cambridge University, where he was ordained subdeacon on 21 December 1454. While a lector in theology he preached a provocative sermon at St Paul's Cathedral on Sunday 16 September 1464, asserting that Christ and his apostles had owned nothing and had begged for their living. Therefore, he argued, the mendicant friars in their way of life were following closest to the model of Christ, and all other priests should renounce their benefices and possessions, and live on alms. This led to a fierce controversy with the secular clergy and a response from Dr William Ive (*d*. 1486), master of Whittington College. Parker was supported by his fellow Carmelites, Thomas Holden and John Milverton (*d*. 1487), and friars from other orders. The three Carmelites were cited for heresy, and in late April or early May 1465 Holden and Milverton fled to Rome. Parker was put into prison by the chancellor, Archbishop George Neville (*d*. 1476), and then handed over to the bishop of London. The following Sunday, he publicly recanted his opinions and, as a contemporary chronicle recounts, pleaded 'that very nede causyd them to saye that Cryste beggyd, by cause that men shulde take the ordyr of fryers most parfytyste of alle orders' (*Historical Collections of a Citizen of London*, 230).

Little is known of Parker's later career except that John Bale, who was prior of Doncaster in the 1530s, asserts in his *Anglorum Heliades* that Parker stayed in Doncaster and that he died and was buried there. It would seem prudent for Parker to have left London after his recantation, and may also explain why Bale mistakenly claims, in a later work, that Parker joined the order in Doncaster. However, Parker was back in London by 1 September 1504 for, during the visit of the prior-general, Peter Terrasse, he was honoured as a jubilarian, having been a member of his order for fifty years, and given leave 'to serve any benefactor' until the next general chapter. Bale lists two works by Parker, one on Aristotle's *On Meteors* and a collection of sermons to the people. Later, in his *Catalogus*, Bale gave the sermons the title *On Christ's Poverty*, and attributed the well-known tract *Dives et pauper* to Parker. Although many have followed Bale in this latter claim, H. G. Richardson has convincingly shown that Parker cannot have been the author. RICHARD COPSEY

Sources J. Bale, BL, Harley MS 3838, fols. 38*v*, 102*v*–103 • Bale, *Cat.*, 1.609 • F. R. H. Du Boulay, 'The quarrel between the Carmelite friars and the secular clergy of London, 1464–1468', *Journal of Ecclesiastical History*, 6 (1955), 156–74 • Emden, *Cam.*, 442, 680 • H. G. Richardson, 'Dives et pauper', *The Library*, 4th ser., 15 (1934–5), 31–7 • R. Copsey, 'The visit of the prior general, Peter Terrasse, to England in 1504–5', *Carmel in Britain*, ed. P. Fitzgerald-Lombard, 1 (1992), 188 • H. G. Pfander, 'Dives et pauper', *The Library*, 4th ser., 14 (1933–4), 299–312 • S. Tahney, 'The manuscripts and editions of *Dives et pauper*, a medieval treatise on the ten commandments', MA diss., Catholic University of Washington, 1950 • J. Bale, BL, Cotton MS Titus D.x., fols. 182*v*, 185 • 'William Gregory's chronicle of London', *The historical collections of a citizen of London in the fifteenth century*, ed. J. Gairdner, CS, new ser., 17 (1876), 55–239, esp. 228–32 • *Commentarii de scriptoribus Britannicis, auctore Joanne Lelando*, ed. A. Hall, 2 (1709), 452 • J. Pits, *Relationum historicarum de rebus Anglicis*, ed. [W. Bishop] (Paris, 1619), 660 • Tanner, *Bibl. Brit.-Hib.*, 574

Parker, Henry, **tenth Baron Morley** (**1480/81–1556**), nobleman and translator, was the son of Sir William Parker (*d.* *c.*1504) and Alice Lovel (1452–1518). His father, who was knighted by Richard III on 24 July 1482, was the latter's standard bearer at Bosworth Field, and may as a result have spent some time in prison in Henry VII's reign. His mother was sister and heir of Henry Lovel, eighth Baron Morley. After her first husband's death she married Sir Edward Howard, son of Thomas Howard, later duke of Norfolk. According to the brass memorial erected to him by his grandson in the parish church at Great Hallingbury, Morley died at the age of eighty, which would make 1475 or 1476 the year of his birth. In fact much of the information on the six brasses of which this forms part is inaccurate, and by Morley's own account he was fifteen at new year 1496, which would mean that he was born in 1480 or 1481. His chief residence was Hallingbury Place at Great Hallingbury, Essex, which was demolished in 1924, and he also signed correspondence from Mark Hall, Essex. His portrait of 1523 by Albrecht Dürer forms part of the British Museum collection.

Upbringing and early career Parker's boyhood was spent in the household of Lady Margaret Beaufort where he acted as her sewer and personal attendant. From her he acquired a deep piety, and he remained conservative in religion for the rest of his life. On new year's day 1496 he marshalled twenty-five knights at her table and gave a detailed account of the ceremony more than half a century later. In 1507 Lady Margaret paid for him to go to London and watch a joust, almost certainly the May day tournament at Kennington. He was her cup-bearer at the time of Henry VIII's coronation. She was a generous patron to him and after his mother's second marriage she paid Howard 500 marks to redeem his lands. She arranged his marriage with Alice (*c.*1487–1553), daughter of John St John of Bletsoe, who was her uterine great-niece, and between 1499 and 1503 received £120 from William Parker's estates for Alice's jointure. Lady Margaret may also have paid for

Henry Parker, tenth Baron Morley (1480/81–1556), by Albrecht Dürer, 1523

Parker to attend Oxford, but there is no documentary evidence for this. Of his children, three—Henry, Margaret, and Jane—later came into some prominence in their own right and the names of two others—Elizabeth and Frances—are found in BL, Harley MS 4775, a manuscript owned by their father.

After his mother died in 1518 Parker was created tenth Baron Morley with precedence of the barony to which he was heir. He was present at the Field of Cloth of Gold in 1520 in attendance on Katherine of Aragon and in 1521 he served on the panel of peers which tried the third duke of Buckingham. This was the first of six treason trials of peers in which he took part in Henry VIII's reign; he was the only peer to have an unbroken record of participation on such occasions. In 1522 he was one of the lords attending Henry at the latter's meeting with the emperor Charles V. He first sat in parliament in 1523 and in the same year Thomas Wolsey named him to a mission to take the Garter to Ferdinand, archduke of Austria. The ceremony took place on 8 December in Nuremberg, and a sketch of the four ambassadors dining with the archduke is found in College of Arms, Vincent MS 152, fol. 178. Morley also sent four letters describing the trip back to England: one to Henry from Cologne and three to Wolsey from Mechlin (presumably), Cologne, and Nuremberg. In these he described his meetings with civic authorities and charted the spread of Luther's ideas in Germany. Although disapproving of Luther, Morley himself appears to have shown a mild anti-clericalism and sent back to Henry caricatures of the pope and clergy which were circulating in German, 'which I think your highness will laugh at' (*LP Henry VIII*, 3/2, no. 3390). By February 1524 he was back in England.

In spite of his flattering comments to Henry and Wolsey in these letters Morley cannot be shown to have achieved any further distinctions during the rest of the decade, although he was granted the manor of Hasilbach in 1526 and was at court at new year's day 1529. He was present at a great council in 1530 and was one of the signatories of the letter supporting the king's divorce which the peers sent to Clement VII. He was appointed a JP for Essex in December 1530, and for Hertfordshire in February 1531. Other commissions followed, almost invariably associated with Essex or Hertfordshire. In 1534 he obtained a judgment giving him precedence over William, Lord Dacre of Gilsland, and this was upheld in 1536. In 1536 he was also made steward of Hatfield Regis.

The Boleyns and Thomas Cromwell Morley was connected to the Boleyns through his mother's second marriage. The two families were neighbours in Essex, and about 1525 Morley contracted a marriage between his daughter Jane and George Boleyn, for which Henry VIII provided a portion of the jointure of 2000 marks. Another daughter, Margaret, married Sir John Shelton, whose mother, Anne, was the sister of Anne Boleyn's father. The alliances brought benefits to the Morley family during the ascendancy of the Boleyn faction and Morley's grandson Henry *Parker, later eleventh Baron Morley, was dubbed knight of the Bath on the eve of Anne Boleyn's coronation.

As early as 1531 Morley was referring to Thomas Cromwell as 'my singular good friend and old acquaintance' (*LP Henry VIII*, 5, no. 23) and Cromwell supported him in various endeavours. In 1537 he was involved in a vitriolic dispute with the prior and chapter of Norwich concerning the dissolved priory of Aldeby and he petitioned both Sir Thomas Wriothesley, his former companion on the mission to the Archduke Ferdinand, and Cromwell to lend him their aid. Although a letter dated 25 March makes it clear that Cromwell had done something for Morley, the monks continued to offer resistance and the chapter wrote a letter of protest to Cromwell on 15 April. On 21 April Morley wrote again to Cromwell 'praying your Lordshipp further to goo thorowe with me and not to forsake me in this my sute' (*LP Henry VIII*, 14/1, no. 822). Ultimately Morley triumphed and the estate was recorded among his properties by 1547. On another occasion Morley asked Cromwell to act as his advocate in his attempt to acquire Beeston Priory in Norfolk, of which he claimed to be patron, but his petitions brought him no reward. In 1543 he purchased lands from the king and in 1544 he received property in Essex and Hertfordshire, some formerly monastic and some formerly belonging to the marchioness of Exeter and to Cromwell. He supplied men for the army in 1543 and 1544; he himself did not take part in the French campaign, but his son represented him.

In 1537 Morley complained to Cromwell that the Norwich monks were expressing doubts about the value of his bonds should he be attainted—a pointer to the precariousness of his position during these years. In 1536 the Boleyns fell and Morley sat on the panel which convicted his own son-in-law, now Lord Rochford, of treason. In the same year he was required to furnish 100 men to quell the Pilgrimage of Grace and in 1537 he was one of the peers who tried barons Darcy and Hussey. For Morley this was a period of real risk since he could easily have been associated with the conservative lords behind the rebellion. Morley was also vulnerable in 1538, at the time of the so-called Exeter conspiracy. In 1542 his daughter, who had regained favour after Rochford's death, was deeply implicated in Thomas Culpeper's allegedly adulterous liaison with Queen Katherine Howard; when she was attainted Morley remained present in the lords for each reading of the bills of attainder.

Conservative peer Although he voted for the first Act of Uniformity in 1549, Morley opposed the Bill for Clerical Marriage (1549), the Bill for Abolishing Sundry Books and Images (1550), and he took part in the prosecution of Edward Seymour, duke of Somerset, in 1550. He was absent from parliament in 1552 for the passing of the second Act of Uniformity, but in the same year he obtained land formerly belonging to Waltham Abbey and the portion of the tithes in Great Hallingbury once possessed by the Benedictine abbey of Colchester. Opposing the extreme religious measures of Edward's advisers, Morley nevertheless showed himself consistently loyal to the young king and in 1549 he declared himself ready to defend him in person.

The first reference to Morley's acquaintance with Mary Tudor comes in June 1536 when Morley visited her at Hunsdon, perhaps with his wife and daughter, significantly just a matter of weeks after the execution of Anne Boleyn and her brother. There is no definite evidence that he knew her before this and their acquaintanceship could equally have originated from the proximity of Great Hallingbury to Hunsdon. A friendship ripened quickly, however, and in 1537 Mary acted as godmother to Morley's grandson. Morley's devotion to Mary seems to have been a genuine one and he was regular in his presentation of literary works to her for the rest of his life. He was present at her coronation and in his writings addressed her in terms of respect and admiration. Like the biblical Simeon he expressed himself ready to depart in peace after she had brought England back into the fold of religious orthodoxy under the firm hand of her cousin Reginald Pole, thanking her in January 1556 for giving him the 'libertye to ende myne olde dayes in quyet' (BL, Add. MS 12060, fol. 20*v*). He died at Great Hallingbury on 27 November following and was buried on 3 December at St Giles's Church, Great Hallingbury.

Translations: dedications to Henry VIII Morley is chiefly remembered for his translations from Latin and Italian, presented to patrons as new year gifts, and these give a sense of the complex strands of his alliances. Of the manuscripts he gave to Henry VIII six survive and at least two others have been lost. Perhaps his first work was a translation of Petrarch's *Trionfi* undertaken for Henry some time in the late 1520s or earlier in imitation of a translation of this work into French by Simon de Bourgouyn, *valet-de-chambre* to François I. The presentation copy has been lost, but a description of it survives in Morley's dedicatory epistle to Henry FitzAlan, Lord Maltravers, which prefaces the undated printed version of about 1553 to 1556. Morley deemed the king well pleased with his efforts and produced other translations for him. Several were renderings from Plutarchian lives which had been published in Latin translation in the fifteenth century. First came the 'Lives of Scipio & Haniball', written no later than 1535 and now BL, Royal MS 17 D. xi; then the 'Life of Thesius', written between 1542 and 1546 or 1547, now BL, Royal MS 17 D. ii; and finally the 'Lyfe of Paulus Emelius', also written between 1542 and 1546 or 1547 and now Bodl. Oxf., MS Laud misc. 684. Morley also presented Henry with two books translated from Italian: his 'Commentarys of the Turke' taken from Paolo Giovio's *Commentario de le cose de' Turchi*, written between 1536 and 1541, now BL, Arundel MS 8, and his 'Tale from Massuccyo Salernytano', a translation of the forty-ninth tale from Masuccio Salernitano's *Novellino*, written between 1544 and 1546/7, now BL, Royal MS 18 A. lxii.

Although all these manuscripts have one or two strapwork initials with decorations they are not deluxe works—unlike Morley's translation of the first forty-six lives from Boccaccio's *De claris mulieribus*, now in the duke of Devonshire's collection at Chatsworth, which is of an entirely different order of magnitude and contains decorated initials on almost every one of its forty-seven folios. This much grander production was almost certainly presented to Henry on new year's day 1543, and, as the preface makes clear, it represents an oblique repudiation of his own daughter whose execution had occurred ten months previously. Morley's one really original piece of writing also came as a response to a politically charged situation. In 1539 Thomas Berthelet, the king's printer, published Morley's *Exposition and Declaration of the Psalme, 'Deus ultionum dominus'* using as his copy text a now lost manuscript presented to Henry probably in the same year. A violent attack on the political role of the papacy, the 'seate of Sathan', the *Exposition* was composed in the wake of the Exeter conspiracy in order to emphasize Morley's loyalty to the crown in spite of his conservative views in religion and his friendship with Henry's eldest daughter. It was also a very useful propaganda tool for Cromwell and may even have been commissioned by him.

Presentations to Queen Mary and others Morley presented at least eight books to Mary. Six can be dated between 1537 and 1547. One of these, BL, Royal MS 2 D. xxviii, is a fifteenth-century copy of Richard Rolle of Hampole's Latin psalter with prefatory letter. The other five are all translations from Latin: BL, Royal MS 17 C. xvi of texts of the angelical salutation and portions of the *Epistola Lentuli* (ascribed to Anselm); BL, Royal MS 18 A. xv of Johannes de Turrecremata's exposition of psalm 36; BL, Royal MS 17 A. xlvi of Erasmus's *Paean virgini matri dicendus*; BL, Royal MS 17 C. xii of Athanasius's preface to the exposition of the psalms; BL, Royal MS 17 A. xxx of extracts from Seneca's *Epistulae morales* (letter 91 linked to a passage from letter 120). From Edward's reign only one gift to Mary survives, a translation of the *Somnium Scipionis*, now BL, Royal MS 18 A. lx. BL, Add. MS 12060, presented at new year 1556, contains an account of the miracles of the sacrament. Modelled on John Fisher's *De veritate corporis et sanguinis Christi in eucharistica* (1527) it also borrows heavily from Hartmann Schedel's *Liber cronicarum* (1493) and includes personal reminiscences as well. It is as strikingly pro-papal as the *Exposition* was anti-papal; after the experiences of Edward's reign Morley had realized the dangers of dispensing with papal obedience.

Cromwell received a greyhound from Morley in 1535 and in February 1537 (or possibly 1539) Morley sent him copies of Machiavelli's *Istorie Fiorentine* and *Il principe*. He suggested that Cromwell show the books to Henry and in order to make things easier he annotated them in the margin at places where the author 'touches any thing consernyng the Bysschop of Rome' (Wright, xxxi). Probably on new year's day 1538 Morley presented Cromwell with a copy of the life of Agesilaus attributed to Plutarch (in fact by Xenophon), now National Library of Wales, MS 17038C. Morley's gifts to Cromwell all relate to the latter's potential as a patron, and, in the letter accompanying the copies of Machiavelli, Morley specifically requests Cromwell to 'tender' him favours.

Morley wrote some lyric poetry, including a translation 'in an Italion Ryme called Soneto' of the *Carmina de utilitate psalmorum* attributed to Maffeo Vegio da Lodi. According to Bale's *Index* Morley also wrote plays, but this is almost certainly inaccurate. A transcription and partial translation of Jacques Lefèvre d'Etaples's *Epistres et evangiles des cinquante de deux sepmaines de l'an* presented to Anne Boleyn in 1532 or 1533, now BL, Harley MS 6561, has been attributed to Morley, but in fact it is the work of Lord Rochford. A commentary on Ecclesiastes dedicated to Edward Seymour, duke of Somerset, highly evangelical in tone and now surviving as BL, Royal MS 17 D. xiii (1547–50), was written by a Henry Parker, knight, but this individual should not be confused with Lord Morley.

James P. Carley

Sources M. Axton and J. P. Carley, eds., *'Triumphs of English': Henry Parker, Lord Morley, translator to the Tudor court* (2000) • J. P. Carley, 'Presentation manuscripts from the collection of Henry VIII: the case of Henry Parker, Lord Morley', *Order and connexion: studies in bibliography and book history*, ed. R. C. Alston (1997), 159–76 • J. P. Carley, 'Plutarch's life of Agesilaus: a recently located new year's gift to Thomas Cromwell by Henry Parker, Lord Morley', *Prestige, authority and power in late medieval manuscripts and texts*, ed. F. Riddy (2000) • H. G. Wright, ed., *Forty-six lives translated from Boccaccio's 'De claris mulieribus' by Henry Parker, Lord Morley*, EETS, original ser., 214 (1943) • D. D. Carnicelli, ed., *Lord Morley's 'Tryumphes of Fraunces Petrarcke'* (Cambridge, MA, 1971) • GEC, *Peerage*, new edn, 9.221–4 • *LP Henry VIII* • BL, Add. MS 12060, fol. 20v • Bale, *Index* • Emden, *Oxf.*, 4.431–2 • H. M. E. M. Cocks, *The great house of Hallingbury* (1988) • R. Axton, 'Lord Morley's funeral', *'Triumphs of English': Henry Parker, Lord Morley, translator to the Tudor court*, ed. M. Axton and J. P. Carley (2000), 213–24

Archives BL, letters to Henry VIII and Thomas Wolsey, Cotton Vitellius B.xx

Likenesses A. Dürer, pencil drawing, 1523, BM [*see illus.*] • T. Wriothesley, coloured sketch, 1523, Coll. Arms, Vincent MS 152, p. 178

Parker, Henry, eleventh Baron Morley (**1531/2–1577**), Roman Catholic exile, was the eldest son of Sir Henry Parker (*d.* 1552) and his first wife, Grace (*c.*1515–*c.*1549), daughter and heir of John Newport of Pelham Furneux. Educated at Gonville Hall, Cambridge, he was made a knight of the Bath at the coronation of Queen Mary on 6 October 1553. On the death of his grandfather Henry *Parker, tenth Baron Morley, on 27 November 1556 he succeeded to the barony and was first summoned to parliament on 6 December 1557. In 1560 he was made lord lieutenant of Hertfordshire and oversaw a certificate of general musters for the county. In 1561, the year in which Queen Elizabeth stayed with him at Great Hallingbury, Essex, for two days, he was described in a letter of Alvaro de la Quadra to King Philip of Spain as 'one of the best and most Catholic gentlemen of this kingdom and much attached to your Majesty's service' (*CSP Spain, 1558–67*, 123).

In 1569 Morley refused to subscribe to the Act of Uniformity on the plea of being a nobleman; he was also linked with the rising of the northern earls. As a result he fled England in early June 1570 and established himself in Bruges, writing to the queen on 8 June asking permission to have his wife and children join him, sending a copy of the letter to the earl of Leicester. He wrote again on 31 August, beseeching the queen's pardon and explaining that he left the kingdom without licence as a result of a scruple of conscience. On 30 October Elizabeth commanded him to return, but he did not do so and remained abroad for the rest of his life. On 4 March 1573 he wrote to Burghley from Bruges, thanking him for his kindness to his wife and son, and asking him to intercede with the queen on his behalf. In March 1574 he was in Madrid, where he and his brother Edmund were received by Philip II and given a gift of 600 ducats. On 4 April 1574, Palm Sunday, his wife, Elizabeth, daughter of Edward Stanley, earl of Derby, was arrested (along with a daughter, her second son, and her daughter-in-law) while hearing mass in her London house. On 17 November 1574 Morley wrote again to Burghley, this time from Lisbon, wondering if earlier letters had been intercepted. He was in Paris in January 1575 and in Venice in May, where he wrote asking licence to live in Germany for two or three years in order to retrieve his debts. According to a note of English fugitives dated 6 July 1575, he had returned to Spain. His wife, daughter, and youngest son arrived in Antwerp in September 1575, and in 1576 he and his wife were at Maastricht. Morley died in Paris on 22 October 1577, and his eldest son, Edward, who had been committed to the Fleet in April 1573, succeeded him as twelfth Baron Morley. His estates, which had been taken into the hands of the crown in 1572, were restored to Edward on 6 May 1578. His widow remained abroad and administration of her effects was granted to her daughter Anne Brunker on 4 February 1591.

Sir Philip Parker (*d.* 1604) was the son of Sir Henry Parker and his second wife, Elizabeth, daughter of Sir Philip Calthorpe of Erwarton, Suffolk, and a younger grandson of Henry Parker, tenth Baron Morley. He inherited the manor of Erwarton from his mother and was knighted in 1580. One of the leading protestant gentlemen of Elizabethan Suffolk, he served as a deputy lieutenant and muster commissioner, and was sheriff of Suffolk in 1578. He married Catherine, daughter of Sir John Goodwin of Winchendon, Buckinghamshire; they named their eldest son Calthorpe. Parker died in 1604.

James P. Carley

Sources GEC, *Peerage*, new edn, 9.225–6 • J. Strype, *Annals of the Reformation and establishment of religion … during Queen Elizabeth's happy reign*, new edn, 2/2 (1824), 551 • *CSP dom.*, *1547–80*, 153, 356, 380–81, 383, 391, 395, 397, 458, 485, 488, 494, 500, 503 • *CSP Spain*, *1558–67*, 184; *1568–79*, 158, 183, 247, 414, 477 • Cooper, *Ath. Cantab.*, 1.378 • H. M. E. M. Cocks, *The great house of Hallingbury* (1988), 9 • D. MacCulloch, *Suffolk and the Tudors: politics and religion in an English county, 1500–1600* (1986) • *DNB*

Parker, Henry [*called* the Observator] (**1604–1652**), political writer, was the fifth son of Sir Nicholas *Parker (*d.* 1619) of Ratton, Sussex, and Sir Nicholas's third wife, Katherine, daughter of Sir John Temple (*d.* 1603) of Stowe, Buckinghamshire. Parker matriculated at St Edmund Hall, Oxford, on 3 February 1626; within a few days he proceeded BA. He proceeded MA on 25 June 1628. Admitted to Lincoln's Inn on 11 February 1630, Parker was called to the bar on 30 January 1638. On 14 February 1634 he and Jane Cannon received from the bishop of London a licence to marry without banns, an indication that both were marrying outside their home parishes. They had two children, Henry and Anne.

Early years The Parkers of Ratton were an important Sussex family. Henry's father Sir Nicholas sat for the county in the parliament of 1597 and served as sheriff and deputy lieutenant. Sir Nicholas's heir, Sir Thomas Parker, sat for Seaford in the Long Parliament. The family's connections were broad, ranging from papist to puritan; during the civil war, some of the Parkers were conservative parliamentarians, others royalists. Henry seems to have drifted towards his indubitably puritan uncle, William Fiennes, Lord Saye and Sele. Lord Saye was one of a number of highly placed friends and patrons that Parker would serve; others were the earl of Essex, John Pym, Henry Ireton, and Oliver Cromwell.

In spite of his legal training, Parker seems never to have developed a practice at common law—indeed his writings display attitudes towards the common law ranging from scepticism to marked hostility. Parker's political and polemical activities in the 1630s are largely unknown, although his call to the bar came at a time when the rule requiring communion within the established church was being enforced, and points to at least that measure of conformity. A suggestive but inconclusive case can be made that Parker wrote *Divine and Politike Observations* (1638), a reply to Archbishop Laud's Star Chamber speech at the sentencing of Prynne, Bastwick, and Burton. In 1640–42 Parker appeared notably but partly anonymously upon the public stage through the first political and ecclesiological writings that can be confidently attributed to him.

His friend the London bookseller and pamphlet collector George Thomason credited Parker with two of the most incisive tracts of the first year of the Long Parliament, *The Case of Shipmony* (1640) and *A Discourse Concerning Puritans* (1641). The first quietly but unmistakably revealed the outlines of Parker's politics: the supremacy of parliament combined with an unexpected tolerance for the idiom of necessity and the reason of state usually associated with the absolutists—as Parker's statements became more forthright his tolerance grew into a strong acceptance. *A Discourse Concerning Puritans*, ostensibly a defence of puritans against calumny (and probably a defence of Lord Saye in particular), moved to a surprising attack upon the clerical presbyterians as well as the defenders of *jure divino* episcopacy. Parker continued to explore ecclesiological themes in *The Question Concerning the Divine Right of Episcopacy* (1641); *The True Grounds of Ecclesiastical Regiment* (1641), which used the still unprinted eighth book of Richard Hooker's *Of the Laws of Ecclesiastical Polity* to assert the royal supremacy over the church but also to tie that supremacy to that of the sovereign people; and *The Altar Dispute* (1641), in which H. P. identified himself as Saye's 'allies-man' (sig. A2*v*).

The Observator The pamphlet that Parker wrote on the eve of civil war was the one that established him (though anonymously) as a major figure on the public stage. *Observations upon some of his Majesties Late Answers and Expresses*, which appeared early in July 1642, gave Parker his moniker in the pamphlet wars, the Observator. Its argument—which clarified but adhered closely to parliament's official position in the war of words with the king—was a forthright statement of a species of bicameral parliamentary sovereignty. While *Observations* conceded that legislation was an activity that required the assent of king, Lords, and Commons, emergency actions undertaken by the houses, functioning as the king's great council, could serve the same turn. The houses could do anything necessary that served *salus populi*, a position that both mirrored and reversed earlier royalist argument and which provoked the constitutional royalist position as a predictable counter. *Observations* generated an armada of royalist replies, and the Observator was widely accepted as an unofficial spokesman of the parliamentary case. In the Commons a snide comment to that effect from Sir Simonds D'Ewes brought the wrath of the house upon him (Steele Young and Snow, 3.256). D'Ewes later privately noted that Parker had a 'hand' in 'many seditious pamphlets' (BL, Harl. MS 165, fol. 210*v*, comment in cipher). Indeed Parker was simultaneously filling two other insiders' roles, as secretary to the earl of Essex and to the committee of safety, positions that seem to have overlapped and were in large measure fiscal. His work at the committee put him in constant contact with the men who were running the war effort, including Saye, Essex, and Pym. So trusted that at one point he was issuing small payment warrants solely on his own signature, Parker was privy to the formation of war policy and the payments made to spies, as well as to financial transactions involving members of the committee. As the committee of safety wound down in late 1643 and was replaced by the committee of both kingdoms, and as the earl of Essex's political and military stances distanced him from the centre of public power, Parker's star, once so bright, shone more dimly. Though Essex promoted Parker's petition to the Commons for further employment, in particular Parker's effort to secure the registrarship of the prerogative court of Canterbury (later the prerogative office), the member of parliament Michael Oldisworth and his patron the earl of Pembroke stymied Parker. After years of struggle, in which Oldisworth continued to hold the office and Parker strove to wrest it from him, the two finally came to share the office in 1649.

Despite his set-backs, Parker remained useful to the parliament. On 26 June 1645 he was brought in to join the parliamentary secretary John Sadler as an official analyst and draughtsman; later the other parliamentary secretary Thomas May joined them. The trio's focus increasingly fell on producing an annotated text of the king's papers captured at Naseby. The resulting publication, *The Kings Cabinet Opened* (1645), was almost as damaging to the royalist cause as Charles's attempt on the five members. For his efforts in this and related tasks Parker was voted £100 on 19 January 1646. Parker also continued his non-official pamphleteering. Most notable were two tracts that provided Parker with the opportunity to defend and amplify the outlook and positions of *Observations*. The *Contra-Replicant* (1642, 1643) made the case for the primacy of the 'Statesman' over the 'Lawyer': 'Reason of state is something more sublime and imperiall then Law' (p. 19). Parker also dared to view the earl of Essex's role as that of a 'temporary Dictator' in the Roman sense (p. 27). *Jus populi* (1644), written in response to James Maxwell's *Sacro-sancta regum majestas* (1644), provided Parker with an occasion for the most theoretical and forthrightly egalitarian statement of his politics, as much in respect of family relations, primogeniture, and gender, as in politics narrowly understood.

In 1647 Parker went to Hamburg to serve there as secretary to the Merchant Adventurers. He travelled back frequently to England, still fighting for the registrarship of the prerogative office, and writing occasional pamphlets as well, including a series against the royalist judge David Jenkins, and *Of a Free Trade* (1647), a tract in defence of the Merchant Adventurers' privileges from the assault made upon them by the levellers. That pamphlet was the most notable of a number of commissioned tracts that Parker wrote for private interests in the 1640s, including an apologia for some of the Vintners (1641), a tract on behalf of the Stationers (1643), and a curious narration of an English hydraulic engineer's tribulations in the Netherlands, *Mr. William Wheeler's Case from his Own Relation* (1645).

Parker submitted reports on foreign matters to Speaker William Lenthall in 1648 and early 1649. After returning to England (probably by mid-May 1649) on 18 July Parker finally succeeded in getting a share of the registrarship of the prerogative office, which was henceforth to be held jointly by him and Michael Oldisworth. He also began work as secretary to Oliver Cromwell and to Henry Ireton in Ireland. Traces of his work there are to be found in public papers, but Parker also seems to have been in London for part of the time. He resumed his pamphleteering, writing vigorously on the behalf of, and against the opponents of, the new Commonwealth: John Lilburne was attacked in *A Letter of due Censure and Redargution* (1650), royalist historical claims were debunked in *The True Portraiture of the Kings of England* (1650), which Parker disingenuously claimed to have discovered but not to have written, and the Commonwealth's Scottish and presbyterian opponents derided in *Scotland's Holy War* (1651). Parker's last publication, a defence of Henry Ireton's actions entitled *The Cheif Affairs of Ireland Truly Communicated* (1651), was dated by Thomason on 5 February 1652.

Assessment Parker's outlook, sometimes contradictory, reflected his role as agent or confidant ('privado' was a term used by him and others to describe the role) as well as the perplexities engendered by his commitment to bicameral parliamentary sovereignty. A younger son of a leading family, Parker could never definitively harmonize the aristocratic and egalitarian impulses within him. Perhaps his greatest consistency was that of state supremacist. He believed in the supremacy of the general welfare over private interests, the ultimate authority of the state over the clergy, and the bicameral parliament as the embodiment of the nation. But even the last view, a hallmark of *Observations*, was strained in the later 1640s and early 1650s as Parker, who sided with the Independents, supported the victorious army's claims to leadership.

As the Observator, Parker was the central figure in the pamphlet wars of the early and middle 1640s. The slogans of *Observations*—that the prince was 'singulis major, universis minor' ('greater than any but less than the whole') and the odder 'quicquid efficit tale est magis tale' ('the cause of something is greater than the effect')—shaped several years of public discourse and were not soon forgotten. The former maxim and three of Parker's tracts were among those singled out for condemnation in 1663 in Roger L'Estrange's *Considerations and Proposals in Order to the Regulation of the Press* (1663). George Thomason held or acquired the rights to a number of Parker's pamphlets, which in 1681 were transferred (with many others) by Thomason's executors to Thomas Newcomb. Under various titles *The True Portraiture of the Kings of England* was republished twice in the later seventeenth and once in both the eighteenth and nineteenth centuries, yet Parker's relative anonymity obscured the full extent of his contribution to the thought of the day, and would not be remedied until the Thomason collection's riches (including Thomason's many attributions) became more generally known.

Parker indirectly alluded to his poor health from 1649 until his death in 1652, and in *Reformation in Courts in Cases Testamentary* (1651) referred to the 'pangs inexpressible' of the 'nephirticall malady' and to 'the stoppage of the stone in the uritories' (pp. 7, 9). Anthony Wood reported that he learned from Fabian Philipps that Parker had died distracted, an assertion that lacks confirmation. Parker's published writings and letters exchanged between him and Lady Hester Temple of Stowe show no sign of mental imbalance (Hunt. L., MS 16439), although his physical sufferings apparently were considerable. Parker was buried in Kensington, London, on 21 May 1652. The domestic egalitarianism of *Jus populi* was put into practice in his will: his wife, Jane, was named sole executor and administrator until their two children reached their majority and the three were each to have equal shares of his apparently small estate—a codicil refers to a fee farm rent in Sussex, which Jane was authorized to dispose of by sale. After Parker's death Jane Parker continued the struggle to hold onto the registrarship of the prerogative office.

MICHAEL MENDLE

Sources M. Mendle, *Henry Parker and the English civil war* (1995) • *DNB* • Thomason tracts [BL] • G. K. Fortescue and others, eds., *Catalogue of the pamphlets, books, newspapers, and manuscripts relating to the civil war, the Commonwealth, and Restoration, collected by George Thomason, 1640–1661*, 2 vols. (1908); repr. (1969) • W. K. Jordan, *Men of substance: a study of the thought of two English revolutionaries, Henry Parker and Henry Robinson* (1942) • M. A. Judson, 'Henry Parker and the theory of parliamentary sovereignty', *Essays in history and political theory in honor of Charles Howard McIlwain*, ed. C. F. Wittke (1936) • L. Glow, 'The committee of safety', *EngHR*, 80 (1965), 289–313 • G. E. Aylmer, *The state's servants: the civil service of the English republic, 1649–1660* (1973), 261 • PRO, SP 28/261–264 *passim* • PRO, SP 16/503 pt 2/28; 16/510/79; 16/539 pt 1/100; 16/539 pt 2/129 • PRO, SP 18/1/121 • House of Lords main papers, 26 July, 28 July, 1 Sept, 14 Dec 1642; 12 May 1643 • *JHC*, 2 (1640–42), 685 • *JHC*, 3 (1642–4), 313, 677, 687–8 • *JHC*, 4 (1644–6), 187, 189–90, 411, 414 • *JHC*, 7 (1651–9), 268–9, 326 • *JHL*, 5 (1642–3), 206, 208 • *JHL*, 7 (1644–5), 121 • Bodl. Oxf., MS Tanner 54, fols. 50*r*–52*v*, 74*r*–75*v*, 81*r*–82*v* • Bodl. Oxf., MS Tanner 56, fol. 92*v* • *CSP dom.*, 1649–50, 158, 185, 238, 364; 1651, 258; 1652–3, 108; 1653, 217, 280; 1654, 162 • *CSP Ire.*, 1647–60, 378 • M. A. E. Green, ed., *Calendar of the proceedings of the committee for advance of money, 1642–1656*, 2, PRO (1888), 686–9 • Hunt. L., MS 16439 • will, PRO, PROB 11/222, sig. 139 • BL, Harleian MS 165, fol. 210v • A. Steele Young and V. F. Snow, eds., *The private journals of the Long Parliament*, 3: *2 June to 17 September 1642* (1992), 256 • G. E. B. Eyre, ed., *A transcript of the registers of the Worshipful Company of Stationers from 1640 to 1708*, 3 vols. (1913–14), vol. 3, pp. 103–7 • Wood, *Ath. Oxon.*, 2nd edn, 3.451–2 • *GM*, 1st ser., 35 (1765), 109 • H. R. Mosse, *The monumental effigies of Sussex* (1931), 161 • W. P. Baildon, ed., *The records of the Honorable Society of Lincoln's Inn: admissions*, 1 (1896), 210 • W. P. Baildon, ed., *The records of the Honorable Society of Lincoln's Inn: the black books*, 2 (1898), 244–5 • R. M. Glencross, ed., *A calendar of the marriage licence allegations in the registry of the bishop of London*, 1, British RS, 62 (1937), 116 • H. Parker to Sir R. Verney, 21 Nov 1644, Claydon House, Verney MSS [Yale Center for Parliamentary History, microfilm reel 6] • Verney to Parker, 6/16 Dec 1644, Claydon House, Verney MSS [Yale Center for Parliamentary History, microfilm reel 6] • HoP, *Commons, 1558–1603* • F. N. MacNamara and A. Story-Maskelyne, eds., *The parish register of Kensington, co. Middlesex, from AD 1539 to AD 1675*, Harleian Society, register section, 16 (1890)

Archives Bodl. Oxf., MS Tanner 54, fols. 50*r*–52*v*, 74*r*–75*v*, 81*r*–82*v* • Bodl. Oxf., MS Tanner 56, fol. 92*v* • Claydon House, Buckinghamshire, Verney MSS, corresp. with Sir Ralph Verney [Yale Center for Parliamentary History microfilm reel 6] • HLRO, House of Lords, main papers • Hunt. L., MS 16439 • PRO, SP 28/261–264 *passim* • PRO, SP 16/503 pt 2/28, 16/510/79, 16/539 pt 1/100, 16/539 pt 2/129 • PRO, SP 18/1/121

Wealth at death apparently modest: will, PRO, PROB 11/222, sig. 139

Parker, Henry Perlee (1795–1873), portrait and genre painter, was born at Plymouth Dock, Devonport, Devon, on 15 March 1795 and baptized on 15 June at Stoke Damerel, Devon, the son of Robert Parker (1748–1830), teacher of marine and mechanical drawing, and his wife, Mary Elizabeth. His first work as an artist followed a brief period as tailor and coachmaker and consisted of portraits and of drawings for his father's pupils to copy. About 1813 he was employed by C. T. Gilbert to produce illustrations for the latter's *Historical Survey of the County of Cornwall* (1815). This required him to tour Cornwall with Gilbert, and brought him into contact with paintings in the private collections of noblemen. On 14 June 1815 he married at Maker, Cornwall, Amy Morfey (*d.* 1844) of Woodbridge, Suffolk, and established himself in Plymouth as a professional portrait painter. His work was much admired, but discouraged by his meagre income he decided to stay with relatives at Sunderland, co. Durham, to see what opportunities as a portrait painter might be offered in that area. He initially earned his living giving drawing lessons, but after visiting Newcastle upon Tyne on several occasions he found he liked the town and settled there for a quarter of a century. His period from 1815 to 1841 in Newcastle saw him become one of the north-east of England's best-known artists, and after painting a portrait of the local fruit painter George Gray in 1816 he attracted so many commissions that he and his wife were able to move into one of the town's most fashionable streets. He also took on pupils and soon made several important friendships among local artists, including Thomas Miles Richardson, later collaborating with Richardson in the foundation of the Northumberland Institution for the Promotion of the Fine Arts (1822) and the Northern Academy (1828). In 1817 he exhibited his first of twenty-three works at the Royal Academy: *Dead Game*, and after selling his popular *Principal Eccentric Characters of Newcastle* to the local member of parliament, Charles John Brandling, he began to be patronized by some of the most important men on Tyneside. In 1822 he was appointed to the committee of the Northumberland Institution, showing thirteen works at its first exhibition in that year. He also in 1822 showed his first works at the British Institution: *Fishermen Selling Fish to a Cottage Girl, Coast of Devon*, and *Celebration of the coronation of His Most Gracious Majesty George IV, on the Sand-Hill, Newcastle upon Tyne, July 19, 1821*, which latter was purchased by the town for 100 guineas and placed in the Mansion House. In the following year he again exhibited at the Royal Academy, sent a further work to the British Institution, and exhibited in Edinburgh, Carlisle, and Newcastle. From this point forward he continued to exhibit his work widely, his last exhibits appearing at the Royal Academy in 1859; the British Institution in 1863; Edinburgh in 1839; and Carlisle in 1833. Many of his exhibits between 1826 and 1850 were smuggling subjects, proving so numerous that he was given the nickname 'Smuggler Parker'. Another favourite subject was local pitmen at play. However, he painted a wide variety of other works recording important occasions in the north-east of England. One of his best known works is *William and Grace Darling Going to the Rescue of the Forfarshire Survivors*, painted jointly with John Wilson Carmichael in 1838.

As the result of the success of one of his historical pictures, the *Wesleyan Centenary Picture* (1839), painted in anticipation of the John Wesley conference held in Newcastle in 1840, he was in 1841 offered the post of drawing master at Wesley College, Sheffield. He accepted the post and, taking his wife and family to Sheffield, never returned to Newcastle again. While working at the college he continued to paint and exhibit his work, and gave private drawing lessons, but became increasingly involved in a move to establish a school of design at Sheffield. This was established in 1845, the year following the death of Parker's wife, and when he was not offered a post at the school he became increasingly disillusioned with Sheffield and in 1847 decided to move to London. Little is known of his remaining years except that he remarried, and, while still continuing to exhibit his work, led a penurious existence until his death at his home, 1 Blenheim Villas, Goldhawk Road, Shepherd's Bush, on 9 November 1873. His work is represented in the Victoria and Albert Museum, London, and the National Portrait Gallery, London, and in various provincial art galleries including the Laing Art Gallery, Newcastle, Sheffield Art Gallery, Sunderland Art Gallery, and the Grace Darling Museum, Bamburgh. MARSHALL HALL

Sources M. Hall, *The artists of Northumbria*, 2nd edn (1982) · N. Johnson, ed., *Henry Perlee Parker* [1969] [exhibition catalogue, Laing Art Gallery, Newcastle, 1969–1970] · P. Usherwood and K. Bowden, *Art for Newcastle: Thomas Miles Richardson and the Newcastle exhibitions 1822–1843* (1984) [exhibition catalogue, Laing Art Gallery, Newcastle upon Tyne, 11 Oct – 2 Dec 1984] · R. Welford, *Men of mark 'twixt Tyne and Tweed*, 3 vols. (1895) · H. P. Parker, 'An artist's narrative', MS, Newcastle Central Library · H. P. Parker, *Critiques on paintings by H. P. Parker … together with … etchings shewing the compositions, &c.* (1835) · *DNB* · *CGPLA Eng. & Wales* (1873) · *IGI*

Archives Bodl. Oxf., autobiography · Newcastle Central Library, MS, 'An artist's narrative'

Likenesses H. P. Parker, self-portrait, repro. in John Bell's commonplace book, priv. coll. · R. H. Parker, oils, NPG · drawing, Sheffield City Museum · portrait, repro. in *Newcastle Weekly Chronicle* (22 Aug 1891) · wood-engraving (after photograph), repro. in *ILN* (1874)

Wealth at death under £8000: probate, 18 Dec 1873, *CGPLA Eng. & Wales*

Parker, Henry Victor [*real name* Henry Victor Parker Saunders] (**1910–1978**), guitarist, was born on 5 November 1910 at 144 Clare Road, Cardiff, the only child of Henry Parker (*d.* in or before 1935), a ship's steward in the merchant service, and Edith Ethel May Saunders, a domestic servant. Both parents were Barbadian. He grew up between Butetown, where he attended South Church Street school, and Cathays, where he went to Gladstone School and Cathays high school. He was a child when his mother returned to Barbados, leaving responsibility for raising him to his maternal aunt Beatrice Saunders. His first instrument was the trombone, which he played in the Salvation Army's Junior Band, and he would have been a brass player had he not moved to the Docks, where the guitar was the prominent instrument. It was there he began to play stringed instruments, his first guitar lessons being given to him by his aunt. He learned technique and material from Caribbean and west African seamen, and also took lessons from

George Glossop senior, the most accomplished local guitarist, before joining a band of strolling stringed instrument players, for whom he provided the bass-line. At sixteen he went to sea briefly, then formed a guitar duo with George Glossop's son, also George, to play Hawaiian music for a touring show for which they travelled to London. There they busked the theatre queues and worked in various dives before Parker returned to Cardiff. With Don Johnson playing mandolin, he provided music for the denizens of dockland's cafés and shebeens but may have travelled to London again where, as an itinerant musician, he claimed to have met, and possibly played with, Louis Armstrong.

Parker returned to Cardiff to marry Georgina Waith (1912–1973), a domestic worker, on 19 January 1935. Their five children, Veronica Melinda Diana (*b.* 1934), Beryl Yvonne (*b.* 1936), Josephine Myrna (*b.* 1937), Graham Victor (Nick; *b.* 1942), and Janis Marilyn (*b.* 1947), were all born in Cardiff, and he continued to work with Don Johnson and Hawaiian guitarist Benny Canning between visits to London, where he earned a living in dance bands and learned to play jazz. With the accordionist Tony Chadgidakis (later Dakis) he attempted to introduce jazz sessions at Butetown's Great Windsor Hotel, but the city, even with its cosmopolitan demographics, was not yet ready to embrace what was still there a new music.

Parker remained in London during the war, and in 1940 at Bond Street's Embassy Club played accordion and double bass with Don Marino Barreto. He can be seen in Barreto's band accompanying Cicely Courtneidge and Jack Hulbert during a nightclub sequence in the musical film *Under your Hat* (1940). He worked with trumpeter Denis Walton's band and (1944–7) with pianist Francisco Condé, playing in nightclubs and at concerts, and broadcasting regularly and establishing himself as a resourceful Latin-American guitarist. He created an impact on the guitar world at a concert of the National Society of Banjoists, Mandolinists, and Guitarists, where his material included 'old West Indian and African airs'. A reviewer commended his style, reminiscent of the African American blues artists Lonnie Johnson, Leadbelly, and Josh White, noting the 'fine rhythm' he achieved, playing with or without a plectrum. 'In his finger-style solos he introduced a continual bass vamp with his thumb on the beat, while his complicated and highly figurative off-beat melodies were a joy to hear' (Burnham, 162). After touring the Welsh valleys with Cardiff pianist Spadie Lee (Lillian 'Lily' Jemmott), he continued to participate in London jam sessions with Chadgidakis and the Deniz brothers, where he played with the pianist George Shearing, members of Geraldo's orchestra, and young saxophonists Johnny Dankworth and Tommy Whittle. He was offered work with the coming bandleaders Edmundo Ros and Eric Winstone but rejected these offers and the chance of wider fame because he wanted to return to Cardiff for health reasons.

In 1947 Parker settled in Butetown, where he earned his living as a railway shunter while playing music nightly for local dances and at a succession of dockland hostelries. With fellow guitarist Ray Noman he established jazz in the city with sessions at the Custom House Hotel and the Great Windsor Hotel, at the same time making the difficult switch from the acoustic instrument to electric guitar. At the Quebec Hotel he and Noman developed what grew into one of the city's most celebrated venues and a virtual school for aspirant musicians. There, attracting traditional jazz exponents as well as the student crowd, Parker began playing previously unfamiliar material from the repertoire of New Orleans revivalism.

Despite his legendary London sojourns, Parker built his reputation in the community where he was born. Named 'a father figure of jazz in Cardiff' (*South Wales Echo*, 10 Feb 1978), a tribute shared with Chadgidakis, his true function was as a heroic community musician, a ubiquitous figure

Henry Victor Parker (1910–1978), by unknown photographer, 1967 [centre, performing at the Old Quebec, Cardiff]

who played for the people of Butetown at street parties and carnivals and provided a continuum and link with the city's Caribbean and African past. Responsible for teaching many local guitarists over several decades, he had a prodigious knowledge of tunes—which he also passed on—and as a Cardiff 'character' was assured of local fame. He appeared on radio and television, and was filmed and interviewed, even after retiring from public performance in 1975. He was found dead on 9 February 1978 at his home in Nelson House, Loudon Square, having suffered a gastro-intestinal haemorrhage due to a chronic peptic duodenal ulcer and coronarary thrombosis. He was given a New Orleans-style funeral, with a marching band heading the cortège as it passed through the streets of Butetown and an estimated 500 mourners following. He was buried at Thornhill cemetery, Cardiff. The funeral, widely reported, was filmed by BBC Wales, and Parker was the subject of a radio tribute. Although he never recorded commercially under his own name, his composition *All Birds Looks Like Chickens to Me* became a standard in Cardiff musicians' repertoire. An image of him wearing his trademark trilby hat and playing guitar, once part of a substantial mural on the site of the former docks, is now housed in the Butetown Community Centre in Bute Street. VAL WILMER

Sources R. Burnham, '"Jeffrey Bros." recital', *B. M. G.: a Journal Devoted to the Banjo, Mandoline, and Guitar* (June 1944), 162 • J. Scantlebury, 'And all that jazz', *The Cardiff Book*, ed. S. Williams, 3, 65–80 • 'Jazzman Vic, of the Quebec, found dead', *South Wales Echo* (10 Feb 1978), 1 • 'Jazzman is given musical send-off', *South Wales Echo* (18 Feb 1978) • personal knowledge (2004) • private information (2004) • b. cert. • m. cert. • d. cert. • interview with Parker, *Western Mail* (*c*.1960)

Likenesses B. Hardy, photograph, 1950, priv. coll. • B. Hardy, photographs, 1950, Hult. Arch. • photographs, 1967, *South Wales Echo* picture library [*see illus.*] • photographs, priv. coll.

Parker, Sir Henry Watson (1808–1881), politician in Australia, was born on 1 June 1808 at Lewisham, Kent, the fourth son of Thomas Watson Parker and his wife, Mary (*b. c*.1786), daughter of John Carnell of Sevenoaks and Carrendon, Hadlow, Kent. After being educated privately by a Dr Waite, domestic chaplain to Princess Sophia of Gloucester, Parker joined the East India Company and served in India, China, and South Africa. After later travelling extensively through Europe, he was employed in 1837 as private secretary to Sir George Gipps, the newly appointed governor of New South Wales, and he arrived in the colony with the governor's party on 24 February 1838.

Becoming Gipps's 'protégé' (Foster, 58), Parker frequently acted as go-between on 'sensitive matters' between the governor and leading figures in the colony (Milliss, 875). Parker's links to 'powerful and conservative colonial groups' (Nairn, 397) were consolidated by his marriage on 21 November 1843 to Emmeline Emily (1808–1888), youngest daughter of Australian wool industry pioneers John and Elizabeth Macarthur. They had no children. In 1846, just before Gipps left the colony, he appointed Parker to the legislative council. He became council chairman of committees, a post he held for ten years. In 1856 New South Wales was granted responsible government, and Parker won the legislative assembly seat of Parramatta in the first general election in March that year. He was nominated by the conservative-dominated government for the position of speaker, but his defeat, by one vote, emphasized the unpredictable nature of this first parliament.

Shifting political alliances saw two ministries fall in the first five months of parliament's sitting. In this chaotic atmosphere Parker was invited to attempt to form a government, with his reputation as a more moderate conservative recommending him as the 'most likely man to conciliate parties' (Serle, 215) and able to gain the necessary support of independent members. He became premier on 3 October 1856. But his authority as leader was questioned by opponents who claimed that the 'controlling genius' behind the ministry (Foster, 145) was in fact Edward Deas Thomson, the very popular former chief administrator of the colony, who had become vice-president of the executive council and representative of the government in the legislative council. The new ministry received its greatest praise because of Thomson's inclusion, and Parker 'was generally credited with administrative ability but obviously lacked the power of political leadership' (Ward, 360). His attempts to legislate on the contentious issues of land and electoral reform 'provoked unrest, abstention and opposition amongst his followers' (Loveday and Martin, 28). Parker's government was defeated on the electoral bill, and he resigned on 4 September 1857.

Parker, as was shown in his period with Gipps, was a 'proficient and shrewd official' (Nairn, 398), yet he was perhaps lacking the political instincts and popular touch necessary to be successful in the new democratic, and increasingly party-political, environment. Remembering him after his death, *The Bulletin* characterized his ministerial career as having had its 'chief incident' in the 'public horsewhipping he received in the Botanic Gardens, from some political malcontent' who was later imprisoned (*The Bulletin*, 9 April 1881, 13).

Parker was knighted in 1858, and in that year retired and returned to Britain. He continued his political involvement by standing, unsuccessfully, as a Conservative against Gladstone in Greenwich in the 1868 general election. In 1879 and 1880 he was a commissioner for the Melbourne and Sydney exhibitions. He died on 2 February 1881 at his home, Stawell House, Richmond, Surrey.

MARC BRODIE

Sources B. Nairn, 'Parker, Sir Henry Watson', *AusDB*, vol. 5 • S. G. Foster, *Colonial improver: Edward Deas Thomson, 1800–1879* (1978) • R. Milliss, *Waterloo Creek: the Australia day massacre of 1838, George Gipps and the British conquest of New South Wales* (Sydney, 1994) • *Gipps–La Trobe correspondence, 1839–1846*, ed. A. G. L. Shaw (1989) • P. Loveday and A. W. Martin, *Parliament, factions and parties: the first thirty years of responsible government in New South Wales, 1856–1889* (1966) • J. M. Ward, *Earl Grey and the Australian colonies, 1846–1857: a study of self-government and self-interest* (1958) • *The Bulletin* (9 April 1881) • P. Serle, *Dictionary of Australian biography*, 2 vols. (1949) • A. W. Martin and P. Wardle, *Members of the legislative assembly of New South Wales, 1856–1901* (1959) • F. Johns, *An Australian biographical dictionary* (1934) • P. Mennell, *The dictionary of Australasian biography* (1892) • *IGI*

Likenesses miniature, watercolour, Mitchell L., NSW; repro. in Milliss, *Waterloo Creek*

Parker, Hubert Lister, Baron Parker of Waddington (**1900–1972**), judge, was born on 28 May 1900 at Thursley, Surrey, the youngest in the family of three sons and two daughters of Robert John *Parker, later Baron Parker of Waddington (1857–1918), a lord of appeal in ordinary, and his wife, Constance (*d.* 1937), daughter of John Trevor Barkley, a civil engineer. He was educated at Rugby School and at Trinity College, Cambridge, where he obtained a first class in both parts one (1921) and two (1922) of the natural sciences tripos. His special subject was geology and he thought of pursuing a career in oil, but abandoned it to read for the bar. He joined Lincoln's Inn, was called to the bar in 1924, and entered the chambers of Donald Somervell. On 10 November 1924 he married Loryn, daughter of Oscar Tilton-Bowser of Covington, Kentucky, USA. They had no children.

Parker gradually built up a substantial practice in civil cases, primarily in commercial matters. His advocacy was marked by fairness, clarity, and good temper—passionate rhetoric was not for him. In 1945 he succeeded Valentine Holmes as junior counsel to the treasury in common law matters. Such an appointment usually leads to a High Court judgeship, and such was his competence that he was very soon under consideration for the bench. He was first approached by the lord chancellor, Viscount Jowitt, in 1948 because Jowitt had been particularly impressed by his 'intellectual distinction'. Parker, however, was a man of integrity, replying that as 'Treasury Devil' he was 'really part of government' and that he had 'just become fully useful in the Labour government's legislative policy. Another 12–18 months should result in the solution of these problems … the right course [is] to complete, as it were, the work' (Stevens, *The Independence of the Judiciary*, 84). By 1950 the time was obviously right and Parker was promoted and given the traditional knighthood.

The work of a king's bench judge entailed his entering fields in which he had had little or no experience at the bar. He had to sit as an assize judge, spending much of his time presiding over criminal trials. He said that the first summing-up in a criminal case that he heard was one he delivered himself. He was, however, regarded as a good judge, both in civil and criminal matters, exhibiting the accepted judicial virtues.

In 1954 Parker was promoted to the Court of Appeal and was given the traditional membership in the privy council. His gifts and temperament were well suited to the work of the Court of Appeal. He was a sound lawyer, with a considerable capacity for identifying the essentials of a case, stating the problem and his answer to it in the fewest possible words—and usually getting the answer right. In 1957 he presided successfully over a tribunal which inquired into alleged malpractices in connection with the bank rate.

In 1958 Lord Goddard retired as chief justice, the presiding judge in the most important division of the High Court, the Queen's Bench Division, as well as being regarded outside the profession as the spokesman of the judiciary. While Goddard had attracted much sycophantic

Hubert Lister Parker, Baron Parker of Waddington (1900–1972), by Sir William O. Hutchison, *c*.1962

praise, he was an unpleasant human being, whose attitudes, most obvious in his enthusiasm for hanging and flogging, increasingly represented a bygone era. Harold Macmillan was in a quandary about whom to appoint as his successor. At the time, the tradition that the attorney-general had the right of reversion to the post was still strong. The attorney-general, however, was Sir Reginald Manningham-Buller, who was almost universally unloved and whose attitudes bore a striking similarity to those of the retiring chief justice. Macmillan's eye then lit upon his lord chancellor, Viscount Kilmuir. Such a move, lateral at best, would have been thought most odd and Kilmuir replied that 'I should prefer to remain by your side so long as you think I am of any use to you and your Government' (Heuston, 178). Such loyalty was mistaken, for Kilmuir was unceremoniously ejected from office in 1962 in the 'night of the long knives'. Kilmuir's sensitivities, however, led to the appointment of Hubert Parker as lord chief justice. He was made a life peer and took the same title as his father.

After the turmoil of the Goddard years, Parker brought calm, although for a while he continued the Goddard enthusiasm for corporal punishment. As chief justice he was an admirable leader of his team of judges, always approachable and ready to help them with their problems. The courts in which he mainly presided were the divisional court and the court of criminal appeal (the latter replaced in 1966 by the criminal division of the Court of Appeal). It may be that in the divisional court the years he had spent as 'Treasury Devil' had caused him to have a greater tendency to support the actions of the executive than had been the case with some of his predecessors. He was, for instance, much criticized when, as the result of the Vassall tribunal, he sentenced two journalists to prison for refusing to disclose their sources, with the observation—much quoted out of context—that 'the citizen's highest duty is to the State', noting also that 'the judiciary is the handmaiden of the executive' (Abel Smith and Stevens, *Lawyers and the Courts*, 308).

Overall, however, Parker was a breath of fresh air as the leader of the judiciary. He was helped by increasing morale as more judges were approved by parliament, which also, at long last, agreed to increases in judicial salaries. The Judicial Pensions Act (1959) finally provided a mandatory retiring age of seventy-five. Yet Parker was proactive. He attempted to modernize the assize system, he described the legal aid scheme (in contrast to his predecessor) as an 'indispensable and … valuable social service' (ibid., 311), and during his time criminal legal aid came to be well remunerated. He thought fault was an increasingly archaic basis for compensation and was attracted by the Saskatchewan compensation scheme. It was Parker who also began systematic training for JPs and endorsed some form of training for all judges—the forerunner of the Judicial Studies Board. He put his support behind the Law Commission after it was established and expounded such radical views as allowing partnerships at the bar. He began judicial conferences on sentencing, and judges were encouraged to visit prisons. It was not without significance that, when the Beeching committee on the courts was appointed, his memorandum to the committee was more radical than that of his judges. He, however, chose to retire as the committee issued its report, in 1971, deciding that a younger chief justice was needed to implement its recommendations.

Parker was a relatively frequent speaker in the legislative sessions of the House of Lords, averaging some four speeches a year. Perhaps his most significant was on the War Damage Bill in 1965, designed to overrule a decision of the House of Lords retrospectively, thus depriving the plaintiff of the award it had won. Parker was 'infuriated' and had a 'complete abhorrence' of the bill. He noted that the courts respected the intentions of the legislature and he had always hoped 'the legislature, in turn, would respect and uphold the standards of justice adopted by the courts' (*Hansard 5L*, vol. 264, 777–8, 23 March 1965). It was all to no avail.

Rather surprisingly, Parker's judgments have not, in general, survived, at least in terms of importance. His only House of Lords case was *Director of Public Prosecutions* v. *Smith* (1960), where the lord chancellor spoke for the law lords in a decision which was admired neither by academics nor by Commonwealth judges. After retirement he sat in a few privy council cases and he wrote the report of the committee of privy counsellors on the authorized procedures for the interrogation of terrorist suspects in Northern Ireland (1972).

Parker was greatly attached to his old school, Rugby, and was for some years chairman of governors. A new science building there was named after him. He enjoyed, among other activities, collecting books and antiques, shooting, fishing, watching birds, and building garden walls. He was a quiet, unassuming man, never well known to the public but liked by those who knew him. During most of his marriage (which was said to be happy and lasted for forty-eight years), he and his wife ran a farm, first in Sussex and later in Essex, specializing in cattle breeding. Parker died on 15 September 1972 at Donhead St Andrew, Wiltshire.

D. A. S. CAIRNS, *rev.* ROBERT STEVENS

Sources *The Times* (8 April 1971); (16 Sept 1972) • personal knowledge (1986, 2004) • private information (1986, 2004) • R. Stevens, *Law and politics: the House of Lords as a judicial body, 1800–1976* (1978) • B. Abel Smith and R. Stevens, *Lawyers and the courts* (1967) • B. Abel Smith and R. Stevens, *In search of justice* (1968) • R. Stevens, *The independence of the judiciary* (1993) • R. F. V. Heuston, *Lives of the lord chancellors, 1940–1970* (1987) • L. Blom-Cooper and G. Drewry, *Final appeal* (1972)
Archives FILM BFI NFTVA, news footage
Likenesses N. Hepple, group portrait, oils, 1958 (*A short adjournment*), Lincoln's Inn, London • W. O. Hutchison, oils, *c*.1962, Lincoln's Inn, London [*see illus.*] • G. Argent, photograph, 1968, NPG
Wealth at death £13,325: probate, 13 Nov 1972, *CGPLA Eng. & Wales*

Parker, Sir Hyde, fifth baronet (1714–1782/3), naval officer, younger son of Hyde Parker (*d*. 1726), rector of Tredington in Worcestershire, and his wife, Mary, daughter of John Reeves, was born at Tredington on 1 February 1714. His grandfather, Sir Henry Parker, alderman of London, created a baronet in 1681, married Margaret, daughter of Alexander Hyde, bishop of Salisbury, and first cousin of the first earl of Clarendon. In 1734 Hyde Parker married Sarah, daughter of Hugh Smithson; they had two sons: Harry (1735–1812), who succeeded to the baronetcy, and Sir Hyde *Parker (1739–1807), admiral.

Parker served for several years in the merchant service before entering the navy at the comparatively ripe age of twenty-four. He then served in the *Antelope* as able seaman, in the *Swift* and *Pearl*, with Captain Matthew Michell, and in the *Centurion*, with Commodore George Anson. He passed his examination on 16 January 1745, and on the same day was promoted lieutenant of the *Harwich*, in which he went out to the East Indies; he was moved by Commodore Barnett to the *Preston*, and in 1747 to the *Princess Mary* by Commodore Griffin, who on 24 March 1748 promoted him captain of the *Lively*, which he brought home in 1749. In November 1751 he was appointed to the *Vanguard* for harbour duty, and in February 1753 to the sloop *Cruiser* engaged in the protection of the North Sea fisheries and the prevention of smuggling. In October 1755 he commissioned the *Squirrel*, and in 1756 was sent out on a special mission to negotiate a treaty with the ruler of Morocco, and to obtain the release of European slaves. During 1757 the *Squirrel* was employed in the North Sea, and in October Parker was appointed to the *Brilliant*, which in the following year formed part of the squadron on the coast of France under Richard, Earl Howe.

In November 1759 Parker commissioned the *Norfolk*, which in January 1760 sailed for the East Indies. On his arrival on the station he was moved by the commander-in-chief, Rear-Admiral Charles Steevens, into the *Grafton*, in

Sir Hyde Parker, fifth baronet (1714–1782/3), by George Romney, in or before 1782–3

which he took part in the operations against Pondicherry, ending in its surrender on 15 January 1761, and against Manila in 1762. He was then moved by Vice-Admiral Samuel Cornish to the *Panther*, and sent out, with the frigate *Argo* in company, to look out for the yearly ship from Acapulco. On 31 October 1762, after very slight resistance, they captured what they took to be that vessel, but it proved to be the return ship from Manila to Acapulco, the *Santissima Trinidad*, which had been compelled to turn back in consequence of damage sustained in a storm. Although not so valuable as the Acapulco ship she was still very rich, and yielded about £30,000 to each of the two captains. Parker returned to England in 1764 in the *Norfolk* and had no employment for the next twelve years. In November 1776 he was appointed to the *Invincible* in the channel. On 23 January 1778 he was promoted rear-admiral; shortly afterwards he hoisted his flag on the *Royal Oak*, as second in command in the squadron going out to North America with Vice-Admiral John Byron. With six of the squadron in a shattered and disabled state, Parker arrived at New York on 29 August, d'Estaing having fortunately withdrawn the French squadron just before. In December Parker went with Byron to the West Indies, and on 6 July 1779 he commanded the rear division in the battle off Grenada, but he saw little action.

In August, after d'Estaing's fleet had departed, Byron and Samuel Barrington sailed for England, leaving Parker to command the British fleet on the Leeward Islands station. Parker, now in the *Princess Royal*, declined to follow d'Estaing or to attempt the recapture of the British islands which had been lost to the French. Instead he kept his fleet at St Lucia to watch the French at Martinique. Parker's ships captured most of two convoys arriving at Martinique from France in September and December 1779 and at the end of the year he captured a force of three French frigates trying to reach the island. However, he could not prevent small French squadrons under de Grasse and La Motte Piquet from reaching Martinique.

In expectation of the arrival of troops from England under General Vaughan, Parker began preparations in early 1780 for an attack on Puerto Rico. However, when Vaughan arrived he preferred to postpone that operation until Admiral Rodney arrived with naval reinforcements. In the meantime Parker and Vaughan planned to recapture St Vincent, but on 21 March the Comte de Guichen's fleet reached Martinique, giving the French naval superiority, and they prepared to attack St Lucia. When they appeared off Gros Islet Bay on 26 March they found Parker's fleet within, anchored in line of battle. Guichen decided not to attack, and on hearing that Rodney had arrived at Barbados with naval reinforcements the French withdrew to Martinique.

Rodney took over command of the British fleet, with Parker as second in command. In April 1780 Guichen's fleet put to sea and Rodney pursued them. In the battle off Martinique on 17 April Parker commanded the van division, which failed to carry out Rodney's plan to produce a decisive action. The blame lay with Rodney for failing to explain his plans adequately to his subordinate commanders, and no disciplinary action was taken against Parker. Nevertheless in July Rodney sent Parker back to England with the trade convoy.

On 26 September 1780 Parker was promoted vice-admiral, and in March 1781 he was appointed to command a squadron in the North Sea. He had escorted the trade for the Baltic, and was coming south with a convoy of some 200 merchantmen, when, on the Dogger Bank on 5 August, he met a Dutch squadron convoying their trade to the north. The Dutch force, under Rear-Admiral Johan Arnold Zoutman, had six ships of the line, while Parker, in the *Fortitude*, had a similar force, although several of his ships were in poor condition. After forming line of battle, the two squadrons engaged, but the action proved indecisive. When the Dutch withdrew—later one of their ships, the *Holland*, sank—Parker's ships were too damaged to pursue. Parker thought his squadron could have been strengthened before the battle had the Admiralty willed it, and he made no secret of his belief that such neglect had prevented his obtaining a decisive victory. George III went down to the Nore in an attempt to placate the admiral. However, Parker insisted on resigning his command and told the king that his navy needed younger commanders and newer ships.

On 10 July 1782, after the death of his elder brother, Sir Harry Parker DD, Hyde Parker succeeded to the baronetcy. Shortly before this, under the new Rockingham administration, he had been appointed commander-in-chief in the East Indies. With his flag in the *Cato* he sailed in October 1782, and, after leaving Rio de Janeiro on 12 December, was not heard of again. Later accounts variously reported the *Cato* as having been wrecked on Madagascar, the Maldives, or the Malabar coast, with the survivors killed by natives. However, there was no hard evidence for any of these stories, and it seems more likely the ship caught fire accidentally at sea and blew up.

J. K. Laughton, *rev.* Alan G. Jamieson

Sources J. Charnock, ed., *Biographia navalis*, 6 vols. (1794–8) • A. G. Jamieson, 'War in the Leeward Islands, 1775–1783', DPhil diss., U. Oxf., 1981 • W. L. Clowes, *The Royal Navy: a history from the earliest times to the present*, 7 vols. (1897–1903) • J. R. Bruijn, *The Dutch navy in the seventeenth and eighteenth centuries* (1993) • N. Tracy, *Manila ransomed: the British assault on Manila in the seven years' war* (1995) • P. Mackesy, *The war for America, 1775–1783* (1964)

Archives BL, descriptions of the Philippines, Add. MSS 19295–19296 | PRO, corresp. with Admiral Rodney and Admiralty letters to him, PRO 30/20

Likenesses J. Northcote, oils, 1781, Saltram, Devon • G. Romney, oils, in or before 1782–1783, Melford Hall, Suffolk; version, NMM • G. Romney, oils, second version, in or before 1782–1783, NMM [*see illus.*] • attrib. J. Reynolds, oils, Melford Hall, Suffolk • line engraving (after unknown artist), NPG; repro. in *London Magazine* (Sept 1781)

Parker, Sir Hyde (1739–1807), naval officer, was the second son of Vice-Admiral Sir Hyde *Parker, baronet (1714–1782/3), and Sarah (*d.* after 1782), daughter of Hugh Smithson. He entered the navy in 1751 in the *Vanguard*, commanded by his father, and transferred with him to the sloop *Cruiser* in February 1753. He joined the *Medway*, commanded by Charles Proby, in the summer of 1755, passed his lieutenant's examination on 7 November 1757, and was promoted lieutenant of his father's ship, the *Brilliant*, on 25 January 1758. He followed his father to the *Norfolk* in November 1759 and went with him to the East Indies. Both transferred again to the *Grafton* in June 1760. Parker was present at the operations against Pondicherry and was appointed to the *Lennox* in July 1761. He was appointed to the command of the *Manila* on 16 December 1761 and promoted captain of the *Baleine* on 18 July 1763. His next command was the *Hussar* from December 1766 to May 1769, first on the Irish station and then on the North American station under Commodore Hood.

Parker was next appointed to command the *Boston* in September 1770 and the *Phoenix* in July 1775. In October 1776 he was sent by Lord Howe to New York to occupy the North River, by which supplies were being sent to the rebels. The river was defended by gunboats and shore batteries, and a variety of obstructions. Parker broke through the defences, destroying two of the gunboats and running the remainder ashore. The *Phoenix* continued in American waters and conveyed troops to Savannah in January 1779. After this she returned home to repair and Parker was knighted on 21 April 1779 for his actions at New York. Parker then returned to the West Indies with a convoy for Jamaica and on 4 October 1780 the *Phoenix* was lost in a hurricane off Cuba. Most of her crew got ashore, salvaging provisions and guns from the wreck. A boat was sent to Jamaica for assistance and Parker and his crew were shortly rescued, after which he returned to England and was appointed to the *Latona*. He then joined the North Sea squadron commanded by his father, and was present at the action off the Dogger Bank. His next appointment was to the *Goliath* in October 1781 and he was at the relief of Gibraltar in the following year. About this time Parker married Anne, daughter of John Boteler; they had three sons, including Hyde *Parker, and two daughters. When war with France threatened, Parker was appointed for a short time to the *Orion* in 1787 and later to the *Brunswick* in 1790 when war with Spain seemed likely. When Russia then threatened war in 1791 and a Baltic expedition was prepared, Parker was made first-captain to Lord Hood.

Parker was promoted rear-admiral on 1 February 1793, appointed captain of the Mediterranean Fleet under Lord Hood, and was present at the occupation of Toulon by the British fleet. He was made a vice-admiral on 4 July 1794 with his flag in the *St George*, and was third in command under Admiral William Hotham who had superseded Hood. The *St George* was involved in the actions with the French on 13 March and 13 July 1795, and Parker returned to England early in 1796. With the likelihood of Spain making an alliance with France, Parker was ordered to take a squadron back to the Mediterranean to join Admiral John Jervis. He was issued with additional instructions to pursue Rear-Admiral Richery if he found that the French squadron had eluded Admiral Mann off Cadiz. He was further instructed not to engage the French if they were accompanied by a Spanish squadron.

Arriving off Cadiz, Parker discovered that Richery had sailed on 4 August and had a twenty-day head start. Parker surmised that they had sailed for the West Indies, went in pursuit, and arrived off Martinique in September 1796 only to discover later that Richery had sailed for Newfoundland and then Brest. Parker's prompt action was nevertheless approved by the Admiralty, and he was given the chief command at Jamaica. He remained on this station until 1800, helped establish a base for the fleet at St Nicholas Mole on San Domingo, and was incensed when the island was evacuated 'without the smallest communication of this important event being communicated to me' (Corbett and Richmond, 3.245, 266). From Parker's complaints to the Admiralty, it is apparent that there was little co-operation or communication between the different West Indian commands. However, he had the consolation of commanding a station rich in prize money and is reputed to have made over £200,000 (Pope, 6).

On his return to England in September 1800 Parker was appointed second-in-command of the Channel Fleet under Jervis (now earl of St Vincent). Like many other officers Parker did not measure up to St Vincent's exacting standards; even so, while planning the expedition to the Baltic, St Vincent wrote to Spencer:

> Should the Northern Powers continue this menacing posture, Sir Hyde Parker is the only man you have to face them. He is in possession of all the information obtained during the Russian Armament [1791], more particularly that which relates to the navigation of the Great Belt. (*Letters*, 1.318–19)

Accordingly Parker was appointed to command in the Baltic in January 1801 with Horatio Nelson as his second-in-command. A few weeks previously, on 23 December (his first marriage having come to an end), Parker had married Frances (*d.* 1844), the eighteen-year-old daughter of Admiral Sir Richard Onslow. This undoubtedly contributed to what both St Vincent and Nelson perceived as a lack of urgency on Parker's part. When St Vincent heard that Lady Parker had organized a ball, he dispatched a thinly veiled threat, 'supposing it impossible' that Parker could still be at Yarmouth 'on account of some trifling circumstance' (*Letters*, 1.86). The ball was cancelled, Parker went on the *London*, and the fleet sailed for the Baltic.

Parker disagreed with Nelson about how best to deal with the Danes and the Russians, but consented to Nelson's proposal to bombard Copenhagen with the fleet's smaller ships of the line. This was undertaken at considerable risk on 2 April. During the height of the battle Parker, anchored with his division 3 miles to the north and imagining the worst, made a signal to discontinue the action. This was not a permissive signal made to Nelson alone but a general signal to the entire fleet. It was largely disregarded and Nelson fought on, forcing the Danes to surrender. This ill-judged signal and his failure to push further up the Baltic to engage the Russians proved the ruin of Parker's reputation. He was immediately recalled and was not employed again. In December 1801 he purchased Benhall Manor, near Saxmundham in Suffolk, and made it his residence. He died at his London home at Great Cumberland Place on 16 March 1807 and was buried at Holy Trinity Church, Long Melford, Suffolk.

Despite the many unfavourable comments from Lord St Vincent, Parker had, until the Copenhagen affair, a good professional reputation. He was described as of stern countenance but was not ill natured (Stirling, 1.258). Towards the end of his career he was considered irresolute and dilatory; however, these traits were not apparent in his pursuit of Admiral Richery or the action in America that earned him a knighthood. He was evidently a popular man for as Nelson wrote after Copenhagen:

> We all respect and love Sir Hyde; but the dearer his friends, the more uneasy they have been at his idleness for that is the truth—no criminality. I believe Sir H. P. to be as good a subject as His Majesty has. (*Letters*, 1.78)

As an officer, Parker was an able administrator rather than a great leader and this was to prove a weakness when it came to having both St Vincent as his chief and Nelson as a subordinate. CLIVE WILKINSON

Sources *DNB* · *Private papers of George, second Earl Spencer*, ed. J. S. Corbett and H. W. Richmond, 3, Navy RS, 58 (1924) · *Letters of … the earl of St Vincent, whilst the first lord of the admiralty, 1801–1804*, ed. D. B Smith, 1, Navy RS, 55 (1922) · D. Pope, *The great gamble* (1972) · *Pages and portraits from the past: being the private papers of Sir William Hotham*, ed. A. M. W. Stirling, 2 vols. (1919), vol. 1 · W. H. Dillon, *A narrative of my professional adventures, 1790–1839*, ed. M. A. Lewis, 1, Navy RS, 93 (1953) · W. A. Copinger, *The manors of Suffolk*, 7 vols. (1905–11), vol. 5 · W. A. Shaw, *The knights of England*, 2 (1906) · Burke, *Peerage*

Archives NMM, logbooks · NYPL, order book · PRO, admiral's dispatches, ADM 1/4, 248, 249 · PRO, admiral's journals, ADM 50/65, 30, 40 · PRO, captain's journals, ADM 51/467, 127, 694 · PRO, captain's letters, ADM 1/2301–2309 | NL Scot., corresp. with Lord Balcarres · NMM, Phillips Croker collection, lieutenant's journals, ADM/L/B163, N152 · NMM, letters to Lord Nelson · Yale U., Beinecke L., letters and orders to Sir John Duckworth

Likenesses G. Romney, oils, 1779, Melford Hall, Suffolk · J. Walker, engraving, 1780 (after G. Romney), NMM · J. Chapman, engraving, 1796, NMM

Parker, Hyde (1784?–1854), naval officer, was the son of Admiral Sir Hyde *Parker (1739–1807) and his first wife, Anne, daughter of John Palmer Boteler, of Henley. He entered the Royal Naval Academy on 2 February 1796, and went to sea in September 1799, serving as a volunteer aboard the *Cambrian*. In 1801 he joined the *Narcissus* as a midshipman, and was promoted lieutenant on 24 September 1804. He was particularly noticed for bravery in boat action against beached coasters on 11 July 1804 at La Vadour in the Bay of Hyères. The following year he took part in the capture of the Cape of Good Hope, and joined the *Volontaire* (Captain Joscelyn Percy). On 22 January 1806 he was promoted commander and, after returning to Britain in June, went on half pay.

In March 1807 Parker took command of the sloop *Prometheus* for the Copenhagen expedition, his services being specially noticed, and he was promoted captain on 13 October. In 1811 he commanded the *Monmouth*, flagship of Sir Thomas Foley, and in April 1812 the frigate *Tenedos*, whose crew he drilled to a high level of efficiency, on the North American station. He served with distinction throughout the Anglo-American War of 1812–14, blockading Boston with his friend Philip Vere Broke, HMS *Shannon*, before leaving the area to permit Broke to engage the USS *Chesapeake* in single combat. On 21 May 1813 he captured an American privateer. In April 1814, in company with the *Junon*, he drove the USS *Constitution* into Marblehead harbour, and would have followed her in had he not been recalled by his superior officer. In September 1814 he commanded the naval forces at the reduction of Machias, the last American-held town between Penobscot and Passamaquoddy Bay. On 15 January 1815 he took the surrender of the USS *President*.

Parker returned to Britain in August 1815. Between 1818 and 1821 he commanded the *Iphegenia* on the North American station, losing one third of his crew to yellow fever. On 16 July 1821 he married Caroline Eden, daughter of Sir Frederick Morton *Eden, bt, and sister of Captain Charles Eden, a whig cousin of Lord Auckland. They had several children, and one son joined the navy. In 1830 he commanded the *St Vincent*, as flag-captain to Sir Thomas Foley at Portsmouth. On 5 September 1831 he was appointed extra aide-de-camp to William IV.

In 1831–2 Parker commanded the *Asia* on the Lisbon station, where he astonished Sir Edward Codrington by his ignorance of signals, tactics, and squadron sailing, before returning to command the *Victory* at Portsmouth. In 1835 he commissioned the *Rodney* for the Mediterranean, where he remained for four years, confirming his reputation as a brilliant seaman and an outstanding captain. He was created CB in April 1839. On 23 November 1841 he was promoted rear-admiral. Between August 1842 and the end of 1847 Parker served as admiral superintendent of Portsmouth Dockyard. His term was interrupted by command of the Evolutionary squadron in 1845, which demonstrated his tory politics and aversion to Sir William Symonds's ships, rather than any attempt at impartial assessment.

In March 1852 Parker was appointed senior naval lord in the earl of Derby's ministry, having been selected by the first lord, the duke of Northumberland. On 5 June 1852 he reached the rank of vice-admiral. The board was riven by the attempts of the tory government to reverse the work of Lord Auckland, which removed political patronage from dockyard appointments; Parker, who supported the naval professional approach, spent most of his time persuading the surveyor, Sir Baldwin Walker, not to resign, and keeping the peace between the political secretary, Stafford O'Brien, and the first lord's private secretary, Captain Frederick Pelham. At the same time this board agreed that all future warships should be propelled by steam, increased the size of the active fleet, and began work on additional steam battleships. Although a tory, Parker was retained as senior naval lord by Sir James Graham on account of his whig connections and lack of ambition. Graham used Parker's ill health to ignore the board in developing strategic planning for the war with Russia.

Parker was already a cipher when war broke out in March 1854. He died at his home in Ham, Surrey, on 25 May 1854. His wife, whose prolonged ill health had added to his worries, survived until 10 November. Their son Captain Hyde Parker (1824–1854) was killed storming the Russian batteries in the Sulina Channel of the Danube on 8 July 1854. Parker had made his son up to captain at a very early age, and secured him a steam command. His own early career had been made by his father, but his service afloat, and later at Portsmouth Dockyard, demonstrated a high degree of skill and competence. His elevation to the post of senior naval lord in 1852 reflected his politics, and the lack of alternatives. The problems of 1852 and the demands of 1853–4 revealed his limits, and exacerbated his ill health. ANDREW LAMBERT

Sources O'Byrne, *Naval biog. dict.* • *Annual Register* (1854) • P. Padfield, *Broke and the Shannon* (1968) • NMM, Codrington MSS • Cumbria AS, Carlisle, Graham MSS • S. M. Eardley-Wilmot, *Life of Vice-Admiral Edmund, Lord Lyons* (1898) • A. D. Lambert, *The Crimean War: British grand strategy, 1853–56* (1990) • Bodl. Oxf., Dep. Hughenden • B. S. Mends, *The life of Sir W. Mends* (1899) • J. H. Briggs, *Naval administrations, 1827 to 1892: the experience of 65 years*, ed. Lady Briggs (1897) • 'Select committee on dockyard appointments', *Parl. papers* (1852–3), vol. 25, no. 511 • University of Cape Town, South Africa, Walker MSS • W. James, *The naval history of Great Britain, from the declaration of war by France in 1793 to the accession of George IV*, [8th edn], 6 vols. (1902), vol. 3 • T. Roosevelt, *The naval war of 1812* (1882) • W. S. Dudley, ed., *The naval war of 1812: a documentary history*, 2 (1992) • Burke, *Peerage* (1927)

Parker, James (1757–1805), printmaker, was born in September 1757 in the parish of St Mary-le-Strand, London, the son of Paul Parker, a corn chandler. He was apprenticed to James Basire (1730–1802) in August 1773. A fellow student was William Blake, with whom Parker shared similar tastes in Ossianic literature, as well as the facility to engrave in a combination of the line, stipple, and roulette manner. In 1783—while living at 19 Little Drury Lane—Parker exhibited *Fingal Preparing to Revenge the Death of Fainafollis* at the Society of Artists; he also sent a proof of the same subject to the Free Society. In 1784 he and Blake became business partners in a printselling and publishing concern. Only two plates are known to have been published by them, and the partnership ended after three years, Parker retaining the print stock and the accommodation above the shop at 27 Broad Street, Carnaby.

Most of Parker's plates were book illustrations; they included a pair after James Northcote, in stipple, entitled *Sterne Conducting Maria into Moulines* (1786) and *Sterne in the Glove Shop* (1789). For John Boydell's *Shakespeare*, he engraved eleven small plates for the letterpress edition (1802) and, in line, a large plate after Richard Westall's *Macbeth*, for which he received £157 10s. Other principal plates included a portrait of *Henry Addington* (1803, after William Beechey), 'engraved in stroke and executed in a very masterly style' (*Monthly Magazine and British Register*, 1 May 1803, 351), *The Revolution of 1688* (1790, after Northcote), and *The Landing of the Prince of Orange* (1801). Parker's particular talent for outline engraving was eminently suited to reproducing John Flaxman's designs: he engraved twenty of the sculptor's compositions for *The Odyssey* and contributed to *The Iliad* (both published in 1805). Flaxman praised him highly as an engraver 'of distinguished merit' and 'a punctual honest Man' (Bentley, 155).

Parker, who lived at Spring Place, Kentish Town, from about 1800, became a governor of the Society of Engravers and was remarkable to his contemporaries for 'his equability of temper, his suavity of manners, and integrity' (*GM*, 75, 1805, 586). He died suddenly, and was buried in the churchyard of St Clement Danes, London, on 26 May 1805. VIVIENNE W. PAINTING

Sources *DNB* • *GM*, 1st ser., 75 (1805), 586 • Free Library of Philadelphia, Philadelphia, Pennsylvania, Autographs of engravers collection • P. Cannon-Brookes, ed., *The painted word: British history painting, 1750–1830* (1991) • G. E. Bentley, *Blake records* (1969) • Graves, *Artists* • A. M. Hind, *A history of engraving and etching*, 3rd edn (1923); repr. (1963) • P. Ackroyd, *Blake*, another edn (1996) • R. N. Essick, *William Blake, printmaker* (Princeton, NJ, 1980) • S. C. Hutchison, 'The Royal Academy Schools, 1768–1830', *Walpole Society*, 38 (1960–62), 123–91, esp. 123

Archives Free Library of Philadelphia, Autographs of engravers collection

Parker, Sir James (1803–1852), judge and vice-chancellor, was born in Glasgow, the son of Charles Steuart Parker and his wife, Margaret, *née* Rainy, both of Blochairn, near Glasgow. He was educated at Glasgow grammar school and Glasgow College before matriculating on 11 June 1821 at Trinity College, Cambridge, where he became seventh wrangler and graduated BA in 1825 and MA in 1828. He was admitted as a student to Lincoln's Inn on 19 May 1824 and called to the bar on 6 February 1829. Specializing as an equity draughtsman and conveyancer, he practised on the northern circuit, took silk in July 1844, and was involved in the investigation of the chancery commission of 11 December 1850. On 2 June 1829 he married Mary (*d.* 1858), daughter of Thomas Babington MP; they had several children, including two sons, Henry and Charles.

On 30 July 1847 Parker failed to win a seat in parliament as a Conservative candidate for Leicester. Although his opponents, Walmsley and Gardner, were later impeached for bribery, he did not again contest the seat. Notwithstanding his political opinions and connections (his father-in-law was MP for Leicester), the whig ministry made him vice-chancellor on 8 October 1851. He was knighted on 23 October of the same year.

A zealous advocate of chancery reform, Parker filled Lord Granworth's vacated seat with great ability and at once proved himself an excellent judge. He was known as patient and courteous, the most important case which he tried being *Lumley* v. *Wagner* (on the question of injunctions). Unfortunately, however, his career as a judge was cut short after only ten months in office by his death, from heart failure, at his home at Rothley Temple, Leicestershire, on 13 August 1852. He was buried in the adjoining chapel on 20 August. SINÉAD AGNEW

Sources Venn, *Alum. Cant.* • *GM*, 2nd ser., 38 (1852), 426 • W. P. Baildon, ed., *The records of the Honorable Society of Lincoln's Inn: admissions*, 2 (1896), 108 • Boase, *Mod. Eng. biog.* • Ward, *Men of the reign*, 700 • E. Foss, *Biographia juridica: a biographical dictionary of the judges of England … 1066–1870* (1870) • Foss, *Judges* • *Law Magazine*, 48 (1852), 321–2 • *ILN* (21 Aug 1852), 130, 222 • *ILN* (18 Sept 1852) [will details] • *Morning Chronicle* (16 Aug 1852), 5 • 'Report into the process, practice, and system of pleading in the court of chancery' (1852), vol. 21, no. 1437 [incl. suppl., p. 333, no. 1454] • *DNB*

Archives Lpool RO, corresp. • Mitchell L., Glas., Glasgow City Archives, corresp. • Trinity Cam., family corresp.

Wealth at death under £10,000: *GM*, 426

Parker, John (1532/3–1592), Church of England clergyman, is of unknown origins. A connection with Archbishop Matthew Parker is possible, but has yet to be demonstrated. He studied first at Peterhouse, Cambridge, but in 1552 migrated to Christ Church, Oxford, where he graduated BA on 26 January 1555, proceeding MA on 20 October 1558. On 28 January 1564 he was incorporated MA at Cambridge and was admitted to Peterhouse, where he is found as fellow-commoner during the following Michaelmas term. He proceeded DTh on 12 March 1583. In 1557 Parker had been collated to the rectory of Shipdham, Norfolk, but in 1560, at the collation of Richard Cox, bishop of Ely, he became rector of Fen Ditton, Cambridgeshire. At an unknown date not earlier than March 1565 he was further collated to the first prebend in Ely Cathedral, and on 21 October 1568 to the archdeaconry of Ely, to which the rectories of Haddenham and Wilburton were annexed.

In 1569 Parker married Winifred, daughter of William Turner, dean of Wells; they had several children, including the antiquary Richard *Parker. At about the same time Bishop Cox married Turner's widow. The family link thus created was advantageous to Parker, who on 24 September 1570 was collated by Cox to another Cambridgeshire rectory, that of Stretham, which he held until his death. He resigned Fen Ditton in 1571, but in 1573 received that of Bluntisham, Hertfordshire, also at Cox's hands, resigning it in 1585. In 1581 Parker was left money in Cox's will, but the story (apparently deriving from Thomas Fuller) that he was subsequently offered the bishopric, and refused it because of the scandalous conditions involved, is unlikely to be true.

Parker was the author of a primer entitled *A Pattern of Pietie, Meete for All Christian Housholdores*, which was published in the last weeks of his life. He died on 26 May 1592, aged fifty-nine, and was buried four days later in the chancel of Stretham church. STEPHEN WRIGHT

Sources Venn, *Alum. Cant.*, 1/3.306 • Foster, *Alum. Oxon.* • Cooper, *Ath. Cantab.*, 2.124 • *Fasti Angl.*, 1541–1857, [Ely] • A. Gibbons, ed., *Ely episcopal records: a calendar and concise view of the episcopal records preserved in the muniment room of the palace of Ely* (privately printed, Lincoln, 1891) • J. Strype, *Annals of the Reformation and establishment of religion … during Queen Elizabeth's happy reign*, new edn, 3 (1824) • *VCH Huntingdonshire*, 2.157 • T. A. Walker, *A biographical register of Peterhouse men*, 1 (1927), 241

Parker, John (*d.* 1656x8). *See under* Parker, John (*fl.* 1631–1680).

Parker, John (*d.* 1681), Church of Ireland archbishop of Dublin, was born in Dublin, the son of John Parker (*d.* 1643), Church of Ireland clergyman, and dean successively of Leighlin (1618–37) and of Killaloe (1637–43). He may have been the John Parker who was a scholar of Trinity College, Dublin, in 1636. He received deacon's orders in 1638, and in 1642 was made a minor canon of St Patrick's Cathedral, Dublin, and at some point he held the prebend of Rathangan, diocese of Kildare. In 1643 he was appointed prebendary of Maynooth, attached to St Patrick's Cathedral, a living once held by his father, and to which he was presented by Bishop Sibthorp of Limerick, to whom the advowson had been conceded by the earl of Kildare. He also became prebend of St Michan's, attached to Dublin's other cathedral, Christ Church, in 1643, again a post once held by his father, and succeeded him as dean of Killaloe, though he appears to have resided in Dublin during the war years and acted as chaplain to the lord lieutenant, the earl of Ormond. In 1649 the parliamentarian authorities stripped him of his ecclesiastical offices and imprisoned him as a suspected royalist spy, though Ormond secured his release in a prisoner exchange some months later. When Ormond left Ireland in 1650, Parker went to England and resided there until the Restoration, apparently continuing to use the prayer book in services.

Parker was one of the clergymen associated with Ormond who secured preferment in 1660, being nominated to the bishopric of Elphin on 6 August, and was one of the bishops consecrated in Dublin on 27 January 1661, being awarded a DD by the University of Dublin the previous day. He was on the committee of the Irish House of Lords which drafted the May 1661 declaration upholding the episcopal and prayer book basis of the Church of Ireland and requiring conformity thereto, though the same month he preached before the Irish parliament, apparently seeking to woo 'moderate' presbyterian opinion to a policy of protestant unity (Greaves, 67). By August 1661 he had been chosen, alongside the bishop of Cork, to present convocation's case on the ecclesiastical state of Ireland to the king, and he remained in London, agitating on such matters as Irish church property, until at least March 1662.

Parker had married Mary, daughter of Thomas Clarke of Fermoyle, co. Longford, and had at least one daughter, Mary (*d.* 1668), who in 1666 married Murrough Boyle, Viscount Blesington, son of the lord chancellor and future primate Michael Boyle. Parker was translated to the archbishopric of Tuam, with the attached sees of Annaghdown and Kilfenora, on 9 August 1667. In 1678 Ormond recommended him, 'a man of prudence, piety and courage', for the Irish primacy or for the archbishopric of Dublin, 'a considerable promotion' (*Ormonde MSS*, 6.147, 196). He was translated to the latter on 28 February 1679 and held a batch of other livings in combination with it, including the treasurership of St Patrick's Cathedral, the chancellorship of Clogher, and the prebend of Desertmore, diocese of Cork. He died at Dublin on 28 December 1681, and was buried three days later in Christ Church, within the communion rails.

J. T. Gilbert, *rev.* Jason Mc Elligott

Sources *The whole works of Sir James Ware concerning Ireland*, ed. and trans. W. Harris, 2 vols. in 3 (1739–45, [1746]) • J. D'Alton, *The memoirs of the archbishops of Dublin* (1838) • H. Cotton, *Fasti ecclesiae Hibernicae*, 6 vols. (1845–78) • A. Ford and others, eds., *As by law established: the Church of Ireland since the Reformation* (1995) • Burtchaell & Sadleir, *Alum. Dubl.*, 2nd edn • 'Blesington', GEC, *Peerage* • *CSP Ire.*, *1660–69* • *Calendar of the manuscripts of the marquess of Ormonde*, new ser., 8 vols., HMC, 36 (1902–20), vol. 6 • H. J. Lawlor, *The fasti of St Patrick's, Dublin* (1930) • R. L. Greaves, *God's other children: protestant nonconformists and the emergence of denominational churches in Ireland* (1997)

Archives Hunt. L., corresp.

Wealth at death left £132: will, D'Alton, *Memoirs of the archbishops*

Parker, John (*fl.* 1631–1680), judge, was son and heir of Richard Parker, of Shorne, Northfleet, Kent, a master of the Utter Bar and JP, and Priscilla, daughter of Robert Edolph of Hinxhill, Kent. Clark refers to a controversy between Thomas Digges and a John Parker in east Kent who may have been Parker's grandfather. Parker was admitted to the Middle Temple on 28 February 1631.

Parker was recorder of Gravesend, and gave a muted testimonial to a sequestered minister, Kenelm Manwaig, who had been resident minister for sixteen years at Gravesend since the 1630s. Parker says 'having himself lived at Gravesend divers years when the petitioner was minister he observed no evil in him' (*CSP dom.*, *1658–9*, 29). He was recorder by 1632, although he was not called to the bar until 8 June 1638. In 1646 Parker was writing to William Prynne about the Kentish committees and was himself then appointed to the county committee. Alan Everitt is therefore in error in considering him a newcomer to the county. On 16 April 1649 the council of state demanded the attendance of Mr Parker, recorder of Gravesend.

Parker was used by the council of state in a variety of sensitive cases relating to Kent, and became one of a small group of trusted local gentlemen. In 1653 he was one of the commission selling estates forfeited for treason, and was one of the trustees for the lands that belonged to the crown in 1635, and for the sale of forest lands and houses and parks which had belonged to the royal family. Even so he may not have been the John Parker made a militia commissioner for Kent on 7 May 1650 or the John Parker who was attempting to purchase the White House and gardens in Greenwich park.

Parker represented Rochester in the parliaments of 1654 and 1656, and when an upper house was formed he was summoned as an assistant. He was created a serjeant in 1655, when he joined the Fleet Street Inn. On 14 November 1655 petitions were to be discussed with the Lord Chief Baron, Serjeant Parker, and the counsel learned. He is subsequently listed as a serjeant-at-law and baron of the exchequer, but his formal appointment is dated 11 February 1656 (C 66/2914). By 1657 as baron he heads the list for the Kentish assessments and was concerned with issues of poor prisoners, prisoners in London, and deafforestation. In 1659 he was one of the judges to go on circuit. Parker was reappointed baron on 29 September 1658 by Richard Cromwell and by parliament from May 1659 to 30 June 1659, from 25 June 1659 to 20 November 1659, and on 19 January 1660, but he was removed at the Restoration although reappointed a serjeant. He survived various challenges to his judgments as baron and lived until the early 1680s, when his name disappears from the serjeants' lists.

This John Parker has often been confused with **John Parker** (*d.* 1656x8), judge, father of Samuel *Parker, bishop of Oxford. According to Anthony Wood this John Parker was one of the assistant committee men in Northamptonshire, of the high court of justice which tried Lord Capell, the earl of Holland, and the duke of Hamilton in 1649, and that on 22 June 1655 was sworn serjeant-at-law, 'being a member of one of the Temples' (*Life and Times*, 4.225). This John Parker was admitted to Gray's Inn in 1611 as of Weylond Underwood in Buckinghamshire, a mistranscription for Weston Underwood, where he still had property at his death. Bearing arms which were first granted to the Parkers of Fryth Hall, Essex, he was called to the bar on 26 June 1617, and followed the usual *cursus honorum*. In March 1647 he was appointed a judge of Brecknockshire and sent by the Commons to try the rioters in the county. Made a serjeant by parliament on 30 October 1648, he joined the Chancery Lane Serjeants' Inn. He was thereafter prominent in the Northamptonshire parliamentary commissions and in the Northampton quarter sessions. Parker's will, dated 24 December 1656, was not proved until 1668 after his daughter had obtained a writ of administration as for an intestate, but Northampton records show that he was dead by June 1658, when deeds were being executed to put into effect some clauses in that will.

Which John Parker wrote the *Government of the People of England, Precedent and Present* (1650) remains unclear.

Sybil M. Jack

Sources *The life and times of Anthony Wood*, ed. A. Clark, 4, OHS, 30 (1895), 255 • Foss, *Judges* • R. J. Fletcher, ed., *The pension book of Gray's Inn*, 2 vols. (1901–10) • Baker, *Serjeants* • J. Wake, ed., *Quarter sessions records of the county of Northampton* (1924) • P. Clark, *English provincial society from Reformation to revolution* (1977), 256 • *CSP dom.*, *1623–5* • R. Pocock, *History of Gravesend* (1797) • A. Everitt, *The community of Kent and the great rebellion, 1640–60* (1966) • *CSP dom.*, *1649–59* • C. H.

Firth and R. S. Rait, eds., *Acts and ordinances of the interregnum, 1642–1660*, 3 vols. (1911) • W. R. Douthwaite, *Gray's Inn: its history and associations* (1886) • will, PRO, PROB 11/326, sig. 52, fols. 407r–408v • PRO, E 159/498, Mich. rec. 14; C 231/6, p. 433; E 159/499, Trinity rec. 3; E 159/499, Hilary rot. 3

Archives Northants. RO, Northampton Library catalogue, NPL 2553, 2554 • PRO, chancery rolls, C 66/2914, C 231/6 • PRO, Exchequer Kings Remembrances memoranda roll, E 159/498, 499

Parker, John [*known as* Colonel Parker] (*b*. *c*.**1651**, *d*. in or after **1719**), army officer and Jacobite conspirator, was born in London, the youngest son of perhaps ten children of William Parker (1610–1678), physician, and Judith (*b*. 1619, *d*. after 1678), daughter of Roger Beckwith of Aldborough, Yorkshire. Parker's father, a gentleman farmer's son from Margate, Kent, had supported the roundhead cause as an administrator in Yorkshire and London, being commissioner of excise in 1650–54. John Parker was presumably, like his sister Eleutheria in 1644, baptized an Independent. As with many Restoration figures, his career was a reaction against such origins.

Parker claimed to have been an ensign at sixteen. He fought in the duke of Monmouth's infantry regiment in French service in the 1670s, during which time he was promoted captain (1676) and gained a lifelong distrust of French political aims. He returned home in 1678 and, after being captain in a short-lived regiment in 1678–9, he became a lieutenant in the Horse Guards (the equivalent rank) in 1681. Despite his later boasts of cavalier relatives, his parents and the Worcestershire family of his first wife (of four), Johanna Rouse (*b*. *c*.1646, *d*. after 1685), whom he married in 1674, had continuing nonconformist and roundhead links. His marriage produced at least three sons and one daughter. During the exclusion crisis he gained court favour by becoming a tory duelling bravo, most notably fighting and wounding Thomas Tollemache in 1682. His sex life, vigorous even for Restoration Whitehall, earned him the nickname 'the Towne Bull' (*Le Fleming MSS*, 276). During Monmouth's rebellion he fought well at Keynsham and Sedgemoor. In reward, he was made major of the earl of Arran's cavalry regiment, becoming its lieutenant-colonel in 1687.

Having followed James II to Ireland in 1689, Parker raised a new cavalry regiment, partly from English Catholics; several survivors joined in his later English plottings, including Robert Charnock and Robert Lowick. He trained them remarkably swiftly, though his financial extortions made him unpopular. At the battle of the Boyne in 1690, his was one of the four cavalry regiments which made repeated charges against the main Williamite attack. He was badly wounded, most of his officers were killed, and only thirty men escaped unhurt. He reappeared that winter in France as a brigadier-general, and served in Flanders in 1691. The confession of the sieur de Grandval, executed next year for an implausible plot to assassinate William there, implicated him deeply; but he apparently had alibis for the dates given.

During the 1692 French invasion attempt Parker, with his training abilities and northern links, and now a Roman Catholic (*pace* his great-nephew Speaker Arthur Onslow), was sent to command the cavalry regiments which the Lancashire Catholics had been organizing since 1689. Crossing to Kent in April, he was captured but escaped, and made his headquarters at Standish Hall, near Wigan. Parker recruited more cavalry and dragoon regiments in Lancashire, Yorkshire, and the north-east, finally commanding (theoretically) nine. His own regiment was divided between the north and London, where captains included Charnock, George Porter, Cardell Goodman, and, temporarily, Sir William Parkyns, with Lowick as its major. Parker corresponded with and supported James's extremist minister John, earl of Melfort. Having narrowly escaped capture in London in May 1693, he was arrested there on 21 May 1694 and sent to the Tower. The Benedictine monk Henry (Joseph) Johnston, his London arms supplier raised £300 to bribe the warders, and Parker escaped on 16 August and crossed to France. A £400 reward was offered for him. Meanwhile, investigation of a 'Lancashire plot' mixing falsehood and truth disrupted his regiments. He married his second wife, a Miss Trinder (*c*.1673–1696), during this mission; they had two sons.

Parker's return to England for the proposed 1696 rising was delayed by seniority disputes with his intended subordinate, Sir George Barclay. James, duke of Berwick, returning from London, met Parker in Kent and carried him back to France. Parker's story that Berwick's carelessness had endangered him was invented during later quarrels. His London captains, under Barclay, led the assassination plot of February 1696, and £1000 was offered for his capture.

Indirect Williamite pressure made the Jacobite court bar Parker from St Germain in 1698, and he resentfully made a first offer to defect. After James II's death, Parker's enemy Charles, earl of Middleton, had him imprisoned in the Bastille during 1702–4 on a wild charge of plotting to kidnap the young James III (James Francis Edward Stuart). Exiled thereafter to Chalons and Saumur with a small French pension, he several times during 1704–6 secretly proposed to a Huguenot spying for England to change sides and reconvert. About 1706 Parker's third wife, Marie Millenges, died. They probably had children, though further details are unknown. Recalled to St Germain and some favour in 1708, he married in 1711 (by then a major-general) Anne (*d*. in or after 1730), daughter of Sir Richard Bulstrode. Notwithstanding Parker's improved reputation at the Stuart court, when he attempted to return to England in 1713 with James's permission the French detained him at Amiens. He was not employed in the Jacobite rising of 1715, despite claiming to retain Lancashire and Yorkshire contacts, and lost his pension. Extreme poverty forced him in 1716 to retreat to Montargis. His begging and complaining letters cease in mid-1719, when William Dicconson, a former Lancashire subordinate, refused to relieve him, and he probably died soon after. His widow married the grandson of Sir Edward Hales, Jacobite earl of Tenterden.

Parker was a short, thin, fair, long-visaged man, soft-spoken and smiling, with a limp from his wound at the Boyne. He habitually exaggerated genuine past exploits when petitioning for help. Onslow imagined that he was driven by perverted loyalism, but Matthew Prior's 1698 summary, '"no purchase, no pay" is his motto and his interest is his principle' (*Bath MSS*, 3.295), seems juster. Some assassination plots against William of which he was accused were imaginary, but, even so, his persistent reappearance in this context seems suspicious.

Of Parker's two surviving sons by his first marriage, Gervase (1675–1750) escaped from him in France, entered the English army in 1695, and, with Williamite relatives' initial assistance, rose to be lieutenant-general and commander-in-chief in Ireland. Christopher (*c.*1678–1765) joined the navy in 1696 and became a superannuated rear-admiral in 1747. He was the father of Admiral Sir Peter *Parker (1721–1811). PAUL HOPKINS

Sources P. A. Hopkins, 'Aspects of Jacobite conspiracy in England in the reign of William III', PhD diss., U. Cam., 1981 • T. C. Porteus, ed., 'New light on the Lancashire Jacobite plot, 1692–4', *Transactions of the Lancashire & Cheshire Antiquarian Society*, 50 (1934–5), 1–62 • *State trials*, vols. 12–13 • *The manuscripts of S. H. Le Fleming*, HMC, 25 (1890) • *Calendar of the Stuart papers belonging to his majesty the king, preserved at Windsor Castle*, 7 vols., HMC, 56 (1902–23) • *Calendar of the manuscripts of the marquis of Bath preserved at Longleat, Wiltshire*, 5 vols., HMC, 58 (1904–80), vol. 3 • *Report on the manuscripts of Allan George Finch*, 5 vols., HMC, 71 (1913–2003), vol. 4 • F. Ravaisson, ed., *Archives de la Bastille*, 19 vols. (1866–1904), vol. 10 • N. Luttrell, *A brief historical relation of state affairs from September 1678 to April 1714*, 6 vols. (1857) • C. E. Lart, ed., *The parochial registers of St Germain en Laye: Jacobite extracts*, 2 vols. (1910–12) • *Bishop Burnet's History*, vol. 4 • Parker to Cardinal Gualtiero, BL, Add. MS 20310, fols. 157–8, 165–8, 192–7, 242–51 • J. Hunter, *Familiae minorum gentium*, ed. J. W. Clay, 4 vols., Harleian Society, 37–40 (1894–6), 3.1073–4 • J. Hunter, *South Yorkshire: the history and topography of the deanery of Doncaster …*, 2 vols. (1828–31), 1.303, 394 • J. D'Alton, *Illustrations historical and genealogical of King James's Irish army list (1689)*, 2nd edn, 2 vols. (1861), 1.246–70 • J. Parker, letter to duke of Shrewsbury, 7 Aug 1694, Northants. RO, Buccleuch papers, vol. 77, no. 49 [Sept.] • D. Nairne, journal, NL Scot., MS 14266, fols. 102*v*–106*v*

Archives BL, Gualtiero MSS, Add. MS 20310 • Royal Arch., Stuart MSS • Wigan Archive Services, Leigh, Lancashire, Standish MSS, Lancashire Plot papers

Wealth at death in debt

Parker, John (*d.* 1765), history painter, was probably from London, where his father lived for some years. He was said in 1764 to have spent twenty-three years in Rome, so he must have arrived there about 1740. In 1749, when he was living on the Corso, he tried unsuccessfully to succeed Mark Parker (*c.*1698–1775)—no relation—as the principal British antiquary in Rome. In 1752 'John Parker, History Painter' became director of the English Academy at Rome, an enterprise sponsored by the fourth Viscount Charlemont (later first earl of Charlemont) and his friends. It soon became 'an asylum for artistic scamps' (Waterhouse, 66) and, while Parker was laid up with an injury to his leg in Naples, Charlemont closed it down in 1755. Parker, however, continued as Charlemont's agent and secretary. There was a rancorous episode with Piranesi, who had promised to dedicate one of the plates in his *Antichità Romane* to Charlemont but who, following Parker's officious interference, withdrew his offer, and mischievously portrayed Parker as 'a fat fellow, with a swelled leg' (*Charlemont MSS*, 1.245).

As a painter, Parker was the pupil of Marco Benefial (*d.* 1764) in Rome. In 1754 he was elected to the Accademia del Disegno in Florence and in 1756 to the Accademia di San Luca in Rome. His unprepossessing altarpiece for the church of San Gregorio, Monte Celio, Rome, remains *in situ*, but his other works are known only through his letters. In May 1756 he had almost finished two subjects taken from Milton for Lord Charlemont and by October 1758 he had completed seven large classical history pieces. Parker acquired pictures, statuary, and medals for Charlemont's houses in Ireland, but a commission from Sir William Stanhope to buy pictures, received in May 1756, was withdrawn in February 1759. Parker then told Charlemont he was 'without friends or money … My condition is deplorable. If I stay here, I have no other prospect but misery' (*Charlemont MSS*, 1.252). Parker apparently stayed in Rome until at least 1761, the date inscribed on his portrait in the Accademia di San Luca, Rome, attributed to Benefial.

In 1763 Parker exhibited, at the Free Society in London from an address in Paddington, *His Own Portrait* (conceivably that ex Christies, 17 July 1992) and *The Assassination of David Rizzio*. He died soon after, his books being sold by Thomas Davies of Covent Garden in July and September 1764 and April and June 1765. A drawing by Parker, *The Death of Cleopatra*, dated Rome, 1748/9, is inscribed 'returned to England about the year 1762—Died at Paddington 1765' (British Museum). JOHN INGAMELLS

Sources *The manuscripts and correspondence of James, first earl of Charlemont*, 1, HMC, 28 (1891), 218–19, 221–8, 245–8, 250–54 • J. Ingamells, ed., *A dictionary of British and Irish travellers in Italy, 1701–1800* (1997), 738–40 • E. Edwards, *Anecdotes of painters* (1808); facs. edn (1970), 16 • E. K. Waterhouse, 'The British contribution to the neo-classical style in painting', *PBA*, 40 (1954), 57–74, esp. 66–7 • Paul Mellon Centre, London, Brinsley Ford archive • Vertue, *Note books*, 5.89 • *St James's Chronicle* (10–12 July 1764), 1

Archives Paul Mellon Centre for Studies in British Art, London, Brinsley Ford archive

Likenesses M. Benefial?, portrait, 1761, Accademia di San Luca, Rome • J. Parker, self-portrait; Christies, 17 July 1992, lot 67

Parker, John (*fl.* 1762–1776), landscape painter, of whose parents nothing is known, studied for some time in the duke of Richmond's gallery of casts in London. He then went to Chichester in 1765, where he studied under the brothers George and John Smith, landscape painters. On returning to London he lived in Stangate Lane, Lambeth, near Westminster Bridge. He exhibited still lifes, paintings of birds, and landscapes at the Free Society of Artists between 1762 and 1773 and won premiums for drawing from the Society of Artists in 1762–3. In 1768 he went to Rome, but had returned to London by 1770, when he exhibited a landscape at the Royal Academy. He exhibited again at the Royal Academy in 1771 and his name appears for the last time as a Royal Academy exhibitor in 1776. Between 1772 and 1775 he was again in Rome and was accompanied by his wife. He was 'the only English artist who had consented to have his child christened' (Ingamells, 739). He was elected to the Accademia del Disegno, Florence, on 12 January 1772. One of his landscapes, dated 1775, remains in the Accademia di San Luca, Rome. In 1776 he was living at 26 Portman Street, London.

L. H. CUST, *rev.* KATE RETFORD

Sources Redgrave, *Artists* • Waterhouse, *18c painters*, 266 • Graves, *Artists*, 210 • Graves, *RA exhibitors*, 6 (1906), 57 • M. H. Grant, *A dictionary of British landscape painters, from the 16th century to the early 20th century* (1952) • J. Ingamells, ed., *A dictionary of British and Irish travellers in Italy, 1701–1800* (1997) • Bryan, *Painters* (1903–5)
Likenesses attrib. M. Benefial, oils, Accademia di San Luca, Rome

Parker, John, first earl of Morley (1772–1840), politician, born on 3 May 1772, was the only son of John, first Baron Boringdon (*d.* 1788), and his second wife, Theresa, daughter of Thomas Robinson, first Baron Grantham. The family came originally from Warwickshire, but their seat was transferred from Boringdon to Saltram, near Plymouth, in the seventeenth century.

Parker succeeded his father, a former MP for Bodmin and Devon and a notable art connoisseur, in April 1788. In September 1788, aged sixteen, he entertained George III and Queen Charlotte at Saltram. He matriculated at Christ Church, Oxford, on 7 April 1789, and was created DCL on 18 June 1799. He was gazetted lieutenant-colonel of the North Devon militia on 1 June 1794, and colonel on 1 November 1799. He was elected FRS as early as 1795.

From an early age Boringdon took an active part in the debates in the House of Lords, and until the death of Pitt he supported the ministerial home and foreign policy. When, on 30 April 1800, Lord Holland moved to insert in the provisions for the union with Ireland a clause providing for the removal of Roman Catholic disabilities, he successfully opposed the proposal. After the death of Pitt he acted with Canning and claimed to have been Canning's earliest adherent in the House of Lords; they corresponded continually and intimately on political matters. Boringdon voted with the whigs in 1811 on Lansdowne's amendment for removing the restrictions on the regent, and on that relating to the removal of the officers of the household, both of which were carried by narrow majorities against ministers. On 19 March 1812 Boringdon, acting in concert with the whigs and moderate tories, moved an address to the regent for the formation of an efficient administration, the object in view being a coalition government, with Lord Wellesley as its chief. An amendment expressing general confidence in the government was carried by a large majority.

In the following session Boringdon introduced in the House of Lords a bill for more effectually preventing the spread of infection from smallpox by provisions for vaccination, but withdrew it after the first reading, on the representation of the lord chancellor that 'the alterations confessedly to be made by the noble lord were more numerous than the whole of the rest of the bill'. In 1814 he introduced a similar bill, but withdrew it on the lord chancellor's stating that the spread of infection was punishable at common law. In a speech delivered on the question of Catholic emancipation on 26 February 1810, whose substance was published the same year, he declared himself favourable to the principle of relief, and characterized the notion of indefinite postponement as 'absolutely horrible', but protested against concessions made in fear or owing to the convenience of the moment. On 29 November 1815 Boringdon was created earl of Morley and Viscount Boringdon. He supported the repressive measures of 1819, but opposed the bill of pains and penalties against Queen Caroline in all its stages. After Canning's death he drifted into whiggism and became a firm supporter of parliamentary reform.

John Parker, first earl of Morley (1772–1840), by John Downman, 1805

Morley not only made great improvements on his own Devon estate (the family bought the Morley estate just in time to use its name for the title), but also gave great assistance to public works in the neighbourhood. He received a gold medal from the Society of Arts, and another from the board of agriculture, for an embankment on the coast. At Catwater harbour he constructed dry docks and fixed moorings for ships, and a flying bridge connecting Plymouth and the adjoining country was due to his enterprise. Cyrus Redding describes Morley at the age of forty as a tall, well-proportioned man, with regular and handsome features, pallid complexion, and sedate physiognomy. He spoke French and Italian fluently, and had considerable taste in the fine arts. The hospitality of Saltram, the largest house in Devon, was lavish: when George III stayed there a hundred beds were made up.

Morley was married twice. On 20 June 1804 he married Lady Augusta Fane (*b.* 1786), the second daughter of the tenth earl of Westmorland. She despised her husband and eloped with Sir Arthur Paget on 18 May 1808, whom she married immediately after her husband divorced her in February 1809. Mrs Henry Wood's *East Lynne* (1861) was based on their romance. Morley and his first wife had one son, Henry (1806–1817), who died in Paris from swallowing a stalk of rye. Morley's second marriage, on 23 August 1809, was to Frances (*d.* 1857), daughter of Thomas Talbot, a surgeon, of Wymondham, Norfolk, with whom he had a son and a daughter. His second wife had 'beauty, virtue, talents, and temper' (Farington, *Diary*, 12 Oct 1809). Morley died at Saltram on 14 March 1840.

Morley's surviving son (from his second marriage), **Edmund Parker**, second earl of Morley (1810–1864), politician and courtier, was born on 10 June 1810, matriculated at Christ Church, Oxford, on 21 January 1828, and graduated BA on 11 November 1830. On 8 January 1845 he was gazetted colonel of the South Devon militia. In politics Morley was a Liberal, but, having been attacked by paralysis in early life, he was prevented from taking much part in public affairs. He was, however, gentleman of the bedchamber to Prince Albert (1840–41), and lord-in-waiting to the queen from 24 July 1846 to February 1852; in October 1852 he was appointed special deputy warden of the stannaries. He married, on 1 March 1842, his second cousin, Harriet Sophia (*d.* 1897), daughter of Montagu Edmund Parker of Whiteway, Chudleigh, Devon, and Harriet Newcombe of Starcross; she was the widow of William Coryton of Pentillie Castle, Cornwall. Their son and Morley's successor was Albert Edmund *Parker, third earl of Morley. Morley died on 28 August 1864.

G. Le G. Norgate, *rev.* H. C. G. Matthew

Sources GEC, *Peerage* • C. Redding, *Fifty years' recollections, literary and personal*, 2nd edn, 3 vols. (1858) • Farington, *Diary*

Archives BL, corresp., papers, and journals, Add. MSS 48218–48251 • BL, Morley MSS • Plymouth and West Devon RO, Plymouth [Edmund Parker] | Beds. & Luton ARS, corresp. with Frederick Robinson • BL, corresp. with Lord Holland, Add. MS 51598 • BL OIOC, letters to William Pitt Amherst, MS Eur. F 140 • Hants. RO, letters to Frederick Robinson • PRO, letters to first Earl Granville, PRO 30/29 • W. Sussex RO, letters to fifth duke of Richmond • W. Yorks. AS, Leeds, corresp. with A. G. Stapleton • Wilts. & Swindon RO, corresp. with Thomas Flindell

Likenesses J. Reynolds, oils, exh. RA 1773, Saltram House, Devon • J. Northcote, oils, *c.*1781, Melford Hall, Suffolk • J. Reynolds, double oils, 1781 (with his sister, Theresa), Saltram House, Devon • J. Downman, chalk and wash drawing, 1805, Saltram House, Devon [*see illus.*] • W. Say, mezzotint, pubd 1831 (after F. R. Say), BM • D. Gardner, gouache drawing (as a child), Saltram House, Devon • G. Hayter, group portrait, oils (*The trial of Queen Caroline, 1820*), NPG • J. Nollekens, marble bust; formerly at Saltram House, Devon • H. W. Phillips, portrait • F. R. Say, portrait • G. Stuart, oils (as a boy), Saltram House, Devon

Parker, John (1798–1860), architect, was born on 3 October 1798, the second son of Thomas Netherton Parker (*d.* 1854) of Sweeney Hall, Shropshire, and his wife, Sarah. He was educated at Eton College and at Oriel College, Oxford, where he matriculated on 31 January 1816, and graduated BA on 9 June 1820, before proceeding MA on 9 June 1825. He entered the church and on 7 November 1827 became rector of Llamyrewig in Montgomeryshire.

Parker had long been interested in architecture, and favoured the Early English style when adding a tower, south porch, and 'other embellishments' to his church (*GM*, 675). In 1830 he visited Palestine with his sister Mary, two years before her marriage to Sir Baldwin Leighton, bt, of Lotar Hall, Shropshire. Some of Parker's sketches are in the National Library of Wales. In 1835 he advised on the construction of Holy Trinity Church, Oswestry, to a budget of £3000–4000, acting as architect for the chancel and apse. In 1844 he became vicar of Llan-y-Blodwell, Shropshire, where he rebuilt the church at his own expense, not only using his own designs, but also carving the altarpiece himself. About 1858 he added a new school and master's house, also in the Early English style, which he regarded as the best for contemporary buildings 'if modified according to the practical requirements of the age' (ibid.).

Parker was local secretary of the Cambrian Archaeological Association, a knowledgeable botanist, and a skilful draughtsman: he drew flowers as well as landscapes and architectural subjects. He demonstrated his enthusiasm for the countryside and architecture in writing *The Passengers* (a dialogue between three tourists in north Wales), first published in the *Cambrian Quarterly Magazine*, and then in 1831 as a volume illustrated with engravings from his own drawings. Parker died at his vicarage, Llan-y-Blodwell, on 13 August 1860. At the time of his death he was rural dean of Llangollen, and was the owner of the Sweeney Hall estate, which he inherited from his father or elder brother in 1854.

M. A. Goodall

Sources Boase, *Mod. Eng. biog.* • *GM*, 3rd ser., 9 (1860), 675 • Allibone, *Dict.* • *A compendium of Pevsner's Buildings of England*, ed. M. Good (1995) [CD-ROM] • J. Parker, *The passengers* (1831) • Foster, *Alum. Oxon.* • *CGPLA Eng. & Wales* (1860) • *IGI* • Mallalieu, *Watercolour artists*

Wealth at death under £9000: resworn probate, Feb 1861, *CGPLA Eng. & Wales* (1860)

Parker, John (1799–1881), politician, the eldest son of Hugh Parker (*d.* 1861) of Tickhill, near Doncaster, and Mary, the eldest daughter of Samuel Walker of Masborough, Yorkshire, was born at Woodthorpe, near Sheffield, on 21 October 1799, and was educated at Repton School. He matriculated from Brasenose College, Oxford, on 6 March 1817, graduated BA 1820, and MA 1823. He was called to the bar at Lincoln's Inn on 1 July 1824, and went on the northern circuit.

Parker was whig MP for Sheffield from December 1832 until July 1852, when he was defeated by J. A. Roebuck and George Hadfield. He served as a lord of the Treasury from 18 July 1837 to 23 June 1841, as first secretary of the Admiralty from 9 June 1841 to 10 September 1841, as joint secretary of the Treasury from 7 July 1846 to 22 May 1849, and again as secretary of the Admiralty from 21 May 1849 to 3 March 1852. He was sworn of the privy council in 1854.

Parker married, on 8 February 1853, Charlotte Eliza, the second daughter of George Vernon of Clontarf Castle, Dublin. No children have been traced. He died at his home, 71 Onslow Square, London, on 5 September 1881, and was buried at Healaugh, near Tadcaster. His wife survived him. G. C. BOASE, *rev.* H. C. G. MATTHEW

Sources *The Times* (7 Sept 1881) • *Law Times* (1 Oct 1881), 366 • J. Haydn, *The book of dignities: containing rolls of the official personages of the British empire* (1851)

Archives Borth. Inst., corresp. with Sir Charles Wood • Claydon House, Buckinghamshire, letters to W. E. Nightingale • Notts. Arch., letters to E. V. Pegge Burnell; corresp.

Wealth at death £100,271 0*s*. 8*d*.: probate, 5 Nov 1881, *CGPLA Eng. & Wales*

Parker, John [*formerly* Jacob Solomons] (**1875–1952**), theatre historian, was born Jacob Solomons in New York on 28 July 1875, the only child of David Solomons and his wife, Florence Joel. His father was a native of Warsaw, but all family links with Poland were lost after his death by drowning in 1881; some sources described him as a sailor, though for his marriage certificate his son recorded his occupation as cashier in an insurance office. The widow, who had been born in Cardiff, decided to return to the United Kingdom where some of her family still lived; choosing to keep both her son and her independence, she took the post of caretaker at Clarence Chambers, King William Street, in the City of London, and enrolled her son at the Whitechapel foundation school, where he was a fellow pupil of Herman Finck.

After a short period as an office boy Jacob Solomons accepted the offer of a commercial acquaintance to return to the United States to improve his prospects, but within a few months he found himself stranded and obliged to work his passage back to England. It was about this time that he decided, on the advice of his mother, to adopt the name John Parker, which he legalized in 1917. While working as a commercial clerk he married, on 8 February 1899, Edith Maud Pizey (1875/6–1942), daughter of Montague Belfield Pizey, schoolmaster. They had a daughter and a son.

There is evidence that between the years 1892 and 1903, while employed in various capacities, Parker had made a start in journalism; he soon became sufficiently well informed on theatrical matters to be able to write to the eminent critic Clement Scott of the *Daily Telegraph* and point out errors of fact where they occurred in his columns. This enthusiasm and passion for accuracy appealed to Scott, who allowed the boy the pleasure of carrying his copy to the newspaper office, encouraged his talent for research, and from 1900 published regular contributions from him in his weekly paper the *Free Lance*. In 1903 Parker was appointed London manager, critic, and correspondent of the *New York Dramatic News*, a post which he held for seventeen years, and in the same year he was made the London correspondent of the *New York Dramatic Mirror*. From 1901 until his death, Parker managed to divide his time between his business as a shipping agent and his work for the theatre which was his first love.

During the nineteenth century several reference works of dramatic biography appeared, but none of these was to reach more than two issues. For the 1907 edition of the *Green Room Book* Parker was invited to provide additional information for the biographies and to contribute the entire section on the American theatre. He then succeeded as editor but was able to bring out only two more editions (1908 and 1909) before it came to an end with the death of the publisher.

Parker's reputation as a theatre historian had by this time become well established, and in 1912 Sir Isaac Pitman & Sons published his new venture, *Who's Who in the Theatre*. The success of the very first edition brought from Sir Herbert Beerbohm Tree the commendation 'As a monument of industry, *Who's Who in the Theatre* seems to me to be absolutely pyramidal. … It is a work which assuredly deserves the gratitude of everyone connected with the theatre'. Over a period of forty years, until his death, and surviving the publishing hazards of two world wars, Parker compiled eleven editions of his *Who's Who* almost single-handed, an astonishing achievement in view of the ever-expanding spheres of the theatre with the growth of the cinema and television. His success as an editor lay in the accuracy and balance of his records. The motto which headed his editorial stationery, *Sine timore, aut favore*, indicated his inflexible rule, a rule which made him a number of enemies in the profession, principally by his refusal to allow his subjects to falsify their ages. It is conceivable that the unsolved mystery of the burglary of his study in September 1928 was the work of some aggrieved actor. All Parker's notes and all the copy for his sixth edition, then ready for press, were stolen. After his first shock had subsided, he rewrote in his own hand all the new material, including more than 450 new biographies.

Parker also found time to give active support to the Critics' Circle, of which he was a founder member, honorary secretary (1924–52), and in one year president. In 1937 he represented the Critics' Circle as British delegate at the International Congress of Critics in Paris. He was also the honorary editor of the *Critics' Circular*.

With little time to spare for the more conventional recreations, Parker had one passing hobby and one sport, albeit as a spectator. He was an accomplished illuminator, and spent many a Sunday morning, during 1905 and 1906, in nightshirt, silk dressing gown, and smoking cap, designing and carrying out, in all their elaborate colour and gold leaf, two 'vellums' for presentation to Lionel Brough and Ellen Terry, respectively, on the celebration of their stage jubilees. His enthusiasm for cricket—he was a member of the Surrey County Cricket Club—was lifelong, but chiefly as a spectator.

Parker was fastidious in both dress and speech. At one time he took lessons in elocution and delighted in imparting what he had learned to his family. His son by his first marriage produced a twelfth edition of *Who's Who in the Theatre* in 1957. In 1944 Parker married, second, Doris Mary, daughter of George Sinclair. He died in a nursing home, 9 Westbourne House, Richmond Road, Twickenham, Middlesex, on 18 November 1952, and was cremated at Mortlake crematorium in London on 24 November.

FREDA GAYE, *rev.*

Sources *The Times* (20 Nov 1952) • J. Parker, ed., *The green room book, or, Who's who on the stage* (1909) • private information (1971) • m. cert.

Parker, John Henry (1806–1884), writer on architecture and publisher, was born at his parents' home, 157 Strand, London, on 1 March 1806, the son of John Parker, businessman, and his wife, Caroline Elizabeth Ryder. He was educated at the Manor House School, Chiswick, and in 1821 was apprenticed to his uncle Joseph Parker, bookseller and publisher, who was in partnership with W. Hanwell in Turl Street, Oxford. Joseph Parker acted as agent for the university Bible Press from *c.*1814, and also secured the agency for the sale of books on the learned side of the university press, an agreement which continued to 1862. John Henry Parker matriculated as 'bibliopola privilegiatus' on 4 February 1832, enabling him to trade as a bookseller in Oxford, and following the retirement in that year of his uncle he took over the business in Turl Street, which had in 1823 expanded to include a further shop in Broad Street. Under his direction from 1832 to 1847 the business was styled 'John Henry Parker, Broad Street, Oxford', and during this period he continued to act as agent for the university press. The business expanded in 1847 to include a printing office in Crown Yard, and a London house, which was opened at 377 Strand. Between 1847 and 1855 the firm was styled 'John Henry Parker (Oxford and London)'; in 1850 a warehouse was taken in Paradise Square. Parker married Frances Mary, daughter of J. W. Hoskyns, fellow of Magdalen College, Oxford, and rector of Appleton, Berkshire; they had a son, James Parker (1833–1912), whom he took into partnership from 1855 until his retirement in 1866. During this period, the firm was styled 'John Henry and James Parker, Oxford and London'. In 1862 John Henry retired from active work and the agency for the university press was transferred to Macmillan & Co. James Parker took over the business, which was then styled 'James Parker & Co., Oxford and London'.

For the prime movers of the Oxford Movement, John Henry Newman, Edward Pusey, and John Keble, Parker published from 1834 numerous *Tracts*, writings on Anglo-Catholicism, and the libraries of the early fathers. He was strongly sympathetic to the Tractarian movement, particularly as it related to ecclesiology. He was a friend of Cardinal Newman. A local journalist recorded that concerning 'Newman's reply to the Protest made by the "Four Tutors" against the famous Tract &c … both the Protest and the reply were forwarded through Mr. Parker, and even after the fateful Oct 9, 1845, when at Littlemore Dr Newman renounced allegiance to the Anglican Church … the great Cardinal's friendship with Mr. Parker was maintained' (H. Painting, 'Some famous Oxford booksellers', *Oxford Chronicle*, 30 Jan 1914).

Parker's main interest was historic architecture and in 1836 he published *A Glossary of Terms used in Grecian, Roman, Italian, and Gothic Architecture*, which went through five editions by 1850 and ten by 1900. An abridged form, *A Concise Glossary*, was reprinted many times between 1846 and 1896. In 1841 he issued *A Companion to … a Glossary of Terms used in Gothic Architecture*, which was followed, in the field of local history, by *A Guide to the Architectural Antiquities in the Neighbourhood of Oxford* (1842), *A Handbook for Visitors to Oxford* (1847), *The Medieval Architecture of Chester* (1858), and *The Architectural Antiquities of the City of Wells* (1866). His *Dictionary of Architecture* (3rd edn, 1840) and his editing in 1848 of the fifth edition of Thomas Rickman's *An Attempt to Discriminate the Styles of English Architecture from the Conquest to the Reformation* (1817; 7th edn, 1881), together with his own *Introduction to the Study of Gothic Architecture* (1849), led *The Bookseller* to declare that Parker had 'done more, perhaps, to popularize a knowledge of architecture in this country, than any other Englishman' (*The Bookseller*, 133, 1 Feb 1869, 105). Several of these works included illustrations by the engraver Orlando Jewitt, who resided at Old Headington, Oxford. His firm also published the popular series of Oxford Classics.

On 7 June 1849 he was elected FSA, and between 1851 and 1855 he contributed to the *Archaeologia* a series of papers on 'Ancient churches in the west of France'. Among his other contributions to the *Archaeologia* he regarded as the most important 'The English origin of Gothic architecture' (*Archaeologia*, 43, 1813, 273) and 'The architectural history of St. Hugh's choir in Lincoln Cathedral' (*Archaeologia*, 47, 1817, 41). In 1851 he edited and published Thomas Hudson Turner's *Some Account of Domestic Architecture in England*, from the Norman conquest to the end of the thirteenth century, a work which Parker himself continued, from Edward I to Richard II, and published in 1853.

Parker knew Sir Stephen Glynne and W. E. Gladstone; the latter had frequented his bookshops while an undergraduate at Christ Church, and later recommended Parker to be Queen Victoria's guide for knowledge of Windsor Castle. Parker stayed at the deanery at Windsor 'working up the subject', but when he became ill with rheumatic fever his duties were transferred to another and in 1866 he went to Rome for his health. He was able to pursue his interest in Roman archaeology and founded the British Archaeological Society in Rome. His studies of ancient remains resulted in *Mosaic Pictures in Rome and Ravenna* (1866) and *The Archaeology of Rome* (1874–6). He also supervised production of *A Catalogue of 3,300 Historical Photographs of Antiquities in Rome and Italy*, which he published in several series between 1867 and 1879; a revised and enlarged edition appeared in 1883.

The scholarly reception of Parker's writings on Rome was more critical. They were censured by John Henry Middleton, in *The Remains of Ancient Rome* (1892), as containing baseless theories and inaccuracy, and in his review of Parker's *Via sacra* in *The Academy* (23 February 1884, 136) Henry Francis Pelham considered Parker uncritical in his handling of ancient authorities and too ready to treat legend as history. Despite his undoubted architectural knowledge, Parker's zeal for the restoration rather than preservation of ancient buildings, so much opposed by John Ruskin, was sometimes considered over-enthusiastic and to have had a less than beneficial influence (*The Athenaeum*, 9 Feb 1884, 191). His pirating of editions of other authors' work, notably John Britton's *Dictionary of the*

Architecture and Archaeology of the Middle Ages (1831–8), also attracted criticism.

On 27 June 1867 the University of Oxford conferred on Parker an honorary MA. In 1869 he endowed the keepership of the Ashmolean Museum, Oxford, with a sum yielding £250 a year and was appointed its first keeper in 1870, a post he retained until his death; his inaugural lecture on 2 November 1870 on the museum's history was noticed in *Notes and Queries* (4th ser., 6, 1870, 429).

Parker was vice-president of the Oxford Architectural Society, and of the British and American Archaeological Society of Rome, and for many years participated in the annual congresses of the Archaeological Institute. He was made CB (civil division), on Gladstone's recommendation, on 30 October 1871. Abroad, he was a member of the Société des Antiquaires de Normandie, the Société Française d'Archéologie, and the Société Française pour la Conservation des Monuments. For his Roman researches Parker was decorated by Umberto I, king of Italy, created a knight of the Italian order of SS. Maurizio e Lazzaro in April 1869, and was awarded a gold medal by Pope Pius IX.

Parker died, aged seventy-seven, at his home, 21 Turl Street, Oxford, on 31 January 1884, and was buried in St Sepulchre's cemetery at Jericho, Oxford, on 5 February. He left an estate valued at just over £12,500.

RICHARD RIDDELL

Sources Allibone, *Dict.* • *Men of the time* (1875) • Boase, *Mod. Eng. biog.* • *The Bookseller* (1 Feb 1869), 105 • *The Athenaeum* (9 Feb 1884), 191 • H. F. Pelham, 'Parker's *The via sacra*', *The Academy* (23 Feb 1884), 136–7 • J. H. Middleton, *The remains of ancient Rome* (1892) • N. Pevsner, 'The Cambridge Camden Society and the ecclesiologists', *Some architectural writers of the nineteenth century* (1972), 123–33 • *N&Q*, 4th ser., 6 (1870), 429 • *IGI* • *CGPLA Eng. & Wales* (1884) • F. Madan, 'Papers relating to the Parkers of Oxford', 1914, Bodl. Oxf., 2581 f.1 • C. J. Parker, *The Parkers of Oxford* (1914)

Archives BL, corresp. with W. E. Gladstone, Add. MS 44270 • Bodl. Oxf., letters and bills to Sir T. Phillipps • Limerick University Library, letters to third earl of Dunraven

Likenesses wood-engraving, NPG; repro. in *ILN* (16 Feb 1884)

Wealth at death £12,523 11*s*. 10*d*.: probate, 10 April 1884, *CGPLA Eng. & Wales*

Parker, John Oxley (1812–1887). *See under* Parker, Christopher Comyns (1774–1843).

Parker, John William (1792–1870), publisher and printer, was the son of John Parker, an army officer. He began working for the London printer William Clowes in childhood and was formally apprenticed to him at fourteen. On completing that apprenticeship in 1813 he remained with Clowes as an accountant. About 1818 he married; the couple were to have two sons and two daughters. Both sons were to join him in the printing business. When the duke of Northumberland complained that Clowes's new-fangled steam-driven press was a nuisance and bought him out, Clowes moved from Northumberland Court, the Strand, to Duke Street, London, taking over premises and equipment formerly belonging to Augustus Applegarth, the improver of Friedrich Koenig's steam press.

Placed in charge of the new operation, Parker developed a reputation for sound management that soon reached Cambridge University Press, which had fallen behind its counterpart at Oxford. In 1828 Parker was sent by Clowes to Cambridge, where, as *de facto* superintendent of the press, he thoroughly modernized all aspects of its operation. In 1832 Parker left Clowes to found a publishing firm in his own name, John W. Parker, at 445 Strand, London. Besides retaining his Cambridge assignment, which included the publication of classical, mathematical, and theological textbooks, Parker was immediately appointed as an official publisher of the Society for Promoting Christian Knowledge (SPCK). Under SPCK auspices Parker inaugurated in July 1832 the penny per copy *Saturday Magazine*, intended to counter disreputable journals directed at the poorer classes.

On 15 November 1836 Parker was elected official printer to the University of Cambridge, following the retirement of John Smith. He held the post until 1854 at an annual salary of £400. His most famous book in this capacity was William Whewell's *Philosophy of the Inductive Sciences* (1847). Many of the titles he printed for Cambridge included cheap (because done on steam-powered presses) editions of the Bible, the Book of Common Prayer, and other religious works. The Bible Society at Cambridge originally objected to such inexpensive editions, but the quality and popularity of Parker's eventually changed their minds. At William IV's request, Parker also designed and published the red-ruled 'King's Bible', which was a great success.

In 1843 Parker's son John William Parker (1820–1860), educated at King's College, Cambridge, joined his father's firm—which became John W. Parker & Sons—as general manager. Within a few years his mother and his brother Frederick were dead. On 12 February 1848 at Holy Trinity Church, Islington, London, his father married Ellen Maria Mantell (*b*. 1818), daughter of the well-known geological writer Gideon Algernon Mantell (1790–1852); they were to have a son and two daughters. The firm's name was changed again, to John W. Parker & Son. Its authors included Charles Kingsley (*Yeast* and *Hypatia*), Richard Chenevix Trench, Sir Arthur Helps, F. D. Maurice, and John Stuart Mill (*On Liberty* and *Utilitarianism*). Under the management of the younger Parker, John W. Parker & Son became a bastion within the London publishing establishment of liberal Christianity, and eventually of Christian socialism. One major expression of the new stance was a significantly realigned *Fraser's Magazine for Town and Country*, under the editorship of Parker junior, begun in July 1847. Its most effective authors included Henry Thomas Buckle, Carlyle, Kingsley, Lewes, Mill, Maurice, Ruskin, and Tennyson.

On 6 May 1848 John W. Parker & Son published the first issue of *Politics for the People*, a monthly journal of sixteen pages intended for lower- and middle-class readers. Its appearance marked the beginning of the Christian socialist movement. The journal's position was that the exploitation of the lower classes by supposedly Christian capitalists was fundamentally contradictory. It ceased publication in June, lacking subscriber support.

Parker's concern for the availability of books to lower-income households made him one of the leading figures in the free-trade controversy of 1852. In May of that year he solicited, compiled, edited, and published *The Opinions of Certain Authors on the Publishing Question*, composed of one hundred eminent authors' views as to whether or not the 'underselling' of books below the established retail price was desirable. They responded overwhelmingly in the affirmative and restrictions on printing were eliminated later in the year.

John W. Parker & Son published none of the major Victorian novels except those of Kingsley. The firm's most notorious non-fiction book, *Essays and Reviews* (1860), developed from its *Oxford and Cambridge Essays*, published annually from 1855 to 1859. *Essays and Reviews* had no named editor. In it seven contributors, all but one of them clergy, argued that traditional Christianity must accept the so-called higher criticism of the Bible and the implications of modern natural science, particularly those of geology. The controversy surrounding its publication was intense. A letter condemning the book was signed by every Anglican bishop in Great Britain, and two of the contributors were suspended from their clerical duties until reinstated by the privy council.

In the midst of this turmoil the younger John W. Parker died on 9 November 1860. His father had just taken a long-time employee, William Butler Bourn, into partnership, but Parker, Son, and Bourn lasted only three years, being sold to Longmans in 1863 for £20,000. Following the sale of his firm, Parker entered into partnership with Thomas Richard Harrison as printers in St Martin's Lane. Their arrangement continued until Parker's death from bronchitis at his home, Warren Corner House, near Farnham, Surrey, on 18 May 1870. He was buried in Highgate cemetery, Middlesex. At once high-minded and practical, Parker was of major consequence as a social and religious reformer. DENNIS R. DEAN

Sources D. R. Dean, 'John W. Parker', *British literary publishing houses, 1820–1880*, ed. P. J. Anderson and J. Rose, DLitB, 106 (1991), 233–6 · H. Curwen, *A history of booksellers, the old and the new* (1873), 317–24 · J. J. Barnes, *Free trade in books: a study of the London book trade since 1800* (1964) · S. C. Roberts, *A history of the Cambridge University Press* (1921) · S. C. Roberts, *The evolution of Cambridge publishing* (1956) · *The Bookseller* (1 June 1870), 491–2 · I. Ellis, *Seven against Christ: a study of 'Essays and reviews'* (1980) · m. cert. · d. cert.

Archives U. St Andr. L., corresp. with James David Forbes · UCL, letters to Society for the Diffusion of Useful Knowledge

Likenesses lithograph (after daguerreotype), BM, NPG

Wealth at death under £40,000: probate, 11 June 1870, *CGPLA Eng. & Wales*

Parker, Joseph (1830–1902), Congregational minister, was born on 9 April 1830 in the Market Place, Hexham, Northumberland, the only child of Teasdale Parker, stonemason, and Elizabeth Dodd, his wife. He was educated at local schools. At fourteen years of age he was set to learn his father's craft, but soon tired of it and was sent back to school. Until he was twenty-one years old he devoted himself, as he said, to 'self-culture'. The Congregational church where his father was a deacon was divided over the introduction of evangelical Arminian ideas by the new minister, James Frame, and the stricter Calvinists,

Joseph Parker (1830–1902), by Sir Emery Walker

including Teasdale Parker, withdrew and (somewhat incongruously) joined the Methodist church.

During his youth Joseph Parker was fascinated by the ideas and speeches of such radical reformers as Edward Miall (1809–1881) and Joseph Cowen (1800–1873). From the age of fourteen Parker had participated in local debates and boys' meetings, but it was as a supporter of the temperance movement that he was given his first opportunity to exercise his gifts in public. In June 1848 he preached his first sermon on the village green and was enrolled as a lay preacher in the Methodist circuit. The family returned to the Congregational church and Parker felt that he was called into the Christian ministry. He wrote for guidance to Dr John Campbell (1794–1867) of Whitefield's Tabernacle, Moorfields, and in his reply Campbell invited him to preach at his church for three Sundays. He left home for London on 8 April 1852. Such was the impression that he made that he was appointed assistant minister.

After Parker had spent nine months in London, where he attended lectures at University College, he accepted a call to the Congregational church at Banbury, where he was ordained minister on 8 November 1853. The congregation, initially of fifty members, soon became too large for the building and a new church had to be built. Parker also caused some consternation and some physical danger to himself by initiating open-air services on the cricket ground. He drew wider attention by challenging the formidable secularist George Jacob Holyoake (1817–1906), and holding his own against him in public debate. It was at Banbury, too, that he began to publish books and articles, an activity that he was to continue vigorously throughout his career.

Among the numerous churches that now sought his services it was the prestigious Cavendish Street Congregational Church, Manchester, that persuaded Parker to become its minister. He accepted its call on 10 June 1858 and began his ministry at the end of the following month. Success attended him again and by 1863 there were over 1000 members in the church, including many wealthy leaders of commerce and industry. All 1700 seats in the church were occupied at the Sunday services.

On 1 October 1860 courses began at Cavendish College (later the Nottingham Congregational Institute), founded by Parker to provide basic training for men who had been deprived of educational opportunities. He shared the teaching with J. B. Paton and J. Radford Thomson of Heywood. After a clash over the expulsion of a student, Parker withdrew from teaching before the end of the first session and resigned from the board of management in 1862.

On 19 September 1869 Parker began his ministry at the oldest nonconformist church in London, the Poultry Chapel, Cheapside. It was not in a flourishing condition but was soon filled with eager congregations. On 23 September he began to hold a lunchtime service for city workers on Thursdays. Average attendance exceeded one thousand, and it attracted people of all denominations and made a significant contribution to ecumenical understanding, despite the fact that prominent Anglicans were officially inhibited from accepting his invitations to address the congregations. It continued for thirty-two years. From 1871 until 1874 he conducted an institute of homiletics to improve the standard of preaching. Parker's success made a new building necessary. The Poultry Chapel was sold for £50,000 and the last service was held there on 16 June 1872. Services continued in temporary accommodation until the new church, erected at Holborn Viaduct and known, significantly, as the City Temple, was dedicated on 19 May 1876. Its marble pulpit was the gift of the corporation of the City of London. Here Parker ministered for the remainder of his life. The City Temple became the most powerful centre of nonconformist influence in the city and indeed far beyond, not least in the United States, a country which Parker visited five times. It was this transatlantic influence that prompted Dr T. L. Cuyler's dictum that 'the back galleries of the City Temple were in the Rocky Mountains' (Adamson, 126).

In 1867 Parker was chair of the Lancashire Congregational Union and was twice elected chair of the Congregational Union of England and Wales, in 1884 and 1901. Between 5 and 8 February 1887 he was in Edinburgh where he lectured and preached at several venues, including the church of St Giles, and he was in Scotland again from 30 July to 16 August 1888 conducting a preaching mission. Then in May 1894 he addressed the general assembly of the Free Church of Scotland and spoke to the thousand ministers who were present on his objections to the higher criticism of the Bible. By these visits he became a familiar name to the Scots. In 1862 he was granted an honorary DD from the University of Chicago. On 4 October 1887, while on a visit to the United States, he delivered at the Brooklyn Academy of Music the eulogy on his friend Henry Ward Beecher, who had died on 8 March 1887, and that event, he confessed, 'was the most memorable public occasion in which I have taken part' (Adamson, 192). His enthusiastic reception on his various visits to the United States sparked off rumours that he would be invited to succeed Beecher. But Parker had no thought of emigrating.

Parker's consistent interest in contemporary politics led him to publish a manifesto as a parliamentary candidate for the City of London in the general election of March 1880. In it he supported disestablishment of the Church of England, abolition of the traffic in liquor, and an extension of peasant proprietorship of land. Although 1200 electors had promised their support, Samuel Morley MP (1809–1886) and others persuaded him to withdraw his name, which he did.

Parker was twice married. On 15 November 1851, at Hexham Congregational Church, he married Ann, the daughter of William Nesbitt, farmer, of Horsley. She died in 1863. A stained-glass window was erected in her memory at Horsley Congregational Church in 1899. On 22 December 1864 Parker married Emma Jane, daughter of Andrew Common JP, banker, of Sunderland. She died on 26 January 1899 and was buried at Hampstead cemetery. In her memory stained-glass windows were installed at City Temple and Union Congregational Church, Sunderland. At Sunderland, too, Parker founded in her memory the Parker Memorial Home for Girls. He never recovered from this bereavement and confessed that he did not find it unfitting to pray to her. There were no children. Parker died at his home at 14 Lyndhurst Gardens, Hampstead, on 28 November 1902 after a debilitating illness and was buried at Hampstead cemetery.

Parker was a prolific author and his published books amount to more than sixty titles. He also wrote a large number of articles and edited journals. His attempt to launch a daily newspaper, *The Dial* (1860–64), failed. His most ambitious publication was *The People's Bible* (1885–95), which ran to twenty-five volumes and consists of the material used in his sermons over a period of years. *Ecce Deus* (1867) was a reply to J. R. Seeley's *Ecce homo* (1865). His *Six Chapters on Secularism* (1854) represents his polemics against the kind of views espoused by Holyoake. His interest in improving the standard of preaching is demonstrated in *Ad clerum: Advices to a Young Preacher* (1870). Bible exposition was a passionate interest of his and permeates most of his writing. *Tyne Chylde: my Life and Teaching* (1883) and *A Preacher's Life* (1899) are autobiographical. His ineffectual attempts at fiction are seen in *Springdale Abbey* (1868) and *Weaver Stephen* (1886). Most of what he published soon sank into oblivion. His verbose and overheated prose proved not to be to the taste of a later generation, while his biblical studies, although often perceptive and moving, suffered from the lack of a firm basis in scholarly precision. Even so, his *Pulpit Bible* (1901) found a welcome in many churches.

Parker was a communicator of genius. The huge congregations that he attracted in England, Scotland, and the United States testified to a rare ability to make the Christian message relevant to his own generation. It put him in the front rank of English preachers. It is not easy for a later generation to account for his influence. In theology he was an evangelical, but not of a dogmatic kind. When C. H. Spurgeon initiated the 'downgrade controversy', Parker commented that Spurgeon's hostility to theological change showed lack of trust in God's providence, and to believe that the age was in decline was to be an atheist (*The Freeman*, Aug 1887). He combined his fairly conservative theological emphasis with a passionate Liberalism in politics. His leonine head and bold stance gave him an imperious presence in the pulpit. Most of his preaching was extemporary, and that enticed him to make unexpected outbursts that both astonished and attracted his congregations, as in his imprecation, 'I say, God damn the Sultan', delivered in his address on the tercentenary of the birth of Oliver Cromwell, 25 April 1899, or his assertion that 'the Stock Exchange is the bottomless pit of London', which came in his tirade against gambling in 1900. His sonorous voice, with its surprising modulations, as well as his dramatic delivery, his humour, his use of dialect, and his freshness, combined to make his oratory unique in the London of his day. Added to this were the puzzling contradictions in his personality. He could be brusque and gentle, sarcastic and mellifluous, full of self-esteem and yet dependent on the kindness and even flattery of those about him.

Parker's career illustrates powerful tendencies in Victorian nonconformity. He began as a radical and republican, but as he came more into contact with rich and influential people he developed into a defender of the social and economic establishment as well as the monarchy. Although claiming to be a defender of Congregationalism in its stricter Independent form, in his speeches from the chair of the Congregational Union in 1901 he advocated a centralized form of Congregationalism. The plans he advocated aroused controversy, but he seems to have been intent on creating a united nonconformist church that would eventually embrace all denominations and be able to compete for social and religious pre-eminence with the Church of England. In his development he embodies the ambition to transform dissent into a powerful movement that would be socially respectable, morally influential, spiritually prophetic, and politically powerful. It was to be an unfulfilled hope.

R. TUDUR JONES

Sources W. Adamson, *The life of the Rev. Joseph Parker, DD* (1902) • J. Parker, *A preacher's life* (1899) • G. H. Pike, *Dr Parker and his friends* (1904) • *Congregational Year Book* (1903), 208b–e • R. R. Turner, 'Cavendish Theological College, 1860–63', *Transactions of the Congregational Historical Society*, 21 (1971–2), 94–101 • J. H. Taylor, 'Joseph Parker's United Congregational church', *Transactions of the Congregational Historical Society*, 19 (1960–64), 91–6 • A. Peel, *The Congregational two hundred, 1530–1948* (1948), 208–9 • J. Parker, *Tyne chylde: my life and teaching* (1883) • *Congregational Year Book* (1885), 33–98 • *Congregational Year Book* (1902), 17–50 • *BL cat.*

Archives DWL | BL, corresp. with W. E. Gladstone, Add. MSS 44446–44520 • LPL, corresp. with A. C. Tait

Likenesses C. B. Birch, plaster bust, 1883, NPG • R. Gibb, portrait, 1894, RSA • J. Adams-Acton, bust • Ape [C. Pellegrini], chromolithograph caricature, NPG; repro. in *VF* (19 April 1884) • H. Furniss, caricatures, pen-and-ink sketches, NPG • E. Walker, photograph, NPG [*see illus.*] • photograph, repro. in Adamson, *Life of the Rev. Joseph Parker* • photograph, repro. in Parker, *Tyne chylde* • stipple and line print, NPG

Wealth at death £289 3*s*. 5*d*.: probate, 17 Jan 1903, *CGPLA Eng. & Wales*

Parker, Sir Karl Theodore (1895–1992), art historian and museum curator, was born on 2 July 1895 at 13 Welbeck Street, Marylebone, London, the younger son of Robert William Parker (1842–1913), a distinguished consulting surgeon, and his wife, Marie Amélie, *née* Lüling. He came from a very cosmopolitan background: his father had joined the Anglo-American medical mission for the relief of casualties on both sides of the Franco-Prussian War (later established at Zürich as the Red Cross); his mother was the daughter of a New Yorker of German extraction married to a lady of French origin and settled in New Orleans; and his elder brother, Robert Lüling Parker (1893–1973), became professor of petrology at the Swiss Federal Institute of Technology and the University of Zürich. He was educated at Bedford School, the Lycée St Louis in Paris, and the universities of Freiburg, where he studied chemistry, and Zürich, where he presented a doctoral thesis on Oliver Cromwell's reputation traced through English literature. As he later acknowledged, his real education came from studying old master drawings in the print room at Basel while he was a student, and visiting most of the main print rooms of Europe after he had completed his studies. During these travels he also began to build up the network of friends which stood him in such good stead throughout his career.

After publishing his first articles, on Hans Baldung Grien and early Alsatian drawings, Parker returned to England in 1924, and became a volunteer in the print room of the British Museum; a year later, he was appointed assistant keeper. His colleagues included A. M. Hind, A. E. Popham, Laurence Binyon, and Arthur Waley, under the keeper, Campbell Dodgson. Parker's area of research expanded dramatically to cover the whole field of old master drawings, and he published widely: in addition to two volumes in the Drawings of the Masters series, of which he was general editor, his book on Watteau (1931) demonstrated his unique ability to combine continental 'scientific' methods of connoisseurship with the feeling for works of art native to the amateur. He was also the founder editor of the periodical *Old Master Drawings: a Quarterly Magazine for Students and Collectors*, to which he contributed 114 short articles on a wide range of continental artists between 1926 and its demise in 1940. Meanwhile, on 14 January 1928 he married Audrey Isabel (1906/7–1976), daughter of Henry Ashworth James, of Herstmonceux Place, Herstmonceaux, Sussex. They had two daughters, Lavinia and Caroline.

Sir Karl Theodore Parker (1895–1992), by Oscar Nemon, 1960

In 1934 Parker succeeded Kenneth Clark as keeper of the department of fine art in the Ashmolean Museum; as the most senior head of a department, he served additionally as keeper of the whole museum from 1945 until he retired in 1962. He was also elected a fellow of Oriel College, joining the increasingly cosmopolitan common room to which numerous refugees were attracted by the provost, Sir David Ross. His career at the Ashmolean was one of the most remarkable in any museum. The collections in his care had been acquired largely by gift, and included a disparate and uneven group of paintings, Renaissance objects from the Fortnum collection, and distinguished old master drawings and prints, notably the greater part of the drawings by Raphael and Michelangelo from the collection of Sir Thomas Lawrence. Realizing that he could never afford to purchase outstanding old master paintings, but that drawings of comparable quality were relatively cheap, Parker set about building on the nucleus and, with an almost infallible feeling for quality quite independent of fashion, he bought over 3000 drawings over the next thirty years. Although they covered all available schools, his purchases naturally concentrated on Italian drawings, which were most numerous on the London market, and he acquired distinguished groups by Parmigianino, Guercino, and the eighteenth-century Venetians Guardi, Piranesi, and the Tiepolos. Moreover, despite his often repeated epigram that the only thing worse than an English watercolour was a faded English watercolour, he acquired important groups of drawings by David Wilkie, J. F. Lewis, and, especially, a representative group of works by Samuel Palmer, including the unique sepia drawings of 1825. Nor did he neglect completely the paintings, preferring oil sketches and documentary works to obvious and expensive machines, and securing the Tallard Madonna, generally attributed to Giorgione, in 1936. In addition to his purchases on behalf of the museum, he added considerably to its collections through his own personal gifts, which included items given to him by the executors of Henry Oppenheimer and by Hugh Cobb, and the greater part of his own library.

The Ashmolean had published no catalogues of its fine art collections for several decades, and Parker began to rectify this immediately on arrival: his first volume, covering the northern schools, came out in 1938, followed in 1956 by that on the Italian schools. Both volumes were written in the lapidary style favoured at the British Museum but were remarkable for being quite personal, and for suggesting numerous attributions which were subsequently confirmed by documentary research. The Ashmolean had never had a fully equipped print room but, thanks to a substantial donation from the second Lord Bearsted, a new wing was built on Beaumont Street and opened in 1950. It housed for the first time in England an integrated print room, library, and seminar room. The study of drawings as documents was reinforced when Parker accepted for the Ashmolean the family collections of Lucien Pissarro, which included not only a dozen paintings and scores of drawings and prints by his father, Camille, but also much of his surviving correspondence, as well as the documentary and artistic estate of Lucien himself and his brothers. The new energy and Parker's charm attracted other gifts, from the executors of Dr Grete Ring and M. V. Braikevitch, giving the Ashmolean unique strengths in nineteenth-century German and Russian drawings respectively.

Parker's achievements were recognized outside Oxford by his election as a fellow of the British Academy in 1950, and by appointments as CBE in 1954 and knight bachelor in 1960. While his outward appearance lived up to his worldly success—he was always immaculately dressed, habitually wearing a black tie after the death of his mother—to his close colleagues and friends he was a man of great charm, his habitually lugubrious manner hiding a wry sense of humour and a modesty unusual in a figure of such distinction. While he claimed that his fluency in French, German, and English left him equally unable to express himself properly in any one of those languages, he wrote clearly and with admirable concision.

After leaving Oxford, Parker retired to Eastbourne. He served as a conscientious and valued trustee of the National Gallery between 1962 and 1969, and returned to Oxford to receive an honorary doctorate in 1972, but his projected work on the portraits of the Venetian doges was never completed, and his activities in retirement were confined to writing letters and looking after his beloved Pekinese. He died at The Gates, 2 Rosebery Avenue, Eastbourne, East Sussex, on 22 July 1992, after suffering a stroke. He was survived by his two daughters. A memorial service was held in the chapel of Oriel College, Oxford, on 31 October 1992. COLIN HARRISON

Sources J. Byam Shaw and I. Robertson, 'Sir Karl Parker and the Ashmolean', *Burlington Magazine*, 104 (1962), 428–32 · H. Macandrew, introduction, *Ashmolean Museum, Oxford: catalogue of the collection of drawings*, 3: *Italian Schools: supplement* (1980), xiii–xvi · H. Macandrew, 'Karl Parker, 1895–1992', *Burlington Magazine*, 134 (1992), 810 · J. A. Gere, 'Sir Karl Parker (1895–1992)', *Master Drawings*, 31 (1993), 71–3 · J. Byam Shaw, 'Karl Theodore Parker, 1895–1992', *PBA*, 82 (1993), 431–8 · *The Times* (28 July 1992) · *The Times* (4 Aug 1992) · *The Times* (20 Aug 1992) · *The Independent* (27 July 1992) · *Daily Telegraph* (3 Aug 1992) · *The Guardian* (6 Aug 1992) · *WWW* · personal knowledge (2004) · private information (2004) · b. cert. · m. cert. · d. cert.

Archives Tate collection, corresp. with Lord Clark

Likenesses V. Hammer, pencil, red chalk, and wash drawing, 1933, AM Oxf. · B. Elkan, pencil drawing, 1941, AM Oxf. · H. A. Freeth, red-brown ink and watercolour drawing, 1952, AM Oxf. · O. Nemon, plaster bust, 1960, AM Oxf. [*see illus.*] · photograph, repro. in *The Times* (28 July 1992)

Wealth at death £428,088: probate, 1 Oct 1992, *CGPLA Eng. & Wales*

Parker, Louis Napoleon (1852–1944), musician and playwright, was born at Luc-sur-Mer in Calvados, France, on 21 October 1852, the only son of an American, Charles Albert Parker, and his wife, Elizabeth Moray, an Englishwoman. His grandfather, Isaac Parker (1768–1830), had been chief justice of the supreme judicial court of Massachusetts; his father was a lawyer too, but in 1840, at the age of thirty-nine, he abandoned his profession and began a wandering life in Europe, seldom caring to remain more than a year in any one place. He was temporarily absent when his son was born, and as the child was thought to be dying and the mother could then speak no French, the Frenchman who baptized him named him after the then ruler of France, Louis Napoleon. In his eventual English career these names, together with the dark hair and skin which he inherited from his mother, gave him an exotic stamp, despite his intense pro-English feeling.

Parker's first fourteen years were spent with his parents, wandering in Italy, Germany, Switzerland, Belgium, and France—though chiefly the first two. His autobiography, *Several of my Lives* (1928), contains vivid descriptions of those countries before 1866. The boy's first language was Italian, to which he soon added German and French; English was a later acquisition. His regular education was inevitably haphazard, but from his earliest years he was taken constantly to operas and plays, and so obtained an intimate sense of the stage and an everyday familiarity with music. In 1866 his parents took him to England, but still kept wandering, and his first settled education began when he was seventeen, when he was sent to the Royal Academy of Music, of which the principal was then William Sterndale Bennett. In 1898, after retiring from his musical career, Parker became a fellow of the Royal Academy.

At the academy Parker quickly came to the fore, as singer, pianist, and organist. In 1873 Sterndale Bennett, whose son James was director of music at Sherborne School in Dorset, asked Parker to go there for six weeks as locum tenens for the piano master. He went, and stayed there for nineteen years, succeeding James Bennett as organist and director of music in 1877. On 7 August 1878 he married Georgiana Bessie Calder (*c.*1853–1919), the eldest daughter of Charles Calder, a merchant, in Sherborne Abbey church. They had two daughters, Elsa and Dorothy, of whom the latter attained some distinction on the stage. Parker spent many eventful years in Sherborne, for he not only raised the school's music to a higher level than any public school had until then attained, he also made the town a musical centre whose influence radiated far over Somerset and Dorset. He was one of the first English Wagnerians, an early member of the original Wagner Society and, after it ended, president of its successor. He was also a composer with a distinct vein of his own: he equipped Sherborne School with a remarkable set of school songs; of his three cantatas, two, *Silvia* (published 1880) and *Young Tamlane*, best display his gift for melody. But two things ended this career—a temporary but disastrous decline of Sherborne School and, more serious, the onset of deafness. The latter left him no future in teaching, conducting, or choir-training.

Fortunately another occupation lay ready for Parker. For some years his dramatic bent had impelled him to attempt plays and, before he left Sherborne for London in 1892, he had had three successes with short pieces and two long ones accepted. Yet his new career was very uphill. Only dauntless tenacity and fertility carried him through. In November 1893, with *Gudgeons* (in collaboration with Murray Carson), he attained big box-office success both in London and in America, which he first visited in 1897. In 1896 *Rosemary* (again with Carson) became equally popular, and for the next twenty years Parker was one of the best-known playwrights in both countries. His most famous plays were *The Cardinal* (1903), *Disraeli* (1911), *Drake* (1912), *Joseph and his Brethren* (1913), and (with W. W. Jacobs) *Beauty and the Barge* (1904); to which may be added *Pomander Walk* (1910), which for years broke records in America, though (through bad casting) it failed in London. Parker was also an admirable translator, as demonstrated by *L'Aiglon* and *Rosmersholm*, and adaptor, as seen in *David Copperfield*, *Cyrano de Bergerac*, and *The Monkey's Paw* by Jacobs. Many of his London triumphs were obtained at His Majesty's Theatre under Sir Herbert Tree, but they were often preceded by great successes in America.

Parker's third career—pageant-making—overlapped with the second. It began in 1905 with the pageant at Sherborne. Parker had never ceased to love the town, and the precincts of its ruined Norman castle gave him a perfect arena. The success of this pageant—which with 900 participants achieved seven performances—was quite outstanding; and requests poured in from elsewhere. By 1909 he had organized five more pageants on a great scale—at Warwick, Bury St Edmunds, Colchester, York, and Dover—besides a few smaller ones. His pageants essentially expressed the settled, prosperous life of England as it was before the world wars. He himself became a British subject two months before the outbreak of war in 1914.

From 1907 until then he organized and greatly improved the historical section of the lord mayor's show.

The last two decades of Parker's very long life were spent chiefly at Bishopsteignton in Devon. In 1936, when he was eighty-four, two things pleased him very much—the very successful filming of his play *Disraeli*, written for George Arliss, and the choice of his *Lily of France* (Joan of Arc) by the city of Nancy for its annual production, which, though interrupted by the Second World War, was afterwards resumed. His last published work was a poem, 'Fathers and Sons', in *The Times* of 21 September 1939. He died at Inverteign, Bishopsteignton, on 21 September 1944. R. C. K. ENSOR, *rev.* NILANJANA BANERJI

Sources L. N. Parker, *Several of my lives* (1928) • *The Times* (22 Sept 1944) • *WWW* • W. Browne and E. de Roy Koch, eds., *Who's who on the stage, 1908* (1908) • B. Hunt, ed., *The green room book, or, Who's who on the stage* (1906) • J. Parker, ed., *The green room book, or, Who's who on the stage* (1907), 277 • J. Parker, ed., *The green room book, or, Who's who on the stage* (1908), 334 • D. Hines and H. P. Hanaford, *Who's who in music and drama* (1914) • A. Rothe, ed., *Current Biography Yearbook* (1944) • personal knowledge (1959) • private information (1959) • d. cert.
Archives Col. U., Rare Book and Manuscript Library, corresp. and papers • Theatre Museum, London, letters
Likenesses P. Burne-Jones, oils, Garr. Club • H. Furniss, caricature, pen-and-ink sketch, NPG • C. Roberts, pencil drawing, priv. coll. • portrait, repro. in Parker, *Several of my lives*, frontispiece
Wealth at death £4750 3*s*. 6*d*.: probate, 16 Dec 1944, *CGPLA Eng. & Wales*

Parker [*née* Walker], **Margaret Eleanor** (1827/8–1896), temperance activist and campaigner for women's rights, was probably born in Bolton, Lancashire, and was the daughter of William Walker, owner of one of the largest tanning establishments in Lancashire. She was educated at a private school in Sheffield, and married on 9 July 1851 Edward Parker (*d.* 1887), the son of the former provost of Dundee, Charles Parker (1796–1867), and a member of the family firm, Charles Parker & Sons, spinners and manufacturers of Dundee. She had five sons and one daughter, all of whom survived her. Margaret and Edward Parker were Wesleyan Methodists, both coming from families strongly committed to that denomination, and Margaret Parker's first public work was to help to secure a new chapel in Dundee.

Mrs Parker's interest in the temperance movement began after hearing G. B. Gough, the American temperance orator, lecture in Dundee in the mid-1850s. She was involved in the Good Templars movement in Dundee from its inception and gave her first public address in presenting a banner to the Olive Leaf Lodge of Good Templars. She became well known for her platform speaking and worked incessantly on behalf of the movement. In 1875 she visited the United States of America as a representative of the grand lodge of Scotland Independent Order of Good Templars, making the acquaintance of 'Mother' Stewart (Eliza Daniel Stewart), the president of the Springfield Women's League, Ohio, and a remarkable worker in the 'women's whisky war' of 1873–4, and induced her to visit Scotland.

On her return Margaret Parker wrote a popular book about her experiences, *Six Happy Weeks among the Americans*, and helped to organize the visit of Mother Stewart and Mary C. Johnson, president of the Brooklyn Women's Crusade, to the United Kingdom in the spring of 1876. Their lecture tour addressed large audiences throughout the country. Margaret Parker's American trip had shown her the value of organization as demonstrated by the temperance crusades run by American women; she determined to establish a British women's temperance organization. Under the auspices of the Women's National Temperance Union of America, Margaret Parker and Mother Stewart summoned a meeting of representative women from all over the United Kingdom at Newcastle upon Tyne on 21 April 1876 during the meeting of the English grand lodge of Templars. The British Women's Temperance Association, a total abstinence society, was established, with Margaret Parker as its first president. She was president for two years and remained on the executive committee of the association until her death. The association was widely influential and became well established, with many branches being formed. In 1876 Margaret Parker was sent as its delegate to the Women's International Convention at Philadelphia, where she was elected president of the International Christian Women's Temperance Union, a post which she held until 1879.

Besides her platform work both in Britain and America, Margaret Parker was a regular contributor to the magazine and newspaper press and corresponded regularly with the leaders of many popular movements. In addition to working for the temperance cause she was an ardent advocate of women's rights, and took a leading part in campaigns for women's suffrage, addressing the New York State Women's Suffrage Association in 1886. At the time of the death of her husband in 1887 she was in Los Angeles, California. In 1893 she attended the first Congress of the International Council of Women in Chicago and was introduced as the woman who was instrumental in calling the congress.

Margaret Parker continued her public speaking and canvassing until her death, which took place at her son's house, 3 Blackness Crescent, Dundee, on 8 November 1896; she was sixty-eight. The obituary in the *Scottish Women's Temperance News* described her as 'a gifted woman, highly intellectual and an indefatigable worker. She was a brilliant journalist, took an active part in politics and in the women's suffrage movement, and was a most assiduous contributor to the press on social subjects'.

LESLEY M. RICHMOND

Sources *Dundee Yearbook* (1896), 78–9 • *Scottish Women's Temperance News* (15 Dec 1896), 13–14 • P. T. Winskill, *The temperance movement and its workers*, 4 vols. (1891–2), vols. 3–4 • m. cert. • d. cert.
Archives Huntly House Museum, Edinburgh, BWTA (Scottish Christian Union)
Likenesses portrait, repro. in *Dundee Yearbook*, 79 • portrait, repro. in Winskill, *The temperance movement*, pl. 27 no. 4
Wealth at death £1699 14*s*. 6*d*.: confirmation, 28 Dec 1896, *CCI*

Parker, Martin (*fl.* 1624–1647), ballad writer, is an obscure figure. He was probably a Londoner, as his writings were most closely associated with metropolitan culture, though his stories are populated by northern lasses, and were read throughout England. On 16 January 1629 Parker was brought before the Bridewell governors in London, accused as a balladeer and vagrant, along with Richard Kempson and several others. They were suspected of involvement in a theft. Parker was released on bail, while the others were detained.

The earliest extant ballad with Parker's initials is a tale of a murder in Cornwall printed about 1624; the last work he wrote seems to have been a chapbook printed in 1647; he was probably dead before 1656, when a mock elegy was written for him. Parker's fame rests on nearly a hundred ballads and quarto chapbooks that bear his initials or name or have otherwise been attributed to him. The size of his canon is uncertain, as his initials may have been fostered upon other men's labours by a canny bookseller—particularly Francis Coles or Francis Grove—who saw the commercial value of Parker's name. Parker was emphatic about the mark of his authorship in his most personally revealing work, *The Poet's Blind Mans Bough, or, Have among you my Blind Harpers* (1641), verses responding to the recent effusion of pamphlets, in some of which his own work had, he felt, been maligned. He asserts that authors should accept responsibility for their work:

> Then he who writes (what e're be his pretence)
> His name should justifie what he hath done
> This maxim I have alwaies thought upon
> What ever yet was published by mee
> Was knowne by *Martin Parker*, or M. P.
> (sig. A4*r*)

In the same work he alludes to his predecessors as Chaucer, Spenser, and Surrey, suggesting a familiarity with literary traditions not otherwise evident in his verse.

Parker's early ballads are talented performances in a highly formulaic genre (hence the difficulty in attribution). They tender moralistic tales of inconstant men and long-suffering or patient women, of cunning and virtue rewarded (*The Desperate Damsells Tragedy, or, The Faithless Young Man*, 1630?; *Good Counsell for Young Wooers*, 1633). They are told in conventional ballad metre, and were published in pairs on blackletter broadsides illustrated with woodcuts. Several exist in multiple editions, and, given the catastrophic survival rate of early seventeenth century broadsides, this suggests that his works were highly popular. Parker told moral tales, and recycled old stories for new audiences, but also utilized the ballad form for tidings of recent events. One broadside, *Lord have Mercy upon Us* (1636), included verse and prose prayers, the former signed M. P., and mortality statistics for plague years. *A Lamentable Relation of a Fearfull Fight at Sea, between the Spaniard and the Hollander* (1639) reported recent news; *A Description of a Strange and Miraculous Fish, Cast upon the Sands in Worwell* (1635?) offered a providential account of a wonder. The ballad was seen as a popular news genre, if limited in accuracy and detail. Henry Peacham wrote in a 1641 pamphlet: 'For a peny you may have all the Newes in England, of Murders, Flouds, Witches, Fires, Tempests, and what not, in one of Martin Parkers Ballads' (H. Peacham, *Worth of a Penny*, 1641, sig. D1*r*).

Parker also wrote chapbooks, and he may have been the first ballad writer to translate comic, moral tales into octavo pamphlet format. The relationship between the two was quite fluid, and among his chapbooks were *Robin Conscience, or, Conscionable Robin* (1635), a moral tale in verse; and *An Abstract of the Historie of the Renouned Maiden Queen Elizabeth … in English Meeter* (1631). In a preface to one of these, the jestbook *Harry White his Humour* (1637), Parker suggests very widespread distribution, though he probably exaggerates: 'thus wishing that thy humour may be satisfied with tenne thousand two peny customers, I commit thee to thy humour' (sig. A4*r*).

Although these earlier works are not very revealing of Parker's political or religious opinions, from 1640 a sentimental pro-royalist politics emerges in his writings. His news ballads were used as propaganda. *An exact description of the manner how his majestie went to the parliament, the thirteenth day of April* (1640) reports the opening of the Short Parliament; *Good Newes from the North* (1640) reports on the bishops' war, with anti-Scottish sentiments. More galling to Scottish pride was *Britaines Honour* (1640), a ballad telling the story of 'two valiant *Welchmen*, who fought against fifteene thousand *Scots*'. These writings intervened in the burgeoning pamphlet debate about prerogative, episcopacy, and the covenant, and provoked some responses. Two retaliatory publications reveal a little about Parker the man. The first, *The Popish Proclamation* (1641), accused Parker, in the company of John Taylor the water poet and George Herbert, of popery. This was not an uncommon charge against the king's supporters in these years, yet it perhaps draws attention to the worldly leanings of Parker's ballads, which had lost the more intense godly gloss of those of the previous century. There is a considerable distance between the Elizabethan ballad writer William Elderton and Parker.

The second attack appeared in an anonymous dialogue pamphlet (perhaps by Richard Overton) presenting news and opinion of the Scottish war, *Vox Borealis, or, The Northern Discoverie* (1641). Reporting the ill success of several 'Ballad-makers, and Pamphlet writers imployed this yeare', the author names:

> One *Parker*, the Prelats Poet, who made many base Ballads against the *Scots*, sped but *little better*, for he, and his *Antipodes* were like to have tasted of Justice *Longs liberalitie*: and hardly he escaped his Powdering-Tubb, which the vulgar people calls a Prison. (*Vox Borealis*, sig. Bv)

This suggests that Parker had run into trouble with the parliament—Justice Long—for something in one of his ballads, though there is no confirmation of this. Furthermore 'now he sweares he will never put pen to paper for the Prelats againe, but betake himselfe to his pitcht Kanne, and Tobacco Pipe; and learne to sell his frothie Pots againe, and give over Poetrie' (ibid., sig. B2*r*). This is a common enough mode of abuse, but it may indicate that Parker was formerly an alehouse keeper, not a very humble occupation, and one compatible with the qualifications of the ballad writer: literacy, some business sense, connections with news, gossip, and stories. The pamphlet notes Parker's association with the king's cause, and the anti-covenanting tenor of his recent ballads.

This was among the pamphlets to which Parker responded in *The Poet's Blind Mans Bough*, suggesting that the 'Borealist' had sought to:

bring me in disgrace; as though I had,
Bin punisht heretofore for writing bad,
Calling me th'Prelats Poet and such tearmes,
Which nothing but his spight at all confirmes,
For I ne're wrot ith' Bishops cause so much,
As now I have on this occasion touch.
(sig. B4*r*)

The imputation of his commitment to episcopacy does not seem an unlikely one. He further claimed that he:

never wrot but in the Just defence,
Of's King and Countrey.
(sig. A2*r*)

Parker became an important figure in popular literary culture, a symbol of traditional royalist allegiance. The position was firmly consolidated by his most famous ballad, 'When the king enjoys his own again', written, as internal evidence indicates, after 1644. The ballad regrets the damage to the country exacted by the civil war and the dishonouring of the king, and looks forward to the orderly restoration of his throne. Parker refers dismissively to the parliamentarian *Bloody Almanack* (from 1643), attributed to John Booker but actually by John Napier. The first edition of the ballad is apparently not extant; there is, therefore, no certainty over Parker's authorship, though many contemporaries attest to it. The first allusion to it appeared in *Gossips' Feast* in 1647; thereafter its title, words, or tune became a staple reference in royalist propaganda. Indications that other ballads should be sung 'to the tune of *When the King*' created a complex mode of intertextuality. Likewise the ballad's reference to 'The Man in the Moon' who

may run out his shoon
By running after Charles his wain

initiated a strain of visual imagery in royalist writing, culminating in the newsbook *The Man in the Moon* (April 1649 – June 1650).

Parker subsequently produced two miscellanies, *The Figure of Five* (1645?) and *The Figure of Seven* (1647), serving a fleeting trend in the market for cheap print; but his productivity had declined rapidly in the 1640s. Some contemporary newsbooks suggested that Parker was involved in editing the polemical royalist newsbook *Mercurius Melancholicus* in 1647–8. Credibility may be given to this proposal by the fact that the main editor, John Hackluyt, was imprisoned without affecting the weekly production of the journal. His involvement remains ambiguous, however: the assertions by hostile newsbooks might be interpreted as evidence that Parker had become symbolic of the sentiments and hopes of the royalist cause, of the nostalgia for a lost, happier world, and a passive anticipation of a felicitous restoration of the old order. If Parker had never lived, royalist and parliamentarian writers would have invented him.

Parker was inactive long before an elegy for him was published by S. F. in *Death in a New Dress, or, Sportive Funeral Elegies* (1656), which implied that he had been dead for some time. The mock elegy was a stock comic pamphlet genre, but it seems likely that the tidings of his death were not premature. Referring ironically to 'Martin Parker the famous Poet' (title-page), the elegy suggests his continuing fame, as his:

Canzonets … are
Yet extant on each Market-day or Fair
… was not every Song
Of thine applauded by the thirsty throng.
(sig. A4*r*)

Parker is also commended for versifying history which had hitherto been buried in 'Dull prose', now fit 'for the solace of great Lords and Earls', an unusual assessment of Parker's audience. Asking the Muse how Parker was so inspired, the author answers himself:

I have't; He alwayes bath'd his Beak in Ale,
Toping whole Tubs off, like some thirsty Whale.
(sig. A4*r–v*)

Alcohol-based inspiration was a familiar topos in portraits of ballad writers, and need not be accepted as biographical fact.

Parker's fame lived on. In John Dryden's *Sir Martin Marr-All*, a character offered money exclaims: 'Hang your white Pelf: sure, Sir, by your largess you mistake me for *Martin Parker*, the Ballad-Maker, your Covetousness has offended my Muse, and quite dull'd her' (J. Dryden, *Comedies, Tragedies, and Operas*, 2 vols., 1701, 1.217). It was particularly through Parker's most celebrated ballad that he was remembered: 'When the king enjoys his own' was reprinted and commemorated at the Restoration; it became a Jacobite song after the revolution of 1688, and was still in use in 1715 and 1745. JOAD RAYMOND

Sources *STC, 1475–1640* · Wing, *STC* · S. F., *Death in a new dress* (1656) · T. Watt, *Cheap print and popular piety, 1550–1640* (1991) · *N&Q*, 2nd ser., 10 (1860), 212 · GL, Bridewell court minutes 7, fol. 105 [microfilm]

Parker, Mary (*d.* 1692). *See under* Salem witches and their accusers (*act.* 1692).

Parker, Mary Ann (1765/6–1848), traveller, was a physician's daughter but her parents' names are unknown. Nothing is known of her early life save that she lived three years in Spain as a very young child. She was evidently a well-educated woman who had travelled widely in Europe and was fluent in Spanish. She was originally reputed to be beautiful in face and figure, but smallpox left its marks on her. Before 1790 she married John Parker (1749?–1794), captain in the Royal Navy, and they had four children. Their two sons died early but their two daughters survived. John Parker was a veteran of the siege of Gibraltar (1779–83) and in 1791 he was sent on the *Gorgon* to relieve the starving convict colony at Port Jackson, New South Wales. Mary Parker accompanied him on a journey which took them around the world before they returned to London by June 1792.

On 4 August 1794 John Parker died of yellow fever off Martinique leaving Mary Parker and their children in very difficult circumstances. She began to write an account of her experiences to raise money. An adroit publicity campaign was engineered on her behalf by Joseph Budworth with the help of John Nichols, publisher of the *Gentleman's Magazine*. Budworth, a Sloane Street neighbour in London, and like John Parker a veteran of the siege of Gibraltar, drew attention to Mary Parker's situation with the publication of his *Siege of Gibraltar: a Poem* (1795) for her benefit, advertising her forthcoming narrative and filling her subscription list. The list was substantial, and drew on literary, naval, and militia connections, and on loyalist sentiment of a sometimes intensely particularist kind, finding tight pockets of local patriotism in Sloane Street and the Lancashire town of Blackburn. Surviving distinguished veterans of the siege signed up, as did dozens of navy pay-office employees; Budworth's London sociability provided members of the Society of Antiquaries, the Trent Club, and others in the highly charged loyalist atmosphere of the time.

Parker's *Voyage Round the World, in the Gorgon Man of War* appeared in 1795. The author presented herself as the conventional private, financially embarrassed, reluctant woman writer, and apologized for the book's 'brevity and other greater demerits', attributing these faults to her predicament as 'nurse, and being obliged to attend so much to her domestic concerns' (Parker, preface). Despite her frank admission that she was publishing for money, Parker was no sensationalist. Constrained by her genteel persona, she did not dwell on the sufferings of her long journey, though she was immediately so violently seasick that she was close to 'desert[ing] … & waver[ed] between Husband & Children', noticed the officer John Gardner; nor did she ever emphasize the 'rare circumstance', as a reviewer put it, of seeing 'a female name in the list of circumnavigators' (*Monthly Review*, 20, 1796, 112). Instead, her narrative is brisk, matter of fact, and entertaining, enlivened by the 'little dash of satire' in her personality observed by Gardner. At ports of call—Tenerife, Cape Town, Port Jackson—she gives a lively account of her social life, interspersed with descriptions of the personalities of her many hosts and hostesses, and observations on landscape, local customs, and manners. The second half of the book is given over to Port Jackson, where she left the impression of 'a very amiable intelligent Woman' (*Journals and Letters of Elizabeth Macarthur*, 34). Sections of her husband's log, minutes, and reports are included, as are his whaling notes; his eyewitness government report on the dreadful condition of Third Fleet transportees; and details of the spectacular electrical storm which greeted the *Gorgon*'s arrival, where Parker memorializes her husband and Gibraltar, likening the latter to 'a besieged garrison' (Parker, chap. 5). She praises Governor Phillip's regime as benign and paternal, devoting a chapter to the natives of New Holland.

A Voyage was well received thanks to Nichols but, despite proceeds from it, her pension, and Budworth's book, within a year Parker, in 'great distress', was receiving money from the Literary Fund. Happily, Nichols, Budworth, and several subscribers were also Literary Fund committee members, and her appeals were repeated through to 1804, when she lost her house and was confined for debt, 'within the Gloomy Walls of a prison'—the Fleet—'this horrid abode' (*Archives of the Royal Literary Fund*, Case 39: a, 6, 8). Little is known of her later life. She died aged eighty-two at the house of her son-in-law Robert Vincent, in Connaught Terrace, Edgware Road, London, on 30 August 1848. DEIRDRE COLEMAN

Sources M. A. Parker, *A voyage round the world, in the Gorgon man of war: Captain John Parker. Performed and written by his widow; for the advantage of a numerous family* (1795) [facs. edn (1991)] • *GM*, 1st ser., 64 (1794), 1128–9, 1193–7 • *GM*, 1st ser., 65 (1795), 941–2 • *GM*, 1st ser., 85/2 (1815), 391 • *GM*, 2nd ser., 30 (1848), 441 • committee meeting minutes, *Archives of the Royal Literary Fund, 1790–1918* (1984), case 39 [microfilm] • N. Cross, *The Royal Literary Fund, 1790–1918: an introduction … with an index of applicants* (1984) • J. Gardner, 'Account of the voyage of HMS Gorgon from England to Australia and return to England', 1791–2, Mitchell L., NSW, Dixson M.S.1 (CY2758) • J. Spilsbury, *A journal of the siege of Gibraltar, 1779–1783*, ed. B. H. T. Frere (1908) • Farington, *Diary*, vol. 17 • *Lady's Magazine* (Dec 1781), 666–7 • R. L. Brown, *A history of the Fleet prison, London: the anatomy of the Fleet* (1996), 141–54, 183–7, 331–5 • 'Captain's log of HMS Gorgon', PRO, ADM 51/383 • 'Lieutenants' passing certificates, John Parker', 20 Feb 1783, PRO, ADM 107/9 • 'Master's log of HMS Woolwich', PRO, ADM 52/3546 • 'Pay book of widows' pensions', 1795, PRO, ADM 22/116 • *The journals and letters of Elizabeth Macarthur, 1789–1798*, ed. J. N. Hughes (1984), 34 • J. E. Cookson, *The British armed nation, 1793–1815* (1997), 24–7 • Nichols, *Lit. anecdotes*, 9.140, 158 • D. Coleman, ed., *Maiden voyages and infant colonies: two women's travel narratives of the 1790s* (1999) • J. Budworth, *The siege of Gibraltar: a poem* (1795)

Archives Royal Literary Fund, London, archives, 1790–1918 (1984), reel 1, case 39 'Mrs. Mary Ann Parker'; reel 25, 'Minutes of committee meetings'; reels A1, A2, 15 [microform]

Parker, Matthew (1504–1575), archbishop of Canterbury and patron of scholarship, was born, according to his own account, in the parish of St Saviour, close to the heart of Norwich, on 6 August 1504. One of six children, he was born into armigerous families on both sides. His father, William Parker (1467/8–1516), a well-to-do worsted weaver with property in Norwich, was the grandson of Nicholas Parker, registrar to successive archbishops of Canterbury between 1450 and 1483. The family of his mother, Alice Monins or Monings (1469/70–1553), originated in Kent (she was possibly related to Anne Boleyn). Following her husband's death she married John Baker of Norfolk, and their son, also John, was sufficiently close to Archbishop Parker to be nominated one of his executors. The archbishop's attachment to his parents' memory caused him to provide for the care of their graves. He also made some provision for his own commemoration. Parker himself kept a parchment roll on which he recorded personal and familial landmarks (Corpus Christi College, Cambridge, Parker Library, MS 583), and in addition he commissioned his Latin secretary John Joscelin to produce two 'semi-autobiographical' accounts of his employer's life, the so-called *Historiola* (Corpus Christi College, Cambridge, MS 489, 71–89) and *Matthaeus*. The latter, a retitled version of the former, was printed in 1572 and reprinted by John Strype in 1711; it also formed the basis of a satirical attack on Parker, *The Life off the 70. Archbishopp off Canterbury*, published by radical opponents in 1574 (ESTC 19292a). The existence of these personal sources, together with Joscelin's laudatory *Historiola Collegii Corporis Christi* (Corpus

Matthew Parker (1504–1575), by Remigius Hogenberg, 1572

Christi College, Cambridge, MS 488, MS 489, 33–74), help to explain the generally good press that Parker has received from posterity.

Cambridge and religious reform Although brought up in the Norwich parish of All Saints at Fye Bridge, Parker relates that he was educated in the parish of St Clement at Fye Bridge. Six men, mostly clerics, taught him reading, writing, singing, and grammar. It is also possible that he was tutored at home. It was certainly at his mother's expense, with the help of a Mr Bunge of Norwich, that Parker was sent to Corpus Christi College, Cambridge, probably in 1520. At first he lived in St Mary's Hostel, but his election as a college bible clerk in March 1521 gave him a modest stipend and enabled him to move into the college's main precinct. He graduated BA in 1525, turning down Cardinal Wolsey's invitation that year to become a member of Cardinal College, Oxford. He was ordained subdeacon on 22 December 1526, and deacon and priest on 20 April and 15 June 1527 respectively. In 1527 he also proceeded MA and was elected a fellow of Corpus. He then embarked upon the serious study of theology, eventually proceeding BTh in July 1535 and DTh in July 1538.

There is no evidence that Parker went to university as anything other than a traditionally pious Catholic. Suggestions that contacts made in Norwich led him towards Lollardy seem unfounded, but religious debate was certainly rife in Cambridge. Erasmus's last visit (1512–14) must still have been fresh in many minds. The summer of 1521 saw the beginning of the English campaign against Martin Luther, launched on 12 May by the promulgation of the papal bull of condemnation and a public burning of books. This development did not deter the growth of a small and clandestine Cambridge community interested in Lutheran ideas. Little can be said of it—its famous association with the White Horse tavern rests upon a single reference in Foxe's *Actes and Monuments*—and it is not known whether Parker belonged to it. Nevertheless it seems clear that there were a few in Cambridge who were attracted to the new ideas, and the star in this firmament was undoubtedly Thomas Bilney of Trinity Hall.

Bilney was neither a Lutheran nor an old-fashioned Lollard. His religious position has been designated by J. F. Davis as 'evangelism', the principal features of which included giving doctrines of faith precedence over the penitential system of the late medieval church, claiming primacy for scripture over ecclesiastical authority, and stressing the importance of preaching, sermons being seen as more important than ceremonies. Evangelism might well provide a fitting definition for Parker's beliefs in the late 1520s. He is not known to have been a dogmatic Lutheran controversialist (unlike Robert Barnes, for instance), but he was certainly present at Bilney's martyrdom just outside Norwich on 19 August 1531, later making his personal testimony available to John Foxe, who was anxious to refute claims that Bilney had recanted. Furthermore Parker carefully preserved some of Bilney's letters, eventually bequeathing them to Corpus. Particularly intriguing is the possibility that Parker actively supported Bilney in his evangelical labours. Foxe records that before Bilney left for London in 1527 he and others converted Robert Barnes 'to the gospell of Jesus Christ … with the assistance of master Fooke of Benet Colledge and maister Soud maister of the same Colledge to whom also wer then associate, Maister Parcker and Maister Powry' (Foxe, *Actes*, sig. Uu7*r*). In this context it is suggestive that the Corpus steward's accounts show Parker to have been away from Cambridge for several extended periods in 1530–31 (March to April and July to August 1530, and October 1530 to January 1531). Preaching tours in East Anglia, inspired by Bilney's example, furnish a plausible explanation for these absences.

Entry into royal service Even if Parker's connection with Bilney was common knowledge it did not inhibit his career, for in 1532–3 he was appointed to a university committee headed by the vice-chancellor, responsible for deciding upon dispensations and graces. During Advent 1533, moreover, he 'entered on the office of preaching', giving one sermon in Cambridge and four in neighbouring villages (*Correspondence*, vii). His formal licence to preach was probably revoked under Archbishop Cranmer's provincial order of November 1534 but restored under the auspices of Hugh Latimer, who led the preaching campaign to promote the royal supremacy and attack 'superstitious' practices associated with the cults of saints and the doctrine of purgatory. He was assisted by a team of able preachers from all over the country. Circumstantial evidence suggests that Parker was one of them, and he himself records that he preached at Balsham, Cambridgeshire, in late 1534, during the primary visitation of Thomas Goodrich, bishop of Ely.

Thus, perhaps, Parker came to the attention of Queen Anne Boleyn, then arguably the leading English lay evangelical, and her circle. By his own account he was called to court on 30 March 1535 and was thereafter appointed one of the queen's chaplains. It was a decisive turning point in his career, setting him on the road to Canterbury. The rewards of royal preferment began modestly in October 1535 with the gift of a doe, but on 4 November Anne presented him to the deanery of the Suffolk college of Stoke by Clare. Some time in 1535 Parker preached before the infant Princess Elizabeth at Hunsdon, Hertfordshire, and in that or the following year preached before the king. Otherwise his precise role in Anne's household remains obscure until, in a conversation that occurred only days before her arrest in May 1536, she commended Elizabeth to Parker's spiritual care. Whatever the real significance of Anne's words they were the last she addressed to him, and a powerful sense of obligation, to both mother and daughter, stayed with him for the rest of his life.

Parker survived Anne's fall, and in February 1537 he was ordered to court to be admitted one of the king's chaplains. Parker later recorded his admission on 1 March, and it was as a royal chaplain that on the 26th he was licensed to preach by Thomas Cromwell, the king's vicegerent in spirituals. The functions of his chaplaincy remain obscure. But it was probably his status, rather than simply his competence in the pulpit, which explains why Parker was invited by Cromwell to preach at Paul's Cross in September 1537, and why he preached before Prince Edward in 1539 and before Princess Elizabeth in 1540. He was still described as a royal chaplain in November 1544, presumably retaining that office until Henry VIII's death, though he does not appear among the chaplains who took part in the king's funeral on 16 February 1547.

Dean of Stoke by Clare Rather more is known of Parker's activities as dean of Stoke by Clare. Originally an alien priory, Stoke had been secularized as the college of St John the Baptist and was governed by statutes of 1423. It was the richest of the Suffolk colleges. The dean had considerable responsibilities, both liturgical and administrative, as well as wide discretion to interpret or even to alter the statutes. When Parker took up office he found an accumulation of difficulties, including the exploitation of the college's resources by its members, neglect of its valuables, dilapidated buildings, accumulated arrears of rent, falling revenues, and recent cases of immorality.

In the first known demonstration of his powers of organization Parker revitalized Stoke, turning it from an institution largely devoted to prayers for the dead into one which served the community at large. He revised the statutes, prescribing that the dean and prebendaries should preach the word of God 'continually' and at least once a year in every parish whose tithes supported the foundation. Within the college there was to be a biblical lecturer who would lecture four days a week. Each hour-long exposition was to be bilingual, the first half in English, the second half in Latin. Moreover he founded a grammar school for 'the youths of the countrye about the college', where poorer children were to be received free of charge (Bjorklund, 123). Parker tackled the college's financial problems robustly, at one point seeking legal advice from his friend Nicholas Bacon, then a Gray's Inn lawyer. Net annual income rose from £324 4*s*. 1*d*. in 1535 to £383 2*s*. 6*d*. by 1548, and Parker was able to indulge his passion for building. As well as erecting the grammar school within the precincts he also transformed an old house into a hall for the dean, prebendaries, and vicars.

The activities of this new broom, which included securing a considerable turnover of college staff, aroused hostility, manifested above all in a conservative attack on sermons preached by Parker in 1536 and 1537, led by Dr John Stokes, prior of Norwich's Austin friary. Parker's efforts to settle an essentially theological dispute peacefully were rebuffed, but the intervention of the secular authorities, including Thomas Cromwell, brought him at least a temporary respite, while Stokes was sent to prison. When the college came under pressure following the Chantries Act of 1545 Parker sought the protection of Queen Katherine Parr, on the grounds that dissolution would give the king a paltry £300 a year, and that in any case the college was now doing a splendid job, especially in providing education. Parker's petition was successful, but the reprieve was short-lived. Another chantries act in 1547 doomed the college, which was dissolved in 1548, though the intervention of Sir Anthony Denny, a leading evangelical courtier, secured a pension of £40 for Parker. There is no doubt that he loved Stoke by Clare: when the college was suppressed he removed a stained glass panel depicting the founder's arms and set it up in the master's lodge at Corpus.

Cambridge Parker's Cambridge career had also been developing. Already valued for his preaching, he was elected master of Corpus on 4 December 1544 following the intervention of the king. Because of his reforms there he came to be regarded as the college's second founder. Making a priority (as at Stoke by Clare) of placing the institution on a sound financial footing, he drew up a model form—adopted from 1545—for new annual accounts, intended to provide clear records of receipts, outgoings, and arrears. By 1550, moreover, he had begun compiling a meticulous book of audits to supplement the general accounts. To eradicate inefficiency and fraud Parker also drew up a complete statement of the college's estates, with the rents due from them, and made a determined effort to recover arrears. He tried, too, to improve the profits of the college's holdings. Within the college precincts he introduced modest increases in room rentals, ensuring that rooms were used more intensively than in the past. In addition, he arranged for inventories to be made of all moveable goods belonging to the college, these inventories to be audited triennially. The restoration of Corpus's financial health enabled Parker to embark on a programme of repair and augmentation. He had a two-storey gallery constructed near the master's lodge, with stone steps leading down into a garden, extended the walls, and erected a dove house. It also became possible to maintain two additional fellows on the foundation.

Above all Parker revised the college statutes, assisted by William May, president of Queens'. Reducing the old emphasis on priestly functions Parker laid down that only between a third and a half, instead of all, the fellowship need be clerics. No mention was made of traditional intercessory and propitiatory obligations. Instead Parker urged the fellows to preach, and provided monetary rewards for the diligent. The reformist character of the amended statutes is underlined by their abrogation under Mary and immediate reinstatement under Elizabeth.

Parker's administrative abilities led in January 1545 to his election as vice-chancellor by a sweeping majority. His tenure was marked by two significant episodes. The first, in the spring, arose from Thomas Kirchmeyer's Latin play *Pammachius*, performed by members of Christ's College in Lent term, which mercilessly satirized the abuses of the Roman Catholic church and especially the failings of the popes. A complaint to the university's chancellor, Stephen Gardiner, bishop of Winchester, a conservative in religion, led to Parker's being asked to investigate. Although the bishop was incensed when Parker sent him a text of the play as corrected for performance, Gardiner's attempts to involve the privy council came to nothing, and the affair ran into the sand.

The second episode, of far greater significance, concerned the fate of the entire university. The Chantries Act of December 1545, by raising the prospect of another round of rich pickings by laymen from ancient endowments, posed a real threat to all colleges, including those of Oxford and Cambridge. At Cambridge not only did the university's friends prevail upon Queen Katherine Parr to intercede with the king: they also successfully proposed that Henry VIII should delegate the task of surveying the property at issue to Cambridge men, rather than to external royal agents. Parker, as vice-chancellor, was one of three commissioners named on 16 January 1546. He helped to construct a survey which presented most of the colleges as so impoverished that the king declared that 'he had not in his realm so many persons so honestly maintained in living, by so little land and rent', adding that 'pity it were these lands should be altered to make them [the colleges] worse' (*Correspondence*, 35–6). Thus were the colleges of Cambridge and Oxford saved.

In February 1548, a year after the accession of Edward VI, Parker was again elected vice-chancellor, almost unanimously. Thus he was involved in preparations for the important royal visitation of 1549, taking part in many of its proceedings as surrogate for his successor, William Bill. In 1549–50 he was engaged in scrutinizing the university accounts, while in 1551–2 he helped search the muniments for information concerning university patronage.

Theological foundations: Parker, Bucer, and Cranmer From 1549 Parker came under the influence of Martin Bucer, the Strasbourg reformer who had been obliged to flee that city in 1548. His works were by then known within educated circles in England, and he had been corresponding with Archbishop Cranmer since at least 1537. At Cranmer's invitation Bucer arrived in England in April 1549 and in the following December was appointed regius professor of divinity at Cambridge. He rapidly became an intimate friend of Parker, who advised the foreigner how to arrange his lectures, presented him to the authorities for his honorary degree of DTh, entertained him to dinner, and lent him money. When Bucer died, on 28 February or 1 March 1551, Parker preached the English funeral sermon, subsequently published as *Howe We Ought to Take the Death of the Godly* (ESTC 19293). A Latin version of the sermon was printed in Bucer's *Scripta Anglicana* (1577). Parker also served as one of Bucer's executors, and in that capacity became heavily involved in complicated negotiations with his widow over the disposal of her late husband's effects. He thereby obtained possession of a substantial portion of Bucer's books and papers, which he continued to study. Bucer's manuscript *Florilegium patristicum*, a compendium of excerpts from the church fathers, was continued after his death until about 1558 by Parker himself. So great was Parker's contribution that its twentieth-century editor published the text under the names of both its compilers. In July 1560, moreover, Parker organized an elaborate public service in Cambridge, designed to restore to a place of honour what was left of Bucer's mortal remains after they had been exhumed and burnt as those of a heretic in February 1557.

Bucer's impact on England was particularly important in four respects. His writings constituted a major source for English liturgical revision. He was heavily involved in the revision of the first Book of Common Prayer, and contributed to the production of the 1550 English ordinal, the one major component of the liturgy not covered by the 1549 prayer book. Finally, in a treatise of applied theology, *De regno Christi*, written in 1550 as a gift for Edward VI, Bucer set out his mature vision of 'Christian discipleship within a loving, responsible *respublica*' (Collinson, *Godly People*, 23). Despite its publication in Latin, and in French and German translations in the following few years, this seminal treatise was only fully translated into English in the 1960s—which in part explains why 'there is no evidence that the book was widely known to the post-Edwardian generation' in England (ibid., 26).

Yet Bucer's work certainly influenced Parker and Grindal. If John Calvin's theology was theocentric Bucer was primarily concerned with 'the well being of the people of God' (Collinson, *Godly People*, 21), and he has been dubbed 'the principal spokesman for the moderate Protestants in Europe, those who sought ecumenical solutions in a time of confessional conflict' (Steinmetz, 85). Both Parker and Grindal fell into that category, but the extent to which their actions as leaders of the conservatively protestant settlement of religion in 1559 were influenced by Bucer's eirenicism remains hotly debated by historians and theologians alike. While claims that Grindal was more truly Bucer's disciple remain unproven, there are stronger grounds for arguing that Parker, who seems in some respects consciously to have modelled his primacy on that of the much more radical Thomas Cranmer, may even have striven to combine the ideals of both Bucer and Cranmer and to impose this somewhat uneasy blend of reformed churchmanship on Elizabethan England.

Advancement under Henry VIII and Edward VI During the 1540s Parker started to accumulate ecclesiastical preferments. On 10 September 1541 the king's charter of refoundation appointed him canon of the second prebend in Ely Cathedral. To this he added the Essex rectory of Ashen, valued at £8 per annum, in February 1543 (resigned by 9 February 1546), the Norfolk rectory of Burlingham St Andrew, valued at £12 per annum, in April 1544 (resigned by 15 November 1550), and the Cambridgeshire rectory of Landbeach in December 1545. It is not known whether Parker resided at any of his benefices.

In 1547, aged forty-three, Parker took a momentous personal step. Since about 1544 he had been living with Margaret Harleston (1519–1570) of Mattishall in Norfolk, and in June 1547 they married, well before the legislation of December 1549 legalizing clerical marriage. They had four sons, two of whom, John (*b.* 1548) and Matthew (*b.* 1551), reached adulthood. Then in June or July 1549, while visiting his native Norfolk, Parker was caught up in Kett's rebellion. Entering the rebel camp on Mousehold Heath outside Norwich he courageously preached submission to the authorities for the sake of the common good. A heckler shouted that Parker had been paid by the gentry to say such things and the crowd turned ugly until the singing of the *Te Deum* in English distracted attention and enabled Parker to slip away. Much later Parker commissioned his secretary Alexander Neville to write a detailed account of the rising, published in 1575 as *De furoribus Norfolciensium Ketto duce*.

In October 1551 Parker became involved in the Edwardian regime's abortive attempt officially to adapt the ancient canon law to current English usage. Although he was not nominated to the committee which finally drafted the *Reformatio legum ecclesiasticarum*, which Cranmer presented to the House of Lords in March 1553, that draft survives (as BL, Harley MS 426) and Parker certainly possessed a fair copy. It is now lost but he made it available to John Foxe, who published it in 1571.

Further preferment followed on 9 June 1552 when Parker was presented by the crown to the deanery of Lincoln and to the prebend of Corringham in Lincoln Cathedral. The deanery was valued around £200 per annum, the prebend £38 16*s.* 6*d.* He was dean for too short a period to make his mark at Lincoln but during his tenure became involved in an important constitutional experiment, when in February 1553 he and three other prebendaries were nominated by chapter to represent them in what appears to have been an *ad hoc* hybrid session of parliament, its membership carefully controlled so that it could authorize two radical measures, namely the new catechism and the forty-two articles of religion. It is significant that Parker should have been sufficiently trusted by his Lincoln colleagues to be nominated their proctor in this controversial business. Indeed his involvement confirms that he was perceived as a coming man in the Edwardian years.

Marian retirement Although Parker had no real involvement in the duke of Northumberland's attempt in 1553 to divert the succession away from Mary Tudor to Lady Jane Grey, he suffered as a married clergyman from the repeal of the Edwardian religious legislation. He noted his gradual demotion with what looks like increasing bitterness, recording how in December 1553 he resigned the mastership of Corpus to Laurence Mopted, 'whom, under constraint, I had myself chosen as my successor', and then how on 2 April and 21 May 1554 respectively he was 'Deprived of my prebend in the Church of Ely' and 'Despoiled of my deanery of Lincoln' (*Correspondence*, viii). (In fact he had been deprived of his prebend and deanery by 27 March and 19 April respectively.)

And yet after this enforced relinquishment of the burdens of office Parker almost immediately felt a curious sense of elation, recording how, though without an income, he:

> lived as a private individual, so happy before God in my conscience, and so far from being either ashamed or dejected, that the delightful literary leisure to which the good providence of God recalled me yielded me much greater and more solid enjoyments, than my former busy and dangerous kind of life had ever afforded me. (*Correspondence*, viii)

The 1574 *Life* records that he 'lurked secreatlye … within the house off one off his frindes leading a poore life whithout any mans aide or succour' (sig. A5*r*). References in two Cambridge wills suggest that he took refuge in that vicinity, and at some point he was obliged to flee in the night 'from such as sought for me to my peril' (*Correspondence*, 59). In the process he fell from his horse and suffered severe injury.

Wherever he was living Parker applied himself to three literary endeavours. One was the continuation of Bucer's *Florilegium patristicum*. In addition he produced a metrical version of the psalter in English, prefaced by verses addressed to the reader and a seventy-four stanza poem on 'the Virtue of the Psalms', each psalm preceded by a prose statement of the devotional argument and followed by a collect. There then follows a verse translation of the canticles, the Athanasian creed, and 'Come Holy Ghost'. An appendix contains nine tunes by Thomas Tallis (one of them the basis for Ralph Vaughan Williams's *Fantasia on a Theme by Thomas Tallis*). According to Parker himself he was urged by friends to make more widely available a production originally intended only for his personal use, a claim not necessarily contradicted by the existence of an early manuscript draft (Inner Temple Library, London, misc. MS 36) showing how he adapted the psalms 'for use by a congregation in corporate worship' (Bjorklund, 198), the rhyme and vocabulary kept simple to ensure that the book was usable by those who lacked musical training. *The Whole Psalter translated into English Metre* was finally printed by John Day, probably in 1567.

Parker's third literary project was a defence of clerical marriage. In this, however, he acted primarily as the midwife for the work of John Ponet, who had died in 1556 before he could complete his response to a tract published two years earlier by Thomas Martyn. *A Defence of Priestes Mariages* (1562; ESTC 17519) was based upon an unfinished draft of Ponet's work, and the exact extent of Parker's contribution is uncertain. He claimed to 'have written a defence of the marriage of priests against Thomas Martin' (*Correspondence*, ix), but the violence of the language in the published text seems much more in keeping with Ponet's style than Parker's, suggesting that the latter's role was essentially editorial.

Elevation to Canterbury Both Queen Mary and Reginald Pole, archbishop of Canterbury, died on 17 November 1558. On 9 December Nicholas Bacon, soon to be made lord keeper of the great seal, and Sir William Cecil, the new queen's principal secretary, sent Parker an informal summons to London. Parker knew what this overture portended, and in a lengthy reply declared that his abilities were not commensurate with such responsibilities. Moreover, he did not wish to disappoint his patrons' expectations of his competence. In any case his health was poor. All he wished for was a prebendal income sufficient to enable him to preach God's word 'amongst the simple strayed sheep of God's fold in … destitute parishes' (*Correspondence*, 50–51). When not active as an itinerant preacher he hoped to spend most of his time in Cambridge. If he had any ambition it was to return to Cambridge as master of Corpus; it was there that he could best serve the commonwealth.

Notwithstanding these protestations Bacon and Cecil again ordered Parker to London in two further letters; his compliance is suggested by his preaching before the queen at Paul's Cross on 10 February 1559. But on 1 March he wrote another long letter, again protesting his inadequacy. He did, however, offer Bacon his thoughts on the qualities requisite in a primate, hoping that the primacy would be bestowed on a man who was not arrogant, fainthearted, or covetous. An arrogant man would 'sit in his own light' and 'discourage his fellows to join with him in unity of doctrine, which must be their whole strength'. A fainthearted man would be 'too weak to commune with the adversaries, who would be the stouter upon his pusillanimity'. A covetous man would be 'profitable for no estate in any Christian commonwealth, to serve it rightly' (*Correspondence*, 57). Bacon informed Parker in mid-May that he could not avoid promotion: he exactly fitted the description he had so helpfully supplied.

Parker's elevation to Canterbury proved a tortuous affair. On 6 June an Italian resident in London reported hearing that Parker had been made archbishop, which probably merely meant that he had accepted nomination to the see. Only on 18 July was a *congé d'élire* issued to the dean and chapter ordering his election, which took place on 1 August. Letters patent for his consecration were issued on 9 September to four surviving Marian bishops and the deprived Edwardian diocesans John Scory and William Barlow. At least three of the Marians refused to officiate and thus, under the terms of the Appointment of Bishops Act of 1533, Parker's consecration proved technically impossible, another archbishop assisted by two bishops, or four bishops acting in concert, being required. Compromise was effected, however, by recourse to a committee of senior canon lawyers, under a commission dated 6 December, and Parker was finally confirmed to the primacy on 9 December and consecrated on the 17th. Meanwhile there had been a serious showdown over the government's attempt to enforce the 1559 Act of Exchange, by which the crown was entitled, during vacancies of sees, to retain episcopal temporalities in exchange for impropriate rectories. From this débâcle Parker and his fellow bishops-elect emerged bloody but unbowed.

One side-effect of Parker's consecration was a long-lasting controversy over the validity of orders within the Church of England. In 1896 Pope Leo XIII's bull *Apostolicae curae* declared all Anglican orders invalid on the grounds of alleged defects in the Edwardian ordinal, used not only at Parker's consecration but also at those of other early Elizabethan bishops. Parker's consecration has been attacked from other directions. The Nag's Head fable, relating that Parker was consecrated at a mock service held in the Nag's Head tavern in London's Cheapside, is not recorded before 1604 and has been long discredited. Of greater substance are reservations concerning the legal status of the Edwardian ordinal, added to the second Book of Common Prayer in 1552. By an oversight the ordinal did not form part of the restored prayer book of 1559, and was consequently without parliamentary sanction when Parker was consecrated. Parker and Cecil were aware of the problem, and devised an ingenious solution. When the second commission was issued for Parker's consecration it contained a clause whereby Elizabeth invoked her royal supremacy to supply any defects in her mandate arising out of the special circumstances of the case. This measure might plausibly be taken to validate the ordinal, which finally achieved a secure legislative status in 1566.

Parker's archiepiscopate: problems of perception Archbishop Parker has all too often been misrepresented as a man whose passionate early concern for reform fizzled out somewhere along the road, leaving behind a weary determination to find a *via media* between the extremes of Catholicism and some form of protestantism. In fact he retained impeccable reformist credentials. Though he did not go into exile under Mary and return 'radicalized', as many did, he was well informed about continental religious developments, as might have been expected of a friend of Martin Bucer, and in any case there is good evidence that he co-operated with former exiles in the period 1559–63 in planning further reformation. For him, as for his colleagues, the Elizabethan church settlement represented a starting point, not a terminus, and informed contemporaries knew well that what was being restored from 1559 was a protestant church, indeed a church of Reformed protestantism, for Lutheranism had been effectively discarded under Edward VI. The Edwardian regime provided two alternative models to be followed. One, personified by Cranmer and Nicholas Ridley, stood for gradual protestant reform, willing to make concessions initially to conservative opinion. The other, represented by John Hooper, stood for rapid and decisive change, without concessions to popery. The difference between the two positions was not over the desirability of continued reformation, but between a willingness to recycle the usable elements of England's Catholic heritage for the sake of stability, and a desire to make a clean break, with all its attendant risks to stability.

These two models still jostled for position in 1559, and the tensions between them erupted in the vestiarian controversy of 1565–6. Their persistence, stemming from the ambiguities of the Elizabethan religious settlement, led to the emergence of a radical movement which drew its strength from a sense of betrayal that the principles espoused by Hooper had not been adopted as the basis for further reform. In fact there was always a danger that, in attempting to please everybody through equivocation and compromise, the Elizabethan regime would end up pleasing nobody. Parker's own position was essentially Cranmerian, but whereas Cranmer had aspired to salvage certain re-usable features of Catholicism, if only temporarily, his Elizabethan successor wished to save re-usable features of Cranmer's church, again not necessarily immutably, and to make accommodation not with Catholicism but with different visions of a Reformed church. Thus Parker conceded in 1563 that 'divers of my brethren will rather note me … too earnest in moderation, which towards them I have used, and will still do, till mediocrity shall be received amongst us' (*Correspondence*, 173). This desire for 'mediocrity' may have arisen from a wish to conciliate, but it was also forced on him by the queen's unshakeable conservatism. He admitted as much at the end of his life, writing that he cared nothing 'either for cap, tippet, surplice, or wafer-bread', though 'for the laws so established I esteem them' (ibid., 478). As events showed, Parker proved too Erastian for his own good.

The Elizabethan church settlement Parker is usually hailed as one of the chief architects of the Elizabethan religious settlement. Its creation was protracted, lasting until the Canterbury provincial convocation of 1563, but its legislative foundations were laid in Elizabeth's first parliament (January–May 1559). From the Roman Catholic side the government faced the threat of papal excommunication, the opposition of the remaining Marian bishops, fortified by conservative lay peers, and the possibility of foreign invasion which might coincide with domestic risings on behalf of the old faith. On the protestant side, where memories of recent martyrdoms were fresh, the ranks were divided between men, like Parker himself, who had lived in retirement under Mary, those who had reluctantly conformed to Catholicism, those who had belonged to underground protestant congregations, and those who had gone into voluntary exile. Among these last some were prepared to accept the 1552 prayer book, while others, inspired by the example of continental Reformed churches, looked for further purges of 'popish' impurities. To reconcile elements so diverse was an almost impossible task. Parker's reluctance to accept the primacy is understandable.

An additional problem lay in Parker's relations with the queen. Though undoubtedly protestant by education and conviction, Elizabeth was conservative in her religious sympathies. It has been argued, on the evidence of liturgical texts from the early months of the reign, that she originally intended to restore the 1549 prayer book. If so she was disappointed, for the same 1559 parliament which enacted an Act of Supremacy, giving her the title of supreme governor of the Church of England, also passed an Act of Uniformity legislating for the use of a slightly amended version of the 1552 prayer book. But where vestments were concerned this second statute, probably at the queen's behest, returned to the usage of 1549, which commanded the use of the alb, with either the chasuble or the cope. Parker's letters suggest that he was neither in London nor at court between March and May 1559, and so cannot have been directly involved in the discussions which led to this ecclesiastical legislation. But he was probably at court by 6 June, and thenceforward his participation in political affairs increased.

An immediate manifestation of his involvement was a change in policy over vestments, where Elizabeth's stance put her at odds with the emergent church hierarchy. By 13 June injunctions had been drawn up for a royal visitation of the entire national church later that summer, including an order prescribing the vestments in use at the death of Edward VI, that is, the surplice for priests and the rochet for bishops and archbishops. It seems likely that Parker, probably supported by Richard Cox (soon to be bishop of Ely), had insisted on the alteration. The injunction concerning vestments is certainly strikingly Parkerian. It emphasizes that seemly vestments must be worn by those admitted into 'any society of learning in either of the universities, or elsewhere', as well as into 'any vocation ecclesiastical' (Frere, *Visitation Articles*, 3.20). It is the only one to quote a supporting biblical text, and that in Latin. Parker's English prose is often larded with Latin phrases, including learned quotations. Thus, far from remaining aloof, Parker may have become closely involved in formulating the vestiarian component of the injunctions.

Further differences with the queen arose over images. Between 21 June and 28 September 1559, while Elizabeth was away from London, unknown persons removed the crucifix and other ornaments from the Chapel Royal. Her subsequent insistence on their restoration sparked off a major dispute over images. Parker and his colleagues were horrified by the queen's order. Probably early in 1560 either he or Grindal prepared a written remonstration to Elizabeth, and the privy council planned a formal debate at which Parker and Cox would dispute with Jewel and Grindal. In the event the crucifix and other ornaments remained in the Chapel Royal for years to come, but the price the queen paid for her victory was a major concession on a related issue, the abandonment of her earlier insistence that rood screens and their accompanying statuary be replaced in parish churches. Edwin Sandys, bishop of Worcester, a radical hardliner, expressed pleasure at this outcome, and declared that only vestments—'I mean the copes'—remained a stumbling block (Robinson, 1.74).

The synods of 1560–1561 Perhaps it was a sign of growing confidence on the part of Parker and the bishops that in 1560, probably in March or April, they held a synod at Lambeth. Its most significant outcome was the document now known as the 'Interpretations' of the bishops. Elaborating and commenting variously upon the 1559 injunctions and the same year's Book of Common Prayer, it includes a series of twenty-three Latin doctrinal articles based upon the forty-two articles of 1553, and was probably produced by the bishops for their own use, though parts of it were more widely circulated. When the synod ended the bishops informed the queen that they had 'of late in our consultations devised certain orders for uniform and quiet ministration in religion', and expressed the hope that she would not disapprove (*Correspondence*, 130).

Another episcopal synod assembled the following year. At its first session, probably held at Lambeth in March 1561, the bishops agreed a revised version of the 'Interpretations', now entitled 'Resolutions and orders taken by … the bishops, for the present time until a synod may be had for … maintenance of uniformity in matters ecclesiastical throughout … both provinces'. By 'synod' the bishops meant 'convocation'. They probably also pondered a text which had been called for a year earlier—a 'brief … declaration' of the essentials of 'our religion', which was to be read by clerics at their first entry to a living and twice a year thereafter. This declaration was printed later in 1561 as *A declaration of certain principal articles of religion, set out by the order of both archbishops … and the rest of the bishops, for the unity of doctrine to be taught* (Corpus Christi College, Cambridge, MS 106, 421–2). Although the precise authorship is obscure Parker probably played a leading role in its preparation. It was resolved that 'the declaration devised for unity of doctrine may be enjoined to be used throughout the realm uniformly' (Kennedy, *Interpretations*, 43). When the second session of the synod convened at Lambeth on 12 April the decision to promulgate the declaration was explicitly reaffirmed, and in exactly the same words.

Behind these documents lay the efforts of the bishops to find a *modus vivendi* with a church settlement in whose creation they had had little part, and whose legal standing was not always clear. Parker was energetic in assuming a co-ordinating role on a national scale. Following the presumed ratification of 'Resolutions and orders' in April 1561 efforts were made to implement them. Bishop Thomas Bentham of Coventry and Lichfield wrote to one of his archdeacons on 15 April ordering the execution of 'certane resolutions' agreed by Parker and the bishops 'for the better understandynge and observynge of the Quenes Majesties injunctions' ('Letter-book of Thomas Bentham', 211–12). In another letter, dated 7 May, Bentham revealed his concern that his chaplain, then visiting London, should obtain 'the table of the degrees of mariedge' (ibid., 226), suggesting that Parker had already produced the 'Table set forth by the Archbishop of Canterbury' referred to in 'Resolutions and orders'. In the event, however, it was not officially published by Parker until 1563.

Where vestments were concerned Parker may have succeeded in ensuring that the 1559 royal injunctions pointed towards the vestiarian practices of 1552–3, but the 1559 Act of Uniformity (and the corresponding rubric in the 1559 prayer book) none the less prescribed the usage of 1549. In synod the bishops resolved to impose article 30 of the injunctions upon pain either of deposition or sequestration of income, intending, through a reintroduction of the vestments 'most commonly and orderly received' in 1552–3 (Frere, *Visitation Articles*, 3.20), to render the clergy easily identifiable both within and without church. But two causes of confusion arose. The bishops failed at this time to spell out exactly what was acceptable practice and what was not, while by retaining the usages of 1549, which left ministers free to choose whether or not they would wear the surplice at such times as they were not formally robed for the administration of holy communion, they licensed clerics to disregard precisely that concern for vestiarian distinctiveness which their other measures after 1559 were designed to uphold. The resulting uncertainty and diversity of practice offended the queen and landed Parker in trouble.

The Canterbury provincial convocation of 1563 The synodal documents of 1560–61 show that the bishops expected their resolutions to be placed before a convocation, where, they hoped, they would become official canons following approval by convocation and the queen. Parker co-ordinated preparations for the first convocation to meet (January 1563) under the conditions of the 1559 settlement. Two important documents were drawn up in advance: 'Certen Articles in substance, desired to be granted by the Quenes majestie' and 'Gennerall notes of matters to be movid by the Clergie in the nexte Parliament & Synod', the latter being a reworking of the former. These did not, as was once believed, originate in convocation's lower house, but were episcopal creations; based on the synodal papers of 1560–61, they advocate a strongly radical programme and reveal the extent to which Parker and his colleagues were themselves proponents of further reformation. 'Gennerall notes', for example, asserts that 'the use of vestment[es], Copes and Surplesses' must be 'frome hensfurth taken awaye' (Inner Temple Library, London, Petyt MS 538/47, fol. 421*v*).

This lurch to the left may reflect the increased influence of the returned exiles, but may also have been prompted by the diocesan visitations conducted from 1560 onwards and by Parker's first provincial survey of the ministry, carried out between November 1560 and summer 1562. The findings of these inquiries concerning the quality of the clergy appalled the hierarchy. Parker's systematic attempt to obtain detailed information concerning the qualifications and activities of the clergy is particularly important as evidence for the extent to which he saw England as a confessional state, in which the institutional structures of the pre-Reformation church had effectively become the religious arm of the queen's government, to be deployed for the imposition of uniform standards of belief and practice. He needed such information to improve the calibre of his clerical rank and file.

Parker prepared carefully, ensuring that he was fully briefed about convocation's procedure and that its prolocutor (the liaison officer between its two houses) was his own nominee—Alexander Nowell, dean of St Paul's. Effective management helped to achieve one major success: the promulgation, after lively debate, of the articles of religion, a confessional statement replacing the twenty-three Latin articles of 1560. These new articles were submitted to Elizabeth some time after 10 February 1563, receiving her approval only after modification and resubmission. Parker and the bishops eventually persuaded her to accept their revisions, and in 1571 thirty-nine articles, based on the forty-two Edwardian ones, were ratified by parliament. The effect of the changes made in 1563 was to condemn Catholic tenets more strongly than in 1553, and to define more closely the sacrament of the eucharist. Subscription to this text was required of those clergymen who had not been ordained according to the protestant ordinal, of all candidates for orders, and of all seeking admission to benefices.

The convocation enjoyed more success with doctrine than with discipline. A 'book of discipline' was presented by the lower house to the bishops on 26 February and referred to a committee chaired by Parker. After 5 March it disappears from the formal record, but almost certainly survives at Corpus (MS 121, 267–355), with the heading, in Parker's hand, 'Articles drawn out bi som certen and wer exhibited to be admytted bi authorytie, but not so allowed'. The only authority by whom such articles could have been disallowed was the queen. Thus the fate of this book of discipline reveals that by 1563 Elizabeth had already set her face against further reformation. It was a decision that had dire consequences for the peace of the church, plunging Parker into a succession of crises from which only death released him. The signs appeared all the more ominous in the light of petitions and articles presented by militant reformers during the convocation. Parker and many other bishops were largely sympathetic to the militants, but the queen's implacable hostility to radical measures threatened to place them in an increasingly uncomfortable position, between royal obduracy and evangelical pugnacity.

The vestiarian controversy: programmes and strategies The vestiarian controversy was a defining feature of Parker's troubled archiepiscopate. At its heart lay uncertainty over legal practice, over the location of ultimate authority in the church, and over the precise significance of vestments, and whether or not they constituted *adiaphora*, or 'things indifferent'—points of ritual or organization unnecessary for salvation but representing custom and established order. Much anguish might have been avoided if a revised version of the prayer book incorporating the changes introduced through the 1559 royal injunctions had been issued, but that would have entailed passing a new act of uniformity, with its attendant risks for the entire religious settlement, and was surely ruled out by the queen. Furthermore the deep biblicism of the 'hotter sort' of protestant aroused grave misgivings as to the queen's authority, implicit in the royal supremacy, to prescribe clerical usage concerning vestments, the more so because the former radicals regarded them not as *adiaphora*, but as conjuring up:

> images of the Roman, and ultimately of the Jewish priesthood, clean contrary to the gospel and to the general tenor of scripture; they were therefore snares for the simple, not matters of indifference, and no human authority could require their use. (Collinson, *Elizabethan Puritan Movement*, 69)

By late 1564 pressure for action over vestments could no longer be contained, despite the efforts of Robert Dudley, earl of Leicester (a leading patron of precisians, and as such a constant thorn in Parker's side), to have the issue dropped. On 25 January 1565 a royal letter, ordering Parker to impose conformity, finally precipitated a crisis. The missive can hardly have come as a surprise, for circumstantial evidence suggests that a draft text, composed by Cecil, had been sent to the archbishop ten days earlier. Parker may even have procured the letter in order to bring matters to a head. On 30 January he communicated the substance of the queen's directive to Grindal, charging him to transmit the command to his fellow bishops. Diocesan certificates detailing instances of diversity in doctrine, ceremonies, or clerical behaviour were to be returned by 28 February. Parker also set up a small working party, headed by himself, to compile what he hoped would be a definitive statement of policy on a range of issues. But when the completed articles were submitted to Elizabeth she twice vetoed them. Parker wrote a despondent letter to Cecil lamenting that the bishops were inhibited from setting out any provincial orders without licence, but then at the queen's instigation he amended the articles, making it clear that they were being issued by the ecclesiastical commissioners. They were printed in March 1566, under the title *Advertisements partly for due order in the publique administration of common prayers and usinge the holy sacramentes, and partly for the apparrell of all persons ecclesiasticall* (ESTC 10026).

Of the five sections of the *Advertisements* three concern vestments. In one respect they represent a notable retreat by the bishops from their earlier position, for they restricted the use of the cope to cathedral and collegiate churches. Officiating ministers elsewhere were expected to wear only a surplice. But the general thrust of vestiarian policy was unchanged: uniformity was to be maintained, and clergymen must remain easily distinguishable from the laity by their attire. Thus clarity was at last achieved on the issue of outward apparel, detailed provision being made for the garments which all clergymen should wear at all times. The last section comprises a long list of 'protestations' to which anyone admitted to ecclesiastical office was required to subscribe, among them the undertaking to 'use sobriety in apparel, and especially in the church at common prayers, according to order appointed' (Gee and Hardy, 467–75). Such a drive for conformity, at a time when radical attitudes were hardening over ceremonies, made the concession over copes irrelevant, ensuring that the *Advertisements* was a dead letter from the start.

The vestiarian controversy: campaigns Alongside his efforts to define policy over vestments went Parker's assault upon individual nonconformists, a tactic that brought him so much opprobrium that he came to fear for his life. At first his approach was conciliatory. In December 1564 he summoned two heads of Oxford colleges, Laurence Humphrey and Thomas Sampson, the academic ringleaders of vestiarian resistance, to a meeting at which he hoped to negotiate a solution to the problem. But though they agreed that the garments were permissible they refused to use them on the grounds that they were inexpedient. Knowing that to punish them would be to stir up trouble for himself Parker hoped for the backing of the secular authorities, but was left dangerously exposed by the reluctance of the government to associate itself with a divisive ecclesiastical policy. It did not help that on 20 March 1565 Sampson and Humphrey joined eighteen other divines, including John Foxe and Alexander Nowell, in petitioning Parker and his fellow ecclesiastical commissioners for liberty to follow their consciences. On the evidence of the document's endorsement, bishops Grindal, Horne, and Cox—three of its five recipients—accepted the appeal. Thus only Parker and Bishop Guest of Rochester appear to have dissented. But the archbishop could not now turn back. He had already told Cecil, 'Better not to have begun, except more be done' (*Correspondence*, 234–5), and, after a final attempt at persuasion on 29 April, Sampson was deprived by 26 May of the deanery of Christ Church, though Humphrey managed to retain his presidency of Magdalen.

At Cambridge, too, there were difficulties, initiated early in 1565 by sermons preached against images by George Withers of Corpus and against vestments by William Fulke of St John's. Parker neutralized Withers by depriving him of his preaching licence. More troublesome was the extensive disobedience at St John's. Dealing with it was largely the responsibility of Cecil, as chancellor of the university, but Parker became involved and in December sought to push Cecil into decisive action, in a letter revealing his increasingly hardline approach, as well as his feverish state of mind:

> [If] you their chancellor, of the privy council and in such place and credit as ye be, will suffer so much authority to be borne under foot by a bragging brainless head or two, in mine opinion your conscience shall never be excusable … Execution, execution, execution of laws and orders must be the first and the last part of good governance. (*Correspondence*, 246)

By the end of the month Fulke had been expelled, and shortly afterwards Andrew Perne, master of Peterhouse, assured Parker that 'yowr Grac[e] and Mr Secretarie [Cecil] … have brokyn the wilfull disorderid that are wise in their owne conceites' (Collinson, *Godly People*, 331).

Early in 1565 the ecclesiastical commissioners began an offensive against nonconformist ministers in the city of London. Their first target was Edward Brocklesby, vicar of Hemel Hempstead, Hertfordshire, but also apparently a chaplain in the Southwark household of Bishop Guest of Rochester. Since Parker himself had trouble over vestments with his chaplain Robert Cole, rector of St Mary-le-Bow, it looks as if the bishops planned to begin tackling the London vestiarian problem by turning those chaplains of their own who sympathized with the scruples of the precisians. Cole was induced to conform, but Brocklesby was not. Appearing before Parker at Lambeth on 8 May he was the first minister to be deprived of his benefice for refusing the surplice.

The London campaign resumed in 1566. In late January Grindal is said to have met the entire London clergy at St Sepulchre, where all but a handful of conservatives accepted a compromise whereby they would wear the surplice in church and outside it a round cap and a 'turkey' gown. But Parker would tolerate nothing less than the vestiarian programme as set out in the *Advertisements*, and he had the support of the queen. When he told her that the precisians were prepared to go to prison for their beliefs she urged him to proceed. Accordingly it was decided on 20 March to summon the London clergy *en masse* to Lambeth for examination as to their conformity over vestments. There they would be asked to subscribe to their willingness to conform to all vestiarian requirements. Beneficed non-subscribers would have their livings sequestrated. If they did not submit within three months they would be deprived. Many refusals were expected.

The climax came at Lambeth on 26 March 1566. For several days Parker and Grindal had been trying to secure the presence of members of the privy council in order to demonstrate government solidarity (Parker's own exclusion from it was one of his difficulties). In the event Cecil stayed away, but Bacon may have been present, to join with Parker, Grindal, and Dean Goodman of Westminster as representatives of authority in facing ninety-eight London ministers. Robert Cole modelled the prescribed vestments. A hostile account records that the company was addressed in peremptory tones:

> the Council's pleasure is that strictly ye keep the unity of apparel like to this man here … Ye that will presently subscribe, *Volo—I will*—so write: you that will not subscribe, *Nolo—I will not*. Be brief; make no words: so is the order. (Frere, *The English Church in the Reigns of Elizabeth and James I*, 1904, 119)

Sixty-one ministers subscribed. The thirty-seven who did not were suspended and the fruits of their benefices sequestered. Parker defended his actions by referring not to the *Advertisements* (perhaps not yet printed) but to the 1559 Act of Uniformity, which, he reminded Cecil, stipulated that the bishops had 'full power and authority to reform, and punish by censures of the church, all and singular persons which shall offend' (*Correspondence*, 273). He was also able to claim success. Suspension and sequestration, with deprivation to follow, were bitter pills for nonconformist ministers, many of whom had families to support. Some of them, moreover, had struggled long and hard to obtain their benefices. By the end of 1566 only a hard core of eight incumbents, three lecturers, and three or four curates remained obdurate.

The vestiarian controversy: pyrrhic victory Meanwhile pamphlet warfare had broken out in the capital. Its progenitor was the talented and versatile Robert Crowley, vicar of St Giles Cripplegate, who was among the nonconformists suspended on 26 March. A week later he fell foul of authority again, harassing choristers who wore surplices in procession to a funeral in his church. When Parker heard the case on 4 April he discovered that Crowley would not allow a conforming minister to officiate at St Giles during his suspension and deprived him on the spot, consigning him to house arrest. Crowley quickly retaliated. Having procured written statements from the other suspended ministers, he turned them into a polemical diatribe, published (anonymously) by 10 May 1566 as *A briefe discourse against the outwarde apparrell and ministring garmentes of the popishe church* (ESTC 6078). Its impact is shown by the speed with which it provoked an official rejoinder, in print by the same date. Entitled *A briefe examination for the tyme, of a certaine declaration, lately put in print in the name and defence of certaine ministers in London, refusing to weare the apparell prescribed by the lawes and orders of the Realme* (ESTC 10387) this lengthy and systematic refutation is commonly attributed to Parker himself. It ridiculed the writings of the nonconformists as 'superfluous brawlings of men perverse in hart' (Primus, 116), reflecting his characteristic view that when scripture does not speak, the prince may do so. It was not a position calculated to win over the radicals, and the war of words continued.

In expending so much energy in confronting the London nonconformists Parker was concurring with Cox's judgement that 'if London were reformed, all the realm would soon follow' (*Correspondence*, 270). The perception generated a certain ruthlessness, reinforced by desperation at the privy council's failure to support him. On 12 April 1566 the archbishop reported that he had spent the whole week dealing with 'brabbling matters', and that his health was beginning to fail: 'my age will not suffer me to peruse all the parishes … an ox can draw no more than he can … Must I do still all things alone?' (ibid., 277–9). By the 28th he had reached the end of his tether, protesting to Cecil that he always seemed to be waiting either for the queen's 'toleration' or for 'further aid', neither of which materialized: 'can it be thought, that I alone, having sun and moon against me, can compass this difficulty?' Struggling to understand why the councillors could not 'consult in time to prevent so many miseries', he bluntly informed Cecil that he discharged himself of 'my allegiaunce, duty, and conscience to you in such places as ye be' (ibid., 280–81). Here, surely, was a good man brought to his lowest ebb.

Two considerations finally roused the council to action—the proliferation of polemical tracts and the fact that five suspended ministers had continued to preach in their various parishes, 'yewsynge words of great vehemencie agaynst ye ordar … set forthe, as also agaynst ye quene, counseyll, and byshops' (Gairdner, 138–9). Shortly before 6 June 1566 the council took steps to remove the offending preachers from the metropolis, but by then it was too late to salvage Parker's reputation. As he himself appreciated, he had been too diligent for the nonconformists' mud not to stick; hence his references to his doings having been 'vilely reported' and his honesty 'foully traduced' (*Correspondence*, 279, 284).

For both church and archbishop the long-term effects of the vestiarian controversy were serious. Clandestine separatist conventicles began forming in London. If in 1566 Parker won the battle, in that hardly any true radicals were then left in possession of London livings, his victory was arguably a pyrrhic one; in 1566 he unwittingly lit the fuse that in 1572 ignited the conflagration known as the admonition controversy; by prosecuting his drive for conformity so rigorously he drove some moderate nonconformists into open revolt. The disaster of 1566 was all the more tragic because Parker's hopes of achieving conformity were bound to be frustrated by the jurisdictional complexities of the early Elizabethan church, by the nonconformist predilections of many who held authority within it, and by the shortage of preachers. Several of the disaffected were still able to achieve promotion surprisingly quickly, while others, drummed out of London benefices, continued to minister in country livings. Hamstrung by a ramshackle administrative structure and by endemic pluralism, Parker emerged from the conflicts of the mid-1560s with his primacy crippled, while his antagonists lived to fight another day.

Bills, books, and homilies Hardly had the vestiarian controversy reached its climax than Parker faced further difficulties in parliament. Late in 1566 six bills on religious issues were introduced into the House of Commons (known as the alphabetical bills because they were distinguished by the letters A to F). There can be no doubt that they originated with Parker and the bishops, smarting under three recent setbacks: the queen's rejection of the prospective canons drawn up by convocation in 1563, her failure to give unambiguous support for the *Advertisements*, and their inability to contain the increasingly militant puritan threat. Bill A, read on 5 December, sought statutory confirmation of the doctrinal articles of 1563. The texts of the other five are lost, but the Commons journals reveal that they concerned such matters as the order of ministers and the residence of pastors. Altogether they constituted a further attempt at a package of reforming measures. They were probably introduced through the Commons in the hope of concealing the bishops' involvement in their preparation, so making it harder for the queen to reject them. But Elizabeth got wind of what was afoot and checked the progress of bill A, whereupon bills B to F died as well. This parliamentary débâcle can only have depressed Parker further. At the end of the month he was too ill to venture to court.

Amid Parker's failures a notable triumph was the publication in 1562, doubtless with his support, of John Jewel's *Apologia Ecclesiae Anglicanae*, the first systematic defence of the Church of England. The archbishop was probably instrumental in organizing the English translation which Anne, Lady Bacon, published in 1564. Another milestone was the production of a quasi-official Latin catechism. Composed by Alexander Nowell and approved by the 1563 convocation, it was submitted to Cecil and then scrutinized by an unidentified commentator. Nowell revised it in the light of the latter's suggestions and Parker, having consulted the new recension, decided on publication. The *Catechismus* appeared in print shortly before 16 June 1570. A third achievement was the issue of a second Book of Homilies in 1563–4, with the archbishop acting as general editor. His contributions cannot easily be identified because the texts were printed unsigned. Elizabeth had probably given the volume her grudging approval by 25 March 1564—the first four editions all bear the date 1563.

Parker gave particular attention to the so-called Bishops' Bible, which has been called his brainchild; he was so pleased with it that he gave an account of its gestation in the *Matthaeus*. By the mid-1560s the pressing need for English bibles in parish churches was gradually being met by the 1560 Geneva version, available from 1562 in a folio format. The work of Marian exiles, it provided an accurate translation, but many of its marginal glosses and explanatory notes advocated theologically (and politically) unwelcome aspects of Calvinist doctrine. The suggestion that a new folio bible be produced for public use in church probably originated with Bishop Cox, but Parker assumed overall direction of the project. Instructing his team of translators to follow the 1539 Great Bible, except where it 'varieth manifestly from the Hebrew or Greek original', he ordered that 'Bitter notes upon any text' were to be eschewed, as was 'any determination in places of controversy'. Passages judged unedifying—genealogies, for instance—were to be marked out so that they could be avoided in public reading. Any words in the old translation tending to 'lightness or obscenity' were to be replaced by inoffensive alternatives (*Correspondence*, 336–7 n. 1).

Although the work was divided among at least eleven bishops (assisted by perusers), the dean of Westminster, and three other scholars, the lion's share was undertaken by Parker himself. As well as various introductory sections (for example, prefaces to the psalter and to the New Testament), he contributed Genesis, Exodus, the gospels of Matthew and Mark, all of Paul's epistles except for Romans and I Corinthians, and the epistle to the Hebrews. Work probably began late in 1565. By 22 September 1568 the substance of the book had been finished. Shortly afterwards, on 5 October, a presentation copy of the initial folio printing (now in the Folger Shakespeare Library, Washington DC) was ready for the queen. The text contains many blunders and misprints. The publication of a quarto edition in 1569 provided an opportunity to correct them, especially in the Old Testament. The New Testament was carefully revised in the second folio printing of 1572 (when, oddly, the Old Testament was reprinted from the text of 1568, rather than the 1569 revision).

Modern assessment of the Bishops' Bible has been unkind, perceiving a 'complete lack of any editorial policy' which allowed the text of the Great Bible to be mangled when it was altered at all, and judging the overall result to be 'either a lazy and ill-informed collation of what had gone before, or, in its original parts, the work of third-rate scholars and second-rate writers' (Hammond, 142–3). Parker must have felt similar misgivings, for in 1572 the Great Bible's rendering of the psalter was reproduced alongside the new version, while in all subsequent editions save one it was printed alone. The sumptuous illustrations of the Bishops' Bible, by contrast, have been universally acclaimed. Apart from maps and tables there are three fine copper engravings, depicting Elizabeth, Cecil, and the earl of Leicester (though only in editions published before 1574), and 124 woodcut illustrations. The latter, the work of the Nuremberg artist Virgil Solis, had first appeared in 1560 in two books printed at Frankfurt-am-Main, one of them Luther's German Bible. They proved so successful that they were reproduced in German and Dutch Bibles published at Cologne. Parker somehow acquired these copies of the original Solis blocks, but had them doctored for use in the Bishops' Bible, with the large blocks in which God was depicted being reworked so that the deity was represented instead by the Hebrew tetragrammaton—the four-lettered name of God. Some of the smaller images of God escaped such censorship, inevitably arousing puritan criticism. The author of *A Second Admonition to the Parliament* (1572; ESTC 4713, 10849) acidly observed that there was 'such a sight of blasphemous pictures of God the father, as what they deserve for it, I will referre them to none other judge than their owne note uppon the 15 verse of the fourth of Deuteronomie' (Aston, 272). The note in question forecasts plagues for those rash enough to represent God by means of images. By then, with a second folio edition of the Bishops' Bible in prospect, Parker faced a dilemma: he wished to incorporate illustrations, while avoiding further puritan criticism, but he had lost control of the woodcut blocks, returned to Germany by 1570–71. He resolved it, no doubt at some expense, by commissioning a new set of blocks based on the Solis designs in which all delineations of God were replaced by the tetragrammaton.

Ten folio editions of the Bishops' Bible were published, the last in 1595. Six quarto editions appeared between 1569 and 1584. Only in the fifth edition, published in folio in 1574, does the title-page proclaim that the work had been 'Set foorth by aucthoritee', revealing that once again the queen had been slow to support Parker's efforts. The Bishops' Bible was a success in that it replaced the Great Bible (last reprinted in 1569) in churches, to the exclusion of the Geneva version. But the latter continued to be read in protestant homes and became the foundation of the Authorized Version.

Climacteric, 1569–1572: the crisis over discipline The northern rising of 1569, the last serious attempt to bring down a central government from a feudal power base in the provinces, shook the nerves of Elizabeth and her leading councillors and led to a fundamental rethinking of political and ecclesiastical priorities. Before the crisis Parker was essentially proactive, seeking to advance the cause of religious reform in spite of frequent rebuffs by the queen. Thereafter he became increasingly reactive, his ambitions limited to the protection of an imperfect *status quo* against attacks from resurgent Catholicism and radical protestantism alike. In its efforts to counter these threats the hierarchy was greatly hampered by its inability to establish an authoritative code of ecclesiastical discipline to replace that of the pre-Reformation church. All its efforts to this end earlier in Elizabeth's reign had been frustrated, often by the queen herself.

The resulting strain manifested itself in part in a controversy over dispensations. The power to dispense from the requirements of canon law, assumed by the crown as part of the royal supremacy, was usually exercised by the court of faculties, controlled by the archbishop of Canterbury. Of the 216 types of dispensation available, that which enabled an incumbent to hold more than one living was particularly contentious. To many people the very fact that church livings could be occupied by non-resident pastors was a scandal to be deplored and resisted. Parker showed that he was sensitive to the issue in July 1569, when he ruminated on ambiguities surrounding the crown's dispensing power and expressed himself careful 'not to extend my sleeve beyond mine arm' (*Correspondence*, 351). But he became circumspect only after Edward Dering's sermon, preached before the queen on 25 February 1570, in which the court of faculties was denounced as the mother and nurse of all abominations. By April Cecil was taking an interest in the debate which Dering had sparked off, requiring Parker to supply details of every dispensation for plurality that he had granted since the beginning of his primacy. The archbishop himself admitted that he had had more grief than gain through the court of faculties, and described it as an offensive institution which should be wholly suppressed. But nothing was done about this running sore until parliament next met in April 1571.

The parliament had important secular business, having been summoned to deal with the ramifications of the northern rising and the publication in 1570 of the papal bull *Regnans in excelsis*, in which Pius V excommunicated Elizabeth and released her subjects from their allegiance. Parker was probably involved in the production of *An Homelie against Disobedience and Wylfull Rebellion* (1570), included in editions of the second Book of Homilies published from 1571. He was instrumental in securing the publication of Heinrich Bullinger's diatribe against the bull, *Bullae papisticae*, presenting a copy to Elizabeth in September 1571 and subsequently arranging for its translation into English. In November 1569 the bishops had been rebuked by the privy council for the alleged laxity of the clergy, in a letter asserting that because ministers were not earnest enough in their pastoral care the people were not resorting to their parish churches, and were consequently falling into dangerous errors and libertarian lifestyles. The bishops were ordered to procure more diligent preaching and also to certify the names of recusants. Ultimately the bishops and the privy council together tackled these problems through parliamentary legislation, a bill 'for cominge to service and receavinge the communion' being introduced into the House of Commons on 4 April 1571. All subjects must attend their parish churches at least once a quarter, or face a fine of at least 30s., and take communion yearly. The bill passed in both houses but was vetoed by the queen, presumably as an encroachment on the royal supremacy.

At the same time the issue of church discipline was again arousing controversy. On 6 April William Strickland, MP for Scarborough, spoke against ecclesiastical abuses, and specifically dispensations and simony. To remedy them he called for the enactment of the Edwardian *Reformatio*. In the ensuing debate reference was also made to the alphabetical bills of 1566, which were formally read next day. No more was heard of the *Reformatio*, and only two of the alphabetical bills, both with short enacting clauses which suggest official backing, became law. Bill C, an attempt to regulate pluralism and non-residence, passed in the Commons but was killed off in the Lords. Bill A, which sought to give statutory confirmation to the articles of religion, also passed swiftly through the lower house, but was stopped in the Lords by the queen. In committee, bill A gave rise to a famous, and telling, altercation between Parker and the radical Peter Wentworth. On 25 April a deputation of six members was appointed to attend Parker and answer his questions. When the archbishop asked why certain articles had been omitted Wentworth replied that the Commons had been too preoccupied with other business to find time to examine how the missing articles 'agreed with the word of God'. Amazed, Parker declared 'surely yow mistooke the matter; yow will referr your selves wholly to us therein'. Wentworth retorted, 'wee will pass nothing before we understand what it is, for that were but to make yow popes: make yow popes who list … for we will make yow none' (Hartley, 1.432). To add to Parker's discomfiture another radical, George Carleton, introduced a bill attacking the primate's power to grant dispensations, but it got no further than a Lords' committee.

Largely thwarted in his hopes of religious reform through parliament, Parker turned instead to convocation. Here he enjoyed greater success. First the articles of religion authorized by Elizabeth were revised and their number restored to thirty-nine. The lower house having signified its consent the alterations were approved by the queen. Second the upper house produced a series of disciplinary articles setting out the responsibilities of every rank of ecclesiastic and dealing with such issues as ordination, preaching, pluralism, and residence, sabbath observance, recusancy, and the admonishment of those leading immoral lives. These articles had originated in the synods of 1560 and 1561, and there was probably a substantial overlap between them and some of the alphabetical bills; Parker may have decided to push for further reform in both parliament and convocation, in the hope that at least one avenue would prove fruitful, or he may have transferred his programme to convocation once it became clear that most of the alphabetical bills were doomed. This time Elizabeth was not hostile, although declining to give formal written assent as supreme governor. Since the lower house was not even consulted, probably for fear of objections from precisians, Parker was taking something of a liberty when he published the articles in 1571 as *A Booke of Certaine Canons, concernyng some Parte of the Discipline of the Churche of England*; canons, in a strictly legal sense, they were not, nor did they become so. Nevertheless they were swiftly absorbed into episcopal and archiepiscopal articles and injunctions.

Finally, Parker drew up rules which gave him greater scope for supervision of the court of faculties. For instance no dispensation was to be issued unless it had been through the hands of either the archbishop himself or the master of the faculties. But although these rules seem to have been implemented puritan sensibilities continued to be offended by the huge range of dispensations still available. A much more drastic pruning was needed, as Parker's successor recognized. In 1576 Grindal recommended to the privy council that just six or seven types of dispensation be retained.

Last confrontations, 1572–1575 In 1572 a further crisis engulfed Parker and the Church of England after Thomas Cartwright was ejected from Cambridge for preaching presbyterian doctrines. For Cartwright and his disciples disputes about Catholic survivals like the surplice were irrelevant. What mattered was implementing major structural change. It was against this background that on 17 May 1572 an unofficial bill 'concerning dispensations for rites and ceremonies' was introduced into the House of Commons. Aimed at protecting godly ministers from enemies who took advantage of trivial deviations from the Book of Common Prayer to get them into trouble at the assizes, it proposed that such clergymen, once suitably licensed by their bishops, should be exempted from the provisions of the Act of Uniformity. In effect they were to be allowed to emulate London's 'stranger churches'—Calvinist congregations established by Dutch and French exile communities, which with Grindal's consent as bishop of London had adopted Reformed constitutions, disciplinary regimes, and liturgies. To license English clergy to copy the stranger churches was to introduce presbyterianism by the back door. Committed at its third reading the bill was promptly replaced by a new bill, read for the first time on 21 May, which left the substance unchanged but rendered the preamble less offensive. Elizabeth demanded to see the texts of the two bills, and then peremptorily forbade any measures concerning religion to be brought into the House of Commons without the prior consent of the bishops. Reform lay dead in the water.

The result for Parker was yet more woe, as a younger generation of puritan zealots, enthused by presbyterianism, broke away from their more moderate leaders. Early in June they enjoyed a huge propaganda coup when John Field and Thomas Wilcox published *An Admonition to the Parliament* (ESTC 10847–9), savaging the bishops as unjust, tyrannous, proud, blind, and pope-like. Parker himself is excoriated as 'this pettie pope', the court of faculties as 'the filthy quaevemire, and poysoned plashe of all the abhominations that doe infect the whole realme' (Frere and Douglas, 30, 32). Ostensibly addressed to parliament but really a presbyterian manifesto for public consumption, this sensational tract was soon the talk of the city. To add to the archbishop's humiliation, preparations for his response (surviving as Inner Temple Library, London, Petyt MS 538/47, fols. 426*r*–427*v*, 462*r*–464*v*, 466*r*–467*v*) fell into the hands of his adversaries, who published these notes later in 1572 with a mordant commentary of their own as *Certaine articles collected and taken (as it is thought) by the byshops out of a litle boke entituled an admonition to the parliament wyth an answere to the same, containing a confirmation of the sayde booke in shorte notes* (ESTC 10850). Gleefully seizing the opportunity to reiterate their arguments, they also demonstrated both that the bishops' security had been breached and that their opponents could not even take notes from the *Admonition* without misrepresenting it.

Parker delegated the task of making further ripostes against the presbyterians first to Thomas Cooper, bishop of Lincoln, who preached at Paul's Cross on 27 June, and then to John Whitgift. When Cartwright involved himself in the controversy in 1573, publishing his *Replye* (ESTC 4711–2) to Whitgift's *An Answere to a Certen Libel* (ESTC 25427), the archbishop declined to respond, observing that 'I am a principal party, and an offendicle to him' (*Correspondence*, 454). Instead he worked behind the scenes, in particular by preparing papers for the benefit of Cecil, now Lord Burghley. But government support for the embattled bishops was slow to materialize, and Parker knew perfectly well why. As he wrote in March 1573, 'The comfort that these puritans have, and their continuance, is marvellous; and therefore if her Highness with her council (I mean some of them) step not to it, I see the likelihood of a pitiful commonwealth to follow' (ibid., 418–19). Edwin Sandys, now bishop of London, reported in April that he was being deluged by letters from noblemen on behalf of Field and Wilcox, who had been imprisoned. In May Parker and Sandys attended an unsatisfactory meeting of the privy council at which Edward Dering and three other leading radicals were interrogated. Burghley and the bishops were agreed that the extremists should be silenced, but they also feared the obloquy that would inevitably follow if they took the necessary steps. Consequently the preaching continued, although Parker did obtain a royal proclamation designed to suppress presbyterian writings.

Published on 11 June 1573, the proclamation was wholly ineffectual: not a single copy of the *Admonition* was surrendered to the authorities. A tougher successor, issued on 20 October, although cruelly blaming all disorders on the negligence of the bishops as having 'dissembled and winked' at abuses (Hughes and Larkin, 2.380), also insisted on the rigorous enforcement of the Act of Uniformity. Accordingly on 8 November the privy council instructed the bishops to proceed. The resulting episcopal inquisition was not implemented consistently, but it did lead to suspensions and then deprivations, particularly in London, thus adding to the tally of disgruntled ministers who had been deprived in recent years for refusing to subscribe to the articles as confirmed in 1571. Repression could indeed be counter-productive:

> the wholesale deprivation of puritan ministers could not in itself pacify the Church; its effect normally was to intensify the schismatic tendencies of the presbyterian movement by diverting the preachers from the comparatively harmless pastoral preoccupations of their own parishes. (Collinson, *Elizabethan Puritan Movement*, 152)

By raising the stakes so high the champions of presbyterianism tarnished the cause of moderate reform. Hence the official disfavour visited upon 'prophesyings', the name given to gatherings of clergymen (though sometimes with a considerable lay attendance) for sermons, discussion, and mutual criticism. Parker himself probably approved of them, being convinced of the importance of preaching and of clerical training, and the inauguration of several prophesyings in eastern Kent in 1572 is unlikely to have occurred without his acquiescence, or even encouragement. The queen, however, was overtly hostile, and in 1574 demanded their suppression. Not for the first time Parker's evangelical instincts conflicted with Elizabeth's retrograde demands, and he was reluctant to implement her orders. Some bishops were commanded only to deal with disruptive prophesyings, others received no instructions at all. As a result many prophesyings survived, to bring ruin on Archbishop Grindal in 1577.

Misfortune dogged Parker to the end of his archiepiscopate. In the late spring of 1574 a confidence trickster named Humphrey Needham, who had earlier provided the bishops with genuine intelligence about clandestine presses, obtained forged letters purportedly written by radical ministers, among them Cartwright. Their contents, setting out plans for every kind of subversion, religious and political, including the murder of Lord Burghley, completely deceived Parker: 'This deep, devilish, traitorous dissimulation, this horrible conspiracy, hath so astonied me, that my wit, my memory, be quite gone' (*Correspondence*, 461). He gave money to Needham on the understanding that it would secure Cartwright's arrest. When the plot was uncovered Parker declared himself glad to learn that William Bonham and Nicholas Standen, two godly ministers who had been imprisoned on the basis of the forgeries, had been released from gaol, even suggesting that the counterfeiters should pay them compensation. But his own reputation had suffered. Robert Beale, a fervently godly clerk of the privy council, later described the whole affair as 'a lewd and malicious practice of Archbishop Parker of Canterbury and his brethren' (Collinson, *Elizabethan Puritan Movement*, 155). The accusation was baseless but the mud stuck.

Parker soldiered on. Late in 1574 there appeared a formidable exercise in presbyterian ecclesiology, the *Ecclesiasticae disciplinae* of Walter Travers, published at Heidelberg with a preface by Cartwright; there was also an English translation. Having tried in vain to persuade John Aylmer to write a confutation, the archbishop told Grindal in March 1575 that he would exercise more judgement before commissioning somebody else to undertake the task. On 11 April, confined to his bed, he wrote his last extant letter, informing Burghley that he was 'stricken with mine old disease more sharply than ever I was'. The tone is that of a man who knows that he has not long to live. He reflects with resignation how 'divers of my brethren partly are gone from me, partly working secretly against me, for the satisfying of some of their partial friends; but I see men be men'. There is some bitterness, too, at the invidious position in which he had so often been placed: 'To dance in a net in this world is but mere vanity.' More poignant still is his rhetorical question, with all its implications for his relations with the queen, and his difficulties which arose from them: 'Her Majesty told me that I had supreme government ecclesiastical; but what is it to govern cumbered with such subtlety?' (*Correspondence*, 477–9). It was a fair comment.

Parker as collector of books and manuscripts In his declining years Parker increasingly retreated into antiquarian studies, in part motivated by the need to find evidence for the existence of protestantism in the remote British past, and so to answer the question tauntingly put to English reformers by Catholic adversaries: 'where was your church before Luther?' Quite apart from providing evidence that powerful men in England were no less devoted to learning and the record of their country's glorious past than to other forms of display, the archbishop's possession of a substantial library assisted him in his task of securing the new religious establishment by providing it with historical foundations. In John Foxe's words, Parker collected books to show that 'religion presently … is no new reformation of things … but rather a reduction of the Church to the Pristine state of old conformity' (*Gospels of the Fower Evangelists*, 1571, sig. 9iir–v).

Parker had been collecting printed books long before 1559, and his earlier concerns are reflected in the contents of his library. Hence his possession of patristic and humanist texts, including his Aldine editions and the works of Erasmus, the writings of reformers like Luther and Zwingli, and controversial tracts. His Venetian edition of Boccaccio's *De genealogia deorum* and *De montibus* had belonged to his college at Stoke by Clare, and books bequeathed to Corpus Christi College by Peter Nobys, master from 1516 to 1523, were also absorbed into Parker's collection.

The Parker register of books bequeathed to Corpus lists more than 800 printed volumes; seventy-five were given to Cambridge University Library in 1574, and more are to be found in Gonville and Caius College and elsewhere. Parker continued to expand his collection to the end, acquiring more than twenty titles printed between 1573 and 1575, along with many complimentary copies given to him as archbishop, such as *The Woorkes of Geffrey Chaucer* (1561), presented by their editor, John Stow. He also purchased pre-1559 titles in his latter years. Thus his copy of the St Albans printer's 1483 *Chronicles* reflects his late interest in English chronicle history. Identification of Parker's early books often depends on his own annotations, and the same applies to his manuscripts. What has been described as 'the small, neat script characteristic of his earlier years' (Graham) has been identified in only one manuscript (Corpus Christi College Cambridge, MS 321), a commentary on Matthew by the Franciscan Petrus Joannis Olivi, whose writings had been condemned as heretical in 1326. If his possession of this manuscript suggests an interest in precedents for church reform, others show him gathering evidence for the progress of reform in his own lifetime, and for his own involvement in it. Parker's gift to Corpus included bound records from his earlier career, along with papers formerly belonging to Martin Bucer.

In the years before 1558 Parker was not the 'mighty Collector' of manuscripts described by John Strype (Strype, *Parker*, 2.497). It was a letter sent to him on 14 July 1560 on the queen's behalf by Sir William Petre which marked the beginning of the archbishop's serious work in this field. It forwarded a request from a group of German protestant historians in Magdeburg, led by Matthias Flacius Illyricus, for English materials for their *Ecclesiastica historia* (1559–74). The categories of material that Parker undertook to find for the Magdeburg 'Centuriators' were also relevant to the archbishop's researches on behalf of English protestantism: Reformed tenets in the practices of the early church and in the decisions of its councils, medieval evidence for papal usurpation and clerical corruption, and early translations of scripture.

By 18 July Parker's own version of the Magdeburg request had reached John Bale, whose response, a list of book titles and owners against the archbishop's own 'regestre' of topics, along with further lists drawn up by the primate's Latin secretary John Joscelin, casts valuable light on Parker's antiquarian purposes—in the archbishop's own words, 'spying and searching [for] credible information, among other things, in whose hands the great notable written books … should remain' (*Correspondence*, 186). To that end Parker and his assistants constructed a record of authors whose texts were deemed important, and of owners of copies of those texts, finding them impartially among public servants, ecclesiastics, nobles, merchants, and townspeople. Nobody was too humble—the list included William Carye, a clothmaker, and the widow of John Ducket, shoemaker. And when books were found Parker was equally diligent in procuring them, writing to many men of his acquaintance, especially churchmen, who might be able to send him texts.

Most of the responses to Parker's appeals date from between 1565 and 1568; dated accessions to the Parker Library at Corpus Christi College also cluster round these years. It was between 1565 and 1567, moreover, that Joscelin supplemented Bale's register of books. Henceforward Parker apparently used these lists as finding aids, for example in obtaining a manuscript of Roger of Howden's *Chronica* from William Carye (MS 138), and a copy of Eadmer's *Historia* from the civil lawyer Dr Henry Johns (MS 452). The archbishop also made use of Bale's 1560 description of the latter's own library, although his efforts to acquire some of Bale's books met with limited success. Indeed, Parker faced a number of obstacles in his pursuit of texts. He and his servants seem to have had only limited access to books and information about libraries in the north of England and the universities, and private ownership of many monastic spoils further hampered their investigations. Those who needed the archbishop's patronage might try to bribe him with presents of books, but Parker had no option but to bargain with those who did not. He did, however, look to the government for assistance, and especially to Cecil, another notable collector. In 1568 the privy council issued a printed letter to 'sundry private persons' with 'auncient recordes and monumentes, written … from divers Abbeyes'. Proclaiming the queen's support for Parker's antiquarian programme, the letter required that those who had books should 'gently impart' them to him. It also offered reassurance that the intention was not to 'withdrawe them from your ryght & interest unto them, but after a tyme of perusying the same … to make restitution of them agayne' (MS 114, fol. 49*r*). In many cases this promise can be shown to have been kept.

More than 500 manuscripts owned by Parker have been identified. Among the most notable items in the collection are the Parker text of the Anglo-Saxon Chronicle (MS 173), the letters of Thomas Becket (MS 295), the Corpus glossary, comprising the first dictionary in English (MS 144), and two famous examples of English Romanesque illumination, the Dover and Bury bibles (MSS 2–4). All but the last of these came from Canterbury monasteries. Many others originated at Norwich, Worcester, and Exeter cathedrals, while Parker obtained from St Albans the best text of the thirteenth-century *Chronica majora* by Matthew Paris (MSS 16 and 26). He also made a representative collection of Anglo-Saxon prose texts, including the only surviving Old English romance, *Appolonius of Tyre* (MS 201); gathered Latin manuscripts from before 800 which included the Canterbury gospels traditionally said to have been brought to England by St Augustine in 597 (MS 286); and acquired important early examples of manuscript chronicles and histories of England, including the ninth-century *Historia Brittonum* attributed to Nennius (MSS 139 and 363). He also collected vital papers concerning the English Reformation.

Parker's treatment of his manuscripts would not be considered appropriate by present day archivists. A single manuscript may contain material from more than one book: in MS 173, for instance, the Anglo-Saxon Chronicle is bound with a much earlier text of the *Carmen Paschale* of Sedulius. In some cases materials bound together were selected for consistency of size alone. Other books were trimmed and rebound, enlarged by manuscript additions, and corrected and commented upon by Parker or his servants. When textual material was added, Parker's scribes often imitated the original hand. Some volumes were valued principally for display, leading to illuminations being cut from one book and added to another. But textual content was also important to the archbishop. Because some quires were missing from his own copy of Aelfric's grammar (MS 449), he had transcriptions made from another one (BL Royal MS 15 B. xxii) to fill the gap. Most of his books were intended for use, and a high proportion of them were given tables of contents, indexes, and marginalia;

thus a note on MS 342, fol. 110r, records a late thirteenth-century married clerk in Parker's own hand. Such annotations provide significant evidence that he was among the keenest readers of his own books.

Parker filled his household with scholars and skilled artisans who worked on his behalf: 'I have within my house in wages, drawers and cutters, painters, limners, writers, and bookbinders', he wrote in 1572 (*Correspondence*, 426). In 1566 he claimed that one of his scribes named 'Lylye' could have 'counterfeited in antiquity' material missing from one of Cecil's books (ibid., 253–4); probably this was Peter Lily, registrar of Parker's consistory court. The scholars employed by Parker were headed by Joscelin and by Stephan Batman, who claimed to have collected 6700 (presumably printed) books for the archbishop. Other members of Parker's scholarly entourage included William Lambarde, George Acworth, a former fellow of Peterhouse, Alexander Neville, the archbishop's secretary, and Thomas Yale, his vicar-general. Parker's steward Thomas D'Oyly also made notes for his master, as did the latter's son John.

John Foxe and John Stow were among the writers patronized directly by Parker; their work pinpoints the intersection of the archbishop's activities as a collector of books and manuscripts with his endeavours as a propagandist for church and state. Lambeth Palace MS 959, a Parkerian copy of *De antiquitate Britannicae ecclesiae*, contains a list of books published at 'the gages' of the archbishop. They include the Anglo-Saxon *Gospels of the Fower Evangelists* (ESTC 2961), for which Foxe provided a preface, while Stow was involved in several editions of texts: Paris's *Chronica majora* (ESTC 19209), Thomas Walsingham's *Ypodigma Neustriae* and *Historia Anglorum* (ESTC 25004–5), the works of the supposed Matthew of Westminster (ESTC 17652–3), as well as his own *Annales* (ESTC 23333–6). Such editions can be grouped with others, including the *Testimonie of Antiquitie* (ESTC 159—writings by Aelfric), *Aelfredi regis res gestae* (ESTC 863—an interpolated text of Asser), and Joscelin's new edition of Gildas's *De excidio et conquestu Britanniae* (ESTC 11893–4), which all demonstrate the archbishop's concern to proclaim the antiquity of the church of England. To the same end he sponsored the first printed editions of Matthew Paris (whose unconcealed loathing for the papacy appealed to Parker) and other chroniclers, and oversaw the production of *De antiquitate Britannicae ecclesiae* (1572, ESTC 19202), tracing the fortunes of the church in Britain from the time of Joseph of Arimathea, over 500 years before the arrival of St Augustine.

For all these productions Parker's library furnished material. For the edition of Paris's *Chronica majora* MS 16 was collated and marked up for a compositor, probably in Reyner Wolfe's printing house. For works like *De antiquitate*, or, *A Defence of Priestes Mariages* (ESTC 17518–19) material was compiled from many manuscripts which still show signs of use for this purpose. Parker's reasons for publishing from the contents of his books and manuscripts were thus barely separable from his motives in collecting them. For subsequent scholarship the effects of his endeavours were also far reaching for, as well as helping to locate the Elizabethan church in a laudable, historical tradition, Parker's insistence that his manuscripts be read, interpreted, and given new, printed form, initiated the sustained study of Anglo-Saxon. He commissioned the printer John Day to arrange for the casting of the first Anglo-Saxon types by continental typefounders, and used them for the first time in *Testimonie of Antiquitie* (1566 or 1567). Joscelin is credited with the preface explaining that the text had been 'set oute in such forme of letters … as was used when they were written'. The new fount, along with Joscelin's pioneering vocabulary, gave this and Parker's other Anglo-Saxon editions an appearance of verifiable antiquity.

Parker's efforts to conserve his priceless collection for posterity are well known. In 1574 he was the most generous of several benefactors to Cambridge University Library, at Andrew Perne's suggestion giving 100 printed and manuscript books. A tripartite indenture between Parker, the university, and Corpus arranged for the maintenance of this collection. In the same year he had a quadripartite indenture drawn up, disposing of most of the rest of his collections. The manuscripts were to go to Corpus, where they were to be carefully catalogued, their use closely controlled, and their conservation monitored. Each year the masters of Gonville and Caius College and Trinity Hall were to audit the library against their own copies of the Parker register. Missing leaves entailed a fine, missing books their replacement. If gross negligence was discovered the entire collection was to be moved to Gonville and Caius; if that college proved remiss, to Trinity Hall; then if necessary back to Corpus, and so on. These precautions have proved effective. But not all Parker's books were covered by the 1574 gifts and indentures. A number of them, sometimes surprisingly important, seem to have passed to the archbishop's sons and have since been widely dispersed.

Metropolitan and diocesan In addition to providing leadership for the Church of England, Parker was often required to be present on state occasions: thus in September 1559, even before his consecration, he attended the obsequies of Henri II of France in St Paul's Cathedral. Busy whenever parliament or convocation was in session, he was also regularly involved in choosing ministers to preach the lenten sermons delivered at court. Given his residence at Lambeth, the archbishop naturally took an interest in London affairs. Thus in 1561 he started the campaign to restore St Paul's after it was badly damaged by fire. Occasionally he had to take responsibility for state prisoners, particularly when an outbreak of plague in the city caused their removal from the Tower. He also sometimes interrogated recusants, like the Lancashire gentleman Sir John Southworth, whom he examined to no avail in 1568. By virtue of his office he was visitor of two Oxford colleges, All Souls and Merton.

The exercise of patronage was a continual concern. The appointment of new bishops is a frequent topic in his correspondence with Cecil. When sees in the province of Canterbury fell vacant, the primate was responsible for their administration. *Sede vacante* ordinations and institutions are copiously recorded in his register. Visitation articles for the entire southern province were written in 1560, separate articles for the cathedrals of the province in that year and in 1567. Parker also conducted a number of extraordinary visitations—for instance of Ely Cathedral in 1563, of the diocese of Norwich in 1567, and of the diocese of Winchester in 1567. Between March 1565 and 1569 he issued about 250 preaching licences.

Parker was also diligent in the role of diocesan. Sets of articles survive from Canterbury visitations undertaken in 1563, 1569, and 1573, and he issued visitation injunctions to his cathedral in 1560, 1570, and 1573–4. A shortage of adequate clergy made pluralism rife throughout the 1560s but Parker had begun to curtail this abuse by 1575. His measures included the appointment of a suffragan: Richard Rogers was consecrated bishop of Dover in 1569. The ordinary church courts were making heavy weather of imposing protestant discipline and the two men were probably behind the creation of a local ecclesiastical commission in 1572. Parker also took a close interest in educational provision within Kent. In 1563 he helped Roger Manwood to found a grammar school at Sandwich, while a year later he was called upon to approve orders for Tonbridge School.

Family and household Parker seems to have enjoyed a contented domestic life. His wife was clearly regarded as quite a catch: in 1551 Nicholas Ridley concluded a letter with his commendations to Mistress Parker, 'whom, although I do not know, yet for the fame of her virtue in God I do love' (*Correspondence*, 45–6), and according to Strype was later so taken with her charm, seriousness, and prudence that he asked whether she had a sister, implying that he might himself be tempted into matrimony. The *Matthaeus* praises Margaret Parker for the grace and self-effacement with which she met the heavy demands placed upon her as the wife of a busy archbishop. His happy home life probably helps explain Parker's angry response to the queen's order of August 1561 forbidding the wives of cathedral and collegiate clergy to reside with their husbands in the precincts; a stormy interview with Elizabeth followed, after which Parker confessed to Cecil that he regretted accepting high office. (He transmitted the injunction to the cathedrals of his province, but there is little evidence of its enforcement.) Calling her 'dearly beloved and virtuous', Parker recorded that Margaret died 'right Christianly' on 17 August 1570 (ibid., x). Their surviving sons both married the daughters of bishops. In 1566 John married Joanna, daughter of Richard Cox of Ely, and in 1569 Matthew married Frances, daughter of William Barlow of Chichester. Parker maintained a substantial household, estimating in 1563 that it was not much under 100 strong. That same year he was licensed to retain forty liveried men as well as his ordinary household servants and ecclesiastical officers. In the nature of the case many of the latter, especially the chaplains, were destined for high preferment in the church, but by comparison with most of his contemporaries Parker can hardly be accused of either favouritism or nepotism.

The internal appearance of Lambeth Palace is recorded in the detailed probate inventory made in May 1575, which lists the contents of forty-six rooms, principal apartments as well as servants' quarters. The archbishop's picture collection was extensive, and its portraits covered a wide religious spectrum from Zwingli to Sir Thomas More. All the Tudor sovereigns except Mary were represented, but only two of Henry VIII's wives—Anne Boleyn and Jane Seymour. Notwithstanding the grief that the privy council often caused him, Parker possessed likenesses of several councillors of puritan bent led by the earl of Leicester, together with representations of William Cecil, Nicholas Bacon, and the first earl of Pembroke. Some paintings added an international dimension: there were pictures of the holy Roman emperor and his wife, of the prince de Condé and the admiral of France, and even of 'The greate Turke' (Sandys, 11). Parker's three immediate predecessors as primate were represented: Reginald Pole, Thomas Cranmer, and William Warham, the last of these, valued at £5, being by far the most valuable item in the entire collection. Other clerical figures included Erasmus, Wolsey, Pietro Martire Vermigli (Peter Martyr), John Jewel, and Melanchthon. There were also scenes from the lives of Wyclif and Zwingli and images drawn from scripture.

The paintings were supplemented by an impressive assemblage of maps. Some were religious or allegorical—'the peregrination of Christe', or 'the Lande of Promise' (Sandys, 12). But most were practical: representations of Britain, Kent, Norwich, and London, and depictions of lands overseas which attest the informed curiosity of their owner. Maps of the Holy Land, France, Germany, Flanders, and the Netherlands accompanied a representation of the whole of Europe, and even of America. There were also six musical instruments in the palace, including four pairs of virginals and an organ in the private chapel. A Bible was available for consultation in the palace's great chamber; another, covered with black velvet, lay in the presence chamber. One room is designated 'the Schole house' (ibid., 16). Parker's apparel included a parliament robe, a convocation robe, a mourning gown, four doublets, and three cloaks. There was no cope among his numerous clerical vestments; indeed, the only reference to one suggests that it had been turned into a bed tester. The archiepiscopal wine cellar held five casks of Gascon wine and a butt of sack. The stables accommodated twelve horses and also two coaches, now just coming into fashion.

Getting and spending Parker died a wealthy man. His probate inventory records the contents of Lambeth Palace as worth £1208 15*s*. He had £1200 in ready money and was owed a further £200. His possessions at Croydon Palace were valued at £52 1*s*. 2*d*., the armour at Lambeth and Canterbury at a total of £168 6*s*. 10*d*. Although Tudor arithmetic often proves inaccurate, the final figure for the entire inventory—£2766 10*s*. 11*d*.—seems plausible. In husbanding an income from which he was expected to maintain the dignity of his office, Parker had to confront the encroachments of the crown. In 1559 he had joined in protesting against the inequable exchanges permitted by that year's Act of Exchange, and in the end his see was one of those least affected by it. Yet his predecessors had granted so many long leases of archiepiscopal estates that few terminated during his tenure, giving him little opportunity to benefit from entry fines, or to profit from higher rents as leases fell in. Parker granted only twelve leases between 1561 and 1575, whereas Archbishop Whitgift was able to issue 105 in the period 1584–1600. Parker also faced the difficulties inherent in acting as a collector of diocesan tenths and subsidies, which entailed the risk of becoming a crown debtor because taxpayers defaulted, or because the collected monies did not reach the exchequer. Knowing that the dishonesty of undercollectors lay at the root of the problem, Parker carefully monitored their activities. Businesslike in all things, he also tried to ensure that he received what was due to him, and where possible to increase his rents. He endeavoured, too, to make the most of his diocesan and metropolitan rights. Grindal later claimed that Parker had prospered partly by conducting *sede vacante* visitations at the beginning of Elizabeth's reign: bishops could make a great deal of money from the traditional dues known as synodals and procurations.

John Parker later estimated that his father's annual income at the end of his life had been £3128. If his revenue was substantial, so were his outgoings. In 1573 the archbishop calculated that he spent £160 a year on the poor. Another £237 went on ministerial stipends and relief for learned strangers. It is impossible to estimate how much he spent on repairs to the thirteen churches, five mansions, and various farms for whose upkeep he was responsible. Subsidies, rents, and new year gifts consumed £400, annuities and fees a further 400 marks. £100 were set aside for liveries and £250 for wages. The largest single item of expenditure was food for the household, a staggering £1300–1400 per annum. Besides all this there were numerous incidental payments for such items as clothing, bedding, medicines, and transport.

Hospitality constituted a heavy burden which all prelates were expected to shoulder. After the restoration of his palace at Canterbury in 1565, at a cost of £1400, Parker's house-warming dinner for the assize judges was also attended by many Kent gentry. On Trinity Sunday 1566, after administering communion himself in the cathedral he entertained the entire cathedral staff and a number of local worthies. The queen frequently enjoyed the archbishop's hospitality. During Lent 1573 she spent a night at Lambeth with a huge entourage; Parker bore the whole charge of the visit. Later that year Elizabeth was lavishly entertained at Canterbury for fourteen days, whereupon Grindal remarked that 'it shall be hard for any of our coat to do the like for one hundred years, and how long after God knoweth' (Nicholson, 347). But although he was a generous host Parker is said by the *Matthaeus* to have eaten sparingly, drunk little, and dressed in silks only when necessary. Indeed, the archbishop was allegedly:

> a mortified man to the world, and the things of it; yet his disposition led him to do things agreeable to his … condition, wherein God had placed him. And therefore, though he was above the affection of magnificence, yet he used magnificent hospitality, and great housekeeping, befitting his rank. (Heal, 'Canterbury', 556)

Some of these claims are conventional to sixteenth-century biography, but many of them ring true in Parker's case.

Death, burial, and commemoration Parker made his will on 5 April 1575, signing it with a shaky hand. It was proved on 1 October. He named five supervisors: Richard Rogers; Sir William Cordell; Thomas Wotton; Dr Thomas Yale; and John Bungey. His five executors were Peter Osborn, John Parker, Richard Wendesley, Andrew Pearson, and John Baker. He died, of unknown causes, at Lambeth Palace on 17 May 1575 and was ceremonially buried on 6 June. The sermon was preached by Bishop Thomas Cooper. Parker's viscera, placed in an urn, were interred near his wife's remains in the Duke's Chapel of Lambeth parish church. The rest of his body was laid to rest under a plain black slab in the palace's private chapel. The epitaph was composed by Walter Haddon. During the Commonwealth the archbishop's tomb was desecrated on the orders of Matthew Hardy, joint purchaser of Lambeth Palace, who sought to recover the lead in which the corpse was wrapped. The bones were allegedly thrown into a dunghill. After the Restoration, Archbishop William Juxon's chaplain, Robert Pory, petitioned the House of Lords to have the perpetrators of this indignity punished. Once the bones had been discovered they were solemnly reinterred in their proper place.

Although no effigy ever commemorated Parker his likeness survives in engravings and paintings. The earliest known representation seems to be an engraving by Remigius Hogenberg, apparently intended for inclusion in copies of *De antiquitate Britannicae ecclesiae*. Dated 6 August 1572, the half-length image shows the primate seated, reading a book, and gives his age as sixty-nine. Hogenberg's pattern was followed by the anonymous artist responsible for the well-preserved portrait miniature found on the inner cover of Corpus Christi College, Cambridge, MS 582. Its oval surround bears the date 6 August 1573, gives his age as seventy, and quotes Parker's motto, taken from 1 John 2: 17: *Mundus transit, et concupiscentia eius* ('the world passeth away and the lust thereof'). Despite the curious reversal of dates it is possible that the engraving derives from the miniature. Several later paintings survive, deriving either from Hogenberg or from two other likenesses unknown before the seventeenth century.

Parker's memory is principally preserved by his benefactions. Pride of place obviously goes to his unparalleled gift of manuscripts and printed books to Corpus. Less well-known are his gifts of plate to the college made between 1569 and 1571. They include a tall covered cup, a rose-water dish, a great salt, and a set of spoons representing Christ and the apostles. Throughout his career, moreover, Parker sought to augment educational opportunities. His financial reforms as master enabled Corpus to found six new scholarships in 1548. He also raised money as a supervisor of the estate of John Mere, establishing a scholarship for a Cambridgeshire man. In 1567 he made arrangements with Norwich corporation to found three scholarships, their holders to be chosen by the mayor and aldermen from schoolboys either from the city or from Aylsham. Another annuity was presented to Corpus in 1569 to fund two more scholars and two more fellows, all of whom were to have originated in Norfolk. By a complex series of property transactions he also enabled the chapter of Canterbury to nominate three scholars to Corpus. Under the archbishop's will his son John gave an annuity of £10 to the college to establish three further scholarships for students from Canterbury, Aylsham, and Wymondham. This is not an exhaustive list of Parker's benefactions.

Historiography and assessment Parker's spectacular benefactions have helped to ensure his high standing in the eyes of posterity. His career, however, has often been misunderstood and, following a process of re-evaluation which began in the last quarter of the twentieth century, a biography that meets the exacting canons of modern historical scholarship is urgently required. Four book-length studies have hitherto held the field. John Strype, whose *Life and Acts of Matthew Parker* was published in 1711 (reprinted 1821), has earned the gratitude of subsequent historians for the documents he printed, some of which have since been lost, but they accompanied an uncritical and biased assessment of his subject. In particular Strype largely originated the image of Parker as the founding father of Anglicanism as it developed after 1660, embodied in a national church which had deliberately taken up a position between the extremes of Roman Catholicism and radical dissent. Strype's anachronistic view of Parker's religious position was repeated by W. M. Kennedy, who in his *Archbishop Parker* (1908—tellingly it appeared in a series entitled Makers of National History) likewise recast Parker in his own image, ignoring the evidence for the archbishop's radical leanings and slighting his links with the English reformers of the 1520s and 1530s. This approach was carried to extremes by Edith Perry, whose *Under Four Tudors: being the Story of Matthew Parker* (1940) was an exercise less in historical biography than in hero worship, portraying the archbishop as 'a conservative, semi-Roman Catholic who battled against Protestants only' (Bjorklund, 11). V. J. K. Brook's *Life of Archbishop Parker* (1962) was a more sober affair but hardly more comprehensively researched; Parker's exploitation of the resources of his archbishopric and his diocesan and provincial administration were barely discussed, and the coverage of his antiquarian interests was inadequate.

No book-length life of Parker has appeared since Brook's, leaving a biographical gap made all the more evident by the radical reappraisal of the context in which the archbishop's career developed. Since the 1960s the notion that the late medieval church was corrupt and moribund, and that protestantism was simply waiting in the wings, has been effectively destroyed. Rather, the later English church has come to be seen as developing out of a series of evangelical initiatives, not all of them inherently anti-papal, which both shaped and were shaped by a developing sense of national identity, and which gradually moulded a form of church government which eventually emerged—though only after 1660—as specifically Anglican. From this perspective Parker's traditional reputation as the father of Anglicanism has been dealt a mortal blow. That said, it has to be acknowledged that the uneven progress of late-twentieth-century research makes it much easier to decide what sort of figure, historiographically, Parker was not, than it is either to say what manner of man he was, or to evaluate his achievement.

At Stoke by Clare, and then at Corpus, Parker had proved himself a first-rate administrator and a committed evangelical leader. But despite his apparently excellent qualifications the prospect of the primacy of all England, under a new queen of whose conservative predilections he must have been very well aware, seems to have made his blood run cold. It is abundantly clear from his correspondence that his alternative berth—a return to Cambridge as its most senior college head, with a brief to launch the university into a truly protestant future and the chance to indulge his passion for historical research—was infinitely more appealing. It was not to be, and through his subsequent correspondence there seems to run a vein of continuing resentment that Cecil and Bacon had forced him into a position of eminence which he found profoundly and increasingly uncomfortable. In 1567 Bacon formally severed relations with Parker for weeks over the archbishop's visitation of Norwich Cathedral, so bitterly had the two men fallen out.

In the last analysis Parker seems to have been a man who reserved what warmth he had for his immediate family and had little truck with those outside it. There is scant evidence in the records to suggest that he was particularly close to any of his episcopal colleagues except Guest of Rochester and Cox of Ely. With Grindal of London and then of York he had, perforce, to make many accommodations. Horne of Winchester, undoubtedly something of a fifth columnist in his attitude to nonconformity, he may have regarded as a thorn in his side. James Pilkington, far away in Durham, went his own way. It cannot be shown that Parker was ever in regular contact with such energetic diocesans as William Alley of Exeter and John Best of Carlisle. Like Cecil and Bacon he lost patience with the vague and ineffective John Parkhurst of Norwich; seems to have ignored Bentham of Coventry and Lichfield; and regarded Cooper of Lincoln primarily as a fellow scholar rather than as an episcopal colleague. On the continent Parker appears to have been an unknown quantity, and he won no praise there for his reforming endeavours, no doubt because radicals who made or maintained contacts with Zürich and Geneva regarded him as their adversary. As targets of his vigorous campaigns against nonconformity they would have found posterity's attribution to him of qualities of moderation and conciliation hard to understand.

It hardly needs stressing that it was not easy to be archbishop of Canterbury under Elizabeth, and that the difficulties that often made Parker's primacy miserable united to wreck completely that of his successor, Edmund Grindal. Parker retained sufficient flexibility, or guile, to avoid Grindal's calamity, but when all allowances have been made it is hard to see that he achieved much more than that; the note of self-pity which increasingly colours his correspondence suggests that he himself fully appreciated the extent of his own defeat, one which was accentuated with the passage of time. His conscientious loyalty to the queen had never earned him many favours, while after the northern rising his advice over major promotions appears to have been largely ignored. Thus Parker was left—perhaps Margaret's death was instrumental—in gloomy and self-imposed isolation at Lambeth, where both Cecil and Bacon may finally have come to regard him as a drag upon, rather than an asset to, Elizabeth's 'but halfly reformed' church as it staggered uncertainly through the 1570s. Only in Cambridge (along with his wife, surely his greatest love), where his munificence to Corpus set a standard of scholarly patronage that few have rivalled, is it possible to find an unequivocally positive memorial to the virtues of Archbishop Matthew Parker.

DAVID J. CRANKSHAW and ALEXANDRA GILLESPIE

Sources CUL, Peterborough MS 30 • CUL, department of manuscripts and university archives, MS collect. admin. 22 • CCC Cam., archives, MS XL A48 • LPL, carte miscellanee, 13, document 57 • LPL, MS 2002 • Lincs. Arch., episcopal register 27 • lord chamberlain's department, records of special events, PRO, LC 2/2 • will, PRO, PROB 11/57 fol. 306*r–v* • state papers domestic, Elizabeth I, PRO, SP 12/5/25 • PRO, SP 12/71 • *The life off the 70. archbishopp off Canterbury presentlye sittinge Englished and to be added to the 69. lately sett forth in Latin: this numbre off seventy is so compleat a number as it is great pitie ther shold be one more, but that as Augustin was the first so Mathew might be the last* (?Heidelberg, 1574) • N. C. Bjorklund, 'Matthew Parker and the reform of the English church during the reigns of Henry VIII and Edward VI', PhD diss., U. Cal., Irvine, 1987 • R. Bowers, 'The Chapel Royal, the first Edwardian prayer book, and Elizabeth's settlement of religion, 1559', *HJ*, 43 (2000), 317–44 • V. J. K. Brook, *A life of Archbishop Parker* (1962) • *Correspondence of Matthew Parker*, ed. J. Bruce and T. T. Perowne, Parker Society, 42 (1853) • J. Josselin, *Historiola Collegii Corporis Christi*, ed. J. W. Clark, Cambridge Antiquarian RS, 17 (1880) • P. Collinson, 'Episcopacy and quasi-episcopacy in the Elizabethan church', *Miscellanea historiae ecclesiasticae*, ed. B. Vogler, 8 (1987), 229–38; Bibliothèque de la Revue d'Histoire Ecclésiastique, 72 • P. Collinson, *Archbishop Grindal, 1519–1583: the struggle for a reformed church* (1979) • P. Collinson, *The Elizabethan puritan movement* (1967) • P. Collinson, *Godly people: essays on English protestantism and puritanism* (1983), 19–44 • D. J. Crankshaw, 'Preparations for the Canterbury provincial convocation of 1562–63: a question of attribution', *Belief and practice in Reformation England: a tribute to Patrick Collinson from his students*, ed. S. Wabuda and C. Litzenberger (1998), 60–93 • D. J. Crankshaw, 'The Elizabethan faculty office and the aristocratic patronage of chaplains', *Patronage and recruitment in the Tudor and early Stuart church*, ed. C. Cross, Purvis Seminar Studies, Borthwick Studies in History, 2 (1996), 20–75 • C. Cross, ed., *The royal supremacy in the Elizabethan church*, Historical Problems, Studies and Documents, 8 (1969) • J. I. Daeley, 'Pluralism in the diocese of Canterbury during the administration of Matthew Parker, 1559–1575', *Journal of Ecclesiastical History*, 18 (1967), 33–49 • J. I. Daeley, 'The episcopal administration of Matthew Parker, archbishop of Canterbury, 1559–75', PhD diss., U. Lond., 1967 • J. Foxe, *Actes and monuments* (1563) • H. Gee, *The Elizabethan prayer-book and ornaments, with an appendix of documents* (1902) • B. Hall, 'Martin Bucer in England', *Martin Bucer: reforming church and community*, ed. D. F. Wright (1994), 144–60 • G. Hammond, *The making of the English Bible* (1982) • *The letter book of John Parkhurst, bishop of Norwich*, ed. R. A. Houlbrooke, Norfolk RS, 43 (1974–5) • W. S. Hudson, *The Cambridge connection and the Elizabethan settlement of 1559* (1980) • J. Ingamells, *The English episcopal portrait, 1559–1835: a catalogue* (privately printed, London, 1981) • N. L. Jones, *Faith by statute: parliament and the settlement of religion, 1559* (1982) • W. P. M. Kennedy, ed., *The 'Interpretations' of the bishops and their influence on Elizabethan episcopal policy (with an appendix of the original documents)*, Alcuin Club Tracts, 8 (1908) • W. P. M. Kennedy, *Archbishop Parker* (1908) • D. R. Leader, *A history of the University of Cambridge*, 1: *The university to 1546*, ed. C. N. L. Brooke and others (1988) • D. MacCulloch, *Suffolk and the Tudors: politics and religion in an English county, 1500–1600* (1986) • D. MacCulloch, 'The myth of the English Reformation', *Journal of British Studies*, 30 (1991), 1–19 • D. MacCulloch, *Thomas Cranmer: a life* (1996) • D. MacCulloch, *Tudor church militant: Edward VI and the protestant Reformation* (1999) • R. I. Page and G. H. S. Bushnell, *Matthew Parker's legacy: books and plate* (1975) • M. Parker and others, *Advertisements partly for due order in the publique administration of common prayers and usinge the holy sacramentes, and partly for the apparrell of all persons ecclesiasticall* (1566) • [M. Parker and others], *A booke of certaine canons, concernyng some parte of the discipline of the Churche of England* (1571) • [M. Parker], *A briefe examination for the tyme, of a certaine declaration, lately put in print in the name and defence of certaine ministers in London, refusing to weare the apparell prescribed by the lawes and orders of the realme* (1566) • [M. Parker and J. Joscelyn], *De antiquitate Britannicae ecclesiae et privilegiis ecclesiae Cantuariensis cum archiepiscopus eiusdem 70* (1572) • H. C. Porter, *Reformation and reaction in Tudor Cambridge* (1958) • J. H. Primus, *The vestments controversy: an historical study of the earliest tensions within the Church of England in the reigns of Edward VI and Elizabeth* (Kampen, 1960) • H. Robinson, ed. and trans., *The Zurich letters, comprising the correspondence of several English bishops and others with some of the Helvetian reformers, during the early part of the reign of Queen Elizabeth*, 2 vols., Parker Society, 7–8 (1842–5) • V. Sanders, 'The household of Archbishop Parker and the influencing of public opinion', *Journal of Ecclesiastical History*, 34 (1983), 534–47 • W. Sandys, ed., 'Copy of the inventory of Archbishop Parker's goods at the time of his death', *Archaeologia*, 30 (1844), 1–30 • F. J. Shirley, *Elizabeth's first archbishop: a reply to Mr J. C. Whitebrook's 'Consecration of the most reverend Matthew Parker' (A. R. Mowbray & Co., 1945)* (1948) • M. VanderSchaaf, 'Archbishop Parker's efforts toward a Bucerian discipline in the Church of England', *Sixteenth Century Journal*, 8 (1977), 85–103 • M. Aston, 'The *Bishops' Bible* illustrations', *The church and the arts*, ed. D. Wood, SCH, 28 (1992), 267–85 • J. Block, 'Thomas Cromwell's patronage of preaching', *Sixteenth Century Journal*, 8 (1977), 37–50 • W. D. J. Cargill Thompson, *Studies in the Reformation: Luther to Hooker*, ed. C. W. Dugmore (1980), 192–201, 251–3 • E. J. Carlson, 'Clerical marriage and the English Reformation', *Journal of British Studies*, 31 (1992), 1–31 • C. Clair, 'The Bishops' Bible 1568', *Gutenberg Jahrbuch* (1962), 287–90 • R. E. G. Cole, ed., *Chapter acts of the cathedral church of St Mary of Lincoln*, 3, Lincoln RS, 15 (1920) • D. J. Crankshaw, 'Elizabethan and early Jacobean surveys of the ministry of the Church of England', PhD diss., U. Cam., 2000 • J. F. Davis, 'The trials of Thomas Bylney and the English Reformation', *HJ*, 24 (1981), 775–90 • B. Dickins, 'The making of the Parker library', *Transactions of the Cambridge Bibliographical Society*, 6/1 (1972), 19–34 • G. R. Elton, *The parliament of England, 1559–1581* (1986) • T. S. Freeman, '"The Reformation of the Church in this Parliament": Thomas Norton, John Foxe and the parliament of 1571', *Parliamentary History*, 16 (1997), 131–47 • W. H. Frere, *The English church in the reigns of Elizabeth and James I* (1904) • W. H. Frere and C. E. Douglas, eds., *Puritan manifestoes: a study of the origin of the puritan revolt, with a reprint of the 'Admonition to the parliament', and kindred documents, 1572* (1907); repr. (1954) • W. H. Frere and W. P. M. Kennedy, eds., *Visitation articles and injunctions of the period of the Reformation*, 3, Alcuin Club, Collections, 16 (1910) • J. Gairdner, ed., *Three fifteenth-century chronicles*, CS, new ser., 28 (1880) • S. Gaselee, *The early printed books in the library of Corpus Christi College, Cambridge* (1921) • H. Gee and W. J. Hardy, eds., *Documents illustrative of English* *church history compiled from original sources* (1896) • T. Graham, 'Matthew Parker's manuscripts: a study of an Elizabethan library and its use', *Cambridge history of the book in Britain*, ed. J. Barnard and E. Leedham-Green, 4 [forthcoming] • *The recovery of the past in early Elizabethan England: documents by John Bale and John Joscelyn from the circle of Matthew Parker*, ed. T. Graham and A. G. Watson (1998) • W. W. Greg, 'Books and bookmen in the correspondence of Archbishop Parker', *The Library*, 4th ser., 16 (1935), 243–79 • C. Haigh, *English reformations: religion, politics, and society under the Tudors* (1993) • C. P. Hall, 'The Gild of Corpus Christi and the foundation of Corpus Christi College: an investigation of the documents', *Medieval Cambridge: essays on the pre-Reformation university*, ed. P. Zutshi (1993), 65–91 • T. E. Hartley, ed., *Proceedings in the parliaments of Elizabeth I*, 1: *1558–1581* (1981) • W. P. Haugaard, *Elizabeth and the English Reformation: the struggle for a stable settlement of religion* (1968) • F. Heal, 'The bishops and the Act of Exchange of 1559', *HJ*, 17 (1974), 227–46 • F. Heal, *Of prelates and princes: a study of the economic and social position of the Tudor episcopate* (1980) • F. Heal, 'The archbishops of Canterbury and the practice of hospitality', *Journal of Ecclesiastical History*, 33 (1982), 544–63 • P. L. Hughes and J. F. Larkin, eds., *Tudor royal proclamations*, 2: *The later Tudors* (1553–1587) (1969) • E. W. Ives, *Anne Boleyn* (1986) • M. R. James, *A descriptive catalogue of the manuscripts in the library of Corpus Christi College, Cambridge*, 2 vols. (1909–12) • N. L. Jones, ed., 'An Elizabethan bill for the reformation of the ecclesiastical law', *Parliamentary History*, 4 (1985), 171–87 • N. L. Jones, *The English Reformation: religion and cultural adaptation* (2002) • N. L. Jones, 'Matthew Parker, John Bale, and the Magdeburg Centuriators', *Sixteenth Century Journal*, 12 (1981), 35–49 • M. Parkes, 'Archaizing hands in English manuscripts', *Books and collectors, 1200–1700: essays presented to Andrew Watson*, ed. J. P. Carley and C. C. G. Tite (1997), 101–41 • N. R. Ker, *Medieval libraries of Great Britain*, 2nd edn (1964) • J. Lamb, ed., *A collection of letters, statutes and other documents … illustrative of the history of the University of Cambridge during the Reformation* (1838) • D. MacCulloch, *The later Reformation in England, 1547–1603* (1990) • M. C. McClendon, *The quiet Reformation: magistrates and the emergence of protestantism in Tudor Norwich* (1999) • M. McKisack, *Medieval history in the Tudor age* (1971) • P. Milward, *Religious controversies of the Elizabethan age* (1977) • W. Nicholson, ed., *The remains of Edmund Grindal*, Parker Society, 9 (1843) • P. J. Lucas, 'A testimonye of verye ancient tyme? Some manuscript models for the Parkerian Anglo-Saxon type-designs', *Of the making of books: medieval manuscripts, their scribes and readers. Essays presented to M. B. Parkes*, ed. P. R. Robinson and R. Zim (1997), 147–88 • J. C. T. Oates, *Cambridge University Library: a history from the beginnings to the Copyright Act of Queen Anne* (1986) • 'The letter-book of Thomas Bentham, bishop of Coventry and Lichfield, 1560-1561', ed. R. O'Day and J. Berlatsky, *Camden miscellany, XXVII*, CS, 4th ser., 22 (1979) • R. I. Page, *Matthew Parker and his books, Sandars lectures in bibliography … 14, 16, and 18 May 1990 at the University of Cambridge* (1993) • A. Peel, ed., *The seconde parte of a register*, 2 vols. (1915) • E. W. Perry, *Under four Tudors: being the story of Matthew Parker* (1940) • R. Rex, *Henry VIII and the English Reformation* (1993) • E. G. Rupp, *Studies in the making of the English protestant tradition* (1947) • J. J. Scarisbrick, 'Henry VIII and the dissolution of the secular colleges', *Law and government under the Tudors: essays presented to Sir Geoffrey Elton*, ed. C. Cross, D. Loades, and J. J. Scarisbrick (1988), 51–66 • H. Schilling, 'Confessional Europe', *Handbook of European history, 1400–1600: late Middle Ages, Renaissance and Reformation*, 2: *Visions, programs and outcomes*, ed. T. A. Brady jun., H. A. Oberman, and J. D. Tracy (1995), 641–81 • D. C. Steinmetz, *Reformers in the wings: from Geiler von Kaysersberg to Theodore Beza*, 1st edn (1971); 2nd edn (2001) • S. Strongman, 'John Parker's manuscripts: an edition of the lists in Lambeth Palace MS 737', *Transactions of the Cambridge Bibliographical Society*, 7 (1977–80), 1–27 • J. Strype, *Annals of the Reformation and establishment of religion … during Queen Elizabeth's happy reign*, 2 vols. (1709); new edn, 4 vols. (1824) • J. Strype, *The life and acts of Matthew Parker* (1711); new edn, 3 vols. (1821) • B. Usher, 'Edward Brocklesby: "the first put out of his living for the surplice"', *From Cranmer to Davidson: a Church of England miscellany*, ed. S. Taylor (1999), 47–68 • B. Usher, 'Expedient and experiment: the Elizabethan lay reader', *Continuity and change in Christian worship*, ed. R. N. Swanson, SCH, 35 (1999), 185–98 • B. Usher, 'The deanery of Bocking and the demise of the vestiarian controversy', *Journal of Ecclesiastical History*, 52 (2001), 434–55 • B. Usher, *William Cecil and episcopacy* [forthcoming] • C. E. Wright, 'The dispersal of the libraries in the sixteenth century', *The English library before 1700*, ed. F. Wormald and C. E. Wright (1958), 148–75 • C. E. Zinberg, 'The usable dissenting past: John Strype and Elizabethan puritanism', *The dissenting tradition: essays for Leland H. Carlson*, ed. C. R. Cole and M. E. Moody (1975), 123–39 • P. Clark, *English provincial society from the Reformation to the revolution: religion, politics and society in Kent, 1500–1640* (1977) • P. Collinson, 'The protestant cathedral, 1541–1660', *A history of Canterbury Cathedral*, ed. P. Collinson, N. Ramsay, and M. Sparks (1995), 154–203 • *Registrum Matthei Parker, diocesis Cantuariensis*, AD *1559–1575*, ed. W. H. Frere and E. M. Thompson, 3 vols., CYS, 35–6, 39 (1928–33) • *Fasti Angl., 1541–1857*, [Lincoln] • *Fasti Angl., 1541–1857*, [Ely] • S. E. Lehmberg, *The reformation of cathedrals: cathedrals in English society, 1485–1603* (1988)

Archives BL, Lansdowne MSS, papers • BL, Harley MSS, corresp. and papers • BL, grants of arms and inventory, Egerton MSS 2580–2581 • Bodl. Oxf., MSS and annotated printed books • CCC Cam., Parker Library and college archives, papers • CUL, corresp. and papers • Inner Temple, London, Petyt MSS, corresp. and papers • LPL, estate book and papers (including archiepiscopal register) • LPL, corresp. • Trinity Cam., MSS and annotated printed books | BL, correspondence, Add. MSS • PRO, correspondence, state papers domestic, Elizabeth I, SP12

Likenesses R. Hogenberg, line engraving, 1572, BM, NPG [*see illus.*] • portrait, miniature, 1573?, CCC Cam., MS 582 [dated 6 Aug 1573] • G. Vertue, line engraving, 1729, NPG • portrait, LPL

Wealth at death moveables worth approx. £2770 at death; annual income assessed at £3128 p.a.: probate inventory

Parker, Sir Nicholas (*d.* 1619), soldier, is first mentioned as commanding the soldiers on board the galleon *Leicester* in a trading expedition in 1582 led by the renowned military and naval commander Edward Fenton to the Moluccas and China by way of the Cape of Good Hope, nominally to discover the north-west passage. He afterwards served in the army that Elizabeth I dispatched to the Low Countries following the treaty of Nonsuch in 1585. He was given command of a company of 100 horsemen in Bergen op Zoom and 'did do very valiantly' in its defence, as Lord Willoughby reported to Lord Burghley in 1588 (*CSP for., July–Dec 1558*, 209). He was knighted by Willoughby later that year, after the siege was raised. Parker also served in France: in 1589 he was master of the ordnance for Willoughby's forces there, and was dispatched to Brittany in 1594, by which time he was 'somewhat skilled in the French tongue', as Sir Thomas Bodley commented (PRO, SP 84/4, fol. 239). In 1592 he commanded 100 lances in the Low Countries, and still had the same command in April 1597.

Parker won the respect of senior officials both at court and in the Netherlands. Upon his departure from the Netherlands, Count Maurice of Nassau commended him to the queen, Sir William Cecil, and the earl of Essex, noting that he had served him well. Essex, for his part, observed that Parker had 'donne ever valiantly in all incounters' (BL, Lansdowne MS 78, fol. 138). In 1597 he commanded a company of troops in the islands' voyage under Essex. The following year he was appointed deputy lieutenant of Cornwall and governor of Pendennis Castle;

he apparently continued in the latter post until his death. Between 1598 and 1603 he reported many sightings of Spanish ships off the Cornish coast, and in spring 1602 noted a rumour 'that there is now a great armado preparing in Lisbone' (*Salisbury MSS*, 12.93). He wrote frequently to Sir Robert Cecil and the privy council begging for more funds and supplies to strengthen the Cornish defences, and lamented: 'I find it a burden over heavy for my poor estate' (ibid., 10.244). He was appointed governor of Plymouth on a temporary basis from 1601 to 1603, in succession to Sir Ferdinando Gorges. In 1602 he was named in the charter of the Virginia Company as one of the adventurers; and another of them, Adrian Moore, married his daughter Anne. His third wife, Katherine, daughter of Sir John Temple of Stowe, Buckinghamshire, bore him a number of children, including the political writer Henry *Parker (1604–1652). Parker died in 1619. T. BORMAN

Sources *CSP for., July–Dec 1588*, 209 • *Calendar of the manuscripts of the most hon. the marquis of Salisbury*, 24 vols., HMC, 9 (1883–1976) • *Report on the manuscripts of Lord De L'Isle and Dudley*, 6 vols., HMC, 77 (1925–66) • *Report on the manuscripts of the earl of Ancaster*, HMC, 66 (1907) • *Calendar of the manuscripts of the marquis of Bath preserved at Longleat, Wiltshire*, 5 vols., HMC, 58 (1904–80) • *CSP dom., 1558–1625* • E. van Meteren, *A true discourse historicall, of the succeeding governors in the Netherlands, and the civill warres there begun in the yeere 1565* (1602) • E. G. R. Taylor, ed., *The troublesome voyage of Captain Edward Fenton, 1582–1583*, Hakluyt Society, 2nd ser., 113 (1959) • A. L. Rowse, *Tudor Cornwall: portrait of a society* (1941)

Archives BL, Cotton and Egerton MSS • Nationaal Archief, The Hague, liassen Engelandt, liassen Lopende • PRO, state papers, foreign series, especially SP 84, SP 78

Parker, Sir Peter, first baronet (1721–1811), naval officer, third son of Rear-Admiral Christopher Parker (*d.* 1765), was probably born in Ireland. He was promoted lieutenant in 1743, and was present in the *Barfleur* at the action off Toulon on 11 February 1744. On 6 May 1747 he was posted captain of the *Margate*, and thereafter he served in home waters and the Mediterranean until 1749. In March 1755 he was appointed regulating captain at Bristol and in May he commissioned the *Woolwich* at Portsmouth. Parker went to the West Indies in 1757 and transferred to the *Bristol* two years later, where he took part in the capture of Guadeloupe. In 1760 he returned to England in the *Buckingham* and in 1761 he took part in Commodore Augustus Keppel's capture of Belle Île. About this time he married Margaret (*d.* 1803), daughter of Walter Nugent; they had more than one child. After the peace Parker lived for the next ten years apparently in Queen Square, Westminster. He was knighted on 10 June 1772 when proxy for Sir John Moore at the installation of the knights of the Bath, and in October 1773 he was appointed to the *Barfleur* at Portsmouth.

In October 1775 Parker was given command, as commodore in the *Bristol*, of a small squadron going out to North America. It did not sail until February 1776 and bad weather prevented its reaching the Carolinas until May. Parker and General Henry Clinton decided to attack Charles Town, intending first to take the fort on Sullivan's Island at the harbour entrance. Troops were landed, but were unable to approach the fort, so Parker decided to reduce it by naval bombardment. On 28 June 1776 he led his squadron against the fort. Unfortunately three frigates ran aground, one being burned later when it could not be refloated, and Parker's flagship was badly damaged by enemy fire, with heavy casualties.

After this repulse Parker joined Admiral Lord Howe at New York and took part in the capture of Long Island. In December 1776 he was detached with a small squadron which captured Rhode Island, where he remained for most of 1777. He was promoted rear-admiral on 20 May 1777 and was later appointed commander-in-chief at Jamaica, although he did not reach the island in the *Bristol* until early 1778.

Among the officers Parker found at Jamaica was Horatio Nelson, nephew of the comptroller of the navy, Captain Maurice Suckling. Parker favoured Nelson by taking him on board the flagship as one of his lieutenants. Before the end of 1778 Parker had raised Nelson to commander and in June 1779 posted him as captain of a frigate. Since Suckling had died in mid-1778, Parker's continued support of Nelson reflected recognition of ability as much as patronage, and the young captain was closely associated with the admiral and his wife.

Parker, who became vice-admiral on 29 March 1779, did not have easy relations with the governor of Jamaica, General John Dalling, but after Spain joined the war in 1779, he provided naval support for expeditions organized by Dalling against Spanish Central America. The attack on Omoa in Honduras in October 1779 was a success, but the expedition to the San Juan river in Nicaragua in 1780 eventually ended in failure. Nelson came back to Jamaica gravely ill from the latter expedition and partly recovered during a stay at the admiral's house.

In 1781 it was alleged that Parker's failure to send assistance to Pensacola, West Florida, led to its falling to a Franco-Spanish force in May. Similarly Parker's reluctance to send some of his ships of the line to North America was said to have been one of the causes of the British defeat at the battle of the Chesapeake in September. However, Parker's first concern was always the safety of Jamaica, the most valuable single colony in the British empire at that time. It was understandable that he was unwilling to detach ships from his squadron when every year the enemy seemed to pose a new threat to the island.

The enemy threat in 1782 was removed by Admiral George Rodney's victory at the Saints (12 April), after which he brought his fleet to Jamaica. In July Parker sailed for England, with his flag on the *Sandwich*, carrying with him the count de Grasse and the principal French officers taken prisoner during the battle.

Parker's services were rewarded with a baronetcy on 13 January 1783; later he was MP for Seaford (1784–6) and Maldon (1787–90). He was promoted admiral on 24 September 1787, and appointed commander-in-chief at Portsmouth in 1793, a post in which he continued until 16 September 1799, when he was promoted admiral of the fleet. At Nelson's funeral in 1805 he was chief mourner as the senior officer of the navy rather than as an early patron and friend of the hero. In the previous two years he had suffered the death of his wife (18 January 1803) and one of his children, **Christopher Parker** (1761–1804), naval officer. Christopher had at an early age been promoted commander (7 December 1778) and captain (7 March 1779) by his father. He had commanded the *Lowestoft* at the capture of Omoa in October 1779, when he was wounded. In the 1790s he served in the West Indies under Admiral Sir John Jervis and in the channel under Admiral Lord Howe; and he was promoted rear-admiral on 1 January 1801. He died on 26 May 1804. He had married Augusta-Barbara-Charlotte (*d.* before 1804), daughter of Admiral John Byron and aunt of the poet; among their children were two sons, Sir Charles *Parker and Sir Peter *Parker, both distinguished naval officers.

Parker himself died in Weymouth Street, London, on 21 December 1811 and was buried at St Margaret's, Westminster on 28 December. At the time of his death he was deputy grand master of the Society of Freemasons and owned an estate at Bassingbourn, Cambridgeshire, and a plantation in Antigua. ALAN G. JAMIESON

Sources T. Pocock, *Young Nelson in the Americas* (1980) · D. Syrett, *The Royal Navy in American waters, 1775–1783* (1989) · P. Mackesy, *The war for America, 1775–1783* (1964) · *The private papers of John, earl of Sandwich*, ed. G. R. Barnes and J. H. Owen, 4 vols., Navy RS, 69, 71, 75, 78 (1932–8) · GEC, *Baronetage* · will, PRO, PROB 11/1528, sig. 549 [28 Dec 1811]

Archives NMM, corresp. with Lord Sandwich · PRO, corresp. with Admiral George Rodney, PRO 30/20

Likenesses portrait, probably NMM

Parker, Sir Peter, second baronet (1785–1814), naval officer, was the grandson of Sir Peter *Parker (1721–1811) and the eldest son of Vice-Admiral Christopher Parker (*d.* 1804) and his wife, Augusta, the daughter of Admiral John *Byron. He was thus first cousin of the poet George Gordon Byron, sixth Lord Byron. As early as 1793 he was on the books of the *Blanche*, then in the West Indies, and afterwards on those of the *Royal William*, guardship at Portsmouth from 1795 to 1799. Whether he was ever on board either seems very doubtful. However, from April 1799 to January 1801 he served as a midshipman on the *Lancaster* with Sir Roger Curtis at the Cape of Good Hope, and from January to April 1801 on the frigate *Arethusa*. On 4 May 1801 he passed his examination, being certified as upwards of twenty-one, and on 21 October he was promoted lieutenant of the *Alexander*. After serving in several ships on the Mediterranean and home stations he was appointed on 7 October 1803 to the *Victory*, Nelson's flagship before Toulon, from which he was promoted to the rank of commander on 8 May 1804. From October 1804 to April 1805 he commanded the hired ship *John*; he was then appointed to the brig-sloop *Weazel* (18 guns), which in October was with the fleet before Cadiz and stationed close in shore. On the evening of the 19th she was not more than 4 miles from Cadiz lighthouse. At six o'clock on the morning of the 20th she saw the enemy's fleet getting under way, and signalled to the *Euryalus*. She was then sent by Blackwood to carry the news to the ships at Gibraltar and to Rear-Admiral Louis. Before she returned to the fleet the battle of Trafalgar was over, but Collingwood was so pleased with the dispatch Parker had made that he promoted him captain, dating from 22 October 1805, the day after the battle. He was then appointed to the frigate *Melpomene* (38 guns) and sent to cruise in the Mediterranean.

Parker remained attached to the Mediterranean Fleet until the summer of 1808, when he was sent to Vera Cruz to bring back treasure—worth $3 million—for the Spanish government; this he landed safely at Cadiz. Unfortunately there were many cases of yellow fever on board the ship; she was sent to Portsmouth, and there Parker himself was dangerously ill. On 11 February 1809 he married Marianne, the daughter of Sir George Dallas bt; they had one son, who succeeded to the baronetcy. That same year the *Melpomene* was sent to the Baltic, where Parker was forced to take sick leave. From March 1810 to June 1811 he was tory MP for the borough of Wexford. He took his seat on 9 March 1810, and the same day made a spirited short speech in support of a grant to Portugal. Hostile to radicals, he was in favour of Roman Catholic relief. In May he was appointed to the *Menelaus* (38 guns), and in July was sent to St Helena to convoy home the East India fleet. He found the island much alarmed by the news of the loss of the frigate squadron at Mauritius, and undertook to go on as a reinforcement to Commodore Rowley. He sailed at once for Bourbon, and, finding the fleet had left, followed, and joined it in time to take part in the capture of Mauritius. He was then sent home with the news and, his conduct having been approved by the Admiralty, was again ordered to St Helena, whence he brought home a large convoy in August 1811. On 21 December he succeeded his grandfather, and became second baronet.

In October 1811 Parker took out Lord William Bentinck as ambassador to the king of Sicily, and in January 1812 he joined Sir Edward Pellew at Port Mahon, where he remained for the greater part of the year, attached to the in-shore squadron before Toulon. There he had more than one opportunity of distinguishing himself in a brilliant skirmish with the enemy's advanced ships. On 28 May he endeavoured to cut off the 40-gun frigate *Pauline*, with a 16-gun brig in company, returning from the Adriatic, and relinquished the attempt only when the *Menelaus*'s foretopmast was almost cut in two by a shot from the batteries and two ships of the line were standing out for the *Pauline*'s protection. On 13 August, having chased a brig laden with government stores into the port of San Stefano in the Bay of Orbitello, he cut her out from under the batteries, an affair which was spoken of as dashing at a time when cutting-out expeditions were not uncommon. In December the *Menelaus* was ordered to Malta and sent home in charge of convoy. She arrived at Portsmouth in May, and after refitting was sent to cruise westwards, in company with the *Superb*. She returned to Portsmouth in December, and after a short interval was ordered to join Lord Keith off Brest. On 14 February 1814, off Lorient, she retook a richly laden Spanish ship, a prize to the French frigates *Atalante* and *Terpsichore*, the latter of which had been captured some days before by the *Majestic*. The *Atalante* deserted her consort and escaped. On 25 March the *Menelaus* fell in with her, and chased her into Concarneau Bay; and, as her captain showed no intention of leaving his anchorage, Parker, on the 28th, sent him a note under a flag of truce, inviting him to come out to meet a frigate of equal force. The challenge was declined.

Shortly afterwards the *Menelaus* was ordered to North America, where, in the latter part of August, she was sent up the Chesapeake. On the 30th Parker had information of a strong party of American militia encamped in his neighbourhood. Towards midnight he landed with 134 men, seamen, and marines, and followed the enemy, who had retired to a position some 4 miles off. With rash bravery Parker led on his men to the attack, but fell, mortally wounded by a buckshot, which divided the femoral artery. Forty others were killed or wounded, and the party drew back to their ship, carrying with them the body of their captain, which was afterwards sent to England and buried in St Margaret's, Westminster. A brave and resourceful officer, Parker committed the greatest of all errors in war, that of underestimating his enemy.

J. K. Laughton, *rev.* Andrew Lambert

Sources T. Roosevelt, *The naval war of 1812* (1889) • D. Syrett and R. L. DiNardo, *The commissioned sea officers of the Royal Navy, 1660–1815*, rev. edn, Occasional Publications of the Navy RS, 1 (1994) • G. Dallas, *A biographical memoir of the late Sir Peter Parker* (1814) • Naval records, PRO • W. James, *The naval history of Great Britain, from the declaration of war by France, in February 1793, to the accession of George IV in January 1820*, 5 vols. (1822–4) • *GM*, 1st ser., 84/2 (1814), 378

Likenesses I. Jones, print, 1793, NPG • Ridley, print, 1804 (after V. Green), NPG • J. Hoppner, oils, 1808–9, NMM • C. Prosperi, relief sculpture (at his death), St Margaret's, Westminster, London

Parker, Sir Philip (*d.* 1604). *See under* Parker, Henry, eleventh Baron Morley (1531/2–1577).

Parker, Richard (1572/3–1629), antiquary, was born at Ely, the son of John *Parker (1532/3–1592), archdeacon of Ely, and his wife, Winifred Turner. He attended school in Ely from 1586, and was admitted to Gonville and Caius College, Cambridge, in March 1590, when he was said to be seventeen years of age. He proceeded BA in 1594, MA in 1597, and BD in 1620. He was successively scholar (1590–95) and fellow of Caius (1595–1611), holding a series of college offices, including a term as dean in 1600 and as bursar in 1608–10. He was rector of Little Wenden, Essex, from 1610, and of Littlebury, Essex, from 1615—'where he served God and the Muses, grew old and died a bachelor', as William Moore said of him (J. Venn, ed., *Annals of Gonville and Caius College*, 1904, 224). Moore (writing *c.*1650) thought highly of Parker and claimed that his work for British antiquities made him very acceptable to William Camden and many other illustrious men. But there is no trace of him in the records of the Elizabethan College of Antiquaries of which Camden was a central figure: Parker was perhaps too young to make his mark in it. Thomas Fuller says of him:

> Our Parker was bred in, and became fellow of Caius-Colledge, an excellent herald, historian and antiquary, author of a short, plain, true, and brief manuscript, called *Skeletos Cantabrigiensis*, and yet the bare bones thereof, are fleshed with much matter, and hath furnished me with the nativities of severall bishops who were masters of colledges. (Fuller, 159)

Truth to say, there is strangely little flesh on the bones. It is ostensibly based on Matthew Parker's 'Academiae historia Cantabrigiensis', appended to his *De antiquitate Britannicae ecclesiae* (1572), to which it adds little, and it is odd that Richard Parker seems to have made no use of the fuller version of Matthew Parker's skeletal account in John Caius, *Historiae Cantabrigiensis academiae* (1574). Some other manuscripts in the Caius Library contain notes in his hand; they show him to have been a keen compiler of material relating to the baronage and confirm a strong interest in heraldry. These, and some congratulatory verses in Camden's *Britannia* and elsewhere, are the sum of his *œuvre*. He appears to have been a keen but uncreative student of antiquities. He died at Littlebury in February 1629.

C. N. L. Brooke

Sources J. Venn and others, eds., *Biographical history of Gonville and Caius College*, 1: 1349–1713 (1897), 138 • *DNB* • Fuller, *Worthies* (1662), 1.159 • R. Parker, 'Skeletos Cantabrigiensis', in *Joannis Lelandi antiquarii de rebus Britannicis collectanea*, ed. T. Hearne, 5 (1770), 185–257 [also Gonville and Caius MSS 592/361, 173/94, pp. 1–177] • N. Cantalupus and R. Parker, *The history and antiquities of the University of Cambridge* (1721) [incl. Eng. trans. of R. Parker, 'Skeletos Cantabrigiensis'] • gesta, 1669–1716, Gon. & Caius Cam., GOV/03/01/04 • exiit books, 1618–78, 1678–1747, Gon. & Caius Cam. • notes on baronage etc., and index of coats of arms, Gon. & Caius Cam., MSS 569/327, pp. 1–62 and 561/320, pp. 1–34 [probably in Richard Parker's hand] • C. Hall, 'College officers: the bursars, stewards and registraries of Gonville and Caius College', *The Caian* (1989–90), 114–26 • G. Camdeno [W. Camden], *Britannia, sive, Florentissimorum regnorum, Angliae, Scotiae, Hiberniae*, later edn (1607) [incl. congratulary verse by Richard Parker in preface]

Archives Gon. & Caius Cam., history of University of Cambridge, genealogical and heraldic MSS • Norfolk RO, genealogical notes, poems, and other papers | BL, biographical collections relating to University of Cambridge, SI MS 1765, Lansdowne MS 965 • Bodl. Oxf., genealogical collections relating to the Peyton, Berners, and Fairfax families • Suffolk RO, Ipswich, pedigrees of the Berners and related families

Parker, Richard (1767–1797), seaman and mutineer, was born on 16 April 1767 at St Peter's churchyard, Exeter, Devon, and baptized on 24 April at St Mary Major, Exeter, the third child of Richard Parker, a successful Exeter baker and corn factor, and Sarah, 'a woman of good family and connections in that neighbourhood', who died when he was young (Althorp papers, G197). He had an older sister Sarah and an older brother John who took over the family business in 1787. 'Brought up in the fear of God' and tutored by the Revd Mr Marshall, 'Grammarian at Exeter' (ibid.), Parker, aged twelve, chose a naval career, and he learnt navigation from Mr Osborne, the quay master at Topsham, Devon.

On 10 April 1782, through the influence of his cousin Lieutenant Arthur, Parker joined the *Mediator*, a 5th rate (Captain Luttrell), as a volunteer. He was rated able seaman and paid a bounty of £5 and two months' advance of £2 5*s*. In April 1783 he transferred to the *Ganges*, 3rd rate; and in September 1783 he joined the sloop *Bulldog* (Captain Marsh), sailing to the Gambia. He arrived back in Portsmouth in April 1784, and was sent to Haslar Hospital, Gosport, in June. He returned to Portsmouth in July but did not accompany the *Bulldog* to the West Indies, instead transferring to hospital at Plymouth. After serving briefly on the *Blenheim*, a 2nd rate, he was discharged in August. He then sailed on Exeter merchant ships to the Mediterranean and to the East Indies until 1793.

In 1793 Parker recruited men for the *Hebe*, a 5th rate (Captain Alexander Hood), but the ship needed repairs, so he joined the *Sphynx*, 6th rate (Captain Lucas), at Woolwich; however, as he later admitted, 'a slight misfortune fell on me, which prevented my joining the Sphynx previous to her sailing' (Althorp papers, G197): the *Sphynx*'s paybooks indicate he was sent to Newgate prison, London, on 15 May 1793. In July, 'After extricating myself from the misfortune alluded to', Parker joined the *Assurance*, 5th rate (Captain Berkeley), at Chatham, 'to do the duty of an officer until the arrival of the Sphynx'. In August he became midshipman, but claimed he was 'kept contrary to my interest in the Assurance'. In November First Lieutenant Richards requested Parker's court martial after he disobeyed an order to take up his hammock to be aired, claiming it would 'disgrace' him as 'an officer' (ibid.). He was court martialled in December, 'disrated', and returned to the *Assurance*. Nevertheless the *Hebe*'s captain requested him, and Parker served as a foremast hand until he went back to Haslar with severe rheumatism in April 1794. He entered the *Royal William* in May, but was immediately rehospitalized. In August he re-entered the *Royal William* until his discharge on 26 November. Parker had leave 'for some particular purpose on Shore' and was reported 'arrested by the Civil Power for Debt' (PRO, ADM 1/1023, 17 June 1797).

Parker returned to his father's home in Exeter and on 10 June 1795 married Ann McHardy, a farmer's daughter from Braemar, Aberdeenshire. One son, John Charles, had already been christened in Braemar in October 1794. Another, John, was christened in Exeter in March 1796, and Parker recorded another child born in May 1796. Ann's brother made Parker an allowance, but he was arrested in Edinburgh for a debt of £23 and to escape prison joined the navy for a bounty of 20 guineas. He joined the Leith tender on 31 March 1797 and entered, as an able seaman from the Perth quota, *Sandwich*, 2nd rate (Captain James Robert Mosse), on 30 April. The ship was anchored at the Nore, off Sheerness, Kent.

The Nore mutiny of 1797, in which Parker played a leading role, started on 12 May in support of the mutiny at Spithead, but lacked its unity and discipline. The ships awaiting stores and men were not a fleet and new recruits from the quotas had diluted naval discipline. Once the North Sea Fleet arrived at the end of May and enlarged their force to thirteen battleships, the Nore mutineers expected their grievances would be met, but the replacement of Admiral Buckner's flag by the red flag of mutiny on 23 May, fears of invasion from Dutch ships, suspected revolutionary involvement, and the mutineers' blockade of the Thames on 2 June alienated merchants and parliament. Gradually ships abandoned the mutiny, disenchanted and deprived of provisions.

The *Sandwich*'s crew surrendered on 13 June and Parker was confined. He was court martialled on the *Neptune* between 22 and 26 June, with Vice-Admiral Sir Thomas Pasley presiding. Captain Mosse prosecuted, charging Parker with 'Making and endeavouring to make mutinous assemblies on board Sandwich … on or about the 12th of May; disobeying the lawful orders of his superior officers, and treating his superior officers with disrespect' (*Portsmouth Gazette*, 26 June 1797). He sought to prove that Parker had led the mutiny and ordered the *Director* to fire on the escaping *Repulse* on 9 June. It was established that Parker was president of the committee from 14 May, had been actively involved in its decisions and punishments, and directed the firing. Was he the real leader? The committee was established before he became involved, but his behaviour clearly shaped and prolonged the mutiny. Parker insisted that he had only obeyed the delegates' commands, had prevented more violence, and was neither Jacobin nor traitor. But the Admiralty secretary Evan Nepean, George III, and Pasley wished his immediate execution and his body to be hung in chains. After sentence was passed Parker asked 'that my death may atone to the Country' (PRO, ADM 1/5486).

Parker's wife watched him on the *Sandwich* from a small boat before, dressed in a suit of mourning, he was hanged from the yardarm on 30 June. He was immediately interred in the naval 'new burying ground' at Sheerness. Ann Parker, who had hoped to bury him 'like a gentleman, as he had been bred' ('Impartial … account', BL, G14560, 20), was not permitted to remove his body, but she secretly retrieved his coffin and took it to Rochester, and then to the Hoop and Horseshoe tavern, Little Tower Hill, London. Crowds gathered to see him, and his head and shoulders were sketched. The magistrates, fearing riots, ordered his burial in St Mary Matfelon vault, Whitechapel, on 4 July. Later his widow, impoverished, had to ask for charity: reportedly in 1840 she was seventy and blind.

There have been different views of Parker the mutineer. His own account correctly summarized his naval service but glossed over moral lapses. Lieutenant Watson of the Leith tender testified to his boastfulness, eloquence, and liking for drink. The 'Impartial account' portrayed a quixotic hero. Brenton described him as 'of a robust make, dark complexion, black eyes, about five feet eight inches high, and a very good-looking person' (Brenton, 1.296–7). Ann Parker had told the Admiralty that he was 'at times in a state of insanity', claiming his 1794 discharge was due to 'mental derangement' (*Portsmouth Gazette*, 26 June 1797). Parker perceived himself as a gentleman and consistently rated himself higher than his actual rank. He was undoubtedly volatile, arrogant, and lacking in self-discipline but Mosse reported that he died 'decent & steady' (PRO, ADM 1/728).

ANN VERONICA COATS

Sources Parker, admiral of mutineers 1797, executed 30 June 1797, BL, Althorp papers, G197 • naval paybooks, PRO, ADM 34/509, ADM 35/179, ADM 35/253, ADM 35/1475, ADM 35/1651, ADM 35/1684, ADM 35/9636, ADM 36/10420, ADM 36/10613, ADM 36/11246, ADM 36/11621, ADM 36/13347 • admiralty correspondence, PRO, ADM 1/727, ADM 1/728, ADM 1/1023, 17 June 1797, ADM 1/1517, ADM 1/3685, ADM 1/5486 • captains' logbooks, PRO, ADM

51/41, ADM 51/144, ADM 51/381, ADM 51/431, ADM 51/567 • admiralty rough minutes, PRO, ADM 3/137 • *IGI* • G. E. Manwaring and B. Dobrée, *The floating republic: an account of the mutinies at Spithead and the Nore in 1797* (1935) • C. Gill, *The naval mutinies of 1797* (1913) • 'An impartial and authentic account of the life of Richard Parker', 1797, BL, G14560 • *Portsmouth Gazette and Weekly Advertiser* (26 June 1797) • Royal Naval Museum, Portsmouth, Admiralty Library, MS 248/4, pt 1 • *Private papers of George, second Earl Spencer*, ed. J. S. Corbett and H. W. Richmond, 2, Navy RS, 48 (1924) • E. P. Brenton, *The naval history of Great Britain, from the year 1783 to 1836*, 1 (1837) • *The Times* (23 June 1797) • May–July 1797, BL, Althorp papers, G197 • Lord Keith to Lord Spencer, June 1797, BL, Althorp papers, G195 • C. Cunningham, *A narrative of occurrences that took place during the mutiny at the Nore in the months of May and June 1797* (1829) [copy in BL] • *DNB* • J. Dugan, *The great mutiny* (New York, 1965)

Archives BL, Althorp papers, G197 • NMM, Northesk collection • PRO, ADM 1/727, ADM 1/728, ADM 1/1023, ADM 1/1517, ADM 1/3685, ADM 1/5486 • PRO, ADM 3/137 • PRO, ADM 34/509 • PRO, ADM 35/179, ADM 35/253, ADM 35/1475, ADM 35/1651, ADM 35/1684, ADM 35/9636, ADM 36/10420, ADM 36/10613, ADM 36/11246, ADM 36/11621, ADM 36/13347 • PRO, ADM 51/41, ADM 51/144, ADM 51/381, ADM 51/431, ADM 51/567 • Royal Naval Museum, Portsmouth, admiralty library and manuscript collection, MS 248/4, pt 1

Likenesses W. Bromley, stipple, pubd 1797 (after S. Drummond), BM • Harrison & Co., line engraving, pubd 1797 (after W. Chamberlaine), BM • G. Murray, line engraving, pubd 1797 (after I. Cruikshank), NPG • Sanson, stipple, pubd 1797 (after Bailey), BM, NPG • engraving (after posthumous sketch), BL • group portrait (with delegates in counsel), NMM • stipple (labelled Robert but is Richard Parker), NMM • two etchings, NMM

Parker, Robert (*c.*1564–1614), religious controversialist, was probably born in Wilton, Wiltshire; his parents' names are unknown. He was educated at Magdalen College, Oxford, entering as a chorister in 1575, graduating BA in 1582, and proceeding MA in 1587. Between 1585 and 1593 he was a fellow of Magdalen. While at Oxford, Parker began moving in a nonconformist direction; the authorities had to punish him for not wearing the required robes, and he tried by every means to avoid clerical subscription to church canons. After finally subscribing in 1591, and with the support of Henry Herbert, second earl of Pembroke, whom he served as chaplain, he gained positions in the church. From 1591 to 1593 he was rector of Patney and master of the hospital of St Nicholas, Salisbury, and then from 1593 to 1607 he was prebendary of Stanton St Bernard.

Parker's conformity was always very marginal and in 1607, with the publication in the Netherlands of his *Scholasticall discourse against symbolizing with Antichrist in ceremonies, especially in the signe of the crosse*, his nonconformist convictions were totally revealed. The work warned about the ceremonial sign of the cross during baptism, because it was abhorrent to God's sense of simplicity and not compatible with scripture. The sign of the cross produced sins such as idolatry, superstition, hypocrisy, impiety, injustice, soul murder, adultery, wrong, slander, and concupiscence. Puritans welcomed the book as unanswerable truth, but Parker's bishop was not pleased. Parker was quickly suspended from his ministry, and 'fled from the storm' by going across to the Netherlands (Brook, 2.239). His flight probably occurred in 1607, but some reports say he travelled across with William Ames in 1610.

Parker's trail reappeared in 1610 in Leiden, where John Robinson's separatist church provided sustenance for a while to Parker and other destitute refugee puritans, such as William Ames and Henry Jacob. For several years Parker had no visible means of support and could not find a pastorate or chaplaincy. By this time he had a wife, Dorothy, and children to provide for, though initially they stayed in England. Secret funds, however, were coming in from sympathetic, puritan-minded merchants so that he could write more fiery, puritanical books; they seem to have sent him and Ames abroad expressly 'to write against the English hierarchy' (Nethenus, 4). However, Parker's second book, *De descensu domini nostri Jesu Christi ad inferos* (1611), a continuation of a work begun by Hugh Sanford, dealt with erudite arguments about Christ's descent into hell, and did not draw much attention.

The period of Parker's residence in the Netherlands corresponded with sharp puritan debates about church polity. Both Leiden and Amsterdam had two English churches, one for the separatists (Brownists) and the other for the non-separatist presbyterian English and Scots. Parker clearly rejected the separatists as schismatics, as is evident from a letter printed in Christopher Lawne's *Prophane Schisme of the Brownists* (1612), yet neither was he fully in tune with the presbyterian position. Instead, he was part of a third or new grouping called the Jacobites or the Amesians—non-separatist (or, said some, semi-separatist) congregational puritans, who included Ames and Jacob. They refused to use the language of separatism, thus remaining loosely within the bounds of the Church of England, but argued for the autonomy of the local congregation.

In 1611 Parker moved on to Amsterdam, where Pastor John Paget of the English Reformed church took him into his home, like a 'member of the same family and living under the same roofe' (Paget, pt 1, 105). Parker joined the English church on 4 January 1612, and the church elected him elder the same year. His family arrived, and his wife became a church member on 17 October 1612. His powerful preaching endeared him to the congregation and soon there was a move to appoint him co-pastor with Paget. Although Parker welcomed the call, Paget was lukewarm—an ardent presbyterian, Paget had been taken aback at Parker's talk that synods were for advice and counsel only, and concluded that Parker was 'somewhat confused' (ibid., 105). He worked to reconvert Parker to presbyterian polity but, when the English government protested against advancement of such an outspoken nonconformist, the city magistrates vetoed his pastoral appointment.

With the doors closed in Amsterdam, in 1613 Parker retreated eastward: the Lord would provide, 'who I know will be my God as well out of Amsterdam as in it' (Paget, ****2). Finally, he found work as a chaplain to English troops and pastor of the tiny English church in the frontier city of Doesburg in Gelderland—not a choice position, but he had no alternative. In accordance with Dutch practice, he presented his ministerial documents to the Dutch classis of Zutphen in September of 1613 and received approval to serve. In the early summer of 1614, after only eight months' service, he died. He was survived by his wife, Dorothy, and three children, Sarah, Thomas, and Elizabeth. Thomas *Parker studied at Leiden University and, with the support of William Ames, graduated MA from Franeker University in 1617; he was later pastor at Newbury, Massachusetts.

Two further works by Parker appeared after his death. *Exposition of the Pouring out of the Fourth Vial* was not published until 1650 (in the Netherlands, like all the others, because permission was not forthcoming to print them in England), but *De politeia ecclesiastica Christi, et hierarchica opposita, libri tres*, his most controversial work, written in Latin for an international audience of scholars, was printed by William Brewster and his Pilgrim Press at Leiden in 1616 (two versions). Two further editions, to which many printers contributed, followed in 1621 and 1638. The book, on church government, still exhibited some ecclesiological vagueness. Parker approved of both primary congregations and the use of synods (but with rather limited authority for the latter). Although John Paget proclaimed himself satisfied that the book was in line with presbyterian puritanism, the chapters about the primary power of congregations appealed greatly to congregational-minded puritans. A favourite text, much quoted by congregationalists, was that 'all ecclesiastical power is always in the whole congregation' (*Politeia ecclesiastica*, bk 3, chap. 6). New England congregationalists especially revered Parker as a founder of the faith: according to Cotton Mather, Parker was 'in some sort the *father* of all the *non-conformists* in our age' (Mather, 1.480).

KEITH L. SPRUNGER

Sources A. C. Carter, *The English Reformed church in Amsterdam in the seventeenth century* (1964) • K. L. Sprunger, *Dutch puritanism: a history of English and Scottish churches of the Netherlands in the sixteenth and seventeenth centuries* (1982) • F. B. Carr, 'The thought of Robert Parker (1564?–1614?) and his influence on puritanism before 1650', PhD diss., U. Lond., 1965 • F. B. Carr, 'Parker, Robert', Greaves & Zaller, *BDBR*, 9–10 • B. Brook, *The lives of the puritans*, 2 (1813), 237–40 • J. Paget, *A defence of church government* (1641) • J. Lane, 'Arent Corsz Hogenacker (ca. 1579–1636): an account of his typefoundry and a note on his types', *Quaerendo*, 25 (spring 1995), 83–113 • consistory register, English Reformed Church of Amsterdam • M. Nethenus, 'Praefatio introductoria', *William Ames*, ed. and trans. D. Horton, 1 (1965) • P. Miller, *Orthodoxy in Massachusetts, 1630–1650* (1933) • W. Bradford, 'A dialogue, or, The sume of a conference between som younge men borne in New England and sundery ancient men that came out of Holland and old England *anno domini* 1648', *Publications of the Colonial Society of Massachusetts*, 22 (1920), 115–41 • *DNB* • W. H. Burgess, *John Robinson, pastor of the Pilgrim Fathers* (1920) • C. Mather, *Magnalia Christi Americana*, 3rd edn, 7 bks in 2 vols. (1853–5)

Parker, Robert (*b.* **1665x8**, *d.* in or after **1718**), army officer, was born near Kilkenny in Ireland, the son of a protestant farmer. Educated in Kilkenny, he joined a militia company of protestant schoolboys formed by James Butler (later second duke of Ormond), and acquired as a result of their rudimentary exercises with arms a taste for military life. In October 1683 Parker enlisted into Captain Frederick Hamilton's company of foot, which soon afterwards was drafted into Lord Mountjoy's regiment. In 1687 Parker was dismissed from the army on account of his religion, but when in London in April 1689 he enlisted under Major Hamilton into Edgeworth's regiment. Edgeworth was soon cashiered and the regiment became the earl of Meath's regiment of foot. Parker fought at the battle of the Boyne (1690), at the sieges of Limerick and Athlone (where he was wounded), and at the battle of Aughrim (1691).

Campaigning with his regiment in the Spanish Netherlands during the Nine Years' War, Parker was present at the siege of Namur, and was awarded in December 1695 a commission as colour ensign for his gallantry at the storming of the breach at the Terra Nova on 20 August 1695. Following the peace of Ryswick (September 1697) Parker was stationed on garrison duty in Ireland, and he married in June 1698. He was made lieutenant in 1702.

During the War of the Spanish Succession Parker was present with his regiment, now entitled the Royal regiment of Ireland, in most of Marlborough's campaigns. He fought at the Schellenberg and Blenheim (1704), Ramillies (1706), and Oudenarde (1708). He became captain-lieutenant on 1 May 1706 and was wounded at the siege of Menin in that year when serving as adjutant. In August 1708, as captain of grenadiers, Parker was sent to Ireland, at the request of Lieutenant-General Ingoldsby, to teach the recruits there the tactical firing discipline in use in the allied army in Flanders. He was reluctant to undertake this task, but remained in Ireland for two years and was presented by the government with a gratuity of £200 on his return to Flanders in 1710. Although he was not present at the battle of Malplaquet (1709), his memoirs recount the exploits of his regiment and provide a graphic contemporary description of the fighting in the woods that day.

At the end of the war Parker went to London on behalf of his brother officers to speak at the board of general officers convened to consider what regiments should be retained on the peacetime establishment. Despite assurances to the contrary from his old acquaintance, the duke of Ormond, the Royal regiment of Ireland was numbered 18th in the line, to the disappointment of many who considered that a more senior number was appropriate. Parker then served with the 18th as part of the garrison of Ghent, while the new frontier between the United Provinces and the Austrian Netherlands was settled. In April 1716 the regiment returned to garrison duty in Oxford, and in April 1718 Parker sold his commission to a nephew of his old benefactor, Lieutenant-General Frederick Hamilton. He settled with his wife and children near Cork in Ireland. The date of his death is not known.

Robert Parker's *Memoirs*, taken from a journal kept while on campaign and written in retirement, were published posthumously by his son in 1746, the year after the duke of Ormond's death. Although Parker claimed to have been passed over for promotion owing to Marlborough's favouritism to others, he obviously held him in high regard, but his opinion of Ormond was less favourable. The memoirs are a valuable detailed account of the trials of a marching officer during Marlborough's campaigns.

James Falkner

Sources R. Parker, *Memoirs of the most remarkable military transactions from the year 1688 to 1718* (1746) • *Robert Parker and Comte de Mérode-Westerloo: the Marlborough wars*, ed. D. Chandler (1968) • N. B. Leslie, *The succession of colonels of the British army from 1660 to the present day* (1974) • W. S. Churchill, *Marlborough: his life and times*, 2 vols. (1947) • C. Dalton, ed., *English army lists and commission registers, 1661–1714*, 6 vols. (1892–1904)

Likenesses oils, NAM; repro. in Parker, *Memoirs*, frontispiece

Parker, Robert John, **Baron Parker of Waddington** (**1857–1918**), judge, was born on 25 February 1857 at Claxby rectory, Lincolnshire, the second son of the Revd Richard Parker, incumbent of Claxby, and his wife, Elizabeth Coffin. His sister Ellen [*see* Pinsent, Dame Ellen Frances] became a leading promoter of mental health services. He was educated at Westminster School and Eton College, where he was Newcastle medallist, before matriculating on 13 October 1876 at King's College, Cambridge. There he became a scholar in 1876 and a fellow in 1881 at an unusually young age. He won the Browne's medal for the Greek ode in 1878 and in 1880 was bracketed fifth in the first class of the classical tripos; he obtained his BA in the same year and his MA in 1888.

Parker was admitted as a student to Lincoln's Inn on 3 November 1883 and was called to the bar on 17 November in the same year. He first read under and later worked with Ingle Joyce. He soon developed a thriving practice, was esteemed for his pleadings and later had many pupils of his own. He never took silk, preferring to remain as junior counsel to the Treasury, a position he held from 1900, when Joyce was made a judge. On 9 September 1884 he married Constance (*d.* 1937), only child of John Trevor Barkley, civil engineer; they had three sons, Trevor, John, and Hubert Lister *Parker, a future lord chief justice, and two daughters, Vivien and Gwendoline.

Parker remained relatively obscure until 1906 when he was made a Chancery judge. He began to make his mark in trying patent cases and in settling the practice under the Patents and Designs Act (1907). Having delivered a judgment in a case relating to Marconi's 'wireless telegraphy' patents in 1913, he was appointed chairman of a technical committee to advise the postmaster-general as to the choice to be made among the five then competing systems. On 1 May 1913 the committee reported in favour of Marconi's.

The death of Lord Macnaghten on 17 February 1913 had made a vacancy for a lord of appeal, for which a leading equity lawyer was required. As a Chancery judge Parker had often sat as an additional member of the Court of Appeal, and on 4 March was promoted to the House of Lords. He was duly sworn of the privy council and took the title of Baron Parker of Waddington in Yorkshire, from the younger branch of the Parkers of Browsholme, to which his family belonged. It was most unusual for a junior barrister to be promoted so rapidly to the House of Lords. Even Lord Blackburn, who was similarly promoted, had sat on the bench for many years. From the outset the profession recognized Parker as a great addition of legal strength to the House of Lords and he gained an authoritative position as a judge of final appeal during the years in which he sat there. His ability to assimilate new law and make it his own was very clear, especially in relation to the prize appeals heard during the First World War. Although the subject was novel to a Chancery lawyer and would have tested the best Admiralty practitioner, Parker was quick to familiarize himself with the decisions and to grasp the intricate practice which prevailed at that time under Lord Stowell. Parker remained on the board of appeal until shortly before his death, taking over as president after Lord Mersey. His ability to harmonize the precedents of past wars with the exigencies of the First World War was obvious, especially in the *Roumanian* and *Zamore* cases.

Parker acted as deputy high steward of Cambridge University between 1915 and 1918, a time when he also sat as the president of the judicial committee and the privy council (appointed to succeed Lord Mersey in 1916). Examples of his characteristic methods of proceeding, both as an ordinary judge and as a lord of appeal, as well as of his remarkable range, can be found in his verdicts on *Johnson* v. *Clark* (a local custom of Kendal); *Fitzhardinge* v. *Purcell* (sporting rights on the foreshore of the Severn); *Jones* v. *Pritchard* (rights and obligations as to party-walls); *Monks* v. *Whiteley* (equitable doctrine of merger); *Barry* v. *Minturn* (an early House of Lords judgment which Parker's colleagues were satisfied to adopt without additions); *Attorney-General for the Commonwealth* v. *Adelaide Steamship Company* (combinations in restraint of trade); *Kreglinger* v. *New Patagonian Company* (clogging the equity of redemption); *Trim School* v. *Kelly* (murder as an accident arising out of and in the course of a schoolmaster's employment); *Stickney* v. *Keeble* (of what contracts time is of the essence); *Tamplin Steamship Company* v. *Anglo-Mexican Company* (frustration of a commercial adventure); *Continental Tyre Company* v. *Daimler Company* (the doctrine of enemy character as applied to British incorporated companies during war); *Admiralty Commissioners* v. *SS America* (the right to sue in respect of another person's loss of life); *Bowman* v. *Secular Society* (illegality of anti-Christian associations); and *Banbury* v. *Bank of Montreal* (authority of agents to bind principals by representations to third parties).

The most striking characteristic of Parker's judgments was their intellectual compactness. He was always more interested in substance than in form and his method was to state a legal principle and to bring the case within it. He was concerned not only with the correctness of a decision but also with the reputation and independence of the tribunal. For example, in a case which concerned the interests of working men, the house was divided as four to three (the four being of one political party and the three of the other). Parker, who was in the minority, thought that the result would cast the judiciary into disrepute, and so suggested to one of his colleagues on the other side that they should read one another's judgments, an offer which was declined.

When the First World War broke out, Parker was one of the first to see the danger of allowing prices and the cost of living to increase rapidly and unreasonably; and, at the time of the 'business as usual' cry, he took steps to urge his views on ministers privately. He met with no success. During 1915 he gave much thought to the problems of post-war reconstruction and brought the subject before the House of Lords in an elaborate and characteristically condensed address on 14 December 1915. During the passage of the Representation of the People Bill of 1918 he took up the cause of those women who had passed university examinations but been denied the right to take up their degrees, and, speaking both as an alumnus and deputy high steward of Cambridge University, pressed on the House of Lords the right of women to vote for the representation of their university in parliament. In this he was successful.

Parker's most noteworthy contribution to debate on public affairs was made in 1918, shortly before he died. On the occasion of a motion by Lord Parmoor on 19 March 1918 in favour of a league of nations, Parker brought before the house a detailed scheme, which went far beyond mere utopian sentiment to suggest practical details of how such a league might be formed; his plan contained twenty articles by which a league could be refined.

Parker's health at this stage, however, was already beginning to fail. He continued to work until the summer of 1918, but died after a short illness near Lurgashall, in Sussex, on 12 July at Aldworth, at the first Lord Tennyson's old home, where he had lived since 1914. As well as maintaining Browsholme Lodge in Haslemere, Surrey, he and Constance had lived at 3 Buckingham Gate in London. Constance and his three sons and two daughters survived him. Lord Parker was one of the most esteemed judges of the early twentieth century. SINÉAD AGNEW

Sources Venn, *Alum. Cant.* • J. Foster, *Men-at-the-bar: a biographical hand-list of the members of the various inns of court*, 2nd edn (1885), 352 • L. G. Pine, *The new extinct peerage, 1884–1971: containing extinct, abeyant, dormant, and suspended peerages with genealogies and arms* (1972), 213–14 • W. P. Baildon, ed., *The records of the Honorable Society of Lincoln's Inn: admissions*, 2 (1896), 408 • H. Cox, *Who's who in Kent, Surrey, Sussex* (1911), 243–4 • *CGPLA Eng. & Wales* (1918)

Archives King's Cam., Browning MSS • UCL, Pearson MSS

Likenesses G. F. Watt, portrait, 1913, King's Cam.

Wealth at death £48,098 14*s.* 1*d.*: probate, 24 Aug 1918, *CGPLA Eng. & Wales*

Parker, Ronald William (1909–1996), accountant and manager of nationalized industries, was born at 29 Hillside Street, Edinburgh, on 21 August 1909, the son of Ernest Edward Parker (*c*.1869–1954), accountant of court, and his wife, Margaret, *née* Henderson (1877–1958). He was educated at the Royal High School, Edinburgh (1914–26), and became a chartered accountant in 1933, after being articled to J. G. Wells & Co. of Edinburgh, and being sent by them to the London office of Thompson McLintock. There he was introduced to Garfield Weston, who developed great confidence in him. In 1935 he became secretary of the Weston Group (later Associated British Foods), which was rapidly expanding in the food industry. Parker (who later became a director) acted for Weston in many acquisitions and mergers. On 23 July 1937 he married Phyllis Mary (*b.* 1913), daughter of Walter E. Sherren, master contractor; they had two sons.

During the Second World War Parker's work shifted towards basic industry. In 1942 he was brought into the Ministry of Fuel and Power as assistant director of finance. Then in 1947, after a brief spell as partner in a firm of accountants, J. Aikman, Smith and Wells, he began a long association with the newly nationalized coal industry in Scotland as finance director of the National Coal Board's Scottish division. He became a passionate supporter of successful public ownership and was chairman of the Scottish division from 1955 to 1968. As chairman he obtained exceptional finance for development including the Hurst seam, and the Longannet pit and power station. Such Scottish coups did not endear him to other areas of the coal industry, but they probably made it possible for him to preside without serious disruption over a fall from over 100,000 Scottish miners to fewer than 50,000. This took place when the National Union of Mineworkers was in its heyday. It was Parker's misfortune that he ultimately had to manage a Scottish industry in rapid decline.

Parker did not become chairman of the National Coal Board, as some had predicted, and in 1968 he left the coal industry to become, from 1968 to 1974, chairman of the Scottish Gas Region. He became a JP for the city and county of Edinburgh in 1972. He retired from management in the public sector in 1974. His later appointments included being a director of Sidlaw Industries and chairman of its growing oil services subsidiary, Aberdeen Service Co. Ltd (1974–83). He died of heart failure at Murrayfield Independent Hospital, Edinburgh, on 9 October 1996 and was cremated at Mortonhall crematorium, Edinburgh, on 17 October. He was survived by his wife and two sons. ARTHUR GREEN

Sources *The Independent* (15 Oct 1996) • *Glasgow Herald* (17 Oct 1996) • *WWW* • private information (2004) [Nicholas Parker] • b. cert. • m. cert. • d. cert.

Likenesses double portrait, photograph, 1956 (with Queen Elizabeth II), repro. in *The Independent*

Wealth at death £322,685.77: confirmation, 20 Feb 1997, NA Scot., SC/CO 981/201

Parker, Samuel (1640–1688), bishop of Oxford, was born at Northampton in September 1640, the second son of John *Parker (*d.* 1656x8) [*see under* Parker, John (*fl.* 1631–1680)], judge. Parker was 'puritanically educated' at Northampton grammar school before entering Wadham College, Oxford, on 30 September 1656. He matriculated on 29 October 1657. Anthony Wood records that Parker, under the supervision of a presbyterian tutor, led a 'strict and religious life', becoming a member of a group known as 'grewellers' owing to their ascetic diet of oatmeal and water. Parker was also reputed to frequent presbyterian meetings hosted by the laundress Bess Hampton. At the time, according to Wood, Parker was 'so zealous and constant a hearer of the prayers and sermons there held forth, a receiver of the sacraments and such like, that he was esteemed one of the preciousest young men in the university' (Wood, *Ath. Oxon.*, 4.226). Parker graduated BA on 28 February 1659.

After the Restoration, Parker fell out with the warden of Wadham, Dr Walter Blandford, on account of his puritanical views and he transferred to Trinity College, where he proceeded MA on 9 July 1663. At Trinity, Parker fell under the influence of Ralph Bathurst, who he later claimed had 'first rescue[d] him from the chains and fetters of an unhappy education' (Parker, *Free and Impartial Censure*, sig. A3*v*). Under Bathurst's guidance Parker became a keen Anglican, and was ordained the following year. Parker subsequently spent some time in London, possibly as a domestic chaplain.

Parker's first published work was an important theological essay, *Tentamina de Deo* (1665), dedicated to Gilbert Sheldon, archbishop of Canterbury, and Charles II. Here Parker sought to show that natural philosophy, far from leading to atheism, constituted an effective means of combating it. Parker became a fellow of the Royal Society on 13 June 1666, nominated by John Wilkins. Although enthusiastic about the Royal Society in all his books Parker was never an active member and his name ceases to appear on membership lists after 1684. It would appear that he was expelled in 1685 for non-payment of his subscription. Parker developed the arguments from the *Tentamina* in two subsequent works addressed to his friend Nathaniel Bisbie. The first, *A Free and Impartial Censure of the Platonick Philosophie* (1666), developed the argument of the last chapter of the first book of the *Tentamina* in attacking Platonism. The second piece, published in 1667, was *An Account of the Nature and Extent of the Divine Dominion and Goodness*. This controversial work defended the view that God's dominion was founded in his power rather than his goodness, as well as attacking the Origenian hypothesis concerning the pre-existence of the soul.

Parker's polemical ability attracted the attention of the archbishop of Canterbury, and Sheldon recruited Parker as a domestic chaplain in November 1667, a move which ensured his rapid promotion. In 1667 he received the rectory of Chartham in Kent and incorporated his MA at St Catharine's College, Cambridge. From June 1670 it appears that Parker succeeded William Sancroft as archdeacon of Canterbury. In July 1671 Parker became rector of Ickham in Kent, being admitted DD and perhaps DM at Cambridge *per literas regias* on 26 November of the same year. The following year Parker was installed a prebendary of Canterbury by royal mandate on 12 November. He also became master of the Eastbridge Hospital (St Thomas the Martyr) in Canterbury on 29 August 1673.

Parker's years in Sheldon's service saw him earn a reputation as one of the most aggressive opponents of religious toleration. His most notorious work was *A Discourse of Ecclesiastical Polity* which, although dated 1670, appeared in 1669. The book generated a storm of controversy for its vitriolic style and its absolutist argument. Parker claimed that the magistrate had absolute power to arbitrate over religious disputes and to determine religious worship in the manner most appropriate for civil peace. Although Parker attempted to make clear his own opposition to the tenets of Thomas Hobbes, his nonconformist critics made the case that Parker himself was a Hobbist. Parker replied to such criticism with a renewed assault upon nonconformists in *A Defence and Continuation of Ecclesiastical Polity* in 1671, and also in his preface to Bishop John Bramhall's *Vindication of himself and the Episcopal Clergy from the Presbyterian Charge of Popery* (1672). The latter provided the occasion for Andrew Marvell to attack Parker in his celebrated *Rehearsal Transpros'd*, in which Parker and his ideas were relentlessly satirized. Parker replied in *A Reproof to the 'Rehearsal Transpros'd'* in 1673, subjecting Marvell to violent personal abuse. Marvell responded with an even more savage *Second Part of the Rehearsal Transpros'd*, which effectively ended the debate. Anthony Wood comments that it was generally thought, even by Parker's friends, that Parker 'thro' a too loose and unwary handling of the debate (tho' in a brave, flourishing and lofty stile) laid himself too open to the severe strokes of his snearing adversary, and that the odds and victory lay on Marvell's side' (Wood, *Ath. Oxon.*, 4.231). At about the same time Parker's activities as a licenser also got him into trouble after he approved a spurious account of the murder and flaying of a New England minister named Baxter by four Anabaptists. The work was investigated and found to be fictitious. Parker was forced to produce a penitential testimonial to the falsehood of *Mr Baxter Baptiz'd in Blood* and this was printed in *Forgery Detected and Innocency Vindicated* (1673).

Perhaps predictably after these reverses, and the death of his patron Sheldon in November 1677, Parker adopted a lower public profile during the later 1670s. He had married Rebecca Pheasant in May or June 1673; their two surviving sons were Gilbert and Samuel *Parker. Parker maintained his interest in science and combating atheism, producing his magnum opus in 1678, *Disputationes de Deo et providentia divina*. This continued and expanded the themes addressed in the *Tentamina de Deo*; attacking Epicureanism, Hobbes, Descartes, and the use of ancient philosophy. A further development of Parker's interests in this respect was *A Demonstration of the Divine Authority of the Law of Nature and of the Christian Religion* (London, 1681), which was designed as a continuation of the *Disputationes de Deo*, and was dedicated to Ralph Bathurst. Parker combined the recent natural law theory of Richard Cumberland with more traditional sources to provide evidence that natural law was obligatory and represented the will of God.

As the early 1680s witnessed a reaction against religious and political dissent Parker re-entered the political fray. In a series of works, beginning with *The Case of the Church of England Briefly and Truly Stated* (1681), Parker developed his ecclesiological position, which has often been misunderstood. Far from being straightforwardly Erastian, Parker claimed (against Edward Stillingfleet) that the episcopal form of the church was established by divine right. He also attempted to prove that episcopacy was the practice of the primitive church in *An Account of the Government of the Christian Church* (1683). In *Religion and Loyalty* (in two parts, 1684 and 1685), Parker argued that post-Reformation protestantism had gone too far in reacting to the inflated clerical claims of the Roman Catholic church. Parker claimed that the separate jurisdictions of church and state could co-exist to their mutual advantage. However, he made it clear that absolute obedience was owed to the sovereign in this world for the sake of peace.

This position recommended Parker to James II who nominated him to become bishop of Oxford upon the death of John Fell in 1686. Parker had resigned his prebendal stall at Canterbury in 1685 but was allowed to retain his archdeaconry *in commendam* with his bishopric and was consecrated at Lambeth on 17 October 1686 with Dr Thomas Cartwright, bishop of Chester. Both appointments were designed to assist in easing conditions for James's co-religionists and Parker was one of the few bishops to accept James's declaration of indulgence of April 1687. Although Parker could not stomach dissenters' demands for toleration by right, the granting of indulgence through royal prerogative was nevertheless consistent with his ultra-royalism. He was, however, unsuccessful in persuading his suspicious clergy to subscribe to an address on 30 May expressing gratitude and loyalty to the king for his promise to secure the clergy's religion and their possessions.

As James moved ahead with his plan to impose Roman Catholics upon the colleges of Oxford and Cambridge, Parker's health and his political authority deteriorated. When the fellows of Magdalen College, Oxford, rejected the Roman Catholic Anthony Farmer for the vacant presidency, the king nominated Parker in his place on 14 August 1687. Bedridden at his episcopal palace at Cuddesdon, Parker asked to be admitted by proxy but the fellows refused him and elected John Hough. The deadlock which ensued was only ended on 25 October when the commission for ecclesiastical causes intruded Parker by force. The ailing bishop came into residence on 2 November and twenty-five fellows were expelled on 16 November, to be replaced by Roman Catholics on successive mandates from the king. Parker's *Reasons for Abrogating the Test* appeared on 16 December and his argument, which questioned the motives behind the original anti-Catholic Test legislation and queried the Anglican position on transubstantiation, heightened suspicion on all sides that Parker was a closet Catholic.

However it is far from clear that Parker, now severely ill, ever intended to change his faith. In spite of more expulsions (fourteen demies followed in January), Parker declared his continued adherence to the Church of England before the fellowship and forbade the celebration of Roman Catholic mass in the college. When in March James ordered Parker to admit nine more Roman Catholics, Parker was alleged to have raged against the king and his policy and then to have fallen into a convulsive fit, which may have been a stroke. During the fatal illness that followed Parker was said to have rejected the ministrations of Roman Catholic priests and received the sacraments from an Anglican clergyman. He died on the evening of 20 March 1688 in the president's lodgings, and was buried by torchlight on 24 March on the south side of the ante-chapel, without a memorial.

For Gilbert Burnet, undoubtedly a prejudiced witness, Parker was 'full of satirical vivacity, and was considerably learned; but was a man of no judgement, and of as little virtue, and as to religion rather impious' (*Bishop Burnet's History*, 1.260). Anecdotes abound to support Burnet's verdict; when asked 'What was the best body of divinity?' Parker is said to have answered, 'That which would help a man to keep a coach and six horses was certainly the best' (*Enquiry into the Reasons*, 2). But if Parker was undoubtedly ambitious and ideologically flexible he was also, as more recent scholarship has emphasized, a wide-ranging intellectual who was at once a champion of the new science, an innovative natural law theorist, and a sophisticated defender of the Anglican church. JON PARKIN

Sources *DNB* · Wood, *Ath. Oxon.*, new edn, vol. 4 · Foster, *Alum. Oxon.* · Venn, *Alum. Cant.* · R. B. Gardiner, ed., *The registers of Wadham College, Oxford*, 1 (1889) · *Fasti Angl., 1541–1857*, [Canterbury] · A. Marvell, *The rehearsal transpros'd*, ed. D. I. B. Smith (1971) · S. Parker, *A free and impartial censure of the Platonick philosophie* (1666); repr. with introduction by K. Robinson (New York, 1985) · *Bishop Burnet's History of his own time: with the suppressed passages of the first volume*, ed. M. J. Routh, 6 vols. (1823), vol. 1 · [G. Burnet], *An enquiry into the reasons for abrogating the test imposed on all members of parliament offered by Sa Oxon* (1688) · J. R. Bloxam, ed., *Magdalen College and James II, 1686–1688: a series of documents*, OHS, 6 (1886) · J. R. Bloxam, *A register of the presidents, fellows … of Saint Mary Magdalen College*, 8 vols. (1853–85), vols. 1–5 · R. Ashcraft, *Revolutionary politics and Locke's two treatises of government* (1986) · G. Schochet, 'Between Lambeth and Leviathan: Samuel Parker on the Church of England and political order', *Political discourse in early modern Britain*, ed. N. Phillipson and Q. Skinner (1993), 189–208 · G. Schochet, 'Samuel Parker, religious diversity and the ideology of persecution', *The margins of heterodoxy: heterodox writings and cultural response, 1660–1750*, ed. R. D. Lund (1995), 119–48 · J. G. A. Pocock, 'Thomas Hobbes, atheist or enthusiast? His place in Restoration debate', *History of Political Thought*, 11/4 (1990), 737–49 · J. Parkin, 'Liberty transpros'd: Andrew Marvell and Samuel Parker', *Marvell and liberty*, ed. W. Chernaik and M. Dzelzainis (1999), 269–89 · J. Parkin, 'Hobbism in the later 1660s: Daniel Scargill and Samuel Parker', *HJ*, 42 (1999), 85–108 · L. Brockliss, G. Harriss, and A. Macintyre, *Magdalen College and the crown: essays for the tercentenary of the restoration of the college, 1688* (1988) · S. Parker, *Religion and loyalty, or, A demonstration of the power of the Christian church within itself* (1684) · S. Parker, *Reasons for abrogating the test imposed on all members of parliament, anno 1678* (1688) · *Biographia Britannica, or, The lives of the most eminent persons who have flourished in Great Britain and Ireland*, 7 vols. (1747–66), vol. 5 · S. Parker, *Disputationes de Deo et providentia divina* (1678) · H. A. Wilson, *Magdalen College* (1899) · *Hist. U. Oxf.* 4: *17th-cent. Oxf.* · J. Spurr, *The Restoration Church of England, 1646–1689* (1991) · J. Black, 'The unrecorded second edition of Samuel Parker's "A discourse of ecclesiastical polity"', *N&Q*, 242 (1977), 187–9 · *The life and times of Anthony Wood*, ed. A. Clark, 5 vols., OHS, 19, 21, 26, 30, 40 (1891–1900)

Archives BL, letter, Add. MS 21092, fol. 24 · Bodl. Oxf., letters, MSS English letters c.28, fols. 3–5, e.1, fols. 188–89; MSS Tanner 29, fol. 148; 30, fol. 157; 31, fols. 113, 114, 166, 176, 177, 206; 32, fols. 26, 136; 34, fol. 240; 35, fols. 102, 122; 36, fols. 223, 255; 37, fols. 19, 20; 39, fol. 194; 123, fols. 175, 177, 179, 181, 188; 124, fols. 63, 65; 147, fol. 66; 290, fol. 202; 314, fol. 38 · LPL, letter, MS 674, fols. 27–9 · LPL, letter, MS 942, fol. 23

Parker, Samuel (1681–1730), nonjuror and theological writer, second son of Samuel *Parker (1640–1688), later bishop of Oxford, was born at Chartham in Kent, where his father was rector. He matriculated on 6 June 1694 at Trinity College, Oxford. Sympathizing with the nonjurors from an early age, he took no degree, but lived on quietly in Oxford, 'well esteemed for several valuable qualifications, particularly his art of pleasing in conversation' (Lathbury, 375), and 'ever a compassionate and hearty Friend to the Afflicted and Poor' ('Life of Samuel Parker', 5.xi). Although scruples about the oaths of allegiance caused Parker to decline offers of preferment, he did not seek to perpetuate the schism in the Church of England and was grateful, like all but the most rigid nonjurors, for the guidance provided by Henry Dodwell's treatise *The Case in View, now in Fact* (1711). Contemporaries suspected that he had been encouraged also by the example of his wife, whom he had married about 1705. She was the daughter of Henry Clements, an Oxford bookseller and the publisher of Dr Sacheverell's works, and she had gone back to worshipping with the conforming church. Nevertheless, Parker's large circle of acquaintance continued to include prominent nonjurors, such as George Hickes, Jeremy Collier, Charles Leslie, Henry Dodwell, Robert Nelson, and Francis Cherry, and he was alluded to repeatedly by Thomas Hearne. He was also consulted frequently by 'learned foreigners, who were generally recommended to him' (*Remarks*, 11.439). Although he may for some time have held a post in the Bodleian Library, Parker derived most of his income from providing lodgings to visitors to Oxford, and from acting as a tutor to young gentlemen preparing for matriculation in the university. Several of these pupils had Jacobite connections, and this sometimes brought Parker under suspicion.

Despite such distractions Parker remained an energetic scholar, with impressively varied interests. Early works, such as *Essays Philosophical Moral and Metaphysical* (1700) and *Silva, or, Familiar Letters upon Occasional Subjects* (1701), reveal his interest in experimental science to have been combined, perhaps surprisingly, with vehement hostility towards the philosophical systems of Locke and Descartes. Translations of works by Homer and Cicero were published in 1700 and 1702 respectively; an *Essay on the Duty of Physicians* appeared in 1715, and he produced a Latin edition, later translated, of a contemporary historical commentary by his father. However, above all, Parker was a theologian: it was said that 'the very Name of Orthodox, Catholic and Primitive, ever sounded harmonious in his Ear' ('Life of Samuel Parker', 5.x). Like Jeremy Collier and Charles Leslie he was an energetic student of early church history and believed that rediscovery of the church's 'primitive face' might correct the failings of a 'loose and vicious age' (ibid., vii). His translation and abridgement of Eusebius, published in 1703 and dedicated to Robert Nelson, was followed by similar collections from Socrates, Sozomen, and Theodoret in 1707 (3rd edn, 1729), and an abridgement of Evagrius (1729). His great *Bibliotheca biblica*, commenced in 1720 but completed only as far as the end of the Pentateuch, employed prodigious patristic learning in an attempt to confute heretical interpretations of scripture. His most able work was *Censura temporum: the good or ill tendencies of books, sermons, pamphlets, &c, impartially consider'd*, written in monthly periodical instalments between January 1708 and March 1710. In this the political and theological assertions of writers such as Benjamin Hoadly, John Locke, and William Whiston were subjected to sustained critical scrutiny.

Parker died at Oxford on 14 July 1730 of dropsy, aggravated by exhaustion brought on by his work on the *Bibliotheca biblica*; he was buried on 17 July at St Peter-in-the-East in Oxford. He left his wife and a large family. His son Richard, who was also a nonjuror, followed his father's literary profession and went on to become the founder of a famous Oxford bookselling and publishing business.

RICHARD SHARP

Sources *Remarks and collections of Thomas Hearne*, ed. C. E. Doble and others, 11 vols., OHS, 2, 7, 13, 34, 42–3, 48, 50, 65, 67, 72 (1885–1921) • 'Life of Samuel Parker', in S. Parker and others, *Bibliotheca biblica*, 5 vols. (1720–35), vol. 5 [preface] • Foster, *Alum. Oxon.* • *DNB* • T. Lathbury, *A history of the nonjurors* (1845) • A. Chalmers, ed., *The general biographical dictionary*, new edn, 32 vols. (1812–17)

Archives Bodl. Oxf., letters to T. Smith DD

Likenesses G. Vertue, line engraving (after H. Green), BM, NPG

Parker, Samuel William Langston (1804/5–1871), surgeon and venereologist, was born in Birmingham, the son of William J. Parker, a medical practitioner of Aston Road, Birmingham, and medical officer to the Aston Union. Parker was educated at Heathfield Road School, Handsworth, under the Revd Daniel Walton. He afterwards attended the medical and surgical practice of the Birmingham General Hospital, and obtained his more scientific training in the school of medicine at the corner of Brittle Street, Snow Hill, where W. Sands Cox lectured. He then went to St Bartholomew's Hospital, London, to attend the lectures of John Abernethy. Parker completed his studies in Paris and became a member of the Royal College of Surgeons in 1828. He started his professional life assisting his father, and then began his own practice in St Paul's Square, Birmingham. In 1830 he married Mary Adams of Derbyshire, who died shortly after childbirth on 20 July 1832. He became a fellow of the Royal College of Surgeons in 1843 when the 300 founding fellows were selected from surgeons of good standing.

Parker took a keen interest in the establishment of Queen's College, Birmingham, and was the professor of comparative anatomy, and of descriptive anatomy and physiology for quarter of a century. He was honorary consultant to the Associated Hospital from its foundation in 1840; he was made consultant surgeon when he retired twenty-five years later. He was also consultant surgeon to the Leamington Hospital for Diseases of the Skin. Parker was the first surgeon in Birmingham to use an anaesthetic (ether), the patient being his own son. He was an active supporter of the Birmingham Philosophical Institution in Cannon Street, where in 1835–6 he gave a course of lectures entitled 'On the effects of certain mental and bodily states upon the imagination', in which madness was discussed. He was a member of the Royal Medico-Chirurgical Society of London.

Parker began his career as a general practitioner, subsequently became a surgeon and wrote on diseases of the stomach, and eventually devoted his best efforts to the study of venereal disease. His main contribution was the administration of mercury, used in the treatment of syphilis, by mercury vapour baths with carefully regulated heat and moisture. In retrospect, it seems unlikely that this was a significant advance. His main work, *The Modern Treatment of Syphilitic Diseases*, ran to five editions between 1839 and 1871.

Parker was a kindly and genial man, with cultivated musical tastes. He was well read, an amateur poet and an able French and Italian scholar. An independent nonconformist in religion, Parker attended Carr's Lane Chapel until his love of the theatre led him to quarrel with the minister and move to the Church of England. Parker developed gastric pains about a year before his death. However, he was well enough to see a patient on the evening before he died, from bronchitis, on 27 October 1871, at his home, 17 Paradise Street, Birmingham. He was buried on 1 November in the family vault at Aston. Parker was survived by his third wife and his son, Samuel Adams Parker, who was a dental surgeon.

D'A. POWER, *rev.* GEOFFREY L. ASHERSON

Sources W. Bates, *BMJ* (4 Nov 1871), 540–41 • *The Lancet* (4 Nov 1871), 659 • S. W. L. Parker, *On the effects of certain mental and bodily states upon the imagination, especially as illustrated by Shakespeare and other poets*, ed. W. Bates (1876) • d. cert. • *CGPLA Eng. & Wales* (1871) • V. G. Plarr, *Plarr's Lives of the fellows of the Royal College of Surgeons of England*, rev. D'A. Power, 2 vols. (1930) [incl. list of pubns] • P. J. Wallis and R. V. Wallis, *Eighteenth century medics*, 2nd edn (1988)

Likenesses T. H. Maguire, lithograph, 1855, RCS Eng. • photograph, repro. in Bates, ed., *On the effects of certain mental and bodily states*

Wealth at death under £4000: probate, 29 Dec 1871, *CGPLA Eng. & Wales*

Parker, (James) Stewart (1941–1988), playwright and writer, was born on 20 October 1941 at 86 Larkfield Road, Sydenham, Belfast, the son of George Herbert Parker (1912–1996), tailor's cutter, and Isobella, *née* Lynas (1913–1987), who had been a bookbinder before her marriage. His parents were both Northern Ireland protestants. Stewart Parker was educated at Strand primary school, Ashfield Boys' School—where he was taught by a charismatic schoolmaster, John Malone—and Sullivan Upper School. From 1959 until 1964 he studied English literature at Queen's University, Belfast, first with Professor Peter Butter and then with Philip Hobsbaum. He graduated BA with upper second-class honours in English literature in 1963, and MA in 1966 with a dissertation on non-realistic elements in the plays of W. B. Yeats, T. S. Eliot, and E. E. Cummings; his external examiner was Professor Peter Ure.

Parker's studies at Queen's University were impeded by the onset of cancer, apparently initiated by a kick on the kneecap while playing football. He spent most of a year in hospital, during which he suffered the amputation of his left leg. Previous to this, he had been keen on amateur theatricals. With his sturdy build, cherubic countenance, and rich baritone voice, he might well have made his way as a performer. The voice, at least, never left him; he was always a notable reader of his own—and other people's—work.

Parker early on gained a local reputation as a poet and was a key figure in the Belfast group, a creative writing workshop whose prominent members in the early 1960s included Seamus Heaney and James Simmons and, later, Michael Longley. Parker's contributions to the works that were discussed week by week included several chapters of a novel, *The Tribulations of S. T. Toile*. This, published only in part during Parker's lifetime, is to be brought out by Blackstaff Press, Belfast. The novel is a work of black humour, involving a school where everybody is malformed, neurotic, spiteful, or otherwise deranged. Poems on similar themes, notably 'Crutch' (an excerpt from *S. T. Toile*) and 'Coming Out' (from hospital), appeared in *Young Commonwealth Poets '65*, edited by P. L. Brent. 'Paddy Dies' and 'Health' appeared in *British Poetry since 1945* (1970), edited by Edward Lucie-Smith. A long poem, *The Casualty's Meditation*, was published in 1970 as a pamphlet in a much sought-after series, Belfast: Festival Publications. There are probably sufficient pieces of Parker's verse to make up a creditable collection.

Parker's main interest, however, was to lie in drama. On 26 August 1964 he had married a student teacher, Kathleen (Kate) Ireland, and in that year went with her to Clinton, New York. Here he became an instructor in English and creative writing at Hamilton College. Always a collector of strange names, Parker was delighted to find that among his colleagues were Gerald Commissar, Homer Snavely, and Channing Richardson Bullfinch III. After several unsuccessful attempts to gain academic posts back in the United Kingdom, Parker moved in 1967 to Cornell University. He seems, however, to have found that teaching impeded his creative effort, so in 1969 he returned to Belfast, determined to earn his living as a writer. He arrived in Northern Ireland the same week as the British army. This circumstance, together with his exile abroad, seems to have sharpened his sense of things Irish, and he involved himself in studying Irish language and culture. His early concern with his maimed body gradually broadened into dramatizing the pains of Ireland itself.

Parker began a regular pop music review column in the *Irish Times* and contributed articles on literary and theatrical subjects to that and to several other newspapers and journals. His main source of income at this juncture seems to have been BBC radio. *The Iceberg*, a play about the *Titanic*, was broadcast on 7 January 1975, and one about a Belfast showband musician, *I'm a Dreamer, Montreal*, on 20 July 1977. A televised version of the latter was transmitted by Thames on 6 March 1979 and was awarded that year's Christopher Ewart-Biggs memorial prize. Other plays pioneered on radio included the wonderfully titled *The Kamikaze Ground Staff Reunion Dinner* (1979), which won the Giles Cooper award for 1980, and *The Traveller* (1985), about the existential crisis of a travel writer. The first of these was transmitted as a television play by the BBC in 1981.

Parker had already had a play about a Belfast songwriting team, *Catchpenny Twist*, first staged at the Peacock Theatre, Dublin, in 1977, adapted in the same year for BBC television in the Play for Today series. This was based on the true story of a couple of Queen's University students who wrote a Eurovision song contest entry for their idol, the then famous singer Sandie Shaw. It included a song,

'Ziggy-Zaggy', performed not by the protagonist but by the comedian Peter Kelly, that might well have won the contest in reality as an entry in its own right. It is the case of a parody persuasive enough to be capable of literal acceptance.

However, Parker's main ambition was for success on the stage. He served for a time as resident playwright at the King's Head Theatre, Islington. Here an Irish-Caribbean musical entitled *Kingdom Come*, written in collaboration with the composer Shaun Davey, was first performed on 17 January 1978. A stage play about a Belfast bicycle salesman had already been produced at the Dublin theatre festival in October 1975, where it was an unexpected and runaway success. This had been revived at the King's Head in 1976, and when it won Parker the *Evening Standard* most promising playwright award, it was transferred to the Vaudeville Theatre in London's West End in February 1977. *Spokesong* also opened at the Long Wharf Theatre in New Haven, Connecticut, on 9 February 1978. This production was brought to the Circle in the Square Theatre on Broadway on 15 March 1979. It represented Parker's breakthrough as a writer.

In 1982 Parker, who had separated from his wife, moved to London, where he was to spend what were to be his few remaining years with a fellow playwright, Lesley Bruce, *née* Barnett (*b.* 1944). By now, his impact was mainly through television. *Iris in the Traffic, Ruby in the Rain* (1981) shows two women whose paths intersect during a drizzly day in Belfast. Each pursues her own path and they meet only at the end when Ruby, a Catholic psychologist, discovers that the distressed old lady she has picked up in her car is mother of the protestant clerk, Iris.

The influence of Joyce's *Ulysses*, with its two wandering protagonists, is manifest here. It is no coincidence that this television play was followed in 1982 by another: *Joyce in June*, commissioned for the Joyce centenary. In addition, *Blue Money*, about a taxi driver who absconds with a briefcase full of cash belonging to a customer, was screened in 1984, and *Radio Pictures* in 1985. This latter, written for and produced on television, shows a radio play, 'Mr Deadman and Miss Goodbody', being rehearsed. During rehearsals the actors and production staff interact and react, their conflicts acting as a commentary on the radio play and vice versa. The whole constitutes an ingenious discourse on the nature of imagination. Here, as elsewhere, Parker owed a good deal to his producer and actors—in this case, Nicholas Renton, Frances Tomelty, and Dinsdale Landen, among others. However, it is equally true that Parker had given them a wealth of material with which to work.

Stewart Parker had become a famous name in television and was entrusted with the script of a series. *Lost Belongings*, directed by Nicholas Bicat, was screened in six hour-long episodes starting in April 1987. This had been twenty years in gestation: an early draft had been entered in the Irish Life Drama competition for 1967. It is a recension of the Deirdre myth, in which a child fostered by the king of Ulster as a prospective bride runs off instead with a young minstrel. The whole story has been updated to contemporary Belfast; however, the outcome is basically the same. Deirdre eventually returns to Ulster but, as had been foretold in the legend, brings disaster upon the place, and dies ignominiously.

The summit of Parker's achievement may be three stage plays produced, respectively, in Belfast (1984), Birmingham (1986), and Derry (1987), and published under the collective title *Three Plays for Ireland* (1989). The first of these, *Northern Star*, is an account of the late eighteenth-century protestant reformer Henry Joy McCracken. This politician had been instrumental in founding the United Irishmen, a movement involving protestants and Catholics alike, whose common goal was to free Ireland from British rule. The consequent uprising culminated in the unsuccessful siege of Antrim in 1798, after which McCracken was tried and executed. Parker seems to have identified with McCracken's politics. The play has a framework of dialogue between McCracken and his mistress, which is interspersed by seven scenes in the form of flashbacks, each taking over the style of a major Irish playwright: George Farquhar, Dion Boucicault, Oscar Wilde, G. B. Shaw, J. M. Synge, Sean O'Casey, and Brendan Behan. Parker may well have seen these as his mentors.

The second play in this presumed trilogy, *Heavenly Bodies*, deals with the life of one of these same playwrights, the nineteenth-century Irish-American Dion Boucicault. The cast consists of two main performers, one of them playing Boucicault and the other an interlocutor, with a group of students acting out multifarious minor roles. The play is really a series of sketches presenting Boucicault as an indomitable Irishman, a kind of Faust-figure. As with all Parker's plays, music is very important—not as mere decoration, but as an integral part of the action.

One of the characters in the third play, *Pentecost*, plays the trombone; another toys with the banjo; there are distant Lambeg drums; and a strategically placed hymn. The action evokes the squalid events of 1974, when a protracted strike organized by protestant extremists brought Belfast to a standstill. Trapped in a semi-derelict house are two Catholics, two protestants, and a ghost—also a protestant—whose age exactly spans the troubled century. The interpolations of Lily, the ghost who in life gave away an illegitimate child fathered by an Englishman, enable Parker to rise to heights of rhetoric. Here she is raging at the Catholic mother whose child has died:

> I haven't noticed you bringing up any youngsters. What right does a hussy like you have to question God's will? Why would he bless the fruit of your womb more than of mine, look at this place, you have it like a pigsty … are there not enough runty litters running the streets, whelped by your kind, reared with a half-brick in their fists, and the backsides hanging out of their trousers?

The play is replete with images of sterility but also with implications of human forgiveness. Pentecost is a season when even ordinary people prophesy. The derelict house—which, after all, has belonged to the ghost—represents an Ireland in which these competing tribes have to co-exist. A central figure Marian, the bereaved mother, says 'I want this house to live. We have committed sacrilege enough on life, in this place, in these times.'

After writing this last play—his own masterpiece and a major work of Irish drama—Stewart Parker again contracted cancer, this time in the stomach. He died, at the height of his powers, on 2 November 1988 in the Westminster Hospital, aged forty-seven. In accordance with his wishes, his body was cremated, and his ashes scattered into the Irish Sea. At his funeral, Parker's colleagues in the making of a new Irish literature—among them Seamus Heaney, Michael and Edna Longley, Derek Mahon—paid their respects to the passing of this latest in a line of Irish playwrights, playwrights whom he had loved and from whom he had sought to learn. A two-volume edition of his complete plays was published in 1999.

PHILIP HOBSBAUM

Sources M. J. Richtarik, projected biography [forthcoming] · 'Irish spokesperson', *The Guardian* (6 Oct 1984) · B. Nightingale, 'Voices in the wilderness', *The Times* (9 Sept 1996) · J. Peter, 'Divided we fall', *Sunday Times* (15 Sept 1996) · *The Times* (5 Nov 1988) · *The Guardian* (5 Nov 1988) · personal knowledge (2004) · private information (2004) · d. cert.

Archives SOUND BL NSA, recordings of readings of his own work by Stewart Parker (1973–80)

Wealth at death £147,693: probate, 25 Jan 1989, *CGPLA Eng. & Wales*

Parker [*née* Robinson], **Theresa** (1745–1775), art patron, was born in Vienna on 1 January 1745, the daughter of Thomas *Robinson, first Baron Grantham (1695–1770), then ambassador to the Habsburg court in Vienna, and Frances Worsley (1716–1750). She was named for her godmother Empress Maria Theresa of Austria. She probably had a traditional aristocratic education at home that included drawing; a picture-puzzle letter that she drew in 1761 is preserved in Leeds (W. Yorks. AS, VR6015), and two etchings of landscapes that she made before her marriage are in the British Museum. On 18 May 1769 at Twickenham, Middlesex, she married, as his second wife, John Parker (1734/5–1788), MP for Bodmin in 1761–2 and for Devon from 1762 until 1784, when he was created Baron Boringdon.

In 1768 John Parker inherited extensive family estates in the west country, including Saltram House in Devon. While her husband was gambling, hunting, shooting, racing, or otherwise occupied with politics Theresa Parker focused her attentions on Saltram. She had a close relationship with her elder sister Anne (Nanny) and brothers Thomas *Robinson, second Baron Grantham, and Frederick (Fritz), and much of what is known about her character and views on life, and the decoration of Saltram, comes from her lively and engaging letters to them. She was a warm, intelligent woman whose 'amiable disposition, her softness and gentleness of manners, endeared her to every one that had the happiness of knowing her' (Reynolds, 'Character', 75) and whose sophisticated taste transformed Saltram into one of the showpieces of south-west England.

In 1768 Robert Adam, then at the height of his career, was commissioned to design two grand new rooms—the saloon and the library (now the dining room)—for the east wing; in 1772 he also designed the stag lodges and a ceiling for the Parkers' Sackville Street house in London. Adam's design extended to the carpets, fittings, and some of the furniture for the rooms. The Parkers spent about £10,000 on the saloon alone. The Saltram account books record payments to Thomas Chippendale in 1771 and 1772, and the suite of furniture in the saloon was probably designed and made by him; Matthew Boulton made the four six-branch candelabra in 1772. The velvet drawing room leading into the saloon was redecorated in 1770, when Theresa 'with her usual taste orderd all the mouldings, & parts of the Capitals of the Columns to be Gilt, which makes the Room much chearfuller & handsommer'; mirrors and tables designed by Adam were added about 1772 (Johnson, 11).

Theresa Parker (1745–1775), by Sir Joshua Reynolds, 1770–72

Theresa Parker chose many of the decorative objects for the house, including ceramics—she had a preference for unglazed black Wedgwood—and designed some pieces in silver herself. In 1772 Grantham wrote to Nanny of an inkstand: 'I am delighted with her Design, and am choaking with Jealousy and Admiration of it' (Johnson, 47). Grantham, a noted connoisseur and amateur architect, commissioned copies of works by Murillo for Saltram while he was ambassador to Spain, and designed the summer house known as The Castle in 1771. Theresa oversaw the landscaping and planting of the grounds, and the creation of hothouses, kitchen gardens, lodges, and a greenhouse; in 1774 she described how she wanted to decorate the new orangery with 'good Medallions and Bas Reliefs in Artificial Stone, which properly arranged over Niches may make it clever' (ibid., 60).

Sir Joshua Reynolds was a close friend of the Parkers. He grew up in nearby Plympton, and according to family tradition John Parker's mother gave Reynolds his first drawing pencil. Reynolds enjoyed hunting and gambling at Saltram, and advised the Parkers on paintings for the house; two are known to have belonged to him. The Parkers purchased paintings by Philippe Jacques de Loutherbourg and George Stubbs, as well as old masters and copies. Other works were commissioned from artists such as Antonio Zucchi, who provided the ceiling paintings for the new rooms, and Angelica Kauffman, who painted Theresa's portrait in 1773 (priv. coll.). Theresa claimed responsibility for acquiring at least four history paintings by Kauffmann for Saltram in a letter to Fritz of 24 August 1775.

There are thirteen paintings by Reynolds at Saltram, including a studio replica; three others were sold in the late nineteenth century. He painted a full-length portrait of Theresa Parker between 1770 and 1772. In 1773 Theresa wrote to Grantham:

> I have some thoughts (that is) Mr. Parker talks, of having the little Boy [her son, John] put into the half length [of] Sir Joshua's which remains just as you left it, only in bright yellow, which he is very fond of at present but I do not approve of. (Lummis and Marsh, 32)

A sitting that year was unproductive; the painting lay unfinished until a more successful result was achieved in 1775. Her son was John *Parker, first earl of Morley (1772–1840).

After contracting a fever Theresa Parker gave birth to a girl prematurely on 20 September 1775; she died of complications following the birth on 21 December and was buried at Plympton St Mary, Devon. Her daughter, Theresa, later married the Hon. George Villiers, and died in 1856. In the obituary of Mrs Parker written by Reynolds (BL, Add. MS 48252, fol. 15) and published anonymously in the *Gentleman's Magazine* he says that her death was:

> occasioned by a stroke of the palsy, which happened soon after her lying-in of a daughter. Of this she appeared to be recovering; but receiving a second stroke, and soon after that a third, it put an end to the life of one of the most valuable of women. (Reynolds, 'Character')

He continued his tribute:

> In so exalted a character it is scarce worth mentioning her skill and exact judgment in the polite arts. She seemed to possess, by a kind of intuition, that propriety of taste and right thinking, which others but imperfectly acquire by long labour and application.

ARIANNE BURNETTE

Sources C. Johnson, *Saltram, Devon* (1998) [NT guidebook]; rev. edn (2001) • [J. Reynolds], 'Character of the late Hon. Mrs Parker, promised in our last magazine', *GM*, 1st ser., 46 (1776), 75 • T. Lummis and J. Marsh, *The woman's domain: women and the English country house* (1990) • R. Fletcher, *The Parkers at Saltram, 1769–89: everyday life in an eighteenth-century house* (1970) • D. Mannings and M. Postle, *Sir Joshua Reynolds: a complete catalogue of his paintings* (2000) • GEC, *Peerage*, new edn, vol. 5 • B. Baumgärtel, *Retrospektive Angelika Kauffmann* (1998) [exhibition catalogue, Angelika Kauffmann, 1741–1807, Retrospektive, Kunstmuseum Düsseldorf, 15 Nov 1998 – 24 Jan 1999; later at Munich and Chur] • E. Waterhouse, 'Reynolds, Angelika Kauffmann and Lord Boringdon', *Apollo*, 122 (Oct 1985), 270–74 • D. Dodd, *Saltram, Devon* (1988) [NT guidebook] • [N. Neatby?], *Saltram House, Devon* (1957) [NT guidebook] • N. Neatby, ed., *The Saltram collection* (1977) • C. Musgrave, 'Saltram House: an Adam house of the west country', *Connoisseur*, 191 (Jan 1976), 20–29 • G. Wills, 'Robert Adam at Saltram', *Connoisseur Yearbook* (1958), 2–7 • H. Avray Tipping, 'Saltram, Devonshire: the seat of the earl of Morley', *Country Life*, 59 (23 Jan 1926), 124–33; (30 Jan 1926), 160–70 • J. Cornforth, 'Saltram, Devon', *Country Life*, 141 (27 April 1967), 998–1001; (4 May 1967), 1064–8; (11 May 1967), 1160–64 • J. Cornforth, 'The making of the Saltram landscape', *Country Life*, 142 (14 Sept 1967), 594–7 • St J. Gore, 'A patron of portrait and landscape: the picture collection at Saltram House, Devon', *Country Life*, 139 (2 June 1966), 1386–8 • HoP, *Commons, 1754–90* • *The letters of Sir Joshua Reynolds*, ed. J. Ingamells and J. Edgcumbe (2000) • A. Griffiths and C. Hartley, 'Prints at Saltram', *Print Quarterly*, 9/4 (Dec 1992), 357–61 • Foster, *Alum. Oxon.*

Archives Beds. & Luton ARS, papers, including family corresp. of Lucas family of Wrest Park, Silsoe, including corresp. of Thomas Robinson, second Baron Grantham • BL, official and family papers of the Parker family, incl. the earls of Morley, incl. corresp. of Theresa Parker, obituary notice, and visiting card, Add. MSS 48218, 48252 | Beds. & Luton ARS, corresp. of Frederick Robinson • BL, corresp. and papers of Thomas Robinson, second Baron Grantham, Add. MSS 24157–24179 • Plymouth and West Devon RO, Exeter, corresp. of the Parker family, including the earls of Morley; corresp. of Frederick Robinson and Thomas Robinson, second Baron Grantham • W. Yorks. AS, Leeds, Newby Hall family and estate archive; Robinson family corresp.; marriage settlement, 13 May 1769

Likenesses J. Reynolds, oils, 1770–72, Saltram, Devon [*see illus.*] • J. Reynolds, oils, 1772–5 (with her son), Saltram, Devon • A. Kauffmann, oils, 1773, priv. coll. • T. Watson, mezzotint, pubd 1773 (after oil painting by J. Reynolds, 1770–72), BM, NPG • S. W. Reynolds, mezzotint, pubd 1824 (after J. Reynolds, 1772–5), BM, NPG • R. B. Parkes, engraving, 1877 (after J. Reynolds, 1772–5) • S. W. Reynolds, mezzotint (after J. Reynolds, 1770–72), BM, NPG • possibly F. Talbot, oils on wood (after J. Reynolds, 1772–5); Christies, 25 April 1980, lot 100

Parker, Thomas (*fl.* **1535–1581**), Roman Catholic priest, is first recorded in the year 1535–6, when he graduated BA at Cambridge. Having proceeded MA in 1540/41, he may have become a vicar-choral in Lincoln Cathedral, but had presumably returned to Cambridge by 24 December 1546, when he was named as one of the fellows of Trinity College in its foundation charter. He proceeded BTh in 1548. A conservative in religion, in June 1549 he was one of the spokesmen for Catholic orthodoxy in a disputation on the sacraments held in Cambridge before the king's visitors. In July 1555 he subscribed articles of religion affirming Catholicism, and was present at Ely on 9 October when Wolsey and Pigot were condemned as heretics. On 26 February 1556 he was admitted Lady Margaret preacher to the university, and was re-elected in 1558. On 17 April 1556, moreover, he was presented by the crown to the vicarage of Mildenhall, Suffolk. He was present in Cambridge during Cardinal Pole's visitation of 1556–7, his own arrival in the town being noted on 21 February 1557.

Parker went abroad after the accession of Elizabeth, and seems to have taken a doctorate at an overseas university—in January 1576 Henry Mason, an English spy who had also taken an oath of allegiance to the king of Spain, referred to a 'Dr Parker and the other English Louvainists', whose secrets he undertook to discover and report to Lord Burghley. However, the identification cannot be regarded as certain, since Parker's name does not appear in the published records of Louvain. He is recorded as living in Milan in 1581, but nothing further is known of him.

RONALD BAYNE, *rev.* ANDREW A. CHIBI

Sources Venn, *Alum. Cant.*, 1/3.308 • Cooper, *Ath. Cantab.*, 1.452–3 • C. H. Cooper and J. W. Cooper, *Annals of Cambridge*, 5 vols. (1842–1908) • J. Lamb, ed., *A collection of letters, statutes and other documents … illustrative of the history of the University of Cambridge during the Reformation* (1838)

Parker, Thomas (1595–1677), minister in America, was born in Newbury, Berkshire, on 8 June 1595, the son of Robert *Parker (*c*.1564–1614), then vicar of Stanton St Bernard, Wiltshire, and his wife, Dorothy Stevens. He began his studies at Magdalen College, Oxford, but as a consequence of his father's having fled to the Netherlands in 1607 to avoid prosecution for nonconformity, he left. In Michaelmas 1610 he matriculated at Trinity College, Dublin, where James Ussher had an impeccable Calvinist reputation as professor of theology. However, when it became evident that there would be no negative consequences for Parker as a result of his father's situation he returned to Magdalen, probably in 1613, when a Thomas Parker is recorded as having subscribed on 23 April. When his father died in 1614, Thomas left Oxford to join his family in the Netherlands. He registered as a student at the University of Leiden, where his studies were supervised for a time by the distinguished puritan theologian William Ames, who had been a friend of his father. Ames recommended that he move on yet again, to the University of Franeker, a new foundation which had attracted many religious exiles from throughout Europe. There Parker studied with a Polish theologian known as Johannes Maccovius and was awarded the degree of MPhil in 1617.

At Maccovius's prompting Parker had prepared a set of seventy theological theses, which were published as *Theses theologicae de traductione hominis peccatoris ad vitam* (1617; reprinted in England in 1657), dedicated to Paul Baynes, John Paget, and William Ames. The Calvinist world, particularly in the Netherlands, was at that time involved in theological controversy, primarily over the modifications to predestinarian doctrine advanced by the Dutch theologian Jacob Arminius. A rival of Maccovius at Franeker, Sibrandus Libertus, accused Maccovius of heresy based on the theses of his pupil Parker, which presented stern views of God and man and an almost mechanistic outlook on salvation. Although Parker had already left for England the charges were debated in the Synod of Dort, with Ames successfully defending Maccovius and Parker.

On returning to England, Parker assisted William Twisse in ministering to the church in his home town of Newbury and served as schoolmaster. A weekly fast brought him into regular contact with his cousins James and Nicholas Noyse. He had evidently tired of scholastic theology and never held a living in the English church. In 1634 he emigrated to America, where he first assisted Nathaniel Ward, the minister in Ipswich, Massachusetts. In 1635 he was, with his cousin James Noyse and his nephew Benjamin Woodbridge, a founder of the adjoining town of Newbury, Massachusetts, and he became pastor of its congregation; Noyse joined him in the ministry as teacher. Their lack of previous parochial involvement with communities of believers perhaps made the two clergymen reluctant to go as far as other colonial clergy customarily did in sharing authority with their congregation (a tendency that in Parker's case would have been reinforced by his friendship with John Paget in the Netherlands). Their presbyterian views led to the elders of Newbury church exercising unusual authority, and the last years of Parker's pastorate were disturbed by some friction within the congregation. However, since Parker and Noyse were almost alone in New England in their presbyterianism there was never any question of establishing a form of governing synod in the region, although Parker, respected for his scholarship, was a participant in the non-governing synods held in New England in 1643 and 1662.

Like many colonists Parker paid close attention to events in England during the 1640s and 1650s. He prepared *The true copy of a letter written by Mr. T. Parker … declaring his judgment touching the government practised in the churches of New England* (1644) as a critique of New England's congregationalism designed to warn the Westminster assembly about the dangers of the New England way. His views were widely employed by advocates of a presbyterian settlement such as Robert Baillie. On the other side, the supporters of congregationalism used Parker's continuing presence in New England to demonstrate that the two polities could co-exist. Parker denounced the execution of Charles I and expressed approval of the restoration of Charles II. His *The Copy of a Letter … to his Sister, Mrs. Elizabeth Avery* (1650) was a reprimand for her adopting Quakerism and publishing her convictions. His letter denounced Quaker views but also took his sister to task for 'printing of a Book, beyond the custom of your Sex'.

Parker himself never married. Shortly after settling in New England he lost most of his sight but this did not prevent him from continuing in his ministry, preparing his published works, and developing elaborate interpretations of biblical prophecies, some of which were published as *The Visions and Prophecies of Daniel Expounded* (1646). He lived with the family of his cousin Noyse. When Noyse died in 1656, Benjamin Woodbridge replaced him as Parker's pastoral assistant. Meanwhile Parker also undertook the responsibility of preparing youths for Harvard, teaching them Latin, Greek, and Hebrew, often having a dozen in his charge. The most famous of his pupils was Samuel Sewall. Parker died at Newbury on 24 April 1677.

FRANCIS J. BREMER

Sources S. E. Morison, 'The education of Thomas Parker', *Publications of the Colonial Society of Massachusetts*, 27 (1932), 261–7 • J. Coffin, *A sketch of the history of Newbury* (1845) • F. J. Bremer, *Congregational communion: clerical friendship in the Anglo-American puritan community,*

1610–1692 (1994) · M. R. McCarl, 'Parker, Thomas', *ANB* · *DNB* · Foster, *Alum. Oxon.* · Burtchaell & Sadleir, *Alum. Dubl.*

Parker, Thomas, first earl of Macclesfield (1667–1732), lord chancellor, was born on 23 July 1667 at Leek, in Staffordshire, the only son (and apparently the only child) of Thomas Parker (1629–*c*.1689) and his wife, Anne (1637/8–1699), a daughter of Robert Venables of Nuneham, Cheshire. He was descended from a minor gentry family who, in the early seventeenth century, were established at Norton Lees Hall in Derbyshire. Parker's beginnings were modest and not without struggle. His father practised as an attorney at Leek and had land and property at nearby Sneyd Hamblett and an interest in several local coalmines, which together produced an annual rental of £100. Young Thomas was sent to grammar school in the neighbouring town of Newport, Shropshire, where he spent three years, and in 1680 he was moved to a school in Derby. Aware of Thomas's superior academic ability, his father endeavoured about 1684 to enlist financial support from Robert Venables so that his son might pursue a university education. However, Thomas Parker's elopement years previously with Anne Venables, prior to their marriage in 1663, had not been forgiven, and money from that quarter was not forthcoming.

Early career By this stage Thomas had been articled for a while to his father, who had transferred his attorney's office to the busier town of Newcastle under Lyme. The course of his subsequent education is, however, a little uncertain. The Inner Temple records show his admission to the inn in February 1684, while in October the following year he entered Trinity College, Cambridge, as a pensioner, where he matriculated on 17 December 1685. Local tradition has it that Parker practised as an attorney at Derby before being called to the bar; although this has been dismissed as apocryphal, it would not have been unlikely, given the absence of any formal programme of legal training at this time, for Parker to have combined an attorney's practice while maintaining the obligatory ties with an inn of court in London. Inheritance of his father's lands and property in or about 1689 may have eased the financial constraints of his situation. At all events, he received his call to the bar on 24 May 1691, having a few weeks previously, on 23 April, married his second cousin Janet (*c*.1666–1733), a daughter and coheir of Charles Carrier of Wirksworth, Derbyshire. They later had a daughter and a son, George *Parker, astronomer and politician.

In his early years as a barrister Parker worked mainly on the midland circuit. His reputation as a clever and accomplished counsellor soon set him apart from many of his fellow circuiters, and in 1696 the corporation of Derby nominated him as their recorder. Not surprisingly, he was drawn into local politics, where he figured as a staunch whig, and in January 1701 he involved himself in the whig campaign in the Derbyshire election. It was from about this time, however, that the focus of his attention shifted to the London courts, and he was probably in permanent residence in the city by 1702, the year in which his name first begins to appear in the law reports.

Thomas Parker, first earl of Macclesfield (1667–1732), by George Vertue, 1712 (after Sir Godfrey Kneller, *c*.1710–12)

Once established in London, Parker made rapid progress. His first appearance before the House of Lords occurred in February 1703, although appropriately it was to argue the corporation of Derby's case in support of a bill for the navigation of the River Derwent. Politics also began to claim his attention. He made a favourable impression among the whig lawyer-politicians, who saw him as a useful recruit to their party's cause. In November 1704 he was selected to defend the whig printer John Tutchin, who was under crown prosecution for libelling the tory ministers in *The Observator*. Although Tutchin was found guilty, he was saved from punishment by an objection from Parker concerning the regularity of the jury system, a piece of technical brilliance which assured him of official advancement under any future whig ministry. Admirers were already giving him 'a mighty character' as one of 'the most learned lawyers of the age' (*London Diaries of William Nicolson*, 251).

Despite his rising prominence in London, Parker had maintained his links with Derby, and at the general election of May 1705 he successfully contested one of the town's parliamentary seats. Whig gains in this election compelled Lord Treasurer Godolphin to offer various *douceurs* among the whig MPs, and Parker was one of the first beneficiaries. Having been elected a bencher of his inn, the Inner Temple, early in May, he was made a serjeant-at-law and then given the rare distinction of queen's serjeant, with precedence over all QCs, early in June. On 9 July he was knighted at Windsor Castle. He had been particularly befriended by the junto whig lawyer William Cowper, and the latter's appointment as lord keeper in

October proved of additional value to Parker's career. Another junto politician with whom Parker was closely associated was Lord Wharton, and it was primarily as a junto spokesman under Wharton's direction that Parker made his debating appearances in the House of Commons. Parker gave early demonstration of his ability to provide highly effective expression to ministerial policy in the 'Church in danger' debate early in December 1705 and in the proceedings that followed on the Regency Bill which Wharton had initiated in the Lords. Alongside his parliamentary career, advocacy in the London courts continued to preoccupy much of his time.

Upon the resignation of Sir Simon Harcourt as attorney-general in February 1708, Parker was thought likely to take the junior law office of solicitor-general, but the expected vacancy did not arise. Loftier prospects were aired only a few weeks later when Lord Chief Justice Holt fell seriously ill. The whig polemicist and confidante of the Marlboroughs, Arthur Maynwaring, saw Parker as an eminently suitable successor, in possessing 'the character of a very good lawyer and an honest man, and is more considerable out of the House of Commons than there' (BL, Add. MS 61459, fol. 114). Holt recovered, however, but in June the duke of Somerset, another of Parker's patrons and a senior figure at court, actively promoted him (though without success) for the still unfilled post of attorney-general.

Parker was one of several prominent barrister MPs and politicians employed by the ministry in the trial of the high-church divine Henry Sacheverell. Sacheverell's inflammatory sermon on the text 'the perils of false brethren', delivered at St Paul's Cathedral on 5 November 1709, and subsequently enjoying a disturbingly high print run of 100,000 copies, was seen in ministerial circles as a dangerous assault on church and state, questioning the very legality of the revolution of 1688 and implicitly arguing for a Jacobite restoration. Following the ministry's decision to impeach Sacheverell in a trial designed to reassert 'revolution principles', Parker was included on the committee appointed on 14 December ordered to draw up the articles of impeachment. He was afterwards given the task of speaking to the fourth and final article, in which Sacheverell was charged as having suggested that the queen's administration was a danger to the constitution. Thus scheduled to speak on what was in effect the central issue in the trial, Parker was seen by the managers as their star performer. When he rose to his feet in Westminster Hall on 1 March 1710 he was recovering from a severe cold which had indisposed him for several days previously, but the inaudibility of his voice ensured that the highly charged atmosphere remained dramatically hushed. For the next hour or so Parker revealed his superb mastery of a complex brief, and with devastating effect he scythed through the ambiguities of Sacheverell's tract to show that these had been carefully contrived and could be read as a clear denunciation of the queen's ministers as enemies of the constitution. Not only did he show that his powers of analysis were quite stunning, he also displayed a singular command of biblical text. With his audience captive, Parker went on to expose Sacheverell's sermon as a preconceived design to undermine church and state by inciting violence and rebellion. Although Parker addressed the audience in Westminster Hall again on 10 March in reply to arguments put forward by the defence on the fourth article, and concluded the case for the prosecution, it was his earlier performance which was most memorable. 'None of the managers', commented Bishop Burnet, 'had treated Sacheverell so severely as he had done' (*Bishop Burnet's History*, 5.446–7).

Lord chief justice No sooner had these proceedings ended (which now awaited the verdict and sentence of the House of Lords) than it was announced on 11 March that Parker had been appointed lord chief justice following the recent death of Sir John Holt. The announcement, made even before Holt's burial, caused much surprise, but it was an opportunity shrewdly seized upon in order to signify the queen's approval of the impeachment and dispel rumours that she secretly supported Sacheverell. Parker's superbly executed brief for the ministry made him the obvious choice for this most senior place on the judicial bench, and the recommendation for his appointment appears to have come from two leading ministerial figures who were also personally acquainted with him, the dukes of Somerset and Devonshire. He was sworn in to office on 13 March, thus relinquishing his seat in the House of Commons, and on the 29th he was sworn a member of the privy council.

It was perhaps ironic that the only crown case of any significance over which Parker presided as lord chief justice arose from the whigs' prosecution in April 1710 of three men who had been ringleaders in the Sacheverell riots. He was subsequently criticized for delivering an overtly partisan summing-up that led to verdicts of high treason against two of the men, but he later took pains to secure their pardon. Parker's personal conduct on the bench did not endear him to members of the bar. Barristers whose arguments he found flawed or pedestrian were often the butt of his notoriously sharp temper, while others were exasperated by his open courtesy and favouritism to a privileged few, such as the young Philip Yorke and John Fortescue-Aland, who impressed him with their arguments.

Quite apart from his preoccupations with the law, Parker was a man of vigorous intellect. His fondness for scholarly enquiry took radical and unexpected directions, and his generous patronage of clerics, scholars, and authors, many of whom in their various ways were free-thinking controversialists, gave him an 'aetheistical' reputation. He took particular pleasure in the conversation of Bernard Mandeville, whose cynical vision of society, *The Grumbling Hive*, had first appeared in 1705. He was drawn to the writings of the deist John Toland, as also to those of Thomas Burnet, who subjected Old Testament texts to radical new interpretations, and of David Wilkins, a pioneer in oriental studies and the study of Anglo-Saxon texts. Other scholarly acquaintances included the nonjuring minister George Hickes, the Huguenot journalist Pierre Desmaizeaux, whom for a while Parker employed as tutor to his son, and Zachary Pearce, whom Parker later appointed as his personal chaplain. Parker's interests also extended to science and mathematics and in March 1712 were publicly acknowledged in his election as a fellow of the Royal Society. Chief among his scientific friends was the astronomer-mathematician Edmond Halley, whose appointment as astronomer royal he was to procure in 1721.

Parker was said to have resisted Robert Harley's invitation to become lord chancellor in the new tory ministry after the resignation of Lord Cowper in September 1710, preferring the securer status of lord chief justice, which he technically held *quamdiu se bene gesserit*, the principle which had been laid down for senior judicial commissions by the Act of Settlement of 1701. He thus found himself able to assist his party, both by defending whig pamphleteers who came under tory prosecution, and by punishing high-church journalists, though when Jonathan Swift roundly attacked him for this in his *Public Spirit of the Whigs*, published in 1712, no action was taken. For the most part, Parker was excluded from the business of the cabinet council, but at the formalities connected with the peace settlement in April 1713, and in the presence of the queen, he antagonized the tory ministers by criticizing the terms; at the end of the month it was rumoured that the ministry was to seek his removal from office by parliamentary process. But it was his intervention in June 1714 that struck a defining blow against the badly divided administration of Lord Oxford. On being approached by Lord Wharton with evidence that Jacobite agents were arriving in England to recruit support, Parker issued a warrant for their arrest, a turn of events which forced the secretary of state, Lord Bolingbroke, to issue a proclamation offering a £5000 reward for the Pretender's arrest if he should land in Britain. By this particular act the government publicly set its face against a Jacobite solution to the succession question, of which it had been widely suspected, and helped to weaken Viscount Bolingbroke's power base in the Commons and signify the ineffectuality of any ministry he might attempt to lead.

Following Queen Anne's death just weeks later, in August 1714, Parker was one of the seven lords justices appointed by virtue of his office (under the 1706 Regency Act) to carry on the government until the arrival of her successor, George I; and when the new king landed at Greenwich on 18 September, Parker was among the chief officers of state who greeted him. With the inauguration of a whig administration, Parker was now able to participate fully in the enjoyment of office both as a politician and as a courtier. He was especially popular with the senior members of the king's German retinue, and on 10 March 1716 he was made a peer, a rare honour for a lord chief justice, taking the title of Baron Parker of Macclesfield. As a further mark of favour he was also given, on top of his recently augmented salary, a pension of £1200. Already an acquisitive purchaser of land, it was only a matter of months before he matched his new social status with the purchase of the Shirburn estate and its castle in Oxfordshire for £18,350. At court he was seen as a desirable, and perhaps more amenable, alternative to Lord Cowper as lord chancellor, and Cowper himself grew increasingly apprehensive on this account, complaining of 'the remarkable manner in which Lord Townshend [secretary of state] has raised Lord Parker to be a kind of coadjutor to the [lord] chancellor'; not only had Parker's 'craving nature' obtained material honours, but he had secured for himself a regular place at cabinet discussions, unprecedented since the days of the infamous Lord Jeffreys (Cobbett, *Parl. hist.*, 9.169).

On those occasions when he spoke in the Lords, Parker was a stalwart supporter of the Sunderland–Stanhope ministry. In his maiden speech, upon the repeal of the Triennial Act in April 1716, he expressed contempt for the electorate, stating that 'it was not fit they should trust the choice of the House [of Commons] to such brute beasts and drunken country esquires' (*Stuart Papers*, 2.124). Parker's further, but unrecorded, remarks on this occasion apparently forced Cowper to intervene. At the impeachment proceedings against Lord Oxford in June 1717, while at pains to remind his fellow peers of their duty to observe the rules and forms of hearing evidence practised in all other courts of judicature, he concluded that, in Oxford's case, this would be a mere formality. More important, however, was his role in the unseemly dispute between the king and his heir, George, prince of Wales, out of which had arisen the painful question of whether the king had the right to direct arrangements concerning the prince's children. In January 1718 Parker was instrumental in obtaining support from most of the judges for an opinion that the king did indeed have control over the education, upbringing, and marriages of the prince's children (although not over their care), an outcome which established Parker still further in royal favour.

Lord chancellor Parker's appointment as lord chancellor on 12 May 1718, following Cowper's not unexpected resignation the previous month, caused some surprise, given his lack of experience in the chancery court. He struck a particularly shrewd, not to say financially advantageous, deal: in addition to the £4000 salary and the usual £2000 for his 'equipage', he was given a cash sum of £14,000 by the king, plus the promise of a tellership of the exchequer for his son. Parker immersed himself in his new office with his usual industry, and those who doubted his suitability were quickly proved wrong. The verdict of the nineteenth-century jurist Lord Campbell upon Parker as lord chancellor was that not only was he 'entitled to the equivocal compliment that none of his judgements were reversed, but his authority upon all points, whether of a practical or abstruse nature, is now as high as that of Nottingham, Somers, or Hardwicke' (Campbell, 4.523).

One of the distinctly political aspects of Parker's new position was his supervision of the commissions of the peace, and it was here that he made an appreciable contribution to the whig supremacy of the early and mid-Hanoverian years. He was far less willing to retain tory justices than Cowper had been, and by the time he left office in 1725 most of the commissions were dominated (though not totally monopolized) by whig gentlemen. Furthermore, he greatly simplified the procedures for remodelling commissions, and he revived the use of summary powers to oust justices guilty of misconduct. Parker, of course, shared his ministerial colleagues' keenness to crack down on political dissension. His own specific concern was with the universities, which he saw as 'infected with principles of sedition' (Williams, 456). In 1717 he had drafted a bill to place them under the direct control of the government, but Cowper, who was still lord chancellor, had advised against it.

Parker continued to enjoy close ties with George I, and in 1719 he performed a further significant service for the king when he chaired a special committee of legal experts to consider the constitutional position regarding the king's wish for the future dissolution of the dynastic union between Britain and Hanover. The committee was forced to conclude, however, that such an expedient, though theoretically desirable, could not possibly be achieved without risking the future security of the protestant succession. The ministerial reconstruction of March–April 1721 in the aftermath of the South Sea Bubble left Parker in a secure position, and in September he felt no compunction in asking the king for advancement to an earldom. On 15 November he was duly created earl of Macclesfield. Among his ministerial colleagues he remained a committed member of the faction led by Lord Sunderland, and after Sunderland's demise in April 1722 he showed similar attachment to his successor, Lord Carteret. The new first lord of the Treasury, Robert Walpole, eyed him cautiously, however, envious of the chancellor's great intimacy with the king and the Hanoverian ministers. Initially, Macclesfield's greatest difficulties appeared in the Lords, where the deep enmity between himself and his one-time patron Cowper, now leading the opposition peers, was openly demonstrated in several unpleasant clashes. His latitudinarian religious views were exhibited in January 1722, when he spoke in favour of the Quakers' Affirmation Bill.

The factional rivalry within the administration, between Carteret and his followers on the one hand and the Townshend–Walpole group on the other, intensified during 1723, and by the end of the year, as Townshend and Walpole appeared to gain ground, it was widely reported that Macclesfield was soon to be displaced. At first the removal of Carteret from the secretaryship of state to the politically less important office of lord lieutenant of Ireland in April 1724 seemed to strengthen Macclesfield's position once more. But the respite was only temporary. Having successfully sidelined Carteret, Walpole was now anxious to engineer the removal of the most prominent of Carteret's followers from the cabinet council. Macclesfield was one of several obvious targets, and in his case a pretext was conveniently at hand.

Impeachment and last years For some time there had been disturbing rumours that the masters in chancery had been misusing suitors' money in their custody, a practice which Macclesfield himself was believed to have encouraged. In November 1724, seemingly in response to what had developed into a public outcry, Walpole instigated an inquiry by committee of the privy council and by mid-December had produced a report. Its exposure of considerable financial abuse in several of the masters' offices implicated Macclesfield deeply and unequivocally. Walpole was now only too willing to assuage the rising tide of public indignation by discarding Macclesfield, and there was emphasis upon the ministry's wish to avoid being seen to harbour or 'screen' a corrupt colleague. It was in any case clear on less partisan grounds that Macclesfield could not remain as lord chancellor in the light of such grave accusations. He himself quickly acknowledged this, and on 4 January 1725 he surrendered his seals of office. But amid pressing demands for the restitution of missing funds, estimated at £60,000, the ministry's opponents ensured that he did not escape parliamentary trial. The ministry was ready to assist in this process, anxious that further investigations be kept within acceptable limits. A petition to the Commons on 23 January complaining of the disappearance of large sums placed in chancery belonging to the estate of one of the suitors, the dowager duchess of Montagu, commenced the process that led to his impeachment.

No fewer than twenty-one articles of impeachment were exhibited against Macclesfield by the House of Commons. He was portrayed as having a particular lust for wealth, and, despite generous rewards from the king, was said to have misused his office to amass further sums of money. It was alleged that he had sold vacant chancery masterships; received hefty bribes for agreeing to the sale and transfer of offices; and admitted to office several masters of insufficient financial means whom he had allowed to pay for their places out of suitors' money. Macclesfield resolutely asserted his innocence, however, continuing to enjoy royal goodwill, and claiming that his 'constant disinterested services to the King have exasperated one set of men' (*Various Collections*, 8.380). His response to the articles, in which he insisted he had done no worse than his distinguished predecessors, was indignantly rejected by the Commons on 23 April as a subtle attempt 'to disguise the crimes laid to his charge' (*JHC*, 20.503). The trial at the bar of the House of Lords lasted from 6 to 25 May. Its managers presented evidence establishing beyond doubt that not only had Macclesfield sold masterships, but that he had maximized his gain by selling to the highest bidders, while suitors had suffered as a consequence of their money being used by masters in investments in order to recoup the exorbitant sums paid. Macclesfield's counsel denied that the lord chancellor had acted criminally in taking 'presents' of cash during these transactions, on the premise that he had merely conformed with what he took to be the usual practices of his office. Macclesfield himself concluded with an intricate refutation of each of the articles, but his masterly performance could not conceal the fact that his defence had failed to establish that the sale of masterships under his two immediate predecessors had been as regular a practice as Macclesfield claimed and had not, therefore, been legitimized by prescription.

On 25 May Macclesfield was found guilty by a unanimous vote of ninety-three peers, and two days later he was sentenced to pay a fine of £30,000 and to imprisonment in the Tower until the sum was paid. Macclesfield's cleverly argued disclaimers were generally regarded as specious; evidence, even, of his generosity and patronage to poor scholars in mitigation of his apparent avariciousness made no impression on his fellow peers. Lord Campbell, considering whether Macclesfield had been too severely judged, and whether the faults of the system over which he presided had been unjustly loaded upon him, reminds us that 'his contemporaries could form a more correct opinion than we can, and we should be slow to accuse them of harshness' (Campbell, 4.555). Instead of carrying on the process begun by his predecessors lords Harcourt and Cowper, of divesting themselves of some of the more flagrant money-taking perquisites of the Lord Chancellor's Office, Macclesfield had taken advantage of the scope offered for additional gain and had exploited his prescriptive rights to the full. It was here that Macclesfield's particular guilt was seen to lie.

Macclesfield's public disgrace was completed on 31 May 1725, when his name was struck from the roll of privy councillors. He remained in the Tower for six weeks until the money for his fine was raised. During his remaining years he resided chiefly at Shirburn, where he pursued his literary and scientific interests, visiting London only occasionally, as he did in March 1727 when he was pallbearer at the funeral of Sir Isaac Newton. He was noted for his hospitality to young scholars, several of whom he employed in his household as chaplain or librarian. George I had been most reluctant to part with him from the ministry, and had promised to refund from the privy purse the sum he had been fined. At the time of the king's death in June 1727, however, only £1000 had been paid. In 1730 George II, whose wrath as prince of Wales Macclesfield had incurred, restored to him his pension of £1500.

Macclesfield died of strangury at the house of his only son, George, in Soho Square on 28 April 1732, and was buried at Shirburn. George, well known in scientific circles for his interest in astronomy, succeeded him as second earl.

A. A. Hanham

Sources *DNB* • J. Campbell, *Lives of the lord chancellors*, 4th edn, 10 vols. (1856–7), vol. 4, pp. 501–66 • HoP, *Commons, 1690–1715* [draft] • GEC, *Peerage* • *JHC*, 20 (1722–7), 453–9, 478–84, 503 • Cobbett, *Parl. hist.*, 7.305, 486, 942, 960–61; 8.414–81; 9.169 • *Report on manuscripts in various collections*, 8 vols., HMC, 55 (1901–14) • *The manuscripts of his grace the duke of Portland*, 10 vols., HMC, 29 (1891–1931), vol. 6, pp. 1–8; vol. 7, pp. 393–5 • D. F. Lemmings, 'Lord Chancellor Cowper and the whigs', *Parliamentary History*, 9 (1990), 163–74 • R. Hatton, *George I* (1978), 167, 369 • G. S. Holmes, *The trial of Dr Sacheverell* (1973), 149–55, 201–6 • L. K. J. Glassey, *Politics and the appointment of justices of the peace, 1675–1720* (1979), 256, 261 • B. Williams, *Stanhope* (1932), 401–2, 456 • BL, Stowe MS 750 • BL, Stowe MS 780, fol. 150 • *The London diaries of William Nicolson, bishop of Carlisle, 1702–1718*, ed. C. Jones and G. Holmes (1985) • *Calendar of the Stuart papers belonging to his majesty the king, preserved at Windsor Castle*, 7 vols., HMC, 56 (1902–23)

Archives BL, account of conference concerning succession to Hanover and England, 1719, Stowe MS 248 • BL, corresp. and papers • BL, papers as lord chancellor, Stowe MS 416 • BL, précis of the Atterbury trial, 1723, Add. MS 34713, fols. 34–78 • CUL, Cholmondeley (Houghton) MSS, papers relating to impeachment • Shirburn Castle, Oxfordshire, papers | U. Nott. L., corresp. with father-in-law; corresp.

Likenesses G. Vertue, line engraving, 1712 (after G. Kneller, *c.*1710–1712), BM, NPG [*see illus.*] • oils, *c.*1718 (after G. Kneller), Althorp, Northamptonshire • B. Ferrers, group portrait, oils, *c.*1725 (*The court of Chancery*), NPG • studio of G. Kneller, oils, Royal Court of Justice, London • oils (after G. Kneller), NPG

Wealth at death rentals from lands and properties in Oxfordshire, Staffordshire, Berkshire, Wiltshire, Cheshire, and Warwickshire, amounted to £3000 p.a. in 1725; some of these assets would have been sold off in order to raise money for fine of £30,000: G. Holmes, *Augustan England*, 133

Parker, Sir Thomas (*c.*1695–1784), judge, was the second son of George Parker of Park Hall, Staffordshire, and a nephew of Thomas Parker, first earl of Macclesfield. At Lichfield grammar school he was a contemporary of two future judicial colleagues, Richard Lloyd and William Noel. Instead of attending university he went directly from school into the office of a London solicitor called Charles Salkeld, where he began a lifelong friendship with Philip Yorke, later Lord Hardwicke. However, on 3 May 1718 he was admitted to the Inner Temple, where in 1724 he was called to the bar. This step may have been prompted by his uncle's appointment as lord chancellor, which took effect on 12 May 1718. At any rate, his uncle soon afterwards wrote to Sir Philip Yorke seeking the position of clerk of the patents for him, saying: 'He is a very diligent young man and of very good understanding' (BL, Add. MS 35584, fol. 206).

Parker's success at the bar was marked by his receipt of the coif from Lord Chancellor Talbot at the last general call of serjeants, in June 1736, with the immediate rank of king's serjeant; one of his patrons at the creation was Hardwicke. After only two years he was appointed a baron of the exchequer, in 1740 he was translated to the common pleas, and in 1742 he returned to the exchequer as chief baron, with a knighthood. These appointments were the gift of Lord Hardwicke, who in rejecting the duke of Somerset's candidate for the last of them (Sir Thomas Bootle) wrote that Parker:

> is a near relation to my late Lord Macclesfield, to whom I had the greatest obligations in the beginning of my life … he is in every way deserving, and has gained a very high character for ability and integrity since his advancement to the bench. (BL, Add. MS 35587, fol. 39)

Although Parker was offered a transfer to the common pleas on the death of Chief Justice Willes in 1761, if the law officers should waive the promotion, in the event it was taken up by Sir Charles Pratt; and so Chief Baron Parker continued to preside over the court of exchequer for thirty years, the longest tenure of the office since William Hody's (from 1486 to 1524). He married, first, Anne, daughter and coheir of James Whitehall of Pipe Ridware. The couple had two sons and two daughters. Second, he married Martha, daughter and coheir of Edward Strong of Greenwich; and this marriage produced another two daughters.

Parker's closeness to Hardwicke gave him a more prominent position than was usual for a chief baron, and among other things he was entrusted with the very sensitive business of managing the trials of the 1745 rebels at Carlisle. Hardwicke frequently sought his legal advice, and the friendship continued with his son, Charles Yorke. Parker nevertheless justified his position by his own merits. His extensive collection of legal manuscripts, dispersed from Park Hall during the twentieth century, shows that he took a keen interest in the law, practice, and history of the court of exchequer, and in 1776 he published his own reports of revenue cases from 1743 to 1767. The contract provided for 1000 copies to be printed for sale at 18*s.* a volume of which Parker was to receive 10*s.*, but as a result of the 'enormous price' it is recorded that 'the sale did not answer their expectation' (T. Cunningham, *History of the Inns of Court*, 1780, xii). An industrious judge, in 1754 he advised Dudley Ryder that if assize business was pressing it was proper to sit as early as five in the morning, 'and if the attorneys are not ready you go on without them' (Harrowby MS, Sandon Hall, Staffordshire; Lemmings, 53). On 28 October 1772 he retired on the ground of old age, with a pension of £2400 a year, though he continued to attend appeals in the privy council into the 1780s. He died at South Weald, Essex, on 29 December 1784, and was buried in the family vault at Park Hall.

J. H. BAKER

Sources Baker, *Serjeants* · Sainty, *Judges* · Foss, *Judges* · Inner Temple, London · BL, Yorke corresp., Add. MSS 35584–36223 · J. H. Baker, *English legal manuscripts in the United States of America: a descriptive list*, 2 (1990), 276 · G. Harris, *The life of Lord Chancellor Hardwicke*, 3 vols. (1847) · *DNB* · *GM*, 1st ser., 55 (1785), 77 · MS contract between John Murray, William Flexney, and Thomas Parker [sold at Sothebys, 24 Feb 1976, lot 259] · D. Lemmings, *Professors of the law* (2000), 53 n. 109

Archives Indiana University, Bloomington, Lilly Library · UCL, just book of evidence · William Salt Library, Stafford, legal notes, etc. · William Salt Library, Stafford, papers | BL, corresp. with earls of Hardwicke, Add. MSS 35586–35638, *passim*

Likenesses J. Tinney, mezzotint (after portrait by T. Hudson), BM, NPG

Parker, Thomas Lister (1779–1858), antiquary and collector, born at Browsholme Hall, Yorkshire, on 27 September 1779, was the eldest of the eight sons of John Parker (1755–1797) of Browsholme, MP for Clitheroe, Lancashire, and his wife, Beatrix (*b.* 1749), daughter of Thomas Lister of Gisburne Park, Yorkshire. He was educated at the Royal Grammar School, Clitheroe, under the mastership of the Revd Thomas Wilson BD, and at Christ's College, Cambridge.

On the death of his father on 25 May 1797, Parker succeeded to the Browsholme estate. He went on his grand tour in 1800, visiting France, Italy, and Russia, and returned home in 1801 with a collection of paintings, drawings, and prints. In 1805–7 he altered the sixteenth-century Browsholme Hall, using Jeffry Wyatt (later Sir Jeffry Wyatville) as architect to rebuild and extend the west wing: this provided a new drawing-room and dining-room, suitable for the display of his growing picture collection. Landscape gardening and forestry also engaged his interest. In the house he displayed a collection of antiquities, a feature of which was the creation of interiors evoking Browsholme's mainly Jacobethan past. The hall and other rooms contained appropriate arms and armour, oak furniture, turned chairs, stained glass, tankards and jugs, horns and antlers, and other suitable antiquarian objects. Parker was the dedicatee of Henry Shaw's *Specimens of Ancient Furniture* (1836), and was described therein as 'a gentleman whose devotion to the arts of the middle ages and kindness to those engaged in their illustration is universally acknowledged'.

Parker formed a good library of manuscripts and printed books, the latter mostly seventeenth-century plays and tracts and eighteenth-century books on architecture as well as antiquities, topography, heraldry, history, travels, poetry, and contemporary literature. The library was recorded in a manuscript catalogue (priv. coll., London) dated 1808 and made by the bookseller William Ford of Manchester, who seems to have acquired the library before 1824. Parker owned four Caxtons, which he sold in 1810.

Parker's early interest in pictures was predominantly for the old masters: his earliest recorded purchase, in 1799, was a landscape by Claude. At Sir William Hamilton's sale in 1801 he bought the portrait of Juan de Pareja by Velázquez (Metropolitan Museum, New York). By 1807 the gallery at Browsholme contained over fifty paintings, chiefly Dutch and Italian, and in that year he compiled a seven-page catalogue of paintings in the gallery at Browsholme. It recorded four paintings by British artists: one landscape each by Gainsborough and Wilson, and *The Shrimpers*, painted by Callcott in 1806, and *A View off Sheerness*, painted by Turner in 1807, two pictures which indicated the future direction of his taste.

In 1808 Parker sold most of his old masters (partly owing to financial pressures) and thereafter concentrated on patronage of contemporary British artists. He had first patronized Turner in 1798 and probably introduced the painter to Sir John Fleming Leicester of Tabley, Cheshire, his first cousin once removed, and to his friend Walter Fawkes of Farnley. Turner drew Browsholme in 1799, and his subsequent watercolour drawing (priv. coll., England) was engraved for the *History of Whalley* (1801), written by Parker's friend Thomas Dunham Whitaker. Parker sold Turner's *Sheerness* in 1811 (National Gallery, Washington, USA) but commissioned a copy from Augustus Wall Callcott. Parker was an enthusiastic patron of James Northcote (1746–1831) and commissioned a large number of portraits and landscapes between 1810 and 1820. He also commissioned or bought works by Sawrey Gilpin, William Havell, George Morland, John Opie, William Owen, Ramsay Richard Reinagle, Robert Smirke, Henry Thomson, William Turner of Oxford, and James Ward.

In 1815 Parker privately printed *A Description of Browsholme Hall … and of the Parish of Waddington*, illustrated with twenty plates drawn and etched by John Chessell Buckler, which show antiquarian interiors contrasting strangely with the elegant and comfortable Wyatt rooms. The volume provides more information about Parker's antiquarian interests than his activities as a collector, and is devoted mostly to the transcription of the collection of seventeenth-century letters and tracts then in the Browsholme library.

Parker was elected FSA in 1801, and afterwards FRS. He was high sheriff for Lancaster in 1804. He had the sinecure post of trumpeter to the queen and held the office—hereditary in his family for many generations—of bowbearer of the Forest of Bowland, Lancashire.

From 1813 to 1817 Parker had a London house at 10 South Audley Street, of which Buckler did drawings in 1813. However, the cumulative effect of spending on pictures, books, building, and landscaping led to a crisis, and in 1824 he sold Browsholme, its contents, and estate to his cousin and heir Thomas Parker of Alkincoats, who on dying without children in 1832 bequeathed the property to his nephew Thomas Goulburne Parker. After 1824 Thomas Lister Parker lived a nomadic existence, staying at the houses of his friends, including Tabley. Towards the end of his life he lived at The Star inn in Deansgate, Manchester, where he died unmarried on 2 March 1858. He was buried on 9 March in his family chapel in Waddington church, Yorkshire. There are two portraits of Parker by Northcote, one of them (reproduced in his *Description of Browsholme Hall*) representing him at the age of twenty-five. Some of his letters are printed in T. R. Raine's *Miscellanies: being Selections from the Poems and Correspondence of the Rev. Thomas Wilson* (1858).

CHARLES SEBAG-MONTEFIORE

Sources T. L. Parker, *A description of Browsholme Hall … and of the parish of Waddington … also a collection of letters from original manuscripts in the possession of Thomas Lister Parker of Browsholme Hall Esq.* (privately printed, 1815) • T. D. Whitaker, *An history of the original parish of Whalley*, rev. J. G. Nichols and P. A. Lyons, 4th edn, 1 (1872), 336–9 • S. Jervis, *Browsholme Hall* (1992) • T. L. Parker, *Catalogue of the paintings in the gallery at Browsholme, the seat of Thomas Lister Parker* (1807) • D. Brown, 'Turner, Callcott and Thomas Lister Parker: new light on Turner's *Junction of the Thames and Medway* in Washington', *Burlington Magazine*, 117 (1975), 721–2 • 'Catalogue of the library at Browsholme, the seat of Thomas Lister Parker Esq, arranged by William Ford, bookseller, Manchester 1808', priv. coll. • *GM*, 3rd ser., 4 (1858), 446 • *DNB*

Likenesses J. Northcote, oils, 1804, Browsholme Hall, Lancashire • J. Northcote, oils, 1804, Tabley House, Cheshire

Wealth at death under £450: administration, 17 July 1858, *CGPLA Eng. & Wales*

Parker, William. *See* Malvern, William of (1485x90–1539).

Parker, William (*d.* 1618), privateer and merchant, appears to have been born into the minor ranks of the Elizabethan gentry, although his parentage has yet to be traced. His brother John was a man of property in Southampton. On 18 June 1590 William Parker married Willmot Rogett at St Andrew's Church, Plymouth, and the parish registers subsequently record the baptisms of their children Margery, Mary, Elizabeth, Nicholas, Willmot, Prudence, and John. Three other children died in infancy. Parker first came to prominence in 1587 when he served as one of Drake's captains in the expedition to Cadiz. During the years 1590 to 1595 he undertook privateering voyages in the *Richard*, backed by letters of reprisal issued by the high court of admiralty. He seized several Spanish prizes and captured Puerto de Caballos in Honduras by daring raids in 1594 and 1595. Recalled to royal service in 1596, Parker was captain of the *Rainbow* for the second Cadiz expedition. He resumed privateering in November of that year, sailing to the Caribbean with his own ship, the *Prudence*, and the barque *Adventure*. His lively account of the voyage was published by Hakluyt. Having captured Puerto de Caballos jointly with Sir Anthony Sherley in April 1597, Parker sacked Campeche, the main town of Yucatan, and was shot through the chest by a bullet which remained lodged in his back. The Spanish retaliated by taking the *Adventure*, executing the captain and thirteen men. Parker arrived back in Plymouth in July 1597.

The most celebrated of Parker's exploits was the capture of Porto Bello in Panama during his Caribbean expedition of 1600–01. Parker's narrative in *Purchas his Pilgrimes* dates the voyage as 1601–2, but evidence from Spanish documents and records of Parker's activities in Plymouth point to this being an error. The *Prudence*, *Pearl*, and three smaller ships set sail in November 1600, capturing and pillaging St Vincent in the Cape Verde Islands, winning a fierce battle at Cubagua, and seizing a Portuguese slave ship. Parker arrived at Porto Bello on a moonlit night in February 1601 and concealed his identity long enough to overcome the town in a surprise attack. To his disappointment, the treasure house stockpile was only 10,000 ducats, which he kept for himself, allowing his soldiers to share the rest of the spoils. Parker withdrew the following evening but was shot through the arm by a musket ball as the fleet sailed away.

After returning home in May 1601, Parker busied himself sending out his ships on privateering voyages until the accession of James I in 1603 brought peace with Spain. Parker then turned to less adventurous merchant trading and property investment. He served on Plymouth corporation, holding the office of mayor for a year from October 1601. He proved to be as confrontational in his civic duties as he was at sea. Sir Robert Cecil received bitter complaints that Parker was hampering the work of royal officials, on one occasion sending men to play hurling on Plymouth Hoe to evade impressment. In 1604 he was suspended from the corporation and imprisoned for his 'sinister malice' in creating trouble between the mayor and the captain of the Fort. In 1605 Parker and fellow Plymouth merchants agreed to back a trading voyage to Virginia by George Waymouth. This scheme failed, but Parker is named in the first Virginia charter of 1606 as one of the four patentees for the northern colony. He invested in the *Richard* which set out for Virginia in August 1606, only to be seized by the Spanish.

Having been passed over when nominated in 1614 and 1615, Parker was chosen by the East India Company in November 1617 as vice-admiral for a voyage to the Moluccas. Serious doubts were expressed about his suitability, not least because he had long since given up seafaring. Parker was described as fat, unwieldy, hot-tempered, and too strict with his men. His supporters prevailed, however, and Parker prepared for his journey by making a will distributing his Plymouth properties and the bulk of his belongings and wealth between his wife, sons, and daughters. The passage of the *Sampson* was dogged by death and sickness. Parker wrote from the Cape in July 1618 complaining of bad beer and beef, and the want of fresh provisions and warm clothing. On 24 September 1618 William Parker died on the voyage to Bantam, lamented as a good commander: an unremarkable end, hardly befitting one who had led such a dashing life.

MARGARET MAKEPEACE

Sources R. Hakluyt, *The principal navigations, voyages, traffiques and discoveries of the English nation*, 10, Hakluyt Society, extra ser., 10 (1904); repr. (1969) • S. Purchas, *Hakluytus posthumus, or, Purchas his pilgrimes*, bk 16 (1625); repr. Hakluyt Society, extra ser., 29 (1906), chap. 9; bk 18 (1625); repr. Hakluyt Society, extra ser., 31 (1906), chap. 1 • W. Parker, 'Captain Parker's own account of the taking the town of Porto Bello in the year 1601', in D. Gonzalez Carranza, *A geographical description of the Spanish West Indies* (1740) • K. R. Andrews, *Elizabethan privateering: English privateering during the Spanish war, 1585–1603* (1964) • *Calendar of the manuscripts of the most hon. the marquis of Salisbury*, 24 vols., HMC, 9 (1883–1976), vols. 11–12, 16 • K. R. Andrews, ed., *English privateering voyages to the West Indies, 1588–1595*, Hakluyt Society, 2nd ser., 111 (1959) • *CSP col.*, vols. 2–3 • R. N. Worth, *Calendar of the Plymouth municipal records* (1893) • *CSP dom.*, 1598–1603 • M. C. S. Cruwys, ed., *The register of baptisms, marriages and burials of the parish of St Andrew's, Plymouth, co. Devon*, Devon and Cornwall RS, 26 (1954) • S. Wignall, *In search of Spanish treasure: a diver's story* (1982) • will, PRO, PROB 11/134, sig. 112 • *Report and Transactions of the Devonshire Association*, 105 (1973)

Archives BL, Add. MS 36767, fol. 17 • BL, Lansdowne MS 142, fols. 163–4

Parker, William, **thirteenth Baron Morley and fifth or first Baron Monteagle** (**1574/5–1622**), discoverer of the Gunpowder Plot, was the son and heir of Edward Parker, twelfth Baron Morley (1551?–1618), and Elizabeth (*d.* 1585), regarded by contemporaries as *suo jure* Baroness Monteagle, daughter of William Stanley, third Baron Monteagle, and his wife, Anne Leybourne, daughter and heir of Sir James Leybourne. William Parker was summoned to parliament as Lord Monteagle in 1604. The creation of the barony originated in a proclamation of Henry VIII in 1514 and it is not known whether letters patent were issued restricting the succession to heirs male of the body; if so the summons of 1604 would constitute a new creation. From his father's death he was summoned as Lord Morley and Monteagle.

Monteagle was knighted by the earl of Essex at Dublin on 12 July 1599, one of many knights created during that ill-fated expedition. In June 1600 he appears to have visited the Low Countries to experience campaigning there. The association with Essex led him into rebellion in February 1601. Monteagle was imprisoned in the Tower after Essex's revolt, and, as one of the principal participants, was examined by the privy council on 16 February. He was fined £4000 in May and released from the Tower three months later, though his movements were initially restricted to a 4 mile radius about the house of his cousin Sir John Leventhorpe at Shinglehall, Epping.

Monteagle was brought up a Catholic. During Elizabeth's reign he was closely associated with the extremist

William Parker, thirteenth Baron Morley and fifth or first Baron Monteagle (1574/5–1622), attrib. John de Critz the elder, *c.*1615

Catholic faction which looked for a Spanish military intervention in support of their co-religionists. He was one of those who arranged Thomas Winter's mission to Spain in 1602, but at the accession of James I he told his erstwhile colleagues that he had 'done with all former plots' (Hatfield MS 112/91), and wrote to the new king declaring his intention to conform to the state religion. Rather disingenuously, he argued that earlier errors were a direct result of his upbringing—'I knew no better' (BL, Add. MS 19402, fol. 146). His religious views remained suspect, and his wife, Elizabeth Tresham (*b.* 1573, *d.* 1647/8), sister of the gunpowder conspirator Francis Tresham, whom he had married in 1589, appears to have remained a recusant all her life. Nevertheless, it seems as if he meant what he said.

There are immediate signs that Monteagle was accepted into favour with the new regime. He was one of the thirty-nine English commissioners who signed the projected treaty of union with Scotland on 6 December 1604. Nevertheless, he still had friends and connections among the extremist Catholic gentry. Tresham, the last recruit to the Gunpowder Plot, was 'exceeding earnest' to ensure that his brother-in-law escaped the projected destruction of the House of Lords, and it is almost certain that Tresham wrote the anonymous letter which Monteagle received while at dinner at his house in Hoxton on 26 October. As he was eating, Monteagle handed this to one of his servants, a friend of Thomas Winter, or a friend of a friend, asking him to read the message aloud. The letter contained a thinly disguised warning of some explosive enterprise against the opening of parliament, and its substance was duly passed on to the plotters. Winter was, indeed, well known in the Monteagle household: he had served Monteagle as a secretary of some sort for several years, and had attended the prorogation of parliament on 3 October 1605 in Monteagle's entourage. The so-called Monteagle letter survives at the Public Record Office (SP 14/216/2).

Monteagle hastened to Whitehall, where he found some of the most prominent members of the privy council—the earls of Salisbury, Nottingham, Northampton, Suffolk, and Worcester—at supper. Not surprisingly they suspected foul play, though still with half an eye to some hoax or fantasy. When the king returned at the end of the month from hunting at Royston he was inclined to believe that mischief was afoot. The vaults under the House of Lords were searched on 4 November by the lord chamberlain, Suffolk, with Monteagle in attendance. They met Guy Fawkes, posing as Thomas Percy's servant and standing guard over the gunpowder, which was concealed under firewood. Monteagle, who knew Percy well, and who paid an annuity to his wife, Martha, and daughter, derived from an advance of £500, voiced his suspicions. A further search that night, which was left to Sir Thomas Knyvett and other Westminster officials and servants, surprised Fawkes at his post, dark lantern in hand.

When in the Tower, Robert Winter told Fawkes how he had heard rumours that Monteagle had sought pardons for three of the imprisoned traitors, but this seems to have been nothing more than desperate gossip. It is unlikely that Monteagle would have risked opprobrium in asking, and quite certain that any request would have been refused. Instead, he basked in carefully orchestrated glory. For passing on the warning, Monteagle received public praise, lands worth £200 a year, and an annual pension of £500. His part in the Spanish treason of 1602 was glossed over in the published account of the Gunpowder Plot and in the trials of conspirators, and still more damaging accusations laid by the imprisoned Jesuit provincial, Henry Garnett, in March 1606 were similarly ignored. Garnett maintained that he had discussed the possibility of armed rebellion in England with Tresham and Monteagle as late as 1605, Monteagle arguing that drastic steps might indeed have to be taken, the king being 'so odious to all sorts' (Gardiner, 511).

Nevertheless, the gratitude was bounded within distinct limits. It may or may not be significant that, in presenting the prosecution case against the gunpowder plotters at their trial, Sir Edward Coke, the attorney-general, apparently contrived to 'forget' specific instructions from the earl of Salisbury to clear Monteagle from slanderous rumours then circulating, at least insofar as the scanty reports of Coke's words permit us to judge. When a bill of thanksgiving for the delivery from the Gunpowder Plot was hurried through parliament early in the 1606 session, an attempt by Sir Henry Poole to include Monteagle in the congratulations was blocked by fellow MPs, ostensibly on the grounds that mention of his name would detract from the paramount role accorded King James in the discovery.

A regular participant in the gaming at court, Monteagle also satisfied his appetite for gambling in other, rather more constructive, speculations. He was among the earliest to adventure money in the Virginia Company, becoming a member of its council in May 1609. The same year he staked £500 in the East India Company, while in 1612 his name is found among those investing in an attempt to discover a north-west passage. The present whereabouts of a portrait by Van Somer, last exhibited at South Kensington in 1866 and then in the collection of Mr John Webb, are unknown. Monteagle died at his Essex residence, Great Hallingbury, on 1 July 1622, where he was also buried. He was succeeded by his son Henry, and a further five children—William, Charles, Frances, Elizabeth, and Katherine—are mentioned in his will, drawn up shortly before his death. MARK NICHOLLS

Sources PRO, SP 14/216, SP 14/19 • PRO, E 134 [esp. E 134/7 James I Easter/39 E 134/miscellaneous James I/24] • Hatfield House, Hertfordshire, Salisbury–Cecil MSS • BL, Add. MS 19402 • GEC, *Peerage* • M. Nicholls, *Investigating Gunpowder Plot* (1991) • *The letters of John Chamberlain*, ed. N. E. McClure, 2 vols. (1939) • S. R. Gardiner, 'Two declarations of Garnet relating to the Gunpowder Plot', *EngHR*, 3 (1888), 510–19 • *The parliamentary diary of Robert Bowyer, 1606–1607*, ed. D. H. Willson (1931) • PROB 11/139, quire 9, fols. 71r–72 • M. E. Finch, *The wealth of five Northamptonshire families, 1540–1640*, Northamptonshire RS, 19 (1956)

Likenesses attrib. J. de Critz the elder, portrait, *c*.1615, Denver Art Museum, Colorado [*see illus.*] • Van Somer, portrait, exh. 1866; formerly in possession of John Webb, in 1866

Wealth at death considerable property and money: will, PRO, PROB 11/139, fols. 71r–72

Parker, William (*bap.* **1714**, *d.* **1802**), theologian and Church of England clergyman, was baptized in Coventry on 9 June 1714, the eldest of the five children of Moses Parker and Hannah, *née* Lovett. His father was churchwarden of St Michael's Church, Coventry. He matriculated at Balliol College, Oxford, on 6 July 1731 and graduated BA in 1735, MA in 1738, BD in 1751, and DD in 1754. He was elected a fellow of Balliol on 29 November 1737 and remained so until 1750–51. His first appointment beyond the university was to the vicarage of St Katharine Cree, London, on 17 April 1752. He held this post until his death; in 1753 he also held the rectory of Little Ilford, Essex.

Parker's early career, spent mainly in Oxford, remains shadowy, but it was one of considerable intellectual achievement. An early recognition of his talents was his election as a fellow of the Royal Society on 19 February 1746. He took part in the closing stages of the deist debates, and staunchly defended revealed religion and the Mosaic history against Thomas Morgan, Conyers Middleton, and Henry St John, first Viscount Bolingbroke. In *The expediency of some divine interpositions, during the first ages of the Christian fathers, consider'd* (1749) he argued against Middleton that divine interpositions had continued from the apostolic into the patristic age to ensure 'the quiet establishment of Christianity in the world' (p. 6). He went further by suggesting that miracles might occur again. In his *Two Discourses* [*on 2 Corinthians 11: 3*] *on the Mosaick History of the Fall Consider'd* (1750) he contended that since the apostles treated the fall as a fact it was inadmissible for later critics to deem it a fable. The work that brought him attention was *Two discourses* [*on John 18: 38*] *before the University of Oxford: in which are contained remarks on some passages in the writings of the late Lord Viscount Bolingbroke* (1754); Bolingbroke had been dead three years but his writings, in which his deism was revealed, were newly published. Perhaps as a result Parker was made chaplain to George II, on 15 August 1754, an appointment that was renewed in 1760 by George III. In *The Scripture Doctrine of Predestination Stated and Explained* (1759) he insisted that God 'hath made no vessels absolutely and necessarily predetermined to dishonour in another life, without their own fault in this' (p. 42).

Theological controversy was not Parker's only route to preferment. Some accrued through his connection with Hereford, where he had preached at the Three Choirs festival in 1753 and dedicated the sermon to the bishop, Lord James Beauclerk. On 14 March 1757 he was collated to the prebend of Pratum Minus in Hereford Cathedral, and on 23 April 1760 he was appointed treasurer of Hereford Cathedral, with the rectory of Bockleton, in that diocese, as part of the treasurer's endowment. Parker was esteemed by more influential prelates than Beauclerk, including Bishop Richard Trevor of Durham and Bishop Richard Osbaldeston of Carlisle. It was his good fortune that the rectory of St James's, Piccadilly, fell vacant a few months after Osbaldeston had been named bishop of London in 1762; Parker was his chaplain and was presented by the bishop to this sought-after benefice on 18 November 1763, to forestall the pressure coming from John Montagu, fourth earl of Sandwich, to award it to the scandal-mired Revd John Kidgell. Parker retained the post for the rest of his life and consolidated his reputation as a pulpit orator. It was at St James's, on 3 May 1768, that he married Mary Whitwell (1728–1799) sister of Lieutenant-General Sir John Griffin *Griffin (formerly Whitwell), MP and later fourth Baron Howard de Walden. This was an advantageous match, bringing Parker the immediate sum of £6000 and the opportunity of further preferment. He succeeded in obtaining the prebend of North Kelsey in Lincoln Cathedral (installed 28 September 1776) but the influence of his brother-in-law was insufficient to win him a bishopric. In any event his rectory was worth an estimated £1600 p.a. in 1802.

On 27 May 1797 Parker's wife succeeded to a large fortune on the death of her brother (she was his fifth and only surviving sister) and assumed the name of Griffin, by royal licence, of 3 June of that year. She died at Bath on 22 July 1799. The couple (who had no children) had been entitled to the Griffin estates at Audley End, Essex, for their joint lives and reportedly enjoyed an income of £3000 p.a. from the property. Neither chose to reside there, however, which allowed Mary Griffin's distant cousin and heir, Richard Griffin, second Baron Braybrooke, to live in the house.

William Parker died on 22 July 1802, at his rectory in Piccadilly, and was buried in a vault under St James's Chapel, Hampstead Road. His ministry at St James's was a modest success but it cut short what could have been a luminous academic career. He took little part in politics; he once praised the Three Choirs festival for the way that it was never interrupted 'by any swellings of party' (*The Pleasures of Gratitude and Benevolence Improved by Church Musick*, 30). He printed a total of sixteen sermons; most were collected in *Several discourses on special subjects, preached before the University of Oxford, and upon other occasions* (1790).

NIGEL ASTON

Sources *GM*, 1st ser., 38 (1768), 246 · *GM*, 1st ser., 63 (1793), 639 · *GM*, 1st ser., 64 (1794), 452 · *GM*, 1st ser., 69 (1799), 1005 · *GM*, 1st ser., 72 (1802), 694 · *GM*, 1st ser., 84/1 (1814), 247 · *GM*, 1st ser., 84/2 (1814), 488 · *IGI* · W. Reader, *Description of St. Michael's Church, Coventry* (1830) · Coventry City Archives, BA/A/G/2/3 · Foster, *Alum. Oxon.*, *1500–1714*, 3.1069 · G. Hennessy, *Novum repertorium ecclesiasticum parochiale Londinense, or, London diocesan clergy succession from the earliest time to the year 1898* (1898) · Hereford Cathedral Library, RS3/PB/21/5, 6; RS3/DT/11, 12 · *Fasti Angl.* (Hardy), 1.491, 526; 2.199 · T. Thomson, *History of the Royal Society* (1812), xliv · Nichols, *Lit. anecdotes*, 6.365; 8.239, 244; 9.658–9, 690 · Lord Braybrooke [R. Griffin], *History of Audley End* (1836), 53, 129 · W. Addison, *Audley End* (1953), 155, 164 · GEC, *Peerage*

Archives BL, Add. MSS 4438, fol. 194; 35608, fol. 99; 35611, fol. 4; 35616, fol. 92

Likenesses J. Parker, portrait, Audley End House, Essex

Parker, Sir William, first baronet (1743–1802), naval officer, was born on 1 January 1743, the son of Augustine Parker of Queenborough in Kent and Elizabeth, eldest daughter of William Beal of Shorles, near Minster in the Isle of Sheppey. Augustine held the honorary title of commander of one of the king's yachts and had at one time been mayor of the borough. In his turn William married Jane (*d.* in or after 1803), daughter of Edward Collingwood of Greenwich, on 28 December 1776 at Queenborough. William and Jane had a large family of seven daughters and one son, William George, together with five other children who died in infancy.

William Parker entered the navy in 1756, probably in November, joining first the *Portland* from which he was speedily discharged into the *Ipswich* in December. From the *Ipswich* he moved to the *Centurion* (Captain Mansell) on 18 February 1757, and he stayed with her as midshipman and master's mate for almost the next six years. In the *Centurion* he was present in the fleet before Louisbourg in 1757, at the capture of Louisbourg in 1758, and Quebec in 1759. In 1760 the *Centurion*, under the command of Captain James Galbraith, was on the Jamaica station in the squadron of Rear-Admiral Charles Holmes, remaining there until 1762. She played a small part in the assault on Havana and then returned to Britain with Sir James Douglas as escort for the first Jamaica convoy.

On his return to England, and with six years' service, Parker passed his lieutenant's examination on 3 November 1762, but he did not receive his promotion until 29 November 1766. For much of his time as lieutenant he was employed on the Newfoundland station in the frigates *Niger* and *Aldborough* and the schooner *Egmont*. He was promoted commander on 25 June 1773 and in March 1775 commissioned the *Martin*, again for service on the Newfoundland station. His first command on reaching post rank on 28 August 1777 was the *Deal Castle* (24 guns). In December 1778 he sailed in her to the West Indies in the reinforcement squadron commanded by Commodore Joshua Rowley, joining the Hon. John Byron at St Lucia. He later moved to the *Maidstone* (28 guns) and then, in 1782, to the *Iphigenia* which was paid off early in 1783. He was next appointed to the *Dictator*, guardship in the Medway, and, after commanding her for three years, was commodore and commander-in-chief on the Leeward Islands station (1787–90) with his broad pennant in the *Jupiter* (50 guns). In the Spanish armament of 1790 he commanded the *Formidable* which was paid off in the autumn.

In December 1792 Parker commissioned the *Audacious* (74 guns) for service in the Channel Fleet under the command of Richard, Earl Howe. On 28 May 1794, when the British and French fleets were in sight of each other, Howe detached part of the fleet under Rear-Admiral Thomas Pasley to concentrate on the enemy rear which he did 'with peculiar firmness and attacked a three-decker ship [the *Revolutionnaire*, 120 guns], the sternmost in the enemy's line'. The *Leviathan* with 'good judgement and determined courage pushed up alongside … and was supported by Captain Parker of the *Audacious* in a most spirited manner' (Howe's dispatch, PRO, ADM 1/100, fol. 367). The *Leviathan* moved on to the next ship in the French line while the *Audacious* continued her fire and the French ship, being unsupported, struck to her. Parker was unable to take possession of the *Revolutionnaire* as the *Audacious* 'was so much disabled in sails and rigging as to render the ship ungovernable' (PRO, ADM 51/54). Instead the *Audacious* limped into Plymouth and the *Revolutionnaire* was repossessed by the French and towed into La Rochelle. This was a notable action on the part of Parker as, had the *Revolutionnaire* been in good order, she was capable of demolishing the *Audacious*. The outcome of this spirited exchange was that in the battle of 1 June 1794 the French were deprived of a 120-gun ship, the British of one of 74 guns.

On 4 July 1794 Parker was promoted rear-admiral of the blue and in the following February he was appointed commander-in-chief in Jamaica with his flag in the *Raisonnable*. While there he was promoted rear-admiral of the red on 1 June 1795. A severe illness compelled him to return to Britain in the summer of 1796. In January 1797, his health recovered, he was ordered with a squadron of five ships of the line to reinforce Sir John Jervis, commanding the Mediterranean Fleet which at this time was off the Tagus. Flying his flag in the *Prince George* (98 guns) Parker joined Jervis on 6 February in time to take an active part in the battle of Cape St Vincent on 14 February. The *Prince George* was the third ship in the British line and came early and effectively into the action. Subsequent accounts of the battle made much of the boarding and capture by Horatio Nelson of the *San Nicolas* and the *San Josef*. There is no doubt, though, that the fire of the *Prince George*, together with that of the *Captain*, *Culloden*, and *Blenheim*, had already caused considerable damage to the *San Josef* before she was fouled by the *San Nicolas*. The likelihood is that the two disabled Spanish ships were already defeated before they drifted down towards the *Captain* and surrender to Nelson. Parker was aggrieved that so much credit on this occasion went to Nelson and he drew up his own narrative of the event. In the heat and confusion of battle it is difficult for any individual to be fully aware of the actions of the ships around him and it is likely that both Parker and Nelson were convinced of the accuracy of their versions of the capture. The overall boldness of Nelson in leading his ship out of the line near the start of the engagement rightly attracted more attention than was given to Parker. Jervis had no doubt, however, of the extent and value of this 'essential victory' and praised all concerned in bringing it about when he acknowledged George III's approbation of 'the gallant behaviour of all the officers and men who were in the action with me, more especially the vice admirals Thompson and Waldegrave and rear admiral Parker and commodore Nelson' (ADM, 1/396).

As third in command at this vital and outstanding victory, Parker was made a baronet and presented with the freedom of the city of London. In common with the other admirals and captains, he received the thanks of both houses of parliament and the gold medal. Parker remained with Jervis (now Lord St Vincent), becoming second in command on the recall of Vice-Admiral Thompson. In the summer of 1798 he regarded himself as slighted by the appointment of Nelson, his junior, to a detached and semi-independent command in the Mediterranean. He apparently allowed his name to be linked with a pamphlet published by Sir John Orde in which excessive language was used to criticise Jervis's detachment of Nelson to the Mediterranean. Jervis's fury can be seen in his letter to Evan Nepean, secretary to the Board of Admiralty, where he referred to 'misrepresentations, partial statements and gross falsehoods more especially the two [conversations] between Sir William Parker and me. Every other conversation is most abominably twisted and distorted for the express purpose of stabbing my character' (BL, Add. MS 31167, fol. 16). Relations between St Vincent and Parker became icy in the extreme; on 19 December 1799 St Vincent wrote, 'this is the last correspondence I shall hold with you of a private nature' (BL, Add. MS 31166, fol. 202)—but Parker remained with the fleet until 1799 and was with Lord Keith in the pursuit of the French out of the Mediterranean and into Brest, after which he went to Spithead and struck his flag.

Parker was appointed commander-in-chief of the Halifax station in March 1800 but was recalled in the following year for having sent two of his ships to the West Indies contrary to orders from the Admiralty. He demanded a court martial for what was essentially a technical offence and was acquitted of misconduct. However, the court suggested that his orders had been indiscreet, an admonition which Parker found hurtful but which a further appointment might well have smoothed away. However, peace with France was on the point of being signed and Parker remained on shore during 1802. On 31 December 1802 he died suddenly of apoplexy at Ham in Surrey, where he was buried.

Parker's will, signed on 14 June 1800 and proved in London on 8 February 1803, indicates a man of quite considerable wealth. Apart from all his household and estate goods which he left in trust to his wife, Jane, and after her to his son, William George, he details bequests amounting to over £50,000 in various stocks and annuities. All of this is left in various proportions to his children but all in trust with requirements as to its distribution after their decease. William George was ultimately to succeed to the house and the estates and to have any residue left after the individual bequests. An interesting insight to the meticulous nature of Parker's will is to be found in a codicil in which he lists his daughters Harriet, Ann, Mary, and Elizabeth as having 'in his absence overrun their quarterly allowance' and directs that the amount and interest 'should be deducted from their inheritance as an act of fairness to their brother and sisters' (ibid.). William George followed his father into the navy, succeeded to the baronetcy, retired with the rank of captain, and died in 1848. KENNETH BREEN

Sources *DNB* • admiralty in letters, PRO, ADM 1 • admiralty out letters, PRO, ADM 2 • admiralty muster books, PRO, ADM 36 • admiralty list books, PRO, ADM 8 certificates • lieutenants' passing, PRO, ADM 107 • captains' logs, PRO, ADM 51 • wills and probate, PRO, PROB 11/1387 • *IGI* • D. Syrett and R. L. DiNardo, *The commissioned sea officers of the Royal Navy, 1660–1815*, rev. edn, Occasional Publications of the Navy RS, 1 (1994) • R. Beatson, *Naval and military memoirs of Great Britain*, 3 vols. (1790) • W. James, *The naval history of Great Britain, from the declaration of war by France in 1793, to the accession of George IV*, [4th edn], 6 vols. (1847) • *Debrett's Peerage* (1824), 1.951

Archives NL Scot., corresp. with Lord Balcarres

Likenesses Worthington and Parker, group portrait, line engraving, pubd 1803 (after *Naval victories, commemoration of the 14th February 1797* by R. Smirke), BM, NPG

Wealth at death over £50,000 in stocks and annuities, in addition to estates and property: will, PRO, PROB 11/1387

Parker, Sir William, first baronet (1781–1866), naval officer, was born on 1 December 1781, the third son of George Parker of Almington, Staffordshire, who was the second son of Sir Thomas *Parker, lord chief baron of the exchequer, and first cousin of John Jervis, first earl of St Vincent, who married George Parker's sister Martha. William Parker entered the navy in February 1793 as captain's servant on board the *Orion*, with Captain John Thomas Duckworth. After a voyage to the West Indies his ship joined the Channel Fleet under Lord Howe, and took part in the battle of 1 June 1794. In March 1795 Parker followed Duckworth to the *Leviathan* and again went to the West Indies, where, in October 1796, he was appointed by Duckworth, while in temporary command of the station, acting lieutenant of the *Magicienne*, a frigate employed during the next eighteen months in active and successful cruising. In May 1798 he was appointed to the *Queen*, flagship of Sir Hyde Parker (1739–1807), but still as an acting lieutenant; he was not confirmed in the rank until 5 September 1799. On 1 May 1799 he was appointed by Sir Hyde acting captain of the *Volage* (24 guns), in which during the next few months he cruised with notable success in the Gulf of Mexico and on the coast of Cuba. His commission as commander was confirmed on 10 October, but he had previously been moved into the sloop *Stork*, in which in the following year he returned to England; after nearly a year in the North Sea, or attached to the fleet off Brest, he was promoted captain on 9 October 1801.

In March 1802 he was appointed to the *Alarm*, one of the few ships kept in commission during the peace, and in November he was moved to the frigate *Amazon* (38 guns), which he would command for upwards of eleven years. Initially the *Amazon* was attached to the fleet off Toulon, under Lord Nelson, and took part in the chase of Villeneuve to the West Indies. She was afterwards detached on a cruise westward, and was absent when Nelson sailed from Portsmouth to fight the battle of Trafalgar. In December 1805 the *Amazon* was attached to the squadron under Sir John Borlase Warren, which on the following 14 March captured the French *Marengo* and *Belle Poule*. The *Belle Poule* was brought to action by the *Amazon*, and surrendered to her: Warren publicly expressed his appreciation of Parker's conduct. During the following years the *Amazon* was employed mostly on the coast of Spain and Portugal, almost constantly on the move; the work was very harassing, and gave no opportunities for distinction. In May 1810 she was sent home for a thorough refit and, on her arrival in Plymouth Sound, Parker obtained three months' leave of absence. On 10 June he married Frances Anne (*d.* 1871), youngest daughter of Sir Theophilus Biddulph; they had two sons and six daughters. At the close of the three months Parker rejoined his ship, and sailed again for the coast of Spain. During 1811 the *Amazon* was attached to the fleet off Brest and in the channel. By the beginning of 1812 she was quite worn out, and was paid off on 16 January.

Parker was now glad to have a spell on shore. The great opportunities, he believed, were at an end, and the war was not likely to last much longer. He had acquired a competent fortune from prize money and bought a place—Shenstone Lodge—near Lichfield, and there, for the next fifteen years, he led the life of a country gentleman. Though a whig and a deputy lieutenant of the county, he took little part in politics and seldom interfered in the business. During this period ashore he lost the sight of one eye in a hunting accident. On 4 June 1815 he was nominated a CB.

In 1827 Parker was offered by the duke of Clarence the command at the Cape of Good Hope, with a commodore's broad pennant. He replied that his uncle had always maintained that no one ought to serve as a flag officer who had not commanded a ship of the line, and that he would prefer an appointment as captain. He was accordingly appointed to the *Warspite*, in which he went out to the Mediterranean and acted during 1828 as senior officer on the coast of Greece. In September Sir Edward Codrington hoisted his flag on board the *Warspite* for a passage to England, and in December Parker was appointed to command the royal yacht *Prince Regent*.

On 22 July 1830 Parker was promoted rear-admiral, and in April 1831 was appointed second in command of the channel squadron, under Sir Edward Codrington, with his flag in the *Prince Regent* (120 guns). In September he was detached on an independent command to the Tagus, where, with his flag in the *Asia*, he remained until June 1834, protecting British interests during the bitter civil war with a tact and success that were acknowledged by his being nominated a KCB on 16 July. That month he returned to England, and was immediately appointed one of the lords of the Admiralty under Lord Auckland. On the change of ministry in December he went out of office, but in April 1835 was reappointed; Lord Auckland was again the first lord. He remained at the Admiralty for six years under Lord Minto, leaving only on his appointment on 12 May 1841 as commander-in-chief in China, where the troubled state of affairs demanded the presence of an officer in whom the government had full confidence.

Parker assumed command of the squadron at Hong Kong on 10 August; after capturing Amoy (Xiamen), Ningpo (Ningbo), Woosung (Wusong), and Shanghai he brought matters to a successful issue by seizing Chinkiang (Zhenjiang) and closing the entrance of the Grand Canal on 21 July 1842. Parker was rewarded for the subsequent peace by being made a GCB on 18 May 1843, by a good-service pension of £300 a year on 26 April 1844, and by a baronetcy on his return to England on 18 December 1844. He had attained the rank of vice-admiral on 23 November 1841, and in February 1845 was appointed commander-in-chief in the Mediterranean.

In May 1846 it was thought advisable, both as a concentration of force and on account of his long experience of Portugal and Portuguese politics, to appoint Parker also to the command of the Channel Fleet. This brought him from Smyrna and Constantinople to Cork, where he arrived on 13 July, to receive a pressing invitation from Lord Auckland to join the Admiralty board as first sea lord. Parker declined: his health, he thought, would not stand the work, and his remaining sighted eye threatened to give out if pressed by candlelight.

In the next few months the squadron visited Lisbon, Lagos, Cadiz, Tetuan, and Gibraltar, and while many of the ships remaining in the Mediterranean wintered at Athens, Parker, with several more, was at anchor in the Tagus, and continued there during the first half of 1847. Parker then returned to the Mediterranean, where the turmoil of revolutions kept him busily occupied during 1848 and the following years. The difficulties he had to contend with were mostly diplomatic, though his actual share in the diplomacy was small: what he had to do was to keep an effective force, and show that British interests were adequately protected. The Mediterranean Fleet then improved its already high standards of naval drill.

In September 1849 Parker moved his flag to the *Queen* to begin a unique second consecutive term as commander-in-chief in the Mediterranean. This situation reflected both his own success and the lack of any suitable senior officer to replace him. Throughout his six years on station Parker was fully occupied with a succession of diplomatic crises, ranging from the troubles of Portugal in 1846–7 and the Italian revolutions of 1848–9 to the Hungarian refugee crisis of 1849 and the Dom Pacifico affair of 1850. As the executor of British diplomacy Parker proved a safe and reliable officer, though he lacked initiative and sophistication. His decision, taken on local advice, to enter the Dardanelles in 1849, in breach of the 1841 Straits convention, was particularly unfortunate. Parker's other concern was a succession of sailing trials that attempted to resolve the bitter political debate on the merits of the large sailing ships designed by Sir William Symonds. Parker could hardly be impartial, having been largely responsible for ordering the majority of these ships while at the Admiralty under Lord Minto. His decision to fly his flag in Symonds's masterpiece, the *Queen*, indicated his preferences.

On 29 April 1851 Parker attained the rank of admiral but continued in the command until March 1852, when he was relieved by Rear-Admiral J. W. D. Dundas and returned to England. He resigned his command at Spithead on 28 April. In July he was nominated chairman of a committee to inquire into the manning of the navy, which had been made a crucial question by the recent repeal of the navigation laws. It was from the recommendations of this committee that the system of continuous service came into being, though at first, and for many years, only partially and tentatively. In October 1853 Parker was offered the command of the Baltic fleet, which was to be assembled in spring for war with Russia. He refused, on grounds of age, ill health, and the sheer labour of drilling a new fleet. From May 1854 to May 1857 he was commander-in-chief at Devonport, and was repeatedly consulted confidentially by successive first lords. Among other points on which he was privately consulted were Lord Dundonald's plan for the destruction of the enemy's fleet, regulations concerning Roman Catholics' attendance at mass, and the conduct of the Second Opium War. During this time he signed the nomination papers for John Arbuthnot Fisher, forming the bridge between Nelson and the navy of 1914.

After his retirement Parker lived principally at Shenstone Lodge. On 20 May 1862 he was appointed rear-admiral of the United Kingdom, and on 27 April 1863 was promoted to be admiral of the fleet. He died of bronchitis on 13 November 1866 at Shenstone Lodge. He was buried privately in his parish churchyard, and a handsome monument to his memory was erected, by subscription, in Lichfield Cathedral.

No officer of Parker's day made so deep an impression on the navy, by reason not of extraordinary talent but of exceptional fixity of purpose. In his youth he was considered by St Vincent and by Nelson a first-rate officer. As an admiral—in Portugal, in China, in the Mediterranean—his conduct was distinguished by skill and tact. But it was as a disciplinarian that his name was best known, not only in his own time, but to the generation that followed him; strict, but not harsh, with a fervent sense of religion and zeal for the service, ever bearing in mind the example of his distinguished uncle, he made everything bend to his idea of what was right. Some of his ideas appeared in his day capricious: he disliked smoking, for instance, and took care that no officer should remain in the flagship who was guilty of the habit. His family connections and whig politics dominated his career: they explain his lack of sea service between 1812 and 1827, his service on the profoundly political Admiralty board of Lord Minto, and his appointment to command in Portugal and China. A deeply religious man, Parker possessed an uncommon degree of self-control and will-power, qualities that enabled him to function successfully in difficult situations where civil and military authority were in conflict. His command in China revealed a certain grasp of the problems of power projection and riverine amphibious warfare; he exploited steam power and worked well with his military and civil colleagues. More than any other officer of his generation, the calm, confident, and courteous Parker represented the navy at the mid-nineteenth century. J. K. Laughton, *rev.* Andrew Lambert

Sources A. Phillimore, *The life of Admiral of the Fleet Sir William Parker*, 3 vols. (1876–80) • NMM, Parker MSS • NMM, Minto MSS • G. S. Graham, *The China station: war and diplomacy, 1830–1860* (1978) • A. D. Lambert, *The last sailing battlefleet: maintaining naval mastery, 1815–1850* (1991) • J. H. Briggs, *Naval administrations, 1827 to 1892: the experience of 65 years*, ed. Lady Briggs (1898) • C. J. Bartlett, *Great Britain and sea power, 1815–1853* (1963) • H. W. V. Temperley, *England and the Near East: the Crimea* (1936) • J. S. Bromley, ed., *The manning of the Royal Navy: selected public pamphlets, 1693–1873*, Navy RS, 119 (1974) • S. Lane-Poole, *The life of … Stratford Canning*, 2 vols. (1888) • E. D. H. E. Napier, *The life and correspondence of Admiral Sir Charles Napier*, 2 vols. (1862)

Archives BL, journal, Add. MSS 42844–42845 • NMM, corresp., letter-books, and papers • NYPL, corresp., and annotated copy of admiralty regulations • Staffs. RO, trust and estate papers | BL, corresp. with Charles Napier, Add. MSS 40020–40045 • BL, letters to Lord Nelson, Add. MSS 34921–34931 • BL OIOC, letters to Lord Tweeddale, MS Eur. F 96 • Cumbria AS, Carlisle, corresp. with Sir James Graham • NL Scot., corresp. with Sir Thomas Cochrane • NL Wales, letters, memoranda, and orders to Horatio James • NL Wales, letters to Joseph Nias • NMM, letters to Lord Minto • NMM, letters to Sir Henry Codrington • priv. coll., letters to Henry Duncan • PRO, corresp. with Stratford Canning, FO352 • PRO, corresp. with Henry Pottinger, FO705 • U. Southampton L., letters to Lord Palmerston • Woburn Abbey, letters to Lord George William Russell

Likenesses attrib. M. Thomas, oils, 1882, repro. in HMS, *Mercury* • Drummond, portrait, exh. 1891; formerly in possession of W. Biddulph Parker • Severn, portrait, exh. 1891; formerly in possession of W. Biddulph Parker • portrait, repro. in Phillimore, *Life of Admiral Sir William Parker*

Wealth at death under £90,000: probate, 15 Jan 1867, *CGPLA Eng. & Wales*

Parker, William Kitchen (1823–1890), comparative anatomist and zoologist, was born on his parents' farm at Dogsthorpe, near Peterborough, Northamptonshire, on 23 June 1823. He was the second son of Thomas Parker, a yeoman farmer and Wesleyan of the old school, and his wife, Sarah Kitchen, who had literary tastes. Parker's parents lost six children in infancy. His early education at the parish school, to 1838, was undertaken in the intervals of work on the farm, but he was early devoted to reading, and acquired a skill as a draughtsman which never deserted him. As he grew older his enjoyment of literature increased. At fifteen he spent about nine months at the Peterborough grammar school, where he learned some Latin and Greek, and during this period he developed a religious fervour which remained with him.

After leaving school, in 1839, Parker was apprenticed for three years to a druggist at Stamford, under conditions which involved fifteen hours' work a day. A love of wild flowers had characterized his boyhood, and during the first years of his apprenticeship he collected, named, and preserved, during the small hours of the morning, some five hundred species of plants. While still a druggist's assistant he read physiology for the first time, and at the end of the apprenticeship, in 1842, he was articled to a surgeon at Market Overton in Rutland, with whom he remained for two years. His enthusiasm for anatomical study grew. He dissected every animal that he could obtain, and made a valuable series of notes and drawings, the greater part of which remains unpublished. In 1844 he left Market Overton for London and became resident assistant to a Mr Booth, a general practitioner in Little Queen Street, Westminster. In that year he entered Charing Cross Hospital as a student, and was later appointed assistant to R. B. Todd, physiologist at King's College. While a medical student he attended the lectures of Richard Owen at the Royal College of Surgeons. It was not, however, until he came under the influence of Todd's colleague William Bowman, the oculist and physiologist, that his exceptional capacity was recognized or that he received any real encouragement to pursue anatomical research.

In 1849 Parker became a licentiate of the Society of Apothecaries, and on 1 January 1850, at St John's, Westminster, he married Elizabeth (1825–1890), youngest daughter of Thomas Jeffrey, clerk to the Vauxhall Bridge Company; he commenced married life as a general practitioner in Pimlico. Parker lived in that neighbourhood until his retirement from practice in 1883, moving in succession from Tachbrook Street to Bessborough Street and Claverton Street. It was only in 1889 that he received a small civil pension. Although Parker cared greatly for biological research, he did not neglect his patients, and much of his best research was accomplished in the intervals of an arduous practice.

Parker's practice had not earned him enough to allow him to retire and devote himself to zoology. He was an acknowledged expert on the development of vertebrate forms of life. Large sums were spent by scientific societies to illustrate his papers with his lithograph prints. For this he received, through the Royal Society, many payments from the Government Grant Fund for the Encouragement of Scientific Research. In 1861 he was an unsuccessful candidate for the curatorship of the Hunterian Museum at the Royal College of Surgeons.

In 1873 Parker was made Hunterian professor of comparative anatomy at the Royal College of Surgeons, having first been admitted a member of the college after a formal examination. He delivered ten courses of lectures in the theatre of the college. But his utterances were more fervid than perspicuous. He was liable to long digressions and was at times incoherent. Of these courses, the last only, given in 1885, was published in book form as *On Mammalian Descent* (1885). It exhibits all Parker's defects as a lecturer. His eldest son said of it that it is 'unsatisfactory enough if one goes to it with a view of getting a succinct statement of our present knowledge as to the mutual relations and phylogeny of the mammalia'. 'Full of quaint fancies and suggestive illustrations' (Parker, 81) it is a collection of moral lessons interspersed with poetic effusions and outbursts of intense enthusiasm, rather than a scientific treatise.

Parker published ninety-nine scientific memoirs. The first thirty-six were confined to the Foraminifera, and were mostly written in conjunction with his friends professors T. Rupert Jones and H. B. Brady, and published between 1858 and 1869 in the *Annals and Magazine of Natural History*, the *Journal of the Geological Society*, and elsewhere. He was joint author with W. B. Carpenter and Rupert Jones of the *Introduction to the Study of the Foraminifera* (1862). Parker's *The Structure and Development of the Shoulder-Girdle and Sternum in the Vertebrata* (1868) included numerous drawings from original preparations made by Parker himself. His observations confirmed the view that the forelimb is attached to the trunk by an arch consisting of a coracoid or anterior, and a scapular or posterior element, at the meeting point of which the humerus is always articulated. It showed that Richard Owen's view that the forelimb consists of a number of outlying apophyses of one of the imaginary vertebral segments of the skull is untenable, even supposing that the skull be allowed to consist of a series of vertebrae.

Parker's most extensive work as an anatomist was that on the skull. His research was published over a period of twenty-five years (mostly in the *Transactions* of the Royal, Linnean, and Zoological societies) in a series of lengthy and copiously illustrated pages. His work on the skull was reduced into book form by G. T. Bettany as *The Morphology of the Skull* (1877) and gives the best conception of the breadth and nature of Parker's labours. His papers on the bird's skull are perhaps the best. Both his earliest and his last researches were on the avian skeleton. His knowledge of the habits, taxonomy, and general anatomy of birds was so extensive that he once spoke for four hours continuously on the lower jawbone of the raven without saying anything that was other than valuable.

Parker's works on the shoulder girdle and skull were largely derived from the work of Rathke, Huxley, and others. His results respecting the skull elaborated the principles laid down in Huxley's Croonian lecture delivered before the Royal Society in 1858. Parker recorded with immense labour, after protracted observations of representative members of each of the great groups of vertebrates, embryological data which confirmed Huxley's conclusions and refuted the vertebral theory of the skull, as elaborated by Owen. Parker's conclusion was that the cephalic scleromeres were not vertebrae. The old vertebral theory was mainly deduced from the detailed comparison of the skull of mammals with the segments of the backbone. But the resemblances between the two were shown by Parker to vanish among the lower vertebrata. Parker's published work occasionally closely paralleled that of his German fellow workers, but his work was original, although some of the more striking of his latterly discovered details in the cranial anatomy of the mammalia had been long anticipated by Hagenbach.

Parker was exceptionally industrious. His life was wholly absorbed in his research and he was content, for the most part, to record his investigations, and to leave his successors to test and generalize from them. Parker's detailed discoveries were based upon the dissection of embryos of all classes of vertebrated animals over a period of more than twenty years. His own fine illustrations of his dissections enhanced his works. Although he was a diffuse, obscure, and rambling writer, his works constitute a mine of carefully observed facts. Huxley, who was Parker's chief scientific friend and adviser, gave him an encouragement and guidance which helped to keep in check his discursive habits.

Parker was elected to the fellowship of the Royal Society in 1865, and in 1866 was awarded its gold medal. He later received the Baly medal of the Royal College of Physicians. In 1864 he was elected a fellow of the Zoological Society with exemption from fees, and the Linnean Society paid him the same compliment. In 1871 to 1873 he acted as president of the Royal Microscopical Society. In 1876 he was elected an honorary fellow of King's College, London. He was an honorary member of the Academy of Natural Sciences, Philadelphia, of the Imperial Society of Naturalists, Moscow, and of the Cambridge Philosophical Society.

Parker died suddenly on 3 July 1890, of heart failure, at 74 Llandaff Road, Cardiff, where he was staying with his second son. He was buried beside his wife at Wandsworth cemetery on 7 July. The grief caused by her death in March 1890 hastened his own. Seven children survived them—four sons and three daughters. Two of their sons followed in their father's footsteps and held professorships in biological science: Thomas Jeffery Parker, at the University of Otago, New Zealand, and William Newton Parker, at the University College of South Wales and Monmouthshire, Cardiff. ROGER HUTCHINS

Sources T. R. J. and J. E. H., *PRS*, 48 (1890), xv–xx • *BMJ* (12 July 1890), 116–17 • [J. E. Harting], 'Memoir of the late W. K. Parker, FRS', *The Zoologist*, 3rd ser., 14 (1890), 302–6 • T. J. Parker, *William Kitchen Parker* (1893) • *CGPLA Eng. & Wales* (1890)

Archives CUL, letters to Sir George Stokes • ICL, letters to Thomas Huxley • Wellcome L., letters to Henry Lee

Likenesses photograph, repro. in Parker, *William Kitchen Parker*, frontispiece

Wealth at death £2095 16*s*. 3*d*.: probate, 26 July 1890, *CGPLA Eng. & Wales*

Parkes, Sir Alan Sterling (1900–1990), reproductive biologist, was born on 10 September 1900 in Bank House, Castleton, near Rochdale, the younger son and third of four children of Ebenezer Thomas Parkes, bank manager, and his wife, Helena Louisa, daughter of Jonas Banks, brass-founder, of Willenhall. He was educated at Hulme grammar school in Oldham and Willaston School in Nantwich, Cheshire. After he failed his school certificate he went for a year to Harper Adams Agricultural College in

Newport, Shropshire. He was called up in 1918 and did a brief period of military service in the Manchester regiment.

After demobilization Parkes went in 1919 to Christ's College, Cambridge, which waived entrance examinations for servicemen. He studied agriculture and obtained a second-class pass degree in 1921. After this inauspicious start, the opportunity to read for a PhD degree (1923) in the University of Manchester on the mammalian sex ratio opened new doors into the world of biology and experimental research. Professor A. V. Hill, his internal examiner, invited him to University College, London, in 1923, where he became Sharpey scholar in the department of physiology and subsequently Beit memorial research fellow (1924–30) and Foulerton student of the Royal Society (1930–34). He gained his Cambridge DSc in 1931.

Parkes had a clear and analytical mind and exceptional ingenuity as an experimentalist, and was an indefatigable and versatile worker. He was appointed in 1932 to the staff of the Medical Research Council, National Institute for Medical Research, Mill Hill. There his adventures in biology ranged from experimental endocrinology to setting up international standards for hormone preparations on the initiative of the director, Sir Henry Dale. Distinguished in appearance, of average height, sturdy in build, and with a shock of white hair from an early age, he returned to Cambridge in 1961 as the first holder of the Mary Marshall and Arthur Walton chair of the physiology of reproduction (until 1967). He was a fellow of Christ's College from 1961 to 1969 and an honorary fellow from 1970.

Parkes's most influential research concerned the survival of cells, tissues, and whole animals at low temperature. He played a major part with Audrey Smith and Christopher Polge in developing the technique of storing and transporting at very low temperatures spermatozoa for artificial insemination, and in discovering that certain small rodents could survive cooling to low temperatures without showing apparent physiological or psychological impairment. Such work led to the formation of a new scientific society and the establishment of the journal *Cryobiology*, a name he and his colleagues coined 'to fill an etymological vacuum'.

Parkes's research into many aspects of reproductive physiology led to articles describing the patterns of reproduction in a number of wild and laboratory mammals, several of them written with his wife, Ruth, whom he married in 1933. She was the daughter of Edward Deanesly, surgeon, of Cheltenham, and they had one son and two daughters. He published freely on the effects of X-rays on reproductive functions, the hormonal control of secondary sexual characteristics of birds, and, with Hilda Bruce, the remarkable capacity of certain pheromones to block the course of pregnancy. After his retirement from Cambridge he became consultant to the world's first sea turtle farm on Grand Cayman Island (1973–80). Always retaining a very broad interest in biology, he was deeply involved in associated social and ethical questions, particularly those relating to human populations. His views about sensitive issues such as women's right to abortion, costly transplant surgery compared to simpler operations, and the quality of human populations are reflected in *Sex, Science and Society* (1966). Other important publications are his *The Internal Secretions of the Ovary* (1929) and *Patterns of Sexuality and Reproduction* (1976).

Parkes gave numerous distinguished named lectures in different countries, and held presidencies, chairmanships, and medals of various learned societies. He was editor and prime mover of new journals and monumental primary volumes in the science he sought to foster. His devastating incisiveness and dynamism took him at an early age to fellowship of the Royal Society (1933), and to a CBE (1956) and a knighthood (1968). His lively sense of humour is displayed in two light-hearted and highly entertaining autobiographies, *Off-Beat Biologist* (1985) and *Biologist at Large* (1988). One of the founders of modern reproductive biology, he died on 17 July 1990 in Shepreth, Cambridgeshire. He was survived by his wife.

R. B. HEAP, *rev.*

Sources A. S. Parkes, *Off-beat biologist* (1985) · A. S. Parkes, *Biologist at large* (1988) · R. W. J. Keay, *The Biologist*, 37 (1990) · personal knowledge (1996) · *The Independent* (25 July 1990) · *The Times* (20 July 1990) · *CGPLA Eng. & Wales* (1990)

Archives Wellcome L., corresp. and papers | CAC Cam., corresp. with A. V. Hill

Wealth at death £167,797: administration with will, 30 Nov 1990, *CGPLA Eng. & Wales*

Parkes, Alexander (1813–1890), chemist and inventor, was born on 29 December 1813, fourth son among the nine children of James Mears Parkes (1788–1871), a brass lock manufacturer, of Suffolk Street, Birmingham, and his wife, Kerenhappuch Childs (*d.* 1866). He was apprenticed to Messenger & Sons, brass-founders, Birmingham, and subsequently went to work for Elkington & Co. (from 1842 Elkington, Mason & Co.), in whose works he had charge of the casting department. His attention was soon directed to the new process of electroplating, then being introduced by his employers as an alternative to the old process of making Sheffield plate by cold rolling. In 1841 he secured his first patent (No. 8905) for the electrodeposition of works of art. He described himself in his earlier patents as an artist, but subsequently as chemist. The deposition of metals, especially silver, by electricity interested him almost to the end of his life, and on one occasion, when giving evidence in court, he was referred to as 'the Nestor of electrometallurgy'.

Among the ingenious processes which Parkes devised in connection with electrometallurgy was his method of electroplating flowers and fragile natural objects with gold, copper, or silver, which was included in a patent granted in 1843. On the occasion of a visit to the Elkington works at Birmingham, Prince Albert was presented with a spider's web which had been coated with silver.

Parkes was an exceedingly prolific inventor, filing sixty-six patents over a period of forty-six years. They relate mostly to metallurgy. He was one of the earliest to suggest the introduction of small quantities of phosphorus into metallic alloys for the purpose of giving them additional

Alexander Parkes (1813–1890), by unknown photographer, 1875

strength. In 1841 he patented a process for waterproofing fabrics by the use of a solution of indiarubber in carbon disulphide. By that time Elkingtons was in partnership with Sir Josiah Mason—founder of Mason College, now Birmingham University—and they worked the process for some years. The patent was eventually sold to Charles Macintosh who had for some years previously been manufacturing in Manchester waterproof fabric by a similar process of rubber impregnation, but using naphtha as the solvent.

From 1850 to 1853 Parkes was at Pembrey, south Wales, superintending the erection of copper smelting works for Elkington and Mason, and to this period belongs his method of using zinc for the desilverization of lead, which was first patented in 1850. It was perhaps one of the most important of his inventions. After some early technical problems had been overcome it was widely adopted, especially on the continent and in America, largely displacing the crystallization process invented by Hugh Lee Pattinson in 1833. It remains in use more than a century later although other lead purification processes, including electrolytic ones, have been developed.

In 1858 Parkes began to turn his attention to the manufacture of seamless metal tubes and cylinders for calico printing. He took out several patents but his tube drawing process was superseded by that of Reinhard Mannesmann in 1885.

Parkes was married; his wife, who survived him, was named Mary Ann. He had a son, Alex. Though in his own day Parkes's reputation rested largely on his considerable contributions to metallurgy, he was also notable as a founder of the modern plastics industry and as the inventor of the first man-made plastic. In the 1860s the burgeoning electrical industry was looking for a better insulator than natural products such as gutta-percha and Parkes believed that cellulose nitrate—explored by C. F. Schönbein in the 1840s as a high explosive—would fulfil this need if its high inflammability could be overcome. This he eventually achieved by plasticizing it with camphor. He demonstrated a variety of small articles made from 'parkesine', as he called his plastic. He was awarded prize medals when he exhibited them at the London Exhibition of 1862 and the Paris Exhibition of 1867. However, his various attempts at the commercial development of parkesine were less successful, despite the backing he received from George Spill & Co. His Parkesine Company (founded in association with Spill and others in 1866) was liquidated in 1868, a year before J. W. Hyatt in the United States patented celluloid, laying the foundation for the modern plastics industry. Its successor company, eventually called the British Xylonite Company Ltd, vigorously pursued the American manufacturers of celluloid in the courts on the basis of Parkes's patents, but to no avail. Nevertheless the Xylonite Company survived into the twentieth century; its factories were still manufacturing celluloid in the 1980s.

Parkes left Birmingham about 1881, and went to live in south London. He died at 2 Penrhyn Villas, 61 Rosendale Road, West Dulwich, on 29 June 1890.

R. B. Prosser, *rev.* Trevor I. Williams

Sources *Engineering* (25 July 1890), 111 • *Mining Journal* (26 July 1890) • F. Sproxton, 'The rise of the plastics industry', *Chemistry and Industry* (25 June 1938), 607–16 • F. Sproxton, 'Alexander Parkes', *Chemistry and Industry* (29 July 1944), 278–9 • ICI, *Landmarks of the plastics industry, 1862–1962* (1962) • *Birmingham Daily Post* (5 July 1890) • M. Kaufman, *The first century of plastics* (1963) • P. J. T. Morris and C. A. Russell, *Archives of the British chemical industry, 1750–1914: a handlist* (1988) • R. Friedel, 'Parkesine and celluloid: the failure and success of the first modern plastic', *History of Technology*, 4 (1979), 45–62 • d. cert. • *CGPLA Eng. & Wales* (1890)

Archives Plastics Historical Society, London, diaries

Likenesses photograph, 1875, Sci. Mus. [*see illus.*] • portrait, repro. in Kaufman, *First century of plastics*

Wealth at death £62 10s.: probate, 22 Aug 1890, *CGPLA Eng. & Wales*

Parkes, David (1763–1833), schoolmaster and antiquary, was the son of John Parkes, of an old family in reduced circumstances. He was born on 21 February 1763 in Cakemore, near Halesowen, Shropshire.

After being educated in the village school, he was apprenticed to a japanner at Birmingham, but soon set up a small school at Mucklow Hill, near the Quintain. He was afterwards made apprentice to William Dunn, master of the free school at Belbroughton, and after seven years obtained a situation as usher in a private school run by the Revd John Harrold, a dissenting minister, of West Bromwich. He meanwhile cultivated a natural love of art, and became proficient in French.

Parkes moved to Shrewsbury, where he established, in a house called the Franciscan Friars, a school for children from commercial families which obtained some repute and was subsequently transferred to larger premises in Castle Street. He married Elizabeth Morris, the eldest daughter of a tradesman and small freeholder of Hadnall, Shropshire, with whom he had three sons and three daughters.

Parkes spent his leisure in travelling about his native county, making innumerable drawings of antiquities and picturesque objects. He thus accumulated an important collection of books, prints, and antiquities connected with Shropshire. He was a frequent contributor to the *Gentleman's Magazine*, and was a prominent citizen at Shrewsbury. As church warden to the parish he improved relief to the poor and reduced the rates. Parkes died in Shrewsbury on 8 May 1833, saddened by the early deaths of two of his sons; his library and collections were sold in the following August. Of his sons, **James Parkes** (1793/4–1828) practised as a drawing master in Shrewsbury and assisted his father in his archaeological drawings. He died on 31 March 1828. Twelve etchings by him of views of monastic and other remains in Shropshire were published posthumously in 1829. The younger son, John Parkes (1804–1832), also practised as a drawing master.

L. H. Cust, *rev.* C. A. Creffield

Sources *GM*, 1st ser., 103/1 (1833), 567 • *GM*, 1st ser., 98/1 (1828), 376 • *GM*, 1st ser., 102/2 (1832), 578 • Redgrave, *Artists*, 2nd edn
Archives BL, monumental inscriptions, Add. MSS 21010–21016, 21180–21181 • Harvard U., Houghton L., 'Antiquities etc' (1 vol.) • Shrops. RRC, memoranda and notes of persons and events
Likenesses miniature, Shrewsbury Borough Museums

Edmund Alexander Parkes (1819–1876), by Barraud

Parkes, Edmund Alexander (1819–1876), physician and hygienist, was born in Bloxham, Oxfordshire, on 29 March 1819, one of the sons of William (1788–1840) and Frances *Parkes, *née* Byerley (1786–1842) [*see under* Byerley, Maria], of Warwick. His father was a textile manufacturer and his mother, the daughter of Thomas Byerley, a nephew and business partner of Josiah Wedgwood, was well known as an author of self-help books aimed at the housewife. The best known of these, entitled *Domestic Duties*, passed through several editions. Parkes spent most of his childhood in Warwick, where his family was active in reformist and Unitarian circles. He was educated at the Blue Coat School in Warwick and, later, at Christ's Hospital in London, after his parents moved to the capital. It was in London that the young Parkes first began to show an interest in medicine, assisting his uncle, Dr Anthony Todd Thompson, at his laboratory. This experience stood him in good stead for his studies as a medical student at University College, London, where he distinguished himself in anatomy, physiology, chemistry, and materia medica. He was awarded his MB degree in 1841. In 1840 he became a member of the Royal College of Surgeons.

After graduating Parkes decided to enter the Army Medical Service, and he was gazetted assistant surgeon to the 84th (York and Lancaster) regiment in 1842; the reason for his decision to join the army is unknown. After spending three years on tour with the army in Burma and India, he retired to take up a position as assistant physician at University College Hospital, London. But though the duration of his military service was brief, Parkes's firsthand experience of cholera, hepatitis, and dysentery had a profound and lasting impact on his career. Immediately after leaving the army he published several original pieces of research into the aetiology, pathology, and treatment of these diseases. The first was *The Dysentery and Hepatitis of India* (1846), in which he expressed the opinion that there was a link between the two disorders. The second was a version of his MD thesis, awarded by the University of London in 1846, and published as *Researches into the Pathology and Treatment of Asiatic or Algide Cholera* (1847). This study confirmed the recent tendency in medical circles to see cholera as primarily a disease of the blood, but it also suggested that respiratory problems caused by disordered blood were 'the proper and distinctive symptoms of the disease' (p. 4).

Parkes's purpose in elucidating the pathology of cholera was to improve diagnosis and to pave the way for future research, should cholera return to Britain. In the short time between the publication of his thesis and the next epidemic of cholera in 1849, Parkes had established himself as an authority on the disease. Indeed, the newly formed General Board of Health commissioned him to conduct an investigation into the first few cases of cholera as they appeared in London. Parkes's brief was to consider the question of the contagiousness of cholera—whether or not it was capable of being spread from person to person. Parkes had already expressed his opinion, on the basis of observations made in India, that this was not the case. The London epidemic only confirmed his view, since he was unable to find any connection at all between the cases he examined. Parkes was a believer in what he termed a 'modified' theory of contagion, which held that there was a specific agent causing cholera, but that certain atmospheric and other local conditions were necessary if it was to assume epidemic proportions. Parkes's emphasis on the local causes of cholera was very much in line with that of the General Board of Health, which stressed that cholera was primarily caused by filth and poor sanitation.

Parkes's professional standing was now such that he was promoted in 1849 to the post of first physician of University College Hospital and to the chair of clinical medicine at University College. He was barely thirty years of age. In the coming years he took on still more professional responsibilities, including the editorship of the *British and Foreign Medico-Chirurgical Review* between 1852 and 1855. He also found time to write a number of original articles on diseases of the heart and skin, and the effects of alcohol upon health. In 1855 he was chosen as Goulstonian lecturer to the Royal College of Physicians, and spoke on the subject of pyrexia. Little is known of his private life at this time, except that he was married on 1 August 1850 to Mary Jane (*d.* 1873), daughter of Thomas Chattock, a solicitor of Solihull.

Had it not been for the Crimean War of 1854–6, it is unlikely that Parkes would have returned to the field of military medicine, an area in which he was to make some of his most important contributions. However, public outrage at the poor medical arrangements made for British soldiers in the Crimea led to several initiatives to reform and expand hospital accommodation, including the shipment of an entire hospital designed and prefabricated by the engineer Sir Isambard Kingdom Brunel, and the War Office requested that Parkes superintend the formation and management of the hospital established (on Parkes's recommendation) at Renkioi, in the Dardanelles.

After the war Parkes became involved in an advisory capacity in the reform of military medicine and, in particular, in the creation of an army medical school. He was induced to leave his post at University College to take the chair of military hygiene at the school, which was established in 1860 at Fort Pitt, Chatham, and he continued to hold this post after the school moved to Netley, near Southampton, in 1863. Parkes was an immensely popular teacher, beloved by students and staff alike. A particularly full account of his influence was given by one of his more prominent pupils, William Jenner. He also remained an active researcher, and was regularly engaged in investigations into the suitability of military rations, clothing, and equipment. In addition to this work he pursued independent research into other subjects such as human excretion. His distinguished record in research earned him a fellowship of the Royal Society in 1861.

However, it is for his work as a hygienist that Parkes is most usually remembered and, in particular, for his *Manual of Practical Hygiene: Prepared Especially for Use in the Medical Service of the Army*, which was first published in 1864. The *Manual*, which went through eight editions (the last in 1891), was regarded by military medical services around the world as the definitive text on the subject. It was also used extensively by civilian sanitary officers, especially in British India and the colonies. The *Manual* made use of the latest scientific research to inform practical sanitation and clearly illustrates Parkes's 'contingent-contagionist' position on the causation of diseases such as cholera. It outlines measures to prevent the entrance of disease agents into the human body (directing attention to the contamination of food and water supplies, for example), while stressing the need for more general environmental controls, including the removal of filth and refuse. Like most of his contemporaries Parkes also believed that an individual's daily habits played an important role in either guarding against or predisposing to infection. In a phrase which exhibits something of his religious convictions, as well as his approach to hygiene, Parkes wrote of the need to 'combine the knowledge of the physician, the schoolmaster, and the priest', and to 'train the body, the intellect, and the moral soul in a perfect and balanced order' (p. xvi).

Although Parkes was an ardent advocate of 'state medicine', with its preventive legislation, and of utilizing the very latest techniques afforded by science, he had not abandoned older views of hygiene, which emphasized the importance of bodily equilibrium. His ardent belief in the need to regulate body, mind, and environment was expressed very clearly in his last two works, both of which were published shortly after his death. The first of these, a pamphlet written for the Society for the Promotion of Christian Knowledge, *On Personal Care of Health* (1876), was directed at the layperson and outlined the modes of life most appropriate to the preservation of health at different ages. The second work, *Public Health* (1876), dealt exclusively with 'state medicine', and is notable chiefly for its advocacy of sanitary reform in rural areas and a stricter interpretation of existing sanitary legislation.

The last months of Parkes's life were spent in a state of continual ill health, which was noted with concern in all the leading medical journals. Parkes finally succumbed to what was later revealed to be acute tuberculosis, though he had suffered persistently from respiratory problems and phlebitis since 1860. He died on 15 March 1876 at his home, Sydney Cottage, St Mary Extra, Bitterne, Southampton, aged only fifty-seven, and was buried on 21 March at Solihull beside his wife, who had died three years before. Friends who had gathered at his bedside said that Parkes accepted death peacefully and bravely, unshaken in his belief that there was an afterlife. He and his wife left no children, but his nephew, L. C. Parkes, followed in the footsteps of Parkes as a writer on hygiene and public health. After his death members of the Army Medical Service contributed generously to a memorial fund which established the Parkes memorial prize, awarded triennially for the best dissertation on military hygiene.

Although he had never received the knighthood that many of his contemporaries felt he deserved, Parkes's professional standing was indicated by his membership of the General Medical Council, the council of the Royal Society, and of the senate of the University of London.

Parkes was an uncommonly popular man, respected as a scientist and a practical hygienist, and for what the *British Medical Journal* called his 'wisdom, moderation and gentleness of character'. He was regarded by many contemporaries as the 'father of modern hygiene' and as a pivotal figure in the development of military medicine.

MARK HARRISON

Sources *Edinburgh Medical Journal*, 21 (1875–6), 1057–8 • *BMJ* (25 March 1876), 397–8 • *The Lancet* (25 March 1876), 480–82 • M. Pelling, *Cholera, fever and English medicine, 1825–1865* (1978) • D. E. Watkins, 'The English revolution in social medicine, 1889–1911', PhD diss., U. Lond., 1984 • *DNB* • M. Harrison, *Public health in British India: Anglo-Indian preventive medicine, 1859–1914* (1994) • *CGPLA Eng. & Wales* (1876) • m. cert.

Archives BL, corresp. with Florence Nightingale, Add. MS 45733 • Wellcome L., papers and corresp. with Thomas Longmore and Florence Nightingale

Likenesses E. Davis, marble bust, 1862, UCL • Barraud, photograph, Wellcome L. [*see illus.*] • Barraud and Jerraud, oils, Royal Army Medical College, Millbank, London • Beynon & Co., colour lithograph, Wellcome L. • marble bust; formerly in Hygiene Museum, London, 1882 • wood-engraving, NPG; repro. in *ILN* (1 April 1876)

Wealth at death £18,000: resworn probate, Sept 1876, *CGPLA Eng. & Wales*

Parkes, Edmund Samuel (1834–1887), banker, was born on 11 July 1834 in Devonport, Devon, the youngest son of Edward Parkes, and his wife, Elizabeth, eldest daughter of Robert and Elizabeth Tozer. On the death of his mother in 1836 Parkes was adopted by Captain James Considine, 22nd light dragoons and lieutenant-governor of Pendennis Castle, Falmouth, Cornwall, where Parkes spent his boyhood. He was educated at Hyde Side House, a boarding-school at Edmonton, Middlesex, where he was a prizewinner in 1847. He began work with a hop merchant, and then with a firm of London shipbrokers.

On 16 December 1852 Parkes was appointed as a teller with the important London and Westminster Bank, becoming assistant chief clerk in 1859. He resigned in 1862 to join the newly formed Alliance Bank of London and Liverpool Limited as manager at Southwark, subsequently becoming joint manager of that bank's head office. In 1867 the Alliance Bank, which rapidly emerged as one of England's largest joint-stock banks, was in difficulties, and in July the chairman reported to shareholders that Parkes had resigned to save the cost of his salary. While in London Parkes met and married Nancy Penrose Lawry (1831–1886), twin daughter of John Lawry, farmer, of Cornwall, and Mary Penrose. Parkes was recruited to the Bank of Australasia in 1867, and he, Nancy, six children, mother-in-law, and two sisters-in-law arrived in Melbourne on board the *Damascus* on 17 November 1867. A further four children were born in Australia.

The appointment of Parkes was not popular with the colonial staff of the bank, who resented the entry of an outsider. As chief inspector, the bank's second most

Edmund Samuel Parkes (1834–1887), by Johnstone, O'Shannessy & Co., *c*.1886

senior official, Parkes was brought into the bank to strengthen the colonial administration, and was seen as the man to introduce 'best practice' technique and procedure learned in British branch banking. Appointed initially for five years, his contract was renewed until, in 1876, he was appointed superintendent of the bank in Australasia. Following years of indecisive management by his predecessor, Parkes was seen as a 'severe martinet dealing with the whole service as a chess player does with his pieces' (Turner, 191). A strict disciplinarian with high standards, he was intelligent and capable, with great force of character. He was well educated and widely read, with a large private library, and his extensive knowledge of banking law and practice was applied unstintingly both in the bank and as an adviser on banking generally. He emerged as a major figure in Australian banking, playing a key role in the Associated Banks (Victoria). Yet he never formally held the chair of that organization, becoming acting chairman only, for five months in 1884–5.

Parkes's time as head of his bank coincided with the development of a boom in the Australian economy. His concern over the dangers implicit in the boom did not, however, inhibit cautious expansion; seventy-nine new branches were opened, deposits and advances more than doubled, and his bank's deposit position improved relative to other Australian banks, raising it, by the time of his death, to the second largest in Australia and one of the largest British-controlled overseas banks. A constant search for efficiency led him to introduce electricity to the bank's Melbourne head office. He also installed type-writers and appointed Australia's first woman bank employee.

In private life Parkes was genial and hospitable and a keen and skilful tennis player, who enjoyed riding a tricycle in the morning between six and seven when nobody was about. Outside the bank he was a member of the influential Melbourne Club and a staunch member and vestry man of Holy Trinity Church of England, Balaclava, Victoria. He was also a member of the council of the Melbourne Church of England grammar school, where four of his sons were educated.

In 1881 Parkes and his Melbourne manager were involved in a railway accident in which they came close to death. The death of his wife in 1886 was a severe blow, and he often expressed a wish to follow her to the afterlife. Ironically, his own death came less than a year later, when he was critically injured in a second railway accident. He died at his home, Irona, Carlisle Street, Balaclava, Victoria, on 11 May 1887, from complications following surgery to amputate his legs, and was buried on the 13th in the St Kilda cemetery, Victoria. T. J. HART

Sources Group Archive, Melbourne, Australia, Australia and New Zealand Banking Group Ltd • Australia, family records • *The Australasian Insurance and Banking Record* (14 May 1887) • Group Archives, London, National Westminster Bank • H. G. Turner, 'Fifty years' banking reminiscences', *The Australasian Insurance and Banking Record* (19 March 1900) • *The Australasian* (24 July 1886) • cemetery records for St Kilda cemetery, Victoria • probate with will, Victoria, Australia

Likenesses Johnstone, O'Shannessy & Co., photograph, *c.*1886, ANZ Group Archive, Melbourne, Australia [*see illus.*] • stained-glass window, Holy Trinity Church of England, Balaclava, Victoria, Australia

Wealth at death £15,870: probate, Australia

Parkes [*married name* Belloc], **Elizabeth Rayner** [Bessie] (**1829–1925**), campaigner for women's rights and journalist, was born in Birmingham on 16 June 1829, the daughter of Joseph *Parkes (1796–1865), a lawyer and politician, and of Elizabeth Rayner Priestley (1797?–1877), who was the granddaughter of Joseph *Priestley, the philosopher and scientist. The Unitarian background of both parents, her father's political connections, and the culture of radical dissent inherited from her mother's family meant that her upbringing was less circumscribed intellectually than might have been expected for a young woman of the affluent middle class of her day. From the age of eleven she attended a boarding-school run by the Unitarian Revd William Field at Leam House, near Warwick, where his daughter Lucy was the first of a number of highly intelligent women to make an impact on the impressionable Bessie, as she was universally known. In 1833, on her father's appointment as secretary to the commission on municipal corporations, the family moved to London, to the first of three London residences in Great George Street, Westminster.

Joseph Parkes was a dominant influence on his daughter. Family life was outwardly conventional, but an unspoken and irrevocable rift developed between her parents. Elizabeth Parkes's sympathies were with their son,

Elizabeth Rayner [Bessie] **Parkes** [Belloc] (**1829–1925**), by Constantin, early 1860s

Priestley, whose developing consumption led them in 1847 to take a house in Pelham Crescent, Hastings, on the Sussex coast, in the hope that sea air would prove beneficial. It was in Hastings that the Parkes family met the unorthodox family of Benjamin Leigh Smith and his five children. There Bessie formed one of the most significant friendships of her life, with Barbara Leigh Smith, later Bodichon, whom she was later to describe as 'the most powerful woman I have ever known' (M. Belloc Lowndes, *A Passing World*, 1897, 21). Their relationship was one of creative interaction. They were a source of mutual education; they read and travelled together, and when apart wrote to one another about what they read—an impressive catalogue of literature and philosophy from Shakespeare, Bacon, and John Stuart Mill through to the work of contemporaries such as Harriet Martineau, Tennyson, and George Sand. In 1848 they began to contribute articles and reviews to two local newspapers with which they had connections, the *Hastings and St. Leonards News* and the *Birmingham Journal*.

Another significant if less intense friendship was formed at the same time with Marian Evans, whom Bessie had met in Coventry through their mutual friend Sara

Hennell. The future George Eliot was beginning her career as a translator and journalist and Joseph Parkes had been the principal contributor to a fund established to publish her translation of J. F. Strauss's *Leben Jesu*. Marian Evans was a much sought-after guest in the Parkes's household, and Bessie memorably described the young George Eliot in retrospect in an article in the *Contemporary Review* (February 1894; repr. in *In a Walled Garden*, 1895). To Marian Evans, Bessie Parkes was one of a number of admiring younger women by whom she was to be surrounded for much of her life. It was nevertheless to her that she confided her decision to live with George Henry Lewes shortly before their departure for the continent in 1854 and it was to Bessie, more than a quarter of a century later, that she wrote one of her last letters.

In Barbara Leigh Smith, Bessie Parkes had a friend who was more of an equal, in age and in family background. They were bound by their creative ambitions: Barbara's to be a painter, and Bessie a poet. They were bound together, too, by a conviction that women's lives were unnecessarily restricted—legally, and in terms of the possibilities for education and employment.

> I believe that now, as in all ages of the world, the substantial equality of nature renders the two sexes of equal weight and value in the moral world, and that their action upon each other in every relation of life is far too complex to admit of any great difference between them in any given rank

Bessie wrote in the introduction to her *Essays on Women's Work* (1865). That principle was at the heart of a decade's vigorous campaigning for more equality of opportunity for women.

Bessie Parkes's *Remarks on the Education of Girls*, published by John Chapman in 1854, outlined the need to extend women's education by encouraging wider, uncensored reading, and by introducing women to the study of subjects such as social and political economy to enable them to participate meaningfully in public affairs. In 1855 Barbara Leigh Smith and Bessie Parkes formed a committee to submit a petition in support of a Married Women's Property Bill then before parliament. The petition failed but their appetite for action was whetted. In October 1856, while on a visit to Edinburgh, Bessie's attention was caught by the *Waverley Journal*, a fortnightly 'edited and published by ladies for the cultivation of the memorable, the progressive, and the beautiful', to which she contributed and also briefly edited. Eventually, in consultation with Barbara Leigh Smith and with Anna Jameson, who was a sympathetic supporter of the two younger women, it was decided to establish an entirely new periodical based in London, the *English Woman's Journal*, whose premises at 19 Langham Place were to become the focus of a number of interconnected enterprises devoted to widening education and employment opportunities for women. The *Journal* was established as a joint-stock company, with Barbara Leigh Smith as the major shareholder and Bessie and Matilda Mary (Max) Hays, actress, novelist, and translator, as co-editors. It sold for a shilling, and subscribers were entitled to the use of a reading- and meeting-room at Langham Place.

Bessie Parkes was the major single contributor to the *Journal* and her views effectively shaped its policies. George Eliot declined to contribute, pleading total commitment to her novel writing, but became a subscriber and adviser. 'The more business you can get into the journal—the more statements of philanthropic movements and social facts, and the less literature, the better', she counselled Bessie (*George Eliot Letters*, 2.379). Bessie was in complete agreement. The journal was never intended to compete with major literary organs of the day. 'Such an idea would have been perfectly hopeless and absurd, and indeed self-destructive', she wrote later (*Essays on Woman's Work*, 63). Of philanthropic movements and social facts there were plenty, particularly on women's employment and on women's education, where the combined influence of Jessie Boucherett, Maria Rye, Adelaide Anne Procter, Isa Craig, and Emily Faithfull, among others, filtered through. On the question of women's suffrage there was virtually nothing, Bessie believing it an impracticable aim.

Bessie was temporarily replaced as editor for six months in 1862 by Emily Davies but returned in 1863. Eventually the journal foundered, riven by internal debates and differences—personal, religious, and political—among its chief supporters. The entire management was transferred to Bessie in August 1864, but soon after the company was officially dissolved. It continued in spirit as the *Alexandra Magazine and English Woman's Journal* until 1865, when Jessie Boucherett refashioned it as the *Englishwoman's Review*, which lasted until 1903.

Bessie's career as a poet, meanwhile, had made a modest beginning. A volume of *Poems* was published by Chapman in 1852 and dedicated to Barbara Leigh Smith. G. H. Lewes reviewed it in *The Leader* (8 January 1853), and both he and George Eliot were encouraging. *Summer Rambles and other Poems* (1854) followed, also published by Chapman, and noticed by the *Westminster Review*. Notable among her subjects were female friendship, other women poets ('For Adelaide' [Procter], 'For Elizabeth Barrett Browning'), and the difficulties which beset women poets ('To an Author who Loved Truth more than Fame'). In *Summer Sketches* there was an attempt to tackle aspects of the 'woman question', in advance of Barrett Browning's *Aurora Leigh*. Other poems celebrated places familiar to her childhood, 'To Birmingham', 'Kenilworth', 'Stoneleigh', and 'Up the River', which began 'I am on the lilied Avon'. Still others introduced direct political messages, on subjects such as public health ('My Old House'), a colliery disaster, and the death of the prince consort ('The palace and the colliery'), and the poet's political mission ('Poets of 1848').

From the early 1860s Bessie had become increasingly attracted to the Roman Catholic faith, possibly encouraged by her friendship with Adelaide Procter, and influenced crucially by a meeting with Cardinal Manning in 1864. She was received into the faith later the same year. Her *Essays on Woman's Work*, many of them collected from the *Journal*—eloquent, informed, and passionate on the subject of more meaningful lives for middle-class women, and more tolerable and varied working conditions for working women—were published in 1865, dedicated to the memory of Anna Jameson. The *Essays* in effect brought to an end Bessie's public contribution to the women's movement, and her conversion to Catholicism heralded a dramatic shift in her life.

In the spring of 1867 Bessie and Barbara Bodichon, returning from a holiday in the south of France, took a chalet on the estate of Louise Swanton Belloc, a journalist, translator, and writer of children's books, and the widow of the French portrait painter Hilaire Belloc. An immediate rapport developed between Bessie and Madame Belloc, and, what was more unlikely, between Bessie and Louis Belloc (1830–1872), her semi-invalid son, who was a barrister. Bessie's ten-year engagement to her cousin Samuel Blackwell had recently ended and she had also refused a proposal of marriage from the blind Liberal MP Henry Fawcett, later the husband of Millicent Garrett. To the surprise of Madame Belloc and the consternation of her friends and family Bessie announced her intention of marrying Louis Belloc, which she did on 19 September 1867. This unlikely union proved to be brief and extremely happy. Two children were born in quick succession, Marie, later the novelist Marie Belloc *Lowndes, and Hilaire *Belloc, the essayist and poet.

The marriage engendered in Bessie, whose French was already fluent, a love affair with all things French which transmitted itself to both her children. According to Marie Belloc Lowndes, she described the five years of her marriage, and nine further years spent at La Celle St Cloud, the Belloc home 12 miles from Paris, as the happiest of her life. The five years of her marriage included the Franco-Prussian War of 1870–71, the dramatic evacuation and near devastation of La Celle St Cloud, and a flight to London, movingly described through Bessie's letters in Belloc Lowndes's memoir, *I, too, have Lived in Arcadia: a Record of Love and of Childhood* (1941). Louis Belloc died suddenly in 1872 from the effects of sunstroke. An inheritance from her uncle Josiah *Parkes, a successful engineer, in 1871 enabled Bessie to live comfortably in the early years of her widowhood, moving between London and France with her children. Then, in 1877, an investment unwisely entrusted to the son of a friend who had become her lodger failed, leaving her for the first time in her life in financially precarious circumstances. She withdrew from London to Slindon Cottage, the dower house of the Slindon estate in Sussex, brought to her notice by Lady Georgiana Fullerton, a move which delighted her son but appalled her daughter, who pronounced her mother unsuited to country life. She none the less made Slindon her English home for the rest of her life.

Widowhood brought with it the resumption of old friendships, in particular that with Barbara Bodichon, but not the resumption of an active public life. Bessie's ties with her French family were strengthened, particularly with her mother-in-law and two of her late husband's sisters. She continued to write intermittently. *La belle France* (1868) and *Peoples of the World* (1870) were commissioned in the first years of her marriage. *In a Walled Garden* (1895) and *A Passing World* (1897), two collections of reminiscences and historical sketches, contain fragments of autobiography and family history and record her interlocking circles of acquaintances and friends. Her last collection of poems, *In Fifty Years*, was published in 1904. In some ways the most remarkable of all her writings are her letters, preserved along with a manuscript diary and reminiscences at Girton College, Cambridge, and published selectively in *I, too, have Lived in Arcadia*. Her children embarked on successful literary careers and remained close to her. She died peacefully on 29 March 1925, aged ninety-five, and was buried in the churchyard of the Roman Catholic church at Slindon.

JOANNE SHATTOCK

Sources M. Belloc Lowndes, *I, too, have lived in Arcadia: a record of love and of childhood* (1941) • J. Rendall, '"A moral engine"? Feminism, liberalism and the *English Woman's Journal*', *Equal or different: women's politics, 1800–1914*, ed. J. Rendall (1987), 112–38 • J. Rendall, 'Friendship and politics: Barbara Leigh Smith Bodichon (1827–91) and Bessie Rayner Parkes (1829–1925)', *Sexuality and subordination: interdisciplinary studies of gender in the nineteenth century*, ed. S. Mendus and J. Rendall (1989), 136–70 • P. Hirsch, *Barbara Leigh Smith Bodichon: feminist, artist and rebel* (1998) • *The George Eliot letters*, ed. G. S. Haight, 9 vols. (1954–78) • G. S. Haight, *George Eliot: a biography* (1968) • P. Nestor, 'A new development in women's publishing: the *English Woman's Journal* and the *Victoria Magazine*', *Victorian Periodicals Review*, 15 (1982), 93–106 • R. Speaight, *The life of Hilaire Belloc* (1957) • M. Belloc Lowndes, *A passing world* (1948) • W. West, *The history, topography, and directory of Warwickshire* (1830)

Archives Girton Cam., corresp. and papers

Likenesses Constantin, photograph, 1860–64, Girton Cam. [*see illus.*] • photograph, repro. in Speaight, *Life of Hilaire Belloc*, facing p. 16 • portrait, repro. in Belloc Lowndes, *I, too, have lived in Arcadia*, frontispiece

Wealth at death £3688 6*s*. 7*d*.: probate, 30 July 1925, *CGPLA Eng. & Wales*

Parkes, (James Christopher) Ernest (1861–1899), colonial administrator and diplomatist, was born in Freetown, Sierra Leone, the son of Thomas Parkes (*b*. *c*.1812, *d*. 1884), and Jane Maitland (*d*. 1892). Thomas Parkes had been taken there as a boy from Guadeloupe by his father, a disbanded African army sergeant, and had then served for forty years in various government clerkships. Ernest Parkes probably attended the Wesleyan Boys' High School, Freetown, and he spent two years as a clerk in the queen's advocate's office before leaving for England in 1878 to study law. There his health broke down. He returned in 1881, causing a small sensation in this staunchly protestant colony by becoming a Roman Catholic, and was appointed clerk to the commandant of Sherbro, the coastal area to the south, annexed in 1861 to the Sierra Leone colony. He accompanied the commandant on missions inland and, unusually in a Sierra Leone Krio of his class, interested himself in the locality.

In 1884 Parkes returned to Freetown to the aborigines branch of the colonial secretariat to assist its head, Thomas George Lawson. Lawson, son of a chief in modern Togo, had been brought to Freetown as a boy, and for over thirty years, though styled only government interpreter, was the trusted diplomatic intermediary between the government and the neighbouring rulers. Over the years he had collected a mass of information about the surrounding country to the north which Parkes edited for him, adding archival information he had collected about the Sherbro. It was sent to the Colonial Office and published as a confidential print (PRO, CO 879/25). Although not always easy to follow, it remains the primary source for the orally transmitted history of the Sierra Leone hinterland.

In 1888 Lawson retired and Parkes became head of a separate aborigines department. In April 1893 he married Louise Bernice, daughter of George Briggars Williams, a prominent Freetown businessman; they had three children. Small in stature, intellectual in appearance with his high domed forehead, and indeed an occasionally published poet and author of a school geography of Sierra Leone, Parkes nevertheless participated actively in the numerous small frontier campaigns of the period, giving valuable advice on strategy—even in 1889 leading a small party of police and burning a town in the Limba country. Moreover he was able to take over Lawson's role as government intermediary with the ruling chiefs who gave him the trust they had given Lawson, even though he spoke no native language, relying on his long-experienced interpreter, Momadu Wakka. He became indispensable to the successive governors, not only for his diplomatic skills, but for drawing up substantial, well-informed policy memos which impressed the Colonial Office. In 1890 he was made head of a separate department of native affairs.

At this time the Sierra Leone colony consisted of an amorphously defined strip of coastline. In 1890, with the French advancing from inland, the Colonial Office at long last agreed to take over the adjoining, still independent, hinterland. A paramilitary frontier police force under British officers was recruited to keep order. Parkes, uneasy about giving this new, ill-disciplined force administrative powers, proposed it be reduced in size and civilian 'political agents' appointed, to supervise the chiefs' own administrations. The Colonial Office was interested—until it was realized that his proposed agents would be educated Africans. Then Parkes's proposal was turned down. When in 1896 a formal protectorate was proclaimed over the area it was administered by white district commissioners.

During this period, Samori Touré, a Mandinka warlord, built up an empire round the upper Niger, latterly in conflict with the French. He sometimes bought arms in Freetown and the government kept in touch with him through Parkes. But when in 1893 his forces ravaged what was believed to be the British sphere, the head of the frontier police, Captain Edward Lendy, backed up by the officer commanding the troops, Colonel A. B. Ellis, both eager to win renown in battle, demanded a punitive expedition be sent. Parkes advised against. Ellis retaliated by denouncing Parkes to the War Office as Samori's paid agent, and the expedition was sanctioned. Lendy was killed, Ellis died as a result of it. His charge that Parkes had taken money from Samori was investigated and found to be groundless.

Sir Frederic Cardew, appointed governor in 1894, found in Parkes an ideal associate. They travelled together over hundreds of miles on successive tours round the entire protectorate. But though he was rewarded with the title secretary for native affairs, Parkes's administrative and diplomatic duties were now bypassed by the district commissioners. They took control of their districts without reference to his department and were responsible for the events that led to the hut tax war of 1898. Meanwhile his health broke down and on 10 August 1899 at his home, Battery House, Freetown, he died of renal failure. He was buried in Freetown later that month. It is hard not to see his early death as good fortune: the white-ruled British Africa of the early twentieth century would have had no place for an African with Parkes's talents.

CHRISTOPHER FYFE

Sources references in the relevant governors' dispatches and enclosures, PRO, CO 267/365–451 • J. D. Hargreaves, 'The evolution of the native affairs department', *Sierra Leone Studies*, new ser., 3 (1954), 168–84 • C. Fyfe, *A history of Sierra Leone* (1962) • Freetown newspapers of the period, BL, Colindale • 'Particulars relating to the tribes and districts of Sierra Leone …', 1887, PRO, CO 879/25 • J. C. E. Parkes, *Geography of the colony of Sierra Leone and its hinterland* (1894) • *Les Missions Catholiques* [Lyon], 15 (1883), 147

Archives PRO, CO 267/365–451

Likenesses F. Cardew, photograph, repro. in *GJ*, 10 (1897), p. 389

Parkes, Frances (1786–1842). *See under* Byerley, Maria (1787–1843).

Parkes, Sir Harry Smith (1828–1885), diplomatist, was born on 24 February 1828 at Birchills Hall in the parish of Bloxwich, north of Walsall, Staffordshire, the youngest of the three children, and the only son, of Harry Parkes (*d.* 1833), a Wolverhampton bank clerk turned ironmaster, and his wife, Mary Ann (*d.* 1832), daughter of George Gitton, bookseller, postmaster, and printer of Bridgnorth. His grandfather John Parkes (*d.* 29 February 1796), reportedly the son of a farmer of Mucklow Hill, had been the Anglican curate in Halesowen, then in Shropshire. After their father's death the Parkes children became the wards of their uncle John Parkes, a retired naval officer, and subsequently of his wife, Mary Ann, in Birmingham. Parkes attended a boarding-school at Balsall Heath, and in May 1838 entered the King Edward VI School in Birmingham, being placed in the 'English' department, which offered a modern rather than a classical curriculum. In August that year his sisters left England for Macao to join their cousin Mary Gützlaff, wife of the missionary and explorer Karl Friedrich *Gützlaff (1803–1851), and in June 1841 Parkes, probably having left the Birmingham school by December 1840, also sailed for China. On arrival in Macao in October 1841 Parkes prepared for employment in the office of John Robert Morrison, secretary and first interpreter of Sir Henry Pottinger, British plenipotentiary and chief superintendent of trade in China. Parkes learned the rudiments of Chinese, and in May 1842 joined Morrison in Hong Kong.

Early career, 1842–1856 Pottinger was engaged in concluding the First Opium War, and when on 13 June 1842 he embarked on the expedition to Nanking (Nanjing), Parkes sailed as part of his suite. He participated in foraging and

Sir Harry Smith Parkes (1828–1885), by Sir Thomas Brock, 1887

in actions against junk traffic on the Yangtze (Yangzi) and, having become a favourite of Pottinger, witnessed the attack on Chinkiang (Zhenjiang) on 21 July in his company. He was present at the signing of the treaty of Nanking on 29 August.

Gützlaff was appointed civil magistrate in Chusan (Zhoushan) following the British occupation of the island, and from September 1842 until August 1843 Parkes acted as his clerk and continued the study of Chinese under his tuition. He passed the consular examination in Chinese in Hong Kong in August 1843. The treaty of Nanking opened five ports to British trade, each requiring consular personnel, and over the next twenty-two years Parkes took his turn in some capacity at most of them. In September 1843 he was appointed interpreter at Foochow (Fuzhou), but owing to a delay in opening the port served instead at the Canton (Guangzhou) consulate and as assistant to the Chinese secretary at Hong Kong. At Canton in January 1844 he assisted the treasurer of Hong Kong in the receipt and shipment of an instalment of $3 million of war indemnity. In June 1844 he was appointed interpreter at Amoy (Xiamen) and in March 1845 he and his consul, Rutherford Alcock, were together transferred to Foochow. Unrest was common at this port: Parkes was attacked by stone-throwing Manchu soldiers on 4 October 1845, and in June 1846 he helped Alcock to secure compensation of $46,163 from the Fukien (Fujian) authorities for British property plundered and destroyed during a riot.

In August 1846 Alcock and Parkes were again transferred in tandem to Shanghai, where Parkes was to be acting interpreter. His services here included the settlement of purchases of land and supervision of the building of a beacon at sea. In 1847 he began the study of Japanese. In March 1848 he accompanied the British vice-consul at Shanghai to Nanking to negotiate the punishment of the assailants of three British missionaries at Tsingpu (Qingpu), following which he was appointed interpreter at Shanghai on 9 April 1848 and received an expression of approval of his conduct from Lord Palmerston. After a period of leave in Europe in 1850–51 Parkes took up the post of interpreter at Amoy, to which he had been appointed in July 1849. He was involved in acquiring a site for British commercial purposes at this port, and visited Formosa (Taiwan). On 21 November 1851 he was appointed interpreter at Canton, proceeding there in February 1852. For several months from March 1853 Parkes acted as consul in Canton during the absence of Sir John Bowring, and his resolute response to a diplomatic incident provoked by the erection of a French flagstaff in the public gardens in March 1853 won him the approbation of Lord Clarendon. In August 1853 he was placed temporarily in charge of the Canton vice-consulate.

Parkes achieved the rank of consul, posted to Amoy, with a commission dated 10 August 1854. In 1855 he accompanied Bowring to Siam as joint secretary to a mission to conclude a commercial treaty with that kingdom, signed in Bangkok on 18 April. Parkes returned to England with the treaty for ratification, delivering it on 1 July, and was received by the queen on 9 July. For the remainder of the year he assisted the Foreign Office on Chinese and Siamese business, and made tours in England and Scotland. In November 1855 he met Fanny Hannah Plumer (1831/2–1879), the fifth daughter of Thomas Hall Plumer, son of Sir Thomas *Plumer (1753–1824), master of the rolls. They were married at St Lawrence's Church, Whitchurch, Middlesex, on 1 January 1856, and were to have two sons and five daughters. On 9 January the couple left England. Parkes exchanged the ratified Siamese treaty in Bangkok on 5 April 1856, negotiated a supplementary agreement there, signed on 13 May, and in June arrived in Canton where he was to act as consul during Alcock's absence.

War and government in Canton, 1856–1859 On 8 October 1856 Chinese officials boarded the lorcha *Arrow* in Canton and arrested the Chinese members of its crew. The *Arrow* had until a few days before been registered at Hong Kong, and remained entitled to fly the red ensign. Parkes accordingly considered the Chinese action to be a violation of treaty rights, and sent dispatches to Bowring, now governor of Hong Kong, portraying the episode as an outrageous insult to the British flag. The demands for public redress which he made on the governor-general of Kwangtung (Guangdong), Ye Ming-ch'en, could not be acceded to without loss of face, and Parkes rejected all lesser propitiation. Bowring saw an opportunity to enforce the British right to enter the city of Canton, established under the treaty of Nanking but hitherto denied, and the deliberate escalation of the *Arrow* incident into war, in which Parkes took a major part, had the object of forcing the removal of impediments to trade and diplomatic intercourse in Canton. Minor reprisals having secured no capitulation from Ye, on 29 October the Royal Navy breached the city wall, and Parkes accompanied Rear-Admiral Sir Michael Seymour in entering the governor-general's yamen. The British were too few permanently to occupy Canton, but they retained ships on the river and artillery positions overlooking the city. In the following weeks, while hostilities continued around him, Parkes remained at the consulate to draft dispatches, correspond with the Chinese authorities, and issue proclamations to the population of Canton. On 16 December 1856 the Chinese set fire to the European settlement outside the city, and Parkes retreated to Hong Kong, where he spent almost a year of relative inactivity attending to consular business. Defeat in the House of Commons on Cobden's motion of censure on the *Arrow* affair led Palmerston to call a general election, and Parkes was severely criticized in parliamentary debate: on 26 February 1857 the earl of Malmesbury declared in the Lords that 'If it were not for the serious consequences involved in this matter, I do not know that I have ever met anything which I should consider more grotesque than the conduct of Consul Parkes throughout these transactions' (*Hansard* 3, vol. 144, 1857, p. 1350, col. 2).

In November 1857 British reinforcements, delayed on their way to China by the Indian mutiny, assembled in Hong Kong. The earl of Elgin had been appointed high commissioner and plenipotentiary in China, and the British acted in co-operation with the French, who sought to avenge the killing of a missionary. Parkes was attached to Seymour's staff, and on 12 December was one of the party which delivered an ultimatum to Ye's officials. He was then engaged in distributing notices in Chinese throughout the suburbs of Canton. No satisfactory response to the ultimatum being received, the bombardment of Canton was begun on 28 December, and the walls secured on 29 December. On 5 January 1858, when the city was entered in numbers, Parkes led a party of sailors which captured Ye. On 9 January the Chinese governor of Canton, Po-kuei, was nominally reinstated, with the actual civil government of the city being assumed by a European commission. Parkes was one of its three members, and, as the only Chinese speaker, became its effective leader. The commission's principal duties were 'to watch the temper of the Chinese authorities and people' (command paper 2571, 1859, 160) and to maintain order. It established a court, administered a police force, and on 10 February reopened the port. Throughout 1858, and despite the signing of the treaty of Tientsin (Tianjin) on 26 June, the Chinese authorities in Kwangtung remained actively hostile to the allies in Canton, mobilizing militia and placing a bounty of $30,000 on Parkes's head. On expeditions to Shektsing in January 1859, and to the Fayuen district and the West River in February, Parkes assisted allied military columns in demonstrations of strength intended to pacify the Canton hinterland. During 1859 he negotiated the lease on a quit-rent of land by the Shameen forts on which to rebuild a British mercantile settlement outside Canton, and he improved the conditions of the coolie trade by establishing an 'emigration house', opened in November, for Chinese labourers seeking work in the British West Indies. Parkes was appointed CB on 6 December 1859.

The Peking (Beijing) campaign, 1860 The violent repulse at Taku (Dagu) on 25 June 1859 of the British and French plenipotentiaries in their attempt to carry the ratified Tientsin treaty to Peking caused a renewal of large-scale hostilities between the allies and China. On 21 March 1860 Parkes concluded the lease from the local Chinese authorities of the Kowloon peninsula, opposite Hong Kong island, for use as a depot by the arriving British force, and a few days later he withdrew temporarily from the Canton commission. On 27 March he sailed for Shanghai where he advised Frederick Bruce, the British plenipotentiary, and on 20 April he acted as interpreter during the unopposed occupation of Chusan. He then returned to Canton, where he extended the system of military and naval patrols in the hinterland. On 22 June he met Elgin, the British ambassador extraordinary, in Hong Kong, and on 6 July received a request to join him in the Gulf of Pechihli. He sailed on 21 July, and was appointed Elgin's joint Chinese secretary, with Thomas Wade as colleague.

On 1 August 1860, attached to General Sir James Hope Grant's suite, Parkes waded ashore near Pehtang (Beitang), was sent ahead into the town, and took possession of the evacuated fort. He engaged in reconnaissance in the advance to the Taku forts, delivered a letter from Elgin to the viceroy Hang-fuh on 18 August, and, after the successful assault on the main north fort in the early morning of 21 August, assisted in negotiating the surrender of the remaining Chinese positions. He arrived in Tientsin on 24 August, arranged for the provisioning of the allied forces, and conducted interviews with the Chinese imperial commissioners. Following the discovery during an interview conducted by Parkes and Wade on 6 September that the commissioners at Tientsin did not, as believed, hold plenipotentiary powers from the emperor, the allied armies advanced towards Tungchow (Tongzhou). Parkes went ahead of the force and parleyed with the Chinese authorities at Tungchow on 14 September and again on 17 September, obtaining an agreement that the armies should advance to a position about 5 miles from the city. On 18 September he left Tungchow to mark out the position of the intended British encampment, near Changkia-wan. Observing a large Chinese military force assembling at the site, Parkes returned to Tungchow to remonstrate with the commissioners, and, receiving a hostile response, attempted to return with his party to the British headquarters. Before they could clear the Chinese lines a general engagement began, and Parkes and his companions, although protected by a flag of truce, were made prisoners by enemy cavalry. After encountering the Manchu general Senggerinchin (Seng-ko-lin-ch'in), Parkes was conveyed with Elgin's private secretary Henry Brougham Loch, a Sikh sowar named Nal Singh, and two French soldiers to Peking. There Parkes was brought before the board of punishments, put in a common prison in heavy chains, and subjected to numerous interrogations, initially under duress. On 29 September, at the direction of Prince Gong (I-hsin), Parkes and Loch were removed to less uncomfortable quarters in a temple, where they were pressed into intervening in negotiations with the British commanders. Elgin later commended Parkes's 'consistent refusal to purchase his own safety by making any pledges, or even by addressing to me any representations, which might have embarrassed me in the discharge of my duty' (command paper 2754, 1861, 226). On 8 October Parkes, Loch, and six others were released, shortly before the delivery of an order from the emperor for their execution. Other prisoners taken under flag of truce on 18 September died in captivity, and in retaliation for this the emperor's summer palace, Yuen-ming-yuen, was destroyed. On 13 October 1860 Parkes returned to Peking to conduct the surrender of the Anting (Anding) gate to Sir Robert Napier. He left the city on 9 November and sailed from Taku for Shanghai on 28 November.

Britain and China, 1861–1865 Parkes returned to his commission at Canton in January 1861. From 16 to 19 January he was occupied in Hong Kong arranging the cession of the Kowloon peninsula to the crown. The treaty of Tientsin opened three ports on the Yangtze to trade, and between February and April 1861 Parkes accompanied Vice-Admiral Sir James Hope in an expedition on the river, establishing consulates at Chinkiang, Kiukiang (Jiujiang), and Hankow (Hankou), and attempting to reach an understanding with the Tai'ping rebels at Nanking. Parkes declared the Yangtze open between Chinkiang and Hankow by a notification dated 9 March. In April he visited Peking and in June travelled to Nanking to treat further with Tai'ping leaders. On 21 October 1861 the allies returned Canton to Chinese authority, and Parkes's duties as a commissioner terminated. In November he travelled to Shanghai and in December met Tai'ping leaders again, at Ningpo (Ningbo). In January 1862 he departed for England, where his fortitude in captivity had made him famous. On 19 May 1862 he was made a KCB. He took a house in Hampstead, travelled in Scotland and Switzerland, joined the 3rd Middlesex volunteers, and was widely lionized. He left England in January 1864 and on 3 March arrived in Shanghai to take up the consulship to which he had been appointed on 21 December 1858. During his tenure he put the Shanghai municipal council's understanding of its own jurisdiction on a proper footing, and took a vigorous interest in the 'camp of instruction' established at Fenghuang-shan to train the irregular military forces previously commanded by Charles George Gordon. In May 1865, during a trip to the Yangtze ports, Parkes received notification, in a letter from Lord John Russell dated 27 March, of his appointment as envoy and minister to Japan, in succession to Alcock. He thereby advanced from the consular to the diplomatic service.

Minister to Japan, 1865–1883 When Parkes landed at Nagasaki on 27 June 1865 he entered the political affairs of a country undergoing rapid change. The Tokugawa shogunate, which had long held the executive functions of government, was being undermined by the rising strength of feudal clans supportive of the emperor's court at Kyoto, making it unclear to foreign diplomats where effective power lay. Parkes arrived at the British legation in Yokohama on 8 July. In October 1865, pursuing instructions received from Lord John Russell, he proposed to other Western representatives that they partially remit the indemnity payable by Japan on account of fighting between the Choshu clan and western forces at Shimonoseki in 1864; in return, Osaka and Hyogo were to be opened promptly, a regularized import tariff instituted, and the treaties made in 1858 ratified by the emperor himself. On 4 November 1865 a naval squadron carrying Parkes and the French, Dutch, and United States representatives arrived off Osaka, where the shogun was temporarily resident, to negotiate these changes. The proximity of Osaka to Kyoto prevented the shogun's government, or *bakufu*, from disguising its weakness in relation to the imperial court, and Parkes's resolve, backed by the warships, duly enforced the emperor's ratification, received on 24 November. Imperial sanction of the treaties increased the security of the privileges obtained by them, regardless of shifts of power between clans and shogun, and Parkes's leading role in the expedition established his primacy among foreign representatives in Japan.

During 1866, as the strength of the rebellious clans of Satsuma and Choshu waxed, the likelihood of civil war in Japan grew more apparent. Parkes initially regarded the clan leaders as illiberal, and was concerned that their interest in trade might be limited to the procurement of contraband armaments. However, the British came to recognize that the clans' hostility to the treaties of 1858 had primarily been due to the shogun's official monopoly of foreign commerce, and the tariff convention with the *bakufu* negotiated under Parkes's leadership and signed on 25 June 1866 removed the restrictions on clansmen trading at the opened ports. Parkes was under instructions from London to retain neutrality, but British merchants such as Thomas Glover in Nagasaki had already embarked on business ventures which purposefully strengthened the clans, and Parkes's own consular subordinates Ernest Mason Satow and Algernon Bertram Mitford, substantially on their own initiative, were in the process of establishing the close and sympathetic ties with the clan leadership which greatly benefited British diplomacy after the Meiji restoration. In July and August 1866 Parkes travelled to Satsuma and Uwajima to meet clan leaders, but he also moved the British legation from Yokohama to the shogun's capital, Yedo, in November, and, visiting the recently appointed shogun Keiki in Osaka in April 1867, observed growing cordiality from the *bakufu*. In July 1867 he visited the western coast of Japan by ship to reconnoitre possible further ports for trade and to investigate the political allegiances of the clans.

On 3 January 1868 the new emperor Mutsuhito abolished the shogunate by decree, instituting a government dominated by five clans. Civil warfare ensued. On 4 February 1868, when a group of imperialist Bizen clansmen fired on foreigners in Kobe, Parkes personally led a party in pursuit, and in concert with other envoys seized Japanese shipping in Hyogo harbour as a guarantee of reparation. Parkes arranged a meeting between the envoys and a deputation from the emperor, held in Hyogo on 8 February, at which the continuing validity of the commercial treaties was confirmed. A notice of neutrality and non-intervention in the hostilities, issued by Parkes to British subjects on 18 February, indirectly favoured the imperialists. Swift imperial agreement to demands for reparation for the murder of French sailors at Sakai in March 1868 contributed further to Parkes's confidence in the new government, and he assented to an audience with the emperor. On 23 March, as he processed through Kyoto to the imperial palace, his party was attacked by renegade swordsmen and ten of the British escort and two Japanese officials were wounded. On 26 March the audience took place, the imperial government having offered compensation and apologies for the outrage. On 22 May 1868 Parkes formally presented his credentials to the emperor in Osaka.

Parkes's chief work following the Meiji restoration was to assist the new government in fostering industry and commerce. Currency irregularities hampered trade; Parkes encouraged the purchase by the government of coining machinery from Hong Kong, and the order of 4 August 1868 setting a fixed rate of exchange between the ichibu and the Mexican dollar reflected his influence. On 9 February 1869 Parkes withdrew his neutrality proclamation, thereby recognizing the new regime's hegemony, and when amicable national relations were cemented by the duke of Edinburgh's visit to Japan in August and September, it fell to Parkes to negotiate the many delicate questions of etiquette. Parkes promoted the use of British capital and personnel in the building of railways, lighthouses, and telegraphs, and when in 1870 the government mint was opened in Osaka under the management of a Briton, Lady Parkes struck the first coin.

On 22 May 1871 Parkes left Japan for leave in Britain, travelling via the United States. He settled with his family in Sussex and later in London and Chislehurst, being fully engaged in Foreign Office work. On 9 February 1872 he met, with Lord Granville, a deputation from the Evangelical Alliance concerned about Japanese intolerance of Christianity, and in April 1872 gave evidence to a committee of the House of Commons on the constitution of the diplomatic and consular services. On 14 June 1872 his eldest daughter, Ellen Mary, died. The Iwakura mission of senior members of the Meiji government, sent to the United States and Europe to study Western systems of government, commercial institutions, and education, arrived in Britain on 17 August 1872. Parkes escorted its senior members on several occasions in the succeeding four months, including a visit to the queen on 5 November and an interview with Granville on 27 November. On 16 January 1873 Parkes departed for Japan, arriving there on 26 March.

After the Iwakura mission, as Japan became less reliant on the advice of foreign diplomats to determine its domestic policy and more active in its international relations, Parkes's influence in the country waned. His often testy and haughty demeanour, a source of embarrassment to his junior colleagues, helped to make Parkes's advice unpalatable to Japanese leaders. He obstructed but could not avert Japanese assertions of sovereignty in matters such as the movement of foreigners in the interior, game laws, and the administration of the Japanese post office, and he could not dissuade the Japanese government from its policy of replacing British technical advisers with native employees. The arrest and beating by Japanese police of a British constable of Parkes's escort on 6 May 1874 sparked a wrangle over reparations and was considered symptomatic of official hostility. In October and November 1874 Anglo-Japanese relations warmed when Parkes's co-operation with Wade, now British minister in Peking, enabled Japan to exact humiliating concessions from China to avoid hostilities in Formosa, and a long-standing source of friction was removed when the British garrison in Yokohama was withdrawn in 1875. However, the abiding discontent of the Japanese lay with the treaties of 1858, particularly respecting tariff autonomy and extraterritoriality, and Parkes tenaciously resisted erosions of British privilege. In 1878 and 1879, when the boundaries of Japanese and foreign jurisdictions were tested by disagreements over quarantine law, he refused to allow the application of Japanese regulations to British ships. The failure of British crown law officers fully to sustain his position reflected a temporary decline in the confidence Parkes enjoyed in official circles, and there were newspaper accusations that his intransigence had contributed to cholera mortality.

Parkes left Japan on 11 October 1879 after learning that his wife was gravely ill in London, and arrived there on 16 November. Lady Parkes had died four days earlier. His own health was poor, and he remained in Britain until December 1881, residing variously at Torquay, Sevenoaks, and Chertsey, but passing winter months in London advising the Foreign Office on Japanese, Korean, and Chinese policy. In February 1881 the Japanese minister in London presented proposals for a revision, amounting effectively to the replacement, of the 1858 treaty, and Parkes successfully advocated their rejection. Radical opinion in Britain was sympathetic to Japan, and in June 1881 Parkes exchanged ill-tempered letters in *The Times* with the Liberal MP Sir Edward Reed. Parkes had restored his standing with his Foreign Office superiors, and on 26 November 1881 was appointed GCMG. He returned to Yokohama on 27 January 1882, and an address of welcome signed by 400 foreign residents there expressed fulsome endorsement of his services. Until its conclusion on 27 July 1882 Parkes participated in the Tokyo conference on treaty revision. He led the European opposition to Japanese moves to overthrow extraterritoriality, and on this issue, and on the question of free foreign trade in the interior, the conference foundered.

From mid-1882 Parkes concentrated much of his attention on Chinese and Korean affairs. Attempts by the Western powers and Japan to bring Korea within the sphere of international relations had been under way since the 1870s. Parkes had no large expectations of the prospects of Korean trade, but recognized the strategic importance of the country with regard to Russian expansion in the Far East. His 1875 recommendation that Port Hamilton (in the Nan-how islands, south of Korea) be annexed as a British naval station had been rejected by the Foreign Office, and his dispatch in 1878 of his second secretary Ernest Satow on an exploratory mission to Quelpart and Pusan had also been viewed coolly in London. Parkes nevertheless remained vigilant on Korean matters and sharply criticized the disadvantageous treaty signed by Admiral George Ommanney Willes in the summer of 1882. On 1 July 1883 Parkes was appointed envoy-extraordinary and minister plenipotentiary to the emperor of China, and he left Japan at the end of August.

Minister to China and Korea, 1883–1885 Parkes arrived in Shanghai on 6 September 1883 to an enthusiastic welcome from the foreign community, and departed for the legation in Peking on 14 September. He was immediately engaged in making an acceptable treaty with Korea, the British government having decided not to ratify the one negotiated by Willes. Parkes arrived in Seoul on 27 October and in co-operation with the German diplomat Edward Zappe drafted a satisfactory treaty, signed on 26 November. Three Korean ports were opened to commerce, and trade regulations and a tariff of duties were established. On 27 February 1884 Parkes was additionally appointed envoy-extraordinary and minister plenipotentiary to the king of Korea, and returned there for the exchange of ratifications on 28 April.

Parkes's tenure of the Peking legation was preoccupied by business arising from the settlement of claims to compensation for damage to British property at the Shameen site in Canton during a riot in September 1883, and by the undeclared war between China and France over Annam. In September 1883 Parkes unofficially broached the terms of a possible settlement of the Annam question with Li Hongzhang, but his main involvement was limited to ameliorating the effects of the conflict on British interests. He liaised with the Royal Navy over the question of protection of the treaty ports, reminded the Chinese government of its obligation to protect foreign civilians, and reported to the Foreign Office on the instances of popular anti-foreign aggression which did occur. On 15 September 1884 a proclamation was issued by Chinese authorities in Canton calling on Chinese in Singapore, Penang, and elsewhere to destroy French vessels and poison French subjects. Parkes regarded this not only as offensive on legal and humanitarian grounds but also as an affront to British sovereignty at those places, and he successfully pressed the government in Peking for an imperial decree disapproving the proclamation and censuring its authors. This duly appeared in the *Peking Gazette* of 30 September.

Parkes died at the British legation in Peking on 22 March 1885, of a remittent typhoid fever exacerbated by fatigue. His secretary of legation, Nicholas O'Conor, wrote that 'in fact he died from the unceasing strain put on a brain requiring long rest and repose' (Lane-Poole, 2.428). His remains received abundant tribute in China, and on 26 June were interred alongside those of his wife in a vault adjoining St Lawrence's Church, Whitchurch, Middlesex. A bust by Thomas Brock was placed in the crypt of St Paul's Cathedral in 1887, and a statue on the foreshore of the Bund in Shanghai was unveiled by the duke of Connaught on 8 April 1890. Parkes had possessed a short, lean frame, with a large head, thinning fair hair descending to full sideburns, and bright blue eyes. His quick gait and alert features were tokens of a brusque and irritable temperament. He was a zealot for official work and could barely endure passive recreation. He was never an orientalist or scholar, publishing only a handful of unofficial articles, but he encouraged such work in his subordinates and served terms as president of the north China branch of the Royal Asiatic Society and of the Asiatic Society of Japan. His deeply felt Anglican protestantism reflected an ardent nationalism; in 1843, aged fifteen, he had thought it a 'great disgrace upon us' that a Roman Catholic chapel had preceded a protestant church at Hong Kong. His diplomacy was part and parcel of his personality, and the irascibility which could give him great force in argument also made him insensitive to reasonable disagreement. He was a hero to the British traders whose privileges he defended (in the 1860s a merchant vessel was named after him), but he came to be damagingly disliked by the governments to which he was accredited. A two-volume biography, published in 1894 with financial subsidy from his family, was hagiographic. Twentieth-century scholarship treated Parkes more severely, judging that his conviction that the peoples of China and Japan must themselves benefit from closer intercourse with the West neither justified the belligerence, nor redeemed the arrogance, of his dealings with their leaders. JOHN WELLS

Sources S. Lane-Poole and F. V. Dickins, *The life of Sir Harry Parkes K.C.B., G.C.M.G. sometime her majesty's minister to China & Japan*, 2 vols. (1894) • G. Daniels, *Sir Harry Parkes: British representative in Japan, 1865–83* (1996) • *Papers relating to the proceedings of her majesty's naval forces at Canton* (1857) [command paper 2163, 1857, XII] • *Correspondence respecting affairs in China, 1859–60* (1861) [command paper 2754, 1861, LXVI] • *Correspondence relative to the earl of Elgin's special missions to China and Japan, 1857–1859* (1859) [command paper 2571, 1859, XXXIII] • G. Fox, *Britain and Japan, 1858–1883* (1969) • 'Memorandum respectfully submitted to the Right Hon[oura]ble Viscount Palmerston…by Mr H. S. Parkes', 1851, CUL, Parkes MSS, 32/1 • 'Early services of Sir Harry Parkes', in or after 1854, CUL, Parkes MSS, 32/2 • letters and dispatches concerning Parkes's services, 1852–61, CUL, Parkes MSS, 27 • E. Satow, *A diplomat in Japan* (1921) • J. Y. Wong, *Deadly dreams: opium, imperialism, and the Arrow War (1856–1860) in China* (1998) • O. Checkland, *Britain's encounter with Meiji Japan, 1868–1912* (1989) • *FO List* (1864–5) • *Further papers relating to the proceedings of her majesty's naval forces at Canton* (1857) [command paper 2206, 1857, XLIII] • *Correspondence respecting the state of affairs in China* (1885) [command paper C.4245, 1884–5, LXXXVII] • J. K. Fairbank, ed., *Late Ch'ing, 1800–1911*, pt 1 (1978), vol. 10 of *The Cambridge history of China*, ed. D. Twitchett and J. K. Fairbank • J. K. Fairbank and Kwang-ching Liu, eds., *Late Ch'ing, 1800–1911*, pt 2

(1980), vol. 11 of *The Cambridge history of China*, ed. D. Twitchett and J. K. Fairbank · *Papers relating to the rebellion in China, and trade in the Yang-tze-kiang river* (1862) [command paper 2976, 1862, LXIII] · *Correspondence respecting the opening of the Yang-tze-kiang river to foreign trade* (1861) [command paper 2840, 1861, LXVI] · *Correspondence respecting emigration from Canton* (1860) [command paper 2714, 1860, LXIX] · 'Sir Harry Parkes' services in Japan', 1881, CUL, Parkes MSS, 32/13 · memorials, St Lawrence's Church, Whitchurch, Little Stanmore, Middlesex · D. Moore Kenrick, 'A century of Western studies of Japan: the first hundred years of the Asiatic Society of Japan, 1872–1972', *Transactions of the Asiatic Society of Japan*, 3rd ser., 14 (1978) · H. Cortazzi, 'The pestilently active minister: Dr. Willis's comments on Sir Harry Parkes', *Monumenta Nipponica*, 39/2 (summer 1984), 147–61 · A. McKay, *Scottish Samurai: Thomas Blake Glover* (1993) · *CGPLA Eng. & Wales* (1885)

Archives BL, corresp. and MSS, Add. MSS 39109–39110, 39116, 52400, 52402, 52414, 58222 · CUL, corresp. and MSS · RGS, articles and corresp., Jnl Mss Central Asia 1854, Jnl Mss S.E. Asia 1856, RGS Corr. Bl. 1851–60, RGS Corr. Bl. 1861–70 | CUL, Jardine Matheson archive, corresp. and MSS · NA Scot., Loch muniments, letters to H. B. Loch, GD 268 · PRO, letters to Lord Hammond, FO 391 · PRO, official MSS, FO 17, 46, 69, 93, 97, 228, 230, 233, 262, 344, 363, 663, 671, 682, 796; Satow papers, PRO 30/33 · PRO NIre., corresp. with H. S. Wilkinson, D.1292.A.1

Likenesses S. Suzuki, photograph, 1883, repro. in Lane-Poole and Dickins, *Life of Sir Harry Parkes*, 1, frontispiece · T. Brock, marble bust on monument, 1887, St Paul's Cathedral, London [*see illus.*] · T. Solari?, bronze statue, Shanghai; now lost, probably destroyed by Japanese in the Second World War · wood-engraving (after photograph by Negretti and Zambra), NPG; repro. in *ILN* (22 Dec 1860), 587

Wealth at death £8833 7*s*. 6*d*.: probate, 21 May 1885, *CGPLA Eng. & Wales*

Parkes, Sir Henry (1815–1896), politician and journalist in Australia, was born on 27 May 1815 at Motthouse, Canley Hamlet, Warwickshire, the youngest of the six children of Thomas Parkes (*b*. 1773), a tenant farmer, and his wife, Martha, *née* Faulconbridge (*d*. 1838), neither of whom could read or write. In 1823 debt forced the family off their farm and, after moving to Glamorgan in search of work, they gravitated to Birmingham. Here Henry took labouring jobs before being apprenticed to a bone and ivory turner, John Holding. Bent on self-improvement, he attended classes at the Birmingham Mechanics' Institute, and avidly read political tracts and poetry. He joined Thomas Attwood's Birmingham Political Union, founded on the belief that 'the interests of masters and men are one' and that they should 'knock at the gates of the Government and demand redress of their common grievances' (Briggs, 191). Parkes never forgot the exciting mass meetings which the union organized at Newhall Hill in the last stages of the fight for the 1832 Reform Bill, and he eagerly followed its leaders into commitment to Chartism.

Marriage and migration to Australia On 11 July 1836, at Edgbaston, Parkes married Clarinda, the 23-year-old daughter of a prosperous whip maker, Robert Varney, who disapproved of the marriage and disowned the bride. After completing his apprenticeship Parkes set up an independent workshop in Birmingham. But the times were difficult; he contracted debts and at the end of 1838 went with Clarinda to London to try to establish himself there. He failed, and the couple decided to emigrate to New South

Sir Henry Parkes (1815–1896), by unknown photographer

Wales. In March 1839 they sailed as assisted migrants on the *Strathfieldsaye*, which reached Sydney on 26 July. Two days before Clarinda had given birth to a daughter, Clarinda Sarah—'our little blue-eyed ocean child' (Parkes, *Emigrant's Home Letters*, 87).

Parkes's first experience of the colony was not happy. The only work he could find was as a labourer on Sir John Jamison's Regentville, a model property 36 miles from Sydney. After six trying months there, he returned to the town and worked first in an ironmonger's store and subsequently with a firm of brass-founders. Then, late in 1840, things looked up when he acquired the post of tide waiter in the customs service, a position which gave him both security and spare time to indulge his writing talent. This talent introduced him to the poet Charles Harpur and to W. A. Duncan, the cultivated editor of the *Australasian Chronicle*, who opened his columns generously to literary aspirants such as Parkes and who had already published much of the verse which in 1842 Parkes collected in a slim volume entitled *Stolen Moments*. Having acquired a lathe, Parkes began working at his old trade on the side. By 1846 he felt secure enough to resign from the customs service and establish a shop selling turned goods, imported toys, and fancy goods in a newly developing small business area.

Entry into politics Parkes's shop soon became a meeting place where like-minded neighbours, mostly small businessmen and journalists, and mostly immigrants of radical bent, discussed the affairs of the day. The group came into the open in 1848, when they promoted the barrister Robert Lowe as the first 'democratic' candidate for the colony's part-elective legislative council. Lowe's subsequent election under a property franchise high enough to exclude two-thirds of the adult male population was a tribute to the organizing ability that Parkes and his friends had brought with them from their radical English backgrounds. Together with the colony's more respectable liberals, they went on to fight against British proposals to resume convict transportation, discontinued to New South Wales in 1840. When in 1849 a convict ship, the *Hashemy*, entered Sydney harbour they were behind a mass demonstration, at which Lowe and Parkes were the principal orators. Parkes subsequently became one of the founders of an Association for Preventing the Revival of Transportation, whose message to advise imperial compliance Governor FitzRoy conveyed to Earl Grey.

Through the political reputation he had managed to win by 1850 among substantial Sydney liberals—chiefly merchants and bankers—Parkes obtained loans that enabled him to establish *The Empire*, a newspaper which Parkes and his supporters saw as both mouthpiece and rallying point for the colony's liberals. For him personally the paper represented a happy reconciliation of his desire to spread his political wings and his duty to support his growing family. He wrote later of being 'intoxicated with the hard and exciting mission of a propagandist' (Parkes, *Australian History*, 83–4), and expected, moreover, to make a fortune out of the venture. The paper's quality and Parkes's political skills were rewarded when in 1854 he was elected to the legislative council as the chief antagonist to the conservative Constitution Bill, which a committee chaired by William Charles Wentworth had produced in response to a British invitation to frame the institutions for a grant of responsible government.

After being approved in London, the constitution, which provided for a legislature of two houses, came into effect in 1856, and Parkes was one of four liberals elected for the premier Sydney City seats in the lower house, the legislative assembly. Using *The Empire* forcefully to back up his work with the liberal leader in the house, Charles Cowper, Parkes played an important part in a major victory whereby the constitution was liberalized in 1858 to provide manhood suffrage and vote by ballot. But then disaster struck: *The Empire*, always financially precarious, collapsed in bankruptcy. Parkes was left 'to begin life afresh with a wife and five children to support, a name in a commercial sense ruined and a doubt of the practical character of my mind' (Diary, 19 Oct 1858, Parkes correspondence, A1011). At the age of forty-three he decided to abandon politics and make a new career in the law. But determination wilted in the face of hard study and he resolved to re-enter politics, living on his salary when in office, and off his friends when not. In June 1859 he was back in parliament, representing East Sydney in the legislative assembly.

By 1860 Parkes was emerging as the rival of the established liberal leadership; but poverty made him vulnerable, and in 1861 Cowper temporarily bought him off with a year's appointment, at a salary of £1000, as a government lecturer touring England to encourage emigration. Parkes sent back to Sydney regular press articles on contemporary scenes and problems, and these writings, published in 1869 as *Australian Views of England*, are among his most attractive. In Birmingham he established, with his sister Maria as his English agent, a new fancy goods importing business, which he was sure would soon 'provide for the rest of our lives' (Parkes to Maria, 24 Oct 1863, Parkes correspondence, A1044).

Home again, Parkes entered parliament once more, at a by-election early in 1864. By then parliamentary divisions in New South Wales had settled into a faction mould. The old conservatism which Wentworth represented had long since been defeated, and most members considered themselves 'liberals' dedicated, in the parlance of the day, to advancing 'the good of the community as a whole'. The colony's politics were driven not by ideology, but by the struggle for office between leaders of fluctuating personal followings. With his immense self-confidence and a touch of amorality, and his political skills as speaker and intriguer in parliament and the electorates, Parkes won ascendancy in this milieu, and was appointed colonial secretary (1866–8) in the government of James Martin. Bankrupt again in 1870, when his importing business failed, he had to resign his parliamentary seat. But his attitude to this set-back was very different from that of 1858. He assured his sister that he would be

> reelected to the Legislature whenever I choose to offer myself, and strange as it may seem two-thirds of the mercantile classes will vote for me. They have got a notion that I am wholly unfit for business, but the fittest of all men for Parliament. (Parkes to Maria, 24 March 1871, Parkes correspondence, A1008)

Parkes as premier Parkes returned to parliament in 1872 to become premier (1872–5). His chief rival was John Robertson: they were Spartan kings, it was said at the time, who alternately reigned. Parkes was briefly in office in 1877, then in 1878 formed a surprise coalition with Robertson and was premier until 1883. The land reforms of his successor, Alexander Stuart, brought budgetary crises and an unsettled period when the colony's revenue needs for the first time fostered a serious protectionist movement. Parkes swept back to power on the cry of Free Trade in 1887, when his premier's salary helped him through a third bankruptcy. But the new Free Trade/Protectionist division presaged the coming of something like a party system based on competing ideologies, and Parkes, skilled at exploiting the freewheeling liberty of a faction chief, was ill at ease. The Free-Traders whom he led to victory at the next election in 1889 made it clear that his freedom of manoeuvre was in future to be restricted by the needs of party, in which they, as well as he, must have a say. The faction period was virtually at an end. Parkes told his daughter that he had lost much of his 'former relish for parliamentary work' (Parkes to Annie Parkes, 15 June 1889, Parkes correspondence, A1044), and was considering acceding to pressure to put himself at the head of a movement to federate the Australian colonies.

Parkes's principal contribution to his adopted homeland was clean and efficient administration during his five premierships. But the statute book gave much evidence of his creativity in measures ranging from hospital reform and the introduction of Nightingale-trained sisters in the 1860s to his celebrated measures of 1866 and 1880 to extend education to all children in the colony and reduce the unhappy effects of competition between rival sectarian and non-religious educational systems. In the late 1880s his governments amended the bankruptcy and criminal laws, carried out major reforms in public works administration and railway management, and defied imperial authority by legislating for drastic restriction of Chinese immigration. Parkes played a major diplomatic role in promoting the federal conference of 1890 and the federal convention of 1891, at both of which, in Alfred Deakin's words, he was 'first and foremost in every eye' (Deakin, 24). The Constitution Bill produced by this first federal initiative was a major starting point for the deliberations of the conventions which, after Parkes's death, led to the formation of the Australian commonwealth.

Second marriage, death, and reputation Parkes was appointed KCMG in 1877 and GCMG in 1888. Clarinda died on 2 February 1888, leaving seven children (five others had died in infancy). On 6 February 1889 Parkes married the English-born migrant Eleanor Dixon, who at thirty-one had already borne him three children and would have another two before she died of cancer in July 1895. On 24 October of that year, Parkes married for a third time; his new wife was the 23-year-old Julia Lynch, born in co. Cavan, Ireland, a servant in the household. By then, aged eighty, he was out of politics after pettish refusal to accept that his days of leadership were over, and steeped in poverty which was forcing him to sell personal possessions to buy food and firewood. Politicians—both friends and foes—were preparing to make a parliamentary grant to him when, on 27 April 1896, at his home in Annandale, Sydney, he died suddenly of heart failure after an attack of pneumonia. He was buried at Faulconbridge, New South Wales, beside his first wife.

The largest figure of nineteenth-century Australian politics, Parkes also remains the most enigmatic. In a celebrated obituary, William Astley saw him merely as a 'master of the art of seeming great' (*AusDB*); more sensitively, Alfred Deakin felt that 'there was in him the substance of the man he dressed himself to appear' (ibid.). Parkes's papers add other dimensions which indicate a personality moulded over a long and changeful life by inner conflict, as he sought to reconcile deeply held principles, an immense drive for self-realization, and the compromises which were the price of success. His vanity and craving for recognition were matched by a fiery integrity which showed in his scorn for the world's judgement of his marital and financial affairs, and enabled him to weather crises which would have destroyed lesser men. Bearded after 1861, he was physically impressive ('leonine' was the contemporary description), and, though uncertain about aspirates, he had few peers among colonial contemporaries for studied oratory. A. W. MARTIN

Sources A. W. Martin, *Henry Parkes: a biography* (1980) • A. W. Martin, 'Parkes, Henry', *AusDB*, vol. 11 • Mitchell L., NSW, J. D. Lang MSS • Mitchell L., NSW, Windeyer MSS • Mitchell L., NSW, Parkes MSS and correspondence • A. Briggs, 'Thomas Attwood and the economic background of the Birmingham Political Union', *Cambridge Historical Journal*, 9 (1947–9), 190–216 • H. Parkes, *An emigrant's home letters* (1896) • H. Parkes, *Fifty years in the making of Australian history* (1892) • A. Deakin, *The federal story: the inner history of the federal cause*, ed. H. Brookes (1944) • parish records, Stoneleigh, Warwickshire [births and baptisms], 27 May 1815 • personal knowledge (2004)

Archives Mitchell L., NSW | BL, corresp. with Florence Nightingale, Add. MS 47757 • LPL, Palmer MSS • LPL, corresp. with Lord Selborne • Mitchell L., NSW, J. D. Lang MSS • Mitchell L., NSW, Windeyer MSS • NL Scot., letters to Thomas Carlyle • priv. coll., letters to Saul Samuel [microfilm] • U. Durham L., corresp. with third Earl Grey

Likenesses J. R. Ashton, pencil drawing, 1891, NPG • J. Ashton, oils, National Memorial School of Arts, Tenterfield • J. R. Ashton, portrait, Art Gallery of New South Wales, Sydney, Australia • J. H. Chinner, oils, NL Aus. • T. Cowen, bust, Art Gallery of New South Wales, Sydney, Australia • N. Illingworth, bust, NL Aus. • T. Roberts, oils, National Gallery, Adelaide, Australia • M. Stoddard, oils, legislative council chamber, Sydney, Australia • A. Streeton, oils, Howard Hinton Collection, Armidale, New South Wales, Australia • photograph, State Library of Victoria, Melbourne, Australia [*see illus.*]

Wealth at death virtually nil

Parkes, James (1793/4–1828). *See under* Parkes, David (1763–1833).

Parkes, James William (1896–1981), historian and theologian, was born at Les Fauconnaires, Guernsey, on 22 December 1896, the younger son and second of three children of Henry Parkes, an English civil engineer who had settled in Guernsey to grow fruit, and his wife, Annie Katharine, *née* Bell. He was educated at Elizabeth College, Guernsey, and, after the First World War, at Hertford College, Oxford, where he was an open classical scholar. He took a second in classical honour moderations in 1921 and an *aegrotat* in theology in 1923. He returned to Oxford for a term of postgraduate work in 1931 (and for a term in both 1932 and 1933) as a closed scholar of Exeter College, and was awarded the DPhil in 1934 for a thesis which was immediately published and became one of his most influential and durable works, *The Conflict of the Church and the Synagogue* (1934).

Parkes was permanently marked by his experiences during the First World War, in which he was gassed in the Ypres salient, and encountered (as he later put it) the 'alternating black and white' of hierarchical incompetence and human solidarity, as well as ample outlets for his own brand of good-natured and often unconventional practicality. At Oxford he became involved in the League of Nations Union, and took the decision to enter the church (he was ordained priest in 1926). In March 1923 his life took a decisive turn with an invitation to join the staff of the Student Christian Movement, and from then on he devoted himself body and mind to the cause of fighting against prejudice and conflict. In addition to his work for the SCM, he was actively involved in the British (later Royal) Institute of International Affairs, the National Union of Students, the League of Nations Union, and the

Committee for European Student Relief of the World's Student Christian Federation. In 1926 he became warden of Student Movement House, a club for (mainly foreign) students in London.

In March 1928 Parkes joined the staff of the International Student Service in Geneva, and with the rise of Nazism he found his work increasingly dominated by the problem of antisemitism (Parkes insisted that the word should be spelt in this way, regarding the form 'anti-semitism' as itself antisemitic). He remained in Geneva until 1935; just before he left he narrowly escaped an assassination attempt by Swiss Nazis. From then until 1964 he lived in the village of Barley, a few miles south of Cambridge, and it was here, with the financial backing of Israel M. Sieff and others, that his library evolved into a research centre on antisemitism and the history of Christian–Jewish relations which attracted scholars from all over the world. It was also in Barley that the first steps were taken towards the foundation of the Council of Christians and Jews, with which Parkes remained closely associated. In 1964, when Parkes and his wife 'retired' from Barley to a small cottage in Dorset, a home was found for the Parkes Library in the University of Southampton, which agreed to keep the library up to date and also established a Parkes Library fellowship in the field of Christian–Jewish relations.

Parkes was a prolific writer. His solidly based investigations of antisemitism and of the history of Christian–Jewish relations opened a new chapter in the study of this difficult and sensitive subject. Parkes argued that antisemitism, although a modern political phenomenon, cannot be detached from centuries of hostile Christian preaching which wilfully misrepresented the true nature of Judaism and directly contributed to the group hatred which is at the root of the isolation and persecution of the Jews. This view, which later seemed banal, was novel in the 1930s and was deeply resented in certain quarters. Side by side with a historical approach, Parkes developed a theological perspective which found a positive place for the Jews within the divine economy and reinterpreted the Christian Trinity as a functional description of God's activity, rather than a definition of his nature. In 1940 he published *Good God*, a kind of popular biography of God, under the pseudonym John Hadham; it was followed by other theological writings and broadcasts under the same name.

Parkes was a soft-voiced and deceptively gentle man, with a relentless inner energy and an impish sense of humour. His voice he lost completely at the end of his life, and also the use of his hands, impaired by Dupuytren's contracture. He had previously derived great pleasure from tapestry making and from gardening. He was a keen student of architecture, and assembled a remarkable collection of architectural photographs. He also collected English brass candlesticks, on which he became a recognized authority.

Parkes was president of the Jewish Historical Society of England (a rare honour for a Gentile) from 1949 to 1951. He was made an honorary fellow of the Hebrew University of Jerusalem in 1970, and received honorary doctorates from the Jewish Institute of Religion, New York, and the University of Southampton.

In 1942 Parkes married Dorothy, daughter of Frank Iden Wickings, an agricultural merchant, of Hildenborough, and his wife, Emily. She had been helping him secretarially and continued to support him in his work to the end of his life. He died in Bournemouth on 6 August 1981. N. DE LANGE, *rev.*

Sources J. Parkes [J. Hadham], *Voyage of discoveries* (1969) • S. Sugarman and D. Bailey, *A bibliography of the printed works of James Parkes with selected quotations*, ed. D. A. Pennie (1977) • personal knowledge (1990) • *CGPLA Eng. & Wales* (1981)

Archives BLPES, corresp. • U. Southampton L., corresp. and papers | Georgetown University, Washington, DC, Lauinger Library, letters to Christopher Sykes • St Ant. Oxf., Middle East Centre, corresp. with Cecil Edmonds • U. Southampton L., corresp. with general manager and editor of *Jewish Chronicle* • U. Warwick Mod. RC, corresp. with Victor Gollancz • Wellcome L., corresp. with Charles Singer

Wealth at death £25,729: probate, 26 Oct 1981, *CGPLA Eng. & Wales*

Parkes, Joseph (1796–1865), election agent and reformer, was born on 22 January 1796 in Warwick, the fourth son of John Parkes, worsted manufacturer, and his wife, Sarah. His brother was Josiah *Parkes, the agricultural and civil engineer. Parkes was brought up in the traditions of moderate dissent. His father, a trustee of the Unitarian church in Warwick High Street, was well connected in local whig circles and on intimate terms with Basil Montagu and Dr Samuel Parr, the latitudinarian clergyman, who enjoyed a mutual friendship with the family minister William Field. Parr took 'a great interest' in the young Parkes, and 'directed his studies, and recommended a course to which he rigidly adhered' (*GM*, 645). After attending Warwick grammar school, Parkes followed his elder brother Josiah to the college at Greenwich run by Parr's former pupil Dr Charles Burney. Like many of the whigs who served as his early models, he completed his education in Scotland, at the University of Glasgow, where he entered the logic class of George Jardine in 1811. There is no record of his graduation. In 1817, after a spell in the office of a Warwick solicitor, he moved to London where, during the course of a five-year clerkship with Messrs Amory and Coles of 25 Throgmorton Street, he was introduced by a fellow Unitarian to Jeremy Bentham, with whom he established an affectionate and lasting correspondence. He also met George Grote, James Mill, and Francis Place, whom he later wrote of as his 'political father', from 'whom I early (a raw miseducated boy) learned much *sound* and *honest*' (BL, Add. MS 35150, fol. 99).

Supplementing his income through parliamentary reporting, Parkes was destined for the bar, but following the collapse of the family business he moved to Birmingham in 1822 and established a solicitor's practice specializing in election work. He soon secured employment as clerk on the committee of inquiry into the borough of Camelford, Cornwall. At the general election of 1826 he served as an agent to William Evans, a whig candidate at Leicester, and in December 1826 he was 'principal agent' to Richard Spooner, a Birmingham banker, who stood as a tory in the Stafford by-election. Thereafter he was regularly engaged on the whig interest in the counties of Worcester and Warwick, and at Stamford in Lincolnshire (*Parl. papers*, 1835, 8.92, 110). Carlyle later recalled how, on one of his Warwickshire visits, he met Parkes, 'then a small Birmingham attorney', who was 'a rather pleasant talking, shrewd enough little fellow, with bad teeth, and a knowing lightly satirical way' (Carlyle, 302). On 2 June 1824 Parkes married Elizabeth Rayner, eldest daughter of Joseph Priestley of Cradley, Staffordshire, and granddaughter of Dr Joseph Priestley, the theologian and chemist, who had taken his family to America; they had two children.

Parkes was a familiar figure in Birmingham politics, advising its improvement commission in 1827–8, campaigning on dissenting and educational issues, and, in a series of articles and pamphlets, urging the necessity of local legal reforms. A regular contributor to the Benthamite *Jurist* from 1827 to 1833, in 1828 he published a *History of the Court of Chancery*, which was described by Henry Brougham, who was later lord chancellor, as 'one of the ablest and most instructive books published of later years' (*Hansard* 2, 18, 1828, 243–4). He played a leading role in assisting Charles Tennyson in his abortive attempt to enfranchise Birmingham between 1827 and 1830, and was extremely active in the movement for parliamentary reform from 1830 to 1832, writing frequent articles in the national press and providing 'an important link of connection between the steady-going Whigs and the swifter-going Radicals' (*The Times*, 12 Aug 1865). He condemned the formation of the Birmingham Political Union as 'ill-contrived and worse timed', referring to it as 'a burning lava of red hot radicalism devastating the fair appearance of the field of reform' and suspecting Thomas Attwood, its founder, of trying to promote his currency reform schemes (Parkes to Tennyson, 2 Feb 1830, Tennyson D'Eyncourt MS H/53/2). Having failed to prevent its formation, however, he willingly proffered his professional services and helped to moderate its activities. When, in November 1831, at the height of the reform crisis, Attwood proposed re-organizing the union on a semi-military basis, it was Parkes who, fearing that the bill might be jeopardized, acted as the Grey ministry's unofficial intermediary, meeting Lord Althorp in secret at his London home and persuading the union leaders to back down.

Thereafter Parkes, who assured the radical George Grote that he was 'not flattered by, but honoured with unsought letters from Lord Althorpe and Lord John Russell', was consulted by the whigs on various technical aspects of the bill, including the proposed qualifications for the borough franchise (BL, Add. MS 35149, fols. 117–19). He was vociferous in campaigning for peerage creations in early 1832, and in emphasizing the threat of violent revolution during the days of May, when he briefly joined the union. After the passage of the Reform Act he considered standing for election, either in Birmingham or in the new constituency of Dudley, where he 'could have cut *in for life* and no expence' (Parkes to Tennyson, 30 March 1832, Tennyson D'Eyncourt MS TdE H/31/20). Without an independent income, however, he was forced to resume his work as 'an obscure country attorney', as he informed E. J. Littleton, 'sunk in the low and to me disgusting occupation of a country lawyer's office' (Parkes to Littleton, 2 Jan 1833, Hatherton MSS).

Parkes played a prominent part in the closely related movement for municipal reform. His experience of contests at Stafford and Leicester had made him acutely aware of the electoral influence possessed by the closed corporations. Adopting the methods used by reforming lawyers like John Campbell and Charles Flint, in December 1826 he successfully initiated legal proceedings against the corporation of Warwick, which led to a case in the court of chancery and the reconstitution of its charter. The following year, in a historical account of the Warwick charter dedicated to Brougham, Parkes called for a complete overhaul of the entire municipal system. During a brief lull in politics in February 1832, he met Lord Melbourne and discussed proposals for 'a general and well considered reform of our Municipal institutions', beginning with the establishment of a royal commission (Parkes to Tennyson, 15 Feb 1832, Tennyson D'Eyncourt MS 4TdE H/53/48). He was appointed by Brougham as its secretary on 18 July 1833, and moved his family to 21 Great George Street, Westminster, where he set up an office for himself and the twenty itinerant commissioners on the ground floor. Following the presentation of their report to the Commons in April 1835, Parkes assisted in the passage of the Municipal Corporations Act, helping to draft many of its clauses, working with Brougham to counter the ultra-tory opposition led by Lord Lyndhurst in the Lords and, after the original bill had become compromised, trying to dampen radical misgivings. 'Far from perfect as the Corporation Act was', he pointed out to Place, 'and reduced as was its original degree of perfection, yet it has done or rather will in its effects *do the business*' (BL, Add. MS 35150, fols. 99–101). His tory critics included Benjamin Disraeli, Lyndhurst's young protégé, who dubbed him 'Pisaller Parkes' in a series of savage attacks in the *Morning Post* (Thomas, 283). Parkes, who received £1650 for his work, continued to assist Brougham on the related Charity Commission, revived in October 1835, and in drawing up the new municipal boundaries, before leading the campaign to have Birmingham incorporated in 1837–8.

Parkes later claimed that 'the circumstances of 1832 and my relation to the Corporation Commission' had given him 'a wider insight into and connection with the Liberal Party of the Country than any man living' (Parkes to Durham, 21 July 1835, Lambton MSS), and he was to prove of great use to the whig party managers at general elections, although his advice was sometimes considered too advanced; even Edward Ellice was forced to ask 'has he a care for all his vigor?' (Ellice to Durham, 30 Aug 1836, Lambton MSS). He was constantly pushing for new and more permanent forms of central and constituency organization, to be active between elections, and was a founder member of the Westminster Reform Club, established on 7 March 1834 as a radical alternative to the whig meeting-place at Brooks's. As both advocate and agent, he was acutely aware of the need to 'register Reformers' and 'oppose foul registered Tories' in the new registration courts where, contrary to the spirit of the Reform Act, annual legal contests to enfranchise supporters and disfranchise opponents had begun to develop (Parkes to Durham, 18 Jan 1835, Lambton MSS). Appalled at the lack of preparation by the 'lazy supine Whigs' in the unexpected election of 1835, he and Lord Durham, with whom he became increasingly aligned, were instrumental in persuading Ellice to establish a national Reform Association, to stimulate and systematize Liberal registration activity in the constituencies (Parkes to Durham, 23 Oct 1835, Lambton MSS). It was officially founded on 21 May 1835, and Parkes became its driving force, personally overseeing the dramatic revision of October 1835, regularly advising Melbourne on Liberal electoral prospects, and keeping the association's paid secretary, James Coppock, 'up to scratch' (Parkes to Stanley, 9 Oct 1836, Parkes MSS). Six months later Parkes, an unceasing proponent of greater whig-radical unity, initiated a scheme to establish a new 'Liberal Union Club', which the whig party managers were effectively forced to accept and adopt at a meeting held at his house on 5 February 1836 (Parkes to Brougham, 12 Feb 1836, Brougham MSS). The Reform Club, as it became known, officially opened on 24 May 1836.

Thereafter, although Parkes remained active in Liberal electioneering and election petition work, he became increasingly disillusioned with the Melbourne ministry, especially its cautious approach to registration, for which he complained there was a 'great want' of 'funds' (Parkes to Durham, 19 July 1836, Lambton MSS). He strongly criticized the whigs' opposition to further electoral reform, without which he warned that 'the representative system' would 'pass annually more and more into the hands of the Tories' (Parkes to Stanley, 3 Aug 1837, Parkes MSS). Liberal losses in the 1837 general election deepened his despondency, which turned to despair following Lord John Russell's finality speech of November 1837, and he was drawn into sympathetic support for the emerging extra-parliamentary movements of the period. After flirting briefly with the Chartists, whose aims he admired but whose methods he abhorred, he gave the full benefit of his electoral expertise to the Anti-Corn Law League of Richard Cobden, who thought him 'one of the cleverest men I have ever met' (Morley, 1.149). He was a leading architect of their national registration campaign, which was to prove so effective against the Conservatives in the 1840s. In 1847, after ill health forced him to cease legal and political work, the whigs rewarded him with the salaried post of a taxing master in chancery.

Like many of the philosophic radicals with whom he is often associated, Parkes retired to scholarly and literary pursuits. His memoir of Sir Philip Francis, whom he believed to be the author of the *Letters of Junius*, was completed and published posthumously by Herman Merivale in 1867. The bulk of his writing, however, remains in the form of anonymous political pamphlets and leaders, particularly in the *Morning Chronicle*, *The Times*, and *Birmingham Journal*, of which he was co-proprietor from 1832 to 1844. He was an assiduous and highly entertaining correspondent, whose frank and fruity letters to leading whigs and radicals have survived in telling quantity. A lifelong admirer of the legal and political system of America, the birthplace of his wife, he was 'by relationship and otherwise' in regular communication with many of its 'eminent public men' (*Parl. papers*, 1835, 8.107–8). His close literary friends included George Eliot, whose *Felix Holt, the Radical* (which fictionalized an election campaign) was completed shortly after his death. His daughter, Elizabeth Rayner (Bessie) *Parkes, herself a prominent writer and campaigner on social and women's issues, was the mother of Hilaire *Belloc (1870–1953).

Parkes never achieved his 'sole *political* object' which, as he once explained to Durham, was 'to gain enough of pecuniary independence to go into the House of Commons free from all personal temptation and place', but he played an important role in the reforming movements and electoral developments of the early nineteenth century (Parkes to Durham, 1 May 1836, Lambton MSS). 'Perhaps no man', commented *The Times*, 'was better acquainted than he with the secret history of politics during the last thirty of forty years' (12 Aug 1865). He shifted, as the occasion took him, between the stance of a dissenting whig and a demagogic radical, but he was never entirely comfortable in either camp. 'Although I am a Radical', he declared, and 'may be a Republican in the year 1900, if by the grace of God I so long live—I am a great advocate for the respect of caste and order' (Parkes to Tennyson, 24 May 1831, Tennyson D'Eyncourt MS TdE H/31/1). He died at his home, 17 Wimpole Street, in London on 11 August 1865, allegedly after contracting a chill while travelling to Warwick to register his vote, and was buried on 17 August at Kensal Green cemetery. He was survived by his wife.

PHILIP J. SALMON

Sources W. Thomas, *The philosophic radicals: nine studies in theory and practice, 1817–1841* (1979) • G. Finlayson, 'Joseph Parkes of Birmingham, 1796–1865: a study in philosophic radicalism', *BIHR*, 46 (1973), 186–201 • J. Buckley, *Joseph Parkes of Birmingham* (1926) • G. B. A. M. Finlayson, 'The municipal corporation commission and report, 1833–35', *BIHR*, 36 (1963), 36–52 • P. Salmon, 'Electoral reform at work: local politics and national parties, 1832–41', DPhil diss., U. Oxf., 1997 • G. Finlayson, 'The politics of municipal reform, 1835', *EngHR*, 81 (1966), 673–92 • D. Close, 'The elections of 1835 and 1837 in England and Wales', DPhil diss., U. Oxf., 1967 • C. Flick, *The Birmingham Political Union and the movements for reform in Britain, 1830–1839* (1978) • N. Gash, *Politics in the age of Peel* (1953) • J. Morley, *Life of Cobden* (1908) • T. Carlyle, *Reminiscences*, ed. K. J. Fielding and I. Campbell, new edn (1997) • priv. coll., Lambton MSS • UCL, Parkes MSS • Lincs. Arch., Tennyson D'Eyncourt papers • BL, Place MSS, Add. MSS 35148–35154, 37949 • UCL, Brougham MSS • Staffs. RO, Hatherton papers • *DNB* • *The Times* (12 Aug 1865) • *GM*, 3rd ser., 19 (1865), 645 • *CGPLA Eng. & Wales* (1865)

Archives U. Birm. L., special collections department, corresp. and papers relating to his work on the Junius letters • UCL, corresp. and papers | Birm. CA, letters to Thomas Russell • BL, corresp. with Thomas Atkinson, Add. MS 45047 • BL, corresp. with John Bright, Add. MS 43388 • BL, corresp. with Francis Place, Add.

MSS 35148–35154, 37949, *passim* • Borth. Inst., corresp. with Sir Charles Wood • Girton Cam., corresp. with his daughter, Bessie Parkes, and others • Lambton Park, Chester-le-Street, co. Durham, letters to first earl of Durham • Lincs. Arch., Tennyson D'Eyncourt MS, corresp. • NA Scot., letters to second Lord Panmure • NL Scot., corresp. with Edward Ellice sen. and Edward Ellice jun. • PRO, corresp. with Lord John Russell, PRO 30/22 • Royal Arch., Melbourne MSS, corresp. • Staffs. RO, letters to first Lord Hatherton • U. Durham L., letters to third Earl Grey • W. Sussex RO, corresp. with Richard Cobden

Likenesses miniature, priv. coll.; repro. in Thomas, *Philosophic radicals*, 243

Wealth at death under £2000: probate, 8 Dec 1865, *CGPLA Eng. & Wales*

Parkes, Josiah (1793–1871), agricultural and civil engineer, was born on 27 February 1793 at Warwick, the third son of John Parkes, a wool-carding and wool-spinning mill owner in Warwick, and his wife, Sarah. His younger brother was Joseph *Parkes (1796–1865), an election agent and reformer. Parkes was educated at Dr Burney's school, Greenwich, and at seventeen he went to work in the machinery department of his father's mill. With the mill's failure in 1820 he moved to Manchester where, in the company of the Quaker chemist John Dalton, he occupied himself with inventions for smoke prevention. In 1823 he was elected an associate of the Institution of Civil Engineers, and he became a member in 1837. He abandoned his Manchester activities to undertake work near Woolwich in Kent on a new process for salt refining. In 1825 he moved to Puteaux-sur-Seine, France, to develop his engineering interests, but the revolution in Paris in 1830 ruined his business, and he returned to England.

After his return Parkes was employed in 1833 by Mr Heathcote to drain and reclaim by steam cultivation part of Chat moss in Lancashire. The steam cultivation failed, but in the attempt to drain the mossland Parkes became convinced of the effectiveness of deep draining in removing excess water from soils. Drains laid at a depth of 4 feet or more in a regular, parallel fashion prevented the water table from rising after rainfall and provided a sufficient depth of soil for productive cultivation. Such an arrangement ran contrary to contemporary opinion, which favoured the shallow, parallel system of draining advocated by James Smith of Deanston.

In 1843 Parkes was appointed first consulting engineer to the recently formed Royal Agricultural Society of England, a position he held until 1847, and in a series of papers in the society's journal he propounded his views on the advantages of his system of deep thorough draining ('Report on drain-tiles and drainage', *Journal of the Royal Agricultural Society of England* [*JRASE*], 4, 1843, 369–79). While he allowed that there could be no fixed rule for the depth and frequency of drains, he argued that it was his own practice to undertake drainage schemes at between 4 and 6 feet, the results of which were consistently beneficial ('On draining', *JRASE*, 7, 1846, 249–72).

At the same time Parkes advocated the use of the drainpipe as a cheap and durable conduit. Having seen handmade pipes used for draining in Kent and Sussex and Thomas Scragg's pipe-making machine for their mass production, Parkes claimed that the great majority of wet agricultural land could be drained effectively using his deep thorough draining system and 1 inch diameter drainpipes, at a cost of about £3 per acre, a rate comparable to the less reliable shallow draining systems with stones or tiles and soles ('On reducing the cost of permanent drainage', *JRASE*, 6, 1845, 125–9; 'Report on the exhibition of implements at the Shrewsbury meeting in 1845', *JRASE*, 6, 1845, 303–23).

Although there was debate over the merits of different depths, some commentators favouring shallower depths for certain soils, and doubts over the ability of 1 inch diameter pipes to maintain an open channel underground (2 inch diameter pipes being preferred), Parkes's principles of under-draining were generally accepted as the most approved method. In evidence to the 1845 select committee on draining, Parkes, one of the chief witnesses, assured the committee that his draining system would not only bring an increase in yields and reduce cultivation costs but also last for ever. The government after the repeal of the corn laws in 1846 sought to encourage the diffusion of agricultural drainage with a £4 million advance under the Public Money Drainage Acts (1846 and 1850). With the establishment of land improvement companies 'inclosure commissioners' were appointed to implement the legislation, and by 1875 Parkes's system had been applied to the £4½ million spent on under-draining in England under the legislation. Only in the last two decades of the nineteenth century was the requirement to use his system relaxed. Parkes was even appointed an assistant (or inspector) to the inclosure commissioners in 1846, and he supervised the adoption of his methods on many estates which borrowed funds under the land-improvement legislation for the purpose of under-draining. He was employed directly by many more landowners to superintend the draining of their estates, not only in England but also in France.

In 1860 Parkes resigned as an assistant inclosure commissioner, and from then on he was less frequently employed as a draining adviser. His last major work was the draining and fixing of the sea slopes in the fortifications at Yaverland and at Warden Point, Isle of Wight, between 1862 and 1869. He died at The Glen, Freshwater, Isle of Wight, on 16 August 1871, of kidney disease.

During his lifetime Parkes made a notable contribution to agricultural engineering. Against a background of the widespread problem of waterlogged agricultural land, in the early 1840s he developed a system of deep thorough draining, making use of the newly introduced, mass-produced drainpipe for fill. His claims for this new draining technology in terms of efficiency, durability, and productivity led to its adoption as the dominant method employed in the great expansion of under-draining of agricultural land in England between 1846 and 1875.

A. D. M. Phillips

Sources *PICE*, 33 (1871–2), 231–6 • d. cert. • 'Select committee of the House of Lords on entailed estates', *Parl. papers* (1845), 12.7–22, no. 490 [charges for drainage] • review, *QR*, 103 (1858), 390–436, esp. 411–13 • A. D. M. Phillips, *The underdraining of farmland in England during the nineteenth century* (1989), 158–64, 206–11 • N. Goddard, 'Information and innovation in early-Victorian farming systems', *Land, labour and agriculture, 1700–1920*, ed. B. A. Holderness and M. Turner (1991), 184–9 • *CGPLA Eng. & Wales* (1871)

Archives UCL, corresp. | BL, corresp. with Sir Robert Peel, Add. MSS 33456, 40574–40599

Wealth at death under £14,000: probate, 12 Oct 1871, *CGPLA Eng. & Wales*

Parkes, Richard (*b.* 1558/9), Church of England clergyman, was a native of Lancashire, but nothing is known of his parents. He was elected king's scholar of Brasenose College, Oxford, in 1574, and matriculated there on 20 December 1577. He graduated BA on 26 February 1579 and MA in 1585. He was ordained when BA, and, according to Wood, 'became a godly divine' and a 'noted preacher' (Wood, 2.27).

Anonymously in 1604, and in his own name in 1607, Parkes entered a controversy over the meaning of Christ's descent to hell. His first work, *A briefe answere unto certaine objections and reasons against the descension of Christ into hell*, attacked an unpublished paper of Andrew Willet that had asserted, following Calvin, that the descent referred to Christ's inwardly suffering the torments of hell while on the cross. Also in 1604, Willet included a rejoinder to Parkes in *Limbomastix*, an attack on the Roman Catholic doctrine of the limbo of the fathers. Parkes responded in 1607 with *An apologie: of three testimonies of holy scripture, concerning the article of our creed, (He descended into hell)*. This reprinted his earlier work along with much new material, and was answered by Willet's *Loidoromastix: that is, a Scourge for a Rayler* (1607). Amid invective Parkes and Willet learnedly discussed scriptural and patristic passages. Parkes denied that he was defending the release of the patriarchs from limbo, affirming that Christ's soul descended to the hell of torments to perfect, by an act of triumph, the redemption purchased on the cross. This view, associated with Lutheran theologians whom Parkes cited, had been maintained in 1599 and 1604 by Bishop Thomas Bilson of Winchester, but Parkes also claimed Calvin in his support.

Parkes exemplifies both the attempt of some conformists to differentiate themselves doctrinally from nonconformists and a continuing strain of conformist expression of alarm concerning puritans. He asserted that Willet was a 'Puritane' (conformists Parkes called 'Protestants') whose captain was Thomas Cartwright, that like Cartwright he was intent on replacing bishops (whom Parkes considered successors of the apostles) with a 'Pretended holy Discipline' which would make 'everie Artizan, an Arbiter of holy Scripture' (*An Apologie*, sigs. C3*v*, Cc2*r*, Aa3*r*), and that Willet was a heretic for his denial of an article of the apostles' creed, a denial which disclosed that puritan objections to ceremonies were but the thin end of a wedge of schism and heresy. Parkes argued that such puritanism was an affront to the king and should be punished. The date of Parkes's death is unknown.

DEWEY D. WALLACE, JUN.

Sources Wood, *Ath. Oxon.*, new edn, 2.27 • Foster, *Alum. Oxon.* • D. D. Wallace, jun., 'Puritan and Anglican: the interpretation of Christ's descent into hell in Elizabethan theology', *Archiv für Reformationsgeschichte*, 69 (1978), 248–87

Parkes, Samuel (1761–1825), chemist, was born at Stourbridge, Worcestershire, on 26 May 1761, the eldest son of Samuel Parkes (1734/5–1811), a grocer, and his first wife, Hannah, daughter of William Mence of Stourbridge. He went to an infant school in Stourbridge, sharing classes for some months with Sarah Kemble, afterwards the actress Mrs Siddons. In 1771 he went to a boarding-school at Market Harborough, Leicestershire, under Stephen Addington, and after four years joined his father's business, while still enjoying much freedom to study.

In 1790 Parkes was one of the founders, and for some years manager, of a public library at Stourbridge. About 1793 he moved to Stoke-on-Trent, Staffordshire, where he followed his great-grandfather's trade as a soap maker. His desire to improve the manufacturing process led him to the serious study of chemistry that was henceforth his chief professional interest. He married, on 23 September 1794, Sarah (1766–1813), eldest daughter of Samuel Twamley of Bromsgrove, Worcestershire. Their only child, Sarah Mayo (1797–1887), was married, on 25 May 1824, to Joseph Wainwright Hodgetts, who lost his life in an explosion at a chemical works in Manchester on 14 February 1851.

In 1803 Parkes settled in London, as a manufacturing chemist, first at Shacklewell Street, Shoreditch, and finally at larger premises in Goswell Road, Islington, where he produced an impressive range of industrial chemicals. His name became known to a wide public and noticed by the learned societies through his manuals of chemistry. The *Chemical Catechism* (1806) went through thirteen English editions (the last two after Parkes's death), several American editions, and was translated into French, German, Spanish, and Italian. The *Rudiments of Chemistry* (1809; 4th edn 1825), an abridgement of the *Catechism*, was intended for school use. Both works enjoyed such success that several pirated editions had to be suppressed by injunctions in chancery. His *Chemical Essays* (1815; 3rd edn 1840) aimed at promoting chemical technology, and earned him international renown, including the approbation of the tsar of Russia, in the form of a valuable ring. Parkes also published miscellaneous papers on original research, one in collaboration with W. T. Brande on the spa waters of Cheltenham (*Journal of Science and the Arts*, 3, 1817, 54–71).

In 1817 the Highland Society voted Parkes a silver inkstand for an essay on kelp and barilla. He joined Sir Thomas Bernard in agitating (1817) against the salt duties (repealed 1825); he appeared as the principal scientific witness before the parliamentary committee inquiring into the question, wrote two influential pamphlets on the subject, and received a silver cup from the Horticultural Society of Scotland for a paper on the uses of salt in gardening. In 1820 he was prominent, as a chemical expert, in a notable case between Severn, King & Co. and the insurance offices. His tastes were liberal; he collected a large library, which included prints and autographs, and brought together a unique set of the works of Joseph Priestley. He

Samuel Parkes (1761–1825), by Parker, pubd 1822 (after Abraham Wivell)

was also a good numismatist and was the first British chemist to investigate the metallic composition of imperial Roman brass coins (*Journal of Science*, 22, 1826, 301–19). He was a member of twenty-one learned societies, English and foreign.

Parkes was a zealous Unitarian and friend of the Revd Robert Aspland, for over forty years the distinguished minister of the Unitarian chapel in Hackney, where Parkes worshipped. He also maintained close relations with Richard Taylor, the nonconformist founder of the firm of Taylor and Francis who over twenty years published and printed Parkes's books. Parkes was a dedicated traveller in pursuit of knowledge of the latest chemical manufactures in all parts of the kingdom, and gave a delightful account of his visit to Birstal, Priestley's native place (*Monthly Repository of Theology etc*, 11, 1816, 274–6). During a visit to Edinburgh in June 1825 Parkes was attacked by a painful disorder, which proved fatal. He died at his home at 30 Mecklenburgh Square, London, on 23 December 1825, and was buried in the graveyard of the New Gravel Pit Chapel, Hackney. His funeral sermon was preached by William Johnson Fox.

ALEXANDER GORDON, *rev.* FREDERICK KURZER

Sources [J. W. Hodgetts], *Monthly Repository*, 20 (1825), 752 • H. [J. W. Hodgetts], *Monthly Repository*, 21 (1826), 120–21 • J. W. Hodgetts, 'Sketch of the life of the late Samuel Parkes', *Quarterly Journal of Science, Literature, and the Arts*, 22 (1827), 1–11 • [R. Aspland], *Monthly Repository*, 21 (1826), 703–4 • [J. Watkins and F. Shoberl], *A biographical dictionary of the living authors of Great Britain and Ireland* (1816), 262, 444 • F. Kurzer, 'Samuel Parkes: chemist, author, reformer—a biography', *Annals of Science*, 54 (1997), 431–62 • F. Kurzer, 'Samuel Parkes' lost analyses of Roman imperial brass coins', *Journal of the Historical Metallurgy Society*, 32 (1998), 47–53 • *DNB*

Archives LUL, letters | St Brides Printing Library, Fleet Street, London, Taylor and Francis MSS, corresp. with his publishers

Likenesses Parker, stipple (after A. Wivell), BM; repro. in *Imperial Magazine* (1822) [*see illus.*] • A. W. Warren, portrait (after drawing by Wageman; after unknown portrait), repro. in *Chemical catechism*, 12th and 13th edns, prefixed • Wivell, Parker, portrait (after drawing by Wivell; after unknown portrait), NPG; repro. in *Annals of Science*, 54 (1997), 459

Wealth at death attained, from very modest beginnings, increasing affluence; towards the end of life lived in large house in Mecklenburgh Square; was attended, during last illness, by Sir Astley Cooper, who counted the king among his patients

Parkes, W. (*fl.* 1612), satirist, was the author of a tract in verse and prose entitled *The Curtaine-Drawer of the World* (1612). He described himself on his title-page as a 'gentleman and sometimes student of Barnard's Inne', and nothing more is known of him. The tract contains some interesting contemporary allusions, such as the reference to the dramatic entertainment called 'England's Joy', which had been written by Richard Venner, and performed at the Swan Theatre in 1603. At pages 50–51 Parkes introduced Sir John Davies's riddle 'Upon a Coffin', and some lines by 'S. R.' (probably Samuel Rowlands).

Nineteenth-century commentators differed greatly in their estimation of Parkes's work. Francis Douce described him as a man of 'great ability and poetic talents' (F. Douce, *Illustrations of Shakespeare*, 1807, 2.75), an opinion seconded by A. B. Grosart in his edition of the work published in 1876. He added that Parkes displayed the 'whip of a genuine satirist' and had some touches 'almost Shakespearian' (Grosart, vi). J. P. Collier, however, found the work tedious, and the *Dictionary of National Biography* concluded that 'though he possesses some strength as a satirist, he lacks invention, and his work is put together without rule or system'. Parkes attracted very little attention in the twentieth century.

GORDON GOODWIN, *rev.* ELERI LARKUM

Sources A. B. Grosart, introduction, in W. Parkes, *The curtaine-drawer of the world*, ed. A. B. Grosart (1876), v–vii

Parkes, Mrs William. *See* Parkes, Frances (1786–1842), *under* Byerley, Maria (1787–1843).

Parkhurst, Ferdinando (*b. c.*1621), translator and writer, has left little trace of his early life. Nothing is known about his parents: Blekiston's suggestion that he was related to the Surrey-based family of John Parkhurst (1563–1639) finds some support in Parkhurst's residence in Epsom, but any connection appears to have been slight. The details of his education are as obscure as those of his early career. Between 1656 and 1657 he acted as registrar to the Commonwealth's commissioners for discoveries: his politics were, however, sufficiently flexible that in 1660 he could join the royalist side and act as prosecutor for the recovery of properties.

Parkhurst is better remembered for his writings than for his deeds. His first work, an almanac for the year 1648, was followed by a translation of some works of Paracelsus

(*Medicina diastatica*, 1653), dedicated to the earl of Denbigh and with a preface by the astrologer William Lilly. In 1660 appeared the first part of *Masorah, seu critica divina*, dedicated to Charles II, a 'synopticall directorie on the sacred scriptures': whether through indolence or for some other reason, the remaining parts of the work never appeared. Parkhurst's loose translation of George Ruggle's comic Latin play, *Ignoramus, or, The Academical Lawyer*, was first performed at some point between 1660 and 1662 at the Cockpit in Drury Lane; on 1 November 1662 it was performed before the king and queen at Whitehall 'with great applause' (preface), but Parkhurst's translation seems to have been less popular than its rivals by Robert Codrington (1662) and Edward Ravenscroft (1678). Scenes from another comic play by Parkhurst survive, but it appears to have remained uncompleted. In 1667 he produced a scientific treatise, the *Meteorographia*. Parkhurst's works display enough erudition to justify the backhanded congratulatory verse of 'P.T.':

> who can say
> Thou art not read in All, though some may
> expose their Genius more to publick sight.
> (*Medicina*, preface)

On 24 August 1671, aged about fifty, Parkhurst married his second wife, Elizabeth Powell (*c*.1643–1674) (his first wife may have been called Sarah). A succession of Ferdinando and other Parkhursts in Epsom in the next century suggests that the line continued: Parkhurst himself died at some unknown point after his wife's death in November 1674. A. R. POLLEY

Sources E. F. J. Tucker, *Ferdinando Parkhurst's 'Ignoramus, the academical-lawyer': a critical edition* (New York, 1987) • *CSP dom.*, *1655–6*, 16 April 1656; *1656–7*, 31 July 1656; *1658–9*, 27 July 1658 • W. A. Shaw, ed., *Calendar of treasury books*, 1, PRO (1904), 1 (1660–67), 6 Oct 1660 • E. F. J. Tucker, 'The Harvard manuscript of Parkhurst's "Ignoramus"', *Harvard Library Bulletin*, 19 (1971), 5–24 • H. E. D. Blekiston, 'Parkhurst, John (1564–1639)', *DNB* • B. M. Wagner, 'John Rhodes and 'Ignoramus'', *Review of English Studies*, 5 (1929), 43–8

Parkhurst, John (1511?–1575), bishop of Norwich, was the son of George Parkhurst of Guildford. He attended Magdalen School, Oxford, where he was a pupil of Thomas Robertson. He was elected a bachelor fellow of Merton College on 14 June 1529, and was a full fellow there from 1530 to 1537, serving as first bursar in 1533 and second bursar in 1536. He graduated BA on 24 July 1528 and MA on 17 February 1533, and was created DTh on 30 October 1566. His ordination as acolyte, on 11 March 1536, was followed in 1538 by his ordination as subdeacon on 16 March, deacon on 6 April, and priest on 20 April. On 14 March 1537 he was admitted to the rectory of Little Wittenham, Berkshire, which he vacated by January 1551.

Parkhurst studied Coverdale's and Tyndale's translations of the New Testament with John Jewel, his pupil at Merton. In 1537 he helped welcome to Oxford the Zürich scholar Rudolf Gwalther, who recalled in 1559 that Parkhurst had then begun to profess the pure faith in Christ which he had maintained thereafter. In April 1539 Parkhurst, then a resident of Alban Hall, was reported, with other members of the university, as eating meat during

John Parkhurst (1511?–1575), by unknown artist

Lent in the house of an Oxford bookseller. In 1540 he wrote a poem attacking Stephen Gardiner on the occasion of the burning of Robert Barnes, William Jerome, and Thomas Garrett.

Parkhurst became domestic chaplain to Charles Brandon, duke of Suffolk, in 1542, and over the next few years wrote verses praising the Brandons and their children, including an epitaph on the duke and a prayer for the duchess's recovery from illness. In 1543 he addressed Latin verses to Henry VIII, designed to be fixed to the gates of King Henry VIII College, Oxford, on the occasion of a royal visit which was cancelled. Queen Katherine appointed him her domestic chaplain some years later, and in 1547 presented him to the rectory of Pimperne, Dorset, which he held until 1548. Parkhurst was at Katherine's deathbed in September 1548. Her then husband, Thomas, Lord Seymour of Sudeley, presented him to the rich rectory of Bishop's Cleeve in Gloucestershire, to which he was admitted on 1 December 1548. There he received John Jewel and his friends and gave generously to poor students. It was almost certainly while at Cleeve that Parkhurst got to know the famous Gloucestershire evangelical Richard Tracy, whom he claimed to love like a father. When Bishop Hooper visited Gloucester diocese in 1551, Parkhurst was described as notably learned.

Parkhurst married, presumably in Edward's reign, a woman some years older than himself, whose father (Parkhurst claimed) disapproved of his religious beliefs. Her parentage is unknown, though the younger Rudolf

Gwalther of Zürich rendered her forename 'Margaris' in Latin (Gwalther, 6). Deprived of his benefice in 1554, Parkhurst had fled to Strasbourg by 9 July, and before October reached Zürich. There he was the guest of Rudolf Gwalther, and made many other friends among the leading Zürich scholars, with whom he corresponded after his return to England. He received, helped, and advised Gwalther's son, also Rudolf, during the latter's time in England (1571–4). Experience of the church of Zürich convinced Parkhurst that it was the perfect model for England. When Parkhurst left Zürich in January 1559, Gwalther wrote to Elizabeth I, the earl of Bedford, and Richard Master, a former Merton friend of Parkhurst's and physician to the queen, recommending Parkhurst's preferment. In May Parkhurst reported to Heinrich Bullinger that he was shortly to go to Guildford to preach against Arian heretics. Restored to Bishop's Cleeve on 2 September 1559, Parkhurst wrote in December to Josias Simler that he had so far kept his neck out of the halter of a bishopric. He was, however, nominated to the see of Norwich on 27 March 1560 and consecrated on 1 September, vacating Bishop's Cleeve in 1563.

Parkhurst proved unequal to the challenges he met in his huge diocese, where religious nonconformity was widespread. He believed 'that the rough and austere forme and maner of ruling doth the least good' (Houlbrooke, 222), but to his critics his gentleness seemed weak. He began his primary visitation in May 1561. On 12 August, during the queen's progress through East Anglia, William Cecil relayed to Archbishop Parker complaints of Parkhurst's slackness in ordering his clergy and dealing with religious radicals. He was one of the bishops who avoided the strict enforcement of Parker's *Advertisements* in 1566, and it was to Parkhurst that Rudolf Gwalther addressed on 11 September 1566 a criticism (which Parkhurst thought insufficiently sharp) of the implementation of Parker's policy. In 1570 he angered the queen by failing to punish certain prebendaries of puritan sympathies who had allegedly broken organs in Norwich Cathedral. Early in 1574 Parkhurst had to send to the archbishop lists of clergy who had refused to wear the surplice. On 7 June, on Parker's explicit instructions, the bishop reluctantly ordered the suppression of all exercises of prophesying in his diocese. He had authorized the establishment of such an exercise at Bury St Edmunds as recently as 16 February 1573. Parkhurst was also insufficiently rigorous in dealing with gentlemen of conservative religious leanings. In 1569 the privy council discovered that two gentlemen of the diocese had not been to church for four or five years; a third had not received communion for ten or eleven. The privy council thereupon castigated Parkhurst for his 'evill governance' (PRO, E 135/25/31, fol. 13) and threatened that if he did not reform these great disorders, the queen would see to his own reformation.

Parkhurst faced at first a severe shortage of adequately qualified clergy. Even after it became less acute, some lay patrons still presented unsuitable candidates. Parkhurst's refusal to admit such men sometimes resulted in litigation. Simony, another abuse of patronal rights which Parkhurst tried to combat, was, according to Archbishop Parker, especially widespread in Norfolk. In 1567 Parker ordered a metropolitical visitation of the Norwich diocese, in the course of which the visitors initiated proceedings against sixty-one long-term non-resident clergy and heard serious charges against George Gardiner, a cathedral prebendary. A royal commission was issued in 1568 to investigate disorders and decays in the cathedral. Parkhurst and other prominent local men to whom it was directed reported serious shortcomings in every aspect of the chapter's activities.

Parkhurst was described in 1570 as insufficiently careful in choosing subordinate officers 'mete for gravite, lerning and dexterite in Government' (PRO, SP 12/73/171). None of the four men whom he appointed as his chancellors was fully satisfactory, and many abuses in his courts were reported to him. Parkhurst was unable to appoint any archdeacons of his own choosing. He regarded the archdeacons of Norwich who held office before 1572 as 'popishe lawyers or unlerned papistes' (Houlbrooke, 207). It was, however, the incompetence of another official appointed before his arrival, George Thimelthorpe, collector of clerical tenths and subsidies, that dealt Parkhurst his heaviest blow. Thimelthorpe's arrears led to the bishop's being declared a debtor to the crown, though a statute against the deceits of under-collectors of clerical tenths and subsidies was passed in 1572. The total size of the debt, and how much of it Parkhurst paid off, are both uncertain, but in February 1578 the arrears outstanding on Parkhurst's death were stated to be £632 4*s.* 9*d.* in respect of the year ending at Christmas 1569, and £1116 11*s.* ½*d.* from 1570. Parkhurst was forced to make drastic household economies, a step especially mortifying for a bishop whom Thomas Becon praised for his charity and hospitality.

The settlement of Dutch and Walloon religious exiles in Norwich in 1565 pleased Parkhurst, who allowed the Walloons to use the chapel of his Norwich palace for their worship. But when in 1571 he issued a commission to the mayor of Norwich and others to deal with disputes within the Dutch church, some of the exiles accused the mayor of infringing spiritual jurisdiction, and peace was restored only by the intervention of the high commission.

A renowned classicist, Parkhurst wrote a collection of Latin poems which was prepared for the press at Zürich in 1558, and published as *Ludicra, sive, Epigrammata juvenilia* in London in 1573. He also contributed to the verses published in 1552 on the deaths of Charles and Henry Brandon, and to John Sheprey's verse *Summa … novi testamenti* published at Strasbourg in 1556.

Parkhurst was plagued by the stone and a severe pain in his leg during the early 1570s. He made his will on 1 February 1573 (codicil added 30 December, witnessed 1 February 1574 or 1575, proved 4 March 1577). Among other legacies, he bequeathed items of plate to Merton College, the town of Guildford, the Students' Stove of the city of Zürich, the two Gwalthers, the mayor of Norwich, Peregrine Bertie (son of his former patron the duchess of Suffolk), the preachers John Walker, George Gardiner, and Henry

Birde, and some of his servants and relatives. His best coverlet made by the Netherlands' religious exiles in Norwich was to go to the Gwalthers as an heirloom. He left most of his Latin books to the library adjoining Guildford School, and made various charitable bequests. Two brothers and four sisters were among his legatees. His will says nothing of his wife, though she was certainly alive on 30 June 1574, long after it was made.

Parkhurst died on 2 February 1575, probably at Ludham in Norfolk and aged sixty-three (on 6 February 1574 he had recorded having almost completed his sixty-third year). He was buried on the south side of Norwich Cathedral nave, where his monument was erected. Brasses were removed during the civil war, but a memorial inscription by George Gardiner survives. The two Gwalthers commemorated him in epicedia published at Zürich in 1576, with the younger Rudolf describing Mrs Parkhurst's grief at her husband's deathbed. RALPH HOULBROOKE

Sources *The letter book of John Parkhurst, bishop of Norwich*, ed. R. A. Houlbrooke, Norfolk RS, 43 (1974–5) • CUL, MS Ee.2.34 • J. Parkhurst, *Ludicra, sive, Epigrammata juvenilia* (1573) • Emden, *Oxf.*, 4.433–4 • exchequer, king's remembrancer, ecclesiastical documents, PRO, E 135/25/31 • PRO, PROB/11/59/76 • exchequer, first fruits and tenths office, miscellaneous records, PRO, E 347/2, part 6, item 437 • F. Blomefield and C. Parkin, *An essay towards a topographical history of the county of Norfolk*, [2nd edn], 11 vols. (1805–10) • H. Robinson, ed. and trans., *The Zurich letters, comprising the correspondence of several English bishops and others with some of the Helvetian reformers, during the early part of the reign of Queen Elizabeth*, 2 vols., Parker Society, 7–8 (1842–5) • *Correspondence of Matthew Parker*, ed. J. Bruce and T. T. Perowne, Parker Society, 42 (1853) • R. Gwalther and R. Gwalther, *In D. Ioannis Parkhursti Episcopi Nordouicensis in Anglia dignissimi obitum epicedia* (1576) • *Reg. Oxf.*, vol. 1 • D. MacCulloch, *Suffolk and the Tudors: politics and religion in an English county, 1500–1600* (1986) • J. Gairdner, 'Bishop Hooper's visitation of Gloucester, 1551', *EngHR*, 19 (1904), 98–121 • state papers domestic, Elizabeth I, PRO, SP 12/73/171 • Norfolk RO, DN/REG/13/19 • S. J. Gunn, *Charles Brandon, duke of Suffolk, c.1484–1545* (1988) • C. H. Garrett, *The Marian exiles: a study in the origins of Elizabethan puritanism* (1938)

Archives BL, corresp., Harley MSS • Norfolk RO | CUL, MS • PRO, E 135/25/31

Likenesses oils on panel, Bishop's House, Norwich [*see illus.*]

Wealth at death £1808 12*s.* 4*d.*—incl. £756 14*s.* of debts due: PRO, E 135/25/31, fol. 33

Parkhurst, John (1563–1639), Church of England clergyman, was baptized at Holy Trinity Church, Guildford, Surrey, on 5 October 1563, the second of four sons of Henry Parkhurst of Guildford and his wife, Alice, daughter of James Hills. He matriculated from Magdalen Hall, Oxford, on 25 February 1581, aged seventeen, and became a demy of Magdalen College in 1583. He graduated BA on 12 November 1584, became a fellow in 1585, and proceeded MA on 10 July 1590. In the 1590s he taught natural and moral philosophy. He served as proctor in 1597–8, proceeded BD on 22 November 1600, and was college bursar in 1602.

At some point Parkhurst was chaplain to Sir Henry Neville, the politician, iron-founder, and (from 1599) ambassador to Paris. In 1602 Neville, at that time imprisoned in the Tower, presented Parkhurst to the rectory of Shellingford (or Shillingford), then in Berkshire. He proceeded DD on 8 July 1610 and on 22 August 1611 married Sarah Brooks (*d.* 1661), widow, daughter of Anthony Tisdale, an Abingdon notable. The couple had at least four children: Henry (*bap.* 1612), Thomas (*bap.* 1614, *d.* 1639), Dorothy (*bap.* 1615, *d.* 1634) and Mary (*d.* 1627).

Parkhurst's other patrons were George Abbot, archbishop of Canterbury, and his brother Robert Abbot, also natives of the parish of Holy Trinity, Guildford. The former he served as chaplain at unknown dates; the latter he succeeded in 1617 as master of Balliol College, Oxford, a promotion perhaps designed to secure for the college substantial educational endowments left in 1610 by Sarah Parkhurst's kinsman Thomas Tisdale of Glympton. Parkhurst was given unconditional leave of absence, and probably spent much of his twenty-year tenure of office at Shellingford, where in 1625 he presided over far-reaching architectural improvements; he was also presented to the rectories of Newington, Oxfordshire, in 1619 and Little Wakering, Essex, in 1623. In his history of the college Henry Savage recalled Parkhurst as 'a Man of singular Learning, gravity and Piety, frequent in Preaching, and vigilant in the Government of this Colledge' (Savage, 126). On the other hand John Evelyn, an admirer of the Laudian innovations of Parkhurst's successor and naturally antipathetic to the religious and political stance of the Abbots, commented on the 'extraordinary remissenesse of discipline [which] much detracted from the reputation of that Colledg' at his arrival in 1637 (Evelyn, 2.18). That year Parkhurst resigned the mastership.

Parkhurst drew up his will at Shellingford on 1 January 1639, leaving £20 to Balliol to buy books and property in Guildford and St Alphege parish, London, to his wife and son Henry. Mourning rings were to go to his surviving brothers, Henry and Thomas (*d.* 1639); his brother-in-law William Purslow; and his nephew Robert Parkhurst, former student at Balliol, sometime MP for Guildford, and the son of his brother Robert (*bap.* 1570, *d.* 1636), lord mayor of London in 1634–5. Parkhurst died soon afterwards and was buried, as he had requested, in Shellingford church on 29 January.

Parkhurst has been identified with the Mr Parkhurst mentioned in letters exchanged between John Chamberlain, Sir Ralph Winwood, and Sir Dudley Carleton as a secretary of Sir Henry Wotton, who in 1613 undertook unauthorized negotiations with the Swiss cantons. Although it is possible that a reference in a 1606 letter to Winwood is to John of Shellingford, the 1613 negotiator seems to have been William (later Sir William) Parkhurst, Wotton's secretary at Venice between 1604 and 1610.

VIVIENNE LARMINIE

Sources Foster, *Alum. Oxon.* • J. Jones, *Balliol College: a history*, 2nd edn (1997), 92 • V. M. Howse, *Shellingford: a parish record* (1978) • H. Savage, *Balliofergus, or, A commentary upon the foundation, founders and affaires of Balliol College* (1668), 126 • Evelyn, *Diary*, 2.18 • *IGI* [Holy Trinity, Guildford, parish register] • will, PRO, PROB 11/180, sig. 69 • G. Baker, *The history and antiquities of the county of Northampton*, 1 (1822–30), 1.228 • *Memorials of affairs of state in the reigns of Q. Elizabeth and K. James I, collected (chiefly) from the original papers of … Sir Ralph Winwood*, ed. E. Sawyer, 3 vols. (1725), 2.56; 3.464, 469 • *The letters of*

John Chamberlain, ed. N. E. McClure, 2 vols. (1939), 1.312, 464, 467; 2.384 · *DNB*

Parkhurst, John (1728–1797), biblical lexicographer, was born in June 1728, the second son of John Parkhurst (1700/01–1765) of Catesby House, a former priory near Daventry, Northamptonshire, and Ricarda (1697/8–1770), second daughter of Robert *Dormer, a judge. He was educated at Rugby School and Clare College, Cambridge, where he graduated BA in 1748 and MA in 1752, and was elected fellow. Soon after Parkhurst was ordained, the death of his elder brother, Dormer, made him heir to large estates at Catesby and at Epsom, Surrey. For some time he acted as curate for a friend, but did not seek preferment. In 1785 he presented the family living of Epsom to Jonathan Boucher, simply because he had preached loyal doctrine to 'a set of rebellious schismatics' in America (Parkhurst, iv). He was a considerate landlord, who reduced his tenants' lease-rent, and once refunded payment based on what he considered an over-evaluation.

In 1754 Parkhurst married Susanna (1731/2–1759), daughter of John Myster (or Misters) of Epsom. They had two sons, John (*d.* 1781) and Charles (*d.* 1792), and a daughter, Susanna (*d.* 1813), who married the Revd James Altham (*d.* 1800). Parkhurst's first wife died on 8 December 1759, and in 1761, probably on 28 April, he married Millicent (1720/21–1800), the daughter of Thomas Northey of London. They had a daughter, Millicent, who married (22 September 1791) the Revd Joseph Thomas of Epsom.

Parkhurst devoted his entire life to intensive study, rising at five and working long hours, despite poor health. His principles of biblical exegesis followed those of John Hutchinson (1674–1737), though he admitted Hutchinson's faults as a writer. His first work, 'A serious and friendly address to the Rev. John Wesley' (1753), questioned Wesley's views on 'assurance'. His own scholarly achievement comprised two works, often reprinted, both providing detailed exegesis of scripture and many illustrations drawn from travels and general literature. *An Hebrew and English Lexicon without Points … to which is Added a Methodical Hebrew Grammar* (1762; last edn, 1830) employed unpointed Hebrew, a practice of which Samuel Sharpe (1799–1881) was probably the last reputable advocate. *A Greek and English Lexicon to the New Testament … Prefixed by a … Greek Grammar* (1769) discarded accents and smooth breathings. An edition of 1798 was edited by his learned daughter Millicent Thomas, and a last edition of 1851 by H. J. Rose and J. R. Major. His reply to Joseph Priestley's unitarian views in *The divinity and pre-existence of our Lord and Saviour Jesus Christ … in answer to … Dr. Priestley's introduction to his history of early opinions concerning Jesus Christ* (1787) is a lengthy exposition of trinitarian doctrine. Parker viewed his works as a defence of protestantism from 'the abominable errours and superstitions of *Popery* on the one hand, and from the unscriptural, absurd, and wicked reveries of the *enthusiastic, self-illuminated Sects* on the other' (*A Greek and English Lexicon*, 1769, preface, 45).

Parkhurst's later years were spent at Epsom, where he continued to revise and correct his works. He was short in stature and erect in bearing, 'irritable and quick, warm and earnest in his resentments, though never unforgiving' (Parkhurst, vi). After a painful illness of ten months he died on 21 February 1797, and was buried at Epsom in the same vault as his first wife. His lengthy will shows the same painstaking attention to detail as his works. His monument by Flaxman in Epsom church has an inscription by his friend the Revd William Jones of Nayland.

John D. Haigh

Sources J. Parkhurst, *An Hebrew and English lexicon without points* (1823), iii–vi · *GM*, 1st ser., 67 (1797), 347–8; 70 (1800), 487–8 · G. Baker, *The history and antiquities of the county of Northampton*, 1 (1822–30), 287–91 · will, PRO, PROB 11/1287, sig. 190

Likenesses J. Smart, miniature, 1765, V&A · Flaxman, monument, Epsom church, Surrey

Parkhurst, Nathaniel (1643–1707), Church of England clergyman, was born in St Clement's parish, Ipswich, one of the sons of godly parents, Benjamin Parkhurst (1616–1684), master mariner, and his wife, Martha, *née* Mercy (*b.* *c.*1624, *d.* in or after 1684). About that time Benjamin's father, George, clothier of Ipswich, emigrated to New England with several other children, settling in Watertown and Boston. It seems that Nathaniel's parents eventually joined them, for Martha was left a widow when Benjamin died at Elizabethtown, New Jersey, in March 1684.

At first intended for a maritime career, Nathaniel Parkhurst showed such promise at Ipswich School under its master Cave Beck that he was sent up to Queens' College, Cambridge, matriculating as a sizar, aged thirteen, at Easter 1657; he graduated BA in 1660 and proceeded MA in 1664, the year he received deacon's orders. In 1665 he became chaplain to the widowed Lady Elizabeth Brooke, and had lodgings in the gatehouse of her mansion, Cockfield Hall at Yoxford. Through Lady Elizabeth Bedingfield of Darsham Hall, Lady Brooke obtained the advowson of Yoxford for Parkhurst and helped him build a new vicarage in Brook Street. When she died aged eighty-one in July 1683 Parkhurst's sermon, *The Faithful and Diligent Christian Described*, was the first of his many published works. The sermons which he preached at the funerals of friends, for the Independent minister Samuel Fairclough of Haverhill (*d.* 1691), and for William Burkitt, reviver of the lectureship at Dedham (*d.* 1703), were printed (usually with lives) without delay, as were several other memoirs and collections of discourses. From 1704 to 1707 three of Parkhurst's volumes were printed for 'Thomas Parkhurst at the Bible and Three Crowns, near Mercers Chappel in Cheapside'; perhaps Thomas was a relation.

Parkhurst's works, as indeed the very fact of his delivering a sermon for a nonconformist clergyman, say something of his churchmanship—a strong commitment to the communion of the Church of England which included a regret at the divisions which excluded so many pious men from that church. His sermons from the 1690s and 1700s show a concern with moral and religious reformation and its importance in preserving England from her enemies: 'Renounce … God's Enemies, the Devil, the World and the Flesh; and live Soberly, Righteously and Godly, and so you shall be good Subjects, and Blessings to the Queen and the Kingdom' (Parkhurst, *Ten Select Discourses*, 157–8). His own theology may have been Calvinist but he emphasized that 'Running into too much of Controversie in Religion, hinders Prayer. Much disputing, unless for Fundamental Truths feedeth the Head, but starveth the Heart, and brings coldness, and promotes Wandrings in Prayer' (ibid., 186–7).

Parkhurst was over fifty when on 28 June 1694 he married Priscilla Grome (1658/9–1712) of Stratford St Mary, Suffolk, at nearby Great Wenham; she was thirty-five. Her father, James Grome, gentleman, of Rattlesden, supplied his pedigree to Bysshe at the 1664 visitation showing Priscilla as the fourth of five surviving daughters; her mother was Joan Mayes, the daughter of George Mayes of Higham, near Wenham. Her grandfather George Mayes, a prosperous chandler of Bury St Edmunds, retired to Rattlesden where, Matthias Candler records, 'he preached in a malthouse' (BL, Add. MS 15520, fol. 56). Although there were no children of the marriage, Parkhurst was still hoping for some when he wrote his will in 1700. He arranged to leave his considerable property in Badingham (near Yoxford) and St Clement's, Ipswich, to his 'well-beloved wife' and his nephew and namesake; failing these two, a host of nephews and nieces and their children would benefit, none bearing the names of Parkhurst or Grome (Suffolk RO, Ipswich, IC/AA1/137/98). Parkhurst died on 8 December 1707 and was buried on the 12th under a ledger slab opposite the pulpit in the nave of the church he had served for forty-two years. His funeral sermon was published in 1708 by J. S., who had to consult closer friends for personal details. The dedication was to Priscilla Parkhurst, who spent her last five years at Stratford; five days after she died, on 24 February 1712, she was buried with her husband. His funeral tribute describes Parkhurst as calm and unassuming, a man of few but effective words, a strong protestant and a firm Anglican, content with the church and state settlements of 1689. Happy in his comparatively obscure rural situation, he wrote and preached with clarity and conviction and, as an opponent of gloomy religion, taught his hearers that 'the servants of God should be as merry as [the wicked], abating the madness and the profaneness of their mirth' (J. S., *Of Sleeping in Jesus*, 57).

J. M. Blatchly

Sources E. S. Jones, 'The family of George Parkhurst', *New England Historical and Genealogical Register*, 68 (1914), 370–75 • M. Morfey, *Ipswich school: an alphabetical list of Ipswichians … to 1857*, 2nd edn (1988) • J. S., *Of sleeping in Jesus* (1708) [funeral sermon of Nathaniel Parkhurst] • will, Suffolk RO, Ipswich, IC/AA1/137/98 • R. T. L. Parr, 'Yoxford yesterday', 6 vols., Suffolk RO, Ipswich • W. H. Rylands, ed., *The visitation of the county of Suffolk, begun … 1664, and finished … 1668*, Harleian Society, 61 (1910), 183

Wealth at death property at Badingham and St Clement's, Ipswich; £4 to the poor of Yoxford: will, Suffolk RO, Ipswich, IC/AA1/137/98

Parkhurst, Thomas (*c.*1632–1711), bookseller, son of John Parkhurst, clergyman of Little Wakering, Essex, was bound to John (II) Clarke on 1 September 1645, having commenced his apprenticeship on 24 June. He became a freeman of the Stationers' Company on 3 July 1654, a liveryman on 2 May 1664, was underwarden in 1689, and was elected master in 1703, though he did not actually serve. On 29 January 1689 he married Priscilla Holden, a widow. Parkhurst published from the George in Little Britain, the Golden Bible on London Bridge, and the Bible and Three Crowns in Cheapside. In 1705 he was described by John Dunton, a former apprentice, as 'the most eminent Presbyterian bookseller in the three kingdoms', and a specialist in 'practical' divinity (Dunton, 281).

By the date of this tribute Parkhurst was close to the end of a long career, during much of which the publication of dissenting books had to be carried out with circumspection. In the 1660s and 1670s there had been a vigorous attempt, led by Roger L'Estrange as surveyor of the press, to suppress all but the most innocuous examples. This was just as vigorously resisted by the Stationers' Company, whose leading figures were often themselves involved in surreptitious publication. Dunton notes that Parkhurst had 'met with very strange success, for I have known him sell off a whole impression before the book has been almost heard of in London' (Dunton). One aspect of this statement is clarified in Oliver Heywood's carefully recorded account of his experiences as a Parkhurst author. In effect Heywood would purchase a substantial part of the edition himself, bound and at a discount, for gratis distribution to his Yorkshire hearers, sometimes receiving a further allowance of copies in lieu of payment. An alternative interpretation is suggested by L'Estrange in describing the practice of dispatching a 'libel' to the country 'with an impression of them or two, before it appears about the town' (*The Observator*, 1/256, 2). Parkhurst was certainly involved in a number of whig printings of the Popish Plot period, including Titus Oates's *A True Narrative of the Horrid Plot* and *The Witch of Endor*, both co-published in 1679 with Thomas Cockerill.

For Presbyterian ministers who, like Heywood, had been ejected from their livings in 1662, Parkhurst provided an essential professional service on very favourable terms. Heywood did not expect Parkhurst's approval of new work to be automatic: the publisher's practice was the modern one of circulating manuscripts to readers, who seem to have included John Howe (another star author) and Matthew Henry. In at least two cases recorded by Heywood, Parkhurst 'expunged' passages likely to cause political offence. In 1691 he published Matthew Mead's *Two Sticks Made One*, a sermon to celebrate the 'happy union' of Congregational and Presbyterian ministers. The most distinguished of his publications for conformists was Samuel Bradford's series of Boyle lectures for 1699.

Dunton praises Parkhurst's scrupulous honesty and kindness as a master, respecting 'something in him above the common rate of mankind'. In the course of a long career he published close to a thousand books, often advertising them in the *Term Catalogues* in blocks of twenty or more. As master elect in 1703 he established a fund to allow each new apprentice to be given a Bible. He sold up his stock in 1711. Parkhurst was buried in the great vault of St Mary Colechurch, Poultry, London, on 9 June 1711.

Harold Love

Sources J. Dunton, *The life and errors of John Dunton … written by himself* (1705) • H. Love, 'Preacher and publisher: Oliver Heywood and Thomas Parkhurst', *Studies in Bibliography*, 31 (1978), 227–35 • D. F. McKenzie, ed., *Stationers' Company apprentices*, [2]: 1641–1700 (1974) • private information (2004) [M. Treadwell] • *IGI*
Archives Stationers' Company, Stationers' Hall, London, Stationers' Company archives

Parkin, Charles (1690–1765), antiquary, born on 11 January 1690, was the son of William Parkin, a London shoemaker. His uncle was William Hutchinson of Clement's Inn; nothing further is known of his parentage. He was educated at Merchant Taylors' School, London, and admitted sizar to Pembroke College, Cambridge, on 5 July 1708. He graduated BA in 1712 and proceeded MA in 1717. He was ordained deacon on 25 September 1715 and priest on 23 September 1716. In 1717 he was presented to the livings of Boughton and Oxborough, Norfolk, by Mary Meriton (*d.* 1732), widow of the previous rector, John Meriton (1662–1717), whom he subsequently married. They apparently had no children and after Mary Parkin's death in 1732, he resided at Oxborough for the remainder of his life, with a Miss Parkin, presumably an unmarried sister.

By 1730 Parkin was preparing a history of Fincham deanery, Norfolk, but three years later he agreed to assist Francis Blomefield on his county history. Parkin contributed the accounts of Grimeshoe and South Greenhoe hundreds during Blomefield's lifetime, both of which were detailed and competent. He had almost completed Claclose at Blomefield's death in 1752. In 1744 he published an attack upon William Stukeley's account of the origins of the caves at Royston, Hertfordshire, published in the first number of *Palaeographica Britannica*. Stukeley scornfully replied in 1746, which elicited a spirited response from Parkin in 1748. He also published *An Impartial Account of the Invasion under William Duke of Normandy*, in 1756.

When Blomefield died he had covered about one third of Norfolk. Thomas Martin tried to persuade Parkin to complete the work, using the Le Neve manuscripts in his custody. Parkin, then aged sixty-three, considered it 'a work of too much trouble'. Martin therefore suggested that he 'proceed in a more concise and agreeable manner than Mr Blomefield' (Stoker, 125). On 29 July 1755 Parkin eventually agreed to undertake the task. He worked rapidly and completed the work by October 1762, although if he wrote an account of Great Yarmouth it was lost. According to John Chambers, this was through the predations of a pet magpie. Parkin's continuation of Blomefield was published posthumously (1767–75) by the Lynn bookseller William Whittingham. The missing account of Yarmouth was supplied from an abridgement of Henry Swinden's history of the town, prepared by an employee of Whittingham. Parkin's reputation suffered through the careless way in which the work was ultimately completed.

Parkin's account of Freebridge, including Lynn, was republished by Whittingham as a separate work in 1772 (with the incorrect date of 1762). The history of Yarmouth, wrongly attributed to him, was republished without author's name in 1776. In 1778 Whittingham also published the first volume of an abbreviated history of Norfolk, covering the city of Norwich. This was a commercial failure, and no further volumes were published. The sheets were reissued in 1783 as Charles Parkin's *History of Norwich*, although he had had no part in it.

Parkin died on 27 August 1765, and bequeathed moneys to Pembroke College for exhibitions for scholars from his own school, Merchant Taylors', and Bowes Free School, Yorkshire, which had been founded by his uncle William Hutchinson. DAVID STOKER

Sources D. Stoker, 'Mr Parkin's magpie, the other Mr Whittingham, and the fate of Great Yarmouth', *The Library*, 6th ser., 12 (1990), 121–31 • *The correspondence of the Reverend Francis Blomefield, 1705–52*, ed. D. Stoker, Norfolk RS, 55 (1992) • [J. Chambers], *A general history of the county of Norfolk*, 2 (1829), 1157 • F. Blomefield and C. Parkin, *An essay towards a topographical history of the county of Norfolk*, [2nd edn], 11 vols. (1805–10), vol. 6, pp. 194–6 • Mrs E. P. Hart, ed., *Merchant Taylors' School register, 1561–1934*, 2 vols. (1936) • *VCH Yorkshire North Riding*, 1.48 • Nichols, *Lit. anecdotes*, 9.409, 424 • *DNB*
Archives BL, collections for a history of Norfolk, Add. MSS 8844, 5819, 4959 • Bodl. Oxf., MS of his continuation of Blomefield's *History of Norfolk* • Bodl. Oxf., MS of the *History of Great Yarmouth* • CUL • Pembroke Cam., MS collection relating to Cambridgeshire antiquities, coins, heraldry, etc. | Norfolk RO, letters to Thomas Martin relating to Peter Le Neve's collections and Norfolk history • Norfolk RO, Norfolk and Norwich Archaeological Society deposit • Pembroke Cam., Pembroke Hall MSS

Parkin, Sir George Robert (1846–1922), educationist and imperialist, was born on 8 February 1846 on a farm near Salisbury, New Brunswick, Canada, the youngest of the thirteen children of John Parkin, a Yorkshire farmer who emigrated in 1817, and his wife, Elizabeth McLean, a Nova Scotia-born loyalist.

Education and early career Parkin recalled his parents' 'hand to hand struggle with the forest and soil'—a life striking for its 'bareness', with 'little music, few books, [and] not much polished society'. His mother gave him a love of literature, however, and young George attended school whenever time could be 'snatched from the hoeing of potatoes, making hay, [or] chopping wood'. These early glimmers of a distant world of learning awakened

> a burning desire to *know* and a longing to see with my own eyes the places one read about, to meet men who wrote books or did things, to get in touch with the world of which the faint echoes only came to one's country life. (National Archives of Canada, George R. Parkin and Annie Parkin MSS, 'Social problems', 24597; autobiographical fragment, 37594)

Parkin followed this desire first to the normal school at Saint John, New Brunswick (1862–3), where he received rudimentary training as a teacher, and then to positions in rural primary schools at Buctouche and Campobello Island. He attended the University of New Brunswick in Fredericton (1864–7), where he imbibed the liberal gospel of mid-Victorian progress and optimism from Macaulay and through the direction of his professors. He was accepted into Fredericton society, thereby acquiring the social skills he would need in later life. After graduating *magna cum laude* and gold medallist, he taught at the Gloucester county grammar school in Bathurst (1867–71)

Sir George Robert Parkin (1846–1922), by Walter Stoneman, 1920

before his appointment as principal/headmaster of the Fredericton Collegiate (1872–89).

Parkin formed in these years his lifelong conviction, expressed in his normal school notebook, that 'the degree of civilization attained by any nation' is a direct result of its standard of education, and that the teacher has enormous power by forming 'the morals and manners of those … whose influence for good or bad will be extensively felt' (Parkin MSS, 25619–25620). This belief underpinned his later work not only in education, but also in his public campaigns for imperial unity, social regeneration, and Christian responsibility. He honed his effective public-speaking techniques in a series of local lectures on temperance, education, democracy, history, and imperial unity. Yet these were troubled years for Parkin. His careful reading of Carlyle challenged the liberal notions of his university days, and his close friendship with John Medley, the high-church Anglican bishop of Fredericton, undermined the individualistic evangelical Baptist faith of his youth for a more learned, collective approach to religion. Not knowing which way to turn to reconcile his conflicting liberalism and conservatism, or his evangelicalism and high Anglicanism, he suffered a severe identity crisis and nervous breakdown. Medley stepped into the breach and sponsored Parkin for a year at Oxford University in 1873–4.

This year set the direction for Parkin's life. As an older student with considerable experience in public speaking he was a great success at the Oxford Union, and was accorded the unusual honour for a non-degree freshman of being elected its secretary. In a famous debate he defeated H. H. Asquith over the issue of imperial unity, when he affirmed its desirability against the then widespread prevalence of Little Englandism. The resultant acclaim solidified his earlier belief in a united British empire as a force for good in the world. During his Oxford year he was also deeply impressed by Edward Thring, headmaster of Uppingham, and saw in Thring's ideals for the English public school a necessary corrective to the lower standards of pioneer schools in Canada. Thring was equally charmed, and after many years of friendship assigned Parkin the task of writing his biography (published in 1898).

Parkin was attracted to the idealism that animated much late nineteenth-century British and Canadian life. He absorbed this from Thring as well as from personal contacts with the brilliant circle at Balliol College, including Benjamin Jowett, T. H. Green, and Lewis Nettleship, and from John Ruskin, who gave influential lectures that year. Parkin accepted idealism, as did many of his fellow students, as a practical creed rather than a philosophical system, a belief that a moral community in the world would result from the ethical character of citizens moved by a sense of selfless public service rather than by a desire for material gain or demagogic approval. In idealism (and in the related National Church movement to which he was also drawn), Parkin found a resolution of his identity crisis. His evangelical energy was rechannelled into a lifelong mission to promote the central tenets of Christian idealism in the empire, school, church, and society.

Parkin spent the next fifteen years teaching in Fredericton. He tried in his own school, and in a connected residential establishment he founded, to implement Thring's concept of building citizenship through the regimen of residential school life and a classical education under a committed headmaster. These initial experiments were not successful. While disappointed, Parkin remained a master teacher. He has been credited, for example, through his imaginative classroom methods, with nurturing the Fredericton school of poets led by Bliss Carman and Charles G. D. Roberts. On 9 July 1878 he married Annie Connell Fisher (1858–1931), his former student at the Fredericton Collegiate, an accomplished classical scholar, and the daughter of William Fisher, a leading civil servant, loyalist, and Anglican. Theirs remained a love match, and Annie was a vital practical and emotional support in all Parkin's work. Together they had six daughters (four survived infancy) and one son.

After leaving Fredericton for the more opportune position of headmaster of Toronto's Upper Canada College (1895–1902), Parkin took a moribund institution and, explicitly following Thring's methods, succeeded in making it the premier private school in Canada. While he ably raised money, added buildings, engaged better masters, and reformed the curriculum, his core aim at the college remained the production of Christian gentlemen. He poured his energy into his own Sunday evening addresses to the boys and into his overall direction of the masters and work. He remained convinced that 'nothing stamps a school as really great save the power of turning out men of high and noble character' (*Upper Canada College Times*, Christmas 1902, 12).

Spokesman for a united empire Parkin's main avenue for the realization of Christian idealism was not the school, however, but the British empire. Throughout his life, but especially during the years 1889–95, he was the leading advocate of imperial unity. His campaigns through thousands of speeches, hundreds of articles, and several books were wide-ranging. In the employ of the Imperial Federation League, he left Fredericton to stump across New Zealand and Australia throughout 1889. Based on the reputation he gained there, he was able to settle with his family in England and undertake five steady years of freelance lecturing and writing for the imperial cause all across Britain, sometimes sponsored by friends, the league, or other organizations, often working from personal contacts. His principal manifesto appeared as *Imperial Federation: the Problem of National Unity* (1892), and a school textbook, *Round the Empire* (1892), sold 200,000 copies and went through four editions up to 1919. He published a large wall map that effectively illustrated the unity of Britain's oceanic empire. He also lectured extensively across Canada, and began then his long affiliation with *The Times*, for which he wrote a series of extensive letters on Canadian history and geography (published as *The Great Dominion*, 1895). These were often difficult campaigns for Parkin—quite aside from the dire personal financial circumstances from which he operated. Many Canadian imperialists were wary of being too closely tied to a formally federated British empire where Britain by force of numbers would have the controlling hand. Yet many British imperialists felt that the colonies were not paying their fair share of imperial defence and other burdens. Parkin had to bridge these two positions. Controversy arose: there were celebrated disputes with the veteran Canadian politician and high commissioner Charles Tupper, which forced the dissolution of the Imperial Federation League in 1893, and a series of attacks on Goldwin Smith's anti-imperialism and North American continentalism.

Despite the spiritual motivation of Parkin's imperialism, he did not ignore the practical arguments favouring imperial unity. Influenced by J. R. Seeley and A. T. Mahan, Parkin pointed out to the British that, as an oceanic empire, their world influence rested on sea power. Given the realities of steamship distances, and the resultant dependencies on coal supplies and coaling bases, the empire desperately needed to retain, for commerce or defence, the quadrilateral of Australasia, South Africa, Canada, and the United Kingdom, and all the connecting islands and waterways. Trade, communications, military power, and cultural and religious influence depended on this geopolitical configuration. Without it, Britain would sink within fifty years, he presciently remarked, into the ranks of the second-class powers before the rising land-based empires of Russia and the United States; the fates of Spain and Portugal were suggestive. Similarly, Parkin pointed out to Canadians and Australians that, without the empire, the individual dominions would be battered about the world stage by aggressive superpowers; the recent experiences of Venezuela and Cuba were instructive. Self-interest, then, combined with the communications revolution of fast steamships, the telegraph, undersea cables, and connecting railways and canals across an 'all-red' route ably defended, combined with common language, literature, and culture, made a united empire possible.

Parkin naturally articulated Canada's position in a united empire. He sought to consolidate his native country's imperial place, especially in the face of a then hostile and continentalist United States. For Parkin imperial unity was never a subsuming of Canada's interests to British colonial administration, but rather a chance for Canada's fledgeling national ambitions to have reasonable scope on the world stage. Indeed, as the oldest and senior dominion, as the geopolitical linchpin in the all-red route, as a nation built on loyalty to the empire, with open spaces for immigrants, bountiful natural resources, and the wellspring of racial vigour engendered by northern climate, Canada was the 'keystone' of empire. He urged Canada, based on these Canadian traditions and characteristics, to accept its destiny and mature from weak colony to strong imperial partner. In Canada he effectively lobbied for practical measures to unite the empire: all-red-route telegraph cables, imperial penny postage, more effective colonial conferences, trade preferences, and, following especially vocal public pressure on his part in 1899–1902, sending Canadian contingents to fight in the Second South African War.

The pan-Britannic union was not an end in itself, however, or a means for jingoism, militarism, or financial profiteering. Rather, Parkin saw a stronger empire, much as he viewed education, as a vehicle for the realization of idealist principles. With imperial power came moral responsibility. In an entirely characteristic speech, he noted in 1894 that the Anglo-Saxon race 'has temptations of an exceptional kind to yield itself to mere materialism, to forget that the things of the spirit are what endure and conquer in the end'. Anglo-Saxons must not 'lose the great moral purposes of life in the race for gain'. They must view the empire as a means of spiritual regeneration:

> The more clearly we realize the growing power, the ever widening influence, the increasing prestige of the empire, the more surely will the thought turn us to self-examination and self-improvement. … Once realize what the expansion of our race in new lands means, and we cannot but turn with new earnestness to grapple with the moral and social problems which lie all around us. (Parkin MSS, 'The Christian responsibilities of empire', 22987–22990, 22970)

A strong, united empire would be a vehicle for pan-Britannic idealism, leading to the moral reform especially of the imperialists at home threatened by growing materialism and social declension, as well as to the uplift of subject peoples abroad. In a telling phrase, he saw himself as 'a wandering Evangelist of Empire'. He was also labelled an 'apostle', 'missionary', or 'lay preacher' of empire.

Parkin's imperial campaigns eventually won his family moderate prosperity and social respectability. He became the confidant of prime ministers, leading educators, governors-general, and world-class thinkers. He personally influenced the imperial ideas of Asquith, Rosebery, Milner, Churchill, and Amery, and moved tens of thousands of others to cheering support. His name was coupled by contemporaries with those of Seeley, Kipling, and Rhodes as the leading advocates of the 'new imperialism', and his personal papers contain scores of newspaper clippings and private letters assigning to him the key role in swaying public opinion to the imperial cause.

The Rhodes Scholarship Trust Because of his long educational and imperial experience, Parkin was invited in 1902 to be the first organizing secretary of the Rhodes Scholarship Trust. He travelled all over the empire and the United States several times before his retirement in 1920, and established the scholarships on a permanent and prestigious basis. His home at Goring-on-Thames became a meeting place for current and former Rhodes scholars as well as for a host of empire-wide visitors. From this position he continued his imperial speaking and writing, publishing biographies of John A. Macdonald, the first prime minister of Canada (1908), and—within a larger account of the scholarships—Cecil Rhodes (1912) which emphasized their subjects' imperial virtues. He campaigned vigorously during the First World War to keep idealism's lessons front and centre and to build on the imperial unity being concretely demonstrated by the dominions on the battlefields. In 1917–18 the British government asked Parkin to use his Rhodes scholarship contacts to lecture all over the United States to counter anti-British or neutralist sentiment there. After the war he readily accepted the new definitions of dominion autonomy which evolved from the peace conference, for his imperialism had always favoured the moral and spiritual unity of empire, displayed so clearly in the war, over any formal, constitutional arrangement. At the end of his life he devoted ever more time to reform of the Church of England, in which he was a prominent lay leader, to meet its National Church and imperial potential. Many honours came his way—honorary doctorates from several universities, including his beloved Oxford, a CMG in 1898, and a KCMG in 1920.

Parkin was a tall man, with a thin, somewhat tired-looking face. Sporting a moustache, narrow side whiskers, and shaggy brown hair, he had piercing, grey-blue eyes that suggested his enormous physical energy and moral earnestness. His remarkably deep and reasonant voice easily filled a hall of ten thousand people before the age of microphones, and the torrential rate of his delivery, often for two hours, held his audiences transfixed. Intense in public life, he exhibited a private sense of humour, with a great capacity for personal friendship and small kindnesses, and took much solace in quiet family times. Parkin died at his home, 7 Chelsea Court, London, of influenza on 25 June 1922, and was buried at Goring-on-Thames in the old churchyard overlooking the garden of his former house. TERRY COOK

Sources T. Cook, '"Apostle of Empire": Sir George Parkin and imperial federation', PhD diss, Queen's University, 1977 • T. Cook, 'George R. Parkin and the concept of Britannic idealism', *Journal of Canadian Studies*, 10 (Aug 1975), 15–31 • T. Cook, 'A reconstruction of the world: George R. Parkin's British empire map of 1893', *Cartographica*, 21 (winter 1984), 53–65 • C. Berger, *The sense of power: studies in the ideas of Canadian imperialism, 1867–1914* (1970) • A. B. McKillop, *A disciplined intelligence: critical inquiry and Canadian thought in the Victorian era* (1979) • R. B. Howard, *Upper Canada College, 1829–1979: Colborne's legacy* (1979) • J. Willison, *Sir George Parkin* (1929) • D. Cole, 'Canada's "nationalistic" imperialists?', *Journal of Canadian Studies*, 5 (Aug 1970), 44–9 • *DNB* • *CGPLA Eng. & Wales* (1922) • private information (2004)

Archives CUL, letters and papers • NA Canada, corresp. and papers | Bodl. Oxf., Lord Milner MSS • Bodl. RH, corresp. with Sir Francis Wylie • NA Canada, George T. Denison MSS • NA Canada, Raleigh Parkin MSS • NA Canada, W. L. and Maude Grant MSS • NA Canada, Lord Minto MSS • NA Canada, Sir Sandford Fleming MSS • Queen's University, Kingston, Ontario, Bliss Carman MSS

Likenesses W. Stoneman, photograph, 1920, NPG [*see illus.*] • F. Varley, oils, 1921–2, National Gallery of Canada, Ottawa • E. Whitney Smith, bust, exh. RA 1928, Bodl. RH • photographs, NA Canada, Parkin family papers

Wealth at death £6227 8s. 4d.: probate, 5 Aug 1922, *CGPLA Eng. & Wales*

Parkinson, Sir Albert Lindsay (1870–1936), builder and contractor, was born on 24 February 1870 at Hastings Place, Lytham, Lancashire, the second of the four sons in the family of seven children of Jacob Parkinson (*d.* 1902), joiner, and his wife, Mary Anne Hall, who later ran a boarding-house in Blackpool. He left school at fourteen to join his elder brother working with their father, who had moved the family to Blackpool in 1873, and had built up a joinery business, registered as Jacob Parkinson & Co. in 1877, working from a small shed in Central Drive, Blackpool. As the business expanded into the building trade, the Parkinsons built a sawmill and joinery works to supply timber for their projects, and moved into the new premises in Kent Road in 1896, the year in which Albert Parkinson took control of the company. After the death of Jacob Parkinson in 1902, it became a limited company, with Albert Parkinson as managing director.

With his brother William in charge of the day-to-day running of the business, Parkinson soon established a reputation for getting things done quickly and on time. Taking advantage of the rapid development of Blackpool as a holiday resort, he built the Talbot Hotel in seven weeks, and after he had built the Theatre Royal, Newcastle upon Tyne, in six months, the company won contracts for more theatres, including the Princes Theatre in London, also built in six months, in 1905, and the interior of the Lyceum. He also built several roller-skating rinks, including one in Paris. He opened offices in Newcastle in 1902, and London in 1905, and in 1911 won his first major contract, to build the new asylum at Whalley for Lancashire county council, completed in 1914 at a cost of £1 million. In 1905 the company built the Blackpool racecourse, the first time it had used reinforced concrete in construction. Parkinson's first wife, whose name is not known, died about 1908 and on 21 February 1911 he married his second wife, Margaret (*b.* 1886/7), daughter of Jackson Robert Singleton, a corporation official and one of Parkinson's partners. He had three sons from his first marriage and one from his second.

During the First World War the Blackpool works supplied shell boxes and joinery for the war department, while Parkinson won contracts to build two aerodromes in 1916 and 1917, and to extend others. During the war he developed the Parkinson–Kahn reinforced concrete house, which he used in several large housing estates in Lancashire and other parts of the north in the 1920s. The firm also built office blocks in London, including Aldwych House (1920–21); the Poland Street garage (1924), the first in Britain to be built with a circular ramp; cinemas such as the Odeon, Temple Fortune, London (1929); the Miners' House in Blackpool (1924–7); the Collegiate School for Girls, Blackpool (1928); and Oddendino's Hotel, Regent Street, London (1927–8). As well as a number of industrial buildings such as the new fish dock in Grimsby (1930–34), the firm undertook road-building contracts, including a section of Western Avenue in London (1929–33), the Barnet by-pass (1928–9), and, most importantly, the Liverpool and East Lancashire Road (1929–33), 25 miles of arterial road between Liverpool and Manchester, the largest new road project ever undertaken in Britain. Government contracts included new RAF aerodromes at Bicester and Heyford (1926–7) and the headquarters of the Royal Corps of Signals at Aldershot. At the same time Parkinson bought several local businesses in Blackpool, including Louis Tussaud's waxworks, and expanded into the ownership of breweries and hotels elsewhere. In 1927 he split the company into two, separating the building and contracting side of the business from the property management side.

Although the headquarters of the company was in London, Parkinson remained closely involved in local activities in Blackpool. A member of the town council from 1905 to 1919, he was mayor of Blackpool from 1916 to 1919, and served as MP for Blackpool from 1918 to 1922, as a coalition Unionist. After he was knighted in 1922, he changed the name of the company to Sir Lindsay Parkinson & Co. Ltd. He declined a baronetcy in 1934.

Parkinson claimed to be the first person in Blackpool to own a private motor car, and his interest in flying led him to organize the country's first aviation meeting in Blackpool in 1909. A keen sportsman, he played for the South Shore Football Club in 1885, and later for Blackburn Rovers as an amateur, and had several offers from league clubs to turn professional. He also played cricket for Blackpool from 1890, and for a number of years took a team to Ireland. In 1924 he and his brother William gave Blackpool a cricket ground and pavilion which later became the county ground, and at his death he was chairman of the Blackpool United Football Club and president of the cricket club. In the 1920s he became a successful greyhound owner, and from 1929 a less successful racehorse owner. He also built up a large art collection, which included the Romanov imperial Russian art collection.

Sir Lindsay Parkinson died on 3 February 1936 at his home, Royal Bank, Preston Old Road, Marton, Blackpool, and was buried in Marton cemetery on 8 February. He was survived by his wife. He had transformed a small local business into a major national company, but after the Second World War it lost its leading role in the building industry, and was sold in the early 1970s.

ANNE PIMLOTT BAKER

Sources *This way forward: a resumé and a record of building and civil engineering construction during seventy-five eventful years*, Sir Lindsay Parkinson & Co. Ltd [1955] • S. M. Gaskell, 'Parkinson, Sir Albert Lindsay', *DBB* • R. Ainsworth, *History of the Parkinson family of Lancashire* (1936), 214–19 • *The Times* (4 Feb 1936) • *Blackpool Gazette and Herald* (8 Feb 1936) • *West Lancashire Evening Gazette* (4 Feb 1936) • b. cert. • m. cert. • d. cert. • *CGPLA Eng. & Wales* (1936) • *WW*

Likenesses photograph, 1916–19, repro. in Sir Lindsay Parkinson & Co. Ltd, *This way forward* • photograph, repro. in Ainsworth, *History of the Parkinson family*

Wealth at death £111,369 13*s*. 6*d*.: probate, 1 Sept 1936, *CGPLA Eng. & Wales*

Parkinson, Sir (Arthur Charles) Cosmo (1884–1967), civil servant, was born on 18 November 1884 at Wimborne Minster, Dorset, the only son and younger child of Sidney George Parkinson, a surgeon, and his wife, Elizabeth Trench. He went to Epsom College, which he left as head prefect, having won a number of prizes; he then went up to Magdalen College, Oxford, as a demy and obtained first-class honours in classical moderations (1905) and *literae humaniores* (1907). In 1908 he entered the civil service and was posted to the Admiralty. The next year he transferred to the Colonial Office where his first assignment was as secretary to the tropical African entomological research committee, and later to a committee investigating the relationship between wild animals and trypanosomiasis (sleeping sickness). This experience gave him an interest in tropical medicine which lasted all his life.

In 1914 Parkinson was appointed assistant private secretary to the secretary of state, but in May 1915 he was released for military service and commissioned as a second lieutenant in the Inns of Court Officers' Training Corps. He served with the King's African rifles in east Africa from 1917, becoming deputy assistant adjutant-general and temporary major. He was appointed OBE in 1919.

On reverting to the Colonial Office in 1920 Parkinson was promoted principal in the east African department, but later that year he was appointed private secretary to the secretary of state. In 1924 he was moved to the dominions division of the Colonial Office and, when the two departments were separated in 1925, he was promoted assistant secretary in the Dominions Office. In 1928 he returned to the Colonial Office as head of the east African department; in 1929 he was awarded the brilliant star of Zanzibar, third class. His promotion to assistant under-secretary of state, supervising the Middle East, Cyprus, and Aden departments, and his CMG came in 1931. He was advanced to KCMG in 1935, and in 1937 was appointed permanent under-secretary of state, with a KCB in 1938.

Parkinson was cast in a scholar's mould, with a keen sense of history and pride in tradition. Himself a perfectionist he expected perfection in others. He was a bachelor and lived for the office. But a consequent concern, perhaps over-fastidious, with the niceties of procedure and style was combined with a wide-ranging ability and insistence on upholding Britain's obligations to the colonial peoples. This, together with his invariable personal kindness and humanity, held the admiration and affection of his colleagues. Nevertheless, with war approaching, ministers evidently felt that a more dynamic leadership was needed. A change had been planned for the autumn of 1939 but was deferred because of the outbreak of war until February 1940. Parkinson was then appointed permanent under-secretary of state for the Dominions Office and Sir George Gater took his place at the Colonial Office.

The staff were frankly sceptical about the substitution of an officer from outside who, whatever his personal abilities, had little experience of central government and none of colonial affairs.

In May 1940 Gater was released on loan to the Ministry of Supply and Parkinson resumed, on an acting basis, the post to which he had been substantively appointed in 1937. It was therefore Parkinson who piloted the Colonial Office through the dark days of 1940–42, covering the spread of the war to Africa and the loss of British Somaliland, and the loss of Hong Kong, Malaya, Singapore, and the Borneo Territories—military defeats which, however, the contemporary press widely attributed to deficiencies in colonial administration. Parkinson's calmness and comradeship did much to sustain morale during this difficult period of blitz at home and losses abroad.

In 1942 Gater returned to the Colonial Office and Parkinson was seconded for special duties, being 'made available to visit colonies from time to time as opportunity offers, to discuss local problems with Governors as the Secretary of State's personal representative'. There was admittedly a case for such an appointment, since personal contacts had perforce been disrupted by the war. But many people felt that others could have filled it equally well, and questioned the wisdom and equity of again displacing such a wise and experienced administrator.

Parkinson himself accepted his new duties with dignity and threw himself into them wholeheartedly. He visited the Caribbean and Bermuda in 1942–3; the Gambia, Nigeria, Kenya, Northern Rhodesia, Nyasaland, Mauritius, Seychelles, Aden, and British Somaliland in 1943; and Ceylon and Gibraltar in 1944. He retired at the end of 1944, but was re-employed during 1945 as adviser on the post-war reorganization of the colonial service. In that capacity he visited Fiji and the other Pacific colonies. He had been promoted GCMG in 1942.

Parkinson remained active after his retirement, publishing *The Colonial Office from within* in 1947. He served on the Epsom College council from 1932 to 1965, being chairman of the executive committee from 1947 to 1961. He was a member of the governing body of University College Hospital, Birkbeck College, and the Old Vic; and as a crown trustee of the City Parochial Foundation from 1951 never missed a meeting until failing eyesight compelled him to resign in 1966. From 1948 to 1966 he served on the delegacy of King's College, London, being a member of the finance committee from 1950 to 1963. From 1956 to 1964 he chaired the court of governors of the London School of Hygiene and Tropical Medicine. He received an honorary LLD from St Andrews.

After his retirement Parkinson moved to Bournemouth to be near his sister. Although he became totally blind in one eye his mind and memory remained fresh to the last. He died suddenly and peacefully in Bournemouth on 16 August 1967. According to an obituary in *The Times*, although 'one of the most efficient of civil servants, he never lost sight of the fact that public affairs were concerned with human beings' (*The Times*, 17 Aug 1967).

HILTON POYNTON, *rev.*

Sources personal knowledge (1981) • private information (1981) • *The Times* (17 Aug 1967) • *WWW* • *CGPLA Eng. & Wales* (1967)
Archives BL OIOC, corresp. with Sir Findlater Stewart, MS Eur. D 174 • Bodl. Oxf., corresp. with Alfred Milner • Bodl. RH, corresp. with Sir Harry Batterbee
Wealth at death £38,336: probate, 25 Oct 1967, *CGPLA Eng. & Wales*

Parkinson, Cuthbert [*name in religion* Anthony] (**1668–1728**), Franciscan friar, was probably the son of Robert Parkinson of Blindhurst, Lancashire. He entered the Franciscan monastery of St Bonaventure at Douai, where he was professed in 1686, taking Anthony as his name in religion. He was ordained priest in 1693, having been appointed professor of philosophy the previous year. He went to England in 1695, and was superior of the Franciscan residences at Warwick from 1698 to 1701 and Birmingham from 1701 to 1710. He was also titular guardian of Worcester and Oxford between 1704 and 1713. In 1713 he was elected provincial of the English Franciscans and again in 1722, and subsequently became titular guardian of Coventry. For many years he resided with the Eyston family of East Hendred, Berkshire. While provincial he attended the general chapter of the order in Rome in May 1723. He was highly thought of by Bishop Matthew Prichard, vicar apostolic of the western district, who had been a contemporary of his at Douai, and by Thomas Hearne, the Oxford antiquary, who was a friend of the Eystons and who spoke of him as 'a very learned worthy man, and of an excellent good-natured temper' (T. Hearne, *Reliquiae Hearnianae*, 2nd edn, 1869, 2.245). Parkinson died at East Hendred on 30 January 1728.

Parkinson was the author of *Collectanea Anglo-minoritica, or, A collection of the antiquities of the English Franciscans, or friers minors, commonly call'd gray friers, in two parts, with an appendix concerning the English nuns of the order of St. Clare*. The second volume contains an account of the colleges and churches of the Franciscans 'heretofore in England'. Parkinson informed Hearne that he compiled this work by the help of books in the study of Charles Eyston of East Hendred. He also compiled *Statuta Fratrum Minorum recollectorum almae provinciae Angliae pro missione* (1713).

THOMPSON COOPER, *rev.* G. BRADLEY

Sources Gillow, *Lit. biog. hist.*, 5.243–4 • Father Thaddeus [F. Hermans], *The Franciscans in England, 1600–1850* (1898) • D. A. Bellenger, ed., *English and Welsh priests, 1558–1800* (1984), 94 • J. Kirk, *Biographies of English Catholics in the eighteenth century*, ed. J. H. Pollen and E. Burton (1909), 176 • P. Guilday, *The English Catholic refugees on the continent, 1558–1795* (1914)

Parkinson, Cyril Northcote (**1909–1993**), writer and historian, was born on 30 July 1909 at 45 Galgate, Barnard Castle, co. Durham, the younger son of (William) Edward Parkinson (1871–1927), art master at the North East county school, and his wife, Rose Emily Mary, *née* Curnow (*b.* 1877). Parkinson attended St Peter's School, York, his father having been appointed principal of the York School of Arts and Crafts in 1913, and won an exhibition to read history at Emmanuel College, Cambridge, in 1929.

Graduating three years later Parkinson was torn between a career as an artist and as a historian but was given access by the family to the Exmouth papers at the

Cyril Northcote Parkinson (1909–1993), by Godfrey Argent, 1969

new National Maritime Museum at Greenwich, and in 1934 published a detailed biography, *Edward Pellew, Viscount Exmouth, Admiral of the Red*, to commemorate the centenary of the distinguished admiral's death. This research stimulated a lifelong interest in maritime history of the eighteenth and early nineteenth centuries. In 1934 he also joined the 22nd London regiment (the Queen's) as a territorial. 1935 was a golden year for Parkinson: he commanded a company of infantry at the jubilee of George V; in June he was elected to a fellowship at Emmanuel College; in October he was awarded a PhD by King's College, London; and in December won the Julian Corbett prize for his two-volume doctoral thesis which he later developed into well-received scholarly books: *Trade in the Eastern Seas, 1793–1815* (1937) and *War in the Eastern Seas, 1793–1815* (1954). During his three years as a research fellow he commanded the infantry unit of the Cambridge University Officers' Training Corps. In 1938 he was appointed senior history master at Blundell's School in Tiverton and the following year became an instructor at the Royal Naval College, Dartmouth. Commissioned as a captain in the Queen's Royal regiment in 1940, he held a variety of instructional and staff appointments in Britain. In 1943 he married Ethelwyn Edith Graves (*b.* 1915), a nursing tutor at Middlesex Hospital. They had two children. Parkinson was demobilized with the rank of major in 1945.

As a lecturer at Liverpool University from 1946 to 1949, Parkinson continued research into naval and maritime history, publishing *The Rise of the Port of Liverpool* (1952). Meanwhile, in 1950 he was appointed Raffles professor of history at the recently established Singapore-based University of Malaya. Responding quickly to the political ferment of Malayan nationalism, Parkinson expanded student numbers to meet demands for rapid localization of the public services and diverted the focus of teaching from European to Asian history. He set his department to produce a Malayan Historical Studies series to cover the little studied history of Malaya from the earliest recorded times and himself published the first of these intended volumes, *British Intervention in Malaya, 1867–1877* (1960). When the newly independent Federation of Malaya demanded its own university, Parkinson campaigned in vain to preserve a united institution based in Johor Bahru, which was within the federation but just across the causeway from colonial Singapore. Hospitable and gregarious, Parkinson brought town and gown together in his own home, where, at informal evening gatherings, he introduced students to aspiring local politicians. But his strong views and abrasive personality clashed with more conservative colleagues and the university establishment.

After divorce from Ethelwyn, in 1952 Parkinson married Oxford-educated writer and journalist (Elizabeth) Ann Fry (1921–1983), who for more than thirty years was a gracious hostess, adapting cheerfully to her husband's changing lifestyle and supporting him enthusiastically until her death. They had two sons and one daughter. The publication of *Parkinson's Law, or, The Pursuit of Progress* in 1958 changed Parkinson's life. Originating in an anonymous light-hearted article in *The Economist* in November 1955, Parkinson's 'recently discovered law' was based on the premise that 'work expands to fill the time available for its completion', and specified that 'administrators are more or less bound to multiply', since 'an official wants to multiply subordinates, not rivals' and 'officials make work for each other'. Pseudo-mathematical formulae and 'scientific proofs' gleaned from Admiralty and Colonial Office statistics showed the numbers of officials spiralling as ships and colonies dwindled. Sharing G. K. Chesterton's view that humour was the most effective way to communicate strong opinions, Parkinson chose the serious *Economist* rather than the satirical *Punch* to unveil his law, followed over the next two years by corollary 'laws' on cabinet government, committees, and 'how to get rid of the boss'.

The articles stimulated favourable correspondence, other than from the director of public relations at the War Office, who pointed to a 2000 per cent statistical error (*The Economist*, 8 Feb 1958), but first appeared in book form in the United States because of the initial reluctance of British publishers. The London edition, published by John Murray in 1958, a small book of little more than 100 pages with illustrations by Osbert Lancaster, was an immediate best-seller and Parkinson, arriving in England in the summer of 1958, an obscure professor from the Far East, was amazed to find himself an instant celebrity, lionized even by those he lampooned. His friend and admirer Enoch Powell compared him to 'a man who found an oil-well in his back garden' (*The Independent*, 12 March 1993). The Institute of Directors organized a reception in his honour in June 1958, and although Parkinson was disappointed when Walt Disney refused the film rights, the BBC produced a musical version with an overture scored for typewriters, and the *Law* was translated into many languages. It proved especially popular in communist countries, notably China and Poland, and in 1988 the Czechoslovakian Theatre Company performed a dramatization in Brno.

Parkinson was visiting professor at Harvard University in 1958 and at the universities of Illinois and Berkeley,

California, in 1959–60. He published *The Evolution of Political Thought* in the same year as *Parkinson's Law* and a comparative study of civilization in 1963. But *Parkinson's Law* effectively ended its author's academic career. He happily resigned from the University of Malaya and threw himself into the independent lifestyle of celebrity, writer, lecturer, and after-dinner speaker. Parkinson was short, squat, and rather comical looking, his physical appearance matching his cynical humour, and for the next thirty years he travelled in the United States, Europe, India, Australia, New Zealand, Japan, and Polynesia, often lecturing to huge audiences.

Parkinson's publications numbered more than sixty, including two biographies of fictional characters—C. S. Forester's Hornblower and P. G. Wodehouse's Jeeves—several historical plays about Guernsey, and eight novels. The latter comprised a series of six novels concerning the exploits of a Guernsey naval officer in the Revolutionary and Napoleonic Wars, one story for children, also partly based in Guernsey, and a final novel about the Isle of Man in the Second World War. In 1971 he launched an unsuccessful Anglo-American publishing company called Leviathan, specializing in big business, and himself wrote several works on business management. He wrote easily and quickly, but sequels to *Parkinson's Law* lacked the freshness and sparkle of the original. In later years he found it increasingly difficult to get books accepted for publication but continued to contribute regularly to British and American newspapers and journals.

Parkinson received honorary degrees from several American universities and was elected professor emeritus and honorary president of Troy University in 1970. A member of the French Académie de Marine, the United States Naval Institute, and the archives commission of the government of India, he took special delight in his honorary titles of lieutenant-colonel of the Kentucky militia, and admiral of the navy of the (land-locked) state of Nebraska.

The runaway financial success of *Parkinson's Law* and its spin-off forced him into tax exile. In 1960 he bought Les Caches Hall at St Martin's in Guernsey and made the island his base for the next twenty-six years, owning a number of fiefs, holding seigneurial court meetings, and revelling in feudal history and customs. Living in considerable style, he took up painting, decorated Les Caches with his own colourful murals, and built a theatre there to stage his own and other plays. Later he restored derelict Annesville Manor.

In old age Parkinson waxed ever more provocative and outspoken about his prejudices, notably government extravagance, punitive taxation, and modern feminism. While he often claimed there was little place for women outside the home except as biddable industrial employees who would not strike, in practice he was more harmonious, constructive, and supportive in his relationship with female colleagues and subordinates than with their male counterparts. And he appreciated intelligent wives. In 1985, two years after the death of his second wife, he married Iris Hilda Waters (*d.* 1994), whom he always called Ingrid, and moved to the Isle of Man in 1986. This did not suit them, and in 1988 they settled in Ingrid's home town of Canterbury, where Parkinson died in a nursing home on 9 March 1993. C. M. TURNBULL

Sources *WW* · *Guernsey Press* (11 March 1993) · *The Times* (11 March 1993) · *Daily Telegraph* (11 March 1993) · *The Independent* (12 March 1993) · C. N. Parkinson, 'A law unto myself', priv. coll. [Unpublished typescript autobiography] · C. N. Parkinson, *Guernsey Press* (April 1983) [obit. of Ann Parkinson] · C. N. Parkinson, *Parkinson's law, or, The pursuit of progress* (1958) · 'Parkinson's law', *The Economist* (19 Nov 1955), 395–7 [also 3 Nov 1956, 16 Feb 1957, 23 Feb 1957] · personal knowledge (2004) · private information (2004) · C. N. Parkinson, *The rise of the port of Liverpool* (1952) · C. N. Parkinson, *War in the eastern seas, 1793–1815* (1954) · C. N. Parkinson, *British intervention in Malaya, 1867–1877* (1960) · C. N. Parkinson, *A law unto themselves* (1966)

Archives Emmanuel College, Cambridge, papers · priv. coll., autobiography · priv. coll., diaries | SOUND BL NSA, BBC Sound Archives, talk, 'Parkinson's law, the law itself', 14 June 1958; interview re *Mrs Parkinson's law*, 10 Oct 1968; Desert Island Discs, 10 July 1979; interview in *About politics* series, 16 April 1974; Robin Day in *World at one*, 15 Nov 1979 · BL NSA, Jupiter recordings 1959 'Some negative aspects of the administrative process'; with John Watnough, 5 March 1962 (no details); Argo, 'Jeeves: a gentleman's person', 1980 cassette

Likenesses G. Argent, photograph, 1969, NPG [*see illus.*] · photograph, repro. in *The Times*

Wealth at death under £125,000: probate, 11 May 1994, *CGPLA Eng. & Wales*

Parkinson, Henry Thomas (1852–1924), Roman Catholic priest and social scientist, was born on 30 January 1852 at Cheadle, Staffordshire, the son of Henry Parkinson, a barber, and his wife, Isabella Millward. He went to Sedgley Park School, Staffordshire, in 1865 and then in 1868 to Douai in France, where he began his ecclesiastical studies, which he continued in 1873 at St Bernard's, Olton, the Birmingham diocesan seminary. In 1874 he proceeded to the English College, Rome, and was ordained priest on 26 May 1877, obtaining a doctorate in divinity at the Gregorian University. On completing his studies he returned to Olton as vice-rector and professor of philosophy. After ten years in this post, in 1887, he had his first and only taste of work in a parish, but it was at St Chad's Cathedral in Birmingham and it gave him an insight into the life of the poor in an industrial city.

When, in 1889, St Mary's College, Oscott, ceased to be a school for lay boys and became exclusively a seminary for the training of future priests Parkinson became professor of philosophy and vice-rector to Bishop Ilsley. He was to spend the rest of his life at Oscott but these thirty-five years were to witness a remarkable development. Although his family background and education might be considered very traditional, if not parochial, he became increasingly aware of a wider context. In 1897 Oscott became a central seminary for the whole of the south of England and this prompted Parkinson to think at a national level. His aims were broadened and he set out not only to make the outside world known to his students but also to make the outside world aware of Oscott and the English Roman Catholic tradition. It was a time when the University of Birmingham was in its beginnings and his interest in the relationship of science to religion led him to make contacts not only with fellow religionists like Sir Bertram Windle but other leading lights including Sir Oliver Lodge. They not only visited Oscott but they considered the possibility of students of the college attending some of the courses at the university.

In his own studies Parkinson never lost touch with the official views of Rome and he was always prepared to adapt to any change at the top level even to the extent of forsaking some of the ideas he had imbibed as a student when they fell out of favour in Rome. When the Central Seminary collapsed in 1907 and Oscott reverted to being mainly a diocesan seminary Parkinson did not lose his breadth of vision. Interest in social matters and the effects of the industrial revolution had been the concern of many Christians throughout the previous century but Parkinson was responsible for awakening the conscience of English Roman Catholics who were lagging behind their co-religionists on the continent in these matters. He gave a regular course of lectures at Oscott on social study and incorporated it into the ethics section of the philosophy course. He was particularly attentive to Pope Leo XIII's encyclical Rerum novarum and he promoted the study of papal teaching on the condition of the working classes among the laity at parish level. When the Catholic Social Guild was founded in 1909 Parkinson became its first president and later he was patron when a Catholic labour college was founded at Oxford in 1921. This was to develop into the Catholic Workers' College and eventually Plater College.

A Primer of Social Science was published in 1913; it proved to be popular and was reprinted several times after Parkinson's death. He was not only associated with international Catholic conferences and meetings abroad, in Belgium and France, but he addressed public meetings at home. In 1909–10 he spoke in Birmingham on behalf of the national committee for the prevention of destitution at a meeting chaired by Henry Russell Wakefield, later the Anglican bishop of Birmingham, and he corresponded and shared platforms in Leeds and London with Sydney and Beatrice Webb. He also wrote pamphlets concerning poor law reform. He continued to attend to his duties as professor of philosophy and rector of Oscott, publishing, in Bruges, two works in Latin: *Definitiones philosophiae universae* (1894), a glossary of philosophical terms, and *Refectio spiritualis* (1906), a two-volume collection of meditations. He had great musical gifts and personally took charge of the college music and liturgy. He was a member of the reviewing staff of *The Tablet* and accepted an invitation from the Catholic University of America to contribute articles to the *Catholic Encyclopedia*.

Parkinson was able to get through an immense amount of work by reason of his strict daily timetable from which he rarely deviated. He had a strong sense of duty. Although he was not an original thinker, he was able to transmit the benefits of his experience and wide reading to his students and the growing number of laity who were taking an interest in social matters. He remained active up to the end. Parkinson was taken ill, removed to hospital, and operated on for peritonitis, but died on 22 June 1924 at Woodlea Nursing Home, Wylde Green, Birmingham. He was buried in the cemetery at Oscott College three days later.

MICHAEL E. WILLIAMS

Sources corresp. and MSS, Birmingham archdiocesan archives, Birmingham, St Mary's College archives • *The Oscotian*, 3rd ser., 24/72 (autumn 1924) • D. Evans, 'Henry Parkinson: philosopher-rector', *Oscott College, 1838–1988: a volume of commemorative essays*, ed. J. F. Champ (1988), 157–67 • *Birmingham archdiocesan directory* (1925) • *The Tablet* (28 June 1924), 890 • corresp., Plater College archives, Oxford • *CGPLA Eng. & Wales* (1924) • b. cert. • parish register, Cheadle, Staffordshire, St Giles [baptism], 8 Feb 1852

Archives Birmingham archdiocesan archives, Birmingham, corresp. and papers • Plater College, Oxford, corresp.

Likenesses Beyaert, portrait, Birmingham archdiocesan archives, Birmingham • photographs, Birmingham archdiocesan archives, Birmingham

Wealth at death £343 14*s*. 1*d*.: probate, 19 July 1924, *CGPLA Eng. & Wales*

Parkinson, James (1653–1722), polemicist, son of James Parkinson, was born in Witney, Oxfordshire, on 3 March 1653. He matriculated from Brasenose College, Oxford, as a servitor on 2 April 1669 and migrated in 1671 to Corpus Christi College with a scholarship. Parkinson soon displayed his characteristic propensity to discord, accusing Robert Newlyn, the president, of nepotism. He was ejected from Corpus in 1674, and moved to Gloucester Hall, where he took his BA degree, and then, in the same year, to Hart Hall. Parkinson gained a reputation as an orator; having impressed with a speech of some note at encaenia in 1674, he was elected to a fellowship at Lincoln College. In 1675 Parkinson proceeded MA and was ordained.

In spite of, or possibly because of, his success as a tutor—he was said to have more pupils than the rest of the Lincoln fellows together, and to have an income of £120 per annum from tuition—Parkinson soon incurred the displeasure of his colleagues with his whiggish and republican opinions. By 1683 their disapproval reached a peak; five of the fellows drew up a list of twelve articles against Parkinson arguing that he maintained 'unwarrantable and seditious principles' (*Life and Times of Anthony Wood*, 69). At a time when the university was actively demonstrating its loyalty to the crown, Parkinson's views were unpopular. The fellows, receiving no encouragement from the rector, Thomas Marshall, took their complaint to the secretary of state, Sir Leoline Jenkins, who in turn contacted the pro-vice-chancellor, Timothy Halton, provost of Queen's College. Parkinson was summoned before Halton on 20 August 1683 and was bound over to appear at the next assizes on a bail of £2000. He duly appeared on 3 September 1683 and was ordered to reappear at the assizes in the following spring. However, the next morning he was summoned by Halton and expelled from the university. He was deprived of his fellowship, in spite of his protests that it was his freehold, by the college visitor, Bishop Thomas Barlow, as soon as the proclamation of expulsion had been posted on 6 September. Parkinson's expulsion was received with some pleasure by many in the university including John Fell, dean of Christ Church, who expressed his hopes that Parkinson's fate would be noted both within and beyond the university. Like Strange Southby and John Locke, Parkinson was a victim of the university's reaction against whiggery.

Parkinson lived in London, remaining an outcast from the university, until 1689 when vice-chancellor Gilbert Ironside renewed his membership. Feeling his republican opinions vindicated by the nation's response to James II, Parkinson campaigned vigorously to be restored to his fellowship, writing a pamphlet published in 1689 entitled *An Account of Mr Parkinson's Expulsion from the University of Oxford*. His efforts were unsuccessful. However, through whiggish pamphlets such as his *An Examination of Dr Sherlock's Book … the Case of the Allegiance due to Sovereign Powers* (1691), Parkinson attracted the favourable attention of the whig archbishop John Tillotson, and the future lord chancellor John Somers. Through their patronage he was appointed chief master of King Edward's School in Birmingham, first appearing in the minutes of the governing body on 4 January 1695. In 1698 Parkinson married the daughter of Philip Freher, proprietor of The Swan inn in New Street, Birmingham, and his wife, Sarah. They had five children, four of whom—James, Elizabeth, Catherine, and Ann—were baptized in St Martin's Church between September 1700 and November 1704.

Parkinson's career as a schoolmaster was no more tranquil than that at Oxford had been. The governors of the school, under the leadership of the Birmingham lawyer Samuel Eden, tried in vain to dislodge him through an action in chancery, alleging that he was allowing the school to decline in numbers and in reputation, and that he had misused the school's endowment for his rebuilding schemes. In 1705 the governors succeeded in withholding that part of the endowment which paid the headmaster and usher but the governors' battle to have Parkinson removed was stymied by Eden's earlier success on their behalf when the school's original charter, voluntarily given up by the governors to Charles II, was restored in 1692: the charter forbade the exclusion of any master by the governors. In spite of chancery's finding in Parkinson's favour in 1711, the arguments between the headmaster and the governors dragged on until his death eleven years later. At least part of the governors' case was justified: the numbers of boys admitted to the school did drop during Parkinson's headship; local gentleman were reluctant to expose their sons to his notorious political views manifested, for instance, in his *A Loyal Oration*, published in the town in 1717.

Parkinson died in Birmingham on 28 March 1722 and was buried near the altar steps in St Martin's Church, Birmingham. He was survived by his son James, who was educated at his father's school and then at Wadham College, Oxford, graduating BA in 1721 and proceeding MA on 11 May 1724. He was elected subdean of Wadham that year but died on 28 December. J. H. CURTHOYS

Sources V. Green, *The commonwealth of Lincoln College, 1427–1977* (1979) • *Hist. U. Oxf.* 4: *17th-cent. Oxf.* • A. Trott, *No place for fop or idler: the story of King Edward's School, Birmingham* (1992) • *The life and times of Anthony Wood*, ed. A. Clark, 3, OHS, 26 (1894) • *VCH Warwickshire*, vol. 2 • T. Fowler, *Corpus Christi* (1898) • W. A. L. Vincent, *The grammar schools: their continuing tradition, 1660–1714* (1969) • T. W. Hutton, *King Edward's School, Birmingham, 1552–1952* (1952) • *An account of Mr Parkinson's expulsion from the University of Oxford* (1689) • J. Wallis, letter, 19 Sept 1683, Bodl. Oxf., MS Add. D. 105

Parkinson, James (*bap.* 1730, *d.* 1813), land agent and museum proprietor, was born in Shrewsbury, where he was baptized at St Mary's Church on 28 February 1730, the son of James Parkinson and his wife, Jane Birch. His family was settled in Ireland in the reign of Charles I, but his parents had been based in Shrewsbury since 1723. He was first brought up as a law stationer, and then became a land agent and accountant. In 1769 he helped settle the tangled estates of Sir Thomas Robinson, first baronet (1703–1777), at Rokeby, Yorkshire, after he had incurred 'very great expenses in building and in costly entertainments' (GEC, *Baronetage*, 1906, 5.69). Parkinson became agent or steward to many noblemen's estates, and was noted as a skilful and upright man of business. He later became one of the proprietors of the Ranelagh Gardens in London. He married Sarah, some time before 1775.

In 1784 Sir Ashton Lever was granted an act of parliament to enable the disposal of his famous museum in Leicester Square by lottery, hoping thereby to recoup the enormous expenses he had incurred in gathering it together. It comprised the rarest productions of the animal, vegetable, and mineral kingdoms, with works of art and various artefacts of native peoples in North and South America, Tahiti, Australia, and other places, brought back by Captain James Cook and others. Lottery tickets at 1 guinea each went on sale from October 1784, but only 8000 (of the 36,000) were sold. On 23 March 1786 the draw was held. Parkinson only later realized that he held the winning ticket, his—by now deceased—wife having purchased two unknown to him in December 1784 and given one away. Parkinson generously allowed Lever to continue to exhibit his collections at the museum until September 1786. The publicity regarding the poor sales of Lever's tickets had been immense, and only now did this help to make Lever's museum truly popular.

Parkinson at first attempted to dispose of the entire museum, and the empress of Russia and the queen of Portugal were named as potential purchasers. When none came forward Parkinson decided to form a company to build a new home in which to reopen a rejuvenated museum to the public. He first appealed for new materials to augment the already vast collections in December 1786. The naturalist Dr George Shaw (1751–1813) read lectures on natural history at the museum in May 1787. Parkinson finally closed the Leicester Square museum in September 1787, and soon opened his large new, appropriate building, the Rotunda, occupying nearly 1000 square yards on the Surrey side of the Thames, near Blackfriars Bridge, in December 1787. This had been designed by himself and James Burton, alias Haliburton (1761–1837), who was its builder. The entrance fee was 2*s.* 6*d.*, which some thought too low for a building which had seventeen different apartments. Its grand saloon was illustrated in the never-completed *Companion*, which Parkinson started publishing in 1790. Although this site proved to be 'most injudicious, since it was completely out of the mighty stream of human beings which never ceases to flow through the centre of the metropolis' (Swainson, 246), as Robert Jameson's 1793 diary demonstrates, it did prove a wonderful oasis for London's naturalists and dealers; there they could study nature through the specimens being continually added, and meet each other. Also, as the American Charles Willson Peale noted, 'the trouble to obtain a sight of the British Museum renders it of less value to the public than a private collection belonging to Parkinson called the Leverian Museum' (C. Willson Peale, *Discourse Introductory to a Course of Lectures on the Science of Nature*, 1800, 20).

Parkinson's activities in acquiring so much new material, whether in natural history, mineralogy, or ethnography, and promoting its display, were impressive. His friend George Shaw published descriptions of many specimens in his *Musei Leveriani explicatio*, of select specimens from the museum, but of which only volume 1 and a part of volume 2 were published between 1790 and 1796, by Parkinson. Many other drawings of its contents, by Sarah Stone (*c*.1760–1844), also survive. There is no doubt that throughout the museum, and especially in mineralogy, where Parkinson was helped by his elder son, John, real efforts were made to describe and classify the material. The *Companion*, when dealing with minerals, specifically lamented that the backward state of 'this most useful study should in England be so very far behind other European nations' (pt 2, 'Minerals', 55). So when the journalist William Jerdan (1782–1869) later described the museum as 'a most heterogenous medley of stuffed animals, without order or classification', and that 'as a means for solid or lasting instruction its miscellaneous and aimless character rendered it useless' (Altick, 30), he was describing a museum in its death throes. Jerdan had arrived in London only in the spring of 1806, long after Parkinson was contemplating how best to dispose of his museum.

It was already rumoured in 1798 that Parkinson had been offered £12,000 and a German baronetcy in exchange for these collections. But he was then intending to move the museum to Bond Street, more in the centre of London, since it was not paying the interest on the sum borrowed to build its Blackfriars site. Parkinson finally decided to dispose of the entire collection about 1804. He first offered it to the second administration of William Pitt (1804), who referred it to Henry Dundas, Viscount Melville; the latter, however, accused of having corruptly used public money elsewhere, did nothing. Parkinson next offered it to the second Grenville administration (1806), and Lord Henry Petty approved his proposal that it be purchased for £20,000, or less if it were valued at a lower price. Ministers referred this to Sir Joseph Banks, but he 'disapproved purchasing it. Parkinson says Sir Joseph hated Sir Ashton Lever, therefore hates the Collection' (Farington, *Diary*, 9 July 1806, 8.2807). So the museum closed in April 1806 and its auction sale, first mooted in September 1805, was entrusted to the London auctioneers King and Lochee, on the premises. It proved a great event, lasting sixty-five days, from 5 May to 19 July 1806, and comprising nearly 8000 lots, described in an enormous *Sale Catalogue*. But the total sum now realized was only £6600. Purchasers came from all over Europe, with more than 180 different bidders intent on augmenting collections or establishing museums elsewhere.

Parkinson died on 25 February 1813 at his home, 5 The Polygon, Somers Town, London, leaving estate under £3500. He and his wife had had a daughter and two sons. The elder son, John Parkinson (*bap.* 1775, *d.* 1847), was a good mineralogist, and had helped his father. He later became active as a diplomat, from at least 1819, first in Europe and then as British consul—initially in Pernambuco, Brazil, and later in Mexico. He was elected FRS in 1840 and died in Paris. The younger son, **Joseph T. Parkinson** (*bap.* 1782, *d.* 1855), had an equally significant career as an architect. He was first articled to William Pilkington. He then became a member of James Burton's Loyal British Artificers, acting on behalf of refugees from revolutionary France. He next designed a castellated house as Burton's residence, and converted his father's Blackfriars Rotunda building for use by the Surrey Institution, with a new chemical laboratory and library, which opened in 1808. He was later surveyor to the Union Fire Assurance Company, and was district surveyor of Westminster. He died in May 1855 in London, and was buried in Kensal Green cemetery. H. S. TORRENS

Sources *GM*, 1st ser., 83/1 (1813), 291–2 · W. J. Smith, 'Sir Ashton Lever of Alkrington and his museum', *Transactions of the Lancashire and Cheshire Antiquarian Society*, 72 (1965), 61–92 · Farington, *Diary*, vol. 8, 1806–7 · *A companion to the museum, late Sir Ashton Lever's*, Leverian Museum (1790); repr. (1979) · *Catalogue of the Leverian Museum* (1806); repr. (1979) · M. S. von La Roche, *Sophie in London, 1786* (1933) · A. Newton, 'Notes on some old museums', *Report of proceedings … of the Museums Association* (1891), 28–48 · D. Lysons, ed., 'Collectanea, or, A collection of advertisements and paragraphs', BL, C.103.k.11 [cuttings from newspapers dated 1660–1825], vol. 2, fols. 110–18 · J. M. Sweet, 'Robert Jameson in London, 1793', *Annals of Science*, 19 (1963), 81–116 · W. Swainson, *Taxidermy: with the biography of zoologists* (1840) · D. Murray, *Museums: their history and their use*, 3 vols. (1904), 1.175–7; 2.325–6 · W. Hone, *The Every-day Book and Table Book*, 2 (1838), 985–94 · H. M. Colvin, *A biographical dictionary of British architects, 1600–1840*, new edn (1978), 621 [Joseph Parkinson] · *Register of St Mary's, Shrewsbury* (1911), 308 and 333 · J. C. H. King, 'New evidence for the contents of the Leverian Museum', *Journal of the History of Collections*, 8 (1996), 167–86 · C. E. Jackson, *Sarah Stone: natural curiosities from the new worlds* (1998) · E. Colby, *The life of Thomas Holcroft*, 2 vols. (1925) · W. Jerdan, *Men I have known* (1866) · R. D. Altick, *The shows of London* (1978), 30–32 · *DNB* · *IGI*

Wealth at death under £3500: administration, 1813, PRO, PROB 6/189, fol. 292*v*

Parkinson, James (1755–1824), surgeon and palaeontologist, was born on 11 April 1755 at 1 Hoxton Square, Shoreditch, London, one of the three children of John Parkinson (*c*.1725–1784), surgeon, and his wife, Mary. He was apprenticed to his father and about 1776 trained at the London Hospital. A year later he was awarded the honorary silver medal of the Royal Humane Society for resuscitating an attempted suicide. His first publication, *Observations on Dr H. Smith's Philosophy of Physic*, appeared in 1780. The following year he married Mary Dale at St Leonard's

Church, Shoreditch. They had three daughters and three sons. During 1784–5 he attended lectures by John Hunter and was awarded the diploma of the Company of Surgeons in 1784.

By the mid-1790s Parkinson had become involved in radical politics. A member of the Society for Constitutional Information (formed 1780), he later became a member of the *London Corresponding Society, and was friendly with John Thelwall and the publisher Daniel Isaac Eaton. His involvement with radical politics led him to produce a number of pamphlets, many under the pseudonym of Old Hubert. These included *An Address to E. Burke from the Swinish Multitude*. Following the arrest in 1794 of Thomas Hardy and others on a charge of high treason Parkinson produced *Revolutions without Bloodshed, or, Reformation Preferable to Revolt* (1794), the proceeds from which were to go to the defendants' families. His *Vindication of the London Corresponding Society* was published at about the same time. As a result of his activities Parkinson was invited to become a member of the committee of the Corresponding Society. In September 1794 an attempt was made on the life of George III, in the so-called Popgun Plot. Parkinson was summoned to appear before the privy council as he knew one of the defendants. Questioned about his membership of the committee Parkinson explained that he had been invited to join:

> Because they believe me firm in the cause (Mr Pitt smiled) of *Parliamentary Reform*, and because I had just produced a little tract for the benefit of the wives and children of the persons imprisoned on charges of High treason. (Smith, 60)

His interrogation by the privy council was published in J. Smith's *Assassination of the King!* (1795). Parkinson's political activities after this date are unknown. By 1799 he was publishing on medical topics again with the appearance of *Medical Admonitions Addressed to Families*. This was followed by two other medical advice books. He also published *The Hospital Pupil* (1800) and *Observations on the Nature and Cure of the Gout* (1805).

Parkinson's other great interest was the study of geology and fossils. The publication of the first volume of his *Organic Remains of a Former World* in 1804 was the result of research begun in or before 1798. Among those acknowledged by Parkinson in the book were the surgeons Sir William Blizard and Henry Cline, and the naturalist Sir Joseph Banks. Epistolary in form, the work was aimed at a general readership. In volume 1 on the vegetable kingdom, he discussed the process of fossilization and argued that the present position of fossils was the result of a great flood. This was part of the larger endeavour 'to find out the ways of God in forming, destroying, and reforming the Earth' (Parkinson, *Remains*, 13). The study of fossils assisted in this by providing evidence of living forms wiped out by the deluge and whose remains were now a source of utility and beauty, as with coal and precious metals. He also believed that nature was in a constant process of transformation and that the earth would continue to undergo regular changes. This led him to ask whether 'may it not thus become fitted for the reception of beings of higher susceptibilities and power?' (ibid., 468). Two further volumes appeared: *The Fossil Zoophytes* (volume 2, 1808) and *Fossil Starfish, Shells, Insects and Mammalia* (volume 3, 1811). It has been described as 'the outstanding event in the history of our scientific knowledge of fossils' (Thackray, 457). Parkinson was a founder member of the Geological Society in 1807, serving on its council from 1813 to 1815, and on its committee of maps in 1809. In the same year he was elected a member of the Wernerian Natural History Society. He was also an honorary member of the Imperial Society of Moscow Naturalists.

In 1817 Parkinson published what was to become his best-known work, *An Essay on the Shaking Palsy*. The book was the product of several years' research, and in it he gave details of six cases which he had studied. Parkinson identified 'Shaking Palsy' as a degenerative disease of the nervous system which caused 'Involuntary tremulous motion, with lessened muscular power' (Parkinson, *Essay*, 1). He achieved this despite having been unable to carry out any anatomical examinations. He also succeeded in identifying the 'shaking palsy' as a specific disease, as until then 'some have regarded its characteristic symptoms as distinct and different diseases, and others have given its name to diseases differing essentially from it' (ibid., ii). It did not, however, become known as Parkinson's disease until 1876 when the French neurologist J.-M. Charcot wrote of the 'maladie de Parkinson'.

Parkinson was an active citizen in his neighbourhood. In 1799 he was made a trustee for the poor of the liberty of Hoxton, he was secretary to the Sunday school at St Leonard's, believing that 'a mere literary education without the inculcation of moral and religious principles would prove highly injurious' (Morris, 17), and for twenty-five years was medical attendant to the private madhouse at Holly House, Hoxton. In 1813 he became surgeon-apothecary and man-midwife to the poor of St Leonard's. A contemporary described him as being 'rather below middle stature, with an energetic intellect, and pleasing expression of countenance, and of mild and courteous manners' (ibid., 18). Parkinson died following a stroke at his home, 3 Pleasant Row, Kingsland Road, Hoxton, on 21 December 1824. MICHAEL BEVAN

Sources A. Morris, *James Parkinson* (1989) • J. Thackray, 'James Parkinson's *Organic remains of a former world* (1804–1811)', *J. Soc. Biblphy. Nat. Hist.*, 7 (1976), 451–66 • J. Smith, *Assassination of the king!* (1795) • J. Parkinson, *Organic remains of a former world*, 1 (1804) • J. Parkinson, *An essay on the shaking palsy* (1817) • *IGI*
Archives RCS Eng., letters

Parkinson, John (1566/7–1650), apothecary and herbalist, was apprenticed from Christmas 1585 for eight years to a London apothecary, Francis Slater, a member of the Grocers' Company; he gained his freedom in 1593. Like many apothecaries in the Grocers' Company, Parkinson felt the importance of his work was given insufficient recognition and that he and others had not enough power within the company. Consequently he supported those who wished to form their own separate company, and joined the Society of Apothecaries when it was established in December 1617; he was a member of its first court of assistants.

Parkinson became so well respected in his profession that he was one of the five apothecaries who were consulted by the College of Physicians during the compilation of the first *Pharmacopoeia Londinensis*. He was also actively involved in obtaining for the new society a grant of arms and in drawing up a schedule of all medicines which should be stocked by an apothecary. In August 1620 he was elected junior warden, but he was not interested in climbing higher up the administrative tree and in the new year of 1622 he asked for permission to leave the court of assistants. In view of the help he had given to the Society of Apothecaries this was, most unusually, granted.

This left Parkinson free not only from committees but also to work at what was now his consuming interest—that of tending his garden in Long Acre, whence he had moved from Ludgate Hill some years earlier. His first and best-loved book was *Paradisi in sole paradisus terrestris, or, A Garden of All Sorts of Pleasant Flowers … with a Kitchen Garden … and an Orchard* (1629). The book of more than 600 pages was dedicated to Queen Henrietta Maria, for which Charles I gave him the title of *botanicus regius primarius*. This was the first work published on English gardening, and it had descriptions of almost 1000 plants, with many of the entries giving evidence of cross-breeding and careful selection.

Parkinson's second work, which occupied him for many years, was *Theatrum botanicum* (1640), with more than 1700 pages. This described some 3800 plants and showed his extensive reading of the period's authorities; of particular value was the almost entire incorporation of Caspar Bauhin's *Pinax*, for its synonyms. Parkinson divided plants into seventeen 'tribes', based partly on their medicinal qualities and partly on habitat. William How in 1655 roundly accused him of plagiarizing the work of Matthias L'Obel, but Parkinson had acknowledged his debt to him, and as one historian wrote, 'He has taken very little, for the simple reason that very little was worth taking' (Raven, 268). Certainly John Ray did not despise the work, for he termed it 'the most full and comprehensive book of that subject extant' (Raven, 272), and frequently quoted from it.

Parkinson died in the summer of 1650, and was buried, appropriately, at St Martin-in-the-Fields, London, on 6 August. His name was commemorated by Plumier in the Central American genus of leguminous trees *Parkinsonia*.

JUANITA BURNBY

Sources Grocers' Company of London, admissions, bindings, and accounts, GL • court minutes, Society of Apothecaries, GL, MS 8200/1 • G. S. Boulgar and E. Hawks, *Pioneers of plant study* (1928) • C. E. Raven, *English naturalists from Neckham to Ray: a study of the making of the modern world* (1947); repr. (1968) • C. R. B. Barrett, *History of the Society of Apothecaries* (1905) • C. Wall, H. C. Cameron, and E. A. Underwood, *A history of the Society of Apothecaries of London*, 1 (1963) • L. G. Matthews, *The royal apothecaries* (1967) • J. Burnby, 'Some early London physic gardens', *Pharmaceutical Historian*, 24 (Dec 1994), no. 4, 2–7

Likenesses W. Marshall, line engraving, BM, NPG; repro. in J. Parkinson, *Theatrum botanicum* (1640) • C. Switzer, woodcut, BM, NPG; repro. in J. Parkinson, *Paradisus terrestris* (1629) • stipple, Wellcome L. • watercolour drawing, NPG • woodcut, Wellcome L.

Parkinson, Joseph T. (*bap.* **1782**, *d.* **1855**). *See under* Parkinson, James (*bap.* 1730, *d.* 1813).

Parkinson, Norman [*formerly* Ronald William Smith] (**1913–1990**), photographer, was born in Roehampton, London, on 21 April 1913, the second of three children and younger son of William James Parkinson Smith, barrister and councillor of the borough of Wandsworth, and his wife, Louise Emily Cobley. Evacuated to the countryside during the First World War, he returned to live in the family home at 32 Landford Road, Putney. Educated at Westminster School (1927–31), he described himself as 'scholastically abysmal', but received the encouragement of the art master, Henry S. Williamson, and was awarded the school's Henry Luce art prize. In 1931 he was apprenticed to the distinguished Bond Street court photographers, Speaight & Son. With a solid, if traditional, grounding in his craft he was able to set up in 1934 (initially in partnership with Norman Kibblewhite) the Norman Parkinson Portrait Studio at 1 Dover Street, London. It was after this that he adopted the name Norman Parkinson.

His earliest photographs, many of which were published in the *Bystander*, were principally of débutantes, but a chance meeting in 1935 with P. Joyce Reynolds, editor of *Harper's Bazaar*, changed the course of his career. Invited to try fashion photography, he was persuaded by the magazine's art director, A. Y. McPeake, to photograph outdoors. Parkinson became a pioneer in the genre, rejecting the static, posed artificiality of the studio and appropriating the naturalism and immediacy of contemporary news photography. He was also broadening his range, and notable early portraits include those of Noël Coward, the Sitwells, and Edward James, a patron of the arts. His regular contributions of current affairs photographs to the *Bystander* included a report on unemployed Welsh miners and a weekly series, from 1937, on the armed forces preparing for war. Parkinson combined a modern style with traditional content in collaborating with the experimental photographer Francis Bruguière on photo-murals for the British pavilion at the 1937 Paris Universal Exhibition, images of quintessential 'Britishness' anticipating his neo-Elizabethan iconography of the post-war years. During the Second World War he combined farming, at Bushley, Worcestershire, with photography.

Parkinson's long association with *Vogue* began in 1940. Its art editor, John Parsons, was another catalyst in Parkinson's career, redirecting him to sources within the history of English painting and architecture. His photographs offered the solace of the English rural idyll during wartime deprivations, and served as a reaffirmation of enduring values in the years of post-war austerity. War damage destroyed most of his pre-war negatives.

From 1949 to 1955 Parkinson spent summer months in New York, working for American *Vogue*. He began to photograph increasingly in colour, in exotic locations throughout the world, a development which became a cornerstone of his later style. His contract with *Vogue* having expired in 1959, he became photographer and associate editor from 1960 to 1964 on *Queen* magazine, a base

Norman Parkinson (1913–1990), by Trevor Leighton

from which he launched his alternative view of the culture of the 1960s. In 1963 he bought a house in Tobago, subsequently dividing his time between there and Twickenham. It was in Tobago that he became a pig breeder and manufactured his well-known sausage, the Porkinson banger. In 1968 he was elected an honorary fellow of the Royal Photographic Society.

Parkinson combined hard work and perfectionism with a keen sense of humour. Six feet five inches tall, slim and mustachioed, he was an imposing figure, and his elegant if often unconventional mode of dress, which included a Kashmiri wedding cap, regularly gained him a place on British and international lists of best dressed men. He returned to *Vogue* from 1965 until he severed his connection with the Condé Nast organization following a dispute in 1978. His twenty-first birthday photographs of Princess Anne, in 1971, and his coverage of her engagement and wedding, in 1973, were widely considered a breakthrough in the glamorous and informal portrayal of royalty. Many similarly acclaimed commissions followed, including the queen mother's seventy-fifth birthday photographs, and the triple portrait with her daughters to mark her eightieth birthday.

Now recognized as a doyen of British photography, Parkinson was elected a fellow of the Institute of Incorporated Photographers in 1975, and in 1981 he was appointed CBE. His first major museum retrospective opened in London's National Portrait Gallery later in the same year. In 1978 he began regular assignments photographing the wealthy and famous for *Town and Country* magazine, which again brought his name to prominence in the USA. In 1983 he received the American Society of Magazine Photographers' lifetime of achievement award.

In November 1935 he married Margaret, daughter of Sir Reginald Mitchell Banks, county court judge. The marriage was dissolved and in 1942 he married Thelma Woolley, daughter of George Blay, timber merchant. There were no children from either marriage. In 1947 Parkinson met Wenda (*d.* 1987), second daughter of William Albert Rogerson FRCP FRCS, of the Royal Army Medical Corps, and she became for many years his favourite model and muse. Together they raised her son by a previous marriage, Simon (*b.* 1945), as Simon Parkinson. Parkinson suffered a stroke while on assignment in Borneo, and died two weeks later in Singapore, on 14 February 1990.

MARTIN HARRISON, *rev.*

Sources N. Parkinson, *Lifework* (1983) · *The Times* (16 Feb 1990) · *The Independent* (16 Feb 1990) · *The Independent* (17 Feb 1990) · private information (1996) · *CGPLA Eng. & Wales* (1990)

Likenesses photographs, 1980–85, Hult. Arch. · M. Boxer, caricature, pen and ink, 1981, NPG · T. Leighton, photograph, NPG [*see illus.*]

Wealth at death under £100,000: probate, 5 March 1990, *CGPLA Eng. & Wales*

Parkinson, Richard (*bap.* **1747**, *d.* **1815**), agriculturist, is probably identifiable with the Richard Parkinson baptized on 31 August 1747 in the parish of Belleau and Aby, Lincolnshire, the son of Abraham Parkinson, a farmer. At the age of nine, he was sent to school, and at the age of eighteen he made a tour of Craven, Lancashire. Parkinson, like his father, became a farmer, probably first farming near Doncaster, Yorkshire. He wrote *The experienced farmer: an entire new work, in which the whole system of agriculture, husbandry, and breeding of cattle, is explained* (1798), and was recommended, in or about 1798, to George Washington by Sir John Sinclair, then president of the board of agriculture. Washington had recently sent proposals to Sinclair for letting land at his estate at Mount Vernon, Virginia, to English or Scottish farmers, and Parkinson negotiated with Washington by letter to rent one of the Mount Vernon farms on the understanding that he would view the property before accepting.

On 3 September 1798 Parkinson set sail from Liverpool with his wife, six children, and a cargo which included cattle, hogs, and horses, including the race horses Phenomenon and Cardinal Puff. The passage to America took ten weeks, in which time he lost eleven horses, including Phenomenon; he arrived at Norfolk, Virginia, on 11 November 1798. After journeying up the Potomac River he finally arrived at Mount Vernon, where he found that Washington was away from home and was instead met by a steward. On docking at the town of Alexandria, where his ship could be cleared, Parkinson hired a horse and travelled back to Mount Vernon, to view his prospective farm. However, he found the land unsuitable, decided not to accept, and instead chose a farm at Orange Hill, 3 miles from Baltimore. There he attempted dairy farming and cultivated turnips (with which he found some success by sowing with plaster of Paris), Indian corn, and peaches.

Parkinson returned to England, probably before publication of his *The experienced farmer's tour in America exhibiting the American system of agriculture and breeding of cattle, with its recent improvements* (1805). He expressed his hope, at the front of his work, that publishing an account of his 'disappointments in America, should have the desired effect—that of preventing my countrymen from running headlong into misery, as myself and others have done'. A further edition of *The experienced farmer's tour* appeared in the same year, entitled *Tour in America in 1798, 1799, and 1800, exhibiting sketches of society and manners, and a particular account of the American system of agriculture.* His work detailed his tours (which included visits to Philadelphia, New York, Brunswick, and the Chesapeake peninsula), his experiences in America, and his views on the American system of agriculture.

Parkinson spent two years farming in Ireland (possibly between 1801 and 1803) where he greatly improved an estate of 500 acres belonging to Lord Conyngham at Slane, co. Meath. On this experience he based his work *The English practice of agriculture exemplified in the management of a farm in Ireland belonging to the earl of Conyngham, at Slane … with an appendix: containing … a comparative estimate of the Irish and English mode of culture* (1806). Parkinson was also author of *General View of the Agriculture of the County of Rutland* (1808), *Practical Observations on Gypsum, or, Plaster of Paris as a Manure* (1808), *Treatise on the breeding and management of live stock … with an appendix containing tables of prices* (1810), *General View of the Agriculture of the County of Huntingdon* (1811), and *General View of the Agriculture of Buckinghamshire* (1813), co-written with St John Priest. Parkinson died at Osgodby, Lincolnshire, on 23 February 1815.

Yolanda Foote

Sources W. Pitt, *General view of the agriculture of Leicestershire* (1811) • J. C. Loudon, *An encyclopaedia of agriculture* (1831), 1211 • J. Donaldson, *Agricultural biography* (1854), 83 • J. G. Wilson and J. Fiske, eds., *Appletons' cyclopaedia of American biography*, 4 (1888), 657 • P. L. Haworth, *George Washington—farmer* (1915) • R. Parkinson, *The experienced farmer's tour in America …*, 2 vols. (1805) • [J. Watkins and F. Shoberl], *A biographical dictionary of the living authors of Great Britain and Ireland* (1816) • *DNB*

Parkinson, Richard (1797–1858), Church of England clergyman, the son of John Parkinson and his wife, Margaret Blackburne, came from a yeoman family long settled in north Lancashire, and was born at Woodgates, Admarsh, near Lancaster, on 17 September 1797. He was educated at the grammar schools of Chipping, Hawkshead, and Sedbergh, and at St John's College, Cambridge, where he matriculated in December 1815. At Sedbergh he was the last pupil who studied mathematics under the well-known John Dawson, and at Cambridge his tutor was Dr Thomas Calvert, later warden of Manchester. He graduated BA in 1820, proceeding MA in 1824, BD in 1838, and DD on 10 December 1851.

On leaving Cambridge in 1820 Parkinson was for a short time master of Lea School, near Preston. He edited the *Preston Sentinel*, a conservative newspaper, during its one year's existence (1821), and was a frequent contributor to its successor, the *Preston Pilot*. He wrote also for *Blackwood's Magazine*, one of his pieces (November 1820) being an amusing parody on 'Young Lochinvar'. In 1823 he was ordained by G. H. Law, bishop of Chester, and became curate of St Michael's-on-Wyre, Lancashire. In the summer of 1826 he was appointed theological lecturer or tutor at St Bees College, Cumberland, a theological college founded by Law in 1816. His *Sermons on Points of Doctrine and Rules of Duty* appeared in two volumes (1825, 1832). He obtained the Seatonian prize at Cambridge in 1830 for his poem 'Ascent of Elijah'. In the same year he was appointed perpetual curate of Whitworth, near Rochdale, Lancashire, but never resided there, leaving his clerical duties to his curate, Isaac Gaitskell, who was a descendant of Robert Walker ('Wonderful Walker'), the curate of Seathwaite commemorated by Wordsworth, and the subject of Parkinson's popular work *The Old Church Clock* (1843; 5th edn, 1880). In 1841 Parkinson resigned the Whitworth living. He had married in 1831 Catherine (*d.* 1860), daughter of Thomas Hartley of Gill Foot, Cumberland, and had two sons and two daughters.

In 1833 Parkinson preached at Bishop Sumner's visitation at Manchester, and the sermon had the effect of obtaining for the preacher election (on 20 May 1833) as fellow of the collegiate chapter. He resigned his lectureship at St Bees. In 1837, and again in 1838, he was Hulsean lecturer at Cambridge. He regarded these lectures, *Rationalism and Revelation* (1837) and *The Constitution of the Visible Church of Christ* (1838), in which he set out his view of the established church in England as the nearest approximation to a church based on the scriptures, as his best work. He was strongly committed to the principles of the Reformation, preaching on the third centenary of the Reformation (4 October 1835) and touring the midlands on behalf of the Protestant Reformation Society in 1841. He published sermons in defence of Anglican doctrine (1839, 1840). Parkinson was a founder of the Chetham Society, and was one of its first vice-presidents in 1843. He edited for the society *The Life of Adam Martindale* (1845), *The Autobiography of Henry Newcombe* (2 vols., 1851–2), and *The Private Journal and Literary Remains of John Byron* (1853–8). He was elected FSA in 1847.

In September 1846 he accepted from Lord Lonsdale the perpetual curacy of St Bees and the principalship of St Bees College, partly because of his wife's ill health. But his retention as a non-resident of the fellowship (afterwards canonry) of Manchester, where he had previously been a popular leader of the clergy, caused great bitterness, and the ensuing controversy led to the Manchester Parish Division Act, which assigned local parochial responsibilities to the canons. His pluralities included the perpetual curacy of Northaw, Hertfordshire, to which he was appointed in 1847. He had ambitious plans for St Bees, unsuccessfully proposing that it should be incorporated to grant degrees. He devolved much of the teaching, apart from his lectures on the Thirty-Nine Articles, to his subordinates. Remembered as a kindly and genial figure by some students, the less well-born found him more distant; he was closely involved with the local Lowther family interest. He spoke with a north country burr: 'In stature he was above the middle size; his carriage was erect, his step stately and slow as became a dignitary' (Huntington, 266). His occasional public offers of benefactions and his commission to William Butterfield to restore the priory church of St Bees gained him a reputation for munificence, though the evidence for actual donations by him is slender.

On 1 March 1857 Parkinson was suddenly seized with an attack of paralysis while in the pulpit of Manchester Cathedral, and, although he resumed his duties, his constitution received a permanent shock. On 28 January 1858 he had a second paralytic seizure at St Bees, and died there on the same day. He was buried on 3 February 1858 at the priory church of St Bees.

C. W. SUTTON, *rev.* M. C. CURTHOYS

Sources R. Parkinson, *The old church clock*, ed. J. Evans, 5th edn (1880) • F. R. Raines, *The fellows of the collegiate church of Manchester*, ed. F. Renaud, 1, Chetham Society, new ser., 21 (1891) • Boase, *Mod. Eng. biog.* • Venn, *Alum. Cant.* • G. Huntington, *Random recollections* (1893) • T. Park, *St Bees College, 1816–1895* (1982) • A. Boutflower, *Personal reminiscences of Manchester Cathedral, 1854–1912* (1913) • J. Wolffe, *The protestant crusade in Great Britain, 1829–1860* (1991)
Archives BL, corresp. with Sir Robert Peel, Add. MSS 40490–40565
Likenesses C. Mercier, portrait, *c.*1858, St Bees College, Cumbria
Wealth at death £18,000: probate, 24 March 1858, *CGPLA Eng. & Wales*

Parkinson, Stephen (1823–1889), mathematician, was born at Keighley in the West Riding of Yorkshire and baptized on 7 September 1823, the seventh child in a family of eight children of Stephen Parkinson, a land agent, who died in the boy's infancy, and his wife, Mary, *née* Ogden, who had to bring up her family on a reduced income.

Parkinson entered St John's College, Cambridge, as a sizar on 25 February 1841. With John Hymers as his college tutor, he was elected to a scholarship of the college. His performance in the mathematical tripos of 1845 excited an unusually lively interest among fellow undergraduates, since the remarkable speed and accuracy of his work resulted in his beating into second place the expected senior wrangler, William Thomson (later the distinguished mathematical physicist Lord Kelvin). However, the order of the two competitors was reversed in the subsequent examination for the Smith's prizes.

After less than two months, in March 1845, Parkinson became a fellow of his college, later proceeding to the degrees of MA (1848), BD (1855), and DD (1868). He also examined for the mathematical tripos in 1849 and 1852. Among his private pupils were the senior wranglers of 1850, 1853, and 1857 (W. H. Besant, T. B. Sprague, and G. B. Finch), and the second wrangler of 1855 (L. H. Courtney).

Parkinson was the author of two mathematical textbooks, *Elementary Treatise on Mechanics* (1855; 6th edn, 1881) and *A Treatise on Optics* (1859; 4th edn, 1884). Neither contained any original methods or procedures, being designed to remove difficulties encountered by his students in these subjects. The two works became extremely popular among students and were the standard books on these subjects in use at Cambridge for about a quarter of a century, until superseded by texts with newer methods and presentation.

Parkinson was also college lecturer in mathematics, being gifted with unusual lucidity. One of his pupils later recalled: 'He was the most courteous of lecturers, and though I didn't mean to read mathematics, I felt bound to do my best in return for all his politeness' (Bowling, 356–62). In 1864 he succeeded J. B. Mayor as college tutor, in which capacity he was remembered by his pupils as a skilled and energetic pedagogue, candid and good-natured, but strict if the occasion demanded. Indeed, it was claimed that in all his years at Cambridge he never made a real enemy.

His marriage to Elizabeth Lucy, daughter of John Welchman Whateley of Birmingham, on 15 August 1871 should have resulted in his vacation of the post but, owing to his great success, he was immediately re-elected, remaining until he retired in 1882. In the eighteen years of his tutorship nearly a thousand pupils passed under his care, and 'Parkinson's side' was an important factor in the prosperity of the college.

By virtue of his frankness, sincerity, and academic expertise, Parkinson's standing in the college was extremely high, and on many points 'the Doctor's' opinion was regarded as almost infallible by those who consulted him. A mark of the high esteem in which he was held was his election, in 1865, to the administrative office of college president, although he declined to be a candidate for the more elevated mastership in 1881.

Parkinson took a leading part in university affairs, and was one of the most vigorous and powerful opponents of reform and innovation. He was senior proctor in 1864, and was elected three times in succession to the council of the university senate, on which he accordingly served from 1866 to 1878. He was also a fellow of the Royal Society from 1870. He died at his home, The Hermitage, Newnham, on 2 January 1889, and was buried in Madingley churchyard. His widow married Gerard Francis Cobb, fellow and junior bursar of Trinity College, in 1893. ADRIAN RICE

Sources E. W. Bowling, *The Eagle*, 15 (1889), 356–62 • *Cambridge Review* (24 Jan 1889), 148–9 • E. J. R., *PRS*, 45 (1888–9), i–iii • Venn, *Alum. Cant.* • C. A. Bristed, *Five years in an English university*, 1 (1852), 318–27 • private information (1895)
Wealth at death £112,444 13*s.* 1*d.*: resworn probate, April 1889, *CGPLA Eng. & Wales*

Parkinson, Sydney (*d.* 1771), natural history artist, was born in Edinburgh, one of three children and the younger son of Joel Parkinson, a brewer and leading Quaker of that city, and his wife, Elizabeth (*c.*1700–1771). His birth year is uncertain: 1745, the traditional estimate, is twelve years after his brother's and by then his mother was in her mid-forties, so it appears suspect.

His father's early death in 1749 left Parkinson's family impoverished. Parkinson clearly received a good schooling none the less, after which he was apprenticed to a woollen draper, probably following his brother (who became an upholsterer). Already, though, he had shown a talent for drawing natural history subjects and the quality of his surviving work suggests he may have studied under

Sydney Parkinson (*d.* 1771), by James Newton, pubd 1773

William de la Cour, who opened a publicly funded art school in Edinburgh in 1760.

The family having moved to London, flower paintings by Parkinson were exhibited there by the Free Society of Artists in 1765–6 and a fellow Scottish Quaker, James Lee, engaged Parkinson to draw plants in his Hammersmith nursery and teach flower painting to his thirteen-year-old daughter, Ann. Through Lee, commissions followed from Sir Joseph Banks to depict in watercolours from the preserved material some of the creatures collected on his 1766 expedition to Labrador and Newfoundland, and to make copies for him of paintings of Indian mammals and birds made for Gideon Loten, a former governor of Ceylon (some of which were reproduced in Pennant's *Indian Zoology* in 1769). The parallel botanical commissions went to the veteran Ehret, by whose superlative work Parkinson was patently much influenced.

Parkinson's evident ability and conscientiousness led Banks to recruit him as one of the two professional artists in his private entourage who were to sail with him and Captain Cook to the south seas in the *Endeavour* in July 1768. Parkinson was to be responsible for the natural history drawings, Alexander Buchan for the topographical ones and portraits; in the event, though, Buchan, who turned out to be epileptic, died relatively early on, throwing a heavy extra burden on Parkinson, though a competent amateur sketcher among the crew, Herman Spöring, was able to relieve him in part.

With great diligence and flair Parkinson had made at least 1300 drawings, many more than Banks had expected, including the first in Western history of an Australian landscape and of its inhabitants at first hand, as well as compiled vocabularies of the languages spoken in Tahiti and New Holland, by the time the ship called at Batavia for repairs on the voyage home. There he contracted malaria and dysentery, from which he died soon after at sea, on 26 January 1771. As he was not officially a crew member, his effects were put in Banks's charge. They included a journal in which publishers were likely to be interested, for it contained much colourful detail not in those kept by Cook and Banks. The dying Parkinson had expressed the wish that this be read by his friend Lee, but on hearing of that Parkinson's brother, Stanfield, accused Banks of seeking to deprive him and his sister of what he saw as legally theirs under the will Parkinson had made before leaving England. As Parkinson's employer Banks considered the right to publish his papers lay with him, but under a solemn promise by Stanfield not to copy or publish any of the journal he consented to lend it for the family to read. Convinced the family had the better claim, Stanfield defiantly then arranged for its publication, forcing John Hawkesworth, entrusted with editing the official narrative of the voyage, to take out a forestalling injunction. John Fothergill, a friend of the Parkinson family from Edinburgh days, was brought in to mediate and effected a compromise whereby Banks paid Parkinson's executors £500 for balance of salary due in return for retaining all Parkinson's papers and any specimens not duplicated in his own collections. Once Hawkesworth had published, in June 1773, the injunction was lifted and Stanfield's publisher thereupon brought out the journal—with a preface ghosted by a Dr Kenrick scurrilously misrepresenting Banks's actions. Appalled by Stanfield's abuse of his good offices, Fothergill bought up some 400 copies remaining of the imprint and, following Stanfield's insanity and death, obtained the rights to the journal, which at his request was republished after his death by his friend Lettsom in 1784, complete with a measured riposte to the earlier preface.

Parkinson's artistic legacy was meanwhile lost to sight. Three-quarters of the pencil sketches he had made on the spot were still only partly coloured when he died but five other artists back in England were able to complete those, aided by his careful notes on colouration and by actual specimens. Banks then hired eighteen of the best engravers available to produce copperplates from the collection but, after thirteen years and with over £7000 spent, publication did not proceed beyond trial proofs. Banks was caught up in multifarious other matters and his finances were under pressure. The British Museum inherited the fifteen volumes of botanical illustrations and three of zoological ones along with Parkinson's sketchbook, but for two centuries the most the world saw was 319 inferior lithographs of Australian plants, produced in 1900–05 from the trial proofs. Eventually, a Natural History Museum project culminated in the 1980s in the issue of 738 of the botanical engravings as a sumptuous part-work under the title *Banks' Florilegium*. Though previously admired by specialists, only then did Parkinson's achievement receive its proper due. A species of fig was named *Ficus parkinsoni* by W. P. Hiern in Parkinson's honour. D. E. ALLEN

Sources D. J. Carr, ed., *Sydney Parkinson, artist of Cook's Endeavour voyage* (1983) • A. W. Anderson, 'Sydney Parkinson', *Gardeners' Chronicle*, 3rd ser., 135 (1954), 24–5 • A. M. Lysaght, 'A letter from Sydney Parkinson in Batavia to Dr. John Fothergill', *Notes and Records of the Royal Society*, 36 (1981–2), 79–82 • W. Colenso, 'Manibus Parkinsonibus sacrum', *Transactions and Proceedings of the New Zealand Institute*, 10 (1877), 108–34 • H. B. Carter, *Sir Joseph Banks* (1992)
Archives BL, *Endeavour* sketchbook, Add. MS 9345 • BL, two pencil sketches by him of flying proa copied from Anson's *Voyage*, Add. MS 23920 • BM, watercolours of zoological specimens collected by him in Newfoundland and Labrador • NHM, London, drawings | NHM, Richard Owen MSS, zoological drawings
Likenesses J. Newton, engraving, pubd 1773, NPG [*see illus.*] • oils, NHM

Parkinson, Thomas (*b.* 1744), portrait painter, was born on 10 December 1744; of his parents nothing is known. He entered the Royal Academy Schools on 30 November 1772. He is known chiefly as a painter of theatrical figures and groups, but also practised regularly as a portrait painter, exhibiting at the Free Society of Artists, the Society of Artists, and the Royal Academy between 1769 and 1789. His portraits include likenesses of Admiral Balfour (1781; ex Christies, 5 December 1952) and Dr William Balmain (engraved by Richard Earlom), as well as less reputable characters such as the forger Jonathan Britain (engraved by John Raphael Smith). The Garrick Club has a number of his works in oil on canvas including *Thomas Weston as Billy Button in 'The Maid of Bath' by Samuel Foot* (exh. Society of Artists, 1772) and *Maria Smith as Sylvia in 'Cymon' by David Garrick* (exh. RA, 1775, lot 217). The latter was originally a double portrait, subsequently cut down to remove a male figure. His *Garrick Led off the Stage by Time with Tragedy and Comedy* was engraved by R. Laurie in 1779. A number of Parkinson's small theatrical portrait drawings are in the Burney Collection (department of prints and drawings in the British Museum). Some of these were engraved for editions of John Bell's *Shakespeare*. PAUL A. COX

Sources Graves, *Artists* • Graves, *RA exhibitors* • Graves, *Soc. Artists* • L. Binyon, *Catalogue of drawings by British artists and artists of foreign origin working in Great Britain*, 4 vols. (1898–1907) • G. Ashton, *Pictures in the Garrick Club*, ed. K. A. Burnim and A. Wilton (1997) • S. C. Hutchison, 'The Royal Academy Schools, 1768–1830', *Walpole Society*, 38 (1960–62), 123–91, esp. 139

Parkinson, Thomas (1745–1830), mathematician and Church of England clergyman, was born on 14 June 1745, at Kirkham, Lancashire, the son of Adam and Elizabeth Parkinson. He was educated at Kirkham Free Grammar School under a Mr Threlfal and entered Christ's College, Cambridge, on 11 October 1764, with an exhibition of £34 per annum. His father, who disapproved of his going to university, refused to support him. To eke out his income he, together with (Richard?) Williams, worked under Israel Lyons the younger in calculating the series of tables of parallax and refraction for the board of longitude; the results were edited by Anthony Shepherd and published in 1772. In 1769 he became senior wrangler and second Smith's prizeman, dividing the honours with George Atwood, third wrangler and first Smith's prizeman. He proceeded MA in 1772, and then financially supported his brother Robert, who entered Emmanuel College the next year. He was for twenty years (1771–91) fellow, and for fourteen tutor, of his college. He was also university proctor in 1786–7.

Parkinson was patronized in particular by George Pretyman (later Tomline). In 1775 he became vicar of Meldreth; in 1789 rector of Kegworth in Leicestershire; in 1794 archdeacon of Huntingdon; and a doctor of divinity in 1795. According to Venn, he had a love affair with a Miss Charlotte Bridge, of Harston, and they were engaged in 1789. However, finding his prospects too poor, she deserted him for a Mr W., whom she married. Subsequently she left her husband and 'sank into the depths', from which Parkinson rescued her by granting her an annuity. In 1798 Parkinson became prebendary of St Paul's Cathedral. From 1804 he was chancellor of the diocese of Chester, and in 1812 became archdeacon of Leicester. He was instrumental in establishing in Leicester a school on the Madras system. He was always a firm opponent of any accommodation with Catholicism.

Parkinson was elected a fellow of the Royal Society on 23 February 1786. Besides a few sermons, he published a two-volume *System of Mechanics* (1785, 1789), the second volume with *hydrostatics* added to the title. Patents 2369 of 1800 and 2568 of 1802 in these fields could be his. Of middle height, he was said to be well disposed and benevolent (*GM*, 88). He died at Kegworth on 13 November 1830, and was buried on 20 November at Kegworth church.

CHARLES PLATTS, *rev.* RUTH WALLIS

Sources *GM*, 1st ser., 101/1 (1831), 85–9 • Venn, *Alum. Cant.* • J. Nichols, *The history and antiquities of the county of Leicester*, 3 (1800–04), 856; facs. edn (1971)

Parks [Parkes; *née* Archer], **Frances Susanna** [Fanny] (1794–1875), author, was born on 8 December 1794 at Conwy in north Wales, the daughter of Captain William Archer, formerly of the 16th lancers, and his wife, Ann, daughter of William Goodhew. The family later moved to Lymington in Hampshire, where on 25 March 1822 she married Charles Crawford Parks (1797/8–1854), a civil servant in the East India Company. Her elder sister Anne Augustine married a clergyman, Henry Allen, and lived in south India during the early years of Fanny's residence in the country.

Fanny and Charles Parks sailed for Calcutta in June 1822, finally leaving India in August 1845. Her account of her years in India, *Wanderings of a Pilgrim in Search of the Picturesque*, largely based on the journal which she kept for her mother, was published in 1850. The focus of the book was India, its people, and their culture. It thus gains momentum when, in 1826, the Parkses left Calcutta, where life was largely confined to British society, to live 'up country' in Allahabad. Here Charles spent almost all his time. Fanny, however, travelled extensively: she sailed by herself in their pinnace, the *Seagull*, up the Jumna River to Agra, and up the Ganges to Fatehgarh, and spent nearly a year visiting Cawnpore, Meerut, Delhi, and Landour in the

Himalayas. Exploring was a delight: 'Oh! the pleasure of vagabondizing over India' (Parks, 2.192). Her husband, whom she describes as kind and considerate, encouraged her travels. The couple had no children, and he probably realized that, in a society which saw a woman's natural focus as her family, she needed an alternative outlet for her energies. These were considerable: she was characterized by remarkable physical stamina, and indefatigable enthusiasm and curiosity about every aspect of Indian life. Everywhere she went she sketched. She studied and noted every aspect of the peoples she met, and the plant, animal, and insect life she encountered, preserving with arsenical soap specimens for her renowned 'cabinet of curiosities', which also housed a heterogeneous assortment of interesting objects, especially Hindu figures. Her fluent Hindustani enabled her to penetrate Indian life, and she adopted some Indian customs, signing her writing and drawings in Persian script (the transliteration of which produced the common misspelling of her surname as Parkes), and playing the sitar. She admired the dignity and grace of Indian life, in which she considered European ways were often an ugly intrusion. Although an Anglican, she was sceptical about attempts at religious conversion and the effect of some European philanthropic endeavours.

Her friendships with Indian women led to a deeper understanding of Indian life. It had always been her ambition to penetrate the zenana: this she achieved through her friend Colonel William Gardner (1771–1835), who had married a Muslim princess. She also became a close friend of the Baiza Bai, the ex-queen of Gwalior. Such relationships enabled her to take part in marriage and other ceremonies normally barred to Europeans, and to gain first-hand understanding of Indian religious beliefs and practices, particularly Hinduism, in which she had a deep interest. Her knowledge of Indian women's life strengthened her sense of the universal exploitation of women, whether in Asia or England, in which latter she condemned the injustice of the educational and legal systems.

Her enthusiasms and interest in Indian life were a source of amusement to her friends. Others, through misunderstanding or jealousy, could be hostile. Fanny Eden, travelling with her brother Lord Auckland, the governor-general, recorded in 1838 how intrusive they found her inescapable presence. In the only known description of her appearance in India, Fanny Eden also wrote, 'She has been a beauty and has the remains of it and is abundantly fat and lively' (Dunbar, *Tigers, Durbars and Kings*, 106).

Fanny Parks's book, which was extensively illustrated with drawings by herself, her friends, and Indian artists, was lavishly produced and won wide acclaim. Reviewers noted the accuracy, detail, and range of observation—as well as the unusual character of the authoress. She followed it in 1851 with the commentary to a *Grand Moving Diorama of Hindostan*, which was based on sketches by distinguished amateur artists in India. Accompanying the diorama was a museum, which contained items from her 'cabinet of curiosities'.

The Parks were by then living in London. Charles Parks died there in August 1854. Fanny survived until 21 December 1875, when she died of shingles at her home, 7 Cornwall Terrace, Regent's Park. She was buried on 28 December in Kensal Green cemetery in the same grave as her husband. ROSEMARY CARGILL RAZA

Sources F. Parks, *Wanderings of a pilgrim in search of the picturesque, during four-and-twenty years in the East with revelations of life in the zenana*, 2 vols. (1850) • J. Dunbar, *Tigers, durbars and kings: Fanny Eden's Indian journals, 1837–1838* (1988) • J. Dunbar, *Golden interlude: the Edens in India, 1836–1842* (1955) • d. cert. • census returns for Westbourne Park Terrace, London, 1851 • census returns for Cornwall Terrace, Regent's Park, London, 1861–75 • *Blackwood's Lady's Magazine*, 32 (Jan 1852), 195–9 • parish register, Conwy, NL Wales [baptism] • *Notes and Queries*, 12th ser., 6 (1920), 190, 233

Wealth at death under £18,000: probate, 14 Jan 1876, *CGPLA Eng. & Wales*

Parkyn, Robert (*d.* 1569), Church of England clergyman and writer, was probably born in the early 1520s to a landed Yorkshire family, probably at Owston. There is no evidence that he attended a university. By 1541 he was in orders and not long after this became curate at Adwick-le-Street in the West Riding where he remained until his death. Parkyn's writings suggest that he retained Catholic sympathies throughout his career. His major work was a metrical *Life of Christ* extant in MSS Eng. poet. b.1 and Eng. poet. e.59 in the Bodleian Library, both in his hand. Bodleian Library, MS Lat. theol. d.15, another holograph, includes several of his poems of varying lengths, including a chronicle and short religious works, as well as a prose narrative of the Reformation. It also contains copies by Parkyn of prose works by Richard Rolle, poems by John Lydgate, and prayers in verse and prose by Thomas More. Parkyn also composed some brief prose devotional works and made a Bible concordance which all survive in Aberdeen University, MS 185. He died on 23 March 1569. His will includes bequests of a number of books, chiefly theological. A. S. G. EDWARDS

Sources A. G. Dickens, ed., *Tudor treatises*, Yorkshire Archaeological Society Record Series, 125 (1959) • A. G. Dickens, 'Robert Parkyn's life of Christ', *Bodleian Library Record*, 4 (1952–3), 67–76 • A. G. Dickens, ed., 'Robert Parkyn's narrative of the Reformation', *EngHR*, 62 (1947), 58–83 • A. G. Dickens, 'The last medieval Englishman', *Christian spirituality: essays in honour of Gordon Rupp*, ed. P. Brooks (1975), 141–82 • A. S. G. Edwards, 'Robert Parkyn's transcript of More's "Prayer of Picus Mirandula unto God … "', *Moreana*, 27 (1990), 133–8 • will, Borth. Inst., prob. reg. 19.66, 54*v*–55

Archives U. Aberdeen, MS 185

Parkyns, Mansfield (1823–1894), traveller in Africa, was born on 16 February 1823 in Caen, Normandy, France, where his parents were visiting at the time. He was the second son of Thomas Boultbee Parkyns (*d.* 1833), a landowner, and his wife, Charlotte Mary (*d.* 1838), the eldest daughter of George Smith of Edwalton, Nottinghamshire, and Foelall, Cardiganshire. His father was a nephew of Thomas Boothby Parkyns, first Baron Rancliffe (1755–1800), and a grandson of Sir Thomas Parkyns, third baronet (1728–1806), of Bunny, the son of Sir Thomas Parkyns (1664–1741). Always known as Mansfield Parkyns, he has the additional forenames Harry and Isham in some sources. Mansfield Parkyns was sent to Uppingham School in 1833, but left shortly thereafter to go to a tutor at Woolwich. He was destined for the Royal Military Academy there, but for unknown reasons instead went to Trinity College, Cambridge, from where he matriculated on 14 October 1840. He left Cambridge after what he described as 'a scrape' and others 'a row', the details of which are unknown, and in 1842 set off on the travels for which he was to gain fame.

Parkyns went first to the continent, where he met Richard Monckton Milnes, who had earlier been at Trinity College, and joined him on his journey to Constantinople and then Cairo. In Cairo, Parkyns decided to go to Abyssinia. He was initially fairly aimless, though as he travelled he formulated a plan for crossing the continent from east to west. He evidently enjoyed himself hugely, rambling around Abyssinia and the Sudan, and visiting areas largely unknown to Europeans. He travelled without a large baggage train and mostly with no other Europeans (though he joined John Bell and Walter Plowden for the first part of the journey). Wearing local dress and picking up the local languages as he went, he mixed happily with the local people, who found him non-judgemental and unruffled by events which would have unnerved most other Europeans. He so far acclimatized himself that in 1843 he married by local rites Tures, a villager from Addi Harisho, in a particularly remote part of Abyssinia, and with her had a son, John, who died in Eritrea about 1916—Parkyns's plan to bring him to England having come to nothing. Later (1846–7) he spent more than a year with the nomadic Kababish tribe as they roamed in the area around al-ʿUbayd in the Sudan, and he acquired his own camels. In between he entertained in his mud hut in Khartoum a party from Trinity College consisting of Francis Galton, Montague Bolton of the engineering family, and Hedworth Barclay of the banking family.

For reasons which are not clear Parkyns resolved in 1848 to return home and, after a stay of some months in Cairo, where he met James Outram, the Indian army officer and political agent then recuperating in Egypt, he reached England in the summer of 1849; he brought with him his journal of his travels, such bird and animal skins of his collection as had survived the depredations of middlemen and the rigours of the journey, and a manuscript history of the Sudan which he had commissioned or obtained (published in 1970 as *On the Frontiers of Islam*, ed. Richard Hill). In London he found himself regarded as an authority on the source of the Nile and instantly offered himself to the Royal Geographical Society of London (after 1859 the Royal Geographical Society) to pursue this question. This idea, however, came to nothing, and he reverted to his earlier ambition of crossing the African continent. In the mean time he settled to the more practical questions of getting his skins stuffed and preparing his journal for publication. In 1850 he left again for Constantinople, having, probably through the influence of Richard Milnes, managed to get himself appointed assistant secretary to the embassy there. He was to act as interpreter in an attempt to dispense with the services of the Levantine dragomans. However, he proved scarcely more to the taste of the ambassador than the Levantines and was back in London by 1851 (though he continued to appear on the Foreign Office list until his death). He completed his book, published in 1853 as *Life in Abyssinia* (2 vols.), which was widely but rather poorly reviewed, being out of step with the contemporary heroic notions of exploration—as indeed were his travels themselves. But those closely interested in the region recognized the value of the book, which contained considerable amounts of new information, and Parkyns was, albeit briefly, an active member of the Royal Geographical Society, serving on its council in 1854 and lecturing to and regularly attending meetings. A second enlarged edition of the book followed in 1868, when the region was again in the public eye. The Sudanese part of his journey was described only in a lecture to the Royal Geographical Society (published in the *Journal of the Geographical Society of London*, 20, 1850, 254–75), which shows his laconic sense of humour and his powers of observation.

Parkyns's adventurous youth came to an abrupt end. Apparently having fallen deeply in love, he married and settled to the life of country squire, husband, and father. His wife was Emma Louisa (*d.* 1877), the third daughter of Sir Richard Bethell QC, solicitor-general and later lord chancellor, and they married on 14 September 1854 at Winslade, Hampshire. They lost their first child, a son, but went on to have eight daughters, all of whom survived. Parkyns enjoyed the life of a country squire from his estate at Woodborough Hall, Nottinghamshire, where he spent his time building up his estate, with his family, wood-carving, pursuing his interest in genealogy, and playing at soldiers with the Sherwood Forester militia battalion. As his family increased so did his need for an income, and in 1858, through his father-in-law's influence, he became assignee in bankruptcy, first in Exeter and then in London; then, without any obvious qualification for the post, he served for twenty years as comptroller of the bankruptcy court (1864–84), living in Bayswater Square, London, to attend to his duties, and escaping to his family in Nottinghamshire when he could. His wife died on 2 December 1877, and he carved new choir stalls in Woodborough church in her memory. (His flirtation in Africa with Roman Catholicism after he had met some impressive missionaries came to nothing and he retained his allegiance to the Church of England.) In 1884 he retired to Woodborough, where he died on 12 January 1894; he was buried in Woodborough church.

Abyssinia Parkyns, as he was known in geographical circles, seems to have been a particularly adaptable person, finding as much enjoyment in the life of a Nottinghamshire squire as in that of an Abyssinian peasant, and buckling to the routine of office life when he needed the money. It was this adaptability which made him such a good traveller. In *Memories of my Life* (1908) Galton described him as 'the traveller most gifted with natural advantages for that career' and added that 'he easily held his own under difficulties, won hearts by his sympathy, and could touch any amount of pitch without being himself defiled' (Cumming, 127). Samuel Baker, who was the next European to visit some of the areas where Parkyns had been, found that he was still fondly remembered after an interval of some fourteen years.

ELIZABETH BAIGENT

Sources D. Cumming, *The gentleman savage: the life of Mansfield Parkyns, 1823–1894* (1987) · M. Parkyns, *Life in Abyssinia*, 2 vols. (1853) · C. R. Markham, *The fifty years' work of the Royal Geographical Society* (1881) · Burke, *Peerage* (1907) · Venn, *Alum. Cant.* · GEC, *Peerage* · *CGPLA Eng. & Wales* (1894) · *IGI* · d. cert. · *DNB*

Archives RGS, journal and MSS relating to Abyssinia and Sudan · U. Nott. L., corresp. relating to family history · U. Nott. L., journal, incl. account of travels on the Upper Nile and his residence in Ethiopia

Wealth at death £8762 15*s.* 8*d.*: probate, 9 Feb 1894, *CGPLA Eng. & Wales*

Parkyns, Sir Thomas, second baronet (1664–1741), writer on wrestling, was born at Bunny in Nottinghamshire; he was the second son of Sir Thomas Isham Parkyns (1639–1684), of Bunny, who became first baronet in 1681, and Anne, only daughter and heir of Thomas Cressey and his wife, Elizabeth, daughter of Sir Thomas Glemham. He was educated at Westminster School under Richard Busby and Thomas Knipe, and in 1680 entered Trinity College, Cambridge, as a fellow-commoner. On leaving Cambridge he entered Gray's Inn, as a student, on 18 May 1682. In 1684 he succeeded his father to the baronetcy and began to improve the estate at Bunny, building four almshouses and a school, and restoring the church. A competent mathematician with a good knowledge of the principles of architecture and hydraulics, Parkyns was his own architect and engineer, creating an aqueduct and erecting a curious tower at Bunny Hall. His interest in education was demonstrated in his *Practical and Grammatical Introduction to the Latin Tongue* (1716). He was also an active JP and sat on the commissions for the counties of Leicester and Nottingham from 1684 until his death; in this connection he published a number of pamphlets, and a book entitled *A method proposed for the hiring and recording of servants in husbandry, arts, misteries, …* (1721). Among the many talents attributed to him was the ability to 'throw a tenant, combat a paradox, quote Martial or sign a mittimus with any man of his own age or county' (*Retrospective Review*, 11.161).

Parkyns's first wife, Elizabeth, the only daughter of John Sampson of Breaston, Derbyshire, and granddaughter of John Sampson of Huby, Yorkshire, alderman of London, was described as an 'excellent woman, clever at recipes for strains' (ibid., 165). She bore Parkyns two sons, Sampson (*d.* 1713) and Thomas (*d.* 1706), and two daughters. Parkyns married, as his second wife, Jane (*d.* 1740), daughter of George Barnat of York, in 1727. They had three children: Thomas, later third baronet, George, an army officer, and Anne. A descendant was the explorer Mansfield Parkyns.

Parkyns is principally known as the author of *The Inn-Play, or, Cornish-Hugg Wrestler*, which appeared in 1727 and was dedicated to George II. The book sought to restore the practice of old sports that had been so vital in fostering

Sir Thomas Parkyns, second baronet (1664–1741), by unknown engraver, pubd 1713

military strength against the French, thus making 'all your subjects more useful to your army' (p. ii). In addition to the military value of wrestling Parkyns 'hoped parliament will establish a stage in every market-town at which gentlemen wearing swords can settle their affronts every month at single-stick' (ibid., v). The book was one of the earliest practical manuals on fencing and wrestling, and stemmed from Parkyns's noting down every lesson that his instructor, Mr Cornish, had given him at Gray's Inn. While Parkyns emphasized the importance of pursuing the correct programme of instruction, the most notable aspect of his work was the way in which he fused very practical advice with ponderous scientific terminology. He extolled the necessity of applying mathematics to sport, thanking *en passant* Isaac Newton. Such a fusion resulted in portentous expositions of the obvious, such as 'a greater impetus is required to move a greater weight some space, than to move a less weight the same space' (ibid., 27). The work also exudes xenophobia: the ancient Greeks are dismissed as a 'poxy race' (ibid., 7), and foreign foods, particularly 'spicy meals', criticized. Parkyns favoured the consumption of beef but urged practitioners to avoid exercising on a full stomach and to 'take light liquids of easy digestion' (ibid., 12). There was a good deal of practical advice on sports, including dress—'wear linen drawers, not tight breeches' (ibid., 37)—as well as copies of indented articles, listing rules, referees, stakes, and such like. Parkyns's influence continued long after his death; the wrestling competition at Bunny Park that he established in 1712 lasted until 1810, offering an annual 22 guinea prize. In 1825 a second edition of *The Inn-Play* was published, and his rules continued to be used, notably in a 50 guinea match that was reported in *Bell's Life in London* on 27 April 1828.

An extremely fit man who never suffered a day's illness in his life, Parkyns remained a vigorous runner and change-ringer until middle age. He died at Bunny on 29 March 1741 and was buried in the chancel of Bunny church in a stone coffin that he had himself selected. He had long been a collector of stone coffins, which he stored in Bunny churchyard, leaving the remainder to his fellow parishioners. Such was Parkyns's love of sport that he had a statue of a man, wrestling, erected in the chancel of Bunny church; this attracted much criticism from the clergy during his lifetime but Parkyns rejected such objections, insisting that the figure was sanctioned by the writings of St Paul.

THOMAS SECCOMBE, *rev.* ADRIAN N. HARVEY

Sources R. Chambers, ed., *The book of days: a miscellany of popular antiquities in connection with the calendar*, 2 vols. (1863–4) • C. Brown, *Lives of Nottinghamshire worthies* (1882) • J. Foster, *The register of admissions to Gray's Inn, 1521–1889, together with the register of marriages in Gray's Inn chapel, 1695–1754* (privately printed, London, 1889) • *GM*, 1st ser., 7 (1737) • *GM*, 1st ser., 11 (1741) • *Retrospective Review*, 11 (1825), 161, 165 • Burke, *Peerage*

Archives U. Nott. L., papers

Likenesses J. Vanderbank, portrait; last known at Bunny Hall, Nottinghamshire, 1895 • etching (after unknown artist), NPG; repro. in *The inn-play, or, Cornish-hugg wrestler* (1713) [*see illus.*] • woodcut (after unknown artist), NPG

Parkyns, Sir William (*bap.* **1649**, *d.* **1696**), lawyer and Jacobite conspirator, was baptized on 21 December 1649 at Bulkington, Warwickshire, the eldest son of William Parkyns (1615/16–1684), squire of Marston Jabbett, Warwickshire, and his wife, Elizabeth (*fl.* 1641–1685), daughter and coheir of Robert Reynes of Stanford, Nottinghamshire. He had four older sisters and three brothers. He may have been the William Parkyns who became a pensioner at Trinity College, Cambridge, on 20 June 1665, without matriculating. He was admitted to the Inner Temple, apparently on 6 May 1665 as of 'Christ's College', and was called to the bar on 3 February 1673. On 26 June 1673, at St Mildred, Bread Street, London, he married Susanna (*b.* *c.*1651, *d.* in or after 1721), daughter of Thomas Blackwell, a London merchant tailor, with £2500 dowry; they had at least eight children, six sons and two daughters, of whom five survived in 1700. His wife later claimed (after 1696, to save the estate, but with confirmation from leading gentry) that he ill-treated her so grossly as to provoke lifelong intermittent attacks of insanity, exploited these to mortgage her jointure rights in Marston Jabbett, and by threatening further mistreatment, extorted large sums from her mother.

On 8 March 1675 Parkyns purchased from Sir Cyril Wych the profitable post of one of the six clerks in chancery. This was executed by trained deputies, not even requiring legal knowledge in the principal; but Parkyns was actively involved, practised as a lawyer, and included among his acquaintance Sir John Holt, who was to preside at his trial. In 1677 his wife and sister-in-law inherited from a cousin a manor house and two-thirds (£80 a year) of Bushey Manor, Hertfordshire, which became his seat; he bought his sister-in-law's share in 1685 for £1240, though—characteristically—he never completed the payment. By 1678 he was also resident in St Giles-in-the-Fields parish, London.

During the exclusion crisis Parkyns became a leading 'abhorrer' who went 'violently into the passions and interests of the court' (*Bishop Burnet's History*, 4.312), and in reward was knighted at Whitehall on 10 June 1681. He was seen as a reliable tory justice of the peace during the early 1680s. He had a £600 legacy—left for Richard Baxter to distribute among nonconformist ministers—confiscated, and petitioned for half as a reward. He was made a nonresident alderman of St Albans under James II's charter of 2 March 1685, cancelled in 1689.

At the revolution Parkyns took the oaths to William and Mary to preserve his six clerks post. In early 1691 David Lloyd listed him among lawyers who supported James, but he apparently remained inactive until after selling the post on 10 February 1693. His fellow toper the brewer Sir John Friend helped involve him; both were 'Melfordians' (a term derived from the title of James's secretary of state John Drummond, first earl of Melfort), believing that only fighting would bring a restoration. Possibly William's turn to the whigs in 1693–4 drove Parkyns towards a Jacobitism more violent than Friend's. A deed of trust in March 1694 may have been a related precaution. Despite suffering from gout in hands and feet, Parkyns became a captain in Colonel John Parker's Jacobite cavalry regiment after Parker had listed his captains at the start of 1694. Two of these, Robert Charnock and George Porter, became his closest fellow plotters.

Parkyns and other Jacobites trusted his spendthrift nephew Matthew *Smith (who had sold the reversion of his mother's estates to Parkyns) because dismissal from William's army had impoverished him. In reality, from late 1694 Smith spied for the government. He reported that Parkyns had concealed arms for a cavalry troop at Marston Jabbett; but, just after the 'Lancashire plot' fiasco, it was politically impossible to search there. Lacking this confirmation, ministers largely ignored Smith's often accurate reports on Parkyns's circle, including the assassination plot.

Parkyns was active in the discussions among Parker's captains in early 1695 about kidnapping or assassinating William. Sir John Fenwick later claimed, implausibly, that only his arguments and delays had prevented Charnock, Porter, and Parkyns from attacking the king just before he crossed to the Netherlands in April 1695. Parkyns attended the meetings in May 1695 with Thomas Bruce, second earl of Ailesbury, and other important Jacobites, which agreed to send Charnock to France to ask James to invade with only 10,000 men, promising to meet him on landing with 2000 horse. Parkyns did more than the others to fulfil this. According to Porter and Smith, he now had his own regiment: in January 1696, at Leicester, he met Jacobites from as far away as Yorkshire, some probably his captains. James wrote to him personally, promising a winter invasion. Robert Ferguson, then writing the preparatory propaganda, visited Bushey. But Parkyns and Charnock, with whom he lodged when in London, were also planning William's assassination as a preliminary stroke. They persuaded Sir George Barclay, who had crossed from France to head the London rising, to organize it. Parkyns alone saw Barclay's general commission from James, perhaps to confirm that it could be interpreted to cover killing William; Porter later claimed or pretended that he said it was specifically for this. Parkyns attended the planning sessions, and provided men, horses, and intelligence for the proposed attempts on 15 and 22 February 1696, though gout and his duties as colonel prevented him from taking part. A £1000 reward was offered for him in the proclamation of 23 February. After searches in Warwickshire and Hertfordshire, which prompted the mob to sack both manor houses, Parkyns was captured hiding in the Inner Temple on 10 March 1696 by a party under a senior bencher.

The lord keeper, Sir John Somers, warned Parkyns on 12 March that this was his last chance to confess. Parkyns said he was willing to tell Charles Talbot, duke of Shrewsbury, secretary of state, what became a gentleman. Gilbert Burnet reported that for four days he seemed amenable, until his eldest daughter, Susanna, encouraged him to stand firm. His trial was then hurried on, and took place, despite his repeated protests, at the Old Bailey on 24 March 1696, the day before the new act on treason trial procedure came into force. Porter was the chief prosecution witness. Parkyns's skilled defence led the judges to intervene against him, but the arms discovered at Marston Jabbett, having been moved about during the plot, were solid evidence, and the jury convicted him in half an hour. His execution, and that of Friend, was delayed until both had been interrogated by a Commons committee: Parkyns's refusal to save himself by naming anybody he had recruited for the rising, or even for the assassination, aroused some admiration, but, despite Lady Parkyns's efforts, no pardon. He repented the faults of his private life to Simon Patrick, bishop of Ely, and to the nonjuror Jeremy Collier. The latter, with Shadrach Cook and William Snatt, attended when the two men were hanged at Tyburn on 3 April 1696, before an enthusiastic crowd, and pronounced absolution. This created outrage, particularly since Parkyns's last paper, while denying that James knew of the assassination, expressed no public regret for his own admitted involvement. The Williamite hierarchy published an attack on the three nonjurors, and the government prosecuted them.

Parkyns's head and quarters were set up on Temple Bar, arousing some pitying revulsion. William granted his Bushey property to Lady Parkyns (not surprisingly, a Williamite) on 12 March 1701, and Marston Jabbett was her jointure. But the debts forced Sir William's heir Blackwell Parkyns to sell both—the latter to the South Sea Company's deputy cashier, from whom it was confiscated after the Bubble.

Ailesbury described Parkyns as 'a most honest moral man, a good gentleman in his country, … and a man of a sweet temper naturally, but too much addicted to the bottle' (*Memoirs of … Ailesbury*, 1.370). Burnet, however, claimed that he had a very bad reputation (perhaps mainly for his marital conduct). The public was startled that an Anglican gentleman should be among the most vehement leaders of the assassination plot.

PAUL HOPKINS

Sources *State trials*, vols. 12–13 • J. Garrett, *The triumphs of providence: the assassination plot, 1696* (1980) • P. A. Hopkins, 'Aspects of Jacobite conspiracy in England in the reign of William III', PhD diss., U. Cam., 1981 • M. Smith, *Memoirs of secret service* (1699) • T. B. Macaulay, *The history of England from the accession of James II*, new edn, ed. C. H. Firth, 6 vols. (1913–15) • *CSP dom.* • W. A. Shaw, ed., *Calendar of treasury books*, 10–16, PRO (1933–8) • PRO, T1/72/50, T1/68/60, T1/71/38 • W. H. Rylands, ed., *The visitation of the county of Warwick … 1682 … 1683*, Harleian Society, 62 (1911) • parish register, Warwickshire, Bulkington, Warks. CRO, DR 198/1 • W. Trumbull, cabinet minutes, BL, Add. MSS 72566–72567 • P. Le Neve, *Pedigrees of the knights made by Charles II*, ed. G. W. Marshall, Harleian Society, 8 (1869) • *The life of James the Second, king of England*, ed. J. S. Clarke, 2 vols. (1816) • *Bishop Burnet's History* • 'Mr Davis's mem[orial]', [1681], Westm. DA, Old Brotherhood papers, 3.223 • *Memoirs of Thomas, earl of Ailesbury*, ed. W. E. Buckley, 2 vols., Roxburghe Club, 122 (1890) • W. Dugdale, *The antiquities of Warwickshire illustrated*, rev. W. Thomas, 2nd edn, 2 vols. (1730) • will and inventory, Staffs. RO [W. Parkyns, father] • *VCH Hertfordshire* • T. D. Hardy, *A catalogue of lords chancellors, keepers of the great seal, masters of the rolls and principal officers of the high court of chancery* (1843) • G. Longman, *Bushey then and now: politics and religion, 1550–1684* (1968) • A. E. Gibbs, ed., *The corporation records of St Albans* (1890) • *The autobiography of Sir John Bramston*, ed. Lord Braybrooke (1845) • Bushey manor deeds, Herts. ALS, Acc 103, MSS 37572–37579 • parish register, Bushey, Herts. ALS, D/P26 1/1 • J. L. Chester and J. Foster, eds., *London marriage licences, 1521–1869* (1887) • Evelyn, *Diary* • D. Nairne, journal, NL Scot., MS 14266, fol. 82 • Inner Temple, London, Inner Temple records, ADM 1/3, BAR 1/4

Likenesses German etching, 1696, NPG • German etching, 1697, repro. in Garrett, *Triumphs of providence*

Wealth at death none; attainted traitor; previously owned estate at Marston Jabbett, Warwickshire, £250–£260 p.a.; £1360 mortgage; estate at Bushey, £80 p.a.; large mortgages, some perhaps fraudulent; reversion of £100 p.a. lands in Coventry, Warwickshire, and Leicestershire; £325 goods after large-scale plundering of goods, horses, etc.: PRO, T1/71/38, T1/72/50

Parliament Joan. *See* Alkin, Elizabeth (*c*.1600–1655?).

Parmenius, Stephen [István Budai] (*d.* **1583**), Latin poet and explorer in America, was probably born in Ráckové, Hungary, the son of István Budai, a name he also bore himself. He was probably educated at the Unitarian College in Kolozawer, Transylvania. He matriculated from Wittenberg University on 29 September 1579, and may have gone from there to other Calvinist places of learning. In the dedication of his work of 1582 he writes that he spent almost three years visiting the 'universities of the Christian world' (Quinn and Cheshire, 76–7).

Parmenius entered Christ Church, Oxford, in 1581 and shared accommodation with Richard Hakluyt the younger, then a student of Christ Church. Hakluyt and Jean Hotman introduced him to the intellectual circle around William Camden in London. Early in 1582 Parmenius published an elegant 'thanksgiving' *Paean on Psalm 104* in Latin verse honouring the queen and her country. He then attached himself to Sir Humphrey Gilbert, who was at that time preparing a colonizing expedition to North America. In June 1582 he published an 'embarkation poem', also in Latin hexameters, eulogizing Gilbert's venture (*De navigatione … H. Gilberti … carmen*). Here he indicated his wish to go on the voyage and thus become the English Camões, and celebrate England's discoveries in epic style as Camões had Portugal's in the previous decade (Camões, *Lusiados*, 1572). Parmenius joined Gilbert's squadron as a passenger in the *Swallow* in June 1583, landing at St John's harbour on 4 August. His brief visit disillusioned him, as his surviving letter to Hakluyt of 6 August shows. The land was wholly unpromising and the colourful native people wholly absent.

> The maner of the Countrey, and people remaine nowe to be spoken of. But what shall I say, my good Hakluyt, when I see nothing but a very wildernesse? … Whether there bee any people in the Countrey I knowe not, neither have I seene any to witnesse it. (Hakluyt, 3.162–3)

Whether further exploration of Newfoundland changed his mind is not known. Parmenius sailed on towards the American mainland on the leading vessel, *Delight*, but on 29 August 1583 the ship ran aground on Sable Island and Parmenius was lost. Edward Hayes, narrator of the expedition, gave Parmenius high praise as a 'rare poet of our time' (Hakluyt, 3.156). Neil M. Cheshire translated Parmenius's Latin writings in 1972, with a full commentary. DAVID B. QUINN

Sources R. Hakluyt, *The principal navigations, voyages, traffiques and discoveries of the English nation*, 2nd edn, 3 vols. (1598–1600) • F. Hotomannorum and J. Hotomannorum, *Epistolae* (1764) • *The new found land of Stephen Parmenius: the life and writings of a Hungarian poet, drowned on a voyage from Newfoundland, 1583*, ed. and trans. D. B. Quinn and N. M. Cheshire [1972] • T. Klaniczay, 'A contribution to the Stephen Parmenius research', *Acta Litteraria Academiae Scientiarum Hungaricae*, 18 (1976), 191–200 • D. B. Quinn, 'Stephan Parmenius, Hungarian pioneer in North America', *Explorers and colonies: America, 1500–1625* (1990), 225–38 • lists of Hungarian students who are known to have studied at universities outside Hungary, National Library of Hungary, MSS Department, Budapest • G. Gömöri, 'Hungarian students and visitors in … England', *Hungarian Studies* (1985), 31–50 • J. Hotman, 'Epistola ix', in *Francisci et Joannis Hotomanorum … et clarorum virorum ad eos epistolae*, ed. J. W. Meel (1700)

Parmentier, James (1658–1730), decorative painter, was the nephew and pupil of the French artist Sebastien Bourdon, with whom he studied until 1671. However, nothing is known of Parmentier's parentage except that he was born in Paris, and the details of his early career, until his second visit to England in 1680, are unclear. Fortunately George Vertue recorded in his *Note Books* a significant amount of information about Parmentier's work after this date, based on his conversations with the painter, who was principally a decorative artist, working in oil on plaster, often producing feigned architectural and sculptural ornament.

Parmentier was one of the artists employed by Ralph, first duke of Montagu, to decorate his new London house (Montagu House, Bloomsbury, subsequently the first home of the British Museum) under the direction of Charles de Lafosse between 1689 and 1691. His general role was to assist in 'laying the dead Colours for Monsr Lafosse. and the Architecture. &. some bass relieves at bottom' (Vertue, *Note books*, 2.85). He was responsible for feigned sculpture on the walls and ceilings of the antechamber, saloon, and staircase, such as reclining 'statues' of the Nile and Tiber flanking an urn. Some of this work is visible in George Scharf's watercolour of the staircase of 1845 (British Museum).

In 1694 Parmentier was sent by William III to assist Daniel Marot with the decoration of the palace of Het Loo in the Netherlands. During this period he executed his most important extant work, the ceiling of the anteroom to the Trèveszaal in the Binnenhof, in The Hague, to Marot's designs. However, 'being passionate & rather sarcastical' (Vertue, *Note books*, 3.39) he quarrelled with Marot and returned to England in 1700.

Parmentier was in Yorkshire from 1700 until 1721, during which time 'he painted several large Historical works. for several Noblemen & Gentlemen' (Vertue, *Note books*, 3.45). The most significant surviving work from this period is the altarpiece of the last supper in Holy Trinity Church, Hull, 'which he made a present in gratification and acknowledgment to that Town or City. for that he had met with great favour and employment having in one year painting Portraits only gaind above 300 pounds' (ibid.). Lost works include the altarpiece and ceiling of St Peter's in Leeds, and his best work of the period, according to Vertue (ibid., 3.35), the staircase of Worksop Manor for the duke of Norfolk, painted in 1709.

Parmentier was a member of the circle of virtuosi at York (of which Francis Place, William Lodge, and Ralph Thoresby were also members) and a member of the Rose and Crown Club of artists, which met weekly in a tavern in Covent Garden. He was unsuccessful on his return to London, and two weeks before his death he told Vertue that he intended to move to Amsterdam 'where his workes were in good esteem' (Vertue, *Note books*, 3.46). He died in London on 2 December 1730 and was buried on 4 December in St Paul's, Covent Garden.

Of the smaller-scale works that Parmentier is known to have painted, a portrait of the wit and courtier Charles de Saint-Evremond survives in two versions (NPG and priv. coll.). Also an allegorical portrait of Charles II on copper (NPG) is thought perhaps to be by Parmentier as it may carry his signature. KATHRYN BARRON

Sources Vertue, *Note books* • E. Croft-Murray, *Decorative painting in England, 1537–1837*, 2 vols. (1962–70) • *DNB* • D. Piper, *Catalogue of seventeenth-century portraits in the National Portrait Gallery, 1625–1714* (1963) • L. Dussieux, *Les artistes français à l'étranger*, 3rd edn (Paris,

1876) • [M. Rogers], *John Closterman: master of the English baroque* (1981), no. 4 [exhibition catalogue, NPG, 24 July – 4 Oct 1981]

Parminter, Jane (1750–1811), architect, came from a Huguenot family and was born in Lisbon, Portugal. Her parents were John Parminter (*b.* 1712), a successful Devon wine merchant who owned coffee houses in London and a glass factory in Lisbon, and his wife, Jane Arboyne or Arbouin (*b.* 1712). She spent the first five years of her life in Lisbon, but was sent to London when the Lisbon earthquake of 1755 destroyed her father's business. Her cousin **Mary Parminter** (1767–1849), architect, was the daughter of Richard Parminter (1736–1779) and his wife, Mary (Polly) Walrond (1747–1772). By the time she was twelve she was an orphan and apparently came under the guardianship of the family of her cousin Jane. Perhaps the deaths of all their parents created a bond between the two cousins, for they spent the rest of their lives together. Following the death of Jane's father they embarked in 1784 on a ten-year tour of the continent, Jane's invalid sister Elizabeth and a friend from London, Miss Colvill, accompanying them. They travelled through France, visiting churches and châteaux, and went on to Italy, Germany, Switzerland, and beyond. They returned from their travels in 1795, and Elizabeth Parminter died in Malmesbury the same year.

It was after their return that Jane and Mary Parminter began the plans for their house, overlooking the Exe, just outside the town of Exmouth in Devon. Although at the time no women were professionally engaged in architecture, family tradition has always maintained that Jane designed the house herself. More recent research has suggested that the design was by a Mr Lowder. Exactly who Mr Lowder was is unclear; he may have been a property developer in Bath, possibly an uncle of Jane's. Equally he may have been her cousin John Lowder (1781–1829), who later became an architect and who would probably have been serving his apprenticeship at the time the house was built. Whoever designed the house, it is likely that the misses Parminter had some input into its design, as it was inspired by the chapel of San Vitale visited by them in Ravenna during their grand tour. The house, named A la Ronde, has sixteen sides, with wedge-shaped interconnected rooms fitted round a central octagonal hall. Regency architecture (*c.*1790–1830) encompassed a wide variety of styles, including Greek revival, Gothic revival, and Chinese and Indian styles. During this period there was also a growing interest in the 'picturesque', particularly in landscape and garden design. A la Ronde is an example of a *cottage orné*, an architectural expression of this interest in the picturesque. *Cottages ornés* were small rustic houses, usually thatched and often built as rural retreats for the middle classes, or as dwellings for estate workers. The interior design and decoration of A la Ronde certainly shows a feminine touch. The Parminters were skilled in the handicrafts commonly practised by women of the time, and the walls of the rooms are covered with their paintings and shell pictures, the borders and friezes are decorated with the feathers of game birds, and the furniture with découpage and semi-precious stone inlay. The rooms also house souvenirs and relics brought back from the Parminters' grand tour. The most extraordinary feature of the house is its shell gallery above the octagonal hall, which took the Parminters ten years to complete. It is encrusted with shells, lichen, glass, mica, pottery, stones, bones, and paint.

When Jane Parminter, who remained unmarried, died in 1811 she was buried in a vault beneath the tiny chapel that the two cousins had had built in the house grounds. The Parminters may also have had a hand in the design of this one-storey chapel, known as Point in View; it is flanked by almshouses, intended for elderly spinsters, and a school for girls, all under the same roof. At the time a special licence from the bishop of the diocese was required before nonconformists could use any building for public worship; this was granted to Mary Parminter in 1812.

Inscribed above the door of the chapel is 'Some Points in View we all pursue'. The point the Parminters had in mind was the conversion of Jews to Christianity, and on Jane's death Mary set up a charity known as the Mary Parminter Trust, or the Point in View Trust. The trust's deeds spell out how the chapel and its adjoining buildings were to be

Jane Parminter (1750–1811), by Francis Torond, 1783 [left, with members of her family: (left to right) Elizabeth Parminter, Mr Frend, John Parminter, and Marrianne Frend]

used: the almshouses were intended to house four unmarried women over the age of fifty years, and the school intended for the instruction of six poor female children. In the case of the almshouses preference would be given to Jewish women who had converted to Christianity; places in the school would be given to girls of Jewish parents. In 1829 a manse was built close to the chapel to house its minister, who had previously lived in one of the chapel's rooms. Although the school is no longer in use, the almshouses still afforded shelter to poor spinsters of the area until relatively recently. They have now been converted into meeting-rooms for the chapel, which is still in use.

Mary Parminter died, unmarried, at A la Ronde in 1849, and she too was buried in the chapel's vault. Under the terms of her will the house and estate passed to unmarried female relatives only, but changes in the law meant that it could be passed on to the Revd Oswald Reichel (1840–1923) in the 1880s. He made several changes to the house, including the replacement of the original thatched roof, the installation of central heating, and the addition of extra windows. After his death the house was put up for sale and was bought at auction by his niece Margaret Tudor (*d.* 1969). In 1935 the house was opened to the public, and it was eventually sold to the National Trust in 1991. KAYE BAGSHAW

Sources H. Mellor, *A la Ronde, Devon* (1991) [National Trust Guide, rev. 1997] • *A la Ronde, Exmouth, and the Parminter collection* [n.d.] [official guide] • J. Cornforth, 'Gentle preoccupations', *Country Life* (14 Feb 1991), 38–41 • C. Hussey, 'A la Ronde, Exmouth, Devon', *Country Life*, 83 (1938), 448–52 • S. J. Forder, 'A very perculiar place', *National Trust*, 64 (1991), 26–8 • D. R. Barber, *A short history of the Mary Parminter charity known as the Point in View Trust* (*c.*1935) • O. J. Reichel, *Extracts from a Devonshire lady's notes of travel in France in the eighteenth century* (1902) • S. Morris, 'Wise virgins', *Antique Collector*, 62 (1991), 54–9 • M. Binney, *Country Life* (12 July 1990), 71

Likenesses F. Torond, group portrait, silhouette, 1783, A la Ronde, Devon [*see illus.*] • portraits, A la Ronde, Devon

Parminter, Mary (**1767–1849**). *See under* Parminter, Jane (1750–1811).

Parmoor. For this title name *see* Cripps, Charles Alfred, first Baron Parmoor (1852–1941); Ellis, Marian Emily [Marian Emily Cripps, Lady Parmoor] (1878–1952).

Parnel [Parnell], **James** (*bap.* **1636**, *d.* **1656**), Quaker martyr, was born at East Retford, Nottinghamshire, where he was baptized on 6 September 1636 as the son of Thomas and Sarah Parnel. He had at least one sibling, Sarah, who was born two years earlier.

Little is known of Parnel's early life. He said that he was educated in the 'humane schools of learning', probably at the local grammar school in East Retford. This experience Parnel described as profitable for learning 'human wisdom' but of no assistance in attaining the desired 'heavenly wisdom and learning' (*Collection of the Several Writings*, 231–32). He was apprenticed to his father, possibly as a shoemaker and farmer. However, by his early teenage years he had become deeply disenchanted with the local church. After undergoing a crisis of faith he claimed that he was 'as perfect in sin and iniquity as any' where he lived (*Collection of the Several Writings*, 233). Parnel's disengagement from the church gave rise to bitter disagreement with the local priest, who thought him deluded; Parnel was also rejected by his family. At about fifteen he joined a band of religious seekers whom some have identified as the Quakers at Tickhill and Balby. George Fox, imprisoned at Carlisle in 1653, noted Parnel among his visitors, and with this meeting began Parnel's relationship with the Society of Friends.

Parnel soon found himself called to the Quaker ministry. Because of his youth and slight appearance opponents derisively nicknamed him the 'Quaking boy' (*Collection of the Several Writings*, xxi–xxii). However, he was effective both as a preacher and a polemicist in print, so much so that a critic, Thomas Drayton, doubted whether one so young could be the author of the tracts attributed to him. Like other Friends, Parnel recognized that print was an important tool for evangelism, and his writings, though often ferocious in their criticism of the church and secular authorities, display a deep biblical knowledge and his skills at argument. Particularly effective is his presentation of the Quaker case on church doctrine, scripture, tithes, rates, and social customs. In 1654, he published *A Trial by Faith*, a pamphlet which was reprinted five times, including in Dutch. In the same year he visited Friends at Cambridge, where he was imprisoned by the mayor, William Pickering, for publishing two papers against the magistrates and ministers. In gaol 'for the space of two sessions', he was tried by a jury who failed to find him guilty of publishing seditious and scandalous pamphlets (*Collection of the Several Writings*, 237).

The year 1655 saw the publication of a number of Parnel's tracts, including *The Watcher*, which challenged Baptist theology and detailed debates that Parnel had had with leading Baptists, such as Richard Elligood at Fenstanton, Joseph Doughty at Cambridge, and John Ray at Littleport in the Isle of Ely. The most startling of the works produced by Parnel in this year, however, was *The Trumpet of the Lord Blowne*, an extraordinary denunciation of the rich and their values, a work in which Parnel showed himself to be perhaps more of a social radical than any of the other early Quakers. It openly attacked what Parnel saw as the unjustified customs, luxuries, and indolence of the lords and gentry, and was bound to earn the young Quaker their enmity. In June Parnel journeyed into Essex, where he became the county's first Quaker evangelist. Quickly gaining support in the northern half of the county at Halstead, Coggeshall, Witham, and Felsted, he preached to more than a thousand people from John Furly's hayloft in Colchester. There he made many notable converts including Furly himself and Stephen Crisp, who was to become a prominent figure in the movement.

On learning that a feast day had been called in the town of Great Coggeshall when special prayers were to be said against the 'errors' of the Quakers, Parnel returned there on 12 July. He spoke in the parish church after a local minister—Priest Willis of Braintree—had ended his sermon. Parnel wrote later that Willis spoke a 'Divination of his own Brain, and not from the Mouth of the Lord' (*Collection *of the Several Writings*, 240). After leaving the church Parnel was arrested and charged with violently entering the church, accusing the minister of blasphemy, promoting a breach of the peace, and living a disorderly and unsettled life. Refusing to provide sureties Parnel was sent to gaol at Colchester Castle, where—except for a march to the assizes at Chelmsford and back—he spent the rest of his life.

Despite being directed by the judge to find Parnel guilty the jury acquitted him; none the less, he was fined £40 for contempt of magistrates and the church, and was returned to gaol. The judge ordered that he was to be denied visits from fellow Quakers. On his return to Colchester, Parnel was cruelly treated by the gaoler, Nicholas Roberts, and in particular by his wife. She was described by Friends as having 'set her man to beat him, and Swore she would have his blood' (Penney, 92). The gaolers sometimes withheld from Parnel 'any Victualls, and at other Times would Set the Prisoners to take away such as was brought to him' (Penney, 92–3). When some Friends procured a 'trundle bed' for Parnel it was denied him, with the result that he was forced 'to Lye on the Stones which in a Wet Season would Run down with Water' (Penney, 93). Other Friends who tried to visit him were abused with, for example, 'piss and water' thrown over them by the gaoler's wife, or when allowed to speak to Parnel, as Thomas Creek of Coggeshall found, it was only through the lock of a door (*Lambs Defence*, 9–10). Parnel was moved to the 'Hole', a space 12 feet up in the castle wall which could be reached only by way of a ladder and a rope, from which he fell injuring himself, 'being very much Bruised in his head and Arms, and taken up for dead' (Penney, 92). He was then taken to the 'Oven', a spot significantly more accessible, though uncomfortable, because of its small size and lack of air; some said that they had 'seen a baker's oven much bigger' (*Lambs Defence*, 4). Several Friends tried to offer assistance during his imprisonment—Thomas Talcot pledged a bond of £40 in order that he might nurse Parnel at home; another offered to take Parnel's place until he recovered—but the authorities refused to countenance any thought of release until his fine was paid.

Parnel died at Colchester Castle on 10 April 1656; his last words were 'Here I dye innocently' and 'Now I go' (*Lambs Defence*, 12). Such was the notoriety surrounding Parnel and the Quakers in general that Ralph Josselin, the vicar of Earls Colne, remarked that following Parnel's death his followers went to Colchester to witness his 'resurrection' (*Diary of Ralph Josselin*, 367). In the inquest that followed the authorities wanted to impress that Parnel's death was not their responsibility but instead had been caused by illness and his apparently wilful hunger strike, (a claim partly supported by the admission of Thomas Shortland, who was present during the prisoner's last night, that Parnel had just ended a ten-day fast). Prominent in promoting this case was Henry Glisson, a Colchester minister and opponent of Quakerism, in his pamphlet, *A True and Lamentable Relation* (1656); the eventual verdict of the coroner and jury agreed with him. In response Friends gave their interpretation of events in *The Lambs Defence Against Lies* (1656), which pointed to the cruel actions of the gaolers and the indifference of the authorities. There is no doubt that Parnel died in cruel circumstances but his prominence in the movement and in particular the manner of his death at a young age led to his subsequent celebration as a Quaker martyr. His body was not returned to the Friends but was buried in an unmarked grave in the castle grounds on account of there being no burial fees paid. A compilation of Parnel's writings was published in 1675.

ADRIAN DAVIES

Sources *A collection of the several writings given forth: from the spirit of the Lord, through the meek, patient, and suffering servant of God, James Parnel* (1675) • C. F. Smith, *James Parnel* (1906) • J. Besse, *A collection of the sufferings of the people called Quakers*, 2 vols. (1753) • N. Penney, ed., *The first publishers of truth* (1907) • A. Davies, *The Quakers in English society, 1655–1725* (2000) • H. Glisson, *A true and lamentable relation of the most desperate death of James Parnel, Quaker* (1656) • *The lambs defence against lies* (1656) • T. Drayton, *An answer according to truth* (1657) • W. C. Braithwaite, *The beginnings of Quakerism*, ed. H. J. Cadbury, 2nd edn (1955) • *Diary of Ralph Josselin, 1616–1644*, ed. A. Macfarlane (1976) • H. Barbour, 'Parnell (or Parnel), James', Greaves & Zaller, *BDBR*, 3.10

Parnell, (Catherine Maria) Anna Mercer (1852–1910), Irish nationalist and artist, was born on 13 May 1852 at home at Avondale, co. Wicklow, the tenth of eleven children and fifth daughter of John Henry Parnell (1811–1859) and Delia Tudor, *née* Stewart (1816–1896). Her older brothers were John Henry Parnell MP and Charles Stewart *Parnell MP, leader of the Irish nationalists. Her older sister Fanny *Parnell (1848–1882) also was involved in Irish politics. The Parnells were part of the protestant ascendancy, a number having established 'patriot' reputations, while Delia Stewart came from a line of distinguished Americans.

Following her father's death in 1859, Anna Parnell and her mother had to abandon the family home, Avondale, and resided first in a number of locations in the southern suburbs of Dublin, then in Dublin and, from the mid-1860s, in Paris. Her formal education was erratic, being mainly in the hands of English governesses who equipped her with an ascendancy accent, but her upbringing allowed her more independence than was customary for young women at the time. At the age of eighteen she returned to Dublin, where she studied art at the Royal Dublin Academy of Art; in the spring of 1875 she moved to London to attend the Heatherley School of Art. Two of her paintings were accepted in exhibitions by the Royal Society of British Arts in 1874 and a third was displayed the following year.

During the mid- and late 1870s Anna Parnell followed the career of her older brother Charles closely, and was in the Ladies' Gallery of the House of Commons during his efforts to 'obstruct' parliamentary business in 1877. Subsequently, in 1880, she published a three-part article describing the scenes. Her mother settled in 1874 in Bordentown, New Jersey, where, after the conclusion of the 1877 parliamentary session, Anna Parnell joined her. Her own political interest was sharpened by the agrarian crisis and Land League agitation in Ireland at the close of the 1870s. Her brother became president of the Irish National Land

(**Catherine Maria) Anna Mercer Parnell (1852–1910)**, by Henry O'Shea, *c.*1878

League in October 1879 and toured North America between January and early March 1880 to solicit funds. She helped to organize the Irish Land League Famine Relief Fund which was set up in New York. After March, when he began the United States Land League, she was soon immersed in its work as well. During this period she became acquainted with Michael Davitt, the founder of the Irish Land League. In late summer 1880 Anna Parnell returned to Ireland and she was the leading force in the Ladies' Land League when it was founded on 31 January 1881, serving as an honorary secretary. She addressed numerous Irish audiences on behalf of the movement, and sometimes faced considerable hostility. Both she and the Ladies' League became increasingly prominent during autumn 1881, especially following the suppression of the Land League in October. During the next few months, while her brother was in Kilmainham gaol, Anna Parnell emerged as a major figure in nationalist circles. Disliking aspects of Land League policy, she opposed Gladstone's Land Act of 1881 and viewed with disdain the 'Kilmainham treaty' between the Liberal ministry and her brother. Soon after his release, in August 1882, Charles extinguished the Ladies' Land League. From this time Anna Parnell was utterly estranged from her brother and never spoke to him again.

By the mid-1880s Anna Parnell was living and painting in Cornwall. In 1885 she re-emerged in politics briefly when she attended a rally in London for the political activist Helen Taylor. During the O'Shea divorce crisis of 1890–91 she was sympathetic to her brother's plight as co-respondent, but took no part in his last campaign. By the turn of the century she was living in straitened circumstances in north Devon. Though largely detached from politics, she sent the Irish nationalist Maud Gonne a contribution for the Patriotic Children's Treat organized as a protest against Queen Victoria's visit to Dublin in 1900. Publication of Michael Davitt's *The Fall of Feudalism in Ireland* in 1904 kindled her interest in Irish affairs once more. She was enraged by Davitt's treatment of the Ladies' Land League and sought to correct the record. During 1907 she set down her own counter-version of events entitled *The Tale of a Great Sham*, which, however, remained unpublished until 1986. At the beginning of 1908 she campaigned in Ireland on behalf of Sinn Féin's first and unsuccessful parliamentary candidate in the North Leitrim by-election. This was her last public involvement. Anna Parnell, who was living under an assumed name, accidentally drowned at Ilfracombe, north Devon, on 20 September 1910 and was buried in Holy Trinity cemetery, Ilfracombe, on 23 September. ALAN O'DAY

Sources A. Parnell, *The tale of a great sham*, ed. D. Hearne (1986) • J. M. Côté, *Fanny and Anna Parnell: Ireland's patriot sisters* (1991) • J. Côté and D. Hearne, 'Anna Parnell', *Women, power and consciousness in 19th-century Ireland: eight biographical studies*, ed. M. Cullen and M. Luddy (1995) • R. F. Foster, *Charles Stewart Parnell: the man and his family* (1976) • M. Ward, *Unmanageable revolutionaries: women and Irish nationalism*, new edn (1995) • T. W. Moody, *Davitt and Irish revolution* (1981) • T. W. Moody, 'Anna Parnell and the Land League', *Hermathema* (1974), 5–17 • A. J. Kettle, *The material for victory* (1958) • K. Tynan, *Twenty-five years: reminiscences* (1913) • R. Sawyer, *'We are but women': women in Ireland's history* (1993)

Archives London School of Economics, Helen Taylor MSS

Likenesses H. O'Shea, photograph, *c.*1878, priv. coll. [*see illus.*] • portrait, repro. in Côté, *Fanny and Anna Parnell*

Parnell, Charles Stewart (1846–1891), politician and landowner, was born on 27 June 1846 at Avondale, co. Wicklow, the seventh of the eleven children of John Henry Parnell (1811–1859), deputy lieutenant and high sheriff for co. Wicklow, and his wife, Delia Tudor (1816–1896), daughter of Admiral Charles Stewart (1778–1869), of Bordentown, New Jersey, USA. He had four brothers and six sisters; two of these siblings—(Catherine Maria) Anna *Parnell and Fanny *Parnell, the 'patriot sisters'—were to make significant concurrent interventions of their own in Irish political life.

Family and early life The Parnells of Avondale were descended from an English merchant family, which came to prominence in Congleton, Cheshire, early in the seventeenth century. These Parnells were active in local politics, and father and son each held the office of mayor of Congleton, and during the civil war they were parliamentarians. Thomas Parnell established the Parnell family in Ireland, when soon after the Restoration he bought an estate in Queen's county. The family produced a number of noted figures, including Thomas Parnell (1679–1718),

Charles Stewart Parnell (1846–1891), by Sydney Prior Hall, 1888–9 [at the Parnell commission inquiry]

the poet, and the better-known Sir John Parnell (1744–1801), who became chancellor of the exchequer in Grattan's parliament. Sir John Parnell lost office in 1799, when he opposed the Act of Union; this gave him a reputation for patriotism, which was qualified by his refusal to support Catholic emancipation. Charles Stewart Parnell's grandfather William Parnell (1780–1821), who inherited the Avondale estate in 1795, was, however, a genuinely liberal patriotic MP for Wicklow from 1817 to 1820, and his father, John Henry, though a rather strict protestant, had similarly amiable political views but no public ambitions; he was the first of the line for five generations not to become an MP. In fact, his son's parliamentary colleague Frank Hugh O'Donnell made a point of describing the Parnell home as 'idle' and 'uncultured', like so many gentry homes of this period.

When Charles Stewart Parnell was six years of age, his parents decided to separate. The young Parnell left the family home—where his sisters had nicknamed him Butthead, because of his high spirits which would not 'brook control'—to obtain an education in England. According to convention, he had an unhappy youth at school and university: he attended first a girls' school in Yeovil, Somerset; in later years he was a pupil at the Revd Whishaw's private school at Chipping Norton. Like much else, this conventional wisdom should be treated with reserve. In 1886 at Plymouth he made a point of praising 'the very excellent teaching which I received in my earlier years—to which I shall always look back with the greatest reverence, affection and respect … in the neighbouring county of Somerset'. Recent disclosure about his time at Magdalene College, Cambridge (1865–9), necessitates revaluation of that period as well. Rather than being isolated, Parnell was forced by the troubled financial circumstances of his estate in Wicklow to be absent a good deal. Nevertheless, he enjoyed a friendly relationship with his contemporaries and his college and looked forward to resuming his studies there. After being rusticated from Cambridge following a brawl, he never returned to complete his degree. He stayed at Avondale for a while, but in 1871 he joined his elder brother John Howard on an extended tour of the United States. Their travels took them mostly through the south and apparently the brothers neither spent much time in centres of Irish immigration nor sought out Irish-Americans. Before 1872 Parnell's Irish experience was circumscribed by the region in and around Dublin and a social circle drawn from his own order. He demonstrated no public interest in politics. The main accretions of youth were a marked upper-class English accent, an interest in horses, hunting, and cricket, and the manners of a gentleman. He stood well in the estimation of his own class, was regarded as a retiring country gentleman of politically rather conservative tendencies, and was noted as an improving landowner who played an important part in opening the south Wicklow area to industrialization.

Parnell became an officer in the Wicklow militia, in part because he felt the elegant uniform improved his appearance at Dublin Castle balls. In 1874 he also became high sheriff of co. Wicklow and was chosen as a member of the synod of the disestablished Church of Ireland. While he was to drop away from formal church attendance in later years, he always held firm, if rather general, religious convictions. He was never, however, to be tempted by Roman Catholicism despite his admiration for its spiritual qualities: following his spell in Kilmainham gaol in 1882 he left all the Roman Catholic devotional material sent to him by well-wishers with the prison governor.

> At dinner … Parnell happened to observe that he was a Protestant, upon which my friend remarked: 'But I hope you won't die one, Mr Parnell'. Parnell at once flushed up and said: 'Certainly I will, most certainly'. (Mullin, 191)

Another account suggests that the eyes 'blazed with indignation' in response to a similar proposition from an Irish party MP (J. Valentine, *Irish Memories*, 1928, 10).

In one important respect, however, Parnell differed from mainstream sentiment in his new class. While at Cambridge—he later insisted—he had taken an interest in the Fenian rising of 1867; his brother and sisters all testified that the execution of the Manchester martyrs (three Fenians hanged in 1867 for killing a policeman while they were trying to rescue Fenian prisoners) made a most marked impression on him. Slowly, and partly as a consequence of lack of success in other enterprises, including a rebuff from a rich heiress (Miss Woods) in Paris, he drifted into the world of patriotic politics. The Irish political scene in the mid-1870s was dominated by Isaac Butt's Home Rule League, which had been formed in 1873. Butt and the majority of his followers devoted their energies to an unfailingly polite and almost totally ineffective parliamentary campaign to advance the Irish case for a moderate degree of self-government. Whatever his reservations about this line of action, Parnell, on deciding to enter politics in the nationalist interest, had little choice but to attempt to become a home-rule MP.

Entry into politics In 1874 Parnell made his initial foray into politics when he sought to contest Wicklow at the general election. As high sheriff of the county he was disqualified, however, and John Howard Parnell became the surrogate candidate in the family interest. The Home Rule

League was surprised to discover that the Parnells professed home-rule principles: no Parnell then belonged to the league or had given notice of self-government sympathies. In the event John Howard finished bottom of the poll. Nevertheless, the campaign fired Parnell's political ambitions; the Home Rule League lost no time enlisting so prized a recruit. After his term as high sheriff ended, he stood in the home-rule interest at the County Dublin by-election in March 1874. His lacklustre campaign did not fill observers with visions of a future leader in the making. Despite a huge defeat and only a modest display of talent, he was quickly given a prominent place in league affairs. He had the origins sought by leaders of the home-rule movement—a protestant landlord, the epitome of ascendancy respectability. His political aspirations were soon fulfilled. In April 1875 his opportunity came when the league executive endorsed him for the County Meath seat, vacant through the death of the revered John Martin. Unusually, the league abrogated its policy of neutrality between competing home-rulers and placed pressure upon a local parliamentary hopeful to withdraw. Parnell was not an ordinary nationalist but one carefully groomed for political honours: a man above all with a family name to cash in on. As his address claimed:

> Neither are my name and family unknown in the history of Irish politics … My ancestor, Sir John Parnell, in the old Irish Parliament was the active and energetic advocate of the removal of the disabilities which affected his Catholic fellow-countrymen. In the evil days of corruption, which destroyed the independence of Ireland, he lost a great office, and refused a peerage to oppose the fatal measure of Union. His successor, Sir Henry Parnell, rendered in the British Parliament services to the cause of Catholic emancipation and to Ireland which the Irish people have not forgotten.
>
> If you adopt me, I will endeavour, and I think I can promise, that no act of mine will ever discredit the name which has been associated with these recollections. (*Meath Herald*, 10 April 1875)

Parnell's intermediary in obtaining the blessings of the committee which selected him as candidate for County Meath was Patrick Egan, a figure who later acquired an extremist and even sinister reputation. Egan had been a Fenian since the 1860s and was to be linked with political violence in the 1880s. However, it should be remembered that in the 1870s Egan, like many other former Fenians, was willing to give the home-rule movement a serious and honest try. His convictions on this point were clear. It would be difficult to overemphasize the umbrella nature of the movement which Isaac Butt led. Furthermore, Patrick Egan performed services not only for Parnell but also for many other home-rule figures, including Colonel King-Harman, later a Conservative under-secretary for Ireland, for whom he wrote election addresses. Not too much should therefore be made of the 'extreme' nature of Parnell's early sponsorship.

As a young politician, Parnell was quite exceptionally nervous: delivering his first election address, he was so wretched a speaker as barely to be able to make himself understood. Moreover, the decision to enter politics had its bad side. Parnell's family had a reputation for mental disorder as well as patriotism: 'Madness', he often said, was not a word the Parnells used lightly, and self-control was achieved only with enormous effort. After his first unsuccessful campaign for Dublin, he collapsed with a nervous illness for six weeks. His closest colleagues noted a tendency to clench his fists so hard while speaking as to leave the marks of his nails on his palms. He was also intensely superstitious, and refused to stay in hotel rooms marked 13, or to support bills with only thirteen clauses: he had been thirteen years old when his beloved father died. Another part of his superstition was a loathing for the colour green. This was an ironic difficulty for an Irish leader who frequently had to speak from public platforms draped with green flags and decorations (the House of Commons was upholstered in the same offensive hue). He refused also a green casket presented to him by an admirer while he was incarcerated. In short, the young Parnell appeared to be a bundle of barely controlled contradictions. He was febrile, tense, and yet withal assertive.

It would be a mistake, however, to overstate the neurotic aspects of Parnell's personality. He seems to have regarded his public nervousness as merely something that had to be overcome. In the end he evolved an effective speaking style, slow and clear on open-air platforms, faster and more exciting at indoor meetings. There is no sign that he was given to agonizing bouts of self-appraisal. Indeed, his colleagues marvelled at his apparent lack of self-consciousness. T. P. O'Connor described him as

> neither expansive nor introspective. It is one of the strongest and most curious peculiarities of Mr Parnell, not merely that he rarely, if ever, speaks of himself but that he rarely, if ever, gives any indication of having studied himself … It is a joke among his intimates that to Mr Parnell the being Parnell does not exist. (T. P. O'Connor, *Charles Stewart Parnell*, 1891, 150)

Parnell, it should be stressed, was an upper-class country gentleman, with much of the assurance—and occasional toughness—of his class. He had a more than healthy respect, as Michael Morris, the mighty Catholic lord chief justice, pointed out, for serious Irish revolutionaries, but he was disdainful in his attitude towards his more run-of-the-mill nationalist colleagues. As James Mullin's memoirs recorded, he lied casually and badly to them about small matters of comfort. A favourite trick was to pay more attention to his beautiful red setter, Grouse, than to the political conversation at his host's dinner table. As Labouchere's obituary noted:

> A selfish man Parnell certainly was, but he was good-naturedly selfish. If anyone stood in his way, he would sacrifice him without a moment's hesitation, nor would he go greatly out of his way to serve a friend. When, however, his own interest was not concerned, he would not put himself out to do either friend or foe an injury. Politeness has been defined as good nature in little things, and this sort of good nature he had. (*Truth*, 15 Oct 1891)

A combination of boredom and disappointment seems to have pushed Parnell into politics. Once involved, he brought to bear considerable qualities of determination, though not, it was said, imagination. 'The strength of Parnell was character rather than intellect', wrote T. P. O'Connor in a typical phrase (*Charles Stewart Parnell*, 1891, 221). John Morley in a similar fashion called him a 'man of temperament, of will, of authority, of power, not of ideas or ideals, or knowledge or political maxims, or even of practical reason in its higher sense' (A. Robbins, *Parnell: the Last Five Years*, 1926, 18). It is true that Parnell was no intellectual in the way that O'Connor and Morley were. He avoided the 'arts' and much preferred dogs, horses, and the sports and pastimes of the countryside as a means of relaxation. His pleasures were as uncomplicated as those of any country squire. A high proportion of those MPs who remained loyal to him after 'the split'—for example, John and Willie Redmond, W. J. Corbett, or J. J. O'Kelly—were men who had enjoyed picnics with him in the beautiful Wicklow hills. It is hard to imagine a man more different from those who were to be his principal lieutenants—Justin McCarthy, Tim Healy, T. P. O'Connor, Thomas Sexton, John Dillon, and William O'Brien. While they were (apart from Dillon) sociable, articulate speakers and inveterate scribblers, Parnell was the reverse. And yet, although he was no intellectual in this conventional sense, he was not, as is so often suggested, a mere technician of power. He made a contribution to Irish political debate which was as important as it was unique.

Parnell's early impact on the House of Commons was slight. On 22 April 1875 he took his seat in the house. Four days later he made his first speech, opposing a committee on a bill for the preservation of peace in Ireland. He maintained that 'in the neglect of the principles of self-government lay the root of all Irish trouble' and 'that Ireland was not a geographical fragment, but a nation' (*Hansard 3*, 223, 1878, 1643–6). On fourteen other occasions he spoke during the session, but made no particular impression. Barry O'Brien recorded that he remained 'chiefly a calm spectator of the proceedings of the House of Commons, watching, learning, biding his time' (B. O'Brien, *Life of … Parnell*, 1898, 85). In 1876 he did, however, suddenly come before the public eye. In a famous interruption of the chief secretary he claimed that the Fenians who had accidentally killed a policeman in Manchester in 1867 while attempting to rescue two of their comrades had committed no murder. Despite the ensuing English uproar, Parnell pressed on with his chosen course of action. In particular, he made it his business to cultivate Fenian sentiment, not only in Ireland but also, and even more assiduously, in England and Scotland. The Home Rule Confederation of Great Britain was largely composed of *sotto voce* republicans and Parnell did his best to become their favourite.

In the parliamentary session of 1877 Parnell threw himself into the project known as 'obstruction'. In itself there was nothing particularly original about the idea of delaying parliamentary business by prolonged and irrelevant speech-making during debates. Even Isaac Butt, the moderate home-rule leader, had condoned the practice in 1875 on the occasion of an Irish coercion bill. However, despite Butt's reproofs, Parnell and his allies, the ungracious Belfast pork merchant Joseph Gillis Biggar and the pock-marked 'work-house boy' John O'Connor Power (both of whom were under sentence of expulsion from the Irish Republican Brotherhood at this time for their participation in constitutional politics), did not restrict themselves to blocking Irish legislation but widened the scope of the tactic to cover imperial concerns. This defiant activity reached its high point in July 1877 with a twenty-six-hour sitting on the South Africa Bill.

Thanks to such work it was clear by early or mid-1877 that Parnell was the effective leader of the Irish in England and Scotland. His deposition of Butt as president of the Home Rule Confederation of Great Britain in the autumn merely ratified this situation.

The New Departure Obstruction did not disappear during 1878. Its force was muted by the ministry's promise of legislation on Irish intermediate education. That subject was then left for consideration until late in the session. Ireland would receive this boon if time remained. It was incumbent upon the 'obstructionists' to restrain delaying procedures or face losing an Irish reform. By mid-1878 relations between Butt and Parnell had reached a nadir; each sought to claim that the education legislation had been enacted because of his own tactics.

Parnell reiterated that his was not a policy of obstruction at all; it was really a policy of independent and strenuous opposition to the government of the day 'all along the line' upon every question. This high-profile defiance of the British government and moderate home-rulers in the House of Commons naturally attracted favourable attention from the Fenians. Parnell's active flirtation with Fenianism was linked to a series of private meetings with Irish republican leaders. As early as August 1877 he had managed to make a very favourable impression on a prominent figure, James J. O'Kelly, who declared to John Devoy: 'He has many of the qualities of leadership—and time will give him more. He is cool—extremely so and resolute' (W. O'Brien and D. Ryan, eds., *Devoy's Post-Bag*, 1948–53, 1.267–8). By the beginning of 1878 he had managed to convince Dr William Carroll, another American-based leader, of his adherence to the principle of absolute independence while avoiding any commitment to the Fenian movement as such. In fact, the increasing hopelessness of the traditional militarist dream of an armed uprising to drive out the English predisposed the more realistic separatists to give him a good hearing. Not that he was saying much. At a second meeting in March 1878 he remained largely silent. He could afford to. The separatists were gradually dropping the idea of making Parnell one of their number. Instead they were beginning to think in terms of how they could most profitably assist him.

John Devoy, the most capable and serious of the Irish-American militants, made this clear in a telegram on 25 October 1878, when he offered Parnell the 'New Departure' package. Parnell had just been re-elected president of the Home Rule Confederation of Great Britain with Fenian support, and Devoy felt—wrongly, as it turned out—that this was a moment of crucial importance. However, the important thing to note is that he offered Parnell the support of American militants on certain conditions: abandonment of the federal demand and substitution of a general demand in favour of self-government; vigorous agitation of the land question on the basis of a peasant proprietary, while accepting concessions tending to abolish arbitrary eviction; exclusion of all sectarian issues from the platform; collective voting by party members on all imperial and home questions, the adoption of an aggressive policy, and energetic resistance to coercive legislation; and advocacy of all struggling nationalities in the British empire or elsewhere.

Parnell made no public response to this package offer. A few days later he decided to accept an invitation from the Ballinasloe Tenants' Defence Association to speak in the west of Ireland. Poor harvests in the late 1870s and falling agricultural prices had created the preconditions for such gatherings. Shrouded as he was in an aura of republican conspiracy, it is hardly surprising that Parnell had yet to become a completely respectable figure in Irish politics. Outside Meath the clergy regarded him warily. As James Kilmartin, the president of Ballinasloe Tenants' Defence Association, later recalled: 'The priests would not then identify with Parnell. None of them would take the chair, and only two took places on the platform' (Bew, 25).

At Ballinasloe, Parnell declared himself in favour of a peasant proprietary as a principle. He could afford to do so: after all, Gladstone's speech in Dublin in 1877 had advocated the multiplication of small agricultural properties in Ireland. Two weeks later, however, Parnell addressed the Kerry Tenants' Defence Association at Tralee, at their invitation, on the land question. Here, while still in favour of the peasant proprietorship principle, he seemed to accept that as a practical strategy, the moderate Bullite approach, which laid greatest emphasis on fair rents and fixity of tenure, was the way forward. *The Nation* (23 November 1878) reported Parnell's careful words, that:

> unless they went in for a revolution he confessed he did not see how they were going to bring about a radical reform of the system of land tenure in this country. For his own part … he was disposed to devote his energies to endeavouring to obtain a settlement on the basis laid down by Mr Butt's Fixity of Tenure Bill as introduced in 1876.

The meeting was infused by a dominant tone of moderation, though the presence of more militant themes cannot be denied. A voice from the crowd challenged Parnell: 'The land is ours.' He replied carefully: 'We do not wish to interfere with the proprietorial rights of the landlord … there are many good landlords.' Another voice cried out: 'Aren't you a landlord yourself?' Someone replied from within the crowd: 'He is, and a good one.' A 'somewhat exhilarated' individual called out 'Butt to the devil', but was promptly 'silenced'. Another voice called out for 'total separation'—and provoked a chorus of 'no, no' and 'yes, yes'. Parnell was clearly still keeping his options open. But, in the midst of all this conjunctural manoeuvring, the Kerry speech did contain one key theme which was to represent the core element of consistency in Parnell's approach to the problem of the relationship between the land and the national question:

> He had heard some people, say 'Oh, I am not a Home ruler—I am a tenant righter'. He had to say to such a man, 'I don't care what you are' … there was no antagonism between them and there could be none. Settle the land question on a firm basis, give the tenant farmers the right to live on their farms, level the barriers that divided class from class, and there would be no interest sufficiently strong to retain English misgovernment and they would then have Home Rule (cheers). (*The Nation*, 23 Nov 1878)

Everything that Parnell said at Kerry was pervaded by one key assumption: it was possible to win a major land reform by energetic pressure on the British parliament. 'They will give us nothing' said a voice in the crowd; but this was not Parnell's message.

Nevertheless, the Fenians continued to work to their own agenda. At a secret meeting in March 1879 in Claremorris, the Fenians decided to support an agrarian movement, provided that they retained control of its county and provincial organization. It is clear, too, that they acted on a key strategic assumption: the British parliament was a 'parliament of landlords'—it would not, therefore, sponsor serious land reform. Any substantial mass Irish peasant agitation would, therefore, at some stage have to challenge the framework of the union, either by insurrection or, at least, by secession of MPs from Westminster.

President of the Irish National Land League Not surprisingly, in the face of these currents, Parnell's early involvement in the land agitation was marked by an obvious hesitancy. Even after the success of a meeting held at Irishtown, co. Mayo, on 20 April 1879 had indicated the obvious potential, he still held back. It required a special effort of persuasion from Michael Davitt, at that time a separatist activist beginning his involvement in land reform, to persuade him to attend the second key meeting at Westport, co. Mayo, on 8 June 1879. Even then he was not fully committed. In fact, it was not until early November, some days after the Irish National Land League was set up in Dublin on 21 October 1879, that Parnell as the new organization's president committed himself fully. He did this by signing a militant Land League address which left no doubt that he stood with the new movement. At the age of thirty-two, after four and a half years in parliament, he had put into place a political coalition without precedent in Irish politics.

Parnell was propelled by his new allies into a frantic bout of activity. In December 1879 he left for the United States to obtain financial support for the new movement, while the neo-Fenians organized a series of mass demonstrations and other confrontations with landlord power in the west of Ireland. The scale of these confrontations—in one celebrated example an entire village, Carraroe in co. Galway, turned out in December to resist an eviction—depended both on the special poverty of the smallholders of the west and the local organizational strength of Fenianism. Inevitably, violence and assassinations against those—landlords, agents, or backsliding tenants or labourers—who opposed the 'popular' will accompanied this movement. Parnell addressed a sparsely attended house of representatives and had an audience with the American president on 4 February. He spoke in sixty-two cities to largely Irish-American audiences and allowed himself more than a few rhetorical indulgences: most notably when in Cincinnati on 20 February 1880 he spoke of breaking the 'last link which keeps Ireland bound to England'. In later years he recalled this tour with loathing and by implication discounted some of the rhetoric. At the time, however, he was clearly anxious to retain Fenian support. In a conversation with a New York journalist on the outward voyage, Parnell insisted that while personally he could not join a secret society, he none the less needed the support of Fenianism.

The announcement of the general election of April 1880 brought Parnell's labours in America to an abrupt end. He hurried home. Overall the election saw the triumph of Gladstone's Liberal Party over the Conservative government. Parnell achieved the personal triumph of being returned for three seats in Cork, Mayo, and Meath. He chose to sit for the Cork seat. However, most of the notable successes for Parnell's supporters were obtained in the province of Connaught. It was clearly revealed that the Land League was still very much a Connaught phenomenon and that while Parnell had a personal influence in the other provinces, it was still limited. On 17 May he was elected leader of the Irish Parliamentary Party, but by a mere twenty-three votes to eighteen. There were, it should be remembered, a total of fifty-nine nominal home-rule MPs.

In August 1880 the House of Lords seemed to set its face against even mild reform by rejecting a very moderate Compensation for Disturbance Bill. Ireland prepared for a turbulent winter. The scene was set for the league's expansion into the more prosperous regions of Leinster and Munster.

In July 1880 Parnell had met Mrs Katharine O'Shea (1845–1921) [*see* Parnell, Katharine], the wife of a somewhat 'whiggish' member of the Home Rule Party, Captain William Henry *O'Shea (1840–1905) [*see under* Parnell, Katharine]. She was a woman well connected with the Liberal Party, being the niece of Lord Hatherley, Gladstone's first lord chancellor, and the sister of Sir Henry Evelyn Wood, commander of the troops in South Africa. By 17 October Parnell was writing to her as 'My dearest love'. The Parnells as a family tended towards the unconventional, both in affairs of the heart and domestic arrangements—Charles's eldest sister, Delia, had eloped at the age of sixteen. It should be remembered also that Parnell's own parents had separated when he was six, and that his famous grandfather Admiral Stewart had lived openly with his mistress for many years.

In Parnell's view Mrs O'Shea had been deserted by her husband for several years. The O'Shea marriage was a fiction. On the other hand Parnell, as a lonely, sensitive man who hated 'social life', found himself in the midst of a storm of greater proportions than he could possibly have expected when he entered politics. Augustus Moore, who lived in the same house in Keppel Street, recorded Parnell returning—armed with a pistol—from bitter parliamentary conflicts and then seeking relaxation from the stresses of the day by playing with a boy's train set. Parnell had an alleged history of casual sexual encounters with social inferiors but this lifestyle was soon to be replaced in favour of Mrs O'Shea at her home at Eltham in Kent. She, too, was well satisfied: 'For a woman of my temperament Parnell was the ideal lover', she later told reporters (Foster, *Paddy and Mr Punch*, 128).

Did O'Shea know of his wife's liaison, which was a subject of gossip in London political circles from 1881? In an able series of letters he later denied that he had firm knowledge of his wife's *affaire*. But it is unlikely that he was telling the truth. In 1881 the two men almost came to the point of fighting a duel. By 1882 Parnell had had a cricket pitch laid out at Eltham. He was soon to establish a study and a laboratory there so that he could continue to practise his favourite hobby. As Katharine herself said in an interview with Henry Harrison after the publication of her memoirs: 'Did Captain O'Shea know? Of course he knew … There was no bargain; there were no discussions; people do not talk of such things. But he knew, and he actually encouraged me in it at times' (H. Harrison, *Parnell Vindicated*, 1931, 123). In short, Captain O'Shea calculated that Parnell's relationship with his wife might issue in some political advancement for himself.

However, in the early weeks and months the O'Shea liaison was of little political importance. Much more important was the fact that Parnell was swept along by what became a truly national agitation. Moreover, while the bulk of the newly attracted stronger farmers in the south and west were supporters of legalistic forms of struggle—some of it highly expensive and rather ineffective, as his activist sister Anna pointed out in her book *The Tale of the Land League: a Great Sham*, serialized in the *Irish People* in 1907—agrarian outrage grew from 863 incidents in 1879 to 2590 in 1880. Parnell agreed publicly with his sister's analysis at Waterford in October 1881 but nevertheless remained the figurehead of an organization packed with revolutionary organizers, violent assassins on the fringe, and a solid core of sensible farmers looking to make gains out of the reduction in landlord power. Serjeant Sullivan noted acutely that 'the threat to his power levelled by the combination of Fenianism and the Land League compelled him to associate with men of a social and intellectual order that he must have disliked'. But he also noted that this was precisely 'the dispensation'—'hard to understand' though it was—by which Parnell became the 'hero of the *bourgeoisie*' (A. M. Sullivan, *Old Ireland*, 1927, 47).

Parnell never accepted the revolutionary premises of his neo-Fenian allies. He believed in the possibility of a major land reform; he aspired to satisfy the tenantry on terms which were not disadvantageous to the landlords—the whole process to be subsidized by a generous contribution from the British tenantry. He wanted to bring the younger and more progressive landlords into the home-rule movement so as to give it sufficient cachet to convince British legislators in London. But he was not able to set the limits of a popular agitation: his advocacy of the boycott and other forms of social ostracism did not satisfy his most militant supporters. Interestingly, however, the unionist *Irish Times* insisted that while Parnell committed a 'flagrant injustice' against his 'own social class', the fact that the land movement fell into 'extremes' was due 'less to the leader's incapacity than the madness of portions of those that followed him' (*Irish Times*, 8 Oct 1891).

Inevitably the government had to act; charges of seditious conspiracy were laid by the Irish attorney-general against Parnell and the Land League executive in November 1880, and the trial began in Dublin in December 1880. After a hearing of nineteen days there was a disagreement of the jury and the case was dismissed. Thus frustrated, the government brought in a coercion bill on 24 January 1881. Its provisions practically suspended the Habeas Corpus Act.

The coercion debates that followed in February 1881 were notable primarily because they had a remarkable effect in helping to transform the Irish Parliamentary Party into a specifically Parnellite party. The Irish MPs who opposed the legislation had no hope of ultimate success, but they fought their corner admirably. Not only did Parnell find himself working with more Irish representatives than ever before, but also a new level of parliamentary unity and combativity was attained. Irish orators who had been unsure of their ground on the agrarian issue found their voices wonderfully when the issue became the more general one of the constitutional liberty of Irishmen. It was a field in which these young men, many of them budding lawyers, were natural experts. It was for the new young Parnellite lieutenants an intoxicating experience in which they decisively proved themselves. As Stephen Gwynn later put it: 'What was new in Parnell's movement was the linking of fierce ebullience to a constitutional machinery' (*Freeman's Journal*, 29 Sept 1906). In the midst of all this clamour Parnell himself made major attempts to explain to British politicians the relatively conservative ethos that lay behind his apparently aggressive public pronouncements. Not surprisingly, his efforts were greeted with incomprehension.

On 7 April 1881 the Liberal government introduced a measure which gave full recognition to tenant-right throughout Ireland and established a new tribunal, a land court, to fix 'fair rents'. Parnell immediately recognized in private that Gladstone had done enough, but in public he maintained a critical stance. Before Gladstone's proposal became law in August, Parnell had relatively few problems in dealing with it. To maintain agitational feeling was the easiest way of ensuring amendments to make the legislation even more favourable to the Irish tenants. However, with the passing of the act (which Gladstone intended should undercut the Land League) the context changed. Refusal to wind down the agitation implied the note of imprisonment and the loss of 'moderate' support in Ireland. On the other hand, refusal to maintain the agitation would have alienated Irish-American feeling and the radical wing of the Land League. Parnell presided at a league convention at which it was resolved that the 'Act should be tested' by selected cases. He was present thereafter at several large Land League demonstrations in opposition to it, and on 13 October he was arrested and conveyed to Kilmainham gaol.

The 'Kilmainham treaty' On the occasion of his arrest at Morrison's Hotel in Dublin, Parnell behaved, as the authorities acknowledged, 'like a gentleman'. He was surprised but perfectly composed, and asked leave to post three letters. One, of course, was to Mrs O'Shea: 'Politically it is a fortunate thing for me that I have been arrested, as the movement is breaking fast, and all will be quiet in a few months when I shall be released' (O'Shea, 1.207).

The management of a mass agitation is no easy business. Parnell had to retain a notion both of the lines of fissure in the British cabinet and within the Irish tenantry. This he did, never allowing himself to be deluded by the rhetoric of the former or the latter. In particular, he was well aware that members of the Liberal cabinet—in particular, Joseph Chamberlain—had doubts about the new policy of mass internment of suspects. Through Captain O'Shea, Parnell kept open his lines of communication to Chamberlain. Partly in consequence he was released on parole on 10 April 1882, having been given permission to attend the funeral of his nephew Henry in Paris. On his return from the funeral he also visited Mrs O'Shea, who placed his dying child Claude Sophie (*b*. 16 February) in his arms, which can only have increased his desire to get permanently out of prison and return to Mrs O'Shea's side. This was made very much easier by the increasing isolation within the cabinet of the chief secretary for Ireland, W. E. Forster, and his policy of repression. The predicted improvement in social conditions in Ireland never seemed to materialize. Coercion was increasingly distasteful to the Liberal Party, especially now that it did not appear to be working.

Parnell informed Captain O'Shea that if the government settled the arrears question on the lines he proposed, he and his colleagues had every confidence that they would be able to exert effective influence against outrages. In a succeeding paragraph, which was not disclosed at the time, he told the cabinet that the arrangement would 'enable him to co-operate cordially for the future with the Liberal party in forwarding liberal principles' (Bew, 57). To promote the settlement of the west of Ireland, Parnell urged the release of Sheridan and Boyton, organizers of the league in the west, and their employment in the work of pacification. The offer shocked W. E. Forster, but it impressed Gladstone. Accordingly, on 2 May 1882 Gladstone informed the House of Commons of the release of Parnell but also of the resignation of Forster. Gladstone always denied that there had been a 'Kilmainham treaty', though he accepted that 'we have obtained information'.

The significance of the release was well understood by Forster, who had argued:

such a course would be a tremendous step towards home rule. It would be equivalent to admitting that these men are what they claim to be and the Government releases them in order to effect what it can not accomplish itself—the pacification of Ireland and the maintenance of law and order. (*Florence Arnold-Forster's Irish Journal*, 467)

In fact, Parnell appears to have been concerned that radical nationalists would feel that he had made a discreditable deal with the enemy. Immediately upon his release, following a chance meeting with P. J. Sheridan in Dublin, one later report records that he allowed that mild-mannered fanatic to swear him into the Irish Republican Brotherhood in the incongruous setting of the library of Trinity College, Dublin. Parnell had offered to join the brotherhood at least once before, in conversation with Patrick Egan, but this time he seems to have actually taken the oath, on condition that his doing so would be kept a secret during his lifetime. Hard on the heels of this incident, on 6 May 1882, Lord Frederick Cavendish, Forster's replacement as chief secretary, along with his permanent under-secretary, Thomas Burke, was stabbed to death in Phoenix Park by the Invincibles, a group of nationalist assassins. Of particular concern to Parnell was the fact that P. J. Sheridan was later to claim a leading role in this body. All accounts agree that Parnell was shaken to the core—and beyond—by the assassination, even to the extent of writing to Gladstone offering to resign as an MP. Instead, a different course was resolved upon: Parnell and Gladstone were to work more closely together. On 23 May 1882 Parnell opened up a correspondence with Gladstone via Mrs O'Shea which was to last for some years.

It seems likely that, added to a genuine growing moderation of political outlook, there was a real element of fear that Parnell's full connection with Sheridan would be revealed, especially after Forster's revelation of Parnell's use of Sheridan's name as part of the ploy to gain his release. Parnell was to be fortunate, however; after the Phoenix Park murders those Land Leaguers who had the most pronounced connections with extremist violence—men such as the treasurer, Patrick Egan, the secretary, Thomas Brennan, and the organizers M. M. O'Sullivan, P. J. Sheridan, and Michael Boyton—fled to the USA. In effect, this flight of the radicals broke the links which existed between Parnellism and crime. It also made it easier for Parnell to reconstruct the nationalist movement; the Land League, banned in October 1881, was replaced in October 1882 by a new highly centralized body, the Irish National League, which at Parnell's insistence laid great emphasis on its legal and constitutional character; also agrarian objectives were downplayed in favour of the pursuit of home rule. Parnell devoted more and more of his time to Westminster: indeed, he spoke only once in the west of Ireland between October 1881 and January 1885, in marked contrast to the frequent visits of 1879–81.

It became known early in 1883 that Parnell was in financial difficulties and that his co. Wicklow estates were heavily mortgaged. This was by no means simply on account of his involvement in the Irish cause: he had been in debt long before his entry into politics. However, the sentiment developed that the Irish people ought to reimburse Parnell for his troubles. By May the papal attitude of disapproval for this scheme was announced. The result was the opposite of that intended. Subscriptions soon flooded in, key leaders of the Irish church, such as Archbishop Croke, ignored the papal prohibition, and Parnell received in December a huge cheque for over £37,000 from the lord mayor of Dublin. The sum is a remarkable index of Parnell's personal popularity.

Towards home rule? By the mid-1880s British parties had adjusted to Parnellism and it to them. Nationalism had been accommodated within the Westminster framework. Also, the high level of attendance and participation of the Parnellites in the House of Commons lifted their influence. Gladstone appreciated that Irish votes ordinarily supplemented Liberal numbers in divisions. There was common ground, in particular, between Parnellism and the progressive section of the Liberal Party. Conservatives, too, discovered that on some questions (such as education, Irish land, and religion) an alliance with the Irish party yielded desirable benefits. Irish votes were valued particularly by that group of tories searching for means to rein in unbridled radicalism. In June 1885 the Irish and Conservative parties joined in toppling Gladstone's second ministry. During the summer and autumn co-operation between the two for future purposes seemed a possibility worth exploring. On land, education, and local government some important Conservatives expressed views compatible with those of nationalists.

With the consent of the new Conservative premier, Lord Salisbury, a secret meeting on 1 August 1885 was arranged between Parnell and the Irish lord lieutenant, Lord Carnarvon. Carnarvon had a certain sympathy for the concept of Irish home rule. It is much more important to note, though, that the vast majority of tories were not prepared to go as far as Carnarvon. The tory leadership as a whole seems to have been anxious to keep Parnell as sympathetic to their side for as long as possible for largely opportunist reasons. At the same time, Parnell was, through Mrs O'Shea, still in contact with Gladstone, who, through the summer of 1885, requested Parnell to state what in practical terms he meant by home rule. On 1 November 1885, Parnell sent his 'proposed constitution for Ireland' to Gladstone who, two weeks later, drafted a home rule bill.

It soon appeared as if this tactic had achieved excellent results. On the eve of the general election on 21 November 1885, having failed to draw Gladstone into the bidding for Irish support, Parnell took the step of issuing a manifesto advising the Irish voters in Britain to vote against the Liberals. It has often been argued that this was a major tactical error. His intervention, it is claimed, deprived the Liberals of just that amount of support which would have enabled them to pass a satisfactory measure of home rule. In fact such an assessment of Parnell's policy is too harsh. Parnell must have assumed that the closer the totals of the two main parties, the greater his own influence. Certainly it is simplistic to assume that a Liberal landslide in 1885 would have guaranteed home rule, and indeed a Liberal landslide in 1906 was brutally to expose this illusion. The reality at the time of the election in 1885 was that neither majority party accepted the principle of a Dublin parliament. However, even if a convincing defence of Parnell can be offered, it should not obscure the element of wishful thinking in his strategy. If anything, Parnell felt, the tories were more likely to deliver. He was certainly being encouraged by Gladstone to believe that they offered the best prospect of getting a home rule bill through both houses. He placed too much reliance on the sympathetic views of Carnarvon and, at this time, Lord Randolph Churchill. He did not adequately analyse the balance of forces within the Conservative Party as a whole. Some of his nationalist colleagues also felt that Parnell's preference for a Conservative alliance reflected his growing determination to deliver a tory version of home rule which reconciled the landlords: 'aristocratic home rule' as he put it to Andrew Kettle (Bew, 74).

Having urged the Irish voters in Britain to vote against the Liberals, Parnell then turned his energies towards the electoral campaign in Ireland itself. Here the expected nationalist electoral triumph was achieved. Parnell won every seat outside eastern Ulster and the University of Dublin. He now had eighty-six MPs at his back 'pledged' to 'sit, act and vote' with the party and to resign if a majority of the party felt that obligations had not been fulfilled. In terms of actual votes cast, for home rule and against, the result was perhaps less stunning. Nevertheless, the electoral map of Ireland now seemed to show an almost complete Parnellite dominance. For the first time the majority of the Irish electors had clearly declared for home rule. Parnell was in an exceptionally strong moral position. But what was the reaction of the leadership of the two main British parties? To put it briefly, the Conservatives turned against the Irish, while the Liberals moved towards them.

The overall result of the election could hardly have suited the Irish purpose better. Outside Ireland the Liberals won eighty-six seats more than the Conservatives, but since eighty-six was also the number of Parnellite MPs, the nationalists now held the balance of power. The consequences were soon apparent. The Conservatives realized that Parnell's delivery of the Irish vote in England—which Chamberlain estimated as giving them twenty-five seats—had not given them a majority. They were quick to end the flirtation with Parnell. Lord Salisbury's government announced to the new parliament in January 1886 that a return to coercion in Ireland was in prospect. By combining with the Liberals, Parnell immediately threw them out of office.

Meanwhile Gladstone's son Herbert had in December 1885 (after the election was over but before parliament had met) flown the famous 'Hawarden kite': a press declaration by Herbert that his father was moving towards home rule. By 28 January 1886 Lord Salisbury's government had resigned; on 1 February Gladstone saw the queen, and explained his intention of introducing a home-rule measure. On 4 February he made a public statement which was perceived to be a commitment to some form of autonomy for Ireland. A Liberal government, depending on the votes of Parnell's parliamentary party, and generally believed to be intending a measure of home rule, was now in office. The reasons for Gladstone's 'conversion' to home rule are clear. During the agrarian crisis of 1879–82 he had persistently overestimated the potential of the 'liberal centre' in Ireland. (In this respect he was more naïve than his cabinet colleagues, notably W. E. Forster.) By 1882 Gladstone had realized that his hopes were misplaced and his disappointment was consequently all the greater. Even before the nationalist landslide of 1885 he dismissed Irish Liberalism (R. B. O'Brien, *Life of Parnell*, 1898, 2.104). By implication, Parnell was clearly the man to talk to about the social and political condition of Ireland.

It was at this propitious moment for the Irish leader that a remarkable episode occurred, which threatened to impair fatally the unity of his party both in parliament and in the country. For Parnell announced his intention to support Captain O'Shea as an 'unpledged' parliamentary candidate for the vacant seat of Galway City. For the first time Parnell's liaison with Mrs O'Shea appeared to have forced its way onto the political stage. Why did Parnell act as he did? The implication must be that O'Shea was again blackmailing Parnell and that the threat of exposure was responsible for Parnell's dictatorial action.

But there was a price to be paid. In the course of riding roughshod over opposition, he publicly put down one of his lieutenants, Tim Healy, and disoriented the two most significant ones, John Dillon and William O'Brien. In short, Galway was a harbinger of the fatal crisis to come. Such a price was only justifiable on the assumption that Parnell's leadership was an absolute necessity. This indeed seems to have been accepted by Parnell and his party, with only Biggar in opposition. Just as Parnell's greatest contribution to Irish nationalism had been to bring unity to previously divided forces, so that unity, once established, became the greatest reason for keeping him in the leadership.

Having survived the Galway crisis, Parnell was able to return to London to study the unfolding of Gladstone's hand. It was a supreme test: Parnell was now unchallenged as party leader, but how would he stand up as a statesman? Gladstone's guiding concept was to link his planned Home Rule Bill with a land bill and thus to deal with the political and social questions simultaneously. The sheer magnitude and complexity of his project have rarely been grasped. There were an enormous number of considerations to be taken into account. The premier had to bear in mind the difficulties of setting up a subordinate legislature. In this area alone there was a difficult question: how to preserve the sovereignty of Westminster and yet make Irish autonomy a worthwhile proposition? (This presented particular difficulties in the fiscal sphere.) But he also had to think about the future social order and peace of Ireland. He had, in particular, to think of ways of reconciling the substantial protestant and unionist minority in Ireland to the new arrangements. This in itself divided into two parts. In the south the protestants were a privileged minority with heavy representation in the landlord class; in the north-east they were a majority and well represented in all the social classes, including the tenantry. It is probably beyond the wit of anyone to produce a legislative proposal that could embrace satisfactorily all these problem areas. It is certain that it was impossible to do so when hindered by the spirit of financial caution which was the hallmark of Gladstone's party.

But despite these disputes over financial matters, the thought of Parnell and Gladstone was converging on one fundamental matter: the future of the land question. Both wanted to find a way out for the Irish landlords. Speaking in Wicklow in October 1885, Parnell had warned that

> The new Democratic Parliament won't be at all so tender of the right of landlords as the last one was … Would it not be a very wise thing for the Irish landlords to recognize the situation in time—to see that if they don't be reasonable they will be chucked overboard altogether? (*The Nation*, 17 Oct 1885)

There is no doubt of Parnell's interest in conciliating the Irish landlords at this juncture. He ascertained their views, tried to meet them, and indeed tried to get Gladstone to meet them. In a document concerning a land-purchase proposal which Mrs O'Shea passed on to Gladstone he wrote:

> A communication, the substance of which I append, has been forwarded to me by the representatives of one of the chief landlord political associations in Ireland. It is thought that if this arrangement were carried out there would remain no large body of opinion amongst the landowning class against the concession of a large measure of autonomy for Ireland, as the Protestants, other than the owners of land, are not really opposed to such concession. (Bew, 81)

This clearly reveals that Parnell was in contact with Irish landlord leaders. It reveals also, of course, a rather foolish reduction of the problem of the protestant minority to that of the problem of the landlord minority. But the main thing to note is Parnell's determination to reach some workable compromise with the Irish landowners. He wanted to get them out of their difficulties on the best possible terms.

On 8 April 1886 Gladstone introduced his Government of Ireland Bill (Home Rule Bill). His object was to establish an Irish legislature, although large imperial issues were to be reserved to the Westminster parliament. By the end of May it was clear that the opposition of the radical and 'whig' wings of the Liberal Party was sufficiently strong to prevent the bill passing the lower house. On 28 May Gladstone announced that the bill, even if passed, would be withdrawn and introduced with important amendments. In June the Home Rule Bill was defeated by forty votes on the second reading. Despite this set-back, it was clear that Parnell's leadership had advanced dramatically a cause which had been drifting aimlessly in the mid-1870s. Home rule was now endorsed by a Liberal premier and it seemed that its eventual triumph was certain.

'Parnellism and crime' The ensuing phase of 1886–90 is perhaps the least understood of Parnell's political career. He had the task of keeping together a movement, and a country, through a period of powerlessness. He needed to keep the Gladstonian Liberals to their bargain, while mitigating as best he could Unionist opposition to home rule. That opposition was intensifying rather than diminishing. Home rule was now the polarizing issue in British politics, that which separated Gladstone's Liberals from the tories and their allies. In Ireland unionist resistance, especially in Ulster, became increasingly organized. Parnell pursued a moderate and conciliatory policy on land purchase, and still hoped, against the flowing tide towards peasant proprietorship, to retain a significant landlord presence under home rule. Parnell therefore opposed any ideas which jeopardized the home-rule movement's new-found respectability, as when William O'Brien, a political lieutenant, launched a renewed land agitation, the Plan of Campaign, designed to unsettle the policies of the tory and Unionist government which had been returned in the general election of July 1886.

In December 1886, when the Plan of Campaign was still in its infancy, Parnell summoned William O'Brien. The two men met behind Greenwich observatory, which was cloaked in thick fog. Parnell pointed out to O'Brien the risks involved in the plan and suggested that he limit it to the estates where it was already in operation. Coercion of the plan might create some bad publicity for the Conservative government, but it was far more likely that an intensive anti-rent agitation would place great strain on the Liberal–nationalist alliance. The general drift of Parnell's remarks made it clear that, as far as he was concerned, the political objective of home rule was far more important than any agrarian considerations. Incidentally, the eccentricity of this occasion was typical of Parnell in this period. The effects of ill health and the desire for secrecy—he frequently used assumed names—gave his movement and appearance a rather marked peculiarity. Sir Robert Anderson, a very senior police officer, later recorded: 'His habit of midnight prowling, his renting houses under assumed names and other like way and deeds, give rise to sinister suspicions of one kind or another'. Anderson added: 'But all suspicions were baseless. The man was eccentric' (R. Anderson, *Sidelights on the Home Rule Movement*, 1906, 146). Reviewing Anderson's book in *Truth* (18 August 1906), Parnell's friend Henry Labouchere admitted that Parnell did cut rather an odd figure as he moved around London late at night wearing a sort of Ulster coat and carrying a black bag: 'I remember one occasion explaining to him that he would do well to keep clear of the scenes of Jack the Ripper's exploits otherwise he would be arrested on suspicion'.

Parnell's moderation and relative inactivity were no protection against his enemies. They were determined to link him with the unacceptable violent face of Irish nationalism. In the spring of 1887 the attack came. On 18 April *The Times*, at the end of a series of articles on the theme of Parnell's links with crime, published a letter purporting to have been written by Parnell, seeking to excuse, under the plea of necessity, his public condemnation of the Phoenix Park murders. The amazing document, dated 15 May 1882, ran as follows:

> Dear Sir,
> I am surprised at your friend's anger but he and you should know that to denounce the murders was the only course open to us. To do that promptly was plainly our best policy.
> But you can tell him and all others concerned that though I regret the accident of Lord F. Cavendish's death I cannot refuse to admit that Burke got no more than his deserts.
> You are at liberty to show him this, and others whom you can trust also, but let not my address be known. He can write to House of Commons.
> Yours very truly,
> Chas. S. Parnell

It was a dangerous crisis in his career, yet Parnell's response was amazingly relaxed. In the early days, when the chance of being able to expose the forgeries seemed faint indeed, he never lost hope and maintained a serene and imperturbable calm of mind that made his friends marvel. He discussed the conspiracy with detachment, as if it concerned some third party and as though he took only an academic interest in it. The Irish leader took up detective fiction with enthusiasm. Parnell was even spotted at the Lyceum Theatre watching a melodramatic crime play. It was reported that he hugely enjoyed the unmasking of the unfortunate fictional forger! It is almost as though, having lived in fear of an attack, Parnell was relieved when it actually came. He was put out of his suspense at least temporarily. On 9 July 1888 Parnell asked the government for a special committee of the house to inquire into the matter. In response the government set up a special commission of three judges to inquire into all the allegations made in *The Times*. On 25 February 1889 Richard *Pigott (1828–1889), who had forged and then sold the incriminating letters to *The Times*, broke down under cross-examination and then fled to Madrid, where he committed suicide. This tragic event decided the issue in Parnell's favour; he must, nevertheless, have been privately grateful that all the efforts made to get P. J. Sheridan to testify before the special commission met with failure. The Liberals were delighted by the turn of events. On 8 March 1889 Parnell attended the Eighty Club to receive the homage of a vastly relieved Liberal alliance. He symbolized the Parnell–Liberal alliance publicly by shaking hands with Lord Spencer, the lord lieutenant of Ireland at the time of the Phoenix Park murders.

All that remained, it seemed, was for Parnell and Gladstone to work out the details of a new home rule bill to set against the day when the tories inevitably fell from office. Gladstone discussed these matters at two meetings with Parnell, in London on 8 March 1888 and at Hawarden on 18–19 December 1889. On each occasion Parnell's demands were entirely within the accepted parameters of Liberal thinking. After the first conversation, Gladstone noted: 'Undoubtedly his tone was very conservative', and after the second, 'He is certainly one of the best people to deal with that I have ever known' (Matthew, 311). Parnell discussed the meeting the next day with a friend, Edward Byrne of the *Freeman's Journal*, and gave no hint of any unease. But such confident pre-eminence was not destined to last. Four days later Captain O'Shea petitioned for divorce. Parnell won time for himself by assuring his colleagues that he would not be damaged anyway.

The divorce crisis In the early months of 1890 Parnell still had the confidence to advance a position on the land question; it offended substantial sections of his own party, because he now appeared to be concerned to defend the interests of the middling gentry and, as far as the tenantry were concerned, to be in favour of discriminating in favour of the smaller tenants. But soon his capacity to direct the nationalist movement along these lines was to be fatally undermined.

The divorce case began on 15 November 1890. No defence was entered, and the trial lasted a mere two days. The evidence presented the two lovers in the most squalid light: most ludicrous of all, it was alleged that Parnell had on occasions evaded the captain by departing rapidly down a fire escape. A decree *nisi* was granted on 17 November. On the following day the Dublin branch of the National League passed a resolution upholding Parnell's leadership. The meeting of the party to elect their sessional leader, the technical title of the Irish leader, was fixed for Tuesday 25 November. Meanwhile everyone held their breath. Then events took a sudden twist.

Parnell was at the height of his power, and it was difficult for any Irish force to move against him. The bishops were silent, some of them explicitly declaring the issue to be purely political, a fact Parnell was to exploit in 1891, when the bishops rediscovered their capacity for moral leadership. It was rather the 'nonconformist conscience' in England which first openly rebelled against Parnell. The Liberal leader, Gladstone, found that a large proportion of his own supporters would no longer support an alliance with the Irish if the Irish were led by Parnell. Gladstone then sent for Justin McCarthy, generally regarded as Parnell's second in command, and, while paying tribute to Parnell's work, told him that Parnell's retention of the leadership would mean the loss of the next election and would mean also the putting off of home rule until a time when he (Gladstone) would no longer be able to lend a hand in the struggle. In order to avoid the charge of 'dictation', Gladstone had resolved not to convey this directly to Parnell himself, but he authorized McCarthy to pass on these opinions to Parnell when he next saw him. McCarthy attempted to contact Parnell, but without success or, at any rate, impact.

On 25 November Parnell managed temporarily to control his party. It re-elected him to the chair but at this stage the members did not know of Gladstone's assessment of the situation. When this became clear, angry party members pressed for a new meeting. In retaliation, on 29 November Parnell issued a manifesto *To the People of Ireland*. Its theme was a simple one: a section of the Irish party had lost its independence. The Liberal alliance, Parnell said, had been desirable but this had evolved into a fusion. He then rather unprofessionally attempted to make damaging revelations about his visit to Gladstone at

Hawarden in December 1889, when, he said, Gladstone had confided to him the details of the home-rule proposals which the next Liberal administration would introduce.

These included, according to Parnell in a rather different version from Gladstone's carefully documented record, the reduction of the Irish representation in the imperial parliament from 103 to 32; the reservation to the imperial parliament of power to deal with the land question; and the maintenance under imperial control of the constabulary for an indefinite period, and of judges for ten to twelve years. With so much reserved to the imperial parliament, Parnell was unwilling to consent to a reduction of the Irish representation at Westminster. Parnell had told Gladstone that he would try to 'reconcile Irish opinion' on the constabulary and judges, but he dissented from the reduction of the representation and from the absence of a land settlement. The feeble nature of the Liberal proposals had a definite implication. The Irish party must retain its independence at all costs. Even if an 'independent' policy led to the defeat of the Liberals at the next general election, 'a postponement would be preferable to a compromise of our national rights by the acceptance of a measure which would not realise the aspirations of our race' (Bew, 116).

On 1 December the 'requisitioned' meeting of the party opened a new debate on the leadership in committee room 15 at Westminster. An early indication in the balance of forces was given when Colonel Nolan's motion to postpone the issue was defeated by forty-four votes to twenty-nine. During the first two days of the lengthy debate the standard of discussion was surprisingly high. There was, however, one symptomatic moment of bitter personal conflict when Tim Healy accused Parnell of misrepresenting the interview with Gladstone at Hawarden. 'I will not stand an accusation of falsehood from Timothy Healy', Parnell exclaimed angrily, and Healy was prevailed upon to withdraw. Desperately the party tried to achieve a compromise. It sought guarantees from Gladstone of a satisfactory home-rule measure if Parnell was to retire. But Gladstone refused to be pressurized in this way, and the party was thrown back on its own resources. These resources—of tolerance and goodwill, at least—were wasting away in the course of the long debate. Finally, when one of Parnell's supporters, John Redmond, referred to 'the master of the party', Tim Healy could not resist the malevolent quip: 'Who is to be the mistress of the party?' Parnell bitterly retorted by describing Healy as that 'cowardly little scoundrel … who dares in an assembly of Irishmen to insult a woman'. 'I made no reply', Healy said later, 'being contented with the thrust that will stick as long as his cry about Gladstone's "dictation" continues' (Bew, 118). The split tore the country apart. Parnell vehemently insisted that the independence of the Irish party could not be compromised either by Gladstone or by the Catholic church. Healy counter-attacked with a devastating series of polemics in which he attacked Parnell ('Mr Landlord Parnell') and Katharine O'Shea with a chauvinistic, moralizing virulence. In articulating an aggressively Catholic nationalism, he defined one of the dominant idioms of modern Irish politics. Parnell, on the other hand, insisted in a major speech in Belfast: 'It is undoubtedly true that until the prejudices of the [protestant and unionist] minority are conciliated … Ireland can never enjoy perfect freedom, Ireland can never be united' (*Northern Whig*, 23 May 1891). The bitterness of the split did not abate with the death of Parnell. His supporters were inconsolable: the writings of W. B. Yeats and James Joyce bear witness to the intensity of their allegiance in the split.

On 10 December Parnell arrived in Dublin to a hero's welcome. He was to retain the capital's loyalty to the end, but most rural nationalists turned against him. Parnell lost bitterly in contested by-elections in North Kilkenny on 22 December 1890, in North Sligo on 3 April 1891, and in Carlow on 9 May 1891. An Orange tory, Lord George Hamilton, could only express admiration for his loyalty to Mrs O'Shea, which showed that there was an 'element of great tenderness in his character' (*Parliamentary Reminiscences and Reflections, 1868–85*, 1916, 222). But most nationalists did not see things in this way. Michael Davitt condemned Parnell's 'sensuous' nature to Arthur Lynch; above all, mainstream Catholic Ireland felt only a profound sense of shock when Mrs O'Shea broke the vows of her previous Catholic marriage by marrying Parnell on 25 June 1891 in Steyning register office, after Parnell had unsuccessfully sought permission for a church wedding. In this last year Parnell's health faded visibly. He returned to the exhausting life of an Irish public agitator, a life he had effectively abandoned in 1881, and at his last public meeting subjected himself to a severe soaking in Creggs, co. Roscommon, rather than disappoint his supporters in the west. His last speech stressed the futility of political violence: 'I have never pledged myself to adopt extreme courses and the man who pledges himself to adopt extreme courses without powder and shot attempts to delude the Irish people' (*Roscommon Messenger*, 3 Oct 1891). This was to take great risks with his health, for Parnell was suffering from a serious kidney disease. On 6 October 1891, on his return, he died, of heart failure and in the arms of his wife, Katharine, at 10 Walsingham Terrace, Brighton. On 11 October he was buried at Glasnevin cemetery, Dublin.

Assessment Was Parnell at heart an Irish rebel? He certainly walked on 'the verge of treason/felony' in the years from 1876 to 1882; he gave good reasons for the fears of moderate home-rulers, let alone unionists. But even in these years of political enthusiasm Parnell's differences with the revolutionary agenda were clear enough. As the extremist Transatlantic of the *Irish World* (1 June 1881) commented on Parnell's view that the younger landlords would throw their lot in with the home-rule cause if the land question was settled by purchase: 'Individual landlords are well fitted to take their place as leaders of the Irish nation. Who are these landlords, Mr Parnell? Except yourself, I see not one in the crowd'. In later years the double effect of the Phoenix Park trauma and the O'Shea affair undoubtedly reinforced the conservative side of his nature.

Unionists complained about Parnell's betrayal of his own class. 'Mr Parnell', wrote W. Hart Westcombe in 1886 in his *The Irish Question: a Monograph in the Form of a Letter to the Prime Minister*, 'was compelled to join the crusade against the class to which he himself belonged. I don't know and I don't care whether Mr Parnell was sincere in his landlord *hetze*'. W. O'Connor Morris discussed Parnell's conciliatory course in the later 1880s towards Irish unionist opinion as merely a trick to lure Gladstone deeper into the home-rule trap: 'His success in Ireland with the classes he sought to conciliate was hopeless, because they knew him well; but Mr Gladstone and those who acted with him were deceived' (Callanan, 303). Three years later he softened the judgement, acknowledging that he never knew Parnell and may have done 'less justice' to his 'motives' than he deserved (W. O'Connor Morris, *Ireland from 1798–1898*, 1898, vii).

But nationalist opinion increasingly portrayed Parnell as a patriot but also a tory and a landlord. With even greater insight, Francis Hackett wrote that Parnell was 'amenable to liberal considerations but utterly immune from liberal sympathies' (F. Hackett, *Ireland: Study in Nationalism*, 1918, 330). This catches the political temper of 'the Chief' exactly: the Irish *ancien régime*, he felt, could not survive the combination of the economic crisis of the late 1870s and the democratization of the mid-1880s without drastic change. He saw it as his role to bring about that change on the most conservative basis available. As his radical friend Henry Labouchere put it, 'Home Rule apart, he was himself a Tory'. Augustus Moore agreed: 'My father, [George Henry Moore] always was a strong supporter of Mr Disraeli on all except Irish politics. Parnell's policy was my father's policy' (A. Moore, 'Parnell and George Henry Moore', *Tuam Herald*, 17 Oct 1891). His brother Maurice George Moore made the same point but more darkly: 'Parnell appreciated the situation … correctly … but he was hampered by the crimes that clung around the Land League, and by the opposition of the landlords, naturally exasperated by attacks on their property' (M. G. Moore, *An Irish Gentleman: George Henry Moore*, 1900, 884).

It is worth noting that the *Irish Times* went against its tory unionist grain, and gave Parnell a most generous obituary:

> It was somewhat of a phenomenon—this man stepping from the ranks of his class to champion the cause of those whom, justly or not, he considered to be the victims of the mistaken system of government and so it was that his personality became invested with a certain romance, which even the sordid and shameful incidents of later times have not wholly divested it of. (*Irish Times*, 8 Oct 1891)

PAUL BEW

Sources F. S. L. Lyons, *Charles Stewart Parnell* (1977) • R. F. Foster, *Paddy and Mr Punch: connections in Irish and English history* (1995) • R. F. Foster, *Charles Stewart Parnell: the man and his family* (1976) • P. Bew, *C. S. Parnell* (Dublin, 1981) • Gladstone, *Diaries* • E. Byrne, *Parnell: a memoir*, ed. F. Callanan (Dublin, 1991) • F. Callanan, *The Parnell split* (1992) • *Florence Arnold-Forster's Irish journal*, ed. T. W. Moody and others (1988) • J. Mullin, *The story of a toiler's life* (Dublin, 1921) • R. Kee, *The laurel and the ivy: the story of Charles Stewart Parnell and Irish nationalism* (1993) • D. G. Boyce and A. O'Day, eds., *Parnell in perspective* (1991) • K. O'Shea, *Charles Stewart Parnell*, 2 vols. (1914) • H. C. G. Matthew, *Gladstone, 1875–1898* (1995)

Archives BL, Gladstone MSS, Add. MSS 44269, 44315–44316 • Boston College, Massachusetts, British Land League MSS • NL Ire., letters to agent in Ireland • NL Ire., corresp. with T. C. Harrington • TCD, corresp. with J. Dillon

Likenesses W. Lawrence, carte-de-visite, 1881, NPG • S. P. Hall, drawings, 1888–9, NPG [*see illus.*] • engraving, pubd 1889, NPG • J. D. Reigh, pencil drawing, 1891, NG Ire. • H. C., oils?, 1892, Magd. Cam. • S. P. Hall, oils, 1892, NG Ire. • R. Barter, bronze sculpture, 1893, NG Ire. • F. C. Gould, caricature, ink sketch, NPG • M. Grant, bronze bust (posthumous), NPG • M. Grant, bronze bust, High Lane Municipal Gallery of Modern Art, Dublin • S. P. Hall, drawings, NG Ire. • C. Laurie, etching, NPG • F. Pegram, pencil sketches, V&A • L. Prosperi, group portrait, oils (*The lobby of the House of Commons, 1886*), NPG • T [T. Chartran], chromolithograph caricature, NPG; repro. in *VF* (11 Sept 1880) • R. Taylor, wood-engraving (after W. Wilson), BM; repro. in *ILN* (4 May 1889)

Wealth at death £11,774 7*s*. 3*d*.: administration, 7 Dec 1891, *CGPLA Eng. & Wales* • £6074 14*s*. 10*d*.: administration, 12 March 1892, *CGPLA Ire.*

Parnell, Fanny Isabel (1848–1882), Irish nationalist and poet, was born on 4 September 1848 at Avondale, co. Wicklow, the eighth child and fourth daughter of John Henry Parnell (1811–1859) and his wife, Delia Tudor Stewart (1816–1896), daughter of Commodore Charles Stewart of the US Navy. Educated by a succession of governesses and tutors, she spent her youth at Avondale until her father's death in 1859, after which the estate was let to tenants and the family moved to Dalkey and then in 1860 to Dublin. In 1865 Fanny accompanied her mother to Paris, where they resided, except for brief visits to Ireland, with her uncle Charles Tudor Stewart until his death in 1874. Fanny, her mother, and sister Anna then moved to Ironsides, the Stewart family estate in Bordentown, New Jersey, where she lived—except for travels in America on behalf of the Ladies' Land League, which she founded in 1880—until her death.

Fanny Parnell's intellect and the range and impact of her activities belie her reputation as a 'romantic poetess'. Like her brother Charles Stewart *Parnell and sister (Catherine Maria) Anna Mercer *Parnell, she became an ardent Irish nationalist. Their nationalist views, once attributed to the influence of their American mother, actually originated in their own reading and experiences. The trend of Fanny Parnell's social thought was more radical than her brother's and, unlike him, she ardently espoused the Fenian cause and attended the celebrated trial of O'Donovan Rossa in 1865. Her passionate nationalist verses began appearing in the Fenian newspaper *Irish People* in May 1864 under the pen-name Aleria. In Paris, where her anti-British views put her at odds with anglophile expatriates in the élite social circles in which she moved, she was known for her beauty and wit. Fanny Parnell's iconoclastic critical intelligence was apparent in the sardonic portraits of Paris snobbery, gossip, and fortune- and title-hunting that she published in the *American Register* in 1874.

After her experience in Paris working with the American Ambulance, the temporary hospital installation in which ladies of high social position served as

Fanny Isabel Parnell (1848–1882), by unknown photographer, *c.*1878

nurses, and in New York volunteering for the Irish Famine Relief Fund, in 1880 Fanny Parnell founded the Ladies' Land League to collect funds in the USA for the Land League in Ireland, which had been founded the previous year by Michael Davitt to reform the land system. Her writings expressed her commitment to social justice and the Land League. Her pamphlet *The Hovels of Ireland*, which went through several editions in a few months in 1880, demonstrated her wide reading in history, economics, politics, and philosophy, and in French, English, and American literature. Her Land League poems, published in the *Boston Pilot* and *The Nation*, were reprinted widely in Ireland, England, and America, and were collected in 1882 under the title *Land League Songs*, with proceeds going to the Land League.

Fanny Parnell's poetry heroicized the land agitation and its leaders in emotional, often violent, language that created powerful and popular propaganda but mediocre and conventional poetry. Her most well-known poem, and one of her best, was 'Hold the harvest', which Davitt called the 'Marseillaise of the Irish peasant'. Like her political activism, her poetry was criticized by some as vulgar and unfeminine. Nevertheless, her Ladies' Land League activities and her 'varses', as she called them, made her a celebrity with stature almost equal to her famous brother's before her sudden death in Bordentown from heart failure on 20 July 1882. Thousands witnessed her elaborate funeral procession from Bordentown to Boston via Philadelphia. She was buried in the Tudor family vault in Mount Auburn cemetery in Cambridge, Massachusetts, where her grave was the site of an annual pilgrimage for many years. MARY HELEN THUENTE

Sources J. M. Côté, *Fanny and Anna Parnell: Ireland's patriot sisters* (1991) · R. F. Foster, *Charles Stewart Parnell: the man and his family* (1976) · M. Hughes, 'The Parnell sisters', *Dublin Historical Record*, 21/1 (1966–7), 14–27 · M. O'Neill, 'The Ladies Land League', *Dublin Historical Record*, 35/4 (1981–2), 122–33 · M. Ward, *Unmanageable revolutionaries: women and Irish nationalism*, pbk edn (1983) · *Celtic Magazine*, 1 (1882), 280–92 · M. Leahy, 'Fanny Parnell, poet and patriot', *Ireland-American Review*, 1 (1939), 248–52 · M. Davitt, *The fall of feudalism in Ireland, or, The story of the Land League in Ireland* (1904)

Likenesses photograph, *c.*1878, NL Ire. [*see illus.*]

Parnell, Henry Brooke, first Baron Congleton (1776–1842), politician, born on 3 July 1776, was the second son of Sir John *Parnell, second baronet (1745–1801), and his wife, Letitia Charlotte (*d.* 1783), second daughter and coheir of Sir Arthur Brooke, bt, of Colebrooke, co. Fermanagh. He was educated at Eton College (1791–3) and Trinity College, Cambridge (1794), but did not take any degree. In 1797 he entered Lincoln's Inn. At the general election in the summer of 1797 he was returned to the Irish House of Commons for Maryborough. He spoke in support of the Regency Bill on 11 April 1799, and followed his father, the former chancellor of the Irish exchequer, in voting against the union.

On the death of his father in December 1801 Parnell succeeded to the family estates in Queen's county, which had been settled upon him in consequence of his brother's disabilities by an act of the Irish parliament passed in May 1789. He succeeded to the baronetcy on his brother's death in July 1812. He married, on 17 February 1801, Lady Caroline Elizabeth Dawson, eldest daughter of John, first earl of Portarlington. They had three sons and three daughters: John Vesey, second Baron Congleton [*see below*]; Henry William, third Baron Congleton; George Damer (*d.* 1882), vicar of Long Cross, Chertsey; Caroline Sophia (*d.* 1858), who became the wife of Charles Thomas Longley, archbishop of Canterbury; Mary Letitia (*d.* 1881), who was married, first, to Lord Henry Seymour Moore (*d.* 1825) and, secondly, to Edward Henry Cole of Stoke Lyne, Oxfordshire; and Emma Jane (*d.* 1884), who married Edward, fifth earl of Darnley (*d.* 1835). He was the grand-uncle of Charles Stewart Parnell. Lady Congleton survived her husband many years, and died at Paris on 16 February 1861, aged seventy-eight.

In April 1802 Parnell was elected to the parliament of the United Kingdom for Queen's county, which he represented until the dissolution in June of that year. He was returned for his brother-in-law's borough of Portarlington at the general election in July 1802, but retired from parliament in November, when the seat was sold to a friend of the prince of Wales. Out of parliament he devoted himself to the study of political economy. At a by-election in February 1806 he was again returned for Queen's county, which he then continued to represent until December 1832.

Irritated by what he saw as Pitt's failure to recompense him for his father's past services and for his own talents, Parnell veered towards opposition. He was appointed a commissioner of the Treasury for Ireland in the 'ministry of all the talents' in April 1806, and made his first Commons speech in the debate on the Irish budget on 7 May. He retired from office on Lord Grenville's downfall in March 1807, and while in opposition spoke frequently on Irish and financial matters. On 18 April 1809 he brought forward a resolution for assimilating the currency of Ireland with that of Great Britain, which was, however, negatived without a division. He argued subsequently that the amalgamation of the two treasuries would promote Irish development and check executive abuses.

Parnell took a particular interest in the subject of Catholic relief and Irish tithe reform. His annual motions for inquiries into the tithe system in the years 1809–12 were opposed by the government and defeated. He supported Grattan's motion respecting the Roman Catholic petitions on 1 June 1810, and in 1811 defended the legality of the Catholic convention. He had better relations with Daniel O'Connell and the Catholic board than had Henry Grattan, and in 1815 he temporarily assumed the lead in introducing the relief motion of that year. This was defeated by a majority of eighty-one on 30 May. He subsequently continued to support the relief motions introduced by Grattan and Plunket, and was an advocate of the 'security' of a state veto over Catholic episcopal appointments.

In February 1810 Parnell was appointed a member of the bullion committee chaired by Francis Horner, and on 8 May 1811 he made an elaborate speech in defence of its report. As chairman of the select committee on the corn trade of the United Kingdom, he drew the attention of the house to their report on 15 June 1813. Unlike other Irish landowners, Parnell favoured agricultural protection at this time on primarily theoretical grounds. Like William Huskisson, he argued from bullionist premises for a protectionism that was transitional, deflationary, and tending to increase production. He hoped that Ireland would be transformed by such means into a granary for Great Britain. While he was disappointed at the unco-operative attitudes of some ministers towards his specific proposals, Parnell's report formed the basis of the 1815 corn law.

On 25 May 1819 Parnell supported Peel's resolutions with respect to the resumption of cash payments, and in July following he brought forward a series of forty-seven resolutions concerning the retrenchment of the public expenditure. Parnell remained critical of the weight of Irish taxation and the manner in which the country was governed. In December 1819 he called for the abolition of the lord lieutenancy as 'a useless piece of pageantry'. In 1820 he introduced a successful bill making it easier for Irish freeholders to qualify for the vote. Ever a critic of coercive measures, on 24 June 1823 Parnell asked for the appointment of a committee to inquire 'into the extent and object of the disturbances existing in Ireland', but was only supported by thirty-nine votes. On 10 February 1825 he opposed the introduction of the Irish Unlawful Societies Bill, and asserted that there could be 'no other termination to its destructive operation but insurrection and rebellion'. In the same month he introduced a bill 'to amend the law in Ireland respecting the subletting of tenements' and a bill 'to regulate the office of justice of the peace in Ireland'.

On 15 February 1828 Parnell was appointed a member of the select committee on the state of the public income and expenditure of the United Kingdom, of which he was subsequently nominated chairman. Parnell used this position to advance his view that the repeal or reduction of taxes on industry, of excise duties and of tariffs on raw materials was a higher priority than the reduction of the national debt.

On 15 November 1830 Parnell's motion for referring the civil list to a select committee was carried against the government by 233 votes to 204, and on the following day the duke of Wellington resigned. Parnell succeeded Charles Watkin Williams-Wynn as secretary for war in Lord Grey's administration on 4 April 1831, and was sworn of the privy council on the 27th of the same month. By entering into an unauthorized negotiation with the French post office, and by encouraging Joseph Hume to bring a motion against the British Post Office, he exasperated the postmaster-general (the duke of Richmond), and narrowly escaped dismissal. The ministry declined to concur in his proposed reduction of the army estimates, which he calculated would save the nation £600,000 a year, and he was shortly afterwards dismissed from office for his refusal to support the ministry in the division on the Russian-Dutch loan on 26 January 1832.

Parnell in 1831 pressed upon Melbourne the necessity of gratifying O'Connell, and at the same time engaged Bishop Doyle to sound out the 'Liberator'. Despite vague assurances from Lord Grey, there was little enthusiasm for such an alliance, and in December O'Connell firmly rejected the idea of taking office. On 23 May 1832 Parnell called the attention of the house to the state of Queen's county, and moved for a select committee to inquire into the general efficiency of the law in Ireland for repressing outrages and disturbances. He was now attacked in the nationalist press as a 'whig Judas', mainly for his part in drafting the highly limited Irish Reform Bill in 1832. After refusing to take the repeal pledge he was defeated in Queen's county at the general election in December 1832. However, on 27 March 1833 he was appointed a member of the excise commission of inquiry, and at a by-election in April 1833 he was returned for Dundee, which he continued to represent until his elevation to the House of Lords.

On the formation of Lord Melbourne's administration Parnell was appointed treasurer of the navy (22 April 1835) and paymaster-general of the forces (14 May 1835). In 1836 these offices were consolidated with those of the paymaster and treasurer of Chelsea Hospital and treasurer of the ordnance, and the duties transferred to a new official styled the paymaster-general, a position that Parnell filled until 1841. By the mid 1830s he had become convinced that protection was no longer desirable. In 1835 he defined his political objects as:

> perfect freedom of labour and capital; the speedy abolition of the corn laws, and in the meantime a fixed duty; the abolition of all unequal taxes, and the substitution of a property tax … the repeal of the septennial act, the ballot, an extension of the franchise, if found necessary; abolition of flogging and of impressment. (*GM*, 2nd ser., 17, 1842, 202)

On 15 March 1838 he spoke in favour of the abolition of the corn laws, and declared that 'there was no one interest in the country which derived any advantage from the corn laws but the landowners'. In March 1839 and in May 1840 he again supported Villiers's motion. He spoke for the last time in the House of Commons during the debate on the sugar duties on 14 May 1841. He was created Baron Congleton of Congleton on 20 August 1841, and took his seat in the House of Lords on 23 August, but never took any part in the debates. After suffering for some time from ill health, he committed suicide by hanging himself in his dressing-room in Cadogan Place, Chelsea, on 8 June 1842, and was buried on the 14th of the same month in the burial-ground of St George's, Hanover Square, where in 1842 a tablet was erected in the chapel to his memory.

Congleton was an active member of the most liberal section of the whig party. He was a fluent but monotonous speaker. While judged a poor administrator by contemporary observers, he achieved a high reputation as a political economist and as a writer on finance. In the art of giving a plain, lucid statement of complex financial matters he had few superiors. In his treatise *On Financial Reform* (1830), which had a considerable influence on public opinion, he laid before the country the financial and fiscal policy that Sir Robert Peel and W. E. Gladstone afterwards carried out. He published a number of other works on currency and banking, on the corn laws, and a *History of the Penal Laws Against the Irish Catholics* (1808).

John Vesey Parnell, second Baron Congleton (1805–1883), evangelist, born in Baker Street, Marylebone, Middlesex, on 16 June 1805, was educated first in France, and afterwards at Edinburgh University, where he took a prize for mathematics. Though intended by his father for the army, he joined the Plymouth Brethren and in May 1830 he established their first Irish meeting-room in Aungier Street, Dublin, which he is said to have built with his own hands. In September 1830 he set out as a missionary to Baghdad, in company with Professor F. W. Newman and Dr Edward Cronin. The mission proved a failure, and Parnell, after two years' residence at Baghdad, went on to India, where he was equally unsuccessful. He returned to Britain in 1837, and spent the remainder of his life in travelling over the country on preaching tours, and in endeavouring to spread the doctrines of the Brethren. He was minister of Orchard Street Chapel, London (1849–60), and of Welbeck Street Chapel (1860–83).

John Vesey Parnell succeeded his father as second Baron Congleton in June 1842, but did not take his seat in the House of Lords until 4 November 1852, as he felt himself unable to take the necessary oaths. He sat on the cross-benches, and spoke only three times in the house. He married, first, in 1831, at Aleppo, Nancy, the sister of his colleague, Edward Cronin. She died at Latakia the following year, from the hardships to which she had been exposed while travelling. He married, secondly, at Baghdad, on 21 May 1833, Khatun, younger daughter of Ovanness Moscow of Shiraz and widow of Yusuf Constantine of Bushehr. She died on 30 May 1865, aged fifty-seven. He married, thirdly, on 21 February 1867, Margaret Catherine, only daughter of Charles Ormerod of the India board, who died in 1910, and with whom he had an only daughter, Sarah Cecilia, born on 5 August 1868. He died at 53 Great Cumberland Place, Hyde Park, on 23 October 1883, aged seventy-eight, and was buried in Kensal Green cemetery on 29 October, when numbers of the Brethren from all parts of the country attended the funeral. He was succeeded in the title by his brother Henry William, third Baron Congleton (1809–1896). Besides several tracts on various religious subjects, he published *The Psalms: a New Version* (1860). G. F. R. BARKER, *rev.* PETER GRAY

Sources HoP, *Commons* • *WWBMP*, vol. 1 • A. P. W. Malcomson, *John Foster: the politics of the Anglo-Irish ascendancy* (1978) • B. Hilton, *Corn, cash, commerce: the economic policies of the tory governments, 1815–1830* (1977) • A. D. Macintyre, *The Liberator: Daniel O'Connell and the Irish party, 1830–1847* (1965) • *Annual Register* (1842) • *GM*, 2nd ser., 17 (1842) • GEC, *Peerage*

Archives Glos. RO, bills, inventories, and receipts • U. Southampton L., corresp. and papers | BL, letters to Macvey Napier, Add. MSS 34621–34622 • BL, letters to Sir Robert Peel, Add. MSS 40226–40399 • Inst. CE, letters to Thomas Telford • NL Ire., letters to Denis Scully • UCL, letters to Lord Brougham • UCL, letters to Society for the Diffusion of Useful Knowledge • W. Sussex RO, letters to duke of Richmond

Wealth at death £7014 17*s.* 10*d.*—John Vesey Parnell: probate, 1884

Parnell, James. *See* Parnel, James (*bap.* 1636, *d.* 1656).

Parnell, Sir John, second baronet (1745–1801), politician, the only surviving son of Sir John Parnell, first baronet (1717–1782), MP, and Anne Ward (*d.* 1795), daughter of Michael *Ward, was born on 25 December 1745. He was educated successively at Harrow School (1758) and Eton College (1759–60) and he entered Trinity College, Dublin, on 20 September 1762 (BA 1766). He continued his education at Lincoln's Inn, entering on 7 January 1766, and he obtained the degree of LLB in 1770. He was called to the Irish bar in 1774 and became a bencher of the King's Inns in 1786. He married on 19 July 1774 Letitia Charlotte Brooke (*d.* 1783), second daughter and coheir of Sir Arthur Brooke MP of Brookeborough, co. Fermanagh. They had five sons, including William *Parnell, and one daughter. The eldest son was mentally and physically handicapped from birth and two private members' bills were passed to provide guardianship and an income of £200 p.a. for his maintenance, as well as to entail the estate on his other brothers and their heirs successively.

Parnell came into the Irish parliament in 1767 for Bangor, where his mother's family, the Wards of Castle Ward, controlled one seat in the borough, but when parliament was dissolved in the following year he did not seek re-election. After the next general election in 1776 he was returned by purchase for Innistiogue, co. Kilkenny. He succeeded his father as second baronet in 1782 and from 1783 until his death in 1801 he sat for Queen's county. In 1785 he succeeded John Foster, when Foster was elected speaker, as Irish chancellor of the exchequer. The following January he was sworn of the Irish privy council and in October he was also sworn a British privy counsellor.

Parnell had spent some time on the continent, with the object of preparing for the diplomatic service, but did not follow this career. In general his political position was

Sir John Parnell, second baronet (1745–1801), by Pompeo Batoni, *c.*1767–8

that of a conservative independent and from his abilities and his background he was a natural recruit to the 'men of affairs' whose support was essential for the day-to-day operation of government. Furthermore he had the additional and very important virtue of being a good parliamentary speaker. Parnell gave government consistent support, but he opposed Catholic relief both in the late 1770s and in the 1790s; although he fell into line with the 1792 and 1793 relief bills, even then he managed to convey his disapprobation of them and voted against emancipation in 1795.

As chancellor of the exchequer Parnell struggled with trying to control the increasing chaos of Ireland's finances. In February 1788 he introduced a bill for reducing the interest on the national debt from 6 per cent to 5 per cent. On one occasion the lord chancellor, Camden, wrote to Pitt asking for £30,000 in cash and insisted that Pitt help Parnell borrow 'at least a million in addition to the £30,000 which has been borrowed'. He also showed a keen and consistent interest in encouraging the development of the economy. He was anxious to improve the port of Dublin and like so many of his contemporaries he was anxious to develop the amenities of the capital; to this end he served on commissions for paving and lighting the streets of Dublin. For many years he was a leading government spokesman on economic affairs. For example, he wrote to Chief Secretary Pelham on 31 December 1783 that:

> the imposition of duties on English goods is very popular as it is seen as a remedy for every distress; and Ireland with constitutional independence, is jealous of duties which derogate it from equality of commerce and consider it nefarious that no advantage in commerce has arisen from independence. (Kelly, 79)

Parnell was above all an Irish nationalist in the Anglo-Irish sense of that word, and as such he was a strong supporter of the protestant interest: in 1792 he said in the House of Commons that 'I rise to rescue the Protestants of Ireland from the calumnies which have been thrown upon them. I rise to rescue the memory of our forefathers from the unjust and unfounded aspirations that have been cast upon them' (Foster, 5). In 1793 he expressed his doubts about a legislative union and concluded that 'England thinks that the connection can be better preserved by a change of system' (McDowell, 416). Lord Cornwallis advised the duke of Portland at the time of the union that:

> on my finding from a conversation which I had with Sir John Parnell soon after he landed, that he was determined not to support the Union, I have notified to him his dismission from the Office of Chancellor of the Exchequer, and I shall pursue the same line of conduct without favour or partiality, whenever I may think that it will lead to promote the success of the measure. (*Correspondence of … Cornwallis*, 3.38)

There is some evidence that Parnell may have misunderstood the determination of the government over the union. His advance in power and influence had hitherto been steady and there is evidence that his dismissal came to him as a shock, although it made him a hero with the opposition and their popular supporters. Parnell supported Sir Lawrence Parson's amendment to the address on 15 January 1800 expressing satisfaction with the constitution of 1782 and its finality. On the decisive debate of 5 February he declared that 'the great majority of the people of Ireland were decidedly adverse to a Union', and he fought a rearguard action against it; on 15 March he moved that the king should be addressed to dissolve parliament and hold an election on the issue but he was defeated by 150 to 104 votes (*A Report of the Debate … 22nd and 23rd Jan. 1799, on the Subject of an Union*, 1799, 169). Sir Jonah Barrington declared that:

> though many years in possession of high office and extensive patronage, he showed a disinterestedness almost unparalleled; and the name of a relative or of a dependant of his own, scarcely in a single instance, increased the place or the pension lists of Ireland … His conduct at the Union did him honour, and proved how warmly he was attached to the interests of his country, and on this account he was dismissed. (J. Barrington, *Rise and Fall of the Irish Nation*, 1833, 30)

Parnell, or his estate, received £7500 for his half of the disfranchised borough of Maryborough.

In the short period that Parnell sat in the united parliament at Westminster he took a leading part in debates on Irish financial affairs. He spoke on the Irish Martial Law Bill and in June 1801 defended the Irish distillers against their English competitors. During the October session he again spoke, mainly on matters of Irish finance and trade. He collapsed and died on 5 December 1801 in Clifford Street, London, and was buried in the burial-ground of St George's, Hanover Square. He was, by Irish standards, a wealthy man and was reputed to be 'plain, frank, cheerful and convivial', especially the latter, and a man who 'generally preferred society to trouble' (J. Barrington, *Historic Memoirs of Ireland*, 2nd edn, 1833, 1.119–20). He was the great-grandfather of Charles Stewart Parnell.

E. M. JOHNSTON-LIIK

Sources E. M. Johnston-Liik, *History of the Irish parliament, 1692–1800*, 6 vols. (2002) • R. F. Foster, *Parnell: the man and his family* (1976), 4–11 • R. B. McDowell, *Ireland in the age of imperialism and revolution, 1760–1801* (1979), 398, 403, 416 • *Correspondence of Charles, first Marquis Cornwallis*, ed. C. Ross, 2nd edn, 3 vols. (1859), vol. 3 • A. Aspinall, 'Parnell, Sir John', HoP, *Commons, 1790–1820* • Burke, *Peerage* (1900), 350 • J. L. J. Hughes, ed., *Patentee officers in Ireland, 1173–1826, including high sheriffs, 1661–1684 and 1761–1816*, IMC (1960) • *Index to privy counsellors, 1711–1910 (and partially from 1660)* [n.d.] • Burtchaell & Sadleir, *Alum. Dubl.* • *The correspondence of the Right Hon. John Beresford, illustrative of the last thirty years of the Irish parliament*, ed. W. Beresford, 2 vols. (1854), vol. 1, p.139 • J. T. Gilbert, *History of the city of Dublin*, 3 vols. (1861), vol. 3, p. 153 • R. A. Austen-Leigh, ed., *The Eton College register, 1753–1790* (1921) • W. T. J. Gun, ed., *The Harrow School register, 1571–1800* (1934) • W. P. Baildon, ed., *The records of the Honorable Society of Lincoln's Inn: admissions*, 1 (1896), 458 • J. O'Hart, *Irish pedigrees, or, The origin and stem of the Irish nation*, 5th edn, 2 (1892), 340 • B. J. Cantwell, *Memorials of the dead*, 10 (1986) • private members' bills, Dublin University Library, 186.s.39, 186.s.40 • J. Kelly, *Prelude to Union: Anglo-Irish politics in the 1780s* (1992)

Archives BLPES, account books and travel journals • LUL, account books and travel journals • PRO NIre., T3166/IC • U. Southampton L., corresp. and papers | NL Ire., Congleton MSS

Likenesses P. Batoni, oils, *c*.1767–1768, Castle Ward, co. Down [*see illus.*] • Irish school, group portrait, stipple, pubd *c*.1795 (*The Rt. Hon. Henry Grattan's answer to the Roman Catholic Address* …; after portrait by G. C. Stuart, *c*.1790), NG Ire. • Irish school, oils, NG Ire. • F. Wheatley, group portrait, oils (*The Irish House of Commons, 1780*), Lotherton Hall, West Yorkshire

Wealth at death dispersed estates: partial calculation, Foster, *Parnell*

Parnell, John Vesey, second Baron Congleton (1805–1883). *See under* Parnell, Henry Brooke, first Baron Congleton (1776–1842).

Parnell [*née* Wood; *other married name* O'Shea], **Katharine** (1845–1921), political intermediary and wife of Charles Stewart Parnell, was born on 30 January 1845 at Glazenwood, Essex. She was the thirteenth child of Sir John Page *Wood (1796–1866) [*see under* Wood, Sir Matthew], formerly chaplain and secretary to Queen Caroline, a 'thoroughgoing Whig', who was latterly vicar of Cressing in Essex and rector of St Peter's, Cornhill. Her mother was Emma Caroline, *née* Michell (1802–1879), a watercolourist, book illustrator, and romantic novelist (a pursuit which another of her daughters, Anna, came to share). Her uncle William Page *Wood (later Baron Hatherley) was lord chancellor in Gladstone's first administration and Sir Evelyn *Wood, soldier and colonial administrator, was her brother. She passed her youth at Rivenhall Place, the family home, where a cultured society, including Anthony Trollope, compensated for the lack of a formal education. At Belhus, the country seat of her brother-in-law Sir Thomas Barrett-Lennard, she met **William Henry O'Shea** (1840–1905). Then a cornet in the 18th hussars, O'Shea was the son of a Limerick-born solicitor who practised in Dublin, and a Catholic. They were married at Brighton on 23 January 1867.

Katharine Parnell [O'Shea] **(1845–1921)**, by unknown artist

The O'Sheas passed their first year of marriage in Madrid, where William had taken a partnership in his uncle's bank. He next tried his hand at breeding racehorses. Losses, combined with gambling debts, led to bankruptcy. While his affairs were subsequently settled, Katharine's prodigiously wealthy aunt Mrs Benjamin Wood ('Aunt Ben') took a house for her at Brighton, where Katharine gave birth to a son, Gerard. Residing together in Beaufort Gardens in London, the O'Sheas briefly cut a dash as a married couple. There their second child, Norah, who was to be Katharine's chief support in her declining years, was born. Katharine bore O'Shea a further daughter, Carmen.

The O'Sheas drifted steadily and respectably apart. Katharine became from the middle of the decade the companion of her aunt, whose seclusion at the Lodge, Eltham, was punctuated by the weekly visits of George Meredith, who received a stipend of £300 per annum to read to her from works other than his own, which she did not esteem. Mrs Wood purchased Wonersh Lodge, just across the park, for Katherine. William was at the time spending some eighteen months in Spain on a mining venture, of which Katharine resignedly commented 'he always drew up an excellent prospectus'.

In the wake of commercial failure, statesmanship urgently beckoned. O'Shea was returned for County Clare at the 1880 election under a home-rule flag of convenience. The exigencies of his political career resuscitated the marriage to some degree, at least in its public aspect, as he sought to further his prospects with a series of political dinners. Determined to procure the attendance of

Charles Stewart *Parnell (1846–1891), the 'uncrowned king of Ireland', Katharine drove to Westminster with her sister Anna to seek him out. Her memoirs describe the *coup de foudre* in Palace Yard:

> He looked straight at me smiling, and his curiously burning eyes looked into mine with wonderful intentness … In leaning forward in the cab to say good-bye a rose I was wearing in my bodice fell out on my skirt. He picked it up, and touching it lightly with his lips, placed it in his buttonhole. (O'Shea, 1.135–6)

Parnell was then thirty-four, she eighteen months older. By October he was writing to her as 'my own love'.

Parnell was incarcerated in Kilmainham gaol, Dublin, from 13 October 1881 to 2 May 1882. Thence he continued to correspond with Katharine, perfecting a system of interlineating letters in invisible ink. On 16 February 1882 Katharine gave birth to a daughter, the short-lived Claude Sophie. That the child was Parnell's has never seriously been disputed, although Captain O'Shea may well have believed it to be his own. Parnell, on temporary release from Kilmainham, was at Eltham when Claude Sophie died on 22 April, as was the captain. Katharine bore Parnell two more daughters in each of the ensuing years: Clare (1883–1909), who bore a haunting resemblance to him, and Katharine (1884–1947).

The extent of the deception practised upon O'Shea by his wife and Parnell has long been a vexed question. As early as 1881, O'Shea had, according to Katharine, irately dispatched Parnell's portmanteau from Eltham to Charing Cross Station, and challenged Parnell to a duel (which did not proceed). While O'Shea appears to have been given assurances as to his wife's relations with Parnell, it is difficult to resist the conclusion that their principal value to him was in permitting him to maintain a sedulously cultivated posture of wounded innocence. His character was a curious combination of vanity, calculation, and naïvety. There was also very possibly an element of willed self-deception at work. Until the end of 1886 he seems to have retained a degree of tenderness towards Katharine, reciprocated by a measure of exasperated fondness that lingers even in her memoirs. Yet the rhythm of his estrangement can be graphed against the seepage into political currency of rumours of his wife's relations with Parnell.

W. H. O'Shea was for Parnell a rapidly escalating political liability. His appetite for *haute politique* was insatiable, his aptitude negligible. In the negotiations which led to the 'Kilmainham treaty', which permitted Parnell's release, and in the aftermath of the Phoenix Park murders which swiftly followed, O'Shea disported himself with a uniquely provoking combination of arrogance and ineptitude. Parnell thereafter sought to bypass O'Shea in his dealings with Gladstone. Mrs O'Shea displaced her husband as a conduit of Parnell's thinking. Her role developed from that of a confidential amanuensis to Parnell into that of an intermediary, acting at Parnell's close direction, in correspondence and to a very limited extent in person. Gladstone found her businesslike to deal with, and her role as go-between was a convenience both to the prime minister and to the Irish leader. She was important in 1886 in extracting from Parnell and sending to Gladstone the former's 'proposed Constitution for Ireland', on receipt of which in November the latter shortly after drafted a home rule bill. In her memoirs she underscored the role she had played, for the purpose of levelling against the late Liberal leader the crude if understandable charge of hypocrisy in his repudiation of Parnell in the divorce crisis.

In a reckless but astonishingly concentrated display of authority, Parnell imposed O'Shea as the member for Galway in February 1886. The political enmity between Parnell and O'Shea became manifest on the defeat of the Home Rule Bill (on which O'Shea abstained), and the secession of Joseph Chamberlain, whom O'Shea had enlisted as a mentor, from Gladstone's Liberal Party. O'Shea testified against Parnell before the special commission set up in 1887 to inquire *inter alia* into the authenticity of the letters published by *The Times* implicating Parnell in the Phoenix Park murders. Parnell obdurately believed that O'Shea lay behind the forgeries, prompting Henry Labouchere's observation that Parnell went to his grave the only man who did not believe that Richard Pigott had forged *The Times'* letters.

The death of Mrs Benjamin Wood (who might have disinherited Mrs O'Shea, had she been touched by scandal) cleared the way for the institution by Captain O'Shea of divorce proceedings on 24 December 1889. She and Parnell pursued an uncertain course, which involved both the levelling of counter-allegations (including one of adultery with Katharine's sister Anna Steele) and the contemplated pursuit of a settlement. The fact that Mrs Wood's will in favour of her had been challenged meant that they were unable to fund the settlement which they, probably too sanguinely, believed could have been achieved. The fixed point in their strategy was Parnell's insistence that once the issue had been engaged there should be a divorce. On 17 November 1890, after two days of damaging and uncontested evidence, W. H. O'Shea obtained a decree nisi of divorce against his wife.

A sordid competition in moralistic fervour underpinned the political argument of the 'Parnell split'. Parnell's nationalist opponents in Ireland, marshalled by T. M. Healy, were determined not to be outdone in their denunciations of Parnell by either the dour plangencies of the 'non-conformist conscience' or tory derision. Parnell charged that the anti-Parnellites had been overborne by 'dictation'. Healy retorted that Parnell had succumbed to the embraces of Katharine O'Shea, the 'Brighton banshee', to whose sinister influence he attributed Parnell's furious quest to reassert his lost supremacy. He lithely parodied Parnell's stance:

> She says I must fight for my station,
> Or forfeit her high admiration,
> To obey her will be
> Quite a pleasure for me,
> So sweet is her English dictation.

Assailed in Ireland as 'Kitty O'Shea', Katharine was in some degree shielded by the fact that it was not a name to which she had ever answered: Parnell's familiar names for her were 'Katie', 'Wifie', or 'Queenie'. On the death of Mrs Wood the couple moved in to 10 Walsingham Terrace, Brighton, a corner residence which the *Brighton Gazette* described as 'away from the bustle of the town at a distance from the resorts of men, exposed to south-westerly gales and immediately overlooking the sea'. On the other side the landscape fell away in cornfields towards Shoreham. In the split Parnell spent the weekends campaigning in Ireland and repaired to Brighton during the week. Once the divorce decree was made absolute, they married at the register office at Steyning on 25 June 1891, two days short of Parnell's forty-fifth birthday. The rigours of the split had taken their toll of what had always been a fragile constitution. His wife was by his side when he died at Walsingham Terrace on the night of 6 October 1891.

Katharine survived her second husband's death by thirty years, in remorselessly deteriorating circumstances. While the proceedings in relation to her aunt's estate had been settled, not altogether advantageously, in 1892, the proceeds were later embezzled by a solicitor. Though prey to bouts of what might mildly be termed eccentricity, she retained unbroken the imperiousness of temperament she shared with Parnell. Her fortunes were partially restored by the appearance in 1914 of her *Charles Stewart Parnell: his Love Story and Political Life*, published under the name of Katharine O'Shea—which carried the requisite *frisson* of notoriety—with 'Mrs Charles Stewart Parnell' in parentheses and diminutive type. While, evidently at the direction of Gerard, Captain O'Shea was characterized as a wronged husband wholly unaware of her infidelity, the account she gave of her relations with Parnell rendered this inherently improbable. The influence of her son and publishers notwithstanding, her memoirs carry the ring of conviction and her dates when compared with Gladstone's detailed records are usually correct. Certainly the veracity of her account was doubted by none of Parnell's surviving lieutenants (then in late middle age), whose transfixed reading of the text plunged them traumatically back a quarter-century in time and produced (as well as varying degrees of disgust) a startled recall of Parnell's mesmeric power. Her two volumes reinstated—and perhaps even invented—the private Parnell. She insisted that, rather than the profession of love for his colleagues and the Irish people ascribed to him in public myth, his last words were the more impressive 'Kiss me, sweet Wifie, and I will try to sleep a little.'

Katharine O'Shea died at 39 East Ham Road, Littlehampton, on 5 February 1921, less than a year before the country she had never visited (but on whose history she had made such an ineffaceable impact) gained its independence. W. H. O'Shea predeceased her on 22 April 1905, at Hove.

FRANK CALLANAN

Sources K. O'Shea [K. W. Parnell], *Charles Stewart Parnell: his love story and political life*, 2 vols. (1914) • J. Marlow, *The uncrowned queen of Ireland: the life of 'Kitty' O'Shea* (1975) • R. Kee, *The laurel and the ivy: the story of Charles Stewart Parnell and Irish nationalism* (1993) • H. Harrison, *Parnell vindicated: the lifting of the veil* (1931) • F. Callanan, *The Parnell split* (1992) • F. Callanan, *T. M. Healy* (1996) • R. F. Foster, *Paddy and Mr Punch: connections in Irish and English history* (1993) • F. S. L. Lyons, *Charles Stewart Parnell* (1977); repr. (1978) • Gladstone, *Diaries* • H. C. G. Matthew, *Gladstone, 1875–1898* (1995) • *DNB*

Archives NL Ire. | BL, Gladstone MSS

Likenesses miniature, repro. in O'Shea, *Charles Stewart Parnell*, vol. 2 [*see illus.*]

Parnell, Thomas (1679–1718), poet and essayist, was born in Dublin and baptized on 14 September 1679 at St Catherine's, Dublin, the first of two sons of Thomas Parnell (*d.* 1685), of Congleton, Cheshire, and subsequently St Michan's, Dublin, merchant, and Anna Grice (*d.* 1709), of Kilosty, co. Tipperary, and subsequently St John's, Dublin, who were issued with a licence to marry in Dublin on 18 April 1674. His brother, John Parnell, an Irish judge, was the ancestor of Charles Stewart Parnell (1846–1891), the Irish nationalist politician. His father had supported Oliver Cromwell and left for Ireland after refusing to swear loyalty to Charles II. Parnell was educated by Dr Jones at a school in Dublin, but before he went to university he and his mother had become involved in the attainder of the protestants in 1689. He was admitted to Trinity College, Dublin, in 1693, graduating BA in 1697 and MA on 9 July, 1700. He was ordained deacon in 1700 by Dr William King, bishop of Derry, who had become a guardian. His sense of his vocation unresolved, he was not ordained priest until 1704.

On 16 August 1704 Parnell was installed as minor canon of St Patrick's Cathedral, Dublin, and there he met Jonathan Swift, who held another minor office at the cathedral, the prebend of Dunlavin. Their friendship appears to date from this time. On 9 February 1706, with the support of Dr King, Parnell became archdeacon of Clogher, to which the parish of Clontilibret was attached. His first visits to London may have been made in 1706. Dr King, now the archbishop of Dublin, wrote on 6 March 1706 advising him on the seriousness of his priestly life. His marriage to Anne (*d.* 1711), daughter of Thomas Minchin of co. Tipperary occurred soon afterwards, although no date has emerged. She appears in his poetry, notably 'Song' ('My Days have been so wondrous Free'), where he uses her nickname ('charming *Nancy*') (*Collected Poems*, 113–14). They had two sons, who died before their father, and one daughter. Parnell's mother died in 1709 and left him land in co. Armagh. In 1709 he became involved in the deliberations of the Church of Ireland on the conversion of the native Irish, which lasted until 27 August 1711.

The death of Parnell's wife in August 1711 led to a long period of grief, which apparently inspired the much anthologized 'A Night-Piece on Death' on bereavement. While he had travelled to London before his wife died, he now became a regular visitor, meeting the whigs Joseph Addison and Richard Steele, possibly through Swift. He began to publish, in *The Spectator* (nos. 460, 501), in Steele's *Poetical Miscellanies*, at the end of December 1713, and *The Guardian* (nos. 56, 66). He became BD and DD of the University of Dublin in 1712 but he moved away from his low Anglican, whig background and supported the tories, newly in power and open to the employment of writers. His poem 'On Queen Anne's Peace' dates from 1713, after the treaty of Utrecht. Swift, now a tory pamphleteer, was able to arrange meetings with the leading politicians. He suggested that Parnell add some compliments to Henry St John, Viscount Bolingbroke, the rival of Robert Harley, earl of Oxford, the tory leader, to his *Essay on the Different Styles of Poetry*. Bolingbroke was pleased and then suggested some corrections on 31 December 1712. The poem was published on 24 March 1713. On 31 January 1713 Oxford asked to meet Parnell, a request which pleased Swift.

After Swift had been offered the deanery of St Patrick's, he successfully requested, on 30 April 1713, that Parnell become prebend of Dunlavin. Parnell, however, was absorbed by the Scriblerus Club, which emerged later in 1713 from the intellectual companionship that developed among Swift, Alexander Pope, John Gay, Dr John Arbuthnot, Oxford, and others. Parnell's contribution remains unknown, although Pope said that he, Dr Arbuthnot, and Parnell wrote the 'Essay concerning the origin of the sciences' (*Memoirs*, 41). Parnell helped Pope with his translation of Homer, staying at Binfield and later at Bath with him in 1714. His 'Essay on the life, writings and learning of Homer' was published in Pope's *Iliad* (1715). The fall of Oxford on 27 July 1714 and the death of Queen Anne on 1 August 1714 led to the dissolution of the Scriblerians and the dispersal of friends. Parnell returned to Ireland in 1714, where Archbishop King presented him with the vicarage of Finglas on 31 May 1716. He then resigned as archdeacon of Clogher.

Parnell returned to London in the summer of 1718 for a brief reunion with some of the Scriblerians, leaving for Ireland in October. Falling ill at Chester, he died on 24 October and was buried in the Holy Trinity churchyard.

Parnell's *Poems on Several Occasions* (1722), edited by Pope, appeared on 11 December 1721 and *The Posthumous Works of Dr Thomas Parnell* in 1758 from manuscripts apparently presented to Benjamin Everard by Parnell himself. His ecclesiastical and literary careers were unresolved. Although he knew the conviviality of the leading literary figures and wits of his time, much of his private life was likewise unresolved. There is anecdotal evidence of his drinking but its meaning is difficult to determine. He was the first of the Scriblerians to die but he was also the first to publish, with *Homer's Battle of the Frogs and Mice*, in May 1717. He had to wait until 1989 for a collected edition of his poems. BRYAN COLEBORNE

Sources *DNB* • T. M. Woodman, *Thomas Parnell* (1985) • *Collected poems of Thomas Parnell*, ed. C. Rawson and F. P. Lock (1989) • *Memoirs of the extraordinary life, works, and discoveries of Martinus Scriblerus*, ed. C. K. Miller (1950) • *The correspondence of Alexander Pope*, ed. G. Sherburn, 5 vols. (1956) • S. Johnson, *Lives of the English poets*, ed. G. B. Hill, [new edn], 3 vols. (1905) • *Collected works of Oliver Goldsmith*, ed. A. Friedman, 5 vols. (1966) • *The Twickenham edition of the poems of Alexander Pope*, ed. J. Butt and others, 11 vols. in 12 (1939–69) • M. Mack, *Alexander Pope: a life* (1985) • M. Mack, *The garden and the city: retirement and politics in the later poetry of Pope, 1731–1743* (1969) • I. Ehrenpreis, *Swift: the man, his works and the age*, 3 vols. (1962–83) • *The prose writings of Jonathan Swift*, ed. H. Davis and others, 14 vols. (1939–68) • *The correspondence of Jonathan Swift*, ed. H. Williams, 5 vols. (1963–5) • *The poems of Jonathan Swift*, ed. H. Williams, 3 vols. (1937) • *The poems of Jonathan Swift*, ed. H. Williams, 2nd edn, 3 vols. (1958); repr. (1966)

Archives Columbus Academy, Ohio, papers • Hunt. L., corresp. • TCD, corresp. • TCD, notebooks and corresp. • Yale U., Beinecke L., papers | TCD, corresp. with William King

Likenesses J. Dixon, mezzotint, pubd 1771, BM, NPG • J. Basire, engraving, repro. in T. Parnell, *Poems on several occasions*, new edn (1773) • J. Hopwood, stipple (after G. Kneller), BM, NPG; repro. in *Poems* • E. Smyth, marble bust, TCD • engraving (after painting), repro. in Mack, *Alexander Pope*, facing p. 237

Wealth at death possibly retained land in Armagh; donated profits from publication of *Homer's battle of the frogs and mice*, 1717

Parnell, Valentine Charles (1892–1972), theatre manager and impresario, was born at 7 Trelawney Road, Hackney, London, on 14 February 1892, one of six sons of Thomas Frederick Parnell, journalist, and his wife, Elizabeth White. His father was for a time editor of the *Hackney Gazette* but was better known as a ventriloquist who used the name Fred Russell to avoid association with the Irish politician Charles Parnell. With his puppet 'Coster Joe', he was much in demand as a music-hall act between 1896 and 1930 and was honoured with an OBE.

Val Parnell was educated at Godwin College, Margate, but at the age of thirteen he began work in the offices of Sir Walter de Frece's expanding circuit of music-halls. In 1914 he enlisted in the Queen's Own 20th regiment and served with this throughout the war. In 1918 he rejoined de Frece, and when the circuit was taken over by Charles Gulliver's London Theatres of Variety (LTV) in 1919, Parnell became booking manager for ten of Gulliver's provincial theatres. Finding he was unable to book top acts because of the competition of the more powerful Moss Empires circuit, Parnell responded by booking a greater number of acts for shorter turns, thus providing a show which ran faster than those of his rivals. He was later to use the same 'high-speed variety' technique—though this time with big names—to revive the fortunes of the London Palladium.

In 1928 LTV's circuit was bought by Sir Walter Gibbons who, with the financier F. A. Szarvasy, was establishing the General Theatres Corporation (GTC) as a nationwide circuit of cinemas and music-halls. Parnell became booking manager for GTC's variety theatres, but the corporation proved to be an ill-starred venture and was rapidly swallowed by the rival Gaumont-British Picture Corporation. George *Black assumed responsibility for GTC's variety halls, and also from November 1932, for about thirty Moss Empires which Gaumont-British had bought up to forestall them being converted into cinemas. With Parnell as his assistant, Black set out to make the London Palladium, the most impressive of GTC's halls, the flagship of a substantial circuit devoted to live entertainment within a corporation set up to exploit the potential of the cinema. Together the two men kept alive the British music-hall tradition for a period of thirty years after the coming of the 'talkies' had seemed to spell its doom.

After seeing a revue at the Nottingham Hippodrome where comedians Jimmy Nervo and Teddy Knox persistently disrupted the acts of the other performers, Parnell had the idea of teaming them with two other comic duos, Charlie Naughton and Jimmy Gold and Billy Caryll and his

Valentine Charles Parnell (1892–1972), by unknown photographer, 1948 [right, with the American actress Betty Hutton at the Palladium]

wife Hilda Mundy in a 'Crazy Week' at the Palladium. Other 'Crazy Weeks' followed and by the middle of 1932 the classic *Crazy Gang team had been assembled with Bud Flanagan and Chesney Allen, and the French-talking juggler Monsewer Eddie Gray, replacing Caryll and Mundy. The Crazy Gang were to be the mainstay of the Palladium programmes until 1940 when for a time they went their separate ways and George Black introduced a series of wartime revue shows.

In March 1945 Black died and Parnell succeeded him as managing director of Moss Empires and director of GTC in charge of their variety halls. At the Palladium Parnell restored classic twice nightly variety bills, but with a major innovation: most of his top of the bill artists were American and many of them were Hollywood film stars. The new policy began unpromisingly with Mickey Rooney, whose brash egocentricity offended austerity-ridden British audiences. It was triumphantly vindicated by Danny Kaye, in 1948 only a minor film star but one whose abilities as a live performer attracted great admiration in Britain. Parnell chose his acts carefully, relying either on performers who had a background in vaudeville as well as the cinema, or on artists like Frank Sinatra with a wide experience of live performance. Parnell was criticized for neglecting home-grown talent, but there were few British artists who could fill the 2200 seats of the Palladium, and Parnell was responsible for the return of one of those who could—Gracie Fields.

In 1955 Parnell began a new career as a television executive, becoming managing director and subsequently chief executive of Associated Television, for which company he produced the hugely successful 'Sunday Night at the London Palladium'. At its height in the early sixties the show reached an audience of over twenty million people. In September 1962 Parnell resigned from his television posts to give younger executives a chance. He was already over seventy and was succeeded by his deputy, Lew (later Lord) Grade.

Val Parnell divorced his first wife, Dolly, in 1914 and married Helen Howell, a dancer, in 1938; this marriage was dissolved in 1963. Three years later he married the singer Aileen Cochrane. He also had a long-term relationship with the actress (and star of ATV's *Crossroads*) (Joan) Noel *Gordon (1919–1985). Parnell had one adopted son. He died from a heart attack on 22 September 1972 at 64 Portsea Hall, Portsea Place, London, aged eighty. A big man—6 feet 2 inches tall with the stature of a heavyweight boxer—Val Parnell was renowned as a tough but fair businessman. He dressed very modestly, and his appearance was said to suggest success in banking rather than in the theatre. A gift from Frank Sinatra bearing the inscription 'To the real star of the Palladium, Val Parnell' indicates the admiration he commanded in the field of show business.

'For forty years', commented Parnell's obituary in *The Times*, 'much that was best in variety and light entertainment passed through his hands to be presented with skill, speed, slickness and panache' (*The Times*, 25 Sept 1972).

ROBERT MURPHY

Sources I. Bevan, *Top of the bill: the story of the London Palladium* (1952) · P. Pilton, *Every night at the London Palladium* (1976) · G. J. Mellor, *The northern music hall* (1970) · private information (2004) · b. cert. · d. cert. · *WWW* · *The Times* (25 Sept 1972)

Likenesses double portrait, photograph, 1948, Popperfoto, Northampton [*see illus.*]

Parnell [*later* Parnell-Hayes], **William** (*c.*1780–1821), political author, was the third son of Sir John *Parnell (1745–1801), and his wife, Letitia Charlotte, second daughter and coheir of Sir Arthur Brooke of Colebrooke, co. Fermanagh. He attended Eton College and Trinity College, Dublin, and on inheriting the property of Avondale, Rathdrum, co. Wicklow from his father, Parnell legally assumed the name of Hayes to commemorate his second cousin, an earlier owner of Avondale. He never, however, really used the name, publishing and corresponding as William Parnell. As a young man, he began to move in literary circles, forming close friendships with the popular poets Mary Tighe, who dedicated a sonnet to him, and Thomas Moore, who wrote the famous 'The Meeting of the Waters' while visiting him at Avondale. In 1802 he published in London *Julietta, or, The Triumph of Mental Acquirements over Personal Defects*, a didactic novel which met with little success.

Although part of the protestant ascendancy class, Parnell opposed the union and was a staunch defender of the Catholics. He maintained good relations with his tenants at a time when land agitation was almost endemic. In 1804 he published *An Inquiry into the Causes of Popular Discontents in Ireland*, a partly satirical pamphlet calling for Catholic emancipation, which ran to three editions by 1805. In 1806 he responded to the controversy it had provoked in *Observations explanatory and critical, on a pamphlet entitled, 'An inquiry into the causes of popular discontents in Ireland'*, also published in pamphlet form in London and Dublin.

A year later Parnell expanded his argument for Catholic emancipation in a book dedicated to the duke of Bedford, *An Historical Apology for the Irish Catholics*, which argued that persecution was the cause of Catholic disaffection. By 1808 three editions had appeared, and the Revd Samuel

Smith in the *Edinburgh Review* ended a highly favourable review 'most cordially recommending his work to the attention of the public' (*EdinR*, 1807, 299–306). F. S. L. Lyons commented that Parnell in these pamphlets:

> put his finger unerringly on some of the factors which were still to be dominant when his grandson came on the scene some sixty years later—the race memory of the Irish, the degraded position of the peasantry, the friction between different religious denominations and of course the Union itself. (Lyons, 20)

In 1810 Parnell married Frances (*d.* 1813), daughter of the Hon. Hugh Howard. The couple had two children, John Henry, father of Charles Stewart Parnell (1846–1891), and Catherine, who married George Vicesimus Wigram. Parnell was elected Liberal MP for Wicklow in 1817, and held his seat until his death. In 1819 he published anonymously *Maurice and Berghetta, or, The Priest of Rahery*, a reiteration in fiction of his political arguments, and dedicated to 'The Catholic priesthood of Ireland'. A scorching review by the editor of the *Quarterly Review*, who dismissed the novel as 'mischievous and absurd' (21.471–86), prompted him to publish another pamphlet, *A Letter to the Editor of the Quarterly Review* (1820) in vigorous protest. The *Quarterly Review* responded (23.360–73), but the controversy was cut short by Parnell's death on 2 January 1821 at Castle Howard, co. Wicklow.

A second edition of *Maurice and Berghetta*, bearing Parnell's name, appeared in London, Boston, and Dublin in 1825, but he was better known as a pamphleteer. The *Gentleman's Magazine* paid tribute to his pamphlets' 'elegance of style, the statesmanlike principles which they enforce and the pure patriotism of the author' (*GM*).

Katherine Mullin

Sources F. S. L. Lyons, *Charles Stewart Parnell* (1977), 20–21; repr. (1991) • Allibone, *Dict.* • *Memoirs, journal and correspondence of Thomas Moore*, ed. J. Russel, 7 (1856), 109 • reviews, *QR*, 21 (1819), 471–86; 23 (1820), 360–73 • *GM*, 1st ser., 91/1 (1821), 86 • *EdinR*, 10 (1807), 299–306 • A. M. Brady and B. Cleeve, eds., *A biographical dictionary of Irish writers*, rev. edn (1985) • D. J. O'Donoghue, *The poets of Ireland: a biographical dictionary with bibliographical particulars*, 1 vol. in 3 pts (1892–3) • Burke, *Gen. GB* • R. Johnston, *Parnell and the Parnells: a historical sketch* (1888) • G. P. Judd, *Members of parliament, 1734–1832* (1955) • *DNB*

Archives NL Ire., letters to Denis Scully • Sheff. Arch., corresp. with Earl Fitzwilliam

Parning, Sir Robert (*d.* 1343), justice and administrator, was a member of a Cumberland family; his father, Robert, was still alive in 1337. He was acting as counsel before 21 July 1315 and became a serjeant-at-law in 1329, serving as king's serjeant from Easter term 1333 to Michaelmas term 1339. He maintained interests in his native county and was knight of the shire for Cumberland in the parliaments summoned for 18 November 1325, 15 September 1327, 7 February 1328, 30 September 1331, and 16 March 1332. He was retained as legal counsel by the knights hospitallers in 1338, and he had close personal and perhaps professional links with Bishop Kirkby of Carlisle. Throughout the 1330s Parning was employed as a justice of assize and gaol delivery and on commissions of oyer and terminer. On 23 May 1340 he was appointed one of the justices of the court of common pleas; on the following day he was knighted and awarded an annuity of 50 marks. On 24 July 1340 he was made chief justice of the court of king's bench, and on 15 December 1340 treasurer, being one of the first laymen to hold the latter office. On 28 October 1341 he was made chancellor. He received a fee of £500 a year for the upkeep of the household of chancery and a further discretionary grant of £200 for associated expenses. Although chancellor, he continued to attend in the court of common pleas.

Parning's London residence was in Aldermanbury, though he also resided at the town house of the bishop of Worcester, and at the time of his death he held extensive estates in Cumberland, Northumberland, and Westmorland. He married, before 1329, Isabel; on his death, his property was divided between his sisters, Joan and Emma. He died in London on 26 August 1343, the great seal having been in commission for the previous eight days. Parning's period at the chancery witnessed important procedural changes which contributed significantly to the development of that institution as a court of equity.

C. L. Kingsford, *rev.* W. M. Ormrod

Sources G. O. Sayles, ed., *Select cases in the court of king's bench*, 7 vols., SeldS, 55, 57–8, 74, 76, 82, 88 (1936–71) • Baker, *Serjeants* • B. Wilkinson, *The chancery under Edward III* (1929) • *CIPM*, 8, no. 458 • J. Raine, ed., *Historical papers and letters from the northern registers*, Rolls Series, 61 (1873) • W. M. Ormrod, 'The origins of the *sub poena* writ', *Historical Research*, 61 (1988), 11–20 • *Chancery records* • *CPR*, *1327–30*, 404 • Tout, *Admin. hist.*, vol. 6

Paroissien, James (1784–1827), military surgeon and diplomatist, was born on 25 November 1784 at Barking, Essex, the son of Lewis Paroissien, a schoolmaster, whose Huguenot grandfather had been naturalized in 1709, and his wife, Mary. His half-brother, George, was educated at Cambridge and served as curate in Hackney for thirty-six years. Little is known about Paroissien's education save that he acquired a proficiency in surgery and medicine and had some knowledge of chemistry.

In December 1806 Paroissien sailed for Montevideo, at that time occupied by British troops, to engage in trade there. After the defeat of Sir John Whitelocke's attack on Buenos Aires in June 1807, he retired to Rio de Janeiro. In Brazil, thanks to Dr Saturnino Rodríguez Peña, an Argentine patriot, he became embroiled in a plot to install Princess Carlota Joaquina, the daughter of Charles IV of Spain and wife to Dom Joâo, the prince regent of Portugal, as queen in Buenos Aires. Unwisely returning to Montevideo in May 1808, Paroissien was imprisoned by the colonial authorities and transferred to Buenos Aires where he was not released until 11 June 1810, following the May revolution which ended Spanish rule in Argentina. By then he had attracted the support of Juan José Castelli, who named him physician when he led an armed expedition to liberate Upper Peru. Present at the battle of Huaqui, where Castelli was defeated by the Peruvian royalists, Paroissien then served with the forces commanded by Juan Martín de Puerreydón. In recognition of his courage and dedication in caring for the wounded he was granted naturalization papers on 25 November 1811. In Córdoba he opened and directed a gunpowder factory and became lieutenant-colonel of artillery, only narrowly escaping death when the factory exploded in 1815.

On 24 September 1816 Paroissien was named surgeon-general of the army of the Andes, the force raised and led by General José de San Martín for the liberation of Chile. Present at the battles of Chacabuco and Maipú, he was further praised for his dedication, promoted colonel, and made a member of the Chilean Legion of merit. On 4 June 1820 San Martín appointed him aide-de-camp for the expedition to liberate Peru. It fell to Paroissien to mediate between Admiral Thomas Cochrane, the imperious commander of the Chilean navy, and San Martín; but although he admired Cochrane's naval exploits he complained of his avarice. On 22 December 1821 he was appointed brigadier-general of the Peruvian army and became a founder member of the order of the Sun, honours awarded by San Martín acting as protector of Peru. Such was San Martín's confidence in him that on 24 December 1821 Paroissien, together with Juan García del Río, was appointed as an envoy to Europe, charged with the mission of finding an emperor for the throne of Peru.

From September 1822 to April 1825 Paroissien and García del Río maintained a Peruvian legation in London, but displayed more concern with obtaining recognition of Peruvian independence than in pursuing San Martín's monarchical project. The two envoys also sought to raise a loan of £1,200,000 for Peru, a project which foundered owing to constant changes in government in Lima. Renouncing diplomacy, on 27 April 1825 Paroissien helped launch the Potosí, La Paz, and Peruvian Mining Association, and in the same year returned to South America to direct the enterprise. But the company was mismanaged, the mines required extensive renovation, and the capital available was soon exhausted. In Lima, Paroissien found himself ruined and, ill from dropsy, died on 23 September 1827 on board the *Olive Branch*, a ship sailing for Valparaiso. A man of wide interests, whose qualities attracted the patronage of successive Spanish American leaders, Paroissien never married and left no known descendants. CELIA WU

Sources R. A. Humphreys, *Liberation in South America, 1806–1827: the career of James Paroissien* (1952) • C. P. Moreyra, *La Deuda Anglo-Peruana, 1822–1890* (1983) • B. Hall, *Extracts from a journal, written on the coast of Chili, Peru, and Mexico, in the years 1820, 1821, 1822*, 3 vols. (1824) • parish register (baptism), Barking, St Margaret
Archives Essex RO, Chelmsford, corresp. and journals
Likenesses J. G. de Castro, portrait, 1819, Chilean embassy, London

Parr family (*per. c.*1370–1517), gentry, played a leading role in Westmorland in the fifteenth century. The family was founded by **Sir William Parr** (*c.*1350–1404), who held one-eighth of the vill of Parr in the parish of Prescot, Lancashire. In May 1370 Parr was pardoned his part in a murder because he was going overseas in the service of John of Gaunt, duke of Lancaster. Parr remained in Gaunt's service until the duke's death, first as a soldier, and later as a trusted member of the ducal retinue. It was probably under Gaunt's aegis that about 1380 Parr married Elizabeth Roos (*d.* 1392x6), the heir of her grandfather Thomas, although the Parrs themselves were later to tell another story. According to Sir William *Parr (*d.* 1547) one of his ancestors was clerk of the kitchen to Lord Roos, fell in love with his daughter, and married her against her father's wishes. However the marriage was achieved, it was to establish the Parrs as a force in the north-west, bringing William a quarter of the barony of Kendal, including the castle, on Thomas Roos's death in 1390. By then Parr was one of Gaunt's knights bachelor, receiving an annual fee of £50. His closeness to Gaunt was to be marked by further patronage, including land in Gascony, and he was one of the duke's executors. On Gaunt's death Richard II took him into his service, a move perhaps aided by Parr's second marriage (before October 1396) to Margaret, widow of the Cheshire knight Lawrence Dutton, who had been a retainer of Richard II's father, Edward, the Black Prince.

In spite of his Lancastrian background, Parr did not benefit particularly from the accession of Henry IV, although he became one of the king's knights. He died on 3 October 1404, leaving as his heir his son **John Parr** (*c.*1382–1408), who at about this time married Agnes Crophill (1371–1436). She was a considerable heiress, and although she already had a son from her first marriage to Sir Walter Devereux (*d.* 1403), which meant that any children with Parr were unlikely to inherit, she brought Parr a life interest in her estates, including Weobley, Herefordshire, as well as her Devereux dower. The Parrs, however, scarcely had time to benefit from the marriage. John died on 25 July 1408, leaving as his heir his son with Agnes, Thomas [*see below*], who was less than a year old. Any chance of further family advancement was thus inevitably postponed. Within ten days of John's death, his son's wardship had been disposed of by the crown, and in 1413 it passed to Sir Thomas Tunstall of Thurland, Lancashire, who married the heir to his daughter Alice, presumably before his death in 1415.

When **Sir Thomas** [i] **Parr** (1407/8–1461) entered his inheritance in 1429 he thus had to rebuild the family's influence, but he started with the advantage of an estate worth between £80 and £100 p.a. For the next thirty years Thomas successfully built up his authority in Westmorland, although curiously he did not use his influence to secure suitable brides for his three sons, who were all still unmarried at his death. Within a year of his coming of age Thomas was escheator of Cumberland and Westmorland. By the mid-1430s he was acting as under-sheriff of Westmorland for the hereditary sheriff, Lord Clifford, which gave him a major role in the administration of the shire. In 1441 Henry Bellingham complained that he could not get justice against Parr because 'the coroners of the same Shire bene his meynyall men' (Storey, 77). Parr was also extending his landed influence by leasing royal estates in the county. His greatest acquisition was two-thirds of the crown's share of the barony of Kendal, which he leased in 1438. This more than tripled his income, and he cannot have been pleased when, in 1443 (half-way through the term of his lease), the lands were granted to John Beaufort, duke of Somerset. The grant did, however, bring Parr into closer contact with Richard Neville, earl of Salisbury, who was made steward of the lands by his cousin Somerset in 1444. By the 1450s Parr was one of the earl's leading retainers, and with the coming of civil war followed Salisbury into the Yorkist camp. He was with the earl at Bloreheath and Ludlow in 1459, which led to his attainder in the Coventry parliament, and he was evidently with the earl at the battle of Wakefield at the end of 1460, for several chroniclers list him among the dead. He survived the battle, however, to enter the service of Edward IV, and died at the end of November 1461.

Unlike his father, Parr left an adult heir, and one who already stood high in the king's favour, so there was no break in the family's ability to benefit from the Yorkist victory. Sir William *Parr (1434–1483) worked closely with his younger brother John *Parr [*see under* Parr, Sir William] (his heir until his death in 1475) to maintain the family's influence in the north-west, and—a new departure—at court. Their efforts paid off, and William came closer than any other Parr to securing possession of the crown's share of the barony of Kendal (representing half the total barony), which had been used throughout the earlier part of the century to endow members of the royal family. In 1471, as a reward for his loyalty to Edward IV in the crisis of 1470–71, William was granted the reversion of the third part of the crown share, held by the dowager duchess of Bedford—a reversion that materialized less than a year later. The crown also brokered an agreement whereby Margaret Beaufort, the holder of the other two-thirds, granted the land to Parr in return for £190 p.a.

William was surely close to being ennobled as lord of Kendal, and his prospects of advancement looked even brighter in 1483 when Richard, duke of Gloucester, with whom Parr had been associated throughout Edward IV's second reign, became king. It must have seemed a crushing blow when Parr himself died at the end of the year, leaving a five-year-old as the head of the family, without even an adult uncle to steer the family fortunes: John had died in 1475 and the youngest brother, Thomas [ii], on 14 April 1471. The minority did at least mean that, when Richard III was defeated at Bosworth in 1485, the Parrs were able to avoid the penalties that might have followed too close an attachment to his cause, but the family was clearly vulnerable, and it was a shrewd move by William's widow, Elizabeth Fitzhugh (1462–*c*.1505), to marry Nicholas *Vaux (*d.* 1523) of Harrowden, Northamptonshire, who had grown up in the household of the new king's mother, Margaret Beaufort. The marriage, accomplished by 1487, was arranged by Margaret, whose own territorial interests in Kendal (ceded to Sir William Parr in 1471) had now been restored by Henry VII. The marriage drew Margaret's potential rivals into her own circle, while offering them protection.

From the Parrs' perspective, Elizabeth's marriage reaped rewards, although it meant a shift of interest for the family. Vaux secured good marriages for all his stepchildren, but within his own sphere of influence rather than in the north-west. **Sir Thomas** [iii] **Parr** (1478–1517) and his younger brother William *Parr (*c*.1480–1547) grew up in the Tudor court circle, and Thomas in particular was an early intimate of Henry VIII, although he was not to live long enough to enjoy the full benefits of royal favour. When Thomas entered his inheritance in 1499 the family's gains from Yorkist patronage had been resumed by the crown, but Thomas's own acquisitions more than compensated for their loss. In 1508 he married Maud, the younger of the two daughters and coheirs of Sir Thomas Green of Greens Norton, Northamptonshire. Green had been a friend of Nicholas Vaux, who married the elder daughter himself. In 1513 Thomas inherited, through his mother Elizabeth, a moiety of the Fitzhugh lands. There was apparently some discussion of Thomas's becoming Lord Fitzhugh, but the Dacres (the recipients of the other moiety) moved to block the proposal on the grounds that they were descended from the senior heiress, and nothing came of the idea.

Thomas's northern interests remained important to him. His first major piece of royal patronage, secured from Henry VIII just a month after his coronation, was the stewardship of the king's share of Kendal, and he continued to purchase land in Westmorland to round off his holdings there. He also seems to have valued his status as patron of Jervaulx, which came to him from the Fitzhughs. But his choice of burial place reveals the family's shift of interest. Earlier Parrs had presumably been buried in their chapel in Kendal parish church, but Thomas and his wife (who died on 1 December 1531) sought burial in the church of the Blackfriars, near their London home.

Thomas [iii] Parr must have been a strong candidate for ennoblement had he lived longer. However, his son William *Parr (1513–1571) was created Baron Parr in 1539, earl of Essex in 1543 (on the same day, 23 December, that his uncle, Thomas's brother William, was created Baron Parr of Horton), and finally marquess of Northampton in 1547. Both men owed their elevation to the marriage, some five months earlier, of Thomas's daughter *Katherine (1512–1548) to Henry VIII. The family arms were argent, two bars azure, a bordure engrailed sable, and their motto *Amour avecque loiaulté*. ROSEMARY HORROX

Sources *Chancery records* • W. Farrer, *Records relating to the barony of Kendale*, ed. J. F. Curwen, 1, Cumberland and Westmorland Antiquarian and Archaeological Society, record ser., 4 (1923) • S. E. James, 'Sir Thomas Parr, 1407–1461', *Transactions of the Cumberland and Westmorland Antiquarian and Archaeological Society*, [new ser.], 81 (1981), 15–25 • M. A. Rowling, 'William de Parr: king's knight to Henry IV (c. 1350–1404)', *Transactions of the Cumberland and Westmorland Antiquarian and Archaeological Society*, new ser., 56 (1957), 87–103 • R. L. Storey, 'Disorders in Lancastrian Westmorland: some early chancery proceedings', *Transactions of the Cumberland and Westmorland Antiquarian and Archaeological Society*, new ser., 53 (1954), 69–80 • M. K. Jones and M. G. Underwood, *The king's mother: Lady Margaret Beaufort, countess of Richmond and Derby* (1992) • S. E. James, 'The Parrs of Kendal, 1370–1571', PhD diss., U. Cam., 1977 • GEC, *Peerage*

Parr, Bartholomew (1750–1810), physician and medical author, was born at Bedford House, Exeter, the son of Bartholomew Parr (1713–1800) and his second wife, Johanna

Burgess. His father, one of the first surgeons to the Devon and Exeter Hospital, was a pupil of William Smellie and a skilful accoucheur, who served the hospital for fifty-four years. Parr was educated at Exeter grammar school and Edinburgh University, where he graduated MD in 1773. His inaugural dissertation, *De balneo*, was pronounced best of the year, and obtained the honour of a lengthy analysis in *Medical and Philosophical Commentaries* (1.297). He then returned to Exeter and was appointed physician to the Devon and Exeter Hospital on the retirement of Thomas Glass, on 16 February 1775.

Parr was a member of a literary society in Exeter (the Society of Gentlemen) founded in 1792 by Dr Hugh Downman. It numbered John Sheldon, Richard Polwhele, and Isaac D'Israeli among its members, and it published a volume of essays in 1796. Parr was married first to Maria, daughter of John Codrington; she died aged thirty-three in 1803. They had a daughter, Maria (*d.* 20 Feb 1797), and three sons: Bartholomew (*d.* 20 May 1812), Codrington, and Samuel. Secondly he married Frances Robson, on 27 May 1809; she left him after six weeks but continued to correspond affectionately with his sons.

Parr was elected a fellow of the Royal Society of Edinburgh on 26 January 1789, and of the Royal Society of London on 23 March 1797. He gave important literary assistance to his friend Andrew Duncan the elder, editor of the *Medical and Philosophical Commentaries* and *Annals of Medicine*. A large number of the critical reviews in these publications were from his pen. To the tenth volume of the former he contributed the interesting 'Account of the influenza as it appeared in Devonshire in May 1782'. His reputation rests mainly on his *London Medical Dictionary* (2 vols., 1809). This large work testifies to the enormous breadth of Parr's medical learning and was completed in less than two years. In addition to anatomy and medicine, Parr wrote authoritatively on natural history, chemistry, general literature, and criticism, and would, it was said, review anything from a treatise on geometry to the flimsiest romance—always being a master of his subject, whatever it might be. With Dr Daniell he occupied the principal medical position in Exeter, following the death of Glass in 1786. He was considered acute in medical perception, and decisive and correct in practice.

There was, however, another side to Parr's character, principally revealed by two lectures given by him to the literary society at Exeter in 1795—*Biographical Anecdotes of the Late Dr Glass of Exeter*—afterwards lodged in manuscript at the Royal College of Physicians in London. While factually correct about the principal details of Glass's life, the overall effect is a spiteful denigration of his character and attainments. He also spoke disparagingly about a number of other eighteenth-century Exeter physicians of whom he had no direct knowledge. It is not immediately obvious why he attacked Glass, who was held in such great affection and esteem in the Exeter of his day. Some of his statements betray an almost pathological jealousy towards his subject, and some were so strong that he deleted them from the manuscript of his lectures. In his younger days Glass had been something of a hero to Parr; the two families were neighbours at Bedford House and Parr's MD dissertation *De balneo* was a topic in line with Glass's interest in hot and cold bathing, and it was dedicated to Glass in fulsome terms. Unlike Glass, however, Parr was not an admirer of Boerhaave, and he evidently considered the 'ancients' (such as Hippocrates and Galen) overrated. Evidence from Joseph Farington suggests that Parr's own personality was flawed. Farington claimed that, despite Parr's literary knowledge and considerable medical practice: 'His disposition was avaritious, and He gave way to much sensuality, even to low, impure connections … selfish and narrow in his mind; an epicure in his living; and to risk His constitution to gratify His passions' (*Farington Diary*, ed. Greig, 23 Nov 1810). The brief duration of his second marriage would seem to endorse this.

Parr was a nonconformist (probably presbyterian), his grandfather John Parr (1691–1779) having been a dissenting minister. He was proposed in 1809 for election to the city chamber but had to stand down on account of this. Parr died in Bedford Circus, Exeter, on 20 November 1810, and was buried there at St Stephen's Church on 26 November. He was said to be a wealthy man, deriving about £1500 per annum from his professional practice, and amassing a fortune of £80,000–£100,000 from other sources. His will indicates legacies in excess of £58,000.

Alick Cameron

Sources W. Munk, 'Medical worthies of Devon', *Western Times* (1 Dec 1855) • *DNB* • *GM*, 1st ser., 80 (1810), 595 • *GM*, 1st ser., 81/1 (1811), 184 • J. D. Harris, *The Royal Devon and Exeter Hospital* (1922) • P. C. de la Garde, *Presidential address to south western branch of the British Medical Association* (1871) • *The Farington diary*, ed. J. Greig, 6 (1926) [23 Nov 1810] • A. Cameron, *Thomas Glass, MD: physician of Georgian Exeter* (1996) • *London Devonian Yearbook* (1910), 201–2 • *The western antiquary* (1881–3)

Archives RCP Lond.

Wealth at death approx. £90,000 incl. legacies in excess of £58,000: *The Farington diary*; Exeter Central library, Oswyn Murray collection 8/36

Parr, Elnathan (1577–1622), Church of England clergyman and religious writer, was born and baptized on 3 March 1577, the son of Richard Parr, vicar of Steeple Claydon, in Buckinghamshire. Educated first at Eton College, he was admitted on 17 September 1593 as a scholar of King's College, Cambridge, and was a fellow of the college from 1596 to 1600; he graduated BA in 1598 and MA in 1601. Ordained as a priest in the diocese of Lincoln on 13 January 1600, he was instituted in that year to the rectory of Palgrave, Suffolk; in 1615 he proceeded BD and acquired a second rectory, at Thrandeston in the same county.

In 1613 Parr was involved in negotiations over the marriage of Jane (*née* Meautys), Lady Cornwallis, whose family presented to his rectory of Palgrave, and Sir Nathaniel Bacon, acting, as he put it 'as an instrument in this weighty business', and reporting that 'of Lady Cornwallis, her favour towards me, though I had great cause to fear the loss of it, yet … I have it as amply as ever I had, I humbly thank God for it' (*Private Correspondence*, ed. Braybrooke, 4–5). By this year Parr himself had married: Lady Cornwallis made reference to his wife, though nothing is known of her. About October 1613, while the discussions continued, Parr fell ill; having thus been 'made unserviceable for my public duty', he spent the time compiling his 'ragged notes and scattered papers' into *The Grounds of Divinitie* (1614) 'A short and plain exhortation to the study of the word', which when published contained a preface to Sir Nathaniel and his new wife. In compiling this work, Parr had:

> striven to be plain, or at least, having no skill in finer cookery, have dressed it as I was able, after our homely and country fashion, for the stomachs of the unlearned, who relish and like better of that which is plain and easy, than either learned and deep treatises … For thee therefore which art but a beginner I have laboured. (preface)

He also published *Abba Father* (1618), a manual on prayer, and two commentaries on Paul's letter to the Romans. Parr died in 1622 at Thrandeston and was buried there on 14 November. A 'corrected and enlarged' edition of *The Grounds of Divinity* appeared in 1632, as did a collected edition of his works. STEPHEN WRIGHT

Sources W. Sterry, ed., *The Eton College register, 1441–1698* (1943) • Venn, *Alum. Cant.* • *The private correspondence of Jane, Lady Cornwallis, 1613–1644*, ed. Lord Braybrooke (1842) • R. Bullen, 'Catalogue of beneficed clergy of Suffolk (1551–1631)', *Suffolk Institute of Archaeology and Natural History*, 22 (1934–6), 294–333

Parr, George (1826–1891), cricketer, born at Radcliffe-on-Trent, Nottinghamshire, on 22 May 1826, was the son of Samuel Parr (1780–1857), a gentleman farmer whose ancestors had farmed their own land for more than 200 years, and his wife, Mary, *née* Martin (1794–1867). He came from a cricketing family, two of his brothers, Henry (1838–1863) and James (1820–1873), briefly playing for Nottinghamshire. He first appeared at Lord's for the North against the MCC in 1845, the year in which he began his long association (1845–70) with Nottinghamshire. He was also recruited to William Clarke's All England eleven, succeeding Clarke as captain in 1857, by which time he was also captain of his county. He introduced (1857) the annual matches between the All England eleven and its great rival, the United All England eleven. Parr's leadership qualities were outstanding and he captained every team with which he was involved. He took the first ever English team overseas, in 1859, to Canada and the United States. By drawing on players from the two England elevens he paved the way for representative England sides and the dawn, in 1877, of test cricket. His side returned unbeaten, as did the one he took to Australia and New Zealand in 1863–4. According to William Caffyn, Parr was less successful as a passenger, being 'nearly out of his mind' when a jib-boom broke on the way home from America and 'paralysed with alarm' at a collision at sea near Sydney.

Parr had represented the Players against the Gentlemen in 1846 and continued to represent them, although not regularly, until 1865, the year in which W. G. Grace first appeared for the Gentlemen. Parr's best scores in these matches, in which he was almost always successful, were 77, 73, 60, and 46 not out. He also produced many good performances for Nottinghamshire, of which the best was probably an innings of 130 played, without conceding a chance, against the powerful Surrey eleven in 1859. He was also highly successful for the All England eleven in matches against 'odds', having several centuries to his credit.

Parr's last appearance at Lord's was in 1870, for the North against the South, in which, according to *Wisden*, he played a fine innings of 41 without a chance. His last first-class match for his county was in the same year, and he resigned his captaincy of the All England eleven at the same time. His last match of all was at Trent Bridge in 1871, when he scored 32 not out and 53 for Nottinghamshire, against fourteen gentlemen of the county, twenty-seven years after first playing in the same fixture.

For about twelve years Parr was undoubtedly the finest batsman in England, a title previously enjoyed by Fuller Pilch. He combined a very strong defence with powerful attacking shots all round the wicket and was thought by John Lillywhite to be 'the finest leg hitter we have ever had' (Lillywhite). He also drove in fine style and his square and late cutting was superb. A tree he frequently hit at Trent Bridge was named after him. In his early days he was able to throw over a hundred yards.

Known as the 'Old Lion of the North', Parr had a benefit match in 1858. The French ambassador gave £1 but no other figures have survived. Twenty years later a match between the North and the South in which Grace played brought him £300. Parr was a shrewd, businesslike man, but Richard Daft thought him prone to forgetfulness and would handle some of his correspondence for him. He was chivalrous and kind by nature but could display a bucolic bluntness if necessary. After his retirement he occupied himself with farming and shooting. Caffyn thought he 'preferred a day's shooting to a season's cricket'. In 1890 Parr married his housekeeper, Jane Smalley. He died on 23 June the following year, after a long illness, at his home, Ivy House, Bingham Road, Radcliffe-on-Trent, and was buried in the town cemetery. He had lived all his life in Radcliffe. J. W. ALLEN, *rev.* GERALD M. D. HOWAT

Sources [A. Haygarth], *Frederick Lillywhite's cricket scores and biographies*, 3 (1863) • *The Times* (24 June 1891) • F. S. Ashley-Cooper, *Nottinghamshire cricket and cricketers* (1923) • A. W. Pullin, *Talks with old English cricketers* (1900) • *Wisden* (1878) • *Wisden* (1892) • *Baily's Magazine*, 1 (1860), 215–20 • R. Daft, *A cricketer's yarns*, ed. F. S. Ashley-Cooper (1926) • W. Caffyn, *Seventy one not out* (1899) • R. Daft, *Kings of cricket* (1893) • E. V. Lucas, *A hundred years of Trent Bridge* (1838) • F. Lillywhite, *Guide* (1865) • R. S. Holmes, *Cricket* (25 Feb 1892) • P. Bailey, P. Thorn, and P. Wynne-Thomas, *Who's who of cricketers*, rev. edn (1993) • A. Haygarth, F. S. Ashley-Cooper, and A. L. Ford, *M.C.C. cricket scores and biographies*, 15 (1925)

Likenesses W. Bromley, oils, *c*.1850, Marylebone Cricket Club, London • photograph, *c*.1850, repro. in Lucas, *Hundred years of Trent Bridge* • F. Lillywhite, lithograph, 1859 (after J. C. Anderson), Marylebone Cricket Club, Lord's, London • double portrait, photograph, *c*.1860 (with R. Daft), Marylebone Cricket Club, Lords, London, ref. 58 • photograph, *c*.1860, repro. in Daft, *A cricketer's yarns* • photograph, *c*.1860, repro. in *Baily's Magazine* • sketch, *c*.1870, repro. in Holmes, *Cricket* • J. Brown, stipple (after photograph by Kilburn), BM, NPG; repro. in *Baily's Magazine* (1860)

Wealth at death £356: administration, 18 July 1891, *CGPLA Eng. & Wales*

Parr, Harriet [*pseud.* Holme Lee] (**1828–1900**), novelist, was born at York on 31 January 1828, one of six children. She was the daughter of Mary Grandage (*d.* *c.*1863) of Halifax, Yorkshire, and William Parr, a travelling merchant of silks, satins, and coloured kidskins who died when she was a child, leaving the family destitute. She attended local day schools in York and then, in exchange for her education, became a servant at a local boarding-school, and thereafter a governess, a profession she pursued for twelve years and which made Charlotte Brontë her favourite author. In these early years reading was her only pleasure, and she published her first poems at sixteen, using the proceeds to buy works by Thomas Carlyle and Shakespeare. No novel appeared, however, until 1854, when she published, under the pseudonym Holme Lee, *Maud Talbot*, a story of mill life containing forgery, murder, and social problems which none the less did little to beguile the reader. Undismayed, Parr sent her second novel, *Gilbert Massenger*, to Charles Dickens, who wrote her an extraordinary letter about the 'vigour and pathos' it possessed, saying that 'It moved me more than I can express' (*Letters of Charles Dickens*, 688). Although its length prevented its appearance in *Household Words*, Dickens helped her find a publisher, and in 1855 it came out as a single volume. She became a contributor to *Household Words* and *All the Year Round* and was later to remark that Dickens had been her 'first encourager' (ibid.).

The story of doomed rustic life told in *Gilbert Massenger* was so popular that the novel was translated at once into French and Italian, and Parr was invited to give a lecture tour in France, Germany, and Belgium. Her success soon enabled her to retire from teaching and buy a small house at Shanklin, on the Isle of Wight, where she taught Sunday school and acted as a ministering angel to the local population. (In fact, she was often mistaken for a Sister of Mercy.) She wrote thirty more novels, all of which are refined in tone, somewhat sentimental, and written in an easy, unaffected style which appealed to the sense of decency of the Victorian reader. These merits, supplemented by the enthusiastic support of Charles Edward Mudie, secured her considerable popularity as a writer for children. She did, however, publish four non-fiction works under her own name: a series of depressing autobiographical essays, *In the Silver Age: Essays—that is, Dispersed Meditations* (1864), *The Life and Death of Jeanne d'Arc* (1866), *Maurice and Eugénie de Guérin* (1870), and *Echoes of a Famous Year* (1872). Her last novel, *Loving and Serving*, appeared in 1883.

Parr never married, and she lived alone with her cats and her servant of forty years until her death from a lung complaint at her home, Whittle Meade, Shanklin, Isle of Wight, on 18 February 1900.

A. F. POLLARD, *rev.* KATHARINE CHUBBUCK

Sources H. Parr, *In the silver age: essays—that is, dispersed meditations*, 2 vols. (1864) • J. Sutherland, 'Parr, Harriet', *The Longman companion to Victorian fiction* (1988), 490–91 • *The Times* (20 Feb 1900) • review of *The beautiful Miss Barrington* by Holme Lee, *The Athenaeum* (15 July 1871), 79 • review of *Her title of honour* by Holme Lee, *The Athenaeum* (16 Sept 1871), 368 • review of *Country stories* by Holme Lee, *The Athenaeum* (1 June 1872), 687 • *The letters of Charles Dickens*, ed. M. House, G. Storey, and others, 7 (1993) • *CGPLA Eng. & Wales* (1900)

Likenesses G. Lance, oils, 1898; formerly priv. coll.

Wealth at death £2060 6*s*. 2*d*.: probate, 28 Aug 1900, *CGPLA Eng. & Wales*

Parr, Helena, marchioness of Northampton. *See* Gorges, Helena, Lady Gorges (1548–1635).

Parr, Sir Henry Hallam (**1847–1914**), army officer, was born on 24 July 1847, the second son of Thomas Clements Parr, a barrister, and Julia, eldest daughter of Sir Charles Elton, bt, of Clevedon. He was educated at Eton College and Sandhurst and commissioned in the 13th light infantry on 8 September 1865. Regimental service took Parr to Ireland, Gibraltar, Malta, and South Africa, with promotion to a lieutenancy on 30 October 1869.

While serving at the Cape in 1874 Parr was appointed district staff officer for Natal, and Sir Garnet Wolseley, then high commissioner, recommended him as private secretary to J. A. Froude, who was being sent out to organize a conference on South African federation. The conference did not take place, but in 1877 Parr became successively aide-de-camp and military secretary to the high commissioner for South Africa, Sir Bartle Frere. Promoted captain on 23 January 1878, Parr was responsible for inspecting colonial units during the Cape Frontier War of 1877–8. Frere then released him to act as assistant staff officer to the ill-fated No. 3 column for the invasion of Zululand. Fortunately for Parr, he accompanied that part of the column absent from camp at Isandlwana when it was overwhelmed by the Zulu on 22 January 1879. Parr returned to Frere's staff in April and took part in Frere's negotiations with Boer representatives in the Transvaal. Apparently due to opposition from the commander-in-chief, George, duke of Cambridge, Parr failed to receive a brevet for his services in South Africa, but he was created CMG.

With Frere's recall, Parr briefly rejoined his regiment but, following the death of Sir George Colley's private secretary in action at Ingogo on 8 February 1881 during the First South African War, he was sent for as a replacement. However, Colley himself was killed at Majuba before Parr reached Natal, and he then acted as chief staff officer in Natal before taking charge of the remount depot. Parr commanded an experimental mounted infantry unit in the closing stages of the war before returning to England in May 1882. Almost at once, Wolseley appointed him to command the mounted infantry for the Egyptian campaign on 2 August. Parr was severely wounded in the leg at Tell al-Mahuta on 24 August but, on recovering, commanded the mounted police in occupied Egypt as provost marshal, receiving his brevet majority on 18 November 1882.

Subsequently, Parr transferred to the reorganized Egyptian army, and in February 1884 went to Suakin to command a mixed force of Turkish cavalry and Sudanese infantry. He was present at Tamai and received his brevet lieutenant-colonelcy on 21 May 1884. After commanding at El Shallal, he became adjutant-general of the Egyptian army, becoming colonel on 24 November 1886 and an aide-de-camp to the queen. However, his health broke in 1887 and, after declining appointment as military attaché both at Berlin and in Australia, he became assistant adjutant-general to southern command in October 1889. In 1888 Parr married Lilian, daughter of George Monck Gibbs. His eldest son died of fever while serving with Parr's former regiment on Malta in February 1910 and his second son was killed with the same regiment in December 1914.

Command of his former battalion came in November 1890 and Parr served with it in Aldershot, Gibraltar, and India, as well as being briefly attached to Sir Charles Ewan-Smith's mission to Fez in early 1892. He was made CB in 1893 and, having turned down the post of assistant adjutant-general in India, he took the appointment of assistant inspector of ordnance at the War Office. In 1898 he went to the Shorncliffe command and was promoted major-general on 1 July 1899. Parr was mentioned as a possible chief of staff to Sir Redvers Buller at the outbreak of the Second South African War, but his health was not considered sufficiently robust, and from Shorncliffe he went to command the south-east district. He moved to the north-west district in 1902 but recurring health problems led to early retirement in November 1903.

In retirement, Parr became a deputy lieutenant for Somerset and a justice of the peace in Dorset. With the creation of the Territorial Force in 1908, Parr joined the county Territorial Association for Somerset and commanded the county's contingent of the national reserve. He was made KCB in 1911. He died, shortly after writing to *The Times* to support the incorporation of the Ulster Volunteer Force within the Territorials, on 4 April 1914 at his residence, Chaffeymoor House, Bourton, in Dorset.

IAN F. W. BECKETT

Sources *Major-General Sir Henry Hallam Parr: recollections and correspondence*, ed. C. Fortescue-Brickdale (1917) • H. H. Parr, *A sketch of the Kaffir and Zulu wars* (1880) • *Army List* • *WWW* • I. Knight, *Zulu: Isandlwana and Rorke's Drift* (1992) • J. H. Lehmann, *The First Boer War* (1972) • *CGPLA Eng. & Wales* (1914)

Wealth at death £1560 0s. 7d.: probate, 20 June 1914, *CGPLA Eng. & Wales*

Parr, John (*c.*1382–1408). *See under* Parr family (*per. c.*1370–1517).

Parr, Sir John (*d.* 1475). *See under* Parr, Sir William (1434–1483).

Parr, John (*d.* 1716), nonconformist minister, was probably a Lancashire man. In the will of the regicide John Bradshaw, dated 20 March 1653, he is mentioned as 'my chaplain Mr. Parr', to whom the testator allowed '24 li. yearly for 5 years to enable him in his studies'. By a codicil of September 1655 Bradshaw revoked the legacy (Earwaker, 2.76). Parr matriculated at Trinity College, Cambridge, in 1659 and graduated BA in 1662. At some date unknown he married, and he and his wife, Elizabeth, had at least two daughters.

Parr returned to Lancashire as a ministerial candidate. In 1669 he was recorded as one of four nonconformist preachers at Darwen and other chapels in the parish of Blackburn. On the declaration of indulgence in 1672 he was licensed as a congregationalist teacher as of Farington (south-east of Preston), and preached both at Walton and Preston. In common with other nonconformists, he preached in many places throughout the 1670s and 1680s. On several occasions his activities drew the attention of the local magistrates. In January 1685 he was charged, with others, with attending a meeting in the house of Thomas Holland of Heath Charnock in the parish of Standish for the purpose of 'Exercise of religion in other maner than according to the Liturgy of the Church of England' (Nightingale, 165). He was fined £6 15*s*. He does not appear to have been ordained as a nonconformist minister until 1687. He then succeeded Thomas Key as minister of Walton Chapel in the same year. In 1689 Elswick chapel was certified for John Parr and his congregation.

On 20 October 1690 Henry Newcome recorded a visit to Preston where he met friends, one being John Parr, who was still actively preaching in Preston and Walton as well as conducting worship at Hoghton Tower. When an association of congregationalist and presbyterian ministers was established in Lancashire on the model of the 'Happy Union' in London, from 6 August 1695 onwards Parr attended the meetings as representative of the northern district, often acting as moderator. Also in August 1695, Parr was one of eight nonconformist ministers who attested that fits suffered by one Richard Dugdale, of Surey, near Whalley in Lancashire, were the result of demoniac possession, which, it was claimed, were subsequently cured by divine intervention.

In 1714 Parr was succeeded by John Turner as minister at Preston and Walton. He died in April or May 1716—Preston parish register records the burial of 'Mr. John Parr' on 4 May 1716. Administration of his estate was granted later in the same year. In his will he made generous bequests to friends and family. He bequeathed the sum of 50*s*. per annum for the poor of Preston during the life of his wife.

CATHERINE NUNN

Sources B. Nightingale, *Lancashire nonconformity*, 6 vols. [1890–93] • G. L. Turner, ed., *Original records of early nonconformity under persecution and indulgence*, 3 vols. (1911–14) • B. Nightingale, *Early stages of the Quaker movement in Lancashire* (1921) • *Calamy rev.* • A. Gordon, ed., *Freedom after ejection: a review (1690–1692) of presbyterian and congregational nonconformity in England and Wales* (1917) • *VCH Lancashire* • T. Jolley, *A vindication of the Surey demoniack* (1698) • J. P. Earwaker, *East Cheshire: past and present, or, A history of the hundred of Macclesfield*, 2 vols. (1877–80) • will, Lancs. RO, WRW/A, 1716 • *The autobiography of Henry Newcome*, ed. R. Parkinson, 2 vols., Chetham Society, 26–7 (1852) • W. A. Shaw, ed., *Minutes of the Manchester presbyterian classis*, 3 vols., Chetham Society, new ser., 20, 22, 24 (1890–91)

Wealth at death approx. £600—bequests: will, Lancs. RO, WRW/A

Parr, Katherine. *See* Katherine (1512–1548).

Parr [*née* Taylor], **Louisa Sarah Ann** (1848?–1903), novelist, was born in London, the only child of Matthew Taylor, a naval officer. She spent her early years at Plymouth, where she was educated. Her writing career began in 1868, when she published a story, 'How it all happened', under the pseudonym of Mrs Olinthus Lobb, in *Good Words*. It proved popular, appearing in a French version as a *feuilleton* in the *Journal des Débats*, the editor apologizing for departing from his rule of never printing translations. At the request of the queen of Württemberg it was translated into German, and it was issued in the United States in pamphlet form. On 16 November 1869 she married George Parr, a surgeon and collector of china, prints, fans, and early editions, and the couple settled down to a comfortable life in Kensington, London.

In 1870 Louisa Parr published *Dorothy Fox*, a novel of Quaker life, which created such a frenzy in the United States that one publisher paid £300 for the advance sheets of her next novel, *The Prescotts of Pamphillon* (1874). But neither *The Prescotts* nor its successor, *The Gosau Smithy* (1875), compared with what is generally recognized as her *tour de force*, *Adam and Eve*, published in 1880. A story of Cornish smuggling life about the roguish Adam, and Eve, his London cousin, Parr's plot is founded on incidents related in Jonathan Couch's *History of Polperro* (1871), and it was written on location in Cornwall after extensive trips through Italy, Algeria, and France. She followed this success with four more novels—*Robin* (1882), *Loyalty George* (1888), *Dumps and I* (1891), and *The Squire* (1892)—before writing her last, *Can this be Love?* (1893), the story of a young woman persecuted by her snobbish lover and his vulgar relatives. Parr also contributed stories to magazines—most notably 'The Neap Reef' to *Good Words* in 1871—and she composed a short life of her fellow novelist Dinah Mulock Craik, which appeared in *Women Novelists of Queen Victoria's Reign* (1897). The main characteristics of her work are a sense of humour and a pleasing style, though she could write pointedly about women's oppression. However, she was always at her best in dealing with the sea.

Louisa Parr died, after a week's illness, from bronchitis on 2 November 1903 at her home at 18 Upper Phillimore Place, Kensington, London. Her husband had predeceased her; they had no children.

ELIZABETH LEE, *rev.* KATHARINE CHUBBUCK

Sources H. C. Black, 'Mrs Parr', *Pen, pencil, baton and mask: biographical sketches* (1896), 57–64 • J. Sutherland, 'Parr, Louisa', *The Longman companion to Victorian fiction* (1988) • Blain, Clements & Grundy, *Feminist comp.*, 834 • R. L. Wolff, 'Parr, Louisa', *Nineteenth-century fiction: a bibliographical catalogue based on the collection formed by Robert Lee Wolff*, 3 (1984), 249–50 • *The Athenaeum* (14 Nov 1903), 653 • *The Times* (7 Nov 1903) • m. cert. • *CGPLA Eng. & Wales* (1904)

Wealth at death £6473 3*s*. 7*d*.: probate, 4 Jan 1904, *CGPLA Eng. & Wales*

Parr, Nathaniel (*d.* 1751). *See under* Parr, R. (*fl.* 1736–1751).

Parr, R. (*fl.* 1736–1751), engraver, is said to have been Remigius Parr, born in 1723 at Rochester, Kent, but, since he had engraved at least twenty-five prints of horses by 1739, this date of birth and the forename Remigius that accompanied it may be regarded with suspicion. The engraver of modest talent who signed himself 'R. Parr' usually worked with 'N. Parr', sometimes as 'Messrs. Parr' or, more commonly, 'Parr', for the leading printsellers and booksellers on a wide variety of subjects. N. Parr was undoubtedly the engraver Nathaniel Parr [*see below*] who died in 1751, and it is likely that R. Parr was the brother, Richard, who survived him. Richard Parr, born about 1707, was the son of John Parr of Weymouth and was apprenticed to William Hulett in 1722. In 1736 James Thornhill had his Weymouth church altarpiece engraved by R. Parr: 'a young man that he [Thornhill] forwarded in graving or put him prentice to it' (Vertue, *Note books*, 3.78). For John and Thomas Bowles, R. Parr engraved portraits of horses and the sea pieces after Peter Monamy and views of games after Francis Hayman that decorated Vauxhall Gardens. He engraved a large number of maps and plates for architectural books published by Robert Sayer and others. In 1747 he engraved his most ambitious prints, a pair of large views of London seen through the arches of Westminster Bridge and of the bridge with the lord mayor's show that were based on paintings by Canaletto. In that year he also produced a huge print of the trial of Lord Lovat in Westminster Hall. He did not long survive Nathaniel, although the date of his death is unknown.

Nathaniel Parr (*d.* 1751), engraver, was one of a large family; three sisters and two brothers survived him. Some of his prints are signed 'N. Parr', but his work is commonly signed 'Parr' or 'Messrs. Parr'. Nathaniel Parr emerged from anonymity in November 1749, when he was interrogated about his part in engraving a political satire, *The Agreeable Contrast*. He claimed that he had engraved 'part only' and had 'refused to be concerned further when some of the offensive part was proposed' (Atherton, 80). He engraved portraits, bookplates, maritime views, naval engagements, architectural works, and topographical views, including a set of Florence after Giuseppe Zocchi. Parr, then resident in the parish of St Clement Danes, Westminster, died between 3 December 1751, when he signed his will, detailing bequests of over £1000, and 9 December, when it was proved.

TIMOTHY CLAYTON and ANITA MCCONNELL

Sources T. Dodd, 'History of English engravers', BL, Add. MS 33403 • H. Atherton, *Political prints in the age of Hogarth* (1974) • will, PRO, PROB 11/791, sig. 340 [Nathaniel Parr] • parish register, Bunhill, PRO, R 4/372 [burial] • E. Harris and N. Savage, *British architectural books and writers, 1556–1785* (1990) • Vertue, *Note books*, 3.78 • I. Maxted, *The British book trades, 1710–1777: an index of the masters and their apprentices* (1983)

Wealth at death bequests of over £1000; Nathaniel Parr: will, PRO, PROB 11/791, sig. 340

Parr, Richard (1591/2–1644), bishop of Sodor and Man, was born of unknown parentage in Lancashire, probably in a southern parish. On 2 September 1609 he entered Brasenose College, Oxford, and matriculated as a plebeian on 24 November in the company of two of the younger sons of Sir Peter Legh of Lyme, and two of their Molyneux cousins. He graduated BA on 17 June 1613, was elected fellow on 25 January 1615, and proceeded MA on 19 April 1616. In 1616 he was also ordained, and according to James Chaloner was 'very painful to my knowledge … in reading the Arts to young Schollers'. With Thomas Legh, who had at times doubted his own calling, Parr was admitted BD on 10 June 1624.

On 16 November 1624 Parr was granted a license to

marry Elizabeth (Chicken) Raymond (*b.* 1593/4) of Peckham, Surrey, daughter of Thomas Raymond of Guildford, gentleman; the marriage apparently produced no children. Parr's reputation as a teacher may have prompted his appointment as chaplain to Thomas Wriothesley, who had that same month, at the age of sixteen, become fourth earl of Southampton. To him Parr dedicated *Concio ad clerum habita Oxoniae in comitiis* (1628), an address in Latin on a text from Revelation 3: 4, given to Oxfordshire clergy on 12 July 1625.

On 25 August 1626 Parr was instituted rector of Ladbroke, Warwickshire, close to the Spencer estates at Wormleighton and Althorp, probably through the good offices of Southampton's sister Penelope, wife of William, the future second Baron Spencer. On 6 November 1627 Parr preached plainly but effectively at the funeral of Robert, first Baron Spencer, at Great Brington, commending his patron's godliness and sense of duty, and acknowledging his own indebtedness to him. As *The End of a Perfect Man* (1628), this was the second and last of his published works.

In 1629 Parr exchanged livings with Dr Edward Brouncker, rector of Eccleston, near Chorley in Lancashire, which was then worth about £160 a year and at the disposal of the crown through the minority of Richard Lathom; he was instituted on 6 February. His ministry was soon tested by the severe plague of 1630 to 1631 in and around Preston (JRL, Legh MSS).

Having proceeded DD on 14 July 1634 (at the same time as Thomas Legh), on 10 June 1635 Parr was consecrated bishop of Sodor and Man, retaining Eccleston *in commendam*. On Man, which increasingly preoccupied him, he found it hard, despite the support of James, Lord Strange, to raise the quality of the ministry and restore the see's revenues (no more than £150 a year) and fabric. He wrily recalled one of his tutors arguing that a bishop's primary duty was to superintend—'a doctrine which goes well downe these dayes'—but, as he assured Thomas Legh in August 1638, he remained 'sure … I cannot away with preachinge' (JRL, Legh MSS). In 1641 he rebuilt Ramsey Chapel.

In October 1643 Parr was sequestered from his Eccleston living, which was given to his kinsman, and well-liked curate there in the 1630s, the presbyterian Edward Gee. He died at Bishop's Court, Peel, Isle of Man, on 23 March 1644, and was buried on 26 March in the grave of Bishop John Phillips in St German's Cathedral.

Brian Quintrell

Sources R. Parre, *Concio ad clerum habita Oxoniae in comitiis* (1628) · R. Parre, *The end of the perfect man: a sermon preached at the buriall of the Right Honorable Sir Robert Spencer* (1628) · R. Parr to T. Legh, 28 Nov 1631–3 Aug 1638, JRL, Legh MSS · state papers, domestic, Charles I, PRO, SP 16/259/78, 265/45, 271/68–9, 345/85i, 412/45i, 441/93, 1633–4, 1638–9 · J. Chaloner, *A short treatise of the Isle of Man*, ed. J. G. Cumming, Manx Society, 10 (1864) · [C. B. Heberden], ed., *Brasenose College register, 1509–1909*, 2 vols., OHS, 55 (1909) · J. L. Chester and G. J. Armytage, eds., *Allegations for marriage licences issued by the bishop of London*, 2, Harleian Society, 26 (1887), 146 · J. E. Bailey, 'Richard Parr DD., Bishop of Sodor and Man', *The Antiquary*, 9 (1884), 118–21 · B. Coward, *The Stanleys, lords Stanley and earls of Derby, 1385–1672: the origins, wealth and power of a landowning family*, Chetham Society, 3rd ser., 30 (1983) · Lady Newton [E. C. Legh], *The house of Lyme* (1917) · *VCH Lancashire*, 6.160 · H. Fishwick, ed., *Lancashire and Cheshire church surveys, 1649–1655*, Lancashire and Cheshire RS, 1 (1879) · J. Arrowsmith, ed., *The registers of the parish church of Eccleston in the county of Lancaster: christenings, burials, and weddings, 1603–1694*, Lancashire Parish Register Society, 15 (1903) · W. Harrison, *An account of the diocese of Sodor and Man*, Manx Society, 29 (1879), 19, 65 · PRO, SP 16/265/45

Archives JRL, Legh MSS, letters to Thomas Legh

Wealth at death almost certainly modest; probably under £200 p.a.; see was worth max. £150 p.a., of which archdeacon took £60: PRO, SP 16/265/45, Hugh Cannell's report, 1633 · Eccleston value approx. £160 by 1650, but had curate from 1636; minister at Parbold chapel, Eccleston Park, got £55 p.a., 1650: Fishwick, ed., *Lancashire church surveys*, 116

Parr, Richard (1616/17–1691), Church of England clergyman, was born at Fermoy, co. Cork, where his father, Richard Parr, was curate. According to his contemporary the antiquary Sir James Ware, Parr's mother was fifty-five years old when he was born. He learned Latin at a priest's school in Ireland before entering Exeter College, Oxford, at the age of eighteen as a servitor in 1635, matriculating on 6 November, graduating BA on 13 June 1639, and proceeding MA on 23 April 1642. In 1641 he was chosen as chaplain fellow on the nomination of the rector, John Prideaux, a post which he held until 1649. When James Ussher, archbishop of Armagh, found refuge in Oxford in 1642, and stayed at Exeter College, he met Parr, who at the end of 1643 accompanied him as chaplain on his journeys around England and Wales seeking shelter from the forces of parliament. Finally, in June 1646 the countess of Peterborough offered Ussher accommodation, first in London, and then in her house at Reigate in Surrey. Parr accompanied Ussher and was appointed to Reigate vicarage by its patron, Roger James, in 1646. In 1649 he married James's sister, a rich widow, Elizabeth Royse. According to his own account Parr ended his association with Ussher in 1655, a year before the primate's death.

In 1653 Parr became vicar of Camberwell, Surrey, where he served as a preacher until his death. At the Restoration he was offered due reward for his loyalty to the Anglican church, declining the deanery of Armagh and an Irish bishopric, but accepting a canonry at Armagh, and gaining an Oxford DD (30 October 1660). From about 1676 to 1682 he seems to have held Camberwell with the living of Bermondsey, Surrey. He was a popular preacher, reportedly breaking two nonconformist churches at Camberwell by 'outvying the presbyterians and Independents in his extemporary preaching' (*Whole Works of Sir James Ware*, 2.206). He died at Camberwell on 2 November 1691, aged seventy-four.

Parr's most lasting achievement was his life of Ussher, which was printed in 1686 together with a lengthy selection from the primate's letters. Parr's purpose was somewhat different from that of Ussher's previous biographer, his other chaplain, Nicholas Bernard. Where Bernard had emphasized Ussher's Calvinism and friendly relations with puritans Parr sought to establish Ussher as a moderate protestant, even an Anglican, defending the Church of

England against both nonconformity and, more especially, Roman Catholicism. The latter, of course, was especially controversial in the 1680s, with a Catholic king threatening the security of the protestant establishment. Parr pointedly stressed Ussher's anti-Catholic theological works and his dislike of toleration for Catholicism, relating how the primate as a young man 'was deeply touched with the sense of the evil of such an indulgence' (Parr, 9). He had, as a result, considerable difficulty in getting the book past the censors. Faced with a considerable delay he appealed to Archbishop Sancroft, but eventually had to make a series of cuts, removing offending passages. Parr's remained the standard edition of the letters and the fullest life until that of Elrington and Todd in the mid-nineteenth century. ALAN FORD

Sources Foster, *Alum. Oxon.* • Wood, *Ath. Oxon.*, new edn, 4.172, 341 • Bodl. Oxf., MS Tanner 483 • R. Parr, ed., *The life of the most reverend father in God, James Usher … with a collection of three hundred letters* (1686) • *The whole works of Sir James Ware concerning Ireland*, ed. and trans. W. Harris, rev. edn, 2 (1764), 206–7 • *The whole works of … James Ussher*, ed. C. R. Elrington and J. H. Todd, 17 vols. (1847–64), vols. 1, 15–16

Archives Bodl. Oxf., letters | BL, letters to E. Borlase, Sloane MS 1008

Parr, Sir Robert John (1862–1931), promoter of children's welfare, was born on 12 April 1862 at Merton Lodge, Torquay, Devon, son of John Parr, a working gardener who never earned more than £3 a week, and his wife, Miriam Grace Tucker. Parr attended Trinity School, an elementary school in Torquay. He was greatly impressed by its master, Thomas Raikes, who seldom resorted to physical chastisement. After leaving school at twelve Parr worked as a gardener and attended night classes in Torquay. Taken on as a clerk by a local coal merchant he learned accountancy, then became a tax assessor. Parr learned public speaking through his involvement in the local parliamentary debating society, where he was a whip.

Parr had a strong social conscience, and despite his other activities served as honorary secretary of the local committees of several voluntary organizations. A fellow member of the local Charity Organization Society branch was Lady Fitzgerald, who was also a member of the central executive committee of the National Society for the Prevention of Cruelty to Children (NSPCC). Founded in 1884 as the London Society for the Prevention of Cruelty to Children, to protect children at risk of abuse and to support families in crisis, the NSPCC had recently come under investigation into its financial management. Its founder and first director, the Revd Benjamin Waugh, needed someone with financial training to assist him. Lady Fitzgerald recommended Parr for the task, and he started work on 10 April 1899. At first Parr was designated a speaker, often standing in for Waugh at NSPCC meetings throughout the country. He was made assistant secretary in 1901. Three years later the NSPCC obtained its important and unique 'authorized status', enabling its inspectors to remove children from abusive or neglectful homes without police involvement, as long as a justice of the peace consented. When Waugh retired in June 1905, Parr succeeded him as director.

Sir Robert John Parr (1862–1931), by unknown photographer, *c*.1925

Parr's time as director of the NSPCC saw the passing of several landmark pieces of legislation in which the society was involved. The 1907 Probation of Offenders Act enabled minor offenders to serve probation rather than imprisonment, helping to prevent the unnecessary imprisonment of a family's wage-earner. NSPCC inspectors often supervised probations relating to child abuse and neglect. The first juvenile courts were set up as a result of the 1908 Children Act. The 1908 Punishment of Incest Act made sexual abuse within families a civil, rather than ecclesiastical, matter. In addition Parr brought submissions to the royal commission on the care and control of the feeble-minded in 1909, and in 1913 to the royal commission on divorce and matrimonial cases. Keen to promote international collaboration in child protection, he addressed the International Humane Conference at Washington, DC in October 1910. He visited the USA again in 1913, and Cape Town in 1926–7. The NSPCC started a medical branch in 1920, which provided London children with free transport to and from hospital. In 1910 Parr had written in his pamphlet *Canal Boat Children* that they generally lived in appalling conditions, and received no education. An NSPCC inspector was appointed in 1920 specifically to help them. From 1922 NSPCC officers provided advice and practical help on the care of children, in addition to investigating cruelty.

In addition to his administrative duties Parr wrote widely on child protection issues, and was the author of more than fifty monographs and nineteen journal articles. He was appointed OBE in 1917 and elected to a fellowship of the British Empire Exhibition in 1924. Parr received a knighthood on 22 February 1926. During his career he acted as the legal guardian of hundreds of young people, with whom he kept up correspondence long into their adulthood. He never married.

Because of ill health Parr stood down from some duties as director in June 1924, retiring in May 1927. However, he continued to act as consulting director of the society until he died at his home, Oak Lodge, Crouch Oak Lane, Addlestone, Surrey, on 10 April 1931. There was a memorial service at St Martin-in-the-Fields, London, the same day, and he was cremated at Woking on 15 April.

NICHOLAS MALTON

Sources R. J. Parr, 'In the days of my youth', undated manuscript autobiographical account, National Society for the Prevention of Cruelty to Children Archive, London, ref. 246/31/1 • A. Morton, *The directorate of Sir Robert Parr* (1954) • R. J. Parr, untitled autobiographical account of how he came to work for the NSPCC, National Society for the Prevention of Cruelty to Children Archive, London, ref. 246/31/2 • 'Death of Sir Robert Parr', *Child's Guardian*, 41/5 (May 1931), 33–5 • 'A historical note: 1899, 1905, 1927', *Annual Report* [National Society for the Prevention of Cruelty to Children] (1927), 5–6 • 'In memoriam: Robert John Parr, knight, director 1905–1927', *Annual Report* [National Society for the Prevention of Cruelty to Children] (1931), 4 • R. J. Parr, *Canal boat children* (1910) • R. J. Parr, *International federation* (1910) • *CGPLA Eng. & Wales* (1931) • b. cert. • d. cert.

Archives National Society for the Prevention of Cruelty to Children Archive, London, MSS

Likenesses photograph, *c.*1925, National Society for the Prevention of Cruelty to Children Archive, London, 195/4/3 [*see illus.*]

Wealth at death £9278 13*s.* 9*d.*: probate, 9 July 1931, *CGPLA Eng. & Wales*

Parr, Samuel (1747–1825), schoolmaster, was born on 15 January 1747 at Harrow on the Hill, the elder of the two children of Samuel Parr (1712–1766), surgeon and apothecary, and his first wife, Anne (*bap.* 1711/12, *d.* 1762), daughter of Leonard and Elizabeth Mignard. His father had been apprenticed to Mignard, a Huguenot surgeon, and moved with him to Harrow and succeeded to the business on his death. His family claimed to be descended from the family of Henry VIII's wife Katherine Parr, but their earliest definite ancestry began when they settled in Leicestershire in the later seventeenth century, with a succession of high-church clergymen who were tories and Jacobites. Among these was his grandfather Samuel Parr, vicar of Hinckley (1704–20); Parr's father upheld the family tradition by giving in 1745 some £800 (nearly all his early savings) to the Young Pretender (Charles Edward Stuart). This financial loss led him to abandon his Jacobitism, though he remained a firm tory.

School and university Parr's father was a determined and educated man who taught his only son Latin grammar at the age of four. Parr was a precocious child and later stated that he could recall being suckled by his mother. Three months after his fifth birthday he became a home-boarder at Harrow School, then achieving a national reputation

Samuel Parr (1747–1825), by George Dawe, *c.*1813 [replica]

through its patronage by leading whig families, and there he was converted to whiggism. Two of his friends there were William Bennet, later a bishop in Ireland, and the future Sir William Jones, the orientalist. Though rivals in the schoolroom they shared literary interests, writing tragedies and imitations of Swift, Addison, and Johnson, becoming rulers of imaginary Greek states in the fields around Harrow, and even disputing in logic and metaphysics. Parr was flogged only once at Harrow, for bad handwriting, and to no effect. His writing remained atrocious all his life, so much so that on an occasion when he wrote to ask for 'two lobsters' his friend read the words as 'two eggs'. He was an excellent pupil, making his first Latin verses at the age of eight, and was top of the school when he was fourteen, but in the spring of 1761 he was taken away to become his father's apprentice.

Parr found rolling pills and compounding potions tedious, could not endure surgical operations, and derided the Latin of the prescriptions without making them up properly. He sought to continue his education by propping his Latin and Greek books against his gallipots and obtaining notes of the school lessons from Jones and Bennet until they went to university. His mother died on 5 November 1762, and within a year his father married Margaret Cox, daughter of the dissolute Dr James Cox, who was dismissed from the headmastership of Harrow. His stepmother wanted him away from the house and persuaded his father to allow him to go to Cambridge to prepare for ordination, which had been his wish since he had played at preaching sermons as a child.

Although his stepmother disliked the expense, Parr

eventually matriculated from Emmanuel College, Cambridge, as a sizar in Michaelmas 1765, but his father died suddenly of apoplexy on 25 January 1766, and his stepmother's allowance would not pay his bills. A founder's exhibition from the Harrow School governors kept him in residence throughout 1766, but then he had to go down. He kept his name on the college books intending to become a 'ten-year man', which meant that as a clergyman of ten years' standing he would then qualify under a university rule to become a bachelor of divinity.

Ordination and teaching Parr was helped in his career by Robert Sumner, his old headmaster, who in November 1766 appointed him first assistant in Harrow School. Parr began work in the post in January 1767 and enjoyed an income of about £100 p.a., consisting of £50 salary and about the same amount in fees from private pupils. He was ordained deacon by Richard Yerrick, bishop of London, on Christmas eve 1769, and for a short time he served curacies at the neighbouring parishes of Willesden and Kingsbury. Under Sumner's able headship numbers at the school rose from 80 in 1760 to 250 in 1771; Richard Brinsley Sheridan was one of the more illustrious pupils. William Beloe, the classical scholar and translator, who was a pupil of Parr, declared that he was 'a great dragon of learning', but a 'severe, wayward and irregular' schoolmaster (Derry, 29). Parr was as devoted to flogging as any contemporary master, but his use of the rod varied according to his inconsistent temper. Sometimes it was unused; at other times it was continually in his hand. When he was in a whipping mood he would birch boys in advance, promising them that their next fault would go unpunished, an often forgotten assurance. Yet he took a keen interest in his pupils and was ready to help them in time of need. Lord Holland recounted that he had heard Sheridan say 'with tears in his eyes that he never met with kindness at school but from Dr. Parr' (Lord Holland, *Further Memoirs of the Whig Party*, ed. Lord Stavordale, 1905, 240). The boys even boasted of his prowess with the rod, and he was popular with them.

On 12 September 1771 Sumner died suddenly. Parr's colleagues agreed that he should apply for the post of headmaster. As a master's degree was required for this, he successfully petitioned the duke of Grafton, chancellor of Cambridge University, for this *per litteras regias*. Influential parents supported him, particularly William Legge, second earl of Dartmouth, who had three sons at the school. The governors, however, appointed an Eton master, Benjamin Heath. Parr's youth probably told against him, though he himself blamed his having voted for John Wilkes at the Middlesex election. The news of the governors' action resulted in a riot among the Harrow boys. The governors were threatened with bludgeons, and one of them had his chaise broken in pieces and another his windows smashed. A ringleader, Thomas Grimston, recounted that Parr 'thanked us for the great love we bore to him, which, he said, was made too plain, he was afraid by our mischief on his account … A great many boys were in tears' (*Du Cane MSS*, 231).

The indignant Parr decided to establish a rival school. Supported by loans from Harrow parents, including £2000 from William Sumner, brother of Robert Sumner, he opened this in a large house at Stanmore on 14 October 1771. He was joined by David Roderick, the second assistant from Harrow, and by forty of his former pupils. He now began to wear a wig and to don clerical attire, which made him look a dozen years older; according to Roderick he sometimes appeared ridiculous:

> by riding in high Prelatical pomp through the streets, on a black saddle, bearing in his hand a long cane, such as women used to have, with an ivory head like a crosier, which was probably why he liked it,

yet at other times he went 'stalking through the town in a dirty striped morning-gown' (*Works*, 1.75). In November 1771 Parr married Jane (1747–1810), only daughter of Zechariah Marsingale of Carleton, Yorkshire, and his wife, the eldest daughter of Timothy Mauleverer. Parr's biographer John Johnstone stated, 'The marriage was managed for him by Dr. Askew. Mrs. Askew was the intimate friend of Miss Marsingale, and the prudence of the young lady was supposed a necessary support to the young scholar in his establishment' (ibid., 1.644). The marriage was unsuccessful. Mrs Parr was hot-tempered and sarcastic, and publicly criticized her husband. Parr told Jeremy Bentham that 'their mode of living together' was 'cohabiting in one sense and no longer in another' (Barker, 2.32–3). The Parrs had three daughters: Sarah Anne, who was born at Stanmore on 31 December 1772; Eliza Jane, born at Colchester on 26 May 1778 and died at Norwich on 29 May 1779; and Catherine Jane, born at Norwich on 13 June 1782. In addition Parr maintained and educated for several years his orphaned godson, Samuel Parr Foster, and helped to support his widowed sister, Dorothy, and her young daughter.

Parr followed at Stanmore the usual classical curriculum, with some innovations. His was the first English school to act a Greek play. He organized this after hearing from Thomas Sheridan that his father, Swift's schoolmaster, had got his pupils to perform a Greek play in Dublin. He chose the play *Oedipus Tyrannus* (though without the choruses) and borrowed costumes from Garrick. This was so successful that he then produced the *Trachiniae* of Sophocles. He allowed the boys to compose English poetry instead of classical verses, with the threat of flogging if the English were bad. When boys quarrelled he encouraged them to fight each other where he could see them from his study window. And he arranged social meetings at which the boys engaged in literary discussions, and unusually encouraged them to engage in athletic sports and cricket matches, which he watched while smoking his pipe.

The Stanmore School, however, did not succeed. It never had more than sixty pupils, including those from Harrow, who were mostly approaching the age to leave school, and there were no new admissions when they left. Parr closed the school in 1777 and obtained the mastership of Colchester grammar school. He secured through Bennet Langton a recommendation from Dr Johnson, who appeared to know him personally. He had been ordained priest on 15 March 1775 and at Colchester served as curate to Dr Nathaniel Forster, rector of All Saints, with whom he became a firm friend, as he did also with Thomas Twining, curate of Fordham. Parr took some twenty pupils with him to Colchester, but the school did not flourish, and he quarrelled with the trustees.

Parr was elected headmaster of Norwich grammar school in August 1778, and went there early the next year. 'Parr's fame for severity', stated a Norwich pupil,

> spread a sort of panic through the city, especially among the mothers, who would sometimes interpose a remonstrance, which occasioned a ludicrous scene, but seldom availed the culprit, while the wiser were willing to leave their boys in his hands. (Barker, 1.227–8)

But Twining, advising his brother Richard, the tea merchant, to send his son to Norwich, wrote, 'I have been told that he flogs too much, but I doubt those from whom I have heard it think *any* use of punishment too much' (*Works*, 1.100). Parr's daily teaching was interrupted at midday by his sending a boy to the pastry-cook's across the road for a pie, which he ate by the schoolroom fire; he ended the afternoon's lessons by birching those promised this punishment during the day.

Soon after going to Norwich, Parr decided to acquire a doctorate. As this was easier to do in civil law than in divinity, he prepared two Latin theses and in 1781 defended them in the law schools at Cambridge. These exercises gained him the degree of LLD and were highly praised by the professor of civil law, but were never published. His first publication, in 1780, consisted of two sermons he preached while a curate at Norwich, and these increased his reputation.

A parish priest In spring 1780 Lady Trafford, the mother of one of Parr's pupils, presented him to the perpetual curacy of Asterby in Lincolnshire, worth, after payment of a curate, £36 a year. In 1783 she presented him to the perpetual curacy of Hatton in Warwickshire, worth about £100 a year, whereupon he resigned Asterby in favour of his curate. He resolved to settle at Hatton and to take private pupils, and so resigned the headmastership of Norwich at Michaelmas 1785. It was stated that this meant that 'an object of terror was gone, but the glory of the place had gone with it' (Derry, 48). Parr lived at Hatton for the remaining thirty-nine years of his life. During that time he became widely known for engaging in disputation, scholarship, and politics, but he also devoted himself to the pastoral care of the parish, which resulted 'in the improved manners of his parishioners, in their habits of industry and regularity and in the exercise of that peaceable and neighbourly disposition' (Barker, 1.64).

Parr performed his ministry in a sober, old-fashioned style, condemning the evangelicals as 'inflammatory'. He accepted no current churchmanship. While friendly with Martin Routh, he disliked his high-church theology. His outlook was latitudinarian, and he upheld both the church and religious liberty. His sermons were often too academic for his rural hearers, but he diligently visited the sick and helped the poor. He made the May Day festivities the village's great annual celebration. To the church he added a new peal of bells, with the help of subscriptions from his pupils and friends; a chandelier and a painted window in the chancel; and a vestry in which he smoked his pipe before and after services.

To Hatton parsonage Parr added studies, bedrooms for his pupils, and a library for his four thousand books, which were to increase to over ten thousand. He took in seven pupils at a time and charged them £100 p.a., which formed the large part of his income. Wearing his old dressing gown and red nightcap, he taught his pupils each morning in the library. Among his pupils at Hatton were Richard Sheridan's son Tom, Augustus Legge, John Johnstone, and John Bartlan, who later became Parr's companion and amanuensis. Although never formally his tutor, Parr was the mentor and friend of Walter Savage Landor. Despite being able to attract enough pupils, Parr was on the look-out for further preferment in the church. Lord Dartmouth sought for him a prebend at Norwich in the gift of Baron Thurlow, the lord chancellor, who refused with a characteristic oath, but Dartmouth did persuade Robert Lowth, his former diocesan at Colchester and by then bishop of London, to collate Parr in 1783 to the prebend of Wenlock Barnes in St Paul's Cathedral, which was worth only £20 a year.

Controversy At this time Parr became involved in three controversies which brought him celebrity. Henry Homer, a classical scholar, wished to publish a new edition of three treatises by William Bellenden, a sixteenth-century Scottish professor and diplomat, and asked Parr to write a Latin dedication and preface for the book. Bellenden's unfinished treatise 'De tribus luminibus Romanorum' suggested to Parr that Britain had its own luminaries, and Homer agreed that the venture should be used to support the contemporary whig cause by having the treatise dedicated to the 'tria lumina Anglorum'—Burke, North, and Fox. The preface was then enlarged into a political tract supporting the coalition of these three politicians and attacking the younger Pitt and his government. The *Praefatio ad Bellendenum* appeared anonymously in 1787, but gradually the authorship became known first to scholars and then was more widely publicized when the work was translated into English.

Parr's next publication came in 1789. The year before, Richard Hurd, a Pittite and Parr's own diocesan as bishop of Worcester, published the works of his friend William Warburton, bishop of Gloucester, but omitted two early tracts which detracted from Warburton's reputation. Parr had disliked Hurd since hearing that he had contemptuously described his preaching at Norwich as 'Parr's long vernacular sermons' (Barker, 2.331–2). Parr's anonymously published *Tracts by Warburton and a Warburtonian, not admitted into the collection of their respective works* consisted of the two tracts by Warburton together with two youthful pamphlets by Hurd, which he wanted to suppress, and an acrimonious epistle dedicated to Hurd. Parr's mischief-making met with general condemnation, but before his tracts appeared he inadvertently became involved in another literary dispute.

Dr Joseph White, Laudian professor of Arabic at Oxford,

was appointed in 1783 to deliver the Bampton lectures. He asked for help in preparing them from Parr, who agreed; but Parr did not know that White had already obtained assistance from Samuel Badcock, the minister of a dissenting congregation in Devon. White gave the lectures very successfully in 1784, but, the year after Badcock's death in 1788, White was accused of having engaged him to write them. Parr in astonishment asserted that he had written a part. A meeting in Parr's house, attended by White, resulted in 1790 in White's publication of a 'statement' that Badcock had written rather more than a third of them and Parr, excluding corrections, about a fifth.

Parr's increasing reputation brought him no important ecclesiastical post. His origins were too humble to give him family connections and patronage, and he lived too late for his whiggism to bring him preferment. His incumbency at Hatton might have appeared to proceed on an eighteenth-century course, for in 1789 he exchanged his perpetual curacy for the rectory of Wadenhoe in Northamptonshire, but this was purely a legal arrangement to enable the rector, Nathaniel Bridges, to accept a benefice in Warwickshire which could be held in plurality only with a perpetual curacy. Parr retained his parsonage and the pastoral care of Hatton, calling himself resident minister or deputy curate. Bridges, as the legal incumbent, had to preach on certain Sundays each year. He was an evangelical, whom Parr termed a 'Methodistical Enthusiast'; on one Sunday, after his departure, Parr warned the congregation about his sermons, saying 'think of them no more, forget them, reject them' (Derry, 166).

For some years Parr was in financial difficulty, and about 1798 he gave up taking pupils, as his support of the French Revolution had caused a decline in their numbers. Early in the nineteenth century, however, his circumstances improved. Although John Horne Tooke and Parr disliked each other, Horne Tooke nevertheless declared he would present him to the rectory of Graffham in Northamptonshire because of his learned reputation. However, Sir Francis Burdett considered Horne Tooke not sufficiently wealthy to be such a great patron, and so bought the advowson and in 1802 presented Parr to the living, which was worth £200 a year. In 1804 Parr gained possession of the expired lease of the estate endowing his prebend at St Paul's Cathedral. It was in an expanding part of northern London, and he succeeded, through leasing out the increasingly valuable land, in raising his prebendal stipend to £900 by 1820.

Political involvement In 1789 Parr preached a charity sermon in Birmingham parish church. In it he made a pioneering reference to the evils of child labour, and the need for the education of the poor, but he startled the congregation by praising Joseph Priestley, the radical minister of the New Meeting-House in Birmingham, as 'one of the brightest ornaments of the age', who, though holding 'dangerous tenets upon a few controversial subjects', was yet 'a profound philosopher, a philanthropic Citizen and a pious Christian' (Derry, 131). Parr had first met Priestley in the previous July at the induction of his Unitarian friend (and future biographer) William Field to the High Street Chapel in Warwick, and become a close acquaintance. In July 1791 a crowd wrecked Priestley's house, destroying nearly all the books, papers, and scientific apparatus, which made Parr fear that his parsonage at Hatton might also be attacked. His books were taken in farm carts to be stored for several weeks at Magdalen College, Oxford. Soon afterwards he was asked at a function to propose the toast of church and king. He did so 'with my own comment', saying, 'Once it was the toast of Jacobites; now it is the toast of incendiaries. It means a Church without the Gospel and a King above the laws' (Field, 1.309).

Parr was now known for supporting reformers and philanthropists on such issues as religious toleration, legal reform, and slavery, but he once more became embroiled in literary disputes. For several years he had assisted Henry Homer and Dr Charles Combe, a Harrow schoolfellow, to produce an edition of Horace. After Homer's death in 1791, Combe continued the work on his own, but when it appeared in 1793, he advertised that it had been overseen by Parr. Anxious to maintain his scholarly reputation, Parr reviewed the work for the *British Critic* (January–April 1794) and criticized in great detail the quality of Combe's editing. Combe responded by publishing *A Statement of Facts* (1794), in which he accused Parr of swindling Homer, and Parr was forced to defend himself in *Remarks on the Statement of Dr. Charles Combe* (1795). Parr certainly courted controversy, and he took the opportunity to attack modern moralists, particularly William Godwin, when he was invited to preach the Spital sermon before the court of aldermen at Christ Church Greyfriars, London, on Easter Tuesday in 1800. Gracing the occasion with a new sermon and a new wig, he preached for two hours; the lord mayor, a Foxite, declared that he had liked all he had heard except the quarters chimed by the church clock. Parr's main theme was to attack Godwin's theory of universal benevolence as expressed in his *Concerning Political Justice* (1793), which held that, since mankind is by nature good, man could attain perfection if not subject to external restraint and allowed by government to exist on a voluntary basis. Godwin replied vehemently to the criticisms in a pamphlet published in 1802.

For some twenty years Charles James Fox was a political hero to Parr, who became nicknamed the Jacobinical Parson. When Fox died in 1806, Parr followed the bier at his funeral in Westminster Abbey and commemorated him by publishing in 1809 the heterogeneous two volumes of *Characters of Charles James Fox*. The first volume comprises newspaper obituaries of Fox, funeral sermons by whig divines, his own eulogy of Fox from the *Praefatio ad Bellendenum*, and finally a long letter upon Fox by Parr to Coke of Holkham. The second, larger volume consists of a multiplicity of notes, notes upon notes, extra notes and additions to notes, and then a discursive review of Fox's history of James II.

These curious volumes were Parr's last work. He was now facing family troubles. On 22 November 1805 his youngest daughter, Catherine Jane, died of tuberculosis, and he grievously missed her gentleness and amiability. His eldest daughter, Sarah Anne, had eloped in 1797 with one of his pupils, John Wynne, the son of a Welsh country gentleman, but in 1808, after the birth of three daughters, they separated. She went to live at Shrewsbury, but her health broke down, and she was taken to Teignmouth in Devon by her mother. Mrs Parr was called upon to give evidence at the trial in Shrewsbury of Wynne, who was being sued by his landlord for unpaid bills; on her return journey she caught a chill, and died at Teignmouth on 9 April 1810. Sarah Wynne's youngest daughter died on 26 May and she herself on 8 July at Hatton. Her two surviving daughters came to Hatton several times until 1813, when their father insisted on keeping them entirely to himself.

On 17 December 1816 Parr married Mary Eyre (1765–1848), daughter of John and Mary Eyre of Coventry. She was the sister of his old friend James *Eyre (1748–1813), for whom Parr had obtained the benefice of Winterbourne in Wiltshire when it was offered to himself by Lord Chedworth in 1801. This marriage proved successful, and Parr enjoyed greater domestic ease than ever before. His son-in-law, Wynne, also married again, and Parr's two surviving granddaughters were now able to spend much of their time at Hatton parsonage.

Last years George IV's accession late in January 1820 brought Parr into public affairs for the last time when the new king ordered the privy council not to include Queen Caroline's name in the church services. Parr entered a formal protest in the prayer book at Hatton, and after her return to England he constantly attended her. She made him her chaplain, and he persuaded her to make his friend Robert Fellowes her secretary to answer the numerous public addresses reaching her. When her solicitor-general, Thomas Denman, was to appear for her before the House of Lords, Parr spent hours with him in the library of Holland House finding classical allusions for his speech.

Meanwhile, early in January 1820 Parr caught a cold which was complicated by erysipelas, and despite his robust constitution he never recovered completely. Nevertheless, he insisted on celebrating his seventy-third birthday among his numerous friends. With bandaged hands he could not dine with them on the turbot, venison, game, and pie, but he joined in the toasts, a servant holding the glass of wine to his lips, and a village boy held his pipe. Then he retired to bed with a basin of gruel. He became well enough, however, to resume his correspondence and his excursions: he made several trips to Cambridge, where he enjoyed being taken by the provost of King's College on a coach drive to the Gog Magog Hills, and dining on sucking-pig at high table. On the third Sunday in January 1825 he took not only the regular services but also a christening and a funeral, and he again caught a cold and developed erysipelas. He bore a long illness with patience and piety, and died at Hatton parsonage on 6 March 1825. The funeral service was conducted by Rann Kennedy, a master at King Edward's School, Birmingham, and a sermon was preached by Samuel Butler, later bishop of Lichfield. Parr was buried in the chancel next to his first wife, and the mural monument bears an epitaph which he wrote for them both. He chose to be remembered solely for the service he had given his parish for nearly forty years.

Parr has commonly been known as the Whig Johnson. He usually dressed as slovenly as Johnson and his chief power lay in his conversation. Bennet Langton recorded that he spent an evening with Johnson, who 'was much pleased with the conversation of that learned gentleman' (Boswell, *Life*, 4.15). However, though Parr did not have the benefit of a Boswell, his conversation was apparently very inferior to Johnson's. He was famous for his forceful personality and vast erudition, though his learned English writings are marked by mannerism and verbosity which make them largely unreadable, and they have proved to be of no lasting interest. He acquired a contemporary reputation as a Latin scholar without leaving any work to account for this. He excelled in writing Latin epitaphs—notably the epitaph which he was asked to compose for Dr Johnson's monument in St Paul's Cathedral. His interest in public affairs and prominent pamphleteering made him a minor ecclesiastical and political figure. Probably his greatest success was as a schoolmaster in his earlier life. LEONARD W. COWIE

Sources W. Derry, *Dr Parr: a portrait of the whig Dr Johnson* (1966) · H. G. Bohn, *Bibliotheca Parriana* (1827) · W. Field, *Memoirs of the life, writings and opinions of the Rev. Samuel Parr*, 2 vols. (1828) · T. Harwood, *Aphorisms … of the late Dr. Parr* (1826) · *The works of Samuel Parr … with memoirs of his life and writings*, ed. J. Johnstone, 8 vols. (1828) · *Parriana, or, Notices of the Rev. Samuel Parr*, ed. E. H. Barker, 2 vols. (1828–9) · E. Calcraft, *A sketch of the late Rev. Samuel Parr* (1825) · *The collected writings of Thomas De Quincey*, ed. D. Masson, new edn, 14 vols. (1889–90), vol. 5 · P. Colson, *Private portraits* (1948) · H. J. Nichols, *Great scholars* (1881) · *DNB* · *IGI*

Archives Bodl. Oxf., corresp. and papers, MSS Eng. misc. 379–549 | BL, letters to T. Burgess, Add. MSS 34583–34586, 46847 · BL, corresp. with S. Butler, Add. MSS 34583–34585 · BL, corresp. with Lord Holland, Add. MSS 51651–51652 · Bodl. Oxf., letters to E. H. Barker · CKS, letters to William Pitt · Holkham Hall, Norfolk, letters to T. W. Coke · Magd. Oxf., corresp. with M. J. Routh, MSS 462–491 · Staffs. RO, corresp. with Lord Dartmouth, D. 742–4544, *passim* · UCL, letters to John Parkes and Samuel Parkes · Yale U., corresp. relating to epitaph for Samuel Johnson, C505

Likenesses J. Sayers, caricature, etching, pubd 1787, NPG · G. Romney, oils, 1788, Emmanuel College, Cambridge · J. Sayers, etching, pubd 1800 (after his earlier work), NPG · W. Say, mezzotint, pubd 1804 (after W. Artaud), BM, NPG · L. de Longastre, print, 1805 (after engraving by W. Skelton), repro. in Bohn, *Bibliotheca Parriana*, frontispiece · J. Opie, oils, exh. RA 1807, Holkham Hall, Norfolk · T. Kirkby, oils, 1811, Harrow School · G. Dawe, oils, 1813, St John Cam. · G. Dawe, oils, replica, *c*.1813, NPG [*see illus.*] · J. Lonsdale, oils, *c*.1823, FM Cam. · A. Chisholm, lithograph, BM, NPG

Wealth at death £30,000 to Caroline Lynes; £10,000 to Augusta Wynne; £4000 and £300 p.a. to Mrs Parr: Bodl. Oxf., Eng. misc. c. 397 e (1819)

Parr, Susanna (*fl.* 1650–1659), religious writer, is of unknown parents and background. Nothing is known of her early life, but by 1654 she had married a Mr Parr. What is known of Susanna is chronicled in six or more pamphlets documenting religious disputes in Exeter in the 1650s. As the author of at least one of these pamphlets she had evidently received some degree of education.

By her own account Susanna Parr had longed during the 1640s for a more 'thorough Reformation' of religious life.

Impressed with the New England model of congregational polity, in 1650 she joined a new meeting held in Exeter Cathedral. This tiny Independent congregation called Lewis Stucley as minister in the same year, and Susanna remained in active fellowship with it for a number of years. However, about 1654 she fell away from the meeting, having come to doubt the validity of separating from the 'true church', and began to attend the congregation of the presbyterian minister Thomas Ford. Stucley responded by initiating proceedings against Susanna. Messengers were sent to persuade her to stop attending Ford's church. When she did not comply, Stucley held public meetings in order to charge her with 'contention' and 'hearing another preacher' (Parr, *Susanna's Apologie*, 17), which according to an elder 'the church neither could nor would bear' (ibid., 18). Stucley continued publicly to reprove Susanna, proclaiming a day of humiliation and fasting against her. When she protested at the injustice of his actions, Stucley replied that she 'should have her affections tied up in their society [alone]' (ibid., 21), and declared that in hearing another preacher she 'might as well delight in another man that was not [her] husband' (ibid., 25). Objecting to this 'gross disorder' Susanna avowed that marital relationships were altogether different from those of church members to their pastor. She then sent letters to the church asking for reconciliation according to biblical principles. Her requests were met with silence.

Susanna turned her attention toward the ministers of Exeter, desiring to be admitted into fellowship and communion with them. Thomas Ford and John Barlett ruled that Stucley's charges against her had been 'partly doubtful, partly proofless, and partly frivolous' (Parr, *Susanna's Apologie*, 39–40) and welcomed her into their church. However, Stucley's church continued to hound Susanna and the dispute was reignited in 1657. In that year Mary Allein, another female member of Stucley's congregation with strong religious convictions, became uncomfortable when a petition calling on Cromwell to reject the offer of the crown and dissolve parliament was circulated at the meeting. Arguing that as a church they had no right to meddle in secular affairs, Mary ceased to attend the meeting. Soon afterwards Susanna and Mary each received notice that unless they satisfied the church Stucley's congregation would excommunicate them on charges of contentiousness, censoriousness, and lying, even though no charge had ever been proven and despite their withdrawal from the meeting. Significantly, Mary's husband, Toby Allein, a prominent local politician who had withdrawn from the congregation under the influence of his wife, was never threatened with a similar charge.

Susanna Parr and Mary Allein wrote a joint reply to be read before Stucley's congregation in which they answered the charges against them. They requested an impartial hearing, that they be shown their errors from scripture, and that the church reconsider such a rash action. When Stucley received the letter, he read, folded, and pocketed it without sharing its message with his flock. He then proceeded with a sermon of excommunication against the women, 'Upon pronouncing of which Sentence the Church made a hideous howling cry, that did even astonish divers then present' (Allein, *Truths Manifest*, 20). In response came the 114-page *Susanna's Apologie Against the Elders, or, A Vindication of Susanna Parr, Composed by her Self* (1659), the author certain that by contesting her innocence in the public arena, she was 'in danger of losing more in all likelihood, rather than regaining what is already lost' (Parr, *Susanna's Apologie*, sig. A2). Nothing more is known of the courageous Susanna Parr. However, what she gained through her apologia was a platform from which to express a theological, rational defence in a manner that justified her actions during the dispute as perhaps the most prudent and spiritually motivated of them all. KAREN O'DELL BULLOCK

Sources S. Parr, *Susanna's apologie against the elders* (1659) · T. Allein, *Truths manifest* (1658) · T. Allein, *Truths manifest revived* (1659) · E. T., *Diotrephes detected, corrected, and rejected* (1658) · P. Crawford, *Women and religion in England, 1500–1720* (1993), 152–9

Parr, Sir Thomas (1407/8–1461). *See under* Parr family (*per. c.*1370–1517).

Parr, Sir Thomas (1478–1517). *See under* Parr family (*per. c.*1370–1517).

Parr, Thomas [*called* Old Parr] (*d.* **1635**), supposed centenarian, was reputedly the son of John Parr, husbandman, of Winnington in the parish of Alberbury, Shropshire. He came to public notice in 1635, when John Taylor, the 'Water Poet', published a colourful account of Parr's life in a pamphlet entitled *The Old, Old, Very Old Man*; this was accompanied by two anonymous broadsides in which the story of Parr was further elaborated.

According to these accounts, Parr was born in 1483. He entered service at the age of seventeen, and eighteen years later succeeded his father as a husbandman in Winnington, subsequently being granted—by successive members of a family named Porter—three twenty-one-year renewals of the lease of his holding, and finally a lease for life. He remained a bachelor until he was eighty, when he married Jane, daughter of John Taylor (no relation to the Water Poet). They had a son, John, and a daughter, Jane, both of whom died in infancy. At the age of 105 Parr did penance in a sheet in Alberbury church for committing adultery with Katherine Milton. His wife died after they had been married for thirty-two years. Parr remained a widower for a decade and then, at the age of 122, married Jane, widow of Anthony Adda, of Guilsfield, Montgomeryshire, and daughter of John Lloyd (or Floyd).

By 1635 Parr was blind and had only one tooth, but his beard was neat, his hearing and digestion were good, and he slept well. In that year the great collector Thomas Howard, fourteenth earl of Arundel, visiting his estates in Shropshire, learned of this 'remarkable piece of antiquity' and decided to add him to his collection (Taylor, sig. 4). He paid for Parr to be brought to London on a litter, accompanied by a female companion, Lucy, whom Taylor puzzlingly identifies as Parr's daughter-in-law, and 'an antique-fac'd fellow called Jacke, or John the Foole'

Thomas Parr (*d.* 1635), by unknown artist, *c.*1635

(ibid., sig. 4*v*). The journey was made in easy stages, admiring crowds turning out *en route* to gape at the old man.

In London, Parr was put on show. He had his portrait etched by Cornelius van Dalen and was presented to Charles I. Disappointingly, he proved able to recall very few of the public events of his long lifetime, being more interested in the price of corn, hay, cattle, and sheep. Six weeks after his arrival in London he died suddenly, on 14 or 15 November 1635.

At the king's command, the royal physician, William Harvey, conducted an autopsy. Uncritically accepting that Parr really had been 152, Harvey noted that his organs of generation were in a healthy state; this seemed consistent with the story of his adultery and with his second wife's report that he had had regular sexual intercourse with her until about twelve years previously. Harvey attributed Parr's death in part to his sudden exposure to rich food and strong drink after a lifetime's diet of cheese, buttermilk, and coarse bread; but he identified the main cause as the effect of London's atmosphere, polluted by people, animals, and the smoke of coal fires, upon someone accustomed to the healthy air of Shropshire.

Parr was buried in Westminster Abbey, where an inscription declared that he had lived through the reigns of ten monarchs. Taylor's tract went into several editions and a Dutch version was published in 1636. Portraits of Parr were widely reproduced, and the story of his longevity entered popular folklore. In the eighteenth century various alleged centenarians were spuriously identified as his descendants. In Shropshire, Old Parr's Cottage, a half-timbered structure at the Glyn, Alberbury, remained an object of popular curiosity until it was burnt down in 1959.

In 1841 a much embroidered biography was published in chapbook form as *The Extraordinary Life and Times of Thomas Parr*; its main purpose was to promote an all-purpose herbal medicine called Parr's Life Pills, authenticated by the recent 'discovery' of Parr's last will and testament, which allegedly contained the formula. In 1906 this tract, issued by the publishers of *Old Moore's Almanack*, claimed to be in its seventy-third edition and was still advertising Parr's Life Pills for Health, Strength and Beauty.

Taylor's account of Parr's life appears to have been based on local tradition, backed by the testimony of some (unnamed) Shropshire gentry, but it lacked documentary support, there being no parish registers at the time of Parr's alleged birth. In 1869 the antiquary W. J. Thoms declared the story incredible, and called for a systematic search of local records to see whether anything relating to Parr's story, corroborative or otherwise, could be found. As yet nothing has been discovered, save for a deed of 1588, granting Parr and his wife Jane a lease for their joint lives of the tenement and lands he occupied at Winnington (Shropshire Records and Research Centre, Shrewsbury, deeds 6000/2809). This corroborates one episode in Taylor's account of Parr's life, but throws no light on his likely age.

In a semi-literate society the exaggeration of age was a common practice, particularly when it brought people attention and respect. As Thomas Fuller wrote in 1647, 'many old men … set the clock of their age too fast when once past seventy, and growing ten years in a twelvemonth, are presently fourscore; yea, within a year or two after, climb up to a hundred' (Fuller, 261). Parr's contemporaries included 'the old countess of Desmond' (Katherine Fitzgerald, second wife of Thomas, eleventh earl), who died in 1604 at the supposed age of 140, and Henry Jenkins (*d.* 1670), who claimed to have been born in 1501. The French virtuoso Nicolas-Claude Fabri de Peiresc (1580–1637) noted that Parr's record was far surpassed by a man in Persia, who was believed by 'credible persons' to be aged 400 (Gassendus, 2.140).

John Taylor gave Parr's supposed longevity a moralistic slant: Parr was an emblem of old England, subsisting on a simple diet and hard physical labour, and uncorrupted by metropolitan luxury. His sudden demise on arrival in London proved that it was intemperate living which explained why people could no longer emulate the longevity of the biblical patriarchs. In the age of the French Revolution the story of Parr's death was reinterpreted in a tract for labouring people (*Cheap Repository. Old Tom Parr: a True Story*, 1797?), to show the folly of seeking to depart from one's allotted station in life. Keith Thomas

Sources J. Taylor, *The old, old, very old man* (1635) [and later edns] • [T. Heywood?], *The wonder of this age* (1635) • [T. Heywood?], *The three wonders of this age* (1636) • W. Harvey, 'Anatomia Thomae Parri … cum Gulielmi Harvae … observationibus', in J. Betts, *De ortu et natura sanguinis* (1669), 319–25; trans. in G. Keynes, *The life of William Harvey* (1966), repr. (1978), 220–25 • Shrops. RRC, SPL deeds 6000/2809 • *GM*, 1st ser., 84/1 (1814), 217 • *Cheap repository. Old Tom*

Parr: a true story (1797?) • *The extraordinary life and times of Thomas Parr* (1841?) • P. Gassendus, *The mirrour of true nobility and gentility*, trans. W. Rand (1657), vol. 2, p. 139–40 • G. C. Lewis, 'Centenarians', *N&Q*, 3rd. ser., 1 (1862), 281–2 • W. J. Thoms, *Human longevity* (1873), 85–94 • W. J. Thoms, 'Old Parr', *N&Q*, 4th ser., 3 (1869), 594–5 • K. Thomas, 'Age and authority in early modern England', *PBA*, 62 (1976), 205–48 • T. Fuller, *The historie of the holy warre* (1647)

Likenesses P. P. Rubens, oils, *c.*1620, Atkins Museum of Fine Art, Kansas City • C. Van Dalen, line engraving, 1635, BM, NPG; repro. in Taylor, *The old, old, very old man*, frontispiece • oils, *c.*1635, AM Oxf. [*see illus.*] • G. Glover, group portrait, engraving, 1636 (*The three wonders of this age*) • J. Caulfield, engraving, 1797 (after oil painting, *c.*1635) • T. and H. Rodd, engraving, 1821 (after oil painting, *c.*1635) • J. Condé, line engraving (*Old Parr*; after P. P. Rubens), BM, NPG; repro. in *European Magazine* (1793) • G. Powle, drypoint (after P. P. Rubens), BM, NPG • oils, second version, NPG

Parr, Sir William (*c.*1350–1404). *See under* Parr family (*per. c.*1370–1517).

Parr, Sir William (1434–1483), knight, was the eldest son of Sir Thomas Parr of Kendal, Westmorland, and Alice, daughter of Sir Thomas Tunstall of Thurland, Lancashire. William succeeded at his father's death late in November 1461. Thomas Parr had been a follower of Richard Neville, earl of Salisbury, and in the 1460s William maintained the link with the Nevilles, now headed by Salisbury's son Richard, earl of Warwick. Parr was with Warwick during the Lincolnshire rising of 1470, and was sent by the earl to the king on 19 March with a request for safe conduct and guaranteed pardon. Edward IV refused, and charged Parr on his allegiance to leave Warwick and Clarence if they refused to surrender, and to urge his fellows to do the same.

Parr appears to have acted on the command. On 6 May the king appointed him lieutenant of Carlisle and of the western march, where Warwick had been captain and warden since 1465, and he does not appear in the list of the earl's adherents drawn up after Warwick's flight. During the readeption of Henry VI, Parr was dropped from the commissions of the peace for Cumberland and Westmorland. On Edward's return from exile in 1471 he joined him at Nottingham. Both his brothers were also in the Yorkist camp and the youngest, Thomas, was killed fighting for the duke of Gloucester at Barnet. Parr became a knight of the king's body, and in July 1471 was rewarded with an extensive land grant, including the castles of Burgh, Pendragon, and Appleby, and with control of a third part of the crown share in the barony of Kendal. He was a royal councillor by 1472, and regularly served on embassies to Scotland. He was made a knight of the Garter in 1474. In 1475 he accompanied the king on his French campaign, and was one of the executors of the will Edward made before his departure. In 1481 his closeness to the king was further recognized when he succeeded Sir Robert Wingfield as controller of the household. Like many of Edward's northern servants he also built up links with the duke of Gloucester, who had succeeded to the Nevilles' northern lands and to their pre-eminence in the north-west. Parr was one of the commissioners to whom the duke's office of constable was committed in 1482.

Parr played a leading role in the burial of Edward IV at Windsor. He and his second wife, Elizabeth, attended the coronation of Richard III: she as a gentlewoman of Queen Anne, he as one of the knights who held the canopy over the king during his anointing. Parr did not live long enough to benefit from the accession of his patron. He was dead by 3 December 1483. His first wife was Joan Trusbut, the widow of Thomas Colt, esquire. Colt died late in 1467 and Joan had married William by July 1468. The marriage was probably arranged under the aegis of Parr's lord the earl of Warwick, for Colt (whose father had come from Carlisle) was also a Neville associate, and Warwick headed the feoffees for the marriage settlement. Joan was a considerable heiress in her own right and brought her husband, among other land, the manor of Netherhall in Roydon, Essex. She died in 1473, and William initially enjoyed the custody of her lands and those of her son by Colt, but in February 1476 they were transferred to John Elrington, the treasurer of the king's household. By June 1475 Parr had married Elizabeth (1462–*c.*1505), one of the daughters of Henry, Lord Fitzhugh, and Alice Neville, daughter of the Parrs' former patron, the earl of Salisbury. She was the mother of all William's children: Sir Thomas *Parr (1478–1517) [*see under* Parr family]; William *Parr, Baron Parr of Horton; John; and Anne.

William Parr worked closely with his younger brother **Sir John Parr** (*d.* 1475). The two brothers shared all Edward IV's land grants and John Parr strengthened the family influence in Westmorland by his appointment (in May 1462) as hereditary sheriff of the county. Both combined their northern interests with a place in the king's household, but the emphasis was different, with John much more of a courtier than his brother. John was a king's esquire by December 1461 when he was appointed steward of the forfeited Clifford lands in Westmorland. He was with the court in East Anglia in 1469, when the news broke of disaffection in the north, and he remained loyal to Edward IV throughout the crisis which followed. He was knighted by Edward on the field at Tewkesbury and became a knight of the king's body. By March 1475 he was the king's master of horse, perhaps partly in tribute to his tourneying skills: he had been among the courtiers who had jousted at Eltham in 1467. He had then been in the team of William, Lord Hastings, with whom he shared several grants of ecclesiastical patronage. He was much involved in preparations for the war with France. In March 1474 he was appointed to muster troops being sent to Burgundy, and in January 1475 he travelled to Flanders to buy horses and armour. He was among those retained for the campaign, and was paid the first instalment of his wages, but he was dead by 1 June 1475 when William Parr succeeded him as sheriff of Westmorland.

In the redistribution of local authority which followed Edward IV's return in 1471, John Parr was apparently cast for a role in Warwickshire. He was constable of Kenilworth from June 1471 to May 1474, and was named to the Warwickshire commissions of the peace from 1471 until his death. His southern base seems, however, to have been the Colt manor of Netherhall and it was only after John's death that William surrendered the Colt lands. John Parr married a daughter of Sir John Young or Yonge, mayor of London. To judge by a jocular reference in a letter from John (III) Paston, the marriage was still recent in June 1472. Paston then wrote to his brother:

> I prey yow recomand me to Syr John Parre wyth all my seruys, and tell hym by my trouthe I longyd neuer sorer to se my lady then I do to se hys mastershepe. And I prey God that he aryse neuer a mornyng fro my lady his wyff wyth-owght it be ageyn her wyll tyll syche tyme as he bryng hyr to Ouyr Lady of Walsyngham. (Davis, 1.574)

ROSEMARY HORROX

Sources PRO · *Chancery records* · N. Davis, ed., *Paston letters and papers of the fifteenth century*, 2 vols. (1971–6) · A. R. Myers, ed., *The household of Edward IV: the black book and the ordinance of 1478* (1959) · A. F. Sutton and P. W. Hammond, eds., *The coronation of Richard III: the extant documents* (1983) · K. Dockray, ed., *Three chronicles of the reign of Edward IV* (1988) · J. C. Wedgwood and A. D. Holt, *History of parliament*, 1: *Biographies of the members of the Commons house, 1439–1509* (1936) · C. L. Scofield, *The life and reign of Edward the Fourth*, 2 vols. (1923) · S. E. James, 'Sir Thomas Parr, 1407–1461', *Transactions of the Cumberland and Westmorland Antiquarian and Archaeological Society*, [new ser.], 81 (1981), 15–25 · P. Holland, 'The Lincolnshire rebellion of March 1470', *EngHR*, 103 (1988), 849–69 · R. Horrox and P. W. Hammond, eds., *British Library Harleian manuscript 433*, 2 (1980), 43–4 · J. R. L. Nicholls, *Kendal parish church guide* (1960)

Parr, William, **Baron Parr of Horton** (*c.*1480–1547), soldier and courtier, was the second of four children of Sir William *Parr of Kendal (1434–1483) and his second wife, Elizabeth (1462–*c.*1505), daughter of Henry, Lord Fitzhugh of Ravensworth, and his wife, Alice Neville. Although his family's lands lay in Westmorland, Parr was raised in the Northamptonshire household of his stepfather, Sir Nicholas *Vaux of Harrowden. In 1505 he married Mary (1484–1555), daughter of William Salisbury and his wife, Elizabeth, daughter of Thomas Wylde of Bromham, Bedfordshire, who brought him Horton manor in Northamptonshire. The couple had four daughters: Matilda, or Maud (married Ralph Lane) [*see* Lane, Maud]; Anne (married Sir Thomas Tresham); Mary (married first John Digby and then Henry Brooke); Elizabeth (married Nicholas Woodhull).

Parr succeeded to much of his stepfather's influence in Northamptonshire, serving on numerous commissions, as knight of the shire in parliament from 1529 to 1540, and as sheriff (1517, 1522, 1533, and 1537). An avid hunter, between 1505 and 1523 he secured royal grants for the keeping of the great and little parks at Brigstock, the park at King's Cliffe, and the forest and castle of Rockingham, as well as the stewardship of all royal lands in Pembrokeshire. In 1537 he was granted one-quarter of the manor of Kendal in Westmorland, part of a parcel of lands he received from the late duke of Richmond's northern holdings.

Parr began his court career in Henry VII's household as one of the king's spears and as squire for the body (by 1506), an office he retained under Henry VIII until March 1512. He fought in the vanguard of the English army during Henry VIII's expedition to France in the summer of 1513, and on 25 September was knighted in the cathedral at Tournai. An excellent soldier, between April and June 1523 he fought in several skirmishes along the Scottish border under the earl of Surrey, who mentioned Parr's courage in battle in several letters to the king. During the 1536 Pilgrimage of Grace, Parr, swearing he would 'put the offenders in despair and dread' (PRO, SP 1/107/115), led a company of men into Lincolnshire to pacify the rebels, helping to secure and hold Stamford.

A bluff, proud, quarrelsome man, Parr was happier on the battlefield than at court, but quickly realized that there was more profit in court politics than in storming castles. In 1515 he was briefly appointed chamberlain to the household of Margaret Tudor, dowager queen of Scots. In 1520 he attended the king at the lavish ceremonies of the Field of Cloth of Gold in France. Through Wolsey's influence Parr was in July 1525 made chamberlain for the newly formed household of the king's illegitimate son, the duke of Richmond, established at Sheriff Hutton in Yorkshire. To Parr this looked like a golden opportunity for advancement, but he quickly discovered that the office was neither as lucrative nor as powerful as he had hoped. Bitter quarrels with one of Richmond's tutors, Richard Croke, did much to increase Parr's disenchantment. By 1530 he had resigned and returned to Horton, although he held a place on the duke's council until Richmond's death in 1536.

An avid supporter of the new religion, albeit probably more for political than spiritual reasons, Parr became Cromwell's chief agent for the dissolution of the monasteries in Northamptonshire which led to several virulent quarrels with disaffected churchmen, particularly the abbot of Peterborough. In 1538 he received as reward a parcel of six lucrative rectories from dissolved religious foundations and the former monastery of Pipewell. After Cromwell's death, he found a new patron in his niece, *Katherine or Kateryn, the daughter of his brother Sir Thomas *Parr (1478–1517) [*see under* Parr family (*per. c.*1370–1517)]. When she married the king on 12 July 1543, he became chamberlain of her household. On 23 December following he was created Baron Parr of Horton and in February 1544 received a substantial grant of lands in Bedfordshire and Northamptonshire, including Kettering and Pytchley manors.

During the summer of 1544, at the queen's request, Parr was named to her regency council while Henry VIII was in France. In failing health, Parr apparently retired instead to Horton, as his name does not appear in the council minutes. He nevertheless remained an important adviser to the queen and messages passed between them regularly. In the summer of 1546, during the plot by religious conservatives against the queen, Parr returned to court and helped to foil the conspiracy by smuggling proscribed books out of her garderobe. He died at Horton the following year, probably on 10 September, and was buried in Horton church, where he is commemorated by a marble effigy.

SUSAN E. JAMES

Sources S. E. James, *Kateryn Parr: the making of a queen* (1999) · *LP Henry VIII* · will, PRO, PROB 11/32, sig. 6 · N. H. Nicolas, ed., *Proceedings and ordinances of the privy council of England*, 7 vols., RC, 26 (1834–7), vol. 7, p. 223 · exchequer, king's remembrancer, accounts various, PRO, E101/424/12, fol. 157 · PRO, E101/426/3, fol. 21 ·

exchequer, court of augmentations, miscellaneous books, PRO, E315/161, fols. 117, 165 · PRO, E101/56/25 · G. R. Elton, *Policy and police* (1972) · W. T. Mellows, ed., *Peterborough local administration: the last days of Peterborough monastery*, Northamptonshire RS, 12 (1947), xxxv–lxxxiv · PRO, state papers Henry VIII, general series, SP 1/107/115

Archives PRO, state papers, letters

Likenesses marble effigy, *c*.1547, Horton church, Northamptonshire

Wealth at death approx. £1500 in bequests; plus plate: 1548, will, PRO, PROB 11/32, sig. 6

Parr, William, marquess of Northampton (1513–1571), nobleman and courtier, was born on 14 August 1513, probably at Blackfriars, London, the third child and only surviving son of Sir Thomas *Parr of Kendal (1478–1517) [*see under* Parr family] and his wife, Maud Green (1492–1531), daughter of Sir Thomas Green and his wife, Jane Fogge. On his father's death Parr was left in the custody of his mother, who lived at Rye House, Hertfordshire. In July 1525, aged eleven, Parr joined the household of Henry Fitzroy, duke of Richmond, at Sheriff Hutton in Yorkshire, studying under such tutors as John Palsgrave.

In 1527 Lady Parr went into debt to buy her son's marriage to Lady Anne Bourchier (1517–1571), heir of Henry Bourchier, earl of Essex. A marriage licence was issued on 9 February 1527, and shortly afterwards the thirteen-year-old William married ten-year-old Lady Anne in the Bourchier chapel at Stanstead Hall, Essex. Parr received livery of his lands on 20 June 1535. Knighted in late 1538 and created Baron Parr on 9 March 1539, Parr believed his marriage would ultimately bring him the earldom of Essex, but when his father-in-law died on 3 March 1540, Cromwell appropriated the title for himself. The following year Lady Anne eloped with 'one Hunt or Huntley' (Baker, 2.60), leaving her husband bereft of wife and title. Parr obtained a legal separation from her in 1542, and when she gave birth to her lover's child secured a bill in parliament (March 1543) barring any child of Anne's from inheriting either her estates or his own. Unable to obtain a formal divorce, Parr was left without an heir or freedom to remarry. In December 1543 he began an affair with one of the queen's ladies, Elizabeth Brooke (1526–1565), daughter of George Brooke, Baron Cobham.

Blond, blue-eyed, elegant, and charming, William Parr was an enthusiastic scholar and Francophile, an avid hunter and musician. He was the co-author of a work on hare coursing (1562), played the virginals, and patronized a family of court musicians, the Bassanos. He maintained a long relationship with Cambridge University which granted him the honorary degree of MA (18 March 1571), and sponsored the founding of Guildford grammar school (1553).

On 23 April 1543 Parr was elected to the Order of the Garter and in the same month named lord warden of the western marches towards Scotland. Hoping that success in that office would gain him the earldom of Essex, in abeyance since Cromwell's execution in 1540, Parr left for the north with high expectations. He was, however, politically naive, argumentative, and arrogant, and his tenure lasted barely six months. His sister *Katherine became

William Parr, marquess of Northampton (1513–1571), by Hans Holbein the younger, 1541–2

queen of England on 12 July and by mid-October he had returned to London. Through her influence he was elevated to the earldom of Essex on 23 December 1543 and about this time, too, was made captain of Henry VIII's honorary royal bodyguard, the gentlemen pensioners, whom he led into France as part of the king's invasion force in the summer of 1544. Parr also served on the privy council from May 1545.

Parr's adherence to the reformed religion during the last years of Henry VIII's reign placed him in the political faction led by the earl of Hertford and by John Dudley, Lord Lisle. Named as an assistant councillor in Henry's will, after the king's death he took part in the coup engineered by Hertford that made the latter protector and duke of Somerset. As his reward Parr was created marquess of Northampton on 16 February 1547. He jousted at Edward VI's coronation four days later. In April he petitioned for the setting up of a commission to deliberate upon a divorce from his wife, but impatient with the slowness of its proceedings (it was headed by Cranmer, who devoted much time and thought to it) he took matters into his own hands and probably late in the summer secretly married Elizabeth Brooke. The commission finally ruled in his favour, but the decision was highly controversial, with no precedent in canon law, and when Somerset learnt of the clandestine marriage he expelled Northampton from the privy council on 28 January 1548 and ordered him to separate permanently from Elizabeth. Alienated from the protector as a result, Northampton may have been fortunate to escape arrest in February along with his brother-in-law Sir Thomas Seymour, who was subsequently executed for treason.

Somerset's political misjudgements led to a series of revolts against the government, the most serious being that in Norfolk led by Robert Kett in 1549. Somerset appointed Northampton to lead a force against the rebels, but on 30 July the marquess disobeyed instructions to keep out of Norwich and his men were repulsed, making the rising worse. The Norfolk rebellion was only crushed the following month by Dudley, now earl of Warwick, with Northampton under his command, and by October the two men were back in London and involved in the moves to oust Somerset. The coup led to the protector's arrest on 14 October 1549, after which Northampton became one of the king's six lords-in-waiting. Four months later, on 14 February 1550, Warwick, now president of the council, made Northampton great chamberlain and granted him substantial lands in six shires, including Sudeley Castle, Gloucestershire, in return for his support. By 1553 Northampton's annual income exceeded £5500 and he had a leading position. He had achieved this despite being neither as politically acute nor as aggressively ambitious as many of his contemporaries. It seems clear, however, that he valued his position at court and the opportunities for shaping policy which it offered. His connections with powerful allies like John Dudley, as well as with his sister the queen and his brother-in-law the earl of Pembroke, enabled him to exert an influence on the course of political events greater than his natural talents might have permitted.

During the summer of 1551 Northampton was sent by Northumberland to France, ostensibly to invest Henri II with the Order of the Garter and to arrange a marriage between the five-year-old French princess Elizabeth and Edward VI. Secretly it was hoped that he could find a means to upset the betrothal of Mary, queen of Scots, to the French dauphin. But although he did arrange the Anglo-French betrothal, he was unable to undermine the Franco-Scottish one. At the end of October he was in charge of the reception of Mary of Guise, dowager queen of Scots, at Hampton Court.

Northampton was luckier in his private life. On 31 March 1551 he succeeded in having both a private bill of divorcement passed in parliament and his marriage to Elizabeth Brooke legalized, managing in the process to hold on to most of his first wife's inheritance. With the failure of Edward VI's health in the spring of 1553, both his second marriage and his political position were in jeopardy. Bitterly opposed to the succession of Princess Mary, Northampton joined with Northumberland and the marquess of Dorset in their attempt to place Lady Jane Grey on the throne. This failed and he was committed to the Tower on 26 July and arraigned for treason on 18 August under the new queen, Mary. She stripped Parr of lands and titles, rescinded his divorce (24 October), and made Lady Anne Bourchier one of her ladies-in-waiting. To protect her own rank and position, Anne was forced to plead for her husband's life. On 13 January 1554 Mary pardoned him, but shortly afterwards the outbreak of Wyatt's rebellion saw him returned briefly to the Tower. He was released on 24 March for lack of evidence.

In May 1554 Parr was restored in blood but not in honours, and in the following January, Mary granted back some of his lands in Northamptonshire. Gradually over the next three years he was given back more of his estates, and on 6 August 1558 he was absolved of debts to the crown incurred before his attainder. Shortly after the accession of Elizabeth, on 25 December 1558, he returned to the privy council, with a grant of £500 p.a. from the crown, while on 13 January 1559 he was officially reinstated as marquess of Northampton. He also recovered many of the stewardships of royal lands in Northamptonshire and Buckinghamshire that he had held under Edward VI. His divorce was reimplemented, and by the summer of 1560 he enjoyed an income of roughly £1700—a measure of his losses since 1553. On good terms with the queen, Northampton frequently attended council meetings. He took part in negotiations with the French in 1559, 1563, and 1564, and received a number of other appointments. In 1559 he was lord high steward at the trial of Thomas, Lord Wentworth, for the loss of Calais, and was a commissioner for the royal visitation of the dioceses of Oxford, Coventry and Lichfield, Peterborough, and Lincoln. Ten years later he was named to the commission for the trial of the fourth duke of Norfolk. His second wife died on 2 April 1565, and his first on 26 January 1571. In May 1571 he took a third wife, Helena Snakenborg [*see* Gorges, Helena, Lady Gorges (1548–1635)], a Swedish lady who had come to England in 1565 in the retinue of the margravine of Baden. Suffering acutely from gout, Northampton died childless on 28 October 1571 in Thomas Fisher's house in Warwick, and was buried on 5 December in the chancel of St Mary's Church there, at the expense of Queen Elizabeth. SUSAN E. JAMES

Sources S. E. James, *Kateryn Parr: the making of a queen* (1999) • *LP Henry VIII*, vols. 4–8, 10, 12–21, *addenda* • household accounts, 1553, PRO, exchequer, king's remembrancer, accounts various, E101/520/9 • survey of lands, 1571, PRO, exchequer, trustees for crown lands and fee farm rents, parliamentary surveys, E317 • *APC*, 1542–75 • *CPR*, 1547–75 • J. Bain, ed., *The Hamilton papers: letters and papers illustrating the political relations of England and Scotland in the XVIth century*, 1, Scottish RO, 12 (1890) • *CSP Spain*, 1538–53 • T. Hoby, 'The travels and life of Sir Thomas Hoby', ed. E. Powell, *Camden miscellany, X*, CS, 3rd ser., 4 (1902) • bills to Parr for musicians, 1541–2, PRO, duchy of Lancaster, cartularies etc., DL 42/133 • J. Nicolson and R. Burn, *The history and antiquities of the counties of Westmorland and Cumberland*, 2 vols. (1777) • G. Baker, *The history and antiquities of the county of Northampton*, 2 (1836–41) • GEC, *Peerage*, new edn, 9.669–74 • D. MacCulloch, *Thomas Cranmer: a life* (1996) • T. Kemp, ed., *The Black Book of Warwick* [1898] • C. A. Bradford, 'Helena, marchioness of Northampton', Bodl. Oxf., MS Rawl. A. 112, 66b, 67b

Archives BL, political corresp., Add. MSS 32649–32652, *passim* • PRO, estate survey, E317 • PRO, holograph letters among the state papers • PRO, household accounts, 1553, E101/520/9

Likenesses H. Holbein the younger, chalk drawing, 1541–2, Royal Collection [*see illus.*] • miniature, *c*.1546–1547, Sudeley Castle,

Gloucestershire · S. van Herwijck, silver medal, 1562, priv. coll. · T. Athow, watercolour drawing, NPG · Stephen of Holland, silver medal, BM

Wealth at death more than £1700, incl. lands; widow's third in Cumbria in 1571 valued at approx. £368, which indicates that Parr's lands there were worth approx. £1200: PRO, E317; *CPR*, 2.155; 4.382

Parratt, Sir Walter (1841–1924), organist, was born on 10 February 1841 at 6 South Parade, Huddersfield, the second son and fifth child of Thomas Parratt (1793–1862), organist of Huddersfield parish church from 1812 to his death, and his wife, Sarah Elizabeth (1807–1891), daughter of William Perkins. Parratt was educated principally by his parents, though he spent a brief period at Huddersfield collegiate school. From an early age he showed evidence of a prodigious musical memory and at the age of ten played the whole of J. S. Bach's *Das wohltemperirte Clavier* by heart in two sittings. In 1852 he was appointed organist at Armitage Bridge, near Huddersfield, at a salary of £10 per annum. Later the same year he attended the choir school of St Peter's Chapel, Charlotte Street (now Palace Street), London, where he acted as organist, at the same time taking lessons from George Cooper at St Sepulchre's, Holborn. In 1854 he succeeded his brother Henry as organist of St Paul's Church, Huddersfield.

At the instigation of Sir Frederick Gore Ouseley, in 1861 Parratt became private organist to the earl of Dudley and organist of Great Witley church, Worcestershire, at a salary of £100 per annum. During his seven years at Great Witley, he spent much time at St Michael's College, Tenbury, in Ouseley's company. On 1 June 1864 he married Emma Gledhill (1842/3–1931), the daughter of Luke Gledhill, a Huddersfield merchant. From 1868 to 1872 Parratt was organist and choirmaster of Wigan parish church, and during this time the first of five children (one son and four daughters) was born to him and his wife. In 1872, aged thirty-one, he succeeded John Stainer as organist of Magdalen College, Oxford, a position he held until 1882. At Oxford, where he lived at 17 St Giles', he conducted the choirs of Jesus and Trinity colleges, the musical societies of Exeter, Jesus, and Pembroke colleges, the Oxford Choral Society, and the Trinity College Glee Club. On 15 May 1873 he graduated as bachelor of music. From this time he became known increasingly as a recitalist: he gave a series of recitals in the Albert Hall, London, in 1873 and took part with S. S. Wesley in the opening of the Victoria Rooms, Bristol, in 1874.

Parratt's first significant composition was his incidental music to Aeschylus' *Agamemnon*, produced for two performances at Balliol College in 1880. The following year he was organist at the first Huddersfield festival, but declined to accept the post of organist at Salisbury Cathedral. In August 1882 he succeeded Sir George Elvey as organist of St George's Chapel, Windsor, a post which he retained until his death. At Windsor the organ was rebuilt in consultation with Ouseley by the firm of Gray and Davison, and Parratt reformed the scope and quality of the music sung, so that after some years there were more than 450 anthems in regular performance. He also conducted the Windsor and Eton Madrigal Society and founded and conducted the Windsor and Eton Orchestral Society. In 1883 he composed music for a performance of *The Tale of Troy* at Cromwell House and in 1886 music for *The Story of Orestes* at Prince's Hall. The additional responsibility of professor of organ at the newly formed Royal College of Music, London, was taken on in 1883, leading to friendships with its director, Sir George Grove, and fellow professors Hubert Parry and Charles Villiers Stanford. In 1892 he was knighted and made private organist to the queen, and in 1893 succeeded Sir William Cusins as master of the queen's music, a position he was to retain under Edward VII and George V. Parratt was awarded an honorary DMus at Oxford in 1894, and received the same degree from Cambridge in 1910 and Durham in 1912. In 1898 he travelled to Russia with W. J. Birkbeck, visiting Moscow and St Petersburg. For the queen's eightieth birthday (1899) he composed the madrigal 'The Triumph of Victoria' ('O happy hour'), published in his compilation of works by distinguished British writers and musicians, *Choral Songs in Honour of Her Majesty Queen Victoria* (1899). He was created MVO by Edward VII in 1901, and George V created him CVO (1917) and KCVO (1921). For the coronation of Edward VII in 1902 he composed his anthem 'Confortare' ('Be strong and play the man'), which was repeated at the coronation of George V in 1911.

Sir Walter Parratt (1841–1924), by Hills & Saunders

In 1905 Parratt became dean of the faculty of music at London University, and from 1905 to 1909 he held the position of president of the Royal College of Organists. In 1906 he was elected an honorary fellow of Magdalen College, and in 1908 he succeeded Parry as Heather professor of music at Oxford, a post he held until his resignation in 1918. Also in 1908 he received the degrees of MA and DMus. During the First World War, Parratt maintained the choral services at Windsor, despite the absence of lay clerks on service. He was greatly affected by the death of his daughter Amy in 1917. On his eightieth birthday in 1921 he received many tributes, including a celebration at the Royal College of Music.

Parratt was regarded as the greatest exponent and teacher of the organ of his day, seeming to Paul Benecke (Knights, 141) 'to be for the organ what Joseph Joachim was for the violin', with a style founded on technical accuracy, clarity of phrasing, and simple registration. He held a position of great influence in English church music, and succeeded in raising both the standard of organ playing and the status of the organist. He was important in the promotion of the works of Bach and the music of contemporary Britons: out of 211 compositions directed by Parratt at Buckingham Palace during the reign of Edward VII, fifty-three were by British composers. His pupils (listed in Tovey and Parratt, 166) included almost all the notable British organists and composers of church music in the succeeding generation. His compositions include an impressive setting of the Obiit service, several anthems, many hymn tunes and Anglican chants, and some twenty songs and partsongs. He wrote the article on music in Humphry Ward's *The Reign of Queen Victoria* (1887) and contributed ten articles to the second edition of Grove's *Dictionary of Music and Musicians* (1904–10).

F. G. Shinn's *Musical Memory and its Cultivation* (1898) was dedicated to Parratt as 'a natural memorizer'. Parratt's chief hobby was chess, a pursuit suited to his innate talent: he performed several documented feats of blindfold chess and was the first captain of the Oxford University Chess Club, founded in 1873. Tall (5 feet 11 inches), with a spare frame and erect carriage, Parratt possessed an energetic personality, and was highly strung but self-controlled in his strict adherence to everyday duties. A charcoal portrait by John Singer Sargent (1914) in the Royal College of Music was said by his son and biographer Geoffrey to show him at his best; another portrait by Gerald Moira (1892) hangs in Magdalen College. He appears with Stainer in William Holman Hunt's painting *May Morning on Magdalen Tower* (1888–91), in the Lady Lever Art Gallery, Port Sunlight.

Parratt suffered a heart attack on 19 October 1923, but recovered to continue his duties as organist, playing for the last time at St George's Chapel on 2 March 1924. He died at his home, 12 The Cloisters, Windsor Castle on 27 March 1924 and, after a brief service at St George's Chapel, was cremated at Woking on 31 March. The following day a memorial service was held in the chapel and his ashes were buried near the organ-loft stairs.

ROSEMARY FIRMAN

Sources D. F. Tovey and G. Parratt, *Walter Parratt, master of music* (1941) • F. G. E. [F. G. Edwards], 'Sir Walter Parratt, master of the king's musick', *MT*, 43 (1902), 441–50 • F. Hudson and R. Williamson, 'Parratt, Sir Walter', *New Grove*, 2nd edn • F. Knights, 'Three Magdalen organists: Paul Benecke's reminiscences of John Stainer, Walter Parratt and John Varley Roberts', *The Organ*, 68 (1989), 137–45 • *British Musician*, 7 (1894), 37–8 • F. G. Shinn, *Musical memory and its cultivation* (1898), 70 • H. C. Colles and J. Cruft, *The Royal College of Music: a centenary record, 1883–1983* (1982) • *MT*, 65 (1924), 401–2 • *Saturday Review*, 137 (1924), 343 • m. cert. • d. cert.

Archives Elgar Birthplace Museum, Broadheath, near Worcester, letters to Elgar

Likenesses W. H. Hunt, oils, 1888–91, Lady Lever Art Gallery, Port Sunlight • E. M. Ellison, pastel drawing, *c.*1890, NPG • G. Moira, oils, 1892, Magd. Oxf. • J. S. Sargent, charcoal drawing, 1914, Royal College of Music, London • W. Rothenstein, sanguine and white drawing, *c.*1921, NPG • K. A. Coward, watercolour drawing, Royal College of Music, London • Hills & Saunders, photograph, NPG [*see illus.*]

Wealth at death £9472 9*s.* 7*d.*: probate, 21 May 1924, *CGPLA Eng. & Wales*

Parris, Edmund Thomas (1793–1873), architect and painter, was born on 3 June 1793 in the parish of St Marylebone, Middlesex, the son of Edward and Grace Parris. He showed early artistic talent and was apprenticed to learn enamel painting and metal chasing with the jewellers Ray and Montague, and he studied mechanics in his free time. In 1816 Parris entered the Royal Academy Schools, where he worked for three years and studied anatomy under Dr Carpue. On 9 October 1819 he married, at St James's, Paddington, Mary Ann, daughter of John Field. Parris exhibited *Christ Blessing Little Children* (painted for St George's Church, Sheffield) at the Royal Academy in 1824.

While repairs were being made to the ball and cross on top of St Paul's Cathedral a land surveyor, Thomas Horner, made 100 sketches from this height of London and the surrounding country. Horner, the owner of the Colosseum (a panorama and place of public entertainment designed by Decimus Burton and situated in Regent's Park, on the site of Cambridge Gate), commissioned Parris, assisted by others, to paint from these sketches a gigantic panorama of London for the Colosseum. Begun in 1825, it covered nearly an acre of canvas, was 400 feet in circumference and 100 feet in height. The project was a financial disaster for Horner, who fled to America, leaving debts of £60,000. Horner's creditors commissioned Parris to complete the panorama, which was finished in November 1829. In 1832 Parris designed and erected the building in which William Daniell RA showed his panorama of Madras. Parris also built a full-scale model of Shakespeare's house for the Crystal Palace at Sydenham in south London (1864).

Parris gained a reputation for portraying female beauty and for some years was a fashionable portrait painter. In 1832 his picture *The Bridesmaid* was exhibited at the British Institution and purchased by Sir Robert Peel; it became popular through the mezzotint after it by J. Bromley. Many of Parris's single figures and groups, in the same weak, sentimental style, were engraved in *The Keepsake* and similar publications. In 1836 and 1838 plates from his drawings were published, with verses by Lady Blessington.

Edmund Thomas Parris (1793–1873), by unknown engraver, pubd 1873 (after James Russell & Sons)

Parris assisted Sir Robert Smirke in preparing Westminster Abbey for the coronation of William IV and painted the architectural screen set up before the organ loft. He was involved in decorative schemes in country houses, including stained-glass windows, carpets, and screens. He worked for the dukes of Sutherland and St Albans, Lord Prudhoe, Lord Downshire, the Earl de Grey, the marquess of Lansdowne, and for Sir Roger Palmer in Portland Place. He painted four scenes with Romantic old-time figures for Johnstown Castle, co. Wexford (1847). Decorations with Tudor royal figures at Scarisbrick Hall, Lancashire, are attributed to him. In 1832 he was appointed historical painter to Queen Adelaide. The publisher Henry Graves arranged for Parris to be hidden in the orchestra pit in November 1837, to draw Queen Victoria on her first state visit to Drury Lane Theatre. Parris painted a small portrait from his sketch (priv. coll.), which was engraved by C. E. Wagstaff and published by Hodgson and Graves (April 1838). He was commissioned by the same firm, in 1838, to paint Queen Victoria's coronation. The queen sat to Parris, saw his picture, and decided that there was 'not one good likeness and a great deal of bad drawing' (Royal Archives, Windsor Castle, Queen Victoria's journal, 4 April 1839). He had sittings from many of the seventy-seven figures who appear in the picture (engraved by Wagstaff, 1842). Parris also painted the funeral of the duke of Wellington (engraved by Wagstaff; published 1 March 1842 by Moon).

Parris had studied fresco technique since 1821 when he delivered a paper before the Royal Institute of Architects. In 1843 he won a £100 prize in the fresco cartoon competition for Westminster Hall with his design *Joseph of Arimathea Converting the Britons*. In 1824 a proposal had been put forward to restore Sir James Thornhill's paintings in the inner dome of the cupola of St Paul's Cathedral. Parris had devised an ingenious apparatus to gain access to these and his scheme had attracted much attention. Lack of funds caused the scheme to be abandoned, but in 1852 the project was revived. Parris was put in charge of repairing the eight very dirty and damaged monochrome wall-paintings of the life of St Paul, with figures 14 feet high—a restoration later considered by some to be a disaster. It was carried out between 1853 and July 1856 using the scaffolding that Parris had designed, on which eight workmen could be simultaneously employed on different levels, while the stonework was also being repaired.

From 1816 to 1874 Parris exhibited historical and fancy pictures at the Royal Academy, and also showed work at the British Institution, at the Society of British Artists, and at the New Society of Painters in Water Colours. He also held a life-drawing school at his house in Grafton Street, Bond Street. He invented a substance known as 'Parris's Medium', which, when mixed with oil, produced a dull fresco-like surface. Parris prepared a model for a tapestry, 40 feet long, of *Christ and the Apostles*, after statues by the Danish sculptor Bertel Thorvaldsen, for the Paris Exhibition of 1867. He died unexpectedly at his home, 27 Francis Street, Tottenham Court Road, London, on 27 November 1873. He was unusually versatile and had enormous energy and a cheerful and kindly temperament.

F. M. O'DONOGHUE, *rev.* DELIA MILLAR

Sources *DNB* • E. Croft-Murray, *Decorative painting in England, 1537–1837*, 2 (1970) • *The Builder*, 31 (1873), 973, 979–80, pl. 69–72 • *Art Union*, 1 (1839), 47 • *Art Union*, 4 (1842), 82 • *Art Union*, 6 (1844), 315 • *Art Journal*, 36 (1874), 45 • *ILN* (9 Aug 1856), 146 • *Strand Magazine*, 1 (1891), 227–8 • *CGPLA Eng. & Wales* (1874) • *IGI*

Archives Royal Arch.

Likenesses E. T. Parris, self-portrait, NPG; repro. in *ILN* [pl.] • wood-engraving (after James Russell & Sons), BM, NPG; repro. in *ILN* (1873) [*see illus.*]

Wealth at death under £200: probate, 2 Feb 1874, *CGPLA Eng. & Wales*

Parris, Elizabeth (*b.* 1682/3). *See under* Salem witches and their accusers (*act.* 1692).

Parris, George van (*d.* 1551), religious radical, was one of only two protestant dissenters executed for unorthodox views during the reign of Edward VI (the other being Joan Bocher). Van Parris was a foreign immigrant to London, a Fleming, though little is in fact known of his background and life before he fell foul of the London authorities. The scant records of his life suggest that he was a surgeon, who had fled his native Flanders and settled in France before journeying on to London. Here he is thought to have joined the London stranger church, founded in 1550, and he was certainly granted papers of denization on 29 October 1550, at the same time as many of the church's first members. It was most likely his denunciation by that congregation which precipitated his trial and execution, though the precise circumstances that led to his arrest and examination by the newly established commission charged with examining heresy remain obscure. The records of the London foreign churches make no mention of van Parris: he is not included in their surviving membership list, and the correspondence of the leading members of the church makes no mention of him—perhaps a reflection of their acute embarrassment that a disciplinary procedure initiated by their church should bring one of their number to the fire. Nevertheless, the *Chronicle of Edward VI* is explicit on the question of van Parris's membership of the church ('April 7: A certain Aryan of the

Strangers, a Dutchman, being excommunicated by the congregation of his countrymen, was after long disputation condemned to the fire'; Jordan, *Chronicle*, 58) and there is no real reason to doubt the church's complicity.

Van Parris was arraigned before Cranmer and other commissioners in April 1551. With Miles Coverdale acting as interpreter, he was examined on his views, and most especially the belief that 'God the Father is only God, and that Christ is not very God'. His refusal to recant sealed his fate, and he was condemned for Arianism on 7 April and consigned to execution. Sentence was finally carried out at Smithfield on 24 April 1551.

The execution of van Parris, and of Joan Bocher the previous autumn, left a legacy of embarrassment within both the foreign community and the Edwardian establishment. The leaders of the stranger church, a church born of persecution, took no pride in their part in his destruction, and John Foxe was moved to express his own distaste for the business in the first Latin edition of his martyrology (*Commentarii rerum in ecclesia gestarum*, Strasbourg, 1554). His account, in fact, introduces some quite conflicting biographical information. According to Foxe, 'George the German', as he calls him, was an unlettered and uneducated man (hardly possible for a man of his profession), and he was executed despite intercession from his master, 'a nobleman of Mainz'. Perhaps the embellishment owes more to Foxe's natural sympathy than real knowledge of the facts. Later, discretion and ideological self-discipline prevailed, and the tale of van Parris was edited out of subsequent English editions of the *Acts and Monuments*. But a tradition flourished of van Parris's personal asceticism, cultivated (no doubt mischievously) by the Catholic author Miles Hogarde. He wrote of van Parris that he:

> lived in such continence and holiness of life, that before going to meat, he would fall prostrate upon the ground, and give thanks to God the Father; his diet was so moderate, that in two days space he used but one meal, and at the time of his death he was so frollicke, that he fared much like our martyrs, in embracing the reed, kissing the post, singing and other such joys. (Hogarde, fol. 46*v*)

ANDREW PETTEGREE

Sources I. B. Horst, *The radical brethren: Anabaptism and the English Reformation to 1558* (Nieuwkoop, 1972) • A. Pettegree, *Foreign protestant communities in sixteenth century London* (1986) • *The chronicle and political papers of King Edward VI*, ed. W. K. Jordan (1966) • W. K. Jordan, *Edward VI*, 2: *The threshold of power* (1970) • *CPR*, *1549–51*, 249 • J. F. Mozley, *John Foxe and his book* (1940), 36 • M. Hogarde, *The displaying of the protestantes* (1556) • J. Foxe, *Commentarii rerum in ecclesia gestarum* (1554)

Parris, Samuel (**1653–1720**). *See under* Salem witches and their accusers (*act.* 1692).

Parron, William (*b.* before **1461**, *d.* in or after **1503**), astrologer, calls himself in his Latin works Master William Parron 'Placentinus', and the duchy of Milan his homeland, implying that he or his family came originally from Piacenza. In his treatise of 1499, *De astrorum succincte vi fatali* ('On the ineluctable power of the stars'), Parron notes that in his fortieth year he had suffered a serious illness (which he had survived by prescribing for himself a diet of lemons and lettuce); this places his birth in 1460 or earlier. In the same treatise he describes his profession as physician and professor of astrology. His almanac for the year 1500 describes him as doctor of medicine and professor of astrology; his almanac for 1502 and his royal horoscope written in 1502 call him doctor of arts and medicine. The king's privy purse accounts for 6 March 1499 record the payment of £1 to 'Master William Paronus, an astronymyre'.

According to Parron's account in *De astrorum succincte vi fatali*, he was working in England by the late 1480s, for he was consulted professionally by Edward Frank, a Yorkist conspirator, some time between the latter's release from the Tower after his attainder in November 1487 and his rearrest for treason in December 1489. Parron claims to have warned Frank to stay out of trouble and to have prophesied a 'bad end' for him, a prophecy duly fulfilled in 1490, when Frank was executed.

By the later 1490s Parron was producing an annual printed almanac and prognostication. Such printed predictions may have been available on the continent as early as 1469, but Parron was among the first to publish them in England. In 1499 he wrote that he had produced an almanac three years before (1496 or 1497), and editions survive for the years 1498 (fragment), 1500, 1502, and 1503. The text for 1498 (printed by Wynkyn de Worde) is in English, but refers to similar publications by the author in Latin for that year and the previous year (1497); the three later publications (all printed by Richard Pynson) are in Latin and are dedicated to Henry VII.

Parron's prognostications, like those of the Flemish astrologers Johan and Jasper Laet, whose almanacs were also translated for the English market, include descriptions of forthcoming eclipses, floods, droughts, plagues, wars, and other perils; and predictions for the sovereign and for foreign princes, other great personages, nations, and principal cities. Like many astrologers of his day Parron claimed special expertise in long-range weather prediction. In *De astrorum succincte vi fatali*, in which he defends judicial astrology and gives an *apologia* for his own life, he boasts that his almanac had correctly predicted the heavy rains of 1499 and takes issue with the most authoritative contemporary critic of astrology, the Florentine Giovanni Pico della Mirandola.

De astrorum succincte vi fatali, written for Henry VII and completed on 15 October 1499 (seven months after Parron's appearance in the king's privy purse accounts on 6 March), may have signalled Parron's achievement of royal patronage. In it he ingratiatingly refers to Edward IV's supposed premonition of Henry's succession, cites an ominous vision in an almanac for 1473 of a white rose falling into the Thames, and pronounces that the stars had determined the destruction of Edward IV's sons and Henry's victory at Bosworth. He also provides veiled but unmistakable justifications for Henry VII's imprisonment and (in 1499) execution of Edward, earl of Warwick, writing that a prince may, without sin, imprison another prince out of fear of insurrection and that it is better for one man to die than for an insurrection to destroy many.

Parron then dedicated his next almanac, dated 24 December 1499, to the king, announcing in it that his subsequent almanacs would be similarly dedicated and mocking his critics as supporters of Perkin Warbeck (executed 23 November 1499). He also claimed to have written a warning, based on his horoscope, for Ludovico Sforza, duke of Milan, in the year of the duke's overthrow (1499).

Parron's last known work, a horoscope of Prince Henry (afterwards Henry VIII) and his parents, Henry VII and Elizabeth of York, contains some rashly concrete predictions. It was written hastily, following the death of Henry's elder brother Arthur, prince of Wales, on 2 April 1502 and was probably completed the following Christmas. For Prince Henry, Parron predicts a future of religious devotion and a successful reign distinguished by a happy married life and numerous surviving sons; for Elizabeth of York he foretells a life of eighty or ninety years. Her almost immediate death on her thirty-seventh birthday (11 February 1503) may have driven Parron not only from the court, but also from England, since he disappears from English records. He probably returned to the continent, but his later career is unknown.

MARTHA CARLIN

Sources W. Parron, 'De astrorum succincte vi fatali hominum et particulariter cuiusdam nati ac adversus detestantes astrologiam iudicialem', 1499, Bodl. Oxf. • W. Parron, 'Liber de optimo fato nobilissimi domini Henrici Eboraci ducis et optimorum ipsius parentum', 1502, BL, Royal MS 12 B.vi • Bibliothèque Nationale, Paris, MS latin 6276 [another presentation copy of the 'Liber de optimo fato'] • J. Armstrong, 'An Italian astrologer at the court of Henry VII', *Italian Renaissance studies: a tribute to the late Cecilia M. Ady*, ed. E. F. Jacob [1960], 433–54; repr. in C. A. J. Armstrong, *England, France and Burgundy in the fifteenth century* (1983), 157–78 • E. F. Bosanquet, *English printed almanacks and prognostications: a bibliographical history to the year 1600*, Bibliographical Society, Illustrated Monographs, 17 (1917), 20, 79–80, pls. V–VI • H. M. Carey, *Courting disaster: astrology at the English court and university in the later middle ages* (1992), 161–3 • *STC, 1475–1640* • A. F. Pollard, ed., *The reign of Henry VII from contemporary sources*, 3 vols. (1913–14); repr. (1967), vol. 1, p. 205n.; vol. 2, p. 231 • G. F. Warner and J. P. Gilson, *Catalogue of Western manuscripts in the old Royal and King's collections*, 2 (1921), 12 • D. C. Allen, *The star-crossed Renaissance: the quarrel about astrology and its influence in England* (1941); repr. (1973), 194–5 • I. Arthurson, *The Perkin Warbeck conspiracy, 1491–1499* (1994) • J. D. North, *Horoscopes and history* (1986) • H. S. Bennett, *English books and readers, 1475 to 1557: being a study in the history of the book trade from Caxton to the incorporation of the Stationers' Company*, 2nd edn (1969), 118–20 • K. Thomas, *Religion and the decline of magic* (1971), 289 • P. Kibre, 'Giovanni Garzoni of Bologna (1419–1505), professor of medicine and defender of astrology', *Isis*, 58 (1967), 504–15; repr. in P. Kibre, *Studies in medieval science: alchemy, astrology, mathematics and medicine* (1984), chap. 19

Archives Bibliothèque Nationale, Paris, MS Latin 6276 • BL, Royal MS 12 B.vi • Bodl. Oxf., 'De astrorum succincte vi fatali'

Parrot, Henry (*fl.* 1601–1626), epigrammatist, published five books of epigrams between 1606 and 1626. These volumes contain over 950 epigrams, mostly of four or six lines, making Parrot the most prolific author of this time in the genre. Each epigram is prefixed with a Latin title; it has been suggested that this may reflect the practice of the day in Winchester College and other grammar schools where students were set Latin epigrams to write on particular topics (Hudson, 149). Though a competent Latinist, Parrot does not appear to have attended a university or the inns of court. A 'Satyr' on 'wolvish Envie' included in *The Mastive* (1615) provides evidence that he held a position as senior clerk in the court of exchequer. An acquaintance is represented as claiming

He cannot write a Booke in such a fashion,
For well I wote t'was nere his Occupation.
Besides by *Checquer-Clarks* that oft have seene him,
I nere could heare of Schollership was in him,

and a 'Mungrell home-spun Clarke' says he

knowes by whome this *Epigram* was made,
He's just saith hee a man of mine owne Trade.
(*The Mastive*, sig. I1 *r–v*)

Further evidence is provided by a mock epitaph on himself in *Cures for the Itch* (1626), in which he speaks of himself as 'living long a Clarke' (sig. G5*r*). There are numerous references to greedy lawyers and ignorant clerks in Parrot's epigrams: these may be conventional, but suggest close involvement with the legal profession.

In 1601 Parrot is recorded as living in London, at an address in 'Aldrichegate streete in the parish of St. Buttolph without Aldrichgate' (Eccles, 387). It is possible that Parrot was a government spy or informer between 1597 and 1601. Jonson in 'Inviting a Friend to Supper' refers to 'Poley' and 'Parrot' as treacherous spies (elsewhere calling them two 'damn'd Villans'). One of the two men thus characterized is Robert Poley, a notorious informer, and the other may be Henry Parrot. 'One *Parrat*' is identified as an informer attempting to extort money from a prisoner in Newgate in 1600 (Eccles, 385–8; *CSP dom., 1598–1601*, 140–41). An attack on Parrot by John Taylor in 1614 describes Parrot as having been at one point 'in prison' (Williams, 'Borrowed feathers', 1026–7).

Jonson's epigram 'On Court-Parrot' accuses Parrot of attempting to 'pluck down' Jonson but only succeeding 'to praise' his rival ''gainst his will'. Several epigrams by Parrot attack Jonson: epigram 94 in *The Mous-Trap* (1606) is ambivalent in characterizing a theatregoer who disliked *Volpone* as 'a goose', where epigram 163 uses the same epithet for Jonson himself, saying that a bricklayer's 'Morter' is more suitable for him than a dramatist's 'Buskins'. A third epigram, published in *The Mastive* ('Olde *Publius Naso* hath compoz'd a Play'), treats Jonson as past his prime as a dramatist, pleasing 'few or none' (sig. E1*v*). Another poet exchanging insults with Parrot is John Taylor the water poet, satirized as a 'poor *Mechanick*' in *Laquei ridiculosi, or, Springes for Woodcocks* (1613); he responded in two epigrams published the following year.

Two of Parrot's titles allude to *Hamlet*, and probably capitalize on the play's popularity, rather than suggesting any closer association with Shakespeare. The first of the collections is *The Mous-Trap* (1606), containing 100 epigrams. In one of them, Parrot praises 'that rare and matchlesse *Martial*' as the greatest of poets and as his model (epigram 46). *Epigrams, by H. P.* (1608) reprints seventy-five poems from *The Mous-Trap* and adds eighty-three more. A recurrent theme in these and subsequent volumes is the instability of 'squint-eyde fortune', arbitrary and 'partiall in her gifts' (epigram 12); social mobility and the sudden rises and falls within the crowded urban landscape are frequent topics in Parrot's epigrams. Captain Ferdinand, 'so wont to swagger and carrowse', now hiding from his creditors, the 'wondrous rich' Rufus who 'lives obscurely like a water Rat', the proud disdainful man unwilling to admit that his father was 'once a man of trade' are characteristic figures (*The Mous-Trap*, epigrams 36, 63, 69). In prefatory epistles and several epigrams, Parrot affects a stance of independence, refusing to court popularity and seeking only to please the 'deeper judgements' of 'the wise':

> I write not to the rusticke rablement,
> Nor fawne upon the curious kinde of men.
> (*Epigrams*, sig. A2*r*)

Parrot's third book of epigrams, *Laquei ridiculosi, or, Springes for Woodcocks* (1613) contains 440 epigrams, of which 247 are new. Several poems in *Springes* are defences of the epigram as a form and of his own practice in devoting himself exclusively to the epigram ('few have writ more *Epigrams* then I'):

> *Epigrams*, are fitted to the season
> Of such as best know how to make *rime reason*.
> (epigrams 41 and 139)

The Mastive, or, Young-Whelpe of the Olde-Dogg (1615), with 184 epigrams, all new, and four satires, is the first collection by Parrot to contain poems other than epigrams. The satires rehearse themes familiar in the epigrams, as in the lines on a 'Gallant' whose deceptive '*Outside*' allowed him to be 'taken for a Knight' though 'His Father liv'd by gaming to defraude' and 'His Mother was an Ale-wife and a Bawde' (sig. I2*r*). The last of Parrot's five volumes is *Cures for the Itch* (1626), which contains 13 prose characters as well as 319 epigrams (58 of them reprinted from earlier collections) and 73 two-line epitaphs, mostly satiric. A prefatory epistle contrasts 'judicious' readers with 'prouder upstarts that would be wiser then their ancestors, because a little bolstered up since their forgetfull base beginnings' (sig. A3*v*). *Cures for the Itch* is entered under Parrot's name in the Stationers' register with the title *Wittes Storehouse of Invencons* (Williams, 'Epigrams', 25). Two other books which have been attributed to Parrot, *The More the Merrier* (1608) and *The Gossips Greeting* (1620), have been shown to be by other authors (ibid., 16–18; Pitman, 134). WARREN CHERNAIK

Sources F. Williams, 'The epigrams of Henry Parrot', *Harvard Studies and Notes in Philology and Literature*, 20 (1938), 15–28 • F. Williams, 'Henry Parrot's borrowed feathers', *Publications of the Modern Language Association of America*, 52 (1937), 1019–30 • M. Eccles, 'Jonson and the spies', *Review of English Studies*, 13 (1937), 385–91 • L. Manley, 'Proverbs, epigrams, and urbanity in Renaissance London', *English Literary Renaissance*, 15 (1985), 247–76 • M. Pitman, 'The epigrams of Henry Peacham and Henry Parrot', *Modern Language Review*, 29 (1934), 129–36 • H. H. Hudson, *The epigram in the English Renaissance* (1947) • *Poems of Ben Jonson*, ed. I. Donaldson (1975) • *CSP dom.*, 1598–1601

Parry, Benjamin (1634–1678), Church of Ireland bishop of Ossory, was born in February 1634 in Dublin, the second surviving son of Edward *Parry (*d.* 1650), bishop of Killaloe, and younger brother of John *Parry, bishop of Ossory. He matriculated at Trinity College, Dublin, on 5 December 1648 but moved to Jesus College, Oxford, where he graduated BA in February 1652. Elected reader in Greek and fellow of Corpus Christi College, Oxford, in 1654, he proceeded MA from the college in May of that year, and BD in 1662 and DD in 1670. After being ordained into the Church of England he became the prebend of Knaresborough and a canon of York from 1664 to 1673, a position to which he added the rectorship of Hope in Flintshire in 1666, the rectorship of Godington in Oxfordshire in 1668, and the rectorship of St Antholin's in London in 1671.

In 1672 Parry was selected by Arthur Capel, first earl of Essex, the newly appointed lord lieutenant of Ireland, as one of his chaplains. He obtained the prebend of St Michan's in Dublin in 1672 before resigning upon becoming dean of Ossory in May 1674, a position he also held with the rectory of Callan and Aghaboe. He was compensated for the loss of St Michan's through his appointment to the prebendary of Castleknock. He married Elizabeth Barrington (*d.* 1679) some time after his arrival in Ireland, but Wood recorded that it was 'not to his content' (Wood, *Ath. Oxon.*, 3.1172); nevertheless, the couple had three sons: Benjamin, Thomas, and James. Parry's first act in Kilkenny was to arrange for the 'plastering and whitening the whole cathedral church, chapels and aisles, except the chancel, and for stopping up the south window of St. Mary's chapel' (Graves and Prim, 47).

In 1675 Parry was presented by letters patent to the deanery of St Patrick's, Dublin, after a hastily arranged meeting of selected members of the cathedral chapter. His election to St Patrick's was controversial, since the deanery had never before been conferred by letters patent. It appeared that the idea had belonged to his brother, John, who, 'without doubt, attempted to betray the rights of the Cathedral' (Mason, 25) to rush Benjamin into the position. Two juries later found that the crown had no authority to make such an appointment.

Parry edited a manual of devotion by Brian Duppa, the bishop of Winchester, which was published in London in 1674. After the death of his brother on 21 December 1677 he was consecrated as bishop of Ossory, under the advice of Ormond, by the archbishop of Armagh on 27 January 1678. He also succeeded to his brother's positions as rector of Llaniestyn in Anglesey, and of St Andrew's, Dublin. He died nine months later at the bishop's palace in Kilkenny on 4 October 1678 and was buried on 7 October alongside his father and brother in St Audoen's Church, Dublin.

H. T. WELCH

Sources J. B. Leslie, *Ossory clergy and parishes* (1933) • Wood, *Ath. Oxon.*, new edn, 3.1172 • *The whole works of Sir James Ware concerning Ireland*, ed. and trans. W. Harris, rev. edn, 2 vols. in 3 (1764) • J. Graves and J. G. A. Prim, *The history, architecture, and antiquities of the cathedral church of St. Canice, Kilkenny* (1857) • H. Cotton, *Fasti ecclesiae Hibernicae*, 4 vols. (1878) • W. M. Mason, *The history and antiquities of the Collegiate and Cathedral Church of St. Patrick, near Dublin, from its foundation in 1190, to the year 1819, etc.* (1820) • Foster, *Alum. Oxon.*, 1500–1714, 3.1119 • 'The pedigree of the Parry family of Newry, Co. Down and the city of Dublin, *c.*1560–1735', NL Ire., MS 173, fol. 87 • 'The Parry monument, St. Audoen's Church', *Irish Ecclesiastical Journal*, 5/107 (June 1849), 282 • *DNB* • J. B. Leslie, ed.,

Clergy of Dublin and Glendalough: biographical succession lists, rev. W. J. R. Wallace (2001)

Parry, Blanche (*c*.1508–1590), courtier, was the daughter of Henry Parry of Newcourt, Bacton, Herefordshire, and Alice Melborne of Tillington in the same county. She nursed the infant Princess Elizabeth, 'whose cradell saw I rockte' (as her monument in Bacton church has it), and was a lady-in-waiting by the time Elizabeth was three years old. She was probably introduced to the court by her aunt and namesake, Lady Herbert of Troy, who became principal lady of Elizabeth's household in 1536. Blanche was made a gentlewoman of the privy chamber on Elizabeth's accession, with a salary of £33 6*s*. 8*d*., and in 1565 she succeeded Kate Astley as chief gentlewoman. The master of the jewel house was John Astley, but the queen entrusted the custody of her personal jewellery to her gentlewomen, and Blanche served as keeper in succession to Lady Knollys and Mistress Norris from an undisclosed date until she relinquished the charge to Mary Radcliffe in 1587. A similar arrangement seems to have obtained with respect to the queen's library. Roger Ascham is sometimes described as the queen's librarian, and John Fortescue, keeper of the great wardrobe, was designated 'master of the library' in the coronation list of 1559, but it was Blanche who took charge of books presented to the queen. It has been plausibly suggested that she had literary and historical interests of her own. In his *Historie of Cambria* (1584) David Powel reproduces the treatise on the Norman conquest of Glamorgan by Sir Edward Stradling of St Donats, and acknowledges in the preface that he had received it from Blanche Parry, 'a singular well willer and furtherer of the weale publike' of Wales. The treatise had been written at the request of Lord Burghley, who had presented it to the queen. Blanche's own new year gifts to the queen were modest items of silver, jewellery, and clothing. As reward for her loyal service she was granted wardships and leases of crown lands in Wales, Herefordshire, and Yorkshire.

When in 1566 the earl of Leicester annoyed his royal mistress by absenting himself from court because of Elizabeth's prevarication over a land grant, Blanche Parry proved to be a useful intermediary. John Dudley assured the earl that, in the absence of Dorothy Broadbent, she was 'our best friend in the privy chamber' (*CSP dom., addenda, 1566–79*, 3). She used her influence to gain crown offices for her kinsmen in Wales, including a place in the queen's guard for her cousin Rowland Vaughan of Bredwardine Castle. She was also able to gain a favour for the city of Hereford. In his book *Most Approved and Long Experienced Waterworkes* (1610) Vaughan describes her as having belonged to a 'trinity of Ladies able to work Miracles' (Lady Warwick and Lady Scudamore were the others), who 'in little Lay-matters, would steal opportunity to serve some friends' turns … because none of these (near and dear ladies) durst intermeddle so far in matters of commonwealth' (Bradford, 22–3). There is some evidence to confirm this assessment of her limited influence in affairs of state. In a letter to William Cecil of 17 December 1584 Rowland's father, Watkyn Vaughan, mentions that he had sent 'instructions' for two bills in parliament to Blanche Parry, one to 'bridle papists' and the other to reform the abuses of 'base captains' in the array of the militia. If the intention was to engage the interest of the queen through an intermediary at court in the adoption of the proposals as 'official' legislation, the stratagem failed in its purpose: the only measure enacted in this session of parliament which answers these descriptions is the act against Jesuits and seminary priests. On the other hand, her nephew John Vaughan of Sutton-on-Derwent, a member of the council of the north, successfully appealed to Parry and Burghley to use their influence to relieve him of the additional burden of serving as sheriff of Yorkshire in 1569. Blanche was instrumental in obtaining for John Dee a grant in reversion to an ecclesiastical benefice, and was godmother of Dee's son (her proxy at the baptism was Mistress Aubrey, another member of the Welsh coterie at court), but there is no substance in the claim made by romantic historians that Blanche shared with Dee an interest in the occult. Rowland Vaughan refers to the sway Blanche had exerted over the household, but 'my spirit being too tender to indure the bitterness of her humour, I was by her careful (though crabbed) austerity forced unto the Irish wars' (Bradford, 18–22). That she took an interest in those engaged in Irish service emerges from letters to Burghley in 1580 and 1586 from Sir Nicholas White, master of the rolls in Dublin. Mistress Parry is mentioned as a contact at court who afforded direct access to the queen, which suggests that she may have been more effective than the other gentlewomen in exercising some measure of political influence.

Like her mistress, Parry was attached to conservative religious ceremonies, and in her effigy in Bacton church she is depicted wearing a pectoral cross. She took active steps to soften the blow to the family fortunes of the recusant Shelleys of Michaelgrove, Sussex. Burghley helped to draw up her will, dated 1589, several drafts of which survive in his hand. She died on 12 February 1590 and was buried in St Margaret's, Westminster. Her great-niece Lady Burgh was the chief mourner at her funeral, and at the queen's orders the obsequies conducted were those reserved for a baroness. The monument of marble and alabaster set up for her in St Margaret's in 1595–6 records her charity to the poor, that she was 'Beneficial to her kinsfolke and countrymen', and that she was 'never no man's wife'. The monument to her at Bacton church is of stone and alabaster; it displays the figures of Queen Elizabeth and, kneeling beside her, Blanche Parry, clasping a book. Pevsner noted that 'the idea is really a secular version of the medieval motif of the worshipper on his monument kneeling before the Virgin—only it is the Virgin Queen here'. There is an accompanying inscription; in twenty-eight lines of verse of somewhat eccentric orthography, probably of her own composition, she records her lifelong service to the queen:

> That traenyd was yn prynces courts with gorgeous wyghts
> … Preferringe styll the causys of eache wyghte
> As farre as I doorse move her grace hys heare

or to rewarde decerts by course of ryghte
As needs ressytte of sarvys doonne eache wheare.
(Pevsner, *Herefordshire*, 69–70)

PETER R. ROBERTS

Sources C. Merton, 'The women who served Queen Mary and Queen Elizabeth: ladies, gentlewomen and maids of the privy chamber, 1553–1603', PhD diss., U. Cam., 1992 · C. A. Bradford, *Blanche Parry, Queen Elizabeth's gentlewoman* (1935) · *The historie of Cambria, now called Wales*, ed. D. Powell, trans. H. Lhoyd [H. Llwyd] (1584) · J. M. Traherne, ed., *Stradling correspondence: a series of letters written in the reign of Queen Elizabeth* (1840), 235 · *Herefordshire*, Pevsner (1963), 69–70 · A. J. Collins, ed., *The jewels and plate of Queen Elizabeth I: the inventory of 1574* (1955) · *CSP dom., addenda, 1566–79*, 3 · *Draft calendar of patent rolls, 27 Elizabeth I, 1584–1585* (1990) · *Draft calendar of patent rolls, 28–29 Elizabeth I, 1585–1587*, 2 vols. (1991)
Archives BL, Catherine Howard's book of the queen's jewels, Sloane MS 814, fol. 35 · BL, Lansdowne MS 59, fol. 43 · *DWB*

Parry, Caleb Hillier (1755–1822), physician, born at Broad Gates, Gloucester Street, Cirencester, Gloucestershire, on 21 October 1755, was the first child of Joshua *Parry (1719–1776), Presbyterian minister, and his wife, Sarah (*d.* 1786), daughter of Caleb Hillier (1686–1753) of Cirencester. Their daughter Amelia married Sir Benjamin Hobhouse. Parry attended Cirencester grammar school, where he met Edward Jenner, who was later to dedicate his book on vaccination to Parry. In 1770 Parry entered the dissenters' academy at Warrington, Lancashire, and three years later went to Edinburgh to study medicine, but from about 1775 spent two years in London, where he resided with Thomas Denman and attended lectures by William Hunter and John Hunter. Returning to Edinburgh in 1777 he served as president of the students' medical society and was one of those responsible for obtaining its unique royal charter.

After graduating MD in June 1778 with a dissertation, 'De rabie contagiosa', and being admitted as licentiate of the Royal College of Physicians, Parry married Sarah Rigby (1749–1831), daughter of Sarah and John Rigby and sister of the physician Edward Rigby, at Palgrave in Suffolk on 23 September 1778. They had nine children, four boys and five girls. Parry settled in Bath in November 1779 at 13 Catharine Place. He attended the Pauper Charity and Casualty Hospital, joined local scientific societies, and developed a large practice. He was one of the earliest in England to fly a hydrogen balloon (10 January 1784). In 1786 Parry inherited his mother's estates, and built a house and established a farm near Bath. Six years later he sold the Hillier properties and bought a plantation in British Guiana, which was a failure.

Many of Parry's patients became his friends, the most notable being Edmund Burke. John Hunter was also among his patients. Parry worked long hours, sometimes attending autopsies at 6 a.m., or working at his microscope after midnight. He recorded an exceptional number of original observations and deductions. He was the first president of the short-lived Fleece Medical Society. In 1799 he joined the staff of the Bath General Hospital; in 1800 he was elected a fellow of the Royal Society and moved to 27 Circus, Bath, where a plaque commemorates him and his youngest son, Admiral Sir (William) Edward *Parry, the Arctic explorer. His eldest son was the physician Charles Henry *Parry.

Caleb Hillier Parry (1755–1822), by Charles Robertson

Parry kept detailed notes of his patients and requested permission for autopsy on patients who had died. The symptoms of angina pectoris had been described by William Heberden, but the pathology was not understood. Parry's *An Inquiry into the Symptoms and Causes of the Syncope Anginosa commonly called Angina Pectoris* (1799) was the first monograph on the subject. He gave Jenner credit for being the first to demonstrate obstruction of the coronary arteries in fatal angina. Parry recognized that angina was intermittent, although the 'malformation' of the coronary arteries was constant, and was the first to conclude that the pain was due to insufficiency of the coronary circulation. In the same book he demonstrated that pressure on the carotid artery slowed the pulse. In an earlier paper he had shown that carotid pressure relieved the pain of hemicrania: the same paper included the first account of tetany associated with hyperventilation, and of histamine cephalgia. In *An Experimental Inquiry into the Nature, Cause and Varieties of the Arterial Pulse* (1816) he provided the first correct explanation of the mechanism of the pulse, and concluded that with each cardiac contraction the blood forced into the aorta produced an impulse which was transmitted along the whole length of the arterial system. His description of two unusual cases of purpura (1809) is probably the first record of polycythaemia. Parry's *Cases of Tetanus and Rabies Contagiosa* appeared in 1814 and *Elements of Pathology and Therapeutics* in 1815. The latter contains the first description of reactive hyperaemia. In 1786 he had taken part in a clinical trial of three varieties of rhubarb, which he tested on each patient in random order—an early comparative clinical trial.

In 1825, three years after Parry's death, his son Charles produced two volumes of *Collections from the Unpublished Medical Writings of the Late Caleb Hillier Parry*, which contain the earliest account of thyrotoxicosis, seen in 1786. Sir William Osler named the condition Parry's disease. Other first observations of Parry's are: a case of idiopathic dilatation of the colon, diagnosed at autopsy; two cases of aneurysmal dilatation of the auricle in mitral stenosis, also diagnosed at autopsy; facial hemiatrophy; and the first description of hay fever.

By crossing Ryeland ewes with merino rams Parry produced wool as fine as pure merino. To prove it he made the first accurate measurements of the diameter of wool fibres. In 1800 he published *Facts and Observations … of Producing in the British Isles Clothing Wool Equal to that of Spain*; and seven years later, *An Essay on the Nature, Produce, Origin, and Extension of the Merino Breed of Sheep*, for which he was awarded a prize by the board of agriculture. In addition, from 1786 onward Parry contributed papers to the *Transactions of the Bath and West Society of Agriculture*, and in 1812 to the *Farmers' Journal*. He won many prizes at the Bath and West shows for his sheep and their wool.

On 24 October 1816 Parry suffered a stroke which paralysed his right side and impaired his speech. In 1817 he was awarded the Bedfordian gold medal for his work on sheep. He died on 9 March 1822 at his home, 7 Sion Hill Place, Bath, and was buried on 15 March in Bath Abbey, where his colleagues erected a monument to his memory. His wife survived him. Parry's library is now housed in the History Room of the Bristol University Medical Library.

S. Glaser

Sources [W. MacMichael and others], *Lives of British physicians* (1830), 275–304 • T. Lewis, *Proceedings of the Cardiff Medical Society* (1940–41), 71–89 • private information (2004) • S. Glaser, *The spirit of enquiry: Caleb Hillier Parry MD FRS* (1995) • Munk, *Roll* • parish register (marriage), 23 Sept 1778, Suffolk RO, Ipswich • Bath City Archives

Archives Scott Polar RI, corresp. and reminiscences • University of Bristol Library, Parry collection | University of Bath, Bath and West of England Society collection

Likenesses Mrs Lightfoot, silhouette, *c*.1780, priv. coll. • C. Robertson, portrait, *c*.1780 (after miniature), NPG • P. Audinet, prints, 1804 (after unknown portrait) • J. H. Bell, portrait, 1804 • Hamlet, silhouette, 1812, priv. coll. • L. Gahagan, bust, 1822, Bath Royal Literary and Scientific Institution, Bath • P. Audinet, engraving (after J. H. Bell), Wellcome L. • C. Robertson, miniature; Sothebys, 16 Dec 1974, lot 131 [*see illus.*] • line engraving, NPG

Parry, Charles Henry (1779–1860), physician, eldest son of Caleb Hillier *Parry (1755–1822) and his wife, Sarah (1749–1831), a sister of Edward *Rigby (1747–1821) of Norwich, was born at Broadgates, Gloucester Street, Cirencester, on 3 July 1779. The Arctic explorer Sir (William) Edward *Parry (1790–1855) was his brother. After an education at Bath grammar school (1786-95) and in London, Parry studied medicine at Göttingen—in 1799 he was one of Samuel Taylor Coleridge's companions in the Harz Mountains; later he travelled in Scandinavia with Clement Carlyon. On 24 June 1804 he graduated MD at Edinburgh, where he became acquainted with Henry Brougham. He was admitted licentiate of the Royal College of Physicians on 22 December 1806, and elected FRS in 1812.

Parry practised at Cheltenham from 1807 to 1815, where he was befriended by Edward Jenner. On 17 July 1809 he married Emma Mary Bedford, and in 1815 he moved to Bath, where the following year he took over his father's practice. He was physician to the general hospital at Bath from 1818 to 1822.

Parry's importance rests primarily on his publication in 1825 of the *Collections from the Unpublished Medical Writings of the Late Caleb Hillier Parry*, to which he added a prolix introductory volume; secondly on two short biographies of his father—a chapter for John Britton's *History and Antiquities of Bath Abbey Church* (1825) and a longer article in William Macmichael's *Lives of British Physicians* (1830)—both unsigned but acknowledged by Charles Parry in his unpublished autobiography; and thirdly on the presentation to Bath General Hospital of his father's library (later housed in the medical library at the University of Bristol). Parry's *Additional Experiments on the Arteries* (1819) added little to his father's work *An Experimental Inquiry into … the Arterial Pulse* (1816). In 1801 Parry published a translation entitled *On Fever and its Treatment in General*, from the original by G. C. Reich. Parry's graduation thesis, *Synocho tropico*, came out in 1804, and his biography of his grandfather the Revd Joshua Parry was edited and published in 1872 by Sir J. E. Eardley-Wilmot. Other publications by Parry include a book on the corn laws, a chronological list of the parliaments and councils of England, and various articles and letters.

Parry retired to Brighton in 1849, where he died at his residence, 5 Belgrave Place, on 21 January 1860. He was buried at All Saints' Church, Weston, near Bath. His wife survived him.

S. Glaser

Sources C. H. Parry, MS autobiography, Bodl. Oxf. • private information (2004) • C. Carlyon, *Early years and late reflections* (1843) • *Bath directories* • *Collected letters of Samuel Taylor Coleridge*, ed. E. L. Griggs, 1 (1956), letter to Sara Coleridge, 17/5/1799 • R. Holmes, *Coleridge: early visions* (1989), 219, 228–30, 233, 236–7 • Munk, *Roll*

Archives Bodl. Oxf., letters and memoirs | UCL, letters to G. B. Greenough

Wealth at death under £6000: resworn probate, April 1860, *CGPLA Eng. & Wales*

Parry, Charles James (1824–1894). *See under* Parry, Joseph (1744–1826).

Parry, David Henry (1793–1826). *See under* Parry, Joseph (1744–1826).

Parry, Sir David Hughes (1893–1973), university administrator, was born on 3 January 1893 at Llanaelhaearn, Caernarvonshire, the eldest of three sons and of four children of John Parry JP, a farmer, and his wife, Anne Hughes, great-great-niece of Griffith Davies, the actuary. Childhood on a hill farm from which a living could be wrested only by unremitting labour left an indelible mark on him. The family and community in which he grew up were both Welsh-speaking and deeply religious; Hughes Parry started to learn English only when he went to school and

Sir David Hughes Parry (1893–1973), by Kyffin Williams, 1964

he became a full member of his local chapel at an early age and a lay preacher.

Educated at Pwllheli county school, Hughes Parry won a scholarship to the University College of Wales, Aberystwyth, in 1910, graduating four years later with first class honours in economics. He was commissioned in the Royal Welch Fusiliers in 1915 and, after active service on the western front, was invalided out of the army in 1919. After demobilization he went to Peterhouse, Cambridge, of which he became an honorary fellow in 1956, and was placed in the first class of part two of the law tripos in 1920. In that year he became a lecturer in law at Aberystwyth. He was called to the bar in 1922 by the Inner Temple, of which he later became a bencher (1952), and took silk in 1955. In 1923 Hughes Parry married Haf (1898–1965), only daughter of Sir Owen Morgan *Edwards, man of letters and inspector of education for Wales. They had no children. In a sense Hughes Parry lived in his father-in-law's shadow. His wife inherited her father's house at Llanuwchllyn, which remained their Welsh home from 1923 onwards. She herself was uncompromisingly Welsh.

From 1924 to 1928 Hughes Parry was lecturer in law at the London School of Economics and Political Science, and from 1928 to 1930 reader. He was appointed professor of English law in 1930 in succession to Edward Jenks. He built up a law department which, by the time he retired in 1959, was second to none in the country. His other outstanding academic achievement was to create in the University of London the Institute of Advanced Legal Studies which became an international centre for legal research. He was its part-time director from 1947 to 1959.

Hughes Parry combined academic work with part-time practice in chambers at the Chancery bar from 1924 to 1946, being the joint editor of important works of reference such as the eleventh (1927) and the twelfth (1932) editions of *Wolstenholme and Cherry's Conveyancing Statutes*. His skill in the drafting and construction of documents was of great value to the many organizations with which he was connected. He was no stranger to the criminal law and was deputy chairman of Caernarvonshire quarter sessions from 1950 to 1966.

At the University of London, Hughes Parry had a unique career, holding practically every important elective office open to him, including the vice-chancellorship in 1945–8 and the chairmanship of the court in 1962–70. He played a leading part in the provision of adequate social and athletic facilities for students on a university, as opposed to a college, basis and a university hall of residence fittingly bears his name.

Hughes Parry remained devoted to Aberystwyth in spite of being passed over twice for the principalship (which affected him more deeply than he cared to admit) and was its president from 1954 to 1964. His early years in that office were clouded by a controversy within the college connected with the principal, Goronwy Rees, but, after Rees resigned in 1957, under Hughes Parry's guidance there was a remarkable growth in facilities and student numbers. He was also very influential on the court and council of the University of Wales and successfully championed retention of its federal structure.

Hughes Parry was deputy chairman of the National Council of Social Service from 1948 to 1962. From 1953 to 1963 he was a member of the lord chancellor's committee on legal reform, on which he did invaluable service for he was not only careful and scholarly but also had a genuine legal imagination. He was also a member of departmental committees on subjects as diverse as war damage, the remuneration of doctors and dentists, colonial universities, and post-war reconstruction in Wales. Indeed his non-legal and non-academic activities were centred on Wales with which he never lost touch; he and his wife retained their Welsh house at Llanuwchllyn, near Bala, while they lived in London and returned to it after retirement.

From 1963 to 1965 Hughes Parry chaired the committee on the legal status of the Welsh language which reached a common-sense compromise (later given statutory force) that Welsh should have equal validity with English. He was also closely connected with the Welsh League of Youth (founded by his brother-in-law) for over a quarter of a century and for even longer with the eisteddfod, of which he was chairman for the last three years of his life. He was an elder of the Presbyterian Church of Wales in 1927, moderator of the North Wales Association in 1963–4, and moderator of the general assembly in 1964–5, an honour previously accorded to only one layman.

Though a devout Christian, Hughes Parry found it hard to obey the injunction in the Lord's prayer to forgive, particularly those who did not live up to his own high standards—or Welshmen who could but would not speak their native tongue. His generosity to others and to the institutions with which he was connected was in sharp contrast to the frugality of his own way of life which sometimes bordered on parsimony, and yet in his later years he took great pleasure in driving expensive motor cars. A puritan by nature, he had a distaste for the pleasures of the table. He was an imposing figure—tall, spare, and in his later years with a shock of white, wavy hair which marked him out in any company.

In London, Hughes Parry was greatly liked and admired, not least for the skill with which he mediated between opposing groups and encouraged compromise solutions often of his own devising. In Wales the reaction to him was mixed and he had his critics to whom he appeared vain and obstinate. Perhaps he allowed his justified pride in his many achievements to come a little too often to the surface while his passionate devotion to Wales tended to blunt his judgement in the controversies, often denominational, in which he became involved.

Hughes Parry was the recipient of many honorary degrees, of which he prized most highly those of Wales (1947), Western Ontario (1948), Cambridge (1953), and London (1963). He was knighted in 1951. Hughes Parry died at his home, Neuadd Wen, Llanuwchllyn, Merioneth, on 8 January 1973. D. W. Logan, *rev.*

Sources D. Hughes Parry, *O bentref Llanaelhaearn i Ddinas Llundain* (privately printed, 1973) ['From the village of Llanaelhaearn to the City of London'] · D. M. Clitheroe, *Impressions of David Hughes Parry* (1974) · private information (1986) · *CGPLA Eng. & Wales* (1973) · personal knowledge (1986)
Archives NL Wales, corresp. and papers | NL Wales, letters received relating to Calvinistic Methodist bill · NL Wales, letters to Thomas Iorwerth Ellis and Annie Hughes Griffiths
Likenesses K. Williams, oils, 1964, U. Wales, Aberystwyth [*see illus.*]
Wealth at death £96,222: probate, 14 March 1973, *CGPLA Eng. & Wales*

Parry, Edward (*d.* **1650**), Church of Ireland bishop of Killaloe and author, was born in Newry, co. Down, the son of Rhys Parry (*d.* 1617), a Welsh merchant. He entered Trinity College, Dublin, in 1616, and graduated BA in 1620, proceeding MA in 1623 and BD in 1630. On 24 November 1624 he was elected a fellow of the college. At a visitation held in 1628 it was found that, contrary to the statutes of the college, Parry held a living more than 3 miles from the college. Subsequently, he was dismissed from his fellowship. This living was the prebendary of Tipperkevin in St Patrick's Cathedral, Dublin. He had been collated to this living in 1627 and held it until 1636, when he resigned it in favour of the prebendary of Stagonil in the same cathedral. From 1624 to 1630 he was vicar of St Kevin's, and in a visitation of 1630 he was recorded as vicar of St Bride's, Dublin. In that year he also served the cure of St Nicholas Without, a living that he still possessed in 1648.

On 29 May 1634 Parry received letters patent for the treasurership of Christ Church, Dublin, and he was installed two days later. In 1638 he broke a long lease of that dignity's estate and orchards. He was appointed to the high commission for ecclesiastical causes on 11 February 1636 and was one of its most conscientious members, attending twelve of the sessions. On 16 March 1638 he was appointed by letters patent to the deanery of Waterford. Here he set about recovering cathedral properties, which had been alienated on long leases with small rents reserved, by claiming that the leases had been forged. By letters patent dated 28 April 1640 he was appointed dean of Lismore, and he was installed in the cathedral on 7 May 1640. He spent less than a week there, during which time he visited Ballydecane, co. Waterford. This was a townland that formed part of the ancient inheritance of the deanery and by 1640 had come into the possession of the earl of Cork. Parry was appointed to this living to recover the deanery's endowment. In this he was unsuccessful because of the demise of the earl of Strafford in 1640 and the outbreak of the Irish rising in 1641.

During the 1640s Parry found a new patron in the earl of Ormond. In 1643, upon his resignation of the prebendary of Stagonil, he was made archdeacon of Glendalough. He retained these livings, along with the treasurership of Christ Church, *in commendam* when he was promoted to the bishopric of Killaloe in 1647. His letters patent were dated 20 March, and the archbishop of Dublin and the bishops of Kildare and Cloyne in Christ Church, Dublin, consecrated him on 28 March. Killaloe, situated in co. Clare, was at this time occupied by the Confederate Roman Catholic forces, and it would appear that he never visited his diocese nor drew an income from it. Hence, he was allowed to hold his former livings *in commendam*. He continued to live in Dublin, where he had a house in St Stephen's Street and held a lease of Chichester House on College Green.

During the 1640s Parry was a defender of the rights and privileges of the established church. In 1641 he was a signatory to a petition to the lords justices that complained about the 'boldness' of the Roman Catholic clergy and sought to defend the financial gains made by the church in the 1630s at the council board. He was also a signatory to a petition, the writing of which has been attributed to him, dated 9 July 1647, to the commissioners from the parliament in England to Ireland. This defended the use of the Book of Common Prayer, which had been prohibited in favour of the *Directory for the Publique Worship of God*. He also defended the church in his posthumous work *David restored, or, An antidote against the prosperity of the wicked and the afflictions of the just* (1660). In this he argued that the divisions and sects that had emerged in the late 1640s would let atheism 'creep in, get ahead, and turn all religion out of doors' (p. 134). Furthermore, something of Parry's theological bent can also be seen in this work in his equating God with the terms majesty, mercies, comforts, and beauties.

The name of Parry's wife is not known. He had at least three children: one daughter, Elinor, who married Robert Hawkshaw, and two sons, John *Parry (*d.* 1677) and Benjamin *Parry (1634–1678). They both followed their father into the Church of Ireland and both of them became bishops of Ossory. Parry died of the plague in Dublin on 20

July 1650 and was buried later that year in St Audoen's Church, Dublin, where a monument was erected to his memory. CIARAN DIAMOND

Sources 'Canon Leslie's typescript succession lists, Killaloe', Representative Church Body Library, Dublin, MS 61.2.10 • *The whole works of Sir James Ware concerning Ireland*, ed. and trans. W. Harris, 1 (1739) • P. Dwyer, *History of Killaloe, from the Reformation to the close of the eighteenth century* (1878) • Burtchaell & Sadleir, *Alum. Dubl.*, 2nd edn • *Irish Builder*, 28 (1886), 307, 308, 320 • J. D. McCafferty, 'John Bramhall and the reconstruction of the Church of Ireland, 1633–1641', PhD diss., U. Cam., 1996 • J. P. Mahaffy, *An epoch in Irish history: Trinity College, Dublin, its foundation and early fortunes, 1591–1660* (1903) • J. W. Stubbs, *The history of the University of Dublin, from its foundation to the end of the eighteenth century* (1889) • J. Morrin, ed., *Calendar of the patent and close rolls of chancery in Ireland, of the reign of Charles I* (1863) • R. Lascelles, ed., *Liber munerum publicorum Hiberniae ... or, The establishments of Ireland*, 2 vols. [1824–30] • H. Cotton, *Fasti ecclesiae Hibernicae*, 5 vols. (1845–60), vols. 1 and 2 • H. J. Lawlor, *The fasti of St Patrick's, Dublin* (1930) • R. Gillespie, *The first chapter act book of Christ Church, Dublin* (1997) • 'Copy chapter acts of Christ Church Cathedral, 1633–1670', Representative Church Body Library, Dublin, MS C.6.1.8.2 • Waterford Cathedral Archives, Representative Church Body Library, Dublin, A. 23 • 'Calendar of Chatsworth/Boyle Manuscripts', NL Ire., MS 12, 813, vol. 3 • *CSP Ire., 1647–60* • T. Sweeney, *Ireland and the printed word: a short descriptive catalogue of early books ... relating to Ireland, printed, 1475–1700* (Dublin, 1997) • 'Archbishop Bulkeley's visitation of Dublin, 1630', ed. M. V. Ronan, *Archivium Hibernicum*, 8 (1941), 56–98 • *DNB* • monument, St Audeon's Church, Dublin

Archives Representative Church Body Library, Dublin, Christ Church Cathedral Archives; Waterford Cathedral Archives

Likenesses J. Dickson, line engraving, BM, NPG; repro. in E. Parry, *David restored or an antidote against the prosperity of the wicked and the afflictions of the just shewing the different ends of both in a most seasonable discourse on the seventy-third psalm* (1660) • J. Dickson, line engraving, repro. in Dwyer, *History of Killaloe*

Parry, Sir (William) Edward (1790–1855), naval officer and Arctic explorer, fourth son of Caleb Hillier *Parry (1755–1822), physician, and Sarah, *née* Rigby (1749–1831), was born at Bath on 19 December 1790. After briefly attending Bath grammar school, he entered the navy in 1803 on board the *Ville de Paris*, the flagship of Admiral Cornwallis, before Brest. He afterwards served in the North Sea and the Baltic in the long war with France. He was promoted to the rank of lieutenant on 6 January 1810 and was appointed to the frigate *Alexandria*, which was employed during the next three years in protecting the Spitsbergen whaling fleet. During this time Parry paid much attention to the study and practice of astronomical observations, and constructed several charts of places on the coast of Norway, and of Balta Sound in the Shetland Islands, for which he received the thanks of the Admiralty. His little treatise, *Nautical Astronomy*, was privately printed by his father.

Since 1812 Britain had been at war with the United States. In June 1813 Parry joined the *La Hogue* (74 guns) at Halifax, Nova Scotia, and in her and other ships continued on the North American station until 1817, when he returned to England on hearing that his father had suffered a stroke. He was at home on half pay when appointed in 1818 to command the *Alexander*, a hired brig, under the orders of Captain John Ross in his expedition to the Arctic seas. With the return of peace, the Admiralty (at the instigation of John Barrow) had decided to resume the search for a north-west passage to the Pacific. The results of this first voyage were meagre, but early in 1819 Parry (still only a lieutenant) was appointed to the sturdy bomb-vessel the *Hecla*, in command of another expedition to discover the passage, and sailed from Deptford in May, with the brig *Griper* in company. His instructions, which were necessarily conditional and vague, were to go up the west side of Baffin Bay, through Lancaster Sound (which Ross had reported land-locked), and so, if possible, to Bering Strait. After a clear run westward through Lancaster Sound he reached Melville Island (one of the later named Parry Islands) and wintered there, hoping to resume the voyage in the following season. This aim was frustrated by pack ice. The two ships returned safely, and came into the Thames in mid-November 1820, with much scientific material. Parry's dispatches, sent in advance by a whaler, had reached the Admiralty on 4 November, on which date he was promoted to the rank of commander. He received the freedom of his native city and many other honours; in the following February he was elected a fellow of the Royal Society and, with the officers and men of the expedition, he received the parliamentary grant previously offered as a reward for those who should first pass the meridian of 110° W within the Arctic circle.

Sir (William) Edward Parry (1790–1855), by Samuel Drummond, in or before 1820

Parry's care for his men, his solution of many of the problems of wintering in the ice, and his meticulous scientific work set a pattern of Arctic exploration for a generation. Many of his young officers (notably James Clark Ross) went on to be famous explorers themselves.

The overland explorations of his good friend John Franklin were intended to be complementary to Parry's expeditions.

Another expedition was resolved on soon after Parry's return to Britain, and on 30 December he was appointed to the *Fury*, which in May 1821 sailed from the Nore in company with her sister ship the *Hecla*, commanded by George Francis Lyon. Passing through Hudson Strait and Foxe Channel on this his longest voyage, he examined Repulse Bay, proved the accuracy of the observations made by Christopher Middleton, passed one winter at Winter Island and another at Igloolik (enlivened by the presence of the local Inuit), and traced Fury and Hecla Strait to its western end. Through the summers of 1822 and 1823 this strait was blocked by ice, and, as symptoms of scurvy were beginning to appear, Parry judged it inadvisable to attempt a third winter in the ice. The ships returned to Britain and were paid off at Deptford on 14 November 1823.

Parry had meantime been advanced to the rank of post captain (8 November 1821) and was now appointed acting hydrographer (1 December 1823). A few weeks later he was entrusted with the command of a third expedition in the *Hecla*, accompanied by the *Fury* (Lieutenant Henry Hoppner), which sailed from Deptford on 8 May 1824; again attempting the passage by Lancaster Sound, he wintered at Port Bowen. On 1 August 1825 both ships were forced ashore in Prince Regent inlet, and, though they were refloated, it was found necessary to abandon the *Fury*. All the men were put on board the *Hecla*, but there was no room for the stores, and Parry accordingly returned to England forthwith. In November 1825 he was confirmed as hydrographer to the Admiralty, an office not then held in high esteem.

On 23 October 1826 Parry married Isabella Louisa (1801–1839), daughter of John Thomas Stanley, first Baron Stanley of Alderley; their surviving children were two daughters and two sons. The elder son, Edward *Parry, became suffragan bishop of Dover; the younger, Charles, a commander in the navy, died at Naples in 1868.

In April 1826 Parry had proposed to the first lord an attempt to reach the pole from Spitsbergen by travelling with sledge-boats over the ice or through any spaces of open water. The proposal was referred to the Royal Society, on whose approval he was appointed again to the *Hecla* and sailed from the Nore on 4 April 1827. The ship was secured in Treurenberg Bay and on 21 June the boats started under Parry's command. After an exhausting struggle across wet and broken ice floes they turned back when Parry realized from his observations that the ice was drifting south almost as fast as they could travel north. His furthest north (lat. 82°43′32″ N) stood as a record for nearly fifty years.

Parry now resumed his duties as hydrographer. He pressed on with preparing surveys for publication, and initiated the exchange of hydrographic material with other nations and also the regular withdrawal of charts for replacement or amendment at the end of every ship's commission. His frustration at the parsimony of the Admiralty brought him into conflict with its first (or political) secretary, John Wilson Croker. Parry and Franklin were knighted on 29 April 1829, and on 13 May, Parry resigned in order to accept the unexpected offer of employment as commissioner of the Australian Agricultural Company. This joint-stock company had been founded in 1824 to breed sheep and employ convicts, but had never paid a dividend. During his four years in Australia, Parry greatly improved the company's prospects by persuading the government to allow it to exchange part of its grant of 1 million acres for better grazing inland.

After a spell as assistant poor-law commissioner for Norfolk (1835–6), Parry, who had done all his exploring in sailing ships, was controller of steam machinery at the Admiralty from April 1837 to December 1846. He had already been called in to reorganize the packet service (overseas mail), which had been transferred from the Post Office to the Admiralty in January 1837, and was responsible for negotiating contracts with steamship companies for carrying the mails to India and elsewhere.

Parry's first wife died in 1839, and on 29 June 1841 he married Catharine Edwards (1808–1896), daughter of the Revd Robert Hankinson and widow of Samuel Hoare, with whom he had twin daughters and a son who died as a Harrow schoolboy.

Parry was captain-superintendent of Haslar Royal Naval Hospital, Hampshire, from December 1846 to 4 June 1852, when he was promoted to the rank of rear-admiral. At this time he was much involved, with others, in planning the search for Franklin. In November 1853 he was appointed lieutenant-governor of the Royal Naval Hospital, Greenwich. During the autumn and winter of 1854 his health was failing, and in the summer of 1855 he went for medical treatment to Ems, Germany, where he died on 8 July. His body was brought to Greenwich, and buried there on 19 July in the mausoleum of the hospital burial-ground.

Parry was the author of *Journal of a voyage for the discovery of a north-west passage from the Atlantic to the Pacific; performed in the years 1819–20 in his majesty's ships Hecla and Griper* (1821). This and the journals of his subsequent voyages were all published by John Murray with the authority of the Admiralty. The memoirs written by his son Edward and published in 1857 dwell on the religious side of Parry's character, which was strongly marked.

J. K. Laughton, *rev.* A. K. Parry

Sources W. E. Parry, *Journal of a voyage for the discovery of a north-west passage from the Atlantic to the Pacific; performed in the years 1819–20, in his majesty's ships Hecla and Griper, under the orders of William Edward Parry, R.N., F.R.S., and commander of the expedition* (1821) • W. E. Parry, *Journal of a second voyage for the discovery of a north-west passage from the Atlantic to the Pacific* (1824) • W. E. Parry, *Appendix to Captain Parry's journal of a second voyage for the discovery of a north-west passage from the Atlantic to the Pacific* (1825) • W. E. Parry, *Journal of a third voyage for the discovery of a north-west passage from the Atlantic to the Pacific* (1826) • W. E. Parry, *Narrative of an attempt to reach the north pole, in boats fitted for the purpose, and attached to his majesty's ship Hecla, in the year 1827, under the command of Captain William Edward Parry, R.N., F.R.S.* (1828) • Scott Polar RI, Parry MSS • PRO, Admiralty MSS • Hydrographic Office, Taunton • A. Parry, *Parry of the Arctic* (1963) • E. Parry, *Memoirs of Rear-Admiral Sir W. Edward Parry, kt., F.R.S.* (1857) • C. R. Markham, 'Parry and his school', *The lands of silence*

(1921), chap. 23 • R. E. D. Ryder, 'Naval participation in the discovery of the north-west passage', *Polar Record*, 4 (1943–6), 309–14 • R. N. Rudmose Brown, 'Sir William Edward Parry', *Arctic*, 12/2 (1959), 98–112 • W. G. Ross, 'Parry's second voyage', *History Today*, 10 (1960), 100–05 • W. E. Parry, Australian journal, 1829–34, Mitchell L., NSW

Archives BL, accounts of voyages, Add. MSS 42089–42092 • Hydrographic Office, Taunton, Admiralty Library, journals • Mitchell L., NSW, Australian journal • NL Aus., letter-books as commissioner for Australian Agricultural Company • NMM, meteorological journals • Scott Polar RI, corresp., journals, and papers | Derbys. RO, letters to Sir John Franklin • NMM, corresp. with Matthew Liddon • NMM, letters to Lord Radstock • PRO, Admiralty MSS • RS, corresp. with Sir John Herschel • Scott Polar RI, corresp. with John Richardson

Likenesses W. Beechey, oils, 1819, priv. coll. • W. Beechey, oils, 1819, NMM • S. Drummond, oils, in or before 1820, NPG [*see illus.*] • S. Drummond, oils, 1823?, priv. coll. • T. Phillips, oils, 1827, Scott Polar RI • S. W. Reynolds, mezzotint, pubd 1827 (after W. Haines), BM • C. Scottowe, oils, exh. RA 1838, NMM • S. Pearce, group portrait, oils, 1851 (*The Arctic Council planning a search for Sir John Franklin*), NPG • H. Allard, engraving (after watercolour by G. Richmond, 1842) • S. Pearce, study, oils, NPG • H. Perry, lithograph, BM

Parry, Edward (1830–1890), bishop-suffragan of Dover, eldest surviving son of Rear-Admiral Sir (William) Edward *Parry (1790–1855), the Arctic explorer, and his wife, Isabella Louisa, *née* Stanley (1801–1839), was born on 14 January 1830, at Sydney, New South Wales, where his father held a temporary appointment from 1830 to 1834. In 1840 he was sent to a Mr Brown's school at Cheam, and towards the close of 1843 to Rugby School, under the headmastership of A. C. Tait. His housemaster, George Edward Lynch Cotton, later bishop of Calcutta, remained a staunch friend throughout his life. In 1846 Parry had reached the 'sixth', and in 1849, after winning many prizes, was awarded a university exhibition of £60 a year. He was head of the school during Tait's last year (1848–9) and, from that time, as he said in later years, Tait proved himself almost a second father to him. Owing to ill health Parry was prevented from trying for a scholarship at Balliol College, Oxford, but in October 1849 he went there as a commoner. In December 1852 he took a first class in *literae humaniores* in the last class list under the old system; he graduated BA in 1852, MA in 1855, and DD in 1870. Being ineligible for almost all Oxford fellowships, by reason of his alien birthplace, he went in January 1853 as tutor to Durham University. In 1854 he was ordained deacon and in 1855 priest, and undertook a long-vacation curacy among the Norham pitmen.

At the close of 1856 Parry left Durham to become curate under Hugh Pearson at Sonning, but in the Easter of 1857 Tait, who had recently been transferred to the see of London, selected him to be his first domestic chaplain. Parry was thus thrown into the very centre of London church life. His secretarial duties were severe, but he found time to continue some parochial work in Marylebone, under Thomas Garnier, later dean of Lincoln, and to take a part in starting the London Diocesan Home Mission. In February 1859 Tait appointed him to the rectory of St Mary's, Acton, and made him one of his examining chaplains. In May of the same year Parry married Matilda, eldest daughter of Benjamin Williams of Limpsfield, Surrey. At this time Acton was developing from a small country hamlet into a populous metropolitan suburb. To meet its growing spiritual needs Parry rebuilt St Mary's Church, enlarged the schools, obtained sites for two new churches, and erected two school churches. In 1863 he became rural dean of Ealing. In the spring of 1869 Tait, who had just become archbishop of Canterbury, appointed him archdeacon and canon of Canterbury.

Tait's active archiepiscopate and the new life of the Anglican church, at home and overseas, had greatly increased the work at Lambeth Palace. The act of 26 Hen. VIII c. 14, for creating suffragan bishops to assist the diocesan bishops, although still extant, had been disused since the reign of Elizabeth. But in 1869, after an attack of an almost fatal illness, Tait obtained the assent of W. E. Gladstone, the prime minister, to the nomination of Parry as his suffragan in accordance with the provisions of the ancient statute. A few weeks later Parry was consecrated in Lambeth Chapel, on Lady day 1870, as fourth bishop of Dover (his predecessor in title, Richard Rogers, died in 1597).

The revival of so archaic an office was received with apathy, even disfavour. But in his double capacity of bishop and archdeacon Parry threw himself into his new work with characteristic thoroughness, relieving Tait of most of his diocesan burdens. The annual number of confirmations under Parry's regime rose at once from under thirty; he toured hitherto neglected parishes regularly and his annual visitation at Canterbury allowed him to meet both clergy and laity. Within the cathedral city the parochial system was strengthened through his efforts by the grouping of the too numerous and ill-endowed parishes under fewer incumbents, and he energetically assisted local charities and institutes. In the lower house of convocation his judgement was highly esteemed. 'I rejoice to think', Archbishop Tait once said in the House of Lords,

> that in my diocese I have had the help of a suffragan who is beloved by the clergy among whom he has laboured; and one effect of his labours among them has been very greatly to increase both my efficiency and the efficiency of the church in the diocese of Canterbury.

Parry declined various offers of promotion, including, in November 1882, that of the bishopric of Sydney with the office of metropolitan of Australia. A fortnight later Archbishop Tait died, but Parry continued the work which he had himself originated, at the cordial invitation of Tait's successor, Archbishop E. W. Benson. Owing to declining health, he resigned his suffragan's commission in November 1889, and died at St Leonards on 11 April 1890, survived by his wife and six children. He was buried in the churchyard of St Martin's, Canterbury. The fine recumbent effigy in the nave of Canterbury Cathedral; the replica in Lambeth Palace of the portrait by H. von Herkomer RA, presented in 1886 by the Kentish clergy and laity to his wife; the Parry Library in the King's School,

Canterbury; and the Parry prize fund at the Clergy Orphan School marked his standing in the diocese. Memorial tablets were also erected in Rugby Chapel and in St Mary's Church at Acton.

Though allied by his early surroundings to the evangelical school, Parry was no doctrinaire or party man. The keynote of his visitation charges is catholic tolerance, fairness, and generous sympathy with good persons of all schools. In his opinion it was the duty of the clergy to master the bearings of modern research on the Bible, while basing their main principles on the divinity and personal work of Christ. Though influenced by Tait, he was more tolerant than that prelate. For many years he was librarian to the chapter, and any point of antiquarian or architectural interest was always sure of his attention. By his personal character and example he formed and fulfilled the ideal of a new and high office in the English church.

His published works were the lives of his father and sailor brother: *Memoirs of Rear-Admiral Sir W. E. Parry* (1857) and *Memorials of Charles Parry, RN* (1870).

F. S. PARRY, *rev.* H. C. G. MATTHEW

Sources *The Times* (12 April 1890) • *The Guardian* (16 April 1890) • *Kentish Observer* (17 April 1890) • W. Benham and R. T. Davidson, *Life of Archibald Campbell Tait*, 2 vols. (1891) • *CGPLA Eng. & Wales* (1890)
Archives Scott Polar RI, journals and notes | Bodl. Oxf., corresp. with Lord Kimberley • LPL, corresp. with A. C. Tait • LPL, letters to E. W. Benson
Likenesses H. von Herkomer, portrait, presented in 1886; replica, at LPL in 1895 • R. T., wood-engraving, NPG; repro. in *ILN* (19 April 1890) • effigy; at Canterbury Cathedral in 1895 • wood-engraving (after photograph by Mason & Co.), NPG; repro. in *ILN* (9 April 1870)
Wealth at death £16,259 0s. 7d.: resworn probate, Dec 1892, *CGPLA Eng. & Wales* (1890)

Parry, Sir (William) Edward (1893–1972), naval officer, was born in London on 8 April 1893, the elder child and only son of Sir (Frederick) Sydney Parry (1861–1941), civil servant, and his wife, Anna Mary, daughter of William Henry Fremantle, a canon of Canterbury and fellow of All Souls and Balliol colleges, Oxford, and later dean of Ripon. His paternal grandfather, Edward *Parry (1830–1890), was archdeacon of Canterbury and later suffragan bishop of Dover. Parry came of a family with a long and distinguished naval tradition, going back almost 200 years. His great-grandfather, Admiral Sir (William) Edward Parry (1790–1855), was the well-known Arctic explorer, and Admiral Sir Thomas Francis Fremantle (1765–1819), one of Nelson's captains at Trafalgar, was a great-great-grandfather.

Parry entered the Royal Naval College, Osborne, as a naval cadet in September 1905 and quickly showed great intellectual ability. He passed out of the Royal Naval College, Dartmouth, top of his term four years later and gained five prizes. As a lieutenant Parry specialized in the torpedo branch which then included responsibility for all the navy's electrical equipment. In the First World War he served as torpedo officer of the cruiser *Birmingham* in the Grand Fleet. In 1922 Parry married Maude Mary Douglas-Hamilton (*d.* 1971), whose first marriage had been annulled, daughter of Dr Arthur Charles de Beauvoir Phillips. They had a son and a daughter who were twins.

Parry was promoted commander in 1927 and in 1934, after a very successful commission as executive officer and second in command of the aircraft-carrier *Eagle* on the China station, he was promoted captain. His first command was the anti-submarine school at Portland, 1936–7, after which he took the Imperial Defence College course. In 1938 he was lent to the Royal New Zealand Navy for command of the cruiser *Achilles*, and in that appointment he took part in the battle of the River Plate (13 December 1939), in which he was wounded but continued in command. The battle resulted in the self-destruction of the formidable German 'pocket battleship' *Admiral Graf Spee* off Montevideo four days later. Parry was appointed CB (1939) for his part in that action, and in 1940–42 served as commodore commanding the New Zealand squadron and first naval member of the New Zealand naval board.

After returning home Parry took command of the recently modernized battle cruiser *Renown*, which among other duties carried Winston Churchill and his staff to Canada and Egypt for the second Quebec and Cairo conferences. In 1944 he was promoted rear-admiral and for the invasion of Normandy (June 1944) he was in command of one of the two 'follow-up' forces. After a period as deputy head of the naval division of the Allied Control Commission for Germany, in 1946 he was appointed director of naval intelligence, an important post which he held for two difficult years of peacetime retrenchment. In 1948 he was promoted vice-admiral and was lent to India as commander-in-chief of the Royal Indian Navy. His task was a very taxing one as not only had it recently been riven by mutinies but 'Indianization' of the service was rapidly being carried out and the British withdrawal from the subcontinent was imminent.

In 1950 Parry was advanced to KCB and he was promoted admiral in the following year. He retired in 1952 and took up fruit farming in Kent. His daughter later wrote biographies of her Parry and Fremantle ancestors. His wife was of great help to him both in New Zealand, where they won the confidence of the Labour politicians then in power and of the naval personnel, and in India where they were equally successful with the congress leaders and became friends of Jawaharlal Nehru. Parry died in London on 21 August 1972.

STEPHEN W. ROSKILL, *rev.*

Sources S. W. Roskill, *The war at sea, 1939–1945*, 3 vols. in 4 (1954–61) • S. D. Waters, *The Royal New Zealand Navy* (1956) • E. Millington-Drake, *The drama of Graf Spee and the battle of the Plate* (1965) • personal knowledge (1986) • *CGPLA Eng. & Wales* (1973) • *The Times* (22 Aug 1972) • *WWW*
Archives IWM, diaries, corresp. and papers | SOUND IWM SA, oral history interview
Likenesses W. Stoneman, photograph, 1947, NPG
Wealth at death £35,131: probate, 28 March 1973, *CGPLA Eng. & Wales*

Parry, Sir Edward Abbott (1863–1943). *See under* Parry, John Humffreys (1816–1880).

Parry, Henry (1561–1616), bishop of Worcester, was born in 1561 about 20 December, in Wiltshire, probably at Salisbury, the son of Henry Parry, chancellor of Salisbury Cathedral. In November 1576 he was elected a scholar of Corpus Christi College, Oxford. He graduated BA in October 1581, proceeded MA in April 1585, and was elected a fellow in April 1586, holding the position of Greek reader in the college. At Oxford, Parry was prominent in the theological debates of his time. He published in 1587 a catechism, *The Summe of Christian Religion*, which was widely used in the university in subsequent years, and *Victoria Christiana* (1594), a 1591 sermon. He was admitted BTh in April 1592 and DTh in February 1596 and intervened decisively on the Calvinist side in the Lambeth articles controversy of 1595–7. During the 1590s Parry was presented to a succession of Kent parishes by Archbishop John Whitgift—Monkton (1591–4), Great Mongeham (1594–6), and Chevening and Sundridge (1596–1610)—but retained a close connection with his college. When Richard Hooker died in 1600 Parry was one of those Corpus men responsible for preserving and resolving to edit his unpublished theology. At some date, probably in the 1590s, he married; his wife's name was Elizabeth.

In 1602 and 1603, by which time Parry had been made a royal chaplain, his personality was recorded in the diary kept by John Manningham, a student of the Middle Temple in London. Parry is found reminiscing about his upbringing, discussing sermons, passing on gossip from the court, providing the diarist with a recipe for making 'ale for the spring' and recommending a new hallucinatory drug available from his brother-in-law, the physician Peter Turner, which 'will for a tyme lay a man in a sweete trans [trance]' (*Diary of John Manningham*, 82). Manningham heard Parry preach on 23 March 1603 as Queen Elizabeth lay on her death bed, his delivery being 'soe fervent and effectuall' that he left 'few eyes drye'. That night over dinner and the following day Parry related to Manningham full details of the death bed scene, in which he elicited from Elizabeth 'a signe … that shee beleeved that fayth which shee hath caused to be professed, and looked faythfully to be saved by Christes merits and mercy only, and noe other meanes' (ibid., 206–7).

Parry prospered under James I: at the court he was 'greatly respected and reverenced', the view being that 'it was not possible to deliver sounder matter, nor with better method' (Harington, 2.205). In August 1605 he was installed as dean of Chester and the following year in August he preached so powerfully before James I and Christian IV of Denmark at Rochester that James—a connoisseur of sermons—professed 'he seldom heard a better' preacher and Christian presented Parry with a valuable ring. In June 1607 Parry was elevated to the bishopric of Gloucester.

As a bishop Parry epitomized the dominant strain of Jacobean prelacy: preacher, pastor, and patron. At Gloucester he drew up the schedule for his primary visitation of the diocese when still bishop-elect, provided a new pulpit for the cathedral in 1609, and personally led the visitation of 1610. It was also his practice to examine or

Henry Parry (1561–1616), by unknown artist, 1614

license curates himself rather than delegate the task to his chancellor. In July 1610 he was translated to Worcester, where he died 'of a palsy' (Wood, *Ath. Oxon.*, 2.193) on 12 December 1616 and was buried in his cathedral. The inscription on Parry's tomb celebrated his 'assiduous preaching of God's word' but he was also a benefactor and investor in the New World. He gave £20 per annum to the destitute of Gloucester while bishop there, contributed £40 to the erection of the arts schools at Oxford, and, in 1612, subscribed £13 6*s.* 8*d.* to the refinancing of the Virginia Company. His will, dated 26 November 1614, left legacies totalling £1500 to his children, Henry, Richard, George, and Martha, but occasioned a dispute between his widow, Elizabeth, the executrix, and eldest son, Henry, acting with his cousin Samuel Turner.

WILLIAM RICHARDSON

Sources Wood, *Ath. Oxon.*, new edn • Foster, *Alum. Oxon.* • *The diary of John Manningham of the Middle Temple, 1602–1603*, ed. R. P. Sorlien (Hanover, NH, 1976) • K. Fincham, *Prelate as pastor: the episcopate of James I* (1990) • C. J. Sisson, *The judicious marriage of Mr Hooker and the birth of 'The laws of ecclesiastical polity'* (1940) • *Hist. U. Oxf.* 3: *Colleg. univ.* • N. Tyacke, *Anti-Calvinists: the rise of English Arminianism, c.1590–1640* (1987) • J. Harington, *Nugae antiquae*, ed. T. Park and H. Harington, 2 vols. (1804) • *VCH Gloucestershire*, vol. 4 • B. Willis, *A survey of the cathedrals*, 3 vols. (1742) • A. Brown, ed., *The genesis of the United States*, 2 vols. (1890) • PRO, PROB 11/129, fols. 289v–290v

Archives BL, corresp., Add. MS 36294, fol. 7 • Bodl. Oxf., corresp., MS Eng. Lett. 41100, fol. 29 • Bodl. Oxf., corresp., MS Rawl. D 47, fols. 58b, 60b, 62, 62b, 163, 192 • Bodl. Oxf., corresp., MS Rawl. D 1175, fol. 83b | Bodl. Oxf., corresp., MS James 13

Likenesses oils, 1614, Hartlebury Castle, Worcestershire [*see illus.*] · effigy, Worcester Cathedral
Wealth at death over £1500: PRO, PROB 11/129, fols. 289*v*–290*v*

Parry, Henry Hutton (1827–1893). *See under* Parry, Thomas (1795–1870).

Parry, Sir (Charles) Hubert Hastings, baronet (1848–1918), composer and historian of music, was born on 27 February 1848 at 2 Richmond Terrace, Bournemouth, the sixth of six children of Thomas Gambier *Parry (1816–1888) of Highnam Court, Gloucestershire, painter and art collector, and his first wife, (Anna Maria) Isabella (1816–1848), the second daughter of Henry Fynes *Clinton and his wife, Katherine.

Early years and education, 1848–1870 Hubert Parry grew up at Highnam Court in the company of his elder brother Charles Clinton (*b.* 1840) and his sister Lucy (*b.* 1841). His mother died in Bournemouth from consumption twelve days after his birth. In memory of her and three infant sons, Francis Gambier (*b.* and *d.* 1843), Edward Clement Hervey (1844–5), and Henry (*b.* and *d.* 1846), his father built a church in the grounds of Highnam. The church, perhaps one of the finest examples of the nineteenth-century Gothic style, was also a monument to Thomas Gambier Parry's enthusiasm for the high-church ecclesiological movement. In 1851 he married Ethelinda Lear (1826–1896), the second daughter of Francis Lear, dean of Salisbury, and Isabella Mary Majendie. By this marriage he had a further six children, who took the surname Gambier Parry.

Hubert Parry's education began in January 1856 at a preparatory school in Malvern, where he stayed until the summer of 1858. From there he moved to a school at Twyford, near Winchester, where, owing to the sympathetic encouragement of its headmaster, George William Kitchin, and the acquaintance of S. S. Wesley at Winchester Cathedral, his interest in music began to develop significantly. During the school holidays he studied the piano and took rudimentary harmony lessons with Edward Brind, organist at Highnam church. Parry went with Brind to the Hereford Three Choirs festival in 1861, an experience which left a deep impression and which marked the beginning of a lifelong association with the festival. In 1861 Parry followed his elder brother to Eton College, where, despite the early signs of heart trouble, he entered with great alacrity into the sporting life of the school, playing in the oppidan wall eleven and the field school eleven. In 1866 he became head keeper of the field and second keeper of the school wall team. More formal musical instruction began in 1863 with Sir George Elvey, organist at St George's Chapel, Windsor, under whom Parry produced a series of anthems and motets, pieces for organ and piano, partsongs, madrigals, and several songs. Some of these pieces were performed at the Eton College Musical Society, which he helped to found in 1863 with his friends Edward Hamilton and Spencer Lyttelton. In December 1866, as the youngest ever successful candidate, he took the Oxford BMus degree examination, submitting a cantata, *O Lord, Thou hast Cast Us out*, as his exercise. After Eton he matriculated in 1867 as a commoner at

Sir (Charles) Hubert Hastings Parry, baronet (1848–1918), by Emil Otto Hoppé, 1915

Exeter College, Oxford, where, with John Stainer, he participated to the full in the Exeter College Music Society (of which he became president in 1869) and in the playing of chamber music.

While at Oxford, Parry studied law and history but received only sporadic tuition in music. Probably the most significant period of instruction was with Henry Hugo Pierson in Stuttgart during the summer of 1867, in which Parry studied orchestration and composition. Under Pierson he orchestrated the slow movement of his early sonata in F minor for piano duet, the *Allegro religioso*, which was performed at the Gloucester festival in September 1868 under S. S. Wesley's baton. Although it had become apparent at Oxford that Parry wanted to pursue a career in music, his father was candidly against the idea. An important purpose of the visit to Stuttgart was to learn German, and in 1868 a visit to Liège was organized for Parry to practise French; both sojourns abroad were calculated to smooth the way for a life in the world of commerce. Moreover, Parry had fallen in love with Lady (Elizabeth) Maude Herbert (1851–1933), the second daughter of Sidney *Herbert, first Lord Herbert of Lea, whose family were also averse to his serious pursuit of music, particularly after his clandestine engagement to Maude in the spring of 1870. Parry therefore resolved to embark on a career as an underwriter at Lloyd's and to study music in his spare time, a course of action which he hoped would placate his father and convince Maude's family that he could support her. It had the desired effect, and they married at St Paul's, Knightsbridge, London, on 25 June 1872.

Years of struggle, 1870–1880 While working at Lloyd's, Parry took lessons with Sir William Sterndale Bennett, but found them insufficiently critical, so he made enquiries through his friend Walter Broadwood and through Joseph Joachim to study with Brahms in Vienna. This came to nothing, so Parry applied to Edward Dannreuther, a renowned pioneer, champion of Wagner, and piano virtuoso. At first study with Dannreuther was in the form of piano lessons, but later these developed more in analytical and compositional directions and included an introduction to the music of Wagner.

The period 1870 to 1876 proved to be an important formative time for Parry. Exposed to the concert life of London, the opera, the sub-editorship of George Grove's new *Dictionary of Music and Musicians* (from 1875), for which he provided numerous articles, and the second cycle of *The Ring* tetralogy at Bayreuth in 1876, Parry rejected the Mendelssohnian aesthetic of his early works for a more progressive musical language influenced by both Wagner and Brahms. Dannreuther, whose role was one of artistic mentor and counsellor, provided Parry both with an introduction to London's influential musical circles and a vital platform for his new compositions with a series of chamber concerts at Dannreuther's home at 12 Orme Square, Bayswater. Nearly all Parry's chamber works—the *Grosses duo* in E minor, the three piano trios, the wind nonet, the *Fantasie-Sonata* for violin and piano, the piano quartet, the string quartet no. 3, and the string quintet—were composed for Orme Square. In 1877, during the Wagner festival in London, Parry met Wagner while he was staying at Orme Square. He was also introduced to Hans Richter, who was soon to establish himself as the capital's premier conductor. Parry's first important orchestral work, the overture *Guillem de Cabestanh*, was performed at the Crystal Palace in March 1879, followed a year later by two performances of his piano concerto in F♯ major conducted by August Manns and Richter, both with Dannreuther as soloist. This brought Parry's name to prominence, as did the more controversial performance of his first choral commission, *Prometheus Unbound*, for the Three Choirs festival at Gloucester in September 1880.

The importance of *Prometheus Unbound*, with its overt Wagnerian rhetoric, has perhaps been overstated as a milestone in the so-called English musical renaissance. Nevertheless the choice of Shelley's text signified much in the context of Parry's developing philosophy and political outlook. Since leaving Oxford, where he had been profoundly influenced by John Ruskin and Charles Darwin and later by the writings of Matthew Arnold, Samuel Butler, George Eliot, and Herbert Spencer, Parry, like his brother before him, steadily found himself rejecting the traditional Christian dogma of his upbringing. By 1873 he was forced to declare his unbelief, which, coupled with his support for Gladstone and the reforming policies of the Liberals, caused a period of alienation from his father.

In 1876 Maude gave birth to their first daughter, Dorothea, named after their favourite character in George Eliot's *Middlemarch*. The strain of childbirth took its toll on Maude, who was slow to recover. Her health, which continued to be a cause for concern to Parry throughout his life, eventually forced him to spend six months in Cannes from November 1876 until April 1877. Here, isolated from London's musical life, he developed a close working relationship with the violinist Edward Guerini. After arriving back in London, Parry ceased working at Lloyd's in order to pursue music full time. The following year there was a further addition to the family with the birth of their second daughter, Gwendolen (named after the character in George Eliot's *Daniel Deronda*).

Years of renown, 1880–1902 After the publicity gained by the piano concerto and *Prometheus*, Parry's reputation in London and the provinces began to increase substantially. His first symphony in G, initially commissioned by Richter, was conducted by the composer at Birmingham in August 1882 and by Manns at the Crystal Palace in 1883. Charles Villiers Stanford, who had performed *Prometheus* at Cambridge in 1881, commissioned some incidental music for the Amateur Dramatic Club's production of Aristophanes' *The Birds* and also a second symphony in F (the 'Cambridge') for the Cambridge University Musical Society. Both were performed in 1883, as was Parry's second commission for the Gloucester festival, the ode *The Glories of our Blood and State*. The same year Parry received an honorary doctorate from Cambridge University in recognition of his work as a composer and scholar. Perhaps more auspiciously, he took up his post as professor of music history at the newly founded Royal College of Music. In sharp contrast to the satisfaction brought by his professional achievements, 1883 also brought news of the death in Sydney, Australia, of his elder brother, which affected him deeply. Clinton Parry, a brilliant scholar at Oxford, yet sent down in disgrace, had squandered large sums of his father's money in South Africa, had become an alcoholic and a danger to his wife and family, and had been a liability to his father.

A sign of Parry's increasing success was marked by the completion in 1881 of 'Knight's Croft', a seaside home at Rustington, near Littlehampton, designed by the architect Norman Shaw. Maude spent much time in Rustington, and for Parry it proved to be a refuge from the vicissitudes of life in London as well as an important base for his chief recreation, sailing. Pressures were indeed mounting in the form of teaching and lecturing at the Royal College of Music, at Oxford (where he was choragus and from which he received an honorary doctorate in 1884), and at Cambridge and Birmingham, which inevitably restricted the possibilities for composition. In 1884 Parry began work on his opera *Guenever*, but the following year his worsening heart trouble (probably a combination of angina and rheumatic fever) led him to take an extended holiday on a cruise around the coast of South America in the company of Sedley Taylor. For Parry these periods of convalescence rarely had their desired effect. Always motivated by a sense of duty and mission, he could not be prevented from resuming work at the earliest opportunity. In 1886, a year which marked his removal to 17 Kensington Square, he completed *Guenever*, but it was refused by Carl Rosa and, despite Stanford's efforts, failed to be taken up on the continent. This experience inevitably dented Parry's confidence, leaving him embittered and disillusioned by a genre which he never attempted again.

And yet within a few months Parry's fortunes were transformed with the triumph of his setting of Milton's *Blest Pair of Sirens*, commissioned by Stanford for the Bach Choir's celebration of Queen Victoria's golden jubilee in 1887. Almost immediately there was an insatiable demand for new works: the oratorio *Judith* was composed for Birmingham in 1888, the *Ode on St Cecilia's Day* for Leeds in 1889, and two symphonies, no. 3 in C (the 'English') for the Philharmonic Society, and no. 4 in E minor for Richter, were both given in 1889. In acceding to the public demand for choral music, and particularly for oratorio, Parry found himself in something of a dilemma. He was loath to turn down commissions from choral festivals, and yet he disliked the conventional Old Testament oratorio form which he knew would be expected. Indeed, for the Birmingham commission of 1888 he considered a variety of subjects ranging from the Albigensians to the story of Columbus, but had to capitulate to the Birmingham committee, who wanted a work with sufficient choral participation. *Judith* was an immediate success with the public, who clamoured for more. *Job*, a shorter work whose text indicates a shift away from a historical subject towards philosophical allegory, was written for Worcester in 1892 and *King Saul* for Birmingham in 1894. Bernard Shaw, who admired the creative vigour of *Prometheus* and of the cantata *L'allegro ed il penseroso*, written for Norwich in 1890, severely criticized Parry's oratorios on the grounds that he believed the genre did little to draw out the composer's natural gifts for 'absolute music'. These gifts for instrumental music did momentarily surface in 1897 with two fine orchestral works, the *Symphonic Variations* and the *Elegy for Brahms*, but the demand for choral music remained intense.

With the *Invocation to Music*, written to mark the bicentenary of Purcell's death in 1895, Parry entered into the first of several collaborations with the poet Robert Bridges. The relationship was never easy, but it did not prevent them from working together on *A Song of Darkness and Light* for Gloucester (1898), on a *Memorial Ode* for Eton College (1908), and, during the war, on a naval ode, *The Chivalry of the Sea* (1916), one of the composer's finest choral essays. He was also expected, as the country's unofficial composer laureate, to respond to official occasions of national significance. In celebration of the queen's diamond jubilee in 1897 he produced a setting of the Magnificat for the Hereford festival, and in commemoration of the achievements of the British forces in South Africa he wrote a splendid Thanksgiving Te Deum (1900). The anthem 'I was glad', composed for the coronation of Edward VII in 1902, is one of the most impressive and enduring pieces of ceremonial music ever written.

In January 1895 Parry succeeded Grove as director of the Royal College of Music. Although Frederick Bridge, Walter Parratt, Stanford, and Franklin Taylor had also been strong candidates, the college council unanimously recommended Parry. The appointment was testimony to his extraordinary charisma. An eminently likeable man, he was generous, open, and able to engender inspiration, vision, sympathy, and self-belief, particularly among the young. Behind the face presented to the world lay a nervous and depressive temperament, but his public profile was one of immense warmth, happiness, and geniality, and his conscientiousness, selflessness, and sense of duty were unshakeable. Even Bernard Shaw feared meeting him, lest he should come under his spell. In recognition of his contribution to the nation's musical life he was knighted in 1898, in 1902 was created a baronet, and in 1905 invested with the CVO.

Away from the public gaze, Parry's domestic life was less happy. Arthur Ponsonby, his son-in-law, recalled that Maude

> never cared for his music, never shared his life, was no companion, and with her funny arrested development and self-centred smallness of vision was no help or comfort to him at all. His devotion to her was pathetic and yet it always seemed as if he were unaware that he could never win her. She hampered him, irritated him, bullied him [and] was a drain on him. (Ponsonby, diary, October 1918)

The resultant inner loneliness, Ponsonby maintained, 'gave him the note of melancholy which came out in his music'. The affection he craved from his wife came instead from his elder daughter, Dorothea. She married Ponsonby in 1898, and their home after 1902 at Shulbrede Priory on the north Sussex border became a favourite haunt. Gwen, his younger daughter, married Harry Plunket Greene, the famous baritone, in 1899. With the death of his stepmother in 1896 Parry also inherited Highnam Court. After a bitter dispute with his half-brother Ernest Gambier Parry over the management of the estate, which was in severe financial trouble, Parry took up residence at Highnam. Ernest moved out, and a lifelong rift between the two brothers ensued.

Later works, 1903–1914 *A Song of Darkness and Light*, written for the Norwich festival in 1898, marked the beginning of a series of choral works in which Parry hoped to express something of his own heterodoxy. Works such as *War and Peace* (1903), *Voces clamantium* (1903), *The Love that Casteth out Fear* (1904), *The Soul's Ransom* (1906), *A Vision of Life* (1907), and *Beyond these Voices there is Peace* (1908) express his profound commitment to humanitarianism. These ethical oratorios, with texts partly written by the composer and partly compiled from the Bible, had their advocates, among them Elgar, Vaughan Williams, Walford Davies, and Howells, but the unfocused philosophical message of the works left audiences unmoved. Only his setting of Browning's *Pied Piper of Hamelin* (1905) stands out, as the most successful large-scale choral work of this period.

At this time Parry began to suffer a series of breakdowns in his health. He took several holidays abroad, but he was too stubborn to desist from his work at the Royal College for long. A more serious breakdown occurred in 1908, when he felt compelled to give up his position as professor of music at Oxford, a post he had held since 1900. His severance with the university was a powerful blow, for his closeness to academic life found voice not only in scholarship and lectures, but also in incidental music written for the Oxford University Dramatic Club's productions of Aristophanes' *The Frogs* (1892) and *The Clouds* (1905).

Resignation from Oxford combined with the failure of his ethical choral works induced Parry to reassess his creative objectives. He fulfilled a desire to write a book on his idol, J. S. Bach (1909), added to his Darwinist historical perspective in *The Art of Music* (1893; rev. 1896), and published a compilation of his Oxford lectures in *Style in Musical Art* (1911). Presented with new opportunities from the Philharmonic Society, he extensively revised his fourth symphony (1909–10), and produced his fifth symphony in B minor in four linked movements (later renamed *Symphonic Fantasia '1912'*), perhaps his masterpiece, for the Philharmonic's centenary celebrations in 1912. This Indian summer of compositional activity was also underlined by his last choral work for the Three Choirs festival, *Ode on the Nativity* (Hereford, 1912) which, with its intricate structural and motivic organization, reflected the concentrated thinking of the fifth symphony.

Decline and death, 1914–1918 Parry's last orchestral work, *From Death to Life* (1914), a symphonic poem with a strong ethical programme, was composed during the first months of the First World War. Its mixture of lament and optimism articulated many of his conflicting emotions and beliefs. Even with the deterioration of the international situation Parry, a pro-Teuton, genuinely believed that Germany would not go to war, a view that was clear from the incidental music he wrote for *The Acharnians* in February 1914, in which he sought, by means of popular tunes from the street and music-hall, national anthems, and other patriotic songs, to parody those in government and elsewhere who were whipping up panic and hysteria. Therefore, when hostilities did break out, the shock was devastating. During the war he watched a life's work of progress and education being wiped away as the male population—particularly the new fertile generation of composing talent—of the Royal College dwindled. Sailing, his chief form of pleasure, was forbidden, so instead he devoted his time to the Music in Wartime movement, providing funds for concerts in schools, hospitals, and camps as well as for ailing choral societies. To meet the War Office's demand for rifle butts, many of the trees on his beloved Highnam estate were felled. Another casualty of the war was his relationship with Stanford, which, after a serious altercation at the end of 1916, became strained to the point of estrangement.

Most of Parry's last works, organ preludes, piano pieces, and songs, were small-scale. The overwhelmingly popular 'Jerusalem', a setting of William Blake's poem which has earned Parry's music the national distinction of concluding each year the last night of the Proms, was written originally for Francis Younghusband's Fight for Right society in 1916 and was taken up by Millicent Fawcett and the National Union of Women's Suffrage Societies in 1917, an organization to which Parry and his wife (a keen suffragist) gave their support. Most substantial was his naval ode, *The Chivalry of the Sea* (1916), a dark, brooding choral elegy, and a cycle of six unaccompanied motets, the *Songs of Farewell*, which, as well as being some of the finest romantic *a cappella* music, are perhaps the most eloquent and personal disclosures of his unorthodox credo. His last literary work, *Instinct and Character*, a kind of philosophical apologia, was rejected by Macmillan and remains unpublished.

Though heart trouble had dogged Parry all his life, his death was caused by blood poisoning and influenza. He died at Rustington on 7 October 1918, a month before the armistice. At the suggestion of Stanford he was buried, nine days later, in the crypt of St Paul's Cathedral. A memorial tablet, with an inscription by Bridges, was unveiled in Gloucester Cathedral during the Three Choirs festival in 1922.

Parry's importance can be measured in several branches of the music profession. As a scholar he was an original thinker on a wide variety of historical, theoretical, and aesthetic issues which are promulgated in his books, articles, and lectures. Parry believed that music and life were inseparable and this he communicated almost evangelistically to his students. As an academic and administrator he did much to promote the status and welfare of the musician, though, much to his frustration, he was unable to establish the condition of residence as part of the Oxford BMus degree (as Stanford had done at Cambridge in 1893), which he felt had held back the acceptance of music as a major academic discipline. Yet it must be as a composer that Parry should be remembered. Although his creative life was to some extent hindered by administration, teaching, and examining, his finest choral and instrumental works were enormously influential. His broad, muscular diatonic language, as revealed in works such as *Blest Pair of Sirens*, 'I was glad', the *Songs of Farewell*, 'Jerusalem', and the five symphonies set a powerful precedent for later British composers. Parry's distinctive style provided a tangible link between Wesley and Stainer of the mid-nineteenth century and those that followed him, such as Elgar, Vaughan Williams, Walton, and Finzi. JEREMY DIBBLE

Sources J. Dibble, *C. Hubert H. Parry: his life and music* (1992) • C. L. Graves, *Hubert Parry*, 2 vols. (1926) • C. H. H. Parry, *College addresses* (1920) • A. Ponsonby, 'Brief glimpses' • A. Ponsonby, MS diary, Shulbrede Priory, Lynchmere, Sussex • R. O. Morris, *Hubert Parry, music and letters*, 1 (1920), 94–103 • J. A. Fuller-Maitland, *The music of Parry and Stanford* (1934) • A. E. F. Dickinson, 'The neglected Parry', *MT*, 90 (1949), 108–11 • W. M. A. Hadow, 'Sir Hubert Parry', *Proceedings of the Musical Association*, 45 (1918–19), 135–47 • H. Howells, 'Hubert Parry', *RCM Magazine*, 65/3 (1969), 19–23 • J. C. Dibble, 'The music of Hubert Parry: a critical and analytical study', PhD diss., U. Southampton, 1986 • G. Greene, *Two witnesses* (1930) • b. cert. • Burke, *Peerage*

Archives Bodl. Oxf. • Royal College of Music, London, papers • Shulbrede Priory, Lynchmere, Sussex | BL, Philharmonic MSS • BL, corresp. with Macmillans, Add. MS 55239 • BL, letters to Sir Edward Walter Hamilton, Add. MS 48621 • BL, letters to F. G. Edwards, Eg MS 3090 • Bodl. Oxf., letters to Dannreuther • Elgar Birthplace Museum, Broadheath, letters to Edward Elgar • FM Cam., letters to W. Barclay Squire • King's Cam., Dent MSS • McMaster University, Hamilton, Ontario, letters to William Hannam • RA, letters to Helen Richmond • U. Reading L., letters from Robert Bridges | SOUND BL NSA

Likenesses photographs, 1861–1917, Shulbrede Priory, Sussex · H. von Herkomer, portrait, 1889 · H. von Herkomer, sketch, 1891, repro. in *Daily Graphic* (17 June 1891) · photograph, *c.*1895, Royal College of Music, London · H. S. Rathbone, portrait, 1897 · W. Rothenstein, chalk drawing, 1897, NPG · W. Rothenstein, pencil drawing, 1897 · C. Mellili, miniature statue, 1906, Shulbrede Priory, Sussex · C. E. M. Pollock, bronze bust, *c.*1910, Royal College of Music, London · E. O. Hoppé, photograph, 1915, NPG, Royal College of Music, London [*see illus.*] · W. & D. Downey, woodburytype photograph, NPG; repro. in W. Downey and D. Downey, *The cabinet portrait gallery*, vol. 4 (1893)

Wealth at death £31,127 16*s*. 6*d*.: probate, 19 June 1919, *CGPLA Eng. & Wales*

Parry, James (*c.*1805–*c.*1871). *See under* Parry, Joseph (1744–1826).

Parry, John (*d.* 1677), Church of Ireland bishop of Ossory, was born in Dublin, the eldest son of Edward *Parry (*d.* 1650), later bishop of Killaloe, and older brother of Benjamin *Parry, later bishop of Ossory. He attended Trinity College, Dublin, from where he graduated BA, and was one of those who listened to the farewell sermon of the archbishop of Dublin, Launcelot Bulkeley, in St Patrick's Cathedral in November 1649. Bulkeley gave the sermon shortly after he had been released from gaol, where he had been imprisoned for resisting the act which had prohibited the use of the Book of Common Prayer. Parry moved to Oxford, where in March 1651 his degree was incorporated, and was elected a fellow of Jesus College, proceeding MA in June 1653.

In 1660 Parry was appointed to the rectorship of Hope in Flintshire, which he held until 1666, when he was succeeded by his brother Benjamin. He also became a chaplain to James Butler, marquess (later duke) of Ormond, who had recently become the lord lieutenant of Ireland, and returned to Ireland, where he proceeded BD at Trinity College, Dublin, in January 1661 and DD in 1662. Parry was appointed as treasurer of Christ Church, Dublin, in February 1661, but later that year returned to Oxford, where he was incorporated to the degree of BD on 25 June 1661. On 19 February 1662 he was installed as the prebendary of Bugthorpe near Stamford Bridge in Yorkshire, and in July 1664 he was appointed to the rectorship of St John of Jerusalem in the diocese of Cork. In 1665 Sir James Ware's biographical work on Irish bishops, which was later translated into English by Walter Harris in 1739, was published, and Parry's 'Epistola ad Jacobum Waraeum' was included as a preface.

In April 1666, through the patronage of Ormond, Parry was installed as dean of Christ Church, Dublin, and precentor of St Patrick's, Dublin, where he remained for the rest of his life. He was also rector of St Andrew's, Dublin, from 1666 to 1677, and held the deanery of Cork for St John of Jerusalem for the same period. In August 1667 he preached on Nehemiah 13: 14 at Christ Church before the earl of Ossory, who was deputizing as lord lieutenant for his father, the duke of Ormond. The sermon, which was published in 1667, favourably compared Nehemiah's godly governorship of Jerusalem through difficult times with Ossory's and Ormond's governorship of Ireland. Parry was consecrated as bishop of Ossory by the archbishop of Dublin on 28 April 1672. About this time he was appointed to the rectorship of Llaniestyn in Anglesey, a position he held until his death. Sir James Ware recorded that during his time as bishop Parry was considered 'a prelate of very good abilities in point of learning, a great benefactor to his church and a patron and encourager of his clergy' (*Whole Works*, 428). He contributed much to the diocese, organizing the restoration of the fabric of St Canice's and in December 1672 entering into a contract on behalf of the local dean and chapter with a local builder to 'help maintain and repair, and keep all timber and carpentry work of the several roofs of the cathedral of St. Canice, Kilkenny for twenty one years' (Graves and Prim, 46). He also contributed to the installation of a new peal of bells in the cathedral and is said to have partly abrogated the monument in St Canice's to David Rothe, the previous Roman Catholic incumbent of the bishopric.

Parry married Constance, daughter of Sir Richard Kennedy, bt, of Newmountkennedy, co. Wicklow, second baron of the exchequer of Ireland, with whom he had two sons, George and Benjamin. In 1674 he was directly involved in a successful attempt to secure the deanery of St Patrick's, Dublin, through a letter patent, for his brother Benjamin. The election was somewhat controversial since the deanery had never before been conferred by a letter patent and was pushed through by a hastily arranged meeting of selected members of the cathedral chapter. Parry died in Dublin on 21 December 1677 and was buried on 26 December at his father's side in St Audoen's Church, Dublin. His will instructed that many charitable causes were to be supported by his estate, such as a number of poor scholars or sizars of Trinity College, Dublin, as well as Christ Church, Dublin, and Jesus College, Oxford, which both received money for plate.

H. T. Welch

Sources J. B. Leslie, *Ossory clergy and parishes* (1933) · Wood, *Ath. Oxon.*, new edn · *The whole works of Sir James Ware concerning Ireland*, ed. and trans. W. Harris, rev. edn, 2 vols. in 3 (1764) · J. Graves and J. G. A. Prim, *The history, architecture, and antiquities of the Cathedral Church of St. Canice, Kilkenny*, 3 vols. (1857) · H. Cotton, *Fasti ecclesiae Hibernicae*, 4 vols. (1878) · W. M. Mason, *The history and antiquities of the Collegiate and Cathedral Church of St. Patrick, near Dublin, from its foundation in 1190, to the year 1819, etc.* (1820) · Foster, *Alum. Oxon.* · 'The pedigree of the Parry family of Newry, co. Down and the City of Dublin, *c.*1560–1735', NL Ire., MS 173, fol. 87 · Burtchaell & Sadleir, *Alum. Dubl.*, 2nd edn · 'The Parry monument, St. Audoen's Church', *Irish Ecclesiastical Journal*, 107/5 (June 1849), 282 · *DNB* · J. B. Leslie, ed., *Clergy of Dublin and Glendalough: biographical succession lists*, rev. W. J. R. Wallace (2001), 956

Parry, John [Parry Ddall, Blind Parry] (**1710?–1782**), musician, was born at Bryncynan, near Nefyn on the Llŷn peninsula. It is not clear whether he was born blind, but he certainly appears to have been blind from a very early age. He became the outstanding player of the triple harp of his day, though his most significant contribution to Welsh music was his three published collections of Welsh and British airs. He learned to play the harp with a relative, Robert Parry of Llanllyfni, and with Stephen Shon Jones of Penrhyndeudraeth. He was harper to Sir Watkin Williams

John Parry [Blind Parry] (**1710?–1782**), by William Parry, *c.*1760–80

Wynn of Wynnstay, Ruabon, and for some time to Sir Watkin's father. Edward Jones (Bardd y Brenin) mentions a harp-playing contest with Huw Sion Prys, of Llandderfel, which Parry won.

By about 1741 Parry was spending much of his time in London, playing for Wynn's circle, and here he associated with some of the greatest figures of the age. His playing was, for instance, noticed and admired by both Handel and the prince of Wales. He also became one of the first members of the Honourable Society of Cymmrodorion, the patriotic London-Welsh society founded in 1751 by Richard Morris and his brothers, Lewis and William. The Morrises urged Parry to apply for the position of court harper to the prince of Wales when it fell vacant in 1750, but he does not seem to have been an ambitious man, and there is no record that he chose to do so.

It is said that Parry inspired Thomas Gray's poem 'The Bard', which it is claimed was begun on a visit by Gray to Wynnstay Hall. A recital by Parry in Cambridge in 1757 apparently prompted Gray to complete the poem, after a break in its writing. In a letter dated May 1757, Gray says that Parry 'scratched out such a ravishing blind harmony, such tunes of a thousand years old', that he 'put my Ode in motion again, and has brought it at last to a conclusion'.

In the course of his career Parry played both in aristocratic homes and at public concerts, chiefly in London, but also across Britain and Ireland. He is known, for instance, to have played in Dublin in 1736 and in Leeds in 1742. However, by 1781 he had retired from the concert scene and returned to Ruabon. He died there on 7 October 1782 and was buried in the churchyard.

His celebrity was such that, following his death, an engraved portrait appeared in the *Gentleman's Magazine* (1782), with the words 'John Parry (Blind Parry), "The Famous Blind Harper of Wynnstay"'. He was responsible for drawing Welsh music to the attention of a wider public than ever before, both through his performances and his publications.

With Evan Williams, Parry edited *Antient British Music* (1742), considered to be the first published work to record Welsh music. It was subtitled 'A collection of tunes, never before published, which are retained by the Cambro-Britons, (more particularly in north-Wales) and supposed, by the learned, to be the remains of the music of the antient Druids, so much famed in Roman history'. A second part was planned but not completed. Parry also edited *A Collection of Welsh, English and Scotch Airs* (1761), which includes 'Four new lessons for the harp or harpsichord composed by John Parry', a work which remains in the harp repertory. His third publication, *British Harmony* (1781), is regarded as the best of the three collections, and is dedicated to Sir Watkin Williams Wynn. His son, William *Parry (1744/5–1791), profited from John Parry's long and brilliant connection with the Wynn family. Under Wynn's patronage he became a pupil of Sir Joshua Reynolds, and a successful portrait painter.

TREVOR HERBERT

Sources H. Williams, *John Parry (1710?–1782)* (1982) • A. Griffiths, 'John Parry: ei gefndir, ei fywyd a'i waith', *Welsh Music/Cerddoriaeth Cymru* (summer 1982), 6–14 • J. L. Williams, *Y tri thelynor* (1945) • R. T. Jenkins and H. M. Ramage, *A history of the Honourable Society of Cymmrodorion* (1951) • O. Ellis, *The story of the harp in Wales* (1991) • A. Rosser, *Telyn a thelynor: hanes y delyn yng Nghymru, 1700–1900* (1981) • *DWB* • M. Stephens, ed., *The Oxford companion to the literature of Wales* (1986) • *GM*, 1st ser., 52 (1782), 550

Likenesses W. Parry, portrait, *c.*1760–1780, NMG Wales [*see illus.*] • W. Parry, etching, BM • engraving, repro. in Williams, *John Parry* • line engraving, BM

Parry, John (**1776–1851**), instrumentalist and composer, was born in Denbigh, north Wales, on 18 February 1776, the son of Thomas Parry, a stonemason. He showed early indications of musical talent, and received some lessons in theory and on the clarinet from a local dancing-master; he also studied the harp. In 1793 he joined the Denbighshire militia band, and having had lessons from Rakeman, the bandmaster, he became its leader in 1795. He held that position for ten years, during which time he learned to play many instruments; the feat which he acquired of playing on three flageolets at once led to his appearing at Covent Garden. He performed there for the benefit of Mrs Thomas Dibdin in 1805, and in 1807 he settled in London as a teacher of the flageolet.

Parry had already written some poetry and songs, and in 1809 he was first engaged to produce songs for Vauxhall Gardens; he continued to write for the manager of the gardens for several years. From 1814 he composed and arranged music for operatic farces and other theatre pieces, sometimes writing the libretto as well as the music. His first works were *Fair Cheating*, for William Lovegrove's benefit at Drury Lane on 15 June 1814, and the music for Thomas Dibdin's *Harlequin Hoax* (Lyceum, 16

John Parry (1776–1851), by Abraham Wivell, 1830

August). These were followed by nine others, including *Oberon's Oath* (Drury Lane, 21 May 1816), *High Notions* (Covent Garden, 11 February 1819), *Helpless Animals* (Covent Garden, 17 November 1819), and *Two Wives, or, A Hint to Husbands* (Drury Lane, 2 June 1824). Parry's version of Scott's *Ivanhoe* was given at least five times in London in 1820, the version at Covent Garden being the most successful (2 March), in part on account of his song 'The Lullaby'. Parry was also a keen collector and arranger of Welsh melodies. He composed six collections of Welsh airs (1804–48) and numerous songs, ballads, and catches, published separately and in contemporary anthologies, as well as pieces for harp, piano, flageolet, flute, and violin. Two Scottish songs, 'O merry row the bonnie bark' and 'Smile again, my bonnie lassie', were particularly popular, as was the duet 'Flow gently Deva'.

Parry regularly conducted cymrodorion and eisteddfods, notably at Wrexham in 1820 and Brecon in 1822; at the Powys eisteddfod of 1820 he received the title of Bardd Alaw ('master of song'). He was one of the chief promoters of the Cambrian Society, and became its registrar; on 24 May 1826 his contribution to the society was recognized with a complimentary concert. He was honorary secretary of the Melodists' Club, and from 1831 to 1849 was treasurer of the Royal Society of Musicians. He wrote several books on musical subjects, including *An Account of the Rise and Progress of the Harp* (1834) and *An Account of the Royal Musical Festival Held in Westminster Abbey in 1834* (1834, having himself been secretary of the festival). He was one of the original contributors to the *Musical World*, was music critic of the *Morning Post* from 1834 to 1849, and for a time worked as music editor of the *Sunday Times*. In June 1837 he gave a farewell concert, when he sang his own popular ballad 'Jenny Jones', accompanied on the harp by his son, John Orlando *Parry. He died in London on 8 April 1851; nothing is known of his wife, Maria.

J. C. HADDEN, *rev.* DAVID J. GOLBY

Sources P. Crossley-Holland and N. Temperley, 'Parry, John (ii)', *New Grove* • A. Nicoll, *A history of early nineteenth century drama*, 2 vols. (1930) • *DWB* • *MT*, 4 (May 1851) • *GM*, 2nd ser., 6 (1836), 80

Likenesses A. Wivell, pencil drawing, 1830, NPG [*see illus.*] • AW, pencil drawing, 1847, Royal Society of Musicians, London • H. Furniss, pen-and-ink drawing, NPG • E. Morton, lithograph (after miniature), BM; repro. in *Welsh Harper* (1839) • oils, possibly Royal Society of Musicians, London • plaster bust, Royal Society of Musicians, London • portrait, Harvard TC

Parry, John Docwra (*bap.* **1800**, *d.* in or after **1845**), topographer, was born in Bedford and baptized on 25 December 1800, the son of John Parry, vicar of Woburn, and his wife, Mary. He was admitted pensioner of Peterhouse, Cambridge, on 15 October 1818 and matriculated in Michaelmas term 1819, graduating BA in 1824 and MA in 1827. He took orders, and in 1827 was serving the curacy of Aspley, Bedfordshire. Parry published several works, including *Select Illustrations, Historical and Topographical, of Bedfordshire* (1827), a partial coverage, since there were apparently insufficient subscribers to permit further volumes, *The Legendary Cabinet: a Collection of British National Ballads* (1829), *The History of Woburn and its Abbey*, published under the patronage of the ninth duke of Bedford in London in 1831, and *An Historical and Descriptive Account of the Coast of Sussex* (1833). Parry also tried his hand at poetry and a reprint of his sylvan eclogue appeared in *Gentleman's Magazine* in 1831.

In January 1833 Parry was living in Brighton, but his situation is obscure. He may have been defrocked, and was apparently the owner–editor of the *Portsmouth Herald*, which he ran as a conservative paper. However, the cost of publishing his 1833 work on the Sussex coast seems to have ruined him, and he was forced to relinquish the paper. He was still alive, and in circumstances of some distress, in July 1845, when he wrote a begging letter to Peel, the prime minister. The date of his death is unknown.

GORDON GOODWIN, *rev.* JOANNE POTIER

Sources H. R. Luard, ed., *Graduati Cantabrigienses*, 7th edn (1884), 397 [for the years 1800–1884] • *GM*, 1st ser., 101/1 (1831), 634 • P. Croot, 'Bedfordshire', *English county histories: a guide*, ed. C. R. J. Currie and C. P. Lewis (1994), 32–41 • Allibone, *Dict.* • Venn, *Alum. Cant.*, 2/5.36 • *IGI*

Archives BL, Peel MSS, Add. MSS 40408, 40511, 40596

Parry, John Humffreys [John Humphreys] (**1786–1825**), antiquary and lawyer, son of the Revd Edward Parry (1752–1805) and his wife, Anne Wynne, was born on 6 April 1786 at Mold, Flintshire. His father was then rector of Llangar, but held this living with the curacy of Mold, where he resided and kept a school; he moved from that town in 1790, when he became rector of the neighbouring parish of Llanferres. Parry was educated at Ruthin grammar school, and then entered the office of his uncle Mr Wynne, a solicitor at Mold. After inheriting some property through the death of his father, he was in 1807 admitted into the Temple, and in 1811 called to the bar. He practised for a time in the Oxford circuit and the Chester great sessions, but appears to have neglected his profession, encumbered his property, and to have finally turned to literature for a livelihood.

In September 1819 Parry started the *Cambro-Briton*, a magazine for the discussion of topics connected with Welsh history and antiquities; only three volumes appeared (London, 1820, 1821, 1822). A member of the Gwyneddigion Society, he also took an active part in the re-establishment of the Cymmrodorion Society in 1820, and edited the first volume of the society's transactions in 1822. When in 1823 steps were taken to carry out the decision of the government to publish an edition of the ancient historians, the Welsh section of the work was entrusted to Parry. In the same year he won prizes at the Carmarthen eisteddfod for essays on 'The navigation of the Britons' and 'The ancient manners and customs of the Britons' (printed, with a third prize essay, at Carmarthen in 1825). In 1824 he published *The Cambrian Plutarch*, a collection of biographies of Welsh worthies. On 12 February 1825 he was attacked and killed in North Street, Pentonville, London, by a bricklayer named Bennett, with whom he had quarrelled in the Prince of Wales tavern. He left a widow (daughter of John Thomas, a solicitor in Llanfyllin) and five children. The Gwyneddigion and Cymmrodorion societies succeeded in raising more than £1000 on their behalf. Parry's eldest son, John Humffreys *Parry, became a well-known barrister. J. E. LLOYD, *rev.* BETI JONES

Sources *DWB* • *Annual Register* (1825) • W. D. Leathart, *The origin and progress of the Gwyneddigion Society of London* (1831) • *Seren Gomer* (April 1825)

Parry, John Humffreys (1816–1880), serjeant-at-law, son of John Humffreys *Parry (1786–1825), antiquary, and his wife, a daughter of John Thomas of Llanfyllin, was born in London on 24 January 1816. He received a commercial education at the Philological School, Marylebone, and spent a short time in a merchant's office in London; but his literary talents made commerce distasteful to him, and he accepted a post in the printed book department in the British Museum. While thus occupied he attended lectures at the Aldersgate Institution and studied for the bar. He was called to the bar in June 1843 by the Middle Temple. He joined the home circuit, and soon obtained a good criminal business, becoming prominent at the central criminal court and the Middlesex sessions. His appointment as a serjeant-at-law, in June 1856, gave him access to better work in the civil courts, where, thanks to an admirable appearance and voice, great clearness and simplicity of statement, and the tact of a born advocate, he was very successful in winning verdicts. He was also prominent in compensation cases, especially for the London, Brighton, and Coast Railway. He obtained a patent of precedence in 1864 from Lord Westbury after lords Campbell and Chelmsford had refused it on the mere ground of his being a serjeant (Ballantine, 207), and he afterwards led the home circuit. In November 1878 he was elected a bencher of the Middle Temple. He was best-known for several notorious cases: the trial of Manning in 1849; of Müller, for the murder of Mr Briggs, in October 1864; the Overend and Gurney prosecution in 1869; the indictment of Arthur Orton, the Tichborne claimant, in 1873–4; and *Whistler* v. *Ruskin* in November 1878. In the last he appeared for Whistler, his own rather melodramatic court style fitting the odd nature of the case and helping to secure a verdict which did not punish his client.

In politics Parry was an advanced liberal. At the time of the first Chartist movement he sympathized with the more moderate of their views, and knew many of their leaders, and assisted William Lovett in his latter days. Parry was also one of the founders of the Complete Suffrage Association in 1842. In 1847 he unsuccessfully contested Norwich against Lord Douro and Sir Samuel Morton Peto and in 1857 was beaten in Finsbury by Tom Duncombe and William Cox, coming third at the poll, and spending £790.

Parry published *Lord Campbell's Libel Act* (1844) and *A Letter on Feargus O'Connor* (1843). He was twice married: first to Margaret New, who died on 13 September 1856; and afterwards to Elizabeth Mead, daughter of Edwin *Abbott (1808–1882); she predeceased him by a few hours. Parry died on 10 January 1880 at his house, 66 Holland Park, Kensington, of congestion of the lungs, aggravated, it is said, by the faulty drainage of the house. He was buried at Woking on 15 January 1880. He had two sons, of whom the elder, John Humffreys, an actor, died in 1891. The second was **Sir Edward Abbott Parry** (1863–1943), judge and author, who was born on 2 October 1863. He was a barrister and, from 1894 to 1911, a county court judge based in Manchester, later becoming prominent for chairing tribunals. He was knighted in 1927. Parry was also a prolific author and dramatist and a theatre producer, describing his varied life in *My Own Way* (1932). He was twice married: first to Helen (*d.* 1932), daughter of Thomas Hart; second, in 1936, to Ellen Ann Page. He died on 1 December 1943. J. A. HAMILTON, *rev.* H. C. G. MATTHEW

Sources *The Times* (12 Jan 1880) • *The Times* (17 Jan 1880) • *Law Times* (17 Jan 1880) • *Law Journal* (17 Jan 1880) • *Solicitors' Journal*, 24 (1879–80), 214 • *WWW* • E. A. Parry, *My own way* (1932) • *The life and correspondence of Thomas Slingsby Duncombe*, ed. T. H. Duncombe, 2 vols. (1868) • *The life and struggles of William Lovett, in his pursuit of bread, knowledge, and freedom* (1876) • M. Williams, *Leaves of a life*, 2 vols. (1890) • W. Ballantine, *Some experiences of a barrister's life*, 2nd–5th edns (1882) • L. Merrill, *A pot of paint: aesthetics on trial in Whistler v. Ruskin* (1992)

Likenesses Spy [L. Ward], caricature, watercolour study, NPG; repro. in *VF* (13 Dec 1873)

Wealth at death under £16,000: probate, 28 Jan 1880, *CGPLA Eng. & Wales*

Parry, John Orlando (1810–1879), actor and singer, the only son of the instrumentalist and composer John *Parry (1776–1851) and his wife, Maria, was born in London on 3 January 1810 and at an early age was taught by his father to sing and to play the harp and the piano. He also studied the harp under Robert Bochsa, and appeared as a performer on that instrument as 'Master Parry' in May 1825. As a singer he made his début on 7 May 1830 at a concert given by Franz Cramer at the Hanover Square Rooms, when he performed Handel's 'Arm, arm, ye brave!' with great success. His voice was described as a baritone of fine and rich, though not powerful, quality. After receiving lessons from Sir George Smart in sacred and classical music, he was in great demand at the Ancient and Philharmonic concerts, and also at musical festivals much further afield. Sigismund Neukomm composed 'Napoleon's Midnight Review' for him, and several other songs, but his voice was best suited to simple ballads. In 1833 he visited Italy and received instruction from Luigi Lablache in Naples, where he resided for a while. At Posilippo he gave a concert in a theatre belonging to the impresario Domenico Barbaja, the second part of which consisted of a burlesque on *Othello*; Lablache sustained the part of Brabantio, Calvarola took the Moor, and Parry was Desdemona, dressed à la Madame Vestris, and sang 'Cherry Ripe'. He also appeared before the king and queen of the Two Sicilies, and gave imitations of Lablache, G. B. Rubini, and Maria Malibran in a mock Italian trio.

By now fluent in Italian, Parry returned to England in 1834, and on 30 June 1835 married Anne, the daughter of Henry Combe, a surgeon. In July 1836 he gave his first benefit concert at the Hanover Square Rooms, when Malibran sang for him, and, demonstrating his comic talent, he joined her in Mazzinghi's duet 'When a Little Farm we Keep' and mimicked Harley. Having been persuaded to try the stage, he appeared at the St James's Theatre (which had just been built by his father's old friend John Braham) on 29 September 1836, in a burletta called *The Sham Prince*, written and composed by his father. He was well received, and on 6 December the same year he appeared in John Poole's *Delicate Attentions* and in a burletta, *The Village Coquettes*, written by Charles Dickens with music by John Hullah. He was then at the Olympic for a brief season. In 1837 he performed his 'Buffo trio italiano', accompanying himself on the piano, in which he successfully imitated Giuliz Grisi Ivanov, and Lablache. He accompanied his father on the harp at the latter's farewell concert in June of the same year, and in 1840 introduced his song 'Wanted, a Governess', with words by George Dubourg.

In 1842 Parry abandoned the stage for the concert room, and began singing, with Anna Thillon and Joseph Staudigl, in pieces written for him by Albert Smith (*The Athenaeum*, 10 June 1843, 556). He then accompanied Camillo Sivori, Liszt, Sigiomend Thalberg, and others in a concert tour around the United Kingdom, during which his powers as a pianist and his originality as a buffo singer were widely recognized. In 1849 Albert Smith wrote an entertainment entitled *Notes, Vocal and Instrumental*, which Parry produced on 25 June 1850 at the Store Street Music Hall, Bedford Square, London, and illustrated with his own large watercolour paintings. In it he indulged in monologue, sang in different voices, played the piano, and made rapid costume changes. The entertainment was a great success and proved more acceptable to the audience than any one-man show since the time of Charles Mathews the elder. Parry then appeared at Crosby Hall, Bishopsgate Street, at Willis's Rooms, King Street, St James's, and in the provinces. On 17 August 1852 he brought out a new solo entertainment at Store Street, called *The Portfolio for Children of All Ages* (*Sunday Times*, 23 May 1852, 3), which he continued with much success until August 1853 (*The Athenaeum*, 13 Aug 1853, 970). The strain of such a schedule had proved too much, however, and the fits of nervous hysteria from which he had suffered for some time left him no option but to retire from public performance. Having partially recovered, he later became organist of St Jude's, Southsea, and gave lessons in singing. On 4 June 1860 he joined Thomas German Reed and his wife, Priscilla, at the Gallery of Illustration, Regent Street, London. He entertained the public there for nearly nine years with a series of droll impersonations and marvellous musical monologues, treating the comic song as a comedy scene with musical illustrations. He invented his own entertainments, composed his own music, and played his own accompaniments. During a period of nearly forty years he composed or compiled several songs and ballads. Many of these won prizes from the Melodists' Club, including 'Fair Daphne' (1840) and 'The Flying Dutchman' (1848). Some of his songs were arranged as quadrilles by L. Negri in 1842, and L. G. Jullien's *Buffa Quadrilles* (1844) were also based on his tunes. Among Parry's other works were glees and much music for the piano, especially polkas.

On 15 July 1869 a complimentary benefit was given for Parry by a distinguished party of amateurs at the Lyceum Theatre, and on 7 February 1877 he took a farewell benefit at the Gaiety Theatre, which included the appearance of all three members of the Reed family and raised £1300. His later years were embittered by the loss, in 1877, of the greater part of his forty years' savings through malpractice by his solicitor. He died, leaving an estate valued at under £100, at the residence of his daughter, Maria, at Pembroke Lodge, East Molesey, Surrey, on 19 February 1879, and was buried in East Molesey cemetery on 25 February. His widow died on 4 January 1883. Their daughter was married twice, first, in 1857, to Lieutenant Francis Walton of the Royal Marines, and secondly, in 1872, to Henry Hugh Lang, an employee of the Inland Revenue.

G. C. Boase, *rev.* David J. Golby

Sources W. H. Husk and N. Temperley, 'Parry, John Orlando', *New Grove* · *The Athenaeum* (10 June 1843), 556 · *The Athenaeum* (13 Aug 1853), 970 · *Sunday Times* (23 May 1852), 3 · *The Era* (20 Feb 1879), 7 · *Morning Advertiser* (22 Feb 1879), 5 · private information (1895) · *CGPLA Eng. & Wales* (1879)

Archives NL Wales, diaries and papers · NL Wales, journals and papers

Likenesses Maclise, miniature, 1895; in possession of Horace N. Pym in 1895 · C. Baugniet, lithograph, BM · D. Maclise, oils, NMG Wales · Nelson, carte-de-visite, NPG · H. Watkins, carte-de-visite, NPG · portrait, repro. in *ILN*, 4 (1844), 389 · portrait, repro. in *Illustrated Sporting News*, 4 (1865), 657 · portrait, repro. in *Illustrated Sporting and Dramatic News*, 10 (1879), 572, 574 · prints, Harvard TC · wood-engraving (after photograph by Samuel Fry & Co.), NPG; repro. in *ILN* (17 March 1877)

Wealth at death under £100: probate, 26 March 1879, *CGPLA Eng. & Wales*

Parry, Joseph (1744–1826), painter, was born in Liverpool, Lancashire, the son of a master pilot. He was initially apprenticed as a ship and house painter, pursuing his talents as an artist during the intervals between work. He appears to have been self-taught and it is unclear when he finally relinquished his trade to practise as a professional artist. In 1787 he sent four works to the exhibition of the Society for Promoting Painting and Design in Liverpool. A number of dated canvases suggest that he was active in Liverpool until 1788. It is thought that about 1790 he moved to Manchester, where he established himself swiftly, contributing to the gradual consolidation of an artistic centre in the city. His work exercised considerable influence in Manchester, where, up to that time, the practice of art had been almost exclusively confined to those who paid short visits during their provincial tours. He submitted work to the Royal Academy in 1803. It was the only occasion on which he did so, his address simply listed as Manchester. In 1810 he exhibited at the Liverpool Academy show on Marble Street and was elected an academician by that body, a position he held for two years.

Parry's range was broad, incorporating large historical compositions together with pictures of shipping and landscapes. His best pictures, however, are familiar scenes of everyday life, such as *The Village Fair* (1819) and *Eccles Wakes*, both in Manchester City Galleries. *Eccles Wakes* contains 200 figures, all separate studies from nature. Parry had considerable practice as a portrait painter, his subjects including the performing artist and Egyptologist Giovanni Belzoni, the publisher John Boydell, and William Henry Betty, the actor. A number of these, engraved by A. Von Assen and published by Parry in 1804, are in the British Museum. Parry died in Manchester in 1826, leaving four sons.

Joseph Parry's son **James Parry** (*c.*1805–*c.*1871) was born in Manchester, Lancashire. He was represented by three works in the first exhibition of the Royal Manchester Institution when it opened at Daniel Jackson's gallery on Market Street in 1827 and continued to exhibit similar works until 1856. His address in 1828 was given as 12 Mulbery Street, but he seems to have lived mainly at 5 Grove Street, Gartside Street. Like his father's, his practice extended to landscapes, portraits, miniatures, and figure subjects. He also engraved many plates from his own and his brother's work. In 1825 he prepared most of the plates in John Corry's *History of Lancashire* (1825), many of them from his own drawings. He also drew and engraved *View of Manchester from Strawberry Hill*, published in 1818, and in 1821 *Manchester College*, and a view of the *Collegiate Church*. His portrait, kit-cat size, which was painted by himself in oil, is in the Royal Salford Museum. In later life he lived 'in very poor circumstances' and received hospitality from the landlord of the Crown and Anchor Hotel in Cateaton Street. He died in the Manchester workhouse about 1871.

Joseph Parry's second son, **David Henry Parry** (1793–1826), born in Manchester, Lancashire, on 7 June 1793, studied in his father's studio, and soon gained for himself a reputation as a portrait painter. He married in 1816 Elizabeth Smallwood of Macclesfield; they had three sons. He was involved in the establishment of the Associated Artists of Manchester in September 1823, the precursor to the Royal Manchester Institution. His local success encouraged him to relocate to London in May 1826, and his practice was beginning to thrive when he died on 15 September 1826; his wife survived him. He was buried in the churchyard of St Martin-in-the-Fields, London. Examples of his portraiture include *Dr. John Hull, F.L.S.*, of which the British Museum holds an engraved version by S. W. Reynolds.

D. H. Parry's youngest son, **Charles James Parry** (1824–1894), was educated at the Manchester grammar school, and began his professional life in the wool industry. He practised as an amateur painter, being the third generation of the Parry family to support a devotion to the arts. He married Alice, youngest daughter of Thomas Southern of Wheathill, Salford; they had two sons—Charles James, who practised as a landscape and sea painter, and David Henry, a painter of military subjects and a writer. Charles James Parry died in London on 18 December 1894.

TINA FISKE

Sources 'Notes & queries', *Manchester City News* (20 June 1891), 2 · 'Notes & queries', *Manchester City News* (27 June 1891), 2 · 'Notes & queries', *Manchester City News* (4 July 1891), 2 · 'Notes & queries', *Manchester City News* (11 July 1891), 2 · 'Notes & queries', *Manchester City News* (25 July 1891), 2 · T. Fawcett, *The rise of English provincial art: artist, patron and institution outside London, 1800–1830* (1974) · E. R. Dibdin, 'Liverpool art and artists in the eighteenth century', *Walpole Society*, 6 (1917–18), 59–91 · W. P. Carey, *Cursory thoughts on the state of the fine arts occasioned by the founding of the Liverpool Academy* (1810) · *DWB* · T. M. Rees, *Welsh painters, engravers, sculptors (1527–1911)* (1912) · H. C. Marillier, *The Liverpool school of painters: an account of the Liverpool Academy from 1810 to 1867, with memoirs of the principal artists* (1904) · B. Stewart and M. Cutten, *The dictionary of portrait painters in Britain up to 1920* (1997) · *Concise catalogue of British paintings*, Man. City Gall., 1 (1976) · *Engraved Brit. ports.* · D. Foskett, *A dictionary of British miniature painters*, 2 vols. (1972) · Graves, *RA exhibitors* · *Gore's Liverpool Directory* (1790), 36 · *IGI* · *DNB*

Archives Man. CL, family MSS, incl. notes and sketchbook of D. H. Parry | Man. CL, Royal Manchester Institution MSS, corresp. concerning the art treasures exhibition hosted by the institution in 1851

Likenesses D. H. Parry, group portrait, chalk drawing · D. H. Parry, self-portrait, oils (D. H. Parry); in possession of his grandson, D. H. Parry, 1895 · J. Parry, self-portrait, etching, BM · J. Parry, self-portrait, oils (James Parry), Royal Salford Museum

Parry, Joseph [*pseud.* Pencerdd America] (**1841–1903**), composer, was born on 21 May 1841 at 4 Chapel Row, Georgetown, Merthyr Tudful, the second son of Daniel Parry and his wife, Elizabeth (*née* Richards). Daniel Parry, a finer at the local ironworks, was illiterate, which may account for some confusion over the rendering of his name in official documents: though he is Daniel on Joseph's birth certificate and his own marriage certificate, the 1841 and 1851 censuses wrongly record him as David. He and his wife came from west Wales; Elizabeth Parry was reputed to be a good musician. At the time of the 1851 census—the last before the family emigrated—Joseph had an elder brother, Henry, and two younger sisters, Elizabeth and Jane.

Parry had little early education and began work in a coal mine at the age of nine. Three years later he moved to the Crawshay family's Cyfarthfa ironworks, where he was a puddler. In later life he claimed to have acquired his first taste for music by listening to the Cyfarthfa band rehearsing outdoors. In 1853 his father emigrated to America, and the rest of the family followed a year later. They settled in Danville, Pennsylvania, where there was a large Welsh community. At Danville, Parry took a job in an iron mill, where he remained until 1865, but learned music, including harmony and counterpoint, while working at the mill. His teachers, John Abel Jones and W. J. Price, were both emigré Welshmen, the latter from Tredegar. In May 1862 he married at Danville, Jane, the daughter of Gomer Thomas. They had five children: Joseph Haydn, Mendelssohn, William Sterndale, Annie, and Dilys.

In 1860 Parry won a composition prize at the Danville eisteddfod with a work called *Temperance Vocal March*, and it was about this time that he began sending works to Welsh eisteddfodic competitions. He won prizes at Swansea in 1863 and Llandudno in 1864. He attended the Aberystwyth eisteddfod in 1865 and it was there, following his induction to the gorsedd (the Welsh eisteddfodic bardic society), that he was conferred with the bardic title Pencerdd America. His eisteddfod successes and the popularity of some of his publications caused a public subscription fund to be set up to enable him to study at the Royal Academy of Music, which he attended between 1868 and 1871. He was a composition pupil of Sterndale Bennett and learned vocal technique from Manuel García. In 1871 he received the MusB from Cambridge University, the first Welsh person to do so. On leaving the academy he returned to Danville, where he set up a private music school or, as he preferred it to be known, a 'musical institute'.

Three years later Parry returned to Wales to become professor of music at the newly opened University College of Wales at Aberystwyth. In 1880 he resigned. Several reasons have been given for the brevity of this appointment: the college could not accept Parry's insistence that women should be allowed to become undergraduates (so that there would be an appropriate supply of female voices for his choirs), but there were other issues. The college was in some financial difficulty and its managers were in frequent dispute with their professor of music, who was less respected as an administrator and teacher than as a composer. In addition, there is evidence to suggest that Parry himself was not an easy man to deal with. None the less, while at the college, he was awarded a MusD by Cambridge University. A male voice choir travelled from Aberdâr to Cambridge to perform his composition exercise, a cantata called *Jerusalem*, in King's College chapel. Parry's national reputation was consolidated during his period at Aberystwyth, and he spent a great deal of time travelling around Wales, conducting and promoting his own works. He was much sought after as a conductor of the *cymanfa ganu* (singing festival).

Between 1881 and 1888 Parry lived in Swansea, where he established and ran the Musical College of Wales. He left Swansea in order to become lecturer and head of the music department at the new University College of South Wales and Monmouthshire at Cardiff. At this time he established yet another private music school, the South Wales School of Music. He bought a house called Cartref in Victoria Road, Penarth on the outskirts of Cardiff, and died there on 17 February 1903. He was buried at St Augustine's churchyard, Penarth.

Parry's output was considerable and included six operas, of which *Blodwen* (first performed in concert at Swansea, 1878) was the first Welsh-language opera and is said to have had five hundred performances by the end of the century, although its first staged version was given in Colwyn Bay on 29 April 1919. He also wrote two oratorios—a third was in preparation at the time of his death—and a number of cantatas and orchestral and vocal works. His *Tydfil Overture*, written and arranged for the Cyfarthfa band, is probably the earliest original work for brass band written by a significant musical figure. Parry's work has never been properly catalogued or assessed, but there is no doubt that he, more than any other Welsh composer before him, successfully engaged with the main forms and traditions of Western art music while preserving a distinctively Welsh identity. His hymn tunes, particularly 'Aberystwyth', have enduring popularity, and his partsong 'Myfanwy' can confidently be cited as the most popular and performed piece written to a Welsh text for male voice choir. In 1893 he co-edited *Cambrian Minstrelsie*, a national collection of Welsh songs. He wrote and lectured widely on Welsh music and was at the forefront of many initiatives to improve musical education in the principality. His obituaries properly described him as the most important Welsh musician of his generation. Parry's life was romanticized in Jack Jones's novel *Off to Philadelphia in the Morning* (1947), which was made into a popular television serial by the BBC.

One of Parry's sons, **Joseph Haydn Parry** (1864–1894) was also a composer. He wrote three operas, *Cigarette* (Cardiff, 1892), *Miami* (London, 1893), and *Marigold Farm* (as yet unperformed). In the 1890s he was a professor at the Guildhall School of Music in London. His works are light in character. Although he possessed much of his father's entrepreneurial ability, he did not have the same musical talent or celebrity. TREVOR HERBERT

Sources *DWB* · facsimiles of official documents, Merthyr Library · *Western Mail* [Cardiff] (18 Feb 1903) · E. K. Evans, *Cofiant Dr Joseph Parry* (1921) · O. T. Edwards, *Joseph Parry, 1841–1903* (1970) · b. cert. · P. Crossley-Holland and N. Temperley, 'Parry, Joseph', *New Grove* [also Joseph Haydn Parry] · A. Loewenberg, *Annals of opera, 1597–1940* (1943) · *CGPLA Eng. & Wales* (1894)

Archives NL Wales, letters and papers · NL Wales, vol. of hymn tunes gathered by Joseph Parry · U. of Wales, Cardiff, Bute Resource Centre, Welsh music archive | NL Wales, letters to W. T. Rees (Alaw Ddu)

Likenesses photograph, 1874, NL Wales · portrait, repro. in Edwards, *Joseph Parry*

Wealth at death £440: probate, 10 June 1903, *CGPLA Eng. & Wales* · £563 5s.—Joseph Haydn Parry: probate, 18 July 1894, *CGPLA Eng. & Wales*

Parry, Joseph Haydn (1864–1894). *See under* Parry, Joseph (1841–1903).

Parry, Joshua (1719–1776), Presbyterian minister and writer, was born at Llan-gan, in Pembrokeshire, on 17 June

1719. The Parry family had long owned considerable property in Wales; but by the time Joshua's father was born, the family wealth had decreased substantially. Little is known about his mother or father, other than that his father was one of twenty-one children. Both parents died when he was an infant. Parry first began his formal education at a private academy under the guardianship of a Mr Davis in Haverfordwest. He then moved to Moorfields, continuing his studies as a pupil at a dissenting academy under the direction of Mr John Eames, a fellow of the Royal Society and friend of Sir Isaac Newton. In 1738 he went to live in London with a Mr Ryland, a merchant and friend of Samuel Johnson. It was in the heady intellectual atmosphere of London that Parry first began to dabble in literary pursuits, publishing pieces in a number of periodicals.

In 1741 Parry received his first ministry post as a preacher at Midhurst in Sussex. Then on 3 March 1742 he took up residency as a minister at the Presbyterian congregation in Cirencester, Gloucestershire. Apart from acting as supply minister to Gloucester from 1749 to 1751, he spent the rest of his life serving the Cirencester congregation founded by Alexander Gregory in 1662, and declining subsequent offers from Crosby Square, London, in 1748, and in 1757 and 1766 to succeed Samuel Chandler at the Old Jewry dissenting meeting in London. During his thirty-four-year ministry in Cirencester he cultivated the friendship of a number of distinguished people, none more important than that of Allen Bathurst, first Earl Bathurst, whose letters from London kept him informed of political events.

In 1752 Parry married Sarah (*d.* 1786), the daughter of Caleb Hillier, who made his living in the wool trade and possessed a considerable amount of land in Withington, Gloucestershire, and in Upcott, Devon. The numerous letters Parry wrote to his wife indicate that the marriage was a happy one, full of love and deep devotion. Together they had ten children, four of whom survived their parents. In 1753 he inherited the valuable estates of Upcott and Withington on the death of his father-in-law. He was now a wealthy man of independent means, which enabled him to spend the rest of his life engaged in his ministry, and as an accomplished man of letters.

Parry was a polymath who was prolific in literary output, producing many essays on a number of political, theological, and moral topics, and writing poetry. He often published under a variety of pseudonyms, including, but not limited to, 'James Wright, Manchester' and 'Philopatria'. Some of the more significant works were: *Political Essays and Satires* (1742), *Evidences of Christianity* (1742), and the essays that were appended to the posthumous memoir of his life. He also wrote tributes to two of his friends: the article on Lord Bathurst for the *Biographia Britannica* and *A Poem to the Memory of Major-General James Wolfe* (1759); he had first known Wolfe when he was a lieutenant-colonel quartered at Cirencester. *Seventeen Sermons on Practical Subjects* (1783) was published posthumously.

Although on many occasions he was offered higher ecclesiastical appointments through the influence of well-connected friends and acquaintances, Parry steadfastly refused to subscribe to the Thirty-Nine Articles of the Church of England. By all accounts he was a deeply pious man who believed in the need for religious tolerance in a rational and enlightened society. His criticism was directed not only at the Church of England, but also at Calvinism and Roman Catholicism. Though he was liberal in his tolerance for other Christian denominations, in 1757 he wrote his 'Confession of faith', the content of which erases any doubts about his firm commitment to the main tenets of orthodox Christianity. On 6 September 1776 Parry died in Cirencester of an apoplexy, or massive stroke. He was buried in the ground attached to his chapel, where a plain stone without an inscription marks his grave. His eldest son, Dr Caleb Hillier *Parry (1755–1822), and his grandson Dr Charles Henry *Parry (1779–1860), were both physicians to the Bath General Hospital. His other grandson of note was Sir William Edward *Parry (1790–1855), the rear-admiral and Arctic explorer.

CHARLOTTE FELL-SMITH, *rev.* JOHN W. CLARKE, JR.

Sources C. H. Parry, *A memoir of the Revd Joshua Parry* (1872) • J. Murch, *A history of the Presbyterian and General Baptist churches in the west of England* (1835), 10, 28–30 • review of J. Parry's *Seventeen sermons*, *Monthly Review*, 69 (1783), 443–4 • *GM*, 1st ser., 46 (1776), 436

Likenesses Ferguson, pencil drawing, *c.*1750, repro. in Parry, *Memoir*

Wealth at death upon marriage received fortune enough to allow comparative independence; inherited estates of Upcott and Withington (several hundred valuable acres) from father-in-law, 1753: Parry, *Memoir of the Revd Joshua Parry*, 33, 34

Parry, Sir Love Parry Jones (1781–1853), army officer, born in London on 28 November 1781, was the son of Thomas Jones of Lwyn Onn, Denbighshire, who acquired the estate of Madryn Park, Caernarvonshire, by his marriage with his cousin Margaret Parry, and, together with his children, took the additional surname of Parry in 1807. Love Parry Jones entered Westminster School in 1796, and obtained a scholarship at Trinity College, Cambridge. Preferring Oxford, he entered as a gentleman commoner at Christ Church on 8 May 1799 (BA 1803, MA 1811). In 1802 he also entered as a student at Lincoln's Inn.

Meanwhile Jones was a captain in the army on half pay, having been appointed ensign, lieutenant, and captain in the 81st regiment in 1794 at the age of twelve, and immediately afterwards placed on half pay of a disbanded regiment under the name Parry Jones. On 28 August 1804 he was appointed major of the 90th regiment (Perthshire volunteers). In 1806 he was returned MP for Horsham, Sussex, as a whig, on the eleventh duke of Norfolk's interest, and made his first speech in support of Windham's bill for introducing short service in the army. He was returned for Horsham in 1807, but was unseated on petition in 1808. After serving with the 2nd battalion 90th for some years, he became brevet lieutenant-colonel on 4 June 1811, and was appointed major of the 103rd regiment in America. He commanded a brigade on the Canadian frontier during the Anglo-American War (1812–14), had a horse shot under him at the battle of Lundy's Lane (Niagara) on 18 December 1813, and was mentioned in dispatches. In 1815 he retired as lieutenant-colonel half pay 6th garrison battalion. He had married, in 1806, Sophia, only daughter of Robert Stevenson, banker, of Binfield, Berkshire, and they had a son and three daughters. He married for a second time on 15 December 1826; his new wife was Elizabeth, only daughter of Thomas Caldecott (formerly Reid) of Lincoln, and they had sons and one daughter.

Jones Parry became colonel in 1825, major-general in 1837, and lieutenant-general in 1846. He was made a knight bachelor in 1835 and KCH in 1836 (but his knighthood was erroneously omitted from the army list). He was MP for Caernarfon boroughs from 1835 to 1837 and sheriff of Anglesey 1840–41. In 1841 he unsuccessfully contested Shrewsbury, Disraeli being one of his opponents. He died on 23 January 1853 at Madryn Park, Pwllheli, Caernarvonshire, and was buried in the family vault at Llanbedrog church on 1 February.

Parry's brother, William Parry Jones Parry, who afterwards took the name of Yale, served through the Peninsular War with the 48th regiment and received a gold medal for, as a captain, commanding a battalion at the battle of Albuera in 1811.

H. M. CHICHESTER, *rev.* JAMES FALKNER

Sources *Army List* • Burke, *Gen. GB* • *GM*, 2nd ser., 39 (1853), 312 • Foster, *Alum. Oxon.* • J. Welch, *The list of the queen's scholars of St Peter's College, Westminster*, ed. [C. B. Phillimore], new edn (1852) • HoP, *Commons* • Boase, *Mod. Eng. biog.*

Parry, Richard (1560–1623), bishop of St Asaph and biblical translator, was the son of John ap Hari or Parry of Pwllhalog in the parish of Cwm, Flintshire, and of Ruthin, and his wife, Elen, daughter of Dafydd ap John of Dyffryn Clwyd. He was born at Pwllhalog in 1560 and educated at Westminster School under William Camden. Elected a student of Christ Church, Oxford, in 1579, he matriculated there on 20 November 1580 and graduated BA on 5 February 1584. On 1 May 1584 he was ordained deacon at Bangor by Bishop Nicholas Robinson, and on 4 May was instituted to the comportion of Llanelidan in Bangor diocese, the endowment of Ruthin Free School. While master at Ruthin, Parry proceeded MA in June 1586. He was made chancellor of Bangor on 24 December 1592—a dignity he resigned on 6 January 1595. He became vicar of Gresford, Denbighshire, on 1 January 1593 and graduated BD in March 1594. In November 1597 he received the degree of DD, and he was installed dean of Bangor on 11 April 1599, having married, probably during 1598, Gwen, daughter of John ap Rhys Wyn of Llwyn Ynn. They subsequently had four sons and seven daughters.

When Bishop William Morgan of St Asaph died in 1604 Parry succeeded him as bishop, being consecrated on 30 December 1604, and, in accordance with recent custom there, followed him as archdeacon. He continued to hold the vicarage of Gresford until 1609. Other livings in the diocese held by him *in commendam* were Rhuddlan (1605–18), Cilcain (1605?–1622), Cwm (1610–16), and Llanrwst (1616–23). He was a good bishop, an experienced scholar and preacher, solicitous for the welfare of his clergy, active in the House of Lords, and a scourge of Roman Catholic recusants. His report of 1611 shows his deep concern over lay impropriation and the lack of a learned resident ministry. Although he became embroiled with Sir John Wynn over a land dispute, he also consulted with him concerning the need for a complete Welsh translation of the book of Psalms. He is chiefly remembered, however, for his revised Welsh translation of the Bible (1620) and the Book of Common Prayer (1621). He sought to do for William Morgan's Bible of 1588 what the revised version of 1611 had achieved for the English Bible. In his dedication to James I, Parry made no mention of any author other than himself, but some of his own contemporaries, as well as modern scholars, have convincingly suggested that he was greatly helped by his chaplain and brother-in-law, the learned grammarian Dr John Davies (*d.* 1644) of Mallwyd, in the work of translating both volumes and seeing them through the press.

Parry died at his house at Diserth (where he had moved in 1609) on 26 September 1623 and was buried two days later at his cathedral. He left a pension of £6 per annum at Jesus College, Oxford, for a poor scholar of Ruthin. His wife survived him and married again.

J. E. LLOYD, *rev.* GLANMOR WILLIAMS

Sources Wood, *Ath. Oxon.*, new edn • W. Browne, *A survey of … St Asaph* (1801) • *CSP dom., 1603–18* • *DWB* • J. G. Jones, 'Richard Parry, bishop of St Asaph: some aspects of his career', *BBCS*, 26 (1974–6), 175–90 • D. R. Thomas, *Esgobaeth Llanelwy: the history of the diocese of St Asaph*, rev. edn, 3 vols. (1908–13) • R. G. Gruffydd, ed., *Y gair ar waith* (1988) • I. Thomas, ed. and trans., *Y Testament Newydd Cymraeg, 1551–1620* (1976) • I. Thomas, *Yr Hen Destament Cymraeg* (1988) • *Letters of William Morgan and Richard Parry* (1905) [privately printed] • W. P. Griffith, *Learning, law and religion: higher education and Welsh society, c.1540–1640* (1996) • A. I. Pryce, *The diocese of Bangor in the sixteenth century* (1923) • J. Y. N. Lloyd, *History … of Powys Fadog*, 6 vols. (1881–7) • R. F. Roberts, *Llên Cymru*, 2 (1952–3), 1–35, 92–110 • *Heraldic visitations of Wales and part of the marches … by Lewys Dwnn*, ed. S. R. Meyrick, 2 vols. (1846) • D. R. Thomas, ed., *Y cwtta cyfarwydd* (1883) • J. E. Griffith, *Pedigrees of Anglesey and Carnarvonshire families* (privately printed, Horncastle, 1914)

Archives Denbighshire RO, Ruthin, treatise addressed to James I relating to William Morgan's Bible translation • NL Wales, corresp. with Wynn family, etc.

Likenesses portrait (in episcopal robes); formerly at Goodrich Court, Herefordshire

Wealth at death exact sum unknown: will, PRO, PROB 11/143/9, fols. 65–6

Parry, Richard (1722–1780), theological writer, son of Hugh Parry, was born in Bury Street, St James's, London. He went to Westminster School in 1736, and in 1740 was elected a student at Christ Church, Oxford; he graduated BA in 1744, MA in 1747, BD in 1754, and DD in 1757. He was appointed rector of Hawkhurst, Kent, by the dean and chapter of Christ Church, Oxford, in 1748. On 7 June 1750 he was made chaplain to Lord Vere, and in 1754 preacher at Market Harborough, Leicestershire. He was later presented by Richard Fleming to the rectory of Witchampton, Dorset (instituted 5 December 1757). On 31 December 1757 he married Mary Anne, eldest daughter of Admiral Gascoigne; they had nine children, of whom five sons and two daughters survived him.

Parry published various theological pieces. In *A Defence of the Lord Bishop of London's Interpretation of the Famous Text in the Book of Job* (1760) he supported Thomas Sherlock against William Warbuton in the debate about the interpretation of the book of Job. He was a magistrate for the county of Leicester, and interested himself in local politics. He also wrote two pamphlets on local issues in Leicester. He died on 9 April 1780 at Market Harborough, and was buried on the 16th in the church of St Mary-in-Arden, the mother church of the town, where there is a flat stone to his memory.

CHARLOTTE FELL-SMITH, *rev.* EMMA MAJOR

Sources B. W. Young, *Religion and Enlightenment in eighteenth-century England: theological debate from Locke to Burke* (1998) • J. Lamb, *The rhetoric of suffering: reading the book of Job in the eighteenth century* (1995) • *GM*, 1st ser., 50 (1780), 203 • *ESTC* • *Old Westminsters* • Foster, *Alum. Oxon.* • J. Hutchins, *The history and antiquities of the county of Dorset*, 3rd edn, ed. W. Shipp and J. W. Hodson, 4 vols. (1861–74) • E. Hasted, *The history and topographical survey of the county of Kent*, 4 vols. (1778–99) • J. Nichols, *The history and antiquities of the county of Leicester*, 4 vols. (1795–1815) • A. Chalmers, ed., *The general biographical dictionary*, new edn, 32 vols. (1812–17)

Parry, Sir Richard Gambier- (1894–1965), army officer and intelligence signals officer, was born on 20 January 1894 at Highnam Court, Highnam, Gloucestershire, the son of Sidney Gambier-Parry, architect, and his wife, Grace Denman, of Duntisbourne Rous, near Cirencester. He was a descendant of Thomas Gambier-Parry (1816–1888), the art collector, and a close relative of Sir Hubert Parry, the musician (to whom he bore a strong physical resemblance). He followed his elder brother Michael Denman Gambier-Parry to Eton College briefly, and like him was commissioned into the Royal Welch Fusiliers, with whom he served in France in 1914–15. He was wounded three times and twice mentioned in dispatches, and later served with the Royal Flying Corps.

On 26 September 1919 Gambier-Parry married a 33-year-old widow, Diana Marian Agnes Williams Andrews (*b.* 1885/6), daughter of Alfred Reginald Norrington, a manufacturer. They later divorced, and on 7 November 1931 he married Phyllis Mary, daughter of Henry Thomas Gomm, a music librarian. After the war Gambier-Parry worked in the public relations department of the BBC from 1926 to 1931. He developed an interest in amateur radio and was also employed by Philco, the radio manufacturers.

In April 1938 Gambier-Parry was recruited by Admiral Hugh Sinclair, a former director of naval intelligence and successor to Mansfield Cumming as chief of the Secret Intelligence Service (SIS), to form Section VIII, the communications branch of the service. Sinclair had realized that SIS's lack of rapid and secure communications would make it vulnerable in a fast-moving war. Hitherto SIS representatives abroad had depended (as did the UK missions where they normally served as passport control officers) upon cipher telegrams sent by cable and subject to delay. Agents reporting direct to London, like those of Claude Dansey's Z Organization, used a cumbersome system of telegraphic and postal addresses. All this led Sinclair to tell Gambier-Parry on the day he joined 'I get a great deal of valuable information, they drive it round Europe in a *carrozza* before it reaches me. Your job here will be to do something about it' (private information).

In the eighteen months that remained before the outbreak of war in 1939, Gambier-Parry energetically set about creating the communications facilities that SIS required. A wireless station was established at Woldingham near Croydon and clandestine transceivers were designed and manufactured at the SIS workshops in Lonsdale Road, Barnes. One of these, described by Gambier-Parry as obsolescent, was acquired by the Germans during the Venlo incident of November 1939. They claimed to be unimpressed by it. Gambier-Parry also negotiated with the Foreign Office for the dispatch of emergency sets, manned by SIS operators, to a number of missions overseas. The reluctance of some heads of mission to accept the sets, on the grounds that their operation infringed the Vienna Convention, taxed his patience to the full.

Nevertheless, by the outbreak of war a substantial number of missions abroad had received sets, those in Prague and Warsaw becoming the only reliable link to London during the events of 1939. The SIS station and set in Oslo accompanied the Norwegian general staff as the Norwegian forces withdrew northwards after the German invasion in April 1940 and was the channel for the Norwegian government's appeal for British help.

SIS's inhibited approach to the use of radio (possibly grounded in an awareness of its vulnerability gained through its own penetration of Comintern communications in the 1930s) meant that, despite Gambier-Parry's efforts, it entered the war seriously inexperienced in the techniques of successful clandestine radio communication. Some early agents on the continent in 1940–41 thus spent too long on the air, to the fatal detriment of their security. However, by 1943 the situation had changed radically, and a German security study acknowledged that continuous improvement in equipment and procedures had much reduced the chances of detection. Nevertheless, the fall of France in June 1940 had found SIS with only a handful of agents in Europe communicating with Section VIII's base station at Whaddon Hall near Stony Stratford. At the same time there was a national shortage of trained operators, and the armed services demanded the lion's share. Never a man to shirk a fight, Gambier-Parry was forced to battle for the resources he needed, not only to provide SIS's communications with its agents abroad, but also to disseminate the product of Bletchley Park's decryption of German communications—Bletchley Park still then being a limb of the SIS. This product, known as ULTRA, was handled by Gambier-Parry's special communications units using, where necessary, unorthodox operating techniques which prevented the enemy identifying a line of traffic based on intercepts. His conviction that SIS signals activity was beyond the remit of Whitehall communications authorities brought him into conflict with the Wireless Telegraphy Board, but he successfully fought off any outside oversight.

Gambier-Parry was a signals officer rather than an intelligence case officer. Certainly, in the early days, he valued scarce equipment above the individual and needed persuading that the agent was paramount. Described by

Andrew Hodges in his biography of Alan Turing as a 'genial paternalist' (Hodges, 270) and affectionately known to his staff as 'Pop', Gambier-Parry was, nevertheless, a vigorous and often belligerent protagonist of the causes, such as the use of ultra high frequency radio communication between aircraft and agents on the ground, that he espoused. While accusations of empire building would not have been misplaced, his was an organizational imperialism bred of necessity, without which SIS would have been hard put to meet the challenges presented by the war. In particular, it is arguable that the success of Gambier-Parry's preparations contributed substantially to the survival of SIS as an independent service. His proprietorial attitude thus had some justification and the borders of his signals empire encompassed not only SIS, but also projects such as the technical operation of Aspidistra, and other stations which broadcast 'black' propaganda on behalf of the government. By the end of the war in 1945, Gambier-Parry controlled an organization which he had created from scratch and which was itself larger than the SIS he had joined in 1938.

In 1947 Gambier-Parry was appointed director of communications for the Foreign Office and SIS jointly, an appointment which symbolized the major role he had played in building the technical and administrative infrastructure which supported both diplomatic and clandestine communications for several decades thereafter. He married lastly, in 1944, Elizabeth Clare, daughter of Colonel H. B. Towse, Royal Scots Greys, who survived him. Promoted colonel in 1939 and brigadier in 1942, he was appointed CMG in 1945 and KCMG in 1956. In retirement he was a generous vice-president of the Milton Keynes cricket club. He died on 19 June 1965 at Abbots Close, Milton Keynes, Buckinghamshire. A. O. BLISHEN

Sources private information (2004) • C. Andrew, *Secret service: the making of the British intelligence community* (1985) • A. Hodges, *Alan Turing: the enigma* (1983) • *WW* (1962) • *CGPLA Eng. & Wales* (1965) • b. cert. • m. cert. [D. M. A. W. Andrews] • m. cert. [P. M. Gomm] • d. cert.
Likenesses photograph, *c*.1950, Bletchley Park Museum
Wealth at death £5366: probate, 2 Sept 1965, *CGPLA Eng. & Wales*

Parry, Robert (*b.* **1563**, *d.* in or after **1613**), diarist and writer, was born on 30 July 1563 at Tywysog, in the parish of Henllan, Denbighshire, north Wales, the second son of Harry ap Robert and Elin, daughter of Rhys Wynn ap Gruffydd of Ffynogion, Llanfair Dyffryn Clwyd, Denbighshire. Robert Parry married Dorothy, daughter of John Wynn Panton.

It is surprising to read early in his diary, '1563 This yere the 30 daye of Julie … I Robert Parry was borne' (NL Wales, Plas, Nantglyn MS I). The diary is leather bound, decorated with gold, stamped on the front and back with a lion rampant between the letters 'R' and 'P' in gold (the lion rampant may still be seen above the front door of Tywysog and on an arch in one of the drawing rooms). It gives valuable information about his family and local and national events; it ends in 1612. Parry served Sir Henry Townshend, second justice of the north Wales and Chester circuit, and brought letters from the privy council to him. On the death of Katheryn of Berain (connected by marriage and friendship), there appeared a manuscript book of verses by Sir John Salisbury of Lleweni and an elegy of ninety-two lines on Katheryn's death by 'Robert Parry gentleman' (Christ Church, Oxford, MS 184).

In 1595 Robert Parry dedicated a prose novel to Henry Townshend—*Moderatus: the most Delectable and Famous Historie of the Black Knight*, signed 'R. P. Gent.'. In 1597 there appeared a small volume of poems, *Sinetes passions uppon his fortunes, offered for an incense at the shrine of the ladies which guided his distempered thoughtes*. This, dedicated to Sir John Salisbury of Lleweni, contains much of John Salisbury's own work but Robert Parry is described as being the author; and it has been suggested that Parry was the 'R. P.' who assisted Margaret Tyler with some translation from the Spanish into English of parts 2, 3, and 4 of *Myrrour of Princely Deeds and Knighthood* by D. Ortunez de Calahorra, P. la Sierra, and M. Martinez. All nine parts were published by 1601.

Parry's diary reveals his sympathy for the Roman Catholic cause. Both he—'Robert Parry gent'—and 'Dorothy Panton his wife' are named on the recusant roll for 1 November 1605 to 9 September 1606. Each was fined £120. They had two children, a son and a daughter. Foulk, the son, became a Jesuit priest, and the Valladolid register records the names of his parents as Catholics. The daughter, Lucy, the heir, married John Vaughan of Moel Ewig Park near Denbigh, and was alive in 1633. Richard Parry (heir to Tywysog) and John Parry, his son, were also fined as recusants. On 28 June 1613 Richard Parry made his will, giving £4 to his brother Robert Parry 'towards redeeming his tenement'. Richard Parry also deals with the 'reversion of lands bought of my brother Robert in Eriviat, Bodleye, Derwen, Llanarth, and Garth Gynau' ('Robert Parry's diary', 137).

Three *cywyddau* and a number of *englynion* are attributed to a certain Robert ap Harri, who was, clearly, of the same area and period as Robert Parry. Two of the *cywyddau* are to members of the Salisbury family and a third seems to be a Catholic defence of the sacrament of the altar. Before the poet is equated with the author of the diary, however, further evidence is desirable. D. ANEURIN THOMAS

Sources R. Parry, diary, 1559–1612, NL Wales, Plas Nantglyn MS 1 • 'Robert Parry's diary', *Archaeologia Cambrensis*, 6th ser., 15 (1915), 109–39 • J. Y. W. Lloyd, *The history of the princes, the lords marcher, and the ancient nobility of Powys Fadog*, 6 vols. (1881–7), vol. 4, p. 82; vol. 6, p. 432 • F. H. Pugh, 'Recusancy in the diocese of Llandaff during the late sixteenth and early seventeenth centuries', MA diss., Cardiff University, 1953, NL Wales, 1953/41, vol. 3 • recusant rolls, E377/15, E 179 220/186, E 179, E 220/187–8 • M. Cleary, 'Catholic resistance in Wales, 1568–1678', *Blackfriars*, 38/444 (March 1957), 111–25 • E. G. Jones, *Cymru a'r hen Ffydd* (1951), 69
Archives NL Wales, diary

Parry, Robert Williams [*pseud.* Bardd yr Haf] (**1884–1956**), Welsh-language poet, was born on 6 March 1884 at Rhiwafon, 37 Station Road, Tal-y-sarn, Caernarvonshire, the fifth of the six children, and only son, of Robert Thomas Parry (1847–1924), a shipping agent employed in the loading of slate, of Carmel in the same county, and Jane Parry (1849–1932), daughter of the Revd William Hughes of Tal-y-sarn.

Unusually, the child's birth was registered twice within a fortnight. His paternal grandfather, Thomas Parry Williams (1815–1888), also a quarryman like his father before him, married three times and had children by all three wives: the distinguished writers T. H. Parry-Williams and Thomas Parry had the same grandfather as Robert Williams Parry; they were the sons of three half-brothers and therefore cousins. This complicated family connection (compounded by the fact that the various branches of the family did not make consistent use of their surnames) was not without its tensions, but out of it the mature poet was to draw some typically wry humour.

The life of Bob Parry, as the poet was known to his family and friends, was outwardly without great incident. He attended the village school at Tal-y-sarn and the grammar schools at Caernarfon and Pen-y-groes. He left school at the age of fifteen, and after three years as a pupil teacher at primary schools in his native village, at Cefncoedycymer near Merthyr Tudful, and in Hereford entered the University College of Wales, Aberystwyth, in 1902 to follow a two-year teacher's course. For three years he taught briefly at higher-elementary schools in Wales and England. In 1907 he enrolled at the University College of North Wales, Bangor, where he took a pass degree in Welsh and English in the year following. For the next two years he was Welsh and English master at Llanberis county school, then returned to Bangor to write a thesis entitled 'Some points of contact between Welsh and Breton', for which he received the degree of MA in 1912. Teaching posts were to follow at Cefnddwysarn in Merioneth (1912–13), at Barry in Glamorgan (1914–16), and in Cardiff, where he taught English. At first rejected by the army on account of his poor eyesight, he was accepted as A1 in November 1916, enlisted, and spent the rest of the war years at camps in Berkhamsted and Winchester and at an anti-aircraft gun station in Billericay, defending London against Zeppelins. Having declined an invitation to join the Board of Education as an inspector of schools in 1919 (this almost certainly out of pique, for he had been turned down four years earlier), in 1921 he became headmaster of Oakley Park, a country school near Llanidloes in Montgomeryshire, but remained in that post only until his appointment, in the same year, to an assistant lectureship of the University College, Bangor, where he shared his duties between the Welsh department under Sir John Morris-Jones and the work of the tutorial classes committee, a post in which he was to remain for eight years. He married Elizabeth Myfanwy Davies (1898–1971) of Rhosllannerchrugog on 4 July 1923 and they set up home at 18 Ffrydlas Road in the nearby slate village of Bethesda; they later moved to Heulfryn, also known as Tŷ'r Ysgol, Carneddi, and then to 10 Coetmor estate, and finally to 3 Coetmor estate, Bethesda. There were no children of the marriage.

In 1929 Parry's academic career was marred by a misunderstanding over the conditions of his employment, and this experience was to disturb him deeply. By this time a poet and literary critic of the highest standing, he felt keenly that the college had discriminated against him because he had not published any substantial body of research work and was, above all, a creative writer. He retaliated by withholding from the prestigious Gregynog Press permission to publish a finely printed selection of his poetry, turned his back on the literary world, obdurately refusing to publish any more poetry, to broadcast, review, edit, adjudicate, or sit on committees of any kind, and—as if in parody of those he despised—threw himself into the writing of notes on medieval Breton and Cornish and on the causal conjunction *pan* in Middle Welsh.

This unhappy and barren phase of Parry's life came to an abrupt end in September 1936 when the RAF bombing school which was being built at Penyberth in the Llŷn peninsula was burnt, in a symbolic act of arson, by Saunders Lewis, D. J. Williams, and Lewis Valentine, prominent members of the Welsh Nationalist Party, after a long public campaign against it. The poet, a supporter of the party, was incensed by the decision of the University College, Swansea, to dismiss Lewis from his lecturer's post even before he had been sentenced to a term of imprisonment in Wormwood Scrubs for his part in the arson. Parry wrote some of his most mordant poems attacking the Laodiceanism of Welsh political life and in response to what he saw as a blatant injustice to the most distinguished literary figure in Wales at that time. Thus stimulated, he resumed the writing of verse.

A plain account of Parry's life hardly suggests the rich inner life of the poet. He had come to prominence as early as 1910, at the age of twenty-six, when he won the chair at the national eisteddfod with his poem 'Yr haf' ('The summer'), an attempt to face the problem of death by a man who was unable to believe in personal resurrection, in which summer is the symbol of life's joy and transience; the recurring theme is *carpe diem*. The poem, written in the traditional metres of Welsh prosody and expressed with singular charm, gave its title to the author's first volume, *Yr haf a cherddi eraill* (1924), and thereafter he was known in literary circles as Bardd yr Haf ('Poet of Summer'). The volume also includes a number of fine sonnets and, in particular, a series of *englynion* in memory of the young poet Hedd Wyn (Ellis Humphrey Evans), who was killed at Pilkem Ridge in 1917, which is among his most famous elegiac works.

Parry published only one other collection: *Cerddi'r gaeaf* ('Poems of Winter') in 1952, which contains his most mature work. If the number of poems he wrote is comparatively small, they nevertheless include about fifty which are among the finest written in Welsh during the twentieth century. They are, for the most part, highly sensuous, superbly crafted poems in celebration of the beauty of the natural world, the wonder and brevity of human life, the loss of youthful innocence, the rigours of old age, and the inevitability of death, and are written from a deeply agnostic but stoical point of view which is unremitting in its intensity and has no place whatsoever for the Christian orthodoxies, rather as in the verse of A. E. Housman, which the Welsh poet greatly admired. Many of these poems are to be found in the major anthologies of

Welsh poetry and are familiar to all who read the language.

Parry, for all his shyness, complex personality, and keen independence of spirit, was a much loved figure among the few who were privileged to know him. He retired at the age of sixty in 1944, and two years later was awarded the honorary degree of DLitt by the University of Wales in recognition of his achievement as a poet. Although his latter years were plagued by ill health, which may have affected the balance of his mind, he was not without friends. Although much concerned with the function of the poet in the modern world, rarely did he speak about his own work, and he shunned the company of other writers. He had a puckish sense of humour and delighted in boyish pranks. He was particularly sympathetic towards the underdog, the marginalized, and the dispossessed. On the darker side, there was his hypersensitivity, claustrophobia, hypochondria, and, towards the end of his life, his melancholy and sheer terror of death—out of which his most powerful poems came.

Parry died of a stroke on 4 January 1956 at his home, 3 Coetmor estate, Bethesda, and was buried five days later in Coetmor cemetery. His grave, which bears a bas-relief carving of Y Lôn Goed, a tree-lined track whose serenity is celebrated in one of his most famous poems, has become a place of literary pilgrimage for his many admirers. There is a memorial to the poet in the centre of Tal-y-sarn and a plaque on the house where he was born. The accolade of publication by the Gregynog Press was bestowed posthumously with the appearance of the volume *Cerddi Robert Williams Parry* (ed. T. Parry, 1980). A selection of his prose writings was published as *Rhyddiaith R. Williams Parry* (ed. B. L. Jones, 1974), and his complete poems, edited by Alan Llwyd, appeared in 1998. MEIC STEPHENS

Sources b. cert. • m. cert. • d. cert. • B. L. Jones, *Robert Williams Parry* (1972) • A. Llwyd, ed., *R. Williams Parry* (1979) • B. L. Jones, *R. Williams Parry*, ed. G. Thomas (1997) • M. Stephens, ed., *The new companion to the literature of Wales*, rev. edn (1998) • T. Parry, 'Preface', *Cerddi Robert Williams Parry* (1980) • A. Llywd, 'Preface', *Cerddi R. Williams Parry: y casgliad cyflawn* (1998) • R. G. Jones, 'Like foolish boys: some thoughts on the poetry of two cousins', *Seeing Wales whole*, ed. S. Adams (1998) • T. Parry, 'Parry, Robert Williams', *Y bywgraffiadur Cymreig, 1951–1970*, ed. E. D. Jones and B. F. Roberts (1997) • private information (2004)

Archives NL Wales, letters and postcards to W. J. Gruffydd [in Welsh] • U. Wales, Bangor, letters to Sir Thomas Parry-Williams [in Welsh]

Likenesses photographs, repro. in T. Emyr Pritchard, *R. Williams Parry* (1998)

Parry, Sefton Henry (1832–1887), theatre manager, was the youngest member of a theatrical family. His versatility was remarkable: he could paint scenery, cut out dresses, and do stage carpentry. In 1859 he went to Cape Town to conduct dramatic performances, and was practically the first to give professional theatrical entertainments in the colony. His wife and a young female dancer assisted him, but the rest of the cast consisted of members of amateur dramatic clubs. After leaving Cape Town he travelled, with a small company, in various parts of the world, and made some money. On returning to England he took part in the construction of several London theatres, for which he prepared the plans and undertook the preliminary management. No new theatre had been added to the places of entertainment in central London since the erection of the Princess's in 1840 until Parry built, on the site of an old coach house and stables, the first of the new theatres, called the Holborn, after the thoroughfare in which it was situated. It was opened on 6 October 1866 with Boucicault's drama *The Flying Scud*, which, with a real horse and George Belmore as Nat Gosling the old jockey, was a great success. Parry remained lessee of the house until 1872. It burnt down on 4 July 1880, and the First Avenue Hotel was later erected on the site. In 1868 Parry built on a portion of the ground of Old Lyon's inn in Newcastle Street, Strand, a house which he christened The Globe. It was opened on 28 November 1868 with H. J. Byron's comedy *Cyril's Success*, but no other piece of much mark was produced there during Parry's management, which lasted until 1871. The third theatre which he built was the Avenue, at the corner of Craven Street, facing the Thames. This was inaugurated on 11 March 1882, under the management of Burke, with Offenbach's opera *Madame Favart*, in which Florence St John took the title role. Parry was connected with the erection of the Greenwich Theatre, and was the proprietor of theatres at Hull and Southampton. He wrote *The Bright Future*, a drama produced at the opening of the Grand Theatre, Islington, on 4 August 1883. He died, after much suffering, from a paralytic attack, at his home, Cricklewood Lodge, Cricklewood, London, on 18 December 1887, aged fifty-five, and was buried in the old Willesden churchyard on 23 December. He left a widow, son, and daughter.

G. C. BOASE, *rev.* NILANJANA BANERJI

Sources *The Era* (24 Dec 1887) • *The life and reminiscences of E. L. Blanchard, with notes from the diary of Wm. Blanchard*, ed. C. W. Scott and C. Howard, 2 vols. (1891)

Wealth at death £33,976 12*s*. 1*d*.: probate, 24 March 1888, *CGPLA Eng. & Wales*

Parry, Sir Thomas (*b*. in or before **1515**, *d*. **1560**), administrator, was the son of Sir Henry Vaughan of Tretower, Brecknockshire, and his wife, Gwenllian, daughter of William ap Grono of Brecon. He was born into a much intermarried group of Anglicized Welsh gentry who flourished under the Tudors; the fact that he was known by the Christian name of his father (though he later softened the form from ap Harry to Parry in order to secure acceptance at the court of Edward VI) probably indicates that he was born and brought up in Wales. He is first recorded in 1536, when he entered the service of Thomas Cromwell, very likely also a Welshman by birth. A protestant in religion, he was employed in that year and later to visit religious houses with Cromwell's instructions for their dissolution. In 1539 or 1540 he married Anne Fortescue (*née* Rede or Reade, former married name Greville), whose husband, Sir Adrian Fortescue, had been executed for treason, apparently connected to the so-called 'Courtenay conspiracy'. His wife's inheritance gave him an interest in Hertfordshire, and may thereby have also brought him to the

Sir Thomas Parry (*b*. in or before 1515, *d*. 1560), by Hans Holbein the younger

attention of Princess Elizabeth, whose childhood homes were clustered in that county.

It is uncertain when Parry entered Elizabeth's service, but it seems likely to have been before 1547. By 1548 he had become her cofferer, and as such her principal business manager. Early in Edward's reign Elizabeth came into informal possession of most of the lands that formed her endowment under Henry VIII's will, despite the hostility of Protector Somerset. Parry helped to improve and add to her properties, for example by acquiring Ewelme in Oxfordshire. Until 1549 Elizabeth had been living off relatives and friends with no independent household, and she and Parry were able to build up a substantial cash surplus. In the years 1551–2 Parry handled sums totalling £4600, and after paying for the previous and current years' expenditure he was still able to hand back to the princess £1500 for her own use.

Parry's intimate knowledge of Elizabeth's household affairs extended beyond finance. In autumn 1548 Kate Ashley, the princess's principal gentlewoman, expressed to Parry her concerns about the sexual attentions to which the princess was being subjected by her guardian and stepfather, Thomas Seymour, Baron Seymour of Sudeley, the younger brother of Protector Somerset, and now husband of Queen Katherine Parr. Kate had seen Seymour embracing Elizabeth, and despite her complaining to Katherine, the abusive relationship continued; on one occasion the husband and wife together visited the princess in her bed and tickled her, on another they cut her dress into pieces. Parry swore himself to secrecy: 'He would rather be pulled with horses than he would disclose it' (Starkey, 73). The dowager queen died on 5 September 1548, and Seymour's thoughts turned to marrying the princess. After Christmas he talked to Parry about the state of her finances, and asked whether the property due to her under Henry VIII's will had been finally conveyed to her by letters patent. Parry replied that they had not. Nevertheless the two men discussed the savings that could be made by pooling and rationalizing the resources disposed of by Seymour and the princess. These transactions, combined with Seymour's political ambitions, placed Parry's mistress in a potentially very dangerous position. Parry even questioned Elizabeth about her attitude towards marriage with Seymour, asking her 'whether she would marry with him' and assuming that the legal conditions for marriage established by her father's will were fulfilled. In one of the most important conversations of her life she replied: 'when that comes to pass, I will do as God shall put in my mind' (Starkey, 72). Elizabeth's cool head and vague replies saved her life and Parry's.

Seymour was arrested on 17 January 1549 for plotting to overthrow the protector's government; rumours of a proposed marriage with Elizabeth formed an important part of the accusations. Parry and Kate Ashley were taken to the Tower for questioning by Sir Robert Tyrwhitt, master of the horse in the household of Katherine Parr. Although (according to Tyrwhitt) a secret pact had been made between Parry, Ashley, and the princess, 'never to confess to anything to the incrimination of the other' (ibid., 74), Parry panicked and rushed up to his room, saying to his wife: 'would I had never been born, for I am undone' and tearing off a chain of office from his neck and the rings from his fingers (Haynes, 70). Under interrogation, on 9 February 1549 he revealed all about Seymour's romps with the princess. But on the crucial point concerning Elizabeth's intentions regarding marriage to Seymour (and so defying the terms of Henry VIII's will) the investigators could find nothing. Nevertheless Seymour was attainted by parliament and executed on 20 March. Parry's confession earned him the scorn of Kate Ashley, who then made a similar confession. When Elizabeth was informed in February 1549 that Parry had told the council about his conversation with Seymour about her estates and disclosed more intimate details of her relationship with Seymour, she kept her head, calling Parry a 'false wretch,' and reaffirmed quite truthfully that she had observed the clauses of her father's will.

Despite Parry's abject betrayal, Elizabeth remained loyal to him. He was reinstated at Hatfield by September 1549, when he wrote his first letter to William Cecil, Elizabeth's future minister, in which he made professions of friendship that may imply that he had introduced this distant kinsman and fellow Welshman to the princess's service. Parry and Elizabeth both benefited from Somerset's fall, for on 17 February 1550 the council issued instructions for the settlement of her lands on Elizabeth. Parry, who had been acquiring property of his own in Berkshire—he established himself at Wallingford, which he represented three times in parliament between 1547 and 1555—had become so indispensable in the management of the princess's finances, that when she was placed under arrest after Sir Thomas Wyatt's rising and sent to Woodstock Palace on 23 May 1554 her gaoler, Sir Henry Bedingfield, insisted that the cofferer continue to take financial responsibility for her household, even though the council wished to separate the two. Consequently Parry took up residence at The Bull inn in Woodstock. Elizabeth was responsible for paying for her own imprisonment and upkeep, which included paying the wages of her gaoler and his servants, as Parry frequently reminded Bedingfield. Up to forty people a day, Bedingfield complained, visited Parry at The Bull. The latter's task was to keep Elizabeth's estates intact as a functioning administrative unit, one whose survival was imperilled by Elizabeth's imprisonment, since she was not even allowed to issue a warrant over her own signature. Parry moved swiftly to enforce her rights. Rents were demanded and stocks of deer in her parks were protected.

Parry now showed a courage and audacity that redeemed his earlier cowardly conduct. As Bedingfield complained, 'it was a marvellous and colourable place to practice in' (Starkey, 155). Parry defied Queen Mary's specific instructions by keeping Elizabeth in touch with the outside world and so maintaining her political connections. He even allowed Francis Verney, a notorious protestant conspirator, to stay at The Bull, and used him as Elizabeth's special messenger to Mary's court.

On 18 October 1555 Elizabeth was allowed to take possession of her estates and she returned to Hatfield with Parry. As Mary's health deteriorated Parry's plotting, stockpiling of weapons, and building up of a network of support did much to ensure a smooth transition of power for Elizabeth. Thus in October 1558 he sent three letters to Sir John Thynne at Longleat which secured the latter's support in Wiltshire. He also summoned the soldier Thomas Markham to Brocket Hall, now the command centre of the princess's operations, where he appeared with written undertakings from the captains of the garrison at Berwick upon Tweed to supply Elizabeth with 10,000 men for the maintenance of her royal title and dignity.

Parry had mobilized Elizabeth's following for a possible coup; but the transfer of power was peaceful, giving precedence to the administrative talents of Sir William Cecil. Nevertheless on 20 November 1558, three days after Elizabeth's accession, Parry (by now a knight) was made controller of the new queen's household, and with Cecil, now the queen's secretary, was a member of the privy council which presided over a protestant religious settlement that restored the royal supremacy. The Spanish ambassador, the count of Feria, saw Parry as the most moderate of the council on religious questions: 'although he is not so good a Catholic as he should be, he is the most reasonable of those near the queen' (*CSP Spain*, 1558–67, 37–8). When John Boxall, formerly Queen Mary's secretary and a committed Catholic, made representations to the queen about the 1559 religious settlement, Parry acted as intermediary.

Parry played an important part in the 1559 parliament (in which he sat for Hertfordshire), sending at least fifteen bills to the Lords. He was also one of the few to know of Elizabeth's secret negotiations with the Scottish rebels in the late summer of that year. As a privy councillor he had been appointed on 6 February to a committee to consider a petition from the Commons to the queen that she should marry, and according to an agent of the English ambassador in Paris he was the chief advocate of a proposal for Elizabeth to marry Lord Robert Dudley; but by November 1559 Cecil's opposition to the plan was beginning to be felt. Soon afterwards, on 15 December, Parry died suddenly, intestate. The Spanish ambassador attributed his death to grief at the course of the affair between Elizabeth and Dudley. He had probably been losing ground to Cecil. Feria thought he detected hostility between the queen's two chief advisers, writing in March 1559 that Cecil 'governs the Queen in spite of the treasurer, for they are not all good friends and I have done what I can to make them worse' (*CSP Spain*, 1558–67, 10).

Inevitably Parry was not popular at court. Tyrwhitt had suspected him of embezzling Elizabeth's money, while Holbein made an unflattering portrait of him, confirmed in physical terms, at least, by Feria, who described him to Philip II in November 1558 as the queen's 'late cofferer, a fat man, whom your majesty will have seen at Hampton court' (*CSP Spain*, 1558–67, 2). But Parry himself would probably have chosen as his epitaph the words he used when writing to Sir John Thynne before Elizabeth's accession: 'I have found thee a faithful and good servant' (Starkey, 223). He was buried in Westminster Abbey. His son Sir Thomas *Parry served as ambassador to France from 1602 to 1606 and became a privy councillor under James I.

JONATHAN HUGHES

Sources D. Starkey, *Elizabeth: an apprenticeship* (2000) • M. Perry, *The word of a prince* (1990) • C. R. Manning, ed., 'State papers relating to the custody of the Princess Elizabeth at Woodstock', *Norfolk Archaeology*, 4 (1855), 133–231 • 'The miraculous preservation of the Lady Elizabeth', J. Foxe, *Actes and Monuments*, ed. J. Pratt, 8 vols. (1877), vol. 8, pp. 600–625 • J. E. Neale, 'The accession of Elizabeth I', *The age of Catherine de Medici* (1963) • S. Haynes, ed., *A collection of state papers, 1542–1570* (1740) • *CSP dom.*, 1548–53 • Longleat House, Wiltshire, Marquess of Bath MSS, Thynne MSS • *CSP Spain*, 1558–67 • HoP, *Commons, 1509–58*, 3.63–5

Archives BL, autograph, Add. MS 33924, fol. 3 • BL, autograph, Add. MS 34079, fol. 5

Likenesses H. Holbein the younger, chalk drawing, Royal Collection [*see illus.*]

Parry, Sir Thomas (1544–1616), administrator, was the eldest son of Sir Thomas *Parry (*b.* in or before 1515, *d.* 1560) and Anne, daughter of Sir William Reade of Boarstall, Buckinghamshire, and widow of Sir Giles Greville and of Sir Adrian Fortescue. A scholar of Winchester College in 1558, Parry continued his education in 1560 in the household of Sir Thomas Gresham at Antwerp and in the next year travelled in Italy. His father, comptroller and treasurer of the household to Queen Elizabeth, was granted in

1560, for his loyal service, the manor of Hampstead Marshall, Berkshire. Though Parry was elected MP for Bridport in 1571, probably as a nominee of the earl of Bedford, it was at Hampstead Marshall that he settled; and, as his official appointments show, he became one of the leading gentlemen of the county. Appointed to the Berkshire commissions of the peace and musters in 1573, he was sheriff in 1576–7 and 1588–9, and knight of the shire in 1586; and he became a deputy lieutenant in 1593. In 1580 and subsequent years Parry extended his estates with the purchase of manors in the vicinity of Hampstead Marshall. His election for Berkshire in 1586 was a confirmation of his standing in the shire. At an unknown date he married Dorothy Brooke (*d.* 1624), a former maid of honour to Queen Elizabeth.

It was after the post of ambassador to France had been frequently declined by others that, in 1601, Elizabeth made the surprising choice of Parry and conferred on him a knighthood. Doubts about his suitability for the post were raised when Parry delayed his departure to reach a settlement with his creditors. His reluctance to travel displeased the queen and it was not until 1602 that he arrived in France. His major problem was a long-running dispute between English merchants trading with France and the French authorities which escalated in 1604 with the seizure of English goods at Rouen. Publicly Parry demanded justice for the English merchants but in his letters to the earl of Salisbury he urged negotiations and an end to retaliatory action. Sir Thomas found the slow negotiations tortuous and in June 1605 he was delighted when a successor was appointed to relieve him of the burdens of office. His successor did not arrive until the end of the year, by which time Parry had made an important contribution to the treaty of February 1606, in which the French agreed to the withdrawal of the penalties on English merchants, an end to local taxes, and the reopening of trade.

In October 1607 Parry was granted, after the death of his half-brother Sir John *Fortescue, the succession to the chancellorship of the duchy of Lancaster. In comparison with the vast majority of his Tudor predecessors Parry lacked administrative experience when he became chancellor in December 1607. He inherited long-serving and experienced senior officers and an effective administration which began, in 1608, an inquiry into the particulars of church property in the duchy. Parry, appointed a privy councillor in December 1607, was an occasional attender at the board. His only important administrative duty was to serve on the commission appointed in July 1612 to devise projects and means to increase the king's revenue. An unwelcome task which began in July 1610 was his responsibility for the custody of Lady Arabella Stuart.

Parry was elected MP for St Albans in 1610 but is not recorded as speaking in the house. It was in the parliament of 1614, when Parry was a member for Berkshire, that the investigation of his activities during the Stockbridge election dominated the house for a time. Despite his threatening letters, the electors in the duchy borough of Stockbridge continued their tradition of returning Hampshire gentry with their election of Henry St John and Sir Richard Gifford. After Parry had failed to persuade St John to stand down, the bailiff obeyed the chancellor's orders and returned Sir Walter Cope and Sir Henry Wallop. On the authority of his warrant, burgesses opposed to these proceedings were arrested, though a different pretext was given. When Parry's letters and warrants were produced in the House of Commons his defenders could only plead that his age and service might excuse his actions and that it was a prescriptive right of the chancellor to nominate a member in the duchy towns. The Commons declared the return invalid and suspended Parry from the Commons. James, who had explicitly denied there was an undertaking to pack the Commons, responded on 11 May by suspending Parry from the privy council. It was a short suspension, for Parry attended the council on 29 June 1614 and continued a regular attender in the summer and autumn of 1614. In the following year he made a brief contribution to the debate about the ways to reduce the king's debts and expenditure. Parry died in London without issue and intestate, and was buried in Westminster Abbey on 1 June 1616. He was survived by his wife, Dorothy. P. R. Seddon

Sources M. Jansson, ed., *Proceedings in parliament, 1614 (House of Commons)* (1988) • M. Lee, *James I and Henry IV* (1970) • BL, Cotton MSS Caligula E x, xi, xii; Titus C vi • BL, Stowe MSS 167, 168 • R. Somerville, *History of the duchy of Lancaster, 1265–1603* (1953) • R. Somerville, *Office holders in the duchy and county palatine of Lancaster* (1972) • HoP, *Commons, 1558–1603* • *VCH Berkshire*, vols. 2–4 • *The letters of John Chamberlain*, ed. N. E. McClure, 2 vols. (1939) • J. E. Neale, *The Elizabethan House of Commons* (1949) • *The letters and life of Francis Bacon*, ed. J. Spedding, 7 vols. (1861–74), vols. 4–5 • *CSP dom.*, 1603–18 • E. R. Foster, ed., *Proceedings in parliament, 1610*, 2 vols. (1966) • *APC*, 1613–15 • *CSP for.*, 1560–61 • BL, Add. MS 29975 • *Calendar of the manuscripts of the most hon. the marquis of Salisbury*, 11–12, HMC, 9 (1906–10)

Archives BL, corresp., Stowe MSS 167, 168 | BL, register of corresp. with Sir Robert Cecil, Add. MS 38138 • BL, Cotton MSS, corresp. • PRO, state papers, 78/49–52

Parry, Thomas (1768–1824), East India merchant, was the seventh of the eight children of Edward Parry (*d.* *c.*1769), of Leighton Hall, near Welshpool, Montgomeryshire, and his wife, Ann. His father was described as a farmer, and a 'hereditary burgess sworn'. Nothing is known about his early life, but by 1788 Parry had arrived in Madras, probably at the stimulus of his brother-in-law, Gilbert Ross, a senior partner of Messrs Ross and Burgie, London East India merchants. The first of his twelve partnerships, formed with Thomas Chase, an East India Company servant, in 1789, initiated the characteristic pattern of his business activity—engagement in a partnership while trading in parallel on his own account. In his last partnerships, between 1819 and 1824, those with John Dare, Parry found a talented associate ensuring that the firm Thomas Parry & Co. would outlive its founder. It survived beyond Indian independence.

Parry's career illustrates the broad vista of opportunity and the immense difficulties encountered in amassing an East Indian fortune. The company's administration of the Madras presidency offered the possibility of lucrative office. Parry became examiner to the mayor's court in

1796 and in 1813 he was appointed cashier and accountant of the government bank. The British business community provided additional fertile ground and he was able to secure the secretaryship of the Carnatic Insurance Company in 1796. Further afield, impecunious Indian princes were in dire need of financial skills. It was not surprising that the nawab of the Carnatic, Omdat-ul-Omrah, should recruit Parry as 'captain' to supervise his treasury's revenue collection. The expansion of British influence enabled Parry's business to 'follow the flag': shortly after the seizure of Dutch possessions in 1796 he established a branch at Trincomalee and a shipbuilding business in Cochin, which by 1820 numbered the Royal Navy among its major customers. In further exploiting the presence of a military establishment with its need for boots and accoutrements Parry established a tannery at San Thomé in 1805. Within a year it employed 350 people.

Rewards were high, but then so were the risks. Trade volumes suffered from tariffs erected to protect the home market against Indian piece-goods, and shipping activities were constantly dogged during the Napoleonic wars by French privateers operating from Mauritius. Rivalry between the company and the 'free merchants' left Parry in bad odour with authority. The inglorious affair of the 'Carnatic debt', where the company had assumed responsibility for the debts of the Carnatic's rulers, almost saw him banished twice from Madras, in 1800 and in 1809. Originally suspected of compromising the company by secretly helping to raise loans for his notoriously spendthrift former employer, the nawab, he later challenged the judgment of the commissioner investigating the forgery of the nawab's bonds. On several occasions his business came close to failure. A particularly bad year was 1806–7: poor monsoons and famine resulted in the failure of several agency houses. A fire on the ship *Marquis of Wellesley*, of which Parry was a part owner, almost administered a *coup de grâce*.

Nevertheless Parry made his imprint on Madras. A generous charitable subscription in 1801 assisted the dependants of soldiers killed in the Anglo-Mysore War, and in 1812 he joined the committee of management of the Native Poor Fund and Infirmary. The gold cup presented to him by 'the several respectable Hindu Inhabitants of Madras' in 1824 testified to his local popularity.

Although the owner of seven houses, including Parry's Castle at San Thomé, domestic happiness eluded Parry. In 1794 he married a widow, Mary Pearce, who returned to England with their children, John and Eliza, for health reasons by 1808. Parry subsequently found solace with Mary Ann Carr, an Anglo-Indian, with whom he had two sons, Thomas William (*b.* 11 Dec 1821) and Edward. All his children predeceased him.

The Indian climate took a severe toll on Parry's health, and in 1807–8 a debilitating illness almost forced a return to England. He finally succumbed to cholera and died on 14 August 1824 while visiting his indigo works at Porto Novo, South Arcot. He was buried in the mission church at Cuddalore, and a tablet sculpted by Francis Chantrey stands as his memorial in St George's Cathedral, Madras. The founder of an exceptionally important British firm in India, he had helped to lay the foundations of its subsequent economic development. Fittingly his name endured in Madras's urban topography—'Parry's Corner'.

PHILIP K. LAW

Sources G. H. Hodgson, *Thomas Parry* (1938) · H. Brown, *Parry's of Madras* (1954) · *New Oriental Register and East India Directory* (1788–1802) · *East-India Register and Directory* (1803–24) · *Madras Courier* (1788–1824) · parish register (marriage), 1794, St Mary's Cathedral, Madras

Likenesses C. Nash, miniature, 1787, repro. in Hodgson, *Thomas Parry* (1938), frontispiece; formerly at Parysland Museum?, Welshpool, in 1938 · crayon drawing, 1805, repro. in Hodgson, *Thomas Parry*, 98

Wealth at death est. over £10,000: will, 1824, Hodgson, *Thomas Parry*

Parry, Thomas (1795–1870), bishop of Barbados, fourth son of Edmund Parry, rector of Llanferres, Denbigh, was born in Denbighshire in 1795. He matriculated from Oriel College, Oxford, taking a first in mathematics and second in *literae humaniores* at Michaelmas 1816, and became fellow and tutor of Balliol College. In 1817 he took orders, and received the college living of St Leonard's, Colchester, while still continuing his tutorial duties. He proceeded MA in 1819.

Chosen in 1824 by Bishop Coleridge as archdeacon of Antigua, Parry lived there for some years working for slave emancipation. He was transferred in 1840, as archdeacon, to Barbados. On 21 August 1842 he was consecrated to the bishopric in Westminster Abbey, receiving at the same time the degree of DD. Although the diocese of Barbados was at this date shorn of the Leeward Islands, it still included the whole of the Windward Islands and Trinidad, and this involved the bishop in much travelling. An account of one of his tours, in the *Colonial Church Chronicle* of 1848, gives a good idea of the energy which he threw into the work of his scattered diocese. After nearly twenty years of such work he was suddenly struck down by illness. Returning to England for rest, he tried to arrange for retirement on a pension, but as the difficulties in the way appeared insuperable, he went back to his post for some years longer, having his son Henry [*see below*] as his archdeacon from 1861, and obtaining his consecration as bishop-coadjutor in 1868. After his health broke down again in 1869 he returned to England and settled at Malvern, Worcestershire, where he died on 16 March 1870. He was buried at West Malvern.

Parry was physically far from robust, but he possessed indomitable will, singleness of purpose, and a cheerful disposition. He was a moderate high-churchman. He published several sermons and tracts, the chief of which are *Parochial Sermons Preached in the West Indies* (1828), *A Practical Exposition of the Epistle to the Romans* (1832), *The Apostleship and Priesthood of Christ* (1834), and *Codrington College, Barbados* (1847).

Parry was married to Louisa, daughter of Henry Hutton, rector of Beaumont, Essex. Their son, **Henry Hutton Parry** (1827–1893), bishop of Western Australia, was educated at Rugby School and Balliol College, Oxford, where he graduated BA in 1851. He was ordained the same year, and went out to his father's diocese as curate of Holy Trinity, Trinidad. In 1855 he went to Barbados as tutor of Codrington (Theological) College; in 1861 he was made archdeacon of Barbados, and on 10 May 1868 was consecrated as bishop-coadjutor to his father. On 20 May 1876 Parry was appointed to the see of Perth, Western Australia, and died at Bunbury, on a visitation, on 16 November 1893. Especially concerned with women's education and with the Aboriginal population, he was an active and effective bishop. He was twice married, first to Elizabeth Mary Thomas (*d.* 1877) and second to Mary Suzanna, *née* Leake, who survived him.

C. A. Harris, *rev.* H. C. G. Matthew

Sources *The Times* (19 March 1870) • *Colonial Church Chronicle*, 24 (1870) • R. Erickson, ed., *Dictionary of Western Australians, 1829–1914*, 4 (1985) • *AusDB*
Archives U. Birm. L., letters to Church Missionary Society

Parry, Sir Thomas (1904–1985), scholar of Welsh and academic administrator, was born at Brynawel, Carmel, Caernarvonshire, on 4 August 1904, the eldest of three children (all sons) of Richard Edwin Parry (1870–1942), a quarryman, and his wife Jane, *née* Williams (1877–1957), from Llangwnnadl on the Llŷn peninsula. Richard Parry had in his youth sailed before the mast and later cultivated a small-holding as well as working in the quarry. All three sons were given a university education and the youngest, Gruffudd, became a prose writer of distinction.

Thomas Parry was educated at Penfforddelen primary school, Groeslon (where he befriended John Gwilym Jones, later a distinguished dramatist and literary critic), Pen-y-groes county grammar school, and the University College of North Wales, Bangor (1922–6), where he graduated with first-class honours in Welsh together with accessory Latin, despite having lost two terms during his second year because of a bout of scarlet fever and diphtheria. Although his teacher, Professor Ifor Williams, was anxious for him to pursue research in Bonn under Rudolf Thurneysen, he was immediately appointed to a lectureship in Welsh and Latin at the University College of South Wales and Monmouthshire, Cardiff, where he stayed for three years. There he was a colleague of the great Welsh scholar Griffith John Williams, and there too he met his wife, Enid Picton Davies (1911–1998), the daughter of a newspaper editor, whom he married on 20 May 1936. The marriage, although childless, sustained them both for nearly fifty years, one bond between them being a shared love of music.

Parry returned to Bangor as a lecturer in Welsh in 1929. All his teaching was based on wide reading and rigorous research. The topic for his MA thesis (1929) was the Renaissance grammarian John Davies of Brecon, 'Siôn Dafydd Rhys', but he then moved on to consider the Welsh ballads of the eighteenth century, on which he published a classic monograph, *Baledi'r ddeunawfed ganrif*, in 1935. He next undertook an account of the whole of Welsh literature from its sixth-century beginnings to 1900: this was published in 1945 as *Hanes llenyddiaeth Gymraeg hyd 1900* ('A history of Welsh literature up to 1900'), an English translation of which, by H. I. Bell, followed in 1955. It remains an indispensable work. A short treatment of the period 1900–45 and an adaptation of the greater work for a more popular readership were published in 1945 and 1948 respectively. Parry became professor and head of department when Sir Ifor Williams retired in 1947, and the department's predominantly linguistic emphasis under Williams was gradually replaced by a more balanced approach. In 1949 Parry published his well-crafted verse play *Lladd wrth yr allor*, a translation of T. S. Eliot's *Murder in the Cathedral*. From 1929 onwards, Parry was also working steadily on his *magnum opus*, an edition of the great fourteenth-century poet Dafydd ap Gwilym, which finally appeared in 1952 (and for which, together with *Hanes llenyddiaeth Gymraeg hyd 1900*, he received the degree of DLitt in 1953). Parry's edition revolutionized the study of the poet and has stood the test of time remarkably well.

In 1952 Parry was appointed librarian of the National Library of Wales, Aberystwyth, and in 1954 he published a second verse play, *Llywelyn Fawr* ('Llywelyn the great'). In 1958 he was appointed principal of the University College of Wales, Aberystwyth, following the acrimonious departure of his predecessor, Goronwy Rees. He had already displayed rare administrative acumen at Bangor, and that acumen was deployed to the full at the national library, where he oversaw the completion of the main building and the steady build-up of the collections (which he encouraged his staff to investigate), and at the University College of Wales, where the Robbins expansion necessitated the construction of a new campus and where language protesters (with whose aims he fully sympathized) and the prince of Wales (who attended the college for a term before his investiture) vied for his attention. He was made a fellow of the British Academy in 1959 and in 1962 he produced his acclaimed *Oxford Book of Welsh Verse*. Parry's chief endeavour at Aberystwyth, however—as in the federal University of Wales, whose vice-chancellor he was (1961–3 and 1967–9), and which he steered through a particularly divisive episode—was the promotion of the highest academic standards, to which he saw his chairmanship from 1963 to 1967 of the University Grants Committee's committee on libraries as a necessary contribution. He was awarded honorary doctorates from the National University of Ireland (1968) and the University of Wales (1969). In 1969 he retired to Bangor, assuming the presidency successively of the National Library of Wales (1969–77) and of the Honourable Society of Cymmrodorion (1978–82). He had been awarded the society's medal in 1976. In his retirement Parry also, in 1975, published (with Merfyn Morgan) *Llyfryddiaeth llenyddiaeth Gymraeg* ('A bibliography of Welsh literature') and was able almost to complete his survey of the language of the new Welsh translation of the Bible, which was published in 1988. Parry was awarded a knighthood in 1978. He died of cancer at his home in Bangor on 22 April 1985, and was buried at Tŵrgwyn Presbyterian Chapel, Upper Bangor, on 25 April 1985.

Parry's students regretted that administration had claimed him so early, because he was a peculiarly gifted and inspiring teacher, aided by a commanding presence (with a voice to match), a mind of remarkable orderliness, and a gift for lucid and often eloquent exposition.

R. GERAINT GRUFFYDD

Sources J. E. C. Williams, 'Thomas Parry, 1904–1985', *PBA*, 73 (1987), 567–99 • *WWW* • *The Times* (24 April 1985) • T. Parry, *Amryw bethau* (1996) • *Ysgrifau beirniadol* [whole issue], 10 (1977) • m. cert.
Archives NL Wales, papers, incl. notebooks relating to 'Gwaith Dafydd, ap Gwilym' • U. Wales, Bangor, MSS | NL Wales, letters to Thomas Iorwerth Ellis • NL Wales, corresp. with Emyr Humphreys • NL Wales, letters to Sir Thomas Parry-Williams
Likenesses A. Janes, oils, 1969, U. Wales, Aberystwyth • K. Williams, oils, 1977?, NL Wales • S. Nisbett, oils, U. Wales, Aberystwyth
Wealth at death £143,165: probate, 5 Sept 1985, *CGPLA Eng. & Wales*

Parry, Thomas Gambier (1816–1888), benefactor and art collector, was born on 22 February 1816 in Cadogan Place, Belgravia, London, the only child of Richard Parry (1776–1817) and Mary Gambier (*d.* 1821), daughter of Samuel Gambier and niece of James, Admiral Lord Gambier. His father and his grandfather, Thomas Parry of Banstead, Surrey, were wealthy directors of the East India Company. Brought up by two maiden Gambier aunts, he went to Eton College (1829–33) and then Trinity College, Cambridge, where he took a BA in 1837, proceeding MA in 1848. He was taught watercolour painting by William Evans, the drawing-master at Eton, and later by Peter DeWint; Henry Warren (1794–1879) and Sir John Gilbert taught him oil painting.

In 1838 Parry purchased Highnam Court, an 1811-acre estate near Gloucester, which he considerably improved; it remained his lifelong home. He established a pinetum in 1844, encouraged by the collector and arboriculturist Robert Stayner Holford, and in 1848, in memory of his first wife, Anna Maria Isabella (Isabel) Clinton (1816–1848), whom he had married on 13 August 1839, he commissioned Henry Woodyer, a pupil of the architect William Butterfield, to design the church of the Holy Innocents at Highnam in the Decorated Gothic style. Parry paid for and endowed the church (consecrated 29 April 1851), the school, the church lodge, and the rectory. A keen high-churchman, he joined the Cambridge Camden Society (founded 1839 and later renamed the Ecclesiological Society), to whose publications he contributed important papers on church decoration. He embarked on a scheme of decoration for the church of the Holy Innocents (1859–61, 1870–80), having perfected the 'spirit fresco' technique, which consisted of pigment mixed into a medium of bleached wax, Elemi resin, spike lavender, and copal varnish. The advantages of this method were its durability, resistance to change, and dull finish; similar processes had been tried by early nineteenth-century French and German artists and had been researched by Parry's friend, Sir Charles Eastlake. In 1880 Parry published an official account of *Spirit Fresco Painting* (2nd edn, 1883), and the process was used by Frederick, Lord Leighton, in his two large frescoes *The Arts of War and of Peace* (1878–80 and 1884–6, Victoria and Albert Museum, London).

Thomas Gambier Parry (1816–1888), by Margaret Sarah Carpenter, 1833–5

Parry was an inveterate traveller, and in 1851–2 he journeyed extensively in France, Germany, and Italy, where he saw murals by the German Nazarene artists Friederich Overbeck, Peter von Cornelius, and Julius Schnorr von Carolsfeld. Although he had begun collecting while at Cambridge, it was not until 1851 that he became interested in trecento and quattrocento Italian masters, and from his journals, account books, and inventories we can accurately track his acquisitions. By 1863 he had bought several important paintings either in Italy or in London, including Lorenzo Monaco's *Coronation of the Virgin*; three predella panels by Fra Angelico, *The 'Imago pietatis' Flanked by Saints*; and Bernardo Daddi's polyptych of 1348. If not a pioneer in this field, he bought with discrimination; nor did he confine himself to paintings, buying medieval ivories, maiolica, Limoges enamel, Venetian and German sixteenth-century glass, and Islamic metalwork. Almost all of these collections were bequeathed by his grandson, Mark Gambier-Parry, to the Courtauld Institute of Art, London, in 1966.

Parry became a leading authority on decorative painting and was asked to complete the eastern six bays of the nave ceiling of Ely Cathedral (1862–4). He also decorated St Andrew's Chapel in Gloucester Cathedral (1866–8) and the lantern (octagon) of Ely Cathedral (1874–5), and in 1878 he painted the ceiling of the Ely baptistery (all executed at his own expense). His style owed much to the Italian trecento, but in his love of richly coloured, stylized naturalism, he is close to William Morris and William Burges.

Parry's second wife, Ethelinda (Ethel) Lear (*d.* 1896),

daughter of Francis Lear, dean of Salisbury, whom he married on 5 August 1851, accompanied him on his travels. The couple had five children: their eldest son, Ernest Gambier-Parry (1853–1936), invalided from the army in 1885, became the family archivist. Ethel also took care of her surviving stepchildren: Charles Clinton Parry (1840–83), Lucy Parry, and Sir (Charles) Hubert Hastings *Parry (1848–1918), who later became a distinguished composer.

Parry was life president of the Gloucester School of Science and Art (1858–88), and he founded and endowed the orphanage St Lucy's Home, and the Free Hospital for Children, Gloucester, in 1866. Of medium height, square-built, and reserved in manner, he was a keen horseman, antiquary, linguist, and musician. He died of a heart attack at Highnam Court on 28 September 1888 and was buried on 3 October in the churchyard of the church of the Holy Innocents, Highnam. A large collection of his drawings, watercolours, and mural cartoons belong to descendants. DENNIS FARR

Sources priv. coll., T. G. Parry MSS [diaries and journals] • priv. coll., E. Gambier-Parry MSS • *The Times* (1 Oct 1888) • *Gloucestershire Chronicle* (6 Oct 1888) • D. Farr, ed., *Thomas Gambier Parry, 1816–1888, as artist and collector* (1993) • A. Blunt, 'Thomas Gambier Parry: a great art collector', *Apollo*, 81 (1965), 288–95 • A. Blunt and others, 'The Gambier-Parry bequest to the University of London', *Burlington Magazine*, 109 (1967), 111–77 • *The Gambier-Parry collection: provisional catalogue*, Courtauld Institute of Art (1967) • *DNB*

Archives Glos. RO, compilation of work on the Highnam Court estate, etc. | Courtauld Inst., corresp. of Anthony Blunt and Mark Gambier-Parry

Likenesses M. S. Carpenter, oils, 1833–5, priv. coll. [*see illus.*] • M. S. Carpenter, drawing (as young man), BM • M. Knight, oils (aged three or four), priv. coll. • carte-de-visite (in old age), priv. coll. • photograph (in middle age), priv. coll.; repro. in Farr, ed., *Thomas Gambier Parry* • photograph, priv. coll.

Wealth at death £164,307 5*s.* 4*d.*: probate, 22 Jan 1889, *CGPLA Eng. & Wales*

Parry, William (*d.* 1585), spy and conspirator, was the son of Harry ap David or Bethels (*d. c.*1566), guard in the royal household, of Northop, Flintshire, and his wife, Margaret. According to Parry, his mother was a Conway of Bodrythan, according to his enemies 'the reputed daughter of a priest' (Holinshed, 1392). If Raphael Holinshed was correct, then this man was perhaps Peter or Piers Conway, rector of Northop and also archdeacon of St Asaph; it is unlikely that Parry's mother was legitimate. According to Parry, his father served Henry VIII and then Princess Mary.

Education and early life Parry was supposedly educated at Chester with John Fisher, who 'had some small skill and understanding in law', and at the grammar school (Holinshed, 1392). Like his social standing, his education was later denigrated to make a mockery of his continental doctorate. Supposedly, he went to London about 1560, perhaps for some further legal training. Parry married the widow Powell (*d.* in or before 1571), daughter of Sir William Thomas of Carmarthenshire, and served William Herbert, first earl of Pembroke, until 1570, when he managed to attach himself to the royal household. By March 1571 he had married Katherine, widow of Richard Heywood, a king's bench official, and acquired lands in Lincolnshire and Kent worth £80 per annum to add to his Flintshire inheritance of £20 per annum. In his own account in 1582, Parry, who had serious debts, doubled this landed income to £200 per annum. John Somers wrote after Parry's arrest that he had 'known him ever since he married old Mistress Haywood, my neighbour in Fleet Street, of whom he made as much as he could, besides abusing her daughter' (*CSP Scot.*, *1584–5*, 585).

In early 1577 Parry travelled to Rome and Siena, sending unsolicited letters to William Cecil, Baron Burghley, whose patronage he continued to seek on his return. By early 1580 Parry had fled his creditors and reached Paris. He tried to rehabilitate himself with Burghley by sending intelligence, but incongruously took it upon himself to recommend pardons for individuals as notorious as the rebel Charles Neville, sixth earl of Westmorland. Burghley was willing to consider Parry fit company for his nephew Anthony Bacon. Parry was agreeable to this and willing to borrow money from Bacon; according to a later account, Robert Dudley, earl of Leicester, used this acquaintance as a reproach against Burghley, which led to the latter 'engaging that his nephew should not be shaken either in religion or loyalty by his conversation with Parry' (Birch, 1.13). The ambassador, Sir Henry Cobham, wrote doubtfully to Burghley that he would consider Parry suspect except that 'he pretendeth to depend on your lordship's good favour' (*Salisbury MSS*, 2.331).

Parry returned to financial troubles in England. After an altercation in the Inner Temple with his creditor Hugh Hare on 2 November 1580 involving a scuffle and a broken door, he was sentenced to death for burglary and attempted murder, complaining 'that the Recorder spake wyth the jury, and that the forman did drinke' (BL, Lansdowne MS 43, fol. 124*r*). He received a royal pardon, only to land in debtors' prison (the Poultry), with bonds of £2000 to keep the peace added to Hare's debt of £1000. Parry's sureties included Sir John Conway, Sir William Drury, and Edward Stafford. In July 1582 he left the country, this time licensed.

Spy or traitor, 1582–1585 If Parry had been recruited as a spy it could explain his ambiguous behaviour. That, or debts. He was received into the Roman Catholic church at Paris and became involved in the politics of Catholic exiles in France. He claimed, hyperbolically, to Burghley in May 1583 to have 'shaken the foundacon of the English semynary in Rheyms and utterly overthrowen the credite of the English pensioners in Rome'. Allegedly, 'if I were well warranted and allowed I would either prevent and discover all Romayne and Spaynish practises against our state, or lose my life in testymony of my loyalty to the queens maiestie' (BL, Lansdowne MS 39, fol. 128*r*). It is difficult to determine whether or not he was an English spy or a traitor. From whatever motive, he declined 'to be troubled or tyed to th'advertisement of ordynary occurrents' to the privy council (BL, Lansdowne MS 40, fol. 55*r*). For Catholic consumption meanwhile, finding it useless to deny that he had 'a project assigned to me' by the

English government, Parry rejected it as 'little to my honour' and resolved 'to employ all my strength and industry in the service of the Catholic Church' (Hicks, 348).

Parry 'conceived a possible meane to relieve the afflicted state of our Catholikes' and in the second part of 1583 went to Italy to tell people about it (Holinshed, 1385). He wrote to the Spanish ambassador at Rome, Enrique de Guzman, count of Olivares, to Giovanni d'Aragon, duke of Terranova, governor of Milan, and to Ptolomeo Galli, cardinal of Como and Gregory XIII's secretary of state, from whom (after a brush with the Milanese Inquisition) he sought a safe conduct to go to Rome. By the time he got it, he was returning to Lyons, meeting there the Jesuit William Crichton. Parry seemed keener to get into correspondence with Galli than to use the safe conduct and then asked the cardinal for a plenary indulgence in view of his 'dangerous enterprise … for the restoration of England to its ancient obedience to the apostolic see and the liberation of the queen of Scotland [Mary, queen of Scots], the only true and undoubted Catholic heiress of the crown of England' (Hicks, 352).

It is unknown whether these early discussions related to Elizabeth I's assassination, though Parry's conversations with Crichton certainly centred on tyrannicide. Crichton said in 1611 that he had agreed that the pope might authorize assassination, but Parry might not kill Elizabeth speculatively in the hope of subsequent approval. When Parry and Crichton were both in English hands in 1585, they concurred that the latter had opposed tyrannicide. Crichton—like Girolamo Ragazzoni, the nuncio in France—wrote to Galli, warning him against Parry; but Crichton conceded he had 'very good qualities' (Hicks, 358). Parry's published confession was that on returning from Lyons to Paris he still proposed 'killing the greatest subject in England, whom I then … hated' (Holinshed, 1385)—he probably meant Leicester, whose enmity had appeared in the matter of Bacon—and that Thomas Morgan suggested Elizabeth as a better target.

At the beginning of 1584 Parry, having acquired a doctorate of law in Paris, returned to England, followed by the indulgence sent by Galli and an encouraging, but soon notorious, letter. Although it is not recorded how Parry explained his intentions, Galli accepted the prospect of Elizabeth's assassination and there is no reason to suppose he would have objected to any such proposal of Parry's. Parry showed the letter to the queen, doubtless to indicate his aptitude as a spy and future prospects for infiltration.

Parry then suggested 'yt were a small matter for the quene to avow my service' with the mastership of St Catharine's Hospital and no other candidate would 'adventure more then I have done in her service' (BL, Lansdowne MS 43, fol. 13*r*). According to Sir Christopher Hatton 'the qweene offered Parrey a pension of a hundred powndes by yere which Parrey refused' (Hartley, 2.88). Such a refusal would have been so uncharacteristic that the *True and Plaine Declaration* (1587) thought it best to assume he had taken the pension, while Phillip Stubbes believed that Parry was 'no doubt bountefully rewarded' for success on behalf of 'her grace over seas in very waightie affaires' (Stubbes, sig. A2*v*). Stubbes carelessly forgot to claim that Parry's dealings, if officially prompted, had been pursued in earnest and tacitly accepted he had only started to conspire afterwards.

Parry was still in debt and probably expected greater reward from the queen. In summer 1584 he resumed discussions as to the desirability of assassinating Elizabeth, this time with Edmund *Neville (*b.* before 1555, *d.* in or after 1620), a putative accomplice. He had supposedly missed opportunities to do the deed himself but now planned his subsequent escape. Arguably Parry had taken upon himself the role of *agent provocateur* to revive his languishing career as intelligencer; if so, it was literally suicidal to let treasonable discussions drag on without proceeding to denunciation. The attempt to incriminate Neville, whom Parry called cousin, might seem a bid to please Burghley—Neville had an inheritance claim against Burghley's son, Thomas Cecil—unless of course Parry was sincere and chose an opponent of the Cecilian *status quo*.

Parry later explained his next, parliamentary, folly as an experiment as to whether, if he protested in the House of Commons, Elizabeth might 'be wrought to deale more gratiously with Catholikes' (Holinshed, 1386). Parry was elected in November 1584 as MP for Queenborough, on the strength of the Heywood Kentish lands, with the support of Sir Edward Hoby and probably with the concurrence of William Brooke, tenth Baron Cobham. On 17 December, 'to the offence of the whole companie', Parry denounced 'the bill of Jesuits … *ex abrupto*, sainge that it caried no thinge with it but bloud, daunger, terror, dispaire, confiscation and that not to the queene's commodytie, but to other men's'. The wrath of the Commons was increased by Parry's pretension to explain himself to Elizabeth alone. A lone claim was noted that they should 'suffer men freelie to utter their conseites of both sides', but Parry spent the night in the custody of the serjeant-at-arms. He saw the privy council, not the queen: she declared herself satisfied with Parry's secondhand explanations but he had to apologize kneeling at the bar of the house, and to profess parliamentary inexperience (Hartley, 2.158–60).

Arrest, trial, and execution, 1585 Neville finally denounced Parry on 8 February 1585. Sir Francis Walsingham, the principal secretary, allegedly suggested Parry reveal anything he knew of plots against Elizabeth and even, specifically, whether he 'himself had let fall anie speech unto anie person (though with an intent onely to discover his disposition) that might draw him into suspicion, as though he himself had anie such wicked intent' (Holinshed, 1383). Parry's vacillations became fatal. He confessed too late and then repudiated the confession as induced by threats of torture. The Commons punningly voted on 18 February that he should be 'dismembred', that is expelled, and then pressed for 'more severe punishment' than hanging, drawing, and quartering (Hartley, 2.116, 184). On the 25th Parry was finally tried in Westminster Hall. He had suggested to Burghley and Leicester that his 'rare and strange' 'enterprise upon such ground &

by such a warrant' might be a dangerous example, better hushed up (BL, Harley MS 787, fol. 107*r*). He also wrote to Elizabeth that he hoped 'most graciously (beyond all common expectacion) to be pardoned', concluding: 'Remember yor infortunate Parry, chiefly overthrowen by yor hard hand. Amend yt in the rest of yor servantes, for yt is past with me yf yor grace be not greater than I looke for' (BL, Lansdowne MS 43, fols. 117*v*–118*r*). He was indeed executed on 2 March in Westminster Palace Yard. Parry made a few gestures towards the expected admission of guilt, but denied much of his confession. He proclaimed Elizabeth's graciousness, but required her to answer for his blood. Officially—his Catholicism having apparently been sufficiently underlined—he died without any religious sign, 'like an atheist and a godlesse man' (Holinshed, 1392). It was an unpublished account that had him asserting 'no salvacon but onelie in the free meryte of Christ'; later, still alive 'when his bowelles were taken out, he gave a great groane' (BL, Lansdowne MS 43, fol. 127*v*).

Parry's self-contradictions have made him a historical conundrum. Catholic writers especially, noting his indubitable involvement in government espionage and the suspect nature of his continental discussions in 1583, have declared all his plots bogus. Robert Persons believed that finally Parry plotted in earnest with one of his friends to kill the queen. Crichton—doomed if Parry had implicated him—thought Parry, abandoning spying, sought 'to atone for the wrongs he had done to Catholics' by removing Elizabeth and letting in Mary (Pollen, *Mary*, 165). In fact, however, Parry became an anti-Marian *cause célèbre* in the passage of the bill for the queen's safety; and, though Elizabeth failed to have Morgan extradited, at Mary's eventual trial the charge reappeared of 'favoring and mainteyning' Morgan, 'the principall perswader of Parry to attempt that most wicked act' (Read, *Bardon Papers*, 73).

Parry prayed that Elizabeth would not regret executing him. Not content to be an agent, he perhaps aspired to be a Walsingham and expose conspiracies on his own. His letter scrawled to Elizabeth from the Tower of London had an excursus (cut from the printed accounts) didactically advising a reconstruction of foreign policy: the queen could not trust France, was 'dishonoured' by supporting Philip II's enemies, and should 'cherish' Mary, her 'undoubted heyre in succession' (BL, Lansdowne MS 43, fols. 117*r*–118*r*). He made a last announcement on the scaffold:

> he had wrytten to the queene and councell, who was lawfull successor to the crowne of England, that place was not fytt to name the partie in. It sufficed her majestie and the councell knewe it and their tytle whom he had named to them was just and lawfull. (ibid., fol. 127*v*)

Officiousness as a spy seems to have ended in megalomania. Perhaps he was really confused as to his own loyalties, but his willingness to admit technical guilt to treason in 'persuading' Neville though 'never intending to kill Queene Elizabeth', might also be true (Holinshed, 1394). Parry got no second royal pardon, but the government need not have been surer of his motives than later writers have been. JULIAN LOCK

Sources L. Hicks, 'The strange case of Dr William Parry: the career of an *agent provocateur*', *Studies: an Irish Quarterly Review of Letters, Philosophy, and Science*, 37 (1948), 343–62 • HoP, *Commons*, *1558–1603*, 3.180–84 • J. H. Pollen, 'Mary, queen of Scots, and the Babington plot: 1. Dr Parry', *The Month*, 109 (1907), 356–65 • J. H. Pollen, 'Plots and sham plots: 2', *The Month*, 100 (1902), 71–87 • J. H. Pollen, *Mary, queen of Scots, and the Babington plot*, Scottish History Society, 3 (1922) • R. Holinshed, *Chronicles* (1587) [incorporating *A true and plaine declaration of the horrible treasons practised by William Parry*] • P. Stubbes, *The intended treason of Dr Parrie and his complices* [1585] • BL, Lansdowne MSS 25, 29, 31, 34, 39, 40, 43, 46 • state papers France, PRO, SP 78/8–10, 13 • queen's bench, baga de secretis, PRO, KB 8/46 • *Report of the Deputy Keeper of the Public Records*, 4 (1843), appx. 2, 273 • C. Read, ed., *The Bardon papers: documents relating to the imprisonment and trial of Mary, queen of Scots*, CS, 3rd ser., 17 (1909) • J. Strype, *Annals of the Reformation and establishment of religion … during Queen Elizabeth's happy reign*, new edn, 4 vols. (1824) • T. Birch, *Memoirs of the reign of Queen Elizabeth*, 2 vols. (1754) • *Calendar of the manuscripts of the most hon. the marquis of Salisbury*, 24 vols., HMC, 9 (1883–1976) • T. E. Hartley, ed., *Proceedings in the parliaments of Elizabeth I*, 3 vols. (1981–95), vol. 2 • J. Bossy, *Under the molehill: an Elizabethan spy story* (2001) • C. Read, *Mr Secretary Walsingham and the policy of Queen Elizabeth*, 3 vols. (1925) • C. Read, *Lord Burghley and Queen Elizabeth* (1960) • J. R. Lock, '"Strange usurped potentates": Elizabeth I, the papacy, and the Indian summer of the medieval deposing power', DPhil diss., U. Oxf., 1992, chap. 7

Archives BL, letters and papers, Harley MSS | Archivio Vaticano, Vatican City, corresp. with Cardinal Galli, Nunziatura di Francia 17 • BL, Lansdowne MSS, letters to Lord Burghley • Hatfield House, Hertfordshire, Cecil papers, letters to Lord Burghley

Parry, William (*fl.* 1597–1601), traveller, who refers to himself as 'gentleman', makes his first appearance in the train of twenty-four officers and men attached to Sir Anthony Shirley at the end of 1597. Shirley was dispatched by the earl of Essex to Italy to assist the duchy of Ferrara against the pope. The expedition, which Parry describes in his only known work, *A new and large discourse of the travels of Sir Anthony Sherley, knight, by sea, and over land, to the Persian empire* (1601), departed from Southwold in Suffolk and made its way through the Netherlands to Germany. In Augsburg, Shirley discovered that Ferrara had submitted and that his services were no longer needed. He and his company therefore set off for Venice, where he decided to travel to Persia in the hope of persuading Shah Abbas to form an alliance with the Christian powers against the Turks.

The party, now including an interpreter and some Persian servants, left Venice late in May 1598 bound for Syria. Parry's impression of the Levant, after a stay of six weeks in Aleppo, was unfavourable. He hated the Arabs and the Turks, 'whose behaviours in point of civility (besides that they are damned infidels and sodomitical Mahomets) do answer the hate we Christians do justly hold them in. For they are beyond all measure a most insolent, superbous, and insulting people' (Parry, 107), and it was with a sense of relief that, having spent October in Baghdad, he accompanied Shirley through Kurdistan to reach Qazvin in Persia in the first week of December. In Persia they were warmly received. 'We thought we had been imparadised', wrote Parry, 'finding our entertainment to be so good and the manner of the people to be so kind and courteous, far differing from the Turks', especially when they heard we came of purpose to their King' (ibid., 115).

From Qazvin, Parry and Shirley followed Shah Abbas to Esfahan, where Shirley had himself appointed ambassador to the Christian rulers. He set out on his mission in late April or early May 1599. In order to circumvent Ottoman territory he chose the land route through Russia, and Parry provides interesting details about their poor treatment in Moscow by the tsar, Boris Godunov. They then went on to Archangel, where Shirley entrusted Parry with letters for England, the one to Sir Robert Cecil being dated 10 June 1600. They separated on the island of Vlieland. Shirley made for Prague to confer with Rudolph II. Parry returned to England.

Parry himself vanishes after the publication of his *New and Large Discourse* in November 1601. Appended to the text was a sonnet by the poet and writing-master from Hereford John Davies, the affectionate tone of which suggests that the two men may have been friends. Parry's work served as a source for the play by John Day, William Rowley, and George Wilkins, *The Travailes of the Three English Brothers* (1607), and the last part of his book, on the journey through Russia, was reproduced in Samuel Purchas's *Pilgrimes* (1625). Lively, amusing, and generally observant, it is the best description of Shirley's visit to Shah Abbas, but as an account of the Middle East it is strongly prejudiced and occasionally misleading. The conclusion that the Persians 'have not many books, much less great libraries amongst their best clerks. They are no learned nation, but ignorant in all kind of liberal or learned sciences, and almost of all other arts and faculties' (Parry, 121–2) implies a grave lack of information. Parry was also ready to credit the most fanciful legends about Muhammad, such as his being buried in Mecca in a magnetically suspended coffin—a myth which would be exploded within twenty years. Parry's is thus one of the last medieval descriptions of the Muslim world rather than one of the first modern accounts.

ALASTAIR HAMILTON

Sources E. D. Ross, *Sir Anthony Sherley and his Persian adventure* (1933) • W. Parry, *A new and large discourse of the travels of Sir Anthony Sherley, knight, by sea, and over land, to the Persian empire* (1601) • *DNB* • S. Purchas, *Purchas his pilgrimes*, 4 vols. (1625), 1407–10

Parry, William (*bap.* **1687**, *d.* **1756**), antiquary, the son of Devereux Parry and his wife, Margaret, was baptized at St John's Church, Hereford, on 2 May 1687. Having matriculated from Jesus College, Oxford, on 19 February 1706, he graduated BA in 1709, MA in 1712, and BD in 1719. He was elected to a fellowship in his college, and on 27 September 1712 was appointed rector of Tellisford, Somerset. He resigned in 1715, and in 1726 he was instituted rector of Shipston-on-Stour, Worcestershire. He died on 14 September 1756 and was buried at Shipston on 16 September.

Parry's elegant hand, resembling the italic print, was much admired. Contemporaries considered some of his manuscripts to be so neatly written that they might be mistaken for well-executed typography. Several manuscripts transcribed by him are extant in the Bodleian Library, and a beautiful transcript which he made of the statutes of his college is preserved among its archives. A volume of his letters to Thomas Rawlins is also preserved in the Bodleian, and an account of a similar collection was communicated by John Greswell to the *Gentleman's Magazine* (1st ser., 77, 1807, 502). In both series Parry frequently mentioned a work on which he was actively engaged, an alphabetical catalogue of ancient and modern coins, compiled from secondary sources. Most of his letters to Rawlins were accompanied by copies of verses. A note in the volume records that Rawlins sent Parry's transcripts to his friends as specimens of calligraphy. Many of Parry's verses appeared in the *Gentleman's Magazine*.

THOMPSON COOPER, *rev.* MARY CLAPINSON

Sources J. Greswell, 'Rev. W. Parry', *GM*, 1st ser., 77 (1807), 502–5 • letters to Thomas Rawlins, Bodl. Oxf., MS Ballard 29 • parish records, Warks. CRO, DR 446 • Foster, *Alum. Oxon.* • F. W. Weaver, ed., *Somerset incumbents* (privately printed, Bristol, 1889), 198 • *IGI* • [J. Walker and P. Bliss], eds., *Letters written by eminent persons in the seventeenth and eighteenth centuries*, 2 vols. (1813) • W. H. Black, *A descriptive, analytical and critical catalogue of the manuscripts bequeathed unto the University of Oxford by Elias Ashmole*, 2 vols. (1845–66)

Archives Bodl. Oxf., literary collections | Bodl. Oxf., letters to Thomas Rawlins

Parry, William (**1744/5–1791**), portrait painter, was the son of John *Parry (1710?–1782), the celebrated blind Welsh harpist. He studied at William Shipley's drawing school on the Strand, London. While a pupil there in 1761 and 1762 he won premiums awarded by the Society of Arts for drawings from antique statuary and from the living model. These drawings are still preserved by the society. According to James Northcote the praise heaped on Parry for his drawings and the attendant prizes 'had the unpleasant effect of relaxing his studies and exertions, instead of stimulating him to attempt approaching nearer to perfection' (Northcote, 1.159). Parry subsequently studied at the duke of Richmond's sculpture gallery. There he not only made drawings of the various antique casts but a drawing of the gallery itself, now lost. Parry was also a student at the St Martin's Lane Academy. In 1762, then living at Market Street, St James's, London, he exhibited with the Free Society of Artists. He exhibited there again in 1763. In 1766, by which time he was a pupil of Joshua Reynolds, he exhibited with the Society of Artists. At that time he recorded his address at Reynolds's home in Leicester Square. In February 1769 he was admitted to the Royal Academy Schools. It was presumably about this time that Parry became a protégé of Sir Watkin Williams-Wynn.

Northcote states that as a result Parry 'retired to Wales', presumably referring to Wynnstay, Williams-Wynn's seat in Denbighshire (Northcote, 1.159). Among the portraits he produced at that time was that of Watkin E. Wynn, signed and dated 1770 (ex Sothebys, London, 17 July 1981, lot 43). Other Welsh sitters included Mr and Mrs Richard Parry Price of Emral Hall, Flintshire, and Mr and Mrs Thomas Puleston (ex Sothebys, London, 12 November 1997, lots 77 and 78). In 1770 he travelled to Italy, where Williams-Wynn provided him with a pension of £150 a year. At Easter 1771 Parry, described as 'Monsu Pari Inglese', a painter aged twenty-six, was recorded as living on the via Babuino, Rome. If this age is correct Parry must have been born in 1744 or 1745, rather than about 1742, the date previously given. In Rome, Parry established a reputation as a copyist. In 1774 he copied Raphael's *Transfiguration* in San Pietro in Montorio several times, selling two such copies to Williams-Wynn, the larger for 400 guineas. In the same year Parry travelled to Naples, and in April 1775 he left Rome for Parma. In addition to copies Parry also painted portraits, including one of the dwarf Baiocco, which he also sold to Williams-Wynn.

In 1775 Parry returned to England, settling in Duke Street, St James's, London. During that year he married a daughter of the architect Henry Keene and he was elected associate of the Royal Academy; from then until 1779 he exhibited at the academy, principally small whole-length portraits, including *Heiva, Chief Mourner of Otahiete* (1776), a portrait of his father, John Parry (1778), playing draughts, and *Peter the Wild Boy* (1779). About 1776 he also painted a historically important group portrait of Sir Joseph Banks, Daniel Charles Solander, and the young Polynesian Omai (priv. coll.). In 1779 Parry's wife died in childbirth but their son, Simon, survived. It was to the loss of his wife that Northcote presumably alluded when noting the 'unhappy family occurrences' which caused Parry to leave London for Wales at this time (Northcote, 1.159). By 1783 he was once more living in London, where he exhibited a *Drawing of a Boy* with the Free Society of Artists. He exhibited for the last time at the Royal Academy in 1787 and 1788, when he recorded his address as 17 Haymarket. Parry returned to Italy probably in 1789. His presence in Rome was recorded by 26 May. In the following year his profession was listed as history painter, resident at the Casa di Battoni, near the Strada Condotta. In a letter to Sir Roger Newdigate, dated 1 September 1790, he noted having made copies of Michelangelo's *Last Judgement*, Raphael's *Madonna della sedia*, and Rubens's *Mars and Venus*. He intended to make further copies on his journey home via Florence and Bologna. By this time, however, he was in poor health. He died on 13 February 1791, shortly after his return to England. He bequeathed his assets to his teenage son, then under the guardianship of his uncle David Parry. F. M. O'Donoghue, *rev.* Martin Postle

Sources E. Edwards, *Anecdotes of painters* (1808); facs. edn (1970) · J. Northcote, *The life of Sir Joshua Reynolds*, 2nd edn, 2 vols. (1819) · J. Ingamells, ed., *A dictionary of British and Irish travellers in Italy, 1701–1800* (1997) · Graves, *RA exhibitors* · Graves, *Artists* · Royal Academy catalogues (1776–88) · Society of Artists catalogues (1766) · Free Society of Artists catalogues (1762–3) · Free Society of Artists catalogues (1783) · Waterhouse, *18c painters* · Redgrave, *Artists* · administration, PRO, PROB 6/167, fol. 219*v*

Likenesses E. Edwards, etching, 1804, BM, NPG

Parry, William (1754–1819), Congregational minister and tutor, was born on 25 November 1754 at Abergavenny, Monmouthshire, where his father was a Baptist deacon. About 1760 the family moved to Stepney, Middlesex. Here, his first work was in the woollen trade, like his father, but in 1774, on the advice of the minister of the Congregational church at Stepney, Samuel Brewer, Parry entered Homerton Academy to train for the ministry. In 1780 he was ordained to the pastorate of Little Baddow, Essex. On 24 May 1780 he married Rachel King Hickman (1760–1791), daughter of Edward Hickman, minister of Back Street Independent Chapel, Hitchin. She died in childbirth on 17 May 1791, in which year two of their infant children also died. He married, secondly, in 1793, Susannah Lincoln, daughter of William Lincoln, a Congregational minister at Bury St Edmunds; she survived him.

Although the minister of a small country church, Parry was regarded at the time as one of the ablest and most accomplished ministers of the day. Appalled by the poverty of his predecessor's widow, he helped establish in 1789 the Benevolent Society for the Relief of Necessitous Widows and Children of Protestant Dissenting Ministers in Essex and Hertfordshire, and he was one of the prime movers in the formation, in 1798, of the Essex Congregational Union. He was a controversialist in the cause of dissenters' civil liberties, publishing most notably, in 1790, three letters to Lord Aylesford, chairman of a meeting of gentlemen and clergy held at Warwick to oppose the repeal of the Test and Corporation Acts. His religious publications included *A Vindication of Public and Social Worship* (1792) and *An Enquiry into the Inspiration of the Apostles* (1797), an anti-Socinian work, commended by the bishop of Winchester. His *Strictures on the Origins of Moral Evil* (1807) prompted a response by Thomas Hill and was followed by *Vindication of the Strictures* in 1808. He also published three ordination sermons.

About 1794 Parry's congregation fell off, owing to the emigration to North America of many of its leading members. Their departure may have influenced him to accept the tutorship of the dissenting academy established by the Coward Trust at Wymondley House, near Hitchin, Hertfordshire, in 1799. His lectures there were noted for their simplicity and avoidance of technical terms. Seventeen volumes of them in manuscript are at Dr Williams's Library. Having kept only a school hitherto, Parry spent long days in concentrated study to compose the lectures, and this affected his health. The Coward trustees sent him 'wine for his infirmities' (Stoughton, 60) and dispatched him to the sea for the air, but his ill health persisted, and must have been a factor in the academy's lack of success. It proved difficult to attract students in the early years. Nor, at first, could Parry keep his assistants. The free enquiry method of theological teaching and the absence of doctrinal tests for students on admission—both Coward traditions and upheld by Parry—made for lack of cohesion and led to disputes; and social pressures, due to the wars with France, were also unsettling. Parry, an easygoing, scholarly man, lost without his notes in lecture room and pulpit, was ill at ease with the tensions which resulted.

A reputation for Socinianism, which had closed Wymondley's predecessor, hung over the academy, denying it the support of local churches. In time, it even hung over Parry himself. In 1818 he felt obliged to publish in the *Evangelical Magazine* a dignified denial that he had changed his belief in the divinity of Christ. A study of his lectures bears him out. Later that year Parry fell seriously ill—evidently as a result of a stroke—and died nine weeks later, on 9 January 1819. He was buried in ground adjoining the Congregational church at Hitchin on 21 January.

JOHN HANDBY THOMPSON

Sources *London Christian Instructor, or, Congregational Magazine*, 2 (1819), 127, 257–61, 321–8, 385–92 • W. Chaplin, *Admonitions from the dead* (1819) [funeral sermon] • S. Newth, 'Memorials of the academical institutions sustained by the Coward Trust … to 1850', *c.*1890, DWL, fols. 118–25 • E. E. Marks, *A brief history of the Congregational church at Little Baddow* (1930), 20–23 • T. W. Davids, *Annals of evangelical nonconformity in Essex* (1863), 354 • W. Urwick, *Nonconformity in Hertfordshire* (1884), 606, 633, 650 • W. Bennet, letter, *Evangelical Magazine and Missionary Chronicle*, 26 (1818), 172 • *Congregational Magazine*, 17 (1834), 132 • R. W. Dale, *History of English congregationalism*, ed. A. W. W. Dale (1907), 596–7 • H. McLachlan, *English education under the Test Acts: being the history of the nonconformist academies, 1662–1820* (1931), 70, 172 • J. Stoughton, 'History of the Coward Trust', *c.*1889, DWL • *DNB* • *IGI*

Archives DWL, corresp., MS lectures, and papers | DWL, Coward Trust MSS, minutes and corresp.

Parry, William (1773–1859), memoirist, is of obscure origins. Nothing is known of his early life beyond what can be gathered from his book, *The Last Days of Lord Byron* (1825): he lived in east London; had a wife and two young sons; and was 'rather corpulent'. He first trained as a shipwright but claimed to have spent most of his life in the army and navy.

In 1823 Parry was recruited from a post at the Woolwich naval dockyard by the London Greek committee and invited by Thomas Gordon to produce a plan for an artillery brigade and explosives laboratory to be sent to Greece. Parry's original plan was scaled down by the committee, so that he was dispatched in November 1823 as fire master (the artillery officer responsible for explosives), with a clerk, foreman, six craftsmen and supplies adequate to set up the laboratory, plus a battery of mountain guns, but without any artillerymen. This rather disappointing equipage eventually reached Missolonghi on 7 February 1824.

That day, Byron wrote to Charles Hancock, 'Parry seems a fine rough subject … he and I will (I think) be able to draw together … he complains grievously of the mercantile and en*thusymusy* … part of the Committee—but greatly praises Gordon and Hume' (Marchand, 11.108).

Although according to later accounts Parry was 'never quite sober' (Trelawny, 235), Byron clearly enjoyed his company. But he was no gentleman, and one German officer snobbishly refused to serve under him. When a Swiss officer was killed by a Suliote, Parry's six craftsmen panicked and insisted on going home, only three weeks after their arrival. Stanhope, later wildly hostile to Parry, reported at the time that 'Parry, Hodges, and Gill … with the assistance of the natives, can perform all the work required of them by the committee' (*Greece in 1823 and 1824*, 119).

After Stanhope's departure, Byron depended heavily on Parry, employing him as his adviser and occasional amanuensis. On 30 March Byron wrote, 'Capt. Parry is doing all that circumstances will permit in his department, and indeed in many others, for he does *all* that is done here, without any aid except the Committee's and mine' (Marchand, 11.145). But according to later accounts, Parry, although promoted to major, achieved very little.

Parry saw Byron regularly during his fatal illness, and like Byron opposed the doctors' bloodletting treatment. When, too late, they wanted the patient to take Spanish bark (a source of quinine), they turned to Parry to persuade him. It was Parry who heard what were probably Byron's last coherent words.

After Byron's death in April, Parry fell sick and withdrew to Zante, where he quarrelled with Stanhope over the decision to allow Trelawny to make off with his artillery to eastern Greece. Since his services were no longer wanted, he returned home, to be reviled publicly and privately by members of the London Greek committee.

Parry's book, fiercely loyal to Byron and highly critical of Stanhope, Blaquiere, and other members of the Greek committee, gave rise to fierce controversy, particularly because of its hilarious account of Jeremy Bentham. In 1827 Parry sued John Hunt, who in *The Examiner* had described him as 'a slanderer, a sot, a bully, and a poltroon' who 'cannot write ten words of English' (*The Examiner*, 380). The libel was proved, but he was awarded only £50 instead of the £1000 claimed. Although it appears from the evidence that Thomas Hodgskin 'ghosted' Parry's reminiscences, the book's vigorous style makes it the most convincing account of Byron's time at Missolonghi.

Parry's final years were dark, but Trelawny's cruel and oft-quoted account of his end must now be modified. After spells in other institutions, Parry was admitted to Hanwell Lunatic Asylum on 31 October 1841, aged sixty-eight, and remained there until he died, aged eighty-five, on 22 April 1859.

CHARLES PLOUVIEZ

Sources W. Parry, *The last days of Lord Byron* (1825) • *Byron's letters and journals*, ed. L. A. Marchand, 11 (1981) • *The Examiner* (17 June 1827), 375–6, 380–82 • W. St Clair, 'Postscript to *The last days of Lord Byron*', *Keats–Shelley Journal*, 19 (1970), 4–7 • *The Times* (15 June 1827) • LMA, Hanwell Asylum archive, H11/HLL/B3/2 and B10/2 • *Greece in 1823 and 1824, being a series of letters by the Honourable Colonel Leicester Stanhope*, ed. R. Ryan (1824) • D. Crane, *Lord Byron's jackal: the life of Edward John Trelawny* (1998) • E. J. Trelawny, *Recollections of the last days of Shelley and Byron* (1858) • J. Millingen, *Memoirs of the affairs of Greece* … (1831) • W. St Clair, *That Greece might still be free* (1972) • P. Gamba, *A narrative of Lord Byron's last journey to Greece* (1825)

Likenesses I. Clark, engraving (after drawing by R. Stymour), repro. in Parry, *Last days of Lord Byron*

Parry, William John (1842–1927), labour leader and businessman, was born on 28 September 1842 at 58 High Street, Bethesda, Caernarvonshire, the only child of John Parry (1803–1850), quarryman and deacon, and his second wife, Elizabeth (1804–1864), daughter of John Jones, joiner. From 1854 to 1856 he attended Llanrwst grammar school, where he acquired fluency in English, which enabled him to act as interpreter and letter writer for the Welsh-speaking quarrymen. Influenced by the Revd Rowland Williams (Hwfa Môn), Parry developed literary and musical interests and became deacon of Bethesda Chapel. A bearded, stocky figure in adulthood, in 1864 he set up a business as accountant, general merchant, and dealer in explosives, and became a chartered accountant in 1880.

William John Parry (1842–1927), by unknown photographer

Parry was married three times: in 1864 to Jane Roberts, in 1878 to Mary Pugh, and in 1902 to Mary Guy. There were four sons (one died young, in 1867), and a daughter. One son committed suicide in 1898, another was a financial liability, and Parry's need for money drove him into a wide range of businesses. By 1895 he was not only a chartered accountant, but also the land agent for the Cefnfaes estate, Bethesda; a merchant of brick, cement, timber, iron, fuse, and oil; the agent for two shipping lines; and an insurance agent. By 1901 he was also a registered money-lender in the Gwynedd Loan and Discount Company, based in Bethesda.

From 1863 to 1879 Parry was Liberal agent for Bethesda, taking part in the campaign for the election in 1868, when George S. G. Douglas-Pennant lost his seat to T. Love D. Jones-Parry, the Liberal candidate. In 1874 Douglas-Pennant regained his seat, and Parry, depressed by the 'servility' of the quarrymen, took no part in the 1880 election when the Liberal C. J. Watkin Williams won the seat. Parry moved into Coetmor Hall, Bethesda, in 1884, and became a shareholder and director of the company which took over a group of radical Welsh newspapers. In 1888 he was editor of *Y Genedl Gymreig* and of *Y Werin*, giving up the post in 1892, when the Welsh National Press Company, of which he was a director, took over.

In 1888 Parry gave evidence to the select committee on town holdings; in 1892 he gave evidence before the royal commission on labour; and in 1893 he gave evidence before the royal commission on land in Wales and Monmouth. He advocated the disestablishment of the Anglican Church in Wales and supported home rule for Wales. When the University College of North Wales was established in Bangor in 1884, he laid the foundations of its Welsh library by appealing for books and manuscripts, donating over 1500 books himself. He was the author of books and pamphlets in English and in Welsh, and wrote in a powerful style. His ambition to become an MP was never achieved; but he travelled to the USA and Canada to research better conditions for quarrymen. He went to Patagonia in 1893 and again in 1894 in a vain search for gold and personal wealth, as he was involved in the Welsh Patagonian Gold Fields Syndicate (1892), which was dissolved in 1907.

Parry's most controversial role was as 'quarryman's champion'. In 1865 he helped to negotiate the end of a strike at Penrhyn quarry, causing Lord Penrhyn to describe him, in 1870, as a 'troublesome fellow … a thoroughly bad one' (University of Wales, Bangor, Archives of trade unions at Penrhyn quarry). In 1874 Parry took the lead in the formation of the North Wales Quarrymen's Union; he served as its secretary from 1874 to 1876. He organized an appeal in 1874 for the Penrhyn quarrymen on strike, describing the struggle as 'right against might'. In November 1874 the quarrymen gained the Pennant Lloyd agreement, which gave them higher wages, a committee to be appointed by the employees to hear grievances, and a reorganization of the Penrhyn Quarry Benefit Club, of which Parry became secretary at £80 per annum. Arthur Wyatt, the chief manager, gave him the monopoly of supplying explosives to the quarry, said to be worth £2000 per annum.

In 1885 Lord Penrhyn's son, George Douglas-Pennant, took over the quarry and in 1886, when his father died, George, now Lord Penrhyn, appointed E. A. Young (1860–1910), a London chartered accountant, as chief manager. Wyatt was dismissed and the Pennant Lloyd agreement was ended. Parry's contract was not renewed. Lord Penrhyn made it clear that he would not tolerate interference by union members between employer and employed. Parry was president of the union from 1877 to 1879 and was re-elected annually as president from 1884 to 1889. In 1893 the union gave him an illuminated address and a cheque for £440 for his services to the 'sons of toil' (minute book, Gwynedd Archives Service, PQ Add. MS). In 1893 Parry failed to get a post in the new labour department of the Board of Trade and on 14 October 1896 his warehouse was destroyed by fire, causing him financial hardship. In 1896–7 he emerged to play the part of peacemaker in the negotiations at the end of the ten-month strike at Penrhyn quarry, but the employees gained no concessions. Parry failed to get back his contract for explosives, and he severed relations with the union in 1898, declaring himself 'nearly broken by disappointment and hopes blasted' (University of Wales, Bangor, Coetmor MS 66, 16 July 1898).

By 1900 the slate industry was depressed and labour relations at Penrhyn quarry were deteriorating. The Penrhyn dispute (1900–03) began in October 1900, with outbreaks of violence by the quarrymen against two contractors in the quarry. The men were locked out until 11 June 1901, when 'loyal' quarrymen were taken back. Parry became secretary of the relief committee, which raised

£46,763 for dependants of those not eligible for union pay. He saw the struggle not as a national one, but as 'one Tyrannical Feudal Lord' against himself and the men (*Daily News*, 1 July 1901). In 1901 he called Lord Penrhyn 'the greatest enemy I have on earth' (*Penrhyn v. Parry*, Gwynedd Archives Service, PQ Add. MS). He won over the *Daily News* to the strikers' cause. In 1901 he became manager of Pantddreiniog quarry, run on co-operative lines, but it failed and was closed by 1911. In March 1903 Lord Penrhyn won a libel action against Parry for his false statements printed in *The Clarion* on 22 June 1901. Parry was ordered to pay £500 damages and costs amounting to £2508, and was saved from bankruptcy only by the Parry Defence Fund, which paid the sum. The quarrymen, without funds, surrendered on 14 November 1903; few of them were re-employed and Bethesda remained divided and impoverished.

Parry continued to sit on public bodies and was made a CBE in 1920. He died at Coetmor Hall, Bethesda, on 1 September 1927, a fallen idol, lonely and embittered. He was buried in Maes-y-groes churchyard near Penrhyn Castle.

JEAN LINDSAY

Sources J. Roose Williams, *Quarryman's champion: the life and activities of William John Parry of Coetmor* (1978) • *DWB* • R Merfyn Jones, *The north Wales quarrymen, 1874–1922* (1981) • W. J. Parry, *Chwareli a chwarelwyr* (1897) • W. J. Parry, *The Penrhyn lock-out, statement and appeal* (1901) • W. J. Parry, *The cry of the people* (1906) • W. J. Parry, *Cyfol y jiwbili, eglwys Bethseda Arfon* (1900) • J. Lindsay, *A history of the north Wales slate industry* (1974) • J. Lindsay, *The great strike: a history of the Penrhyn quarry dispute of 1900–1903* (1987) • C. Parry, *The radical tradition in Welsh politics: a study of liberal and labour politics in Gwynedd, 1900–1920* (1970) • J. Lindsay, '"Not Eldorado": W. J. Parry and the Welsh Patagonian gold fields syndicate', *Transactions of the Honourable Society of Cymmrodorion*, new ser., 3 (1997), 136–63 • J. Grigg, *The young Lloyd George* (1973); repr. (1990) • archives of trades unions at Penrhyn quarry, U. Wales, Bangor [unlisted] • unlisted minute book, NWQU, 1 May 1893, Gwynedd Archives, Caernarfon, PQ Add. • unlisted evidence of draft proof of *Penrhyn v. Parry* libel case, Gwynedd Archives, Caernarfon • *Daily News* (1 July 1901) • U. Wales, Bangor, Coetmor MSS • d. cert.

Archives Gwynedd Archives, Caernarfon, corresp. • NL Wales, corresp. and papers • U. Wales, Bangor, corresp. and papers | Gwynedd Archives, Caernarfon, M 1311/18 • Gwynedd Archives, Caernarfon, PQ Add. • NL Wales, letters to T. E. Ellis • U. Wales, Bangor, archives of trades unions at Penrhyn quarry

Likenesses oils, 1874, Gwynedd Archives, Caernarfon • photograph, 1874 (with Lord Penrhyn; after portrait), Gwynedd Archives, Caernarfon • photograph (with family), Gwynedd Archives, Caernarfon • photograph, Gwynedd Archives, Caernarfon [*see illus.*]

Wealth at death £230 2*s*. 0*d*.: probate, 28 Sept 1927, *CGPLA Eng. & Wales*

Pars, Henry (1734–1806), draughtsman and drawing-master, was born in 1734, and baptized on 25 August of that year at St Anne's, Soho, London, the son of Albertus Pars, a chaser, and his wife, Mary. He was the elder brother of the artist William Edmund *Pars (1742–1782); another brother, Albert Pars (*b*. 1745), was a successful modeller in wax. Pars began his working life following his father's trade, but when this declined he took over, about 1763, the drawing school founded in 1754 by William Shipley, the originator of the Society of Arts. The school, near Beaufort Buildings in the Strand, emphasized both the practical and fine arts; Pars, who had been a pupil of Shipley's school, continued it along the lines envisaged by its founder. Although some academies then used life models, Pars's students were set to work copying prints and antique casts. After gaining a degree of proficiency the better students were then allowed to work in the duke of Richmond's renowned gallery. Thomas Jones, who was a student at the school in 1761–2, remembered that he was 'reduced to the humiliating Situation of copying drawings of Ears, Eyes, Mouths and Noses among a group of little boys of half my age who had the start of me by two or three years' (King, 18). The school was nevertheless considered the best of its day, and students went there to be prepared for the academy in St Martin's Lane. Many well-known painters, sculptors, and architects attended it, some returning as teachers, and among its pupils were William Henry Pyne and William Blake; the latter went there at the age of ten to learn drawing. Pars worked until his death on 7 May 1806. He was buried in the churchyard of Pentonville chapel, Islington.

W. C. MONKHOUSE, *rev*. MARK POTTLE

Sources W. T. Whitley, *Art in England, 1800–1820* (1928) • J. King, *William Blake: his life* (1991) • R. N. Essick, *William Blake, printmaker* (Princeton, NJ, 1980) • D. Bindman, *Blake as an artist* (1977) • Redgrave, *Artists* • J. L. Roget, *A history of the 'Old Water-Colour' Society*, 2 vols. (1891) • *IGI*

Pars, William Edmund (1742–1782), topographical watercolour painter, was born in London on 28 February 1742, the son of Albertus Pars, a metal-engraver, and his wife, Mary, and trained at William Shipley's drawing school in the Strand. He won a number of awards from the Society of Arts, notably, in 1764, third premium for an ambitious history, *Caractacus before the Emperor Claudius* with life-size figures, exhibited at the Free Society that year. He began showing portraits with the Society of Artists in 1760, and it was as a portrait painter that he advertised in 1763, giving his address as the Twisted Pillars, Strand. He was a member of the St Martin's Lane Academy, formed in 1760; his likeness is probably recorded in an anonymous drawing of its members now in the British Museum. In 1761 he was assisting his brother Henry *Pars (1734–1806) as a teacher at Shipley's school.

In 1764 the Society of Dilettanti commissioned Pars to accompany an expedition to record the classical monuments of western Turkey, led by Dr Richard Chandler, with the architect Nicholas Revett. The expedition sailed for the Dardanelles on 24 June 1764. Over the next two years they investigated and recorded sites in Asia Minor and Attica, returning to England in August 1766. The Dilettanti published Chandler's *Ionian Antiquities* in two volumes in May 1769. The drawings that Pars made on this journey are among the earliest professional views of Greece; his studies of the Parthenon marbles and other Greek sculpture are pioneering works of neo-classicism. Seven of the views were shown at the Royal Academy in 1769, and that winter he entered as a pupil at the academy's schools. The next spring his view of the Parthenon was exhibited, and on 27 August he was elected an associate academician. The Greek views were to be put to various uses. James Stuart used them as illustrations in the second volume of his *Antiquities of Athens*, where Pars's drawings became the standard record of the Parthenon marbles. In 1776 Paul Sandby was given permission to make aquatints from the watercolour views, and in 1781 John Thomas Serres made a series of copies of them. Various drawings of sculptures were engraved for other publications.

In 1769 another of the Dilettanti, Henry Temple, second Viscount Palmerston, took Pars with him to Switzerland. Once again he was a pioneer: his Swiss views are among the earliest visual responses to the Alps. Five of them were engraved by William Woollett; eight appeared at the Royal Academy in 1771. That year he accompanied Palmerston to Ireland and the Lake District. He now worked for various patrons, executing portraits, watercolour views, and copies of paintings by other artists. He added figures to a large view by William Hodges of the interior of the Pantheon in Oxford Street, opened in January 1772. For Horace Walpole he made views of Strawberry Hill, some of which were engraved for Walpole's *Description of Strawberry Hill* (1784). In October 1775 Walpole supplied him with a letter of introduction to Sir Horace Mann in Florence, for the Dilettanti now awarded Pars a bursary of £60 a year to pursue his studies in Italy for three years. He arrived in Rome on 21 September, having lost 'his portmanteau … & all his money & drawings' (Walpole, *Corr.*, 5.26, 48) on the way. He travelled with the wife of the miniaturist John Smart. 'Mrs Pars' died of consumption in 1778, and was buried in the protestant cemetery.

Pars became a member of the circle of British artists in Rome that included John Warwick Smith and Thomas Jones, whose *Memoirs* supplies colourful details of Pars's personality and activities. He describes a young woman who was a neighbour when he and Pars shared rooms in Salvator Rosa's house in strada Gregoriana, with whom the two men flirted. 'Instead of attending his Studies at the Rospogliosi [*sic*] palace, Pars would cling to the grating of her window for hours together, broiling in the Sun like a Lizard' (Oppé, 89). In 1779 he made a full-size copy of the Rospigliosi *Aurora* by Guido Reni for the earl of Bristol's house at Downhill; in 1780 he visited Naples to copy Titian's *Danaë* at Capodimonte. At Albano he drew the tomb of the Horatii for the background of his portrait *John Coxe Hippisley*. A large canvas, *General Simcoe, John Burridge Chadwick and Archdeacon Andrew* shown in front of a tomb in an Italian landscape, is now in the University of Toronto.

In autumn 1782 Pars contracted pleurisy while drawing with his feet in water in the Grotto of Neptune at Tivoli. He died in October, after a short illness. Jones mourned him with the comment: 'though he was rather hasty and sometimes indeed Violent in his Temper—He was a Warm and sincere friend' (Oppé, 116). His identified works, with the exception of a few oil paintings including a handful of portraits, are views of the far-flung places he visited. The drawings submitted to the Dilettanti were transferred to the British Museum in 1799, the views placed in the department of prints and drawings, the studies of sculpture in the Greek and Roman department. The Swiss watercolours done for Palmerston are also in the British Museum print room. The rest of his output is widely scattered. ANDREW WILTON

Sources A. P. Oppé, ed., 'Memoirs of Thomas Jones, Penkerrig, Radnorshire', *Walpole Society*, 32 (1946–8) [whole issue] • R. Chandler, *Travels in Asia Minor*, ed. E. Clay (1971), with an appreciation of William Pars by Andrew Wilton • A. Wilton, *William Pars: journey through the Alps* (Zürich, 1979) • F. Russell, 'A connoisseur's taste: paintings at Broadlands—1', *Country Life*, 171 (1982), 224–6 • Walpole, *Corr.* • *IGI*

Parsell, Thomas (1674–1720), headmaster, was born on 23 August 1674, the son of Thomas Parsell of London. He was admitted into Merchant Taylors' School, London, on 11 September 1684. In June 1693 he was elected to a scholarship at St John's College, Oxford, whence he graduated BA (1697), MA (1701), BD and DD (1706). On 6 June 1701 he was appointed first under-master of his old school, and on 30 April 1707 headmaster, having been chosen without hesitation by the company. The following month, on 25 May 1707, he married Frances Shipp at Lambourne in Essex; eight children were baptized at St Laurence Pountney, London, between 1708 and 1717.

Parsell owed his election as headmaster to his reputation as 'an eminent grammarian', and he seems to have printed a school edition of William Lilly's *Compendium syntaxis Erasmianae* in 1702. His chief literary work was a translation of the Book of Common Prayer into Latin. The first edition, in 1706, was published as *Liturgia, seu, Liber precum communium in ecclesia Anglicana receptus*. The psalms, epistles, and gospels are described as being taken from Sebastian Castellio's version; the rest was Parsell's translation. A second edition appeared in 1713, a third, dedicated to his schoolfriend Sir William Dawes, archbishop of York, in 1720, and by 1759 it had reached its seventh edition. Parsell also edited, for school use, the *Panegyricus* of the younger Pliny; published in 1716 it was taken chiefly from the Delphin edition. Parsell died on 7 July 1720 and was buried at St Mary Abchurch, London.

J. H. LUPTON, *rev.* S. J. SKEDD

Sources H. B. Wilson, *The history of Merchant-Taylors' School*, 2 vols. (1814) • C. J. Robinson, ed., *A register of the scholars admitted into Merchant Taylors' School, from AD 1562 to 1874*, 2 vols. (1882–3) • Foster, *Alum. Oxon.* • *N&Q*, 5th ser., 8 (1877), 148 • *IGI* • J. Greenwood, *An essay towards a practical English grammar*, 2nd edn (1722), 228

Parsley, Osbert (1510/11–1585), composer and singer, is of unknown parentage and place of birth. But his birth date can be deduced from the memorial tablet marking the place of his burial in the nave of Norwich Cathedral: it states that he was aged seventy-four at his death, and also that he spent fifty years as 'a Singing-man' at the cathedral. Parsley is first mentioned in the extant cathedral accounts for 1538–40 as a lay clerk, and he continues to appear in subsequent documentation until his death. Between 1558 and 1583 he and his wife, Rose, owned a house in St Saviour's parish.

Parsley composed sacred music to both Latin and English vernacular texts. His Latin music is fluent and attractive, the expressive psalm *Conserva me, domine* being especially noteworthy for its elegant polyphonic style. His five-part Lamentations (his most famous work) differs from the settings by his more famous contemporaries in the restricted compass of the top part. Both psalm and Lamentations were probably intended for domestic devotional use. Parsley's English church music, which comprises two four-part settings of the morning service and one anthem, and possibly a setting of the evening canticles, is less imaginative than his Latin music. A small quantity of instrumental music, presumably for viols, also survives; mostly this occurs in manuscripts in the British Library, but one piece, a well-crafted three-part canonic setting of *Salvator mundi*, was printed by Thomas Morley in 1597.

Parsley's will, which was made on 9 December 1584, was proved by his widow on 6 April of the following year; he left bequests valued at about £75. That he was well respected by his contemporaries, for his musical ability and his personal character, is attested by his memorial.

IAN PAYNE

Sources J. Morehen, 'Parsley, Osbert', *New Grove* • I. Payne, *The provision and practice of sacred music at Cambridge colleges and selected cathedrals, c.1547–c.1646* (1993), 200–01 • H. Benham, *Latin church music in England, c.1460–1575* (1977), 169 • T. Morley, *A plain and easy introduction to practical music*, ed. R. A. Harman (1952), 178–9 • E. H. Fellowes, ed., *Tudor church music*, 10: *Hugh Aston, 1480?–?, John Marbeck, 1510–85?, Osbert Parsley, 1511–85* (1929)

Wealth at death approx. £75 bequests: will, 6 April 1585, episcopal consistorial court of Norwich, register 1585–6, fol. 6; Fellowes ed., *Tudor church music*

Parson [*née* Rooker], **Elizabeth** (1812–1873), hymn writer, daughter of William Rooker (1772–1852), Congregational minister of Tavistock, Devon, and his wife, Elizabeth Angas of Bridport, was born at Tavistock on 5 June 1812. From 1840 to 1844 she conducted a class for young people in her father's chapel, and for them she wrote several hymns, which came into use in a number of collections, which included the Baptist *Hymns and Psalms* (1858). Eighteen of her hymns were also printed by one of her pupils for private circulation, under the title of *Willing Class Hymns*. Two were very popular among her contemporaries, 'Jesus, we love to meet' and 'O happy land! O happy land!': W. Garrett Horder found them 'full of melody and movement' (Horder, 442). Elizabeth Rooker also wrote several hymns for adults, but these were printed only for private use. On 8 February 1844 she married Thomas Edgecombe Parson, a solicitor, and she died at 36 Torrington Place, Plymouth on 6 May 1873.

J. C. HADDEN, *rev.* ROSEMARY MITCHELL

Sources J. Julian, ed., *A dictionary of hymnology*, rev. edn (1907) • W. Garrett Horder, *The hymn lover* (1889), 442 • *Congregational Year Book* (1853), 225–8

Parson, Thomas (*b.* 1631, *d.* in or after 1668), clergyman and ejected minister, was born in London, the son of Thomas Parson of London. He matriculated as a pensioner from Pembroke College, Cambridge, on 19 June 1647 under the mastership of Richard Vines, took his BA in 1650, and was nominated to the fellowship by Oliver Cromwell in the same year. After taking his MA in 1654 he was ordained by the fourth London classis at St Benet Gracechurch, London, on 24 May 1654. Parson first took the cure of souls at the parish church of Chingford in Essex but resigned when he was elected rector of St Michael Wood Street, London, on 12 October 1655.

At Wood Street, Parson continued the presbyterian discipline instituted by his predecessor, Arthur Jackson. He attended meetings of the sixth London classis and, from May 1657, was a delegate to the London provincial assembly where he served variously as scribe, assessor, and a member of the ruling grand committee. At the twenty-fifth provincial assembly (November 1658–May 1659) Parson and Abraham Pinchbecke, Thomas Manton's assistant at St Paul's Covent Garden, were ordered to draw up a letter to be sent to the presbyterian ministers in the province. It has been assumed that the letter was published as *A seasonable exhortation of sundry ministers in London to the people of their respective congregations*; this tract, published on 23 January 1660, warned against the dangers of popery and heresy and was signed by many of the London presbyterian ministers, including Parson. However, this attribution is probably incorrect as a different manuscript exhortation specifically addressed to the ministers and ruling elders of the province exists in the provincial assembly's manuscripts. This document berates the City's ministers for lacking the zeal to implement the presbyterian discipline in the London parishes. Whichever attribution is correct, Parson was committed to the establishment of a presbyterian church in England. He also joined his fellow ministers in early 1660 to preach a sermon on Acts 16: 31 at the morning exercises at St Giles-in-the-Fields, Middlesex, on the topic of saving faith. He was ejected from St Michael Wood Street on Black Bartholomew's day, 24 August 1662. The parish vestry seems to have parted on good terms with him, paying him an advance on money owed and appointing a committee to collect the tithes owed to him by parishioners. Calamy reports that after Parson's ejection much of his time was spent editing the first edition of Francis Gouldman's *Dictionary* to which he wrote the epistle and the index.

Before 1667 Parson moved to Dublin, where he continued as a presbyterian minister. In July 1668 he became embroiled in a dispute with Independents over the administration of holy communion to informal gatherings. In the same month Parson, along with Daniel Rolls, John Hooke, and Noah Bryan, wrote to the leading presbyterian ministers in London asking for them to resolve the dispute. It is unknown when Parson died. Although the *Dictionary of National Biography* describes a Thomas Parson who was buried at St Mary Aldermary, London, on 10 April 1681 as the presbyterian minister, this attribution is doubtful, as the Aldermary Parson was a goldsmith. It is more probable that Parson died in Ireland in or after 1668.

E. C. VERNON

Sources minutes of the London provincial assembly, DWL, MS 201.12 • Venn, *Alum. Cant.* • *Calamy rev.*, 382 • *The nonconformist's memorial … originally written by … Edmund Calamy*, ed. S. Palmer, 1

(1775), 167 • *Calendar of the correspondence of Richard Baxter*, ed. N. H. Keeble and G. F. Nuttall, 2 (1991), 54, 56 • *A seasonable exhortation of sundry ministers in London to the people of their respective congregations* (1660) • T. Case, *The morning exercise methodized* (1660)

Parson of Rothiemay, the. *See* Gordon, James (1617–1686).

Parsons, Abraham (*d.* **1785**), traveller and commercial consul, was born probably in Bristol, the son of a merchant captain. In early life he visited many countries in command of merchant vessels, an occupation that suited a man 'naturally fond of novelty, and remarkably inquisitive' (Parsons, iii). He then set up in business as a merchant at Bristol, but was not successful. In 1767 the Turkey Company appointed him their consul and marine factor at Iskenderun (Scanderoon), the port for Aleppo, a post he held for six years before resigning on account of the unhealthiness of the climate. He began travelling for commercial speculation, making several journeys in Asia Minor in 1772–4, and travelling from Iskenderun through the mountains to Aleppo. From there he crossed the desert to Baghdad, where he stayed between May and October 1774. He travelled up the Euphrates to Hillah and down-river to Basrah, where he was during the siege by a Persian army in 1775. He next visited Bombay, and then—ever inquisitive—made a lengthy voyage along the west coast of India as far as Goa, returning to Bombay early in 1776. In 1778 he travelled via the Red Sea and Egypt, and visited Mocha, Suez, Cairo, and Rosetta. Having returned to Europe in the same year he retired to Leghorn, where he died in 1785.

Parsons bequeathed a manuscript narrative of his travels to his brother-in-law, the Revd John Berjew of Bristol, whose son, the Revd John Paine Berjew, edited it and published it in 1808 as *Account of Travels in Asia and Africa*. In it Parsons provided details of the trade at Iskenderun, of the town and its surroundings, and of the journeys he made in the area. He attentively observed other towns and cities and the routes between them. Of his time at Aleppo he wrote that he had 'little else to do but walk about and make observations', and thus saw more than others who lived there many years. As a consul he was interested in and described the lifestyle of other consuls. He recorded a detailed and lively account of his desert journey in 1774 from Aleppo to Baghdad. His observations give insights into the various places that he visited, including Bombay, Mocha, and Cairo. Everywhere he took much interest in commerce, government, and ways of life. He gave a detailed account of the preparations for the inundation and its impact on Cairo, and described the 216 groups making up the grand procession of pilgrims to Mecca. A paper by Parsons, 'A phenomenon at Bussorah (March 1775)', appeared in *Nicholson's Journal of Natural Philosophy* for 1808. It describes a dust storm which plunged the town into total darkness.

H. M. Chichester, *rev.* Deborah Manley

Sources A. Parsons, *Account of travels in Asia and Africa*, ed. J. P. Berjew (1808) • *GM*, 1st ser., 78 (1808), 517

Parsons, Alfred William (**1847–1920**), landscape painter, illustrator, and garden designer, was born at Beckington, Somerset, on 2 December 1847, the second son of Joshua Parsons, surgeon, of Beckington. He was educated at private schools and entered the savings bank department of the Post Office as a clerk in 1865, but two years later (1867) he gave up his career in the civil service and devoted himself to painting. He trained briefly at the South Kensington School of Art.

Parsons exhibited widely, showing oils, watercolours, and pen-and-ink drawings. Early in his career he showed at the Dudley Gallery. The first appearance of his work at a Royal Academy exhibition was in 1871 and he continued to exhibit there until his death. He also contributed to exhibitions of the Royal Institute of Painters in Water Colours (and sat on the council of that body), the Royal Society of Painters in Water Colours, and the Royal Society of Artists in Birmingham. He submitted works to the Walker Art Gallery autumn exhibitions and the Manchester City Art Gallery exhibitions of watercolour drawings, as well as to international exhibitions, such as the world fair at St Louis (1904), where he was also responsible for arranging the display of British art works. He also showed with commercial galleries, including the Leicester Galleries, the Grosvenor Gallery, the New Gallery (where he also sat on the consulting committee), and the Fine Art Society. At the society he held a number of important one-man exhibitions, including 'Gardens and orchards' in 1891, for which the American writer Henry James wrote an exhibition catalogue essay.

Parsons also participated in the late nineteenth-century arts and crafts movement. In 1881 he joined William Morris's Society for the Protection of Ancient Buildings and helped to found the Art Workers' Guild in 1884. Through his friendship with the American painter Edwin Austin Abbey, he participated in the American Tile Club. Abbey and Parsons were associated with the 'Broadway group', an informal gathering of painters and writers, including Henry James, F. D. Millet, and John Singer Sargent, who sojourned at Broadway, Worcestershire in the 1880s and 1890s. A member of many artistic organizations, Parsons joined the New English Art Club in 1886. Elected associate of the Royal Academy in 1897, he attained full membership in 1911. In 1899 he was elected associate of the Royal Society of Painters in Water Colours, and he became a full member in 1905. Parsons was chosen president of the society, in succession to Sir Ernest Albert Waterlow, in 1913, and held that office until his death. In 1910 he joined the Imperial Arts League.

A very important section of Parsons's artistic output is formed by his work as a book illustrator, much of which appeared in *Harper's Magazine*. He also contributed the illustrations to *The Genus Rosa* by Ellen Willmott (1910), and collaborated with Edwin Austin Abbey in illustrating Robert Herrick's *Hesperides* and *Noble Numbers* (1882), *She Stoops to Conquer* (1887), *Old Songs* (1889), and *The Quiet Life* (1890), and with F. D. Millet in providing the illustrations for Millet's book *The Danube, from the Black Forest to the Black Sea* (1893). In 1892–4 Parsons paid a visit to Japan; he published his impressions of that country, with illustrations, in his book *Notes in Japan* (1896). Parsons also provided illustrations for several editions of William Robinson's *The Wild Garden* (1881, 1894), as well as for several of Robinson's gardening magazines and other publications.

In 1899 Parsons embarked on a career as a professional garden designer in partnership with Captain Walter Croker St Ives Partridge and Charles Clement Tudway. Extant examples of his work include Wightwick Manor, Staffordshire, and Great Chalfield, Wiltshire. His keen interest in gardens and flowers was reflected not only in his paintings and designs but also in his participation as judge at the Chelsea flower show.

Henry James claimed that Parsons possessed 'an inexhaustible feeling for the country in general, [and] his love of the myriad English flowers is perhaps the fondest part of it' (H. James, 'Our artists in Europe', *Harper's Magazine*, 79, 1889, 59). Parsons's landscape paintings embodied the naturalistic trend in nineteenth-century British landscape painting and reflected the influence of the French Barbizon school. In 1887 Parsons's painting of an orchard in springtime, *When Nature Painted all things Gay* (exh. RA, 1887; Tate collection), was purchased by the trustees of the Chantrey fund. His botanical illustrations were regarded as learned and correct. Collections holding examples of his work include the Art Gallery of New South Wales, the Royal Academy of Arts, the Royal Collection, and the Royal Society of Painters in Water Colours. Parsons, who was unmarried, died at his house, Luggershill, at Broadway, Worcestershire, on 16 January 1920 and was cremated at Golders Green on 20 January.

TANCRED BORENIUS, *rev.* ANNE HELMREICH

Sources A. L. Helmreich, 'Contested grounds: garden painting and the invention of national identity in England, 1880–1914', PhD diss., Northwestern University, Illinois, 1994 • N. Milette, 'Landscape-painter as landscape-gardener: the case of Alfred Parsons, R.A.', DPhil diss., University of York, 1997 • 'The Society of Painters in Water Colours: a list of members, associates and honorary members from its foundation, November 30, 1804', [n.d.], Royal Water Colour Society, London • S. Houfe, *The dictionary of British book illustrators and caricaturists, 1800–1914* (1978) • Graves, *RA exhibitors* • A. Robins, *The New English Art Club centenary exhibition* (1986) • M. S. Young, 'The Tile Club revisited', *American Art Journal*, 2 (1970), 81–91 • R. G. Pisano, *The Tile Club and the aesthetic movement in America* (1999) [exhibition catalogue, Stony Brook, NY, New London, CT, and Pittsburgh, PA, 9 Oct 1999 – 13 Aug 2000] • *The Times* (21 Jan 1920) • M. Simpson, 'Windows on the past: Edwin Austin Abbey and Francis Davis Millett in England', *American Art Journal*, 22 (1990), 65–89 • A. L. Helmreich, 'Re-presenting nature: ideology, art and science in William Robinson's "Wild Garden"', *Nature and ideology: natural garden design in the twentieth century* (1997), 81–111 • N. Milette, *Parsons, Partridge, Tudway, an unsuspected design partnership, 1884–1914* (1995)

Archives Hunt. L., corresp. • Worcs. RO, corresp.

Likenesses Elliott & Fry, photograph, 1915, NPG • A. W. Parsons, self-portrait, pencil drawing, NPG • woodcut, repro. in H. James, 'Our artists in Europe', *Harper's Magazine*, 79 (1889), 59

Wealth at death £18,401 10s. 1d.: probate, 27 March 1920, *CGPLA Eng. & Wales*

Parsons, Andrew (1615/16–1684), nonconformist minister, was the son of John Parsons of Milton, Somerset. He matriculated from Christ Church, Oxford, on 20 June 1634, aged eighteen, graduated BA on 8 July 1635, and proceeded MA on 20 April 1638. Ordained deacon in Wells on 24 September that year, Parsons was beneficed in Somerset, though the precise location is no longer known. A strong supporter of parliament, with the outbreak of the civil war Parsons was forced to flee to London. When parliament's leaders were looking to supply parishes under their control with ministers, Parsons was asked to go to Wem, Shropshire, because the rector, Nicholas Metcalfe, had been ejected by the parliamentary garrison in October 1643. The rectory in Wem was formally sequestered on 23 June 1646, and Parsons was presented to it by the committee for plundered ministers. Financial arrangements for Metcalfe's family were controversial, and on 29 October 1647 the committee for plundered ministers ordered Parsons to pay a fifth of the revenues to Metcalfe's wife, Margaret, in spite of Parsons's protestations that Metcalfe was at that time rector of Hinstock. In 1648 Parsons signed the *Testimony* of Shropshire ministers. During the Commonwealth he was a member of the Shropshire classis of Prees and in 1654 he served as an assistant to the Shropshire commission. He was formally re-presented to Wem by Robert Corbet of Stanwardine in 1655. In 1659 he contributed a horse and arms in support of Sir George Booth's rising in Cheshire.

However, following the Restoration, Parsons was prosecuted in August 1660 for seditious preaching against the king. He was alleged to have said that more sins had been committed in a month than in the previous twenty years, implying that the king's 'murder' was no sin, but when witnesses against him failed to appear he was discharged without fees. He was arrested again in November 1661 for preaching in the parish church even after the churchwardens had attempted to lock him out. Though he was later released after promising not to travel more than 5 miles away, he was rearrested and, after eight weeks' imprisonment, was tried on 28 May 1662 before Lord Newport and nine justices on charges drawn from a sermon he preached on 13 October 1661. Parsons was convicted and sent to prison until a £200 fine could be paid. At this time his living at Wem was also sequestered by the chancellor of Lichfield. After three months his fine was remitted by the king at the intervention of Lord Newport, and on 11 September 1662 he was released from prison, but he was deprived of his living, and his successor was instituted on 26 November 1662.

Parsons remained in Shropshire for a few months until he moved to London in 1663. Once in London he exercised a preaching ministry among the many illegal nonconformist conventicles. He was reported to be the preacher at one such meeting at the Rose, Cheapside, on 6 May 1665, and he became Thomas Wadsworth's assistant in the presbyterian congregation that met in Globe Alley, Southwark, though both the date he began and the details of his ministry there are no longer known. After Charles II's indulgence Parsons was licensed as a presbyterian to preach on 2 April 1672 at his house in Deadman's Place, Southwark. His partnership with Wadsworth continued until the latter's death on 29 October 1676. Parsons was then called as pastor to the congregation meeting in White Hart Yard, Bridge Street, Covent Garden. Richard Baxter agreed to take on preaching and pastoral responsibilities for Wadsworth's congregation during the interim, though he declined to become their pastor. After 1677 Baxter assisted Parsons with the White Hart Yard congregation. In response to the great fire that devastated Wem on 3 March that year Parsons published *Seasonable Counsel to an Afflicted People* (1677) and organized a collection for the town's relief. He continued to be periodically harassed by the authorities. At Middlesex sessions on 31 August 1682, he was fined £80 for preaching twice in August in the parish of St Paul's, Covent Garden.

In his will, drawn up in the parish of St Martin-in-the-Fields on 10 January 1683, Parsons named his wife, Sarah—of whom nothing is known except that during his ministry in Covent Garden she contributed towards their sustenance by making gold and silver lace—son, Thomas, three daughters, Mary Porter, Phebe, and Hannah, and a daughter-in-law Mary Parsons, to each of whom he left a shilling. By the winter of 1683–4 Baxter noted that Parsons had been 'long ill of the stone in the bladder' (Keeble and Nuttall, 2.257). His poverty led Baxter to give him 50s. from money donated by the earl of Bedford before 14 June 1684. Parsons died on 1 October that year and was buried in London. W. A. SHAW, *rev.* J. WILLIAM BLACK

Sources *Calamy rev.*, 381–2 · Foster, *Alum. Oxon.* · W. Wilson, *The history and antiquities of the dissenting churches and meeting houses in London, Westminster and Southwark*, 4 vols. (1808–14), vol. 3 · *Walker rev.* · M. Henry, *The life of the Rev. Philip Henry, A.M. with funeral sermons* (1698) · *Calendar of the correspondence of Richard Baxter*, ed. N. H. Keeble and G. F. Nuttall, 2 vols. (1991) · archdeaconry of Middlesex, 3 Nov 1684, LMA, X1/177

Parsons, Sir Anthony Derrick (1922–1996), diplomatist, was born at Pont Street Nursing Home, London, on 9 September 1922, the younger son of Colonel Harold Archer James Parsons (*b.* 1895), of the Royal Corps of Signals, and his Anglo-Irish wife, Irene, *née* Hall-Dare. Emerging from King's School, Canterbury, in 1940, he joined the Royal Artillery, winning a Military Cross in Italy in 1944. The war over, he spent three years in Palestine seconded to the Transjordanian frontier force until Britain's withdrawal from the mandate. On 5 June 1948 he married Sheila Emily Baird, with whom he enjoyed nearly fifty years of a supremely happy marriage. They had two sons and two daughters.

In 1949 Parsons secured War Office permission to take a degree in oriental studies at Balliol College, Oxford, obtaining in 1951 first-class honours in Arabic and Turkish. In May 1954, after three years as assistant military attaché in Iraq, he transferred to the diplomatic service. He used his language skills to great effect, first in Ankara, involved not least with the Cyprus problem, and then in a series of Arab posts. In Cairo in 1961 he helped to restore full relations, broken since the Suez invasion, with the government of Gamal Abdul Nasser. After a two-year break in the Latin American department in London, busy

Sir Anthony Derrick Parsons (1922–1996), by unknown photographer, 1982

with the decolonization of the Caribbean and the Cuban missile crisis, he returned in 1964 to the Arab world as head of chancery in Khartoum. His time there covered the violent ousting of General Abboud's dictatorship by a massive popular uprising. In the course of this uprising the previously planned visit of the queen was only sanctioned in London thanks to the ambassador, Sir Ian Dixon Scott (with Parsons as interpreter), prevailing on the assembled revolutionary leaders in the nick of time to call off their bloodstained rioting. Parsons's favourite memory of the welcome then given to the queen was of the communist leader stumbling up to her at a reception (on a historic Nile steamboat), raising his glass, and saying 'Please accept this toast from Your Majesty's loyal Communist Party of the Sudan' (personal knowledge).

Parsons was posted next as political agent in Bahrain in 1965, at the height of Nasser's charismatic anti-British domination of the Arab world. At the end of the 1967 Six Day War his agency building was on the point of being sacked by the mob when the diminutive ruler, Sheikh Eissa, drove up unescorted, and from the bonnet of his car persuaded the crowd to stop their attack and go home. Parsons's genuine friendship with the ruler and many other Bahrainis survived even London's decision to withdraw in three years its protection of the gulf, reversing a contrary assurance given to the rulers two months before by the same embarrassed visiting minister of state. In 1969 Parsons was sent on promotion to the United Nations mission in New York in the pivotal role of its head of chancery for two years, followed by three as assistant under-secretary in the Foreign Office, dealing, appropriately enough, with United Nations affairs and the Middle East. His five subsequent years as ambassador in the then key post of Iran, from 1974 to 1979, were dramatic in the extreme. For the first three the chairmen of companies from all over the industrial world poured into Tehran looking for contracts in a country made wealthy by OPEC's tripling of crude oil prices in 1973. Dozens of those from Britain had to sleep on beds laid side by side in the

Hilton ballroom. Then disaster began to strike the confidence of the shah in his liberal authoritarianism; a populace discontented with his disastrously over-rapid development plans and urged on by the powerful Shiʿi clerics hostile to his secularism broke into a crescendo of strikes and riots. Faced, as Parsons advised him, with a no-win situation, the shah surrendered to history, and the Pahlavi monarchy was replaced by the Islamic republicanism of Ayatollah Khomeini, who returned from exile in triumph. In his book *The Pride and the Fall* (1984), Parsons gave a revealing account of the whole episode from personal experience.

After a short spell as deputy under-secretary in London, Parsons spent his final three years in the diplomatic service, from September 1979 to August 1982, as permanent UK representative to the United Nations, a post for which he was by now pre-eminently qualified. Being (in his own words) 'the embodiment of Decolonisation Man' (personal knowledge), he was able to gain the trust of formally non-aligned Commonwealth colleagues when dealing with such thorny issues as the Rhodesian problem, Namibian independence, the Soviet invasion of Afghanistan, and finally the Falklands War. In all of these his gift for listening understandingly in private to many potential opponents and bringing them round by quiet argument to support the British stance in public had signal reward. Even with his Soviet colleague at the United Nations he enjoyed the rough and tumble of debate; on the first of the few occasions he felt obliged to veto a Security Council resolution, the Russian concerned, who sat next to him, whispered as he sat down, 'Don't worry, Tony. It's like adultery. The first time you commit it, it's rather shaming. But after a while it's great fun' (personal knowledge). The pair broke into hilarious laughter and, to Parsons's embarrassment, were caught doing so by the television cameras. During these hectic years he found time to publish a vivid memoir of his time in the Middle East, entitled *They Say the Lion* (1986).

On Parsons's retirement in 1982, when he was promoted GCMG (he had been appointed LVO in 1965, CMG in 1969, and KCMG in 1975), he was invited by the prime minister, Margaret Thatcher, to occupy a new post as her personal adviser on foreign affairs. He accepted for a year on the understanding that it would involve co-operating with the Foreign Office and not, in the Thatcher manner, competing with it. She and he disagreed on many matters but established a remarkable degree of mutual liking and respect. His favourite memory was of Thatcher chiding him in one of their sessions, 'Thank goodness, Tony, I don't belong to your class'. 'What class are you putting me in, Prime Minister?' he replied. 'Upper middle-class intellectuals: they see everyone else's point of view and have none of their own' (personal knowledge). He had of course strong views on every subject, but his firm expression of them was always marked by good humour and a total rejection of pomposity. Only on one occasion, the Suez aberration of 1956, was his loyalty to her majesty's government severely tested.

Parsons retired to Devonshire, looking forward to pursuing his wide literary enthusiasms, not least his special interest in the influence of Conrad on T. S. Eliot. He accepted, however, the modest role of research fellow and lecturer on the Middle East at Exeter University, and was in constant demand from the media as a commentator on international affairs. He also served on the boards of various institutions, including the British Council, of which he was a fervent supporter. Two successive tragedies which visibly crushed him in the early 1990s were the unexpected deaths of both of his gifted sons, but he resolutely continued his busy and ostensibly cheerful life. His last book, *From Cold War to Hot Peace: UN Interventions, 1947–1984* (1995), a unique analysis of the subject, was written while he was recovering from a near-fatal cancer, and he maintained a flow of impressive public think-pieces (and of hilarious private reminiscences) until the day of his own sudden death from heart failure at his home, Highgrove, Ashburton, Devon, on 12 August 1996. His remains were cremated on 14 August at Exeter. He was survived by his wife and two daughters.

GLENCAIRN BALFOUR-PAUL

Sources British Diplomatic Oral History, interview with Sir Anthony Parsons, CAC Cam., 22 March 1996 • private information (2004) • personal knowledge (2004) • *The Times* (14 Aug 1996) • *The Guardian* (14 Aug 1996) • *Daily Telegraph* (14 Aug 1996) • A. Parsons, *The pride and the fall* (1984) • A. Parsons, *They say the lion* (1986) • A. Parsons, *From cold war to hot peace: UN interventions, 1947–1984* (1995) • *The Independent* (14 Aug 1996) • *WWW* [forthcoming] • *FO List*

Archives Bodl. Oxf., papers as permanent UK representative to the UN • NRA, priv. coll., papers | CAC Cam., British Diplomatic Oral History

Likenesses G. Bruce, photograph, 1979, Hult. Arch. • photograph, 1982, News International Syndication, London [*see illus.*] • photograph, 1994, University of Exeter • photograph, repro. in *The Independent* • photograph, repro. in *The Guardian* • photograph, repro. in *Daily Telegraph*

Wealth at death minimal: private information

Parsons, Bartholomew (*c.*1574–1642), Church of England clergyman, was born in Somerset into the same family as Robert Persons (Parsons), the Jesuit, and entered Oriel College, Oxford, in 1590, aged about sixteen. He graduated BA from the college on 29 January 1600, and proceeded MA on 9 July 1603. Two years later he was instituted to the rectory of Manningford Bruce, Wiltshire. At the time of his admittance BD on 28 May 1611, Parsons is believed to have been acting as chaplain to Bishop Henry Cotton of Salisbury. Certainly in that year he was instituted to the vicarage of Collingbourne Kingston, in the diocese of Salisbury, and in 1620 he acquired the adjoining Wiltshire rectory of Ludgershall; he held both benefices until his death. Parsons married, though nothing is known of his wife. Of his children, the eldest known survivor—also named Bartholomew—was born in 1617 or 1618, for he matriculated aged sixteen from Gloucester Hall, Oxford, on 7 November 1634. A daughter died in infancy in 1620, and a second son, John, was admitted to Queen's College, Oxford, in 1638, aged sixteen.

Parsons was an enthusiastic exponent of the divine

right of kings. In his sermon *The Magistrates Charter Examined* (1616), preached at Salisbury assizes, he attacked the view that:

> a king is instituted of God, constituted of the people; the kingdom is given him of God, delivered him of the people; that he reigneth from God, delivered him of the people; is chosen of God, confirmed of the people.

Such ideas 'make civil magistrates, even kings, the supreme homagers to both people and pope, and give them both power to pull off their crowns, and cast them out of their thrones' because 'the civil power, which is immediately in the people, and but in the magistrate precario, by courtesy from them, may, nay must, be taken from Kings by the people in case of infidelity and heresy' (*Magistrates Charter*, 9). The arguments of Cardinal Bellarmine and the resistance theories of the Huguenot Philippe Duplessis de Mornay are both explicitly condemned on the same basis.

Parsons's *The First Fruites of the Gentiles* (1618) contains a preface to Buckingham, 'such a King as for his intellectual, moral, political and theological virtues, and endowments, the globe of the Earth hath not borne till this present'; but he asks that the duke use his influence with James I 'not with Absalom to popular insinuations and applauses, nor with Haman, to make yourself terrible by procuring decrees against opposites, but with Nehemiah, to do good amongst your people and seek the welfare of them' (preface, A2*v*). Parsons, indeed, seems to have cultivated close relations with the magistracy in his county: his *Dorcas, or, A Perfect Pattern of a True Disciple* (1631) is prefaced 'from my house at Collingbourne' to 'my loving friend, Sir Francis Pile, baronet' and to his wife, 'who are met together as another Cornelius and Dorcas abounding in the work of the Lord' (sig. A2). On 8 December 1635 Parsons preached at the funeral of Sir Francis, reporting he had known him for twenty years. From his *Boaz and Ruth Blessed* (1633) it appears that he had recently officiated at the wedding of 'my much respected friends' Peregrine Thistlethwaite the younger, esquire, and his wife, Dorothy. His *A Romane Centurion Becomming a Good Souldier of Jesus Christ* (1635) contains a preface to Mr John Popham, signed from 'my rectory in Ludgershall' 30 March 1634.

In his *Honos and onus Levitarum* (1637), a sermon preached at Marlborough on 10 October 1636 on the occasion of the archdeacon's visitation, Parsons claimed that of 9284 English parishes, impropriations 'have devoured 3895, almost half the number, and far above the half in value and goodness'. For impropriate ecclesiastical livings, he hoped that God would prompt bishops, cathedral chapters, and colleges to provide for the poor clergy who laboured in them, 'but to dream of any restitution of them from lay possessors … were as the poet saith, a dream or a shadow', despite honourable exceptions; he urged his readers to pray that 'the vessels that are left in the house of the Lord go not to Babylon' (*Honos*, 24–5). Parsons died in 1642 'aged sixty-seven' and was buried in the chancel of the church at Ludgershall, Wiltshire, on 27 February.

STEPHEN WRIGHT

Sources Foster, *Alum. Oxon.* • C. L. Shadwell, ed., *Registrum Orielense*, 1 (1893) • Wood, *Ath. Oxon.*, new edn • *VCH Wiltshire*, vols. 9, 11, 15 • T. Phillipps, *Institutiones clericorum in comitatu Wiltoniae* (1825)

Parsons, Benjamin (1797–1855), Congregational minister, was born on 16 February 1797 at Nibley in Gloucestershire, the son of Thomas Parsons (*d.* 1803), who was from a family of yeomen farmers at Uley in Gloucestershire, and his wife, Anna Stratford (*d.* 1812), also of an old farming family. After attending the parsonage school at Dursley and the grammar school at Wotton under Edge, he was apprenticed for seven years to a tailor at Frampton-on-Severn. During his apprenticeship he studied Latin, and in 1815 became a teacher at the Sunday school in Frampton. He joined the church in the Countess of Huntingdon's Connexion at Rodborough Tabernacle in 1821. He studied at Cheshunt College 1821–5.

After preaching in Swansea for nine months in 1825, and a short stay at Rochdale, in 1826 Parsons was ordained to the Congregational church at Ebley, near Stroud in Gloucestershire, and remained there for the rest of his life. On 3 November 1830 he married Amelia, daughter of Samuel Fry of Devonport. They had several children, including Anna [*see* Lloyd, Anna Shatford]. Although there had been a chapel in Ebley since 1797, there was no school, and Parsons devoted himself to the education of the inhabitants. He lectured to the men in the evening, established a night school in a little chapel at Paken Hill, and started a provident fund in 1832. A day school was opened in 1840. To support himself and his family he also ran a fee-paying school. A militant teetotaller and sabbatarian, Parsons also supported the abolition of slavery and the repeal of the corn laws, and was drawn towards Chartism, strong in nearby Monmouthshire. He was a keen advocate of voluntarism in education.

Parsons's many publications, which exhibit considerable humour and, on occasion, scathing sarcasm, include *Anti-Bacchus: an Essay on the Evils Connected with the Use of Intoxicating Drinks* (1840), *The Wine Question Settled* (1841), *The Mental and Moral Dignity of Women* (1842), *Education, the Birthright of Every Human Being* (1845), *A Letter to Richard Cobden on the Impolicy and Tyranny of State Education* (1852), and *A Letter to the Earl of Derby on the Cruelty and Injustice of Opening the Crystal Palace on the Sabbath* (1853). Parsons died at his home, the Chapel House, Ebley, on 10 January 1855, and was buried at Ebley.

BERTHA PORTER, *rev.* ANNE PIMLOTT BAKER

Sources R. Tudur Jones, *Congregationalism in England, 1662–1962* (1962) • Boase, *Mod. Eng. biog.* • E. P. Hood, *The earnest minister: a record of the life of Benjamin Parsons* (1856) • review, *Evangelical Magazine and Missionary Chronicle*, new ser., 34 (1856), 711
Likenesses portrait, repro. in Hood, *The earnest minister*, frontispiece

Parsons, Sir Charles Algernon (1854–1931), engineer and scientist, wad. s born at 13 Connaught Place, Hyde Park, London, on 13 June 1854, the youngest of the six sons of William *Parsons, third earl of Rosse (1800–1867), and his wife, Mary *Parsons, countess of Rosse (1813–1885), photographer, elder daughter of John Wilmer Field, of

Sir Charles Algernon Parsons (1854–1931), by Walter Stoneman, 1919

Heaton Hall, Yorkshire. His eldest brother was Laurence *Parsons, later fourth earl of Rosse. William Parsons provided a stimulating environment for his sons at Birr Castle, Parsonstown, Ireland; he engaged tutors of high scientific calibre, and encouraged the boys into his workshops and observatory, where Charles developed a taste for mechanics. This mechanical aptitude had one unfortunate outcome; conveying friends on their home-made steam car at 7 m.p.h. one day, with Charles as stoker, the boys' cousin Lady Bangor fell from the vehicle and was killed. Before William Parsons's death the family cruised each year on their yacht *Titania*; afterwards they took a summer vacation in the alpine region.

At the age of seventeen Parsons entered Trinity College, Dublin, where he spent two years before proceeding to St John's College, Cambridge, in 1873. There was then no engineering school at Cambridge, but Parsons attended lectures on mechanism and applied mechanics, and he studied mathematics with such effect that in 1877 he graduated as eleventh wrangler. He later recalled, of these five years of pure and applied mathematics, 'that the strain was more severe than anything in business life, and luckily for me, boat racing interfered with reading' (Clarke).

Parsons at once began his engineering training by a four-year apprenticeship at the works of Sir William Armstrong & Co. at Elswick, Tyneside. This was followed by two years (1881–3) with Kitson & Co. of Leeds, where he developed a four-cylinder high-speed epicycloidal steam engine that he had patented, and he also occupied himself with experiments on the propulsion of torpedoes by means of rockets. In 1883 he married Katherine (*d.* 1933), the daughter of William Froggatt Bethell of Rise Park, East Riding of Yorkshire. They had a son and a daughter.

In 1884 Parsons acquired a junior partnership in the firm of Clarke, Chapman & Co. of Gateshead, and assumed charge of their newly organized electrical department. In those days electric dynamos were small machines driven usually at 1000 to 1500 revolutions per minute by a belt from the flywheel of a reciprocating engine. Parsons set about designing a high-speed generator and then developing a steam turbine to drive the dynamos directly. It occurred to him that, by dividing the expansion of steam into a number of pressure drops, it should be possible to run a turbine at a moderate speed and at the same time secure a proper relationship between the steam speed and blade speed. His first patents, taken out in 1884, show how thoroughly he considered all the difficulties in the path for the construction of such a high-speed turbine and the steps which he proposed to take to overcome them. The principle of subdividing the whole expansion of the steam into a number of stages, so that only comparatively moderate velocities have to be dealt with, still forms the basis of all efficient turbine design. The first Parsons turbo-dynamo, constructed in 1884, developed an output of 7.5 kW when running at a speed of 18,000 revolutions per minute, and was an immediate success. Many such machines were constructed almost exclusively for ship lighting, and by 1888 about 200 were in service.

Realizing the possibilities of the new type of prime mover, and in order to develop it to its fullest extent, Parsons dissolved his partnership and in 1889 founded the firm of C. A. Parsons & Co. He bought back his patent rights, and established a small works at Heaton on a site about 2 miles from the centre of Newcastle upon Tyne. The first power station in the world to employ turbo-generating plant was the Forth Banks power station at Newcastle. This station went into commission in January 1890 with an initial equipment of two 75 kW Parsons turbo-alternators. Other public lighting companies quickly followed this lead, and turbo-alternators were installed at Cambridge and Scarborough. The Cambridge station went into commission in 1892 with three 100 kW units. These machines were the first turbine units to be operated with condensers, and tests showed their efficiency to be comparable with that of the best reciprocating engines of equal power.

As the size of turbo-alternators for power station work gradually increased, so the efficiency of the sets was improved. Parsons lived to see an output of more than 200,000 kW delivered by a single turbo-generator and the reciprocating steam engine completely superseded by the turbine for central station work.

The growth of electricity supply consequent upon the invention of the turbine created a demand not only for larger generating units but also for higher transmission voltages, in order that more extensive areas might be economically served. In the early days the practice had been to generate at about 2000 volts, and to increase the pressure when required by transformers. By 1905 Parsons had constructed turbo-alternators generating at 11,000 volts, and this voltage became the usual generating pressure for many years. In 1928 he again attacked the problem of generating at higher voltages and produced a 25,000 kW turbo-alternator generating directly at 36,000 volts. The machine was entirely successful and Parsons had set a new standard in power station practice. Many of the most important power stations, both in Great Britain and abroad, adopted the practice of generating directly at 36,000 volts, thereby eliminating the large and costly step-up transformers necessary with the previous method.

Parsons's patent of 1884 had referred to steam-turbine propulsion of ships, but it was not until 1894 that he decided to attack this problem. He established a separate organization with works at Wallsend, and formed a separate company, which was later known as the Parsons Marine Steam Turbine Company. A small vessel, the *Turbinia*, with a length of 100 feet and a displacement of 44 tons, was constructed and fitted with turbine machinery, and after much experimental work attained a speed of 34 knots. At the naval review held in 1897 to celebrate the diamond jubilee of Queen Victoria, the *Turbinia* created a sensation by racing down the lines of warships at a speed greater than that of any other vessel afloat, as at that time the fastest destroyers could hardly exceed 27 knots. In 1899 the Admiralty entrusted Parsons with the construction of a 30 knot turbine-driven destroyer, the *Viper*, which attained a measured speed of over 37 knots. A second destroyer, the *Cobra*, was also fitted with turbine machinery, but shortly afterwards both these ships were lost at sea by accidents.

In 1901 the first turbine-driven passenger vessel, the *King Edward*, was built for service on the River Clyde, followed by the sister ship *Queen Alexandra*, and within the next year or two the cross-channel boats *Queen* and *Brighton* were fitted with turbines. The Parsons Marine Steam Turbine Company, in order to demonstrate to the Admiralty once more the advantages of turbines for warships, laid down in 1901 another turbine-driven destroyer, which was acquired in 1903 by the fleet under the name of *Velox*. This was followed in 1902 by the first turbine-driven cruiser, the *Amethyst*, which was one of four cruisers then under construction. The performance of the *Amethyst* was so remarkable that the last prejudices against turbine machinery in the Royal Navy were overcome, and the way was open for its general adoption. In 1905 a committee on naval design appointed by the Admiralty advised that in future turbine machinery should be used exclusively in all classes of warships; the dreadnoughts were the first class of battleship to be affected by this decision. The Cunard Company was first among the merchant fleets to install turbines, in 1905 in the 30,000 ton liner *Carmania*. The *Lusitania* and *Mauretania* followed in 1906, the latter vessel holding the 'Blue Riband of the Atlantic' for nearly a quarter of a century.

There remained yet to be met the demand of the immense fleets of low-speed tramp steamers and cargo vessels. Parsons realized that the only satisfactory solution was the introduction of mechanical reduction gearing between the turbine and the propeller shaft, thus enabling each vessel to run at its most efficient speed. In order to test this he bought in 1909 an old cargo vessel, the *Vespasian*, and replaced the 750 hp triple expansion engines by geared turbines; after exhaustive tests the new machinery was proved to be entirely successful. This was another great advance, for not only did it diminish the size of the machinery and increase its efficiency, but it enabled the ordinary cargo vessel to profit equally by the employment of turbines.

Lastly, after the First World War the competition of the marine oil engine had to be met. Parsons felt very strongly that marine engineers ought to take advantage of the economies in fuel resulting from the use of higher pressures and temperatures as obtained in installations on land. Knowing that a practical demonstration was the surest and quickest way to convince the sceptics, he accordingly equipped a small passenger vessel, the *King George V*, with high-pressure geared turbines. This vessel was the pioneer of high-pressure steam at sea, and thereby opened up a new field for marine engineers.

Parsons took a keen interest in all matters connected with optics, and when he established the Heaton works in 1889 he organized a special department for the production of searchlight reflectors. He built up what was probably the most important business devoted to the manufacture of such reflectors. In January 1921 he acquired a controlling interest in the optical firm of Ross Ltd, of Clapham. Here he introduced various improvements in the methods of glass-grinding, but soon turned his attention to the much larger question of the manufacture of optical glass itself. The following July he purchased the Derby Crown Glass Company, and under the name of the Parsons Optical Glass Company produced about a hundred different kinds of glass for optical purposes. Parsons made many scientific and mechanical improvements in the processes employed in the manufacture of the glass. In 1925 he purchased the firm of Sir Howard Grubb & Sons, makers of large astronomical telescopes, and under the name of Sir Howard Grubb, Parsons & Co. built new works for it at Walkergate, adjacent to his turbine works at Heaton. Many notable instruments were constructed there, including 36 inch reflecting telescopes for the Royal Greenwich Observatory and for the Royal Observatory, Edinburgh, and two 74 inch reflectors, one for Toronto and the other for Pretoria.

Parsons also invented an 'auxetophone', a loudspeaker for increasing the sound of stringed instruments, particularly of the double bass. This was used at the Queen's Hall in 1906, and was generously supported by Henry Wood, but was otherwise not accepted by the musical profession. Of Parsons's many inventions and experiments, an attempt to make diamonds was the only one in which he failed to achieve his aim.

Parsons was appointed CB in 1904 and KCB in 1911, and

was admitted to the Order of Merit in 1927. He was elected fellow of the Royal Society in 1898, and was vice-president in 1908 and Bakerian lecturer in 1918. He received the Rumford medal in 1902 and the Copley medal in 1928. From the Royal Society of Arts he received the Albert medal in 1911, and from the Institution of Electrical Engineers, the Faraday medal (1923) and the Kelvin medal (1926). He was elected an honorary fellow of his college in 1904, and received honorary degrees from the universities of Oxford, Cambridge, Edinburgh, Glasgow, Dublin, Durham, Liverpool, and Sheffield. In 1911 he delivered the Rede lecture at Cambridge, and he was president of the British Association in 1919. The city of Newcastle upon Tyne made him a freeman in 1914. He died on 11 February 1931 on board the *Duchess of Richmond* at Kingston, Jamaica.

Parsons is considered to be the most original engineer whom this country has produced since the days of James Watt. He lived to see the fruit of his labours in the complete transformation of the method of producing power from steam, on both land and sea. He took out more than 300 patents. Outside his work, he was an enthusiastic fisherman; in society, he was shy and retiring.

Parsons's son was killed in action in 1918. His daughter, Rachel, was one of the first women members of the Institution of Naval Architects. A keen racehorse owner, she was murdered at Newcastle racetrack in 1956.

CLAUDE GIBB, *rev.* ANITA MCCONNELL

Sources J. F. Clarke, *An almost forgotten great man* (1984) • *The Times* (13 Feb 1931) • R. Appleyard, *Charles Parsons: his life and work* (1933) • J. A. E., *PRS*, 131A (1931), v–xxv • *Scientific papers and addresses of the Hon. Sir Charles A. Parsons*, ed. G. L. Parsons (1934) • R. H. Parsons, *The steam turbine and other inventions of Sir Charles Parsons* (1942) • A. Richardson, *The evolution of the steam turbine* (1911) • *Reminiscences and letters of Sir Robert Ball*, ed. W. V. Ball (1915) • private information (2004) • F. Heath, *Nature*, 127 (1931), 315–16 • *CGPLA Eng. & Wales* (1931)

Archives Birr Castle Archives, Offaly, corresp. and papers • CUL • Institution of Mechanical Engineers, London, notebook and drawings • Sci. Mus., corresp. and papers • St John Cam., papers | St John Cam., letters to earl of Rosse

Likenesses W. Stoneman, photograph, 1919, NPG [*see illus.*] • W. Orpen, oils, 1921, Laing Art Gallery, Newcastle upon Tyne • M. Codner, oils, Institute of Mechanical Engineers, London

Wealth at death £810,395 8*s.* 9*d.*: probate, 2 May 1931, *CGPLA Eng. & Wales*

Parsons, Edward (1762–1833), Congregational minister, was born in Stepney, Middlesex, on 16 July 1762 into an Irish family. He became one of the earliest students at the countess of Huntingdon's college at Trefeca, and on leaving became a minister in the Countess of Huntingdon's Connexion, firstly in Tunbridge Wells and subsequently in Norwich. After a brief ministry in Bristol he formed a congregation at Wigan, spent 1781 at the chapel at St Saviour's Gate, York, and in 1784 took charge of the chapel in Mulberry Gardens, Wapping, for a brief time.

Parsons left the Countess of Huntingdon's Connexion and joined the Congregationalists, for whom he preached for some months at Canon Street, Manchester. He then became assistant at the White Chapel, Leeds, succeeding John Edwards as minister in 1785. The frequently enlarged

Edward Parsons (1762–1833), by Thomas Goff Lupton, pubd 1819 (after James Northcote)

chapel became too small for the congregation, and it was under Parsons that Salem Chapel was built in 1791. From 1786 he preached at Tottenham Court Chapel annually for forty years. Parsons was prominent in the formation in 1795 of the London Missionary Society, and was a director for some years. In August 1813 he helped to organize a branch of the society at Leeds. He was a trustee of the *Evangelical Magazine* from its inception in 1793 until his death.

Parsons published many sermons and tracts, and edited the works of several of nonconformist luminaries, including Philip Doddridge (1802–5, 1811) and Jonathan Edwards (1806). In 1801–2 he engaged in a pamphlet controversy with William Atkinson. Under the pseudonym Vindex he wrote to vindicate dissenters 'against the charge of democratic scheming'. A popular and eloquent preacher, his last published work was an address entitled *On Self-Possession in Preaching* (1833). He retired from Salem Chapel in 1832.

Parsons was twice married. With his second wife (*d.* 1820), a daughter of James Hamilton MD of Dunbar and of Winterfield Hall, Belhaven, he had a large family. He died at Douglas, Isle of Man, on 29 July 1833.

His eldest son, **Edward Parsons** (1797–1844), was also a Congregational minister. He studied at Homerton College from about 1812 until 1817, and was ordained to the ministry of Sion Chapel, Halifax, in 1818. From 1821 he assisted John Clayton at the Weigh House Chapel in London, and succeeded him as minister (1826–9). From November 1836 to April 1839 he was minister at the newly formed chapel in Harley Street, Bow. In the latter year Salem Chapel, Mile End Road, was built for him, and he remained there until his life was cut short by a fall down stairs. He was the author of a number of historical and geographical works, including *History in All Ages* (1830), which reached a twenty-ninth edition in 1861, and *The Tourist's Companion … from Leeds and Selby to Hull* (1835), and published several sermons. He died at 31 Assembly Row, Stepney, on 19 November 1844. His second son, James *Parsons (1799–1877), also became a Congregational minister.

BERTHA PORTER, *rev.* J. M. V. QUINN

Sources J. G. Miall, *Congregationalism in Yorkshire* (1868) · J. Morison, *The fathers and founders of the London Missionary Society*, new edn [1844] · private information (1895) · d. cert. [Edward Parsons (1797–1844)] · C. Binfield, *So down to prayers: studies in English nonconformity, 1780–1920* (1977)

Likenesses J. Ogborne, stipple, pubd 1789 (after H. Singleton), BM, NPG · T. G. Lupton, mezzotint, pubd 1819 (after J. Northcote), BM, NPG [*see illus.*] · J. Thomson, stipple, pubd 1829 (after W. Derby), BM, NPG · portrait, 1844, repro. in Morison, *Fathers and founders of the London Missionary Society*, 429 · Parker, stipple (after J. R. Wildman), BM, NPG; repro. in *Evangelical Magazine* (1827) · portrait, repro. in *Evangelical Magazine* (Oct 1797)

Parsons, Edward (1797–1844). *See under* Parsons, Edward (1762–1833).

Parsons [*née* Phelp], **Eliza** (1739–1811), novelist and playwright, was born in Plymouth, Devon, the only daughter of John Phelp, a wine merchant of Plymouth, and his wife, Robora. At an early age she married Mr Parsons, a turpentine merchant of Stonehouse, near Plymouth. In consequence of losses in business caused by the American War of Independence, they moved to London (1778–9). There, at a house near Bow Bridge, formerly known as the Bow China House, Parsons built warehouses and workmen's dwellings, and for three years had every prospect of success. In 1782, however, his property was destroyed by fire, and it is said that only Eliza Parsons's presence of mind saved the whole of Bow from destruction. She courageously ordered the workmen's houses to be pulled down, and thus the fire was prevented from spreading. Her husband then left business, and obtained an appointment in the lord chamberlain's office at St James's. Through the favour of the marchioness of Salisbury, Eliza Parsons was granted a small place in the same department.

At her husband's death (*c.*1790) Eliza Parsons turned to novel writing as a means of providing for her children. Her first book, *The History of Miss Meredith*, in two volumes, appeared in 1790. It was dedicated to the marchioness of Salisbury, and among the subscribers were the prince of Wales, Mrs Fitzherbert, Elizabeth Montagu, and Horace Walpole.

In 1792 Eliza Parsons wrote a play, *The Intrigues of a Morning, or, An Hour at Paris*. It was acted at Covent Garden on 18 April, for the benefit of Mrs Mattocks, and repeated for Mr Hull's benefit at the same theatre. Munden and Fawcett took part in its performance. The play, a farce in two acts, was a poor version of Molière's *Monsieur de Pourceaugnac*.

Eliza Parsons wrote nineteen multi-volume popular novels, mostly in the Gothic tradition, and of little enduring literary merit. Besides the works already mentioned, her publications include *The Errors of Education* (1792); *Woman as she should be, or, The Memoirs of Mrs Menville* (1793); *The Castle of Wolfenbach: a German Story* (1793); *The Voluntary Exile* (1795); *The Mysterious Warning* (1796); and *Women as they are* (1796). *The Castle of Wolfenbach* and *The Mysterious Warning* were among the novels of horror read by Isabella Thorpe in Austen's *Northanger Abbey*. Both were reprinted in 1968 in the *Northanger Set*, edited by Devendra P. Varma. Eliza Parsons's *Murray House* (1804) has also been attributed to Mary Meeke, another prolific Gothic novelist.

Eliza Parsons benefited from several small sums from the Royal Literary Fund and its assistance in 1803 in obtaining her release from debtors' prison. In 1804 she translated six of La Fontaine's *Tales*, under the title of *Love and Gratitude*. She died on 5 February 1811 at Leytonstone in Essex. Of her eight children, three sons and one daughter predeceased her, and four daughters, all married, survived her.

ELIZABETH LEE, *rev.* REBECCA MILLS

Sources Blain, Clements & Grundy, *Feminist comp.* · J. Todd, ed., *A dictionary of British and American women writers, 1660–1800* (1984) · D. E. Baker, *Biographia dramatica, or, A companion to the playhouse*, rev. I. Reed, new edn, rev. S. Jones, 1/2 (1812), 561; 2 (1812), 328 · J. Shattock, *The Oxford guide to British women writers* (1994), 331–2 · *GM*, 1st ser., 81/1 (1811), 195 · *N&Q*, 3rd ser., 4 (1863), 373 · *N&Q*, 7th ser., 1 (1886), 113 · Watt, *Bibl. Brit.*, vol. 2 · *IGI* · N. Cross, ed., *Archives of the Royal Literary Fund, 1790–1918* (1982–3) [microfilm]

Parsons, Elizabeth [*called* the Cock Lane Ghost] (1749–1807), impostor, was born at Cock Lane, in the City of London, an obscure turning between Newgate Street and West Smithfield. She was the elder of two daughters of Richard Parsons, deputy parish clerk of St Sepulchre's, who supplemented his income by letting out rooms in the Cock Lane house. One lodger in 1759 was William Kent from Norfolk. Kent's wife had died in 1756, shortly before his arrival in London, where in Parsons's house he continued a relationship with his deceased wife's sister Frances Lynes, known as Fanny. On one occasion, when Kent was absent in the country, Fanny had Elizabeth Parsons, described as a 'little artful girl about eleven years of age', to sleep in her bed. In the night they were disturbed by extraordinary noises, which Fanny interpreted as a warning of her own death. Neighbours were called in to hear the sounds, which continued to be heard in an intermittent fashion until Kent and his sister-in-law left Cock Lane, and went to live at Bartlett Court, off Red Lyon Street, Clerkenwell. There Fanny died on 2 February 1760, her death having been diagnosed as due to smallpox.

The noises at Cock Lane ceased for a year and a half after Fanny left the house, but they recommenced in January 1762, shortly after Kent had successfully sued Parsons for the recovery of a debt. Elizabeth Parsons, from whose bedstead the sounds apparently emanated, suffered fits, and the household was continually disturbed by unexplained noises, likened at the time to the sound of a cat scratching upon a cane chair. Richard Parsons attributed these manifestations to the presence of a ghost, which he proceeded to interrogate by means of knocking on the bedpost. In this way it was ascertained that the spirit was that of the deceased lodger Fanny Lynes, and that she had been poisoned by a dose of 'red arsenic' administered by Kent in a glass of purl. The story was widely reported and drew numerous visitors, including the duke of York, to the dimly lit room where the manifestations were supposed to take place. During séances conducted by a female relative of Parsons named Mary Frazer, the ghost signified its displeasure at any expressions of incredulity by tapping and scraping, for which it was dubbed Scratching Fanny. The sceptics among the visitors had to conceal their opinion, 'or no ghost was heard, which was no small disappointment to persons who had come for no other purpose' (*GM*, 44). Horace Walpole was openly dismissive of 'a ghost, that would not pass muster in the paltriest convent in the Apennine' (Walpole to H. Mann, 29 Jan 1762, Walpole, 22.3). He visited the house on the following day, where he 'stayed until past one, but the ghost was not expected until seven, when there are only 'prentices and old women'. The Methodists, he added, had promised contributions to the ghost's sponsors: 'provisions are sent in like forage, and all the taverns and alehouses in the neighbourhood make fortunes' (Walpole to G. Montagu, 2 Feb 1762, Walpole, 10.6).

On 1 February 1762 the Revd Dr Aldrich of St John's, Clerkenwell, assembled in his house a number of gentlemen and women, having persuaded Parsons to let his child be brought to the house and tested. The child was put to bed by the women at ten o'clock, and shortly after eleven the company, which included Samuel Johnson, assembled in the girl's bedroom, and with great solemnity requested the spirit to manifest its existence. However, although the girl declared that she felt the spirit like a mouse upon her back, no sounds were heard, and Dr Johnson expressed the opinion of the whole assembly that the child had some art of making or counterfeiting a particular noise, and that there was no supernatural agency at work. The account of this investigation, published by Johnson in the *Gentleman's Magazine*, gave the imposture its death blow. Shortly afterwards Elizabeth Parsons was moved to another house, and threats were held out that her father would be imprisoned in Newgate if she did not renew the rappings. Scratchings and rappings were heard during the course of the night. Unlike previous manifestations, which were probably caused by ventriloquism, the sounds on this occasion were found to issue from a piece of board which the girl had concealed in her clothing. On 10 July 1762 Richard Parsons, his wife, and Mary Frazer were tried at the court of king's bench before Lord Mansfield and a special jury, and were convicted of conspiracy. A clergyman named Moore and one Mr James, a tradesman, who had given countenance to the fraud, agreed to pay William Kent £600 as compensation, and were dismissed with a reprimand. Parsons was sentenced to appear three times in the pillory, and to be imprisoned for two years; his wife and Mary Frazer were sentenced to hard labour in Bridewell for one year and six months respectively. The popularity of the imposture was shown by a public subscription made on behalf of Parsons, and by the calm demeanour of the mob when he stood in the pillory in February 1763.

The affair was the occasion of the well-known satirical poem 'The Ghost', by Charles Churchill, in which Johnson, or Pomposo, was falsely accused of being fooled by the hoax. A plan by Samuel Foote to transfer the caricature to the stage in his play *The Orators* (1762) brought the threat of a beating from Johnson. The imposture was also ridiculed by William Hogarth in his famous engraving of 1762 entitled *Credulity, Superstition, and Fanaticism*. Elizabeth Parsons, who is thought to have been twice married, secondly to a market gardener, died at Chiswick in 1807 (*London Scenes*, 184).

THOMAS SECCOMBE, *rev.* HEATHER SHORE

Sources O. Goldsmith, *The mystery revealed, containing a series of transactions and authentic memorials respecting the supposed Cock Lane ghost* (1762) • G. W. Thornbury and E. Walford, *Old and new London: a narrative of its history, its people, and its places*, 6 vols. (1873–8) • J. Timbs, *Romance of London: strange stories, scenes, and remarkable persons of the great town*, 3 vols. (1865) • H. B. Wheatley and P. Cunningham, *London past and present*, 3 vols. (1891) • Aleph [W. Harvey], *London scenes and London people: anecdotes, reminiscences, and sketches of places, personages, events, customs and curiosities of London city, past and present* (1863) • A. Lang, *Cock Lane and common-sense* (1894) • D. Grant, *The Cock Lane ghost* (1965) • *GM*, 1st ser., 32 (1762), 43–4, 81–4 • *Annual Register* (1762) • E. Chatten, *Samuel Foote* (1980) • Walpole, *Corr.*

Likenesses W. Hogarth, etching and engraving, 1762, BM • portrait, 1762, repro. in Grant, *Cock Lane ghost* • J. W. Archer, print, repro. in Grant, *Cock Lane ghost* • print, repro. in Grant, *Cock Lane ghost*

Parsons, Elizabeth. *See* Parson, Elizabeth (1812–1873).

Parsons, Francis (*d.* 1804), portrait painter, was a student at the drawing academy in St Martin's Lane, London. In 1763 he exhibited at the Society of Artists' exhibition in Spring Gardens portraits of an Indian chief and of Miss Davies, an actress. The former was presumably that of Cunne Shote, a Cherokee chief, engraved in mezzotint by James McArdell, and now in the Gilcrease Institute, Tulsa, Oklahoma. Parsons was a member of the Incorporated Society of Artists, and served as director in 1775 and the following years, and as treasurer in 1776. His portrait of the engineer James Brindley (National Portrait Gallery, London) was engraved in mezzotint by R. Dunkarton in 1770. As he did not succeed greatly in portraiture, Parsons latterly kept a shop as a dealer and restorer of pictures. He exhibited for the last time in 1783 and died early in 1804 at his home in Piccadilly, London, leaving a wife, Hannah. The list of bequests made in his will, including £80 to one John Smart (presumably the miniature painter) in respect of a joint annuity which failed, suggests that Parsons was a kind-natured man. L. H. CUST, *rev.* PAUL A. COX

Sources Graves, *Artists* • Graves, *Soc. Artists* • E. Edwards, *Anecdotes of painters* (1808); facs. edn (1970) • J. C. Smith, *British mezzotinto portraits*, 4 vols. in 5 (1878–84) • exhibition catalogues (1763–83) [Incorporated Society of Artists] • will, 1804, PRO, PROB 11/1405, sig. 129

Parsons, Geoffrey Penwill (1929–1995), pianist and accompanist, was born on 15 June 1929 in Sydney, Australia, one of three sons of Francis Hedley Parsons and his wife, Edith Vera Buckland. He was educated at Canterbury high school, Sydney, and continued to the State Conservatorium of Music there as a pupil of Winifred Burston. His career as a pianist was launched when he won the Australian Broadcasting Corporation's concerto competition in

Geoffrey Penwill Parsons (1929–1995), by Malcolm Crowthers

1947, which led to his first concert tour of Australia the following year (and, he later noted, his thirtieth tour there in 1993). While at the conservatorium he was encouraged by Vern Bartlett, a family friend who was also the leading accompanist in Sydney at that time, to give serious thought to making his own career in this role.

Some trial recitals in this capacity with local singers suggested that Parsons should work further in this direction and brought him to the attention of Peter Dawson (1882–1961), a popular bass-baritone ballad singer, with whom he toured Australia and New Zealand in 1949. Dawson was due to make another of his tours of Britain, taking in Canada *en route*, and invited Parsons to join him. The Canadian dates fell through, but Parsons spent his last £60 on a passage to England in the hope of joining up with Dawson again. He arrived in England in 1950, and remained in the country for the rest of his life, first facing a personal crisis of no work or prospects when his dates with Dawson were restricted to six. Knowing, through Dawson, only some contacts working in the variety theatres, Parsons turned to them in the hope of obtaining work. 'I kept going along to the piers and being accompanist for mouth organs, bones I remember I played for, a piano accordion, jew's harp; I really did play for the lot', he later recalled (Askonas, 17). In addition he found some concert work rather in the shadow of Gerald Moore, then the first-choice accompanist for leading international singers. In 1955 it transpired that Moore could not be available to appear with the prominent German lieder singer Gerhard Hüsch on the latter's first return to Britain since the end of the Second World War. Parsons was approached to replace Moore, and the event was so successful that Hüsch engaged him again the following year and thereafter invited him to become his permanent accompanist.

Although Hüsch was then nearing the end of his performing career, Parsons seized the chance to visit him in Munich for serious daily work on the lieder repertory. 'We worked virtually all day', said Parsons: 'the best possible school for me that I could have had. My interest in Lieder was good before that, but it became all-absorbing' (Askonas, 17). Word soon spread that Parsons had exceptional accomplishment as a gifted partner for a singer, bringing him an invitation from the recording executive Walter Legge to accompany his wife, the celebrated soprano Elisabeth Schwarzkopf, at London's Royal Festival Hall in 1961. They worked through seven three-hour rehearsals in preparation for the concert, and thereafter Parsons was in the forefront of his specialized profession.

His investment of time and patience in meticulous preparation was a major component of Parsons's success in working with Schwarzkopf and other famous singers from many countries. Following the opening of London's new Barbican Hall in March 1982 he was invited to put together his own series of song recitals, no doubt to demonstrate the hall's suitability for small-scale events as well as orchestral concerts. In October of that year 'Geoffrey Parsons and friends' presented, within a single month, memorable themed programmes by individual singers, the 'friends' including Victoria de los Angeles, Dame Janet Baker, Nicolai Gedda, Felicity Lott, and Margaret Price, to whom were added on other occasions Elisabeth Harwood, Hans Hotter, Sena Jurinac, and Jessye Norman, to name but a few. Parsons wrote a programme article for his Barbican series, 'The art of the accompanist', wherein he defined his artistic ideal as 'producing a cushion of basically rich sound, on which the singer feels supported and borne along in utter safety' (Barbican Hall, 12 Oct 1982). He added, in the same article, 'We are expected to know all the "standard" songs, and most of the unusual ones, in keys not only high, low and medium, but also appropriately higher, lower or more medium, printed or not'. Parsons did not confine his attentions to singers, but worked also with violinists such as Ida Haendel, Nathan Milstein, and Wanda Wilkomirska, and with the cellist Paul Tortelier. It was all part of what he called 'a life of unceasing and stimulating challenge' (ibid.), in which he invariably combined courtesy and regard for the artist he was accompanying with a justified sense of his own worth. Roger Vignoles, a fellow accompanist and occasional duet and two-piano partner, declared that the only word to do justice to Parsons in performance was 'immaculate' in relation to 'the seamless fluency of his playing' (Vignoles).

Vignoles also testified to Parsons's 'unfailing generosity', not least to 'the dozens of younger musicians who came to his London home in West Hampstead', where 'he was an excellent and famously hospitable cook' (Vignoles). He enjoyed good food, fine wines, books, and paintings, liked to visit the theatre and always enjoyed opera, leaving an enduring memory of his playing for rehearsals of *Der Rosenkavalier* at Glyndebourne one summer, just because he loved the work so much. He would converse as affably with an off-duty critic as he did with his own circle, which included his long-time domestic partner, the singer and voice teacher Erich Vietheer (who predeceased him in 1989). He was a committed Anglican, a benefactor of both St Albans Abbey and St Cyprian's, Clarence Gate, where he worshipped regularly and endowed a stained-glass window. He accumulated honours from London music colleges, was appointed OBE in 1977, and received the Order of Australia in 1990. His death from cancer on 26 January 1995, in the Middlesex Hospital, London, followed mercifully soon after the onset of the disease. NOËL GOODWIN

Sources L. Askonas, 'Somewhere I managed to practise', *Classical Music* (16 Jan 1982), 17 · *WW* (1995) · N. Goodwin, *The Independent* (28 Jan 1995) · *The Times* (28 Jan 1995) · R. Vignoles, *The Independent* (6 Feb 1995) · personal knowledge (2004) · d. cert.
Likenesses group portrait, photograph, *c.*1965, Hult. Arch. · M. Cosman, pen-and-ink drawing, 1981, repro. in Askonas, 'Somewhere I managed to practise' · M. Crowthers, photograph, repro. in *The Times* [*see illus.*] · photograph, repro. in Goodwin, *The Independent*
Wealth at death £699,685: probate, 12 May 1995, *CGPLA Eng. & Wales*

Parsons [*née* Hext]**, Gertrude** (1812–1891), novelist, was born at Restormel, Cornwall, on 19 March 1812, the fourth daughter in the family of nine children of Captain John Hext (1766–1838) of Trenarren, Cornwall, an infantry officer, and his wife, Elizabeth (*d.* 1851), youngest daughter of Thomas Staniforth of Liverpool. In 1844 she joined the Roman Catholic church. On 8 April 1845 she married Daniel Parsons (1811–1887), son of John Parsons, the vicar of Sherborne, Dorset. Educated at Oriel College, Oxford (where he was taught by J. H. Newman), he had taken holy orders and served several curacies before his conversion to Roman Catholicism in 1843. After their marriage, the couple lived at Begbrooke, Frenchay, near Bristol, and Stuart Lodge, Malvern Wells. A deeply religious woman, Gertrude Parsons was charitable to the poor and a leading benefactor of the mission at Little Malvern.

Gertrude Parsons's enthusiastic commitment to her adopted faith was most apparent, however, in many of her published works. *Thornberry Abbey* (1846), in which the heroine and her clergyman fiancé are both converted to Catholicism, is clearly semi-autobiographical. In another early novel, *Edith Mortimer, or, The Trials of Life* (1857), a young Roman Catholic convert learns to conquer her pride, breaking off her engagement to a rich protestant cousin. In the 1860s Gertrude Parsons wrote four tract tales for Burns and Oates's Tales and Narrative series, which was aimed at a working-class audience; these included *Lent Lilies* and *The Muffin Girl*.

Gertrude Parsons's concern to provide suitable reading matter for working-class Catholics was further evidenced in the *Workman, or, Life and Leisure*, which she initiated, and which she edited from January to December 1865. At first a weekly publication, it included serial fiction, poetry, various light factual articles, and church news. Although other writers, such as the prolific Catholic author and journalist Emily Bowles, were contributors, Gertrude Parsons seems to have written the bulk of the pieces. This may explain the editorial decision in June to turn the magazine into a monthly publication with the revised title the *Literary Workman*. Although better presented and less paternalist than other similar Catholic journals, it seems also to have had difficulty in attracting a committed readership. When the *Literary Workman* ceased publication, Gertrude Parsons continued to write for the Catholic *Lamp*, as well as other periodicals as diverse as *Notes and Queries* and *London Society*.

Gertrude Parsons's publications in *London Society* reflected the character of much of her later fiction. She continued to publish Catholic tales such as *The Sisters of Ladywell* (1881), and she also wrote hagiographical biographies of Ignatius of Loyola (1860) and Saint Colette of Corbie (1879). But many of her later novels were romances of variable quality, aimed at a wider reading public and touching little on religion. *Ursula's Love Story* (1869) is a charming and well-written domestic romance. But a later work, *Under Temptation* (1878), is a weak and wordy sensation novel, in which the portrait of the elderly and eccentric Lady Grafton is the only redeeming feature.

Gertrude Parsons died at Teignmouth, Devon, on 12 February 1891, leaving no children, and was buried at the priory church, Little Malvern, on 17 February.

ROSEMARY MITCHELL

Sources *The Tablet* (28 Feb 1891), 348 · Gillow, *Lit. biog. hist.* · Boase & Courtney, *Bibl. Corn.*, 2.425–7; 3.1301–2 · G. C. Boase, *Collectanea Cornubiensia: a collection of biographical and topographical notes relating to the county of Cornwall* (1890), 654 · S. Acheson, 'Catholic journalism in Victorian Catholic society, 1830–70, with special reference to *The Tablet*', MLitt diss., U. Oxf., 1981 · M. Maison, *Search your soul, Eustace: a survey of the religious novel in the Victorian age* (1961) · Burke, *Gen. GB* (1914)
Wealth at death £16,707 8*s.* 5*d.*: resworn probate, April 1892, *CGPLA Eng. & Wales* (1891)

Parsons, Humphrey (*c.*1676–1741), brewer and politician, was the third and only surviving son of Sir John Parsons (1613–1717), and his wife, Elizabeth, daughter of Humphrey Beane of Epsom. John Parsons, from a London brewing family, prospered as proprietor of the Red Lion brewery in East Smithfield, London. The large scale of his operations included some exportation and naval contracting. Knighted by James II, he was an impressive figure in the London civic world: alderman (from 1689), lord mayor (1703–4), and MP. Sir John left the brewery to his son Humphrey, who in turn was to leave it to his son, John.

Sir John was a pronounced tory with Jacobite leanings, but always prudent. A native of Surrey, he acquired a major political interest at Reigate by the acquisition of The Priory property there. This facilitated his election as member for that borough in 1685, and almost continuously between 1689 and his death. Humphrey followed in his father's political footsteps and also became an alderman (1721), sheriff (1722–3), and twice lord mayor of London (1730, 1740), as well as master of the Grocers' Company (1726–31) and president of both the Bethlem and the Bridewell hospitals. Although unable to retain his late father's seat at Reigate in 1717, he was nevertheless able to sit in the House of Commons for Harwich (1722–7) and for London (from 1727 until his death). His great personal popularity in London added significantly to his political importance as its member of parliament.

The Red Lion's business continued to grow under Humphrey Parsons, making it one of the four largest breweries in the capital in the second quarter of the eighteenth century. This prosperity enabled Humphrey to maintain a 'brilliant stable'. According to an oft-repeated tale, he took some of his impressive mounts with him on a visit to France and was invited to join a royal hunt. When one of his horses was admired by Louis XV, Alderman Parsons, the story goes, grandly presented it to the king, who reciprocated by conferring on him some privilege relating to the importation of beer into France. Neither the terms of the privilege nor the amount of beer involved is known, but the mere rumour of royal rewards added lustre, even political glamour, to Parsons's name (Hughson, 2.195; HoP, *Commons*).

On 16 April 1719 Parsons married Sarah (*d.* 1759), daughter of Sir Ambrose *Crowley MP, a great ironmonger and munitions manufacturer and a prominent tory. Her brother, John Crowley, was detained during the 1715 rebellion as a suspected Jacobite activist. Humphrey and Sarah raised one son, John, and two daughters, Sarah and Anne. In 1745 Anne married Sir John Hynde Cotton, who succeeded as fourth baronet in 1752 and was an even more prominent tory leader.

Humphrey Parsons was much less cautious than his father in avowing his tory commitments and Jacobite sympathies. After 1713 he was a frequent visitor to France, and he became one of the Pretender's most valued correspondents in London. It is not clear precisely what services he was able to render to the Pretender beyond acting as a conduit for the introduction of Jacobite tracts, but, when elected alderman and MP for London, he was conspicuous and effective in his opposition to the Walpole regime. Irregularities in his supervision of the election of a sheriff were alleged by ministerialists, and cited as justification for the City Election Act of 1725. All the more impressive, therefore, was his success in obtaining election to parliament from London in 1727—the only tory that year. He played a leading part inside and outside the house in stopping Walpole's Excise Bill in 1733, and was triumphantly returned to the House of Commons by grateful City voters at the head of the poll in 1734.

Parsons died on 21 March 1741 during his second term as lord mayor, and was buried at Reigate. His popularity is suggested by a number of engravings published about the time of his death. The British Museum possesses four mezzotint portraits of him, including one engraved by John Faber junior, after a portrait by John Ellys.

The careers of Humphrey Parsons and his father, Sir John, illustrate ways in which an older higher stratum in the City, whose prosperity and political importance predated the revolution, could, in the changed world after 1688, both maintain their economic position and provide leadership to popular toryism.

Charles Welch, *rev.* Jacob M. Price

Sources HoP, *Commons* • N. Rogers, *Whigs and cities: popular politics in the age of Walpole and Pitt* (1989) • P. K. Monod, *Jacobitism and the English people, 1688–1788* (1989) • O. Manning and W. Bray, *The history and antiquities of the county of Surrey*, 3 vols. (1804–14) • *Notes on families and individuals of the name 'Parsons' etc.* (*Calendar of 'Parsons' Wills and Administrations*), 2 pts, Army and Navy Cooperative Society, 02.8 (1903) • 'Boyd's Inhabitants of London', Society of Genealogists, London, 238 • P. Mathias, *The brewing industry in England, 1700–1830* (1959); repr. (1993) • *GM*, 1st ser., 1 (1731), 79 [King of France presents subject with his picture] • *GM*, 1st ser., 11 (1741), 164 • D. Hughson, *London: being an accurate history and description of the British metropolis*, 6 vols. (1805–9), vol. 2, p. 195 • will, PRO, PROB 11/708

Likenesses J. Faber junior, engraving (after J. Ellys), BM • J. Faber junior, mezzotint, BM • W. P., print, BM • line engraving, NPG • mezzotint (after unknown artist), BM, NPG

Wealth at death see will, PRO, PROB 11/708

Parsons, Ian Macnaghten (1906–1980), publisher and anthologist, was born on 21 May 1906 at 28 Pont Street, Chelsea, London, the only son of Edward Perceval Parsons, a stockbroker, and his wife, Mabel Margaret, *née* Macnaghten. After prep school he went to Winchester College; a contemporary remembered him as 'an unbelievably handsome … and godlike figure … with his golden hair haloed by his straw boater with its blue-black-blue ribbon' (R. W. David, memorial address). In 1925 he entered Trinity College, Cambridge, as a pensioner (commoner). Two years later he became a senior scholar on the strength of a first in English. This was the last year English was not on offer as part three of the tripos. In his third year Parsons read psychology, which did not carry a class mark. His first, in English part two, stood as his final class. Parsons was one of the Cambridge 'guinea pigs' who attended I. A. Richards's sessions on practical criticism. He edited the *Cambridge Review* and published some of F. R. Leavis's earliest criticism, as well as poetry by his contemporaries, who included Richards's pupil William Empson.

In 1928 Parsons found employment with the publishers Chatto and Windus as a typographer. Two years later Harold Raymond, the chairman, appointed Parsons as a junior partner. In that year Parsons also made his début as an author with *Shades of Albany*, a slim illustrated volume he described as 'a facetious phantasy' inspired by the chambers in Piccadilly.

The young writer-publisher was now in a position to bring the work of his Cambridge contemporaries to the attention of the world at large. Empson's *Seven Types of Ambiguity* (1930), Leavis's *New Bearings in English Poetry: a Study of the Contemporary Situation*, and his wife Q. D. Leavis's *Fiction and the Reading Public* (both in 1932) were the first of a steady stream of critical books published by Chatto under Parsons's aegis from the 1930s to the 1970s.

Parsons suffered a misfortune over publication of *Ultramarine*, the first novel by the writer Malcolm Lowry, a Cambridge contemporary. After it had been appraised by Oliver Warner, the firm's reader in succession to Frank Swinnerton, and given to Parsons, the typescript was stolen from a suitcase he left unattended on the seat of 'an old open 3 litre Bentley of which in my salad days I was the proud possessor', as Parsons later explained (*TLS*). Lowry had no carbon copy and after he had painfully reconstructed the text from a draft he defected to Jonathan Cape. The 3 litre Bentley was often pointed towards the Lake District and Scotland during Parsons's holiday periods. Though bookish he was also vigorously athletic; off duty he enjoyed long walks and climbs. He once visited Lapland simply 'in order to get away from civilisation, to get right away to an obscure part of the world where there's no chance whatever of running into anybody you've ever met before' (*The Listener*, 28 March 1934).

Parsons managed to find time to review and lecture as well as publish. He took classes at the Working Men's College and was part of the team of broadcasters who in the BBC's early days reviewed new books for the Home Service. Parsons's talks, reprinted in *The Listener* in the first quarter of 1934, reveal his wide-ranging literary inquisitiveness. However serendipitous he was as a reviewer, Parsons always remained faithful to poetry, his first literary love, and to his aim of making it more accessible to the general reader. He began with *The Poet's Corner* (1930), a collection of what he considered to be 'the hundred most popular poets in English'; in 1936 came *The Progress of Poetry: an Anthology of Verse from Hardy to the Present*, which included poems by Eliot, Auden, Day-Lewis, Spender, MacNeice, and Empson. Parsons was an excellent reciter of poetry as well as an accomplished after-dinner speaker.

On 30 August 1934 Parsons married Marjorie Tulip Brooker, *née* Ritchie (*b.* 1902), known as Trekkie, an artist who had done illustrative work for the Hogarth Press. They lived in Victoria Square, Belgravia.

Parsons worked closely with Norah Smallwood on *Night and Day*, a weekly magazine of which he was managing director and Graham Greene the editor. Parsons and Smallwood hoped the magazine would prove to be a British rival to the *New Yorker*. It was launched by Chatto on 1 July 1937 but lasted only six months, undone by a libel action involving Greene's review of Shirley Temple's film *Wee Willie Winkie*.

In 1939 when war broke out both Parsons and Trekkie joined the Auxiliary Fire Service and in 1940 Parsons took a commission in the Royal Air Force volunteer reserve. Although at thirty-four he was declared too old for flying duty, he served in intelligence in France with the British expeditionary force until Dunkirk; and then after D-day with Supreme Headquarters Allied Expeditionary Force. On demobilization he held the rank of wing commander and was awarded the OBE.

Back in civilian life in 1945 Parsons returned to Chatto. In 1946 Chatto took over the Hogarth Press. Leonard Woolf retained his editorial sovereignty but financial control of the imprint remained with Chatto. Their combined lists represented much that was most significant in modern literature. From the Hogarth stable came Virginia Woolf, Vita Sackville-West, Henry Green, and Christopher Isherwood; and from Chatto, Aldous Huxley, Julian Huxley, Richard Hughes, Compton Mackenzie, V. S. Pritchett, Rosamond Lehmann, T. F. Powys, Sylvia Townsend Warner—to mention only some of the most eminent names.

Parsons had originally met the Woolfs in 1935 when he approached them for permission to reprint some of Virginia's novels in the Phoenix Library, pocket editions published by Chatto. That had come to nothing but in 1942, after he had been bombed out of Mecklenburgh Square, Leonard came to live next door to the Parsons in Victoria Square and a friendship ripened between the three of them. The Parsons' marriage became complicated by a growing intimacy between Leonard and Trekkie. Trekkie divided her time between Monk's House (Woolf's weekend house in Rodmell, Sussex) and the Parsons' home of Juggs Corner in Kingston, near Lewes, and went on visits abroad with Leonard. Parsons accepted the situation without demur or fuss, not allowing it to interfere with his and Woolf's business interests. An unpublished letter from Parsons to Woolf asks Leonard to remit half of the cost of a winter coat they had agreed jointly to give Trekkie as a present.

In 1953 Chatto became a limited company. In 1954 Raymond retired and Parsons took over as chairman. Under his guidance the company extended its reputation as an imprint notable for publishing works of contemporary literature. Fiction and biography were keenly cultivated, while Parsons's work as a promoter of poetry continued with his *Poetry for Pleasure* anthology, eight volumes published between 1952 and 1956; *Men who March Away*, a pioneering collection of First World War poetry to which he wrote an introduction in 1965; and his important edition of *The Collected Works of Isaac Rosenberg* (1979).

Of the post-war generation of authors published by Parsons the most prolific was Iris Murdoch, whose first novel, *Under the Net*, was brought out by Chatto to great acclaim in 1954. In the field of translation the major contribution came from the works of Freud: the Hogarth Press had begun this before the war, and the work of Alix and James Strachey was now completed by Angela Richard. Likewise Parsons inherited translations of Stendhal and of Proust by Scott Moncrieff. The Proust volumes were reissued with illustrations by Philippe Jullian, and the cult received a further boost from George D. Painter's two-volume life of Proust in 1959 and 1965, a landmark in modern literary biography.

If Parsons did not personally engineer the boom in books about Bloomsbury, he proved to be its ideal impresario. *A Writer's Diary*, a one-volume edition of Virginia Woolf's journals edited by Leonard, appeared as the curtain-raiser in 1953. The publication of Leonard's own autobiography in five volumes from 1960 to 1969, revealing much that was new about his wife's state of health, whetted the public's appetite for still more. This was satisfied for a while by the publication of Quentin Bell's life of Virginia Woolf (his aunt) in 1972. In 1977 came *A Marriage of True Minds: an Intimate Portrait of Leonard and Virginia Woolf*, which Parsons wrote with George Spater, the American Woolf scholar.

Resources were now in place to publish Virginia's letters and diaries in full, something that Leonard had initially resisted. The mammoth task, edited by Anne Oliver Bell (Quentin Bell's wife), Nigel Nicolson, and others, was carried out in sets of six and five volumes respectively, throughout the 1970s and early 1980s. The outspoken candour of Virginia's comments on her friends sometimes shocked Parsons. On reading the typescript of one early volume he strongly objected to including some disparaging remarks about Raymond Mortimer which he felt would prejudice the book's being reviewed in the *Sunday Times*. The editors appealed to Mortimer himself who said that the remarks were 'Virginia's truth' and should be printed exactly as they stood—and they were.

Meanwhile, Parsons became president of the Publishers' Association (1957–9) and a staunch upholder of the net book agreement, which was already under threat. Conditions became more and more difficult throughout the 1960s for an independent publishing company of Chatto's limited financial base to stand on its own, and in 1969 Chatto merged with Jonathan Cape. In 1972 Parsons defended Helen Bannerman's *Little Black Sambo*, which came under attack for its alleged racism. A pressure group, Teachers Against Racism, were urging that it should be withdrawn from circulation. This was one battle that Parsons lost. When the Bodley Head became part of Chatto in 1973, Parsons was made joint chairman. He retired in 1975 and was succeeded by Smallwood. Parsons also held directorships with the Edinburgh printers Hunter and Foulis, the Reprint Society, the Scottish Academic Press, and the Sussex University Press. He was made a CBE in 1971 and court assistant to the Stationers' and Newspaper Makers' Company in 1977.

Outside his work Parsons led a full social life, hosting many convivial gatherings at Juggs Corner. He was a popular member of the Garrick and the Beefsteak clubs. He gardened when in Sussex, took a keen interest in sport, especially rugby and cricket as a member of the MCC. He died at his home in Kingston near Lewes, Sussex, on 29 October 1980. ANTHONY CURTIS

Sources *The Times* (31 Oct 1980) · *WWW, 1981–90* · text of the addresses given by J. A. Adam and R. W. David at the memorial meeting for Ian Parsons at the Stationers' Hall, London, 10 Dec 1980 · register, 1974, Trinity Cam. · *TLS* (10 April 1967) · *DNB* · *The Listener* (Jan–March 1934) · O. Warner, *Chatto & Windus: a brief account of the firm's origin, history and development* (1973) · U. Sussex, Leonard Woolf collection · *Letters of Leonard Woolf*, ed. F. Spotts (1990) · U. Reading L., special collections, Chatto & Windus and Hogarth Press archives · personal knowledge (2004) · b. cert. · m. cert. · d. cert.

Archives IWM, papers as literary executor of Isaac Rosenberg · U. Reading, Chatto & Windus and Hogarth Press archive | U. Sussex, Leonard Woolf collection

Likenesses photographs, U. Reading L., Chatto & Windus archive

Wealth at death £107,718: probate, 6 Jan 1981, *CGPLA Eng. & Wales*

Parsons, James (1705–1770), physician and antiquary, was born in March 1705 at Barnstaple, Devon. He was brought up in Ireland, his father having received the appointment of barrackmaster at Bolton. Parsons received his general education in Dublin and acted for a short time as tutor to Lord Kingston, before going to Paris to study medicine. There he studied under the most eminent professors of the day, and by virtue of their attestations he was given leave to take the degree of doctor of medicine in any university in France, which he chose to do, for financial reasons, at Rheims, on 11 June 1736.

In July 1736 Parsons moved to London, where he remained for most of his life. He received employment first as an assistant to the anatomist James Douglas, before being appointed physician to the public infirmary of St Giles in 1738; he also developed an extensive obstetric practice. In the following year he married, at St Andrew's, Holborn, Elizabeth Reynolds (*d.* 1786), with whom he had two sons and a daughter, all of whom died young. Parsons lived with his wife in Red Lion Square and his house became a regular meeting place for those who moved in London's scientific and antiquarian circles. Parsons was himself elected to the fellowship of the Royal Society on 7 May 1741, acted as its foreign secretary from 1751 to 1762, and succeeded his mentor Douglas in delivering the Croonian lectures, which he gave for three years in succession from 1744. He was also a member of the Society of Antiquaries and of the Society of Arts, and he was admitted a licentiate of the Royal College of Physicians on 1 April 1751. Described as 'cheerful and decent in conversation', Parsons was a flute-player and a good draughtsman.

As his thirty-one papers in *Philosophical Transactions* and eight separately published volumes testify, Parsons had a wide range of interests, with medicine and natural history chief among them, followed closely by the painterly arts and antiquarianism. His expertise as a physician, which was founded on a careful anatomical approach, centred on the human urinary and reproductive systems: his first three published works all dealt with such matters. The third, *A Description of the Human Urinary Bladder: Animadversions on Lithontriptic Medicines* (1742), was less concerned with the subject of its title than that of its subtitle, particularly the then popular but controversial remedies of Joanna Stephens, the efficacy of which he attempted to disprove by means of several case studies.

Lying somewhere between medicine and natural history was Parsons's interest in anatomical abnormalities in humans and other animals. Cases which he investigated included two joined female children, a sheep with a monstrous horn growing out of its throat, a purported mermaid foetus displayed as a freak at Charing Cross, an alleged hermaphrodite from Angola (which he exposed as a fraud in *A Mechanical and Critical Enquiry into the Nature of Hermaphrodites*, 1741), and whatever else was then making 'some noise in town' (*Philosophical Transactions*, 47.142).

Unusual, if not abnormal, subjects of natural history were also favourites, among the more exotic being the Indian rhinoceros that arrived in England in 1739; on this animal Parsons wrote a paper for *Philosophical Transactions*—there being 'no place more proper for recording truth in natural history'—which was later translated into both French and German. Of the more conventional subjects of natural history, sea life was a recurrent theme in his published papers, although it was plants that received a volume of their own, in *The Microscopical Theatre of Seeds* (1745). Issued in parts, this contained detailed microscopical descriptions of seeds accompanied by their uses and virtues, etymology, and synonyms; but this proved less than successful, being discontinued after only one volume, an outcome which might have been different had Parsons not, as one contemporary commentator noted, 'added to each description, under the title of *Uses*, the farrago of properties attributed to them by various authors, without sufficiently distinguishing the results of experience from the effects of imagination' (Nichols, 479).

Complementing Parsons's approach to medicine and natural history was his skill at depicting the subjects of his studies. Few of his papers were unaccompanied by detailed plates drawn faithfully from life with his own hand. This concern with the scientific representation of nature not only supported his work but also influenced its direction, most notably in the 1746 Croonian lecture which he gave on the subject of the muscles of the face. Published as *Human Physiognomy Explain'd* (1747), it attempted to explain 'by what mechanisms the several muscles of the face impress upon it the various sentiments of the soul, and mostly leave indelible traces of the reigning passions'—fear, terror, scorn, love, and desire among them—with the intention that 'any one, versed in the art of designing, may be able to represent the passions of the mind upon the face, by dint of his knowledge of muscular structure' (85). It is in the context of these investigations, and their implications for the emerging genre of history painting in British art, that Parsons is believed to have formed a close association with the artist William Hogarth, an association which, it has been argued, led Parsons and Hogarth to draw on each others' work in art and science for their own ends.

Along with a paper in *Philosophical Transactions* on the comte de Caylus's method of imitating ancient painting in burnt wax, Parsons's last published work is representative of his antiquarian interests. It is entitled *The Remains of Japhet* (1767) and he used it to attempt to show that the source of many of the European tongues was originally Irish and Welsh—languages he had learned as a boy.

In June 1769 Parsons sold his library and natural history collection and retired to Bristol, owing to failing health. However, he returned to London soon afterwards and died in his house in Red Lion Square on 4 April 1770, aged sixty-five. He left his estate to his wife and was buried in the family vault in Hendon, Middlesex, but not until seventeen days after his death. This was because of his request that he should not be buried until some change had appeared in his corpse. GILES HUDSON

Sources Nichols, *Lit. anecdotes*, 5.472–89 • S. West, 'Polemic and passions: Dr James Parsons' *Human physiognomy explained* and Hogarth's aspirations for British history painting', *British Journal for Eighteenth-Century Studies*, 13 (1990), 73–89 • L. C. Rookmaaker, 'Two collections of rhinoceros plates compiled by James Douglas and James Parsons in the eighteenth century', *Journal of the Society of the Bibliography of Natural History*, 9 (1978–80), 17–38 • Munk, *Roll* • B. Henrey, *British botanical and horticultural literature before 1800*, 2 (1975), 41–2 • Desmond, *Botanists*, rev. edn, 538 • *GM*, 1st ser., 40 (1770), 90 • *GM*, 1st ser., 56 (1786), 715 • *DNB*

Likenesses B. Wilson, oils, 1762, NPG • R. Dighton, engraving (after Wells) • Wells, portrait, NPG

Parsons, James (1724–1779), planter and politician in America, was born in Dublin; details of his parents and upbringing are unknown. By 11 May 1750 he was living in South Carolina, where he presumably had studied law, as he was admitted on that date to practise in the colony's court of common pleas. By the following year he owned two plantations, Winnoes and Kilkeny, in St Paul parish, Colleton county. He eventually acquired five additional plantations in Ninety-Six District as well as houses in Charles Town and Jacksonborough; altogether he acquired more than 22,355 acres in three counties. Included among his landholdings were 10,618 acres in the backcountry, suggesting that he had faith in the growth and stability of the region. While residing in South Carolina as a planter, he held 376 slaves.

Parsons's political and public service career began following a special election in 1751 when, despite his recent arrival in the colony, he was elected to a seat in the royal assembly. He was re-elected for a dozen sessions, serving during the years 1752–75; following the break with Britain his service to South Carolina continued unabated for terms in the first three sessions of the general assembly, followed by service in the first and second provincial congresses and the first three meetings of the new general assembly. He was speaker of the initial meeting of the general assembly. This period witnessed the transition from royal government to local legislative control.

On 28 May 1753 Parsons married Susannah Miles (*d.* 1799), described in the *South Carolina Gazette* as 'a handsome young lady, with a genteel fortune and other accomplishments'; they had two sons: James O'Brien, who died in 1769 while a student at Westminster School, London, and George, who died in 1778. During his twenty-five years in public life Parsons served in a variety of other posts, including justice of the peace, ensign and lieutenant colonel in the militia, vestryman of St Michael parish, hemp inspector, commissioner for building an Exchange and Customs House in Charles Town and courthouses elsewhere, and vice-president of South Carolina. He also took many young men in charge to train for the law. Over a number of years he was an active member of both the St Andrew's Society and the Charles Town Library Society. His sentiments towards the American colonies were displayed in his support of the Stamp Act Congress (1764–5), service on the committee of correspondence (1766–70, 1772–3) and councils of safety (1775 and 1776), and reaction to the Virginia 'resolves' and the Massachusetts 'circular letter' (1768) for which he was the reporting member. Parsons continued his accustomed law practice until near the end of his life, when he resigned from the assembly because of declining health. He died on 1 October 1779 in Charles Town and was buried in the town's St Michael's churchyard. He was survived by his wife, Susannah, who died in October 1799. She had come into possession of her late husband's extensive property, valued in excess of £1,981,331, including a large library. In time much of Parsons's property was received by cousins and other relatives of hers. In 1791, when President George Washington toured the south, he was entertained in the splendid home that James Parsons had built for his family.

WILLIAM S. POWELL

Sources W. B. Edgar and N. L. Bailey, eds., *Biographical directory of the South Carolina house of representatives*, 2 (1977) • N. L. Bailey and others, eds., *Biographical directory of the South Carolina senate, 1776–1985*, 2 (1986) • *South Carolina Historical and Genealogical Magazine*, 16 (April 1915), 90; 50 (1949) • B. Glover, *Narratives of Colleton county, South Carolina* (1969) • J. H. Easterby, *History of the St. Andrew's Society of Charleston* (1929) • A. S. Salley, ed., *Marriage notices in the South Carolina 'Gazette'* (1902)

Wealth at death over £1,981,331

Parsons, James (1762–1847), Church of England clergyman, was the son of the Revd James Parsons of Cirencester. He entered Trinity College, Oxford, but subsequently migrated to Wadham College, from which he matriculated on 16 December 1777. He graduated BA in 1781 and MA in 1786. In 1800 the corporation of Gloucester presented him to the perpetual curacy of Newnham with Little Dean, Gloucestershire. He proceeded BD in 1815 from St Alban Hall, Oxford, of which he was for some years vice-principal. Parsons was married; his eldest daughter, Sophia, married, on 28 May 1823, Alexander *Nicoll.

Parsons was a good classical and oriental scholar. Shortly after 1805 he returned to Oxford, at the invitation of the delegates of the Clarendon Press, to undertake the continuation of the Oxford Septuagint, which had been interrupted by the death of its projector, Robert Holmes (1748–1805). He completed this substantial labour in 1827 and retired to his living in Gloucestershire. He published a learned volume entitled *Sermons, Partly Critical and Explanatory* (1835), with a useful preface and notes, and edited in 1830 the sermons of his son-in-law, Alexander Nicoll, regius professor of Hebrew at Oxford, with a memoir of Nicoll's life. Parsons died on 6 April 1847 and his library was sold in June 1847.

GORDON GOODWIN, *rev.* H. C. G. MATTHEW

Sources *GM*, 2nd ser., 28 (1847), 103 • *Clergy List* (1847) • Foster, *Alum. Oxon.*

Parsons, James (1799–1877), Congregational minister, second son of Edward *Parsons (1762–1833), a Congregational minister, and his second wife, a Miss Hamilton (*d.* 1820), was born in Leeds on 10 April 1799. After attending the school of the Revd William Foster of Little Woodhouse, Leeds, he was articled, in 1814, to the firm of Tottie, Richardson, and Gaunt, solicitors, in Leeds. In 1818 he accompanied one of the partners to London, where he studied literature and practised oratory at debating societies. On the death of his mother he abandoned the law in favour of the Congregational ministry, and in the autumn of 1820 entered the academy at Idle. During his two-year course of study he preached not only in the neighbouring villages but also at the Finsbury Tabernacle and Tottenham Court Chapel in London.

In 1822 Parsons accepted a call to Lendal Chapel, York, where his sermons attracted large congregations. Since no further enlargements were possible to Lendal Chapel, the new Salem Chapel was erected and was opened on 25 July 1839. Parsons remained there throughout his active career, until in 1870 his eyesight began to fail him, and he retired from Salem Chapel to settle at Harrogate, where he took occasional pulpit duties. He had married, in 1828, Mary Mullis, daughter of John Wilks (attorney in London and for many years MP for Boston in Lincolnshire). They had one son, who died young, and four daughters, who survived him. In 1873 he was elected the first president of the Yorkshire Congregational Union and Home Missionary Society.

'James Parsons of York' was the most remarkable pulpit orator of his time. Trained for the law, he addressed his congregation as an eloquent barrister would a jury, and he enthralled his hearers. Many of his sermons were published in *The Pulpit* between 1824 and 1864. Always carefully prepared, they demonstrated his detailed knowledge of scripture, and were repeatedly used by other preachers. He also published *Excitements to Exertion in the Cause of God* (1827) and *Sermons, Critical and Explanatory* (1830), which reached a fourth edition in 1837. Parsons died in Harrogate on 20 October 1877, survived by his wife, and was buried in York six days later.

BERTHA PORTER, *rev.* J. M. V. QUINN

Sources J. G. Miall, *Congregationalism in Yorkshire* (1868) • *York Herald* (22 Oct 1877) • *Leeds Mercury* (22 Oct 1877) • *The Congregationalist*, 6 (1877), 748–53 • *Congregational Magazine*, 14 (1831), 229–40 • J. W. Williams, *Pulpit memorials*, ed. E. J. Evans and W. F. Hurndall (1878), 343–80 • H. R. Reynolds, 'In memoriam—James Parsons', *Evangelical Magazine and Missionary Chronicle*, [4th ser.], 7/[2] (1877), 726–9 • *CGPLA Eng. & Wales* (1877) • Boase, *Mod. Eng. biog.*

Likenesses W. J. Ward, mezzotint, pubd 1825 (after G. Marshall), BM • T. Blood, stipple (after J. R. Wildman), BM, NPG; repro. in *Evangelical Magazine* (1825) • J. Cochran, stipple and line engraving (after photograph by S. Haggard), NPG • attrib. P. Westcott, oils, City of York Art Gallery • portrait, repro. in *The Pulpit*, vol. 25 • portrait, repro. in Williams, *Pulpit memorials*, 343

Wealth at death under £5000: probate, 20 Nov 1877, *CGPLA Eng. & Wales*

Parsons, John (*c.*1575–1623), organist and composer, is said to have been the son of Robert *Parsons (*c.*1535–1572), musician, a claim which seems unlikely given the date of Robert Parsons's death. He married Jane in 1600 and with her had three children—William, Dorothy, and Thomasine. Parsons became master of the choristers at Westminster Abbey in the year 1612–13. From 1616 he combined this with the role of parish clerk and organist of St Margaret's, Westminster. He became organist and master of the choristers at the abbey on 7 December 1621. He received a house in the almonry and £16 per annum as organist and £36 13*s.* 4*d.* for looking after the choristers.

A small amount of sacred vocal music by Parsons survives. His four-part setting of the burial service was published in Edward Lowe's *A Review of Some Short Directions* (1664) and performed at the funeral of Charles II. Parsons himself was buried on 3 August 1623 in Westminster Abbey cloisters; probate of his will was granted to his wife, Jane, on 21 December. An epitaph to him recorded in the

1674 edition of William Camden's *Remains Concerning Britain* pays tribute to his skill as an organist:

Death passing by and hearing Parsons play,
Stood much amazed at his depth of skill,
And said, 'this Artist must with me away'
(For Death bereaves us of the better skill),
But let the Quire, while he keeps time, sing on,
For Parsons rests, his service being done.
(Camden, 549)

L. M. Middleton, *rev.* David S. Knight

Sources P. Oboussier, 'Parsons, John', *New Grove* • grant of office of organist, Westminster Abbey Library and Muniment Room, WAMS 9837 • W. Camden, *Remains concerning Britain*, ed. J. Philipot and W. D. Gent, 7th edn (1674) • I. Spink, *Restoration cathedral music, 1660–1714* (1995) • H. W. Shaw, *The succession of organists of the Chapel Royal and the cathedrals of England and Wales from c.1538* (1991) • probate act, City Westm. AC, Acc.120, act book 3, fol. 82v • register, Westminster Abbey [burial]

Parsons, John (1742–1785), physician and anatomist, son of Major Parsons of the dragoons, was born at York. He was educated at Westminster School, being admitted a king's scholar in 1756. In 1759 he was elected to Christ Church, Oxford, where he matriculated on 19 June. He graduated BA on 27 April 1763 and MA on 6 June 1766. As an undergraduate he contributed a Latin ode to the *Oxford Poems* (1761) on the death of George II. He subsequently studied medicine at London, Edinburgh, and Oxford, developed a preference for natural history and botany, and while at Edinburgh in 1766 was awarded the Hope prize medal for the best *hortus siccus*. In 1767 he became the first holder of the readership in anatomy founded by Matthew Lee at Christ Church, Oxford, though still without a medical degree. He graduated BM on 12 April 1769, and DM on 22 June 1772. In the same year he married Miss Anne Hough. He was elected reader in anatomy in the university in 1769, physician to the Radcliffe Infirmary on 6 May 1772, and first clinical professor on Lord Lichfield's foundation, 1780–85. His first course of clinical lectures was announced in *Jackson's Oxford Journal* in October 1781. Under his direction a substantial anatomy school was built at Oxford. Parsons was an enterprising physician who also lectured on philosophy and medical chemistry (see his *Plan for a Course of Lectures in Philosophical and Practical Chemistry*, 1770). In addition, he accumulated a large collection of specimens to illustrate his lectures, which provided the basis for a museum which was augmented subsequently by minor additions bought by the Lee trustees at the request of the readers. Parsons was admitted a candidate of the Royal College of Physicians on 30 September 1774, and fellow exactly a year later, 30 September 1775. In 1784 he delivered the Harveian oration.

Parsons died of fever on 9 April 1785, and was buried in Christ Church Cathedral, Oxford, where a white marble gravestone was placed in his memory. On 17 March 1791 Parsons's widow married John Grosvenor, who had assisted her late husband in his anatomical lectures.

W. A. Shaw, *rev.* Michael Bevan

Sources C. Webster, 'The medical faculty and the physic garden', *Hist. U. Oxf.* 5: *18th-cent. Oxf.*, 683–723 • *GM*, 1st ser., 42 (1772), 390 • *GM*, 1st ser., 61 (1791), 380 • Munk, *Roll* • J. Welch, *A list of scholars of St Peter's College, Westminster* (1788) • A. Wood, *The history and antiquities of the University of Oxford*, ed. J. Gutch, 2 (1796), 886 • Foster, *Alum. Oxon.*

Parsons, John (1761–1819), bishop of Peterborough and college head, was the son of Isaac Parsons, butler of Corpus Christi College, Oxford, and his wife, Alice (both of whom are buried in the cloisters of that college). The family were prominent bankers in Oxford; his brother, Herbert, and cousin, John Parsons, were both mayors of the city. Born in the parish of St Aldates, Oxford, he was baptized in St Aldates Church on 6 July 1761. He received his early education, first at the school attached to Christ Church, and subsequently at Magdalen College School. He was admitted at Wadham College on 26 June 1777, and was elected a scholar there on 30 June 1780. He graduated BA in 1782, MA in 1785, and BD and DD in 1799.

Having taken holy orders, Parsons was elected fellow of Balliol on 29 November 1785. He was a regular contributor to the *Monthly Review* and was responsible for the preliminary work on the Oxford edition of Strabo (published in 1807). In July 1797 he was presented by the college to the united livings of All Saints' and St Leonard's, Colchester. On 22 January 1798 he married Elizabeth Parsons (*d.* 1827), probably a cousin, at St Aldates Church, and on 14 November 1798 he was elected master of Balliol. He held that office until his death. From 1807 to 1810 he was vice-chancellor of the university.

With Parsons's mastership the real revival of Balliol, and, it may be said, of the university generally, began. He made the college examination a reality, and thus, in conjunction with John Eveleigh, provost of Oriel, he gave the lead to the university in making the examinations, which had degenerated into a discreditable farce, also a reality. With Eveleigh he elaborated the new examination statute of 1801, by which university honours were for the first time awarded for real merit, and he was one of the first examiners, the earliest class list under the new system appearing in 1802. He was for many years 'the leading, or rather the working, member' of the hebdomadal council. By the success of the experiment at Balliol he may be said to have laid the foundation of the collegiate tutorial system. He had great sympathy with the undergraduates, and he was much respected by them. Benjamin Jowett recalled that when Parsons first became master:

> the junior common room was reported to be in a very bad state. He sent for the 'book of rules', and, after examining it, put it on the fire, sending for the leading members of the junior common room to see it burning, and thus put an end to the institution.

Richard Jenkyns, who succeeded him as master, was tutor under him, and when Parsons was made a bishop was appointed vice-master, vigorously seconding his administration of the college.

Although he was a warm advocate of all reforms calculated to promote the welfare of his college and of the university, Parsons held strong tory principles. He was vigorously opposed to all 'innovations', either in the university or in national politics. He was the senior of the three heads of houses who, on the death of the duke of Portland in 1809, proposed the tory Lord Eldon for the chancellorship of the university, to which the whiggish Lord Grenville was elected.

This and other services rendered to the tory party in the university marked Parsons out for preferment. In 1810 he was appointed dean of Bristol, and in 1812 he was presented to the chapter living of Weare in Somerset, which he held until his death. In 1813, mainly through Eldon's influence, he was raised to the bishopric of Peterborough. Both as dean of Bristol and as bishop of Peterborough, Parsons was active in the establishment and promotion of the National Society for Promoting the Education of the Poor. In conjunction with Eveleigh he advanced its interests at Oxford; and, together with Joshua Watson, he is credited with drawing up in 1812 the terms of union for the district committees of the provincial schools. In September 1818 he was appointed one of the commissioners for inquiring into educational charities.

Parsons seldom spoke in the House of Lords, but he was very useful on committees, and especially improved the Consolidation Bill and the Church Building Bill. He died at Oxford on 12 March 1819, of rheumatic gout, and was buried, quietly, by his own desire, in the chapel of Balliol College, where there is a monument to him. He left no children.

Parsons was a preacher of a high order, with a dignified and emphatic delivery, though only his sermons to the Commons (20 March 1811) and to the Society for the Propagation of the Gospel (1818) were published. All his manuscript sermons were burnt after his death, by his express request. In the acrimonious controversy concerning the Bampton lectures of Dr Joseph White, the Arabic professor, of which the Revd Samuel Badcock was asserted to have been the author, and portions of which were claimed by Dr Samuel Parr, Parsons was appointed one of the arbitrators, but declined to act; it was believed that he also had 'a considerable right of property in the lectures, which his honour or his kindness obliged him to dissemble', and that Parr in some of his claims was 'trespassing on ground he knew to be his own' (*De Quincey's Works*, 157).

Parsons is described by the Revd E. Patteson, in a letter to Sir William Scott, as 'a second founder' of his college, 'a reformer of the abuses of the university, an enforcer of its discipline, an able champion of its privileges, and a main pillar of its reputation' (*Annual Biography*, 1820, 431). He had vigorous colloquial powers, and was both witty and gay when conversing with congenial companions; but in general society he was grave and reserved.

EDMUND VENABLES, *rev.* M. C. CURTHOYS

Sources *Annual Biography and Obituary*, 4 (1820) • *Christian Remembrancer*, 1 (1819), 384–5, 670–72 • *GM*, 1st ser., 88/2 (1818), 525 • *GM*, 1st ser., 89/1 (1819), 481 • G. V. Cox, *Recollections of Oxford* (1868) • J. Britton, *The history and antiquities of the abbey and cathedral church of Peterborough* (1828) • E. Churton, ed., *Memoir of Joshua Watson*, 2 vols. (1861) • C. J. Abbey and J. H. Overton, *The English church in the eighteenth century*, 2 vols. (1878) • *De Quincey's works*, ed. D. Masson, 2nd edn, 16 vols. (1862–71), vol. 5 • private information (1895) • J. Jones, *Balliol College: a history, 1263–1939* (1988) • *VCH Oxfordshire*, 4.246

Archives Bodl. Oxf., accounts, corresp., diaries, and papers | BL, corresp. with Lord Grenville, Add. MS 69111

Likenesses W. Owen, oils, exh. RA 1818, Balliol Oxf.; copy, Wadham College, Oxford

Parsons, John Henry (1890–1981), cricketer and Church of England clergyman, was born on 30 May 1890 at St John's Street, Oxford, the second of the six children of William Parsons (1854–1931), chef at Brasenose College, Oxford, and later a hotel manager, and his wife, Kate Horn (*d.* 1919). The family moved to the midlands in 1898 and Parsons attended Bablake School in Coventry. There he became captain of cricket and football before finding employment at the Humber car factory in the city, where he quickly advanced to the responsible role of a car tester. Footballing and cricketing performances on the sports field led to trials with both Coventry City Football Club and Warwickshire County Cricket Club. In August 1910, within one week, he went from being a net bowler with the county to playing first-class cricket, via a double century on his début for the second eleven. The press comment that 'Warwickshire seem to have struck something good' (*Sporting Argus*) led him to make the first of several brave decisions. This was to accept professional terms with a county which had serious financial problems and abandon a career in the prosperous car industry. In the four years before the First World War broke out Parsons was a member of the team which, against all expectations, won the county championship in 1911. He made the first of his thirty-eight centuries in 1913 and appeared for the Players against the Gentlemen in July 1914. His name was pencilled in for the next MCC tour of Australia and it was said he would 'go straight to the top of the tree' (*Wisden*, 1915, 124).

The outbreak of war put paid to these cricket prospects. Parsons served in the Warwickshire yeomanry and took part in the battle of Suvla Bay at Gallipoli before being commissioned in the Worcestershire yeomanry. Both regiments took part in the attack on Huj, near Gaza, in November 1917, when he was one of 181 men who routed a Turkish and Austrian force of over 2000. It proved to be the last cavalry charge in British military history. Success paved the way for General Allenby to take Jerusalem and Parsons was awarded the Military Cross.

There followed five years serving with the Indian army on the north-west frontier during which Parsons married, on 19 April 1922, Gwendoline Ellen (Gwen) Bassett (1894–1964), a nursing sister in Quetta. They had a son and a daughter. Soon afterwards he took another brave decision: to leave the army and resume a career as a cricketer. The bravery lay in hoping he could re-establish himself in the Warwickshire side. In the social context of the time he was turning his back on a life as an Indian army officer to play cricket as Parsons, J. H.—a professional.

In the twelve years which followed (1924–36) Parsons completed a first-class career which yielded 17,969 runs (average 35.72). He toured India with the MCC in 1926–7, while innings of 161 against the 1928 West Indians and 190 against the 1931 New Zealanders again brought press suggestions that he be picked for England. The nearest he got, however, was selection for the Gentlemen against the Players, when in four appearances (1929–31) he averaged

40.12. For the professional had, in 1928, made yet another brave decision when he sought ordination in the Church of England. He trained at St Aidan's Theological College, Birkenhead. While serving his title at Rugby and supervising soup kitchens during the depression, Parsons continued to play occasional first-class cricket as an amateur, and sometimes captained Warwickshire. He 'led a disciplined side and knew what he wanted', recalled his county colleague E. J. 'Tiger' Smith (Howat, *Cricketer Militant*, 83).

Shortly after war broke out in 1939—by which time he was vicar of Liskeard in Cornwall—Parsons volunteered to be an army chaplain. Two brigadiers recalled those years: 'What a pearl of great price the unit had as their padre' and 'I wish I could strip him of his black buttons and make him one of my company commanders' (Howat, *Cricketer Militant*, 92). After the surrender of Italy in 1943, he became senior chaplain at Taranto, where his spiritual and practical concern for the allied forces, German prisoners of war, and displaced Italian civilians brought him a mention in dispatches.

On his return to Liskeard after the war (to a parish which had hardly known him) Parsons's incumbency was significant for the fervour of his evangelism and for the size of his congregations, together with his ability to run youth clubs and to raise money. Yet underlying all these—as in his chaplaincy at Taranto—was the need for reconciliation. In 1946 he had the sword he had carried at Huj against the Turks made into a ploughshare, echoing the book of Micah. With it he ploughed the field, sowed the seed, reaped the corn, and baked the bread which 'I used at the Communion Service' (Howat, *Cricketer Militant*, 104). He was appointed to a canonry of Truro Cathedral in 1953 and subsequently (1959–65) served the rural parish of Birlingham, near Worcester, while still able to make 65 (with four sixes) against Solihull School when over seventy.

Jack Parsons died at 11 De La Hay Avenue, Plymouth, on 2 February 1981 and was cremated at St Martin's, Liskeard, three days later. The seriousness of purpose and the fulfilment of aims—his philosophy of life—were reflected in his cricket. There was perfection of technique in his batting and he belonged, in essence, to the classical era of cricket in the grace and formalism of his approach.

GERALD M. D. HOWAT

Sources G. Howat, *Cricketer militant: the life of Jack Parsons* (1980) • *Wisden* (1982), 1207–8 • *Daily Telegraph* (3 Feb 1981) • *The Times* (3 Feb 1981) • G. Howat, 'The last of the Romans', *The Times* (29 May 1980) • *Sporting Argus* (5 Aug 1910) • private information (2004) [Kate Parsons, daughter]

Archives Warwickshire County Cricket Club, Birmingham, minute books of the general and executive committee

Likenesses photographs, repro. in Howat, 'The last of the Romans'

Parsons, Sir John Herbert (1868–1957), ophthalmologist and physiologist, was born in Bristol on 3 September 1868, the youngest of the five children of Isaac Jabez Parsons, grocer, and his wife, Mary Goodhind Webb. He was educated at Thomas Turner's private school, at Bristol grammar school, and at University College, Bristol, where he studied arts, science, and medicine. His entry into the college was aided by his gaining a Gilchrist scholarship and his medical studies by a Stewart scholarship, and he won the first entrance scholarship to Bristol Royal Infirmary. Parsons left Bristol in 1889 and pursued medicine further at University College, London, where he graduated BSc with honours in physiology (1890). He completed his medical course in St Bartholomew's Hospital, where he graduated MB in 1892. He thereupon returned to University College as Sharpey scholar and assistant and demonstrator in physiology to E. A. Schafer (later Sharpey-Schafer). He married in 1894 Jane Roberta (*d.* 1911), daughter of John Hendrie of Uddingston, Lanarkshire; a son and a daughter survived him.

Parsons settled in London, and after a short period in general practice in Finchley he found himself compelled to return to his initial interest in physiology; through this he took up ophthalmology and became a clinical assistant at Moorfields Eye Hospital. He qualified FRCS in 1900 and was elected pathological curator and librarian at Moorfields Hospital. In 1904 he was elected to the consulting surgical staff of that hospital and of University College Hospital, both of which he served throughout his working life; he was also for a time consulting surgeon to the Hospital for Sick Children, Great Ormond Street. At the same time he conducted a large ophthalmic practice at a house in Queen Anne Street.

Parsons's concern was the working of the eye and its behaviour in health and disease. After his own studies ceased he encouraged others to continue this work. His first book was a small manual, *Elementary Ophthalmic Optics* (1901), an attempt to impress on the student that it was wrong to test a patient's vision or examine him or her clinically without a thorough understanding of the optics of the methods he was using. Simultaneously he undertook research work on the physiology of the eye in the department of physiology of University College, beginning with the innervation of the pupil and the lacrimal gland. His fundamental work on the control of the intra-ocular pressure was summarized in his second book, *The Ocular Circulation* (1903). For these researches he obtained the degree of DSc (London, 1904). Thereafter Parsons turned his attention to ocular pathology, and from his laboratory at Moorfields he published a series of original papers; the whole subject was also correlated and integrated for the first time in his classical treatise, *The Pathology of the Eye* (4 vols., 1904–8). With its appearance Parsons became a world authority and his hospital clinics a Mecca for students from abroad. At the same time his maturing clinical experience was reflected in the appearance of a comprehensive and yet concise clinical textbook, *Diseases of the Eye*, which, soon after its appearance in 1907, became the most popular work of its type; it went through ten editions before passing to other editorial hands.

Parsons's interests then turned to the psychology of vision and perception; in this vast field his main thesis was that perceptive phenomena could be analysed only on a factual basis; that the only safe approach to their understanding was a materialistic one, through physiological experimentation; and that introspective psychology divorced from biology was dangerous. Endowed with untiring energy, unusually wide knowledge, critical ability, and scientific honesty, Parsons attained a unique place in the scientific world by the publication of four books on this wide subject. Two of them were classical, *An Introduction to the Study of Colour Vision* (1915) and *An Introduction to the Theory of Perception* (1927); and two of them were small and incidental, *Mind and the Nation: a Précis of Applied Psychology* (1918) and *The Springs of Conduct* (1950)—the latter being a summary of Parsons's neuropsychological creed, written when he was eighty-two.

Parsons had wide interests in public, professional, and cultural life. He served on several government commissions, his greatest contribution in this respect being in the adequate lighting of factories, a subject gravely neglected at the time. During the thirty-one years of the activities of the departmental committee set up by the Home Office on factory lighting, he played a prominent part; and he was one of the founder members of the Illuminating Engineering Society, of which he was the first chairman of council, its president in 1924, and honorary member in 1943. In professional societies Parsons participated wholeheartedly. To the Ophthalmological Society of the United Kingdom, which he joined in 1900, he made some 140 contributions, and he was its president in 1925. He was president of the Royal Society of Medicine (1936–8) and honorary fellow (1942).

Parsons also took a prominent part in international ophthalmology, directing his influence towards the resumption of friendly relations between ophthalmologists throughout the world after the First World War. He helped to create the International Council of Ophthalmology (1927) and to arrange the very successful 13th International Congress of Ophthalmology in Amsterdam (1929). He was chairman of the editorial committee of the *British Journal of Ophthalmology* from its foundation in 1917 to 1948. He was one of the founder members of the British Council of Ophthalmologists and was largely responsible for its substitution by the Faculty of Ophthalmologists to serve as the co-ordinating and academic custodian of the specialism. Of the greatest importance was his association with the Medical Research Council on which he served from 1929 to 1932; to his influence was largely due its efforts to maintain an interest in research in visual problems in the period between the two world wars. In the first of these he served initially with the rank of captain as ophthalmic surgeon to the 3rd London General Hospital, between 1916 and 1917; he then took the rank of colonel as ophthalmic consultant to the home forces between 1917 and 1918; and thereafter he served in an advisory capacity to the army, the navy, and the Royal Air Force. In 1919 he was appointed CBE, and he was knighted in 1922.

The Royal College of Surgeons invited Parsons to give the Arris and Gale lectures in 1903–4; from the British Medical Association he received the Middlemore prize in 1904 and again in 1914. From the Ophthalmological Society he received the Nettleship gold medal (1907) and the Bowman lectureship (1925); from the Oxford Ophthalmological Congress he was awarded the Doyne medal (1919); and from the American Ophthalmological Society he was given the Howe medal (1936). He was made honorary DSc of his own university, Bristol, in 1925, and LLD at Edinburgh in 1927. In 1921 he was elected FRS, and he served on the society's council in 1926–7 and 1941–3, and became a vice-president in 1941–2. On his eightieth birthday he was presented with his portrait, painted by John Gilroy, by the Faculty of Ophthalmologists and the Ophthalmological Society; and the same occasion was marked by the appearance of a special number of the *British Journal of Ophthalmology* consisting of contributions made by his scientific and clinical pupils and associates.

Parsons's life was full of work, but he also enjoyed leisure. He appreciated good company and was a delightful host, particularly to the young, on whom he lavished much kindness, assisting them freely in their work and professional troubles. He had a great appreciation of music and used to go to the opera armed with a score. His knowledge of languages was wide and Persian literature and art interested him greatly. Golf was an absorbing hobby most of his life and he enjoyed periodic holiday cruises.

At the outbreak of war in 1939 Parsons left London and retired from practice, lending his London house to the French Red Cross. He went to live in Leeds with longstanding friends, though he visited London frequently. In his later years progressive deafness, an annoying tremor, and cardiac troubles—disabilities exasperating to a nature so forceful and active—gradually curtailed his activities. He died in University College Hospital, Grafton Way, London, on 7 October 1957.

STEWART DUKE-ELDER, *rev.*

Sources personal knowledge (1971) • E. T. Collins, *The history and traditions of the Moorfields Eye Hospital: one hundred years of ophthalmic discovery and development* (1929) • D. M. Albert and D. D. Edwards, eds., *The history of ophthalmology* (1996) • S. Duke-Elder, *Memoirs FRS*, 4 (1958), 205–14 • *WWW*

Likenesses W. Stoneman, photograph, 1931, NPG • J. Gilroy, oils, U. Lond., Institute of Ophthalmology

Wealth at death £58,135 19*s*. 4*d*.: probate, 27 Jan 1958, *CGPLA Eng. & Wales*

Parsons, John Meeson (1798–1870), art collector, was born on 27 October 1798 in Newport, Shropshire, the youngest son of Thomas and Elizabeth Parsons. He was taught by the Revd Richard Thurstfield of Pattingham and later by the Revd Francis Blick of Tamworth before studying privately at Oxford but he had to give up because of inflammation of the eyes, supposedly brought on by too much reading. He settled in London, and became a member of the stock exchange. He became interested in railways, and was elected an associate of the Institution of Civil Engineers on 5 February 1839. He was a director of the London and Brighton Railway Company from 1843 to 1848, and chairman from 1843 to 1844; he was also a director of the Shropshire Union railway from 1845 to 1848.

Parsons lived for many years at 6 Raymond Buildings, Gray's Inn, and spent much of his time collecting pictures and works of art. He married a daughter of John Mayhew; they had one daughter, but his wife died soon afterwards. He moved to 45 Russell Square, Bloomsbury, in 1869, and died there on 26 March 1870.

By the time of his death Parsons had acquired a valuable collection of pictures, mainly of the German and Dutch schools, and watercolour drawings by English artists. In his will he offered up to 100 of his oil paintings to the National Gallery, London: the trustees chose only three—J. M. W. Turner's *Fishing Boats in a Breeze off the West*, and two paintings by the Belgian painter P. J. Clays. He also stipulated that if the National Gallery did not accept the whole gift, the Department of Science and Art at South Kensington (later the Victoria and Albert Museum) should be able to choose some oil paintings, and he gave them the opportunity to choose up to 100 of his watercolours, or sepia or charcoal drawings. In 1870 the department chose ninety-two oil paintings and forty-seven watercolours. Parsons also left a number of engravings to the British Museum.

G. C. Boase, *rev.* Anne Pimlott Baker

Sources *PICE*, 31 (1870–71), 252–3 • *List of the bequests and donations to the department of science and art for the South Kensington Museum* (1889), 15 • S. Redgrave, *A descriptive catalogue of the historical collection of water-colour paintings in the South Kensington Museum* (1877), 82 • 'Department of science and art: eighteenth report', *Parl. papers* (1871), 24.xxx, 44, 387, 404, C. 397 • *CGPLA Eng. & Wales* (1870)
Archives V&A
Wealth at death under £120,000: probate, 4 May 1870, *CGPLA Eng. & Wales*

Parsons, Laurence, **fourth earl of Rosse** (1840–1908), astronomer and engineer, was born on 17 November 1840 at Birr Castle, Parsonstown (Birr), King's county, Ireland, the eldest of the four surviving sons of William *Parsons, third earl of Rosse (1800–1867), astronomer, engineer, and politician, and his wife, Mary, *née* Field (1813–1885) [*see* Parsons, Mary, countess of Rosse], daughter of John Wilmer Field of Heaton Hall, Yorkshire. His youngest brother, Sir Charles Algernon *Parsons, invented the marine steam turbine. Known in his youth by the courtesy title of Lord Oxmantown, Laurence was educated at home by tutors and under the close supervision of his parents. His father achieved fame by completing in 1845 the great 6 foot reflecting telescope which was to remain the largest in the world for seventy years. The countess of Rosse combined the roles of loving mother, architect, and pioneering photographer. Laurence and his brothers enjoyed a healthy though severe regime at Birr which combined an open-air life with practical work in their father's well-equipped workshops. They had opportunities to meet many of his distinguished friends at Birr or in London. Laurence graduated from Trinity College, Dublin, in 1864 as a non-resident student.

Oxmantown's first scientific paper, entitled 'Description of an equatoreal clock', appeared in the *Monthly Notices of the Royal Astronomical Society* in 1866 and described a hydraulic device to drive a telescope at a constant rate; his propensity for such ingenious inventions never left

Laurence Parsons, fourth earl of Rosse (1840–1908), by Frederick Sargent, 1870s

him. There followed a memoir which appeared in the *Philosophical Transactions of the Royal Society* giving an account of observations of the Orion nebula made at Birr from 1848 to 1867. The work collated drawings made over seven seasons with the 3 foot and 6 foot telescopes by several assistant observers (B. B. Stoney, S. Hunter, and R. S. Ball) and by Oxmantown himself. The centrepiece of the paper was a detailed engraving which was judged by J. L. E. Dreyer as being 'always of value as a faithful representation of the appearance of the Orion nebula in the largest telescope of the nineteenth century' (Dreyer, 251). The advent of photography soon rendered such painstaking work unnecessary.

The third earl died in October 1867 and Oxmantown succeeded to the title and the estates. That same year he was elected a fellow of the Royal Society and of the Royal Astronomical Society; he was also appointed high sheriff of King's county. In 1868 he became a representative peer for Ireland. On 1 September 1870 he married Frances Cassandra Harvey-Hawke (1851–1921), only child of the fourth Baron Hawke and his second wife, Frances Fetherstonhaugh. They had three children: William Edward, who inherited as fifth earl and died of war wounds in 1918, Geoffrey, and Muriel.

The fourth earl is best remembered for his work on the radiant heat of the moon which he started in 1868 and continued more or less for the rest of his life, although much of the later work was carried out by his observing assistant, Dr Otto Boeddicker. Lord Rosse was the first to make infra-red measurements of any astronomical body other than the sun and he recognized the importance of compensating for heat emitted by the telescope and by the sky. He detected the radiant heat with a pair of thermocouples at the focus of the 3 foot reflector. He studied how the radiant heat varied with the phase of the moon, and measured how the atmospheric attenuation increased with the distance of the moon from the zenith. He was the first to use an infra-red filter which took the form of a glass plate; by placing the plate in front of the detector he was able to block radiation with wavelengths longer than eight microns. He estimated the temperature of the lunar surface by comparing filtered and unfiltered temperature rises from the moon, the sun, and a blackened reference source of heat. An account of the lunar investigations was delivered to the Royal Society in the Bakerian lecture of March 1873, and he continued to improve his techniques. His initial estimate of 500 °F (260 °C) was revised to 247 °F (119 °C) and later to 197 °F (91.7 °C). A reanalysis of the data by W. M. Sinton in 1958 gave a value of 158 °F (70 °C), in excellent agreement with later observations. Boeddicker remarked that 'the results of these investigations were treated with considerable coolness by the scientific world' and that the lack of recognition 'was a life-long disappointment to him' (Boeddicker, 375).

Lord Rosse was a gifted inventor and never happier than when he was busy in his own workshops. As commercial thermocouples were not sensitive enough for the lunar heat observations he made his own and with infinite patience gradually refined their design. In 1869 he fitted a clock drive to the massive 6 foot telescope which allowed it to be used more efficiently. In 1874 the old wooden mounting of the 3 foot telescope was replaced by an equatorial mounting of metal, designed in consultation with B. B. Stoney and W. G. Strype and built by W. Spence of Dublin. Other unpublished work at Birr included observations with a heavy Browning spectroscope, and photography of the Orion nebula and the Milky Way.

Lord Rosse took a keen interest in the development of the steam turbine which was invented by his brother Charles and he served as chairman and director of both the Marine Steam Turbine Company formed in 1894 and the Parsons Marine Steam Turbine Company formed in 1897. He seldom missed a meeting, often crossing from Ireland specially for the occasion. Charles frequently sought his advice on both technical and business matters. In recognition of his services he was made an associate of the Institution of Naval Architects in 1899.

Lord Rosse was elected chancellor of the University of Dublin in 1885 and remained in office until his death. In 1903 he played a key role in persuading Lord Iveagh to donate a capital sum to provide new buildings and equipment for the departments of experimental physics and botany. Apart from contributing generously to the building fund himself, he made a bequest to the scientific departments in the university. The fourth earl was made a knight of the Order of St Patrick in 1890 and was lord lieutenant of King's county from 1892. He served as president of the Royal Dublin Society (1887–92) and of the Royal Irish Academy (1896–1901). The University of Oxford conferred the honorary degree of DCL in 1870 and Dublin and Cambridge universities that of LLD in 1879 and 1900 respectively. He was made an honorary member of the Institution of Mechanical Engineers in 1888.

Insight into Lord Rosse's character comes from the testimony of Boeddicker who was his assistant for twenty-eight years. He attributed 'a strong reticence and shyness' (Boeddicker, 374) to his relatively sheltered childhood. Lord Rosse himself occasionally mentioned 'the effort it cost him to mix in public life, and especially to preside and speak at public meetings' (ibid., 375). On the other hand Boeddicker described him as 'a man of extraordinary tenacity of purpose, whom no failure could turn away from a project he once considered feasible' (ibid.) and added 'he was a man of absolute rectitude, with a strong sense of duty, a true friend, a sound and conscientious adviser' (ibid., 376). After a decline in health lasting two years, the fourth earl died at Birr Castle on 29 August 1908 and was buried in the old churchyard of Birr on 2 September.

I. Elliott

Sources Lord Oxmantown [L. Parsons], 'Description of an equatoreal clock', *Monthly Notices of the Royal Astronomical Society*, 26 (1865–6), 265–7 • L. Parsons, fourth earl of Rosse, 'The Bakerian lecture: on the radiation of heat from the moon, etc.', *PTRS*, 163 (1873), 587–627 • Lord Rosse [L. Parsons], 'Temperature of moon's surface', *Nature*, 16 (1877), 438 • W. M. Sinton, 'A history of infrared astronomy from 1868 to 1960', *Publications of the Astronomical Society of the Pacific*, 98 (1968), 246–51 • D. Taylor and M. McGuckian, 'Lunar temperature measurements at Birr Castle', *Science in Ireland, 1800–1930*, ed. J. Nudds and others (1988), 115–22 • R. Appleyard, *Charles Parsons: his life and work* (1933) • J. L. E. D. [J. L. E. Dreyer], *Monthly Notices of the Royal Astronomical Society*, 69 (1908–9), 250–53 • J. J. [J. Joly], *PRS*, 83A (1909–10), xv–xix • O. Boeddicker, *The Observatory*, 31 (1908), 374–6 • *Nature*, 78 (1908), 448–9 • *Royal Irish Academy, Abstract of Minutes* (1908–9), 1, 8 • *The Times* (31 Aug 1908) • *The Times* (17 Dec 1908) • *Irish Times* (3 Sept 1908) • *Reminiscences and letters of Sir Robert Ball*, ed. W. V. Ball (1915) • Burke, *Peerage* • d. cert.

Archives Birr Castle, Offaly, corresp. and papers | CUL, corresp. with T. R. Robinson and G. Stokes • RAS, letters to RAS • TCD, letters to John Joly

Likenesses M. Rosse, group portrait, photograph, *c*.1854 (with his three brothers), repro. in D. H. Davison, *Impressions of an Irish countess: the photographs of Mary, countess of Rosse* (1989) • F. Sargent, pencil drawing, 1870–79, NPG [*see illus.*] • A. de Brie, oils, Birr Castle, Offaly • photograph, Birr Castle archives, Offaly • portrait, TCD • wood-engraving (after photograph by J. Hughes), NPG; repro. in *ILN* (7 Feb 1880)

Wealth at death £80,178 8*s*. 11*d*.: probate, 3 Dec 1908, *CGPLA Eng. & Wales* • £48,290 18*s*. 0*d*.—in England: Irish probate sealed in England, 14 Dec 1908, *CGPLA Eng. & Wales*

Parsons, Sir Lawrence, first baronet (*c*.**1637–1698**), landowner and local politician, was the eldest son of William Parsons (*d*. 1652) of Birr, King's county, and his wife, Dorothy, daughter of Sir Thomas Philips of Newtownlimavady, co. Londonderry. William was the son of Sir Lawrence Parsons, second baron of the Irish exchequer, and a nephew of Sir William Parsons, lord justice of Ireland. In the 1641 rebellion he served in the king's army as governor of Birr, which he held against attack from the confederate forces until he surrendered to General Preston on 20 January 1643. He later joined the parliamentarian army, became the quartermaster-general to General Poyntz, and played a crucial part in the battle of Rowton Heath on 24 September 1645. He died in 1652 from 'a petrifaction in one of his kidneys, which is said to have been completely converted into stone' (Cooke, 107). The kidney was donated to the museum of Trinity College, Dublin.

Lawrence Parsons succeeded to the estates at Birr on his father's death and after the Restoration served as a sheriff for King's county, commanded a militia troop at Birr, and sat on the commission responsible for the payment of arrears of pay to those officers who had served in the army of Charles I. He was created a baronet in 1677. He married Frances (*d.* 1701), youngest daughter of William Savage of Castle Rheban, co. Kildare.

Following the accession of James II in 1685, there was a radical shift of power away from the protestant landowning class. In April 1687 the situation was so altered that when Lady Parsons was accused of treason by an illiterate servant, Sir Lawrence took his family to the safety of England. Before leaving he appointed Hewar Oxburgh, who had worked for the family for thirty years, to collect his rents and run his affairs in his absence. When, contrary to his instructions, Oxburgh failed to send the rent he was collecting to England, Sir Lawrence left his family in Manchester and returned to Birr in April 1688. He found Oxburgh had been made the sheriff of King's county and the colonel of a regiment which had been paid for by the estate rents.

In February 1689, following a reign of terror in the county by a tory called Fannin who threatened to attack and burn Birr, Parsons allowed eighty local protestants to take refuge in Birr Castle. This in turn prompted Oxburgh to insist that the castle be garrisoned with men of his regiment. Parsons locked him out and Oxburgh ordered his men to undermine the walls. Realizing his position was hopeless, Parsons surrendered, was locked up, and was taken to the assizes at Philipstown (now Daingean) on 27 March 1689. Sir Henry Lynch directed the jury to find him guilty of high treason for keeping a garrison against King James, and sentenced him to death. Those convicted with him were shackled, 'but Sir Lawrence being lame with the gout, it was unnecessary to bolt him' (Cooke, 127). Parsons was further attainted as a traitor by King James's Dublin parliament in May 1689, and his estates were confiscated and conferred on Oxburgh, who sat in that parliament as a member for King's county.

Parsons was reprieved five times, but was held in the gaol at Birr with twelve others for thirteen months. In May 1690 he was taken to Dublin where it was hoped to exchange him for prisoners held by King William. In Dublin he contacted Patrick Sarsfield, whose intervention secured him bail on the condition that he live in the city with his solicitor.

Parsons was freed when Dublin fell to King William's troops after the battle of the Boyne (1 July 1690). He was made high sheriff of King's county and in early August travelled with a small party to Birr with supplies for the garrison that had recently been established there. Outside Birr on 11 August 1690 he survived an ambush in which his friend, Theobald Burke, was killed. Later that day Birr itself was threatened with attack by a larger Irish force which only withdrew on being given provisions by the townspeople. Parsons returned to Dublin on 2 September 1690, two weeks before Birr Castle was attacked by forces commanded by the duke of Berwick.

Parsons returned to Birr in December 1691 to find the town devastated by the garrison sent to defend it. He spent his last years petitioning for compensation and for the discharge of his debts to the crown, claiming that he had kept and defended Birr Castle for King William 'until he was forced by want of arms and ammunition to surrender' (Shaw, 316). He died in 1698 and was succeeded by his son, Sir William Parsons, who served as a captain of militia in 1690, and who represented King's county in every parliament except one from 1692 until his death in 1741.

PIERS WAUCHOPE

Sources T. L. Cooke, *The picture of Parsonstown* (1826) · MS account of the siege of Birr, Birr Castle, Rosse MSS, muniment room, summary list ref. A/24 · GEC, *Baronetage*, vol. 4 · *A further narrative of the late victory obtained by Colonel Points against his majesties forces near Chester* (1645) · *Calendar of the manuscripts of the marquess of Ormonde*, new ser., 8 vols., HMC, 36 (1902–20), vol. 3 · W. A. Shaw, ed., *Calendar of treasury books*, 12, PRO (1933) · *CSP dom., 1697* · *DNB*

Likenesses oils, *c.*1680, priv. coll.; repro. in W. B. Parsons, earl of Rosse, *Birr Castle* (1982)

Parsons, Lawrence, second earl of Rosse (1758–1841), politician, was born on 21 May 1758, the eldest son of Sir William Parsons, fourth baronet (1731–1791), landowner and politician, of Birr Castle, King's county, Ireland, and Mary Clere of Kilburry, co. Tipperary. He was admitted from Mr Warburton's school in Dublin to Trinity College, Dublin, in 1777; he graduated BA in 1780 and subsequently took the degrees of LLB (1783) and LLD (1790). He registered in Lincoln's Inn in 1782. As his attendance while a student at the gallery of the Irish House of Commons and his membership of the volunteer corps, founded at Birr in April 1776, suggests, Parsons was politically precocious. His sympathies were with the patriots, and he made his first noteworthy contribution in 1780 when he published what one well-placed commentator, probably Edward Cooke, the under-secretary at Dublin Castle, deemed 'a tolerable pamphlet' (NL Ire., MS 2098), entitled *Observations on the Irish Mutiny Bill*. The case Parsons made was not original, but the pamphlet served, along with his election in 1781 to the auditorship of the Trinity College Historical Society, to give him a high profile in the institution, and he was the preferred choice of 'the younger part' of the electorate of fellows and scholars when a by-election was called in July 1782 to return a member of parliament for the college constituency (Johnston, 197).

On entering the House of Commons, Parsons was drawn to Henry Flood's brand of radical patriotism, and the two men soon became fast friends. It was never a relationship of equals; Parsons was very much the student and Flood the mentor, but they were bound by mutual respect as well as by mutual need. Guided by Flood, Parsons joined

Lawrence Parsons, second earl of Rosse (1758–1841), by James Heath, pubd 1810 (after John Comerford)

with him at the beginning of the 1783–4 session in seeking to convince MPs to curb the accumulating national debt by cutting expenditure. He had few opportunities to impress in the Irish Commons for some years thereafter, as he spent most of the mid-1780s in England promoting Flood's efforts to secure a parliamentary seat at Westminster. Among other incidents, this involved Parsons acting as a go-between in an affair of honour in 1784, and standing with Flood as a candidate for the constituency of Seaford in 1785. Back in Ireland in the late 1780s Parsons took the same independent stance that Flood adopted at Westminster. He also continued to be guided by him, as instanced by the Regency crisis, when he memorably dismissed Henry Grattan's proposal that the Irish parliament should offer the prince of Wales a regency on terms different from those acceptable at Westminster as 'an idle gasconade which may alarm England and cannot by any possibility serve ourselves' (*The Parliamentary Register*, 9.121). The animus that Parsons directed at Grattan in their exchange on 3 March 1789, which nearly precipitated a duel between the two men, was personal as well as political. It partly reflected the antipathy with which Parsons (and Flood) regarded the politics of party and it ensured that he showed no disposition to join the Irish Whig Club, in which Grattan was a leading light, when it was formed to concert opposition activity in the wake of the Regency crisis.

As a result of his election in 1790 to represent King's county, and of the death in 1791 of Henry Flood and his father, following which he became fifth baronet, Parsons came into his own as an independent political voice. His instincts remained strongly disposed towards financial and constitutional reform, which won him the admiration of political radicals, including Wolfe Tone, outside parliament, but there were definite limits to his radicalism. These were manifest in 1793 when he recommended that the elective franchise should not be extended to any Catholic who was not possessed of a freehold of £20 per annum. This disposition to favour moderate over radical change was underlined in his pamphlet *Thoughts on Liberty and Equality* (1793), in which he argued against the egalitarian thrust of the French Revolution. However, despite his unease with the extent of the reforms being agitated, Parsons continued to act 'distinctly and independently' (Rosse MS F/21). His stand against the war with France during the 1794 session was looked upon with virtually as much disquiet by the leaders of the opposition as it was by Dublin Castle, but he persisted regardless. He maintained 'no connection with Lord Fitzwilliam's administration' but disapproved strongly of the lord lieutenant's precipitous recall (ibid., F/21). He opposed the introduction of the Insurrection Act in 1796 and contended that what he later described as 'the imbecillity of its operations' contributed to 'the progress of popular discontents' (ibid., F/19). Paradoxically, he contemplated a rapprochement with the administration in 1797 on the grounds that he should 'do more good' by 'consenting in general to co-operate with it' (ibid., D/2/6) than by opposing it, but upon the eve of the 1798 rising he offered a powerful plea in support of 'the adoption of such measures as would tend to conciliate the affection of the people to government' (ibid., F/21). Given his history of independent activity, it is hardly surprising that Lord Cornwallis's expectation that Parsons would support a legislative union that was based on 'fair and equitable principles' proved unfounded (*Correspondence of … Cornwallis*, 3.197). Parsons was among the most vocal opponents of the union and he proposed the crucial amendment to the address to the crown expunging the reference to a union that was carried by 109 votes to 104 on 24 January 1799.

Although Parsons was unable to prevent the ratification of the Act of Union, his stand on the issue improved his political profile. Moreover, it dovetailed with the accretion in political influence deriving from his marriage on 5 April 1797 to Alice Lloyd (1779–1867), daughter of John Lloyd and Jane Le Hunte, of Gloster, King's county, to ensure his election for King's county to the imperial parliament in 1801. Parallel with this, his wish to hold high office prompted a palpable moderation of his political viewpoint. Instead of the independent stand which he had adopted in the Irish parliament, he co-operated closely with the government at Westminster, and consequently he was made one of the lords of the Treasury in Ireland in March 1805. His absence from the Commons during the Fox–Grenville ministry did not enamour him to the ministry, but since it virtually coincided with the death of his father's half-brother, the first earl of Rosse, and his elevation to the peerage as second earl of Rosse on 20 April 1807, it did him no harm. Indeed, with ministerial support in 1809 he became a representative peer and resigned the Treasury lordship for the position of Irish postmaster-general. He spent twenty-two years in this office, and he proved an attentive and reforming postmaster.

Because he disliked travelling to London, Parsons seldom spoke in the House of Lords. When he did, his contributions were largely confined to economic and to religious matters. It was the latter, particularly, which displayed his mounting unease with the implications of the demand by Catholics for full admission to the political process. Convinced by the early 1820s that 'notions of aboriginal possession … as well as religion … are always working in the minds of the Catholics against the connection' (Redesdale MS T3030/13/3) with Great Britain, and that the level of agrarian violence in the country and the popularity of Pastorini's prophecies, the millenarian hopes promulgated by the Catholic bishop Charles Walmesley, did not preclude a repeat of the 'massacre of … 1641' (ibid., T3030/13/2), his outlook became increasingly reactionary. He was no less disturbed by the thought that Catholic emancipation would 'drive away the upper classes of Protestants' (ibid., T3030/13/3) but he did not publicly oppose it. He was more forthcoming in his opposition when O'Connell launched a campaign to repeal the Act of Union in 1830, and was profoundly disquieted by the Church Temporalities Act in 1833 (on which he made his last Lords speech) on the grounds that it represented a further attack on the power and position of Irish protestants.

Parsons devoted the final years of his life to the intellectual pursuits that, following the publication of his *Observations on the Bequest of Henry Flood* (1795) in defence of Flood's attempt to leave his estate to Trinity College, assumed a prominent place in his life. The presence in his personal papers of a variety of political memoirs, fragments towards a biography of Flood, poetry, and the publication in 1834 of *An Argument to Prove the Truth of Christian Religion* bear ample witness to his efforts and to his abilities. They also bear testament to the fact that he was a thoughtful, intelligent man whose personal political odyssey from reformism to conservatism was emblematic in so many ways of much of the protestant community of which he was a part. He died on 24 February 1841 in Brighton, Sussex, twenty-six years before his wife, and was succeeded as third earl of Rosse by his son William *Parsons (1800–1867), the celebrated astronomer. JAMES KELLY

Sources Birr Castle, Offaly, Rosse MSS • PRO NIre., Redesdale MSS, T 3030/13/1–7 • A. P. W. Malcomson, 'Sir Lawrence Parsons', *Offaly: history and society*, ed. T. O'Neill (1998) • N. D. Atkinson, 'Sir Lawrence Parsons, 2nd earl of Rosse, 1758–1841', PhD diss., University of Dublin, 1961 • E. M. Johnston, 'Members of the Irish parliament, 1784–7', *Proceedings of the Royal Irish Academy*, 71C (1971), 139–246 • *Correspondence of Charles, first Marquis Cornwallis*, ed. C. Ross, 3 vols. (1859) • J. Porter, P. Byrne, and W. Porter, eds., *The parliamentary register, or, History of the proceedings and debates of the House of Commons of Ireland, 1781–1797*, 17 vols. (1784–1801) • GEC, *Peerage* • A. Aspinall, 'Parsons, Sir Lawrence', HoP, *Commons, 1790–1820* • J. Kelly, *Henry Flood: patriots and politics in eighteenth-century Ireland* (1998) • R. B. McDowell, *The Irish administration, 1801–1914* (1964) • list of the Irish parliament, 1783, NL Ire., MS 2098 • *The manuscripts of J. B. Fortescue*, 10 vols., HMC, 30 (1892–1927), vol. 8 • *DNB* • Burtchaell & Sadleir, *Alum. Dubl.* • Burke, *Gen. Ire.* (1976)

Archives Birr Castle, Offaly, corresp. and papers | Balliol Oxf., letters to Alicia Conroy • BL, corresp. with Robert Peel, Add. MSS 40213–40346 • Glos. RO, Redesdale MSS • NRA, priv. coll., letters to Lord Lansdowne • Royal Irish Acad., Burrows MSS • U. Nott. L., letters to countess of Charleville

Likenesses J. Heath, stipple, pubd 1810 (after J. Comerford), BM, NPG [*see illus.*] • J. Heath, stipple, pubd 1810 (after J. Comerford), NG Ire. • portrait, Birr Castle, Offaly

Parsons, Sir Leonard Gregory (1879–1950), paediatrician, was born at Kidderminster, Worcestershire, on 25 November 1879, the son of Theophilus Lessie Parsons and his wife, Sarah, daughter of Timothy Sharpe, a farmer who migrated to the United States. Parsons came of a Worcestershire farming family and was devoted to Wesleyan Methodism. He grew up at Aston in a home in which devout living was inculcated through parental example, education was liberal, and hospitality generous. He attended the King Edward VI Grammar School for five years, where his enthusiasm for chemistry and rugby football were encouraged. In 1896 he entered Mason College, Birmingham, to study zoology; later he turned to medicine, winning many scholarships and acting for a time as a prosector of anatomy. He qualified MB BS (London) in 1905. During his university years he was involved with the Student Christian Movement and missionary activities. He also developed his talent as a shot and a sprinter and played tennis and rugby with great enthusiasm.

In 1908 Parsons married Ethel May (*d.* 1955), daughter of the Revd Dr John Gregory Mantle, a Wesleyan Methodist minister. He had known her since childhood. They had one son, who also became a paediatrician, and one daughter.

Parsons held junior hospital appointments at Birmingham and London and practised for a few years at Bromsgrove. His habit of self-criticism and inquiry, and an unusual skill with children, diverted him to paediatrics. Postgraduate training at the Hospital for Sick Children, Great Ormond Street, London, followed by his election to the staff of the Birmingham Children's Hospital as physician to out-patients in 1910, culminated in an active term of service as lecturer in diseases of children and paediatrics at the University of Birmingham. During the First World War Parsons served in Greece and Serbia and was appointed consulting physician to the Serbian army. In 1917 he received the order of St Sava.

During the post-war years Parsons established himself as a kindly, diligent doctor. He was greatly in demand as a consultant and personal attendant to doctors throughout the midlands and his appointment in 1928 as first professor of child health in the University of Birmingham came as no surprise. The following year he was elected subdean of the medical faculty. New buildings and equipment were added to the Children's Hospital as Parsons's fame grew and research workers flocked to his busy clinic. His personal influence in Birmingham was such that by 1930 he was able to gather together representatives from various hospitals, the university, and the city council in an active campaign for the prevention of children's diseases; despite serious interruption with the outbreak of war in 1939 this great project resulted in the opening of the Leonard Parsons infants' block at the Children's Hospital in October 1945 and the establishment of the Institute of Child Health in that year. The outbreak of war also saw Parsons appointed group officer for the Emergency Medical Service in Birmingham. All through these years, too, Parsons served his university and medical school in many capacities. He supported the hospitals centre plan, from which came the fine medical centre at Edgbaston; and he discharged carefully his administrative responsibilities, which were considerable after he was appointed dean of the medical faculty in 1941. Yet he found time for all who sought his advice on medical education, child welfare, or the practice or problems of post-war medicine. He retired from his professorship in 1946.

Parsons was elected FRCP in 1923, he was knighted in 1946 for his work for children during the war, and in 1948 he was elected FRS for investigations into child health and the wasting disorders of children. He lectured widely, served as president of many conferences and scientific associations, and received the honorary fellowship of numerous societies for the study of children's diseases. Parsons was a physician who combined great clinical acumen and original talent for scientific investigation with an eminently practical outlook on everyday affairs. He left his mark on medical affairs in Birmingham, while the medical research conducted in his laboratory brought it an international reputation. By means of painstaking chemical and clinical studies of the blood of children, his team tracked down the origin of a serious type of jaundice in the newborn infant, which he proved to result from excessive destruction of the red corpuscles and the consequent stimulation of production of new blood cells in various regions of the body. A serious wasting disease of infants was shown to set up complicated symptoms because fats and vitamin D are absorbed with difficulty from the intestines. Parsons also added significantly to our knowledge of rickets, which through the emphasis he placed upon environment and diet he did much to prevent and cure. Finally, he brought clarity to paediatrics by stressing the importance of antenatal factors. He saw clearly that deficient diet for, or infection of, the mother might well result in serious disability of the child. By his insistence on the need for quantitative chemical investigation of problems often enough dismissed as peculiar to the child, Parsons greatly helped to raise paediatrics to a high scientific level and opened up hitherto unrealized fields of investigation. Together with Seymour Barling he wrote *Diseases of Infancy and Childhood* (1933).

A simple, rather shy man, Parsons had a quick sense of humour and delighted in the company of a wide circle of friends. He was a devout Methodist who read his Bible morning and evening, neither smoked nor drank alcohol, and attended chapel with great regularity. It was shortly after returning to his home, Hillfield, Wentworth Road, Four Oaks, Warwickshire, from the morning service at the Four Oaks Methodist chapel that he died suddenly from cerebral haemorrhage on 17 December 1950.

G. R. CAMERON, *rev.* MICHAEL BEVAN

Sources G. R. Cameron, *Obits. FRS*, 7 (1950–51), 453–67 · J. Peel, *The lives of the fellows of the Royal College of Obstetricians and Gynaecologists, 1929–1969* (1976), 302–3 · *The Lancet* (30 Dec 1950), 936–7 · *BMJ* (30 Dec 1950), 1498–500 · *CGPLA Eng. & Wales* (1951)

Likenesses W. Stoneman, photograph, 1946, NPG · photograph, repro. in *The Lancet* · photograph, repro. in *BMJ*

Wealth at death £33,838 18*s*. 3*d*.: probate, 12 June 1951, *CGPLA Eng. & Wales*

Parsons [*née* Millo], **Marguerite Lena** [Daisy] **(1890–1957)**, suffragette, was born at 64 High Street, Poplar, London, on 21 May 1890, the daughter of Alfred Albert Millo, a dealer in jewellery, and his wife, Emily Elizabeth, *née* Moxley. Her father was in poor health, and her mother worked as a charlady to help make ends meet. After leaving school at twelve, Daisy did housework for neighbours and looked after her younger brothers before getting a job as a cigarette packer at a factory in Aldgate. The work was sweated labour: for packing 1000 cigarettes she was paid 3*d*. On some days she earned less than 1*s*. She noticed how male workers, with trade unions to back them and with the power conferred by the parliamentary franchise, enjoyed superior working conditions and privileges. She married Robert Stanley (Tom) Parsons, a fitter and driver in a powerhouse, and by 1914 they had three daughters, as well as bringing up an orphaned niece. As a mother she experienced one effect of women's being denied full citizenship. Objecting to compulsory vaccination, she applied to a magistrate for an exemption order for her eldest child and was told by the magistrate that the father alone was empowered to make such an application; mothers had no say in such matters directly affecting the upbringing of their children.

Daisy Parsons became a local organizer of the East London Federation of Suffragettes, founded in 1913 by Sylvia Pankhurst to involve the working women of the East End in the women's suffrage cause. Living at 94 Ravenscroft Road, Canning Town (her home until her death), Parsons was honorary secretary of the South West Ham district of the federation. She came to prominence as a member of a deputation of six working women from the East End, led by Julia Scurr, whom the prime minister, H. H. Asquith, agreed to meet at 10 Downing Street on 20 June 1914, following a protest in the House of Commons by Sylvia Pankhurst, who had threatened to continue her hunger strike unless the deputation was given a hearing. Addressing the prime minister in support of the suffrage demand, Parsons cited her own experiences as a working mother. 'We feel that it is an insult to us. When we bring children into the world we at least should be able to say what is good for them' (Bodl. Oxf., Asquith MS 89, fol. 143). At the outbreak of war she took charge of a baby clinic founded by the federation in response to the extra wartime hardships faced by mothers.

In 1922 Parsons was elected a member of West Ham borough council, having been involved in Will Thorne's

National Socialist Party, a splinter group of the Social Democratic Federation, which had taken a patriotic line in relation to the war. She had been co-opted in 1919 as a member of the council's recently established maternity and child welfare committee, which among other things distributed milk to expectant and nursing mothers. Politically she combined an assertion of women's rights of citizenship as mothers and workers with a strong sense of working-class identity, and the right of all to have decent homes and a healthy environment in which to bring up children. She stressed the importance of the domestic sphere, extolling the virtues of housework which she believed, from her own early working life, to be preferable to the exploitation which women endured in factory labour. An alderman of West Ham from 1935, she was the first woman mayor of West Ham (1936–7). In her year of office she was depicted cheerfully vacuuming a carpet in an advertisement by the municipal electricity supplier showing the benefits of electricity to housewives. Among her other public engagements as mayor, she drove the first trolleybus in the borough from its depot and opened the Beckton Lido. During the Second World War she chaired the education committee which oversaw the evacuation of children from the borough. As a local politician she was remembered for ‘her solid support for the people and the fact that she was always most outspoken and there when needed’ (Bloch, 109). In 1951 she was awarded an MBE for her public service. Parsons died, survived by her husband, at Queen Mary's Hospital, Stratford, on 29 September 1957. TIM WALES

Sources *Woman's Dreadnought* (27 June 1914) • R. Taylor, *In letters of gold: the story of Sylvia Pankhurst and the East London Federation of the Suffragettes in Bow* (1993) • E. Crawford, *The women's suffrage movement: a reference guide, 1866–1928* (1999) • *West Ham, 1886–1986* (1986) • J. Marriott, *The culture of labourism: the East End between the wars* (1991) • b. cert. • d. cert. • F. Primrose Stevenson's notes of the deputation to Asquith from the East London Federation of Suffragettes, 20 June 1914, Bodl. Oxf., MS Asquith 89, fols. 128 ff. • H. Bloch, ed., *Canning Town voices* (1998) • H. Bloch and N. Harris, eds., *Canning Town* (1994) • *Annual Report* [East London Federation of Suffragettes], 1 (1914–15)

Archives Newham Archive and Local Studies Library, London, corresp., photographs, and cuttings

Likenesses cartoon, 1936, West Ham Electricity Department; repro. in Bloch and Harris, eds., *Canning Town*, 106 • N. Smyth, group portrait, photograph, repro. in Taylor, *In letters of gold*, 14

Wealth at death £481 6*s*. 11*d*.: probate, 7 Jan 1958, *CGPLA Eng. & Wales*

Parsons [*née* Field], **Mary, countess of Rosse** (1813–1885), photographer, was born on 21 July 1813 at Heaton Hall, Bradford, the elder daughter of John Wilmer Field (1775–1837), landowner, and his first wife, Ann Wharton-Myddleton (*d*. 1815). She and her younger sister, Delia, were educated at home by their governess, Susan Lawson, who is reputed to have encouraged Mary's inquiring mind and wide-ranging interests. After 1827 the family spent most of the year at the London house in Hanover Square. On 14 April 1836 she married William *Parsons, Lord Oxmantown (1800–1867), who, on the death of his father in 1841, became third earl of Rosse and inherited his family estates and Birr Castle, King's county. The first of her eleven children, a daughter, was born in 1839, but only four sons, Laurence *Parsons (1840–1908), Randal (1848–1936), Clere (1851–1923), and Charles *Parsons (1854–1931), survived beyond childhood.

Mary Parsons's marriage settlement and substantial inheritance enabled her to pursue her scientific and artistic interests and to participate in those of her husband, who was president of the Royal Society (1849–54) and a commissioner for the Great Exhibition of 1851. She is said to have mastered sufficient astronomy to assist him with calculations, and supported him practically and financially in the construction of his giant telescope, completed in 1845. This was to feature repeatedly in some of her most successful and evocative photographs, one of which, *Mouth of the Great Rosse Telescope at Parsonstown*, was reproduced as the engraved frontispiece to *Curiosities of Science* (1858). Others, such as *Lord Rosse's Three-Foot Telescope* (Castle Ward album) and the various stereoscopic images of the early 1860s, were more technically informative and were reproduced in *Philosophical Transactions of the Royal Society* (1861) and exhibited at the Dublin International Exhibition of 1865.

Early in 1854 Lady Rosse took her first photographs, initially using the waxed paper process and then working extensively with collodion, which she applied to portraiture, photographing both notable figures, such as the mathematician and astronomer Sir Thomas Romney Robinson, and finely composed informal groups of her family and friends, images that are paralleled in the photography of the ladies Nevill at Eridge Park, Kent, and the early work of Lady Hawarden at Dundrum in neighbouring co. Tipperary, in common with whom she used shadow as a compositional element. She was proposed as a member of the Dublin Photographic Society (later the Photographic Society of Ireland) in November 1856 and in 1859 was awarded the society medal for the best paper negative. From the grounds of Birr, she created picturesque views of the castle, the River Camor, and the town of Birr: the sort of images she might have contributed to the Amateur Photographic Association of which she became a member in 1863. She experimented too with photography from the yacht *Titania*, which the family chartered for seven years.

Lady Rosse was a woman with great energy and determination. In a successful attempt to alleviate local poverty during the Irish potato famine of 1845, she initiated extensive work to provide local employment; in collaboration with her uncle Richard Wharton-Myddleton she redesigned and organized the rebuilding of the castle demesne. Subsequently she built a nursery wing, a stable block, gatehouse, and entrance gate. She was also responsible for the design and on-site manufacture of cast-iron and bronze gates, with heraldic embellishment to the keep gates. She recorded the new building photographically and frequently used the arch of the keep gate as a background for group portraits. Her design ability is also evidenced by a massive oak armorial sideboard, a Gothic bedroom suite, and a Gothic monument to the memory of her father in St Paul's Church, Shipley.

Early portraits of Mary Parsons portray her as a slim, elegant, dark-haired woman; later she appears more formidable, but seldom without a smile. She excelled as a hostess, was devoted to her sons, and played a major part in their upbringing and education. After the death of her husband in 1867, she left Birr to spend the rest of her life at 10 Connaught Place, London. Always an independent woman, she maintained interests in her Heaton and Shipley estates and in global investments, particularly railway stock. She died on 22 July 1885 in her London home, and was buried at Birr. Many of her photographs are in the collection of the Birr Scientific Foundation, Offaly.

CAROLYN BLOORE

Sources D. H. Davison, *Impressions of an Irish countess: the photographs of Mary, countess of Rosse* (1989) • W. Cudworth, *Mannington, Heaton and Allerton, townships of Bradford* (1896) • H. Hind, *Bradford remembrancer* (1972) • T. R. R., *PRS*, 16 (1867–8), xxxvi–xlii [obit. of William Parsons, 3rd earl of Rosse] • C. W. Foster and J. J. Green, *History of the Wilmer family* (1888) • *Photographic Journal*, 5 (1858–9), 96–7 • *Photographic Journal*, 8 (1862–4), 263–4 • *Photographic Notes* [15 Sept], 220 • L. Walker, *Drawing on diversity: women, architecture and practice* (1997) • D. H. Davison, '10. Mary, countess of Rosse: pioneer photographer', *Some more people and places in Irish technology* (1990), 28–9 • J. Timbs, *Curiosities of science* (1858) • W. Parsons, third earl of Rosse, 'On the construction of specula of six-feet aperture', *PTRS*, 151 (1861), 681–745 • vault, Birr Castle, Offaly, Ireland • stained-glass windows, St Barnabas, Heaton • christening register, Bradford parish church cathedral • private information (2004)

Archives Birr Castle, Offaly, MSS | Castle Ward, scrapbook

Likenesses watercolour, *c*.1836, Birr Castle, Offaly • silhouette, *c*.1840, Birr Castle, Offaly • S. C. Smith, oils, *c*.1850, Birr Castle, Offaly • M. K. Ward, watercolour, 1851, Castle Ward, co. Down • attrib. W. P. Parsons, collodion photograph, *c*.1856, Birr Castle, Offaly • carte-de-visite, after 1860–1869, Castle Ward, co. Down

Wealth at death £25,229 7*s*. 5*d*.; annual income of Heaton and Shipley estates £3000: Rosse MSS, G19, Birr Castle, Offaly

Parsons, Philip (1594–1653), college head, was born in December 1594 in London; his parents are unknown. Educated at Merchant Taylors' School, London, from 1607 to 1610, he was elected probationary fellow of St John's College, Oxford (matriculating on 26 June 1610), graduated BA on 6 June 1614, and proceeded MA on 9 May 1618 (incorporated at Cambridge in 1622). He dedicated his Arcadian comedy in Latin, *Atalanta* (BL, Harley MS 6924), to William Laud, the college president. Unsuccessful in the 1624 proctorship election—'the greatest canvas (as 'twas thought) in the memory of Man' (Wood, *Ath. Oxon.*, 1.227)—Parsons went to Padua for his MD (incorporated at Oxford on 20 June 1628), and back in England professed 'our true Religion' before parliament on 2 April 1628 (*JHC*, 1.878). A letter to a patient on the stone—'your tormenting Inmate'—is interesting evidence of his medical practice (Bodl. Oxf., MS Tanner 314, fol. 73*r*).

On 15 April 1633 Parsons was admitted, on Laud's nomination, as principal of Hart Hall. On 6 January 1634 he married Elizabeth Langley at St Peter-in-the-East, Oxford. Latin poems by Parsons appear in Oxford's anthologies *Solis Britannici perigaeum* (1633) and *Coronae Carolinae quadratura* (1636). He was a delegate providing for Sir John Byron's troops in Oxford in August and September 1642; another delegacy met at his lodgings in November 1647 to direct those called before the parliamentary visitors. For whatever reason, Parsons did not appear before the visitors. On 3 March 1649 he was to be summoned before the committee for the advance of money to answer for Hart Hall's unpaid rent. Parsons died on 1 May 1653 and was buried at Great Barrington church, Gloucestershire. Letters of administration were granted to his widow on 28 January 1654.

HUGH DE QUEHEN

Sources S. G. Hamilton, *Hertford College* (1903) • Foster, *Alum. Oxon.* • Mrs E. P. Hart, ed., *Merchant Taylors' School register, 1561–1934*, 2 (1936) • Wood, *Ath. Oxon.*, 2nd edn • F. Madan, *Oxford literature, 1450–1640, and 1641–1650* (1912), vol. 2 of *Oxford books: a bibliography of printed works* (1895–1931); repr. (1964) • Venn, *Alum. Cant.* • transcript of marriage register of St Peter-in-the-East, Oxford, Society of Genealogists • parish register, Great Barrington, Glos. RO • M. A. E. Green, ed., *Calendar of the proceedings of the committee for advance of money, 1642–1656*, 1, PRO (1888) • admon., PRO, PROB 6/29, fol. 280v

Parsons, Philip (1729–1812), Church of England clergyman and schoolmaster, was born at Dedham, Essex, the son of William Parsons, an attorney of Dedham who originated from Hadleigh, Suffolk, and his wife, whose maiden name was Smythies. His father died when Parsons was young and he was brought up by his grandmother. He was educated at Lavenham grammar school, under his maternal uncle the Revd Thomas Smythies, and matriculated from Sidney Sussex College, Cambridge, in 1748; he graduated BA in 1752, as third junior optime, and proceeded MA in 1776. Having been ordained deacon on 23 February 1752 and priest on 24 March 1754, he worked as usher at Oakham grammar school. He left in 1761, on being presented by Lord Winchilsea to the mastership of Wye College, Kent, and the perpetual curacy of Wye. It is thought that his *jeu d'esprit* 'On advertising for curates', which was published in *The World* in 1756, brought him to Winchilsea's attention. Parsons founded a Sunday school at Wye and helped to establish others elsewhere in the county by preaching and publishing on the subject.

In 1775 Parsons was presented to the rectory of Eastwell, Kent, by Winchilsea and to the rectory of Snave, also in Kent, by Frederick Cornwallis, archbishop of Canterbury, in the following year. He also served as domestic chaplain to Lewis Thomas Monson, Baron Sondes. He continued to live in Wye, from where he published a variety of serious and humorous works; they included a treatise on the heat and light of planets and a collection of essays and letters. His principal publication was *Monuments and painted glass in upwards of one hundred churches, chiefly in the eastern part of Kent* (1794), to which he added an appendix on three other churches that were well known to him: Hadleigh, Lavenham, and Dedham. Many copies of this work were destroyed in the disastrous fire at Nichols's printing office in 1808.

Parsons was married and had several children, only two of whom, Robert and Philip, are mentioned in his will. Blind and in considerable pain in his last months, he died at Wye College on 12 June 1812.

GORDON GOODWIN, *rev.* S. J. SKEDD

Sources *GM*, 1st ser., 88/1 (1812), 671; 88/2 (1812), 291–2 • Venn, *Alum. Cant.* • J. R. Smith, *Bibliotheca Cantiana: a bibliographical account of what has been published on the history, topography, antiquities, customs,* *and family history, of the county of Kent* (1837) • will, PRO, PROB 11/1536, sig. 392

Parsons, Richard (1641/2–1711), ecclesiastical judge and antiquary, was born at Birchanger, Essex, the son of William Parsons (1599x1604–1671). William Parsons was a scholar of Winchester College from 1614, and a fellow of New College, Oxford, from 1622, graduating BCL in 1629. William was rector of Birchanger from 1641. During the civil war he escaped deprivation, despite continuing to read the Book of Common Prayer, but was gaoled for nineteen weeks at Cambridge. At the Restoration he became a prebendary of Chichester and acquired the Essex livings of Lambourne and Dunmow.

In 1654 Richard Parsons was elected, at the age of twelve, to a scholarship at Winchester College, as founder's kin, succeeding to a fellowship at New College, Oxford, in 1659 and matriculating on 25 October of the same year. He vacated his fellowship in 1665. He graduated BCL on 8 April 1665 and was created DCL on 25 June 1687. Late in 1670 or in 1671 he married Mary Izod. After she died of a fever on 26 October 1690 Parsons remarried, becoming the third husband of Susanna, the daughter of Sir Edward Bathurst of Lechlade. He became vicar of Driffield, Gloucestershire, in 1674. In 1677 he became chancellor of the diocese of Gloucester (as also of the two peculiars of Withington and Bibury and acting as a surrogate in the archdeacon of Gloucester's court). He served both as vicar and chancellor until his death, and it seems, also acted as JP.

As chancellor Parsons presided over the consistory court and conducted annual diocesan visitations. Responsible for the preservation of good order and orthodoxy within the diocese he made his mark as a stern suppresser of dissent, a duty which he may have exercised with all the more vigour from memories of the treatment of his father. He deployed his power behind the tory Anglicans of Tewkesbury in their struggle with their questionably conformable minister, Francis Wells. According to Edmund Calamy, when another precariously conforming clergyman, Nicholas Billingsley, preached a visitation sermon criticizing the lives of the clergy Parsons plucked him by the hair in the open street, calling him a rogue and threatening to bind him over. The life of the Quaker John Roberts recalled a similar example of Parsons's anger, when the chancellor broke in on a meeting of Quakers gaoled in Gloucester Castle and grabbed the man by the hair and tried to stop his mouth. The control that Parsons exercised over the church courts also raised controversy. Thomas Hyde, the absentee archdeacon of Gloucester, twice wrote to Archbishop Sancroft alleging that Parsons had taken bribes and complaining about his ruthless domination of the church courts at Gloucester. In 1695 Parsons's hardline attitude towards religious dissent and his reputation for corruption came together and brought him before the court of exchequer when a bill was laid against him for having laid unduly heavy fines on dissenters which he had then retained in 1678, 1681, 1683, and 1685.

During his professional rounds of Gloucester, Parsons, encouraged by Sancroft's chaplain Henry Wharton, compiled extensive notes for an intended history of the cathedral and diocese. Ill health prevented Parsons from writing this, but he did send information about Gloucestershire to Edmund Gibson for the latter's new edition of William Camden's *Britannia* (1695). His notes were also made use of, though with little acknowledgement, by Sir Robert Atkyns in his *Ancient and Present State of Glostershire* (1712). Parsons's court records survive in the Gloucestershire Record Office. A large volume of notes for his intended history (another volume is now lost) passed after his death into the possession of Jonathan Colley, chaplain and chanter of Christ Church, Oxford, thence into the library of Peter Le Neve, and in 1729 into that of Thomas Martin of Palgrave. It was sold in 1730 to Richard Rawlinson, and so came into the possession of the Bodleian Library in 1755 (Bodl. Oxf., MS Rawl. B. 323). A manuscript by Parsons concerning impropriations in Gloucestershire, dated 8 July 1704, is in the British Library (BL, Lansdowne MS 989, fols. 38–9).

Parsons died on 12 June 1711 at his home, the Common Kitchen, in Gloucester Cathedral Close, and was buried two days later in the family vault which he had had made in the lady chapel of Gloucester Cathedral. Already buried there were his first wife, Mary; two sons, Robert (1674–1676) and Thomas (1685–1689); and three daughters, Anne (1679–1707), Mary (1672–1698), who married William Bayly of Frethern Lodge in 1694, and Honour (baptized in January 1677 and died in London in 1693). The only children to outlive both Richard and Mary were Jane, baptized in March 1681, and Richard, baptized in May 1683, a scholar of Winchester College from 1695 until, in 1704, he followed his father and grandfather to New College. They and his second wife, Susanna, were the beneficiaries of his will, proved on 7 September 1711; Jane was appointed sole executor. A new lease of Parsons's house in the Cathedral Close (now 3 Millers Green), where much of his business had been carried out, was granted to Jane in 1715.

SUZANNE EWARD

Sources Gloucester Cathedral chapter act book 1, 1616–87, Gloucester Cathedral Library • Gloucester Cathedral chapter act book 2, 1688–1739, Gloucester Cathedral Library • Gloucester Cathedral register of baptisms, marriages, and burials, 1661–1717, Gloucester Cathedral Library, MS 37 • 'A register of the dean and chapter of Gloucester beginning at Michaelmas 1672: and containing the severall leases set by the church since that time', [1672–1776], Gloucester Cathedral Library, D936 E 16 • list of benefactors to the library of the College (King's) School, Gloucester, 1686–1712, Gloucester Cathedral Library, MS 206 • Hockaday abstracts, Glos. RO, Gloucester diocese • will, Glos. RO • 'A parochiall visitation of the diocesse of Gloucester', Bodl. Oxf., MS Rawl. B. 323 (SC 11662) • Foster, *Alum. Oxon.* • Wood, *Ath. Oxon.*, 2nd edn, 2/1.990; 2/2.132, 230 • T. F. Kirby, *Winchester scholars: a list of the wardens, fellows, and scholars of … Winchester College* (1888) • I. Gray, *Antiquaries of Gloucestershire and Bristol* (1981) • *DNB* • D. Roberts, *Some memoirs of the life of John Roberts* (1747) • E. Calamy, ed., *An abridgement of Mr. Baxter's history of his life and times, with an account of the ministers, &c., who were ejected after the Restauration of King Charles II*, 2nd edn, 2 vols. (1713), vol. 2, p. 358 • D. Beaver, 'Conscience and context: the Popish Plot and the politics of ritual, 1678–1682', *HJ*, 34 (1991), 297–327

Archives BL, Lansdowne MS 989, fols. 38–9 • Bodl. Oxf., letters to Antony Wood

Wealth at death see will, 21 Oct 1707, proved 7 Sep 1711

Parsons, Richard Godfrey (1882–1948), bishop of Hereford, was born at Pendleton, Lancashire, on 12 November 1882, the only son of William Parsons, merchant, of Calcutta, who became secretary of the Bengal chamber of commerce, and his wife, Bertha Best, of Thetford, Norfolk. Educated at Durham School (1895–1901), he became in 1901 a demy of Magdalen College, Oxford, obtaining in 1903 a second class in honour moderations and in 1905 and 1906 first-class honours in *literae humaniores* and theology, and being elected to a Liddon studentship. Postgraduate work in Germany was followed by residence at the deanery, Westminster, as the pupil of the dean, J. Armitage Robinson, and at Cuddesdon College.

Ordained deacon and priest at London in 1907, with a curacy at Hampstead parish church, Parsons returned to Oxford the same year as fellow, praelector, and chaplain of University College. There he showed the combination of his intellectual command of theological matters and his desire for reform, and he 'dabbled with modernism' (Stephenson, 89). In 1911 he was made principal of Wells Theological College, and in 1912 was associated with B. H. Streeter, William Temple, and others in the publication of *Foundations*, a book on liberal theology which at the time made a considerable stir, and in which Parsons was one of the joint authors of an essay, 'The interpretation of the Christ in the New Testament'. In 1912 he married Dorothy (*d.* 1953), only daughter of Francis Gales Streeter, of Littlehampton, Sussex. They had two sons, the elder of whom died of wounds in Egypt in 1942.

The war had by 1916 practically emptied the college at Wells, and in 1916–17 Parsons served as a temporary chaplain to the forces in London. In 1916 he became vicar of Poynton, Cheshire, and in 1919 rector of Birch in Rusholme, near Manchester. He combined with his parish activities teaching and organizing work for the University of Manchester, in which in 1929 he became dean of the faculty of theology. He had in 1924 taken the degree of DD at Oxford. In collaboration with A. S. Peake he prepared for publication and saw through the press the English edition of *An Outline of Christianity* (1926), a work in five volumes originally planned and produced in America.

Consecrated in 1927 as suffragan bishop of Middleton, Parsons combined this with his other commitments until 1931, when he became residentiary canon and subdean of Manchester. In 1932 Parsons became bishop of Southwark, one of the heaviest and most arduous dioceses in England. Although intellectually extremely able, he had his greatest satisfaction perhaps as a 'grass-roots' churchman given to working for the needy of a parish rather than to great oratory. This came to the fore in his new south London diocese, with large numbers of the poorer working class, and particularly during the winter of 1940 when the diocese suffered heavy bombardment from the air. Parsons's efforts and the strain of this time told on his health. He became bishop of Hereford in 1941. There he remained, and contributed more broadly to church matters, particularly in the immediate post-war years. He paid visits to Romania and Yugoslavia; he acted as chairman in 1947 of an inter-church conference between theologians of the Anglican church and theologians from Denmark and Iceland. He was described in his obituary in *The Times* as 'no merely academic scholar, but a man of wide outlook in public affairs and with a lively interest in housing and kindred social questions'. He also had a 'passionate' desire to see Christianity applied to corporate, and state, conduct. He was made an honorary fellow of University College, Oxford, in 1942 and an honorary DD of the John Hus faculty at Prague in 1946. He died at the General Hospital, Hereford, on 26 December 1948 and was cremated at Cheltenham on 30 December.

A. E. J. Rawlinson, *rev.* Marc Brodie

Sources *The Times* (28 Dec 1948) • *The Times* (31 Dec 1948) • A. M. G. Stephenson, *The rise and decline of English modernism* (1984) • *WWW* • personal knowledge (1959) • [C. S. Earle and L. A. Body], eds., *A register of Durham School from January 1840, to December, 1907: with some entrances before 1840: and a list of king's scholars from AD 1558* (privately printed, Durham, [1908]) • *CGPLA Eng. & Wales* (1949)

Archives LPL, autobiographical notes and papers | BL, corresp. with Albert Mansbridge, Add. MS 65254 • Lancs. RO, letters to T. H. Floyd

Likenesses W. Stoneman, two photographs, 1940–45, NPG • T. B. Gibbs, oils, 1942, bishop's palace, Hereford • photograph, NPG

Wealth at death £2326 7s. 1d.: probate, 29 June 1949, *CGPLA Eng. & Wales*

Parsons, Robert (*c.*1535–1572), musician and composer, is of unknown parentage. An upbringing in the music of the church may be presumed, and all known details of his adult career associate him with the Chapel Royal. At both Michaelmas and Christmas 1560 he was authorized by Richard Bower, master of the choristers of the Chapel Royal, to report to the exchequer to collect the quarterly allowance due for the maintenance of the choirboys. His immediate predecessor in this function, Richard Needham, had borne the title of usher to the children, indicating that he held some unestablished post as assistant to the elderly Bower in training and looking after the boys. In every likelihood Parsons had already been Needham's junior colleague for some time, and he succeeded to the latter's responsibilities when he departed, apparently early in 1560, to become master of the choristers at St George's Chapel, Windsor.

Parsons's association with the Chapel Royal continued until a more permanent position became available with the appearance of a vacancy suitable for his voice among the singing-men. On 17 October 1563 he was appointed to the junior position of epistoler, and on 8 January 1564 to the full office of gentleman, which thereafter he occupied for the rest of his life. His services to the Chapel Royal were recognized by his receipt on 30 May 1567 of reversions to crown leases of three Lincolnshire rectories. By November 1571 he was married to Helen (*d.* in or after 1572), with a house at Greenwich.

Slightly younger than William Mundy and Robert White, Parsons completed with them the generation of major composers immediately preceding William Byrd, on whose early music Parsons's influence can occasionally be detected. Among his Latin vocal works, the *alternatim*

Magnificat for six voices is fully liturgical and extremely elaborate. Engaging extended examples of canon and much sonorous division of the constituent voices, it is a young man's showpiece of compositional dexterity, distinguished especially by its assurance in contrapuntal technique. Also for the Catholic liturgy, and likewise for a large six-voice choir such as that of Mary I's Chapel Royal, is the *alternatim* hymn 'Iam Christus astra ascenderat'.

Parsons's subsequent composition for the Elizabethan liturgy, extending to two extant vernacular anthems, the seven movements of the First Service, and another service now fragmentary, reflects the conditions obtaining in the Chapel Royal in the first few years of the new reign. The conception underlying the seven-voice First Service is as grand as that informing the Magnificat, but more compressed in execution through taming of the use of melisma (a group of notes sung to a single syllable) in the interests of comprehensibility of the words. Its supply of music for morning prayer, ante-communion, and evening prayer on a great festival takes its texts from the 1549 prayer book, and appears certain to have been composed in the opening months of Elizabeth's reign when the restoration of that prayer book was still her preferred choice. Of the anthems, the six-voice 'Deliver me from mine enemies' engages canon two-in-one throughout and achieves a monumental grandeur that rendered it one of the most frequently copied anthems of its period.

Parsons's remaining Latin vocal music is non-ecclesiastical. Among those trained in the traditions of composition for the Latin rite, only the most fervent convert would cease to compose in its successor styles when the national church became protestant, and, writing in 1597, Thomas Morley included Parsons in a list of composers who surreptitiously, he suggested, owed their skill to their preservation of Catholic values. Elizabeth's own injunctions effectively precluded the use of Latin music in the Chapel Royal after June 1559, so performances now could only be domestic. Parsons set as through-composed motets three texts associated with the Latin burial service and matins of the dead; the motivation for their composition is unknown. More conventional in their choice of text for items of domestic devotional music in Latin were the two psalms 'Domine, quis habitabit' and the rather old-fashioned 'Retribue servo tuo', and two prayers, 'O bone Iesu' (setting the 'Verses of St Bernard' found in pre-Reformation primers) and the striking and now very popular 'Ave Maria'. The winsomeness of the last of these owes much to its adoption of a texture commonly associated with the early consort song, its highest voice articulating an affectingly simple melody above a busy contrapuntal accompaniment.

Most of Parsons's vocal composition exhibits a characteristically English spaciousness animated and propelled by controlled use of suspended and passing dissonance. This, coupled with a profusion of imitative points framed to the natural rhythm (though in no way to the meaning) of the words, generates a fluidity of sonority and invention which compensates amply for the prevailing absence of harmonic experimentation, and also of flexibility in the pulse of the harmonic rhythm, that may be found in the music of John Sheppard and Thomas Tallis.

As befitted a court musician, Parsons produced a considerable body of instrumental works for viols. He contributed particularly to the emancipation of instrumental style from its vocal origins, the fantasias entitled 'De la court' and 'The Songe called Trumpetts' generating a vigour of expression genuinely instrumental in character. Parsons contributed at the same time to expansion in the conventions of the In nomine. His four or five consort songs for solo voice and viols include examples apparently written for performance in the course of the plays intermittently acted by the Chapel Royal boys for the entertainment of the queen. 'Pour down, ye powers divine', from a play entitled *Pandolpho*, makes a poignant response to the words that elevates it to a position among the finest of its kind.

On 25 January 1572 Parsons drowned in the River Trent at Newark, leaving a widow, Helen, but no known children. In all likelihood the occasion of his journey had been to recruit choristers for the Chapel Royal from the town's still thriving parish church choir, and to take seisin of two of his rectories due to lapse to him on 24 February. The anthologist Robert Dow presently composed these hexameters to lament his early death:

> Qui tantus primo Parsone in flore fuisti,
> Quantus in autumno ni morerere fores.
> ('Parsons, you who were so great in your first flourishing, how great you would be in your autumn, had you not died.')

Roger Bowers

Sources *Robert Parsons: Latin sacred music*, ed. P. Doe, Early English Church Music, 40 (1994) • A. Ashbee, ed., *Records of English court music*, 9 vols. (1986–96), vols. 6–8 • P. Phillips, 'Broadening horizons: Robert Parsons's *O bone Iesu*', *MT*, 139 (1998), 18–23 • P. Oboussier, 'Parsons, Robert (i)', *New Grove*, 2nd edn • P. Brett, ed., *Consort songs*, 2nd edn, Musica Britannica, 22 (1974), 9–10 • P. Doe, ed., *Elizabethan consort music*, 1, Musica Britannica, 44 (1979), nos. 20, 32, 33, 56, 62, 106, 136, 148, 150

Parsons, Robert. *See* Persons, Robert (1546–1610).

Parsons, Robert (1646/7–1714), Church of England clergyman, was the son of John Parsons of Southampton. Parsons matriculated at University College, Oxford, on 10 December 1663 aged sixteen, and graduated BA on 27 June 1667 and MA on 22 April 1670. It was while Parsons was at Oxford that evidence first appears of his connection with John Wilmot, second earl of Rochester, a connection that was to shape Parsons's life and career; Rochester wrote to Joseph Williamson 'to get a *mandamus* drawn for Rob. Parsons to be chosen squire bedel [a minor but lucrative academic post], as the king has promised' (*CSP dom.*, *1670*, 673). In 1670 or 1671 Parsons took holy orders and was installed curate to William Beaw (later bishop of Llandaff) at Adderbury, Rochester's estate near Banbury, Oxfordshire. He was appointed chaplain to Rochester's mother, Anne Wilmot, dowager countess of Rochester, and married Joanna van Beverweerd, daughter of Louis de Nassau, lord of Beverweerd, and sister to the wives of both the earl of Arlington, secretary of state, and the earl of Ossory. About the same time Parsons was appointed chaplain to

Thomas Lamplugh, successively bishop of Gloucester and archbishop of York. In August 1671 Dr Thomas Vyner, dean of Gloucester, wrote to Williamson

> asking him to use his influence with Arlington … to procure [the rectory of Stonehouse, Gloucestershire] for his wife's sister's husband, Mr. Parsons, chaplain to the Bishop of Gloucester, a good scholar, and yet but meanly preferred. (*CSP dom.*, *1671*, 439)

Parsons was instituted vicar of Shabbington in Buckinghamshire on 8 March 1672 and rector of Shabbington a year later. On 24 March 1679 Parsons received a dispensation to hold the rectory of Enmore, Somerset (*CSP dom.*, *1679–80*, 108), the ancestral estate of Elizabeth Malet, Rochester's wife.

After a serious illness in 1678 Rochester left London on horseback in April 1680 to visit his mother in Adderbury and his wife at Enmore. He became so weak that he had to return by coach to his residence at the High Lodge at Woodstock Park, 6 miles from Adderbury, where 'he concluded he could hardly recover' (Burnet, 128). Parsons, as curate of Adderbury, was in attendance upon Rochester for nine weeks, from 26 May to 26 July 1680. Parsons's reading of the suffering servant passage in Isaiah 52: 13–53: 12, with its startling parallels in the New Testament—'he was wounded for our transgressions' (Isaiah 53: 5)—which Rochester memorized, may have contributed to Rochester's celebrated deathbed conversion. Together with Rochester's mother, Parsons witnessed Rochester's dying remonstrance 'to burn all his profane and lewd writings … all his obscene and filthy pictures' (Parsons, 28–9), a sad loss to English literature and art history. Finally, 'according to the Directions he received' from Rochester (Burnet, 130), Parsons on 9 August 1680 preached Rochester's funeral sermon, one line of which, 'when all the trophies of wit and gaity are laid in the dust' (Parsons, 48), Alexander Pope did not disdain to remodel.

The sermon was a best-seller: versions and reprints of it included twenty-four separate editions in England before 1800, twelve more with Burnet's *Some Passages of the Life and Death of the Right Honourable John Earl of Rochester* (1680), four German translations, and cheap reprints by the Religious Tract Society of Baltimore in 1818. It is strange that the 'good scholar' published nothing more. 'Robert Parsons' on the title-page may be the most successful of Rochester's impersonations.

After Rochester's death Parsons continued to accumulate benefices. He was instituted a canon of Llandaff Cathedral in Glamorgan in June 1681, in which incumbency he was succeeded in October 1703 by his eldest son, Robert. He became a portionist rector of Waddesdon, Buckinghamshire, in April 1682; rector of Oddington, Gloucestershire, in 1687, when he resigned Shabbington; and archdeacon of Gloucester in March 1703. On 9 December 1705 Thomas Hearne remarked that when Anthony Addison preached before the circuit court in St Mary's, Oxford,

> one Robin Parsons (formerly of University College … who preach'd mad Ld. Rochester's Funeral Sermon) hearing Mr. Addison, when he came out of the Church said, He was an impudent Fellow for stealing before the Judges. For, says he, this Sermon was my Friend Mr. Pindar's of University College: w[ch] was certainly true. (*Remarks*, 1.120)

Parsons's clerical witticism alludes to Romans 2: 21: 'thou that preaches a man should not steal, dost thou steal?' Parsons died on 18 July 1714, leaving his wife and two surviving sons, Robert (*b.* 1678) and Bainton (1691–1742). He was buried at Oddington. Administration was granted to his son Robert on 6 September, his widow having renounced. FRANK H. ELLIS

Sources *DNB* · G. Lipscomb, *The history and antiquities of the county of Buckingham*, 4 vols. (1831–47) · Wood, *Ath. Oxon.*, new edn · *CSP dom.*, *1660–1702* · G. Burnet, *Some passages of the life and death of the Right Honourable John earl of Rochester* (1680) · R. Parsons, *A sermon preached at the funeral of the Rt Honourable John earl of Rochester* (1680) · *Fasti Angl.* (Hardy) · J. Le Neve, *Monumenta Anglicana*, 5 vols. (1717–19) · Foster, *Alum. Oxon.* · *Fasti Angl.*, *1541–1857*, [Bristol] · *Remarks and collections of Thomas Hearne*, ed. C. E. Doble and others, 11 vols., OHS, 2, 7, 13, 34, 42–3, 48, 50, 65, 67, 72 (1885–1921) · V. Barbour, *Henry Bennet, earl of Arlington* (1914) · N. Fisher, 'Rochester's funeral sermon', *Book Collector*, 39 (1990), 265–7 · T. F. Kirby, *Winchester scholars: a list of the wardens, fellows, and scholars of … Winchester College* (1888) · parish registers, Adderbury, Oxfordshire

Parsons, Samuel Holden (1737–1789), revolutionary army officer in America, was born on 14 May 1737 in Lyme, Connecticut, the third son of the Revd Jonathan Parsons (1705–1776) and Phebe Griswold (*d.* 1770). The conversion of Samuel's father from Old Light to New Light Congregationalism during the Great Awakening led to the family's resettlement in Newburyport, Massachusetts, in 1746. Samuel attended Harvard College, graduating with the class of 1756, and then returned to his birthplace to read law with his prominent uncle, Matthew Griswold. In September 1761 he married a Griswold neighbour, Mehetable Mather (1743–1802), with whom he had eight children. His family connections and growing reputation as a lawyer ensured his repeated election as a Lyme representative to the general assembly from 1762 until he moved to New London in 1774, following his appointment to the colony's newly constituted committee of correspondence and as king's attorney for New London county in 1773. Though without firsthand military experience, by 1775 he had also risen to the rank of lieutenant-colonel in the 3rd regiment of the Connecticut militia.

When hostilities broke out, Parsons helped to plan and facilitate the capture of Fort Ticonderoga before assuming command of Connecticut's 6th regiment raised for the siege of Boston during 1775. Parsons's regiment arrived too late to participate in the battle of Bunker Hill (17 June), but served for the remainder of the year in the Boston area until the men's enlistments expired in December.

George Washington turned to Parsons to recruit as many from the 1775 regiments into the 1776 line as possible. Though his efforts met with mixed results, Parsons's new regiment, the 10th, was present when the British evacuated Boston in March 1776. In April he was ordered to New York and on 9 August congress appointed him brigadier-general. During the battle of Long Island on 27

August Parsons acquitted himself with distinction, holding, as ordered, a key position until completely surrounded before making his way back to the American lines. After the retreat to New York city, his brigade was deployed to meet the British assault at Kips Bay on 15 September, but fled at the sight of the enemy. During the remainder of the campaign he commanded continental units in Westchester County, along the Hudson River, and in northern New Jersey.

Congress's effort to raise a long-term army consumed much of Parsons's energy during the first half of 1777. Initially Washington stationed Connecticut's regiments along the state's western border to encourage enlistments. But in early April he ordered all recruits to the Hudson. Parsons remained in New Haven overseeing the completion of Connecticut's regiments. On 15 April he learned of an imminent British attack on the state, but when the Danbury raid occurred on 25 April he was as unable as the continental units on the Hudson to participate in the state's response. The event highlighted a tension between the strategic needs of the continent and Connecticut's security that remained unresolved throughout the war.

Parsons's chief military contribution lay in mediating this tension. Initially, he advocated taking the offensive against Long Island and New York, but these initiatives usually resulted in failure. Fortunately for Parsons his immediate superior, Israel Putnam, took the responsibility. By the time Putnam retired from active command in 1779, British raiding had put Parsons on the defensive. His primary objective became maintaining the loyalty of the Connecticut line and the state's civilian population. These circumstances made him less a field than a political general.

Parsons's political talents first became evident in a vehement public letter he addressed to Governor Tryon of New York in November 1777 accusing Tryon of responsibility for atrocities against civilians in a recent raid along the Hudson River. This led to a much-publicized exchange between the two in which Parsons turned the continental army's inability to protect civilians into a claim of moral superiority. Tryon's role in raids against New Haven, Fairfield, and Norwalk led Parsons to strike a similar pose in 1779. Parsons was actually able to deploy 150 continentals under his personal command in Norwalk's defence. But the British capacity to strike the coast wherever they chose with little warning made Norwalk the exception rather than the rule.

In trying to manage the *petite guerre* that afflicted Connecticut's coastline, Parsons also became involved in espionage. One of his agents, William Heron, in turn teased the British with the possibility that Parsons's loyalty might be bought. The prospect seemed plausible because Parsons's military career had impoverished his family. At the beginning of the war he had sold his estate on the coast and invested the proceeds in depreciating continental money and securities. After 1778 Parsons repeatedly tried to resign his commission because of financial hardship and ill health. Washington and congress valued his services sufficiently to refuse these requests, but Parsons remained a brigadier until after Benedict Arnold's treason, only being promoted major-general on 23 October 1780. Partially because of this promotion he stayed with the army until July 1782.

After his military retirement Parsons settled in Middletown, which elected him alderman and representative to the general assembly. In 1781 Yale had also awarded him an honorary degree. But he needed more lucrative honours and in June 1785 accepted appointment as congressional commissioner to liquidate some Virginia accounts and subsequently as an American Indian commissioner. A western trip in 1785–6 alerted him to the potential of the Ohio region. On returning home, he organized a syndicate to purchase several townships in Ohio, and, after the passage of the northwest ordinance, he was appointed chief justice of the new territory. Before setting out again for the west, he participated in Connecticut's ratifying convention, strongly urging the adoption of the new constitution. During the summer of 1788 he drafted a basic code for the Northwest Territory with the aid of a fellow Harvard graduate, James M. Varnum. He perished in a canoeing accident while descending the Big Beaver River on 17 November 1789 before he could redeem his family from the impoverishment the War of Independence had brought upon them. RICHARD BUEL JUN.

Sources S. H. Parsons, corresp. to Governor Jonathan Trumbull, Connecticut State Library, Hartford, Connecticut, Jonathan Trumbull MSS • R. Buel jun., *Dear liberty: Connecticut's mobilization for the revolutionary war* (1980) • C. S. Hall, *Life and letters of Samuel Holden Parsons* (1905) • C. K. Shipton, 'Samuel Holden Parsons', *Sibley's Harvard graduates: biographical sketches of those who attended Harvard College*, 14 (1968) • L. J. Cappon, 'Parsons, Samuel Holden', *DAB* • S. H. Parsons, letters to George Washington, L. Cong., manuscript division, George Washington MSS • N. Calhoun, *Connecticut's revolutionary war leaders* (1973) • *Magazine of American History*, 11 (1884), 257 • G. B. Goring, 'A vindication of General Samuel Holden Parsons', *Magazine of American History*, 20 (1888), 286–303 • J. Trumbull and J. G. Woodward, *Vindications of patriots of the American revolution* (1896)

Archives Connecticut State Library, Hartford, Connecticut archives: Revolutionary War, Jonathan Trumbull MSS • L. Cong., George Washington MSS • U. Mich., Sir Henry Clinton MSS

Wealth at death insolvent; initial inventory of £276 had £3794 of claims exhibited against it: Connecticut probate estate papers, Hartford, Connecticut State Library

Parsons, Theophilus (1750–1813), revolutionary politician and jurist in the United States of America, was born on 24 February 1750 in Byfield, Massachusetts, the third of three children of Moses Parsons (1716–1783), a Congregational parish minister, and Susan Davis (1719–1794), daughter of Abraham Davis and his wife, Anne. As a child he attended Byfield Academy, studying hard and doing mathematics for fun and relaxation; he graduated from Harvard College in 1769. From 1770 to 1773 he taught school at Falmouth while reading law with Theophilus Bradbury. He began to practise law in Falmouth in July 1774, but returned to Byfield in October 1775 after British warships destroyed Falmouth. There he continued his legal studies under the guidance of Judge Edmund Trowbridge, an eminent lawyer who possessed loyalist sympathies and the largest law library in New England. He also established a flourishing legal practice in Newburyport; having worked himself to exhaustion he recovered only by taking long horse rides.

During the American War of Independence, Parsons served the patriot cause by helping to establish a republican government for Massachusetts. In 1778 he was one of the Essex Junto, a group of New Englanders who campaigned against a proposed Massachusetts constitution because the members believed it too democratic in tone and not adequate to guarantee property rights. He published the junto's views in a pamphlet entitled *The Essex Result*, and a year later served as a member of the convention that produced the Massachusetts constitution of 1780. This document, which called for a strong governor, a senate elected on the basis of property, and a privileged position for the Congregational church, reflected the thinking of Parsons and his friends. On 13 January 1780 Parsons married Elizabeth Greenleaf; they had twelve children, five of whom died in infancy. Also in 1780 he moved to Newburyport, where he resided and practised law for the next twenty years. He was elected to the state legislature in 1787 and served there until 1791; he was re-elected in 1805. But his forte was not politics. A man of stern rectitude who spoke his mind even when his words were unpopular, he preferred to practise law and meditate on constitutional principles.

In 1788 Parsons attended the Massachusetts state convention that ratified the federal constitution. An ardent proponent of the constitution, he worked to persuade others to his point of view. Hoping to convince a number of delegates that the new national government would not overawe the states, he wrote a conciliatory speech that was delivered by John Hancock, chairman of the convention. In the speech he and Hancock proposed as a condition of ratification several constitutional amendments, three of which were later incorporated into the Bill of Rights. Parsons continued to practise law, and his reputation as one of New England's foremost legal scholars grew. In 1800 he moved to Boston, where he attracted many promising law students to study with him. The jealousy of his colleagues was aroused, and they established a rule limiting to three the number of an attorney's pupils. Six years later he was appointed chief justice of the supreme judicial court of Massachusetts, a position he retained until his death. Under his guidance the court established a number of important legal precedents, formalizing rules of procedure and firmly embedding the principles of English common law in American jurisprudence.

In his leisure time Parsons pursued many interests besides law. He wrote papers on mathematics and astronomy, and he conducted chemical and electrical experiments in his home. A student of Greek, he wrote an unpublished Greek grammar, and he was proficient in French. He also dabbled in carpentry. He helped found the Social Law Library and the Boston Athenaeum, and he was chosen a fellow of Harvard College in 1806. A family man, he remained close to home throughout his life, and entertained large numbers of guests in an oversized dining-room. He died of hydrocephalic apoplexy on 30 October 1813 in Boston. PAUL DAVID NELSON

Sources T. Parsons, *Memoir of Theophilus Parsons* (1859) · R. K. Osgood, ed., *The history of the law in Massachusetts: the supreme judicial court, 1692–1992* (1992) · E. J. Bellefontaine, 'Theophilus Parsons as a legal reformer', *Boston Bar Journal*, 36 (1992), 14–19 · G. J. Clark, *Life sketches of eminent lawyers*, 2 (1895) · T. Parsons, *Commentaries on American law* (1836) · W. G. Ross, 'Parsons, Theophilus', *ANB* · *New England Palladium* [Boston] (4 Nov 1813) · F. G. Cook, 'Theophilus Parsons', *Great American lawyers*, ed. W. D. Lewis, 2 (1907)

Likenesses G. Stuart, oils, repro. in E. Hayward and B. Hayward, eds., *Dictionary of American portraits* (1967), 474

Parsons, Sir William, baronet (*c*.1570–1650), political administrator and promoter of the plantation of Ireland, was the eldest son of James Parsons, second son of Thomas Parsons of Disworth Grange, Leicestershire, and his wife, Catherine, daughter of Henry Fenton of Fenton, Nottinghamshire, and Cicely, daughter of John Beaumont of Cole Orton, Leicestershire.

Surveyor-general of Ireland Some time after 1588 Parsons entered the service of his uncle Sir Geoffrey Fenton, surveyor-general of Ireland, and he succeeded to that office himself on 26 December 1602. According to Thomas Carte, he was 'plodding, assiduous, and indefatigable, greedy of office, and eager to raise a fortune' (*DNB*). He also appears firmly to have believed in the need to entrench protestantism in Ireland through vigorous plantation, of which he was 'in theory and practice the prime mover' (Treadwell, 301). His post and a succession of plantation commissions involved him intimately in the wholesale redistribution of land ownership during the settlement of the English interest in Ireland during the early Stuart era. In 1625 Parsons referred to the 'English empire' in Ireland (*CSP Ire.*, *1625–32*, 56–8). Inasmuch as there was such an entity by then, it was in large part due to Parsons, who helped do for land ownership in Ireland what Sir John Davies did for the kingdom's legal system.

On 24 October 1603 Parsons was appointed a commissioner to inquire into the dissolved monasteries in Tyrconnel, and on 20 December 1605 he was made a commissioner for the apportionment and erection of the county of Wicklow. He was deeply engaged as a commissioner in the plantation of Ulster from 1610, obtaining as an undertaker 1000 acres of arable in the precinct of Clogher, co. Tyrone, which he dubbed the manor of Cecil. As a servitor he also obtained 1000 acres in Dungannon. He subsequently obtained another 1000 acres in the precinct of Tullagha in co. Cavan. In 1611 he received a pension of £30 in consideration of his services in the settlement of Ulster.

Election to parliament It was largely due to his establishment of such a prominent interest there that Parsons secured election as one of the representatives for the county of Armagh in the parliament of 1634, having sat for the borough of Newcastle, co. Dublin, in the 1613–15 parliament. As an undertaker in the plantation of Wexford from 1618, he obtained 1500 acres at an annual rent of

£8. He also had a hand in the settlement of Longford and Ely O'Carrol in 1619.

Having long supported the active confiscation of Irish estates and plantation of English landlords, at the end of 1619 Parsons found it convenient for purposes of promotion to drop his opposition to the less confrontational policy of surrender and regrant in Connaught. This commended him to Buckingham, whose courtly associates stood to profit from the proceedings in the west of Ireland, and in 1620 Parsons found a warm enough welcome when he went to London. An introduction was effected by Parsons's reasonably proximate kinsman by marriage, Richard Boyle, the earl of Cork, whose wife was Parsons's cousin Catherine Fenton. William and his brother Laurence, attorney-general and admiralty judge in Munster, had both obtained knighthoods already, conferred by Buckingham's creature Lord Deputy St John on 7 June at Dublin. William now also obtained grants of land (including the manor of Tassagard in co. Dublin and other properties amounting to an annual rental of £100), one of the earliest Irish baronetcies (1620), and a seat in the Irish privy council. In addition, he succeeded in commending to Buckingham a policy of continuous plantation which restored some of the momentum to that project. The granting of huge estates to a handful of individuals had singularly failed to secure adequate levels of protestant settlement in Ulster and the Irish midlands, and enthusiasm had waned at court. But Buckingham was attracted by the prospect of carving up substantial portions of Irish real estate among his own increasingly importunate dependants, and lent his weight to hastening the dubious, not to say illegal, plantation of Leitrim through the English privy council. The plantation of Leitrim in 1620 brought Parsons another 800 acres. Parsons also persuaded the marquess of the utility that lay in establishing an Irish court of wards, of which he was himself created master on 6 September 1622.

Master of the court of wards The court formalized the existing *ad hoc* arrangements for the slow erosion of the Catholic nobility in Ireland, providing for the protestant instruction of aristocratic orphans, and requiring of them the oath of supremacy as a condition of their eventual succession. The creeping progress of this attempt at élite conversion was of secondary importance by comparison with the more pressing objective of separating heirs from their inheritances as a means of reducing in some measure the annual subvention of £20,000 which was paid out of English coffers towards the government of Ireland. But the Irish court of wards did not simply answer the needs of the English government, and its institution probably had just as much to do with the ambitions of Sir William Parsons, whose mastership of the court placed extensive powers of patronage at his personal disposal, as well as an annual salary of £300. It also laid the foundations for further plantations, placing under the master's control a host of invaluable Irish muniments. In particular Parsons helped prepare the ground for Buckingham's plantation of upper Ossory and protected the scheme, which would see the marquess secure 'the largest single grant *de novo* of prime Irish land of the reign', from the persistent opposition of Buckingham's rival at Whitehall, the earl of Middlesex (Treadwell, 240). Parsons's personal land acquisitions also continued, with the addition of large new estates in Wicklow in 1628 and Fermanagh in 1630.

By this time, Parsons was associated with the faction which supported the lord deputy, Falkland, and was centred on the earl of Cork, and Roger Jones, Lord Ranelagh. They were opposed by Lord Chancellor Loftus, vice-treasurer Annesley, and Lord Wilmot. Discredited by a scandal over the expropriation of Phelim McFeagh O'Byrne in the course of a Wicklow plantation in which Parsons himself had a hand, Falkland, Buckingham's creature, was recalled within a year of his patron's death, and the balance of power in Ireland shifted against the Boyle group. The decisive moment was the arrival of the new lord deputy in 1633. Temporarily pursuing a policy of mollifying Catholic interests, largely in order to shift the financial burden of the military establishment onto Old English shoulders, Sir Thomas Wentworth turned against their protestant persecutors in Dublin Castle. Parsons managed to shed his connections with the discredited earl of Cork, however, and retained his own position of power in the court of wards. This probably reflected his responsibility for the implementation of a new regime in the court as part of the agreement reached between the king and his Old English subjects in 1628 known as 'the graces'. One of the concessions granted included the right to sue for livery in the court of wards without taking the oath of supremacy. This became a key feature in the policy of appeasing the king's Catholic subjects which accompanied Wentworth's initial implementation of his 'thorough' regime. But Parsons also played a role in another limb of the new lord deputy's administration which was eventually turned to uses much more destructive of the Catholic interest, namely the commission for defective titles. Used to force less secure tenures at greatly increased rents on innocent crown tenants, the commission became a source of immense resentment among both Old English and Gaelic proprietors. Stating their grievances in 1643, the Anglo-Irish confederation of Catholics specifically attacked Parsons and two other commission members for having 'voided 150 letters patent' in the course of a morning's work (Kearney, 82). Additionally, it is possible that commission members, like the officials of the court of wards, exploited their position to obtain land at an undervaluation.

Appointment as lord justice In 1640 Parsons represented the county of Wicklow in the Irish parliament. On the death of Vice-Deputy Sir Christopher Wandesford on 3 December 1640, he and Robert, Lord Dillon of Kilkenny, Strafford's brother-in-law, were appointed lords justices of the kingdom. When Dillon's appointment was protested, a fresh commission was issued appointing Parsons and Sir John Borlase, and they were sworn on 10 February 1641. Borlase being 'old and indolent' (*DNB*), Parsons now assumed primary responsibility for Irish affairs. He was fortunate not to suffer as a result of his association with the Straffordian regime, and eyed developments in the

Irish parliament nervously as the Dublin MPs, taking their lead from Patrick Darcy's *Argument*, attempted to assert their rights of judicature and impeachment. His government, particularly after the outbreak of the Irish rising, has been severely criticized, and it has been said that the jealousy with which he regarded the Catholic gentry of the pale was directly responsible for their combination with the rebels of Ulster. It is even claimed that he purposely stimulated the rising in order to furnish an excuse for a fresh conquest and 'a new crop of confiscations' (ibid.). His letters certainly show that he saw an opportunity to turn the rising to advantage 'by settling here very great multitudes of the English', and that he was convinced 'that a thorough destruction must be made before we can settle upon a safe peace' (ibid.).

When civil war subsequently broke out in England, Parsons regarded the Westminster parliament as the best hope for the recovery of the English interest in Ireland. It was Parsons who secured permission for the representatives of that assembly to sit in the Irish privy council from 2 November 1642, which they continued to do until the king ordered their expulsion the following February. By then Charles was already bypassing the lords justices, preferring to act through Ormond, Clanricarde, and others, whom he had authorized to meet with the Catholic rebels, rather than Parsons and Borlase, who had blocked the confederates' attempts to communicate their demands to the king, including the request that Parsons himself be dismissed for continuing the Straffordian policy of confiscation. The lord justice strenuously opposed Ormond's policy of discriminating between the gentry of the pale and the Gaelic Irish, and it was on account of the opposition he offered to the proposals for a reconciliation between the former and the king that he was removed from office on 31 March 1643—'a fair recompense', he wrote bitterly to the earl of Cork:

> for all my zealous and painful toil to the crown, which God knows was heartily done. The ground is, as I find, because I have endeavoured to be sharp to those damnable rebels, who now seem in a fair way to evade all their villainey. (*DNB*)

On 3 April a royal commission appointed Sir Henry Tichborne as lord justice in place of Parsons, who was kept under restraint at Dublin Castle in November 1643, but released on bail. By August 1645 he had apparently fallen into rebel hands, his name being one among several mentioned by the parliamentary committee for Irish affairs in a proposal for an exchange of prisoners held at Drogheda. But it was subsequently remarked that Parsons did not at that time wish to be involved in the exchange. He was in London by December 1646. Although it is claimed that 'he did not meet with the reception he thought he deserved' in England (*DNB*), in November 1647 the committee for Irish affairs at Derby House recommended that parliament pay his £500 annual pension. The following January he was appointed one of the commissioners for raising £50,000 for the Irish service, and in March 1648 it was proposed that he go to Dublin to assist Colonel Michael Jones in organizing the defence of the city. In May 1649 the lord president of the council of state erected in the aftermath of regicide personally recommended publishing the former lord justice's thoughts in a tract on Irish affairs, as the new executive put together the propaganda campaign for the forthcoming expedition into Ireland. It is also evidently noteworthy that, after his death, Parsons was buried with all due honour on 2 March 1650 in the church of St Margaret, Westminster. At an unknown date he had married Elizabeth (*d.* 1640), eldest daughter of John Lany, alderman of Dublin. They had several children, but it was one of their grandchildren, Richard, subsequently created baron of Oxmantown and Viscount Rosse in 1681, who succeeded to Parsons's title and estate.

SEAN KELSEY

Sources *DNB* · *CSP Ire.* · T. W. Moody and others, eds., *A new history of Ireland*, 3: *Early modern Ireland, 1534–1691* (1976) · H. Kearney, *Strafford in Ireland: a study in absolutism* (1989) · V. Treadwell, *Buckingham in Ireland* (1998) · parish register, St Margaret's, Westminster, City Westm. AC, 2 March 1650 [burial] · GEC, *Baronetage*

Archives BL, corresp. and papers, Add. MSS 46921–46932 | Chatsworth House, Derbyshire, letters to earl of Cork

Likenesses S. Paul, or S. De Wilde, mezzotint, 1777, BM, NG Ire., NPG · oils (in middle life), known to be at Parsonstown Castle in 1895

Parsons, William (1658–1705), army officer and publisher, was the youngest of the two sons of Sir William Parsons of Langley, Buckinghamshire, who was created baronet in 1661, and his wife, Elizabeth, daughter of Sir Laurence Parsons, knight. He matriculated from Christ Church, Oxford, on 28 April 1676 and joined the 1st regiment of foot guards as an ensign in 1682, rising to captain in 1686 and, briefly in 1687, to lieutenant-colonel.

In November 1688 Parsons was a captain in Tollemache's regiment of foot in the Netherlands when it took part in the prince of Orange's descent on England. He was then 'Unfortunately Depriv'd of the Happy Station I then enjoyed, And by an Absolute Necessity Forc'd (Durum Telum Necessitas!) to Turn my self to another Sort of Affair' (Parsons, dedication). This involved laying out money to prepare an English edition of Guillaume Marcel's *Tablettes chronologiques* (1686), a popular pocket book listing the dates of the rulers of church and state. He commissioned John Sturt to engrave some forty-three copper plates for publication, and in November 1689 licensed his *Chronological tables containing the successions of all ye popes, emperours, and kings which have reigned in Europe from ye nativity of our Saviour to ye year 1688*. The success was such that the booklet went through three impressions within the first two years, with further editions up to and after his death.

Parsons was appointed the major of Colonel Edward Lloyd's regiment of foot on 10 December 1693 and on 16 March 1695 was promoted to lieutenant-colonel of Colonel Fairfax's regiment which served that year in Flanders. He nevertheless continued to interest himself in publishing, and in 1698 he commissioned another engraver, Tauuel, to begin work on plates for a book to contain 600 monograms of Parsons's own design. Thomas Tuttell (*d.* 1702), a maker of mathematical instruments and globes, of Charing Cross, dedicated his *Description and Uses of a New Contriv'd Eliptical Double Dial* (1698) to Parsons, describing him as 'the Great Encourager of Artists' (sig. A3). Of the *Chronological Tables*, Tuttell wrote: 'At present the greatest part of our *Nobility* and *Gentry* are, by use, and *Your* Instructions, become themselves such *Judges* in what is *Curious*, This, *Sir*, is wholly owing to YOU, who at once Revive *Art* and the *Artist*' (sig. A4). Parsons went into partnership with Tuttell to produce a new globe (at 25*s*.), although, as no such globes exist, it appears that the scheme came to nothing. Parsons's address at this time was given as 'at the Caesar's Head in the Old Palace of Westminster' (*Proposals*).

The first five impressions of the *Chronological Tables*, priced at 4*s*., sold 4000 copies by 1703. In that year Parsons published *The Tent of Darius Explain'd, or, The Queens of Persia at the Feet of Alexander*, his translation from the French of André Félibien's description of the painting by Charles Le Brun. The book was illustrated by Simon Gribelin's engraving of the painting and dedicated to 'the Nobility and Gentry' as a way 'of expressing my gratitude' for 'the Success of my *Chronological Tables*' (dedication). In 1704 he produced Tauuel's plates of monograms in *A New Book of Cyphers; More Compleat and Regular than any yet Extant*, which was sold either in book form or at 6*d*. a sheet. It included a frontispiece by Joseph Nutting, some new plates by Gribelin and an advertisement for Gribelin's *New Book of Ornaments*, which had been dedicated to Parsons.

His success in directing engravers to carry out his ideas prompted Parsons in August 1704 to apply for the post of engraver to the Royal Mint but, not being an engraver, he was deemed unsuitable. He married Thomasina, a daughter of Sir John Barker, bt, of Grimston Hall, Suffolk; she survived him when he died, childless, in 1705. He was buried at St Margaret's, Westminster, on 26 May.

PIERS WAUCHOPE

Sources J. Burke and J. B. Burke, *A genealogical and heraldic history of the extinct and dormant baronetcies of England, Ireland and Scotland*, 2nd edn (1841); repr. (1844) · *A biographical history of England, from the revolution to the end of George I's reign: being a continuation of the Rev. J. Granger's work*, ed. M. Noble, 3 vols. (1806) · Foster, *Alum. Oxon.* · C. Dalton, ed., *English army lists and commission registers, 1661–1714*, 6 vols. (1892–1904) · T. Tuttell and W. Parsons, *Proposals … for a new pair of globes* [n.d., 1700?] · A. Félibien, *The tent of Darius explain'd, or, The queens of Persia at the feet of Alexander*, trans. W. Parsons (1703) · P. Hofer, ed., *A book of ornaments engraved by Simon Gribelin* (1941) · W. A. Shaw, ed., *Calendar of treasury books*, 19, PRO (1938) · J. Redington, ed., *Calendar of Treasury papers*, 3, PRO (1874) · J. de la Crose, 'Chronological tables', *Works of the Learned* (Feb 1692), 290–91 · T. Tuttell, *The description and uses of a new contriv'd eliptical double dial* (1698) · *DNB* · will, PRO, PROB 11/491, sig. 264 · parish register, St Margaret's, City Westm. AC [burial]

Likenesses S. Gribelin, line engraving, *c*.1705 (after P. Berchet, 1696), BM, NPG · S. Gribelin, line engraving, BM

Parsons, William (1736–1795), actor, was born on 29 February 1736, the son of William Parsons, a carpenter in Bow Lane, Cheapside, and his wife, Elizabeth, and educated at St Paul's School, to which he was admitted on 7 April 1749. His mother came from Maidstone, according to the June 1795 number of the *Gentleman's Magazine*, which also claims Maidstone as his birthplace and that his parents were people of some property from whom he inherited a small estate. Although this journal suggests he was apprenticed to an eminent apothecary, most accounts state that at the age of fifteen he was settled by his father as a pupil under Sir Henry Cheese, a surveyor. As a youth he allegedly performed in spouting clubs and eventually determined on a career as an actor. He was not entirely without resources, as he was also employed, according to Bellamy, by several picture dealers to paint small landscapes.

Parsons's first professional engagement was at York in the mid-1750s. Around 1757 or 1758, he moved to Edinburgh, where he came into possession of old men in comedy, 'a line of characters which best suited his figure, feelings and cast of features' (Gilliland, 2.891). At Edinburgh, after walking several miles through heavy rain to appear at the theatre one evening, he developed the asthma which was to affect him for the rest of his life. In 1762 Garrick, requiring an actor to play Filch in *The Beggar's Opera*, offered him an engagement, and both Parsons and his wife, Mary (*d*. 1787), whom he had met in Edinburgh, and who acted as Mrs Price, made their first London appearances at Drury Lane on 21 September 1762. Parsons's attachment to Garrick, who instructed him in acting, was such that he resisted subsequent inducements to engage at Dublin and at Covent Garden. However, he did join the company at the Haymarket, and made his début there as Robin in Samuel Foote's *The Patron* on 13 June 1764. He acted there in the summers of 1765, 1772–3, 1775–9, 1782–8, and 1790–94. In November 1772 he purchased a part share in the Bristol theatre, where he appeared during the next three summers, after which he relinquished his share. He also acted at the Liverpool theatre for several summers.

Parsons was 'excellent in every part he performed; I do not think that a conspicuous failure is recorded', wrote Adolphus (1.353). 'Whatever he once touched became his property during life' said Boaden (1.62), and it was generally conceded no one could compete with him in these roles. Among his most notable parts were Sir Hugh Evans, in Congreve's *The Double Dealer* (which O'Keefe thought his best role), Dorus, in David Garrick's *Cymon*; and Moneytrap, in Vanbrugh's *The Confederacy*. John Litchfield believed that it was in old men that the actor's claim to excellence lay, but particularly singled out the buffo characters, such as Sir Fretful Plagiary, in Sheridan's *The Critic*, and Corbaccio, in Jonson's *Volpone*. As Foresight, in Congreve's *Love for Love*, 'the tottering knee, the sudden stare, the plodding look, nay, the taking out of his handkerchief, evinced such a perfect knowledge of man in his dotage that we despair of ever seeing anything at all approaching it' (Gilliland, 2.894). 'I have repeatedly enjoyed this rich treat, and became sensible how painful laughter might be, when such a man as Parsons chose to throw his whole force into a character', claimed Boaden of his Sir Fretful Plagiary:

> When he stood under the castigation of Sneer, affecting to enjoy criticisms which made him writhe in agony; when the tears were in his eyes, and he suddenly checked his unnatural laugh, to enable him to stare aghast, upon his tormentors; a picture was exhibited of mental anguish and

> frantic rage, of mortified vanity and affected contempt, which would almost deter an author from the pen, unless he could be sure of his firmness under every possible provocation. (Boaden, 1.63)

Parsons thought his best part was Corbaccio, but said that all the merit he had in it he owed to Edward Shuter. Boaden describes the physical basis of this performance, in which his expression was confined not merely to his face,

> but every passion circulated in him to his extremities, and spoke in the motion of his feet, or the more striking intelligence of his hands: the latter became the claws of a harpy, when they crawled over the parchment which blasted all his hopes. (ibid., 1.62)

Parsons was a born comic actor. 'He was an undoubted ORIGINAL', wrote Litchfield,

> both in conception and manner; and if any performer could be said to found a *school of acting*, PARSONS would be the first to lay claim to such an honour; with a fund of genuine *English* Humour he combined the *Italian* GESTICULATION and the *French* LOCOMOTION. (Bellamy, 54)

Gilliland tells us that:

> His face was long; and possessed astonishing flexibility: his eyes were dark and large; and what constituted the great merit of his countenance, was its power of expressing every passion with which comedy abounds … every movement of a muscle expressed the feelings of the sentiment he was about to deliver. His face alone did not play; his whole frame supported a correspondent motion which the passion of his countenance so intelligibly communicated to his audience. (Gilliland, 2.893)

Parsons knew how to use his whole body to enhance his performances, even harnessing his breathing difficulties to the effectiveness of his delivery. He 'immersed' himself in his character, using not only his face and arms, but also his whole system: 'he wrapped himself up in a part, and deluded himself by a singular process, into the notion that he was *in reality*, the man he only *feigned* to represent' (Bellamy, 58).

Although Parsons could also play country characters, his forte was that of old men in comedy, a talent that he owed as much to his skill and his judgement as to his physical advantages. Boaden states that he

> had a figure, a gait, a countenance, a voice that marked him out as the actor of old men in comedy. Whether he exhibited their avarice or their fondness, their insensibility or their weakness, he never lost the character for a moment. (Boaden, 1.62)

In such representations, according to *The Thespian Dictionary*, 'he possessed a greater portion of art than nature; but in his art he displayed such consummate judgement that he never failed in extorting true applause'. For Bellamy, however, it was in his use of nature that this judgement was exercised: 'As … [he] acted from Nature his ideas were ever taken from objects that moved in her circles, and not from those of Fancy' (Bellamy, 36). His achievement was to give prominence and respectability to a line of characters that had previously lacked these attributes. For, 'by studying the pettish peevishness and other passions of old men, and contemplating very probably, in real life, what effect these had on the voice, the face, nay the very gait', Parsons 'gave so faithful a portraiture of nature, that though the subject was not handsome, it was universally admired for its extraordinary similitude' (Bellamy, 62). Parsons made interesting parts that had previously seemed insubstantial, and authors, including Garrick, soon started to write especially for him.

That Parsons was more than a buffoon or grimacer, suggested Litchfield, was due to the variety of the roles he played and the sureness of touch with which he characterized this variety. The exercise of judgement and the skilled use of a consummate technique, to which observation and physical transformation were central, seem to be behind this ability. However, Charles Dibdin had doubts about his delivery. He felt Parsons was too anxious to stress or emphasize words to clarify their importance and that he was also over-anxious to be audible. Frederick Reynolds, however, considered Parsons maintained his ground more through mental than vocal powers. He certainly had great power over his audiences: 'Nobody can forbear laughing either *with* him or *at* him, whenever he opens his mouth', claimed Thomas Davies (Russell, 172). Not only were the spectators convulsed, but his fellow actors themselves were sometimes incapable of performing further.

In private life Parsons was a gentlemanly and companionable individual. In conversation Dibdin found him something of a freethinker and considered that 'on philosophical subjects he certainly took too large a latitude' (Bellamy, 74), being too influenced by Voltaire and Rousseau. Michael Kelly records his fondness for 'that exquisite actor' Parsons, recalling how he frequently dined with him 'in a band-box of a house' (Kelly, 314) in Lambeth, which he called Frog Hall, or in a little eating-house almost opposite the Drury Lane stage door, where he indulged his fondness for fried tripe after almost every performance. Parsons, says Dibdin, 'loved truth, and detested hypocrisy'—he was 'warm and sincere in his friendships, affectionate and attentive in his domestic situation, and upright and honest in his decidings' (Bellamy, 76). An artist of considerable merit, he was also an astute judge and collector of the paintings of others. His favourite artist was the landscape painter Richard Wilson, on whose work he reputedly modelled his own. He was also a talented painter of still lifes—particularly fruit—and a good musician. A facility for composing impromptu verses—especially on the charms of Elizabeth Inchbald—is evident in surviving manuscripts.

Parsons was very thin and much afflicted by asthma. For some years before his death he was frequently unable to act, weakened by the strain of performing to the enlarged auditorium of the rebuilt Drury Lane. Shortly after the death of his first wife, on 29 November 1787, he had married Dorothea Stewart, who was, according to the *Gentleman's Magazine* of June 1795, one of the three daughters of the Hon. James Stewart, MP for Wigton burghs. They had two sons, one of whom died young. Parsons was determined to leave adequate means for the support of his family. On 19 January 1795, after playing Sir Fretful Plagiary with some difficulty, he told his wife that he would act no more and returned to his home, Stangate, in Mead's Row, St George's Fields, Lambeth, where he died on 3 February 1795. He was buried at St Margaret's Church, Lee, Kent, on 15 February. Charles Dibdin wrote the following epitaph for his tombstone:

> Here PARSONS lies. Oft on Life's busy stage,
> With nature, reader, hast thou seen him vie.
> He friendship knew; knew Science; knew the age;
> Respected knew to live—lamented die.
> (Bellamy, 47)

Another tribute to Parsons occurred in George Colman's *New Hay at the Old Market* (1796):

> CARPENTER: We want a new scaffold for the *Surrender of Calais*.
> PROMPTER: Ah, where shall we get such another hangman? Poor fellow, poor Parsons! the old cause of our mirth is now the cause of our melancholy; he who so often made us forget our cares, may well claim a sigh to his memory.
> CARPENTER: He was one of the comicalest fellows I ever see.
> PROMPTER: Ay, and one of the honestest, Master Carpenter. When an individual has combined private worth with public talent, he quits the bustling scene of life with twofold applause, and we doubly deplore his exit.

Parsons was survived by his wife and son; his son died in the East Indies. Dorothea married her son's tutor, the Revd Mr Davis, in August 1795, but was deserted after he spent Parsons's legacy. JIM DAVIS

Sources T. Bellamy, 'Life of William Parsons', *Miscellanies in prose and verse* (1795) • J. Boaden, *Memoirs of the life of John Philip Kemble*, 2 vols. (1825) • T. Gilliland, *The dramatic mirror, containing the history of the stage from the earliest period, to the present time*, 2 vols. (1808) • *GM*, 1st ser., 65 (1795), 527 • *The thespian dictionary, or, Dramatic biography of the present age*, 2nd edn (1805) • Genest, *Eng. stage* • *European Magazine and London Review*, 27 (1795), 147–9 • M. Kelly, *Reminiscences*, 2 vols. (1826) • J. Adolphus, *Memoirs of John Bannister, comedian*, 2 vols. (1838) • J. O'Keeffe, *Recollections of the life of John O'Keeffe, written by himself*, 2 vols. (1826) • *Theatrical biography, or, Memoirs of the principal performers of the three Theatre Royals*, 2 vols. (1772) • W. C. Russell, *Representative actors* [1888] • F. Reynolds, *The life and times of Frederick Reynolds, written by himself*, 2 vols. (1826) • G. Colman, *New hay at the old market* (1796) • W. Hawkins, *Miscellanies in prose and verse, containing candid and impartial observations on the principal performers belonging to the two Theatres-Royal, from January 1773 to May 1775* (1775) • Highfill, Burnim & Langhans, *BDA* • *IGI*

Archives Harvard TC, corresp.

Likenesses J. Zoffany, oils, 1766, Garr. Club • J. Zoffany, oils, *c.*1768, Wolverhampton Art Gallery • B. VanderGucht, oils, exh. RA 1775, Garr. Club • J. Roberts, line engraving, pubd 1776 (after his earlier work), BM, NPG • Paul, mezzotint, pubd 1777 (after unknown artist), BM • R. Laurie, mezzotint, pubd 1779 (after R. Dighton), BM, NPG • G. Carter, oils, *c.*1782, Royal Shakespeare Theatre, Stratford upon Avon • J. Zoffany, portrait, *c.*1788, Birmingham Museum and Art Gallery • W. Loftis, watercolour drawing, 1789, Folger • S. De Wilde, three portraits, oils, 1791–3, Garr. Club • coloured aquatint, pubd 1793 (after unknown artist), BM, NPG • gouache drawing, *c.*1793, Garr. Club • J. Parker, stipple, pubd 1795 (after S. Harding), BM • E. Bell, mezzotint, pubd 1796 (after S. De Wilde), BM • J. Parker, stipple, pubd 1796 (after S. Harding), BM • J. R. Smith, mezzotint, pubd 1796 (after S. De Wilde), BM • S. De Wilde, watercolour drawing, 1802, Theatre Museum, London • T. Jonson, etching, pubd 1820 (after G. Cruikshank), BM • S. De Wilde, engraving, repro. in Bellamy, 'Life of William Parsons', frontispiece • S. De Wilde, oils (as Colonel Oldboy in *Lionel and Clarissa*), Garr. Club • S. De Wilde, oils, Garr. Club • S. De Wilde, oils • S. De Wilde, pencil drawing, Harvard TC • R. Dighton, pencil, pen, ink, and watercolour drawing (as Moneytrap in *The confederacy*), Garr. Club • attrib. Noad, pencil, pen, ink, and watercolour drawing (as Lope Tocho in *The mountaineers*), Garr. Club • J. Roberts, drawing, BM • T. Rowlandson, pen and watercolour drawing, BM • W. Spicer, pencil and watercolour drawing, Garr. Club • J. Zoffany, oils (as Sheepface in *The village lawyer*), NPG • ink and wash drawing, BM • portrait (after S. De Wilde), City of Leicester Museum and Art Gallery • prints, BM, NPG

Wealth at death estate valued at £400 p.a.: Bellamy, 'Life of William Parsons', P. Highfill, 'Actors' wills', *Theatre Notebook*, 15/1 (autumn 1960), 9

Parsons, Sir William (1745/6–1817), musician and composer, was possibly born in London. He became a chorister at Westminster Abbey, under Benjamin Cooke, which may have led to appearances in the choruses at theatres and in the concerts of the Academy of Ancient Music. Before 1768 he applied unsuccessfully for an engagement at Covent Garden Theatre, and subsequently travelled to Italy for the improvement of his vocal and composing skills. Unfortunately, no further details of this sojourn survive. On his return he achieved great success as a singing and harpsichord master. On 21 November 1778, at St Marylebone, he married Charlotte Sophia (*bap.* 2 Sept 1761), daughter of the organist John *Worgan and his first wife, Sarah. On the recommendation of F. Ashley he became a member of the Royal Society of Musicians on 2 March 1783. He had a three-year-old daughter at this time.

Parsons acted as an assistant director for the great Handel commemorations in Westminster Abbey and the Pantheon in 1784, and, following the death of John Stanley in 1786, procured the post of master of the king's music, which he held until his death. His first composition in this role was a setting of an ode by Thomas Warton the younger, *In Rough Magnificence Array'd*, performed at court to celebrate the new year 1787. Unfortunately, the music for court odes composed by Parsons appears to be lost. *Court Minuets for His Majesty's Birthday* (1794) was among a handful of works Parsons published around this time, including ballads, theatre music, arrangements, and *A Selection of Solfeggi, for the Use of those who are Learning to Sing* (1790?). In 1793 his salary was £200 as 'Master of the Musick' and £100 as 'Conductor of the Musick', the band including eminent figures such as Charles Burney and William Shield. Doane gives both Shepherd's Bush and Somerset Street as London addresses for Parsons at this time.

On 26 June 1790 Parsons was admitted BMus and DMus at Oxford. On his visiting Dublin in 1795, he attended the lord lieutenant, John Jeffreys Praft, second Earl Camden, who knighted him. He appears to have been the first professional musician so honoured in Great Britain, although this was perhaps on account more of 'the score of his merits' than of 'the merits of his scores' (Brown & Stratton, *Brit. mus.*). In 1796 Parsons was appointed instructor to the princesses. However, music was not his only interest, and his name was on the commission of the peace. For many years Parsons attended Bow Street police court as a kind of subsidiary magistrate, and he was later promoted to stipendiary magistrate at Worship Street, or, according to some, Great Marlborough Street. He died of apoplexy at his home in Somerset Street, Portman Square, London, on 19 July 1817, aged seventy-one. His will of 16 January 1816 left his whole estate to his wife, Charlotte Sophia, who proved the will on 2 August 1817.

Parsons was a professional member of the Catch Club, an honorary subscriber to the New Musical Fund, and a fellow of the Society of Antiquaries. He was an early patron of Michael Kelly and harmonized several of his songs, and also some by the composer and singer Charles Edward Horn. Evidently a gregarious character, Parsons was able to count eminent individuals such as members of the royal family and Joseph Haydn among his circle of friends. L. M. Middleton, *rev.* David J. Golby

Sources Highfill, Burnim & Langhans, *BDA* · *GM*, 1st ser., 87/2 (1817), 92 · Brown & Stratton, *Brit. mus.*, 312 · J. Doane, ed., *A musical directory for the year 1794* [1794]

Likenesses C. Wilkin, engraving, pubd 1790, U. Oxf., faculty of music; repro. in Highfill, Burnim & Langhans, *BDA*, p. 228 · C. Wilkin, oils, *c.*1790, U. Oxf., Examination Schools · Ridley and Blood, stipple (after drawing by F. Wilkins junior), NPG; repro. in *European Magazine* (1806) · oils, Royal Society of Musicians, London

Wealth at death left whole estate to widow: will, 1817

Parsons, William (*fl.* 1785–1824), poet, was a member of the group later known collectively as the Della Cruscan school, after the pseudonym of Robert *Merry (1755–1798), the most famous of their number; the group printed a number of verses in *The World* magazine during the mid to late 1780s. During that period Parsons was living in Florence, and he is mentioned by Hester Lynch Piozzi as being a flattering and agreeable member of her coterie in that city (*Autobiography*, 1.278). In the *Florence Miscellany* of 1785, the joint production of Mrs Piozzi, Robert Merry, Bertie Greatheed, and others, Parsons had the lion's share. His free translation from Dante set the Italianate tone of the collection, but did not draw the critical fire provoked by the stylistic excesses of Merry. According to William Gifford, Parsons was considerably nettled at not being included, 'though an undoubted Bavian', in the first edition of the *Baviad*, Gifford's scornful verse treatment of the vogue for the poetry of the Della Cruscans, a group that he had once referred to as a 'knot of fantastic coxcombs' (Gifford, ix). Parsons 'accordingly applied to me', maintained Gifford:

> (in a circuitous method, I confess), and as a particular favour was finally admitted … But instead of gratifying [his] ambition, as I fondly expected, and quieting him for ever, this reference had a most fatal effect upon his poor head, and from an honest, painstaking gentleman converted him in imagination into a minotaur. (ibid., 8–9n.)

Parsons's attempts at retaliation in *The Telegraph* and other London papers were deemed by one contemporary account mere 'pins and needles, shot at the javelin-proof armour' of Gifford (*Literary Memoirs*, 2.115).

Parsons adopted the deliberate pose of a gentleman amateur in *A Poetical Tour in the Years 1784, 1785, and 1786. By a Member of the Arcadian Society at Rome* (1787), in which 'the effusions of momentary impressions' are eked out by imitations, translations, and complimentary verses to Mrs Piozzi and Mrs Elizabeth Montagu. In November 1787 Parsons was elected a member of the Royal Society, and subsequently published only sporadically. His *Ode to a Boy at Eton* (1796) is addressed to the son of his fellow Della Cruscan Greatheed and was intended to 'counteract the gloomy conclusions' of Gray's better-known ode. *Fidelity, or, Love at First Sight: a Tale [in Verse], with other Poems* (1798) was a contribution to the contemporary fashion for Arthurian romance. Parsons's last known publication was *Travelling Recreations* (1807), in which he defined his ambition as 'merely to be classed among the mob of gentlemen who wrote with ease', but Gifford's satire had done irreparable damage, and subsequent generations classed him only among the acolytes of a once fashionable school of poetry. Although it is known that Parsons died before 2 March 1850, the exact date and place of his death are unknown; throughout his lifetime he appears to have resided mainly at Bath, however, when not travelling in Europe. Thomas Seccombe, *rev.* Corinna Russell

Sources W. Gifford, *The Baviad, and Maeviad*, new edn (1797), *passim* · *Autobiography, letters, and literary remains of Mrs Piozzi*, ed. A. Hayward, 1 (1861), 278 · [D. Rivers], *Literary memoirs of living authors of Great Britain*, 2 (1798), 115 · R. Marshall, *Italy in English literature, 1755–1815* (1934), 1.74–80 · *British Critic*, 7 (1796), 548–9 · T. Thomson, *History of the Royal Society from its institution to the end of the eighteenth century* (1812), appx 60 · *N&Q*, 1 (1849–50), 273

Parsons, William, third earl of Rosse (1800–1867), astronomer, was born on 17 June 1800 in York. He was the eldest son of Lawrence *Parsons, second earl of Rosse (1758–1841), and succeeded him in the courtesy title Lord Oxmantown in 1801. His mother was Alice (1779–1867), daughter of John Lloyd of Gloster, King's county, Ireland. He entered Trinity College, Dublin, in 1819, and transferred to Magdalen College, Oxford, where he matriculated in February 1821. He showed distinction in mathematics there and graduated in December 1822. From 1821 until 1834 he was member of parliament for King's county, where his father had his seat at Birr Castle in Parsonstown. He was made lord lieutenant of the county in 1831 and colonel of its militia in 1836. In 1836 he married Mary Field (1813–1885) [*see* Parsons, Mary, countess of Rosse], elder daughter of the wealthy John Wilmer Field of Heaton Hall, near Bradford in Yorkshire. She proved an energetic manager of the Parsons household and became a fine and prolific photographer. When the ailing second earl retired to Brighton to convalesce the newly-weds established their home at Birr Castle. Their first child, Alice, was born in 1839, but died at the age of eight. Of their eleven children only four, Laurence, Randal, Clere, and Charles, reached adulthood.

In 1824 Lord Oxmantown joined the Astronomical Society. He was fascinated by optical and mechanical engineering, especially the challenges of large reflecting telescopes. William Herschel had pioneered their design,

William Parsons, third earl of Rosse (1800–1867), by Stephen Catterson Smith, exh. Royal Hibernian Academy of Arts 1860

using a copper–tin alloy known as speculum metal for the mirrors, with triangular wooden altazimuth stands to hoist the tube and raise the observing platform. Oxmantown set out to perfect these techniques and, unlike Herschel, render them public, initially in the *Edinburgh Journal of Science* from 1828. He assembled a local team led by the blacksmith William Coghlan. Local peat bogs supplied the fuel for his well-controlled ovens. In his first experiments at Birr from 1827 Oxmantown made composite objective mirrors with disc and annular sections which could be adjusted longitudinally to bring together the rings' mean foci, so reducing spherical aberration. He also designed and publicized a 2 hp steam-driven mirror polishing machine. In 1831 he was elected to the Royal Society and in 1836 offered to build for his friend the London astronomer James South an equatorial telescope to replace that by Troughton, which the irascible South notoriously judged worthless. In 1839 Oxmantown completed a 3 ft diameter objective of sixteen radial sections for a Newtonian reflector with a focal length of 27 ft, and sent the Royal Society a full account of his techniques. His method for supporting the 3 ft mirror was borrowed from the capable Dublin instrument maker Thomas Grubb, who in turn adopted Oxmantown's careful recipes for casting the speculum. The following year Oxmantown at last produced an objective of the same size in one casting, and gave up experiments with composite mirrors. The Dublin natural philosopher William Rowan Hamilton was first to point the 3 ft reflector at a celestial object. In autumn 1840 Oxmantown invited South and the Armagh astronomer Thomas Romney Robinson to Birr to observe with the telescope. Robinson, in particular, prematurely announced that it could resolve many apparently gaseous nebulae first described by Herschel into congeries of stars. Robinson was confident that such resolutions would be more apparent with an even more powerful reflector and would thus undermine the fashionable nebular hypothesis, which claimed that suns and planets evolved naturally by the condensation of a celestial nebulous fluid. In late 1840, at the Royal Irish Academy, Robinson proclaimed Lord Oxmantown's successes and his telescope's potentially devastating consequences for nebular evolution.

Lord Oxmantown succeeded to the earldom on his father's death in February 1841, then launched his largest and most expensive telescope project, the construction of a Newtonian reflector with a 6 ft aperture and a 4 ton mirror. This instrument, known as 'the monster telescope' or 'Leviathan of Parsonstown', completed in 1844, was the largest telescope in the world for over six decades. Its total cost of £12,000 was principally met from the income of Lady Rosse's Yorkshire estates. Casting the mirror was a dramatic and well-publicized engineering achievement. The new earl commissioned a huge foundry with three peat-fired furnaces 4 ft in diameter for iron crucibles each holding 1.5 tons of alloy, and an annealing oven where the metal, having been emptied by cranes into a huge mould, was carefully cooled over a period of sixteen weeks. Only after five trials did his team produce a perfect casting for transfer to the grinding and polishing machine, but by early 1843 they managed to grind surface imperfections off the second casting to make two usable mirrors. Because polishing was slow and tarnishing fast it was preferable to repolish one mirror while observing with another. The Leviathan's tube and hoist were fixed between two massive Gothic meridian walls, 56 ft high and 72 ft long. A central stone pier carried a cast-iron universal joint for the mirror cell. The 56 ft wooden tube was controlled by winches, chains, and counterweights. The motion between the walls allowed a displacement of only 15° controlled by a screw linked to a 40 ft radius meridian arc. The observing platform for low elevations rose on staging at the south end of the walls; for higher altitudes a long gallery carried on the west wall moved across the central space to follow the tube's lateral motion. At least three assistants were needed to help the observer by moving the winch, giving the tube an east–west motion, and shifting the gallery.

The Leviathan was immediately treated as marvel and tourist attraction. During the meeting of the British Association for the Advancement of Science at Cork in 1843 Rosse as president organized a prestigious visit to his own observatory. William Lassell, who visited from Liverpool in 1844, was prompted to build his own large telescopes. In early 1845 Rosse purchased a more powerful Manchester steam engine for his polishing machine. Observations by Rosse, South, and Robinson began with the 6 ft telescope in February 1845. By April they had already achieved the telescope's most spectacular result, the discovery of the spiral structure of the whirlpool nebula Messier 51. Rosse showed drawings of this astonishing structure at the Cambridge meeting of the British Association in June 1845. Between Christmas 1845 and March 1846 Rosse's team even concluded that sections of the great Orion nebula could be resolved into stars, a claim damaging for the nebular hypothesis. Guidebooks and newspaper articles helped establish the earl's astronomical and technological repute. Some public reports distinguished between the world before and after Rosse. Through his West Riding connections Rosse had close links with the embattled Anglican minister in Bradford, the evangelical philosopher William Scoresby. Scoresby visited Birr Castle and lectured on Rosse's great telescope during a tour of the United States in 1848. The Glasgow astronomy professor John Pringle Nichol, another visitor to Birr and proponent of the nebular hypothesis, publicized Rosse's achievements on a similar lecture tour, and also lobbied the premier, Robert Peel, to give Rosse a British earldom. But the Birr Castle observatory was never quite able to fulfil such grand expectations. The claimed resolutions of Orion (Messier 42) were eventually firmly rejected by astronomers. The Irish climate often frustrated observers and visitors, the mirror's performance changed as it tarnished, and the Leviathan proved hard to manage.

In 1845 Rosse was elected an Irish representative peer and sat in the House of Lords in the Conservative interest. During the great famine public works schemes were directed at Birr Castle by Lady Rosse, while in 1847 Rosse himself sent letters to *The Times* recommending large-scale emigration and an end to the subdivision of inherited land to prevent further dearth and revolt. He discussed these views with his friend Nassau Senior and government officers. His duties and interests took him to London each year for the period of the summer social season. In 1848, on Edward Sabine's persuasion, he successfully put himself forward as president of the Royal Society, though concerned by loss of valuable time at the telescope. He won the society's royal medal in 1851, membership of the Imperial Academy of St Petersburg in 1853 and was made chevalier of the Légion d'honneur in 1855. He resigned the Royal Society's presidency in 1854. His efforts to shift its main activities to the period of the social season failed. So did his insistence that its council should include a significant number of political and aristocratic members, such as the Conservative Sir Robert Inglis, men whose close governmental connections were, he judged, vital for the president's power as lobbyist. These difficulties were graphically illustrated in 1852 when Rosse, long an enthusiastic partisan of Charles Babbage's plans to construct calculating machines, failed to persuade the chancellor of the exchequer, Benjamin Disraeli, to fund Babbage's difference engine. Rosse also held that the annual government grant to the society, inaugurated in 1849, should be spent on new experimental projects, not as reward for past achievements in the sciences. Rosse helped direct a substantial part of the 1849 grant to the publication of Robinson's Armagh observations. With Robinson's backing Rosse also led the society's committee, set up in 1852, to oversee the construction of a large reflector in the southern hemisphere. Rosse's committee began negotiations with Thomas Grubb to build such a telescope before the costly plan was abandoned at the outbreak of the Crimean War.

When he accepted the Royal Society's presidency Rosse discussed with Sabine and Robinson the staffing of his Birr observatory. The Leviathan was to be used for the selective re-examination of recorded nebulae, not discovery of new objects. After the disuse of the telescope during the famine Robinson arranged the repolishing of the objective and revived the observational programme. Robinson's nephew, William Rambaut, started work at Birr in 1848, as did the Dublin physicist George Johnstone Stoney and, from 1850, his brother, the engineer Bindon Blood Stoney. In 1850 the Pulkovo astronomer Otto Struve visited the earl to plan joint stellar observations between Birr and the Russian observatory, but the plans came to nothing. Rosse published major surveys of the nebulae in Herschel's catalogues in the *Philosophical Transactions of the Royal Society* and continued active experiments on his mirrors, including the substitution of silver for speculum metal, new kinds of suspension, and better ways of automating polishing. In autumn 1852 he chaired a British Association committee on standardized methods for mapping the moon. In 1852 both Stoney brothers left Birr Castle, and from 1853 Struve and other eminent astronomers began publicly to question the nebular resolutions claimed by Rosse's team. During the 1860s Rosse employed the artist Samuel Hunter to make improved drawings of Orion, and, from 1865 retained the astronomer Robert Ball, who also acted as tutor to his three younger sons. Rosse and Ball visited the astronomer William Huggins in London to learn about new spectroscopic techniques which they soon adopted at Birr, and which eventually demonstrated the truly gaseous quality of Orion and many other nebulae. Rosse continued to the end to maintain his eminence in the astronomical community and was a major patron of artisans and engineers through his expenditure on telescope development. Plans for a large southern hemisphere telescope were revived in 1862, and in 1866 Rosse joined the new committee to oversee Howard Grubb's work in constructing the great Melbourne reflector. Rosse also kept up his political and administrative activities. In 1862 he became chancellor of the University of Dublin and in 1867 published a further collection of essays on Irish land reform. Once again he endorsed emigration and estate consolidation, and attacked the political economy of writers on Irish affairs such as J. S. Mill. Isaac Butt, active defender of home rule, responded fiercely to the earl's views. Rosse died on 31 October 1867 as a consequence of an operation on his knee, and was buried at St Brendan's Church, Parsonstown. Lady Rosse died on 22 July 1885. Their eldest son, Laurence *Parsons, who as Lord Oxmantown had long taken an active role in his father's astronomical programme, inherited both the title and active management of the telescopic work. Their youngest son, Charles Algernon *Parsons, became a renowned engineer and inventor of the marine steam turbine. J. A. BENNETT

Sources H. C. King, *The history of the telescope* (1955) • P. Moore, *The astronomy of Birr Castle* (1971) • *Monthly Notices of the Royal Astronomical Society*, 29 (1868–9), 123–30 • *The scientific papers of William Parsons, third earl of Rosse, 1800–1867*, ed. C. Parsons (1926) • J. A. Bennett, *Church, state, and astronomy in Ireland: 200 years of Armagh observatory* (1990) • *Reminiscences and letters of Sir Robert Ball*, ed. W. V. Ball (1915) • R. B. McDowell and D. A. Webb, *Trinity College, Dublin, 1592–1952: an academic history* (1982) • I. S. Glass, *Victorian telescope makers: the lives and letters of Thomas and Howard Grubb* (1997) • M. B. Hall, *All scientists now: the Royal Society in the nineteenth century* (1984) • A. Chapman, *The Victorian amateur astronomer: independent astronomical research in Britain, 1820–1920* (1998) • J. R. Nudds, *Science in Ireland 1800–1930: tradition and reform* (1988) • E. G. Forbes, ed., *Human implications of scientific advance: the 15th International Congress of the History of Science* [Edinburgh 1977] (1978) • Burke, *Peerage*

Archives Birr Castle, Offaly, corresp. and papers | BL, letters to Charles Babbage, Add. MSS 37192–37201, *passim* • CUL, letters to Sir George Stokes • Lpool RO, letters to fourteenth earl of Derby • RS, corresp. with Sir J. F. W. Herschel

Likenesses Bosley, lithograph, pubd 1849 (after daguerreotype), BM • S. C. Smith, oils, exh. Royal Hibernian Academy of Arts 1860, RS [*see illus.*] • J. H. Foley, statue, 1874–6, St John's Place, Birr, Ireland • Maull & Polyblank, photograph, NPG

Part, Sir Antony Alexander (1916–1990), civil servant, was born on 28 June 1916 in Chelsea, London, the only son of Alexander Francis Part, barrister and company director, from a Lancashire family, and his second wife, Una Margaret Reynolds Snowdon, from Yorkshire. He had a younger sister, an older half-brother and half-sister, and a younger half-brother. His early childhood years were spent in happy and prosperous family surroundings in Chelsea, but his adolescence was overshadowed by his parents' divorce. After a good grounding in classics at a preparatory school he entered Harrow School with a scholarship at the age of twelve and later specialized in French and German. He won a scholarship to Trinity College, Cambridge, where he achieved first-class honours in both parts of the modern and medieval languages tripos (1935 and 1937).

Part entered the Board of Education in 1937 through the competitive examination for the administrative class of the home civil service. Though he was soon lent to the newly created Ministry of Supply, a keen interest in education and training motivated the greater part of his civil service career. In 1940 he married a ballet dancer, Isabella (Ella), daughter of Maurice Bennett, businessman. His marriage was happy and although they had no children he and his wife maintained a close relationship with his siblings and their children.

Part joined the Royal Ulster Rifles in 1940, but his knowledge of German quickly led to a commission in the intelligence corps, where by 1943 he had gained rapid promotion to lieutenant-colonel, serving in the western desert campaign and later in the Twenty-First Army group headquarters preparing for the invasion of France. His personality was changing. At school he had been shy and retiring. University had built his self-confidence. Finding in the army that he was thought somewhat over-assertive, he learned an important lesson about leadership which he never forgot.

Recalled to the Ministry of Education at the end of 1944, Part became principal private secretary to three successive ministers. His first major opportunity came in 1946 when he and the chief architect of the department as joint heads set up a new branch to assist education authorities to build the new schools needed to meet the demands of the rising birth rate and the raising of the school leaving age. The programme they developed was so effective in enabling good schools to be built quickly at acceptable cost that it earned international reputation. As a Commonwealth Fund fellow in the USA in 1950–51, Part found leading American experts in school building eager to learn from him about these British methods. He contracted tuberculosis in America and did not return to work until spring 1953.

Promoted to under-secretary in 1954 as head of the schools branch and later of the further education branch, Part was active in the initiatives to improve and expand technical training at all levels through technical colleges and colleges of advanced technology. He became deputy secretary in 1960, covering teacher training and further education, served as a departmental assessor on the committee on higher education (1961–4) chaired by Lord Robbins, and seemed well positioned by ability and experience to achieve his growing ambition to become permanent secretary of the Ministry of Education.

There were, however, other plans for Part. In March 1963 he was moved to the Ministry of Works to organize a merger of departments into the Ministry of Public Building and Works, of which he became permanent secretary in 1965. It was as permanent secretary of the Board of Trade in 1968, of the newly created Department of Trade and Industry in 1970, and of the Department of Industry from 1974 to 1976 that he had the greatest scope for the exercise of his talents and experience. He worked hard to establish an industrial department as a major force in Whitehall and was greatly upset by the decision of the Labour government to split the Department of Trade and Industry into three in 1974. His strengths were his vision, his genuine interest in manufacturing industry, his ability to work constructively with most businessmen, trade unionists, and politicians, and his flair for public speaking. He exhibited great energy and determination in everything he undertook, whether in the fields of education or trade and industry. He put into practice his strong conviction that public administration should be efficient and financially prudent.

After retiring from the civil service in 1976, Part took up a new career as a non-executive director of a number of firms, including chairmanship of Orion Insurance Company. He continued his active interest in education as deputy chairman of the court of governors of the London School of Economics. Part was appointed MBE (1943), CB (1959), KCB (1966), and GCB (1974). He received honorary degrees from Brunel (1966), Aston (1974), and Cranfield (1976), and an honorary fellowship of the London School of Economics (1984). In his prime he was tall and dark with a confident bearing. However, he had poor health all his life and this greatly affected his appearance in his last years in the civil service and thereafter, major heart surgery causing him to have a pronounced stoop and to move very slowly. He enjoyed the performing arts, but his main interests were in his work in both public and private sectors, which despite his ready wit he took very seriously. Part, who lived latterly at Flat 5, 71 Elm Park Gardens, London, died of heart failure in Westminster Hospital, London, on 11 January 1990. A memorial service was held at St Margaret's, Westminster, on 22 February 1990. He was survived by his wife. Douglas Croham, *rev.*

Sources A. Part, *The making of a mandarin* (1990) • *The Times* (15 Jan 1990) • *The Times* (25 Jan 1990) • *The Independent* (16 Jan 1990) • *CGPLA Eng. & Wales* (1990)
Archives CAC Cam., corresp.
Wealth at death £150,096: probate, 27 April 1990, *CGPLA Eng. & Wales*

Partington, Charles Frederick (*fl.* 1820–1835), writer and lecturer on technology and practical science, is of obscure origins. Nothing is known either of his personal life. The first edition of his *History and Descriptive Account of the Steam Engine* appeared in 1822 and he then began an active period as a lecturer on such practical subjects. Between 1823 and 1830 he lectured regularly at the London Institution, in some cases offering broad (although brief) surveys of such subjects as natural or experimental philosophy, at other times focusing on a relatively narrow subject such as the nature and properties of water. He lectured to the London Mechanics' Institution in 1825 and 1833, appeared at the Russell and Surrey institutions, and was regularly employed by the mechanics' institutes of Yorkshire and Lancashire; he commanded the highest fees paid to a lecturer by the Stalybridge Mechanics' Institution.

At the London Institution in December 1823 Partington delivered a group of lectures on mechanical philosophy specifically for young people, a practice he repeated the following year as well. While the idea of science lectures for the young had been widely touted since the eighteenth century Partington's lectures were among the earliest offered within a London institutional setting, for the famous youth lectures by Michael Faraday at the Royal Institution did not begin until December 1827. For a time Partington was employed as an assistant librarian at the London Institution, although his salary was paid by the librarian, William Maltby; this arrangement ended in 1832. In his publications he sometimes entitled himself 'of the London Institution'; the Institution's management objected to that practice and insisted that such references cease. Like many popular lecturers of his time, Partington was chiefly dependent on the fees paid him for individual courses by different organizations and on whatever income his writing produced.

Partington's writings and lectures particularly emphasized the steam engine, manufacturing processes, and construction technology. In addition to his treatises on the steam engine, his *Mechanics' Library, or, Book of Trades* (first published in 1825) was his most substantial work, and some of its components enjoyed a long period of influence; *The Engravers' Complete Guide* continued to be cited in twentieth-century discussions of engraving technique. He edited a *British Cyclopedia* (in ten volumes) in 1835, a *Scientific Gazette* in 1825–6, and co-edited the influential *London Journal of Arts and Sciences* between 1828 and 1834. He also wrote on London topography; one of his first publications was a *Brief Account of the Royal Gardens Vauxhall* (1822), and one of his last was a *National History and Views of London* (1834). An intense practicality and appeal to utility dominated his writings, but historical interests also characterized his work: in 1825 he prepared an edition of the marquess of Worcester's *Century of Inventions* (1663), praising its anticipation of the principles of the steam engine, as well as an edition of James Ferguson's eighteenth-century lectures on various physical subjects. His lectures included these practical and historical emphases, and he took particular pride in the large collection of working models with which he illustrated his lectures on manufacturing processes and steam engines.

Partington's enthusiasm for technology in general, and for the steam engine in particular, was characteristic of the group of popular lecturers and writers to which he belonged.

> Without the aid of the steam engine, the commercial industry of this country must instantly sink before the competition which would then ensue with the rest of Europe. And though it throws many of the operative classes out of employ, it opens new channels for their productive industry. (*Popular and Descriptive Account of the Steam Engine*, 3rd edn, 1836, xiii)

Partington is not known to have taken part in research activity, nor did he figure in the early professionalization of science manifested in the scientific societies of the early nineteenth century. His main significance is as a pioneering popular lecturer, influential editor, and textbook writer. He has not attracted much attention from historians. As an expositor of the steam engine he was overshadowed by the more successful Dionysius Lardner. His career seems to have ended in the mid-1830s. It is not known when he died. J. N. Hays

Sources J. N. Hays, 'Science in the City: the London Institution, 1819–1840', *British Journal for the History of Science*, 7 (1974), 146–62 • J. C. Cutler, 'The London Institution, 1805–1933', PhD diss., University of Leicester, 1976 • J. N. Hays, 'The London lecturing empire, 1800–1850', *Metropolis and province: science in British culture, 1780–1850*, ed. I. Inkster and J. Morrell (1983), 91–119 • M. Tylecote, *The mechanics' institutes of Lancashire and Yorkshire before 1851* (1957)

Partington, James Riddick (1886–1965), chemist and historian of science, was born on 20 June 1886 at 194 Morris Green Lane, Middle Hulton, Lancashire, the only son and first of the three children of Alfred Partington, bookkeeper of Bolton, and his wife, Mary Agnes, daughter of Adam Riddick, tailor, of Dumfries. He was educated at Southport Science and Art School and became articled to the public analyst in Bolton after his parents returned there in 1901. By private study he qualified for entrance to Manchester University in 1906. After obtaining first-class honours in chemistry in 1909 he did research in physical organic chemistry under Arthur Lapworth, held a Beyer

James Riddick Partington (1886–1965), by Ruth Partington

fellowship (1910–11), and was awarded the MSc in 1911; his DSc followed in 1918.

An 1851 Exhibition scholarship enabled Partington to work on the specific heats of gases under H. Walther Nernst in Berlin from 1911 to 1913. Nernst's belief that mathematics was indispensable to the physical chemist inspired Partington's first book, *Higher Mathematics for University Students* (1911; 4th edn, 1931), while Nernst's grasp of theory and consummate experimental abilities gave Partington a model for his own academic career. Like Nernst, Partington wrote an influential *Textbook of Thermodynamics* (1913; 4th edn, 1950). He was an assistant lecturer and demonstrator in chemistry at Manchester University from 1913 to 1919, when London University appointed him professor of chemistry at East London College (renamed Queen Mary College in 1934). On 6 September 1919 Partington married Marian (*d.* 1940), daughter of Thomas Jones, brickworks manager, of Buckley, Chester. They had one son and two daughters.

Partington's reputation had grown during the First World War. Soon after it started he joined the army and saw active service as an infantry and engineer officer, becoming a captain. For some time he purified water for the troops on the Somme, working on a barge with fellow chemist Eric K. Rideal. In 1916 they were transferred to the munitions inventions department of the Ministry of Munitions and, in the chemistry department of University College, London, headed by F. G. Donnan, joined a team developing a method of manufacturing nitric acid, needed for explosives, from atmospheric nitrogen. Partington's war experiences of applied chemistry led to two further books, *The Alkali Industry* (1918; 2nd edn, 1925) and, with L. H. Parker, *The Nitrogen Industry* (1922). He was appointed MBE (military) in 1918 and thereafter always adopted a military air.

Until retiring in 1951 Partington remained at Queen Mary College, which elected him a fellow in 1959. He continued research on specific heats of gases, electrochemistry, thermodynamics, and other topics, mainly in inorganic physical chemistry, and spent much time writing and revising textbooks on inorganic and physical chemistry for students at different levels. Despite a dazzling output of research papers it was these influential textbooks rather than his experimental work that made his name familiar to all chemists. His monumental *An Advanced Treatise on Physical Chemistry* (5 vols., 1949–54) contains a wealth of data in 1.5 million words and is of lasting value.

Partington's historical writings, which had begun in 1928 with a monograph, *The Composition of Water*, constitute his most enduring work. A meticulous scholar, he taught himself ancient and modern languages, used primary sources wherever possible, and produced a steady stream of books and articles on the history of chemistry. His *Origins and Development of Applied Chemistry* (1935) is a massive study of the production and uses of materials in the Near and Middle East to the end of the Bronze Age, the date at which previous historians of science had started. His military experience added weight to his criticism of earlier writings on the subject in *A History of Greek Fire and Gunpowder* (1960). His fine *A Short History of Chemistry* (1937; 2nd edn, 1948) was the forerunner of the encyclopaedic *A History of Chemistry* (4 vols., 1961–70). Volumes 2–4 are a richly documented account of the period since 1500; Partington did not complete volume 1, part of which appeared posthumously, so his final views on alchemy remain unpublished.

During the Second World War Partington's college was evacuated to Cambridge. He lived there until 1964, then moved to Northwich, Cheshire, to be near his sister. His house was full of books, and in his study he could smoke his favourite strong tobacco, but he was often seen in London or Cambridge libraries, reading with intense concentration, constantly writing on slips of paper which he subsequently edited and pasted together to form the manuscript for a tolerant printer. A blunt and outspoken critic of contemporaries whose achievements seemed to him inadequate, he nevertheless gave praise where it was due. He was highly regarded in the 1920s and 1930s for his wide and scholarly knowledge of chemistry, his integrity, precision, and good sense, and those who knew him only as a historian in later years remember a reserved man with a dry sense of humour which reveals itself in the prefaces of some of his books.

Partington was the first chairman (1937–8) of the Society for the Study of Alchemy and Early Chemistry; now the Society for the History of Alchemy and Chemistry, it awards the triennial Partington prize to a young historian. From 1949 to 1951 he was president of the British Society for the History of Science. He received the American Chemical Society's Dexter award for history of chemistry in 1961 and the Sarton medal of the American History of Science Society shortly before his death.

Partington died on 9 October 1965 in the Grange Hospital, Weaverham, Cheshire. He bequeathed his fine library to Manchester University.

W. A. Smeaton, *rev.* W. H. Brock

Sources F. H. C. Butler, *British Journal for the History of Science*, 3 (1966–7), 70–72 • F. W. Gibbs, *Chemistry and Industry* (22 Jan 1966), 151 • *The Times* (11 Oct 1965) • *The Times* (15 Oct 1965) • *WWW* • J. C.

Poggendorff and others, eds., *Biographisch-literarisches Handwörterbuch zur Geschichte der exacten Naturwissenschaften*, 7b, pt 6 (Berlin, 1980), 3870–73 · J. R. Partington, 'Nernst Memorial Lecture', *JCS* (1953), 2853–72 · b. cert. · m. cert. · d. cert.

Archives JRL, notebooks

Likenesses R. Partington, photograph, Queen Mary and Westfield College, chemistry department [*see illus.*] · photograph, repro. in *Chemistry and Industry* (6 May 1932), p. 394 · photograph, repro. in Gibbs, *Chemistry and Industry*

Wealth at death £56,539: probate, 15 Dec 1965, *CGPLA Eng. & Wales*

Partridge, Sir (John) Bernard (1861–1945), cartoonist and illustrator, was born in London on 11 October 1861, the sixth child and third son of Richard *Partridge FRS (1805–1873) and his wife, Frances Janette (Fanny) Turner. His father was professor of anatomy at the Royal Academy and later president of the Royal College of Surgeons, and his uncle, John *Partridge (1789–1872), was portrait painter-extraordinary to Queen Victoria. He was educated at Stonyhurst College, Lancashire, and later studied at the West London School of Art. For a brief period he worked as a stained-glass designer and as a decorator of church interiors. At about the same time he acted professionally under the name of Bernard Gould with Henry Irving and Johnston Forbes-Robertson. He also played the part of Sergius Saranoff in the first performance of *Arms and the Man* by George Bernard Shaw in 1894. In 1897 he married Lydia Faith, the daughter of Edward Harvey. They had no children. He had joined the staff of *Punch* in 1891 on the recommendation of George Du Maurier and served as junior cartoonist under Edward Linley Sambourne, succeeding him as second cartoonist in 1901 and as principal cartoonist in 1910. For some years he contributed chiefly joke and theatrical cartoons but in 1899, not without misgivings, he turned to political caricatures. His final political cartoon was published on 18 April 1945, so that his career in this area was almost as long as that of Sir John Tenniel while his years of service to the pages of *Punch* were still longer. Ninety-four years of *Punch* cartoons were covered by these two draughtsmen.

The influence of the theatre was frequently evident in Partridge's drawings, and he sometimes seemed to make his cartoons a stage on which he mounted any scene and setting whether tragic or comic, carefully delineated, and appropriately costumed. He used shading and often rendered the minutest details. He was perhaps less vivacious than Tenniel, but his secure draughtsmanship and his knowledge of historical periods and their right setting made almost any subject safe in his hands. A famous example, *Unconquerable*, of Kaiser Wilhelm II and Albert, King of the Belgians, published on 21 October 1914, shows his talent in depicting facial expressions. He seldom burlesqued his characters, though he could do so with considerable power when the occasion demanded: his general fidelity to truth saved him from the difficulty sometimes experienced by cartoonists when called upon to deal with tragic events, or to administer encouragement rather than rebuke. His likenesses were excellent, and he made regular use of a strong image drawn with academic correctness and a constant emphasis on symbolism. By the time of his death his style was decidedly old-fashioned in appearance, especially when compared to contemporaries such as David Low.

Sir (John) Bernard Partridge (1861–1945), by Emil Otto Hoppé, 1915

Partridge was probably at his best in heroic or grandiose scenes, and many of his cartoons during the first and second world wars were strikingly powerful, dignified and memorable. However, it is perhaps regrettable that his lively early book illustrations and social cartoons were overshadowed by his political drawings. Handsome and courteous, he was often spoken of by his colleagues as one of the last of the Victorians. He painted in oils, watercolours, and pastels and exhibited at the Royal Academy and the New English Art Club. He drew for many other magazines, including *Moonshine*, *Lady's Pictorial* and *The Sketch*. In 1925 he was knighted. Partridge died on 9 August 1945 at his home, 10 Holland Park Road, Kensington, London. His wife survived him. A collection of his drawings, *Mr. Punch's Personalities, 1926–1929*, is in the National Portrait Gallery, Kensington, London, where there is also a self-portrait in chalk and wash on paper. There are drawings by him in several public collections, including the British Museum, Victoria and Albert Museum, and Imperial War Museum, London, some municipal art galleries, and the University of Kent at Canterbury.

E. V. KNOX, *rev.* PAUL GOLDMAN

Sources M. Bryant and S. Heneage, eds., *Dictionary of British cartoonists and caricaturists, 1730–1980* (1994) · S. Houfe, *The dictionary of 19th century British book illustrators and caricaturists*, rev. edn (1996) · D. P. Whiteley, 'Bernard Partridge and *Punch*', *Image*, 8 (1952), 48–59 · D. Low, *British cartoonists, caricaturists and comic artists* (1942) · J. Johnson and A. Greutzner, *The dictionary of British artists, 1880–*

1940 (1976), vol. 5 of *Dictionary of British art* • B. Dolman, ed., *A dictionary of contemporary British artists* (1929) • R. G. G. Price, *A history of Punch* (1957) • *CGPLA Eng. & Wales* (1945) • *The Times* (11 Aug 1945) • personal knowledge (1959) • private information (1959)

Archives BL, corresp. with T. A. Guthrie, Add. MSS 54263–54267 • CUL, letters to Austin Dobson • Richmond Local Studies Library, London, corresp. with Douglas Sladen

Likenesses J. Russell & Sons, cabinet photograph, *c.*1885, NPG • Bassano, photograph, *c.*1885–1886, NPG • Elliott & Fry, cabinet photograph, *c.*1886, NPG • E. O. Hoppé, photograph, 1915, NPG [*see illus.*] • H. Coster, photographs, 1930, NPG • W. Reynolds-Stevens, metal bust, 1937, NPG • B. Partridge, self-portrait, chalk and wash drawing, NPG • R. Peacock, oils, NPG

Wealth at death £13,596 1*s.* 6*d.*: probate, 30 Nov 1945, *CGPLA Eng. & Wales*

Partridge, Eric Honeywood [*pseuds.* Corrie Denison, Vigilans] (**1894–1979**), lexicographer and etymologist, was born on 6 February 1894 on a farm in the Waimata valley near Gisborne, North Island, New Zealand, son of John Thomas Partridge, grazier, and his wife, Ethel Annabella Norris. In 1907 the family moved to Brisbane in Australia. Thanks to a literary father, he had been able to use dictionaries—'those … sources of sober, never-disillusioning entertainment' (Partridge, 66)—from the age of seven, and he became an enthusiastic teenage writer. He left Toowoomba grammar school at sixteen and, after working as a trainee teacher, won a scholarship to the University of Queensland to read classics, before switching to French and English. In April 1915 he joined the Australian infantry and served in Egypt, at Gallipoli, and on the western front, where he was wounded.

Back in Australia, Partridge took his BA degree. He then departed for Oxford University, where he read for his University of Queensland MA in eighteenth-century English romantic poetry and an Oxford BLitt in comparative literature. He taught briefly at a Lancashire grammar school, and then at the universities of Manchester (1925–6) and London (1926–7). In 1925 he married Agnes Dora (1893–1978), daughter of Arthur James Vye-Parminter, an architect. They had a daughter.

Never a comfortable public speaker, Partridge abandoned teaching in 1927, newly styling himself 'a man of letters'. To this end Partridge founded the Scholartis Press ('scholarly' plus 'artistic'), on capital of £100; it survived until 1931 when it foundered in the depression, leaving Partridge bankrupt. Of the list's 100 titles—including three novels by Corrie Denison (Partridge's pseudonym)—few made any mark, but three of them indicated the editor-in-chief's future: *Songs and Slang of the British Soldier*, edited by Partridge with John Brophy (1930); the British edition of Godfrey Irwin's *American Tramp and Underworld Slang* (1930); and Partridge's edition of Francis Grose's *Classical Dictionary of the Vulgar Tongue* (1931).

In 1933 came Partridge's first attempt at lexicology: *Words, Words, Words!* This was swiftly succeeded by his first essay at the topic that dominated his professional life: slang. Having been commissioned by Routledge, where the publisher Cecil Franklin had noticed the language-related Scholartis publications, *Slang Today and Yesterday* appeared in 1933; the book that sprang from these relatively tentative explorations, *A Dictionary of Slang and Unconventional English*, was published in 1937. *A Dictionary of the Underworld*, dealing with British and American cant, appeared in 1949; *Origins*, an etymological dictionary, in 1958. All were to be revised. Partridge was a wide-ranging, prolific author, driven both by his desire, almost literally, to 'preach the word', and by the need for cash. Dictionaries aside, he published *Shakespeare's Bawdy* (1947), *Chamber of Horrors*, 'a glossary of official jargon' by Vigilans (1952), and *Comic Alphabets* (1961). *You Have a Point There* (1953) dealt with punctuation, and *Usage and Abusage* (1942) aimed to topple Fowler's *English Usage* from its dominance of the field.

Partridge joined the army education corps in the Second World War (1940–41), and later moved to the correspondence department of the RAF (1942–5). Demobbed in 1945, he returned to a career that left him unrivalled as Britain's leading solo lexicographer. A good cricketer and tennis player, he was a regular at Lord's, the Oval, and Wimbledon, and wrote professionally on tennis. He died at Moretonhampstead, Devon, on 1 June 1979, a resident of a nursing home, Holcombe House, working on the revision of his *Dictionary of Catch Phrases*, first published in 1977.

In an age of teams, of academic sinecures, and of publishing-house reference departments and substantial advances, Partridge remains in many ways the classic lexicographer of his time. Like 'Webster' and 'Johnson', 'Partridge' stands among the dictionary's eponyms. Even Murray, other than for a brief period when a few Oxonians talked of 'Murray's dictionary', cannot claim that honour.

As well as scholarship Partridge invariably offers a human dimension. He was, it has been recalled, with perhaps a little overstatement, the classic 'nutty professor': the big overcoat, the cigarette, the long white hair adrift, the undisputed occupation of seat K1 at the British Library. No one could have been further from the corpus-based productions (and producers) of today's dictionaries. He had, in a discipline where wit is at a premium, a sense of humour. As Anthony Burgess put it, he was not a linguist but a philologist, quite literally a 'lover' of words. Cheerfully refusing to admit linguistics into his lexicography, he always wanted to make some kind of statement. For him something was always better than nothing—even if that something might err towards guesswork. He could also, as with his etymology of 'phoney', be quite inspired.

What Partridge did was to amass a lexicon of English slang that will inevitably be overtaken, but will never be surpassed. Like any modern slang lexicographer, he was essentially a linguistic voyeur—kneeling at the keyhole to scribble down the vocabularies of worlds in which he would take no active part—but his eyesight was surpassing in its clarity and breadth of vision. Incorporating the whole range of his predecessors, from the sixteenth century onwards, he unified a vocabulary that might otherwise have vanished. His own first efforts were based on J. S. Farmer's and W. E. Henley's seven-volume work of the 1890s, passed on to him for revision by his publishers, but he moved far beyond them. Unlike them he had the *Oxford*

English Dictionary against which to assay his discoveries and theories, but—as his many citations in the second edition make clear—the debts were mutual.

JONATHON GREEN

Sources E. Partridge, 'Genesis of a lexicographer', *From Sanskrit to Brazil* (1952) · D. Crystal, ed., *Eric Partridge in his own words* (1980) · *DNB* · J. Green, *Chasing the sun: dictionary-makers and the dictionaries they made*, pbk edn (1997) · A. Burgess, *A mouthful of air* (1992) · *CGPLA Eng. & Wales* (1979) · m. cert.

Archives University of San Francisco, California, corresp., literary MSS, and papers | BL, letters to R. F. L. Bancroft, Add. MSS 62551, 63520 · CUL, letters to E. H. Blakeney · King's Lond., Liddell Hart C., corresp. with Sir B. H. Liddell Hart · RIBA, letters to Philip Tilden · U. Birm. L., letters to C. T. Onions · Warks. CRO, letters to R. E. H. Duke

Likenesses photograph

Wealth at death £82,678: probate, 18 Dec 1979, *CGPLA Eng. & Wales*

Partridge, John (*fl.* 1566–1582), translator and poet, was the author of three long poems, two household books, and several shorter texts. His three major poems, *Lady Pandavola*, *Astianax and Polixena*, and *The Worthie Hystorie of … Plasidas*, were all printed in 1566. *Lady Pandavola* narrates the love of Pandavola and Alfyne, and culminates in the tragic deaths of the two lovers. The story is followed by three poems—a dedicatory poem to Thomas Baynam, verses in praise of faithful friends, and a final poem against flattery—which highlight the major themes of the romance: faithfulness, love, treason, and tyranny. The poem, of 969 lines, is written in alternating lines of iambic hexameter and heptameter, with epistles and poems in different verse forms interspersed. The theme of treason also figures prominently in *Astianax*, written in 121 couplets of iambic heptameter. It narrates the sacrifices of Polixena (the Trojan princess) and Astianax (Hector's son), in order to show 'of warre the cruell fate' (l. 8). *Astianax* appears to be based on Jasper Heywood's translation of Seneca's *Troades*, Ovid's *Metamorphoses*, and Lydgate's *Troy Book*. Partridge's third long poem, *Plasidas*, comprises 632 rhyming couplets of iambic heptameter and is a generic mixture of romance and hagiography. Partridge uses this very popular story (earlier versions appear in Caxton's *Golden Legende* and in the *Gesta Romanorum*) to instruct his readers about divine providence and the virtue of patience. It is dedicated to Arthur Dwabene, a 'marchaunt venturer' to whom Partridge is 'servante and dayly oratour' (dedicatory letter). *Plasidas* is embellished with classical and biblical allusions, vivid descriptions of nature, and animal imagery and symbolism.

Partridge's two household books—*The Treasurie of Commodious Conceits* (1573) and *The Widowes Treasure* (1582)—are very similar; but while *The Treasurie* contains mostly recipes, the contents of *The Widowes Treasure* are more medical than culinary. The former is dedicated to Master Richard Wistow, assistant to the Company of Barbers and Surgeons, and the latter to an unnamed gentlewoman. These were Partridge's most popular compositions: *The Treasurie* went through thirteen editions from 1573 to 1637; and between 1582 and 1639 *The Widowes Treasure* was printed ten times. Partridge also composed a pamphlet entitled *The Ende and Confession of John Felton*. Felton was a papist who denied Elizabeth's supremacy. The pamphlet contains an account of Felton's crimes and execution, the proclamation read at his execution, and a warning poem (of sixty-six rhyming couplets in alternating lines of iambic hexameter and heptameter) to other papists of their fate if they continue to disobey queen and church. *An Admonition of Warning to England* comprises twenty-four rhyming couplets in alternating lines of iambic hexameter and heptameter. It is an emotional plea to England to repent before disaster strikes. The poem was written to accompany, and was published with, an account of the 1565 Neapolitan earthquake, and presents natural disaster as a form of divine punishment. Partridge may also have penned the ballad *A Mervaylous Straunge Deformed Swyne*. It is signed I. P. and has been variously attributed to Partridge, John Pitts, and John Phillips.

JOYCE BORO

Sources *Hystorie of the moste noble knight Plasidas and other rare pieces: collected into one book by Samuel Pepys, and forming part of the Pepsyan Library at Magdalene College, Cambridge*, ed. H. G. Gibbs (1873) · D. Bush, *Mythology and the Renaissance tradition in English poetry* (1932) · *DNB*

Partridge, John (1644–1715), astrologer and almanac writer, was born on 18 January 1644 in East Sheen, Surrey, the son of John Partridge, a Thames waterman who was also a sidesman and assessor of the parish, and Elizabeth, who died in January 1661 and was buried in the Mortlake parish churchyard. East Sheen was then a rural area, and it is evident from Partridge's will, where he asked to be buried there or in a neighbouring riverside parish, rather than in London where he lived, that he retained a lifelong attachment to that area, and its associated 'country' virtues. His first employment was as a cobbler, but he soon taught himself Latin, and some Greek and Hebrew. He also studied medicine and astrology, and was instructed in the latter by a Dr Francis Wright.

Astrological and political activities, 1677–1694 About 1677 Partridge moved to Covent Garden, London (in James or Henrietta Street), where he issued his first publication, *Calendarium Judiacum, or, An Almanack* (1678). This was quickly followed the next year by five astrological works: *Mikropanastrōn, or, An Astrological Vade Mecum*; *Ekklēsialogia: an Almanack* (1679); *Vox lunaris*, 'being a philosophical and Astrological Discourse of two Moons which were seen in London on 11 June 1679'; an essay on the nativity of Louis XIV; and *Prodromus*, 'an astrological essay'. Increasingly, however, he devoted most of his efforts to his annual almanac. At its beginning in 1681 the annual title was *Mercurius Coelestis*. In 1683 it changed to *Mercurius Redivivus*. Finally, from 1690 he opted for *Merlinus Liberatus*, which encapsulates his simultaneously mystical and political concerns. It also invoked William Lilly's earlier and highly influential almanac, *Merlinus Anglicus*.

In politics Partridge was a passionate and radical whig, to the point of open republicanism, who claimed membership in the notorious Calves Head Club. In religion he was equally strongly dissenting, anti-Catholic and anti-clerical. 'Priest! P— on the name, I loathe the very smell' (*Almanack for the Year of our Redemption*, sig. A4) he wrote in

John Partridge (1644–1715), by unknown engraver

his almanac for 1687. His relentless promotion of his extreme beliefs, with corresponding attacks on James II, tories, and the church, all expressed in colourful and often violent language, frequently placed him in danger of imprisonment and even execution. Like his civil war predecessors he used the stars to discover, authorize, and express these radical sentiments; the advantages of such implied divine sanction and apparently disinterested insights were legion.

Partridge's astrology, at the same time, was not simply a useful tool, cynically employed as propaganda. He was also equally concerned with effecting a revolution in his subject, a return to putative roots. He sought to re-establish the astrological tradition founded by Ptolemy in the second century AD, and to rescue his craft from what he considered to be modern decadence. His two major books are both efforts in that direction, and they were as ambitious and vigorously polemical as his more topical almanacs. Before taking up this project in earnest, the political events of the day intervened. During the exclusion crisis and in its aftermath he lashed the tories and 'papists', and thus by the time of James II's accession in 1685 he was already a well-known opponent of the new regime. That same year he prudently removed to the Netherlands. (He claims to have acquired a Dutch medical degree at this time; whether this was earned, purchased, or simply invented is difficult to establish. On his tombstone it is claimed that the doctorate was from Leiden.)

Partridge's almanacs for 1687 and 1688 dropped their usual titles for something more dramatic—*An Almanack for the Year of our Redemption* (1687) and *Annus mirabilis* (1688). Produced under the transparent alias John Wildfowl and printed in the Netherlands, they fiercely denounced James II's government, and proclaimed that 'a commonwealth's the thing that kingdoms want' (*Almanack for the Year of our Redemption*, 1687, B4v).

Placing himself in the tradition of biblical prophecy, Partridge used *Mene Tekel* (1688) to predict James's death for that year, and in the November he returned to England with the forces of William III, to be present at the latter's accession. He did not produce an almanac for 1689 but that year's *Mene Mene, Tekel Upharsin* included a prognostication and set the seal of the stars on the revolution of 1688 claiming vindication in the flight of James as 'a civil death'.

Some elements of Stuart censorship of almanacs survived the revolution, and Partridge continued to test its limits by, for example, omitting the death of Charles I (normally printed in red ink, as befits a martyr) from the section on saints' days. Archbishop Tillotson immediately reprimanded the Company of Stationers, and threatened further measures. However, such direct censorship expired with the Printing Act of 1695.

The reform of astrology In the 1690s, Partridge took up residence at the sign of the Blue Ball, Salisbury Court, Blackfriars. His almanac was now well on the way to becoming the Company of Stationers' best-selling title, and for that reason, the most frequently copied. Partridge complained that three or four fake editions were available every year. In February 1694 he married Jane Kirkman, who was said to be the widow of one of the duke of Monmouth's tailors, and independently wealthy.

In the main, however, Partridge's energies in this decade were devoted to astrological battles. He was the acknowledged leader of a programme to reform astrology, which he viewed as corrupted (also a whig and republican theme), and which he intended to restore to its former glory by 'Reviving the True and Ancient Method laid down for our Direction by the Great Ptolemy'. He announced his aim in *Opus reformatum* (1693). For Partridge and his principal ally, John Whalley, Ptolemy had provided something very like the equivalent of the whigs' 'Ancient Constitution' for astrologers.

This reform project recognized the disrepair and sinking estate of astrology in England since 1660. It placed the blame on the popular, magical, and ostensibly decadent practices of 'Magick-Mongers, Sigil-Merchants, Charm-Broakers, &c.' (J. Partridge, *Defectio geniturarum*, 1697, BV). The remedy, according to Partridge, was a reform of astrology along strictly rational lines, as 'no otherways than as a Branch of Natural Philosophy' (*Opus reformatum*,

1693, viii)—not in the sense adhered to by the Royal Society, but rather using principles of 'Motion, Rays, and Influence' (ibid.) formulated in the Aristotelian tradition, mathematically adumbrated, and resulting in precise (and indeed, testable) predictions.

Partridge and Whalley were responding not only to the declining reputation of astrology but to a slightly earlier and very different reform programme with the same broad aim. This was inspired by the new experimental philosophy of Francis Bacon, and was opposed to Aristotelian rationalism. Its main exponents were Joshua Childrey, John Goad, and John Gadbury, all, as it happens, tories and Anglicans, if not crypto-Catholics.

Partridge thus had a double set of reasons to hate these competing reformers, and he set about attacking them with his usual polemical gusto. His principal target was their leader, Gadbury, who had already been the butt of Partridge's libellous *Nebulo Anglicanus* in 1693. Gadbury's pioneering *Collectio geniturarum* (1662) attempted to approach the subject of nativities systematically and comparatively. Partridge's next book was duly entitled *Defectio geniturarum* (1697), 'Being an Essay toward the Reviving and Proving the True Old Principles of Astrology'. It attacked Gadbury as an 'ignorant Reformer' along with his data, his methods of interpretation, his colleague George Parker, the innovations of Kepler, and the heliocentric astrology with which several of the Baconian reformers had experimented. Instead Partridge offered a narrowly internal, puritanically pure, and thoroughly traditional astrology, rational and naturalistic in the Aristotelian sense. There is no mistaking his sense of urgency: 'never did Astrology stand in need of a speedy Reformation more than at this time … Astrology is now like a dead Carkass' (*Defectio geniturarum*, B2R).

Partridge continued the dispute with an attack on Parker in *Flagitiosis mercurius flagellatus* (1697), in which he accused Parker of wife-beating, adding that he 'whipped her too the heliocentric way' (p. 28). Parker returned the favour, asserting (for example) in his almanac for 1706 that Partridge's real family name was Hewson, and calling him 'a Junior Hewson' (Mayhew, 41), clearly a reference to Colonel John Hewson (*d.* 1662), a particularly ruthless soldier and judge under Cromwell, also originally a cobbler, who was still remembered in the early eighteenth century. (But not, it seems, by a later biographer of Partridge, Bishop Thomas Percy of Dromore, writing in *The Tatler* in 1786, who took Parker's reference literally.)

Partridge's programme to rescue astrology was a failure. The sharp decline in respect for that subject was due to political developments and broad social changes, especially since about 1660, which were quite out of the control of any individual astrologers and any merely internal reform. His Ptolemaic astrology was taken into the early nineteenth century by John Worsdale, with equal rigour but equal lack of general acceptance.

Partridge and Swift, 1707–1714 The failure of Partridge's broader intellectual programme did not hinder his personal success. At the start of the eighteenth century he was the best-known and most widely read astrologer in England. That was undoubtedly why he was chosen by Jonathan Swift to be the victim of a hoax that extended his fame still further, although not in a way he would have sought. First, however, it should be noted that Partridge had already received the satirical attentions of Tom Brown, who produced a parody in 1690 entitled *Prophecies out of Merlin's Carmen*, and in 1700 published weekly instalments of another parody, *The Infallible Astrologer*, by 'Mr Silvester Partridge'. There is no doubt that Swift read Brown.

Towards the end of 1707, a month or two after the publication of *Merlinus Liberatus* for the following year, there appeared a new star in the annual astrological firmament: *Predictions for the Year 1708*, which described itself as 'Written to prevent the people of England from being further imposed upon by the vulgar Almanack makers, by Isaac Bickerstaff, Esq.' Its writer claimed to be in possession of a new technique, the precision and infallibility of which he contrasted with the ambiguity of those of other astrologers, and with which he would rescue the reputation of astrology. In keeping with (genuine) astrological tradition, which favoured death as an event about which there can be no dispute, he would demonstrate its efficacy by predicting the impending demise of several eminent people, including the cardinal de Noailles and—'upon the 29th of March next, about eleven at night, of a raging Feaver' (*Predictions for 1708*, 4)—John Partridge.

Inured to professional infighting, Partridge ignored this upstart. On 30 March 1708, however, there appeared *The Accomplishment of the First of Mr. Bickerstaff's Predictions*, 'being an account of the death of Mr. Partridge the almanack-maker upon the 29th instant'. Swift, purporting to be an anonymous member of the gentry who happened to be present at the time, supplied a graphic and detailed description of the scene at Partridge's deathbed. However, in another convincing touch which reveals his familiarity with real astrological discourse, he criticized Bickerstaff for being almost four hours astray in his timing, Partridge having breathed his last 'about Five minutes after Seven'. *The Accomplishment* concluded with an abusive 'Elegy on the Death of Mr. Partridge', including the famous epitaph:

> Here five feet deep lies on his back
> A cobbler, starmonger and quack
> Who to the stars in pure good will
> Does to his best look upward still:
> Weep, all you customers that use
> His pills, his almanacs, or shoes.

Partridge now wrote, protesting indignantly (if redundantly) that he was not only alive but had not died on 29 March. But word of the joke had spread, even to the continent, where both of Swift's pamphlets were quickly translated. When the *Merlinus* for 1709 appeared, Swift countered with a pseudonymous *Vindication of Isaac Bickerstaff, Esq. Against what is Objected to him by Mr. Partridge*, in which he insisted that the astrologer was no more. The reasons he gave included the fact that 'no Man alive ever writ such damn'd Stuff as this', and that the only other denial had been that of the cardinal de Noailles. Were we then, Swift asked, to accept the word of a Frenchman and a papist against that of the loyal English protestant author? (By implicitly bracketing Partridge with the cardinal, Swift, who knew Partridge's politics very well, was of course simply twisting the knife.)

By now Partridge was the laughing-stock of educated and patrician circles all over Europe. London's metropolitan literati quickly joined in. Steele borrowed 'Bickerstaff' for *The Tatler*, which he was starting up in April 1709, and aided by Congreve, Dr Thomas Yalden, pretending to be Partridge, issued *Squire Bickerstaff Detected, or, The Astrological Impostor Convicted*, in which he complained comically about his difficulties persuading people that he was still alive.

There is no doubt about the quality of Swift's celebrated joke on Partridge, or the extent of its fame. (It was imitated by Benjamin Franklin in the 1730s with an American astrologer, Titan Leeds.) However, it is necessary to be cautious in drawing further conclusions. For example, the fact that Partridge's almanac then failed to appear in 1710, and only a satiric *Partridge's Almanack* appeared for 1711–12, has often been attributed to its effects on a 'dazed' or disheartened Partridge. In fact, however, the Company of Stationers was already engaged in a dispute with the author of its chief money-spinner. Partridge had sold his edition for 1710 to another and higher bidder, and the company promptly obtained an injunction forbidding its publication. Partridge appealed, and after the court of queen's bench failed to produce a verdict, they agreed in 1713 on a new annual fee of £100 (he had asked for £150). *Merlinus Liberatus* thus resumed publication for the year 1713.

A second and even more common mistake is to assume that Swift's satire was the end of astrology, a fatal intervention marking its death. That would be a gross exaggeration. There is no evidence that it had any effect—nor any reason why it would—on the sales of Partridge's almanac (let alone others) to a largely plebeian readership; the company, which operated along strictly profitable lines, continued his imprint into the last decade of the century. In addition, Partridge left over £2000 in his will, so his personal fortunes can hardly have suffered much either.

What the Bickerstaff episode does symbolize is the 'death' of astrology as a respectable pursuit among the relatively well-educated and largely urban upper and middle classes, and especially professionals. Partridge was the perfect target for such an attack, because he combined a 'levelling' demotic politics with astrology. Moreover, in his case astrology, strongly identified with the sectarian strife and radicalism of the civil war, went together with the attributes (through both his first trade, which Swift constantly harped on, and his country origins) of the common people who were thought to be the natural home of such misguided and contemptible beliefs.

All this is plainly evident in the deathbed speech which Swift put into Partridge's mouth:

> I am a poor ignorant fellow, yet I have sense enough to know that all pretences of foretelling by astrology are deceits, for the manifest reason that all the wise and learned, who alone can judge whether there be any truth in this science, do unanimously agree to laugh at and despise it, and that none but the ignorant vulgar give it any credit. (*The Accomplishment*, 1708, 3)

The reference to 'agreeing' to laugh at astrology is especially apt; this was no casual or spontaneous assault.

Partridge eventually discovered the identity of his tormentor, and *Merlinus* for 1714 commented adversely on his character. It also hailed the accession of George I in the customary manner as a further deliverance from 'popery, French slavery and English traitors'. On 3 December, however, Partridge also wrote out his will, in which he sought by generous provisions for a handsome tombstone and the local poor to persuade the Mortlake parish to overlook his reputation as an enemy of the church, and permit his burial there.

Partridge died in London on 24 June 1715, and was interred on 30 June. His tomb, with black marble top and white marble sides, is in the south portion of the churchyard of St Mary the Virgin, Mortlake. The Latin inscription is no longer legible, but a transcription was made by 'D. L.' and published in the *Gentleman's Magazine* for January 1785. Obviously written with an eye to posterity, it describes Partridge in misleading and highly respectable terms as an astrologer and doctor of medicine who practised medicine for two kings and one queen, namely Charles II, William III, and Queen Mary, and was made a doctor of medicine at Leiden in Holland.

PATRICK CURRY

Sources *DNB* • G. P. Mayhew, 'The early life of John Partridge', *Studies in English Literature*, 1 (1961), 31–42 • P. Curry, *Prophecy and power: astrology in early modern England* (1989) • B. S. Capp, *Astrology and the popular press: English almanacs, 1500–1800* (1979) • *Entered at Stationers' Hall: a sketch of the history and privileges of the Company of Stationers* (1871) • *The last wills and testaments of J. Partridge, student in physick and astrology; and Dr Burnett, master of the Charter-House, London* (1716) • *GM*, 1st ser., 55 (1785), 107–8 • tombstone, St Mary the Virgin, Mortlake, Surrey

Likenesses R. White, line engraving, BM, NPG; repro. in Partridge, *Mikropanastrōn, or, An astrological vade mecum* (1679) • R. White, line engraving, repro. in H. Davies, ed., *The prose writings of Jonathan Swift*, 2 (1939), facing p. 137 • R. White, line engraving, BM; repro. in A. Mynsicht, *Thesaurus and armamentarium medicochymicum, or, A treasury of physick*, trans. J. Partridge (1682) • engraving, AM Oxf. [*see illus.*]

Wealth at death over £2000—legacies: *Last wills and testaments of J. Partridge*

Partridge, John (1789–1872), portrait painter, was born in Glasgow on 20 November 1789, the second son of Samuel Partridge (1746–1832), merchant, and his second wife, Catherine Stuart (1767–1837). He was the elder brother of the surgeon Richard *Partridge (1805–1873) and uncle of the cartoonist and illustrator Sir (John) Bernard *Partridge (1861–1945). About 1814 he became a pupil of Thomas Phillips, and in 1815 he first exhibited at the Royal Academy a portrait, *Miss Foote as Lucilla*. In the following year he was admitted to the Royal Academy Schools and exhibited his first picture at the British Institution. In 1820 Partridge married his cousin Clementina Sarah Campbell (*d.* 1880), but they had no children. The artist painted himself and his wife in the midst of the Partridge family at his

John Partridge (**1789–1872**), self-portrait, *c.*1838

Brook Street home in London (late 1820s; Museum of London). Perhaps to advance his burgeoning career by a prolonged study of the old masters, Partridge departed in 1823 for Italy, where he gained influential patrons including Viscount Sandon, later second earl of Harrowby, 'Lady Bute and Lord Francis Egerton'—probably Frances Coutts, dowager marchioness of Bute (*d.* 1832), and Francis Henry Egerton, eighth earl of Bridgewater (1756–1829) (Ormond, 'John Partridge', 397). He returned to London in 1827 and was one of the first artists to settle close to his clientele, choosing Brook Street for his studio home.

Partridge soon became a successful and prosperous portrait painter, with patrons from the aristocracy and gentry, often Scottish, such as the fifth duke of Buccleuch and the Malcolms of Poltalloch. His sitters included the fifteenth duke of Norfolk, the second duke of Sutherland, the second marquess of Westminster, the maharaja Duleep Singh, and the sculptor John Gibson. Partridge's commission from the king of the Belgians in 1836 led Queen Victoria to see his pictures. Her patronage began in 1838, and in 1840 he painted portraits of the queen and of Prince Albert, which were exhibited at the Royal Academy the following year. These works were successful, were soon copied several times for the royal couple, and were later engraved. In 1843 Partridge was appointed portrait painter-extraordinary to Queen Victoria and Prince Albert, and exhibited at the Royal Academy a portrait of the queen for presentation to Louis-Philippe, king of France. However, his success with the royal family was short-lived, and he was eclipsed by the German-born court painter F. X. Winterhalter, who arrived in London in 1842 to paint for the queen.

In 1846 Partridge sent to the Royal Academy portraits of Lord and Lady Beauvale, later Viscount and Viscountess Melbourne, which were hung so obscurely that he decided never to exhibit there again. He had discovered in 1833 that he had enemies in the academy, probably incited by Ramsay Richard Reinagle, whom he had upset by altering one of the latter's portraits at the request of the owner. From then on his pictures had been badly hung, and against expectations he had never been elected an associate member of the Royal Academy. He remained silent until 1864 when a government report on the academy gave him the chance to publish a pamphlet, *On the Constitution and Management of the Royal Academy.*

This brought to light the evils of the institution's monopoly, as illustrated by his own unhappy example:

> Thus in the midst of my career, I found myself driven from the position I held in public estimation and employment, with the consequent sacrifice of my professional income, as the penalty for maintaining any degree of self-respect and independent feeling. (J. Partridge, *Constitution and Management*, 30)

Partridge's rejection of the prime outlet for his work reduced the number of his portrait commissions. He recorded in his sitters' book 228 portraits between 1827 and 1845 but only seventy-six in the twenty years afterwards. Like other such excluded painters, he set up a gallery in his studio. His only major attempt to regain popular acclaim was his large painting *The Fine Art Commissioners in 1846* (1846–1850s, ruined; oil study and key; all NPG), incorporating twenty-eight eminent figures responsible for the decoration of the new Palace of Westminster. Despite exhibiting at his gallery in 1851 large finished studies of these public figures (for example, Viscount Melbourne, 1844, and Viscount Palmerston, 1846; both NPG), little public interest was shown in his project, and the finished painting was never sold. After his death a contemporary authority considered his portraits 'carefully drawn and painted, his likeness good', but despite his popularity as a portraitist 'he did not attain to the first rank' (Redgrave, *Artists*, 322).

Besides portraits, Partridge exhibited subject pictures. He showed some of these at the Royal Academy, and also in Liverpool and Dublin, but most at the British Institution between 1816 and 1861. To the last of these he additionally contributed small studies, but also on occasion larger works, like *Satan* in 1829 and *L'allegrezza* in 1833. Such paintings encompassed literary, Italian, and Scottish themes, genre, and landscapes, and often depicted children. Little is known of the artist's character or personal life. In 1835 William Powell Frith, whom Partridge encouraged, found that 'his manners were delightful, copied, I was told afterwards, a good deal on those of Sir Thomas Lawrence' (W. Frith, *My Autobiography and Reminiscences*, 2nd edn, 3 vols., 1888, 1.25). He had private means, and at the height of his success in 1841 earned £2762 from his portraits alone. Partridge died at his home, 60 Brook Street, Grosvenor Square, London, on 25 November 1872. At the end of his life he donated a number of paintings to the National Portrait Gallery, London, and the remaining contents of his studio were subsequently sold at Christies on 15 June 1874. R. E. GRAVES, *rev.* CHARLES NOBLE

Sources Graves, *RA exhibitors* • Graves, *Brit. Inst.* • J. Partridge, notebooks, NPG, Heinz Archive and Library • C. Partridge, correspondence with NPG, NPG, Heinz Archive and Library, registered packet 342 • [J. Partridge], *On the constitution and management of the Royal Academy* (1864) • R. Ormond, 'John Partridge and the fine art commissioners', *Burlington Magazine*, 109 (1967), 397–402 • O. Millar, *The Victorian pictures in the collection of her majesty the queen*, 1 (1992), 194–7 • O. Millar, *The queen's pictures* (1977), 170–71 • R. Ormond, *Early Victorian portraits*, 2 (1973), 398 • F. H. W. Sheppard, ed., *The Grosvenor estate in Mayfair*, 2: *The buildings*, Survey of London, 40 (1980) • Redgrave, *Artists* • B. Stewart and M. Cutten, *The dictionary of portrait painters in Britain up to 1920* (1997), 361 • private information (2004) • Wood, *Vic. painters*, 3rd edn, 1.397 • Bryan, *Painters* (1903–5) • bap. reg. Scot. • *CGPLA Eng. & Wales* (1872)
Archives NPG, MS notebooks
Likenesses J. Partridge, oil detail, 1827–9, Museum of London • J. Partridge, oil study, 1836 (for his group portrait of the Sketching Society), NPG • J. Partridge, self-portrait, oils, *c*.1838, NPG [*see illus.*] • J. Partridge, group portrait, ink and wash (*A meeting of the Sketching Society*), BM
Wealth at death under £20,000: probate, 23 Dec 1872, *CGPLA Eng. & Wales*

Partridge, Joseph (1724–1796), schoolmaster and antiquary, was born at the Red Lion, Nantwich, Cheshire, and baptized on 1 May 1724, the son of Joseph Partridge (*d.* 1756), waggoner and landlord of the Red Lion, and Sarah Tew (*d.* 1771/2). He succeeded to his father's business as a waggoner, and had married his wife, Mary (1726/7–1806), by 15 August 1757, when their only child, Jane, was baptized at Nantwich. When about forty-two years of age Partridge qualified for the Church of England without going to the universities. On 26 August 1766 he obtained a licence from the bishop of Chester to become master of the free grammar school at Acton, Cheshire. At about the same date he became curate of Baddeley and chaplain of Woodhey, both of which posts he retained until his death. He demonstrated his religious orthodoxy in his didactic poem published in 1766, *The Anti-Atheist*.

Partridge left Acton to become master, in August 1772, of the Nantwich charity school, where he succeeded Joseph Hilditch (*d.* 1772). Known as the Blue Cap School, it educated forty poor boys of the town in reading and writing. Partridge, who remained master until his death, found time to work on the first history of his home town, published in 1774 as *An Historical Account of the Town and Parish of Nantwich*. In addition to a sermon printed in 1778 he had brought out in 1754 a pamphlet connected with some personal controversy with Thomas Burrow of Manchester.

Partridge died on 25 October 1796, probably at Nantwich, and was buried on 29 October in Nantwich churchyard. He was survived by his wife, who died on new year's day in 1806, aged seventy-nine, and was buried with her husband. C. W. SUTTON, *rev.* S. J. SKEDD

Sources J. Hall, *A history of the town and parish of Nantwich, or Wich-Malbank, in the county palatine of Cheshire* (1883); repr. (1972), 380 • E. Lloyd, *Nantwich and Acton grammar school, 1560–1960* (1960) • J. P. Earwaker, ed., *Local gleanings relating to Lancashire and Cheshire*, 2 vols. (1875–8), vol. 1, pp. 103, 113 • *IGI*

Partridge, Sir Miles (*d.* 1552), courtier and soldier, is said to have been a relative of William Partridge of Wishanger in Miserden, Gloucestershire, but his name does not appear as a member of that family in the visitation of 1623. It is likely, however, that he was connected to the numerous Gloucestershire Partridges, as he held a number of offices in that county including sheriff (1547) and commissioner for the collection of a relief granted by parliament (1550). His wife, Jane, and his two daughters, Margery and Katherine, survived his death. One daughter married William Stokebrege, a London grocer. Partridge had a brother Hugh who was described as a gentleman.

Towards the end of the reign of Henry VIII, Partridge began to acquire land, some of it former monastic property. In 1544 he was granted Almondsbury, Gloucestershire, and in 1548 he and his brother received a very large grant of former monastic land in Bristol. The next year he was granted a house, garden, and 8 acres in Kew, Surrey. In 1550 he granted two manors in Kent to William Sharington, and he had other property in London and Devon.

Partridge made himself notorious as a gamester, and on one occasion, when playing with Henry VIII, staked on one throw of the dice £100 against the bells of Jesus Chapel in St Paul's Churchyard. Partridge won and had the bells taken down and broken. His gaming companions included Sir Thomas Palmer, Sir Ralph Bagnall, and Edward Underhill.

After Edward VI's accession Partridge attached himself to Edward Seymour, duke of Somerset and lord protector; he accompanied the protector to Scotland in 1547, fought at the battle of Pinkie on 28 September, and was knighted at Roxburgh. At court he was chief master of the king's games, pastimes, and sports, and he held the reversion of the office of groom porter. Partridge's career declined rapidly after the fall of Somerset in 1549. In October he was charged with embezzling goods belonging to Somerset. According to information presented to the council 'certain stuff' had been conveyed to Kew, but it was uncertain where it now was since Somerset had two other servants living there.

Partridge became implicated in the failed plot against John Dudley, earl of Warwick, and other members of the council; on 7 October 1551 he was accused by Sir Thomas Palmer of having earlier in the year undertaken to raise London and seize the great seal with the help of apprentices. He was arrested on 16 October and imprisoned in the Tower. Later, because of alleged ill health, he was moved to the lieutenant's house on Tower Hill where his wife was allowed to attend him. A commission was appointed for his trial on 29 November. When Somerset stood trial in December he repudiated Partridge's testimony that he had had armed men in his chamber at Greenwich. Partridge himself protested his innocence of crimes against the king or council, but was convicted of felony at Westminster on 5 February 1552 and hanged at Tower Hill on 26 February. He was buried at the Tower. After his execution an act of parliament decreed the forfeiture of all his properties and rights of inheritance. Sir Henry Gates was granted Partridge's goods and chattels, but his widow received an annuity and the Devon manor of Kenn. In 1553 his daughters obtained restitution by act of parliament.

An ambitious man who lived in dangerous times, Partridge made the fatal mistake of backing the wrong man. He was apparently a man of some learning and distinct protestant leanings. His forfeited possessions at Kew included a Bible, a psalter, a New Testament, and a prayer book, and while he was in the Tower he was given spiritual comfort by the radical evangelical John Bradford.

A. F. Pollard, *rev.* Barrett L. Beer

Sources Burke, *Gen. GB* (1894) • J. Stow, *A survey of London*, rev. edn (1603); repr. with introduction by C. L. Kingsford as *A survey of London*, 2 vols. (1908); repr. with addns (1971) • *The chronicle and political papers of King Edward VI*, ed. W. K. Jordan (1966) • W. K. Jordan, *Edward VI*, 2: *The threshold of power* (1970) • W. Patten, 'The expedition into Scotland … 1547', *Tudor tracts, 1532–1588*, ed. A. F. Pollard (1903), 53–157; repr. (1964) • *CPR, 1547–53* • *CSP dom., 1547–53* • *Literary remains of King Edward the Sixth*, ed. J. G. Nichols, 2 vols., Roxburghe Club, 75 (1857) • C. Wriothesley, *A chronicle of England during the reigns of the Tudors from AD 1485 to 1559*, ed. W. D. Hamilton, 2, CS, new ser., 20 (1877) • J. Stow, *The annales of England … untill this present yeere 1601* (1601); repr. (1605)

Partridge, Peter (*c.*1385–1451), theologian and churchman, originated in the diocese of London, but had probably become a master of arts of Oxford when he was ordained as subdeacon on 22 December 1408 to the title of St Frideswide's Abbey in Oxford, and as deacon on 2 March 1409; he was bachelor of theology by 1414 and doctor by 1421. In his youth he was, like many Oxford masters, sympathetic to the ideas of John Wyclif (*d.* 1384); according to the Czech writer Peter Ňemec of Žatec, Partridge was later reminded, at the Council of Basel, that he himself had introduced the younger master Peter Payne (*d.* 1455/6?) to Wyclif's writings, but had then abandoned Wycliffism himself at the prospect of preferment in the church. This Hussite debating point is lent support by Partridge's early notebook (Bodl. Oxf., MS Digby 98), into which he copied numerous pieces of anti-mendicant propaganda, and some of Wyclif's polemical letters, later excised.

This early radical phase, datable to *c.*1405–1410, was succeeded by a long period during which Partridge taught and preached at Oxford, residing there at least seasonally. He was licensed to preach in the Oxford archdeaconry on 23 March 1413, and was present at the convocation summoned by the bishop of Lincoln to investigate the persistence of heresy in the university (4 March 1414). He rented Wilby Hall in Oxford, presumably as its principal, in 1421 and 1428. During this time, like many contemporary Oxford masters, he acted in numerous useful capacities on behalf of the university, the bishop of Lincoln, and perhaps the bishop of Salisbury; as a representative probably of one of these authorities he was present at the Council of Constance, and served in 1417 on a conciliar committee to resolve a dispute at Bayonne. He represented Oxford in a delegation to Archbishop Henry Chichele (*d.* 1443) sent to discuss the promotion of graduates (appointed 7 July 1421), and was in turn appointed by Chichele in 1423 to a commission of theologians deputed to witness and give judgment on the heretical utterances of William Taylor (*d.* 1423). The minority government of Henry VI on 13 July 1428 sent him to Rome to treat with the king of Germany, Sigismund (*r.* 1410–37), Alfonso V of Aragon (*r.* 1416–58), and Pope Martin V (*r.* 1417–31), and in 1432–3 he represented the archbishop of Canterbury and the bishops of his province at the Council of Basel, where he made an official protest or *provocatio* against the council's organization.

It is likely that not only Partridge's ordinary activity in ecclesiastical matters, but also his personal acquaintance with surviving Wycliffite masters was valued by the authorities, both at Taylor's trial and in debate with the Hussite delegates, who included Payne, at Basel. The English tactic seems to have been, in deference to the conciliatory attitude of the council, to exploit the latent divisions of the Bohemian delegates by discrediting Payne as already a heretic and traitor before his defection to Prague, and Partridge's memory of Payne's influence on the Lollard leader Sir John Oldcastle (*d.* 1417) and activities in Oxford before the Lollard rising were clearly embarrassing to his opponent. Payne countered by reminding Partridge of his own forsaken radical beliefs, to which Partridge responded by recalling his attempt to wean Payne from Wycliffism. These exchanges on 31 March and 6 and 7 April 1433 were inconclusive, but indicate Partridge's useful role in argument with educated Lollards and Hussites.

Partridge was amply rewarded for these services with numerous benefices, of which the earliest known is the rectory of West Kington, Wiltshire, before 1419, but the most valuable of which was the chancellorship of Lincoln in 1424. He held it in plurality with only one other benefice, at Biddenden, Kent, which he resigned in 1436 to take up another rectory in Lincoln diocese, at Castle Ashby, Northamptonshire. By then he probably resided mainly at Lincoln, where he was involved in a long dispute with Dean John Macworth, and was attacked, on 28 June 1435, by the dean's henchmen during vespers. He nevertheless was at one with the quarrelsome dean in resisting Bishop William Alnwick's revision of the cathedral statutes in 1441. He died there on 10 January 1451 and was buried in the cathedral. His will does not survive, but gifts of logical and philosophical texts to All Souls College, Oxford, are recorded in its earliest catalogue, and two of his gifts to his cathedral library remain, a text of Augustine (Lincoln Cathedral Library, MS 72) and another, evidently in his own hand, of Richard Snettisham's abbreviation of Robert Cowton's commentary on the *Sentences* and John Sharp's abbreviation of the *Quaestiones Quodlibetales* of Duns Scotus (BL, Royal MS 11 B.i).

Partridge's only works (apart from his *provocatio*) appear to be *tabulae* or indices of the latter two books, which appear in his own hand in the Royal manuscript. The *tabula* to Snettisham is attributed, while that to Sharp may have only been copied. Both are included, together with the former's attribution, in the texts of Snettisham and Sharp in Balliol College, Oxford, MS 192. The collection of texts in Bodleian, MS Digby 98, written out by Partridge, provides evidence of his concerns of about 1405–10:

numerous grammatical, logical, astronomical, and mathematical texts, including several of Robert Grossesteste (*d.* 1253), are probably the teaching aids of a master of arts, while items of anti-mendicant propaganda and pamphlets by Wyclif (later excised, but noted in the contents) testify to views which were fairly current in Oxford at that time. JEREMY CATTO

Sources *Tabulae*, BL, Royal MS 11 B.i · Partridge's notebook, Bodl. Oxf., MS Digby 98 · *Provocatio* at Basel, Bodl. Oxf., MS Digby 66 · Petri Zatecensis, *Liber diurnus de gestis Bohemorum in concilio Basiliensi*, ed. F. Palacký (Vienna, 1857), 1/3 of *Monumenta conciliorum generalium saeculi XV*, 344 · H. E. Salter, ed., *Cartulary of Oseney Abbey*, 3, OHS, 91 (1931), 223, 230 · Rymer, *Foedera* · F. Peck, ed., *Desiderata curiosa*, new edn, 2 vols. in 1 (1779), 313 · A. H. Thompson, *The English clergy and their organization in the later middle ages* (1947), 90–1 · Emden, *Oxf.*

Archives Balliol Oxf., MS 192 · BL, Royal MS 11 B.i · Bodl. Oxf., MS Digby 98 · Bodl. Oxf., MS Digby 66

Partridge, Richard (1805–1873), surgeon, the tenth child and seventh and youngest son of a family of twelve, was born on 19 January 1805 at Ross, Herefordshire, to Samuel Partridge (1746–1832), merchant, and his second wife, Catherine Stuart (1767–1837). He was apprenticed in 1821 to his uncle, W. H. Partridge, who was in practice in Birmingham, and during his apprenticeship he acted as dresser to Joseph Hodgson at Birmingham General Hospital. In 1827 he entered St Bartholomew's Hospital in London, to attend the lectures of John Abernethy. He was admitted a member of the Royal College of Surgeons on 20 April 1827, and in the following October he became a licentiate of the Society of Apothecaries. He acted for some time as demonstrator at the Great Windmill Street school of medicine, and in 1831, on the foundation of the medical faculty at King's College, London, he was appointed the first demonstrator of anatomy. He resigned from this post in 1836, when he was appointed professor of descriptive and surgical anatomy in succession to Herbert Mayo. In 1831, while demonstrator at King's College, Partridge's name came to public attention in connection with the murders committed by the 'London Burkers', Bishop and Williams, when they attempted to sell him the body of the Italian boy who was their last victim.

On 23 December 1836 Partridge was appointed visiting or assistant surgeon to the Charing Cross Hospital; he became full surgeon there on 8 January 1838, and resigned the office on 13 April 1840, on his appointment as surgeon to the newly established King's College Hospital. He remained surgeon to King's College Hospital until 1870.

In 1837 Partridge was elected a fellow of the Royal Society. He held all the chief posts at the Royal College of Surgeons, having been a founder fellow in 1843; he became a member of the council in 1852, examiner in 1854, Hunterian orator in 1865, and president in 1866. In 1853 he was appointed professor of anatomy at the Royal Academy, where he succeeded Joseph Henry Green of St Thomas's Hospital. Partridge had prepared himself for this post many years previously by taking lessons in drawing from his brother John *Partridge, the portrait painter. In the Royal Medical and Chirurgical Society of London, Partridge served at every level. Elected a fellow in 1828, he was secretary (1832–6), a member of council (1837–8, and again in 1861–2), vice-president (1847–8), and president (1863–4).

In the autumn of 1862, at the request of Garibaldi's friends in England, Partridge travelled to Spezia in Italy to attend the general, who had suffered a severe gunshot wound in his right ankle. Partridge, who had had no experience of gunshot wound, overlooked the presence of the bullet, which was afterwards detected by Professor Nélaton and removed by Professor Zanetti.

Partridge was a fluent lecturer, and sketched well. As a surgeon he was a nervous operator, but an admirable clinical teacher. He also paid close attention to the aftercare of the patients on whom he had operated. He published only one article, entitled 'The face', in R. B. Todd's *Cyclopaedia of Anatomy and Physiology* (2, 1839); he made a few contributions to the *Transactions* of various medical societies; and he wrote a work on descriptive anatomy, but never printed it. Partridge died on 25 March 1873 at his home, 18 Wimpole Street, Cavendish Square, London. He left a widow, Frances Janette (Fanny), *née* Turner. Their third son was the cartoonist and illustrator Sir (John) Bernard *Partridge. D'A. POWER, *rev.* B. A. BRYAN

Sources *Medical Times and Gazette* (29 March 1873), 347–8 · *The Lancet* (29 March 1873), 464 · *Proceedings of the Royal Medical and Chirurgical Society*, 7 (1871–5), 231–2 · R. Richardson, *Death, dissection and the destitute*, pbk edn (1988) · private information (1895) · *CGPLA Eng. & Wales* (1873) · *IGI*

Archives CUL, corresp. with Joseph Bonomi

Likenesses P. H. Maguire, lithograph, 1845; at Royal Medical and Chirurgical Society, London in 1895 · Barraud & Jerrard, photograph, 1873, Wellcome L. · R. Burgess, group portrait (with doctors and scientists), Wellcome L. · E. Edwards, photograph, NPG; repro. in *Portraits of men of eminence*, 3 (1865) · F. Holl, engraving (after drawing by G. Richmond) · S. Lulles, mezzotint, Wellcome L. · Mayer & Pierson, carte-de-visite, NPG · E. Moira, carte-de-visite, NPG · Moira & Haigh, photograph, Wellcome L. · G Richmond, drawing · wood-engraving (after photograph by Barraud and Jerrard), NPG; repro. in *ILN* (5 April 1873)

Wealth at death under £5000: administration, 4 June 1873, *CGPLA Eng. & Wales*

Partridge, Seth (1603/4–1686), mathematical writer, is probably identical with the Seth Partridge who was born about 1603 and is buried in the church at Hemel Hempstead, Hertfordshire, where there is an inscription to his memory. He described himself as a surveyor, but his time seems to have been mostly occupied in teaching various branches of mathematics, including arithmetic, astronomy, land measuring, gauging of vessels, trigonometry, navigation, and cosmography.

For the use of his pupils Partridge prepared some notes on 'Napier's bones', which he published in 1648 under the title *Rabdologia, or, The Art of Numbering by Rods*. Its object is to explain in an easy manner the use of this popular counting aid. On 1 August 1657 he completed another mathematical work, entitled *The Description and Use of an Instrument called the Double Scale of Proportion*. This book was published in 1661 and was the first text to describe a slide-rule incorporating a slide—that is, a central ruler sliding between two fixed rules. Partridge died on 25 February

1686 aged eighty-two, and was buried at Hemel Hempstead; his son (1635–1703) and grandson (1675–1748), a citizen and goldsmith of London, both of whom were also named Seth Partridge, were also buried there. No details of a wife are known. A. F. Pollard, *rev.* H. K. Higton

Sources E. G. R. Taylor, *The mathematical practitioners of Tudor and Stuart England* (1954) • F. Cajori, *A history of the logarithmic slide rule* (1909) • J. E. Cussans, *History of Hertfordshire*, 1 (1870) • A. De Morgan, *Arithmetical books from the invention of printing to the present time* (1847), 42, 51 • Nichols, *Lit. anecdotes*, 9.507

Parvo Ponte, Adam de. *See* Balsham, Adam of (1100x02?–1157x69?).

Parys, William (*d.* **1609**), schoolmaster, matriculated as a pensioner of Peterhouse, Cambridge, in June 1582, graduated BA in 1586, and proceeded MA in 1589. On 9 January 1595 he was elected master of St Olave's Grammar School in Southwark, and held the post until his death in 1609. He left a widow and three children.

Despite no evidence that Parys wrote anything at all, he has been conjectured to be the W. P. who wrote or translated the following books: *Foure Great Lyers, Striving who Shall Win the Silver Whetstone* (1585?); *The most pleasaunt and delectable historie of Lazarillo de Tormes, a Spanyard … translated out of Spanish and into English, by W. P.* (1596); *A booke of secrets: shewing divers waies to make and prepare all sorts of inke, and colours … Translated out of Dutch into English, by W. P.* (1596); *John Huighen Van Linschoten his Discours of Voyages into ye Easte & West Indies* (1598). The *Short-Title Catalogue* accepts none of the above conjectures.

Gordon Goodwin, *rev.* Matthew Steggle

Sources Venn, *Alum. Cant.* • J. Ames, *Typographical antiquities, or, An historical account of the origin and progress of printing in Great Britain and Ireland*, ed. W. Herbert, 3 vols. (1785–90), 1144, 1281, 1286, 1327 • *STC, 1475–1640* • Cooper, *Ath. Cantab.*, 2.529

Paschal, John (*d.* **1361**), bishop of Llandaff, was a native of Suffolk who became a Carmelite friar at Ipswich. He was sent to study at Cambridge, where he was said to have graduated as a doctor of theology. Afterwards he returned to Ipswich where he attracted the attention of William Bateman who, after his elevation to the see of Norwich, procured from the pope in 1344 the consecration of Paschal as titular bishop of Scutari. On 20 February 1344 Pope Clement VI also conferred upon him the see of Llandaff, while the incumbent, John Eaglescliffe, was still alive. In England he acted as Bateman's suffragan, consecrating the churchyard of the Carmelites at Norwich in 1344, but he was in Avignon in 1347 when Llandaff fell vacant. While Clement consecrated Paschal as bishop, the chapter at Llandaff chose as bishop their archdeacon, John Coventry, with the approval of Edward, prince of Wales. Clement promptly set this election aside and provided Paschal on 3 June. Paschal did not take up residence immediately, because he was given a commission to consecrate churches in the diocese of Canterbury in 1348, among them the church of Cliffe-at-Hoo, Kent. At Llandaff in 1354 he issued an ordinance against those laymen who were guilty of gravely abusing the leases entered into between them and the clergy. He died on 11 October 1361 and was buried in his cathedral. He was a man with a considerable reputation for learning. It may be his homilies on the saints that survive in the British Library, Royal MS 7 B.i, but none of his other works is extant.

C. L. Kingsford, *rev.* Marios Costambeys

Sources Emden, *Cam.* • G. Williams, *The Welsh church from conquest to Reformation* (1962)
Archives BL, Royal MS 7 B.i

Paschall, Andrew (1631?–1696), Church of England clergyman and advocate for a universal language, was born in Soper Lane, London. He matriculated at Queens' College, Cambridge, in 1647, proceeding BA in 1651, MA in 1654, and BD in 1661. A fellow of Queens' from 1653 to 1663, he was a university preacher from January 1658. He was obliged to demand readmittance to his fellowship at the Restoration, which was granted in August 1660. Three years later he resigned it when presented to the living of Chedzoy in Somerset, by Sir Francis Rolle. Here he remained until 1689 when he moved first to Bristol and thence to Wells as chancellor of the cathedral (25 March 1689), prebendary (25 December 1690), and canon residentiary (September 1693).

At Cambridge, Paschall had connections with the Cambridge Platonists through John Smith, fellow and later dean of Queens', or John Worthington. From them he derived an insistent rationality and a commitment to learning as a way of recovering true, pre-lapsarian knowledge which would heal religious schism and its resultant social disorder. Paschall was imbued with the idea that man's duty to God meant that he must labour for moral and social improvement. His favoured tool for effecting such social reform through learning was the universal language of John Wilkins in the mastering, improving, and propagation of which he spent several decades.

Paschall's research into a universal language was carried out in the context of group activity on the subject orchestrated by John Aubrey in a circle of correspondents that included Paschall himself, Francis Lodowick, Robert Hooke, John Ray, and Thomas Piggott. Inspired by this and by the Royal Society, Paschall, in association with Joseph Glanvill, tried to establish a 'Clubb for Philosophicall Correspondence' in Somerset. Although this functioned only briefly, in 1669–70, Paschall continued to pursue its twin aims of promoting a universal language and amassing observations for a general natural history. In the 1680s he proposed the writing of a natural history of Somerset modelled on the county natural histories produced by Robert Plot. Although nothing came of such projects, and Paschall himself published nothing, his career reveals the force of the intellectual, idealistic social reform movement of the century, in Paschall's case interestingly combined with a staunch church tory political position. In August 1694 Paschall was appointed steward for two years at Wells, and he died soon after the term of this office, before November 1696. A. J. Turner

Sources A. J. Turner, 'Learning and language in the Somerset levels: Andrew Paschall of Chedzoy', *Learning, language and invention: essays presented to Francis Maddison*, ed. W. D. Hackmann and A. J. Turner (1994), 297–308 • V. Salmon, 'John Wilkins' *Essay* (1668):

critics and continuations', *Historiographia Linguistica*, i, 2 (1974), 147–63 • R. T. Gunther, *Early science in Oxford*, 12: *Dr Plot and the correspondence of the Philosophical Society of Oxford* (1939) • *The correspondence of Henry Oldenburg*, ed. and trans. A. R. Hall and M. B. Hall, 7 (1970) • Venn, *Alum. Cant.*

Archives Bodl. Oxf., letters to John Aubrey, incl. scheme for universal writing based on phonetic principles • RS, MS LB. P.

Pasco, John (1774–1853), naval officer, was born on 20 December 1774, the eldest son of John Pasco, a caulker of Plymouth Dockyard. In June 1784 he entered the frigate *Druid*, and in 1786 was servant of the midshipmen's berth in the frigate *Pegasus*, commanded by Prince William Henry. He was afterwards in the *Penelope* on the Halifax station, and from 1790 to 1795 in many different ships in the channel. In 1795 he went out to the West Indies with Sir John Laforey, who promoted him on 15 June to be lieutenant of the *Beaulieu* under his son Captain Francis Laforey, formerly a midshipman of the *Pegasus*. From 1796 to 1799 he was in the *Raisonnable* in the channel and at the Cape of Good Hope, and from December 1799 to October 1802 in the *Immortalité* with Captain Henry Hotham on the coast of France.

In February 1802 Pasco's father, by then a foreman of caulkers, was dismissed from Plymouth Dockyard, presumably for involvement in the petitions for increased pay organized during the near-famine of the previous year, which Lord St Vincent's Admiralty board regarded as subversive. Pasco imperilled his career by protesting to the Admiralty, and was lucky to be appointed in April 1803 to the *Victory*, which went out to the Mediterranean as Lord Nelson's flagship. He remained in the *Victory* during her whole commission, in the blockade of Toulon, in the chase of the French fleet to the West Indies, and in the battle of Trafalgar. During the latter part of the time he acted as signal officer, including at Trafalgar. According to Pasco himself, the signal which Nelson ordered him to make as the battle was about to begin was 'England confides that every man will do his duty', but he pointed out to the admiral that, as 'confides' was not in the signal book, time would be saved by substituting 'expects', which was. To this Nelson assented (*Dispatches and Letters*, 7.150). Early in the battle Pasco was severely wounded in the right arm, and was carried below.

For his wound, Pasco received a grant from the patriotic fund, and was later awarded a pension of £250 a year; but his promotion to the rank of commander was not dated until 24 December 1805, and he was not posted until 3 April 1811. This was on account of the death of Nelson, who followed the unusual practice of making his junior lieutenant act as first lieutenant and his senior take charge of signals, as a result of which Pasco missed the customary promotion of first lieutenants after the victory. For nearly three years after his promotion to commander's rank, Pasco remained unemployed. In November 1809 he was appointed to the store ship *Hindostan*, which he took out to New South Wales. With him he took his wife, Rebecca, the daughter of J. L. Penfold of Plymouth Dockyard, whom he had married on 1 September 1805. A son was born at sea the following year—one of six sons (two of whom died in infancy) and three daughters. Afterwards Pasco commanded the *Tartarus* on the North American station, and from 1811 to 1815 was captain of the frigate *Rota* on the Lisbon station. After the peace (1815–18) he had command of the *Lee*, a small frigate employed in the channel for the suppression of smuggling. Like most officers of his generation, Pasco had little employment during the peace, but in 1846 he commanded the *Victory* at Portsmouth, and was promoted to flag rank on retirement, on 22 September 1847. He married again in 1843. His second wife was Eliza, the widow of Captain John Weaver RN. He died at Stonehouse, Devon, on 16 November 1853.

Pasco's naval career was creditable but unremarkable. He is chiefly remembered now as the man who made Nelson's famous signal, but in his own day he was pointed out as an example of the sort of rise from humble circumstances, once commonplace in the navy, which was becoming increasingly rare.

J. K. Laughton, *rev.* N. A. M. Rodger

Sources O'Byrne, *Naval biog. dict.* • *Letters and papers of Admiral of the Fleet Sir Thos. Byam Martin, GCB*, ed. R. V. Hamilton, 1, Navy RS, 24 (1903), 28–9 • *Naval Chronicle*, 24 (1810), 437 • R. Morriss, 'Industrial relations at Plymouth dockyard, 1770–1820', *The new maritime history of Devon*, ed. M. Duffy and others, 1 (1992), 216–23 • PRO, ADM 1/2345, Cap. P. 300; ADM 106/3006; ADM 106/2979 [father's career] • service book, PRO, ADM 11/1, 284 • *The dispatches and letters of Vice-Admiral Lord Viscount Nelson*, ed. N. H. Nicolas, 7 vols. (1844–6)

Likenesses oils, NMM

Pascoe, Francis Polkinghorne (1813–1893), entomologist, was born on 1 September 1813 at Penzance, Cornwall, the only child of William Pascoe (*d.* 1817), and his wife, whose maiden name was Polkinghorne. He was educated at the grammar school in Penzance, and afterwards served with Mr Berryman, a surgeon in that town. He subsequently attended St Bartholomew's Hospital, London, as a student, and was admitted MRCS in 1835. In the following year he entered the navy as an assistant surgeon, and in June 1836 sailed for Australia in the *Buffalo* with Captain John Hindmarsh (1785–1860), who had been appointed the first governor of South Australia. Pascoe later went to the West Indies and the Mediterranean.

After the death of a relative in March 1843 Pascoe inherited some property and retired from the navy. On 28 November of the same year he married Mary (*d.* 1851), second daughter of William Glasson, of Falmouth. The couple settled near St Austell, Cornwall, near a property producing kaolin. They had one son (*d.* 1872), who became a lieutenant in the navy, and at least three daughters, with whom Pascoe travelled extensively across Europe and Africa. After the death of his wife at Montpellier in 1851 Pascoe moved to London, and devoted his time to natural history, and in particular entomology. Gradually he formed the great entomological collections which later passed to the British Museum (Natural History) in South Kensington.

Pascoe's first paper was published in Henfrey's *Botanical Gazette* in 1850, but the remainder of his work dealt with entomology (primarily the Coleoptera). He made about seventy contributions to various scientific publications including his article 'Longicornia Malayana' (vol. 3, 3rd ser.) which appeared in the *Transactions of the Entomological Society of London* (1864–9), and his subsequent work on the Colydiidae, and the Curculionidae. He was also author of *Zoological Classification* (1877, later edn. 1880), *Hints for Collecting and Preserving Insects* (1882), and *The Student's List of British Coleoptera* (1882). Although a firm believer in evolution and admirer of Charles Darwin, Pascoe was a persistent opponent of the theory of natural selection, about which he wrote in *Notes on Natural Selection and the Origin of Species* (1884), and *The Darwinian Theory of the Origin of Species* (1886). A further subject he became interested in, during his later years, was the animal kingdom, about which he issued the compilations *List of British Vertebrate Animals* (1885) and *Analytical Lists of the Classes, Orders … of the Animal Kingdom* (1886).

Pascoe was elected a fellow of the Linnean Society in June 1852, and was also a member of the Ray and Horticultural societies. He joined the Entomological Society of London in 1854, becoming its president for the years 1864–5. He was made a member of the Société Entomologique de France in 1862, and belonged to a number of other foreign societies. In 1891, owing to failing health, he was advised to leave London (Paddington) and move to the country, which advice he duly followed, moving first to Tunbridge Wells, and then on to Brighton. Pascoe died on 20 June 1893, while he was staying at 30 Marine Parade, Brighton, and was survived by three daughters: Flora, Kate, and Maude.

B. B. WOODWARD, *rev.* YOLANDA FOOTE

Sources Boase & Courtney, *Bibl. Corn.*, 2.427–9, 3.1302 • *Entomologist's Monthly Magazine*, 29 (1893), 194–6 • *Natural Science*, 3.159 • private information (1895) [Miss Pascoe] • *Catalogue of scientific papers*, Royal Society, 19 vols. (1867–1925) • *BL cat.* • Boase, *Mod. Eng. biog.* • *Proceedings of the Entomological Society of London* (1893), 55–6 • *CGPLA Eng. & Wales* (1893)

Archives Oxf. U. Mus. NH, Hope Library, corresp., entomological scrapbook, and notebooks

Wealth at death £17,114 2*s.* 8*d.*: probate, 22 Aug 1893, *CGPLA Eng. & Wales*

Pashe, William (*fl.* 1513–1537), composer, is of unknown parentage and upbringing. In 1513 he was working in or around London and was admitted to the Confraternity of St Nicholas, the city's guild of church musicians and parish clerks; the death of his wife, Embryth, was notified to the guild in 1517. At least by about 1519 he had become a lay vicar-choral of the choir of St Paul's Cathedral; he was still in office there in 1526, but in 1527 and 1528 occurs as a singing-man, and probably master, of the choir of the musically ambitious parish church of St Peter Westcheap, London. In 1514/15 and 1536/7, as 'Mr Passhe of London', he was engaged as organ consultant by the parish of Kingston, Surrey. His date of death is unknown.

Thomas Morley placed 'Mr Pashe' at the head of the list of composers whose works he consulted when writing his *Plaine and Easie Introduction to Practicall Musick* (1597). Regrettably, only three works have survived: a votive antiphon *Sancta Maria, mater Dei*, a Magnificat, and the mass *Christus resurgens* for the Easter period, all for full choir of five voices. All are ornate, extended, and virtuosic, fully matching the vocal resources available in so prominent a choir as that of St Paul's; while not outstanding in quality, they are crafted in a style characteristic of the many routinely competent contemporaries of John Taverner.

ROGER BOWERS

Sources H. Baillie, 'Some biographical notes on English church musicians, chiefly working in London (1485–1569)', *Royal Musical Association Research Chronicle*, 2 (1962), 18–57 • R. Bowers, 'Pasche, William', *New Grove* • H. B. Walters, *London churches at the Reformation* (1939), 563–71 • GL, St Paul's Cathedral MSS • register of Guild of St Nicholas, GL • *William Pashe: Magnificat for five voices*, ed. N. Sandon (1999) • *William Pashe: Sancta Maria, mater Dei*, ed. N. Sandon (1999) • R. Bowers, 'The playhouse of the choristers of Paul's, *c.*1575–1608', *Theatre Notebook*, 54 (2000), 70–85 • N. Sandon, 'F G A B flat-A: thoughts on a Tudor motif', *Early Music*, 12 (1984), 56–63 • T. Morley, *A plain and easy introduction to practical music*, ed. R. A. Harman (1952), 321

Archives CUL, compositions • Gon. & Caius Cam., compositions | St John Cam., compositions

Pashfield, Robert (*fl. c.*1600). *See under* Bruen, John (1560–1625).

Pashley, Robert (1805–1859), lawyer and traveller, the son of Robert Pashley of Hull, was born, probably at York, on 4 September 1805, and was educated at Mansfield, Nottinghamshire, under a Mr Williams. He was admitted at Trinity College, Cambridge, on 3 May 1825, and was elected to a scholarship in 1828. He took a double first class in 1829, and was elected a fellow of Trinity in the following year. In 1832 he proceeded MA, and, as travelling fellow of Trinity, undertook in 1833 a tour in Greece, Asia Minor, and Crete. Through the influence of Sir Francis Beaufort, he received from the Admiralty a free passage in the vessels employed in the Mediterranean survey. On his way home he spent some time in Venetian archives preparing an appendix to his travels which appeared in 1837, in two volumes, as *Travels in Crete*. Contemporaries judged the work to be scholarly and attractively written, but unfortunately a great part of the impression, together with Pashley's library and collections of antiquities, was destroyed in the fire at the Temple in 1838.

Pashley was admitted to Lincoln's Inn in 1825 and the Inner Temple in 1837. He was called to the bar in 1837 and obtained a large practice on the northern circuit. He acquired so great a reputation as a settlement lawyer, that the act for regulating appeals, which gave the court the power of amendment, was known as 'the act for the better suppression of Pashley'. In 1851 he became QC, and was elected a bencher of the Inner Temple. In 1852 he was an unsuccessful candidate for parliament both at York and at King's Lynn. He published works on pauperism in 1852 and 1854. To try to set the poor law on a more rational geographical footing, he advocated the removal of the law of settlement and the raising of two-thirds of the money needed by a national levy on property. From 1856 to his death he was assistant judge of the Middlesex sessions. He died after a short illness, at his home, 16 Manchester Square, London, on 29 May 1859 and was buried in Kensal Green cemetery. Nothing is known of his wife, but he had a son Robert Edmund (1857–1878).

RICHARD GARNETT, *rev.* ELIZABETH BAIGENT

Sources *GM*, 3rd ser., 7 (1859), 191–3 · Venn, *Alum. Cant.* · Boase, *Mod. Eng. biog.* · private information (1895) · *CGPLA Eng. & Wales* (1859) · d. cert.

Wealth at death under £16,000: probate, 8 July 1859, *CGPLA Eng. & Wales*

Pask, Edgar Alexander (1912–1966), anaesthetist, was born on 4 September 1912 at 188 Kedleston Road, Derby, the second son of Percy Pask (1880–1957), fruit importer, and his wife, Mary (1885–1952), daughter of Alexander Speedie of St Marks, Isle of Man, and his wife, Mary, *née* McCutcheon. He won an open scholarship from Rydal School to Downing College, Cambridge, and in 1934 he obtained first-class honours in the natural sciences tripos. In 1937, after study at the Royal London Hospital, he graduated MB BCh and was admitted MRCS, and LRCP. After house appointments at the London, where he became interested in anaesthesia, he was appointed house anaesthetist at the Radcliffe Infirmary, Oxford. In February 1940 he became junior assistant to Professor MacIntosh of Oxford. He also obtained the diploma in anaesthetics in 1940.

In May 1941 Pask volunteered for service with the RAF. At the physiological laboratory at Farnborough (which became the Institution of Aviation Medicine) he undertook research which frequently necessitated dangerous experiments on the human subject. He studied the efficiency of methods of artificial respiration and, because anaesthetized subjects had to be used, Pask himself was deeply anaesthetized many times. To discover whether RAF crew could survive if they bailed out of an aircraft at altitude, Pask also carried out experiments which involved his exposure to low oxygen levels, equivalent to those which exist at increasing heights. He then related the effects, especially on his level of consciousness, to actual descents. He showed that 35,000 feet was the greatest height from which escape by parachute could be made without oxygen with any chance of survival. He risked his life on each of many occasions.

Of Pask's work at Farnborough the best-known relates to the design of flotation jackets. It was discovered that the Mae West would not support an unconscious subject with his head out of the water, and instead often turned the individual face-down. The only way to test improved prototypes was on unconscious volunteers, and Pask was anaesthetized many times wearing different jackets and then immersed in the pool at Farnborough, while the results were recorded on film. With MacIntosh he designed a new breathing system which allowed him to float in an unrestricted fashion while MacIntosh and the anaesthetic machine remained on the poolside. This (coaxial) breathing system was ahead of its time, and many years later a similar device was 'invented' and used in clinical practice. Pask's thesis for his MD was based on the life-jacket work. To test clothing for aircrew who might have to survive exposure, Pask parachuted into freezing seas off Shetland. He maintained that only in this way could he be sure that a particular idea would come up to expectation. His bravery was recognized by appointment as an OBE (military division) in 1944.

Edgar Alexander Pask (1912–1966), by unknown photographer

After the war Pask was appointed reader in anaesthetics to the Newcastle division of the University of Durham, with the appointment delayed so that he could first spend time in the USA and Canada. He took up his post in May 1947, and was awarded a personal chair on 8 February 1949, thus becoming only the second professor of anaesthetics in the country. His research produced innovations in lung ventilator design, and an established chair was created on 26 October 1959. He married on 13 October 1954 Muriel Mary O'Brien (1913–1997), a nurse; a daughter, Susan, was born in 1955.

Pask was a founder member of the Faculty of Anaesthetists and eventually vice-dean; he was also a member of council of the Association of Anaesthetists. He delivered several prestigious lectures and wrote many papers, and was the third recipient of the Association of Anaesthetists' John Snow medal. In 1965 he served as president of the section of anaesthesia of the Royal Society of Medicine.

Pask had a charismatic personality and was truly a leader, being able to inspire all who worked with him and instil into them the same principles of utter dedication and care which were his own hallmarks. This influence ensured that several of his staff later attained great distinction. He was meticulous and gained a reputation for challenging questioning combined with requests for evidence to support any statement made. His incisive mind allowed him to make great contributions, and he was much sought-after as a member of committees.

Although he insisted on the highest standards Pask was a kind and most considerate man, and closer acquaintance revealed an acute sense of humour. He was surprisingly small and of slender build with a craggy face and, usually, an enigmatic expression. His sudden and unexpected death after a heart attack at his home in Mitchell Avenue, Jesmond, Newcastle upon Tyne, on 30 May 1966 followed a spell of deteriorating health. He was buried at West Road cemetery, Newcastle. JOHN S. INKSTER

Sources R. R. MacIntosh and W. W. Mushin, 'Anaesthetics research in wartime', *Medical Times* (Sept 1945) • H. E. Wittingham, 'Progress of aviation medicine in the RAF', *BMJ* (13 July 1946), 39–45 • minutes of senate, U. Newcastle, no 148, 8 Feb 1949 • R. R. MacIntosh and E. A. Pask, 'The testing of lifejackets', *British Journal of Industrial Medicine*, 14 (1957), 168–76 • *The Journal* [Newcastle upon Tyne] (31 May 1966) • *Anaesthesia*, 21 (1966), 437–9 • *The Lancet* (11 June 1966), 1330–31 • *Annals of the Royal College of Surgeons of England*, 39 (1966), 131–2 • E. M. Gibson and M. H. Harrison, *Into thin air: a history of aviation medicine in the RAF* (1984) • A. Taylor, 'Professor Edgar Alexander Pask', *Current Anaesthetics and Critical Care*, 9 (1998), 156–60 • private information (2004) [Susan Walker; Mary Pask registrar of U. Newcastle] • personal knowledge (2004) • m. cert.

Archives Royal Victoria Infirmary, Newcastle upon Tyne, department of anaesthesia, B. W. Welsh collection, MD thesis and reprints of many publications | FILM BFI NFTVA, original film of tests at Farnborough (Lifejackets) [copies on videotape at Association of Anaesthetists, Bedford Square, London, and in Department of Anaesthesia, Newcastle upon Tyne]

Likenesses photograph, *c.*1954, U. Newcastle, medical school • photograph, Hult. Arch. [*see illus.*]

Wealth at death £14,270: probate, 4 July 1966, *CGPLA Eng. & Wales*

Paske, Thomas (*d.* 1662), Church of England clergyman, was probably born in Cambridge, a younger brother of William Paske (*d.* 1639), who was admitted as a scholar from Eton College to King's College, Cambridge, about 1594, and who graduated BA in 1599 and proceeded MA in 1602. Thomas was a scholar of Clare College, Cambridge, who graduated BA in 1602 or 1603, was elected a fellow at Christmas 1603 and proceeded MA in 1606. He succeeded William as vicar of Hendon, Middlesex, on 9 September 1611 and became chaplain to James Hamilton, marquess of Hamilton. He resigned his fellowship in 1612, but returned to Cambridge to proceed BD in 1613.

Both brothers gained steady preferment. William Paske, who had proceeded BD from Clare in 1609, became chaplain to the bishop of London and in 1618 proceeded DD and became a prebendary of St Paul's Cathedral. On 31 December 1620 Thomas Paske was elected master of Clare. He was incorporated DD in 1621, and two years later became vice-chancellor of the university. He was instituted to the vicarage of St Mary Magdalen, Bermondsey, Surrey, in 1624, although he retained Hendon until 1626. In 1625 he became a prebendary of Canterbury Cathedral and succeeded Thomas Aylmer both as archdeacon of London and in the living of Much Hadham with Little Hadham, Hertfordshire. Following his presentation to the prebend of Ulles-kelf in York Minster on 10 November 1628 the fellows of Clare petitioned for, and obtained from Charles I some time before 2 September 1640, permission to elect a successor as master of the college, but no such appointment was made. Paske continued to be active in the southern province: several sets of his visitation articles as archdeacon of London survive. By the later 1630s he had taken up residence in Canterbury. In the spring of 1640 he was one of those delegated by Convocation to the difficult task of revising the book of subsidies. Absent from the November 1640–February 1641 session of Convocation, he was present again in April and May 1641.

By 1641 Paske had married his wife, Anne; a daughter, Elizabeth, was baptized at Canterbury Cathedral on 12 February 1641 or 1642. Following the outbreak of the civil war, as subdean of Canterbury he complained on 30 August 1642 to Henry Rich, earl of Holland, about the ruthless treatment of the cathedral by troopers of Colonel Sandys's regiment. In the dean's absence Paske had been ordered by the parliamentary commander, Sir Michael Lindsey, to deliver up the keys, upon which 'soldiers entering the church giant-like began a fight with God himself' (*Fifth Report*, HMC, 45). His communication to Lord Holland was published on 9 September as *The Copy of a Letter Sent to an Honourable Lord, by Dr Paske, Subdeane of Canterbury, London*, but he told the House of Lords on 17 September that it had appeared without his knowledge.

By 16 May 1643 pressure from parishioners at Bermondsey had succeeded in having Paske replaced by the lecturer there, Jeremiah Whitaker, and by 20 December that year Paske had also been sequestered from Hadham. In 1645 he was ejected from Clare College in favour of Ralph Cudworth; he also lost his prebends. David Lloyd states that Paske 'suffered cheerfully for his majesty and his son for eighteen years' (Lloyd, 504); he evidently had means to support himself and his family. His wife, Anne, and four children (including Elizabeth and Thomas, baptized in 1643) were awarded a fifth from Much Hadham in September 1644. The following year Paske was assessed at £400 by the committee for the advance of money, but the family were later reported to have moved to a house in Hadham which was better than the rectory, and the committee for compounding failed to oust him; at least three further children were born in the parish—Theophila (*bap.* 1644 or 1645), Judith (*bap.* 1646), and George (*bap.* 1650). Articles were exhibited against Paske for using the prayer book at ceremonies for the family of local landowner and royalist leader, Arthur Capel, Lord Capel (*d.* 1649).

At the Restoration, Paske was reinstated in the rectory of Hadham, in his two prebends and archdeaconry, and in the mastership of Clare, but he surrendered his right of restitution to the last to the ejected master, Theophilus Dillingham, who, on 30 March 1661, married Paske's daughter Elizabeth. The same year Paske also resigned his York prebend to his son-in-law. On 24 June he attended the lower house of Convocation, but in December, probably because of illness, he subscribed by proxy. He issued visitation articles for his London archdeaconry in 1662, but drew up his will on 12 September and died within weeks; probate was granted on 19 November. The main beneficiary was his son Thomas, but there were bequests to three younger children and to the poor of Much Hadham;

his wife was the executor. Paske was reputed to be eminent in learning, judgement, and piety, to be a great teacher, to have modestly refused a bishopric, and to have accepted unwillingly his other preferments. According to Lloyd, in one day during his final illness he was visited by three bishops, four privy councillors, two judges, and three physicians, all former pupils.

CHARLOTTE FELL-SMITH, *rev.* S. L. SADLER

Sources *CSP dom.*, 1627–8, 304; 1637–8, 230; 1640, 580; 1640–41, 6 · M. A. E. Green, ed., *Calendar of the proceedings of the committee for advance of money, 1642–1656*, 2, PRO (1888); repr. (1967), 634 · *Fifth report*, HMC, 4 (1876), 26, 45–6 · *Ninth report*, 1, HMC, 8 (1883), 122 · PRO, PROB 11/309, fols. 301–2 · Venn, *Alum. Cant.* · *Walker rev.*, 202 · D. Lloyd, *Memoires of the lives … of those … personages that suffered … for the protestant religion* (1668), 504 · J. Barwick, *Queraela Cantabrigienses* (1647), 7 [34] · *Mercurius rusticus* (1685), 118–20 · W. Kennet, *A register and chronicle* (1728), 480, 615, 754, 777, 792 · J. Le Neve, *Fasti ecclesiae anglicanae* (1716), 188, 422 · R. Newcourt, *Repertorium ecclesiasticum parochiale Londinense*, 1 (1708), 63 · E. Carter, *The history of the University of Cambridge* (1753), 53, 56, 59, 412 · C. H. Cooper, *Annals of Cambridge*, 3 (1845), 187–8 · J. B. Mullinger, *The University of Cambridge*, 3 (1911), 57 · *VCH Cambridgeshire and the Isle of Ely*, 3.200, 346 · J. Twigg, *The University of Cambridge and the English Revolution, 1625–1688* (1990), 21, 22n., 98, 101 · J. Davies, *The Caroline captivity of the church: Charles I and the remoulding of Anglicanism, 1625–1641* (1992), 227, 256, 320 · K. Fincham, ed., *Visitation articles and injunctions of the early Stuart church*, 2 vols. (1994–8) · *IGI* [parish registers of Canterbury Cathedral and Much Hadham]

Archives GL, 4383/1/350 · LPL, MS 943/599

Paslew, John (*d.* 1537), abbot of Whalley, was probably from the Paslew family of Wiswell in Whalley, Lancashire. He became a Cistercian monk, but nothing is known of him until he was elected abbot in 1507, when he was apparently in his late thirties. Surprisingly, he was not ordained priest until 1518. Whalley was in the second rank of Cistercian houses: not one of the greatest, but large, fairly well endowed, and successful. Paslew was ambitious for himself and for the abbey. He rebuilt the abbot's lodgings, added a lady chapel to the church, and probably built the north-east gateway. He travelled widely across the north and to London; he assumed a mitre, was summoned to the Canterbury convocation in 1529, and acted as a collector of clerical taxation in 1532. But Paslew's achievements had a price, and in 1530 he began to sell abbey plate, and to pursue tithes and fees more aggressively in the appropriated parishes, that is, those where the monastery appointed the vicar and received the most valuable tithes.

Paslew's pride was to be followed by a dramatic fall. With a gross annual revenue of £541 and twenty-seven monks, the abbey was outside the terms of the 1536 Act of Suppression, which was directed against the smaller monasteries, and seemed safe: paradoxically, it was brought down by the Pilgrimage of Grace, the movement which aimed to save the monasteries. In the autumn of 1536 Paslew and his monks were caught between the northern insurgents and a force raised for the king by the earl of Derby. The earl planned a muster at Whalley on 30 October, but rebels from Yorkshire had got there first. On 23 October, after a brief and perhaps token resistance, the abbey opened its gates to the rebels and Paslew and eight of his monks took the rebel oath to protect the church and the commons. Paslew was summoned by the rebel leadership to conferences at York and Pontefract, but did not attend and seems to have taken no further part in the rebellion. Nevertheless, and despite a general pardon, after the failure of the rising he was tried for treason by royal commissioners at Lancaster. Old, ill, and apparently in despair, Paslew seems to have expected fulfilment of a dream that he would die in 1536–7: he pleaded guilty to five counts, and was executed at Lancaster on 10 March 1537. The precise grounds for his conviction are not known, but the crown used it as a pretext for closing the abbey. A month after Paslew's execution his monks were ejected and his house was no more.

CHRISTOPHER HAIGH

Sources *LP Henry VIII* · J. E. W. Wallis, 'The narrative of the indictment of the traitors of Whalley and Cartmell, 1536–7', *Miscellanies, V*, Chetham Society, 90 (1931) · C. Haigh, *The last days of the Lancashire monasteries and the Pilgrimage of Grace*, Chetham Society, 3rd ser., 17 (1969) · W. S. Weeks, 'Abbot Paslew and the Pilgrimage of Grace', *Transactions of the Lancashire and Cheshire Antiquarian Society*, 47 (1930–31), 199–223 · A. C. Tempest, 'Nicholas Tempest, a sufferer in the Pilgrimage of Grace', *Yorkshire Archaeological and Topographical Journal*, 11 (1890–91), 246–78 · *VCH Lancashire* · T. D. Whitaker, *An history of the original parish of Whalley*, rev. J. G. Nichols and P. A. Lyons, 4th edn, 2 vols. (1872–6) · Borth. Inst., reg. 27, Wolsey · T. N. Toller, ed., *Correspondence of Edward, third earl of Derby*, Chetham Society, new ser., 19 (1890)

Pasley, Charles (1824–1890), army officer and engineer, the eldest son of General Sir Charles William *Pasley (1780–1861), and his second wife, Martha Matilda Roberts (*d.* 1848), was born at Brompton barracks, Chatham, Kent, on 14 November 1824. He was educated at the King's Grammar School, Rochester, Kent. He entered the Royal Military Academy at Woolwich in February 1840, and was commissioned second lieutenant in the Royal Engineers on 20 December 1843. He went through the usual course of professional instruction at Chatham, where his father was head, and proved so good a surveyor and mathematician that for some months he temporarily held the appointment of instructor in surveying and astronomy.

After serving at several home stations Pasley was promoted first lieutenant on 1 April 1846, and in June was sent to Canada. He was employed on ordinary military duties until 1848, when he was appointed to assist in the survey of the extensive and scattered ordnance lands on the Rideau Canal. The outdoor survey was done in the winter to enable the surveyors to chain over the frozen lakes, and to avoid the malaria and mosquitoes of the swamps.

In 1849 Pasley was sent to Bermuda, where he oversaw the deepening of the channel into St George's harbour. In November 1850 he returned to England on account of ill health, and in February 1851 he was selected to join the staff of the Great Exhibition.

In 1853 Pasley was appointed colonial engineer of the colony of Victoria. After arriving in Melbourne in September he found himself at the head of a large office, responsible for port improvements and various public works, later including roads. He was promoted captain on 17 February 1854, and on 16 October he was nominated to the legislative council. In December 1854, when very serious disturbances took place at the goldfields of Ballarat, he volunteered his services to the military forces, and, acting as aide-de-camp to the officer commanding, Captain J. W. Thomas, took part in the assault on the Eureka stockade. Convinced of the need for firm action, he none the less maintained discipline among the soldiers to protect prisoners, and his help was acknowledged in dispatches.

In November 1855 Victoria became a self-governing colony, and in the first responsible ministry Pasley took office as commissioner of public works. Encouraging local designers and using Melbourne basalt, he oversaw the construction of many important public buildings in Melbourne, as well as urban roads, high roads, and railways. In 1856 he was elected for South Bourke, but he lost ministerial office in 1857 and resigned his seat that year.

In 1856 Pasley was also appointed trustee of the Melbourne and Mount Alexander Railway, which had been purchased by the government. In 1858 he was a member of a commission to inquire into the defences of the colony. He lost his post in a reorganization of the public works department in 1859 and decided to return to military duty. He was about to embark for England in July 1860 when, hearing of the chance to see action in the New Zealand wars, he volunteered his services and set off for Taranaki. He was initially assistant military secretary to the commanding officer, General Pratt, but in October he was put in charge of the trenches for an attack on a Maori fort at Kaihihi. Although the attack was successful, Pasley was severely wounded in the thigh. He was invalided to Melbourne in November 1860, and remained there until he was able to embark for England in May 1861. He was mentioned in dispatches and awarded a pension of £100 per annum, and on 28 January 1862 he received a brevet majority for his services in the campaign. He also received the New Zealand war medal.

On arrival in England in August 1861 Pasley was appointed commanding royal engineer at Gravesend. At Hampton, Middlesex, on 29 March 1864, he married his cousin Charlotte Roberts. They had no children. From 1864 to 1868 he was special agent for Victoria, and dealt with the equipment of the ironclad *Nelson*, and the design, construction, armament, and dispatch of the turret-ship *Cerberus*, which the Victorian government bought from the British government for the defence of Melbourne.

In October 1865 Pasley was appointed to take charge of the great extension of Chatham Dockyard, with which he had made considerable progress when he was appointed, in 1873, director of works at the Admiralty. He was promoted lieutenant-colonel on 6 July 1867, and brevet colonel on 6 July 1872. In 1870 he was appointed secretary to and in 1871 member of the committee on designs for ships of war.

From 1873 to 1882 Pasley was director of engineering works and of architecture at the Admiralty, and visited various British and foreign dockyards and military ports. He was made a civil CB on 23 April 1880. From 1880 to 1882 he was acting agent-general for Victoria and chairman of its board of advice. His advice was sought by British and overseas governments on matters of engineering, such as the best means of improving the entrance to the harbour of Alexandria.

The more important works designed under his superintendence at the Admiralty were the entrance locks at Chatham Dockyard, with their ingenious sliding caissons, the two first-class dry docks at Devonport and Haulbowline, the naval barracks and college for naval engineers at Keyham, the alterations of Greenwich Hospital to fit it for a naval college, and the extension of Chatham and Portsmouth dockyards. He was an associate member of the Institution of Civil Engineers, on whose council he briefly served.

Pasley retired from the army on 27 August 1881, with the honorary rank of major-general, and as director of works at the Admiralty in September 1882. He died at his house, at 7 Queen Anne's Grove, Bedford Park, Middlesex, on 11 November 1890, being survived by his wife. He was an excellent administrator, well liked by both colleagues and superiors, and conscientious and original in his profession. R. H. VETCH, *rev.* ELIZABETH BAIGENT

Sources J. Stokes, 'Major-General Charles Pasley', *Royal Engineers Journal* (2 Feb 1891) • *AusDB*, 5.409–11 • War Office records • Admiralty records • *CGPLA Eng. & Wales* (1891)

Archives NL Scot., diaries and family corresp. • NL Scot., family corresp. | Mitchell L., NSW, letters to his father

Wealth at death £6243 16*s.* 11*d.*: probate, 14 Jan 1891, *CGPLA Eng. & Wales*

Pasley, Sir Charles William (1780–1861), army officer, was born at Eskdalemuir, Dumfriesshire, on 8 September 1780. Nothing is known of his parents. He was privately educated by Andrew Little of Langholm and progressed so rapidly that at the age of eight he could read the Greek testament. Four years later he wrote a history of the wars between the boys on either side of the River Esk, the Langholmers and the Mucklemholmers, translating it into Latin in the style of Livy. He also wrote a poem about Langholm Common riding, which brought some profit to the publisher. In 1794 he was sent to school at Selkirk with five cousins; four Malcolms—Sir James, Sir John, Sir Pulteney, and Sir Charles—and Sir James Little. They and Pasley were styled in later life the six knights of Eskdale. Pasley entered the Royal Military Academy at Woolwich on 29 August 1796, and on 1 December 1797 was commissioned second lieutenant in the Royal Artillery. He was transferred to the Royal Engineers on 1 April 1798, and on 28 August 1799 was promoted first lieutenant.

Between 1799 and 1807 Pasley served in Minorca, Malta, Naples, and Sicily. During 1804 he was sent by the governor, Lieutenant-General W. A. Villettes, from Malta to communicate with Lord Nelson, and he advanced to second captain on 1 March 1805. In April and May 1806 he served in the defence of Gaeta against the French, and then at the battle of Maida on 4 July. He took part in the siege of Copenhagen in 1807 and was promoted captain on 18 November. He joined Major-General James Leith in September 1808 at Oviedo in the north of Spain, where he was employed, firstly, to reconnoitre the Asturian frontier and then to communicate with the British commander at

Sir Charles William Pasley (1780–1861), by unknown artist, 1810

Reinosa in November. Pasley left Soto on the 15th at night, as the French entered it. Three days later he was appointed by Lieutenant-General Sir David Baird as an extra aide-de-camp due to his knowledge of Spanish. On the 25th he joined Lieutenant-General Sir John Moore's staff in a similar capacity, and was with Moore during withdrawal to, and at the battle of, Corunna (16 January 1809). During the retreat Pasley lent his horse to a lame soldier and afterwards had to proceed on foot, for part of the time wearing only one shoe.

In August 1809 Pasley accompanied the expedition to Walcheren in the Netherlands, was employed in reconnoitring the coasts of Cadzand and Walcheren under the fire of enemy batteries, and took part in the battle of Flushing. At his own suggestion he led a storming party, in the middle of the night of 14 August, to capture and spike the guns of a prominent French battery on the dike. The attack succeeded in its aim and took fifty prisoners; but Pasley was wounded, first by a bayonet in his thigh, and then, after reaching the top of the dike, by a shot through his body fired by a French soldier from below. The bullet injured his spine, and he was seriously disabled for a year, during which he learned German. He received the silver war medal with two clasps for Maida and Corunna, and a pension for his wounds.

In November 1810 Pasley published the first edition of his *Essay on the Military Policy and Institutions of the British Empire*, which ran into a fourth edition in November 1812. It was favourably reviewed (reputedly by George Canning) in the *Quarterly Review* of May 1811 as one of the most important political works that had come to the anonymous reviewer's notice. While in command of the Plymouth company of the Royal Military Artificers in 1811, Pasley endeavoured to improve the practice of military engineering. He visited a Lancastrian school in August of that year, and began a course of instruction for his non-commissioned officers. He composed an elaborate treatise on a similar principle to the systems of Andrew Bell and Joseph Lancaster to enable the non-commissioned officers to teach themselves and their men without the assistance of mathematical masters, and to go through their course of geometry in the same manner as their company drills or their small-arms exercises. This system was so successful that in March 1812 it was laid before a committee of Royal Engineers, who reported favourably upon it to the inspector-general of fortifications, and it was afterwards introduced on an extended scale into the engineering schools at Chatham. While Pasley was at Plymouth he was, temporarily, commanding royal engineer of the district, a position which, although so junior an officer, he held for nearly two years and received an unprecedented special allowance.

Pasley's energy and success, backed by the representations of Wellington from the Peninsula as to the defective condition of military engineering in the field, resulted in the formation of an establishment for field instruction at Chatham, and in Pasley's appointment to the office of its director, by General Lord Mulgrave, in June 1812, with the rank of brevet major, antedated to 5 February 1812. He was promoted brevet lieutenant-colonel on 27 May 1813, and became a regimental lieutenant-colonel on 20 December 1814 without apparently ever holding a majority in the corps. At Chatham he married, on 25 June 1814, Harriet, daughter of W. Spencer Cooper; however, she died after several months. His second marriage, at Rochester on 30 March 1819, was to Martha Matilda Roberts (*d.* 1848). The couple had six children, three of whom survived their father. One, Charles *Pasley (1824–1890), became an officer of the Royal Engineers.

In 1814 Pasley published the first of three volumes of *Military Instruction*; the last appeared in 1817. The first contained the course of practical geometry drawn up at Plymouth; the two latter, a complete treatise on elementary fortification, including the principles of the science and rules for construction, many of which apply to civil as well as to military works. In 1817, finding that his men had been 'most grossly ill-treated by the army bread contractor', he began to examine in detail how the army was supplied with provisions. He printed and circulated in 1825, but abstained from publishing, the results of his investigations into the system of general or commissariat contracts and his recommendation that it be abolished in favour of regimental purchases. His suggestions were partly the means of introducing better arrangements. In 1818 he published a volume of standing orders which contained a complete code of military rules for the duties of all ranks in the army.

During Pasley's tenure of office as head of the instructional establishment at Chatham, he organized improved systems of telegraphing, sapping, mining, pontooning, and exploding gunpowder on land and in water, and laid down rules for such explosions founded on careful experiment. He also prepared pamphlets and courses of instruction on these and other subjects. A volume on *Practical Architecture* was especially valuable. In his leisure time he learned the Welsh and Irish languages from Welsh and Irish privates of the Corps of Royal Sappers and Miners. His work, *Practical Operations of a Siege*, of which the first part was published in 1829 and the second in 1832, proved authoritative and was the best contemporary textbook written in any language on that subject. Every aspect of a siege was treated separately, and Pasley exposed various mistakes into which French and German authors had fallen. The book was translated into French, and published in Paris in 1847.

Pasley was promoted brevet colonel on 22 July 1830 and regimental colonel on 12 November 1831. During 1831 he was appointed CB and began a volume of 320 pages (completed in May 1834) on the expediency and practicability of simplifying and improving the measures, weights, and money used in Great Britain without materially altering the current standards. Through this work he hoped to bring about the result that, in the words of section 2 of statute 27 Geo. III, c. 10, there should be 'only one weight, one measure, and one yard throughout all the land'. He advocated the adoption of the decimal system but opposed introduction of French units.

In May 1836 Pasley began a work, *Limes, Calcareous Cements, Mortar, Stuccos and Concretes, and … Cements* (1838; 2nd edn, 1847), containing several discoveries—the result of experiments at Chatham—which led to the manufacture in large quantities of artificial cements such as Portland, patent lithic, and blue lias. Between 1803 and 1829, but especially during his time at Chatham, he published a further ten books, including *Description of the Universal Telegraph for Day and Night Signals* (1823) and *Rules, Chiefly Deduced from Experiments, for Conducting the Practical Operations of a Siege* (1829). He also contributed to three volumes of the Royal Engineers' *Professional Papers*.

In connection with experiments on the explosion of gunpowder under water, Pasley carried out the removal of the brig *William* and the schooner *Glenmorgan* from the bed of the Thames near Gravesend in 1838. For this service he received the thanks of the municipal authorities and was presented with the freedom of the City of London in a gold casket valued at 50 guineas. During six successive summers (1839 to 1844) he cleared away the wreck of the *Royal George* from the anchorage at Spithead, and that of the *Edgar* from St Helens on the Isle of Wight. The value of the materials recovered was greater than the expense incurred.

The successful military application of Pasley's professional work was also publicly acknowledged. In the debate in the House of Commons on 6 February 1840, on the vote of thanks to the army after the capture of Ghazni, Major-General Sir Henry Hardinge stated that the invention with which the gates of Ghazni were blown open had been developed by Pasley. The easy and bloodless capture of the native pas in the New Zealand War of 1846–7 was elsewhere ascribed to the adoption by officers of the use of explosives, and to the systematic employment of the spade, as taught by Pasley at Chatham.

Pasley remained at Chatham until his promotion to major-general on 23 November 1841, at which time he was appointed inspector-general of railways. He received the honorary degree of DCL at Oxford in 1844, and, on relinquishing the appointment of inspector-general of railways in 1846, he was made a KCB. He held the appointment of public examiner at Addiscombe College in Surrey for sixteen years (up to 1855) and took an active part in its management. In 1816 he had been elected FRS and had joined the Astronomical, Geological, and Royal Geographical societies, and the Statistical Society of London, among others.

Pasley held no public office after 1855, but occupied himself chiefly in re-editing his works, in superintending the construction of pontoon equipages, and in other matters connected with his profession. He was promoted lieutenant-general on 11 November 1851, appointed colonel-commandant of the Royal Engineers on 28 November 1853, and became general in the army on 20 September 1860. He died on 19 April 1861 at his home, 12 Norfolk Crescent, Hyde Park, London, from congestion of the lungs. R. H. VETCH, *rev.* JOHN SWEETMAN

Sources *Army List* • W. Porter, *History of the corps of royal engineers*, 1 (1889) • J. Kane, *List of officers of the royal regiment of artillery from the year 1716 to the year 1899*, rev. W. H. Askwith, 4th edn (1900) • *The dispatches of … the duke of Wellington … from 1799 to 1815*, ed. J. Gurwood, 12: *France and the Low Countries, 1814–1815* (1838) • Boase, *Mod. Eng. biog.*

Archives BL, diary and papers, Add. MSS 41961–41995 • NL Scot., corresp., diaries, and papers • Royal Engineers, Chatham, Kent, records of various operations executed at the Royal Engineers establishment and elsewhere • Royal Engineers Museum, Gillingham, papers | NA Scot., corresp. with Lord Dalhousie

Likenesses portrait, 1810, repro. in C. W. Pasley, *The military policy and institutions of the British empire* (1914) [*see illus.*] • Eddis, portrait, Royal Engineers Brompton barracks, Chatham, Kent

Wealth at death £14,000: resworn probate, June 1862, *CGPLA Eng. & Wales* (1861)

Pasley, Sir Thomas, first baronet (1734–1808), naval officer, was born at Craig, near Langholm, Dumfriesshire, on 2 March 1734, the fifth of eleven children of James Pasley (1692/3–1773) of Craig, and Magdalen (*fl. c.*1700–1775), daughter of Robert Elliot of Middlemiln (or Middleholm Mill), Roxburghshire, eldest brother of Sir Gilbert Elliot. He entered the navy in 1751, on the *Garland* (24 guns). From 1753 he served on the Jamaica station in the sloop *Weasel* (16 guns), and in the *Dreadnought* (60 guns) until 1757. At the beginning of his career he served under Captain Maurice Suckling and Captain the Hon. Robert Digby, an early patron. When Digby was promoted captain of the *Bideford* (28 guns) he took Pasley with him, as acting lieutenant; and when the *Bideford* was ordered to England carrying £300,000 in bullion, Pasley was sent to London with the treasure and a guard of marines. After passing his examination on 1 August 1757 he returned to Portsmouth, and on 10 October he was appointed lieutenant of the *Dunkirk* (60 guns; Captain Digby), part of Admiral Edward Hawke's fleet in the unsuccessful expedition against Rochefort of that year. His ability attracted attention and he was given command of the fireship *Roman Emperor* (16 guns); from her, at his own request, he moved to the newly built fir frigate *Hussar* (28 guns), whose captain, John Elliot, was Pasley's cousin. Although only a year older than Pasley, Elliot had been, thanks to family interest, a post captain since 5 April 1757. The *Hussar* was his first independent command. On 24 November Elliot sank the French *Alcyon* (50 guns) and on 8 January 1758 he took the *Vengeance*, a large French privateer. As a result he was in November appointed to the newly launched *Aeolus* (32 guns), and he took Pasley with him. In a cruise in the Basque Roads in March 1759 the *Aeolus* chased two French frigates, *Blonde* (36 guns) and *Mignonne* (20 guns), capturing the latter on 22 March. At the beginning of 1760 the *Aeolus*, part of Hawke's fleet watching the French coast, had been blown off station and had put into Kinsale for provisions; on hearing of the French privateer François Thurot's landing of 1000 French troops at Carrickfergus on 21 February, he promptly moved to meet this threat with two other frigates, the *Pallas* (32 guns) and the *Brilliant* (32 guns), then also at Kinsale. Elliot was the senior captain of this tiny squadron which on 28 February found the French force of three frigates, off the Isle of Man. In the succeeding battle Thurot was killed, and the French ships surrendered. During the battle Pasley boarded Thurot's ship, the *Marlschal de Belle Isle* (44 guns), and hoisted the British flag; he was promoted first lieutenant of the *Aeolus* in the succeeding appointments. He remained in the *Aeolus*, first cruising in the channel and taking prizes and, at the end of August, off the coast of Spain near Cape Ray in the Bay of Aviles.

On his return to England, Pasley found he had been promoted commander and appointed to the sloop *Albany* to protect the coastal trade between Dublin and Plymouth, a task he proceeded to carry out until February 1763. For most naval officers peace normally meant unemployment, but Pasley, perhaps through Elliot family influence, was appointed to the *Ranger* (8 guns) on 10 February 1763 and employed for three years with the hopeless task of preventing smuggling between England and Ireland. In March 1769 he was appointed to command the *Weasel* (16 guns) and sent to Guinea on the west African coast, carrying four engineers who were to report on the state of the fortifications there. A delay in sailing meant that the *Weasel* arrived in the most unhealthy season; all the engineers and many of the crew died of fever, so that Pasley was compelled to press men out of the merchantmen there to enable him to return home. Returning to Guinea with a new crew in February 1770 he had better fortune. On his return he was given the *Pomona* (18 guns), and in the winter of 1770–71 he was sent to Greenock to raise men as a result of the Falkland Islands crisis. Promotion to post rank finally came on 21 January 1771 when he was appointed to the *Seahorse* (20 guns) in the West Indies. He returned to England in May 1772 and was put on half pay. Two years later he married Mary (*d.* 1788), daughter of Thomas Heywood, chief justice and deemster of the Isle of Man. Pasley's published journals show them to have had an affectionate marriage; they had two daughters.

Pasley remained on half pay until 6 September 1776 when he was appointed to the *Glasgow* (20 guns). In December he convoyed the outward-bound West Indian merchant fleet so successfully that he received the thanks of the merchants, who presented a piece of plate to his wife in Pasley's absence. Between February 1777 and July 1778 he was on the Jamaica station, taking several prizes; and he came home in August 1778 with another large Jamaican convoy. On 30 October 1778 he was appointed to the *Sybil* (28 guns), then still on the stocks at Buckler's Hard, Hampshire. She was launched in January 1779; Pasley declared, 'the most Elegant Frigate I ever saw on the water is—my Sybil' (*Private Sea Journals*, 70), and at the end of March he convoyed merchant ships to Newfoundland. He left there in October with the homeward bound ships for Lisbon. At Lisbon he was under the command of Commodore George Johnstone, cruising off Cape St Vincent in January 1780; and on his return to England he was sent, on 10 February, to the Cape of Good Hope to protect two homeward-bound East India Company ships. At the Cape, Pasley found the *Resolution* and the *Discovery*, returning home from Captain Cook's last voyage, and gave passage home to Nathaniel Portlock who was bringing duplicates of Cook's journals and drafts; they arrived at Falmouth on 27 August 1780.

Later that year Pasley was appointed to the *Jupiter* (50 guns), one of a squadron, first under Admiral Digby and then in 1781 under Johnstone, which took part in the action against the French admiral Suffren in Porto Praya roadstead, in the Cape Verde Islands, on 16 April 1781, and at the subsequent burning of Dutch East-Indiamen in Saldanha Bay in south-west Africa. Pasley returned to England in 1782, and in May took Admiral Hugh Pigot to the West Indies. Cruising off Havana, in company with an armed brig, Pasley took five out of a force of thirteen enemy vessels. The Spanish admiral in Havana sent two line-of-battle ships to take the *Jupiter*, which had been damaged going aground. But so spirited was the defence she put up that, on turning to face her pursuer, she caused the Spanish vessel *Tiger* to move away and allow Pasley to escape. He made his way to Antigua dockyard for necessary repairs, capturing a mast ship *en route*.

Peace once again brought unemployment. The *Jupiter* returned to Chatham to be decommissioned and broken up, and Pasley saw no further service until 1788. On 26 April of that year his wife, who had suffered from 'extreme sensibility' (*Private Sea Journals*, 72), died at Avignon. He was then made commander-in-chief in the Medway, with a broad pennant in the *Vengeance* (74 guns), and afterwards he moved to the *Bellerophon* (74 guns) in which he joined the Channel Fleet in 1790 during the Spanish armament. With the outbreak of the French Revolutionary War he was in 1793 again appointed to the *Bellerophon*, and on 12 April 1794 he was promoted to the rank of rear-admiral of the blue. Pasley commanded a reconnoitring squadron in the days leading up to the battle of the Glorious First of June. On 28 May he was ordered to attack the French rear to prevent their escape, and he engaged the French *Revolutionnaire* alone for a considerable time before other ships came to his help. The *Bellerophon* played a distinguished part in the van on 1 June during which Pasley lost a leg. He was granted a pension of £1000 for the wound. He was promoted rear-admiral of the red on 4 July 1794 and created a baronet on 26 July. In common with the other admirals present at the battle he was presented with a gold medal and chain, while the committee for the relief of wounded seamen presented him with a pair of goblets, valued at £500. This was not the end of his active service. On the anniversary of the battle in 1795 he was promoted vice-admiral of the white and three years later he was appointed commander-in-chief at the Nore. On 14 February 1799 he was promoted vice-admiral of the red and in March appointed commander in-chief at Plymouth. He became admiral of the blue on 1 January 1801 but saw no further service, although he was promoted admiral of the white on 9 November 1805. Pasley died on 29 November 1808 'at his seat near Winchester, of dropsy of the chest' (*Private Sea Journals*, 288). The baronetcy descended, by special provision, to his grandson, Thomas Sabine *Pasley, the child of his elder daughter, Maria, and Major John Sabine.

Pasley's career followed a traditional pattern, with family connections and naval interest playing their part at the beginning, and ability and good fortune contributing an increasing share as he grew older. He was a courageous and highly professional seaman and an able though not a distinguished commander. Several of his nephews achieved eminence in the navy, notably the two brothers Admiral Sir Pulteney *Malcolm and Admiral Sir Charles *Malcolm, and Peter *Heywood. P. K. Crimmin

Sources J. Ralfe, *The naval biography of Great Britain*, 1 (1828), 425 et seq. • *Naval Chronicle*, 4 (1801), 349–65 • *The private sea journals kept by Admiral Sir Thomas Pasley, bart., 1778–1782*, ed. R. M. S. Pasley (1931) • D. Syrett and R. L. DiNardo, *The commissioned sea officers of the Royal Navy, 1660–1815*, rev. edn, Occasional Publications of the Navy RS, 1 (1994) • GEC, *Baronetage* • Burke, *Peerage* (1890) • W. L. Clowes, *The Royal Navy: a history from the earliest times to the present*, 7 vols. (1897–1903), vols. 3–4 • D. Lyon, *The sailing navy list: all the ships of the Royal Navy, built, purchased and captured, 1688–1860* (1993) • O. Warner, *The glorious first of June* (1961)

Archives NMM, journal | Yale U., Osborn MSS, corresp.

Likenesses L. F. Abbot, oils, 1795, NMM; repro. in Pasley, ed., *Private sea journals*, facing p. 273 • C. Townley, mezzotint, pubd 1795 (after W. Beechey), BM, NPG • Bartolozzi, Landseer, Ryder and Stow, group portrait, line engraving, pubd 1802 (*Commemoration of the victory of June 1st 1794*; after R. Smirke), BM, NPG • W. Ridley, stipple, 1805 (after M. Brown), BM, NPG; repro. in *European Magazine* (1805) • W. Beechey, portrait, repro. in Pasley, ed., *Private sea journals*, frontispiece • engraving (after portrait by L. F. Abbot, 1795), repro. in *Naval Chronicle*; formerly in priv. coll.

Pasley, Sir Thomas Sabine, second baronet (1804–1884), naval officer, was born Thomas Sabine on 26 December 1804. He was the only son of Major John Sabine of the Grenadier Guards (brother of Sir Edward Sabine), and his wife, Maria, elder daughter of Admiral Sir Thomas *Pasley, first baronet. On the latter's death, on 29 November 1808, he succeeded to the baronetcy, and in the following year assumed the surname and arms of Pasley. He attended Dr Pearson's school in East Sheen, and Burnfoot School in Durham, and entered the Royal Naval College in August 1817. In December 1818 he joined the *Rochefort* (80 guns) going out to the Mediterranean as flagship of Sir Thomas Francis Fremantle, and afterwards of Sir Graham Moore. In October 1823 he joined the brig *Redpole*, and a few months later the *Arachne*. On 16 March 1824 he was promoted lieutenant, and in April was appointed to the *Tweed*, going out to the Brazilian station.

Pasley married, on 10 June 1826, Jane Matilda Lily (*d.* 15 May 1869), eldest daughter of the Revd Montagu John Wynyard; they had seven sons and two daughters. After his Brazilian service, he served in the West Indies, and in the Mediterranean as flag-lieutenant to his cousin and guardian, Sir Pulteney Malcolm. On 17 September 1828 he was promoted commander. He commanded the brigs *Cameleon* and *Procris*, and, as acting captain, the frigates *Rattlesnake* and *Blonde*; he was confirmed as captain on 24 May 1831. From February 1843 to January 1846 he commanded the *Curaçao* on the Brazilian station; from June 1849 to June 1854 he was superintendent of Pembroke dockyard; from October 1854 until 31 January 1856, when he was promoted rear-admiral, he commanded the *Royal Albert* and then the *Agamemnon*, in the Black Sea. From December 1857 to December 1862 he was superintendent of Devonport Dockyard. He was promoted vice-admiral on 23 March 1863, and admiral on 20 November 1866. From 1866 to 1869 he was commander-in-chief at Portsmouth; and on 24 May 1873 was nominated a KCB. He died on 13 February 1884, at his home, Moorhill, Botley, Southampton, Hampshire, and was buried at Shedfield churchyard. His eldest son predeceased him in 1870; he was succeeded in the baronetcy by his grandson, Thomas Edward Sabine Pasley.

A competent and hard-working officer, Pasley was brought up in the service by his cousin, Sir Pulteney Malcolm, and then accepted a number of demanding and unattractive posts to provide, both financially and in promotion opportunities, for his large family.

J. K. Laughton, *rev.* Andrew Lambert

Sources L. M. S. Pasley, *Memoir of Admiral Sir Thomas Sabine Pasley* (1900) • A. C. Dewar, ed., *Russian war, 1855, Black Sea: official correspondence*, Navy RS, 85 (1945) • A. D. Lambert, *The Crimean War: British grand strategy, 1853–56* (1990) • Burke, *Peerage* • *CGPLA Eng. & Wales* (1884)

Likenesses portrait, repro. in Pasley, *Memoir*

Wealth at death £33,973 15*s.* 0*d.*: resworn probate, Sept 1884, *CGPLA Eng. & Wales*

Pasmore, (Edwin John) Victor (1908–1998), artist, was born on 3 December 1908 at Chelsham House, Chelsham Road, Surrey, the eldest son of Edwin Stephen Pasmore (1866–1927), physician and specialist in mental diseases, and Gertrude Eva Screech (1884–1974), amateur painter. His early life was comfortable, and the milieu in which he grew up was artistic—not only did his mother paint, but his father was a man of taste who collected objects of

(**Edwin John) Victor Pasmore (1908–1998)**, by Ida Kar, 1954

virtu. His younger brother Stephen recalls him single-mindedly drawing battleships and aeroplanes in the nursery during the First World War. Pasmore's evident passion for painting was encouraged to such an extent that while at Harrow School (1922–6) he painted a competent copy of Landseer's *Dignity and Impudence*.

The art master at Harrow, Maurice Clarke, proceeded to introduce Pasmore to the work of the French impressionists, but the boy was equally impressed by Rembrandt and the late works of Turner, and was fascinated by the conceptual side of art as instanced in Leonardo's notebooks and Joshua Reynolds's *Discourses*. He tried to paint what he saw, mainly landscape and still life. The sudden death of his father in 1927 deprived Pasmore of all immediate hopes of becoming a professional artist, and he became a clerk in the public health department of the London county council.

Pasmore worked for the London county council for ten years, refusing all promotion so that he might reserve his energies for painting in his spare time. From 1927 until 1931 he attended evening classes at the Central School of Arts and Crafts under A. S. Hartrick, a cosmopolitan figure who had known Van Gogh, Gauguin, and Lautrec. In 1931 he began to show with the London Group, and in 1932 he joined the London Artists' Association. Pasmore continued his self-education largely through copying the masters, at this point taking the Fauve paintings of Matisse and Bonnard as examples, and holding his first solo show. He began to mix with the British avant-garde, made lasting friendships with William Coldstream and Claude Rogers, and experimented with abstraction rather before he properly understood it, participating, with Ivon Hitchens and Ceri Richards among others, in a ground-breaking exhibition, 'Objective abstractions', at Zwemmer's Gallery (1934).

Although impressed by the abstractions of Ben Nicholson, Pasmore returned to traditional naturalism, under the influence of Sickert and Bonnard, and destroyed his early abstract efforts. The depression of the 1930s saw the development of realistic art with a social conscience, and Pasmore soon became involved with his friends Rogers and Coldstream in founding the *Euston Road School to teach these new principles. Pasmore, however, was more drawn to the discipline of measuring with a plumb line, that is to say towards a science of objective picture making, than to any specific social or political stance. He was now able to give up his job with the London county council, largely because of the enlightened patronage of Kenneth Clark, newly appointed director of the National Gallery, who undertook to pay Pasmore a stipend in return for paintings. This open show of support made all the difference to the young artist, and his work assumed increasing authority.

On 3 June 1940 Pasmore married the artist Wendy Blood (*b*. 1915), with whom he had two children. At the outset of the Second World War, the Euston Road School was dissolved and Pasmore registered as a conscientious objector. None the less he was conscripted in October 1941, trained as an NCO and earned something of a reputation as a marksman. He was subsequently sent for guards officer cadet training at Sandhurst, whereupon he once more proclaimed himself a conscientious objector and walked out of barracks. He was declared a deserter and imprisoned for six months. Finally, in September 1942, after appearing before a number of tribunals, he was completely exempted from military service and allowed to get back to his painting.

The influences of Whistler, Conder, and Japanese prints are discernible in Pasmore's work of this period, but Chinese painting, particularly of the Song dynasty, was also a key inspiration. Bombed out of their flat in Ebury Street in 1941, the Pasmores stayed with friends and Victor buried himself in the writings of Cézanne, Gauguin, and Van Gogh. He pondered colour theory and was fascinated by what he saw as the gap between the paintings and the ideas of the post-impressionists. His own work developed. The apparently pointilliste paintings of the Thames at Chiswick, with which he rapidly made a name for himself, have strong curvilinear frameworks that suggest a spiral movement. This may owe something to Turner, and it was a motif to which Pasmore returned.

In 1943 Pasmore took up the post of visiting teacher at Camberwell School of Arts and Crafts. He was an inspiring tutor, remembered with affection by such diverse students as Terry Frost and Euan Uglow, and continued working there until 1949, after which he worked at the Central School for five years. In 1954 he was appointed director of painting in the School of Fine Art, King's College, University of Durham, a post he held until 1961. Meanwhile his painting had undergone what many saw as a 'road to Damascus' conversion: Pasmore had 'gone abstract'.

Pasmore's landscape paintings had become increasingly tentative and abstract, and the seminal Picasso exhibition at the Victoria and Albert Museum (1945–6) had emphasized what he interpreted as the crisis in modern painting. Instead of returning to fauvism or cubism, however, Pasmore pursued a more independent abstract mode after the example of Klee, Mondrian, and Ben Nicholson. The period 1947 to 1951 was largely transitional, with Pasmore making and exhibiting abstract paintings and collages. Then in 1951 he made his first abstract reliefs, announcing that easel painting was dead. Shock was general. The influential critic and general arbiter of taste Herbert Read called it the most revolutionary event in post-war British art, and opinion was split. Pasmore, a gifted public speaker with a touch of the prophet, enjoyed the notoriety, and in writing, lecturing, and teaching, set about the promulgation of his revised views.

Pasmore showed considerable courage in 'going abstract' just at the point when he was establishing a reputation as a realist painter. In fact his work had become increasingly concerned with structure and pattern, light and space, shape and colour, and the only way forward he could detect was in terms of abstract form. He became even more active as a teacher, running a department at Durham specifically devoted to research and experiment into the language of abstract form. His influence, combined with that of his colleagues Harry Thubron and Richard Hamilton, changed art education. Even more concretely, Pasmore was appointed consultant architectural designer (1955–77) for the development of part of Peterlee New Town, co. Durham, which enabled him to design constructivist art on a scale one could walk through.

Pasmore had too restless an intelligence to sit for long on his laurels. By the mid-1960s he felt that geometrical reliefs were too limiting, and he returned to painting. He thought of himself as a modern romantic, and always talked of the modern revolution in painting which involved for him a synthesis of objective representation with subjective freedom of expression. To this end he developed a rich abstract language of line and colour, taking universal symbols from nature such as the spiral and interlocking shapes (derived from waves and swirling snow), and employing a variety of marks from the stippled to the sprayed, but generally suggestive of organic form. His work was lyrical, essentially musical, intuitive, full of clouds of evocative colour and a wandering though exact line.

In 1964 Pasmore made his first graphics, and for the rest of his life printmaking was a central part of his working practice. Unfailingly inventive, he worked with a number of different print workshops in London and in Rome, producing a steady stream of etchings and screen prints. Sometimes these were combined with the mystical or romantic poetry he liked to write. He was never idle, acquiring a house and studio in Malta in 1966, and making environmental paintings in the courtyards there from piled blocks of rough-hewn honey-coloured stone, daubed paint on walls, and a painted swimming-pool in which, on occasion, would float a solitary orange from an overhanging tree. One courtyard became a refuge for all the stray cats of the island, others were open-air studios. Towards the end of his life Pasmore reintroduced figurative imagery into his paintings, making copies of pictures by Picasso and Turner, and creating allegories of man's relationship with his environment. He never ceased to experiment and push beyond the boundaries of his art, and this was his lasting strength.

Pasmore was rewarded with international sales and celebrity, and with honours in Britain. In 1959 he was made CBE and in 1981 Companion of Honour, and he was elected a Royal Academician in 1983. Among his many exhibitions were retrospectives at the Tate Gallery in 1965 and 1980, at the Yale Center for British Art in 1988, and at the Serpentine Gallery in 1991. In 1990 he selected 'The artist's eye' at the National Gallery. He was not noted for his diplomatic skills. When he first met Kenneth Clark, who became one of his staunchest supporters, Clark was trying a new frame on one of the Turners in the National Gallery. Pasmore told him abruptly that he had no taste. Yet they became friends. For all his brusqueness and quasi-military bearing—the gruff delivery and the barking laugh—Pasmore could be immensely charming. There was humour in his bright black eyes, as well as intelligence. If there was obstinacy in his make-up, it was the very quality which ensured that his career took the unusual and rewarding course that it did. He died, survived by his wife, at his home, Dar Gamri, at Gudja in Malta, on 23 January 1998, and was cremated at Kensal Green four days later. His work is held in many public collections including the Tate, Manchester City Art Gallery, Leeds City Art Gallery, Wakefield City Art Gallery, the Ashmolean Museum, Oxford, Aberdeen Art Gallery, the Arts Council, Walker Art Gallery, Liverpool, the Museum of Modern Art, New York, and the Art Gallery of South Australia, Adelaide. ANDREW LAMBIRTH

Sources C. Bell, *Victor Pasmore* (1945) · A. Bowness and L. Lambertini, *Victor Pasmore* (1980) · N. Lynton, *Victor Pasmore* (1992) · private information (2004) · personal knowledge (2004) · *The Guardian* (24 Jan 1998) · *The Times* (26 Jan 1998) · *The Independent* (26 Jan 1998) · *Victor Pasmore: selected works, 1926–1954* [exhibition catalogue, Arts Council, 1955] · *Victor Pasmore: the image within* (1977) [exhibition catalogue, Marlborough Fine Art Ltd, London, Sept–Oct 1977] · *Victor Pasmore* [exhibition catalogue, Yale U. CBA, 16 Nov 1988 – 8 Jan 1989] · *Victor Pasmore: new work* (1995) [exhibition catalogue, Marlborough Fine Art Ltd, London, 13 Sept – 21 Oct 1995] · *Victor Pasmore: a print retrospective, 1951–1997* (2001) [exhibition catalogue, Marlborough Graphics Gallery, London, 1–24 Feb 2001] · b. cert. · m. cert.

Archives priv. coll. · Tate collection, album of Christmas cards | Tate collection, corresp. with Lord Clark · Tate collection, letters to Sir William Coldstream | FILM BBC · Channel 4 · priv. coll. | SOUND BL NSA

Likenesses R. Moynihan, oils, 1939, Royal College of Art, London · two photographs, 1951, Hult. Arch. · I. Kar, photograph, 1954, NPG [*see illus.*] · W. Pasmore, photograph, 1995, repro. in *Victor Pasmore: new work* · J. Pasmore, photograph, repro. in *The Guardian* · Snowdon, photograph, repro. in B. Robertson, *Private view* (1965), p. 56

Pasold, Eric Walter (1906–1978), textile and clothing manufacturer, was born in Fleissen, in the Austro-Hungarian empire (after 1918 it became Plesná, in Czechoslovakia), on 19 June 1906, the eldest of the four children of Max Walter Pasold and his wife, Berta, *née* Geipel. The family, Lutheran and German-speaking, had long been connected with textiles. Eric Pasold was educated at a state school in Fleissen and a textile college in Asch. His involvement in the family business took him on visits to England, and in 1932 he bought a site near Slough and built a small knitting factory. His younger brother, Rolf, joined him, and from 1932 to 1939 they shuttled between England and Czechoslovakia, running both the new venture and the old family firm. The brothers identified themselves with Britain by becoming naturalized British subjects in 1936 and 1937. The Slough business specialized in children's knitted clothing marketed under the trademark Ladybird. Output rose during the war and soared thereafter, and the communist take-over in Czechoslovakia in 1948 ensured that the family enterprise, by then extremely successful, was concentrated in Britain.

In 1957 Pasolds became a public company, though almost all the capital remained in family hands. Problems of marketing, management, and succession loomed, however; the much expanded firm needed something other than the old techniques of family direction. Eric, always the dominant partner in the business, sought a link with one of the big textile groups. The outcome was that in 1965 he sold 54 per cent of the Pasold equity to Coats Paton Ltd. He joined that company's board but resigned after three years. In 1971 Coats Paton bought the remainder of the Pasold equity.

Pasold's approach to business was strongly influenced by the political upheavals of his lifetime. In his twenties he found himself a citizen of a new country whose language he did not speak and whose nationalistic aspirations he did not share. The original family business came to be controlled by the Nazis after Hitler's annexation of the Sudetenland in 1938; a decade later it was confiscated by the communists. Pasold's business success sprang from a combination of technical expertise, an eye for markets, a search for efficiency in an integrated plant, and a tough management style. Characteristically, he conducted much of his international commuting in the 1930s piloting his own aeroplane. During the war he served on numerous textile industry committees. Disillusionment set in during the 1960s; England, he believed, was succumbing to socialism. Devoted to free enterprise, adventurous and individualistic, he had little love for the interventionist ways of trade unions, civil servants, and governments generally.

Pasold had a strong personal interest in the history of textiles and especially of knitting. In 1964 he established the Pasold Research Fund, and in 1968 a lectureship in textile history at Nottingham University was financed. His services to exports were recognized by an OBE in 1961, and his work in education by an honorary MA from Nottingham University in 1977.

In 1969, with his health deteriorating and having sold all his British assets, Pasold retired to Switzerland. He died at 51 Haldenstrasse, Lucerne, on 5 January 1978.

D. C. Coleman

Sources E. W. Pasold, *Ladybird, ladybird: a story of private enterprise* (1977) • personal knowledge (2004) • private information (2004) • K. G. Ponting, 'Pasold, Sir Eric Walter', *DBB* • *Textile History*, 9 (1978)
Archives U. Nott. L.
Likenesses photographs, repro. in *Textile History* • photographs, repro. in Pasold, *Ladybird, ladybird*

Pasor, Matthias (1599–1658), linguist and philosopher, was born on 12 April 1599 at Herborn, Germany, the first son of Georg Pasor (1570–1637) and Apollonia Hendsch (*d.* 1614). His father was a philologist who became a professor at the universities of Herborn and of Franeker, Netherlands. He had a younger brother, Johann Jacob, who survived him. He attended the *gymnasia* of Herborn and Siegen, and received his master's degree in philosophy on 20 February 1617 at Heidelberg, where he had matriculated on 13 April 1616 after having studied at Herborn and at Marburg.

In Heidelberg, Pasor studied theology, which he combined with giving private lectures. His reputation led, in 1619, to his appointment as extraordinary professor of natural philosophy, and in April 1620 as professor of mathematics. He left Heidelberg on 6 September 1622 when the town was sacked by the Bavarian army. Without any possessions he arrived in October in Herborn, where he resumed his private lectures. Early in 1624 the ongoing Thirty Years' War led Pasor to flee Germany, first for a month to Leiden, and then to Oxford, where he was incorporated as master of arts on 5 June 1624 on the strength of his Heidelberg degree. Again he gave private lectures, in Hebrew and mathematics. Later in 1624 he accompanied some Hamburg students to Paris as their private tutor in mathematics, and while there studied Arabic and Syriac with the Lebanese-born professor of languages and royal interpreter, Sionita. In the spring of 1625 he returned to Oxford and settled in Exeter College. On 25 October 1626 he accepted the chair of oriental languages (his inaugural lecture was published), and later he combined it with lectures in Hebrew at St Mary Hall. The appointment enabled him to decline the invitation of Bishop James Ussher to go to Ireland.

In 1629 Pasor went to Groningen, where the university had invited him to occupy the chair of moral philosophy. From 1635 onwards he also taught mathematics there. In 1645 he switched to the chair of theology.

Pasor was reluctant to publish. His will reveals that his notes were written under the pressure of time, and were in a disorderly state. He requested that if his heirs (his younger brother in Germany with children Anna Margaretha and Matthias) should be unable to administer his estate, it should fund three chairs called 'Professiones Pasorianae' at the University of Herborn, whose holders would be expected to edit and publish his notes; however, his family inherited his estate, and so there were no Pasorian professors. Although Pasor did not publish himself he made considerable efforts to publish the works of

Matthias Pasor (1599–1658), by Steven van Lamsweerde, 1645

his father, and there also exist a series of printed disputations which were defended under his presidency, dealing with theology and ethics. No mathematical work has been found.

At Groningen, Pasor took part in the general duties of the senate, and in the discussions about Cartesianism he supported Descartes. He contributed to the biographies and portraits of Groningen professors in *Effigies et vitae* (1654), probably supplying his own biography as well. The 'Programma funebre', in which his death was announced, described him as a 'strong, independent man, who never married, incorruptible, pious and peaceful, a good colleague, a faithful friend and well-liked by all'. He died at Oude Boteringestraat, Groningen, on 28 January 1658, and was buried on 4 February in the nearby Academy church.

JAN VAN MAANEN

Sources *Effigies et vitae professorum Academiae Groningae & Omlandiae* (Groningen, 1654); repr. (1968) • testament, Jan 1658, Rijksarchief Groningen, Archief Rijksuniversiteit, no. 89 • 'Programma funebre', Rector Academiae L. S., 4 Feb 1658, Groningen University, department of precious works • handwritten agreement, 16 Feb 1635, Rijksarchief Groningen, Resoluties van gedeputeerde staten, 125.11 • W. J. A. Jonckbloet, *Gedenkboek der Hoogeschool te Groningen* (1864) • *Oeuvres de Descartes*, ed. C. Adam and P. Tannery, new edn, 11 vols. in 13 pts (Paris, 1974–89), vol. 4 • Wood, *Ath. Oxon.* • P. A. G. Dibon, 'L'Enseignement philosophique dans les universités Néerlandaises à l'époque pré-Cartesienne, 1575–1650', PhD diss., Leiden, 1954 • G. Toepke, ed., *Die Matrikel der Universität Heidelberg*, 2 (Heidelberg, 1884); repr. (Nendeln, Liechtenstein, 1976) • J. S. Ersch and J. G. Gruber, *Gelehrten lexikon* (1840), section 3, vol. 13, i.v. Pasor

Archives University of Groningen, Netherlands

Likenesses S. van Lamsweerde, line engraving, 1645, NPG [*see illus.*]

Wealth at death substantial; promised high wages, indicating large capital: 'testament', Jan 1658, Rijksarchief Groningen, Archief Rijksuniversiteit, no. 89

Pasquali, Francis (*fl.* 1743–1795). *See under* Pasquali, Nicolò (1717/18–1757).

Pasquali, Nicolò [Niccolò] (**1717/18–1757**), musician and actor, was born in Cosenza, Italy. Little is known of his life until he arrived in London about 1743, accompanied by his younger brother **Francis Pasquali** (*fl.* 1743–1795), also a musician, as well as a publisher, scene designer, and impresario, who may have been his pupil. The older Pasquali worked as a violinist and composer and became a member of the Royal Society of Musicians on 3 April 1743; he published his *Sonate a violino e basso* op. 1 in London in 1744. A concert at the Haymarket Theatre (1 April 1745) featured Nicolò performing a violin solo and Francis (commonly known as 'Pasquali, Jr', or 'Pasqualino') playing a concerto on the violoncello. Both Italians were rated as 'principal performers' (Burney, *Hist. mus.*, 1008) on their respective instruments around this time. Nicolò also led an opera directed by Francesco Geminiani at the Haymarket six days later and may too have played in the band at the King's Theatre. The brothers' joint appearances included a concert at Coopers' Hall, Bristol, on 11 September 1747.

Next came a move to Ireland, and in October 1748 the elder Pasquali became the director of Thomas Sheridan's band at Smock Alley Theatre in Dublin, where he remained for three seasons. He composed three masques for Smock Alley, at least one of which, *The Temple of Peace* (9 February 1749), used machinery and scenes designed by his younger brother. He also conducted the Irish première of Giovanni Battista Pergolesi's *Stabat mater* (3 October 1749) and directed concerts for the Fishamble Street Charitable Musick Society, including his oratorio *Noah* (27 March 1750 and 21 January 1751; now lost). The Smock Alley band played at other venues and for charitable events, although these appear to have conflicted with Sheridan's interests and theatre business on occasion.

Pasquali was able to travel to England during this period, first in 1750 (his *Six Sonatas for Two Violins* and *XII English Songs*, taken from the masques, were among the works published in London around this time) and again in 1752, when he led several London concerts. A benefit concert for him at the Little Theatre in the Haymarket (3 February 1752) is recognized as one of the first times the piano was ever played in public in Britain.

Pasquali left Dublin in 1752 for Edinburgh, an increasingly popular location for foreign musicians, where he appeared as leader and soloist at the Canongate theatre and musical society, taught, and composed. He made his acting début in his own whimsical farce, based on Hogarth's print, entitled *The Enrag'd Musician, or, The Tempest Rehearsed* (Canongate, 2 February 1753). Other works include a popular *Stabat mater* (lost), many songs and minuets, at least two cantatas (both lost), contributions to *The*

Harpsichord Miscellany (1763), and another oratorio, *David* (the harpsichord part to which was sold in 1868 and now belongs to the Royal College of Music). Pasquali's few surviving works suggest the influence of Handel and reveal a great deal of natural ability, and may have influenced William Boyce. However, he made his most enduring impact through theoretical writings. The figured-bass teaching manual *Thorough-Bass Made Easy*, published in Edinburgh in 1757, achieved unusual success for a pedagogical work in English during this period, appearing in at least four further British editions (including nineteenth- and twentieth-century examples) and, most significantly, translations into French and Dutch (published in Amsterdam). *The Art of Fingering the Harpsichord* was published posthumously by Robert Bremner in Edinburgh in 1758 and also enjoyed further editions.

Contemporary commentators, including Mary Delany and Charles Burney, spoke favourably of Pasquali's qualities as a man, musician, and teacher. He died in Edinburgh, suddenly, on 13 October 1757, aged thirty-nine.

The younger brother, Francis, was active in London following his return from Dublin. From about 1760 he was a music publisher in Poland Street, near Great Marlborough Street, and also achieved prominence as a double bass player. In 1772 he opened the New Rooms for Concerts and Assemblies on Tottenham Street, which were successful as home to the concerts of ancient music from 1776 and received royal patronage in 1785. He was also connected with the King's Theatre during the 1780s, possibly as an assistant to his son-in-law Michael Novosielski (husband of his daughter Regina), in the scene department. Pasquali's fortunes took a serious turn for the worse when the concerts of ancient music moved to the King's Theatre in 1794. No details of his death are known. He was living in St Pancras in 1786 and is listed as 'delinquent' (Highfill, Burnim & Langhans, *BDA*) in the rate books of 1795.

DAVID J. GOLBY

Sources Highfill, Burnim & Langhans, *BDA* • D. Johnson, 'Pasquali, Niccolò', *New Grove*, 2nd edn, 19.185–6 [incl. list of works] • Burney, *Hist. mus.*, new edn, 2.844, 1008, 1014 • S. McVeigh, *The violinist in London's concert life, 1750–1784: Felice Giardini and his contemporaries* (1989), 66–7 • *General Advertiser* (11 March 1752) • *The autobiography and correspondence of Mary Granville, Mrs Delany*, ed. Lady Llanover, 1st ser., 3 vols. (1861); 2nd ser., 3 vols. (1862) • [J. S. Sainsbury], ed., *A dictionary of musicians*, 2 (1824), 269 • H. D. Johnstone and R. Fiske, eds., *Music in Britain: the eighteenth century* (1990), vol. 4 of *The Blackwell history of music in Britain*, ed. I. Spink (1988–95), 217 • D. Baptie, *A handbook of musical biography* (1883), 174 • C. Ehrlich, *The music profession in Britain since the eighteenth century* (1985), 26

Wealth at death Francis Pasquali was listed as 'delinquent' in the rate book of 1795: Highfill, Burnim & Langhans, *BDA*

Pass, Simon. *See* Passe, Simon de (1595–1647).

Passano, Giovanni Gioacchino di [John Joachim de Passano] (*fl.* **1520–1547**), diplomat, was probably a native of Genoa. He is first recorded in 1520, when he attended the Field of Cloth of Gold as the secretary of Ottaviano Fregoso, the Genoese resident ambassador at the French court. He then entered the service of Louise of Savoy, the mother of the French king, François I, as *maître d'hôtel*, and it was as her representative, having become seigneur de Vaux, that he first came to England in June 1524. Although ostensibly on a business trip, he negotiated with Cardinal Wolsey, who provided him with a lodging at Blackfriars. In spite of false reassurances put about by Wolsey, the emperor, Charles V, became so alarmed by the length of Passano's stay that on 20 October he demanded his dismissal. The defeat and capture of François I at the battle of Pavia (24 February 1525) effectively nullified Passano's mission, which had been intended to drive a wedge between Henry VIII and the emperor.

As Louise assumed the regency of France in her son's absence, Passano assisted her efforts to gain Henry VIII's help in securing François's release from prison. On 6 August 1525 he was commissioned to oversee the payment of French pensions to members of the English court, a duty which he continued to discharge for several years thereafter. His contacts in the banking world fitted him well for the task, for he not only lent money of his own to the king of France, but also persuaded some of his Italian relatives and friends to do likewise. On 30 August 1525 Passano and Jean Brinon signed the treaty of the More in which Louise promised to pay Henry 2 million gold crowns in annual instalments. Following François I's release from captivity in March 1526, Passano became his *maître d'hôtel*. Between 1526 and 1532 he served three times as the French resident ambassador in England: from April 1526 until July 1527; from January 1530 until January 1531; and from March 1531 until January 1532. His reputation as a 'worker of diplomatic miracles' was frequently acknowledged by his imperial rival, Chapuys (Pollard, 269). During his second embassy in England, Passano witnessed the final disgrace of Wolsey. Relations between the two men had become strained once Wolsey realized that he could not count on French aid. Late in 1530, as Wolsey tried to recover his position, Passano sent a report to François which Sir Francis Bryan described as 'of verye good sort, in disclosinge the mysdemeanour of the sayd cardinall' (*State Papers, Henry VIII*, 7.213—there misdated to 1529).

Despite his close involvement in English affairs, Passano remained in contact with his native land. Thus, in September 1527 he was sent by François I to Marshal Lautrec's camp outside Naples. On his way there, he visited Piacenza, Parma, Genoa, and Ancona. From October 1538 until May 1539, he served as French resident ambassador in Venice, lending money to various agents for the purchase of books and 'antiquities' for the king and for the hire of book-copyists. The French royal accounts contain numerous warrants ordering reimbursement of Passano's travel and other expenses, as well as substantial gifts of cash in reward for his services. Little is known about his private life. In December 1527 his natural daughter, Perrette, born of a liaison with Madeleine de Marignano, was legitimized by the king, and in March 1540 letters of naturalization and permission to acquire fiefs, lordships, and benefices were granted to Passano's wife, Katherine Sault, and to his children, Antoine and

Anne. In 1547, under Henri II, Passano was living in retirement in Padua, whence he offered unsuccessfully to arbitrate in the dispute between England and France over the possession of Boulogne. His date of death is unknown.

R. J. KNECHT

Sources *Catalogue des actes de François 1er*, 10 vols. (Paris, 1887–1908) · *LP Henry VIII* · *State papers published under … Henry VIII*, 11 vols. (1830–52) · A. F. Pollard, *Wolsey*, rev. edn (1953) · G. Jacqueton, *La politique extérieure de Louise de Savoie* (1892) · F. Decrue, *Anne duc de Montmorency* (1889)

Passe, Simon de (1595–1647), engraver, was born in Cologne, the son of Crispijn de Passe (1564–1637) and his wife, Magdalena de Bock (1555–1635). Crispijn de Passe, born in Arnemuiden in Zeeland, was a prominent engraver, draughtsman, and print publisher who obtained his training in Antwerp and was active there for several years. He was forced to leave Antwerp because of his Anabaptist faith and settled in 1589 in Cologne, where all his five children were born. Crispijn the younger (1594–1670), Simon, Willem [*see below*], and a daughter, Magdalena (1600–1638), all became professional engravers. In Cologne, Passe set up a productive and distinguished print publishing house, producing countless portraits of the European nobility, religious, mythological, and allegorical prints, and print books, which found a ready market in the whole of Europe. In 1611 the family was exiled from Cologne and took refuge in Utrecht. With the assistance of his children, Passe soon managed to start a prosperous business again. Even before Simon and Willem left for England he was producing prints for the English market, in the 1590s in co-operation with the London bookseller and publisher Hans Woutneel.

Simon de Passe's first dated prints were made in 1612. He soon developed into a gifted portraitist, and in 1616 he settled in London in order to pursue a career of his own. His early prints were published by Compton Holland, the later ones by John Sudbury and George Humble. One of his first prints portrays Queen Anne on horseback (1616). He contributed portraits to Henry Holland's *Baziliologia* (1618) and made a number of portraits of the royal family and of English noblemen and scholars, among them the duke of Buckingham (1617), Lucy Harington, countess of Bedford, Francis Bacon, and William Perkins—a total of fifty-seven prints, mostly drawn after life, and with a new type of auricular frame. One of Passe's specialities was the engraving of silver (and, in a few cases, gold) roundels with portraits of royalty: subjects included James I, Queen Anne, Charles, the French King Henry IV with his wife, Maria de' Medici, and the family of Frederick V of the Palatinate. Dated examples were made between 1615 and 1618. These roundels were probably never intended for printing, but were used as medals or could be worn on a chain.

In 1621 Passe's younger brother **Willem de Passe** (1597/8–1636/7) joined him in London. Willem and his sister Magdalena had engraved the sixty-five portraits of famous English scholars in Henry Holland's *Herōologia*, published by their father in Utrecht in 1620. In London, Willem produced a total of seventeen portraits of princes and noblemen, most of them after life: among other prints were a double portrait of James I and Charles (1621), Frederick of Bohemia and his family (1621, after a drawing made from life in The Hague), and the family of James I (1622, showing his wife, Anne, his children, and his grandchildren, including those who were deceased). This copper plate, published by John Bill with a royal privilege, was updated several times by the addition of later offspring.

Around 1622–3 Willem de Passe married Elisabeth Jenner, probably a relation of the print publisher Thomas Jenner, who published most of his prints. This marriage must have been the reason why Willem gave up his Mennonite faith and was baptized in the Dutch Reformed church in Austin Friars on 6 April 1624. The couple's son Crispijn was baptized there two days later, and a daughter, Elisabeth, in 1625; these two children died young. According to a document of 1647, drawn up in Holland after Willem's death, his only heir was his nineteen-year-old son Crispijn, who must have been born in 1628.

Simon de Passe left London in 1622; his last engravings in England were portraits of the Spanish ambassador, the count of Gondomar, and Charles I and his then fiancée, Maria of Spain (published in Utrecht). He worked for two more years in Utrecht where among other works he made a posthumous portrait of Antoine de Pluvinel for the *Maneige royal* (1623) of his elder brother Crispijn, who had started a career of his own in Paris in 1618. Simon de Passe was baptized in the Calvinist church on 28 October 1624, one day before he left for Denmark, where he was offered the job of royal engraver to Christian IV. In 1637 the king made him responsible for the co-ordination of a large but unfinished series of eighty-four drawings which were to represent scenes from Danish history; in 1639 he was asked to organize a large series of paintings for the banquet hall at Kronborg Castle, which were commissioned from Netherlandish painters. On 17 January 1641 Simon de Passe married Elizabeth Rasmusdatten. He died in Copenhagen on 6 May 1647.

Crispijn de Passe the younger returned from Paris to the Netherlands in 1629, while Willem stayed in London for the rest of his life. The latter's last dated print, an equestrian portrait of the duke of Buckingham, is from 1625. The reason for his inactivity during the remainder of his life (he died between October 1636 and December 1637) is unknown.

ILJA M. VELDMAN

Sources A. M. Hind, *Engraving in England in the sixteenth and seventeenth centuries*, 2 (1955), 245–301 · J. Verbeek and I. M. Veldman, *Hollstein's Dutch and Flemish etchings, engravings and woodcuts, c. 1450–1700*, ed. K. G. Boon, 16 (1974) · I. M. Veldman, *Crispijn de Passe and his progeny (1564–1670): a century of print production*, trans. M. Hoyle (Rotterdam, 2001) · A. Griffiths and R. A. Gerard, *The print in Stuart Britain, 1603–1689* (1998) [exhibition catalogue, BM, 8 May – 20 Sept 1998] · D. Franken, *L'œuvre gravé des van de Passe* (Amsterdam, 1881); repr. (1975) · H. D. Schepelern, 'Simon de Pas og andre kobberstikkere omkring Christian IV', *Kunstmuseets Aarsskrift*, 38 (1951), 1–45 · W. J. C. Moens, ed., *The marriage, baptismal, and burial registers, 1571 to 1874, and monumental inscriptions of the Dutch Reformed church, Austin Friars, London* (privately printed, Lymington, 1884), 56 · S. Muller, *Bijdragen en medeelingen van het Historisch Genootschap gevestigd te Utrecht*, 10 (1887), 54

Passe, Willem de (1597/8–1636/7). *See under* Passe, Simon de (1595–1647).

Passele, Sir Edmund (*b.* in or before 1267, *d.* 1327), lawyer and justice, took his surname from Pashley in the parish of Ticehurst in east Sussex. He was not related to the members of the quite separate Passelewe family. Edmund was the son of Robert of Pashley and his wife, Sarah, and cannot have been born any later than 1267. His father was the son of Ralph of Alderstead, from Merstham in Surrey, and both he and Edmund held lands there. Robert probably took the surname Pashley only after his marriage to Sarah put him in control of lands she had inherited at Pashley. Robert was steward of the rape of Hastings in 1285, was knighted between 1292 and 1295, and then served as knight of the shire for Sussex in 1295 and 1300, in addition receiving judicial commissions in 1304, 1305, and 1306. Edmund, who was his eldest son and heir, probably received a university education in Roman law (possibly at Oxford), for in 1307 Hervey Stanton specifically referred to him as a 'legist'. Other common-law serjeants of the period can be shown to have possessed some knowledge of the learned laws, but none seems to have achieved Passele's level of expertise. His first known employment is as steward of the rape of Hastings (in 1298). He later served as steward of the liberty of the archbishop of Canterbury between 1298 and 1302. This overlapped with the beginning of two decades of activity as one of the leading serjeants of the common bench. Passele was among those called to the bar in Michaelmas term 1299, and remained an active and prominent serjeant until 1318. Among the clients paying him retainers were the king (though only in 1309) and the city of London (as from 1310). He was appointed a justice of the London eyre of 1321 soon after it opened, and seems to have been knighted shortly before he took his seat on the bench. He sat as a baron of the exchequer from the beginning of Michaelmas term 1323 to the end of Michaelmas term 1326, and died not long before 27 March 1327.

Passele's first wife (to whom he was married by 1288) was Maud, the daughter and heir of John of Kitchenour. She was the mother of his eldest son, William, who predeceased his father, of his second son and heir, John, and possibly of a third son, Edmund, who was murdered at Coulsdon in Surrey in 1328. Maud was dead by 1318, and Passele is subsequently found as the husband of Margaret, the posthumous daughter of Thomas de *Normanville (*d.* 1295) and his wife, Denise, the daughter of John de Lovetot, a justice of the common bench disgraced in 1290. She had previously been married to William Basing, who had died in the summer of 1316. Margaret and Passele had three sons (Edmund, Robert, and Thomas), all of whom benefited from property settlements made by their father, and a daughter (Margaret). After Passele's death, in the early 1330s a third woman called Joan appeared, who claimed to be his legitimate widow. The bishop of London certified that she had indeed gone through a marriage ceremony with Passele at St Mary Magdalen, Old Fish Street, in London, and the implication is that the marriage to Margaret (if such took place) was a bigamous one. Joan also later alleged that Margaret had been responsible for the deaths not just of Passele's eldest son, William, and third son, Edmund, but also of her 'husband' Edmund himself in order to prepare the way for her children to succeed to Edmund's lands. But Margaret was acquitted in king's bench in 1329 of involvement in the younger Edmund's death, and the other charges against her were never proved. PAUL BRAND

Sources *Chancery records* • N. H. MacMichael, 'The descent of the manor of Evegate in Smeeth with some account of its lords', *Archaeologia Cantiana*, 74 (1960), 1–47 • PRO, CP40, CP25 (1), JUST 1 [court of the common pleas, plea rolls; court of common pleas, feet of fines; justice itinerant, eyre and assize rolls] • unprinted and printed law reports • *CIPM*, 7, no. 32

Wealth at death see *CIPM*

Passelewe, Robert (*d.* 1252), administrator, began his career in royal government by 1214 under the patronage of Peter des Roches, bishop of Winchester. By 1218, and perhaps by 1216, he was also serving the papal legate Guala. After Guala's departure from England in December 1218 Passelewe travelled frequently to Rome to deliver instalments on Guala's English pension. On one of these visits, in the spring of 1222, des Roches commissioned Passelewe to request from the pope a declaration that the fifteen-year-old King Henry was of full age. The following spring Passelewe returned from yet another mission to Rome with the requested declaration. This earned him the undying enmity of Hubert de Burgh, des Roches's chief political opponent in the king's minority government. In December 1223 Passelewe was sent to Rome again by des Roches, against the wishes of both de Burgh and Archbishop Stephen Langton, to request the appointment of a papal legate to England. In 1224–5 he was yet again in Rome, this time to plead with the pope for the reinstatement of Falkes de Bréauté, exiled from England after the siege of Bedford Castle, whom Passelewe had served since at least 1222. The *querimonia*, the statement of his grievances which Bréauté presented at the curia, was almost certainly Passelewe's work.

Passelewe suffered along with his patrons from de Burgh's political ascendancy. In 1224 his property was confiscated and he was exiled from England. Although he recovered his property in early 1226, helped by a papal petition on his behalf, he remained out of favour at court until 1232, when des Roches displaced de Burgh and returned his own faction to power. From January 1233 until May 1234 Passelewe was one of the four key figures in des Roches's government, serving as deputy treasurer to Peter de Rivallis, as chief official at the exchequer, and as senior justice of the exchequer of the Jews. Passelewe profited handsomely from his position at court, acquiring a number of custodies and wardships (including control over eight of Hubert de Burgh's former manors), and extorting money from Jewish communities under his control. When des Roches's regime fell, however, Passelewe was an obvious target. His family manor at Swanbourne, Buckinghamshire, was attacked and burnt by Richard Siward, and in May 1234 the Council of Gloucester deprived Passelewe of all the offices and most of the property he had acquired since 1232.

In 1235 Passelewe offered 600 marks to recover the king's grace, and in 1240–41 is recorded as pleading in a *quo warranto* proceeding on behalf of the crown. It was not until the eve of the king's departure for Poitou in May 1242, however, that Passelewe was reappointed to any royal office, this time as sheriff of Hampshire and supervisor of the works at Westminster Abbey. For the next eight years Passelewe would be a ubiquitous figure in the king's administration. Rewards quickly followed. In November 1242 he received the prebend of Sneating, in the king's gift by reason of the vacancy in the bishopric of London. Within a year he had exchanged Sneating for Nesden, and Nesden for Caddington, all prebends of St Paul's Cathedral. In March 1244 the king appointed him archdeacon of Lewes in the vacant bishopric of Chichester, and in April attempted, unsuccessfully, to promote him to the bishopric itself. Perhaps to compensate him for the loss of the bishopric, in 1245 the king granted him the church of St James, Northampton, which Passelewe thereafter held in plurality with his London prebend and his archdeaconry.

Passelewe remained sheriff of Hampshire until 1249. His administrative responsibilities, however, extended well beyond the boundaries of his shire. Passelewe organized and led the famously oppressive forest eyre of 1244–5. Assisted by his protégé Geoffrey Langley, Passelewe assessed heavy amercements, fines, and rents on persons judged guilty of encroaching upon the forest boundaries. Among those convicted on this eyre was John de Neville, chief justice of the southern forests. Along with a number of other royal foresters Neville was dismissed and heavily amerced. From February 1246 to April 1250 Passelewe himself served as chief justice of the southern forests, until he was replaced by Langley. Passelewe also conducted inquiries into serjeanties alienated without licence, and served as custodian of several vacant abbeys during these years.

Because sheriffs and forest justices could imprison suspects and punish malefactors, such offices were generally considered inappropriate for clerics to exercise. Passelewe's willingness to hold these offices, despite his clerical status, aroused the ire of many churchmen, including Robert Grosseteste, bishop of Lincoln. In April 1244, when Passelewe was elected bishop of Chichester by the cathedral canons, it was probably his role as sheriff that persuaded Archbishop Boniface of Canterbury to oppose his election and send him for theological examination by Grosseteste. Passelewe failed the examination, and his election was eventually quashed by the pope. In 1245 it was Passelewe's service as justice of the forest that rendered him unfit, in Grosseteste's eyes, for the cure of souls. Grosseteste therefore refused to institute Passelewe to the church of St James, Northampton, to which he had been presented by the king. This time, however, Passelewe succeeded in persuading the archbishop of Canterbury to institute him, Grosseteste's objections notwithstanding.

In December 1246 Passelewe received yet another prebend, this time in the vacant bishopric of Salisbury. Only in December 1249, however, did he accept ordination as a priest, whereupon the bishop of Ely presented him to the church at Dereham, Norfolk, formerly held by the royal clerk Jeremy of Caxton. This caused a breach with the king, who had wanted the living for his half-brother, Aymer de Lusignan. Passelewe was dismissed from his forest offices in April 1250, whereupon he retired from royal service. Relations with the king were restored at Christmas 1250, however. Gifts followed, and in October 1251 Passelewe received the king's permission to make his will, along with formal acquittance from all accounts that might in future be demanded from either himself or his brother Hamo. Passelewe died at Waltham on 6 June 1252.

Robert Passelewe had two brothers, Hamo, who served as sheriff of Norfolk and Suffolk, and Simon *Passelewe, royal clerk and justice of the exchequer of the Jews. His sister married William of Holwell, sheriff of Hertfordshire. Their son Stephen entered the church, assisted by his uncle Robert, who secured a valuable benefice for him. His heirs are not recorded, but were presumably his brothers, both of whom outlived him.

ROBERT C. STACEY

Sources *Chancery records* • Paris, *Chron.*, vols. 3–5 • *Ann. mon.* • *Fasti Angl., 1066–1300*, [St Paul's, London] • *Fasti Angl., 1066–1300*, [Salisbury] • *Fasti Angl., 1066–1300*, [Chichester] • N. Vincent, *Peter des Roches: an alien in English politics, 1205–38*, Cambridge Studies in Medieval Life and Thought, 4th ser., 31 (1996) • N. C. Vincent, 'Jews, Poitevins, and the bishop of Winchester, 1231–1234', *Christianity and Judaism*, ed. D. Wood, SCH, 29 (1992), 119–32 • C. A. F. Meekings, *Studies in 13th century justice and administration* (1981) • D. A. Carpenter, *The minority of Henry III* (1990) • *Roberti Grosseteste episcopi quondam Lincolniensis epistolae*, ed. H. R. Luard, Rolls Series, 25 (1861) • *The letters and charters of Cardinal Guala Bicchieri, papal legate in England, 1216–1218*, ed. N. Vincent, CYS, 83 (1996) • *Curia regis rolls preserved in the Public Record Office* (1922–), vol. 16

Passelewe, Simon (*d.* **1269/70**), administrator, was a brother of Robert *Passelewe. He was a royal clerk by 6 May 1242, when the king promised him an ecclesiastical benefice worth 40 or 50 marks, as soon as one became available. In December 1243 he was sent with Gilbert of Preston to scrutinize records of Jewish debts at Cambridge; a few months later he was appointed keeper of the vacant bishopric of Chichester. In 1248 the king appointed Passelewe warden of the Stamford fair, and assigned him to tallage the royal demesne in Essex and Hertfordshire. By January 1253, when the king granted him annual robes, he was probably already an exchequer clerk. In February 1253 he may have served briefly as a justice of the Jewish exchequer, but in October 1253 and July 1254 he was sent to Gascony with shipments of treasure for the king. His continuous service as justice of the Jewish exchequer had begun by 19 February 1255, and continued until at least June 1258, and perhaps until June 1259. It fell to Passelewe, therefore, in November 1255, to appraise the chattels of the Jews of Lincoln who had fled or been executed or arrested following allegations that they had crucified Hugh, a boy of Lincoln. Although apparently out of office between June and September 1259, he was reappointed to the Jewish exchequer on 30 September 1259, and served as justice until between February and June 1262.

Passelewe's service at the Jewish exchequer during these years was frequently interrupted by other duties. In the spring of 1258 the king sent him to raise money from several monastic houses, without success. On 4 May 1258 he was sent as a royal messenger to Richard, earl of Cornwall, in Germany, almost certainly to report the king's agreement two days before to appoint a committee of twenty-four magnates to reform the realm. In May 1260 he was sent to borrow money from Louis IX; in August he was in the Welsh marches, trying to make peace with Llywellyn ap Gruffudd. Although briefly estranged from the king in July 1262, Passelewe accompanied him to France, and in January 1263 was the king's proctor at Paris, having been sent there with Master John of Chishall and Imbert de Montferrand to try to make peace between King Henry and Simon de Montfort.

After that time, however, Passelewe's movements are poorly recorded. In February 1266 he was sent on a second mission to Louis IX, and in February 1268 he was in Paris again, this time as King Henry's proctor in negotiations for a truce between Gascony and Navarre. By Trinity 1268 he was a baron of the exchequer. Although still alive on 21 October 1269, he was dead by October 1270, and probably by March, when his daughter Katherine Passelewe and his son and heir, John of Middleton, were engaged in a complex series of transactions involving lands inherited from their father in Compton, Surrey. Information about their mother (or mothers) is nowhere recorded.

ROBERT C. STACEY

Sources *Chancery records* • C. A. F. Meekings, 'Justices of the Jews, 1216–68: a provisional list', *BIHR*, 28 (1955), 173–88 • Paris, *Chron.* • *Close rolls of the reign of Henry III*, 14, PRO (1938), 253, 301, 402

Passfield. For this title name *see* Webb, Sidney James, Baron Passfield (1859–1947) [*see under* Webb, (Martha) Beatrice (1858–1943)].

Paston family (*per. c.*1420–1504), gentry, who were made famous by the survival of the 'Paston letters'—and by the enthusiasm for them of Horace Walpole (1717–1797)—were from north-east Norfolk and of humble origin.

Rise into the gentry **Clement Paston** (*d.* 1419) was 'a good pleyn husbond[man]' of Paston, Norfolk (Davis, 1.xli); his wife, Beatrice (*d.* 1409), may have been 'a bond womanne' (ibid., 1.xlii), but her brother Geoffrey Somerton (*d.* 1416) had made a career for himself as a local solicitor. Geoffrey saw the promise in his nephew William (I) *Paston (1378–1444), the son of Clement and Beatrice, and paid for his education at a grammar school and the inns of court. It was William (I) who elevated the family into the gentry class. He had a successful legal career, which culminated in 1429 with his appointment as chief justice of common pleas. William negotiated two advantageous marriages, one for himself, the other for his son and heir, John (I) *Paston. His own marriage took place in 1420; his wife was **Agnes Paston** (*d.* 1479), daughter and coheir of Sir Edmund Barry (*d.* 1433); Agnes brought her husband three manors in East Anglia and, coming from a well-established family, graced the Pastons with the distinction they had hitherto lacked. The marriage William made for his eldest son in 1440 was even more of a coup. Margaret Mautby [**Margaret Paston** (1421/2–1484)] was also from a good Norfolk family and she too was an heiress, bringing with her nine manors in Norfolk and Suffolk; it was, however, her connections that counted for most. Her mother was a Berney of the Reedham branch of that family, and the Berneys of Reedham were related to Sir John *Fastolf of Caister (*d.* 1459), the grandee of north-east Norfolk between 1430 and his death in 1459. William (I) had used his privileged position to buy land cheaply; he had also nurtured a relationship with the dukes of Norfolk. Hence when he died in 1444 all seemed set fair for the firm establishment of the family within the local hierarchy.

Thwarted ambitions: the 'war of Fastolf's will' This was not to be. There was a gap of a generation before the Pastons were accepted into East Anglian society. There are a variety of reasons for a delay that so easily might have been a disaster. John (I) Paston, who had received a university education at Cambridge, prospered as a legal dogsbody principally for Sir John Fastolf, although he was also found serviceable by the earls of Oxford and the dukes of Norfolk (among others). There was trouble between him, his mother, and his brothers over his father's will, but that did not debilitate the family while things were going smoothly. William and Agnes had had five children who reached maturity: John (I) (1421–1466), Edmund (1425–1449), Elizabeth (*c.*1429–1488), William (II) (1436–1496) [*see below*], and Clement (*b.* 1442, *d.* in or before 1479). The marriage of Elizabeth was also a contentious issue between Agnes and John (I) during the 1450s until she was at last married, aged about thirty, to Robert Poynings in 1459. It was, however, the death of the childless Sir John Fastolf on 5 November of that year and the almost simultaneous outbreak of civil war that derailed the Pastons. John Paston claimed that Fastolf, in a nuncupative will, had made him his sole heir. Such a claim—as the old soldier had died not only extremely wealthy but in possession at Caister of one of the most desirable contemporary houses in the country—was contested by John Paston's fellow executors. The 'war of Fastolf's will' drained the resources of a divided Paston family and was to all intents and purposes lost by them when William Waynflete, bishop of Winchester, was called in to make peace in 1470.

Peace had its price. Fastolf's soul, as well as the Paston family, paid it. The college of priests and poor men to be founded at Caister to pray for the childless Fastolf—the major preoccupation of his declining years—was the principal casualty: the college remained unbuilt. Virtually all the Fastolf property was appropriated by others, notably Alice Chaucer, the dowager duchess of Suffolk (*d.* 1475), and Waynflete himself (for the endowment of his new foundation at Oxford, Magdalen College, which was no substitute, where prayers were concerned, for Caister College). The dukes of Norfolk had taken Caister, but through the unexpected death of John (VII) Mowbray, the fourth duke, in 1476 and the support of Edward IV and of William, Lord Hastings (under whom John (II)—see below—served at Calais as a member of the garrison), the family did acquire that plum in the Fastolf pudding. What had undone their efforts in the contest was the refusal of John (I) Paston, who died in 1466, to compromise; their lack of powerful allies, as the over-mighty of East Anglia in the 1460s (like the dukes of Norfolk and Suffolk) were either determined to get the Fastolf estates for themselves, or (like the earls of Oxford) were politically impotent; their turning to new patrons—George Neville, archbishop of York, and the Woodvilles—just at the time when they were about to lose their influence at court; and the feeling in Norfolk county society that they were, especially being a 'new' family, overreaching themselves. Besides, the Pastons had plenty of old enemies in the locality who were ready to help propel them downwards; Thomas Tuddenham had gone in 1462, but John *Heydon remained to assist in their discomfiture. In 1469, when the duke of Norfolk besieged Caister and it had to be surrendered to him, they came close to being entirely struck down.

Family fortunes restored How did the Pastons survive? Two members of the family were its saviours. The first was Sir John (II) *Paston (1442–1479), John (I)'s eldest son, whose connections in the court and household of Edward IV, held throughout even the readeption, when he and his younger brother, John (III) [*see below*], took up arms against Edward, his court, and his household at the battle of Barnet in 1471, and whose buoyant personality carried him and the family through the hardest of hard times. Moreover, he was not only a man of the world; he was also a man of sound sense. The second family saviour was John's uncle, **William (II) Paston** (1436–1496), who, alienated to some degree as he was from the main stem of the family, yet supported his nephew, mainly financially, after John (I) Paston's death. Without William's loans the family would have foundered as John (II) was in possession of the barest minimum of Paston property, most of it controlled by his grandmother Agnes (*d.* 1479) and his mother, Margaret (*d.* 1484), who was a parsimonious and reluctant lender. There was, almost predictably in such circumstances, disagreement between mother and son about provision for the other children of herself and John (I); they had had seven: Sir John (II) (1442–1479), **Sir John (III) Paston** (1444–1504), Edmund (*d.* in or before 1504), Margery [**Margery Calle** (*c.*1450–*c.*1479)], Walter (*c.*1456–1479), Anne (*d.* 1494/5), and William (III) (*b. c.*1459), who became insane about 1503. The major family scandal of this generation was Margery's marriage to her lover, Richard Calle, the man who ran the Paston estates efficiently, but who was none the less of a lower class and without land (as well as a servant). The marriage, which the lovers had entered into clandestinely and with a determination born of desperation, took place in 1469, a catastrophic year for the family; the union could not be overturned, even by the bishop of Norwich, called in by the distraught Margaret, and Margery and her husband were, therefore, banished. The banishment was only temporary in the case of Richard Calle, as good (and loyal) administrators were hard to find, but may not have been in the case of Margery, a daughter who had demeaned the family. There was also squabbling over Walter's maintenance and education; all that was forgotten in the grief at his death in August 1479, a few weeks after he had graduated BA at Oxford.

The Pastons rise into high society William (II) Paston was a London-based man of business who served a whole host of patrons and clients; his thoroughgoing success was barely interrupted by his Lancastrian leanings. William's commitment to his nephew, even if it sometimes wavered, and his loans, even if they were (or were said to be) sometimes grudging, were crucial to the survival of the Pastons in the years between 1467 and 1476. It was only after the unlooked-for death of John (II) in the plague year of 1479 that William (II) fought his younger nephew John (III) for those estates that he claimed his father, William (I), had bequeathed him in 1444. That subsidiary contest lasted until the mid-1490s and was costly; if politics had not altered to the family's advantage in 1485, the dispute might have been more damaging than it was. The triumphant return of Henry Tudor was only slightly more remarkable than that of John de Vere, earl of Oxford. The Pastons once again had a local patron, one who ruled the roost in East Anglia until his death in 1513. John (III) fought at the battle of Stoke in 1487 to defend the new dynasty and his own good fortune; he was knighted on the field. Already de Vere's councillor, he remained his dependable servant, associate, and client until he died in 1504. A century after Clement Paston had ridden to the mill 'on the bar horsbak wyth hys corn under hym' (Davis, 1.xli), the Pastons had finally arrived in high society.

The Paston letters With the encouragement of Horace Walpole, John Fenn (1739–1794), an antiquarian of East Dereham, Norfolk, published a selection of the Paston letters in two volumes in 1787: 'the most curious papers of the sort I ever saw' (Davis, 1.xxiv), according to Walpole. A further two volumes followed in 1789 and after Fenn's death a fifth volume he had prepared was brought out by his nephew William Frere (1775–1836) in 1823. The fame of the Pastons had been launched: that it was so was for two other reasons than Walpole's taste for gothick curiosities. The first was the 'vast debts' (ibid., 1.xxv) of the last of the Pastons, William *Paston, earl of Yarmouth (*d.* 1732) [*see under* Paston, Robert, first earl of Yarmouth], who sold some of the family papers. The second was that the earl's death was timely; it coincided with the life of Francis Blomefield (1705–1752), who in the 1730s was preparing his great work, *Essay towards a Topographical History of the County of Norfolk*, published between 1739 and 1775. After the earl had died Blomefield examined the family papers in the muniment room at Oxnead and his interest helped preserve what at that time were regarded as the more important of them, namely letters—sackfuls of the less important papers, namely financial and estate documents, appear to have been burnt. Other East Anglian scholars besides Blomefield were involved in the collecting of Paston letters—Peter Le Neve (1661–1729), Thomas

Martin (1697–1771), and John Ives (1751–1776), for example; some of their collections were acquired by John Fenn; others were not. The subsequent publishing history of the Paston letters has been briefly told by their third editor, Norman Davis, in the introduction to his two-volume edition of the 1970s. The sufferings of the second editor, James Gairdner (1828–1912), verged on tragedy when, having already prepared his three-volume edition (published in the 1870s), Gairdner was told by the owner of a number of the manuscripts that they were indeed in his attic as Gairdner had believed them to be: by then it was too late for him to make use of them. Although Gairdner was able to use those manuscripts when adding a fourth volume to a new edition of 1901, he still had not seen the manuscripts of John Fenn's first two volumes; those had turned up in 1889 but were unavailable for consultation until purchased by the British Museum in 1933. Not, therefore, until Norman Davis's edition of the 1970s, some 200 years after they had received Horace Walpole's excited attention, did the original and complete texts of the Paston letters come before the general reader—complete because John Fenn had omitted from a number of letters material that he had considered uninteresting. The story does not, however, end there. Norman Davis had contemplated a third volume, as his two volumes do not include all the letters and papers reckoned to be among the Paston letters, but the content of such a volume is hard to determine. Defining a 'Paston letter' is not easy once letters to and from the Pastons themselves and the most obviously related documents—the contents of Norman Davis's two published volumes—have been dealt with.

The bulk of the original manuscripts are in the British Library; there are, however, 'strays' in the Bodleian Library, the Pierpont Morgan Library, the Norfolk County Record Office, and elsewhere. Although there are few Paston letters as such at Magdalen College, Oxford, the Fastolf papers at the college are an indispensable source for an explorer of the Paston universe. Moreover, most of Sir John Fastolf's own letters, about seventy in number and almost all of them among the Paston manuscripts in the British Library, have yet to be properly edited or even published in full. The Paston letters cover the years from *c.*1420 to *c.*1500; by far the greater number were written in the forty years between 1440 and 1480, the years when members of the family were in different locations—John (I), John (II), and William (II) usually in London; Margaret Paston and John (III) normally in Norfolk—and when they were struggling to advance in society; much of the writing concerns the greatest of the struggles, that over Fastolf's will. The first Davis volume, which is of letters and documents written by the Pastons themselves, contains 421 items. The most prolific writer by far was Margaret (over 100 letters written by clerks on her behalf: Paston women did not write their own letters), or rather, it was her letters that were most carefully preserved, by her husband and two eldest sons; John (II) and John (III) also wrote a great deal, much to each other, but more to the point they saved one another's letters. In the second volume are 444 letters to various Pastons from a variety of non-Paston correspondents: relatives, friends, servants, clients, and patrons. The overwhelming majority (over 250) are to John (I) Paston; most of the remainder (more than 100) are to John (II) and John (III). Evidently keeping letters, drafts of letters, and other papers was—or became, possibly under the influence of the topographer William Worcester (*d.* 1480x85)—a Paston habit.

The Paston letters tell much more about the Pastons than the story of their uneven social ascent. They are the richest source there is for every aspect of the lives of gentlemen and gentlewomen of the English middle ages, and for that very reason have been more readily exploited by treasure-seekers and sensationalists, of whom Horace Walpole was the first and most forgivable, than they have been by assiduous searchers after knowledge of such lives from day to day, month to month, and year to year. It is in those respects that the Pastons may be regarded as typical English gentry. The history of the family in the fifteenth century is theirs alone. COLIN RICHMOND

Sources N. Davis, ed., *Paston letters and papers of the fifteenth century*, 2 vols. (1971–6) • *The Paston letters, AD 1422–1509*, ed. J. Gairdner, new edn, 6 vols. (1904) • C. Richmond, *The Paston family in the fifteenth century: the first phase* (1990) • C. Richmond, *The Paston family in the fifteenth century: Fastolf's will* (1996) • C. Richmond, 'The Pastons', *History and Archaeology Review*, 2 (spring 1987), 21–5 • R. Barber, *The Pastons: a family in the Wars of the Roses* (1981) • R. Virgoe, ed., *Illustrated letters of the Paston family: private life in the fifteenth century* (1989)

Archives BL, letters and papers, Add. MSS 28212, 33597, 35251, 39848–39849, 43488–43491, 45099, 54210 | Norfolk RO, WKC I/43, 44, 45

Paston, Agnes (*d.* **1479**). *See under* Paston family (*per. c.*1420–1504).

Paston, Clement (*d.* **1419**). *See under* Paston family (*per. c.*1420–1504).

Paston, Clement (*c.***1515–1598**), sea captain, was the fourth surviving son of Sir William *Paston (1479?–1554) of Paston, Caistor, and Oxnead, Norfolk, and his wife, Bridget, the daughter of Sir Henry Heydon of Baconsthorpe. He followed his brothers Thomas *Paston (*c.*1517–1550) [*see under* Henry VIII, privy chamber of] and John *Paston (*c.*1510–1575/6) into the royal service, where all three were gentlemen pensioners by 1545. Clement is mentioned as a gentleman in 1544, but received his first payment only on 8 February 1545. By that time he had already acquired sufficient seafaring experience to be appointed to the command of the *Hone of Hamburgh*, a rented Hanseatic ship of 250 tons, in October 1544. In 1545 he transferred to the *Pellican of Dansick* and in May 1546 was in command of the *Anne Gallant*, when he captured a French ship, probably the galley *Mermaid*, commanded by the baron of St Blanchard. Although there was a dispute over whether the galley was a 'good prize', Paston seems to have kept most of the plunder, and Blanchard became his prisoner until he was ransomed for 7000 crowns (about £1600).

In 1547 Paston fought at the battle of Pinkie and was twice wounded. When the duke of Northumberland called upon the gentlemen pensioners to support the claim of Jane Grey in July 1553, Paston and his brother John were among those who responded, remaining with the duke until his cause collapsed. As a result, Queen Mary sent them into the custody of their father in Norfolk, but influence or further information brought them back to court in time to attend her coronation in their proper places on 1 October. Shortly afterwards Paston was awarded an annuity of £20 over and above the £50 that he received as a pensioner, and he remained a member of the band until his death. Early in Elizabeth's reign he was associated with the duke of Norfolk, and it was Norfolk who proposed his election as MP for the county in the by-election of 1566. This was to be his only parliamentary experience. He avoided involvement in Norfolk's fall, and on the death of his brother John succeeded in 1577 to his place on the commission of the peace at the advanced age of over fifty. He was of the quorum by 1583. He also served as a commissioner for the musters in 1579, but a lack of enthusiasm for the religious developments of the reign probably prevented further local preferment. He was noted as 'backward' in religion in 1587. His last appearance at court was in the second quarter of 1589, and he seems to have spent the last few years of his long life in retirement. His last recorded sea service was in 1586.

Paston married late (after 1567) Alice, the daughter of Humphrey Packington of London, and widow of Richard Lambert, also of London. They appear to have had no children, but Alice brought him a considerable fortune, and it was with her money that he rebuilt Oxnead, which was his inheritance from his father. Paston made his will on 1 September 1594, leaving his lands to his nephew, Sir William Paston, £1000 to his wife (who, however, predeceased him), and valuable bequests to Roger Manners and to the earl of Rutland. He died on 18 February 1598, aged over eighty, at Oxnead, and was buried in the church there, where a lengthy monumental inscription celebrates his long life and many virtues. DAVID LOADES

Sources *LP Henry VIII*, vols. 19–21 • *APC*, *1542–50* • HoP, *Commons*, *1558–1603* • A. F. Pollard, ed., *Tudor tracts*, *1532–1588* (1903) • F. Blomefield and C. Parkin, *An essay towards a topographical history of the county of Norfolk*, 5 vols. (1739–75) • W. J. Tighe, 'The gentleman pensioners in Elizabethan politics and government', PhD diss., U. Cam., 1984 • BL, Lansdowne MS 52, 69 • will, PRO, PROB 11/91, fols. 206*v*–211*v*

Wealth at death substantial: will, March 1598, PRO, PROB 11/91, fols. 206*v*–211*v*

Paston, Edward (*bap.* **1550**, *d.* **1630**), music collector, was baptized on 15 February 1550, the second son of Sir Thomas *Paston (*c.*1517–1550) [*see under* Henry VIII, privy chamber of], a gentleman of the privy chamber, and his wife, Agnes, daughter of John Leigh of Stockwell. Edward VI was his godfather. No information about his education has come to light, but, as described in his epitaph in Blofield church, Norfolk (where he was buried on 24 March 1630), he was 'most skillfull of liberall Sciences especially musicke and Poetry as also strange languages'. He married first Elizabeth, daughter of Richard Lambert, sheriff of London, who left no children when she died. He and his second wife, Margaret (*d.* 1640), daughter of Henry Berney of Reedham, had six sons and three daughters.

Paston's life was spent away from court tending his family: he remodelled his father's manor house at Thorpe-next-Norwich in 1590 and built a substantial house at Appleton, near Sandringham, in or after 1596 and another at Town Barningham in 1612. A Roman Catholic, he maintained a mass centre at Appleton—his niece Mary Berney recounted the hair-raising tale of its near discovery. Bartholomew Young mentions Paston's travels in Spain, while Geoffrey Whitney attests uncritically to his prowess as a lutenist 'who LINUS, & AMPHION staynes, and ORPHEUS farre excelles' (Whitney, 186). Paston was one of the most avid and industrious collectors of music in his generation; in his will his collection is described in some detail, and the surviving items, some identified by name, others by bindings, contents, and scribal hands, may be found in English and North American libraries. They indicate a broad interest in continental music and an unusual historically oriented taste in English music. They are chiefly important, however, as the sole source of certain compositions by William Byrd, who appears to have written songs celebrating events in the Paston family life, as well as settings of sententious verses on the fall of monarchs that Paston himself is likely to have written.

PHILIP BRETT

Sources P. Brett, 'Edward Paston (1550–1630): a Norfolk gentleman and his musical collection', *Transactions of the Cambridge Bibliographical Society*, 4 (1964–8), 51–69 • will, PRO, PROB 11/157, sig. 43 • E. B. Burstall, 'The Pastons and their manor of Binham', *Norfolk Archaeology*, 30 (1947–52), 101–29 • F. Blomefield and C. Parkin, *An essay towards a topographical history of the county of Norfolk*, [2nd edn], 11 vols. (1805–10), vol. 6, p. 489; vol. 8, pp. 99, 330 • A. Hamilton, ed., *The chronicle of the English Augustinian canonesses regular of the Lateran*, 2 (1906), 101–2 • H. Spelman, *The history and fate of sacrilege … 1632* (1698), 253 • B. Young, trans., *The Diana of George of Montemayor* (1598) • G. Whitney, *A choice of emblemes* (1586) • R. Hughey, *The correspondence of Lady Katherine Paston, 1603–1627* (1941), 40–41, 43, 60–63, 68–9 • BL, Harley MS 1583, fol. 378 • *The manuscripts of his grace the duke of Rutland*, 4 vols., HMC, 24 (1888–1905), vol. 1, p. 223 • *Visitation of Norfolk, 1664*, Norfolk RS, 5 (1934), 159 • monument, Blofield church, Norfolk

Wealth at death see will, PRO, PROB 11/157, sig. 43

Paston, Edward (**1641–1714**), Roman Catholic priest, was born in Norfolk, the younger son of William Paston, landowner and high sheriff of Norfolk in 1637, and Agnes Paston, *née* Everard, of Appleton Hall, Flitcham, Norfolk. He was sent to the English college at Douai when only ten years of age, arriving there on 24 September 1651. He was ordained priest at Bruges on 10 April 1666, was a co-founder of St Gregory's Seminary in Paris, but returned to Douai in 1670 to teach philosophy, being made a DD in 1681. On 11 June 1682 he left for England, but finding mission work uncongenial he resumed his teaching career at Douai in May 1683. On the accession of James II he revisited England and lived privately in London until June 1688, when he was chosen president of Douai College in the place of Dr James Smith, who had become bishop in England. Paston's arrival in Douai on 22 July heralded a long but stormy presidency. Known to be pious and studious, he provoked immediate unrest when he tried to

Edward Paston (1641–1714), by unknown artist

introduce a new code of discipline based on Sulpician methods in vogue elsewhere. Despite the expulsion of several students, the president had to abandon his reforms. In his defence, it may be said that the new rules later introduced by Rome without any disturbance reflect some of his own ideas. To add to his difficulties, it was during his presidency that long-standing critics of the college brought a charge of Jansenism against its superiors. This charge was never substantiated and Paston himself was exonerated. Nevertheless, Dr Edward Hawarden, his vice-president and one of the most learned priests of the time, was forced to resign from the college in 1707. Paston died suddenly at the college in Douai on 21 July 1714.

THOMPSON COOPER, *rev.* D. MILBURN

Sources G. Anstruther, *The seminary priests*, 3 (1976), 160–61 • P. Guilday, *The English Catholic refugees on the continent, 1558–1795* (1914), 330–37 • *The memoirs of Gregorio Panzani*, ed. and trans. J. Berington (1793), 401–4 • C. Dodd [H. Tootell], *The church history of England, from the year 1500, to the year 1688*, 3 (1742), 479 • J. Fendley, 'The Pastons of Horton and the Horton Court library', *Recusant History*, 22 (1994–5), 501–28 • A. F. Allison, 'The origins of St Gregory's, Paris', *Recusant History*, 21 (1992–3), 11–25, esp. 19 • E. H. Burton and E. Nolan, *The Douay College diaries: the seventh diary, 1715–1778*, Catholic RS, 28 (1928)

Likenesses oils, Douai Abbey, Woolhampton, Reading • oils, Burton Constable, East Yorkshire [*see illus.*]

Wealth at death two estates in Gloucestershire: Anstruther, *Seminary priests*, 161

Paston, Elizabeth, countess of Yarmouth. *See* Wiseman, Elizabeth, Lady Wiseman (1647–1730).

Paston, George. *See* Symonds, Emily Morse (1860–1936).

Paston, Henry. *See* Howard, Henry (1684–1720).

Paston, John (I) (1421–1466), landowner and letter writer, was the eldest son of William *Paston (1378–1444) of Paston in Norfolk, justice of common pleas, and his wife, Agnes (*d.* 1479), daughter and coheir of Sir Edmund Barry of Orwellbury, Hertfordshire. He was born on 10 October 1421. Paston followed in his father's footsteps by training in the law, spending time at both Trinity Hall and Peterhouse in Cambridge, and being admitted to the Inner Temple by 1440. It was also in 1440, between April and November, that he married Margaret *Paston (*d.* 1484) [*see under* Paston family], daughter and heir of John Mautby of Mautby, Norfolk—a very good match for the son of a professional lawyer, which did much to consolidate the family's position in Norfolk society in terms both of land and of status. The fact that Margaret later chose to be buried at Mautby, beneath a tombstone emblazoned with the Mautby arms, suggests that she retained a clear sense of the social superiority of her own family over that into which she had married.

East Anglian politics The significance of John Paston's career stems from the survival of substantial amounts of his family's correspondence from the mid-1440s onwards, letters that form an unrivalled source for the study of gentry life, and for the state of local and national politics, in a period where informal evidence of this kind is extremely rare. Judge William, the son of a husbandman, used the money and connections he made through his successful legal career to buy estates in his native northern Norfolk, which established his family among the region's gentry. His influence and standing allowed him to advance his family's interests with success, despite the disputes over title which were always likely to attend the rapid accumulation of a substantial estate by purchase. After his death, however, the family suffered a series of reverses in the later 1440s, and their experiences—portrayed in compelling detail by the letters—have often been held to demonstrate the extent to which gentry society in East Anglia suffered from the depredations of the followers of William de la Pole, duke of Suffolk, who dominated the region during those years. Suffolk, it is argued, exploited his influence over the malleable Henry VI both to establish himself at the head of government and to oust the duke of Norfolk from his rightful place as the dominant lord in East Anglia. In this view, Suffolk's leading servants, in particular Sir Thomas Tuddenham and the lawyer John Heydon of Baconsthorpe, were unscrupulous thugs who, with Suffolk's backing, were able during the 1440s to terrorize the region's gentry, and particularly those associated with the duke of Norfolk, of whom the Pastons have been seen as an archetypical example.

However, there are problems with such an interpretation of the Pastons' experiences. It is clear that Suffolk was not in fact an intruder into local power structures, but had established himself during the 1430s at the head of a powerful political network, based around the duchy of Lancaster estates in Norfolk, which had dominated the region without controversy since the beginning of the century. Further, although the Mowbray dukes of Norfolk had held substantial estates in Suffolk since the beginning of the century, they had had no sustained opportunity to establish themselves as active participants in East Anglian politics, so that it was Norfolk rather than Suffolk who was trying to break into existing structures of regional power in the 1440s. In this context, it is possible to examine the Pastons' difficulties in terms of the particular circumstances within local political society in which they found themselves in the later 1440s, rather than as a paradigmatic example of the effects of a universal reign of terror by Suffolk's East Anglian affinity.

Certainly, the death of William Paston in 1444, and the succession of John Paston as a young man of only twenty-two, left the family suddenly vulnerable—vulnerability evident in 1445 in the loss of the manor of East Beckham in northern Norfolk, a purchase that William seemed to have secured shortly before his death after a ten-year dispute with Edmund Winter, head of a neighbouring gentry family. Edmund Winter's son-in-law, and another near neighbour and rival of the Pastons in northern Norfolk, was John Heydon of Baconsthorpe; he, like William Paston before him, was a successful lawyer seeking to establish himself among the leading gentry of the region. Heydon's local influence was growing rapidly, because of his association with the duke of Suffolk, at the very point when William Paston's death dealt a severe blow to the influence which his family could muster in defence of their interests. It seems to have been not any generalized oppression of local society by the duke of Suffolk, but the particular enmity of John Heydon—rooted in territorial rivalry within a small corner of northern Norfolk, and underpinned by the previous ten years of conflict between the Pastons and the Winters—that played a key role in determining both the political associations that John Paston forged for himself in the later 1440s, and the reverses he suffered. It was almost certainly on Heydon's initiative that the courtier Robert Hungerford, Lord Moleyns, asserted his wife's claim to the Pastons' manor of Gresham in northern Norfolk by seizing the property in February 1448, despite the fact that William Paston's purchase of the estate in 1427 had been legally watertight. In October 1448, when John Paston's initial attempts to recover the property through negotiation and legal action had proved fruitless, he sent his wife to occupy a 'mansion' in the town. In January 1449 Moleyns's men mounted an assault on the house, which was badly damaged in the attack, and expelled Margaret Paston. In all, Moleyns was able to retain possession of the estate for three years.

The fact that Heydon and Moleyns were associated with the duke of Suffolk does seem to have precluded the possibility that John Paston might look for help within the duke's powerful and wide-ranging regional affinity, despite the fact that his father had been associated with this network. Instead, his search for support from other quarters led him to associate himself with Thomas Daniel, an esquire of the royal household originally from Cheshire, who was attempting to break into power structures in Norfolk in the later 1440s in opposition to Suffolk's affinity. However, Daniel's lordship afforded Paston no practical help, and neither of the men who were to be his chief patrons in the following decade—his wife's kinsman Sir John Fastolf and John (VI) Mowbray, duke of Norfolk—seems to have offered any effective political support at this point. Neither is even mentioned in Margaret Paston's letter discussing their difficulties, in May probably of 1449, in which she reported local opinion that 'but if ze have my lord of Suffolkys godelorchyp qhyll the werd is as itt is ye kan never leven in pese wyth-owth ye have his godelordschep' (*Paston Letters and Papers*, 1.236), and recommended that her husband—who was in London for most of the time during these years—should therefore try to obtain Suffolk's goodwill.

Suffolk's fall at the beginning of 1450 seemed to offer an opportunity finally to make some headway. Early in 1451 John Paston succeeded in regaining possession of Gresham from Lord Moleyns, and he was closely involved in the efforts led by the duke of Norfolk, the earl of Oxford, and Sir John Fastolf during 1450–51 to undermine the local power of Suffolk's servants. However, by the spring of 1451 it was becoming clear that these efforts would be unsuccessful, and the Suffolk affinity re-emerged, relatively unscathed, as the dominant force in local politics under the leadership of the dowager duchess and of Thomas, Lord Scales, leaving John Paston once again on the wrong side of regional power structures.

Indeed, the next major problems that confronted him did not come from within the Suffolk affinity, but instead demonstrated the deficiencies of the lordship to which he had attached himself. In 1452–3 Paston and a large number of other gentlemen, including many of his former opponents, united in complaint about the activities of one Charles Nowell and his associates, who had been responsible for a series of assaults, robberies, and forced entries in 1452, including an attack on Paston himself. Nowell and his men were associated both with Thomas Daniel, Paston's lord in the late 1440s, who seems to have been a generally disruptive force in the region, and with the duke of Norfolk, for whom this was one in a series of political misjudgements in his handling of his local following. Paston's association with Daniel does not seem to have survived this episode, but he did subsequently return to Norfolk's political orbit, certainly by 1455.

Fastolf's will By the mid-1450s, however, Paston was much more closely embroiled in matters that were to dominate the rest of his career—the affairs of the ageing, wealthy, and childless Sir John Fastolf. In 1450 Paston was one of a number of lawyers and administrators employed by Fastolf, but the relationship subsequently became much closer; by 1455 Paston was one of his most influential advisers. In June 1459 Fastolf made a will in which he ordered his executors to carry out his long-planned intention of founding a college at his home at Caister, to consist of seven monks or priests and seven poor men to pray in perpetuity for his soul and those of his family. However, when Fastolf died in November of that year, Paston claimed that he had made another nuncupative will two days before his death, according to which Paston alone was to have responsibility for founding the college, and the administration of the estate was to be undertaken by Paston and Fastolf's chaplain, Thomas Howes, rather than by all ten executors (who included William Waynflete, bishop of Winchester, John, Lord Beauchamp, Justice William Yelverton, and Fastolf's secretary, William Worcester). In return for the fulfilment of these responsibilities, Paston claimed, and on payment of a sum of 4000 marks, he himself was to have in fee simple all Fastolf's lands in Norfolk and Suffolk. Whether this was a genuine reflection of Fastolf's last wishes, or whether it was opportunism on Paston's part—or, perhaps most likely, some combination of the two—Paston's ambitious claim to the extensive and valuable estates was never likely to go unchallenged.

This was also, of course, a time of major upheaval in national politics. John Paston's hostility to the enduring influence of the court-connected Suffolk affinity and his links with the duke of Norfolk meant that he associated himself with the Yorkist cause. Having been named as a JP on only three previous occasions (in 1447, 1456, and 1457), he was appointed to the Yorkist commission of the peace in Norfolk in November 1460, and served consistently thereafter. He also represented the shire in the last, Yorkist-dominated parliament of Henry VI's reign, and in the first parliament of Edward IV. However, conflict with Sir John Howard, sheriff in Norfolk at the start of the new reign, also meant that Paston spent some time in the Fleet prison in 1461.

Nevertheless, John Paston's major preoccupation remained the Fastolf inheritance. He had taken possession of the estates immediately after Fastolf's death, but it rapidly became clear both that some of the other executors would challenge Paston's claims about Fastolf's last wishes, and that other claimants would take the opportunity to challenge his possession of several of the properties. The duke of Norfolk, for example, seized Caister itself for some time in 1461. Paston struggled to maintain his possession of the manors of Cotton and Caldecott Hall in Suffolk against William Yelverton and Gilbert Debenham. In 1465 the duke of Suffolk laid claim to Hellesdon and Drayton, two Norfolk manors close to his own property at Costessey, and in October of that year, after months of legal and physical skirmishes, Suffolk's men attacked, ransacked and robbed the manors, causing much destruction. In January 1466 Anthony Woodville, Lord Scales, forced the seizure of Paston's property in Norwich in the king's name, claiming that Paston was a serf of the crown. In 1464 and 1465, in the course of these various disputes, Paston was twice more imprisoned in the Fleet. The legal challenge to Paston's version of the will brought by his co-executor William Yelverton began in the Canterbury court of audience in 1464; no decision was reached before Paston's death.

John Paston's was not an easy career, in the 1440s and 1450s because the enmity between himself and John Heydon placed him on the outside of the political networks that dominated his region, and in the 1460s because of the repercussions of the gamble he took in claiming the Fastolf inheritance. Nor was his family life, of which the letters provide such vivid evidence, always untroubled: his partnership with his wife, Margaret, seems to have been a successful one, but his relationship with his eldest son, John (II) *Paston, was stormy. John (I) Paston died in London on 21 or 22 May 1466, at the age of only forty-four—an early death which Margaret blamed on the conflict over Fastolf's lands—and was buried during Whitsun week at Bromholm Priory, Norfolk (although his son and heir had still not managed to complete his father's tomb there by the time of his own death in 1479). Paston was survived by his wife, who died in 1484. He was succeeded by John (II) Paston, the eldest of their family of five sons—John (II), John (III) *Paston [*see under* Paston family], Edmund, Walter, and William—and two daughters, Margery *Calle [*see under* Paston family] and Anne.

HELEN CASTOR

Sources N. Davis, ed., *Paston letters and papers of the fifteenth century*, 2 vols. (1971–6) • *The Paston letters, AD 1422–1509*, ed. J. Gairdner, new edn, 6 vols. (1904) • C. Richmond, *The Paston family in the fifteenth century: the first phase* (1990) • C. Richmond, *The Paston family in the fifteenth century: Fastolf's will* (1996) • H. Castor, *The king, the crown, and the duchy of Lancaster: public authority and private power, 1399–1461* (2000) • *Chancery records* • K. B. McFarlane, 'William Worcester, a preliminary survey', *England in the fifteenth century: collected essays* (1981), 199–225

Paston, Sir John (II) (1442–1479), landowner, was born before 15 April 1442, the eldest son and heir of John (I) *Paston (1421–1466) of Paston, Norfolk, and his wife, Margaret *Paston (*d.* 1484) [*see under* Paston family], daughter and heir of John Mautby of Mautby, Norfolk. It is clear from his letters that he was educated well, although nothing is known of the details; an inventory of his books, in his own hand, survives from the later 1470s.

The defining feature of Paston's career was the struggle to make good his father's claim to inherit the estates of Sir John Fastolf. It was in order to press his father's case that he was sent to join Edward IV's household in 1461. He was knighted when he came of age in 1463. In November of that year his relationship with his father was stretched to breaking point when he left home without his parents' knowledge or permission, probably to join the king in the north. As a result, his father—who described him as a drone among bees—refused to help him or to receive him at home until May 1465, although his mother remained in contact with him and worked to effect a reconciliation.

In May 1466 his father died, and Sir John became head of the family. In the following years he spent much of his time in London, and maintained his connections with the court. In April 1467, for example, he took part in a tournament at Eltham with the king and Lord Scales. In June of the following year, he and his brother John (III) *Paston [*see under* Paston family] were members of the retinue which accompanied the king's sister Margaret to Bruges for her marriage to the duke of Burgundy. He also occasionally held local office, as MP for Norfolk in 1467–8 and as JP in 1469–70.

The main business that occupied him, however, was the

continuing dispute over the Fastolf estates. In July 1466 the king confirmed his possession of Caister and other lands that his father had held, and in August 1467 he secured probate of Fastolf's will, together with Fastolf's chaplain Thomas Howes. However, Howes defected to the opposing camp—those among Fastolf's trustees who were challenging the Paston claim to inherit—and in October 1468 some of these trustees, including Howes and William Yelverton, sold Caister to John (VII) Mowbray, duke of Norfolk. The duke's father had already made one attempt to seize the property by force in 1461, and in August 1469 Norfolk took advantage of the developing crisis in national politics to assert his new claim by besieging the manor for five weeks, eventually forcing the defenders, led by Paston's brother John, to surrender.

In 1470 Sir John finally reached an agreement with William Waynflete, bishop of Winchester, the most eminent of Fastolf's trustees—a compromise that his father had always refused to make. Paston was to have Caister, Hellesdon, Drayton, and some other properties, while Waynflete would take possession of the rest of the estate in order to provide for the priests and poor men who were to pray for Fastolf's soul—not, as Fastolf had intended, in the foundation of a college at Caister, but as part of Waynflete's new college of St Mary Magdalen in Oxford. However, the agreement could not immediately be put into effect, since Caister remained in the hands of the duke of Norfolk.

In the autumn of 1470 Henry VI was restored to the throne by Lancastrian forces under the earl of Warwick. Paston had associations with the earl of Oxford, who was constable of England under the new regime, and in December these connections paid off when Norfolk surrendered possession of Caister. Paston and his brother John both fought on the losing Lancastrian side at the battle of Barnet in April 1471; two months later Norfolk again seized Caister. The next few years were difficult—despite the agreement with Waynflete; for example, Drayton was lost to the duke of Suffolk—but the family's fortunes were not completely destroyed. Both brothers were pardoned after the battle, and between 1473 and 1477 Sir John spent substantial amounts of time in Calais serving under the command of Lord Hastings. Finally, in January 1476 the duke of Norfolk died, and six months later Sir John was at last able to make good the Paston claim to Caister.

In October 1479 Sir John Paston was in London, 'in suche feere of the syknesse', as he wrote to his mother, Margaret (*Paston Letters and Papers*, 1.515). His fear was well founded; he died there in the following month, and was buried in the Whitefriars Priory, as he had requested in his will. To his mother's disappointment, he never married; in 1469 he had become engaged to Anne Haute, a cousin of Queen Elizabeth Woodville and her brother Lord Scales, but the betrothal was eventually broken off in 1477. This was not the only cause his mother had to reproach him; perennially short of money, he never completed his father's tomb at Bromholm Priory, which, Margaret wrote in 1471, 'is a schame, and a thyng that is myche spokyn of in thys contre' (*Paston Letters and Papers*, 1.359). The relationship between mother and son, and that between Paston and his brother John, are among the personal details revealed most vividly by the letters of the 1460s and 1470s. He left an illegitimate daughter, Constance, probably by Constance Reynforth. He was succeeded by John (III) Paston, the eldest of his four brothers, who—having looked after much of the family's business in Norfolk during his brother's absences in London and Calais—went on to consolidate the family's position within local landed society over the next twenty-five years. HELEN CASTOR

Sources N. Davis, ed., *Paston letters and papers of the fifteenth century*, 2 vols. (1971–6) • *The Paston letters, AD 1422–1509*, ed. J. Gairdner, new edn, 6 vols. (1904) • C. Richmond, *The Paston family in the fifteenth century: the first phase* (1990) • C. Richmond, *The Paston family in the fifteenth century: Fastolf's will* (1996) • H. S. Bennett, *The Pastons and their England* (1922) • *Chancery records*
Archives Magd. Oxf., Fastolf MSS

Paston, Sir John (III) (**1444–1504**). *See under* Paston family (*per.* c.1420–1504).

Paston, John (*c.*1510–1575/6), courtier, was the third son of Sir William *Paston (1479?–1554), of Caister and Oxnead, Norfolk, and Bridget, daughter of Henry Heydon of Baconsthorpe, Norfolk. Clement *Paston [*see under* Paston family] was his younger brother. Nothing is known of John Paston's early life, and it is at Doncaster in October 1536, attending his brother-in-law, Thomas Manners, earl of Rutland, that details of him are first recorded. The occasion was certainly dramatic as the young Paston, one of the 6000 men led by the earls of Shrewsbury, Huntingdon, and Rutland, faced the prospect of battle with the rebel forces of the Pilgrimage of Grace, whose numbers were possibly five times greater. In the event a truce was agreed and battle avoided, and the next thirteen years of Paston's service to the Manners family continued on a considerably more even keel. From 1536 to 1543 Paston served as a gentleman usher to the earl, and he performed the same office for his son until 1549. No doubt due to his connections with the Manners family, he gained election to parliament in 1547 as one of the two MPs for Nottingham—the second earl of Rutland was constable of Nottingham Castle.

Concurrently with his later years of service to the earls of Rutland, Paston joined the household of Henry VIII. From at least 1542 to 1569 he held office as a gentleman pensioner. Formed in 1539 and drawn exclusively from the gentry, the gentlemen pensioners served both as a further adornment to the Tudor court and as the king's bodyguard. It was in this capacity that Paston accompanied Henry to France in 1544 and joined the king in his successful siege of Boulogne, captured in September. Perhaps in acknowledgement of this service, in 1545 Henry granted Paston an annuity of £20. Paston seems to have performed his courtly duties with flair, since he was later remembered as 'a gallant courtier … with rarest virtues adorned, to courtiers all a glass' (HoP, *Commons, 1509–58*, 3.67).

Paston attended both Henry's funeral and Edward's coronation. Although almost nothing is known of his activities during the young successor's brief reign, Paston was in November 1550 awarded the stewardship of the duchy of Lancaster for the counties of Cambridgeshire, Norfolk, and Suffolk, previously held by his brother Thomas. This would suggest he was at least *persona grata* with the duke of Northumberland's regime, as would his fortunes in 1553. Probably one of the gentlemen pensioners on duty at court when Northumberland made his bid to install Lady Jane Grey as queen, Paston fell briefly into disgrace when the attempt failed. On 31 July he and his brother Clement were ordered to retire to their father's house until Mary's further pleasure should be known, and their names were at first struck from the list of those summoned to attend the new queen's coronation. They were recalled to court on 24 August, however, and both were present when Mary was crowned on 1 October, but Paston lost his stewardship to Sir Richard Southwell in November, and his apparent absence from court for much of Mary's reign may imply a less than cordial relationship with her. Although he retained the office of gentleman pensioner for ten years after Mary's death, he is last recorded in attendance at court at her funeral on 14 December 1558. It seems highly likely that one reason for his final removal from his post as gentleman pensioner in 1569 was his close association with Thomas Howard, fourth duke of Norfolk. However, despite government suspicions, noted in 1570, that Paston might well harbour Roman Catholic sympathies, no further action was taken against him.

Paston married twice. With his first wife, whose name is not known, he had one daughter. By 1565 he had remarried, and it may have been this second marriage, to Anne, daughter of Christopher Mowlton and widow of a Mr Arrowhead, that enabled Paston to retire to Suffolk and purchase farmland with a herd of 1200 sheep. With Anne he had another daughter, Bridget, who in 1582 married Edward Coke, later lord chief justice of both the court of common pleas and court of the king's bench. Paston made his will on 4 September 1575, leaving the greater part of his possessions to his wife and daughters. He had died by 30 May 1576, when his will was proved, and he was buried in the chancel of Huntingfield church, Suffolk.

LUKE MACMAHON

Sources *LP Henry VIII*, vols. 17–21 • HoP, *Commons*, *1509–58*, 3.67–8 • D. MacCulloch, *Suffolk and the Tudors: politics and religion in an English county, 1500–1600* (1986) • M. Bush, *The Pilgrimage of Grace: a study of the rebel armies of October 1536* (1996) • *Suffolk*, Pevsner (1961) • W. Rye, ed., *The visitacion of Norffolk … 1563 … 1613*, Harleian Society, 32 (1891) • W. J. Tighe, 'The gentlemen pensioners, the duke of Northumberland, and the attempted coup of Lily 1553', *Albion*, 19 (1987), 1–11 • N. Williams, *Thomas Howard, fourth duke of Norfolk* (1964)

Wealth at death possessions to family and others: will, 30 May 1576

Paston, Margaret (1421/2–1484). *See under* Paston family (*per.* *c.*1420–1504).

Paston, Robert, first earl of Yarmouth (1631–1683), politician, was born on 29 May 1631 at Oxnead Hall, Norfolk, the eldest son of Sir William Paston, first baronet (*c.*1610–1663), and Lady Katherine (*d.* 3 Jan 1636), daughter of Robert Bertie, first earl of Lindsey. The Pastons were a leading county family, and Oxnead was one of Norfolk's finest houses, assessed at forty-five hearths in 1664. Both Sir William and his son were avid collectors of books, paintings, jewellery, and curios. Although not a strong royalist, Sir William had to compound for his estates, and his wife had to give £1100 worth of plate to the earl of Manchester for the eastern association army, as Sir Robert reminded the king when Manchester accompanied him to Oxnead in 1671.

Robert Paston was educated at Westminster School and Trinity College, Cambridge (where he was admitted fellow-commoner on 10 March 1646), and then travelled abroad. On 15 June 1650 he married Rebecca Clayton (*d.* 1694), daughter of a London merchant, Sir Jasper Clayton; they had six sons and four daughters, several of whom died in their father's lifetime. He was a devoted husband and father. He was too corpulent for field sports and suffered from persistent ill health, notably gout: walking was difficult and he was seldom free from pain. He also had chronic financial problems, stemming from his and his father's habit of spending more than they could afford, but exacerbated by his father's wartime losses and his own large family. He continued to embellish Oxnead, building a banqueting house for the royal visit in 1671. Meanwhile the estate dwindled, as he mortgaged more manors and sold off part of his collection. His letters are full of complaints about the miseries of debt and schemes for making money; his library contained many works on alchemy, astrology, and magic. His financial, health, and family problems left him melancholy at times, although he found solace in a firm Anglican faith. The bishop of Norwich thought that Paston and his wife had made the church at Oxnead as beautiful as any in the diocese. Although he remarked that parsons could be silly animals, Paston and his wife were patrons of some of the most militant 'high-flying' clergy in the county.

Despite having been sequestered, Sir William held local office throughout the 1650s and Robert became a JP in 1659. In 1660 Robert was elected MP for Thetford and was knighted; he succeeded his father as second baronet in 1663. In 1661 he was returned for Castle Rising, on the interest of Henry Howard, later sixth duke of Norfolk. He was not an active member, but made a name for himself in December 1664 by proposing the unprecedented sum of £2.5 million for the king's supply. Amid general astonishment the proposal was accepted, and Paston prepared to capitalize on the king's gratitude. He hoped for a title, but above all for some grant which would solve his financial problems. In 1666 he was granted the farm of a range of customs duties, but this proved less profitable than anticipated. He was created Viscount Yarmouth on 19 August 1673; the creation was generally linked to the marriage the previous year of his eldest son, William [*see below*], to Charlotte Howard, the king's illegitimate daughter (*c.*1650–1684) with Elizabeth, Viscountess Shannon. The appointment of his wife's kinsman, Thomas Osborne, earl of Danby, as lord treasurer, did little to improve his fortunes either, despite repeated letters from Yarmouth begging for favour.

Although Yarmouth had been a deputy lieutenant since 1661, he had played little active part in Norfolk affairs. Then, on 6 March 1676, he was appointed lord lieutenant, thanks to Danby, who bitterly resented the opposition of the previous lord lieutenant, Horatio, Baron Townshend, to the election of his son-in-law as MP for King's Lynn in 1675. The Lynn election had been followed by an even more bitterly fought by-election for the county, in which Townshend's preferred candidate had been vigorously opposed by the county's numerous Anglican clergy and an emergent 'church party'. As lord lieutenant, Yarmouth tried to remain on good terms with everyone, but the county was too deeply divided and he was forced to become a party leader. Opponents of the church party were removed from the lieutenancy and the commission of the peace. Opposition to the election of his son William as MP for Norwich led him to attempt to purge his opponents from the corporation as well. During the exclusion crisis he used his authority as lord lieutenant in support of anti-exclusionist candidates throughout the county. His loyalty was rewarded with promotion to an earldom on 30 July 1679. He encouraged a series of loyal addresses from the county, carefully noting who had subscribed and who had not, but his proposal to collect money for the king found little support. He presided over the proceedings against Norwich's charter, which had not yet been declared forfeit when he died on 8 March 1683. He was buried at Oxnead.

William Paston, second earl of Yarmouth (1653/4–1732), did not succeed his father as lord lieutenant, but James II appointed him treasurer of the household in February 1687. The following month he married his second wife, Elizabeth *Wiseman (1647–1730), daughter of Dudley *North, fourth Baron North, and widow of Sir Robert Wiseman, and converted to Catholicism. He reconverted in 1689, but refused to swear allegiance to William and Mary. Suspected of Jacobite activity, he was imprisoned twice, but in 1696 he took the oath and was admitted to the Lords. His debts continued to mount, made worse by a series of imprudent speculative ventures. He was barely able to afford a servant or a horse, while his goods were seized and his lands mortgaged, sold, or forfeited. He died at Epsom on 25 December 1732, aged seventy-eight, the last of his family: his siblings and their sons had predeceased him. All his goods and lands were sold, but even then his creditors were to receive a little more than 11*s.* in the pound. JOHN MILLER

Sources R. W. K. Cremer, *Norfolk portraits* (1944) • R. W. K. Cremer, *Norfolk assembly* (1957) • HoP, *Commons, 1660–90* • *Sixth report*, HMC, 5 (1877–8), 363–90 • R. W. Ketton-Cremer, *Norfolk in the civil war: a portrait of a society in conflict* (1969) • J. Miller, 'A moderate in the first age of party: the dilemmas of Sir John Holland, 1675–85', *EngHR*, 114 (1999), 844–74 • R. Wenley, 'Robert Paston and the *Yarmouth collection*', *Norfolk Archaeology*, 41 (1990–93), 113–44 • V. L. Stater, 'Continuity and change in English provincial politics: Robert Paston in Norfolk, 1675–83', *Albion*, 25 (1993), 193–216 • J. M. Rosenheim, *The Townshends of Raynham* (1989) • P. Gauci, *Politics and society in Great Yarmouth, 1660–1722* (1996) • PRO, PROB 11/373, fol. 118*r–v* • PRO, PROB 11/693, fols. 291*v*–292*v* • M. Chan, *Life into story: the courtship of Elizabeth Wiseman* (1998) • GEC, *Peerage*

Archives BL, corresp., Add. MSS 27447–27448, 27959, 28621 • Norfolk RO, state letters • PRO, state papers, domestic, 1660–83 | BL, Egerton MSS, letters to Danby • BL, Townshend MSS • BL, Wyndham MSS, Add. MS 37911 • Bodl. Oxf., Tanner MSS, Hobart MSS, and other MSS • Norfolk RO, Townshend MSS • Norfolk RO, Wyndham MSS, WRC 7/6 • Raynham Hall, Townshend MSS

Likenesses B. Reading, line engraving, NPG • P. Vanderbank, line engraving, BM, NPG

Paston, Sir Thomas (*c*.1517–1550). *See under* Henry VIII, privy chamber of (*act.* 1509–1547).

Paston, William (I) (1378–1444), justice, was born at Paston in north-east Norfolk, the only son of Clement *Paston (*d.* 1419) [*see under* Paston family] and his wife, Beatrice Somerton (*d.* 1409). Twenty years after William's death his son was accused of being descended from serfs. The Paston pedigree and documents, partly preserved in a seventeenth-century copy, which persuaded Edward IV to grant a declaration that the Pastons were 'gentlemen discended lineally of worship blood sithen the conquest hither' (*Paston letters and Papers*, 2.549) need to be treated with some scepticism, but there is little doubt that Clement came from a family long-established in the region and of the peasant élite. His will shows that he and his wife were buried within Paston church, a sign of some status. It may be true that his wife came of villein stock, but if so her family had certainly risen in the world—her brother, Geoffrey (*d.* 1416), was a successful attorney who, being childless, left much of his property to his nephew, William, whose education he had apparently financed.

William Paston none the less was the real founder of the family fortunes. By 1406 he was acting as an attorney in the court of common pleas, and during the next few years his abilities—for there is no evidence of aristocratic patronage at this stage—earned him a wide variety of legal posts and fees in East Anglia. By 1411 he was retained as counsel to both the city and cathedral priory of Norwich, and was probably also acting for Bishop Alexander Tottington, who appointed him executor of his will in 1413. Tottington's successor, Richard Courtenay (*d.* 1415), appointed Paston chief steward of his estates, and by 1415 he was also chief steward of Bromholm Priory, Norfolk. He was probably already acting as counsel for Great Yarmouth, where he was made JP in 1415; soon afterwards he became first counsel, then chief steward, for Bishop's Lynn. He became a JP for Norfolk in 1418, and by 1420 he was retained as counsel by the duchy of Lancaster and by the earl marshal, soon to be duke of Norfolk. He had already been, and was to continue to be, an executor and feoffee for many East Anglian gentlemen, and was appointed to many commissions in Norfolk.

Probably in 1418 Paston was called to the degree of serjeant-at-law and he begins to appear frequently in the year-books, his contributions being extensively reported, and seeming to have a clarity and force that help to explain his professional success. On 15 October 1429 he was raised to the bench as one of the justices of the common pleas, and continued to perform the duties of this office until a few months before his death, though in 1437 he received an exemption on the grounds of long service and great age from all offices and commissions outside Norfolk; thereafter he ceased to ride the assize circuits.

Paston married late and well. His wife, Agnes (*d.* 1479), was the daughter and coheir of Sir Edmund Barry of Orwellbury, near Royston, Hertfordshire. They were married in 1420, when Paston was forty-two; Agnes was no more than twenty. She outlived her husband by thirty-five years and never remarried. Agnes was undoubtedly a loyal widow, even if she may not have been a loving wife—she chose to be buried not beside her husband, but beside her parents, grandparents, and Clement Paston, her youngest son who predeceased her, in the White Friars at Norwich. Presumably William Paston had to wait until he was an established man of law before being able to marry a young woman who brought him three East Anglian estates; her jointure was, perhaps had to be, generous: the valuable manor of Oxnead, Norfolk, which Paston had purchased a year or two previously, possibly with this marriage in mind. He was also generous when assigning Agnes her dower, leaving property to her, which, together with her jointure and her own inheritance, was valued at £100 per annum. One consequence was that Agnes became a wealthy woman at her husband's death. Another was that William's eldest son, John (I) *Paston, not as well provided for, was far less than generous, indeed less than just, in his dealings with his three younger brothers and younger sister. Nor were Paston family relationships improved by William's dithering on his deathbed; the incisiveness he had shown as a judge deserted him when he had to put his own affairs in order.

Those affairs had been highly successful. William Paston put together an imposing estate from the proceeds of office, carrying his family into the front rank of Norfolk landed families. Except for the Cambridgeshire manor of Snailwell, he did not buy at all outside Norfolk, and he bought when he could in the north-east of the county, for example the important manors of Cromer before 1426 and Gresham in 1427. Some of his ten purchases were bought from widows, for instance Swainsthorp and East Beckham; he may have behaved high-handedly to these vulnerable ladies, and in one case may even have been tyrannical and callous. Once he had been made a justice William Paston was a domineering as well as a dominant personality in north Norfolk. Sometimes he overreached himself, as with the manor of East Beckham, nominally acquired from the widowed Joan Mariot in 1434, but not secured by the Pastons for another seventy years. But that was exceptional, not least in that the trouble at Gresham was manufactured by a particularly unsavoury and unscrupulous nobleman, Robert Moleyns, Lord Hungerford (*d.* 1459).

At Paston itself William set about creating a manor from the miscellaneous properties he inherited, purchased, or exchanged in the neighbourhood; it was essential for a man clambering so vigorously upwards to be lord of the place after which he was named; less than gentry origins needed to be obscured. The process of creation had to be completed by John Paston. William Paston also modernized the house at Paston, as he did at Oxnead; in both cases he had to get a licence to move a road in order that he might live in the grand style. He wished also to be stylishly dead. William Paston died on 13 August 1444 in London, and was buried in the lady chapel of Norwich Cathedral. Although he wished for a perpetual chantry to be founded there for him, his eldest son made off with the cash deposited by Paston's executors as an earnest of intent to found the chantry, and made no effort to provide for prayers for his father's soul. Probably there was no tomb for Paston's body either. 'No chantry' is a suitable epitaph for a man as this-worldly as William Paston. His other epitaphs are those those small sheets of paper he covered with notes and memoranda in three languages, his 'scribbling papers', as they have been called. There are two that are of real consequence: one concerns East Beckham and is in the Norfolk Record Office; the other, in the British Library, is more varied but does contain a recipe for 'faire holsom drynk of ale' which he had from Sibyl Boys, a Norfolk gentlewoman and near neighbour: it humanizes him a little. COLIN RICHMOND and ROGER VIRGOE

Sources N. Davis, ed., *Paston letters and papers of the fifteenth century*, 2 vols. (1971–6) • *The Paston letters*, AD *1422–1509*, ed. J. Gairdner, new edn, 6 vols. (1904) • C. Richmond, *The Paston family in the fifteenth century: the first phase* (1990)

Archives BL | Norfolk RO, W. Ketton-Cremer collection

Wealth at death landed income est. to be approx. £250–£300 p.a.: Richmond, *The Paston family*, 34

Paston, William (II) (**1436–1496**). *See under* Paston family (*per. c.*1420–1504).

Paston, Sir William (**1479?–1554**), landowner, was the son of Sir John *Paston the younger (1444–1504) [*see under* Paston family] of Paston, Norfolk, and his wife, Margery, daughter of Sir Thomas Brews of Sturton Hall in Sall, Norfolk. Sir John succeeded his brother as head of the family in 1479, and was sheriff of Norfolk in 1485. He was in favour with Henry VII, was knighted at Stoke, and was a knight of the king's body by 1501. He died in 1504. William Paston was a student at Cambridge in 1495, but it is not known for how long, as he appears to have taken no degree. He may have trained as a lawyer, because his advice in that connection was acknowledged on one occasion by the borough of Yarmouth. His father probably introduced him to the court, where he became an esquire of the body to Henry VII, and was present in that capacity at his funeral. His main service, however, was to be in his home county of Norfolk, where he first appears as a commissioner of array in 1511. In 1512 he was listed among those gentlemen who were to provide soldiers for the forthcoming war, although there is no evidence that he served himself. In 1513 he received a joint grant of the castle and lordship of Eye in Suffolk from the crown as a reward for some unspecified service, and was sheriff of Norfolk and Suffolk in 1517. He continued his occasional attendance at court, being listed among those from Norfolk who went to the Field of Cloth of Gold in 1520. He was also among those who received the emperor Charles V in England later that same year. He was knighted between 4 December 1518 and 7 June 1520, but there is no record of the circumstances.

Paston served on numerous Norfolk commissions, appearing on the commission of the peace (seemingly for the first time) in 1522. In the same year he was with the army on the Scottish border, and submitted accounts for part of that operation in June. In 1524 he had the unenviable job of subsidy commissioner, again in Norfolk, and was at court to welcome the papal ambassador in September. He also acted as an executor of the estate of Sir Thomas Lovell, who died in that year. For the next thirty years he appears regularly in similar roles. In 1528 he was sheriff again. In October 1536 he was instructed to raise 150 men to serve under the duke of Norfolk against the Pilgrimage of Grace, although it is not clear whether he led them in person. In 1537 he appeared on the Norfolk commission for the dissolution of the lesser monasteries, and in 1539 was involved in a fracas over a parliamentary election, in which he was apparently acting on behalf of the duke. In the same year he was a commissioner for the defence of the east coast, and in January 1540 was at court to welcome Anne of Cleves.

When Paston was granted the manor of Caister Berolf and other Norfolk properties on 4 May 1544, for a payment of just over £200, he was described as the king's councillor, but he was never a member of the privy council, and this seems to have been an honorific designation. By January 1547 he was the senior member of the Norfolk bench, and was named first in the jury convened at the Guildhall in London for the trial of the earl of Surrey, the son of Paston's former patron. Later that year he was instructed to provide two great horses for the campaign against Scotland, but was now too old to serve in person, and was specifically listed among those who should remain at home for the defence of their countries in 1548. His only recorded part in the Norfolk rising of 1549 was to send two cannon for the defence of Norwich, which promptly fell into rebel hands. There appears to have been no trouble in his immediate neighbourhood at Caister, and his son Sir Thomas *Paston [*see under* Henry VIII, privy chamber of (*act.* 1509–1547)] represented the family in the royal army.

Probably about 1500 Paston married Bridget, the daughter of Sir Henry Heydon of Baconsthorpe, also in Norfolk. They had ten children—five sons and five daughters. The eldest son, Erasmus, died in 1538, having married and left children, including Sir William *Paston (1528–1610); Henry probably died in infancy; Thomas was a gentleman of the privy chamber by 1542, had been knighted by 1549, and succeeded on his father's death. John *Paston and Clement both served as gentlemen pensioners from 1544, and Clement *Paston was later an MP and a well-known sea captain. Of the five daughters, Margery, who was probably the eldest, became a nun at Barking, and may have died before the dissolution. Eleanor married Thomas Manners, thirteenth Baron Ros, at some point between 1520 and 1525, and became countess of Rutland on his elevation to the earldom in the latter year. Her eldest son, Henry, later the second earl, was born on 23 September 1526. Thomas Manners died in 1543, and a few affectionate letters survive from Eleanor to her father, who gave her both emotional and practical support in her bereavement. The last of these is dated February 1544; in it she sends greetings to her mother, who was clearly still alive at that date. Anne, Elizabeth, and Margaret, the remaining daughters, all survived into adulthood, and married into Norfolk gentry families.

Sir William Paston died at Paston about 20 September 1554, and was buried there on the 26th. His will, made on 28 June, was proved on 4 December in the same year. His wife had predeceased him, and there is no mention of Thomas, all dispositions being referred to his executors (unnamed). John, Clement, and Margaret also survived him, and received bequests. There were legacies to Erasmus's sons, William and Edmund, a provision that the latter be trained in 'the lawes of Englond', and substantial sums amounting to some £2000 to his servants and the poor of the neighbourhood. Although he had been, up to a point, both a courtier and a soldier, and had excellent court connections, Sir William's main service to the crown was within his own county, where he was active in all forms of local government for about half a century. The fact that he never sat in parliament probably says more about his relations with the duke of Norfolk, and possibly about his rather old-fashioned view of that institution, than it does about either his loyalty or his industry in Norfolk.

David Loades

Sources *LP Henry VIII*, vols. 1–7, 10–21 · *CSP dom.*, 1547–53 · F. Blomefield and C. Parkin, *An essay towards a topographical history of the county of Norfolk*, [2nd edn], 11 vols. (1805–10) · W. Rye, ed., *The visitacion of Norffolk … 1563 … 1613*, Harleian Society, 32 (1891) · heraldic visitation pedigree, 1573, Oxburgh Hall, Norfolk · will, PRO, PROB 11/37, fols. 111*r*–112*r* · HoP, *Commons*, 1509–58, 3.67–9 · Emden, *Cam.*, 444

Archives Oxburgh Hall, Norfolk, Bedingfeld papers · PRO, domestic state papers, SP 1, SP 10

Wealth at death bequests of over £2000: will, PRO, PROB 11/37, fols. 111*r*–112*r*

Paston, Sir William (**1528–1610**), benefactor, was the son of Erasmus Paston (*d.* 1538), landowner, and Mary (*d.* 1590), daughter of Sir Thomas Wyndham of Felbrigg, Norfolk; Sir William *Paston (*d.* 1554) was his grandfather. He may have attended the monastic school supported by the convent of St Benet of Hulme, in North Walsham, Norfolk, which was lost at the Reformation. He matriculated from Gonville Hall, Cambridge, in 1546. On 5 May 1551 he married Frances, daughter of Sir Thomas Clere of Stokesby, Norfolk. Their eldest son and heir was named Christopher; other children included a second son, Wolfstan, and a daughter, Anne. In 1554 he inherited his paternal grandfather's estate, thus becoming one of the richest men in Norfolk. He played little part in national affairs but took a prominent role in the government and political life of his native county and was known as a careful administrator and a 'just and painstaking magistrate' (Forder, 1). Under the patronage of Thomas Howard, fourth duke of Norfolk, he was sheriff of Norfolk and Suffolk in 1565–6. He was knighted on 22 August 1578.

A supporter of Edmund Freake, bishop of Norwich (1575–84), Paston was involved in the bitter conflict between the bishop and the puritans for control of the chancellorship of the diocese in 1578. He was described by

Bishop Scrambler as an 'observer of law' which has been taken to mean that his religious views were either conformist Church of England or impartial (Smith, 214). In 1597 he moved to the new house which his uncle, Sir Clement Paston, had built at Oxnead. Known for his liberality, hospitality and benefactions, Paston is chiefly remembered for the founding and endowment of North Walsham grammar school (the Paston School), in 1606. The school has a portrait of him by an unknown artist, which shows him 'venerable in his civilian attire of sober black' (Forder, 11). He made his will in 1610, declaring himself to be 'in good health and perfect remembrance' but died on the 20 October of that year. He was buried in the chancel of the church of St Nicholas at North Walsham, in a black marble tomb by John Key, adorned by an alabaster effigy of a reclining man in armour. A Latin epitaph on his tomb records some of his many acts of munificence. He settled £40 per annum on his newly founded school, with £10 for a weekly lecturer, and he was also a benefactor of Gonville and Caius College, Cambridge, Bath Abbey, Norwich Cathedral, and the poor of Yarmouth. Sir William's life was not without tragedy, since his son Christopher had become insane by 1609. JUDITH FORD

Sources Venn, *Alum. Cant.*, 1/3.317–18 • C. Forder, *A history of the Paston School*, 2nd edn (1975), 1–11 • A. Hassell Smith, *County and court: government and politics in Norfolk, 1558–1603* (1974), 16, 68, 106, 214, 221, 251, 284 • will, 1610, PRO, PROB 11/116, sig. 98 • F. Blomefield and C. Parkin, *An essay towards a topographical history of the county of Norfolk*, [2nd edn], 11 vols. (1805–10), vol. 6, pp. 488–90 • *CSP dom.*, *1603–10*, 528 • *The papers of Nathaniel Bacon of Stiffkey*, ed. A. H. Smith, G. M. Baker, and R. W. Kenny, 1: *1556–1577*, Norfolk RS, 46 (1979), 186–7, 250, 271

Archives BL, family corresp., Add. MSS 27443–27446, 33597, 34888–34889, 43488–43491, 45099; Add. Ch 14253–14256 • Bodl. Oxf., letters and papers

Likenesses J. Key, alabaster effigy on monument, 1610, St Nicholas's Church, North Walsham, Norfolk • W. C. Edwards, etching (after portrait), BM, NPG • oils, Paston School, North Walsham, Norfolk

Paston, William, second earl of Yarmouth (1653/4–1732). *See under* Paston, Robert, first earl of Yarmouth (1631–1683).

Pastorini, Benedict (*d.* 1806x10), draughtsman and engraver, was born in Italy, and at an early age moved to England, where he was employed as a decorator of ceilings. He also studied stipple engraving under Francesco Bartolozzi: in 1786 a visitor to Bartolozzi's studio, Sophie von la Roche, met an Italian and two English pupils. He executed some very successful plates in this manner, mostly subjects after Angelica Kauffmann, Antonio Zucchi, J. F. Rigaud, and others, but including a full-length portrait of Mrs Billington after Sir Joshua Reynolds. Between 1762 and 1774 Pastorini was employed to engrave the plates for the brothers Adams' *Works in Architecture* (1778–1822). He published in 1775 a set of ten engravings, entitled *A New Book of Designs for Girandoles and Glass Frames in the Present Taste*. He exhibited two drawings for ceilings at the Royal Academy in 1775 and 1776. He also engraved a frieze-caricature in aquatint. When the Society of Engravers was formed in 1803 to protect engravers and their widows and orphans, Pastorini was one of the first governors, the qualification being the contribution of a plate worth 75 guineas. This society was the precursor of the Artists' Benevolent Fund, founded in 1810; as Pastorini's name does not appear among the governors then, it is probable that his death had taken place between this date and his last recorded work of 1806—two caricature heads engraved after works in the Royal Collection attributed to Leonardo. Two members of his family, F. E. Pastorini and Joseph Pastorini (1772/3–1839), practised as miniature painters, and exhibited at the Royal Academy from 1812 to 1834. The latter painted a series of miniatures of Harrow schoolboys (Harrow School collection). He died in Newman Street, London, on 3 August 1839, aged sixty-six. L. H. CUST, *rev.* J. DESMARAIS

Sources Redgrave, *Artists* • J. Pye, *Patronage of British art: an historical sketch* (1845) • A. W. Tuer, *Bartolozzi and his works*, 2 vols. (1881) • T. Clayton, *The English print, 1688–1802* (1997) • E. Croft-Murray, *Decorative painting in England, 1537–1837*, 2 (1970) • Bryan, *Painters* (1886–9) • Thieme & Becker, *Allgemeines Lexikon* • C. le Blanc, *Manuel de l'amateur d'estampes*, 3 (Paris, 1858–88) • Graves, *Artists* • S. T. Prideaux, *Aquatint engraving* (1909)

Pastorius, Francis Daniel (1651–1719/20), German settler in America, was born on 26 September 1651 in Sommerhausen, Bavaria, Germany, son of Melchior Adam Pastorius, a judge and burgher of the neighbouring town of Windsheim, and his wife, Magdalena Dietz Johenn. After graduating from Windsheim's Latin school in 1668, Pastorius entered the University of Altdorf where he studied theology and classics, and then went on to study languages and law at the universities of Strasbourg, Basel, Jena, and Regensburg. In 1676 he received his doctorate in law from the University of Nuremberg and briefly practised as a lawyer in Windsheim, after which he took up a position as a lecturer in law at the University of Frankfurt.

During his sojourn in Frankfurt, Pastorius grew intensely interested in the pietist religious movement and developed a friendship with the influential pastor Philip Jacob Spener. At Spener's recommendation he spent 1680 and 1681 accompanying a young aristocrat, Johannes Bonaventura von Rodeck, on his travels through England, Ireland, France, and Italy. While visiting England, Pastorius met William Penn, who had returned briefly from America to spread the word about the opportunities for plentiful land and religious freedom offered by the Pennsylvania colony, and became a convert to Quakerism. Upon his return to Frankfurt in 1682 Pastorius became convinced that religious nonconformists such as pietists, Mennonites, and Quakers would never be able to practise their religion freely in central Europe and, in co-operation with pietist friends, devised a plan to create a pietist settlement in Pennsylvania. The group purchased 25,000 acres from Penn but abandoned the idea of colonizing the land themselves. Instead, Pastorius was commissioned by his associates, who in 1683 organized themselves as the German or High German Company, later the Frankfurt Land Company, and by a group of merchants from the nearby town of Crefeld, who had acquired a 15,000 acre tract of their own, to conduct a group of German and Dutch Mennonites and Quakers to settle in Pennsylvania.

Pastorius arrived in Pennsylvania on 20 August 1683, settled on the company's tract of land located between the Schuylkill and Delaware rivers, and on 24 October began to lay out the village, which he wished to name 'Germanopolis' but which soon became known more demotically as Germantown. He immediately affiliated himself with the Quakers of nearby Philadelphia and, as a friend of Penn and a devout and highly educated man, gained respect and influence simultaneously among the Germantown settlers and the Quaker élite. On 26 November 1686, he married Anneke Klostermann, the daughter of Dr Johann Klostermann of Muhlheim, one of the original Germantown settlers. The couple had two sons, John Samuel (*b.* 1690), and Henry (*b.* 1692), with whom they lived in the house Pastorius had built at 6013 Germantown Avenue.

Pastorius soon emerged as the leading citizen of Germantown, which itself became the starting point of German settlement in North America, functioning as its lawgiver and spiritual leader as well as holding numerous offices. He was commissioned a justice of the peace by Penn in 1684, was elected as Germantown's first bailiff in 1691, and served for many years as the town's clerk. He founded and served as the master and primary teacher of Germantown's school, at which lessons were conducted in English. Pastorius was intensely aware and proud of his and his community's German heritage, but he also had a profound belief in the importance of adapting to one's circumstances, reminding his son in a letter that 'each of you [is] an *Anglus Natus* an Englishman by Birth. Therefore, it would be a shame for you if you should be ignorant of the English Tongue' (Wolf, 140). As a tireless promoter of settlement in Pennsylvania he wrote, at William Penn's request, a widely circulated pamphlet entitled *A Particular Geographical Description of the Lately Discovered Province of Pennsylvania* (1700), which encouraged thousands of its readers to emigrate to the colony. In 1687 he was elected to the assembly of Pennsylvania, and in 1692 he played a significant role in the assembly's successful attempt to bar the state's council from levying a tax on landed property. Equally at home among the Germantown settlers and the Penns, Logans, Lloyds, and other prominent early Philadelphia families, Pastorius became through his activism, learning, and piety one of the colony's leading citizens.

In addition to his many other achievements, Pastorius was a major early opponent of the institution of slavery. On 18 February 1688 he drew up a memorial against slaveholding, 'Resolutions of the German Mennonites', in which he criticized slavery on the basis that it contradicted the 'Golden Rule': as 'this [slavery] is not done in the manner we would be done at', white people have no moral right to enslave Africans (Pennypacker, 197). Pastorius's document was adopted by the Germantown Quakers and sent on to the monthly meeting, by which it was approved and forwarded to the yearly meeting at Philadelphia, which declined to support it. It is noteworthy as the first protest made by a religious body against slavery, marking the beginnings of Quaker agitation against the American slave trade, and is the subject of John Greenleaf Whittier's poem 'The Pennsylvania Pilgrim'.

Pastorius died at his home in Germantown, 6013 Germantown Avenue, between 26 December 1719 and 13 January 1720, the dates respectively of the making and proving of his will. Many of his works, including the *Young Country Clerk's Collection* of legal texts and the *Bee Hive*, a collection of his writings on religion, slavery, and horticulture, are preserved as manuscripts in the rare book room of the Van Pelt Library of the University of Pennsylvania and at the Germantown Historical Society in Philadelphia.

NATALIE ZACEK

Sources *DNB* • M. S. Wokeck, 'Pastorius, Francis Daniel', *ANB* • W. T. Parsons, 'Representation of ethnicity among colonial Pennsylvania Germans', *A mixed race: ethnicity in early America*, ed. F. Shuffelton (New York, 1993) • M. D. Leamed, *Life of Francis Daniel Pastorius* (Philadelphia, 1908) • S. G. Wolf, *Urban village: population, community, and family structure in Germantown, Pennsylvania, 1683–1800* (Princeton, NJ, 1976) • O. Kuhns, *The German and Swiss settlements of colonial Pennsylvania* (New York, 1901) • W. F. Dunaway, *A history of Pennsylvania* (New York, 1946) • G. B. Nash, *Quakers and politics: Pennsylvania, 1681–1726* (Princeton, NJ, 1968) • R. Wood, ed., *The Pennsylvania Germans* (Princeton, NJ, 1942) • J. E. Illick, *Colonial Pennsylvania: a history* (New York, 1976) • J. J. Kelley, *Pennsylvania: the colonial years, 1681–1776* (1980) • J. T. Scharf and T. Westcott, *History of Philadelphia, 1609–1884* (Philadelphia, 1884) • J. G. Whittier, *The Pennsylvania pilgrim* (Boston, 1873) • S. W. Pennypacker, *The settlement of Germantown, Pennsylvania, and the beginning of German immigration to North America*, Proceedings of the Pennsylvania-German Society, 9 (1899) • www.geocities.com/Heartland/Prairie/6508 [Pastorius Home association website]

Archives Germantown Historical Society, Philadelphia, Pennsylvania, MSS

Likenesses A. Jaegers, monument, 1908, Vernon Park, Germantown, Pennsylvania

Pataudi. *See* Khan, Muhammad Iftikhar Ali, nawab of Pataudi (1910–1952).

Patch, Sir Edmund Leo Hall- (1896–1975), civil servant, was born at 90 Arthur Street, Chelsea, London, on 4 March 1896, the youngest of the three sons (there were no daughters) of William Hall-Patch (earlier known as Hall) and his Irish wife, Honora Riley. His father, who became—with his children—a convert to Roman Catholicism, had started life in the Royal Navy and, after a period as majordomo at the legation in Brussels, was then a verger at the Brompton Oratory. Edmund never married and his family was important to him. When his second brother, an engineer rear-admiral, was killed in 1945, Hall-Patch assumed the guardianship of his children and, after his father's death, did much for his widowed stepmother.

As a child Hall-Patch was delicate and was sent to a religious house in the south of France. Both these experiences—France and a Roman Catholic education—strongly influenced his life. In France he became bilingual and he always felt quite as much at ease in France and in Europe as he did in England, while the only home he ever owned and to which, but for financial and legal difficulties, he would later in life have emigrated was in the south of France. And wherever in the world he worked he was always close to the Catholic hierarchy.

After a spell at school in England, Hall-Patch returned at sixteen to Paris to train as a professional musician. He got a union card—later to be of great value to him—but soon decided he was not good enough. By 1914 he was studying French at the Sorbonne; he joined up, was commissioned in the Royal Artillery, won the Croix de Guerre with palms, was gassed, medically downgraded, and ended the war as a captain and railway transport officer near Paris.

In 1919 Hall-Patch was earning his living in the band of a Paris cabaret when he met Frederick Leith-Ross of the Treasury who, with his family, became a lifelong friend and patron. Leith-Ross found him a job first with the Supreme Allied Economic Council and then in 1920 with the reparations commission. There he prospered and from 1925 to 1929 was head of its finance section. When this came to an end he went to Siam as financial adviser to the government. He greatly enjoyed it, learned the language, and steeped himself in the life of the country. But it was not an easy assignment for so scrupulous a man—and in 1932, unable to approve the Siamese government's financial policies and at loggerheads with the Bank of England whose expectations he regarded as unrealistic, he resigned.

There were few jobs in the depression. Hall-Patch tried America, living in a smart hotel and playing the saxophone at night. Back in London he was a successful if intrepid and often injured riding instructor. By 1933, however, he was back on course, as financial adviser to a British group in Turkey and in 1934 in Romania as British member of a League of Nations commission of economic experts. All this was prelude. In 1935 Leith-Ross invited him to join the Treasury as an assistant secretary, to accompany him on a mission to China, and then to stay on from June 1936 as financial adviser to the British embassy. He was a great success there and in Japan, which was soon added to his bailiwick. In 1938 he was appointed CMG and in 1940 became the government's financial commissioner throughout the Far East.

By 1941 war had closed in and Hall-Patch returned to the Treasury to keep an eye on the Far East and be involved in negotiations, on such matters as lend-lease, with the United States. In 1944 he was promoted to assistant under-secretary and transferred to the Foreign Office to direct and lay enduring foundations for its growing economic work. In 1946 he was promoted to deputy under-secretary and in the following year knighted as a KCMG. As the principal economic adviser to Ernest Bevin he played a central and demanding role in the British response to the Marshall plan. In 1948 he was promoted again—this time to become ambassador and leader of the British delegation to the nascent Organization for European Economic Co-operation. For the next four years he was chairman of its executive committee, working and travelling prodigiously, popular with his colleagues—American and European—and seen by them, and perhaps by himself, as the champion of closer British ties with Europe. In 1951 he was appointed GCMG. But by then the job was done; by 1952 Marshall aid was over and in Britain the initial attraction and impetus of the European ideal had faded. Hall-Patch handed over to his deputy, and went, a little sadly but still as ambassador, to be the British executive director of the International Monetary Fund and the International Bank for Reconstruction and Development in Washington. In 1954 he retired from the public service, and joined Leith-Ross on the board of the Standard Bank of South Africa, succeeding him as chairman from 1957 to 1962. The wind of change was blowing in Africa and under Hall-Patch the bank prepared itself to ride the storm and made a start on the sweeping changes which were mainly carried through by his successor and friend, Sir F. Cyril Hawker. By 1962 his health was declining and he retired. In the years that followed he retained financial interests in Britain and the USA, wrote occasional articles, was on the board of Lambert International in New York, and travelled often to America and France.

Hall-Patch's career was as surprising as it was successful. He had a brilliant, but rather tortuous and pessimistic mind, perhaps more French than English. He was a very private person and cultivated an air of myth and mystery; even to his family he tended to appear and disappear like a magician. Stories abounded—seldom confirmed, but few were finally denied; stories of sorrows and romances, of the anonymous authorship of a daring French novel, or of popular music for film or revue, of unusual friends—Chou En Lai and Syngman Rhee, Yvonne Printemps and Sacha Guitry. His dress, slightly theatrical and antique, with stocks and stick-pins, an unscrutable air behind thick spectacles, and a tendency to break suddenly into French all added to the enigma.

A cheerful and charming companion, Hall-Patch had many and various friends; he was always kind and ready to help—and a special delight to children. He enjoyed his material pleasures and everything French—food and wine, his music, and the rewards of his success. But he never felt quite at home in Whitehall and this diminished his influence and effectiveness. Perhaps exaggeratedly, he felt he had experienced life and taken its buffets at the grass roots and always saw himself as an outsider looking into the establishment, impelled by an austere conscience to warn his more sheltered and unwary colleagues against facile optimism or complacency. Bevin valued him and was amused by his Cassandra role. 'Morning 'all-Patch', he would say as he saw Hall-Patch lowering ominously in the corridor 'and what's the snags to-day?' When he had heard, he felt forearmed against the worst.

What, perhaps, was most surprising was that with his sceptical and traditional cast of mind, Hall-Patch often seemed a pioneer and even a rebel involved in great changes. His most lasting achievements were the pioneering and strengthening of the economic side of the Foreign Office and the handling of all the European developments arising from the Marshall plan, with Britain very much in the lead. He was often a fervent, and some even thought an intemperate, advocate of attenuating Britain's diminished position in the world by closer involvement in Europe rather than by the more traditional and fashionable alternatives of closer Commonwealth ties and a special relationship with the USA. In this he was ahead of his time—and if he was disappointed that his views did not prevail, he accepted this loyally and played, with real distinction, a constructive and significant part in developments of great moment for the future of his country. He died of bronchopneumonia at Ascot Nursing Home, Ascot, on 1 June 1975. HENNIKER, *rev.*

Sources personal knowledge (1986) • private information (1986) • b. cert. • d. cert. • *WWW* • *The Times* (4 June 1975)
Likenesses W. Stoneman, photograph, 1952, NPG
Wealth at death £62,658: probate, 22 Aug 1975, *CGPLA Eng. & Wales*

Patch, Richard (1770?–1806), murderer, was born at Heavitree, near Exeter, Devon. His father was a small farmer who resorted to smuggling, for which he was imprisoned in Exeter, subsequently becoming the turnkey there. Richard, who was the eldest son, was early used to having money to spend. He was apprenticed to a butcher in Ebford, a village notorious for the immorality of its inhabitants, where he was said to have learned bad habits. On his father's death he inherited the farm and rented another nearby. He was not successful in this occupation and had to mortgage the farms. He quarrelled with the local rector and refused to pay his tithes, soon departing to London to avoid an action in this regard. He went into the service of Isaac Blight, a ship-breaker in Rotherhithe, where his sister and a brother were already employed.

In the summer of 1803, in order to protect himself against his creditors, Blight executed an instrument conveying his property to Patch and entered into a partnership agreement with him in August 1805. For this Patch paid £250 out of £350 he had managed to raise by the sale of his farms, and promised a further £1000 by 23 September 1805. This sum he must have known that he had no prospect of raising. On the evening of 23 September shots were heard in Blight's house by passers-by and Blight was found dead the next morning of pistol-shot wounds. No one had been seen leaving the house after the shots were fired, and it was therefore assumed that Patch, who had been in the house, had killed Blight.

Patch was tried for the murder on 5 April 1806 at the sessions house in Horsemonger Lane before Lord Chief Baron Macdonald. The trial was attended by the royal dukes of Cumberland and Sussex, for whom a special royal box was installed, and by the duke of Orléans and a throng of titled individuals. Patch was dressed in a good black suit and, having challenged three jurors, pleaded not guilty with equanimity to the charge of murder. It was said at the trial that 'he began his career of guilt in a system of fraud towards his friend, continued it in ingratitude and terminated it in blood'. Circumstantial evidence was skilfully marshalled by the prosecution, and he was found guilty, but he never confessed to the crime. He wept bitterly when visited in his cell by relatives (including his wife's brother), but subsequently remained calm and resigned. He was hanged on 8 April 1806 by Ketch, along with Benjamin and Sarah Herring who had been condemned for coining, outside the new prison, in Southwark. As was usual, his body was then dissected. Patch was described as having the appearance of a decent yeoman of athletic build, being about 5 feet 7 inches tall, with a florid face.

W. W. WROTH, *rev.* J. GILLILAND

Sources C. Pelham, *The chronicles of crime*, [another edn], 2 vols. (1886) • A. Knapp and W. Baldwin, *The Newgate calendar, comprising interesting memoirs of the most notorious characters*, 4 vols. (1824–8) • J. L. Rayner and G. T. Crook, eds., *The complete Newgate calendar*, 5 vols. (privately printed, London, 1926) • 'Account of the trial of Richard Patch, for the wilful murder of Mr Isaac Blight', *Lady's Magazine* (April 1806), 211–16 • *Kirby's wonderful … museum*, 6 vols. (1803–20), vol. 4, pp. 46–97 • *GM*, 1st ser., 76 (1806), 375 • *The Times* (7 April 1806)
Likenesses etching, 1806, NPG • etching and acquatint, pubd 1806, NPG • etching and stipple, 1806 • stipple, pubd 1806 (after G. Simpson), BM • etching, BM • portrait, repro. in Pelham, *Chronicles of crime* • portrait, repro. in *Kirby's wonderful … museum*, 4.46–97

Patch, Thomas (*bap.* 1725, *d.* 1782), artist and physiognomist, was baptized on 31 March 1725 at St Paul's, Exeter, the second of the three children of John Patch (1691–1746), a surgeon, and his wife, Hannah Miller. He studied medicine in Exeter and in London with Dr Richard Mead, but after a short time abandoned his studies and travelled to Italy with Richard Dalton. In 1747 he is recorded in Rome, where he met Sir Joshua Reynolds (who may have sparked his interest in caricature), Matthew Brettingham, Joseph Wilton, and Simon Vierpyl. While he was working in the studio of Claude-Joseph Vernet he was commissioned by the earl of Charlemont to paint views of Rome and Tivoli (1750–51); in 1752 he was making copies for Ralph Howard. He became a member of the short-lived British Academy in 1753, but at Christmas 1755 he was banished from the city for a homosexual incident. He moved to Florence, where he was soon accepted, and, apart from trips to Venice and Pola (1760) and Rome (1772), he remained there for the rest of his life.

Patch soon began to paint views of Florence, copying old masters as well as producing decorative landscapes based on Vernet's work. Visitors on the grand tour bought his paintings, and, with additional help from dealing in pictures and antiquities, he was able to indulge other interests. One of his caricature groups shows Patch holding a volume inscribed *Le regole del fisonomizare* (1774, Floors Castle); this, with additional documentary evidence, shows that he was working on a systematic physiognomical study that may have been illustrated with heads and figures, eventually etched (some in soft ground) and hurriedly published in 1770. If this assumption is correct, the painted caricature groups should be considered a humorous by-product of a substantial body of research. The finest pair shows Lord Stamford with fellow travellers in Florence and Pola (1760, Dunham Massey), and the largest, *The Golden Asses*, includes thirty-seven figures (1761, Chatsworth and Lewis-Walpole Library). Preparatory drawings and the series of etched caricatures have helped to identify some of the figures in the paintings.

In the 1770s Patch planned to publish sets of engravings after 'every celebrated author' (*Life of Masaccio*, title-page), but—like his studies in physiognomy—this overambitious scheme was abandoned. None the less, his aim was to trace the development of early Renaissance art: he published etchings after Masaccio (1770) and Fra Bartolommeo and Giotto (both 1772), and, in collaboration with Ferdinando Gregori, the baptistery doors by Ghiberti (1774). The volume dedicated to Giotto records frescoes (now attributed to Aretino Spinello) which were destroyed by fire in 1771, fragments of which were salvaged by Patch. His status as a connoisseur is shown in Johan Zoffany's *Tribuna*, where he is portrayed discoursing on Titian's *Venus of Urbino*. In January 1778 Patch sustained a stroke and, but for the constant companionship of Horace Mann, little is known of his activities. Four years later he suffered a second stroke, and he died, unmarried, on 30 April 1782 in Florence. HUGH BELSEY

Sources F. J. B. Watson, 'Thomas Patch', *Walpole Society*, 28 (1939–40), 15–50 • F. J. B. Watson, 'Thomas Patch: some new light on his work', *Apollo*, 85 (1967), 348–52 • J. Ingamells, ed., *A dictionary of British and Irish travellers in Italy, 1701–1800* (1997), 745–6 • A. Wilton and I. Bignamini, eds., *Grand tour: the lure of Italy in the eighteenth century* (1996) [exhibition catalogue, Tate Gallery, London, Oct 1996 – Jan 1997 and Palazzo delle Esposizioni, Rome, Feb–Apr 1997] • M. Chiarini and A. Marabottini, eds., *Firenze e la sua immagine* (Venice, 1994) [exhibition catalogue, Forte di Belvedere, Florence, 29 June – 30 Sept 1994] • F. Russell, 'Thomas Patch, Sir William Lowther, and the Holker Claude', *Apollo*, 102 (1975), 115–19 • B. Ford, 'Thomas Patch: a newly discovered painting', *Apollo*, 77 (1963), 172–6 • G. K. S. Edwards, 'Thomas Patch', *Apollo*, 26 (1937), 217–21 • E. A. Maser, 'Giotto, Masaccio, Ghiberti and Thomas Patch', *Festschrift Klaus Lankheit zum 20 Mai 1973* (1973), 192–9 • Walpole Mann correspondence, 25.272

Likenesses J. Reynolds, group portrait, oils, 1751 (*Parody on Raphael's school of Athens*), NG Ire. • T. Patch, self-portrait, 1760, Dunham Massey, Greater Manchester • portrait, before 1760, NPG • T. Patch, self-portrait, 1760–61, priv. coll. • T. Patch, self-portrait, 1761, Yale U., Farmington, Lewis–Walpole Library; version, Chatsworth House, Derbyshire • T. Patch, self-portrait, 1761, priv. coll. • T. Patch, self-portrait, 1763–4, Petworth House, Sussex • T. Patch, self-portrait, 1765, Yale U. CBA • T. Patch, two self-portraits, *c.*1765, Yale U., Farmington, Lewis–Walpole Library • T. Patch, self-portrait, 1767–8, Tissington, Derbyshire • T. Patch, self-portrait, 1769, Yale U., Farmington, Lewis–Walpole Library • T. Patch, self-portrait, etching, 1769, BM; repro. in T. Patch, *Caricature* (1768) • J. Zoffany, oils, 1772–9, Royal Collection • T. Patch, group portrait, self-portrait, caricature, 1774, Floors Castle, Scottish Borders • T. Patch, self-portrait, caricature, oils, Royal Albert Memorial Museum, Exeter • T. Patch, self-portrait, drawing, Royal Albert Memorial Gallery, Exeter • T. Patch, self-portrait, etching, BM; repro. in T. Patch, *Caricature* (1768) • miniature, NPG

Pate, John (*d.* 1704), singer, first gained notice in 1692; nothing is known of his early life. In May that year he was in the first performance of Henry Purcell's *The Fairy Queen*, as Summer and the shepherdess Mopsa, and he also sang the spirit Kalib in John Dryden's *The Indian Emperor*. He is named as the singer of the florid countertenor solo ''Tis nature's voice' in Purcell's manuscript for his 1692 St Cecilia ode. On 30 April 1695 Pate and the bass Reading sang in the première of William Congreve's *Love for Love* and that June the two singers were dismissed from the playhouse on the lord chamberlain's orders after their involvement in a Jacobite celebration at the Dog tavern, Drury Lane, which ended in a riot. Pate performed an Italian song in *The Female Wits* at Drury Lane in the summer or autumn of 1696.

Pate then seems to have travelled to Italy. In January 1698 Dr Arbuthnot wrote to the master of University College, Oxford, that Mr Pate had brought music back from Italy, and on 30 May that year John Evelyn, hearing him at Samuel Pepys's house, noted that he was 'lately come from *Italy*, reputed the most excellent singer, ever England had' (Evelyn, 289); his programme on that occasion included 'many rare Italian Recitatives' and several of Purcell's compositions. After appearing in concerts at York Buildings in May and June 1698, Pate sang for two seasons at Drury Lane, where his performance of Giovanni Bononcini's 'Pastorella' was received 'with great Applause' (*Mercurius Musicus*, 138). In his preface to *The Island Princess* (1699) Peter Motteux praised 'Mr Pate's admirable Performance, which … gives life to the whole Entertainment' (Motteux).

On 17 September 1700 'Letters from France say, that Mr. Pate, who belonged to the playhouse here, and sung so fine, is committed to the Bastile at Paris for killing a man, and that he is condemned to be broke on the wheel' (Luttrell, 4.687). However, Pate is named in the play-text as singing in Richard Steele's *The Funeral*, premièred in December 1701, and in February 1703 he performed in Italian and English at a concert at Drury Lane, 'having recover'd his Voice' (*Daily Courant*, 10 Feb 1703). He died at Hampstead in January 1704 and was buried there, in the churchyard of St John's Church, on 14 January.

OLIVE BALDWIN and THELMA WILSON

Sources W. Van Lennep and others, eds., *The London stage, 1660–1800*, pt 1: *1660–1700* (1965) • *Daily Courant* (10 Feb 1703) • *LondG* (7–11 Dec 1699) • *Post Boy* (19–21 Sept 1699) • *Post Man* (4–7 June 1698) • Evelyn, *Diary*, vol. 5 • N. Luttrell, *A brief historical relation of state affairs from September 1678 to April 1714*, 3–4 (1857) • G. A. Aitken, *The life and works of John Arbuthnot* (1892) • C. L. Day and E. B. Murrie, *English song-books, 1651–1702: a bibliography with a first-line index of songs* (1940) • D. Hunter, *Opera and song books published in England, 1703–1726* (1997) • O. Baldwin and T. Wilson, 'Purcell's stage singers: a documentary list', *Performing the music of Henry Purcell* [Oxford 1993], ed. M. Burden (1996), 275–81 • *The female wits* (1704) • *Mercurius Musicus* (July 1699) • P. A. Motteux, *The island princess, or, the generous Portuguese* (1699) • R. Steele, *The funeral* (1702) • J. Milhous and R. D. Hume, 'Dating play premieres from publication data, 1660–1700', *Harvard Library Bulletin*, 22 (1974), 374–405 • O. Baldwin and T. Wilson, 'Alfred Deller, John Freeman and Mr Pate', *Music and Letters*, 50 (1969), 103–10 • register, Hampstead, St John, 1704 [burial]

Pate, Richard. *See* Pates, Richard (1503/4–1565).

Pate, Richard (1516–1588), lawyer and refounder of Cheltenham grammar school, was born on 24 September 1516 at Minsterworth, Gloucestershire. He was admitted as a scholar at Corpus Christi College, Oxford, on 26 September 1532, but had vacated his place by 1536; there is no record of his having taken a degree. On 10 August 1541 he was admitted to Lincoln's Inn, where he was accused on 19 November 1546 of producing a satire against the benchers of the inn. By 1547 he had married Matilda or Maud (*d.* 1598), daughter of John Rastell, mayor of Gloucester, and

Richard Pate (1516–1588), by unknown artist, 1550

widow successively of Henry Marmion (mayor in 1533 and 1541) and Thomas Lane, first recorder of Gloucester (*d.* 1544).

It may well be true, as he later claimed, that Pate was 'an ancient professor of the gospel' (HoP, *Commons, 1558–1603*, 3.185), but zealous protestantism fitted snugly with his material interests. An agent in managing and evaluating former ecclesiastical property and its appropriation by the state, he was able to exploit such commissions for private gain. The process seems to have begun in 1544 with his appointment as under-steward and keeper of the manorial courts pertaining to Cirencester Abbey. Other similar responsibilities followed. On 14 February 1546 Pate was appointed a royal commissioner of chantries in Gloucester and Bristol, and on 24 November 1547 he was granted the lease of the manor of Hartpury, Gloucestershire. By July 1545 he had become friendly with the wealthy and influential Sir Thomas Chamberlain, and on 27 February 1549 the two men paid to the office of augmentations the very large sum of £1154 for chantry properties valued at more than £100 per annum which the government had placed on the market.

A justice of the peace from 1547, Pate was appointed escheator of Gloucester on 5 December 1548, and in 1556 became its recorder. Such advancement is not to be explained by his status in the legal profession, since he was not called to the bar until 10 February 1558. Probably his early rise to high position may be attributed to a combination of growing private prosperity and his very judicious marriage. Despite his elevation Pate may justifiably have felt that his record made him vulnerable during the reign of Mary. In 1557 he was called before the commissioners for refusing to make loans of £100 which the government had demanded. No action was taken, however, and it did his reputation no harm in the long term.

By the time of Elizabeth's accession Pate was one of the most important and influential men of Gloucester and had set about building a residence to match his status. Maud had inherited from her second husband the manor of Matson, a suburb of Gloucester formerly owned by Llanthony Priory, which after her death was to revert to his son Thomas. In 1561 Pate acquired a 200 year lease on the reversion, and set about rebuilding the old manor house, Matson House. In that year too he was confirmed in the recordership by the new charter, which established the position as Gloucester's principal legal office, to which the town clerk was deputy. Indeed the recorder's significance increased during Elizabeth's reign, as the legal disputes in which the corporation became involved grew more frequent. Pate was also Gloucester's representative in the first two Elizabethan parliaments. In 1571, however, he was defeated in a contested election by the town clerk, Thomas Atkyns, who won much support from lesser men of the town; Sir William Cordell, master of the rolls, wrote to William Cecil, Lord Burghley, urging that Pate, 'a good parliament man and very diligent and painful there', had been unfairly excluded and citing a precedent to show that recorders sat as a matter of course. Cecil refused to intervene. The following year Atkyns won again, Pate alleged, 'by gathering together of a multitude by great labour, and by some threatening words, contrary to the law' (Neale, 263). But a new appeal to Cecil also failed.

Pate represented Gloucester once more, in 1586. His retirement as recorder in that year gave rise to even sharper conflict. Pate nominated as his successor William Oldsworth, who may have bought the office from him. Oldsworth secured the support of the aldermen, but the mayor, Luke Garnons, an associate of Atkyns, refused to appoint him, arguing that the right of election belonged to the common council of the city, not to the aldermen alone. For almost a year Garnons stood firm in the face of a string of angry letters from the council, instructions from the lord lieutenant, and even a judgment of the chief justices. Not until November 1587, after the end of his mayoral term, did Oldsworth and Pate get their way.

Pate was important also for his benefactions, and is remembered especially for his role in the refounding of Cheltenham grammar school. A school already existed in the town by the time of the Chantries Act of 1547, and its continuance as a grammar school is recorded in the crown accounts for Gloucestershire up to and just after the accession of Mary. It is likely that the school was restarted on

Elizabeth's accession, and that Richard Pate, the former commissioner of the chantries with which it had been associated, was somehow involved. By 7 January 1574 Pate had already 'built a house in Cheltenham, co Gloucester, sufficient as well for the instruction of boys as for a dwelling for the schoolmaster' (PRO, patent rolls, Elizabeth, no. 1560). The patent recognized this school and granted property of St Katherine's and Our Lady's chantries in Cheltenham and other former ecclesiastical property to be used for an almshouse in the town. Pate's grammar school and hospital at Cheltenham were endowed by him in an indenture dated 6 October 1586. By this document Richard Pate and Corpus Christi College, Oxford, agreed that, in return for administering the school and hospital and looking after his property in Cheltenham and Gloucester, the college should receive a quarter of its revenue. The president and senior fellows were to be responsible for managing the property and the school. They were to select the master, an MA aged not less than thirty, who was to be assisted by an usher and paid at least £16 per annum. Detailed provisions were made as to the number of the scholars and the standards they were expected to reach; if these were not met, the teachers' stipends were to be reduced. Prizes were to be provided for outstanding pupils.

Pate did not make it easy to secure hospitality at his almshouse. Inmates were required to have been born in Cheltenham parish. They were either to be at least sixty years old, or to be incurably (but not infectiously) ill, 'and shall also be able to rehearse without book and by memory the Lord's prayer, the articles of our belief, and the ten commandments of God'; should any of those admitted prove 'a common drunkard, scold, swearer, hedge breaker, or otherwise a common troubler of the company there … or suffer any light person to haunt his company' they would, after three warnings, be permanently excluded (*Pate's Grammar School*, 22–3).

Richard Pate died on 29 October 1588. His wife survived until 1598, but of their children only Margaret attained adulthood, marrying one Richard Brooke. On 25 April 1577 Pate and his wife had granted the young couple a lease of 150 years of Matson House and the lands belonging to it, but both Margaret and Richard died very soon after; their orphaned daughter Susan appears as Pate's executor and, with Maud, co-beneficiary of his will. Richard Pate was buried in the south transept of Gloucester Cathedral, where a monument which represents also his wife and four children depicts him in the dress of a lawyer. His portrait is at Corpus Christi College, Oxford; it depicts him aged thirty-four, with a short beard and moustache, cap, white frilled shirt, gown with brown fur lining, and gold chain. STEPHEN WRIGHT

Sources A. L. Browne, 'Richard Pates, MP for Gloucester', *Transactions of the Bristol and Gloucestershire Archaeological Society*, 56 (1934), 201–25 • Emden, *Oxf.*, vol. 4 • *VCH Gloucestershire*, vols. 2, 4 • HoP, *Commons, 1558–1603* • J. E. Neale, *The Elizabethan House of Commons* (1949) • *Pate's grammar school and hospital charity* (1898) • 'Matson in Tudor and early Stuart times', *Transactions of the Bristol and Gloucestershire Archaeological Society*, 46 (1924), 325–51 • T. Fowler, *The history of Corpus Christi College*, OHS, 25 (1893) • will, PRO, PROB 11/73, sig. 4

Likenesses oils, 1550, CCC Oxf. [*see illus.*] • monument, Gloucester Cathedral • oils, Folk Museum, Gloucester

Pate, William [*called* the Learned Tradesman] (**1666–1746**), draper and writer, was the son of William Pate and a direct descendant of John Pate (*b.* 1557) of Brin in Essex, the great-uncle of Sir John Pate, bt (1585–1652), of Sysonby, Leicestershire. Pate may have matriculated at Trinity College, Cambridge, in 1683. This claim, made in John Nichols's *Literary Anecdotes*, was disputed by the *Dictionary of National Biography* on the ground that Pate travelled instead to Italy. However, the *Dictionary of National Biography* mistakenly identifies Pate as the subject of a letter written by the satirist John Arbuthnot (January 1698) in which he is said to have travelled abroad and to have returned with an impressive collection of music. It is now thought that Arbuthnot referred to the singer John Pate (*d.* 1704). None the less William Pate did indeed enjoy a friendship with Arbuthnot and was certainly a person of some considerable learning. Charles King, writing to Humfrey Wanley in 1693, for example, alludes to Pate as a young man newly set up, 'yet probably master of the best study of books and the best scholar of his age I know'.

During the 1690s Pate inherited his father's prosperous woollen draper's business and house opposite the Royal Exchange, London. It was here that Arbuthnot lodged before going to Oxford University. Pate then enjoyed many friendships at Oxford and had presented a portrait of the courtier and scientist Sir Kenelm Digby to the Bodleian Library in 1692. Two years later he gave Arbuthnot a letter of introduction to Arthur Charlett, master of University College, in which Pate spoke of his friend's honesty, discretion, and merit. In return it was probably through Arbuthnot's influence that Pate became a familiar figure on the early eighteenth-century literary scene. He was on good terms with Jonathan Swift who, while staying in London in January 1709, wrote of Pate as a 'bel esprit and a wollen-draper' (Swift to R. Hunter, 12 Jan 1709, in *Correspondence of Jonathan Swift*, 1.120). During the autumn of the following year they renewed their acquaintance: on 17 and 24 September 1710 Swift dined with Pate at his house at Lee Grove, Kent, while on 6 October Swift, Pate, and Sir Andrew Fountaine visited a chophouse and 'sauntered in booksellers' and china shops' (Swift, *Journal*, 1.43). Through Swift Pate also met Alexander Pope who, writing to John Hughes in 1714, enclosed 'a proposal for his Homer' to Pate as someone who might promote the subscription. It is highly likely that Pate was the subject of the *Guardian* essay (no. 141, 22 Aug 1714) in which Richard Steele praised the civility, learning, and business acumen of a 'woollen draper' acquaintance. Others knew Pate as the Learned Tradesman.

About 1710 Pate had started his own essay periodical, the *Lacedemonian Mercury*, with Tom Brown as a rival to John

Dunton's *Athenian Mercury*. Despite the venture's failure, Pate retained the friendship of Brown who in 1710 dedicated his *Memoirs of the Present State of the Court and Councils of Spain* to his 'honest friend, Mr Pate'. In 1734 Pate served as a sheriff of the City of London. He died, unmarried, at Lee Grove on 9 December 1746 and was buried in the old churchyard there. He dictated the following apophthegm to be inscribed in gold letters on his tomb: 'Epicharmion illud teneto nervos atque artus esse scientiae'. In his will Pate bequeathed his estate to his nephews, Robert Pate, fellow of Gonville and Caius College, Cambridge, and William Pate of Cornhill, London.

THOMAS SECCOMBE, *rev.* PHILIP CARTER

Sources *The correspondence of Jonathan Swift*, ed. H. Williams, 5 vols. (1963–5) · J. Swift, *Journal to Stella*, ed. H. Williams, 2 vols. (1948) · G. A. Aitken, *The life and works of John Arbuthnot* (1892) · *N&Q*, 8th ser., 4 (1893), 346 · PRO, PROB 11/751, fol. 269*r–v* · Venn, *Alum. Cant.*

PICTURE CREDITS

Osborne, Dorothy (1627–1695)—© National Portrait Gallery, London
Osborne, Ethel Elizabeth (1882–1968)—Dr Mary Goodson, Leeds (private collection)
Osborne, Francis, fifth duke of Leeds (1751–1799)—private collection; photograph National Portrait Gallery, London
Osborne, John James (1929–1994)—© National Portrait Gallery, London
Osborne, Malcolm (1880–1963)—© reserved; collection National Portrait Gallery, London
Osborne, Ralph Bernal (1808?–1882)—© National Portrait Gallery, London
Osborne, Lord Sydney Godolphin (1808–1889)—© National Portrait Gallery, London
Osborne, Thomas, first duke of Leeds (1632–1712)—© National Portrait Gallery, London
O'Shanassy, Sir John (1818–1883)—La Trobe Picture Collection, State Library of Victoria
O'Shea, Teresa Mary (1913–1995)—© Capstack Portrait Archive; collection National Portrait Gallery, London
Osler, Sir William, baronet (1849–1919)—courtesy of the College of Physicians, Philadelphia
Ostenaca (*d.* before 1780?)—© Bodleian Library, University of Oxford
Ó Súilleabháin, Muiris (1904–1950)—© reserved; by courtesy of the National Gallery of Ireland
Otis, James, senior (1702–1778)—The Roland P. Murdock Collection, Wichita Art Museum, Wichita, Kansas
Otis, James, junior (1725–1783)—© reserved; The Frick Collection, New York
Otter, William (1768–1840)—Ashmolean Museum, Oxford
Ottley, Sir Francis (1600/01–1649)—courtesy and copyright of Shrewsbury Museums Service, U.K.
Otway, Thomas (1652–1685)—University of London Library, Sterling Library; photograph National Portrait Gallery, London
Oudh, nawab wazirs of (*act.* 1754–1814)—© Photo RMN - G. Poncet
Oughtred, William (*bap.* 1575, *d.* 1660)—© Copyright The British Museum
Ouseley, Sir Frederick Arthur Gore, second baronet (1825–1889)—© National Portrait Gallery, London
Ouseley, Gideon (1762–1839)—© National Portrait Gallery, London
Outram, Sir James, first baronet (1803–1863)—© National Portrait Gallery, London
Ouvry, Frederic (1814–1881)—Society of Antiquaries of London
Overall, John (*bap.* 1561, *d.* 1619)—© National Portrait Gallery, London
Overton, Robert (1608/9–1678/9)—© National Portrait Gallery, London
Owen, Daniel (1836–1895)—by courtesy of the National Library of Wales
Owen, John (1563/4–1622?)—© Copyright The British Museum
Owen, John (1616–1683)—© National Portrait Gallery, London
Owen, John (1766–1822)—© National Portrait Gallery, London
Owen, Sir Richard (1804–1892)—© The Natural History Museum, London
Owen, Robert (1771–1858)—© Manchester City Art Galleries
Owen, Robert Dale (1801–1877)—Wisconsin Historical Society WHi-4853
Owen, Wilfred Edward Salter (1893–1918)—© National Portrait Gallery, London
Oxberry, William (1784–1824)—unknown collection / Christie's; photograph National Portrait Gallery, London
Oxenden, Ashton (1808–1892)—Notman / National Archives of Canada / C-051995
Oxford, Sir Kenneth Gordon (1924–1998)—© News International Newspapers Ltd
Paddy, Sir William (1554–1634)—The President and Fellows of St John's College, Oxford
Page, Sir Francis (1660/61?–1741)—© National Portrait Gallery, London
Paget, Sir Arthur (1771–1840)—Plas Newydd, The Anglesey Collection (The National Trust). Photograph: Photographic Survey, Courtauld Institute of Art, London
Paget, Sir Bernard Charles Tolver (1887–1961)—© National Portrait Gallery, London
Paget, Dorothy Wyndham (1905–1960)—© Empics
Paget, Sir Edward (1775–1849)—© National Portrait Gallery, London
Paget, Sir George Edward (1809–1892)—private collection
Paget, Henry William, first marquess of Anglesey (1768–1854)—Plas Newydd, The Anglesey Collection (The National Trust). Photograph: Photographic Survey, Courtauld Institute of Art, London
Paget, Sir James, first baronet (1814–1899)—St Bartholomew's Hospital Archives and Museum. Photograph: Photographic Survey, Courtauld Institute of Art, London
Paget, Dame (Mary) Rosalind (1855–1948)—© National Portrait Gallery, London
Paget, Violet [Vernon Lee] (1856–1935)—© Tate, London, 2004
Paget, William, first Baron Paget (1505/6–1563)—Plas Newydd, The Anglesey Collection (The National Trust). Photograph: Photographic Survey, Courtauld Institute of Art, London
Paine, James (*bap.* 1717?, *d.* 1789)—Ashmolean Museum, Oxford
Paine, Thomas (1737–1809)—Gift of Marian B. Maurice, Photograph © 2004 Board of Trustees, National Gallery of Art, Washington
Paisley, Robert [Bob] (1919–1996)—Getty Images - Hulton Archive
Pakenham, Sir William Christopher (1861–1933)—© private collection; photograph The Imperial War Museum, London
Pakington, Sir John (1549–1625)—© reserved
Pakington, John Somerset, first Baron Hampton (1799–1880)—© National Portrait Gallery, London
Palairet, Sir (Charles) Michael (1882–1956)—© National Portrait Gallery, London
Paley, William (1743–1805)—© National Portrait Gallery, London
Palgrave, Sir Francis (1788–1861)—© National Portrait Gallery, London
Palgrave, Francis Turner (1824–1897)—© National Portrait Gallery, London
Palgrave, William Gifford (1826–1888)—© National Portrait Gallery, London
Palles, Christopher (1831–1920)—by kind permission of the Board of Trinity College Dublin
Palliser, Sir Hugh, first baronet (1723–1796)—Los Angeles County Museum of Art, Marion Davies Collection
Palliser, Sir William (1830–1882)—© National Portrait Gallery, London
Palmer, Barbara, countess of Castlemaine and *suo jure* duchess of Cleveland (*bap.* 1640, *d.* 1709)—© National Portrait Gallery, London
Palmer, Sir Charles Mark, first baronet (1822–1907)—© National Portrait Gallery, London
Palmer, Edwin James (1869–1954)—© National Portrait Gallery, London
Palmer, John (1742–1818)—© National Portrait Gallery, London
Palmer, John (1744–1798)—Garrick Club / the art archive
Palmer, Mary (1716–1794)—private collection; photograph National Portrait Gallery, London
Palmer, (Beatrix) Maud, countess of Selborne (1858–1950)—The de László Foundation; Witt Library, Courtauld Institute of Art, London
Palmer, Roger, earl of Castlemaine (1634–1705)—National Trust Photographic Library / John Hammond
Palmer, Roundell, first earl of Selborne (1812–1895)—© National Portrait Gallery, London
Palmer, Samuel (1805–1881)—Ashmolean Museum, Oxford
Palmer, William (1740–1816)—The British Library
Palmer, William Waldegrave, second earl of Selborne (1859–1942)—© National Portrait Gallery, London
Panizzi, Sir Anthony (1797–1879)—© National Portrait Gallery, London
Pankhurst, Dame Christabel Harriette (1880–1958)—© National Portrait Gallery, London
Pankhurst, Emmeline (1858–1928)—© National Portrait Gallery, London
Pankhurst, (Estelle) Sylvia (1882–1960)—© National Portrait Gallery, London
Panton, Thomas (1731/2–1808)—© National Portrait Gallery, London
Paoli, (Filippo Antonio) Pasquale (1725–1807)—photograph by courtesy Sotheby's Picture Library, London
Papworth, John Buonarotti (1775–1847)—© National Portrait Gallery, London
Papworth, Wyatt Angelicus van Sandau (1822–1894)—RIBA Library Photographs Collection
Pardoe, Julia (*bap.* 1804, *d.* 1862)—© National Portrait Gallery, London
Pares, Sir Bernard (1867–1949)—© National Portrait Gallery, London
Pares, Richard (1902–1958)—photograph reproduced by courtesy of The British Academy
Paris, Matthew (*c.*1200–1259)—The British Library
Parish, Sir Woodbine (1796–1882)—© National Portrait Gallery, London
Park, Sir Keith Rodney (1892–1975)—© National Portrait Gallery, London
Park, Mungo (1771–1806)—© National Portrait Gallery, London
Parke, Daniel (1664/5–1710)—The Virginia Historical Society, Richmond, Virginia
Parke, Mary Winifred (1908–1989)—Godfrey Argent Studios / Royal Society
Parke, Thomas Heazle (1857–1893)—© National Portrait Gallery, London
Parker, Agnes Miller (1895–1980)—© reserved; Scottish National Gallery of Modern Art, Edinburgh
Parker, Charles Stuart (1829–1910)—© National Portrait Gallery, London
Parker, Henry, tenth Baron Morley (1480/81–1556)—© Copyright The British Museum
Parker, Henry Victor (1910–1978)—© South Wales Echo, Cardiff, 1967
Parker, Hubert Lister, Baron Parker of Waddington (1900–1972)—Estate of the Artist; The Honourable Society of Lincoln's Inn. Photograph: Photographic Survey, Courtauld Institute of Art, London
Parker, Sir Hyde, fifth baronet (1714–1782/3)—© National Maritime Museum, London, Greenwich Hospital Collection
Parker, John, first earl of Morley (1772–1840)—Saltram, The Morley Collection (The National Trust). Photograph: Photographic Survey, Courtauld Institute of Art, London
Parker, Joseph (1830–1902)—© National Portrait Gallery, London
Parker, Sir Karl Theodore (1895–1992)—© Estate of Oscar Nemon; collection Ashmolean Museum, Oxford
Parker, Matthew (1504–1575)—© National Portrait Gallery, London

Parker, Theresa (1745–1775)—Saltram House, National Trust
Parker, Thomas, first earl of Macclesfield (1667–1732)—© National Portrait Gallery, London
Parker, William, thirteenth Baron Morley and fifth or first Baron Monteagle (1574/5–1622)—The Berger Collection at the Denver Art Museum, TL-17738, © Denver Art Museum 2004
Parkes, Alexander (1813–1890)—Science & Society Picture Library
Parkes, Edmund Alexander (1819–1876)—Wellcome Library, London
Parkes, Edmund Samuel (1834–1887)—reproduced with the permission of Australia and New Zealand Banking Group Ltd
Parkes [Belloc], Elizabeth Rayner [Bessie] (1829–1925)—The Mistress and Fellows, Girton College, Cambridge
Parkes, Sir Harry Smith (1828–1885)—St Paul's Cathedral; © reserved in the photograph
Parkes, Sir Henry (1815–1896)—La Trobe Picture Collection, State Library of Victoria
Parkes, Samuel (1761–1825)—© National Portrait Gallery, London
Parkhurst, John (1511?–1575)—Bishop's House, Norwich; photograph National Portrait Gallery, London
Parkin, Sir George Robert (1846–1922)—© National Portrait Gallery, London
Parkinson, Cyril Northcote (1909–1993)—© National Portrait Gallery, London
Parkinson, Norman (1913–1990)—© Trevor Leighton / Camera Press; collection National Portrait Gallery, London
Parkinson, Sydney (*d.* 1771)—© National Portrait Gallery, London
Parkyns, Sir Thomas, second baronet (1664–1741)—© National Portrait Gallery, London
Parminter, Jane (1750–1811)—A La Ronde, Exmouth, Devon; photograph National Portrait Gallery, London
Parnell, (Catherine Maria) Anna Mercer (1852–1910)—© reserved
Parnell, Charles Stewart (1846–1891)—© National Portrait Gallery, London
Parnell, Fanny Isabel (1848–1882)—National Library of Ireland; photograph National Portrait Gallery, London
Parnell, Sir John, second baronet (1745–1801)—Castle Ward, The Bangor Collection (The National Trust). Photograph: Photographic Survey, Courtauld Institute of Art, London
Parnell [O'Shea], Katharine (1845–1921)—photograph National Portrait Gallery, London
Parnell, Valentine Charles (1892–1972)—© Popperfoto
Parr, Sir Robert John (1862–1931)—NSPCC Archive
Parr, Samuel (1747–1825)—© National Portrait Gallery, London
Parr, Thomas (*d.* 1635)—Ashmolean Museum, Oxford
Parr, William, marquess of Northampton (1513–1571)—The Royal Collection © 2004 HM Queen Elizabeth II
Parratt, Sir Walter (1841–1924)—© National Portrait Gallery, London
Parris, Edmund Thomas (1793–1873)—© National Portrait Gallery, London
Parry, Caleb Hillier (1755–1822)—photograph by courtesy Sotheby's Picture Library, London
Parry, Sir David Hughes (1893–1973)—The University of Wales, Aberystwyth
Parry, Sir (William) Edward (1790–1855)—© National Portrait Gallery, London
Parry, Henry (1561–1616)—by kind permission of the Bishop of Worcester and the Church Commissioners; photograph: The Paul Mellon Centre for Studies in British Art
Parry, Sir (Charles) Hubert Hastings, baronet (1848–1918)—by permission of the E. O. Hoppé Trust, Curatorial Assistance, Inc., Los Angeles; collection National Portrait Gallery, London
Parry, John [Blind Parry] (1710?–1782)—© National Museums and Galleries of Wales
Parry, John (1776–1851)—© National Portrait Gallery, London
Parry, Sir Thomas (*b.* in or before 1515, *d.* 1560)—The Royal Collection © 2004 HM Queen Elizabeth II
Parry, Thomas Gambier (1816–1888)—in the collection of T. Fenton
Parry, William John (1842–1927)—Gwynedd Archives and Museums Service
Parsons, Sir Anthony Derrick (1922–1996)—© News International Newspapers Ltd
Parsons, Sir Charles Algernon (1854–1931)—© National Portrait Gallery, London
Parsons, Edward (1762–1833)—© National Portrait Gallery, London
Parsons, Geoffrey Penwill (1929–1995)—© Malcolm Crowthers
Parsons, Laurence, fourth earl of Rosse (1840–1908)—© National Portrait Gallery, London
Parsons, Lawrence, second earl of Rosse (1758–1841)—© National Portrait Gallery, London
Parsons, William, third earl of Rosse (1800–1867)—© The Royal Society
Partington, James Riddick (1886–1965)—Queen Mary & Westfield College, University of London
Partridge, Sir (John) Bernard (1861–1945)—by permission of the E. O. Hoppé Trust, Curatorial Assistance, Inc., Los Angeles; collection National Portrait Gallery, London
Partridge, John (1644–1715)—Ashmolean Museum, Oxford
Partridge, John (1789–1872)—© National Portrait Gallery, London
Pask, Edgar Alexander (1912–1966)—Getty Images - Hulton Archive
Pasley, Sir Charles William (1780–1861)—© National Portrait Gallery, London
Pasmore, (Edwin John) Victor (1908–1998)—© National Portrait Gallery, London
Pasor, Matthias (1599–1658)—© National Portrait Gallery, London
Paston, Edward (1641–1714)—The Burton Constable Foundation. Photograph: Photographic Survey, Courtauld Institute of Art, London
Pate, Richard (1516–1588)—Corpus Christi College, Oxford / Bridgeman Art Library